DICTIONARY *for* THEOLOGICAL INTERPRETATION *of the* BIBLE

KEVIN J. VANHOOZER
GENERAL EDITOR

CRAIG G. BARTHOLOMEW, DANIEL J. TREIER, *and* N. T. WRIGHT
ASSOCIATE EDITORS

Baker Academic
Grand Rapids, Michigan

© 2005 by Baker Book House Company

Published in North America by Baker Academic
a division of Baker Publishing Group
P.O. Box 6287, Grand Rapids, MI 49516-6287
www.bakeracademic.com

and in Great Britain by the Society for Promoting Christian Knowledge
36 Causton Street
London SW1P 4ST

Printed in the United States of America

Library of Congress Cataloging-in-Publication Data
Dictionary for theological interpretation of the Bible / Kevin J. Vanhoozer, general editor ; Craig G. Bartholomew, Daniel J. Treier, and N. T. Wright, associate editors.
     p.   cm.
   Includes bibliographical references and index.
   ISBN 10: 0-8010-2694-6 (cloth) (U.S. edition)
   ISBN 978-0-8010-2694-2
   1. Bible—Theology—Dictionaries. 2. Bible—Criticism, interpretation, etc.—Dictionaries.
 I. Vanhoozer, Kevin J. II. Bartholomew, Craig G., 1961– III. Treier, Daniel J., 1972–
 IV. Wright, N. T. (Nicholas Thomas)
 BS440.D495   2005
 220.3—dc22   2005015484

British Library Cataloguing-in-Publication Data
A catalogue record of this book is available from the British Library.

ISBN 0-281-05780-X (U.K. edition)

The internet addresses, email addresses, and phone numbers in this book are accurate at the time of publication. They are provided as a resource. Baker Publishing Group does not endorse them or vouch for their content or permanence.

14 15 16 17 18   11 10 9 8 7 6

CONTENTS

CONTRIBUTORS

Anderson, Ray S. Ph.D., University of Edinburgh. Professor of Theology and Ministry, Fuller Theological Seminary. **Practical Theology**

Bacote, Vincent E. Ph.D., Drew University. Assistant Professor of Theology, Wheaton College. **Justice**

Badcock, Gary D. Ph.D., University of Edinburgh. Associate Professor of Theology, Huron University College. **Calling/Vocation; Holy Spirit, Doctrine of the**

Baker, William R. Ph.D., University of Aberdeen. Professor of New Testament, Cincinnati Bible Seminary. **James, Book of**

Bartholomew, Craig G. Ph.D., University of Bristol. H. Evan Runner Chair in Philosophy, Redeemer University College. **Biblical Theology; Deconstruction; Ecclesiastes, Book of; Postmodernity and Biblical Interpretation**

Barton, Stephen C. Ph.D., King's College London. Reader in New Testament, University of Durham. **Social-Scientific Criticism**

Beck, John A. Ph.D., Trinity Evangelical Divinity School. Associate Professor of Hebrew, Concordia University Wisconsin. **Geography**

Begbie, Jeremy. Ph.D., University of Aberdeen. Vice Principal, Ridley Hall, University of Cambridge. **Music, the Bible and; Worship**

Benson, Bruce Ellis. Ph.D., Katholieke Universiteit Leuven. Associate Professor of Philosophy, Wheaton College. **Poststructuralism; Structuralism**

Bimson, John J. Ph.D., University of Sheffield. Tutor in Old Testament, Trinity College, Bristol. **Chronology and the OT; Ezra, Book of; Nehemiah, Book of**

Blocher, Henri A. G. Diplôme d'Etudes Supérieures de Théologie, Faculté Libre de Théologie Protestante of Paris. Professor of Systematic Theology, Faculté Libre de Théologie Evangélique. **Atonement; Original Sin**

Block, Daniel I. D.Phil., University of Liverpool. Professor of Old Testament, Wheaton College. **Deuteronomy, Book of**

Bock, Darrell L. Ph.D., University of Aberdeen. Research Professor of New Testament Studies, Dallas Theological Seminary. **Messiah/Messianism; Miracle**

Boersma, Hans. Th.D., State University of Utrecht. James I. Packer Professor of Theology, Regent College. **Violence**

Bowald, Mark A. Ph.D., University of Toronto. Assistant Professor of Religion and Theology, Redeemer University College. **Grace; Objectivity**

Brady, Christian M. M. D.Phil., University of Oxford. Assistant Professor and Director of Jewish Studies, Tulane University. **Lamentations, Book of; Targum**

Bray, Gerald. D.Litt., University of Paris-Sorbonne. Anglican Professor of Divinity, Beeson Divinity School. **Allegory; Medieval Biblical Interpretation**

Briggs, Richard S. Ph.D., University of Nottingham. Tutor in New Testament and Hermeneutics, University of Durham. **Speech-Act Theory**

Brown, Jeannine K. Ph.D., Luther Seminary. Assistant Professor of New Testament, Bethel Seminary. **Chronology and the NT**

Bryan, Christopher. Ph.D., University of Exeter. C. K. Benedict Professor of New Testament, University of the South School of Theology. **Passion Narratives; Romans, Book of; Sermon on the Mount**

Burnett, Richard E. Ph.D., Princeton Theological Seminary. Associate Professor of Systematic Theology, Erskine Theological Seminary. **Historical Criticism**

Burridge, Richard A. Ph.D., University of Nottingham. Dean of King's College and Honorary Lecturer in New Testament Studies, King's College London. **Biography**

Buth, Randall. Ph.D., University of California Los Angeles. Director, Biblical Language Center, Hebrew University and Biblical Language Center. **Language, Linguistics**

Chaplin, Jonathan. Ph.D., University of London. Associate Professor of Political Theory, Institute for Christian Studies. **Political Theology**

Charry, Ellen T. Ph.D., Temple University. Margaret W. Harmon Associate Professor of Systematic Theology, Princeton Theological Seminary. **Earth/Land; Human Being, Doctrine of; Incarnation**

Chilton, Bruce. Ph.D., University of Cambridge. Bernard Iddings Bell Professor of Religion, Bard College. **Temple**

Cole, Graham A. Th.D., Australian School of Theology. Professor of Biblical and Systematic Theology, Trinity Evangelical Divinity School. **God, Doctrine of; Lord's Supper; Sanctification**

Cook, John A. Ph.D., University of Wisconsin. Lecturer, University of Wisconsin. **Lexicons, OT**

Cummins, S. A. D.Phil., University of Oxford. Associate Professor of Religious Studies, Trinity Western University. **John, Book of; Oral Tradition and the NT**

Davids, Peter H. Ph.D., University of Manchester. Scholar-in-Residence, Vineyard Church, Stafford, TX. **Jude, Book of; 2 Peter, Book of**

Dawn, Marva J. Ph.D., University of Notre Dame. Theologian, Christians Equipped for Ministry. **Powers and Principalities**

de Gruchy, John W. Ph.D., University of South Africa. Robert Selby Taylor Professor of Christian Studies, University of Cape Town. **Bonhoeffer, Dietrich**

deSilva, David A. Ph.D., Emory University. Professor of New Testament and Greek, Ashland Theological Seminary. **Apocrypha**

Enns, Peter. Ph.D., Harvard University. Associate Professor of Old Testament, Westminster Theological Seminary. **Exodus/New Exodus; Pseudepigrapha**

Escobar, Samuel. Ph.D., Universidad Complutense de Madrid. Thornley B. Wood Professor of Missiology, Eastern Baptist Theological Seminary. **Liberation Theologies and Hermeneutics**

Evans, Craig A. Ph.D., Claremont Graduate University. Payzant Distinguished Professor of New Testament, Acadia Divinity College. **Jewish Exegesis**

Evans, Mary J. M.Phil., CNAA. Vice Principal, London School of Theology. **Hosea, Book of**

Farrow, Douglas. Ph.D., King's College London. Associate Professor of Christian Thought, McGill University. **Ascension; Church, Doctrine of the**

Felch, Susan M. Ph.D., Catholic University of America. Professor of English, Calvin College. **Dialogism**

Fowl, Stephen E. Ph.D., University of Sheffield. Professor of Theology, Loyola College in Maryland. **Virtue**

Frame, John M. D.D., Belhaven College. Professor of Systematic Theology and Philosophy, Reformed Theological Seminary. **Apologetics; Logic**

France, R. T. Ph.D., University of Bristol. Principal of Wycliffe Hall (Retired), University of Oxford. **Kingdom of God; Relationship between the Testaments**

Gagnon, Robert A. J. Ph.D., Princeton Theological Seminary. Associate Professor of New Testament, Pittsburgh Theological Seminary. **Sexuality**

Garland, David E. Ph.D., Southern Baptist Theological Seminary. Associate Dean of Academic Affairs and Professor of New Testament, Truett Theological Seminary. **1 Corinthians, Book of**

Gow, Murray D. Th.D., Australian College of Theology. Minister, St. Paul's Cooperating Parish, Kamo, New Zealand. **Ruth, Book of**

Gracia, Jorge J. E. Ph.D., University of Toronto. Samuel P. Capen Chair of Philosophy and State University of New York Distinguished Professor, State University of New York at Buffalo. **Meaning**

Green, Joel B. Ph.D., University of Aberdeen. Dean of Academic Affairs and Professor of New Testament Interpretation, Asbury Theological Seminary. **Commentary; Context; Dictionaries and Encyclopedias; Narrative Theology**

Greene-McCreight, Kathryn. Ph.D., Yale University. St. John's Episcopal Church, New Haven, CT. **Interpretation, History of; Literal Sense; Mary; Rule of Faith**

Grenz, Stanley J. D.Theol., University of Munich. Late Pioneer McDonald Professor of Theology, Carey Theological College. **Community, Interpretative**

Griffiths, Paul J. Ph.D., University of Wisconsin. Arthur J. Schmitt Professor of Catholic Studies, University of Illinois at Chicago. **Reading; Religion**

Groves, J. Alan. Ph.D. candidate, Free University of Amsterdam. Professor of Old Testament, Westminster Theological Seminary. **Judges, Book of**

Gundry, Robert H. Ph.D., Manchester University. Scholar-in-Residence and Professor Emeritus, Westmont College. **Jesus, Quest for the Historical; Matthew, Book of**

Gundry-Volf, Judith. Th.D., University of Tübingen. Adjunct Associate Professor of New Testament and Research Scholar, Yale University. **Pauline Epistles**

Harlow, Daniel C. Ph.D., University of Notre Dame. Associate Professor of New Testament, Early Judaism, and Early Christianity, Calvin College. **Dead Sea Scrolls; Jewish Context of the NT**

Harrison, Carol. Ph.D., University of Oxford. Professor of Historical Theology, University of Durham. **Augustine**

Hart, Trevor A. Ph.D., University of Aberdeen. Professor of Divinity and Dean of the Faculty of Divinity, University of St. Andrews. **Imagination**

Hess, Richard S. Ph.D., Hebrew Union College. Professor of Old Testament, Denver Seminary. **History of Israel; Kings, Books of; Oral Tradition and the OT**

Hill, Andrew E. Ph.D., University of Michigan. Professor of Old Testament Studies, Wheaton College. **Genealogy**

Hill, Daniel. Ph.D., Kings College London. Lecturer in Philosophy, University of Liverpool. **Philosophy; Proposition; Warrant**

Holmes, Stephen R. Ph.D., University of London. Lecturer in Theology, University of St. Andrews. **Creed; Image of God; Salvation, Doctrine of**

Horton, Michael S. Ph.D., University of Coventry; University of Oxford. Professor of Theology and Apologetics, Westminster Theological Seminary in California. **Historical Theology; Sacrament**

House, Paul R. Ph.D., Southern Baptist Theological Seminary. Associate Dean and Professor of Divinity, Beeson Divinity School. **Haggai, Book of; Obadiah, Book of**

Humphrey, Edith M. Ph.D., McGill University. Associate Professor of New Testament Studies, Pittsburgh Theological Seminary. **2 Corinthians, Book of; Infancy Narratives; Jesus and Scripture; New Creation**

Hurtado, Larry W. Ph.D., Case Western Reserve University. Professor of New Testament Language, Literature, and Theology, University of Edinburgh. **Monotheism**

Jacobs, Alan. Ph.D., University of Virginia. Professor of English, Wheaton College. **Love**

Jacobs, Mignon R. Ph.D., Claremont Graduate University. Associate Professor of Old Testament, Fuller Theological Seminary. **Malachi, Book of; Micah, Book of**

Jeanrond, Werner. Ph.D., University of Chicago. Professor of Systematic Theology, Lund University. **Text/Textuality**

Jeffrey, David Lyle. Ph.D., Princeton Theological Seminary. Distinguished Professor of Literature and Humanities, Baylor University. **Western Literature, the Bible and**

Keesmaat, Sylvia C. D.Phil., University of Oxford. Associate Professor of Biblical Studies and Hermeneutics, Institute for Christian Studies. **Colossians, Book of**

Kelly, Brian E. Ph.D., University of Bristol. Dean of Chapel, Canterbury Christ Church University College. **Samuel, Books of**

Kille, D. Andrew. Ph.D., Graduate Theological Union. Consultant. **Psychological Interpretation**

Knapp, Henry M. Ph.D., Calvin Theological Seminary. Associate Pastor, First Presbyterian Church, Beaver, PA. **Protestant Biblical Interpretation**

Koptak, Paul E. Ph.D., Garrett-Evangelical Theological Seminary; Northwestern University. Paul and Bernice Brandel Professor of Communication and Biblical Interpretation, North Park Theological Seminary. **Intertextuality**

Laansma, Jon C. Ph.D., University of Aberdeen. Associate Professor of Ancient Languages and New Testament, Wheaton College. **Hebrews, Book of**

Lane, Anthony N. S. B.D., University of Oxford. Professor of Historical Theology and Director of Research, London School of Theology. **Justification by Faith; Tradition**

Lauber, David. Ph.D., Princeton Theological Seminary. Assistant Professor of Theology, Wheaton College. **Yale School**

Lee, Moonjang. Ph.D., University of Edinburgh. Professor of Theology and Missions, Trinity Theological College, Singapore. **Asian Biblical Interpretation**

LeMarquand, Grant. Th.D., University of Toronto. Associate Professor of Biblical Studies and Mission, Trinity Episcopal School for Ministry. **African Biblical Interpretation**

Longman, Tremper, III. Ph.D., Yale University. Robert H. Gundry Professor of Biblical Studies, Westmont College. **Song of Songs**

Lucas, Ernest C. Ph.D., University of Kent; Ph.D., University of Liverpool. Vice Principal and Tutor in Biblical Studies, Bristol Baptist College. **Daniel, Book of**

MacDonald, Neil B. Ph.D., University of Edinburgh. Senior Lecturer in Theology, University of Surrey Roehampton. **Language-Game**

Magallanes, Hugo. Ph.D., Drew University. Associate Dean and Associate Professor of Church in Society, Asbury Theological Seminary. **Racism**

Marshall, I. Howard. Ph.D., University of Aberdeen. Honorary Research Professor of New Testament, University of Aberdeen. **Johannine Epistles; 1 Timothy, Book of; 2 Timothy, Book of; Titus, Book of**

Martin, Francis. S.S.D., Pontifical Biblical Institute. Chair for Catholic-Jewish Theological Studies, Pope John Paul II Cultural Center. **Spiritual Sense**

Mattox, Mickey L. Ph.D., Duke University. Assistant Professor of Theology, Marquette University. **Luther, Martin**

McCann, J. Clinton, Jr. Ph.D., Duke University. Evangelical Professor of Biblical Interpretation, Eden Theological Seminary. **Psalms, Book of**

McConville, J. G. Ph.D., Queen's University, Belfast. Professor of Old Testament Studies, University of Gloucestershire. **Jeremiah, Book of; Joshua, Book of; Prophetic Writings**

McGrath, Alister E. D.Phil., University of Oxford. Professor of Historical Theology, University of Oxford. **Doctrine**

McIntosh, Mark A. Ph.D., University of Chicago. Associate Professor of Theology, Loyola University Chicago. **Mysticism, Christian**

McKnight, Scot. Ph.D., University of Nottingham. Karl A. Olsson Professor in Religious Studies, North Park University. **Apostasy; Covenant; Israel**

Millard, Alan R. M.Phil., University of London. Emeritus Professor of Hebrew and Ancient Semitic Languages, University of Liverpool. **Archaeology**

Moberly, R. W. L. Ph.D., University of Cambridge. Reader in Old Testament, Department of Theology, University of Durham. **Exodus, Book of; Jewish-Christian Dialogue; Patriarchal Narratives**

Möller, Karl. Ph.D., University of Gloucestershire. Lecturer in Theology and Religious Studies, St. Martin's College. **Amos, Book of; Prophecy and Prophets in the OT; Rhetoric; Rhetorical Criticism**

Moritz, Thorsten. Ph.D., London University. Professor of New Testament, Bethel Seminary. **Critical Realism; Mark, Book of**

Motyer, Stephen. Ph.D., King's College London. Lecturer in New Testament and Hermeneutics, London School of Theology. **Anti-Semitism**

Murphy, Francesca Aran. Ph.D., King's College London. Reader in Systematic Theology, University of Aberdeen. **Revelation, Book of**

Murphy, Nancey. Ph.D., University of California Berkeley; Th.D., Graduate Theological Union. Professor of Christian Philosophy, Fuller Theological Seminary. **Epistemology**

Noll, Mark A. Ph.D., Vanderbilt University. McManis Professor of Christian Thought, Wheaton College. **History**

Noll, Stephen F. Ph.D., University of Manchester. Vice Chancellor, Uganda Christian University. **Angels, Doctrine of**

Nolland, John. Ph.D., University of Cambridge. Academic Dean and Director of Postgraduate Studies, Trinity College Bristol. **Form Criticism and the NT**

Nordling, Cherith Fee. Ph.D., University of St. Andrews. Director of Spiritual Leadership Development, Calvin College. **Feminist Biblical Interpretation**

O'Connor, Robert. Ph.D., University of Notre Dame. Associate Professor of Philosophy, Wheaton College. **Pragmatism; Science, the Bible and**

Osborne, Grant R. Ph.D., University of Aberdeen. Professor of New Testament, Trinity Evangelical Divinity School. **Genre; Redaction Criticism**

Pao, David W. Ph.D., Harvard University. Assistant Professor of New Testament, Trinity Evangelical Divinity School. **Prophecy and Prophets in the NT**

Parry, Robin. Ph.D., University of Gloucestershire. Commissioning Editor, Paternoster Press. **Ideological Criticism; Narrative Criticism; Reader-Response Criticism**

Paul, Ian. Ph.D., Nottingham Trent University; St. John's College. Director of Partnership Development, St. John's College Nottingham. **Metaphor**

Perrin, Nicholas. Ph.D., Marquette University. Assistant Professor of New Testament, Wheaton College. **Gnosticism; Gospels; Nag Hammadi**

Peterson, Eugene H. M.A., Johns Hopkins University. Professor Emeritus of Spiritual Theology, Regent College. **Prayer; Spirituality/Spiritual Formation**

Rae, Murray A. Ph.D., King's College London. Senior Lecturer, University of Otago. **Anthropomorphism**

Redditt, Paul L. Ph.D., Vanderbilt University. Professor of Old Testament, Georgetown College. **Esther, Book of; Leviticus, Book of; Source Criticism**

Reese, Ruth Anne. Ph.D., University of Sheffield. Assistant Professor of New Testament, Asbury Theological Seminary. **Male and Female**

Reno, R. R. Ph.D., Yale University. Associate Professor of Theology, Creighton University. **Sin, Doctrine of**

Renz, Thomas. Ph.D., University of Bristol. Lecturer in Old Testament, Oak Hill College. **Ezekiel, Book of; Habakkuk, Book of; Nahum, Book of; Zephaniah, Book of**

Richards, Kent Harold. Ph.D., Claremont Graduate University. Executive Director and Professor of Old Testament, Society of Biblical Literature. **Societies, Scholarly**

Riches, John K. M.A., University of Cambridge. Hon. Research Professor, Department of Theology and Religious Studies, University of Glasgow. **Galatians, Book of**

Riddell, Peter G. Ph.D., Australian National University. Professor of Islamic Studies and Director of the Centre for Islamic Studies and Muslim-Christian Relations, London School of Theology. **Language, Grammar and Syntax; Semiotics**

Rodgers, Peter R. B.Litt., University of Oxford. Adjunct Professor, Fuller Theological Seminary. **Lexicons, NT; 1 Peter, Book of; Textual Criticism**

Rogerson, John W. D.D. Emeritus Professor of Biblical Studies, University of Sheffield. **Liberal Biblical Interpretation**

Rosner, Brian S. Ph.D., University of Cambridge. Senior Lecturer in Biblical Studies and Ethics, Moore Theological College; Macquarie University. **Salvation, History of**

Rota, Michael W. Ph.D. candidate, Saint Louis University. **Thomas Aquinas**

Rowland, Christopher. Ph.D., University of Cambridge. Dean Ireland Professor of the Exegesis of Holy Scripture, University of Oxford. **Apocalyptic**

Ryken, Leland. Ph.D., University of Oregon. Professor of English, Wheaton College. **Literary Criticism**

Schreiner, Thomas R. Ph.D., Fuller Theological Seminary. Professor of New Testament, Southern Baptist Theological Seminary. **Assurance**

Schultz, Richard L. Ph.D., Yale University. Armerding Chair of Biblical Studies, Wheaton College. **Form Criticism and the OT; Isaiah, Book of**

Scott, James M. Th.D., University of Tübingen. Professor of Religious Studies, Trinity Western University. **Exile and Restoration**

Seerveld, Calvin. Ph.D., Free University of Amsterdam. Professor Emeritus of Aesthetics, Institute for Christian Studies. **Art, the Bible and**

Seitz, Christopher. Ph.D., Yale University. Professor of Old Testament and Theological Studies and Dean of the Faculty of Divinity, University of St. Andrews. **Canonical Approach**

Snodgrass, Klyne. Ph.D., University of St. Andrews. Paul W. Brandel Professor of New Testament Studies, North Park Theological Seminary. **Exegesis**

Sparks, Kent L. Ph.D., University of North Carolina. Associate Professor of Biblical Studies, Eastern University. **Numbers, Book of**

Spencer, Stephen R. Ph.D., Michigan State University. Blanchard Professor of Theology, Wheaton College. **Hope; Last Things, Doctrine of**

Spinks, Bryan D. D.D., University of Durham. Professor of Liturgical Studies, Yale University. **Liturgy**

Stiver, Dan R. Ph.D., Southern Baptist Theological Seminary. Professor of Theology, Hardin-Simmons University. **Method**

Streett, Daniel R. Ph.D. candidate, Yale University. Adjunct Professor of New Testament, Criswell College. **Philemon, Book of**

Stylianopoulos, Theodore G. Th.D., Harvard University. Professor of New Testament, Holy Cross Greek Orthodox School of Theology. **Orthodox Biblical Interpretation**

Sundberg, Walter. Ph.D., Princeton Theological Seminary. Professor of Church History, Luther Seminary. **Enlightenment; Princeton School**

Sung, Elizabeth Yao-Hwa. Ph.D. candidate, Trinity Evangelical Divinity School. **Culture and Hermeneutics**

Tennison, D. Allen. Ph.D. candidate, Fuller Theological Seminary. Adjunct Professor, Azusa Pacific University. **Charismatic Biblical Interpretation**

Thiselton, Anthony C. Ph.D., University of Sheffield. Professor Emeritus of Christian Theology, University of Nottingham. **Hermeneutical Circle; Hermeneutics**

Thompson, John L. Ph.D., Duke University. Professor of Historical Theology, Fuller Theological Seminary. **Calvin, John**

Throntveit, Mark A. Ph.D., Union Theological Seminary Virginia. Professor of Old Testament, Luther Seminary. **Chronicles, Books of**

Torrance, Alan J. Dr. Theol., University of Erlangen-Nuremberg. Chair of Systematic Theology, University of St. Andrews. **Analogy**

Travers, Michael E. Ph.D., Michigan State University. Professor of English, Southeastern College at Wake Forest. **Formalism; Poetry**

Treier, Daniel J. Ph.D., Trinity Evangelical Divinity School. Assistant Professor of Theology, Wheaton College. **Concept; Creation; Faith; Jesus Christ, Doctrine of; Model; Philosophy; Proof Text; Scripture, Unity of; Theological Hermeneutics, Contemporary; Typology; Wisdom**

Trueman, Carl R. Ph.D., University of Aberdeen. Associate Professor of Church History and Historical Theology, Westminster Theological Seminary. **Illumination**

Turner, Max. Ph.D., University of Cambridge. Professor of New Testament Studies, London School of Theology. **Ephesians, Book of; Utterance Meaning**

Urban, David V. Ph.D., University of Illinois at Chicago. Assistant Professor of English, Calvin College. **Hero Story; Imagery; Irony**

VanGemeren, Willem. Ph.D., University of Wisconsin. Professor of Old Testament and Semitic Studies, Trinity Evangelical Divinity School. **Joel, Book of**

Vanhoozer, Kevin J. Ph.D., University of Cambridge. Research Professor of Systematic Theology, Trinity Evangelical Divinity School. **Intention/Intentional Fallacy; Providence; Ricoeur, Paul; Systematic Theology; Truth; Word of God**

Van Leeuwen, Raymond C. Ph.D., University of Toronto. Professor of Biblical Studies, Eastern University. **Proverbs, Book of; Translation; Wisdom Literature**

Verhey, Allen. Ph.D., Yale University. Professor of Christian Ethics, Duke University. **Ethics**

Wainwright, Geoffrey. D.D., University of Cambridge. Cushman Professor of Christian Theology, Duke University. **Trinity**

Walton, John H. Ph.D., Hebrew Union College; Jewish Institute of Religion. Professor of Old Testament, Wheaton College. **Ancient Near Eastern Background Studies; Etymology; Jonah, Book of**

Walton, Steve. Ph.D., University of Sheffield. Senior Lecturer in Greek and New Testament, London School of Theology. **Acts, Book of**

Wanamaker, Charles A. Ph.D., University of Durham. Associate Professor, University of Cape Town. **1 Thessalonians, Book of; 2 Thessalonians, Book of**

Ward, Timothy. Ph.D., University of Edinburgh. Vicar, Holy Trinity Church, Hinckley, Leicester, UK. **Scripture, Sufficiency of**

Webb, William J. Ph.D., Dallas Theological Seminary. Professor of New Testament, Heritage Seminary. **Slavery**

Webster, John. Ph.D., University of Cambridge. Professor of Systematic Theology, University of Aberdeen. **Barth, Karl; Canon; Gospel; Scripture, Authority of**

Wenham, Gordon J. Ph.D., King's College London. Professor of Old Testament, University of Gloucestershire. **Genesis, Book of; Law**

Westphal, Merold. Ph.D., Yale University. Distinguished Professor of Philosophy, Fordham University. **Onto-Theology**

Williams, Stephen N. Ph.D., Yale University. Professor of Systematic Theology, Union Theological College. **Revelation**

Williamson, Peter S. S.T.D., Pontifical Gregorian University. Assistant Dean, Sacred Heart Major Seminary. **Catholic Biblical Interpretation**

Wilson, Lindsay. Ph.D., University of Melbourne. Vice Principal and Lecturer in Old Testament, Ridley College, Melbourne. **Job, Book of**

Wolters, Albert. Ph.D., Free University of Amsterdam. Professor of Religion, Theology, and Classical Languages, Redeemer University College. **Metanarrative; Worldview; Zechariah, Book of**

Wolterstorff, Nicholas P. Ph.D., Harvard University. Noah Porter Professor Emeritus of Philosophical Theology, Yale University. **Authorial Discourse Interpretation**

Wood, Susan K. Ph.D., Marquette University. Professor of Theology and Associate Dean, St. John's University. **Baptism**

Wright, N. T. D.Phil., D.D., University of Oxford. Bishop of Durham. **Philippians, Book of; Resurrection Narratives; Resurrection of the Dead; Roman Empire**

Wright, Stephen I. Ph.D., University of Durham. Director, College of Preachers, Spurgeon's College. **Luke, Book of; Parables; Preaching, Use of the Bible in**

Yarbrough, Robert W. Ph.D., University of Aberdeen. Associate Professor of New Testament, Trinity Evangelical Divinity School. **Tübingen School**

Yocum, John. D.Phil., University of Oxford. Fellow in Christian Doctrine, University of Oxford. **Scripture, Clarity of**

Young, Frances M. Ph.D., University of Cambridge. Edward Cadbury Professor of Theology, University of Birmingham. **Patristic Biblical Interpretation**

ABBREVIATIONS

Bible Texts and Versions

AT	Author's Translation
BH	*Biblia Hebraica*. Edited by R. Kittel and P. Kahle. 3d ed. Privileg. Württ. Bibelanstalt, 1937
BHS	*Biblia Hebraica Stuttgartensia*. Edited by K. Ellinger and W. Rudolph. Deutsche Bibelgesellschaft, 1983
DH	Deuteronomic History
ESV	English Standard Version
ET	English translation/version(s)
KJV	King James Version
GNB	Good News Translation
JB	The Jerusalem Bible
LXX	Septuagint (Greek OT)
MT	Masoretic Text (Hebrew Bible)
NA[27]	*Novum Testamentum Graece*. Edited by Eberhard and Erwin Nestle, and K. Aland. 27th rev. ed. Deutsche Bibelstiftung, 1993
NIV	New International Version
NJB	The New Jerusalem Bible
NKJV	New King James Version
NRSV	New Revised Standard Version
NT	New Testament
OT	Old Testament
PN	Passion Narrative
Q	*Quelle*, hypothetical source of material common to Matthew and Luke but missing in Mark
P.Oxy.	Papyrus Oxyrhynchus
RSV	Revised Standard Version
SP	Samaritan Pentateuch
Tanak	Acronym for the Hebrew Bible: *T*orah (Law), *N*evi'im (Prophets), *K*etubim (Writings)
TNIV	Today's New International Version
UBS[4]	*The Greek New Testament*. Edited by K. Aland et al. 4th rev. ed. United Bible Societies, 1983
Vulg.	Vulgate (Latin)
WL	Wisdom Literature

Old Testament Books

Gen.	Genesis
Exod.	Exodus
Lev.	Leviticus
Num.	Numbers
Deut.	Deuteronomy
Josh.	Joshua
Judg.	Judges
Ruth	Ruth
1–2 Sam.	1–2 Samuel
1–2 Kings	1–2 Kings
1–2 Chron.	1–2 Chronicles
Ezra	Ezra
Neh.	Nehemiah
Esther	Esther
Job	Job
Ps. (Pss.)	Psalms
Prov.	Proverbs
Eccles.	Ecclesiastes
Song	Song of Songs
Isa.	Isaiah
Jer.	Jeremiah
Lam.	Lamentations
Ezek.	Ezekiel
Dan.	Daniel
Hos.	Hosea
Joel	Joel
Amos	Amos
Obad.	Obadiah
Jon.	Jonah
Mic.	Micah
Nah.	Nahum
Hab.	Habakkuk
Zeph.	Zephaniah
Hag.	Haggai
Zech.	Zechariah
Mal.	Malachi

New Testament Books

Matt.	Matthew
Mark	Mark
Luke	Luke
John	John
Acts	Acts
Rom.	Romans
1–2 Cor.	1–2 Corinthians
Gal.	Galatians
Eph.	Ephesians
Phil.	Philippians
Col.	Colossians
1–2 Thess.	1–2 Thessalonians
1–2 Tim.	1–2 Timothy
Titus	Titus

Philem.	Philemon
Heb.	Hebrews
James	James
1–2 Pet.	1–2 Peter
1–3 John	1–3 John
Jude	Jude
Rev.	Revelation

Apocrypha

Add. Dan.	Additions to Daniel
Bel.	Bel and the Dragon
Pr. Azar.	Prayer of Azariah
Song of Thr.	Song of the Three Young Men
Sus.	Susanna
Add. Esth.	Additions to Esther
Bar.	Baruch
1 Esd.	1 Esdras
2 Esd.	2 Esdras (= 4 Ezra)
Jdt.	Judith
Let. Jer.	Letter of Jeremiah (Bar. 6)
1–4 Macc.	1–4 Maccabees
Pr. Man.	Prayer of Manasseh
Ps. 151	Psalm 151
Sir.	Sirach (Ecclesiasticus)
Tob.	Tobit
Wis.	Wisdom (of Solomon)

OT Pseudepigrapha

Apoc. Ab.	*Apocalypse of Abraham*
Ascen. Isa.	*Ascension of Isaiah*
1 En.	*1 Enoch (Ethiopic Apocalypse)*
2 En.	*2 Enoch (Slavonic Apocalypse)*
3 En.	*3 Enoch (Hebrew Apocalypse)*
Jub.	*Jubilees*
L.A.B.	*Liber antiquitatum biblicarum (Pseudo-Philo)*
Liv. Pro.	*Lives of the Prophets*
Pss. Sol.	*Psalms of Solomon*
T. Judah	*Testament of Judah*
T. Levi	*Testament of Levi*
T. Mos.	*Testament of Moses*
T. Naph.	*Testament of Naphtali*

Dead Sea Scrolls and Related Texts

CD	*Cairo Damascus Document (cf. 4Q265–273; 5Q12; 6Q15)*
DSS	Dead Sea Scrolls
1QH	*Thanksgiving Hymns*
1QIsaᵃ	Isaᵃ
1QM	*War Scroll*
1QpHab	*Commentary on Habakkuk*
4QMMT	*Miqtsat Ma'ase ha-Torah = 4Q394–399*
1QS	*Community Rule*
4Q158	*Reworked Pentateuch*
4Q174	*Florilegium = 4QFlor*
4Q252	*CommGen A*
4Q285	*Sefer ha-Milkhamah*
4Q500	*papBened*
4QSamᵃ	4Q51

4QSamᵇ	4Q52
11Q19–20	*Temple Scroll*

Tractates of the Mishnah, Tosefta, and Talmud

Mishnah

m. 'Abot	'Abot/Avot
m. Demai	Demai
m. Git.	Gittin
m. Meg.	Megillah
m. Ned.	Nedarim
m. Sanh.	Sanhedrin
m. Šabb.	Šabbat
m. Sotah	Sotah
m. Sukkah	Sukkah
m. Yad.	Yadayim
m. Yoma	Yoma

Tosefta

t. Sanh.	Sanhedrin

Jerusalem Talmud

y. 'Abod. Zar.	'Abodah Zarah
y. Pe'ah	Pe'ah
y. Pesakh.	Pesakhim
y. Ta'an.	Ta'anit

Babylonian Talmud

b. B. Bat.	Baba Batra
b. Khag.	Khagigah
b. Hul.	Khullin/Hullin
b. Meg.	Megillah
b. Mo'ed Qat.	Mo'ed Qatan
b. Nid.	Niddah
b. Pesakh.	Pesakhim
b. Šabb.	Šabbat
b. Sanh.	Sanhedrin
b. Yoma	Yoma

Other Rabbinic Works

'Abot R. Nat.	'Abot/Avot de Rabbi Nathan
Gen. Rab.	Genesis Rabbah
Lev. Rab.	Leviticus Rabbah

Other Jewish Works

Josephus

C. Ap.	*Contra Apionem (Against Apion)*
A.J.	*Antiquitates judaicae (Jewish Antiquities)*
B.J.	*Bellum judaicum (Jewish War)*
Vita	*Vita (The Life)*

Philo

Abr.	*De Abrahamo (On the Life of Abraham)*
Cher.	*De cherubim (On the Cherubim)*
Contempl.	*De vita contemplativa (On the Contemplative Life)*
Det.	*Quod deterius potiori insidari soleat (That the Worse Attacks the Better)*
Hypoth.	*Hypothetica (Hypothetica)*
Plant.	*De plantatione (On Planting)*

Prob.	*Quod omnis probus liber sit* (*That Every Good Person Is Free*)
QG	*Quaestiones et solutiones in Genesin* (*Questions and Answers on Genesis*)
Spec.	*De specialibus legibus* (*On the Special Laws*)

Nag Hammadi Tractates

Gos. Thom.	*Gospel of Thomas*
Gos. Truth	*Gospel of Truth*

Apostolic Fathers

Barn.	*Barnabas*
1–2 Clem.	*1–2 Clement*
Did.	*Didache*
Herm. *Vis.*	Shepherd of Hermas, *Vision*
Ign. *Eph.*	Ignatius, *To the Ephesians*

Other Early Christian Literature

Athanasius

Inc.	*De incarnatione* (*On the Incarnation*)
C. Ar.	*Orationes contra Arianos* (*Orations against the Arians*)
C. Gent.	*Contra gentes* (*Against the Pagans*)

Augustine of Hippo

Bapt.	*De baptismo contra Donatistas* (*Baptism*)
Civ.	*De civitate Dei* (*The City of God*)
Conf.	*Confessionum libri XIII* (*Confessions*)
Doctr. chr.	*De doctrina christiana* (*Christian Instruction*)
Enarrat. Ps.	*Enarrationes in Psalmos* (*Ennarations on the Psalms*)
Enchir.	*Enchiridion de fide, spe, et caritate* (*Enchiridion on Faith, Hope, and Love*)
Faust.	*Contra Faustum Manichaeum* (*Against Faustus the Manichaean*)
Quaest. Hept.	*Quaestiones in Heptateuchum*
Spir. et litt.	*De spiritu et littera* (*The Spirit and the Letter*)
Trin.	*De Trinitate* (*The Trinity*)

Clement of Alexandria

Paed.	*Paedagogus* (*Christ the Educator*)
Strom.	*Stromata* (*Miscellanies*)

Cyprian

Ep.	*Epistulae* (*Epistles*)

Eusebius

Dem. ev.	*Demonstratio evangelica* (*Demonstration of the Gospel*)
Hist. eccl.	*Historia ecclesiastica* (*Ecclesiastical History*)

Gregory of Nazianzus

Ep. ad Cled.	*Epistula ad Cledonium* (*Letters* 101–2)
Or.	*Orationes*

Irenaeus

Epid.	*Epideixis tou apostolikou kērygmatos* (*Demonstration of the Apostolic Preaching*)
Haer.	*Adversus haereses* (*Against Heresies*)

John Chrysostom

Hom. 2 Cor.	*Homiliae in epistulam ii ad Corinthios*
Hom. Matt.	*Homiliae in Matthaeum*
Hom. Rom.	*Homiliae in epistulam ad Romanos*

Justin (Martyr)

1–2 Apol.	*Apologia i–ii* (*First–Second Apology*)
Dial.	*Dialogus cum Tryphone* (*Dialogue with Trypho*)

Lanctantius

Inst.	*Divinarum institutionum libri VII* (*The Divine Institutes*)

Origen

Cels.	*Contra Celsum* (*Against Celsum*)
Comm. Jo.	*Commentarii in evangelium Joannis*
Comm. Matt.	*Commentarium in evangelium Matthaei*
Princ.	*De principiis* (*Peri archōn*) (*First Principles*)

Tertullian

Marc.	*Adversus Marcionem* (*Against Marcion*)
Praescr.	*De praescriptione haereticorum* (*Prescription against Heretics*)
Prax.	*Adversus Praxean* (*Against Praxeas*)
Spect.	*De spectaculis* (*The Shows*)
Virg.	*De virginibus velandis* (*The Veiling of Virgins*)

Classical and Hellenistic Sources

Aristotle

Metaph.	*Metaphysica* (*Metaphysics*)
Rhet.	*Rhetorica* (*Rhetoric*)

Herodotus

Hist.	*Historiae* (*Histories*)

Plato

Leg.	*Leges* (*Laws*)
Theaet.	*Theaetetus*

Pliny the Elder

Nat.	*Naturalis historia* (*Natural History*)

Pliny the Younger

Ep.	*Epistulae* (*Letters*)

Seneca

Ep.	*Epistulae morales* (*Letters*)

Sophocles

Oed. col.	*Oedipus coloneus*

Suetonius

Aug.	*Divus Augustus*

Medieval Sources

Gregory the Great

Hom. in evan.	*Homiliae in evangelia*

Moral.	*Expositio in Librum Job, sive Moralium libri xxv (Moralia)*	BSac	*Bibliotheca sacra*
		BSL	Biblical Studies Library
		BT	*The Bible Translator*
Thomas Aquinas		BTB	*Biblical Theology Bulletin*
QQ	*Questiones quodlibetales*	BU	Biblische Untersuchungen
ST	*Summa theologiae/theologica*	BZAW	Beihefte zur Zeitschrift für die alttestamentliche Wissenschaft
Additional Abbreviations		CahRB	Cahiers de la Revue biblique
A1CS	The Book of Acts in Its First Century Setting	CBC	Cambridge Bible Commentary
		CBQ	*Catholic Biblical Quarterly*
AAR	American Academy of Religion	CCSL	Corpus Christianorum: Series latina. Turnhout, 1953–
AB	Anchor Bible		
ABD	*Anchor Bible Dictionary.* Edited by D. N. Freedman. 6 vols. Doubleday, 1992	*CD*	*Church Dogmatics*, Karl Barth
		Chm	*Churchman* [Watford, Herts, UK]
		ChrLit	*Christianity and Literature*
ACCS	Ancient Christian Commentary on Scripture	*CJT*	*Canadian Journal of Theology*
		Comm	*Communio*
ACCSNT	Ancient Christian Commentary on Scripture: New Testament	*CoS*	Hallo, W. W., and K. L. Younger, eds. *The Context of Scripture.* Vol. 1, *Canonical Compositions from the Biblical World.* Vol. 2, *Monumental Inscriptions from the Biblical World.* Brill, 1997–2000
ACCSOT	Ancient Christian Commentary on Scripture: Old Testament		
AGJU	Arbeiten zur Geschichte des antiken Judentums und des Urchristentums		
AJSL	*American Journal of Semitic Languages and Literature*	*CQ*	*Classical Quarterly*
		CRINT	Compendia rerum iudaicarum ad Novum Testamentum
AJT	*Asia Journal of Theology*		
AnBib	Analecta biblica	*CTJ*	*Calvin Theological Journal*
ANET	*Ancient Near Eastern Texts Relating to the Old Testament.* Edited by J. B. Pritchard. Princeton, 1950. 3d ed., 1969	*CurBS*	*Currents in Research: Biblical Studies*
		DBI	*Dictionary of Biblical Imagery.* Edited by L. Ryken, J. C. Wilhoit, and T. Longman III. InterVarsity, 1998
ANF	*Ante-Nicene Fathers.* Edited by A. Roberts and J. Donaldson. 10 vols. 1885–96. Reprint, Eerdmans, 1986–89	*DBSJ*	*Detroit Baptist Seminary Journal*
		DJG	*Dictionary of Jesus and the Gospels.* Edited by J. B. Green and S. McKnight. InterVarsity, 1992
AThR	*Anglican Theological Review*		
AUSS	*Andrews University Seminary Studies*	ÉBib	Études bibliques
BA	*Biblical Archaeologist*	ECC	Eerdmans Critical Commentary
BAR	*Biblical Archaeology Review*	*EDBT*	*Evangelical Dictionary of Biblical Theology.* Edited by W. Elwell. Baker Books/Paternoster, 1996
BASOR	*Bulletin of the American Schools of Oriental Research*		
BBR	*Bulletin for Biblical Research*	*ÉgT*	*Église et théologie*
BDAG	Bauer, W., F. W. Danker, W. F. Arndt, and F. W. Gingrich. *Greek-English Lexicon of the New Testament and Other Early Christian Literature.* 3d ed. University of Chicago Press, 2000	EKKNT	Evangelisch-katholischer Kommentar zum Neuen Testament
		EncJud	*Encyclopaedia Judaica.* 16 vols. Encyclopaedia Judaica, 1972
		ErJb	*Eranos-Jahrbuch*
BEATAJ	Beiträge zur Erforschung des Alten Testaments und des antiken Judentum	ET	English translation/edition
		EvQ	*Evangelical Quarterly*
BECNT	Baker Exegetical Commentary on the New Testament	*EvT*	*Evangelische Theologie*
		ExAud	*Ex auditu*
BETL	Bibliotheca ephemeridum theologicarum lovaniensium	FC	Fathers of the Church. Catholic University of America, 1947–
Bib	*Biblica*	FCB	Feminist Companion to the Bible
BibInt	*Biblical Interpretation*	FF	Foundations and Facets
BIS	Biblical Interpretation Series	FOTL	Forms of the Old Testament Literature
BKAT	Biblischer Kommentar, Altes Testament. Edited by M. Noth and H. W. Wolff	FThSt	Freiburger theologische Studien
		GBS	Guides to Biblical Scholarship
		HAT	Handbuch zum Alten Testament
BN	*Biblische Notizen*	*HBT*	*Horizons in Biblical Theology*
BNTC	Black's New Testament Commentaries	*HS*	*Hebrew Studies*

HSM	Harvard Semitic Monographs
HTKNT	Herders theologischer Kommentar zum Neuen Testament
HTR	*Harvard Theological Review*
HUCA	*Hebrew Union College Annual*
HUT	Hermeneutische Untersuchungen zur Theologie
IBC	Interpretation: A Bible Commentary for Teaching and Preaching
ICC	International Critical Commentary
IDB	*The Interpreter's Dictionary of the Bible*. Edited by G. A. Buttrick. 4 vols. Abingdon, 1962
IJST	*International Journal of Systematic Theology*
Inst.	John Calvin. *Institutes of the Christian Religion*. Edited by J. McNeill. Translated by F. L. Battles. 2 vols. Westminster, 1960
Int	*Interpretation*
JAAR	*Journal of the American Academy of Religion*
JAOS	*Journal of the American Oriental Society*
JBL	*Journal of Biblical Literature*
JETS	*Journal of the Evangelical Theological Society*
JNES	*Journal of Near Eastern Studies*
JPS	Jewish Publication Society
JPT	*Journal of Pentecostal Theology*
JPTSup	Journal of Pentecostal Theology: Supplement Series
JR	*Journal of Religion*
JSJ	*Journal for the Study of Judaism in the Persian, Hellenistic, and Roman Periods*
JSJSup	Journal for the Study of Judaism Supplement
JSNT	*Journal for the Study of the New Testament*
JSNTSup	Journal for the Study of the New Testament: Supplement Series
JSOT	*Journal for the Study of the Old Testament*
JSOTSup	Journal for the Study of the Old Testament: Supplement Series
JSS	*Journal of Semitic Studies*
JTS	*Journal of Theological Studies*
JTSA	*Journal of Theology for Southern Africa*
KEK	Kritisch-exegetischer Kommentar über das Neue Testament (Meyer-Kommentar)
LCC	Library of Christian Classics
LCL	Loeb Classical Library
LWorks	Martin Luther. *Luther's Works*. Vols. 1–30 edited by J. Pelikan, 31–54 by H. Lehman. 55 vols. Concordia/Fortress, 1955–1986
MTS	Marburger theologische Studien
NAC	New American Commentary
NBf	*New Blackfriars*
NCB	New Century Bible Commentary
Neot	*Neotestamentica*
NHS	Nag Hammadi Studies
NIB	*The New Interpreter's Bible*. Edited by L. Keck. 12 vols. Abingdon, 1994–2002
NIBCNT	New International Biblical Commentary on the New Testament
NIBCOT	New International Biblical Commentary on the Old Testament
NICNT	New International Commentary on the New Testament
NICOT	New International Commentary on the Old Testament
NIDNTT	*New International Dictionary of New Testament Theology*. Edited by C. Brown. 4 vols. Zondervan, 1975–85
NIDOTTE	*New International Dictionary of Old Testament Theology and Exegesis*. Edited by W. A. VanGemeren. 5 vols. Zondervan, 1997
NIGTC	New International Greek Testament Commentary
NIVAC	NIV Application Commentary
NovTSup	Novum Testamentum Supplements
NPNF[1]	*Nicene and Post-Nicene Fathers*, Series 1. Edited by P. Schaff. 14 vols. 1886–90. Reprint, T&T Clark/Eerdmans, 1979–
NPNF[2]	*Nicene and Post-Nicene Fathers*, Series 2. Edited by P. Schaff and H. Wace. 14 vols. 1890–1900. Reprint, Hendrickson, 1994
NSBT	New Studies in Biblical Theology
NTAbh	Neutestamentliche Abhandlungen
NTC	New Testament in Context
NTG	New Testament Guides
NTS	*New Testament Studies*
NTT	New Testament Theology
NTTS	New Testament Tools and Studies
ÖBS	Österreichische biblische Studien
OBT	Overtures to Biblical Theology
OED	*Oxford English Dictionary*. Prepared by J. A. Simpson and E. S. C. Weiner. 2d ed. 20 vols. Clarendon/Oxford University Press, 1989
OiC	*One in Christ*
OTG	Old Testament Guides
OTL	Old Testament Library
PG	Patrologia graeca [= Patrologiae cursus completus: Series graeca]. Edited by J.-P. Migne. 162 vols. J.-P. Migne, 1857–86
ProEccl	*Pro ecclesia*
PRSt	*Perspectives in Religious Studies*
PTMS	Pittsburgh Theological Monograph Series
QD	Quaestiones disputatae
QR	*Quarterly Review*

RAC	*Reallexikon für Antike und Christentum*. Edited by T. Klauser et al. A. Hiersemann, 1950–
RACSup	*Supplements* to *RAC*. Edited by T. Klauser. A. Hiersemann, 1971–
RelS	*Religious Studies*
RelSRev	*Religious Studies Review*
RevExp	*Review and Expositor*
RevQ	*Revue de Qumran*
RHPR	*Revue d'histoire et de philosophie religieuses*
RHR	*Revue de l'histoire des religions*
RTR	*Reformed Theological Review*
SAC	Studies in Antiquity and Christianity
SBB	Stuttgarter biblische Beiträge
SBL	Society of Biblical Literature
SBLDS	Society of Biblical Literature Dissertation Series
SBLMS	Society of Biblical Literature Monograph Series
SBLSCS	Society of Biblical Literature Septuagint and Cognate Studies
SBLSP	*Society of Biblical Literature Seminar Papers*
SBLSymS	Society of Biblical Literature Symposium Series
SBS	Stuttgarter Bibelstudien
SBT	Studies in Biblical Theology
SBTS	Sources for Biblical and Theological Study
SC	Sources chrétiennes. Paris: Cerf, 1943–
SCA	Studies in Christian Antiquity
SE	*Studia evangelica*
SemeiaSt	Semeia Studies
SHR	Studies in the History of Religions (supplements to *Numen*)
SHS	Scripture and Hermeneutics Series
SJLA	Studies in Judaism in Late Antiquity
SJT	*Scottish Journal of Theology*
SNTSMS	Society for New Testament Studies Monograph Series
SP	Sacra pagina
SR	*Studies in Religion*
SSN	Studia semitica neerlandica
ST	*Studia theologica*

TDNT	*Theological Dictionary of the New Testament*. Edited by G. Kittel and G. Friedrich. Translated by G. W. Bromiley. 10 vols. Eerdmans, 1964–76
TDOT	*Theological Dictionary of the Old Testament*. Edited by G. J. Botterweck and H. Ringgren. Translated by J. T. Willis, G. W. Bromiley, D. E. Green, and D. W. Stott. Eerdmans, 1974–
Them	*Themelios*
ThTo	*Theology Today*
TJ	*Trinity Journal*
TNTC	Tyndale New Testament Commentaries
TOTC	Tyndale Old Testament Commentaries
TS	*Theological Studies*
TSAJ	Texte und Studien zum antiken Judentum
TynBul	*Tyndale Bulletin*
TZ	*Theologische Zeitschrift*
TZTh	*Tübinger Zeitschrift für Theologie*
VE	*Vox evangelica*
VT	*Vetus Testamentum*
VTSup	Vetus Testamentum Supplements
WA	*D. Martin Luthers Werke: Kritische Gesamtausgabe* (Weimarer Ausgabe). Ed. J. F. K. Knaake et al. 57 vols. H. Böhlau, 1883–
WBC	Word Biblical Commentary
WC	Westminster Commentaries
WCC	World Council of Churches
WMANT	Wissenschaftliche Monographien zum Alten und Neuen Testament
WTJ	*Westminster Theological Journal*
WUNT	Wissenschaftliche Untersuchungen zum Neuen Testament
YNER	Yale Near Eastern Researches
ZAW	*Zeitschrift für die alttestamentliche Wissenschaft*
ZNW	*Zeitschrift für die neutestamentliche Wissenschaft und die Kunde der älteren Kirche*
ZPE	*Zeitschrift für Papyrologie und Epigraphik*
ZTK	*Zeitschrift für Theologie und Kirche*

INTRODUCTION

What Is Theological Interpretation of the Bible?

Kevin J. Vanhoozer, General Editor

Of the making of dictionaries there would seem to be no end. What, then, could possibly justify adding one more item to an already well-stocked inventory? Neither the editors nor the contributors are under the illusion that a new reference work will change the world. Nevertheless, we believe that the time is ripe for a resource that combines an interest in the academic study of the Bible with a passionate commitment to making this scholarship of use to the church. *DTIB* aims to provide clarification, analysis, and evaluation of the various approaches to biblical interpretation currently in the marketplace, with a view to assessing their theological significance—in particular, their value for reading Scripture in and for the community of the faithful.

What Theological Interpretation Is *Not*

Initially, it is easier to say what theological interpretation of the Bible is *not* rather than what it is.

Theological interpretation of the Bible is not an imposition of a theological system or confessional grid onto the biblical text. By theological interpretation, we do not intend to urge readers to return to a time when one's interpretation was largely dominated by one's particular confessional theology (e.g., Lutheran, Reformed, Roman Catholic, et al.). While it may be true that exegesis without theological presuppositions is not possible, it is not part of the dictionary's remit to take sides with a specific confessional or denominational tradition. (On the other hand, we do affirm the ecumenical consensus of the church down through the ages and across confessional lines that the Bible should be read as a unity and as narrative testimony to the identities and actions of God and of Jesus Christ.)

Theological interpretation is not simply what dogmatic theologians do when they use the Bible to support their respective doctrinal positions. Although so-called precritical interpretations took biblical authority seriously and sought to read for the church's edification, they may be vulner-able at three points: They may fail to take the text seriously in its historical context. They may fail to integrate the text into the theology of the OT or NT as a whole. They may be insufficiently critical or aware of their own presuppositions and standpoints (Wright).

Theological interpretation of the Bible is not an imposition of a general hermeneutic or theory of interpretation onto the biblical text. Theological interpretation is also not simply a matter of imposing a *general* hermeneutic on the Bible as if the Bible could be read "like any other book." There are properly theological questions, such as the relationship of the OT and NT, that require more than what is typically offered in a general hermeneutic (Watson). Stated more strongly, there are some interpretative questions that require theological, not hermeneutical, answers: "The turn to hermeneutics as a general discipline . . . has not so much offered a resolution of older theological questions, historically considered, as it has changed the subject" (Seitz 42). There is something left for interpreters to do after reading the Bible like any other book. At the same time, we believe that certain biblical and theological themes have implications not only for biblical interpretation, but for general hermeneutics as well.

Theological interpretation of the Bible is not a form of merely historical, literary, or sociological criticism preoccupied with (respectively) the world "behind," "of," or "in front of" the biblical text. Those who seek to renew biblical interpretation will incorporate whatever is true, noble, right, admirable, and useful in the various historical, literary, and sociological approaches used to describe the world "behind" the text (e.g., in the past), the world "of" the text (e.g., its plot and literary form), or the world "in front of" the text (e.g., the way in which readers receive and react to it). Theological interpretation may not be reduced to historical or to literary or to sociopolitical criticism, but it is not less than these either. For God has been active in history, in the composition of the biblical text, and in the formation of a people to reveal and redeem. Yet each of these disciplines, though ancillary to the project of interpreting the church's Scripture, stops short of a properly theological criticism to the extent that it brackets out a consideration of divine action.

Why "Theological" Interpretation of the Bible?

DTIB responds to two crises precipitated by Enlightenment and post-Enlightenment developments in biblical interpretation respectively: to the modern schism between biblical studies and theology, and to the postmodern proliferation of "advocacy" approaches to reading Scripture where each interpretative community does what is right in its own eyes. The primary purpose of this dictionary is to provide biblical interpreters with a tool that would help make sense of the diverse interpretative approaches and evaluate these approaches as to their contribution toward a theological interpretation of the Bible. Our hope is that this work will provide an important new resource for recovering biblical studies as a properly theological discipline.

The "ugly ditch" in modern biblical interpretation: between exegesis and theology. The critical approach to biblical interpretation that has come to dominate the modern study of the Bible, especially in the university but also in seminaries, was developed in order to protect the Bible from what was thought to be its "dogmatic captivity" to confessional and theological traditions. For some two hundred years now, Christian faith has not been thought to be either necessary or relevant in the attempt to discover "what it meant." Theology thus came to be of only marginal importance for biblical studies as practiced in university and divinity school settings. Indeed, modern biblical studies has become a virtual "theology-free zone." Even scholars who identify themselves as Christians have to check their theological convictions at the door when they enter the academy (Fowl xii–xxx).

The divide separating biblical studies and theology was nothing less than Lessing's famous "ugly ditch": the gap between reason and faith, between publicly ascertainable history on the one hand and privately valued belief on the other. The goal of biblical studies for the typical modern scholar was to understand the texts by restoring them to their original historical contexts and by reading them on their own terms, namely, as (human) products of particular times and places, cultures and societies. In this interpretative framework, the Bible tended to be studied as evidence of a historically developing "religion," as evidence of how ancient Israelites—and later, Jesus and his followers—tended to think about God, the world, and themselves. To study "religion," however, is to study human beings and human history—in contrast to "theology" as the study of God and the mighty acts of God.

The problem was not so much with modern biblical scholarship's interest in reconstructing historical contexts and the history of the text's composition. The bigger problem was its tendency to treat the biblical texts as sources for reconstructing human history and religion rather than as texts that testify to God's presence and action in history. To treat the Bible as a source—as evidence for some natural phenomenon "behind" it—is to deflect attention away from what the texts are saying (as testimony) in favor of a hypothetical reconstruction of "what actually happened." History here trumps exegesis.

Interpreted theologically, the ugly ditch may be nothing less than the perceived gap between "nature" and "grace." Reason, together with its many critical children—source, form, tradition, redaction criticism, and so on—is qualified to interpret the Bible as a historical and human text. But to read the Bible as the word of God is to make a leap into the realm of "grace" that either opposes, crowns, or outflanks reason (Wolters).

The "muddy ditch" in postmodern biblical interpretation: between exegesis and ideology. The Bible-theology relation in the late modern or postmodern era is less an ugly ditch, across which it is impossible to leap, than it is a "muddy ditch"—the quagmire of history, language, tradition, and culture—out of which it is impossible ever to extricate oneself. Postmoderns typically deny that we can escape our location in history, culture, class, and gender. Our readings of the biblical text will be shaped, perhaps decisively so, by our particular location and identity. The goal of interpretation is therefore to discover "what it means to my community, to those with my interpretative interest." Postmodern readers come to Scripture with a plurality of interpretative interests, including (perhaps) the theological, though no one interest may claim more authority than another. The postmodern situation of biblical interpretation gives rise to a pluralism of interpretative approaches and hence to a legitimation crisis: Whose interpretation of the Bible counts, and why?

Biblical interpretation in postmodernity means that there are no independent standards or universal criteria for determining which of many rival interpretations is the "right" or "true" one. A host of postmodern thinkers has slain the giant assumption behind much modern biblical scholarship that there can be objective, neutral, and value-free reading of biblical texts. Postmodern thinkers have charged modernity's vaunted historical-critical method with being just one more example of an ideologically motivated approach. The critical approach only pretends to be objective, neutral, and value free. Modern biblical critics are as rooted in the contingencies of history and tradition as everyone else. Indeed, biblical criticism is itself a *confessional* tradition that begins with a faith in reason's unprejudiced ability to discover truth. The question postmoderns raise for historical critics is whether, in exorcising the spirit of faith from biblical studies, they have not inadvertently admitted even more ideological demons into the academic house.

Whereas the temptation of historical criticism is to offer only "thin" descriptions of the world behind the text or of the process of the text's composition, the temptation of ideological criticism is to offer only thinly veiled echoes of one's own voice. To be distracted by what is "behind" or "before" the text, however, is to miss its message; such nontheological biblical criticism is like music criticism by the deaf and art criticism by the blind.

What Is Theological Interpretation of the Bible?

DTIB attempts to provide resources for understanding and engaging the contemporary crises in and around biblical interpretation and for proceeding toward a more constructive engagement with Scripture. Three premises undergird our approach to the theological interpretation of the Bible.

The theological interpretation of the Bible is not the exclusive property of biblical scholars but the joint responsibility of all the theological disciplines and of the whole people of God. It was Gerhard Ebeling who once declared that church history is essentially the history of biblical interpretation. To the extent that this is so, the present crisis in biblical interpretation—the confusion not only over what the Bible means but also over how to read it—is also a crisis for the church. The study of church history can itself be a theological discipline insofar as it helps the present church to learn from previous ways of interpreting Scripture. Indeed, one reason for the increased interest in theological interpretation of the Bible is the recent rehabilitation of the reputation of the church fathers as profound exegetes. Some have even touted "the superiority of pre-critical exegesis" (Steinmetz).

Is biblical studies a theological discipline? By and large, the resounding answer, at least in the setting of the modern university, has been *Nein!* Modern biblical scholars insist that biblical studies must be autonomous in order to be critical (Barr). Yet some degree of involvement with theology seems to be inevitable, for three reasons. First, biblical scholars must have recourse to theology in order to make sense of the text's claims (Jeanrond). Readings that remain on the historical, literary, or sociological levels cannot ultimately do justice to the subject matter of the texts. Second, biblical studies needs theology (especially the latter's analysis of contemporary culture) in order to be aware of the aims, intentions, and presuppositions that readers invariably bring to the biblical text (Wright). Third, biblical studies needs theology in order to provide a sufficient reason for the academy's continued engagement with the biblical text. Only the assumption that these texts say something of unique importance can ultimately justify the depth of the exegete's engagement (Levenson).

A word about biblical theology is in order, for on the surface this discipline seems a likely candidate to mediate the divide between biblical studies and theology. However, some (e.g., Barr; Fowl) see biblical theology as one more symptom of modern biblical scholarship's assumption that it is possible neutrally and objectively to describe the religious beliefs of the biblical writers. The results of this study—"what it meant" to *them*, back then—are of more antiquarian than ecclesial interest and are offered to the academy, not the church. Yet others (e.g., Watson; Rosner) view biblical theology as an activity that is practically identical with the theological interpretation of the Bible in its concern for hearing the word of God in the church today.

If exegesis without presuppositions is impossible, and if some of these presuppositions concern the nature and activity of God, then it would appear to go without saying that biblical interpretation is always/already theological. One's view of God, for instance, will influence which biblical statements about God one considers literal and which statements one takes as figurative. The inevitability of employing theological categories, however, does not automatically license a wholesale appropriation of any one theological system. Nevertheless, readers with a theological interest, whether in the academy or the church, will at least seek to go further than describing what *others* have said or thought about God. Theological interpreters want to know, on the basis of Scripture and in light of contemporary concerns, what *we* should say and think about God.

Finally, practical theology takes part in biblical interpretation when it inquires into how the people of God should respond to the biblical texts. The way in which the church witnesses, through its language and life, is perhaps the most important form of theological interpretation of the Bible.

The theological interpretation of the Bible is characterized by a governing interest in God, the word and works of God, and by a governing intention to engage in what we might call "theological criticism." Can theological interpretation be "critical," and if so, in what sense? Historical and literary criticism we know, but with regard to theological criticism, we may be tempted to ask, "Who are you?"

A theological interpretation of the Bible is more likely to be critical of readers than of biblical authors or biblical texts. It is not that text criticism and other forms of criticism have no role; it is rather a matter of the ultimate aim of reading. Those who seek to interpret Scripture theologically want to hear the word of God in Scripture and hence to be transformed by the renewing of their minds (Rom. 12:2). In this respect, it is important to note that God must not be an "afterthought" in biblical interpretation. God is not simply a function of a certain community's interpretative interest; instead, God is prior to both the community and the biblical texts themselves. A properly theological criticism will therefore seek to do justice to the priority of God. One way to do so is to guard against idols: images of God manufactured by the interpretative communities.

The dictionary editors believe that the principal interest of the Bible's authors, of the text itself, and of the original community of readers was theological: reading the Scriptures therefore meant coming to hear God's word and to know God better. *DTIB* therefore aims not to impose yet another agenda or ideology onto the Bible, but rather to recover the Bible's original governing interest. On this view, biblical interpretation takes the form of a *confession* or acknowledgment

of the work and word of God in and through Scripture.

One should not abandon scholarly tools and approaches in order to interpret the Bible theologically. On the contrary, modern and postmodern tools and methods may be usefully employed in theological interpretation to the extent that they are oriented to illumining the text rather than something that lay "behind" it (e.g., what actually happened) or "before" it (e.g., the ideological concerns of an interpretative community). At the same time, a theological vantage point calls into question the autonomy of the realm of "nature," and the autonomy of so-called critical approaches to reading the Bible, in the first place. Neither "nature" nor "knowledge" is ever religiously neutral; from the standpoint of Christian doctrine, "nature" is a divine creation, and "knowledge" is inseparable from some kind of faith. The challenge, therefore, is to employ critical methods, but not uncritically. Critical tools have a ministerial, not magisterial, function in biblical interpretation. The aim of a properly "confessional criticism" (Wolters) is to hear the word of God; a theological criticism is therefore governed by the conviction that God speaks in and through the biblical texts.

The strongest claim to be made for theological interpretation is that only such reading ultimately does justice to the subject matter of the text itself. Because biblical texts are ultimately concerned with the reality of God, readers must have a similar theological interest (Jeanrond). Theological *text* genres (e.g., Gospels, prophecies, apocalyptic, etc.) call for theological *reading* genres, for styles of reading that proceed from faith and yet seek theological understanding. To read the biblical texts theologically is to read the texts as they wish to be read, and as they should be read in order to do them justice.

In sum, DTIB *provides a Christian theological evaluation of the contemporary issues and approaches pertaining to biblical interpretation with a view to assessing how they enable the church better to hear what God is saying to church and world today.* DTIB thus promises to be a key resource for those involved in the contemporary renaissance of what has come to be known as the "theological interpretation of Scripture."

The theological interpretation of the Bible names a broad ecclesial concern that embraces a number of academic approaches. At present, no one model of theological interpretation of the Bible holds sway in the church. The editors of *DTIB* recognize that there is more than one way of pursuing an interest in theological criticism. Because we are only in the initial stages of recovering a distinctly theological interpretation of Scripture, it would be unwise to preempt discussion of how best to read the Bible in the church. In choosing the various contributors, the editors were careful to invite representatives of different theological backgrounds, denominations, and interpretative approaches. Nevertheless, it is possible to discern at least three distinct emphases, more complementary than contradictory, that help us begin to distinguish types of theological interpretation.

Some interpreters have an interest in divine authorship, in the God-world relation "behind" the text as it were. This first type recognizes that our doctrine of God affects the way we interpret the Scriptures, while simultaneously acknowledging that our interpretation of Scripture affects our doctrine of God. Indeed, this two-sided problematic has been designated a matter of "first theology" (Vanhoozer). The focus here is less on establishing "what actually happened" than on reading the Bible in terms of divine authorship or as divinely appropriated human discourse (Wolterstorff). Interpreting Scripture as divine discourse opens up interesting possibilities for discerning the unity among the diversity of biblical books and for relating the two Testaments. Theological assumptions about God's involvement with the production of Scripture play an important role in how interpreters take or construe the text and in how they deal with thematic developments as well as apparent historical inconsistencies.

A second group of theological interpreters focuses on the final form of the text rather than on questions of human or divine authorship. For these interpreters, it is the text as a finished literary work or narrative that serves as the prime theological witness. One discovers who God is by indwelling the symbolic world of the Bible. Proponents of this second approach seek to interpret the Bible on its own terms, whether these terms be literary (e.g., narrative) or properly religious (e.g., canon). Theology is a matter of "intratextual" reading (Lindbeck) that patiently unfolds the world of the text in order to learn what God was doing in Israel and in Jesus Christ. The God-world relation as depicted in the text thus becomes the framework for understanding today's world too.

Still other interpreters of Scripture identify the theologically significant moment with the reading and reception of the Bible in the believing community today. The divine action that counts for these interpreters is the work of the Holy Spirit, which they locate as much in the present as, if not more than, in the past. What makes biblical interpretation theological is a function of the aims and interests of the community of readers for which the Bible is "Scripture" (Fowl). The focus here is on the world of the Christian community and its members, who seek to live before God and to worship faithfully. The theological interpretation of Scripture is a distinct practice *of the church*, and hence it is regulated by the goods at which that practice aims. The primary concern with the *outcome* of biblical interpretation affords an interesting vantage point from which to assess the relative contribution of various types of biblical criticism and interpretative approaches.

The Format of *DTIB*

DTIB is intended as a resource for all readers interested in the theological interpretation of Scripture, not merely for those who advocate a particular approach. One purpose of the dictionary is to heal the debilitating breach that all too often prevents biblical scholars and theologians from talking to each other, or even from using the same reference books. If the dictionary accomplishes the purpose for which it was commissioned, it should appeal to biblical scholars, theologians, and pastors alike. Indeed, it should become an indispensable resource for any serious student of the Bible who also regards it as Scripture—a word from God about God. And this leads to the second purpose: to provide a resource for scholars in other disciplines to employ as they seek to promote biblical wisdom in and for their own disciplinary domains. The theological interpretation of Scripture is as important for scientists and sociologists as it is for exegetes and theologians proper—for all of us need a biblically and theologically informed framework for understanding God, the world, and ourselves.

Articles in the dictionary are arranged alphabetically from A to Z. Many headings are cross-referenced to other topics. Some readers may be interested to know how the editors formulated the list of topics. *DTIB* contains four basic types of articles.

Texts. Articles under this heading will focus on the various books of the Bible as well as certain textual features (e.g., canon) that have theological significance. Articles on books of the Bible focus on the message of the text rather than the process of its composition. They also pay special attention to issues of theological significance that have arisen in the history of interpretation and highlight special problems and/or contributions that particular books of the Bible make with regard to doctrine and theology.

Hermeneutics. Some articles under this heading will treat issues pertaining to the theory of interpretation; other articles will examine the theories themselves. Articles in this category will also evaluate the suitability of general interpretative approaches for a theological interpretation of the Bible. Articles in this section include philosophical and literary approaches or concepts that have made an impact on biblical studies (e.g., deconstruction, genre).

Interpreters and Interpretative Communities. Articles under this rubric will focus on the persons or communities doing the interpreting (e.g., Barth; African biblical interpretation). This category includes topics relating to the interests, presuppositions, ideologies, and traditions of interpretative communities as well. Several articles will focus on certain qualities of the reader that contribute to "theological interpretation of Scripture" (e.g., virtue).

Doctrines and Themes. Finally, one group of articles treats explicitly theological concerns, especially as these can and have been brought to bear on the practice of biblical exegesis (e.g., covenant) and vice versa. These articles move in both directions: doctrinal themes arise out of reflection on biblical texts yet these doctrines in turn afford new lenses through which to interpret the text (McGrath). As we have already argued, assumptions about God have an important bearing on our biblical interpretation. Yet other doctrines too are particularly relevant to how one conceives the task of biblical interpretation. What, for instance, are the effects of sin on biblical interpretation? What is the role of the Holy Spirit in biblical interpretation? More importantly, how does our Christology affect our reading of Scripture (and vice versa)? Questions such as these indicate how the worldview implied in Scripture in turn affects how we think about, and engage in, biblical interpretation.

Conclusion: Reading to Know God

Of the making of dictionaries there is no end. Quite so! Yet the "end" of *DTIB*, its most important raison d'être, is to help promote the knowledge of God, the good, and the gospel via the practice of biblical interpretation. The ultimate justification for *DTIB* is its utility in helping to promote the knowledge of what God has done in Israel and in Jesus Christ for the good of the world.

The principal thrust of theological interpretation is to direct the interpreter's attention to the subject matter of Scripture—God, the acts of God in history, the gospel—rather than to a particular theological tradition or, for that matter, to some other topic (e.g., the history of the text's composition, the secular history "behind" the text, the structure of the text, etc.). The dictionary will explore all these other elements in interpretation with a view to assessing their contribution to helping the reader grow in the knowledge of God.

Theological interpretation of the Bible, we suggest, is biblical interpretation oriented to the knowledge of God. For much of their history, biblical studies, theology, and spirituality were all aspects of a single enterprise, that of knowing God (McIntosh). Knowing God is more than a merely academic exercise. On the contrary, knowing God, like theological interpretation of the Bible itself, is at once an intellectual, imaginative, and spiritual exercise. To know God as the author and subject of Scripture requires more than intellectual acknowledgment. To know God is to love and obey him, for the knowledge of God is both restorative and transformative.

Theological interpretation of the Bible achieves its end when readers enter into the world of the biblical texts with faith, hope, and love. When we make God's thoughts become our thoughts and God's word become our word, we begin to participate in the world of the text, in the grand drama of divine redemption. This is perhaps the ultimate aim of theological interpretation of the Bible: to know the triune God by participating in the triune life, in the triune mission to creation.

No one denomination, school of interpretation, or hermeneutical approach has a monopoly on reading the Bible for the word of God. Insights from the whole body of Christ—a body animated and guided by the Spirit of Christ—are needed if Christians are to display the mind of Jesus Christ.

In sum, the aim of this dictionary is to provide the resources necessary to respond to what for Johann Albrecht Bengel (1687–1752) was the biblical interpreter's prime directive: "Apply yourself wholly to the text; apply the text wholly to yourself." Interpreting Scripture theologically is the way to read the Bible "for a blessing" (Kierkegaard), for the sake of human flourishing, for the individual and social "good." Dictionaries are not schools of sanctification, of course; yet the ultimate aim of the present work is to commend ways of reading Scripture that lead to the blessing of knowing God and of being formed unto godliness.

Bibliography

Barr, J. *The Bible in the Modern World*. SCM, 1973; Fowl, S., ed. *The Theological Interpretation of Scripture*. Blackwell, 1997; Jeanrond, W. *Text and Interpretation as Categories of Theological Thinking*. Crossroad, 1988; Levenson, J. *The Hebrew Bible, the Old Testament, and Historical Criticism*. Westminster John Knox, 1993; Lindbeck, G. "Postcritical Canonical Interpretation: Three Modes of Retrieval." Pages 26–51 in *Theological Exegesis*, ed. C. Seitz and K. Greene-McCreight. Eerdmans, 1999; McGrath, A. *The Genesis of Doctrine*. Eerdmans, 1990; McIntosh, M. *Mystical Theology*. Blackwell, 2000; Rosner, B. "Biblical Theology." Pages 3–11 in *New Dictionary of Biblical Theology*, ed. T. D. Alexander and B. Rosner. InterVarsity, 2000; Seitz, C. "The Theological Crisis of Serious Biblical Interpretation." Pages 40–65 in *Renewing Biblical Interpretation*, ed. C. Bartholomew et al. SHS. Zondervan/Paternoster, 2000; Steinmetz, D. "The Superiority of Pre-Critical Exegesis." Pages 26–38 in *The Theological Interpretation of Scripture*, ed. S. Fowl. Blackwell, 1997; Vanhoozer, K. *First Theology*. InterVarsity, 2002; Watson, F. *Text, Church, and World*. T&T Clark, 1994; Wolters, A. "Confessional Criticism and the Night Visions of Zechariah." Pages 90–117 in *Renewing Biblical Interpretation*, ed. C. Bartholomew et al. SHS. Zondervan/Paternoster, 2000; Wolterstorff, N. *Divine Discourse*. Cambridge University Press, 1995; Wright, N. T. *The New Testament and the People of God*. SPCK, 1993.

A

Acts, Book of

History of Interpretation

Acts is arguably one of the most complex books of Scripture for the interpreter because of its multiple dimensions. It is a narrative that locates the growth of the early Christian movement in particular geographical and historical settings. As Luke's second volume (Acts 1:1), it is unique in the NT in continuing the story of Jesus into the story of the church. But in it Luke also presents a portrait of the church designed to persuade (the purpose enunciated in Luke 1:1–4 covers both volumes), so students of Acts need to ask what Luke seeks to persuade his readers about. Hence, for a book so full of references to God and the Spirit, that necessarily involves asking about the book's theology. Because of its multiple layers, Acts has been a laboratory for most types of critical study, although many are theologically disappointing.

The earliest full commentary on Acts is that of John Chrysostom, a series of sermons displaying a strong concern to relate Acts to Christian life and faith in his day—at times to the exclusion of the historical focus of twentieth-century scholarship. Similar concerns can be seen in the sixteenth-century commentaries of Luther and Calvin, who regard Acts as speaking to the issues of their day.

However, it took the nineteenth-century missionary movement for Acts to become seen as a resource for the church's *mission* in the contemporary world. Most notably, Roland Allen, a High Church Anglican, challenged the burgeoning missionary societies of the early twentieth century to adopt a strategy more like that portrayed of Paul in Acts, developing indigenous leadership for nascent churches and handing responsibility over to local leaders. It was only in the later twentieth century—with honorable exceptions—that Allen's plea began to be heard.

Mainstream academic study of Acts, meanwhile, was strongly focused on historical criticism. Three German scholars are pivotal: Dibe-lius, Conzelmann, and Haenchen. Their studies focus on Luke's theology, in the sense that they believe that Luke put his own stamp on his material, in both his selection and shaping of the stories. They combine studying Acts by using the tools of redaction criticism with a thoroughgoing historical skepticism, assuming that many parts of the story did not take place as Luke described them. In large measure, they do so because they believe that Luke was reinterpreting early Christian history to come to terms with the "delay of the parousia"—the collapse of the expectation that Jesus would return soon.

Conzelmann, in particular, develops a view of Luke-Acts that centers on a threefold division of time into the time before Jesus' coming, the time of his ministry (called "the middle of time," the German title of his seminal work *The Theology of St. Luke*), and the time of the church; he sees this threefold division in Luke 16:16. Conzelmann proposes that Luke replaced the imminent expectation of the earliest generation with a theological interpretation of continuing history, which Conzelmann calls "salvation history" (German: *Heilsgeschichte*), including moving the return of Jesus into the remote future.

The debate over the "delay of the parousia" dominated Lukan scholarship for most of the second half of the twentieth century, with the result that historical questions were foreground in debate and theological questions tended to be sidelined. Thus, O'Neill's *The Theology of Acts* is subtitled *In Its Historical Setting*; it begins with a chapter on the date of Acts, and then reads the book against O'Neill's reconstructed historical setting in the first third of the second century. A shining exception to this trend is Marshall, *Luke*, who argues cogently that salvation is a, if not the, central theme of Luke-Acts.

In the 1980s narrative criticism grew in prominence, applied to Luke-Acts first by Johnson and later by Tannehill. Their work reset the agenda of Acts scholarship and led to more theological readings of Acts. Notably, narrative criticism's emphasis on studying the "final form" of texts, rather than hypothetical sources, means that Acts is seen holistically. Of course, analyzing Luke's presentation in Acts does not compel a scholar to agree with Luke's view (e.g., Tannehill [3] disagrees with what he understands to be Luke's view, that Christians should call Jewish people to become followers of Jesus). But it does produce a "level playing field," where scholars can discuss together what Luke's theology is. Thus, in more recent times there are stimulating and helpful studies of the theology of Acts (not all from a narrative-critical perspective).

The Message of Acts

There are numerous proposals for the theological center of Acts; in particular, "salvation" is widely seen as Luke's major theme across his two volumes (Marshall, *Historian*; Green 19–22). Here is a typical statement: "Salvation is the principal theme of Acts, its narrative centrally concerned with the realization of God's purposes to bring salvation in its fullness to all people" (Green 19). Although salvation is very important, and the book of Acts is the story of salvation spreading "to the ends of the earth" (1:8), a careful reading shows that God is the one who drives the story along and takes the initiatives that lead to the expansion of the believing community. And so we consider the message of Acts from this perspective.

In Acts, God is *purposeful*. Luke presents the church's growth as fulfilling Scripture, with a particular stress on Isaiah and the Psalms (e.g., "fulfillment" language is prominent in the key speech in 13:27, 29, 33–35, 41, citing Psalms, Isaiah, and Habakkuk; see Pao). God is now bringing about these purposes (Peterson; Squires), manages events to his own ends, and directs his servants to be in the right place at the right time to bring others to know God (e.g., 8:26, 29, 39).

Acts portrays God as *a missionary God*, seeking first Jewish people to come to know him through Jesus the Messiah, and then drawing in Gentiles too, carrying out the program of 1:8. In the earlier sections Acts focuses on evangelism among Jews (e.g., 2:5–11; 3:11–26), and throughout the book the mission goes to Jewish people first, whether in synagogue (e.g., 17:1–3; 18:4) or a (Jewish) place of prayer (16:13–16). At the end, Paul is seeking to persuade Jewish people in Rome to become followers of Jesus (28:17–23). This shows that Acts should not be read as the story of God abandoning the Jewish people, but rather as God redefining the nature of his people (Jervell, esp. 18–25, 34–43).

As the book progresses, God pushes the believing community out among the Gentiles. At crucial points, God intervenes to direct the believers. Thus, it is God's initiative that creates and progresses Philip's encounter with the Ethiopian eunuch (8:26, 29)—a man whose castration would not permit him to take a full part in Jewish worship (Deut. 23:1). God engineers Peter's meeting with the Roman centurion Cornelius, sending an angel to Cornelius's house, using a vision to overcome Peter's reluctance to go to the home of a Gentile, and speaking by the Spirit to Peter (10:1–8, 9–16, 17–21). Then God pours the Spirit on the Gentiles, thus overcoming any outstanding hesitancy from both Peter and the Jerusalem believers (10:44–48; 11:15–18). When Barnabas and Saul leave the pioneering Jew-Gentile community in Antioch, it is God who calls them to do this by the Spirit (13:1–3, presumably speaking through a prophet in the gathering). When Paul and his colleagues cannot find the right way to go, God is actively preventing them from going in wrong directions (16:6–8), and God then communicates the right direction by a vision (16:9–10). Again and again Acts highlights that the redefinition of God's people is happening at God's initiative.

God acts and calls people through a number of agents: angels (10:3–6), the Spirit (8:29), people (Peter, Stephen, Philip, and Paul are particularly prominent), and his word, which can be almost personified (over fifty times Acts uses "the word," frequently qualified by "of the Lord/God," esp. in 6:7; 8:14; 11:1; 12:24; 13:49; 19:10, 20).

In all of this activity God is a *saving God* (Green 19–22; Marshall, *Historian*), a wide-ranging category that includes physical healing (3:1–10 with 4:9; 14:9), reconciliation with God (2:21, 40, 47), forgiveness (5:31), and deliverance from a storm (27:20, 31). Throughout, God is the one who accomplishes these things, through Jesus (2:22; 10:38; 15:11; 16:31), who is the Savior (5:31; 13:23). Humans receive salvation by responding to the message in believing trust in Jesus (2:44; 3:16; 14:9; 16:31–32, 34) expressed in repentance and water baptism (2:38; 16:33; 22:16), resulting in becoming part of the believing community (2:39–42). Acts stresses the believers' unity (e.g., the use of *homothymadon*, "with one accord," in 1:14; 2:46; 4:24; 5:12; 15:25).

The believing community is presented warts and all, to the extent that believers can be a barrier, or at least resistant, to the new moves God is making. Thus, the Jerusalem believers criticize Peter for visiting Cornelius (11:2) and are persuaded otherwise only because they see that God is acting (11:18). The argument does not go away, for more Judean believers argue that circumcision and torah-observance are necessary for salvation (15:1, 5). When this question is debated, there is repeated emphasis on what *God* is doing, to make clear that this is no human project (15:7–11, 12, 14–19).

So where does *Jesus* fit into this development? While he is not entirely absent from the narrative (e.g., 9:34), in Acts we generally hear *about* Jesus rather than encounter him acting personally. Jesus is the center of the apostolic preaching, especially his resurrection (2:24, 32; 3:15; 4:10; 5:30; 10:40–41; 13:30, 34, 37; 17:3, 31), which is stressed rather more than his death. Because of his resurrection and exaltation, Jesus is able to pour out the Spirit (2:32–33). Indeed, his resurrection shows that Jesus is truly Israel's Messiah and Lord (2:36), the fulfiller of Israel's hopes and God's promises (13:32–33), and it is on the basis of his resurrection that people are summoned to repentance and faith (2:38; 17:30–31).

The question of responsibility for the death of Jesus in Acts is strongly debated, particularly because of Sanders's claim that Luke holds the Jews responsible as a race. Though there are passages in which the apostles hold "you" responsible for Jesus' crucifixion, albeit in ignorance (e.g., 2:23, 36; 3:13–15, 17; 4:10), these passages are always found in and around Jerusalem locations. By contrast, when the evangelists speak to Jews from outside Jerusalem, it is "they" (the Jerusalemite Jews and their leaders) who are responsible for the death of Jesus (10:39; 13:27–29). Luke's view becomes clear in 4:27, where a combination of Herod, the Gentiles, and the Jewish people of the city are responsible for the death of Jesus. Thus Luke hints not only that God's salvation reaches to the whole world, but also that the whole world needs God to save them (on this issue, see Weatherly, esp. ch. 2).

In Acts, God is encountered personally most frequently by *the Holy Spirit*—when people turn to God, they receive the Spirit (2:38, a programmatic verse whose emphasis recurs in 9:17; 10:43–44; 11:15–17; 15:8; 19:1–7). Considerable debate exists over the nature of the Spirit's ministry in Acts, especially whether the Spirit exclusively brings empowerment for mission. Menzies argues that a soteriological ministry of the Spirit is a Pauline emphasis not found in Luke-Acts. Others assert that the Spirit also brings people into the experience of salvation and transforms them ethically (Dunn; Turner, *Power*—both agreeing with Menzies that the empowerment for witness theme

is the major emphasis of Luke's pneumatology, but denying that it is exclusively so). That the Spirit's work likely includes more than witness is shown by, for example, the lack of any emphasis on witness among the Samaritan converts after they receive the Spirit (8:14–24)—indeed, Peter and John are the ones who preach in the other Samaritan villages (8:25).

A second important issue is whether the Spirit comes "once and for all" to believers at conversion or whether there is a subsequent "gateway" experience (frequently called "baptism in the Holy Spirit" by today's writers, although this is not a phrase found in the NT; on the wider issue, see the helpful compact discussion in Turner, *Baptism*). Pentecostal scholars appeal to accounts such as the delay in the Samaritan believers receiving the Spirit (8:14–17; Menzies 204–13), or the Ephesian "disciples" who had not heard of the Spirit (19:2; Menzies 218–25). However, others note the uniqueness of the Samaritan situation, where the gospel was reaching new territory (Turner, *Power*, 360–75), and the fact that Paul baptizes the Ephesian dozen in water in the name of Jesus (19:5), suggesting that previously they were not Christians, but disciples of John the Baptizer (19:3–4; Turner, *Power*, 388–97).

Acts in the Biblical Canon

Acts is properly to be read as the continuation of Luke's Gospel, and many seeds planted in the Gospel come to fruition in Acts. Thus, the hints of Gentile inclusion found in the infancy narratives (e.g., Luke 2:32) become a major theme in Acts. The new exodus motifs found in Luke, notably the use of Isa. 40–55 (e.g., Luke 3:4–6; see Pao, esp. ch. 2; Turner, *Power*, 244–50), are fully developed in the renewal and restoration of Israel in Acts (Pao, ch. 4), which now becomes a worldwide, ethnically inclusive community (note the echo of Isa. 49:6 in the key verses Acts 1:8; 13:47). The Lukan emphasis on the Spirit as the power of Jesus' ministry (Luke 1:35; 3:16, 21–22; 4:1 [twice], 14, 18; 10:21; 11:13) leads to Jesus promising the Spirit's power for the apostles' ministry (Luke 12:12; 24:49; Acts 1:5), and to the Spirit's coming to equip the believers for mission and ministry (Acts 2:1–4, 16–21, 38; etc.). To read Acts apart from Luke is to impoverish and badly skew one's reading of Acts (see Walton; Wenham and Walton, chs. 11, 13).

Reading Luke and Acts together, on the other hand, can explain some puzzles. Such an approach is suggestive for Luke's apparently diminished emphasis on the death of Jesus in Acts, for Luke has told this story clearly in his Gospel and, while writing Acts, can count it as read and known. The clear statement of Acts 20:28, seeing the blood of Jesus as "obtaining" his people, is the tip of a large iceberg of understanding of Jesus' crucifixion found in the Gospel, notably in Luke 23 (Wenham and Walton 235).

As Wall (26–32) highlights, the canonical location of Acts, sandwiched between the fourfold Gospel and the Epistles, also suggests a double relationship with the four Gospels on the one hand, and the Epistles, especially the Pauline Epistles, on the other. This location highlights the uniqueness of Acts within the canon, as telling the story of the earliest believers as a continuation of the story of Jesus, and as a preparation for reading the Epistles. Without Acts, the canon would provide a diminished understanding of both the divine power behind mission and the divine passion for mission, which together drove the growth of the earliest communities. Without Acts, we would lack models of how mission works out in different situations, for we would be left trying to reconstruct events from the even more fragmentary accounts in the Epistles. Without Acts, we would find it much harder to envisage a framework for the writing and events of the Pauline Epistles (although it must be said that it is hardly easy *with* Acts!). Equally, Acts provides insight into the varieties within earliest Christianity, such as in the Jerusalem meeting (15:6–29), which shows up tensions between believers who emphasize their Jewishness and those wanting to be open to Gentiles—tensions that can also be seen in the Pauline corpus (e.g., Galatians, Romans, Ephesians) and elsewhere (e.g., the Jewishness of James or Hebrews), but whose landscape would be harder to reconstruct without Acts.

Theological Significance of Acts

A major issue in interpreting Acts is the extent to which it is prescriptive, saying how the church is always meant to be, or descriptive, telling us how the church was at this particular period (Marshall, *Acts*, 101–5). One helpful tool in deciding case by case about this issue is to consider how far Luke presents clear patterns of events. For example, 2:38–42 presents a fivefold pattern of what it means to become a Christian, involving repentance from sin, water baptism, receiving forgiveness and the gift of the Spirit, and joining the renewed people of God. This pattern keeps reappearing in Acts, not always in the same sequence as in 2:38–42, but with the same elements present (e.g., 8:12–17; 10:44–48;

19:1–20). Using this "patterning" tool, we may identify three themes that address the theology and practice of today's churches.

First, Acts compels us to ask, and keep asking, what *God* is doing in our churches and our lives. At times the voice of God prevents believers from going the wrong way (e.g., 16:6–8), and at other times the divine call seems surprising (e.g., 8:26, taking Philip away from a growing new congregation in Samaria and to the desert). As we have seen, at times the church's instincts are misguided (e.g., 11:2; 15:1, 5).

The radical theocentricity of Acts highlights the constant temptation to anthropocentricity today, whether seen in advertising that panders to human self-centeredness or "tribalism" that will not act outside the parameters of our community. In practice, churches—and theologians—find it all too easy to believe that they need not pay attention to asking what God is doing, and therefore fall into the dangers of making God in their own image and limiting what they consider he can do to the parameters of their experience. Acts calls us to real and continuing openness to God and his agenda, and highlights the prayerfulness of the believing community, for that is how their dependence on God is expressed and experienced (e.g., 1:14, 24; 2:42; 3:1; 6:4; 9:40; 10:9; 12:5; 13:1–3; 14:23; 16:25; 20:36; 21:5; 28:8).

Second, Acts encourages an expectation that God will act and speak in order to bring people to himself. The emphasis on the expansion of the believing community "to the ends of the earth" (1:8) shows this theme on a large scale, and numerous individual incidents show God reaching out to people. Among Jews, most notably God touches the life of Saul, the persecutor of the church, and turns him round to become a passionate advocate of the faith that he attacked (9:1–22). Among Gentiles, God reaches beyond the bounds of the believing community by using angels (10:1–6) or guiding the missionaries into unexpected places (16:6–10)—and in the case of the journey to Philippi, they find themselves in prison when they follow this clear divine leading (16:19–24), a sign that to follow the divine voice and participate in the divine mission is far from an easy path. In this expansion God uses a variety of agents—most prominently the Spirit, as we noted above, but also angelic and human agents.

Western churches and theological thinkers today can easily have a low expectation that God actively seeks to draw people to himself, whereas such expectation can be stronger and fuller in parts of our world where the church is growing. Acts offers a challenge and encouragement that God truly is active in his world and has not abandoned it to its own devices in deistic fashion. Acts thus invites the construction of a *theo*-logy that sees God as its subject and not merely its passive object. Recent developments in pneumatological thought suggest that this emphasis is in the process of being recognized.

Third, the evangelistic speeches in Acts focus on the resurrection of Jesus, suggesting a corrective to today's evangelistic message and preaching. The speeches highlight the fact and implications of the resurrection of Jesus. A case that he has been raised from the dead is rarely offered. Most often, the evangelists are interested in communicating that it is God who has raised Jesus—the verbs used, *egeirō* and *anistēmi*, are found with God as their subject (e.g., 2:24; 17:31)—and that God's action in raising Jesus confirms Jesus' identity as Israel's Messiah and the world's Lord and judge (e.g., 2:36; 17:31). It is because of who Jesus is now known to be, postresurrection, that people are summoned to repent and turn to God (e.g., 2:38; 17:30).

This emphasis contrasts with the near-exclusive emphasis found in much of today's evangelistic preaching and christological thinking on the death of Jesus. While the cross is by no means unimportant to the evangelists of Acts, it is not the sole focus of their preaching and reflection in a way that 1 Cor. 1:23–24; 2:2 might suggest, if read in isolation from the rest of that letter and the NT. Resurrection from the dead is by no means easy to proclaim to skeptical, scientifically trained, Western ears, but today's Westerners, like their contemporaries in the east and south, are increasingly open to "spiritual" dimensions to reality, and Acts encourages today's evangelists to give greater attention to the resurrection of Jesus in their proclamation. It also invites christological reflection that sees the exaltation of Jesus, in his resurrection and ascension, as a key factor in understanding who he truly is, both then and now.

Bibliography

Allen, R. *Missionary Methods*. Robert Scott, 1912; Conzelmann, H. *The Theology of St. Luke*. Faber & Faber, 1960; Dibelius, M. *Studies in the Acts of the Apostles*. SCM, 1956; Dunn, J. D. G. *Baptism in the Holy Spirit*. SCM/Westminster, 1970; Green, J. "Acts of the Apostles." Pages 7–24 in *Dictionary of the Later New Testament and Its Developments*, ed. R. P. Martin and P. Davids. InterVarsity, 1997; Haenchen, E. *The Acts of the Apostles*, trans. R. M. Wilson. Blackwell, 1971; Jervell, J. *The Theology of the Acts of the Apostles*. Cambridge University Press, 1996; Johnson, L. T. *The Literary Function of Possessions in Luke-Acts*. SBLDS 39. Scholars Press, 1977; Marshall, I. H. *The Acts of the Apostles*. NTG. JSOT, 1992; idem. *Luke*. Paternoster, 1970; Menzies, R. *Empowered for Witness*. JPTSup 6. Sheffield Academic Press, 1994; O'Neill, J. C. *The Theology of Acts in Its Historical Setting*. SPCK, 1961; Pao, D. *Acts and the Isaianic New Exodus*. Baker, 2002; Peterson, D. "The Motif of Fulfilment and the Purpose of Luke-Acts." Pages 83–104 in *The Book of Acts in Its Ancient Literary Setting*, ed. B. Winter and A. Clarke. A1CS 1. Paternoster/Eerdmans, 1993; Sanders, J. T. *The Jews in Luke-Acts*. SCM, 1987; Squires, J. T. "The Plan of God in the Acts of the Apostles." Pages 19–39 in *Witness to the Gospel*, ed. I. H. Marshall and D. Peterson. Eerdmans, 1998; Tannehill, R. *The Narrative Unity of Luke-Acts*. Vol. 2 of *Foundations and Facets*. Fortress, 1990; Turner, M. *Baptism in the Holy Spirit*. Grove, 2000; idem. *Power from on High*. JPTSup 9. Sheffield Academic Press, 1996; Wall, R. "The Acts of the Apostles." NIB 10:1–368; Walton, S. "Where Does the Beginning of Acts End?" Pages 448–67 in *The Unity of Luke-Acts*, ed. J. Verheyden. BETL 142. Peeters, 1999; Weatherly, J. *Jewish Responsibility for the Death of Jesus in Luke-Acts*. JSNTSup 106. Sheffield Academic Press, 1994; Wenham, D., and S. Walton. *A Guide to the Gospels and Acts*. Vol. 1 of *Exploring the New Testament*. SPCK/InterVarsity, 2001.

Steve Walton

Aesthetics *See* Art, the Bible and; Formalism; Literary Criticism; Music, the Bible and; Western Literature, the Bible and

African Biblical Interpretation

For most of the first two millennia of Christian history, the geographical center of Christianity has been the northern hemisphere. During this century a radical shift has been taking place. Most of the Western world is now secularized, with church membership shrinking drastically and Christian influence on the wane. The situation in the southern hemisphere, and particularly in Africa, is quite different. The churches have grown at an amazing rate such that there are now almost a half a billion Christians on the continent. As Christians in Africa have taken responsibility for the many dimensions of their common life, there has emerged a vibrant biblical scholarship, most of which is little known outside of Africa.

Patristic Exegesis

Biblical scholarship is not a new thing on the African continent. Some of the most important biblical exegetes from the patristic period lived and worked on African soil. "African fathers" like Origen and Augustine are considered an important memory for modern African Christians to reclaim. Although the ancient North African and

Nubian churches are now gone, the ancient Coptic and Ethiopian Orthodox Churches continue to thrive in difficult circumstances. More work is needed to help us to understand this tradition of exegesis.

Missionary Exegesis

In the modern period Western missionaries brought Christianity to Africa. This missionary heritage is an ambiguous reality for modern Africans. Although grateful for those who sacrificed much to carry the gospel message, most Africans are also suspicious of the Western cultural baggage, which informed missionary readings of Scripture. One cannot spend many days in Africa before one hears this story: "When the white men came, they told us that our way of praying was wrong—one should not pray with one's eyes open but with one's eyes closed. So we closed our eyes to pray. When we opened our eyes, we had the Bible but the white man had the land." The missionary who came with the Bible was also the interpreter of the Bible. Many African clergy and biblical scholars today (at least from the so-called "mainline" or "mission-founded" churches) were trained by white teachers who, to one degree or another, have used Western methods of exegesis and engaged the text with Western presuppositions. Many of the Bible versions available in African languages were translated by missionaries with an inadequate grasp of African languages and cultures. Most textbooks in African theological colleges and universities today were written in the West and reflect those needs and interests. Few African interpreters consider this "missionary" exegesis to be adequate.

White South African Exegesis

White South African exegetes have tended to concentrate on text-critical and literary-aesthetic issues. The racist apartheid system, which formed the basis of South African society for much of the twentieth century, was sometimes defended by biblical interpreters (Smit). There is now, however, a growing community of biblical scholars in the white community in South Africa who are supportive of exegesis that is engaged in the struggle for what Gerald West calls "survival, liberation and life" (West, *Academy*, 114).

Liberation Exegesis in South Africa

Sharing much in common with American black theology and Latin American liberation theology, liberation exegesis in South Africa has found its primary motivation in employing the Bible as a liberating tool. Black biblical scholars living under apartheid could not ignore the fact that they lived within an oppressive system. Some (Boesak; Tutu) have focused on the text itself, finding liberative themes such as the story of the exodus and Jesus' concern for the poor. Others (Mosala) have looked behind the text for the ideology that produced it, claiming that the Bible and its readers need to be liberated from the Bible before it can be a liberative tool (cf. West, *Hermeneutics*).

Biblical Exegesis in Independent Africa

A growing corpus of biblical interpretation is emerging in independent sub-Saharan Africa. Little of this literature is satisfied with the historical-critical paradigm that tries to sever exegesis from the hermeneutical task. While often using Western exegetical tools, African readers always make the attempt to relate the text to their contemporary situation. The context of the reader (the world "in front of" the text) tends to be a higher priority than the context of the text (the world "behind" the text).

Actually, this individualistic way of stating the issue needs correction. No African would consider the individual alone as the interpreter. John Mbiti sums up the worldview of the African with the words "I am, because we are" (Mbiti, *Religions*, 108). The dialogue, therefore, is not so much between *reader* and text as between community and text. The African reader of the text cannot be separated from her or his context in the community.

Biblical interpretation in sub-Saharan Africa is done in the context of mission, culture, suffering, and faith. African Christians are aware of having been "evangelized," of having received the gospel message from the West. This gospel came in a package that included Western church structures (and denominational divisions) and assumptions. In short, even the best missionary endeavors had an imperialistic dimension. It has been a concern of African interpretation to discern the difference between the gospel and Western cultural imposition. To take a notoriously difficult example, when missionaries came to Africa, some condemned polygamy as un-Christian and unbiblical. When the Bible was translated into African languages, it did not escape notice that many of the great heroes of the faith had more than one wife. Examples of this kind can be multiplied. One of the first attempts to deal with the "missionary" context was Mbiti's Cambridge doctoral thesis published as *New Testament Eschatology in an*

African Background. The original title "Christian Eschatology in Relation to Evangelisation of Tribal Africa" reveals how crucial the mission context is for African interpretation (cf. Okure, "Parables").

Closely related is the reality that African interpretation is done within the context of African culture. Exegesis comparing African cultural practices and ideas with similarities found in Scripture makes up the largest part of the growing corpus of published African exegesis (LeMarquand, "Bibliography"). It has long been noted that there are similarities between the biblical world and the African world. African OT scholars in particular have highlighted the continuity, as well as the discontinuity, between the two worlds. On the basis of linguistic and cultural similarities, a few have tried to trace genealogical relationships between the Bible and Africa. Most are content to see analogical relationships between these cultures and to mine the similarities in order to illumine the text or find biblical principles for dealing with analogous issues in the modern African context. Some African scholars argue that finding parallels between biblical and African traditions serves an apologetic purpose: if the biblical world is similar to our African world, then the Bible must be a good thing! Others have a more kerygmatic approach, seeing the purpose of comparison in the heuristic value that the elucidation of similarities has for helping African readers to understand the text: moving from African tradition (the known) to a biblical text (the unknown) enables biblical understanding.

Examples of this comparative approach abound. For example, does the Kikuyu taboo on counting help us to understand the guilt that, according to 2 Sam. 24:1–10, David felt after conducting a census (Githuku), or does the story of the Gerasene demoniac in Mark 5 help African church leaders to deal with problems of spirit-possession in Africa today (Avotri)? A major problem felt by interpreters in the West—the presence in the biblical text of stories of miraculous occurrences—is not considered to be an interpretative problem by most African interpreters. The latter usually assume belief in the unseen world and its effects on the visible world (LeMarquand, "Relevance").

Suffering is pervasive in modern Africa. War, hunger, exploitation, and tyranny cannot be bracketed out of interpretation. In an eloquent plea for a "relevant" exegesis, Nigerian scholar Teresa Okure argues that exegesis without hermeneutics is useless. To urge the exegetical community never to forget that exegesis must always be the servant of the community, she appeals to the Nigerian proverb that says, "The legs of the bird that flies in the air always point to the ground" (Okure, "Parables"). The exegete cannot ignore human need.

In the West, scholarship has been done primarily within the academy. In the interest of "objectivity," critical methods are used to uncover the meaning of the text in its original context. The faith stance of the reader is considered to be irrelevant (or problematic) in the "unbiased" search for truth. In Africa, there is more of an attempt to acknowledge the place of the faith of the biblical scholar. Almost all exegesis in Africa is "confessional" and written for the edification of the believing community. The meetings of the Pan-Africa Association of Catholic Exegetes, for example, open with prayer and include the daily celebration of the Eucharist on their agenda. Papers are discussed not only in the light of critical exegetical methods and relevance to the African situation, but also in the light of the *regula fidei*.

Problems and Emerging Concerns

The most pressing problems for African biblical exegesis are practical. There is rarely enough money for African scholars, seminaries, and universities to buy books. Most scholars are writing in their second or third language. Publishing houses in Africa have a small market for scholarly books. War, political unrest, and lack of clean water play havoc with the running of theological institutions.

On the other hand, biblical studies in Africa is beginning to garner attention, both inside and outside of the continent. The Society of Biblical Literature has encouraged the interaction of scholars from the global community, including Africa. *The African Journal of Biblical Studies* (published in Nigeria), *The Bulletin for Old Testament Studies in Africa* (published in Norway), and a number of helpful monographs and collections of essays by African scholars provide vehicles for disseminating biblical scholarship. The global exegetical community can no longer ignore African scholarship. African contributions provide enriching biblical readings for scholarship and for the body of Christ.

Within the exegetical community in Africa are a number of emerging concerns (Dube): Can the liberationist perspective from South Africa and the more culture-focused questions of the rest of the continent be mutually beneficial? How can the readings of "ordinary" or "popular" readers enrich scholarship? How can scholarship best be a help to the Christian community? Will postcolonial models of interpretation be of benefit?

Beneath these readings from Africa, a unifying theological issue can be discerned. The search for common ground between the Bible and African culture raises the issue of general revelation. In the face of African colonial and missionary history, which often tended to vilify African cultural and religious practices, many contemporary African theologians and Bible scholars are concerned to show that God had not abandoned Africa before the missionaries came. Just as God was at work in the cultures of the Bible, so he was at work in Africa. Some on the more radical side have even suggested that African culture should be considered "the OT" for Africans, God's special revelation for African peoples (see the essays in Mukonyora, Cox, and Verstraelen). Most have not taken this road, however. Several African scholars appeal to the story of Paul's preaching in Athens as a model (Acts 17:16–34). In this text Paul begins his preaching from the culture of Athens, showing how God was close to all people and known to all, at least to some limited degree. Likewise, Africans can be assured that the God they had known and worshiped for millennia was not an evil God, but the same God who has now fully manifested himself in Jesus Christ. The same God who in the past provided rain, food, children, and health in response to the prayers of African peoples has now been fully revealed in the person of Jesus Christ. Certainly there is discontinuity between African religion and the biblical revelation since all cultures (and Africans are quick to point out that this includes Western cultures) participate in the fall. Biblical revelation is unique and necessary but not completely new. God's work in Christ is seen as a completion of God's kindness, which was always known in African societies, in which God did not leave himself without a witness (Acts 14:17).

See also Augustine; Culture and Hermeneutics; Liberation Theologies and Hermeneutics

Bibliography

Avotri, S. "The Vernacularization of Scripture and African Beliefs: The Story of the Gerasene Demoniac among the Ewe of West Africa." Pages 292–310 in *The Bible in Africa*, ed. G. West and M. Dube. Brill, 2000; Boesak, A. "The Relationship between Text and Situation, Reconciliation and Liberation, in Black Theology." *Voices from the Third World* 2, no. 1 (1979): 30–40; Dickson, K. "Continuity and Discontinuity between the Old Testament and African Thought and Life." Pages 95–108 in *African Theology en Route*, ed. K. Appiah-Kubi and S. Torres. Orbis, 1979; Dube, M. *Postcolonial Feminist Interpretation of the Bible*. Chalice, 2000; Githuku, S. "Taboos on Counting." Pages 113–17 in *Interpreting the Old Testament in Africa*, ed. M. Getui, K. Holter, and V. Zinkuratire. Peter Lang, 2001; LeMarquand, G. "A Bibliography of the Bible in Africa." Pages 631–800 in *The Bible in Africa*; idem. "An Issue of Relevance: A Comparative Study of the Story of the Bleeding Woman (Mk 5:25–34; Mt 9:20–22; Lk 8:43–48) in North Atlantic and African Contexts." Th.D. diss., Wycliffe College/University of Toronto, 2002; Mbiti, J. *African Religions and Philosophy*. Heinemann, 1969; idem. *New Testament Eschatology in an African Background*. Oxford University Press, 1971; Mosala, I. *Biblical Hermeneutics and Black Theology in South Africa*. Eerdmans, 1989; Mukonyora, I., J. L. Cox, and F. J. Verstraelen, eds. *"Rewriting" the Bible: The Real Issues*. Mambo, 1993; Okure, T. "'I Will Open My Mouth in Parables' (Matt 13.35): A Case for a Gospel-Based Biblical Hermeneutic." *NTS* 46 (2000): 445–63; idem. *The Johannine Approach to Mission*. Mohr/Siebeck, 1988; Smit, D. "The Ethics of Interpretation—and South Africa." *Scriptura* 33 (1990): 29–43; Tutu, D. "Some African Insights and the Old Testament." *JTSA* 1 (1972): 16–22; West, G. *The Academy of the Poor*. Sheffield Academic Press, 1999; idem. *Biblical Hermeneutics of Liberation*. Cluster, 1991.

Grant LeMarquand

Alexandrian Interpretation   *See* Allegory; Hermeneutics; Jesus Christ, Doctrine of; Literal Sense; Patristic Biblical Interpretation

Allegory

Allegory is primarily a method of reading a text by assuming that its literal sense conceals a hidden meaning, to be deciphered by using a particular hermeneutical key. In a secondary sense, the word "allegory" is also used to refer to a type of literature that is expressly intended to be read in this nonliteral way. John Bunyan's *Pilgrim's Progress* is a well-known example of allegorical literature, but it is doubtful whether any part of the Bible can be regarded as such. The parables of Jesus come closest, but they are not allegories in the true sense. The apostle Paul actually used the word *allegoria*, but arguably this was to describe what would nowadays be called "typology" (Gal. 4:24). The difference between typology and allegory is that the former attaches additional meaning to a text that is accepted as having a valid meaning in the "literal" sense, whereas the latter ignores the literal sense and may deny its usefulness altogether. Paul never questioned the historical accuracy of the Genesis accounts of Hagar and Sarah, even though he regarded them as having an additional, spiritual meaning as well. Other interpreters, however, were often embarrassed by anthropomorphic accounts of God in the Bible, and sought to explain away such language by saying that it is purely symbolic, with no literal meaning at all. It is in this latter sense that the word "allegory" is generally used today.

Allegory began in the Hellenistic world as a means of interpreting the Homeric poems. The obvious immorality of so many of Homer's divine heroes could not be accepted as the basis for instructing children in morality, and so the commentators of Alexandria devised ways of interpreting it figuratively. The fornication of the gods was understood to picture cosmic events that could not easily be described. By the first century BCE it had become a standard hermeneutical tool, and was widely used by Philo of Alexandria (d. 50 CE), a Jew who wanted to demonstrate that the OT was the true source of Greek philosophy. Perhaps the most famous of his allegorical conjectures is the way in which he interpreted the meeting of Abraham with the three men (or angels) at the terebinths of Mamre (Gen. 18). Noting that Abraham addresses them in the singular as "Lord," Philo supposed that this indicates the presence of a triad in God. The Pythagoreans believed that three was the perfect number, and so finding this number in the divine being was part of demonstrating God's perfection.

Philo did not believe that God was three, of course, but later Christian exegetes took up what he said and used it as an indication that God had revealed himself, even in the OT, as a Trinity of persons. Such recycling reveals one of the major motives for allegory among early Christian exegetes, who needed to find a Christian meaning in every OT passage. Interestingly, their main hermeneutical principle was one still regarded by many people today as valid, that the clearer parts of Scripture must be used as the basis for determining the meaning of the harder parts. Allegory was not used to establish Christian doctrine, but merely to discover it in texts that, on the surface, appear to be talking about something else.

The *locus classicus* for Christian allegory was the Song of Solomon, which became and remained a favorite of medieval interpreters. It was universally agreed that the literal sense of the Song could not possibly be its "real" meaning, since God would not have inspired a tale of seduction. Given that assumption, and the belief that the Scriptures speak of Christ, those who interpreted the Song had to find a way of reading it that would reflect the relationship between Christ and his church. Two main strands of allegory sprang up: one stressed the identity of the woman

as the church, and the other said that she stood for the soul of the individual believer. These strands were frequently interwoven, so the text could be applied to either the individual Christian or the body of the church, depending on what seemed most likely in the eyes of the interpreter.

The Song of Solomon rapidly established itself as one of the most popular OT books and inspired many great spiritual classics. Bernard of Clairvaux (d. 1153) preached eighty-six sermons on it, which are still in print and widely read today. In the nineteenth century the missionary Hudson Taylor wrote *Union and Communion*, which remains a staple devotional book among evangelical Christians. So deeply entrenched was the allegorical reading that when it was challenged, George Burrows actually wrote a commentary defending it (1859), which is also still in print! The power of this tradition is perhaps best seen in the popularity of a modern chorus: "He brought me to his banqueting table, and his banner over me is love" (Song 2:4 KJV). Almost everyone automatically interprets this as referring to Christ and the fellowship of his church, even though it apparently has nothing to do with either.

Theologically speaking, allegory relied on the belief that Scripture was an object analogous to the human body. Just as we are composed of flesh, soul, and spirit, so the Bible has a corresponding literal, moral, and spiritual sense. This was the teaching of Origen (ca. 185–254), which became the basis for all future interpretation. Origen believed that it was essential to get the literal sense right, because only it could provide the clues needed to interpret the other senses correctly. When the literal sense was clear, it did not need any elaboration, but when it was not, interpreters had to take recourse to one or both of the other possible meanings. Origen did not limit the use of this technique to obscure passages only, but applied it to any that lacked an immediate pastoral application. For instance, in Origen's view the episode of Jesus cleansing the temple, while it might have been historical, could not be taken literally as an example of appropriate Christian behavior, and so he allegorized it into the purification of the soul from all evil thoughts and desires. Given that the NT teaches that our bodies are temples of the Holy Spirit, this interpretation seemed merely to be using a well-known spiritual principle as a means to interpret an otherwise inapplicable text.

It is often difficult to distinguish the moral from the spiritual sense of interpretation, but broadly speaking, the former deals with our life on earth and the latter with our relationship with God. Jacob's ladder, for example, was to be interpreted in the spiritual sense, because it was the way of ascent to God. Jacob (Israel) failed to climb it because he—the OT people of God—was asleep in God's house (Bethel). In this way, the story came to symbolize both the apostasy of Judaism and the spiritual blessing given to Christians, who are privileged to stand with the angels in the presence of God.

Allegorical interpretation is often fanciful but seldom harmful because it is generally based on theological truths that can be proved from the clearer parts of Scripture. Only at a late stage did it become the basis for certain doctrinal formulations, like those of Roman Catholic Mariology, which Protestants uniformly reject. In the late twentieth century, a new form of "postmodern" allegory made its appearance, based largely on psychological archetypes supposedly present in our subconscious. It differs from classical allegory partly because of its fixation with particular symbols (many of which are assumed to be sexual) but mainly because it is oriented toward a secular, humanist interpretation of reality and eschews the divine dimension of traditional theology. In some respects, and particularly in its interpretation of sexual symbolism, postmodern allegory is more rigid than its classical counterpart, which enables its proponents to claim that it is "scientific," though this has been disputed by its detractors, many of whom are theologians and biblical scholars.

In sum, allegory as a hermeneutical method has generally fallen into disfavor since the eighteenth century, but it can still be found at the popular level, and recent interest in literary criticism has revived interest in it, at least to a limited extent. It is even conceivable that allegory may be a valid way to interpret certain parts of the Bible, though it is most unlikely ever to become a general hermeneutical principle.

See also Medieval Biblical Interpretation; Parables; Patristic Biblical Interpretation; Spiritual Sense; Typology

Bibliography

Daniélou, J. *From Shadows to Reality*. Burns & Oates, 1960; Edwards, M. J. *Origen against Plato*. Ashgate, 2002; Fletcher, A. *Allegory*. Cornell University Press, 1964; Hanson, R. P. C. *Allegory and Event*. 2d ed. Westminster John Knox, 2002; Whitman, J., ed. *Interpretation and Allegory*. Brill, 2000.

Gerald Bray

Allusion   *See* Intertextuality; Relationship between the Testaments

Amos, Book of

The book of Amos is widely regarded as the earliest legacy of the "writing prophets" and as a paradigm of the prophetic genre. Amos's main theological contributions are the uncompromising censure of the social injustice prevalent in Israelite society in the eighth century BCE, together with the concomitant threat of a severe divine punishment.

History of Interpretation

"Precritical" Readings. The members of the Qumran community were particularly interested in passages that illuminated their own beliefs and practices. These include Amos's reference to David's "fallen tent" (9:11), which was reinterpreted in line with their own missionary expectations (4QFlor 1.11–13), and the threat of Israel being exiled beyond Damascus (5:26–27), which was seen to justify the community's own existence "in the land of Damascus" (CD 7.14–21).

In the Talmud, a range of passages from the book of Amos is used for a variety of ceremonial, ethical, paraenetic, and apologetic purposes (see *y. 'Abod. Zar.* 39a, 40 on Amos 4:4; *b. Nid.* 65 on 4:6; *b. Mo'ed Qat.* 25b, 28b on 8:9; and *b. Hul.* 59b–60a on 3:8).

With Origen's commentary (see Eusebius, *Hist. eccl.* 6.36.2) having been lost, Jerome's work of ca. 406 CE is the earliest and most important commentary of the patristic period. Jerome offers primarily historical exegesis, paired with a christological understanding of the prophet's message. Theodore of Mopsuestia and Theodore of Cyrrhus, exponents of the Antioch school, while aware of the text's metaphorical and salvation-historical dimensions, similarly favored literal readings. Even Cyril of Alexandria, who was strongly indebted to Jerome, sought to avoid the excesses of mystical-allegorical interpretation associated with the school of Alexandria (Dassmann 340–44).

In the patristic writings, quotations from Amos were often restricted to the same dozen verses. For instance, 4:13 played an important role in dogmatic discussions about the creatureliness of the Holy Spirit (advocated by the Pneumatomachs), and 8:9 was frequently understood to refer to the darkness that came over the land at Jesus' death. Amos 5:18–20 was interpreted as referring to the horrors of the final judgment, 9:6 and 9:11–12 were understood christologically, and 8:11 was used by preachers to instill in their audiences a hunger and thirst for God's word (Dassmann 344–50).

Amos in Modern Perspectives. Modern research on Amos shows the same trends as the scholarly investigation of the OT prophets generally. From the 1880s to the 1920s, scholars focused on the innovative impetus of the prophet, understood as an "ethical monotheist," whose task it was to announce the divine ethical imperative (Wellhausen; Duhm). This stress often went hand in glove with a search for Amos's ipsissima verba, the very words of the prophetic genius.

From the 1920s onward, form and tradition critics reversed this trend. They focused on the social and institutional settings (such as the Israelite cult or certain wisdom circles) of the speech forms used by Amos and understood the prophet largely as a transmitter of traditional theological convictions (Reventlow).

While these approaches were most concerned with the oral stages of the prophet's words, redaction criticism, which originated in the 1960s, attends to the book's literary prehistory and attempts to trace its stages of growth (Wolff). Contrary to their predecessors, redaction critics affirm the value of redactional contributions, rejecting pejorative labels such as "secondary" or "inauthentic" (Jeremias).

Simultaneously with the redaction-critical quest, other scholars have begun to focus on the text's final form, investigating the structure, poetics, or rhetorical nature of the book (Carroll R., *Contexts*; Möller, *Prophet*). Yet another recent trend is to concentrate on the contribution made by the reader in the generation of meaning.

The Message of Amos

As with every text, our appreciation of Amos's message depends on a variety of hermeneutical decisions. One of these is well illustrated by Brevard Childs's comment, made vis-à-vis redaction criticism's interests in the text's literary prehistory, that historical interpretation of the redactional layers of Amos often runs counter to the perspective demanded by the literature itself (408). Thus, while redaction critics might regard some material as later additions to the prophet's message, the book's canonical form invites a reading that treats the text as what it purports to be: the words of the eighth-century prophet Amos (1:1).

We should also recognize that the book is addressed to subsequent Judean readers, who would have seen Amos's struggle—and ultimate failure—to convince his Israelite audience of the imminent divine punishment in the light of the catastrophic events of 722 BCE. Read from this "past-fulfillment perspective," the book thus becomes a powerful warning, admonishing its readers not to repeat the stubborn attitude of their northern brothers and sisters, lest they too face the divine judgment.

An Outline of Amos's Message. Following the superscription (1:1) and motto (1:2), a series of oracles threatens Israel's neighbors with a divine punishment for their atrocious war crimes (1:3–2:5). Yet, the series eventually culminates in a judgment speech against Israel (2:6–16). Amos thus singles out God's people as the prime target of punishment, which is presented as the divine response to Israel's oppression of the weak and marginalized.

The book then gives the ensuing debate between Amos and his complacent audience (5:14; 6:1–3; 9:10; Möller, *Prophet*), who reject his message of judgment, relying instead on their cherished theological traditions. Amos's reinterpretation and subversion of concepts like the exodus (2:9–10; 3:1–2; 9:7) and the day of Yahweh (5:18–20), his "hymns" extolling God's destructive powers (4:13; 5:8–9; 9:5–6), and the acerbic criticism of Israel's religious activities (4:4–5; 5:21–23)—these are all best understood from the polemical perspective demanded by this dialogical context.

Amos 3–6 contains five judgment speeches (chs. 3 and 4; 5:1–17, 18–27; ch. 6) introduced by "hear this word" or "woe to you who . . ." They reiterate the threat of a divine punishment, arguing that its annunciation was unavoidable (3:3–8). They also corroborate God's verdict (3:9–11; 4:6–12; 5:10–13) and underline the absurdity of the social injustice prevalent in Israelite society (6:12).

The visions in Amos 7:1–8:3—together with the embedded narrative report of Amos's clash with the priest Amaziah, which confirms the hostile attitude of Amos's audience (7:10–17)—underline that the punishment, while not desired by Amos, will not be averted (7:8; 8:2). Another judgment speech (8:4–14), introduced by "Hear this," repeats some of Amos's charges before giving way to various announcements of judgment.

In the final vision (9:1–4), this judgment is depicted as actually occurring, while 9:8–10, in line with the book's implied distinction between culprits and victims, identifies the "sinful kingdom" and "all the sinners among my people" as the prime targets of the divine punishment. An image of future restoration, agricultural abundance, and security in the land concludes the book (9:11–15).

Amos and the Canon

Amos and the Twelve. Recent scholarship has stressed the unity of the Book of the Twelve. On this view, echoes such as that of Joel 3:16a (4:16a MT) in Amos 1:2 are understood as indicating a deliberate linkage and juxtaposition of the two writings. Yet from a canonical perspective Amos's message of judgment might just as fruitfully be compared with a passage like Hab. 1:12–17. While Amos readily depicts the divine judgment as an enemy invasion, Habakkuk, in raising the question of theodicy, offers an intriguing canonical counterperspective.

Amos and the OT. Regardless of the historical relationship between the prophets and the Torah, in canonical perspective Amos is presented as presupposing some of Torah's stipulations (cf. 2:8 with Exod. 22:26; 3:12 with Exod. 22:13). As Douglas Stuart has shown (xxxi–xlii), Amos also frequently employs the language of the pentateuchal blessings and curses.

Amos in the NT. The NT quotes Amos twice. In Acts 7:41–43, Amos 5:25–27 is understood as referring to the Israelites' idolatry during the wilderness period. In Acts 15:13–18, James applies the rebuilding of David's fallen tent (Amos 9:11–12) to God forming a new people for himself from among the Gentiles.

Some statements in the letter of James about the rich and their treatment of the poor (James 2:6–7; 5:1–6) also show a connection with Amos's message or, more likely, that of the OT prophets generally.

Amos and Theology

There has been a tendency to regard Amos as the harbinger of an inescapable and all-encompassing divine judgment. Others have rejected this construal of the prophet as the messenger of a nation-murdering God, arguing that the prophetic proclamation is instead aimed at repentance. A possible way out of this impasse is suggested by sociolinguistic approaches like rhetorical criticism and speech-act theory, which can help to demonstrate that the possibilities of inescapable doom and of mercy invoked by repentance both inhere in the use of prophetic judgment oracles (Möller, "Words").

Yet our construal of Amos's theology is also affected by judgments about the authenticity of passages such as the salvation oracle in 9:11–15, which is frequently understood to contradict the prophet's uncompromising message of judgment. From a canonical perspective, the oracle does represent an important contribution to the book's theology. Since recent sociolinguistic approaches refute historical criticism's literalistic fixation on the supposed discrepancies of the surface text, they actually invite us to regard this salvation oracle as an integral part of the prophet's original message.

A "full" theological reading thus entails an appreciation not only of Amos's denunciation of the social injustice prevalent in Israelite society and the concomitant threat of an impending divine punishment. It also includes the prophet's vision of a restored people, who once again will fully enjoy life in the land. The oracles against foreign nations (Amos 1–2), furthermore, point to God's sovereign control of this world and his determination to hold the nations responsible for their oppressive and inhumane treatment of the weak and powerless.

In current theological discussion, Amos has been inspirational particularly for Latin American theologies of liberation. They have appropriated its message in an attempt to change existing political and economic structures and create a society marked by solidarity with the poor and "sacrificial service in the struggle to eradicate oppression" (Carroll R., *Contexts*, 19).

See also Prophecy and Prophets in the OT; Rhetorical Criticism

Bibliography

Carroll R., M. D. *Amos*. Westminster John Knox, 2002; idem. *Contexts for Amos*. JSOT, 1992; Childs, B. *Introduction to the Old Testament as Scripture*. Fortress, 1979; Dassmann, E. "Amos." *RACSup* 1 (2001): 334–50; Duhm, B. *Die Theologie der Propheien*. Marcus, 1875; Jeremias, J. *The Book of Amos*. Westminster John Knox, 1998; Möller, K. *A Prophet in Debate*. Sheffield Academic Press, 2003; idem. "Words of (In-) Evitable Certitude?" Pages 352–86 in *After Pentecost*, ed. C. Bartholomew et al. SHS. Zondervan/Paternoster, 2001; Reventlow, H. G. *Das Amt des Propheten bei Amos*. Vandenhoeck & Ruprecht, 1962; Stuart, D. *Hosea–Jonah*. Word, 1987; Wellhausen, J. *Die kleinen Propheten*. 4th ed. De Gruyter, 1963; Wolff, H. W. *Joel and Amos*. Fortress, 1977.

Karl Möller

Anagogical Sense   *See* Medieval Biblical Interpretation

Analogy

At the very heart of Scripture there appear to stand contradictory axioms—what Frederick Ferré has described as "the *prima facie* conflict between repeated Biblical warnings that God is wholly incommensurable with his creation and

... explicit statements on the Deity's purposes, emotions, and characteristic modes of behaviour" (94). On the one hand, the Bible appears to imply that God must so utterly transcend finite created reality that statements with God as referent must mean something different from what they would if their referent belonged to the created order. On the other hand, the Bible clearly suggests that human creatures (operating with a creaturely vocabulary and conceptuality) can *indeed* refer to God and understand that to which they are referring on the basis of his Self-revelation to contingent and finite human minds. So how can the same terms refer to both domains?

When we affirm that the apostle Paul loves, Mother Teresa loves, and God loves, are we really saying the same thing of the transcendent and eternal God that we are saying of the apostle Paul or Mother Teresa? This poses a dilemma. If we assume that the word "love" is used univocally of humans and also God, we seem to risk the charge of anthropomorphic projection—treating God as if "he" were simply another human creature. If, on the other hand, we suggest that when the word is used of God it means something radically different from when it refers to the human context, one has to explain how using human language of God does not amount to sheer equivocation. The latter suggests agnosticism with respect to the meaning of our terms when they refer to the Deity and condemns Christian reference to God and his purposes to an "Alice in Wonderland" world. In sum, is it possible to assume semantic continuity in applying our terms to the two contexts? If so, on what grounds?

Theology has traditionally rejected univocal predication (which leads to anthropomorphism) and equivocal predication (which implies agnosticism) in favor of analogy as a means of referring to God.

In Western thought, this theory has been associated primarily with the thought of Thomas Aquinas as interpreted by Cardinal Cajetan. This tradition argued that when a quality is predicated analogically of two or more different beings (Paul and God), it is intrinsically possessed by each *but not in the same way*. It is possessed by each *in proportion to the being that each kind of reality has* (Phelan). Love is possessed intrinsically by human beings, by angels, and by God, but not in the same way. The way in which human beings love is proportionate to the being that humans have, the way in which angels love is proportionate to the being that angels have, and likewise, the way in which God loves is proportionate to the being that God has.

This means we can affirm analogically that "God loves" without ascribing human loving to God, thereby avoiding the anthropomorphic trap. The divine incommensurability with the created order is thus respected.

But this solution is flawed. The "analogy of proper proportionality," as this is called, makes two claims simultaneously: First, it claims that the relevant quality can be affirmed analogically of both the created and the Creator. Second, it claims that a further analogy exists between the two proportionalities that exist between the analogates—there is an analogy between the *relationship* between God and God's loving and the *relationship* between humans and their loving. But this second statement does not help the first. It simply makes a further analogical statement of the same kind as the first but referring now to the relationships rather than the qualities. Suggesting an analogical proportionality between the two relationships is irrelevant. It does nothing to solve the fundamental problem as to how love or goodness or wisdom can refer (and be understood) within the created realm while also being predicated appropriately of *God*.

The recent scholarship of J. B. Mondin and others has claimed that Aquinas does not advocate any such analogy of proper proportionality but affirms *direct* (analogical) similarity between perfections attributed to God and those same perfections attributed to humanity. Theological claims are possible because there is an intrinsic likeness between the divine and the contingent realms. This is what undergirds the semantic continuity that makes God-talk possible. Integral to Aquinas's theory are two key principles. First, the utilization of a term of God and humanity must invariably recognize the priority of that term's application to God and the posterior or derivative applicability of that term to the human (God-talk is *per prius et posterius*). Second, given that God does not belong to a class (*Deus non est in genere*), analogical statements must never serve to subsume God and humanity under some third generic concept (e.g., wisdom, goodness, or love). Perfections are predicated primarily and properly of God and are only predicated of human beings because these qualities derive from God. (Predication is always *unius ad alterum* as opposed to *duorum ad tertium*.)

Here, however, a further problem emerges. The metaphysical principle that undergirds and sustains God-talk conceived in these terms is, as

Mondin explains, the scholastic principle that *there is a universal similarity or likeness between agents or causes and their effects*. ("Omne agens agit simile sibi.") This provides the grounds of Aquinas's affirmation that the creation possesses an intrinsic likeness to its Creator. If God is an agent, then there must be an intrinsic similarity or likeness between the Creator and what is created—and thus semantic continuity between statements attributing perfections to God and similar affirmations relating to features of the created order.

This solution, however, seems to contravene the principle at the very heart of Aquinas's theory, that God must not be subsumed within a class. Not only has he subsumed God within the class of agents, but also he has extrapolated to the divine from assumptions that apply to the universal class of agents, assumptions that effects necessarily (for some reason) resemble their causes.

This brings us to one of the most fundamental and important questions for biblical theology. Is there an alternative, consistent ontological ground that provides warrant for the assumption of semantic continuity?

Whereas the West has assumed that Aquinas was the father of analogy, the concept of *analogein* is central to Athanasius's theology (Heron; Torrance, *Reconstruction*, and *Reconciliation*). In debate with Arianism, Athanasius distinguished between the anthropomorphic projection (*mythologein*) of mere human concepts (*epinoiai*) on to the divine and *theologein* or *analogein*. In *theologein* (God-talk proper), human terms can transcend their ordinary context of use (*ana-logein*) such that they refer veridically (*alēthōs*) or appropriately to the reality of God.

The condition of this is the twofold *homoousion*—that the incarnate Word of God to humanity (the *skopos* [goal] of the Scriptures) is of One Being with God the Father, and that the Spirit, in whom we recognize the incarnate Logos and who transforms our thinking, speaking, and understanding, is also of One Being with the Father. In and through the reconciliation and reschematization of our thinking and concepts (*noiai*) divine truth is discerned in such a way that the vocabulary of a world alienated in its thinking is thereby commandeered (Jüngel) to refer to God. Theology supposes, therefore, a semantic shifting of our concepts in parallel with the transformation of our minds (Rom. 12:2) through the witness of the Spirit to the incarnate Logos so that they might truly and appropriately refer to God. In sum, *theologein*, valid or truthful (*alēthōs*) refer-

ring to God, is grounded in the reconciliation of our conceptualities, paradigms, and language-games such that, as we have the mind that is in Christ Jesus, we are given to participate in the new, transformed semantics (or "language-games"—*rhēmata*) of the Body of Christ. The ontological ground of theological analogy, therefore, is the participation of our *logoi* in the incarnate *Logos* where, by grace, our human language and thought-forms are given to refer meaningfully to the transcendent God.

"I have revealed you to those whom you gave me out of the world. . . . I gave them the words [or 'speech'—*rhēmata*] you gave me and they accepted them" (John 17:6, 8).

Bibliography

Ferré, F. "Analogy in Theology." In vol. 1 of *The Encyclopaedia of Philosophy*, ed. P. Edwards. 2 vols. Macmillan, 1967; Heron, A. I. C. "Homoousios with the Father." Pages 58–87 in *Incarnation*, ed. T. F. Torrance. Handsel, 1981; Jüngel, E. *Doctrine of the Trinity*. Eerdmans, 1976; Phelan, G. B. *Saint Thomas and Analogy*. Marquette University Press, 1941; Torrance, T. F. *Theology in Reconciliation*. G. Chapman, 1965; idem. *Theology in Reconstruction*. Eerdmans, 1979.

Alan J. Torrance

Analogy of Faith   See Protestant Biblical Interpretation; Rule of Faith; Scripture, Unity of

Analytic Philosophy   See Philosophy

Ancient Near Eastern Background Studies

For over a century comparative studies between the OT and the ancient Near East have hovered at the fringe of hermeneutics and exegesis. Since at times critical scholars have exploited these studies for polemical attacks against the biblical text, conservatives were long inclined to avoid or even vilify them. Borrowing or adapting was viewed as incompatible with Scripture's inspiration. Even as these interpreters in recent decades have grown more interested in tapping into the gold mine of comparative data, the results have often been considered tangential to the ultimate theological task. The influence from the ancient world has been identified with all that Israel was supposed to reject as they received the revelation from God that would purge their "worldview" (or, if this word is used precisely in a theological sense, "world-picture") of its pagan characteristics. Comparative studies were seen as serving only as a foil to the theological interpretation of the text. Consequently, comparative studies have been viewed as a component of historical-critical analysis at best, and more often, as a threat to the uniqueness of the literature of the Bible.

In the process something very important has been lost. We have come to think of the material provided by comparative studies as anti-theological when in reality it has the potential to serve as a guide to understanding some of the theology of the text. Here is the extended syllogism:

If:

(a) comparative studies provide a window to the ancient worldview; and

(b) Israel in large measure shared that ancient worldview; and

(c) revelation was communicated through that worldview; and

(d) that revelation embodies the theological teaching of the text;

Then: comparative studies become crucial to the theological understanding of the OT. This syllogism will be explored in five theses.

1. God did not reject the entire world-picture of Israel's neighbors, but used much of its structure as a framework for revelation

The revelation that Israel received typically concerned the nature and acts of God, the condition of humanity, and the relationship between God and the people that he had created. This revelation, penetrating and reformational as it was, did not change other aspects of Israel's worldview. (Again, for sake of space, I use "worldview" loosely here to encompass understanding of the structure of the world, as well as a wide array of cultural perspectives, societal institutions, and philosophical assumptions.) God left unchanged much of the way Israel learned about the shape of their world. He offered no new information about geography, astronomy, physics, physiology, medicine, or biology. In short, he left Israel operating and thinking in terms of Old World, premodern science. They did not know that there was more than one continent, that people think with their brains, that illness is caused by bacteria, or that a spherical earth rotates and revolves around a spherical sun. The truth of God's revelation of himself did not depend on changing those concepts. Furthermore, God worked within Israel's concepts (shared with her neighbors) of how time and history worked, of the corporate solidarity that was shared by groups in community, of the social structures relating to tribal and monarchic governments, and of how what was sacred should be protected and respected. Theologically, these

may well be understood within the framework of creation, fall, and providence, but our concern here is to track the impact that these correlations might have on the interpretation of various aspects of the biblical text. In addition, God's communication used the established literary genres of the ancient world and often conformed to the rules that existed within those genres. All of these issues are critical to the proper interpretation of the text and require comparative studies to clarify them.

Perhaps the best example of this is found in the concept of the three-tiered cosmos. In the ancient Near East the heavens were understood to be made up of three superimposed disks with pavements of various materials. Flowing all around this cosmos were the cosmic waters, held out by mountains at the fringes of the land and held back by the sky, on which the earth floated. Similar views of the structure of the cosmos were common throughout the ancient world and persisted in popular perception until the Copernican revolution and the Enlightenment. The language of the OT text reflects this view, and there is no revelation in the Bible that seeks to correct it. Without revelation to the contrary, we must consider it likely that this is the view of the cosmos that Israel would have held in common with her neighbors.

Our theological understanding of the text and our doctrine of Scripture both must accommodate this information. Specific texts that would be affected might include Exod. 24:10 and Gen. 1:6–8. The former will now be understood better, but it is the latter that will have potentially far-reaching effects. We may understand the text, in its cultural context, to be saying that God put the *raqi'a* in place, which the Israelites understood to be something solid in substance ("firmament/expanse/dome"; cf. Ezek. 1:22–26), holding back the cosmic waters above. If in contrast we do not believe that anything solid is or ever was up there, our resulting theological interpretation of Scripture needs careful nuancing. Such nuance will of necessity have ripple effects into the way we formulate our doctrine of Scripture, which, in the long run, this must not weaken. Such information is no more a threat to the integrity of the text than the fact that we do not think with our hearts (as people in the ancient world, including Israel, believed). But if we fail (or refuse) to recognize the cultural dimension of the text in Gen. 1, our theological interpretation will be affected. Devising an alternative explanation of *raqi'a* would require attaching to it a meaning contrary to how the Israelites understood the word. Our doctrine of Scripture would be jeopardized if we felt free to conform the meanings of words to make them more comfortable to us.

Furthermore, understanding that God was not trying to give a modern description of the structure of the cosmos can allow us to focus on the part of the teaching of the text that is most pertinent theologically, the functioning of the cosmos as established in the purpose of the Creator.

2. God often used existing institutions and converted them to his theological purposes

Many of the theologically laden concepts and institutions in the OT were not devised as new ideas in heaven and delivered via theophany to the Israelites. Numerous examples can be cited of where they were adapted from contemporary cultural practice, perhaps the most obvious being circumcision. Circumcision was practiced widely in the ancient Near East as a rite of puberty or marriage. It was used as a rite of passage to mark individuals as members of a particular community. In Genesis it is also a rite of passage used to identify the newborn infant as a member of the covenant community. This is how Israelites would have understood this practice when it was prescribed for Abraham and his descendants, and many of the nuances that it held in society were carried across into the theological meaning, though others were radically changed. This is an important example to show clearly that theological initiatives are not necessarily devoid of cultural history. At the same time, the recognition of a cultural bridge does not rule out the providential activity of God within those cultures. Once we know that theological initiatives can come across a cultural bridge, we can begin asking what other institutions or initiatives might have cultural bridges.

Consider the Israelite institution of sacrifice. When the details of the Israelite sacrificial system are finally laid out in Lev. 1–7, sacrifice has already been a regular practice in the ancient Near East and among Israel's ancestors for millennia. Yet the OT offers no other text instituting this practice or giving guidelines for it. Theologians seeking to rectify this gap often found themselves, in Gen. 3, suggesting that God's provision of clothing for Adam and Eve would have required an animal to be killed, and therefore could have served as an opportu-

nity to give instructions about sacrifice. Little confidence can be achieved by inferring such a major institution from such a small gap of silence in the text.

The sacrifices offered by Cain and Abel, Noah, and the patriarchs are similar to those found throughout the rest of the ancient Near East. They focus on thanksgiving, dedication, or petition. It is not surprising that there is nothing in pre-Sinai Israelite practice to compare to the purification or reparation offerings described in Lev. 4–6 since they involve cleansing of the sancta and therefore would have no function prior to the construction of a sanctuary to define sacred space.

If we ask where the pre-Mosaic practice of sacrifice derived from, we would have to take the silence of the text as suggesting that it was of human invention, guided by Providence. When we accept that it was developed through divine providence rather than through more direct revelation, we give the culture a much larger role. Such a conclusion implies that a study of the culture must be undertaken to grasp the theological dimensions that finally emerged in Israel's practice, and received the divine stamp of approval with modifications and additions.

3. Revelation did not always counter ancient Near Eastern concepts, but often used them in productive ways

When Israel was instructed to build the tabernacle, and thus define sacred space, ancient Near Eastern concepts were behind the entire undertaking, and they gave shape to the theology of sacred space. The orientation toward the east, the centering of the most important objects, the creation of zones of increasing sacredness, the ideas about what materials would be most appropriate to sacred space, and the rules for access to sacred space—all these draw heavily from the ancient Near East and comprise the theology of the temple.

We would entirely miss the mark to allegorize the architectural features of the temple, trying to give them "theological" meaning rather than finding meaning in the ancient Near Eastern background, as the Israelites would have. That they *can* be given allegorical meaning is arguably demonstrated in Hebrews. That the theological interpretation in the text is meant to be found in allegory or that we have the freedom or ability to pursue such an approach with confidence is questionable.

4. Literary connections do not negate inspiration of Scripture

Ever since the discovery of the Babylonian flood and creation accounts, a major building block of the platform of critical scholarship has been to demonstrate that the OT is derivative literature, a disadvantaged stepsister to the dominant cultures of the ancient Near East. The attempt has been made to reduce the OT to converted mythology whose dependency exposes its humanity. For confessing orthodoxy, there is no room for the conclusion that the OT is simply man-made theology. If the flood is simply a human legend made up by people and borrowed into Israelite thinking, if the covenant is merely Israel's way of expressing their optimism that God has specially favored them by making a treaty agreement with them, if the prophets never heard the voice of God but were simply mimicking their ancient Near Eastern counterparts—then we are greatly to be pitied for having been duped in what would have to be considered the greatest hoax in history.

In contrast, however, there is nothing inherently damaging to a high view of Scripture if its authors interacted at various levels with the literature current in the culture. All literature is derivative relative to its culture—it must be if it intends to communicate effectively. For the text to engage in polemic and correction, it must be aware of current thinking and literature.

In our modern world, if God were to reveal his work in creation, he would have to explain how it related to the big bang or to evolution. His revelation would focus on the origins of the physical structure of the universe because that is what is important in our cultural perspective. In the ancient world, physical structure was relatively insignificant. They were much more interested in the aspect of bringing order out of chaos and the divine exercise of jurisdiction demonstrated in giving everything a role and a purpose. Written in this context, the creation account would be presented with these ancient ideas in mind. The text formulated its discussion in relation to the thinking found in the ancient literature. It would be no surprise, then, that areas of similarity will be found. This is far different from the contention of some critics that Israelite literature is simply derivative mythology. There is a great distance between borrowing from a particular piece of literature and resonating with the larger culture that has itself been influenced by its literatures. When Americans speak of the philosophy of "eat, drink, and be merry, for tomorrow we die," they are resonating with an idea that has penetrated society rather than borrowing from the writings of Epicurus.

In like manner, it is no surprise that OT genres show marked similarities to those same genres in the larger culture. Whether we are looking at wisdom, hymnic, historical, or legal literature, we will find generous doses of both similarities and differences. Insofar as we are convinced that genre understanding contributes to legitimate theological interpretation, we must become familiar with the mechanics of the genre in the ancient Near East. But similarities do not jeopardize inspiration. Even if the OT had the very same law or the very same proverb that was found in the ancient Near East, inspiration would be involved in the author choosing to incorporate that law or proverb into the canonical collection and to nuance it properly in the appropriate context.

Where there are differences, it will be important to understand the ancient Near Eastern genres because the theological points will often be made by means of contrast. The theology behind the book of Job, for example, is built primarily on the distinctives of the ancient Near Eastern view (represented in the arguments of Job's friends), which was based on an appeasement mentality. The book's message is accomplished in counterpoint. If we are unaware of the contrasts, we will miss some of the nuances.

In fact, then, we must go beyond the simple identification of similarities and differences to articulate the relationships on a functional level. Similarities could exist because Israel adapted something from ancient Near Eastern culture or literature or, as previously mentioned, because they simply resonated with the culture. Differences could exist as the Israelites reject some ancient Near Eastern perspective or could emerge in Israelite polemics (Rodriguez 62–63). In all such cases, the theology of the text may find its nuances in the cultural context. Thus, even in cases of borrowing institutions, practices, literary forms, and so on from surrounding cultures, Israel would have had the fallen direction (fallenness) of these structures corrected by revelation, and we may appreciate their development within the frame of creation and providence.

5. Spiritualized explanations must not be chosen when cultural explanations are readily available

Without the guidance of comparative studies, we are bound to misinterpret the text at some points. If a text is a complex of ideas linked by threads of writing, and interpreters have the task of filling in the gaps, it is theologically essential that we fill them appropriately. Distortion or misinterpretation will result if we fill gaps with contemporary theological trajectories when they ought to be filled with cultural understanding. Consider the following examples.

In the account of the tower of Babel in Gen. 11, the traditional interpretation that goes back to the rabbis and the early church fathers suggested that the tower was a means by which the people were attempting to *get up* to God. Some suggested a specific objective such as overthrowing God or replacing him with an idol. Others proposed that the people were acting out their hubris and overstepping divinely established boundaries. In contrast, analysis against the background of urbanization in early Mesopotamia identifies the tower as a ziggurat. In turn, a study of ziggurats demonstrates that they were not designed so that people could go up to the heavens or in an attempt to transgress divine boundaries. Instead, a temple was built next to the ziggurat and the idea was that the god would *come down* and visit his temple and people. There his needs would be met and, as a result, he would bring blessing and prosperity. Thus, Gen. 11 indicates that the tower was built, as all Mesopotamian ziggurats were, with its head in the heavens. Then it tells us that God did indeed come down, but not with the expected results. Rather than being pleased and bringing blessing, he was disturbed and reacted with punishment.

It is only through this understanding that the theological purpose of Gen. 11 comes through as introducing the development of the principal religious ideals of the ancient Near East. In Genesis, this comes at the climax of Gen. 1–11, where the sin of humankind has progressed from the initial act of disobedience by Adam and Eve, through the corrupt behavior of all people at the time of Noah, and now to the more insidious distortion of Deity. Having failed to become like God, people have regressed into making Deity in their own image—a being with needs, who can be manipulated. It is in this context that the covenant is initiated as God's program of revelation to correct the distortions of Babel. The history of interpretation shows that without the necessary cultural data, the theological interpretation of the text has pursued blind alleys. Not only was the account itself thereby misunderstood, but also the bridge between the two parts of Genesis was lost.

A second illustration can be found in Josh. 10. How could the sun and moon stop? Those committed to literal interpretation have just suggested that people of faith simply have to accept the plain statement of Scripture, not recognizing that they have already changed it. After all, it is not hard for the sun to stand still when it is not even moving. They have changed the "literal" interpretation to a statement that the *earth* stopped moving. Here interpreters since the Copernican revolution have been content to fill in the gaps in the text with physics. Or, unpersuaded that physics could be so tamed, they have offered alternative suggestions, such as protection from the heat of the sun, with little conviction that the text was thereby well represented. Again, we must try to penetrate the ancient worldview, where we will find that Josh. 10 operates in the world of omens, not physics. We cannot ask what these terms mean to us; we must ask what they meant to an Israelite in their cultural context.

In the ancient Near East the months were not standardized in length, but varied according to the phases of the moon. The beginning of a month was calculated by the first appearance of the new moon. The full moon came in the middle of the month and was identified by the fact that the moon set just minutes after the sun rose. The day of the month on which the full moon occurred served as an indicator of how many days the month would have. It was considered a good omen if the full moon came on the 14th day of the month because then the month would be the "right" length and all would be in harmony. If "opposition" (moon and sun simultaneously on opposite horizons) occurred on the 14th it was considered to be a "full-length" month made up of full-length days (cf. Josh. 10:13). People observed the horizon very carefully in the middle section of the month, hoping for this opposition of sun and moon to come on the propitious day (14th). Opposition on the wrong day was believed to be an omen of all sorts of disaster, including military defeat and overthrow of cities. Thus, great significance was attached to these omens. In Josh. 10, since the sun is over Gibeon (east) and the moon is over Aijalon (west), it is clear that it is near sunrise in the full-moon phase.

The Mesopotamian celestial omens use verbs like "wait," "stand," and "stop" to record the relative movements and positions of the celestial bodies. When the moon and/or sun do not wait, the moon sinks over the horizon before the sun rises and no opposition occurs. When the moon and sun wait or stand, it indicates that the opposition occurs for the determination of the full-moon day. The biblical text does not suggest that the astronomical phenomena were unique; instead, Josh. 10:14 says plainly that what was unique was the Lord accepting a battle strategy from a man ("the LORD listened to a man"). Joshua's knowledge of the Amorites' dependence on omens may have led him to ask the Lord for one that he knew would deflate their morale—for the opposition to occur on an unpropitious day.

Thus our theological reading of the text does not require us to defend an astronomical occurrence such as heavenly bodies actually pausing in their movements. This does not change the general idea that God fought on behalf of Israel, but it does give the interpreter a more accurate picture of the way in which God did so, which is surely an important aspect of the theological reading of the text.

In conclusion, then, as our theological interpretations require us to fill in the gaps, we have to be careful to consider the option that those gaps may be filled from the cultural context before we leap to fill them with strictly theological significance. As we make this transition, we have to expand the focus of our comparative studies. Too often in the past, focus has been limited to either individual features (e.g., birds sent out from the ark) or the literary preservation of traditions (e.g., creation accounts, vassal treaties) and has been conducted with either apologetics (from confessional circles) or polemics (against confessional traditions) in mind. As theologians interested in the interpretation of the text, we should recognize the importance of comparative studies that focus on conceptual issues to illuminate the cultural dynamics behind the text.

See also Archaeology; Worldview

Bibliography

Hallo, W. "Biblical History in Its Near Eastern Setting: The Contextual Approach." Pages 1–26 in *Scripture in Context*, ed. C. Evans et al. Pickwick, 1980; idem. "Compare and Contrast: The Contextual Approach to Biblical Literature." Pages 1–19 in *The Bible in Light of Cuneiform Literature*, ed. Hallo, Jones, and Mattingly. E. Mellen, 1990; Horowitz, W. *Mesopotamian Cosmic Geography*. Eisenbrauns, 1998; Rodriguez, A. M. "Ancient Near Eastern Parallels to the Bible and the Question of Revelation and Inspiration." *Journal of the Adventist Theological Society* 12 (2001): 43–64; Saggs, H. W. F. *The Encounter with the Divine in Mesopotamia and Israel*. Athlone, 1978, 1–29; Seely, P. "The Firmament and the Water Above." *WTJ* 53 (1991): 227–40, and 54 (1992): 31–46; idem. *Inerrant Wisdom*. Evangelical Reform, 1989; Talmon, S. "The Comparative Method in Biblical Interpretation: Principles and Problems." *VTSup* 29 (1977): 320–56; van der Toorn, K. *Sin and Sanction in Israel and Mesopotamia*. Van Gorcum, 1985, 1–9; Walton, J. *Ancient Israelite Literature in Its Cultural Context*. Zondervan, 1989; idem. *Genesis*. NIVAC. Zondervan, 2001; idem. "Joshua 10:12–14 and Celestial Omens of the Ancient Near East." Pages 181–90 in *Faith, Tradition, History*, ed. A. Millard, J. Hoffmeier, and D. Baker. Eisenbrauns, 1994; idem. "The Mesopotamian Background of the Tower of Babel and Its Implications." *BBR* 5 (1995): 155–75; Walton, J., V. Matthews, and M. Chavalas. *IVP Bible Background Commentary: Old Testament*. InterVarsity, 2000.

John H. Walton

Angel of the Lord   *See* Angels, Doctrine of

Angels, Doctrine of

Are angels a theme or a doctrine in biblical theology? Since Schleiermacher's time, angels have been seen as liturgical and aesthetic embellishments. In classical times, they were given a place in the dogmatic syllabus (see Grudem). While granting that angels are found primarily in narrative settings, a case can be made that the Bible has an angelology, a consistent portrayal of angelic existence, character, and activity.

Angels in the Biblical Texts

The term "angel" itself (Hebrew: *mal'ak*; Greek: *angelos*) is functional, denoting a messenger, whether human or spiritual. Hence, a survey of biblical texts must cast its net wider and consider other designations of spiritual beings. Within the OT these include the gods or sons of God, holy ones, and several lesser terms. The admission of demigods as angelic raises a further issue: whether Satan and the fallen angels must be treated in a similar fashion. The admission of evil angels and spirits then broadens consideration to include NT references to "principalities and powers." Perhaps the overarching category for theological interpretation would be "spiritual beings," whether faithful or rebellious (cf. Heb. 1:14).

OT Creation Accounts. In contrast to later interpretation (e.g., Milton, *Paradise Lost*), the OT creation account makes no mention of the creation of angels or their activity in heaven or on earth until Gen. 3:24, which speaks allusively to cherubim with flaming sword. The OT creation account must be read both as a polemic against ancient Near Eastern mythologies of origin and as a realistic description, similar to the view of the Wisdom literature, of life under the firmament of heaven. In other places, the

OT makes reference to the divine council of the "sons of gods" (Hebrew: *bene 'elim*), suggesting that heaven is populated by spiritual beings, whether they are loyal servants or not (Ps. 82). However, the primary function of these beings is to set off the incomparability of the One God of Israel (Labuschagne).

Human nature is also implicitly contrasted with the angelic realm. The first woman is tempted by the hope of becoming like God or the gods (*'elohim*), who know good and evil. Three post-Edenic accounts—of the marriage of the sons of God (Gen. 6:1–4, the font of the Enoch myth), of the assault on heaven at Babel, and of the attempted rape of angels at Sodom—all raise questions about the relation of human nature to the angelic world. Most explicit, however, is the psalmist's marveling inquiry: "What is man that you are mindful of him, the son of man that you care for him? You made him a little lower than the heavenly beings and crowned him with glory and honor" (Ps. 8:4–5). The implied answer is that humanity in the image of God surpasses the ranks of the angelic world.

OT Salvation History. The "angel of the Lord" (*mal'ak Yahweh*) is best known from appearances to Hagar, Abraham, and Jacob. The angel of the Lord appears sometimes as a distinct messenger, at other times as virtually interchangeable with God himself (Gen. 32:24–30). In a highly suggestive passage, the Lord appears to Abraham at Mamre as three men, two of whom are later explicitly called angels (Gen. 18:1–2; 19:1).

At the time of the exodus, the angel of the Lord acts as the leader of God's people (Exod. 23:20–22). He identifies himself as "the captain of the Lord's host" (Josh. 5:13–15 KJV). The idea of angels fighting for Israel and executing God's judgments appears in later narrative (2 Kings 6:17) and in the eschatological visions of the prophets (Ezek. 8–9). In an apocalyptic development of the tradition, Daniel sees angelic princes fighting for God's saints and accompanying "one like a son of man" in judgment (Dan. 7:9–14; 10:13). Some interpreters see the Son of Man as himself an angel, but this seems unlikely.

OT Evil Powers. The OT reticence to speak of evil angels and Satan in particular is of a piece with its "apophatic angelology" (Noll). Nevertheless, the apocalyptic tradition and the NT are not mistaken in discerning an evil spirit in Eden's "ancient serpent" (Rev. 12:9; 20:2). Likewise, the Adversary (*ha-satan*) of God's court in Job manifests the same rebellious character. The mythol-ogy of divine and human hubris reappears in the prophets, particularly in the "Day Star, son of Dawn," who is cast down to the underworld (Isa. 14:12 NRSV).

NT Christology. Despite the centrality of Christ in NT theology, angels continue to appear throughout. In the Gospels they provide the "framework of mystery" (Barth) around the entry of the Son of God into the world of flesh and his return to heaven. They announce Jesus' birth and his resurrection and ascension but are strangely absent from his earthly ministry. Jesus himself makes clear that angels accompany the work of salvation (Luke 15:10) and will accompany the Son of Man when he comes in glory (Mark 8:38).

In the Christology of the Epistles, angels provide a foil to set off the exclusive deity of Christ (1 Cor. 8:4–8). Paul sometimes lumps "angels" and "principalities" together as representatives of the intermediary realm over which Christ reigns (Rom. 8:38). The Letter to the Hebrews devotes two chapters to a comparison of Christ and the angels. It concludes that Christ is both above and below them, "the radiance of God's glory and the exact representation of his being," and also true man, for a little while being made lower than angels (Heb. 1:3; 2:9).

Prince of This World. Satan is more prominent in the NT than the OT, apparently being flushed out by the appearance of Christ (Rev. 12:9). He is the "prince of demons," whose forces are routed by Jesus (Mark 3:22). He is also "the prince of this world," who is judged even as he appears to win victory at Calvary (John 12:31). He is the spirit infecting the "principalities" and "powers" (KJV) so that they can be described as "the spiritual forces of evil in the heavenly realms" (Eph. 6:11–12).

John's Apocalypse. The angelology of the OT and NT climax in the final book of the Bible. In chs. 4–5, John from a heavenly vantage point describes the drama of creation and redemption. The angels of creation ask: "Who is worthy?" and they acclaim the slain Lamb, who steps forward with choruses of praise. In chs. 12–14, the theme of conflict and combat in the heavenly realm is represented in the battle between the dragon, the beast, and the false prophet on one side, and the Lamb and his witnesses on the other. The final victory is acclaimed in three antiphonal "Hallelujah" choruses to God and the Lamb (19:1–8), echoing the praise in chs. 4–5.

Angels in the Practice of Theological Interpretation

Angelology provides a kind of litmus test in detecting changes in theological interpretation through the ages, since there have been radically different evaluations of the meaning and importance of the biblical texts about spiritual beings.

The Classical Synthesis. The two most important sources of classical theology in the East and West are Pseudo-Dionysius and Augustine, respectively, who synthesized biblical angels with the Platonic realm of the mind. The former author, a Neoplatonist of the fifth century CE, portrayed a complex "celestial hierarchy" of nine angelic ranks, using various terms from Scripture. His account, thought for centuries to be apostolic, forms the basis of Eastern Orthodox angelology. Augustine's thought takes more seriously the biblical focus on angels as messengers of salvation, but he also exegetes the creation accounts and sees angels as rational creatures who turned to (and from, in the case of Satan's host) God's grace. Rational deduction about angels reaches its zenith in Thomas Aquinas, who argues for the logical necessity of an order of "minds without bodies." Thomas bases much of this rationalization on the thin biblical thread of Ps. 104:4.

The Reformation Reserve and Modernist Rejection. The Reformers reacted against the speculative nature of scholastic angelology. John Calvin in particular limited discussion of angels to positive texts. In his view, the function of angels is limited to the economy of salvation. One may wonder whether Calvin's minimalism opened the door to the outright skepticism of the Enlightenment. René Descartes and John Locke, for instance, do not reject angelology outright, given its scriptural authority, but they claim that angelic existence and character is unknowable. It is only a small step for one to conclude that "heaven may be left to angels and sparrows."

Romantic and Postmodern Recoveries. From the Renaissance onward, angels became increasingly humanized in Western art as chubby cherubs, having virtually no resemblance to their biblical namesakes. The last serious attempt to treat angels in a narrative context is John Milton's *Paradise Lost*. While this epic goes behind the biblical texts, it represents a serious attempt to grasp the intermediate nature of angels in the drama of creation and redemption. Later aesthetic treatments, like that of William Blake, blur the biblical distinction between good and evil spirits and move toward a kind of pantheism. Among current theologians, Walter Wink follows the same tack in a postmodern recovery of principalities as "symbolic of the 'withinness' of institutions, structures and systems."

Karl Barth deserves special mention as a postcritical "angelic doctor." Barth's own angelology begins with rejection of the Thomistic synthesis but devotes more attention to the biblical texts than Calvin does. For Barth, heaven with its angels represents the Whence of salvation in Christ, and Barth shares with the psalmist the marvel that "in Jesus Christ [God] has not taken to himself heaven and the angels in their majesty but man and the earth." For all his serious treatment of angels as servants, Barth dismisses texts about evil angels "with a swift, sharp glance," interpreting John 8:44 to imply that "the devil never was an angel."

Theological Significance of Angels

The first and most pertinent question to ask is, Must we accept the biblical testimony that angels exist? Karl Barth answered this question bluntly: "To deny the angels of God is to deny God himself." Confession of "things visible and invisible" seems indeed to be the dogmatic position of the historic catholic faith. Yet it seems that many evangelical Protestants have put angels and angelology out of sight and out of mind.

Angels and the Biblical Canon. The "canonical approach" to biblical theology pioneered by Brevard Childs opens the door to a contemporary angelology derived from Scripture. Three features stand out in such a canonical approach. The first is a willingness to explore the tradition underlying biblical portrayals of angels without succumbing to the genetic fallacy, that the final form is simply the background writ large. For instance, the divine council of gods may be accepted as reality in many OT references without undermining the exclusive monotheism of the Torah.

A second feature is attention to the discrete witness of both Testaments while seeking a holistic doctrine to emerge. So, for instance, the virtual absence of Satan in the OT can be acknowledged while understanding his full-fledged appearance in the Gospels as concomitant with the coming of the Son of God, as explained allegorically in the war in heaven (Rev. 12:1–5).

A third feature is the shape given an angelology by the christocentric character of the canon. The unanswered questions of the OT—"What is man that you are mindful of him?"—are only answered by the appearance of One who stands on the divine side of heaven's throne and who has descended lower than the angels. Similarly, the surprised angelic paeans at the announcement of the slain Lamb's coming to redeem creation are completed by the victory songs that accompany his second coming, to usher in a new creation.

Such a canonical angelology makes space for the various kinds of questions asked by the angelic doctors of the Jewish and Christian tradition, while reminding interpreters of the limits of piercing the mysteries above the firmament of heaven.

See also Powers and Principalities

Bibliography

Bandstra, A. *In the Company of Angels*. CRC Publications, 1995; Barth, K. *Church Dogmatics*. Vol. III/3. T&T Clark, 1960; Bauckham, R. *The Climax of Prophecy*. T&T Clark, 1993; Childs, B. *Biblical Theology of the Old and New Testaments*. Fortress, 1992; Forsyth, N. *The Old Enemy*. Princeton University Press, 1987; Garrett, S. *The Demise of the Devil*. Fortress, 1989; Grudem, W. *Systematic Theology*. Zondervan, 1995; Hurtado, L. *One God, One Lord*. Fortress, 1988; Kreeft, P. *Angels (and Demons)*. Ignatius, 1995; Labuschagne, C. J. *The Incomparability of Yahweh in the Old Testament*. Brill, 1966; Noll, S. *Angels of Light, Powers of Darkness*. InterVarsity, 1998; Paige, S. *Powers of Evil*. Baker, 1995; Rowland, C. *The Open Heaven*. Crossroad, 1982; Russell, J. B. *The Devil*. Cornell University Press, 1977; Wink, W. *Unmasking the Powers*. Fortress, 1986.

Stephen F. Noll

Anthropomorphism

Anthropomorphism is the portrayal of God in human form. In the biblical literature we find individual parts of the human body attributed to God, such as hands (1 Sam. 5:11; Heb. 10:12), eyes (Ezek. 7:4; 1 Pet. 3:12), ears (1 Sam. 8:21; 1 Pet. 3:12), face (Gen. 32:30; 1 Pet. 3:12), and so on. The text attributes to him physical actions such as laughing (Ps. 2:4), smelling (Gen. 8:21), and whistling (Isa. 7:18). In addition to these portrayals of God with bodily characteristics, God is also depicted as experiencing hatred (Deut. 16:22; Rom. 9:13), anger (Exod. 22:24; John 3:36), vengeance (Deut. 32:35), sorrow (Gen. 6:6), and a range of other human passions. The attribution of passions to God is more specifically referred to as anthropopathism.

Such anthropomorphic depictions of God are used freely in the Scriptures, yet those same Scriptures also warn against conceiving of God in human terms. In Exod. 20:4 the prohibition of idolatry carries with it the implication that the infinite God cannot be represented through any finite form, nor conceived according to the measure of the natural world. Israel is reminded that they saw no form when the Lord spoke at Sinai (Deut. 4:12, 15). God's unlikeness to human beings is thus asserted: God does not sleep (Ps. 121:4); he is not a human being that he should lie or change his mind (Num. 23:19; 1 Sam. 15:29); nor will he exercise wrath like a mortal (Hos. 11:9). The transcendence of God is a constant theme, and his surpassing of all human understanding is frequently enjoined upon those who would speak of him.

The Theological Tradition

Out of deference to the transcendence of God and under the influence of Hellenistic philosophy (Heraclitus and Xenophanes were relentless critics of anthropomorphic talk of God), both the Jewish and Christian traditions have sought at times to downplay the anthropomorphic language of Scripture. Aramaic translations of the OT avoid all anthropomorphisms, and the Septuagint frequently removes or moderates the attribution of human characteristics to God in the Hebrew texts (e.g., LXX, Josh. 4:24; Exod. 15:3). The Jewish philosopher Philo was typical of many who were eager to stress the allegorical interpretation required in the face of biblical anthropomorphism. He was followed in this by Maimonides, who drew on the philosophy of Aristotle to counter all anthropomorphic conceptions of God. Caution about the anthropomorphic portrayal of God emerged early in Christian tradition. Clement of Alexandria, for instance, denied that God experiences emotions such as joy, pity, or grief (*Strom.* 2.16, 72). When encountering biblical anthropomorphism, therefore, we must not suppose that these terms express passions of God. "Reverence rather requires that from these expressions an allegorical meaning should be extracted" (*Strom.* 68.1–3). This advice is followed by Gregory of Nazianzus, who interprets reference to God's "face" as his oversight and to his "hand" as indicating God's provision (*Or.* 31.22). Theodoret understands God's "face" as his benevolence, his restoration of freedom, and his care (on *Daniel* 3:41), while John of Damascus gives allegorical explanations for each of the biblical anthropomorphisms that attribute parts of the body to God (*Exact Exposition of the Orthodox Faith* 1.11).

If, in order to avoid naive conceptions of God, anthropomorphic expressions may be substituted by more abstract allegorical explanations, what is to be said about their appearance in the Bible? According to these patristic authors, anthropomorphic expressions are a divine concession to the weakness of human understanding. Calvin takes up this line and writes of God's accommodation to the capacities of the human mind and heart. The important point to note here is that it is God who so accommodates himself. Human thought and language has no capacity from itself to speak of God. The possibility of human speech, even indeed of anthropomorphic speech, bearing witness to God is entirely a matter of God's blessing (Gollwitzer 151).

Gollwitzer is among those who further point out that all language is anthropomorphic insofar as it relates everything to humanity itself. The deficiency of anthropomorphism, if it be regarded as such, can only be removed, therefore, by having language remove itself (Jüngel, *God*, 260). Such is the approach of apophatic theology.

Revelation

There is, however, an alternative. The correctness of the tradition's caution against all human attempts to represent God must not be allowed to obscure the central affirmation of Scripture that God makes himself known. God presents himself in ways that enable human beings to know and to speak of him. All the language we use of God will be inadequate and cannot attain to the full mystery and transcendence of God; yet the treasure of God is entrusted—*by God himself*—to earthen vessels. God reveals himself and makes eloquent the witness of faith, so that even inadequate human words and concepts may be the means by which God makes himself known. This takes place most especially in the incarnation. The divine Word takes human form. This is the most significant anthropomorphism, for by this means God enables human beings, in speaking of one who is like them in all respects, but without sin, to speak truly of God himself. Naive anthropomorphism is banished; God is not *like* a human being (Jüngel, *God*, 297), but here we may speak of God by speaking of him *as* a human being.

The meaning of all theological speech, in consequence, is to be determined by reference to Christ. In his light human beings may learn what it means to say that God is "Father" or that he is "angry" or that he "rejoices" or that he inclines his "ear" toward humankind. They may do this not by projecting human images onto God, for that is idolatry, but by attending to revelation humanity is enabled to speak truly of God. The incarnation confirms, furthermore, that the OT speaks correctly of God when it speaks not in remote and abstract terms but in anthropomorphic terms of the living God, who is present in person. The reality of God's personal presence with humanity must not be sacrificed to a form of deference for the infinity and transcendence of God that would preclude us from speaking of God at all.

See also Analogy; Revelation

Bibliography

Caird, G. B. *The Language and Imagery of the Bible*. Duckworth, 1980; Calvin, J. *Ins*. 1.12; Eichrodt, W. *Theology of the Old Testament*. Vol. 1, trans. J. A. Baker. SCM, 1961; Gollwitzer, H. *The Existence of God as Confessed by Faith*, trans. J. W. Leitch. SCM, 1965; Jüngel, E. "Anthropomorphism." Pages 72–94 in *Theological Essays*, trans. J. Webster. T&T Clark, 1989; idem. *God as the Mystery of the World*, trans. D. Guder. Eerdmans, 1983; Kuitert, H. M. *De mensvormigheid Gods*. Kampen, 1962. German translation by E.-W. Pollman. C. Kaiser, 1967; Prestige, G. L. *God in Patristic Thought*. 2d ed. SPCK, 1952; Torrance, T. F. *The Christian Doctrine of God, One Being Three Persons*. T&T Clark, 1996.

Murray A. Rae

Anti-Judaism *See* Anti-Semitism

Antiochene Interpretation *See* Hermeneutics; Jesus Christ, Doctrine of; Literal Sense; Patristic Biblical Interpretation; Typology

Anti-Semitism

The term "anti-Semitism" came into public use as recently as 1879, when Wilhelm Marr, a German political agitator, founded the "League of Anti-Semites." He was a racist who had earlier replaced "Jews" with "Semites" in his writings, in order to make his point that Jewish identity is first and foremost *racial* rather than *religious*. The "League" quickly failed as a political organization, but the term took root, and since then "anti-Semitism" has been used to denote "all forms of hostility manifested toward the Jews throughout history. It is often qualified by an adjective denoting the specific cause, nature, or rationale of a manifestation of anti-Jewish passion or action: e.g., 'economic anti-Semitism,' 'social anti-Semitism,' 'racial anti-Semitism,' etc." (*EncJud* 3:87). Its origin in Marr's racist theories means that the term always connotes hatred of Jews as a people, even if it also covers opposition to Judaism as a religion or cultural phenomenon.

This raises an important question, whether the NT can be called "anti-Semitic" just because in various ways it rejects the *religion* of the Jews.

Does theological argument against *Judaism* constitute hostility toward *Jews*? Some significant Jewish writers in this area (e.g., Cohn-Sherbok) do not distinguish between anti-Semitism and anti-Judaism, because they regard a theology that treats Jesus as the fulfillment of the Scriptures, and salvation as by faith in him (rather than through membership in Israel and obedience to Torah), as implicitly anti-Semitic. In fact, this is the predominant Jewish reaction to the NT, with Berkowitz, for instance, describing the NT as "the most dangerous antisemitic tract in history," providing the theoretical basis for actual anti-Semitic hatred throughout time (Berkowitz 325).

If this is so, then Christianity is inherently anti-Semitic—much more clearly so than Hinduism or Buddhism, because it takes the sacred Scriptures of Judaism and rereads them around Jesus Christ. Some Christian theologians have taken up this view. Ruether, for instance, argues that the "christological hermeneutic" of the NT must be rethought, because it disallows the *Jewish* interpretation of the Scriptures. Christians must repent of such imperialism, she argues, and recognize that Jesus was just a Jewish prophet, giving *hope* of the kingdom rather than the kingdom itself. The theologies of John, Paul, and Hebrews come in for particular criticism, with their apparently *replacementist* attitude toward Judaism. To rescue something of original Christianity, this view employs the critical procedure known as *Sachkritik*, whereby a conception of the NT's basic message is used to criticize other aspects of NT theology. In this case, the simple proclamation of the kingdom by Jesus forms the essential heart. He called his hearers to a new life of love and service as they waited for the kingdom morning to dawn. But then (in this view) the NT writers made Jesus the personification of divine Wisdom (John 1), or the temple in person (John 2; 1 Cor. 3), or the "true" vine of Israel (John 15), or the real recipient of the Abrahamic promises (Gal. 3), or the heavenly High Priest who alone makes atonement (Heb. 9). Thus they took the simple message of Jesus and turned it against the Judaism to which he belonged, implicitly disallowing the Jewish covenant with God. The real dynamic of such theology appears, we are told, when the NT gives vent to rabidly anti-Jewish sentiments, such as "Ye are of *your* father the devil" (John 8:44 KJV), or Matthew's damning "His blood be on us and on our children!" (Matt. 27:25)—two NT texts which have certainly been used to fuel hostility toward Jewish people.

So we are faced with three questions. First, is there a proper distinction to be drawn between anti-Judaism and anti-Semitism? Second, is the NT view of Jesus essentially anti-Semitic? And third, what are we to say about the so-called "anti-Semitic" texts in the NT, like those quoted above?

Anti-Judaism and Anti-Semitism?

We must surely say that a distinction between these is vital. All anti-Semitism is anti-Jewish, because hatred of Jewish people is hardly compatible with love of their religion. But not all anti-Judaism is anti-Semitic, because it is fully possible to disagree with tenets of Judaism while still loving Jewish people. In fact, it is highly likely that this is what we encounter in the NT. All the NT writers, with the possible exception of Luke, were Jewish. Tomson, in his major treatment, argues that Jews by definition cannot be anti-Semitic. This is a passion that can only be felt and expressed by Gentiles, he argues. Statements that would be anti-Semitic on Gentile lips must be regarded as "argument within family" when uttered by Jews to fellow-Jews. Otherwise the OT prophets themselves, and Jesus, would have to be accused of anti-Semitism simply for directing strongly worded polemic at Israel (see, e.g., Isa. 1:2–15; Hos. 8; Matt. 23). In theory we may imagine a completely apostate Jew consumed with hatred for the people of his or her birth, but we do not meet this anywhere in the Bible.

NT Christology?

Is it *essentially anti-Semitic* to regard Jesus as the "meaning" of the OT Scriptures? That the NT writers held this view of Jesus and the OT is clear—taking their inspiration, apparently, from Jesus himself (Luke 24:27). Here the vital issue is to ask after their *intention*. Not long after the NT we encounter, in the *Epistle of Barnabas*, a hateful polemic against the Jews based on "Jesus fulfills the OT": they have never understood their own Scriptures, they have always been idolatrous and rebellious, and now they refuse to see the truth. The *Epistle of Barnabas* begins a long and sorry catalog of the Christian "use" of the basic convictions about Jesus to denigrate and demonize the Jews: because they do not believe, they show themselves to be "of the devil" and worthy of exclusion from Christian society. One of the most shameful was Luther's horrible diatribe against the Jews, in which he urged German Christians to burn Jewish houses and throw them out: this was motivated precisely by Luther's belief that the Jews had shown themselves to be finally unresponsive to the Christian gospel. The NT view of Jesus thus became a weapon by which to judge them.

But in the NT itself the desire to interpret the OT around Jesus arises from three humble convictions, held "within family," and argued-for within that context: (1) Jesus really is the Messiah. (2) The "Old Testament" (as we call it) is still the faithful word of God, and Israel his covenant people. (3) Through Christ God has again poured out the Spirit of prophecy, enabling a prophetic rereading of the old texts. The NT writers shared the second conviction with their fellow-Jews; the argument flowed around and out of the other two. It gave rise to some passionate polemic, both from Jesus himself (e.g., Mark 13) and from Paul (e.g., Rom. 11:9–10; 1 Thess. 2:14–16), announcing the judgment of God on an apostate nation, in prophetic style. It produced dramatic rereadings of OT themes: For examples, the exodus and Passover are reinterpreted around Jesus (John 6). The Melchizedek priesthood is highlighted as undermining the cult and pointing to Jesus (Heb. 7). Deuteronomy 32—the famous "Song of Moses"—is understood to explain the conversion of *the Gentiles* to Christ (Rom. 10:19–11:12). And the longed-for restoration of Israel (e.g., Amos 9:11–12) is understood to *include* the Gentiles (Acts 15:13–18)!

None of these points—and many others like them—is made with hostility or hatred toward fellow Jews who still read the Scriptures in the traditional way. But taken out of this original context, into a Gentile environment in which there is already a sharp social distinction between Jews and dominant Gentile cultures, the words of the NT can ring very differently.

Anti-Semitic Texts?

This brings us to those awkward texts, such as Matt. 27:25 and John 8:44 (quoted above; cf. also Rev. 2:9; Acts 7:51). The approach to these must be the same as the approach to the broader christological reinterpretation of the OT. They are not ontological judgments on the essential character of the Jews, but *warnings within family* that, if hostility to Jesus persists, then their relationship with God is radically changed. "You are of your father the devil" (John 8:44) is, in context, a *warning* that, if "the Jews" persist in plotting Jesus' death, or in regarding it as justified, they will forge a moral kinship with the devil, who is a murderer. This challenge is all part of John's subtle argument framed around the debate:

was the death of Jesus the legally justified execution of a blasphemer, or the illegal murder of a prophet? Similarly Matt. 27:25 ("His blood be on us and on our children!") is an appeal to the "children" of the speakers—now contemporary with the evangelist—*not* to accept the verdict of their parents, that Jesus' execution is a "safe bet" before God.

Anti-Semitism has been the scourge of Christian history, a terrible blot on the name of Christ, and a grave distortion of Christian Scriptures. Yet, when we listen to those Scriptures carefully, we hear a very different message.

See also Ideological Criticism; Israel; Jewish-Christian Dialogue

Bibliography

"Antisemitism." *EncJud* 3:87–160. Keter, 1972; Berkowitz, E. In *Judaism* 27 (1978): 325; Cohn-Sherbok, D. *The Crucified Jew.* HarperCollins, 1992; Luther, M. "On the Jews and Their Lies" (1543), trans. M. Bertram. *LWorks* 47:122–306; Motyer, S. *Antisemitism and the New Testament.* Grove Books, 2002; idem. *Your Father the Devil? A New Approach to John and 'the Jews.'* Paternoster, 1997; Ruether, R. R. *Faith and Fratricide.* Seabury, 1974; Tomson, P. *'If This Be from Heaven . . .'* Sheffield Academic Press, 2001.

Stephen Motyer

Apocalyptic

"Apocalypticism" is a word derived from *apokalypsis*, Greek for "unveiling," or "revelation," and is the term found at the start of the book of Revelation (Rev. 1:1). Apocalypticism is a strand of religion in Second Temple Judaism (though found in different forms in other religions in antiquity) and refers to the discernment of divine secrets by dream, vision, or audition. Prime among the unveiled secrets are those concerning the future and the fulfillment of the divine promises for history. This is an important feature in the two canonical examples of this kind of literature, the books of Daniel and Revelation. In addition to these canonical works, typical apocalypses would include those attributed to Enoch (*1, 2,* and *3 Enoch*), 2 Esdras (*4 Ezra*), the *Apocalypse of Abraham*, the *Ascension of Isaiah*, the Shepherd of Hermas. In addition, there are many apocalyptic fragments in nonapocalyptic texts, such as the account of Levi's visionary ascent to heaven in the Greek version of the *Testament of Levi* (2).

An apocalypse is a particular type of revelatory literature found in ancient Judaism, characterized by claims to offer visions or other disclosures of divine mysteries concerning a variety of subjects.

But apocalypticism is also widely used to describe a religious phenomenon whose characteristics evince many of the eschatological features of the apocalypse. There are radical differences between this age and the age to come, angelic mediation, symbolic form, and the cataclysmic events that must take place before the new age can come about. This differentiation is crucial for any understanding of the contemporary discussion. On the one hand, there is the view that apocalypticism is determined by the revelatory character of this literature. On the other hand, there is the view that the religion is determined entirely by the (mainly eschatological) contents of these texts. This difference explains the great variety in definitions that modern literature on the subject offers of this phenomenon.

Apocalypses vary in the degree of mystery they contain in their contents. Some include explanations of their imagery by means of an authoritative angelic interpreter. The book of Daniel functions in this way, as also do parts of 2 Esd. 11–13. By contrast, Revelation differs from these in not having such a pattern of symbolic vision followed by interpretation. Martin Luther—in his 1535 preface to the book of Revelation (his earlier preface had been much more dismissive of the religious value of the book)—observed the difference between Daniel and Revelation. Daniel's dream visions are followed by an accompanying angel's interpretations (e.g., Dan. 7:15–28). This feature is almost completely lacking in the Apocalypse. Revelation 17, in which one of the angels of the seven bowls accompanies John and explains the vision of Babylon, offers a solitary exception.

The discovery of fragments of the Enoch apocalypse at Qumran reminds us that apocalyptic was a widespread phenomenon in Second Temple Judaism. The fact that the earliest parts of this text antedate the book of Daniel by at least a century suggests that the phenomenon had a long history in Judaism. It has obvious links with the prophetic texts of the OT, particularly to the future of hope and the visionary insight of the prophets. The emergence of a visionary tradition, with evocations of heavenly visions and extravagant symbolism, suggests a change even beyond the prophecy in Ezekiel and the early chapters of Zechariah.

The concern with human history and the vindication of Jewish hopes in the apocalypses echo prophetic themes, several of which have contributed to Revelation's language, particularly Ezekiel, Daniel, and Zechariah. It is possible that a change took place in the form of that hope in the prophetic literature, when the future hope comes to be placed on another plane, the supernatural and otherworldly (e.g., Isa. 65–66; cf. Rev. 21; 2 Esd. 7:50). The cataclysmic upheavals described in Zech. 8–14 and Isa. 24–27; 55–66 have similarities with those described in Revelation. Apart from prophetic texts, antecedents of apocalypticism have also been found in the Wisdom tradition of the Hebrew Bible. This literature shows special interest in understanding the cosmos through the discernment of the meaning of dreams, oracles, astrology, and the ability to divine mysteries concerning future events. These were the activities of certain wise men in antiquity, as evident from Dan. 2. The book of Job, with its opening apocalyptic insight into the doings in the heavenly world and its concluding divine theophany, suggests a work that uses the theme of revelation to contribute a solution to the problem of human suffering.

The book of Revelation is the classic apocalypse. Not only is it described as "an apocalypse of Jesus Christ" (Rev. 1:1 AT); it is also "prophecy" (22:18). The first three chapters of Revelation describe the call of John the seer on the isle of Patmos. This is followed by a series of seven letters to the angels of the seven churches in Asia Minor. In chapter 4, a door is opened for the seer to behold a vision of God, lauded by the host of heaven. Into that heavenly world comes a Lamb "standing as though it had been slain" (5:6 AT), which also receives worship. The opening of a sealed book in God's hand sets in train a catalog of destruction and judgment. Between chapters 4–5 and 21 the visions are dominated by three sequences—seven seals, seven trumpets, seven bowls. These sequences are interspersed with other visions that focus on the role and cost of witness (e.g., ch. 11), the threat from the demonic power and its earthly embodiment in the state (chs. 12–13), in which Revelation continues the political symbolism found in Dan. 7. Throughout these visions there is a challenge to readers to opt for the way of witness rather than compromise with the diabolically inspired imperial culture. The book concludes with visions of the messianic reign on earth, which precedes the last assize, the descent of the new Jerusalem, and resolution of the dualistic contrast between heaven and earth, good and evil. A major theme of the book is the overcoming of the stark contrast between God and the world, most graphically expressed in the early chapters, but overcome at the climax of the book when God's presence is on earth, dwelling in a renewed creation and in the new Jerusalem.

There are two basic types of interpretation of Revelation. The first involves presenting the meaning of the text in another, less-allusive form, showing what the text *really* means, usually with great attention to the details of the text and their meaning, often relating them to historical events or persons. The Apocalypse only occasionally prompts the reader to "decode" the meaning of the apocalyptic mysteries (17:9, 18; cf. 1:20; 4:3).

A second form of interpretation refuses to translate the images but instead uses them metaphorically. Thus, it applies the image to another situation or person, not by way of equating the two, but by a process of juxtaposition, casting light on that to which the image has been applied. The imagery of the Apocalypse is juxtaposed with the interpreter's own circumstances, whether personal or social, so as to allow the images to inform understanding of contemporary persons and events. Such interpretation has deep roots in the Christian tradition, going back at least to the time of the fifth-century writer Tyconius, whose work was so important for Augustine. Revelation thereby becomes a resource not just for the generation of the last days but also for the religious life in every generation. Finally, there is appropriation by visionaries, where the words of the Apocalypse either offer the opportunity to "see again" things similar to what has appeared to John, or prompt new visions related to it.

In early Christianity visionary insight played an important part (Mark 1:10; Acts 10–11). Paul, for example, writes about the centrality of the divine revelation (Gal. 1:12, 16). For many NT writers, vision equips them with insight hidden from others and privileges them to enjoy a role in history denied even to the greatest figures of the past. First Peter is typical of the outlook of many other NT documents in its emphasis on the privilege of the writer's time: "It was revealed to [the prophets] that they were serving . . . you, in regard to the things that have now been announced to you, . . . things into which angels long to look!" (1:11–12 NRSV).

Even the Gospel of John, which has few explicit references to visionary experience, is permeated with the theme of the apocalypses—revelation. Thus, at the conclusion of the prologue, the evangelist speaks of the Son in the following way: "No one has ever seen God; the only Son, who is in the bosom of the Father, he has made him known" (1:18 AT). Jesus proclaims himself as the revelation of the hidden God, when he tells Philip, "Whoever has seen me has seen the Father" (14:9 NRSV). The vision of the invisible God is related to Jesus. The vision of God, which is reserved in the book of Revelation for the fortunate seer (Rev. 4) and for the inhabitants of the "new Jerusalem," who will see God face-to-face (22:4), is found, according to the Fourth Evangelist, in the person of Jesus of Nazareth.

Despite attempts over the years to play down the importance of apocalypticism in early Christianity, the indications suggest that its thought forms and outlook were more typical of early Christianity than is often allowed. In the earliest period of Christianity, resort to the apocalyptic language and genre enabled the NT writers to have access to the privilege of understanding the significance of events and persons from the divine perspective. Apocalypticism, therefore, was the vehicle whereby the first Christians were able to articulate their deepest convictions about the ultimate significance of Jesus Christ in the divine purposes.

See also Hope; Last Things, Doctrine of

Bibliography

Bauckham, R. *The Theology of the Book of Revelation*. Cambridge University Press, 1993; Charlesworth, J. H., ed. *Apocalyptic Literature and Testaments*. Vol. 1 of *The Old Testament Pseudepigrapha*. Doubleday, 1983; Collins, J. *The Apocalyptic Imagination*. Crossroad, 1984; idem, ed. *The Origins of Apocalypticism in Judaism and Christianity*. Vol. 1 of *The Encyclopedia of Apocalypticism*. Cassel & Continuum, 1998; Hellholm, D. *Apocalypticism in the Mediterranean World and the Near East*. 2d ed. Mohr, 1989; Kovacs, J., and C. Rowland. *The Book of Revelation*. Blackwell, 2004; McGinn, B., ed. *Apocalypticism in Western History and Culture*. Vol. 2 of *The Encyclopedia of Apocalypticism*. Cassel & Continuum, 1998; Rowland, C. *The Open Heaven*. SPCK, 1982; idem. *Revelation*. NIB 12. Abingdon, 1998; Stein, S., ed. *Apocalypticism in the Modern Period and the Contemporary Age*. Vol. 3 of *The Encyclopedia of Apocalypticism*. Cassel & Continuum, 1998; Stone, M. E. "Apocalyptic Literature." Pages 383–441 in *Jewish Writings of the Second Temple Period*, ed. M. E. Stone. Fortress, 1984.

Christopher Rowland

Apocrypha

The OT Apocrypha are books written during the later Second Temple period (between ca. 300 BCE and 100 CE) in a variety of genres, most patterned after books in the Hebrew Scriptures. This collection is considered canonical, and thus the object of theological interpretation, by Roman Catholic and Eastern Orthodox communions (the latter having an even more inclusive definition of the corpus than the former), but noncanonical by Jews and Protestant Christians. The stance of several Reformation-era Protestant bodies was that the books of the Apocrypha were suitable for private reading for instruction in ethics and manners, but not for the establishing of any doctrine.

Nevertheless, the apocryphal books are important for both Jews and Christians of all denominations as texts that are themselves rich with the theological interpretation of the Hebrew Scriptures, shaping, preserving, and extending the theology of the OT. Moreover, the leading voices of the early church clearly recognized the contribution these texts could make to the formation of Christian theology.

The Theological Interpretation of the OT in the Apocrypha

The Apocrypha continue to proclaim God as a God of covenant faithfulness, both in dealing with individuals and with the nation. Recurrent themes are the following: God's choice of Israel as God's inheritance and special portion (Add. Esth. 13:15–17), selection of Jerusalem as the place where people (specifically, Israel) can have access to the unapproachable God (3 Macc. 2:9, 15–16), special connection with the fortunes of Israel such that the honor of God and the nation of Israel are inseparably associated (Bar. 2:11, 14–15; 3:5; 3 Macc. 2:16), and God's commitment to protect the Jews against their enemies, who thus become God's enemies (3 Macc. 2:3–10; 6:3–9, 15, 28; 7:6, 9).

God's grace toward Israel is especially manifested in the giving of the Torah (the embodiment of Wisdom) exclusively to Israel (Sir. 24:1–23; Bar. 3:36–4:4). The law is not a means of earning God's favor—it is a manifestation of God's favor. It is regarded as the path to life, virtue, and the continued experience of God's favor now and hereafter (Sirach; 4 Maccabees; Wisdom). It may present a challenge, but it is not too difficult for human beings (2 Esdras; Sirach). Far from a burden, it is the God-given provision for virtue and immortality, for a properly ordered human existence, fulfilling God's intentions for humanity in our creation (4 Macc. 2:21–23). The fact that God gave the commandment proves that it can be observed, providing the antidote for sin. In this regard, it is quite instructive to contrast 4 Macc. 2:4–6 and Rom. 7:7–10.

The doing of Torah is placed entirely within a reaffirmation of Deuteronomy's theology of his-

tory and covenant: obedience leads to the experience of God's promised favors, transgression leads to chastisement of Israel at the hands of Gentile nations, and repentance and recommitment to Torah lead to restoration of God's favor toward God's people. This is consistently reaffirmed throughout the literature in light of new challenges (deSilva 207, 229, 274–75). Across this literature, Deuteronomy's basic theology is expanded to include the afterlife and the enjoyment of covenant rewards or experience of punishment in light of the failure of this life to bring "justice for all" (see 2 Macc. 7; Wis. 1–5; 4 Maccabees, passim; 2 Esdras, passim). This assures that God will be just not only to the nation, but also to each individual Jew.

Out of this literature also comes a more advanced theology of suffering. It may come as punishment or chastisement for sins (Tob. 3:3–5; 2 Macc. 6:12–16; 7:18; Bar. 1:15–18; Pr. Azar. 3–9), but this is an insufficient explanation in many cases, as when individual righteous people suffer. In such cases, suffering becomes a test of the righteous (Tob. 12:13–14; Wis. 3:5; 4 Macc. 11:12) or even an opportunity to atone for the nation (2 Macc. 7:37–38; 4 Macc. 6:28–29; 17:21–22).

The way in which the authors of the Apocrypha interpret biblical prophecy shows that they already follow a hermeneutic whereby no prophecy of God can fail (Tob. 14:4), and whereby earlier prophecies of restoration following some past disaster can continue to be applied to new situations of exile or domination. God's faithfulness, justice, and sovereignty must therefore lead to the regathering of Israel from the Dispersion and the fulfillment of Isaiah's vision of Jerusalem's ascendancy (Tob. 13–14; Sir. 36:13, 16). As 2 Esdras shows, the concept of the "two ages" becomes ever more important for rescuing covenant theology and the doctrine of election as the people face disconfirmation by historical infelicities.

In addition to meditating on texts speaking about God's special relationship with Israel and the righteous, the Apocrypha develop traditions about creation in significant ways. The belief that God created the cosmos ex nihilo is attested in 2 Macc. 7:28, a belief that will provide further support for the conviction that God is capable of re-creating a person's life in the resurrection. The created order, indeed, ought to prove sufficient to lead people to the knowledge of God, but remains ineffectual for the Gentiles (Wis. 13:1–9). God displays his sovereignty and providence in that every created thing has a purpose (Sir. 39:16–21, 33–35). This sovereignty extends to the lives of human beings, who are "clay in the hand of the potter," to be done with as the potter decides (Sir. 33:10–13 NRSV); the government of the nations (Add. Esth. 13:9–11; 16:16); and timely interventions on behalf of God's people (Wis. 11–19; 3 Maccabees, passim; Sus. 44–46).

These authors also show lively engagement with the Adamic traditions as they struggle with the human predicament. Wisdom of Solomon understands God to have created humankind for immortality, after God's own image/eternity. Death only came in as a result of sin and of the devil's envy (Wis. 1:16; 2:21–24), clearly developing Gen. 3. Second Esdras takes this further, lamenting the fact that the "evil inclination" took root in Adam and has spread like a "disease" through all the human race (2 Esd. 3–14; see 3:20–22; 4:30; 7:118–119). This expresses a doctrine of "original sin" quite similar to that developed earlier by Paul (Rom. 5:12–21). As in Paul, however, it is held in tension with human responsibility for striving against the evil inclination and eagerly pursuing righteousness (2 Esd. 7:92, 127–29; Rom. 2:6–10).

Finally, the Apocrypha contribute significantly to the growth of angelology and demonology. Demons are the source of affliction for individuals, with exorcism and the binding of the demon bringing relief (as in Tob. 3:7–8, 17; 8:1–3). Angels act on behalf of God's people and are expected to intervene in the lives of individuals, whether taking human prayers before God as messengers or bringing assistance or revelations from God to human beings (as in Tob. 3:16–17; 12:12–15, 18).

The Theological Interpretation of the Apocrypha in the Early Church

The influence of apocryphal books on the early church is considerable. We must ignore the stunning examples of how the Apocrypha have shaped the ethics, the imagery, and the expression of the NT and focus solely on major points of theological influence.

As early Christian leaders reflected upon the person and work of Jesus, they showed a special indebtedness to Wisdom of Solomon and the traditions of the Maccabean-era martyrs found in 2 and 4 Maccabees. The Christology of Hebrews, Colossians, and John builds upon previous traditions about the person of "Wisdom," God's partner in creation, the mediator through whom God made the cosmos and continues to order and govern it (Wis. 8:1; 9:1–2, 9). "Wisdom" is no longer a created being, but an emanation of God—"a

pure emanation of the glory of the Almighty, . . . a reflection of eternal light, a spotless mirror of the working of God, and an image of his goodness" (Wis. 7:25–26 NRSV).

Reflecting on the person of Jesus, NT authors interpret him in light of these traditions about "Wisdom." Now it is Jesus who is "the image of the invisible God" (Col. 1:15), the "reflection of God's glory and the exact imprint of God's very being" (Heb. 1:3 NRSV), God's agent in the creation of all that is (John 1:1–3; Heb. 1:2–3; Col. 1:16–17), and the mediator by which people come into relationship with God (John 1:10–13; cf. Wis. 7:27). These wisdom traditions, then, gave the early church a theological language with which to express their convictions about their encounter with God in the person of Jesus. The impact of Wisdom of Solomon continues to be felt throughout the first four centuries. It contributes to the church's development of the doctrines of the Son's eternal generation by the Father, the Father and the Son sharing in the same essence (*homoousios*), and the Trinity and the equality of the three persons.

Another important contribution to Christology concerns the sacrificial interpretation of Jesus' death on the cross. The Torah does not prepare one to regard a human death in such terms, but the Apocrypha offer reflection on the deaths of the martyrs, who chose torture and death out of obedience to God and to Torah rather than apostasy and release. These texts provide an important bridge between the "Suffering Servant" song of Isa. 52:13–53:12 and the broad spectrum of concepts used to express the meaning of Jesus' death. In 2 Maccabees, the seven brothers embrace death as a means of bringing "to an end the wrath of the Almighty" that fell upon the "whole nation" (2 Macc. 7:37–38 NRSV). They allow God's anger, in other words, to expend itself fully upon them so that the nation would not continue to suffer. In 4 Maccabees, the language of "purification," ransom, exchange, and "atoning sacrifice" is added to speak of the deaths of these martyrs: "Let our punishment suffice for them. Make my blood their purification [*katharsion*], and take my life in exchange for theirs" (4 Macc. 6:27–29 NRSV); the martyrs have "become, as it were, a ransom for the sin of our nation. And through the blood of those devout ones and their death as an atoning sacrifice [*hilastērion*], divine Providence preserved Israel" (4 Macc. 17:21–22 NRSV). All of these concepts are used in the NT to interpret the significance of Jesus' crucifixion, and the basic theories of atonement all have their roots in these martyrological texts.

The belief in the physical resurrection of the dead, in the possibility of going to "be with the Lord" upon death, in the certainty of postmortem reward and punishments, and in the judgment of all people by God beyond death—these are found throughout the NT and the writings of successive generations of Christians. These convictions, however, are nurtured more by the Apocrypha than by the Hebrew Scriptures, which are slight in their references to postmortem existence (and ambiguous in most places where an afterlife might be too readily assumed by Christian readers). Nowhere in the Hebrew Scriptures does one find visions of God's postmortem vindication of the righteous and of God's indictment and punishment of the wicked such as one finds in Wis. 1–5 or 2 Macc. 7. It is these texts that resonate so well with the personal and cosmic eschatology of Jesus, Paul, and the other voices of the NT.

The theological influence of these apocryphal books can also be seen in smaller ways. Examples are the frequent attribution of the introduction of sin and death to the devil's envy (first posited in Wis. 2:24; see *1 Clem.* 3.4; Augustine, *Trin.* 4.12.15), and the dualistic anthropology in which the physical body is devalued as an impediment to the soul and its perception of spiritual realities (Wis. 9:15; see Augustine, *Trin.* 4.5, 10; 8.2; 17.28; 24.44).

Theological Interpretation of the Apocrypha among Protestants?

The Protestant position regarding the Apocrypha as a basis for theological reflection stems from two major concerns about these books. First, there was never a clear, unanimous agreement in the early church concerning their canonicity, though the majority position by the early fifth century was clearly for their inclusion in the OT. The same objection, however, could be made against most of the General Epistles and Revelation. The second concern, and probably the more serious, was the manner in which certain passages in the Apocrypha were used to establish doctrines that were especially objectionable to the Protestant Reformers.

The intercession of the "saints" in heaven on behalf of God's people here in this life is most clearly evidenced by 2 Macc. 15:12–14. There the deceased high priest Onias III and the prophet Jeremiah pray to God on behalf of the Jewish nation in its struggle against the Seleucid armies. The belief that atonement could be made for the sins of the deceased, to release them from the consequences of their sins, was clearly supported by 2 Macc. 12:39–45. Finally, we find the doctrine that virtuous deeds built up a "treasure" against a future day of necessity and could have cultic value as an offering (Tob. 4:8–11; Sir. 29:9–12). This easily lays a foundation for the "treasury of merits" and support for the belief that these merits, once accumulated, could be passed on to others (including the departed, as in 2 Macc. 12:39–45). These were key issues in the Protestant Reformation, and key texts that supported them were to be found in the books whose canonicity had never been officially decided. Hence, it was inevitable that the Reformers should revive the arguments of Jerome and others that the church should follow the shorter OT canon received from the synagogue.

What, then, are Protestant Christians interested in theological interpretation to do with the Apocrypha? First, the Apocrypha are indispensable to understanding the theological environment of the first century CE. They provide a witness to the ways in which OT theological traditions were being selected, weighed, and modified or extended in the centuries after the return from exile, and thus being made available to Jews at the turn of the era. Through attention to these texts, we arrive at a much better informed understanding of what was at stake theologically in the confession of Jesus as Messiah and in the questions addressed by early Christians (e.g., the inclusion of Gentiles without the requirements of circumcision and keeping kashruth [Jewish dietary laws]).

Second, these texts were resources that made significant contributions to early Christian theology, especially in the areas of Christology, personal eschatology, anthropology, and martyrology. If Protestants exclude them from their study, they are without access to books that were highly valued by their theological parents and highly formative for the faith they confess.

Finally, Protestants can continue to appreciate their raising of, and wrestling with, questions of perpetual interest to theologians. Sirach raises the problem of divine sovereignty and human responsibility for sin (15:11–15; 33:11–13). Second Esdras raises the perennial questions of God's justice and of the struggle to rise above our own bent to sinning. Wisdom posits the relationship of a defective ethics with the crumbling of the Jewish (and Christian) worldview, a strangely (post-) modern problem as well. All Christians would profit from engaging the apocryphal books at least as worthy conversation partners, if not as canonical authorities.

Bibliography

Charles, R. H. *Apocrypha*. Vol. 1 of *The Apocrypha and Pseudepigrapha of the Old Testament in English*. Oxford University Press, 1913; Collins, J. *Jewish Wisdom in the Hellenistic Age*. Westminster John Knox, 1997; deSilva, D. *Introducing the Apocrypha*. Baker, 2002; Harrington, D. J. *An Invitation to the Apocrypha*. Eerdmans, 1998; Longenecker, B. *Eschatology and the Covenant*. JSOT, 1991; Metzger, B. *An Introduction to the Apocrypha*. Oxford University Press, 1957; Nickelsburg, G. W. E. *Resurrection, Immortality, and Eternal Life in Intertestamental Judaism*. Harvard University Press, 1972.

David A. deSilva

Apologetics

Apologetics is the theological discipline that defends the truth of the Christian message. One important subject of recent debate among apologists has been the relationship between apologetics and Scripture. All apologists seek to defend the biblical message, and they usually defend their apologetic method as itself in accord with Scripture. But they disagree on questions such as these: (1) Does the Bible teach anything specific about apologetics, or about related topics such as epistemology (see, e.g., the debate in Cowan, 208–19, 256, 350–51)? (2) What does it teach about apologetics? (3) How should Scripture itself be used (alongside other tools such as general revelation, logic, reason, et al.) in the work of apologetics? For purposes of this dictionary, it is also important to consider (4) *how* Scripture teaches us about apologetics and (5) how apologetic concerns may affect our interpretation of Scripture more generally. The discussion below will address these topics, not necessarily in sequence.

The Bible does not discuss apologetics as an academic discipline, but it does speak about defending the faith. The term "apologetics" comes from the Greek *apologia, apologeisthai*, which in the NT usually refers to an individual's defense of his conduct, as in 1 Cor. 9:3, and sometimes against legal charges, as in Acts 19:33; 22:1; 24:10. In the Acts passages, however, Paul defends himself by defending his message. So in Phil. 1:7, 16 *apologia* refers explicitly to a defense of the gospel, and in 1 Pet. 3:15 to a defense of the Christian hope.

Moving beyond the *apologia*-vocabulary, we can see that defense of the gospel appears frequently in the Bible. There is a strong apologetic element in the "signs" of the fourth gospel (John 20:30–31), and in Luke's attempt to impart "certainty" to Theophilus (Luke 1:4; cf. "proofs" in Acts 1:3). Paul's epistles contain much defense of his gospel against objectors. This emphasis on defense goes back to Jesus' own confrontations with opponents and, still earlier, to God's prophetic indictments of unfaithful Israel. (In these cases especially, we should bear in mind the maxim that often the best defense is a good offense.)

All of this suggests the broader thesis of Ezra Hyun Kim, that from one perspective the whole Bible is *apologia*. For in the Bible God presents his truth over against error, speaking it into a sinful world, always having in view the objections of his opponents. The authors of the Bible, divine and human, seek to present their message cogently, rationally, persuasively. This is not to say that the Bible is a collection of rational syllogisms, but that in all its genres, even in its poetic, narrative, and wisdom teaching, it seeks to present God's message as right, true, and persuasive.

Defending the faith, therefore, is a biblical practice. The discipline of apologetics seeks to instruct Christians in such defense. As analysis of a biblical practice, apologetics is a properly theological discipline. If theology is "the application of Scripture to all areas of life," then apologetics is "the application of Scripture to unbelief" (Frame, *Knowledge of God*, 81, 87), including the unbelief that remains in Christian hearts.

As with all theology, the Bible is normative for apologetics. It does not teach apologetics in a focused or systematic way, even to the extent that it teaches about justification in Rom. 1–5, the resurrection in 1 Cor. 15, or the events of the last days in 1 Thess. 4–5. However, it has much to say about the theistic worldview; the nature of the gospel, knowledge, wisdom, the noetic effects of sin, and regeneration; the opposition of belief and unbelief; the Spirit's illumination; God's revelation in the natural world; and the role of Scripture itself as our authority for all areas of human life.

My own reading suggests that a "biblical apologetic" would take this general shape: "The fear of the LORD is the beginning of knowledge" (Prov. 1:7) and "wisdom" (9:10); indeed, wisdom and knowledge are summed up in Jesus Christ (1 Cor. 1:30; Col. 2:3). Though God is known through his creation, people repress this knowledge (Rom. 1:18–32) until God's grace renews their minds (12:2). The apologist should press upon the non-

Christian the evidence that God is clearly revealed in nature. But he should present it in the context of a biblical worldview, with an epistemology reflecting what the Bible says about knowledge. And he should present the gospel in God's own authoritative voice, using Scripture's own arguments (as 1 Cor. 15:1–11) and other arguments that follow scriptural leads. As an example of the latter, when Scripture says that God is revealed in creation, it authorizes us to find evidence in creation to use in apologetic witness (as Acts 14:15–18; 17:22–31). When it says that the events of redemption occurred at specific times and places, it authorizes us to find apologetic resources in the historical study of those times and places (Acts 26:26).

Having learned from Scripture what we can about apologetics, it is natural that those conclusions influence our reading of Scripture in other areas. All theological conclusions serve as hermeneutical grids in this sense. But there are dangers. For example, apologists have sometimes drawn a sharp distinction between miracle and providence, for the sake of the "argument from miracle." Miracles must be distinct from other events, it is said, so that we can identify them for use in apologetic argument. In my judgment, however, Scripture itself does not make such a sharp distinction (Frame, *Doctrine of God*, 241–73). The implication for apologetics is not that the argument from miracle is faulty, but that both providence and miracle reveal God to human beings in somewhat, though not sharply, different ways. We need to hold loosely enough to our theological/apologetic conclusions that we will be able to revise them in the light of further study of Scripture. There must be a true hermeneutical circle: our theological conclusions influencing our exegesis, and our exegesis influencing our theological conclusions. Openness to revision in both directions requires humility as well as perspicacity.

Cornelius Van Til's work in apologetics led him to a model similar to the one sketched earlier. This model, in turn, inclined him toward theological interpretations of Scripture that emphasized the sovereignty and authority of God, the authority and sufficiency of Scripture, the ontological Trinity, the fullness of wisdom in Christ, and the foolishness of unbelief. His apologetic creativity influenced his theological creativity, and the reverse. On the whole, I think his work is a good example of fruitful hermeneutical reciprocity between these disciplines.

Bibliography

Boa, K., and R. Bowman Jr. *Faith Has Its Reasons*. NavPress, 2001; Cowan, S., ed. *Five Views of Apologetics*. Zondervan, 2000; Frame, J. *Apologetics to the Glory of God*. P&R, 1994; idem. *Cornelius Van Til*. P&R, 1995; idem. *Doctrine of God*. P&R, 2002; idem. *Doctrine of the Knowledge of God*. P&R, 1987; Kim, E. H. "Biblical Preaching Is Apologia: An Analysis of the Apologetic Nature of Preaching in Light of Perspectivalism." D.Min. project, Westminster Theological Seminary (CA), 2000; Van Til, C. *Introduction to Systematic Theology*. P&R, 1962.

John M. Frame

Apology   *See* Apologetics

Apostasy

Apostasy is a theological category describing those who have voluntarily and consciously abandoned their faith in the God of the covenant, who manifests himself most completely in Jesus Christ. As a category, it cuts across significant philosophical and theological ideas, including freedom of the will, the sovereignty of God, the perseverance of the saints, the relationship of faith and works, eternal security and assurance, as well as how one understands the nature of genuine faith. Christian theologians, since Augustine but also even more intensely since John Calvin and Martin Luther, have vigorously disputed not so much the *reality* of apostasy as the validity of the category for *genuine believers* (Pinnock). Apostasy, as Christians have understood it, pertains to the orientation of the heart, to moral behavior, and to theological orthodoxy (which technically is "heresy"). Furthermore, many theologians distinguish between "backsliding" (forgivable lapses of the believer) and "apostasy" (permanent, unforgivable lapses).

Apostasy in the OT

Analogous to, but not identical with, apostasy are the various cataclysmic sins of Adam and Eve (Gen. 3), Cain (ch. 4), Lot's wife (19:15–29), Esau (25:29–34), and even Saul (1 Sam. 13) and Solomon (1 Kings 11). More significant, however, are (1) the sin of Israel in the wilderness, where Israel tests Yahweh and Yahweh disciplines Israel; and (2) the perpetual disobedience of Israel in the land, which leads to covenantal discipline in exile (e.g., Exod. 32; Num. 14; 25; Judges; 2 Kings 17; Ps. 78; Isa. 3:6–12). One of the fundamental themes of the prophets (e.g., Hosea; Isa. 1–39; Jeremiah) is the warning to turn (*shuv*) away from sin and back to covenantal fidelity. Those who fail to turn are deemed covenantal apostates. Forgiveness, however, remains the divine promise for those who do turn back to Yahweh (Hos. 1–2; 11:1–4).

Apostasy in the NT

The NT speaks of apostasy in numerous passages and under a variety of terms (e.g., Luke 22:22; 2 Thess. 2:3; 1 Tim. 4:1–3; 2 Tim. 4:10; Marshall). Jesus speaks of the "unforgivable" sin as blasphemy against the Holy Spirit (Matt. 12:31–32), which is overt and conscious denunciation of the work of God's Spirit in Jesus Christ (cf. Lev. 24:15–16). There are similar descriptions and attitudes found in Acts 13:8, 45; 14:2; 18:6; 19:13–16, and one might argue that the "sin that leads to death" (1 John 5:16–17) is another instance of apostasy, or perhaps an irrecoverable form of backsliding. Apostasy and sin (in general) are set in a powerful theological context by the apostle Paul; though he certainly counts sin as a tragedy in Christian existence, God's eternally faithful grace and forgiveness continue to abide for those who are faithful (Rom. 8). Paul, however, clearly states the necessity of perseverance (Col. 1:21–23; Volf).

Early Christian thinking on apostasy receives a powerful statement in the Letter to the Hebrews, where warning passages punctuate the text with rhetorical potency (McKnight). In each warning passage, we find (1) the *subjects* or *audience* in danger of committing the sin, (2) the *sin* that leads to (3) the *exhortation,* which if not followed, leads to (4) the *consequences* of that sin. These passages are 2:1–4; 3:7–4:13; 5:11–6:12; 10:19–39; 12:1–29. In brief, they have several elements: (1) The subjects appear to be believers. (2) The sin is apostasy, understood as deliberate and public refusal to submit to God and his will for persons in Jesus Christ. (3) The exhortation is to repent and to follow faithfully and obediently. And (4) the consequence for apostasy is eternal punishment.

Apostasy in the Practice of Theological Interpretation

Because apostasy is disputed among Christian theologians, it must be recognized that one's overall hermeneutic and theology (including one's general philosophical orientation) shapes how one reads texts dealing with apostasy. One set of theologians understands apostasy as sinful behaviors of a permanent nature that only nonbelievers or those who are on the edge of saving faith can commit (Ortlund; Schreiner and Ware). Another set believes the biblical evidence sets

forth the case that some genuine believers can repudiate their faith and jeopardize their standing before God.

Apostasy candidly recognizes the responsibility of humans before the covenant God: humans are created by God in his image, are fallen, but can also be reconciled by faith to that Creator-covenant God through his gracious act of forming a covenant with them. Without ever suggesting that obedience must be perfect, apostasy warns that the covenant member has an obligation to live within its terms. Such responsibility is framed by a biblical theology of grace, sin, justice, and final judgment. Humans who violently and voluntarily violate the terms of the covenant are in danger of final judgment. Again, however, this responsibility is not about perfection (which the Day of Atonement and the offer of forgiveness completely deny) but about the pattern of life: covenant members who fail to live responsibly are in danger.

Most importantly, *apostasy is theo-fugal.* Apostasy is neither casual sin, nor even a specifically violent sin (e.g., murder, adultery, etc.). Instead, apostasy is settled and voluntary rejection of God's will: it is a *departure from the Fatherhood of God.* Apostasy is not about violating civil or moral law (though it probably involves such behaviors) but about repudiating the lordship of God (Heb. 3:12) over the life of a person living in a relation to God through the covenant that God has made in Jesus Christ. This leads to the idea that apostasy is not only *theo-fugal* but also *Christo-fugal*—it is a *departure from Jesus Christ,* the agent of salvation (Heb. 6:4–6). We can go further: the statement of Jesus about blasphemy reveals that apostasy is also *Pneuma-fugal*: it is departure from the Holy Spirit, the very source of life and sanctification (Matt. 12:31–32).

Yet, it needs to be noted that *apostasy is compatible with God's sovereignty and election.* Apostasy does not somehow threaten God's sovereign will (as if the apostate successfully resists what God is fighting for; cf. Cottrell; Craig). It is *within* God's will, somehow within God's covenantal plan of redemption, for the covenant person to carry responsibility for his or her life before God. Furthermore, *within* the biblical notion of election (e.g., Rom. 8; 1 Pet. 2:9–10) there is an understanding that those elected by God are called to perseverance and obedience. If the "elect" repudiate God's sovereign claim on life, that election is shown to be compatible with apostasy.

How so? Election, to begin with, must be defined in its biblical, rather than modern English, sense. Thus, it needs to be understood as an expression of God's preemptive and sustaining grace that is sufficient both to rescue his people from sin and sustain them in a life of obedience. "Sufficient" should not be understood to mean "inevitable." Some argue that election itself is only an election *of Christ,* and that all who are in him become the elect by virtue of *his* election (but only in that relationship to him; Shank; Forster and Marston). Thus, apostasy as a category must be given a voice in determining what "election" means. Election does not rule out apostasy, nor does apostasy make light of God's sovereign election.

Pastorally, apostasy needs to be muted by the sufficiency of God's work in Christ and through his Spirit while it is held up as a rare, but real, possibility. Apostasy ought not to be used as a continual threat so much as an occasional warning of the disaster that Christians may bring upon themselves if they do not examine themselves. As a warning, apostasy can function as a moral injunction that strengthens commitment to holiness as well as the need to turn in complete trust to God in Christ through his Spirit. It needs to be remembered that God's grace is sufficient to sustain his own (Jude 24).

See also Assurance; Covenant

Bibliography

Cottrell, J. "The Nature of the Divine Sovereignty." Pages 97–119 in *The Grace of God, the Will of Man,* ed. C. Pinnock. Zondervan, 1989; Craig, W. "Middle Knowledge: A Calvinist-Arminian Rapprochement?" Pages 141–64 in *The Grace of God, the Will of Man,* ed. C. Pinnock. Zondervan, 1989; Forster, R., and V. Marston. *God's Strategy in Human History.* Tyndale, 1973; Gundry-Volf, J. *Paul and Perseverance.* Westminster John Knox, 1990; Marshall, I. H. *Kept by the Power of God.* Bethany, 1969; McKnight, S. "The Warning Passages of Hebrews: A Formal Analysis and Theological Conclusions." *TJ* 13 (1992): 21–59; Ortlund, R., Jr. "Apostasy." Pages 383–86 in *New Dictionary of Biblical Theology.* InterVarsity, 2000; Pinnock, C. "From Augustine to Arminius: A Pilgrimage in Theology." Pages 15–30 in *The Grace of God, the Will of Man,* ed. C. Pinnock. Zondervan, 1989; Schreiner, T., and B. Ware, eds. *Biblical and Practical Perspectives on Calvinism.* Vol. 1 of *The Grace of God, the Bondage of the Will.* Baker, 1995; Shank, R. *Elect in the Son.* Westcott, 1970.

Scot McKnight

Aquinas, St. Thomas *See* Thomas Aquinas

Archaeology

In the nineteenth century the discovery of ancient Egyptian and Assyrian monuments and inscriptions with occasional references to events also mentioned in the Bible led to an expectation that more could be found in the biblical lands, which some hoped would "verify" the Scriptures in the face of biblical criticism. Throughout the twentieth century, excavations in the Near East have added enormously to the wealth of material found by the Victorian pioneers. Most discoveries have no direct relevance to the Bible; though bringing more details to knowledge of the ancient world, many offer general information about the background of the biblical writings, and some aid interpretation more specifically. Obviously, ancient texts tend to give the most precise help. The reader of any book written in a different age or environment from his or her own is likely to face concepts that are strange, hard to understand, or even appear incredible.

The OT

Only acquaintance with the context in which a work was composed can lead to a sensible explanation of it, and this is where archaeology helps to interpret the OT. Its contribution can be divided into four areas: (1) historical background; (2) historical complements; (3) cultural analogies; (4) cultural correlations.

Historical Background. While the biblical writings and Greek and Latin authors preserved some facts and traditions about Assyria, Babylonia, Egypt, and Persia, recovery of original documents and artifacts has enabled extensive histories of those powers to be written, revealing the kingdoms of the Hittites, the Aramaeans, and other neighbors of ancient Israel. The varying periods of strength and weakness enjoyed by the great powers on the Tigris, Euphrates, and Nile over more than two millennia provide the setting for OT history, while briefer spells of glory enjoyed by lesser monarchies are analogous to Israel's.

By Abraham's time, ca. 2000 BCE, urban civilization, with written records, was over a thousand years old. The accounts of the patriarch and his descendants fit well with the Middle Bronze Age period in the Levant, when abandoned cities were refounded and Egypt was making its strength felt in the area. People were moving, or being moved, from there into Egypt, and they eventually seized control as the Hyksos rulers. The Egyptian New Kingdom provides the setting for Moses and the exodus, with its power in Canaan declining during the twelfth century BCE as Israel took over the promised land. The half century or so of the Israelite empire under David and Solomon can be understood once the weakness of Egypt and Assyria at the time is recognized. Then the aggressive new regime in Damascus, followed by resurgent Assyrian forces pushing westward, reduced Israel to a local state and ultimately to incorporation in the Assyrian provincial system (720 BCE). Judah survived until Nebuchadnezzar sacked rebellious Jerusalem in 586 BCE. The "live and let live" policy of Persian kings enabled the Jews to reestablish their center in Jerusalem, within the imperial administrative system. Understanding political events through the centuries aids interpretation of Israel's history and of many prophecies involving other nations; plus, the biblical explanations of events in theological terms gain added perspective.

Historical Complements. Reports composed to glorify Assyrian kings in particular complement the biblical records in especially valuable ways. First, they name kings of Israel and Judah in the same chronological sequence as the Bible, relating some to the same episodes, sometimes to episodes additional to the biblical narratives. Thus, they testify independently to the reliability of the biblical texts and the opposing side's view of events. Second, the Assyrian texts usually supply exact dates, enabling the chronology of the kings of Israel and Judah to be established in terms of world history, something impossible from the biblical texts alone. Later, the Babylonian Chronicle places Nebuchadnezzar's conquest of Jerusalem in 597 BCE, on March 15/16, and offers other entries clarifying events in the last decades of Judah's life and in the career of Jeremiah. Persian history affords similar illumination for the postexilic period. Earlier than Assyria's first contact with Israel, in Ahab's reign, was Pharaoh Shishak's visit, ca. 925 BCE. His list of places visited on his campaign, although incomplete, expands the report of 1 Kings 14:25–26 (see Kitchen 293–300, 432–47, 575, 587). Few historical records have been recovered from Syria-Palestine, and only one certainly reflects a biblical text. That is the Moabite Stone on which Mesha celebrates his conquest of towns held by Gad in Transjordan about 830 BCE (2 Kings 3:4–27; Num. 32; Smelik in *CoS* 2:137–38).

Cultural Analogies. As noted above, when Israel came into being, major cultures were already ancient; she did not, therefore, have to build her culture from nothing. In fact, excavations show that the towns and villages of the monarchy were similar to those of adjacent realms in architecture, masonry, metalwork, and pottery, and so also in economy and lifestyle. Although in the second millennium BCE Babylonian cuneiform script was widely used, with Egyptian hieroglyphic and hieratic current in the Levant, by 1000 BCE, the alphabet was fully formed and replaced those systems there. Being simpler and easier to use, it may have spread more widely through society; but since most documents were written on papyrus or leather, they have perished. Nevertheless, the evidence of scanty texts and situations elsewhere suffices to show that books could have circulated throughout the monarchy period (Millard, "Books").

Israel occupied its promised land as ironworking began to be developed in the Near East. That is well reflected in the Canaanites' fearsome war machine, "iron chariots," presumably chariots armored with iron (Josh. 17:16–18; Judg. 1:19; 4:3; see Millard, "King Og's Bed"), and in the armor and weapons of Goliath, wholly of bronze except for his spearhead (1 Sam. 17:5–7). No trace of the golden decorations of Solomon's temple survives, and the description in 1 Kings 6 seems to make extravagant, exaggerated claims in asserting that the interior was plated with gold. Investigations into the use of gold sheeting in Egyptian temples demonstrate that this was an ancient practice, and Assyrian and Babylonian kings boast of similar pious donations; so Solomon's activity can be comprehended as consistent with the expectations placed on wealthy monarchs.

Conceptual comparisons are helpful, too. In Mesha's inscription (see above) Moab's god Chemosh is "angry with his land" and so allowed Israel to dominate it, then relented and, says Mesha, "delivered me from all kings and let me have victory over all my enemies," phraseology familiar from Judges (2:14; 2 Sam. 8:14; 22:18; etc.). In this and other ways, Hebrew writers commonly employed the ideas of their day.

Cultural Correlations. Discoveries with clear links to biblical texts are less common. One example is the finding of many carved ivory pieces in the palace precinct of Israelite Samaria. They had served as veneer and decoration on wooden furniture and can explain how the "ivory house" of Ahab should be understood (1 Kings 22:39). Amos (6:4) condemned such expensive and useless luxury, widely admired at the time and well attested in Assyrian palaces. At several sites, notably Lachish, heavy destruction can be dated to the Assyrian attack in Hezekiah's reign, pictured in relief on the walls of Sennacherib's palace at Nineveh, described in his annals, and told in 2 Kings 18–19 (Ussishkin). Through archaeological discoveries in various countries of texts in languages closely akin to Hebrew, meanings of terms and expressions in the Bible are more precisely understood. Best known are the small stone weights marked with their value *pim*, by weight two-thirds of a shekel, so explaining the previously unintelligible word *pim* in 1 Sam. 13:21.

The NT

The history of NT times is well known from the works of Greek and Latin authors, so archaeology contributes less in this area than it does for the OT. Yet it can enlarge understanding of details, such as why the titles of Roman officials vary from city to city in Acts (Hemer, *Acts*). The historical geography of the NT has benefited from the definite location of ancient sites and thus of routes taken (notably Derbe; Hemer, *Acts*, 112) and from clarifying local allusions in the letters to the seven churches (Rev. 2–3; Hemer, *Letters*). Knowledge of the Jewish background has gained enormously through the recovery of the Dead Sea Scrolls. They not only open new windows on religious thought and practice (e.g., covenant concepts, eschatology; Schiffman and VanderKam), but also on the state of the Hebrew Scriptures, the reading and writing of other books in first-century Palestine. With other discoveries, they show a wider spread of literacy than often supposed (Millard, *Reading*). Greek papyri found dehydrated in Egypt from the mid-nineteenth century onward yield a continuing stream of examples of the common Greek language of the era (Koine), elucidating words and expressions throughout the NT (e.g., Heb. 11:1, faith as the "title-deeds"; the classic work remains Deissmann).

Cultural Correlations. Material remains offer cultural correlations similar to those for the OT. Large stone jars exemplify those at Cana (John 2:6), stone vessels being less susceptible to ritual impurity (Millard, *Discoveries*, 182–84). The criticism of large, showy phylacteries (Matt. 23:5) becomes intelligible in the light of first-century examples from Qumran less than one inch wide, which would be hardly visible when worn (Millard, *Discoveries*, 196–97). The numerous tombs around Jerusalem have features comparable with the description of Joseph of Arimathea's tomb, making intelligible some of the details (e.g., the disciple bending to look in, John 20:5; Millard, *Discoveries*, 278–95). Phrases in Paul's Letters become more vivid when their ancient connotations are recognized and the physical contexts

perceived (e.g., metaphors from athletics, 1 Cor. 9:24–27). Especially significant are the Greek inscriptions forbidding Gentiles entry to the inner parts of Herod's temple. They not only make plain the crime Paul allegedly committed there (Acts 21:28); they also anchor his picture of the dividing wall Christ has in reality abolished (Eph. 2:14).

Interpretation

Devout Christians and others have used archaeology to try to prove that the Bible is true (e.g., Marston; Keller), while some have claimed it proves the opposite (e.g., Thompson; Finkelstein and Silberman). Both approaches expect more of archaeology than it can yield, and neither takes a balanced attitude to the texts. As a theological work, the Bible cannot be proved by discovery of material remains, nor can they demonstrate it to be erroneous (unless they reveal an indisputable anachronism). Failure to find Canaanite cities destroyed by Joshua's forces, or magnificent buildings erected by Solomon, cannot prove the reports wrong; there may be good reasons for the failure. Such problems arise through lack of evidence, which some scholars take to indicate that biblical assertions are wrong. However, further research has often vindicated the biblical writers (e.g., Belshazzar was considered a fictional figure until inscriptions naming him proved the contrary; the royal letters in Ezra have often been deemed Jewish concoctions, yet original imperial decrees of Persian rulers display comparable attitudes toward local cults).

The Distinctiveness of God's People

In the realm of religion, archaeology helps to clarify the distinction between Israel's faith and her neighbors' beliefs. Texts from the Late Bronze Age provide instructions for rituals and lists of sacrifices (notably at Emar on the mid-Euphrates: Fleming in *CoS* 1:427–43; and at Ugarit: Pardee in *CoS* 1:295–302). They include practices like those in Israelite ritual laws, but directed to a variety of deities. Stone, metal, and pottery figures represent those gods, while texts reveal the extent and problems of polytheism (heavenly quarrels, inconsistent and amoral behavior), emphasizing the distinct nature of Israel's monotheism. Ancient cultures continuously struggled to understand their divinities and their wishes, in contrast to the revelations of divine purpose given in the Hebrew Bible. It was in its faith, archaeology demonstrates, that Israel was unique. As ancient Israel differed little in material matters from its neighbors and held many attitudes in common with them, so Jesus and his followers shared the cultures of their contemporaries. In both cases the differences lay in the largely intangible spiritual and moral tenets, which are not bound by time or place.

Bibliography

Deissmann, A. *Light from the Ancient East*. Hodder & Stoughton, 1927; Finkelstein, I., and N. A. Silberman. *The Bible Unearthed*. Free Press, 2001; Hemer, C. *The Book of Acts in the Setting of Hellenistic History*. Mohr, 1989; idem. *The Letters to the Seven Churches of Asia in Their Local Setting*. Sheffield Academic Press, 1986; Keller, W. *The Bible as History*. Rev. ed. Lion Publishing, 1991; Kitchen, K. A. *The Third Intermediate Period in Egypt 1100–650 BC*. 2d ed. with supplement. Aris & Phillips, 1996; Marston, C. *The Bible Is True*. Eyre & Spottiswoode, 1934; Millard, A. "Books in Ancient Israel." *Palestine Exploration Quarterly*. Forthcoming; idem. *Discoveries from Bible Times*. Lion Publishing, 1997 = *Nelson's Illustrated Wonders and Discoveries of the Bible*. T. Nelson, 1997; idem. "King Og's Bed and Other Ancient Ironmongery." Pages 481–91 in *Ascribe to the Lord*, ed. L. Eslinger and G. Taylor. Sheffield Academic Press, 1988; idem. *Reading and Writing in the Time of Jesus*. Sheffield Academic Press/Continuum and New York University Press, 2000; Schiffman, L. H., and J. C. VanderKam, eds. *Encyclopedia of the Dead Sea Scrolls*. Oxford University Press, 2000; Thompson, T. L. *The Bible as History*. Cape, 1999; Ussishkin, D. *The Conquest of Lachish by Sennacherib*. Institute of Archaeology, 1982.

Alan R. Millard

Argument *See* Utterance Meaning

Art, the Bible and

The Bible itself is art, God-speaking literary art, booked under the Holy Spirit's guidance by very differently skilled persons.

The Bible Charters Human Artistic Activity

The Bible charters human artistry indirectly by assuming that making art is a normal creaturely gift and responsibility in God's world, like becoming married. Although some persons decide not to marry (Matt. 19:3–12; 1 Cor. 7:25–40), marriage is a room in creation provided by the Lord for the enrichment of a person's life, and it is not to be depreciated (1 Tim. 4:1–5). Although not everyone may compose music, write novels, or craft pictures, God has provided us humans, says the Bible, with the ability to speak poems (Gen. 2:23), sculpt ornaments (Exod. 25:9–40), and sing songs (Pss. 33:1–3; 149–150), which can please the Lord and edify the neighbor. Imaginative construction of materials such as metals, wood, and fabrics into lampstands, cherubim statues, and festive clothing as God-honoring symbols can be bona fide, Holy-Spirited work (Exod. 31:1–11).

Older Testament. The Bible documents how, after humankind fell into sin with Eve and Adam's disobedience toward God, artisans like everyone else—parents, political leaders, teachers, prophets—could be true to the way of the Lord *or* revel in the lies of pride, violence, and vanity. Lamech's rhetoric was murderous boasting (Gen. 4:23–24); skyscraping Babel architecture was an idolatrous affront to the Lord (Gen. 11:1–9); and the special praise festivals God's elect people frequently orchestrated stank in God's nostrils (Amos 5:21–24; Isa. 1:10–20). Yet the Lord approved Miriam's dance, choreographed with timbrels for the women of liberated Israel to perform on the banks of the Red Sea (Exod. 15:19–21). It was good of King David to set up a Levite guild of musicians and songwriters (1 Chron. 15:16–24). These, along with the poetry of Isaiah (40; 60–62) and Job (19; 28; 40–41), are incontrovertible evidence that God enjoys literary art.

God has no qualms about the visible, sensible character of artistry and its possible liturgical use. The Lord told Moses to sculpt a bronze snake and raise it up on a pole, so those bitten by vipers could look at it and receive God's healing (Num. 21:4–9). Because the statue eventually became treated as a miracle-working relic, hundreds of years later Hezekiah finally had it destroyed (2 Kings 18:1–8). Art can be a costly offering that God apparently allows (1 Kings 5–6; 7:13–51). Yet King Solomon's opulence and excessive attention to building his own fabulous palaces (1 Kings 7:1–12) signal that the excellent pagan Sidonian artisans hired for producing God's temple fit into Solomon's deteriorating wisdom, headed for luxury, militarism, national bankruptcy, and a lascivious idolatry (1 Kings 9–11). Prizing art—like the desire for knowledge ("philo-sophy") (Gen. 3:1–7; 1 Cor. 1:20–25) and concern for political security (2 Sam. 24:1–10)—can be a temptation to sin as well as a test to exercise one's faithfulness (Judg. 7:2–8; Prov. 1:2–6) in thanking the Lord for such marvelous capabilities (James 1:2–4).

The OT treats the weal and woe of art among God's people and the surrounding nations throughout history. Nomadic tribal cultures have song rituals and tell stories (Num. 10:35–36; Judg. 9:7–20), but it takes a measure of education (e.g., Moses: Exod. 2:1–10; Acts 7:20–22; Heb. 11:23–26) and a sense of peoplehood to develop certain artistry (Exod. 15:1–18; Deut. 32:1–44). A corpus of repeatable Psalms, editing books of Proverbs (Prov. 25:1), composing literature like the Song of Songs, the Lamentations of Jeremiah, and the writings of Job and Ecclesiastes—all these take settled cultural capital and the differentiated institutionalization of professional composers and scribal schools to develop.

NT. The NT is prospecting, as it were, to form a *new* cultural community of believing Jew *and* Greek (Rom. 10:5–13; 1 Cor. 12:12–13; Gal. 3:23–29; Col. 3:5–11) amid a dominant Roman and Hellenistic pagan culture (John 18:28–40; Acts 17:16–34). Hence, it is focused more on the mission of converting unbelievers into the discipleship of realizing Jesus Christ as the promised Messiah and the Savior of all nations (Matt. 16:13–20; Rom. 9–11) than in dealing with artistic problems. However, the Bible is a single continuous and true narrative of the Lord God's great deeds, and the NT also assumes the goodly presence of art and literature as a creaturely way to express human gratefulness to the Lord and to encourage one another on our journey to the *eschaton*.

The Eastern magi gave artistic valuables to baby Jesus and his parents as worship offerings (Matt. 2:7–12). Jesus defended the Mary who spilled precious perfume from an alabaster jar over his body in celebration of his ministry (Mark 14:3–9). It was normal for Jesus and his twelve apostles to sing a hymn after the Passover meal (Mark 14:22–26). According to the Bible, singing psalms and hymns, Spirit-filled songs, *is* redeeming one's time (Eph. 5:15–20), and is part and parcel of the redemptive lifestyle (Col. 3:12–17). Through the educated apostle Paul (Acts 22:3), who was gifted by God's Spirit to book the fervent tour de force of Rom. 1–8, God says: Do not speak in bland generalities, but season your speech with specific salty rhetoric (Col. 4:5–6). Remember, Jesus Christ was a consummate teller of parables, which are NT *meshalim*, a genuine metaphorical artistry of words.

From beginning to end the Bible is positive toward all things bright and beautiful, fascinating and strange. God saw everything God had made, and it all looked good (*tov, kalos*), says Gen. 1. Trees planted near running water, wild animals in jungles, birds nesting in shrubs, whales sporting in the oceans, precious stones hid deep in the earth (Pss. 1; 104; Job 28)—these are God's treasure hunt, for us humans to discover and clothe with artful cultivation. Someday even the glorious art of the nations will be refined, purified, and brought into the city of God (Rev. 21:22–27). The fact that God surprises human expectation (Matt. 25:31–46) suggests that the saints on the

new earth may come to enjoy art they had not noticed in their lifetime.

Art as **Biblia Pauperum**

Once followers of Jesus Christ became a dominant public church institution, after the conversion to Christianity of Emperor Constantine (313 CE), art became a means to bring the Bible story to the many who could not read. Pope Gregory the Great (590–604) enunciated the stand on didactic art in the church environs, which despite occasional waves of iconoclasm became Roman Catholic Church policy for a millennium. The church would use images to teach Bible stories and trained singers to chant biblical texts in a regular lectionary way, thus reinforcing the OT and NT doctrines for the faithful to hear (in Latin).

Meanwhile, skilled monks who recopied parchment manuscripts of the Bible (especially from ca. 900 CE until movable type printing was invented ca. 1450) took time to decorate initial capital letters with fantastic curlicue tendrils. Sometimes these artists illuminated margins of the biblical text, using colorful tempera and gilding gold to portray flowers, monsters, and insects, out of sheer jubilation at the amazingly prolific glory of creatures God has created.

Recent Past History. When the Renaissance popes (Julius II, 1503–13; Leo X, 1513–17) had the resources to live like princes and begin building St. Peter's Church in the Vatican in 1506, art by great painters in papal employ such as Raphael (1483–1520) and Michelangelo (1475–1564) tended to magnify and glorify the patrons (and the artists) more than present the simple gospel of the Bible. Nevertheless, the Bible still often provided the subject matter for the artwork. Art promoted later by the Council of Trent (1545–63) remained catechetical church art, but also mixed in adoration of saints, so that the Bible storytelling focus of quattrocento art mutated into broadly devotional art, inclining viewers to an ecclesiastical piety.

The Eastern (Greek and Russian) Orthodox Church, since the second ecumenical Council of Nicea (787), adopted icons as a special way to have "sacred" art parallel the Bible's mediation of God's word. Because Christ is the image of God (Col. 1:15–20; 2 Cor. 4:1–6), images honor the prototype original they are like. A consecrated painted image of Christ makes God's incarnation as a visible human palpable. So the standardized, almost schematic icon figure simply focuses one's rapt attention, acts as a window beckoning the viewer into the very presence of Christ, and brings the invisible God veritably close to oneself. Just as the God-breathed Bible makes God's will known to humans, so the Holy Spirit uses venerated icons such as sermons in paint to mediate grace: the holy icon serves believers like a sacrament. Art for the Orthodox Church is closely tied to a churchly presence.

In Europe the historic Reformation led by Luther (1483–1546), Calvin (1509–64), and others championed Bible reading and Bible preaching (in the vernacular language) as the principal means of grace; the Bible had become neglected by the institutional church. Art, however, was viewed not as an instrument to be specially adopted by the institutional church, but as a human response to God's grace, for service in the world at large. So art became "unchurched" but was considered a marvelous conduit for believers' faith to be shared and imaginatively bodied forth in the public square.

Luther himself wrote new melodies with stanzaic pattern, so ordinary people could sing songs of faith at home, in school, and at church gatherings. Calvin persisted with poet Clement Marot and songwriters like Louis Bourgeois until there was a complete Genevan Psalter, so the Bible's praise and laments could be artistically voiced by God's people and heard by their enemies. Later Heinrich Schütz (1585–1672), Johann Sebastian Bach (1685–1750), and many other church musicians wrote cantatas and "passions" for choirs to sing at worship services, to highlight celebration of Bible passages bringing the gospel. But it was especially the mundane outreach of art into the nonchurch world that received impetus wherever the centrality of the Bible promulgated by the Reformers took hold.

Group portraits of businessmen fulfilling their nonchurch vocation (Rembrandt, *Syndics of the Cloth Guild*, 1662), spacious atmospheric landscapes filled with Ps. 19 glory (by Jan van Goyen and Jacob Ruisdael), scenes honoring domestic daily life (Vermeer's *Cook* [pouring milk], before 1660), and stunning bouquets of cut flowers with the *memento mori* of a dead bug (by Pieter Claeszoon)—all testify that in the 1600s Dutch artists were looking at God's world outside the church door and presenting imaginative artwork about it with a vision shaped by the Bible.

Current Problems and Opportunities. Since the Enlightenment, European art, like politics and philosophy, has become deeply secularized; the Bible has been largely privatized and downgraded to "a personal choice" rather than experienced as a culture-forming directive. There are,

to be sure, still many outstanding artists, Jews and Christians, whose artwork bespeaks their communion with the Bible.

Throughout the world non-European people have been greatly influenced by Pentecostal Christian missionaries. Their Bible is mainly instruction for us to be saved from this world for heaven, rather than a source of light for redeeming historical acts and re-forming artistry to be a gift of joy and sorrow for believers' neighbors now. Many Bible-believing evangelical Christians today either see little connection between Bible and artistry or restrict art to what is functional for church liturgy, doctrinal beliefs, and devotional practice.

However, if one has a robust faith in the power of God the Holy Spirit to permeate culture—art, political policy, philosophical theory—with the directional message of the Bible, then one can appreciate how the Bible has suffused its light. It broke through, for example, in the novels of Alan Paton (1903–88), the cinematic oeuvre of Robert Bresson (1907–82), and the popular song of Bruce Cockburn (born 1945). The Bible often enters artistry as a leaven in ways one cannot clearly point to so much as taste in the artistic bread distributed (Luke 17:20–21; Matt. 13:33).

Bibliography

Bach, B., ed. *Das Bild in der Bibel*. Claudius, 1991; Chaplin, A., and H. Brand. *Signposts for Christians in the Arts*. 2d ed. InterVarsity, 2001; Drury, J. *Painting the Word*. Yale University Press, 1999; Luttikhuizen, H., and M. Bendroth, curators. *The House of God*. Calvin College Center Art Gallery, 8 January–13 February 2003; Morgan, D., ed. *Icons of American Protestantism*. Yale University Press, 1996; Panofsky, E. "Comment on Art and Reformation." In *Symbols in Transformation*. Princeton University Press, 1969; Paulson, R. *Book and Painting*. University of Tennessee Press, 1982; Rookmaaker, H. *The Complete Works*, ed. Marleen Hengelaar-Rookmaaker. 6 vols. Piquant, 2002–; Seerveld, C. *Bearing Fresh Olive Leaves*. Piquant/Tuppence, 2000; idem. "Christian Aesthetic Bread for the World." *Philosophia Reformata* 66 (2001): 155–77; idem. *Rainbows for the Fallen World*. Tuppence, 1980; Veith, G., Jr. *The Gift of Art*. InterVarsity, 1983; idem. *State of the Arts*. Crossway, 1991; Wolfe, G., ed. *IMAGE*. Quarterly. www.imagejournal.org.

Calvin Seerveld

Ascension

The comic cycle of descent and ascent is to epic narrative what *proodos* and *epistrophē* are to classical cosmology and psychology. Scripture knows little or nothing of the latter, naturally, though later allegorical and anagogical exegesis (such as informs Augustine's *Confessions*, e.g., or Dante's *Comedia*) does. Of the former, however, Scripture already knows a great deal. Its narrative structure is characterized by cycles of descent and ascent, and is ultimately comic. It is the ascension of Jesus that makes it so, and as a resolution of these cycles the basic significance of Jesus' ascension can in turn be grasped.

That being the case, the doctrine of the ascension ought itself to become an organizing principle for the reading of Scripture, even before appeal is made to patristic or medieval exegetical hierarchies. The same conclusion can be reached from consideration of the primitive confession "Jesus is Lord." For in pointing to the culmination of biblical history and all the aspirations of the people of God, that confession offers itself as a universal hermeneutic of the Scriptures. And it is precisely, in the first instance, a confession of Jesus' ascension (cf., e.g., Phil. 2:9; Acts 2:34; Heb. 1:3).

Our first task, then, is to approach the doctrine of the ascension from the standpoint of Scripture, while our second task is to approach Scripture and tradition from the standpoint of the doctrine of the ascension. Obviously, these cannot be strictly sequential activities; they must overlap. Nor can they be pursued successfully in a short space. All that can be done here is to provide a bit more detail about the ascension as a biblical motif, and about the deployment of the doctrine of the ascension.

As Biblical Motif

Irenaeus reminds us that the Word of God has descended and ascended from the beginning of human history, to draw humanity into a life-giving conversation with God. The Bible offers an account of this descent and ascent, and of the corresponding movements of mankind, especially of the covenant people. From the mountain garden of God to the deserts east of Eden; from Ararat to the plains of Shinar, where the great tower was built; from Mt. Sinai to the wilderness wanderings; from Zion to Babylon—the biblical story is one of invitations to communion with God and declensions from that communion. The biblical landscape, in other words, is full of peaks and valleys, of ascents and descents, literally as well as figuratively, historically as well as liturgically. The Prophets and the Psalms (including the songs of ascent) integrate the Edenic aspirations of the people of God with the geography of Zion, the temple liturgy, the spirituality of covenant life, and geopolitics. Psalm 24, for example, becomes

a cipher for the whole biblical vision, Dan. 7 for the full sweep of redemption history.

We are not surprised to encounter, then, at the climax of the gospel story and "the mystery of godliness" (1 Tim. 3:16), the ascension of Jesus into heaven. Here is the "one like a son of man, coming with the clouds of heaven," who approaches the Ancient of Days and is "led into his presence" (Dan. 7:13). Each of the evangelists has his own way of presenting this event, but none overlooks it, for it would be impossible to tell the story of Jesus as part of the story of Israel, or the story of God's universal redemptive purposes, without giving some account of Jesus' ascension. That the ascension, as an event distinct from the resurrection, is often said today to be a Lukan invention represents a mistake in theological interpretation that truncates the story of Jesus and makes difficult any attempt to carry it through to the parousia (Acts 1:9–11). It also makes it difficult to interpret either the church or the world in the eschatological situation of the present age, marked as it is by the tension between the presence and the absence of the ascended Jesus—a point to which we will return.

The NT employs a variety of imagery and allusions in presenting the ascension, each of which contributes something to its theological richness. Individual histories in the OT are taken up typologically: Moses (especially in Matthew); Aaron, Elijah, and David (especially in Luke); Melchizedek (especially in Hebrews, John, and the Apocalypse); and of course Daniel's visionary "son of man" (throughout and especially in Paul). But no single office or image or forerunner provides a paradigm that is fully adequate. Hence, allusions generally come in complex bundles. No one but Jesus, in whose personal history all these others coalesce, can bring to a resolution the cycle of ascent and descent that characterizes fallen humanity. No one but Jesus can complete the victory of God over the nations (cf. Pss. 2, 47, 110) or bring humanity into the very presence of God. No one but Jesus, that is, can mediate eternal life.

Irenaeus, one of the Bible's most theologically astute readers, captures something of the vitality and reach of the ascension motif. He views it from the perspective of Pentecost (cf. John 20:17–23; Acts 2:33–36) and sets it in the cosmic context of Gen. 1–3 (cf. Eph. 4:7–10; Heb. 1:1–14). The ascension of Jesus marks the completion of the divine act of creating humanity in the image of God, through full investiture with the Holy Spirit, thus fitting humans for an eternally refreshing converse with the Father and for stewardship of the renovated cosmos. Through his own U-shaped history (baptism, death, resurrection, and ascension) Jesus recapitulates the entire experience of fallen man and restores the gift of the Spirit, who becomes "our ladder of ascent to God" and to immortality (*Haer.* 3.24.1; cf. 3.17ff.; 4.20; 5.20.2; 5.36). At the parousia the results of this recapitulation will be revealed. Meanwhile the church, as the community of the Spirit, participates eucharistically and through martyrdom in the ministry of Jesus (*Haer.* 4.18; 5.2.3; 5.28.4; cf. John 6:35–66).

As Doctrine and Hermeneutic

The doctrine of the ascension, if anthropological in the sense just stated, is also political, liturgical, cosmic, and spiritual. In each of these dimensions it is—or ought to be—not only an ecclesial doctrine but also an ecclesiological one. And in each of these ways it can teach us to appropriate Scripture more deeply.

The political is developed in connection with the confession of Jesus as Lord. The lordship of the ascended Messiah means that, not only the people of God, but also all powers in heaven and on earth are subjected to him. This means in turn that Caesar can no longer claim lordship over the peoples of the earth except in some limited sense as a temporary steward of justice and good order (cf. Acts 4; Rom. 13; 1 Pet. 3:13–22; etc.). The Son of Man, not Caesar or his equivalent, is the supreme pantocrator. It is vital, however, to recognize that the exercise of his rule, openly declared by and through the church (Eph. 3:10), nonetheless appears on earth during the *saeculum* in the same paradoxical form as it did on the cross. It is the burden of the Apocalypse, in particular, to make this clear. Special sight is required to see the power of the ascended Melchizedekian Christ (Rev. 1:9–20; cf. Acts 7:56), and a special vocation—martyrdom—is required to exercise that power effectively (Rev. 7; 14; cf. 11:11–13; 20:4–6). It is always tempting to overlook this qualification, especially in periods when martyrdom is in decline. But perhaps it is equally tempting, at least in the modern context, to overlook the basic political claim as such. (Oliver O'Donovan presents a recent attempt to recover that claim, through a theological interpretation of Scripture.)

The liturgical also appears in the Apocalypse, where the blood of the saints shed on earth is a witness to the blood of Christ presented before God in the holy of holies (Rev. 4–19). So does

the cosmic, for cosmic renovation is the ultimate consequence of that liturgy (Rev. 20–22; cf. Col. 1). The liturgical and the cosmic likewise come together in Hebrews, as the true backdrop against which political decisions are to be made. Hebrews is structured rhetorically around the Pentecost lections and an invitation to the church to "draw near" to the divine throne on which the ascended Christ has been seated as Priest-King (cf. Heb. 4:16; 8:1–7; 10:19–25; 12:25–29). Later on, with the abatement of political urgency, the liturgical and the cosmic are expressed more optimistically in terms of "the marriage of heaven and earth," which in patristic homilies is especially celebrated in connection with Ascension Day. This becomes the theme of several of Christianity's great theological, liturgical, and architectural structures (witness, for example, the Orthodox liturgies influenced by Pseudo-Dionysius; or, in the West, the building of the St. Denis basilica). Permutations here have much influenced the way in which the Scriptures have been read and understood, as the latter are drawn into the orbit of particular liturgical and cosmological visions, whether more or less distant from those of the biblical authors themselves. Needless to say, not all of these readings are compatible or equally felicitous in their effects.

The spiritual dimension of the doctrine cannot be detached from the other dimensions mentioned if, as Scripture and tradition teach, Jesus' ascension was a bodily event (cf. Acts 1:9–11; Irenaeus, *Haer.* 1.10.1; Gregory of Nazianzus, *Ep. ad Cled.*). Nevertheless, we must speak also of its relevance to the inner life of the soul: from the corporate context of the sursum corda, to personal prayer and the practice of piety, to private meditation and pursuit of the *visio Dei*. Paul points us to all of this, though not only to this, in Col. 3:1–3: "Seek the things that are above, where Christ is, seated at the right hand of God" (RSV). On such passages Origen and Augustine and their respective followers provide many centuries of glosses, often in the vein of Christian Neoplatonism, though other kinds of glosses can be found as well. It may be in this way that the doctrine of the ascension has had the most direct bearing on interpretation of the Bible. For the soul, as it advances toward God, is said to have insight into the Scriptures unavailable to less-refined souls. A hierarchy of meanings thus appears to it in keeping with its advance; grosser interpretations are stripped away along with this-worldly vanities (cf. Origen, *Princ.* 4.2.9).

Though there is most certainly some truth to this Origenist principle, it has its dangers. In the modern context it has been reformulated by Immanuel Kant in *Religion within the Limits of Reason Alone* (bk. 3). Here one may do with the Scriptures what one pleases, if operating on the premises of the Enlightenment and pursuing the course of progress—that is, the putative historical or general ascent of man. This Kantian understanding of the spiritual sense of Scripture may well relieve us of any embarrassing difficulty over the miraculous nature of the ascension. But it also relieves us of most of the traditional wealth of this doctrine, and of its power to confront our own age with the challenge of Jesus' lordship. At the same time, it relieves the church of its obligation to point to the absence of the ascended Christ as well as to persist in the sacramental embodiment of his presence—to bear witness quite concretely to his impending parousia.

Bibliography

Barth, K. *Church Dogmatics*. Vol. IV/2. T&T Clark, 1958; Davies, J. G. *He Ascended into Heaven*. Association, 1958; Dawson, G. S. *Jesus Ascended*. P&R, 2003; Farrow, D. *Ascension and Ecclesia*. T&T Clark, 1999; Kierkegaard, S. *Practice in Christianity*. Princeton University Press, 1991; Lohfink, G. *Die Himmelfahrt Jesu*. Kösel, 1971; Marrevee, W. H. *The Ascension of Christ in the Works of St. Augustine*. Saint Paul University, 1967; Milligan, W. *The Ascension and Heavenly Priesthood of Our Lord*. Macmillan, 1892; O'Donovan, O. *The Desire of the Nations*. Cambridge University Press, 1996; Parsons, M. C. *The Departure of Jesus in Luke-Acts*. JSOT, 1987; Torrance, T. *Space, Time, and Resurrection*. Eerdmans, 1976.

Douglas Farrow

Asian Biblical Interpretation

During the last few decades some Asian theologians have actively engaged in searching for Asian elements in biblical hermeneutics. This article surveys some issues in Asian biblical hermeneutics, and reflects from within the Asian context on the ways the discourse has developed.

Asian Perspectives

In the Asian approach to the Bible, we can identify four stances. Asian theologians have read the Bible from the contextual, pluralist, postcolonial, and religious perspectives.

Contextual Perspective. Asian theologians brought their contextual concerns to the reading of the Bible. Bringing the contextual concerns to the biblical text and excavating themes that would illuminate the distorted historical realities in Asia have been encouraged by the hermeneutical initiative of liberation theologies in Latin America. In Korea, theologians who experienced economic exploitation and political oppression came to interpret the Bible from the *minjung* (the poor and oppressed people) perspective. They eventually developed the *minjung* theology. In Japan, the harsh reality of the *burakumin* people (the defiled indigenous group and the tribals) was used as a hermeneutical lens to focus light from the Bible. Similarly in India, we saw the emergence of the *dalit* (the untouchables outside the caste system) theology, interpreting the Bible from the perspective of *dalit* people. Various other contextual concerns have been brought to interact with the Bible: women, nation building, unification, coexistence with other religious neighbors, social justice, poverty, liberation, and many others.

Pluralist Perspective. Moving beyond the contextual concerns, a few Asian theologians have attempted to bring a pluralist perspective in interpreting the Bible. They accept the cultural-religious texts and stories in Asia as authoritative sources on equal footing with the Bible. In their interaction with the Bible, those Asian theologians using the pluralist perspective seek to juxtapose the Bible (text A) with the Asian sources (text B) for mutual correction and mutual enrichment. Archie C. C. Lee, who is on the front line in advertising this pluralist approach, calls it a "cross-textual" hermeneutics. This cross-textual reading is a new experiment in Asian hermeneutical discourse, though for some time Asian Christians have circulated the idea that the Asian religious traditions and Christianity converge. Archie Lee defines this new adventure in the following way: "A cross-cultural approach aims at going beyond comparative studies and interfaith dialogue. It is a way to do theology which is meaningful to Asian Christians and theologians who have both the identity of being Asian as well as being Christian and who value both their cultural-religious text and the biblical text" ("Biblical"). Asian theologians who propose story theology as an Asian way also espouse the reading of the Bible side by side with the Asian cultural-religious stories/texts.

Postcolonial Perspective. A few Asian theologians have been active in using postcolonial discourse in biblical interpretation. In a nutshell, the postcolonial reading brings the following two hermeneutical perspectives. (1) The postcolonial reading exercises the hermeneutics of suspicion on the texts used to justify the colonial powers. (2) The postcolonial reading pays primary attention to the voices of the colonized and marginalized in the biblical text. We cannot say that the postcolonial reading of the Bible is a unique Asian contribution in the discourse of biblical hermeneutics. But we may have to recognize how, in line with the pluralist approach, it suggests that "other" religious texts that were once suppressed by the colonial power are to be valued equally with the Bible. Kwok Pui-Lan and R. S. Sugirtharajah are on the front line in advertising the postcolonial reading of the Bible.

Religious Perspective. In the Asian circle of biblical hermeneutics, another proposal is to approach the Bible with a religious perspective. This hermeneutical stance attempts to overcome the limits of the much-criticized historical-critical approach, and to read the Bible for awakening, embodying, and transforming the reading subject. Moonjang Lee suggests that readers explore alternatives to the current approaches to the Bible. He points out that the traditional Western approaches tend to be academic and detached, focusing on extracting "themes from the text that can be explained logically and supported factually." The traditional Asian approaches to sacred texts, according to Lee, are more practically engaged and focus on personal transformation, internalizing the messages of the text that are to be grasped intuitively. What Lee is suggesting is a reorientation in the way readers approach the Bible. A reader should approach the Bible as a religious text with the goal to grasp the wisdom and principles that can be perceived. As long as this reorientation of the hermeneutical goal is safeguarded, Asian readers can be open to the various critical reading methods.

Issues in Asian Biblical Hermeneutics

Scriptural Authority. The issue of biblical authority has been the subject of much debate in the West. Most Asian theologians involved in the discourse of Asian biblical hermeneutics readily accept the critical view of the Bible as a book that contains conflicting ideological traditions—the tradition of the oppressors and the tradition of the oppressed. Consequently, Asian theologians do not accept the authority of the *whole* Bible. *Minjung* theologians in Korea regard the Bible as one of the reference books that show aspects of *minjung* movements in particular socioeconomic situations in the past.

Asian theologians have added one more ingredient in relativizing scriptural authority by referring to the multiscriptural environment in Asia. The gist of their argument is that the authority of the Bible is hard to maintain because

the Bible is just one of the sacred scriptures in Asia. The superior status of the Bible in relation to other authoritative scriptures of Asian religions is to be rejected. The following remark by Archie Lee well expresses the so-called new awareness: "The encounter between the biblical text and the religiosity and spirituality expressed in the sacred texts of the living faiths of Asia will re-address the whole question of scriptural authority and absolute truth claims of the Christian faith" ("Biblical"). Other Asian theologians—such as Stanley Samartha, R. S. Sugirtharajah, Kwok Pui-Lan, C. S. Song, and Wesley Ariarajah—strongly endorse the attempt to relativize the authority of the Bible.

There seems to be a legitimate call to rediscover the Bible in the multiscriptural reality in Asia. However, its implications do not seem to have been fully digested by those theologians. A few observations can be made. (1) Every Asian theologian is well aware not only of the existence of the sacred texts in respective religious traditions in Asia, but also of their place within the respective faith community. The sacred texts are given due respect. (2) The sacred texts remain normative for adherents of the respective faith community. Samartha had to admit that the Bible is normative for Christians as other sacred books are normative to their respective adherents: "The Bible remains normative for all Christians in all spaces and at all times, because it bears witness to God's dealings with the whole world and to Jesus Christ, his life and death, and resurrection, his deeds and teachings, thus providing the basis for Christian theological reflection." Within the Christian faith community, the Bible is not seen as "one among many references in the search for truth." The attempt to relativize scriptural authority in the Asian hermeneutical discourse does not seem to be successful because traditional understanding of sacred books in Asia would safeguard the biblical authority within the Christian faith community. In this sense the Asian critique of scriptural authority fails to reflect the Asian religious ethos.

Use of Asian Cultural-Religious Stories. Another major issue in Asian biblical hermeneutics is the use of Asian resources. Some Asian theologians have proposed to juxtapose the Bible with other Asian resources. Their hermeneutical stance can be summarized as follows. (1) The Creator God has always been present in the Asian history, cultures, and religions. (2) Asian cultures and religions have equal status with the Bible, which cannot be regarded as the only reference in the search for the truth. (3) Therefore, Christians should be "open to different religious and cultural insights in the matter of interpreting the texts" (Samartha).

Archie Lee suggests cross-textual hermeneutics as the most appropriate approach to the Bible in Asia. He holds that cross-textual hermeneutics would solve what he calls the dilemma of Asian biblical interpretation, and urges us to accept the Asian cultural and religious text (text B) along with the biblical text (text A). The hermeneutical task in Asia necessarily includes two sides: "On the one hand, [cross-textual hermeneutics] affirms the cultural-historical point of view in order to understand its form and setting-in-life. The text is then applied to and interpreted in contemporary context. It is assumed that the text can enlighten our context. On the other hand, our Asian perspectives must also be brought in to shed light in the interpretation of biblical texts" ("Biblical," 38). Drawing on these perceptions, Lee proposes a creative interpenetration between the gospel and the Asian cultural text as the guiding principle in cross-textual hermeneutics ("Cross-Textual"). Sugirtharajah also fully endorses this initiative by further insisting that "divers textual expressions of human-divine encounter" should be reflected in the interpretative process ("Bible"). He even calls it religious bigotry to claim the uniqueness and superiority of the Christian tradition over others.

This hermeneutical stance is intertwined with the idea of religious pluralism. We may need to have a detailed examination of the relevancy of religious pluralism in Asian biblical hermeneutics to assess this proposal. That task would go beyond the scope of this article. Yet the following comments place their proposal in context. (1) Asian Christians have lived in a multireligious and multicultural milieu for centuries, but their experience of religious plurality needs to be correctly described. In Asia, each religion is a comprehensive system to perceive humanity, nature, and the universe. Each has maintained its respective religious identity and faith community. Hinduism, Buddhism, and Confucianism have their unique religious identity and teachings. (2) An Asian identity by culture must be differentiated from an Asian identity by commitment and allegiance to a particular religion. Asians carry the traditional religious elements in their body, but a multiple simultaneous allegiance to various religions would be something alien to the experience of religious plurality in Asia. (3) The boundaries between faith communities are to be respected. To be a member of a particular faith community is to accept the authority of the religion's unique teachings. The popular religiosity of Asian people expects Christians, Buddhists, and Confucians to be faithful to their respective teachings. In this regard, it may not be plausible to advise the Buddhist scholars or monks to be consciously open to Christian insights while reading their Buddhist sacred books.

Asian Reading Method. In the Asian biblical hermeneutical circle, strange as it may sound, the search for an Asian reading method has been one of the areas least attempted. We saw an embryonic attempt in an Indian Jesuit theologian, George M. Soares-Prabhu. About three decades ago he suggested an Indian way of reading the Bible, reacting critically to historical criticism. Soares-Prabhu made two important observations. (1) The nature of the Bible as a religious text requires reading methods different from the historical-critical approaches. (2) The effectiveness of a method is judged by the hermeneutical concern or interest of the reader. He differentiated the academic interest to obtain exact information from personal transformation through response in faith. The reading method should be devised to suit the hermeneutical concern. Although Soares-Prabhu attempted to pioneer a new territory, we do not see any further development in that line. Though some Asian theologians referred to the existence of hermeneutical traditions in Asia, they did not explore further, to work out ways to employ them in biblical interpretation. More recently, Moonjang Lee proposed to read the Bible in a postcritical way as a religious text and to develop an academic reading of the Bible in Asian ways. But still the traditional reading methods in Asia were not fully appropriated and incorporated in biblical hermeneutics.

Conclusion

Asian biblical hermeneutics are still in the making and challenge Asian Christians to be more creative and original in approaching the Bible. In approaching the Bible with multiple perspectives, Asian readers can have a dialogical partnership with Western readers. In the discourse of biblical hermeneutics, the uniquely Asian contribution will be found in the way(s) in which the traditional reading practices in Asia are appropriated and incorporated in exegeting and perceiving the messages of the Bible.

Bibliography

Ariarajah, W. *The Bible and People of Other Faiths.* WCC, 1989; Lan, K. P. *Discovering the Bible in the Non-Biblical World.* Orbis, 1995; Lee, A. C. C. "Biblical Interpretation in Asian Perspective." *AJT* 7, no. 1 (1993): 35–39; idem. "Cross-Textual Hermeneutics on Gospel and Culture." *AJT* 10, no. 1 (1996): 38–48; Lee, M. "A Post-Critical Reading of the Bible as a Religious Text." *AJT* 14, no. 2 (2000): 272–85; Samartha, S. J. *One Christ—Many Religions.* Orbis, 1991; Soares-Prabhu, G. "Towards an Indian Interpretation of the Bible." *Biblebhashyam* 6 (1980): 151–70; Sugirtharajah, R. S. *Asian Biblical Hermeneutics and Postcolonialism.* Orbis, 1998; idem. "The Bible and Its Asian Readers." *BibInt* 1, no. 1 (1993): 54–66; idem. *The Bible and the Third World.* Cambridge University Press, 2001; idem, ed. *Vernacular Hermeneutics.* Sheffield Academic Press, 1999.

Moonjang Lee

Assurance

Assurance is often limited to subjective feelings of security before God, but if we are to understand assurance in a biblical theology framework, it must be placed on the larger canvas of God's redemptive historical purpose.

Based upon God's Promise

Assurance is rooted in God's saving promise, beginning with the protevangelium, the pledge of victory over the seed of the serpent in Gen. 3:15. The initial promise is then fleshed out in Yahweh's covenants with Abraham, Israel at Sinai, David, and the new covenant. We must grasp the thread of the story line that informs Yahweh's covenant with Israel. The Lord has promised to redeem his people, and indeed the whole world, through the seed of Abraham (Gen. 12:1–3; cf. Gal. 3:16). The blessing promised to Abraham is fulfilled in the gospel of Christ (Acts 3:19–26; Gal. 3:6–9). The covenantal promises all point to the apostolic gospel (Rom. 1:2–4; 16:25–26), which proclaims the crucified and risen Lord (Rom. 4:25; 1 Cor. 15:1–4). Hence, we are not surprised to read that all God's promises find their fulfillment in Christ (2 Cor. 1:20). What Paul says relative to God's word to Israel is true of God's entire saving plan, "But it is not as though the word of God has failed" (Rom. 9:6 ESV).

The fundamental biblical teaching on assurance, therefore, is that believers should be full of confidence since God has promised to bless his people. That which God has pledged shall certainly be accomplished. Nothing can thwart his purposes in redemptive history. Believers can be assured that God will complete the good work that he has begun in them (Phil. 1:6). The love of God in Christ is so powerful that believers will never be severed from God's love (Rom. 8:35–39). God is faithful, and hence he will bring to pass what he has pledged in the lives of his people (1 Cor. 1:9; 10:13; 2 Cor. 1:18; 1 Thess. 5:24; 2 Thess. 3:3; 2 Tim. 2:13). Those whom God has foreknown and called will certainly be glorified on the last day (Rom. 8:28–30; cf. 1 Pet. 1:5). Further, it seems clear from Scripture that God desires his people to have confidence in their final salvation (John 5:24; Heb. 10:19–22; 1 John 3:2; 5:11–13). Still, the scriptural writers insist that assurance must focus on God's objective promises. Assurance does not come fundamentally from introspection, nor are believers summoned to reflect on their own capacity to endure. Assurance rests upon God's promises in Christ, clinging in faith to the work of Christ that secures salvation and brings us into God's presence.

Assurance and Warnings

Through most of its history the Christian church has been divided as to whether genuine believers will truly persevere. The debate centers particularly on the severe warnings in the NT that threaten judgment for those who apostatize (e.g., Rom. 11:22; Gal. 5:2–6; 2 Tim. 2:11–13; Heb. 6:4–8; 10:26–31). Furthermore, other texts refer to those who were part of the church and have since defected (e.g., 1 Tim. 1:18–20; 2 Tim. 4:10; 2 Pet. 2:19–22). Most agree that the problem is remarkably difficult and defies facile answers. Preserving the tension between assurance and warnings is necessary to be faithful to the biblical witness. If we abstract assurance from the warning passages, believers are prone to fall into lethargy and a false sense of spiritual security. If the warnings are sundered from assurance, believers may be overwhelmed by fear and doubt. The tension between these two sets of passages should be plotted against the background of NT eschatology, in which believers are *already* saved in this present evil age, but have *not yet* received the perfection promised.

Some have argued that apostasy is possible for genuine believers (Marshall; McKnight). Others maintain that those whom God has truly saved will persevere to the end (Grudem; Schreiner and Caneday). We should observe that both sets of interpreters believe that good works are *evidence* of genuine saving faith, and both argue that good works as a fruit of faith are necessary for eschatological salvation (cf. James 2:14–26). Furthermore, both would agree that obedience is one indication that a person genuinely belongs to God

(1 John 2:3–6; 2 Pet. 1:5–11). In both instances assurance is not an abstraction that is realized apart from the work of the Spirit in the lives of God's people. Still, it seems that the biblical teaching on assurance is best preserved by acknowledging that those who defected from the church only *appeared* to be genuine believers. Their leaving of the church demonstrates that their faith was not genuine (1 Cor. 11:19; 1 John 2:19).

Witness of the Spirit

Assurance in faith is also inextricably tied to the witness of the Holy Spirit (Rom. 8:16; 1 John 3:24; 4:13). The witness of the Spirit must not be abstracted from the rest of the biblical testimony. Believers have assurance fundamentally because of God's promises, and hence they consider God's objective work on their behalf. But the witness of the Spirit also confirms that believers are the children of God. The Spirit testifies to the hearts of God's people that they are truly God's children. The objective promises of God are now confirmed by the work of the Spirit within. The Spirit ineffably but clearly communicates that believers are in the circle of God's love and that they will never be lost from God's saving grasp.

What role does assurance play in the interpretation of Scripture? The Spirit seals to our hearts as we read that we truly belong to God. The objective promises of God found in Scripture and the internal work of the Spirit coalesce to produce assurance. In turn, the assurance granted by the Spirit informs us as we continue the interpretative task. Scripture is interpreted within the circle of confidence that belongs to the children of God. As we read the word of God, the Spirit assures us that the Father is benevolent to his children. Thus, those who have the Spirit grasp that God's promises are fundamental, and that our works, though important and necessary, can never be foundational or the basis of our right standing with God. The assurance that comes from the Spirit always points believers to Christ as God's wisdom, from whom we receive righteousness, sanctification, and redemption (1 Cor. 1:30).

See also Apostasy; Covenant

Bibliography

Beeke, J. *The Quest for Full Assurance*. Banner of Truth, 1999; Berkouwer, G. C. *Faith and Perseverance*, trans. R. Knudson. Eerdmans, 1958; Carson, D. A. "Reflections on Assurance." Pages 247–76 in *Still Sovereign*, ed. T. Schreiner and B. Ware. Baker, 2000; Eaton, M. *No Condemnation*. InterVarsity, 1995; Grudem, W. "Perseverance of the Saints: A Case Study of Hebrews 6:4–6 and the Other Warning Passages in Hebrews." Pages 133–82 in *Still Sovereign*, ed. T. Schreiner and B. Ware. Baker, 2000; Gundry-Volf, J. *Paul and Perseverance*. Westminster John Knox, 1990; Marshall, I. H. *Kept by the Power of God*. Bethany, 1974; McKnight, S. "The Warning Passages in Hebrews: A Formal Analysis and Theological Conclusions." *TJ* 13 (1992): 21–59; Schreiner, T., and A. Caneday. *The Race Set before Us*. InterVarsity, 2001; Zachman, R. *The Assurance of Faith*. Fortress, 1993.

Thomas R. Schreiner

Assyriology *See* Ancient Near Eastern Background Studies

Atlas *See* Geography

Atonement

"Atonement" (*at-one-ment*) has been, since the sixteenth century, the main English word for that which ensures right or happy relations with the Deity and removes obstacles to that end. Other languages do not offer an exact correspondence—and this may subtly affect theological interpretation as it is carried in different linguistic areas. The semantic spectrum of "atonement" covers both German *Versöhnung* (reconciliation) and *Sühne* (expiation), with some overlap with *Erlösung* (redemption, with emphasis on its effect, liberation). In French and other Latin tongues, the main term is *rédemption* (the thought of the price paid is near at hand), with *expiation* important too, at least in the vocabulary of previous generations. English use offers a distinct advantage: the lexical frequency and weight of "atone" and "atonement" in common versions of Scripture can be compared with that of the verb *kapar* and its derivatives in the Hebrew OT, which they usually render in translation. Intensive Bible reading by a majority of the people over a long time had linguistic effects: under contextual guidance or pressure, the biblical use of *kapar* thus molded the meaning of "atonement." "Atone" is probably perceived with a fair degree of equivalence with *kapar*. Yet, it is to be remembered that correspondence cannot be perfect (e.g., the English reader hardly guesses that there is a close kinship between "atone" and "ransom," *kofer*, a kinship of which the Hebrew reader is marginally aware even when his or her attention is focused elsewhere). One should also realize that there is no NT word to play a similar role—occurrences of *hilaskesthai* (nearest in meaning), "to propitiate," and its derivatives are sparse indeed (Luke 18:13; Rom. 3:25; Heb. 2:17; 1 John 2:2; 4:10).

Whether served by one keyword (*kapar* in the OT), or by none—that is, many (NT)—the theme of atonement could hardly be more prominent than it is in Scripture: the major topic of one book in the Law, the concern of several psalms, an important interest of prophecy. Atonement lies at the heart of the good news. The striking NT feature is its close association with the *death* of Jesus, not only in Paul's evangel (1 Cor. 2:2–13), but also in all strands of apostolic witness (an index could be the amount of space devoted to the passion narrative in the Gospels, or the title "Lamb" in Johannine writings). Since that death is a scandal for Jewish expectations and foolishness to the Greek mind, the problem of interpretation is felt acutely, first in the NT, and also throughout the history of theology. We shall recall how diverse theologies of the atonement have been, sketching the history of interpretation; briefly survey main biblical material; and then investigate the *loci* of decision, in procedure and attitudes—where and why this or that course has been chosen.

Theologies at Variance

With few exceptions, the church fathers were pastors rather than specialized theologians. To communicate the message of the atonement, they freely mingled several schemes, with little concern for systematic ordering. They saw the surrounding pagan world as the playground of demons, and proclaimed the victory of Christ over Satan; often with the thought that God, through the cross, outwitted and duped the Deceiver (Gregory of Nyssa). But that presentation was by no means exclusive, and Aulén went far beyond the evidence when he called it the "classical view." *Logos*-Christologies easily combined with an emphasis on the teaching of heavenly truth and the "true Gnostics" of the Alexandrian school (Clement; Origen) saw revelation as a major component of atonement. The "mystical" view was widespread, basing atonement on the union of flesh and Spirit in the person of Jesus Christ, the infusion of divine life into the body of humankind, with healing and transforming power. Irenaeus's *anakephalaiōsis* (recapitulation) synthesis stressed the role of the new Adam (and the new Eve). Athanasius emphasized the *theōsis* (deification) of human nature as assumed by the One who is very God of very God. At the same time, the fathers freely use the languages of piacular sacrifices and penal substitution, not only the Latin but also the Greek fathers, as Rivière has shown. Athanasius is noteworthy for his effort at systematization (Rivière 94–95): God's veracity demanded that sin be retributed with the death penalty (Gen. 2:17); Christ offered his mortal body

in death as a substitute for ours (*antipsychon hyper pantōn*); thus was our debt repaid (*Inc.* 6.9–10; cf. *C. Ar.* 2.47, 66). Eusebius explicitly identified the principle of sacrificial expiation with vicarious punishment (*Dem. ev.* 10.1). Augustine, as the legitimate heir of the patristic estate, clearly formulated the penal debt interpretation, though it is not in the forefront of his teaching (*Enchir.* 10.33; *Faust.* 14.4).

Anselm's contribution was to concentrate on one scheme, to bind it with Chalcedonian Christology, and fearlessly to bring out its logic. The structure is the same as in Athanasius's argument on divine truthfulness, but the decisive concern is that of feudal honor. Satisfaction obtains through Christ's denial of self as a work of supererogation (it is *not* penal: the *Cur Deus homo* assumes the alternative *aut satisfactio, aut poena*; 1.15). Abelard is known as the pioneer of the subjective, moral influence, view (though he did express the objective and penal one when commenting on Rom. 4:25; as quoted by Tobias Eißler 124n30). Thomas Aquinas highlights Christ's loving and meritorious consecration to the Father, as the Head of the body, but he definitely maintains a penal satisfaction component (*ST* III^a, q. 48, esp. art. 4 and 5; and most precise, *De rationibus fidei* 7).

The Magisterial Reformers made penal expiation central and set forth the once-for-all, finished work of the cross as the foundation of justification by faith alone. Luther preached it with unprecedented force (under the influence of Gal. 3); he taught that the satisfaction of divine justice and the propitiation of God's wrath is the basis of our deliverance from sin, death, and the devil (Eißler 128–29). Calvin marshaled the biblical evidence (Isa. 53 as a key). While Anabaptists stressed Christ's example in the way of martyrdom, Luther's and Calvin's doctrine of atonement became the heart of the evangelical message, and its so-called "crucicentrism," down, for example, to John Stott. Until the middle of the twentieth century, Roman Catholics also commonly held penal substitution as one element in complex theologies.

In the wake of Socinian attacks, Protestant liberalism and Catholic modernism rejected objective theories, especially penal substitution. The "heretical" anthropology of R. Girard has reinforced the trend. Radical feminists have expressed the strongest possible aversion. In the Roman Church, after the critique by Sabourin and Lyonnet and under the climate created by Teilhard de Chardin and Rahner, few scholars of note, if any, have maintained it. K. Barth again proclaimed that Christ was "the Judge judged in our stead" but expressly repudiated the doctrine that he was so punished as to spare us death and to "satisfy" the demands of wrath (*CD* IV/1, §59/2, fine print after about 40 percent of the section). In their later writings Moltmann and Pannenberg have come closer to evangelical language. However, Moltmann denies that God's wrath was appeased (25–26), and Pannenberg, despite strong statements of penal substitution (425–27), claims that "the reconciling death of Christ is not a payment that Christ made to God in place of others" (429; 448, against "satisfaction").

Mapping Biblical Evidence

In the OT, atonement appears as the effect of divine grace, mainly as forgiveness (Ps. 130:3–4) and as the function of sacrifices—God-given to that end (Lev. 17:11). Hope is directed to a total removal of sin (Zech. 3:9), toward which the seventy "sevens" are decreed (Dan. 9:24, using *kapar*). The NT claim to fulfillment centers in Jesus' death. How does it provide atonement? Though the heinous crime of men, the rejection of Light by darkness, it was no accident; it accomplished what God had purposed (Acts 2:23; 4:28; 1 Pet. 1:20) and was the goal of Christ's mission (Mark 10:45; John 12:27; cf. 10:18). It offered the perfect example of meekness and courageous confession (1 Pet. 2:21; 1 Tim. 6:13), but there is no suggestion that it could be *as such* the basis of atonement. It demonstrated the *summum* of love, on Christ's and on the Father's part (John 13:1; 15:13; Rom. 5:8), but since that love is no romantic (suicidal) passion, it remains to be explained why it had to be expressed in death. The clearest answer is that Christ's death was required for our justification, which happens "by his blood" (Rom. 5:9), and specifically—since leaving sins unpunished casts doubts on God's justice—that God may be "both just and justifier" when he acquits the guilty who put their faith in Jesus (cf. 3:26).

How, still, is this achieved? R. W. Dale discerned three pictorial sets or schemes through which the NT accounts for the atoning efficacy of Jesus' death; E. Brunner added two others, which may be regarded as complementary:

1. Sacrifice. The title "Lamb" (at least in part) and references to the blood belong to that presentation. Sacrifice is expressed in Isa. 53 (v. 10, *'asham*); it is found in many NT places, as "propitiatory sacrifice" in 1 John 2:1–2 and 4:10 (cf.

Rom. 3:25), and as sacrifice "for sin" in Rom. 8:3 (possibly the same in 2 Cor. 5:21).

2. Penal Execution. The language of the law court (that also of justification, including the justification of Jesus; 1 Tim. 3:16), with condemnation and curse, and of the legal document that was against us (Col. 2:14) develops that viewpoint. It is dominant in Isa. 53; it is implied in the phrase "to bear sin or iniquity," meaning liability to the corresponding punishment. Christ bore our sins (1 Pet. 2:24), suffered under their condemnation (Rom. 8:3) and the curse we had deserved (Gal. 3:13).

3. Ransom. Redemption implies not only the effect of freedom granted but also the means of price paid (the price is underlined in 1 Cor. 6:20 and 7:23, and how precious the ransom-blood that was given for us in 1 Pet. 1:19). The language of debt is correlative, since our legal debt, we were unable to pay, made us slaves and captives (Gal. 3:23; 5:1–3), the "remission of sins" being the "release of debts" (*aphesis*). Also in the background is the special institution of the kinsman-redeemer, who acts as a substitute for a deceased relative.

4. Victory. Atonement represents a winning battle against the forces and agents of estrangement, against the devil and the powers aligned with him. Christ's Passion as his duel with Satan and the outcome as his triumph is found in several passages (John 12:31; Col. 2:14; Heb. 2:14; Rev. 5; 12).

5. Passover. Jesus told of his imminent death as the fulfillment of the Passover type (Luke 22:15–16). John (19:36) and Paul followed (1 Cor. 5:7). This representation brings together the themes of the Lamb, the new exodus, and the new covenant.

Discerning Critical Issues

Strategic choices on how to deal with biblical material are made on many issues or clusters of issues.

One Biblical Thought? Whether there is a unifying perspective on atonement throughout biblical writings and whether it can guide theological reflection is obviously first rank. There is little hope of a fruitful interpretation of Scripture *as such* if one discards the canonical principle, presupposes that various authors held contrary views, or that their witness lies on a plane altogether alien from the quest of *intellectus fidei*. The presupposition of classic Christianity affirms that all the Scriptures, owing to their common inspiration, reflect the same, homogeneous, *mind*—despite striking differences in angle, aspect, emphasis, vocabulary, *and* conceptual apparatus (in that sense, there are many theologies of atonement in the Bible, but they are not incompatible with one another).

This entails the Reformers' hermeneutical principle: *Scriptura sacra semetipsam interpretans*. It implies several things: The lack of a clear statement of a view in a book should *not* count as a sign of rejection (the absence of evidence is no evidence of absence)—contrary to much current practice. Various presentations should be interpreted as convergent and complementary, not opposed. And theological "hygiene" should banish dichotomies between biblical themes (e.g., initiative of love/appeasement of wrath). Sound method will then extend to the whole of Scripture the import of the more explicit passages, whose "natural" meaning (as Calvin would say) remarkably resists efforts at circumventing it, such as Isa. 53; Rom. 3; 2 Cor. 5; Gal. 3; Heb. 9. Other presuppositions on Scripture and its relationship to theological reason hardly generate similar interpretations.

Mere Disjointed Metaphors? Skeptics of the classical use of Scripture to build the doctrine of atonement often stress the metaphorical nature of the language used; representations are not consistent, signifying that they should not be taken literally (We do not read of the debt being settled. To whom was the ransom paid? There is no resurrection in sacrifices . . .). That the NT uses metaphor is fact—one could argue that the cross was a judicial punishment *literally*, but the statement that *God's* judgment was exercised also involves transference. It is less obvious that these metaphors disagree. On the contrary, writers freely blend several of them in the same verses (the three main schemes intertwined in Rom. 3:24–26), and it is fairly easy to "translate" one into the other, including that of victory. Therefore, the presumption is that they made for a consistent picture. The issue, however, is the cognitive import of metaphors generally. It may be argued that metaphors range from free and ornamental ones, to foundational and revealing ones, tools of knowledge that glide into conceptual status. These play a regulative and even informative role in theology (analogy may then be distinguished from metaphor). Criteria might include frequency, consistency, richness in correspondence, and whether logical consequences are drawn (in the text).

Sacrificial and judicial metaphors may claim a privileged status in Scripture. The NT views the Levitical system as *typical*, foreordained to represent the meaning of Christ's death. Human judges are instituted as the representatives of God, with delegated authority to render judgment in his name (the logic of Rom. 12:19–13:7). Presumably, these institutions yield metaphors (analogies) apt and cognitively useful.

Organic Connections? Within the "body" of divinity, to some extent an organic whole, there must be solidarities between the doctrine of atonement and neighboring ones. Consideration of thematic connections weighs heavily upon the interpretation of atonement material.

The main issues concerned seem to be these: the seriousness of sin and helplessness of human beings (*Cur Deus homo*: "You have not yet considered what is the gravity of sin"), especially the preoccupation with guilt in biblical sensitivity; the validity of retribution (in such doubt in contemporary culture); the reality of divine wrath, and the way it is related to love and mercy; the incarnation, and whether it is understood as salvific in itself or as a preparation and precondition for the work of the cross; the principle of substitution, with the structure of "headship" (for some, "corporate personality"); the relationship of justification and sanctification, with exclusive and inclusive representation.

More or Less Radical? A theological interpretation of Scripture, tending toward an *intellectus fidei*, faces the question of radicality. Is it right to insist that the demands of God's righteousness are so absolute that our best deeds are but "filthy rags" in his sight? That he would deny his word (Athanasius) and himself, if he were to forgive sinners without capital punishment for sin being executed? Or is this a false absolutization of a human idea of divine holiness?

Adjusting Subjective Involvement

When Scripture is interpreted on atonement, the theologian's personal implication is also a *locus* of decision.

Reverence and Responsibility. Against the former myth of neutrality, the role of tradition, which shapes the interpreter's horizon, and of community interests have been increasingly recognized. At the same time, theology would dissolve into tribal propaganda if the theologian relinquishes the responsibility of critical assessment, after objective criteria.

The topic of atonement illustrates the need for that balance. It would be rash to ignore the continuity of patristic, medieval, and evangelical tradition on atonement. Combined with hermeneutical virtues (Vanhoozer), gratitude and reverence for tradition are in order. They may free a theologian from the tyranny of contemporary sentiment, and from the demand (also commercial) that he offer allegedly "new insights," with the assumption that older treatments are obsolete. Yet, tradition itself is not unanimous, and as a fallible human apprehension, it too stands under the word of God. The analysis of present community interests should help in resisting distortions of biblical evidence (vigilance) and also help in highlighting what is most relevant to real needs and adapting pedagogical procedure.

Another kind of reverence and responsible vigilance is called for with contributions from the social sciences—precious indeed, provided the degree of corroboration be appraised and "ideological" twist discerned.

Fear and Faith "Coram Deo." The roots of a theologian's choice go deeper than intellectual tradition and environment. They are spiritual. The way one will interpret the Scriptures is ultimately affected by one's stance "before God." Does one see oneself as God's advocate, called to make the doctrine less repulsive to "cultured people among its despisers"? Does one see oneself as a sinner without a plea, "undone" in the presence of the thrice-holy God, in fear—and faith?

See also Metaphor; Violence

Bibliography

Aulén, G. *Christus Victor*, trans. A. G. Hebert. SPCK, 1961 [1931]; Blocher, H. "*Agnus Victor*: The Atonement as Victory and Vicarious Punishment." In *What Does It Mean to Be Saved?* ed. J. Stackhouse Jr. Baker, 2002; idem. "The Sacrifice of Jesus Christ: The Current Theological Situation." *European Journal of Theology* 8 (1999): 23–36; Brunner, E. *Dogmatics*. Vol. 2, trans. O. Wyon. Lutterworth, 1952; Cousar, C., et al. on Atonement and Scripture. *Interpretation* 52, no. 1 (Jan 1998); Dale, R. W. *The Atonement*. Congregational Union of England and Wales, 1897 [1875]; Eißler, T. In *Warum das Kreuz?* ed. V. Gäckle. R. Brockhaus, 1998; Goldingay, J., ed. *Atonement Today*. SPCK, 1995; Lyonnet, S., and L. Sabourin. *Sin, Redemption, and Sacrifice*. AnBib 48. Pontifical Institute, 1970; Moltmann, J. "The Passion of Christ as the Suffering of God." *Asbury Theological Journal* 48 (1993): 19–28; Morris, L. *The Apostolic Preaching of the Cross*. Tyndale, 1955; Nicole, R. "The Nature of Redemption." Pages 245–82 in *Standing Forth*. Christian Focus, 2002; Packer, J. I. "What Did the Cross Achieve? The Logic of Penal Substitution." *TynBul* 25 (1974): 3–45; Pannenberg, W. *Systematic Theology*. Vol. 2, trans. G. W. Bromiley. Eerdmans, 1994; Rivière, J. *Le Dogme de la Rédemption*. Lecoffre-Gabalda, 1931.

Henri A. G. Blocher

Augustine

Scripture was at the heart of Augustine's conversion and ministry, his theological reflection and personal devotion. At least two-thirds of his works are either commentaries or sermons on scriptural texts (the latter often take the form of sustained commentary, for example his *Tractates on St. John's Gospel* and his *Ennarations on the Psalms*). His other works constantly cite or allude to Scripture, so that it often seems that the language of the biblical author becomes Augustine's own; this is particularly evident in his *Confessions*, which are immersed in the poetry of the Psalms.

It was probably Augustine's devout mother, Monica, who first made him aware of the Christian Scriptures, and it is significant that, fired with an enthusiasm for wisdom after reading Cicero's *Exhortation to Philosophy* at the age of nineteen, he should immediately turn to examine the Scriptures. At this stage they were a great disappointment: they struck Augustine's educated and cultured mind as somewhat crude and badly written, lacking the literary merit of the "majesty of Cicero." It was not just how the biblical authors expressed themselves, but also what they said that troubled Augustine: the OT and NT seemed to be full of discrepancies; the morality and conception of God contained in the former repelled Augustine; the contradictions in the latter undermined their authors' credibility. He discovered that these were reservations that he shared with the dualistic Manichaean sect, which claimed to represent true Christianity; it was to them and their literalistic exegesis that he adhered for the next nine years.

Ambrose, bishop of Milan, whom Augustine heard preach in the mid 380s, was a key figure in Augustine's eventual reconciliation with Christianity and its Scriptures. His allegorical approach, coupled with his Neoplatonic learning, revealed to Augustine the revolutionary possibility that true reality was spiritual, and that Scripture need not be treated with deadening literalism. Instead, it could be interpreted spiritually, with levels of meaning to meet the most demanding literary scholar and rational critic, as well as the devout faithful.

Scripture itself finally tipped the balance for Augustine, the reluctant convert, in Milan in 386. The divinely inspired call, "Take up and read," led to his opening the copy of Paul's letters that he had been reading and taking to heart the text upon which his eyes alighted: Rom. 13:13. From then on

Scripture was to be the hub of Augustine's Christian life and work. When he was unexpectedly ordained in Hippo in 391, he immediately asked his bishop for time free to study the Scriptures. Thenceforth, they were to be his sole resource for the moral, spiritual, and practical guidance of his congregation. They were an arsenal from which to refute heretics and schismatics, the source and inspiration of his theological reflection, and the wellspring of his spiritual life.

Augustine would not have possessed a single-volume Bible; rather, he would have used individual books of Scripture, which, in his mind, together constituted a canon. The text he would have generally used is now known to us as the Old Latin, though he perhaps later used some of Jerome's new Latin translations (which laid the foundations for what we now possess as the Vulgate). He shared with other early fathers the basic presupposition that Scripture was wholly inspired by the Holy Spirit, so that no one part could disagree with or contradict another; Scripture was unified and inerrant. It therefore also possessed for them various levels, which invited different interpretations of the same text, according to whether it was read literally or spiritually. Many of the fathers identified three or four different levels; Augustine, in two texts, enumerates four: the etiological, the historical, the anagogical, and the allegorical. Most important, Augustine and the fathers regarded Scripture as primarily christological; Christ was the key to its interpretation and was to be found in both Testaments as its foundation, meaning, center, and end.

Augustine, in common with other fathers of the church, used various traditional (by his day) methods of interpretation, which had become established due to their usefulness in overcoming the difficulties that the diverse and disparate scriptural texts raised, and in teaching and preaching to their congregations. Typology, which identified "types" or prefigurings of NT persons, events, and sacraments in the OT, allowed them to unify the two Testaments with each other and with the current identity and practices of the church. Allegory, the most popular method of interpretation, allowed Augustine to overcome the difficulties posed by a passage that appeared contradictory, banal, immoral, or obviously figurative and to plumb its spiritual depths. Thereby he could guard its mysteries from the unworthy and reveal them to the worthy, meeting the various members of his congregation at their different levels and enabling them to exercise their minds and, ultimately, delight in the truth they discov-

ered. It also allowed Augustine and his cultured audience to reconcile themselves to Scripture as a text possessing literary merit, able to stand alongside the great works of classical literature on an equal footing. This was obviously an issue to which Augustine was particularly sensitive: his *On Christian Doctrine*, a work on Christian exegesis and preaching, is at the same time a treatise on the relation between Christianity and classical culture and rhetoric. He cannot resist the temptation, in the fourth book, to demonstrate in a detailed and technical way, characteristic of the former rhetor, the literary eloquence and polish of Scripture.

It was ultimately at the level of meaning or intention that Augustine located the unity of Scripture. In his work *On the Harmony of the Gospels*, he argues that the apparent discrepancies in the accounts of the evangelists are merely at the level of personal reminiscence. The Holy Spirit has providentially allowed such discrepancies to provide the reader with different viewpoints. The accounts are the "casualties of their recollections." What is much more important is the truth of the facts they recount and their unified intention: this is what the exegete is obliged to seek out. In *Confessions*, book 12, Augustine goes even further and argues that the meaning and intention that each individual reader finds might be different, but each is equally valid; there are as many meanings as readers. What then are the parameters for acceptable interpretation? For Augustine, it is the double commandment of love of God and neighbor; so long as exegetes do not contradict this basic rule, then their teaching is acceptable. Love is the inspiration and source of Scripture, its meaning and its end.

See also Human Being, Doctrine of; Illumination; Love; Medieval Biblical Interpretation; Patristic Biblical Interpretation

Bibliography

Arnold, D. W. H., and P. Bright, eds. *De Doctrina Christiana*. Christianity and Judaism in Antiquity 9. University of Notre Dame Press, 1995; Bright, P., ed. *Augustine and the Bible*. University of Notre Dame Press, 1986; Duchrow, U. *Sprachverständnis und biblisches Hören bei Augustin*. Vol. 5 of *Hermeneutische Untersuchungen zur Theologie*. Mohr, 1965; La Bonnardière, A.-M. *Biblia Augustiniana*. Études augustiniennes, 1960–75; idem. *Saint Augustin et la Bible*. Beauchesne, 1986; de Margerie, B. *Saint Augustine*. Vol. 3 of *An Introduction to the History of Exegesis*. Saint Bede's, 1993; Pépin, J. "Saint Augustin et la function protréptique de l'allegorie." *Recherches Augustiniennes* 1 (1958): 243–86; Pontet, M. *L'Exégèse de saint Augustin prédicateur*. Aubier, 1944; Van Fleteren, F., and J. C.

Schnaubelt, eds. *Augustine*. Collectanea Augustiniana 5. Peter Lang, 2001.

Carol Harrison

Authorial Discourse Interpretation

The defenders of authorial discourse interpretation claim that such interpretation is what all of us do most of the time when we interpret; for example, it is what we all do when we read history books, scientific texts, legal documents, and instructions for the repair of home appliances. The special contribution that this way of understanding makes to biblical interpretation is that it offers a way to grasp how it can be that God speaks.

Why God's Speaking Has Been Neglected

The claim that God speaks to human beings occurs over and over in the Bible. It likewise occurs throughout history, as Christians and others try to make sense of their experience. In the Christian liturgy, when Scripture reading is introduced with the words "Listen for the word of God," the people respond with the acclamation "This is the word of the Lord."

Yet theologians have paid remarkably little attention to God's speaking. There would seem to be two main reasons for this. For one thing, God's speaking has typically been assimilated, mistakenly so, to other things that God does, and thus given no attention in its own right. In conservative and evangelical circles, God's speaking has traditionally been assimilated to inspiration; God inspires the prophets and the writers of Scripture. That inspiration is not the same as speaking can be easily seen, however. I may in one way or another *inspire* you to say or write what you did; it nonetheless remains the case that it was *you* who said or wrote it, not me. God's inspiring the prophets and biblical writers to speak and write as they did is not the same as *God himself* speaking.

In mainline and liberal circles of the twentieth century, God's speaking has been assimilated to God's self-revelation. God, it is said, reveals or manifests himself; and human beings then put into words what it is that was revealed or manifested. It can easily be seen that revelation is also not the same as speaking. One may reveal something about oneself without saying anything at all; while remaining silent, the person's quaking hands reveal his nervousness. It is no doubt true that when we speak, we always reveal *something* about ourselves; but what we reveal is normally not the content of our speech. A native speaker of English reveals that he is a native speaker but rarely says that he is. It is especially important not to identify such speech actions as asking or commanding with revelation. If you ask me the time of day and I focus all my attention on what that reveals about you, I neglect to respond to your request; indeed, focusing on what your question reveals about you may be a way of evading your request.

The other reason theologians have given remarkably little attention to God's speech as such is that it has been thought that to attribute speech to God is to speak anthropomorphically, just as when one attributes eyes and arms to God. Theologians have asked what it is about God that these supposed anthropomorphisms point to; and their answer, in the case of attributions of speech to God, has been either that it points to God's inspiration or to God's revelation. The conviction that talk about God speaking is anthropomorphic thus contributes to the mistaken assimilation of God's speaking to inspiration or revelation. As we shall see, the theory used to articulate authorial discourse interpretation enables us to understand the attribution of speaking to God as non-anthropomorphic.

Locutionary and Illocutionary Actions

One of the major contributions of the Oxford philosopher J. L. Austin, who did most of his work in the 1950s, was his development of so-called *speech-act theory*. For our purposes here, all we need from speech-act theory is the most basic of all the distinctions that Austin introduced. Suppose that someone makes an assertion about a late train by uttering the sentence, "The train is running late." Austin calls the act of uttering that sentence a *locutionary act*; likewise, the act of inscribing that sentence.

But there is something else the person has done, says Austin, than perform that locutionary act, something else he has done *by* performing that locutionary act, not just in addition to it. He has *asserted* that the train is running late. To see that uttering that sentence is a distinct act from making that assertion, notice that either one can be performed without performing the other. One can utter or inscribe the sentence without asserting that the train is late; for instance, one can utter or inscribe it as an example of some point, which is, in fact, what I did in the preceding paragraph. On the other hand, there are ways of asserting that the train is running late that do not involve uttering or inscribing that sentence. For instance,

I might make that assertion by uttering a synonymous sentence in some foreign language; or I might make it by using smoke signals, pictures, Morse code, and the like. Austin proposed that we call actions that we perform *by way of* performing locutionary actions, *illocutionary actions*, with examples being asserting, warning, asking, and commanding. The locutionary action *counts as* the illocutionary action.

The defender of the priority of authorial discourse interpretation holds that what all of us do most of the times we interpret oral or written discourse is try to identify and understand the *illocutionary acts* that the discourser performed by producing that utterance or inscription. When you turn to me in the station and utter the sentence, "The train is running late," I want to grasp what you said—that is, what illocutionary act you performed. And when I read the repair manual for my lawn mower, I want to grasp what those who issued this manual were saying thereby—what instructions they were giving.

Sometimes we think we know very well what the person said; but we suspect that is not what she *wanted* to say, not what she *intended* to say. As with all intentions, the intention to say something may misfire. You intended to say that the train is running late; but you were somewhat distracted, and what came out was something else. In some situations it is more important to us to know what the person intended to say than what she did say. But obviously, most of us do not misspeak most of the time, or communication would be next to impossible. For the most part, our interest is in what the person did say, not in what she intended to say in case that is different. Our interest is in the illocutionary action she did perform. Interpretation conducted with the aim of discovering and understanding the illocutionary act performed is *authorial discourse interpretation*. (The term was probably first used in Wolterstorff.)

Double Agency Discourse

If we are to employ this conceptuality to understand how God speaks, we must take note of a kind of discourse that neither Austin nor any of his followers took any special note of, *double agency discourse*. (This term too was probably first used in Wolterstorff.) Sometimes one person performs some illocutionary action by way of another person performing some locutionary or illocutionary action; the latter speaks *on behalf of* the former, or *in the name of* the former. One of the most common forms of such double agency discourse in ordinary life occurs when

one person gives to another the right of attorney. Before the day of telephone and electronic communication, it also occurred when a head of state commissioned someone to be his ambassador. It seems clear that this is how the biblical writers understood the relation of God to the prophet; the prophet spoke on behalf of God. The prophet was not merely a communicator of messages from God to human beings; the prophet also spoke in the name of God. By hearing the prophet speak, human beings heard God speak to them there and then—double agency discourse.

Another form of double agency discourse occurs when one *appropriates* the discourse of another for one's own purpose—as when we approvingly quote what someone said, or remark, in response to some speech, "I agree with that" or "He speaks for me too." In such cases there was no prior commissioning; one simply took a piece of discourse that had already occurred and appropriated it for one's own discourse.

The question of anthropomorphism comes down, then, to this: does God need a body to perform illocutionary actions by way of commissioning someone to speak on his behalf or by way of appropriating what has already been said? The answer seems quite clearly to be no. It might be asked whether God needs a body even to perform locutionary actions; why could God not produce inscriptions of sentences on a wall even though God lacks hands, and produce utterings of sentences in the air even though God lacks vocal cords? But what we are interested in is whether God can literally command, warn, reassure, ask, assert, and so forth—all of these being *il*-locutionary actions. And there seems no reason to say that God could not.

Advantages of Thinking in Terms of Double Agency Discourse

When a head of state commissions someone as his ambassador, and when any one of us gives someone power of attorney, the ambassador or attorney does not become a mere mouthpiece of the one who commissions him to speak on his behalf. The ambassador and attorney retain their own individuality. They choose the words they use, their character is reflected in how they speak, their knowledge or lack of knowledge of one thing or another is revealed, and all of that. So too when we appropriate some extant piece of discourse for our own: the appropriated discourse obviously retains its own character. Had we spoken in our own voice, it might well have come out rather differently. The application to

God's speech is obvious. If we think in terms of double agency discourse, we can take due account of all the particularities and idiosyncrasies of what the human being said while at the same time interpreting what God said thereby.

One particular application of this point is of special importance. The Bible comes to us in the form of sixty-six books, plus perhaps a few depending on the canon that one prefers; biblical scholars have argued that a few of these, especially Isaiah, should be seen as two or more books attached to each other. It is common among biblical scholars in the critical tradition to insist that each of these books be read separately, not as parts of one big book, the Bible. To read them as parts of one big book is to fail to recognize the integrity of each. Matthew presents Jesus in a different light from Luke; if we read them together, we miss the richness of those different perspectives.

But now suppose one thinks about the situation in terms of double agency discourse. Sometimes when a person writes a book, he will, along the way, appropriate by quotation one passage from one writer to make his point, another passage from another writer, and so forth. Indeed, it would in principle be possible to write a book of one's own in which one does nothing but quote passages written by others. In many such cases, the point one wants to make by quoting some passage may be somewhat different from the point that the original author made by writing it. On the other hand, often one cannot figure out the point of the quoting writer without first figuring out the point of the quoted text. So too, if we think of Scripture as God's word to us, God's discourse to us. One can both interpret each book by itself, honoring its integrity by trying to discern its particular message, while also interpreting all the books together for God's discourse. Indeed, doing the latter *presupposes* that one has done the former. Scripture is the polyphony of human discourse through the totality of which God's discourse comes to us.

See also Intention/Intentional Fallacy; Meaning; Revelation; Speech-Act Theory; Word of God

Bibliography

Austin, J. L. *How to Do Things with Words*. Clarendon, 1962; Searle, J. *Speech Acts*. Cambridge University Press, 1970; Vanhoozer, K. *Is There a Meaning in This Text?* Zondervan, 1998; Wolterstorff, N. *Divine Discourse*. Cambridge University Press, 1995.

Nicholas P. Wolterstorff

Authorial Intention   *See* Authorial Discourse Interpretation; Intention/Intentional Fallacy

Authorship   *See* Authorial Discourse Interpretation; Pseudepigrapha

B

Bakhtin, Mikhail *See* Dialogism

Baptism

Baptism has multiple meanings reflected in various biblical texts. It incorporates members into the church through baptism into the one body of Christ (1 Cor. 12:13). Through baptism into Christ's priesthood (1 Pet. 2:5, 9; Rev. 1:6; 5:10) the baptized are able to offer spiritual sacrifices acceptable to God and thus are deputed to the public worship of the church. Baptism described as a "spiritual circumcision" indicates participation in the new covenant (Col. 2:11–12 NRSV). It is also a pardoning and cleansing from sin (Acts 22:16; 1 Cor. 6:11; Eph. 5:26; Heb. 10:22), a new birth (John 3:5), and a gift of the Spirit (Acts 2:38). Baptism requires conversion, a new life in Christ, and a renunciation of sin that entails a new ethical orientation (1 Cor. 6:9–11).

In Christian churches the theology of baptism has been influenced by two foundational texts, Rom. 6:3–4 and Mark 1:9–11. The Western churches have primarily stressed baptism as participation in Christ's death and resurrection according to the theology in the Epistle to the Romans. The act of baptismal immersion is the sign of Christ's dying and rising and signifies the new life and Christian identity of the baptized.

The Eastern churches tend to privilege Mark 1:9–11 and parallel texts. They view baptism as the reenactment of Jesus' baptism in the Jordan. The Gospel texts stress the pneumatological and trinitarian aspects of baptism—the gift of the Spirit and the presence of the Father, Son, and Spirit in the water bath in the Jordan. The baptized become adopted heirs of the Father and receive the anointing of the Holy Spirit.

Faith is both required for baptism and an effect of baptism. For example, in Acts 2 those who welcomed Peter's message were baptized. In the early church the rite of initiation included a trinitarian profession of faith in question-and-answer form. For the traditions that have restored the ancient practice of the catechumenate, this period is a time in which the candidates grow in faith. The Rite of Christian Initiation of Adults has made adult baptism normative for an understanding of the theology of baptism. The primary difference between those communions who baptize infants and those who practice believer baptism is not whether faith is present or not, but where faith is located. Baptists and other groups issuing from the Anabaptist arm of the Reformation require a personal profession of faith on the part of the person who is baptized. In the Roman Catholic tradition, as in many other Christian traditions, the godparents and the parents express faith by proxy. In the baptism of infants, the faith of the church precedes the initiation of the child, signifying that all are welcomed into a faith community through baptism. It shows that proclamation and evangelization on the part of a faith community must precede any individual confession of faith, and that faith is God's work in us and not our own.

Evidence for the baptism of infants exists from the end of the second century. Reasons supporting the development of infant baptism include references to the baptism of households (Acts 16:15, 33; 1 Cor. 1:16), a literal interpretation of John 3:3 accompanied by a high mortality rate, and the explanation of Cyprian that the sin of Adam was forgiven in baptism. In addition, Augustine developed the doctrine of original sin, based on his reading of Rom. 5:12–21 and his efforts to counter the Pelagian teaching that free will supported by ascetic practices was sufficient for living a Christian life and attaining salvation.

Swiss Brethren, also known as Anabaptists, hold that baptism represents a public confession of "repentance and amendment of life" by those "who believe truly that their sins are taken away by Christ" (Schleitheim Confession, 1527). Other confessional groups who do not practice infant baptism, although not directly related to the Swiss Brethren, profess similar doctrines. For example, Baptists consider baptism to be a voluntary public profession of Christian faith, which requires candidates old enough to understand its significance and symbols.

More attention needs to be given to the unity of the rites of initiation: baptism, postbaptismal anointing or confirmation, and Eucharist. As the Faith and Order document *Baptism, Eucharist and Ministry* observes, "Participation in Christ's death and resurrection is inseparably linked with the receiving of the Spirit. Baptism in its full meaning signifies and effects both" (WCC §B14). Baptism and the Eucharist are linked as early as 1 Cor. 10:2–4 and perhaps John 19:34 and 1 John 5:6. Both baptism and Eucharist celebrate the same mystery, the death and resurrection of Christ in the power of the Spirit. We are baptized only once, but our regular celebration of the Eucharist recalls the once-and-for-all sacrifice of Christ represented on the altar and enables us to join ourselves to Christ and one another as the body of Christ (1 Cor. 10:16–17). In the Eucharist our communion in the body of the Lord, both in the Christ dead and risen and in his ecclesial body, achieves a repeatable visibility. Our participation in the Eucharist is as profoundly baptismal as our baptism is profoundly oriented to the Eucharist. In baptism we become the priestly people of God, and in the Eucharist we exercise that priesthood. The unity of the rites is most apparent when they are celebrated together as in the Rite of Christian Initiation of Adults. The Orthodox churches also maintain the unity of the rites in the initiation of infants.

Even though there is but one baptism because there is only one Christ, dead and risen, into whom we are baptized (Eph. 4:4–6), the mutual recognition of baptism remains one of the ecumenical tasks of our time. Baptism administered with water and invocation of the trinitarian name together with faith in Christ form the basis of an imperfect communion among Christians. Traditional disputed issues are whether or not baptism is a sacrament and whether a personal confession of faith is required for the sacrament. While Roman Catholics do not require a full understanding of their sacramental teaching by other ministers to recognize their baptisms, those communities who practice believer's baptism do not recognize infant baptisms. More recently, theological debates about the proper language used for God in the trinitarian formula affect mutual recognition. Eucharistic practices relative to sacramental initiation are inconsistent. The Orthodox, Roman Catholics, Lutheran Church–Missouri Synod, and various Baptist groups link full ecclesial community with full sacramental initiation and the Eucharist. Other groups admit all the baptized to the Eucharist. Finally, even though baptism is identified as a significant ground of unity among Christian churches, the ecclesial character of baptism has not been given significant attention, particularly in view of the fact that a person is baptized into a particular ecclesial community within a divided Christianity. All are baptized into the one church of Christ, yet the particular communities into which we are baptized are not always in communion with one another. Since baptism is an unrepeatable act, any practice that might be interpreted as rebaptism must be avoided where there is mutual recognition of baptism.

See also Sacrament

Bibliography

Beasley-Murray, G. R. *Baptism in the New Testament.* Eerdmans, 1973; Buchanan, C. *A Case for Infant Baptism.* 3d ed. Grove, 1984; Hartman, L. *'Into the Name of the Lord Jesus.'* T&T Clark, 1997; Johnson, M. *The Rites of Christian Initiation.* Liturgical Press, 1999; Kavanagh, A. *The Shape of Baptism.* Pueblo, 1978; Pawson, D., and C. Buchanan. *Infant Baptism under Cross-examination.* Grove, 1974, 1976; Wainwright, G. *Christian Initiation.* John Knox, 1969; WCC. *Baptism, Eucharist and Ministry.* Faith and Order Paper 111. WCC, 1982.

Susan K. Wood

Barr, James   *See* Biblical Theology; Concept; Etymology

Barth, Karl

The Swiss Reformed theologian Karl Barth (1886–1968) is by common consent the weightiest Protestant dogmatician since Schleiermacher. His significance for the theory and practice of biblical interpretation and the importance of his biblical exegesis in understanding his theology are, however, commonly underestimated. Because of this, Barth's work remains marginal in contemporary theological hermeneutics, and the corpus of his work is read with insufficient attention to what he regarded as its most essential feature, its reference to the biblical testimony. An informed account of Barth's exegetical labors and of his theology of Scripture and its interpretation is thus essential to any adequate assessment of his work.

Reared in moderately conservative Swiss clerical and academic circles, Barth studied with the leading German theologians in the early years of the twentieth century, and entered the pastorate in 1911, formed in the theological and exegetical culture of liberal Protestantism. This theology proved unworkable in the task of ministry, above all because its focus on human history and moral endeavor lacked a deep sense of the sovereign aseity of God. From around 1915, Barth began to dismantle his heritage and to replace it with an account of the Christian faith centered on God's free, prevenient perfection. The reconstruction was largely undertaken through intensive study of the Pauline corpus; its most enduring literary monument is Barth's *Epistle to the Romans*, first published in 1919 and entirely rewritten two years later.

Barth's *Romans* is often read either as an account of his own developing theological position, or as a hermeneutical manifesto. It is in fact neither; it is intended as a commentary on Paul, which tries to say what Paul's text said and says as a servant of revelation. The commentary takes the form of an elaborate conceptual paraphrase; though it is not always transparent, and sometimes overwhelms Paul's text, Barth's intention was to try to indicate the astonishing reality that he considered Paul to be indicating: the sheer gratuity of God. It was this content, and not any hermeneutical commitments, that shaped Barth's stance toward the dominant conventions of historical criticism (his views are expressed in the prefaces to the various editions of the commentary). Barth considered historical criticism necessary but insufficient. It is necessary because the interpreter must seek to grasp the biblical text as what it is, in all its historical contingency. It is insufficient because the contingent text is defined by its function within revelation. Historical criticism seeks to explain the text without reference to its revelatory function, and consequently it fails to grasp the text as what it is (an instrument of divine speech). Moreover, historical criticism misconstrues the act of interpretation as one performed by an exegete upon a historically distant, inert text, rather than as an attempt to follow the text's indication of the present activity of the divine word. Barth's critics considered his exegesis to be mere practical or spiritual theology; yet this hardly met his challenge that exhaustive historical explanations of the text fail to treat Scripture in accordance with its objective character as an instrument of revelation.

In 1921 Barth took up work as a theological professor in Germany. Most of his teaching in the 1920s was in the fields of Reformed historical theology and NT exegesis. One fruit of his rediscovery of the Reformed tradition was a rearticulation of the Protestant Scripture principle: Scripture is the contingent textual servant of the divine word, though not identical with that word. However, Barth's chief preoccupation was not with questions of the nature or authority of the Bible so much as with its content, expounded in lengthy lecture series on, for example, Ephesians, 1 Corinthians, the Sermon on the Mount, John, James, and 1 Peter. Much of this material has only been published posthumously; its sheer bulk indicates the centrality of biblical exegesis for Barth's theological project.

From 1932 Barth devoted himself increasingly to writing his *Church Dogmatics* (*CD*), a multivolume work of systematic theology unfinished at his death. The work attempts a comprehensive account of the triune God's ways with his creatures, structured around the themes of creation, reconciliation, and redemption, introduced by a treatment of the doctrines of revelation and God. Part of the bulk of the work derives from the presence of a great deal of detailed exegesis, often in the form of lengthy excurses (such as on Gen. 1–3, Job, or the Synoptic presentation of Jesus' ministry). Barth insists that dogmatics is secondary to exegesis, not a conceptual improvement upon Scripture but an attempt to listen to Scripture so as to assist the church's work of proclamation. The *CD* is best read as a set of conceptual variations upon scriptural texts and themes, sometimes explicitly tied to exegesis, sometimes more loose and indirect, but always attempting to indicate what is already proclaimed in the prophetic and apostolic witness.

"Witness" is a key category in Barth's understanding of the nature and authority of Scripture. God's revelation takes place through the testimony of the biblical writings, which are elect witnesses to the divine word. The authority of their witness is not grounded in a static, quasi-material relation between the divine word and an inspired text, but in God's use of Scripture as an auxiliary. Though Barth's account is sometimes misread as unstable actualism, he believed it preferable to older Protestant teaching because it respects both divine freedom and the human character of the biblical witnesses. The category of witness is also central for Barth's understanding of biblical interpretation. To interpret a text is to read it for what it is; but the biblical text *is* a human witness to revelation, and so, if it is to be read as what it is, it must be read with an eye to its function of testifying to revelation. This testimony is not some additional feature alongside other, more "natural" features of the text; it is simply the text's content, that to which it refers and directs its readers.

Within this conception of the nature of the Bible and its interpretation, Barth's exegetical practice in the *Church Dogmatics* is quite varied. Attempts are often made by interpreters of Barth to present one or another strategy as basic, particularly by those who find in Barth a concentration on the christological narratives of Scripture, and on their ability to present the identity of particular agents. Though Barth's use of narrative in Christology is instructive for his insistence that Jesus' significance is not reducible to general attitudes, it by no means exhausts his ways of using scriptural materials, which are varied and unsystematic. Sometimes he gives lengthy exegetical treatment to specific passages; sometimes he generates catenae of biblical quotations with little comment. He produces extensive restatements of biblical stories, arguments, themes, or concepts. At some points his interest is more directly applicative, and at other points scriptural citations are analyzed in the course of seeking warrants for theological proposals. Moreover, the presence of Scripture in the *CD* is as much in its saturation by biblical allusion, citation, and paraphrase as it is by explicit exegesis (in this, Barth is recovering a more ancient mode of theology as meditation on the scriptural sources of faith).

Barth showed little interest in the theoretical questions about hermeneutics that preoccupied many in Bultmann's school in the mid-twentieth century. He thought little would be gained from high theory, and much could be lost—most of all, a sense that the biblical texts are inherently communicative because of their election as witnesses to Christ. He also feared the subjectivism of existential hermeneutics in which the text and its content await the interpreter's act of "realization." Barth was also relaxed about questions concerning Scripture's historical reference, since he did not consider realism dependent upon literalism, and since on theological grounds, he judged, Scripture offered adequate testimony to that of which it speaks.

Barth is the commanding modern example of constructive theology undertaken in the closest relation to the exegetical task. His interpretation of Scripture is undoubtedly not beyond question, especially when he allowed it to be commandeered by doctrinal interests (his late account of the baptismal material in the NT is a case in point). But his achievement is to have offered a theological account of the nature of Scripture and its interpretation that makes appeal to divine revelation rather than interpreting subjects, and to have undertaken a dogmatic work that both recommends and illustrates the deference of doctrine to the Bible.

Bibliography

Barth, K. *Church Dogmatics*. T&T Clark, 1956–75; idem. *The Epistle to the Philippians*. Westminster John Knox, 2002; idem. *The Epistle to the Romans*. Oxford University Press, 1933; idem. *The Resurrection of the Dead*. Hodder & Stoughton, 1933; idem. *Witness to the Word*. Eerdmans, 1986; Burnett, R. *Karl Barth's Theological Exegesis*. Mohr, 2002; Cunningham, M. K. *What Is Theological Exegesis?* Trinity, 1995; Ford, D. *Barth and God's Story*. Lang, 1991; Hunsinger, G. "Beyond Literalism and Expressivism: Karl Barth's Hermeneutical Realism." Pages 210–25 in *Disruptive Grace*, ed. G. Hunsinger. Eerdmans, 2001; Jeanrond, W. "Karl Barth's Hermeneutics." Pages 80–97 in *Reckoning with Barth*, ed. N. Biggar. Mowbray, 1988; McGlasson, P. *Judas and Jesus*. Scholars Press, 1991; Watson, F. "The Bible." Pages 57–71 in *The Cambridge Companion to Karl Barth*, ed. J. Webster. Cambridge University Press, 2000.

John Webster

Being   *See* Onto-Theology

Biblical Criticism   *See* Historical Criticism

Biblical Theology

Introduction: The Pedigree of and Motivation for Biblical Theology

Biblical theology is said to have begun with Gabler's inaugural address in 1787, in which he distinguished biblical theology from systematic theology. This *is* an important milestone in the development of biblical theology as a distinct theological discipline, but biblical theology, in the sense of the search for the inner unity of the Bible, goes back to the church fathers.

In his struggle with Marcion and the Gnostics over the unity of the Bible, for example, Irenaeus articulates the unity of the Bible as a single story:

> Two histories converge in the biblical account, the history of Israel and the life of Christ, but because they are also the history of God's actions in and for the world, they are part of a larger narrative that begins at creation and ends in a vision of a new, more splendid city in which the "Lord God will be their light." The Bible begins, as it were, with the beginning and ends with an end that is no end, life with God, in Irenaeus's charming expression, a life in which one is "always conversing with God in new ways." Nothing falls outside of its scope. (Wilken 63)

With Irenaeus's narrative approach to the Bible, we have an incipient biblical theology seeking to articulate the inner unity of the Bible in response to Marcion. The unity of the Testaments is affirmed—there is one God, who called Abraham, spoke with Moses, sent the prophets, and is also the Father of our Lord Jesus Christ—and is articulated in terms of the story shape of the Bible as a whole. Furthermore, the story is explained in terms of the theme of renewal or re-creation.

Here we see how, from the earliest days of the Christian church, ways are found of expressing the inner unity of the Bible, in the service of reading the Bible as Scripture and relating it to the challenges of the day, producing theological interpretation. At the heart of such interpretation is a highly creative grafting of the new onto the old. We wonder where this development comes from. Henri de Lubac rightly asserts:

> Rather was it the consequence of the fact of the Incarnation on the conscience of some few Jews. In the end what was originally known by intuition was developed into a skilfully constructed theory capable of withstanding Jewish attacks on the one hand and those of Gnostics on the other, at the same time providing the means for preserving the scriptures and using them as a basis. . . . Right from the beginning the essential was there, the synthesis was made, in the dazzling and confused light of revelation. *Novum testamentum in Vetere latet: Vetus nunc in Novo patet.* . . . Very early, of course, separate traditions in the interpretation of scripture were established, different schools arose. . . . But the same fundamental principle compelled the recognition of all. From the beginning "the harmonious agreement of the Law and the Prophets with the Testament delivered by the Lord" was the "rule of the Church." (88)

Lubac here perceptively notes that central to Christian faith from its inception is an intuitive sense of the unity of the Testaments in Christ. In this respect biblical theology originates, as it were, in the Christ event and in the Bible itself. The relationship of the Testaments is *the* issue in (modern) biblical theology (Reventlow), and Lubac helpfully points us to the source of the Christian commitment to, and concern to articulate the logic of, the inner unity of the Bible. Not surprisingly, therefore, this pattern and concern is evident in different ways in catechesis and homiletics from the outset and in all the major Christian thinkers that follow the church fathers, not least Augustine, Aquinas, Luther, Calvin, and others (cf. Childs, *Old and New*).

Barr (*Concept*) thinks it anachronistic to find biblical theology in these Christian thinkers that precede Gabler. Barr is wrong insofar as biblical theology is the search for the inner unity of the Bible, for in this sense it is clearly present from the church fathers onward. But Barr is right in the sense that it is only around Gabler's time that biblical theology is clearly distinguished from systematic theology/dogmatics as a distinct discipline. In the church fathers and the Reformers, biblical theology is not differentiated from theological interpretation or systematic theology. This differentiation of the two in the theological encyclopedia is Gabler's major contribution. (For assessments of Gabler's contribution, see Sandys-Wunsch and Eldredge; Stuckenbruck; Ollenburger.)

Gabler and the Development of Biblical Theology as a Distinct Discipline

Gabler's motivation for the distinction between biblical theology and dogmatics is theological—he wants to help Christians discern what God is really saying. He commences his inaugural with his concern about the variety of views among Christians. One of the reasons he discerns for this is the failure to distinguish biblical theology from dogmatic theology. Gabler contrasts religion with theology: "Religion then, is every-day, transparently clear knowledge; but theology is subtle, learned knowledge, surrounded by a retinue of many disciplines, and by the same token derived not only from the sacred Scripture but also from elsewhere, especially from the domain of philosophy and history" (495). In this contrast, Gabler associates the Bible with religion: "There is truly a biblical theology, of historical origin, conveying what the holy writers felt about divine matters; on the other hand there is a dogmatic theology of didactic origin" (495). Biblical theology remains the same, whereas dogmatics changes all the time.

Gabler's understanding of biblical theology is deeply rationalistic. He argues that we need to separate the things in the Bible that refer to their own times from the "pure notions which divine providence wished to be characteristic of all times and places" (496). Thus, we first need to collect the sacred ideas of the authors and then classify them, after which we should compare them with the universal ideas of reason. From this process biblical theology will appear! In this way Gabler's genuine theological concern is irretrievably skewed by his rationalist philosophy. The Bible is seen as a source of ideas and principles that are separated from their embodiment in Israel, Jesus, and the life of the church. This shadow of alien philosophical concerns has dogged the footsteps of biblical theology to this day. Does this mean that any renewal of theological interpretation should return to a pre-Gabler view, in which biblical theology and theological interpretation are undifferentiated?

Gabler was not original in making the distinction between biblical theology and dogmatics. Rather, he sought methodological clarity on their relationship and "can be said to have done more than any other single figure to make biblical theology a separate discipline" (Sandys-Wunsch and Eldredge 150). Gabler's whole approach is so colored by philosophy that one is tempted to dismiss him out of court, but that would be a mistake. His distinguishing of biblical theology from theology is helpful and an important step in differentiating biblical theology in the "theological encyclopedia." For biblical theology to flourish as an entity in its own right, such a distinction is important, provided we can distinguish it from Gabler's rationalism and other alien philosophies.

Biblical theology is concerned to describe the inner unity of the Bible on its own terms. It therefore is descriptive and historical in a way that theological interpretation and systematic theology are not. In my view, for this component in the theological encyclopedia to flourish, it needed to be differentiated from associated elements, just as with time it had become necessary for the doctrine of the church and eschatology to be distinguished from the doctrine of God. Without accepting one manifestation of this development as wholly true, it is possible to discern here a normative unfolding of theology as a discipline.

What seems to argue against this is Gabler's rationalism, Wrede's development of biblical theology in a history-of-religions direction (Fowl 14), and the fragmentation to which Gabler's distinction led in biblical studies. Bauer was the first to distinguish OT and NT theology, and soon the view arose that the discontinuities between the Testaments were so strong as to defy attempts to articulate their unity. The related stress on the diversity of Scripture that has been central to most historical criticism has haunted biblical theology to this day. The result has been a focus on smaller and smaller parts of the Bible, all with their own theologies, so that nowadays it is quite difficult to take the inner unity of the Bible seriously at all.

Biblical theology has always been motivated at least in part by a concern for theological interpretation: "Most biblical theologians want to be theological" (Fowl 14). But if it inevitably subverts such work, then Fowl and others are right to see it as unhelpful in relation to theological interpretation. "The discipline of biblical theology, in its most common form, is systematically unable to generate serious theological interpretation" (Fowl 1). This is, however, in danger of confusing its philosophical underpinnings with the discipline itself. There are a variety of ways of doing historical and descriptive biblical theology, and it is a mistake to view Gabler and Wrede's approaches as the norm. As Childs says, "The real question is not whether to do Biblical Theology or not, but rather what kind of Biblical Theology does one have" (*Crisis*). We need to learn from the checkered history of biblical theology that it will flourish and develop in very different ways in relation to different theologies and philosophies. Thus, for example, Childs's extensive work on biblical theology demonstrates the fertility of the Barthian tradition in this respect.

The impetus toward biblical theology stems from the gospel itself. Gabler's distinction is helpful in that it enabled biblical theology to develop as a theological discipline in its own right, thereby making possible a deepened understanding of the inner unity of Scripture.

The Possibility of Biblical Theology Today

The growing sense of the diversity of Scripture in modernity (Levenson) and the ideological critique of postmodernity militate against the flourishing of biblical theologies of the Bible as a whole. Indeed, in recent years only two scholars, Childs and Scobie, have produced major theologies of the Bible in the English-speaking world. For many biblical scholars, biblical theology is not a viable possibility.

The more immediate context for (the lack of) contemporary efforts in biblical theology is the rise and demise of the so-called Biblical Theology Movement (BTM). Dates for this movement can be set with precision, from around 1945 to 1961, when publications by Gilkey and Barr are said to have sunk the BTM. Although biblical theology should not be equated with the BTM, it has never fully recovered from its demise. The BTM was strongly Protestant, particularly American, and consciously oriented toward reading the Bible for the church, while acknowledging the legitimacy of historical criticism. The BTM was connected with the emergence of the "neoorthodoxy" of Barth, although it tended to be suspicious of Barth's supposed rejection of historical criticism. Indeed,

Brunner rather than Barth was the greater influence on the BTM.

The BTM in the USA represented a major attempt to break out of the impasse of the modernist/fundamentalist debate about the Bible that had plagued American churches, through a vibrant recovery of biblical theology. Childs (*Crisis*) identifies its major emphases:

1. A recovery of the Bible as a *theological* book. Historical criticism has a legitimate role to play, but it represents the start and not the end; it must lead us to hear God address us through his word, and biblical theology is a major ingredient in this respect.
2. *The unity of the Bible* as a whole. The BTM regarded it as vital that we overcome the chasm that had opened up between OT and NT.
3. The BTM made *God's revelation of himself in history* central to biblical theology. In this respect Israel was regarded as utterly unique, and God reveals his being and will through his great acts, particularly in the OT through his redemption of the Israelites from Egypt.
4. The BTM laid great stress on the distinctiveness of the biblical perspective.

By 1961 the BTM, which manifested such energy and hope for a recovery of the Bible, was verging on collapse. What were the structural deficiencies that facilitated the demise of this great edifice? Childs (*Crisis*) argues that there were a host of unresolved problems in the BTM that eroded it from within and made it vulnerable to attack from Barr and Gilkey from without:

1. According to Childs the BTM never resolved the issue of the Bible and its authority. Fundamentalism was rejected, but so too was Barth's use of the Bible, which was regarded as not taking historical criticism sufficiently seriously. Problematically, no clear alternative emerged to either of these views. For all its emphasis on the Bible, the BTM failed to produce great commentaries and generally seemed to confine its use of the Bible to a few favorite books.
2. Second, the emphases of the BTM were seldom translated into educational and curriculum policy in the seminaries.
3. In the late 1950s and in the 1960s, the church was feeling the need to respond to the modern world and the great diversity of challenges it represented. The BTM appeared to be sorely lacking in this respect. It had not given rise to a new style of preaching, and theological ethics seemed to be getting along quite well without it.
4. The BTM's emphasis on God's acts *in history* appeared to solve many problems, but this apparent success concealed some major cracks in its edifice, cracks that James Barr and Langdon Gilkey exploited ruthlessly.

The arguments that facilitated the demise of the BTM bear close scrutiny. Gilkey argues that the BTM got caught between being half liberal and modern, and half biblical and orthodox: "Its world view or cosmology is modern, while its theological language is biblical and orthodox" (194). In opposition to liberalism, the BTM asserted its belief in revelation through God's mighty acts, thereby understanding God's speech and acts literally and univocally. At the same time it held on to the modern belief in the causal continuum.

A modern understanding of causality means that most of the biblical events did not in fact happen. Instead, they become symbols: "*We* believe that the biblical people lived in the same causal continuum of space and time in which we live, and so one in which no divine wonders transpired and no divine voices were heard" (Gilkey 196). Gilkey probes the writings of the BTM in this respect and finds them riddled with contradictions. He argues that the implication of this tension for the BTM is that the Bible is really a book of great acts the Hebrews believed God to have done, but which we know he in fact did not do. The result is that the mighty acts of God are reduced to God's "inward incitement of a religious response to an ordinary event within the space-time continuum" (201), akin to Schleiermacher's emphasis on religious experience. Gilkey argues that the BTM needs a more sophisticated view of language and a theological ontology. Hebrew recital must be distinguished from our recital; the biblical writers use language *univocally*, whereas we know that we can only speak of God *analogically*.

Living as we do in the light of postmodern undermining of many aspects of modernity, it is remarkable to think how effective was Gilkey's argument. There is an implicit assumption of the modern myth of progress. It is now apparent that Gilkey is assuming the particular perspective of modernity, as well as misrepresenting the biblical and Christian tradition. Even within the Bible there is awareness that its language of God is not univocal. And certainly the Christian tradition is well aware of the complexity of its language for and of God. Already in Aquinas we find a careful distinction between univocal, equivocal, and analogical language.

Barr's critique of the BTM relates to two main areas, the concept of revelation and history central to the BTM (*Interpretation*, 65–102), and its misuse of word studies and the so-called Greek/Hebrew contrast in views of the world. Barr's critique of the historical emphasis of the BTM is similar to that of Gilkey. He focuses on the antinomy or "double talk" between the confession of God's acts in history, and history as the result of critical examination of data. Barr furthermore finds that substantial parts of the Bible do not fit with a historical emphasis.

Barr's better-known critique is of the BTM's persistent failure to take modern semantics into account and thus to be guilty time and again of "illegitimate totality transfer," thereby wrongly reading meanings into words. Barr is critical of the tendency of the BTM to find the distinctive theological content of the Bible in its vocabulary, as exemplified, for example, in the Kittel-Friedrich dictionary (*TDNT*).

There was undoubtedly a need for Barr's critique of the understanding of how language worked in the BTM. However, Francis Watson has rightly argued that Barr's critique of the BTM in this respect is not as devastating as is often suggested by others and by Barr himself. According to Watson, Barr builds his sweeping criticism on a narrow foundation and wrongly suggests that the errors are foundational to the entire project of the BTM. Watson reexamines Cullmann's work on time, a particular object of Barr's critique, and demonstrates how Cullmann is aware of the diverse ways in which the NT words for time are used, but consciously chooses to focus on occasions that are theologically poignant. For Watson, such an approach is quite legitimate. Barr also criticizes Cullmann for his contrast between Hebrew and Greek thought. Cullmann contrasts the NT view of the resurrection with the "Greek" concept of immortality and, as Watson shows, Cullmann is quite right in this respect.

Watson concludes: "There is little basis for his claim that 'biblical theology' as once practised was fundamentally and irretrievably flawed. If biblical theology collapsed, it did not do so because of the overwhelming force of its critics' arguments" (24). Indeed, "there is, then, little or nothing in this piece of modern theological history to deter one from attempting to renew and to redefine biblical theology" (26).

The significant corpus of literature the BTM produced has largely disappeared. While we should not repeat its errors, the positive elements in it need to be retrieved, and not least its sense that biblical theology and theological interpretation are closely allied. What is clear from both Gilkey's and Barr's critiques of the BTM is that they stem from particular theological outlooks. The demise of the BTM is related to the radicalization of modern theology at the time, and Barr appeals regularly to this "progress" as part of his critique. What is lacking in Barr's and Gilkey's approach is a healthy sense of plurality in theology and the way in which different theological perspectives might relate to something like the BTM. Barr's approach, for example, is much that of liberal theology, whereas Childs's is that of a scholar working in the Reformed, Barthian tradition. These contexts orient them toward biblical theology and the BTM in quite different ways. Theological context makes a huge difference when it comes to (the very possibility of) biblical theology.

Biblical Theology and Theological Interpretation

Assuming, therefore, the possibility and importance of biblical theology, how might it relate to theological interpretation?

1. Tota Scriptura. Theological interpretation is concerned with reading the Bible for the church today. In that process it inevitably assumes an understanding of the Bible as a whole. In this respect biblical theology connects not only with *sola scriptura* but also *tota scriptura*. Scripture as a whole is confessed to be God's word. *The* major contribution of biblical theology is to deepen our understanding of the shape, complexity, and unity of Scripture on its own terms. Barr (*Concept*) calls this type of biblical theology "panbiblical" and says that we should not focus on it at the expense of all the biblical theological work done on smaller parts of the Bible. However, the intuition that motivates comprehensive biblical theology stems from the gospel itself, so that discernment of the inner unity of the Bible must remain the goal and crown of biblical theology.

Theological interpretation will inevitably focus on and draw from different parts of the Bible—a strong sense of the macrobiblical theological context will constrain such interpretation against proof-texting and selective myopia. An example of this is the selective use made by some theologians of the exodus motif in the Bible. A sense of the larger context of biblical theology constrains use of this motif in terms of its relation to creation and redemption and their interrelationship (Levenson; O'Donovan).

2. The Relationship between Bible and Theology. Biblical theology and its (im)possibility bear strongly on the relationship between the Bible and theology. In his analysis of the uses of the Bible in theology, Kelsey (158ff.) articulates the question as to whether the *discrimen*—the imaginative construal the reader brings to the Bible so that it functions theologically as Scripture—comes from the community or reader, or whether Scripture norms the *discrimen*. Kelsey argues that the unified appropriation of Scripture for theology results from the *discrimen* the reader brings to Scripture. However, this approach seems to underplay the role of biblical theology in the process. Biblical theology as the attempt to articulate the inner unity of Scripture suggests that Scripture itself may norm the *discrimen*. Certainly this is the case in the work of a theologian such as O'Donovan, about whose work we shall say more below.

It should also be noted that the relationship between biblical theology and theology is not one-way but dialectical. Calvin asserted that the role of a good theology is to lead us back into the Bible so as to hear it better (Childs).

3. The Relationship between the Testaments. This remains *the* key issue for biblical theology. Irenaeus's fight to affirm the identity of the OT "Lord" with the God and Father of our Lord Jesus Christ remains foundational for the practice of a Christian biblical theology. In response to salvation-historical readings of the Bible, Reventlow (14) asserts that by itself the Christ event should not be regarded as a continuation of the OT event; only faith sees it thus. Such a believing assumption is an indispensable starting point for a Christian biblical theology.

Yoder, Hauerwas, and Hays advocate a narrative approach to the Bible, but one in which Jesus' pacifism is central and critically normative in relation to the OT traditions. By comparison, Reformed biblical theology discerns a deeper unity between the Testaments anchored around the themes of covenant and kingdom. Indeed, a major issue today is Christian interpretation of the OT. Childs has become cautious of his earlier use of quotations of the OT in the NT as a means of tracking biblical theology (*Crisis*). He has become more aware of the need to do justice to the discrete witness of the OT and thus to hear the OT on its own terms first (*Old and New*). By comparison, Watson argues for a christological reading of

the OT and finds von Rad a more fecund source in this respect. In response to Watson, Seitz asserts that we instead need a trinitarian hermeneutic that will allow us to hear the voice of the OT on its own terms, as Childs recommends.

4. Appropriate Methods for Biblical Theology. Diverse methods have been proposed in OT and NT theology, methods such as dogmatic, diachronic, cross-section (Eichrodt for the OT), redemptive-historical, topical, and so on (see Hasel, *OT Theology*; Hasel, *NT Theology*). Similarly, certain major models for biblical theology can be discerned today: dogmatic, typological, great themes, redemptive history, narrative, cultural-linguistic, sociological, Jewish biblical theology, and canonical (Childs, *Old and New*). Such methodological pluralism has led some to doubt the rigor and possibility of the discipline itself. However, if we imagine Scripture as a great cathedral, with multiple entrances and rooms, then it is easier to see how a variety of approaches may be legitimate and even complementary, just as a cathedral can be explored in many different ways and from a variety of angles. Thus, there is, for example, no reason why separate OT and NT theologies may not be of great value provided they are part of a broader goal of articulating a biblical theology as a whole. And there is surely room for a range of biblical theologies, operating along topical, dogmatic, great ideas, redemptive-historical, story lines, and so on. Yet, what these approaches will need to share, if they are to fund theological interpretation, is recognition of the Bible as canonical and the ancient sense of its inner unity that comes from Christian faith.

Such a model of diverse but complementary approaches within a canonical framework still leaves open the question of whether or not there is a main entrance to the cathedral of Scripture from which its inner unity can most clearly be discerned. Theologically, such a center would certainly be Christ, and it remains a matter of debate as to how to articulate this more precisely, whether in terms of the kingdom of God or other such expressions.

5. Biblical Theology and God's Address for All of Life. The BTM failed to relate biblical theology to the wide variety of challenges with which modernity presented the church in the twentieth century. This is surprising because any biblical theology attentive to themes such as creation and re-creation (cf. Gunton) will be aware of the comprehensive scope of the Bible. Contemporary theological interpretation needs to wrestle with the scope of the Bible as God's address for all of life in our postmodern context. There are some fine examples of this, such as Brueggemann's work on *The Land*, but the terrain is largely uncharted.

6. Biblical Theology and Theological Interpretation: An Example. Undoubtedly, biblical theology and theology can be related in a variety of helpful ways. An excellent example of how biblical theology might fund theological interpretation is O'Donovan's work in theological ethics. In *Resurrection and Moral Order*, the Pauline insight of resurrection as the reaffirmation of creation provides the construal whereby O'Donovan is able to read the Bible as a whole for theological ethics. In *The Desire of the Nations*, this insight remains but is informed by a redemptive historical sense of God's work in Israel, which climaxes in Jesus of Nazareth. In both cases biblical theology is a vital ingredient that enables O'Donovan to take Scripture in its totality with the utmost seriousness while doing theological work with a high degree of sophistication. Even as theological concepts take hold in his work, O'Donovan continues to do thick, creative readings of the Bible. Thus, that exegesis increases rather than decreases as the Bible is brought to bear on politics.

Conclusion

As the church fathers realized, biblical theology in the sense of discerning the inner unity of the Bible is an indispensable ingredient in theological interpretation if the latter is to take the authority of Scripture seriously. Modern biblical theology has had a checkered history, so it is tempting to separate biblical theology from theological interpretation. This would be a serious mistake since some sense of the unity of Scripture will always be a vital ingredient in any reading of the Bible for the church. Of late, comprehensive biblical theologies have been the exception rather than the rule. It will be vital for a renewal in biblical theology to accompany any renewal of theological interpretation.

Bibliography

Barr, J. *The Concept of Biblical Theology*. Fortress, 1999; idem. *Old and New in Interpretation*. SCM, 1966. 2d ed., 1982; Bartholomew, C. "Biblical Theology and Biblical Interpretation: Introduction." Pages 1–22 in *Out of Egypt*, ed. C. Bartholomew et al. SHS. Zondervan/Paternoster, 2004; Bartholomew, C., et al., eds. *A Royal Priesthood?* SHS. Zondervan/Paternoster, 2002; Brueggemann, W. *The Land*. Fortress, 1977; Childs, B. *Biblical Theology in Crisis*. Westminster, 1970; idem. *Biblical Theology of the Old and New Testaments*. Fortress, 1992; Eichrodt, W. *Theology of the Old Testament*, trans. J. Baker. 2 vols. OTL. Westminster, 1961–67; Fowl, S. *Engaging Scripture*. Blackwell, 1998; Gabler, J. P. "An Oration." Pages 492–502 in *The Flowering of Old Testament Theology*, ed. B. Ollenburger, E. Martens, and G. Hasel. Eisenbrauns, 1992; Gilkey, L. "Cosmology, Ontology, and the Travail of Biblical Language." *JR* (1961): 194–205; Gunton, C. *Christ and Creation*. Paternoster/Eerdmans, 1992; Hasel, G. *New Testament Theology*. Eerdmans, 1978; idem. *Old Testament Theology*. 4th ed. Eerdmans, 1991; Kelsey, D. *The Uses of Scripture in Recent Theology*. SCM, 1975; Levenson, J. *The Hebrew Bible, the Old Testament, and Historical Criticism*. Westminster John Knox, 1993; Lubac, H. de. *Catholicism*. Sheed & Ward, 1958; O'Donovan, O. *The Desire of the Nations*. Cambridge University Press, 1996; idem. *Resurrection and Moral Order*. IVP/Eerdmans, 1986; Ollenburger, B. "Biblical Theology: Situating the Discipline." Pages 37–62 in *Understanding the Word*, ed. J. T. Butler et al. Sheffield Academic Press, 1985; Rad, G. von. *Old Testament Theology*, trans. D. Stalker. Vol. 1, Harper, 1962. Vol. 2, Harper & Row, 1965. Reprint, Westminster, 2001; Reventlow, H. G. *Problems of Biblical Theology in the Twentieth Century*. SCM, 1986; Sandys-Wunsch, J., and L. Eldredge. "J. P. Gabler and the Distinction between Biblical and Dogmatic Theology: Translation, Commentary, and Discussion of His Originality." *SJT* 33, no. 2 (1980): 133–58; Scobie, C. *The Ways of Our God*. Eerdmans, 2003; Seitz, C. "Christological Interpretation of Texts and Trinitarian Claims to Truth." *SJT* 52, no. 2 (1999): 209–26; Stuckenbruck, L. "Johann Philipp Gabler and the Delineation of Biblical Theology." *SJT* 52, no. 2 (1999): 139–57; Watson, F. *Text and Truth*. T&T Clark, 1997; Wilken, R. L. *The Spirit of Early Christian Thought*. Yale University Press, 2003.

Craig G. Bartholomew

Biography

Ancient or Modern?

Our modern world is preoccupied with people, and the development of a postmodern rejection of the "big picture" has only intensified this with its fascination about individuals. Over the last century or so, biography has become a major tool for understanding people within society. Thus at a more academic level, biographies have sought to describe the life and times of significant persons, to set the individual in the context of the major events of his or her period, often at great length. On the other hand, popular literature is full of instant biographies that reflect the current obsession with celebrities, what they look like, and speculations about their private life. Both types are indebted to a post-Freudian interest in "personality," to understand what makes an individual "tick." The problem for the theological interpretation of Scripture occurs when readers today bring these understandings of biography to the books of the Bible, especially the Gospels: to what extent can they be read as biographies of Jesus?

The Interpretation of the Gospels

For much of the ancient and medieval periods, the Gospels, like the rest of the Bible, could be interpreted on several levels: The literal meaning provided facts. An allegorical interpretation applied the text to the story of redemption. Moral approaches gave instructions for behavior. And an anagogical reading related it to the reader's spiritual pilgrimage. The Reformers rejected all levels except the literal, and so the Gospels were interpreted as history—the stories of Jesus, even biographies. They were even used to produce romantic "Lives" such as Ernest Renan's *Life of Jesus* (1863). However, when modern biographers began to explain the personality of someone through the individual's upbringing, schooling, psychological development, and so on, the Gospels looked unlike such biographies.

Uniqueness. During the 1920s, scholars like K. L. Schmidt and Rudolf Bultmann rejected any notion that the Gospels were biographies; the Gospels have no interest in Jesus' personality or appearance, and they tell us little about his life, other than his brief public ministry, concentrating on his death. Instead, the Gospels were seen as popular folk literature, collections of stories handed down orally over time. Far from biographies, the Gospels were described as *sui generis* (Bultmann 371–74). For Bultmann, this interpretation had theological implications: God's unique revelation of his word in Jesus Christ was written in a unique genre.

Historical and Sociological Interpretations. Form-critical approaches meant that the Gospels were no longer read as whole narratives or theological documents. Instead, the concentration on each individual pericope moved the focus to the passage's *Sitz im Leben* in the early church, and traditio-historical analysis replaced theological interpretations. The rise of redaction criticism led to the development of theories and sociological analysis about the groups that produced them, the so-called Johannine or Matthean communities. However, redaction critics did see the writers of the Gospels as individual theologians, and the development of new literary approaches to the Gospels viewed them as conscious literary artists. This reopened the question of the place of the Gospels within first-century literature, with scholars like Talbert and Aune treating them as biographies.

The Gospels as Ancient Biography

Genre Is Central to the Interpretation of Any Text. Communication theory considers the relationship of transmitter, message, and receiver—or author, text, and audience. Discerning the kind of communication is crucial, for both transmitter and receiver must use the same conventions: thus, correct interpretation depends on a correct identification of the kind of communication. One does not listen to a fairy story in the same way as to a news broadcast. Hence, genre is central in both composition and the interpretation. Genre forms an agreement, often unspoken, or even unconscious, between authors and readers, whereby the author writes according to a set of expectations, and readers interpret the work using the same conventions. Genre is identified through a wide range of "generic features," which may be signaled in advance, or embedded in a work's formal and structural composition and content. Taken together, such features communicate the "family resemblance" of a work.

Ancient "Lives." In examining whether the Gospels are a form of ancient biography, we must consider the generic features shared by ancient "lives" or *bioi*—the word *biographia* does not appear until the ninth-century writer Photius. From the formal or structural perspective, they are written in continuous prose narrative, between 10,000 and 20,000 words—the amount on a typical scroll of about 30–35 feet in length. Unlike modern biographies, Greco-Roman lives do not cover a person's whole life in chronological sequence, and they have no psychological analysis of the subject's character. They may begin with a brief mention of the hero's ancestry, family, or city, his birth and an occasional anecdote about his upbringing; but usually the narrative moves rapidly on to his public debut later in life. Accounts of generals, politicians, or statesmen are more chronologically ordered, recounting their great deeds and virtues; lives of philosophers, writers, or thinkers are more anecdotal, arranged topically around collections of their ideas and teachings. Although the author may provide information about his subject, often his underlying aims include apologetic, polemic, or didactic. Many ancient biographies cover the subject's death in great detail, since here he reveals his true character, gives his definitive teaching, or does his greatest deed. Finally, analysis of the verbal structure of ancient biographies reveals another generic feature. Though most narratives have a wide variety of subjects, it is characteristic of biography to focus on one particular person, with a quarter to a third of the verbs dominated by the subject, while another 15 to 30 percent occur in his sayings, speeches, or quotations (Burridge, *What?* 261–74).

Lives of Jesus. Like other ancient biographies, the Gospels are continuous prose narratives of the length of a single scroll, composed of stories, anecdotes, sayings, and speeches. Their concentration on Jesus' public ministry from his baptism to death, and on his teaching and great deeds, is not much different from the content of other ancient biographies. Similarly, the amount of space given to the last week of Jesus' life, his death, and the resurrection reflects that given to the subject's death and subsequent events in works by Plutarch, Tacitus, Nepos, and Philostratus. Verbal analysis demonstrates that Jesus is the subject of a quarter of the verbs in Mark's Gospel, with a further fifth spoken by him in his teaching and parables. About half the verbs in the other Gospels either have Jesus as the subject or are on his lips: like other ancient biographies, Jesus' deeds and words are of vital importance for the evangelists' portraits of Jesus. Therefore, these marked similarities of form and content demonstrate that the Gospels have the generic features of ancient biographies.

Theological Implications

A Christological Claim. It is significant that Jesus was the only first-century Jewish teacher about whom such a *bios* was written. Individual Gospel pericopae can be helpfully compared with rabbinic stories and anecdotes. Thus, the greatest-commandment debate (Mark 12:28–34 et par.) is like the famous story of the differing reactions of Shammai and Hillel when asked to teach the whole law to a Gentile inquirer standing on one leg (*b. Šabb.* 31A). If the Gospels are seen merely as a collection of such stories strung together like beads on a string, we might expect similar works about Hillel, Shammai, or the others. Yet this is precisely what we do not find. Both Neusner and Alexander have explored reasons why there is nothing like the Gospels in the rabbinic traditions. Burridge ("Gospel," 155–56) has argued that to write a biography is to focus on a human person center stage, where only the Torah should be. Therefore, the biographical genre of the Gospels is making an explicit theological claim about the centrality of Jesus, that the full revelation of God is to be found in the life, death, and resurrection of this person.

Focus on Jesus. Since the Gospels are portraits of a person, they must be interpreted in a biographical manner. Given that space is limited to a single scroll—ranging from Mark's 11,250 words to Luke's 19,500—every pericope or passage contributes to the overall picture of Jesus according to each evangelist. Thus, Christology becomes central to the interpretation of the Gospels. Each evangelist builds up his account of Jesus through the selection, redaction, and ordering of material. The key question for the interpretation of any verse or section is what this tells us about Jesus and the writer's understanding of him. Hence, the motif of the failure of the disciples to understand Jesus in Mark is not to be interpreted as polemic against differing groups and leaders within the early church, as often in a more form-critical approach. Instead, it is part of Mark's portrayal of Jesus as hard to understand and tough to follow—and therefore readers should not be surprised to find the Christian life sometimes difficult. Reading the Gospels requires a thorough understanding of the Christology of each evangelist, while every section must be interpreted in the context of its place in the whole theological narrative. Burridge (*Four?*) has attempted to describe the particular Christology of each Gospel writer through the traditional images of the human face, lion, ox, and eagle.

Plurality within Limits. Theological interpretation must also take account of the presence of four Gospels within the canon. The diversity was a problem for ancient pagan critics and comes up in debate today, especially with Muslims. Yet Morgan has argued that this is a theological opportunity to produce "faith images of Jesus," with the four canonical portraits acting as both "stimulus and control" (386). Therefore, we must resist the temptation since Tatian's *Diatessaron* to reduce everything to a single master narrative, or even the amalgam mixing different Gospels' passages, as often found in carol services or Good Friday meditations. The theology of each evangelist needs to be respected, while the canon of all four serves to establish the limits for orthodox interpretations of Jesus. The twentieth-century scholarly consensus about the uniqueness of the Gospels' genre produced a sociohistorical interpretation of them as documents produced "by committees, for communities, about concepts." However, their biographical genre means that they must be interpreted as "by people, for people, about a person" (Burridge, "About," 115, 144). This means paying proper attention to their biographical focus on the person of Jesus Christ and their theological understanding of him as we seek to interpret his significance for today.

See also Gospels; Jesus, Quest for the Historical

Bibliography

Alexander, P. "Rabbinic Biography and the Biography of Jesus: A Survey of the Evidence." Pages 19–50 in *Synoptic Studies*, ed. C. Tuckett. JSNTSup 7. JSOT, 1984; Aune, D. *The New Testament in Its Literary Environment*. Westminster, 1987; Bultmann, R. *The History of the Synoptic Tradition*. Rev. ed. with supplement, trans. J. Marsh. Blackwell, 1972; Burridge, R. "About People, by People, for People: Gospel Genre and Audiences." Pages 113–45 in *The Gospels for All Christians*, ed. R. Bauckham. Eerdmans, 1998; idem. *Four Gospels, One Jesus?* SPCK/Eerdmans, 1994; idem. "Gospel Genre, Christological Controversy and the Absence of Rabbinic Biography: Some Implications of the Biographical Hypothesis." Pages 137–56 in *Christology, Controversy, and Community*, ed. C. Tuckett and D. Horrell. Brill, 2000; idem. *What Are the Gospels?* SNTSMS 70. Cambridge University Press, 1992; Morgan, R. "The Hermeneutical Significance of Four Gospels." *Interpretation* 33, no. 4 (Oct 1979): 376–88; Neusner, J. *In Search of Talmudic Biography*. Brown Judaic Studies 70. Scholars Press, 1984; idem. *Why No Gospels in Talmudic Judaism?* Scholars Press, 1988; Talbert, C. H. *What Is a Gospel?* Fortress, 1977/SPCK, 1978.

Richard A. Burridge

Body *See* Human Being, Doctrine of

Bonhoeffer, Dietrich

In 1925 Bonhoeffer, a young student at the University of Berlin, wrote a seminar paper on "The Historical and Pneumatological Interpretation of Scripture" (*Young*, 285–99) that set out an approach to the interpretation of Scripture to which he adhered throughout his life. While this approach can best be seen in his specifically exegetical writings (e.g., *Creation and Fall;* and *Discipleship*) and sermons, it is implicit more generally in his other theological writings.

The influence of Karl Barth's commentary *The Epistle to the Romans* is evident throughout Bonhoeffer's seminar paper and, behind that, the legacy of the Protestant Reformation. Without rejecting the achievements of historical criticism, Bonhoeffer noted that once it had done its work, the canon of Scripture disintegrated, leaving only debris and fragments behind. Thus, if we are truly seeking to listen to the word of God in Scripture, we cannot be captive to the shifting results of critical study. But pneumatological interpretations of Scripture that make experience the criterion for interpreting Scripture are equally problematic, for they do not take the historicity of revelation seriously. The key issue is therefore the relationship between the letter of Scripture, which historical criticism helps us understand better, and the Spirit, who speaks to us through Scripture as witness to God's revelation. The letter of Scripture is dead unless the Spirit gives it life, awakening our response within the community of faith. Discerning the word of God within the words of Scripture is what the theological interpretation of the Bible is all about. As Bonhoeffer put it in his introduction to *Creation and Fall*: "Theological exposition takes the Bible as the book of the church and interprets it as such. This is its presupposition and this presupposition constitutes its method; its method is a continual returning from the text (as determined by all the methods of philological and historical research) to this presupposition" (22).

Bonhoeffer's approach to Scripture was profoundly affected during his year of study in New York in 1930–31, when he discovered the liberating power of the Bible in relation to his own life. This call to obedience to the word of God in the biblical witness prepared him for his role in the church struggle against Nazism. At an ecumenical conference at Gland in 1932, he declared: "We are more fond of our own thoughts than the thoughts of the Bible. We no longer read the Bible seriously, we no longer read it against ourselves, but for ourselves" (*No Rusty Swords*, 185).

Three further comments are relevant for our discussion. The first is Bonhoeffer's recognition of the importance of the OT in preventing us from falsely spiritualizing the witness of the NT. The second is his rejection of Bultmann's program of demythologization as a liberal reductionism, in which the concrete and contextual character of the biblical message is denied in the interests of some universal truth. The third is his proposal for a "nonreligious" hermeneutics with an emphasis on identifying with Christ in solidarity with the victims of oppression.

Bibliography

Bonhoeffer, D. *Creation and Fall*. Dietrich Bonhoeffer Works 3, ed. J. de Gruchy. Fortress, 1997; idem. *No Rusty Swords*. Collins, 1977; idem. *The Young Bonhoeffer: 1918–1927*. Dietrich Bonhoeffer Works 9, ed. C. Green et al. Fortress, 2002.

John W. de Gruchy

Bultmann, Rudolf *See* Hermeneutical Circle; Hermeneutics

C

Calling/Vocation

The idea of the call of God is deeply rooted in biblical thought. The God of the Bible does not hold himself aloof from the world, but reaches out and establishes relationship with us. One of the more frequent expressions of this outreach is found in narratives of divine calling. In the Bible calling is basically a summons by which a person enters into some relationship with God. As such, it is not infrequently a shattering human experience (Jer. 1:4–10). From the theological point of view, however, the call is grounded in the will of God himself as expressed in his word of grace and command, and as mediated by the power of the Spirit working in human lives.

So important is the idea of God's calling in a variety of biblical contexts that talk of the call of God can actually be synonymous with talk of salvation itself. For example, we read in the prophet Hosea: "When Israel was a child, I loved him, and out of Egypt I called my son" (Hos. 11:1). Here the "call" is shorthand for God's deliverance of the people of Israel in the exodus, and thus refers to the primal salvation story of the OT. Similarly, in what is likely the earliest document of the NT, the "call" again denotes the offer of salvation itself. We are urged to live a life worthy of the God who "calls [us] into his own kingdom and glory" (1 Thess. 2:12 NRSV). Elsewhere, the call is also closely aligned with the concept of election. It is because Israel has been "chosen" that it is also "called" (Isa. 41:8–9); in the NT, by the same logic, it is because the Gentiles have also been chosen by God that they too are called, in order to be included among God's people (Rom. 8:30; 9:24–25).

Calling, Protestantism, and Modernity

The common contemporary use of the words "calling" and "vocation" to refer to the professions or careers upon which a person can embark, therefore, is quite alien to the root meaning of calling in the Bible. The origin of this secular understanding has been much debated since M.

Weber's *Die protestantische Ethik und der "Geist" des Kapitalismus* (1904–5). In this seminal sociological study, Weber argued that the successful rise of capitalism in the early modern period was closely linked with Protestant and, in particular, Calvinist piety. In Weber's interpretation, it was no accident that capitalism first flourished in contexts such as Scotland and New England. In these cultural settings, Calvinism led people to reject any notion of a "monkish" withdrawal from the world, and to believe instead that a life of Christian perfection was both obligatory and attainable in this world. According to Weber, Calvinism accordingly interpreted the world of ordinary work, marriage, and so forth as having full religious significance. Thus, it generated the conditions under which an occupation could be embraced as a "calling" in the religious sense, and under which the generation of wealth could be viewed as a moral obligation. The near-universal recognition of the Weberian phrase "the Protestant work ethic" testifies to the pervasive influence of this thesis.

There is, however, little basis in Scripture for Weber's understanding of calling, so that it is difficult to envisage a strict Calvinist culture giving such a secular twist to the idea. Even 1 Cor. 7:17–24, the text most often cited in this connection, nowhere directly equates an *occupation* with a vocation. Furthermore, virtually every Calvinist in early modern Scotland and New England knew that there was such a thing as an "effectual calling," which in the Westminster Confession of Faith (10.1) was formidably defined as the bringing of the predestined to actual faith and obedience. In strict Calvinist circles, this *doctrine* (for doctrine it emphatically was) is also known as "irresistible grace." The Calvinists of Scotland and New England learned this view of calling by heart from their Shorter Catechism:

Q. 31. What is effectual calling?
A. Effectual calling is the work of God's Spirit, whereby, convincing us of our sin and misery, enlightening our minds in the knowledge of Christ, and renewing our wills, he doth persuade and enable

us to embrace Jesus Christ, freely offered to us in the gospel.

Nor is such a view necessarily restricted to classical Calvinism. A recent Roman Catholic document says in another voice something similar concerning the basic theological sense of calling:

> God, infinitely perfect and blessed in himself, in a plan of sheer goodness freely created man to make him share in his own blessed life. For this reason, at every time and in every place, God draws close to man. He calls man to seek him, to know him, to love him with all his strength. (Catholic Church, 1.1)

Modernity, however, from its beginnings in the philosophical revolutions of the seventeenth century and in the culture that these inspired, has struggled to draw down the kingdom of God to the earth, insisting upon the this-worldly character of "rational" religion. Against its inevitable triumph stood only the ancient deceits of "priestcraft," deceits that could be exposed through reason. It was primarily in this context that the earlier understanding of calling came to be reinterpreted in terms of secular occupations. Such reinterpretation follows from the innermost logic of modernity. The Christian religion is construed in the Enlightened sense, so that righteousness amounts to following the dictates of ordinary human moral sensibility rather than hearing the promise of the gospel with faith. Hence, the point at which a person "hears the call" can only be where one engages in "rational" moral action. Perhaps for this reason, much modern usage of "calling" and "vocation" implies a reference to the caring professions in particular (education, medicine, etc.).

Within liberal Protestantism, Weber's thesis concerning vocation found clear resonance. On the whole the liberals embraced the Enlightened vision, seeking to highlight the moral content of Christian faith and its this-worldly character—though also admittedly attempting to defend against the harsher criticisms of church, theology, and faith that the storm of the Enlightenment brought on. Representative liberal theologians of the early twentieth century, such as Ernst Troeltsch, quickly accepted Weber's thesis, since they held the realization of a this-worldly "Protestant" faith to be the real goal of Christian history. Through the direct and indirect influence of such thinkers, the idea of vocation as occupation found its way into mainstream Protestant thought in the twentieth century. Though later resisted by a few theologians (e.g., Karl Barth), their objections have for the most part gone unnoticed.

Calling in Contemporary Theological Perspective

With the demise of the modernist vision, however, the challenge for theology in a postmodern context must surely be to develop afresh a theological understanding of the ideas of calling and vocation. One interesting option that presents itself in the present context is to reconceive calling with the help of virtue theory. From this point of view, a primary obligation laid upon the churches would be to become communities within which discernment of God's call and obedience to it become matters of attention, habit, and collective wisdom. But to be faithful to the biblical witness, such attention needs to be directed in the first instance to hearing the word of God, responding to the initiative of grace, and living out its implications in a life of godliness, rather than to fulfilling some role in the secular economy.

In a narrower sense, of course, though always within this larger vision, it is possible to speak of a calling to a particular office in the church. Paul was "called to be an apostle of Christ Jesus" just as the Corinthian believers to whom he wrote were "called" to faith (1 Cor. 1:1, 26). The latter, however, remains the normative kind of calling. Not all are apostles, but all are summoned to faith and obedience.

In bearing our witness to the gospel, however, the fulfillment of our calling in leading a life worthy of the Lord must influence life in the public sphere. In this derivative sense, we can fulfill God's calling in an occupation or some social role. In the case of a figure such as Martin Luther King, and in the context of the American South in the 1950s–60s, one might well judge that faithfulness to the call of God needed to take precisely the form it did. But this is not at all the same as to say that such activism was in and of itself King's *calling*. On the contrary, King's work and witness had religious depth precisely because it was so rooted in Christian faith and in the service of our neighbor, which the gospel requires.

Bibliography

Badcock, G. *The Way of Life*. Eerdmans, 1998; Catholic Church. *Catechism of the Catholic Church*. 2d ed. U.S. Catholic Conference, 2000; Hardy, L. *The Fabric of This World*. Eerdmans, 1990; Schuurman, D. *Vocation*. Eerdmans, 2004; Troeltsch, E. *The Social Teaching of the Christian Churches*, trans. O. Wyon. 2 vols. Macmillan, 1931; Volf, M. *Work in the Spirit*. Oxford, 1991; Weber, M. *The Protestant Ethic and the Spirit of*

Capitalism, trans. T. Parsons. 2d ed. Allen & Unwin, 1976; Wingren, G. *Luther on Vocation,* trans. C. Rasmussen. Muhlenberg, 1957.

Gary D. Badcock

Calvin, John

Having joined the "evangelical" or Protestant movement in the early 1530s through what he later called a "sudden conversion," Calvin describes himself, in his rare autobiographical statements, as instilled from childhood with reverence for the church. But his conversion brought a new teachability, fueled by an equally new taste of purer doctrine and true godliness. In his career as a Reformer of both Strasbourg and Geneva, Calvin would retain all these traits as ingredients for the interpretation and application of Scripture.

For Calvin, the virtue of Scripture for the reader lay in its utility or benefit, and the key that unlocked those benefits was an understanding of the *scope* of Scripture—the goal or purpose of the writer. Calvin's instincts as a reader and proclaimer of the Bible were hugely shaped by his absorption of the rhetorical agenda of Renaissance humanism, which sought the truest human knowledge in a return to the classical sources, including the Bible. In Calvin's case, his turning to the classics was concerned less with beauty of expression than with how to ascertain an author's meaning and how to communicate that meaning persuasively.

Accordingly, Calvin's earliest exegetical work, his 1539 commentary on Romans, made his own commitments clear. First, Calvin asserted that the whole point of commenting on Scripture was "to lay open the mind of the writer." To be sure, in the case of Scripture, Calvin was not overly concerned to distinguish between the divine and human authors of any particular text: the rules for interpretation, in either case, were the same. One effect of Calvin's doctrine of inspiration was to confirm the Bible's embeddedness in history and culture. Hence, the best tools for unlocking the mind of the scriptural writer always included a solid understanding of history, geography, and chronology, as well as matters of Hebrew and Greek grammar, genre, and context.

Second, from the outset of his career, Calvin attempted to write commentaries with "lucid brevity"; unlike many of his contemporaries, he usually succeeded. But this particular principle was much more than a plea for clear prose; it was also expressive of his commitment to exegesis in service of the church, including the laity. Here, too, one sees how Calvin always directed his exegesis to discern the benefits of what Scripture reveals and to communicate these benefits persuasively. Even as the Scriptures represent God's accommodation of revelation to human capacity, so also must interpreters accommodate proclamation and teaching to their audiences.

Third, the earliest methodological remarks of Calvin demonstrate that he saw no tension whatsoever between the homiletical orientation of the exegete and the more dogmatic or didactic role of the theologian. Here it is helpful to read his preface to the 1539 edition of the *Institutes* alongside his Romans commentary; it becomes clear that he has in mind a common project served best by a division of genre. Calvin believed that the dogmatic and systematic exposition of doctrine is a natural outgrowth of exegesis. His goal of lucid brevity was strategically supported by reserving what could have been lengthy theological digressions—*loci communes,* commonplaces—for his oft-revised *Institutes.* That work is integrated far more closely with his commentaries than modern editions make known.

Fourth, Calvin's early remarks argue that Scripture is read best in dialogue with one's predecessors and contemporaries. Indeed, despite the common impression that *sola scriptura* signaled Protestants' rejection of tradition, for Calvin the final authority of Scripture by no means warranted neglect of earlier commentators or theologians. Calvin elsewhere went so far as to insist that these ancient writings (Augustine and Chrysostom took pride of place) were providentially arranged aids for our own reading of Scripture, and we would be ingrates to neglect them.

These affirmations of earlier exegetical literature provide a good point of departure for considering some important aspects of Calvin's later exegetical practices. These include not only his relationship to the traditional exegesis of his day, but also the question of how he implemented his own rules for interpreting and applying Scripture as his career unfolded.

If the motto *sola scriptura* is often mistaken as a dismissal of all tradition, the exegesis of early Protestants such as Calvin is just as often wrongly taken as having forsaken allegory in favor of a stark literalism. To be sure, Calvin did reject traditional interpretations that could not find support in what he variously described as the simple, literal, historical, or genuine meaning of the text. And in his more theoretical comments on this point, Calvin displayed a quick and instinctive rejection of allegorical meanings, particularly those attributed to Origen and his successors, but also what he saw as the "fanciful" readings of many of the rabbis.

In practice, however, Calvin could not avoid all allegory nor, it turns out, did he wish to. At least, he had to reckon with the apparent warrant introduced by Paul in Gal. 4:24, where Sarah and Isaac's conflict with Hagar and Ishmael is presented as an *allegoria* of the conflict between faith and works, gospel and law. Forced to reckon with this apostolic allegory, Calvin insisted that here is no fictive or arbitrary metaphor, but simply a comparison between the household of Abraham and the church of Paul's day. The typology is legitimate because it is closely tied to the historical narrative; indeed, Abraham's household literally *was* the church in his day.

In his comments here and elsewhere, Calvin proceeds to retain many traditional typological interpretations of the relationship between the NT and OT and to introduce others of his own coinage. But he does so by establishing such links not as secret or spiritual meanings that upstage the "letter" of the text. Where the traditional allegories or anagogies are retained, they reappear either as adjuncts or extensions of the historical narrative (typological fulfillments, etc.) or as rhetorical devices employed by the biblical narrator (analogies, hyperbole, figures). Calvin can therefore truly be said to be more concerned for the literal sense of the text, but his interpretations are still concerned to find Scripture's application. In maintaining this "churchly" concern, however, he has more in common with the "spiritual" approach of his medieval forebears than with modern historical-critical exegesis.

All these exegetical moves on Calvin's part are governed by one fundamental conviction, still related to what he understood as the scope of Scripture in the broadest sense: Scripture tells of but one people of God, one covenant of grace, one gospel, and one story—the story of a gracious God's tenacious claim on a people called by his name. Most important of all, it is a story that extends *beyond* Scripture, to Calvin's own day, and (he would say) to ours.

Calvin is thus understandably lauded for the way his theological interpretation of Scripture finds a unity throughout the Bible and brings Scripture to bear on the life and faith of its readers, but not all should be counted as easy gain. If Calvin's passion for application brought biblical promises into the present, it also revived biblical antagonists. In his own day and in later centuries, many lamented his frequent polemical outbursts against modern-day heirs of Hagar and Ishmael—especially the Roman Catholics of the sixteenth century, along with Jews and Anabaptists. Any reappropriation of Calvin as a model for theological exegesis has to temper his methods and rhetoric by a sober appreciation of the dangers of a Protestant triumphalism, an appropriate measure of self-criticism, and an awareness of the lessons (good and bad) that might be drawn from modern ecumenism. Nonetheless, Calvin's vision of the unity of Scripture as the good news that draws a sinful people into obedience and hope remains a worthy goal today.

Bibliography

Kraus, H.-J. "Calvin's Exegetical Principles." *Interpretation* 31 (1977): 8–18; Millet, O. *Calvin et la dynamique de la parole*. Bibliothèque littéraire de la renaissance, série 3, tome 28. Editions Slatkine, 1992; Muller, R. "The Hermeneutic of Promise and Fulfillment in Calvin's Exegesis of the Old Testament Promises of the Kingdom." Pages 68–82 in *The Bible in the Sixteenth Century*, ed. D. Steinmetz. Duke University Press, 1990; idem. *The Unaccommodated Calvin*. Oxford Studies in Historical Theology. Oxford University Press, 2000; Parker, T. H. L. *Calvin's New Testament Commentaries*. 2d ed. Westminster John Knox, 1993; idem. *Calvin's Old Testament Commentaries*. T&T Clark, 1986; Puckett, D. *John Calvin's Exegesis of the Old Testament*. Columbia Studies in Reformed Theology. Westminster John Knox, 1995; Steinmetz, D. *Calvin in Context*. Oxford University Press, 1995; Thompson, J. "Calvin's Exegetical Legacy: His Reception and Transmission of Text and Tradition." Pages 31–56 in *The Legacy of John Calvin: Calvin Studies Society Papers 1999*, ed. D. Foxgrover. Calvin Studies Society, 2000; Wright, D. F. "Calvin's 'Accommodation' Revisited." Pages 171–90 in *Calvin as Exegete*, ed. P. De Klerk. Calvin Studies Society, 1995.

John L. Thompson

Canon

The term "canon," originally meaning a measuring rod or rule, and then a catalog or set of standards, has from the fourth century been in general Christian theological usage as a technical term for the list of sacred writings deemed normative for Christian belief and practice. The decline of theological and exegetical appeal to the canonicity of the biblical writings is one of the major indicators of the changed status of Scripture in modernity. Recent attempts in theology and biblical hermeneutics to rehabilitate the notion of canon are among the most important developments in contemporary biblical interpretation.

History of the Canon

The history of the development of the biblical canon is complex and controversial. The full canon of Jewish Scripture is a relatively late development. Though substantially complete at the beginning of the Christian era, it was not finally settled until the beginning of the second century CE. Postexilic Judaism was governed by the Torah, to which were added (possibly from around 400 BCE) the Prophets. These are the Former Prophets—Joshua, Judges, 1 and 2 Samuel, and 1 and 2 Kings; the Latter Prophets—Isaiah, Jeremiah, Ezekiel; and the twelve Minor Prophets. The so-called "Writings"—Psalms, Proverbs, Job, the Song of Songs, Ruth, Lamentations, Ecclesiastes, Esther, Daniel, Ezra-Nehemiah, and 1 and 2 Chronicles—only acquired common acceptance at some later point. In addition, there are a number of postexilic writings in Greek of apocryphal or pseudepigraphical status, widely used by Jews and by Christians in the first centuries of the church. Athanasius's canon of the OT in his Festal Letter of 367 includes, for example, Baruch and the Epistle of Jeremiah. Judith, Tobit, Sirach, 2 Esdras, and the Wisdom of Solomon commonly appear in early Christian lists of what are regarded as the accepted OT writings, indicating wide usage of such texts. In the latter half of the fourth century, Jerome (unlike, for example, Origen, Cyril of Jerusalem, or Augustine) restricted the Christian OT to the thirty-nine Hebrew texts that now constitute the canon as set out by the Protestant Reformers. In the sixteenth century the Council of Trent established the wider list of Hebrew and apocryphal texts as *de fide* for Roman Catholics.

By the middle of the second century, the four Gospels and thirteen letters of Paul were generally accepted by the churches as authoritative apostolic teaching, to be read as Scripture alongside the OT. This can be seen from allusions to NT texts in the writings of the apostolic fathers, and from references to NT readings in public worship. A major stimulus to the development of an NT canon was given by the heretic Marcion, who promulgated a severely restricted list, comprising ten Pauline letters (excluding the Pastorals) and a truncated version of Luke's Gospel. In response, Irenaeus and Tertullian, for example, insisted on acceptance of all four Gospels. Though the core of the NT canon is thus stable by the end of the second century, the full list of writings does not settle for a further two hundred years. The so-called *Muratorian Canon/Fragment* (sometimes dated to the late second century, though it may be much later) lists all the NT books except Hebrews, James, and 1 and 2 Peter, but includes the Apocalypse of Peter and the Wisdom of Solomon. Early in the imperial era, Eusebius gives a list of universally accepted books (the four Gospels, thirteen Pauline letters, 1 John, and 1 Peter), a list of disputed books (including James, 2 Peter, Jude, 2 and 3 John, Hebrews, and Revelation), and a list of rejected texts (the apocryphal gospels and acts, the *Didache*, and others). Athanasius's Festal Letter of 367 lists the current twenty-seven NT books; but the canonical status of some texts (especially Hebrews, 2 Peter, Jude, and Revelation) remained in dispute. The first known full list of both OT and NT writings is that of the so-called Gelasian Decree (originating in the council around 380); this list is reproduced by the Council of Trent.

Theology of Canon

The status of the canon has undergone a drastic shift in modernity. The precise boundaries of the canon, and the relation of canonical writings to nonbiblical tradition, remained matters of confessional dispute after the Reformation. Yet, precritical Christian theology was largely agreed that Christian faith and practice are governed by a set of inspired texts whose antiquity, orthodoxy, and wide usage entitle them to be recognized as prophetic and apostolic Scripture. With the rise of the critical history of Christianity in the eighteenth century, a different account of the status of the canon and the lengthy processes of canonization came to prominence.

On this critical account, canonization is not so much an aspect of the providential ordering of the history of the church, but a set of contingent human undertakings. The effect of this is the "naturalization" of the canon, so that it comes to be regarded as an arbitrary or accidental feature of the Christian religion, to be explained, not transcendentally, but simply in terms of the immanent processes of religious history. This means that the texts of the canon cease to be viewed as categorically different from other noncanonical texts. It means, further, that canonicity is to be defined as the result of an act of choice and authorization on the church's part, apart from any supposed divine warrants for such an act. Moreover, the processes of canonization are not viewed as the church's gradual perception of the inherent status of the biblical texts, but as a product of, and medium for, social and political relations, to be analyzed in terms of the functioning of ideology as a means of social control. Canon, like "orthodoxy," is a product, not recognition. Both in giving an account of the history of early Christianity, and in giving a theological account of the Bible, therefore, canon has been subsumed into the history of religion, and so it has become a concept both more arbitrary and less innocent.

This set of developments has stimulated a variety of responses. Some historically reductive accounts have abandoned any affirmations of the normativity of the canon, since its imposition is merely a transient stage in the routinization of Christianity in the early period, a stage that has no enduring claim upon Christian thought and practice. Some recent theologians have sought to rehabilitate the notion of the canon by a variety of strategies. Most commonly, these involve explicating the social functions of canonical materials. The biblical canon, like other socially authorized collections, is a primary resource in the construction of a social and religious world, an instrument of common sensibility. In effect, these accounts shift the location of the canon away from the theology of revelation and toward the church community, with the canon as a function of its need for identity and persistence. These accounts resist the historical reductionism that makes canon into a matter of arbitrary power. But because their defense of the canon is socially pragmatic, they find it difficult to specify nonarbitrary reasons for the adoption of the canon, such as those that might be given by a theological account of revelation.

A further response to the "naturalization" of the canon would be to make use of more directly theological language to describe both the texts of Scripture and the processes of their canonization. Thereby one could relate them to the revelatory and providential work of God in Christ and the Spirit. This would entail developing claims that the texts to be found in the canonical catalog are revelatory, in that they are appointed by God to be instruments of his communicative activity. The theological conceptuality to describe this feature of the biblical texts can vary (the most usual term is that of "inspiration"). An important feature of any such account, however, will be theological teaching about the present communicative activity of the risen Christ in the power of the Spirit; critical-historical accounts of canon and canonization are frequently vitiated by deistic assumptions that make God's action through creaturely entities difficult to conceive.

On this basis, the process of canonization would be described, not as an arbitrary act of decision or political imposition, but as a Spirit-directed process of discernment and judgment. Canonization thus is to be understood as assent rather than authorization, as an act of reception and submission, and as a pledge to be governed by the textual norm given to the church. Further, a theological account of canon would seek to show that canon is not mere statute, a rule to be invoked only at points of transgression. Instead, it forms the primary discursive habits of the Christian community, especially in public worship, in doctrine, and in decisions concerning the identity of the community. Hence, acceptance of the canon commits the church to the use of the biblical writings as authoritative norm.

Canon and Interpretation

The canon of Scripture is a list of texts to be used. The "use" of Scripture is its deployment as norm by the Christian community. "Use," however, is an activity of a different order from "production": the church's acts of reading and reception of the biblical writings do not constitute the Bible as Scripture; instead, believers seek to hear what is addressed to the church through the mediation of this text. As canon, therefore, Scripture needs to be read fittingly, in the particular ways and with the particular virtues that are appropriate to the nature of Scripture as the church's given norm, and that serve the end of Scripture, which is the instruction and edification of the saints.

As canon, Scripture is authoritative because it is the instrument of divine address. To read and interpret canonical material is therefore to be required to read and interpret faithfully—with attention to the divine speech encountered through the text, and so to read and interpret repentantly—with awareness of the human capacity to resist God's address. In the Christian tradition, such virtues have generally been regarded as the gifts of the Holy Spirit, and the interpretation of canonical Scripture has been considered a spiritual exercise directed by God's illuminating presence. If, further, the end of Scripture is attention to divine speech, then strategies of biblical interpretation will be judged according to their capacity to promote that end. Methods whose primary concern is (for example) the reconstruction of a text's historical or authorial origin, or the generation of affective states in the reader, will be judged less likely to foster attention to revelation as it is presented in Scripture.

To describe Scripture as canon is also to make a claim that the assembled texts constitute a whole, and that their collection is of significance for the interpretation of the constituent parts. Gathered as a canon, the individual texts of the Bible do not simply exist adjacent to each other, and their relations are not simply intertextual (as in the reference of the NT to OT materials). Rather, the canon is a single (though complex) entity whose individual textual elements are both mutually interpretative, and also to be understood in the light of the whole of which they form parts. The texts of the canon are such because they testify to a single overarching work of God in the economy of creation and reconciliation: the canon is a whole because it refers to this unified divine work. This has direct effects on biblical interpretation. Individual canonical units are not to be defined as discrete entities, wholly determined by such factors as provenance, authorship, genre, language, and so forth; they are also determined by the whole to which they belong. Moreover, the canon may be read as a whole, derivative as it is from a single (though manifold) act of divine communication, and its individual texts are to be interpreted with reference to that whole.

Bibliography

Abraham, W. *Canon and Criterion in Christian Theology.* Clarendon, 1998; Barth, K. *Church Dogmatics.* Vol. I/1. T&T Clark, 1975; Berkouwer, G. C. *Holy Scripture.* Eerdmans, 1975; Campenhausen, H. von. *The Formation of the Christian Bible.* Fortress, 1972; Childs, B. *Biblical Theology of the Old and New Testaments.* SCM, 1992; Folkert, K. "The 'Canons' of 'Scripture.'" Pages 170–79 in *Rethinking Scripture,* ed. M. Levering. SUNY Press, 1989; Gamble, H. *The New Testament Canon.* Fortress, 1985; Guillory, J. *Cultural Capital.* University of Chicago Press, 1993; Metzger, B. *The Canon of the New Testament.* Clarendon, 1987; van der Kooij, A., and K. van der Koorn, eds. *Canonization and Decanonization.* Brill, 1998; Webster, J. "The Dogmatic Location of the Canon." Pages 9–46 in *Word and Church.* T&T Clark, 2001.

John Webster

Canonical Approach

A "canonical approach" or a "canonical method" refers to a species of theological interpretation and exegesis pioneered by Brevard Childs. It has had wide application within the disciplines of biblical theology, OT and NT interpretation, commentary, and history of biblical interpretation. It might be helpful to speak of a canonical approach as having three related facets: literary/exegetical, catholic/ecclesial, and theological. It is not possible entirely to isolate these, so beware of areas of overlap in the discussion that follows.

Literary/Exegetical

Canonical reading is derived from historical-critical interpretation of the last two centuries. That is, it is to be distinguished from reader-response or structural/rhetorical modes of reading, which hermeneutically privilege the place of the reader or the preunderstanding (secular or theological) of the community approaching the text. In that sense, it shares a concern for the objective reality of the text and for its intentional direction and ruled character, as this also distinguished historical-critical approaches in their various stages of development (literary-critical, source-critical, form-critical, tradition-critical).

Unlike them, however, canonical reading does not seek authorial intent at the level of the text's prehistory, in an alleged source or form, or tied to an historical audience, as these might be reconstructed using various critical tools of retrieval. At the same time, a canonical approach does believe that the depth dimension uncovered by historical tools is a reality that must be dealt with constructively and with great theological sensitivity. This is so because appeals to things like "single Isaiah authorship" may assert a form of historical rationalism equally at odds with the objective form of the material as it lies before us in its plain-sense presentation. Further, by noting the prehistory of the text—mindful of the speculative and therefore limited nature of such reconstructions—a canonical reading can seek to understand the theology of the final-form presentation as a kind of commentary on the text's prehistory. Through the arrangement and sequencing of the material as we now have it, it is a theological statement made by allowing certain aspects of the prehistory to receive prominence and clarity, and other aspects of that prehistory to recede in importance. Nowhere, for example, is any biography of "deutero-Isaiah" provided by the final form of Isaiah, even as the material may plausibly be connected to such a historical conceptuality. This means that the literary constraints of Isa. 40–55 must be sought in the context of the larger book, and its assertion of a unified or coherent or single "vision." Similarly, while historical analysis may lay bare levels of tradition (Q or the "J Source" or pre-Deuteronomic tradition), it will not have adequate theological or literary warrant for determining which level is to have exegetical priority. It will either conclude that the biblical text is a container of competing and incongruent theological claims, or it will wittingly or unwittingly give precedence to one such claim over another.

The earlier source or form will be privileged because it is closer to the "reality" being conveyed; or the later sources might be privileged because they suit the more mature theology that can only, with the proper passage of time, be grasped and understood.

Canonical reading sees the choices offered by such a historical approach, and yet reckons that the final form is itself a statement, fully competent to judge and constrain the prehistory reconstructed by such methods. Sometimes earlier traditions will be given literary prominence, while on other occasions a later editorial move will seek to constrain the tradition as received, and seek to coordinate interpretation by an extrinsic link to other texts in the canon. Canonical reading is therefore not an exact science, but a theological decision about what the proper parameters for interpretation are: the final-form presentation and the arrangement and sequencing that it exhibits, over against the simple history of the text's development as this is critically reconstructed.

Catholic/Ecclesial

A canonical reading is, self-consciously, a modern form of reading. It takes seriously its own specific location in the history of ideas and in the development of modern historical study. At the same time, because it seeks to honor the final form of the witness, and the associations that the final form has sought to privilege, it is understandably an art of reading kindred to that of many phases of precritical reading. This is most obvious in terms of what it rejects by not giving priority to phases of the text's prehistory (about which most premodern reading is unaware or disinterested). But it is also the case that, insofar as the final form of the witness receives a sensitive and appreciative handling, canonical reading may find itself open to allegorical and figural interpretations, such as emerged in an earlier day. At a minimum, because canonical reading does not believe that a historical approach represents a progressive improvement, but only asks specific kinds of questions of texts, it has a different understanding of what counts for good reading. This makes it open to learn from the past and from the kinds of questions that occupied theological readers in the rich catholic heritage of precritical interpretation. It is not a retrievalist or nostalgic concern that makes this history of interest, but rather the recognition that reading has an ineluctable social component. Premodern exegesis is keenly aware of the history of reading within which it is situated, and it judges this context a blessing as well as a challenge to be faced and dealt with.

Historical approaches tended to believe that the prior history of interpretation was outmoded, irrelevant, wrong, confused, or capable of being transcended by appeal to "historical objectivity." This insistence on being an altogether different species of reading is what marred historical approaches, and it should have put a question mark over the entire enterprise. Canonical reading has always judged the historical-critical questions as interesting and necessary to consider—in the light of the sheer givenness, externality, and materiality of the witness—but as incapable of sustaining a claim to independence or priority.

One other factor is crucial to note. What I am terming "catholic or ecclesial" reading is, in the first instance, Christian reading. Appeal to the "rule of faith" by canonical reading is not an appeal to piety or virtue, in the manner of some recent approaches, but to an assumption of an interlocking and coherent witness, in the material form of the canon. That witness stretches across two Testaments of one Bible (whether in a single Greek language or not). The rule of faith operated in the early church by constraining the church to seek interlocking and associative interpretation. The Creator God of the OT sent his only Son, witnessed to through the medium of the apostolic writings and in the life of the Holy Spirit, given at baptism. This faith was sustained by preaching (from the same two-Testament witness), the sacraments, and the life of prayer. Catholic reading, so understood, cannot read the Testaments apart from one another, because the two different material witnesses have a single subject matter.

It cannot be said ahead of time what kind of pressure a canonical reading must be willing to respond to on this front. There will be times in the church's life when the danger is in conflating the two different witnesses, with the consequence that a "resultant system" (allegorical excess, propositionalism, philosophical abstraction, or something else) obscures the plain-sense witness of the two-Testament witness. At other times, historical differentiation and the search for distinctive individual witnesses within the Testaments, for whatever salutary reasons one might give, make the relationship between Old and New forms of witness impossible to see. Or one may make only extrinsic and artificial linkings in the name of aesthetic harmony or apologetic worries.

Here, attention to readings that take place in Jewish religious life serve an important corrective function; such attention may call the church to a deeper understanding of what a single religious tradition makes out of diverse Scripture, for similar as well as for different reasons. Central to Jewish religious life is the conviction that God is one, and the insistence at this point is not philosophical but exegetical and scriptural. Christians share this theological conviction, even as the material form of their witness is differently diverse: it comes in the dual form of "prophets and apostles."

Theological

Canonical reading exists within a recent history of ideas, concerning especially literary and hermeneutical methods applied to the reading of the Bible. It offers a critical perspective on critical interpretation in the modern academic context.

But it does not assert its literary and catholic distinctives, as these have been described, only to point to deficiencies and attenuations. Indeed, canonical reading is reading in a particular post-historical-critical climate, and it draws positively from this context as well as negatively.

The same is true in some measure for the theological goal and underpinnings of canonical reading. It locates, and then cautions about, the kinds of theologizing that inevitably, if sometimes minimally, appear in historical readings, insofar as these ignore the final arrangement and presentation of the individual writings and collections in the canon, and so foreshorten or historicize or misconstrue genuine theological reflection.

One can defend the appeal to the final form, not just on the grounds that such a presentation has integrity and rationality. The final form—because it is not simply the most recent level of tradition, but is the aggregation of the entire history of the text's development, now in a given form—has a claim to our greatest attention. In other words, there is nothing morally superior about later reflections as over against earlier ones, as is sometimes claimed for a canonical approach's interest in the final form. Only the final forms bear the fullest witness to all that God has said and handed on within the historical community of faith. This point has been made recently by a theologian: "If God is thought of as revealing himself to his people in increasing measure over time, in the course of a teleological process of salvation worked out within history, then there is a prima facie case for privileging the witness of later communities, who were witnesses to the greatest extent of that revelation." He continues: "A reading of the Old Testament which assumes

this view of revelation will naturally give theological privilege to the later compilers of the final form of the canonical texts. It is their historical location, rather than some special moral quality of trustworthiness which they supposedly possessed and earlier writers lacked, which gives their text theological priority" (Ward 249).

What is said here of the OT can be, and is, extended theologically to the entire Christian Bible by a canonical reading. It is all the more crucial to acknowledge the centrality of a two-Testament theological approach, when it is considered that the formation of the second Testament, as a theological witness, took place as commentary on the Old in the light of the gospel, showing Christ to be "in accordance with the Scriptures." The theological work of the NT is intrinsically connected to hearing the full revelation of the OT as accorded and configured in the gospel of Jesus Christ. This happens not as an extrinsic act of piety or hope; it grows out of the testimony of the NT's own witness, which lays claim to the Old Scriptures and sees in them the gospel's preparation and prefiguration.

See also Narrative Theology; Rule of Faith; Yale School

Bibliography

Brett, M. *Biblical Criticism in Crisis*. Cambridge University Press, 1991; Childs, B. "The Exegetical Significance of Canon for the Study of the Old Testament." *VT Supplements* 29 (1977): 66–80; Frei, H. *The Eclipse of Biblical Narrative*. Yale University Press, 1974; Seitz, C. *Biblical Theology of the Old and New Testaments*. Fortress, 1992; idem. *Word without End*. Eerdmans, 1998; Sheppard, G. T. "Brevard Childs." Pages 574–84 in *Historical Handbook of Major Biblical Interpreters*, ed. D. McKim. InterVarsity, 1998; Ward, T. *Word and Supplement*. Oxford University Press, 2002.

Christopher Seitz

Canon within a Canon   *See* Canon; Scripture, Unity of

Catholic Biblical Interpretation

Catholic interpretation—here referring to the Roman Catholic tradition—is best understood in light of the history of interpretation, and of Catholic doctrine about the relation of Scripture to Tradition and the Catholic Church.

History

The first generation of Christians accepted the Jewish Scriptures and the interpretation of them they had received from Jesus and the apostles. The church interpreted the Law, the Prophets, and the other sacred Writings in light of the life, death, and resurrection of Jesus, who "fulfilled" the Scriptures. Disputes about doctrine were resolved by resorting to the judgment of the apostles and elders (Gal. 2:2; Acts 15) or by appealing to the primitive apostolic tradition (Gal. 1:8; 2 Thess. 2:15; 1 John 2:24; Jude 3; 1 Tim. 6:20; 2 Tim. 1:12–14). Second-century Christianity saw the rise of interpretation that rejected the OT and selected from the apostolic writings (Marcion) or radically reinterpreted them (Valentinus and other Gnostics). The church responded by referring to the tradition of interpretation found in the churches established by apostles (Irenaeus, *Haer.* 3.2–3; PG 7:847–48) and by compiling lists of apostolic writings authorized for catechetical and liturgical use—leading eventually to the canon.

The fathers of the church continued the struggle for sound interpretation, seeking to clarify doctrinal questions and feed their flocks by means of the Scriptures and of the traditions they had received. Through the patristic era there was little distinction between exegesis and theology: biblical commentaries were at the same time theological works, and vice versa.

Medieval writers and preachers expounded the four senses of Scripture taught by some church fathers: The *literal* sense reported events and the face-value meaning of the words. The *allegorical* revealed the meaning of OT events in light of Christ. The *moral* explained the implications of the text for Christian behavior. The *anagogical* pointed to the eschatological significance of the text. Other authors, such as Thomas Aquinas, produced theological *summae*, which expressed doctrine in carefully defined propositions and inadvertently introduced a separation between theology and the study of Scripture.

Renaissance humanism paved the way for a renewal of exegesis through its interest in the biblical languages and its advances in textual criticism. The Reformers reoriented theology, preaching, catechesis, and Christian devotion toward Scripture. However, their principle of *sola scriptura* and their rejection of the authority of Tradition and the teaching authority of pope and bishops evoked a strong reaction: the Council of Trent (1546) upheld the authority of both Scripture and the "unwritten . . . traditions concerning both faith and morals, as coming from either Christ's spoken words or from the Holy Spirit" (First Decree). It further asserted "that no one, by relying on their own judgment in matters of faith and morals, . . . shall dare to interpret the Sacred Scriptures in opposition to

what has been and continues to be taught by Holy Mother Church, to whom belongs the capacity to judge the true meaning of the texts, or to the unanimous teaching of the Fathers" (Second Decree). Although Reformation controversies led the Catholic Church to reform in various ways, its leadership became wary of biblical studies and subordinated biblical interpretation to scholastic theology.

Encounter with Modern Biblical Criticism

The Catholic Church's caution about Scripture and Catholic scholarship's isolation from Protestant biblical studies delayed the confrontation with modern biblical criticism. In 1893 Pope Leo XIII's *Providentissimus Deus* encouraged Catholic scholars to study biblical languages and become expert in the new scientific criticism in order to defend against its rationalist forms. However, when some prominent Catholic scholars adopted modernism, the Catholic Church's openness gave way to a reaction against higher criticism that forbade Catholic scholars to question traditional assumptions about authorship, historicity, and the integrity of biblical books (Pontifical Biblical Commission, "Responses"). Fifty years later, after the rationalist threat had subsided, Pope Pius XII authorized Catholic exegetes to pursue critical studies with full freedom. He directed them to pay attention to literary forms and the manners of communication in previous ages and other cultures, so as more clearly to understand the mind of the human authors (*Divino afflante Spiritu*, 1943).

The Second Vatican Council marked an important turning point as the Catholic Church sought to refocus on the sources of its faith in Scripture, patristic writings, and the ancient liturgies. The council's *Dogmatic Constitution on Divine Revelation* (Paul VI, *Dei Verbum* [*DV*]) reformulated Catholic doctrine regarding Scripture and Tradition. It confirmed Pius XII's acceptance of modern biblical studies and exhorted both clergy and laity "to learn by frequent reading of the Divine Scriptures 'the supreme good of knowing Jesus Christ' (Phil 3:8)." The ecumenical orientation of Vatican II opened Catholics to learning from, and cooperating with, biblical scholars outside the Catholic Church.

After the Second Vatican Council, Catholic scholars made up for lost time by immersing themselves in the historical-critical study of Scripture; exegetes such as Raymond Brown, Joseph Fitzmyer, Roland Murphy, and Rudolf Schnackenberg earned the respect of their guild.

However, now complaints began to arise that the historical-critical method was not producing the desired fruit. Historical theologians such as Henri de Lubac and Jean Daniélou judged that the church's tradition of theological interpretation was being lost, arguing for a return to patristic interpretation and a recovery of the spiritual sense of Scripture. Tensions grew between exegesis and systematic theology; some questioned whether scientific exegesis was useful for the church's pastoral ministry. In a 1988 public lecture Joseph Cardinal Ratzinger, head of the Vatican's Congregation for the Doctrine of the Faith, called for a critical examination of the philosophical assumptions that commonly accompany the historical-critical method and spoke of a "crisis" in biblical interpretation.

In response to these criticisms and to new literary and hermeneutical approaches, the Pontifical Biblical Commission, reconstituted as an international consultative body of twenty exegetes, undertook an evaluation of exegesis in the church. Pope John Paul II officially received their study and authorized its publication in 1993, *The Interpretation of the Bible in the Church* (*IBC*). The *IBC* describes the characteristics of Catholic interpretation, confirms—but qualifies—the use of the historical-critical method, and welcomes the use of other methods and approaches, provided they function within a hermeneutic of Christian faith. The Biblical Commission's document emphasizes that Catholic exegesis must "maintain its identity as a theological discipline" (Conclusion, e). This document and *DV* remain the most important church documents for understanding Catholic biblical interpretation.

Since the publication of the *IBC*, Catholic exegesis has continued to reflect the extreme diversity of contemporary biblical scholarship. Nevertheless, a trend in some quarters toward theological interpretation may be detected in arguments for its importance (Johnson and Kurz; Schneiders; Williamson), in some commentaries, and in a renewed appreciation for patristic and medieval interpretation.

Doctrine of Scripture

Catholic biblical interpretation is governed by the belief that Scripture is the word of God expressed in human language. On the one hand, because all Scripture is inspired by the Holy Spirit, God is its principal author. "Since everything asserted by the inspired authors or sacred writers should be regarded as asserted by the Holy Spirit, it follows that . . . Scripture . . . teach[es] firmly, faithfully and without error the truth that God wished to be recorded in the sacred writings for the sake of our salvation" (*DV* 11). On the other hand, God "chose and employed certain men, who . . . made full use of their own faculties and powers . . ." (*DV* 11). The human limitations of the inspired authors were not eradicated by the activity of the divine Author so as to make Scripture inerrant in scientific matters or historical details.

Scripture fulfills a foundational, life-giving, and authoritative role for the church. It is *foundational* for doctrine because Scripture is the word of God and because it witnesses to the events and their interpretation on which Christian faith is grounded. It *communicates life*: "God's word . . . remains the sustaining life-force for her children, the nourishment for the soul and the pure and lasting source of spiritual life" (*DV* 21). Scripture is also *authoritative*: "All the preaching of the Church, as indeed the entire Christian religion, [should] be nourished and ruled by Sacred Scripture" (*DV* 21).

Scripture does not merely recount God's saving words and actions in the past; it also is perpetually relevant, since God continues to speak to his people through it. This always-contemporary attribute of Scripture especially characterizes its reading in the liturgy "since it is Christ himself who speaks when Sacred Scripture is read in the church" (*IBC* IV.C.1.b).

Interpretation

The Role of Tradition. Christ's apostles communicated to the churches they founded what they had received from Christ or learned by the Spirit. "What was handed on by the apostles includes everything that helps the People of God to live in holiness and to grow in faith, and so the Church, in her teaching, life, and worship, perpetuates and hands on to every generation all that she herself is, all that she believes. The Tradition that comes from the apostles develops in the Church with the help of the Holy Spirit, for there is growth in understanding of the realities and words that have been handed down" (*DV* 7). As a communication of divine revelation, *Tradition* must be distinguished from various theological, disciplinary, liturgical, or devotional *traditions* that arise and seek to give expression to it. Sacred Tradition can be understood as the living presence of God's word in the church's life through time.

Scripture and Tradition flow "from the same divine wellspring" (*DV* 9) and "form one sacred deposit of the word of God" (*DV* 10). The relationship between Scripture and Tradition is reciprocal; each acts upon the other. The idea that Scripture should be interpreted in light of Tradition follows from the fact that the canon of Scripture itself is a fruit of Tradition. At the same time, meditation on Scripture nourishes and shapes the development of Tradition. Besides Scripture itself, in varying degrees, the fathers of the church, the creeds, the liturgy, the writings of the saints, the dogmatic definitions, and contemporary teaching of bishops and the pope bear witness to Tradition.

The primary role of Tradition in Catholic exegesis is to provide a deliberately embraced preunderstanding of what it is that Scripture is talking about (*IBC* III.b). Catholic exegesis seeks to avoid the risk of *eisegesis* that preunderstanding poses by distinguishing meanings present in the text from later developments. For instance, one may distinguish what the Gospel of John says about the Father and the Son from later trinitarian dogma, which, though consistent with the gospel, goes beyond it. In pastoral catechesis and preaching, Tradition provides the context in which Scripture is explained (*IBC* IV.C.3.b).

The Role of the Church. Catholics insist that Scripture is entrusted not to individual Christians, but to the whole people of God. Interpretation must occur in communion with the whole church. Differing roles belong to different members of the body of Christ. Biblical interpretation is not the exclusive preserve of scholarly or priestly elites, but belongs to all and, in a special way, to the simple poor who hope in God (*IBC* IV.C.3.m).

The pope and bishops exercise a special role of rendering authoritative decisions if the occasion requires it. "The task of authentically interpreting the word of God, whether in its written form or in the form of tradition, has been entrusted to the Teaching Office of the Church [which] is not above the word of God but serves it by teaching only what has been handed on" (*DV* 10). Historically, the Magisterium has concerned itself primarily with doctrine and has rendered authoritative interpretations of only a handful of texts (Brown and Schneiders 1163–64). Catholics believe that Scripture, Tradition, and the Teaching Office of the church each play necessary and complementary roles.

The OT and the Gospels. Catholic interpretation receives the OT (including the seven books of the LXX not found in the Hebrew canon) as Sacred Scripture and perpetually valid, even though the OT contains some things that are "incomplete and provisional" (*DV* 15). These books bear witness to God's dealings with his chosen people,

Israel, and prepare for the coming of Christ, the universal Redeemer, announcing his coming by prophecy and indicating its meaning by various types (*DV* 15). Catholics interpret the OT in light of the paschal mystery and the NT. Nevertheless, the Catholic Church esteems the literal sense of the OT, its canonical interpretation before the Christian Passover, because it testifies to a stage in salvation history and nourishes the church with teachings about God, sound wisdom about human life, and a treasury of prayers (*DV* 15).

Among all the Scriptures, "the Gospels have a special preeminence, for they are the principal witness to the life and teaching of the incarnate Word" (*DV* 18). The Gospels "faithfully hand on what Jesus, the Son of God . . . actually did and taught for [our] eternal salvation . . ." (*DV* 18). Catholic interpretation recognizes the selective and synthesizing work of the evangelists in keeping with their purpose of proclamation and pastoral care (*DV* 19).

Other Principles. The proper *object of interpretation* is the final canonical text since it alone is the inspired word of God; source criticism is useful insofar as it sheds light on the meaning of the final text. The *aim of interpretation* is to understand the word of God, the meaning of the text for Christian faith, and to pass beyond a cognitive grasp of the words of Scripture to understand the realities to which the words refer (*IBC* II.A.1.d). Exegesis can never be reduced to historical or literary knowledge, which are means rather than the end. Because genuine understanding requires an affinity between text and interpreter, certain qualities should characterize *interpreters*: Christian faith, the grace of the Spirit, a life lived in accord with the message of Scripture, participation in the life of the church, and personal prayer. The *primary task of Catholic exegesis* is to "determine as accurately as possible the meaning of biblical texts in their own proper context, that is, first of all in their particular literary and historical context and then in the context of the wider canon of Scripture," explaining the theological significance where appropriate (*IBC* III.D.4.b).

In carrying out its task, Catholic exegesis seeks the "meaning the sacred writer, in his own historical situation and in accordance with the condition of his time and culture, intended to express and did in fact express with the help of the literary forms that were in use during that time" (*DV* 12). To this end Catholic exegesis makes use of the ordinary scholarly means for interpreting ancient texts, the historical-critical method, while seeking to avoid rationalism, historicism, historical positivism, and other problematic presuppositions that have sometimes accompanied its use. At the same time exegesis freely makes use of literary methods, approaches derived from the history of interpretation or social sciences, and contextual approaches—so long as these methods and approaches are used in a manner consistent with Catholic interpretation's essential principles.

Catholic interpretation seeks to understand what the divine Author wished to communicate, and thus to interpret Scripture "in the light of the same Spirit by whom it was written" (*DV* 12). Valid interpretations of texts must cohere with the meaning of the whole of Scripture and Christian doctrine. Although Catholic exegesis recognizes differing perspectives and interpretations of the same events in Scripture (*IBC* III. A.2.g), it affirms the *essential unity of Scripture* grounded in Scripture's intertextuality, in its divine inspiration, and in the unity of the divine plan. This unity requires interpreting individual texts in light of the whole canon.

Catholic interpretation recognizes various senses of Scripture. The *literal sense*, "that which has been directly expressed by the inspired authors" (*IBC* II.B.1.c), is derived by studying texts in their historical and literary contexts. The *spiritual sense* is "the meaning expressed by the biblical texts when read under the influence of the Holy Spirit in the context of the paschal mystery and of the new life which flows from it" (*IBC* II.B.2.b). The importance of the spiritual sense is most obvious in reference to OT texts that are read christologically, such as 2 Sam. 7:12–13. Typology forms part of the spiritual sense. The *fuller sense* (*sensus plenior*), "a deeper meaning intended by God but not clearly expressed by the human author" (*IBC* II.B.3a), is a special instance of the spiritual sense when the literal and the spiritual sense differ. It is recognized when a later biblical text or an authoritative doctrinal tradition confirms its presence (e.g., Isa. 7:14 and Matt. 1:22–23).

Catholic interpretation insists on the need to bring the meaning of the biblical word into the present (*actualization*) and to embody it in diverse cultures (*inculturation*). By its attention to the theological meaning of Scripture, good exegesis prepares for actualization, a task that belongs to pastoral ministry.

See also Spiritual Sense; Tradition

Bibliography

Béchard, D., ed. *The Scripture Documents*. Liturgical, 2002; Brown, R., and S. Schneiders. "Hermeneutics." In *The New Jerome Biblical Commentary*, ed. R. Brown, J. Fitzmyer, and R. Murphy. Prentice Hall, 1990; Catholic Church. *Catechism of the Catholic Church* (§§74–141). 2d ed. United States Catholic Conference, 2000; Council of Trent. Session IV. First and Second Decrees. Pages 3–6 in Béchard; Daniélou, J. *The Bible and the Liturgy*. University of Notre Dame Press, 1956; Gilbert, M. "Exegesis, Integral." In *Dictionary of Fundamental Theology*, ed. R. Latourelle and R. Fisichella. Crossroad, 1995; Johnson, L. T., and W. Kurz. *The Future of Catholic Biblical Scholarship*. Eerdmans, 2002; Latourelle, R., ed. *Vatican II, Assessment and Perspectives*. Paulist, 1988; Leo XIII. *Providentissimus Deus*. Encyclical. 1893. Pages 37–59 in Béchard; Lubac, H. de. *Medieval Exegesis*, trans. M. Sebanc. Eerdmans, 1998; idem. *Scripture in the Tradition*, trans. L. O'Neill. Crossroad, 2000; Montague, G. *Understanding the Bible*. Paulist, 1997; Paul VI. *Sacred Constitution on Divine Revelation* (*Dei Verbum*). Vatican II, 1965. Pages 19–31 in Béchard; Pius XII. *Divino afflante Spiritu*. Encyclical. 1943. Pages 115–36 in Béchard; Pontifical Biblical Commission. *The Interpretation of the Bible in the Church*. 1993. Pages 244–315 in Béchard; idem. "Responses." 1905–15. Pages 187–208 in Béchard; Ratzinger, J. "Biblical Interpretation in Crisis: On the Question of the Foundations and Approaches of Exegesis Today." Pages 1–23 in *Biblical Interpretation in Crisis*, ed. R. J. Neuhaus. Eerdmans, 1989; Schneiders, S. *The Revelatory Text*. 2d ed. Liturgical, 1999; Williamson, P. *Catholic Principles for Interpreting Scripture*. Pontifical Biblical Institute, 2001; idem. "The Place of History in Catholic Exegesis." In *Behind the Text*, ed. C. Bartholomew et al. SHS. Zondervan/Paternoster, 2003.

Peter S. Williamson

Charismatic Biblical Interpretation

For "charismatic" groups, the communities that emphasize an individual experience of the Holy Spirit as well as an empowerment in spiritual gifts, the Bible is an authoritative revelation from God that must be read, proclaimed, and lived out as it offers the example of the "Spirit-filled" life. At the heart of charismatic biblical interpretation is the expectation of a personal encounter with God's supernatural power. Charismatic Bible reading should lead to charismatic experience.

Charismatic movements are a worldwide phenomenon, yet a lion's share of self-reflection on charismatic hermeneutics comes from North America and Europe. This article reflects a North American and European focus.

The Pentecostal Movement

While there have been charismatic movements throughout Christian history, Pentecostalism is the first such movement in the twentieth century. Two primary convictions for early Pentecostals were the restoration of beliefs and practices of the NT church, and the second coming of Christ. Christians should expect apostolic experiences from miracles to ministry, since a fully realized

Christian life would prepare believers for Jesus' soon return.

Early Pentecostal Hermeneutics. These convictions influenced a hermeneutic that viewed biblical narratives as a paradigm for modern Christian life. Of central importance was the "baptism in the Spirit" as described in Acts 2:1–4; 10:44–46; and 19:1–7. According to Pentecostalism as a whole, Spirit baptism was (and is) an experience subsequent to conversion, evidenced physically by "speaking in tongues," and given for the purpose of empowering the believer to evangelize the world and minister through spiritual gifts.

This particular interpretation of the reception of the Spirit in Acts reflects what has been called Pentecostal "Bible Reading Method," a precritical practice of reading all verses upon a particular subject, then harmonizing those verses into a consistent doctrine. This way of reading the Bible is both literal and immediate, with little awareness of a history behind or after the events and teachings recorded in the text. Pentecostal determination to see apostolic witness and life restored to the church is driven by a theological focus on Jesus as the Savior, Healer, Baptizer in the Holy Spirit, and Soon-Coming King—what many Pentecostals have called the "fourfold gospel" (the first Pentecostals would add "Sanctifier" to that list). It stresses an experiential desire for the Spirit-filled life as exemplified in biblical narratives, or the "full gospel."

Beyond the formulation of doctrine, a Pentecostal hermeneutic is largely typological. Because the text must immediately apply to the life of believers, correlations have been made between biblical narratives and present circumstances without critical exegesis. Pentecostal preaching has disclosed Pentecostal themes throughout the biblical text, from Genesis to Revelation.

Along with a restorationist, Jesus-centric theology (a foundational text was Heb. 13:8—"Jesus is the same yesterday and today and forever"), Pentecostals have understood biblical interpretation to be guided by the Holy Spirit and confirmed by their experience. The role of the Spirit is paramount to Pentecostal hermeneutics. If the Spirit inspired the Bible, its interpretation must depend on the Spirit. When disputing an interpretation, Pentecostals appeal to the Spirit's leading in their Bible reading.

Experience is sometimes viewed as so important to their hermeneutic that Pentecostals have been strongly criticized for exegeting their experience rather than the Bible. However, many Pentecostals understood their experience to be God's confirmation of their interpretation, particularly with regard to spiritual manifestations. Spiritual manifestations during communal worship have been viewed as a sign of God's blessing on whatever had been preached, even if Pentecostals outside of that local community rejected the sermon's message.

Recent Debates in Pentecostal Hermeneutics. Since the mid-twentieth century, the Pentecostal movement has seen its members join the academic community and engage in critical biblical scholarship. Pentecostal scholars have rejected the earlier methods of Pentecostal Bible reading, with a precritical exegesis, while debate continues concerning the function of narrative, and the roles of the Spirit and experience in hermeneutics.

Contemporary works reflect the influence of evangelicalism within Pentecostal scholarship as much of the Pentecostal debate focuses on the comparison and position of a Lukan narrative theology alongside a Pauline didactic theology. Gordon Fee, a well-known Pentecostal exegete, has strongly criticized the didactic value of biblical narratives within Pentecostalism, leading to a critique of Spirit baptism following conversion and "speaking in tongues" as evidence of received baptism. However, other Pentecostal scholars have rejected that critique as an attack on the very basis of Pentecostalism. To answer Fee and others, they include the paradigmatic role of biblical narratives as part of authorial intent and argue for a "charismatic" pneumatology based on Luke-Acts alongside Paul's soteriological pneumatology.

Most recently, scholars have debated the need for a Pentecostal hermeneutic outside of an evangelical framework. Some argue for a postmodern hermeneutic that moves beyond questions of authorial intent to an understanding of the text as capable of multiple meanings in dialogue with the reader. These scholars attempt to build a hermeneutic in dialogue with such thinkers as Paul Ricoeur, Martin Heidegger, Hans-Georg Gadamer, and Jürgen Habermas.

Another discussion concerns what essentials would make a hermeneutic "Pentecostal." The role of the Spirit in interpretation is given primary emphasis, though some scholars worry that it leads to a dualistic hermeneutic. Other essentials include the dialogical role of experience and openness to the authority of biblical narratives.

While Pentecostal scholars work on a hermeneutical method open to Pentecostal experience and acceptable to the academic community as a whole, much of the scholarly discussion has had only a moderate impact on local Pentecostal communities that continue to practice a largely precritical and typological hermeneutic.

The Charismatic Movement

The "charismatic movement" is a term commonly applied to Baptists, Catholics, Episcopalians, Lutherans, Methodists, Presbyterians, Orthodox, and other non-Pentecostal Christians who accepted in whole or in part the Pentecostal message, with a confirming experience of the Spirit, though they did not leave their respective denominations. By the 1960s, this reception became a nationally recognized phenomenon, with charismatic movements found in many historic denominations.

Charismatic Hermeneutics. Since a primary charismatic concern is spiritual renewal within traditional denominations, many charismatics interpret Scripture within their own theological tradition. However, they do bring to the subject of hermeneutics a belief in the personal relevance of Scriptures concerning the Spirit-filled life, especially those that focus on *charisms* (e.g., 1 Cor. 12:8–10). Charismatics also see the paradigmatic value of biblical narratives, though they reject some of the ways Pentecostals have interpreted those narratives. Many do not accept the interpretation of Spirit baptism (this term is also disputed) as a subsequent work of grace or "speaking in tongues" as its necessary evidence.

Charismatic experience has led some to view Scripture in a new way. Many charismatics report a renewed focus on Christ, which has led to a fresh commitment to the authority of the Bible as God's word about Christ. A deeper appreciation of the Spirit's role in interpretation has also been cited as a contribution of the charismatic renewal to more traditional hermeneutical approaches. According to Richard Quebedeaux, Scripture is understood only through the Holy Spirit, who makes known the *"living,* 'dynamic' *word of God,"* to which Scripture is subservient.

Charismatic scholars such as Paul Hinnebusch stress the recovery of a personal meaning in Scripture among charismatics, many of whom prayerfully engage in a "directive use of Scripture," believing that the Bible can give specific answers to personal situations. Mark Stibbe adds that charismatics also rely on "a community of shared experience" in interpreting and applying Scripture to their lives. Drawing on the work of thinkers like Ricoeur, they argue that Scripture can have multiple meanings under the leading of

the Spirit, though these meanings may be valid only to the person reading and may not supersede doctrine or good exegesis. Some scholars, though, want to distinguish between the usage of Scripture and its interpretation. Others such as Clark Pinnock strive to maintain a balance between biblical authority, doctrinal tradition, and the freedom of the Spirit, a balance not always found among other charismatics.

Recent Trends in Charismatic Hermeneutics. Since the 1980s, new types of charismatic groups have arisen with their own unique emphases in Christian spirituality, including "signs and wonders" as a means to evangelism, and "power encounters" with demonic forces. Critics have accused these groups of experimenting with Christian practice and then "proof-texting" various Scriptures to support those experiments—such as the "power encounter" teaching of Charles Kraft. These newer charismatics argue in turn for a more prophetic hermeneutical approach that keeps both the original meaning and the prophetic significance of Scripture in mind. The Spirit that inspired the original biblical authors also leads the charismatic community to recollect Scriptures that apply directly to their situation. There is an analogical correlation between the original meaning and contemporary significance of Scripture that is safeguarded from error by the Spirit and community discernment.

Restoration of the NT church as an eschatological event is also emphasized in some nondenominational groups who, as reflected in the writings of C. Peter Wagner, believe in the renewal of the five offices mentioned in Eph. 4:11, with special attention given to apostles and prophets. Restoration of the Spirit-filled life remains a guiding focus of these charismatic biblical interpreters, who seek to bridge a gap between reading the Bible and living the Bible.

Bibliography

Archer, K. "Early Pentecostal Biblical Interpretation." *JPT* 18 (2001): 32–70; Arrington, F. "Hermeneutics, Historical Perspectives on Pentecostal and Charismatic." Pages 376–89 in *Dictionary of Pentecostal and Charismatic Movements*, ed. S. Burgess and G. McGee. Regency, 1988; Fee, G. *Gospel and Spirit.* Hendrickson, 1991; Kärkkäinen, V.-M. "Pentecostal Hermeneutics in the Making: On the Way from Fundamentalism to Postmodernism." *The Journal of the European Pentecostal Theological Association* 18 (1998): 76–115; Ma, W. "A 'First Waver' Looks at the 'Third Wave': A Pentecostal Reflection on Charles Kraft's Power Encounter Terminology." *Pneuma* 19:2 (1997): 189–206; Martin, G., ed. *Scripture and the Charismatic Renewal.* Servant, 1979; Menzies, W., and R. Menzies. *Spirit and*

Power. Zondervan, 2000; Quebedeaux, R. *The New Charismatics II*. Harper & Row, 1983; Stibbe, M. "This Is That: Some Thoughts concerning Charismatic Hermeneutics." *Anvil* 15:3 (1998): 181–93; Wagner, C. P. *Apostles and Prophets*. Regal, 2000.

D. Allen Tennison

Christian Interpretation of the OT *See* Anti-Semitism; Relationship between the Testaments; Rule of Faith; Scripture, Unity of

Christus Victor *See* Atonement; Powers and Principalities

Chronicles, Books of

The two books of Chronicles were originally written as one by an anonymous author. Known as "The Book of the Events of the Days" in early rabbinic tradition, the translators of the Septuagint divided it in two and, assuming it was a supplement to the earlier history of Samuel and Kings, gave it the misleading title "The Things Omitted." Much of the earlier history is omitted (e.g., the history of the northern kingdom). Other parts are simply summarized (e.g., David's military victories in 1 Chron. 18–20; cf. 2 Sam. 8–23), or presented in significantly different ways (e.g., the account of Manasseh in 2 Chron. 33; cf. 2 Kings 21). The title "1–2 Chronicles" comes from Jerome, translator of the Latin Vulgate, who in the fourth century CE suggested that "a chronicle of all of sacred history" would better describe the contents of a work beginning with Adam and ending with Cyrus.

History of Interpretation

Chronicles has not received the attention it deserves in either Jewish or Christian theological circles for several reasons. In the first place, the LXX's misleading title ("Things Omitted") and its questionable placement among the historical books in subsequent Bibles have led some—who fail to recognize its inherently theological, if not homiletical, nature—to challenge its historical accuracy. Specifically, the question of the historical reliability of these books has dominated the discussion from earliest times. In the precritical period, though synagogue and church alike assumed Chronicles' reliability, its apparent supplementary character rendered it useful only in instances where Samuel–Kings was silent. This, more than any other reason, accounts for Chronicles being the least utilized portion of Scripture.

Second, only a few exemplars of Chronicles have appeared at Qumran. No ancient commentaries have survived the rabbinic neglect of these books that continued into the medieval period. This may be because both the Talmud and Mishnah regarded Chronicles as a book for the sages to ponder, rather than the laity. What pondering was done, however, saw Chronicles essentially as Ezra's midrash on the earlier histories of Samuel and Kings.

Third, the earlier, widespread assumption that any differences between Chronicles and Samuel–Kings were the result of tendentious alteration has been successfully challenged, especially since the critical work of Wilhelm de Wette in the nineteenth century. Text-critical investigation demonstrates the care with which the Chronicler used his sources. The sources were closer to the Lucianic version of the LXX and the parts of Samuel found among the Dead Sea Scrolls (4QSam[a]) than to the Masoretic text of Samuel, as previously thought. Understanding this fact accounts for many of the discrepancies and means that Chronicles must not simply be read as a theologically motivated rewriting of the earlier history.

Fourth, until recently it was supposed that Chronicles and Ezra-Nehemiah comprised two parts of a single composition, relating Israel's history from Adam to the postexilic community under Nehemiah. As a result, Chronicles was read through the theological lens of Ezra-Nehemiah. Today that assumption is questioned. While these books do display similarities of style, language, and general outlook, they differ on a number of key theological matters. These include the nature of "Israel," the Davidic covenant, the function of the Levites, the place and function of prophecy, retributive justice, the Sabbath, mixed marriages, and the significance of the exodus. Though still debated, an emerging consensus recognizes the separate authorship of Chronicles and Ezra-Nehemiah as well as the integral nature of the genealogies in 1 Chron. 1–9 to the work as a whole. This favors a date during the Persian period, somewhere in the fourth century BCE. Decisive here are the lists of David's descendants in 1 Chron. 3:17–24, extending to the late fourth century, and the inhabitants of Jerusalem in 9:2–34, extending to the early fourth century.

Finally, since interpretation depends upon prior decisions regarding setting, extent, and time of composition, the variety of opinion regarding dating of Chronicles and its relationship to Ezra-Nehemiah has generated a corresponding variety in elucidation. For instance, a previous generation, following Noth, interpreted the Chronicler's work as a response to a rival Samaritan faction formed in the wake of the 332 BCE fall of the Persian Empire. Today, however, the schism is placed at the end of the second century, rendering the Chronicler's so-called "anti-Samaritan polemic" anachronistic. Among contemporary scholars, Welten, who continues to maintain the common authorship of Chronicles and Ezra-Nehemiah, has extensively investigated the Chronicler's battle reports and suggests that the early-third-century hostilities between the Ptolemies and the Seleucids are a more appropriate interpretative milieu for Chronicles. Those who reject common authorship are divided in their understanding of the Chronicler's context. Some find a likely backdrop in the early years of the return (529–515 BCE), influenced by the prophetic call of Haggai and Zechariah to rebuild the temple (e.g., Freedman; Newsome; Braun). Others suggest the need for faithfulness amid the tense repercussions of the Persian suppression of the Tennes revolt in 351–348 BCE (Williamson). Japhet, convinced that Ezra-Nehemiah precedes Chronicles, suggests the end of the fourth century, early in the Hellenistic period.

In sum, it is only in the modern period that Chronicles has been read for the very different historical and theological portrayal of Israel that it presents. From the ancient period through the middle of the twentieth century, Samuel–Kings provided the biblical version of that history, with Chronicles providing "supplementary" information. This, in turn, resulted in the substantial neglect of these books in rabbinic, patristic, medieval, and Reformation exegesis.

Context and Message

Comparisons between Chronicles and Samuel–Kings frequently fail to recognize the very different contexts of the two works. Samuel–Kings sought to answer the pressing questions of exiles who had experienced the fall of Jerusalem to Nebuchadnezzar II, the destruction of the temple, the end of Davidic rule, and deportation to Babylon in 587/6 BCE. Chronicles, however, addresses the postexilic community that, following the Persian defeat of the Babylonians under Cyrus in 539 BCE, had returned from Babylon to live under Persian rule and worship in the rebuilt Jerusalem temple. Instead of asking, "Why did this happen to us?" they sought their relationship with the past: "Who are we?" "Are we still the people of

God?" and "What do God's promises to David and Solomon mean for us today?"

Chronicles addresses these questions by retelling the story of Israel and inviting the people to see themselves as living in situations of either "exile" or "restoration." Exilic situations result from unfaithfulness, serving other gods, or failing to seek the Lord. Even if literal exile does not occur, the loss of God's blessing inevitably results in devastating consequences. Blessing can be restored, however, through repentance (2 Chron. 7:14). Thus, Chronicles encourages the struggling postexilic community to seek and serve a loving and merciful God, who awaits their response and hears their prayers.

Contribution to the Canon

Modern versions of the Bible, the LXX, and the Vulgate group 1–2 Chronicles with the historical books, placing them between 2 Kings and Ezra-Nehemiah. In this arrangement, the prophet Malachi's announcement that Elijah will precede the arrival of the Lord immediately precedes the Gospels' portrayal of John the Baptist as the forerunner of the Messiah in the opening books of the NT. In the Hebrew canon, however, these books of Chronicles follow Ezra-Nehemiah in the Writings. This placement at the end of the Hebrew Bible is theologically significant in two ways. First, on the basis of chronology, Ezra-Nehemiah should close the Hebrew Bible. But their presentation of the return from exile soon deteriorates into the familiar problems of the postexilic community, issues only partially resolved in the reforms of Ezra and Nehemiah. The Chronicler's presentation of the return, though confined to a brief citation of the Cyrus Edict, ends with an invitation: "Whoever is among you of all his people, may the LORD his God be with him! Let him go up!" (2 Chron. 36:22–23 NRSV). This conclusion avoids the less-than-optimistic state of affairs found in Ezra-Nehemiah and lets the Hebrew canon end on a note of hope.

Second, the books of Chronicles function as a culminating summary and integration of all that has gone before. This is especially evident regarding worship. Disparate cultic considerations from the Psalter, the institution of Levitical functionaries, and the reorganization found in the Priestly Code are synthesized and brought together, thereby positing worship as the cohesive element lacking in the fragmented postexilic community. A Hebrew canon concluding with Chronicles also explains Luke 11:51, "From the blood of Abel to the blood of Zechariah," as a time frame extending from the murder of Abel (Gen. 4) to the murder of Zechariah (2 Chron. 24:20–22). No other OT book utilizes more biblical material than Chronicles, which draws extensively upon all three sections of the Hebrew canon. While the books of Samuel and Kings serve as the primary source, citations of or allusions to Genesis, Exodus, Leviticus, Numbers, Deuteronomy, Joshua, Judges, Ruth, Ezra, Nehemiah, several psalms, Isaiah, Jeremiah, Lamentations, Ezekiel, Zephaniah, and Zechariah all appear. In this way, Chronicles anticipates aspects of contemporary "inner-biblical exegesis."

Theological Significance

The explication of Chronicles' theological significance begins with recognition of its overall structure. A long genealogical introduction (1 Chron. 1–9) is followed by a presentation of the period of the united monarchy under David and Solomon (1 Chron. 10–2 Chron. 9). A third section discusses the period of the divided monarchy, concentrating upon the kings of Judah (2 Chron. 10–28). The work concludes with an interpretation of the period from Hezekiah to the Babylonian exile as a reunited monarchy (2 Chron. 29–36). Of these four, the long second section is fundamental for the Chronicler's theological position. The reigns of David and Solomon are presented as a unity. Within this unity, two divine promises establish the Chronicler's central theological principles. In the first of these, God promises David that his throne will be established forever, through his descendants (1 Chron. 17:3–14). In the second, God promises Solomon that all who humble themselves, pray, seek God's face, and repent will be forgiven (2 Chron. 7:12–22). The genealogies that precede this crucial section depict the people's original unity. By means of these twin principles of king and cult, the section that follows evaluates the kings of Judah, who ruled during the divided monarchy, following the reign of Solomon. The final section presents Hezekiah as a new David and Solomon, who restores that vision of all Israel, reunited under a Davidic king, and worshipping at the Jerusalem temple following the collapse of the north.

Within this narrative framework, three theological themes are especially important. First, the temple dominates these pages as the primary symbol of God's presence with Israel. The Chronicler's presentation of the reigns of David and Solomon consists, essentially, of David's preparations for and Solomon's construction of the temple. David's preparations for the temple include bringing the ark to Jerusalem (1 Chron. 13–16), military conflicts that consolidate the empire and amass the required wealth (18–20), the purchase of Ornan's threshing floor as the temple site (21:25), and the more-detailed preparations found in chapters 22–29, including numerous lists of temple personnel and God's placement of the blueprint for its construction into David's hands (28:19). Solomon is explicitly designated as the temple-builder (28:6, 10; cf. 28:5; 29:1), and the presentation of his reign has been drastically rewritten to emphasize this role (2 Chron. 1–9). Abijah's programmatic speech (ch. 13), often deemed a compendium of the Chronicler's theological interests, cites the northern tribes' abandonment of the temple and establishment of a rival priesthood as the primary form of their rebellion, in contrast to the faithful worship practiced in the south (13:8–12). Furthermore, every subsequent king is evaluated regarding the faithful preservation of proper worship in the temple. Finally, the Chronicler's concern for identity and continuity, first seen in the genealogies that linked the postexilic community with their roots (1 Chron. 1–9), is intimately tied to the temple. The central presence of the Levites within those genealogies suggests that worship, properly led by the Levites and carried out in the Jerusalem temple, provides the means by which the community connects with the traditions of the past.

"All Israel" is a second theological theme of the Chronicler. Earlier scholarship insisted that the Chronicler was uninterested in the northern kingdom after its fall to Assyria, and that his concept of "Israel" was narrowly exclusive and confined to the southern tribes of Judah and Benjamin, as in 2 Chron. 11:3; 12:1. The situation, however, is more complex than this. In 10:16; 11:13, "all Israel" clearly refers to the north, and in 9:30 both north and south are meant. Actually, the Chronicler's understanding of Israel is quite inclusive and seeks to revitalize the ancient ideal of the twelve tribes by regularly depicting the enthusiastic and unanimous participation of "all Israel" at major turning points in the narrative. These include the accessions of both David and Solomon to the throne (1 Chron. 11:1; 29:20–25), the capture of Jerusalem (11:1–4), the transfer of the ark (13:1–4, 5–6; 15:3; 16:3), and the construction and dedication of the temple (2 Chron. 1:2; 7:8). Consequently, the Chronicler sees the division of the kingdom into north and south as a tragic severing of God's people by Jeroboam's rebellion and Rehoboam's inability to deal with the insurrection (13:4–12). His hope is that "all

Israel," north as well as south, will again be one. To that end, there are frequent calls for the people to return to common worship in Jerusalem, most notably, those of Abijah and Hezekiah that frame the period of the divided monarchy (13:4–12; 30:6–9).

A third theological theme is the Chronicler's so-called "principle of immediate retribution," the view that obedience leads to blessing and disobedience leads to judgment. First Chronicles 28:9 first expresses this: "If you seek him, he will be found by you; but if you forsake him, he will abandon you forever" (NRSV). The blessing/judgment is immediate in that it occurs within the individual king's lifetime. Although many instances are regularly cited, a careful reading of Chronicles indicates that this characteristic principle of the Chronicler is neither as mechanical nor as simplistically applied as previously thought. In 2 Chron. 7:14 God promises Solomon, "If my people . . . humble themselves, pray, seek my face, and turn from their wicked ways, . . . I will forgive their sin and heal their land" (NRSV). When one remembers that judgment is typically preceded by prophetic warning (e.g., 16:7–9; 20:15–17; 36:15–16), and that judgment is withheld after a repentant response to prophetic warning (e.g., 12:5–8; 15:1–15), it is clear that the Chronicler is more concerned with repentance and restoration than retribution.

Bibliography

Allen, L. *The First and Second Books of Chronicles.* NIB. Abingdon, 1999; Braun, R. *1 Chronicles.* WBC 14. Word, 1986; Coggins, R. J. *Samaritans and Jews.* John Knox, 1975; Freedman, D. N. "The Chronicler's Purpose." *CBQ* 23 (1961): 436–42; Graham, M. P., et al., eds. *The Chronicler as Historian.* JSOTSup 238. Sheffield Academic Press, 1997; Graham, M. P., and S. L. McKenzie, eds. *The Chronicler as Author.* JSOT-Sup 263. Sheffield Academic Press, 1999; Japhet, S. *I and II Chronicles.* OTL. Westminster John Knox, 1993; Kalimi, I. *Zur Geschichtsschreibung des Chronisten.* BZAW 226. De Gruyter, 1995; Kelly, B. *Retribution and Eschatology in Chronicles.* JSOTSup 211. Sheffield Academic Press, 1996; Klein, R. W. "Chronicles, Book of 1–2." *ABD* 1:992–1002; Newsome, J. D. "Towards a New Understanding of the Chronicler and His Purposes." *JBL* 94 (1975): 201–17; Noth, M. *The Chronicler's History.* JSOTSup 50. Sheffield Academic Press, 1987; Selman, M. *1 Chronicles* and *2 Chronicles.* TOTC. InterVarsity, 1994; Throntveit, M. "Linguistic Analysis and the Question of Authorship in Chronicles, Ezra and Nehemiah." *VT* 32 (1982): 201–16; idem. "The Relationship of Hezekiah to David and Solomon in the Books of Chronicles." In *The Chronicler as Theologian,* ed. M. P. Graham et al. JSOTSup 371. T&T Clark, 2003; idem. *When Kings Speak.* SBLDS 93. Scholars Press, 1987; Welten, P. *Geschichte und Geschichtsdarstellung in den Chronikbüchern.* Neu-kirchener, 1973; Williamson, H. G. M. *1 and 2 Chronicles.* NCB. Eerdmans, 1982; idem. *Israel in the Book of Chronicles.* Cambridge University Press, 1977.

Mark A. Throntveit

Chronology and the NT

Chronology can refer to the fixed or relative dating of key NT events as well as the dating of NT writings. The goal of this entry will be to evaluate the *importance of chronological analysis for theological interpretation* and to raise some cautions related to the search for chronology. (For lists of proposed dates for key NT events, cf. Caird or Hoehner.)

The Value of Chronological Analysis for Theological Interpretation

To Illuminate the Historical Context of NT Books More Fully. An understanding of the sociohistorical context of the NT is crucial for its theological interpretation. As much as chronology contributes to greater understanding of the social world of the biblical text, to that degree chronology has decided value for theological interpretation. One obvious illustration would be the dating of NT books. Proposals for the dating of the Pastoral Epistles, for example, differ widely, depending on authorship perspectives. It is readily apparent that conclusions regarding the theology of the Pastorals, especially their ecclesiology, will differ quite markedly, depending on determination of their composition dates (with authorship corollary).

For Reconstruction of the Historical Jesus and the History of the Early Church. Since a reconstruction of the historical Jesus or the history of the early church often sits in dialogical relationship with NT theological interpretation, chronology that assists in such reconstruction has value. For example, if the temple incident occurs during Jesus' final days, as recorded in the Synoptics (cf. Mark 11:15–19 et par.), and is the impetus for his execution, then it is likely that John has intentionally moved the temple incident to the early part of his Gospel for theological reasons. Possibly he wants to introduce Jesus as fulfillment of key Jewish festivals by first drawing the analogy of Jesus as temple, the center of Jewish worship. If this is the case, then chronology helps illuminate Johannine theology.

For Intertextual Reading of the NT Writings. An area where chronology has significant impact on theological interpretation is at the level of an intertextual or canonical understanding of the NT. At this level the relative dating of NT books has its greatest interpretative impact. To illustrate, redaction criticism, whose goal is the theological distinctives of the Gospels, is predicated on the hypothesis that Matthew and Luke postdate Mark and use Mark as source material. To use another example, study of the Pauline corpus necessarily involves some determination of the relative chronology of his letters, especially as it clarifies Pauline theology. If one posits theological development in Paul, the relative dating of Paul's letters will necessarily coincide with any particular proposal of development. The view, for example, that Paul moves toward a greater tolerance of the law is based in part on specific sequencing of his letters.

For Affirming or Calling into Question the Historical Reliability of the NT. The determination of a detailed chronology is more often tied to the issue of the historical reliability of the NT than strictly to its theological interpretation. For example, an important issue in Pauline chronology is whether Gal. 2 retells an incident that precedes or postdates the Jerusalem Council of Acts 15, and whether these two portraits of an early church event even agree with each other. In the end, however, determination of this issue is not absolutely necessary for theological interpretation of either Galatians or Acts. Scholars who understand Acts 15 to be contradicting Gal. 2 do not *by necessity* produce a different theological interpretation of these books than those who see the two as coherent. The issue comes down to the *historical reliability* of Acts (or Galatians), which, while important, should not be confused with their *theological interpretation*.

The Need to Evaluate Worth of Chronological Analysis in Particular Instances

These illustrations show that the importance of NT chronology for theological interpretation surfaces on a case-by-case basis. No single perspective on chronology would seem to fit the NT as a whole. It would be most profitable to take our cue from the NT authors themselves regarding chronology. The writers of the Gospels, for example, often favor thematic concerns over those of chronology. Luke transposes the story at Nazareth from placement after several miracle stories, giving it head position at the start of Jesus' ministry (4:16–30; cf. Mark 6:1–6//Matt. 13:54–58). This indicates the importance of this story for his thematic interests: concern for the marginalized in Jesus' ministry. Even when chronological interests are present, theology is often primary.

This may be the case with the three-year ministry of Jesus often derived from John's record of three Passover festivals. In the end, it may be that John is less interested in *three* Passovers (years) than in three *Passovers*, the feast he most carefully emphasizes in his Gospel.

The Danger of Undue Emphasis on Chronology

By forcing chronological precision (a modern vs. ancient value) upon the NT writings, we risk missing or misconstruing their theological message (Stiver 52). It also frequently results in unnecessary harmonization. A classic example involves the three denials of Peter between the Gospel accounts. By neglecting nonchronological interests of the evangelists, some have counted six or even nine denials of Peter in a harmonized version of Jesus' passion. Either case ignores the four evangelists' agreement in attributing three denials to Peter.

More complex and theologically important is the issue of the date of Jesus' crucifixion. The Synoptics seem to indicate that Jesus is killed on Nisan 15, the afternoon after celebration of the Passover meal, while John apparently ties his death to Nisan 14, during the ritual slaughter of the lambs on the day before the Passover meal. The problem with too quickly moving toward harmonization of these two witnesses is potential misinterpretation of one or the other. While proposing that Jesus is crucified on Nisan 14 does not take away significantly from the Synoptics' theological connection between Jesus' death and Passover (in either dating scenario, they are in close affinity), affirming a Nisan 15 date for his death does require major theological maneuvering in John.

John identifies Jesus as the Passover lamb at crucial points. Twice at the beginning of the narrative, the theme is heralded from John the Baptist's lips: "Here is the Lamb of God . . ." (1:29, 36 NRSV). It is also inferred from the day and time of Jesus' crucifixion at 19:14, since the sixth hour was the very time when the slaughter of the lambs commenced on Nisan 14, the Day of Preparation. (For the argument that the reference is instead to Friday, cf. Blomberg 246–47.) It is highly significant that the final scene of the crucifixion climaxes with a fulfillment quotation referencing the Passover lamb: "None of his bones will be broken" (Exod. 12:46; John 19:36). To argue that John is not drawing the analogy between Jesus and the Passover lamb might be the result of an excessive need to harmonize the

Synoptics and John. To miss the analogy would be a theological shame.

In this example, John's theology is based on a specific detail of chronology, the date and time of Jesus' crucifixion, and so this is an example of chronology that has import for theological interpretation. By this example, I am not arguing that the Synoptics can or should be harmonized with John on this issue, although France provides a rather compelling reading of the Synoptics that does just that (France 50–54). The example, however, does illustrate what might be lost if we depart too quickly, and against textual indicators, from an evangelist's theological motive toward chronological harmonization.

Conclusion

Is the determination of chronology important for theological interpretation of the NT? A multifaceted answer is necessary. At times study of chronology is not necessary or even desirable for theological interpretation. In other instances, a general sense of chronology is helpful, but exact chronology proves to be both illusive and more or less irrelevant. There also seem to be situations in which very specific chronological determinations have significance for theology. Whenever possible, we ought to let the NT authors themselves lead the way in determining the importance of chronology for theological interpretation.

Bibliography

Beckwith, R. *Calendar and Chronology, Jewish and Christian.* AGJU 33. Brill, 1996; Blomberg, C. *The Historical Reliability of John's Gospel.* InterVarsity, 2001; Caird, G. B. "The Chronology of the New Testament." *IDB* 1:599–607; Finegan, J. *Handbook of Biblical Chronology.* Princeton University Press, 1964; France, R. T. "Chronological Aspects of 'Gospel Harmony.'" *VE* 16 (1986): 33–59; Hoehner, H. "Chronology." *DJG,* 118–22; Luedemann, G. *Paul, Apostle to the Gentiles,* trans. F. S. Jones. Fortress, 1984; Riesner, R. *Paul's Early Period.* Eerdmans, 1998; Stiver, D. "Ricoeur, Speech-Act Theory, and the Gospels as History." Pages 50–72 in *After Pentecost,* ed. C. Bartholomew et al. SHS. Zondervan/Paternoster, 2001; Vardaman, J., and E. Yamauchi, eds. *Chronos, Kairos, Christos.* Eisenbrauns, 1989; Wedderburn, A. J. M. "Paul's Collection: Chronology and History." *NTS* 48 (2002): 95–110.

Jeannine K. Brown

Chronology and the OT

There is no single, coherent chronology running through the OT, though an interest in chronology is evident at many points. Attempts to add detail and coherence to OT chronology are evident in the surviving fragments of Demetrius the Chronographer (third century BCE), the book of Jubilees (second century BCE), the works of Josephus, and rabbinic writings. A concern to synchronize biblical and secular chronologies first emerges with early Christian writers such as Julius Africanus. The chronology worked out by Archbishop James Ussher in the seventeenth century (which famously dated creation to 4004 BCE) became widely known through its incorporation in some editions of the King James Bible.

The rise of the historical-critical method made many scholars skeptical of the OT's chronological information. Today it is recognized that it cannot all be treated in the same way. For the earliest periods we encounter frequent round numbers and multiples of (e.g.) 60 or 70 (sometimes with the addition of 7), which suggest we are dealing with schematic and symbolic figures rather than historiographic data. This may explain why it is sometimes difficult to reconcile chronological information, such as for the period between the patriarchs and the exodus (cf. Gen. 15:13, 16; Exod. 6:16–20; 12:40–41). On the other hand, the books of 1–2 Kings furnish us with information that can often be shown to be accurate (see below).

There is little evidence that our practice of counting years by eras was known in OT times. There are some indications that the exodus may have provided the starting point for such a reckoning (Num. 33:38; Judg. 11:26; 1 Kings 6:1), but the figures involved are often regarded as schematic.

Partly for this reason, the date of the exodus (and consequently the length of the period of the Judges) has been a notoriously difficult issue for OT historians. According to 1 Kings 6:1, the exodus took place 480 years before the founding of the temple in the fourth year of Solomon's reign. Taken at face value, this dates the exodus around 1450 BCE, in round figures. However, many scholars place greater weight on Exod. 1:11, according to which the enslaved Israelites built the "store cities" Pithom and Raamses for Pharaoh. The name Raamses (or Rameses in Exod. 12:37) recalls the Egyptian Delta capital Pi-Ramesse, built under Ramesses II. Taken with other evidence, this has led many to identify Ramesses II (1279–1213 BCE) as the pharaoh of the exodus and/or the oppression. Hence Exod. 1:11 seems to favor a date no earlier than the thirteenth century BCE for the exodus (Kitchen).

The majority of scholars have adopted a date of around 1260 BCE, explaining the 480 years of 1 Kings 6:1 as either schematic (a multiple of the significant OT figures 12 and 40) or a total obtained by adding periods that actually overlapped. But the earlier date does have its defenders (Bimson; Wood). Proponents of a fifteenth-century exodus would see the name Raamses/Rameses as the work of a redactor who wished to give an ancient site its more "modern" name (a parallel case being the reference to Dan in Gen. 14:14; cf. Judg. 18:29). The reference to Israel in Merenptah's stela is often brought into the debate. This attests Israel's presence in Canaan by 1208 BCE but, unfortunately, tells us nothing about how long Israel may have been in the land before that date.

Far less controversy attends the dating of the monarchic period. For the overlapping monarchies of Israel and Judah, we are given a wealth of chronological information. The editors of 1–2 Kings may well have drawn on actual court annals that were preserved into the exile. Usually we are given the length of a king's reign, a note synchronizing his accession with a particular regnal year of his counterpart in Israel or Judah, and his age on ascending the throne. Early critical scholarship treated this information with the same skepticism that it applied to the data in Genesis, but an appreciation of the wider ancient Near Eastern context has led to its being treated with greater respect.

Even so, it is no easy matter to work the regnal lengths and synchronic references into a chronology that dovetails with extrabiblical sources. Working back from a firm base in the Persian period, a detailed chronology has been pieced together for the preceding Neo-Assyrian and Neo-Babylonian periods. In fact, the Assyrian practice of keeping "eponym lists" (in which each year was given the name of a different official, or eponym) means that Assyrian chronology can be reconstructed accurately, to within a year, as far back as 911 BCE. This provides OT chronology with several cross-references, since the OT refers to five Assyrian kings, and Assyrian texts mention eight kings of Israel and Judah.

Several proposals have been made for harmonizing the biblical data in 1–2 Kings with absolute dates supplied by the extrabiblical material. Many scholars in the English-speaking world have adopted the scheme of E. Thiele. This involves a combination of calendar reforms, coregencies, and different methods of reckoning a king's first year (accession-year and nonaccession-year systems) to produce both internal harmony for the biblical data and synchronisms with the absolute dates derived from Assyrian sources.

Some scholars have rejected Thiele's approach, concluding that some of the information in 1–2 Kings is simply schematic and inaccurate (e.g., Hughes). However, Thiele accounts convincingly for most of the awkward data, and there is little reason to suspect schematization until we reach the reigns of David and Solomon, with their forty years each. Thiele's chronology gives a date of 930 BCE for the end of Solomon's reign.

As mentioned above, we have secure dates for the Neo-Babylonian and Persian periods, so where biblical chronology depends on synchronisms with the specific years of Babylonian or Persian kings (e.g., 2 Kings 25:8; 2 Chron. 36:22; Hag. 1:1), the dates are not usually in doubt.

The OT writers were interested in chronology for the same reason they were interested in history, for it was in the world of concrete events that the will and work of Israel's God could be traced and demonstrated. Figures that appear schematic (e.g., 40 or 70 years and multiples thereof) also serve an important role, though it may not be a historical one. They underline the recurring theme that Israel's history was not just a string of random events; it had shape and purpose, reflecting the sovereignty of Israel's God.

See also History of Israel

Bibliography

Anstey, M. *The Romance of Bible Chronology.* Marshall, 1913; Barnes, W. *Studies in the Chronology of the Divided Monarchy of Israel.* Scholars Press, 1991; Bimson, J. *Redating the Exodus and Conquest.* JSOTSup 5. 2d ed. Almond, 1981; Hughes, J. *Secrets of the Times.* JSOTSup 66. JSOT, 1990; Kitchen, K. A. "Egyptians and Hebrews, from Raamses to Jericho." Pages 65–131 in *The Origin of Early Israel.* Beer-Sheva 12, ed. S. Ahituv and E. D. Oren. Ben Gurion University of the Negev Press, 1998; Thiele, E. *The Mysterious Numbers of the Hebrew Kings.* 3d ed. Eerdmans, 1983; Wood, B. "Did the Israelites Conquer Jericho? A New Look at the Archaeological Evidence." *BAR* 16, no. 2 (1990): 44–58.

John J. Bimson

Church, Doctrine of the

The Bible is the world's most fascinating book, whether from a literary, historical, cultural, or theological perspective. But the Bible is for something more than our pleasure and puzzlement. It is for our instruction in salvation and in good works (2 Tim. 3:15–17). The Bible is about something more than the pattern of our cultural or religious past. It is about "the plan of the mystery hidden for ages in God who created all things," a plan fulfilled in Jesus Christ and made known through the church (Eph. 3:9–10 NRSV). The theological interpretation of the Bible, then, which assumes this "something more," cannot be conducted without reference to Christ and to the church (Col. 1:24–29). Indeed, it cannot be conducted without the church itself as its context and precondition. It is never merely private (2 Pet. 1:20–21).

But what is the church? From whatever angle we approach this subject—and theological interpretation of Scripture invites and demands an approach from many different angles simultaneously—we can hardly fail to say at least this: the church is the community of the new covenant between God and humanity, which is grounded in the self-offering of Jesus Christ. Everything else that is said about the church, particularly that which is believed but not yet seen, is said in this connection. Is the church the people of God, opened now to "the elect from every nation," en route to the promised rest of God (Heb. 4)? Is it the servant of God, the prophet or herald of the kingdom of God? Is it a company of disciples and martyrs, devoted to its Lord and to his Great Commission? Is it a time-embracing but death-defying communion of saints, and is it really "one, holy, catholic and apostolic," as the creed says? Is the church the household of God, the body and the bride of Christ, the temple of the Holy Spirit (1 Cor. 3:9–17; 1 Pet. 2:4–10)? Is it an eschatological mystery, a sacrament of salvation, a mystical fellowship in the divine nature, a corporate *imago Trinitatis*? Is it the city of God, the polis of perpetual peace, the very "pillar and foundation of the truth" (1 Tim. 3:15)? If indeed all of these things, it is what it is by virtue of the new covenant that God the Father effected in Christ and sealed with the Spirit (Eph. 1–3; cf. John 13–17).

Now if the church is a presupposition of theological interpretation, actual ecclesial modes of life—whether more or less true to the nature of the new covenant—shape our interpretative possibilities both in ecclesiology and elsewhere. We can make no pretense to some neutral or ideal standpoint for interpretation. Even the adoption of a basic paradigm is conditioned by our ecclesial experience; moreover, the simultaneity demanded above is attainable only in principle. Theological interpretation of the church is conducted from within the church, and under the conditions of the church militant—which means also under the conditions of the church paradoxically at odds with itself. That is a problem to which we will return, but only after considering the church from the standpoint of its trinitarian foundations and its twofold liturgical life, the life by which it knows and expresses itself as the new covenant community.

Creatura Verbi et Spiritus

The Nature and Purpose of the Church (§9) rightly speaks of the church as *creatura Verbi et creatura Spiritus*. For *lex orandi* agrees with *lex credendi* that "without the Spirit there is no seeing the word of God, and without the Son there is no approaching the Father" (Irenaeus, *Epid.* 7; cf. Rom. 8). The church is that new humanity which God's two hands are molding into the divine image for communion with the Father, which is the church's goal. The Word himself is incarnate as the head of the church, on whose behalf "through the eternal Spirit [he] offered himself unblemished to God" (Heb. 9:14; cf. Eph. 5:25). The Holy Spirit is the church's animator and guide, its cohesive force and fructifying power. What the Word articulates, the Spirit manifests, such that the church, as the body of Christ, becomes "the fullness of him who fills all in all" (Eph. 1:17–23 NRSV; 3:14–21; cf. *Epid.* 5).

Thus the church is indeed the creation of the Word and the Spirit in an altogether unique sense. While not itself a mode of the Trinity's own koinonia or *perichorēsis*, the church has that koinonia and *perichorēsis* as its presupposition. While not itself the incarnation of God (this is where the "bride" metaphor must qualify the "body" metaphor: it is Christ alone who is both divine and human), the church has the Son of God within it. While not itself divine (the Spirit of God is its animator, not its *anima* or *animus*), the church has deification as its destiny. That is, with Christ's return it expects the fullness of the gift of the Spirit, so as to perfect its communion with the Father. It is to keep in view this highest of callings, this ultimate of dignities, that the expression *creatura Verbi et Spiritus* is employed.

The four creedal *notae* (marks) rest on this trinitarian foundation and must be interpreted in this light, for they open up questions of ontology which no lesser mode of analysis can penetrate. But the trinitarian foundation itself is laid through the economy of God in bringing about the birth of the Son in the womb of Israel—literally, of Mary the Theotokos—so as to bring "many sons to glory" (Heb. 2:10). It is laid down as an offering of the triune God to humanity, and of humanity to the triune God, in a mutual history, in a covenanted relationship. This relationship, as extended to the church, is governed and enabled by word and sacrament in their new covenant form.

Creatura Verbi et Sacramenti

Both the liturgy of the word and the liturgy of the sacrament require us to recognize the church as *creatura verbi* in a second, derivative sense, which points simultaneously to three facts: First, the new covenant community is the beginning of the promised new creation: *paradisus in hoc mundo*, as Irenaeus put it (*Haer.* 5.20.2). Second, it is brought into being, like the first creation, by divine fiat; it springs to life under the impact of the command it hears with and from Christ: Rise! *Exsurge!* (Eph. 5:14 Vulg.; cf. Rev. 1:17–20). Third, while the people still dwell in "the land of sepulture" (Irenaeus, *Haer.* 5.31), this divine fiat is mediated to them through the proclamation of the gospel and the exposition of Scripture. As in the awakening, so also in the nourishing and ordering of its life, the church is responsive and responsible to the divine word that is there spoken. In the Scriptures, "the Father who is in heaven comes lovingly to meet his children, and talks with them" (*Dei Verbum* 21). When we have said that the church is *creatura verbi*, we have said that the church does not live out of its own resources but "by every word that proceeds from the mouth of God" (Matt. 4:4 NRSV; cf. John 6:63).

It is not enough, however, to say that the church is *creatura verbi*, not if the church really does live. The living church is not only *creatura verbi* but, if that, then also *creatura sacramenti*. The manna from heaven on which it lives comes to it during its present sojourn not only as word but, epicletically, also as sacrament (John 6:52–65; cf. Irenaeus, *Haer.* 5.2.3). It is by means of the sacraments that the people of God are given a real participation in the self-offering of Jesus Christ, which is a self-offering both of God to man and of man to God. By means of the sacraments they are sealed within the church and as the church, in order to render a thank offering in and for the world. By means of the sacraments they become not merely a priestly people but a "body," participant in that body *quod pro vobis datur* and in the eternal life inherited by it (cf. Luke 22:19; Heb. 10). In other words, there are covenant rites as well as covenant documents in the ecclesial economy: word and sacrament

work together to make the church the firstfruits of the new creation.

Chief among the sacraments are baptism and the Eucharist, which between them form the axis of all other sacramental activity in the covenant community. Taken together, these two sacraments constitute the *forma formans* of participation in the life of Christ and in his royal priesthood (Rom. 6; 1 Cor. 10–15; cf. Irenaeus, *Haer.* 4.17–18; 5.28.4). Baptism effects a once-for-all recapitulation of the believer's own life and thus replaces circumcision as the effectual sign of membership in the covenant community. It liberates believers for the worship of God. The Eucharist continually places in the believer's hands an offering worthy of God while actualizing the ecclesial community as such, locating and maintaining it by divine grace at the intersection of the ages and at the junction between heaven and earth. Just as the old covenant was sealed by a feast on Mt. Sinai, so also the new covenant has its eucharistic feast. In it God's people share "the food of immortality" through communion with him who has passed from death to life, and from this world to the Father (cf. Exod. 24; Heb. 12). It is through these sacraments that the promises fulfilled in Christ and announced to the world are substantiated in and for the church, and that the church appears, to the eye of faith, as the eschatological mystery that it is.

Theological Interpretation and the Sacrifice of Unity

Theological interpretation (whatever its immediate object) is obliged to take into account the church's character as *creatura verbi et sacramenti*, and in particular the eschatological qualification that the sacraments entail. The new covenant community is not merely a community that, aided by the Scriptures, remembers Jesus and hopes for his return. It is a new being determined by a eucharistic becoming—by the Spirit's act of making it present to the Father in and with Jesus. That being the case, authentic theological interpretation is possible only as something implicated in eucharistic activity. It is possible only as gift and gratitude. It may be approached through the faithful sowing and harvesting of words, ideas, and actions, and through the reading and rereading of texts in the company of the faithful, but it cannot be achieved apart from the taking, blessing, breaking, and donating that is God's own act in Christ. With that in mind, we may return to the problem of theological interpretation under the paradoxical conditions of ecclesial disunity and the breaking of eucharistic fellowship.

Disunity contradicts both the headship of Christ and the lordship of the Spirit, just as it contradicts the truth of the divine fatherhood (Eph. 3–4). It thus contradicts the church as such and defies the law of its being as *creatura Verbi et Spiritus*. Not surprisingly, there is a lack of agreement about the causes of the contradiction. Historically, the East charges the West with failing to say *et Spiritus* clearly enough, because in the creed it has already said what it ought not to say: *filioque*. The West reverses the charge. For its own part, however, the West has for some time been divided internally between a word-oriented and a sacrament-oriented ecclesiology. The former tends to epistemology, emphasizing knowledge, individual faith, and the local congregation; the latter to ontology, emphasizing communion, corporate faith, and a catholic institution. This gives rise to Schleiermacher's claim that the latter makes one's relation to Christ depend upon one's relation to the church, while the former makes one's relation to the church depend upon one's relation to Christ—as if this either/or were really conceivable!

If these divisions already owe something to differences in theological interpretation of Scripture, they also profoundly exacerbate the same. Scripture helps to maintain the church as the pillar and foundation of the truth, but if the church really is the pillar and foundation of the truth, then legitimate theological interpretation is jeopardized by the disunity of the church to the same degree that the church itself is jeopardized. Disunity robs authentic interpretation of its main condition of possibility. Church divisions render the intersection between Scripture and church tradition chaotic and the rules that govern it (even those of the Vincentian Canon) unclear. What are we to say that will cast some light on this situation?

What we must not say is that unity is something for us to achieve through ecumenical cooperation. That is really to think of the church merely as a human creation, as *creatura conventus*. Moreover, it may lead to such patent nonsense as we find inserted (§74) into *The Nature and Purpose of the Church*. There it can even be asked, in exploring "the tolerable limits to diversity," not only whether we might safely disagree about the procession of the Spirit, but also whether it is really church-dividing "to understand the resurrection of Christ only symbolically," or "to confess Christ only as one mediator among others," or "to substitute the history of ancient Israel . . . with the pre-Christian history of one's own culture and

people" (§74). What is this if not to ask whether theological interpretation needs to be Christian or churchly at all?

On the other hand, we must not say either that the unity essential for sound theological interpretation can already be found here or there in the church. That claim also trivializes the problem of disunity, and hence of theological interpretation. Whether in Orthodox, Catholic, or Protestant guise, it reproduces the Corinthian error rebuked by Paul.

A third thing we ought not to say is that unity and catholicity are features of the church only in the *eschaton*. The *et sacramenti* disallows this evasion. The integrity of the church, like that of its members, may be something "hidden with Christ in God" (Col. 3:3), but we are not thus relieved of the burden of anticipating it on earth. As John Paul II reminds us, "Concern for restoring unity pertains to the whole Church, faithful and clergy alike. It extends to everyone according to the potential of each" (*Ut unum sint* §101; quoting *Unitatis redintegratio* §5). Or more pointedly (in §96): "Could not the real but imperfect communion existing between us persuade Church leaders and their theologians to engage with me in a patient and fraternal dialogue on this subject, a dialogue in which, leaving useless controversies behind, we could listen to one another, keeping before us only the will of Christ for his Church and allowing ourselves to be deeply moved by his plea 'that they may all be one . . . so that the world may believe that you have sent me' (*Jn* 17:21)?" To refuse such a request, or to adopt a contrary attitude, would be to deny the real presence of Christ in the church militant, and to speak only of his absence from it. Far from affirming an eschatological reserve, it would deny the eschatological situation of the church altogether—the witness of its martyrs as well as of its Eucharists.

It is precisely the eucharistic tension between the presence and the absence of Christ with which we must reckon here. The sin of disunity—of competing creeds and jurisdictions, or of other de facto denials of the ecclesial *notae*—stems in part from the anxiety generated by this tension. The Eucharist places the new covenant people in a posture of waiting. It situates them precariously between Egypt and Canaan, between the *saeculum* and the kingdom of heaven. The apparent insecurity of this position may tempt the church to cling to this or that feature of its secular identity. Insurance policies are then taken out against the eschatological wager; from matters of dress to matters of dogma, identity markers are laid down by the church to secure for itself a unity that it can only receive as a gift. The same markers that comfort the church here, of course, alienate it there; but it does little good to go around collecting the markers and trying to sort out which ones everyone can accept. What is called for instead is a more careful eschatological analysis and the willingness to make what John Paul II calls "a sacrifice of unity" (*Ut unum sint* §102).

What would such a sacrifice look like in eucharistic theology itself? Or in Mariology, that closely related mode of ecclesiological discourse—Mary being the archetype of free participation in the self-offering of Christ—that is likewise plagued by difficulties in eschatology? What would it look like in treating the present relation between the people of the old covenant and the people of the new? What would it look like in treating of the keys and of the Petrine office (Matt. 16:13–20), and hence also of the conduct of the wider Christian mission? Where the unity of the church is concerned, these (together with the *filioque*) are still among the most important challenges facing the theological interpretation of Scripture. And if they are important for the unity of the church, they are important for theological interpretation as such. Only by way of a sacrifice of unity can theological interpretation hope to flourish. Only as the church takes up Mary's "*fiat mihi secundum verbum tuum*" (Luke 1:38 Vulg.) can it hope to see the barriers to unity removed, and the condition of authentic interpretation restored.

See also Catholic Biblical Interpretation; Community, Interpretative; Israel; Orthodox Biblical Interpretation; Protestant Biblical Interpretation

Bibliography

Congar, Y. *The Mystery of the Church*. Helicon, 1960; Dulles, A. *Models of the Church*. Image, 1987; Farrow, D. *Ascension and Ecclesia*. Eerdmans, 1999; John Paul II. *Ecclesia de Eucharistia*. Encyclical. Vatican, 2002; idem. *Ut unum sint*. Encyclical. Vatican, 1995; Journet, C. *The Theology of the Church*. Ignatius, 2004; Küng, H. *The Church*. Sheed & Ward, 1967; Lubac, H. de. *Catholicism*. New American Library, 1964; Minear, P. *Images of the Church in the New Testament*. Westminster, 1960; Newbigin, L. *The Household of God*. SCM, 1953; O'Donovan, O. *The Desire of the Nations*. Cambridge University Press, 1996; Torrance, T. F. *Royal Priesthood*. Oliver & Boyd, 1955; Vatican II. *Dei Verbum*, 1965; idem. *Lumen gentium*, 1964; Volf, M. *After Our Likeness*. Eerdmans, 1998; Watson, F. *Text, Church, and World*. Eerdmans, 1994; WCC. *The Nature and Purpose of the Church*. Faith and Order Paper 181. WCC, 1998; Zizioulas, J. *Being as Communion*. St. Vladimir's Seminary Press, 1985.

Douglas Farrow

Colossians, Book of

History of Interpretation

Throughout the history of Christian thought, Colossians has played a central role, particularly in relation to Christology and soteriology. The church fathers focused primarily on the hymn in Col. 1:15–20, where Paul's description of the Son as the image of the invisible God and the firstborn of all creation (1:15) provided the basis for the doctrine of the preexistence of Christ. This in turn gave rise to the doctrine of the two natures of Christ: "The pre-existent one is also the incarnate one and who yet at the same time bears the whole divine being in himself" (Schweizer 253; Gorday 12–14). Such an emphasis provided the impetus for seeing the work of God in the OT as continuous with the work of Jesus. Calvin later argued that 1:15–20 is not about the two natures but rather describes Jesus as the one who has made God visible to believers. The emphasis shifts, therefore, from Jesus' relation to God to his relation to believers and the result of such a relationship in their lives.

The second major contribution of Colossians in the history of interpretation was to discussions of soteriology, primarily whether salvation includes all of the natural world, the whole of the cosmos, and even all people (Gorday 15–21). More recently, Sittler has carried this theme forward in arguing that 1:15–20 shows that redemption embraces both history and nature and therefore has political, and especially ecological, implications. The radical nature of this redemption for all dimensions of life has continued to shape the soteriological thrust of discussion of Colossians into the present.

Ethically, Colossians initially provided the basis for condemnations of ascetic practice. For much of the history of interpretation, readers paid relatively little attention to the household codes of Col. 3:18–4:1, using them primarily to counteract the abuse of Christian freedom and equality. More recently, however, this passage has played a central role in ethical discussions concerning the role of women and the institution of slavery. Such discussions generally interpret Colossians as endorsing a restrictive social ethic that justifies both slavery and the subordination of women (D'Angelo; Martin). Such interpretations have provided one of the bases for the position that Colossians is post-Pauline. In such a context Colossians is seen to be evidence of a tendency toward a more hierarchical ethic in the development of the early church. While such views on the post-Pauline character of Colossians are widespread, they are by no means unchallenged (Wright, *Colossians*; Cannon).

The Message of Colossians and Its Relation to the Canon

Paul's letter to the Colossians is rooted in the story of Israel and in the story of Jesus. These two stories function as a challenge to the dominant story facing the Colossian Christians: the story of Rome. Such a challenge is evident from the outset of the letter, where Paul describes the gospel as bearing fruit and growing in the whole world (1:6), and later describes the Colossians themselves as bearing fruit and growing in the knowledge of God (1:10).

For the inhabitants of Colossae, the language of gospel (*euangelion*) carried strong imperial overtones. A central claim of Rome was that the empire achieved and guaranteed universal peace, the Pax Romana. The imperial gospel, moreover, assured the Colossians that fruitfulness and fertility was all around them. It was a claim that incessantly called everyone to acknowledge Rome as the source of abundance. Partaking in such abundance in the midst of scarce resources required fidelity to the empire and its structures, oppressive or not.

This was no new claim. Throughout its history, Israel constantly grappled with an empire's claims to be the source of abundance, security, and fertility. But there was also a countertestimony within Israel's story, a witness to an alternative social vision that challenged the claims of empire. The fruitfulness of Yahweh, and the fruit that Israel was called to bear, was central to that countertestimony. Fertility and fruitfulness in the land on the one hand, and peace and security on the other, are rooted in a rejection of the militaristic consumerism of empire and the social and economic practices that support it. The language of such blessing is the language of fruitfulness (Lev. 26:3–6; Isa. 5:1–7; Ezek. 34:25–31; Mic. 4:1–5; Zech. 8:1–16).

These themes come to their climax in Jesus. The community that Jesus envisions is not only judged by its fruit but is itself a manifestation of the fruitfulness of Yahweh. At key points in the narrative—some of them foundational, some of them climactic—we meet the metaphors and language of fruitfulness (Matt. 13:23//Mark 4:20; Luke 8:15; Matt. 7:16–20; Luke 6:43–45).

By using the language of fruitfulness, with all of its overtones from the story of Israel and the preaching of Jesus, Paul in Colossians is proclaiming a different gospel, which bears fruit fundamentally different from the fruit of the empire.

Before Paul discusses that way of life, he describes the cosmic scope of this gospel and the nature of the reconciliation it brings. In 1:15–20 Paul alludes to Adam as the image of God; however, he does so in his description of Jesus, the second Adam. He also alludes to the creation of wisdom in Prov. 8:22, the firstborn of creation. There is a faint echo of Gen. 9:8–17, where God reaffirms the covenant with all living things, and the phrase "all living things" or "all flesh" is repeated nine times in the Greek. In Col. 1:15–20, the repetition of "all things" or "everything" occurs seven times. By confessing that in Jesus God reconciles all of creation to himself, Paul is reaffirming God's most foundational covenantal promise to be faithful to all of creation.

The identification of Jesus with God, and the linking of God's covenant promise to creation with the reconciliation of all things in Jesus through the cross, is a clear challenge to the empire. Not only does the language of image evoke Adam, it also evokes Caesar, whose images were ubiquitous throughout the ancient Roman world both in statues and on coins. The claim that Jesus is above all thrones, dominions, rulers, or powers challenges the throne, dominion, rule, and power of Rome. And while the Pax Romana is achieved and maintained through the public crucifixion of those who challenge Rome's rule, Jesus' blood shed on such a cross radically subverts imperial rule and establishes a more profound peace.

Here Paul is asserting the primacy of the story of Jesus over against the story of Rome. This alternative story line, with its proclamation of a different peace, is rooted deeply within the story of Israel. That story, however, is redefined in Jesus, in whom its central character finds expression.

In Col. 2 Paul reinforces this by describing a worldview that is attempting to capture the imagination of the Colossian Christians. Paul's description of this worldview echoes the scriptural prophetic polemic against idolatry (Walsh 8–9). Perhaps the best way to draw out the parallels is in the form of a chart.

The Colossian Philosophy	Idolatry
1. The philosophy is captivating (Col. 2:8).	1. Idolatry makes repentance and knowledge of God impossible (Hos. 5:4).

The Colossian Philosophy	Idolatry
2. The philosophy is empty deceit (2:8), and a shadow without substance (2:17).	2. Idolatry is worthless, vanity, nothingness (Pss. 97:7; 115:4–7; 135:15–18; Isa. 44:9; 57:13; Jer. 2:5).
3. The philosophy is a human tradition (2:8), a human way of thinking (2:18), that imposes human commands and teaching (2:20).	3. Idols are constructed by human hands (Ps. 115:4; Isa. 2:8; 41:6–7; 44:11; Jer. 10:1–10; Hos. 8:4, 6; 13:2; Hab. 2:18).
4. The philosophy is puffed up without cause (2:18) and deceives people by employing so-called plausible arguments (2:4, 8).	4. Idolatry results in a deluded mind and a fundamental lack of knowledge (Isa. 44:18–20; Hos. 4:6); an idol is a teacher of lies (Hab. 2:18).
5. The philosophy is of no value in checking the flesh (2:23).	5. Idolatry is impotent, without value, and does not profit (Pss. 115:4–7; 135:15–18; Isa. 45:20; 46:1–2; Jer. 2:11; Hos. 7:16; Hab. 2:19).
6. The philosophy disqualifies, insists on self-abasement (2:18), and promotes severe treatment of the body (2:23).	6. Idolatry is a matter of exchanging glory for shame (Ps. 106:20; Jer. 2:11; Hos. 4:7; 7:16; 13:1–3; Rom. 1:23).

In these verses Paul's language evokes the prophetic critique of idolatry, and in so doing his critique of the empire finds a context in larger biblical tradition. For instance, "the proclamation that Christ triumphs over the rulers and authorities on the cross (2:15) is clearly rooted in the prophetic confession that Yahweh is Lord and shares glory with no idols (Isa 42:8; 48:11)" (Walsh 9). These overtones are heightened when put in parallel with Col. 1:15–20. The prophetic critique of idolatry is rooted in the confession that Yahweh, not the idols, is Creator of heaven and earth (Pss. 115:16; 135:5–7; Isa. 40:12–26; 44:9–28; 45:12, 18; Jer. 10:11–16; 51:15–19). So also Paul's critique of the philosophy is rooted in the assertion that Jesus is the one through whom and for whom all things were created (Col. 1:15–17). As the results of such an echo, Paul alludes to empire and asserts that Jesus is the true image, not Caesar. Jesus is over all thrones, dominions, rulers, and powers. He is the head in whom all things hold together, not Caesar. And Jesus is the one in whom the Deity dwells. All of these assertions are rooted in the larger biblical narrative of Yahweh as the one who offers a salvation that defeats the captivity, deceitfulness, vanity, shame, and impotence of idols and the empires that image them.

Here we return to competing stories. If a life directed by idolatry constitutes forgetfulness of Yahweh's covenant in Israel's Scripture (Deut. 4:15–31; 6:10–15; 8:11–20), the succumbing to imperial idolatry means that the Colossian Christians have forgotten that they indwell the story of Jesus. "In Christ" they have died (2:20; 3:3), were buried (2:12), and were raised from the dead (2:12; 3:1). They set their minds on the ascended one (3:2–3) and anticipate his coming (3:4). Christ's death, burial, resurrection, ascension, and return form the narrative heart of the counterimperial ethic Paul elucidates in 3:1–17.

This alternative story and ethic culminate, however, in Paul's description of the "household code" in 3:18–4:1. Here Paul's argument is made or broken. It doesn't matter if Paul uses language that subverts the empire and its violent and oppressive practices, if in the end he affirms a patriarchal household structure that reinscribes economic control and violence. I have argued elsewhere that rather than reinscribing the hierarchy of the household in these verses, Paul is subverting them (Walsh and Keesmaat, ch. 11). Paul's instructions to the household have three surprising and subversive aspects. Many scholars have recognized the first aspect: Paul directly addresses not only the head of the household—husband, father, and master—but also women, children, and slaves. This has the effect of giving the dignity of participation to those who would have seldom been addressed as having status in the relationship.

Second, and often lost in English translation, is Paul's play on the language of Lord, or Master (*kyrios*). This is most striking in the section to slaves, where the rhetorical effect of the constant movement from the "masters according to the flesh" to "the Master" undermines the ultimate legitimacy of these earthly masters.

Third, when Paul tells slaves that they will receive an inheritance (3:24), he is evoking the language of slaves receiving an inheritance in the year of Jubilee (Lev. 25). For those with ears to hear, Paul's language suggests that in the story of Jesus, slaves are to be set free, for they too are to receive an inheritance. As a result, in these verses Paul challenges the most fundamental hierarchy in which power was centralized in the Roman Empire.

These verses are thus shown to be a working out of Paul's words in 3:12 and following. There a self-sacrificing love, manifesting itself in compassion, kindness, humility, meekness, and patience, comes to its culmination in an ethic of forgiveness, love, and the rule of peace. This is not the peace of the empire (the Pax Romana), but the peace of a different ruler, Christ (3:13–15). In light of these verses, and in light of v. 11, where Paul proclaims that "there is no longer Greek and Jew, circumcised and uncircumcised, barbarian, Scythian, slave and free" (NRSV), a subversive word to slaves that proclaims their liberation makes perfect sense.

For the Colossian Christians, Paul's allusions to Israel's Scriptures provide an alternative story line that fundamentally challenges the claims of the story of the empire.

The Theology of Colossians

The challenge that Colossians provides to its imperial context is overwhelmingly rooted in a strong theology of creation. Paul describes himself as the servant of a gospel that "has been proclaimed to every creature under heaven" (1:23). This assertion comes after the hymn of 1:15–20, with its echoes of creational monotheism (Wright, "Poetry") and its repeated affirmation that *all things* in heaven and on earth were created in Christ, through Christ, and for Christ. It is because all things were created good in Christ that all things are now reconciled in Christ.

At the heart of the philosophy was its insistence on self-abasement, asceticism, and severe treatment of the body (2:17, 20–23). As we saw above, Paul describes these practices as idolatrous and emphasizes Jesus as the one who has triumphed over all other thrones and rulers and powers. Thus he asserts that God in Jesus is the true Creator of the heaven and earth, over against the idolatrous forces that seek to enslave the Colossian Christians (2:8). Jesus is the one who is now the Creator of all, and in the face of all that would seek to deny the goodness of his creation, Paul is asserting that as Creator he has not only vanquished all other creation-denying rulers (2:15), but has also renewed the creation.

In addition, not only is Jesus the true image of the Creator God, but those who have clothed themselves with the new self are "being renewed in knowledge according to the image of [the] creator" (3:10). The Colossian Christians themselves bear the image of that Creator and hence witness to the world the forgiveness, love, and reconciling peace that Jesus has achieved through the blood of the cross (1:20; 3:13–15). At the end of this letter, Paul's subversion of the household codes reveals how far-reaching this creational reconciliation goes. The household structure he is describing was the basic economic, social, and political unit of first-century culture. Hence, Paul is daring to assert that those who image the Creator will act differently in social, economic, and political spheres. From what we know of the church in the first century, this was indeed the case.

In a culture such as ours, where the idolatry of the market necessarily results in disregard for almost every creature under heaven, Colossians provides a word of hope. Just as in the first century Paul proclaimed that Jesus, not Caesar, was the one who had reconciled the whole of the world, so Paul proclaims to us that Jesus, not globalization, reconciles the whole of the world. Just as Paul proclaimed to the Colossians that the forces that deny the goodness of this creation are idolatrous, so he proclaims to us today that those economic and political practices that destroy the creation and those in it are idolatrous. And just as Paul proclaimed that the lordship of Christ challenged the imperial structures for familial, social, and economic life, so Paul proclaims to us today that the lordship of Christ challenges our societal structures that shape familial, social, and economic life in service of empire and its oppression.

Paul ends Colossians by asking the believers to remember his chains (4:18). We do well to remember them, for they indicate where such a subversive theology could lead, not only in Paul's time, but also in ours.

See also Powers and Principalities; Roman Empire

Bibliography

Cannon, G. *The Use of Traditional Materials in Colossians.* Mercer University Press, 1983; D'Angelo, M. "Colossians." In *A Feminist Commentary.* Vol. 2 of *Searching the Scriptures,* ed. E. S. Fiorenza. Crossroad, 1994; Dunn, J. D. G. *The Epistles to the Colossians and to Philemon.* NIGTC. Eerdmans, 1996; Gorday, P. *Colossians, 1–2 Thessalonians, 1–2 Timothy, Titus, Philemon.* ACCSNT 9. InterVarsity, 2000; Lincoln, A. *The Letter to the Colossians.* Vol. 9 of *NIB.* Abingdon, 2000; Lincoln, A., and A. J. M. Wedderburn. *The Theology of the Later Pauline Letters.* Cambridge University Press, 1993; MacDonald, M. *Colossians and Philemon.* SP 17. Liturgical Press, 2000; Martin, R. *Colossians and Philemon.* NCB. Eerdmans, 1981; Schweizer, E. *The Letter to the Colossians,* trans. A. Chester. Fortress, 1981; Sittler, J. "Call to Unity." *Ecumenical Review* 14 (1961–62): 177–87; Walsh, B. "Late/Post Modernity and Idolatry: A Contextual Reading of Colossians 2:8–3:4." *Ex Aud* 15 (1999): 1–17; Walsh, B., and S. Keesmaat. *Colossians Remixed.* InterVarsity, 2004;

Wilson, W. *The Hope of Glory*. Brill, 1997; Wright, N. T. *The Epistles of Paul to the Colossians and Philemon*. TNTC. Eerdmans, 1986; idem. "Poetry and Theology in Colossians 1.15–20." Pages 99–119 in *The Climax of the Covenant*. T&T Clark, 1991.

Sylvia C. Keesmaat

Commentary

A commentary on a biblical book provides information, organized schematically in relation to the structure of the book, presumed to be relevant for understanding the book's message. Traditionally proceeding in a verse-by-verse format, the commentator presents interpretative data chosen from a wide array of possibilities, such as philological, grammatical, source-critical, historical, social-scientific, and literary.

Beyond this general characterization, the genre of the biblical commentary today is difficult to describe. This is because the late twentieth century witnessed the genesis of numerous commentary series, each justifying itself by purporting to represent a different approach to the task of commenting on biblical texts. Each attempts to serve an increasingly well-defined audience, and each subtly redraws the boundaries of the genre to meet its own ends.

Generalizations about the commentary are also made problematic by the increasingly pervasive recognition that the enterprise of commentary writing has entered a critical era. How can the sheer number of commentaries flooding the marketplace be justified? With the deluge of secondary literature on seemingly every possible aspect of a biblical text, and with the smorgasbord of methodological approaches wielded among biblical scholars, what hope of taking into account and representing the state of the scholarly enterprise might a commentator nurture? Given the multitudinous questions raised against modern biblical criticism, with its inherent commitment to literal meaning and scientific neutrality, must we not recognize that commentaries have failed in their purported roles as mere servants of the biblical text, wholesalers of authoritative, objective scholarship?

The particular enterprise of theological interpretation of Scripture has not been well served by the spread of commentary writing in the last three centuries. Among the primary interests shaping biblical studies during this period, two are especially inhospitable to theological interpretation of these texts. The first is a heightened concern with the "literal sense" that arose in the wake of the Reformation. In biblical studies as in natural science, focus on "literal interpretation" pressed for commitments to observer neutrality. According to the medieval encyclopedia, both the Bible and the entire sensible world were books written by the hand of God. Both biblical text and all of nature served metaphorically to reveal the Divine Author. Thus, where Luke writes that, after witnessing the ascension of Jesus, the disciples' walk from the Mount Olivet to Jerusalem was "a sabbath day's journey" (Acts 1:12–13 NRSV), the Venerable Bede could comment in the early eighth century:

> Anyone who becomes worthy of an interior vision of glory of the Lord as he ascends to the Father, and of the enrichment by the promise of the Holy Spirit, here enters the city of everlasting peace by a Sabbath journey. There will be for him [*sic*], in Isaiah's words, *Sabbath after Sabbath*, because, having been free of wicked works here [in this life], he will be at rest there in heavenly recompense. (Bede 14)

Prior to the 1600s, then, exegesis of God's two books, cosmos and Bible, proceeded in accordance with the theory of the four levels of interpretation: the literal, the allegorical, the moral, and the analogical. When Protestant interpretation countered this fourfold method of exegesis, in favor of the "literal sense," the work of interpretation, broadly conceived, was loosed from the specifically religious concerns to which it had previously been tethered (Howell).

At the same time, the modern era came increasingly to be characterized by its position vis-à-vis history, and especially by its detachment from what went on before, as though it occupied a new, autonomous cultural space (Schorske). Moderns inhabit one history, the biblical texts another, with the result that the biblical materials could not be read as having direct relevance to modern people. What is more, this perspective segregated "history" and "text" so that the history to which the biblical text gives witness was isolated from the biblical text that provides such a witness. Since biblical studies accorded privilege to "history," the biblical text was viewed with critical suspicion, and interpretation was increasingly construed as a discipline of "validation" (when the biblical text was judged to represent historical events with accuracy) or of "reconstruction" (when it was not).

For many critical scholars, then, even to acknowledge the search for contemporary significance would be enough to poison the water. As one observer has put it, the historical project was to move forward "without any practical interest, be it lessons, devotion, entertainment, or propaganda" (Breisach 323). Therefore, it is no surprise that voices bemoaning the irrelevance of modern biblical criticism to the theological task, to ethical discourse, to homiletics, and the like have become so pervasive and increasingly vibrant. The modern paradigm of study portrayed "the strange world of the Bible" as profoundly remote from our world, rendering as arduous if not impossible the task of shuttling between the world of the Bible and our own world, for the purpose of negotiating good news for God's people. Many commentators who today articulate a real concern for the life of the church nevertheless self-reflectively witness the success of the historical paradigm in the writing of commentaries: "I like to think of commentaries as windows into the world presented by the biblical text" (Perkins 398). "To my mind, the first and main purpose of a commentary is to help the reader to discover *what the text meant* in its original setting" (Hagner 58). It is important that we grasp, though, that this way of construing the enterprise is of relatively recent vintage in relation to the long history of commenting on biblical texts.

The beginnings of commentary are found in the Bible itself—first, in the interpretation of biblical texts within other biblical texts, all within the Hebrew Bible; and then in the interpretation of the Scriptures of Israel within the writings of the NT. Texts were revised and reappropriated, as authoritative tradition, to address changing circumstances. Although these interpretations were not systematized, they nonetheless served as early commentary. A common feature of ancient Judaism was "the realization that there was no pure teaching of Revelation apart from its regeneration or clarification through an authoritative type of exegesis" (Fishbane 4). Moving outside the interpretation of biblical texts among the biblical writers themselves, the translation of the Hebrew Bible into Greek (LXX) and the development of the targumic tradition served further to codify interpretative traditions. The Qumran scrolls evidence a vast exegetical enterprise, with two commitments not so much juxtaposed as intertwined: to the truth and authority of the Scriptures, and to their legitimate interpretation and embodiment in the community of the faithful. Whether through reworking biblical texts or in more substantive exposition, commentators represented among the Dead Sea Scrolls concerned themselves with the contemporary understanding and practice of the Scriptures. The traditions of midrashim similarly engaged in a dialogue with the biblical texts, extending their meaning from the past into the present, with "readers fighting to find what they must in the holy text" (Boyarin 16). Precisely because of the authoritative status of the biblical texts, their immediacy to contemporary readers was a nonnegotiable presupposition; their capacity to speak on God's behalf in the readers' present and to be embodied in their lives was crucial. Commentary, in this sense, was cultivated in the field of contemporary culture while at the same time it plowed the language and theological categories of the biblical witness deep into the imagination of these communities.

The early church was not known for the writing of commentaries, at least not in a form recognizable to twenty-first-century pastors, teachers, and students. In those first centuries, theology was an exegetical enterprise, and the typical forms of "commentary" were the homily and theological treatise, along with catechetical lectures and pastoral letters. Scholarly Christian writing in the first centuries devoted itself to an elaboration of biblical theology—drawing out and schematizing rather than rehearsing biblical texts. Following interpretative patterns found already in the Hebrew Bible, remembered of Jesus, and practiced among the writers of what would become the NT documents, interpreters recontextualized biblical texts, providing an updated rereading in the service of Scripture's messianic and ecclesial message of salvation (Margerie). In the millennium before the Reformation, the growth of the commentary proper pressed less and less in the direction of dialogical engagement with Scripture, depending more and more on handing down the received tradition of interpretation (for a list of commentaries in 650–1000 CE, see McNally 83–117). Bible commentary took a more doctrinal and picturesque form from the twelfth to the fifteenth centuries in the xylograph known as *Biblia pauperum*, with biblical scenes shown, like stained-glass windows, in triptych and produced from wooden blocks carved in relief. With this *Bible of the Poor*, the fundamentals of the faith could be taught to the illiterate through the juxtaposition of images drawn from OT and NT. Type and antitype appeared side by side, as with scenes of Moses receiving the law and Elijah's calling fire down from heaven presented as precursors to the gift of the Spirit at Pentecost (Labriola and Smeltz). Reacting against biblical interpretation in the medieval period, the Protestant Reformers emphasized making the Bible accessible to the people (thus new efforts to translate the Bible in the common vernacular) and determining the one meaning of Scripture (thus the quest for the original meaning of biblical texts). Handbooks for interpretation focused on criteria for achieving legitimate readings, including philology, study of the historical circumstances governing the meaning of words, and reference to the intent of the author (e.g., Griffiths; Steinmetz).

Commentary has thus taken many forms. Each reflects (1) the hermeneutical imperative, which proceeds from the twofold observation that these texts must be interpreted if they are to function as Scripture, and that biblical texts are not self-interpreting; and (2) the interpretative needs and aims of the world within which the commentary was produced.

Today, the major critical commentaries (e.g., AB, Hermeneia, ICC, NIGTC, WBC) are characterized above all by concerns of a philological, grammatical, and historical nature; when engaging concerns of a theological sort, they tend to treat them historically—such as by reporting on Paul's theological concerns with the Corinthian church. Commentary series that are more widely accessible (e.g., NICNT, NAC, SP, NCB, NIBC) may be more strategic and selective in the issues they discuss, but are similarly concerned primarily with establishing meaning "back there and then." Commentators have been "good technicians of the text, but have avoided theology like the plague" (Fee, "Reflections," 389). The commentaries self-consciously concerned with "application" (e.g., NIVAC; Fee, *1 Corinthians*) tend to move at the level of "principles" derived from historical exegesis. They work under the presumption, articulated in the eighteenth century by Johann Philipp Gabler (see Sandys-Wunsch and Eldredge), that one might derive timeless and universal principles of the Bible from the foundations of linguistic and historical analysis. Lacking is a thoroughgoing commitment to the immediacy of the biblical witness, which derives from the theological affirmation that Christian believers who read these texts today and the people of God to whom those texts were first addressed comprise the one people of God, historically and globally. Scripture's theological vision—with its theological claim on our willingness to regard these texts as our Scripture and to inhabit its story as our own—when it is present at all in modern commentary, has typically been relegated to the periphery.

Given the degree to which the modern commentary is the child of scientific exegesis, which aspires to articulate authoritatively the single, historical meaning of the biblical text, some will doubt whether the plasticity of the commentary genre is capable of an authentically theological interpretation of Scripture. If the history of the commentary we have briefly rehearsed is at all suggestive, however, our only concern is not whether but how theological commentary may be written today.

If, in the wake of the Reformation, commentary exists especially to mediate the text to its would-be interpreters (Bruner), who are eager but relatively unskilled, then the pressing question is, What separates the contemporary reader from comprehending the ancient text? Scientific exegesis has answered singularly with reference to the historical rift. Theological exegesis focuses elsewhere, on the degree to which we share the theological claims of the biblical text and in terms of our willingness to "stand under" the Scriptures. It refers to our practices of engaging with Scripture in the context of our commitment to live faithfully before the God to whom the Scriptures witness.

What shape might theological commentary take? First, it would operate on the basis of the theological claim of one people of God, one church. It would hold the hermeneutical motto that the community within which the biblical texts were generated, the community who came to regard these books as canonical, and the community now faced with the need to interpret these texts as Scripture are the same community.

Second, then, it would see the contemporary community served by the commentator as the community to whom the biblical text is addressed. Eco's concept of the Model Reader is helpful here: "To make his text communicative, the author has to assume that the ensemble of codes he relies upon is the same as that shared by his possible reader. The author has to foresee a model of the possible reader (hereafter Model Reader) supposedly able to deal interpretively with the expressions in the same way as the author deals generatively with them" (7). To engage the biblical text in this way is not to objectify its message in a historical moment now distant from our own, and then imaginatively to allow its message to leap forward to our own time. It is, rather, to embrace the persona of the text's audience as our own. We do not invite the text to a transformation of its original meaning into a new application geared toward our thought-forms; instead, the text invites us into a transformation of allegiances and commitments. Such transformation will manifest itself in behaviors appropriate to our social worlds. In the case of 1 Peter, for example, the model readers presumed and sculpted by the text are those who hear their names in the letter's opening, "to the elect who are sojourners of the diaspora" (1:1 AT). Peter's model readers are those who embrace and embody the status of persons whose identity as pilgrims in the world grows out of their experience of the new birth. Their lives are radically marked by their membership in a community defined by their allegiance to Christ, and thus stand in an ambiguous relationship to the mores and values of the world around them. Accordingly, their forms of existence attract opposition from their neighbors. First Peter is addressed to just such people and is read best by those who share its theological assumptions and those who hear its opening as an invitation to embody its world.

This means that the primary agenda of theological commentary would not be the construction of systematic theology, in the now-dated sense of organizing and restating the central doctrines of the Christian faith. Questions would focus elsewhere—such as what sort of world, what sort of community, and what sort of person is this text constructing? Reading these texts as Scripture would thus call for dispositions of humility and expectation before the text, pressing for authentic wrestling with such questions as these: To what life-world is this text pointing? With what vision of reality does it confront us? Taking seriously the narrative shape of the biblical canon has the effect of calling upon its readers to choose sides: Will we embrace and serve the divine aim that presses this narrative forward and surfaces in these texts, or will we resist and oppose it? The result is that engaging with this narrative involves us in a formative and decision-making process. With which characters will we identify? Who are our heroes? How does the divine aim that guides this narrative beckon us? In short, the biblical narrative is present as an alternative framework within which to construe our lives, and so it challenges those who would be Christian by calling for a creative transformation of the stories by which we make sense of our lives and of the world. From this perspective, failure to "stand under" Peter's message would not be the consequence of historical distance, but theological.

Third, theological commentary would locate itself self-consciously within the particularity of an ecclesial community. On the negative side, this means that theological commentary cannot hope to serve an encyclopedic role, documenting and passing on all that is known about a given text. Nor can it proceed as though its basic concern is with the sort of history that might satisfy the world of academe or the interests of the wider public. Nor can it act as though the measure of validity in interpretation can be taken apart from the great creeds of the church, a concern with the "rule of faith," and the history of Christian interpretation and its embodiment in Christian lives and communities (*Wirkungsgeschichte*). What distinguished Karl Barth's commentary on Romans, which deserves pride of place as theological commentary of the modern era, was Barth's self-conscious stance as a theologian. Similarly, Brevard Childs's justly celebrated work on Exodus reflects on this book theologically within the context of the Christian canon, in a deliberate attempt to actualize the text for the church that turns to it as Scripture. What distinguishes Anthony Thiselton's more recent work on 1 Corinthians is not merely its judicious navigation of scholarly opinion on this Pauline letter. We also see his careful attention to how the letter has been read over the centuries and his ability to bring Paul's text into engaging conversation with theological issues that plague us today. François Bovon undertakes his study of Luke "with the sober reserve of a scholar and with the confidence of a believer," realizing that genuine understanding becomes possible "only if God leads me into his Word" (xiii). Writing in a commentary series that describes itself as "critical and historical," where we would have anticipated assertions of scientific objectivity and scholarly neutrality, Bovon lays claim to his theological commitments and ecclesial location not as hindrances to, but as partners in, the interpretative enterprise.

Such contemporary scholars as Childs, Bovon, and Thiselton move in the direction of theological commentary by pressing the limits of the series to which they contribute. Other series are friendlier to the enterprise. The Two Horizons Commentary, now in process, promises theological exegesis in tandem with sustained attention to theological horizons. Some of these horizons are attention to key themes of the writing, elucidation of the book's contribution and relation to biblical theology, and deliberate exploration of the book's significance for constructive theology today (Green and Turner). *The New Interpreter's Bible* provides for each biblical book both commentary and reflection; in his contribution on the Acts of the Apostles, for example, Robert Wall insists that "reading Acts as Scripture seeks to insinuate its narrative world into the changing 'real' worlds of current readers" (28). With reference to the *NIB*, however, it must be admitted that some treatments are more helpful than others in their theological hermeneutic. The Ancient Christian Commentary on Scripture provides stunning access to the theological interpretation of Scripture characteristic of the first eight centuries of the church; here is a signpost toward insights and strategies aplenty for reading Scripture theologically today.

Fourth, to engage in theological commentary would not require that one proceed in an antihistorical or ahistorical fashion. That is, the choice between theology and history is a false one, and so is the choice between theological exegesis and historical inquiry. Barth, myopically criticized for despising historical criticism, had no apparent difficulty in writing for both: "If we rightly understand ourselves, our problems are the problems of Paul; and if we be enlightened by the brightness of his answers, those answers must be ours" (1). In commenting on Romans, Barth says, "I felt myself bound to the actual words of the text, and did not in any way propose to engage myself in free theologizing" (ix). The constraints of working with this historical text and the work of theological interpretation need not be mutually exclusive.

It could not be otherwise. After all, all language is embedded in culture, and whatever else they are, biblical texts are cultural products whose communicative aims are at the same time both constrained and mobilized by the contexts within which they were generated. Moreover, the capacity of the Bible to function as Scripture depends in part on its capacity to expose and thwart our own limited, historical horizons. Our interpretative horizons threaten the domestication of Scripture, so that its strenuous demands are denuded of their challenge. For a well-formulated theological hermeneutic, one needs to secure the status of the biblical text as "subject" in theological discourse, and not only as object. We turn to historical inquiry to help structure a conversation in which values and customs familiar in our communities are juxtaposed with those not simply represented but actually proposed in Scripture. The relativizing of taken-for-granted concepts such as kinship, wealth, and power has the effect of disorienting the reader and altering perception. In this sort of scriptural engagement, communities of interpretation are challenged and formed with respect to their practices; they find their theological horizons expanded, their moral imaginations assaulted and sculpted. Historical inquiry is thus a servant of theological commentary.

No particular method can insure theological interpretation, but any method must be tamed in the light of Scripture's theological aims, and some methods are more relevant and theologically friendly than others. In addition to approaches that situate the voice of Scripture sociohistorically, of special interest in theological commentary would be models of analysis that take seriously the generally narrative content of Scripture. They would also respect the theological unity of Scripture, which takes its point of departure from the character and purpose of Yahweh and gives rise to its historical unity as the narrative of that purpose being worked out in the cosmos. And they would respect the final form and canonical location of the biblical texts.

Bibliography

Barth, K. *The Epistle to the Romans*. Oxford University Press, 1933; Bede, the Venerable. *Commentary on the Acts of the Apostles*. Cistercian Studies Series 117. Cistercian Pubns., 1989; Bovon, F. *Luke 1*. Hermeneia. Fortress, 2002; Boyarin, D. *Intertextuality and the Reading of Midrash*. Indiana Studies in Biblical Literature. Indiana University Press, 1990; Breisach, E. *Historiography*. 2d ed. University of Chicago Press, 1994; Bruner, F. D. "The Why and How of Commentary." *ThTo* 46 (1990): 399–404; Childs, B. *The Book of Exodus*. OTL. Westminster, 1974; idem. *Isaiah*. Westminster John Knox, 2000; Eco, U. *The Role of the Reader*. Advances in Semiotics. Indiana University Press, 1979; Fee, G. *1 Corinthians*. NICNT. Eerdmans, 1987; idem. "Reflections on Commentary Writing." *ThTo* 46 (1990): 387–92; Fishbane, M. "Inner-biblical Exegesis: Types and Strategies of Interpretation in Ancient Israel." Pages 3–18 in *The Garments of Torah*. Indiana Studies in Biblical Literature. Indiana University Press, 1989; Green, J., and M. Turner, eds. *Between Two Horizons*. Eerdmans, 2000; Griffiths, R., ed. *The Bible in the Renaissance*. St. Andrews Studies in Reformation History. Ashgate, 2001; Hagner, D. "Writing a Commentary on Matthew: Self-Conscious Ruminations of an Evangelical." *Semeia* 72 (1995): 51–72; Howell, K. *God's Two Books*. University of Notre Dame Press, 2002; Labriola, A., and J. Smeltz. *The Bible of the Poor*. Duquesne University Press, 1990; Margerie, B. de. *An Introduction to the History of Exegesis*. 3 vols. Saint Bede's Pubns., 1991–95; McNally, R. *The Bible in the Early Middle Ages*. Scholars Press Reprints and Translations. Scholars Press, 1986; Perkins, P. "Commentaries: Windows to the Text." *ThTo* 46 (1990): 393–98; Sandys-Wunsch, J., and L. Eldridge. "J. P. Gabler and the Distinction between Biblical and Dogmatic Theology: Translation, Commentary, and Discussion of His Originality." *SJT* 33 (1980): 133–58; Schorske, C. *Thinking with History*. Princeton University Press, 1998; Steinmetz, D., ed. *The Bible in the Sixteenth Century*. Duke Monographs in Medieval and Renaissance Studies 11. Duke University Press, 1990; Thiselton, A. *The First Epistle to the Corinthians*. NIGTC. Eerdmans, 2000; Wall, R. "The Acts of the Apostles." *NIB*. 10:1–368.

Joel B. Green

Community, Interpretative

We observe a resurgent awareness of one's community of reference in personal identity formation and of one's participation in community and their importance for human existence in general. This has worked with the reemergence of "community" as a value in the postmodern context to occasion a renewed interest among Christians in the role and even the primacy of the faith community in the hermeneutical task. This development has sparked a lively debate about the role of the interpretative community in the theological interpretation of Scripture. Hence, some theorists elevate the communal goal of fostering virtue and human flourishing as providing the hermeneutical key to interpreting Scripture (Fowl). Others look to the role of the community in performing the "drama" set forth in the Bible (Wright). A third group highlights the community's task of bearing faithful witness to what God declares in Scripture (Wolterstorff).

Despite this difference of opinion regarding the precise role of the interpretative community, the communal focus is in keeping with emphases within the Bible itself, which coalesce in the image of the faith community as a people gathered around the text, listening intently for the voice of God. Both the OT and the NT place importance on the public reading of Scripture, on reading the sacred texts within the context of the gathered community. For example, the revival of religious practice that occurred among the Jews who had returned from the Babylonian exile came as a result of the people inviting Ezra to read and expound the Law to the assembled company (Neh. 7:73–8:18). This OT focus is carried over into the NT. Hence, Paul exhorts Timothy to "devote" himself "to the public reading of Scripture, to preaching and to teaching" (1 Tim. 4:13). In the era of the new covenant, the Scripture that is to be read publicly is not limited to the Law of Moses; it also includes the writings of the apostles and other early church leaders, some of whom authored circular letters intended for the hearing of several local congregations. In these gatherings, the believers were not merely silent recipients of the teaching of their leaders. Rather, when prophets spoke the people were to weigh carefully the messages being voiced (1 Cor. 14:29). Above all, however, the goal of that weighing was to discern the voice of the Spirit speaking to the community. The image of the gathered people listening for the Spirit's voice lies behind the exhortation that concludes each of the letters of the risen Lord to the seven churches: "Those who have ears, let them hear what the Spirit says to the churches" (Rev. 2:7 AT; etc.).

In keeping with the biblical image of the community gathered to listen to the Spirit's voice, the Westminster Confession declares that the final authority for the community of faith is "the Holy Spirit speaking in the Scripture" (art. 1.10). Although the context in which it is given suggests a communal orientation, this statement of the "Protestant principle of authority"—to cite Bernard Ramm's apt descriptor—does not explicitly stipulate who constitutes the intended recipients of the Spirit's speaking. Indeed, in the modern era the Spirit was thought to direct the divine message primarily toward individuals, who, in the opinion of specialists in the guild, were to approach the text with the techniques of biblical exegesis.

The recent questioning of the hegemony of historical-critical approaches has raised in the minds of some scholars the specter of subjectivism. What is to prohibit the individual interpreter from reading into the biblical text one's own preferences, thereby confusing the voice of the Spirit with the special pleading of the reader's own inner psyche? This concern suggests one understanding of the primacy of the interpretative community: it provides the basis for placing all private "hearings" of the Spirit within the wider hearing of the community, including the conclusions regarding the content of the Spirit's speaking that have characterized the faith community throughout its history.

Yet, as important as it may be, appealing to the community as a check on potential pitfalls of privately interpreting Scripture does not mark the central significance of the interpretative community in the hermeneutical task. To determine this dimension requires a consideration of the goal of the Spirit's speaking in Scripture. Although the address can take several forms, in keeping with the manifold diversity of writings that constitute the Bible (Goldingay), the overarching goal of the Spirit's speaking is to create a "world" or a "comprehensive universe" (McKnight 262). What the Spirit creates is nothing less than the eschatological world God intends for creation, a new creation centered in Jesus Christ (2 Cor. 5:17). Because above all this world entails a new community comprised of renewed persons, the world the Spirit creates through Scripture is a communal world, a community of the Word, a fellowship of persons who gather around Jesus Christ, who is the Word.

If the goal of the Spirit is the creation of a community, then the Bible is primarily a communal book. It is truly a book of the community. The Bible is the source of the "paradigmatic events" (Coleman 109–10) of the Christian community. These events—at the center of which is the story of Jesus—shape or form the community's way of conceiving the totality of reality, as well as the community's understanding of its ongoing experience. Insofar as their appropriation of these events leads succeeding generations to understand themselves in relationship to the past history of the community and in anticipation of a future that will bring about the actualization of the community's ideals, these events create a meaningful present (O'Dea 43). In this manner, the community gathered around the text becomes the contemporary embodiment of Jesus' narrative, and as such it is "the body of Christ."

The goal of the interpretative community in gathering around the text, therefore, is to embody the biblical narrative to such a degree that it becomes the foretaste of the eschatological new creation that the Spirit is fashioning. En route to this goal, the community reads the text enlivened by the question, "What is the Spirit saying to the churches?" This question is universal and ecumenical, and consequently it demands that the global church read together with the goal of discerning what it means to be the one church in the world today.

At the same time, this question is also highly local in intention. Ultimately, the text is read and the Spirit's voice is heard within the context of local gathered communities. We come to Scripture aware that we are participants in a concrete, visible fellowship of disciples in covenant with each other. We desire to hear what the Spirit is saying to us as a particular congregation of believers who share the mandate of being a fellowship of disciples in this specific setting (Klaassen 10). Sensitivity to reading within community, in turn, extends to our individual interpretative efforts, as our private readings of Scripture are seasoned with the awareness that, even as the church scattered, each of us remains at all times a participant in a gathered community.

Viewed from this perspective, the interpretative community plays a central role in the hermeneutical task. As a gathered community we listen to the voice of the Spirit so as to determine what it means for us to be an embodiment of the one church of Jesus Christ within the specific locale in which God has placed us.

Bibliography

Coleman, R. *Issues of Theological Conflict*. Eerdmans, 1980; Fowl, S. *Engaging Scripture*. Blackwell, 1998; Goldingay, J. *Models for Scripture*. Eerdmans, 1994; Grenz, S., and J. Franke. *Beyond Foundationalism*. Westminster John Knox, 2002; Klaassen, W. "Anabaptist Hermeneutics: Presuppositions, Principles and Practice." Pages 5–10 in *Essays on Biblical Interpretation*, ed. W. Swartley. Institute of Mennonite Studies, 1984; McKnight, E. *Postmodern Use of the Bible*. Abingdon, 1988; O'Dea, T. *The Sociology of Religion*. Prentice-Hall, 1966; Ramm, B. *The Pattern of Religious Authority*. Eerdmans, 1959; Stackhouse, J., Jr., ed. *Evangelical Futures*. Baker, 2000; The Westminster Confession of Faith. In *The Creeds of the Churches*, ed. J. Leith. 3d ed. John Knox, 1982; Wolterstorff, N. *Divine Discourse*. Cambridge University Press, 1991; Wright, N. T. "How Can the Bible Be Authoritative?" *VE* 21 (1991): 7–32.

Stanley J. Grenz

Composition Criticism *See* Redaction Criticism

Concept

The nature and status of "concepts" is a general philosophical debate, entangled in the problem of "universals"—more fittingly pursued in other dictionaries. Concepts have been a problem for biblical interpretation too, however, especially in the use of linguistic evidence for the practice of "biblical theology" and then doctrinal construction.

In 1961 James Barr famously attacked "Kittel," the *Theological Dictionary of the New Testament*, as not in fact a lexicon but a set of concept-studies in linguistic guise. An entire apparatus for biblical theology was perceived to collapse at the same time—sharp distinctions between Greek and Hebrew thought, with the former more abstract and conceptual than the latter, were shown to be simplistic, as were overly tight connections between words and ideas, and so on. Barr noted the tendency to use "concept" in several senses: (1) It can mean a general notion that might be represented by any of several words ("love"). (2) It can be a brief formulation of the main content of a passage ("the Johannine concept of God's love"). (3) It can mean an idea that might not be tied to a specific linguistic expression ("the Johannine concept of God"). These senses might be either favorable or pejorative (Barr 210–11).

Confusion of technical terms with concepts is a related difficulty (Silva 107); however, etymology, semantics, and the like are handled elsewhere. Barr's own linguistic theory now seems dated, and his disjunction between the linguistic and the ideal/philosophical/theological quite sharp. But in any case, he started a revolution that has stood time's test (see, e.g., Cotterell and Turner 106–28). The idea—so dear to a phase of biblical theology and also to fundamentalism—that the Bible might be mined for simple, stable ideas tied to words is untenable in view of authorial diversity and linguistic philosophy.

Most technicalities aside, two points are worth addressing briefly. First, linguistic "commensurability" is at stake in a postmodern context: can verbal meaning cross cultural boundaries, or not? Kevin Vanhoozer has addressed the tension between "canon" and "concept"—between "sameness" and "otherness"—by arguing for the possibility of "conceptual mimesis" involving a degree of "creative imagination." His specific query was the diversity of biblical genres, which invites conceptual redescription while also forestalling any absolute sameness within that. David Yeago provides a helpful example by countering arguments for multiple, widely varying, NT Christologies: similar theological judgments can take different conceptual forms. Words lying behind the concept "incarnation" in John 1 need not appear in Phil. 2 for some kind of conceptual overlap to obtain. Accordingly, a relatively adequate narrative of rough conceptual identity is ingredient to biblical and postbiblical traditioning processes (Treier).

Second, then, with regard to language in practice: while concepts require a degree of framework-independence to achieve relative stability across cultural distance, this does not force us into an antiquated understanding of language. Linguist Kathleen Callow suggests that for explaining translation we need "a mental correlate of words which is not language specific" (Callow 20). She tackles the difficulty of defining concepts and concludes that they should be understood as "habitual events" (mental, in the first instance) acquired "by participation" in activities (which have a social dimension; 53, 55). Concepts have "firm cores" of meaning with vast amounts of detail, some of which we draw upon in any particular thinking event, in any action of referring (57, 64). So "concepts are not what we think about; they are what we think with" (65).

Concepts are learned as social skills; to what extent their patterns of organizing knowledge about the world are universal—even "essential" as the basic categories of reality—is a debate that biblical interpretation is unlikely to solve. Still, the consequences are severe if we remain ignorant of the debate—not only regarding proper conceptual stability and diversity amid the church's theological interpretation, but also regarding what outsiders can or cannot discern about the meaning of Christian teaching.

See also Biblical Theology; Etymology; Systematic Theology

Bibliography

Barr, J. *The Semantics of Biblical Language.* Oxford University Press, 1961; Callow, K. *Man and Message.* UPA/Summer Institute of Linguistics, 1998; Cotterell, P., and M. Turner. *Linguistics and Biblical Interpretation.* InterVarsity, 1989; Silva, M. *Biblical Words and Their Meaning.* Zondervan, 1994; Treier, D. "Canonical Unity and Commensurable Language." Pages 211–28 in *Evangelicals and Scripture,* ed. D. Okholm et al. InterVarsity, 2004; Vanhoozer, K. "From Canon to Concept: 'Same' and 'Other' in the Relation between Biblical and Systematic Theology." *Scottish Bulletin of Evangelical Theology* 12, no. 2 (Autumn 1994): 96–124; Yeago, D. "The New Testament and the Nicene Dogma." Pages 87–100 in *The Theological Interpretation of Scripture,* ed. S. Fowl. Blackwell, 1997.

Daniel J. Treier

Context

Referring generally to the social and linguistic webs within which speech is set and derives its significance, "context" has proven to be a prodigiously elastic term in the hands of biblical interpreters. The term is often used of (1) the sociohistorical setting within which a text was generated, within which the events to which a text provides witness took place, or within which the traditions that came finally to expression in a text were shaped and handed down. Context can mean (2) the portions of something written that precede and follow a word or passage in a text. It can also refer to (3) the situation of the reader, understood in sociohistorical as well as theological terms, which helps to shape how the reader accesses and construes the significance of a text. For persons interested in the theological interpretation of Scripture, none of these species of context is unimportant.

1. Context as Sociohistorical Setting

Various forms of historical criticism of biblical texts have deployed the concept of context. In the early 1900s, the *form critics* sought to classify the individual units of teaching or narrative within a book according to their form (e.g., legend or miracle story), then assign each form to a *Sitz im Leben* (situation in life) within the practices of the community. In an attempt to reconstruct the pre-literary history of biblical literature, form critics inquired into how particular forms of literature functioned in the life of their communities, and answered with reference to such needs as worship, proclamation, instruction, apologetic, settling disputes, and so on (e.g., Gunkel). Similarly, in its concern with the disciplined art of persuasion, *rhetorical criticism* seeks as a necessary step the identification of a rhetorical situation—that is, that complex of persons, events, and relations generating pressure for a verbal response (e.g., Kennedy). *Historical criticism* draws attention to the worlds (chronology, geography, politics, institutions, customs, etc.) within which the biblical texts were written, as well as the aims of the authors of those texts, as the primary determinants of textual meaning. *Social-scientific analysis* has both refined and thickened historical inquiry by seeking to account for the social and cultural conditioning of the writers and their first readers and, then, how and why those texts were designed to function in their sociocultural matrix (e.g., Eilberg-Schwartz). Opening the notion of "context" further, *discourse analysis* concerns itself with the temporal moment of a communicative act. First, this involves the world within which the text first participated at the time of its generation. It thus is focused on such presuppositions as sociocultural scripts assumed, challenged, and/or broadcast by the author, or provided by the author in order to broaden further the presupposition pools of his audience. Second, it examines the new discourse situation within which its readers access the text (see below, §3). In its own way, each of these approaches to interpretation takes seriously the purposeful nature of biblical texts, which were conceived in order to accomplish certain ends. Attention to context, then, urges interpreters carefully to consider the particularity of those texts, whose meaning is tied in some significant sense to the situations motivating their generation.

The relation of authors and their texts to their contexts is rarely straightforward, and this has profound implications for theological interpretation of biblical texts. Robert Wuthnow helpfully notes how cultural products, like texts, often relate in an enigmatic fashion to their social environments: "They draw resources, insights, and inspiration from the environment: they reflect it, speak to it, and make themselves relevant to it. And yet they also remain autonomous enough from their social environment to acquire a broader, even universal and timeless appeal" (Wuthnow 3). Similarly, Stephen Greenblatt draws attention

to the concepts of "constraint" and "mobility," which set the parameters within which textual improvisation is possible. "Constraints" refers to the boundaries set around one's behavior within a given society, to the limits set around acceptable and unacceptable actions. "Mobility" refers to the elasticity or "scope for variation" within those parameters. Between these two poles, works of art, like texts, have an educational or formative purpose. "They do not merely passively reflect the prevailing ratio of mobility and constraint; they help to shape, articulate, and reproduce it through their own improvisatory intelligence" (Greenblatt 229). This means, on the one hand, that textual meaning cannot simply be identified with or reduced to the historical situation of their origins since, from this perspective, cultural products such as texts have the capacity to speak to and also beyond the situations within which they were formed. Even products of cultures distinct from our own may speak to us in our own encultured situations, by means of the juxtaposition of those cultural structures, alien and familiar, that lend certainty to everyday life, with the result that we find ourselves disoriented, our perceptions altered, our imaginations transformed. These texts have the capacity to bring our own conventional wisdom into question, to assail our own pet convictions, to renew our deepest commitments, and to shape our imaginations toward the divine purpose and project to which these texts give witness.

The capacity of texts to improvise in relation to their social environments means, on the other hand, that through attention to context we may follow in the theological footsteps of the writers of biblical texts, tracing how they themselves have engaged in cultural analysis and critique. When read against the horizons of their own, particular sociohistorical environment, what do these texts affirm, deny, reject, undermine, or embrace? How does this text participate in theological and ethical reflection? On what authorities does it build its theological engagement? That is, texts such as Job or Mark do not simply present the world "as it really is" but purposely shape the story in such a way that some aspects of their worlds are undermined and others legitimated. Hence, what vision do they present of the world "as it should be" or as we are to imagine it to be? How does the text speak back to, against, and within its world?

In such ways, attention to "context as sociohistorical setting" has the potential to return to the text its role as subject, and not only object, in theological discourse. We are better enabled to hear the voice of the biblical text itself, rather than that of the church or other authorized interpreter who, like a ventriloquist, has become skilled in controlling the text so that it speaks only as it is allowed.

2. Context as Cotext

"Cotext" refers to the location of an utterance within a string of linguistic data, the sentences, paragraphs, and chapters surrounding and related to a text and within which an utterance finds its meaning. The importance of cotext is signaled by the ambiguity of language. Specific words are often capable of multiple meanings, giving rise to potential uncertainties whether one is reading or hearing words read. Likewise, chunks of texts, whether phrases or sentences or even paragraphs, can be interpreted in diverse ways. Sentences other than the first to appear in a text have their interpretation constrained by the preceding text, as words, sentences, and entire units of discourse are shaped in their significance by the larger cotexts within which they appear. Previous meaning systems can be renewed, nuanced, and even destroyed in new, or even in expanded, cotexts. Accordingly, attending to the cotextual location of a text is an exercise in the control of meaning.

For theological interpretation, exegetical attention to cotext provides an indispensable corrective to the focus on word studies that has plagued biblical studies. Numerous reference works (e.g., especially earlier contributions to *TDNT*, and an older generation of word studies associated with such names as Vincent or Vine) erroneously tied a great deal of theological freight to the appearance of particular terms, quite apart from how those terms were actually used. In a notorious example, Ethelbert Stauffer wrote that, for John, *agapē* (and its cognates) refers to Christian, self-giving love, thus neglecting the fact that we find in the Johannine corpus usages of the term that provide significant evidence to the contrary (e.g., John 3:19; 12:43; 1 John 2:15).

Theological interpretation underscores the importance of cotext, too, when a specifically Christian reading of the Bible is undertaken, since this requires that a text be read in relation to the whole of the canon (within its canonical cotext).

3. Context as Readerly Situation

In the decades leading up to the twenty-first century, the location of the reader as a potent factor in biblical interpretation came increasingly to be recognized. Under the influence of Descartes (1596–1650), who pictured the perception of knowledge in terms of a mind grasping a subject, the interpretative process posited an objective reader in search of the meaning already inherent in the text. In biblical theology, this perspective was expressed in the famous distinction between what a text meant (in its historical context) and what it means (today), with a premium placed on extracting from the biblical materials timeless, universal truths (i.e., "truths" independent of context). Today, however, it is widely acknowledged that we are incapable of grasping the text as it is in and of itself, that texts are construed always in relationship to those engaged in the process of reading.

Although the context of the reader is capable of being parsed in numerous ways relevant to biblical interpretation, of special importance for theological interpretation is the theological location of the reader. According to more moderate forms of reception theory (e.g., Iser; Eco), texts like those in Scripture are characterized by the invitation for readers "to make the work" together with the author. Texts are characterized by gaps that must be filled by readers, and different readers will actualize the text's clues in different ways. Accordingly, texts are capable of a range (though not an infinite number) of possible, valid meanings, depending on who is doing the reading, from what perspectives they read, and what reading protocols they practice.

To some significant degree, what it means to engage, for example, in a Wesleyan reading of Scripture is that those doing the reading have been nurtured in the Wesleyan tradition of according privilege to some theological categories over others—the pursuit of holiness, for example, and the primacy of grace. This does not mean that the readings of Wesleyans (or Anabaptists or Calvinists) are complete, or that they constitute the only possible ways of construing texts, but it does indicate how, from diverse communities of reading, we may hear the same pattern of words in new keys. Neither does it sanction every reading as equally valid, but it does indicate in one significant way how diverse readings of the same text might lay claim to legitimacy. And it underscores the importance for the hermeneutical equation of the theological formation of those engaged in the practice of interpretation.

See also Archaeology; Canonical Approach; Geography; Intertextuality; Liberation Theologies and Hermeneutics; Reader-Response Criticism; Utterance Meaning

Bibliography

Eco, U. *Interpretation and Overinterpretation*. Cambridge University Press, 1992; Eilberg-Schwartz, H. *The Savage in Judaism*. Indiana University Press, 1990; Greenblatt, S. "Culture." Pages 225–32 in *Critical Terms for Literary Study*, ed. F. Lentricchia and T. McLaughlin. University of Chicago Press, 1990; Gunkel, H. *The Folktale in the Old Testament*. Historic Texts and Interpreters in Biblical Scholarship 5. Sheffield Academic Press, 1987; Iser, W. *The Implied Reader*. Johns Hopkins University Press, 1974; Kennedy, G. *New Testament Interpretation through Rhetorical Criticism*. University of North Carolina Press, 1984; *TDNT*; Wuthnow, R. *Communities of Discourse*. Harvard University Press, 1989.

Joel B. Green

Continental Philosophy   *See* Philosophy

Continuity (between the Testaments)

See Relationship between the Testaments

1 Corinthians, Book of

In the effective history of 1 Corinthians, the letter has been primarily mined for its contribution to debates about virginity (7:1–40), the mode of Christ's presence in the Lord's Supper (11:23–26), and the nature of the resurrection (15:1–58). Because Paul seems intent only on settling the practical problems that have arisen in the church, many in recent times think the letter lacks developed doctrine and contains only applied theology. Paul is assumed to be counteracting the Corinthians' spurious beliefs that have caused confusion about the importance of individual leaders, the nature of human sexuality, the nature of spiritual gifts, and the nature of resurrection—all of which have led to their behavioral excesses.

In the last century, these beliefs have been identified as antinomian Gnosticism. The letter became a favorite of later Gnostics in the tradition of Valentinus, who fastened onto Paul's statements about a spiritual body to buttress their view denying the resurrection of flesh and blood, but most are now skeptical of identifying the Corinthian opponents as Gnostics. Others attribute the problems to a Hellenistic Jewish religiosity, akin to Philo's, that focused on *sophia* and *gnōsis*. More recently, some claim that the problems are rooted in an "overrealized eschatology." The Corinthians presumably took literally Paul's statement "Behold, now is the day of salvation" (2 Cor. 6:2 KJV) and developed an overheated, spiritualistic illusion that they were already living in the kingdom come, as if the day of the Lord had come (1 Cor. 4:8; 2 Thess. 2:2). A theology of glory also caused them to downplay the cross.

Other recent studies find the problems in Corinth stemming more from the influence of their cultural setting than from specious theological beliefs. Paul's purpose is not to correct their theology but to get them to think theologically so that they would respond properly to their polytheistic, pluralistic culture. The cross and resurrection form the theological cornerstone of Paul's response. Karl Barth argues: "The discourse of the whole epistle proceeds from a single point and harks back to this point," the resurrection of the dead (113).

Shortly before his assassination, Julius Caesar reestablished Corinth as a Roman colony in 44 BCE. The Romans established colonies to foster the majesty of their culture, religion, and values. When Paul came to Corinth a century later to proclaim Christ's greater majesty, he found a city teeming with commerce as the vital link between Rome and its eastern provinces. This letter should be read against the background of a mercantile society imbued with Roman cultural values that fed a ruthless preoccupation with attaining public status, promoting one's own honor, and securing power. The scramble for scarce honor was as intense as the scramble for scarce wealth. Values of the dominant culture so antithetical to the message of the cross percolated into the church, destroying its fellowship and its Christian witness as some members vainly sought to balance secular mores with Christian norms. These secular values played havoc with Paul's attempt to build a community based on love, selflessness, and the equal worth of every member. Paul corrects their misconduct with carefully wrought ethical exhortations grounded in a correct theology.

Traditionally, the problems that Paul addresses in 1 Corinthians have been attributed to imagined theological disputes swirling around Peter, Apollos, Paul, and the elusive Christ party (1:12). These theological rivalries combined with the Corinthians' attraction to flashy displays of knowledge, wisdom, and spiritual gifts, and a gnostic worldview—all were assumed to be ripping apart the fellowship. A recent trend traces the problems in Corinth back to personality-centered politics and the members' social placement. The discordant factions within the community did not divide over fine points of theological interpretation but grew out of the rivalry of leading figures, who may have hosted different house churches.

The influence of secular ethics and the Corinthians' failure to grasp the full implications of the wisdom of the cross led to their competitive party spirit (1:10–4:21), their suing one another in pagan courts (6:1–11), their dangerous brushes with sexual immorality (5:1–13; 6:12–20), their dallying with idols (8:1–11:1), their humiliation of the have-nots at the Lord's Supper (11:17–34), and their vaunting of particular spiritual gifts (12:1–14:40). A Greek worldview caused them to believe in life after death without a resurrection of the dead (15:1–58). They failed to comprehend how an earthly body that is physical and perishable could be made suitable for a heavenly realm that is spiritual and imperishable.

Paul's letter has its genesis in his dismayed response to oral reports about what is going on in Corinth (1:11; 5:1; 11:18; cf. 16:17–18) and his answers to Corinthian queries in their letter to him (see 7:1). The problems emerge from the complexities of everyday life—a man living with his father's wife (5:1–13), lawsuits against fellow Christians (6:1–11), prostitution (6:12–20), celibacy and marriage (7:1–40), food sacrificed to idols (8:1–11:1), head dress in public worship (11:2–16), divisions at the Lord's Supper (11:17–34), the use of tongues in worship (12:1–14:40). Paul alternates between his reactions to oral reports and his answers to the Corinthian letter:

Oral reports (1:10–4:17 / 4:18–6:20)
Corinthian letter (7:1–40 / 8:1–11:1)
Oral reports (11:2–34)
Corinthian letter (12:1–14:40)
Oral reports (15:1–58)
Corinthian letter (16:1–12)

In each case, Paul draws out the theological implications of their behavior and the necessity of the norm of love and the wisdom of the cross for guiding all that they do, rather than issuing authoritarian directives. The theological core of this letter is his reiteration of the heart of his preaching—the feeble and stupid message of the crucified Christ, which nevertheless proves to have a power and wisdom no human eloquence possesses, since it is the power and wisdom of God himself.

Internal Dissension and the Wisdom of the Cross (1:10–4:21)

Paul first addresses the problem of the internal rivalries among the bigwigs in the church, who were scrambling for position in the community and dividing up Christ into lifeless fragments (1:10–4:17). The breakdown of community is caused by the infusion of "the spirit of the world" (2:12, synonymous with "the wisdom of the world" [1:20; 3:19] and "the wisdom of this age" [2:6]) into their attitudes, judgments, and behavior. Secular wisdom's baneful influence on church members, rather than some overarching theological misconception, lies behind most of the problems that Paul addresses.

To bring an end to the Corinthians' political infighting and to uproot the worldly wisdom driving their behavior, Paul seeks to stimulate theological thoughtfulness that results in a cross-centered community adopting his own cruciform lifestyle (4:16). The death and resurrection of Jesus are the foundational events that determine Paul's vision of the Christian community, but Greco-Roman symbols and mythology competed with the cross to provide a framework for interpreting life. The Corinthians' quarreling reveals that they have uncritically absorbed the ideals and values of the pagan world around them. Paul seeks to replace a pagan paradigm, fascinated by displays of status and power, with God's paradigm, exhibited in the weakness of the cross. He does not sweep the crucifixion under the carpet as an unfortunate episode remedied by the glories of the resurrection but trusts the power of the cross to convict the audience of its truth. For those who claim honor on the basis of worldly wisdom, he offers the foolish wisdom of the cross that overturns human wisdom. For those who crave impressive displays of eloquence, he proclaims Christ's crucifixion in weakness, fear, and trembling, accompanied only by demonstrations of the Spirit's power.

The cross embodies the power of God to absorb all the blind rage of humanity and to avert its deadly consequences, but humanity, both Jew and Greek, fails to recognize that truth because it does not fit their categories and ways of thinking. Human wisdom is circumscribed by its partial knowledge, susceptible to self-deceit, and blinded by its own conceit and pride. Paul cites five passages from Scripture in 1:18–3:23 (1:19; 2:9, 16; 3:19, 20) to make the point that humans cannot grasp God's wisdom through their own effort. God has manifested his power and wisdom in sending his Son, allowing him to be crucified, proclaiming a seemingly weak and foolish message through apostles regarded by the world as weak and foolish, calling into being a church made up of those whom the world regards as nobodies, and uniting them to the crucified Christ, who becomes their righteousness, sanctification, and redemption. This wisdom can only be appropriated through the Spirit, whose most central work is not to be found in the visible things such as healings, glossolalia, and eloquent preaching but in leading believers to the crucified Christ (2:2) and calling believers into community. The Spirit, not an orator's eloquence, reveals the message's truth to the believer (2:4, 13).

For Paul, the message of the cross is the antidote to the human self-glorification poisoning the fellowship. Victory is won by giving up life, not taking it. Selfish domination of others is discredited. Shame is removed through divine identification with the shamed in Christ's shameful death. Paul further undermines the self-aggrandizement of the leading figures in the church by casting himself and Apollos as servants (3:4) and field hands (3:6–9), and he identifies apostles as figures of shame who are indistinguishable from the dregs of society (4:10–13). The image of building contractors (3:10–17) reminds them of their accountability in the final judgment. He expects submission to the cross to quash egoism and to lead all Christians to serve one another, and Christian leaders, in particular, to serve the community from below.

Ethics and Christ's Lordship of the Body (5:1–6:20)

The three issues that occupy Paul in 5:1–6:20 (incest, lawsuits, and visiting prostitutes) complement the previous discussion in chapters 1–4. In these opening chapters he insinuates that the church is riven by unnecessary strife, fed by unjustified spiritual pride. These cases expose their carnality (3:1) and serve to puncture the Corinthians' inflated arrogance. The immorality of church members has not only undermined any grounds for the church's boasting; it has wrecked the church's witness of God's transforming power to change lives. Christianity offers not only a completely new sexual ethos and a new ethos regarding material possessions; it also brings about a complete transformation of individuals through their washing, sanctification, and justification (6:11). God's grace does not simply whitewash sin. It is intended to transform sinners.

Paul's ethical exhortation is grounded in his view of the final judgment of all humanity and the resurrection of Christians. Each passage contains an eschatological affirmation: a hope that the incestuous man's spirit might be saved on the day of the Lord (5:5); an assertion that the saints will judge the world and the angels (6:2); and a reminder that the body will be raised (6:14). Paul seeks to shake them out of their blasé attitude toward sinful conduct and drive home the seriousness of their sin and their need for repentance. He argues that Christians should live in ways congruent with who they are—as those who belong to Christ and are destined to live with Christ (5:7–8; 6:11, 19–20). Christ's lordship lays claim on the Christian's body, which is destined for resurrection, so that those who belong to Christ are not free to do with their bodies whatever they please. Hiring a prostitute for sex essentially denies Christ's ultimate sovereignty by filching what belongs to Christ and handing it over to one who belongs to Satan.

Celibacy, Divorce, and Marriage and God's Calling (7:1–40)

In discussing questions about celibacy, divorce, and marriage in 7:1–40, Paul does not foist his own preference for celibacy on others but leaves room for believers to make their own decisions under Christ (see 7:6–7, 10, 12, 25, 28, 32, 35, 40). Some in Corinth must have regarded celibacy as a higher good, as evidenced by his opening quotation from their letter to Paul (7:1). While he believes celibacy is good, he knows that it is not good for everyone and certainly does not lift one to a higher spiritual plateau. His advice is grounded in his theological conviction that no condition presents an obstacle to living the Christian life, since a Christian is now defined by God's call (1:9) and nothing else. He develops this principle in 7:17–24, which seems from a casual reading to interrupt the discussion. These digressions (see also 9:1–10:22; 13:1–13) provide the theological underpinning guiding his counsel on the practical matters. Here Paul reminds them that the offer of salvation comes to believers without requiring them to alter their ethnic, social, or domestic status. What matters is keeping the commandments of God (7:19), in particular, avoiding fornication (7:2–5). Christians can keep the commandments of God whether circumcised or uncircumcised, slave or free, married or celibate. Any attempt to alter one's status in life for religious reasons gives more importance to that worldly status than it merits and controverts God's calling in Christ based on grace alone.

Again, Paul's advice is suffused with his eschatological perspective. The death and resurrection of Christ and the giving of the Spirit mean that the new age has invaded the present. Christians must evaluate their choices in life from the perspective of the end that has come so near (7:29–31). An end-time awareness should sharpen the focus of their decisions in the mundane matters of this world. Since the end is plainly in sight, Christians should see and judge more clearly what is and is not important and not allow the world's values and opinions (7:22–23) to cast them in the forge of its deadly furnace.

Idol Food and Christological Monotheism (8:1–11:1)

Paul's lengthy discussion of idol food (8:1–11:1) is grounded in his christological monotheism, which defines the people of God over against those who worship many so-called gods and lords in their sundry guises. As a cosmopolitan city, Corinth was a religious melting pot, with older and newer religions flourishing side-by-side. Most persons could accommodate all gods and goddesses into their religious behavior, and they could choose from a great cafeteria line of religious practices. The Christian confession of one God and one Lord, however, requires *exclusive* loyalty to God as Father and to Christ as Lord (8:6). Paul rejects Christians participating in any function that overtly smacks of idolatry because it poses a danger to the Christian with a weak conscience, who might be sucked back into idolatry's clutches (8:7–13). It also compromises the Christian witness to one God, confirms the idolater in his idolatry, and will bring the Christian under God's wrath (10:1–13). The Supper of the one Lord, which unites participants to him, excludes eating idol offerings, which unite participants to idols and their demons (10:14–22). Even a perfunctory or make-believe show of fealty to an idol compromises the loyalty owed only to God and Christ. Christianity breaks down the barriers that classify people by their ethnic identity, social standing, or sexual gender; it also erects barriers that create a distinctive Christian identity (cf. 10:32). Paul teaches that one's presumed rights should be readily forfeited in the interest of saving others. At stake is whether the church will keep religious syncretism at bay so that it can remain holy to God, and whether the believer's allegiance to Christ will override all other attractions and attachments.

Decorum in Public Worship and God's Creation (11:2–16)

Paul's advice on another mundane matter, wearing headdresses in public worship, is grounded in his view of creation and how being "in the Lord" alters how life is to be perceived (11:11). God's saving work through Christ transcends society's gender hierarchy. Paul takes for granted that women may pray and prophesy in the assembly as long as they have an appropriate head covering. But Christians must avoid flouting what is cultur-

ally shameful (11:6; cf. 14:35). Wearing a head covering (11:13) is a sign of personal rectitude for a woman, and its absence implies the opposite. Christians should observe the proprieties of polite society in their public gatherings to avoid bringing unnecessary dishonor to themselves and, concomitantly, to their Lord.

The Lord's Supper and Christ's Sacrifice (11:17–34)

In 11:17–34, Paul seeks to correct the Corinthian desecration of the Lord's Supper. The Lord's Supper should intensify group solidarity, but the Corinthians' supper has become a flash point highlighting their social inequality and alienation. No one ought to feel humiliated at the Lord's Supper, yet the Corinthians' manner of conducting the meal has left the have-nots feeling that they are beneath the notice of their fellow Christians (11:22). Paul appeals to the Last Supper tradition to correct their practice. The Corinthians act selfishly; Jesus acted unselfishly in giving his life for others. The Corinthians' actions will lead to their condemnation (11:29, 32); Jesus' action leads to the salvation of others. The combination of broken bread and cup conveys the nature of Jesus' ultimate sacrifice. Christ gave his body and sacrificed his blood in an expiatory death, which brings the offer of salvation to all persons, and each believer receives an equal share of the benefits of his sacrifice. That reality should be symbolized by what happens during the Lord's Supper. The Corinthians' observance of the Lord's Supper, in which one has more than enough and gets drunk, while another has too little and goes hungry, epitomizes the culture of selfishness and fails to proclaim the meaning of the Lord's death for all. Instead, they are to imitate Christ's example of self-giving, and everything they do in their meal should accord with his self-sacrifice for others. Consequently, Paul urges them to share what they have with each other (11:33).

Spiritual Gifts, Spiritual Persons, and Public Worship (12:1–14:40)

The lengthy discussion of spiritual gifts in 12:1–14:40 reveals that the Corinthians have limited the "spiritual gifts" to a handful of spectacular gifts and placed tongues above prophecy as a clear sign of supernatural power working in a spiritual person. In correcting their unwarranted spiritual pride and disorderly worship, Paul obliquely critiques their infatuation with speaking in tongues. He begins by asserting that all Christians are imbued with the Holy Spirit and are therefore spiritual by virtue of their confession "Jesus is Lord" (12:3), and he broadens the spectrum of grace gifts that manifest the Spirit (12:4–26). As throughout the letter, Paul develops the issue's theological implications, which they have overlooked. He makes clear that there are diversities of gifts, services, and activities, but only one Spirit who distributes them as he wills. Each gift is given to different persons for the common good. Consequently, each person is needed in the community. Inspired speech is only one among many ways the Spirit works in the body of Christ. No one should feel superior because he or she possesses a particular spiritual endowment. The Spirit decides who gets what gift and apportions them according to the need in the community, not according to the value of the recipient. All are gifted by God in some way and encouraged to contribute their gifts in ways that will build up the community. Spiritual gifts are not indicators of one's spiritual status.

The segmentation of the Corinthian congregation into cliques is the by-product of human depravity that spurs individuals to treat their differing spiritual experiences as a pretext for reinstating class divisions—now employing spiritual classifications—so as to elevate themselves over others. The seemingly unrelated digression in 13:1–13 praising love actually lays out the principle by which gifts should be exercised in the church. If any extol their own particular gift(s) as the highest and best, Paul demonstrates how devoid of value these gifts are without love. The question is not which gift is the most beneficial, stimulating, or spiritual. It is, instead, whether love is radiated in exercising their gifts. Though God and Christ are not mentioned, the cross of Christ as the manifestation of God's love for the world defines Paul's understanding. The principle of love embodied in the cross mandates that one should always seek honor for others, which stands in an absolute antithesis to the dominant value, which seeks honor only for oneself out of preening self-indulgence. Since almost every problem in the church is mentioned in 13:4–7, Paul implies that the source of their problems is their lack of love.

Paul holds up what contributes most to "building up" the church (14:3–5, 12, 17, 26) as the touchstone for ranking the relative value of gifts, particularly for public worship. The speech gifts that are intelligible to all, including outsiders, are the most fruitful and should be the most valued. Finally, he gives specific advice and commands on tongues and prophecy in worship (14:26–40),

based on the theological conviction that the Spirit of ardor is also the Spirit of order.

The Resurrection of the Dead and God's Creative Power (15:1–58)

The climax of the letter is Paul's lengthy discussion of the resurrection in chapter 15. The Corinthians did not assume that the resurrection had already occurred (2 Tim. 2:18) but believed in an afterlife without the resurrection of the dead. Their error is not rooted in some deliberate doctrinal rebellion but in honest confusion, given their Greek worldview. They failed to comprehend how an earthly body that is physical and perishable can be made suitable for a heavenly realm that is spiritual and imperishable. Earthly bodies and heavenly existence are therefore deemed to be as different as chalk from cheese. The Corinthians assumed that at death the mortal body is shed like a snake's skin, and the immortal soul continues in a purely spiritual existence. Paul's argument for the bodily resurrection divides into two distinct sections. The first section, 15:1–34, makes the case for the reality of the resurrection. The second section, 15:35–58, explains how the resurrection is possible.

In the first unit recording the resurrection appearances of Christ (15:1–11), Paul is not trying to prove the resurrection of Jesus but arguing from it. Some of the Corinthians are saying that there is no resurrection of the dead (15:12), yet they accepted the unified apostolic proclamation that Christ has been raised. Their denial of the resurrection of the dead is theologically untenable (15:12–19). If there is no resurrection of the dead, Christ has not been raised. If Christ is not raised from the dead, then everything based on that belief collapses in a heap of broken dreams. Paul affirms that as Christ was resurrected from the dead, so also those who are in Christ and pattern their lives after him can hope to be resurrected by God. Jesus is the representative of others who also will be raised so that the end-time resurrection becomes the ineluctable sequel to Jesus' resurrection (15:20–28). This unit reveals why Paul so adamantly defends the resurrection of the dead. If there is none, then death will remain unconquered and still hold sway beyond the End as a power set over against God. This circumstance is theologically incongruous. Since God is all-powerful, death must in the end be vanquished.

Because the Corinthians could not comprehend how resurrection was possible, they assumed it was impossible. In 15:35–58, Paul does not explain how the resurrection happens but only makes the case that it can happen. He grants their assumption that a polarity exists between earth and heaven, and that earthly embodied existence is completely incompatible with heavenly spiritual existence. He makes clear that resurrection is not the resuscitation of the corpse. A body fit to inhabit this world must be changed before it is fit to inhabit the heavenly world. Nature illustrates that there are different kinds of bodies and that dramatic transformation can occur. As the bare seed that is sown is not the plant that miraculously sprouts from the ground, so the earthly body that is sown is not the spiritual body that is raised. As God chooses to give the seed a different body (15:37), so God will give humans, sown with a body animated by soul, a body animated by the Spirit in the resurrection (15:42–44a). As humans were dressed at birth in the clothing of the "man of dust," so Christians will put on the clothing of the "heavenly man" in the resurrection (15:47–49). What is mortal will be changed by the power of God so that those who are raised will be given a spiritual body that is consistent with its new celestial habitat. Divine agency must be accounted for in life and in death. Death is impotent before the power and mercy of God, who wills to forgive sins (15:3, 17) and to raise the dead.

Paul is concerned about the correlation of theology and morality throughout the letter. Bad theology can lead to bad behavior and vice versa. Belief in the resurrection impinges directly on how one is to live (6:12–14; 15:32–34, 58).

Bibliography

Asher, J. *Polarity and Change in 1 Corinthians 15.* HUT 42. Mohr, 2000; Barclay, J. "Thessalonica and Corinth: Social Contrasts in Pauline Christianity." *JSNT* 47 (1992): 49–74; Barth, K. *The Resurrection of the Dead.* Hodder & Stoughton, 1933; Carson, D. A. *Showing the Spirit.* Baker, 1987; Fee, G. *The First Epistle to the Corinthians.* NICNT. Eerdmans, 1987; Furnish, V. P. *The Theology of the First Letter to the Corinthians.* NTT. Cambridge University Press, 1999; Garland, D. *1 Corinthians.* BECNT. Baker, 2003; Litfin, D. *St. Paul's Theology of Proclamation.* SNTSMS 83. Cambridge University Press, 1994; Mitchell, M. *Paul and the Rhetoric of Reconciliation.* Westminster John Knox, 1992; Rosner, B. *Paul, Scripture, and Ethics.* Biblical Studies Library. Baker, 1999; Thiselton, A. *The First Epistle to the Corinthians.* NIGTC. Eerdmans, 2000; Winter, B. *After Paul Left Corinth.* Eerdmans, 2001; Wright, N. T. "Monotheism, Christology, and Ethics: 1 Corinthians 8." In *The Climax of the Covenant.* Fortress, 1992.

David E. Garland

2 Corinthians, Book of

Second Corinthians is complex on several levels. Subtleties in language render it the student's nightmare and the exegete's playground. Because of debates regarding its integrity, it provides a convenient entrée into the ongoing conversation of Pauline scholars. Here, too, Paul deftly joins matters particular to the Corinthian church with larger theological questions. In all this we see the apostle at his most impassioned and his most astute, as he plays pastor, theologian, and even "fool." Throughout he uses a variety of literary and rhetorical strategies, grounding his concerns in the foundational principles of the faith.

History of Interpretation

Today's commentaries normally commence with the onset of the historical-critical method and the controversies sparked by the epistle in the last few centuries. Prior to this time, however, the letter served the church to a degree disproportionate to its size. It is, indeed, from 2 Cor. 3 that we derive the Christian categories of "old" and "new covenant." Augustine devoted an entire book of his *Literal Meaning of Genesis* (12.28, 34) to the intricacies of 2 Cor. 12:1–9. Chrysostom drew upon the letter in order to paint striking word-pictures of his favorite apostle (*Hom. 2 Cor.*). Gregory Palamas dwelt upon the epistle's theme of glory throughout his defense (*The Triads*) of the "hesychasts" who practiced "quietude" and so saw God's energies with natural eyes. Aquinas used 2 Corinthians to argue that, in their final beatific vision, the faithful will behold "the divine essence" (*ST* q. 12. art. 9. obj. 2) and in his discussion of reason and grace (*ST* q. 109. art. 1. obj. 3). Charles Wesley adapted 2 Cor. 3:18 to hymnody in his immortal lines "Changed from glory into glory / Till in heav'n we take our place."

By the late eighteenth century, the profound delight that the letter inspired in its readers was overtaken by more mundane concerns. J. S. Semler (1776) considered that 2 Corinthians must have been composed of at least two letters; A. Hausrath (1870) posited his "four chapters hypothesis" concerning chapters 10–13. The results of their source criticism were further complicated by Windisch (1924), who treated chapters 8 and 9 as two independent administrative letters. Current proponents of partition theories cite the apostle's name at 1:1 and 10:1, and a tonal change between chapters 9 and 10. They further point to ongoing correspondence between Paul and the Corinthians, seen in 1 Cor. 5:9; 2 Cor. 2:3–4, 9; and 7:8, 12. Some have believed that chapters 10–13 comprise the "tearful letter" of which Paul speaks. Most recently, the section 6:14–7:1 has been debated, with some dubbing it an Essene-like interpolation incompatible with Paul's theology, and others arguing for its authenticity (Webb). Such issues of integrity are interconnected with views of Paul's theology, career, and ministry. For convenient descriptions of the debates, see Gilchrist and Kreitzer (esp. 35–36).

Quite recently, some have prescinded from the source debate, turning to sociological, literary, and rhetorical concerns. An interest that links contemporary scholars with their forebears is the question of the identity of Paul's opponents—those "[*hyperlian*] super-apostles" who could, like Satan, "transform themselves" into agents of light (11:5, 14). Chrysostom, in the usual pragmatic manner of the Antiochene school, had identified these opponents as the much-debated "*skolops* [thorn]" in Paul's flesh (12:7; *Hom. 2 Cor.* 26.3–4). Through the years, critics have emerged with various pictures of this group—Judaizers (F. C. Baur [1833] and many others); proponents of Jesus as a miracle-working "divine man," or *Theios Anēr*; "enthusiasts" of various stripes, including early Gnostics (from Bultmann 1985 to F. Watson 1986). These questers have sought to make sense of the issues of apostolicity, gospel, and revelatory signs and wonders that run throughout the letter. (Again, for more players in this drama, see Kreitzer 71–82.) However, others wisely have urged caution in "mirror-reading" the epistle to locate opponents.

Then there is the study of Paul the visionary. Second Corinthians 12, despite its irony, inclines the reader to inquire in this vein. In antiquity, such concern led to the pseudepigraphical *Apocalypse of Paul*, and the use of 2 Corinthians in grounding the insights of spiritual theology. Today, Paul's "spirituality" is studied in an "academic" mode, with its major proponent from the Jewish community. Alan Segal views Paul as our best example of early rabbinic mysticism, followed by others who detect in 2 Corinthians *merkabah* mysticism (visions of the heavenly throne-chariot; cf. Ezek. 1). James D. Tabor likewise sees evidence that Paul privileged visionary experience.

The letter has also been grist for the mill of the literary and rhetorical critic. Richard Hays demonstrates Paul's subtle appeal to echo and allusion in such passages as 3:1–18. Others, beginning with Hans D. Betz, have turned their minds to the apostle's rhetoric, labeling chapters 10–13 a "Socratic apology" (Betz), a "philosopher's apology" (McCant), or a pastoral speech-act (Chevallier).

F. Young and D. F. Ford argued that the entire letter follows the rhetorical template set down by classical rhetorical theoreticians, and so is unified. Paul's moves also have provided an entrée for sociological discussions of inner and external conflict and power-relations (Chow). Some have sought a deliberately integrative approach, such as Ben Witherington, or E. Humphrey, who demonstrates the intricacies of textual, cultural, and historical allusions in 2 Corinthians through an adaptation of V. Robbins's "textural" model.

Issues, Themes, and Messages

Principal themes of the letter include: true knowledge (a theme shared with 1 Corinthians), old and new covenants, suffering and patience, holiness in the authentic Christian life, vulnerable giving and receiving, the importance of the body and body of Christ, the loving resolution of conflict and reconciliation, the use and abuse of authority, and especially, revelation and transformation. Joining these disparate themes together is the person of Jesus himself. He gives knowledge of God, fulfills the old covenant and initiates the new, and is the patient Sufferer par excellence. He is himself the temple of the living God, "God's unspeakable gift" to humanity, and the one by whose body and in whom we become a body together. Through Christ, God reconciled the world to himself, in his life divine power was made perfect in weakness, and through him has come God's new creation. "For it is the God who said, 'Let light shine out of darkness,' who has shone in our hearts to give the light of the knowledge of the glory of God *in the face of Jesus Christ*" (2 Cor. 4:6 NRSV, italics added).

Despite the debates regarding unity, the letter is bound together by what could be called "apocalyptic discourse." With the apocalypses proper, 2 Corinthians presents a cosmic reality so that the life of the Christian community is understood in terms of God's disclosed actions in time, as well as in light of a weighty unseen world. However, Paul further reconfigures the world in terms of the decisive *apokalypsis* of God in the person of Jesus Christ. Hence, knowledge, austerity of life, sacrifice, charitable giving, authority, and even special revelation are not ends in themselves. All are of value because of Jesus, in whom the new creation has been established so that his body grows from glory to glory (3:18). From one perspective, the glory of Jesus is the only light in this letter, that before which every other light-source pales; from another perspective, it is because of his very light that all human endeavors, all struggles in the church, and all members of the new creation are utterly important. Paul calls the apostles "the glory of Christ" (8:23b NRSV), picturing the entire community growing into this likeness (3:18).

By this unflinching focus upon Jesus as the revelation of God, Paul sees human existence as both transitory and bound for glory. Currently we hold "treasures in clay vessels" (4:7 AT); our human and failing eyes have seen "the knowledge of the light of the glory of God in the face of Jesus" (4:6 AT). This visionary possession of Christ's body together is a gift that far surpasses the revelations of those great souls of old. Moses, Elijah, and Ezekiel glimpsed, in special visions, God's glory from afar, and so instructed God's people. But that hazy "appearance *of* the likeness *of* the glory *of* the Lord" (Ezek. 1:28b, italics added) has been eclipsed by the very light of God among us. Jesus, the seemingly "poor" (8:9), with veiled and vulnerable glory that the world thought to extinguish, blazed on the resurrection morning. As a result, the whole world has changed ("There is a new creation!" 5:17 NRSV) and has been granted a surprising fresh dignity. Because of Jesus, the new creation is being prepared.

Things are not as they seem, once it is acknowledged that the greatest apocalypse (Jesus himself) has been revealed. Mundane symbols such as clay jars and mirrors, as well as potentially sacred images such as fragrance and veils, are all taken up into Paul's dramatic vision. Here we are taught not to despise the work of God's hands, nor to overexalt it. Readers of the twenty-first century are reminded, in our time of crazy and undisciplined "spirituality," that if we are truly to live, our spiritual life must be cruciform and lived together in that particular Holy Spirit of God. Present faithful suffering displays the life of Jesus in mortal bodies (4:11) and prepares "an eternal weight of glory beyond all measure" (4:17 NRSV). So it is that the foundational story of Jesus the Messiah—his life, death, resurrection, and exaltation—casts its light upon the everyday and the terrible. So it is that the arduous and irksome life of God's people is assumed into the cosmic drama, taking on great significance. "I will welcome you, . . . and you shall be my sons and daughters, says the Lord Almighty" (6:17b–18 NRSV).

As he concludes a difficult correspondence, Paul summarizes, "For he was crucified in weakness, but lives by the power of God. For we are weak in him, but . . . we will live with him by the power of God" (2 Cor. 13:4 NRSV). In the apostle's own case, this weakness and power would mean a painful rectification of problems with and in Corinth. It would mean looking to see Christ's resurrection power working in difficult interchurch relationships. Our own needs may not be so very different, given the current crisis of authority in many congregations and communions. Be that as it may, we may give thanks for an epistle that is at once heavenly minded and earthly rooted, given to us "for building up and not for tearing down" (13:10 NRSV).

2 Corinthians and Canon

In its description of God's new covenant through Christ, 2 Corinthians exegetes the OT hope for a qualitatively new communion (Jer. 31:31–34; Ezek. 34; 37) between God and humanity, and among the faithful. The historical dynamic Paul offers is essential: we are not to disparage the Mosaic covenant, as though the ancient people of God had erred; we are nevertheless to fully honor the new covenant, made perfect in Jesus. There is both a continuity and a discontinuity, since God's glory has been revealed, first to Israel, and now fully in Christ. This is a historical understanding of the covenants that the church has not always heeded. In early centuries, some Christians missed this dimension of the gospel, forgetting that God "did something new" in Jesus whereby the law was fulfilled. Gnostics, Marcionites, and others in the subapostolic period mocked the ancient Hebrews for taking literally words that God had "intended" only to be taken metaphorically (e.g., Clement of Alexandria, *Paed.* 2.10). Today, the opposite error is in vogue: Christians ignore the finality of the Jesus apocalypse, positing two ways of salvation, one for Jew, one for Christian. Paul will not leave us this option. In 2 Cor. 3–4, as in Rom. 10, he shows an undeniable continuity of the new covenant with the old, but the "veil" is only removed ("apocalypsed!") in Jesus. The Torah possessed a glory meant to be "set aside" (2 Cor. 3:13–14 NRSV) because it would come to completion in the One from whom the very light of God shines (on this, see Wright).

Paul relates this new story of Jesus and God's people by explicit reference to the OT, and also by allusion and echo, deeply inhabiting the old covenant story and demonstrating its new climax. Nor does he despise writings not strictly canonical, since he recalls (not uncritically) movements of Judaism (e.g., rabbinic mysticism) that we have long forgotten. Like the ancient poet Terence, Paul can say, "I consider nothing human to be alien to me"—but this he does with theological reason, for all is his, and he is in Christ, and Christ is God's. Close readings of 2 Corinthians dislodge unexpected allusions and memories of past writings, artifacts, and traditions. These discoveries enrich our own Christian world, so long as we maintain our focus upon the One in whom all things cohere.

2 Corinthians and Theology

The theological drive of 2 Corinthians is that of integration. Above all others, this letter reminds us that the pastoral, academic (scribal), and theological roles are best held together. Paul addresses the particular questions of his beloved church without losing sight of the larger picture. Here, if we will look, are answers to the "New Age" challenge, as Paul holds before us the One for whom new-agers thirst, but whom they do not recognize. Here are methods to resolve problems of authority and church structure—Paul embodies the vulnerable leader who uses his powerful role for the sake of his church. Here is a call to holiness that does not denigrate the body or the physical, but sees even the mundane as "sacramentals" disclosing the Holy One. Here is a written and luminous icon of the one who spoke worlds into being, and through whom has come and is coming and will come God's new creation. Paul does not here fully articulate the doctrine of the divinity of Christ, as he did in his reformulated Shema of 1 Cor. 8:5–6. In 2 Corinthians, that doctrine of Jesus as the LORD (through whom are all things) is assumed. Here Paul builds on that foundation, so as to nurture the common life made possible by "the Lord [who] is the Spirit" (2 Cor. 3:17). It is his lively hope that together we will be transformed into the image of that One who participates by right in the life of the Triune God. In the Spirit, Paul proclaims not himself, but Jesus Christ as LORD.

Bibliography

Baur, F. C. "Die Christuspartei in der korinthischen Gemeinde." Pages 1–76 of *Ausgewählte Werke*, ed. K. Scholder. 1963; Betz, H. D. *Der Apostle Paulus und die sokratische Tradition*. Mohr/Siebeck, 1972; Bultmann, R. *The Second Letter to the Corinthians*, trans. R. A. Harrisville. Fortress, 1985; idem. *Der zweite Brief an die Korinther*, ed. E. Dinkler. KEK 6. Vandenhoeck & Ruprecht, 1976; Chevallier, M.-A. "L'argumentation de Paul dans II Corinthiens 10 à 13." *RHPR* 70 (1990): 3–15; Chow, J. *Patronage and Power*. JSNTSup 75. JSOT, 1992; Fitzmyer, J. "Glory Reflected on the Face of Christ (2 Cor 3:7–4:6) and a Palestinian Jewish Motif." *TS* 42 (1981): 630–44; Gilchrist, J. "Paul and the Corinthians—The Sequence of Letters and Visit." *JSNT* 34 (1988): 47–69; Hays, R. *Echoes of Scripture in the Letters of Paul*. Yale University Press, 1989; Humphrey, E. "Apocalyptic Rhetoric and Intertextuality in 2 Corinthians." Pages 113–35 of *The Intertexture of Apocalyptic Discourse in the New Testament*, ed. D. Watson. SBLSymS 14. SBL, 2002; Kreitzer, L. *2 Corinthians*. Sheffield Academic Press, 1996; McCant, J. "Paul's Thorn of Rejected Apostleship." *NTS* 34 (1988): 550–72; Robbins, V. *Exploring the Texture of Texts*. Trinity, 1996; Segal, A. *Paul the Convert*. Yale University Press, 1990; Tabor, J. *Things Unutterable*. University Press of America, 1986; Watson, F. *Paul, Judaism, and the Gentiles*. Cambridge University Press, 1986; Webb, W. *Returning Home*. JSNTSup 85. JSOT, 1993; Witherington, B., III. *Conflict and Community in Corinth*. Eerdmans, 1995; Wright, N. T. "Reflected Glory: 2 Corinthians 3." Pages 175–92 of *The Climax of the Covenant*. Fortress, 1991; Young, F., and D. Ford. *Meaning and Truth in 2 Corinthians*. SPCK, 1987.

Edith M. Humphrey

Covenant

Covenant—the promissory relationship that Yahweh would be Israel's God and Israel would be Yahweh's people (Rendtorff)—has recently found itself in dispute with "promise" for the central category in Christian thought (McComiskey; Kaiser). Historical critics, with their emphasis upon historical context, development, and diversity within the biblical witness, often fail to engage the Bible as a unity in spite of the largely successful explorations of the covenant theme by a variety of biblical theologians (Baker; Childs; Eichrodt; Fuller; Wright).

Covenant in Biblical Texts

Context for the Covenant. Scholarship has recently recognized that the creation narrative depicts the universe as the temple of God (Watts). Pagans fashioned idols and images for their temples and places of worship, and so constructed an image of God. But the creation account turns pagan worship on its head. Instead of humans fashioning an image of God, the Creator God fashions a human in his own very image (Gen. 1:26–27). He places that very image in the temple of his creation, as its climactic revelation of who he is and what he is like. That image is a male-female (2:18–25; Jewett). However, the male-female image of God has been disputed as to its specific content (Hughes; Sayers). Regardless, it is this perception of humans that cries out the (largely) unheeded summons of "*Ecce homo!*" (John 19:5 Vulg.) in modern civilization.

It is precisely "human as image of God" that falls (Gen. 3), and (as theology unfolds) so the *imago Dei* suffers under sin. Humans apart from God fight with one another, make measly progress, and eventually threaten their own destruction (Gen. 4–11). But in his grace, Yahweh steps into history through a man named Abram/Abraham to form a new relationship with humans. Genesis 1–12, then, establishes not only the justification for covenant, but also a revelation of God as the Covenant Maker, who desires that his creation be established in a proper relationship with him.

Covenant: From Abraham to Jeremiah. With Abraham, Yahweh fashions a (grant) covenant (Gen. 12:1–3; 15; 17; 22), in which God *obligates himself* to Abraham and his descendants as Lord, Savior, and Protector in promising them a place (land, temple), people (Israel), and blessing (spiritual and material). Israel is called to covenant faithfulness (Gen. 15:6), circumcision (ch. 17), and torah obedience (Exod. 19–24; Deuteronomy). Noteworthy in the biblical revelation of covenant is *divine initiative*: humans do not, as pagans do with idols, imagine a covenant; instead, God breaks into history with a revelation of relationship in terms of covenant.

Israel, however, breaks covenant (e.g., Exod. 32). Nonetheless, Yahweh promises that he will remain faithful to the Abrahamic promise/covenant with Israel, if only through the two southern tribes of Judah and Benjamin and, most especially, in the royal promise of an eternal heritage in the Davidic line (2 Sam. 7; Ps. 89). As the flood expressed God's reshaping of his covenantal relationship with humans through judgment, so the exile provokes Yahweh to promise a "new covenant" (Jer. 31:31–34). It will be a covenant where God begins again with a new people (seen here as the restoration of the twelve tribes), an unbreakable covenant that is *internal, democratic*, and marked by forgiveness and peace (Isa. 11:6–9; Jer. 31:27–34; 32:40; Ezek. 34:25, 27).

The New Covenant. The Last Supper of Jesus is the occasion at which that anticipated covenant of Jeremiah is established: "This is my blood of the covenant . . . poured out for many" (Mark 14:24). Jesus' message heretofore concentrated on kingdom (McKnight, *Vision*), and so little is spelled out in this context, but the writer of Hebrews has what can be called a "New Covenant hermeneutic" (Hahn). Jesus is "the mediator of a better covenant" (8:6 NRSV), the "new covenant" (8:8), because it is enacted on the basis of better promises (8:6; cf. 9:15). This covenant renders the old as "obsolete," with its focus on temple, land, and nation (8:13). This author's focus is on the eschatological effectiveness (10:1, 10, 14) of the new covenant because it is effected through the blood of the eternal Son (9:12–14). Once again,

however, covenant faithfulness is required (cf. 6:1–8; 10:29; McKnight, "Warning").

Covenant in the Practice of the Theological Interpretation

Covenant, as a hermeneutical category, is a powerful heuristic tool for comprehending the large sweep of the biblical message, *but it is only one lens*. Not every biblical author sorts out history and God's ways through the lens of covenant. The term is found throughout the OT, but it is relatively rare in the NT. Recognizing the relatively rare use of covenant as a hermeneutical tool for the earliest Christians, however, does not minimize the depth and clarity this category permits those who read the Bible as a whole, to find a center from which the entire can be seen.

Even if Jesus prefers "kingdom" as his "hermeneutic," the term "covenant" at the Last Supper demonstrates that what Jesus means by kingdom can be aptly summarized, and even reshaped, by the category of covenant. *Covenant, then, is in dialectic with other terms*. Thus, "kingdom" focuses upon prophetic expectation of a Davidic restoration and draws the reader into the prophetic corpus to find what Jesus was expecting and doing. "Covenant" leads that same reader to see kingdom in terms of what God was doing from the very beginning—with Adam, with Noah, and especially with Abraham, Moses, and David. Kingdom and covenant, then, are two ways biblical revelation speaks of God's doings in this world. One might grant hermeneutical priority to kingdom (McKnight, "Hermeneutics").

Similar reflections might be made about other terms that shape how the early Christians depicted the relationship of humans with God. Thus, "justification," while it has been given preeminence at times among systematic theologians (e.g., Anselm and those who operate fundamentally with legal and academic categories), can be given a reinvigorated value when understood as *a powerful instance of God's covenant relationship with his people*. One might say that God's relationship with his people is not so much a "legal declaration of being in the right" as God's covenantal act of establishing a right relationship, where the focus of covenant leads the term "justification" in the direction of a relationship rather than a status.

The biblical material on covenant is the discourse of theological anthropology. While humanistic thinking centralizes humans, it also burdens them with an insufferable load and a life-sapping weight. But, biblical thinking on covenant shows humans for what they are: the male-female image of God, now fallen, but restored through a relationship with God. Instead of offering yet another human-created image in the pagan temple of humanism, covenant offers to the world a depiction of humans as God's image placed on earth to nurture his creation and sustain fellowship with one another. Humanism is thus shown for what it is: an attempt by moderns once again to re-create God in their own image. At the deepest level, then, covenant instructs that humans are not what they are meant to be, do not know what they are to know, and do not live as they are to live apart from the covenant.

If God's essential act is one of covenant making, then his people's task is fundamentally to lead others into that covenant relationship and to live faithfully in terms of that covenant. Humans are hereby given the proper place they deserve in God's creation: they are made in the male-female image of God, but they are fallen. In his grace, however, God has provided the path of restoration through a covenant relationship. If God's fundamental relationship to humans can be described as covenantal, then the task of his people is to lead others into that covenant and to live faithfully.

Covenant thinking not only establishes relationship with God. It also summons the human related to God through covenant to *a life of faithfulness*. If the covenant with Abraham fails to address the human need for moral direction, God began to make that clear when he reestablished the covenant with Moses (Exod. 19–24). But even that covenant failed to remedy the human moral condition. So, the expectation of Jeremiah becomes a reality in the death and resurrection of Jesus Christ. This event, in connection with Pentecost and the creation of the church as new-covenant community, establishes that covenant morality is only effective through the blood of the eternal Son and the internalization of the covenant through the Spirit.

What boggles the mind, however, is that God did not write off humans after their rebellion. Judgment does occur (seen in the flood and the exile, both of which anticipate final judgment), but God's last word is not judgment. God's final word to humans is covenant. The image of God is given full range when we reflect on covenant, and *sin* is made out to be what it really is. God makes humans special—and so they are given the responsibility to order, manage, and direct the created orders. So valuable are they to God that he seeks their restoration. But this only makes it clear that covenant theology shows sin for what it is: sin is not just human failing, nor is it just behavioral disturbance. Instead, sin is rebellion against the good guidance of the image-creating God, against God himself.

Covenant also reminds humans of the *patience of God*, for though he calls his people to faithfulness, their sin does not lead to immediate extirpation. Instead, God's patient hand remains stretched out for his people to turn back to him and follow his good guidance. God's patience leads him to permit torah revelation as a preliminary glimpse of his goodwill. Only over time do humans come to terms with their unflagging inability to follow the torah as God would have. So, in his gracious patience, God comes to terms with humans in an *internal work of the heart through his Son and through the indwelling of the Holy Spirit*. All of this is part of God's covenant. What God's patience allows, then, is the gradual unfolding of the one (not two) covenant (not covenants) for the entire world (Holwerda).

Finally, covenant enables us to see that *the end of history is a glimpse of God's intent from the beginning of history*. The end of history finds humans bowing before Jesus Christ (Phil. 2:5–11) and offering God their praises of the worthiness of his Son (Rev. 5). That is the climax of the covenant relationship. It means that from the beginning the telos (goal) of God has been to lead all humans to bow before him in eternal worship and praise. That praise finds its motivation in the blood-stained Lamb, who is also the conquering Lion of Judah.

Bibliography

Baker, D. L. *Two Testaments, One Bible*. InterVarsity, 1991; Childs, B. *The New Testament as Canon*. Fortress, 1985; Eichrodt, W. *Theology of the Old Testament*. 2 vols. SCM, 1967; Fuller, D. *The Unity of the Bible*. Zondervan, 1992; Hahn, S. "Kinship by Covenant." Ph.D. diss., Marquette University, 1995; Holwerda, D. *Jesus and Israel*. Eerdmans, 1995; Hughes, P. *The True Image*. Eerdmans, 1989; Jewett, P. *Man as Male and Female*. Eerdmans, 1975; Kaiser, W. *Toward an Old Testament Theology*. Zondervan, 1978; McComiskey, T. *The Covenants of Promise*. Baker, 1985; McKnight, S. "The Hermeneutics of Confessing Jesus as Lord." *Ex Auditu* 14 (1998): 1–17; idem. *A New Vision for Israel*. Eerdmans, 1999; idem. "The Warning Passages of Hebrews: A Formal Analysis and Theological Conclusions." *TJ* 13 (1992): 21–59; Rendtorff, R. *The Covenant Formula*. T&T Clark, 1998; Sayers, D. *The Mind of the Maker*. HarperSanFrancisco, 1987; Watts, R. "The New Exodus/New Creational Restoration of the Image of God: A Biblical-Theological Perspective on Salvation." Pages 15–41 in *What Does It Mean to Be Saved?* ed. J. Stackhouse Jr. Baker, 2002; Wright, N. T. *The New Testament and the People of God*. Fortress, 1992.

Scot McKnight

Covenant Theology *See* Last Things, Doctrine of

Creation

The developed doctrine of creation ex nihilo emerged, from roots in the Jewish Scriptures, as the early Christian alternative to pagan and gnostic cosmologies. It "is not something self-evident or the discovery of disinterested reason, but part of the fabric of Christian response to revelation" (Gunton 8). Among contemporary rivals to its trinitarian understanding of divine providence, we find materialism and remnants of Deism, varieties of animism and Eastern monism, plus New Age and other adoptions of pantheism and/or panentheism.

Creation as a Matter of Interpretation

On the Christian understanding, creation was an act of divine freedom; the universe had a beginning in time and is limited in space. God's act was not arbitrary, but purposeful as a project of love; creation is in close relation to God, but relatively free to be itself so as to develop in love for God and display divine glory (Gunton). By maintaining the world's relative goodness, Christian tradition resisted the pagan tendency to view matter as evil or deficient, unleashing scientific inquiry since the world became valuable for study in its own right (not simply for symbolizing other ideal structures).

Biblical Narrative and Science? Today, however, biblical teaching and scientific inquiry are widely regarded as polar opposites. Basic approaches to the creation narratives of Gen. 1–2 may be treated on a rough spectrum. (1) Strict creationists, often identified with "creation science" belief in a "young earth" (especially in the USA), interpret Genesis "literally" first and then evaluate science, correlating various details but rejecting mainstream conclusions. (2) At the other end of the spectrum, science is consulted first and Genesis interpreted as thoroughgoing "myth." Naturalistic evolutionists turn science into a worldview; various theistic evolutionists may or may not adopt "methodological naturalism," while some of their "allegorical" understandings take Genesis quite seriously in theological terms. (3) In between, the so-called "gap" theory understood much of evolution to be compatible with an indefinite time period between Gen. 1:1 and 1:3, while (4) the "day-age" theory likewise held to an "old earth," by taking the days of Gen. 1 to be epochs of indefinite length. These views still tended to try correlating particular details between the biblical and scientific narratives. (5) Recently rising in influence among Christian interpreters of Genesis are versions of a "literary framework" approach. Noting that Augustine, for instance, recognized literary patterning in Genesis long before the challenge of modern science, such an approach takes seriously the historical context of the creation narratives as well. (Meanwhile, regarding philosophy, the recent "intelligent design" movement does not necessarily align with a particular reading strategy.)

Literary approaches recognize that Genesis counteracts pagan myths focused on procreation instead of creation (regarding the genealogy of deities rather than nature). Days 1–3, of "preparation," address the darkness, watery abyss, and formless earth of Gen. 1:2; days 4–6, of "population," involve the filling of what God has formed (e.g., Hamilton 54–56); day 7, connecting God via Sabbath to Israel's "workweek" (Exod. 20:8–11), has much-debated theological significance. In any case, scientific theories are open to ongoing Christian consideration, while the biblical texts are interpreted with integrity as authoritative. Theologians debate implications for the nature and origin of evil, cosmology, animal death, and human death. Immortality of the soul in a Greek sense is not the teaching of Genesis, and passages such as Ps. 90 point Christians toward greater appreciation of finitude as divine gift. Yet canonical reading requires that Rom. 1–8 regarding life and death, and the many NT uses of Adam and Eve, be respected so as to maintain the goodness of God's original creation, the specificity of humanity's creation as image of God, and the historicity of the fall. More broadly, creation is a divine act that in the cosmos gives not only "general revelation" of God but also a context connecting biblical interpretation to all of life.

The Triune God and Redemption? Links are strong, then, between creation and the rest of the Christian story. While creation in the OT connects to the rise of monotheism, the universality of Israel's God does not support the many natural, basically unitarian, theologies that arose in the modern age. Though appropriating aspects of the Christian doctrine, these always stay subject to the shifting vagaries of science or even philosophical naturalism; in the context of such new narratives, the doctrine's crucial contributions are rejected or lost.

Hence, creation confronts us with whether or not to achieve biblical theology via strategies of correlation. Accepting Christianity's scandal of particularity does not require obscurantism, but a trinitarian vision of the created world that responds to cultural challenges winsomely, with unique beauty and logic. For instance, when arguing for "genuinely causal" (as opposed to "merely explanatory") gaps in cosmological knowledge, given a distinction between divine and human causality, we do not automatically revert to a discredited "God of the gaps" (DiNoia 72). It has been Gunton's frequent claim that loss of trinitarian distinctiveness weakened the doctrines of creation and providence internally, which has exposed the Christian faith to opposition from the very scientific inquiry it helped to foster.

By contrast, a trinitarian emphasis helps to connect, rather than oppose, creation and redemption. Moreover, trinitarian divine agency enables personal relatedness and creaturely freedom in noncompetitive forms of causality, as we learn most dramatically in the incarnation. The Son gives the cosmos structure and coherence (see, e.g., OT hints about wisdom; John 1; Col. 1; Heb. 1), while the Spirit gives ongoing life and freedom for created particulars to be themselves (e.g., Pss. 33:6; 104:30). The Trinity need not be forced directly into passages such as Gen. 1:26–27 to be a coherent extension of the story at which Scripture—including the OT—hints.

Creation and the Form of Interpretation

Aside from its role as a test case, then, in various ways the doctrine of creation could shape the form of theological exegesis.

"Natural" Order. Creation as sustained by God possesses order, which has been reaffirmed in the resurrection of Christ's body (O'Donovan); we are redeemed as a new creation within the present order, awaiting full transformation that preserves continuity with current identities. Thus, the "structure" of reality has integrity of goodness to which our action responds; it is the "direction" of entities, not their being, which is subject to the order of fall and redemption (Wolters). Interpretation, in a sense parallel to Adamic naming of other creatures, is a God-given responsibility involving meaningful human action, but it also discovers and responds to the "kinds" of things that are.

Biblical interpretation is special given the story of fall and redemption, the unique sort of book(s) being read, and the ministry of Word and Spirit. But we are still reading texts. If space permitted, one could show that understandings of "nature" and "grace" correlate readily with biblical hermeneutics. One example is a Lutheran tendency toward the relative freedom of nature and grace, thereby sharply distinguishing historical criticism and theological exegesis from each other. Another is a "Reformed epistemology," seeking distinctively Christian approaches that transform nature (textual scholarship) by grace (e.g., one's presuppositions).

"Cultural" Development and Diversity. Thus, the created order seems, at minimum, to determine some limits to the possible meanings of biblical texts. From the beginning, though, God has delighted in the variety of creation and its human stewardship. After Pentecost has apparently begun to reverse Babel, cultural development—including interpretative difference tied to human particularity—can produce plurality worth celebrating, and not always problems tied to fallenness (Smith). Variety need not entail violence; it can create the conditions necessary for love and joy. From a Christian standpoint "nature" and "culture" blend form and freedom, givenness and gravenness.

Cultural development is worth celebrating when it connects us with delight to the natural world God has made. Forms of interpretation can be oppressively technical and stifle the freedom of such delight, or can foster the use of technologies that overwhelm nonhuman creatures, natural beauty, and/or cultural difference. This should give Western interpreters pause concerning our scholarly exports and current practices—both hoarding our exegetical resources and hiding from the gifts that others may offer—plus, more mundanely, how much power and paper we consume. Biblical texts require that we take seriously the tangible world where we might embody them, and its rhythms for work and rest.

Creativity and Divine Glory. Concern for the tangible and for time also raises the question of "creativity." Such language can risk blurring the grandeur of God, who creates in a way that humans do not. We rearrange and realize the possibilities of preexisting materials. Yet the fact that "there is nothing new under the sun" (Eccles. 1:9) does not license monotony, but gives measured appreciation of human potential. Ecclesiastes soberly considers the endless proliferation of books and other cultural projects, concluding that pretense to mastery—of knowledge or any other domain of life—would be folly (12:12). Cultural production, including biblical scholarship, has relative value as a way of fostering community and celebration of ordinary life; its goal should be neither to finish a project of mastering texts, nor to create much of the novelty on which our academic programs and reputations currently thrive.

Nevertheless, the doctrine of creation reminds us that we live in a "person-friendly cosmos" (DiNoia). God does glory and receive glory in ongoing cultural efforts, which can be pleasing and make some progress. To the degree we undertake biblical interpretation communally with God, each other, and the nonhuman creation—to the degree that our doctrine of creation leads us to interpret for and from shalom—we will delight in new harmonies of various voices. Joining together to hear biblical texts speak the wonders of our God, we may also look to "the Maker of heaven and earth" for loving help (Pss. 121; 124); because of God's power we need fear nothing else (Seitz).

See also Providence; Science, the Bible and; Worldview

Bibliography

Blocher, H. *In the Beginning.* InterVarsity, 1984; DiNoia, J. A. "By Whom All Things Were Made." Pages 63–73 in *Nicene Christianity,* ed. C. Seitz. Brazos, 2001; Gunton, C. *The Triune Creator.* Eerdmans, 1998; Hamilton, V. *The Book of Genesis Chapters 1–17.* NICOT. Eerdmans, 1990; O'Donovan, O. *Resurrection and Moral Order.* 2d ed. Eerdmans, 1994; Seitz, C. "Our Help Is in the Name of the LORD, the Maker of Heaven and Earth." Pages 19–34 in *Nicene Christianity,* ed. C. Seitz. Brazos, 2001; Smith, J. K. A. *The Fall of Interpretation.* InterVarsity, 2000; Wolters, A. *Creation Regained.* Eerdmans, 1985.

Daniel J. Treier

Creed

Brief summary statements of the heart of the Christian faith, possibly used during baptismal services, can be traced right back to the NT, ranging from the simple assertion "Jesus is Lord" (Rom. 10:9) to fuller assertions (1 Cor. 8:6 or 15:3–5). Even in the canonical writings, these are already being used to regulate belief (there are several examples in 1 John), and so, presumably, to regulate biblical interpretation. Creeds, and their role in the reading of Scripture, might be seen as a development of such indications.

In the early patristic period, there are regular appeals made to the "rule of faith": the essence of Christian truth as taught by the apostles who had been with Jesus is encapsulated in the "rule of faith"; if the Scriptures teach the same apostolic faith, they cannot contradict this rule. For Tertullian, Irenaeus, and other early patristic theologians, the conditional might have been alive, in that they lived before the canon was determined, and so it would have been open to them to object to a particular book on grounds of unorthodox teaching. Historically, although the develop-

ment of both is complex, the ecumenical creeds (Nicene; Apostles'; the Chalcedonian Definition) and the canon of the NT come into being at about the same time. The creeds offer a summary of the central points of faith that cannot be diverged from; these points are developed largely through scriptural exegesis (e.g., Athanasius and the Arians argue as to which of their positions is more faithful to Scripture), but once fixed they become virtually regulative. The creeds were intended to represent binding exegetical decisions: this (in summary and in part) is what the Christian Scriptures say. No theology, and so no interpretation of Scripture, could be judged adequate if it falls outside the creedal boundaries.

Generally, the Christian churches have accepted this decision, at least until recently. The common formulation confessing the faith "contained in the Holy Scriptures and witnessed to in the ecumenical creeds" expresses this decision precisely. On this account, the idea that those who fixed the creeds were wrong is unthinkable. God in his good providence guided his church in this decision, just as he did in the fixing of the canon of Scripture. The creeds remain an authoritative summary of the central dogmatic propositions to which the Scriptures witness. This has profound hermeneutical implications: some interpretations are authorized, and others excluded, if the creedal formulae have interpretative authority. For instance, certain Arian positions concerning the relative status of such Johannine texts as "the Father is greater than I" (14:28) and "I and the Father are one" (10:30) are excluded a priori.

The role and status of Protestant confessions (e.g., the Westminster Confession) are similar, but within a narrower compass. Many Presbyterian churches are still committed to the Westminster standards (and Lutheran churches to the Formula of Concord, etc.). Here the point is explicit: since the confessions often assert that there is no other authority than Holy Scripture, their own role can only be as interpretations, and interpretative tools, for Scripture. Their status as doctrinal standards can only be understood as a corporate insistence that the Scriptures be read this way, and not another, within their traditions. Scripture remains the absolute and unchallengeable basis and norm of all faith and theology. Nevertheless, creeds and confessions act as subordinate norms, codifying and interpreting the teaching of Scripture in an authoritative way.

See also Rule of Faith; Tradition

Bibliography

The most significant creeds and confessions are in Pelikan, J., and V. Hotchkiss, eds. *Creeds and Confessions of Faith in the Christian Tradition*. 4 vols. Yale University Press, 2003 (with *Credo*, a valuable introductory volume by Pelikan). See also Barth, K. *Credo*, trans. J. S. McNabb. Hodder & Stoughton, 1936; Webster, J. "Confession and Confessions." In *Nicene Christianity*, ed. C. Seitz. Brazos, 2002.

Stephen R. Holmes

Critical Realism

In recent years critical realism has made significant inroads in the theological interpretation of Scripture (Meyer; Wright). There are two main reasons why this development is particularly significant. First, it reflects an increasing willingness among biblical scholars to conceive of their interpretive work as a philosophical enterprise based on epistemological choices and frameworks. Second, critical realism has thrown into question many of the underlying positivistic assumptions of naive realism, which have underpinned much theological interpretation, but it has done so without selling out to the relativism inherent in idealist, phenomenalist, and even instrumentalist epistemologies. What are the distinctives of critical realism that have propelled it to the forefront of philosophical reflections on theological interpretation? The critical-realist combination of insisting on the external reality of "the thing known" while acknowledging that human knowledge can only be a subjective appropriation of reality can hardly be accused of having attained esteem by sheer eccentricity. Given the commonsense character that theological realism (Grosshans) or indeed metaphysical realism in general (Alston) has for many, a brief historical contextualization is necessary to account for its rise.

Contextualizing Critical Realism

Modernity has been characterized by approaches to human knowledge largely based on an abstract objectivism and empiricism, a combination that in turn was seen to facilitate the dialogue between religion and science about the cognitive value of epistemological theories. Only in the final thirty years of the twentieth century did critical realism become an essential part of the science-religion dialogue (Barbour; Peacocke; van Huyssteen; Soskice). This is not to deny that critical realism essentially existed along with naive realism as far back as pre-Enlightenment times. But it was only recently that it came to be presented by many as the most plausible way of making sense of scientific theories and religious doctrines as symbolic representations of external reality. As such, they ought to be taken "seriously but not literally" as approximations of reality (Robbins 656). Critical realism thus moves from perceived explanatory success to claims of realism. In the process it lays the ground for theology as epistemically compatible with science (van Huyssteen 258). Robbins and Murphy, however, question critical realism's inherently Cartesian distinction between the mind as an inner realm of representations of reality and the physicality of existence, thus potentially allowing a serious gap between how the world is and how it is perceived (Robbins 655–66; Murphy 287–90). Yet, the avoidance of precisely such a gap by postulating that reality was mind-independent, while accessible in principle (however subjectively), was billed by critical realists as a major selling point over against both relativist and empiricist conceptualizations of truth. Toward the end of the twentieth century, it was especially Alston who questioned the assumption that antifoundationalism required antirealism. However, another challenge comes from those who approach the matter in a strictly verificationist manner. This line of attack denies the possibility of excluding the appearance of future evidence (which would demonstrate the inadequacy of earlier truth judgments). For a theological response, see McGrath (148–50).

Epistemological debates in the natural sciences are paralleled in theological circles, for instance, with reference to the application of religious language to matters of spirituality and God. Is such language—or indeed all language?—strictly metaphorical (Soskice) or does religious language allow us a "real" glimpse into external spiritual realities, including the divine? However, it is in the field of modern theology that some of the most significant debates have taken place. This is perhaps best illustrated by comparing the positions of MacIntyre on the one hand and Torrance on the other. The latter seemingly celebrates objective thinking as based on "facts," whereas the former privileges tradition as the communal dimension of human knowledge. On closer inspection, though, Torrance agrees that knowledge is indeed communal (the "social coefficient of knowledge"—Torrance 102–3), as opposed to being "neutral" in the sense of truth-as-correspondence. Torrance may occasionally use the language of scientific positivism, but in fact he is deeply suspicious of claims about there being logical bridges between ideas and existence (76). Like MacIntyre, he understands the need to utilize intuition and creativity in advancing rational inquiry (Achtemeier 355–74).

It is the Canadian theologian Lonergan whose blend of cognitional theory, epistemology, and metaphysics is profoundly influencing biblical studies, especially through the writings of Meyer and Wright. In light of his relevance for developing a hermeneutic of theological interpretation of Scripture, a closer look at his contribution is warranted.

Lonergan and the Quest for Religious Knowledge

For Lonergan the critical realist, human knowledge involves experience, intelligence, reflection, and deliberation. Experience is the sensing of outer reality and as such is the first step toward knowledge. It generates basic questions about reality such as How? Why? What for? Hypothetical answers are then given. But the pursuit of knowledge requires the move from asking What is it? to Is it? In other words, there is a progression (by way of "understanding") from asking questions incapable of being answered affirmatively or negatively to those that require precisely such a judgment by way of answer. The resulting judgment itself is an approximation of what Lonergan calls the "virtually unconditioned," or certainty. It is refined by asking further questions to ensure that as much data as possible are allowed to inform the judgment.

Knowledge claims are judgments of probability, even in the modern sciences, for such claims are invariably based on, and abstracted from, partial or random evidence. As human beings we are incapable of accounting for the universe in a single ordered sequence of reasoning. Moreover, since knowledge is based on experience, it is inconceivable that sound judgment results from looking "objectively" at the world of experience. Experiential objectivity (i.e., orientation toward experience as an object) as the expression of a crude obsession with sense data (naive realism or empiricism) is therefore not an option. Cognitive meaning cannot be restricted to what is "sense perceptible," for such perception is only preliminary in the acquisition of knowledge. Idealism, on the other hand, is equally deficient in its denial of what is real, for experience is based on precisely what is real, whatever metaphysical realm is reflected by a given reality.

Lonergan's insistence that epistemological judgment is an approximation to the virtually

unconditioned has repercussions for the notion of religious knowledge or theology. As we are not aware of conditions against which the existence of the transcendent can be verified or judged, metaphysical arguments about the transcendent fall short. In other words, since the transcendent is not just "virtually" unconditioned but also "really" so, we have no way of judging its existence independent from our philosophical premises. Religious knowledge evades the constraints of ordinary human knowledge. Knowing God is a function of conversion, not human reasoning. Against Lonergan, it has been pointed out that his brand of critical realism leaves no way of adjudicating between competing religious claims (Stinnett 107). This may be a slightly unfair criticism in the sense that Lonergan does not regard critical realism as a way of solving the philosophical impasse caused by such competing religious claims. Having said that, he seems to claim that the impasse is relativized by privileging prior divine love in the process of attaining religious knowledge (123). What matters in terms of a theological reading of Scripture is that for Lonergan the very act of such a reading ought to foster openness for God's prior love as a condition of developing religious knowledge. The resulting purification of our subjectivity is a precondition for the kind of objectivity that transcends the experiential and moves toward the absolute, that is, the "objectivity" that results from judgment.

Another Canadian scholar, Ben F. Meyer, has digested Lonergan's philosophical contribution to the enterprise of reading Scripture theologically and made it accessible for biblical studies.

Critical Realism and Biblical Theology (Meyer)

Readers of Meyer's two major books on the subject (*Critical Realism* and *Reality and Illusion*) are immediately alerted to his indebtedness to Lonergan's thought. Meyer himself suggests that Lonergan is the master whose work Meyer cannot improve. Instead, he appropriates Lonergan's philosophical approach for the purpose of recovering biblical theology from the clutches of positivism, neo-Kantianism, and the existentialism that has dominated much of German theology (*Reality*, 151ff.). He wants to promote biblical theology as a hermeneutical enterprise that puts a high premium on the author's intentionality as a way of connecting with the extratextual (including transcendent) realities. Yet he does not have illusions of doing so either neutrally (or free from dogma and in that sense "academically") or by reducing the biblical witness to a theological projection of the mind. The interpreter needs to exhibit both historical realism and a prior commitment to the Bible as divine proclamation. The theological truth claims of the biblical text have to be faced, not demythologized or ideologized. For too long historical criticism has been dominated by atheistic ideological paradigms and movements. What is needed is a critical realist cognitional theory that starts with an all-powerful loving God whose prime characteristic is his continued interest in creation as evidenced in his biblical self-disclosure. As such, the Bible is neither just allegorical-figurative (Alexandrian approach) nor literal-historical (Antiochene approach). It is conceivably both, the main adjudicator being the human intentionality embodied in the text. It will not do, for instance, to interpret Romans as an abstract discussion of God's grace, when Paul's intentionality was to speak into the specific social situation of the first-century Roman church. That church was struggling with issues of God's covenantal faithfulness in light of Jewish-Gentile tensions resulting from the law-free admission of Gentiles into the christocentrically defined people of God. Nor will it do to reduce the significance of the Gospels to issues of historicity versus theology when in fact their authors' intentionality was to hold the two together.

Importantly, for Meyer human intentionality in biblical interpretation and theology is not just a key aspect that connects authors and interpreters; it also is equally significant for bridging the gap between the NT kerygmatic claims about Christ and Jesus' historical consciousness. Alluding to what Mussner once called the crux of Christian theology, he asks: "If Christology has no roots at all in the consciousness of the historical Jesus, how in the end could it vindicate its claim to be other than and much more than mere ideology?" (*Critical*, 161). There needs to be significant continuity between the NT authors' intentionalities and that of Jesus. Meyer is deeply suspicious of theological readings of the NT that do not account for or indeed demonstrate such continuity.

The Role of "Story" (Wright)

Meyer's rehabilitation of human intentionality to biblical interpretation lives on in the work of N. T. Wright. The latter's indebtedness to the former is not dissimilar to Meyer's own use of Lonergan. Yet Wright goes significantly beyond a restatement of Meyer's hermeneutics by developing a "story"-based approach to biblical interpretation, which leads to more tangible exegetical results and decisions. His focus on narrative-historical categories is grounded in the conviction that human transformation and intentionality (as expressed in texts) are most fundamentally affected by the stories that make up human reality and relationality. Our worldviews, and therefore our perception of reality, are most directly affected by the stories we live and encounter.

This insight has significant repercussions for biblical interpretation. (1) It forces the interpreter to recover both "story" and "stories" as major factors in our approach to the biblical literature. It is probably no coincidence that the prime genre in the biblical literature is that of storytelling. Far from being intended as vehicles of lightweight doctrinal insights, they have the prime function of drawing the hearer (or reader) into a transformative dialogue in ways that transcend the capabilities of propositionally phrased truth claims. (2) It leads to a recalibration of interpretative priorities. Instead of approaching the task of exegesis from the bottom up (by privileging dictionaries and grammars), the theological interpreter seeks primarily to account for the textually embodied intentionality of the author. One does this by relating it to all of its pertinent levels of story, starting with the biblical grand narrative and moving toward the sociorhetorical situation of the text to be interpreted. Therefore, in contrast to the positivistic objectification of knowledge, human intentionality is now seen against the canvas of the storied knowledge of the communicative partners. Knowledge simply does not exist in a vacuum; neither does intentionality.

(3) It follows that the notion of subjectivity in interpretation per se is not an evil to be rejected or lamented; it is to be welcomed as an aspect of human creationality that allows communication to be transformative, that is, "story-changing." In this sense interpretation has to be subjective to be relevant. Yet critical realism insists that authorial intentionality as an external reality must be the controlling factor in interpretation. Determinate meaning exists, even if it is not objectively accessible. (4) This is not to deny that the intentionality of empirical or historical authors may be partially or entirely obscured. But insofar as a text (or speech for that matter) conveys authorial presence via the implied author—who is the empirical author's creation—authorial intentionality remains the crucial interpretative corrective. The provisionality of an interpretation in itself does not imply a value judgment. All interpretations of a given text are provisional, but relative to the

others, only one of them will have the strongest claim to accuracy.

Summary and Outlook

Critical realism distinguishes between external reality on the one hand and human knowledge on the other. The former exists objectively, but it is only accessible through the grid of knowledge or worldview. Far from being objective, knowledge is in fact more than the merely "factual," for it is the ever-changing matrix that connects mental consciousness to external realities, with the latter holding the former accountable. The matrix itself consists of beliefs and questions about reality, as well as epistemic frameworks for determining what qualifies as proper knowledge discourse. Almost by definition critical realism rejects any dichotomy between scientific and nonscientific knowledge. Put differently, it welcomes cross-disciplinary integration, for the critical realist's configuration of truth has to remain open to further refinement by whatever tools are appropriate to the subject matter. In theory, what qualifies as "appropriate" is determined by worldview. In practice, of course, worldview is a function of religiocultural conditioning and—as the theologian insists—revelation. In constructing representations of reality, the role of revelation is at least twofold: (1) to provide and safeguard biblical discourse, and (2) to empower the interpreter spiritually and transformatively. In recent years speech-act theory has made great strides in bringing precision to our understanding of Spirit-endowed theological interpretation. It should prove fascinating to observe the increasingly significant contributions of speech-act theory to critical-realist hermeneutics, for the subjectivity of theological (or indeed any) interpretation needs to be both captivated and cultivated by the Spirit of God.

See also Epistemology; Objectivity

Bibliography

Achtemeier, P. "The Truth of Tradition: Critical Realism in the Thought of Alasdair MacIntyre and T. F. Torrance." *SJT* 47 (1994): 355–74; Alston, W. *A Sensible Metaphysical Realism*. Marquette University Press, 2001; Barbour, I. *Religion in an Age of Science*. Harper & Row, 1990; Grosshans, H.-P. *Theologischer Realismus*. Mohr, 1996; Lonergan, B. *Method in Theology*. Herder & Herder, 1972; MacIntyre, A. *After Virtue*. 2d ed. University of Notre Dame Press, 1984; McGrath, A. *The Foundations of Dialogue in Science and Religion*. Blackwell, 1998; Meyer, B. *Critical Realism and the New Testament*. Pickwick, 1989; idem. *Reality and Illusion in New Testament Scholarship*. Glazier/Liturgical, 1994; Murphy, N. "From Critical Realism to a Methodological Approach: Response to Robbins, Van Huyssteen, and Hefner." *Zygon* 23 (1988): 287–90; Peacocke, A. *Intimations of Reality*. University of Notre Dame Press, 1984; Robbins, J. "Pragmatism, Critical Realism, and the Cognitive Value of Religion and Science." *Zygon* 34 (1999): 655–66; Soskice, J. M. *Metaphor and Religious Language*. Clarendon, 1985; Stinnett, T. "Lonergan's 'Critical Realism' and Religious Pluralism." *The Thomist* 56 (1992): 97–115; Torrance, T. F. *Reality and Scientific Theology*. Scottish Academic Press, 1985; van Huyssteen, W. "Experience and Explanation: The Justification of Cognitive Claims in Theology." *Zygon* 23 (1988): 247–61; Wright, N. T. *The New Testament and the People of God*. Fortress, 1996.

Thorsten Moritz

Cross-Cultural Interpretation *See* Culture and Hermeneutics

Cultural-Linguistic Theology *See* Culture and Hermeneutics; Language-Game; Narrative Theology; Yale School

Cultural Studies *See* Culture and Hermeneutics

Culture and Hermeneutics

The status of culture as a consequential factor in biblical and theological interpretation is receiving increasing attention, thanks to three major phenomena: theoretical developments related to epistemology; the onset of postmodernism in the West; and the proliferation of Christian communities in the global South, whose theological readings of Scripture and of their situations (postcolonial and other) are becoming more readily available. A host of theological visions now claim attention in their own right. For those pursuing the theological interpretation of Scripture as that which grounds and directs Christian identity and practice, this complexity calls for a reappraisal of the contribution of culture to hermeneutics, the constitution and function of tradition, and the character of theological diversity and unity.

In this discussion, we will sketch the concept of "culture"; identify issues in several important exemplars and proposals; and note the implications these suggest for the church's interpretative practice.

The Culture Concept

Culture is notoriously difficult to define. Noted here are relevant features of several major theoretical orientations and shifts in its conceptual development.

Culture in early anthropology was defined as a "complex whole" encompassing a society's beliefs and values, behavioral norms, institutions, and artifacts (Tylor, in Geertz 4). Among many subsequent modifications, social structure (referring to relatively enduring social arrangements) is differentiated from culture (reserved for the symbolic dimension: the quest to construct and communicate meaning). On a semiotic view, a culture, comprised of "interworked systems of construable signs," is not a causal power but a context calling for "thick descriptions" (Geertz 5, 14). Cultural analysis renders the particular universe of symbolic action (or life-view) of a group at a specific time, expressed in the forms and practices associated with its way of life (Storey).

Other approaches to social description have emphasized structure and function. Earlier theories assumed the closely coordinated relations of forms and practices: culture qua unified system whose reproduction supported the group's persistence over time.

Late- and postmodern sociological conflict theories have criticized such conceptions for construing groups and cultures as static entities; as systems comprised of highly interdependent parts; or as constituted by consensus. They emphasize, rather, contradictions and rival traditions within cultures; intragroup conflicts of interest; and the role of power, ideology, and coercion in organizing social life (Tanner).

Under the present conditions of globalization and postmodernity, the more extensive encounter with cultural pluralism has intensified our awareness not only of variation, but also of the porosity and hybridity of cultures within a continual dialectic between the local and the global (Schreiter, *Catholicity*). The prevailing academic practice treats cultures not in essentialist terms (as consisting in distinctive traits) but in social constructionist ones (as constituted by symbolizing practices occasioning the ongoing production of meaning). Human actors, located within a sociocultural landscape comprised of shifting alignments under continually changing circumstances, are central to this account. Culture's functionality—its contingent, negotiated character—is accentuated.

Culture and Epistemology

Although culture is the medium of human existence, and evidence of complex intercultural relations and processes goes back to antiquity, the theoretical study of culture and an articulated concept as such is a distinctly modern development in the West. Thus, apart from a few exceptions (e.g., Troeltsch; Kuyper; et al.; see Niebuhr), until relatively recently, theological scholarship has not engaged systematically with issues such as cultural production, particularity, and pluralism, and their hermeneutical implications.

Late modern/postmodern developments in the human sciences have established the now widespread recognition that because the world for humans is as much conceptual as concrete, facts are theory-laden. In large measure rationalities are tradition-constituted, rooted in particular symbolic worlds (Berger and Luckmann; MacIntyre). Enculturation and social location substantively fund and shape our capacities for perception and judgment and our consequent social practice, as communities and as individuals.

Thus, the modern notion of objectivity had assumed that "to get genuinely in touch with the object, or to do so in a more reliable way, one must eliminate the particularity of one's perspective" (Wolterstorff 85). Instead, it is the case that "every human community shares and cherishes certain assumptions, traditions, expectations, anxieties, and so forth, which encourage its members to construe reality in particular ways, and which create contexts within which certain kinds of statements are perceived as making sense. There is no such thing as the 'neutral' or 'objective' observer; equally, there is no such thing as the *detached* observer" (Wright 36; Thiselton). Insofar as readers have viewed culture principally as a deforming impediment to theological interpretation, or have sought to confine cultural knowledge to either the tacit dimension of preunderstanding or the "contextualization" stages of the interpretative process, a modification is in order. The particular, partial cultural programming all acquire via primary socialization (and thereafter) is both an enabling and obstructing condition for knowledge, a theological asset and liability. Moreover, readers' culturally situated and specific knowledge cannot be divested; it operates within every phase of biblical and theological interpretation, whether inadvertently or intentionally. The following examples exhibit the mutually implicated relationship of culture and interpretation.

Culture and Biblical Interpretation

General (culturally informed) assumptions about texts and reading initially influence the process and outcome of interpretation. Critical-realist, conservative reader-response approaches acknowledge readers' contributions, but "believe there is something in the text prior to the act of reading—gaps, indeterminacies, instructions, flags, and signals, for example—that governs their response" (Vanhoozer, "Reader," 318). Such readers will follow the text's cues, seeking to understand (via, e.g., grammatico-historical exegesis) before overstanding it (pursuing their own questions, interests, and aims), while more radical methods privilege the reader's freedom to overstand and/or undo it (ideology criticism's proper service; Clines).

In addition to general stances, readers' specific social locations and theological orientations both open up and occlude reception of Scripture. While the yields of self-conscious commitments might be presumed, the actual history of interpretation indicates that readers' particular positions and interests—theological and sociological—may interact in unexpected ways.

In the history of Christian interpretative practice in the United States, readings of the biblical exodus account exemplify several such approaches. They also illustrate the complicated dynamics of interpretation: the initial typological use of the exodus story by European settlers escaping Old World oppressions (Goldingay) was followed by their appeal to the conquest narrative to justify subjugation of Native American peoples and seizure of the land (Warrior). In 1637, New England Puritans, claiming OT warrant for making slaves of captives taken in a "just war," shipped the defeated Pequots to the West Indies in exchange for African slaves (Takaki 58).

As a Native American reflecting on the history of this text's reception and use, Warrior expresses misgivings concerning the church, Scripture, and the methodology of narrative theology (advocated by ethicists, liberationists, and others), in view of the proved capacity of the formerly oppressed to become oppressors (Goldingay). His account is instructive not only as a protest of de facto imperialist hermeneutical practices, but especially as a caveat: faith communities who remain sociohistorically unself-critical and self-referential in their theological and devotional readings of Scripture are susceptible to producing and actualizing ideological interpretations.

These instances also suggest that pursuit of singular interests and/or employment of exclusive methods will circumscribe theological understanding. "What we see in the text, especially in its implications, is what our experience, our gender, our social position, and our political affiliations have prepared us to see" (Elliott 12) in the first instance. Thus, readers' explicit awareness of their personal, social, and ecclesial locations and interests (theological and other), including views represented in the history of interpretation, coupled with intentional interaction with interpreters outside their tradition—all such awareness is needed to help counteract tendencies to docetism and/or ethnocentrism (Craffert). An expanding knowledge of history's ambiguities can discipline and deepen interpreters' social self-understanding, enabling a greater critical-realist grasp of Scripture's narrative and prophetic salience.

The cases above also demonstrate that a selective appropriation of Scripture—whether formally (sole use of any hermeneutical framework) or materially (anything less than *tota Scriptura*)—lends itself to misreading both parts and whole, which may result in the attenuation or inversion of genuine Christian identity and practice.

Culture and Theology

Theological construction—the integrative attempt to articulate the vision and instruction that the world projected by the canonical text provides for the world of lived existence—is another level at which the sociocultural factors contribute considerably to interpretative judgments. Although diverging as "prescriptions," several proposals argue that context and the logic of cultural construction are constitutive of Christian identity and theological discourse.

Local Theologies. Robert Schreiter (*Local*) has called attention to the "local" character of theology, reframing the tradition as a series of local theologies; thus emergent "contextual" theologies can enter a nonpreemptive "gospel dialogue" with the tradition. Formally, many modes for theological reflection comprise the tradition: variations on sacred Scripture, wisdom, and praxis alongside *scientia*, sure knowledge (implying a decentering and supplementation of the academic genre). Materially, Schreiter's proposed process for discerning Christian identity involves a theory relating local performances to the tradition, criteria (cohesion, translatability into worship, orthopraxis, openness to criticism, ability to challenge other theologies), norms (Scripture, creeds, etc.), and conditions for a successful mutual engagement of a theology and the tradition. His process offers evaluative resources, while suggesting further reflection on the status and uses of the tradition's constituents.

Contextual Theologies. Attending to context ("present human experience") as a valid source for theology is an intrinsic Christian imperative, says Stephen Bevans. "Contextual theologies" prioritize variously the gospel, the tradition, a specified culture, and social change, as his fivefold typology shows. The translation model stresses preservation of the tradition; the anthropological, cultural "authenticity"; praxis, the need for social change; the synthetic model, all aspects equally; and the transcendental, the self-expression of a unique historical, cultural subject. Since "exclusive use will distort the theological enterprise" (28), a "healthy pluralism" will select circumstantially among these equally valid options.

Bevans's analysis formally accounts for theological pluralism and highlights the significance of concrete conditions for theology. However, context qua *"locus theologicus"* calls for qualification: though context is an indispensable source for theology, it is problematic that some models assign context revelatory status on a par with Scripture. Because limits, fallibility, and fallenness attend all group life, contexts are not self-interpreting or privileged sources *in se*, but normed by Scripture.

Schreiter observes that under the impact of globalization, the concept of context itself has become increasingly deterritorialized and hyperdifferentiated (*Catholicity*). Notions of social identity and of space are constructed with greater attention to difference and to multiple belonging. These developments clearly add to the complexity and plurality of theological discourse.

Constructed Theologies. The logic of an a priori contextualism is intensified in Kathryn Tanner's proposal appropriating postmodern cultural theory. Its major tenets are a thoroughgoing constructionism and historicism and a neo-Marxian conception of theology as reflection on social practice. Since symbols are "bare essential forms," the theologian is "always ultimately making meaning rather than finding it" (93). Thus, she rejects the claim that Christian identity is the same as a coherent meaning-complex of any depth around which consensus obtains, and also tradition's putatively privileged status. Instead, the markers Christians commonly invoke can be detached from received interpretations, redeployed to criticize conventional practices, and used to argue for the theological sense of emergent markers. The unruled, largely nondetermined character of Christian symbols and practices should produce not worry over disagreements, but an extended argument: "discipleship is an essentially contested notion" (159) precisely because each is to live as a creative, critical, responsible agent. Christian identity, then, is not a given, but a task: "Our lives are our own construction. . . . The way

we live could be different. . . . Established meanings and rules have no power of themselves to resist alteration [but are] held in place through the exercise of human power—by the will of the participants, by human institutions of social control, by the sanctions of human authorities, and by penalties against deviance" (169).

Tanner rightly dispels misconceptions of theology and practice as a monolithic, self-enclosed tradition by emphasizing Christians' participation in wider societal life (hence the assimilability of many practices across permeable "boundaries"). She stresses the tradition's diversity and the underdetermined, culturally adaptive, creative character of Christian practice due to its life- and globe-encompassing aspirations and to changing conditions. Yet, alongside the (related) view of God, the most debatable proposition is the indeterminacy of the symbol; as the object of a historical and living tradition of interpretation, the canonical text possesses both a determinate if complex semantic (historical, linguistic) range, and generative potential tied to the text. The poststructuralist insistence that signifiers may float and be reemployed at will (especially as disarticulated from the Bible's narrative structures) distances itself from characteristic Christian belief and practice (however diversely developed) since the church's inception.

A critical-realist hermeneutic recognizes a moderate form of contextualism and constructionism in our interpretative products, since communities and readers are positioned, conditioned, and invested variously (theologically, culturally, sociologically) with respect to the concrete and the biblical worlds. Still, radical forms of historicism and constructionism (attuned to difference and disagreement, and suspicious of claims of consensus) challenge the project of theological interpretation of Scripture to account for the diversity within the tradition and to demonstrate their theological coherence and convergence. Wherein does the actual unity of Christian interpretation consist, given the multiplicity of local, occasional readings? What are the implications of cultural particularity, partiality, and pluralism for our hermeneutical practice?

Contextual, Canonic, and "Catholic" Theologies. Vanhoozer (*Drama*, esp. ch. 10) argues that theology ultimately aims at a participatory understanding enabling Christian communities to speak, think, and live out the theodrama, the story of what God is doing in Christ for the sake of the world. A sapiential "canonical-linguistic" theology involves exegetical reason but especially practical reason (*phronēsis*: forming fitting judgments about how to act in particular contexts), in order to "live well with others in the world to God's glory" (308). Word and Spirit operate conjointly. The Spirit empowers comprehension and actualization of the word (the canonical text: the church's Scripture and the Christian's script), leading readers into an imaginative grasp of text and context. Thereby the Spirit enables them to "follow the Scriptures into new territory, continuing the 'itineraries of meaning' indicated by the biblical text" (308). As a wisdom-oriented, canonically directed exercise of practical reason, theology is prosaic, expressed and enacted in everyday life. It also is phronetic, making contextually sensitive, biblically faithful, "improvisatory" decisions about rendering the "fit in Christ" in new situations for which there are no guaranteed procedures. And it is prophetic, as countercultural and contextual as the gospel requires.

This canonical-linguistic vision of theology articulates what is definitive for Christian identity (Christianity's core doctrines, rooted in the canon's authority as the triune God's communicative action), and the universality of this assent. It affirms the basic character and translatability of the canonical text as an instantiation of a concrete universal (the embedding of truths of transcultural significance in necessarily particular situations, words, and actions). It also accepts the cross-cultural, contextualizing nature of all Christian proclamation and action, and thus the respective contributions made by a "Pentecostal plurality" of such theologies, rendering and realizing the canon's theological potential (Walls; Sanneh). Moreover, theology's prosaic task of serving contemporary speech-act and moral action in ordinary life proceeds on *phronēsis*—discerning significant similarities between situations, thus reasoning with creative fidelity to Scripture via a theodramatically and canonically instructed metaphorical imagination (Hays).

However, the properly prosaic and phronetic character of a canonical-linguistic approach reintroduces the issue of culture(s) more acutely. The biblical texts preserve "a prosaic wisdom, . . . practical reasoning incarnated" in a plurality of specific social contexts as well as literary genres. Since the Bible's explicit and implicit ethical instruction took the form of culture-specific practices in a series of concrete, changing environments in the ancient world, on many issues the canon represents a genuine dialogue. The diverse perspectives and practices the Bible incorporates are such that determining its teaching as a whole, and discerning its salience in a specific context, is no small task. *Phronēsis*, the next section suggests, is a complex matter, pervasively informed by culture.

Culture and Theological-Ethical Judgment. A major weakness of a "principlizing" approach to biblical ethics is the frequently culturally unself-conscious, inconsistent reasoning underlying judgments about how the culturally embedded biblical texts provide transculturally normative direction (Swartley; Vanhoozer, *Drama*). Aiming to bring greater clarity and coherence to contemporary ethical appropriation, Webb offers a method for interpretative assessment based on a crucial distinction concerning the nature of the Bible's ethical teaching. That teaching is comprised both of the definitive revelation of an "ultimate" social ethic and a historical series of partially realized, concrete instantiations of it. Webb's thesis is that the canonical text embodies and projects a "redemptive movement" hermeneutic, one indicating, in some cases, the possibility of "moving beyond the original application framings" in order to extend the scope of redemption in other contexts. In their given form the biblical utterances are intended to express and implement a further measure of redemption in their original life-settings. Subsequent interpreters, bearing in mind the Bible's redemptive thrust, must distinguish between instances in which the practices detailed in a given text are intended to be reproduced without change in every context, and those intended as instructive paradigms for further redemptive action in their own situations. (A "static" hermeneutic, by contrast, tends to construe the NT's "original application framings" as the limit-situations for actualizing redemption.) Certain postbiblical, sociocultural developments (e.g., in the U.S., institutionalized, mandatory [versus ad hoc, voluntary] changes to the earlier acceptance of slaveholding, many patriarchal practices, primogeniture-based inheritance laws) represent advances most Christians now recognize as more consistent with the biblical vision of creation and redemption. Strictly speaking, however, these practices surpass certain directives intended as first steps toward the fulfillment of the ultimate ethic the Bible envisages. To fulfill Scripture's redemptive intent in and for all (differently configured) cultures, additional hermeneutical clarity is needed.

Webb suggests this might be gained by a cultural analysis of biblical texts, based on three standards of reference: the movement a practice represents in comparison to its "foreign" context (the conventions of the ancient world); the "domestic" context (existing traditions or norms within the immediate covenant community); and the "canonical" context (across major salvation-history epochs, primarily from the OT to the NT). He also identifies sixteen intra- and two extra-scriptural criteria focusing and refining the transcultural/cultural assessment of specific texts on a given topic; further appraisal regarding relative force (from "persuasive" to "inconclusive") yields cumulative patterns. The major test-cases examined are slavery, patriarchy, and homosexual practice: Webb demonstrates, via these criteria, that the biblical presentation of the first two institutions moves redemptively in the direction of reducing restrictions and disparities in status; the last is consistently rejected, despite its acceptance outside the community of faith. The Bible's differing stances show that individual assessment of topics is required.

This proposal's major strengths are the canonic-theological rootedness of the "redemptive movement" thematic, and the heuristic value of the formal and material criteria elicited for the transcultural/cultural assessment of texts. These strengths enable the coherence and trajectories as well as the diversity of biblical teaching to emerge within the metaframework of redemptive history. Extending the contributions of Hays, Swartley, and Longenecker, it invites additional critical and constructive work.

A socially self-aware, contextualizing *phronēsis* recognizes that, in many instances, contemporary readers may not properly appreciate, appropriate, or extend the redemptive and often countercultural force of biblical instruction apart from understanding its salience vis-à-vis the social systems and symbolic worlds within which they were originally specified. Thus, interpretation and practice will be enhanced as readers engage in comparative, thick cross-cultural and structural descriptions and ponder the distinctive ranges of constraint and possibilities God's people have faced and currently face, in the worlds behind, of, and in front of the biblical text.

The theological interpretation of Scripture, then, is essentially contextual, "canonic," and "catholic" (Vanhoozer, *Drama*). Only as the renewed attempts to engage with the canonical dialogue by particularly situated communities are enlarged by catholicity (e.g., seeking cross-cultural validation; Swartley) can interpreters incorporate a mutually instructive enrichment and a critical check on unreflexive ethnocentrism. This will help to ensure that it is the canonical text

(and the redemptive movement of the theodramatic action it projects) that remains the norm and impetus for creative fidelity in a multiplicity of local interpretations.

See also Context; Ideological Criticism; Wisdom

Bibliography

Berger, P., and T. Luckmann. *The Social Construction of Reality*. Doubleday, 1996; Bevans, S. *Models of Contextual Theology*. Orbis, 1992; Clines, D. "Biblical Interpretation in an International Perspective." *BibInt* 1 (1993): 67–87; Craffert, P. "On New Testament Interpretation and Ethnocentrism." Pages 459–68 in *Ethnicity and the Bible*, ed. M. Brett. Brill, 2002; Elliott, J. *A Home for the Homeless*. Fortress, 1981; Geertz, C. *The Interpretation of Cultures*. Basic, 1973; Goldingay, J. "Hermeneutics." Pages 387–401 in *Dictionary of the Old Testament: Pentateuch*, ed. T. D. Alexander and D. W. Baker. InterVarsity, 2003; Gonzalez, J. *Out of Every Tribe and Nation*. Abingdon, 1992; Hays, R. *The Moral Vision of the New Testament*. HarperSanFrancisco, 1996; Larkin, W., Jr. *Culture and Biblical Hermeneutics*. Baker, 1988; Longenecker, R. *New Testament Social Ethics for Today*. Eerdmans, 1984; MacIntyre, A. *Whose Justice? Which Rationality?* University of Notre Dame Press, 1988; Mouw, R., and S. Griffioen. *Pluralisms and Horizons*. Eerdmans, 1993; Niebuhr, H. R. *Christ and Culture*. Harper & Row, 1956; Sanneh, L. *Translating the Message*. Orbis, 1989; Schreiter, R. *Constructing Local Theologies*. Orbis, 1985; idem. *The New Catholicity*. Orbis, 1997; Storey, J. *An Introduction to Cultural Theory and Popular Culture*. 2d ed. University of Georgia Press, 1998; Sugirtharajah, R., ed. *Voices from the Margin*. Orbis, 1995; Swartley, W. *Slavery, Sabbath, War, and Women*. Herald Press, 1984; Takaki, R. *A Different Mirror*. Little, Brown, 1993; Tanner, K. *Theories of Culture*. Fortress, 1997; Thiselton, A. *The Two Horizons*. Eerdmans, 1980; Vanhoozer, K. *The Drama of Doctrine*. Westminster John Knox, 2005; idem. "The Reader in New Testament Interpretation." Pages 301–28 in *Hearing the New Testament*, ed. J. Green. Eerdmans, 1995; Walls, A. *The Missionary Movement in Christian History*. Orbis, 1996; Warrior, R. "A Native American Perspective: Canaanites, Cowboys, and Indians." Pages 277–85 in *Voices from the Margin*, ed. R. Sugirtharajah. Orbis, 1995; Webb, W. "The Limits of a Redemptive-Movement Hermeneutic." *EvQ* 74 (2003): 327–42; idem. *Slaves, Women, and Homosexuals*. InterVarsity, 2001; Wolterstorff, N. "Suffering, Power, and Privileged Cognitive Access: The Revenge of the Particular." Pages 79–94 in *Christianity and Culture in the Crossfire*, ed. D. Hoekema and B. Fong. Eerdmans, 1997; Wright, N. T. *The New Testament and the People of God*. Fortress, 1992.

Elizabeth Yao-Hwa Sung

Custom *See* Ancient Near Eastern Background Studies

D

Daniel, Book of

History of Interpretation

Qumran. The eight manuscripts of Daniel found at Qumran indicate its importance for that community. *Florilegium* (4Q174) 2:3 cites Dan. 11:32 and 12:10, using the same citation-formula as for other biblical prophetic books. The *Community Rule* (1QS) echoes Dan. 11:33–34 in calling a teaching official a *maskil*, and the members of the community the *rabbim*. Although in column 1 it alludes to Dan. 11–12, the *War Scroll* (1QM) does not mention resurrection (Dan. 12:1–3).

Jewish Apocalyptic. In the *Similitudes (Parables) of Enoch* (ca. 50 CE) the figure called "that/the Son of Man" originates from Dan. 7:13. He casts down kings from their thrones, taking his seat on the throne of glory as a judge—probably based on Dan. 7:9–10. He is equated with the messiah in *1 En.* 48:10; 52:4. *First Enoch* 70:1 distinguishes Enoch from the Son of Man, while in 71:14 the two seem to be identified. Some argue that 71:14 is simply comparing Enoch to the Son of Man, others that *1 En.* 71 is a later addition and development of the tradition.

In 2 Esd. 13 (late first century CE) a wind stirs up the sea, out of which comes "the figure of a man" who "flew with the clouds of heaven" (cf. Dan. 7:1, 13). The man takes his stand on a great mountain that was "carved out without hands" (cf. Dan. 2:34). The preceding vision of an eagle that rises out of the sea (2 Esd. 11–12) refers to Dan. 7. The interpreting angel says that the eagle is the fourth kingdom of Daniel's vision, but indicates that identifying it as Rome is an innovation (12:12).

Later Jewish Interpretation. Josephus (*A.J.* 10.10–11) counts the fourth kingdom in Dan. 2 as Rome, but refuses to comment on the stone, probably to avoid offending Roman readers by speaking of Rome's downfall. This may explain why he ignores Dan. 7. Josephus identifies the little horn of Dan. 8 with Antiochus Epiphanes. Also in *Lev. Rab.* 13:5, Rome is the fourth kingdom. Later commentators modify the interpretation to make

Islam the fourth empire. The seventy weeks of Dan. 9:20–27 are usually interpreted as the period between the destruction of the first and second temples. The Talmud (*b. Sanh.* 97b) records a curse on those who try to calculate the date of the End. Nevertheless, various Jewish scholars attempted to do that by using the numbers in Daniel (see Silver).

Christian Interpretation. For Hippolytus (early third century) Christ is the stone in Dan. 2 and the fourth figure in the furnace in Dan. 3. The little horn of Dan. 8 is Antiochus, but the fourth kingdom in Dan. 7 is Rome and the little horn the antichrist. The birth of Christ comes after sixty-nine weeks of Dan. 9:20–27, with the last week referring to the distant future. Most other patristic commentators saw the seventy weeks fulfilled either in the life and death of Christ or in the destruction of Jerusalem. Jerome took the latter view. He defended the historicity and christological interpretation of Daniel against Porphyry. He opposed allegorization of the stories by Alexandrian exegetes such as Origen. Antiochus is the little horn in Dan. 8, and a type of the antichrist, who is the little horn of Dan. 7 and the subject of Dan. 11:24–45. Identification of references to the antichrist in Daniel continued into the Middle Ages. Dissident Catholics, such as Franciscans in the early fourteenth century and Jan Hus (d. 1415), identified the pope with the antichrist (see McGinn).

In Luther's preface to his translation of Daniel, the fourth empire is Rome, living on in the German Empire. Although threatened by the Turks (Muhammad is the little horn in Dan. 7), it would last until the coming of God's kingdom. He saw dual reference to Antiochus and the antichrist in Dan. 8 and 11. The antichrist is the sole subject of 11:36–45, where Luther saw references to the papacy. Luther wrote a more detailed exposition of Dan. 8 in terms of the antichrist/the pope.

John Calvin held that Daniel's visions extended only to the time of Nero. The fourth beast is the Roman Empire. The giving of the kingdom to the holy ones refers to the spread of the gospel.

The little horn of Dan. 8 is Antiochus. The seventy weeks of Dan. 9 end with the coming of Jesus and the Romans' destruction of Jerusalem. Daniel 11:36–45 refers to the Roman Empire.

Late medieval apocalyptic millennialism drew inspiration from Daniel. Thomas Müntzer (ca. 1489/90–1525) defended the German Peasants' Revolt as the coming of the "fifth kingdom," the stone of Dan. 2. The "fifth monarchy men" in mid-seventeenth-century England saw themselves in similar terms. Another kind of apocalypticism is William Miller's (1782–1849) calculation, based on Dan. 8:14, that the world would end in 1843. The dispensational movement based on J. N. Darby's (1800–1882) teaching sees Daniel's prophecies culminating either in the coming of Jesus or in the "end times" yet to come (e.g., the whole or last half of the seventieth week).

A few seventeenth-century scholars, such as Hugo Grotius (1583–1645), argued that the fourth beast was Greece and that Daniel's prophecies refer only to the events of the Antiochene period. In the nineteenth century this was strongly advocated, with a second-century BCE date for the book, in commentaries by Bertholdt (1806), von Lengerke (1835), Hitzig (1850), Ewald (1868), and others. There was a strong response from conservative scholars such as Hengstenberg (1831), Pusey (1864), and Keil (1867). Commentaries by F. W. Farrar (1895) and S. R. Driver (1900) popularized the German critical consensus among English readers. By the turn of the century this was the majority view, though the conservative position continued to be defended down through the twentieth century.

This survey shows that Daniel has often been a center of controversy, particularly over interpretation with regard to eschatology, but also regarding authorship and date. In the midst of this debate, the book's theological message has often been neglected; three approaches combine to help in discerning it. The growth of literary approaches to the OT is helpful, with emphasis on recognizing how different genres convey meaning. The study of intertextuality is particularly useful in Dan. 7–12; recognition of allusions to, or the reuse of, material from elsewhere in the OT provides important indicators of the underlying theology. Third, Childs's canonical approach rightly stresses the importance of understanding an OT text first in its own context, and then also in the context of the revelation of God in Christ in the NT.

The Message of Daniel

Daniel 1:1–2 introduces the theme of human and divine sovereignty. The Babylonian king's capture of Jerusalem and removal of some temple vessels to the treasury of his gods might evidence the superiority of Babylon's gods. Daniel 1:2 counters this. The Lord, the God of Israel, "gave" the king of Judah and the temple vessels into Nebuchadnezzar's power—for reasons not specified. The Lord is the ultimate sovereign, who "sets up kings and deposes them" (2:21a) and has a goal for history, the establishing of "a kingdom that will never be destroyed" (2:44). Nebuchadnezzar confesses that "he does what he wills with the host of heaven and the inhabitants of the earth" (4:34–35 NRSV) and, importantly, that "all his works are truth, and his ways are justice" (4:37 NRSV). God's rule is morally determined. The Ancient One judges the world powers, taking sovereignty from the bestial, subhuman powers and giving it to "one like a human being" (7:9–14 NRSV; NIV: "son of man"). In God's kingdom humanity reaches its full potential. Salvation history culminates in the achievement of God's purpose in creation—a world in which sovereignty is given to human beings (Gen. 1:26–28). However, God's people will experience suffering before receiving the kingdom (Dan. 7:21–22). The cry "How long?" (8:13) reinforces this point. Why does God's purpose sometimes seem to be frustrated? Daniel 9–11 provides a partial answer, countering any idea that God's sovereignty makes humans merely puppets. Daniel's prayer explains why the Lord gave Judah into the power of Babylon. This was a moral act, arising from Judah's persistent unfaithfulness to God. The prayer assumes that God responds to human behavior. Daniel 11 balances allusions to God's sovereignty (vv. 27, 29, 36, 45) with statements that, within limits, a human sovereign can "do as he pleases" (vv. 3, 16, 36).

Daniel 1 introduces a second major theme: human and divine faithfulness. Kings are prone to hubris, believing they can exercise a godlike sovereignty. As a result, those committed to God are challenged to a lifestyle of faithfulness. In Dan. 1 the issue is personal integrity. Daniel's stand is made privately and diplomatically. The Jews in Dan. 3 have to oppose idolatry publicly. The plot in Dan. 6, motivated by jealousy, is targeted at Daniel's religious practice because that seems the best way to succeed. Daniel could still pray to God secretly, but since his piety was well known, that would have been to compromise. In each case God is faithful to the faithful Jews.

The stories emphasize the Jews' preservation *in* the furnace or lions' den and not just their being saved *from* it. They are preserved because an angel mediates God's presence to them. In the context of the whole book, these stories are not simplistic promises of divine deliverance, but prepare the way for the intimations of suffering, persecution, and martyrdom of the faithful in chapters 7–12. They assert that God is faithful to his people and that his purposes will triumph.

In Dan. 1 God rewards Daniel's faithfulness by giving him exceptional wisdom. The stories emphasize the superiority of Daniel's wisdom over that of the Chaldeans. But God does not reveal things to satisfy curiosity. Nebuchadnezzar's dream about the tree is a warning against hubris and an opportunity to repent. The writing on the wall is a judicial sentence on Belshazzar's idolatrous blasphemy. The visions of Dan. 7–12 encourage the faithful to remain firm until the triumph of God's purpose. Those given wisdom are to use it to instruct others and to "lead many to righteousness" (11:33; 12:3).

Talk of angels enables talk about God's involvement in the world while preserving God's transcendence. Daniel 10:13 and 10:20–11:1 describe a struggle between heavenly beings, called the "princes" or "leaders" of Persia, Greece, and Israel. The main theological points expressed here are that history has a transcendent dimension, and that there is a synergy between events in heaven and on earth. What happens in heaven does not totally determine what happens on earth, and vice versa.

Daniel and the Canon

Given the different Hebrew and Greek forms of Daniel, canonical interpretation raises the question: Which canon? Childs argues for the primacy of the Hebrew canon, on the ground that only this corpus is common to both Jews and Christians, and so provides the theological bridge between the peoples of the two covenants. In practice, Daniel's inclusion in "the Writings" rather than "the Latter Prophets" in the Hebrew Bible is of little theological significance, since Jews usually treat Daniel as a prophetic book alongside those in the Latter Prophets.

Daniel and the OT. Daniel 4 echoes tree imagery in Ezek. 17, 19 (vine), and 31. Daniel 10 has verbal links with the theophanies in Ezek. 1–3 and 9–10. Daniel 9 contains parallels in thought and vocabulary with Lev. 26:27–45, a passage about sabbatical years and divine wrath. Daniel 9:2 refers explicitly to Jeremiah. Second Chronicles 36:20–21 understands Jeremiah's seventy years symbolically, as ten sabbatical cycles. This suggests that Dan. 9:24–27 is a symbolic, not a chronological, schema. The theological basis of the symbolism is the jubilee cycle (forty-nine years, seven sabbatical cycles, Lev. 25:8–12) as the prelude to release from slavery. In Daniel's schema one jubilee cycle leads to release from Babylon. This foreshadows the ultimate release after ten jubilee cycles (for more detail, see Lucas). Daniel 11:40–45 has verbal links with the prophecies about Assyria in Isa. 8, 14, 28, 37, and others in Ezekiel and Zechariah. Maybe it is not a detailed prediction about Antiochus's end, but a promise that that end will come, using the language of earlier prophets about the downfall of Assyria.

Daniel and the NT. Luke 20:18 concludes the parable of the Wicked Tenants with, "Everyone who falls on that stone will be broken to pieces; and it will crush anyone on whom it falls" (NRSV), alluding to Isa. 8:14–15 and Dan. 2:34–35. Jesus is identified with the stone that crushed the statue, and thus with the kingdom of God.

Scholars disagree about the background of the phrase "Son of Man" as used by Jesus, and how far the Synoptics reflect Jesus' own usage or develop it. The Synoptic sayings fall into three groups: (1) those about the future "coming" of the Son of Man with clouds and/or angels; (2) those about his suffering, death, and resurrection; (3) a small number about the present authority of the Son of Man. There is wide agreement that Dan. 7:13 lies behind the first group. These identify Jesus with the figure in Daniel who finally receives the kingdom, the coming of which was a central theme of Jesus' preaching. The idea of the Son of Man suffering may arise from his association with the suffering "people of" (7:27) "the holy ones of the Most High" (7:18, 22, 27 NRSV). Those who suffer martyrdom are promised resurrection and vindication (12:1–3). The third group may reflect the "dominion" given to the "one like a son of man" in 7:13.

Revelation's major antichrist figure is "the beast" that rises out of the sea and is a hybrid of Daniel's four beasts (Rev. 13:1–4). It shares features with the little horn in Dan. 7 and 8. The time for which it exercises authority (Rev. 13:5) seems based on Dan. 8:14. This is a reapplication of the theological significance of the little horn without any attempt to treat what Daniel says of it as detailed predictions about the antichrist.

Daniel and Theology

Daniel presents a salvation-history metanarrative that integrates and interprets the smaller narratives within history. Postmodernists are averse to metanarratives, claiming that they are "oppressive." However, Daniel's metanarrative empowers the oppressed by challenging the metanarrative of the oppressor, who in his hubris seeks to shape history according to his will.

Although Daniel exposes the hubris of human rulers and the divine judgment it attracts, it also states that God gives rule and dominion to humans. Daniel 4:10–12 paints a picture of the good that can be achieved by human rulers. When humans *image* God, they have the right to rule in his name. When they try to *be* God, they forfeit that right and may become "bestial." Those who recognize God's rule *over* them are in a position to allow God to rule *through* them.

Because God allows rulers enough freedom to become bestial, the faithful sometimes suffer. Daniel's stories encourage the faithful to become involved in a pagan world, with the hope of some measure of success and effective witness, even if there are risks. In the visions this seems impossible. God's sovereignty means that the faithful cannot take his response to their situation for granted. Belshazzar's blasphemous conduct meets with swift retribution. That of the little horn is allowed much longer before being ended. The faithful may be delivered *from* death in a fiery furnace (ch. 3) or *through* death in the fires of persecution (ch. 12).

The references to "the wise" and the "many" whom they influence (Dan. 11:33; 12:3) may allude to the Suffering Servant of Isa. 52:13–53:12. If so, this emphasizes that the way to glory is faithful service, even through the suffering that this may bring. The response to the cry "How long?" is a call to endurance, trusting in the faithfulness of God and holding to hope of resurrection. Jesus, the Son of Man, exemplified this.

See also Apocalyptic

Bibliography

Archer, G. *Jerome's Commentary on Daniel.* Baker, 1958; Beale, G. *The Use of Daniel in Jewish Apocalyptic Literature and in the Revelation of St. John.* University Press of America, 1984; Calvin, J. *A Commentary on Daniel.* Banner of Truth, 1986 (reprint of the Calvin Translation Society edition of 1852–53); Childs, B. *Introduction to the Old Testament as Scripture.* SCM, 1979; Collins, A. Y. "The Influence of Daniel on the New Testament." Pages 90–112 in *Daniel* by J. Collins; Collins, J. *Daniel.* Hermeneia. Fortress, 1993; Collins, J., and P. Flint, eds. *The Book of Daniel.* 2 vols. Brill, 2001; Dunn, J. D. G. "The Danielic Son of Man in the New Testament." Pages 528–49 in vol. 2 of *The Book of Daniel,* ed. J. Collins and P. Flint; Fewell, D. *Circle of Sovereignty.* Abingdon, 1991; Goldingay, J. *Daniel.* WBC. Word, 1989; Knowles, L. "The Interpretation of the Seventy Weeks of Daniel in the Early Fathers." *WTJ* 7 (1944): 136–60; Lucas, E. *Daniel.* Apollos OT Commentary. Apollos/InterVarsity, 2002; McGinn, B. *Visions of the End.* Columbia, 1979; Russell, D. S. *Daniel.* Saint Andrew Press, 1989; Silver, H. *A History of Messianic Speculation in Israel.* Macmillan, 1927.

Ernest C. Lucas

Dead Sea Scrolls

Discovered in 1947–56, the Dead Sea Scrolls (DSS) preserve the library holdings of a group of Essenes who established themselves at Qumran around 100 BCE. There are around a hundred thousand scrolls, yet all but a handful of them survive only in fragments. Together they represent some 930 manuscript copies of approximately 350 different literary compositions that may be divided into three general categories: (1) *Biblical texts.* Among the biblical scrolls and fragments are copies of virtually every book of the Hebrew Bible, with the sole exception of Esther and possibly Nehemiah, although the latter may be represented in absentia if Ezra and Nehemiah were originally one book. (2) *Parabiblical texts.* From a modern point of view, the Apocrypha and Pseudepigrapha may not be canonical, but some of these books had scriptural status among various Jewish groups. Besides fragments of previously known works such as Tobit, Ben Sira, the Epistle of Jeremiah, all parts of *1 Enoch* except for the *Similitudes,* and *Jubilees,* the DSS have yielded new texts associated with such figures as Noah, Jacob, Levi, Rachel, Joseph, Qahat, Amram, Joshua, Samuel, David, and Daniel. Many of the pre-Qumran works in this category survive in Aramaic instead of Hebrew. (3) *Sectarian texts.* These works represent the in-house literature not just copied but also composed by and for members of the Qumran community. A variety of genres are represented under this heading, including (a) rule books such as the *Community Rule,* the *Damascus Document,* and the *Messianic Rule;* (b) hymns and poetic works such as the *Thanksgiving Hymns* and *Songs of the Sabbath Sacrifice;* (c) calendrical and liturgical texts (e.g., priestly courses, calendric signs, and *Words of the Heavenly Luminaries*); (d) apocalyptic works (e.g., 11Q Melchizedek, 4Q521 Messianic Apocalypse, 4Q246 Aramaic Son of God text); (e) Wisdom literature (e.g., 4Q525 Beatitudes); (f) commentaries on scriptural texts (e.g., the pesharim associated with several books of the Prophets); and (g) midrashic reworkings of biblical works (e.g., *Reworked Pentateuch* and *Genesis Apocryphon*).

For interpreting the theological message of Scripture, the DSS shed considerable light on the textual form, canonical shape, and exegesis of the Hebrew Scriptures at the turn of the eras. They also provide comparative leverage for appreciating the distinctive theology of the NT writings.

The Scrolls and the OT

The biblical manuscripts among the DSS number around 220, a little over a fourth of the library. The majority (140) come from cave 4. As with the library in general, the state of their preservation varies widely. The oldest biblical manuscripts (4QSam[b], 4QJer[a], 4QExod[b]) date to the end of the third century BCE and are therefore more than a thousand years older than the oldest previously known manuscripts. Among their library holdings, the Qumran Essenes had multiple copies of most scriptural books, the most popular being the Psalms (36 copies), Deuteronomy (30), and Isaiah (21). These happen to be the very ones most often quoted in the NT.

The biblical scrolls from Qumran have helped to clarify that there was no "Bible" before the end of the first century CE. There were collections of sacred writings ("scriptures") but no official canon, no fixed collection of books accepted as authoritative and normative for all Jews. And there was no fixed textual form for each book up until about 100 CE or even as late as the end of the second Jewish revolt against Rome (132–35 CE).

The biblical DSS may be grouped into at least four broad textual categories (Tov). (1) *Proto-Masoretic* texts resemble the text of a particular book in the developing MT tradition. By one calculation, some fifty-seven, 47 percent, of the Qumran biblical scrolls fall in this category, including 1QIsa[b], 4QJer[a, c], and 4QEzra. The actual figure, however, may be much lower, since twenty of the twenty-four Pentateuchal texts in this category are equally close to the Samaritan Pentateuch (SP). (2) *Proto-Samaritan* texts are those bearing affinities with the text of the SP. Qumran Scrolls in this category comprise around 6.5 percent of the Qumran pentateuchal manuscripts, or 2.5 percent of all the biblical scrolls and include such manuscripts as 4QpaleoExod[m], 4QExod-Lev[f], and 4QNum[b]. (3) *Septuagintal* texts are those that look like the putative Hebrew text behind the Greek translation of a particular book in the LXX. Texts in this group represent only some 3 to 4 percent of

the Qumran biblical scrolls and include 4QDeut[q], 4QSam[q], and 4QJer[b]. (4) *Nonaligned* texts have no strong affinity with any of the above text types. This group is, in fact, a broad rubric for numerous forms of the biblical text. Qumran scrolls that fall into this category number approximately fifty-seven, or 47 percent, including 4QDeut[b, c, h], 4QIsa[c], and 4QDan[a].

Several books of the Hebrew Scriptures seemed to have existed in multiple literary editions (Ulrich). The identification of a distinct literary edition centers on recognizing large-scale patterns in the variants in a manuscript or manuscripts. Many biblical books evidently were the product of a long, complex literary process involving numerous authors, editors, and copyists through several generations and even centuries. Among the biblical scrolls from the Judean desert, variant literary editions are most evident for Exodus, Numbers, Joshua, Jeremiah, and Psalms. The sheer variety of textual forms exhibited among the biblical DSS suggests that the Essenes at Qumran—and likely other Jewish groups in the Second Temple period—did not assign sacred status or authority to only one textual form of certain scriptural books, but to the book or tradition as such. Their various methods of interpreting Scripture, from rewriting it to reading it as prophecy pointing toward their own history and experience, show that they regarded Scripture as a living tradition and treated it as such.

The official rabbinic canon (Tanak) eventually had three divisions: the Law (Torah), the Prophets (Nevi'im), and the Writings (Ketubim). Such a threefold division, or perhaps even a fourfold one, may be attested, albeit not very clearly, in the halakic document 4QMMT. This pre-Qumran work from the second century BCE speaks of "the books of Moses" and "the books of the Prophets" and mentions "Davi[d]" (a reference to the Psalter?) and "[the events] of ages past" (a reference to the historical books Joshua–2 Kings and/or Chronicles, Ezra, and Nehemiah[?]). By the latter part of the Second Temple period, most Jews recognized the Torah or Pentateuch as authoritative, and this was certainly the case at Qumran. But not all Jewish groups necessarily limited the Mosaic Torah to only five books (Genesis to Deuteronomy). The Qumran Essenes evidently regarded *Jubilees*, the *Temple Scroll*, and the *Reworked Pentateuch* as sacred books of Moses. Most Jewish communities also recognized the books of the Prophets as sacred Scripture. Here again, the Essene group at Qumran was no exception, as both the number of copies of prophetic books and the existence of commentaries on them attest. However, it is not clear which books and how many books each group put in this category, or in what order they put them. It is also unclear whether a third distinct category of books (such as the Writings in the rabbinic canon) existed before about 100 CE. If it did, it did not necessarily contain only the books included in the rabbinic canon (Psalms to Chronicles).

The Scrolls and the NT

The community of Essenes who copied and composed the DSS overlapped with the early Jesus movement for a period extending about four decades. Most of the DSS, though, are pre-Christian, and all of them are non-Christian. Despite the idiosyncratic claims of a few scholars, no NT figures are mentioned or alluded to in the Scrolls. Still, the DSS have shed welcome light on the Jewish matrix of Christian origins by providing parallels to the NT in terminology, conceptuality, literary genres, biblical interpretative methods, religious practices, and theological beliefs. Some of the parallels in theological terminology and belief are especially noteworthy.

Terminology. Both the Essenes of Qumran and the early Christians referred to themselves as members of "the Way" (Acts 9:2; 19:9, 23; 22:4; 24:14, 22; cf., e.g., 1QS 9.17–18; CD 1.13). The expression "(the) many/majority" (2 Cor. 2:6; cf. Mark 14:24 et par.) to designate the community or congregation appears as *ha-rabbim* several times in the community rules 1QS and CD. The word *ha-mebaqqer*, "guardian, overseer," a title found in the sectarian rule books (e.g., 1QS 6.13; CD 13.5–7; 15.5–6, 10–11), may be the Hebrew equivalent of *episkopos*, "bishop, overseer" in the NT (Acts 20:28; Phil. 1:1; 1 Tim. 3:2; Titus 1:7). The phrase "poor in spirit" (Matt. 5:3) surfaces in 1QM 14.7 and 1QH 14.3, and the antithetical formulation "You have heard that it was said, . . . but I tell you" in the Sermon on the Mount (Matt. 5:21–48) resembles the rhetorical structure "You know, . . . but we think/say" now found in 4QMMT. Furthermore, not a few expressions familiar from the letters of Paul have parallels in the Scrolls. Among them are "the righteousness of God" (Rom. 1:17; 3:5, 21, 22; 10:3; 2 Cor. 5:21; 1QM 14.5–6; 1QS 10.25; 11.12), "righteous/just judgment" (Rom. 2:5–6; 1QH 1.23, 30), "Spirit of holiness" (Rom. 1:4; 1QS 4.21; 8.16; 9.3; CD 2.12; 1QH 7.6–7; 9.32), "sinful flesh" (Rom. 8:3; 1QS 11.9; cf. 1QM 4.3), and "mystery" in the sense of divine secret (Rom. 16:25; 1 Cor. 2:7; 1QpHab 7.5).

Righteousness and Faith. The concepts of righteousness and faith have featured in discussion of the theological appropriation of a particular OT verse in Paul and the DSS. According to Hab. 2:4b NRSV, "The righteous [will] live by their faith [or: faithfulness, *'emunah*]." Paul applies the verse to those who have faith in Christ: "The one who is righteous will live by faith" (Rom. 1:17 NRSV; Gal. 3:11). The *Habakkuk Commentary* from Qumran quotes the same verse and comments: "Interpreted, this concerns all those who observe the Torah in the house of Judah, whom God will free from the house of judgment on account of their suffering [or: their toil/work, *'amlam*] and their faith in [or: their fidelity to, loyalty to, *'emunatam*] the Teacher of Righteousness" (1QpHab 8.1–3). Understood as loyalty or fidelity, the faith of believers in Christ may not be that much different from the Qumran sectarians' faith in their founder, the Teacher of Righteousness, insofar as both involve commitment. Two differences are notable, though. First, the Qumran text applies the Habakkuk verse to the sectarians' Torah observance, which may also be the referent of *'amlam* understood as "their observance"; this strikes a decidedly different note than Paul's emphasis on faith apart from Torah observance. Second, the Teacher of Righteousness apparently was not for the Essenes the object of faith as Jesus was for his followers. However much they revered the Teacher, the Jews at Qumran did not attribute any saving significance to his death or see themselves as mystically united to him. The DSS therefore speak not so much of faith in the person of the Teacher of Righteousness as of faith in or fidelity to the path he had marked out for them and to the divinely revealed approach to Scripture he had mediated.

Works of the Law. One of the most important parallels is the expression "works of the law." Paul uses the phrase (*erga nomou*) in Rom. 3:20, 28; Gal. 2:16 (3x); 3:2, 10. It occurs nowhere in the Hebrew Bible or rabbinic literature, and before the discovery of the Scrolls it was considered a Pauline neologism. Now it is found in the *Florilegium* (4Q174 1.1–2.i.7; cf. 1QS 5.21; 6.18 for the formulation "his observances in the law") and, most revealingly, in the halakic document 4QMMT (C 29). The abbreviation for this writing is an acronym derived from its use of the expression *miqtsat ma'ase hattorah*, "some of the works of the law." This document appears to be a manifesto of the Essenes or their progenitors before they left Jerusalem and before they or an offshoot of them moved to Qumran. It contains a calendar that may or may not be original to it, a list of more than twenty legal issues on which they and their opponents disagree, and an exhortation to a person ("you") whom they try to win over to their position. Three parties are thus in view, a "we" party, a "you" (singular) party, and a "they" party. The document was initially identified as a letter from the Teacher of Righteousness to the "Wicked Priest," the sect's principal opponent. Yet it does not have the form of a letter, and the precise identity of both the senders and the recipient is unclear, though the addressee may well have been the current high priest, perhaps even the one who would become the Wicked Priest.

Eschatology and Messianism. Both the Qumran Essenes and the members of the early Jesus movement had an intense awareness that they were living in the last times (e.g., 1QpHab 2.5–6; 1QS^a 1.1; Acts 2:17). Early Christians located themselves further along the eschatological time line than did the covenanters of Qumran. For the Christians, the new age had already dawned, the kingly rule of God in the earth had already begun, and the Messiah had already come. Yet both groups had a charismatic founder, and both read and interpreted Scripture in actualizing ways while seeing their respective movements as the fulfillment of biblical prophecy. Both could speak of themselves as children of light and of everyone else as children of darkness. Both viewed themselves as predestined by God to their elect status and their final salvation.

Although the Qumran Essenes were, like the earliest Christians, an apocalyptic movement, and though they composed works with apocalyptic features and copied older apocalypses such as *1 Enoch* and *Jubilees*, they evidently did not compose any full-blown apocalypses themselves. Yet one of the works found in fragments at Qumran and Masada, the *Angelic Liturgy* or *Songs of the Sabbath Sacrifice*, shares with the NT Apocalypse (Revelation) of John particular themes. Examples are the heavenly temple and heavenly worship, and specific motifs, such as silence in heaven (Rev. 8:1; 4Q403 1.i.40–46) and an animate heavenly altar (Rev. 9:13–14; 4Q405 frag. 20, 2.21–22 [= 11 Q17], lines 12–13). One of the major sectarian scrolls, the *War Rule* (1QM and cave 4 fragments), has in common with Revelation the expectation of an end-time battle between the forces of good and evil. And the pre-Qumran *New Jerusalem* text shares with Rev. 21 an extensive reliance on Ezek. 40–48. Both have a heavenly guide who measures the architecture and offers occasional explanations, a gargantuan size for the city, an emphasis on the twelve tribes of Israel, and an interest in precious stones and metals.

Messianic expectation also features in both the DSS and the NT but with some profound differences. The Essenes of Qumran may have expected the Teacher of Righteousness to have an eschatological counterpart in a priestly messiah, who would function as "Interpreter of the Law" and "teach righteousness at the end of days." But they did not regard the Teacher as a messiah, they attached no redemptive significance to his death, and they did not expect him to come back from the dead or down from heaven as God's final agent of redemption. Nor did they worship him. For their part, most early Christians did not pull out of mainstream society and retreat to the isolation of the desert, as the Qumran Essenes did. The Christian movement was open to Jews of all persuasions and to Gentiles as well. Not so with the Qumran Essenes. What is more, the Qumran Jews were devoted to the ideals of celibacy, ritual purity, and Torah observance in a way that did not characterize most forms of Christianity. Then, too, messianism was and remains much more prominent a belief in Christianity than it has ever been in Judaism or ever was at Qumran.

The Scrolls anticipate a division of messianic labor and envisage the one coming of multiple messiahs, whereas the NT speaks of the two comings of the one messiah and of several messianic tasks being performed by Jesus alone. It is customary to speak of two messiahs at Qumran: the royal, Davidic "messiah of Israel" and the priestly "messiah of Aaron" (e.g., 1QS 9.11; 1Qsa 2.14, 19–20; CD 12.23; 14.19; 19.10 [= ms. B, 1.10]; 20.1 [= ms. B, 2.1]). The "messiah of Israel" is also given other, biblically derived titles such as "Branch of David" (e.g., 4Q174; 4QpIsa^a; 4Q285; 4Q252) and "Prince of the Congregation" (e.g., CD 7.19–20; 4Q285). His main job is to play the role of conquering warrior at the end of days. The priestly messiah of Aaron always takes precedence over the royal messiah; his eschatological functions include providing atonement and giving instruction in and proper interpretation of the Torah. He is probably the referent of the titles "the Interpreter of the Law" (e.g., 4Q174; CD 7.18) and the one "who will teach righteousness at the end of days" (CD 6.11). Besides these two figures, however, the Scrolls speak about an eschatological figure known as the Prophet (1QS 9.10–11; the same figure may be in view in 11QMelch 2.18; 4QTest 5–8, citing Deut. 18:18–19). And 4Q521 seems to envision an Elijah-type prophet-messiah. Further, two key scrolls invest the archangel Michael with a major role in eschatological salvation (1QM 17; 11QMelch). In view of the functions served by these various eschatological figures, then, it may be proper to speak of not two but four messiahs in Qumran expectation, even if only two are regularly called *messiah*. Overall, the distinctive feature of NT messianism is that it applies variations of all four paradigms—royal, priestly, prophetic, heavenly—to a single figure.

Conclusion. Familiarity with the DSS has become indispensable for a well-rounded theological interpretation of both the OT and NT. For interpreters of the OT, the DSS provide an invaluable glimpse into the state of the text and canon of the Hebrew Scriptures at the turn of the eras, as well as insight into how one Jewish group interpreted and applied those Scriptures to themselves. For readers of the NT, the DSS provide a treasure trove of parallels in theological beliefs. In all this they supply a crucial historical contextualization of the witness of Scripture, in respect to both the continuities and discontinuities of Christianity's relation to early Judaism.

Bibliography

Abegg, M., P. Flint, and E. Ulrich. *The Dead Sea Scrolls Bible.* HarperSanFrancisco, 1999; Charlesworth, J., ed. *Jesus and the Dead Sea Scrolls.* Doubleday, 1992; idem. *John and the Dead Sea Scrolls.* Reprint, Crossroad, 1991; Collins, J. *The Scepter and the Star.* Doubleday, 1995; Fitzmyer, J. *The Dead Sea Scrolls and Christian Origins.* Eerdmans, 1999; Flint, P., and J. VanderKam, eds. *The Dead Sea Scrolls after Fifty Years.* 2 vols. Brill, 1999; Murphy O'Connor, J., and J. Charlesworth, eds. *Paul and the Dead Sea Scrolls.* Reprint, Crossroad, 1990; Schiffman, L., and J. VanderKam, eds. *The Encyclopedia of the Dead Sea Scrolls.* 2 vols. Oxford University Press, 2000; Stegemann, H. *The Library of Qumran.* Eerdmans/Brill, 1998; Stendahl, K., with J. Charlesworth, eds. *The Scrolls and the New Testament.* Reprint, Crossroad, 1992; Tov, E. *Textual Criticism of the Hebrew Bible.* 2d ed. Van Gorcum/Fortress, 2001; Ulrich, E. *The Dead Sea Scrolls and the Origins of the Bible.* Eerdmans/Brill, 1999; VanderKam, J., and P. Flint. *The Meaning of the Dead Sea Scrolls.* HarperSanFrancisco, 2002; Vermes, G. *The Complete Dead Sea Scrolls in English.* Penguin, 1997.

Daniel C. Harlow

Death *See* Creation; Last Things, Doctrine of; Original Sin; Sin, Doctrine of

Decalogue *See* Ethics; Law

Deconstruction

Deconstruction is far more than another "neutral" method of interpretation. It involves a critique of Western philosophy and of the entire hermeneutical tradition. Consequently, to begin to grasp the implications of deconstruction we must suspend any idea of deconstruction as just another dish on the hermeneutical smorgasbord. Here we explore its theoretical roots and shape before examining more closely its implications for theological interpretation.

"Deconstruction" is the word that has come to describe Jacques Derrida's philosophy. Derrida (1930–2004) derived the term "deconstruction" from Heidegger's *Destruktion*:

> When I made use of this word, I had the sense of translating two words from Heidegger at a point where I needed them in the context. These two words are *Destruktion*, which Heidegger uses, explaining that *Destruktion* is not a destruction but precisely a destructuring that dismantles the structural layers in the system, and so on. The other word is *Abbau*, which has a similar meaning: to take apart an edifice in order to see how it is constituted or deconstituted. (Derrida, *Ear,* 86–87)

Naming his philosophy "deconstruction" was not his choice; according to Derrida, the word was seized upon by some of his readers. For most English readers, Derrida's thought is so difficult when first encountered that it is easily seen as wholly new, but this is not the case. Paul de Man and Derrida are the major figures in deconstructive postmodernism, but its roots push down into the soil of phenomenology, structuralism, Heidegger, and Nietzsche.

A chance hearing of a broadcast about Camus led Derrida to enroll at the École Normale for philosophy classes. His main early influence was Sartre. By 1957 Derrida was planning a doctorate on "The Ideality of the Literary Object," inspired by the reading of Husserl and phenomenological aesthetics, but this was never completed. At his thesis defense in 1980 Derrida explained some of the reasons for not completing the original project. Most important was his reading of Husserl, which led him to discern problems with *phenomenological inquiry*, problems with writing and the literary aspects of philosophy.

In the process of developing his critique of phenomenology and of Husserl in particular, Derrida came to share Heidegger's criticism of the metaphysics of Western philosophy and of ontotheology. Such a critique is anticipated in Nietzsche, and though "he has refrained from offering a comprehensive commentary on Nietzsche's thought, Derrida often avails himself of Nietzschean motifs, and Nietzsche is either named or implicated in virtually every work to which Derrida has appended his signature"

(Schrift 95). In Derrida's critique of Husserl, signs play a central role, and Derrida's *deconstruction* of Saussure, the father of structuralism, is fundamental to his project.

Much could be written about metaphysics, ontotheology, and presence. Briefly and simply put, they refer to strategies of finding an Archimedean point amid the flux of history, whereby one discerns the true meaning of things, texts, and so on. This point might be Plato's ideas or Husserl's consciousness, but they all have in common the promise of an absolute and secure knowledge. In that knowledge we would be able to see the world *sub specie aeternitatis*, to peek over God's shoulder, as it were, from a standpoint far away from the play of the world.

Regarding hermeneutics, Derrida sees the approach of seeking to decipher the true meaning of texts as a manifestation of *the metaphysics of presence*. At the well-known ending of his essay "Structure, Sign, and Play," Derrida (*Writing*, 292–93) discerns two types of interpretation. "The one," he says, "seeks to decipher, dreams of deciphering a truth or origin which escapes play and the order of the sign, and which lives the necessity of interpretation as an exile. The other, which is no longer turned toward the origin, affirms play and tries to pass beyond man and humanism, the name of man being the name of that being who, throughout the history of metaphysics or of ontotheology—in other words throughout his whole history—has dreamed of full presence, the reassuring foundation, the origin and end of play."

In terms of philosophy of language, a helpful way to understand what is at stake in deconstruction is to attend to the role of *ideality* (Wolterstorff). The doctrine of ideality, which comes from Frege in particular, distinguishes between authorial intention and the element in language that remains constant and fixes meaning: ideality. Gadamer and Ricoeur distance themselves from strong connections between authorial intention and meaning but retain a doctrine of ideality. Derrida problematizes ideality, especially in *Speech and Phenomena*, by exposing its aporia. An ideal meaning is never a pure presentation to begin with; it is a re-presentation. Thus, there can be no purely "ideal" meaning; there is only an endless series of reverberations. What presents itself is the representation of nonpresence, what Derrida calls "otherness," "difference," or "alterity," thereby opening meaning up to flux and play and endless deferral.

The implications of this deconstruction of ideality are radical, and Derrida develops an arsenal of techniques for setting texts in play. However, it is important to note that Derrida's problematizing of ideality, and thus the metaphysics of presence, never means finally abandoning ideality or the metaphysics of presence for an alternative position, which for Derrida does not exist. The result is that there are always two poles or two ways in Derrida's thought. Authorial intent is that indispensable guardrail for interpretation (metaphysics of presence), but it never "opens" a reading (play and flux). The logic of deconstruction leads one toward flux and play, but Derrida always tries to hold on to both at the same time.

Theologically, responses to Derrida have varied considerably, ranging from Mark Taylor and Caputo to Ward, Milbank, Pickstock, and others. Taylor and Caputo are much enamored with Derrida and reshape theology along the lines of deconstruction. Ward argues that deconstruction supplements Barth's theology with an adequate postmodern philosophy of language. A fascinating aspect of Derrida's work is his regular engagement with the Bible. He often refers to biblical texts and motifs, and he has focused in particular on the tower of Babel narrative and the Akedah (Binding of Isaac; Gen. 22). But Ward's argument is belied by a comparison of Derrida's actual handling of biblical texts with Barth's theological interpretation.

Take Derrida's reading of the tower of Babel narrative, for example. For Derrida, it is a metanarrative, the narrative of narratives. Derrida takes the narrative to be about the origin of the multiplicity of mother tongues. For what, Derrida asks, does God punish the Shemites? It is for having desired and sought by themselves a singular and universal genealogy. Derrida understands God's punishment in terms of the misunderstanding that results from a multiplicity of tongues. He sums this up in terms of translation: God imposes, as it were, the necessity and impossibility of translation. Out of God's jealousy and resentment against that single and unique lip of men, says Derrida, Yahweh violently imposes *his name*. Derrida takes *Babel* to be God's name, which God proclaims over the city! Derrida connects God's name "Babel" with Yahweh, observing that the text says this YHWH, an unpronounceable name, descends toward the tower. And the war God thus declares has already raged in God's name, Babel. Babel is a proper noun and simultaneously, according to Derrida, functions as a common noun signifying confusion.

Derrida's performative setting of the tower of Babel narrative in play is intriguing in the way it brings the story of Babel into relationship with language and translation. But the story is not read in its canonical context, and the interpretation of Babel as the name of God is exegetically wrong and theologically a serious distortion (Bartholomew). Likewise, his secularized reading of Kierkegaard's reading of Gen. 22 in *The Gift of Death* is also miles away from Barth's positive style of theological interpretation of the Bible. Ward may be right that Barth's theology of language does require a supplement, but certainly not a Derridean one.

In my view the most insightful theological analysis of deconstruction is that by George Steiner (*Real Presences*). He acknowledges Derrida's great contribution toward dismantling the fortress of consciousness so utterly central to modernity. However, for Steiner deconstruction confronts us ultimately with a religious choice; either nihilism—the ultimate destination of Derrida's work—or "In the beginning was the Word." If Steiner is right, then it will be apparent that deconstruction will not be of great help to theological interpretation. Indeed, while there are significant examples of the use of deconstruction in biblical interpretation (see the article on Postmodernity), few of these are examples of *theological* interpretation. We should be grateful for Derrida's critique of modernity and for his engagement with biblical and theological issues such that they are on mainstream philosophical agendas nowadays. But he will provide us with little help in developing a positive theological hermeneutic.

For theological interpretation, Derrida's major challenge is philosophical and especially at the level of philosophy of language. This has implications for theological interpretation in that any contemporary theological hermeneutic will need to account for language better than postmoderns such as Derrida. As Milbank asserts, "If Derrida can give a gnostic hermeneutic of the human text in the light of the gnostic logos, then we should have the confidence to give a Christian hermeneutic in the light of the real one" (79).

Bibliography

Bartholomew, C. "Babel and Derrida: The Challenge of Postmodernism for Biblical Interpretation." *Tyn-Bul* 49, no. 2 (1998): 305–28; Caputo, J. *The Prayers and Tears of Jacques Derrida.* Indiana University Press, 1997; Derrida, J. *The Ear of the Other.* Schocken, 1985; idem. *The Gift of Death.* University of Chicago Press, 1995; idem. *Speech and Phenomena and Other Essays on Husserl's Theory of Signs.* Northwestern University Press, 1973; idem. "Des Tours de Babel." Pages 165–207 in *Difference in Translation,* ed. J. Graham. Cornell University Press, 1985; idem. *Writing and Difference.* University of Chicago Press, 1978; Ingraffia, B. *Postmodern Theory and Biblical Theology.* Cambridge University Press, 1995; Milbank, J. *The Word Made Strange.* Blackwell, 1997; Schrift, A. D. *Nietzsche and the Question of Interpretation.* Routledge, 1990; Steiner, G. *Real Presences.* Faber & Faber, 1989; Ward, G. *Barth, Derrida and the Language of Theology.* Cambridge University Press, 1995; Wolterstorff, N. "The Promise of Speech-Act Theory for Biblical Interpretation." Pages 73–90 in *After Pentecost,* ed. C. Bartholomew et al. SHS. Zondervan/Paternoster, 2001.

Craig G. Bartholomew

Demons   See Angels, Doctrine of; Powers and Principalities

Demythologization   See Hermeneutics; Theological Hermeneutics, Contemporary; Western Literature, the Bible and

Derrida, Jacques   See Deconstruction; Postmodernity and Biblical Interpretation

Descartes, René   See Epistemology

Determinate Meaning   See Meaning; Theological Hermeneutics, Contemporary

Deuteronomistic History   See Deuteronomy, Book of; History of Israel

Deuteronomy, Book of

The theological significance of Deuteronomy can scarcely be overestimated. Inasmuch as this book offers the most systematic presentation of truth in the entire OT, we may compare it to Romans in the NT. On the other hand, since Deuteronomy reviews Israel's historical experience of God's grace as recounted in Genesis–Numbers, a comparison with the Gospel of John may be more appropriate. Having had several decades to reflect on the significance of Jesus, John produced a profoundly theological Gospel, less interested in the chronology of the life of Christ, and more concerned with its meaning. Similarly, according to Deuteronomy's internal witness, Moses has had almost four decades to reflect on the exodus from Egypt and Yahweh's establishment of a covenant relationship with Israel. Like John, Deuteronomy functions as a theological manifesto, calling Israel to respond to God's grace with unreserved loyalty and love.

History of Interpretation

Deuteronomy is the fifth and final book of what Jewish tradition knows as the Torah, and Christians refer to it as the Pentateuch. In popular Hebrew tradition, the book is called *Sefer Devarim*, "Book of Words," which is an adaptation of the official Hebrew name, *'Elleh Haddebarim*, "These are the Words," the first two words of the book. In the third century BCE the LXX translators set the course for its history of interpretation. Instead of translating the Hebrew *To Biblion tōn Logōn*, "The Book of Words," or more simply *Logoi*, "Words," they replaced this with *To Deuteronomion*, "Second Law" (Latin: Deuteronomium). The form of the name seems to be derived from Deut. 17:18, where Hebrew *mishneh hattorah*, "a copy of the Torah," is misinterpreted as *to deutero-nomion*. This Greek heading probably became determinative because the book reiterates many laws found in Exodus–Numbers, and in chapter 5 cites the Decalogue almost verbatim. But the name "Deuteronomy" overlooks the fact that the book presents itself not primarily as law but as a series of sermons. Much of the book reviews events described in the earlier books. Where laws are dealt with (e.g., the central sanctuary law in ch. 12), the presentation is often exposition rather than recital of the laws themselves.

Prior to source criticism, both Jewish and Christian readers assumed Mosaic authorship, a fact reflected in the common designation of the pentateuchal books outside the English world as the Five Books of Moses. For the former, as the work of Moses it came with profound authority (cf. Mark 10:3; 12:19; Luke 20:28; John 5:45; 9:28; etc.). Observing Jesus' manner, some looked upon him as the eschatological prophet like Moses, whom Yahweh would raise up (Deut. 18:15; cf. Matt. 11:9; John 1:21, 25; 6:14; 7:40). While Jesus himself rejected this role (John 1:21), judging by his number of quotations, Deuteronomy was Jesus' favorite book. This impression is reinforced by his distillation of the entire law into the simple command to love the Lord with one's whole being and to love one's neighbor as oneself. In the Pentateuch, although appeals for loving one's neighbor and the stranger occur earlier (Lev. 19:18, 34), the command to love God appears only in Deuteronomy (6:5; 11:1; 11:13; 13:3; 30:6).

Paul repeatedly cites Deuteronomic texts (Rom. 10:19; 11:8; 12:19; 1 Cor. 5:13; 9:9; Eph. 6:2–3; etc.). However, it is clear that Paul interpreted the entire history of God's revelation and also Deuteronomy in light of Christ and the cross (Rom. 10:6–8; 1 Cor. 8:6; Gal. 3:13). He seems to have functioned as a second Moses, not only providing a profoundly theological interpretation of God's saving actions in Christ, but also reminding readers that salvation comes by grace alone. In Romans and Galatians Paul's argumentation addresses those who would pervert the "law" (a narrow legalistic interpretation of Hebrew torah) into a means of salvation, rather than treating it as a response to salvation (cf. Schreiner; N. T. Wright). While on the surface Paul's responses to this heresy often appear to contradict Moses, such statements should be interpreted in context and as rhetorical responses to opponents. In his disposition toward the "law," he was in perfect step with Moses. There is nothing new in Paul's definition of a true Jew as one who receives the praise of God because he is circumcised in the heart (Rom. 2:28–29; cf. Deut. 10:16–21; 30:6), nor in his praise of the law as holy, righteous, and good (Rom. 7:12; cf. Deut. 6:20–25), nor in his distillation of the whole law into the law of love (Rom. 13:8–10; cf. Deut. 10:12–21). Elsewhere, Peter's characterization of Christians as a privileged people, "a chosen race" and "God's own possession" (1 Pet. 2:9), echoes Moses' understanding of Israel (Deut. 4:20; 10:15; 14:2; 26:18–19).

Insofar as the early church used Deuteronomy, on the one hand the fathers and other spiritual leaders tended to follow Paul's christological lead, but in application of the laws often resorted to spiritualizing the details. By marshaling the Shema (Deut. 6:4–5) to defend trinitarian doctrine (Lienhard 282–83), they obscured the original contextual meaning (Block, "How?"). In the Reformers we witness two different dispositions toward the laws of Deuteronomy. Luther tended to read them through Paul's rhetorical and seemingly antinomian statements (Rom. 7:4–9; 2 Cor. 3:6; Gal. 3:10–25) and his own debilitating experience of works-righteousness within the Roman Catholic church. Hence, he saw a radical contrast between the law (which kills) and the gospel (which gives life). His emphasis on the dual function of the law (civic—to maintain external order on earth; theological—to convict people of sin and drive them to Christ; cf. Lohse 270–74) missed the point of Deuteronomy. This book presents the law as a gift to guide the redeemed in righteousness, leading to life (cf. Deut. 4:6–8; 6:20–25). Like Luther, Calvin insisted that no one can be justified by keeping the law. But through the law, Israel is instructed on how to express gratitude for their redemption and bring glory to God (Calvin 363).

These two approaches tended to dominate until the Enlightenment, when the attention of critical scholars shifted from the theological value of Deuteronomy to hypotheses concerning its origin. By the second half of the nineteenth century, the documentary approach to pentateuchal studies was firmly entrenched. Deuteronomy had been isolated as a source separate from J, E, and P. Julius Wellhausen proposed that chapters 12–26 represent the original core, written by a prophet (some suggest Jeremiah) ca. 622 BCE (cf. 2 Kings 22–23) to promote reform of Israel's religious practices (2 Chron. 34–35) and centralize the cult in Jerusalem. The prophet presumably hid the book in the temple so as to be found; it was completed after the exile and combined with Genesis–Numbers (an amalgam of J, E, and P sources).

Convinced that Joshua completed the story of the Pentateuch, Wellhausen and others preferred to interpret Deuteronomy within the context of the Hexateuch. Deuteronomy was crucial for von Rad's OT theology, which found in 26:5–9 an ancient credo confessing the essentials of Israelite faith (e.g., "The Form-Critical Problem," in *Problem*). Martin Noth went in the opposite direction, cutting Deuteronomy from Genesis–Numbers and treating this book as the paradigmatic theological prologue to the Deuteronomistic History (Joshua–Kings). Its purpose is to provide a theological explanation for the events surrounding 722 BCE and 586 BCE, now viewed as the result of Israel's persistent apostasy and worship of strange gods.

Some scholars attribute the bulk of Deuteronomy to country Levites writing shortly before 701 BCE (von Rad, *Studies*), prophetic circles of northern Israel (Nicholson 58–82), or sages in the Jerusalem court (Weinfeld). Recent scholarship tends to interpret the book as a manifesto, written in support of Josiah's efforts to centralize the religion of Israel in Jerusalem. According to Weinfeld, Deuteronomy is not only a remarkable literary achievement, but also represents a profound monument to the theological revolution advocated by the Josianic circles. This revolution involved attempts to eliminate other shrines and centralize all worship of Yahweh in Jerusalem, as well as to "secularize," "demythologize," and "spiritualize" the religion. It sought to replace traditional images of divine corporeality and enthronement in the temple with more abstract, spiritual notions reflected

in its "name theology." In this new religious world, sacrifices were no longer institutional and corporate but personal expressions of faith, and the tithe was no longer "holy to Yahweh" but remained the owner's (14:22–27; Weinfeld, *ABD* 2:177).

Recognizing the strengths of each position, most recently some have proposed that dissidents (scribes, priests, sages, aristocrats) originally produced Deuteronomy. According to Richard D. Nelson (4–9; cf. Albertz 194–231), the book has roots in crisis (seventh century), when loyalty to Yahweh was undermined by veneration of other gods. The well-being of many was jeopardized by exploitative royal policies, and the prophetic institution was out of control, calling for tests of authenticity and limitation of influence. The inconsistencies and ambiguities in the Deuteronomic legislation reflect the varying interests of the dissident groups. On the one hand, virtually all critical scholars agree that Deuteronomy either provides the occasion or is the result of the Josianic reform. On the other hand, they agree that its speeches are pseudepigraphical, fictionally attributed to Moses in support of the parties whose interests are represented (cf. Sonnet 262–67).

Not all are willing to date Deuteronomy this late. J. G. McConville (*Deuteronomy*, 33–40) and others argue that its religious and political vision does not fit the Josianic period as described in 2 Kings. On the contrary, "Deuteronomy, or at least a form of it, is the document of a real political and religious constitution of Israel from the pre-monarchic period" (34). As such, it challenges prevailing ancient Near Eastern royal-cultic ideology, replacing this with a prophetic vision of Yahweh in direct covenant relationship with his people governed by torah. Through the torah the prophetic authority of Moses, the spokesperson for Yahweh, extends to the community. The "Book of the Torah," deposited next to the ark and formally read before the assembly, provides a constant reminder of the will of the covenant Lord. As for the theological revolution envisioned by Weinfeld, this interpretation is coming under increasingly critical scrutiny (Wilson; Richter; Vogt).

Deuteronomy presents itself as a record of addresses delivered orally by Moses on the verge of Israel's crossing over into the promised land, speeches immediately committed to writing (31:9; cf. Block, "Recovering"). However, in accordance with ancient Near Eastern literary convention, strictly speaking, the book as we have it is anonymous. We can only speculate when the individual speeches of Moses were combined, arranged, and linked with their present narrative stitching. Certain stylistic and literary features, the content of historical notes in the book, and the resemblances of the present structure to second millennium BCE Hittite treaty documents suggest that this happened much earlier than many critical scholars admit.

Hearing the Message of Deuteronomy

Because of a pervasive latent Marcionism and adherence to theological systems that are fundamentally dismissive of the OT in general and Deuteronomy in particular, its message has been largely lost to the church. This is a tragedy, not only because—more than any other OT book—the message of Deuteronomy lies right on the surface, but also because few OT books proclaim such a relevant word. How can readers today rediscover the message?

First, it is important to "hear" Deuteronomy. At significant junctures Moses appeals to his people to "hear" the word he is proclaiming (5:1; 6:3–4; 9:1; 20:3). In 31:9–13 he charges the Levitical priests to read the torah that he has just transcribed (i.e., his speeches) before the people every seven years at the Feast of Booths. This statement not only assumes canonical status for the torah Moses has just proclaimed; it also highlights the critical link between hearing his words in the future and the life of the people of God. This link may be represented schematically as follows:

> Reading → Hearing → Learning → Fear → Obedience → Life

A similar relationship between reading/hearing the words of "this torah" and future well-being is expressed in 17:19, where Moses explicitly charges future kings to read the torah so that they may embody the covenant fidelity he has espoused on the plains of Moab.

Second, to hear the message of Deuteronomy, we must recognize its genre and form. At one level, Deuteronomy represents the final major segment of Moses' biography that began in Exod. 1 (cf. Knierim 355–59, 372–79). Accordingly, Deuteronomy may be interpreted as narrative in which lengthy speeches have been embedded.

At another level, the manner in which the first two speeches have been arranged is reminiscent of ancient Near Eastern treaty forms, especially the second millennium BCE Hittite suzerainty treaties (see Thompson; Craigie). Recognition of the fundamentally covenantal character of Deuteronomy has extremely significant implications. Yahweh

is the divine suzerain, who graciously chose the patriarchs and their descendants as his covenant partner (4:37; 7:6–8). He demonstrated his commitment (*'ahab*, "he loved") by rescuing them from Egypt (4:32–40), entering into an eternal covenant relationship with them at Sinai (4:9–32), revealing his will (4:1–8), and providentially caring for them in the desert (1:9–3:29). He is now about to deliver the promised land into their hands (1:6–8; 7:1–26). As a true prophet of Yahweh, Moses challenges Israel to respond by declaring that Yahweh alone is its God (6:4), and by demonstrating unwavering love for him through obedience (6:5–19; 10:12–11:1; etc.). Moses realistically anticipates Israel's future rebellion, leading ultimately to banishment from the land. Yet, Yahweh's compassion and the irrevocable nature of his covenant mean that exile and dispersion among the nations cannot be the last word; Yahweh will bring them back to himself and to the land (4:26–31; 30:1–10). Indeed, Moses perceives the covenant that he is having them renew with Yahweh as an extension of Sinai (29:1), and ultimately an extension and fulfillment of the covenant made with the ancestors (29:10–13).

At a third level, Deuteronomy presents itself as a series of addresses by Moses to Israel immediately before their entrance into Canaan and his own death. The narrative preamble (1:1–5) should determine how we hear its message. Although in later chapters Moses will integrate many prescriptions given at Sinai and afterward into his preaching, contrary to prevailing popular opinion Deuteronomy does not present itself as legislation. Rather, this is prophetic preaching at its finest. The preamble identifies Moses' words as *hattorah hazz'ot*, "this torah" (1:5 AT). The word *torah* should be primarily understood not as "law" (for the book includes much that is not legal), but as "instruction." *Torah* is derived from the verb *yarah*, "to teach," and from the expression *sefer hattorah* (e.g., Deut. 29:21 [20 MT]; Josh. 1:8; etc.): "Book of the Instruction," rather than "Book of the Law." *Torah* was applied to specific aspects of Yahweh's will revealed earlier (e.g., Exod. 12:49; 24:12; Lev. 7:1; Num. 19:14; etc.). Nevertheless, the torah that Yahweh commanded Joshua to read and obey fully (Josh. 1:7–8) and read to the people of Israel as part of the covenant-renewal ceremony at Shechem (8:30–35) was likely the collection of Moses' sermons that constitute the bulk of the present book. Eventually, the scope of torah was expanded to include the narrative sections (Deut. 1:1–5; 27:1–10; 34:1–12; etc.), that is, the entire book of Deuteronomy more or less as we have it. It is widely accepted that the document referred to as "the book of the torah" (*sefer hattorah*, 2 Kings 22:8; 2 Chron. 34:15) and "the book of the torah of Yahweh by the hand of Moses" (2 Chron. 34:14), discovered by Josiah's people in the course of renovating the temple, was some form of Deuteronomy. It represents the heart of the torah, which the priests were to teach and model (Deut. 33:10; 2 Chron. 15:3; 19:8; Mal. 2:6, 9; cf. Jer. 18:18; Ezek. 7:26; Ezra 7:10). Psalmists praised it (Pss. 19:7–14; 119), the prophets appealed to it (e.g., Isa. 1:10; 5:24; 8:20; 30:9; 51:7), faithful kings ruled by it (1 Kings 2:2–4; 2 Kings 14:6; 22:11; 23:25), and righteous citizens lived by it (Ps. 1). In short, Deuteronomy provides the theological base for virtually the entire OT and the paradigm for much of its literary style.

Deuteronomy obviously incorporates prescriptive and motivational material deriving from Sinai (in the Decalogue, 5:7–21; the so-called Deuteronomic Code, 12:1–16:15; the covenant blessings and curses, 28:1–29:1). Yet, specific prescriptions analogous to other ancient Near Eastern law codes tend to be concentrated in only seven chapters (19–25; on legal lists as a genre, see Watts 36–45). But even these are punctuated by strong rhetorical appeals and a fundamental concern for righteousness rather than merely legal conformity. The remainder, even of the second address, bears a pronounced homiletical flavor. Both Deuteronomy and the word *torah* are represented more accurately by Greek *didaskalia* and *didachē*, as used in the NT, than by *nomos*.

This does not mean that what Moses declares in these speeches is any less authoritative than the laws given at Sinai. In 1:3 the narrator declares that Moses functions as the authorized spokesman for Yahweh. Nevertheless, here Moses' role is that of pastor, not lawgiver. Like Jacob in Gen. 49, Joshua in Josh. 24, and Jesus in John 13–16, knowing that death is imminent, Moses gathers his flock and delivers his final homily, pleading with the Israelites to remain faithful. Deuteronomy is therefore to be read primarily as discourse on the implications of the covenant for a people about to enter the promised land (cf. Gen. 15:7–21; 26:3; Exod. 6:2–8).

But hearing the message of Deuteronomy involves more than hearing the words and correctly identifying the genre; it also involves interpreting the book correctly, grasping its theology, and making appropriate application. According to the internal witness, with these addresses Moses sought to instill deep gratitude in the generation that was about to claim the promised land.

At the same time he guided them in applying the covenant made at Sinai to the new situation on the other side of the Jordan. While the Canaanites posed a formidable military threat, the spiritual threat was more serious. Accordingly, throughout the book emphasis is on exclusive devotion to Yahweh, demonstrated in grateful obedience. If they would do so, Moses envisioned the people of Israel and the land they would occupy as flourishing.

How are Christians to read the book today? The following principles may guide in the face of this challenge. First, rather than beginning with what the NT has to say about Deuteronomy, we should read the book as an ancient Near Eastern document that addressed issues current a thousand years before Christ, in idioms derived from that cultural world. Although the NT church accepted this book as authoritative Scripture, Deuteronomy sought to govern the life of Israel, composed largely of ethnic descendants of the patriarchs.

Second, we should recognize the book as a written deposit of eternal truth. Some of these verities are cast in explicit declarative form, as in "Yahweh is God; there is no other [god] besides him" (4:35, 39 AT). Others are couched in distinctive Israelite cultural dress, for which we need to identify the underlying theological principle. For example, "When you build a new house, you shall make a parapet for your roof" (22:8 NRSV). This represents a specific way of demonstrating covenantal love for one's neighbor. The validity of specific commands for the Christian may not be answered simply by examining what the NT explicitly affirms. On the contrary, unless the NT explicitly declares a Deuteronomic ordinance passé, we should assume minimally that the principle underlying the command remains valid.

Third, after we establish the meaning of a passage in original context, we must reflect on its significance in light of Christ, who has fulfilled the law (and the prophets, Matt. 5:17). This means not only that he is the perfect embodiment of all the law demands, and its perfect interpreter, but also that he represents the climax of the narrative. The message of the NT is that the One who spoke on the plains of Moab is none other than Jesus Christ, Yahweh incarnate in human form.

Deuteronomy and the Canon

The written copies of Moses' last addresses to Israel were recognized as authoritative from the very beginning. Not only did Moses prohibit addition to or deletion from his words (4:2), but he also commanded the Levites to place the written torah beside the ark of the covenant. There it was to remain perpetually as a witness against Israel, as the norm by which the nation's conduct in the promised land would be measured. The fact that this Torah was placed *beside* the ark, rather than *in* it (unlike the tablets containing the Decalogue [10:1–9], written down by God himself [5:22; 10:2]), does not suggest lesser authority, but different significance. The Decalogue represented the actual covenant document (4:13; 10:1–4), placed in the ark as a reminder to God of his covenant with Israel. The Deuteronomic torah was Moses' commentary on the covenant, whose terms included not only the Ten Principles, declared directly by God himself, but also the statutes and ordinances (*khuqqim* and *mishpatim*) revealed to Moses at Sinai and then passed on to the people (4:1). Moses' instructions on the covenant were fully inspired and authoritative, for he spoke to Israel "according to all that Yahweh had commanded him [to declare] to them" (1:3 AT).

The theological stamp of Deuteronomy is evident throughout the OT canon and into the NT. If in Deuteronomy the term *torah* applies expressly to the speeches of Moses, eventually it was applied to the entire Pentateuch, for which Deuteronomy represents the conclusion. Many treat Deuteronomy as a dangling legal appendix to the narratives of the patriarchs, Israel's exodus from Egypt, the establishment of covenant at Sinai, and the desert wanderings; yet, some (e.g., Noth) divorce the book from the Pentateuch altogether. However, critical scholars are increasingly recognizing a Deuteronomic flavor in many of the preceding narratives, so that in some the classical JEDP source hypothesis of pentateuchal origins has collapsed into a theory of two sources. One would be Deuteronomic (including most of what was previously attributed to Yahwist and Elohist sources), and the other the reactive P source (Albertz 464–93).

The stamp of Deuteronomy on the so-called "Deuteronomistic History" (Joshua–Kings) is evident not only in the style of these books (many of the embedded speeches sound like Deuteronomy—Josh. 23, 24; 1 Sam. 12; etc.), but also especially in its theology (cf. McConville, *Grace*). Specifically, Solomon's emphasis on the temple as a place for the "name of Yahweh" to dwell (1 Kings 8) harks back to Deut. 12 et passim. More generally, if and when the nation of Israel and her monarchy are destroyed, it is because they have failed in covenant with Yahweh as outlined in Deuteronomy. The influence of Deuteronomy is less obvious on Chronicles and Ezra-Nehemiah, but in the Latter Prophets one hears echoes of Moses' orations throughout. In Hosea and Jeremiah, the links are so direct that scholars often debate which came first, Deuteronomy or the prophet. Prophetic pronouncements of judgment and restoration appear often to be based on the covenant curses of Deut. 28 and promises of renewal in chapter 30. Indeed, the canonical prophets as a whole and Malachi specifically (Mal. 4:4–6) end with a call to return to the "torah of my servant Moses" (AT), which has its base in the revelation at Sinai but, strictly speaking, refers fundamentally to Moses' exposition.

In the Psalms, Deuteronomic influence is most evident in the so-called "torah" psalms (1, 19, 119), which highlight the life-giving purpose of the law, but also in the "wisdom" psalms, with their emphasis on fear of Yahweh (111:10; cf. 34:8–12). Weinfeld has argued that Deuteronomy bears many verbal and conceptual affinities with Proverbs (e.g., emphasis on fear of Yahweh, and presentation of two ways—life/blessing and death/curse)—which point to wisdom influence (*Deuteronomy 1–11*, 62–65; *School*, 244–319). However, it seems more likely that the influence was in the opposite direction.

NT texts like Luke 24:44 suggest that by the time of Christ the expression *Torat Mosheh* (Law of Moses, as in Josh. 8:31) served as the standard designation for the first part of the Jewish canon (alongside "the Prophets" and "the Psalms"). As noted earlier, the pentateuchal location of Deuteronomy, which serves as a theological exposition of the events narrated in the previous books, may have influenced the canonical location of John. However, whereas Christ himself is presented as Yahweh incarnate, the person whose role most closely resembles Moses in Deuteronomy is Paul. This apostle was specially called not only to lead the community of faith in mission, but also to interpret God's saving actions and instruct God's people in the life of covenant faith. In so doing he responded sharply to those who insisted that adherence to the law of Moses was a prerequisite to salvation. Like Deuteronomy, often Paul's Epistles each divide readily into two parts, the first being devoted to theological exposition (cf. Deut. 1–11), and the second to drawing out the practical and communal implications of the theology (cf. Deut. 12–26).

Deuteronomy and Theology

As an overall theme to Deuteronomy, we propose the following: A call to Israel for faithfulness in the land, in response to the grace Yahweh has lavished on them (cf. 6:20–25). In developing this theme, Moses presents a theology that is remarkable for both profundity and scope.

First, Israel's history begins and ends with God. Deuteronomy instructs Israel and all subsequent readers on his absolute uniqueness (4:32–39; 6:4; 10:17; 32:39; 33:26), eternality (33:27), transcendence (7:21; 10:17; 32:3), holiness (32:51), justice and righteousness (32:4; cf. 10:18), passion (jealousy) for his covenant and relationship with his people (4:24; 5:9; 6:15; 9:3; 32:21), faithfulness (7:9), presence (1:45; 4:7; 6:15; 7:21; 31:17), compassion (4:31), and especially covenant love (4:37; 7:7–8, 13; 10:15, 18; 23:5). But none of these are mere abstractions. Yahweh lives in relationship with humans, which explains why Moses never tired of speaking of God's grace—expressed in many different concrete actions toward Israel. Examples include election of Abraham and his descendants (4:37; 7:6), rescue of Israel from the bondage of Egypt (4:32–36), establishment of Israel as his covenant people (4:9–31; 5:1–22; 26:16–19), providential care (1:30–33; 8:15–16), provision of a homeland (6:10–15; 8:7–14), provision of leadership (16:18–18:22), and victory over their enemies (7:17–24).

Second, Deuteronomy offers a comprehensive picture of the community of faith. Externally, the community that stands before Moses consists largely of the descendants of Abraham, and the first-generation offspring of those who had experienced the exodus from Egypt. In Deuteronomy, the doctrine of divine election plays a prominent role. The book speaks of the divine election (*bakhar*, choose) of the place for Yahweh's name to be established and to which the Israelites are invited for worship and communion (12:5; et passim). It also tells of the divine election of Israel's king (17:15), whose primary function is to embody covenant righteousness, and of the Levitical priests (18:5; 21:5), who were to promote righteousness. However, Yahweh's election of Israel to be his covenant people receives special attention. Deuteronomy 4:32–40 places Yahweh's rescue of Israel within the framework of cosmic history, declaring this event to be unprecedented both as a divine act and as a human experience. Lest hearers have any illusions about the grounds of election, Moses emphasizes that Yahweh's election of Israel was based on neither exceptional physical nor spiritual qualifications. Israel was not granted favored status with Yahweh because of its significance as a people, for it was the least (7:6–8), or because of its superior behavior vis-à-vis the nations, for her past is characterized by rebellion (9:1–23). On the contrary, election was an act of sheer grace, grounded in Yahweh's love for the ancestors (4:32–38) and in his inexplicable love for their descendants (7:6–8). In so doing, Deuteronomy presents Israel as an incredibly privileged people. They alone have experienced the strong redeeming hand of Yahweh (4:32–40), have participated in a covenant ceremony (4:9–31), and enjoy vital communion with Yahweh. Thereby he not only hears them whenever they cry out, but in an unprecedented act of revelation he also has made his will known to them (4:1–8; 6:20–25). Their standing with God is characterized directly as that of covenant partners (26:16–19) and a holy people belonging to him alone (7:6; 14:2; 26:19; 28:9). Metaphorically, they are counted as his adopted sons (14:1; cf. the portrayal of God as their father in 1:3 KJV/MT; 8:5; 32:5–6, 18) and his treasured possession (*segullah*, 7:6; 14:2; 26:18). However, although Yahweh had called the nation as a whole to covenant relationship, the true community of faith consists of persons who love Yahweh with their entire being. They demonstrate that love through righteousness (*tsedaqah*, 6:25), which includes repudiating all other gods and compassionately pursuing justice toward others (10:16–20).

Third, no other book in the OT presents as thorough a treatment of covenant relationship as Deuteronomy. Though some draw sharp lines of distinction between the Abrahamic covenant and the covenant that Yahweh made with Israel at Sinai, Deuteronomy perceives these to be organically related. The Sinai/Horeb covenant represents the fulfillment of the covenant Yahweh had made with Abraham and an extension of his commitment to Abraham's descendants (cf. Gen. 17:7). In Deuteronomy, Moses propounds an exposition of the covenant to which the present generation binds itself (26:16–19). Chapters 29–30 do not envision a new covenant, but the present generation's recommitment to and extension of the old.

It is within this covenantal context that we must understand the role of the law. Deuteronomy stresses obedience within that relationship: (1) Obedience was not to be viewed as a burden but as response to the unique privilege of knowing God's will (Deut. 4:6–8), in contrast to the nations who worshipped gods of wood and stone (4:28;

Ps. 115:4–8). (2) Obedience is not a way of salvation, but the grateful response of those who had already been saved (6:20–25). (3) Obedience is not primarily a duty imposed by one party on another, but an expression of covenant relationship (26:16–19). (4) Obedience is the external evidence of the circumcision of one's heart and the internal disposition of fearing God (10:12–11:1; 30:6–9). (5) Obedience involves a willing subordination of one's entire being to the authority of the gracious divine suzerain (6:4–9; 10:12–13). (6) While obedience is not the prerequisite to salvation, it is the evidence of righteousness, which is a precondition to Israel's fulfillment of her mission and blessing (4:24–25; chs. 11, 28). (7) Obedience is both reasonable and achievable (30:11–20).

The last point demands further comment, especially since the book seems to view Israel's failure as inevitable (4:24; 5:29; 29:14–30:1; 31:16–21; 32:14–27). Part of the answer to this dilemma may be found in the frequent alternation of singular and plural forms of direct address. The shifts between "you" singular and "you" plural serve a rhetorical function, recognizing that though Yahweh entered into covenant relationship with the nation, in the end fidelity cannot be legislated and must be demonstrated at the personal level. Yet, this device also recognizes the existence of two Israels. On the one hand, there was a physical Israel, consisting of descendants of Abraham, Isaac, and Jacob. On the other hand, there was a spiritual Israel, consisting of those persons (like Moses and Joshua and Caleb) who demonstrated unqualified devotion to Yahweh. For the latter, obedience was not only possible; it was a delight. But Deuteronomy is both pessimistic and realistic about the former, anticipating a future of rebellion that will lead eventually to the destruction and exile of the nation. According to 30:6–10 this problem of national infidelity will only be resolved in the distant future, when Yahweh brings the people back and circumcises their hearts.

Fourth, Deuteronomy presents a highly developed theology of land. Moses' cosmic awareness is expressed by his appeal to heaven and earth to witness Israel's renewal of the covenant (4:26; 30:19; 31:28). But corresponding to Yahweh's love for Israel within the context of the nations, in 11:12 he declares that the land currently occupied by the Canaanites, set aside for Israel, is the special object of Yahweh's perpetual care (*darash*). Yahweh is delivering this land to the Israelites as their special grant (*nakhalah*, 4:21 et passim), in fulfillment of his oath to the ancestors (1:8 et passim). Yet, the Israelites are challenged to

engage the Canaanites, drive them out (9:3), and utterly destroy them and their religious installations (7:2–5; 12:2–3). However, this land is not given to Israel because the people have earned it (9:1–24), but as an act of grace.

Deuteronomy describes the nation's relationship to the land within the context of the tripartite association of Deity-land-people. Accordingly, the response of the land to Israel's occupation will depend entirely upon the people's fidelity. If they are faithful to Yahweh, the land will yield bountiful produce (7:11–16; 11:8–15; 28:1–14). But if they prove unfaithful, not giving Yahweh the credit for their prosperity and going after other gods, then the land will stop yielding its bounty, and he will sever the tie with it (4:25–28; 8:17–20; 11:16–17; 28:15–26). When the Israelites will be removed from the land because of their sin (which in Moses' mind appears inevitable), this will not represent a cancellation of the covenant, but the application of its fine print (cf. Dan. 9:4–16). Because of Yahweh's immutable covenant commitment to Abraham (Deut. 4:31), he must and will bring Israel back to the land and to himself (30:1–10). Accordingly, within their present literary contexts and the history of God's covenant relationship with Israel, the "new" covenant of which Jeremiah speaks in Jer. 31:31–34 and the eternal covenant of which Ezekiel writes in 16:60 (cf. 34:25–31) should not be interpreted as absolutely new. Instead, they are anticipations of the full realization of God's original covenant made with Abraham (ratified and fleshed out at Horeb), when the boundaries of physical and spiritual Israel will finally be coterminous. (The NT development of this theme in the context of the Lord's Supper [Luke 22:20; 1 Cor. 11:25] and in Hebrews [8:8–13; 9:15; 12:24] recognizes that ultimately God's covenant relationship with his people is possible only because of the mediatorial and sacrificial work of Christ.) Accordingly, Israel's exile cannot be the final word on the land. Because of Yahweh's compassion and the irrevocability of his covenant with Israel (Deut. 4:31), when the people repent he will regather them (30:1–5). However, the book is clear: Israel's occupation of the land and her prosperity are contingent on fidelity to Yahweh.

Fifth, Deuteronomy presents a remarkable approach to government. From beginning to end, Israel is presented as a theocracy, with Yahweh as her divine suzerain (though the kingship of Yahweh receives scant explicit attention; cf. 33:5). The book provides for judicial officials appointed by the people (1:9–15; 16:18), and kings, priests, and prophets appointed and/or raised up by Yahweh (17:14–18:22). Indeed, many scholars interpret 16:18–18:22 as a sort of state "constitution" for Israel, designed to reinforce the centralization of power in Jerusalem under Josiah (cf. McConville, *Deuteronomy*, 78–79). However, this interpretation is extremely problematic, because 17:14–20 presents the monarchy as optional, and interest in the king's real power over the people is eclipsed by concern for his role as a paradigm of covenant faithfulness. This disposition is quite at odds with the nature of Israelite kingship historically. The "constitution" interpretation of 16:18–18:22 also is especially problematic because it tends to overlook the primary concern of the book—to establish a people under the authority of torah and governed by "righteousness" (*tsedaqah*).

Conclusion

For modern readers plagued by a negative view of the OT in general and OT law in particular, Deuteronomy offers a healthy antidote. Through the work of Christ not only is Israel's relationship made possible, but also the church, the new Israel of God, is grafted into God's covenant promises. As with Israel, access to these promises remains by grace alone, through faith alone. However, having been chosen, redeemed, and granted covenant relationship with God, Yahweh's people will gladly demonstrate wholehearted allegiance with whole-bodied obedience (Rom. 12:1–12). Deuteronomy remains an invaluable resource for biblical understanding (1) of God, especially his grace in redeeming those bound in sin; (2) of appropriate response to God, entailing love for God and for our fellow human beings; and (3) of the sure destiny of the redeemed. More than any other book in the OT (if not the Bible as a whole), Deuteronomy concretizes faith for real life. Inasmuch as the NT identifies Jesus Christ with the God of Israel's redemption, in the spiritual and ethical pronouncements of Deuteronomy we find fleshed out both the first and great commandment (Matt. 22:34–40) and "the law of Christ" (Gal. 6:2). A church that has discovered this book will have its feet on the ground, resisting the tendency to fly off into realms of Platonic ideas and inward subjectivity so common in Western Christianity.

Bibliography

Albertz, R. *A History of Israelite Religion in the Old Testament Period*. 2 vols. Westminster John Knox, 1994; Block, D. "How Many Is God? An Investigation into the Meaning of Deuteronomy 6:4–5." *JETS* 47 (2004): 193–212; idem. "Recovering the Voice of Moses: The Genesis of Deuteronomy." *JETS* 44 (2001): 385–408; Calvin, J. *The Four Last Books of Moses*. Vol. 1. Eerdmans, 1950; Craigie, P. *The Book of Deuteronomy*. NICOT. Eerdmans, 1976; Knierim, R. "The Composition of the Pentateuch." Pages 351–79 in *The Task of Old Testament Theology*. Eerdmans, 1995; Lienhard, J., et al., eds. *Exodus, Leviticus, Numbers, Deuteronomy*. ACCSOT 3. InterVarsity, 2001; Lohse, B. *Martin Luther's Theology*. Fortress, 1999; Luther, M. *Lectures on Deuteronomy*. LWorks 9. Concordia, 1960; McConville, J. G. *Deuteronomy*. Apollos/InterVarsity, 2002; idem. *Grace in the End*. Zondervan, 1993; idem. *Law and Theology in Deuteronomy*. JSOTSup 33. JSOT, 1984; McConville, J. G., and J. G. Millar. *Time and Place in Deuteronomy*. JSOTSup 179. Sheffield Academic Press, 1984; Millar, J. G. *Now Choose Life*. Eerdmans, 1998; Nelson, R. *Deuteronomy*. OTL. Westminster John Knox, 2002; Nicholson, E. W. *Deuteronomy and Tradition*. Fortress, 1967; Noth, M. *The Deuteronomistic History*. JSOTSup 15. JSOT, 1981; Olsen, D. *Deuteronomy and the Death of Moses*. Fortress, 1994; Rad, G. von. *Deuteronomy*. OTL. Westminster, 1966; idem. *The Problem of the Hexateuch and Other Studies*. SCM, 1966; idem. *Studies in Deuteronomy*. SBT 9. SCM, 1953; Richter, S. *The Deuteronomistic History and the Name Theology*. De Gruyter, 2002; Schreiner, T. *The Law and Its Fulfillment*. Baker, 1993; Sonnet, J.-P. *The Book within the Book*. Brill, 1997; Thompson, J. A. *Deuteronomy*. TOTC. InterVarsity, 1974; Tigay, J. *Deuteronomy*. JPS Torah Commentary. JPS, 1996; Vogt, P. *Deuteronomic Theology and the Significance of the Torah*. Eisenbrauns, 2006; Watts, J. *Reading Law*. Sheffield Academic Press, 1999; Weinfeld, M. *Deuteronomy 1–11*. AB 5A. Doubleday, 1991; idem. "Deuteronomy, Book of." *ABD* 2:168–83; idem. *Deuteronomy and the Deuteronomic School*. Clarendon, 1972; Wenham, G. "Deuteronomy and the Central Sanctuary." *TynBul* 22 (1971): 103–18; Wilson, I. *Out of the Midst of the Fire*. SBLDS 151. Scholars Press, 1995; Wright, C. J. H. *Deuteronomy*. NIBCOT. Hendrickson, 1996; Wright, N. T. *The Climax of the Covenant*. Fortress, 1993.

Daniel I. Block

Dialectic   *See* Dialogism

Dialogism

Dialogism, as its root "dialogue" suggests, is based on our ordinary experience of face-to-face conversations, but its expanded perspectives on persons, reciprocity, and responsibility offer a rich hermeneutical context in which to read the Bible.

Dialogism was most fully articulated by Mikhail Mikhailovic Bakhtin (1895–1975), a Russian writer arrested in 1929 for alleged activity in the underground Orthodox Church and sentenced to internal exile. Despite poor health and political pressure, Bakhtin survived the Stalinist regime, although he published relatively little in his own lifetime and most of his works remained fragmentary or unrevised. Promoted by a group of graduate students who rediscovered him in 1961, he has subsequently emerged as an important thinker, both in Russia and in the West.

Central to the notion of dialogism is that meaning does not exist in an abstract or singular form; this is in contrast to the dialectical tradition, in which thesis and antithesis are resolved into a synthesis. Dialogism insists on the priority of two or more persons who remain distinct from one another. Thus, it is not words *that* communicate, but we *who* communicate in interactions that require, as a minimum, the irreducible community of two. To illustrate, imagine two people looking at each other: I see you as a whole person, a three-dimensional body situated within a three-dimensional environment. At the same time, I see only bits of myself and a two-dimensional horizon that stretches away from me. I see you better than I see myself, and you see me better than you see yourself. Your excess of vision supplements mine, just as my excess of vision supplements yours. To create meaning, we must each "fill in" the other's horizon by offering our "excess of vision" to each other as a gift. What I offer to you and what you offer to me, in our reciprocal, complementary visions, is what we cannot create for ourselves. And to offer that gift we must remain distinct, outside one another, resisting the temptation to collapse one perspective into the other.

Meaning thus arises from within an irreducible community of two, as part of a dynamic call and response. Dialogism is more than simply a dialogue, two people talking together; it is rather a rich personal context that emphasizes asymmetric reciprocity and responsibility.

Although Bakhtin was not a theologian, dialogism can help us better understand the Bible by focusing in turn on the author, the text, and the reader.

First, the call/response of meaningful language characterizes not only our relationships to other persons, but also our relationship to the infinite Person, to God. Bakhtin puts it this way: "Revelation characterizes the world just as much as natural laws do," and this revelation is itself "characterized . . . by the Person who wants to reveal Himself" (Felch and Contino 219–20). Communication, call/response, or dialogic interchange is thus inscribed into the very fabric of the world. To return to the visual image, God is the one who looks on me, who sees more of me than I can see of myself, who from this excess of vision offers me the gift of meaning. Furthermore, "what I must be for the other, God is for me" (Bakhtin, *Art*, 56). That is, what I should be for others, God already is for me, whether or not I recognize this to be the case.

It is not simply that God's beneficent, and therefore productive, gaze provides a model for meaningful encounters, but also that God's creation of and revelation in the world guarantees the possibility of meaning. God is not a concept, an absolute principle, an inert authoritative dogma. God is the *infinite* person who can in his wholeness guarantee a three-dimensional environment that will sustain a plenitude of meanings. But because he is a *person*, he also initiates the call/response of meaningful language. What this means for the Bible is that inscripturated revelation, along with natural revelation, must be received as a gift that bestows meaning upon me. God's word reveals me to myself, and to submit to its gaze is to accept a meaning-ful gift. To refuse its gaze is to attempt the impossible and the perverse, to create a meaningful event with only one participant, myself. For Bakhtin, such an attempt is not only doomed to failure but also constitutes "a lapse into sin" (Bakhtin, *Art*, 124).

Second, because words are offered as gifts from other people, dialogism takes seriously their shape and form. What this means for the Bible is that its genres and language are not expendable casings that can be updated, discarded, or ignored at will. With the critical realists (cf. Soskice), dialogism insists that there is no such thing as "mere" metaphor: terms such as "shepherd," "king," or "father" do not exhaust the nature of God but neither are they arbitrary. They speak in true, if limited, ways of God's person. Similarly, although the Bible is not identical with God, just as my own words are not identical with my person, it is the ordinary means by which I come to know God and myself. Dialogism thus refuses both bibliolatry and bibliophobia.

Third, dialogic reciprocity requires that the reader actively engage the words of the Bible. To use Bakhtin's terms, we can read the Bible merely as authoritative discourse, as words that come *at* us. Such words can be either recited or rejected, but they remain external to us and therefore lifeless. We can also read the Bible as internally persuasive discourse, as words that come *to* us. Such words are internalized as we chew them, digest them, and make them our own in new and living ways. At best, however, authoritative discourse and internally persuasive discourse become united in the penetrated word that retains its authoritative self-sufficiency without tyranny. As penetrated word, the Bible holds together both horizontal and vertical dimensions; it penetrates us, pushing us toward the truth, and is itself penetrated by God's presence.

Bibliography

Bakhtin, M. M. *Art and Answerability*, ed. M. Holquist and V. Liapunov, trans. V. Liapunov. University of Texas Press, 1990; idem. *The Dialogic Imagination*, ed. M. Holquist, trans. C. Emerson and M. Holquist. University of Texas Press, 1981; idem. *Problems of Dostoevsky's Poetics*, ed. and trans. C. Emerson. University of Minnesota Press, 1984; idem. *Toward a Philosophy of the Act*, ed. M. Holquist and V. Liapunov, trans. V. Liapunov. University of Texas Press, 1993; Coates, R. *Christianity in Bakhtin*. Cambridge University Press, 1998; Emerson, C. "Russian Orthodoxy and the Early Bakhtin." *Religion and Literature* 22 (1990): 109–31; Felch, S., and P. Contino, eds. *Bakhtin and Religion*. Northwestern University Press, 2001; Green, B. *Mikhail Bakhtin and Bible Scholarship*. Society of Biblical Literature, 2000; Mihailovic, A. *Corporeal Words*. Northwestern University Press, 1997; Soskice, J. M. *Metaphor and Religious Language*. Clarendon, 1985.

Susan M. Felch

Dictionaries and Encyclopedias

With important precursors, since the second half of the twentieth century, these reference tools have become increasingly available and important for biblical and theological studies. They now comprise the closest analog we have to the "knowledge base" available on the World Wide Web for industrial and scientific applications. The explosion of research and publishing, together with the ever-more-detailed work of biblical scholarship, has made it virtually impossible for individuals to remain current or to gain currency in any but the most circumscribed fields. As a result, the Bible dictionary and theological dictionary or multivolume encyclopedia has achieved the status of indispensable compendia of contemporary thought. Nevertheless, a general perusal of these reference tools demonstrates the degree to which those engaged in the theological interpretation of Scripture occupy the frontiers of the disciplines of systematic theology and biblical studies. This is because, at their best, dictionaries and encyclopedias gather together and collate the state of play at the time of their publication; due to relative adolescence theological interpretation of Scripture, discussion or exemplars of the discipline are largely absent from the theological reference library.

We turn, first, to theological dictionaries (e.g., Elwell; Ferguson and Wright; Richardson and Bowden), where the centuries-old chasm separating scholarly study of the Bible and systematic theology is plainly on display. Only rarely does one come across serious engagement with biblical scholarship. Often one encounters either evidences of the commitment of the theological enterprise to philosophical foundations and/or the propositional content of systematic theology, or the repetition of some of the failed experiments in biblical theology. The latter is expressed, for example, in the choice of systematic categories as a mold into which one might press or squeeze the biblical witness; in facile descriptions of the biblical witness that grasp for unity at the expense of hearing also the diverse voices of Scripture or making sense of them; in characterizations of the biblical witness that allow one biblical voice to speak for all (in evangelical Protestant traditions, with the Pauline voice often trumping the others); in the aggregation of biblical texts drawn from throughout the canon without reference or attention to literary, historical, or canonical context; and in the deployment of problematic word studies in the service of biblical theology (see below).

This rather dismal portrayal is not so much an indictment of the enterprise represented by theological dictionaries as it is a summary statement of the segregation of the disciplines of theological and biblical studies, each with its own accredited procedures and epistemic base. Concerning the task of theology, Barth remarked: "Dogmatics does not ask what the apostles and prophets said but what we must say on the basis of the apostles and prophets" (16). But two hundred years of biblical studies have left us with little access to the theological immediacy or vitality of "what the apostles and prophets said." Moreover, due to the ways in which the discipline of systematic theology has developed, the genre of theological dictionaries has not been oriented toward producing or representing theological interpretation of Scripture. What we do encounter in these reference works is often a keen sense of the developing theological tradition—an overview of the ways in which the biblical witness has been crystallized in the history of doctrine; and this can prove invaluable in the theological formation of the interpreter of Scripture. In this respect, *The Dictionary of Historical Theology* (T. Hart) especially invites careful attention.

Of course, theological reference works are not without bias, and individual entries do not always move beyond the theological horizons of the tradition and perspective of their contributors (whether Reformed or Lutheran, for example). For this reason, a recent entry into the field of reference works, those books that self-consciously work within and represent a particular tradition are worthy of note. Not surprisingly, for example, *The New International Dictionary of Pentecostal and Charismatic Movements* (Burgess) treats such subjects as healing or glossolalia far more extensively and within different theological assumptions than more traditional theological dictionaries. The same may be said with regard to "ordinances" in the *Dictionary of Baptists in America* (Leonard) and "sacraments" in the *Dictionary of the Presbyterian and Reformed Tradition in America* (D. G. Hart). Even where one finds little in the way of explicit theological interpretation of Scripture, these reference tools provide plentiful evidence of how our formation within a theological tradition and under the influence of wider sociocultural forces helps to shape the character of our theological engagement with the biblical materials.

If, from the side of systematic theology, reference works do not exhibit much in the way of engagement with academic biblical studies, the opposite is, if anything, even truer in the case of Bible dictionaries and encyclopedias, where the concerns of constructive theology seem far from view. This is due above all to the self-imposed agenda of biblical studies since the late eighteenth century, its primary and narrow focus on discerning and explicating the meaning of the biblical text, understood grammatically and historically. Theological concerns, when they surface in biblical studies, are mostly articulated descriptively (e.g., "the theological perspective of the Deuteronomist" or "John's theological stance" designated the domain of biblical scholars who describe themselves especially as historians) rather than constructively (in terms of their contemporary immediacy, regarded as the domain of systematic theologians and ethicists). With respect to this descriptive task, suitable works have multiplied in the last two decades. Discussion of theological motifs is well represented in such reference works as *Dictionary of Jesus and the Gospels* (Green and McKnight), *Dictionary of Paul and His Letters* (Hawthorne et al.), *Dictionary of the Later New Testament and Its Developments* (Martin and Davids), and *Dictionary of the Old Testament: Pentateuch* (Alexander and Baker), as well as in the more traditional one-volume Bible dictionaries (e.g., Freedman, *Eerdmans*).

Conversation with systematic theology in biblical studies reference tools remains scarce; indeed, even descriptive theological work cannot yet be taken for granted. Consider, for example, "the

industry standard": the widely acclaimed, six-volume, 7,035-page *Anchor Bible Dictionary* (*ABD*; Freedman). With more than 6,000 entries, one might think that every conceivable topic pertinent to the biblical studies enterprise would be represented, even exhausted. Although one does find all sorts of biblical minutiae and cognate esoterica, including references to numerous sites and people not mentioned in the Bible, theological concerns are sometimes conspicuously absent. There is no entry on "gospel" ("good news") or "truth," for example, and one looks in vain for biblical-theological treatments of "prayer" or "church." A magnificent achievement in many respects, the *ABD* often finds its home more easily in the department of religious studies than in Christian theological discourse.

The shortcomings of the *Theological Dictionary of the New Testament* (*TDNT*; Kittel and Friedrich) are widely recognized (cf. Barr). With its interest in the distinctive theological significance of NT words, essays in *TDNT*, especially but not exclusively in its earlier volumes, tended to download impressive theological content into *words*, suggesting that the significant unit of meaning was the individual word rather than the discourse within which the word appears. The *New International Dictionary of New Testament Theology* (Brown) often fails to escape the same criticism. Happily, as wordbooks the more recent *Theological Dictionary of the Old Testament* (Botterweck and Ringgren) and *New International Dictionary of Old Testament Theology and Exegesis* (VanGemeren), working from more nuanced linguistic commitments, have advanced beyond their NT counterparts as reference tools suited to the work of theological interpretation of Scripture.

For persons interested in the theological interpretation of Scripture, the bibliography (below) may thus far seem to be of little help. Two recent contributions have begun to mitigate this rather negative assessment, however. Among its offerings, *A Dictionary of Biblical Interpretation* (Coggins and Houlden) provides essays sketching the history of interpretation of biblical books and discussing major biblical interpreters (e.g., Origen and Augustine), interpretative practices (e.g., "Inner-Biblical Exegesis"), and some biblical themes (e.g., "Akedah") relevant to our concerns. Finally, there is the *New Dictionary of Biblical Theology* (Alexander and Rosner), divided into three major sections. The first addresses a range of concerns central to the contemporary biblical-theological enterprise, including the unity and diversity of the biblical materials, the relationship between the Testaments, and even "Systematic Theology and Biblical Theology." The second focuses on major collections of writings in the Bible (the prophetic books, for example, or the Pauline corpus) before turning to entries on individual books. Third, we find a generally well-chosen series of articles on biblical themes. Even here, however, one finds little by way of self-conscious engagement with contemporary theology; the focus is largely descriptive, though from time to time the careful reader will find contributors moving into programmatic comments regarding present-day appropriation.

Bibliography

Alexander, T. D., and B. Rosner, eds. *New Dictionary of Biblical Theology*. InterVarsity, 2000; Alexander, T. D., and D. W. Baker, eds. *Dictionary of the Old Testament: Pentateuch*. InterVarsity, 2003; Barr, J. *The Semantics of Biblical Language*. Oxford University Press, 1961; Barth, K. *Church Dogmatics*. Vol. I/1. T&T Clark, 1975; Botterweck, G., and H. Ringgren, eds. *TDOT*; Brown, C., ed. *The New International Dictionary of New Testament Theology*. 3 vols. Zondervan, 1975–78; Burgess, S., ed. *The New International Dictionary of Pentecostal and Charismatic Movements*. Rev. ed. Zondervan, 2002; Coggins, R. J., and J. L. Houlden, eds. *A Dictionary of Biblical Interpretation*. Trinity, 1990; Elwell, W., ed. *Evangelical Dictionary of Theology*. 2d ed. Baker, 2001; Ferguson, S., and D. F. Wright, eds. *New Dictionary of Theology*. InterVarsity, 1988; Freedman, D. N., ed. *The Anchor Bible Dictionary*. 6 vols. Doubleday, 1992; idem. *Eerdmans Dictionary of the Bible*. Eerdmans, 2000; Green, J., and S. McKnight, eds. *Dictionary of Jesus and the Gospels*. InterVarsity, 1992; Hart, D. G. *Dictionary of the Presbyterian and Reformed Tradition in America*. InterVarsity, 1999; Hart, T. *The Dictionary of Historical Theology*. Eerdmans, 2000; Hawthorne, G., et al., eds. *Dictionary of Paul and His Letters*. InterVarsity, 1993; Kittel, G., and G. Friedrich, eds. *TDNT*; Leonard, B. *Dictionary of Baptists in America*. InterVarsity, 1994; Martin, R., and P. Davids, eds. *Dictionary of the Later New Testament and Its Developments*. InterVarsity, 1997; Richardson, A., and J. Bowden. *The Westminster Dictionary of Christian Theology*. Westminster John Knox, 1983; VanGemeren, W., ed. *New International Dictionary of Old Testament Theology and Exegesis*. 5 vols. Zondervan, 1997.

Joel B. Green

Différance   *See* Deconstruction; Postmodernity and Biblical Interpretation

Discontinuity (between the Testaments)   *See* Relationship between the Testaments

Dispensation(alism)   *See* Daniel, Book of; Last Things, Doctrine of; Revelation, Book of; Salvation, History of

Diversity   *See* Culture and Hermeneutics; Feminist Biblical Interpretation; Racism; Scripture, Unity of

Doctrine

One of the central tasks of Christian theology is to weave together the various strands of the biblical witness, integrating them into a coherent and systematic account of the Christian vision of reality. "Doctrine" is the term generally given to the body of teachings that result from this sustained engagement with Scripture. This process of engagement is complex and involves a number of specific forms of interaction, including the development of a coherent understanding of a given area of thought through reconciling passages that sometimes appear to be in tension. Historically, this has been of particular importance in relation to the areas of Christology (synthesizing biblical statements concerning the humanity and divinity of Christ) and grace (reconciling statements concerning human freedom and divine sovereignty). In recent years, a more general debate over how Scripture is to be interpreted through doctrine has been extended, with particular attention being paid to the different types of biblical genre (especially narratives), and their relationship to the development of doctrine: in what way may a narrative be said to generate doctrines?

At a very early stage in Christian reflection, it was conceded that it was simply inadequate to repeat biblical affirmations and assume that this ended intellectual discussion of the issues they raised. A series of controversies—most notably, the Gnostic controversy of the second century, focusing on Irenaeus—demonstrated the need for a normative interpretation of Scripture as the official teaching of the church. He also stressed the need to accept that certain interpretations of the biblical material were severely deficient and incapable of doing justice to the Christian vision of reality. For Irenaeus, these interpretations were to be defined as heretical, and the church needed to clearly repudiate them as such.

Irenaeus stressed the importance of creeds as public statements of Christian doctrine. These creeds wove together biblical images, themes, and statements to yield a definitive statement of fundamental Christian doctrines. Writing around 350, Cyril of Jerusalem defined the role of creeds as a "synthesis of faith" that set out ". . . to present the one teaching of the faith in its totality, in which what is of greatest importance is gathered together from all the Scriptures. And just as a mustard seed contains a great number of branches in its tiny grain, so also this summary of faith brings together in a few words the entire knowledge of the true religion which is contained in the Old and New Testaments."

Christian doctrine is thus a communal, authoritative interpretation of the totality of the biblical witness. It is to be distinguished from theological opinion by the fact that it is accepted within the church as an authoritative, normative statement of Christian beliefs. Even at an early stage in the long process of Christian engagement with Scripture, it was accepted that not all areas of doctrine were of equal importance. The early church singled out the doctrine of the "two natures" of Christ and the doctrine of the Trinity as being of especial importance, in that they distinguished Christianity from Judaism on the one hand, and from pagan worldviews on the other. The term "dogma"—meaning an essential, nonnegotiable element of Christian belief—was used to refer to these two areas of doctrine, and dogma was contrasted with heresy. However, a degree of latitude was recognized in other areas of doctrine—for example, in relation to understandings of the church or of the last things.

The overall development of doctrine through the centuries is best seen as the gradual unfolding of the fundamental themes of Scripture, in much the same way as a seed grows into a plant. This view is stated in the works of the leading Scottish evangelical theologian James Orr (1834–1913). In his *Christian View of God*, Orr insists that theology must constantly work to ensure that its doctrinal formulations are adequate to the "infinite truth" they seek to mediate, which is revealed in Scripture. One of Orr's most distinctive contributions lies in his recognition of "progress in dogma"—in other words, doctrinal development. Rejecting a static understanding of doctrine, he argues that the entire theological enterprise must be dedicated to developing dogmatic formulations that are adequate to the revelation they seek to express, yet which ultimately transcends them. "The dogmatic molds which were found adequate for one age have often proved insufficient for the next, to which a larger horizon of vision has been granted; and have had to be broken up that new ones might be created, more adapted to the content of a Revelation which in some sense transcends them all."

A similar idea is developed by Charles Gore (1853–1932). He responds to those who argue that the simplicity of the biblical witness to Christ is compromised and distorted by theoretical development within the history of the church, especially during the patristic period. Gore insists that these later theoretical formulations are to be seen as "the apostolic teaching worked out into formulas by the aid of a terminology which was supplied by Greek dialectics." There was no distortion, no misrepresentation—merely the "gradual unfolding of teaching" of "an unbroken stream of tradition."

A number of factors stimulated the development of doctrine in the patristic period and beyond. The most important of these is the outbreak of controversy within the church over a point of doctrine, which forced clarification of this area of theology. The Arian, Pelagian, and Donatist controversies all forced reconsideration of areas of theology (specifically, in the areas of Christology, the doctrine of grace, and the doctrine of the church). In the case of the Arian controversy, issues of biblical interpretation were of central importance. The key question under debate was whether the complex NT witness to the person of Christ could best be understood by asserting that Christ was one of God's creatures, but supreme among those creatures (the Arian position); or whether Christ was the Son of God incarnate (the Athanasian position, which eventually won the day).

A second factor of importance is the need to see the "big picture"—to be able to understand how the various elements of Scripture relate to each other, and how they contribute to the shaping of a Christian worldview. This idea can be seen in the writings of P. T. Forsyth (1848–1921), especially his landmark work *The Person and Place of Jesus Christ*. Here Forsyth argues that doctrine is the "science of faith," in that it sets out to give a coherent and comprehensive account of the Christian understanding of reality as expressed in Scripture.

Yet such an understanding is of more than intellectual importance; it serves to identify the church and safeguard its distinctiveness, so that it might not lose its "saltiness." Forsyth argued that the identity of the church requires definition if it is to continue in existence as a distinct entity. Doctrine, according to Forsyth, is essential to the life of the church, in that it both *arises from* and *expresses* that life. "A Church must always have a dogma, implicit or explicit. A cohesive Church must have a coherent creed. But it must be a dogma the Church holds, not one that holds the Church. The life is in the body, not in the system. . . . The idea of a dogma, as the organized declaration or confession by any Church of its collective doctrine, is only the intellectual counterpart of the idea of the organized Church itself" (Forsyth 213).

There thus exist two pressures that make doctrine inevitable: the human desire to make sense of things and extend the horizons of understanding, and the social need for the church to offer a definition of its identity and boundaries. As Reinhard Hütter points out, there is a clear need for the church to possess a publicly recognizable, binding teaching that transcends individual beliefs or personal interpretations of biblical passages.

The development of doctrine has not been without its critics. For some, doctrine represents an unnecessary and distorting overlay on the Bible. Adolf von Harnack (1851–1930), one of the most significant German liberal Protestant theologians, argued that the development of doctrine or "dogma" was the result of the intrusion of Greek ideas into Christian theology. Harnack drew a sharp and ultimately indefensible distinction between "Hellenistic" and "Jewish" ways of thinking, arguing that doctrine represented the triumph of the former over the latter. Although this view was highly influential in the first half of the twentieth century, it is no longer regarded as acceptable.

Nevertheless, Harnack's concerns remain significant, especially as they raise the question of how improper doctrinal developments may be identified and reformed. Are all doctrinal developments authentic? Certainly not. A good example of the problems arising from unchecked theological expansionism can be seen from the Middle Ages, which witnessed remarkable proliferation in doctrinal speculation, some of which seemed highly questionable. So how can such doctrines be assessed? And how can the situation be remedied? These questions were faced with the utmost seriousness during the Protestant Reformation of the sixteenth century. The mainline Reformers argued that there was an urgent need for the reform of the church. That there existed a Christian church in Europe prior to the Reformation was not to be doubted; it had, however, lost its way at the spiritual, theological, and ecclesiastical levels.

The Reformation is best seen as a demand for the church to set itself in order and return to more authentic and biblical ways of living and thinking.

The use of the word "reform" is of critical importance; it points to the need for the reformation of an existing body: a Christian church existed in the form of the medieval Catholic Church in Europe, before the Reformation. Even though both Luther and Calvin were scathing in their criticisms of that church, their fundamental assumption was that this was a Christian church, even if it was severely distorted and confused.

The fundamental concern of Reformers such as Martin Luther and John Calvin was thus to recall the church to its biblical roots. The Reformers were particularly concerned that a series of beliefs and practices had developed within medieval Christianity that had little biblical basis. Luther and Calvin proposed to eliminate such beliefs and replace them with more biblical themes. The Reformation can be seen as an attempt to reaffirm the priority of Scripture in every aspect of Christian life and thought; it gave a new stimulus to doctrinal reflection.

One of the most important developments of this period was the emergence of works of biblical theology, works stressing that doctrine was directly grounded in Scripture. The most important of these was Calvin's *Institutes*, first published in 1536. "My object in this work," wrote Calvin, "is to so prepare and train students of sacred theology for the study of the word of God that they might have an easy access into it, and be able to proceed in it without hindrance" (preface [1539]). In effect, Calvin set out to provide a detailed work of systematic theology that demonstrated its rooting in Scripture at every point, offering a continuous interpretation of Scripture in doing so.

Although subjected to much criticism in recent years, the concept of doctrine now remains an assured element of Christian life and thought, particularly within evangelical circles. The recognition of the need for communally accepted interpretations of Scripture has been catalyzed by a series of debates, often focusing on the ideas of theological mavericks, which have met with vigorous responses from leading representatives of more orthodox positions. While evangelicals will always wish to insist upon the priority of Scripture over its interpreters, the importance and legitimate place of such communal interpretation is part of Christian intellectual discipleship.

See also Creed; Historical Theology; Rule of Faith; Systematic Theology; Tradition

Bibliography

Betz, H. D. "Orthodoxy and Heresy in Primitive Christianity: Some Critical Remarks on Georg Strecker's

Republication of Walter Bauer's *Rechtgläubigkeit und Ketzerei im ältesten Christentum." Interpretation* 19 (1965): 299–311; Calvin, J. *Institutio Christianae religionis.* 2d ed. V. Ribelius, 1539; Chadwick, O. *From Bossuet to Newman.* Cambridge University Press, 1957; Cyril of Jerusalem, "Of Faith." Vol. 7 of *NPNF*[2]; Forsyth, P. T. *The Person and Place of Jesus Christ.* Independent Press, 1909; Gore, C. *The Incarnation of the Son of God.* John Murray, 1922; Hütter, R. "The Church as Public: Dogma, Practice and the Holy Spirit." *ProEccl* 3, no. 3 (1994): 334–61; McGrath, A. *The Intellectual Origins of the European Reformation.* 2d ed. Blackwell, 2003; Nichols, A. *From Newman to Congar.* T&T Clark, 1990; Orr, J. *The Christian View of God and the World, as Centring in the Incarnation.* Charles Scribner's Sons, 1908; Packer, J. I. "On from Orr: The Cultural Crisis, Rational Realism, and Incarnational Ontology." *Crux* 32, no. 3 (Sep 1996): 12–26; Torrance, T. F. "The Deposit of Faith." *SJT* 36 (1983): 1–28.

Alister E. McGrath

Dogma   *See* Creed; Doctrine; Rule of Faith; Systematic Theology; Tradition

E

Earth/Land

"Earth" and "land" are both translations of *'erets*, one of the most frequently used nouns in the Hebrew Scriptures. The roughly 2,400 references to earth, land, dry land, ground, and soil are a key to understanding both Israelite religion and the transformation of it wrought by Christianity powered by Greek thought.

Part of the lengthy conversation between the Samaritan woman and Jesus at Jacob's well (John 4:20–24) captures the point perfectly.

> "Our ancestors worshiped on this mountain, but you say that the place where people must worship is in Jerusalem." Jesus said to her, "Woman, believe me, the hour is coming when you will worship the Father neither on this mountain nor in Jerusalem. You worship what you do not know; we worship what we know, for salvation is from the Jews. But the hour is coming, and is now here, when the true worshipers will worship the Father in spirit and truth, for the Father seeks such as these to worship him. God is spirit, and those who worship him must worship in spirit and truth." (NRSV)

Jews and Samaritans disagreed on where to worship God, but they agreed that there is an appropriate place to do so because God has a mountain home. John's Jesus opposes the basic notion that where to worship God is even an issue at all. Proper worship is a matter of "spirit and truth," not mountains. A proper relationship with God is not connected to land but to spirit. This made room for the Greek notion that revolutionized religion, leaving Jews, Samaritans, and anyone else who understands God to be connected to earthly events and places gaping in shock.

Christians, however, could not adopt the Platonic notion that meaning resides only in ideas and not in places, because they do not worship the God of the philosophers, but of the Jews, and they so must also attend to Scriptures besides John. Genesis teaches that God created the earth and its contents and blesses it. "The earth is the Lord's" (Ps. 24:1) says that meaning does reside in concrete places, indeed, in every place, because of its origin and owner. Human beings are merely its stewards, authorized both to guard and to use it. Yet Ps. 115:16 puts it forcefully: "Heaven belongs to God, and he has given the earth to mankind" (AT). In this vein, particular territories belong to different tribes and nations. God promises the land of Canaan to Abra(ha)m (Gen. 13:15; 17:8), his son Isaac (26:3–4), his grandson Jacob (28:13), and their offspring forever. Further, portions of the promised land are distributed to each of the twelve tribes from Jacob's sons, except the tribe of Levi, which does not live from the land.

Even though specific lands are designated for various tribes and nations, the land itself ever remains God's possession, with its own theological vocation. It glorifies God by providing a natural order that sustains life and supplies the needs of all living things. By controlling nature, God inspires awe, wonder, and praise at his wisdom and goodness, and we rejoice (Ps. 104). At the same time, the earth is God's tool to reward obedience and punish wrongdoing. At God's command, it can produce famine instead of plenty, or swallow up the disobedient (Num. 16:31–32). If we defile the earth with sexual impropriety and violence, it will vomit us up out of itself to be cleansed (Lev. 18:28).

OT theology teaches that piety is well formed when people properly understand God's relationship to land. Places become memorials to divine grace and power. They are named or renamed after God does striking events in specific places in order to edify future generations. Hagar named the spring where an angel of God promised that her son, Ishmael, would be the father of a mighty nation. Because she had seen the Lord and lived, she named it Beer-lahai-roi, spring where one sees and lives (Gen. 16:7–14). Jacob, for example, renames Luz as Bethel, house of God, after his famous dream in which God reconfirms the promises made originally to Abraham, adding that he would accompany Jacob wherever he goes and bring him back to the land (28:10–22). Next, he named the ford of the Jabbok River as Peniel, the face of God, after wrestling with the angel of God all night in preparation for meeting his brother Esau on the morn (32:24–32).

Perhaps the most striking example of how the Bible grounds religious identity in places is Josh. 3–4, Israel's crossing of the Jordan River. It repeats Israel's crossing of the Red Sea, but with a new generation that had never known Egypt. Here God authorizes Joshua to take Moses' place as leader of the people. God stops the flow of the river and has the priests stand in the middle of the riverbed with the ark of the covenant while all the people file past to safety on the other side. When all have crossed, Joshua has a leader of each of the twelve tribes select a large stone from the riverbed. He sets them up to mark what has happened there as a sign of God's favor, to stand as a reminder forever. According to the OT, the land itself proclaims the story of God and Israel, and the earth preaches Israel's God to the nations.

The NT charts a different path for Christianity by radically reconfiguring the connection between God and the land and people of promise. Physical Israel, both people and land, becomes spiritual Israel by faith, as suggested by John 4. Yet, Christianity cannot let go of the earth, because it is more grounded in the reality of Jesus Christ than in the power of human faith. Augustine of Hippo saw that Plato and his philosophical descendants had powerful insights into human psychology and morality. Still, he could not cut the cord between God and the earth because Jesus Christ has bridged the distance between earth and heaven. For Christians, he is the paramount (if not the only) place of God's grace and wisdom, which comes, not as ideas, but as one formed of the dust of the earth and the blood of human life.

It has proved difficult to hold together the two notions that meaning resides in place and that meaning resides in the power of ideas. Revelation picks up John's spiritualizing move. The argument between Jerusalem and Mt. Gerizim is still won by Jerusalem, but not the city of David. Now Jerusalem comes down from God out of heaven (Rev. 3:12; 21:2); indeed, it is heaven. One wonders whether contemporary postmoderns have retained the theological meaning of place in their zeal for the politics of personal sociological locatedness.

Bibliography

Brueggemann, W. *The Land*. Fortress, 1977; Wilken, R. L. *The Land Called Holy*. Yale University Press, 1992.

Ellen T. Charry

Ecclesiastes, Book of

Ecclesiastes is particularly challenging for theological interpretation. The vigorous debate among Jewish schools in the first century as to whether or not Ecclesiastes "defiled the hands" continues to this day. Now the discussion is about the extent to which Ecclesiastes is good news. A minority of scholars argues that Ecclesiastes affirms joy, while the majority finds it to be pessimistic, even hopeless.

History of Interpretation

By the fourth century CE, allegorical reading of Ecclesiastes was dominant among Jews and Christians, with "eating and drinking" being taken as referring to the Torah or the Eucharist, and the vanity element as a warning against excessive attachment to this world compared to "eternal" life. An allegorical reading of Ecclesiastes remained the dominant mode until the Reformation. It took the revival of literal interpretation by the Reformers to recover, for example, the possibility that "eating and drinking" refers to legitimate enjoyment of the God-given creation. Whether interpreted allegorically or literally, Ecclesiastes, prior to the rise of modern criticism, was read as Scripture, with the epilogue regarded as *the* key to the book.

Siegfried pioneered the source-critical approach to Ecclesiastes, identifying nine different sources in the book. Within English-speaking circles, McNeile and Barton developed more moderate source-critical approaches to Ecclesiastes. As the twentieth century progressed, a radical source-critical approach to Ecclesiastes became rare, and the book has come to be seen more and more as a unity, with the exception of the epilogue, which is almost universally seen as a later addition. The prime legacy of source criticism in the interpretation of Ecclesiastes is the tendency to read the book without the epilogue.

Hermann Gunkel initiated form-critical analysis of Wisdom literature, and the assessment of the forms used in Ecclesiastes has continued to play a fundamental role in the interpretation of the book. However, on the macrolevel of the form of Ecclesiastes, no consensus has been reached with regard to genre and structure. The tradition history of Ecclesiastes has been a matter of concern throughout the twentieth century. Within the OT wisdom tradition, Ecclesiastes has regularly been seen as a negative, skeptical reaction to mainline wisdom as represented by Proverbs. Gese identified Ecclesiastes with a crisis of wisdom in Israel, but scholars remain divided over the existence and extent of this "crisis."

A limited consensus has emerged out of historical-critical interpretation of Ecclesiastes. Few scholars nowadays defend Solomonic authorship; most regard Ecclesiastes as having been written by an unknown Jew around the latter part of the third century BCE. Most regard the book as a basic unity apart from the epilogue. However, there is no agreement regarding Ecclesiastes' structure, message, and relationship to OT traditions and to international wisdom. Historical-critical scholarship differs from precritical readings in its general rejection of the need to harmonize Ecclesiastes with theological orthodoxy. However, this loss of theological constraint has not produced agreement about the message of Ecclesiastes, as, for example, the variety of proposals for translating *hebel* indicates.

In recent decades a variety of new reading strategies have been applied to Ecclesiastes.

Childs's canonical reading has led him to reappropriate the epilogue as the key to the canonical function of Ecclesiastes. Childs reads Ecclesiastes as a corrective within the broader wisdom tradition, comparable to James's relationship to Romans in the NT.

The literary turn in biblical studies in the 1970s resulted in a spate of fresh literary readings of Ecclesiastes. Wright ("Riddle of the Sphinx") has analyzed the structure of Ecclesiastes by means of a close reading along the lines of "New Criticism." The theme of Ecclesiastes is understood to be the impossibility of understanding what God has done. The only advice that Qoheleth (the "preacher" or "teacher" of Ecclesiastes) gives is to enjoy life while one can. Loader (*Polar*) performs a modified structuralist reading of Ecclesiastes, whereby he discerns polar opposites as the heart of its structure. These polar opposites reflect the tension between Ecclesiastes' view and that of general wisdom. However, for Loader, Ecclesiastes finally is negative; he rescues it theologically as a negative witness to the gospel.

Perry approaches Ecclesiastes as the transcript of a debate between Koheleth (K) and the Presenter (P). Perry argues that Ecclesiastes elaborates on the paradigmatic contradiction in Hebrew Scripture that is introduced in the creation story of Genesis. It has to do with the way religious consciousness distinguishes itself from empirical or experiential modes of viewing life. Fox ("Frame") proposes reading Ecclesiastes as a narrative-wisdom text, with openness to distinguishing between narrator, implied author, and

Qoheleth. Longman, Christianson, and others have pursued Fox's narrative proposal in a variety of ways. There are also examples of poststructuralist, feminist, and psychoanalytic (Zimmerman) readings of Ecclesiastes.

Hearing the Message of Ecclesiastes

There is something wonderfully ironic about a book on the enigma of life being terribly difficult to grasp, so that Ecclesiastes enacts its own message. Yet the following hermeneutical steps enable us to discern that message.

First, it is important to read Ecclesiastes and not just "Qoheleth." The legacy of historical criticism is to try to get behind the text to the "real Qoheleth." However, the case for reading the book as a literary whole is compelling; one is always on highly speculative ground when trying to get to the "real Qoheleth." The way forward is to focus on the different voices in Ecclesiastes, inquiring after the perspective of the implied author. Perry, Fox, Longman, and Christianson have done important work in this direction.

Second, reading the text as a literary whole must involve taking the epilogue seriously as part of that whole. An urgent issue in Ecclesiastes scholarship is to reopen the debate about how the epilogue relates to the main body of the text.

Third, Ecclesiastes must be read in the context of the canon of Scripture and especially of the OT Wisdom literature. Fox (*Time*) has done seminal work on the epistemology of Qoheleth in comparison with Proverbs and rightly argues that Qoheleth's epistemology is empiricist, whereas that of Proverbs is not. However, Fox does not note the significance of this for the canonical interpretation of Ecclesiastes. Although Qoheleth goes out of his way to stress that he embarked on his quest by *khokmah* (1:13; 2:3), the key elements of his epistemology are reason and experience alone, and these always lead him down to the *hebel hebalim* ("vanity of vanities") conclusion (1:2; 12:8). Read against Proverbs, in which "the fear of the LORD is the beginning [foundation and starting point] of wisdom" (9:10), it becomes apparent how ironic Qoheleth's description of his epistemology is. In this sense Ecclesiastes is an ironic exposure of an empiricist epistemology as always leading one to a *hebel* conclusion. Further work needs to be done on irony and epistemology in Ecclesiastes.

Fourth, considerable attention needs to be given to the poetics of Ecclesiastes. Only comparatively recently have scholars come to recognize that the Wisdom books are literary compositions in their own right. Repetition, for example, is a significant characteristic of Ecclesiastes. Most significant are the repetitions of the *hebel* (vanity) conclusion and the joy/carpe diem passages. From one angle the history of the interpretation of Ecclesiastes is a sustained attempt to level the book to one or the other of these two poles. Either the joy passages are made subsidiary to the negative *hebel* conclusion, or the *hebel* passages are made subsidiary to the joy conclusion. The crucial question is how the *hebel* passages relate to the joy passages.

My suggestion is that in Ecclesiastes the *hebel* conclusions, arrived at via Qoheleth's empiricism applied to the area he examines, are juxtaposed with the joy passages, which express the positive perspective on life that Qoheleth received from his Jewish upbringing. These perspectives are set in contradictory juxtaposition so that, in the reading, gaps are opened up that have to be filled as the reader moves forward. The book thereby raises for readers the question of how these perspectives are to be related. Especially in the postexilic context in which Ecclesiastes was probably written, it would have been tempting for Israelites to use reason and experience to conclude that life is *hebel hebalim*.

A crucial question is whether or not Ecclesiastes itself gives us clues as to how to bridge the gaps between these perspectives. Understanding the irony of Qoheleth's epistemology is one major clue, telling us that if one starts with reason and experience alone in difficult situations, one will always end up with *hebel*. The other major clues to bridging the gaps come toward the end of the book. Normally in Ecclesiastes, a *hebel* conclusion is reached and then juxtaposed with a joy passage. Toward the end of the book this order is reversed (11:8–10), and particularly important is the exhortation prefacing the final section before the epilogue: "Remember your creator" followed by a threefold "before . . ." (12:1–8). This exhortation to remember is the equivalent of starting with the fear of the Lord. It means developing a perspective integrally shaped by a view of this world as being the Lord's.

Ecclesiastes and the Canon

Read positively, Ecclesiastes complements rather than contradicts Proverbs and Job. Proverbs is already well aware of retributive paradox (Gladson), especially in its latter chapters; Job and Ecclesiastes explore such paradox in detail, Job through a story of terrible suffering, and Ecclesiastes through an intellectual struggle

for meaning. Also, Ecclesiastes, with its affirmation of creation and its understanding of work as toil and life as *hebel*, has strong links with Gen. 1–3.

Ecclesiastes never is quoted in the NT, although Rom. 8:20 perhaps alludes to it, as *mataiotēs* (frustration, futility) is the usual Septuagint word for *hebel*. Ecclesiastes, like Proverbs, hopes for justice, although it manifests no doctrine of the new creation, as do some of the prophets and the whole NT. Like Proverbs, Ecclesiastes contains reflections upon diverse topics such as wealth, pleasure, work, time, injustice, wisdom and folly, and government. Considerable work remains to be done in exploring these themes in relation to the rest of the Bible.

Ecclesiastes and Theology

The theological relevance of Ecclesiastes depends upon one's reading of it. Read as negative and hopeless, Ecclesiastes' only contribution will be as a negative witness to the gospel. However, a positive reading of Ecclesiastes indicates that it has an important positive contribution to make theologically.

Qoheleth's affirmation of joy is an expression of the doctrine of creation. In line with the goodness of creation, Qoheleth celebrates life under the motifs of eating and drinking, working, and enjoying marriage. This is not hedonism in the context of despair, but an affirmation of life as God has made it.

In a fallen world there is much that raises the most serious questions about the goodness of life. The empirical strength of those questions comes into focus in the *hebel* passages and conclusions. In terms of pastoral theology, Ecclesiastes is most important in its juxtaposition of *hebel* and joy in the experience of Qoheleth as he wrestles with the value of life under the sun. Ecclesiastes explores the struggle that believers go through as they endeavor to affirm life amid suffering, injustice, and disillusionment.

Qoheleth's struggle is more intellectual than that of Job. His quest is summed up in a rhetorical question: "What do people gain from all the toil at which they toil under the sun?" (1:3 NRSV). Central to Qoheleth's quest is the issue of how we know in such a way that we can trust the results—epistemology. In my view, Ecclesiastes is an ironic exposure of a way of knowing that depends upon reason and experience alone, as opposed to an approach that starts with remembering one's Creator, with faith and obedience. Ecclesiastes explores these issues in a narrative fashion, telling the story of Qoheleth's quest. It is not a philosophical book. Nevertheless, it does have implications for the theology of epistemology. In line with Proverbs and Job, Ecclesiastes affirms the importance of a theological starting point comparable to "faith seeking understanding." Ecclesiastes' exposure of empiricism and its logical consequences are of great contemporary relevance in the face of the nihilism so common in postmodernism.

Bibliography

Barton, G. A. *A Critical and Exegetical Commentary on the Book of Ecclesiastes.* ICC. T&T Clark, 1912; Childs, B. *Introduction to the Old Testament as Scripture.* Fortress, 1979; Christianson, E. S. *A Time to Tell.* Sheffield Academic Press, 1998; Fox, M. "Frame Narrative and Composition in the Book of Qoheleth." *HUCA* 48 (1977): 83–106; idem. *A Time to Tear Down and a Time to Build Up.* Eerdmans, 1999; Gese, H. "The Crisis of Wisdom in Koheleth." Pages 141–53 in *Theodicy in the Old Testament,* ed. J. Crenshaw. Fortress, 1983; Gladson, J. A. *Retributive Paradoxes in Proverbs 10–29.* University Microfilms International, 1979; Loader, J. A. *Ecclesiastes.* Eerdmans, 1986; idem. *Polar Structures in the Book of Qohelet.* De Gruyter, 1979; Longman, T. *The Book of Ecclesiastes.* NICOT. Eerdmans, 1998; McNeile, A. H. *An Introduction to Ecclesiastes: With Notes and Appendices.* Cambridge University Press, 1904; Perry, T. A. *Dialogues with Koheleth.* Pennsylvania State University Press, 1993; Siegfried, C. *Prediger und Hoheslied.* HAT. Vandenhoeck & Ruprecht, 1898; Wright, A. G. "The Riddle of the Sphinx: The Structure of the Book of Qoheleth." *CBQ* 30 (1968): 313–34; idem. "The Riddle of the Sphinx Revisited: Numerical Patterns in the Book of Qoheleth." *CBQ* 42 (1980): 38–51; Zimmerman, F. *The Inner World of Qoheleth.* Ktav, 1973.

Craig G. Bartholomew

Echo *See* Intertextuality; Relationship between the Testaments

Egyptology *See* Ancient Near Eastern Background Studies

Eisegesis *See* Exegesis

Election *See* Church, Doctrine of the; Covenant; Israel; Violence

Enlightenment

This is a historical designation used initially in English-speaking scholarship to describe the ideological program of the eighteenth-century French *philosophes*, but which became a general descriptor identifying the eighteenth century as a progressive social epoch, promoting secular intellectual freedom and representative government against the oppressive forces of tradition. This broader meaning of the term corresponds to the German concept of *Aufklärung,* defined by Immanuel Kant in 1784 as both a spiritual force and method of truth that rejects "self-incurred tutelage" to authorities that represent old ideas of the past. To be mature and free, a person must analyze the reality of the human condition apart from the conventional wisdom of religious dogma and the divine right of kings. *"Sapere aude,"* said Kant, "'Dare to use your own reason!'—that is the motto of enlightenment."

Kant's essay captured the spirit of an age that had been in formation for over a century. Reacting to the wars of religion that engulfed Europe between the death of Luther in 1546 and the Glorious Revolution of 1688, an intellectual avant-garde felt compelled to examine the rational basis for society and its improvement. This examination was dependent especially upon Thomas Hobbes (*Leviathan,* 1651) and Baruch Spinoza (*Theological-Political Tractate,* 1670), both of whom treated the mutual alliance of religion and politics as the source of corruption and tyranny in the social order. Drawing upon ancient Epicurean thought, Hobbes and Spinoza construed historical religion essentially as "superstition," which manipulates "the fear of the gods" in order that priest and prince may dominate a largely unlettered populace. To make their case, both philosophers interpreted the Bible not as the revelation of a timeless ecclesiastical dogma, whether Catholic or Protestant, but rather as largely the profane story of the human effort to usurp divine sovereignty for political purposes. The corrupting force of political power is the key hermeneutical idea needed to understand Scripture. It is the meaning behind the text. The Bible must be read like any other book: its purposes are defined by the human motivations of its writers.

According to Spinoza, the only exception to this harsh and suspicious interpretation of the Bible is the teaching of Christ. Against religious superstition, Christ teaches that the Law and the Prophets—that is, the essential content of the Bible—are summed up in the commandments to love God and neighbor. These commandments are the foundation of a natural religion of reason. To read the Bible according to Christ is not easy because of the way religious and political authorities use it. The rational interpretation of Scripture requires an educated elite that will exegete the text independently of dogmatic considerations.

A comparable position is advanced in English Deism, which formed its philosophy in reaction to the turmoil of the civil war and its aftermath in the Restoration. John Locke (*A Letter concerning Toleration*, 1689) asserts that religion is a matter of free, private association in which like-minded individuals worship God in their own way. Neither government nor the established church should interfere with this freedom. By noninterference they bear the true "mark" of Christ, which is toleration. "The kings of the Gentiles exercise lordship over them, said our Savior to his disciples, but ye shall not be so, Luke xxii, 25, 26."

On the continent, Pierre Bayle grounded religious toleration not in the teaching of Christ but in methodological skepticism. In his notorious and influential *Historical and Critical Dictionary* (1695–97), Bayle asserts that rational inquiry, because it leads to doubt, serves true religion in that it tests the proper basis of faith: "God does not want [our minds] to find a standing ground too easily and sets traps for it on all sides." No "truth" is so certain that it may be used to suppress the free expression of ideas.

This conviction became a commonplace among the French *philosophes* such as Denis Diderot and Voltaire, and also in the philosophy of Jean-Jacques Rousseau. In their work outright hostility to Christianity is barely disguised. In the *Social Contract* (1762), for example, Rousseau judges Christianity to be the enemy of a just social order, arguing that Christ set up on earth "a spiritual kingdom, which, by separating the theological from the political system, made the state no longer one." Christians cannot be trusted to be good citizens because their allegiance is divided. The effort to de-Christianize France in the fanatical phase of the French Revolution was a direct result of this opinion.

Suspicion of Christianity also underlies the secular impulse of the American Revolution. Reflecting on the significance of the Declaration of Independence, Thomas Jefferson declared it to be "the signal of arousing men to burst the chains under which monkish ignorance and superstition had persuaded them to bind themselves, and to assume the blessings and security of self-government." Jefferson saw the history of Christianity as little more than a "slaughterhouse."

The "enlightened" ideas of tolerance and free inquiry, especially as these ideas are grounded in an Epicurean suspicion of religion, were embraced even among those who ostensibly served the church as pastors and teachers. This is clear in the work of Hermann Samuel Reimarus, whose *Apology for the Rational Worshipers of God* was written in secret and did not appear in print until after his death. In 1777–78, Gotthold Ephraim Lessing anonymously published portions of the manuscript as *Fragments* and caused a sensation. In the *Fragments*, Reimarus claims that the accounts of the resurrection in the Gospels are fraudulent narratives concocted by the disciples for political advantage. Jesus himself was an admirable but disillusioned moral teacher of the imminent kingdom of God, an idea common to Judaism of the time. For the future of modern historical research of the Bible, Reimarus is crucially important. He is the first to place the teaching of Jesus in contextual continuity with Judaism and to see it as reflecting an eschatological worldview. Lessing's ugly broad ditch resulted, between history's accidental truths and the demands of reason.

Perhaps Kant summed up the thrust of the Enlightenment with regard to religion by his understanding of *Religion within the Limits of Reason Alone* (1793). In "moral religion," he says, "it is a basic principle that each must do as much as lies in his power to become a better man." Whether Jesus Christ and Scripture serve this basic principle may have been a matter of debate among the proponents of Enlightenment. What was not in debate among them was the principle itself.

Bibliography

In addition to primary sources mentioned: Harrisville, R. A., and W. Sundberg. *The Bible in Modern Culture*. 2d ed. Eerdmans, 2002.

Walter Sundberg

Ephesians, Book of

No NT writing more joyfully celebrates God's grace in the gospel than does Ephesians, nor does any contain so rich and concentrated a vein of theological gold. This short letter's profound and extensive influence on the church's thought, liturgy, and piety ranks with that of the much longer Psalms, John, and Romans (on the letter's history of influence, see Schnackenburg 311–45). It was Calvin's favorite letter, and Coleridge was later to pronounce it "the divinest composition of man." In more recent times Ephesians has come to be thought pseudepigraphical, and consequently marginalized in Pauline studies. In the meantime, contemporary focus on both *ecumenical* theology and on *canonical* readings of the biblical writings has helped to maintain something of the letter's former prominence.

History of Interpretation

Ephesians has been a central text throughout the history of the church, the subject of many commentaries from Origen, Chrysostom, and Jerome onward, and continually thereafter ransacked for its spiritual and theological treasures. With the Reformation, and the modernist quest that followed it, the letter came increasingly to be read as a unified discourse with its own distinct message. This tendency was radically sharpened by increasing doubts in the nineteenth and twentieth centuries concerning its authenticity and its Ephesian destination.

Increasingly interpreters propose that "Ephesians" was written by an admiring disciple of Paul, late in the first century—one who wrote in a different style from the apostle. This author was far more heavily dependent on Colossians than Paul ever was on his own writings (about a third of the wordings of Colossians, and many of its main themes, appear in Ephesians) and was offering what he saw as the essential legacy of the apostle's theology for a new time and circumstances. It is argued that the (pseudonymous) writer no longer actively hopes for an imminent return of Christ and, indeed, has replaced the whole shape of Paul's largely *future* hope with a realized eschatology, in which believers are *already* raised from death and exalted with Christ into the heavenly places (2:1–10; 1:3–4; allegedly contra 1 Cor. 4:8; 15:1–54; and Rom. 6:1–11; *but* see Col. 2:11–13). It is held that the writer has left Paul's theology of the cross for a theology of glory instead, and that he has given ecclesiology a radical new direction and extravagant prominence as the "universal church" (whereas, it is often asserted, Paul himself uses *ekklēsia* only of *local* congregations; but per contra, see Gal. 1:13; 1 Cor. 10:32; 12:28; 15:9; Phil. 3:6). It is also said that he has moved toward a supersessionist view of Israel and the law, in which the church replaces Israel as the people of God (2:14–18; contra Rom. 9–11; for an accessible account of all these alleged shifts, see, e.g., Lincoln and Wedderburn, ch. 8).

Other interpreters, however, consider Ephesians authentic and see most of the claimed shifts as either exaggerated or already present in its "companion" letter, Colossians (cf. Col. 4:7–8//Eph. 6:21–22), and/or generated by the letter's more general, doxological, visionary, and exhortatory purposes (so, e.g., Arnold, Moritz, and the major commentaries by Barth, O'Brien, and Hoehner).

The Style of Theologizing in Ephesians

Unlike other Pauline letters, Ephesians does not directly tackle some particular local or immediately strategic concerns. Yet it was probably intended primarily to be read *alongside* Colossians in the Lycus valley churches (possibly as the "letter from [nearby] Laodicea," Col. 4:16), and as a partial prophylactic against the danger there of syncretistic veneration of angelic powers (see Arnold). Instead, Ephesians is dominated by (1) blessing of God for the cosmic reconciliation he has begun in Christ (1:3–14 [esp. 1:9–10]; 3:20–21); (2) prayer that the readers might spiritually comprehend this gospel and be fully grasped by it (1:15–2:10; 3:1, 14–21); and (3) an integrally corresponding ethical exhortation to live out that good news *together* in a unity that exemplifies it to the cosmos (4:1–6:17).

The writer deliberately builds important stages in the letter around material already regarded as core "creedal" tradition in the Pauline churches, including a significant vein of OT texts largely read christologically (cf. Pss. 8 and 110 in 1:20–23; Isa. 52 and 57 in 2:14–18; Ps. 68 in 4:8–10; Isa. 26 and 60 in 5:14; Gen. 2:24 in 5:30–32; and Isa. 11, 52, and 59 in 6:10–17: see Moritz, passim; Best, *Essays*, ch. 3). And this short letter is so densely packed with the apostle's major themes that it has been hailed as the "crown" and "quintessence" of Paulinism. But the style of address is not Paul's usual "argument" or expository discourse as much as it is thankful, prayer-filled celebration and exhortation, written with the zeal, idealism, and burning enthusiasm of the visionary. The writer almost certainly feels that he himself powerfully experiences the very "Spirit of wisdom and revelation" which he prays for his readers (1:17), and that the eyes of his own heart have thereby been opened to comprehend the rich glory of the gospel (1:18–2:8; 3:2–10). He senses that by this Spirit he is already deeply united with the ascended Lord (1:3; 2:5–6). By the same Spirit (3:16) he has already begun to know the depths of Christ's love and to be filled with the eschatological fullness of God (3:18–19). And it is as one full of this Spirit (5:18) that he pours out his doxological and edificatory address.

The form and style of address—together with the concrete content of Paul's prayer for his readers in 1:17–2:10 and 3:1, 14–19—underscore that the apostle regards authentic theological understanding (the sort that enlivens and transforms) as *fully possible only* in the *community* (not in mere "individuality") that *experiences the char-*

ismatic self-revealing and transforming presence of God's Spirit.

The Substantive Content, Shape, and Contribution of the Letter's Theology

For the sake of brevity, in what follows I distribute, under separate headings (like so many separated bones, muscles, and other organs), parts that Ephesians holds together in interconnected, full-bodily motion.

Theology. Written from a Jewish-Christian perspective, from the very outset (1:3–14) Ephesians patently blesses *Israel's* God. He is the almighty author of creation and the promised new creation (1:4; cf. 2:15; 3:11 [cf. 4:6]; 4:24), working out his sovereign pretemporal will to the eschatological praise of his glorious grace (1:6, 11–14). That grace focuses on fulfillment in Christ of the promises made to Israel of corporate "sonship" (now, yes, but primarily eschatological: 1:5–6, as in Rom. 8:23); new-exodus "redemption" from slavery/sin (1:7); "sealing" (with the Spirit: 1:13), and final "inheritance," in which God takes full possession of his people (1:14; cf. 1:18). At that point he will bring all things into the open cosmic unity and harmony of reconciliation with himself, which has already begun in the church in and through Christ (1:9–10; cf. 1:22–23; 3:19).

In Pelagian and especially in Reformation and later debates, attention fell on the opening eulogy's emphasis on *God as the sovereign source of election and predestination* (1:3–5, 9–11), and on what it means to affirm that this is accomplished "in Christ." Unresolved is the question whether behind the evident *corporate* nature of the election (the "we"/"us" stands for the *congregation* of God's people in Christ) there is also an implied election/predestination of *individuals* into the church: the latter is exegetically improbable (but not theologically thereby excluded).

But (as with other NT writings) God's identity is *supremely* revealed as "the God and Father *of our Lord Jesus*" (1:3 NRSV, italics added; cf. 1:17)—not so much on the basis of the number of times such expressions are used, as on the letter's profoundly christocentric (proto-binitarian) shape.

Christology. In most ways Ephesians recapitulates the teaching of Paul's other letters, including emphasis on Jesus as (1) the Christ; (2) the unique Lord (exalted to God's right hand, and thence as "head of all things," sharing his cosmic rule: see esp. 1:20–23; cf. 4:6); and (3) the Son of God. As elsewhere, he is also an Adamic figure who is the beginning (1:4), the paradigm

(4:20–24; 5:1–2, 25–32), and the end of God's purposes with humankind (1:10; 4:13, 15–16). As in other Paulines, the Lord is invoked as the *co-source*, with the Father, of "grace and peace" (1:2; cf. 6:23), but uniquely also of "love and faith/ faithfulness" (6:23–24). Paul usually refers to God as providing the "grace" of his apostolate and other ministries, through the Spirit, and Ephesians maintains the same (e.g., 3:2, 7), but much more explicitly than at (e.g.) 1 Cor. 12:5, describes the ascended Christ as the (co-)*giver* of the varied ministry gifts (4:10–12). Similarly, in Ephesians the risen Christ, like God, uniquely "fill[s] all things" (4:10), especially the church (1:22–23). Grasping the infinite love of Christ means to be filled with all the fullness of God (3:17). All this amounts to a deep-level "binitarian" Christology. It is matched by Paul's first explicit exhortation that Spirit-filled congregational worship should regularly involve singing and making melody *to* the Lord Jesus as well as giving thanks to the Father *through* (or "in the name of") the Lord Jesus (5:18–20). To mark Jesus as the expected recipient of full and regular worship, alongside the Father, was thus to include him within the identity of the One God/Lord of Israel (cf. 4:5–6; 1 Cor. 8:5–6; and the Shema [Deut. 6:4], on which they depend). That in turn was self-consciously to move into some form of *binitarian* monotheism (see Hurtado), and to provide the basis for pronounced liturgical developments.

Two more distinctive christological emphases may be mentioned: (1) Eph. 4:8–10 speaks of a descent and ascent of Christ. In conjunction with 1 Pet. 3:18–19, this has been taken (from the fathers onward) as a descent from the cross to hades (e.g., to harrow the imprisoned spirits), followed by resurrection-ascension. But this is exegetically implausible (in both letters!) and breaks the contextually required symmetry of the ascent-descent pattern, which might be ascent to heaven followed by corresponding re-descent (in the gift of the Spirit: so Lincoln; Harris). More probably it is the incarnational descent from heaven to earth, and then to the humiliation of the cross (= "the very lowest parts" AT), followed by corresponding ascent in resurrection-exaltation (see Schnackenburg; O'Brien; Hoehner). (2) The confession of Jesus as "head" of the ecclesial body is said to shift from the image of the local church as a whole body (including head, ears, eyes, etc., in 1 Cor. 12) to a universal church seen as an otherwise headless torso-and-limbs. But more probably as head to the church, Christ is portrayed as a lordly husband to his bride in a "one-body" union (5:22–31).

Pneumatology. The teaching on the Spirit in Ephesians is far more extensive than in its companion letter, Colossians, but also much closer to that of Paul's other letters (contra Adai; see Hui). The Spirit is the self-manifesting, transforming, and empowering presence of God—*and* of Christ—most probably the personal executive power by which both the Father and the Son indwell and "fill" the church (cf. 2:18, 22; 3:16–19), and direct (3:5; 4:30; 6:18), shape (1:17–19; 4:3), inspire (5:18), and empower it (1:17–19; 6:17; cf. 4:10–16). As such, the Spirit is essentially proto-trinitarian in character (Turner, "Trinitarian").

Salvation/Reconciliation/Cosmic Unity. At the theological heart of Ephesians glows the multifaceted jewel of the ineffable "mystery" revealed in the gospel (cf. 1:9–10; 3:3–4, 6–9; 5:32; 6:19; cf. Caragounis). This, while planned in eternity, was "set forth" paradigmatically in the Christ event (1:9 ESV, NRSV) as God's eschatological intention to (re-)unite "all things" in cosmic harmony with himself in Christ (1:10; cf. Col. 1:18–20). Many fathers from Irenaeus onward took the key verb *anakephalaiōsasthai* to mean "recapitulate" (i.e., to restore in the new head, Christ, all that was lost in the old, Adam). Others preferred to see a simpler allusion to 1:23, and took the verb to mean "to bring under (the) one head, Christ" (cf. NJB). The majority, however, recognize the verb means "to sum up/gather up" as under one *kephalaion* (= heading). The background assumption (as at Col. 1:18–20) is that creation has been plunged by sin into a chaos of alienations. Correspondingly, the hoped-for "summing up" takes the specific form of the reuniting of all things (or "reconciling" thereof: so Col. 1:20) in cosmic peace and harmony. *This is the vision that fundamentally stamps all else in the letter* (see Turner, "Mission"). It is a vision the author believes has been decisively inaugurated through Christ's redemptive (1:7), and especially in his *reconciling*, death (2:14–18). In a horizontal dimension the cross tears down (in principle) the wall of alienation dividing the two ancient divisions of humankind (Jew and Gentile), previously generated by the law, and allows the former two to be re-created as one *new* humanity in Christ (2:14–15). But in a vertical dimension the cross also reconciles both these groups *to God* (2:16–17), creating a church that thereby already exemplifies (to the world and to the *heavenly hosts*: cf. 3:10!) the beginnings of the cosmic reunification and messianic peace (2:18) in 1:9–10. That salvation has at least fully

dawned in the transforming faith-union that joins Jew and Gentile with the exalted Lord (2:6, 8); even though it has yet to be consummated.

Eschatology. Contrary to the assertion of some interpreters, the author does *not* believe the vision of 1:9–10 is already fully accomplished. He looks out onto a still largely benighted unbelieving "old" humanity, alienated from God, from the church, and from each other; dead in sin, and under the malign influence of the evil one (cf. 2:1–5; 4:17–20; 5:11–14). Even for the church itself, the days are evil (5:15; 6:13) and beset by encircling hosts of opposing powers (6:10–17; 4:27). Its day of redemption and inheritance (1:11–14, 18; 4:30) still essentially lies in the temporal future, which readers will naturally identify (from Col. 3:4, or from the Pauline tradition more generally) with the parousia. Ephesians does, however, take up the Pauline apocalyptic belief that the eschatological blessings already exist in the heavenly places, and that believers already share in these by virtue of their union with Christ. Ephesians gives distinct emphasis to this (esp. 1:3–14) and in 2:6 can even assert that believers are raised up and enthroned with Christ there (themes closely paralleled in Col. 2:12–13; 3:1–4). But this does *not* mean a shift to an overrealized eschatology, as is so often asserted. It is partly the regular bold assurance of eschatological benediction. More specifically, though, it is joyful affirmation of faith's close, partly reciprocal, indwelling between the believer and the heavenly Lord. Just as experience of the Spirit as "down payment" (1:14) of our inheritance is a foretaste of the eschatological fullness of Christ (1:23; 3:18–19; 4:10), so by the same Spirit we are now present *to* Christ, and so "with him," and share in his exaltation. And this sharing "with" him in the heavenlies is no triumphalism: it does not lift the believer out of earthly existence, with all its individual, household, and community responsibilities to live the cruciform life of openness, meekness, love, and service (see below).

People of God/Church/New Humanity/Ministry. In no Pauline letter is the church so remarkably prominent (see Schnackenburg 293–310, 321–31; Best, *Critical and Exegetical Commentary* 622–41). Ephesians develops many ecclesiological themes present in other Pauline letters, especially Colossians. Thus, the church is the holy "people of God" (= the saints), fulfilling the destiny of Israel. It is the body over which Christ is the head (Eph. 1:22//Col.1:18; 2:10; Eph. 4:15//Col. 2:19). It is God's *ekklēsia* (assembly), probably meaning the multiple and distinct earthly representation of the one heavenly and eschatological assembly (against the view that it is simply the universal earthly church, see O'Brien), the temple he indwells (Eph. 2:20–22; cf. 1 Cor. 3:16–17; 2 Cor. 6:16–18). But Ephesians brings distinctive emphases to bear. The temple is being built on the foundation of the fundamental apostolic/prophetic revelation of its essentially concorporate nature (fusing Jew and Gentile; 2:20–22; 3:5–6).

The church is also portrayed as a single developing body, one growing harmoniously from childhood toward Christlike (eschatological?) maturity, the "complete man." In this growth it is shaped, and held together, by the ministries that the Lord gives (4:10–16). Or to vary the metaphor again (sharply so in gender!), it is a body that is Christ's *bride*, and he is head over it as a husband to his wife (5:22–32; cf. 2 Cor. 11:2, but there the bride is a single congregation, and Paul its "best man"). The church is also the one new-creation humanity (2:15; 4:20–24), which, while not effacing the Jew/Gentile distinction (readers can still be addressed as "You Gentiles," 2:11; 3:1), embraces both in a unity that transcends such distinction (and any other racial division). It has a fundamentally "Israel" bias and shape and fulfills its hopes and destiny (2:11–18, esp. 12–13), but takes its singular most-defining identity from the ultimate *reconciling* self-giving of the (Jewish) Christ (4:20–21, 32; 5:1–2). In a context of Jewish mysticism, where the veneration of the heavenly beings was a potentially divisive threat (see Colossians), the soteriology, eschatology, and ecclesiology of the letter could hardly be more sharply relevant.

Ethics. Not surprisingly, the *one main and urgent task* of the church (as the writer composes his three chapters of ethical exhortation) is to maintain, and *visibly live out*, the cosmic unity/harmony begun in Christ (4:1–3). This means much more than merely ensuring that Gentile converts are treated on fully equal terms with Jewish believers (2:11–20; 3:5–6): it also means that *all* must renounce the old-creation patterns of alienat*ed* and alienat*ing* behavior (4:17–31; 5:3–15). Instead, they must adopt the cruciform virtues that recognize the authentic self, in God's likeness (*not* the smothered self of totalitarian regimes!), as belonging to and for the other. Thus they embrace ways of being/living that build the community's varied relationships and thereby give them previously unimaginable and joyful depth (esp. 4:25, 29; 4:32–5:2; 5:15–20, but throughout: cf. Turner, "Mission," 148–60). No better paradigm can Paul provide than that of

authentic marriage, which models the Christ-church relationship (5:22–32), and none has been more influential. But we would miss the apostle's point entirely if we took it just to be his later, more-considered teaching on marriage than that in 1 Cor. 7: he intends this portrayal of marriage to illumine *all* Christian relationships.

Powers and Spiritual Warfare. No Pauline letter—other than the sister letter, Colossians—gives such attention to principalities and powers. Arnold has argued that this is evoked by Ephesian fears of demonic magical powers associated with the Artemis cult. Perhaps more probable is that Paul fears the influence of Jewish-Christian teaching (primarily in the Lycus valley) about mystical heavenly ascent, and concomitant undue reverence for angelic beings. In terms of the history of interpretation, pride of place has certainly been given to Eph. 6:10–20. But while this passage has regularly been taken as a kind of specialist appendix on how to deal with the evil powers, it is much more convincingly understood as a fitting summary and conclusion to the themes of the whole letter (Lincoln).

Ephesians and the Canon

With relatively few exceptions, those who consider Ephesians pseudonymous still warmly commend its message. Its place in the canon restores a reading of it as complementary to Paul's letters and, indeed, even the "crown of Paulinism," rather than as any kind of substantial reassessment of it. As recognized above, it also dramatically highlights the universal, heavenly, and eschatological nature of the church as a community of cosmic reunification.

Ephesians and Theology

There is hardly a sentence of Ephesians that has not been deeply influential on Christian theology. But it is the letter's ecclesiology of cosmic reunification that has deservedly given it a place of singular import in contemporary theological discussion. Ephesians 2 has sparked important discussion of racial hostility (Rader). Ephesians 4:1–3, 7–16 has profoundly inspired various kinds of ecumenical theology of church and ministry. Many of these constitute a challenge to an evangelical tendency to point to Christ *rather than* to the church (which Ephesians would surely have seen as a false antithesis and even possibly as a betrayal of the church's calling). But the letter also emerges in theology as a challenge to contemporary individualism, and as a call for a radically new and engaging understanding of the "self" and authentic personhood (see, e.g., Ford).

See also Powers and Principalities

Bibliography

Arnold, C. *Ephesians*. Cambridge University Press, 1989; Barth, M. *Ephesians*. 2 vols. AB 34–34A. Doubleday, 1974; Best, E. *A Critical and Exegetical Commentary on Ephesians*. T&T Clark, 1998; idem. *Essays on Ephesians*. T&T Clark, 1997; Caragounis, C. C. *The Ephesian "Mysterion."* Gleerup, 1977; Ford, D. *Self and Salvation*. Cambridge University Press, 1999; Harris, W. H., III. *The Descent of Christ*. Brill, 1996; Hoehner, H. *Ephesians*. Baker, 2002; Hui, A. W. D. "The Concept of the Holy Spirit in Ephesians." *TynBul* 44 (1993): 379–82; Hurtado, L. *Lord Jesus Christ*. Eerdmans, 2003; Lincoln, A. *Ephesians*. WBC 42. Word, 1990; Lincoln, A., and A. J. M. Wedderburn. *The Theology of the Later Pauline Letters*. Cambridge University Press, 1993; Moritz, T. *A Profound Mystery*. Brill, 1996; O'Brien, P. T. "The Church as a Heavenly and Eschatological Entity." Pages 88–119 in *The Church in the Bible and the World*, ed. D. A. Carson. Baker, 1987; Rader, W. *The Church and Racial Hostility*. Mohr, 1978; Schnackenburg, R. *The Epistle to the Ephesians*. T&T Clark, 1991; Turner, M. "Mission and Meaning in Terms of 'Unity' in Ephesians." Pages 138–66 in *Mission and Meaning*, ed. A. Billington, T. Lane, and M. Turner. Paternoster, 1995; idem. "'Trinitarian' Pneumatology in the New Testament?—Towards an Explanation of the Worship of Jesus." *Asbury Theological Journal* 58 (2003): 167–86.

Max Turner

Epistemology

This branch of philosophy, also called theory of knowledge, considers issues such as the sources of knowledge, the means by which knowledge claims can be justified, and the relationship between justification and truth. Though philosophers have addressed it since the beginning, it became the center of philosophical inquiry in the modern era; now, however, there are those who question its necessity or legitimacy.

From Medieval to Modern

Medieval thought recognized two categories of knowledge: *scientia*, based on the model of geometry; and *opinio*, or probable knowledge, based on *approbation* by authority. The rejection of traditional authority as a legitimate source of knowledge has been attributed to the race's "coming of age" and rejecting religious superstition. A more credible account involves the problem of *too many* authorities created by the Reformation (Stout). At the beginning of the seventeenth century, bloodshed due to theological differences challenged epistemologists to provide a rational method for settling disputes (Toulmin). René Descartes (1596–1650), the "father" of modern philosophy, proposed to reject all he had been taught and then rebuild a system of knowledge by means of demonstrative (geometrical) reasoning. In his quest for certitude, he deployed two metaphors that shaped epistemological theories for the next three hundred years: the metaphor of knowledge as a building and the image of the "veil of ideas." It is ironic that these metaphors are a continuing source of skepticism, as seen below.

Foundationalism. It is now common to identify modern epistemology as "foundationalist." Knowledge is a building, which must be constructed by reason upon a set of indubitable (foundational) beliefs. Modern epistemology consisted of a succession of failed attempts to carry out Descartes's project. Descartes took beliefs that appeared "clearly and distinctly" to the mind's eye to be indubitable; he argued from these ideas to the existence of God and the trustworthiness of the senses. Unfortunately, what is clear and distinct to one thinker is often not so to others.

John Locke (1632–1704) countenanced three kinds of knowledge: that, like Descartes's, based on "relations of ideas"; that based on revelation; and that based on ideas derived from sensory experience. In light of his focus on the last of these, he is credited with inaugurating the modern empiricist tradition.

Already in the eighteenth century David Hume (1711–76) showed the futility of the foundationalist's ambitions. Scripture could not provide a foundation for theology because there is no compelling argument for the text to be a product of revelation. With empirical knowledge the problem is construction; one may indeed have certain knowledge of one's own sensory experiences, but attempts to prove anything on this basis (e.g., the existence of unobserved objects) all fail to meet Descartes's standard of truth-certifying reasoning. Thus, in every case either the proposed foundational beliefs turn out to be questionable, or if unquestionable, not suitable for supporting any interesting claims. Philosopher of science Karl Popper concluded that the structure of science is not built on a solid foundation, but is more like a house built on pilings driven into a swamp.

The end of foundationalism came with W. V. O. Quine's metaphor of knowledge as a web of belief. According to this "holist" theory of knowledge, no belief need be immune from revision. When a belief is called into question, it can be supported by reasoning in various directions: "inward" from experiential beliefs near the edges of the web, or "outward" from theories and presuppositions central to the web.

Inside-Out Epistemology. A second metaphor has shaped modern epistemology: "Knowing is seeing." Descartes conceived the mind as an inner theater in which metaphorical objects (ideas) are illuminated by an inner light and observed by a metaphorical spectator. The notion that the true perceiver is in the mind and has access only to its own ideas has been a constant source of skepticism; there is no way to compare one's ideas to the things they are supposed to represent. More recent versions of skepticism or relativism translate this "veil of ideas" into the "veil of language" (Rorty).

Modern Controversies. Immanuel Kant attempted to overcome Hume's skepticism by healing the opposition between rationalism and empiricism. He inaugurated the idealist tradition (the thesis that all of reality is essentially mind-dependent), which dominated philosophy through the nineteenth century. Since then, a new opposition has been established: that between Anglo-American philosophers, who tended to return to empiricism, and Continental philosophers, who tend to operate within the Kantian problematic.

A second dichotomy has been between those who distinguish the human sciences from the natural sciences and those who do not. The distinction between the *Naturwissenschaften* and *Geisteswissenschaften*, based on a dualist account of human nature, was intended to immunize culture from reduction to the deterministic categories of Newtonian physics. A valuable result has been an emphasis on the role of interpretation in understanding human phenomena.

A third opposition is between those who approach epistemology by seeking criteria for justifying a claim itself versus a person's being justified in believing that claim. Much current work in philosophy of religion focuses on the latter; philosophy of science and most (other) epistemology focuses on the former.

Truth and Justification. Descartes saw no distinction between criteria for asserting the truth of a proposition and criteria for its justification. However, once it was recognized that foundations and reasoning therefrom ordinarily produce mere probability, the relation between justification and truth became problematic. One solution was to define both truth and justification in terms of coherence: a belief is justified if it coheres with the rest of a true system of beliefs. This theory of truth contrasts with the theory that truth lies in correspondence with reality. Arguably, neither of these theories has found adequate explication.

The problem of relating truth and justification has been evaded by an important movement in recent epistemology that analyzes the concept of knowledge as justified, true belief. Truth is taken for granted (or handed to the philosophers of language for analysis), and the epistemologist's task is merely to provide an explication of justification.

Recent philosophers of science have judged it impossible to argue from a theory's justification to its truth; furthermore, the question is unimportant given that scientific knowledge is never final.

After Modernity, What?

If modern epistemology began with Descartes (1650), its end is marked by the publication of Quine's "Two Dogmas of Empiricism" in 1951. Since then, developments in holist epistemology have been largely by philosophers of science. Best known is Thomas Kuhn, who argued that scientific paradigms originate with an authoritative text, and they include metaphysical assumptions, guidelines for appropriate scientific methodology, and judgments regarding significant problems, as well as the theories and data that were the focus of earlier philosophy of science. Kuhn's account of science has been exported to other fields of knowledge, including theology (Barbour). These moves have rightly been taken to imply the inevitable particularity and historical location of paradigms, research programs, or traditions; the tradition-dependence of standards of justification (and perhaps theories of truth); and the theory-ladenness of evidence. Whether these problems spell the end of the pursuit of rationality is open to debate.

Current Options. Periods in intellectual history are usually only recognizable with hindsight. There are many who would deny that the epistemological changes since Quine are significant enough to constitute the end of an era. So one option in contemporary epistemology is to keep trying to improve on modern positions. For example, Susan Haack proposes a theory of knowledge that combines the best of foundationalism with a coherence approach to knowledge. Alvin Plantinga dismisses "classical foundationalism" but argues that Reformed epistemologists are entitled to their own judgments about "properly basic beliefs."

In sharp contrast are self-styled postmodernists. This diverse group is difficult to characterize except for their agreement that the modern period has come to an end. Their positions range from the (unexceptionable) claim that there is no universal, God's-eye knowledge to the claim that one can never escape one's class, gender, and cultural location.

Another current option is Richard Rorty's neopragmatism. He diagnoses modernity's preoccupation with skepticism as a consequence of understanding knowledge in terms of representation; instead, he argues that knowledge is to be understood as what is best for us to believe. The method of seeking agreement is not by comparing propositions to some independent reality but by open dialogue.

Finally, there is the option of recognizing the tradition-constituted nature of all human knowledge, but without succumbing to the relativist position that no rational debate is possible between proponents of rival traditions. This account began with the holist philosophy of science mentioned above. Alasdair MacIntyre, its primary proponent, set out to find a method for rational adjudication between competing theories in ethics. He came to the conclusion that such judgments could only be made by tracing the historical development of the theories. This parallels the conclusion that scientific theories can only be judged according to their progress over time. MacIntyre recognizes that large-scale intellectual traditions have particular historical starting points, usually a text or set of texts; a tradition can be understood as a historically extended, socially embodied argument about how best to interpret and apply the community's formative texts. Although competing large-scale traditions contain their own accounts of truth and justification, he argues that nonetheless it is sometimes possible to make objective arguments for the rational superiority of one tradition over its rivals. One may do this on the basis of how each tradition does or does not succeed in overcoming its own intellectual crises, and especially when one tradition is capable of explaining its rival's failures more intelligibly than the rival can itself.

Modern epistemology was preoccupied with the (unsuccessful) quest for universal and certain knowledge; skepticism was a constant threat. If this is indeed the postmodern era in epistemology, the preoccupation of this era can be said to be relativism. There is a spectrum of positions from some postmodernists' acceptance and celebration of relativism, through Rorty's modest proposal for seeking agreement through open discussion, to MacIntyre's claim that rational adjudication between competing traditions is difficult but not always impossible.

Significance for Interpretation of Scripture

To a great extent styles of reasoning in theology and biblical studies have followed developments in epistemology. Foundationalism led to revolutions in theology and biblical studies. Theology came to require its own sorts of foundations, whether rationalist, experientialist, or biblicist. The requirement for indubitability explains why biblicists would want a doctrine of inerrancy; the demand for truth-certifying construction encourages foundationalists to minimize the gap between text and interpretation. The quest for the objective history behind the text is another manifestation of the search for foundations.

What are we to say of current options in epistemology? The postmodernist openness to multiple interpretations may be welcomed by many, especially those whose voices have been marginalized. Yet, lest this openness be pushed to the point of pure relativism, there is much to be said for Rorty's optimism regarding the possibility of reaching agreement on the basis of open discussion, and for MacIntyre's proposal for the testing of rival traditions.

Kuhn's account of the role of authoritative texts in science and MacIntyre's account of the role of texts in all major traditions have important implications for the role of Scripture. In the ancient and medieval periods, theology's basis in authority needed no special pleading; thus, the modern rejection of the epistemology of authority in favor of scientific reasoning based on empirical evidence dealt a blow to theology, from which some would say it has never recovered (Stout). But if Kuhn and MacIntyre are right, the modern rejection of tradition and authoritative texts has been mistaken. All knowledge is "intratextual" (Lindbeck). Stephen Toulmin describes the progress of modern epistemology as omega-shaped: at the end of modernity we have nearly returned to where modernity began. This is certainly correct regarding the role of textual authority.

A consequence of rejecting the modern quest for universal knowledge is an end to the distinction between reading the text as Scripture and studying the text "objectively"; the Enlightenment tradition provides no more conviction-free starting point than the Christian tradition itself (McClendon and Smith).

See also Critical Realism; Method; Objectivity; Philosophy; Warrant

Bibliography

Barbour, I. *Myths, Models, and Paradigms*. Harper & Row, 1974; Haack, S. *Evidence and Inquiry*. Blackwell, 1993; Kirk, J. A., and K. Vanhoozer, eds. *To Stake a Claim*. Orbis, 1999; Kuhn, T. *The Structure of Scientific Revolutions*. 2d ed. University of Chicago Press, 1970; Lindbeck, G. *The Nature of Doctrine*. Westminster, 1984; MacIntyre, A. *Three Rival Versions of Moral Enquiry*. University of Notre Dame Press, 1990; McClendon, J. Wm., Jr., and J. Smith. *Convictions*. Trinity, 1994; Murphy, N. *Anglo-American Postmodernity*. Westview, 1997; Plantinga, A. "Reason and Belief in God." Pages 16–93 in *Faith and Rationality*, ed. A. Plantinga and N. Wolterstorff. University of Notre Dame Press, 1983; Popper, K. *The Logic of Scientific Discovery*. Harper, 1965; Quine, W. V. O. "Two Dogmas of Empiricism." *Philosophical Review* 60 (1951): 20–43; Rorty, R. *Philosophy and the Mirror of Nature*. Princeton University, 1979; Stout, J. *The Flight from Authority*. University of Notre Dame Press, 1981; Toulmin, S. *Cosmopolis*. University of Chicago Press, 1990.

Nancey Murphy

Essenes   *See Jewish Context of the NT*

Esther, Book of

The book of Esther is set in the reign of Ahasuerus (the biblical name for Xerxes, king of Persia 485–465 BCE), though the Septuagint version calls the king Artaxerxes, presumably Artaxerxes I Longimanus (464–424), but possibly Artaxerxes II Mnemon (404–359). The book narrates the life of a Jewish maiden, who is orphaned, reared by her uncle, becomes queen of the Persian Empire, and saves the Jews living in the empire from the scheming of Haman, the Agagite. The Hebrew version cannot be earlier than the time of the events it relates (fifth century), and may be a product of the Greek period (i.e., after 332 BCE). The Septuagint version, which intersperses another 107 verses, probably took its shape in the second or first century BCE.

History of Interpretation

Early Jewish interpretation of Esther took the form of comments on individual verses, which were collected during the Middle Ages in the *Esther Rabbah*. The earliest, extant, complete Jewish commentary on the text was that of Rashi (1040–1105 CE). Generally speaking, Jewish opinion moved in two directions. On the one hand, Jews objected to its lack of specifically religious sentiments, and to its authorization of the Feast of Purim, which they think may well have originated as a pagan festival. On the other hand, because of its treatment of anti-Semitism, Jews through the centuries have often read it as their "story." Early Christian interpretation is relatively sparse, especially in Eastern churches that rejected it as canonical (see below). Nor did the Reformers Luther and Calvin devote much energy to it.

Modern interpretation of Esther has focused first on whether it is a work of historiography or fiction. Those favoring historiography point to places where what is known from other sources seems to corroborate the book of Esther. The dates given in the book fit appropriately in the reign of Xerxes, as do the extent of the Persian Empire from India to Ethiopia, the council of seven nobles, the efficient postal system, the keeping of official diaries, the use of impalement as a means of capital punishment, the practice of obeisance, and reclining on couches at meals. The book also uses Persian words and names (Clines, *Ezra*, 260–61). For example, the name "Marduka" appears in Babylonian sources, though it is not certain that name was equivalent to "Mordecai." The word "Purim" also derives from the Assyrian language (Hallo). The difficulty with that word is that in Esther it refers to one who "casts the lot" (singular) rather than "lots." Despite a variety of attempts to explain the plural term, it may be easiest to recognize that people "cast the lot" several times in the narrative—hence, the use of the plural form "lots."

On the other hand, several features seem historically improbable to scholars. Some find it unlikely that Xerxes orders thousands of Jewish subjects slaughtered for no good reason, then reverses himself and gives the Jews free rein to kill thousands of other Persian subjects. Others note that the elevation of a Jewess to the rank of queen contradicts Herodotus (Clines, *Ezra*, 257–60).

More recently, Craig has argued that the reversals occurring throughout the narrative indicate that the book is "carnivalesque." The dominant characteristic of carnivals is their use of reversals to ridicule the status quo. So in Esther, the Jewess heroine replaces the Persian queen; Mordecai replaces Haman. Parody takes the form of turning King Ahasuerus and Haman into fools, and the "nonreligious" festival of Purim subverts the status quo.

Clines employs a variety of methods of biblical study to find the primary "book" in 1:1–8:17, a book whose plot focuses on the threat to Jews (ch. 3) and its resolution in a decree counterbalancing the first (ch. 8). He takes 9:1–10:3 as a series of additions similar to those in the longer Greek versions of the book.

Feminist readings typically see Esther as forming a context for reflecting on the (in)visibility of women in history and historiography. The book of Esther teaches that danger to the community "can be averted . . . by mixing [physical] attractiveness, sense and faith" (Brenner 13). Nevertheless, this solution carries a price tag: assimilation into Persian culture.

The Message of Esther

First, the efforts of Mordecai and Esther show that Diaspora Jews can serve God through serving foreign leaders. Such service entails temptation to compromise their convictions. Nor is it without danger, as the books of Esther and Daniel both make clear. Governments, however, often influence people's lives so personally that a God-fearing public servant can do great good.

Second, Mordecai's urging Esther to become involved on behalf of her people (4:13–14) shows that holding positions of power carries with it the responsibility to use that power appropriately. Esther's ethnicity might well have enveloped her in the pogrom, too, so her action included the element of self-preservation. Even if it had not, however, she would have had the responsibility to act.

Esther and the Canon

Despite the fact that the book of Esther was composed relatively late, it makes few allusions to the rest of the OT. Yet the Joseph narratives in Genesis form an exception. Hebrew phrases are virtually identical in Esther 1:3 and Gen. 40:20; in 3:4 and Gen. 39:10; in 1:21 and Gen. 41:37; in 2:3 and Gen. 41:35; in 3:10//8:2 and Gen. 41:42; or similar in 4:16 and Gen. 43:14 (Moore, *Studies*, xliii, lxxix nn. 69–70). Another obvious connection is between Esther and 1 Sam. 15, which narrates the execution of Agag by Samuel. That event constitutes the background for Haman's hatred of the Jew Mordecai. The "additions" to Esther in the Greek translations, moreover, contain numerous allusions to other books in the Hebrew Bible.

Esther's place in the Jewish canon seems to have been secured by the second century CE, when it was listed among the books of the Hebrew Bible in the Talmud (*b. B. Bat*. 14b–15a). How much earlier it reached that status is a matter of discussion. No copy of it was found among the Dead Sea Scrolls. Further, Josephus spoke of a Hebrew canon of twenty-two books, rather than the generally recognized number of twenty-four, suggesting that he did not include Esther (or Ecclesiastes).

Probably the reason the rabbis accepted it was that it provided the warrant for the Feast of Purim, the origin of which the book describes. Reasons for debating its canonicity centered on the morality of the book in general and its glee over the slaughter of Persians in particular. Another problem is its failure to mention God even once! Consequently, the additions in the Septuagint mention God frequently, especially in prayers of Mordecai and Esther and in a speech by Mordecai.

The NT makes no allusions to Esther, and early Christians divided over its inclusion in the Bible. Generally speaking, Western churches accepted it, while churches farther to the East did not. As late as the Reformation, Luther could say that he wished the book did not exist at all, because it contained pagan impropriety.

Esther and Theology

One crucial issue in the book of Esther is that of vengeance. The book openly portrays God's people taking revenge on their enemies. Occasionally scholars have tried to mitigate that portrayal by translating the Hebrew verb *naqam* as meaning "to inflict just punishment" instead of "to take revenge." However, the verb appears in Gen. 4:24, where Lamech tells his two wives that he has avenged himself seventy-sevenfold by killing a man who wounded him.

Readers may sympathize with threatened Jews in the Persian Empire and understand their desire for revenge, but neither of those factors mandates that they approve of wholesale slaughter. Such readers do well to remember that the Bible depicts human beings as invariably sinful, so the mere fact that the book of Esther does not call this taking of revenge "sinful" does not mean that God approved the action. Furthermore, Wenham (109) advocates reading narratives like this one not by stressing the actions of the actors, but by stressing the outlook of the book itself. So, what was the theological outlook of the book of Esther?

Remarkably, the Hebrew book of Esther does not mention God explicitly even once, though it does include one possible circumlocution for God (Esther 4:14): "relief and deliverance will rise for the Jews from another place" (Meinhold). Wiebe (413) argues that the phrase actually is a rhetorical question: "If you [Esther] keep silent at this time, *will* relief and deliverance arise for the Jews from another place?" Either way, the omission

195

of any reference to God gives the book what is often referred to as a "secular" tone. Hence, it is necessary to deal with this issue before saying anything about the book's theology. Clines (*Ezra*, 255) argues that so many pieces have to fall into place for the Jews to escape annihilation that an attentive reader will see the book as relating, not a series of remarkable coincidences, but the careful operation of a hidden God working behind the scenes. A survey of the book reveals the following examples: (1) the fall of Queen Vashti, which brings Esther to the attention of King Ahasuerus (1:10–12); (2) Mordecai's help when the king is in danger, followed by palace oversight in not rewarding him (2:21–23); (3) the king's sleeplessness, resulting in his discovery of Mordecai's unrewarded service, precisely while Haman is on duty in the palace and can be tapped to name and extend the reward to Mordecai (6:5); (4) Haman's jealousy of Mordecai, which results in his preparing a gallows for Mordecai—from which Haman himself is hung (5:14; 7:9–10); (5) when Esther discloses to the king the plot of Haman to destroy all Jews, herself among them, the king leaves the room in a rage, but returns just as Haman further compromises himself in the eyes of the king by flinging himself upon the queen to beg for mercy; and (6) the last-minute nature of rescinding the king's order to slay Jews and its replacement with an order to slay those who want to kill Jews (9:1–17). The king of Persia may think he is in control of matters, but the author of Esther knows better. Still, it takes the eyes of faith to see the hidden God, a worthwhile discovery for Jews in a foreign land.

The hidden God protects God's people in Persia, so God is universal, not limited to the land of Palestine. Moreover, God's victory on behalf of the Jews is to be celebrated in a festival. There is no mention of a temple, either in Jerusalem or Persia. (Ackroyd [34] reads Ezek. 11:16 as saying that God had made for the exiles a "temporary sanctuary" or a "sanctuary in small measure," but that translation is uncertain, with no other evidence that Jews built a temple in Mesopotamia or Persia.) The festival described in Esther is not one of the annual festivals mandated in the Torah as times to offer sacrifices to God. Possibly the author advocates a type of celebration of God that involves not sacrifice, but resting and exchanging food.

Also, the hidden God remains faithful to the people of Israel. This conclusion is justified even though there is no reference in the Hebrew version to the patriarchs and no appeal to God's covenant with them or with the people at Sinai because, paradoxically, the identity of the hidden God must be self-evident. In the Septuagint version, moreover, Mordecai prays to God as the "God of Abraham" (Add. Esth. 13:15; cf. Esther's allusion to the call of Abraham in 14:5), and reminds God of God's salvation of the people from Egypt (13:16). Even the pagan king Artaxerxes can recognize Jews as the "children of the living God" (16:16), probably but not necessarily a reference to the God of Israel.

Bibliography

Ackroyd, P. *Exile and Restoration*. OTL. Westminster, 1968; Berg, S. *The Book of Esther*. SBLDS 44. Scholars Press, 1979; Brenner, A. *A Feminist Companion to Esther, Judith, and Susanna*. FCB 7. Sheffield Academic Press, 1995; Clines, D. J. A. *The Esther Scroll*. JSOTSup 30. JSOT, 1984; idem. *Ezra, Nehemiah, Esther*. NCB. Eerdmans/Marshall, Morgan & Scott, 1984; Craig, K. *Reading Esther*. Literary Currents in Biblical Interpretation. Westminster John Knox, 1995; Fox, M. *Character and Ideology in the Book of Esther*. University of South Carolina Press, 1991; Gerleman, G. *Esther*. BKAT 21. Neukirchener Verlag, 1973; Hallo, W. "The First Purim." *BA* 46 (1983): 19–26; Levinson, J. *Esther*. OTL. Westminster John Knox, 1997; Meinhold, A. "Zu Aufbau und Mitte des Estherbuches." *VT* 33 (1983): 435–45; Moore, C. *Esther*. AB 7B. Doubleday, 1971; idem. *Studies in the Book of Esther*. Ktav, 1982; Paton, L. *A Critical and Exegetical Commentary on Esther*. ICC. T&T Clark, 1908; Wenham, G. *Story as Torah*. T&T Clark, 2000; Wiebe, J. "Esther 4:14: 'Will Relief and Deliverance Arise for the Jews from Another Place?'" *CBQ* 53 (1991): 409–15.

Paul L. Redditt

Ethics

"Ethics" may be defined as disciplined reflection on that dimension of human life denoted "moral." Within the Bible is abundant reflection on issues of conduct and character. Among those who would read the Bible as Scripture, as somehow normative for faith and life, reflection on issues of moral conduct and character is disciplined by such reading. The theological interpretation of Scripture must, therefore, attend both to biblical ethics and to its use in the moral deliberation of the churches.

Biblical Ethics

Biblical ethics is inalienably religious, always qualified and disciplined by convictions about the works and ways of God. To abstract biblical ethics from its religious context is to distort it. And biblical ethics is stubbornly diverse, resisting any simple reduction to a timeless set of rules. Within Scripture different particular communities, each with its distinctive cultural and social context and each facing particular concrete questions of conduct and character, are addressed. To reduce this rich diversity to an abstract and timeless unity is to impoverish it. Still, the one God of Scripture provides the unity of biblical ethics.

Ethics in Torah. The one God forms a people as their liberator and ruler. The story was told in recitals of Israel's faith: the God of Abraham heard our cry when we were slaves, rescued us from oppression, and made us a people with a covenant (e.g., Josh. 24:2–18). The covenant was like an ancient suzerainty treaty, acknowledging and confirming God as the great king and themselves as God's people. Like other suzerainty treaties, this covenant begins by identifying the great king and reciting his works (e.g., Exod. 20:2), then continues with stipulations that forbid both loyalty to another king and injustice and violence in the land (e.g., 20:3–17). It ends with provisions for periodic renewal of the covenant plus assurances of blessings upon faithful observance and curses upon infidelity (e.g., 25:22–33).

This story and covenant formed not only a people but a Scripture, providing the framework for gathering stories and stipulations until the literary formation of Torah, the first five books of the Bible, and its acceptance as having Mosaic authority.

"Torah" is usually translated "law," and much of it is legal material. Various collections (e.g., the Decalogue, or Ten Commandments; the Book of the Covenant, Exod. 20:22–23:19; the Holiness Code, Lev. 17–26; the Deuteronomic code, Deut. 4:44–28:46) can be identified and associated with particular periods of Israel's history. The later collections sometimes revisit earlier legislation, displaying both fidelity to, and creativity with, the earlier traditions.

Although there is no tidy differentiation in the Torah between "ceremonial," "civil," and "moral" laws, the traditional rubrics identify significant functions of the law. As "ceremonial," the Torah struggles against temptations to covenant infidelity in foreign cults, and nurtures a communal memory and commitment to covenant. As "civil," the Torah is fundamentally theocratic; this theocratic conviction that the rulers are ruled too, that they are subject to law, not its final creators, has a democratizing effect. As "moral," the Torah protects the family and its economic participation in God's gift of the land, protects persons and property (but persons more than property), requires fairness in disputes and economic transactions, and provides for the care and protection of the vulnerable: widows, orphans, the poor, the sojourner.

The legal materials, however, never escape the story and its covenant. Indeed, "torah" is finally better rendered "teaching." Narrative and covenant set the legal traditions in the context of grateful response to God's works and ways. Moreover, the story forms and informs the law. The story of one God, who heard the cries of slaves, for example, forms statutes that protect the vulnerable.

The narratives of the Torah, of course, are morally significant in their own right. Artfully told, they nurture moral dispositions, forming a vision of a people and a world ruled by God. Noteworthy among them are the stories of creation, affirming as they do that the one God of covenant is the God of creation, too. Nothing God has made is god, but all that God has made is good. The very ethos of the cosmos prohibits idolatry and invites gratitude. If the curse falls heavy on human sin, the God who makes promises and covenant will not let sin or the curse have the last word. He comes again to bless, and the Yahwist stories of the ancestors not only trace the blessing of David's empire to God but also evoke the readiness to use the power of empire to bless the subject nations (e.g., Gen. 12:1–3; chs. 18–19, 26; 30:27–28; chs. 39–41).

Ethics in the Prophets. The one God who created the world, and rescued and established a blessed people within it, spoke to them through the prophets. Their "Thus saith the LORD . . ." was familiar language of diplomacy in the ancient Near East for the "announcement" by a ruler's messenger. The prophets always came with a particular word for a particular time, but always reminded the people of the story and the covenant. They were not social reformers skilled in the craft and compromise of politics; they were messengers of God.

They brought a word of judgment against any infidelity to the covenant. The infidelity of idolatry was never "merely" religious; the claims of Ba'al involved the fertility of wombs and land, and a theory of ownership. The infidelity of injustice was never "merely" moral, for covenant fidelity to God does justice. The welfare of the poor and powerless was the best index of covenant fidelity. So the prophets denounced unjust rulers, greedy merchants, corrupt judges, the complacent rich, and especially those who celebrated covenant in ritual and ceremony without caring about justice, without protecting the powerless, without faithfulness (e.g., Amos 5:21–24). On the other side of God's judgment, the prophets saw and announced God's own good future. God will reign and establish both justice and peace, not only in Israel but also among the nations, and not only among the nations but in nature itself.

Ethics in Wisdom. The will and way of the one God can be known not only in the great events of liberation and covenant, not only in the oracles of God's messengers, but also in the regularities of nature and experience. The moral counsel of Israel's sage did not appeal directly to Torah or to covenant; rather, reflection about moral conduct and character was disciplined and tested by experience.

By careful attention to nature and experience, the sage was able to comprehend the basic principles operative in the world, and to these principles it was both prudent and moral to conform. The one God is the Creator, who established and secures the order and stability of ordinary life. So the sage could give moral advice about eating and drinking and sleeping and working, the way to handle money and anger, the way to relate to friends and enemies and women and fools, when to speak and when to be silent—in short, about everything in experience.

The ethics of wisdom tend to delight both in simple things, like the love of a man and a woman (Song of Solomon), and in the quest for wisdom itself. Experience, however, teaches the hard lessons that there is no tidy fit between prudence and morality, that the righteous sometimes suffer (Job), that wisdom has its limits (Job 28), and that the regularities of nature and experience cannot be simply identified with the cause of God (Ecclesiastes).

Wisdom reflects about moral conduct and character quite differently from the Torah and the prophets, but "the end of the matter," like the beginning of wisdom (Prov. 1:7; 9:10), is a reminder of covenant: "Fear God and keep his commandments" (Eccles. 12:13). That beginning and end keeps wisdom in touch with Torah, struggling mightily to keep Torah in touch with experience, and covenant in touch with creation.

Ethics in the NT. Jesus of Nazareth came announcing that the kingdom of God is at hand, already making God's good future present in words of blessing and works of healing. He called people to repent, to form their conduct and character in response to the good news of that coming (and present) future.

To welcome a future where "the last will be first" (Mark 10:31 NRSV), a future already signaled in Jesus' humble service, is to be ready to be "servant . . . of all" (Mark 10:43–45). To delight in a kingdom where the poor will be blessed is now to be carefree about wealth and to practice generosity. To repent before a kingdom that belongs to children, that is signaled in table-fellowship with sinners, and that is gestured in open conversation with women is now to turn from conventional standards of value to bless children, to welcome sinners, and to treat women as equals.

Because Jesus announced the good future of God, he spoke with authority, not simply on the basis of law and tradition. Because the reign of God demands a response of the whole person and not merely external observance of the law, he made radical demands upon character. A radical demand for truthfulness replaced (and fulfilled) legal casuistry about oaths. A readiness to forgive and be reconciled set aside (and fulfilled) legal limitations on revenge. A disposition to love even enemies put aside legal debates about the meaning of "neighbor." Neither the law nor experience was discarded as moral teacher, but law and wisdom were both qualified and fulfilled in an ethic of response to God's future reign.

Jesus died on a Roman cross, but God raised him up in an act of power that was at once vindication of this Jesus and prelude to God's final triumph. Thus, moral reflection in the NT always looks backward and forward.

The Gospels use the tradition of Jesus' words and deeds to tell his story creatively and faithfully, shaping the conduct and character of particular communities. Mark represents Jesus as calling people to a heroic discipleship, being ready to suffer and die, as well as to live in ordinary relationships with heroic confidence, not in Jewish law or Roman justice, but in God. Matthew represents Jesus as upholding the law, as its best interpreter, even as he demands a righteousness that "exceeds that of the scribes and Pharisees" (5:20 NRSV). Luke emphasizes the requirements of care for the poor and mutual respect of Jew and Gentile. John tells the story quite differently, that his readers might "have life" (20:31) and know that such life requires love for one another.

The Epistles of Paul make little use of the tradition of Jesus' words and deeds. He proclaims the gospel of the cross and resurrection as "the power of God for salvation" (Rom. 1:16 NRSV). Thus, within Paul's churches moral reflection is to be radically affected by the works and way of God made known in the gospel (Rom. 12:1). The power of God enables and requires a response, a life and a common life "worthy of" or fitting to the gospel (Phil. 1:27). The power of God stands in fundamental opposition to the powers of this age. And the one who receives the gospel, the power of God, is freed from their dominion to stand under the lordship of Christ. That "standing" is now always both gift and demand, appropriately treated both as indicative and as imperative (cf. Rom. 5:2; 1 Cor. 16:13).

The Pauline Epistles address and form communities of moral discourse and discernment (Rom. 15:14). Neither Paul nor the churches created moral guidelines and judgments ex nihilo; rather, they utilized existing traditions (of the church, synagogue, and the Greek schools and culture), but tested and modified them. Thus, they discerned a way of life "worthy of the gospel of Christ" (Phil. 1:27). Paul and his churches exercised such discernment in moral reflection about the relations of Jew and Gentile, slave and free, male and female, rich and poor, church and state. The judgments were not "timeless truths" in the style of a philosopher, but timely applications of the gospel to specific problems in particular contexts.

Other NT writings confirm both the inalienably religious character of biblical ethics and its great diversity. Revelation, for example, provides a symbolic universe to make intelligible both the experience of injustice at the hands of Caesar and the conviction that Jesus is Lord, and to call for both patient endurance of suffering and faithful resistance to the values of empire.

The ethical voices are "many and various," but the one God of Scripture still speaks in their midst to renew life, transform identity, sanctify a people, and bring conduct and character and community into coherence with God's reign.

Ethics in Biblical Interpretation

The churches have always commended Scripture as "useful . . . for training in righteousness" (2 Tim. 3:16). But they have not always agreed about *how* Scripture is "useful." There is "an important two-part consensus" that "Christian ethics is not synonymous with biblical ethics," and that "the Bible is somehow formative and normative for Christian ethics" (Birch and Rasmussen 11, 14). Somehow, but how?

Various strategies (see Gustafson) have been proposed to bring Scripture to bear on moral reflection, sometimes privileging one or another of the diverse biblical materials (e.g., law, prophetic social criticism, wisdom), and sometimes privileging one or another mode of reflection (e.g., teleology, deontology, axiology). Such proposals are flawed, as long as they regard the Bible as a little library of ancient religious texts, or ethics as autonomous, founded on reason. Apart from the faith and practices of the church, there can be no constructive relation between Scripture and ethics. There has recently been fruitful attention to the theological interpretation of Scripture for the moral reflection of churches, notably from both Protestant (like Hays; Fowl and Jones) and Catholic scholars (like Spohn; Harrington and Keenan).

Christian communities continue to read the biblical materials not just as an interesting ancient Near Eastern library but as Christian Scripture, not only as curious literary artifacts but as canon, not only as scripted (as written) but also as script to be somehow performed.

The Bible is not a legal code but fundamentally a story. As we read Scripture in Christian community, the Bible has its authority to *remember* the story. This is the "good" that belongs to the practice. Remembering, of course, is not just the disinterested recall of facts, but owning it as our story—as constitutive of identity and determinative for discernment. Without remembering, there is no identity. In amnesia, one loses oneself. In memory, one finds an identity. Without common remembering, there is no community. It is little wonder that the church sustains this practice of reading Scripture and is itself sustained by it.

There are, moreover, certain standards of excellence in reading Scripture to remember: fidelity and creativity, humility and discernment. Fidelity is simply readiness to live with integrity, in faithful remembrance of the story. Fidelity, however, requires creativity; for the past is past and we do not live in it, even if we remember it.

We do not live in David's Jerusalem or in Paul's Corinth, and an effort simply to "preserve" or perform the past is doomed to anachronistic eccentricity. Fidelity requires creativity and change.

Humility is readiness to read Scripture "over against" ourselves rather than in self-serving defense of our own interests and opinions (Fowl and Jones 42). Humility will not simply insist on some "right to private interpretation"; it will participate in the moral discourse of the community. To see the shape of the story and of lives formed to it requires discernment, the ability to recognize "fittingness"—the ability to recognize the plot of the story, to see the wholeness of Scripture, and to order the interpretation of any part toward that whole. It is to recognize how a statute, a proverb, or a story "fits" the whole story. In Christian ethics, discernment is the ability to plot our lives to "fit" the whole of Scripture, to order our lives to be worthy of the story.

The practice of reading Scripture is not a substitute for the practice of moral discourse, but the two are intimately related. The churches are communities of moral discourse and deliberation, "able to instruct one another," because they are communities of discernment—by being communities of memory. Discernment in Christian community depends finally on remembering the story of the one God of Scripture. Scripture is "useful" and indeed critical for that remembering. The greatest danger for the Christian life is still forgetfulness, and reading Scripture together is still the remedy for it.

See also Law; Virtue; Wisdom

Bibliography

Birch, B., and L. Rasmussen, *Bible and Ethics in the Christian Life*. Rev. ed. Augsburg, 1989; Blount, B. *Then the Whisper Put On Flesh*. Abingdon, 2001; Brown, W. *The Ethos of the Cosmos*. Eerdmans, 1999; Cosgrove, C. *Appealing to Scripture in Moral Debate*. Eerdmans, 2000; Fowl, S., and L. G. Jones. *Reading in Communion*. Eerdmans, 1991; Furnish, V. P. *Theology and Ethics in Paul*. Abingdon, 1968; Gustafson, J. "The Place of Scripture in Christian Ethics: A Methodological Study." *Interpretation* 24 (1970): 430–55; Harrington, D., SJ, and J. Keenan, SJ. *Jesus and Virtue Ethics*. Sheed & Ward, 2002; Hauerwas, S. *Unleashing the Scripture*. Abingdon, 1993; Hays, R. *The Moral Vision of the New Testament*. HarperSanFrancisco, 1996; Longenecker, R. *New Testament Social Ethics for Today*. Eerdmans, 1984; McDonald, J. I. H. *Biblical Interpretation and Christian Ethics*. Cambridge University Press, 1993; O'Donovan, O. *Resurrection and Moral Order*. 2d ed. Eerdmans, 1994; Ogletree, T. *The Use of the Bible in Christian Ethics*. Fortress, 1983; Spohn, W. C. *Go and Do Likewise*. Continuum, 1999; Swartley, W. *Slavery, Sabbath, War, and Women*. Herald Press, 1983; Verhey, A. *The Great Reversal*. Eerdmans, 1984; idem. *Remembering Jesus*. Eerdmans, 2002; Yoder, J. H. *The Politics of Jesus*. Eerdmans, 1972. Rev. ed. 1994.

Allen Verhey

Etymological Fallacy *See* Etymology

Etymology

Etymological studies have long been an alluring seductress to students of the Bible. It is not surprising that those who view every word of Scripture as inspired by God should be tempted to seek inspired meaning in each individual word. It is not surprising that those who consider Scripture to represent a mystical union of the Holy Spirit with human authors have been tempted to find a meaning in words that penetrates far deeper than the conscious levels of usage. It is commonplace to believe that even ferreting out every possible nuance behind every word fails to exhaust all the levels of inspired truth. Thus, etymological studies, through no fault of their own, have become a menace to sound interpretation. Those who sometimes maintain only the slightest grasp of the Bible's original languages repeat their clichéd results from pulpits. These expositors desire to offer theological insight, but more often than not the result is exploitation.

The Meaning of Etymology

A word's origin is called its etymology. Speakers and writers do not usually choose to employ a word based on an understanding of its etymology or subsequent history. Most speakers are entirely unaware of the etymology of the words they are using. Even when they *are* aware of it, they realize that they are not using their words in that connection. Linguists refer to the study of the historical development of a word as a *diachronic* approach. The alternative is the *synchronic* approach, the study of the current usage of the word in all its possible contexts. The diachronic study of a word, including its etymology, may help the interpreter to understand by what route a word came to mean what it does mean. Additionally, it may help to alert someone to a subtle nuance of meaning. A synchronic study of a word will help the interpreter know what the word means to the person who has just used it.

Words originate in various ways. A word might arise as a composite of parts (combining two independent words, such as a preposition and a verb). Alternatively, a word might enter speech from another language, or develop out of an already established root (e.g., by using affixes to change the part of speech, e.g., "kindness"). But however words come into a language, they tend to develop over time, and through the whims of usage often wander from their origins. The changes can be morphological (altering the form of the word) or semantic (altering the meaning of the word) or both, but often the current meaning is only vaguely related to the original meaning. For example, though the English word "sinister" originally referred to being left-handed, those who use the word today are rarely even aware of that history. The important point here, and the central point for theological interpretation, is that understanding the meaning of a word, whether theological or otherwise, must derive from its usage, not from its etymology. Synchronic data are essential for interpretation; diachronic data are unreliable.

Understanding the meanings of words, then, is accomplished by understanding how words are used and how meanings are understood by the native speakers who hear or read them. Like any other author, the main reason a biblical author chose a particular word would be because it carried precisely the meaning in contemporary usage that he wanted to communicate. We should not expect that the Holy Spirit altered the laws of communication, but that he operated within those laws to achieve his objective effectively.

This article will not have the space to give positive instruction on carrying out a synchronic approach to arrive at sound exegetical results. Readers will find that aspect developed in *NIDOTTE* (Walton). We will only be able to summarize the most common fallacies perpetrated when the diachronic method is not used cautiously.

Composite Parts

When we analyze word choices, we should not interpret as if the use of a compound word assumes knowledge of or carries the meaning of the parts. For example, in English we would use the word "awful" without even noticing that it is a combination of awe + full. English has many compound words, some easily recognizable, such as "understand," others not as readily noticed, such as "syllabus" (because the compound was devised in Greek rather than in English, and then borrowed whole). In Greek, where compound words are common, interpretation by dissection is a constant temptation. But a moment's thought about English usage should warn us against placing confidence in that type of approach. Returning to the word "understand" we see that our use is not at all influenced or informed by viewing it as a combination of "under" and "stand." One could not arrive at an interpretation of the meaning of that word by evaluating the parts. Furthermore, it would be difficult to sustain an argument that, in addition to the meaning of the word as a whole, additional meaning could be drawn from the parts.

Consequently, it would not be legitimate to build theology by dissecting Greek words. The Greek word translated "church" (*ekklēsia*) is built out of two words that mean "called out," yet we cannot assume that the word was being used with that etymology in mind—it is simply the word for church. Likewise, the fact that the Holy Spirit is described by the Greek term *paraklētos* (a compound of preposition and verb) does not mean that we can understand the nature of the Spirit as "one called alongside" (the meaning of

the parts). With each of these words, the meaning would be determined by how they were used in contemporary Greek literature.

Shared Roots between Parts of Speech

In Hebrew, the problem is not so much compound words as it is the relationship of words that share the same root. In English, we understand that words sharing the same root may be related or may not. For instance, recognition of the root "adult" in "adultery" will not be of any use. Using a more complex and subtle example, one could easily associate "company" and "companion," but when one examined the verb "accompany," only partial success could be achieved. If the verb were being used to speak of joining someone on a walk, there would be no problem; but if the speaker were using the more technical idiomatic sense of accompanying a soloist on the piano, the root relationship would provide little assistance.

Likewise, in biblical languages the interpreter cannot have confidence that the words sharing a common root will also share a common core meaning. We must be aware, therefore, that we cannot use one to shed light on the other unless the relationship can be independently established. For instance, the word for "angel, messenger" (*mal'ak*) shares a root with the Hebrew word for "work, occupation" (*mal'akah*), yet it would be a mistake to try to interpret one in light of the other. In conclusion, reducing a word to its constituent parts or relating it to a common root cannot be expected to provide reliable guidance to establishing meaning or theology.

A well-meaning teacher dealing with Prov. 22:6 was trying to explain to his class what the text meant when it said that the properly trained child would not depart from the parent's teaching "when he is old." He informed the class that since the verb "to be old" also contributed its root to the noun "beard," the text meant that when the son was old enough to grow a beard, he would not depart from the teaching. Such analysis can only mislead and distort—it contributes nothing to sound exegesis.

Shared Roots between Hebrew Stems

A related distinction concerns the verbal stems. Though there is often a level of semantic interrelation between stems (e.g., the Niphal as the passive of the Qal), sufficient examples of deviation urge us to caution. Sometimes stems have developed in entirely different directions. More subtle are the cases where relationship between the stems remains visible yet certain nuances pertain in one but not in the other. So, for example, for the root *s-kh-q* the Qal and the Piel both concern joy, laughter, and fun, but the Piel contains a more negative nuance (making fun of someone) as well as a sexual nuance (Gen. 26:8, caress). The extent of relatedness between verbal stems should be established by applying the synchronic method to each stem individually before the interpreter feels free to classify all the verbal occurrences together in the semantic range.

For example, it is not unusual for the suggestion to be made that the Hebrew word *kipper*, often translated "to atone," "comes from the root" meaning "to cover." *Kipper* is a Piel form in ritual texts. The supposed meaning of the root is drawn from a single occurrence in the Qal in Gen. 6:14, where Noah covers the ark with pitch. The problem is that the meaning "cover" could not be carried confidently from the Qal to the Piel without some independent attestation of that meaning in the usage of the Piel. The situation is exacerbated here in that it is possible that the Qal occurrence comes from a homonymous root, which does not mean simply "to cover," but "to cover with pitch" (based on analysis of the much more frequent Akkadian usage).

Words Confused by English Usage

A problem can occur when an element from the semantic range of an English word is applied to the corresponding Hebrew word, which itself has a more limited semantic range. In a classic example the English word "glory" has in its semantic range the meaning "heaven" (e.g., "gloryland"). The Hebrew word *kabod*, though properly translated "glory," does not have "heaven" in its semantic range. The lay English reader then might be excused for making the mistake of interpreting Ps. 73:24 as a reference to heaven, but linguistically informed interpreters are without excuse.

Another variation can occur when too close an association is drawn between English and Greek words. When a speaker introduces the offering suggesting that we should give "hilariously" because the Greek word in 2 Cor. 9:7 is the word from which our English word "hilarious" derives, an English meaning has been imposed on a Greek word. This phenomenon is also evident when it is commented that we can understand a passage like Acts 1:8 by knowing that the word "power" translates the Greek term from which our word "dynamite" is derived. Again this is an English meaning being imposed on a Greek word that is its ancestor. Linguistically, this constitutes anachronism as it reads back a meaning derived from synchronic analysis of contemporary English onto an earlier diachronic stage in Greek.

Lexical and Contextual Use

The lexical sense refers to those elements of meaning that the word will automatically carry into any of the contexts in which it is used. If there is even one occurrence (in the same category of the semantic range) that does not carry an element of meaning, then that element must be excluded from the lexical sense. So, for instance, one could not include "creation out of nothing" in the lexical sense of Hebrew *bara'* because there are a number of occurrences that clearly do not involve creation out of nothing (e.g., Gen. 5:1–2). This verb has the potential to express creation out of nothing, but that would be up to the *context* to establish. Such a nuanced meaning could be one option available for the *contextual* sense of the verb, but it is not a meaning inherent in the very nature of the word, the *lexical* sense. Neither the contextual sense nor the lexical sense necessarily includes the *etymological* sense, which may not be preserved within the current semantic range of the word at all. We cannot think of the Holy Spirit as adding to the normal semantic range of a word.

Conclusion

We will be better interpreters when we understand words and their usage. Authors make choices in the communication process, and it is our task to understand the choices they have made. Our goal is to be on their wavelength. Word study is a step in the process of exegesis; it does not comprise the whole. The authority of the Scriptures is not found in words, though each word has an important role to play; rather, the authority is embodied in the message.

Bibliography

Barr, J. *Comparative Philology and the Text of the Old Testament*. Eisenbrauns, 1987; idem. *The Semantics of Biblical Language*. Oxford University Press, 1961; Cotterell, P., and M. Turner. *Linguistics and Biblical Interpretation*. InterVarsity, 1989; Klein, W., C. Blomberg, and R. Hubbard. *Introduction to Biblical Interpretation*. Word, 1993; Osborne, G. *The Hermeneutical Spiral*. InterVarsity, 1991; Silva, M. *Biblical Words and Their Meaning*. Zondervan, 1993; Walton, J. "Principles for Productive Word Study." *NIDOTTE* 1:161–71.

John H. Walton

Evangelical Biblical Interpretation

See Charismatic Biblical Interpretation; Princeton School; Protestant Biblical Interpretation

Evil *See* Original Sin; Powers and Principalities; Sin, Doctrine of; Violence

Exegesis

The word "exegesis" is derived from the Greek verb *exēgeisthai*, which can mean "to lead" or "to explain." In biblical literature it is always used in the sense "to explain, interpret, or describe." Acts 21:19 uses the verb to say that Paul *explains* to James and the elders what God has done among the Gentiles (see also Judg. 7:13 LXX; Luke 24:35; Acts 15:12–14). The most illustrative NT use of *exēgeisthai* is in John 1:18, where we are told that "the unique God" (or "the unique Son"—note the textual question) has *explained* (or revealed) the Father. Although no one has seen God, this one who is in the bosom of the Father has explained him—or, in the context of the Gospel of John—the Father is revealed, communicated, and made known in and by the Son. Even so, the use of *exēgeisthai* in the NT gives no hint as to why the word "exegesis" took on such importance. The noun *exēgēsis* is attested in the NT only at Luke 1:1, but it is used elsewhere, including twice in the LXX, at Judg. 7:15 and Sir. 21:16. In nonbiblical Greek, however, *exēgēsis* was used by Jews, Greeks, and Christians for explanation—often careful explanation—of laws and religious ideas. Herodotus, Plato, Philo, and Josephus all use *exēgeisthai* and *exēgēsis* as technical terms in describing the exposition or interpretation of laws or sacred Scriptures (e.g., Herodotus, *Hist.* 1.78; Plato, *Leg.* 7.802c; Philo, *Contempl.* 78; Josephus, *B.J.* 2.162; *A.J.* 11.192). Christians used the words the same way. Clement of Rome asks "Who can *explain* (*exēgeisthai*) the bond of the love of God?" (*1 Clem.* 49:2) and marvels that of love's perfection there is no *explanation* (*exēgēsis*; 50:1). In the Shepherd of Hermas *exēgēsis* is used of the *explanation* of the image of the tower (*Vis.* 3.7.4). Eusebius mentions that five treatises of Papias were extant which have the title "*Interpretation* of Oracles of the Lord" (*Logiōn kyriakōn exēgēseōs*; *Hist. eccl.* 3.39.1).

"Exegesis" then means "explanation," nearly always intended as explanation after careful consideration and usually with regard to Scripture or founding documents. It is the process we go through in explaining any communication, whether written or oral. But usually the assumption associated with "exegesis" is that this analysis is "scientific," that one is trained in understanding words and their relations, that one is careful to analyze correctly and not import meaning illegitimately, and that one is not guilty of *eisegesis* (importing meaning unrelated to the text). More technically, *"exegesis" refers to a linguistic-syntactical analysis to discern communicative intent*. That is, exegesis is the analysis of the significance of words and the relations into which they are set to construct meaning. Meaning is a set of relations for which words are verbal symbols. By placing specific words in specific relations to each other and in specific contexts, meaning is conveyed, and exegesis seeks to analyze the significance of the particular words used and the relations into which they are set to discern the intent of the communication.

For some, the terms "exegesis," "hermeneutics," and "interpretation" are synonymous. In earlier times the terms were distinguished, with interpretation encompassing both other words and including the process of theologizing and application as well. Hermeneutics was seen as the rules and procedures governing interpretation, and exegesis was limited to a search for past meaning. Exegesis focused on historical context and grammatical relations to determine what the text meant at its origin. Today, hermeneutics may well be the most comprehensive of the three terms in that it deals with the whole process of understanding and appropriating texts. Distinctions can and should be made between the three terms but with the realization that the boundaries between them are blurred. Valid exegesis will always involve an attempt to understand the historical and cultural context in which the communication arose, and by necessity it leans more toward an author-oriented hermeneutic. Exegesis is rightly assumed to be a *foundational* task for doing theology. We need to understand the intent of the text before we build theological systems on it, but in reality the implied objectivity often associated with exegesis is misleading. Theology, however primitive, is already at work before we come to the text. We all bring to the text theological assumptions and questions that motivate our work and that both allow and hinder our efforts to see the significance of the relations in the text. Still, the attempt not to impose our theologies on texts is demanded by any fair exegesis. We cannot come to the text without presuppositions, but we can come to the text without presupposing what its meaning is.

The goal of exegesis is not merely information but a "usable understanding." Far too much attention is placed on "meaning" and not nearly enough on the *function* of texts. Texts are the result of action and are intended to produce action (Lundin, Thiselton, and Walhout 43–44), and speech-act theory rightly is gaining prominence in helping us understand how language works (Vanhoozer, *Meaning?* 208–65; "Speech Acts," 1–49). We have not understood a text until we understand what it seeks to accomplish in its hearers, and exegesis is not successful until it knows how the text should be used. Texts may legitimately be used for meditation and reflection beyond their intent, but that is a process quite distinct from interpretation and certainly from exegesis. This is especially true of Scripture that has as its primary intent to change us and give us an identity. "Thus it is simply wrong-headed for us ever to think that we have done exegesis at all if we have not cared about the intended Spirituality of the text" (Fee, *To What End?* 282). Both God and the human authors desire to communicate, and no interpretation can be considered valid that does not listen for and to that communicative intent (Snodgrass 9–32). If we come unwilling to obey the text, we will never fully understand it (cf. John 7:17). If we come assuming we already know what the text says, it does not have a decent chance to address us. The primary task of exegesis is to listen with a willing and obedient heart. Isaiah 6:10 and Matt. 13:15 speak of understanding with the heart for good reason.

Exegesis can be done while using a translation of the Bible, but only with difficulty and at considerable handicap. Translations are the result of someone else's exegetical activity. Translators by necessity interpret a text in order to translate it. Translation is both the first and last step in interpreting a text. A translator must make a preliminary translation to begin to understand the text, but then makes exegetical choices about the text's intent and chooses the best way to communicate those ideas in the receptor language. Translations, therefore, close off options that are present in the text—to say nothing of creating options that are not in the original. Those working only with translations need even more care and effort to make sure they know what is involved in the text. For these reasons, when people think of exegesis, the primary reference is to exegesis of the Hebrew, Aramaic, and Greek texts of Scripture.

The Process of Exegesis

Exegesis involves the careful analysis of the relations of the text at every level—from the macrolevel to the microlevel—to determine communicative intent. Understanding of intent depends on our ability to "locate" a text, to perceive where and how the text takes its existence, and how its component parts relate to each other to form the message. Much of this happens intuitively and without reflection. We understand that Paul's letters were written in the first century, not the fifteenth, to people in cities around the Mediterranean, not to people in China or America. Exegesis seeks consciously to discern the relations within the text and its world, and in doing so focuses attention on specific arenas. The following tasks—each primarily a discerning of relations—are required in doing exegesis.

1. Assess Relevant Textual Variants. Unlike with some documents, the initial task in biblical exegesis involves determining the most likely original wording of the text. Modern editions of the Hebrew and Greek Testaments are wonderful tools, giving not only the likely text but also evidence showing the most important variants. The existence of numerous manuscripts copied by hand has resulted in variant readings, some intentional, some unintentional. Textual criticism is the discipline that assesses these variants to determine the most likely original. It assesses external evidence (the physical evidence of the manuscripts, to determine the quality and date of the manuscripts and the distribution of the readings) and internal evidence (both what scribes are likely to have done in copying and what most likely fits the author's style and theology). Analysis of important textual variants not only provides insight about the original wording; it also provides commentary by showing what scribes did in seeking to understand the text they copied.

2. Learn as Much as Possible about the Historical, Cultural, and Literary Context of the Passage. Broadly conceived, this means learning as much as possible about the world in which the document emerges and is a never-ending task. We bring to the text an assumption—sketchy as it may be—of what its world was like, whether ancient Israel or first-century Palestine and the Greco-Roman world. The more we learn about these entities and the primary sources revealing them, the more opportunity we have to understand the text. It is not that we must study other documents first, however, for the biblical text is itself a primary witness to these worlds.

More narrowly conceived, the concern is to learn as much as possible about the specific context and content of the entire work and then of the specific context of the passage being studied. Exegesis usually focuses on specific passages of a document, but a given pericope can be understood only in light of the whole. Understanding of the whole, however, presupposes understanding the individual parts. This is the horizontal herme-neutical circle; interpretation takes place in the continual movement of knowing the part from the whole and the whole from the part. Attention must be given to the purpose and "location" of the whole document and then to the location within the document of the passage in question. The relation to passages immediately preceding and following the pericope being studied is among the most important relations for understanding. Also involved is the ability to perceive relations to other practices or writings, most importantly, quotations or allusions to the OT, but also cultural aspects of Judaism or the Greco-Roman world (such as attitudes toward impurity or emperor worship). Some people distinguish between the "context" and the "cotext" of a passage, with the former referring to the historical and sociologi-cal setting of the text and the latter referring to the sentences and paragraphs surrounding the passage and related to it (Cotterell and Turner 16). Most, however, refer to historical and social context and to literary context.

3. Determine the Significance of the Genre Both of the Whole Work and of the Individual Passage. Signals are sent about the function of a passage by the genre selected, and determina-tion of genre is one of the most important as-pects of exegesis. This is one more way a text is "located." A promise and a proverb have quite different functions: the former entails a commit-ment, whereas the latter states what is only gener-ally true. A narrative, a psalm, and a letter to a church do not carry the same kinds of authority. Apocalyptic is expected to use certain images and treat certain themes. Recognition of a passage as early-church confessional material puts it in a different category.

4. Determine the Structure of the Passage. Thought is always structured or it is nonsensi-cal. In discerning the structure of a passage, we are able to follow the flow of the author's logic and come to understanding. Some structures are rather set by convention (such as letters) or chronology (such as narratives). Others provide insight through creative arrangement, using such features as parallelism, chiasmus, ring structures, or inclusio. One of the most important questions to keep asking of texts is, What has prominence? What has the author emphasized by repetition, placement, or some other device? The more we understand how an author presents material, the clearer our understanding is.

5. Determine the Syntax of the Passage. If analysis of structure deals with the general flow of thought in a passage, syntax is concerned with the flow of thought in detail and how individual clauses, phrases, and words relate to each other. Particularly with narrative texts, the overall syn-tax may be rather straightforward and obvious. With more discursive material, often the syntax is quite complex, especially for a text like Eph. 1:3–14, which is one long sentence in the Greek text. Where such complexity exists, the effort to diagram the Greek or Hebrew sentence, noting how independent and dependent clauses func-tion, is a tremendous aid to understanding (Fee, *N. T. Exegesis* 31, 60–77).

6. Determine the Significance of Individual Words or Constructions. Discerning how spe-cific words convey meaning is obviously crucial, but exegesis is much more than word studies. In fact, word studies are often misleading. Words do not have meaning that can be assessed by some formula. Words have a conventional range of meanings, ways we expect them to be used. These meanings (the dictionary definitions) make up the semantic field of a word. Any aspect of a word's meaning—but not all of it—may be used in a given context, or the word may even be used creatively in a new way. Word studies show the etymology (the origin) of words, which may be of *no* significance for later meaning, and the variety of ways in which a word has been used. Such work must be done, but it does not show what a word means in a given context. One can only know that meaning by discerning the relations in the context. This also means discerning how words are put together in specific grammatical constructions. Of crucial importance for both Hebrew and Greek is discerning the use of prepo-sitions, infinitives, participles, and the way nouns are connected, especially with the genitive and dative in Greek. By way of example, the meaning of *pistis Christou* (Gal. 2:16 et al.) is notoriously debated both as to the aspect of the semantic field of *pistis* and the kind of genitive with *Christou*. Does the phrase mean "faith in Christ" (as most translations, but yielding a redundancy in the text) or "the faithfulness of Christ"?

7. Summarize the Findings by a Dynamic Translation or Paraphrase. Only after a careful analysis of the relations of and in the text can one think to have done an exegesis, but it is not enough to have dissected the text. Understanding requires that the thought of the text be expressed in a meaningful translation or paraphrase—and then appropriated for life.

Conclusion

The process described above is focused on determining the author's communicative intent, but exegesis also has larger concerns, or at least may be seen in a broader set of relations. Biblical exegesis does not deal merely with individual books but also with the relations between them (doing biblical theology). The understanding of a canonical work is augmented and nuanced when that work is seen in relation to other documents in the canon. This is true for all interpreters but is most obvious in Brevard Childs's emphasis on canon criticism, which seeks to transcend an overly historical-critical approach and focuses on the "canonical meaning" that texts take on by being part of the church's collection. Further, when biblical documents are seen in light of a developed theology, additional light may be shed by a theological exegesis that searches out implications, explains the relevance of texts, *and* uses the text to think theologically. A good example of legitimate theological exegesis is Miroslav Volf's adaptation of the parable of the Prodigal Son to issues of violence and reconciliation among humans (156–65). While much benefit is possible, the danger is that interpreters impose on texts a theology unrelated to their function. Such "spiritual exegesis" was often present throughout the church's history, but is more meditation on the text than exegesis of it.

See also Canonical Approach; Commentary; Context; Genre; Meaning; Textual Criticism; Translation

Bibliography

Cotterell, P., and M. Turner. *Linguistics and Biblical Interpretation*. SPCK, 1989; Fee, G. *New Testament Exegesis*. Westminster, 1983; idem. *To What End Exegesis?* Eerdmans, 2001; Hagner, D. *New Testament Exegesis and Research*. Fuller Theological Seminary, 1992; Hayes, J., and C. Holladay. *Biblical Exegesis*. John Knox, 1982; Kaiser, O., and W. Kümmel. *Exegetical Method*, trans. E. Goetchius. Seabury, 1963; Kaiser, W., Jr. *Toward an Exegetical Theology*. Baker, 1981; Lundin, R., A. Thiselton, and C. Walhout. *The Responsibility of Hermeneutics*. Eerdmans, 1985; Marshall, I. H., ed. *New Testament Interpretation*. Paternoster, 1977; Porter, S. "What Is Exegesis? An Analysis of Various Definitions." Pages 3–21 in *Handbook to Exegesis of the New Testament*, ed. S. Porter. Brill, 1997; Snodgrass, K. "Reading to Hear: A Hermeneutics of Hearing." *HBT* 24 (2002): 1–32; Stenger, W. *Introduction to New Testament Exegesis*, trans. D. Stott. Eerdmans, 1993; Stuart, D. *Old Testament Exegesis*. 3d ed. Westminster John Knox, 2001; Vanhoozer, K. "From Speech Acts to Scripture Acts: The Covenant of Discourse and the Discourse of Covenant." Pages 1–49 in *After Pentecost*, ed. C. Bartholomew et al. SHS. Zondervan/Paternoster, 2001; idem. *Is There a Meaning in This Text?* Zondervan, 1998; Volf, M. *Exclusion and Embrace*. Abingdon, 1996.

Klyne Snodgrass

Exile and Restoration

The themes of exile and restoration occupy a privileged position in any discussion of the theological interpretation of Scripture. They not only pervade biblical texts both directly and indirectly, but also form an organizing principle—a theoretical framework—for the fundamental thought-structures of the Scriptures. Many biblical scholars think that Israel's experience of exile contributed powerfully to the formation of the biblical texts themselves.

The present essay will not try to catalog the extensive biblical material on exile and restoration; that would go well beyond the space available here (see, e.g., Smith-Christopher; Hatina; Scott, *Exile*; Scott, *Restoration*). Instead, this essay discusses an ancient Jewish model of the theological interpretation of Scripture, a model that uses exile and restoration as a crucial part of its overall construct. The "grand narrative" that postmoderns have given up trying to find was much at the forefront of the theological interpretation of Scripture in the Second Temple period.

The Role of the Modern Interpreter

Before turning to antiquity, however, it seems best to begin with ourselves as modern interpreters. Self-awareness is essential to any theological interpretation of Scripture, not least with respect to the themes of exile and restoration. In attempting to interpret the Scriptures "for the church," we must be cognizant of our own proclivities and presuppositions, which filter and, to some degree, determine what we may find in the biblical text and how we may apply it. To this end, we may begin our study of exile and restoration by considering how our own modern interpretative framework may affect our perspective on the issues at hand.

In recent discussion of exile and restoration, two concerns have been raised about the role of the interpreter on these matters. First, Erich Gruen distinguishes what he calls "the gloomy approach" to Jewish dispersion from the less common positive approach. The gloomy view resolves Diaspora into exile (*galut*) and sees salvation exclusively in terms of homecoming, the recovery of a homeland. The positive view sees Jews as "the people of the Book," the text as a "portable temple," and restoration to a homeland as superfluous. In the end, Gruen suggests that both approaches are too simplistic, too stark. "The whole idea of privileging homeland over diaspora, or diaspora over homeland, derives from *a modern*, rather than an ancient, *obsession*" (Gruen 234 [emphasis added]). Whether or not Gruen is correct, we must remain vigilant to detect in ourselves any unwarranted biases that may distort interpretation.

Second, Simon Goldhill argues that Friedrich Nietzsche (1885) is a fundamental starting point for the modern discourse of exile. The interpretative strategies that Nietzsche reveals inaugurate the arguments of much contemporary writing on exile. These strategies include, first of all, the premise that "homesickness" or "nostalgia" (*Heimweh*) is part of the general human condition: all human beings experience alienation, a loss of home, which defines their lot as existentially "exilic." Second, exile is not merely a physical condition of spatial separation from a literal homeland, but rather a metaphor for the loss of an idealized intellectual topography, whether sociopolitical, cultural, moral, or spiritual. In this sense, exile becomes an expression for the "dislocation" and "alienation" that modern human beings (and especially intellectuals within society) *feel* on an existential level. Third, exiles desire to return to the idealized intellectual topography. However, to "return" is not a simple process of merely readopting an earlier intellectual position, because really to "return" requires one to overcome the disenfranchisement that led to exile in the first place. Therefore, "return" always involves reclaiming power (Nietzsche, *The Will to Power*) and setting things right again. For Nietzsche, the intellectual homeland to which he longs to return is pre-Socratic philosophy of ancient Greece, and the way back is by means of "the rainbow bridges of concepts," which he constructs by an intellectual journey "from North to South" (from the Renaissance through Christianity to the pre-Socratics). Fourth, Nietzsche's notion of exile and restoration (return to the pre-Socratics) is inextricably linked with the rise of German nationalism in the nineteenth century, which sought to establish the Dorian race as the founding ancestors of the German people.

Nietzsche's concept of "return" should be seen in light of his "classical" teaching of an "eternal return of the same." As Hubert Cancik (*Antike*; Cancik, "End," 89, 105) has rightly argued, however, this construct was in no way the quintessence of Greek thought (Hesiod's *Works and Days*, for example, never indicates that the golden age

will return). It nevertheless has had a profound effect on modern comparisons between Jewish and Greek religion and philosophy. The favorite image used in this kind of comparison, line and circle—"goal-oriented thought, history, eschatology" versus a "static idea of being, nature, eternal return"—misrepresents the historical facts on both sides.

Nietzsche's influential ideas about exile and return should alert us to possible latent assumptions in our interpretation of these motifs in the Scriptures. We all come to the text with a certain amount of "cultural baggage." Even if we ourselves have not read Nietzsche (and Nietzsche is merely one possible source of "interference"), his influence on us may be indirect and unperceived. Although we can never escape our location in history, culture, class, and sex, careful historical work can help us at least to see our blind spots in these areas and to avoid making ancient texts merely a reflection of our own self-absorbed, modern fantasies.

Learning Theological Interpretation from "Reworked Scriptures"

If we must be sensitive to modern influences that may distort our historical and theological interpretation of the biblical texts, we must consciously open ourselves to ancient influences that may enhance our ability to interpret the same texts. Particularly relevant here are Jewish writings of the Second Temple period, some of which were considered authoritative in their own right, such as *Reworked Pentateuch* (4Q158), the *Temple Scroll* (11Q19–20), and *Jubilees*. These are books that experts usually place under Geza Vermes's rubric "Rewritten Bible," but which James VanderKam argues are better termed "Reworked Scriptures." Hence, it is not presumed from the outset that a particular canon exists at Qumran, with a specific scope and shape.

These "Reworked Scriptures" are especially interesting for several reasons. First, they exemplify the theological interpretation of Scripture as it was practiced during the Second Temple period, the very time in which the NT writings were being formed. Learning from these Jewish sources may therefore contribute to our general understanding of exegetical, traditional, and theological processes at work within the NT, which are often remarkably different from the ones that modern scholars devise.

Second, in the case of the book of *Jubilees* at least, the "Reworked Scriptures" can be shown to have had a direct influence on the NT and other early Christian writings (Scott, *Exile*; Scott, *Restoration*). Therefore, the work we do on the "Reworked Scriptures" may provide not only a general understanding of certain hermeneutical aspects of these early Christian writings. It may also build a traditional bridge between what we call the OT and the NT, a bridge much more substantial and directly relevant than the gossamer "rainbow bridges of concepts" used by Nietzsche.

Third, the "Reworked Scriptures" offer us a model for our own theological interpretation of Scripture, since in many ways we are attempting to do much the same thing as these writings were doing: to help the community of faith, often in a stressful situation, to understand in a comprehensive, coherent, and cogent way the revealed word and works of God. The purpose is so that the people of God can be progressively transformed in the process, thereby responding to God's will for both the community and the world. It would seem absolutely essential that we take these texts seriously as part of the matrix of the NT and other Christian literature, even if their pseudepigraphical form repels us at first. The worldview to which these (and other) Second Temple texts expose us opens up a wholly different mode of thinking and facilitates a contextualized and nuanced theological interpretation of Scripture.

We should be clear, however, that theological interpretation, whether ancient or modern, is a decisively *human* task—a human attempt to bring together disparate pieces into a coherent whole and to see their collective implications for life. In a sense, every theological interpretation of Scripture is a reworking, since the interpreter is actively involved in the process (not merely a passive observer of phenomena). The interpreter always introduces a creative element (insight) into the resultant theological construct that was not necessarily inherent in the discrete biblical texts themselves. Hence, the process can yield differing results depending on (1) which texts are considered (always a selection, since it is impossible to see everything all at once and, in any case, everything cannot be brought into a coherent theological construct), (2) which interpretative framework is used to understand those texts and to correlate them with each other, and (3) how the resulting theological construct is applied to the needs of the interpretative community. Although the theological construct is vulnerable to criticism and correction at any one of these three points, entering into the hermeneutical circle of the part and the whole allows for refinements at any level. This happens as the retroductive process of interpretation continues through successive stages, often either in consultation with the interpretative community or in response to outside pressures.

Exile and Restoration in the Book of **Jubilees**

The book of *Jubilees*, a pseudepigraphon that apparently dates from the middle of the second century BCE, presents itself as divine revelation that Moses received on Mt. Sinai. In the first chapter, God converses with Moses directly. In chapters 2–50, the revelation comes through the mediation of the "angel of the presence," who dictated to Moses from heavenly tablets. Although this divine revelation to Moses reportedly consisted of the whole history of humankind from beginning to end (e.g., *Jub.* 1:4, 26–27, 29; 23:32), the surface narrative of the book focuses on only part of it, from the creation of the world to the arrival of Israel at Sinai. In essence, therefore, *Jubilees* covers the same ground as Gen. 1 to Exod. 24. It appears to be "a rewriting of earlier pentateuchal material, which it places in a new setting (Sinai), and it quotes extensively from a more ancient text of Genesis and Exodus" (VanderKam 287).

Jubilees is a polemical writing with a strong priestly orientation, which seeks to prove the validity of its own position over against other competing perspectives with respect to two main issues—sacred space and sacred time. Like other pseudepigrapha in the Second Temple period, *Jubilees* is vying for predominance in the name of divine revelation transmitted through heroes of the past. To this end, *Jubilees* portrays itself as containing the very revelation given to Moses on Mt. Sinai, the scope of which spanned from creation to new creation. Although the book is firmly based on Israel's Scriptures, it is nevertheless also, at least in part, a radical reworking of those texts. The book seeks to demonstrate the divinely ordained symmetry between the temporal and spatial axes in the space-time continuum.

First, *Jubilees* affirms a rigorous temporal symmetry. All human history is foreordained by God and inscribed in the heavenly tablets, which in turn are revealed through angelic mediation to Moses on Mt. Sinai. In this presentation, historical patterns are adduced to confirm divine providence over earthly events. A striking example of this is found in the correspondence between the *Endzeit* and the *Urzeit*. In *Jubilees*, as in other apocalyptic literature, God intends the world ultimately to conform to his original intention for the creation. But *Jubilees* goes even further by implying a complete recapitulation: the *Endzeit* or restoration will exactly mirror the *Urzeit* or patriarchal period. For just as human longevity progressively declined over the course of the fifty Jubilees from the creation of the world until Israel's entrance into the promised land, so also human longevity will incrementally increase over the course of the fifty Jubilees from Israel's return to the land to the new creation. In other words, the proof of the existence of divine providence—and therefore the correctness of *Jubilees'* version of things—is in its rhythmic working in history: construction, destruction, and reconstruction. All this was decreed from heaven to occur in periods that were equal in length and therefore symmetrical.

According to our reconstruction of *Jubilees'* chronological system, the axis of symmetry on the temporal plane—both the midpoint and low point of all human history—is astonishingly the exile and the destruction of the temple. This occurred at the culmination of the sixtieth Jubilee (AM 2940 [*anno mundi*, "in the year of the world," reckoned from creation] = 588/587 BCE) in a world era totaling 120 Jubilees. On either side of this line of symmetry, human history is essentially a mirror image.

This perfect historical symmetry is a function of the cultic cycles (such as the weekly Sabbath, the 364-day year, the seven-year "week," and the 49-year Jubilee) generated by rhythms of the sun, which were established on the fourth day of creation—the exact middle of the first week. The greater and lesser conjunctions of these cultic cycles divide history into distinct periods, and the intersection of these conjunctions with major events in human history lends the events a particular significance or reveals an interrelationship with other events. For example, the grand Jubilee of Jubilees—the fiftieth Jubilee from creation in AM 2450—is seen, in conformity with the law of Jubilee in Lev. 25 interpreted on a national scale. It is the time for Israel's redemption from the slavery in Egypt and the nation's return to the land that rightfully belongs to it.

Jubilees affirms not only a temporal symmetry between *Urzeit* and *Endzeit*, but also, second, a spatial symmetry between heaven and earth. We have argued that the goal of history in the book is God's original intention for his creation, the total recapitulation of the primeval period before Adam's sin in the Garden of Eden. If this is correct, then we must also notice that the way things will be on earth is the way things are and always have been in heaven. The goal of history, in other words, is that the cultus will be "on earth as in heaven."

Since the earthly cultus operates first and foremost in the land of Israel, and especially in the central sanctuary within the land, the process of recapitulation begins when Israel in exile repents from its previous sins (not least from its previous failure to observe the proper calendar), and God returns the people to the land. At the precise moment of entrance into the land of restoration (to occur ostensibly in 98/97 BCE), the cultic clock starts ticking. In fact, the people are expected to enter the land at the culmination of the seventieth Jubilee (AM 3430), ten Jubilees (= seventy "weeks" = 490 years) after the exile began. From then on, Israel is obligated to observe the entire law, including most prominently the weekly Sabbath, the annual festivals, the sabbatical year, and the Year of Jubilee. Only in so doing can Israel maintain the proper rhythm, which is simultaneously going on in heaven—all oriented on the cycles of the sun and of the cultus.

If the clock of the cultic cycles starts ticking upon entrance into the land, then the exact boundaries of the land need to be precisely defined. Since the Scriptures give differing dimensions, *Jubilees* opts for the tradition that gives the land maximal boundaries to the north and to the east (Gen. 15:18–21; Deuteronomy), corresponding to the ideal extent of the land during the Davidic-Solomonic empire. *Jubilees* apparently holds that the generation of the conquest not only employed a faulty (lunar) calendar, but that they also misconstrued the boundaries of the land as beginning at the Jordan rather than at the Arnon. In this way, Israel radically erred in its cultic practice from the outset and thereby defiled the land, making the exile necessary so that the land would make up the cumulative seventy years of sabbatical rest that had been missed during the 490-year preexilic period (2 Chron. 36:21). Thus, by the end of the corresponding 490-year period of exile, atonement for iniquity would have been made (Dan. 9:24).

In *Jubilees*, recapitulation includes both universal and particular aspects that are integrally interrelated. In keeping with its view of sacred time—a comprehensive chronological framework rooted in the creative order itself—*Jubilees* necessarily contains a complementary vision of sacred space. This vision includes the whole created world and especially the holiest sites, Zion and the land, which will occupy the focal point in the age to come. All times and places will eventually be brought back into conformity with the Creator's will as foreordained in the heavenly tablets.

The foregoing survey of *Jubilees'* temporal and spatial axes goes a long way toward explaining the crucial role of exile and restoration within the book's overall conception of world history. We may add a further observation about the role of exile. There is a striking similarity between Israel's exile from the land and the expulsion of Adam and Eve from the Garden of Eden. In order to appreciate this similarity, we need to see that both places are presented in *Jubilees* as the holiest earth. Thus, *Jub.* 8:19–20 describes the choice territory allotted to Shem as having all the holy sites: "He [Noah] knew that the Garden of Eden is the holy of holies and is the residence of the Lord; [that] Mt. Sinai is the middle of the desert; and [that] Mt. Zion is in the middle of the earth. The three of them—the one facing the other—were created as holy [places]." The Garden of Eden is portrayed as a temple ("the holy of holies," 8:19), just as Zion itself contains the temple (having a "holy of holies," 23:21), which was to be built (1:10, 17) and then rebuilt in the end time (1:28–29). When *Jubilees* speaks about Eden, it is aimed at a future, eschatological temple on Mt. Zion in a new creation, at the time of Israel's return to the land and restoration.

Implications

The vistas that *Jubilees'* treatment of exile and restoration open up have many far-reaching implications for the investigation of the NT and other early Christian literature. For example, *Jubilees* foresees a protracted period of exile that would end only after Israel had turned to God in repentance (1:15, 23). Does this have any relevance for the message of repentance preached by John the Baptist and Jesus? In support of this possibility we may note that the Matthean genealogy of Jesus divides the generations from Abraham to the Messiah into three groups of fourteen, the last of which extends "from the Babylonian exile to the Messiah" (Matt. 1:17 AT). Does this mean that the Messiah brings the end of the exile? According to the summary in Mark 1:14–15, Jesus proclaimed, "The time is fulfilled, and the kingdom of God has come near; repent and believe in the good news" (NRSV). What exactly is "the time" that is proclaimed as "fulfilled"? Paul uses similar language in Gal. 4:4: "But when *the fullness of time* had come, God sent his Son, born of a woman, born under the law" (NRSV, italics added). Are we to think of a periodization of history such as that presented in *Jubilees* as divinely foreordained?

Jubilees may also be helpful in understanding the nature of the restoration. According to Acts 1:6–7, when the disciples ask Jesus after the resurrection, "Lord, is this the time when you will restore the kingdom to Israel?" Jesus replies, "It is not for you to know the times or periods that the Father has set by his own authority" (NRSV). Thereupon, Jesus tells his followers that they will be empowered for mission "to the ends of the earth" (v. 8), apparently assuming that there will be a length of time before the final restoration of Israel takes place. Scholars have long thought that the "delay of the parousia" (the second coming of Christ) was a great embarrassment to early Christians. However, according to our reconstruction of *Jubilees'* chronological system, the book expects an era of incremental restoration to last for fifty Jubilees (2,450 years), corresponding to the length of the first era of incremental decline. In this regard, *Jubilees'* expectation can be compared with that in the Apocalypse of Weeks (*1 En.* 91:11–17; 93:1–10), which looks forward to a similarly long period of restoration. In view of these expectations for a progressive and lengthy restoration, which do not appear to be apologetic in nature, we can ask: Does the delay of the parousia in Christian sources now look less like a dire expedient to explain away an embarrassing situation than like an established tradition regarding the duration of the recapitulation of all things?

Finally, the *Book of Jubilees* provides opportunity to interact with N. T. Wright's reconstruction of the historical Jesus. According to Wright, Jesus should be understood as a Jewish apocalyptic prophet who proclaimed the kingdom of God: (1) the return of Israel from exile, (2) the final triumph of God over evil, and (3) the return of Yahweh to Zion. However, unlike the *literal* expectations of return from exile and restoration found in the OT prophets and in Jewish literature of the Second Temple period, Jesus believed, in Wright's view, that all three elements of the kingdom of God were taking place *figuratively* in and through his own ministry. Thus, for example, Wright states: "[Jesus] believes himself, much as John the Baptist had done, to be charged with the God-given responsibility of regrouping Israel around himself. But this regrouping is no longer a preliminary preparation for the return from exile, the coming of the kingdom; it *is* the return, the redemption, the resurrection from the dead" (132, with author's emphasis). Similarly, in his final journey to Jerusalem, Jesus in his own person was intentionally enacting Israel's return from exile, the final triumph over evil, and the return of Yahweh to Zion.

Although Wright's reconstruction of Jesus' restoration program is vulnerable to critique at many crucial points (cf. Newman), perhaps one of Wright's most controversial statements is that "the great majority of Jesus' contemporaries" understood themselves to be "still in exile, in all the senses that really mattered" (445). It is impossible, however, to know whether "the great majority" held to an ongoing exile mentality, for our evidence of popular conceptions in first-century Judaism is extremely limited. Moreover, behind Wright's idea of exile "in all the senses that really mattered" is the notion that "exile" (normally understood as the state of living in banishment from the homeland) can somehow be redefined (such as the state of living under foreign oppression) to make it applicable to first-century Jews residing in the land of Israel. *Jubilees* shows, however, that already in the mid-second century BCE (before the formation of the Qumran community and its possibly idiosyncratic self-conception of living in exile near the Dead Sea), the concept of a protracted exile in the literal and unvarnished sense of the term was part of a living tradition, at least in one pocket of "Palestinian" Judaism of the "Second Temple period." This raises afresh the issue of whether Jesus himself may have held a similar view (cf. McKnight; Scott, *Geography*).

See also Jewish Context of the NT

Bibliography

Cancik, H. "The End of the World, of History, and of the Individual in Greek and Roman Antiquity." Pages 84–125 in *The Encyclopedia of Apocalypticism*. Vol. 1, *The Origins of Apocalypticism in Judaism and Christianity*, ed. J. Collins. Continuum, 2000; idem. *Nietzsches Antike*. Metzler, 1995; Goldhill, S. "Whose Antiquity? Whose Modernity? The 'Rainbow Bridges' of Exile." *Antike und Abendland* 46 (2000): 1–20; Grabbe, L., ed. *Leading Captivity Captive*. JSOTSup 278. Sheffield Academic Press, 1998; Gruen, E. "Diaspora and Homeland." Pages 232–52 in *Diaspora*. Harvard University Press, 2002; Hatina, T. R. "Exile." Pages 348–51 in *Dictionary of New Testament Background*, ed. C. Evans and S. Porter. InterVarsity, 2000; McKnight, S. *A New Vision for Israel*. Eerdmans, 1999; Newman, C., ed. *Jesus and the Restoration of Israel*. InterVarsity/Paternoster, 1999; Nietzsche, F. *Werke: Kritische Gesamtausgabe*. Pages 412–13 [August–September 1885, frag. 41(4)] in vol. 7.3, *Nachgelassene Fragmente Herbst 1884 bis Herbst 1885*, ed. G. Colli and M. Montinari. De Gruyter, 1967; Ruiten, J. van. "Eden and the Temple: The Rewriting of Genesis 2:4–3:24 in the Book of Jubilees." Pages 63–94 in *Paradise Interpreted*, ed. G. Lut-tikhuizen. Themes in Biblical Narrative: Jewish and Christian Traditions 2. Brill, 1999; Scott, J. "The Division of the Earth in *Jubilees* 8:11–9:15 and Early Christian Chronography." Pages 295–323 in *Studies in the Book of Jubilees*, ed. M. Albani et al. TSAJ 65. Mohr/Siebeck, 1997; idem. *Geography in Early Judaism and Christianity*. SNTSMS 113. Cambridge University Press, 2002; idem. *On Earth as in Heaven*. JSJSup 91. Brill, 2005; Scott, J., ed. *Exile*. JSJSup 56. Brill, 1997; idem. *Restoration*. JSJSup 72. Brill, 2001; Smith-Christopher, D. *A Biblical Theology of Exile*. Overtures to Biblical Theology. Fortress, 2002; VanderKam, J. "Questions of Canon Viewed through the Dead Sea Scrolls." *BBR* 11 (2001): 269–92; Wright, N. T. *Jesus and the Victory of God*. Fortress, 1996.

James M. Scott

Exodus, Book of

The book of Exodus—traditionally ascribed to Moses, the central human figure in the book, but in itself anonymous—is foundational for the biblical understanding both of God, Yahweh, and of the people of God, Israel. Its content sets out parameters for understanding God and Israel, parameters that have always played a major role in the thought and practice of both Jews and Christians, though these differing religious traditions have tended to appropriate the material in markedly different ways. Of enormous significance for Christian theology is God's self-revelation to Moses at the burning bush (Exod. 3); for ethics, the Ten Commandments (Exod. 20); and for spirituality, the pattern of Egypt, exodus, sea, and wilderness read metaphorically in terms of sin, redemption, baptism, and discipleship.

The book is in two main parts, strikingly depicted in its own words. First, Yahweh delivers Israel from Egypt: "You have seen what I did to Egypt and how I bore you upon eagles' wings and brought you to myself" (19:4 NRSV). Second, Yahweh gives torah, a moral and ritual constitution for Israel to enable them to realize their unique vocation: "So now, if you truly obey my voice and keep my covenant, you shall be my special treasure among all peoples. Although the whole earth is mine, you shall be for me a priestly kingdom and a holy nation" (19:5–6 AT).

The preliminary question of the genre(s) of the text, and the difference this might make to its theological interpretation, is complex. What it might mean to take seriously the received form of the text, and yet to recognize its intrinsic diversity and its likely lengthy underlying processes of transmission and discernment, can here only be briefly suggested, rather than argued. First, divine self-revelation and its faithful human recognition could as well take place over an extended period as at a single point of time. Second, the shape and sequence of the material may be meaningful in its own right, even if it does not correspond straightforwardly to the historical development of Israel's religion. Third, there need be no intrinsic reason why the Spirit should not appropriate any meaningful form of human communication. If ancient Israel's genres do not correspond to those of "history" as articulated in modern Western thought, they need be none the worse for that. The challenge is learning to recognize and appreciate the ancient conventions, and to relate them appropriately to our modern ones.

Exodus is well served by modern, theologically oriented commentaries. The outstanding volume remains the one by Childs, both for its reflection on the text and for its giving access to the great Jewish and Christian commentaries down through the centuries. Fretheim and Brueggemann each offer sophisticated but easily readable interpretation. From a Jewish perspective, Sarna is accessible and fascinating, while Jacob is more comprehensive though more polemical.

The richness and complexity of Exodus suggest an approach to its theological interpretation section by section.

1. Setting the Scene, Exod. 1:1–2:22

The growth of Israel into a people has clear resonances with God's mandate at creation and with his promise to Abraham (Exod. 1:7; cf. Gen. 1:28; 12:2), thus clearly contextualizing all that follows within God's overall purposes for his world. Yet human opposition directly threatens this outworking of God's purposes, and the patient overcoming of this opposition is a major concern of the book.

It is striking that the first characters to play a positive role are all women—the midwives, Moses' mother and sister, Pharaoh's daughter—and unsurprisingly feminist interpreters have engaged suggestively with this (Bellis and Kaminsky 307–26).

Moses means well, but his act of violence exposes the double-edged nature and unpredictable consequences of such acts (Childs 27–46).

2. God Calls and Commissions Moses, Exod. 2:23–7:7

The burning bush story is one of the most discussed passages in the whole OT (for an introduction to its symbolic interpretations, see Levine). Fire that burns without consuming is a prime symbol of God; perhaps because fire, as in Otto's famous characterization of holiness as *mysterium*

tremendum et fascinans (Otto), both attracts (by its movement and color) and repels (by its heat if one gets too close). The hearing of God's voice from the fire will characterize Israel's encounter with God at Sinai (Deut. 4:9–13).

God calls Moses to be a "prophet," one who will speak and act for God; God will deliver Israel (3:7–8), which means that Moses is to deliver Israel (3:9–10). Moses feels overwhelmed at the enormity of this and produces a series of excuses, mainly expressing a sense of inadequacy; God takes these difficulties seriously, thereby implying genuine space in relationship with himself (3:11–4:12). Only when Moses tries to decline altogether does God become angry (4:13–14).

Moses' second difficulty relates to the name of God, which God then gives—Yahweh (3:13–15). The wordplay on the verb "to be" (*hayah*), which indicates something of the meaning of the divine name (3:14), has been a focus for Christian theologizing about the nature of God down through the ages, not least in relation to the LXX's rendering: "I am the One who is" (see LaCocque and Ricoeur 307–61). In both Hebrew and Greek, the text envisages a Deity whose nature is not dependent upon other than self—yet who graciously engages with, and indeed commits to, Moses and Israel. The self-revelation that makes God known also in no way removes the intrinsic mystery of God, but rather establishes the principle that, with God, "the more you know, the more you know you don't know." (On the vocalization of the divine name and the appropriate form for Christian use, see Seitz 131–44.)

Moses' initial encounter with Pharaoh is disappointing—far from heeding Moses, Pharaoh responds with cynical brutality; Moses needs to learn that God's ways are not his ways (5:1–23). God reaffirms his new self-revelation as Yahweh, a God who will deliver his people, and a reluctant Moses prepares to try again.

(On the much-discussed technical problem of how Yahweh giving his name to Moses relates to the extensive use of the divine name in Genesis, see Moberly, *Old Testament*.)

3. The Plagues, Exod. 7:8–11:10

Moses' confrontation with Pharaoh and his magicians—who initially can exercise the same kind of power that Moses exercises—raises numerous theological issues. First, why such an extended sequence? Why does not Yahweh, through Moses, simply sweep away the opposition? This is explicitly addressed in 9:14–16, in terms of the plagues serving to enhance recognition of Yahweh. Implicitly also, God's action is appropriately encountered within the familiar constraints of a long struggle.

Second, why does God harden Pharaoh's heart? This is clearly related to the first issue. At least it is clear that Pharaoh also hardens his own heart; thus it is not the case that Pharaoh is wanting to respond positively but is being prevented, but that God confirms him in the course he embraces for himself, and uses this to heighten the significance of Israel's deliverance.

Third, what if one reads this text (and the crossing of the sea) from an Egyptian perspective? Does this not show Yahweh to be, in some sense, a tribal or national deity, less than the one God of all? Interestingly, this question, sharply posed by those who have suffered oppression that has justified itself by appeal to God (Warrior), tends not to bother liberation theologians who are inclined to see an oppressor receiving just deserts. The underlying issue is election, Yahweh's call of Israel, with God consequently making a distinction in how he treats Israel (9:4, 26). Yet election is not just a privilege, for the OT principle is that (in the words of Jesus, Luke 12:48 AT) "much is expected of those to whom much is given" (cf. Amos 3:2).

4. Passover, Exodus, and Crossing the Sea, Exod. 12:1–15:21

The Passover texts have usually been of greater interest to Jews, who have still sought to enact what is prescribed, than to Christians, who have seen them as prefiguring Christ and so have tended to read the texts in a metaphorical mode (cf. 1 Cor. 5:7–8).

The use of the exodus by liberation theologians raises important hermeneutical issues (see Bellis and Kaminsky 215–75). On the one hand, a general OT case can be made that Israel is a model for the nations, and that therefore what applies to Israel can be applied to others also; and deliverance from unjust oppression is clearly a major concern within the text. On the other hand, God is said to be motivated explicitly by his antecedent commitment to the patriarchs (2:24; 6:2–8). The particularity of Israel's election should not be ignored, as also the purpose of the exodus, to make Israel servants/slaves to Yahweh. In general, any responsible Christian use of the material should be refracted through the lens of Christ, where the judgment and redemption of God are definitively revealed. To take the OT seriously both in its own right and in the light of Christ is demanding, but that is the task of Christian theology.

5. Learning in the Wilderness, Exod. 15:22–18:27

The wilderness narratives of Exodus are continued in Numbers, where some of the stories are clearly similar so as to draw a contrast (manna/quails, Exod. 16//Num. 11; rebellion at Meribah, Exod. 17:1–7//Num. 20:2–13). Israel's failings are treated more lightly in Exodus, before the giving of torah at Sinai, than in Numbers, where the post-Sinai context implies that more is expected of those to whom more is given.

In the wilderness Israel has to learn new ways of living—what it means to be Yahweh's people. Exodus 16 is paradigmatic, presenting a form of "Give us each day our daily bread." The hardships of the wilderness lead Israel to complain and to remember Egypt selectively (16:1–3). Yahweh's response is not only to provide for them, but explicitly to test their obedience (16:4–5). After Israel is reprimanded for complaining (16:6–12), God's provision is given (16:13–14) and initiates a didactic sequence. First, when God provides food, the people do not even realize it without Moses' explanation (16:15). Second, God's provision is strictly according to need (not strength)—neither more nor less (16:16–18). Third, it cannot be hoarded, so God's gift must be collected fresh each day (16:19–21). Fourth, the regular daily pattern varies on the Sabbath, for on Sabbath eve double can be collected and some kept; but the people are tempted to disbelieve this just as much as the regular pattern (16:22–30). Finally, some manna is solemnly preserved, presumably as a reminder of its lesson and meaning even in the promised land, where manna no longer needs to be provided (16:31–36).

6. The Covenant at Sinai, Exod. 19–24

As Israel gathers at Sinai, we have the keywords that sum up Exodus as a whole (19:4–6). The awesome nature of Yahweh's presence at Sinai is depicted by the language of storm, earthquake, volcano, fire, and trumpet (19:16–19). The argument that this depicts a live volcano, and therefore attempts to locate Mt. Sinai should search for a volcano, seriously misconstrues the purpose of the language. The text seeks to convey the overwhelming nature of the divine presence by appealing to the most shaking and moving of known phenomena.

In this awesome scene, Moses has uniquely privileged access to God (19:19–20; cf. 19:9; 14:31). Sinai in Exod. 19:24 is like a temple with restricted access: the people stay off/outside; selected leaders, such as priests, come into the holy place and encounter God (24:1, 9–11); Moses, like the high priest, goes alone to God as into the holy of holies (24:2, 15–18). Among other things, this underlines the parallels between Israel's regular worship and its foundational engagement with God; also, it stresses the implicit authority of the legislation associated with Moses. (In a different vein, Moses' ascent of the mountain into the fire and darkness of the divine presence was taken as a model of spiritual life in the suggestive typological interpretation of the early church; see Gregory of Nyssa.)

Yet even Moses is off the mountain when God speaks the Ten Commandments (19:21–20:1), which are presented as the direct, and overwhelming, address of God himself (20:18–19, 22), so as to suggest the conformity of their content to the very nature of God. Moses interprets the giving of the commandments in a key verse, 20:20: they are to *test* Israel, so as to bring about the *fear of God* and *diminish sin*. Obedience to the commandments is demanding but will make Israel into the upright people they are meant to be. "Fear of God" is the prime OT term for appropriate human responsiveness to God. The combination of "test" and "fear" recurs in Gen. 22, in a way suggesting that Abraham's costly obedience in being willing to relinquish Isaac in some way models what Israel's responsiveness to the Ten Commandments should be (Moberly, *Old Testament*, 144–45).

The detailed laws of Exod. 21–23 are, by contextual implication, outworkings in everyday, mundane situations of the fundamental concerns of the Ten Commandments. The Israelites then commit themselves to the covenant explicitly in terms of obedience to the Ten Commandments and the detailed laws (24:3) in a ritual where the blood perhaps symbolizes consecration (24:4–8; cf. 29:20–21), thus marking Israel as Yahweh's holy people (Nicholson 172). On this basis Israel's representatives "see" God (24:9–11). The proximity of access to God that is now possible, on the basis of consecrated covenantal obedience to the will of God, contrasts sharply with the earlier distance from the holy place of God that was enjoined upon Israel (19:10–15, 21–24).

7. Tabernacle and Priesthood, Exod. 25–31

The purpose of the tabernacle is to mediate the presence of Yahweh, so that as Israel moves on from Sinai, the divine presence that came upon Sinai can continue to accompany Israel in this "sacramental" shrine. The ark and the mercy seat are where Yahweh will meet with Moses (25:22), and the regular daily sacrifices will set the con-

text for Yahweh's sanctifying presence in Israel (29:38–46, a key interpretative passage). Subsequent Jewish and Christian practices of morning and evening prayer seek to perpetuate this basic pattern of enabling openness to the divine presence in differing contexts.

The images and symbols within the tabernacle resonate with a wider ancient Near Eastern context (Keel 111–76). Since royal thrones were regularly flanked by fabulous creatures, the flanking cherubim above the ark implicitly indicate the presence of Yahweh's royal throne (25:17–22). The symbolism also acquires meaning from its Israelite context. It is likely that the seven-branch lampstand (25:31–40) is meant to be understood as a stylized representation of the burning bush—a perpetual symbolization of the fundamental encounter at Sinai/Horeb.

8. Covenant Breaking and Renewal, Exod. 32–34

Israel's impatient making of the golden calf is presented as, in effect, a breaking of the first two commandments, and this while Israel is still at the mountain of God; it is rather like committing adultery on one's wedding night. Even if this was not the specific intention of the people (which is open to various less-heinous construals), the text's account of their action is explicit (32:7–10). Aaron's self-exculpatory evasiveness—compare his account to Moses (32:21–24) with the narrator's own account (32:1–6)—suggests deception of self and/or others in a way indicative of a gap between appearance and reality.

Israel's faithlessness almost terminates the covenant at the outset. But Moses remains faithful, and his intercession makes a difference within God's purposes (32:10–14; cf. the importance attached to the role of faithful intercessor in Ezek. 22:30; Isa. 62:6–7). When Yahweh offers to make of Moses another Abraham (32:10b; cf. Gen. 12:2–3), Moses shows his true stature by declining the offer. The intercessory role of Moses is further developed in Exod. 33:11–20. The pattern here is that initially Moses speaks much and Yahweh little; but as the intercession continues, Moses speaks less and Yahweh more, until finally Yahweh alone speaks and Moses recedes from view. Overall, Moses uses his privileged position before God to seek a fuller revelation of God, which is granted in terms of what stiff-necked Israel most needs—grace and mercy (33:19). Yet this deeper engagement with God brings out the intrinsic limits of such engagement: the one with whom Yahweh speaks "face-to-face" (33:11) "cannot see my [Yahweh's] face" (33:20) (cf. Eph. 3:19, where Paul prays for Christians *to know* the love of Christ *that surpasses knowledge*). And the following provisions for Moses' safety in the rock (33:21–23), which stress the limited and partial nature of what Moses will see, paradoxically prepare for the greatest self-revelation of the nature of God, upon Yahweh's own lips, in the whole Bible (34:6–7).

Despite its intrinsic importance for the character of God, 34:6–7 has received less attention in Christian theology than 3:14. By contrast Jewish theology has given prime weight to 34:6–7, even designating it as a revelation of "the thirteen attributes" of God (for enumeration, see Jacob 985). Together the two passages are complementary in a foundational way for the OT understanding of Yahweh. In the context of Israel's sin, the strong emphasis is on divine mercy (see Moberly, "How?" 191–201). The reaffirmation of judgment in 34:7b is striking—since, in context, there is a sense in which Yahweh *is* clearing the guilty—and is most likely meant to safeguard Yahweh's moral nature and requirements, to clarify that the mercy is not leniency or moral indifference. In other words, Yahweh's mercy is meant to lead to renewed practices of faithfulness and integrity (cf. Ps. 130:4), not to a sense that Israel can "get away" with things because God will let them off. If Exod. 19–24 emphasizes God's searching moral demand, Exod. 32–34 stresses his searching grace. Theologically, it is vital to hold these two emphases in tension, and to resist all attempts to play off one against the other.

As a unit Exod. 32–34 offers a fundamental construal of Israel's existence before God, analogous to the construal of the world's existence in the flood narrative (Gen. 6–9). At their very beginnings the world in general and the chosen people in particular commit sin and face destruction (Gen. 6:5–13; Exod. 32:7–10). One person, Noah/Moses, remains faithful, is uniquely said to have "found favor" with Yahweh (Gen. 6:8; Exod. 33:12), and becomes a mediator of God's grace for the future. Faithful Noah and Moses are mentioned at the turning point of the narratives from judgment to renewal (Gen. 8:1; Exod. 33:11). Noah offers sacrifice and Moses prays (Gen. 8:20; Exod. 33:12–18), each to elicit a climactic pronouncement of divine mercy and forbearance toward sin (Gen. 8:21; Exod. 33:19; 34:6–7). And each narrative strikingly emphasizes that the sinful qualities that brought judgment in the first place remain unchanged (humanity's sinful inclinations, Gen. 6:5; 8:21; Israel's being stiff-necked, Exod. 32:9; 33:3, 5; 34:9). So God deals with the world in general, and the chosen people in particular, in the same way (without partiality). And each should know that their continuing existence is because of divine grace toward the unfaithful, grace paradoxically mediated by one who is faithful.

9. The Tabernacle Established and Inaugurated, Exod. 35–40

Israel brings extensive freewill offerings (implicitly a response to grace), and the skilled craft that enables the tabernacle to be constructed is explicitly an endowment from God (35:4–36:7). Everything for the tabernacle and for the vestments of its priests is made as prescribed (39:32–43). Moses is obedient in exactly the same way that Noah was obedient (40:16; Gen. 6:22).

At the end of the book the cloud and glory of Yahweh's presence come to the tabernacle as they earlier came to Mt. Sinai (40:34; 24:15–16). So the one who met with Israel at Sinai will accompany Israel through the wilderness, and will also come to the temple in Jerusalem (1 Kings 8:10–11).

Conclusion

One possible way of reading the book as a whole is to see Exodus as probing the meaning of servitude and freedom, which can be focused on the differing implications of the Hebrew root *'bd* (slave/servant). Israel is delivered from slavery to Egypt (esp. 1:13–14, *'bd*, 5x), a slavery of heartless oppression, so as to become a slave to Yahweh instead. The first of the specific "ordinances" at Sinai is about the Hebrew slave (*'ebed*) who (remarkably) loves his master and chooses to serve him for life in preference to gaining independence (21:2–6). This may well be put in this prime position so as to metaphorically picture Israel in relation to Yahweh, who later says, "For it is to me that the Israelites are slaves" (Lev. 25:55 AT). Such servitude is one of justice and holiness. It is the highest honor elsewhere in the OT for a person to be designated as "servant ['ebed] of Yahweh" (so, e.g., Abraham, Moses, David [Gen. 26:24; Josh. 1:7; 1 Kings 11:13]). Likewise, Paul calls himself the servant/slave (*doulos*, the regular LXX rendering of '*ebed*) of Christ (Rom. 1:1; etc.). The thought underlying all this is well captured in the famous (*Book of Common Prayer*) words, "His service is perfect freedom." Compare the psalmist's linking obedience to torah with living in freedom (Ps. 119:44–45), and Paul's emphasis that Christian freedom is not for self-gratification but for loving service of others (Gal. 5:1, 13). The basic point is the intrinsic conceptual connection between freedom from alien oppression and obedient service to God—a conceptuality that, in a contemporary culture that rather too easily appeals to "freedom" as self-evident in value and meaning, requires careful and sustained attention.

Bibliography

Bellis, A., and J. Kaminsky. *Jews, Christians, and the Theology of the Hebrew Scriptures*. SBL, 2000; Brueggemann, W. "The Book of Exodus." NIB 1:675–981; Childs, B. *Exodus*. OTL. SCM, 1974; Fretheim, T. *Exodus*. IBC. John Knox, 1991; Gregory of Nyssa. *The Life of Moses*, trans. A. Malherbe and E. Ferguson. Classics of Western Spirituality. Paulist, 1978; Jacob, B. *The Second Book of the Bible*, trans. W. Jacob. Ktav, 1992; Keel, O. *The Symbolism of the Biblical World*, trans. T. Hallett. SPCK, 1978; LaCocque, A., and P. Ricoeur. *Thinking Biblically*. University of Chicago Press, 1998; Levine, E. *The Burning Bush*. Sepher-Hermon, 1981; Moberly, R. W. L. "How May We Speak of God? A Reconsideration of the Nature of Biblical Theology." *TynBul* 53 (2002): 177–202; idem. *The Old Testament of the Old Testament*. OBT. Fortress, 1992. Reprint, Wipf & Stock, 2001; Nicholson, E. *God and His People*. Oxford University Press, 1986; Otto, R. *The Idea of the Holy*, trans. J. Harvey. Oxford University Press, 1924; Sarna, N. *Exodus*. JPS Torah Commentary. JPS, 1991; Seitz, C. *Figured Out*. Westminster John Knox, 2001; Warrior, R. "Canaanites, Cowboys, and Indians: Deliverance, Conquest, and Liberation Theology Today." Reprinted in pages 188–94 of *The Postmodern Bible Reader*, ed. D. Jobling et al. Blackwell, 2001.

R. W. L. Moberly

Exodus/New Exodus

Exodus is more than a book of the OT. It is a theological paradigm that resonates, both implicitly and explicitly, in various books of the OT, Second Temple literature, and the NT. In both Jewish and Christian heritage, Israel's exodus has served as a generative model for articulating God's subsequent redemptive acts in new exoduses. This theme is also closely aligned with the new creation; there is a connection between creation and redemption: to redeem is to re-create.

The Book of Exodus

Within the book of Exodus itself, we already begin to see the interpenetration of these themes. In 1:1–7, Israel's life in Egypt is described by using creation language: "The Israelites were fruitful and multiplied greatly and became exceedingly numerous, so that the land was filled with them" (v. 7). Such language is clearly reminiscent of Gen. 1:28 and 9:1. When Pharaoh takes notice that the Israelites have become "much too numerous" (v. 9), he takes it upon himself to counter

that trend first by enslaving them and then by killing the male children at birth. The very thing that is a sign of God's creation-blessing (filling the earth) is what Pharaoh wants to reverse. Such a maneuver pits Pharaoh not so much against Israel but squarely against Israel's God, its Creator and, as the story unfolds, its Redeemer.

Because Pharaoh's actions are an attempt to reverse the blessings of the Creator/Redeemer God of Israel, it is only fitting that God's subsequent dealings in Exodus be couched in the language of creation. Yahweh enacts redemption of Israel through a series of creation reversals. Each plague is, for example, an undoing of the created order. Frogs and insects, rather than maintaining their ordained place in the ecosystem, invade Egypt—chaos results where once there was order. Also, the ninth plague reintroduces the reign of darkness into what God had once ordered light (Gen. 1:3–5); what were once separated in orderly fashion, day and night, are now again joined in chaos. Perhaps most explicit is the parting of the Red Sea. Long ago God had separated the water from the dry land (Gen. 1:9–10). For the Israelites, he does so again: in Exod. 14:16, God divides the water, exposing the dry land so the Israelites can walk through. The army of Pharaoh is not so blessed, however. They attempt to cross, but in the final creation reversal, God brings the waters of chaos crashing down upon the army. In Gen. 1 and Exodus, God employs his creation to bring life. But in Exodus, he reintroduces chaos to punish the enemies of Israel.

This interplay between redemption and creation continues to work itself out throughout Exodus. Israel was redeemed for a purpose, and that purpose begins to come to fruition on Mt. Sinai. Commentators have considered both the giving of the law at Sinai and the building of the tabernacle to be re-creative acts. The completion of Israel's redemption includes the institution of God's order on the level of human conduct toward God and others (social/moral law). Likewise, the tabernacle is the introduction of heavenly order into a chaotic world. Even the dimensions of the tabernacle suggest order: each outer and inner court is 75 by 75 feet square. The curtain is made of blue, purple, and red material, with cherubim interwoven throughout (36:35)—a picture of heaven, so to speak. The tabernacle was constructed on a pattern of six creative days culminating in a Sabbath rest; six times in the tabernacle narrative we find the phrase "The LORD said to Moses" (25:1; 30:11, 17, 22, 34; 31:1), which culminates in a Sabbath (31:12–18). The entire account is punctuated in 40:33; "So Moses finished [*klh*] the work [*ml'kh*]" is reminiscent of the words at the completion of creation in Gen. 2:2 (AT): "So God on the seventh day finished [*klh*] his work [*ml'kh*]." The building of the tabernacle is a mini creative act.

Exodus is not simply about liberating the Israelites from captivity, as it is sometimes expressed in various modes of liberation theology. Rather, taken as a whole the entire exodus story is about God's redemption of Israel, to form a new-creation community, one that is obedient to God and through which God will fulfill his promise to Abraham: "All peoples on earth will be blessed through you" (Gen. 12:3).

Isaiah

The interplay of themes is seen in a number of places in the OT, some more subtle than others. Perhaps the most explicit reflex of the creation/exodus thematic complex is Israel's return from Babylon. The exodus and return from Babylon are bookends to Israel's journeys. She begins her existence by being redeemed from one foreign land, and then, hundreds of years later, at the close of one chapter of her existence and the beginning of another, she is again rescued from exile. Isaiah 43:14–19 refers to Yahweh as Israel's "Redeemer" (v. 14), who is also Israel's "Creator" (v. 15). He announces Israel's imminent release from Babylon by reminding them that it was "he who made a way through the sea, a path through the mighty waters, who drew out the chariots and horses, the army and reinforcements together, and they lay there, never to rise again, extinguished, snuffed out like a wick" (vv. 16–17). Israel's Creator is also its Redeemer. This Redeemer-Creator God who drowned Pharaoh's army is the same God who will now deliver the Israelites from another captivity. The certainty of God's deliverance today is based on what he has done yesterday. The Redeemer-Creator God of Exodus is on the move again: "See, I am doing a new thing!" (v. 19).

Wisdom of Solomon

Jewish writings of the Second Temple period also employ this thematic complex. A good example is the apocryphal Wisdom of Solomon. This book was written during a time of intense persecution (likely during the reign of Gaius Caligula, 37–41 CE), and the writer is attempting to bring encouragement to his readers. The form this encouragement takes is a review of God's (or, for this writer, Wisdom's) care for his people throughout history. For most of the book's second half, the culminating event to which the writer appeals is the exodus (10:15–19:22). The message is that the God of the exodus is "our God" as well (15:1). The author adds a dimension to this theme, however. The deliverance of which he speaks is not primarily escape *from* persecution but *through* persecution, the transition from this life to the next, an "exodus" from one land to another (see 3:1–4, esp. v. 2: *exodus*, "departure"). Perhaps this is why the author chooses Israel's exodus experience as a central topic of conversation in chapters 10–19. The author presents Israel's historical exodus, its passage from "death to life," as it were, as the prime biblical portrait of what wisdom is doing now in the lives of the persecuted Jews to whom he is writing. It is their own passage from death to life, their own exodus.

The New Testament

The NT shows clear evidence of articulating God's work in Christ in exodus-creation language. In fact, it is such a richly attested theme in the NT we can only draw attention to a few central passages. First we have the use of Hos. 11:1 in Matt. 2:15. Much has been made of this passage, mainly in terms of the odd way Matthew seems to be using Hosea. But our point here is more straightforward. By appealing to Hos. 11:1 in conjunction with the boy Jesus leaving Egypt, Matthew is drawing an analogy: as God called the Israelites out of Egypt, so too did God call Jesus out of Egypt as a boy. In some sense Jesus is to be understood as living out Israel's experience. Christ, to put it a bit differently, is the final, concrete, focal point for Israel's experience. He is the "ultimate Israel," and this is shown, according to Matthew's quotation, by the fact that Jesus, like the Israelite slaves, came out of Egypt.

Perhaps nowhere in the NT is the new exodus theme more explicit than in Heb. 3:1–6. The parallel here is between Moses and Christ as deliverer. The main point of this difficult passage is that Jesus is superior to Moses. Although somewhat difficult to discern in 3:1–6, the reasons for this are made clearer in what follows (4:1–13). It is through Christ (the new Moses) that we the church (the new Israel) are delivered from enslavement (to the present world order, characterized by sin, death, and eternal separation from God) and given entrance to heaven (the new promised land).

Paul alludes to the exodus in 1 Cor. 10:1–2: "For I do not want you to be ignorant of the fact, brothers, that our forefathers were all under the

217

cloud and that they all passed through the sea. They were all baptized into Moses in the cloud and in the sea." Paul seems to be recalling the exodus for the benefit of his Christian audience (a point made explicit in v. 11). He says that the Israelites who experienced the exodus were "under the cloud," meaning they were guided and protected by God in the form of the pillar of cloud, and by that guidance they "passed through the sea." What then does it mean that the Israelites have been "baptized into Moses"? Baptism is the Christian's concrete expression that the believer, in Christ, is now leaving behind an old way of life—a life of bondage to sin and death—and entering into a new mode of existence (see also Rom. 6:3–4). It is a symbol of the process whereby we undergo our own exodus, leaving the pattern of this world and joining another way of life under Christ's leadership and authority. This, perhaps, is the point that Paul is making about Israel's passage through the sea. It, too, was a kind of baptism, where God's people leave an old way of life and begin another under Moses' leadership. The Red Sea incident has thus become for Paul a powerful, theologically rich forecast of that final deliverance in Christ, the beginning of a new life, a new mode of existence in a new land, with God as supreme ruler.

The NT also employs creation language to describe the church's redemption in Christ. For example, John 1:1 recounts the birth of Christ in words that clearly echo Gen. 1: "In the beginning was the Word." The coming of Christ is a new beginning. Paul puts it somewhat differently. Christ is the second Adam, in whom all of humanity will have a new beginning (Rom. 5:12–21; 1 Cor. 15:20–28). It is worth noting that Jesus refers to his own "departure" from this life as his "exodus" (Luke 9:31). And through his resurrection, in fact, the creation itself begins to anticipate not only personal but also cosmic implications of what the Creator-Redeemer God has done (Rom. 8:22–23).

The exodus theme in the NT reaches its final stage in the book of Revelation. The coming of Christ, the new Moses, and the deliverance he achieves for his people through his death and resurrection—these are actually the first stage of a two-stage process. The final stage of this exodus journey will take place at his second coming. Revelation speaks a great deal about the destruction of "Babylon." This is certainly not meant to represent any one city, much less the literal city of Babylon, but the present world order as a whole. The status that Egypt achieved

in the OT as the ultimate symbol of worldly opposition to God came to be supplanted during the postexilic and intertestamental period by Babylon. And for generations of Jews living in the shadows cast by this horrific event, it stands to reason that the exile to Babylon would inspire them to use this nation as a shorthand representation for any major opposition to God. We have already seen how Isaiah draws the forceful analogy between Egypt and Babylon. The writer of Revelation, then, stands in a strong tradition.

The destruction of God's enemies in Revelation is marked by a series of plagues and disasters that are clearly reminiscent of the plagues against Egypt. When this world order, with its oppression against God's people, is finally brought to an end, it will be the final act of judgment against God's enemies who would dare harm his servants. In the end, Babylon will, like Pharaoh and his army before them, meet a violent end, like a huge millstone thrown into the sea (Rev. 19:21). Babylon will meet a watery death, in symbolic terms, and the final exodus will be complete. Then a new heaven and new earth will take the place of the old (21:1). The redeemed humanity, re-created in the image of the risen Christ, will return to the garden (note the presence of the tree of life in 22:2) and dwell in the new creation. The last exodus leads to the new creation.

See also Liberation Theologies and Hermeneutics

Bibliography

Enns, P. "Creation and Re-Creation: Psalm 95 and Its Interpretation in Hebrews 3:1–4:13." *WTJ* (1993): 255–80; idem. *Exodus*. NIVAC. Zondervan, 2000; idem. *Exodus Retold*. HSM 57. Scholars Press, 1997; Fretheim, T. *Exodus*. Interpretation. John Knox, 1991; Gowan, D. *Theology in Exodus*. Westminster John Knox, 1994; Janzen, J. G. *Exodus*. Westminster Bible Companion. Westminster John Knox, 1997; Keesmaat, S. *Paul and His Story*. JSNTSup 181. Sheffield Academic Press, 1999; Plastaras, J. *The God of Exodus*. Bruce Pubg. Co., 1966.

Peter Enns

Explanation and Understanding See
Hermeneutical Circle; Hermeneutics

Expository Preaching See Preaching, Use of the Bible in

Ezekiel, Book of

The book of Ezekiel is most famous for its visions, especially of the dry bones (ch. 37) and the new temple (40–48). More recently, the sexually charged language of chapters 16 and 23 has provoked comment. The book is addressed to an audience in the Babylonian exile. It speaks to those who have lost everything and yet have everything to gain, if only they acknowledge their guilt and put their trust in the God of the covenant. Its main concern is the true identity of the people of God, which is not to be found in history or genealogy but in the purposes of God. The theocentric message of the book is reinforced by frequent use of the recognition formula ("then they/you will know that I am Yahweh").

The Argument of the Book

While the book of Ezekiel is the only prophetic book largely written in the first person, the prophet is portrayed not so much as a preacher as someone addressed by the word of God. The prophet is a model for how to receive the word of God, which is contrasted with his audience's lack of receptiveness (2:8–3:11). In fact, the resistance of Ezekiel's exilic audience to the prophetic word is a major theme in the book, and 37:1–14 appears to comment on the fact that the prophetic word will accomplish its task only the second time round, in its written form (Renz, *Function*, 204–9). This task is the reconstitution of the people of Israel, which requires a change of allegiance on the part of the exiles. They must dissociate themselves from their sinful past and identify with the restored Israel that God is about to create—a new people as far as attitudes are concerned, although a branch from the same ethnic stock. The task of dissociation is undertaken primarily in the first part of the book, while the new orientation is offered particularly in chapters 34–48.

There are several subcollections in the first part of the book. They are marked by a narrative portion that includes either a date (1:1–3), a notice about elders approaching the prophet (14:1), or both (8:1; 20:1). In four cycles, which all end on a strong note of finality, the destruction of Jerusalem is justified as deserved punishment for its rebellion, but the argument is developed in specific ways in each cycle. The first cycle, chapters 1–7, presents the basic case: Judah's and Jerusalem's sin will lead to its end. The second cycle, 8–13, strengthens the plausibility of this case by answering possible objections, such as the idea that God could not possibly abandon his people (8–11) or the idea that judgment is for the distant future, not for the present time (12:21–13:23). The third cycle, chapters 14–19, outlines more precisely what the exiles' response should

be to this disaster and includes explicit calls to repentance (14:1–12; 18:1–32). Repentance cannot avert the disaster that will befall Jerusalem, but it offers life for the exilic community, which without repentance is as doomed as Jerusalem. The last section (in the book's first part), chapters 20–24, summarizes the first three cycles and brings the narrative to the point when Jerusalem is laid under siege. Ezekiel's response to his wife's death is a model for how the exilic community should respond to Jerusalem's fall. Public mourning would signal sympathy, which in the case of Jerusalem's deserved judgment, is inappropriate. Instead, the exiles are to accept the judgment and groan over their own sins (24:15–27).

In the compilation of prophecies concerning nations other than Judah in chapters 25–32, three collections can be identified: prophecies against Judah's nearest neighbors (25), prophecies against Tyre (26–28), and prophecies against Egypt (29–32). The following points are made: (1) The fact that the Babylonian king is Yahweh's instrument can be seen not only in the events surrounding the fall of Jerusalem but also throughout Nebuchadnezzar's western campaign. (2) Yahweh does not tolerate malice and self-righteousness, and thus, by implication, he himself does not act out of malice or self-righteousness. (3) No other nation will be allowed to take possession of the land—indeed, seven nations are dealt with before Israel reenters the land (cf. Deut. 7:1). (4) The oracles against Tyre and Egypt affirm that Yahweh deals with rebellious, self-sufficient pride and shows up its futility wherever he encounters it. (5) Egypt will never again be attractive as a substitute for trusting Yahweh. And (6) the frequency of the recognition formula reminds us that in all this God is revealing himself, making each of these events in international affairs "a moment of self-disclosure for Yahweh" (Block 2:12).

The reuse of the watchman motif in chapter 33 forms a closing bracket, paired with its first occurrence in chapter 3, and signals the function of the intervening chapters: to warn of impending danger. The prophet did not return to his homeland to warn Jerusalem, the community most obviously under threat. His ministry was to the exilic community, for whom the warning was not yet too late. Chapter 33 picks up motifs from chapter 18 to remind readers that the proper response to the warning is repentance. The arrival of a refugee from Jerusalem informing the exiles that the city has been destroyed (33:21) changes the rhetorical situation but not the message. Ezekiel reaffirms that physical descent from Abraham is insufficient for reestablishment in the land. At the same time, the chapter gives a discouraging picture of Ezekiel's post-586 audience; only "when this comes—and come it will!—then they shall know that a prophet has been among them" (33:33). The first part of the book has already indicated that "this" includes judgment as well as restoration (20:32–44), and glimpses of judgment are found throughout chapters 34–48.

This last major part of the book is arranged in a palistrophic pattern (ABCDCBA), with the vision of the dry bones in the center (37:1–14), and at the outer ends an affirmation of Yahweh's kingship as the beginning and end of Israel's restoration (chs. 34, 40–48). The first inner ring is formed by two-panel prophecies claiming the land for Israel against other nations (35:1–36:15; chs. 38–39). The second is formed by anthologies summarizing the work of transformation and the blessings resulting from it, with 36:16–38 focusing on the spiritual, and 37:15–28 on the political. The two are aspects of the one transformation brought about by acknowledging Yahweh as king. Yahweh's kingship is affirmed vis-à-vis self-serving human rulers (ch. 34) and in the way space is organized in chapters 40–48, with the temple forming the new center of the nation independent of the palace, confirming Yahweh as absolute power holder (43:7). The messiah plays no part in the nation's restoration, but a new David will guarantee the nation's unity (37:15–28). He will exercise rather than challenge the rule of Yahweh (34:23–24). There is a certain shift from responsibility to passivity in the oracles of salvation. Yahweh will not only bring repentant exiles back to the land but also will himself bring about the repentance. He does this work of transformation through the prophetic word, as the central vision makes plain.

Ezekiel within the Canon

God's sovereignty and glory are central to the book of Ezekiel, but his anguished passion is stressed as well. This combination, together with a focus on the fate of Jerusalem, is also found in the book of Isaiah, but developed in Ezekiel with a greater focus on the Babylonian destruction of the city. There are close parallels to the book of Jeremiah. It is possible that Ezekiel heard Jeremiah and that later material from Jeremiah came to Babylon via people who were in contact with Jeremiah (Vieweger). Ezekiel is characteristically more expansive (cf., e.g., Jer. 23:1–8 with Ezek. 34). Both stress that the future lies with the exiles, even though they deserve no better than the inhabitants of Jerusalem. In the language of Ezekiel, Israel's future lies in God's concern for his name, not in any virtue on the part of the exiles. While the book of Jeremiah has many links with Deuteronomy, Ezekiel borrows priestly language and categories. Common to both traditions is the adultery motif for depicting disloyalty to God. Characteristic for priestly thinking is an emphasis on the polluting effect of sin. By polluting land and sanctuary, sin jeopardizes God's presence among his people and the people's presence in the land. The effect is such that the prophet at one point wonders whether there will be a future for Israel (9:8). The punishment is not so much deportation from the land but death: in the city, in flight, and in exile. It is appropriate that a priestly prophet should draw this stark distinction between life and death, since Israel's cultic system is based on this fundamental contrast. Rebellion against God leads to death, but "I have no pleasure in the death of anyone, declares the Lord Yahweh; so turn, and live" (18:32 AT). Thus, the book of Ezekiel can be read as an illustration of Rom. 6:23: "For the wages of sin is death, but the free gift of God is eternal life in Christ Jesus our Lord" (NRSV).

A vital theme of biblical theology, covenant, is also important in the book of Ezekiel. Ezekiel fulfills a role similar to Moses, renewing the covenant at a time of breakdown of the relationship. In the biblical narrative, Ezekiel is the only person other than Moses to communicate divine laws to Israel (chs. 43–48). The covenant motif stresses the need for loyalty and the catastrophic effect of disloyalty. Zedekiah's disloyalty to Nebuchadnezzar reflects his disloyalty to God (17), and Jerusalem's disloyalty to God is portrayed as a wife's disloyalty to her caring husband (16). The covenant metaphor rests on the concept of an ordered relationship. The heart of the problem is the people's rejection of God's governance. This also explains why the leaders of Judah are often singled out for condemnation: they have usurped God's sovereignty. But God's sovereignty is not founded in the covenant relationship itself, which is why any creature's appropriation of glory rightly belonging to the Creator leads to destruction. Ezekiel demonstrates that judgment begins with the household of God (cf. 1 Pet. 4:17), but also that it does not end there. The Oracles against the Nations in chapters 25–32 focus more narrowly on one set of historical events than those found in Jeremiah and Isaiah. Nevertheless, they presume that divine standards are the same for everyone, and they offer a particularly vivid condemnation of human pretensions to power and self-sufficiency (cf. Rom. 1:18–23).

The definition of God's people as those who submit to God's rule stresses that descent from Abraham does not guarantee inheritance of Abraham's promises (33:23–29); this definition resonates with a similar emphasis in the NT (cf. John 8:39; Rom. 9:8–16; Gal. 3:29; 4:24–31). In both Ezekiel and the NT, submission to God's rule finds expression in how one relates to a specific act of God's judgment. Jerusalem's destruction is for the exiles, who deserve the same judgment, chance, and challenge to repent. Similarly, the cross is an exercise of God's sovereignty and judgment over human pride and rebellion, an exercise that allows others to go free. Yet only Christ's death deals with sin. Ezekiel's concern for accepting Jerusalem's destruction as God's just judgment is consequently transformed in the gospel concern to accept Christ's death as the judgment that makes peace (e.g., Col. 1:20).

Perspectives from the History of Interpretation

The impact of the book of Ezekiel on the postexilic community is visible in the book of Zechariah, though it is less obvious in other postexilic writings. Ezekiel was an inspiration also for the Qumran community (Cothenet). Philo and Josephus paid little attention to Ezekiel, but rabbinic interest in the book was strong in spite of difficulties in making it agree with the Mosaic Torah. Especially after the fall of Jerusalem in 70 CE, Ezekiel's vision of the throne-chariot gained prominence as an attempt to integrate the transcendence and immanence of God without the tangible reality of a temple (*merkabah* mysticism). Maybe to stress the need for communal guidance in reading Ezekiel, parts of the book were apparently declared off limits for Jews under thirty years old, as Jerome noted.

The use of motifs from Ezekiel in the Johannine literature, and especially in the book of Revelation, is well known (see, e.g., Moyise). More recently, Newman traced Ezekiel's influence on the apostle Paul's understanding of divine glory. The early church remained fascinated by the book, and especially the concluding vision as a picture of heaven or the church. The four faces of the creatures bearing the throne-chariot in the opening vision became symbols of the four Gospel writers, and the king of Tyre was identified with the antichrist (both already in Hippolytus). Such luminaries as Origen, Ephraim the Syrian, Jerome, Theodoret of Cyrus, and Gregory the

Great expounded Ezekiel. It was also used outside exegetical and homiletical literature. Along with the chapters stressing repentance (14; 18), other passages (3:17–21; 33:1–9; 34:1–24) were used frequently, especially in expressing a theology of church offices and in dealing with questions such as whether bishops who fled from persecution should be reinstalled. Ezekiel 37 is often cited as a prediction of the eschatological resurrection of the body, most forcefully by Tertullian.

Central to the church's reading of the book is recognition of Christ in Ezekiel. The early church was reluctant to offer a detailed christological interpretation of the figure in the opening vision. Thus, Jerome insisted that the figure primarily represents God the Father, then the Son as image of the invisible God. Nevertheless, after the Council of Chalcedon, the combination of metal and fire in the appearance of the figure in Ezekiel's opening vision (1:26–27) served for defending the doctrine of Christ's two natures (Theodoret, Gregory). It was also popular to find the protective sign of the cross in 9:4, and the shut gate in 44:1–3 was often applied to the Virgin Mary. These are cases where the doctrine rather than the biblical text must bear all the weight of the interpretation. Ezekiel's prophecies of a new David stress divine sovereignty and the unity of God's people, saying little about the new David himself. Most promising is the lead given by commentators such as Origen and Isidore of Seville, who saw Ezekiel himself as a sign of Christ. It is noteworthy that in the *Targum of Ezekiel* "son of man" is rendered as "son of Adam," suggesting that in this early interpretation Ezekiel was seen as the first member of the new creation.

The book of Ezekiel retained its popularity in the Middle Ages among Jewish interpreters (e.g., Rashi, Eliezer of Beaugency, David Kimhi), but the church's interest appears to have waned over time. Indeed, Anselm of Laon used the widespread neglect of the book to justify his lecture series on Ezekiel in 1121–23. Where there was interest, it was often focused on the visions, whether they be understood allegorically (e.g., Rupert of Deuz) or literally (Andrew of St. Victor), an interest also reflected in illustrations and paintings related to Ezekiel, which often combined the throne vision of Ezek. 1 with Isa. 6. With the Reformation, the allegorical reading was more and more sidelined, although it remained popular in the Puritan tradition (Greenhill). John Calvin devoted his last written efforts to Ezekiel, producing a historical and theological exposition of the first twenty chapters.

221

Early modern scholarly interpretation focused on philological matters and poetic style, while the book gained prominence in African-American spirituals ("Dem Bones") and preaching as a message of hope to exiles. The historical-critical method left the book's literary unity and integrity of authorship intact for a long time. Indeed, the book was in favor by some critics for its supposed teaching of individualism, a view based on a misunderstanding of Ezekiel's use of individualistic legal language to affirm generational responsibility (see, e.g., Joyce). But a publication by Hölscher in 1924 opened up an era of wide disagreement about all aspects of the origin and content of the book, with dates suggested from the time of Manasseh to the Maccabean period (for a brief summary, see Childs 357–60).

While the variety of positions held is still striking, three main approaches can be distinguished today. The majority of interpreters identify different levels of growth in the book, with later layers interpreting earlier layers. The material from the Ezekiel "school" is often thought to have been added in exilic and early postexilic times (Zimmerli), but many commentators argue that the book was completed in exile (e.g., Hals; Allen). This is also the view of a number of "holistic" interpreters, who focus on reading the book as a literary whole addressed to the Babylonian exiles (e.g., Greenberg; Block). Theological interpretation is not greatly affected by the disagreements between these first two approaches. A third group of scholars claims to identify up to more than a dozen redactional layers in the book (e.g., Pohlmann). In their view the book of Ezekiel originated over a period of more than 250 years and provides little or no reliable evidence for the existence of a prophet Ezekiel.

Theological interpretation undertaken in this context would look different, but the methodology used appears misguided and unreliable, and its advocates have not yet offered a theological interpretation of the book based on their analyses. Feminist interpretation has raised important issues (Patton) that have entered mainstream study of the book, unlike the attempt at a psychoanalytical interpretation offered by Halperin. More popular interest has focused on the eschatological visions (Lindsey), and the book is sometimes used as evidence for premillennialism (Rooker). Throughout this history, arguably the most successful interpretations have been those that paid attention to the rhetorical force of the book. Thereby readers discover what behavior God punishes and what kind of community he re-creates. They also reflect on the prophetic office and word as a means of establishing the new community.

Ezekiel and the Church Today

Each generation needs to explore afresh how Ezekiel reveals behavior that leads to death. The condemnation of idolatry and false prophecy was transformed in the early church to warnings against heresy and pagan lifestyle. This can still serve us today, if we remember that these judgment passages apply to God's people first of all. The stark alternatives of allegiance to God or rebellion against him, and thus consequences of life or death, must be presented to everyone. Nevertheless, the book's particular thrust is to remind us that we have all been on the way to death and that receiving life in Christ is no cause for self-congratulation. Similarly, the fall of the king of Tyre from a divinely given position of privilege may be seen as illustrative of the fall of the antichrist or Satan, but this should not distract from its application to individual and collective human pride and arrogance. Being a member of God's people presumes proper acknowledgment of the cause of death and the source of life. The original function of the book for the Babylonian exiles, and its use in spirituals, remind us that socioeconomic aspects do not define the people of God. At the same time, finding one's identity in God's purposes ought to influence all aspects of life, including the socioeconomic. Communal life and, by implication, personal life need to be ordered in such a way that nothing compromises God's sovereignty. Given the harsh critique of human pretensions to power and the careful limitation of human power in the concluding vision, any use of Ezekiel to bolster one's own power (e.g., husbands over wives, priests over laity) is an abuse of the book.

Because it is in Christ that the people of God experience death and resurrection, Ezek. 37 is ultimately fulfilled in Christ's death and resurrection. As a second Adam and Moses, the prophet is a type of Christ, who is the ultimate second Adam and Moses, the beginning of a new creation. The central role of the prophetic word in bringing about this new creation prefigures the transformation of God's people through the incarnated Word. Now as then, the word gives life by bringing forth faith in the purposes of God. Like those who saw the return from exile, the church today experiences fulfillment of God's purposes, while awaiting the time when everything will be ordered in a manner that acknowledges God's lordship. The way spiritual and political restoration are intertwined in Ezek. 34–48 and the flexible use of motifs from Ezekiel in the book of Revelation (e.g., Magog changed from person to nation) counsel against identifying a sequence of eschatological events in the latter part of the book, let alone any sequence that separates spiritual from political restoration.

In our contemporary cultures, which often link identity with consumption and marginalize the church, Ezekiel offers the promise of new life in the wilderness for a community that finds its identity in God and his purposes.

Bibliography

Block, D. *The Book of Ezekiel*. Vol. 1, *Chapters 1–24*. Vol. 2, *Chapters 25–48*. NICOT. Eerdmans, 1997–98; Calvin, J. *Ezekiel 1 (Chapters 1–12)*, trans. D. Foxgrover and D. Martin. Calvin's Old Testament Commentaries 18. Paternoster, 1996; Childs, B. *Introduction to the Old Testament as Scripture*. Fortress, 1979; Cothenet, E. "Influence d'Ézéchiel sur la spiritualité de Qumran." *RevQ* 13 (1988): 431–39; Dassmann, E. "Hesekiel." *RAC* 14 (1988): cols. 1132–91; Duguid, I. *Ezekiel and the Leaders of Israel*. VTSup 56. Brill, 1994; Galambush, J. *Jerusalem in the Book of Ezekiel*. SBLDS 130. Scholars Press, 1992; Greenhill, W. *An Exposition of Ezekiel*. Banner of Truth, 1995 (reprint of 1863 ed.; originally published 1645); Halperin, D. J. *Seeking Ezekiel*. Pennsylvania State University Press, 1993; Hölscher, G. *Hesekiel*. BZAW 39. De Gruyter, 1924; Jerome. *Commentariorum in Hiezechielem libri XIV*, ed. F. Glorie. S. Hieronymi presbyteri Opera 1/4. CCSL 75. Brepols, 1984; Joyce, P. *Divine Initiative and Human Response in Ezekiel*. JSOTSup 51. JSOT, 1989; Levey, S. H. *The Targum of Ezekiel*. The Aramaic Bible 13. T&T Clark, 1987; Lindsey, H. *The Late Great Planet Earth*. Zondervan, 1970; Matties, G. *Ezekiel 18 and the Rhetoric of Moral Discourse*. SBLDS 126. Scholars Press, 1990; Mein, A. *Ezekiel and the Ethics of Exile*. Oxford University Press, 2001; Milgrom, J. "Leviticus 26 and Ezekiel." Pages 57–63 in *The Quest for Context and Meaning*, ed. C. A. Evans. Biblical Interpretation 28. Brill, 1997; Moyise, S. *The Old Testament in the Book of Revelation*. JSNTSup 115. Sheffield Academic Press, 1995; Newman, C. *Paul's Glory Christology*. NovTSup 69. Brill, 1992; Patton, C. L. "'Should Our Sister Be Treated Like a Whore?' A Response to Feminist Critiques of Ezekiel 23." Pages 221–38 in *The Book of Ezekiel*, ed. M. S. Odell and J. T. Strong. SBL Symposium Series 9. SBL, 2000; Renz, T. "Proclaiming the Future: History and Theology in Prophecies against Tyre." *TynBul* 51 (2000): 17–58; idem. *The Rhetorical Function of the Book of Ezekiel*. VTSup 76. Brill, 1999; Rooker, M. F. "Evidence from Ezekiel." Pages 119–34 in *A Case for Premillennialism*, ed. D. Campbell and J. Townsend. Moody, 1992; Stevenson, K. R. *The Vision of Transformation*. SBLDS 154. Scholars Press, 1996; Vieweger, D. *Die literarischen Beziehungen zwischen den Büchern Jeremia und Ezechiel*. BEATAJ 26. Lang, 1993.

Thomas Renz

Ezra, Book of

At first sight the book of Ezra is an uneven work that does not yield easily to theological interpretation. More than half of it concerns the first wave of returning exiles, from the decree of Cyrus in 538 to the completion of the temple in 516 BCE. Ezra does not appear until chapter 7, after a gap of almost sixty years. Events of the intervening decades are sketched out of chronological order in 4:6–23. Ezra's return to Judah with another group of repatriates is the substance of chapters 7–10, which cover the events of a single year (458/457). A particular barrier for Christian interpreters is the book's uncompromising Jewishness, expressed in its concern for genealogical purity and restored temple worship.

History of Interpretation

The book of Ezra was originally read as the first part of a longer work that included the book of Nehemiah (as is evident from the earliest listings of canonical books). The division into two books occurred in the early church, for reasons that are not clear, and is first attested in the third century. It is not found in Hebrew Bibles until 1448. The current arrangement should not be allowed to obscure the essential unity of Ezra-Nehemiah, and this article should be read in conjunction with that on the book of Nehemiah.

Precritical Christian interpreters either viewed the books of Ezra and Nehemiah typologically (e.g., the crises over mixed marriages point to the need to keep in mind at all times the distinction between the children of God and the children of this world) or held up the personal piety of the two men as examples to be emulated. Some commentators, taking a lead from Jerome's comment that Ezra means "the Helper" while Nehemiah means "the Consoler sent by the Lord," treated the two books as works of help and consolation in times of trouble. One bishop of the Church of England saw the combined work of Ezra and Nehemiah prefiguring and legitimizing the alliance of church and state, while another clergyman preferred to see the two as examples of the passive and active virtues of religion.

In sharp contrast to rabbinic tradition, which saw Ezra as the father of Judaism, Christian critical scholarship of the nineteenth and early twentieth centuries generally had a negative view of the man and of the book that bears his name. Postexilic Judaism was widely regarded as inferior to the earlier prophetic faith, and this naturally affected assessment of Ezra-Nehemiah. The view of Torrey, that Ezra was a fictional creation of the Chronicler, was an extreme expression of this tendency. Others merely played down Ezra's role or judged him a failure. Recent scholarship has moved toward a more positive assessment, though there are occasional attempts to revive the view that Ezra never existed.

According to the Babylonian Talmud (*B. Bat.* 15a), Ezra was the author of Ezra-Nehemiah and 1–2 Chronicles, and a few modern scholars have defended this view. The majority, however, have held that the anonymous author of Chronicles was responsible for putting Ezra-Nehemiah into more or less its final form (e.g., Clines; Blenkinsopp). This view has affected theological interpretation insofar as a uniform theological stance has been perceived throughout 1–2 Chronicles and Ezra-Nehemiah.

The two works certainly share many points of common interest (summarized by Blenkinsopp 53). However, since the 1970s a number of scholars have put more weight on the distinctive ideas and emphases of Ezra-Nehemiah and have strongly challenged the common authorship theory (notably Williamson, *Israel*, 5–70). The independent authorship of Ezra-Nehemiah has gained ground in recent years, but the issues are complex and by no means resolved.

The Message of Ezra

Because there is particularly clear evidence for diverse sources within Ezra-Nehemiah, interpretation of the work has tended to become bogged down in historical-critical issues (Childs 626–30). Notable exceptions are Eskenazi's attempt to read Ezra-Nehemiah as a literary whole, and Williamson's analysis ("Nehemiah") of the work's "overall theological shape" (see further under Nehemiah). Studies such as these, which focus on the message of the final literary product, facilitate theological interpretation. They show that it is important to read the book of Ezra not only as a literary whole but also as the first part of a larger work. The key theological issue that emerges is the continuity of God's purposes for Israel. Given that the return from exile fell far short of a return to preexilic status, was there any sense in which the earlier "Israel" could still be said to exist? Did its God-given identity and purpose remain intact?

The book of Ezra answers "yes" to these questions in a variety of ways. The opening verse establishes the continuity of God's purpose from before the exile. It is repeatedly emphasized that the temple was rebuilt on its original site (2:68; 3:3; 5:15; 6:7); it was thus to be seen as a reconstruction of, not a replacement for, Solomon's temple (cf. 6:3–4; 1 Kings 6:2, 36). The very same vessels that Nebuchadnezzar had looted from the temple were restored to it (1:7–11). Personnel were appointed according to "the Book of Moses" (6:18). Ezra himself was descended from the chief priests of the preexilic age (cf. 7:1; 1 Chron. 6:14). The genealogies of chapters 2 and 8 also serve to affirm continuity. The returned exiles represented all twelve tribes (6:17; 8:35) and could indeed be called "the people of Israel" (6:16, 21).

The continuation of God's purposes is also affirmed by means of typology (Williamson, *Ezra*, 84–86). The book of Ezra shares with Isa. 40–55 the view that the return from exile was a second exodus. Thus, 1:11b echoes the language of Exod. 3:17; 33:1; and so on, and may also recall a much earlier bringing-out from Babylonia (cf. Gen. 15:7). This exodus typology is not confined to the first wave of returnees. Ezra's own "journey up from Babylon" began on the first day of the first month (cf. 7:9 NRSV). But the party did not actually leave the River Ahava until the twelfth day of that month (8:31), a date that Ezra may have chosen because of its resonance with Exod. 12:2–6.

The use of typology indicates that the God who had created his people from unpromising beginnings and rescued them from slavery could be trusted to act in similar ways again.

Canonical Context

Because of its focus on continuity with the past, Ezra-Nehemiah may seem to stand at the end of a canonical trajectory, looking back rather than forward, and content with the Jewish community's status within the Persian Empire. References to the prophecies of Jeremiah (1:1), Haggai, and Zechariah (5:1; 6:14) might also seem to suggest that a point of fulfillment has been reached.

But this is to miss a powerful strand of discontent and a sense of only partial fulfillment. The attitude toward Persian kings is ambivalent. On the one hand they are God's agents for the reconstruction of the community; on the other, what the people experience under their rule is nothing less than bondage (9:8–9). In Ezra 6:22 the Persian king is called "the king of Assyria," and this is unlikely to be an error; it is probably an "indication that there is in the end little to choose between Empires" (McConville 38).

The restored Israel repeats the sins of earlier Israel (9:10–14), and the list of those who pledged to divorce their foreign wives in Ezra 10 provides no reassurance that the cycle of iniquity and shame is thereby ended. Indeed, the conclusion to Nehemiah provides yet more instances of backsliding after a time of renewed commitment to the covenant laws. These indications of a hope that is only partially fulfilled are reminders that the postexilic community was only one stage in the unfolding of God's purposes.

It is important to remember this when considering that community's exclusiveness. The racial purity established by genealogies, and safeguarded by the dissolution of mixed marriages, sounds like narrow nationalism and exclusive soteriology, but it must be set in both a historical and canonical context. Historically, the concern for continuity and legitimacy can be seen as a reaction to particular circumstances: the identity of the community was precarious and in need of safeguards. Canonically, the tenor of Ezra-Nehemiah is balanced by a more open attitude to Gentiles in other OT narratives (e.g., Gen. 41:50–52; Josh. 6:25; Ruth 4:13–17), and in numerous prophetic texts (e.g., Isa. 49:6; 56:3–8; Zech. 8:20–23). Thus, OT Israel lived within the tension of its election and its priestly role to the nations (encapsulated in Gen. 12:2–3; Exod. 19:5–6). Sometimes one aspect of the polarity is to the fore, sometimes the other.

Theology

Viewed historically, the restoration of Jerusalem and Judah was piecemeal, dogged by setbacks and reversals, and proceeding without any coherent plan. However, the theological perspective of Ezra-Nehemiah invites us to see the guiding hand of Israel's God in seemingly disconnected events. This explains the writer's disregard for chronological order and the fact that gaps of several years, in one case decades, are passed over in silence (see further on Nehemiah).

Related to this perspective is the writer's wish to trace the will of God in the affairs of state. A secular historian might explain the repatriation of Judean exiles and the rebuilding of the temple in terms of the Persian Empire's policy toward the religious life of its subject peoples. Ezra-Nehemiah acknowledges the important role of Persian kings (Ezra 1:1–4; 6:1–12), but wants us to know that it was Yahweh who stirred up the spirit of Cyrus and put a desire to beautify the temple into the heart of Artaxerxes (1:1; 7:27).

Ezra 6:14 is particularly telling. The writer informs us that the temple was completed by "command of the God of Israel and the decrees of Cyrus, Darius and Artaxerxes, kings of Persia." Artaxerxes actually reigned after the period mentioned in vv. 14–15, but he is included because all three Persian kings fulfilled the command of the God of Israel. The eye of faith does not sharply divide the acts of God from the actions of human rulers.

Bibliography

Blenkinsopp, J. *Ezra-Nehemiah*. OTL. SCM, 1989; Childs, B. *Introduction to the Old Testament as Scripture*. SCM, 1979; Clines, D. J. A. *Ezra, Nehemiah, Esther*. NCB. Eerdmans, 1984; Douglas, M. "Responding to Ezra: The Priests and the Foreign Wives." *BibInt* 10 (2002): 1–23; Eskenazi, T. *In an Age of Prose*. SBLMS 36. Scholars Press, 1988; McConville, J. G. "Diversity and Obscurity in Old Testament Books: A Hermeneutical Exercise Based on Some Later Old Testament Books." *Anvil* 3 (1986): 33–47; Torrey, C. *The Composition and Historical Value of Ezra-Nehemiah*. BZAW 2. Ricker, 1896; Williamson, H. G. M. *Ezra and Nehemiah*. OTG. JSOT, 1987; idem. *Israel in the Books of Chronicles*. Cambridge University Press, 1977; idem. "Nehemiah: Theology of." *NIDOTTE* 4:977–82.

John J. Bimson

F

Faith

"Faith" is a significant biblical theme both materially and formally—not only requiring theological exegesis, but also shaping the very form that understanding takes. It exemplifies the need for both a large-scale theological vision, to orient one's gaze upon the various biblical witnesses, and for that vision to be refined through detailed exegesis.

The Biblical Narrative of Faith

The OT narrative, according to Heb. 11, portrays many heroes of faith. Consensus has suggested that the relevant Hebrew noun, 'emunah, is primarily used to designate truth, honesty, or loyalty, especially characteristic of God. The hiphil form of the verb 'mn is used for the appropriate response to God's fidelity, in faithful trust and obedience. For example, Abraham believed God's (seemingly) unbelievable promise so that he obediently set out for a promised inheritance and later was willing to obey the unthinkable and sacrifice Isaac. By contrast, prophetic texts, particularly Isaiah, relate Israel's exile in part to its lack of faith, for the people idolatrously trusted in tactics based only upon what they could see. These prophets nevertheless call upon Israel, once again, to trust in divine deliverance.

Thus, they establish a theological trajectory for the primacy of faith in the new covenant, with its foreshadowing in the old. In the NT faith has been taken to have a more cognitive dimension, relating to persuasion or conviction, while the OT aspect of trust is emphasized over against the priority of postexilic Judaism: faith as fidelity to the Torah. By no means, however, does that trajectory produce a monologic NT use of the term. Its variety, in fact, prepares for the diversity of later developments in Christian theology.

Theological Understandings of Faith

In his important treatment, Avery Dulles develops seven models for how theologians understand faith. On the *propositional* model, faith involves assent to revealed truths on God's authority. A *transcendental* model relates faith to a new cognitive horizon or perspective given by God, distinguishing it from "beliefs" formulated in propositions.

Even less cognitive are the *fiducial* model, which emphasizes trust; and the *affective-experiential* model, which emphasizes faith's relation to experience. So also the *obediential* model, which emphasizes acknowledgment of God's sovereign initiative; the *praxis* model, which emphasizes hopeful action in solidarity with the suffering; and the *personalist* model, which emphasizes personal relationship conferring a new mode of life—these largely exclude cognition in defining faith.

Faith and Knowledge: Epistemological Questions and the Doctrine of Revelation

Undoubtedly, some definitions exclude or deemphasize knowledge because of noncognitive biblical emphases such as trust. But modern theologians have also tended to consider the very possibility of divine revelation incredible. Accordingly, they have prioritized *either* the credible (e.g., human experience) *or* the divine (e.g., God's particular sovereign initiative) in their construals of revelation's corollary, faith.

Biblical teaching that sees faith as response to the proclamation of God's truth, however, seems inescapable at some level. Faith might well involve more than doctrinal assent, but can it involve less? Alternatively, focusing on propositions has often meant neglecting the holistic, personal, and dynamic dimensions of faith. Moreover, can we maintain that faith involves a form of knowledge ("a firm and certain knowledge of God's benevolence toward us," as Calvin put it) without becoming answerable, in a deadly way, to epistemological standards oriented to "sight"? Must we respond to a perceived (but false) dichotomy between faith and reason by emptying faith of revealed truth?

Faith and Works: Soteriological Questions and the Doctrine of Justification

Another theological dilemma in defining faith concerns its place in salvation, especially the doctrine of "justification by faith" and whether or not to add the word "alone." If we accept this doctrine at all, we must then define its terms. On the one hand, if we add to "faith alone" that "the faith which saves is never alone," do we lose Paul's distinction between faith and works? On the other hand, if we understand "faith alone" largely in cognitive terms, do we not fall prey to the faith-works dichotomy, which James criticizes?

Both Paul and James supported their teachings with OT texts (e.g., Gen. 15:6; Hab. 2:4), so that the theology of faith is an important test case regarding canonical unity. Paul captured the thrust of OT eschatology in a way that some Jewish opponents did not: after Israel's exile, covenant life with God would no longer consist in possession of—or proficiency at obeying—the Torah, but trust in God's deliverance through another's fidelity. Accordingly, Paul emphasized that eschatological salvation required God's particular action in the history of Jesus Christ, also excluding Hellenistic overrealizations of that salvation via the Holy Spirit. With faith thus related to love, in light of a particular hope, Paul's teaching would not grant justification to those with the mere "faith" James criticized. The two concepts of "faith" are recognizably different, as are their emphases from common OT texts; nonetheless, the soteriological teachings of Paul and James may be complementary rather than contradictory.

A related dilemma concerns *pistis Christou* and related phraseology in Paul—whether this is an objective genitive designating faith in Christ (an "anthropological" view), or a subjective genitive designating the faith(fulness) of Christ (a "christological" view). The former might be called the traditional approach, at least from the Protestant Reformation onward; the latter has come into favor especially since the early 1980s (with the publication of Hays; favoring the former, see Dunn in Hays's new edition), but has had periodic supporters throughout the modern age. Tradition therefore does not factor *too* strongly; nor are exegetical or hermeneutical arguments knockdown, for one side or the other. Since it is unlikely that dramatic new evidence will surface, the theological interpreter probably must wait for arguments that favor more clearly a pattern of interpreting the evidence we have.

This dilemma already makes clear the need to distinguish words from concepts: *pistis* cannot be read exclusively as "faith" or "fidelity," and cannot have the same sense with regard to God, Abraham, Christ, and us in all the relevant texts. Yet the need to clarify its sense in Rom. 4 with regard to Abraham (and Christ) is very important, if the christological view is to shore up the flow of Paul's argument contra justification by faithfulness via the Mosaic law (so Dunn). Alternatively, the anthropological view must avoid turning human believing into a conditional "work," and show how *God's* faithfulness could be manifest by way of such *human* believing (Rom. 3; so Hays). It is difficult to decide whether in several passages (e.g., Gal. 2:16; Rom. 1:17; 3:22) Paul repeats himself regarding human faith for emphasis (the anthropological view), or kerygmatically moves from divine faithfulness in Christ's faith(fulness) to human response.

Biblical Faith, Covenant Communion, and Theological Interpretation

Thus, despite recent reconciliations of Paul and James (in the judgment of some biblical scholarship), and of Protestants and Roman Catholics (in the theological judgment of some), much work remains. Hays maintains that the newer readings of Paul push us to relate justification by faith and participation in Christ much more closely. There are dangers in that, if we take such participation in an overly mystical or ontological sense (as McCormack notes). However, even if one doubts the newer Finnish readings of Martin Luther as orienting salvation toward "divinization" or participation in the divine life, it still seems that Luther and Calvin depicted faith in a far richer, less individualistic frame than many of our contemporaries. Whatever the exegetical shortcomings, what remains sure is the Reformers' legacy for theological interpretation of faith as involving covenantal union with Christ, the mediator of divine action (so, e.g., Pitkin).

Today we need exegetically informed soteriological articulations of the connection between faith and love, as well as theological epistemologies that take seriously faith's challenge to "sight" (a characteristically "modern" preoccupation) without lapsing into the worst of "fideism" (perhaps a characteristically postmodern tendency). Faith, after all, is oriented very much to hearing instead of sight, since it is a corollary concept of obedient human response to the divine word (e.g., Rom. 10). More particularly, we have only begun to approach biblical exegesis with the goal of "faith seeking understanding"—striving for cogent, defensible interpretations, but also knowing when to justify particular readings on Christian theological terms, and what it means to resist pretenses of eschatological certainty or exhaustiveness. Only in the modern age has such faith seemed fully opposite to reason, a matter of "believing what you know ain't true" (Mark Twain, cited in Springsted 6).

In classic terms, faith involves a tradition that shapes moral action and perception by way of participation in God, the good. Contrary to somewhat artificial dichotomies with reason, Christian faith is "thinking with assent"—not so much "chosen, willed, and judged from a critical spectator's standpoint; it is, rather, thinking and willing and doing from a participant's standpoint" (Springsted 223). Faith is a matter of time, for it is a virtue—not simply an internal property to be acquired, and then momentarily isolated when described or assessed—but an enduring pattern of action in a moral space marked by divine communication. Christian understanding of faith develops not by proof-texting biblical definitions but from reading such texts within an anthropology and a narrative framework shaped by covenant.

Faith's relation to prayer is all too easily obscured or neglected, due to preoccupations with epistemology and soteriology. This emphasis on prayer is true of our Lord in the Gospels (e.g., Mark 11:22–26), and is consistent with faith as "calling on the name of the Lord" (e.g., Rom. 10:13). Recovering prayer as faith's characteristic posture might provide for a covenantal, more holistic understanding than has informed our epistemological and soteriological dilemmas to date. Boldness in prayer is based upon the Spirit's assurance of God's benevolence toward us in Christ, yet we are also warned (e.g., in the OT prophets) not to approach God if we refuse to share that benevolence with others. In this way charity is the form, though not the essence, of faith, as mind and will attend together to God—and others (Springsted 168, 174). Over and over we cry out for forgiveness and grace, being faithful—obeying the gospel and mining its riches—by trusting the Lord. We are not simply called to be good Samaritans, but first are always cared for as wounded travelers (Springsted 251). For this reason theological interpreters ought not only to pray while vigorously seeking understanding, but also to pursue (via mind *and* will) understanding itself as a prayerful activity of faith.

See also Justification by Faith; Virtue

Bibliography

Bultmann, R. "Πιστεύω. . . ." *TDNT* 6:174–228. Eerdmans, 1968; Dulles, A., SJ. *The Assurance of Things Hoped For.* Oxford University Press, 1994; Hart, T. *Faith Thinking.* InterVarsity, 1995; Hays, R. *The Faith of Jesus Christ.* 2d ed. Eerdmans, 2002; John Paul II. *On the Relationship between Faith and Reason (Fides et Ratio).* U.S. Catholic Conference, 1998; McCormack, B. "What's at Stake in Current Debates over Justification? The Crisis of Protestantism in the West." Pages 81–117 in *Justification,* ed. M. Husbands and D. Treier. InterVarsity, 2004; Michel, O. "Faith." *NIDNTT* 1:593–606. Zondervan, 1986; Pitkin, B. *What Pure Eyes Could See.* Oxford University Press, 1999; Springsted, E. *The Act of Faith.* Eerdmans, 2002.

Daniel J. Treier

Female   *See* Male and Female

Feminist Biblical Interpretation

Just as there is no single approach or ideology that encompasses "feminism" as a whole, neither is there a single approach that can legitimately be called "feminist biblical interpretation." One's hermeneutical stance may be womanist, *mujerista*, African, North American, Asian, Latin American, or European. It may be rejectionist, reformist, or loyalist in terms of method. Nevertheless, feminist biblical interpretation generally places women at the center of theological inquiry and, to varying degrees, makes their experience the criterion and norm for theological reflection, critique, reconstruction, and praxis. Despite recent challenges from postmodern, post-structuralist, and certain process feminist theorists and theologians, this appeal to women's experience—particularly the experience of oppression and marginalization by men—is predominant among feminist hermeneutics.

Despite their different social, political, and religious locations and worldviews, most feminist biblical scholars operate from a common set of assumptions. These include the following presuppositions: (1) Language not only expresses the world but helps to shape it. (2) Women's diminution has been aided and abetted by male-centered language, symbols, and structures. (3) The texts reflect the patriarchal, androcentric, and sometimes oppressive forms of hierarchy, which have prevailed in Hebrew and Christian cultures. And (4) all interpretation is "interested" and must necessarily be critiqued according to whose interests are being served by existing systems. This critique generally leads to either a reexamination of text and tradition to offer alternative interpretations, or a revision of the texts, or an outright rejection of the biblical canon.

Broadly defined, these options represent the three primary Western feminist approaches to Scripture. The first is the rejectionist position of feminists like Mary Daly and Daphne Hampson, who judge the Hebrew and Christian texts, and the entire Judeo-Christian tradition, to be hopelessly sexist and patriarchal. These anti- or post-Christian feminists believe this tradition to be a primary source of human oppression. The loyalist (biblicist) or evangelical position takes an opposite approach. These interpreters embrace the biblical canon as a whole without necessarily considering it to be sexist and accept as authoritative its witness to Jesus Christ as the triune God's human self-revelation. However, two different interpretative approaches exist regarding women's ontological and relational identity.

One approach accepts the historically promulgated argument for a hierarchy of order in human creation and thus in gendered relationships, particularly in terms of marriage, family, and in the church. Women's fulfillment is considered found in her submission and dependence on male leadership in each of these spheres—leadership exercised in love that does not diminish women's human uniqueness or freedom. The other approach advocates egalitarianism in all spheres of life such that women and men's diversity and unity are honored and upheld in relationships of equal, mutual submission. This view particularly argues that the full biblical material does not allow for subordination within the Christian community. In the unity and diversity of the body of Christ through the Holy Spirit, divine gifting precedes gender and not the reverse. Women who are loyalist biblical scholars generally read the text *as women* to give an interpretative perspective not often found in the existing literature.

Finally, there is the experience-based reformist approach, which represents the largest and most pervasive influence in feminist biblical interpretation. As their initial interpretative step, reformists such as Elizabeth Schüssler Fiorenza, Letty Russell, Phyllis Trible, and Sandra Schneiders all employ a hermeneutic of suspicion, or what Anthony Thiselton refers to as a "sociocritical hermeneutic." This approach to texts, traditions, and institutions seeks to penetrate beneath their surface function and expose them as instruments of power, domination, or social manipulation. Predominantly influenced by the women's liberation movement and various liberation theologies,

reformists use one chief criterion to judge biblical texts for truth, adequacy, and coherence—or the lack thereof. That criterion is the alignment of such texts with the feminist critical principle of women's full and equal humanity (or in some cases, a view of female ascendancy). At work is the powerful and pervasive Kantian conviction that tradition must be freed from the constraints of what it "actually says" by applying the "inner light of truth" inherent in the human subject, who has final authority over one's own moral sensibility. Hence, modern feminism has a tendency to equate authority with domination and to prioritize the hermeneutic of suspicion.

Functioning as active agents of interpretation and critical construction of religious meaning, reformists employ a variety of methods, including historical-critical, literary, anthropological, sociological, sociopolitical, narrative, and various combinations thereof. Often, however, there is a common methodological pattern to each that includes deconstruction, critical assessment, and reconstruction. The text is first deconstructed to uncover the hidden dynamic of domination. Next, there is the search and retrieval of what are believed to be dormant theological themes, neglected history, and lost female interpretation and experience concerning the texts. If the first question is, "Who currently benefits?" then the second question is, "Can the text be altered in form and/or interpretation to specifically benefit those who have been marginalized?" If the answer is positive, then the final step of reconstruction begins. If a negative judgment is made, the text is deemed not to be "true."

One of two critical stances can generally be found in Western reformist hermeneutics. One is to critique *interpretations* by appealing to the authority of certain texts to judge the interpretation of others. In other words, it advocates an authoritative canon within the canon, which unfortunately often fails to recognize its own interested interpretation and dominating potential. The other views *the text itself* as patriarchal and thus in need of reform based on an a priori, externally derived set of criteria, or what is essentially a normative canon outside the biblical canon. A level of ambiguity is thus inherent in these interpretative approaches as they try to criticize the tradition while correlating women's experience with it. Two seemingly contradictory assumptions arise. On the one hand, the biblical text has the quality of a neutral object set between competing value systems and moral judgments. These values, morals, and worldviews operate to judge certain *interpretations* as oppressive and thus incorrect. On the other hand, given its original context, the text is judged to be *inherently* patriarchal.

In either case, however, feminists admit that the same texts considered to promulgate women's exclusion and subordination have also been the source of hope, formation, and sustenance for centuries of Christian women. Both rejectionists and reformists argue, however, that a loyalist reading of the text (a gendered rather than liberationist reading) is not adequately critical and truly feminist. Such interpretations are viewed as enmeshed in the order of reality established through male domination. Women simply collude com/implicitly with their oppressors in perpetuating existing patriarchal systems, rather than radically undermining them. Loyalists, on the other hand, challenge the totalizing narrative of victimization, the universal experience of oppression, and the villainy of the Judeo-Christian tradition assumed out of hand by reformists and rejectionists.

See also Ideological Criticism; Liberation Theologies and Hermeneutics; Male and Female

Bibliography

Achtemeier, P., ed. *Interpretation* 42, no. 1 (1988); Carr, A. "The New Vision of Feminist Theology—Method." In *Freeing Theology*, ed. C. LaCugna. HarperSanFrancisco, 1993; Collins, A. Y., ed. *Feminist Perspectives on Biblical Scholarship*. Scholars Press, 1985; Fiorenza, E. *But She Said*. Beacon, 1992; idem. *In Memory of Her*. New York, 1983; Johnson, E. "Feminist Hermeneutics." *Chicago Studies* 27 (1988); Martin, F. "Feminist Hermeneutics." In *This Is My Name Forever*. InterVarsity, 2001; idem. *The Feminist Question*. Eerdmans, 1994; May, M. "Feminist Theology." In vol. 2 of *The Encyclopedia of Christianity*. Eerdmans, 2001; Parsons, S., ed. *The Cambridge Companion to Feminist Theology*. Cambridge University Press, 2002; Reno, R. R. "Feminist Theology." In *This Is My Name Forever*. InterVarsity, 2001; Russell, L., and S. Clarkson, eds. *Dictionary of Feminist Theologies*. Westminster John Knox, 1996; Schneiders, S. "The Bible and Feminism—Biblical Theology." In *Freeing Theology*, ed. C. LaCugna. HarperSanFrancisco, 1993; idem. "Feminist Ideology Criticism and Biblical Hermeneutics." *Biblical Theology Bulletin* 19 (1989); Thiselton, A. *The Two Horizons*. Paternoster, 1980; Trible, P. *God and the Rhetoric of Sexuality*. Fortress, 1978.

Cherith Fee Nordling

Figural Reading   *See* Allegory; Literal Sense; Typology

Figure of Speech   *See* Imagery; Metaphor; Poetry

Fish, Stanley   *See* Community, Interpretative; Pragmatism

Folklore   *See* Hero Story; Oral Tradition and the NT; Oral Tradition and the OT

Formalism

Definition

Formalism is a type of literary criticism that concentrates study on the "literary work as an object in its own right" (Murfin and Ray 132–33). It emphasizes careful reading of the text and minimizes such external considerations as author, historical occasion, original audience, and contemporary audience. At its best, formalism attempts to provide an objective analysis of a piece of writing from a literary perspective, including style, rhetorical contexts, and structure. Formalism assigns ontological status to the text, claiming it to be "an object of knowledge *sui generis*" (Wellek and Warren 156). Formalist critics deny that meaning is to be found in the author's intention or the reader's understanding (Wimsatt and Beardsley's "intentional fallacy" and "affective fallacy" respectively). Radically text-based, formalism claims that meaning is intrinsic to the text, not to be found by referencing any external considerations such as history or the author's biography.

History

Philosophically, modern versions of formalism developed out of Immanuel Kant and aesthetically from the Romantic poets of the early nineteenth century (Walhout and Ryken 2). In the United States, formalism received its classic expression in the New Criticism of the mid-twentieth century, in the works of such writers as Cleanth Brooks, John Crowe Ransom, Robert Penn Warren, and William Wimsatt. The term "New Criticism" is to be understood in the context of their wish to move past the historical and biographical study of literature in American university classrooms of the day to a literary criticism that is more text-based. New Criticism quickly became the norm in university literature departments and remained so until the 1960s. On the European continent, formalism was associated with the Russian formalists and the Prague Linguistic Circle (Roman Jakobson and Rene Wellek). In all its expressions, formalism calls attention to the primacy of the text in interpretation.

Formalism began to play an important role in biblical interpretation in the late twentieth century. An influential early article by James Muilenberg reminded us of the importance of the biblical texts themselves. Formalism took on full force with the rise of interest in literary approaches to the Bible in the 1970s and 1980s. Kenneth A. Mathews notes, "While this [new] criticism had a short life among secular literary critics, superseded by structuralism and deconstruction, it has had a stronger hold on biblical studies" (213). Notable examples of works that use formalistic principles include one by M. Weiss and those published by the Sheffield School (*JSOT*). J. Cheryl Exum and David J. A. Clines supply a useful brief overview of "new" and "newest" literary criticisms for biblical interpretation (11–25). Tremper Longman provides a brief survey (25–37). In the early twenty-first century, formalism as a literary approach has given way to a range of reader-centered interpretative strategies, among them feminism, reader-response criticism, and deconstruction.

Usefulness

Understood and used in proper balance, formalism offers valuable insights and necessary tools to biblical interpreters. With its emphasis on the primacy of the text, formalism demands careful analysis of the biblical texts as we have them. In so doing, formalism underscores a high view of inspiration and gives due respect to the details of individual books in the Bible. Further, formalism calls attention to the unity of the text as it is in the canon, thereby vitiating the atomistic tendencies of some historical-critical approaches of the twentieth century. The attention to the text in formalistic readings provides a much-needed antidote to the many reader-oriented interpretative strategies that have held sway in the late twentieth and early twenty-first centuries. Such strategies as postcolonialism, psychoanalysis, and others mentioned above locate meaning in the reader rather than the text or author. At their worst, these poststructuralist approaches, as they are sometimes called, leave too much room for affective, sectarian, and even idiosyncratic readings. Formalism provides a necessary corrective by returning the interpretative focus to the text itself. When used in its moderate forms—shorn of the radical formalists' insistence that meaning has no existential or historical dimensions—and employed alongside other time-proven methods of biblical interpretation, formalism contributes to a balanced hermeneutic.

Limitations

As with any interpretative approach, formalism has its limitations. First, formalism, along with other literary approaches to interpretation, invariably minimizes historical concerns and is sometimes blatantly ahistorical (Exum and Clines 11; *pace* Walhout and Ryken 19). When interpreting the Bible, we must keep one eye on historical backgrounds. Second, formalism denies any correspondence between a literary text and truth; rather, formalism typically affirms a coherence epistemology that ultimately falls short of doing justice to biblical texts. The Bible refers to a "real reality," both transcendent and temporal. Textual coherence as the only epistemological requirement comes short of a comprehensive biblical hermeneutic. Third, formalism sometimes privileges aesthetic concerns in literary analysis over ethical or intellectual issues (Walhout and Ryken 19); while there is much beauty in biblical writings, such beauty is not the raison d'être of the Bible. Finally, formalism implicitly denies the relevance of authorial intention to the text (Longman 26). In effect, formalism denies the relevance of author, reader, and *Sitz im Leben* to interpretation of texts.

Applicability

Even with its limitations, formalism still provides an essential element in a full-orbed interpretative strategy. Its emphasis on the text underscores the unity of the biblical texts as we have them in the canon, thereby providing an antidote to the centrifugal force of many traditional historical-critical methodologies. When interpreters pay due attention to the unity and coherence of the canonical texts, they demonstrate their respect for the inspiration of Scripture. The Bible is not a book of theological proof texts; it is written in literary forms. Formalism focuses attention on genre, structure, and figures of speech, thereby balancing the historical methods of interpretation. Used alone, no single interpretative strategy will do justice to the biblical texts. Taken in its proper context and accompanying other appropriate approaches, formalism illuminates biblical texts in ways no other current methodology can.

See also Deconstruction; Intention/Intentional Fallacy; Poststructuralism; Psychological Interpretation; Reader-Response Criticism

Bibliography

Exum, J. C., and D. J. A. Clines. "The New Literary Criticism." Pages 11–25 in *The New Literary Criticism and the Hebrew Bible.* JSOTSup 143. Sheffield Academic Press, 1993; Longman, T., III. *Literary Approaches to Biblical Interpretation.* Zondervan, 1987; Mathews, K. A. "Literary Criticism of the Old Testament." Pages 205–31 in *Foundations for Biblical Interpretation,* ed. D. Dockery, K. A. Mathews, and R. Sloan. Broadman & Holman, 1994; Muilenberg, J. "Form Criticism and Beyond." *JBL* 88 (1969): 1–18; Murfin, R., and S. M. Ray, eds. *The Bedford Glossary of Critical and Literary Terms.* Bedford Books, 1997; Sternberg, M. *The Poetics of Biblical Narrative.* Indiana University Press, 1987; Walhout, C., and L. Ryken. *Contemporary Literary Theory.* Eerdmans, 1991; Weiss, M. *The Bible from Within.* Magnes, 1984; Wellek, R., and A. Warren. *Theory of Literature.* 3d ed. Harcourt, Brace & World, 1956; Wimsatt, W. K., and M. C. Beardsley. *The Verbal Icon.* University Press of Kentucky, 1954.

Michael E. Travers

Form Criticism and the NT

When we speak or write, we do not just "say what we say." Patterns and conventions of various kinds focus and enhance our communication efforts; it has always been so. What is more, the patterns and conventions we employ in a particular context are typically well chosen for their appropriateness to the aspects of life to which any particular activity of communication is connected. Certain uses of language seem fitting if we are called upon to write a reference; others fit better the telling of a joke, the conduct of an argument, the writing of a poem, or the activity of prayer, and so on. The conventions are not rigid, and there is plenty of overlap. But for the most part, there is a clear connection between the patterns and conventions of language use and the life context for a particular exercise in communication. Form criticism is the study of these forms that are or have been used in communication.

The approach to the NT that claimed for itself the name form criticism (*Formgeschichte*, lit., "history of form") is to be traced to the work of three German scholars who had all studied with H. Gunkel, whose approach to the study of forms in the OT strongly influenced them. The three are M. Dibelius (1919), K. L. Schmidt (1919), and R. Bultmann (1921). The work of Dibelius, and especially Bultmann, has had an enduring impact on NT studies. Typically, before them the study of forms had focused on forms as found in the studied materials themselves. At times this was understood as implying a prehistory, but the focus of interest was in the forms and their functioning. Dibelius coined the new term in connection with the fact that he was concerned not with the "history of forms" (*Formengeschichte*), but with

unearthing the history to which the use of specific forms pointed. Dibelius and the others built upon an important feature of Gunkel's approach. Gunkel believed that each of the primitive forms found in the OT had its original setting in some definite place in the life of Israel, and that in this original setting (*Sitz im Leben*) was a clear and distinct form designed to match the specific setting. Correspondingly, Dibelius assumed that the original oral forms standing behind the Gospel materials would be relatively pure exemplars of forms that corresponded to the specific life-settings in which each originated. Dibelius identified six kinds of material in the Gospels: sermon material, paradigms, tales, legends, passion story, and myth. He believed that, on the basis of form, materials could be dated earlier or later, and that form provided an index to historical reliability. Specifically, the forms in which the artistry of the narration has gained value were secondary (e.g., the miracles stories), and those with mythical elements were relatively late.

The basic contours of Bultmann's inquiry are quite similar to that of Dibelius. But where Dibelius was interested in establishing laws of formation that would account for the structure of the different forms, Bultmann was more interested in the ways in which texts change in transmission. On the basis largely of the changes made to Markan material by the later Gospels, Bultmann formulated "laws of tradition," which he thought could be applied equally well to the oral phase, and would make it possible to remove accretions and restore materials to their original form. Also, compared with Dibelius, Bultmann was more comfortable with the idea that a single story might exhibit the features of more than one form. Bultmann offered a more complete and systematic analysis of the materials of the Gospels and identified a greater range of forms and subforms; partly for this reason he has had a much greater enduring impact. Bultmann was quite skeptical about the likely historicity of Gospel materials. According to his "criterion of dissimilarity," only materials that were distinctive in relation to both the Jewish context and early-church interests can with any confidence be traced to the historical Jesus, though in practice Bultmann was not rigid in the application of this criterion.

Vincent Taylor offered to British scholarship a version of form criticism that was much more optimistic about the historical reliability of the Gospel materials and thus opened up the possibilities of a form-critical method for more conservative scholars.

Form criticism is to be appreciated along a number of fronts. Despite all that is speculative about it, it succeeded in stimulating an imaginative engagement with dimensions of the life of the early church in a period largely otherwise inaccessible to us. It also highlighted the way in which the telling of Gospel stories represented an articulation of the faith of those who had come to an experience of salvation in connection with Jesus. And in the Gospel materials it demonstrated the importance of a range of forms, the identification of which can contribute to the clarification of the intended thrust of the materials. At some level form criticism underlined the importance for the Gospels of their own prehistory. The Gospels represent the witness of the early church to the enduring significance of the historical life, death, and resurrection of Jesus. Unfortunately, the general historical skepticism of the practitioners of form criticism has eviscerated this potential.

The most questionable assumptions of form criticism are these: (1) The earliest form will be the purest form. (2) Oral development closely parallels written development. (3) The use of specific forms points sharply to a specific *Sitz im Leben* (only a measure of correlation is likely). (4) Form is an index to historical accuracy. And (5) development took place under the control of impersonal laws of tradition (without, e.g., a role for key church leaders or for specific eyewitnesses). A different perspective on form-critical judgments would be created by attention to the constraints that the religious integrity of the transmitters of the Gospel material might impose upon their role. In addition, one must respect the investment of God, not only in the ministry of Jesus, but also in the subsequent transmission of knowledge of the events and their significance.

The name form criticism (but probably not *Formgeschichte*) has also been applied to other dimensions of, and approaches to, the study of forms in the NT. Classical form criticism was weak on the aesthetics of literary forms. But at least part of the significance of forms has to do with their capacity for particular kinds of rhetorical impact. A. N. Wilder (1964) and R. Tannehill (1975) and others have provided a lead in this direction. Yet others have sought to use the categories of Hellenistic rhetoric to illuminate the NT. These include H. D. Betz (1979) and K. Berger (1984). And finally we should mention the study of the forms to be found in NT letters. Dibelius made a beginning in 1926; B. Rigaux addressed the topic in 1962; R. Funk did so in 1966; and

there has since been a small flow of monographs and articles exploring particular forms (thanksgiving, benediction, doxology, petition, disclosure, greeting, etc.).

Bibliography

Berger, K. *Formgeschichte des Neuen Testaments.* Quelle & Meyer, 1984; Betz, H. D. *Galatians.* Fortress, 1979; Bultmann, R. *History of the Synoptic Tradition,* trans. J. Marsh. Harper & Row, 1963; Buss, M. *Biblical Form Criticism in Its Context.* JSOTSup 274. Sheffield Academic Press, 1999; Dibelius, M. *From Tradition to Gospel,* trans. B. Woolf. Scribner's, 1933; idem. *Geschichte der urchristlichen Literatur.* De Gruyter, 1926; Funk, R. *Language, Hermeneutics, and the Word of God.* Harper & Row, 1966; Güttgemanns, E. *Candid Questions concerning Gospel Form Criticism.* PTMS 26. Pickwick, 1979; Linnemann, E. *Biblical Criticism on Trial.* Kregel, 2001; McKnight, E. *What Is Form Criticism?* Fortress, 1969; Rigaux, B. *Saint Paul et ses lettres.* De Brouwer, 1962; Schmidt, K. *Der Rahmen der Geschichte Jesu.* Trowitzsch, 1919; Tannehill, R. *The Sword of His Mouth.* Fortress/Scholars Press, 1975; Taylor, V. *The Formation of the Gospel Tradition.* Macmillan, 1933; Wilder, A. N. *The Language of the Gospel.* Harvard University Press, 1964.

John Nolland

Form Criticism and the OT

Form criticism is a historical-critical analytical method that identifies and *compares* conventional structural and content features of biblical texts. Just as modern oral and written forms such as the business letter, fairy tale, and sermon are fairly standardized, so also OT genres such as hymns, laments, proverbs, and prophetic judgment oracles reflect fairly constant formal patterns. Originally, the primary interest of those who used it was sociohistorical; today, their focus is increasingly literary-rhetorical. As a historical-critical tool it is essentially nontheological in its orientation. However, several of its conclusions and entailments have significant implications for the theological interpretation of texts.

History

Hermann Gunkel (1862–1932) is credited with developing the method that became known as form criticism (or form history). However, the Hebrew Scriptures themselves employ some designations for literary types (dirge, psalm, proverb, instruction, song, prayer), and already early Jewish and Christian as well as Reformation-period interpreters gave attention to literary forms in their discussions of biblical style (Buss in Hayes 10–56). Gunkel's primary goal was to reconstruct a "history of Israelite literature" by isolating the individual shorter forms and longer genres contained in the biblical books. This was an undertaking that the then-dominant literary-critical method could not achieve since, in his view, most biblical texts had a long and complex oral prehistory. According to Gunkel, "every ancient genre originally belonged to a quite definite aspect of Israel's life," its so-called life-setting or *Sitz im Leben* (Gunkel 33).

Thus, studying Israelite literary history also entailed studying its social history. Gunkel viewed these forms as relatively stable, but gradually developing from short to long and pure to mixed, also claiming that every genre has only one life-setting (but not vice versa). However, much of the OT was considered to involve the later imitation of earlier oral forms, after the creative Hebrew "spirit lost power" (Gunkel 37). Unfortunately, according to Longman (48; also Knierim 435–40), Gunkel employed a theory of genre that was obsolete even in his own day.

Gunkel applied this new approach to Genesis and the Psalms, while Gressmann and Westermann applied it to the historical and prophetic books, respectively. Gunkel's student Mowinckel argued for the predominantly cultic origin of all Hebrew literature. Later practitioners tended to overextend the method in their effort to categorize every textual segment, frequently engaging in debates over the correct category (e.g., is Ps. 139 an individual complaint, a praise psalm, or a wisdom poem?). Others have domesticated the method, offering little more than structural outlines of texts. (The various FOTL volumes, though well-intentioned, offer examples of both.) Some alleged imitated forms (e.g., Isa. 55:1 as mimicking the water-hawker's sales pitch) may be understood better as merely figurative language. In recent decades, the attempt to reconstruct the history of various forms has largely been abandoned, and greater attention is given to the analysis and comparison of *written* genres than to underlying *oral* forms.

As a new century began, the method was being reassessed and combined with new linguistic, sociological, aesthetic-rhetorical, and postmodern perspectives.

Procedure and Recent Developments

The examination of the sociocultural shaping of linguistic expressions has four basic steps: (1) demarcating the unit and analyzing its structure, (2) comparing individual forms and determining the genre to which they belong, (3) reconstructing the life-setting of the genre, and (4) determining the intention of the genre in general and of this example in particular. Genre categories can be conceived of as a series of concentric circles, in which fewer texts share a greater number of features as one moves toward the center: poetry → psalm → lament → of the individual → with confession of guilt. For Gunkel, three elements were constitutive components of a genre: (1) thoughts and moods, (2) linguistic form, including vocabulary and grammar, and (3) connection with life, more recently described by Ben-Amos as "the cognitive, expressive, and behavioral levels" (Buss in Hayes 1), while Giese distinguishes form, content, and function (Sandy and Giese 9). More simply, one could speak of formal (or structural) and nonformal features. Modern literary theory offers a "communicative-semiotic approach" to genre (Longman 50) that is more useful than Gunkel's theory, which was dependent on the folklore studies of the Grimm brothers. One can consider forms as a literary "menu" from which the speaker/author can choose, although genre selection may be more instinctive than consciously purposeful. More helpful is the comparison of genre with a contract or with the rules of a game that govern the relationship between the sender and receiver of the encoded message. In order for the audience/reader to "get" the message, the speaker/author must adhere to the terms of the agreement, to the regulations that order play. In other words, effective communication must conform to conventional expectations. The bending of genres can be intentional, as in parody, but may result in cognitive dissonance rather than heightened attention.

As one proponent of the method summarizes: "Form criticism had a meteoric rise in the early part of the twentieth century and fell from favor toward its end" (Campbell in Sweeney and Ben Zvi 15). Accordingly, some view form criticism as passé or as having no future; others consider a radical revision to be necessary if it is to survive. According to Campbell, a literary genre is best understood not as the key that unlocks a text's meaning but rather as "a tag that an interpreter can put on a text after its secrets have been explored, . . . that helps situate a text within a general class so that it can be more easily understood" (Campbell in Sweeney and Ben Zvi 24). Focusing on the actual rather than on the hypothetical, on the *Sitz im Text* (textual setting) rather than on the *Sitz im Leben*, on the fluidity and adaptability rather than on the static or ideal nature of genre types—these strategies will rescue form criticism from the abuses and limitations that plagued it during the preceding century. This involves studying the larger literary patterns that connect smaller units into larger compositions, noting the unique as well as the typical features of a text, combining both synchronic and diachronic approaches, and attending to the readership as well as the authorship of texts. Such efforts will integrate this "new" form criticism with other critical methods and lead to new interpretative insights.

Implications for Theological Interpretation

What are the potential implications of the form-critical method for the theological interpretation of biblical texts? As a primarily analytical tool aimed at historical reconstruction, traditional form-critical perspectives can clearly run counter to more synthetic theological-canonical approaches. In its initial failed attempt to facilitate the writing of a history of biblical literature, form criticism served as a handmaiden of historical criticism. Form critics' unproved assumption of evolutionary developments from short to long utterances and simple to complex (mixed) forms, coupled with exclusive ascription of expressions of individual piety to the postexilic period, undercut biblical claims of divinely inspired prophetic spokespersons and authors. Early form critics also denigrated late biblical literature as a "tragedy" when the "genres are exhausted; imitations begin to abound [and] redactions take the place of original creations" on the road to canon (Gunkel 36). Furthermore, listing "saga, legend, tale, novella, and fable" as primary OT narrative genres (Coats) suggests that, although such genres can contain historical elements, any claim that they offer reliable accounts of God's mighty acts is exaggerated. The etiological tale that explains the origin of a current name or practice is normally understood as a fabrication (contrast Childs). Finally, close comparison of Hebrew genres with parallel examples from the ancient Near East (e.g., cosmologies, love songs, prophetic oracles) can lead to downplaying the uniqueness and authority of biblical literature.

A basic premise of form-critical analysis is that form and function are integrally related: the identification of the former can lead to the latter. However, comparison of three lists of even the basic OT genres reveals the difficulty of achieving a consensus in labeling. For example, Sandy and Giese, using standard designations, speak of narrative, history, law, oracles of salvation, announcements of judgment, apocalyptic, lament, praise, proverb, and nonproverbial wisdom. Walton, using ancient literary types, distinguishes cosmology, personal

archives and epics, legal texts, covenants and treaties, historical literature, hymns, prayers, incantations, Wisdom literature, prophetic literature, and apocalyptic literature. Ryken, using modern literary categories, discusses heroic narrative, epic, comedy, tragedy, lyric poetry, psalms, love lyrics, encomium, proverbs, satire, and visionary literature.

To give a more specific illustration, one wonders how useful an interpretative tool form criticism is when the genre of Jonah has been variously analyzed as a fable, didactic novel, prophetic legend, parable, midrash, allegory, prophetic confession, or a mixture of several genres. Each of these labels is also in tension with the book's place within the Hebrew (the Book of the Twelve) and Greek canon as one of a dozen undifferentiated briefer records of prophetic activity. Similarly, no consensus has emerged regarding which OT (or ancient Near Eastern) texts properly belong to the category of "Wisdom literature." Roland Murphy includes Job, Proverbs, Ruth, Canticles, Ecclesiastes, and Esther in his volume on *Wisdom Literature*. However, even though Job addresses questions of theodicy, some have assigned it a nonsapiential genre category such as "lawsuit" or "dramatized lament," while others abandon the attempt, simply concluding that it is a "masterpiece . . . *sui generis*" that draws on numerous genres (Hartley 37–38). Form-critical analyses often run the risk of imposing modern standards of coherence and consistency on ancient texts, having failed to illuminate the nature of the fundamental unit of canonical literature—the biblical "book" (but see Ben Zvi in Sweeney and Ben Zvi).

This is not to suggest that form criticism is a completely flawed tool, unable to assist in the task of theological interpretation. If Longman is correct in claiming that genre identification is the key to the meaning of a text (Longman 61, citing Hirsch), then form-critical analysis is foundational to the interpretative task. Recent modifications of the method, especially by evangelical scholars, have made it more useful in this regard. For example, Giese describes his approach as "genre criticism," which "works with the canonical form of the text and not any form *before* that," focusing on the function of a given genre within the present biblical text rather than on its original oral form and setting in life. Giese dismisses the latter pursuit as unnecessary and too often biased (Sandy and Giese 8). Gunkel's focus on formal conventions served to rescue Psalms studies from one-sided efforts to understand individual compositions on the basis of internal indications of their origin (especially in the postexilic and Maccabean periods). In 1969, James Muilenburg issued a call to give proper attention not only to the conventional features of a group of related texts but also to the unique rhetorical features of individual compositions. Thus, an awareness of the typical form of the community lament helps one to have a greater appreciation of the skill of the author of Ps. 80. He integrated into this structure a refrain that echoes the priestly blessing from Num. 6:24–26 (vv. 3, 7, 19), and developed the extended metaphor of a vine to portray Israel's redemptive history (vv. 8–16).

Genre analysis helps to focus and correct reader expectations in a number of respects. A proper understanding of genre features and functions can prevent a person from unduly seeking precise scientific assertions in poetic or anthropomorphic cosmological texts whose primary purpose is to exalt the sovereign creational activities of Israel's God, especially in contrast to pagan concepts of origins. The comparison of ancient Near Eastern genre parallels with OT texts, far from diminishing the uniqueness of the Bible, serves to highlight it. No ancient annalistic history or prophetic collection is as extensive as the biblical exemplars or clearly displays a deity's sovereign purposes in history for a people or nation (rather than the temporary favoring of a particular monarch). Comparing biblical with Mesopotamian law reveals the higher valuation of life over property and the protection of the poorer classes in the biblical materials. A comparison between the Song of Songs and later Egyptian love poetry not only highlights the biblical demand for exclusive sexual relationships within the context of marriage, but also raises fundamental questions about the validity of predominantly allegorical or typological interpretations. A comparison of Deuteronomy's structure with contemporary international treaty documents not only offers support for a late-second-millennium date of composition but also suggests that God appropriated contemporary literary conventions in portraying his relationship with his covenant people (Kitchen, "Fall and Rise"). Similarly, Kitchen's comparison of the book of Proverbs with forty ancient proverbial collections shows that a form-critical argument can be made for the unity of Prov. 1–24 (consisting of a title, prologue, main body; Kitchen, "Proverbs"). Thus, chapters 1–9 provide the theological context for interpreting the often more "nontheological" individual proverbs in chapters 10–24.

An awareness of genre distinctions also can enrich understanding of biblical inspiration. All biblical genres (psalms, proverbs, historical narrative) are equally inspired (2 Tim. 3:16–17) and therefore profitable, but they do not communicate divine truth in the same manner as prophetic oracles do, nor are their corresponding "truth claims" equally testable. Paul Ricoeur writes (90–91): "A hermeneutic of revelation must give priority to those modalities of discourse that are most originary within the language of a community of faith," which "are caught up in forms of discourse as diverse as narration, prophecy, legislative texts, wisdom sayings, hymns, supplications, and thanksgiving." To express the literary richness and diversity of biblical genres and imagery merely through dogmatic propositions involves unnecessary reductionism.

Though various genres may be capable of "conceptual paraphrase" (to use Vanhoozer's term), it is necessary to approach the Bible both as a literary critic and as a systematic theologian, and to acknowledge that biblical texts are intended to do more than inform us. According to Vanhoozer, applying "speech-act" theory to biblical literature reminds us that, since Scripture does many things with words, its authority is multifaceted: proverbs require thoughtful consideration, while the Ten Commandments require absolute obedience. More expressive genres are needed to supplement more assertive, directive, or commissive genres in order to communicate the nature of an appropriate response to divine revelation (Vanhoozer 93–104). Thus, form criticism, as modified in contemporary genre-criticism theory, not only can aid us in interpreting texts but also can deepen our appreciation of the diversity of Scripture as a whole.

See also Genre

Bibliography

Ben-Amos, D. "Analytical Categories and Ethnic Genres." *Genre* 1 (1968): 275–301; Childs, B. "The Etiological Tale Re-examined." *VT* 24 (1974): 387–97; Coats, G. W., ed. *Saga, Legend, Tale, Novella, Fable.* JSOTSup 35. JSOT, 1985; Gunkel, H. "Israelite Literary History." Pages 31–41 in *Water for a Thirsty Land*, ed. K. C. Hanson. Fortress, 2001; Hartley, J. *The Book of Job.* NICOT. Eerdmans, 1988; Hayes, J. H., ed. *Old Testament Form Criticism.* Trinity University Press, 1974; Kitchen, K. R. "The Fall and Rise of Covenant, Law, and Treaty." *TynBul* 40 (1989): 118–35; idem. "Proverbs and Wisdom Books of the Ancient Near East: The Factual History of a Literary Form." *TynBul* 28 (1977): 69–114; Knierim, R. "Old Testament Form Criticism Reconsidered." *Int* 27 (1973): 435–48; Knierim, R., and G. Tucker, eds. The Forms of the Old Testament Literature [FOTL series]. Eerdmans, 1981–; Longman, T. "Form Criticism, Recent

Developments in Genre Theory, and the Evangelical." *WTJ* 47 (1985): 46–67; Muilenburg, J. "Form Criticism and Beyond." *JBL* 88 (1969): 1–18; Murphy, R. *Wisdom Literature*. FOTL 13. Eerdmans, 1981; Ricoeur, P. "Toward a Hermeneutic of the Idea of Revelation." Pages 73–118 in *Essays in Biblical Interpretation*, ed. L. Mudge. Fortress, 1980; Ryken, L. *How to Read the Bible as Literature*. Zondervan, 1984; Sandy, D. B., and R. Giese. *Cracking Old Testament Codes*. Broadman, 1995; Sweeney, M., and E. Ben Zvi, eds. *The Changing Face of Form Criticism for the Twenty-First Century*. Eerdmans, 2003; Tucker, G. *Form Criticism of the Old Testament*. Fortress, 1971; Vanhoozer, K. "The Semantics of Biblical Literature: Truth and Scripture's Diverse Literary Forms." Pages 51–104 in *Hermeneutics, Authority, and Canon*, ed. D. A. Carson and J. Woodbridge. Zondervan, 1986; Walton, J. *Ancient Israelite Literature in Its Cultural Context*. Zondervan, 1989.

Richard L. Schultz

Foundationalism   *See* Epistemology

Fourfold Sense   *See* Literal Sense; Medieval Biblical Interpretation; Spiritual Sense

Fowl, Stephen   *See* Theological Hermeneutics, Contemporary; Virtue

Frei, Hans   *See* Narrative Theology; Yale School

Fulfillment   *See* Prophecy and Prophets in the NT; Prophecy and Prophets in the OT; Relationship between the Testaments; Salvation, History of

Functionalism   *See* Scripture, Authority of; Theological Hermeneutics, Contemporary; Yale School

G

Gabler, J. P. *See* Biblical Theology

Gadamer, Hans-Georg *See* Hermeneutical Circle; Hermeneutics; Ricoeur, Paul

Galatians, Book of

With an appropriateness that Paul could hardly have anticipated, Galatians is one of the most fruitful writings of the NT. Not only was it the foundational document of the Reformation; it was also widely influential throughout church history. Chrysostom, Jerome, and Augustine all composed commentaries on it within a few decades and a few hundred miles of each other at the turn of the fourth/fifth centuries, as Christianity began to expand under official recognition. Luther's commentary was itself enormously influential (even John Bunyan records his debt in *Grace Abounding*), in contrast to his commentary on Romans, published only in a provisional form in 1908 (critical ed. 1938). The letter is evidently written with deep passion and out of a great sense of care and anxiety for the Galatians, as they are tempted to follow those who argue that observance of the law is a necessary condition for membership in the people of God. It reveals the existence of deep controversy and conflict among the apostles over the issue of observance of the law. By contrast with the proponents of a law-observant Christianity, Paul insists that righteousness is to be found only by those who live by faith in Jesus Christ and who are led by the Spirit. Such people live in hope and out of the experience of the living Christ within them. This is the new life of freedom, which replaces the former life of bondage. Such a radical view of the newness of Christian existence (by contrast with all old ways, not only of the Gentiles but also of the Jews) raises some difficult questions about the relation of the OT to the NT, and of Paul to some of the other NT writers (Matthew and James) who place much greater emphasis on the law. At the same time it raises important questions about the nature of Christians' freedom and guidance by the Spirit.

What weight are the churches to give appeals to the Spirit in the search for guidance and in times of controversy? Paul's assertion of the radical newness of believers' life in Christ also raises acute questions about the place of other forms of religious belief and practice within Christian understanding and practice, not least of members of the Jewish faith.

History of Interpretation

Guidance by the Spirit and Freedom from the Law in Galatians. In his argument with the Galatians, Paul clearly states that the role of the law in their lives (or the lives of the Jews?) was a temporary one. Before faith they were kept under the law, which acted as a custodian; once faith came they were all sons of God, "no longer under a custodian" (3:23–26 RSV). Clearly (not least in the light of the subsequent interpretation of this passage), Paul's use of this metaphor leaves a number of questions open: What precisely was the nature of this custodianship? Once Christian believers were no longer subject to the law as custodian, did that mean that their relationship to the law was then at an end? What was the nature of their new life in the Spirit, in which they had begun their Christian existence, such that the desire to return to practice of the law could be ironically described by Paul as a desire to perfect their new life "in the flesh" (3:3 AT)?

Marcion, one of the earliest commentators on Paul, saw the law as stemming from a different God than the God of Jesus Christ, and believed that the law of the just but cruel creator God had as its principal function the enslavement and punishment of human beings. The gospel brought by the Spirit liberated believers and allowed them to escape from the world of creation. This reading sets a mark for subsequent orthodox interpreters who seek to distance themselves from the teaching of Marcion. For Chrysostom, the law has two functions: the first as a bridle to curb the Jews; the second, more importantly, to teach the Jews the basic grammar of morality. The law is, as it were, a primary teacher who drills on the rudiments of

238

the subject and is left behind when the pupil has learned all that he may and then moves on to be taught by a philosopher. It would be degrading for such a student to go back to his primary teacher, when he is already being taught by one much wiser and more learned. The role of the Spirit is also twofold: regenerating believers in baptism, thus liberating them from the desires of the flesh; also, instructing in the higher morality, so that believers may produce fruit. Augustine introduces a new motif into the understanding of the function of the law: it is there to humble those who seek justification by works, precisely because no one can perform all the works of the law. Thus, people are driven to seek the righteousness that comes by faith in Jesus Christ. The Spirit leads believers in the way of faith, but they constantly have to battle with the effects of original sin. Thomas Aquinas drew together the teaching of the fathers: the law was to restrain sins, to bring people to seek grace, to tame concupiscence, and also to serve as a figure of future grace. This last point allowed a more allegorical reading of the ceremonial aspects of the law.

Luther accepted that the law had a civil (political) use in promoting order and discipline in society; it also had a theological use: following Augustine, he described it as a hammer to break the proud and bring them to Christ. Through faith Christ enters the life of believers and through his Spirit guides and leads them, though they always have to battle with the power of sin in their lives. Until this point, few commentators attributed anything but a quite minor role to the law in the life of believers. At most, it is one source of ethical teaching, though a minor one compared with the teaching of the NT (Aquinas). For Calvin, this became more problematical. Faced with the Radical Reformers—who appealed to the inspiration of the Spirit to justify their pacifist and simple style of living—and inspired by a belief in the unity of the two covenants, Calvin appealed to the law as the true benchmark of Christian ethics. He thus proposes a third use of the law, which is the "principal use and more closely connected with its proper end. It has respect to believers in whose hearts the Spirit of God already flourishes and reigns. . . . That, by teaching, admonishing, rebuking, and correcting, it may fit and prepare us for every good work. . . . The law acts like a whip to the flesh, urging it on as men do a sluggish ass." But it also has a teaching function, even for believers in whose hearts "the Law is written and engraved." For them, "it is the best instrument for enabling them to learn with greater truth

and certainty what that will of the Lord is which they aspire to follow, and to confirm them in this knowledge" (*Inst.* 2.7.12). Thus Calvin exalts the written law of the OT over the law written in the heart. This is taken up by later Puritan commentators such as William Perkins, who see evidence of obedience to the law as a ground for assurance of the believer's election. Perkins gives some remarkable examples of what he sees to be the clear guidance of the written law, which includes not selling one's children into slavery. Among post-Enlightenment commentators, F. C. Baur saw the conflict between Peter and Paul at Antioch as representing the struggle between a law-based, particularist understanding of religion and the new law-free, universalist religion of Christianity, based on a new God-consciousness mediated through the Son. This new (idealist) understanding of Spirit was subsequently attacked by the history of religions school (Heitmüller), which located the understanding of Spirit in popular Hellenistic forms of effervescent religion, though Bousset argued that Paul's true religion of the Spirit transcended the popular cultic form of early Christianity. This characterization of Spirit-led belief as universalist, and Judaism with its own ethical traditions as particularist, easily led into various late-nineteenth-century portrayals of Judaism as legalistic and caught up in extreme forms of casuistry.

Justification by Faith and Not by Works. Commentators see Paul as contrasting two very different types of religious observance; one is based on works, driven by fear of the consequences of failing to obey the law; the other is based on faith in Christ's work in securing our forgiveness, which brings freedom to follow the Spirit (Chrysostom). There are questions, however, about the role of believers in the life of faith, how far they are restored/regenerated and able to act justly and lovingly, how far any such acts of righteousness are themselves the result of God's gracious action. Chrysostom believed both that our crucifixion with Christ in baptism leads to the killing of our passions and so to the end of sin, and also that there was a continuing need for ascetic discipline in the life of the Christian. Thus, he portrayed Paul as the ideal type of the Christian monk. Augustine believed that those who die to the law exchange a carnal for a spiritual understanding of the law. Moreover the law is no longer imposed, for now Christ lives in the believer, who thus acts out of love of justice. Nevertheless, although this might sound like a perfectionist understanding of Christian life, Augustine distinguishes between the present mode of Christ's dwelling in the believer and that which is to come. Now Christ lives in believers by faith only; in the life to come he will live in them by sight. In this life there is still a lack of clarity and certainty about relationship with Christ, which leads Augustine to become less confident in the bond.

For Aquinas, faith itself is a gift of grace and is informed by the gift of love (*fides caritate formata*); in this way God is understood as imparting the fullness of his gifts to believers. God assists our free will by his grace; Christians are released from the written law and instructed and directed by God himself; Christ directs the soul as the soul directs the body. Luther vehemently objected, saying this meant that faith not informed by love and therefore not issuing in works of love was viewed as nonsalvific; such teaching implied a doctrine of justification by works. The righteousness received through faith in Christ was a pure gift and not in any sense dependent on our activity. Christ entering the heart drives out Moses and brings grace and righteousness. With such a view, righteousness is not merely reckoned to the believer but, because it has its roots in the intimate union between Christ and the believer, issues in actual righteousness. In this sense, the believer is freed from the law. Nevertheless, while there is this union in the believers' hearts, they live out their callings in the world, where the law still obtains.

Calvin's reading of Gal. 2:15–21 first attacks the view of Jerome (and Origen) that it was only the ceremonial (as opposed to the moral) law that could not justify. While conceding that the original dispute was about ceremonial matters, he argues that Paul nevertheless moved from the particular to the general because he "was worried not so much about ceremonies being observed as that the confidence and glory of salvation should be transferred to works." He differs importantly from Luther, who takes "Through the law I died to the law" (v. 19) to mean renouncing it and being freed from it. For Calvin, it means rather that the law bears the curse within it, which slays us, not that we are liberated from its sphere. The new life of believers is engrafted into the death of Christ, from which they receive a secret energy. Believers are "animated by the secret power of Christ, so that Christ may be said to live and grow in [them]." The life of Christ in the believer depends on a "true and genuine communication with him" and has two possible senses for Calvin. First is the governance of the believer's actions by

Christ's spirit. Second is participation in Christ's righteousness, so "that, since we cannot of ourselves be acceptable to him [French version], we are accepted in him by God. The first relates to regeneration, the second to the free imputation of righteousness." It is in the second sense that Calvin takes the present passage, though he indicates in the French version of his commentary that he would find it better if it could be taken in both senses. Thus both Luther and Calvin provide support for the dominant Reformed view that the righteousness of faith is an alien righteousness, imputed rather than imparted, a view linked with a negative view of the reality of the believer's sharing in Christ's righteousness. On the other hand, both these Reformers speak powerfully and movingly of the believer as united to Christ: "We so live in the world that we also live in heaven; not only because our Head is there, but because, in virtue of union, we have a life in common with him (John 14.1ff.)" (Calvin, *Galatians*, 42–43; *Commentaires*, 296–97).

Christian Anthropology—the Desires of the Flesh and the Desires of the Spirit: Gal. 5:16–18 and the Ethics of Desire. Paul states that the desires of the flesh and the Spirit are opposed to each other and engaged in struggle with each other in such a way as to bring a certain consequence: "You may not do what you want" (v. 17 AT). This statement is wonderfully ambiguous and has spawned a family of Christian anthropologies of very different temperaments. For dualists like Gnostics and Manichaeans, the flesh is seen as the creation of an alien principle, which holds the pure, incorruptible soul in bondage. The soul can, however, be released through saving knowledge of its plight. This knowledge of the fundamental opposition between flesh and spirit leads to renewal of the soul and a life of abstinence and asceticism, *not doing what one—wrongly—wants*. Such doctrines were vigorously opposed by the orthodox churches but nevertheless were influential and reflected in the adoption and idealization of ascetic lifestyles and the exaltation of virginity. Chrysostom saw flesh and spirit not as two opposed principles but as referring to different states of mind or judgment: those instructed by the Spirit knew clearly what the choices were that faced them and were *able to choose not to do what was wrong*. Again, this meant resisting the desires of the flesh and leading a life of (monastic) asceticism. Chrysostom portrayed Paul as the ideal type of the Christian monk, crucifying the flesh with its passions and desires (5:24). Aquinas follows the fathers in taking "flesh" and "spirit" to refer to different modes of the soul's willing. But rather than seeing fleshly desires as intrinsically wrong, he understands them as natural, wrong only insofar as they are taken to excess or allowed to distract the soul from the pursuit of spiritual, supernatural desires. For Aquinas, there is then a struggle within the Christian life to establish a proper balance between natural and spiritual desires, which means that we *cannot always do the good we want*. This tendency to see the Christian life as one of *continuing struggle in the will between the desires of the flesh and the Spirit* is given greater impetus by Luther, whose deep fears of judgment during his life as an Augustinian friar continued to disturb him later. He remained powerfully convinced of the continuing sinfulness of believers, and at the same time he also believed that those who were united to Christ were able to bear the fruit of the Spirit in their lives. This darker strain in Reformed theology was given yet greater impetus by Calvinist doctrines of total depravity, tendencies that were combated by Methodism and the holiness movements.

View of the Other in Galatians. Finally, we must consider the ways that readings of Galatians have influenced Christians' views of those outside the community of faith. With its sharp contrasts between those who follow the life of the flesh and those led by the Spirit—and between those who believe, are in Christ, and are sons and daughters of Abraham, Christ, and God and those who are not—Galatians can easily lead to a quite negative characterization of all those who are not Christian believers, indeed, to a very negative characterization of all forms of human difference (3:28). Such negative attitudes are clearly evinced in Chrysostom's *Discourses against the Jews* and in Luther's and subsequent Lutheran portrayals of Christianity as a legalistic religion of works and self-redemption. This is further developed in F. C. Baur's portrayal of Judaism as a particularistic, as opposed to a universal, form of religion (cf. Boyarin's reception and critique of Baur). But it is not only Jews who are thus categorized as alien and other: for Luther, all those who do not accept his doctrine of justification by faith are to be seen as pursuing some form of works-righteousness, whether Jews, Turks, schoolmen, philosophers, or monks. The list presumably is extendable.

Place within the Canon

The radical nature of Galatians' theology of the Spirit and its doctrine of the temporary nature of the law raise a number of questions. In the first place, it is argued that Paul's own views of the law change between Galatians and Romans (describing the law as "holy and just and good," in 7:12 NRSV). This does not necessarily entail any contradiction between Galatians and Romans, though there is certainly a difference of tone and emphasis. There are much greater difficulties in plotting the relations between Galatians and works like Matthew and James, which emphasize performing works of the law and doing all that Jesus commanded. Certainly, Luther felt that it was not possible to reconcile Paul and James, which he famously dismissed as an "epistle of straw," just as commentators have continued to see Matthew's emphasis on judgment by works as inimical to Paul's teaching on justification by faith. However, there are similar tensions within Paul's own writings, which should prompt the theological interpreter to question a too-simplistic resolution. Yet Marcion raised more radical questions about the relation of Paul's works (pruned to suit Marcion) to the rest of the canon and in particular to the OT, which for him was testimony to a different, creator God, opposed to the merciful and gentle God of Jesus Christ. Even though orthodox Christian interpreters have fiercely resisted such views, they continue to find powerful supporters. Harnack was one such, and this support for Marcion was coupled with a deeply negative view of Judaism. He saw it as a labyrinthine religion of legalism—transcended by Jesus' teaching of the fatherhood of God and a higher righteousness in the form of an ethic of intention. Even among those who have held that the law plays an integral part in the history of salvation, there is, as recognized, a radical dispute about the nature of its continuing role in the life of the believer.

Galatians presents us with one of the sharpest statements of the giftedness of Christian existence, its dependence not on human effort but on gratitude and faith in God's grace in Christ, a life lived in union with Christ. That life neither springs from nor is subsequently conditional upon human observance of the law of the OT, though it will indeed bear the fruit of the Spirit. Such a vision of the Christian life as a wholly new mode of existence, free from the "bondage" of the old life of the flesh, has never been easy to sustain or indeed to reconcile with the continuing evidence of disharmony, conflict, and other "works of the flesh" in the life of Christian communities. At one extreme are those who have emphasized the perfectionist strand in Paul's thought, asserting the possibility of a new life wholly freed from the flesh, where the soul is free to follow the guidance or instruction of the Spirit. At another extreme are those who have regarded such perfection as something to be achieved only in a future state, since the present life is still dominated by the power of the flesh to create disorder in Christian lives. Hence, the law remains necessary both as a whip to scourge the flesh and as a clear guide for Christian conduct. In this life the human will remains weak; hope, in the face of imminent judgment, resides in the imputation of Christ's righteousness to the believer: "Just as I am, without one plea" (C. Elliott). While perfectionist readings may run up against the hard facts of Christian communal existence, the more negative views seem largely deaf to the promises that Paul makes to Christians in this life and to his despair that those who have once tasted such a life should be willing to turn their backs on it. Readings like those of Aquinas, and to a degree Augustine and Luther, are more alert to the tensions within Christian existence between Spirit-led freedom and the "desires of the flesh," and thus seem more faithful to the text and offer creative ways of appropriating it. In particular, they offer encouragement to Christians to take more seriously their own moral experience as they are led by the Spirit, and to have the courage to explore new ways of living that are governed not by the letter of the law but by the fruit they bear.

See also Justification by Faith; Pauline Epistles

Bibliography

Baur, F. C. *Paul*. Williams & Norgate, 1876; Bousset, W. *Kyrios Christos*. Abingdon, 1970; Boyarin, D. *A Radical Jew*. University of California Press, 1994; Bunyan, J. *Grace Abounding to the Chief of Sinners*. Clarendon, 1962; Calvin, J. *Commentaires de M. Jean Calvin sur toutes les epîstres de l'Apôtre Sainct Paul*. S. Honorati, 1563; idem. *The Epistles of Paul the Apostle to the Galatians, Ephesians, Philippians, and Colossians*. Eerdmans, 1965; idem. *Inst.*; Chrysostom, J. "Commentary on Galatians." Vol. 13 of *NPNF*[1]; Harnack, A. von. *Marcion*. Wissenschaftliche Buchgesellschaft, 1996; Heitmüller, W. *Taufe und Abendmahl bei Paulus*. Vandenhoeck & Ruprecht, 1903; Luther, M. *A Commentary on St. Paul's Epistle to the Galatians*. J. Clarke, 1953; Perkins, W. *A Commentary on Galatians*. Pilgrim, 1989; Plumer, E., trans. *Augustine's Commentary on Galatians*. Oxford Early Christian Studies. Oxford University Press, 2003; Thomas Aquinas. *Commentary on St. Paul's Epistle to the Galatians*. Magi Books, 1966.

John K. Riches

Genealogy

Numerous genealogical records are scattered throughout the OT and NT. Genealogies were one way to demonstrate both historical continuity and sociological relationship(s) in the ancient world. Practically speaking, the inability to bridge past and present through such ancestral records meant a family, clan, tribe, or society was at risk of extinction—since it implied a set of circumstances that imperiled an ongoing genealogical history.

Principal Genealogies in the Bible

The most extensive and complex of the biblical genealogies are found in 1 Chron. 1–9. This prologue to the Chronicler's history selectively traces the generations from Adam (1:1) to the Hebrews who resettled Jerusalem and Judah after the Babylonian exile (9:3–9); it contains more than thirty genealogies. Like most biblical genealogies, they were designed to illustrate the continuity of the postexilic Hebrew community with earlier counterparts. They also linked the divine promises to David and his descendants with the covenant promises made previously to the Hebrew patriarchs. Finally, the Chronicler's genealogies served to legitimize the interim political leadership role of the Levitical priesthood in Jerusalem until such time as the Davidic monarchy was reestablished.

Other significant genealogies are found in Gen. 4:16–24; 5; 10; 11:10–32; 19:30–38; 22:20–24; 25:12–26; 36; 46:8–27; Exod. 6:14–25; Num. 3; 26; Ruth 4:18–22; 2 Sam. 3:2–5; 5:13–16; Ezra 7:1–5; Esther 2:5–6; Matt. 1:1–17; Luke 3:23–38.

Definition

According to Robert Wilson, "A genealogy is a written or oral expression of the descent of a person or persons from an ancestor or ancestors" (*Genealogy*, 9). Particular terminology is sometimes employed to characterize the composition of biblical genealogies, as illustrated in 1 Chronicles:

- breadth, listing a single generation of descendants from a common ancestor (e.g., 2:1)
- depth, listing successive generations, commonly four to six (e.g., 3:10–16)
- linear, displaying depth alone (e.g., 2:10)
- segmented, displaying both breadth and depth (e.g., 3:17–24)
- descending, proceeding from parent to child (e.g., 9:39–44)
- ascending, moving from child to parent (e.g., 9:14–16; further, Wilson, *Genealogy*, 18–26)

Purpose

Literarily, genealogies are important connecting links in the biblical narrative since by nature any such reporting of history must be selective. They may serve a number of purposes, even simultaneously. At times the genealogy may signify social status and legitimize the wielding of certain power by individuals or groups (as in the case of the hereditary offices of kingship and priesthood in Hebrew society). Certain legal rights and duties were associated with the genealogy as well, such as claims for land tenure and military conscription. In agrarian tribal societies, genealogies commonly identified clans and families by means of geographical location and thus were the ancient equivalent of an address book.

According to Satterthwaite, two primary functions of the biblical genealogies may be noted: describing the descent of the nations from Adam through Noah; and tracing the "line of the promise" from Seth to the nation of Israel—culminating in the genealogies of Jesus Christ (656, 662; also, Johnson [77–82] has isolated nine distinct functions).

History of Interpretation

Ancient and Medieval. Generally speaking, early Christian interpretation emphasized spiritualized and symbolic meaning rather than historical and sociological understanding. For Augustine, Cain represented the temporary and corrupt "earthly city," while Adam, Abel, and Seth typified the "heavenly" or "eternal city of God" (ACCSOT 1:111, 116). In the same way, after the tower of Babel episode, the descendants of Abraham continued the legacy of the "city of God" on earth (ACCSOT 1:172).

Sometimes christological prefigurations were attached to certain individuals. For example, Bede taught that the birth of Enoch (as the seventh in the line of descent from Adam) foreshadowed the virgin birth of Jesus the Messiah and the sevenfold gifts of the Holy Spirit that rested in Jesus (ACCSOT 1:118; cf. Rev. 5:6). Augustine did, however, recognize the sociological function of the genealogy in legitimizing an individual or tribe for service in an office, as in the case of Moses and Aaron (ACCSOT 3:37).

At times, the fathers were given over to extensive allegorizing, as in the case of Lot's genealogy (Gen. 19:30–38). Origen equated Lot with the Torah and his wife with the people of Israel who longed for the comforts of Egypt, while Lot's two daughters represented the sins of "vainglory" and "pride." For Irenaeus, the offspring (Moab and Ammon) from Lot's incestuous relations exemplified the two synagogues, Samaria and Judah (ACCSOT 2:80–81).

Finally, the early church fathers sometimes applied numerological interpretations to demonstrate the symbolic affirmation of future fulfillment or the spiritual reality of great theological truths in the OT. Thus Chrysostom connected the number seventy-five (descendants of Jacob who went to Egypt, Gen. 46:27 LXX; seventy in MT and Vulgate) etymologically with the name "Israel" as used in Ps. 75:1 LXX (= 76:1 ET) to show the fulfillment of God's prediction to grow Israel into a great nation.

Reformation. Both Luther (1483–1546) and Calvin (1509–64) read the biblical genealogies at face value, as historical records. The two addressed their historical accuracy and the literary integrity of the Bible in attempts to reconcile apparent discrepancies (e.g., the number of descendants in the genealogy of Jacob, Gen. 46:8–27; see Calvin 1/ii:392; Luther 8:84–88).

Theologically, both affirmed that the genealogies demonstrated God's sovereign and merciful oversight generally of humanity, and especially of his people Israel, in moving history to the Christ event (e.g., Calvin 1/ii:44–45; Luther 2:240). Both perceived evidence of the fulfillment of divine prophecy about the progeny of figures like Jacob and Esau (e.g., Calvin 1/i:253; Luther 1:340). Finally, both emphasized their purpose in identifying Jesus as the "promised Seed" (Calvin 16:80–81; Luther 1:340). More specifically, Calvin interpreted the dual genealogies of Jesus as a twofold verification of his fulfillment of OT prophecies, both as part of the natural lineage of the "son of Adam" (Luke 3:38) and the legal lineage of the "son of Abraham" (Matt. 1:1; Calvin 16:84).

Generally speaking, Luther tended to extract spiritualized meanings more so than Calvin. For example, see his commentary on the glory and success of the "flesh" in the godless lineage of Esau, designed as a foil for the "poor in spirit" character exemplified by the righteous stemming from Isaac through Jacob (Luther 6:310–11; cf. 1:348 on the spiritualizing of Enoch's righteousness). Luther was also highly polemical against the rabbinic interpretation of the OT genealogies (cf. Luther 1:349–50; 8:88–89).

Not long afterward, Archbishop James Ussher published his famous work on biblical chronology (*Annales Veteris et Novi Testamenti* [1650–54]; see Anstey 26–27). Ussher assumed that the genealogies were both historically accurate and complete as linear registers of human descent. Thus, by calculating the number of generations (and assuming a fixed time span per generation), he established a date for the creation of the world at 4004 BCE. Ussher's chronologies were the premodern standard for centuries, largely due to inclusion in the margin of certain editions of the King James Version.

Modern. 1. Post-Enlightenment interpreters tend to assume a skeptical stance. Broadly construed, the reasons for this "hermeneutics of suspicion" are the highly selective and theological nature of the biblical genealogies, and the comparative data provided by ancient Near Eastern parallels and modern sociological and anthropological study (cf. Rendsburg 185). For example, the genealogy of Ezra (Ezra 7:1–5) contains only five links back to Zadok, King David's high priest (a span of five centuries!). Similarly, Exod. 6:14–26 records five generations between Jacob and Moses, whereas 1 Chron. 7:23–27 lists at least ten generations. Matthew's stylized genealogy of Jesus (three sets of names, each with fourteen links) indicates interests more literary and theological than chronological (Matt. 1:17). More than this, Luke traces Jesus' lineage to God himself (Luke 3:38)!

Rendsburg, however, has recently argued for the overall reliability and consistency of genealogies in the Pentateuch (202–4). He has based his conclusions, in part, on the observable pattern of overlapping generations (190–91), so that people of the same age need not be of the same generation. Likewise, an individual may be a descendant of a common ancestor through two different family lines of unequal length (e.g., Jair four generations removed from Judah or five from Joseph, both sons of Jacob; Rendsburg 188; cf. 1 Chron. 2:21). By means of careful internal analysis, Rendsburg has demonstrated that everyone coeval with Moses in Exodus through Joshua is from three to six generations removed from one of Jacob's sons (the exception is Joshua; 193–94; see section "OT Genealogies and Historical Reconstruction" in Satterthwaite 658–59).

2. The emphasis of form criticism on genre identification, literary structure, and social setting has prompted the study of genealogies as a subgenre of biblical narrative. Such study has raised questions concerning issues of orality and fluidity in transmission, and the identification of formal characteristics (see "Definition" above). Overall understanding has been enhanced because form-critical analysis provides an opportunity to study the function of this (sub-)genre in literary and theological context.

3. Various types of literary analysis have also increased appreciation and understanding of genealogies. For example, comparative study of ancient Near Eastern materials reveals that function varies according to circumstances and may be categorized in domestic, political, and religious terms (Chavalas 109). In addition, such literature may combine material from varying time periods, often telescoping several generations, and typically emphasizing legitimation (120–27).

Robinson (601) has noted that the genealogies work to establish the narrative genre of the OT by continuing the theme(s) of the context in which they are embedded (e.g., the genealogy of Seth has links to the creation story; the genealogies of Isaac and Jacob are tied to the Abrahamic covenant). A case in point is the quasi-genealogical Table of Nations (Gen. 10). The purpose is not genealogical. Rather, it serves as a detailed expansion of the statement in Gen. 9:19 (a reference to Noah's three sons as progenitors of all peoples) and a continuation of the divine blessing of Gen. 1:28 (cf. Walton 367, 379).

Beyond this, etymological study of Gen. 1–11 reveals that the names, by means of wordplays, offer an "'onomastic commentary' parallel to the events within the narratives" (Hess, *Studies*, 158). For example, the genealogy of Seth contains names related to ideas like substitution, praise, prayer, and rest, thus supporting the understanding that Seth represents the line of God's promise.

4. Much current NT scholarship sides with the Reformers on the genealogies of Jesus. Matthew portrays Jesus as Son of David, rightful heir to the throne and Israel's Messiah (cf. *DJG* 255). Matthew's Gospel also links the Davidic covenant with the Abrahamic covenant. Luke identifies Jesus not only as the descendant of Abraham, but also in the lineage of Noah, Adam, and ultimately God himself. Luke's Gospel emphasizes the divine sonship of Jesus and his universal ministry as "Son of Man" (cf. *DJG* 256–57). Luke's strategic placement of Jesus' genealogy after his baptism and before his temptation further supports this understanding. Less prominent, but still espoused by some, is the idea that Matthew's genealogy records Jesus as a descendant of David through Joseph, while Luke's reports Jesus as a descendant of David through Mary (see discussion in *NIDNTT* 3:654–56).

Theological Significance

1. The biblical genealogies make subtle but substantial contributions to our understanding

of God and his redemptive plan. For instance, the continuity of his covenantal revelation with successive generations (as the God of Abraham, Isaac, and Jacob) indicates his intention to work with and through humanity (Exod. 3:16). The extensive genealogies spanning many generations verify that God indeed is slow to anger and abounds in love and faithfulness (34:6–7). Implicit in the lists of names, whether belonging to the righteous or to the wicked, is God's providential rule of human activity—overturning evil for good (Gen. 50:20). Ultimately, the genealogies are not about famous or heroic people, but generations of people in relationship with a great God (Pss. 33:11; 102:12; Eph. 3:21).

2. Broadly understood, the genealogies of Genesis attest humanity's fulfillment of the divine commission to "be fruitful and increase in number" (Gen. 1:28). More specifically, the genealogies of Seth, Terah, and Jacob are testimony to God's covenant faithfulness to the Hebrew patriarchs and matriarchs, developing Israel into a great nation (Gen. 12:1–3; 15:5; 26:24; 28:14).

3. The biblical genealogies reflect the culture of the ancient world as well, emphasizing the preservation of individual identity within the group. It is difficult for modern technological societies to appreciate the importance of interrelatedness in agrarian societies, where subsistence living is often the norm. By means of genealogies, however, the ancients placed themselves into this pangenerational solidarity (see Walton, Matthews, and Chavalas 413). Indirectly, this may be a manifestation of the "social likeness" of people made in God's image, a reminder that it is not good to be alone, and an affirmation of cooperation and partnerships for success in life (cf. Gen. 2:18; Eccles. 4:9–12).

4. The process of naming a child was significant in the ancient world. Many times a name reflected circumstances related to birth (e.g., Isaac, Gen. 21:3, 6; Esau and Jacob, Gen. 25:24–26; Jabez, 1 Chron. 4:9). In some instances, the act of naming was an expression of blessing or even a statement of destiny concerning a child's future (e.g., Jesus, Matt. 1:21). Occasionally, a person's name may change to reflect a reversal of fortunes: Jacob, meaning "He grasps the heel," is renamed Israel, "He struggles with God" (Gen. 32:28; 35:10). Naomi, "Pleasant," renames herself Mara, "Bitter" (Ruth 1:20). Many theophoric names (including elements of names of Israel's God like "Jeho-" or "El-") are self-contained statements about God or relationship to God: Jehohanan means "Yah[weh] is gracious," and Elijah,

"My God is Yah[weh]." So instead of serving a primarily historical function, the genealogy often served "to use continuity with the past as an explanation of the current structure and condition of society . . . [and] their current theological situation" (Walton, Matthews, and Chavalas 413).

5. The Chronicler deliberately included Hebrew women and foreigners in his genealogical prologue. This suggests that the writer recognized in Israel's history at least partial fulfillment of God's covenant promise to bless the nations through Abraham's descendants (e.g., 1 Chron. 4:17–19; 7:24; cf. Gen. 12:1–3). In addition, this "inclusivism" may have been both a corrective to the later excesses of the racial "exclusivism" promoted by Ezra and Nehemiah, and an exhortation for Hebrew women to become more active in initiatives for the restoration of postexilic Jerusalem (Hill 100–1, 157–58).

6. The purpose of genealogies generally is both to preserve the ancestral legacy of an individual or family and (or) legitimize an individual or familial claim to some position of leadership or service. The biblical genealogies trace the ancestral legacy of Jesus of Nazareth as both "Son of Man" (or representative human being, Matt. 1:1–16; cf. 12:8, 32, 40) and "son of David" (or rightful heir of the Davidic throne, Matt. 1:1; 20:30–31; cf. Rev. 3:7; 22:16). The Bible's careful identification of Jesus as the Messiah fulfills the "offspring theology" first announced in Gen. 3:15 and then developed through the rest of Scripture. It is no coincidence that biblical genealogies cease in the NT record after the birth of Jesus of Nazareth.

Bibliography

Anstey, M. *Chronology of the Old Testament*. Kregel, 1973; Brown, R. *The Birth of Messiah*. Doubleday, 1977; Calvin, J. *Calvin's Commentaries*. Reprint, Baker, 1979. Vol. 1, *Genesis*, trans. J. King; Vol. 16, *Harmony of the Evangelists, Matthew, Mark, and Luke*, trans. W. Pringle; Chavalas, M. "Genealogical History as 'Charter': A Study of Old Babylonian Period Historiography and the Old Testament." Pages 103–28 in *Faith, Tradition, and History*, ed. A. Millard et al. Eisenbrauns, 1994; Hasel, G. "The Genealogies of Gen 5 and 11 and Their Alleged Babylonian Background." *AUSS* 16 (1978): 361–74; Hess, R. "The Genealogies of Genesis 1–11 and Comparative Literature." *Bib* 70 (1989): 241–54; idem. *Studies in the Personal Names of Genesis 1–11*. Alter Orient und Altes Testament 234. Neukirchener Verlag, 1993; Hill, A. *1 and 2 Chronicles*. NIVAC. Zondervan, 2003; Hillyer, N. "The Genealogies of Jesus." *NIDNTT* 3:653–60; Huffman, D. "Genealogy." *DJG*: 253–59; Japhet, S. *I and II Chronicles*. OTL. Westminster John Knox, 1993; Johnson, M. *The Purpose of the Biblical Genealogies*. SNTSMS 8. 2d ed. Cambridge University Press, 1988; Lienhard, J., ed. *Exodus, Leviticus, Numbers, Deuteronomy*. ACCSOT 3. InterVarsity, 2001;

Louth, A., ed. *Genesis 1–11*. ACCSOT 1. InterVarsity, 2001; Luther, M. *LWorks*. Vol. 1, *Genesis 1–5*, trans. G. Schick; Vol. 2, *Genesis 6–14*, trans. G. V. Schick; Vol. 6, *Genesis 31–37*, trans. P. Pahl; Vol. 8, *Genesis 45–50*, trans. P. Pahl; Malamat, A. "King Lists of the Old Babylonian Period and Biblical Genealogies." *JAOS* 99 (1968): 163–73; Prewitt, T. "Kinship Structures and the Genesis Genealogies." *JNES* 40 (1981): 87–98; Rendsburg, G. "The Internal Consistency and Historical Reliability of the Biblical Genealogies." *VT* 40 (1990): 185–206; Robinson, R. B. "Literary Functions of the Genealogies of Genesis." *CBQ* 48 (1986): 595–608; Sasson, J. "A Genealogical 'Convention' in Biblical Chronography?" *ZAW* 90 (1978): 171–85; Satterthwaite, P. "Genealogy in the Old Testament." *NIDOTTE* 4:654–63; Sheridan, M., ed. *Genesis 12–15*. ACCSOT 2. InterVarsity, 2002; Walton, J. *Genesis*. NIVAC. Zondervan, 2001; Walton, J., V. Matthews, and M. Chavalas. *The IVP Bible Background Commentary: Old Testament*. InterVarsity, 2000; Wenham, G. *Genesis 1–15*. WBC 1. Word, 1987; Wilson, R. R. "Between 'Azel' and 'Azel': Interpreting Biblical Genealogies." *BA* 42 (1979): 11–22; idem. "Genealogy, Genealogies." *ABD* 2:928–32; idem. *Genealogy and History in the Biblical World*. YNER 7. Yale University Press, 1977.

Andrew E. Hill

General Revelation   *See* Creation; Ethics; Philosophy; Revelation; Science, the Bible and

Genesis, Book of

Introduction

By its very position as the first book of the Bible, Genesis (Greek: "origin") has been the focus of more attention than most other parts of the OT. It sets the scene for the rest of Scripture and is one of the books most quoted in the NT. Genesis orients the Bible reader to study the following books with appropriate assumptions about their context and theology. Its narratives have been an inspiration to countless authors and artists. Even in today's secular West, its stories and themes are still familiar.

But familiarity is no guarantee of interpretative integrity. Texts used out of context are liable to be misunderstood and misused, so here, as elsewhere in this dictionary, the aim is to understand Genesis both as a text of its time and as a key witness in the canon of Holy Scripture.

History of Interpretation

"The early chapters of Genesis had arguably a greater influence on the development of Christian theology than did any other part of the Old Testament" (Louth xxxix). Early Christian writers, following the lead of the NT, drew heavily on the opening chapters of Genesis to explain the doctrines of creation and the fall. The typology

of Christ as the second Adam, who triumphed where the first Adam failed, was very important in patristic theology. Vital too was the understanding of humanity created in the image of God. Though this image was marred in the fall, God's ultimate purpose was its restoration in the new creation.

Symbolism was important in early Christian interpretation of Genesis, but that is not to say that they took the stories allegorically. They were accepted as literal accounts of the origin of the cosmos, just as the patriarchal narratives that follow them were understood historically. The problems posed by modern science did not trouble Christian interpreters till the nineteenth century. The Reformers and their immediate successors continued the same essentially literal approach to Genesis, with less emphasis on the symbolic dimensions of the book. Throughout this time it was assumed that Moses was the author of Genesis.

From the seventeenth century and the dawn of the Enlightenment, however, these traditional views began to be questioned. Spinoza in his *Tractatus theologico-politicus* (1670) suggested that Ezra had compiled the Pentateuch from Mosaic materials. A landmark for the discussion of Genesis was Astruc's *Conjectures on the Memoires Used by Moses to Compile Genesis* (1753), which proposed that Genesis was compiled from several parallel sources. This idea that Genesis and the other books of the Pentateuch were composed of various sources was intensely debated throughout the nineteenth century. Thanks to the brilliant advocacy of Julius Wellhausen in *Prolegomena to the History of Israel* (1878), a form of the documentary hypothesis came to be widely accepted by biblical scholars. This approach distributes Genesis into three main sources, J (Yahwist, 950 BCE), E (Elohist, 850 BCE), and P (Priestly, 500 BCE). These three sources were combined successively, so that Genesis reached its final form in the fifth century BCE, about 800 years after Moses. This entailed a quite skeptical approach to the content of Genesis. The accounts of the patriarchs do not reflect their own historical situation, "but only of the time when the stories about them arose. . . . This later age is here unconsciously projected . . . into hoar antiquity, and is reflected there like a glorified mirage" (Wellhausen 319).

While historical skepticism was battering the patriarchs, scientific discovery was undermining the traditional understanding of Gen. 1–11. Early Christian writers read these chapters more as narrative theology than as history, but nevertheless tended to assume that the chronology of Genesis was credible. But the development of geology indicated that the earth originated much earlier than 4004 BCE, as Archbishop Ussher had supposed in the seventeenth century. This made the interpretation of the genealogies of Gen. 5 and 11 problematic. Further discovery showed that the processes of creation had probably taken many millions of years, not six days. And Darwin's *Origin of Species* (1859) led many to conclude not only that the timescale of Genesis was wrong, but also that its ultimate assertion, "God created the heavens and the earth" (1:1), was misleading. Chance mutation was a sufficient explanation of the diversity of life on earth: the idea of a creator was superfluous and indeed just the superstition of a less-enlightened era.

This dismissal of Genesis and its theology as just the misguided notions of an ignorant age seemed to be confirmed by texts from ancient Nineveh of a flood story similar to Gen. 6–9. G. A. Smith deciphered and announced the Gilgamesh tablet 11 in 1872 and published it the next year. Though Smith was no skeptic, works by him and others led many to regard Gen. 1–11 as just another ancient oriental myth, with no more credibility or authority than the creation myths of any other people. The nineteenth-century intelligentsia concluded that Western science is the source of real truth.

The twentieth century was kinder to Genesis. Although for most of the century the documentary hypothesis with its late dating of the sources reigned supreme, there was a concerted attempt by scholars to find early authentic elements in these sources. Alt and Westermann argued that elements of the promises to the patriarchs went back to very early times. Scholars well-versed in archaeology and comparative Semitics (Albright; Speiser; de Vaux) found many parallels between the names and customs of Genesis and those of early-second-millennium Mesopotamia. This allowed them to argue that the stories of Genesis contain more historical information than their date of composition might have led one to expect. Though more skeptical voices (Van Seters; Thompson) have been raised in the late twentieth century, the archaeological evidence still tends to speak in support of Genesis (Millard and Wiseman).

The discovery of yet more ancient texts paralleling Gen. 1–11 (Sumerian King List, Flood Story, and the Atrahasis epic, among others) has led to the recognition that Genesis is not simply reproducing the ideas of surrounding cultures.

At least at the theological level, it is contesting them fiercely (see below on "The Message of Genesis").

Finally, the last quarter of the twentieth century has witnessed many assaults on the documentary hypothesis (e.g., Whybray), so that it is now widely agreed that a better explanation of the growth of the Pentateuch ought to be found. Meanwhile, a vogue for final-form canonical readings has swept through biblical studies, including work on Genesis. This has bypassed much of the debate about sources and led to scholars asking about the structure and message of the books in their extant form. Though some of this work is driven more by literary concerns than by theological interest, it has often revealed some very instructive points about the theology of the book.

The Message of Genesis

Like many other books, Genesis has suffered from attempts to read its parts separately. This is most obvious among commentators who accept the documentary hypothesis. The Yahwist's (J) love of simple anthropomorphic descriptions of God is contrasted with the Priestly writer's (P) lofty transcendental approach. Whereas P tells of God speaking, in the Elohistic (E) source God tends to reveal himself in dreams. In commentators wedded to this theory of distinct sources, it is unusual to find much attempt to describe the theology of the book as a whole, to see these different emphases in polyphonic harmony as opposed to clashing dissonance.

More traditional readers of Genesis have also been guilty of directing more attention to one portion of the book than another. Christian commentators tend to devote disproportionate attention to Gen. 1–11 because of its importance in NT and later theologies. Jewish readers, on the other hand, are more interested in the stories of the patriarchs because they tell of the origins of the Jewish people and their claim to the land of Israel.

If we are to be fair to the text, however, we must be wary of privileging one part of the book over another section. We should look at individual parts, but it is necessary to integrate the message of one part into the overall picture.

The Structure of Genesis

The coherence of the book is demonstrated by its carefully articulated structure. The opening creation account (1:1–2:3) is followed by ten sections, each headed by the same (*toledoth*) title:

"These are the generations/descendants of" (2:4; 5:1; 6:9; 10:1; 11:10, 27; 25:12, 19; 36:1; "story," 37:2 NRSV). The sections alternate between extended narratives, such as chapters 2–4 and 37–50, and terse genealogies, such as chapters 5 and 36. If extended narratives are compared, such as the career of Abraham (chs. 12–25) alongside that of Jacob (chs. 25–35), certain similarities emerge, suggesting a typological reading. This is particularly evident in the comparison of Adam and Noah, where the latter is clearly a second-Adam figure. Like Adam, he is the father of the whole human race; and like Adam, he sins (9:20–27).

Keywords form another device linking and unifying the book of Genesis. The terms "bless" and "blessing" are used more often in Genesis than in any other book of the Bible. At creation, God blesses birds, fish, humankind, and the Sabbath, but it is preeminently the patriarchs who are blessed. Indeed, Abraham's name contains two of the three consonants in the word "bless" (*barakh*), suggesting that he is the incarnation of blessing. A second key term in Genesis is "seed" or "offspring" (*zera'*), first used of human seed in 3:15 and then frequently in the promises to the patriarchs. The third important word is "land/earth," first occurring in 1:1 and often again in the patriarchal promises.

These keywords tie the introductory eleven chapters to the following stories about the patriarchs. They cluster thickly in 12:1–3: "bless/ing" occurs five times, "land/earth" three times, and the whole passage revolves round the promise of descendants: "a great nation." Genesis 1–11 tells of the disarray between the nations; 12:3 declares that in Abraham all the nations will find blessing. The call of Abraham is the answer to the problems of the world.

The Sections of Genesis

To grasp the message of Genesis more exactly, however, we need to examine the contribution of each section in more detail. It falls into three distinct sections:

1. First Exposition: The Hexaemeron, 1:1–2:3
2. Second Exposition: The Protohistory, 2:4–11:26
3. The Core: The Patriarchs, 11:27–50:26

The opening expositions not only give the background to the core; they also foreshadow its themes.

The Hexaemeron. The magnificent overture tells of God creating the cosmos in six days (hence the Greek title "Hexaemeron," "six days [of creation]") and gives the first exposition of the theology of Genesis. Its first verse, "In the beginning God," mentions not a pantheon but only one God, who takes the initiative and orders the whole of creation. Implicitly, this rules out polytheism, the general belief of antiquity.

Second, this one God is sovereign. There is no fight with competing deities, as in other creation myths. God simply speaks, and there is light, dry land appears, and fish swarm in the sea. This is a God whose word effects what is spoken. The God who spoke in creation is the God who spoke to the patriarchs and who will do what he promised them.

Third, not only is this one God almighty, but also the celestial bodies—such as the sun, moon, and stars, worshiped by much of the ancient world—are merely creatures. Indeed, the significance of the attention given to the creation of these bodies and the dry land is that they are vital for human existence.

Fourth, the Hexaemeron climaxes with the creation of human beings in the image of God. Everything builds to this point, and God himself draws the attention of the rest of creation to it by inviting the heavenly host to watch the creation of the human race: "Let us make man in our image" (1:26). Humankind is not only blessed but also encouraged to propagate: "Be fruitful and multiply" (1:28 NRSV).

Here the contrast with Babylonian thought is again evident. In the Atrahasis epic, the creation of humanity is an afterthought, to supply the gods with food; later the gods regret making humans and therefore curb human fertility. Genesis, on the contrary, sees God supplying human beings with food and encouraging their proliferation.

Finally, the Hexaemeron concludes with God resting on the seventh day, another unique feature of this account. The implication is clear: since human beings are made in God's image, they too should rest on the seventh day. The erratic patterns of ancient pagan festivals and holidays are replaced by a weekly Sabbath, on which not only God rests but also his creatures, humankind and beasts (Exod. 20:8–11; Deut. 5:14), must rest as well. The goal of creation is thus rest and peace, not ceaseless activity: this is a vision reaffirmed in Jacob's blessing (Gen. 49).

The Protohistory. The second exposition, or Protohistory (2:4–11:26), simultaneously reaffirms the ideals of Gen. 1 and explains how the present sin-dominated world emerged. The Garden of Eden was a place of harmony, where a benevolent Creator provided all humankind's needs: water, food, animals, and companionship. First, 1:28 urges humankind to be fruitful and multiply; then, 2:21–25 portrays the archetypal marriage, in which God creates the perfect bride and presents her to Adam. Yet in a world where humanity lacks nothing, Adam and Eve break the one injunction given to them, and their cosmos turns to chaos.

Their relationship of mutual help and companionship turns sour. The harmony between humankind and beast now becomes a deadly struggle: "He shall bruise your head, and you shall bruise his heel" (3:15 RSV). Since the serpent will suffer in the head and the man only in his heel, the text clearly predicts the eventual triumph of man over beast, of humankind over the power of evil; but the focus of the text is on the ongoing violence within creation. Humankind will battle not just with animals, but also with plant life while struggling to grow food rather than weeds (3:18). And the result of it all is death (3:19).

Death comes quickly in chapter 4: Cain kills Abel, and Lamech promises seventy-sevenfold vengeance on those who attack him. Fratricidal strife will characterize the families of the patriarchs too (Jacob-Esau in chs. 25–33, and Joseph in ch. 37). But the avalanche of sin continues in Gen. 3–11, culminating in God's remark that "the earth is filled with violence" (6:11, 13). This state of affairs prompts God to send the flood to wipe out all flesh, both humans and animals.

Again, this is an example of Genesis rejecting the theology of the Near East. The Gilgamesh and Atrahasis epics tell of the gods sending a flood simply because there were too many people making too much noise! In Genesis, however, sin, not pique, motivates the divine judgment. Gilgamesh portrays the gods as scared by the catastrophe they have unleashed and as quite unable to halt it; Genesis presents matters as always under God's sovereign control. When God remembered Noah, the flood started to subside (8:1).

The flood is portrayed as a great act of decreation. Not only are all living creatures destroyed, but the water also covered the earth, just as it did before God declared, "Let the dry land appear" (1:2, 9 RSV). This act of decreation is followed by an act of re-creation. Once again, the dry land appears, plants and trees are seen, and the animals and Noah leave the ark to repopulate the earth. Indeed, like Adam and Eve, Noah is told to "be fruitful and multiply" (8:17; 9:1, 7 RSV). He is the new Adam, who by his obedience and

sacrifice has transformed divine wrath into mercy (8:21; cf. 6:5–6).

Unfortunately, Noah, the one perfectly righteous man, also falls (9:20–21), and his sin is compounded by his son's behavior (cf. Cain). So the world enters a downward spiral again, which culminates in another universal act of judgment at the Tower of Babel (11:1–9).

The Patriarchs. The stories of the patriarchs (Gen. 12–50) are five times as long as the opening chapters of the book. This clearly shows where the author's interests lie: he wants to trace the origins of Israel and the twelve tribes. However, he wants to show more than that. He is putting forward the call of Abraham and his offspring as the answer to the problems of humankind set out in Gen. 3–11. The promises in 12:1–3 are more than a conglomeration of keywords such as "blessing"; they declare God's intention to deal with the effects of sin on the human race.

There are four elements to the promises in Gen. 12 and following chapters. First, a land is promised (12:1, 7; 13:14–17). Second, this land will be inhabited by numerous descendants of Abraham (12:2; 13:15–16; 17:4–6). Third, Abraham and his descendants will enjoy a special covenant relationship with God (12:3; 17:4–13). Fourth, through Abraham and his descendants all the families of the earth will be blessed (12:3; 18:18; 22:18). A close reading of all the promise passages shows how the promises develop each time they are repeated. These repetitions make the promises more detailed and specific: "a land" (12:1) becomes "this land" (12:7) and "all the land . . . forever" (13:15). Similar developments are discernible in the other elements of the promise.

The promises are so central to the message of Genesis that David Clines (29) is right in defining the theme of the Pentateuch: "the partial fulfillment—which implies the partial non-fulfillment—of the promise to or blessing of the patriarchs." Nearly all the episodes in Gen. 12–50 may be related to these promises. The patriarchs gradually acquire land rights in Canaan (21:22–33; 23:1–20; 33:19). Slowly and with difficulty they have children (21:1–7; 25:21; 30:1). God's blessing is evident in his protection of the patriarchs despite their folly (12:10–20; 20:1–18; 28:1–22; 34:1–35:5). Finally, through them some foreigners are blessed (14:15–24; 20:17–18; 21:22–24; 39:3–23; 47:13–25). As Clines observes, the fulfillment of these promises within the book of Genesis is but partial: subsequent books of the Pentateuch show a yet more complete fulfillment, and it is not until the book of Joshua that the Israelites eventually acquire the land. Running through the story line is openness to the future, a mood alternating between hope and disappointment.

The promises announce God's solution to the problems painted so graphically in Gen. 3–11. They also reaffirm his original intentions for creation. Abraham, like Noah before him, is a second-Adam figure. Adam was given the Garden of Eden; Abraham is promised the land of Canaan. God told Adam to be fruitful and multiply; Abraham is assured that God will make his descendants as numerous as the dust of the earth (13:16) and the stars of heaven (15:5). In Eden, God walked with Adam and Eve; Abraham is told to walk before God and be perfect (3:8; 17:1; cf. 6:9). Through his obedient and faithful response to these promises, the promise is turned into a divine oath guaranteeing its ultimate fulfillment (22:16–18; cf. 50:24).

The length and detail of the patriarchal narratives show that the origin of Israel and the twelve tribes is the chief concern of Genesis. However, this analysis of the promises and their relationship to the story line shows that Israel's special relationship with God—and through that relationship their connection with land and to the nations—is even more important. It justifies Israel's claim to the land: God promised it to them, and the Canaanites forfeited their right to it through their misbehavior (Gen. 19).

However, a subsidiary theme is particularly apparent in the second half of the book. The two longest stories are about feuds between Jacob and Esau in chapters 25–33 and between Joseph and his brothers in 37–50. Fratricidal strife is also prominent in the Cain and Abel episode of the Protohistory (4:1–16). There is no resolution of the conflict in chapter 4; indeed, the situation degenerates until the whole earth is filled with violence (6:11, 13). But in the case of the later patriarchs, there are quite different endings. Both stories present moving scenes of reconciliation. Esau runs to meet Jacob and throws his arms around him. Joseph declares he has forgiven his brothers: "You meant evil against me, but God meant it for good. . . . So do not fear; I will provide for you and for your little ones" (33:4; 50:20–21 RSV). On a number of occasions Abraham and Isaac act as peacemakers in disputes (13:8–10; 26:17–33).

In all these episodes the patriarchs are depicted as being anxious to make peace and forgive past wrongs. This goodwill shines all the more brightly when set against the unrepentant callousness of Cain and Lamech. The experience of the patriarchs, on the other hand, suggests that forgiveness and reconciliation within families and between nations is not only possible but also desirable. It is an appeal to its readers to forgive and make up with their enemies, whether they be close relatives or people of other races, for it is by so doing that the fulfillment of the promise comes that "through your offspring all nations on earth will be blessed" (22:18).

Genesis in the Canon

As the first book of the Hebrew and Christian canon, Genesis inevitably occupies a most important place. It sets the tone and agenda for the rest of Scripture. The book sets out in clear and simple terms some of the basic affirmations of the Bible. Direct allusion and quotation from it are rare in the OT, but its ideology is pervasive. In the NT direct quotation from it is quite frequent, and its ideas are treated as even more fundamental than the law.

Within the OT canon it heads the first section, the Torah, which is often translated as "the Law." But this English term is too narrow a rendering of the Hebrew: "Instruction" would be better. The narratives of Genesis are profoundly instructive: they explain the nature of God, the role of humankind, God's ideals for human behavior, and so on. Similarly, in the following books of the Pentateuch, it is not just the laws that instruct, but also the narratives in which the laws are given.

There is a particularly close relationship between Genesis and the next four books of the canon: Genesis gives essential background information for readers of Exodus to Deuteronomy. Without Genesis the plot of Exodus to Deuteronomy would be difficult to follow. In particular, the frequent references to the patriarchs and the promises made to them would be most obscure. However, it is difficult to define the relationship between the books of the Pentateuch more decisively.

Exodus to Deuteronomy does look like a biography of Moses. Exodus 2 tells of his birth, and Deut. 34 of his death, while in between he is the most important human character in the story. But Genesis seems almost superfluous to a biography of Moses. On closer reading more connections emerge between Genesis and the following books. The promises to the patriarchs constitute the foundation of Moses' ministry (Exod. 3:6–22). Other experiences of the patriarchs foreshadow episodes in Moses' life. For instance, Abraham's expulsion from Egypt is described in terms suggesting that it was like the exodus. The patriarchal encounters with their future brides at wells prefigure Moses' meeting with his future wife (Gen. 12:20–13:3; 24:15–28; 29:1–14). These features make Genesis more than mere background to the life of Moses: they show his continuity with Israel's founding fathers.

In other ways Genesis sheds light on the teaching of the later books and complements them. Sacrifice figures quite importantly in Exodus to Deuteronomy, and in Genesis the patriarchs are depicted as offering sacrifice at various turning points in their careers. Furthermore, the sacrifices of Cain and Abel, Noah, and Isaac (Gen. 4; 8; 22) serve to teach key principles of sacrifice through narrative, just as the later books of the Law make similar points through precept. Genesis 1 teaches monotheism: the later laws insist that Israelites may worship only "the LORD." Genesis 2 sets out the Pentateuch's approach to relations between the sexes: passages such as Lev. 18 and 20 and Deut. 22 show how these ethical principles apply in some controversial situations.

Themes and personalities from Genesis reappear in many parts of Scripture. Psalms celebrate creation (e.g., 104), lament the sinfulness of God's people (e.g., 106), and retell the patriarchal story (e.g., 105). The same themes reappear in the prophets, who also occasionally mention the patriarchs (Isa. 41:8; Hos. 12). The whole book of Ecclesiastes is a reflection on the state of humankind after the fall, which has made death universal and inevitable (Gen. 3:19).

The NT's debt to Genesis is also huge. In defining his views on marriage, Jesus appeals to Gen. 1:27 and 2:24 (Matt. 19:5). In a similar way Paul uses Gen. 3 to explain the nature of sin and to develop his doctrine of Christ as the second Adam (Rom. 3; 5; 7). Several writers hold up Abraham as a model of faith and obedience (Rom. 4; Heb. 11:17–22; James 2:21–23). And the Bible ends with Revelation's vision of the new Jerusalem, some of whose most notable features—a river, tree of life, gold, and jewels—all hark back to the original Garden of Eden (Rev. 21:1–22:5).

Genesis and Theology

The pervasive influence of Genesis on the rest of Scripture and on early Christian theology has already been mentioned, and it can hardly be explored further here. Suffice it to say that the themes of Genesis are both fundamental and central to biblical theology. That there is but one sovereign God, who created the world and continues to rule it by his power, is apparent from Gen. 1

and is foundational to the whole of Scripture and the theologies that have sprung from it.

Also apparent in the early chapters of Genesis is God's concern for humankind. Inverting the beliefs of the ancient world that humans were designed to supply the gods with food, Genesis declares that God provides both the human and the beast with food. His concern for human well-being is also apparent in Gen. 2. This divine care for God's creatures runs through the OT and in the NT climaxes in the incarnation.

Contrasting with the immorality of ancient deities and the permissiveness of modern gods, however, the God of Genesis is stern in his moral demands. Humanity's sinfulness and particularly its violence lead to three massive acts of judgment: the flood, the scattering of the nations at Babel, and the destruction of Sodom. The rest of Scripture affirms God's moral character: "You are of purer eyes than to see evil and cannot look on wrong" (Hab. 1:13 AT). This divine intolerance of sin is at once both the hope of the world and its greatest problem. It is its hope, in that God will not permit evil ultimately to triumph. It is its greatest problem: Genesis shows that even the most righteous are liable to sin, with disastrous consequences.

Yet Genesis looks forward in hope; the promise to the patriarchs comes to its climax: "In you all the families of the earth shall be blessed" (12:3 NRSV). The book affirms that the offspring of Abraham will ultimately bruise the serpent's head. From pre-Christian times this verse (3:15) has rightly been read messianically. The grim realism of Genesis about the present human condition is lightened by the firm hope of redemption in the future.

Finally, through its accounts of forgiveness and reconciliation in chapters 33 and 50, Genesis points the way forward for human societies. It anticipates our Lord's demand that we should forgive our enemies and demonstrate our discipleship by loving one another.

See also Patriarchal Narratives

Bibliography

Alt, A. "The God of the Fathers." In *Essays on Old Testament History and Religion*. Blackwell, 1966; Brueggemann, W. *Genesis*. Interpretation. John Knox, 1982; Calvin, J. *Commentary on Genesis*. 2 vols. 1554, ed. and trans. J. King. Calvin Translation Society, 1847, 1965. Reprint, Banner of Truth Trust, 1975; Cassuto, U. *A Commentary on the Book of Genesis*. 2 parts. Magnes, 1961–64; Clines, D. J. A. *The Theme of the Pentateuch*. JSOT, 1978; Dalley, S. *Myths from Mesopotamia*. Oxford University Press, 1989; Driver, S. R.

The Book of Genesis. WC. Methuen, 1904; George, A. *The Epic of Gilgamesh*. Penguin, 2000; Gunkel, H. *Genesis*. 3d ed. Göttinger Handkommentar zum Alten Testament. Vandenhoeck & Ruprecht, 1910; Hamilton, V. *The Book of Genesis*. 2 vols. NICOT. Eerdmans, 1990–95; Hartley, J. *Genesis*. NIBCOT. Hendrickson/Paternoster, 2000; Kitchen, K. *The Bible in Its World*. Paternoster, 1977; Louth, A., ed. *Genesis 1–11*. ACCSOT 1. InterVarsity, 2001; Millard, A., and D. Wiseman, eds. *Essays on the Patriarchal Narratives*. InterVarsity, 1980; Moberly, R. W. L. *The Old Testament of the Old Testament*. Fortress, 1992; Rad, G. von. *Genesis*, trans. J. Marks. Rev. ed. OTL. SCM, 1972; Speiser, E. A. *Genesis*. AB 1. Doubleday, 1964. 3d ed., 1979; Van Seters, J. *Abraham in History and Tradition*. Yale University Press, 1975; Vaux, R. de. *The Early History of Israel*. 2 vols. Darton, Longman & Todd, 1978; Wellhausen, J. *Prolegomena to the History of Ancient Israel*. 1878. Meridian, 1957; Wenham, G. *Genesis*. 2 vols. WBC. Word, 1987–94; idem. *Pentateuch*. Vol. 1 of *Exploring the Old Testament*. SPCK, 2003; idem. *Story as Torah*. T&T Clark, 2000; Westermann, C. *Genesis*, trans. J. Scullion. 3 vols. SPCK/Fortress, 1984–86; Whybray, R. N. *The Making of the Pentateuch*. JSOT, 1987; Williamson, P. *Abraham, Israel and the Nations*. Sheffield Academic Press, 2000; Young, D. *The Biblical Flood*. Eerdmans, 1995.

Gordon J. Wenham

Genre

Wellek and Warren say: "Genre should be conceived, we think, as a grouping of literary works based, theoretically, upon both outer form (specific meter or structure) and upon inner form (attitude, tone, purpose—more crudely, subject and audience)" (221). This definition, however, is hotly contested in today's postmodern climate. The current debate centers on whether it is descriptive or prescriptive. Does it provide rules for interpreting a work or merely describe what some works have in common? If it is only descriptive, it cannot function as a category for understanding a literary creation.

History of the Discipline

Plato took a descriptive approach, identifying two types—drama (with action) and epic (centering on people). Aristotle demurred, defining genre as mimesis, or imitation, and arguing that each (comedy, tragedy, epic) was to be interpreted accordingly. The Roman poet Horace went further, arguing that each had interpretative laws governing it (with eight genres—comedy, tragedy, epic, lyric, pastoral, satire, elegy, epigram). For the next several centuries the Platonic view dominated, with some exceptions such as Martin Luther, who built on Aquinas to develop the idea of *sensus literalis*, arguing that a statement can be understood literally on the basis of its generic context. In the neoclassical period (seventeenth–eighteenth centuries), Aristotle was rediscovered, and the view of genre as mimesis came to the fore. Prescriptive laws developed, but they on the whole were arbitrary, and the Romantic period revolted and considered each work an autonomous piece of art in process of becoming. Thus, many abolished all generic classifications.

The tension between the descriptive and the prescriptive has continued to the present and parallels the development of hermeneutical theory. Ricoeur ("Hermeneutics," 112–28) sees three periods: (1) a classificatory approach (classical period); (2) an epistemological understanding following Schleiermacher and Dilthey (nineteenth to early twentieth centuries); (3) an ontological approach, from Heidegger through Gadamer to the present. Representing the classical understanding have been the New Critics (seeing genre as a formal category), literary scholars such as E. D. Hirsch (calling for an "intrinsic genre" in every work that guides interpretation), and John Searle (whose speech-act theory calls for the interpreter to allow the work to guide the interpretation), as well as most evangelical approaches. The autonomous view is upheld by recent schools such as deconstruction and reader-response criticism, which state that genres intermix and cannot be classified (Derrida).

Genre as Classification, Epistemology, and Ontology

The solution to the debate is to recognize that genre contains all three dimensions: it classifies a literary work, is part of the process of coming to understanding (epistemology), and develops a literary world into which one enters (ontology). In literary circles there is also a growing realization that generic categories change on the basis of periods of literary interest. Aune speaks of "the necessity of a diachronic, or historical, study of generic types in addition to a consideration of their internal or external form" ("Problem," 9). The genre of various biblical works, such as apocalyptic, must be determined by the characteristics discovered through meticulous study of the many Jewish apocalyptic writings of 200 BCE–100 CE. Baird notes five criteria for a generic type, characteristics that (1) set it apart from other generic types, (2) recur with enough frequency to distinguish it from others, (3) form a logically coherent pattern within the set, (4) persist in writings before and after the time of writing, and (5) contain a similar style, language, and content (387–88).

The epistemological aspect is identified by Gerhart, who introduces the reader into the process via four aspects: the text determines meaning (Hirsch), leading to a fusion of past and present as the reader is placed within a process of tradition (Gadamer), resulting in a new reality structured by a number of texts (Todorov), thus allowing the reader to produce an individual work from the text (Ricoeur). This of course leads to a polyvalent view of meaning, as each reader constructs his/her own understanding. Here we move into the ontological dimension, in which writing as discourse becomes an event that is autonomous from the author and takes on a life of its own. It develops its own "life-world" and invites the reader to enter that world and unite with the text (Ricoeur, "Distanciation"). Thus, genre is no longer a prescriptive system but simply the matrix that guides interpreters in constructing their own worlds of meaning.

Yet one wonders if these opposed poles are the final word. Gerhart ("Diagnostics," 145–53) provides a bridge from the subjectivist to the objectivist aspects via three stages of interpretation: (1) An initial reflective awareness of the text occurs. (2) Possible meanings (polysemy) are sifted as the interpreter verifies the more likely and constructs the sense and meanings of the text. (3) This opens up new vistas of meaning as the text becomes a model "in front of" the reader. In doing so, she sets Hirsch and Ricoeur side by side. Hirsch uses Wittgenstein's concept of "language-games" to separate meaning (the classification side) from significance (the epistemological and ontological sides) and sees both as valid aspects of interpretation. Vanhoozer (337–50) also weds the three dimensions by calling genre "a rule-governed form of social behavior" (following Searle). Genre as communicative act demands competence in the language-games of the various literary types, and understanding can come only as the reader uses the proper rules according to the sociohistorical location of the literary work. These rules lead to a discovery of the life-world of the text and guide the reader into that textual world. Thus "the concept of genre . . . describes the illocutionary act *at the level of the whole*, placing the parts within an overall unity that serves a meaningful purpose" (341, italics his). In this way genre not only classifies the form but also allows one to experience the world and to connect in a new way with existence. Thereby the different forms of the Bible can not only be understood but also encountered as divine truth. In them God's voice can be experienced anew.

Bibliography

Aune, D. *The New Testament in Its Literary Environment*. Westminster, 1987; idem. "The Problem of the Genre of the Gospels: A Critique of C. H. Talbert's *What Is a Gospel?*" In *Studies of History and Tradition in the Four Gospels*. Gospel Perspectives 2, ed. R. T. France and D. Wenham. JSOT, 1981; Baird, J. A. "Genre Analysis as a Method of Historical Criticism." *SBL Proceedings 1972*. Vol. 2; Cross, A. "Genres of the New Testament." Pages 402–11 in *Dictionary of New Testament Background*, ed. C. A. Evans and S. Porter. InterVarsity, 2000; Derrida, J. "Law of Genre." *Glyph* 7 (1980): 207–9; Genette, G. "Genres, 'Types,' Modes." *Poétique* 8 (1977): 389–421; Gerhart, M. "Generic Studies: Their Renewed Importance in Religious and Literary Interpretation." *JAAR* 45 (1977): 309–25; idem. "Paul Ricoeur's Notion of 'Diagnostics': Its Function in Literary Interpretation." *JR* 56 (1976): 137–56; Hirsch, E. D. *The Aims of Interpretation*. University of Chicago Press, 1976; Osborne, G. "Genre Criticism—Sensus Literalis." *TJ* 4 (1983): 1–27; Ricoeur, P. "The Hermeneutical Function of Distanciation." *Philosophy Today* 17 (1973): 129–41; idem. "The Task of Hermeneutics." *Philosophy Today* 17 (1973): 112–28; Searle, J. *Speech Acts*. Cambridge University Press, 1969; Thiselton, A. *New Horizons in Hermeneutics*. Zondervan, 1992; Vanhoozer, K. *Is There a Meaning in This Text?* Zondervan, 1998; Wellek, R., and A. Warren. *Theory of Literature*. Harcourt, Brace & World, 1956.

Grant R. Osborne

Geography

The geographical investigation of a region typically explores that place either through the lens of physical geography or through the lens of human geography. Physical geography is concerned with the surface of the earth and the processes that change it, pursuing questions related to the geology, topography, hydrology, climate, plants, and animals associated with the region. By contrast, human geography is primarily concerned with the way humans are influenced by the realities of physical geography and the ways they interact with it. This type studies urbanization patterns, use of the land, economic advantages, politics, and transportation within a region.

Because the events and people of the Bible are intimately linked to time and place, both the realities of physical and human geography find their way into its pages. This occurs at several levels. First of all, every inspired author of the OT and NT lived and worked under the realities of a given place. That means that their setting influenced all their daily habits and their perspective on matters such as water, wildlife, and travel. Since this geographical worldview was intimately connected to the way they thought and wrote, we will have a clearer understanding of their perspective on matters like dew and rain when we understand the authors' experience with dew and rain in their cultural context. Second, the events on which these authors reported were also greatly influenced by their geographical setting: for example, the location of battles, the motivation for those battles, and the lines of retreat. Our understanding of those events will grow with our understanding of geography. Third, there are times when the biblical authors intentionally bring matters of geography into the communication process in order to artfully manipulate both the message received by the reader and the reader's emotional response to it. To miss the significance of the geography used in those texts is to miss a portion of the message the author is trying to deliver.

Because the Bible is affected by geography in these three ways, specialists in the land of the Bible carefully pursue these matters to enhance their understanding of the events recorded and the message associated with those events. This pursuit may take one of two forms: historical geography or literary geography. Historical geography inquires into both the physical and cultural geography of the Bible lands to assess its impact on the history and culture of the events reported. Edward Robinson (1838) did the first such scientific investigation of the Holy Land. This work was complemented by the explorations of William F. Lynch (1849), the writings of William F. Thompson (1883), and the monograph by George Adam Smith (1936). Similar investigation of historical geography has been advanced in our own time through scholars like Yohanan Aharoni, Barry Beitzel, Nelson Glueck, Efraim Orni, Elisha Efrat, and Carl Rasmussen.

Historical geography has tirelessly pursued the placement of cities and regions on the map while answering questions that only the study of geography might answer for us. Consider two such examples. In Judg. 4, we find that Jabin, the king of Hazor, has been oppressing the Israelites cruelly for twenty years. He was able to establish and hold this power both at the Lord's indulgence and through the use of nine hundred iron chariots. When the children of Israel turn from their idolatry, the Lord designs a battle plan that will eliminate those chariots and remove Jabin's influence from the region. The Israelite general who is to carry out that plan is named Barak. But when Deborah carries the Lord's instructions to Barak, he responds with stammering hesitation, "If you will go with me, I will go; but if you will not go with me, I will not go" (Judg. 4:8 NRSV). With God's plan in hand, why would Barak hesitate

to advance? The answer to the question lies in the geography reported in the text. Barak was instructed to muster the Israelite forces on Mt. Tabor. This prominent mountain rises dramatically to tower eight hundred feet above the level floor of the Jezreel Valley. Since chariot forces charging down this valley would be unable to mount an attack up this rising terrain, it appears to be the perfect place for infantry to wait for the intruding chariots. But the Lord's instructions call for Barak to leave this natural citadel and charge the advancing chariots. This plan, which defied logic but not faith, causes Barak to hesitate. And when the Lord brings a miraculous rainstorm that floods the plain, disabling the chariots before the charging infantry, logic joins faith in seeing this as a masterful plan. The divine plan requires Barak to step out in faith. His hesitation is directly related to the geography of God's plan and the lack of faith he displays upon hearing it.

Another example may be found in Mark 4:35–41, where a violent windstorm nearly takes the lives of the disciples as they attempt to cross the Sea of Galilee. Apparently, Jesus has been seeking some solitude after a time of intense teaching and ministry on the northwest shore. At evening, Jesus invites the disciples to join him in taking a boat from the west shore of the lake to the east. Along the way, they are met by a furious squall that threatens to swamp the boat. Given the fact that a number of these men are professional fishermen on this very lake, why would they have agreed to set off in weather conditions that could put them in such peril? The answer to that question may again be found in geography. A variety of winds can make their influence felt on the Sea of Galilee. Some are quite predictable; others are not. The *sharquia* (Arabic for "east") wind is an unexpected downdraft that develops in the lake region during the evening hours when the temperature difference between the surface of the lake and the 1,300-foot ridges above the eastern shore is just right. As heat radiates away from those ridges, the cold air from above can accelerate down the slopes to replace the warmer air at the lake's surface. These winds can reach sixty miles per hour, rousing the placid surface into a frothing bath with six-foot waves. Since this wind typically occurs under a clear evening sky only when temperature differences are just right, there is no way the disciples can see it coming. That is why they do not hesitate to follow Jesus into the boat that will become the setting for the dramatic miracle that closes the story.

A second way in which geography plays a role in interpreting the Bible is through what we call literary geography. This form of literary analysis is new to biblical studies but has had a longer history within secular literary analysis under the guise of local-color writing and regionalism. This form of geographical inquiry leans heavily on the insights of the physical and human geographer but then pursues the literary function of those references in the text. A close reading demonstrates that biblical authors and poets strategically use, reuse, and nuance geography in order to influence the emotions, understanding, and perceptions of their readers. Consequently, Bar-Efrat concludes, "places in the narrative are not merely geographical facts, but are to be regarded as literary elements in which fundamental significance is embodied" (194).

The familiar story of David and Goliath (1 Sam. 17) provides an example of geography at work as a literary mechanism. Throughout the book the author is working aggressively at many levels to elevate the reader's perception of David while allowing the stock of Saul to fall. The story of David and Goliath plays an important role in shaping those perspectives, and the geography used in this story strongly influences the way we read this event. The very first words of the narrative occupy the reader with the geographical setting of this classic battle. The Philistine army has gathered at Socoh in Judah, encamped at Ephes Dammim, between Socoh and Azekah, while Saul and his army have camped in the eastern portion of the Elah Valley (17:1). A careful, literary reading of this geography illustrates that the detail and precision are designed to influence the reader's perception of all that follows.

The battle will occur within the Judean Shephelah. The Shephelah lies just to the west of the Judean Highlands, separating the Israelites and the Philistines. Topographically, the Shephelah consists of a series of low ridges and wide U-shaped valleys oriented on an east-west axis. These unassuming valleys are critical both to the economy and defense of Saul's kingdom. This region is noted for its plentiful grain fields and sycamore trees. But what is more, these valleys are the buffer zone that separates Israel from the Philistines. The nation that controls these valleys enjoys both economic advantages and a higher level of national security. As the story begins, the reader is provided with troubling news. The Philistines have made a significant incursion into the Elah Valley, penetrating all the way to Socoh. Earlier, when the Israelites asked Samuel for a king, they may have had just such a scenario in mind. They asked for a king who would go out before them and fight their battles (1 Sam. 8:20). If Saul is going to show his worth, the geography suggests that this is the time to do it. But as the reader meets Saul in this story, we find him to be anything but that kind of leader. Goliath calls for a man to fight with him; Saul is dismayed and terrified, failing to inspire his soldiers to action even in the face of this national crisis (17:11). But David is all that Saul is not. Once he arrives on the scene, things change quickly. David dispatches Goliath and immediately the Israelite army surges forward, chasing the Philistines out of the Elah Valley and plundering their camp on the way. Given any other setting, this would have been a remarkable military victory over the Philistines. But this battle acquires the Elah Valley for the kingdom of Israel, securing both economic and military advantages for the victor. Hence, it is no wonder that David is heralded as a national hero at the expense of King Saul. Thus, the further demise of Saul and the rise of David are enhanced in this story through the careful and strategic use of geography in the storytelling process.

Another example of the literary use of geography is found in the book of Genesis, where the author uses "drought" to compare and contrast the faith of Abraham, Isaac, and Jacob. The life and family of each is threatened by the arrival of a drought: Abraham (Gen. 12:10–20), Isaac (26:1–7), and Jacob (46:1–7). This form of famine was a terrible tragedy for those living in the rain-dependent reaches of the promised land. A drought would typically cause the residents of Canaan to migrate toward greener pastures. But there is more to these stories than the inconvenience of migration, for each man is confronted with the question of whether to leave the promised land. Although these narratives are widely separated from one another in the book of Genesis, careful structuring of each story as well as the issue of drought invites the reader to compare and contrast the responses of these three men to this challenge. In the end, Jacob is the one who demonstrates the highest level of spiritual commitment to the divine plan. He literally has to be pushed out of the promised land by the Lord in a theophany at Beersheba. By contrast, Abram demonstrates the lowest level of spiritual commitment. The narrative shows him rushing from the land with little thought for the consequences to the promises he had received earlier in the chapter. In the end, the author of Genesis uses famine both to link these three stories, to create

255

tension in the plot, and to contrast the spiritual commitment of these three men—yet another example of geography's importance for proper theological interpretation of Scripture.

See also Earth/Land

Bibliography

Aharoni, Y. *The Land of the Bible: A Historical Geography,* trans. A. Rainey. Westminster, 1979; Bar-Efrat, S. *Narrative Art in the Bible.* JSOT Bible and Literature Series 17. Almond, 1989; Beck, J. "Faith in the Face of Famine: The Narrative-Geographical Function of Famine in Genesis." *Journal of Biblical Storytelling* 11 (2002): 58–66; idem. "Geography and the Narrative Shape of Numbers 13." *BSac* 157 (2000): 170–79; idem. "Geography as Irony: The Narrative-Geographical Shaping of Elijah's Duel with the Prophets of Baal (1 Kings 18)." *Scandinavian Journal of the Old Testament* 18 (2003): 291–302; idem. "The Storyteller and Narrative Geography." Pages 165–96 in *Translators as Storytellers.* Studies in Biblical Literature 25. Peter Lang, 2000; idem. "Why Did Moses Strike Out? The Narrative-Geographical Shaping of Moses' Disqualification." *WTJ* 65 (2003): 135–41; Beitzel, B. *The Moody Bible Atlas of Bible Lands.* Moody, 1985; Glueck, N. *The River Jordan.* McGraw Hill, 1968; Lynch, W. *Narrative of the United States' Expedition to the Jordan River and the Dead Sea.* Lea & Blanchard, 1849; Orni, E., and E. Efrat. *Geography of Israel.* 4th ed. Israel Universities Press, 1980; Rasmussen, C. *Zondervan Atlas of the Bible.* Zondervan, 1989; Robinson, E. *Biblical Researches in Palestine and the Adjacent Regions 1838 and 1852.* 3 vols. Universitas Booksellers, 1970; Smith, G. *The Historical Geography of the Holy Land.* Harper & Row, 1966; Thompson, W. *The Land and the Book.* 3 vols. T. Nelson & Sons, 1881.

John A. Beck

Gnosticism

Sometimes used in reference to modern thinkers, "Gnosticism" as a historical term is associated with various heterodox sects that emerged between the second and fifth centuries CE. Some of these sects proved to be of little lasting consequence, others posed serious challenges to the faith of the church, and still others gave way to such important religious movements as Mandaeism and Manichaeism. Reliant on biblical figures and terminology, Gnosticism has sometimes been regarded as a "parasitic religion." The description is aptly ambiguous, for it is often unclear whether a given gnostic sect should be regarded as a variation within Judaism or Christianity, or as a religion in its own right, one that, though building on prior traditions, makes a decisive break from its theological and exegetical heritage. Much of what is commonly considered gnostic seems to reflect an accommodation to the Platonic philosophical orientation of the culture (in this respect, Harnack's edict that Gnosticism represents the "acute hellenization of Christianity" is still apropos) or a radicalization of the demands of the parent religion (resulting most notably in ascetic practices). Both the libertine and ascetic expressions of Gnosticism are rooted, paradoxically, in the common vision of an ontologically debased cosmos.

Sources

For years the most important witnesses to the gnostic teachers have been the church fathers. In this connection, Irenaeus's *Against the Heresies,* written toward the end of the second century, is most important. Other fathers worthy of mention are, in the West, Tertullian (e.g., *The Prescription against the Heretics*) and Hippolytus (*Refutation of All Heresies*); in the East, Clement of Alexandria (*Stromateis*), Origen (*Commentary on the Gospel of John*), and Epiphanius of Salamis (*Panarion*). A handful of gnostic texts have also been preserved in Askew Codex, Bruce Codex, and Berlin Codex. Following the discovery of the Nag Hammadi codices in 1946, the pool of sources has widened considerably. Even more significantly, the Nag Hammadi library has allowed scholars to examine the Gnostics on their own terms and not simply from the testimony of their opponents.

Definition

The most widely quoted definition of "Gnosticism" occurs in a statement prepared at the 1966 Messina Colloquium. Differentiating between "gnosis," which is broadly defined as the "knowledge of divine mysteries reserved for the elite," and "Gnosticism" as a specific phenomenon developing in the second century, the authors of the Messina "Final Document" see the latter as involving

> a coherent series of characteristics that can be summarized in the idea of a divine spark in man, deriving from the divine realm, fallen into this world of fate, birth and death, and needing to be awakened by the divine counterpart of the self in order to be finally reintegrated. Compared with other conceptions of a "devolution" of the divine, this idea is based ontologically on the conception of a downward movement of the divine whose periphery (often called Sophia or Ennoia) had to submit to the fate of entering into a crisis and producing—even if only indirectly—this world, upon which it cannot turn its back. (Bianchi xxvi–xxvii)

While this is adequate as a generalization, methodological objections to this definition have been raised on two levels. In the first place, it is sometimes charged that the Messina document artificially separates second-century Gnosticism from its first-century antecedents. The stipulation that "Gnosticism" was of second-century origin not only may serve to slant subsequent phenomenological analysis of the movement, but also prejudges the question as to its formative influences. Second, although the definition certainly applies to the majority of gnostic teachings, there are important exceptions to the Messina rule. For example, though neither Marcion nor Justin the Gnostic espouse systems of devolution or original divine consubstantiality, both are regularly considered Gnostics.

But a more generalized definition may not be the answer either. For example, Jonas has suggested that Gnosticism simply reflects a soteriological system in which the obtaining of gnosis or knowledge is central. This is hardly useful, for by this definition Judaism, Christianity, and Islam could also count as "gnostic." Thus, the dilemma: on the one side, an overspecific description of "Gnosticism" hazards setting up an uncomfortably narrow Procrustean bed; on the other side, an overly broad definition is in danger of saying at once too much and too little. Perhaps the most useful definition is one that focuses strictly on the characteristically gnostic distinction between the transcendent Deity and the creator-demiurge (cf. Plato, *Timaeus*), the latter being regularly identified with the Creator of Gen. 1–2.

The Gnostic Myth in Outline

Although there is a wide degree of variation in the details of the gnostic myth, a basic outline may be distilled from a representative number of systems. For most Gnostics, humanity is intrinsically good, in fact, consubstantial with the divine. But after being created, humanity falls into a protracted stupor; it forgets its divine origins and is tricked by the malevolent creator into thinking that there is none higher than the creator. Taking pity on humanity, the true God then sends the Redeemer figure down through the heavens in order to reveal knowledge and thereby to awaken the divine spark within humanity. Those who recognize this divine inner spark have secured their redemption, proved themselves among the elect, and transcended the evils of material creation.

Origins

Certainly the most pressing questions in current studies of Gnosticism are those regarding origins: (1) What are the philosophical and religious forces that influenced Gnostic doctrine? (2) In what religious grouping did Gnosticism immediately begin to take shape? To the first question various answers have been offered. Hinduism, Buddhism, Babylonian astral speculation, Iranian mythology, Canaanite religion, Jewish apocalyptic, and Greek mystery religions (to name some) have all been credited at various points for having exerted some kind of influence on Gnosticism. Nor, in the religious ferment of the Hellenistic age, is such a constellation of influences impossible, although some of these theorized backgrounds cancel each other out.

Toward identifying the religious milieu in which Gnosticism arose, the comparative methods employed in the history-of-religions school, which focus on isolated motifs, have proved to be of limited use. More recently, broader comparisons have led to a narrowing of options: pre-Christian Judaism or Christianity. The former was first seriously proposed over a century ago by Friedländer. He points out that Eusebius attests to pre-Christian Jewish philosophers who saw a literal reading of Torah as unnecessary. Philo and Filastrius speak of similar such groups in Alexandria; these also had a developed system of "powers," a strong tendency toward allegorization, and an antinomian stance. Perhaps because much European scholarship of the time was generally disinclined to accept Second Temple Judaism as a formative religious force, these arguments failed to win support for a number of decades. Today, scholars like Quispel, Perkins, and Pearson have vigorously renewed the case for Gnosticism's pre-Christian Jewish origin. The position no doubt receives added support from the Nag Hammadi texts: several writings, for example, the *Apocalypse of Adam* and the *Apocryphon of John*, contain traces of Christian redaction but no evidence that the basic document was anything other than Jewish.

For those who subscribe to the Christian origins of Gnosticism (Yamauchi, Pétrement, Logan), the absence of specifically Christian motifs is no evidence of Jewish origin. The OT was after all the Christians' first Bible. Second, it is argued that the antinomian character of Gnosticism is best understood as an outcome of Christian reflections on law. Finally, a number of stock motifs within Gnosticism (a savior/redeemer figure, realized eschatology, freedom-giving grace) can hardly have had their starting point anywhere else but in Christianity.

Yet some of these arguments that see Gnosticism as strictly a Christian development often seem to presuppose an overly sharp discontinuity between Christianity and Judaism. What is more, the alleged conceptual parallels between the gnostic texts and the NT writings sometimes seem to rely on a dubious and over-Gnosticized reading of the latter. Unavoidably, judgments concerning the origins and nature of Gnosticism are inextricably tied to a (prior) interpretation of the NT, including its cosmology, anthropology, soteriology, and eschatology. To some extent, the present impasse in the question of gnostic origins (and with it the sense that scholars are often speaking past one another) reflects an equally disparate understanding of the nature of early Christianity.

If it is all but impossible to draw a tight and unilinear connection between Gnosticism and its immediate religious context, it is at least possible to explain the emergence of Gnosticism through other categories. There is a good deal of evidence that Gnosticism, at least in its initial form, arose as an interpretive movement that sought to respond to metaphysical and theodicean problems raised by Scripture. Stroumsa and Fossum have convincingly argued that certain Hellenistic Jews, embarrassed by the anthropomorphisms of the Torah, resorted in Platonic fashion to separating the creator god from the Most High God so as to avoid debasing the transcendent Deity. The introduction of the demiurge into the biblical account of creation may also have afforded means of dealing with the question of evil. Without reflecting negatively on the true God, the entrance of sin into the world could thereby be attributed to one who made the less-than-perfect world and was himself morally deficient. On this reconstruction, it is also possible that as those maintaining a demiurgical reading of Genesis came into conflict with the larger community, they continued to galvanize their position so that their portrayals of the demiurge became increasingly negative. So, for example, when in gnostic interpretation the god of Isaiah declares, "Apart from me there is no God" (Isa. 45:5), far from being a statement of the Creator's superiority, the divine assertion only betrays his peevish arrogance and ignorance of transcendent reality. This consistent turning of Scripture on its head, for which the Gnostics are well known, is principally governed by their cosmogony.

If this account of gnostic origins is accurate, then the labeling of gnostic interpretation as "protest exegesis" (Rudolph) risks missing the point. Gnosticism was a protest of sorts, but it was not interested in protest for protest's sake. Instead, it appears that the very first Gnostics were at bottom trying to reconcile the data of Scripture with the philosophical assumptions inherent in their Hellenistic worldview. The resulting synthesis involved not only the development of elaborate mythological systems, but also a thoroughgoing rereading of Scripture. While it is possible, as some suggest, that the rise of this hermeneutical movement was occasioned by a particular social or political crisis (perhaps the failure of the apocalyptic vision and hence a disillusionment with the traditional God of Judaism), this remains only conjecture.

Gnosticism Then and Now

Understanding Gnosticism is an important step toward ascertaining its possible influences on the NT. It has been argued, for example, that Paul's Corinthian opponents adhered to a gnostic-like over-realized eschatology. Gnostic-style dualism has also been said to lie behind the writing of many of the so-called Deutero-Pauline letters (e.g., Colossians, Ephesians); concerns with a particular brand of Gnosticism, docetism, are also apparent in the Johannine corpus (e.g., John 20:27; 1 John 4:2). It remains highly controversial whether and to what degree the earliest church regarded gnostic thought as consistent with normative faith.

By the end of the second century, the church fathers (and rabbis) were eager to refute Gnostic claims. In almost every respect, gnostic teaching stood at odds with emerging orthodoxy. Perhaps there is some truth to Williams's suggestion that it was Gnosticism's thoroughgoing integration of Scripture with prevailing philosophical trends that accounted for its eventual superfluity and demise. Yet the basic ideas of Gnosticism live on to this day, in both conservative and liberal theologies, and in ethical systems that downplay the role of the body and creation. Ancient Gnosticism also anticipates certain strains of modern and postmodern thought. Seeing self-authentication as the means of transcending a hostile universe, Gnosticism has been rightly deemed the forerunner of modern existentialism. It is equally appropriate to compare Gnostic hermeneutics with deconstruction's emphasis on the instability of the linguistic sign: both rely on the metaphysical judgment that creation is fundamentally incoherent. For Gnosticism, existentialism, and deconstructionism alike, salvation/knowledge is obtained individualistically, quite apart from the mediation of communal interpretations and structures.

See also Nag Hammadi

Bibliography

Bianchi, U., ed. *The Origins of Gnosticism*. SHR 12. Brill, 1967; Fossum, J. *The Name of God and the Angel of the Lord*. WUNT 36. Mohr/Siebeck, 1985; Friedländer, M. *Der vorchristliche jüdische Gnosticismus*. Vandenhoeck & Ruprecht, 1898; Grant, R. *Gnosticism and Early Christianity*. Rev. ed. Harper & Row, 1966; Harnack, A. *Geschichte der altchristlichen Literatur bis Eusebius*. 2 vols. Hinrichs, 1893–1904; Jonas, H. *The Gnostic Religion*. 2d ed. Beacon, 1963; King, K. *Images of the Feminine in Gnosticism*. SAC 4. Fortress, 1988; Logan, A. *Gnostic Truth and Christian Heresy*. Clark, 1996; Pearson, B. *Gnosticism, Judaism, and Egyptian Christianity*. SAC. Fortress, 1990; Perkins, P. *The Gnostic Dialogue*. Paulist, 1980; Pétrement, S. *A Separate God*. HarperCollins, 1990; Quispel, G. "Der gnostische Anthropos und die jüdische Tradition." *ErJb* 22 (1953): 195–234; Robinson, J. M. "From Easter to Valentinus (or to the Apostles' Creed)." *JBL* 101 (1982): 5–37; Rudolph, K. *Gnosis*. Harper & Row, 1983; Stroumsa, G. A. G. *Another Seed*. NHS 24. Brill, 1984; Williams, M. A. *Rethinking "Gnosticism."* Princeton University Press, 1996; Yamauchi, E. *Pre-Christian Gnosticism*. Eerdmans, 1973.

Nicholas Perrin

God, Attributes of See God, Doctrine of

God, Doctrine of

What a person believes about God or does not believe about God is of great moment. A. W. Tozer (9) put it powerfully: "The history of mankind will probably show that no people has ever risen above its religion, and man's spiritual history will positively demonstrate that no religion has ever been greater than its idea of God." To seek to understand the biblical ideas of God is no trivial pursuit.

The theological interpretation of the God of Scripture asks normative questions of the biblical deposit. What ought we to believe about God in the light of this portrayal? How ought we to live, given that light? To expect normative answers to such questions assumes an authority of the text and an access to its meaning and an ability to frame its significance in such a way as to bridge the then of the writing and the now of the present reader. A whole cluster of theological terms comes into play to establish the bona fides of such a pursuit: revelation, inspiration, reliability, perspicuity, supremacy, sufficiency, canonicity, and illumination by the Holy Spirit.

God in the Biblical Texts

In the canonical presentation God comes before us in myriad ways. God is the majestic Creator in the creation narrative (Gen. 1:1–2:3), the awesome warrior celebrated in Moses' song (Exod. 15:1–18), the holy God of Leviticus, the righteous God of the proverb (Prov. 20:23), the living God of prophetic claim (Isa. 44:1–20), the heavenly Father of prayer (Matt. 6:7–15), the waiting father in parable (Luke 15:11–32), and the sovereign God of apostolic epistle (Eph. 1:3–12). This list is by no means exhaustive.

With regard to the specifics, the wise course is to follow the Scriptures' own "storied" portrayals of God and thus observe the flow of redemptive history.

The Creator God. The scriptural account begins with God as the majestic Creator of the heavens and the earth (Gen. 1:1–2). Like a king, God says the word and his will is effected. Like a Hebrew worker, a week is the divine rhythm of creation, with six days of labor, and then rest (2:2–3). The created order is good, and with the creation of God's image bearer, very good. The picture is of a number of harmonies—between God and humankind, between man and woman, and between man and woman and other creatures. The primal word is one of blessing (e.g., 1:28). But then comes the rupture and cursing results (e.g., 3:17).

The mystery of evil's appearance is never fully explained. The serpent is like a dark parallel to Melchizedek (i.e., without genealogy). Scripture is non-postulational, not given to theory. It has been up to theologians and philosophers to attempt theodicies (e.g., Irenaeus, Augustine, Leibniz, Hick). The canonical response is to include the story of Job rather than a philosophical treatise. What the biblical account goes on to present is how the good God recovers the creation and fulfills his purposes. Put another way, Scripture is more interested in the survival-of-evil problem than its arrival—"How long, O LORD?" is a frequent question. As in Job, the ending is the key.

The Grieving God. Humankind now lives outside Eden. The divine responses are grief, judgment, and grace (Gen. 6:5–8). A new start is made as Noah and his kin emerge from the flood of judgment (ch. 8). But the declension continues, and Babel represents the nadir (11). Creation needs reclamation. Disorder needs to give way to order. And God has a plan. Importantly, God is portrayed in these events with something analogous to the emotional life of his image bearer. There is divine pathos as A. J. Heschel observed (*Prophets*, 2:3).

The Calling God. God calls Abraham and makes him a promise (12:1–3). The outworking of that promise becomes the spinal column of canonical Scripture. Abraham's name will become a great one, and it has. Some today refer to Judaism, Christianity, and Islam as Abrahamic faiths because of the importance that each places on Abraham as either the paradigmatic man of obedience (Judaism), or the man of faith (Christianity), or the man of submission (Islam).

In addition, a great nation will emerge from Abraham's stock. Through Abraham and his progeny, the whole earth will be blessed. The language of blessing that pertained to the initial creation reappears. The Abraham story will begin a stream of history crucial to the divine project. But as the biblical story line unfolds, the promise comes under threat again and again.

The Redeemer God. The threat to the promise's realization becomes particularly acute during Israel's years in Egypt (Exod. 1–2). With Joseph, Abraham's descendants begin so well in Egypt, but eventually they become an enslaved people. Their oppression by Pharaoh reaches to heaven itself, and God responds by calling Moses to the task of leading Israel to the promised land. God sets his people free. He redeems them from slavery (chs. 3–15). The cluster of events constituting that liberation becomes paradigmatic for so much that follows, whether on view as God's people returning from exile (Isa. 40–55) or as the cross of Jesus (Luke 9:31).

The Gracious and Merciful God. Once beyond Pharaoh's reach, Moses—who led God's people so successfully out of Egypt—asks to see this God's glory (Exod. 33:18). The divine answer comes as close to a systematic articulation of the being and attributes of God as the Scripture provides. God reveals his name, which in effect is a window into the nature and character of the Deity (33:19). He is the gracious and merciful God, the slow-to-anger God, and the forgiving God. However, this God also judges wickedness (34:5–7). This much Moses can know, and yet only the back parts of God are to be seen (33:21–23). There are depths to God that Moses cannot access. This God can only be known on God's own terms, and as the subsequent rendering of God in Leviticus makes plain, approached in worship only on God's own terms.

The One God. The God who created the heavens and the earth, and who is the maker of Israel, has no consort and is part of no pantheon. This is the stand-alone God without rival (Deut. 6:4–5). This was the lesson that God's people had to learn time and time again. So important is this claim that it is to become the heart of Israel's religious pedagogy (6:6–9). A culture shows its values in

what must be passed on to its children. The confession of the oneness of Israel's God is central to its confession of faith and value.

The Triune God. The coming of Jesus requires nothing less than a reconfiguring of the divine name. Disciples are to be baptized now in the one name of God, which is Father, Son, and Holy Spirit (Matt. 28:18–20). The divine oneness—so prominent in the earlier Testament and reaffirmed by Jesus earlier in this very Gospel account—is now seen as complex in its nature (cf. 19:17 and 28:18–20). The story of the one God now involves Father stories, Son stories, and Holy Spirit stories in ways that so overlap as to underline the reality of the oneness and yet preserve internal distinctiveness. And in the case of Jesus, the biblical authors write in such a way as to maintain the reality of his humanity without jettisoning his divinity (as John's testimony shows).

The Forgiving God. The God who forgives is a prominent aspect of the divine name, as noticed in an earlier section. That accent continues in the newer Testament. Jesus commissions his disciples to preach the forgiveness of sins in his name, beginning at Jerusalem but then extending to the ends of the earth (Luke 24:44–47). This emphasis makes little sense unless the scriptural portrayal of God's holiness is given its full gravity.

Moreover, the depths of Christ's achievement on the cross as the God-man cannot begin to be plumbed without an appreciation of how serious is the rupture between God and humanity. A mediator is essential (1 Tim. 2:5–6). The older Testament's sacrificial system was limited in ways that the definitive sacrifice of Jesus surmounts (Hebrews, passim). Jesus is the linchpin in the divine project to reclaim the creation (Col. 1:15–20). Indeed, his resurrection and glorification prefigure the future of the created order (Rom. 8:1–27).

The Consummator God. The resurrection of the God-man and his glorification underline the value of the creation. The groaning creation will be set free (Rom. 8:18–25). The original creation purpose will be effected. God's restored images will reign in a renewed heavens and earth (Rev. 20–22). The scriptural story moves in its canonical unfolding from rupture to restoration, from disorder to order. God's kingly rule will have its uncontested sphere, and God's people of all the ages will be at home there as the sons and daughters of God (1 John 3:1–3). In the end, God's project is revealed to be a family one. The groaning creation and the last days give way to a habitat in which righteousness is at home (2 Pet. 3:1–13). Thus, the survival problem of evil is finally addressed.

The Speaking God. The God who is the maker of his image is not less than his creatures. The image is a speaking and acting reality. So too is the God who made him and her. There is a revelation from God through the created order per se (Ps. 19). But this revelation is sufficient to make idolatry foolish and to stimulate a search for the true God, if only people would heed it (Acts 17:24–31). God has made his will and ways known in a special revelation that reaches its climax in Christ (Heb. 1:1–4). The burden of this special revelation is good news of the forgiveness of sins found through Christ (Luke 24:44–47). The Scriptures are the crystallization of this special revelation. Therefore, the theological interpretation of Scripture—which asks the normative questions about belief and value—is thus of unsurpassed importance to the task of knowing God.

The Worthy God. The ideas of God presented above reveal a God worthy of worship in the classic sense of our expressing in word and deed our sense of the value (worthship) of God. In the light of the gospel, the whole of life can be construed as worship, whether the payment of taxes is in view or Paul's mission to the Gentiles (Rom. 12–15). So too our praise of God is worship, as the description of the heavenly assembly of Rev. 4–5 makes plain. According to Jesus, the Father seeks worshippers. Such worship is predicated on truth. How is God to be understood and approached? God's way is the answer, whether in view are the prescriptions concerning the tabernacle in the OT (Exod. 25–40) or Jesus' linkage of worship and truth in the NT (John 4:24). The theological interpretation of Scripture needs a doxological framework.

God and the Theological Interpretation of Scripture

Theological Interpretation Recognizes That God Still Speaks through Scripture. The theologian observes that for biblical writers, such as the writer to the Hebrews, Scripture is not a fossilized word. As the writer applies Ps. 95 to the consciences of the readers, there is recognition that this is a living contemporary word (Heb. 4:12–13). It is the Holy Spirit speaking (3:7), yet the human instrument is not forgotten. These are also David's words (4:7).

The writer to the Hebrews is not alone in this construal of Scripture. Jesus challenged the Sadducees for knowing neither their Scripture nor its content about the power of God (Matt. 22:29).

Importantly for Jesus, what God said back then was a word addressed to his questioners now (22:31). Paul similarly regarded the ancient Scripture as a contemporary word. God had future audiences in mind in the creation of Scripture. The Romans are to draw hope from that contemporary-though-past word (Rom. 15:4). Likewise, the Corinthians are to be warned in the here and now by what happened to disobedient Israel in the past. These written examples had the Corinthians in view and not just the first readership (1 Cor. 10:11). Significantly, both Jesus' rebuke and Paul's instructions are addressed to groups and not simply to the individual.

Given the above, the believing theologian cannot do theology by appealing to the biblical texts without the existential awareness that he or she may also be addressed. In this light, a cluster of attitudes are appropriate. Reading Scripture about God is a wisdom pursuit that ought to be predicated upon reverence for the God whose Scripture it is (Prov. 1:7 applies here). Reading Scripture about God needs "the skylight" of prayer—to use Karl Barth's happy term (151). In so doing, the theologian learns from the psalmist of Israel (Ps. 119:18). There is an academic engagement with Scripture that is entirely proper. The problematic at the personal and ecclesial levels emerges when that is the only mode of engagement.

To attempt to read Scripture theologically without the appropriate attitudes is a foolish project rather than a wise one. The character of the theological interpreter of Scripture is part of the story. A certain consonance between the character of the interpreter of Scripture and the character of the God of Scripture is needful. As P. T. Forsyth put it (9), "The truth we see depends upon the men [*sic*] we are."

Theological Interpretation Is Aware of the Danger of Bibliolatry. In some of the Christianity of his day, Samuel Taylor Coleridge saw an unhealthy fixation on the text of Scripture as opposed to a healthy devotion to the God of Scripture. He coined the term "bibliolater" to refer to the problem (in Willey 47). The fact that no autographs survive should help to keep the theologian from the idol of text worship. B. B. Warfield even suggested somewhere that this may be the reason that in the providence of God no originals remain. The bronze serpent of the wilderness period later became an idol in Hezekiah's time. The king therefore destroyed it (2 Kings 18:4). In Jesus' day some of the Jews had enormous reverence for the text but had missed the point of the scriptural testimony. Jesus rebuked them for not seeing that he (Jesus) was the subject of the very Scripture they prized. Yet they would not embrace him (John 5:39–40).

The theological interpretation of Scripture needs to be wary, on the one hand, of the danger of idolizing the text, and on the other, aware of the necessity for an appreciation of the burden of the scriptural testimony with its christological focus.

Theological Interpretation Appreciates Extrabiblical Language, Concepts, Distinctions, and Descriptors When Needful. The biblical portrayal of God provides a case in point of the need for other than scriptural language on occasion to secure the claims of the biblical writers. As we have seen, Scripture presents the one God as complex on the inside as Father, Son, and Holy Spirit. Later theological reflection on this scriptural presentation of unity in diversity and the misreading of it by many (e.g., Arianism, to name but one) have led to the need for terminology other than the scriptural to preserve the sense of Scripture. One example is "Trinity," as B. B. Warfield pointed out so helpfully many years ago (*Studies*, 22). The Arian quoted Scripture as did the orthodox. The need for the theological interpretation of Scripture has its genesis in such a problematic and its pastoral ramifications. Addressing the problematic has been a major factor in the rise of theology's own distinctive domain of discourse with its extrabiblical but heuristically enabling concepts (e.g., *homoousios*), distinctions (e.g., infinite and finite), and descriptors (e.g., *ens perfectissimum*).

Theological Interpretation Appreciates the "Storied" Character of Revelation. Scripture, conceived holistically, has a plot line, characters, and drama involving conflict and resolution. The living God of scriptural presentation therefore is not deity in general. This God has a name and stories that explicate that name. Creation stories, revelation stories, redemption stories, and judgment stories are just a few of them. Alan Richardson (59) made an excellent point: "The only kind of linguistic analysis which is useful in elucidating the Christian meaning of the word 'God' is that which is undertaken by scholars on the basis of the original languages of the Bible and related language groups with all the aid of archaeological, philosophical, critical and historical expertise which has been developed over the centuries." What needs to be added is "and with due attention given to the 'storied' nature of the biblical portrayal of God."

A theologian may approach Scripture systematically with his or her normative questions—such as, What ought we to believe about Christ? What ought we to believe about salvation? and so forth—but in so doing needs to be alert to the Scripture's narrative drive and christological accents. The older method of proof-texting in the use of Scripture to build theology needs to give way to a method of contextualized affirmation. With this approach, the text appealed to would be placed in its context in its argument in its book, and in the canon in light of the flow of redemptive history.

Theological Interpretation Discerns the Analogy of Faith. The revelation of the divine name to Moses in Exod. 3 reaches a climax on the heights of Sinai in Exod. 33 and 34. Moses' request to see God's glory is answered with the proclamation of the divine name, "The LORD, the LORD, the compassionate and gracious God, slow to anger, abounding in love and faithfulness, maintaining love to thousands, and forgiving wickedness, rebellion and sin. Yet he does not leave the guilty unpunished; he punishes the children and their children for the sin of the fathers to the third and fourth generation" (34:6–7). This parading of qualities is the nearest Scripture comes to giving a list of the attributes of God.

The importance of this list cannot be overestimated. In whole or in part, these descriptors occur in every major division of the Hebrew Bible and have their echoes in the NT (Num. 14:17–19; Pss. 103:6–14; 145:8–9; Joel 2:12–14; Jon. 4:1–2; John 1:17 and 2 Cor. 13:14, to cite only two NT resonances). It was because God's name reveals God to be like this that Jonah fled his commission to preach judgment to Nineveh. He knew that, since God was like this God, if the Ninevites repented, then God would relent. The very thing he feared happened. So he wanted to die (Jon. 3:10–4:3). Significantly, by the time of prophets like Jonah and Joel, the list has expanded to include God's relenting of judgment. Presumably the content of the divine name has been amplified by the stories of God staying his judgment in the light of repentance, as seen in earlier episodes of God's dealings with his people.

The analogy-of-faith principle works with the biblical accents in construction of theological models. Thus, the doctrine of God—with its classic language such as communicable and incommunicable attributes—needs to factor in the importance of the *middoth* (the qualities) presented above. For example, to follow the *middoth* is to place the emphasis on the grace and mercy of

God and not the divine anger, on the moral attributes of God and not his metaphysical ones (to use traditional categories).

A theological interpretation that is sensitive to the biblical self-presentation in its canonical unfolding will observe the proportion of faith, whether in view is the character of God or the importance of the divine forgiveness of sins. In short, the theological interpretation of Scripture needs to be informed by a biblical theology method that, in Brian Rosner's fine words (10), "proceeds with historical and literary sensitivity and seeks to analyze and synthesize the Bible's teaching about God and his relations to the world on its own terms, maintaining sight of the Bible's overarching narrative and Christocentric focus."

See also Providence; Trinity

Bibliography

Barth, K. *Evangelical Theology*. Fontana, 1969; Childs, B. *Biblical Theology of the Old and New Testaments*. Fortress, 1993; Cole, G. "The Living God: Anthropomorphic or Anthropopathic?" *Reformed Theological Review* 59 (2000): 16–27; Forsyth, P. T. *The Principle of Authority in Relation to Certainty, Sanctity and Society*. 2d ed. Independent, 1952; Heschel, A. J. *The Prophets*. 2 vols. H. Torchbook. Harper & Row, 1969–75; Richardson, A. *Religion in Contemporary Debate*. SCM, 1968; Rosner, B. "Biblical Theology." Pages 3–11 in *New Dictionary of Biblical Theology*, ed. T. D. Alexander and B. Rosner. InterVarsity, 2000; Tozer, A. W. *The Knowledge of the Holy*. J. Clarke, 1965; Warfield, B. B. *Biblical and Theological Studies*. P&R, 1968; idem. *The Inspiration and Authority of the Bible*. P&R, 1970; Willey, B. *Nineteenth Century Studies*. Penguin, 1973.

Graham A. Cole

God, Providence of *See* Providence

Gospel

In the NT, the gospel (*euangelion*) is the good news of salvation in Jesus Christ, especially as a matter for public proclamation. The term has particular prominence in the Pauline writings, where it signifies the christological and soteriological essence of the Christian faith, which lies at the heart of the apostolic mission, and in a polemical context, that by which the authentic Christian faith is distinguished from counterfeits. The latter signification became particularly important in later Protestant (especially Lutheran) theological appeal to the term as indicating the preaching of the justifying work and word of God in Christ over against works righteousness.

The origin of the term "gospel" is disputed. Some derive its Christian usage from the imperial cults, where it refers to announcements of significant imperial decrees or victories; this derivation is insecure, however, and the term may reflect its verbal use in the LXX version of texts such as Isa. 40:9; 52:7; and Nah. 1:15 (2:1 LXX). Its profile in early Christianity is due to its centrality for Paul's theological vocabulary, where it is used to describe both the content of the faith and the basic activity of Paul's apostolic testimony. From this usage, presumably, the term comes to serve in the postapostolic period as the genre designation for the narratives of life and acts of Jesus.

The gospel concerns an interceptive divine action that divides human history and ushers in a decisively new (eschatological) stage of creaturely time. Paul lays much emphasis on the divine origin of the gospel, and thus of his own apostolic mission, which is not grounded in human aspiration or authorized by human tradition, but derivative from the self-manifestation of Christ (Gal. 1:11–12). Accordingly, since the gospel concerns God's saving work in Jesus Christ, it can equally be spoken of as "the gospel of God" (Rom. 1:1; 15:16; 2 Cor. 11:7; 1 Thess. 2:2, 8–9) or "the gospel of Christ" (Rom. 15:19; 2 Cor. 2:12; 9:13; 10:14; Gal. 1:7; Phil. 1:27; 1 Thess. 3:2). In both designations, the genitive is both subjective and objective, because God and Christ are both equally the origin of the gospel and its content.

More closely, Paul describes the gospel as "the power of God for salvation to everyone who has faith, to the Jew first and also to the Greek. For in it the righteousness of God is revealed through faith for faith" (Rom. 1:16–17 NRSV). Originating in God's omnipotent rule over all things, the gospel concerns "salvation," the comprehensive reordering of God's relation to humankind. In the gospel, God is reconciled to sinful creatures, as fellowship is restored through the life, death, and exaltation of Jesus Christ. As such, the gospel is the revelation of God's righteousness: God's character and work as the holy one, who in Christ effects the sinner's acquittal, renewal, and restoration to life in fellowship with the Creator and Savior. Its human correlate is faith, in that the gospel evokes assent and trust from those who renounce self-wrought righteousness and are given to share in the blessings that the gospel pronounces.

The term "gospel" thus embraces both the objective content that forms the substance of Christian faith (Jesus' person and work as saving event), the present effectiveness of that substance as a living determinant of the human situation, and the proclamation of the content and its effect. "The Christ event both precedes the message . . . and continues itself in the message" (Käsemann 9). Thus, for Paul, the gospel reaches into human history in its proclamation. Not only do his preaching and missionary work constitute a presentation of the gospel of Christ (Rom. 1:15; 15:19; 2 Cor. 2:12; 10:14), but also, the congregations that flow from them arise out of the gospel and its proclamation (1 Cor. 4:15; 1 Thess. 2:2–12). Quite naturally, therefore, Paul sees the gospel as both particular and exclusive: because it is the manifestation of God's eschatological judgment in Christ, there cannot be "another gospel" (Gal. 1:6–9).

In the early sixteenth century, Western Christians, eager for the renewal of the church, turned to Paul's account of the gospel and read their own circumstances through its categories. Paul's struggle for the centrality of the gospel of salvation in the church provided a graphic and apostolically authoritative example of the antithesis between authentic Christianity and traditions of human-centered righteousness. This reinterpretation of Paul laid special emphasis on righteousness as pure gift, received in faith, rather than as a principle of moral regeneration. The pastoral consequence of this was a resolution of anxiety about salvation by the gospel's proclamation of acquittal, received in faith rather than earned by religious or moral works (some accounts of the Reformation debates now suggest that Catholics and early Protestants misread one another in this matter). Moreover, the Pauline stress on the gospel as proclaimed shaped the characteristic Protestant emphasis on the preached word as the instrument of the gospel's presentation, to which all other churchly acts and ministries are subordinate. Within the churches of the Reformation, an early distinction arose between Lutherans and the Reformed over the relation of gospel and law. The Lutheran churches emphasized the accusatory function of the law, which, by afflicting the conscience, drives the sinner to the gospel's consolations. In this way, the gospel is in no sense a "new law." The Calvinist churches, though they adopted a Lutheran account of justification as forensic acquittal, saw the relation of gospel and law in integrative rather than confrontational terms. Though works of the law do not justify, they do constitute the shape of the gospel-derived life of sanctification.

In an influential strand of twentieth-century Lutheran theology, "gospel" (especially in its Pauline formulation as the gospel of the justifying word of God) has been made into the hermeneutical key to the NT. In Käsemann or Jüngel, for example, this strand of Pauline theology has served as a "canon within the canon," displaying or perhaps constructing the unity of the NT. Though theologians in this tradition have produced vivid restatements of some parts of the NT's soteriology and anthropology, they have rarely been able to generate a comprehensive account of either Paul or the NT as a whole.

Bibliography

Becker, J. *Paul*, trans. O. C. Dean Jr. Westminster John Knox, 1993; Friedrich, G. "Ευαγγέλιον." *TDNT* 2:721–35; Jervis, A., and P. Richardson, eds. *Gospel in Paul*. Sheffield Academic Press, 1994; Jüngel, E. *Justification*. T&T Clark, 2001; Käsemann, E. *Commentary on Romans*. SCM, 1980; McCurley, F. R., and J. Reumann. *Witness of the Word*. Fortress, 1986; McGlasson, P. *God the Redeemer*. Westminster John Knox, 1993; Pannenberg, W. *Systematic Theology*. Vol. 2. T&T Clark, 1985; Stuhlmacher, P. *Das paulinische Evangelium*. Vandenhoeck & Ruprecht, 1968.

John Webster

Gospels

In the early church the word "gospel" (*euangelion*), meaning "news" or "good news," has a differentiated use. Paul can quite easily speak of the "gospel" of Jesus' death, burial, and resurrection (1 Cor. 15:1–5), even as Jesus is recorded as having preached the "gospel of God" (Mark 1:14 KJV). How these particular uses of the term relate to the now canonical, written Gospels in part depends on what we believe "gospel" meant in the first and second centuries. If "gospel" signified nothing more than a set of timeless truths, then the connection between these written accounts about Jesus and the messages proclaimed by Jesus and Paul is rather tenuous. On the other hand, if "gospel" was specifically understood as the historically rooted, narrative proclamation of the lordship of the *kyrios*, then the apparent incongruity between Paul's gospel, Jesus' gospel, and the four Gospels is largely resolved.

For most of church history, the four Gospels have been received as historically reliable, and indeed, to this day they are recognized as the best available sources for our understanding of the historical Jesus. Without them, the circumstances surrounding his life, ministry, death, and resurrection would be lost to history, as would be the substance of his teachings. As such, they have for centuries served as a wellspring of Christian devotion, an inexhaustible source for artistic and musical inspiration, and the narrative bedrock for theological reflection on the person of Christ.

Genre and Audience

During the heyday of form criticism in the early twentieth century, NT scholars were inclined to view the Gospels as little more than the written residue of the oral kerygma, a subliterary product of ancient folk culture. Despite C. W. Votaw's comparisons between the Gospels and Greco-Roman biographies, K. L. Schmidt's vigorous insistence that the Gospels were a type of *Kleinliteratur* proved to be more compelling. For decades to come, the prevalent tendency was to view the Gospels in nonliterary terms. As a result, at least up until the past three decades, the Gospels were considered *sui generis*; the question as to how these texts might have fit into the first-century literary landscape was tacitly regarded as all but moot.

Once redaction criticism brought about a more earnest appraisal of the Gospel writers as creative and proactive authors, the question of genre eventually re-presented itself more forcefully. Some have argued that the Gospels are most closely akin to the Hellenistic aretalogies, quasi-biographical accounts of divine men. (In an interesting inversion of this view, Weeden holds that Mark employs certain aretalogical elements with a view to creating a kind of anti-aretalogy, subverting the triumphalism inherent in the genre.) Another approach, spurred on by a surging interest in Q (see below) and the *Gospel of Thomas*, conceives of the Gospels as essentially a conglomeration of wisdom sayings ensconced in a historicized, eschatologized narrative framework. Still another view regards the Gospels, Luke-Acts in particular, as a kind of ancient novel. Although undoubtedly the Gospels contain elements of all these genres (as well as others, including Greek tragedy and epic), the closest analogy to the Gospels seems to be the biography. At the same time, the overt theological tenor of the Gospels and their obvious indebtedness to the Hebrew literary tradition warn against overstating the comparison. If it is claiming too little to say that the Gospels show no signs of having been influenced by the genre, it is claiming too much to say that the Gospels are a type of biography. In all these comparisons there is an ever-present danger of forcing the Gospels into a literary mold in which they do not finally belong.

The genre of the Gospels cannot be separated from the Gospel writers' aims and intended readership. It is fairly certain that the Gospels were meant to serve as foundational documents for the early Christian communities by providing some kind of historical background for the early Christians' faith, doctrinal instruction, and perhaps even catechetical material. (Although the view that the Gospels were composed as liturgies has met with little acceptance, there is good evidence that the church used the texts precisely this way, at least by the first half of the second century.) For most of the twentieth century, it has been commonly assumed that the Gospels were written strictly for the benefit of a particular, localized community. But this point is now being scrutinized (e.g., by Bauckham), especially in light of a growing awareness of the broad interconnectedness between the early Christian communities. If this new perspective on the Gospel writers' intended audience proves influential, it will presumably give rise to fresh consideration of how the writers conceived their task. It will also, on a broader level, call into question some of the most basic assumptions of form criticism, which depends so heavily on relating the form in question to the reconstructed *Sitz im Leben*.

The Synoptic Problem

Because so little can be known about the precise dating and origins of the Gospels, other questions have naturally presented themselves. In what order were they written? If the similarities between the Synoptic Gospels are to be explained by some kind of interdependence, how might such dependencies be envisaged?

For centuries, interpreters followed Augustine (and most of the patristic writers) in thinking that Matthew was written first, which in turn was used by Mark. Then followed Luke (who knew both), and finally came John. In the final years of the eighteenth century, however, this paradigm gave way to new models. G. E. Lessing and J. G. Eichorn, for example, supposed that the similarities and differences between the first three Gospels were to be explained by a prior oral tradition. These and other "oral theories" were quickly eclipsed by the thesis of J. J. Griesbach that Augustine was correct in making Matthew first, but mistaken in failing to hold that Mark was written last. The Griesbach hypothesis, still held by some scholars today, would rule German scholarship for the first half of the nineteenth century.

However, by the 1860s, laboring under a stream of steady criticism, the Griesbach theory eventually gave way to a view espoused by H. J. Holtzmann. He relied on C. H. Weisse and argued that Matthew and Luke independently drew on an early version of Mark and a now-lost sayings source. Eventually, within the framework of this theory, canonical Mark was substituted for proto-Mark and the sayings source was redubbed Q (for German *Quelle*, "source"). By the early twentieth century, the now-termed Two-Source Hypothesis would also secure a stronghold in English-speaking scholarship. To this day its dominance has, on the one hand, laid the foundation for a rather extensive field of research into the alleged document Q and its community. On the other hand, it has provoked thoughtful reaction from some who feel that the Two-Source Hypothesis is, despite its popularity, by no means the strongest account for the evidence.

The Emergence of the Fourfold Canon

Since the original Gospels were published anonymously, with superscriptions (*euangelion kata maththaion, euangelion kata markan*, etc.) being added some decades later, the question arises as to when the present names of the evangelists were first associated with their respective texts, and whether these traditional attributions are accurate. Writing at some time in the first third of the second century, the church father Papias knew of texts written by Matthew and Mark, but his statements are, infamously, not without their difficulties (Eusebius, *Hist. eccl.* 3.39.16). Is Papias actually referring to our Gospel of Matthew, an earlier Hebrew version of it, a proto-Gospel sayings collection, or something else altogether? It is impossible to be certain. Fortunately, Papias's testimony regarding Mark is clearer and is for many scholars evidence enough that the author of our second Gospel was in fact John Mark. The authorship of Luke is not attested until Irenaeus (ca. 180), but we also know that in the middle of the second century both Justin and Marcion had access to Luke's text. If the text now attributed to Luke had been known at an earlier point by another name, there would presumably be some indication of that.

Of all four Gospels, the most frequently cited in the early patristic era was Matthew: Clement of Rome and Ignatius of Antioch were already quoting it by the turn of the first century. At the same time, if the apostolic fathers knew Matthew or any other of the Gospels by their present titles, they appear to be averse to using such designations. For example, Clement exhorts his readers to remember "the words of the Lord" (*1 Clem.* 13.1), but does so without mentioning that these words occur in a written Gospel. Likewise, the

Didache (8:1) draws attention to what is written "in the Gospel," but which Gospel exactly seems at least in the author's mind to be neither here nor there. This tendency continues down to Irenaeus. When this late-second-century figure conflates wordings from different Gospels, he nonetheless cites his quotation as coming from "the Gospel." Add to this the witness of those who used or fashioned their own harmonies (Justin and Tatian, respectively), and it becomes apparent that the early Christians' understanding of the Gospels was quite different from the way the same texts are read today. Whereas modern scholarship has tended to focus on the distinctiveness of each evangelist, the ancient believers saw the four Gospels as diverse manifestations of one and the same Gospel. There was one Gospel, because behind the diversity of the four Gospels stood the one unifying Spirit.

In the middle of the second century, it was precisely this notion that armed the church in its defense against the Valentinians; as far as we know, they were the first to search out and pinpoint discrepancies between the Gospel accounts. Origen also preserves the complaint of Celsus. Writing shortly before the time of Irenaeus, Origen has his literary mouthpiece (Celsus) remark that the Christians "alter the original text of the Gospel three or four or several times over, and they change its character to enable them to deny difficulties in the face of criticism" (*Cels.* 2.27.90). Undoubtedly, such charges were felt to have their force, for it is not much later that Irenaeus makes his well-known defense of the fourfold witness. Comparing the four Gospels to (among other things) the four winds of the earth and the four creatures in Revelation, he sees the arrangement of Scripture as being rooted in a principle of natural theology and salvation history (*Haer.* 3.11.8). Some scholars (Cullmann; Gamble) have maintained that the bishop's argument is little more than an ad hoc response to those who criticized the integrity of the church's most important books; others (Hengel; Stanton) see the bishop as simply buttressing a point already widely granted within the church. Since the witness of Irenaeus is equivocal, a proper treatment of the question of the origins of the fourfold collection must look to other considerations: the *Muratorian Fragment*, papyrological witnesses, and other evidence.

***The* Muratorian Fragment.** The author of the *Muratorian Fragment* undoubtedly knew all four Gospels and knew them as a serial collection: the first Gospel, the second Gospel, and so on. This much is undisputed. But what has been fairly recently contested, most notably by A. C. Sundberg and Geoffrey Hahneman, is the conventional dating of the fragment (ca. 170 CE). Locating the *Muratorian Fragment* in the fourth century, Hahneman argues that the ancient author misleadingly set his work in the same time period as the Shepherd of Hermas as part of an attempt to discredit it amid discussions of canonicity. It is also argued that the genre represented by the fragment is no second-century phenomenon: canon lists like this are much more characteristic of the fourth and fifth century. Finally, the witness of the fragment is said to be inconsistent with what can be known about the history of canon. Surely, it is reasoned, it was only with Irenaeus that the church began to speak of the four Gospels.

Although the arguments of Sundberg and Hahneman have won a sizable following, their late dating for the *Muratorian Fragment* has not successfully dislodged the traditional view. If, as Hahneman argues, the author of the *Fragment* really intended to speak negatively of the Shepherd of Hermas, there surely would have been much clearer indications of this. Hahneman has also been criticized for misapprehending the genre of the fragment: rather than being an authoritative canon list, it may simply have been a kind of introduction or annotated table of contents. A form of this sort would not at all have been unusual in the second-century world. Finally, by pressing the alleged incongruity between the seemingly prescient *Muratorian Fragment* and the rather inchoate notion of canon that supposedly prevailed up until Irenaeus's time, the Sundberg-Hahneman thesis—so critics object—runs dangerously close to circular argumentation. Since there is a good deal at stake (the *Muratorian Fragment* has traditionally been taken as strong evidence for the existence of a fourfold Gospel collection prior to Irenaeus), further research will undoubtedly be forthcoming.

Other Considerations in Dating the Fourfold Collection. The above considerations notwithstanding, the question as to whether the fourfold canon emerged earlier or later in the second century remains hotly joined. But the arguments marshaled on either side raise their own sets of methodological questions. To what extent does Hengel's argument regarding the absence of conflicting reports on the naming of the Gospels involve an *argumentum ex silentio*? Or again, does proving an early knowledge of the four Gospels actually require that they existed together as a collection? And on the other side, if the fluidity of second-century textual tradition is an argument

for a late Gospel canon, can we be certain that these second-century writers felt obliged to conserve the exact wording of their tradition? Can it not be argued that the conflating, harmonizing, or other reworking of the Gospel texts presupposes a high view of their authority? Likewise, does the reliance on gospels in addition to the four Gospels (e.g., in Tatian's *Diatessaron*) by itself rule out the possibility of a fourfold canon? Clearly, more work remains to be done on these issues.

Behind this dispute remains an even more basic definitional issue going back to Zahn and Harnack. If Zahn understood the canon in positive fashion, as the compilation of authoritative writings, then Harnack took canonization foremost to mean the act of delimitation and rejection of books that would not share the privileged status of Scripture. To this day, the discussion regarding the formation of the canon of the Gospels (and the NT as a whole) has been dogged by different scholars meaning different things by "canon."

The Gospels in Modern Study

Before the Enlightenment the Gospels were regarded as historically accurate records of the events surrounding Jesus' life, death, and resurrection. With the advent of historical-critical methods, rationalist readings of the Gospels arose only to draw the reaction of theological conservatives who sought to defend the evangelists' roles as historians. D. F. Strauss's *The Life of Jesus Critically Examined* (first ed., 1835), with its mythopoeic reading of the Gospels, not only constituted in his own time an attack on both liberal and conservative wings of the debate. He also forced, for generations to come, the question of how the Gospels may be used as history. The problematic relationship between faith and history, decisively highlighted by Strauss, endures to this day.

Historical and theological investigation into the Gospels has remained undeterred. Form criticism, a methodology (originally borrowed from the discipline of OT study) employed in order to isolate the various forms that make up the Gospels and their original life-settings, has spanned the course of twentieth-century scholarship. But as a trend, form criticism gave way to redaction criticism in the post–World War II years. In some ways the latter tool may be seen as an extension of the former (in that it seeks to differentiate prior tradition from vestiges of editorial involvement); in other ways the renewed consideration given to the individual writers behind the Gospels involves a complete reorientation for NT scholarship.

In recent years, there has been a tendency to steer away from atomizing, source-critical approaches toward a model that takes seriously each Gospel text as a whole. How the Gospels function as literature, the essence of literary criticism, is a question that arises, on one level or another, with increasing frequency in the secondary literature. Rhetorical criticism, structural criticism, reader-response criticism, and discourse analysis are only a few lines of approach subsumed under this larger category.

Finally, mention must be made of the theological relationship between John and the Synoptics. In addition to the perennial source-critical question (did John know one or several of the Synoptic texts?), there are material concerns. Why is it that the first three Gospels share so little with the fourth? What do we make of apparent chronological discrepancies between John and the Synoptics? If the Synoptics primarily present Jesus as the Messiah who announces the kingdom through parables, why does John's Jesus declare himself to be—much more unequivocally—the great "I am!" (8:58)? Many, heartily agreeing with Clement's dictum that John's is the "spiritual Gospel," have largely denied the Fourth Gospel's value as a historical source. From this has often followed a corresponding reduction in John's christological contribution. But neither the historical nor theological skepticism is warranted. In retrospect, the acceptance of a fourfold Gospel collection not only ensured a finely balanced Christology (in the years leading up to Nicea and beyond), but also provided a wealth of metaphors for describing the kingdom.

The precise ways in which the Gospels are to be appreciated as literature and historical documents will no doubt determine the future direction of Gospel studies. In the past, the Gospels have been central to the church's proclamation. It is, after all, the risen Lord whose earthly life is recounted in the Gospel records. Whatever paths are taken in the future, these four texts will remain an invaluable window into Christian origins and a never-ending source of inspiration for those who direct their lives in *imitatio Christi*.

See also Biography; Form Criticism and the NT; Jesus, Quest for the Historical; Redaction Criticism; Source Criticism

Bibliography

Bauckham, R., ed. *The Gospels for All Christians*. Eerdmans, 1998; Campenhausen, H. von. *The Formation of the Christian Bible*. Fortress, 1972; Cullmann, O. "Die Pluralität der Evangelien als theologisches Problem im Altertum." *TZ* 1 (1945): 23–42; Frankemoelle, H. *Evangelium—Begriff und Gattung*. SBB 15. Katholisches Bibelwerk, 1988; Gamble, H. *The New Testament Canon*. GBS. Fortress, 1985; Goulder, M. *Midrash and Lection in Matthew*. SPCK, 1974; Güttgemanns, E. *Candid Questions concerning Gospel Form Criticism*. PTMS 26. Pickwick, 1979; Hadras, M., and M. Smith. *Heroes and Gods*. Harper & Row, 1965; Hahneman, G. M. *The Muratorian Fragment and the Development of the Canon*. Clarendon, 1992; Harnack, A. von. *The Origin of the New Testament and the Most Important Consequences of the New Creation*. Macmillan, 1925; Heckel, T. K. *Vom Evangelium des Markus zum viergestaltigen Evangelium*. WUNT 120. Mohr/Siebeck, 1999; Hengel, M. *The Four Gospels and the One Gospel of Jesus Christ*. Trinity, 2000; Kelhoffer, J. A. *Miracle and Mission*. WUNT 2.112. Mohr/Siebeck, 2000; Koester, H. *Ancient Christian Gospels*. SCM/Trinity, 1990; Kürzinger, J. *Papias von Hierapolis und die Evangelien des Neuen Testaments*. Pustet, 1983; Lemcio, E. E. *The Past of Jesus in the Gospels*. SNTSMS 68. Cambridge University Press, 1991; Sanders, J. N. *The Fourth Gospel in the Early Church*. Cambridge University Press, 1943; Schmidt, K. L. *Der Rahmen der Geschichte Jesu*. Wissenschaftliche Buchgesellschaft, 1964; Skeat, T. C. "The Origin of the Christian Codex." *ZPE* 102 (1994): 263–68; Smith, D. M. "When Did the Gospels Become Scripture?" *JBL* 119 (2000): 3–20; Stanton, G. "The Fourfold Gospel." *NTS* 42 (1997): 317–46; Strauss, D. F. *The Life of Jesus Critically Examined*. Translated from the 4th German ed. by G. Eliot. Fortress, 1972; Sundberg, A. C. "Towards a Revised History of the New Testament Canon." *SE* 4 (1968): 452–61; Talbert, C. H. *What Is a Gospel?* Fortress, 1977; Thiede, C. P. "Papyrus Magdalen Greek 17 (Gregory-Aland P⁴⁶): A Reappraisal." *ZPE* 105 (1995): 13–20; Trobisch, D. *The First Edition of the New Testament*. Oxford University Press, 2000; Votaw, C. W. *The Gospels and Contemporary Biographies in the Greco-Roman World*. Fortress, 1970; Weeden, T. J. *Mark-Traditions in Conflict*. Fortress, 1971; Zahn, T. *Geschichte des neutestamentlichen Kanons*. 2 vols. A. Deichert, 1888–92.

Nicholas Perrin

Government *See* Political Theology

Grace

Grace is unmerited benevolence. A theological understanding of grace begins with the unearned favor that God extends to all humanity and to his chosen people. It concludes in the graciousness expressed between persons in community and in the created *kosmos*. Discussions of grace tend to fall into two types: as a topic for constructive, systematic theology, or as a distillation of relevant passages or themes in Scripture. If these two are brought into closer proximity, neglected areas of discussion are revealed: grace as ingredient to the act of reading Scripture itself and, by extension, grace as a necessary consideration in the hermeneutical description of reading the Bible (see Webster 86–106).

Grace is neglected in hermeneutics insofar as modern debates over the nature of reading often assume a distinction between "nature" and "grace" and are preoccupied with the former to the exclusion of the latter. Biblical hermeneutics tend to accept these terms. As a result, questions related to the Bible as *natural* entity—"text" or "book" or "speech act"—are common, and those related to the Bible as the *gracious* communication of God are rare. Likewise, issues pertaining to the natural status of language as a human expression are featured while those that arise from consideration of Scripture as a sanctified instrument of God's grace are conspicuously absent.

Approaching the question of reading Scripture by means of its natural dimensions, in these ways and others, does not *necessarily* require or account for any unique gracious activity by God. The question of *God's* speech action and of God's gracious enablement of the author and/or reader *could* be read, in these modes, to be superfluous. In modern debates, thus, the question of reading a book and of reading Scripture most often turns on the nature of human beings as communicative. It generally excludes the perennially relevant question of how the human communicative nature is related to, and dependent on, the gracious relationship of humans to their Creator. Also, it usually excludes the additional question of how their communication is affected by their status as alternately sinful and redeemed sanctified creatures. In other words, both traditional notions of general and special grace bear immediately on hermeneutical questions but, in modern discussions, tend not to arise.

Examples of this preoccupation with "natural" hermeneutics can be seen in the dominance of terms driven by the status of the human author, specifically the "authorial intention" question. The preoccupation is also evident in debates over the perennial so-called "problem of historicity" and "distanciation." Historical criticism, structuralism, post-structuralism, narrative criticism, reader-response criticism, and other isms have arisen in response to issues related to either the composition, or reading, of texts as natural entities apart from the questions of sin and grace. As long as the event of reading Scripture is construed in an ambiguous relationship to the grace of God that bears upon all human activity, the graceful reading of Scripture is neglected, inadequately perceived, and ultimately distorted.

By contrast, Scripture itself witnesses to grace as a constituent and antecedent feature of God's dealings and communication with his creatures. This includes the goodness that God exhibits toward all creation (Pss. 33:5; 119:64; 145), God's compassion for the needful and hurting (Pss. 25:6; 103:8; Luke 1:72; 2 Cor. 1:3), his forbearance in the face of human sin and rebellion (Exod. 34:6; Ps. 145:8; Rom. 2:4; 9:22), and especially his redemptive mercy in the salvation provided by Christ (John 3:16–17; Rom. 5; 1 Cor. 15:10; 2 Cor. 6:1; 8:1; 2 Tim. 2:1; Titus 2:11).

The universally necessary and pervasive nature of God's graciousness compels the reconsideration of grace as underwriting the reading of Scripture as the living word of God. In this sense Scripture reading receives its orientation and bearing first and foremost from the prevenient gracious action of God (Hays 219). Thus, the proper way to construe the human act of reading Scripture is as faithful, trusting, and obedient individual and corporate responses to God's grace (Webster 71). This is the hermeneutical stance advocated by Paul in Rom. 3 in contrast to the hermeneutic of distrust indicated by "Israel" toward the oracles of God. For Paul, "God's oracles and promises are interpreted anew, in ways that no one could have foreseen, in light of the experience of grace through the death and resurrection of Jesus" (Hays 220–21).

This hermeneutic of distrust has a modern counterpart in the well-known "hermeneutics of suspicion," which presently contends to be a dominant mode of reading. If employed as a primary or encompassing feature of our stance toward God's word, it is, by its very nature, antithetical to proper reading, which requires the hermeneutic of trust and grace assumed by Paul. Suspicion should not be directed toward the divine Speaker or his sanctified word but toward our own tendencies, as readers and reading institutions, to distort the text in efforts of self-justification (Hays). Moreover, this self-criticism is initiated, maintained, and resolved by God's gracious action of conviction, forgiveness, and restoration.

Rightly grasping the nature of Scripture involves both rational assent and a pious disposition of mind, will and affections. Recognition, acceptance, giving audience, devotion, a checking of distracting desire, faith, trust, a looking to Scripture for consolation: such attitudes and practices are to characterize the faithful reader of Scripture, and their absence denotes a degenerate understanding of what is involved in reading it. (Webster 69)

Reading Scripture is an act of faithful listening: it requires an acknowledgment of the general and particular graciousness of God. Grace is its presupposition and also its intended outcome in the grace extended by acts of forgiveness and love between persons. A hermeneutics of grace, over against a hermeneutics of suspicion, also follows the pattern of thought indicated in Paul's sermon on Mars Hill (Acts 17:24–28a, 30–31). The "unknown god" they worshipped offers an indication of the grace that the one true God has extended to all people in patiently forbearing sinfulness and ignorance. The advent of Christ calls all to repent and to trust in the graciousness of God. All people can now receive salvation and be delivered from their sin and ignorance "in Christ." "In Christ" we also now can listen and attend to the gracious word of God in Scripture. In Christ we then extend grace to each other and to the world, fulfilling the telos of the hermeneutics of faith.

Bibliography

Hays, R. "Salvation by Trust? Reading the Bible Faithfully." *Christian Century*, February 26, 1997, 218–23; Webster, J. *Holy Scripture*. Cambridge University Press, 2003.

Mark A. Bowald

Grammar *See* Language, Grammar and Syntax

Grammatology *See* Deconstruction

Gregory of Nyssa *See* Human Being, Doctrine of

H

Habakkuk, Book of

The book of Habakkuk deals with the question of whether and how the cycle of injustice and violence can be broken. Its most famous assertion is that "the righteous shall live by . . . faith" (2:4b RSV). Across the ages, the interpretation of this phrase has concerned readers. Similar attention has been given to exploring the nature and role of chapter 3, the prayer suggesting that the answer to the problem of suffering and injustice cannot be found apart from the language of worship.

The Argument of the Book

The book is set during the twilight of the Assyrian Empire. It opens with the prophet's complaint (1:2–4) about the prevalence of injustice; 1:5–11 is generally considered to reflect God's response, although others view it as the revelation that caused the complaint (e.g., Floyd). The complaint is intensified in 1:12–17, which suggests that 1:5–11 was not considered an adequate response. If injustice is punished by violence, that only leads to further injustice—where shall it end? In any case, 2:1 marks a break between Habakkuk's argument in chapter 1 and the report of God's reply in 2:2–20, which consists of a statement of principle (2:2–5), followed by its application to the specific situations about which Habakkuk is concerned (2:6–20). The prayer in chapter 3 opens with the confession that the prophet is "alarmed" at what he has heard, combined with a plea for renewal of God's work, which includes mercy in the midst of turmoil (v. 2). The fear is not lost through the prayer (cf. 3:16), but Habakkuk nevertheless concludes with a note of exultation, expressing confidence in God's salvation (3:17–19). The main part recalls the manifestation of God's presence in the exodus event (although without referring to the exodus itself or even to the people of Israel) in 3:3–7, before verses 8–15 address God directly as a fully armed chariot-riding warrior. It concludes with the affirmation that God's "going out" is for the deliverance of his people (vv. 13–15). With 3:16 the prayer moves back to the specific situation addressed in the book.

Chapter 3 is sometimes considered to be the vision of which 2:2–3 speaks (e.g., Andersen), but more likely the vision is set out in verses 4–5 and exposited in the rest of chapter 2. Faith and faithfulness (both seem implied by the Hebrew) are the antithesis to presumptuous desire. The former is the way to life. The latter brings destruction upon the greedy because "wine" (standing in for a number of things being desired; 2:5) is a traitor—too much of it will lead to downfall. Verses 6–20 allow application of this principle beyond greed for conquest. The revelation is guaranteed by the fact that this is how God has organized the universe (cf. 2:13): just as greed will destroy the greedy, violence will fall back on the aggressor (2:17). The end of greed and violence arrives when the whole world submits to Yahweh (v. 20, cf. v. 14) in the way that Habakkuk and the people of God do in praying chapter 3.

Habakkuk within the Canon

Habakkuk follows Nahum canonically and logically. The situation of injustice mentioned at the beginning of the book may well have been caused in part by Assyrian domination, whose end is celebrated in Nahum. The rise of the Babylonian Empire is the solution to the problem of Assyrian domination as well as Judean wrongdoing (1:5–11), but only at the price of further injustice (1:12–17). The hymn with which Nahum opens promises that God will make an end to all ungodly power; until this promise is fulfilled, the hymn with which Habakkuk closes remains pertinent. The righteous live by faith in the faithfulness of this revelation.

A theological reading of the book will take into account not only the immediate canonical context but also the fact that a critical stage in the fulfillment has been reached with the revelation of God's righteousness in the cross and resurrection of Jesus Christ. The object of faith is now defined more precisely (Rom. 1:17; Gal. 2:16; 3:11–12). In Pauline polemic, the emphasis shifts from the righteous "living by faith" to living through "becoming righteous by faith" rather than works of the law. If so, this aligns with Habakkuk's contrast between faith and arrogance in the context of torah's inability to restrain wickedness (1:4) and the revelation of God's wrath in a new deed. The alternative is formulated in John 3:36, "Whoever believes in the Son has eternal life; whoever disobeys the Son will not see life, but must endure the wrath of God" (NRSV; cf. 1 John 5:10–12). Similarly, Paul's address to the synagogue community of Antioch in Acts 13 presumes that the climactic continuation of salvation history in the cross and resurrection of Christ constitutes another divine intervention. It brings such surprise that it separates listeners into those who believe and those who scoff (using the Old Greek translation of Hab. 1:5 in v. 41).

In Hebrews (10:38), Hab. 2:4b is used as an introduction to its famous passage on the nature of faith, emphasizing the need for perseverance in the assurance that the hope for things not yet seen will not be disappointed. The eschatological thrust is thus preserved. The issue of delay introduced in Hab. 2:3 is explained in 2 Pet. 3:9 as due to God's patience. The discussion in 2 Thess. 2:3–12 can be understood in the light of Jewish reflection on what causes final redemption to be delayed, which took its starting point from Hab. 2:3 (see below).

Links between the books of Habakkuk and Isaiah have often been observed (cf., e.g., Hab. 2:1 and Isa. 21:6) but maybe of greater theological significance is the use of the exodus and theophany tradition in ch. 3 (cf. Exod. 15; Deut. 33; Judg. 5; Pss. 68; 77; et al.). The exodus is the archetype of God's deliverance, and the NT use of the exodus tradition in understanding Christ's coming prepared the way for applying Hab. 3 to Christ's coming.

Perspectives from the History of Interpretation

An eschatological understanding of the book of Habakkuk is reflected in the standard Old Greek text and the Barberini manuscript, a translation of chapter 3. Also, within the Qumran community Habakkuk served the sectarian self-understanding as an embattled eschatological community. Especially following the destruction of the temple by the Romans, the interpretation of 2:3 was hotly disputed in apocalyptic writings and rabbinical discussion; the key issue was whether the time of the final redemption was fixed or dependent on human factors (see Strobel). In Christian reception of the verse, as in *1 Clem.* 23:5, the certainty of final redemption is often focused upon; yet there is also discussion of what it is that delays the final redemption (e.g., Hippolytus of Rome and Tertullian). Alongside historical interpretation, a spiritual interpretation is often given, identifying Christ as the righteous one, and Satan or the antichrist as the wicked (e.g., Jerome, Cyril of Alexandria). Augustine belongs to the few who apply the verse to the first rather than the second coming of Christ (*Civ.* 18.31). *Didache* 16.5 still makes a link between this eschatological perspective and the reception of Hab. 2:4, but from then on the two verses (3 and 4) are dealt with independently from each other.

Habakkuk 3 appears to have found its way into Jewish liturgy fairly early, probably in pre-Christian times. Its first use in Christian worship appears to have been in connection with the Easter liturgy, from which it found its way into some weekly liturgies. This may explain that the christological interpretation of this chapter was firmly established, even with commentators who preferred a historical interpretation for the first two chapters (e.g., Theodoret of Cyrus). In the Syrian liturgy, chapters 1–2 were also read during passion week.

Habakkuk and the Church Today

Throughout history it has been obvious to readers of the book that what is said about the Babylonians in Habakkuk also applies to (contemporary) powers from the Roman Empire onward. The claim that God uses military powers to respond to wrongdoing is not unique to Habakkuk, but maybe nowhere else is the problematic side of this arrangement highlighted as much. There is no answer to this problem except for the revelation that violence will not prevail, because the greed that motivates it is self-destructive, and faith in God makes the righteous live. Faithfulness to God is enacted in worship and sustained by the memory of divine deliverance. The implicit claim is that divine use of violence is not unlimited. The NT message adds to this that the defeat of injustice and ungodliness does not occur in demonstration of superior military power but through God allowing violence done to himself. This is surely the most astounding use of injustice for the deliverance of God's people. In keeping with Habakkuk's vision, the supreme expression of human injustice is the beginning of the end of all injustice.

Bibliography

Andersen, F. *Habakkuk*. AB 25. Doubleday, 2001; Floyd, M. *Minor Prophets, Part 2*. FOTL 22. Eerdmans, 2000; Strobel, A. "Habakkuk." *RAC* 13 (1986): cols. 203–26; Thompson, M. E. W. "Prayer, Oracle and Theophany: The Book of Habakkuk." *TynBul* 44 (1993): 33–53; Watts, R. "'For I Am Not Ashamed of the Gospel': Romans 1:16–17 and Habakkuk 2:4." Pages 3–25 in *Romans and the People of God*, ed. S. K. Soderlund and N. T. Wright. Eerdmans, 1999.

Thomas Renz

Haggai, Book of

As is true of most of the OT's shorter books, Haggai research has generally followed in the wake of how larger books have been treated. Early Christian interpreters of Haggai offered several symbolic readings of the book's contents. These included treating Zerubbabel as a type of Christ, the restored temple as a prophecy of the new covenant, and Zerubbabel's signet ring as a symbol of Jesus' kingly power (Ferreiro). Early-twentieth-century historical-critical scholars highlighted Haggai's historical references and the light they shed on the postexilic period. They tended to accept the accuracy of the book's statements and noted the book's links to Zech. 1–8. They also discussed the probability that an editor or chronicler wrote down the prophet's utterances and added them to a brief history of Haggai's activities. Thus, the book was treated as a basically accurate historical treatment of the prophet Haggai's work among the postexilic Israelite community (Mitchell).

In the 1960s and 1970s form and redaction critics tended to accept these findings and sought to further define the book's setting and the levels of the book's editing (Beuken; Wolff). By the 1980s, however, a few historical critics had begun to question the old consensuses and started to posit ways that the book could be read as a unified construction by a single author (Verhoef; Meyers and Meyers), or at least as a substantially unified edited work (Petersen). Of course, some experts tended to agree with earlier historical critics (Redditt). Finally, literary and canonical critics looked for ways to analyze the book in its final form (Childs; House).

A treatment of the book's final form in its overall canonical context indicates that the book's role in the OT is significant. The Law and Prophets emphasize Israel's loss of land due to sin and Yahweh's ultimate restoration of some segment of Israel to the land (Lev. 26; Deut. 27–28; 30; Isa. 4:2–6; Jer. 30–33; Ezek. 36–37; Hos. 11:1–9; etc.).

This restoration is sometimes described in very ideal terms (Ezek. 40–48). Haggai, Zechariah, and Malachi ministered during the tumultuous era in which Israel had begun to return to the land, and each addresses what needs to happen for full national renewal to occur. In particular, Haggai focuses on fulfilled prophecy, on the people's obedience to the prophetic word, on the temple's importance in a renewed community, and on the Davidic covenant's role in Yahweh's continued blessing of Israel.

Fulfilled Prophecy (1:1)

Haggai and Zechariah were near contemporaries. Haggai's messages may be dated ca. 520 BCE, while Zechariah's were delivered during 520–518 BCE. Thus, both prophets work after Persia displaced Babylon as the greatest world power in 539 BCE. This event was itself a fulfillment of promises made in such passages as Isa. 13:1–14:23, Jer. 50–51, and Hab. 2:1–20. Both prophets also ministered in the wake of Cyrus's decree and after the initial return. His edict allowed Jews to return to their homeland, as promised in a variety of texts (Isa. 35; 44:28–45:1; Jer. 29:1–14) and happening in 538–535 BCE (Ezra 1–2). These momentous events could be rightly considered evidence that Israel's seventy years of exile (Jer. 29:1–14) had given way to a new era in which Israel might once again live in the promised land, renew the covenant, and enjoy Yahweh's blessings (Deut. 28:1–14). Prophecy was coming true in Haggai's lifetime, and the question was what that fulfillment would look like in lived experience.

Obedience to the Prophetic Word and Divine Blessing (1:2–15)

Haggai's people may well have expected great blessings because of the pronouncements of earlier prophets (1:9), yet they experienced Yahweh's judgment instead (1:6). Haggai declares that this situation is due to the fact that they have not finished the temple and thus do not honor the God who brought them to the land (1:2–11). Since Yahweh receives no honor, they do not receive the benefits of the land (1:8). They remain a punished people, though in their own land. Haggai's solution is for them to rise and build.

To their credit, the Israelites respond positively. Therefore, Yahweh is with them, renewing, stirring, motivating, and empowering their spirits and bodies (1:13–14). Their response separates this generation from the countless unheeding audiences endured by earlier prophets (2 Kings

17). They recognize that the God who restored them to the land (1:1) and who controls nature (1:2–11) merits the honor a temple symbolizes. They also recognize the inextricable link between obedience and the full presence of Yahweh.

In calling for temple renewal, Haggai concurs with the emphasis on a central sanctuary found in Exodus, Leviticus, Deuteronomy, 1–2 Kings, Isaiah, and Psalms. The temple signifies God's presence in Israel (1:12–14; Exod. 32–34; 1 Kings 8) and demonstrates Israel's commitment and obedience (1:2–6; Exod. 35–40; 1 Kings 5–7). Haggai also agrees with the view of the future displayed in Deut. 28:64–68 and 30:1–10; Isa. 60–62; Jer. 30–33; and Ezek. 40–48. Haggai expects a better future because Yahweh has begun to intervene in history, and he connects temple building to that better future. Thus, Haggai definitely anchors his belief in the events of 520 BCE, yet he also anticipates Yahweh's great future work.

The Temple and the Renewed Community (2:1–19)

As the people build they can easily see that their temple hardly attains to the beauty of, for instance, Ezekiel's envisioned temple (Ezek. 40–48). Thus, the prophet encourages the people with three basic promises. First, Yahweh promises to be with this people the way he was with Israel in the exodus (2:4–5). Yahweh has not forgotten the Sinai covenant or the Sinai covenant partner. Second, Yahweh's Spirit will be among them, thereby removing any need for fear (2:5). Third, the God who fills the earth will fill the temple with the treasures of the nations of the earth (2:6–8). Divine presence and universal sovereignty will make the latter glory of the temple greater than its former glory (2:9). Through the temple, then, Yahweh's glory and Israel's prominence will be evident among all peoples.

But such glory cannot come unless Israel becomes a cleansed people. Before the temple building began, everything Israel did was unclean due to their disobedience (2:10–14). Now, however, Yahweh will bless them as a holy people. All their needs will be met (2:15–19), which reflects a return to the blessing mentioned in Lev. 26:3–13 and Deut. 28:1–14. Yahweh will honor their repentance.

The Davidic Covenant and Renewed Blessing (2:20–23)

With the people, temple, and presence of Yahweh all addressed, it is hardly strange for the prophet to conclude with a message on the importance of the Davidic covenant. After all, the appearance of the perfect Davidic ruler is part of many renewal passages (Isa. 9:2–7; 11:1–9; Jer. 23:1–8; Ezek. 34:20–24; etc.). Haggai claims that Zerubbabel, a Davidic descendant and current leader of Israel, is "like [a] signet ring" on Yahweh's hand (2:23). Haggai does not say Zerubbabel is the coming king. Nonetheless, he is a symbol that the Lord has not abandoned the Davidic covenant (2 Sam. 7). David's line has not been extinguished, so Israel has long-term hope. This text works like 2 Kings 25:27–30, where Jehoiachin, the exiled Davidic descendant, is honored. Jehoiachin is not the promised Davidic ruler, but his existence keeps the Davidic promise alive.

Conclusion

Haggai's theological vision balances the past, present, and future. It is anchored in both the covenant promises and the eschatological vision of previous biblical writers. It thereby links covenant promise and covenant obedience to current trouble and future blessing. It claims that what is to come begins now with obedient servants of Yahweh. In many ways, then, Haggai stresses the "now" and "not yet" aspects of life, promise, and the *eschaton* that mark the whole of Scripture. Thus, there is little difference between the OT and the NT's approach to prophetic promises. Both are more subtle than a simple one-for-one prediction-fulfillment scheme.

Bibliography

Beuken, W. *Haggai–Sacharja 1–8: Studien zur Überlieferungs der frühnachexilischen Prophetie*. SSN 10. Van Gorcum, 1967; Childs, B. *Introduction to the Old Testament as Scripture*. Fortress, 1980; Ferreiro, A., ed. *The Twelve Prophets*. ACCSOT 14. InterVarsity, 2003; House, P. *The Unity of the Twelve*. JSOTSup 97/BLS 16. Sheffield Academic Press, 1990; Meyers, C., and E. Meyers. *Haggai, Zechariah*. AB 25B. Doubleday, 1987; Mitchell, H. G., et al. *Haggai, Zechariah, Malachi and Jonah*. ICC. T&T Clark/Scribner's Sons, 1912; Petersen, D. L. *Haggai and Zechariah 1–8*. OTL. Westminster, 1984; Redditt, P. *Haggai, Zechariah, Malachi*. NCB. Eerdmans, 1995; Verhoef, P. *The Books of Haggai and Malachi*. NICOT. Eerdmans, 1987; Wolff, H. W. *Haggai*. Augsburg, 1988.

Paul R. House

Heaven *See* Last Things, Doctrine of

Hebrews, Book of

The writer of Hebrews is one of the great pastoral theologians of the apostolic period. In spite of its persistent historical and theological difficulties, this summons to a faithful response to the divine voice sounds a clear note to a people that has here no abiding city.

History of Interpretation

By the second century CE the Eastern church, with its emphasis on the pilgrimage of the soul to God, had embraced Hebrews and considered it Pauline (on the history of interpreting Hebrews, see Koester 19–63; Hagner; Greer; Hagen, *Testament*; Hagen, *Commenting*; Demarest). The Western church, however, which boasts the earliest use (*1 Clement*; ca. 95 CE), was more concerned with questions of church order and either ignored Hebrews or disputed its Pauline authorship and authority. A consensus emerged during the christological debates of the fourth and fifth centuries. From texts such as 1:4 and 3:1–2 the Arians argued that the Son was created and *became* greater than the angels; on the other hand, Athanasius (d. 373) found affirmations of the Son's divinity in passages such as 1:3 and 13:8. The latter view won out, though subsequent readings continued to use Hebrews to support differing views of the relationship between Christ's humanity and divinity. At the same time Ambrose (d. 397) argued that 6:4–6 forbids only the *rebaptism* of repenters, solving what had been a key problem for the Western church. Within this consensus the West gradually came to embrace Pauline authorship, although the book's position in lists and collections reflects the view that it stands on the outer margin of Paul's writings. Also during the earliest centuries, the church's leaders had come to be called "priests," and the Mass had come to be understood in terms of a sacrifice; both of these developments drew on and influenced the interpretation of Hebrews.

The disruptions of the sixteenth century affected the reading of much of Scripture, including Hebrews. The humanists reopened questions of authorship—doubts grew about the ascription to Paul—and shifted their attention from the Vulgate to the original languages. Erasmus (d. 1536) believed that Hebrews represented a movement from a lower order of religiosity (the OT) to a higher spiritual and moral order (the New). Luther (d. 1546) suggested Apollos as the author and placed Hebrews after 3 John; his heirs continued to debate its canonical status. Based on Heb. 9:16–17, Luther came to construe the Mass not as a sacrifice offered to God, but as a *testament* that Christ offers to his people, which is received by faith alone. Among the other Reformers, while some affirmed Paul's authorship, Calvin (d. 1564) argued against it but affirmed the

book's place among the apostolic writings. For some, the conviction that the Holy Spirit was ultimately responsible for the book made questions about the human author of lesser consequence. All the Reformers argued strongly that Christ's once-for-all sacrifice precluded any notion of the Mass as a sacrifice. In response, the Council of Trent included Hebrews among the letters of Paul and, using Hebrews in support, reaffirmed that the Mass is a propitiatory sacrifice offered in an unbloody manner by Christ's disciples, whom he established as priests.

With the rise of modern historical criticism in the seventeenth and eighteenth centuries, work focused with ever-increasing intensity on questions surrounding the book's original situation vis-à-vis the historical rise of Christianity.

Answers for such questions can be luminous for interpretation, but in the case of Hebrews evidence is limited. The *author* remains unknown. Suggested names, either as author or editor/translator, include Paul, Clement of Rome, Luke, Barnabas, Apollos, Silas, and Priscilla and Aquila. For centuries it was assumed that the *addressees* were Jews (cf. the book's title, dating to the second century) and their *location* was in Palestine. Many, however, have argued for a Gentile audience. On balance it was probably a mixed audience (Ellingworth 21–27), and the book's single geographical hint (13:24) favors Italy and possibly Rome as the destination (see further Lane 1:liii-lx).

Involved in these decisions are questions of *date* and *occasion*. A date following 70 CE is possible but, taking the internal and external evidence together, a date not long before Nero's persecutions took hold works best (64–65). As to the *problem* being addressed, what we must allow for is the possibility of a complex mix of issues related to the community's history and social setting. In part, it may have been this community's felt need of a cultic means of addressing the consciousness of postbaptismal sins that called forth this address (Lindars 4–15). There appears to have been willingness to trade off true endurance for a compromise with their antagonistic world. It is maintained by many that there was a return—in actuality or spirit—to the temple or synagogue. From the writer's point of view, there has been a failure to grasp the implications of confessions they had made, teachings they had received, and examples they had witnessed. In any event the single most *identifiable* impediment to this community's progress is reluctance to do precisely what the writer repeatedly urges them to do. Through Christ, they need to draw near to God, to "hold fast to" their Christian hope based on God's promise, and to do this in close, daily fellowship with one another (e.g., 10:23–25 NRSV).

Over the last century much of the work done on Hebrews has focused on *backgrounds*, its *use of the OT*, and *literary-rhetorical* analysis.

Hebrews contains substantial parallels with Paul, with the Stephen traditions of Acts 7, and with 1 Peter; there are also allusions to Jesus' earthly career (for the latter, Hughes 75–100; Koester 106–9). Although none of these can make a claim for dependence in literary terms, they evidence the participation of Hebrews in broader currents of apostolic proclamation. In particular, Manson's thesis that Hebrews stands in the stream represented by Stephen and the "Hellenists" has been corrected and refined but has continued to receive support (Hurst 89–106; Lindars 120–21, 124–25; Barrett, "Christology").

Religio-historical work has not only uncovered parallels to isolated elements, but has also endeavored to bring into focus the conceptual background of Hebrews. That Hebrews' imagery and argument involve *both* a vertical, spatial duality of earth and heaven *and* a horizontal, temporal duality of this age and the age-to-come is patent, though the nature of the duality and which orientation (vertical or horizontal) is controlling is not. The very definition of terms is highly problematic, yet the options for Hebrews' pre-Christian background have clustered around Philo, Gnosticism, Qumran, apocalyptic writings, and *merkabah* (throne-chariot) mysticism. On the whole, Hebrews best fits within the Christianized "already–not yet" version of the linear-apocalyptic (Hurst 11) outlook encountered elsewhere in the NT (Barrett, "Eschatology"). Yet the impression remains that the writer had some exposure to the philosophical categories and uses of language that also appear in Philo, and that this has contributed to his manner of expression.

The major *explicit* source of the writer's thought is the *OT*. It is apparent that all of Hebrews' citations are drawn from a Greek *Vorlage*; there is no compelling evidence that he made use of a Hebrew source. Hence, work has proceeded to explore the canonical (and extracanonical) scope of the writer's quotations and allusions, the form of the LXX used, the alterations of the wording of the OT texts, the rationale behind the changes, the rhetorical deployment of the citations within the argument, the exegetical methods employed, and the underlying hermeneutics.

Finally, the *genre* of Hebrews can tentatively (Koester 81) be described as a homily. *Rhetorical* analysis has clarified the high level of skill in the use of the Greek language and in the art of persuasion represented, though the book has finally resisted easy classification according to ancient models of epideictic or deliberative rhetoric. The dominant models employed for understanding the *literary structure* of Hebrews have been structural agnosticism, conceptual analysis, rhetorical criticism, literary analysis, and linguistic analysis. In his text-linguistic analysis Guthrie has argued that by separating the exhortatory units from the expositional, it is possible to identify the distinctive manner in which both of these series of units proceed toward the same pastoral goal.

Hearing the Message of Hebrews

Hebrews is a pastoral theologian's rhetorical effort to shore up the faith of this church and the only work we have from his hand. Judgments about its theology (or theolog*ies*) must therefore be made carefully and only as viewed through the lenses of the book's structure and the writer's pastoral-rhetorical interests (Lindars 1–3, 26–29). Such a reading includes taking seriously its cultic language (e.g., sacred space, blood; see Dunnill) and temple imagery as well as the argument's appeals to emotion (Koester 89–91).

The book unfolds along the parallel tracks of exposition and exhortation (for the present analysis of the book's structure, see Guthrie). The *expository* track has two parts: 1:1–4:13 and 4:14–10:25. Along the way (2:1–4; 3:1–4:13; 5:11–6:20) and following 10:25 (10:26–13:25) the writer drives home the point for this community through direct *exhortations*. These two tracks, though they converge on the same goal, are structured quite differently.

The Goal: Exhortation. The hortatory units, rather than following a logical development, achieve their goal by means of a largely emotional appeal that reiterates key ideas (e.g., sin, faith, endurance, word of God, enter); through these the readers are challenged to persevere.

The series of exhortations as a whole operates within a view of history that locates this audience in the climactic epoch (1:2) of creation's story. In this story the Son is the eschatological heir of all things and the one through whom all things were made—a story whose end is imminent. In this way the readers are made to see that all that has gone before has been oriented to salvation wrought through the Son. To turn away from this salvation is therefore to abandon all hope and worse. And the divine word, having explicitly spoken to this salvation in advance, has also fashioned for them patterns—types—that both instruct and exhort with respect to this salvation.

The writer's concern is ultimately with the fate of the entire community, in keeping with the larger vision of the book, which sees the people of God, past and present together, awaiting the fulfillment of the divine promises. Thus, in 3:7–4:13, the drama within which the readers are to see themselves is that of Num. 14, wherein the apostasy of a *few* led to the apostasy of the *entire* community (cf. Heb. 12:15). Accordingly, though Hebrews does not give expression to a developed ecclesiology, the strategic role of *daily* gatherings (3:13; 10:25) for the community's existence must be noticed.

Salvation itself is projected in local terms, as the "world to come," a resting place, the Most Holy Place, a city, a heavenly homeland, Mt. Zion, even the region *outside* of a sphere (13:13). These images draw heavily on the audience's instinctive understanding of sacred space and its dangers for those to whom sin clings. On the other hand, free entrance into the space of God's presence is an almost indescribable joy, giving them on earth a share in the holiness (12:14) of the temple. Here too, the communal gatherings play a critical role (Lindars 105). This salvation, which they already enjoy in part (6:4–5, 19–20), for the present remains in the form of "promise," and the community is portrayed alternately as a *waiting* (e.g., 10:25) or a *pilgrim* people.

In view of Christian existence as a sojourning and taking for granted the hostility of sinful humanity (12:3), suffering is viewed as the corollary of this faith (e.g., 10:32–39; 11:25–26; 13:11–14) and a universal means of perfecting God's sons and daughters (2:10–11; 5:7–10; 12:4–11). The world external to the church is the inhospitable location within which it sojourns; by going forth *out* of the world (13:13), they are *in* it but not *of* it. The fundamental sin is that of unbelief (= disobedience), and God's enemies (1:13) are those who reject his promise. Apostasy begins where faith falters (2:2; 5:11–14). Full apostasy is presented as a genuine possibility even if the writer believes that his audience is destined for better things. Probably we should read the warning of 5:11–6:12 in the light of the notion of sacred space and corporate conceptions of salvation, such that those who are baptized into the community are viewed as genuinely participating in the realities of salvation. Their subsequent renunciation of faith in full knowledge and understanding of what they are doing (6:6; 10:29) leaves them no possibility of repentance (cf. 12:17). There is

likely some connection with Mark 3:29 (Matt. 12:32) and 1 John 5:16–17, though all of these are difficult texts (cf. also 1 Tim. 1:13). In any event it is doubtful that the writer foresees a situation within which the church itself would enact rules to *enforce* 6:4–6.

The types of exhortations given are both "static" ("hold fast") and "dynamic" ("approach"; "go forth") in nature, and receive their focus in the exhortation to be *faithful* (Attridge 21–22). The description (11:1) and portrayal (11:2–12:3) of faith—the object of which has never changed—presents it as the capacity for the readers to conduct themselves steadfastly in their present world-order and life-situation, even to the point of death. They do so in accordance with a heavenly and yet unseen reality, simply because it is held forth to them in God's word. Their high priest is himself the leader and perfecter of this faith (12:2–3; 2:10; cf. 6:20). A positive agenda of earthly, societal righteousness is the largely unexpressed entailment of this faith; this is not escapist or isolationist.

The Means to the Goal: Exposition. If the hortatory units work together through the reiteration of key motifs, the expositional track of the argument develops along both spatial and logical lines (Guthrie 121–27).

It is likely that the expositional material in 1:1–4:13 is in its core largely traditional and familiar to the readers, even if the writer is giving it a fresh expression. Thus, the use of Pss. 2, 8, and 110, the wisdom Christology of 1:1–3 (Dunn 51–56, 206–9), and the christological descent-ascent pattern are all strongly paralleled elsewhere (e.g., John 1:1–18; Phil. 2:5–11; Col. 1:15–20). It is with 5:1–10:25 that the argument advances into new territory.

Son: 1:4–4:13. On one level, the common thread in this section is the need properly to receive the revelation (word) of God in the Son. Thus, statements of the preexistent and exalted Son's superiority to the prophets, angelic mediators of the old covenant (2:2), and the lawgiver Moses are capped by an extended appeal to receive God's word of promise in obedient faith (3:7–4:11), and finally by a most emphatic affirmation of the ineluctability of God's judging word (4:12–13). All of this summons the readers sharply to attentiveness before the fresh teaching of 5:1 and following.

At the same time this section is channeling all this in the direction of the high priestly teaching. This is done both explicitly (1:3; 2:17–18; 3:1) and indirectly, especially through the sonship idea. In diverse ways Christ—in his nature, status, and history as Son—uniquely and for all time fills the role of high priest. The one identity is metamorphosed into the other through both an internal consistency and an inner textual move: Ps. 110, already in wide currency for the christological implications of its first verse, had also made the pronouncement of verse 4.

High Priest: 5:1–10; 7:1–28. Bookended by the major inclusion of 4:14–16 and 10:19–25, and bracketing out 5:11–6:20, the exposition of Christ's high priesthood runs from 5:1 through 10:18—which divides into two movements, with a brief summary statement in between (8:1–2). Thus, the writer first establishes that Jesus is our high priest (5:1–10; 7:1–28), then develops further implications from his priestly work in the heavenly temple (8:3–10:18).

Taking together 4:14–16 with 5:1–10, the *fact* of Christ's priesthood is substantiated by his history as Son and, most pointedly, by the oracular fusion in 5:5–6 of Pss. 2:7 and 110:4 (109:4 LXX). All of this is correlated and contrasted with human high priesthoods, especially the Aaronic. In the same sentences Christ's priesthood is held forth to the community as a *normative example for them* of faith(fulness) in hardship, as utterly *removed from sin*, and as the *promise* of a *sympathetic* priest by virtue of his total (yet without sin!) identification with them in worldly existence. All these features are pregnant with paraenetic implications.

Hebrews 7:1–28 advances by further developing the nature, need, and benefits of Christ's priesthood, beginning with a discussion of Melchizedek. Melchizedek remains for Hebrews a human figure; what is said represents a christological-typological reading of the canonical *texts* of Gen. 14 and Ps. 110. The point is to define the nature of the priestly "order" to which Ps. 110 makes reference. This exegesis implies that the *type* of Gen. 14:18–20 anticipates Ps. 110:4, that Ps. 110:4 invites such reflection on Gen. 14, and that the orientation of both will come to light in the historical rise of the Son of God. It likewise matters that this priesthood preceded Levi's and that the historical figure of Abraham encountered and acknowledged it; all this anticipates Heb. 11.

If 7:1–10 looks back to Gen. 14, then verses 11–19 (1) note that Ps. 110:4 itself anticipated a new priestly order, and (2) turn their attention forward to the correlative fact of the appearance of the Son. The upshot is that the manifest change of priesthood has brought a change of *law/covenant*, through which *perfection* has come.

The idea of "perfection" is prominent throughout Hebrews. Christ is "perfected"—with respect to vocational fittedness rather than moral development—and is the "perfecter" of faith. The beneficiaries of a covenantal arrangement can also be said to have been or not been "perfected." Ultimately, perfection is everything involved in effecting arrival at the goal of creation's and salvation's history: the approach through Christ to God. Thus, rather than speaking of the "fulfillment" of the OT, Hebrews prefers to show how the imperfect anticipated that which alone brings us to the goal, the perfect (cf. 1:1–4).

This perfection is a function of a change of law. Law is subsumed in *covenant*, the core feature of which is the relationship of this God and his people, and most centrally the right of entrance into the divine presence. In effect the Mosaic law *asserts* the postponement of the revelation of the promised access even as it symbolizes it. With the historical inauguration of the "eternal covenant" (13:20), the goal has been reached. How this writer views the revelatory function of the first covenant is implied by the way in which he uses it to explicate the *perfect* high priesthood of the Christ; discontinuity and continuity thus converge in the notion of perfection. Further, if Ps. 110 ordains a change of priesthood, then we should expect to find that the Scriptures anticipated a change of law/covenant. Of course, they do so in a famous passage (Jer. 31), and the writer will cite it shortly (8:8–12). Thus Jer. 31, which again bespeaks discontinuity *and continuity*, is made to serve the argument of Ps. 110:4, and the scriptural pieces interlock perfectly in the Son (1:1–2).

Finally, before summarizing the argument thus far (7:26–28), it is further supported by focusing on the implications of the divine oath and the inherent weakness of the human priests (vv. 20–25). Merely human priests are not able to usher humanity through eschatological divine judgment and death to the "world to come." Thus, the Son by virtue of his resurrection life "is able to save forever [or, to the uttermost] those who are drawing near to God through him, because he always lives to intercede for them" (v. 25 AT; cf. 2:14–15).

Priestly Ministry in the True Tent (8:1–10:18). If the argument of 5:5–6 proceeded by slipping from Ps. 110:1 down to v. 4, then the direction is reversed in 8:1–2, the hinge text between 5:1–7:28 and 8:3–10:18. The fact of the high priesthood having been established through Ps. 110:4, we follow the lead of Ps. 110:1 into the location and nature of Christ's ministry.

First, it is established that the Melchizedekian order must involve a sacrifice in a temple, and that it must be the "true" sacrifice and temple to which the earthly sacrifices and tabernacle/temple *corresponded* (an ancient and widespread notion, native to the OT) and which they *foreshadowed* as an eschatological reality. All this was indicated by the Scriptures themselves. As to the day of inauguration, Christ's earthly ministry before the cross served to prepare and qualify him vocationally. But his entrance into the office appears to have comprised everything from the cross onward, such that the cross is an aspect of the *heavenly* offering (Milligan 127–33; Peterson 191–95; contra Westcott 227–30).

Having established that Christ, as our high priest (5:1–7:28), has obtained a ministry within the "true tent" superior to that of the Levitical priesthood (8:1–13), the exposition proper concludes with an extended and involved description of that ministry (9:1–10:18). To understand Christ's service, this description proceeds along the lines of a broad utilization of the Levitical priestly service. The centerpiece is going to be the annual Day of Atonement (Lev. 16; cf. 23:26–32; Num. 29:7–11), quite naturally, since the ultimate point of either system is the approach to God, quintessentially expressed in the entrance into the Most Holy Place. Yet the argument slides with ease from there to the daily service and the covenant inauguration ceremony and back, allowing these cultic actions to merge somewhat. Ultimately, the argument is that the *entire* integrated Mosaic cultus (the law) possesses the "shadow of the good things that are coming, and not the very embodiment [or, actual presence] of the realities" (10:1 AT; cf. 8:5). Thus, while the law corresponds to and thus reveals Christ's ministry, providing the categories through which Christ's ministry is to be imagined and understood (continuity), it must be clearly seen that it is *not* the reality and stands in contrast to it (discontinuity).

What should be noticed in this is that the logic of the argument does not work on the basis of a simple material versus immaterial opposition. It is finally the *blood and body* of Christ as fully human that replace the sacrifices of the old covenant. Just exactly what blood signified for the writer is never articulated (cf. Ellingworth 471–74; Attridge 248); likely it was accepted by writer and readers alike as a polyvalent symbol from the OT. Within this argument, Christ's blood alone effects *true* cleansing, forgiveness, and sanctifica-

tion; certainly the opening chapters of Scripture are never far from the writer's mind, suggesting that he views all of this as the answer to the defilement, death, and expulsion of Gen. 3. This in turn assumes a broader understanding of a substitutionary atonement (2:9; 10:12). For this reason, Christ's sacrifice was effective for all sins *from the foundation of the world* (9:15, 26).

Hebrews 10:1–18 constitutes a four-shot finishing salvo, summarizing the general perspective on the law (10:1–3) and underscoring it with three scriptural appeals: Ps. 40:6–8 (39:7–9 LXX, in Heb. 10:4–9); Ps. 110:1 (109:1 LXX, in Heb. 10:11–14); Jer. 31:33–34 (in Heb. 10:15–18). The closing words of 10:18, masterfully chosen, contain within them both promise (10:19–25) and warning (10:26–31).

Hebrews and the Canon

The question of canonization was dealt with above (on what follows, in general see Lindars 119–27). Certainly there are NT parallels to elements within Hebrews' theology (e.g., Attridge 30–31, 102–3; Koester 54–58). Yet, in spite of the call to hold fast to "our confession" of Jesus being "high priest" (3:1; 4:14; 10:23), only in Hebrews is Christ directly called the "high priest" (= "great priest" in 10:21) or even a "priest." Nowhere else in the NT is Melchizedek or his priesthood mentioned or Ps. 110:4 taken up. Moreover, the convergence of sonship (not merely a royal idea in Hebrews) and priesthood, on the one hand, and priesthood and kingship on the other (6:20–7:1) is provocative against the OT background. Unique also is the way in which Hebrews portrays the heavenly cultus, especially in line with the Day of Atonement. All these points, with the exception of kingship, are basic to Hebrews' entire argument.

It has been said of Hebrews' Christology that it provides some of the clearest statements in the NT supporting *both* preexistence *and* adoption (Dunn 52). Related to this, the depictions of the Son's inclusion in the divine identity *and* his full participation in human "blood and flesh" (2:14 AT)—yet without sin—are among the strongest anywhere. Moreover, Hebrews does not hold back from drawing out the implications of the Son's humanity as the leader and perfecter of faith (2:10, 17–18; 4:15; 5:7–10; 12:1–3). Hebrews' definition and illustration of faith itself develops much more richly than James (2:14–26), and in a distinctive fashion develops an aspect of faith that Paul only alludes to (e.g., Gal. 5:6). In its strong warnings against unbelief, Hebrews' "rigorism" (5:11–6:20;

10:26–30, 39; 12:17) has challenged readers since the earliest centuries. Themes such as the word of God, angels, promise/oath, resting place, the new covenant, perfection, and divine discipline receive distinctive treatment here.

Certainly, Hebrews' use of the OT signals a deep investment of this writer's argument in the Scriptures. This facet of the book not only provides one of the chief NT examples of apostolic exegesis; it also represents a highly developed theology of the divine Word in history (Hughes). His approach to the OT takes seriously its historical nature but insists that it speaks directly to the Christian context, sometimes even consisting of words spoken by Christ himself (e.g., 2:12–13; 10:5–7); carefully understood, there is nothing naive or manipulative in his work. Consistent with this is the strategy to show how the OT Scriptures themselves indicate their incompleteness and anticipate the perfect yet to come (Caird, "Exegetical"). The result is that both deep-running *continuity* and sharp *discontinuity* cut across the entire fabric of usage. Certainly this strategy is informed and guided by the writer's Christology, and there can be no question that the Scriptures came to this writer as already interpreted. Yet he gives every indication of conducting an independent, fresh reading of the OT, which is finally to be measured by the implicit claims that this is *truth*. It is true both in terms of what the Scriptures were/are saying (from his own perspective, he is simply articulating the meaning that is in fact *there*, in the text) and in terms of how things are with God and the world, "yesterday and today and forever" (13:8).

Hebrews and Theology

There is something fascinating and unsettling about this book that names neither author nor audience. It cannot have come from any of the disciples, and it has no claim to have been Paul's, yet it represents one of the leading theological voices of the apostolic age. The most "Hellenistic" of NT books, yet known as "to the Hebrews," intensely pastoral and theologically creative, a heavenly summons to a very earthly holiness—it has spent much of its existence on the margins. Its glimpse into the abyss of apostasy has kept the church off balance from the beginning till now. Its cultic logic has puzzled a Gentile-dominated church, derogating the blood sacrifices of animals by insisting on the blood sacrifice of the Son of God, pronouncing obsolete the Mosaic cultus while leaving no alternative but to view Christ's work, encompassing all of creation's story, through the cultic world of Israel's story. In Christ's work, finally, the voice of God has been heard, the gospel of Jesus Christ, the Son of God, our great high priest. As certainly as Hebrews contemporizes the OT Scriptures in the mouth of the Holy Spirit, so also in it the Spirit speaks, as the church has acknowledged.

Without looking over its shoulder, Hebrews has passed beyond questions of Jew-Gentile boundary markers and ethnic derivation to the one God who has spoken to his one historic people, past, present, and future, formerly and incompletely in the prophets, consummately in these last days in the Son. *All* of the readers—presumably Gentiles too—are Abraham's seed (2:16) and heirs of the promise to him (6:13–20). Again, this writer has not been shy to make explicit what was latent in the inherited confession. He fearlessly works out the implications of the Scriptures and thus reveals—not constructs—for the church a wider and clearer vision of a priestly sacrifice and intercessory ministry than is given anywhere else in the canon (regarding the Eucharist, in general and as a sacrifice, and the Christian priesthood, see Koester 127–29; Lindars 136–42).

Centrally, Hebrews is a summons to faith. That its salvation is by divine grace is explicit, and in the world projected by this writer's theology, it could not possibly be otherwise than through faith. That this is a faith with deeds, a faith expressing itself through love, is assumed. But what matters here is that ours is a faith that is "the reality of things hoped for, the proof of things unseen" (11:1 AT). This faith was pioneered and perfected by Jesus Christ, so that through his work authentic faith embodies *his* agonistic story of salvation.

Remarkably, given the nature of its argument, this discourse with studied care avoids a restriction of its challenge to Jewish readers tempted to return to the religion of the temple. Certainly, as Lindars has emphasized (101–18, 134), there is an effective program offered for those who feel the need "to do something practical so as to objectify their inner conflict of emotions" concerning guilt. Yet if, when Hebrews says that "we have here no enduring city" (13:14), this applies to Jerusalem, then, a fortiori, it applies to Rome—or to Kampala—as it does to Jerusalem. Nothing finally requires us to think that the writer's concerns were limited to a threatened return to Judaism; his thoroughgoing appeal to the OT law is due more to his theology of the Word than to the orientation of his audience. His real concern is that his readers "show the same zeal" that they had earlier demonstrated "until the end"—that they continue to stand their ground "in a great contest with sufferings," accepting the seizure of their possessions, because they know that they have a "better and lasting possession."

What this sermon's effect was on the house church for which it was written cannot be known. But for the church catholic this "word of exhortation" has done exactly what it set out to do: encourage and embolden to a faith that will go outside the camp, bearing the disgrace Christ bore. Countless thousands have enacted such a form of existence "to the point of shedding blood," based precisely on this firm demonstration and revelation of the high priestly work of Christ. They did not shrink back.

Bibliography

Attridge, H. *The Epistle to the Hebrews*. Hermeneia. Fortress, 1989; Barrett, C. K. "The Christology of Hebrews." Pages 110–27 in *Who Do You Say That I Am?* ed. M. A. Powell and D. Bauer. Westminster John Knox, 1999; idem. "The Eschatology of the Epistle to the Hebrews." Pages 363–93 in *The Background of the New Testament and Its Eschatology*, ed. W. D. Davies and D. Daube. Cambridge University Press, 1954; Blackstone, T. "The Hermeneutics of Recontextualization in the Epistle to the Hebrews." Diss., Emory University, 1995; Bockmuehl, M. "The Church in Hebrews." Pages 133–51 in *A Vision for the Church*, ed. M. Bockmuehl and M. B. Thompson. T&T Clark, 1997; Caird, G. B. "The Exegetical Method of the Epistle to the Hebrews." *CJT* 5 (1959): 44–51; idem. "Son by Appointment." Pages 73–81 in vol. 1 of *The New Testament Age*, ed. W. C. Weinrich. Mercer University Press, 1984; Demarest, B. *A History of the Interpretation of Hebrews 7,1–10 from the Reformation to the Present Day*. Mohr/Siebeck, 1976; Dunn, J. D. G. *Christology in the Making*. 2d ed. SCM, 1989; Dunnill, J. *Covenant and Sacrifice in the Letter to the Hebrews*. SNTSMS 75. Cambridge University Press, 1992; Ellingworth, P. *The Epistle to the Hebrews*. NIGTC. Eerdmans, 1993; Grässer, E. *Der Glaube im Hebräerbrief*. MTS 2. Elwert, 1965; Greer, R. *The Captain of Our Salvation*. Mohr/Siebeck, 1973; Guthrie, G. *The Structure of Hebrews*. NovTSup 73. Brill, 1994; Hagen, K. *Hebrews Commenting from Erasmus to Bèza, 1516–1598*. Mohr/Siebeck, 1981; idem. *A Theology of Testament in the Young Luther*. Brill, 1974; Hagner, D. *The Use of the Old and New Testaments in Clement of Rome*. NovTSup 34. Brill, 1973; Hughes, G. *Hebrews and Hermeneutics*. SNTSMS 36. Cambridge University Press, 1979; Hurst, L. D. *The Epistle to the Hebrews*. SNTSMS 65. Cambridge University Press, 1990; Käsemann, E. *The Wandering People of God*, trans. R. A. Harrisville. Augsburg, 1984; Koester, C. *Hebrews*. AB 36. Doubleday, 2001; Laansma, J. *"I Will Give You Rest."* WUNT 2.98. Mohr/Siebeck, 1997; Lane, W. *Hebrews 1–8* and *Hebrews 9–13*. WBC 47A–B. Word, 1991; Lindars, B. *The Theology of the Letter to the Hebrews*. NTT. Cambridge University Press, 1991; Loader, W. R. G. *Sohn und Hoherpriester*. WMANT 53. Neukirchener Verlag, 1981; Manson, W. *The Epistle to the Hebrews*. Hodder & Stoughton, 1951; Milligan, G. *The Theology of the Epistle to the Hebrews*. T&T Clark, 1899; Peterson, D. *Hebrews and Perfection*. SNTSMS 47. Cambridge University Press, 1982; Westcott, B. F. *The Epistle to the Hebrews*. Macmillan & Co., 1892.

Jon C. Laansma

Heidegger, Martin   *See* Hermeneutical Circle; Hermeneutics; Onto-Theology

Hell   *See* Last Things, Doctrine of

Hellenism   *See* Jewish Context of the NT; Roman Empire

Hermeneutical Circle

The term "hermeneutical circle" has two separable but closely related meanings. One concerns the relation between understanding the "parts" of the text and understanding it as a "whole." A "circle" arises because each process depends reciprocally upon the other. To understand the parts (grammar, vocabulary, and individual elements in their context), we need to have some inkling of the whole, including what the text is about. Yet to understand this "whole" depends on an apprehension of its elements. These two processes together form a progressive dialectic. Hence, "spiral" might be less misleading than "circle."

A second version of this principle traces a parallel dialectic between the two poles of a "preliminary" understanding or (reflecting the German) of *preunderstanding* (*Vorverständnis*), and a fuller understanding (*Verstehen*), for which this beginning can pave the way. The interpreter begins with what Dilthey calls a prior relationship to "life" (*Leben*), in contrast to what Lonergan terms "the principle of the empty head." The latter leads nowhere. Bultmann suggests an example: to understand a musical text, we need to have some inkling of what music is; to suppress everything that we may know already about music simply ensures an absence of understanding.

This process does not stop here. The fuller (or more accurate) understanding "speaks back" to the preunderstanding to correct and to reshape it. This revision contributes to a better understanding. Hence, to reread a "difficult" book, or even to undertake successive readings, may bring about a deeper understanding of it.

Applications of the First Version in Hermeneutics

Schleiermacher (1768–1834) expounded both versions of the hermeneutical circle and is often credited with its first formulation. However, he himself gives this credit to Friedrich Ast (1778–1841): "The hermeneutical principle which Ast has proposed and . . . developed . . . is that just as the whole is understood from the parts, so the parts can be understood only from the whole." Schleiermacher observes that this principle is "incontestable": "One cannot begin to interpret without using it" (195–96).

It is central to Romanticist hermeneutics that to understand a text the interpreter needs to catch the vision that inspired or motivated the author to give creative expression to it in a text. Thus, Schleiermacher valued "NT Introduction" because on the one hand it engaged with the occasion for writing and the author's distinctive theology, and on the other hand with the grammatical and lexicographical details needed to test or to correct provisional understandings of this larger picture. This also reflects a broad correlation with Schleiermacher's other two poles, the "divinatory" (*divinatorische*) and "comparative" axes of understanding. The divinatory is "the feminine strength in knowing people," and the comparative is the "masculine," scientific, and analytical dimension (150).

Elsewhere I have applied this principle to the understanding of Pauline texts. As Beker urges concerning Paul, a constructive dialectic emerges between the principle of *coherence* and the principle of *contingency*. The first concerns the nature of Paul's theology and his vision as a whole; the second explores the exegesis of passages written for specific occasions. Each facilitates understanding the other (Beker; Thiselton 237–71). This also applies to understanding interpreters themselves.

Applications of the Second Version in Hermeneutics

A positive emphasis upon preunderstanding appears in Schleiermacher, Martin Heidegger (1889–1976), and Hans-Georg Gadamer (1900–2002), but is most widely associated with Rudolf Bultmann (1884–1976). Yet a rudimentary awareness of the hermeneutical circle emerged in the work of Heinrich Bullinger in 1538. He held that a preliminary notion of where the author's argument leads must inform detailed understandings of the language and text. In 1742 Chladenius also stressed the relevance of an initial "perspective" (*Sehe-Punkt*) on the part of an interpreter.

Schleiermacher is more explicit: "The provisional grasp of the whole . . . will necessarily be incomplete; . . . our initial grasp is only provisional" (200). "Even after we have revised our initial concept of the work, understanding is still only provisional. . . . [But] this procedure is indispensable" (201, 203). Bultmann's most widely known account occurs in his essay "Is Exegesis without Presuppositions Possible?" (342–51). Here he discusses W. Dilthey's notion of the interpreter's "life-relation" to the text. Preunderstanding (*Vorverständnis*) comes through experience of life (*Leben*) and equips an initial encounter with a text to lead on to "understanding" (*Verstehen*). Bultmann writes, "Can one understand economic history without having a concept of what economy and society . . . mean? One cannot understand the Communist Manifesto of 1848 without understanding the principles of capitalism and socialism" (347). Exegesis thus "presupposes" a life-relation that constitutes a needed preunderstanding.

Heidegger insists: "Interpretation is grounded in something we have in advance . . . in a fore-conception [*Vorgriff*]" (192). He concedes that the interpreter "must already have understood what is to be interpreted"; but adds, "*If we see this circle as a vicious one, . . . the act of understanding has been misunderstood from the ground up*" (194–95). In Gadamer, this gives rise to a dialectical process of question and answer, and the role of "openness" in inquiry.

Since about 1970 the hermeneutical circle has featured prominently in liberation hermeneutics, in feminist interpretation, and in ideological critiques including Marxist hermeneutics. Juan Luis Segundo appeals to the hermeneutical circle to legitimate a "pre-understanding" of solidarity with the poor (esp. 29), and he cites the work of James Cone as another positive use of the hermeneutical circle to privilege Black consciousness as a condition for liberating interpretation (Cone 53–81). Do these uses, however, compromise the "openness" that Gadamer, Betti, and Ricoeur find essential for a preunderstanding that is not shaped by "interest"?

See also Dialogism; Hermeneutics

Bibliography

Beker, J. C. *Paul the Apostle.* Fortress, 1980; Bultmann, R. *Existence and Faith.* Fontana, 1964; Cone, J. *A Black Theology of Liberation.* Lippincott, 1970; Heidegger, M. *Being and Time.* Blackwell, 1962; Schleiermacher, F. *Hermeneutics.* Scholars Press, 1977; Segundo, J. L. *The Liberation of Theology.* Orbis, 1976; Thiselton, A. *New Horizons in Hermeneutics.* Paternoster, 1992.

Anthony C. Thiselton

Hermeneutics

"Hermeneutics" denotes critical reflection upon processes of interpretation and understanding, especially the interpretation of biblical texts or texts that originate from within other cultures. However, this may include all kinds of communicative processes, from signs and visual art to institutions and literary phenomena.

Introduction: The Shape of the Subject

In premodern times hermeneutics was often defined as the formulation of "rules" of interpretation. However, after Schleiermacher (1768–1834) it was widely recognized that understanding constitutes a creative art, not merely the application of rules. Further, hermeneutics became a transcendental discipline; it explored the very basis and conditions under which understanding becomes possible. After Schleiermacher it also became more significant to distinguish between the actual process of interpretation and a critical and coherent reflection upon this process.

A second turning point came with the work of Hans-Georg Gadamer (1900–2002). Gadamer stressed that all understanding is decisively conditioned not only by the place of texts within given historical horizons, but also by the "situatedness" of interpreters within their own historical horizons. "Historicality" [*Geschichtlichkeit*] conditions all understanding. If differences between these two horizons are simply suppressed, understanding will be illusory or distorted, and we cannot then "listen" to a text on its own terms.

Gadamer uses "method" in a pejorative sense. Method attempts to impose a preformed grid of concepts upon that which we seek to understand. Thereby it speaks before it listens, while hermeneutics listens before it speaks. "Method" reflects the generalizing bias of rationalism. By contrast, Gadamer looks to art, to "worlds" of language, for a more sensitive and fruitful dialectic between historical particularities and truth.

In this light many writers from Gadamer to the present emphasize the role of human fallibility, self-deception, manipulation, and "interest" in interpretation. Paul Ricoeur (b. 1913) begins with an account of the fallibility of the human will and the possibility of self-deception. Hermeneutics addresses the problem of "double meaning." Hermeneutics may counter manipulation and "destroy idols," as well as retrieve meaning. Jürgen Habermas (b. 1929) develops "interest" further. Suspicion of the interpreter or human "subject" reaches a high point in the deconstructionism of Jacques Derrida (1930–2004).

In postmodernism Richard Rorty (b. 1931) tends to reverse the hermeneutical project by transposing it into a version of pragmatic relativism, in which the verdict of the "local" peer-group becomes a criterion of truth. This is a reversal of Schleiermacher and Gadamer, even if Rorty calls it "hermeneutics."

Hermeneutics nurtures respect for "the other." It endeavors to train habits of "listening" to the other (including texts) on its own terms, *before* laying out some conceptual grid into which "the other" must fit. In their original aims, although not always in their programs, liberation hermeneutics, feminist hermeneutics, black hermeneutics, and even Marxist hermeneutics arose as attempts to hear the voice of the marginalized, or "the other." Emilio Betti (1890–1968) believes that hermeneutics should be required in all universities, because it nurtures patience, tolerance, the capacity to listen, and respect for the "otherness" of the other, rather than "mastery" by reason alone.

Hermeneutical Reflection in the Ancient World and the Early Church

It is difficult to draw a clear line between interpretative practices and hermeneutical reflection. Philo of Alexandria (ca. 20 BCE–50 CE) interprets much of the OT in allegorical terms, but it is clear that this results from hermeneutical reflection on the misleading character of anthropomorphisms in language about God. To say "God planted a garden in Eden" is "fabulous nonsense," just as Adam cannot "hide" from God (Philo, *Plant.* 8; cf. Gen. 2:8; 3:8).

Whether Paul uses "allegorical" interpretation in Gal. 4:24–26 may be a matter of interpretative practice rather than "hermeneutics," although modern discussions do elucidate a hermeneutical principle. Otto Michel prefers the term "typology" to "allegory" because allegory suggests parallel ideas, but typology rests on parallel events. In pre-Pauline traditions, the phrase "in accordance with the Scriptures" (1 Cor. 15:3–5 NRSV) denotes an appeal to Scripture as a frame of reference for understanding Christ's death and resurrection, not simply an appeal to some specific text. This coheres with Jesus' two-way use of the OT: Scripture sheds light on his work, while Christology equally offers a frame of reference within which to understand Scripture (Luke 24:26–27).

In the second century Marcion provoked debate about the OT as Scripture. The church rejected his devaluing of the OT. Irenaeus (ca. 130–ca. 200) also raised the question of the status

283

of Christian tradition (*regula fidei*) as a necessary guide for interpretation of the Bible. It is because they ignore such tradition and Christology that gnostic exegesis becomes fanciful and "garbled" (*Haer.* 1.11.1; 2.5.2).

Origen (ca. 185–254) formulated perhaps the first system of hermeneutics. He postulated a "triple sense" of Scripture: the literal, the moral, and the spiritual (*Princ.* 4). However, this is not merely "allegorical interpretation," for Origen grounds his work in an appreciation of symbol, a theology of the incarnation, and a "sacramental" view of the world. The Scriptures are "letters brought to life by the Holy Spirit" (Balthasar xii; Torjesen).

Origen also pays attention to the effects of texts upon readers. When he speaks of the Gospel of John as "spiritual," he is thinking of its transforming power; it is more than "a book of facts." "The words must be brought to life" (*Princ.* 4.1.7). These are God's words, albeit spoken through "earthen vessels" (4.1.6). Origen does not devalue the "literal" meaning. R. W. L. Moberly broadly echoes Origen's perspective when he urges that we should "take with full seriousness the integrity of the biblical text on its own terms, that is, to find the 'spiritual meaning' precisely in the 'literal sense'" (231–32).

This suggests the need for caution against any overly neat contrast between a supposedly allegorizing "Alexandrian" school (Origen and his successors) and a supposedly more literalist "Antiochene" school (John Chrysostom, 347–407, and Theodore of Mopsuestia, ca. 350–428). Chrysostom indeed emphasized the need to study the mind of the writer, and to pay attention to the linguistic context. Why was this passage composed? What is it to effect ("Homily LXIV on Matthew," sect. 3)? However, it may be more accurate to suggest that while Antiochenes looked especially to authors of texts, Alexandrians looked in greater degree to the pastoral effect on readers, although even this is relative.

Features from the Middle Ages to the Eighteenth Century

Gregory the Great (of Rome; ca. 540–604) commended the "four senses" of Scripture: the literal (mainly semantic and historical), the allegorical (often a spiritual or pastoral extension of meaning), the moral, and the anagogical (a context in world-history related to eschatology).

The medieval *Glossa ordinaria*, or standard "gloss," offered brief explanatory notes on given chapters or verses, and could vary in quality from personal intrusions to responsible exegetical comments. Hugh of St. Victor (d. 1141) placed a renewed historical emphasis on the agenda. Thomas Aquinas (ca. 1225–74) endorsed the notion of "the fourfold sense," but also paid special attention to linguistic and theological issues: Scripture uses metaphor, but above all it reveals God.

Luther (1483–1546) and Calvin (1509–64) insisted that Scripture is not so multilayered and polyvalent that it presents only puzzles and uncertainties. Their concern to promote the clarity of Scripture (*claritas Scripturae* in Luther; *perspicuitas Scripturae* in Calvin) and their claims about a "single" meaning belong in this polemical context. These are misunderstood if viewed in the abstract. The many exegetical commentaries that they produced demonstrate that, as H. Bavinck observes, "Clarity does not mean that . . . exegesis would be unnecessary" (cited with approval by Berkouwer 271). Erasmus regarded Scripture as so complex that it was virtually impossible for an interpreter to pass through its puzzles to certain knowledge. Luther replied that the interpreter could always apprehend "sufficient" light for each step of the way for doctrine and action.

Luther and Calvin also offered many guidelines familiar in biblical studies. "We must look and see to whom it has been spoken, whether it fits us" (*LWorks* 35:170). By forcing passages out of context, each "constructs his own Christ" (*LWorks* 40:157). William Tyndale (ca. 1494–1536) stressed the historical and corporate dimensions of hermeneutics, including what today we might call the capacity of Scripture to perform speech acts: it promises, heals, convicts, appoints, pronounces verdicts, and liberates (7–10).

J. C. Dannhauer appears to have been the first to use the actual term "hermeneutics" as a title in 1654. By the eighteenth century, however, hermeneutics had become a broader discipline. In 1713 Christian Wolff produced a general work, in which he emphasized "author's intention." In 1728 Jean Alphonse Turretinus reaffirmed that the goal of interpretation was to place oneself within the surroundings and times of biblical writers. Chladenius (1742) noted the role of interpreters' "perspective" (*Sehe-punkt*). J. A. Ernesti (1707–81) distinguished between hermeneutics as the study of meaning and theology as the study of truth; but J. S. Semler (1725–91) insisted that hermeneutics embraced both.

The Refounding of Hermeneutics as a Modern, Independent Discipline

Friedrich Schleiermacher stands at a decisive turning point in the development of hermeneutics. In his early years he was deeply influenced by Moravian pietism. However, he also discovered and relished the intellectual challenges of university theology and the transcendental philosophy of Kant. Kant had asked not simply, "What do we know?" but also, "On what basis is knowledge possible?" Schleiermacher asked not simply, "How do we understand texts?" but also, "On what basis is textual understanding possible?" Hermeneutics became an independent discipline exploring the problem of "understanding" (*Verstehen*). In the past, he believed, hermeneutics had been subsumed within some prior system, and applied retrospectively to justify an "understanding" already reached. He called such a procedure "regional hermeneutics," in contrast to "universal hermeneutics."

Schleiermacher based hermeneutics on two poles or axes: the divinatory and the comparative. He writes, "The divinatory (*divinatorische*) method seeks to gain an immediate comprehension of the author as an individual." "Divinatory knowledge is the *feminine* strength in knowing people; comparative knowledge, the *masculine*" (150). He illustrates this in *The Celebration of Christmas* (1805). After the Christmas service, the women of the household sing hymns to Jesus, while the men debate the conceptual difficulties of the incarnation. The women "understand" Christmas, which is like "a long, caressing kiss" to the world.

Yet both poles are necessary. To divine intuitively without critical reflection is the way of "the *nebulist*"; to focus narrowly on historical and comparative questions without personal vision is the way of "the *pedant*" (205). These respectively become the key categories of "understanding" (*Verstehen*) and "explanation" (*Erklärung*) in Ricoeur, Apel, and Habermas. *Understanding* reflects Schleiermacher's pietist roots and his interaction with Romanticism; *explanation* reflects his respect for Enlightenment thought and transcendental philosophy.

A divinatory perception of the whole transcends mere "analysis" of the elements of a text. Here Schleiermacher expounds "the hermeneutical circle" in two senses. To understand presupposes a preliminary understanding (or preunderstanding, *Vorverständnis*) of the whole, but this in turn depends on understanding the parts; yet even to commence the process of understanding presupposes such a preunderstanding of what is to be understood. A parallel circular (or spiral) movement characterizes (1) understanding the whole and the parts, and (2) preunderstanding and fuller understanding. Hermeneutics thus requires study of "Introduction to the NT," although not for merely antiquarian purposes. "Only historical interpretation can do justice to the rootedness of the New Testament authors in their time and place" (104). "The interpreter must put himself . . . in the position of the author" (112–13).

Further, the NT can be understood "only by the joint consideration of two factors: the *content* of the text and the *range of effects*" (151, italics added). Although he speaks of "psychological" interpretation, Schleiermacher does not elevate inner "intentions" above language in the public, *inter*subjective world (expanded in Thiselton, *New Horizons*, 204–36, 558–62).

Wilhelm Dilthey (1831–1911) stands as Schleiermacher's successor in hermeneutics in several respects, but also with major differences. Dilthey drew on Hegel's concept of "historical understanding" and placed hermeneutics on the agenda for the social sciences. He extended textual interpretation to interpretation of actions and institutions, and had a stronger perception of the double-sided historical "situatedness" both of interpreters and of what they sought to understand.

Martin Heidegger (1889–1976) radicalized this historical situatedness or "historicality" (*Geschichtlichkeit*). He used the term "being-there" (*Dasein*) in contrast to Being (*Sein*), viewing *Dasein* as "thrown" into a *pregiven* "world," which bounded its horizons of understanding. Although he describes this as "phenomenology," many see it as an existentialist hermeneutics. Heidegger further declares that time is "the horizon for the understanding of Being" (40). Thus, a pregiven temporal "world" determines "possibilities" for *Dasein* and human understanding. It is in terms of this pregiven world that we understand something *as* something (188–90). Hence, "interpretation is grounded . . . in a fore-conception" (*Vorgriff*, 191), and understanding is never without "presuppositions" (191–92).

Rudolf Bultmann (1884–1976) echoes this last phrase and also seeks to formulate an *existential* hermeneutic of the NT. Indeed, his proposals to "demythologize" the NT are largely based on the view that while "myth" purports to describe "objective" states of affairs, in actual practice myth serves to evoke certain attitudes or to generate certain acts of will. More strictly, it might be called a program of de-objectification. He writes, "The real purpose of myth is not to present an objective picture of the world as it is. . . . Myth should be interpreted not cosmologically but anthropologically, or better, existentially" (1:10).

Bultmann offers three definitions of myth, but these do not entirely cohere with one another. Sometimes "myth" denotes an "obsolete" world-view in which miracles occur; sometimes it is virtually equivalent to analogy or metaphor. In this latter case, we could not dispense with myth, and demythologizing would be impossible. The main use of myth is to denote existential language disguised as descriptive *or* "objective" language. Thus, language about creation is not to inform us about events in a remote past, but to summon us to acknowledge our present creatureliness and total dependence upon God. Language about the last judgment is not to describe some future event, but to call us to responsibility before God.

Sometimes this does indeed help to restore "the main point" of certain biblical material. Nevertheless, Bultmann is profoundly mistaken in holding a view of language that ascribes to it only one function at a time (*either* to describe *or* to change our attitude). If he had engaged with J. L. Austin's view of performative language, or with Wittgenstein, or with wider theories of language, Bultmann would have perceived that often it is precisely because language conveys truth about a state of affairs that its force may be performative or life-changing. Jesus can effectively say "I forgive you" because God has authorized Jesus to act in the place of God. Christians can acknowledge Christ as Lord not only in terms of an existential cash-currency of trust and obedience as "slaves of Christ," but also because God has declared that Christ is Lord (as the state of affairs) at the resurrection (Rom. 1:3–4). To be "raised with Christ" *presupposes* that Christ was raised in a more-than-subjective or existential way (1 Cor. 15:3–5; for a detailed critique, see Thiselton, *Two Horizons*, 205–92).

The Late Twentieth Century: From Gadamer to Postmodern Approaches

Gadamer takes us beyond rationalism, but also beyond existentialism. In part 1 of *Truth and Method*, he compares the more fruitful starting points of the classical *sensus communis* and of *Bildung* as "formation"—against a narrower rationalism (Gadamer 9–30). He compares the appropriate historical concerns of Vico with the individualistic rationalism of Descartes. Kant's preoccupation with "autonomy" and the individual self misleads (Gadamer 42–70). Further, aesthetics cannot be transposed into merely abstract concepts without distortion (81–100).

He explores the dynamics of the "world" of the game, "performance" in theatre or festival, and art as ontology. In the "world" of the game, "the primacy of play over the conscientiousness of the player is . . . acknowledged. . . . Play draws him into its domain" (Gadamer 104, 109). What constitutes it as a game determines the world within which the player acts. The game exists only in its performance, just as "a festival exists only in its being celebrated" (124). Musical or theatrical events or games would not be what they are if they merely replicated previous music or games in every possible respect. They "define themselves" in contingent, finite terms "only through the occasion" (147), even if a continuity of tradition makes them performances of *this* music or *this* game. Understanding comes about in changing, contingent events, but also in dialectic with shared traditions.

Gadamer traces the development of the hermeneutical tradition in part 2 of *Truth and Method*. Schleiermacher had focused on "consciousness," but this is "a distorting mirror" (276). Following Heidegger, he explores that upon which consciousness *rests*, historically given traditions and "prejudgments" or "prejudices" (*Vorurteile*). "Tradition is a . . . partner in dialogue" (358). The Enlightenment wrongly opposed reason against tradition or authority. To acknowledge authority is an act of *reason* whereby reason, "aware of its own limitations, trusts to the better insight of others" (279). "Hermeneutical experience" is characterized by "openness." "Anyone who listens is fundamentally open" (361). In openness, I "listen" even to "things that are against me." This recalls the claims of Luther and Bonhoeffer that if we read Scripture only to affirm what we want to hear, its cutting edge will be blunted. Gadamer urges that hermeneutics transforms supposedly fixed, freestanding "problems" into "questions that arise and that derive their sense from their motivation" (377). This forms a fruitful process of dialectic.

Part 3 explores ontology and language and contains some ambiguities. An overready hospitality to *intra*linguistic worlds may be said to invite postmodern perspectives, in spite of Gadamer's emphasis upon historically given traditions. Further, he does not explicitly address the problem of criteria of understanding, not least because these cannot be formulated in advance, or in abstraction from the dialectic of question and answer in its "application." However, his work on linguistic "worlds" retains a constructive role in hermeneutical enquiry.

Paul Ricoeur (b. 1913) is the most creative hermeneutical theorist of our times. With an interdisciplinary approach, he begins with the fallibility of the human will and with the nature of symbol. He writes, "Extension of meaning [is] operative in every symbol" (*Theory*, 55). This also applies to dreams, which both disguise their content from the self through self-deception, yet are potentially revealing. Dreams are "disguised, substitutive, and fictive expressions of human wishing or desire" (*Freud*, 5). "To interpret is to understand a double meaning" (8).

Ricoeur's recognition of deception alongside symbol reaches the heart of his hermeneutics. He writes, "Hermeneutics seems to me to be animated by the double motivation: *willingness to suspect, willingness to listen*; vow of rigor, vow of obedience. In our time we have not finished doing away with *idols* and we have barely begun to listen to *symbols*" (*Freud*, 27, with first italics mine; later italics, his). In his two masterpieces, *Time and Narrative* and *Oneself as Another*, he expounds the continuity of a stable self in terms of accountability and agency, and also temporally in relation to memory, attention, and hope. He expounds the temporal logic of "emplotment," which allows for narrative coherence and responsible agency amid change and pluriformity. In effect, he recognizes certain insights of postmodern thought, including a hermeneutic of suspicion, but resists evaporating human selfhood into mere semiotic performances.

Ricoeur opposes oppressive manipulation. However, it is left to Jürgen Habermas, among others, to formulate a more explicitly sociopolitical hermeneutic. In Christian theology this kind of concern emerged in Gustavo Gutiérrez. Hermeneutics should begin, he argues, with an empathy with the socioeconomic situation of the poor in Latin America, as, in effect, a preunderstanding. He draws on hermeneutical tools associated with Marxist theorists and with Habermas, and focuses on specific biblical texts that handle "liberation," notably that of the exodus. Within this movement Juan Luis Segundo acknowledges that liberation hermeneutics begins with "partiality," and appeals to the hermeneutical circle for methodological justification for this. He claims that "de-ideologizing" is a legitimate parallel with Bultmann's "demythologizing" (7–38, 231–34). Lack of space here prohibits my further discus-

sion, available elsewhere (*New Horizons*, 103–41, 393–410, 430–70, 515–55, and elsewhere).

See also Allegory; Anthropomorphism; Authorial Discourse Interpretation; Deconstruction; Gnosticism; Hermeneutical Circle; Literal Sense; Postmodernity and Biblical Interpretation; Reader-Response Criticism; Theological Hermeneutics, Contemporary

Bibliography

Balthasar, H. U. von. "Preface." In *Origen: An Exhortation to Martyrdom, Prayer, and Selected Works*, ed. R. Greer. SPCK, 1979; Barton, J., ed. *The Cambridge Companion to Biblical Interpretation*. Cambridge University Press, 1998; Berkouwer, G. C. *Studies in Dogmatics: Holy Scripture*. Eerdmans, 1975; Bultmann, R. "New Testament and Mythology." In *Kerygma and Myth*, ed. H.-W. Bartsch. 2 vols. SPCK, 1962–64; Gadamer, H.-G. *Truth and Method*. 2d ed. Sheed & Ward, 1989; Gutiérrez, G. *The Theology of Liberation*. Orbis, 1973; Heidegger, M. *Being and Time*. Blackwell, 1962; Moberly, R. W. L. *The Bible, Theology, and Faith*. Cambridge University Press, 2000; Mueller-Vollmer, K., ed. *The Hermeneutics Reader*. Blackwell, 1986; Ricoeur, P. *Essays on Biblical Interpretation*. SPCK, 1981; idem. *Freud and Philosophy*. Yale University Press, 1970; idem. *Interpretation Theory*. Texas Christian University Press, 1976; idem. *Time and Narrative*. 3 vols. University of Chicago Press, 1984–88; Schleiermacher, F. *Hermeneutics*. Scholars Press, 1977; Segundo, J. L. *The Liberation of Theology*. Gill & Macmillan, 1977; Tate, W. *Biblical Interpretation*. Hendrickson, 1991; Thiselton, A. *New Horizons in Hermeneutics*. Paternoster, 1992; idem. *The Two Horizons*. Paternoster, 1980; Torjesen, K. *Hermeneutical Procedure and Theological Method in Origen's Exegesis*. De Gruyter, 1986; Tyndale, W. *A Pathway into the Holy Scripture*. In *Doctrinal Treatises*, ed. H. Walter. Parker Society/Cambridge University Press, 1848; Vanhoozer, K. *Is There a Meaning in This Text?* Zondervan, 1998; Watson, F. *Text, Church and World*. T&T Clark, 1994.

Anthony C. Thiselton

Hero Story

Hero stories (or heroic narrative) are stories focused on the life and actions of the text's protagonist, who "expresses an accepted social and moral norm" (Ryken 107). He is one whose life "reenacts the important conflicts of [his] community," is able to benefit that community, and whose exploits "capture the popular imagination"; moreover, the hero's narrative "suggests that life has both a significant pattern and an end" (Houghton and Strange xxiii; cf. Campbell). Biblical heroes have exemplary lives but are rarely portrayed as wholly ideal. Rather, they represent the cultural and religious values of their environment. Biblical heroes provide both positive examples to follow and negative examples to avoid; readers of biblical hero stories will see themselves

287

and their own circumstances in these heroes and their exploits.

The Bible abounds with various kinds of hero stories. Leland Ryken outlines different types of heroes: *Idealized heroes* merit respect and emulation. *Tragic heroes*, despite being basically good persons, possess a tragic character flaw that leads to a horrible mistake. And *comic heroes*, albeit imperfect, emerge victorious and sympathetic by dint of perseverance. Ryken notes that most biblical heroes can be considered "heroes of common humanity, or *realistic heroes*"—those who resemble us in both strengths and weaknesses, offering positive examples to follow and negative examples to avoid (108). The realistic and ultimately historical nature of such biblical heroes makes the term "hero story" preferable to the alternative term "legend," a word whose meaning, by 1600, became increasingly associated with unhistorical accounts (*OED*). Heroes also fall under the larger category of *archetypes*—an image or pattern that recurs throughout literature and life, about which Northrop Frye has written extensively in general (*Anatomy*) and in the Bible specifically (*Great Code*; cf. Ryken, Wilhoit, and Longman [*DBI*], xvii–xx). While there are various kinds of archetypal characters (e.g., the virtuous wife, the benevolent ruler, the deliverer, et al.), the one most significant to biblical heroes is the "hero of faith"—a category celebrated in Heb. 11. Biblical heroes are inevitably heroes of faith, and they are inevitably rewarded for their faith even as, conversely, they fall from idealized stature when they exhibit less than unswerving dependence on God.

Heroes of Genesis

Genesis contains various realistic heroes of faith. Noah's righteousness amid a corrupt generation and his unflinching obedience to the Lord seems to identify him as an idealized hero—until his drunken nakedness (9:21–22) reveals his fallibility. In the same way, Abraham's bold obedience to God (e.g., leaving Haran, 12:4; nearly sacrificing Isaac, ch. 22; Auerbach), his courageous rescue of Lot (14:14–16), and his intimate, importunate relationship with the Lord (18:16–33) present us with an idealized figure. At the same time, his misrepresentations of Sarah before Pharaoh (12:10–20) and Abimelech (ch. 20) reveal his own lapses into cowardice and faithlessness, as does his relationship with Hagar (16:1–4). Nonetheless, Abraham's NT representations are those of an idealized hero of faith. His role as the father of believers in God and Christ transcends his role

as the physical father of the Jewish people (cf. John 8:31–59; Rom. 4; 9:7–8; Gal. 3:6–29; Heb. 6:13–15; 11:8–12, 17–19; *DBI*, 4–5).

Unlike the Noah and Abraham narratives, Jacob's narrative features a protagonist whose initially dubious character becomes increasingly heroic. It is initially difficult to sympathize with the conniving and domestic Jacob, who cheats his older twin, Esau, out of both his birthright and blessing. When his father-in-law, Laban, later tricks Jacob into marrying his older daughter, Leah, one senses that Jacob is receiving his just deserts for his own deceptions (Gen. 29:23–27). Even before Laban's bait and switch, however, Jacob begins to grow in faith—the most notable characteristic of his grandfather Abraham (28:10–22). This faith reaches heroic proportions when he wrestles with God (32:22–32). Significantly, this encounter immediately precedes Jacob's reconciliation with Esau. Jacob's ultimate reward for his great faith is (as was Abraham's) his place as a patriarch of the people of Israel, and it is no coincidence that the One with whom Jacob wrestles names him "Israel" after Jacob's successful struggle (32:28).

Jacob's son Joseph follows a more idealistic route to heroism, most notably in the faith he demonstrates while resisting Potiphar's wife and while a prisoner (39:1–41:40). Still, the youthful Joseph's behavior before being sold into slavery may be seen as brash and conceited (37:2–11), and a development in Joseph's character—from self-exalting to unequivocally exalted by God—is evident before he is called to rescue Egypt and his own family from famine.

Moses and Joshua

Moses' story, spanning Exodus through Deuteronomy, is heroic in part because of Moses' decision to leave his place of privilege as the son of Pharaoh's daughter and instead to identify with and champion his own people, the enslaved Israelites (Heb. 11:24–26). As with the Genesis patriarchs, however, he is not an idealized hero, and his own flawed acts—his murder of the Egyptian (Exod. 2:12) and his striking of the rock before the Lord (Num. 20:10–12)—both display self-reliant anger instead of obedient submission to God's direction. Significantly, the first rash act delays Moses' ministry some forty years; the second prevents his entrance into the promised land. Overall, however, Moses is a quintessential hero of faith, obeying God unswervingly before the might of Pharaoh, his armies, and the natural elements.

Moses heroically champions the cause of his people even as he rises above their common failings. Throughout their wanderings, Moses displays faith where the Israelites are faithless, most significantly in his bold responses both to their idolatry before the golden calf (Exod. 32) and their rebellion after the exploration into Canaan (Num. 14). In both these cases, Moses bravely upholds God's righteousness before a disobedient people. Moreover, in both instances, Moses intercedes for the people before a wrathful God, particularly significant in the second case, where God has threatened to destroy the Israelites altogether and make Moses himself "into a nation greater and stronger than they" (14:12). In these instances, Moses shows himself to be God's champion first and Israel's champion second, but there is no doubt that his former status brings about the latter.

Joshua, Moses' successor, can be seen as an idealized hero whose faithful obedience to God's commands enables him to lead Israel's conquest of the promised land (Josh. 1–12). Unlike Moses, he does not lapse into disobedience, and he enters the land as a reward for his faith (Num. 14:6–9, 30). Consequently, Joshua, God's flawless champion, was often portrayed as a type of Jesus, the Flawless One to come (e.g., Milton in *Paradise Lost*, 12:300–14; Flannagan 699nn94–95).

Later OT Heroes

The heroes of Israel continue throughout the OT, each displaying varying degrees of faithfulness to the Lord. Samson is a hero whose consistent lapses into faithless disobedience are transcended by God's faithfulness to his champion (Judg. 13–16; cf. Heb. 11:32). An idealized contrast is Daniel, whose bold faith as a captive in Babylon empowers him to represent the highest ideals of his people's religion in the face of multiple antagonists and ordeals (Ryken 109–14). The OT heroes include the deliverers of Judges, prophets (most notably Samuel, Elijah, and Elisha), a number of the kings of Israel (or Judah, after the kingdom was divided), and the postexilic heroes Ezra and Nehemiah. Saul is the most prominent example of a tragic hero (Good 56–80; Ryken 151–55), although Samson too can rightly be classified as tragic (Ryken 148–51). Displaying the tragic flaw of impiety, Saul fears men before God; this results in his death and the end of his royal line. Saul demonstrates his flaw when he disobeys the Lord's instructions to destroy the Amalekites and all their possessions (1 Sam. 15). When Samuel confronts him, Saul admits that he "was afraid of the people" and succumbed to their demands (15:24). For this sin, God rejects Saul as king and chooses David to replace him (15:26–16:13).

The tragic Saul finds his foil in David, who exhibits heroic faith by slaying Goliath, defeating various enemies, and evading the jealous Saul (1 Sam. 17–2 Sam. 10). Sadly, his adultery with Bathsheba and murder of Uriah (2 Sam. 11) make David's own story largely tragic in his later years. Although his repentance before God and Nathan (2 Sam. 12) saves him from an end like Saul's, the tragic consequences of his actions can be seen in the death of his illegitimate son (12:18). In addition, violent strife and sexual immorality thereafter characterize David's household (2 Sam. 13–18; 1 Kings 2:13–25). Similarly, Solomon indulges in sensuality and idolatry in old age and falls from heroic faithfulness; as punishment, God divides the kingdom after Solomon's death (1 Kings 11:1–13).

Female Heroes

The OT contains a number of hero stories with female protagonists, two of the most prominent being Ruth and Esther. Ruth demonstrates heroic faithfulness to the Lord through faithfulness to her mother-in-law, Naomi, articulated in her declaration, "Where you go I will go, and where you stay I will stay. Your people will be my people and your God my God" (1:16). Ruth's faithfulness is noticed by Boaz, who commends both her dedication to Naomi (2:11) and the upright manner in which she entreats him to marry her and fulfill his role as kinsman-redeemer (3:10). The ultimate significance of Ruth's heroism is revealed in the book's closing verses, which reveal her to be the great-grandmother of King David and (as we may see from Matt. 1:5) a direct ancestor of Jesus. (The NT also celebrates the heroic faithfulness of Boaz's ancestor Rahab; Josh. 2; Matt. 1:5; Heb. 11:31.)

Esther's heroic faithfulness is manifested in her loyalty to the Jewish people and her wise cousin Mordecai. Heeding his admonition that she may well have been raised up as King Xerxes' queen in order to save the Jews from Haman's plot (4:14), Esther wisely acts to rescue her people and expose Haman's treachery.

The heroic faith of Deborah and Israel's unlikely deliverer, Jael, is celebrated in Judg. 4–5 and contrasted favorably with Barak's timidity (4:8). Curiously, Heb. 11 lists Barak while remaining silent about Deborah and Jael (11:32).

289

The feminist critic Phyllis Trible has emphasized the stories of female characters who are marginalized and/or victimized in male-dominated narratives. Although Trible does not focus on heroic faith, at least two of these characters—Sarah ("Genesis") and Hagar (*Texts*, 8–35; cf. Bellis 70–79), both of whose narratives are embedded within Abraham's narrative—can be considered "heroes" in the sense discussed here. Both demonstrate various degrees of faith amid their comparative powerlessness.

Jesus as Hero

The Gospels can rightly be called heroic narratives of Jesus, for they consistently depict him as the ultimate "hero of faith." This characterization extends from his youthful declaration, "I had to be in my Father's house" (Luke 2:49), to his final words on the cross as recorded by Luke, "Father, into your hands I commit my spirit" (23:46; *DBI*, 381). Jesus' most heroic act—his death on the cross for humanity's sins—is portrayed in all four Gospels as an act of faithful obedience to God his Father (Matt. 26:39–46; Mark 14:35–42; Luke 22:42; John 18:11). Jesus also exhorts his disciples to exhibit heroic faith, telling them, "If you have faith as small as a mustard seed, . . . nothing will be impossible for you" (Matt. 17:20), and promising them, "Anyone who has faith in me will do what I have been doing" (John 14:12). It is thus fitting that the author of Hebrews immediately follows his litany of heroes by admonishing his audience and himself: "Let us fix our eyes on Jesus, the author and perfecter of our faith" (12:2). Indeed, the archetypal OT heroes of faith find their fulfillment in the heroic narrative of Jesus; in turn, all believers in Jesus are exhorted to display heroic faith themselves, having Jesus as their ultimate example (12:1–3).

Bibliography

Alter, R. *The Art of Biblical Narrative*. Basic, 1981; Auerbach, E. "Odysseus' Scar." Pages 3–23 in *Mimesis*. Princeton University Press, 1953; Bellis, A. *Helpmates, Harlots, and Heroes*. Westminster John Knox, 1994; Campbell, J. *The Hero with a Thousand Faces*. Bolligen Series 17. Pantheon, 1949; Flannagan, R. *The Riverside Milton*. Houghton Mifflin, 1998; Frye, N. *Anatomy of Criticism*. Princeton University Press, 1957; idem. *The Great Code*. Harcourt Brace Jovanovich, 1982; Good, E. *Irony in the Old Testament*. 2d ed. Almond, 1981; Houghton, W., and R. Strange. *Victorian Poetry and Poetics*. 2d ed. Houghton Mifflin, 1968; Nohrnberg, J. "Princely Characters." Pages 58–97 in *"Not in Heaven,"* ed. J. Rosenblatt and J. Sitterson. Indiana University Press, 1991; Ryken, L. *Words of Delight*. 2d ed. Baker, 1992; Ryken, L., J. Wilhoit, and T. Longman III, eds. *Dictionary of Biblical Imagery* [*DBI*]. InterVarsity, 1998; Sternberg, M. *The Poetics of Biblical Interpretation*. Indiana University Press, 1985; Trible, P. "Genesis 22: The Sacrifice of Sarah." Pages 170–91 in *"Not in Heaven,"* ed. J. Rosenblatt and J. Sitterson; idem. *Texts of Terror*. Fortress, 1984.

David V. Urban

Hillel *See* Jewish Context of the NT

Hirsch, E. D., Jr. *See* Intention/Intentional Fallacy

Historical Criticism

Because both "history" and "criticism" are such protean terms, and have been for nearly two centuries, historical criticism has never been easy to define (notwithstanding the often rather arbitrary distinctions made between so-called "lower" and "higher criticism"). Historical criticism is sometimes narrowly defined as "the study of any narrative which purports to convey historical information in order to determine what actually happened" (Marshall 126). Yet, historical criticism is typically more broadly associated with the (more or less) scientific process of investigating a text's transmission, development, and origins. It includes matters such as the text's linguistic, literary, cultural, religious, political, sociological, psychological, economic, and anthropological context. Source, form, redaction, tradition, and even more recent rhetorical and reader-response criticism are often regarded as specialized types of historical criticism, but these disciplines have different goals even if they share methodological similarities. Historical criticism seeks to answer a basic question: to what historical circumstances does this text refer, and out of what historical circumstances did it emerge?

To some extent, historical criticism has been employed since ancient times, especially in the legal tradition, where questions about the meaning, intent, and authenticity of documents have always been at issue. But ever since Lorenzo Valla in 1440 exposed the spurious origins of the *Donation of Constantine*—a document falsely purported to go back to the early fourth century—and critically compared the Vulgate and the Greek NT, Western scholars especially have been concerned to interpret texts, especially the Bible, according to a systematic process of analysis. Thereby they at every point examine the relationship between what stands in the text and what stands behind it—the connection between the text and the various antecedents that may have shaped it. Renaissance humanism with its cry "Back to the sources!" developed many tools for doing so, and Erasmus's work on the Greek NT was a supremely influential product of this newer, more "critical" approach. In fact, many believe it was this newer, more rigorous approach to the Bible that was the driving force behind the Reformation. Whether or not their approach can be justly called "historical criticism," the Reformers demonstrated a remarkable openness to using practically any tool for understanding what stands in the text. Moreover, they saw their approach to the interpretation of Scripture as a means of liberation not only from allegorical interpretation and many of the dogmatic interpretations of Rome, but also from the entire tradition and history of interpretation. For example, Calvin showed his historical curiosity through his efforts to harmonize the Synoptic Gospels and even wondered—though on the basis of albeit largely linguistic-grammatical analysis—who actually wrote the Epistles of James, Hebrews, and 2 Peter.

Protestants in the seventeenth and eighteenth centuries used an increasingly historical approach to the Bible—the literal sense having gradually collapsed into the historical (Frei 1–50)—in order to continue their battle against Rome and to settle doctrinal disputes among themselves. They also used it to counteract the subjectivizing tendencies of pneumatic and pietistic interpreters. Yet the greatest impetus for such an approach came as a result of the Enlightenment's rationalistic demands. In the face of growing skepticism about the Bible, especially the historicity of many of its narratives, many both within the church (Griesbach, Semler, Michaelis, et al.) and outside it (Spinoza, Reimarus, Lessing, et al.) thought a more "scientific" interpretative method was needed to warrant belief or disbelief in this or that church doctrine. By the nineteenth century highly sophisticated historiographical methods of research had developed. German scholars and others began to draw and insist upon a distinction between the traditional, commonplace definition of history—*Geschichte*, more akin to story—and a newer, more scientific kind of history—*Historie*, which is based on the formal concepts of analogy and probability. Von Hofmann and his followers made valiant efforts to rehabilitate history's formal connection to faith by the development of the concept of *Heilsgeschichte* (salvation history), but the concept never really survived Troeltsch and the history of religions school.

With the rise of historical consciousness, an ever-increasing abundance of information about the past, and a growing confidence in modern man's ability to ascertain it, history—both as an ideal concept and an academic discipline—began to assume almost metaphysical significance (Hegel). Instead of history being a predicate of revelation, revelation became for many a predicate of history. Thus, historical-criticism (now hyphenated to emphasize its power) became all the more important. In godlike fashion, many modern biblical interpreters began to presume a position of unprejudiced, nonparticipatory observation outside or above history even though their judgments were often as prejudiced, speculative, and dogmatic as those they were seeking to overcome. Unaware of the relativity of their own judgments, some approached the Bible with a presupposition of skepticism, especially with regard to miracles. In the name of scientific objectivity, others attempted to place biblical authors under the hot lights of historical criticism and conduct "a disciplined interrogation of their sources to secure a maximal amount of verified information" (Krentz 6). Other more sophisticated interpreters, such as Schleiermacher, claimed that the goal of interpretation was "to understand the author better than he understood himself." Still others, with cruder methods and sensibilities, such as F. C. Baur, D. F. Strauss, and legions after them, searched for the "historical Jesus" as if with "swords and staves" (Matt. 26:47 KJV). But perhaps as significant as this or any hermeneutics of suspicion was historical critics' focus on what lies *behind* the text rather than the text itself. Atomistic preoccupation with individual parts of the biblical witness, especially the various historical-psychological circumstances from which it arose, contributed to confusion over what the biblical witness as a whole is about: its actual content, subject matter, and theme.

Such confusion combined with the tendency to reduce the meaning of biblical texts to their sociohistorical antecedents or to the various psychological conditions of authors. All this led Karl Barth—having been deemed by his contemporaries as "a declared enemy of historical criticism"—to exclaim defiantly in his preface to the second edition of his *Römerbrief* (1922): "The historical critics must be *more critical* to suit me!" Barth's theological revolution was in large part actually a protest against historicism and psychologism. These two great tools of modern theological reductionism were the philosophical and ideological bases for much that was done in the name of "historical criticism" throughout the nineteenth and twentieth centuries. Barth was not content with an explanation of the text that he could not "regard as any explanation at all, but only as the first primitive attempt at one." Nor was he content with a bifurcated, two-stage, "double-entry bookkeeping" approach whereby historical critical "results" stand on one side of the ledger and theological truths on the other, and the task of the exegete is to reconcile the two. Instead, Barth insisted that theological exegesis of the Bible include honest, sober historical-critical analysis. Yet suppose, as Barth also insisted, that the actual subject matter, content, and theme of the Bible is not a historical fact like other historical facts that can be grasped by historical critical investigation. Suppose it is not something a historian qua historian can find behind the biblical witness. Then what role does historical criticism have for the theological exegete?

Despite its misapplication and abuse, historical criticism provides an invaluable service. It offers an initial preparation for understanding what stands in the text. It delivers a disciplined and deliberate rather than arbitrary process for determining what is there. Because what is there is often not only propositional statements or expressions of human piety but also words that point to actual events and circumstances, historical criticism can be useful in reconstructing pictures of such events and circumstances. However, in light of Barth's efforts to promote theological exegesis, two important points should be made.

The first thing to be said about such pictures is that not only are they necessary; they are also inevitable. The witness of the prophets and apostles does indeed have to do with historical situations. Interpreters ineluctably reconstruct these situations in their minds, and do so with or without the help of historical criticism. The question, therefore, is not whether interpreters reconstruct what lies behind the text, but concerning the quality or appropriateness of the pictures they reconstruct. Obviously, some pictures are better, more plausible, and less anachronistic than others. This does not mean, of course, that truthful readings of the Bible are unavailable to "precritical" interpreters, only that "belief in the 'truth' of the Bible cannot be a substitute for historical study" (Marshall 132), any more than historical study can be a substitute for truth. But all interpreters, critical, precritical, or postcritical, do well to remember that the truth at issue in the Bible is one, not two, and cannot be divided up, parceled out, distributed, applied, or treated as some sort of aggregate. It is whole, complete in itself, self-determining and self-actualizing, or it is something else altogether.

Second, the picture that historical criticism helps to form is one solely in the mind of the interpreter. It is not to be confused with the actual events themselves or with the real subject matter, content, and theme the prophets and apostles' words bear witness to: God, truth, or revelation. In other words, historical critics should be wary of the temptation to make idols of such pictures. Because of the sovereign freedom of the Bible's central subject matter, content, and theme, such pictures should be regarded as strictly provisional and subject to continual reform.

Historical criticism can help not only to liberate readers from layers of false presuppositions and conceptions laid upon the text by the history of interpretation or tradition. It can also help to shatter the false images, the inappropriate conjectures and unwarranted constructions modern (and even postmodern) interpreters often bring to the Bible. It can serve to alert readers to the often utterly foreign nature of biblical texts and their various antecedents. By disabusing presumptions of familiarity with the text, it can serve to reinforce, even if only at a human level, the otherness of the text. If genuinely critical, it can neither undermine nor establish faith, but can assist interpreters in being self-critical and therefore modest about their own results.

At its most basic level, historical criticism is a method used to understand the concrete humanity of texts. Because the Bible too is, notwithstanding its divine content, a fully human document, historical criticism is an indispensable tool for analyzing its human character. Written in human speech by specific individuals at specific times in specific places, in specific languages and with specific motives and intentions, the Bible itself requires serious historical investigation, and if "serious," then why not also "critical"? Unless one embraces a docetic understanding of the Bible, Christian interpreters of the Bible can no more ignore the task of its critical historical investigation than they can ignore the humanity of Jesus Christ.

Bibliography

Barr, J. *The Bible in the Modern World*. SCM, 1973; Barth, K. *Church Dogmatics*. Vol. I/2, trans. G. W. Bromiley. T&T Clark, 1958; Bray, G. *Biblical Interpretation Past and Present*. InterVarsity, 1996; Brown, R. *The Critical Meaning of the Bible*. Paulist, 1981; Burnett, R. *Karl Barth's Theological Exegesis*. Eerdmans, 2004; Childs, B. *Biblical Theology of the Old and New Testaments*. Fortress, 1993; Frei, H. *The Eclipse of Biblical Narrative*. Yale University Press, 1974; Gadamer, H.-G. *Truth and Method*, trans. J. Weinsheimer and D. Marshall. Crossroad, 1975; Harrisville, R. A., and W. Sundberg. *The Bible in Modern Culture*. Eerdmans, 1995; Krentz, E. *The Historical-Critical Method*. Fortress, 1975; Marshall, I. H. "Historical Criticism." Pages 126–38 in *New Testament Interpretation*, ed. I. H. Marshall. Eerdmans, 1977; Morgan, R., and J. Barton. *Biblical Interpretation*. Oxford University Press, 1988; Neill, S., and N. T. Wright. *Interpretation of the New Testament, 1861–1986*. Oxford, 1988; Smart, J. D. *The Strange Silence of the Bible in the Church*. Westminster, 1970; Thiselton, A. *New Horizons in Hermeneutics*. Zondervan, 1992; idem. *The Two Horizons*. Eerdmans, 1980.

Richard E. Burnett

Historical Theology

While biblical theology draws a line through redemptive history and systematic theology draws a circle demonstrating the intrasystematic coherence of scriptural doctrines, historical theology reminds both that one never steps outside of the hermeneutical circle, simply exegetes Scripture, and discovers its doctrines in abstraction from a communal history of interpretation. In distinction, then, from both biblical and systematic theology, historical theology may be described as the study of the *history of exegesis* (descriptive) rather than the act of biblical exegesis itself (prescriptive). The goal is not to determine what the church is authorized to say, but to determine what the church has in fact said in its dogmatic formulations through their organic development.

Historical theology is also distinguished from church history. The latter (with precedent since Eusebius's *Ecclesiastical History* or earlier) is concerned with the development of the church per se (incorporating various subdisciplines of historical research, such as social, political, and intellectual history). Historical theology limits its concentration to the development of church dogmas in relation to their environment. Thus, historical theology requires familiarity with both the realm of biblical studies and theology on one hand, and the formal methods of historical research on the other.

Only in the eighteenth century was theological study divided into distinct subdisciplines now familiar in theological education: biblical, systematic, historical, practical, and sometimes also apologetic (philosophical) theology (Farley). In the ancient church period, the term "theology" was sufficient to cover the range of exegesis and extrapolation, and in this enterprise the basic tasks of historical theology (interpretation and analysis of doctrinal precedent) were actively pursued. Origen's *First Things* (*De principiis*, or *Peri archōn*), Lactantius's *Divine Institutes* (*Divinarum institutionum*), John of Damascus's *Accurate Exposition of the Orthodox Faith* (*Ekdosis akribēs tēs orthodoxou pisteōs*), and Augustine's *Enchiridion* became paradigmatic for this topical approach.

In the Middle Ages, theology as "queen of sciences" was regarded as the most comprehensive research program; hence, the attempt to supply a *summa* of knowledge. This included metaphysics, ontology, cosmology, and epistemology as much as the traditional topics of earlier (and later) theological treatises. Increasingly, the *sentence* form of theology also emerged as a gloss on Scripture and the church fathers (as in Peter Lombard's *Sentences*).

Historical theology was anticipated in many respects by the Reformation and Counter-Reformation movements of the sixteenth and seventeenth centuries. In this context, a sophisticated grasp of the sources (biblical, patristic, and medieval) was necessary in order to demonstrate the antiquity and consensual support for one tradition over against another. And while the Protestant Reformers held different views of tradition from those of their Roman Catholic opponents, their humanist training grounded them and their Counter-Reformation rivals in the importance of historical perspective and development. Still, there was a considerable unity of exegetical, systematic, historical, and practical research, commanding equally considerable breadth of learning that later specialization in some respects lacks.

With the Enlightenment, the polemical intent of much historical-theological reflection (a largely interconfessional battle) was regarded as a dead end, since all heteronomous authority was viewed with suspicion. We are only now beginning to recognize modernity as its own form of repressive polemicism, rather than a benign, liberating, and neutral criticism. Historical theology as a distinct subdiscipline emerged out of what was called the "history of dogma" (*Dogmengeschichte*) in the eighteenth century and is associated with the names of G. S. Steinbart, F. C. Baur, Albrecht Ritschl, and especially turn-of-the-century Berlin professor Adolf von Harnack. Nineteenth-century historians of dogma, both conservative and liberal, tended to identify a given figure or period with a central dogma (the Great Idea), which, although more easily summarized, often led to a reductionism that ran roughshod over important nuances. As a rule, more recent historical theologies—across the various Christian traditions—reflect greater appreciation of dialectical subtlety.

In his multivolume *History of Dogma* (German, 1885–90; ET, 1896–) and more popular *What Is Christianity?* (ET, 1901), Harnack succeeded in radicalizing his predecessors' critique of orthodox Christianity, which he identified as a decadent "Catholicism." The grandson of formative historian of dogma Gustav Ewers, Harnack hoped that his work may be "found not unworthy of the clear and disciplined mind which presided over the beginnings of the young science" (*History of Dogma*, xi, American preface). Disguised as a neutral, historical-scientific analysis of Christian backgrounds, historical theology emerged under Harnack's leadership as a learned yet highly critical discipline, presupposing that the earliest faith of Jesus and his followers (always ethical in nature) was corrupted by Hellenism, resulting in the major articles of the Christian creed. Although this thesis has been seen to be reductive at best and a fatal distortion of the evidence at worst, it continues to exercise enormous rhetorical force, especially among some biblical scholars and theologians for whom borrowed philosophical terms constitute declension from the simplest, earliest Christianity. Just as historical studies contributed to the deconstruction of the Christ of faith in favor of the so-called "Jesus of history" in NT studies, so also historical theology (it was thought) would eventually strip away the husk of patristic, medieval, and Protestant orthodox consensus to reveal the kernel of original truth in the teachings and person of Jesus himself.

In the light of its development in the wake of Enlightenment criticism, one may wonder how useful or even appropriate it might be for a recovery of a theological interpretation of Scripture. Two responses come to mind.

First, in its associations with modern criticism, historical theology is no more compromised than biblical studies, and in spite of their particular biases, both fields in the modern period have yielded a considerable body of knowledge that is often taken for granted today. While we must be aware of presuppositions—especially unacknowledged ones—that guide any given proposal, erroneous conclusions do not disqualify the method, which in this case is critical though sympathetic analysis. Historical theology shares with the human sciences more generally the methods and skills advanced in the history of hermeneutics, and those hermeneutical assumptions are as evident in the work of a given historical theologian as in the subject studied.

A second response has to do with the dangers to theology in general that historical theology in particular can help avoid. The dangers include the following: *golden-age thinking*, in which an individual or community selects a favored period, movement, or hero, and treats every other subject and period in relation to it as either a renewal or a declension. While the historical method cannot be the determinative factor in biblical and systematic theology, it must limit the study of the history of dogma. Thus, historical theologians can often serve to critique the description of particular dogmatic formulations offered or assumed by exegetical and systematic theology, holding naive or "straw-man" arguments in check. As Richard Muller counsels, "Rightly or wrongly, Arianism had considerable power and appeal: it is the task of the historian to examine this appeal. The orthodoxy of Nicea must also be examined in its cultural and intellectual context—so that the forms of its doctrinal expression and their adequacy to the needs of fourth-century Trinitarianism can be fully understood" (Muller 99). To a certain extent, therefore, historical theology relativizes and postpones normative evaluations by placing them within a context, while allowing other theological disciplines the freedom to assert the truth of those claims themselves.

In addition to reining in golden-age thinking, historical theology can challenge *a timeless view* of church dogmas. Just as biblical theology traces the development of canonical revelation in concrete historical contexts, historical theology does the same with postcanonical ecclesial reflection. As is the case with the various biblical traditions, church dogmas did not drop out of the sky; they reflect the effects of cultural, linguistic, social, and even political circumstances of their time and place.

Historical theology can also provide a guard against *biblicism*: the tendency to identify one's own interpretation of Scripture with Scripture itself. A biblicist does this to the extent of ignoring, or perhaps even being unaware of, the location of that interpretation both in the interpreter's frame of reference and in relation to the history of interpretation generally. No dogma is an island; any dogma is inextricably linked with other dogmas of varying importance, which themselves also participate organically in an "effective history" (*Wirkungsgeschichte*). This ongoing conversation and its effects condition every exercise in exegesis and systematization (as in any other form of interpretation). Historical theology reminds us that it is as easy for the exegete to impose one's own dogmatic framework on the biblical text as it is for the community to do this in any given place and time.

Finally, historical theology can serve as a helpful corrective to *speculative tendencies*, to which biblical scholarship as well as systematic and philosophical theology are sometimes inclined. While it is not itself immune to this temptation, historical theology is at least equipped to remind its corollary subdisciplines of the (often enormous) skill and energy that the church has expended in identifying its boundary-formulations. This can reduce the frequency with which theological programs repeat the mistakes of the past and provide them with a constant check on innovative or retrogressive construals. As Muller summarizes, "The study of the history of the church and its teachings is not only an objective, external discipline, it is also a subjective, internal exercise by which and through which the life and mind of the church become an integral part of the life and mind of the individual Christian" (107).

See also Tradition

Bibliography

Farley, E. *Theologia*. Fortress, 1983; Harnack, A. *The History of Dogma*. Translated from the 3d German ed. by N. Buchanan. 7 vols. Little, Brown & Co., 1896–1905; Hart, T., ed. *Dictionary of Historical Theology*. Eerdmans, 2000; Muller, R. *The Study of Theology*. Zondervan, 1991; Pelikan, J. *The Christian Tradition*. 5 vols. University of Chicago Press, 1989.

Michael S. Horton

Historicism   *See* History; Historical Criticism

Historiography   *See* History

History

The Christian stake in history is immense. Every aspect of lived Christianity—worship, sacraments, daily godliness, private devotion, religiously inspired benevolence, preaching—and every major theme of Christian theology—the nature of God in relation to the world, the meaning of Christ, the character of salvation, the fate of the universe—directly or indirectly involves questions about how the present relates to the past. Yet despite this superlative importance, theological reflection on historical practices, assumptions, and arguments remains in short supply. And this is not to speak of how persistently questions about the historicity of the Bible—which concern the relation of scriptural narrative to events that may have actually happened—remain in the intellectual background. In the precritical period

questions of the Bible's historicity tended to be subsumed under overarching church dogma: biblical narratives were interpreted as factual, typological, or both, depending upon the theological system as a whole. In modern (Enlightenment) discourse, biblical writers frequently have been understood using contemporary standards of critical verification, and so have been defended by conservatives as "accurate" or relativized by liberals as "myth-making." In postmodern discourse, the assertion is heard that the historicity of biblical writings is in principle a diversionary question, because it takes attention away from the interpretative constructs of contemporary readers and communities. Common in all eras has been the assumption that historical knowledge takes care of itself.

The Bible and Modern Debates about History

Standard accounts of developments leading to current uncertainties about the status of historical knowledge trace a primarily European story, which begins with the emergence of the modern historical seminar at the University of Berlin in the 1820s under the guidance of Leopold von Ranke. Sustained by great personal drive and buoyed by optimism drawn from Enlightenment, Romantic, and Christian sources, von Ranke contended that diligent research in state archives would lay bare the genesis of modern nations and so reveal history "as it really was in its essence" (*wie es eigentlich gewesen*). Over the next 140 years, von Ranke's concentration on elite males as the main actors in political and military narratives was greatly expanded as various forms of social, Marxist, comparative, and quantitative history came in and out of fashion. Yet his ideal of historical investigation as a rigorously critical enterprise ("scientific" in the broad sense of the term) that yields truths about the past—sometimes The Truth—survived. Only with the modern "linguistic turn" was that ideal challenged and the nature of historical knowledge turned into a complex problem.

That problem involves the collapse of three certainties (summarized from Appleby, Hunt, and Jacob). First was a heroic myth about Western history interpreted as—in one account for the United States—the rise of "the successful male white Protestant, whose features were turned into ideals for the entire human race" (135). Against this myth have arisen various forms of historical advocacy that treat once-marginalized populations (women, subalterns, African-Americans,

Orientals, workers, homosexuals) as critical historical actors. The result is sharp contention among advocates speaking for these various groups concerning which of them is most central or important for the truest understanding of the world's real history.

Second was a myth about the intellectual purity of science. So long as this myth survived, historians could dignify their labor by showing how closely careful archival research resembled the research of scientists; it sought verifiable conclusions drawn from facts arranged objectively to tell the truth. Against this myth arose the subversive notion that science too was a social process (or more radically, a social construction), resembling other products of human mental activity such as art, nationalism, or religious belief much more than had previously been thought. Thomas Kuhn's *Structure of Scientific Revolutions* (1962) was the catalyst for this revolutionary assault. The tremors resulting from this work shook the ground on which historians stood. In the new view, scientific procedures were governed by much larger social conventions and did not necessarily yield pristine, irrefragable, objective results. If so, how much less certainty could be produced by history, with its incomplete "data sets," its inability to replicate "experiments," and its lack of "verifiable" proof for conclusions?

Third were myths about the ability of language to reflect reality or, put another way, the unexamined assumption that statements about human conditions were indeed really about those conditions rather than about the ones who made the statements. Here the precipitate of tumult was writing from Europe, often France, suggesting that language revealed much more about how humans perceived ("constructed") their experience than what they found in a supposedly "real" world (Jacques Derrida). Or it proposed that statements about human activities in the past were mostly encrypted devices aimed at solidifying relationships of power in the present (Michel Foucault). For history-writing, such assertions threatened notions about re-creating the past *wie es eigentlich gewesen* as remorselessly as they undercut notions about historians' ability to float free above the political conflicts of their own day.

In extreme forms, the modern attitude toward historical knowledge is dismissive, for example, in the words of Hans Kellner: "History can be redescribed as a discourse that is fundamentally rhetorical. . . . Representing the past takes place through the creation of powerful, persuasive images which can be best understood as created objects, models, metaphors or proposals about reality" (Ankersmit and Kellner 2). The shift such radicals hail is from an ideal of history grounded in the scientism of Carl Hempel—featuring schemes of "verification" and aspirations toward "covering laws"—to one governed by Kuhn's notion of "paradigm."

In all contests defined by modern-postmodern battles over the nature of history, it is important for Christians to affirm that scriptural religion defines its own moral and epistemological universe. Traditional Christian faith, in other words, does not articulate well with the basic coordinates taken for granted by combatants from many sides in contemporary intellectual dispute. Unlike postmodernism—exemplified at its extreme by radical forms of multiculturalism—biblical religion holds forthrightly to the ideal of universal truth. Unlike modernism—exemplified at its extreme by the overweening objectivism of Enlightenment rationality—biblical religion describes truth as a function of personal relationships. In a recent survey of the Western historical canon, Donald Kelley of Rutgers University succinctly summarizes the basic biblical preoccupations: "The term, and perhaps the concept, *history* in a Herodotean sense is not used in the Bible . . . , but . . . the term *truth* appears over a hundred times in both the Old and the New Testament, . . . and *wisdom* . . . over two hundred times. Classical tradition . . . conceived of truth as conformity to fact and proper meaning, which occasionally corresponds to biblical usage. . . . But most often *truth* is the word and law of God, which must be obeyed on the grounds of authority. So it was also in the New Testament, especially in the preaching of Paul, where the truth resides in Christ and, in contrast to human 'fables,' 'traditions,' and 'philosophy,' would set men free" (81).

Over the last several centuries, Western Christians have committed themselves variously to notions of history as simple fact. Christian efforts both to appropriate Enlightenment standards and to take the measure of postmodernist challenges are worthy in themselves. But they will come closer to biblical norms if they remember two overarching realities: (1) In Scripture, God is pictured as both personal and the source of all truth. (2) In a scriptural view, because God truly exists and is always more than the construction of any individual person (or aggrieved group, or ethnic community, or political interest), the personality of truth does not undermine its reality.

More specifically, biblical religion can afford an attitude of intellectual lèse-majesté toward recent debates about historical knowledge. On the one side, this view affirms that the Enlightenment rationalists are correct. Humans may certainly come to learn true things, and to make valid moral judgments, about events or circumstances in the past. The reasons for this confidence, however, rest not on notions of human competence but on an understanding of divine action. God is the source of all things. Through Christ, "all things came into being, . . . and without him not one thing came into being" (John 1:3 NRSV). Not only does the creative activity of the Son of God stand behind the production of all records useful for history, but in that same Son of God "all things hold together" (Col. 1:17), or we might say, sustain their coherence as part of an integrated discourse. Moreover, believers concerned about historical knowledge can take heart from the assurance that God created all possibilities for human culture, art, politics, and social interaction, and so they are "good, and nothing is to be rejected," if they are regarded thankfully as manifestations of God's creating power (1 Tim. 4:4). One of the implications from realizing that humans may appreciate the creation as good must certainly be that we may know it to be good, and even more basically, that we may know it.

Biblical revelation also contains multitudinous statements about the epistemic capacities of humanity that lead to a similar confidence in the possibility of historical knowledge. God created humans with the moral and intellectual capacity to "have dominion" over the physical creation (Gen. 1:26 NRSV). God also is the source of human diversity, since "from one ancestor he made all nations to inhabit the whole earth, and he allotted the times of their existence and the boundaries of the places where they would live" (Acts 17:26 NRSV). But that human diversity, as the entire narrative of Scripture underscores, does not prevent people everywhere from learning the true facts and the proper interpretation of God's ongoing historical action aimed at the redemption of his people.

So what's the problem? When looking at what Christians affirm about the nature of the created universe and the epistemic abilities of human beings, it seems that the Christian faith fully embraces a religious version of Enlightenment confidence in the perspicacity, security, and objectivity of historical knowledge.

The problem is that other parts of biblical revelation look like a quarry for postmodernist assertions undercutting blithe confidence in historical objectivity. Humans are sinners and thus empirical recidivists who "keep listening, but do not comprehend; keep looking, but do not understand" (Isa. 6:9 NRSV). Freely chosen moral corruption darkens understanding (Eph. 4:18); it turns the God-given capacity for knowledge into blindness (Isa. 43:8; Matt. 15:14; 2 Pet. 1:9; and many more). According to these strands of revelation—and they are not insubstantial—humans persistently abandon their capacity for finding the truth in favor of abuses that spring from idolatrous self-interest.

Another and very different strand of Scripture also seems to reinforce postmodernist conclusions. It is the biblical message of the incarnation of the Son of God—at a particular time and place, and into a particular culture with its singular patterns. The very particularity of the incarnation inspires the notion that the vast panoply of human cultural differences—the very differences that so often seem incompatible and, thus, the ground for skeptical theories from the multiculturalists—is a gift of God. Missiologists who study the passage of Christian faith between widely varying cultural groups have put this matter best. So Andrew Walls explains: "Christ took flesh and was made man in a particular time and place, family, nationality, tradition and customs and sanctified them, while still being for all men in every time and place. Wherever he is taken by the people of any day, time and place, he sanctifies that culture—he is living in it. And no other group of Christians has any right to impose in his name a set of assumptions about life determined by another time and place" (217). In sum, from the perspective provided by Christian understanding of the fall, but also the incarnation, there seems to be considerable Christian support for the radical, postmodernist parties in contemporary historical strife.

Yet the point in *beginning* with an effort to view problems of historical knowledge *first* from a Christian angle of vision is not merely to inquire how Christian resources may be exploited by armies active on the field of contemporary intellectual combat. The point is rather to achieve a "Peace of God" (an allusion to the medieval church's provisional efforts at reducing feudal anarchy)—which means, among other things, not taking the current state of discussion as the best way of framing the question.

A Peace of God for history requires a self-consciously Christian form of chastened realism, with the chastening every bit as serious as the commitment to realism. Such a modest realism should be ready to acknowledge that postmodernist critics have accurately described many forms of self-serving distortions or limitations of historical knowledge. At the same time, it can treat the hubris of Enlightenment rationality as a heresy rather than the original sin. This stance does not, of course, solve actual controversies of historical fact, specific problems of historical interpretation, or contested applications of historical knowledge. What it does provide is some reassurance about the potential of grasping actual historical fact, however limited or hedged around by self-limiting qualifications. It offers hope for potential progress in moral evaluation of the past, but only if evaluators are much more attentive to the interpretations of others and much more humble about their own certainties than evaluations usually are. This line of directly biblical reasoning rests, finally, on the awareness—however obscured by idolatrous self-assertion, simple fallibility, or the situatedness of all human existence—that the reason we may come to know something about the past is that the past, like the present, is governed by an all-powerful, all-loving God.

Modern Debates about History and the Bible

Some awareness of modern arguments over the status of historical knowledge would help biblical theologians steer between the Scylla of relativistic postmodernism and the Charybdis of naive Enlightenment positivism. On one side, the extreme application of radical views about history would destroy the Christian faith, and so such an application can be set aside without a qualm. Morality in classic Christian terms rests on a real, God-given natural law, on divine commands like those revealed in the Ten Commandments, or on both. The heart of the gospel is also bound up with a realistic view of history: "If Christ has not been raised, our preaching is useless and so is your faith" (1 Cor. 15:14). Christianity has always displayed an innate tendency toward historical realism, in large part because it depends upon events that Christians—by their creeds, liturgies, dogmatics, preaching, ethics—assert really happened.

Yet, on the other side, the Bible and the great Christian traditions do not offer unambiguous support for the opponents of postmodernism. Individual biblical passages and the great historical summaries of Christian doctrine agree:

- People write history, and people always view the past from the particular vantage point where they stand.

- There are no simple historical facts that are also interesting. Asserting that "there once lived in Judea a rabbi called Jesus" comes close to a simple historical fact, but it is far less interesting and far less complex than the assertion that "Jesus was the Christ of God."

- Although historical knowledge is possible, it is never exhaustive, irreformable, or absolute. The apostle in 1 Cor. 13 was not speaking directly about questions of historical knowledge, but he very well could have been: "For our knowledge is imperfect. . . . For now we see in a mirror dimly. . . . Now I know in part" (13:9, 12 RSV).

- The history inspired by God in Scripture is unique. It contains a full understanding of the divine purpose for human events in a way that no history authored by humans can do. When humans write history as if they were inspired by the Holy Spirit, the result is foolishness (e.g., countless false sightings of the antichrist), disastrous violence (e.g., God is fighting for our side), or a contradiction of the gospel (e.g., the history of only my denomination has been guided by God).

Constructively considered, modern debates about historical knowledge might be helpful for bringing out themes in Scripture and the Christian traditions that are obscured when either rampantly postmodern or unreconstructed Enlightenment assumptions prevail, including themes of contingency, multiple causation, and the personality of truth.

Christian commitment to the notion that research opens a broader pathway to historical insight than does deduction depends upon scriptural intimation of a principle of contingency. In other words, if we want to find out about a theological system, a particular doctrinal possibility, or a proposed exegetical innovation, we must seek out as much evidence as possible about the system, the doctrine, or the innovation. The contingency of the incarnation is the key pointing a way forward for historians in their research (e.g., John 1:46—"Can anything good come from [Nazareth]?" . . . "Come and see"). It might do the same for theologians. If we want to know something, we should not rely upon what we simply take for granted that it must entail, but rather, study that something. We know God by experiencing him; so likewise do we gain reliable knowledge about theological systems, individual doctrines, and specific interpretations of Scripture by studying them.

Historians who attend to the person of Christ—the sum of God's own self-disclosure—expect historical knowledge to be made up of *multiple*, overlapping explanations concerning *causes* for events and circumstances. This understanding is rooted in the duality of orthodox Christology, especially as phrased by the Chalcedonian Definition: "One and the same Christ, Son, Lord, Only-begotten to be acknowledged in two natures, inconfusedly, unchangeably, indivisibly, inseparably, the distinction of natures being by no means taken away by the union, but rather the property of each nature being preserved, and concurring in one person and one subsistence, not parted or divided into two persons, but one and the same Son, and only begotten, God the Word, the Lord Jesus Christ." Christian historians who take to heart Chalcedonian doctrine about the divine and human present in one integrated Person are predisposed to seek knowledge about any historical situation from more than one angle. The wisdom of that expectation is underscored by the fact that it is often illustrated in Scripture.

> This man was handed over to you by God's set purpose and foreknowledge; and you, with the help of wicked men, put him to death by nailing him to the cross. (Acts 2:23)

> And because the gracious hand of my God was upon me, the king granted my requests. (Neh. 2:8//2:18; Ezra 7:6, 9)

These are instances where the biblical authors recognize multiple legitimate skeins of cause and effect, one in the purposes of God, others in the realm of ordinary historical investigation. What Christian historians may derive from Scripture about the possibility of legitimate multiple causation to explain past events could also be put to use by theologians. Discussions of providence, creation, the divine and human agency in salvation, the coming of the kingdom of God—these and many other doctrines would be better understood if historiographical insights were called upon for assistance.

The personality of truth—an important reality underscored for Christian historians with the assistance of postmodern reasoning—is of perhaps even greater use. Debates over whether, for example, Luke was more a theologian or a historian are shown to be jejune by both biblical reasoning and modern historiographical controversy. If all purported history is in some sense ideological, then the pertinent question becomes not whether Luke was more theologian or historian, but what he was trying to do with his historical materials. We explore what in our contemporary assumptions about historicity aids or obscures our understanding of Luke-Acts, and what we will make of Luke's actual writing, rather than what we feel it is possible for him to say.

In sum, modern debates over the nature of historical knowledge are no more a royal road to theological understanding than debates, assumptions, practices, and expectations about history in earlier times. What they do offer, however—and usually in proportion to how upsetting they seem—are goads to more self-conscious and consistently biblical theological construction.

See also Historical Criticism

Bibliography

Ankersmit, F., and H. Kellner, eds. *A New Philosophy of History*. University of Chicago Press, 1995; Appleby, J., L. Hunt, and M. Jacob. *Telling the Truth about History*. W. W. Norton, 1994; Domanska, E., ed. *Encounters*. University Press of Virginia, 1998; Evans, C. S. *The Historical Christ and the Jesus of Faith*. Oxford University Press, 1996; Evans, R. *In Defense of History*. W. W. Norton, 1999; Haskell, T. *Objectivity Is Not Neutrality*. Johns Hopkins University Press, 1998; Iggers, G. *Historiography in the Twentieth Century*. Wesleyan University Press, 1997; Kelley, D. *Faces of History*. Yale University Press, 1998; Kuklick, B., and D. G. Hart, eds. *Religious Advocacy and American History*. Eerdmans, 1997; Murphey, M. *Philosophical Foundations of Historical Knowledge*. State University of New York Press, 1994; Noll, M. "History Wars." *Books and Culture*, May/June 1999, 30–34; July/Aug 1999, 22–25; Sep/Oct 1999, 38–41; Nov/Dec 1999, 42–44; idem. "A Theological Understanding of 'Ordinary History.'" *Christianity and History Newsletter* 19 (2000): 6–16; Spitzer, A. *Historical Truth and Lies about the Past*. University of North Carolina Press, 1996; Walls, A. "Africa and Christian Identity." Pages 212–21 in *Mission Focus*, ed. W. Shenk. Herald Press, 1980; Wells, R., ed. *History and the Christian Historian*. Eerdmans, 1998.

Mark A. Noll

History of Effects *See* Historical Theology; Interpretation, History of; Tradition

History of Israel

A theological interpretation of the biblical history of Israel may review the story of the nation from two polar opposites: The gracious and mighty deeds of God bring about his people's existence and deliver them from destruction. But then, the people themselves have a rebellious nature and thus are constantly at odds with the will of their Deity. These opposite movements find reconciliation in the OT through the covenant that God gives to his people to guide them in their life and faith. Even this, however, proves inadequate so many times. In the end it is the same powerful and loving grace of God, present in the nation's birth, that continues to guide the people—a grace that delays judgment and yet, when that judgment comes, provides a means of salvation and life for a remnant. In the NT period Israel appears composed of many factions, and its responses to the messianic claims of Jesus vary. Nevertheless, the dominant sense is one of the rejection of these claims. God's plan for Israel remains, but alongside that plan emerges the Gentile Christian community, where the message of the gospel flourishes in a largely unforeseen manner.

The history begins with the calling forth of Abram and the promise of Gen. 12:1–3. Abram's repeated demonstration of faith expands the promise in the following chapters until it reaches a point where it includes the entire land of Canaan, offspring as many as the sand of the sea, and blessing to all nations who bless Abram's seed. Although Abram experiences small expressions of this promise—the purchase of the cave of Machpelah (ch. 23), the birth of Isaac (21), and the blessing of Melchizedek (rewarded with Abram's tithe in 14:18–20)—their full realization is postponed beyond the period of Abram and the following three generations. Yet this promise remains the theological key to the interpretation of the narratives of Israel's patriarchs. God reaffirms blessing to Isaac (25:11), who passes it on to his son Jacob (27:28–29). The promise of offspring remains a precarious one throughout Genesis, as it was the most difficult one for Abram to believe and accept. God preserves Jacob despite his brother's hatred. God blesses him in the house of Laban, and when he leaves to return to the promised land, he has many sons to carry on his line. Even here, however, Joseph appears headed for certain death and oblivion (ch. 37). Yet God does not forget his promise, and this younger son is elevated to second in command in Egypt. As a result Jacob and his family are delivered from the famine and thrive there.

The oppression and exodus form the fundamental saving event in God's plan for his people of the OT. Remembered twice in prose and poetry (Exod. 14–15), God's work is nothing less than the creation of a new people for himself, distinct from the other nations of the earth. Neither the power of Pharaoh nor that of the sea is able to hold back this event. Instead, they become the means by which God demonstrates his sover-

eignty in the liberation of his people. The exodus event, as a historic act of redemption, becomes a key element in defining God and his relationship to his people. He is a liberator from slavery, and they are bound in covenant with him. Without the exodus, none of the promises of land, seed, and blessing would be fulfilled. This event transforms the means by which the remainder of Israel's history is understood. The redemption of God sets the stage for a much more complete fulfillment of the earlier promises. God's claim on his people is absolute, and so is their obligation to accept the demands of the covenant relationship. Marred by idolatry and moral failure, that generation does not inherit the land of promise. Instead, their children receive the opportunity. Like their parents they also march across the dry ground of a body of water. This time it is the Jordan, rather than the Red Sea. However, they follow God's leader, and their faithfulness is rewarded with the covenant blessing of the land of promise. In this manner the great stories of conquest should be read as fulfillment. The salvation of Rahab and the Gibeonites represents the reciprocity of blessing promised to those who bless God's people. The settlement throughout the land continues the promise of fruitfulness as Israel expands to occupy the gift God has given them. As at Sinai, the covenant renewal ceremonies (Josh. 8:30–35; 24) reaffirm that these blessings are part of God's ongoing relationship with his people.

The generations after Joshua do not prove as faithful in their life according to God's covenant. Their assimilation to the worship of the gods of surrounding peoples (Judg. 2:9–11) and their marriages with nonbelievers result in a dilution of their power to resist the enemy invaders. The disunity grows worse and worse, and in the end even the divinely appointed judges are unable to prevent the civil war that erupts (chs. 20–21) and the consequent destruction of many Israelites. In this scene the story of Ruth demonstrates the ongoing presence of the faithful, even if in a minority. It is this faithfulness that reasserts the promise of God to Abram and his descendants. The fruitfulness of Ruth continues a line that leads to David and Israelite control of all the land of promise. If the promise to Abram reaches a high point during David's reign, one must for this period also read of God often working behind the scenes. Not so obvious as in previous generations, the divine hand continues to move events according to his will. Thus, the popular Saul is ultimately rejected and replaced with the youthful upstart David. The selection of David and rejection of Saul is not an arbitrary whim introduced by the narrator. Instead, the confessions that David regularly makes before undertaking tasks suggest a vibrant faith in God, a faith not evident in the statements of Saul.

Nevertheless, the human freedom to choose remained, as did the divine willingness to allow people to act on their own moral decisions. As previously in the wilderness generation, the people under the judges, and Saul's hatred of David, so the latter's family and his own generals engage in blood-filled betrayals and battles to usurp power and seek murderous revenge. Without an awareness that the line of good and evil goes through the heart of everyone, it is difficult to understand the terror and carnage that often reigned in the palace. And the family of David was only the first in a long line of the children and spouses of kings who sought to affect the decisions and events of the palace through schemes and force. The Israelite citizenry imitated this pattern of evil. The depravity of human nature and the propensity to turn away from God led to Israel's worship of other gods. This abandonment of the covenant could only mean that God would respond by driving people from the covenantal gift, the land. As he had done with the first couple in driving them from the Garden of Eden (Gen. 3), so God allowed enemies to end the independence of the northern kingdom and, nearly a century and a half later, that of the southern kingdom. Neither nation would repent, and this sinful failure led to the downfall of the nation of Israel. All this is recorded in the books of Kings as the reason for their destruction. As Noth observed, the whole history of Israel as written especially in the books of Kings (but also in the earlier historical books) is a demonstration of the justice of God, in bringing about the destruction of Judah and Jerusalem and the end of the independent monarchy.

Side by side with this depiction of sin and judgment is the story of Israel's history as recorded in the books of Chronicles. Unlike Kings, the Chronicler begins the historical account with a series of genealogies that focus on the good hand of God in his grace, which begins with the first man and woman and proceeds to the present day of the Chronicler. The emphasis on the roles of those who worship and create music for the Jerusalem temple suggests a different purpose of this history. Unlike the books of Kings, Chronicles delights in the positive features of the great kings whose faith and faithfulness inspired the Chronicler to emphasize their best. Thus Saul is glossed over and nothing critical is said of David

or Solomon. The southern kingdom is emphatically the place of God's blessing. The north is condemned from the outset: nothing good can come from there. David is the cult founder of the worship of God in Jerusalem. Once the ideal of unity is compromised, even the good Judean kings fall into sin and experience God's judgment. Theologically, this recounting of Israel's history is less concerned with the sin of the people and more concerned with the right way to worship God. This occurs with the people of God united and praising God in all forms of temple worship. Here the history is understood less in terms of how kings responded to the covenantal requirement to believe in a single Deity, and more in terms of how they worshipped that Deity through the temple and its cult in Jerusalem.

Next to the exodus and the covenants with Israel and David, one of the most reflected-upon events in Israel's history is the destruction of the temple. This destruction—especially after the miraculous deliverance of Jerusalem and the temple from the Assyrian king a century earlier (a miracle recorded in three separate biblical accounts in 2 Kings 18–20; 2 Chron. 32; Isa. 36–39)—brought a greater crisis of faith than any other event in Israel's history. How could the writers see through the sorrow and rejection of God, such as found in the poetry of Lamentations, to affirm God's faithfulness (3:23)? For the inhabitants of Jerusalem, Jeremiah would proclaim that the people had so sinned in their idolatrous pursuits that they could expect nothing but judgment (Jer. 2; etc.). Habakkuk would not try to explain the terrible mystery of a people more idolatrous than Israel destroying the nation, but only counsel a steadfast faithfulness (2:3–4). For those already in exile, Ezekiel would explain how the temple had become thoroughly saturated with idolatry of every kind so that God departed from it and from the land, thereby allowing the terrible judgment to fall (chs. 8–11). Yet almost two centuries earlier Hosea (in speaking of the judgment against the northern kingdom) had affirmed that God's mercy would override his judgment for his people (Hos. 11:7–9), and other prophets had looked forward to a new age (e.g., Isa. 2:1–4 = Mic. 4:1–5).

The history-changing event of the destruction of Jerusalem and the exile brought with it a new interpretation of ancient prophecies. No longer did the people look for the anointed one, the Messiah, in a historical king, but now they began to look for this fulfillment in a golden age in which all the prophecies would be fulfilled. It is no wonder that the returnees from the exile who were old enough to remember the temple before the 586 BCE destruction, wept when they saw the modest foundations of the one that was rebuilt in 517 (Ezra 3:12). Nevertheless, this was neither the end of Israel's history nor the fulfillment. Side by side with the grand expectations of a renewed Jerusalem and temple (Ezek. 40–48; Isa. 56–66) were the prophetic figures who sustained the early returnees with promises of God's blessings for their devotion to rebuilding the temple. At the same time some projected their prophecies beyond the stage of immediate history to an earth-shattering apocalypse (Daniel; Zech. 9–14) that would usher in a new age. Then there were the priestly pragmatists, such as Ezra the scribe; with the leadership of figures like Nehemiah, Ezra reconstituted the postexilic community of the mid-fifth century BCE into a people who were called to a life of holiness centered around the torah, the law of God.

All these trajectories continued into the inter-testamental age. The apocalyptic writers generated a mass of literature that followed world-changing themes. They also formed isolated communities such as the one that produced the Dead Sea Scrolls. John would follow in this literary style with his Revelation, and Jesus himself would be remembered for a similar teaching in his Olivet Discourse (Matt. 24). The prophetic trajectory would also continue. In the teachings of Jesus and his followers, it would combine with messianic fulfillment in the person of Jesus Christ, and in literary allusions in the Gospels that would suggest at last the true return from the exile had come, and the promised age was about to begin. The call to holiness would remain along with its application in the obedience to the torah. In particular, this group formed the center of Judaism in Palestine, with a faith strong enough to endure the persecutions of the second-century (BCE) Hellenizer Antiochus Epiphanes and the oppression of Roman rule that began a century later. While groups such as the Pharisees would debate the meaning of the words of God in the Law, Jesus introduced his authoritative interpretations that penetrated to the heart of the purpose of God's intention (Matt. 5:27–44). Thus, Israel's history was brought to a turning point for all who would take it seriously. There would be those who saw in Christ the fulfillment of the old prophecies and those who sought to follow the law in all its requirements. The small group that attempted to cling to both Christ and the law would not long outlast the division of Christianity and Judaism that emerged by the end of the first century. With the destruction of the temple in 70 CE, the promise to Abram of land, seed, and universal blessing would take on a distinct meaning and provide a different history for Christians and Jews.

Bibliography

Block, D. *Judges, Ruth*. NAC 6. Broadman & Holman, 1999; Clines, D. J. A. *The Theme of the Pentateuch*. JSOTSup 8. JSOT, 1978; Eichrodt, W. *Theology of the Old Testament*, trans. J. Baker. 2 vols. SCM, 1967; Fretheim, T. *Exodus*. Interpretation. John Knox, 1991; George, M. "Yhwh's Own Heart." *CBQ* 64 (2002): 442–59; Hanson, P. "Israelite Religion in the Early Postexilic Period." Pages 485–508 in *Ancient Israelite Religion*, ed. P. Miller Jr., P. Hanson, and S. McBride. Fortress, 1987; Hess, R. *Joshua*. TOTC. InterVarsity, 1996; idem. "Joshua." Pages 165–71 in *New Dictionary of Biblical Theology*, ed. T. D. Alexander and B. Rosner. InterVarsity, 2000; Japhet, S. *I and II Chronicles*. OTL. Westminster John Knox, 1993; Noth, M. *Überlieferungsgeschichtliche Studien*. 2d ed. M. Niemeyer, 1957; Provan, I. *Hezekiah and the Book of Kings*. De Gruyter, 1988; Schniedewind, W. *The Word of God in Transition*. JSOTSup 197. Sheffield Academic Press, 1995.

Richard S. Hess

History of Religions School *See* Religion

Hittitology *See* Ancient Near Eastern Background Studies

Holocaust *See* Anti-Semitism; Jewish-Christian Dialogue; Violence

Holy Spirit, Doctrine of the

It is a measure of its importance to Christian faith that the doctrine of the Holy Spirit has been disputed through the history of Christianity; lesser subjects never prove so controversial. The NT claims that in the outpouring of the Holy Spirit, the risen and ascended Lord Jesus Christ himself continues to be present to us (John 14:16–18; 2 Cor. 3:17). It also claims that in our experience of the Spirit, the fulfillment of God's promises concerning the end of the age can be discerned (Acts 2:14–21). These are, however, monumental claims, the full sense of which was then and is now extraordinarily difficult to grasp.

It was thus inevitable that disagreement should have emerged over how the "work" and "person" of the Spirit should be understood. Even within the NT, evidence of such controversy can readily be identified. In the Acts of the Apostles, the outpouring of the Spirit upon *Gentiles* at first scandalizes the Jewish followers of Jesus. Although ultimately the coming of the Spirit grounds the Gentile mission they themselves undertake (Acts 10:44–11:18; 15:1–21), it would be mistaken to overlook the immense religious upheaval occasioned by the Spirit's work for the first Christians. Again, as a result of this mission, Paul is obliged to regulate the Corinthian church's anarchic expression of the gifts of the Spirit. In his argument he appeals to principles of mutuality in Christ's body, the supremacy of love, and the need for worship to be conducted "decently and in order" (1 Cor. 12:1–14:40 RSV).

There thus is good precedent in the Bible for the difficulty that Christians have subsequently had in negotiating the many claims made concerning experience of the Spirit.

The "Breath" of God in Biblical and Theological Perspective

In the wider biblical context, it is nevertheless notable that references to the Spirit "frame" the total narrative of the biblical canon. In the beginning, the Spirit of God "broods" over the face of the primeval waters; then God speaks and heaven and earth are summoned into being (Gen. 1:2). At the other end of the canon, the Spirit is source for a different act of summons, by which we inherit a new heaven and new earth: "Come" (Rev. 22:17). Though modest reference to the Spirit is made in these texts, the association of the Spirit with both protology and eschatology is significant, for such ideas decisively shape theological understanding. Whether by accident or providence, thus is signaled that the work of the Spirit is a regulative theme in the Bible as a whole. Indeed, Scripture itself is said to be "breathed" by God (*theopneustos*, 2 Tim. 3:16), an expression that involves reference to the Spirit as the "breath" of God.

Such usage, however, demands a certain hermeneutical subtlety that often proves elusive. Christian orthodoxy affirms the deity of the Holy Spirit, but the basic meaning of the Hebrew word *ruakh*, as of the Greek *pneuma*, both of which our word "spirit" translates, is simply "moving air." The temptation is to understand the Spirit in an impersonal and instrumental sense. A recent example is found in the NRSV translation of the *ruakh 'Elohim* of Gen. 1:2 as "a wind from God," rather than more robustly as "the Spirit of God" (as in the footnote).

Though the temptation to free the Bible from ecclesiastical or dogmatic constraint is particularly characteristic of modern historical-critical exegesis, this specific problem is not new. Au-

gustine, among others, wrestled with the ostensibly impersonal connotations of "Spirit," even when employing it in a fully trinitarian sense. The problem was that the name Spirit differs sharply from the personal and relational names of the other two persons, "Father" and "Son." At one point, Augustine substitutes the name "Gift" for "Spirit," since he can make so little of the latter in his theory of relations (*Trin.* 5.11).

In the face of such difficulties, one may well ask why "spirit" should have become a theological word at all, not only in Hebraic thought, but also in a wide variety of human cultures. The answer, undoubtedly, is that as an elemental force of nature, and as the medium of life for everything that breathes, air fascinated ancient peoples. Even today in many human languages, the words "life" and "breath" are closely related or even identical. In English, the connection appears only indirectly, but it is nevertheless significant. "He breathed his last," we say, reflecting not only the experience of anyone who has watched another die, but also the view of ancient medicine, which looked to breath rather than the brainwaves as evidence of life. By extension, the ancients took breath to be significant not only physically, but also religiously. If to have breath is to be alive, then to be alive is to be, potentially or actually, a religious subject—a person capable of relating to God.

Such associations between breath, or spirit, and physical life appear in the Bible, as in "breath of life" texts of Genesis (6:17; 7:15, 22) and in the poetry of the Psalms (104:25–30)—though most spectacularly, in the "valley of dry bones" vision of Ezek. 37: "Prophesy to the breath, prophesy, mortal, and say to the breath: Thus says the Lord GOD: Come from the four winds, O breath, and breathe upon these slain, that they may live. . . . The breath came into them, and they lived, and stood on their feet, a vast multitude" (Ezek. 37:9–10 NRSV).

The biblical link between breath and physical life, however, easily yields in overall significance to the theme of the Spirit's gift of "spiritual" life. Already in Hebrew Scripture, one can find intimations of the future work of the Spirit, such as the words of Joel 2 quoted in Acts 2:14–21. Here the spiritual renewal of the people of God in the end times is associated with a new outpouring of the Spirit. It is, however, above all in the Pauline corpus and the Johannine literature of the NT that this theme is developed.

In the letters of Paul, the Spirit is not only the source of authority in Paul's ministry (Rom.

15:17–19; 1 Cor. 2:4–5, 13), but the whole Christian life is comprehended as life "in the Spirit." It is by virtue of the Spirit's work that we become children of God (Rom. 8:14–17; Gal. 4:5–7), making the confession of faith: "Jesus is Lord" (1 Cor. 12:3). By the Spirit, we are able to overcome our struggle with the principle of sin in ourselves (Rom. 7:5–6; 8:1, 17; Gal. 5:16–17). The Spirit thus bears its fruit in the moral conduct and character of the Christian (Gal. 5:22–23). The Spirit, furthermore, is operative in the worship and existence of the church, in an activity extending from the routine affairs of administration through to the *charismata* of "tongues," prophecy, and the working of miracles (1 Cor. 12:7–11, 27–31).

The Johannine tradition, for its part, not only speaks of the Spirit as "living water" (John 4:13–14; 7:37–39 RSV), thus drawing upon and extending the ancient association between the Spirit and life, but also as "Paraclete" or "Counselor" (John 14:16, 26). It is also the most explicit of all the main pneumatological sources of the NT about the root sense of "Spirit" as breath or wind (John 3:8). In John, however, this breath of God has become also the breath of Jesus himself, for John's "Pentecost" occurs when the risen Lord appears, *breathes upon* the disciples, and says, "Receive the Holy Spirit" (John 20:22).

The Holy Spirit in the History of Doctrine

The subsequent history of pneumatology contains two major foci, around which the doctrine of the Spirit moves. Both involve an explicit trinitarian reference, and both remain living issues in the contemporary theological context.

The Christian writers of the second century had little interest in the Holy Spirit, so that, from the pneumatological standpoint, their writings are a disappointment. The apologists, in particular, concentrate so heavily on the doctrine of the Logos that the Spirit is effectively pushed to the margins. As great a third-century theologian as Origen lives in the shadow of this kind of subordinationism. Even in the protracted debates of the early fourth century occasioned by the claims of Arius the arch-heretic, the sense persisted that a satisfactory treatment of the christological question would be a satisfactory treatment of everything that really mattered. The original Creed of Nicea (325), from which the "Nicene Creed" ultimately derives, managed to affirm only "[We believe] in the Holy Spirit" in its third article, omitting to specify further what the shape of this belief ought to be. The inescapable impression left is that it does not matter greatly.

As in the case of Christology, however, controversy eventually brought the doctrine of the Spirit explicitly to the fore—after the christological question had been mainly resolved. Having been marginalized theologically and politically in deference to christological orthodoxy, a moderate version of Arianism reasserted itself in the middle decades of the fourth century, maintaining that, whatever may be said of the Son in his relation to the Father, the Spirit at least remains a creature. The major responses to this claim came from the bishop-theologians Athanasius of Alexandria, Basil of Caesarea, and Gregory of Nazianzus, in works that still rank among the classic formulations of the doctrine of the Holy Spirit. The answer of Athanasius and Gregory to the new Arian challenge was unambiguous: the Spirit is "consubstantial" with the Father and/or the Son. In both cases, arguments in defense of Nicene Christology that were well established in anti-Arian polemic were adapted to the cause of pneumatology (McIntyre). Basil of Caesarea, in his public writings at least, took a different course. He knew that the Nicene dogma had proved to be so controversial in the past as to be of limited use in the present. So Basil presented his case on the basis of ecclesiastical precedent, arguing that the matter could be resolved by recognizing that the Spirit is the Sanctifier who is, as such, rightly the object of worship. Established liturgical formulae, for example, constitute a major thread of evidence in the case he makes. Ultimately the Council of Constantinople (381) dogmatized the deity of the Spirit in its formulation: "The Lord and giver of life, who proceeds from the Father, who with the Father and the Son is worshipped and glorified." Thereby it employed both a language and a pneumatological "style" that can be traced directly to Basil of Caesarea.

The question of the deity of the Holy Spirit was thus formally resolved by the Council of Constantinople in 381, in its revision of the Nicene Creed (Kelly). What is left unstated, however, is what the relation between the Son and the Spirit might be, or indeed, whether there is any relation at all. This surprising omission unfortunately left a space in which the most far-reaching controversy in Christian history surrounding the doctrine of the Holy Spirit could occur. For reasons relating as much to trinitarian theory as to pneumatological principle, Latin theology from the time of Augustine had maintained that the Holy Spirit proceeds from the Father *and* the *Son*. Augustine, for example, had suggested that the temporal "missions" of the persons are grounded in their eternal "processions," so that the sending of the Spirit by Christ was possible only on the basis of a metaphysically prior procession of the Spirit from the Son. This understanding was then fleshed out in a brilliant theory of trinitarian relationality, and by way of the famous "psychological analogy." By the beginning of the scholastic period, however, the Augustinian thesis had assumed a rigidity in the minds of major representatives of the Latin tradition that was altogether foreign to Augustine's own more tentative approach.

The major outcome of this self-certainty within the Latin tradition was the insertion of the *filioque* phrase into the Latin text of the Nicene Creed on the authority of Pope Benedict VIII in 1014. Hence, *"qui ex Patre filioque procedit* [who proceeds from the Father *and* the *Son]"* now became the Latin confession. Though dogmatizing long-standing Western theory, and universalizing in Latin liturgy something that had for centuries been local liturgical preference, this act was deeply offensive to the Christian East. To the Greeks, it symbolized not only the increasingly chauvinistic claims of the Latins, but also what was wrong with the papacy. In the East the *filioque* has never been seen as a constructive contribution to the Christian doctrine of the Holy Spirit. The result was ironically that the greatest of Christian schisms, that between the Greeks and the Latins (formally dating from 1054), occurred in the cause of the doctrine of the Holy Spirit, the trinitarian person to whom communion is technically appropriated.

Contemporary Problems and Possibilities

The debates of the fourth or the eleventh century may seem distant, but many of the same issues face us today. On the Christian left, from the "pop" theology of John Shelby Spong to varieties of feminist analysis, a running polemic against any idea of a transcendent God who acts redemptively in the world can be identified. It has issued in a treatment of the Spirit as so radically immanent in the several liberative quests of our time as to be indistinguishable from them. As in the philosophy of Fichte, and the theology of the classical liberal Protestant tradition, moralizing praxis here is everything.

On the other side of the coin, the explosive growth of Pentecostal groups globally presents another challenge, some might say an equal and opposite one. If the weakness of the liberal approach is a loss of the lordship of the Holy Spirit, then a major problem in much current Pentecostalism is that the lordship of the Spirit claimed is

irreconcilable with the human good as ordinarily conceived. Of real relevance here is the question of the relation of the Spirit to the word of God, the word that dignifies human reason, and its implications for a fully trinitarian understanding of the Spirit.

A theological hermeneutic of the Spirit for today must endeavor to steer a middle path between these extremes of pure anthropocentrism and pneumatic excess. Ideally, in so doing such an account would leave adequate scope for the satisfaction of both tendencies, humane and ecstatic, within a more comprehensive vision. However, Western theology today lacks the intellectual foundations upon which such an account could, in principle, be given. What is demanded is a theology integrative of the whole, whereas what is offered by virtually all contemporary Western theology is a theology in and of fragments. Perhaps it can only be from the cultural and theological traditions emerging in non-Western Christianity that such integrative insight will come. In such a case, the future of the Christian doctrine of the Holy Spirit may lie in the hands of the emerging churches.

See also Illumination

Bibliography

Anselm. *On the Procession of the Holy Spirit.* In *Trinity, Incarnation, and Redemption,* ed. and trans. J. Hopkins and H. Richardson. Harper & Row, 1970; Augustine. *Trin.*; Badcock, G. *Light of Truth and Fire of Love.* Eerdmans, 1997; Basil of Caesarea. *De Spiritu Sancto.* Herder, 1993; Congar, Y. *I Believe in the Holy Spirit,* trans. D. Smith. 3 vols. Seabury, 1983; idem. *The Word and the Spirit,* trans. D. Smith. Harper & Row, 1986; Del Colle, R. *Christ and the Spirit.* Oxford University Press, 1994; Dunn, J. D. G. *Jesus and the Spirit.* SCM, 1975; Kelly, J. N. D. *Early Christian Creeds.* 2d ed. Longman, 1972; Lampe, G. *God as Spirit.* SCM, 1977; McIntyre, J. *The Shape of Pneumatology.* T&T Clark, 1997; Moltmann, J. *The Spirit of Life,* trans. M. Kohl. SCM, 1992; Mühlen, H. *Der Heilige Geist als Person in der Trinität bei der Inkarnation und im Gnadenbund.* 5th ed. Aschendorff, 1988; Pinnock, C. *Flame of Love.* InterVarsity, 1996; Smail, T. *The Giving Gift.* Hodder & Stoughton, 1988.

Gary D. Badcock

Homiletics   *See* Preaching, Use of the Bible in

Homosexuality   *See* Sexuality

Hope

Hope is waiting in confident expectation for God's promises in Christ, summed up in the gospel. Hope is fundamental because the gospel concerns

God's culmination of his redemptive work, "the grace that Jesus Christ will bring you when he is revealed" (1 Pet. 1:13 NRSV), the "hope of glory" (Col. 1:27). Most of that for which we trust in Christ remains yet future (Rom. 8:24b), for the Spirit's present blessings are "firstfruits." God alone controls fulfillment, so hope is waiting for God to act, graciously and powerfully, on our behalf as in the past.

Christians hope "by faith" (Gal. 5:5). Faith trusts in God's promises, while hope expects what is to come. God's reliability and his promise should foster lively, growing assurance, despite delays and doubts.

Waiting Expectantly for God in Christ

Humans' most pressing need is for the fullness of God's gracious, glorious presence with us, for us. The psalms and the prophets frequently speak of waiting for the Lord (Pss. 25:3, 5, 21; 33:20; 130:5), hoping for and in him (33:18, 22; 131:3; 147:11), and calling him their hope (71:5), the hope of Israel (Jer. 14:8; 17:13) and of all the earth (Ps. 65:5). In turn, "the eye of Yahweh" is on them (33:18 AT). The singleness of biblical hope (62:5–6) should persevere despite perilous circumstances, assured of deliverance and restoration (42:5, 11). God's faithful power favors with his provision those who trust in him, but those who trust in human rulers are hopeless (Ps. 146).

As the only Creator, the living God is the only reliable object of hope. This provides an authentic ("living") hope (1 Pet. 1:3). All promises made in the name of other gods fail (Jer. 14:22).

Christ Jesus, "our great God and Savior," is the hope of all believers (Titus 2:13). The "last days" are already here because the Messiah has come (e.g., 1 Cor. 10:11; Heb. 1:2–3) and will complete what he has begun. As joint heirs with Christ (Rom. 8:17), Christians wait for his return from heaven (1 Thess. 1:10), the glorious manifestation that is the blessed hope (Titus 2:13) and includes resurrection into the eternal kingdom of God (1 Cor. 15:19). The presence of Christ even now dwelling with us and in us by the Spirit constitutes "the hope of glory" (Col. 1:27).

Waiting Confidently

Christians enjoy trinitarian grounds for confidence in "the hope promised by the gospel" (Col. 1:23b NRSV). The "God of hope" covenantally bound his promises, guaranteeing their hope (Rom. 4:18; 15:13). God's character establishes the gospel's promises as utterly reliable (Col. 1:5;

Heb. 10:23; Titus 1:2; Heb. 6:18; 7:20). Likewise, God's past faithfulness to his people gives reason to hope (e.g., Pss. 42:4, 6; 105; 106; Rom. 15:4).

Triumphant over enemies (Col. 2:15), the superlative priest and perfect sacrifice anchors Christian hope (Heb. 6:19). God's supreme "mighty act" was raising Jesus, as the firstfruits (1 Cor. 15:20; cf. Rom. 8:29; Rev. 1:5), assuring believers that he will raise them also (2 Cor. 4:13).

Through the eschatological Spirit, the power of the age to come (Ezek. 36:26–28; 37:5–6, 9–10, 14; Joel 2:28–29), believers "eagerly wait for the hope of righteousness" (Gal. 5:5 NRSV) and abound in hope (Rom. 15:13), having received pledge and seal (Eph. 1:13c–14).

Waiting Expectantly for Remedy

Hope for grace is oriented toward remedying sinfulness, displaying hope's historical character by situating it in the sequence of creation-fall-redemption-reconciliation-consummation. Hope is discontent with the present, personally and structurally, unwilling to remain wounded and wounding. The remedy includes corporate, personal, and cosmic dimensions, all integral to God's salvation (Rom. 8:19, 22). Hope derives from the Messiah's culminative work and thus experiences the tension between present and future blessings.

In this unjust order, the relatively innocent suffer, while the wicked remain unpunished. Justice is not simply punishment of the wicked, for no amount of suffering by the guilty will make things right. The God of justice promises to restore the fortunes of the oppressed (Zeph. 3:19–20), bringing a world in which righteousness dwells (Isa. 65:25; Amos 5:24). In restoration God will make all things new (Rev. 21:4–5).

God's purging and renewal is so extensive as to be "new creation" (2 Cor. 5:17; Gal. 6:15; Isa. 65:17; Rev. 21:1), overturning sin's effects and accomplishing what sin prevented. Sin and Satan will not thwart God from the eternal fruition of his purposes for creation (Rev. 21–22).

Expectant Waiting as Lifestyle

Hope can seem illusory, given rampant evil and appalling suffering. Christian hope rejects triumphalism ("first suffering, then glory," Rom. 8:17–18). Though God's promises sustain hope, God has not fully revealed his purposes, nor do we fully understand what is revealed. Moreover, waiting can undermine confident expectation, echoed by the psalmists: "How long, O Yahweh?"

(Pss. 6:3 AT; 13:1–2; 74:10; 79:5; 80:4; 89:46; 94:3; cf. Rev. 6:10).

Portrayed in vivid images of majestic, soaring eagles and inexhaustible runners, God's magnificent promise (Isa. 40:31) speaks not of hope's ultimate fulfillment, but of its effectiveness before fruition, even during long delays. Unfailingly faithful to his promises, God is unpredictable in his utter reliability. His faithfulness is seen only in faith.

Hope is an essential Christian virtue (1 Cor. 13:13), bestowed by the Spirit on the basis of Jesus' resurrection (Rom. 15:13). Christian hope yields the moral fruits of joyful confidence in God (8:28; 12:12), unashamed patience in tribulation (Rom. 5:3; 12:12), and perseverance in prayer (12:12), anchored to God's steadfastness (Heb. 3:6; 6:18–19). Waiting for God is associated with virtues such as integrity and uprightness (Ps. 25:21) and love (1 Cor. 13:7). Paul admonishes believers not to set their hopes on the uncertainty of riches, but rather on God, who richly provides everything (1 Tim. 6:17)—as exemplified by real widows (5:5).

Hopeful Christians should be diligent servants in the world, manifesting the gospel's hope in their vocations. As new creations foreshadowing *the* new creation, Christians should be means of gracious change to the communities and structures of the age, calling others to join in mercy and justice now and hope for the culminative justice and renewal.

The vice of hopelessness can be presumption ("premature, self-willed anticipation of the fulfillment of what we hope for from God") or despair ("premature, arbitrary anticipation" of nonfulfillment, perhaps as resignation, "humble acquiescence to the present") (Moltmann 23). Both forms deny the pilgrim character of hope (Pieper 47).

Hermeneutical Conclusions

Right reading of Scripture on hope requires understanding what God has promised—to each generation. Reading Scripture for its hopes for believers thus acutely poses how it is both a historically and culturally specific document (or collection) and also the enduringly authoritative word of God for all the church throughout history in every culture.

Christians should not read Scripture's promises as merely descriptive of narrated characters or initial recipients/hearers; neither should they claim "every promise in the Book is mine." Reading Scripture canonically, as God's written word for all the church, still acknowledges distinctions between historically and theologically contextualized promises and later readers' contexts.

Christians' most cherished hope is Christ's personal, bodily return in judgment and blessing. God's character abides infallibly (though without specifying *how* in each situation he will be loving, merciful, faithful, nor what that means for possible peril or blessing). God's people read his promises to earlier generations as God's hopefull word to them as well, but discerning what God thereby says for them in their circumstances. God's narrated past provisions illustrate what he can do (and sometimes does) for believers in need.

Modern biblical scholars and theologians largely abandoned biblical eschatology as mythological. Moltmann's *Theology of Hope* spurred recovery of eschatology as fundamental to Jesus' and the apostles' teaching, and the gospel itself as inescapably eschatological, against the profoundest evils. At an extreme, however, especially among evangelicals, exaggeration abounds, wrongly embellishing with conjecture what God has promised.

Hopelessness refuses to wait for God's promises, insisting "now or never." Hopeless readings (whether presumptuous or despairing) insist on understanding and nurture "now or never," refusing insight that comes slowly, from the Spirit, through diligent, sound practices. In contrast, rather than facile or evasive readings of challenging or puzzling passages, readings that "hope all things" (1 Cor. 13:7c NRSV) trust God's provision of insight and nourishment, if not now, then later, and perhaps only incrementally.

See also Last Things, Doctrine of; Virtue

Bibliography

Bauckham, R., and T. Hart. *Hope against Hope*. Eerdmans, 1999; Moltmann, J. *Theology of Hope*, trans. J. Leitch. Harper, 1967; Moule, C. F. D. *The Meaning of Hope*. Highway Press, 1953. Reprint, Fortress, 1963; Pieper, J. *On Hope*. Ignatius, 1986.

Stephen R. Spencer

Hosea, Book of

History of Interpretation

In earlier times comment on Hosea tended to concentrate on the book's imagery rather than its place in the history of Israel. Special attention was paid to the varied pictures of God's love and judgment, and it was often related in typological fashion to the work of Christ. In recent years

Hosea has not been the focus of as much scholarly interest as some of the other OT prophets. Often literary-critical or historical issues have been of most interest. Questions concerning Hosea's family have occupied a lot of attention: the identity of his wife, Gomer; the nature of her adultery; whether or not she and the wife of chapter 3 are the same person; whether any or all of her children are fathered by Hosea and what the precise significance of their names might be; and whether indeed these are real people or merely literary constructs. Most scholarly articles have concentrated on chapters 1–3. Those who have considered the later chapters have focused on the interpretation of the many and varied images and metaphors used by Hosea to describe Israel's unfaithfulness and God's attitude toward his people. The familiarity with the imagery of bread-making (in ch. 7) and of farming and shepherding has led some to draw conclusions about Hosea's own background.

The question as to the relation of the more positive approach of chapter 14 with the strong judgmental emphasis of chapters 4–13 has occupied the attention of some. So also have other questions relating to the unity and integrity of the book, sometimes relating to the many textual difficulties or to the various canonical links mentioned below. In more recent years feminist scholars have looked again at chapters 1 and 3 and questioned whether Hosea is in fact here portrayed as an obsessive, possessive, power-hungry, and abusive husband—with Gomer in reality the heroine rather than the villain of the piece. Others, in response, have argued that it is not valid to read such a modern agenda into the text.

The Message of Hosea

Hosea speaks directly into the situation of Israel within the eighth century BCE, and it is not really possible to understand what is going on in Hosea without some awareness of that situation. On the one hand, Israel as a whole was economically prosperous and stable during and after Jeroboam's long reign. They were at peace, with the southern kingdom of Judah equally flourishing under their longtime king Uzziah. They benefited economically from their situation on the major trade route between Assyria and Egypt. Assyria had removed surrounding threats but as yet had not really troubled Israel itself. But the prosperity of the nation was not shared by all. Many of the previous generation of small farmers had lost their land after repeated Syrian incursions and several years of drought. A huge, almost unbridgeable gap had developed between rich and poor, with justice almost inevitably the prerogative of the rich.

Religiously speaking, things were going well. Worship of Yahweh was popular; all the required sacrifices and feasts were kept with rigorous attention to detail, great ceremony, and no regard for expense. However, alongside this religiosity, idolatry was rampant, respect for the law was nonexistent, and the people were in effect treating Yahweh as an idol or a baal who could be pacified by presents and bribed into acting on Israel's behalf.

Within this context Hosea takes the imagery used by surrounding nature cults, with a strong emphasis on fertility, and completely transforms it. Chapters 1 and 3 speak of his own fairly disastrous family life. Sandwiched between is a poetic description of the unfaithfulness and adultery of God's people Israel, dramatically pictured here as God's wife, and of the consequences of that unfaithfulness, which puts their identity as the people of God at severe risk. Chapters 4–13 present a series of sermons or oracles using a whole range of methods, pictures, images, and metaphors to set out the reality of Israel's attitudes and actions, the reaction of God to these, and the consequences that had been set in motion. Interspersed within this are insights into the nature of God, his deep love, the hurt he feels at Israel's behavior, his desire for them to return to be his people in reality, but also God's justice and the inevitability of their punishment and destruction if there is no repentance.

Hosea's main aim seems to have been to show Israel that their religious confidence was spurious, their behavior was unacceptable, their understanding of God was quite deficient, and their future was at risk. Hosea 1:1 makes it clear that the book was completed after Hosea's ministry was ended, and 14:9 indicates awareness of future readers. However, in between, certain editorial comments have been incorporated within the messages that Hosea delivered to his contemporaries. The whole is clearly seen as having ongoing relevance, reflecting Hosea's own conviction that history repeats itself. Those from different generations and different situations can certainly be challenged by Hosea's message.

Hosea and the Canon

Hosea's closest links are with Amos, who also spoke out in the northern kingdom during the reign of Jeroboam II. Amos brings to the foreground and extends the picture of Israel's economic and social corruption that is reflected in Hosea, while Hosea extends and develops Amos's portrayal of the idolatry and syncretism that was rife throughout the land. There are also many connections with Isaiah and Micah, the other eighth-century prophets working in the south. The understanding of the covenant presented especially in Deuteronomy and Exodus has a strong influence on Hosea's reflections. In turn, Hosea's exploration of what is involved in being God's people stands as a background to the more event-based account of the period in 2 Kings and to the teaching of the later prophets.

There are few direct references to Hosea in the NT. Yet, Matthew (9:13; 12:7) records Jesus twice quoting from Hosea's clear statement in 6:6 that God desires "mercy, not sacrifice." And Paul uses Hos. 1:9–10 and 2:23 in Rom. 8:14 and 9:25–26, as part of his discussion on who exactly it is that is eligible to be called "my people." It is debatable whether the Israelites' conviction that "on the third day he will raise us up" (Hos. 6:2 NRSV), almost certainly spoken in the context of a spurious repentance, lies behind the references to Jesus' resurrection on the third day in, for example, Matt. 16:21; 17:23; and Luke 9:22.

Hosea and Theology

Hosea's understanding of God, Israel, and the world is founded on the concept of covenant, specifically the covenant between God and Israel. Israel's very existence was bound up with the people's identity as those in covenant relationship with God, whose calling was to represent God before the world. They were Yahweh's people, and he was their God. If the covenant collapsed, then Israel would, in effect, no longer exist. Any kind of relationship is costly. It makes demands in both emotional and behavioral terms. Hosea portrays the covenant requirements incumbent on God's people and the cost that is involved for Yahweh himself. The marriage metaphor, where Israel is pictured as God's wife, was avoided by many of the prophets due to the danger of misunderstanding arising from the widespread use of sexual imagery in the surrounding fertility cults. As in all the prophetic literature, this book totally rejects everything that Baalism stands for and, in particular, the use of sex in magical and cultic fertility rites. However, Hosea's transformation of the image becomes quite appropriate. God had committed himself to Israel as a husband to a wife, and Israel had also committed itself to the covenant. The corollary of this is that both sides must remain faithful. Hosea's point is that just as physical adultery shatters a marriage relationship and in the process causes great pain, so Israel's spiritual adultery will shatter their relationship with God. On the other hand, with evidenced forgiveness and mercy on the one hand and evidenced repentance on the other, even a shattered marriage can be repaired.

God's Love for Israel. The "marriage" between Yahweh and Israel was based on his love for them. Even when they deserted him and served other gods—committed spiritual adultery—he still loved them and longed to have them back. Hosea's own experience helped him to understand God's position, and he therefore strongly attacks Israel's idolatry but also pleads desperately with them to repent and return to God, who in that circumstance will gladly forgive and restore them. The constancy of God's love is a theme that runs through the book. In the past he has blessed and cared for them (2:15; 11:1; 13:4–5). In the present he longs to restore them (7:1; 11:8–9). The future is still in question, depending on their response. God takes them seriously as people and allows them the dignity of taking responsibility for their own actions even when that results in negative consequences. The way they exercise their responsibility will influence their own future. Those who argue that God is portrayed here as abusive and controlling miss this point altogether. He cannot be in relationship with those who are not his people and, if they persist in their refusal to act as his people, then they are inevitably signing their own death warrant (4:6–9; 9:7–9; 13:9–16). However, because of God's ongoing and gracious love, there is still hope for salvation (11:10–12; 14:4–9). This is Yahweh's ongoing and deep desire.

The marriage metaphor is profound, but it is not big enough to tell the whole story. Hosea also portrays God, among other things, as a caring parent (11:1–4), a doctor (7:1; 11:3; 14:4), and a shepherd (11:4; 13:5). The implication is that God is able to supply all their needs.

The Requirements of Relationship. Because of God's nature as "the Holy One" (11:9, 12), relationship with him can only exist on his terms. If Israel is to be his people, they must be a holy people; their commitment to him must be exclusive, and their behavior must reflect his nature. Wholehearted devotion and faithfulness to God are vital, but right behavior toward other people as well as toward God himself is an essential part of being God's people. Hosea does not major on social responsibility in the way that Amos does, but he is very well aware of the importance of justice, righteousness, and compassion as characteristics of God's people (2:19; 6:6; 12:6). Relationship also requires knowledge, and Hosea stresses the importance of Israel studying God's word in order to know what he has revealed about himself. The priests who had been given the responsibility for ensuring the people's knowledge of God therefore come under particular condemnation (4:6–9). God's terms for a restored relationship include their repentance and turning back to him (3:5; 5:4; 11:5, 10–11). Hosea wants Israel to grasp the seriousness of sin (1:2; 2:1–5; 3:1–5). The imagery he uses to describe the faithfulness and betrayal of Israel is almost as varied as what is used to describe the love of God. Israel needs to see itself not just as an adulterous wife or an unresponsive child, but also as a stubborn heifer, a half-baked and half-raw cake, a sick person or a foolish bird (4:16; 5:13; 7:8–12; 9:11; 11:1–3). In Israel there is "only cursing, lying and murder, stealing and adultery" (4:2), prostitution, idolatry, immorality, arrogance, and hypocrisy (2:7–8; 4:10–13; 5:7; 8:2–6; 12:7–8). Like adultery in marriage, Israel's sin is not something that can simply be ignored; it needs to be acknowledged and dealt with. But repentance must be real. Sacrifices without major lifestyle changes are completely unacceptable. Renewed commitment is evidenced not by a renewed demonstration of religious fervor but by transformed lives (6:1–6).

Hosea was apparently not very hopeful that Israel in general would respond to God's pleading with them, but he was convinced that in the end God's love would triumph (11:8–11; 14:4–9). In this way he points forward to the later revelation of God's love revealed in Jesus. The people cannot defeat sin by ignoring or avoiding it, but a way nevertheless does exist to deal with its otherwise inevitable consequences.

Beeby's theological commentary on Hosea brings out strongly the link demonstrated between the love of God and the knowledge of God, providing an illustration of the way in which others have used Hosea to discuss a range of epistemological questions. Several of the essays edited by Vanhoozer helpfully use Hosea to illustrate their understanding of the love of God in today's world. Stuhlmueller, in the book cowritten with Senior, shows how Hosea can provide stimulation for modern mission. Hosea's critique of attitudes toward economics found among his wealthier contemporaries certainly speaks into today's consumer cultures. Hosea has much to say to all who accept the challenge of reflecting theologically on today's world.

Bibliography

Achtemeier, E. *Minor Prophets 1*. Hendrickson, 1996; Bal, M. *Lethal Love*. Indiana University Press, 1987; Beeby, H. D. *Grace Abounding*. Eerdmans, 1989; Birch, B. C. *Hosea, Joel, and Amos*. Westminster John Knox, 1997; Goldingay, J. "Hosea 1–3, Genesis 1–4 and Masculist Interpretation." *HBT* 17 (1995): 37–44; Kidner, D. *Love to the Loveless*. InterVarsity, 1981; Mays, J. L. *Hosea: A Commentary*. OTL. SCM, 1968; Senior, D., and C. Stuhlmueller. *The Biblical Foundations for Mission*. SCM, 1983; Stuart, D. *Hosea–Jonah*. WBC. Word, 1987; Vanhoozer, K., ed. *Nothing Greater, Nothing Better*. Eerdmans, 2001; Ward, J. M. *Hosea*. Harper & Row, 1966; idem. *Thus Says the Lord*. Abingdon, 1991; Williamson, H. G. M. "Hope under Judgment: The Prophets of the Eighth Century BCE." *EvQ* 72 (2000): 291–306; Wolff, H. W. *Hosea*. Hermeneia. Fortress, 1977; Yee, G. A. "Hosea: Commentary and Reflection." *NIB* 7:195–297.

Mary J. Evans

Human Being, Doctrine of

The Bible has no single theological psychology or doctrine of human nature, sometimes also called theological anthropology. These are philosophical generalizations, and the Bible is not a philosophy book. Still, some NT texts do embody philosophical concepts that were prominent at the time of their writing. The Tanak does not contain philosophical concepts. What we have are verses here and there that have been central in the thinking of highly influential philosophical theologians who specifically treated this theme, bequeathing their interpretation of Scripture on this topic to us latter-day Christians. Christian psychology as such took shape in the fourth and fifth centuries.

To speak about theological psychology differentiates the Christian understanding of human nature from secular psychology. It too operates according to assumptions about human behavior that enable us to construct safe and just societies. Christian psychology differs from secular psychology because it posits an undeniable and indestructible link between God and humanity. From a Christian perspective, humanity can never interpret itself in terms of itself, but only in terms of God, its Creator. All religions holding that God created us share this characteristic. Nonreligious interpretations of human life do not bear this constraint. Hence, theological psychology cannot admit that human beings are autonomous, but only and always related to God.

Biblical Foundations

Perhaps the most important verse used in constructing a Christian psychology is Gen. 1:26, "Let us make humankind in our image, according to our likeness" (NRSV). Yet, two chapters later, the first humans disobey God (Gen. 3); in the next chapter (4), we learn of the first murder; and two chapters after that (6), God sees the world so filled with corruption and violence that he regrets having created it altogether. Nevertheless, after the flood, seeing that humanity is morally unstable, God promises that he will never again destroy the world in response to corruption, "for the inclination of the human heart is evil from youth" (8:21 NRSV). In other words, early in the biblical story God reconciles himself to the reality of human moral failing. Perhaps he suffers disappointment. As if not to let us forget for a moment, the remainder of the Tanak teems with stories of deception, idolatry, and violence.

Sin is a prominent theme in Rom. 5–8. Paul draws an analogy between Adam, the first man, and Christ, the new man. The former brought death into the world; the latter, by being resurrected, brought life from death. Later tradition would make the same parallel between Eve, the mother of life, and Mary, the mother of Christ. In Rom. 8, Paul introduces what would become a major theme of Christian psychology. We incline toward either physical things or spiritual things. Those whose cast of mind is toward the former are hostile to God because God is spiritual, while the Spirit of God dwells in those inclined toward spiritual things. We are transformed from the former to the latter by baptism into the death of Christ and called to live that spiritual power thereafter.

Christian psychology has teetered on the point of this paradox: we are in the divine image, yet fatally flawed. Interpreters stress now one side of this tension, and then the other. Theologians who meditate on these Scriptures search for clues as to what God thinks of us. So, to understand how Scripture may be and has been read theologically for our edification and to search out its wisdom, we do well to read behind those who deposited these traces for us.

Since biblically grounded Christians insist on constructing a theological psychology from the biblical materials, we will follow two highly influential Scripture interpreters on this theme, one from Greek-speaking Christianity, Gregory of Nyssa, and one from Latin-speaking Christianity, Augustine of Hippo.

Patristic Formulations

Gregory of Nyssa. Gregory of Nyssa framed Christian psychology for the Greek Christian world with his treatise *On the Creation of Humanity* (*De opificio hominis*), written in 380. It is an interpretation of Gen. 1:26–27 organized around thirty questions that he poses about the intent of God with the creation of humankind. The questions cover the meaning of being in the divine image, the relation of the soul to the body, and the physical likelihood of the possibility of resurrection in response to unbelievers and Christians with whom he seriously disagreed.

Humanity, Gregory teaches, is the summit of creation, created last so that everything was prepared for our enjoyment and well-being. We are superior to other creatures because only we can draw near to God, can be clothed in virtue, and are capable of immortality and drenched in righteousness. We are the royalty of the cosmos.

Being the image of God is a psychological and moral likeness, not a physical one. It means that only we resemble the beauty of God and experience the bliss that he is when we are alienated from all evil, free from unruly emotions. That we manifest the divine beauty is evident in that we have the gift of understanding and are capable of love.

He follows the psychology of his day by identifying three aspects of the soul: physical, sensual, and rational. The soul is created together with the body at conception and animates the body. It is perfected in its higher intellectual functions.

Gregory is most interested in the mind. There is what he calls a spacious "city of the mind" that stores information gathered by the senses to give us knowledge of things. The mind, he believes, is not located in a single organ but is diffused throughout the whole body, producing its proper effect on each part as is appropriate to it. Similarly, the image of God is present in the whole body, but is fullest in the human intellect.

The mind remains good and beautiful as long as it remains like its archetype, but if it departs therefrom, it loses its beauty and goodness and becomes misshapen until the image of God is hidden. The instability of the soul suggests that although we image God, we are quite different from the one who is pure, immortal, and everlasting. Scripture points this out by following Gen. 1:26 with the creation of humanity as male and female. This is a departure from the prototype, God, who is neither male nor female.

The male-female distinction speaks of human passion, which creates the struggle between the unchangeable beauty and goodness that characterize God and his image in us, and our desires that pull us in different directions. Although human nature is created for the beauty and goodness that are God, our emotional instability means that our powers of understanding and deliberation can be swayed by different desires. We are at once brutal and beautiful and endowed with freedom to change.

Marriage was added for procreation, since we humans are mortal and must replace ourselves. And procreation comes from the irrational side of the self, in which we act like animals rather than angels. Thus, the irrational side of our nature is also profitable for the human race. Marriage controls the most irrational and potentially destructive part of us.

Our erratic emotions, however, extend beyond sexual lust and can deteriorate into anger, love of pleasure, fear, greediness, envy, deceit, conspiracy, hypocrisy, and so on. Gregory calls this the "evil husbandry of the mind." These evils can be transformed into virtues when the desire for the good and the beautiful (God) is strengthened. A rightly ordered life enables the divine gift to reappear. Gregory concludes that our personalities are neither fully good, nor fully evil, but caught between nobility and vanity. When vanity becomes ascendant, "life becomes painful and miserable."

All of this will only be worked out, Gregory teaches, with the consummation of history, with resurrection. Following 1 Cor. 15, he looks forward to our transformation from the corruptible and earthly to the impassible and eternal. Then we shall become like the angels.

Augustine of Hippo. The Christian West was deeply influenced by Augustine of Hippo, Gregory of Nyssa's younger contemporary. He was a tremendously prolific writer and returned again and again to the task of articulating his moral psychology. It is found in all three of his major works: his autobiography, the *Confessions*, the second half of his major work on *The Trinity*, and *The City of God*, as well as in his major commentary on Genesis. Bits and pieces are also scattered throughout other works. His understanding of human nature is one of his irrevocable contributions to Western thought and literature.

Augustine, like Basil, took his understanding of human nature from the beginning of Genesis and wrote several commentaries on it. But he was also apparently taken with the great penitential psalm (51), honing in on v. 5: "Indeed, I was born guilty, a sinner when my mother conceived me" (NRSV). From Gen. 1:26 he insisted that being created in the divine image refers to our higher faculties, those that separate us from brute animals. He especially stressed abilities of memory, understanding, will, and the attributes of goodness, love, justice, and wisdom that characterize God and in which we can participate. Growth in spiritual maturity is the gradual recognition that growing into this image is the purpose of human life. The human calling is to discover that we long for the goodness and wisdom that are of God, and that we find these only through Jesus Christ. Augustine's *Confessions* established the fundamental point of theological psychology: we cannot understand ourselves unless and until we understand God. In his book *The Trinity*, he made this point in terms of discovering that the image of God we bear is the image of the triune God. In *The City of God*, he formulated this vision in terms of the Christian pilgrimage to the heavenly city; the human calling is to grow in holiness.

While our self-concept must always be in relation to God, Augustine had to account for the reality round about. The world (the earthly city) is filled with dissension, war, and violence. When he observed children, including recalling his own childhood, Augustine saw that they seem to be naturally selfish; they do not want to share their toys, obey their caregivers, or do their lessons. Adolescents, he said, recalling his own destructive behavior at age sixteen, are no different. We all, he concluded, are rebellious, turned in upon ourselves, self-absorbed. Sin contrasts with the goodness of God that Gregory so exalted in when looking at us.

From Ps. 51:5, one suspects, Augustine drew the conclusion that all human beings are born sinful and that state is somehow transmitted to them at conception. In *The City of God*, he was careful to say that sex itself is not sinful (sex in marriage for procreation is especially good), but the fact that after the fall lust surrounds it renders it dangerous. Augustine's main concern is self-mastery. Our inability to conquer lust—be it sexual, economic, or political—is the reason behind human downfall and the key to understanding human psychology. The observation that we fail of self-mastery is called original sin, and it contrasts with actual sin. The former has nothing to do with our life's story, but is how things are with all of us, while the latter, actual sin, refers to misdeeds that make up our personal narrative.

The irrefragability of sin led to the idea that we are utterly unable to please God, and so have no freedom to avoid sin. This was in contrast to all previous Christian theology that depended on the ability to learn from the goodness of God. Yet the need to assert human freedom in order to render morality possible has plagued this view. Unfortunately, the tradition thought in polar opposites, each side condemning the other, rather than recognizing both individual variation and the contradictions within each human breast. The older view that spiritual growth is a slow process of education empowering the soul for obedience to God was often ruled out.

Lest we conclude that there is no escape from death and corruption of the body, Augustine turned to the sacraments of the church. He created the notion that baptism into the death of Christ so connects us with the Mediator that we are washed clean of original sin. Thereby we gain the opportunity to begin a pilgrimage to the heavenly city, during which we grow into the image of God, which is our true identity. We do this in the companionship of the church.

There are many matters on which we might compare Gregory and Augustine, since their psychology pivots around the same points. In many cases, the differences are of emphasis. Three points of difference between them, however, are worth mentioning. Augustine divided humanity into saints and sinners and laced his psychology with the doctrine of election. He bounced between urging people to aspire to the heavenly holiness and holding that God ordains only some to make up the number of angels in heaven, to complete the proper number lost by the fall of the bad angels. Gregory did not struggle with this tension. He believed that good would naturally vanquish evil, and that human freedom remained pure enough even after the fall to restore us to our divine destiny with God.

A second important difference to note is that while Augustine divided humanity into two sorts, Gregory saw the struggle between what Augustine called the two cities as a struggle within every human heart. We are inclined toward both goodness and evil at the same time.

The third difference between them is the role of Christ. Gregory's treatise does not tie the struggle between good and evil in human life to Christ. Augustine locates the ability to make the pilgrimage to God dependent on being baptized into the Mediator, who bridges the great chasm between earth and heaven.

These two readings of human nature—one stressing the strength of human self-mastery, the other stressing the weakness of the human will—are two judgments about who we really are, what will destabilize us, and what will ennoble us. They are different assessments of human moral strength and character. Does the nobility we inherit from God empower us to overcome the pull of lust and evil that the world offers? Or are our baser desires beyond our control, throwing us utterly on the grace of Christ if it be God's will so to rescue some of us?

These are the major themes of Christian psychology, which at bottom is a moral psychology. Later theologians toy with these themes, and in modern times, secular psychology and ideology has cast them in different lights. In the West, Karl Barth, in a particularly Reformed manner, reinterpreted the *imago Dei* as a divine promise to be eternally in covenant relationship with human beings, a promise signified by Christ, rather than as a human ability to relate to or know God. On this view, moral motivation arises from gratitude for this covenant relationship. Liberation theology, on the other hand, used the Augustinian framework to give theology an especially moral bent by distinguishing oppressed from oppressor in political confrontations.

See also Image of God; Original Sin; Psychological Interpretation; Sin, Doctrine of

Bibliography

Cary, P. *Augustine's Invention of the Inner Self.* Oxford University Press, 2000; Mathewes, C. "Augustinian Anthropology." *Journal of Religious Ethics* 27, no. 2 (1999): 195–222; Young, R. "Gregory of Nyssa's Use of Theology and Science in Constructing Theological Anthropology." *Pro Ecclesia* 2 (Summer 1993): 345–63.

Ellen T. Charry

Hymn *See* Music, the Bible and; Poetry; Psalms, Book of

I

Ideological Criticism

Definitions of "ideology" abound, and arguably all such definitions are themselves ideological. Some interpreters, influenced by Marxist scholarship, use the term negatively to refer to an idea-system that creates "false consciousness" and blinds one to the way things really are. Increasingly the term is used in broader ways. I use it to refer to "a roughly coherent set of ideas, amounting to a world-view" (Clines 8). Ideologies are acquired through processes of socialization, and they function as "glasses behind the eyes," shaping the way reality is perceived and guiding behavior. To those who hold them, they seem obvious and natural, and so are usually unperceived until attention is drawn to them.

At its most basic, ideological criticism is the task of uncovering the hidden ideologies at work in social practices, structures, and texts. Written texts encode ideology, communicating and reinforcing it in ways usually unperceived. It is often said that every ideology serves the interests of certain people and groups while marginalizing others. This would make every ideology, however liberating for some, a potential source of oppression for others. Unmasking the dynamics of such power-relations is central to the work of the ideological critic. With reference to a written text, the critic will employ a hermeneutic of suspicion, seeking to find whose interests are served by the text. For instance, David Clines argues that the Decalogue was written to protect the interests of the older males within the Israelite community.

Ideological critics have also argued that no interpretation of a text is "objective" in a positivist sense. Thus, the project of a neutral interpretation of Scripture, to which some forms of historical criticism have aspired, is every bit as ideologically loaded as a theological interpretation (Segovia). Many evangelicals share this perspective (e.g., Bartholomew). Every reading is itself ideological, and reading therefore is a fundamentally ethical and political act. Ideological critics will openly declare their own position and will (in theory) aspire to subject it to constant critique lest it become absolutized. Thus, ideological criticism of the Bible seeks to critique not only Scripture but also those who have interpreted it.

The Variety of Ideological Criticism

Ideological criticism is a quite diverse reading strategy. It is employed by the many liberation theologies (Latin American, Black, feminist, postcolonial, queer), which all seek to take the experiences of the oppressed group they represent as the critical principle for hermeneutics, the marginal position from which the biblical texts are read. The engagement with Scripture arises from concrete situations, and a passion for justice lies at its root. The liberationist reader will seek out the biases of official interpretations, thus undermining their neutrality and truth-status. They will also identify liberating strands within the Bible (e.g., freedom for the slaves, all humanity in God's image) that feed into their liberating theology. At the same time "toxic texts" (racist, sexist, homophobic ones, etc.) will be identified and thus stripped of authority. For instance, some feminist biblical interpreters argue the following: (1) The teaching that all humans are equally in God's image (Gen. 1:26) is a liberating text that undermines any theology or practice denying the full humanity and equality of women. (2) Paul's teaching that man is the image and glory of God while woman is the glory of man (1 Cor. 11:7) is patriarchal and must be rejected. (3) Traditional Christian teachings of the equality of men and women are patriarchal and oppressive because "equal but different" in practice means "not equal."

The ideological critic will often be aware that an ideology (and theology is seen as an ideology) liberating for one group may be oppressive to another; consequently, no ideology must be absolutized. For instance, the exodus motif, with its focus on freedom for the oppressed and suffering slaves, has been a major inspiration to many diverse liberation theologies. However, the exodus was a stage on the way to the all-important possession of Canaan—a land already inhabited. The Canaanites were the indigenous people who were conquered, subjugated, and killed. The Bible invites readers to identify with the Israelite invaders rather than the Canaanites. A Native American reader may find such texts oppressive and wish to subvert them, especially as such texts were used by European settlers to justify their taking of land (Warrior). Thus, radical pluralism in interpretation is celebrated by many ideological critics, for it stops any one reading strategy from setting itself up as *the* way to read texts. Postcolonial interpretation is especially sensitive to such issues. At the heart of postcolonialism is the criticism that Europe has set the agenda for reading Scripture. Europe has decided the issues that matter and the methods for reading, imposing these on the rest of the world. This is simply an extension of the colonial relationship that existed in the past. Interpreting the Bible postcolonially involves allowing for radical diversity in interpretations arising from the radical diversity of concrete situations in which Scripture is read (Segovia). It means reading Scripture through the eyes of the colonized and not only the colonizer.

Ideological Criticism and Theological Interpretation

The claim that all interpretation is ideological creates a welcome space for the academic acceptability of theological interpretation alongside other academic modes. Also, Christians should not be too quick to dismiss a hermeneutic of suspicion because it finds an analogue in the doctrine of sin. The human heart *is* deceitful, and often our real motivations are hidden even from ourselves. Suspicion thus has its hermeneutical role in a fallen world, although the elevation of suspicion to the driving seat of interpretation is problematic. That move would undermine the very cry for justice that calls forth ideological readings in the first place. *All* notions of "truth" and "justice" would be unmasked, and Christian theology would dissolve in a pool of agnosticism, along with *all* moral and truth-seeking discourse (including liberation theologies). The Christian reader of Scripture will prioritize a hermeneutic of trust and only allow suspicion to play second fiddle. There are good nontheological (Patrick and Scult) as well as theological reasons for such a stance. Indeed, the theological interpreter will see in Scripture the basis for an unmasking of the ideologies of the world. In the dialogical encounter between Bible and present situation, the present situation is decentered and open to reevaluation in light of Scripture, which retains the weight of authority (Thiselton, ch. 16).

One gift that ideological criticism can bequeath theological criticism is that of opening up genuinely liberating dimensions of biblical texts to which we have been blinded by our own ideological limitations. Thus, a middle-class Western Christian may never so much as notice the political implications of the exodus narrative, or the value of the insight that much of the biblical literature was written by people living under the rule of colonial powers. Ideology can blind us to some aspects of the text but also open us to others. There is much to learn from listening to how others "hear" the Bible.

However, most ideological critics wish to argue that the Bible contains numerous conflicting ideologies, many of which are positively oppressive. The Bible contains "texts of terror" that are sexist, racist, homophobic, elitist, and colonialist. At one and the same time, the Bible is a liberating text and a "letter that kills." Numerous problems are raised for theological interpretation. First, Christian theological criticism must see Scripture as *in some sense* being or mediating the word of God. But how can we receive Scripture as the word of God if it contains so many harmful texts? Indeed, many ideological critics have the undermining of biblical authority as one of their declared aims, for as long as Scripture exercises authority, it retains its authority to oppress. Second, theological criticism seeks to read Scripture as a unity; but if it embodies numerous conflicting ideologies, how can we claim that the teaching of any particular text is *the* (as opposed to *a*) teaching of the Bible? Third, ideological criticism often seeks to expose the notion of a canon as itself ideological and suspect. This unweaves the very notion of Scripture that lies at the heart of theological interpretation. Christians need to be careful how they appropriate the tools of ideological criticism.

To get our bearings, Christian theological interpretation must not surrender the notion of canon—indeed, canon provides a fruitful way to address some of the concerns raised by ideological critics. For Christians, the Bible is only authoritative *as a whole*, with all its complex intertextual connections (Parry). Suspicious interpretations are often the result of isolating texts from the canonical context. For instance, reading Abraham's sacrifice of Isaac as a legitimization of child abuse is only possible if the notion of canon is abandoned (Moberly). The biblical canon provides resources for internal critique, so that the critical standpoint from which the unmasking is done is generated by the Scriptures themselves and is not an alien one imposed from the outside. For example, a text like Ruth, told from a female perspective, relativizes the androcentric perspective of many biblical stories without in any way threatening biblical authority or inspiration (Bauckham, ch. 1; Parry). Or the fact that Deuteronomy stands at the head of the history running through to 2 Kings invites a critical interpretation of the stories of Israel's kings (McConville). William Webb has helpfully developed a "redemptive-movement" hermeneutic maintaining that Christian interpreters should trace the canonical trajectories across Scripture when attempting to see which aspects of the Bible transcend cultural contexts and which do not. This enables him to argue, for instance, that even though much of the Bible reflects the patriarchal cultures in which it was written, it would call *us* either to egalitarianism or ultrasoft patriarchy in gender relations. Webb's canonical hermeneutic (1) arises from Scripture itself and (2) retains a strong notion of biblical inspiration and authority while (3) allowing interpreters to recognize the presence of patriarchal ideology in the text. Webb argues that all biblical texts push in a redemptive direction even if many texts do not push *all* the way. Less-conservative canonical strategies for handling ideological critique of the Bible for Christian readers can be found in the work of Walter Brueggemann and Terence Fretheim (with Froehlich).

See also African Biblical Interpretation; Asian Biblical Interpretation; Canon; Feminist Biblical Interpretation; Liberation Theologies and Hermeneutics; Racism; Scripture, Unity of; Slavery

Bibliography

Adam, A. K. M. *What Is Postmodern Biblical Criticism?* Fortress, 1995; Bartholomew, C. "Uncharted Waters: Philosophy, Theology and the Crisis in Biblical Interpretation." Pages 1–39 in *Renewing Biblical Interpretation*, ed. C. Bartholomew et al. SHS. Zondervan/Paternoster, 2000; Bauckham, R. *Gospel Women*. Eerdmans/T&T Clark, 2002; Brueggemann, W. *Theology of the Old Testament*. Fortress, 1997; Clines, D. J. A. *Interested Parties*. Sheffield Academic Press, 1995; Fretheim, T., and K. Froehlich. *The Bible as Word of God in a Postmodern Age*. Fortress, 1998; McConville, J. G. "Law and Monarchy in the Old Testament." Pages 69–88 in *A Royal Priesthood?*, ed. C. Bartholomew et al. SHS. Zondervan/Paternoster, 2002; Moberly, R. W. L. *The Bible, Theology and Faith*. Cambridge University Press, 2000; Parry, R. "Feminist Hermeneutics and Evangelical Concerns: The Rape of Dinah as a Case Study." *TynBul* 53 (2002): 1–28; Patrick, D., and A. Scult. "Rhetoric and Ideology: A Debate within Biblical Scholarship over the Import of Persuasion." Pages 63–83 in *The Rhetorical Interpretation of Scripture*, ed. S. Porter and D. L. Stamps. Sheffield University Press, 1999; Segovia, F. F. *Decolonizing Biblical Studies*. Orbis, 2000; Thiselton, A. *New Horizons in Hermeneutics*. HarperCollins, 1992; Warrior, R. "A Native American Perspective: Canaanites, Cowboys, and Indians." Pages 277–85 in *Voices from the Margin*, ed. R. Sugirtharajah. Orbis, 1995; Webb, W. *Slaves, Women and Homosexuals*. InterVarsity, 2001; "Ideological Criticism." Pages 272–308 in *The Postmodern Bible*. Yale University Press, 1995.

Robin Parry

Ideology *See* Ideological Criticism

Illocutionary Act *See* Speech-Act Theory

Illumination

Illumination is the term that refers to the need for the human mind to be enlightened by God in order to understand the things of God. It finds its scriptural roots in language of God as light, often in contrast to the darkness of the world. Here, God is seen as the one who, as light, dispels the darkness; and human beings are shown as those who yet prefer darkness since it allows their wicked deeds to be hidden (e.g., John 1; 3:19–21). Theologically, however, the concept really emerged not so much in the context of exegeting such passages but rather in discussions of epistemology that took their cue from the kind of issues raised by the Neoplatonic philosophy of Plotinus.

The central issue to which the idea of illumination is addressed is that of knowledge of divine things: given the fact that divine truth is ultimately infinite, perfect, and uncreated truth and human beings are finite and sinful creatures, how can the latter have certain knowledge of the former?

The concept receives its most influential yet enigmatic expression in the writings of Augustine, who regards the idea as resting on three principles: God is light and thus illuminates all human beings to one level or another. Divine truth is intelligible. And human beings can only come to grasp this Divine truth to the extent to which God illumines them. Further, God has endowed human beings with a structure of rationality that reflects the pattern of ideas in the divine mind. This makes knowledge possible, but the human mind still requires light from God. In other words, all knowledge requires the constant presence and action of God himself. By developing his position thus, Augustine is able to safeguard both the finitude of the human mind, the sovereignty and mystery of God, yet also the reality and adequacy of human knowledge of God. Thus, he offers a view of Christian knowledge that maintains the importance of both its objective reality and its subjective appropriation within a context controlled by God's sovereignty.

In the history of theology, significantly divergent interpretations of Augustine's view arose. Thomas regarded the active intellect as the source of illumination, and since God was the cause of the active intellect, so he was, in an ultimate sense, the one who illumines. This involves something of an attenuation of Augustine's own position while still safeguarding his central concerns. Franciscan approaches, however, tended to emphasize the direct role of God himself in illumination via the infusion or impression of divine forms upon the mind.

One influential modern interpretation of Augustine that has enjoyed some influence in Catholic circles is that associated with the neo-Thomism of Etienne Gilson and Frederick Copleston, known as the "formal theory." This view is not dissimilar in some ways to aspects of the Protestant approach, since it is concerned not so much with the origins of ideas as with the way in which they are believed. The formalists regard illumination as providing a quality of certainty and necessity to particular ideas. Where this approach would appear to break distinctly with the older Franciscan notion is in the radical separation it makes between the origin/content of the ideas and their certainty, with only the latter being the proper sphere of illumination.

A further interpretation of Augustine emphasizes the fact that he can talk of illumination in terms of two lights: the divine light of God, and the lesser light of the human intellect. This view has the advantage over that of the neo-Thomism of Copleston in that it is able to offer an account of the human intellect as both passive (in relation to the divine light) and active (in relation to its own power of illumination/cognition). This view has been argued most notably by Protestant philosopher Ronald Nash, who sees three paradoxes lying at the heart of Augustine's teaching: The human intellect is both passive and active in relation to the forms, which are both given to it by God and used by the human mind in knowing. The forms are and are not separate from the human mind (they exist as archetypes in God, in things created after the eternal pattern, and in the human mind). And the human mind is and is not a light that makes knowledge possible.

While Augustine was a profound influence on pre-Enlightenment Protestantism with respect to grace, this was not so marked with respect to illumination. Given its essentially Aristotelian epistemology, the philosophical use of illumination tended to be avoided, with theologians on the whole identifying illumination with the internal testimony of the Holy Spirit. In this context, illumination became a mode of knowing divine truths, which separated it from mere notional assent to the same. Thus, for example, though the sense of the Bible could be grasped by the application of the standard rules of linguistic interpretation, the mode by which these truths were themselves known was radically different in the believer and the unbeliever because of the action of the Holy Spirit. In this way, illumination also played a significant role in those crucial Protestant concepts, certainty and assurance of faith, by testifying not simply that biblical teaching is true in the general sense but also that it is true *for the one who believes it.* Frequently linked to the notion of *filioque,* the Spirit was seen as taking the word and applying it, or making it real, to the person upon whom the Spirit was acting. Furthermore, Protestantism saw illumination as allowing for belief in suprarational truths (such as the Trinity) that were taught in Scripture but seemed nonsensical in comparison with normal categories of logic and coherence. Illumination in context effectively exalted human reasoning powers to a higher level, where such apparently paradoxical ideas could be believed without incoherence.

Several comments are in order relative to the various notions of illumination. First, the abandonment of Neoplatonism as offering an adequate account of human nature inevitably meant that the Augustinian notion of illumination needed to be either replaced or radically transformed in the modern philosophical and psychological context.

Second, even if vestiges of the tradition can be salvaged for the present day, numerous problems persist. There is, for example, always a danger—inherent in use of illumination as focused simply on the certainty with which a belief is held—that a radical separation between the content of belief and the mode of belief is being posited. The maintenance of a strict separation between the origin of a belief and the way in which the belief is held would seem to be a highly problematic position if conceived in terms of illumination in anything approaching the trajectories of Augustinian thought.

Further, notions of illumination that purport to lift the human mind beyond normal rationality are also not without difficulty. On one level, the crisis in criteria of rationality, as posited by much recent thinking, renders the structure of the old arguments about rationality implausible. On another level, when illumination is conceived of in this way, it can come to function simply as a deus ex machina, to be wheeled in at the appropriate time in a manner that allows a coach and horses to be driven through opposing positions while rendering one's own stance impervious to criticism.

This leads to the third point: the relationship of the theological concept of illumination to biblical interpretation is not straightforward. Too much emphasis on illumination as providing the content of Christian belief can render biblical interpretation an essentially gnostic activity, which places the views of those who have been "illuminated" beyond the criticism of those who have not. Thus, any views proposed by the illuminated can be claimed as legitimate biblical teaching no matter what interpretative methods are being used to extract them. Too much emphasis on illumination as the mode of believing, however, can reduce the act of interpretation itself to the level of the nontheological and thus destroy what is distinctly Christian about the act of interpretation. In fact, the linguistic emphasis of modern accounts of knowledge in general and interpretation in particular renders much of the tradition a dead end. With reference to understanding texts, the rise of hermeneutics in the place of epistemology has, in theological discussion, really served to sideline the kinds of issues with which illumination in the classical sense dealt. Having said that, it can perhaps be retained as useful if it is restricted in application to discussion of the mode of belief (faith), when linked to the subjective activity of the Holy Spirit. First Corinthians 2 speaks of the Spirit of God teaching and imparting truth in words not taught by human reason, and of giving understanding of spiritual truths. To the natural person, such things as the Spirit teaches are nonsense and incomprehensible, implying that there is more to biblical interpretation than simply learning the public rules of the game. Clearly, Scripture here is making an implicit connection between the Spirit, faith, and precisely the kinds of questions with which classical theories of illumination attempted to wrestle, and which remain perennially relevant to the church.

See also Epistemology; Holy Spirit, Doctrine of the

Bibliography

Ackworth, R. "God and Human Knowledge." *Downside Review* 75 (1957): 207–14; Bubacz, B. *St. Augustine's Theory of Knowledge*. E. Mellen, 1981; Copleston, F. *A History of Philosophy*. Vol. 2, *Augustine to Scotus*. Burns & Oates, 1962; Gilson, E. *The Christian Philosophy of St. Augustine*. Random House, 1960; Nash, R. *The Light of the Mind*. University Press of Kentucky, 1969; idem. *The Word of God and the Mind of Man*. Zondervan, 1982; Scheutzinger, C. E. *The German Controversy on Saint Augustine's Illumination Theory*. Pageant, 1960; Warfield, B. B. *Calvin and Augustine*. P&R, 1956.

Carl R. Trueman

Image of God

The idea of the image of God both illustrates and tests theological interpretation of Scripture. On the one hand, the near-universal witness of the Christian Church that the distinctiveness of humanity lies in their creation in the image of God is an illustration of how an apparently minor biblical theme can come to have a major role in theological work. On the other hand, the content given to the idea tests whether an account responds adequately to the theological witness of the Scriptures.

On the first point, it is noteworthy that beyond the foundational text in Gen. 1:26–27, and its reprise in Gen. 5:1–3 and 9:6, the phrase never occurs again in the OT. Other indications of the particular place of humanity within God's plan exist (e.g., Ps. 8), but the particular phrase "image of God" is absent. Why, then, should the Christian theological tradition have fastened onto this phrase, and not another, to describe what makes humanity unique within creation?

The answer seems to be a theological judgment concerning both the centrality of the Gen. 1 text and the appropriateness of the phrase for describing humanity's place in the world. Although this term is not central in the sense of being regularly repeated within the biblical witness, there has been a consistent sense among Christian exegetes that the place of Gen. 1:26–27 within the canon makes its assertions of prime importance. Hence, this description of what it is to be human is regarded as far more significant than other phrases that occur more often. Equally, this term, with its implication of a particular resemblance to God, has been judged to get to the heart of what it is that distinguishes humanity from the rest of the creation.

On the second point, the meaning of "the image of God" is not at all clear within the Genesis account. That this is what sets humanity apart from the beasts is clear enough, but what it might denote is much less obvious. Recent historical-critical study claims that the image is a physical resemblance; clearly, from a theological perspective, this is totally inadequate and indeed unacceptable. The majority Christian tradition of reading the image in terms of rationality or some similar intellectual ability appears to owe more to Greek philosophical anthropology than any biblical or theological tradition. In any case, it has the unacceptable consequence of denying true humanity to those suffering from profound learning difficulties, and indeed from young children, the unborn, and certain persons toward the end of their lives.

An alternative approach, hinted at by Augustine but arguably not fully developed until the work of Karl Barth, sees the creation of humanity in the image of God as interpreted by the following text, which emphasizes the gender differentiation in human life: "male and female he created them." This can be spelled out in various ways: the family might be seen as the basic instantiation of society or culture, and so the image of God might be seen as the ability to be social or cultural beings, for instance. The most common reading in recent theology, however, has been to see the mention of male and female as pointing to the irreducibly relational nature of human life. On this account, to be made in the image of God is to somehow share in or repeat God's own relational life as Father, Son, and Holy Spirit (which, as Luther suggested, might be seen hinted at in the text "Let *us* make humanity in our own image" [AT]).

A different and profoundly theological approach is suggested by the ways in which the Genesis phrase is taken up in the NT. It is still used in the same way to indicate the specialness of humanity, as in the Letter of James (3:9), but there is also a new emphasis, with Jesus Christ being described several times as "the image of God," or a similar phrase: Col. 1:15; 2 Cor. 4:4; Heb. 1:3; Phil. 2:6. If a canonical approach to Scripture is adopted, so that this identification is permitted to interpret the earlier use of the phrase in Genesis, the possibility of a family of thoroughly theological readings is opened. At least on this reading, we would want to insist that it is the incarnate Son, the Jewish man Jesus Christ, who shows us what it is to be human. This might be glossed by acknowledging the present fallen state of humanity, and suggesting that it is only in seeing Jesus, unfallen and so unwarped, that we can really give any account of what it is to be human.

It is possible to go further than this, however. Jesus might not just be seen as the one example of humanity available to us, but also as the true pattern of humanity—he is not only created in the image of God, but he is himself the image of God, in which we are all created. Given that he comes "late in time," a theological discussion of how this works will depend on discussions of God's eternity or similar concepts, but it is not difficult to construct an adequate account. An analysis of Paul's language of the "two Adams" is sometimes offered to support such a reading, with Christ as the last, or eschatological, Adam, whose life is as decisive for the nature and possibilities of human life as the first, or protological, Adam. Reflection on the "cosmic Christ" language of several NT letters could lend further support and content to such an idea. If Christ is the "firstborn of all creation," through whom, and for whom, and in whom all else is made, then the reality of his own human nature must interpret the humanity that is created in, for, and through him. (If Wisdom's song in Prov. 8 is read christologically, as it generally was at least in the patristic period, then this text also supports such a reading.) The rich possibilities of a theological reading, so different from the more dominant readings within the tradition, are apparent.

See also Human Being, Doctrine of

Bibliography

Barth, K. *Church Dogmatics*. Pages 183–206 in Vol. III/1, *The Doctrine of Creation*, trans. G. W. Bromiley. T&T Clark, 1958; Berkouwer, G. C. *Man*, trans. D. Jellema. Eerdmans, 1962; Jenson, R. *Systematic Theology*. Vol. 2. Oxford University Press, 53–72.

Stephen R. Holmes

Imagery

Genuine appreciation of imagery is crucial to the theological interpretation of Scripture. As the *Dictionary of Biblical Imagery* (*DBI*) declares, "The Bible is a book that *images* the truth as well as stating it in abstract propositions" (xiii). The *DBI* defines "image" as "any word that names a concrete thing . . . or an action. . . . Any object or action that we can picture is an image." Important terms related to "image" include "symbol," "an image that stands for something in addition to its literal meaning" (xiv); "metaphor," "an implied comparison"; "simile," which "compares one thing to another . . . using the formula *like* or *as*"; "motif," a pattern that recurs throughout a piece of literature; and "archetype," an image or pattern that recurs throughout literature and life (see Frye, *Anatomy*; Frye, *Great Code*).

Motif

The creation account in Gen. 1 is replete with natural images. But God's initial image of creation—light—comes about without a natural source, thus drawing special attention to itself. Supernatural light is a recognizable motif throughout the Bible, seen in the pillar of cloud that guides the Israelites in the desert (Exod. 13:21), the light surrounding the divine figures revealed to Ezekiel (1:27; cf. 43:2) and Daniel (10:6; cf. Rev. 1:14–16), the light radiating from Jesus during his transfiguration (Matt. 17:2), and finally, the light of God's glory that illuminates the new Jerusalem (Rev. 21:23). These concrete images of light are distinguished from instances where God is metaphorically described as being or giving light. But the connection between the concrete and the metaphorical is clear (all being manifestations of the broader archetype of light throughout Scripture), and the former gives meaning to the latter. Other important biblical motifs include ordeal by water (e.g., Noah's ark; the crossing of the Red Sea; Jesus calming the storm and walking on the water) and the honoring of a younger brother over his older brother(s) (e.g., Abel, Isaac, Jacob, Joseph, Ephraim, David, Solomon; and finally Paul, the last-born of the over five hundred "brothers" to see the resurrected Christ [1 Cor. 15:5–8]).

Simile

The OT contains numerous similes, usually offering comparisons to nature. The Psalms and prophetic books employ simile to describe God and his attributes. The psalmist tells God, "Your righteousness is like the mighty mountains, your justice like the great deep" (36:6); both God's "jealousy" and his "wrath" are said to "burn like fire" (79:5; 89:46; cf. Jer. 4:4; Nah. 1:6). Hosea frequently uses simile (Petersen and Richards 50–60), often to describe God's wrath against Israel. God declares, "I will pour out my wrath on them like a flood of water. . . . I am like a moth to Ephraim, like rot to the people of Judah. . . . I will be like a lion to Ephraim, like a great lion to Judah" (5:10, 12, 14; cf. 13:7–8). In response to repentance, however, God will be "like the dew to Israel" (14:5; cf. 14:5–8).

The OT often uses simile to describe those blessed or opposed by God. The righteous man of Ps. 1 is "like a tree planted by streams of water" (v. 3), while the wicked are "like chaff that the wind blows away" (v. 4). Rich men who heed not God are "like sheep . . . destined for the grave" (49:14). The faithful psalmist, conversely, is "like an olive tree flourishing in the house of God" (52:8). Hosea uses similes to describe the rebellious Israel that God will soon judge. Adulterous Israel will be stripped naked "like a desert" (2:3); the Israelites are "like a stubborn heifer" (4:16). As punishment "they will be like the morning mist, like the early dew that disappears, like chaff swirling from a threshing floor, like smoke escaping through a window" (13:3). These foreboding similes can be contrasted to the lush imagery in the similes of the Song of Songs (Landy), a book seen by many interpreters as a celebration not only of human love, but also of the love between God and his people.

The NT abounds in similes, perhaps the most significant being Jesus' parables of the kingdom. In these parables, which function as extended similes (but whose literary elements transcend simple categorization; Ryken 139–53), Jesus combines the imagery of nature and society as he proclaims "the kingdom of heaven" to be "like a man who sowed good seed in his field" (Matt. 13:24), "a mustard seed" (13:31), "treasure hidden in a field" (13:44), "a king who prepared a wedding banquet for his son" (22:2), and "ten virgins who took their lamps and went out to meet the bridegroom" (25:1; cf. 13:45, 47; 18:23; 20:1; 25:14; Luke 13:19–21). Elsewhere, Jesus employs simile, often to admonish or confront. He tells his audience they must "become like little children" (Matt. 18:3; cf. 1 Pet. 2:2); he tells the teachers of the law and Pharisees they are "like whitewashed tombs" (Matt. 23:27).

Paul uses simile to describe the rigors of Christian discipleship, employing imagery from contemporary Greco-Roman culture (1 Cor. 4:9; 9:26; Eph. 6:6; 2 Tim. 2:3) and Jewish ceremonial law (Phil. 2:17; 2 Tim. 4:6). The General Epistles use similes of nature to describe humanity's fleetingness (James 1:10; 1 Pet. 1:24), "the man who doubts" (James 1:6), false teachers (2 Pet. 2:12; Jude 10), God (James 1:17), and the devil (1 Pet. 5:8). Revelation is laden with imagery (Farrer), including similes. Multiple similes, generally drawing upon powerful images of nature or splendid images of refined metals or jewels, describe "someone 'like a son of man'" (1:13; 1:14–16), the four living creatures (4:7), the attacking locusts (9:7–10), and the new Jerusalem (21:11, 21). Revelation's imagery demonstrates the richness of language but also its inability to describe fully the still-unseen things of God. Both despite and because of its powerful imagery, readers of Revelation—and Scripture as a whole—recognize with Paul that for now they "see but a poor reflection," as "in a mirror" (1 Cor. 13:12 NIV/NRSV).

See also Hero Story; Metaphor

Bibliography

Abrams, M. H. *A Glossary of Literary Terms.* 7th ed. Harcourt Brace, 1999; Alter, R. *The Art of Biblical Poetry.* Basic Books, 1985; Farrer, A. *A Rebirth of Images.* Dacre, 1949; Frye, N. *Anatomy of Criticism.* Princeton University Press, 1957; idem. *The Great Code.* Harcourt Brace Jovanovich, 1982; Landy, F. "The Song of Songs." Pages 305–19 in *The Literary Guide to the Bible,* ed. R. Alter and F. Kermode. Harvard University Press, 1987; Petersen, D., and K. H. Richards. *Interpreting Hebrew Poetry.* Fortress, 1992; Ryken, L. *How to Read the Bible as Literature.* Academie, 1984; Ryken, L., and T. Longman III, eds. *A Complete Literary Guide to the Bible.* Zondervan, 1993; Ryken, L., J. C. Wilhoit, and T. Longman III, eds. *Dictionary of Biblical Imagery* (*DBI*). InterVarsity, 1998.

David V. Urban

Imagination

If, as Kevin Vanhoozer noted in the introduction, the theological interpretation of Scripture (and the knowing of God that is its end) is indeed "at once an intellectual, imaginative, and spiritual exercise," then it behooves us to inquire what the particular contributions of imagination might be. Two main reasons render such stock-taking desirable. First, many readers will have only a vague sense of what the words "imagination" and "imaginative" actually connote. Second (and related), many will perhaps have inherited an equally vague sense of disquiet about the imaginative as a disposition, and suspect that they can (and perhaps as good Christian readers of the text even should) get along fine without it. But it is not so. By clarifying some of the vital contributions of human imagination, we will see that "two out of three ain't bad" holds no more water in this context than in trinitarian theology. A reading that is properly "intellectual" and "spiritual" will also necessarily be imaginative, and enhancement of imagination's distinctive contributions to the process can only enhance its other two dimensions as well.

What is imagination? There is no single or simple answer to this question. One recent study of the subject asks whether we ought not to "say of imagination what Augustine once said of time—we think we know what it is but when asked we realize we don't" (Kearney). Having stopped and thought about those activities and phenomena that we intuitively associate with the imaginative, attempts to list its key contributions reveal its basic and pervasive influence on much if not most of what, humanly, we do in the world and experience of it. Hence, Kearney's maxim that "better to appreciate what it means to imagine is . . . better to appreciate what it means to be." Limiting ourselves to a high level of abstraction and a short list, we might venture the following set of contributions explored in the literature. Imagination

- traces and creates patterns of likeness and dissimilarity between things. (Green; Warnock)
- renders presence in the midst of absence. (Casey; Kearney)
- orders the human world even in its empirical manifestation. (Johnson; Llewelyn)
- facilitates our trespass beyond the empirical or the familiar. (Murdoch; Nussbaum)
- reorders the given and enables us to experience the world differently. (Bachelard; Coleridge)
- permits our apprehension of possible futures. (Bloch; Lynch; Steiner)
- is the source of fantasy, falsehood, and delusion. (Nettle; Sartre)

Close attention to these discrete but related aspects reveals each having something to do with a human capacity to make sense of things by locating them within some wider pattern or order. Warnock concludes that imagination is indeed the name we give to ways of engaging with things (whether real or "imaginary" things, and whether in intellection, feeling, or action) that ascribe to them meaning and value. Clearly, then, we should expect imagination to be central to our attempts to make sense of Scripture.

On the whole—and unfortunately—it has been the negative potential of the imaginative that has been noticed most clearly by Christians. In the modern period this negative spin is perhaps inherited partly from the single-minded reservation of the term "imagination" by the translators of the 1611 King James Version of the Bible for use in referring to evil plotting, evil motivation, inclination against and even resistance to God's will, when there were other perfectly good English words available for use (as comparison with any modern translation shows). From Gen. 6:5 to the Magnificat, for 350 years English-speaking Christians had "the imagination of their hearts" etched into consciousness in association with that which displeases God and is a cause for judgment (McIntyre). Little wonder, then, that they treated it at best with suspicion and at worst with disdain. Our point here is not to sanctify imagination in any artificial manner. No doubt sin is something in which imagination is usually complicit in one way or another; but it shares this in common, surely, with the rest of our fallen nature (including the intellect!). And if imagination lies close by the worst products of our humanity, so too its presence and activity must be acknowledged in the very best. This, though, is generally overlooked, as is the fact that God's drawing of the world to himself in Christ and through the Holy Spirit deliberately appropriates forms and strategies, and calls in turn for responses, of a highly imaginative sort. This is true not least with respect to the central role that the text of Scripture plays in this revelatory and redemptive economy.

In several ways imagination is essential to our efforts as readers to trespass beyond the text itself. Such efforts are vital to our understanding of any text, for unless we are to rest content with the text as a more or less attractively bound stack of paper adorned with ink marks, then we naturally assume that it is intended by someone to refer us beyond itself in some sense. Space here compels us to consider only three examples of how this is so.

1. Even the most thoroughgoing literary formalism, which eschews bids to discover the "actual" author/editor or his intention, cannot escape the need to posit a hypothetical author, to treat the text, that is to say, as the result of an intentional act of human communication. In doing so, we generally do not ignore issues of particular context from which the texts emerged. We seek to attune our sensibilities to the expectations to which they were directed, and this sometimes involves an imaginative bid to become surrogate members of a culture or community remote from our own. Moreover, we are sometimes driven (in order to make sense of a particular text) to posit quite specific personal or social situations, to account for peculiar emphases or modifications of the vulgate. The capacity to translate ourselves out of our own circumstance into that of others in this way is vital to our attempts to understand any text, and it is one way in which imagination facilitates understanding.

2. Imagination also permits us to fathom the human depths of Scripture's own world; to resonate with or react against the experiences, actions, and motivations of characters in the stories that the text tells; to indwell vicariously the joys and complaints crystallized in the Psalms; and so on. Imagination provokes (and helps us satisfy) that insatiable curiosity about what is other than ourselves (Murdoch), which fuels our interest in the world of the text and draws us into it with transforming effect.

3. Theological interpretation of Scripture cannot skip over the general levels of interpretation just described, but has nonetheless finally to reckon with the distinctive claim that in this book God has spoken and speaks. This clearly requires us as readers to go beyond the words on the page and discern what God might be saying through the appropriation (Wolterstorff) of human texts. Here if anywhere the spiritual and intellectual levels of reading are both manifest. But such discernment, recognizing God's speech within the already complex patterns of human discourse, appropriating such discourse "as" divine discourse, is also a highly imaginative activity (cf. Green on "as" as the "copula of imagination"). So, the sort of careful historical work that attempts to piece together "what actually happened" in the history of Israel or the ministry of Jesus, to which imagination is also central (Collingwood), is far from being the only—let alone the most important—way in which it facilitates our trespass beyond or behind the text of Scripture as Christian readers.

Imagination is clearly also vital to our approach to the text as it confronts us at various levels on the page as a literary phenomenon. Despite the Christian suspicion of imagination alluded to above, the Bible itself is a text that uses, to the full, highly imaginative genres in the service of divine self-revealing. In this regard the "basic character" (McIntyre) of imagination is indicated by the thoroughly imaginative cast of much of Jesus' own teaching, the characteristically parabolic mode that repeatedly subverts his hearers' (and readers') views of the world, themselves, and how things stand with God. But the poetry of Psalms, the vivid images of the aphorisms of Proverbs, the imaginative visions of God's promised future around which prophetic and apocalyptic writings are structured, the carefully composed narratives of the OT and the Gospels—these are all vital rather than incidental elements of the rich symbolic world that Scripture furnishes for our imaginative indwelling, with a view to our personal reorientation and renewal. This is true of individual portions of the biblical text, but also of our insistence as Christian readers upon taking it as a whole that is greater than the sum of those parts. Those patterns of meaningfulness to which we appeal in our use of such categories as "canon," "typology," and so forth are ones the recognition of which is a highly skilled imaginative exercise.

As theologians have usually recognized, the radical otherness of God with respect to the world he has created renders any and every appropriation of creaturely forms or categories by God in revealing himself inherently analogical, and therefore directed inevitably toward the inculcation of a response on our part at the level of imagination. It is first and foremost through engagement with the textual medium of Scripture that these forms and categories encounter us. In this sense it may justly be insisted that Christian faith as a gift of the Holy Spirit is a matter of having one's imagination taken captive and reshaped, such that one comes to see and taste and feel the world anew (Green)—as one's experience of it collides with that redescription in the light of God's character and activity that Scripture contains.

Bibliography

Bachelard, G. *On Poetic Imagination and Reverie*. Spring Pubns., 1971; Bloch, E. *The Principle of Hope*. Blackwell, 1986; Casey, E. *Imagining*. Indiana University Press, 1976; Coleridge, S. T. *Biographia literaria*. J. M. Dent, 1906; Collingwood, R. G. *The Idea of History*. Oxford University Press, 1948; Green, G. *Imagining God*. Harper & Row, 1989; Hart, T. "Imagination and Responsible Reading." Pages 307–34 in *Renewing Biblical Interpretation*, ed. C. Bartholomew et al. SHS. Zondervan/Paternoster, 2000; Johnson, M. *The Body in the Mind*. University of Chicago Press, 1987; Kearney, R. *Poetics of Imagining*. Edinburgh University Press, 1998; idem. *The Wake of Imagination*. Routledge, 1988; Llewelyn, J. *The Hypocritical Imagination*. Routledge, 2000; Lynch, W. *Images of Hope*. Helicon, 1965; McIntyre, J. *Faith, Theology and Imagination*. Handsel, 1987; Murdoch, I. *Existentialists and Mystics*. Penguin, 1997; Nettle, D. *The Strong Imagination*. Oxford University Press, 2001; Nussbaum, M. "The Literary Imagination in Public Life." *New Literary History* 22 (1991): 877–910; Sartre, J. P. *The Psychology of Imagination*. Methuen, 1972; Steiner, G. *After Babel*. Oxford University Press, 1992; idem. *Grammars of Creation*. Faber, 2001; Warnock, M. *Imagination*. Faber, 1976; Wolterstorff, N. *Divine Discourse*. Cambridge University Press, 1995.

Trevor A. Hart

Incarnation

The incarnation claims that during the Roman occupation of Palestine, when King Herod the Great ruled Judea, the God of Israel became a human person. "God the Son," or the "Second Person of the Trinity," became a Jewish artisan: Jesus of Nazareth, who later came to be called Jesus Christ, meaning "anointed Savior."

Biblical Foundations

Two biblical texts in particular support this shocking claim. One is from Paul, and the other is from the Gospel of John. The earlier text is Phil. 2:5–8. Paul is encouraging the young Christians at Philippi to be steadfast, noble, and firm in their commitment to Christ, expressed through love for one another and utter humility and unity of mind in their dealings with one another. He urges them to imitate Christ himself, who, though in the form (*morphē*) of God, was so humble that he discarded his godliness to become human and even die, mistaken for a common criminal.

The other text that suggests incarnation is the prologue of John's Gospel, 1:1–14, 18. The prologue is set up as a theological interpretation of Gen. 1, giving a rather different account of God's work of creation than presented there. John uses the Greek word *Logos* (itself meaning "word") to signify the order and meaning with which he created the world. He gives this Logos an independent identity, saying that it was with God, and even was God before or as he created the world. The Word has this divine meaning and order, and it is also the light of "all people" (1:4 NRSV), whether individuals are able to recognize it or not. In v. 14, John articulates one of the most compelling yet disconcerting ideas of all time: "Divine Logos became flesh," a person! "Incarnate" is the transliteration of the Latin *incarnatus est* (Nicene Creed), which itself is a translation of *sarx egeneto* (became flesh) of John 1:14, in which the evangelist says that the meaning and order of God became Jesus of Nazareth.

Patristic Formulations

These two passages remain elliptically tantalizing. Much remains unclear. As Christians began praying to Jesus, many both within and without the church asked, "What are they doing?" Worshipping Jesus seemed simply idolatrous. It took two hundred years for the implications of the startling claims raised by the Pauline and Johannine texts to be thoroughly understood, and another 150 years for criticism of them to be clearly answered. Indeed, the incarnation is one of the great mysteries of the faith.

Worshipping Christ raised the question of where to draw the line between God and creature. In the fourth century, a presbyter named Arius (d. 336) objected to considering Christ as God, because anything that is separate from God (as suggested by John's identification of divine speech as separate from God) must be a creature, and therefore could not be God, who is eternal and uncreated. The Word of God, Logos, that resides in Jesus had to be categorized as a creature, and so too Jesus. Arius's position was rejected by the Council of Nicea in 325, John's notion of divine speech was considered to be divine (uncreated), and Christ to be "begotten, not made, of one being with the Father," as the later Nicene Creed would put it.

Some years after the Council of Nicea, the words *sarkōthenta* (became enfleshed) and *enanthrōpesanta* (became human) appear in the second article of baptismal creeds of the Greek-speaking churches. These creeds are first associated with the historian Eusebius of Caesarea (d. ca. 340) and the catechist Cyril of Jerusalem (d. ca. 387). Their creeds were standardized into what was called the Nicene Creed at the Council of Chalcedon in 451, whose 500–600 bishops attributed it to the work of the 150 bishops gathered at the previous Council of Constantinople in 381. The Creed went by the name Nicene because the bishops of these two councils were upholding and, in their turn, elucidating the faith of the earlier Council of Nicea regarding the divine identity of Christ.

Once the church agreed that Christ was God and that Christians were not worshipping a man, as the Romans worshipped the emperor, the question arose, In what sense then was Christ a human being? In the fifth century, the question was, Is becoming enfleshed the same as becoming human? If it is, being human is reduced to having a body, and this was not appealing because it left out human consciousness. The objection was based on the claim that salvation comes from God's having become human. If being human is limited to having a body, then our personalities, our spirits are not saved, and this seemed to undermine the whole point of the incarnation.

Conflict was not resolved until the majority of bishops agreed that John's teaching meant that God became a complete human being, not simply a human body. The debates ended by accepting a great paradox. It was said that Jesus Christ was a thoroughgoing union of divinity and humanity in which divinity took on but did not overpower the humanity and the humanity did not besmirch the divinity. Christ had not simply human flesh, but also human consciousness; the fullness of God assumed the fullness of humanity—body, mind, and spirit. This was stated officially by the phrase "one person, two natures."

This settled, there remained the question of Gospel passages that attributed human emotions to Jesus while seeming to deny his divinity. These were attributed to the human nature in order to protect the divine nature from involvement in human emotions, because God was above these. On the other hand are passages that indicate Jesus knew the future. These were attributed to the divine nature. In short, everything Jesus did had to be attributed to one nature or the other, because there remained deep anxiety about fully embracing the claim that God became a human being. God and "man" still had to keep apart.

Interpretation

Official teaching on the incarnation underwent little change after the fifth century. Christians continue to confess that Christ is truly human and truly divine, God from God, light from light. Our question is, What is its significance for us? There are at least two points to note.

Jesus reveals God to us in his person, not conceptually. Yet Jesus is no pushover. He had a temper. He could dismiss people rudely, and even spoke to his mother smartly. He spoke in riddles, refused to answer pointed questions, and intentionally hid his meaning from his friends. He made incredibly harsh demands of his followers, and taught love of enemies while denouncing his opponents, according to the Gospel accounts. And this, Christians claim, is God enfleshed.

Now, it is perhaps precisely in seeing the "unlovely" sides of Jesus that we learn how utterly human God actually did become. He became a person with all the weaknesses and temptations that we know so well. Indeed, by becoming a person with all sorts of human weakness, his voluntary death, to save both his followers and the entire nation from a bloodbath, appears the more astounding.

God became a man with all the warts of human nature and offered them all to God by dying that others might live. The final act of his life overwhelms all the irritations others endured from him during his short life. Here is where the meaning of the incarnation is revealed. God became like us in every way, and only because of that does his dying on our behalf cancel out the sins that he has taken as his own. In this, he shows us both our greatest unloveliness and our greatest nobility. In this, he ennobles us beyond our sins.

A second important meaning of the incarnation is that the other face of God's becoming human is that a man became divine. God has taken human life, with all its warts, and raised it to accompany himself. Here is the true foundation of human dignity. In Jesus, God takes us into his own nobility, remaking us in his likeness. Jesus not only reveals the wisdom, goodness, and beauty of God, but also again, by representing all of us, shows us the divinization of human life. Through him, human life is remade in the beauty, wisdom, and goodness of God.

See also Jesus Christ, Doctrine of

Bibliography

Barth, K. *Church Dogmatics*. Vol. III/1, *The Doctrine of Creation*, trans. G. W. Bromiley. T&T Clark, 1958; Berkouwer, G. C. *The Person of Christ*. Eerdmans, 1954; Dunn, J. D. G. *Christology in the Making*. Westminster, 1980; Gregg, R. C., and D. Groh. *Early Arianism*. Fortress, 1981; Grillmeier, A. *Christ in Christian Tradition*. John Knox, 1964; Keck, L. "Toward the Renewal of New Testament Christology." *NTS* 32 (1986): 362–77; Kelly, J. N. D. *Early Christian Creeds*. Longman Group, 1972; Norris, F. "Deification: Consensual and Cogent." *SJT* 49, no. 4 (1997): 411–28; Norris, R. *Manhood and Christ*. Clarendon, 1963; Wesche, K. "'Mind' and 'Self' in the Christology of Saint Gregory the Theologian: Saint Gregory's Contribution to Christology and Christian Anthropology." *The Greek Orthodox Theological Review* 39, no. 1 (1994): 33–61; Williams, R. *Arius*. Darton, Longman & Todd, 1987; Young, F. *From Nicaea to Chalcedon*. Fortress, 1983.

Ellen T. Charry

Indeterminacy   *See* Meaning

Infancy Narratives

Matthew 1–2 and Luke 1–2 (with the chronology in 3:23–38) are at once among the most beloved, ignored, and debated Gospel passages. A treasurehouse for the liturgist, they bring the theologian to the edge of mystery, the literary critic to the margins of genre, and the historian to the brink of a headache.

Issues and History of Interpretation

Neither Mark nor John contains infancy accounts, and those of Matthew and Luke differ in outline and detail; it might thus be considered that these four chapters are not strictly necessary. Although other bizarre extracanonical stories (e.g., *Pseudo-Matthew, Infancy Gospel of Thomas*, and *Protevangelium of James*) cast their shadow, these prologues retain an honored place in the canon, providing the church with the Magnificat and the Nunc Dimittis.

Classical Commentators. Earliest commentators evince technical, textual, and theological concerns. For example, the speaker of the Magnificat is identified as Elizabeth in both the second-century Irenaeus and in some Old Latin manuscripts. This difference in detail indicates that there was, even at this stage, debate regarding the more appropriate cantor of a song that echoes the aged Hannah—Elizabeth, the natural choice, is passed over for Mary in our Gospels. A more significant controversy revolved around Matthew's Isa. 7:14 citation, and the meaning(s) of *'almah*—translated *parthenos*, "virgin," in the LXX; but as *neanis*, "young woman," in other Greek translations. The second-century apologist Justin argues in his *Dialogue with Trypho* for the faithfulness of the LXX, which seems to inform Matthew. Again, Origen (*Cels.* 1.28–69) refutes Celsus's charge that the Matthean account is a fabrication (inspired by Jesus' own malingering) and that Mary conceived Jesus out of wedlock by the soldier "Panthera." (Similar illegitimacy stories are found in the writings of the Tannaitic rabbis [see Tertullian, *Spect.* 30] and in the medieval Jewish *Toledoth Yeshu* [lit., *Generations/Lineage of Jesus*].) All these materials, along with John 8:41, reflect ongoing discussion of the irregularity of Jesus' conception.

More frequently the infancy gospels were a source of enrichment for the ancients rather than of contention. For example, John Chrysostom, in introducing the intricacies of the Matthean infancy narrative, exhorts his listeners to "revolve these things" in their minds. "For from taking thought concerning these matters, there springs in the soul some great good, tending unto salvation, . . . that all our members may serve him" (*Hom. Matt.* 2.9). His interpretation of Matt. 1–2 does not shy away from the problems aforementioned, even while he discloses unanticipated mysteries drawn from this "holy vestibule" (*Hom. Matt.* 2.1), meaning Matthew's prologue. In particular, his treatment of the women in the genealogy shows how the incarnate Son assumed human weakness. So also Jerome and Ambrose: "None of the holy women are taken into the Saviour's genealogy, but rather such as Scripture has condemned, that He who came for sinners being born of sinners might so put away the sins of all" (in Aquinas, *Catena aurea* 1.19); "Nor . . . would it shame the Church to be gathered from among sinners, when the Lord Himself was born of sinners" (1.20). Another favorite vignette of the fathers was the offering of the magi's gifts: "It was knowledge and obedience and love that they offered Him . . . as to God" (Chrysostom, *Hom. Matt.* 8.1); "Gold, as to a King; frankincense, as sacrifice to God; myrrh, as embalming the dead" (Gregory the Great, *Hom. in evan.* 1.106). "They bring three gifts, i.e. the faith in the Holy Trinity. Or, opening the stores of Scripture, they offer its threefold sense, historical, moral and allegorical" (*Gloss. Anselm*, in Aquinas, *Catena aurea* 1.77).

The ancient commentators, then, followed Mary, who "kept all these things . . . in her heart" (Luke 2:19 KJV). Such is the case also with the greats since that time. For example, Calvin (*Commentary on a Harmony of the Evangelists*) and John Wesley (*Notes on the Whole Bible*), unstymied by the obvious textual difficulties, stress their theological and anthropological significance. We may be surprised to discover that these Protestant commentators agree with the ancients regarding the ever-virginity of Mary, and explain Matt. 1:25 so as to deny that Jesus' mother had subsequent children! We are less surprised to read Calvin's and Wesley's meditations on God's initiative in the incarnation and humankind's ideal stance in receiving that gift, as embodied in Mary.

Post-Enlightenment Commentators. A spiritualized approach to the narratives emerged in the nineteenth century with D. F. Strauss, who, among others, salvaged an "inner meaning" of Scriptures from what were supposed to be entirely nonhistorical texts. Strauss enthused:

> This is the key to the whole of Christology. . . . In an individual, a God-man, the properties and functions which the Church ascribes to Christ contradict themselves. In the idea of the race, they perfectly agree. Humanity is the union of the two natures—God become man. (*Life*, 2:895)

The infancy narratives about Jesus, then, are to be read by the enlightened as a picture for the greatness of *humanity*.

Scholarship on the infancy narratives has probably never fully recovered from the nineteenth century. Few standard NT introductions tackled the passages until the advent of redaction and literary criticism, when they made a comeback, frequently accompanied by a rationalist distinction between "history" and theological ideas (on this, see Horsley, ch. 1). The recent treatment of Edwin D. Freed (170) closes with the predictable words of J. K. Elliott (17): "For all their apparent historicizing and verisimilitude, the Christmas story provides us with no more real facts about the historical Jesus than Paul himself does."

Freed should have heeded the masterful work of Raymond Brown, who offered, as an exception to the ongoing dichotomized treatment of the infancy narratives, two editions of his comprehensive *The Birth of the Messiah*. His work reminds us of many keen scholars who have read these passages, considering the chapters from within the Catholic tradition, while remaining aware of "contemporary" problems (often anticipated in antiquity!). He places the passages in historical, theological, and literary context, and eschews a simplistic division between "fact" and "theology." Again, he questions the faddish appeal to the "midrash" genre (popularized by Episcopal Bishop John Spong) that now so engages those working on these narratives: the stories cannot be termed "midrash," Brown explains, because they do not aim to comment upon OT texts; instead, they illuminate the identity of Jesus the Christ by echoing the OT.

The welter of newer approaches to the accounts includes the studies of feminist Jane Schaberg, who breathtakingly musters evidence for Mary giving "illegitimate birth" to Jesus. The social historian Horsley finesses the work of Otto Rank (*The Myth of the Birth of the Hero* [1909; ET, 1914]) with an eye to sociological analysis, and concludes that "the birth legends of Jesus have sociopolitical implications" (171) and thus a revolutionary connection with history. Regarding Horsley's attempt to bring the accounts into dialogue with Herod's "oppressive" legacy, Brown wisely comments, "Modernizing the sociopolitical situation of Jesus' time is often a hindrance in discerning what the author wished to convey to his first hearers/listeners" (614). Despite the appeal of Schaberg and Horsley for many early-twenty-first-century readers, the thorough and faithful work of Brown remains an unparalleled standard.

Message and Contribution to the Canon

It is probably inadvisable to distill our four chapters into a single "message," except that of initiating and incarnating God's care for his people. The infancy narratives introduce many significant matters, including the connection of the OT with the NT, the virginal conception (implied in Matt. 1:18–23; stated in Luke 1:34), the provision of Mary as a model of piety and faith, the human growth of Jesus to maturity, and the exquisite artistry of the Gospel writers. Both Gospel writers aptly suit their prologues to the contents that follow. Matthew forges an explicit pattern of "fulfillment" through the genealogy, OT citation, and narrative patterns. Luke, through atmosphere, echo, and structure, subtly impresses upon his readers the climax and turn of the ages in Jesus the Christ. Luke's deft use of the diptych (the intertwined stories of the infants John and Jesus) has been noted by many; Matthew's use of citation is less well understood, since some moderns have dismissed it as proof-texting, without an intimate knowledge of the evangelist's perspective. Readers need to give careful attention to Matthew's role in the nascent conflict with emerging Judaism and to Luke's irenic emphasis.

It is frequently remarked that the infancy narratives present a late stage in the NT understanding of Jesus' divinity—first fixed at the resurrection, then at the baptism, and finally, at the moment of conception. We could add that although the virginal conception might simply have been a "sign" of God's special activity, we may not be in a position to apprehend what was a "necessary" correlative for the genesis of the Second Adam. Brown admits that the quest for the progressive understanding of Christology remains speculative, but sees no conflict between a commitment to the creed and the possibility that the apostolic community "only gradually and in retrospect . . . work[ed] out the christological implications for earlier parts of Jesus' life" (711). However we approach such schemes, Brown provides a model for the faithful reader who refuses to bracket questions of genre and history.

Those concerned about the details of the narratives continue to deliberate over their differences (cf. Freed's chart, 57–59), their parallel to pagan birth narratives (e.g., Suetonius re Augustus, *Aug.* 94.3), the phenomenon of the "star" (supernova? comet? planetary conjunction?), the details of Quirinius's reign and the census, the problem of Jesus' "brothers and sisters," and the status of the "magi" (e.g., Freed 96–100). This latter was a point of discussion among the ancients and has come full circle in the wake of the contemporary "new age" movement. Such quests are not to be despised but to be placed in a larger context, as the student forges a perspective that is at once historical, theological, and literary. The faithful reader will recognize the unique literary flavor of each narrative and approach the relationship between event and text with regard for genre. To be sure, the nativity stories differ from the rest of the Gospels, providing us with poignant stories that are masterfully shaped so as to recall key figures and highly symbolic OT passages. They are not, however, created from whole cloth, and they continue to bear upon historical research.

In the end, we will not want to be so concerned with minutiae that we miss the impact of the stories. Gregory Thaumaturgus recalls God's wondrous actions, unveiled to the eye of the child or the seasoned scholar:

She wrapped in swaddling-clothes Him who is covered with light as with a garment. . . . She laid in a manger Him who sits above the cherubim, and is praised by myriads of angels. . . . In the board from which cattle eat was laid the heavenly Bread, in order that He might provide participation in spiritual sustenance for men who live like the beasts of the earth. Nor was there even room for Him in the inn. He found no place, who by His word established heaven and earth; "for though He was rich, for our sakes He became poor." (*The First Homily on the Annunciation to the Holy Virgin Mary* 34–37; in *ANF*, vol. 6)

Bibliography

Brown, R. *The Birth of the Messiah*. Doubleday, 1993; Caird, G. B. *The Gospel of Saint Luke*. Penguin, 1963; Davies, W. D., and D. Allison. *A Critical and Exegetical Commentary on the Gospel according to Saint Matthew*. 3 vols. ICC. T&T Clark, 1988; Elliott, J. *Questioning Christian Origins*. SCM, 1982; Fitzmyer, J. *The Gospel according to Luke*. Vol. 1. AB 28. Doubleday, 1981; Freed, E. *The Stories of Jesus' Birth*. Sheffield Academic Press, 2001; Horsley, R. *The Liberation of Christmas*. Crossroad, 1989; Marshall, I. H. *The Gospel of Luke*. Eerdmans, 1978; Schaberg, J. *The Illegitimacy of Jesus*. Harper & Row, 1987; Spong, J. *Born of a Woman*. Harper, 1992; Strauss, D. F. *The Life of Jesus Critically Examined*, trans. M. Evans. 2 vols. C. Blanchard, 1860.

Edith M. Humphrey

Inner-Biblical Interpretation *See* Intertextuality

Intention/Intentional Fallacy

Debates about the intentional fallacy date from the mid-twentieth century. Nevertheless, the notion of authorial intention crops up throughout the history of biblical interpretation and has bearing on a number of crucial hermeneutical issues, including the nature of the text, the meaning of meaning, and the aims and norms of reading.

Literary Criticism

In 1946, William Wimsatt and Monroe Beardsley coauthored "The Intentional Fallacy," a manifesto for "New Critics," who believed that an exaggerated concern with the psychology of the poet (e.g., motives and purposes for writing) leads one to overlook the formal features of the literary work itself, thus substituting biography for criticism. The "fallacy" of intentionalism is therefore to mistake a *historical* inquiry about authors for a properly *interpretative* study of texts. In late-twentieth-century biblical studies, much the same charge was leveled against historical critics by exegetes who focused on the Bible's textual properties (its poetic, literary, narrative, and rhetorical features).

E. D. Hirsch led the "intentionalist backlash." His *Validity in Interpretation* (1967) defended "the sensible view that a text means what its author meant." Hirsch argued that the author's intention—the willed verbal meaning—is the only practical interpretative norm, the only scholarly standard for judging right and wrong interpretations. It is the author's will alone that determines which of the possible verbal meanings a sentence (e.g., "He's hot") or text actually bears.

Hirsch built upon Edmund Husserl's phenomenology, holding that intentionality is the essential characteristic of consciousness, which is always consciousness *of* something. To intend, therefore, is to direct one's consciousness in a particular way (e.g., believing, hoping) toward a particular mental content (e.g., a thought, a hope). Understanding is an intentional act directed at an intentional object (e.g., meaning); meaning is what understanding grasps or is about.

Poststructuralists present a new challenge to intentionalism. They argue that the author's will is not "outside" language, directing it this way and that, but is itself subject to language, forced to speak and think in terms of distinctions and relations instituted by diverse language systems. So Paul, the apostle of freedom, continues to think in terms of master/slave even as he asks Philemon to treat Onesimus as a brother in Christ. Language precedes subjectivity and intentions; hence, the so-called death of the author.

Biblical Studies and Theology

For the church fathers, theology was largely a matter of biblical interpretation, and ascertaining the author's intention was often cited as one mark of right interpretation. Athanasius wrote: "Now it is right and necessary here, as in all divine Scripture, faithfully to expound the time which the Apostle wrote, and the person, and the point; lest the reader . . . be wide of the true sense" (*C. Ar.* 1.54). At the same time, biblical passages should be interpreted in light of the entire "scope of Scripture," by its overall message handily summarized in the Rule of Faith.

In Augustine's opinion, it is ultimately more important to arrive at truth than at the intention of the human author. However, "anyone who understands in the Scriptures something other than that intended by them is deceived" (*Doctr. chr.* 1.36.41). Such a person may reach the right destination, but on the other hand, the person may begin to prefer one's own way. Augustine

concludes that such a person "is to be corrected and shown that it is more useful not to leave the road."

Although Thomas Aquinas identified the literal sense of Scripture with the meaning intended by the author, he also held that the ultimate author of Scripture is God (*ST* I.1.10). This is arguably the major point of contrast between medieval and modern interpreters. Biblical scholars after the Enlightenment tend to restrict authorial intention to what the human authors, situated in particular cultural and historical contexts, could have meant. Biblical criticism has contributed much to our stock of knowledge, though it has also resulted in an inability to read the Bible as animated by a divine intention.

The Reformers stand between the medieval and modern periods, concerned with reading for the inspired Word of God yet also concerned to do justice to the grammar and historical context of the text. In the preface to his *Commentary on Romans*, Calvin declared, "It is the first business of an interpreter to let his author say what he does say, instead of attributing to him what we think he ought to say." Calvin was precritical in his insistence that the human authors were divinely inspired. In his interpretation of Ps. 87, he refers to the historical and spiritual intentions interchangeably: "We must consider the intention of the prophet, or rather the object of the Spirit of God, speaking by the mouth of the prophet."

Partly in response to the theological impoverishment of modern biblical criticism and partly influenced by the New Critical reproach of historical criticism, late-twentieth-century interpreters developed an interest in the intent of the text itself. Narrative critics sought the world "of" or "in front of" the text (the self-contained textual world mediated to the reader), not the world "behind" it (the world of the historical author). It is doubtful, however, whether much sense can be made out of textual intent because texts, lacking consciousness, cannot have intentions. Brevard Childs worked an interesting variation on this theme by proposing "canonical intent" as the object of exegetical interest. Those responsible for assembling and transmitting Scripture inscribed their intent into and onto the final form of the canonical texts. It is not the narrative but the properly canonical shape that renders the authoritative subject matter of Scripture. However, to the extent that canonical intent refers not to the final form of the text but to the intentions of the canonizers, one may ask why *their* intentions, rather than those of the original authors or even later interpreters, enjoy pride of place. In response, Childs suggests that what is theological about canonical intention is the subject matter (not the divine authorial intention) to which the final form of the biblical text directs us.

Yet another contemporary approach stresses the aims of the interpretative community. The aim of believers who read Scripture in the church differs from scholars who study the Bible in the academy. Believers read Scripture with the aim of knowing God and of being transformed in order to live and worship faithfully before God; for this end, reading for the intention of the human author is neither necessary nor sufficient (Fowl). The church's interest in edification and doxology overrides its interest in authorial intention.

Intentional Action

Recent philosophy of action has breathed new life into the concept of authorial intent; it has also clarified what is right and what is wrong about the "intentional fallacy." According to Wittgenstein, John Searle, and other analytic philosophers, intention is not a private mental event but an indispensable and public aspect of all human action. Only intention, for example, makes a blink *count as* a wink, the wave of a hand *count as* a greeting—something more than mere bodily movements or physiological events. Similarly, only intention makes marks in the sand *count as* a line from a Shakespeare play rather than random patterns caused by the waves. When confronted with apparently meaningful human behavior or intelligible signs, we cannot help but attribute intentionality (Gibbs).

A text is a set of verbal signs intended by an author to bring about understanding in a reader. Intention pertains to what authors are doing *in tending* to their words. To interpret is to describe what an author is doing in a particular sentence or passage by paying attention both to its formal features (e.g., the words, the structure) and to its broader context, to the text as a whole (e.g., the literary genre). The relevant context is the one that allows one to offer a sufficient description of the author's action, a description that admits of no more relevant questions. Note that what an author does with words may occasionally have little to do with the meaning of the words themselves. We ascribe ironic intentions to authors, for example, not because the verbal meaning demands it but because other relevant contextual clues tip us off as to what the author is really doing. Irony could not exist apart from authorial intention. To generalize: *every* appeal to the text as evidence for one's interpretation turns out to be a tacit appeal to the author's probable intent (Juhl).

Knowing what an author *planned* or *tried* or *wanted* to say is not the same as knowing what an author has actually done. For the intentionalist, meaning is a matter of intentional action, not planning. Again, intention is not a psychological event that precedes an action but an intrinsic aspect of the action that in fact makes the action what it is. A string of words counts as a promise, for example, because a speaker uses the appropriate linguistic conventions (e.g., "I promise") intentionally to make a promise.

Is authorial intent boon or bane to the project of theological interpretation of Scripture? A focus on authorial intent would seem to run counter to the kind of spiritual interpretation of Scripture that Augustine and others felt was necessary for the edification of the church. How, for example, could one read the OT as pointing to Christ if the human authors did not consciously have Christ as the content of their message? Yet some ascription of intentionality to biblical texts appears inevitable, for *someone* is doing something with these words. To understand textual meaning, then, is just to impute intentions; the only question is whose, author's or reader's?

Divine Authorial Intention

Acknowledging Scripture as the word of God does not militate against intentionality but calls for and qualifies it. Specifically, it calls for recognition of dual authorship where the divine intention appropriates, superintends, or supervenes on the human intention. God speaks in Scripture by way of human discourse, but not by outshouting the human authors. God identifies his word with *just these texts* because they already communicate a good number of his intentions. We may legitimately presume that the divine intention corresponds to the human intention unless there is good reason—given the nature of God or the broader canonical context—to think otherwise. Recognizing Scripture's divine authorship ultimately requires us to read the biblical texts as *one book*. As with any action, we can adequately identify what has been done in Scripture only by considering its action as a *whole*. The divine intention most comes to light when God's communicative acts are described in *canonical* context.

What interpreters believe about God affects what they take God's intention to be: "Interpretation of a person's discourse occurs, and can only occur, in the context of knowledge of that person" (Wolterstorff 239). Does this represent a "divine intentionalist fallacy," where biographical criticism (of God!) intrudes on interpretation? It does not. For we know the Word who is God primarily by attending to God's word written. Luther observed that all books are to be interpreted in the spirit of their author, and that an author's spirit is nowhere more on display than in his or her writings. In the case of Scripture, the divine author's spirit is the Holy Spirit; the word is the enactment of the Spirit's communicative intention. To read theologically is to ascertain the intention of the Spirit speaking in and through Scripture.

Conclusion

Whose intentions guide interpretation? To interpret Scripture theologically is to read for the divine intention, and this means reading each part in light of the canonical whole. The canonical context alone forms the proper context for describing what God is doing in his word and for understanding the purpose for which God's word was sent (Isa. 55:11). To limit oneself to recovering only the human authorial intentions is to fall short of theological interpretation. And to impose one's own intentions or the intentions of one's community is to fail to guard oneself from potential idols.

The final word belongs to Jerome: "It was my purpose not to draw the Scriptures to my will but to say what I understood to be the intention of the Scriptures. For it is the duty of the commentator to set forth not what he himself wants but what the one whom he interprets means. Otherwise, if he says contrary things, he will not be so much interpreter as opponent of him whom he attempts to explain" (*Letters* XLVIII.17).

See also Authorial Discourse Interpretation; Canonical Approach; Formalism; Meaning

Bibliography

Childs, B. *Introduction to the Old Testament as Scripture*. Fortress, 1979; Fowl, S. "The Role of Authorial Intention in the Theological Interpretation of Scripture." Pages 71–87 in *Between Two Horizons*, ed. J. Green and M. Turner. Eerdmans, 2000; Gibbs, R., Jr. *Intentions in the Experience of Meaning*. Cambridge University Press, 1999; Gracia, J. *How Can We Know What God Means?* Palgrave, 2001; Hirsch, E. D. *Validity in Interpretation*. Yale University Press, 1967; Iseminger, G., ed. *Intention and Interpretation*. Temple University Press, 1992; Juhl, P. D. *Interpretation*. Princeton University Press, 1980; Vanhoozer, K. *Is There a Meaning in This Text?* Zondervan, 1998; Wimsatt, W. K., with M. Beardsley. *The Verbal Icon*. University Press of Kentucky, 1954; Wimsatt, W. K., and M. Beardsley. "The Intentional Fallacy." *Sewanee Review* 54 (1946): 468–88. In Wimsatt, *Verbal Icon*; Wolterstorff, N. *Divine Discourse*. Cambridge University Press, 1995.

Kevin J. Vanhoozer

Interlocutionary Act *See* Speech-Act Theory

Interpretation, History of

The history of biblical interpretation can refer to a present act of historical research, in which writers from the history of the precritical tradition are examined for content as they engage the biblical texts. This we might call first-order history of biblical interpretation, and it is a basic description of what is said. On the other hand, the phrase "the history of biblical interpretation" can mean the study of modern-period writings about the church's tradition for their hermeneutical and interpretative strategies. We might call this second-order history of biblical interpretation. Modern historical-critical research on the Bible has deemed both these first- and second-order tasks as irrelevant in the search for knowledge of the biblical world, defined in terms of the historical world into which the Bible fits. The first task, while deemed "historical" in its research methods, is itself dismissed as useless for historical-critical research on the Bible. The second task is dismissed, because studying "precritical" hermeneutics is deemed useless for modern historical research—but only useful for contemporary interpretation. That is, both the first task and second task, while historical in their own right, can indeed offer the contemporary church forgotten insights and methods of reading Scripture. Both tasks also call on the interpreter to acknowledge and value the interconnectedness of the canon and the overall narrative that it recounts in its very task. Within the theological disciplines, this then can provide for a contemporary return to recapture riches from the history of biblical interpretation.

From their very beginning the Scriptures have been subject to interpretation. Indeed, interpreting them is a command: "'Son of Man, . . . eat this scroll; then go and speak to the house of Israel.' So I opened my mouth, and he gave me the scroll to eat. . . . So I ate it, and it tasted as sweet as honey in my mouth" (Ezek. 3:1–3). Indeed, the Scriptures themselves are interpretations of events and communication both human and divine. We think here of both narratival recounting of events and prophetic declarations that interpret Israel's action in light of its covenant relationship with its God. We can also see this reinterpretation of the OT within its own pages, for example, in the Psalms' recasting of creation and redemption. And the two covenants in their turn interpret each other, for example, in the NT figural rereading of the OT manna story, which casts Jesus as the Bread of Life (Exodus; Num. 11; John 6). We also see this in the proof-texting of the OT in the NT, such as the Matthean formula quotations "This happened in order to fulfill . . ." "The Old Testament lies within the New, and the New shines forth from the Old" (Jerome). This reliance of the OT on the NT and the NT on the OT raises the question of canon in the history of biblical interpretation. In both the first-order task of the history of interpretation and its second-order task, the canon is seen to be one, not two, much less documents J, E, D, P, Mark, Matthew, Luke, Q, and John. The unity of the canon is assumed, not proved.

Until the last twenty years or so, the debate about the interpretation of Scripture has been centered around how the Antiochene school differed from the Alexandrian school of interpretation. It was once thought that the Antiochenes were more "literal" in their interpretation and the Alexandrians more "allegorical." In addition, these terms themselves were not clearly defined. For the most part, this schema has been set aside. Recently a new thesis has emerged, moving in a much different direction (Young), proposing that in the patristic era the Bible was read for the formation of the Christian culture and people, both individual and collective. This makes Alexandria and Antioch appear much closer to each other than previously assumed.

Recent studies of biblical interpretation have tended instead to focus on the cultural worlds and communities represented by the exegetical works. This includes considering the collection and transmission of the scriptural texts, and examining both social conflict and communal formation arising from the reading of these writings. However, from the earliest times interpretation of the Scriptures became a tool of theological argumentation and formation of the understanding of the "literal sense," or plain sense, its authoritative meaning. An example of this is Justin's *Dialogue with Trypho*, where Scripture's "literal sense" funds the argument, the assumption being that both the speaker and his opponent each understand themselves to be reading according to the literal sense, the authoritative sense, which would ground arguments based on Scripture.

While clearly the history of biblical interpretation of the first order is for the main an investigation of precritical material within a critical scholarship, we can learn more about what exactly precritical might mean by engaging in this task and following their example. A corollary of this is the supposed great hermeneutical divide of the modern period between what the text meant and what it means. For modern interpretation, what the text meant is a question of systematics or even phenomenology. For the history of biblical interpretation, though, both the first- and second-order tasks, the question of what the text meant and what it means, are not two separate matters, with the second prioritized over the first. Again, we can learn from the history of biblical interpretation the wholeness of reading Scripture over against a modern dissection of text and meanings.

Christian history is always written to and for a specific community. This is true also of biblical interpretation of the first order in particular, but potentially for the second order as well. While we are coming to see that Christian history may differ in method and conclusions from its secular companions, likewise we find that biblical interpretation of both the first and second orders will not have the same categories, premises, and goals as secular, modern interpretation. The most important observation to make is that the first order and even second order will not necessarily have the goal of "objectivity," but of transformation of lives. For the purpose of first-order and potentially second-order history of interpretation is laying Christ bare within the straw of the manger, which is the Bible (so Luther).

See also Literal Sense

Bibliography

Bobertz, C., and D. Brakke. *Reading in Christian Communion*. University of Notre Dame, 2002; Margerie, B. de. *Introduction à l'histoire de l'exégèse*. 4 vols. Cerf, 1980–90; ET, *An Introduction to the History of Exegesis*. 3 vols. St. Bede's Pubns., 1994; McKim, D. *Historical Handbook of Major Biblical Interpreters*. InterVarsity, 1998; Old, H. *The Reading and Preaching of the Scriptures in the Worship of the Christian Church*. 4 vols. Eerdmans, 2002; Young, F. *Biblical Interpretation and the Formation of Christian Culture*. Cambridge University Press, 1997.

Kathryn Greene-McCreight

Interpretation in the Church See Catholic Biblical Interpretation; Church, Doctrine of the; Liturgy; Mysticism, Christian; Orthodox Biblical Interpretation; Protestant Biblical Interpretation; Spirituality/Spiritual Formation; Theological Hermeneutics, Contemporary; Virtue

Intertestamental Period *See* Jewish Context of the NT

Intertextuality

In Matthew's account of the crucifixion, all but the women watching from a distance make their assessment of Jesus; everyone close to the scene has something to say. The Roman soldiers post a sign over his head that reads, THIS IS JESUS, THE KING OF THE JEWS. Those passing by also mock him, repeating his words about the temple's destruction. The chief priests, scribes, and elders join in, "He saved others, . . . but he cannot save himself." After three hours of darkness and narrative silence, Jesus finally speaks, quoting the words of another righteous sufferer: "'*Eloi, Eloi, lama sabachthani?*'—which means, 'My God, my God, why have you forsaken me?'" (Matt. 27:37–46). While Jesus' famous use of Ps. 22 has generated much commentary, it should be remembered that every utterance in this scene makes use of words previously spoken in other contexts. Readers who attend to all these citations and their original contexts find that Jesus' cry of abandonment stands as a profound answer to the mockery. Moreover, three aspects of this use of quoted speech touch on matters that interpreters now place under the umbrella term "intertextuality" (inner-biblical exegesis, literary theory, and biblical theology).

Inner-Biblical Exegesis

First, Jesus' quotation of the psalm voiced his anguish by means of scriptural words. Some have suggested that the citation of the lament psalm also proclaims confidence that God will deliver those who trust in him. "For he has not despised or disdained the suffering of the afflicted one; he has not hidden his face from him but has listened to his cry for help" (Ps. 22:24). The cry of dereliction is shorthand for the movement of the whole psalm from a wail of lament to a shout of victory (Perelmuter 14).

Although the church has always studied and expounded the NT's citation of the Scriptures of Israel, a group of recent interpreters has turned its attention to inner-biblical exegesis, the way that OT texts relate to other Scripture texts as a midrash (from Hebrew *darash*, "to seek") or commentary (*traditio*) on already existing texts (*traditum*). Instead of looking at the influence of earlier sources on those that come after, the focus shifts to how later generations interpret and comment on the literary tradition. So Prov. 2–7 can be seen as a commentary or sermon on Deut. 6:7–9 and 11:19 (Buchanan 1–20), and Lev. 25:3–7 as explanatory gloss on Exod. 23:10–11a (Fishbane, *Garments*, 9). In this view, later rabbinic intertextual readings of midrash continue and extend a process that began in the formation of the OT itself (Boyarin). Fishbane (*Biblical*) distinguishes scribal, legal, haggadic (nonlegal ethical), and mantological (prophetic) modes of exegesis. Others, such as Mason, speak of gloss (e.g., contemporizing additions to Amos 2:4–11), arrangement (e.g., 1 Sam. 8–10 juxtaposes positive and negative views of monarchy), directed quotation (e.g., Dan. 9:1–2, 20–27 interprets Jeremiah's prophecy), and theological themes (e.g., David's preparations for constructing the temple in Chronicles resemble Moses and the tabernacle).

While Fishbane did not include the NT in his study, some interpreters find signs of inner-biblical exegesis, for example, in Paul's use of Jer. 9:22–23 to critique "boasting" in 1 Cor. 1:26, 29 (O'Day). Others argue that Christian writers used techniques similar to the covenanters at Qumran, who also believed that their community was the fulfillment of God's promises to Israel. These techniques include typology (Rom. 5:14), allegory (Gal. 4:24; Deut. 25:4), catchword links ("reckon" in Rom. 4; cf. Gen. 15:6; Ps. 32:1–2), quoting from variant texts, altering the quoted text, reading the text in an unorthodox manner (Gal. 3:16 uses singular "offspring"), use of haggadic interpretations of texts (Moses received the law on Sinai from angels), and traditional forms of homiletic argumentation (Jesus answered the lawyer's question, "Who is my neighbor?" by citing texts from the Law and Prophets and illustrating with a story; Moyise 128–31). Some read the Gospels for clusters of Greek words that also appear in the Septuagint (Stegner); others for larger narrative patterns, such as the Elijah/Elisha cycle (Roth) or OT traditions of temple and kingship (Swartley). Arguing that NT texts were composed according to the literary conventions of the day, still others would speak of imitation of OT, intertestamental, and even classical models (McDonald), and adapting citations to speak to new situations (Stanley). In sum, while such approaches rely on historical reconstructions of the Bible's history of composition and run the risk of subjectivity in identifying precursors, they remind the contemporary interpreter that biblical writers were also interpreters of traditional texts.

Theories of Language and Literature

Second, the mockers make sarcastic use of Jesus' words about the temple, misquoting his claim that "not one stone here will be left on another" (Matt. 24:2; cf. 26:60). This verbal recycling points to the dialogical nature of speech acts, that in some sense all the words we speak are a response to a situation or even the answer to the words of another. Based on this insight, another stream of approaches starts with the nature of language itself, incorporating literary theories of intertextuality. The movement may be traced back to T. S. Eliot's insistence that no writer or artist works in isolation from the "dead poets" that have gone before, and Harold Bloom's suggestion that an "anxiety of influence" moves writers to misread those predecessors in order to create something new. Julia Kristeva used Mikhail Bakhtin's dialogical view of language to speak of a text as a "mosaic of quotations," each text the "absorption and transformation of another." Although she is credited with coining the term "intertextuality," Kristeva eventually rejected it as too narrow to describe the intersubjectivity of human discourse. She and other theorists expanded the notion of "text" to encompass all potential interrelationships—historical, cultural, and social—not only written artifacts (see Fewell 11–20; Tanner 1–47).

For many biblical interpreters who use these theories, the network of potential connections is endless, yet exegetical practice requires that some limits on investigation be set. Therefore, questions about the ideology that motivates the interpreter's choice of limits must be raised. Moreover, because the dialogical approach holds that something more can always be said, interpretation is in some way incomplete, and meaning is tentative and decentered. While the very nature of this approach may seem to undercut biblical authority, intertextual study need not presume the "loss of an authoritative Center." Divine authorship does not rule out the possibility for hearing multiple voices in biblical interpretation (Phillips 244), and interrelation with other texts need not rule out authorial intention.

As a "sympathetic critic," Richard Hays uses a form of inner-biblical exegesis to show how Paul reinterprets biblical traditions in the light of God's new work of joining Jews and Gentiles into a community centered in Jesus Christ. Building on that approach, he also uses Hollander's literary theory of poetic echo to distinguish intentional allusion from echoes that do not depend on intention. Such a distinction is difficult because we do not know the minds of the readers Paul addressed; therefore, Hays speaks of the "allusion" of obvious intertextual references, and the "echo" of subtler ones (29). Echoes of Scripture call the reader to evoke aspects of the original context of the textual echo that are not quoted, yet within the echo chamber of a new context as well. Thus, Paul interprets Hosea's "my people" in 2:25 (ET, 2:23) as directed to Gentile Christians, a sign that God indeed has fulfilled his promises to Israel by calling out a people in Christ (Rom. 9:25–26; Hays 66–68). As with studies in inner-biblical exegesis, Hays's approach points to a radical newness in relation to existing texts, a newness that continues and does not supersede the earlier work.

Rhetoric and Biblical Theology

Third, Matthew shows that the mockers also cite the same psalm that Jesus did. The scornful words of the religious leaders recall those of the mockers in Ps. 22:6–8, "He trusts in the LORD; let the LORD rescue him. Let him deliver him, since he delights in him" (v. 8; Matt. 27:41–43). Matthew does not say whether the mockers were aware or unaware that they were recalling ancient words of another. But by assembling these citations, the writer leads readers to identify the religious leaders of Jesus' day with the mockers in the psalm, an identification they would never have embraced. Believing they are on the Lord's side, their own words put them in the place of those who oppose the Lord (cf. Ps. 2). Spoken to bolster their claims of victory, the mockery ironically highlights their defeat. Moreover, Matthew sends readers back to the psalm and the whole Psalter to see that their mockery actually states the truth. Jesus is the King of Israel, he is the Son of God, and most importantly, he will be delivered—all the ends of the earth will hear and worship (Ps. 22:22–31).

In sum, by reporting the words of Jesus and his enemies, Matthew uses the earlier words of Ps. 22 to demonstrate the significance and richness of the scene, and also to show that this story of a crucified teacher is not divorced from the way Israelites understood their own story. As Childs puts it, the radically new is stated in terms of the old (93). Therefore, intertextual study also reveals Matthew's rhetorical purpose, to persuade readers that Jesus is not only a trusting Israelite whom God delivered and vindicated, but also Messiah, Son of God and King of Israel. More than a tracing of possible sources and influences, an intertextual approach illuminates the way writers use earlier texts to enrich meaning and establish authoritative testimony. It helps readers identify and understand the biblical writer's rhetorical strategies.

Finally, if the study of intertextuality offers any promise, it encourages work toward a biblical theology that relates the two Testaments without smoothing over the distinctives of either. It was the juxtaposition of the NT beside the OT that brought about a new reading of Israel's Scriptures, not a modification of the text (Childs 75–79). The older paradigms of promise-fulfillment and salvation history are enriched by the recognition that biblical writers stood in dialectical relationship with their own written tradition. Simply put, interpreters will not only look for what is old in the new; they will also see how the new sheds new light on the old. Moving beyond older evolutionary assumptions that what comes last is best, the approach can break down some of the compartmentalization into theologies of the OT and NT. One can understand the desire to maintain strict boundaries, based as they are in reaction to Christian tendencies to read the OT through "Romans-colored glasses" and leave the witness of the OT writers muted. Yet this distinction is also one of many factors behind the neglect of the OT in the teaching and preaching of the church.

In the best of recent intertextual studies, the two Testaments are seen not as discontinuous, but as part of a story with recurring themes and patterns, facilitating a "more synthetic presentation" (Martens 101). Such a presentation of the whole biblical canon can only encourage greater use of the OT in the church's teaching and proclamation, "to show how the word made flesh is in accordance with the Scriptures" (Seitz 6), and how God addresses the church in God's word to Israel (Achtemeier). Matthew's claim that the God of Israel is at work in Christ and the church is a matter that must be proclaimed and to which hearers may be persuaded, either to believe what they did not believe before or to believe it more firmly and fervently. So also, the study of biblical intertextuality can and should carry over into Christian preaching and teaching, for it is here that congregations are introduced to the "stereophonic witness" (Martens) of the Christian Scriptures.

See also Jewish Exegesis; Relationship between the Testaments

Bibliography

Achtemeier, E. "The Canon as the Voice of the Living God." Pages 119–30 in *Reclaiming the Bible for the Church*, ed. C. Braaten and R. Jenson. Eerdmans, 1995; Boyarin, D. *Intertextuality and the Reading of Midrash*. Indiana University Press, 1990; Buchanan, J. *Introduction to Intertextuality*. E. Mellen, 1994; Childs, B. *Biblical Theology of the Old and New Testaments*. Fortress, 1992; Fewell, D. "Introduction: Writing, Reading and Relating." Pages 11–20 in *Reading between Texts*, ed. D. Fewell. Westminster John Knox, 1992; Fishbane, M. *Biblical Interpretation in Ancient Israel*. Oxford University Press, 1985; idem. "Inner-Biblical Exegesis: Types and Strategies of Interpretation in Ancient Israel." Pages 3–18 in *The Garments of Torah*. Indiana University Press, 1989; Hays, R. *Echoes of Scripture in the Letters of Paul*. Yale University Press, 1989; MacDonald, D., ed. *Mimesis and Intertextuality in Antiquity and Christianity*. Trinity, 2001; Martens, E. "Reaching for a Biblical Theology of the Whole Bible." Pages 83–101 in *Reclaiming the Old Testament*, ed. G. Zerbe. CMBC, 2001; Mason, R. "Inner-Biblical Exegesis." Pages 12–14 in *A Dictionary of Biblical Interpretation*, ed. R. Coggins and J. Houlden. SCM/Trinity, 1990; Moyise, S. *The Old Testament in the New*. Continuum, 2001; O'Day, G. "Jeremiah 9:22 and 1 Corinthians 1:26–31: A Study in Intertextuality." *JBL* 109 (1990): 259–67; Perelmuter, H. *Siblings*. Paulist, 1989; Phillips, E. "Serpent Intertexts: Tantalizing Twists in the Tales." *BBR* 10 (2000): 233–45; Roth, W. *Hebrew Gospel*. Meyer-Stone, 1988; Seitz, C. *Word without End*. Eerdmans, 1998; Stanley, C. *Paul and the Language of Scripture*. SNTSMS 74. Cambridge University Press, 1992; Stegner, W. *Narrative Theology in Early Jewish Christianity*. Westminster John Knox, 1989; Swartley, W. *Israel's Scripture Traditions and the Synoptic Gospels*. Hendrickson, 1994; Tanner, B. *The Book of Psalms through the Lens of Intertextuality*. Studies in Biblical Literature 26. Peter Lang, 2001.

Paul E. Koptak

Intratextuality   *See* Narrative Theology; Yale School

Irenaeus   *See* Patristic Biblical Interpretation; Rule of Faith; Scripture, Unity of

Irony

The Bible contains two major kinds of irony, verbal and dramatic.

Verbal Irony

Verbal Irony Occurs When a Statement's Intended Meaning Differs Significantly from Its Ostensible Meaning. Wayne Booth notes that ironic statements "cannot be understood without rejecting what they seem to say" (1). Such statements, however, are not always easily recognized. A sinister irony accompanies Cain's response to God's inquiry concerning Abel's whereabouts: "Am I my brother's keeper?" (Gen. 4:9). This question is doubly ironic. Cain's intended verbal irony—likely playing upon Abel's role as a keeper of flocks—presupposes the answer "no." But Cain's words also reveal his "ironic failure to perceive his true relationship to his brother" (Good 85).

Verbal Irony Often Produces a Humorous Effect. Abraham recognizes the irony of Ephron's apparent generosity when he offers to give Abraham a burial plot free of charge; the result is that Abraham politely dismisses such pretense and pays a ridiculously high sum for Ephron's field (Gen. 23:8–15). Humorous irony is also evident amid situations as horrific as the Israelites' revelry before the golden calf. The narrator reports that Aaron fashioned the calf "with a tool" (Exod. 32:4), but when he explains the matter to Moses, he tells him that the people "gave me the gold, and I threw it into the fire, and out came this calf!" (32:24). A more self-conscious example of irony is Elijah's sarcastic taunting of the prophets of Baal (1 Kings 18:27).

In Job, Several Speakers Employ Verbal Irony, with Increasing Rhetorical Effectiveness. Irony is evident in Bildad's and Zophar's rhetorical questions regarding the justice of God and Job's inability to understand it (8:3; 11:7). Job's exasperated response displays a more aggressive, biting irony: "Doubtless you are the people, and wisdom will die with you!" (12:2). God himself, however, displays the most powerful irony. He follows a series of questions to Job—all ironic because no one but the Lord could possibly answer them—with this supremely sarcastic declaration: "Surely you know, for you were already born!" (38:21). God then continues his questions, even asking Job if he is able to domesticate and communicate with the fierce leviathan (41:1–5). The power of God's irony here lies in his "treating an obvious impossibility as a possibility" ("Humor," 410).

Verbal Irony Is Also Evident in the NT. Consider Jesus' statement to the Syrophoenician woman who begs him to deliver her demon-possessed daughter: "First let the children eat all they want, . . . for it is not right to take the children's bread and toss it to their dogs" (Mark 7:27). The woman's recognition of Jesus' irony exhibits great faith, and Jesus grants her request. John's Gospel contains plentiful examples of intentionally ironic questions by Jesus and unintentionally ironic questions by others (Duke 63–94). Paul's irony is evident when he taunts the arrogant Corinthians (1 Cor. 4:8, 10), and throughout Galatians (Nanos), which contains his hyperbolic denunciation of his circumcising opponents, whom he wishes "would go the whole way and emasculate themselves!" (5:12).

Dramatic Irony

Dramatic Irony Results from the Audience Sharing with the Author Knowledge Unavailable to One or More Characters. One example is Jacob's indignant address toward Laban after the latter unsuccessfully searches Jacob's fleeing caravan for Laban's stolen household gods (Gen. 31:36–37). Angered by Laban's accusation, Jacob considers his household vindicated when Laban finds nothing. Unknown to either character, but known to the audience, is that Rachel has indeed stolen and successfully hidden the gods (31:19, 33–35). Dramatic irony is central to Joseph's narrative, particularly his interaction with his brothers in Egypt. The audience knows what his brothers only learn later: their attempt to reduce Joseph by selling him into slavery has actually served to fulfill his boyhood dreams that they would bow before him (Gen. 37; 42:6–9).

In the Ehud narrative, the left-handed Ehud's sword, strapped to his right thigh, escapes detection by King Eglon's guards. The audience, however, is well aware of the "secret message" Ehud says he has for Eglon (Judg. 3:19). Ehud plunges the sword into the fat king's belly, and the ensuing phrase can be translated "the offal in his belly came out" (3:22). This translation emphasizes the narrative's irony, for after the escaping Ehud locks the doors of the upper room, Eglon's waiting servants—who had obeyed the king's order to leave him alone with Ehud—speculate that the doors are locked because Eglon "must be relieving himself" (3:24).

Irony also surrounds Haman's downfall in Esther. Thinking King Xerxes means to honor him, Haman unwittingly advises Xerxes to honor Mordecai—even though Haman had come to the king to persuade him to hang Mordecai on a gallows he had built (6:3–11). After being humiliated by Xerxes' honoring of Mordecai, Haman is punished for his treachery by being hung on his own gallows.

Dramatic Irony Is Prominent in the Gospels. Gilbert Bilezikian calls Mark "a drama of mistaken identity" (122). He asserts, "The dramatic irony that permeates the very structure of the Gospel finds its highest expression in the ethnarchs' resolve to destroy Jesus in order to shatter his messianic pretensions, which, when carried out, in fact accomplishes his messianic destiny." Dramatic irony in John is also prominent (Culpepper 165–80; Duke), exemplified by the narrative of the man born blind (9:1–41) and Jesus' trial (18:26–19:16; 19:19–22; Duke 117–37). Duke observes, "The man born blind . . . sees with increasing clarity; the ones who claim sight plunge into progressively thickening night" (118). In a sense, Jesus' entire ministry is fundamentally ironic, for although God's Son, he comes to serve and be sacrificed for humanity (Matt. 20:28); and he bids his followers to humble themselves so that they might be exalted (Luke 14:11; 18:14; cf. Matt. 20:27).

Authorial Intent and Theological Significance

Although characters are often oblivious to the irony in which they participate, the biblical authors consistently present their irony intentionally, thereby displaying the larger intentions of the God who sovereignly orders every narrative. Such sovereignty is equally evident in rare cases where readers suspect they see ironic happenings the human author may have been unaware of.

Bibliography

Bilezikian, G. *The Liberated Gospel.* Baker, 1977; Booth, W. *A Rhetoric of Irony.* University of Chicago Press, 1974; Culpepper, R. A. *Anatomy of the Fourth Gospel.* Fortress, 1983; Duke, P. *Irony in the Fourth Gospel.* John Knox, 1985; Gabel, J. B., C. B. Wheeler, and A. D. York. *The Bible as Literature.* 4th ed. Oxford University Press, 2000; Good, E. M. *Irony in the Old Testament.* 2d ed. Almond, 1981; "Humor." *DBI*, 407–11; Muecke, D. C. *Irony and the Ironic.* Critical Idiom 13. Methuen, 1970; Nanos, M. *The Irony of Galatians.* Fortress, 2002; Ryken, L., and T. Longman III, eds. *A Complete Literary Guide to the Bible.* Zondervan, 1993; Sternberg, M. *The Poetics of Biblical Interpretation.* Indiana University Press, 1985.

David V. Urban

Isaiah, Book of

The book of Isaiah has had a profound effect on Judaism and the Christian church. The prophet Isaiah is often viewed as the most significant of ancient Israel's prophets. Furthermore, due to its well-known messianic prophecies, Isaiah has been known as the "Fifth Gospel" since early in the Christian era (Sawyer 1). Nevertheless, for more than a century, its theological legacy has been obscured by historical-critical claims that, in addition to the eighth-century prophet, two or more major authors or prophetic circles as well as numerous editors and glossators over a period of nearly half a millennium contributed to the book. They supposedly produced a diverse and diffuse anthology with a prophetic voice that,

theologically, makes "an uncertain sound." In recent decades, however, a renewed focus on the book's unity has led to a greater appreciation of its major themes and literary motifs.

History of Interpretation

Isaiah's significance was immediately recognized, becoming the prophetic book most frequently quoted in the NT and cited in the Mishnah, as well as the most copied prophetic book among the Dead Sea Scrolls. Sirach 48:17–25 recounts the events of Hezekiah's reign, just as Isa. 36–39 does. Sirach describes the prophet Isaiah as "great and faithful in vision" (v. 22 AT) and as the one who "by the spirit of might . . . saw the last things and comforted those who mourned in Zion" (vv. 23–24 AT; likely referring to Isa. 61:2–3). The existence of the first-century CE pseudepigraphical book *The Martyrdom and Ascension of Isaiah* also attests to Isaiah's import. The Talmudic tractate *Baba Batra* (15a) claims, "Hezekiah and his colleagues wrote Isaiah."

The LXX translator(s) tended to "personalize" the text, turning third-person references into first- and second-person statements, and to create a "preached text" by turning statements into commands. Jewish nationalism was asserted, contrary to the Hebrew text's "generosity toward the nations" (Baer 278–79). The targum affirmed the messianic understanding of Isa. 9; 11; and 52:13–53:12 (as well as 10:27; 16:1, 5; 28:5; 43:10), but not of 7:14. The targum describes the Messiah not simply as an eschatological figure but as "something of an eternal figure," for there is a "tendency to move from anticipation to actuality in respect of God's action" with regard to Messiah. Israel's "saving response to God is seen as already under way" (Chilton xviii–xix).

Origen (185–254) authored the first known commentary on Isaiah, but it remained incomplete. Early full commentaries were written by Eusebius of Caesarea, Jerome, and Cyril of Alexandria. The importance of the book for the fathers was due primarily to its messianic prophecies, and their interpretation basically followed that of the NT. Patristic commentators emphasized Israel's rejection of the Messiah and consequent judgment, although a remnant would be saved, as well as God's blessing on the nations. They used Israel's legalistic blindness as a warning to Christians to beware of idolatry (McKinion xxi). According to Jerome, Isaiah "should be called an evangelist rather than a prophet, because he describes all the mysteries of Christ and the church so clearly that one would think he is composing a history of what already happened rather than prophesying what is to come" (McKinion 3). A sampling of patristic interpretation illustrates their christological and ecclesiological emphases: Isaiah 2:1–6 refers to the law being first given to the apostles and then delivered to all peoples by them (Theodoret of Cyr). The seven women of 4:1 are the seven churches (Victorinus of Petovium). The branch of 4:2–4 is Jesus (Bede). The angelic cry "holy, holy, holy" displays the Trinity (Jerome). The desolation of the land announced in 6:11 refers to that carried out by the Romans (Eusebius of Caesarea). The animal harmony described in 11:6 depicts the makeup of the church (Chrysostom). And 35:6 refers to the healing ministry of Jesus.

Nine complete commentaries remain from the medieval period. Two medieval interpreters, in particular, helped pave the way for later modernist approaches. Andrew of St. Victor gave exceptional attention to historical concerns, writing a prologue to Isaiah in which he described the prophet's life and character. Unlike his contemporaries, he interacted with both Jerome and the rabbis, citing without refutation the rabbinic interpretation of 7:14 as referring to Isaiah's son, even though affirming the messianic interpretation. In the case of 53:3, however, he accepted the Jewish interpretation that this refers to the Jews in the Babylonian captivity or to the prophet (Smalley 162–65). Another medieval interpreter, Abraham Ibn Ezra, is credited with being the first extant commentator (in 1155) to attribute the second part of the book to an anonymous prophet in Babylon on the eve of the Persian conquest. In this claim, Ibn Ezra by more than six centuries anticipated the similar conclusion of two German scholars, Döderlein and Eichhorn.

Various scholars built on the insights of late-eighteenth-century German scholars. Isaiah 40–66 was viewed as distinctive in three major respects: (1) It addresses a different audience than 1–39, exiles in Babylon anticipating an imminent return to Zion, even naming the Persian ruler Cyrus. (2) It contains different theological emphases, focusing on God as Creator of Israel and sovereign over the nations and on God's servant as the bringer of salvation, rather than on God's exaltation through judgment and through the reign of the messianic king. (3) It has a more flowing and lofty poetic style, making extensive use of repetition and rhetorical questions. This culminated in Bernhard Duhm's influential commentary of 1892, distinguishing three primary authors: one preexilic, associated with chapters 1–39; one late exilic, associated with 40–55; and one postexilic, associated with 56–66. These authors eventually became known as First Isaiah, Second Isaiah, and Third Isaiah. However, these three major sections were hardly to be viewed as unified compositions. According to Duhm, for example, chapters 13–23 were edited in the second half of the second century BCE, 24–27 were composed around 128 BCE, 34–35 stemmed from the Maccabean period, 36–39 were added from 1–2 Kings, and four "Servant Songs" that neither Second nor Third Isaiah had authored were inserted into chapters 40–55. From Duhm onward, more than half a dozen authorial and editorial hands were seen as involved in the production of the final canonical book, with only a few hundred verses being ascribed to the eighth-century prophet.

This "search for the historical Isaiah" essentially eliminated any possibility of a unified theological reading. For nearly a century, those rejecting authorial unity ceased to write on the entire book, commenting instead on critically distinguished subsections thereof. Nor did they give much attention to developing plausible explanations for how all of the diverse writings ultimately came to be included in one prophetic scroll. The focus rather was on discerning those texts that, for various reasons, could *not* have originated with the eighth-century prophet. The prophet ceased to be viewed as a divine spokesperson who received a revelation of God's plan for his covenantal people, both present and future, which he, in turn, communicated to them with passion, persuasion, and poetry with the words "thus says the LORD."

In the late 1970s a new phase of Isaianic studies began, as scholars began to investigate various unifying elements. For the most part they focused on phenomena within the text that generations of conservative scholars had pointed out in support of Isaianic authorship. These scholars variously attributed the observed unity (Schmitt 117–27) to a connecting hinge (Ackroyd), canonical relationships (Childs), thematic patterns (Clements), cultic prophetic activity (Eaton), symbolic structures (Lack), prophetic schools (Mowinckel), unitary editing (Rendtorff and Steck), or editorial insertions and stylistic imitation (Williamson). In addition, a number of "assured results" of Isaianic studies since Duhm have been questioned, including the late dating of much of 13–23, the apocalyptic label for 24–27, the Deuteronomistic origin of 36–39, the distinctiveness of the Servant Songs, and the existence of Third Isaiah (Schultz,

"How Many 'Isaiahs,'" 154). The application of newer rhetorical-literary approaches (such as those of Conrad, Gitay, Melugin, Muilenburg, Polan, and Quinn-Miscall) has also contributed to more holistic readings. Conrad focuses on "repetition in vocabulary, motif, theme, narrative sequence, and rhetorical devices" that creates cohesion (30), while Quinn-Miscall reads Isaiah "as a single work, a vision expressed in poetic language," emphasizing imagery, "the picture displayed by Isaiah" (Quinn-Miscall 169). As a result, the dominant focus has once again shifted to the unity of Isaiah rather than on its many authors and editors. However, now the emphasis is not on the one *prophet* Isaiah, as was the predominant view up until the nineteenth century, but on the one *book* Isaiah.

Hearing the Message of Isaiah

The current focus on the common themes, motifs, and verbal parallels throughout Isaiah, leading to a new focus on the unity of the book, allows one to once again hear the message that has been largely drowned out by more than a century of historical-critical debate. Such a unified reading is not dependent on one's ability to identify the particular "prophetic voice" that is speaking in a given passage (contra Goldingay 2–5); rather, one must trace the development of prophetic thought in the course of the book. One such approach is to follow a macrostructural model for understanding the message. William J. Dumbrell (107) divides the book into eight sections that alternate between *history* and *eschatology*, with the first and final sections containing both elements. W. H. Brownlee, C. A. Evans, and A. Gileadi view the book as following a symmetrical, or "bifid," structure (Evans), dividing Isa. 1–33 and 34–66 up into seven corresponding sections. David Dorsey expounds the book following an ABCDC'B'A' chiastic structure (234). Although each of these proposals reflects recurrent thematic emphases, it is difficult to distinguish clearly between history and eschatology within blocks of prophetic texts or to assume that a competent reader can discern and adequately evaluate elaborate structural patterns. *Therefore, in unfolding the message, it is preferable to proceed through the book sequentially*, synthesizing section-by-section how major themes are developed through the repetition of key words, images, and motifs, intertextual links, and narrative analogies.

Barry Webb notes four indicators of formal and thematic unity within the book ("Zion," 67–72): the title in 1:1, the emphasis on the heavens and the earth at the beginning and end of the book, the role of the Hezekiah narrative in 36–39 within the overall structure, and the focus on Zion/Jerusalem throughout. Each of these indicators will be discussed in our journey. Isaiah 1:1 claims all that follows not simply *includes* but is "the vision concerning Judah and Jerusalem that Isaiah son of Amoz saw during the reigns of Uzziah, Jotham, Ahaz and Hezekiah, kings of Judah," a prophetic ministry spanning more than half a century. The reference to a succession of Davidic kings fully roots the book in the events that unfolded in eighth-century Israel, while the use of the term "vision" (*khazon*) indicates that the prophecy results from divine revelation rather than from human insight. The visionary role of the eighth-century prophet is noted in 1:1; 2:1; and 13:1; no new prophetic figure is explicitly introduced in Isa. 40 or 56 to give legitimacy to the presence of a Second or Third Isaiah.

Chapter 1 offers an introductory indictment of Judah and Jerusalem, announcing both the ongoing beating of God's rebellious child and the future purging of the morally polluted city.

However, a second title introduces a vision not of contemporary Jerusalem but of Jerusalem's future exalted temple mount to which all nations will stream (2:1–4), indicating that the scope of Isaiah's vision extends from the prophet's day to the "last days." The prophet implores the house of Jacob to "walk in the light of the LORD" now, just as all nations will do then. Numerous parallels between the initial chapters (1:1–2:4) and the final chapters (63–66, see Tomasino) form an inclusio (bookends) around the main body: the (present or new) "heavens and earth," the future glorification of Zion, and the reference to God's people as rebels (*pasha'*, 1:2; 66:24). The central section of chapters 1–5 (within an apparent ABCB'A' structure) describes God's judgment against all "the proud and lofty" men and women, humbling them so that the LORD alone will be exalted (2:6–4:1; cf. 2:11–12, 17). The coming devastation is contrasted with the future glory of Mt. Zion (4:2–6//2:1–5), before the section ends with a second indictment against Judah and Jerusalem (5:1–30//1:2–31), this time portrayed not as a rebellious child or harlot but as an unfruitful vineyard.

In Isa. 6, against the backdrop of the end of the half-century reign of Uzziah, Isaiah encounters the LORD of Hosts as the exalted King who sends him to his estranged people, although the prophetic proclamation will result in hardening and judgment rather than repentance and salvation.

Isaiah 7–8 presents the first of three tests within the first half of the book.

King	Object of Trust	Outcome	Text
Test 1: Ahaz	Assyria	Failure	Isa. 7–11
Test 2: Unnamed	Egypt	Unclear	Isa. 28–33
Test 3: Hezekiah	God	Success	Isa. 36–39

In each test, the Davidic king is tempted to trust in foreign alliances rather than in Yahweh's covenantal election of Zion. (The second and third passages are tied to the first by numerous intertextual and thematic links, cf. 7:9 + 28:16; 8:7–8 + 28:17–29; 8:14 + 28:16; 8:15 + 28:13; also 37:1; 7:3 + 36:2; 7:4 + 37:6; 7:11, 14 + 37:30; 38:7, 22.) The prophet's trust (8:17) is in sharp contrast to Ahaz's doubt (7:11–13). In the face of the present Davidic king's failure, Isa. 9–11 announces God's future intervention in history (note the inclusio formed by 5:3 and 8:22, bracketing Isa. 6–8). This is to happen both in judging Assyria (10:24–27) and in the coming of a future Davidic ruler who will not falter (Isa. 9; 11). A hymn caps all this off, celebrating the future victory (Isa. 12, a partial reprise of the Song of the Sea in Exod. 15).

The so-called "oracles concerning the foreign nations" section (Isa. 13–23) affirms God's sovereignty over both the neighboring states (14:28–17:14) and the great powers (chs. 18–21). Accordingly, God's people are neither to fear them nor to trust them. Although these chapters frequently have been ascribed to a much later date, Hayes and Irvine offer a convincing interpretation of them against the backdrop of eighth-century political developments (17–33). In the introductory subsection, Babylon is addressed (13:1–14:23) and is already a major player in Isaiah's day (see 39:1, 5–7). Serving as "a fitting symbol of that arrogant pomp and power of the world," the fall of the king of Babylon is described in hyperbolic poetic terms, anticipating "the eventual fall of the whole world system which stands in opposition to God" (Webb, *Message*, 81). But Zion is equally prominent: the next two subsections begin by affirming Zion's security (14:32; 18:7) and conclude by describing an assault on Zion (17:12–14; 22:1–14; Jenkins 239).

Isaiah 24–27 usually is labeled as "late apocalyptic" and therefore often ignored in tracing Isaiah's message. However, most of its major motifs and emphases can be found in nonapocalyptic prophetic texts, and key apocalyptic elements are lacking in these chapters (e.g., symbolic visions, schematization of history, angelic interpreter). Furthermore, this section displays thematic continuity with Isa. 13–23 in its depiction of a world judgment expressing divine wrath against human pride and national presumption (Isa. 24). Expressions of praise are also prominent: 24:14–16a; 25:1–5, 9–12; 26:1–19. Intertextual links with earlier chapters are striking (25:4 → 4:6; 26:1 → 12:2; 26:15 → 9:3; 27:2–5 → 5:1–7). This section also develops major themes from the preceding chapters: the humbling of the proud and lofty (25:10–12; 26:5–6), rebellion (24:20), faith (26:2–4), and Zion's future (24:23; 25:6–8; 27:13). The focus is on two unidentified cities: the ruined city (*qiryat-tohu*, 24:10) that opposes God, and the strong city (*'ir 'az*, 26:1) that trusts him (cf. 24:10, 12; 25:2 [2x], 3; 26:1, 5; 27:10), thus evoking divine visitation (*paqad*: 24:21–22; 26:14, 16, 21; 27:1, 3). Isaiah 24–27 lacks datable historical allusions, portraying more generally than chapters 13–23 how the fate of the nations ultimately will be determined when God triumphs over his enemies (chs. 24–25) on behalf of his people (chs. 26–27). At the heart of this section is a banquet for all peoples on Mt. Zion, culminating in the cessation of death (25:6–8; on the latter, see also 26:19–27:1).

Isaiah 28–33 is parallel in structure to Isa. 7–11, and contains a series of woe oracles (28:1; 29:1–15; 30:1; 31:1; 33:1) in which the rulers of Judah are once again challenged to trust Yahweh (i.e., Test #2//chs. 7–8). In the course of these chapters, the specific situation becomes clearer. Rather than trusting in the assurances linked to the divine election of Zion (28:16), they are "obstinate children . . . who go down to Egypt without consulting me; who look for help to Pharaoh's protection, to Egypt's shade for refuge" (30:1–2) against "Assyria[, who] will fall by a sword that is not of man" (31:8). Just as in Isa. 7–8, the description of failed human leadership in Zion is juxtaposed with the announcement of a coming ruler who will reign in righteousness and justice (chs. 32–33//9–11; esp. 32:1 and 33:17, but also 33:22, which recalls 6:5). The quietness and trust that was lacking in Isaiah's day will then be experienced forever (cf. 30:15 and 32:17), and the dulled senses will be sharpened (29:9–10, 18; 32:3–4).

Isaiah 34–35 has been variously described as a little apocalypse (Duhm), as poems dislocated from Second Isaiah (McKenzie), as postexilic additions forming a redactional bridge between First and Second Isaiah (Steck), and as the original conclusion of First Isaiah (Clements). However, proceeding from the previously mentioned suggestion that Isaiah has a two-part structure—perhaps supported by the DSS manuscript 1QIsaᵃ, which leaves three blank lines between Isa. 1–33 and 34–66—these chapters are best viewed as introducing the great reversal within the book: the theological transition from judgment to salvation. Seitz (*Isaiah 1–39*, 242) understands Isa. 34–35 as portraying the promise of the ultimate victory of Zion along with the defeat of the representative opponent of God (Edom in ch. 34, similar to the role of Babylon within 13–23 and Moab [25:10–11] within 24–27). The following chapters, 36–38, then offer a concrete historical example of this victory, with Assyria as the foe. Within the structure of Isaiah, these chapters function analogically in announcing eschatological promise and praise: 1–11 + 12; 13–23 + 24–27; 28–33 + 34–35. Chapters 34–35 are in stark thematic contrast. In 34 the garden becomes a desert; in 35 the desert becomes a garden (see the verbal parallels: vengeance, 34:8 + 35:4; streams, 34:9 + 35:6; haunts of jackals, 34:13 + 35:7; abode [*khatsir*], 34:13 + 35:7; will not pass through/journey on it [*'abar*], 34:10 + 35:8). In its introductory function, Isa. 34 anticipates the day of divine vengeance (v. 8), which will be described more fully in the final section (59:17; 61:2; 63:4). More significantly, Isa. 35 introduces numerous images and motifs of salvation and restoration that are prominent in Isa. 40–55 (according to one calculation, nearly 90 percent of the words in the chapter recur in the latter).

Since Duhm, it has been commonplace to assume that Isa. 36–39 has been inserted into the book from 2 Kings when Second Isaiah was added to First Isaiah. However, Seitz has argued that these chapters are more at home within the Isaianic tradition (*Zion's Destiny*, 193–94), especially in its development of God's sovereign control over history (37:26), the giving of a sign to the Davidic king (37:30), and the promise of a remnant from Zion (37:32). Taken together, these chapters serve two functions: (1) They present the third historical test, which King Hezekiah passes. (2) They facilitate the historical transition from Assyrian to Babylonian domination as insolent Sennacherib's doom is both predicted and described (37:21–38) and the prophet makes the first announcement of the Babylonian conquest of Jerusalem (39:5–7). Chapters 38 and 39 are nonchronological in order, both taking place *during* the Assyrian siege of Jerusalem, which is probably the event underlying the initial description of "the Daughter of Zion,

. . . left like a shelter in a vineyard, like a hut in a field of melons, like a city under siege" (1:8). Chapter 38 describes Hezekiah's exemplary trust in God in a time of personal crisis, being rewarded with personal and national deliverance (38:5–6). Then chapter 39 describes his prideful failure in a time of personal recognition, being rebuked by the prophet who announces Jerusalem's coming destruction. These chapters form the climax toward which the entire first half of the book has been heading: the ultimate showdown between Yahweh and Assyria as Yahweh intervenes on behalf of Zion.

However, as a result of the announcement of Jerusalem's ultimate destruction, the question of Zion's future is necessarily raised. Following the transitional sections of Isa. 34–35 and 36–39, the remainder consists of three sections of nine chapters each. The first two end in a refrain-like warning: "There is no peace . . . for the wicked" (48:22; 57:21); the third ends with a graphic description of the ultimate end of the rebels (66:24). The book describes Zion's future restoration in three movements: (1) God's people will first be restored to the land through his anointed political deliverer, Cyrus (chs. 40–48). (2) Israel will be restored to God through the spiritual deliverer, the Suffering Servant (Isa. 49–57). (3) Then once again Zion will be glorified by Yahweh and the nations (Isa. 58–66).

Isaiah 40–48 begins with words of comfort to God's people. Following Sennacherib's western campaign ending in 701, the people of the northern kingdom (Israel) and many of the southern kingdom (Judah) were already in exile. (According to Sennacherib's Annals, he conquered 46 strong cities and countless small villages, leading 200,150 people into captivity.) Thus, reassuring words regarding restoration would have been in order already in Isaiah's day. Isaiah 40 offers the thematic introduction: your incomparable God returns! Paralleling Isa. 6, the prophet receives a fresh commission to announce the new thing about to happen: the coming "salvation." All but one of the major themes are addressed in Isa. 40: the powerful prophetic word, which transforms everything; the unrivaled sovereignty of the Creator God; the futility of idols and the gods they represent; the divine preparation and execution of the return (second exodus); and Jerusalem's comfort. The LORD's servant, the final theme, is developed in the following chapters. In Isa. 41, Yahweh's sovereignty is demonstrated in the calling of Cyrus (still unnamed) from the east, subduing kings before him (41:2). In Isa. 42 the true

Servant of God is introduced and is contrasted by juxtaposition with Cyrus, whose violent ways (41:2, 25) he will not follow (42:2–3). Both Cyrus and God's Servant are called in righteousness (41:2; 42:6), called by name (45:4; 49:1), grasped by the hand (45:1; 42:6), and will accomplish Yahweh's will (44:28; 53:10, both using *khepets*). This servant is also contrasted with the chosen nation, which is blind and unresponsive (42:18–20), in need of redemption (chs. 43–44; cf. 43:1, 14; 44:6, 22–24). In 44:24–45:25, Cyrus is explicitly named and his work is described: he will bring about the destruction of Babylon (chs. 46–47). However, the focus remains on Yahweh rather than on Cyrus: he is the God who has carried and will continue to carry his people—in sharp contrast to the Babylonian gods, which must be carried in carts (46:1–4, each verse using some form of *nasa'*). The anticipatory call for the exiles to "leave Babylon" can already be sounded, for "the LORD has redeemed his servant Jacob" (48:20).

In Isa. 49–57, the coming spiritual deliverance through God's Servant is announced. Three passages describing the Servant's election, opposition, and vicarious suffering and exaltation (49:1–13; 50:4–11; 52:13–53:12) alternate with three extended passages describing Zion's current condition, coming comfort, and glorious future (49:14–50:3; 51:1–52:12; ch. 54). The servant has a twofold mission: to restore Israel, being made a "covenant for the people" (the means of reestablishing their relationship with God); and to "bring my salvation to the ends of the earth" as a "light for the Gentiles" (49:6, 8–9; cf. 42:6–7). The events of Isa. 53 bring about a remarkable shift. In Isa. 54–66, the word "servant" (*'ebed*) occurs only in the plural (11 times): "The work of the individual suffering servant restores the national servant so that individuals within Israel once again can serve God" (Schultz, "Servant, Slave," 1195). The section concludes by offering the free gift of salvation to "all you who are thirsty" (55:1), while also setting forth its demands (chs. 56–57; cf. 55:6–8). However, the new exodus in its fullness will be postponed due to the "failure of Jacob-Israel to fulfil its role" (R. Watts, *New Exodus*, 58–59).

The final section of the book is framed by an indictment of the rebels among the people (*pasha'*, 58:1; 66:24)—not all of them will choose to become God's servants. However, the primary focus is on the glorification of God and Zion (*kabod*, 58:8; 59:19; 60:1–2, 13; 61:6; 62:2; 66:11–12, 18–19, a word that does not occur once in Isa. 49–57; cf. also "splendor," *pa'ar*, 60:7, 9, 13, 19, 21; 61:3,

10; 62:3). In response to God's accusations, the people confess their rebellion (59:12–13; cf. v. 20), and the Divine Warrior, in turn, zealously avenges them (59:15b–19; 63:1–6). His actions frame the description of the resultant blessings: foreigners will help to rebuild and glorify Zion (ch. 60), the mourners will be comforted and made participants in an eternal covenant (61:1–3, 8–9), and God's estranged bride will be restored (62:4–5). The climactic summary announces: "They will be called The Holy People, The Redeemed of the LORD; and you will be called Sought After, The City No Longer Deserted" (62:12). The praise and petition of the prophet (63:7–64:12) evoke the divine promise of judgment against the obstinate people and the creation of a new heaven and new earth, in which a restored Jerusalem rejoices in unmitigated material blessing and peace and an intimate relationship with God (65:17–25). People from all nations will come and see God's glory and worship him (66:18–23), but the rebels will be subjected to unending punishment (66:24).

A close analysis of Isaiah as a whole reveals a carefully edited composition. Each section has its own distinctive structure and emphases; numerous intertextual links serve to connect various sections. Repeated words and images indicate the centrality of Zion and faith, and of judgment followed by salvation. The book develops along a redemptive-historical trajectory, beginning with a portrait of Zion in Isaiah's day as it weathers several political-military crises. Then it moves ahead through the Babylonian exile and restoration under Cyrus to the renewal and glorification of Zion in the context of the new heavens and the new earth.

Isaiah and the Canon

As do most Israelite prophetic books, Isaiah draws frequently on historical traditions: creation (40:26; 42:5; 45:7, 12, 18; 57:16), the flood (24:18; 54:9), Sodom and Gomorrah (1:9–10; 3:9; 13:19), Abraham (29:22; 41:8; 51:1–2; 63:16), the exodus and wilderness rebellions (11:16; 43:14–21; 48:20–21; 51:9–10; 52:11–12; 55:12–13; 63:9–13), Joshua and the judges (1:26; specifically Gideon: 9:4 and 10:26; 28:21), David (28:21; 29:1; 37:35; 38:5; 55:3), and the post-Solomonic split into two kingdoms (7:17). More important are the covenantal foundations of Isaiah's portrayals of rupture and transformation:

1. Creation/Noahic: 24:5–6; 51:3; 54:9–10
2. Patriarchal: 10:22; 41:8–10; 48:19; 49:18–21; 54:1–3; 61:7, 9; 65:9

3. Sinai: 2:3; 4:2–6; 5:18–30; 42:24–25; 56:1–8
4. Davidic: 9:6–7; 11:1–5, 10; 16:5; 32:1; 55:3
5. New: 32:15–20; 33:24; 51:4–7; 61:8

The book's central passage, Isa. 36–39, appears in nearly identical form in 2 Kings 18:13–20:19 (although Hezekiah's written prayer following his illness is without parallel; Isa. 38:9–20). Second Chronicles 32:1–26, 31 summarizes these events much more briefly, offering an intriguing interpretation involving a divine test of "all that was in [Hezekiah's] heart" (v. 31). His heart reflected initial pride and ingratitude, which provoked divine wrath, as well as self-humbling, delaying the consequences of divine wrath (vv. 25–26). There are also similarities between 2 Kings 16:5 and Isa. 7:1. Second Chronicles 26:22 and 32:32 claim that Isaiah wrote accounts of Uzziah's and Hezekiah's reigns.

The verbal and thematic parallels between Isaiah and other prophets, such as with Micah (esp. Mic. 4:1–3//Isa. 2:2–4) or Jeremiah, have often been recognized (Schultz, *Search for Quotation*, 34–42, 290–329), indicating that Isaiah both influenced and was influenced by his prophetic colleagues.

More profound and pervasive, however, is Isaiah's influence on NT writers. According to J. Watts (111; see Sawyer 26–28), 194 NT passages contain allusions to verses from 54 of Isaiah's 66 chapters. Citations are especially frequent in Matthew, Luke/Acts, Romans, Hebrews, and Revelation, with Isa. 6:9–10; 40:3; and 56:7 being quoted three times each. If one analyzes the explicit NT quotations of Isaiah, one can identify four main categories: (1) messianic prophecies, distinguishing (a) texts fulfilled by Jesus (apologetically useful examples of fulfilled prophecy: 9:1–2; 11:10; 42:1–3, 4; 49:6; 53:1, 4, 7–8, 9; 61:1–2) and (b) texts applied (or transferred) to Jesus (54:13; 55:3; 56:7; 62:11); (2) eschatological texts (referring to salvation history and the "last things": 25:8; 27:9; 45:23; 49:8, 18; 59:20–21; 65:1–2); (3) texts applied to the Christian life or used to teach doctrine (22:13; 40:6–8, 13; 45:21; 52:7, 11, 15; 53:12; 59:7–8; 64:4; 66:1–2); and (4) texts pointing to parallels between events or Israel's conduct in the OT and in the NT (1:9; 6:9; 7:14; 8:14, 17; 10:22–23; 28:11–12, 16; 29:10, 13, 14; 40:3–4; 43:20–21; 52:5; 54:1). Going beyond individual citations, scholars have identified the foundational use of Isaiah in various biblical books. R. Watts demonstrates that a "dual perspective of salvation and judgment—both within the context of the INE [= the Isaianic new exodus]—seems to provide the fundamental literary and theological structure of Mark's Gospel," and that the "Markan Jesus apparently understood his death in terms of the Isaianic 'servant'" (*New Exodus*, 4, 384). Similarly, "the entire Isaianic New Exodus program provides the structural framework for the narrative of Acts as well as the various emphases developed with this framework" (Pao 250). According to Hays, Paul quotes Isaiah thirty-one times, since, as is especially evident in Romans, Paul "reads in Isaiah the story of God's eschatological redemption of the world" (223). After examining fifty allusions to Isaiah in Revelation, Fekkes claims that his "interpretation of Isaiah in particular was clearly one of the more important pre-visionary influences which provided the substance and inspiration for the vision experience and for its final redaction" (290). In sum, one must conclude that Isaiah has influenced the NT more than any other OT book.

Isaiah and Theology

Isaiah's potentially rich contribution to systematic and practical theology has been more piecemeal than profound for a number of reasons. For more than a century, historical-critical scholars have divided up the book among various authorial and editorial hands. They thus claim that it is impossible to find—and even inappropriate to seek—a unified theology in the book (Roberts 130–31). Typical of this approach is Hans Wildberger, whose massive German-language commentary on Isa. 1–39 concludes with (fifty pages of) summaries of the theology of both the Isaianic and the non-Isaianic portions, even excluding Isa. 40–66 from consideration. Furthermore, even when synthesizing Isaiah's theology, interpreters commonly turn instinctively to systematic categories such as Yahweh—LORD of the nations, Israel—the people of God, Christology, and eschatology.

Accordingly, theologians typically have mined Isaiah's theological riches in search of raw materials for constructing various doctrines. Two examples offer illuminating illustrations. Following early Christian interpreters, such as Origen, Tertullian, and Gregory the Great, some systematic theologians (such as Henry Thiessen) find in Isa. 14 (especially vv. 12–15) a characterization and description of the fall of Satan, which is linked to Ezek. 28 as well as Luke 10:7–19 and Rev. 12:7–9. Others reject such use of Isa. 14 as "double-meaning" exegesis. However, the former approach ignores the context of the description at the head of Isaiah's Oracles concerning Foreign

Nations (Isa. 13–23). The latter approach disregards the function of Babylon within canonical Scripture as the prototypical foe of God and his purposes in the world, perhaps accounting for its placement as the first of the oracles.

A more significant example is the use of messianic texts drawn from Isaiah to construct an OT Christology or as reading selections for the church year. On the one hand, such approaches often focus primarily on the triad Isa. 7, 9, and 11 as advent texts and on Isa. 53 as a passion text. On the other hand, historical-critical scholars often view the former and the latter as presenting distinctive or even contradictory messianic portraits stemming from different authors and eras. More commonly, historical-critical scholars view the former as too theologically advanced to come from the eighth-century prophet or as simply reflecting idealized poetic portraits of leadership that focused on Hezekiah or Josiah or some other future king of Judah. However, such approaches overlook the placement and intertextual relationship between these texts. As argued above, the Davidic-king texts within Isa. 1–39 and the servant texts within Isa. 40–66 are integral to the progression of thought in their respective contexts (the terms "king" and "servant" therein being uniquely suited as messianic designations). Isaiah 32 and 33 also should be included in christological reflections, since they also mention the future king, functioning similarly to Isa. 9 and 11. Furthermore, in portraying the servant's act of vicarious atonement, Isa. 53 must be viewed as "part of a grander and more comprehensive vision of purification" within the book (Groves 87).

Moreover, these two messianic figures legitimately can be identified (see Schultz, "The King," 157–59). Both possess the Spirit (11:2; 42:1) and are linked to the Davidic covenantal promises (9:7; 11:1; cf. 55:3, with the servant serving as a covenant for the people: 42:6; 49:8). And both are royal figures who establish justice (11:5; 42:3–4), the latter being honored by kings (49:7; 53:12). In fact, Isa. 61:1–3 may be taken as a final "servant" text, especially in light of its use in Luke 4:16–22. However, the Immanuel text of Isa. 7:14, despite its use in Matt. 1, functions within the first historical test of faith as a confession of trust in the divine presence in the midst of a national crisis, rather than as a messianic prediction. Reading this text within its canonical context requires that we see Matthew's fourfold use of "fulfillment" language in Matt. 1–2 (1:20–23 → Isa. 7:14; 2:13–15

→ Hos. 11:1; 2:16–18 → Jer. 31:15; 2:19–23 → Isa. 11:1).

In employing this term, the evangelist apparently is identifying events within the personal biography of Jesus the Messiah that echo events in Israel's corporate history and *fill* these earlier prophetic utterances *full* of meaning. It is therefore legitimate to affirm that "the gospel of earthly Jesus and risen Lord is found in Isaiah, *in nuce*. . . . In its temporal, literary, and theological organization, the Book of Isaiah is a *type of Christian Scripture*, Old and New Testaments" (Seitz, *Figured Out*, 104).

To be sure, Isaiah is neither a dogmatics textbook nor merely an anthology of ancient religious texts; rather, it is a prophetic witness to the divine word addressing the fears and hopes of God's people within the context of their historical situation. Accordingly, a theological synthesis of Isaiah will recognize the centrality of Jerusalem (48x)//Zion (46x) as God's chosen dwelling place, climaxing in its divine deliverance from Sennacherib's siege (Isa. 37:33–37; cf. 36:14–20), an event that may well have been the catalyst for the composition of the present book. Isaiah is thus clearly theocentric in focus. The Holy One of Israel (28x) is variously portrayed metaphorically as a disappointed father (1:2), a vinedresser (5:4–6; 27:3), a king (6:5; 33:22; 43:15; 44:6), a barber (7:20), a sanctuary and stumbling stone and snare (8:14), a banquet host (25:6), a warrior-hero (27:1; 28:21; 30:32; 42:13; 51:9; 59:17), a builder (28:16–17; 34:11), a shepherd (40:11), a pregnant woman (42:14), a husband (54:5), and a potter (64:8). He is Immanuel, the God who is with us (7:14; 8:8–9), standing behind every act of judgment or salvation, regardless of who his immediate agent may be.

In stark contrast to God's holiness is the people's guilt (*'awon*, 24x, as in 1:4), incurred through both idolatry and social injustice. A central sin of Israel as well as of the nations is pride (at least 17x), presenting two options—self-humbling or divine humbling (at least 15x), so that God alone will be exalted (esp. 2:11–12, 17; 5:15–16). God's sovereignty over the nations and over history is demonstrated as expressing his plan (*'etsah*, 5:19; 46:10–11). The nations play a central role in that divine plan (see Seitz, *Zion's Destiny*, 152–57), both as divine agents (10:5, 12) and as those who ultimately will worship and serve the one true God (2:1–4). Sometimes the movement is centripetal (45:5–6, 22–23) and sometimes it is centrifugal (49:6–7; 66:19–21), but throughout it is clear that God's covenantal blessings and salvation are not reserved for Israel alone. Isaiah is about mission. Through his mighty word God asserts his superiority over the gods (10:10–11; 44:9–10, 15, 17) and announces his acts of deliverance through his King, through his Servant, and through his own deeds as Divine Warrior (42:13; 51:9; 63:1–6). Thereby, he brings about the eschatological glorification of Zion on behalf of the remnant (10:20–22; 11:11, 16), so that there is a radical contrast between Zion's immediate and eschatological future (1:27; 2:3; 24:23; 46:13). In terms of the book's central images, the divinely prepared highway will lead the people back to their God (11:16; 19:23; 35:8; 40:3; 42:16; 43:19; 49:11; 57:14; 58:11; 62:10). Then their dulled and limited (spiritual and physical) senses will once again be fully operational (6:9; 29:9–10, 18; 30:10–11; 32:3–4; 33:23; 35:5–6; 42:7, 18–20; 43:8; 44:18; 59:10), and light (*'or*, 27x) will permanently dispel the darkness (*khoshek*, 13x, as in 9:2; 42:16).

These theological claims and assurances call for behavioral changes from God's people: salvation has its demands (55:6–8; chs. 56–58), and confession of sin is in order (59:9–15; 63:15–64:12). Isaiah's vivid portrayal of Israel's ungodly behavior parallels contemporary societal woes (5:8–25; 10:1–4). As modern readers, we are drawn into the "we-words" of Isaiah (Conrad 83–116; esp. 25:9; 26:1, 8, 12–13, 17–18; 33:2; 53:1–6). We, just as the leaders of ancient Judah, are challenged to place our faith and trust in God alone (*'aman*, 7:9; 28:16; 43:10; 53:1; *batakh*, 17x, esp. 26:3–4). It is God alone whom we should fear, rather than fearing people or our circumstances (7:4; 8:12–13; 10:24; 11:2–3; 12:2; 19:16; 33:6; 35:4; 37:6; 40:9; 41:10, 13–14; 43:1, 5; 44:2, 8; 50:10; 51:7, 12; 54:4, 14; 57:11; 59:19), for God is ever with us. This is the abiding message of Isaiah.

Bibliography

Baer, D. *When We All Go Home.* JSOTSup 318. Sheffield Academic Press, 2001; Chilton, B. *The Isaiah Targum.* The Aramaic Bible 11. M. Glazier, 1987; Conrad, E. *Reading Isaiah.* OBT. Fortress, 1991; Dorsey, D. *The Literary Structure of the Old Testament: A Commentary on Genesis–Malachi.* Baker, 1999; Duhm, B. *Das Buch Jesaia.* HAT. Vandenhoeck & Ruprecht, 1892; Dumbrell, W. *The Faith of Israel.* Apollos/InterVarsity, 1988; Evans, C. A. "On the Unity and Parallel Structure of Isaiah." *VT* 38 (1988): 129–47; Fekkes, J. *Isaiah and Prophetic Traditions in the Book of Revelation.* JSNTSup 93. JSOT, 1994; Goldingay, J. *Isaiah.* NIBCOT. Hendrickson, 2001; Groves, J. A. "Atonement in Isaiah 53." Pages 61–89 in *The Glory of the Atonement*, ed. C. Hill and F. James III. InterVarsity, 2004; Hays, R. "'Who Has Believed Our Message?' Paul's Reading of Isaiah." Pages 205–25 in *SBLSP: Part One.* Scholars Press, 1998; Jenkins, A. "The Development of the Isaiah Tradition in Isaiah 13–23." Pages 237–51 in *The Book of Isaiah*, ed. J. Vermeylen. Leuven University Press, 1989; McKinion, S., ed. *Isaiah 1–39.* ACCSOT 10. InterVarsity, 2004; Pao, D. *Acts and the Isaianic New Exodus.* WUNT. Mohr/Siebeck, 2000; Quinn-Miscall, P. *Reading Isaiah.* Westminster John Knox, 2001; Sawyer, J. F. S. *The Fifth Gospel.* Cambridge University Press, 1996; Schmitt, J. *Isaiah and His Interpreters.* Paulist, 1986; Schultz, R. "How Many 'Isaiahs' Were There and What Does It Matter? Prophetic Inspiration in Recent Evangelical Scholarship." Pages 150–70 in *Evangelicals and Scripture*, ed. D. Okholm et al. InterVarsity, 2004; idem. "The King in the Book of Isaiah." Pages 141–65 in *The Lord's Anointed*, ed. P. Satterthwaite et al. Baker/Paternoster, 1995; idem. *The Search for Quotation.* JSOTSup 180. Sheffield Academic Press, 1999; idem. "Servant, Slave." Pages 1183–98 in *NIDOTTE*, vol. 4. Zondervan, 1997; Seitz, C. *Figured Out.* Westminster John Knox, 2001; idem. *Isaiah 1–39.* Interpretation. Westminster John Knox, 1993; idem. *Zion's Final Destiny.* Fortress, 1991; Smalley, B. *The Study of the Bible in the Middle Ages.* University of Notre Dame Press, 1964; Tomasino, A. "Isaiah 1.1–2.4 and 63–66, and the Composition of the Isaianic Corpus." *JSOT* 57 (1993): 81–98; Watts, J. D. W. *Isaiah.* Word Biblical Themes. Word, 1989; Watts, R. "Consolation or Confrontation? Isaiah 40–55 and the Delay of the New Exodus." *TynBul* 41 (1990): 31–59; idem. *Isaiah's New Exodus and Mark.* WUNT. Mohr/Siebeck, 1994; Webb, B. *The Message of Isaiah.* InterVarsity, 1996; idem. "Zion in Transformation." Pages 65–84 in *The Bible in Three Dimensions*, ed. D. J. A. Clines. JSOT, 1990.

Richard L. Schultz

Israel

The fundamental covenant of the Bible is that Yahweh would be Israel's God and Israel would be Yahweh's people (Gen. 17; Exod. 6:2–8; Deut. 32:8–9; Isa. 44:1–2; Ezek. 20:5; Rendtorff). Three affirmations are assumed in this formula: (1) Yahweh is sovereignly active in history; (2) it is this sovereign Yahweh who establishes a relationship with humans; and (3) the relationship gives birth to a specific people who are special to Yahweh (elect Israel; cf. Novak). Fuller revelation provides definition to each: Yahweh reveals himself as Trinity; the relationship with humans is enacted in perfection through the accomplishments of Jesus Christ (life, teachings, death, resurrection, ascension, sending of Holy Spirit); the special, elect people of God is the universal church. Thus, in Christian theology "Israel" refers to the ethnic nation that becomes the spiritual body of Christ.

Israel in Biblical Context

Israel in the OT. God is the Creator; he fashions in the world (his temple) humans in his image and presents humans to the world as an expression of who he is and what he is like (Gen. 1:26–27). Those humans fall (ch. 3) and make chaos of God's good creation. In turn, God judges sinfulness by unlocking the keys of order and returning it to its original *tohu va-bohu* (the formlessness and emptiness of 1:2). He saves only Noah and his family, and from them begins afresh to turn his image-bearers into what they were intended to be. But, once again, they seek to turn other things into images (ch. 11). Hence, God, in his mysterious grace, seeks to re-create his image-bearers through Abraham, father of Isaac, who fathered Jacob, also called Israel (Gen. 12–35). "Israel," then, is technically the progeny of Jacob; at the larger level, however, "Israel" is the line of Abraham through Isaac and Jacob and Joseph.

The story of Israel is a story of survival based on gracious election, responsibility, and discipline: redemption from Egypt (Exod. 12–15); entry into the land (Joshua); leadership struggles before the Davidic dynasty (Judges; 1 Sam. 8–11). The kingdom splits under Rehoboam (2 Chron. 10–12), but God's Davidic promise continues through Judah (2 Sam. 7). Even exile at the hands of Babylon (and Persia) does not break apart the promise to Israel as the successor of Abraham and David (Isa. 40–55; Haggai; Ezra-Nehemiah).

Israel in the NT. Jesus both reenacts and fulfills Israel's history in his baptism at the Jordan (Matt. 3), temptations (4:1–11), refashioning of the torah (chs. 5–7), ten miracles (chs. 8–9), selecting twelve apostles as the new shepherds of Israel (10:1–4), and recapitulation of specific figures in Israel's history, like Son of Man (Dan. 7; Mark 2:8–12; 13:24–27; 14:61–62), Servant (cf. Isa. 52:13–53:12; Mark 1:11; 3:27; 9:9–13; 10:45; Luke 4:16–21; 7:22), and David (Matt. 19:28–30; his use of "kingdom"). Jesus thus is the representative Head as the new Israel, and he thus divides human history into the Adam (old Israel) line and the Christ (new Israel) line (Rom. 5:12–21).

The church is thus the "Israel of God" (Gal. 6:16). More importantly, the Christians' constant appropriation of language formerly used of Israel but now applied to the church shapes this idea. No better expression of this can be found than 1 Pet. 2:9–10. One thinks also of Eph. 2:11–22; Heb. 8:8–10; and Rev. 2:14. "So strong is this sense of solidarity that one must conclude that continuity between the two Testaments is grounded in the fact that both tell the story of how the same God fulfills his covenant promises to the same people" (Minear 72). The most significant early Christian revelation was that the gospel of Jesus Christ was a salvation for anyone and everyone who believes, to the Jew first but also to the Gentile (Gal. 3:6–14; Rom. 1:16; ch. 4). In effect, then, the early Christians *democratized* the atonement and *universalized* the covenant (Gal. 3:28; Rom. 12:1–2; Heb. 8–10).

The question of whether or not early Christian prophecy expected a future for ethnic/national Israel is disputed. One might take Matt. 23:37–39 as a conditional prophecy (Allison), and one might take Rom. 11:26 ("all Israel will be saved") as spiritual Israel (the church). One might take other figures of Israel in prophecy as referring either to the remnant (thus, the followers of Jesus) or as metaphorical—so concluding that the NT does not anticipate a future for ethnic/national Israel. Or, one might focus on the ethnic dimensions of Rom. 9–11 (e.g., 9:1–5, 31; 10:21; 11:1–36), take other supposed metaphorical references as more literal, and conclude that there is in fact an expectation that at the end of history God will again work with Israel as his people.

Israel in the Practice of the Theological Interpretation

Israel Demonstrates the Faithfulness of God to Abraham and David. What God has promised to Abraham and David continues throughout history and finds its embodiment in the gospel of Jesus Christ. The covenant with Abraham, expressed as Yahweh being Israel's God and Israel as Yahweh's people, remains viable, active, and powerful because of the fidelity of God to his word. But it is not just covenant that God grants to Israel: it is also *torah* that Israel bequeaths to the world (Van Groningen). God has chosen to reveal the terms of his covenant and the structure of moral expectations through Israel, his people. Israel's election provides history with an exemplary people, sometimes falling woefully short. Israel is thus God's revelation of justice, peace, and loving-kindness (Wright 68–81).

The role of Jesus Christ in reenacting Israel's history and prophecies concentrates the moment of fulfillment, not so much in the church, as in Jesus Christ himself. Thus, there is a christocentric "replacement" of Israel, rather than an "ecclesial" replacement (Motyer). (Replacement theology, the theory that the church so fulfills the promises to Israel that the promises to ethnic Israel are rendered obsolete, is much disputed by Christian theologians today [Holwerda].) Fulfillment in Jesus Christ leads to a rereading of the OT as a witness to the redemption that is found in Jesus Christ.

Israel Illustrates That God's Work Is through a People, Not Just Individuals. Modern individualism is chased from the room when one reflects on how God has chosen to work in history: his work, while clearly individual at points, is through a people. God works through Israel, and as effected by the gospel of Jesus Christ, that "social organism" explodes into a universal new "social organism," the church. Israel as people also illustrates what the apostle Paul means: "Not all descended from Israel are Israel" (Rom. 9:6, 8; 11:5). As the prophets also anticipated (Mic. 6:6–8), the true people of God are not identical with ethnic Israel. As the NT affirms, the true people of God are those who do the will of God (Matt. 7:21–28; Mark 3:31–35; Rom. 4).

Israel Embodies God's Way of Disciplining a People to Remind Them of His Covenant Expectations. Israel's (and the church's) history, if it tells us anything, speaks not of triumphalism but of the ups and downs of covenant obedience and disobedience, and how God responds to his people in discipline for disobedience. If Israel and the church find themselves powerless, they need either to stand faithfully against the inevitable war of the Seed of Eve with the serpent or to confess that their sin has led to God's discipline. The primary examples of God's discipline remain the Egyptian sojourn, the Assyrian and Babylonian captivities, and the Roman destruction of Jerusalem in 66–73 CE.

Israel Demonstrates the Sovereign Act of God in His Election of a People. Israel did not "deserve" God's election of the people, and neither is the church a body that "deserves" God's grace. Instead, in his mystery God chose to make his redemptive purposes for the entire world known through a wandering man from Ur of the Chaldees (Abraham), through a small group of people in the highlands of the land of Israel, through an oppressed minority in the land of Egypt, through a wandering people in the desert who come to terms with the land of Israel, through an exiled and beaten community, and through a small group of followers of Jesus who become a worldwide church. This choice cannot be explained; it can only be declared that God in his grace has spoken his word through these peoples. Thus, revelation and election, as the Jewish author David Novak has made clear, must be connected.

Choosing Israel Is a Revelation of God as Incarnate. God's form of revelation is not philosophy but a covenant relationship with a people. In other words, choosing Israel anticipates the embodiment of God in human history not only through a people but also in an individual, Jesus Christ. God's revelation thus becomes fundamentally personal and interpersonal, taking part in human realities. This cuts into the mystical flight from earth, as well as the neglect of planet earth and human history in anticipation of "heaven." Even more so, it blasts the arrogance of modern pluralism and cultural postmodernism, where truth is called into question by appeal to variant cultural manifestations. Israel calls moderns to concrete, universal revelation through a people (Israel, church) and in one person (Jesus Christ).

See also Anti-Semitism; Church, Doctrine of the; Covenant; Jewish-Christian Dialogue; Kingdom of God

Bibliography

Allison, D., Jr. *The Jesus Tradition in Q.* Trinity, 1997; Holwerda, D. *Jesus and Israel.* Eerdmans, 1995; Minear, P. *Images of the Church in the New Testament.* Westminster, 1960; Motyer, S. "Israel (Nation)." Pages 581–87 in *New Dictionary of Biblical Theology,* ed. B. Rosner et al. InterVarsity, 2000; Novak, D. *The Election of Israel.* Cambridge University Press, 1995; Rendtorff, R. *The Covenant Formula.* T&T Clark, 1998; Van Groningen, G. "Israel." Pages 379–85 in *Evangelical Dictionary of Biblical Theology,* ed. W. Elwell. Baker, 1996; Wright, G. E. *The Challenge of Israel's Faith.* University of Chicago, 1944.

Scot McKnight

J

James, Book of

James, disparaged by Luther and broken into context-less pieces by Dibelius, has struggled for its theological voice to be heard by the church. Today, as theology is being turned on its head into action items for faithful Christians, James's "wisdom" comes across as theologically cutting edge for people who desire a dynamic relationship with God.

History of Interpretation

The clearest early use of James comes from the Eastern church, specifically from Origen, in the third century, who cites it thirty-six times. Employment of similar language, such as "double-minded" (a term unique to James in the NT), suggests possible knowledge of James in early Western writings, such as *1 Clement*, Shepherd of Hermas, the *Didache*, and the *Letter of Barnabas*. Eusebius reports that Clement of Alexandria, Origen's predecessor, wrote an entire commentary on James, though Clement never cites James in other extant writings.

Despite its early favor in the Alexandrian school, James was not allegorized. More common was quoting statements from James, without regard for their contexts, in support of various teachings. Cyril of Alexandria, who cites James 124 times, for example, isolates James 3:2 ("We all stumble in many ways") from its context about teachers, as support for general human frailty. He also, among many others, promoted 1:17 ("Every good and perfect gift is from above") as a proof for the divinity of Christ.

Chief interest in James—both in the West and in the East throughout the early centuries of teaching and preaching, beginning as early as fourth-century Hilary of Poitier but including Augustine—focused most heavily on the latter half of 1:17 ("who does not change like shifting shadows") as crucial biblical support for God's immutability. Another focal interest was James's intersection with the cosmic struggle of God and the devil in temptation of the believer. Augustine

wrote an unrecovered commentary on James, and his respect for James, shown in his sermons, helped vault it from obscurity in the West. He was interested in the moral teaching of James, especially with regard to speech.

The Venerable Bede, eighth-century author of the best, most influential early commentary on James, carefully explicates 1:13 by explaining that God does test people with "external" temptations, but only the devil tempts with "internal" temptations, which attack the soul. This also helps explain Jesus' temptation, which troubled the early church in light of this verse. Bede, more like commentaries centuries later, combines exacting exegesis with insightful theology and application.

Eleventh-century Theophylact, who is almost certainly dependent on Didymus the Blind and Oecumenius, curiously identifies the "righteous man" of 5:6 (KJV) not only with Christ but as a prophecy of the author's (understood as James, Jesus' brother) own political execution.

Attention did not focus on faith and works in 2:14–26, though the contrast with Paul is recognized. A seventh-century monk, Andreas, is typical in explaining that "faith" in Paul is prebaptismal, whereas "faith" in James is postbaptismal. Augustine proclaims that James explains how Paul should be understood, that good works are to result from justifying faith. Origen and Cyril of Alexandria both similarly bring James into their commentaries on Romans.

In the Reformation era, Luther disdained James's teaching on faith, lack of any teaching about Christ, exaltation of the law (his understanding of "law of liberty" in 1:25 KJV), and lack of logical order. This led him to the dogmatic conclusion that it was not written by an apostle but by a second-generation believer, probably Jewish, who carelessly wrote down some apostolic teaching he had heard but packaged this with his own nonapostolic, even anti-Christian ideas. Even in the early church, the authorship of James was a question mark on its authority, and Eusebius recognized it as a "disputed" book. Origen's connecting it to James, the Lord's brother, had settled the question for most. Though concern over James's authorship troubled others of Luther's era, like Erasmus and even Luther's disputant, Cardinal Thomas de Vio (Cajetan), Luther's radical solution was unique.

None of the other Reformers, such as Tyndale, Zwingli, Calvin, or even Philipp Melanchthon, were influenced to adopt this extreme position, which strikes many as a much-too-convenient way for Luther to subordinate James's theology of faith to salvation by faith alone. The fact that 2:26 was used against Luther in his Leipzig Debate and that 5:14 was the Roman Catholic proof text for the sacrament of extreme unction may be historical factors that prejudiced Luther against James.

In his commentary, Calvin explicitly rejects Luther's unwise precedent, cautioning against imposing uniformity and upholding the value of diversity in the canon. Calvin underscores this by asserting that Paul and James apply faith to different, legitimate facets of justification, Paul to acceptance by God, James to a reality that requires evidence. In fact, a person can even be said to be justified by works in that works are a necessary evidence of saving faith. Calvin makes no mention of divine immutability in 1:17 and Christ in 5:6 and rejects extreme unction in 5:14 on the basis that the gift of healing was a temporary apostolic gift.

Despite the fact that Luther's canonical subordination of James and conjectures about authorship were but a ripple that seemed to disperse quietly in his day, they erupted again like a geyser in the era of critical scholarship and continue to moisten the air of James scholarship. Efforts to resolve the issue of authorship and the related issue of James's relationship to early Christianity occupied nearly all scholarly resources from the mid-1800s to the late twentieth century.

The quest to find historical solutions began with Herder, who postulated that Paul and James had a personal relationship, understanding each other's view of justification and faith. Historical criticism proper began with Kern and De Wette, who, interacting with each other's publications, propelled the notions that Paul and James are totally incompatible on justification (Luther redivivus). They counted James as the pseudonymous voice of a radical, Ebionite, Jewish Christianity of the second century, which opposed domineering Gentile Christianity, and as devoid of any coherence or valuable theological perspective.

This low opinion of James was magnified by those connected to the Tübingen School and reached its pinnacle at the end of the nineteenth century. Then Massebieau and Spitta independently proclaimed James to be a Jewish document, covered with a veneer of Christianity by the introduction of Jesus Christ to 1:1 and 2:1. At the same time, in contrast, Mayor, and also G. Kittel, believed historical-critical methodology implicated James, written by Jesus' brother, legitimately to represent earliest Christianity, pre-apostolic council (49 CE), still heavily flavored with Jewish thought. They even raised evidence to suggest that Paul responds to James on faith and not vice versa.

As the twentieth century began, two scholars focused on the literary aspects of James but with strikingly different conclusions. Ropes, postulating a pseudonymous Palestinian author writing post-70 CE, recognized James's indebtedness to Jewish and Christian thought, and also Jewish Wisdom literature, but nevertheless advocated that the controlling influence is the fourth-century BCE Greek moral form of address, "diatribe." Ropes also recognized James's intelligent use of Greek to create catchwords, particularly in chapter 1. Unlike Ropes, who believed the somewhat-isolated units show progress in thought, Dibelius, operating from a form-critical perspective, put feet on Luther's earlier criticism. He determined that the organization of the pieces in James is totally ad hoc and superficial, that the book is the best NT representative of paraenetic literature throughout, and that each unit must be interpreted independently from its context because no authorial intention holds the book together. All of this leads to his conclusion that James has no theology of its own, only thoughts ripped from other contexts and meaninglessly pieced together.

Nearly all twentieth-century study has attempted to breathe life into James after Dibelius's near deathblow to it. Adamson specifically focuses his commentary on demonstrating the coherence and relevance of James to Christian life. Laws boldly unveils integrity of human character, akin to God's own singleness, as the underlying theological conviction of the book. Davids advanced the study of Francis, and Martin built on the work of Davids, taking the epistolary character of James to its penultimate and contending for an intricate cycle of patterning within. Cargal and Johnson find cohesiveness through rhetorical criticism. Moo suggests that

James be approached as a sermon and defended as a theological document.

The Overall Message

Dibelius's charge of incoherence has quite rightly been set aside as exaggerating the scissors-and-paste construction of James and drawing unfounded conclusions regarding the paraenetic genre. Even if James results from the work of an editor or even a collector, its purpose and intent are communicated at least by the arrangement of the material.

Despite the lack of a direct statement of purpose or a clear statement of its intended audience, James does base its teaching on the author's intimate and authoritative knowledge of a specific community to whom he writes. Yet, exactly how wide or narrow the community is cannot be determined very far. They are Hellenistic Jewish Christians, but as to where in the early Christian Mediterranean world, only conjectures may be offered.

What is clear is that James fits more into a wisdom genre than into the polemics of philosophy or theology. James leads with behavior and relationship to God, for which theological values form an oft-assumed base. James is concerned that his readers live well and more successfully than they currently are. This is the typical concern of Wisdom literature, like Proverbs, or Job, or Sirach.

The general problem the author of James perceives for his readers is that their spiritual development is being hindered by various forces: their own economic and social condition, lack of conviction, poor choices, overconfidence in the security of their position with God, injustices inflicted on them, and the influence of the world around them. The solution is to repent, to turn back from their spiritual wasteland of wandering before it is too late and Christ comes in judgment. The author's overall goal is for his readers to become one in person, in community, and in relationship with God. The proof of this new and continuing orientation is in their behavior with respect to God and others, in and outside the church. The means for this is for them to hear God immediately through the epistle itself, and daily through prayer, worship, and the church.

James's focus on hearing God comes from recognizing the significance of the proverb of 1:19, "Let everyone be quick to hear, slow to speak, and slow to anger" (NRSV), in relationship to the entire epistle. It is commonly recognized that the three parts of this proverb are unpacked in the paragraph that follows: "slow to anger" (1:20–21), "quick to hear" (1:22–25), and "slow to speak" (1:26–27). What is not so often observed is that these three parts of the proverb, broadly conceived, are also developed in the ensuing chapters: correctly hearing the word (ch. 2), the difficulty of controlling the tongue (ch. 3), and the damaging effect of angry speech (ch. 4). The positive effect of hearing God reverberates through every negative issue the author takes up, right through to enabling a wandering believer to hear and respond to the truth of God in 5:19.

Contribution to the Canon

Despite its current location at the back of the NT canon among the "non-Pauline" collection of epistles, reflecting the Western (Roman) ordering, in the Eastern order (also reflecting Athanasius's order in his Festal Letter of 367), James heads the General Epistles, which follow immediately after Acts, before the Pauline Epistles.

How might reading James this far up in the NT canon affect our interpretation of it? First, it would be more obvious that James is a trustworthy representative of Jesus' teaching, particularly the Sermon on the Mount, as also found in the Gospels. Second, it would be more apparent that James showcases concerns of the church in its earlier, pre-Gentile days as seen in the earlier chapters of Acts. Third, it might make it easier to see that Paul, not James, is the innovator in the early church and the one whose teaching requires careful scrutiny and patient explaining.

Deppe documents that while as many as 184 sayings in James have been purported to be allusions from the Synoptic Gospels, those that are most assuredly legitimate (though many others are probable allusions) narrow to eight: James 1:5 and 4:2c–3 (Matt. 7:7; Luke 11:9); 2:5 (Luke 6:20b; Matt. 5:3); 5:2–3a (Matt. 6:19–20; Luke 12:33b); 4:9 (Luke 6:21, 25b); 5:1 (Luke 6:24); 5:12 (Matt. 5:33–37); 4:10 (Matt. 23:12; Luke 14:11; 18:14b). While James never quotes Jesus or one of the Gospels, it showcases how many early Christian teachers may have freely incorporated the very language of Jesus' teaching as they understood it. This allows that teaching to be applied to new situations, as when showing favoritism to the powerful and neglect to the marginal becomes a violation of neighbor love (2:1–4).

James provides a peek into the early church. Whether or not its date is pre-Gentile, its orientation is Gentile-less, with no mention of circumcision or issues of how Jewish law applies to those beyond Jews. It speaks of the assembly of believers as a "synagogue" (2:2 Greek), implying that the church began organizing itself on this Jewish model. It suggests that nonbelievers at times frequented these synagogues (2:2–4). It shows that elders, apparently at least two, provided spiritual leadership, that they visited the sick and sought their spiritual and physical healing through prayer. It also shows that people in the church had spiritual obligations to care for one another through times of nagging sinfulness and even apostasy (5:13–20). Recognition that James draws upon three of the same OT passages as 1 Peter but for different purposes (Isa. 40:6–8// James 1:10–11//1 Pet. 1:24; Prov. 10:12//James 5:20//1 Pet. 4:8; Prov. 3:34//James 4:6//1 Pet. 5:5) suggests that early Christian teachers worked freely from common resources.

With Paul, James shared a desire that people be justified before God through Christ. Yet, James was not concerned about those entering justified status so much as those exiting by default or intention. James would probably have agreed with Paul's adamant position that keeping Jewish traditional laws and rituals has nothing to do with justification in Christ. Nevertheless, he was probably intentionally cautionary about how Paul's teaching on this subject could be easily misused.

However the canon is organized, James stands as an important balance to Paul's presentation of justification, and a needed caution. James has value as the only NT epistle that marshals a theological defense of the poor, a sustained concern about speech-ethics, and reflection on numerous and various aspects of prayer. This makes its canonical weight proportionally much heavier than its slim size.

Theological Significance

James's thoughts about God are typical of anyone raised in a Jewish home in the early first century, and the author assumes his readers share these convictions with him. They rest comfortably beneath the surface of his main points. When 1:17 says that God supplies the good things in people's lives, the author shows his trust that God knows what is good for us and who we are personally, and that he is powerful enough to harness the forces of the universe to our well-being. When 4:3 says that people do not receive everything they pray for because of sinister desires, the author reveals his belief that God knows our motives, good and bad—that we cannot hide anything from him.

Many other ideas about God can be discerned. He is the Creator (1:17–18), making people in his own image (3:9), and his word is powerful enough to give people rebirth (1:18). His character is constant in that he never cavorts with evil (1:13, 17), always keeps his promises (1:12), and has a watchful, discerning eye on the poor and how the powerful treat them (1:9–11; 2:1–7; 5:1–6).

No doubt, James is far more God- than Christ-centered, though what is said about Christ has to count as a quite high Christology. Jesus shares the titles "Lord" (1:1; 2:1; 5:7–8, 14–15) and Judge (5:9) with God; his very name, like God's, is powerful enough to heal (5:14) and significant enough to be blasphemed/slandered (2:8); to him is possibly attributed the Shekinah glory of God (2:1). Christ's return to judge on God's behalf is also pending (5:7–9).

James emphasizes that the fundamental point of human life is to find God, respond to his voice, and relate to him successfully and robustly, now and eternally. As essential as Christ is in this enterprise, James reminds us of something Christianity understandably quite easily forgets, that Christ is the means, perhaps the agent, but not the end of our quest. Our goal is God and a successful relationship with him. To focus solely on Christ in worship is to miss Christ's own purpose of bringing us to God. In this way, James should be prized and heard in the church. Though written to believers, James speaks to Christians first as people, and second as those who believe in Jesus. Thus, it can speak to people beyond the church. James functions as a guide to everyone in their most basic need, to be integrated with others, God, and themselves. James tells us that we can each, like Abraham, be God's friend, and he ours. No message is more needed for the world or for the church than this.

Bibliography

Adamson, J. *The Epistle of James*. NICNT. Eerdmans, 1954; Baker, W. "Christology in the Epistle of James." *EvQ* 74 (2002): 47–57; idem. *Personal Speech-Ethics in the Epistle of James*. WUNT 2.68. Mohr, 1995; Bauckham, R. *James*. New Testament Readings. Routledge, 1999; Bray, G., ed. *James, 1–2 Peter, 1–3 John, Jude*. ACCSNT 11. InterVarsity, 2000; Calvin, J. *Commentaries on the Catholic Epistles*. 1551, trans. J. Owen. Eerdmans, 1948; Cargal, T. *Restoring the Diaspora*. SBLDS 144. Scholars Press, 1993; Chester, A., and R. P. Martin. *The Theology of the Letters of James, Peter, and Jude*. Cambridge University Press, 1994; Davids, P. *Commentary on James*. NIGTC. Eerdmans, 1982; Deppe, D. *The Sayings of Jesus in the Epistle of James*. Bookcrafters, 1989; De Wette, W. M. L. *Historical-Critical Introduction to the Canonical Books of the New Testament*, trans. F. Frothingham. Crosby & Nichols,

1858; Dibelius, M. *James*. Revised by H. Greeven. Hermeneia. Fortress, 1976; Francis, F. "The Form and Function of the Opening and Closing Paragraphs of James and I John." *ZNW* 61 (1970): 110–26; Herder, J. G. *Briefe zweener Brüder Jesu im unserm Kanon*. Meyer, 1775. Herders sämmtliche Werke 7, ed. B. Suphan. Weidmann, 1884; Johnson, L. T. *The Letter of James*. AB. Doubleday, 1995; Kern, F. H. *Der Brief Jakobi untersucht und erklärt*. Fues, 1838; idem. "Der Charakter und Ursprung des Briefes Jacobi." *TZTh* 8 (1835): 3–132; Kittel, G. "Der geschichtliche Ort des Jakobusbriefes." *ZNW* 41 (1942): 54–112; Luther, M. *Luther's Works*, vols. 35–36, 54. Fortress, 1959; Martin, R. P. *James*. WBC. Word, 1988; Massebieu, L. "L'épître de Jacques: est-elle l'oeuvre d'un chrétien?" *RHR* (1895): 249–83; Mayor, J. *The Epistle of St. James*. 1913. Zondervan, 1954; Moo, D. *The Letter of James*. Pillar. Eerdmans, 2000; Ropes, J. *The Epistle of St. James*. ICC. T&T Clark, 1916; Spitta, F. *Zur Geschichte und Literatur des Urchristentums*. Vol. 2, *Der Brief des Jakobus*. Vandenhoeck & Ruprecht, 1896; Wall, R. *The Community of the Wise*. New Testament in Context. Trinity, 1997.

William R. Baker

JEDP   *See* History of Israel; Source Criticism

Jeremiah, Book of

Jeremiah, one of the longest OT books, has given us the most memorable portrayal of a biblical prophet, and is also the source of the idea of the "new covenant."

History of Interpretation

Interpretation of Jeremiah has often focused on the prophet himself. The first great phase of modern study of the book, initiated by B. Duhm, distinguished between its prose and poetry. In isolating the poetry, Duhm was searching for the authentic words of the prophet, and therefore for the true prophetic experience. In this sense, his critical questions were inseparable from a religious interest. Duhm's work gave rise to further studies that pursued strictly historical questions, such as S. Mowinckel's classic division of the book's material into three strands, A (poetic oracles), B (prose sermons), and C (prose narratives about Jeremiah); others manifested religious interest. A supreme example is J. Skinner's treatment, in which the prophet is regarded as a model of prayer and of the individual's experience of God.

As a fruit of this phase in the critical study of the book, Jeremiah became the initiator and parade example of religious individualism, by contrast with the older type of religion in Israel, which was characterized as corporate and ritualistic. Jeremiah's qualification as an example of

personal piety lay particularly in his prayers. A group of these prayers came to be known (inappropriately) as his "confessions" (viz., 11:18–23; 12:1–6; 15:10–14, 15–21; 17:14–18; 18:18–23; 20:7–12, 14–18). These prayers keenly express his pain and protest that arise directly from his call to be a prophet. Their honesty and boldness seemed new and important to the older critical scholars.

In this phase of interpretation, the new covenant (31:31–34) was regarded as a high point in individualistic religion, because of the idea of a transition from written code to knowledge of God that was "written on the heart."

A second important phase in modern interpretation focused, not on the prophet himself, but on the meaning of the book in its final redaction. J. P. Hyatt inaugurated the tendency to see the book as "Deuteronomistic" (or "Deuteronomic"). One theological advantage of this development was that it reinstated the prose sections of the book, which had been devalued in the first phase (and which often still suffer from that legacy). The Deuteronomistic interpretation allowed the accent to fall on the experience of the community in exile, and the capacity for prophecy to be reappropriated in new circumstances. The Deuteronomistic interpretation branched into a variety of models. E. W. Nicholson, for example, saw the prose sermons as the preaching of Jeremiah's message in exile, with developments and innovations. R. P. Carroll and W. McKane think, in contrast, that the book grew rather haphazardly over a protracted period.

In this phase the central theological issue was how the promises of Yahweh might be valid in the wake of the exile, which seemed to have changed everything. The new covenant could now be seen as the key to a new way of thinking about God's activity in Israel. For example, J. Unterman perceived a theological shift from a theology of repentance (in which Israel could avoid judgment by repenting) to one of "redemption," in which Yahweh took a quite new initiative in Israel's salvation, by *enabling* the people to be faithful (32:39–40). (How far the new covenant was really "new," however, was a matter of debate; Carroll.)

A final phase may be identified as that in which the book is regarded as a literary text. An example is T. Polk, for whom the "persona" of the prophet is a figment of the religious community's imagination, and who embodies aspects of their experience. One focus in this context is the parallel between the depicted life of the prophet and the life of Israel. Jeremiah's restoration after suffering becomes an earnest of the community's own restoration (cf. 15:19; 31:18).

In a modern reading of Jeremiah with theological questions, historical, literary, and canonical factors all play a part. In seeking to apply the message to church and individuals, we need to be aware first of its challenge to a Jewish people exiled in Babylon. We should, second, attend to its shape as a whole. In this way its "gospel," in the shape of new covenant and restoration, can be heard along with Jeremiah's analysis of the ills that brought judgment in the first place. The new covenant itself can be heard, not only as foreshadowing salvation in Christ, but also as a challenge to understand the radical nature of covenantal commitment, and of "worship in spirit and in truth." Finally, the ministry of Jeremiah is a model of courage, faithfulness, and true leadership, without becoming a pretext for an unbiblical "individualism."

The Message of Jeremiah

The message of Jeremiah can be traced initially by an account of the book's progression. Following the prophet's call (1:1–19) is a series of poetic oracles of judgment, together with exhortations to repent (2:1–6:30). The people's falseness in worship and faith is characterized, along with Jeremiah's grief over this (7:1–20:18). The failure of Judah's kings is lamented, and we are given initial visions of a wholly new order, including a messianic promise and judgment on Babylon (21:1–25:38). The stubbornness of the people is a major theme in 26:1–36:32, but at the heart of this section, paradoxically, is the Book of Consolation (BC; 30:1–33:26), which in turn is constructed around the new covenant. The fall of Judah and subsequent events are narrated (37:1–45:5). The last main section consists of Oracles against the Nations (OAN) and a further account of the fall of Judah (46:1–52:34).

Such an account is inevitably overly schematic. For example, the division offered above is that of the MT, while the LXX differs, being much shorter, but also having the OAN in the middle of the book rather than at the end. These two redactional types of Jeremiah have adopted different strategies to highlight the OAN, which play an important part in demonstrating a reversal of fortunes by God's grace. The account given is overly schematic in another way, for in drawing attention to the centrality (literally and theologically) of the new covenant, it passes over the fact that from an early stage salvation-notes

are interspersed among passages of judgment (e.g., 3:14–18).

However, this overview does highlight key movements and themes. The first half of the book, up to chapter 25, gives an analysis of the problem with Judah in God's eyes. They have abandoned him for other gods (ch. 2), mistaken a trust in institutions for true religion (7:1–15), and become deeply corrupt as a society, so that no truth or trust is known or practiced (8:22–9:9). For this, God will act against them. His action can be seen as a dismantling of the elements of the covenant: temple, Davidic king, historic land (Stulman). Up to this point the organization of the book shows how such hope as Jeremiah might have originally had for a renewal in Judah closed down as the stubbornness of the people became evident (McConville). Such closure is symbolized by the prohibition placed on Jeremiah's intercessory prayer (7:16; 11:14; cf. 15:1).

In tandem with this systematic undermining of Judah's false trust is a strong theme of God's own empathy with the people, manifested through the portrayal of the prophet. Jeremiah stands on both sides of the issue, feeling the grief of the people that will surely come with the judgment (4:19–22), and also the anger of God because of their perversity (11:11–20). The unity of Jeremiah and God in grief and alienation from sinful Judah is clearly expressed in 8:22–9:3, which grounds Jeremiah's reputation as "the weeping prophet," yet where the true grievance turns out to be God's. On the other hand, the symbolic and representative character of Jeremiah's life is illustrated, for example, by the embargo on marriage placed upon him, as a witness to the tragic brevity of the life now held out to the people (16:2–4).

The emotional burden of this dual role on Jeremiah is extreme and leads to a lament in which he curses his birth (20:14–18). The death he thus seeks corresponds to the "death" that Judah itself must endure; and the continuation of prophet and message into the second half of the book is a token of life beyond that death for the people (Clines and Gunn).

The book is constructed so as to affirm that God's judgment is not the final word. The perspective of salvation beyond judgment occurs sporadically in the first half (3:14–18; 16:14–15), but it is stronger in the second half. Important turning points are the Davidic messianic promise (23:5–6), following hard on the condemnation of the historic kings (ch. 22), God's first promise that he will enable faith among the returned exiles (24:7), and the seventy-year term put on the exile, after which Babylon will be judged in turn (25:12–14). From chapter 24, the challenge to faith becomes the acceptance that God will first act in judgment. The insistence on this, which informs Jeremiah's confrontation with the false prophet Hananiah, for example (ch. 28), is also an insistence that God in the end will vindicate himself and his faithful people, as exemplified by Jeremiah.

A key phrase that expresses God's intention to save after judging is "I will restore your fortunes" (NRSV; "I will . . . bring you back from captivity," NIV), which comes first in 29:14, then seven times in Jer. 30–33 (BC). The core of this idea is God's "turning" (*shub*). Indeed, there is extensive play on this word in Jeremiah, since it can mean repenting and returning (on Israel's part) and a turning (of fortunes) brought about by God. In Jer. 30–33 the dramatic turn from judgment to salvation is vividly depicted. One device is the non sequitur, exemplified in 30:12–17 (picture of sin and judgment, vv. 12–15, followed "illogically" by a declaration of salvation, vv. 16–17). Another is the story of Jeremiah's purchase of a field in the midst of siege (ch. 32), an apparently nonsensical act that signifies a future for Judah against all likelihood.

God's turning Judah's fortunes is depicted as a new miraculous act. Jeremiah declares to God, "Nothing is too hard for you!" (32:17, cf. v. 27), and his intention to save hard-hearted Judah after the Babylonian devastation is put on a par with his primary acts in both creation and deliverance of Israel from Egypt (32:17, 21–22).

In the middle of the Book of Consolation is the famous promise of the new covenant (31:31–34). This covenant has several elements: It will be made "with the house of Israel and with the house of Judah." It will be unlike the former covenant, in that its requirements (the *torah*) will be written "on their hearts." They consequently will need no teacher. And God will forgive their past sins. The agency of God himself in bringing about the renewed faithfulness of the people is prominent in this, and is repeated later in the BC (32:39–40). This becomes an important explanation of how there can be a future for Judah in covenant with God, given that they have so persistently flouted it in the past. The continuity with historic, geographical Judah should also be noted, since the new covenant promise is followed almost immediately by an assurance that the devastated city of Jerusalem will be rebuilt (31:38–40).

After this theological high point, the narrative returns to the account of the fall of Jerusalem and Judah, together with its causes. This account is not strictly chronological, since it embraces both Zedekiah, the last king (597–587 BCE; chs. 34, 37–39), and the earlier king Jehoiakim (609–598 BCE, chs. 35–36). Right to the end, Jeremiah continues to declare God's purpose to punish Judah by means of Babylon, and he is beaten and imprisoned for what is perceived as treason (37:13–16). Following the fall of the city, Jeremiah himself is spared the exile by the Babylonian authorities, but then is taken to Egypt by a party that sought its salvation in that quarter, despite Jeremiah's consistent warnings against this (24:8–10; 42:18–22). Even so, the word of God still comes through Jeremiah to the people in Egypt, implying the possibility of grace even after this new act of disobedience (ch. 43).

In the last main section of the book are the OAN (chs. 46–51). These confirm the commission at Jeremiah's call that he would be a "prophet to the nations" (1:5). Unexpected is the application of the formula "Afterward, I will restore [their] fortunes" (48:47; 49:6, 39) to Moab, Ammon, and Elam. This shows how far the theology of the Book of Consolation affects the structure of the whole book of Jeremiah. The oracles also confirm, however, God's intention to save Judah in the end. The demise of Babylon, accordingly, occupies most space here (chs. 50–51). In saving Judah, God is called their "Redeemer" (50:34).

Jeremiah and the Canon

The canonical importance of Jeremiah is evident not only from its length and its prominent position, but also from its influence on later books. Chronicles, Ezra, and Daniel cite Jeremiah's "seventy years" in their respective assimilations of the idea of a purposeful "exile" followed by salvation (2 Chron. 36:21; Ezra 1:1; Dan. 9:2). The Daniel text in particular shows how the principle established by Jeremiah goes well beyond the immediate historical circumstances for which it was conceived.

Jeremiah also develops themes already present in Hosea: God's faithfulness, the covenant people's unfaithfulness, the prophet's deep involvement in his message, signifying God's personal engagement with his people, and salvation after judgment (note Hos. 14). These then may be seen to have a broad grounding in the prophetic message. In fact, the judgment-salvation pattern, so clearly exemplified in Jeremiah, is embedded deeply in the whole prophetic corpus. While only Jeremiah gives the name of "new covenant" to the decision of God to save out of and in spite of sin, the theme is present in other prophetic books. Ezekiel, for example, also knows of the divine agency in replacing "the heart of stone" with "a heart of flesh" (Ezek. 11:19). (W. Dumbrell has shown how "new covenant," properly understood, is a feature of the prophets in general.) Moreover, Jeremiah's embodiment of the suffering of God is an important OT witness to the incarnation, and it has affinities with the Suffering Servant of the book of Isaiah. The primacy of God in the achievement of Israel's ultimate salvation, therefore, is not a matter of doctrine only, but entails his personal, costly commitment to his purpose.

The pattern of judgment-salvation in Jeremiah is also present in Deuteronomy. That book too knows of a judgment inevitably consequent upon Israel's stubbornness (Deut. 9:4–6; 30:1), and converts an exhortation to "circumcise your hearts" (Deut. 10:16; cf. the metaphor in Jer. 4:4) into a declaration that God himself will undertake to do this (30:6). While critical scholarship does not always recognize the historical priority of Deuteronomy over Jeremiah, the agreement of the two books on the pattern of salvation prohibits any simplistic antithesis between Law and Prophets in canonical terms. Therefore, in any explanation of the new covenant, the contrast between the law "written on stones" and "written on hearts" should not be absolutized into a categorical repudiation of Moses. A rhetorical aspect of the contrast should be recognized. The Law and the Prophets share an analysis of the human problem (persistence in sin), call for thoroughgoing moral and spiritual reconstruction (from the "heart"), and point to the grace of God, ultimately, as the source of reformation.

Jeremiah should also be placed in relation to the books of Kings. This is partly because there is material overlap between the two corpora (esp. in 2 Kings 25 and Jer. 52), reflecting the fact that both account for the same cataclysmic events in the history of Israel and Judah. In canonical terms, they tell the story of the covenant that is set up in Exodus–Deuteronomy, showing how the covenantal curses, threatened in Lev. 26 and Deut. 28, finally fall (Jer. 11:3–4; 2 Kings 17:19–20). While Kings knows that the exile of Judah will not be the end of the covenant between Israel and God (1 Kings 8:46–53), Jeremiah is more explicit on an actual restoration to its full blessings, especially in terms of return to the promised land. In this respect, Jeremiah echoes Deuteronomy more fully than Kings does (Deut. 30:3–5).

Finally, new covenant finds fulfillment in the NT. The Gospels attest to Jesus as fulfilling the "covenant" in his own blood (Mark 14:22–24; Matt. 26:26–28; cf. John 6:54). The sacrificial terminology in the context of a Passover meal comprehends Jesus' covenant-fulfillment in relation to the Mosaic covenant. Some ancient texts insert the word "new" in the Synoptic accounts here, testifying to an understanding in the church that the covenant inaugurated by Jesus was in fact the new covenant. This understanding is found expressly in 1 Cor. 11:25 (cf. 10:16; Rom. 11:27); Heb. 8:8–13; 9:15; 10:16–17; 12:24.

The fundamental NT witness, therefore, is that Jesus fulfills the covenant with Israel. The adoption of the language of new covenant, especially in Hebrews, draws attention to the promise in Jeremiah (and behind it Deuteronomy) that God himself would act decisively to bring about the salvation that had always eluded his people because of their hardness of heart. The coming of Jesus is thus presented as the culmination of that "incarnational" trend, already visible in Hosea and Jeremiah, in which God commits himself, at cost, to the salvation of his people. Since Jeremiah's new-covenant language should not be used to evacuate the Mosaic covenant of force or meaning, as if it were a failed experiment, so its adoption in Hebrews, being part of that book's strong pattern of new replacing old, has a certain rhetorical aspect. "Fulfillment" and "abolition" are both tropes that, if pressed logically, can hardly be reconciled. Rather than postulating an "old" covenant abolished, it is better to think of a combined canonical witness to God's resolve ultimately to make his covenant with humanity effective.

Jeremiah's Theological Significance

Jeremiah tells a story that promises renewed salvation after judgment and names this as a new covenant, which, canonically, leads to fulfillment in God's act of salvation through Christ. However, as a word to the church, it functions not merely as a story with a happy ending. While the story line in Jeremiah depicts the prophet's call to repent as something in the past that went unheeded, a reading of the book paradoxically continues to witness to the perennial need to return to God. The memorable "return [repent], faithless children" (3:14)—where "faithless" is *shobabim*, a play on *shub*, "return/repent"—ironically depicts the moral condition of those who are ever under God's call to obedience, while displaying a tendency at heart to strain in the opposite direction (here Jeremiah is not far from Paul in Rom. 7:14–25). The structure of judgment-salvation, then, can be heard, not only as a once-for-all story leading to the triumph of Christ, but also as a portrayal of an ever-present possibility in God's dealings with people.

The book of Jeremiah helped its first readers to face an unmitigated calamity and come to terms with new acts of God. Its demolition of false objects of trust still speaks to those who have an unhealthy attachment to any particular form of "church," tradition, or any way of being religious that has become entrenched and comfortable. Judah's road to idolatry (Jer. 2) was strewn with the good intentions of much worship of Yahweh in his temple (7:1–15). Modern idolatries too may seem to cohabit easily with the form of religion.

Correspondingly, exile and restoration can call us to readiness for new ways of being in relationship with God. When false attachments are exposed for what they are, the way of faith can seem unsettlingly to lack familiar markers. Change can seem synonymous with chaos. In Jeremiah, salvation is both restoration of the old and exploration of the radically new. The return to land would be no mere recovery of the *status quo ante*; yet it was properly a restoration. The ambivalence is in the idea of "renewal" itself. Whatever shape the new might take, the same God leads and finds us there. With this reassurance we can sit lightly to religion as a familiar set of symbols, and find it again as the worship of God in spirit and truth.

Jeremiah uses "heart" metaphors to speak about this true religion (4:4; 31:33). The specific metaphors (involving circumcision, torah) are based, trenchantly, on elements in the religious tradition. With such language Jeremiah appeals for a loyalty and devotion of will and energies that run through the whole being. This prompts, finally, considerations about individual and community.

As we noticed, the appeal to the "heart" is not a mark of a turn to "individualistic" religion. Rather, in Jeremiah as in Deuteronomy (6:5), it calls for the thorough reformation and renewal of a whole community. There is thus no sanction here for the false polarities of individual versus community, or institutional versus spontaneous (notwithstanding the point about false attachments to institutional forms). Rather, Jeremiah calls the community of faith to be constantly renewed, in its breadth and depth.

What then of Jeremiah as the OT's greatest witness to an individual in communion with God? This individualism is precisely "prophetic." That is, Jeremiah demonstrates by his calling, ministry, and life how an individual can bear the responsibility for the burden of memory and obligation that belongs properly to the whole community. Jeremiah did not willingly choose the lonely path; it was laid on him by the people's abandonment of God, his own attachment to the "ancient paths" (Jer. 6:16), and God's call to him to be a prophet. He is thus not a model of individual piety as such. Rather, as a faithful Israelite, he proved equal to the challenge of standing against the powerful tide of his contemporary "modernity." That is his perennial challenge to believers, whatever form the temptation to compromise and apostasy might take in their time and place.

Bibliography

Carroll, R. P. *Jeremiah*. OTL. SCM, 1986; Clines, D., and D. Gunn. "Form, Occasion and Redaction in Jeremiah 20." *ZAW* 88 (1976): 390–409; Duhm, B. *Das Buch Jeremia*. Mohr, 1901; Dumbrell, W. *Covenant and Creation*. Paternoster, 1984; Hyatt, J. "The Deuteronomic Edition of Jeremiah." *Vanderbilt Studies in the Humanities* 1 (1951): 71–95; McConville, J. G. *Judgment and Promise*. Eisenbrauns, 1993; McKane, W. *Jeremiah*. Vol. 1, *1–25*. Vol. 2, *26–52*. ICC. T&T Clark, 1986–96; Mowinckel, S. *Zur Komposition des Buches Jeremia*. Jacob Dybwad, 1914; Nicholson, E. *Preaching to the Exiles*. Blackwell, 1970; Polk, T. *The Prophetic Persona*. JSOTSup 32. JSOT, 1984; Skinner, J. *Prophecy and Religion*. Cambridge University Press, 1922; Stulman, L. *Order amid Chaos*. The Biblical Seminar 57. Sheffield Academic Press, 1998; Unterman, J. *From Repentance to Redemption*. JSOTSup 54. JSOT, 1987.

J. G. McConville

Jesus, Quest for the Historical

The quest for the historical Jesus seeks to discover Jesus as he was in historical fact as distinct from portrayals of him—however factual or unfactual they may be or have been—in oral tradition, which has long since disappeared, and in early literature that has survived (above all, the canonical Gospels and, in recent study, the *Gospel of Thomas*). The quest is a modern phenomenon, dating from the eighteenth century onward. Up to that century and except for some who resorted to symbolical interpretations, it was generally assumed that at least the canonical Gospels, plus references to Jesus' earthly career elsewhere in the NT, contain historically accurate information, so that differences among them have only to be harmonized for a fuller picture. Underlying this assumption was a belief in the divine inspiration of Scripture and a further, literary assumption that the canonical narratives about Jesus are meant to be taken as entirely factual. Otherwise and unthinkably, God would be lying through the Scripture. Since early accounts of Jesus contain a good deal of the miraculous, acceptance of supernaturalism accompanied this complex of historiographical assumptions and theological belief.

Theological and Philosophical Sources of the Quest

The advent of Deism and rationalism in the eighteenth century shook the foundations of the foregoing traditional view. In concert, Deism and rationalism denied the supernatural intervention of God in history. This denial entailed a rejection of historicity when it came to the accounts of Jesus' virgin birth, miracles, resurrection, ascension, and foreknowledge as the Son of God. Consequently, scholars set about picking and choosing what they thought to be historically acceptable as distinct from myth, folklore, and the like; or in the case of traditionalists, they set about defending historicity in toto. Thus began the quest for the historical Jesus, and it has continued to the present moment.

Effects of the Quest

The history of the quest has often been detailed (see esp. Schweitzer; Brown) and need not be repeated here except insofar as it has affected, and been affected by, theology. The deistic element in the quest—that is, the notion of God as an absentee landlord—led naturally to a wholesale rejection of the incarnation of God in Jesus Christ or, not so radically, to a redefining of Jesus' divinity less in terms of the hypostatic union and more in terms of a closeness to God that is true also of other human beings, though to a higher degree than in their case (so, e.g., Schleiermacher). Consequently, an appreciation of Jesus' humanity came to the fore, in contrast to an earlier emphasis on his deity. The appreciation of his humanity also spread to traditionalists, though they continued to maintain his full deity, but now in a more even balance with the humanity. Across the board, then, the historical Jesus looked more human than before, more rooted in the general human condition and in the particulars of first-century Palestinian geographical, social, political, and economic as well as religious conditions. Insofar as Jesus' deity is neither denied nor diminished and inasmuch as orthodox Christology affirms his humanity, this development counts as a theological plus.

Rationalism had a similarly mixed effect on the way ancient records of Jesus' life were evaluated. On the left hand, a critical eye discovered more and more differences among them—differences that fall into apparently redactional patterns and that to many scholars looked historically unharmonizable—so that the doctrine of scriptural inspiration suffered, as did also opinions regarding the historical reliability of the canonical Gospels even apart from miracle stories. On the right hand, some traditionalists were so convinced of already having the historical Jesus by way of factual reporting in every line of those records that they felt no need to join in the quest, only the need to offer rational harmonizations of reportorial differences. Yet others, however, kept hold of divine inspiration but allowed the differences to make them rethink the question of literary genre to the effect that a Gospel does not have to consist only of historical facts. It may also include unhistorical elaborations—christological, ethical, eschatological, and so on—inspired as such in equal measure with the historical reportage. Those who thought so joined the quest of the historical Jesus, but have come to considerably more positive results than the pure rationalists.

Jesus as Teacher. With the rejection or fading of the supernatural came an emphasis on the historical Jesus as a teacher of individual morality and then, too, of communitarian ethics ("the social gospel"). Meanwhile, the miracles of healing were explained away as psychosomatic, the exorcisms as mental therapy on the insane, and the nature miracles (such as the stilling of a storm) as coincidental (the storm just happened to abate at that moment) or mythological (deriving from OT portrayals of God as treading on the waters or from pagan stories of gods and heroes doing the same). Those parts of the Gospels, such as the Sermon on the Mount, that portray Jesus as a teacher thus came into prominence.

Jesus as Example. The Romantic movement laid weight on human experience, so that under its influence questers after the historical Jesus portrayed him as a human being who experienced God in a specially intimate way—thus as an example to be imitated as well as a teacher by whom to be instructed. His death ceased to be an atonement for sins and became more an example of self-sacrificial love for one's neighbor. Theologians of Abelardian proclivity gravitated to this sort of historical Jesus.

The Mysterious Jesus. Experience can easily slide into mysticism. Hence, when mysticism was combined with the strangeness to modern sensibilities of apocalyptic elements in scriptural portrayals of Jesus, it was only natural that Albert Schweitzer should describe the Jesus of history as so inscrutable that mystery (by no means a divine one, however) engulfs him. Therefore, the exemplary Jesus and the didactic Jesus took their exit just as the uniquely divine and redemptive Jesus had already done for the Deists, rationalists, and Romantics.

Jesus as Preacher. But a Jesus so shrouded in mystery as to be inscrutable can explain the historical phenomenon of early and continuing Christianity even less well than a moralistic teacher and example does. So emphasis shifted to the historical Jesus as a powerful preacher of God's kingdom and, more particularly, of God's claim on human beings in the crises of their everyday existence. This existential theology is often portrayed as uninterested in Jesus as he was in historical fact. Indeed, it focused more on the preached Jesus ("the Christ of faith") than on Jesus the preacher ("the Jesus of history") and drastically minimized the amount of historical factuality to be found in ancient sources, as in R. Bultmann's program of demythologization (shades of D. F. Strauss). Nevertheless, the slimmed-down Jesus was theologically designed to accommodate the distaste of "modern man" for the miraculous and other supernatural ingredients in the scriptural and traditional Jesuanic recipes. Yet at the same time it left some impression of the existential pungency of the historical Jesus' words (hence the designations "word theology" and "crisis theology").

The Kerygma and the New Quest

Such pungency seemed to require a Jesus who left historical memories of more robust proportions, however. So the Jesus of the early Christian *kerygma* (proclamation), as outlined especially by C. H. Dodd, T. W. Manson, and J. Jeremias (among others), acquired a few more historical features derived from the canonical Gospels. Then out of a theological fear that the demythologized Jesus had turned into a docetic Jesus, devoid of tangible humanity, or at least of very much of it, E. Käsemann—a Bultmannian—launched "The New Quest of the Historical Jesus." Skeptical presuppositions of a historiographical sort—for example, that any data about Jesus that tally with his Jewish heritage or with what Christians believed about him must be suspected as unhistorically projected into his life—kept this new quest

from voyaging very far from the port of Docetism in its modern configuration.

The Third Quest

But discovery of the Dead Sea Scrolls aroused a renewed interest in Jesus' Jewish heritage, so that similarities between him and this heritage came to be viewed with greater trust. By the same token, similarities between him and early Christian beliefs about him also came to be viewed with greater trust. This produced a measure of historical continuity from Judaism through Jesus to Christianity (the so-called "Third Quest of the Historical Jesus," though the division into three quests is itself historically suspect). Thus, Jesus came to be seen as a prophet who tried to reform Judaism in a movement of restoration through socioeconomic justice and nonviolence (so in various ways, E. P. Sanders, John P. Meier, and N. T. Wright, among others), or as an apocalypticist who announced the near and cataclysmic inbreaking of God's rule on earth (so Dale Allison Jr.). As a prophet, Jesus would have expected continuity between Jewish history and—given national repentance and obedient faith—the arrival of God's rule. As an apocalypticist, he would have expected a break between that history and the arrival of God's rule, a break marked by a literal coming of the Son of Man on the clouds of heaven (as opposed to a figurative coming at the destruction of Jerusalem in 70 CE) with an accompanying resurrection of the dead and the last judgment. In either case, because the attempt at reform mostly failed or because the fullness of God's rule did not arrive on time, his followers turned the historical Jesus into the founder of a new species of Judaism that rapidly developed into the church, with the heavenly exalted Christ at its head.

Interplay between Theology and Historiography

Theological predilections among early Christians produced different ways of portraying Jesus, whether as a prophet, an apocalypticist, a teacher of practical wisdom, a miracle-worker, a righteous sufferer, the Messiah, or God in human form. Modern theological predilections and animosities have fastened on this or that early portrayal of Jesus as historical at the expense of other such portrayals. This phenomenon has characterized the quest for the historical Jesus from its start; and despite repeated warnings concerning its prejudicial character, it continues to characterize the quest. Thus, for example, there are mar-

357

riages of theological convenience between two parties: One is a modern dislike of apocalyptic expectations for the future and a historical Jesus who only dealt in wise and witty observations about the present human condition (so the Jesus Seminar). The other is a modern concern for economic justice and a historical Jesus who only set about establishing egalitarianism among first-century Palestinian peasants (so liberation theology). Under the influence of postmodernism, particularly with its stress on differences between communities of faith, advocacy theology has exacerbated the tendency to look for Jesus in the well of history and see the reflection of one's own face, or the face of one's community. Thus, theological predilections unite with the desire for simplicity to produce caricatures of the historical Jesus, who in all likelihood was a figure of considerable complexity and to one degree or another fit all his canonical portrayals.

Rejection of Jesus' deity devolves into views of the historical Jesus solely as a prophet, a teacher of wisdom, a charismatic holy man, a shaman, or even a magician. A nontheological history-of-religions approach also tends toward such views. A theological antipathy toward eschatology, which includes a doctrine of bodily resurrection, leads either to rejecting the historicity of Jesus' resurrection, or to redefining it in nonbodily terms and often putting it in a supposedly unhistorical category of eschatology, where it is not subject to historical investigation (against which, see Wright). A theological openness toward eschatology stems these tides; and, in reverse, the conflicting historical judgments affect theological positions.

Conclusion

All in all, then, the history of the quest for the historical Jesus exposes a symbiotic relation between theological positions and historiographical positions taken in the quest. Rejection of divine immanence and a dehistoricizing of the miraculous in Jesus' life feed each other. To the contrary, acceptance of divine immanence and trust in the historicity of the miraculous in Jesus' life feed each other. Full acceptance of Jesus' deity (so-called "Christology from above") undergirds the historicity of his predicting the passion-and-resurrection, the destruction of Jerusalem and the temple, and the second coming, while these predictions in turn support a belief in his deity. On the other hand, rejection of his deity—or a preponderant emphasis on his humanity (so-called "Christology from below")—feeds a dehistoricizing of the predictions and vice versa. At most it al-

lows—in the cases of his passion and resurrection and the destruction of Jerusalem—for prediction by the power of natural human foresight.

Not that the historical Jesus always called on his divine omniscience. No, according to the canonical records he called on it only when necessary for the work of God's kingdom. Otherwise, he asked questions to gain information and used other ordinary means of learning. According to those same records, he similarly called on his divine omnipotence only when it was needed for the work of God's kingdom. Otherwise, he was subject to the same physical needs and limitations that all human beings are subject to. These two examples show how theology—in this case, a Christology of the divine and the human in the one person of Jesus—contributes to the historicity of biblical accounts concerning him, and how these accounts contribute to the Christology concerning him.

See also Biography; Gospels; History; Jesus Christ, Doctrine of

Bibliography

Braaten, C., and R. Harrisville, eds. *The Historical Jesus and the Kerygmatic Christ.* Abingdon, 1964; Brown, C. *Jesus in European Protestant Thought.* 2d ed. Baker, 1988; Bultmann, R. *Jesus and the Word.* Charles Scribner's Sons, 1958; Dodd, C. H. *The Apostolic Preaching and Its Development.* Hodder & Stoughton, 1936; Green, J., and M. Turner, eds. *Jesus of Nazareth, Lord and Christ.* Eerdmans, 1994; Gundry, R. "Recent Investigations into the Literary Genre 'Gospel.'" Pages 97–114 in *New Dimensions in New Testament Study,* ed. R. Longenecker and M. Tenney. Zondervan, 1974; idem. "Reconstructing Jesus." *Christianity Today* 42, no. 5 (April 27, 1998): 76–79; Haight, R. "The Impact of Jesus Research on Christology." *Louvain Studies* 21 (1996): 216–28; Johnson, L. T. *The Real Jesus.* HarperSanFrancisco, 1996; Kähler, M. *The So-Called Historical Jesus and the Historic, Biblical Christ.* Fortress, 1964; Käsemann, E. "The Problem of the Historical Jesus." Pages 15–47 in *Essays on New Testament Themes.* Alec R. Allenson, 1964; Powell, M. A. *Jesus as a Figure in History.* Westminster John Knox, 1998; Robinson, J. M. *A New Quest of the Historical Jesus.* SCM, 1959; Schwarz, H. *Christology.* Eerdmans, 1998; Schweitzer, A. *The Quest of the Historical Jesus.* Macmillan, 1973; Sobrino, J. *Jesus the Liberator.* Orbis, 1993; Wright, N. T. *The Resurrection of the Son of God.* Fortress, 2003.

Robert H. Gundry

Jesus and Scripture

The phrase "Jesus and Scripture" suggests at least two separate studies: the relationship between the incarnate Word and the inscribed word, and the stance of the historical Jesus toward the Scriptures of his own day. Generally, theologians have confined themselves to the first discussion, while biblical scholars have tackled the latter. They are so mutually informative, however, that it is difficult to determine which should be foundational. One could begin "inductively" with Jesus' own attitude toward the Tanak, and then go on to probe the relationship between the Son and Scripture as authorities. However, no such study "from below" is entirely successful without recourse to established traditions or decisions concerning, first, the person of Jesus, and second, the canonicity and accuracy of various Scriptures. The circle or spiral of hermeneutics is encountered wherever we enter, at the level of "history" or "theology"—if, indeed, pursuits of history and theology can ever be fully separated in a Christian enterprise. In this study, we begin with the theological question and then attempt to form a picture of Jesus' own pattern in approaching Holy Writ, as this emerges in the Gospels.

People of the Book; People of the Christ

Christians have been called one of the three "Peoples of the Book." This is, however, less true of Christianity than it is of Islam or Judaism (cf. Barton). Some have assumed that this is because Christians give priority to the (present personal) experience of God over the "written record of experience" from the past. It seems truer, however, to describe Christians as "People of *the Christ*" even more than they are "People of the Book." Though much of "the Book" may have come chronologically *before* an understanding of "the Person," it is to the personal Word, the Son, that we pay our homage; he is the one who illumines both those pages of the Book that have preceded and those that have followed his advent.

Thus, Paul argued that the entire purpose of the Torah was to point to the Christ; its glory was meant to be "set aside" (2 Cor. 3:7, 14 NRSV) so as to give way to his greater glory. Speaking of the first covenant people, he says, "To them belong the . . . glory, the covenants, the giving of the law, the worship, and the promises; to them belong the patriarchs, and from them . . . comes the Christ, *who is over all!*" (Rom. 9:4 NRSV). After the fall of the temple in 70 CE, the Jewish rabbis increasingly extolled the Torah; in Christian circles, that honor was given to the incarnate Word: what the rabbis said about the Torah, the apostles declared true of Jesus. The Book, as it was recognized in the Christian community, was seen to be gathered, Old and New Covenant/Testament, around the One who brings, enacts, and ratifies God's promises. We thus call the Scriptures "the word" in a secondary sense, because in them we find a lifted curtain or "re-velation" of the One who *is* the Word, God-with-Us. But it is Jesus himself who reveals the triune God.

This relationship between the inscribed and incarnate Word is taught, implicitly and explicitly, in the Scriptures themselves. Mark 11:27–12:37 presents the question of authority chiastically, moving between Jesus as authority and Scripture as authoritative:

> A Jesus, in the temple, asked about authority; Jesus approved by crowd, 11:27–33
> > B Rejecting God's word, 12:1–12
> > > C Test 1: What does Torah say about taxes (Pharisees)? 12:13–17
> > > C′ Test 2: What does Torah say about resurrection (Sadducees)? 12:18–27
> > B′ Heeding God's word, 12:28–34
> A′ Jesus, in the temple, asks about authority; Jesus approved by crowd, 12:35–37

Throughout this section, the Gospel weaves together questions of right worship, understanding, and authority, implying a connection between monotheistic worship and the honor of the "Messiah-Lord," and moving from a common deference toward Scriptures to a polarized reaction to Jesus' teaching: "They were afraid"; others "listened . . . with delight" (12:12, 37). These same issues are tackled more directly in the Fourth Gospel. Jesus parries with the scribes: "You search the Scriptures because you believe that in them you possess eternal life: and it is *they* that are witness-bearers concerning me" (5:39 AT). Again, in Luke 14:24, to the friendly ears of his disciples, Jesus is heard to declare: "I tell you that many prophets . . . desired to see what you see, but did not see it, and to hear what you hear, but did not hear it" (NRSV). The author to the Hebrews schematizes all this: "Long ago God spoke to our ancestors in many and various ways by the prophets, but in these last days he has spoken to us by the Son . . . [who] sustains all things by his powerful word" (Heb. 1:1–3 NRSV).

Finally, in visionary mode, the seer John places before our eyes, at the climax of his visions, the Logos: "He has a name inscribed that no one knows but himself. He is clothed in a robe dipped in blood, and his name is called The Word of God" (Rev. 19:12 NRSV). Finally disclosed by the seer as the Logos with the sharp sword coming from his mouth, this One is identified with the Lion/Lamb, who earlier in Revelation displayed unique power to unseal the scroll held in the hand of the Almighty (Rev. 5:1–10). The One who *is* the Word has jurisdiction and interpretative power *over* God's word, and so creates, sustains, and explains all things. It is by him, indeed, that we know the mysterious unnameable One, for he it is who "exegetes" the Father ("has made him known," *exēgēsato*, John 1:18) to those with ears and eyes made new.

For Christians, then, the Word is in the first place a *Person*. Because the Word is a Person and the Son has become human, true human words can be spoken and written, and so collected in the library that we call the Scriptures. Because the Word is a Person, the Word of God is not simply a record of experience, but active (Rom. 10:6–18), near to us, within our hearts, and renewing the world that the Son spoke into existence at the beginning. To understand the primacy of the personal Word may indeed assist in ecumenical debate regarding the manner in which the Scriptures are inspired, and the stance that Christians ought to take toward the written word. Careful reflection will prevent both the use of Jesus' words to critique other scriptural words (as in "material criticism," *Sachkritik*), and also a "bibliolatry" that confuses a certain theory of inspiration with worship of the One who has come among us. Jesus and the Scriptures are both authoritative; yet the latter is an authority because of and on behalf of the former. The One we adore; the other we honor because of that One who is all lovely. In the Scriptures, letters, words, sentences, precepts, propositions, and stories are dignified and pressed into service by that One who is God's first, perfect, and ultimate Word. Again, they come into shape within the context of God's living people ("tradition"). Because of this, God's communication or communion with us is internal and mysterious, as well as transferable one to another. His goal is to make of us "letters," "written on our [corporate] heart" with his own "finger," the Holy Spirit of God (2 Cor. 3:2–18).

Jesus Reads the Scriptures

Thus, by the surprising design of God, we find ourselves in a position to ask that impudent question, "What was Jesus' attitude toward Scripture?" Perhaps it is inevitable that we will not fully understand how the master exegete saw and read the Scriptures. We are constrained, however, to ask these questions, for throughout the Scriptures we encounter Jesus' name and voice alongside references to Holy Writ. While it may be cheeky to speak about Jesus' *attitude* toward Scriptures,

we can surely observe how the Gospels picture Jesus as reading, quoting, and using them.

Synoptic and Johannine studies, as well as the simple recognition that Jesus spoke in Aramaic, not in Greek (the language of the NT), demonstrate that we do not possess many of his ipsissima verba (actual words). No doubt the Gospel writers reflected issues of their own communities as they inscribed the oral traditions in which Jesus used Scripture. Many have tried to isolate what Jesus himself must have said from these later stages in which the faithful community adapted his handling of Scripture to suit their audience(s). Readers interested in this quest may dip into the bibliography below and make their own judgments regarding the various "hermeneutical keys" that have been used. Here we do not attempt a reconstruction but rather consider how Jesus' use of Scripture emerges from reading the Gospels as a whole. In this approach, we show confidence that the writers of the NT were stamped by the mark of the exegete Jesus, imitating his methods (perhaps from within the matrix of the earliest church, rather than directly at his feet), and so informing their own work by the stance that the Lord himself embodied.

History of Interpretation: What Constitutes a "Use of Scripture"?

Ought we to circumscribe our task by referring strictly to outright citations prefaced by formulas such as "as it is written" or "as Scripture says"? Some have done this, arguing that where the text calls attention to Scripture qua Scripture, the citations are more fundamental (e.g., Powery). Here is a major methodological problem: Are references to Scripture found on the lips of Jesus to be traced to the historical events, or are they the portraits of the early church or the Gospel writers? Again, we find a scholarly spectrum. In adjudicating between the various views, the words of Nils Dahl are instructive:

> In no case can any distinct separation be achieved between the genuine words of Jesus and the constructions of the community. We do not escape the fact that we know Jesus only as the disciples remembered him. Whoever thinks that the disciples completely misunderstood their Master or even consciously falsified his picture may give fantasy free reign. (94)

It seems best, then, to approach the study of Jesus' use of Scripture from within the context of an overall picture, seeking his authentic voice—whether this be found in direct reference, allusion, echo, or a cumulative teaching that emerges from combined texts and images.

Although there are functional differences between direct citations, indirect references/allusions, and "echoes" (cf. Hays), direct citations are not necessarily more significant than the less-obvious references. Direct citations may reach a broader audience, but indirect allusions strike a deeper chord. Direct citations call attention to the issue of authority, offering a kind of argumentative trump card; unsignaled references appeal to an acknowledged authority, creating a community of understanding (see Dimant 379–419; Allison). Think of the difference between a lecturer who quotes pedantically and a preacher who represents a beloved personality by echoing "I have a dream!"

Mode: Playful and Serious. In the Gospels, Jesus is depicted as using Scripture, positively and polemically, as a shield and a sword, in playfulness and with utter earnestness. In John 10:34, for example, Jesus engages in controversy over the relationship between humans, the Anointed One, and God, citing Ps. 82:6. Many assume that this passage tells us more about overt theological disagreements between first-century monotheists (Pharisaic versus Christian) than about Jesus. Yet his style is inimitable: pointed questions, allusive reference to Scripture, and the tantalizing "and the scripture cannot be annulled" (10:35 NRSV). Some have taken his phrase as programmatic (cf. Matt. 5:19; e.g., Kuyper), without commenting on the bizarre choice of Scripture and the parenthetical nature of his remark. Others have seen his comment as wholly ironic, descriptive of Pharisaic minute exegesis but not the Jesus way: so the scribes are hoisted on their own petard (Chilton).

There is another option: here Jesus both instructs and corrects, subtly calling the hearer to question what it really means to "break" or "annul" God's Torah. Torah is not "broken" by healing on the Sabbath (John 5:18; 7:23) but by ignoring the shape of Torah's narrative, and its climax in the One before them. Whether or not Jesus had such an overt discussion with his detractors concerning his status is a less important issue than the approach to Scripture—as a coherent whole that transformingly addresses a people (10:35) and that will culminate in God's dramatic transforming action (v. 36). Here Jesus cites an unusual phrase, one that jolts his hearers into thinking about the purpose of God's word.

Approach: Humility and Authority. This approach is consonant with the pattern found in a Synoptic Gospels debate (Matt. 22:23–33// Mark 12:18–27//Luke 20:27–40) variously related.

Here Jesus tackles the disbelief of the Sadducees, humbly submitting to their "canonical" scruples in teaching about the resurrection. Though the Torah itself provides precious little direct teaching on the doctrine, Jesus finds help in the central passage "at the bush," which calls attention to the living and life-giving nature of God. The readers understand the Scriptures when they come to recognize the "power of God" (Mark 12:24//Matt. 22:29): any other reading is limiting and simply "wrong." The Scriptures can be read in an unfruitful manner, whenever they are not seen as providing a window onto the character of the living God. Jesus links the question about doctrine, as in John 10, with the nature of God's power. Especially in Mark's version of the debate, we see the same allusive and devastating interrogative style—this seems to be muted in Matthew and attenuated in Luke, though still discernible.

Use: Direct and Indirect. We have seen Jesus speak about the fruitful reading of Scripture, by citations both exact ("at the bush") and inexact (a psalm is not "Law"). We conclude by considering a passage that offers both an allusion and an echo—Matt. 11:18–30. Wisdom has already been invoked in Matt. 11:19, making the allusions to Sir. 24:19 and 51:23–27 inescapable. Here Jesus speaks with the grace and generosity of personified Wisdom, offering rest, refreshment, humility, and a yoke to "all." He embodies Wisdom, thus (in a style reminiscent of the parables) pointing to himself without engaging in self-assertion. The words function in the same way as his roundabout phrase "Son of Man," intriguing the hungry hearer and offering rest to those who recognize the divine voice. In Sirach, it is the teacher who directs students to take on "Wisdom's" yoke; here, Jesus calls, "Take my yoke." It is up to the hearer to decide whether he is quoting Wisdom, simply offering Wisdom's yoke on God's behalf, or whether it is the special yoke of Jesus to which the listener is called. Who is the one who speaks? What and whose is the yoke promised? How is the carrying of burdens related to rest? The hearer is invited to "come and see."

The Sirach allusion is nourished by echoes of Jer. 5:5, in which God's yoke has been broken, and 6:16, where God himself offers counsel and rest for the soul. The one who comes, follows, and learns humility will be led to the Jesus of the cross, that one who bears burdens and alone can give the Sabbath rest of God. Again, an intriguing voice uses holy books in such a way as to make the hearers question their presuppositions and redirect their gaze toward the Author of life. Even sacred books of dubious authority bend to his purpose, as Jesus with humble authority calls us to the central questions. His method, at once direct and indirect, bears fruit. The one who is concerned for God's yoke of Torah and free offer of Wisdom's feast, will find themselves at the feet of the one whose burden is light. All of Scripture—Torah, Prophets, Deuterocanonicals—accomplishes the purpose of the living God and directs us to the life-giving Word incarnate.

Method: Scripture Fulfilled in the Personal God. We can see that Jesus' method is to point us to the personal God. Ultimately, Jesus handles Scripture so as to illuminate God, to tell God's story, and thus, it seems, to testify (however indirectly) to himself. His skirmishes with the Sadducees indicate that Scripture can be read in an entirely wrong way. Hence, there are limits to hermeneutical freedom! However, his confidence in the word of God seems robust enough that he can use Scripture as a tool, engaging the readers even at their own limited levels. Brief "snapshots" or "still lives" of the Word may bring about life, for the inscribed Word echoes the enlivening Speaker. Though Jesus may have modeled rather than directly stated the relationship between himself and the scriptural story, the general tenor of the Gospels presents Jesus as reading the Torah in a consistent way: Torah (indeed the whole Hebrew Bible) "testifies" to the living God, and so also to him.

This theme of Scripture as "fulfilled" corresponds to Jesus' announcement that the reign of God has arrived. This fulfillment does not, however, point mainly to a subjective "experience" (*pace* Chilton 167), but to the person and activity of God, who shares his life with the new humanity. Because the person and activity of God cannot be tamed, Jesus frequently uses Scripture in surprising ways, thus bringing the reader up short. He is not entirely alone in this enterprise, for by the time of Jesus, Torah was interpreted through debate (cf. the Mishnah), through surprising attention to details of the text (pesharim), through stories creatively retold (midrashim), and through expanded paraphrase (targumim). As with other ancient interpreters of the written word, Jesus exegetes both to correct his hearers and to expand their horizons. Today, we would be remiss not to expect that Jesus' use of Scripture disturbs as well as confirms our human enterprises. Though we have approached his reading of Scripture in terms of drama and story, we must not squeeze the Master Storyteller into our own mold, insisting that he read Scripture according

to our model, be that narratival or otherwise. It may be that the growing edge for our present faith community lies elsewhere, as we note Jesus using Scripture in an ironic, prescriptional, propositional, or concessive mode.

Throughout the Synoptics and John, in various strata and subgenres, clues point unmistakably to the conclusion that Jesus considered himself to be intimately connected with a new divine activity— a new exodus, a new yoked activity, a surprising turn (but also a fulfillment) to God's ongoing dealings with humankind. The range of citations and several references to "Law and Prophets" suggest a certain shaping of the inscribed word, without a confinement of God's Spirit—the texts deemed "apocryphal" can also be used, and Jesus can cheerfully use the restricted canon of Torah where this is necessary. Again, much evidence points to Jesus' habitual use of the Aramaic paraphrases of Scripture (the targumim), which would have been readily understandable to his audience, rather than the Greek translations (LXX) or even the Hebrew (Evans 98; Chilton 57ff.) version of the OT. The revelation of Scripture, then, is translatable, not slavishly depending upon the "originals" or even always hampered by a restricted canon. The Scriptures are authoritative because they disclose the living God; they can, however, also be misread and misused. Here Jesus' ironical use of Scripture must be acknowledged (cf. Mark 4:11–12: "lest they repent and be forgiven" [AT], citing Isa. 6:9–10).

The central strategy in the Gospels' overall interpretation of the OT narrative seems to have been the bringing together of two traditional corporate figures—Suffering Servant (second half of Isaiah) and victorious Son of Man (Dan. 7)—as Jesus' story and person are presented. Some interpreters have assumed that this was the activity of early-church exegetes. However, Jesus himself is the most obvious candidate for a striking move of this sort. As C. H. Dodd put it (in his classic on this subject):

> Creative thinking is rarely done by committee. . . . To account for the beginning of this most original and fruitful process of rethinking the Old Testament we [find] need to postulate a creative mind. The Gospels offer us one. Are we compelled to reject the offer? (110)

Significance for Today

Our two intertwined themes—the incarnate and inscribed word, and Jesus' approach to Scripture—are enormously important for the formation of God's people. Because of God's gifts to us, we hold within our Christ-formed community the treasure of God's word (2 Cor. 4:7). As such, we are living "arks of the covenant," who contain not simply information nor a beguiling story, but the enlivening Word by Whom we enter the divine drama and live within it. The written word is prized because it points to the One who discloses God's very secrets to us. Entering into these mysteries means to be taught by the Jesus of Scripture how to approach, read, and deploy his word, so that we become, under his tutelage, scribes bringing out of the storehouse what is old and what is new, at the appropriate times (Matt. 13:52). To be trained by Jesus means that we will learn how to read the Scriptures in deadly earnest and with celebrative play, that we will model humility and bow to Christ's authority as we direct others to him in our reading of the word, and that we will dwell within the Scriptures daily so that they become a natural part of our allusive and indirect speech, as well as direct authorities to cite. Given the current challenges, we will not allow our concern for the authority of Scripture to become a new idolatry, so that we focus solely on a doctrine of inspiration, or on Christianity as a system. Rather, we will learn from our Lord, who read Scripture as a revelation of the personal and living God, culminating in his great act of taking humanity unto himself.

By a multitude of different words, conventions, and genres, we see before our eyes and hear within our ears news of that One who spoke worlds into existence, and who speaks the new creation into our startled ears. His glory shines in its pages, inscribed word and incarnate Word bound up together. Here is a great humility—that the One who is the Word could become an unspeaking infant. Here is, perhaps, an even greater humility—that the One who is the Word deigned to be inscribed within the written page, stamped upon the product of created vegetation, and made visible by design upon a humanly formed palimpsest. By his light we understand its enlightening words; by this light we approach the One who is the Light. The service of the written word toward us, God's people, is in itself a parable of our vulnerable, incarnate Lord, the Servant of all.

See also Jewish Exegesis; Relationship between the Testaments; Targum; Word of God

Bibliography

Allison, D. *The Intertextual Jesus*. Trinity, 2000; Barton, J. *People of the Book*. Westminster John Knox, 1988; Boring, M. *The Continuing Voice of Jesus*. Westminster John Knox, 1991; Bultmann, R. *History of the Synoptic Tradition*, trans. J. Marsh. Harper & Row, 1963; Chilton, B. *A Galilean Rabbi and His Bible*. Glazier, 1984; Dahl, N. A. "The Problem of the Historical Jesus." In *Jesus the Christ*, ed. D. Juel. Fortress, 1991; Dimant, D. "Use and Interpretation of Mikra in the Apocrypha and Pseudepigrapha." Pages 379–419 in *Mikra*, ed. M. Mulder. Van Gorcum, 1988; Dodd, C. H. *According to the Scriptures*. James Nisbet, 1952; Ellis, E. *The Old Testament in Early Christianity*. Mohr, 1991; Evans, C., ed. *The Interpretation of Scripture in Early Judaism and Christianity*. Sheffield Academic Press, 2000; Fitzmyer, J. "The Use of Explicit OT Quotations in Qumran Literature and in the NT." In *Essays on the Semitic Background of the New Testament*. Sources for Biblical Study. Scholars Press, 1971; France, R. T. *Jesus and the Old Testament*. Tyndale, 1971; Funk, R., R. Hoover, and the Jesus Seminar, eds. *The Five Gospels*. Macmillan, 1993; Hays, R. *Echoes of Scripture in the Letters of Paul*. Yale University Press, 1989; Hooker, M. *Jesus and the Servant*. SPCK, 1959; Hoskyns, E. *The Riddle of the New Testament*. Faber & Faber, 1947; Juel, D. *Messianic Exegesis*. Fortress, 1988; Kimball, C. *Jesus's Exposition of the Old Testament in Luke's Gospel*. JSNTSup 94. Sheffield Academic Press, 1994; Kugel, J., and R. Greer. *Early Biblical Interpretation*. Westminster, 1986; Kuyper, L. *The Scripture Unbroken*. 1978; Moyise, S. *The Old Testament in the New*. Continuum, 2001; Powery, E. *Jesus Reads Scripture*. Biblical Interpretation Series 63. Brill, 2003; Vermes, G. *Jesus the Jew*. MacMillan, 1973; idem. *The Religion of Jesus the Jew*. Fortress, 1993; Wright, N. T. *Jesus and the Victory of God*. Fortress, 1996.

Edith M. Humphrey

Jesus Christ, Doctrine of

It is a Christian truism that Jesus Christ is central when reading the OT and NT as Scripture: he is their basic content, the Word of God; he gives them their form (in a certain sense, *Old* and *New* Testaments); he himself is the aim toward which their reading should be oriented. Such hermeneutical claims surface in diverse places—Luke 24; John 5; Rom. 10; Heb. 1; and so on. Many articles in this volume explore interpretative territory in that light, and more specifically in light of christological material: incarnation, atonement, ascension, Jesus as interpreter of Scripture, and other themes. Meanwhile, many find compelling the statement in John's Gospel that if everything about Jesus were written down, "the whole world would not have room" (21:25). Hence, this essay pursues Christology from a more narrowly hermeneutical vantage point (and, to some degree, vice versa).

Christology's Biblical Foundations

Christian faith has the roots of its storied history in Jewish monotheism. The basic pattern of biblical teaching about God starts with the Shema of Deut. 6:4: "Hear, O Israel: The LORD our God, the LORD is one." What are Christians to make of their worshipping Jesus Christ in view of such OT teaching—the Bible as the early Christians knew it? This remains the perennial question for our faith, especially if we build on the biblical metaphor of Jesus Christ as its foundation (Matt. 7:24–27; 1 Cor. 3:10–17).

How then should we gather biblical materials for christological construction? A popular approach in the past few decades has been to survey the NT titles for Jesus; we then consider NT proclamations of salvation via biblical theology with reference to Christ.

Titles of Christ. "Son of Man," it seems, was Jesus' favorite self-designation. While in the OT this preeminently designates humanity, the Gospels associate it with the entire scope of the Christ-narrative: his service on earth, suffering and death, and exaltation to eschatological glory. By naming himself the Son of Man, Jesus seems to have claimed a messianic role and dignity, avoiding the political hazards of the term "Messiah" while nevertheless acknowledging his mission's supernatural origin and character in some fashion. The latter point remains controversial, especially in tandem with the interpretation of Dan. 7. However, some kind of divine identity may lie in the background. This would legitimate taking the honorific language of Pss. 2 and 110, "whereby Israel's anointed king was thought of as God's son seated at God's right hand," to a new level of significance with respect to Jesus' relation to Israel's God (C. A. Evans 32, in Davis et al., *Trinity*, unfolding various reasons for this).

"Son of God" is not recorded as Jesus' own term, but is a favorite of the Epistles, wherein sometimes it may refer to his preexistence. In the Gospels its emphasis is Jesus' supernatural power over the spirit world (e.g., Mark 3:11; 5:7). Likewise, "Lord [*kyrios*]" does not predominate in the Gospels; it was probably a form of respectful address (perhaps akin to "sir") while Jesus was on earth. After his resurrection and ascension, however, its use as the Greek equivalent of the OT Yahweh becomes significant. A famously crucial instance is Phil. 2:9–11, where Paul uses this name to identify Jesus with Israel's covenant God—in shocking fulfillment of a strong monotheistic text, Isa. 45:21–24. The exaltation of a human being to share in what was, and is now fully revealed to be, Yahweh's identity was a remarkable claim (and a political one, too, according to recent emphases regarding such titles vis-à-vis the imperial cult).

John's Gospel, of course, also identifies Jesus with Yahweh, in particular via repeated "I AM" sayings (cf. Exod. 3:14). The name becomes Jesus' self-identification, often followed by various appellations that link him to the roles of Israel's God: light, shepherd, true vine, and so on. John also identifies Jesus Christ with the Logos, the divine Word, in which the universe has its beginning and structure.

Long debates persist in biblical theology over the existence and coherence of an "orthodox" conceptual substructure underlying these titles. "Christ," or "Messiah [anointed one]," may illustrate this matter. In the OT, anointing simply designates a divinely ordained office within the Israelite theocracy. Although the idea of a particular person fulfilling the role of Davidic king, overthrowing the Romans, and ushering in Yahweh's kingdom was present within first-century Judaism, messianic conceptions were not monolithic. There were skeptics, corporate notions of Israel having a messianic vocation, and various proposals on offer for the renewal of the nation and its full return from exile.

"Messiah" is usually a title in the Synoptic Gospels, where it is only occasionally Jesus' claim (e.g., Mark 14:61–65); moreover, defending that biblical portrayal of his self-attestation to a historian's satisfaction has been somewhat challenging. In any case, the divine identity with which the Gospels associate Christ is not simplistically that of the later creeds (on which, see below). Eventually, however, "Christ" became so associated with Jesus' identity as to tend toward a proper name (e.g., at points in Acts and Paul).

Surrounding biblical theology's struggle with the significance of titles for Jesus Christ, then, two stresses especially have caused vulnerability. (1) The relation of OT and NT and (2) the identification of God in and between those texts receive further treatment below regarding the (perceived) modern collapse of the Christian story's integrity. Meanwhile, we may address a third biblical-theological concern here: the Christologies implied in NT proclamations of salvation. Indeed, the traditional distinction between the "person" and "work" of Christ is quite tenuous or even unhelpful in light of biblical theology; at minimum, the distinction must not become a division. The Bible generally keeps "act" and "being" tightly together.

Proclamations of Salvation. The Synoptic Gospels present Jesus as the bearer of God's kingdom in his person, words, and work. But they do so with variety. Matthew's Jesus comes to save his people from their sins, in a manner especially concerned with functional righteousness—theirs must exceed that of the Pharisees as they learn from the authoritative Teacher what is really crucial for fulfilling Torah. Matthew's Jewish Christians must become people of universal mission, concerned with extending to others the mercy, forgiveness, and healing they have received from God. Mark's Gospel, meanwhile, is action-packed, with Jesus not only teaching but also healing, exorcising demons, and suffering—all the while deflecting attention to Israel's God, whose fulfillment of the Isaianic new exodus has begun, and with it a drama of decision for discipleship. The somewhat cosmopolitan two-volume Luke-Acts too, then, develops considerable Jewish material and emphasizes some of these themes. But Luke's prophetic Jesus has now poured out his Spirit upon a new community, through whom he powerfully continues his work—unhindered, as the last word of Acts emphasizes (Greek/NRSV), despite both internal and external challenges. These Gospels narrate a Jesus whose relationship with Israel's God as Father (e.g., Matt. 6–7) and dependence upon the Spirit (e.g., Matt. 4; Luke 4) are singular—as his resurrection ultimately vindicates—but also paradigmatic for the followers who, given a new form of his presence, will spread his life's work.

That empowering presence of the Spirit of Christ leads us to Paul. If there is a "center" of Pauline theology, then union with or participation in Christ might be the strongest candidate. The baptized drink of the Spirit, whom Jesus outpoured and by whom they are covenanted together as one community, continuing to partake of their nourishing source and to proclaim their unity. Christ and his Spirit may be distinguished but never separated in Paul, and this surely gives us an incipient form of the conceptual apparatus for later trinitarian theology (so Fee, e.g., in Davis et al., *Trinity*; Davis et al., *Incarnation*).

The Johannine Jesus is yet more strongly divine and human—both. He is the Light in whom there is Life, who abundantly illuminates his people already by the Spirit. However extensive its differences from the Johannine writings, the book of Revelation likewise portrays Jesus with both a human and a heavenly face. The Lion of Judah is, of course, paradoxically the slain Lamb, and in this way his people, paradoxically, overcome the world.

So also in other Epistles, especially 1 Peter, the suffering service of Jesus Christ not only accomplishes God's triumph over evil powers and the liberation of his people, but also establishes the pattern for their resistance. Theological interpreters must be careful not to advocate a christological paradigm of passive quietism that further subjugates the victim; instead, they must clarify that Jesus' suffering constitutes active struggle against the devil, sin, and death—as *may* ours. Some have suggested a contrast in 2 Peter and Jude, where focus on the power of the cross gives way to emphasis on future divine judgment. Christ is the Master of believers, but the Judge of people outside his household. What balances this is the OT truth that "judgment . . . begin[s] with the household of God" (1 Pet. 4:17 NRSV). Thus, eschatologically oriented Christology becomes an incentive for Christian virtue—ultimately love (2 Pet. 1), which must be extended even or especially to all whom Christ's community might turn away from pagan immorality (Jude).

The Christology of James is even more indirect, while his concerns are again bound up with communal virtue. Yet God's protective judgment on behalf of the suffering and an implied christological opposition to violence (even or especially verbal violence!) remain evident. Also, for an audience with some Jewish background, Hebrews addresses suffering and communal life. Jesus' suffering richly fulfills Lev. 16: His sacrifice was public and once-for-all. Yet he has triumphantly ascended to the heavenly sanctuary as high priest, where he continually intercedes for us. And he will eventually return to the people and announce forgiveness finished. Metaphors of Jesus as sacrifice and as priest are mixed, to care for all the dynamics of human consciences—both past and postbaptismal sins—in a way that the OT system could not decisively accomplish. Hebrews is replete with typological use of the OT regarding the person and work of Christ, and it is perhaps no coincidence to find there some of the NT's strongest language for both Jesus' preexistent sonship and adoption into sonship.

In short, the NT seems to play out two OT trajectories—the prophetic Servant or Son of Man, and the royal Son of David or Son of God—in identifying Jesus with the anticipated revelation of the Creator Yahweh in redeeming Israel. This foundation put in place a structure for centuries of Christian thought, life, and worship. But did the church build with wood, hay, and stubble; or with gold, silver, and precious stones?

Christology's Traditional Building Blocks

Patristic and early medieval developments are often narrated with reference to successive intellectual environments (Alexandria and Antioch) and the major heresies, which elicited controversy along with (sometimes) creedal consensus. The christological essentials that emerged are chiefly three: Jesus Christ is fully human but also fully the divine Son of God, and these two "natures" are united in one "person" (the "hypostatic union"), though their properties remain appropriately distinct.

Ebionism, for which source material is scant, was probably the earliest post-NT tendency that was deemed heretical. Apparently growing out of Jewish Christianity and perhaps those dubbed "Judaizers" by Paul, Ebionites saw Jesus as a unique human, as the Christ (for a time, anyway) but not divine. They held a form of "adoptionism," in which the human Jesus was assumed into a role within the divine plan. This will, perhaps, be a characteristic temptation of those who take seriously interaction with the OT, the historical Jesus, and Judaism, in their own right.

Alexandrian "Word-Flesh" Christology. As the gospel continued to gain influence in (and be influenced by) the broader Greco-Roman world, Alexandria became an important center of Christian reflection. Alexandrian or "Word-flesh" Christology prioritized the mystical Christ over the historical Jesus (as we think of it now), concerned chiefly with the possibilities of union between the divine Logos and human flesh. Tending toward some form of Platonic dualism between body and soul, material and immaterial, and so on, this approach emphasizes the unity of Christ—at the extreme, a single divinized person to the expense of his human integrity. Such was the environment from the third century on through the ratification and extension of the Nicene Creed (originally developed in 325) at Constantinople in 381.

Docetism, then, names a family of heresies that lost the reality of Christ's humanity in the second and third centuries, protecting the divine from suffering or change. For instance, a sharp distinction was made between Jesus and the Christ (Cerinthus), or it was suggested that Jesus the Christ only appeared to be human (Marcion). In either case, the specter of "patripassianism" (the idea that God directly suffered on the cross) loomed, against which Tertullian notably contended. Meanwhile, Irenaeus led the charge against "gnostic" elements that Docetism reflected. The hermeneutic behind such movements will be manifest more indirectly today. Yet, one might argue that transpositions of passages about Jesus Christ into some more abstract "divine" reality—opened via some philosophical or cultural key—are perennial, as demonstrated by defenses of Gnosticism among some mainline Christians, and de facto Gnosticism among some conservatives.

In the fourth century, *Arianism* erred on the Ebionite side, although in a rather subtle and often compelling way. Saying that Jesus Christ was the Son of God, Arius nevertheless seemed to say that he was the first (and only a) creature. "There was a time when he was not"; hence, Arianism denied the self-existence and eternity of the Son, thereby contending that he was *homoiousios* (of similar substance) but not *homoousios* (of one or the same being, the eventual orthodox formulation) with God the Father. Arius's Christ protected the grandeur of God by, in the end, being nothing more than a mediating creature. Hermeneutical temptations here include again protecting the humanity of the Son in salvation, but more subtly adopting a philosopher's God, with whom the Logos could not be in the beginning.

Athanasius, exiled five times as the church's imperial battle raged back and forth, is the orthodox hero in vanquishing Arianism. For him, the incarnation of the Son was vital because of a *theiōsis* soteriology: God must take on the human substance in order to communicate divine being to humanity. Salvation is a matter of sharing in the power of the risen immortal Christ, not simply a sophisticated human ascent. It might be said that Athanasius's Christology was as "Word-flesh" as Arius's; because of soteriology Athanasius affirmed the divinity of this Word, while Arius did not. Accordingly, a heresy naturally emerged on the other side. *Apollinarianism* saw the incarnation as the Logos replacing the human mind or will of Jesus Christ—in a sense, a form of monophysite (or, one-nature) Christology. The hermeneutical struggle is subtle, for biblical passages do not directly specify when they are speaking of "person" or "nature," or that to which such terms refer.

Antiochene "Word-Man" Christology. By contrast to Alexandria, Antioch would approach Christology more "from below" than "from above." Its hermeneutics were less allegorical and more literal (not in a constricted modern sense but in a richly canonical, typological, or figural sense). More Aristotelian in character, "Antiochene" or "Word-man" thinking saw a necessary connection between body and soul; God would be understood through and not apart from the world, so that the human Jesus was necessary for knowing the divine Logos. Theodore of Mopsuestia popularized the Cappadocian dictum that "what is not assumed is not redeemed"—the Logos must have a human mind or will instead of replacing it.

Once the full divinity and humanity of Jesus Christ had been reaffirmed in 381, Antiochene ascendancy naturally raised the question of their relationship. Although the sources are scant and complex here as well, *Nestorianism* took the Antiochene extreme. Asked to rule on whether it was suitable to call Mary *Theotokos* (God-bearer), Nestorius demurred, worrying that it would imply either Arian or Apollinarian errors. But his position seemed adoptionist, de facto separating the two natures so that they formed only a moral but not an ontological union. As an extreme reaction, then, *Eutychianism* initiated a new monophysitism, in which the one nature was a sort of *tertium quid* that blended divine and human.

Chalcedon and the Later Middle Ages. Drawing heavily on Tertullian and the Eastern leader Cyril of Alexandria, Leo the Bishop of Rome produced his "Tome," a doctrinal letter that substantially informed the Definition of Chalcedon in 451. Chalcedonian Christology became basically the orthodox solution, although monophysite groups in the East (and some Nestorians) have continued to object. Chalcedon's solution was a sort of hermeneutical rule, drawing boundaries outside which the church might not go: the two natures were reaffirmed, and their union in one *hypostasis* without confusion (contra Eutychianism), separation (contra Nestorianism), and so on. The incarnation reveals but does not change the essence of what it means to be God or human.

Subsequently, *monothelitism* (the view that Jesus Christ had only one will) would be condemned (at Constantinople in 680). The coherence of trinitarian and christological dogma would be explored with ever-increasing analytic clarity, or speculation, depending on one's point of view. Thomas Aquinas is an intriguing later medieval figure, not only for the paradigmatic influence of his *Summa*, but also in view of his increased attention to Christ's humanity. Forms of Christ-devotion were ever more burgeoning, and in the West these forms often attended to the human vulnerability of Jesus in new ways (Williams, in Bockmuehl). He was simultaneously a terrifying Judge and a petitioner for sympathy. The earlier and Eastern emphasis on adoration of the cosmic Lord shifted in the West to the eucharistic host. This time period teaches us to pay attention to various kinds of texts, and indeed the variety of media and contexts in which Jesus Christ is rendered; such devotion expresses and may shape theological interpretation.

The Reformation. The Eucharist, in fact, became the center of christological controversy with the rise of the Protestant Reformation. Luther probably saw himself doing nothing new, except recovering a more biblical focus on Christ as God's justifying Word. Still, Philipp Melanchthon's Lutheran dictum "To know Christ is to know his benefits" would, transmogrified variously and in concert with "quests for the historical Jesus" (discussed elsewhere), shape the modern age decisively, as exemplified in Friedrich Schleiermacher and Rudolf Bultmann (Tanner).

The Eucharist debate among the Reformers remains instructive, however. Luther eschewed what he saw as the crudity of "transubstantiation" in Roman Catholicism, along with the excessive speculation of scholasticism's "theology of glory," which retained the dignity of the philosophers' terrifying God in place of the radically self-giving God revealed in Jesus ("theology of the cross"). Yet Luther also retained a bodily presence of Christ "in, with, and under" the sacramental elements, not only based on a "literal" reading of John 6 and "This is my body," but also because he perceived the alternatives to be Nestorian. On his understanding of orthodoxy's *communicatio idiomatum* ("communication of attributes" or "properties"), the human nature of Jesus must share in the divine ubiquity; for Zwingli to insist that Christ's body was only present in heaven was a heretical division of the natures of the God-man.

John Calvin's effort at a mediating position remains complex. The Reformed tradition generally has taken the *communicatio idiomatum* to occur at the level of the person rather than between the natures. Calvin argued against the Lutheran line regarding what literal exegesis of "This is my body" must conclude; regarding biblical texts concerning heaven, divine omnipresence, and their relation to the human; and regarding what view of the Eucharist would be adequately trinitarian, taking the humanity of Christ and a distinct role for the Holy Spirit seriously enough. In the so-called "Extracalvinisticum" he affirmed with Augustine and other forebears that the Second Person of the Godhead remained omnipresent even while incarnate, whether on earth or in heaven.

Calvin also took up from predecessors Christ's threefold office of Prophet, Priest, and King, which has remained influential (see Wainwright's exposition). The foundation he thought was biblical: these were the anointed OT offices that the

Messiah would fulfill—proclaiming the divine Word of wisdom to us, gaining divine favor for us, and strengthening us for eternal victory over evil.

Hermeneutically, the Reformers probably saw themselves as producing kerygmatic and biblical-theological Christologies more than strongly systematic Christologies. Still, for all their commitment to *sola scriptura* and concern about scholastic speculation, they could not avoid logical struggles and appeal to traditional formulations. The Christ-narrative was primary but provoked discussions of necessity, of traditional but biblically tricky items such as the descent into hell, and so on. Karl Barth may add another lesson here: he placed Luther in a line of Johannine emphasis running toward Eutyches, with Calvin following the Synoptic Gospels' focus that heads toward Nestorius (*CD* I/2:24). Accused at points of erring on both sides, Barth felt we must instead pursue a strategy of "juxtaposition" regarding the two approaches, opting to balance them in the long run rather than trying to say the whole truth all at once.

Modern Collapse of Scripture's Christ-Narrative

As hinted earlier, the modern age pressured the "incarnational narrative" both historically and hermeneutically. Rising historical consciousness, embedded in certain philosophical commitments, provoked doubt over the Bible's supernatural claims. Beyond challenges between OT and NT, and within the NT regarding the identity of Jesus Christ in relation to God, incoherence was alleged between the biblical witnesses and the orthodox creeds (e.g., Harnack's legacy).

The response of "liberal" (ever a slippery term) forms of Christianity was generally to accept significant reductions in the historical truth status of the biblical story. Hans Frei has generalized that the early modern English were more willing to deny straightforwardly the Bible's christological narrative, whereas the Germans tended more piously to salvage its truth by understanding its meaning in an alternative conceptual scheme. Jesus has therefore been a great moral teacher, a supreme example of religious consciousness, more recently an egalitarian revolutionary, etc.

Meanwhile, grossly oversimplifying, we may develop two basic lines of response among the confessionally orthodox. Responding with "Nein!" to modern religion, Barth returned the biblical Jesus Christ to the center of dogmatics—to some extent, a revolution in theological content for liberals and conservatives alike. Barth sought a revolution in form as well, suffusing his dogmatics with Christology throughout rather than treating it primarily in a few distinct or even isolated sections. A unique interweaving of reconciliation (his most basic soteriological category) and revelation (the modern preoccupation) was crucial to this, and the architecture of *Church Dogmatics* IV on reconciliation is striking. For example, in his strategy of juxtaposition, Barth tied obedience to the Son of God, exaltation to the Son of Man, and glory to his mediatorial role. The latter refers to narrative identification of the divine and human with/in the concrete person named Jesus Christ, not to a sphere of distinct action such as the other two. That concrete person or "mode of being" is also the revelation per se of "God himself." A singular convergence between God's act and triune being comes in the doctrine of election: in Jesus Christ (as both the electing God, and the elected and rejected human) God has constituted himself as being always for us. Much of Barth's most interesting christological exegesis may be found in that discussion.

While appreciative, Wolfhart Pannenberg has worried with Dietrich Bonhoeffer about Barth's "revelatory positivism." Pannenberg has attempted a new understanding of history in which its meaning is only finalized eschatologically, but Christ's resurrection proleptically enables a certain confidence. Criticizing modern notions that exclude the Christian faith, he has constructed a Christology "from below" that ends up with the creedal Jesus as the Son of God. Emphasis on public historical argument may also be found in the work of biblical scholars such as N. T. Wright, who has learned enough philosophy of history to address the possibilities of "quests for the historical Jesus" theologically. Most recently he has made an argument for the resurrection's high probability, once Jesus is set in the context of first-century Judaism and the development of the early church. By contrast, many have continued in Barth's legacy, especially as extended by Frei, with an emphasis on literary study of how the Gospels identify Jesus Christ, and then on kerygmatic presentation. Others appreciate elements of both strategies and create a variety of nuances along the spectrum.

The Hermeneutics of Contemporary Reconstructions

As we sift through the rubble of postmodern Christologies, perhaps surprisingly we find treasures new and old—possibly even a solid foundation standing firm. Three queries about the legacy of Chalcedon offer a way to organize efforts at reconstruction.

(How) Can We Accept Chalcedon's Content? For some Christians, and surely for Western culture at large, the legacy of Chalcedonian Christology remains incredible. Even if the challenges were adequately addressed regarding its supernatural claims, there would still be the apparent philosophical impossibility of *these* two natures being united in one person, and the temptation of psychological inquiry into what must have been the consciousness of one living such a life. The former continues to receive sophisticated treatment (surveyed, e.g., by C. S. Evans, in Davis et al., *Incarnation*), with "two-minds" or modified "kenotic" Christologies being the most promising alternatives to paradox. Psychology probably influenced the popularity of process-oriented Christologies for a time (e.g., Macquarrie), but the hermeneutical question remains: To what extent can views claim to be faithfully Chalcedonian if they somewhat vaguely aim to fulfill its "governing intention" only?

In a sophisticated treatment of christological models and methodologies, John McIntyre reflects on that question. He rejects not only the more original "anhypostatic" framework that Chalcedon implied (in which the Son's human nature is without *hypostasis*, or impersonal—to avoid adoptionism and the like), but also the subsequent "enhypostatic" framework in which Leontius of Byzantium stated a similar point (the Son's human nature is personal not independently but *in* the divine person of the Logos). In light of perceived philosophical and psychological problems for the Son's full humanity, McIntyre argues for an ontological union of divine and human *hypostases*. He nobly attempts to avoid Nestorianism, but most will have their doubts: should personhood be thought first from the human to the divine, or vice versa? And in any case, is not "person" something Jesus Christ "is," instead of something one "has" ("personality"; tied to "nature")? If the *communicatio idiomatum* is the essential point of the Chalcedonian solution (so Weinandy), and if enhypostatic Christology is ingredient to it, then our options seem limited.

The communication of properties is not an unambiguous hermeneutical rule (as the Reformers testify); indeed, "person" and "nature" are feeble categories with which we talk about the grammar of the biblical story, which is tied to the name Jesus Christ. There are passages hinting at two aspects of his reality (e.g., Phil. 2)—but divinity and humanity are secondary abstractions regarding this singular primary being. We cannot apply preconceived notions to our Lord or to passages about him, so much as use such categories *post facto* for describing the mystery of the incarnation.

(How) Can We Adopt Chalcedon's Categories? What then of Chalcedon's dependence upon substance metaphysics? This relates again to the nature of its claims—and of our own pursuit of truth.

Chalcedon's boundary language—"without . . ."—regarding substances seems static compared to the dynamism of the Gospel narrative. Are these boundaries only analytical—grammatical and hermeneutical—but not metaphysical? Some seize on this issue and take the point further, turning incarnation solely into metaphor; others in a backlash take Chalcedon's language to be straightforwardly literal. Having surveyed these contemporary options, Sarah Coakley suggests instead that Chalcedon is riddle-like, using negatives to point out a horizon of Christian vision while distancing the incarnation from conceptual grasp (in Davis et al., *Trinity*).

In other words, Chalcedon makes metaphysical claims according to a certain theological (rather than post-Kantian) apophatic approach that preserves the divine mystery. Linguistic rules have great value within such an approach. Thus we may fulfill "the law of prayer is the law of faith"—an early church slogan that suggested not only salvation, but also worship, is at stake in Christology.

Recent work on early Christianity has shown how fitting are these rules. Yeago has countered Dunn's representative claims about Paul having a nonincarnational Christology (in contrast to John), by showing that the differences deal with conceptual expression; the underlying theological judgments are similar. Paul's use of Isaiah in Phil. 2:6–11 is a test case in which, with hermeneutical precision about the proper role of concepts vis-à-vis judgments, the conclusions of the Nicene Creed biblically follow.

Moreover, Bauckham counters the widely held scholarly narrative of Jesus Christ's ascent to Hellenistic divinity in the creeds, via intermediate steps, through Jewish angelomorphic or exalted-patriarch Christologies. He replaces the usual disjunction between "ontic" (being) and "functional" (act) Christologies with the Jewish distinction between who may and may not be worshipped: principal angels and exalted patriarchs never properly receive worship, according to almost all first-century Jewish literature. Yahweh alone may be worshipped, and this divine identity is tied to three actions: creation, sovereign rule, and the redemption by which that rule is extended over the whole creation. Again, Isaiah is crucial, anticipating that the Servant of the new creation/exodus will be constitutive for more fully revealing the identity of Yahweh himself. Paul rightly reads the fulfillment of this trajectory to be Jesus Christ the incarnate, resurrected Lord. Bauckham illustrates that narrative christological thinking will continue to raise questions about the traditional divine attributes such as impassibility—although the answers may surprise us if we are respectful of classic incarnational doctrine (so, e.g., Weinandy).

It is intriguing to what extent Chalcedon's approach to theological categories might have broader use. Parallels between the divinity and humanity of Christ, and the doctrine of Scripture, are discussed elsewhere—as are models of christological or trinitarian oneness and multiplicity with reference to other doctrines. The doctrine of God might be especially connected to Christology in the form of its categories—the incarnation is surely singular but also revealing (!) about the relations between God and world, divine act and being, various divine attributes, and the like. This may entail a certain reserve about using models that positively "solve" problems in the doctrine of God, versus instead negating errors and narrating the mystery of salvation so as to make space for proper worship. Christology may teach us a hermeneutic both rigorous and apophatic. In any case, focus on the interconnections between worship and salvation not only brings patristic seeds of theological exegesis back into bloom. It also has borne historical fruit—being broadly consistent with, for example, the recent work of Hurtado on early Christ-devotion in the context of Jewish monotheism.

(How) Can Chalcedon Go Global? Christ-devotion is, of course, burgeoning throughout much of the world and in particular in the global South. Western theological interpreters who neglect the resulting christological harvest shall be malnourished (for survey and some bibliography, see Kärkkäinen); after all, both the junk food and what is healthy, savory fare from the West are themselves local theologies!

To be sure, there are challenges in relating some global Christologies to biblical expressions. In particular, models of atonement are increasingly contested, along with the propriety of problem-to-solution connections between Christology

and soteriology—doctrinal constants that have seemed essential to the biblical narrative until the "New Perspective on Paul" and the plurality of postmodern communities and concerns (Lowe).

However, such melting-pot or mixing-bowl questions have been asked first and foremost of the Bible itself! Following Chalcedon, and associated efforts that protect the mystery of worship and the narrative of salvation with some agreed-upon Christian language, promotes doctrinal freedom within parameters for the variety of local witness. Such a model for theological exegesis will be increasingly important in a world of religiously plural reactions to Jesus (for samples of which, see Ford and Higton). Biblical fidelity and freedom connect when "the law of prayer is the law of faith," while we also maintain "what is not assumed is not redeemed." Global concerns support Wright's mission "to get the question of Jesus back on the agenda when people are talking about Christology" (Wright 49, in Davis et al., *Incarnation*). Liberationists especially have insisted that Jesus' humanity—when this uniquely Christian story of God is taken seriously—forces open Western enclaves while grounding and connecting local projects (for historical examples of the theological point, see Walls).

Attending to the human and the historically particular, as required by Christology, requires accordingly that Christology be developed with attention to the full array of biblical materials. Christological hermeneutics should not substitute generalizations about the form of other subjects for the content of the Bible regarding Jesus Christ and his meaning for those subjects. The biblical story is, for example, strikingly political, but not by way of a generic "incarnational" theme. Instead, we must be humbled by a theology of the cross, face the demand implied by naming him "Lord" in baptism, and so on. Nor is the cross a principle to be wielded by human reason or winsome to cultural sensibilities (1 Cor. 1–2) about advocacy groups; we must have hermeneutics that accept its scandalous biblical particularity.

In Christ, then, theological interpretation connects to both worship and salvation. For the sonship and servanthood that are such prominent christological themes in the Bible connect us to Jesus in faith by way of testing (Moberly). He is Yahweh, condescending to forgive our failure and singularly fulfill the human vocation, but he is again and ultimately forming a people that will live according to his human pattern. Christ is therefore the meeting point in which our interpretations can be acts of humble adoration (wherein we participate in adoration of the Father with him; so Torrance), yet also human acts—seeking faithful understanding. Whether or how we might have our eyes opened, in childlike faith (on which Thompson reflects) to recognize Jesus, itself tests us—even as Christ himself meets us in this too (Moberly). Hence, Luke 24 has been a pinnacle of recent reflection on theological interpretation, and on Christology as its orienting vision. May our communion—both sacramental and ordinary—set the context for interpretation that realizes the true identity of Jesus Christ.

See also Incarnation; Jesus, Quest for the Historical; Jesus and Scripture; Messiah/Messianism; Rule of Faith; Scripture, Unity of

Bibliography

Bauckham, R. *God Crucified*. Eerdmans, 1998; Bockmuehl, M., ed. *Cambridge Companion to Jesus*. Cambridge University Press, 2001; Davis, S. T., et al., eds. *The Incarnation*. Oxford University Press, 2002; idem. *The Trinity*. Oxford University Press, 2000; Dunn, J. D. G. *Christology in the Making*. 2d ed. Eerdmans, 1996; idem. *Jesus Remembered*. Eerdmans, 2003; Ford, D., and M. Higton, eds. *Jesus*. Oxford Readers. Oxford University Press, 2002; Frei, H. *The Eclipse of Biblical Narrative*. Yale University Press, 1974; Grillmeier, A. *Christ in Christian Tradition*, trans. J. Bowden. 2 vols. in 3. John Knox, 1975–96; Hunsinger, G. "Karl Barth's Christology." Pages 127–42 in *Cambridge Companion to Karl Barth*, ed. J. Webster. Cambridge University Press, 2000; Hurtado, L. *Lord Jesus Christ*. Eerdmans, 2003; Kärkkäinen, V.-M. *Christology: A Global Introduction*. Baker Academic, 2003; Lowe, W. "Christ and Salvation." Pages 235–51 in *Cambridge Companion to Postmodern Theology*, ed. K. Vanhoozer. Cambridge University Press, 2003; Macquarrie, J. *Jesus Christ in Modern Thought*. SCM, 1990; McIntyre, J. *The Shape of Christology*. 2d ed. T&T Clark, 1998; Moberly, R. W. L. *The Bible, Theology, and Faith*. Studies in Christian Doctrine. Cambridge University Press, 2000; Powell, M. A., and D. Bauer, eds. *Who Do You Say That I Am?* Westminster John Knox, 1999; Tanner, K. "Jesus Christ." Pages 245–72 in *Cambridge Companion to Christian Doctrine*, ed. C. Gunton. Cambridge University Press, 1997; Thompson, W. *The Struggle for Theology's Soul*. Crossroad, 1996; Torrance, A. "Being of One Substance with the Father." Pages 49–61 in *Nicene Christianity*, ed. C. Seitz. Brazos, 2001; Wainwright, G. *For Our Salvation*. Eerdmans, 1997; Walls, A. *The Cross-Cultural Process in Christian History*. Orbis, 2002; Weinandy, T. *Does God Suffer?* T&T Clark, 2000; Wright, N. T. *The Resurrection of the Son of God*. Christian Origins and the Question of God 3. Fortress, 2003; Yeago, D. "The New Testament and the Nicene Dogma." Pages 87–100 in *The Theological Interpretation of Scripture*, ed. S. Fowl. Blackwell, 1997.

Daniel J. Treier

Jesus Christ, Return of *See* Hope; Kingdom of God; Last Things, Doctrine of

Jesus Christ, Titles of *See* Jesus Christ, Doctrine of

Jewish-Christian Dialogue

Until about a generation ago, Jewish-Christian dialogue hardly featured in the context of theological interpretation of Scripture. One would expect to find such dialogue primarily in relation to Israel's Scriptures, since these texts are both Jewish Scripture (Tanak) and Christian Scripture (OT). Yet, if one looks at the landmark OT theologies of Walther Eichrodt (1961) and Gerhard von Rad (1965), Jewish-Christian dialogue simply does not feature. If comments about Judaism are found, they are regularly of a pejorative kind (see the memorable picture of a Jewish boy encountering biblical criticism in Chaim Potok's *In the Beginning*), very much in the tradition of Wellhausen (see Levenson 1–61). The sphere of NT study was hardly different in this regard. Bultmann had little to say about Judaism (except with regard to the influence of Hellenistic Judaism upon NT thought), and what he did say was rarely complimentary. Occasional works considering both Jewish and Christian perspectives can be found, such as Martin Buber's *Two Types of Faith*; though this a little too easily reads as a Jew repaying in kind to Christians the kind of sophisticated misrepresentation and pejorative assessment that Christians have regularly directed toward Jews.

The contemporary situation is different, at least in most scholarly contexts (though Christian disinterest in, or negative assessments of, Jewish faith—and vice versa—can still be found in many contexts). There are various reasons for this—horror at the Holocaust, the pressures of secularized indifference to Christianity and Judaism, a growing number of Jewish participants in academic biblical study, the recognition that Christians have often misrepresented Judaism (Sanders, among others, has been influential here). Whatever the reasons, Christians and Jews are realizing that, for all their differences, they share greater common ground than they have sometimes realized, and that therefore the perpetuation of older attitudes and assumptions is at best ignorance and at worst sin. Not only Christians (see, e.g., Braybrooke, *Time to Meet*) but also Jews (see, e.g., *Dabru Emet*, with responses by Christians, in Pannenberg et al.) are trying to articulate fresh ways of understanding and relating to the sibling faith in constructive dialogue.

Dialogue, properly understood, should not (though unfortunately sometimes it does) mean marginalizing or downplaying the distinctive beliefs and practices of Christians and Jews. Rather, it represents an attitude of respect and constructive engagement, whose aims are understanding and friendship, and whose long-term outcome cannot be predicted.

Within OT studies the transformed ethos is evident in the way von Rad's former pupil Rolf Rendtorff has made Jewish-Christian dialogue into a focal point for theological interpretation. The two most influential Christian OT theologians of recent years, Brevard Childs and Walter Brueggemann, both (in different ways) take seriously Jewish interpretations of those biblical texts they themselves interpret as Christians. From a Jewish perspective Jon Levenson has argued in theory and demonstrated in practice the kind of difference that should (and should not) be made by interpreting the biblical text within the wider context of Judaism.

Childs's and Levenson's accounts of the difference that a Jewish-Christian perspective may make are instructive. Both recognize the legitimate anxiety that theological perspectives may too quickly prejudge interpretive issues in favor of understandings congenial to traditional Jewish or Christian theologies; so they both insist on the disciplines of philological and historical criticism to promote self-critical scholarly integrity. But both see as crucial the wider context, or frame of reference, within which such disciplined work is done. The believer can simultaneously inhabit a tightly defined academic context, in which certain faith-related questions and concerns may be bracketed out, and a more broadly defined community-of-faith context, where a wider range of texts, practices, understandings, and experiences creates resonances and insights that would not otherwise be possible. Just as a faith perspective can be both bracketed out and incorporated in relation to a nonfaith perspective, so can a Christian perspective be both bracketed out and included in relation to a Jewish perspective, and vice versa. Childs and Levenson thus each revive—though only in a fundamentally reconceived way—the ancient and medieval affirmation of different senses, or multiple level readings, of Scripture.

Childs, for example, says: "Because of the experience of the Gospel, a Christian rightly renders the Old Testament ultimately in a different way from the Jew" (*Biblical*, 335). "But how can one claim to read Isaiah as the voice of Israel in the Hebrew Scripture and at the same time speak of its witness to Jesus Christ? It is not only possible, but actually mandatory for any serious Christian theological reflection. Because Scripture performs different functions according to distinct contexts, a multi-level reading is required even to begin to grapple with the full range of Scripture's role as the intentional medium of continuing divine revelation" ("Does?" 63).

Levenson, for example, says:

In the realm of historical criticism, pleas for a "Jewish biblical scholarship" or a "Christian biblical scholarship" are senseless and reactionary. Practicing Jews and Christians will differ from uncompromising historicists, however, in affirming the meaningfulness and interpretive relevance of larger contexts that homogenize the literatures of different periods to one degree or another. Just as text has more than one context, and biblical studies has more than one method, so scripture has more than one sense, as the medievals knew and Tyndale, Spinoza, Jowett, and most other moderns have forgotten. As the context gets larger, Jews and Christians can still work together, as each identifies imaginatively with the other's distinctive context. But imagined identities are only that, and if the Bible (under whatever definition) is to be seen as having coherence and theological integrity, there will come a moment in which Jewish-Christian consensus becomes existentially impossible. (104)

In terms of the differences that such perspectives can make to specific exegesis, Moberly on Gen. 22 offers a reasonably detailed case study (71–161, esp. 154–61). There is a growing dialogical literature, of which Bellis and Kaminsky (215–385) provide an instructive example.

See also Anti-Semitism; Israel; Relationship between the Testaments

Bibliography

Bellis, A., and J. Kaminsky. *Jews, Christians, and the Theology of the Hebrew Scriptures*. SBL, 2000; Braybrooke, M. *Time to Meet*. SCM/Trinity, 1990; Buber, M. *Two Types of Faith*, trans. N. Goldhawk. Routledge & Kegan Paul, 1951; Childs, B. *Biblical Theology of the Old and New Testaments*. SCM, 1992; idem. "Does the Old Testament Witness to Jesus Christ?" Pages 57–64 in *Evangelium, Schriftauslegung, Kirche*, ed. J. Adna et al. Vandenhoeck & Ruprecht, 1997; Eichrodt, W. *Theology of the Old Testament*, trans. J. Baker. 2 vols. SCM, 1961; Frymer-Kensky, T., et al. *"Dabru Emet."* *ProEccl* 11 (2002): 5–7; Levenson, J. *The Hebrew Bible, the Old Testament, and Historical Criticism*. Westminster John Knox, 1993; Moberly, R. W. L. *The Bible, Theology, and Faith*. Cambridge University Press, 2000; Pannenberg, W., et al. "A Symposium on *Dabru Emet*." *ProEccl* 11 (2002): 8–19; Potok, C. *In the Beginning*.

Knopf, 1975; Rad, G. von. *Old Testament Theology*, trans. D. Stalker. 2 vols. SCM, 1965; Rendtorff, R. *Canon and Theology*, trans. M. Kohl. Fortress, 1993; Sanders, E. P. *Paul and Palestinian Judaism*. SCM, 1977.

R. W. L. Moberly

Jewish Context of the NT

An understanding of the Jewish context of early Christianity is essential for the theological interpretation of Scripture, particularly the NT. Jesus was a Jew, his first followers were Jews, and the movement he initiated was Jewish. Many of the NT authors were Jewish, and until the end of the first century, Jews continued to make up a significant proportion of the many Christian communities that sprang up around the Mediterranean. It was only in the second century that the Christian movement parted ways with Judaism, but even then the new faith continued to find much of its theological inspiration in the Jewish Scriptures and in Jewish traditions of interpreting those Scriptures.

Historical Overview

The Persian Period (539–333 BCE). Judaism emerged during the exile of Judah in Babylon (586–539 BCE), where the ancient religion of Israel underwent a transformation. When the decree of Cyrus the Persian allowed Judean exiles to return to their homeland, only a modest number took the opportunity. Among the major events of the early postexilic period were the final editing and codification of the Torah; the rebuilding of the temple (520–515 BCE), though on a much humbler scale than the temple of Solomon; the religious and social reforms of Ezra, who promulgated the Torah as the law of the land and put an end to mixed marriages; the rebuilding of Jerusalem's walls under the direction of Nehemiah, a Persian-appointed Babylonian Jew; and the emergence of the high priesthood as the locus of leadership. Several late books of the Hebrew Bible were written during this period, including historical, prophetic, and possibly some of the wisdom books.

Ancient Israelite religion was tied to the land, the status of nationhood, and the monarchy. It was based on ancestral traditions that were not yet in their definitive written form. Postexilic Judaism, however, developed in totally changed circumstances: the people of Israel-Judah had lost control of their land, which became a province in a succession of foreign empires, with no status as an independent nation and no native kingship. What they did have, though, was a definitive

written code of instruction, the Torah of Moses. The changed political situation also brought with it a change in religious understanding. Specific theological beliefs, either absent or undeveloped in the religion of Israel, came to develop. These included the apocalyptic notions of resurrection and eternal life, with postmortem rewards and punishments, as well as developed thinking about Satan, angels, and demons. The touchstone of Israelite religion, worship of only one God, took on a more decisive form beginning in Babylon (Isa. 40–55), to become in the postexilic period a full-fledged monotheism, the chief hallmark of Jewish theology.

The Hellenistic Period (333 BCE–63 BCE). The next great watershed in Jewish history came with Alexander the Great's conquest of the ancient Near East, from Greece to western India, including Palestine (333–323 BCE). After defeating the Persian Empire, the young Macedonian fostered a fusion of Greek and oriental cultures (Hellenism). The Greek polis and its institutions—gymnasia, racetracks, amphitheaters, public baths—sprang up all over the East. After his death, Alexander's generals divided up his empire. Palestine was ruled at first by the Ptolemies (301–198 BCE), a dynasty of Greek kings based in Egypt, where a large and influential Jewish community was established and where the Hebrew Scriptures were translated into Greek, beginning in the third century BCE. The Jewish Diaspora in Egypt also produced a variety of Greek literature in classical genres, such as epic poetry, tragedy, and philosophical treatises. Writings produced by Jews in the eastern Diaspora include Esther, Tobit, and possibly the court tales in Dan. 1–6.

After the Ptolemies, Palestine fell under the sway of the Seleucids (198–142 BCE), a line of Greek rulers headquartered in Syria. The first real crisis faced by Palestinian Jews in the Hellenistic era came in the form of an unprecedented persecution by the Seleucid ruler Antiochus IV "Epiphanes" (175–164/3 BCE), whose motives remain puzzling. The backdrop of the persecution involved struggles between factions of Hellenizing and pious Jews in Jerusalem, and rival claims to the high priesthood. In 167 BCE Antiochus effectively outlawed the practice of Judaism by having copies of the Torah destroyed, forbidding circumcision and sacrifices, banning Sabbath observance and holy days, and forcing Jews to make offerings to pagan gods. After erecting and garrisoning a fortress in Jerusalem, he committed the ultimate blasphemy by entering the innermost sanctuary of the Jerusalem temple, erecting an altar to Zeus there, and ordering the sacrifice of pigs on it (1 Macc. 1:41–64; 2 Macc. 6:1–11).

This act touched off a revolt in 167 BCE led by a priest named Mattathias and his sons, dubbed the "Maccabees" after the nickname Maccabeus, "the Hammerer," given to Mattathias's son Judas (1 Macc. 2). After three years of guerrilla warfare and victories over the Syrians, Judas took control of Jerusalem and rededicated the temple in 164, an event celebrated to this day in the festival of Hanukkah (1 Macc. 4:36–61). Many scholars think that Dan. 7–12 was written and the entire book put into final form during the temple crisis. For the next twenty years or so, periods of armistice and renewed fighting alternated until Jewish military rule passed to the brothers of Judas: Jonathan (152–142 BCE) and Simon (142–134 BCE).

For a brief eighty-year period (142–63 BCE), the Maccabees established an independent Jewish state, the only time in the Second Temple age when Jews ruled themselves. The dynasty bears the name "Hasmonean," after an ancestor of Mattathias named Hashmon. In 142 Judas's brother Simon crowned himself king and assumed the office of high priest. By investing both offices in himself, he enacted something that had never been done before. Eventually the dynasty was weakened by squabbles over succession; it came to an end when the Romans conquered Palestine in 63 BCE. Through the Hasmoneans may have been popular with the masses, many pious Jews resented them because they adopted Hellenistic ways and ruled like pagan monarchs, and because they combined the offices of king and high priest.

The Roman Period (63 BCE–135 CE). By the first century BCE, Jews were a visible minority in the Roman Empire, numbering some five or six million in a population of fifty to sixty million. After conquering Jerusalem, the Roman general Pompey installed the Hasmonean John Hyrcanus II (63–40 BCE) as high priest and *ethnarch* ("ruler of the people"). Palestine now became a puppet state of Rome. As their client king, the Romans eventually appointed Herod the Great (37–4 BCE), an Idumean who through a series of massive construction projects left the most indelible mark on the land of any Jewish ruler. Among his extensive building programs were a refurbished Jerusalem temple and the seaside resort city of Caesarea Maritima. Infamous for political cunning and ruthlessness, he had three of his sons and one of his wives executed. After his death,

Herod's kingdom was divided among his three surviving sons: Herod Archelaus (4 BCE–6 CE) got Judea, Idumea, and Samaria; Herod Antipas (4 BCE–39 CE) received Galilee and Perea; and Herod Philip II (4 BCE–34 CE) ruled in the area northeast of Galilee. From 6 CE to the outbreak of the first Jewish revolt against Rome in 66, the Romans ruled Judea through their own prefects, the most notorious of whom was Pontius Pilate (26–36 CE).

A host of factors led the Jews of Palestine to revolt against the Romans in 66–70 CE. Among them were economic hardship and accompanying social unrest fueled by famine and the oppressive tax policies of the Romans, which took upward of 30 percent of the income of the typical Jewish farmer. Also significant was Jewish nationalist sentiment fomented by revolutionary groups like the Zealots, and heightened end-time hopes and messianic expectations fueled by royal pretenders and would-be messiahs. Last but not least was the offensive leadership of the Roman procurators, such as Florus, who in the year 66 CE pilfered the temple treasury and permitted his troops to ransack the city as he tried to gain control of the temple.

An unofficial declaration of war ensued when the lower priests and revolutionary leaders in Jerusalem terminated the sacrifices offered on behalf of Rome and the emperor, much to the consternation of the chief priests and leading Pharisees, whose opposition sparked a civil war among pro- and anti-Roman factions. The historian Josephus provides a most circumstantial account of the conflict in *The Jewish War*; his other great work, *The Jewish Antiquities*, is a major source for our knowledge of the entire Second Temple period. Though the Romans largely quelled the insurrection by the year 70, when they destroyed Jerusalem and the temple, it was not until 73 that the last Jewish rebels perished, after taking refuge atop the Judean mountain fortress of Masada. A second Jewish revolt, put down by the Romans in 132–35 CE, was led by a self-proclaimed messiah, Simon Bar Kosiba, who took the messianic title *Bar Kochba*, "Son of the Star." The Romans crushed the rebellion and turned Jerusalem into a pagan city. Jewish life in Palestine shifted northward to Galilee.

Unity and Diversity: Common Theology and the Various Groups

The Four "Pillars": Monotheism, Covenant Election, Torah, Temple. Jews stood out in the Greco-Roman world by virtue of the antiquity of their religion, adherence to a religion of the book, and observance of ritual practices such as circumcision, Sabbath rest, and dietary restrictions. By the first century, Judaism was a diverse religion with several interest groups competing to represent the true heritage of Israel and its sacred traditions. With the exception of the Qumran Essenes, we cannot speak of "sects" since the very notion presumes deviations from an official, normative form of the religion—something that did not exist in the first century. There was, however, a Jewish common theology. The single most important belief was monotheism. Also important was the notion of covenant election: God had entered into a solemn pact with Israel at Mt. Sinai, choosing them to be his special possession and agents of redemption in the world, and graciously giving them his instruction in the (written) Law. As a token of his presence and favor, God had given Israel the land and caused his name to dwell in the temple, the one place where they were to offer sacrifices.

God, election, Torah, and temple: these constitute the core of common beliefs shared by virtually all religiously minded Jews; yet each of the four major tenets, and much else besides, was understood and applied in often competing ways. For example, many Jews expected God to act more or less directly in eschatological salvation, gathering the scattered tribes of Israel, bringing Gentiles to worship in Jerusalem, and establishing his universal reign of righteousness. Others, however, believed that God had used various mediator figures to accomplish his work in creation and history and that he would do so at the end of the age. The personified divine attributes of "word" and "wisdom" feature in Hellenistic Jewish texts as God's agents in creation. Also, a variety of intermediary figures—principal angels like Michael, exalted patriarchs such as Enoch, and four types of messiahs, royal, priestly, prophetic, and heavenly—play a role in the eschatological tableau of the Pseudepigrapha and the Dead Sea Scrolls (DSS). The notion of covenantal election was also embraced in a variety of ways. The Qumran Essenes, for instance, held a very exclusive, sectarian form of this doctrine. Likewise, the interpretation and implementation of the Torah was conceived quite differently among various Jewish groups, particularly on matters of ritual purity and sacrifices.

The temple itself was widely regarded as the center of the nation, the navel of the universe, the focus of identity for Jews living in the land of Israel as well as a source of pride for those in the Diaspora. Diaspora Jews such as Philo of Alexandria, however, often spiritualized the temple and its sacrificial system; even devout Jews in the homeland viewed the institution with ferocious ambivalence. On the one hand, it was the locus of God's presence, worth defending and even dying for in the threat of its profanation. On the other hand, it was run by priests whose manner of doing so met with vehement objections and whose very legitimacy was often questioned. In the eyes of fervently nationalist Jews, the temple was the seat of collaboration with Rome, corrupt beyond fair use. Some Jews expected it to be destroyed and replaced by a temple made by God in the new age. Others thought it was dispensable even in the present age. It is amid this variety of religious conviction and theological understanding that the various Jewish groups are to be placed.

Pharisees. The Pharisees were a lay movement whose name may mean something like "separatists." They devoted themselves to the exact interpretation of the written Torah and to the promulgation of their "oral Torah," traditions of interpreting and applying the written text (*B.J.* 2.162; *A.J.* 13.297; 17.41; *Vita* 91; cf. Mark 7:5; Matt. 15:2; Acts 22:3; 23:6–8). A key element of their social program was to extend the priestly regulations of ritual purity mandated in Leviticus to all Jews in all spheres of life. We have little specific knowledge of their internal organization or their social status and roles, but they seem to have formed themselves into a voluntary association, stood above the peasant and artisan classes, and functioned in a variety of administrative and educational settings. That they exerted an informal, popular influence is undeniable, but they never had control of either governmental or religious affairs. Only in the decades after 70 CE did they attain true predominance, since they were the only integrated Jewish group to survive the first revolt against Rome and to reconstitute Judaism on a new footing.

Next to Josephus, the apostle Paul is the only literary figure of the first century who can confidently be identified with Pharisaism. In a recitation of his pre-Christ Jewish pedigree, he says that he was "as to the Law, a Pharisee" (Phil. 3:5). Elsewhere he comments, "I advanced in Judaism beyond many among my people of the same age, for I was far more zealous for the traditions of my ancestors" (Gal. 1:14 NRSV). In both of these passages, Paul connects his former persecution of the Jesus movement with his zeal for the Torah, but his Pharisaism as such would hardly account for his violent acts. Acts portrays the apostle as a Christian Pharisee who maintained his devotion to the Torah. This portrait stands in some tension with the testimony of Paul's letters (e.g., Gal. 2:15–21; Phil. 3:7–11; Rom. 3:21–26; 10:4) without being totally at odds with it (e.g., 1 Cor. 9:19–21).

The Pharisees appear in the Synoptic Gospels, often coupled with the scribes (learned men, typically Pharisees [Mark 2:16; Luke 5:30], but not necessarily), as the principal antagonists of Jesus during his Galilean ministry. They debate with him over such halakic matters as Sabbath, fasting, tithing, food purity, and divorce (Mark 2:18–22, 23–28; 3:1–6; 7:1–23; 10:2–9; et par.). These issues are the very ones that figure in the earliest (pre-70 CE) traditions about the Pharisees in rabbinic literature. In the Synoptics the Pharisees also question Jesus' association with tax collectors and "sinners," demand a prophetic sign to validate his authority, and try to entrap him with a question about paying taxes to the Romans (Mark 2:15–17; 8:11–13; 12:13–17; et par.).

Even so, the Pharisees were probably the Jewish group to whom Jesus was the closest in his stance on matters of Torah piety. Matthew's portrayal of them as petty legalists and hypocrites (ch. 23) owes much to controversies between Pharisaic Jews and Christian Jews in the evangelist's own milieu. The exact reach of their influence in the time of Jesus is portrayed variously, with Mark limiting their appearance to the villages of Galilee, while Matthew expands their role and locates them in Judea and Jerusalem as well. Luke sustains the element of hostility between Jesus and the Pharisees but includes unique traditions favorable to them (e.g., Luke 13:31; Acts 5:34–39; 23:6–9). The Fourth Gospel places them in both Galilee and Judea (e.g., John 1:24; 3:1; 4:1; 7:32–52), virtually equates them with "the Jews," enlarges their leadership role in national and synagogue life (e.g., John 9), and allies them with the chief priests and Sanhedrin (11:46–47; 12:19, 42; 18:3). Missing in John are most of the debates over Torah piety; instead, objections to Jesus' healing on the Sabbath develop into charges that he makes himself out to be "equal to God" (John 5:18; cf. 8:13–30).

Sadducees. Sad to say, we know even less about the Sadducees than the Pharisees. The label probably derives from the name Zadok, the high priest in the time of David and Solomon. Many, perhaps most, of the Sadducees belonged to the Jerusalem aristocracy; at least a few high priests came from their ranks. There is no basis, though, for assuming that all aristocrats were Sadducees,

that all Sadducees were priests, or that the Sadducees made up the majority of the Sanhedrin. This common portrait represents a generalization drawn from a few modest statements in Josephus and Acts.

Another misleading but oft-repeated claim derived from Josephus is that the Sadducees recognized the authority of only the Pentateuch, the written Torah of Moses, with the implication that they did not accept the books of the Prophets or any of the books later included among the Writings. What Josephus actually says is that they rejected those laws of the Pharisees "not recorded in the laws of Moses" and that they observed nothing "apart from the laws" (*A.J.* 13.297; 18.17). What this probably means is simply that the Sadducees rejected (many of) the Pharisees' halakic positions. The Sadducees themselves surely propounded their own (stricter, more conservative) traditions of interpreting and applying the Torah—their own "oral torah," in effect. At any rate, there is no good reason to suppose that they acknowledged only the books of the Torah as authoritative.

Oddly enough, every tenet of Sadducean theology highlighted in the ancient sources entails a negative. According to Josephus (*B.J.* 2.164–65), the Sadducees rejected the idea of fate while affirming the free will and moral responsibility of human beings, as opposed to the Pharisees, who accepted both. They also (in contrast to the Pharisees) denied that the soul continues after death and therefore dispensed with the notion of postmortem rewards and punishments (*B.J.* 2.165; *A.J.* 18.16). This might mean that they believed in the extinction of the soul at death, but it might rather indicate that they subscribed to the ancient Israelite belief in Sheol as the realm where all the dead, just and unjust alike, go to lead the same shadowy existence. In the Synoptic tradition and Acts, their disbelief in the resurrection of the dead stands out (Mark 12:18–27 et par.; Acts 23:6–8). The formulation of Acts 23:8 is particularly striking: "The Sadducees say that there is no resurrection, or angel [*angelon*], or spirit [*pneuma*]; but the Pharisees acknowledge all three" (NRSV). A denial of angels would be odd in a group that accepted the Torah, and Josephus says nothing of this matter. Perhaps all that is meant is that they did not entertain the elaborate angelologies typical of some Jews (the Qumran Essenes, for instance). But if the words *angelon* and *pneuma* are taken as adverbial accusatives, the verse may be understood to suggest that they denied resurrection *as* or *in the form of* an angel or spirit.

The Sadducees appear far less frequently in the Synoptics than do the Pharisees. Matthew sometimes pairs the two groups against Jesus (16:1, 6, 11–12). The similarity of a few halakic positions registered in the DSS with stances attributed to the Sadducees in rabbinic literature—particularly those relating to the transmission of ritual impurity in liquid streams in 4QMMT and *m. Yad.* 4:7—has led some scholars to suggest that the Qumran sectarians were Sadducees and not Essenes. More likely, however, the priestly roots shared by both groups led to some shared halakic judgments. Besides, the developed angelology and strong determinism of the core sectarian texts among the DSS render a Sadducean identity for the Qumran group highly unlikely.

Essenes. Thanks to the DSS, we are better informed about the Essenes than any other Jewish group, and Josephus devotes more attention to them than to the others (*B.J.* 119–61; *A.J.* 18.18–22). Rather surprisingly, though, they are never mentioned in the NT, at least under a label that we can confidently associate with them. Most scholars regard the Scrolls as the library holdings of Essenes who installed themselves at Qumran off the northwest shore of the Dead Sea around 100 BCE. This consensus has survived several competing explanations posed over the last decade.

Pliny the Elder locates the Essenes off the northwest shore of the Dead Sea (*Nat.* 5.73), which is where Qumran lies. He notes that they were without women, renounced sexual desire, did without money, and lived in isolation. Josephus describes their procedures for admitting new members (*B.J.* 2.137–42), and both he and Philo comment on the communal ownership of property among the Essenes (Jos., *B.J.* 2.122; cf. Philo, *Prob.* 77) as well as their celibacy (Jos., *B.J.* 2.120–21; Philo, *Hypoth.* 11.14). All of these features, along with other parallels, are attested more or less clearly in the Qumran *Community Rule* (1QS).

The Essenes at Qumran may have been a breakaway group or else a subset of the wider Essene movement, which emerged in the middle of the second century BCE and whose membership Josephus places at four thousand. A celibate group with priestly origins and leadership, they pulled out of Jerusalem sometime in the mid to late second century BCE, protesting how the temple was being run. The DSS indicate that they objected to the temple's worldliness, the calendar in use there, the stance on ritual purity taken

by its leadership, and the illegitimacy and impiety of the Hasmonean high priesthood (e.g., CD 3.12–17; 4.13–19; 20.22–23 [= ms. B, 2.22–23]; 4QMMT). They eventually withdrew to the desert to practice an ascetic lifestyle in preparation for the end of the age. These Essenes devoted themselves to communal prayer, study, worship, meals, and ritual purity, as a surrogate temple in whose midst prayer and praise functioned as substitute sacrifices that would atone for the sins of the land (e.g., 1QS 5.4–7; 8.4–10; 9.3–6). An apocalyptic sect with a strongly dualistic and deterministic worldview, they considered themselves the only true Israelites, whom God would vindicate and exalt when he visited the earth in judgment. They expected a great final battle (1QM), and anticipated God using a variety of redemptive agents, including two messiahs, a priestly one and a royal one; a prophet; and the archangel Michael. The Qumran Essenes were wiped out in the summer of 68, although a few of them may have joined the last vestiges of Jewish resistance atop Masada.

The Essenes are particularly relevant to theological interpretation of the NT since Jesus and his followers shared much of the same apocalyptic worldview, minus the stark determinism and the sectarian withdrawal from mainstream society. The messianism of the DSS provides an important comparative vantage point from which to appreciate NT Christology. Three notable similarities between Essene and early Christian practice include the communal sharing of goods; the Essenes' daily ritual immersion in water and John's baptism; and the communal meals at Qumran and the Christian Lord's Supper. Each of these practices was undertaken with different theological understandings and took on distinctive forms, so the parallels should not be exaggerated. The DSS and the NT also share several parallels in terminology (e.g., "poor in spirit," "the Way," "works of the Law," and "the righteousness of God"), theological conceptions such as dualism, doctrines like justification by grace, and the expectation of a final battle and a new Jerusalem.

Fourth Philosophy and Other Resistance Movements. After his account of the Pharisees, Sadducees, and Essenes in book 18 of his *Jewish Antiquities*, Josephus devotes a section to a group he calls "the fourth philosophy." He identifies Judas the Galilean as the leader and notes that "this school agrees in all other respects with the opinions of the Pharisees, except that they have a passion for liberty that is almost unconquerable, since they are convinced that God alone is their leader and master. They think little of submitting to death in unusual forms and permitting vengeance to fall on kinsmen and friends if only they may avoid calling any man master" (*A.J.* 18.23). Judas and his followers regarded taxation as slavery and submission to it as a denial of God's sovereignty. With the aid of a Pharisee named Saddok, Judas incited a revolt in response to a census undertaken by Quirinius, the Roman legate of Syria, after Herod Archelaus was removed from office in 6 CE (*A.J.* 18.4–5; cf. *B.J.* 2.18; cf. Acts 5:37).

Josephus recounts several instances of social banditry during Herod's reign, during periods of especially harsh economic conditions. He also devotes considerable attention to royal pretenders who emerged after the death of Herod. At the start of the first Jewish revolt in 66 CE, two messianic movements took shape. Manahem captured the arsenal at Masada, proclaimed himself king in Jerusalem, and organized a siege of the palace. He was later murdered, but some of his followers returned to Masada. Simon bar Giora took control of Jerusalem from the Zealots and John of Gischala. After decking himself out in a white tunic and a purple cape, he was captured and executed in Rome. The most overtly messianic of the royal pretenders was the leader of the second Jewish revolt in 132–35, Simon bar Kosiba, who took the name bar Kochba, "son of a star," and minted coins bearing the inscription "Year 1 of the Redemption of Israel."

Josephus mentions a variety of popular prophets. Some of them engaged in symbolic actions regarded as tokens of eschatological salvation (such as leading people across the Jordan River); others delivered oracles of either deliverance or doom.

A group of urban assassins known as the Sicarii (after the Latin name for their weapon of choice, a small curved dagger known as a *sica*) began practicing their craft in Jerusalem in the 50s. According to Josephus, "This group murdered people in broad daylight right in the middle of the city. Mixing with the crowds, especially during the festivals, they would conceal small daggers beneath their garments and stealthily stab their opponents. Then, when their victims fell, the murderers simply melted into the outraged crowds, undetected because of the naturalness of their presence. The first to have his throat cut was Jonathan the high priest, and after him many were murdered daily" (*B.J.* 2.254–56). The targets of the Sicarii were the ruling elite in Jerusalem and pro-Roman members of the aristocracy who lived in rural areas. Hostage taking was also part of their strategy.

The Zealots came on the scene in the year 67 CE. So-called because of their revolutionary zeal, this movement originated among peasants in Galilee who fled to Jerusalem a year into the first Jewish revolt. In their effort to gain control of the city, they attacked members of the Herodian nobility and priestly aristocracy who wanted to sue for peace with the Romans, competed with other revolutionary factions, and of course joined in battling the Romans during the final siege. At one point, the Zealots were compelled by the forces of Ananus and Jesus son of Gamala, both chief priests, to take refuge in the inner court of the temple. They were eventually freed by outside supporters from the Idumeans, who killed Ananus and Jesus, and took vengeance on their enemies, including members of the nobility (*B.J.* 4.197–333). By the time the Romans laid their final siege to Jerusalem, the Zealots were the smallest of the rival revolutionary groups.

Priests. Josephus does not include the priests in his discussion, but they were the chief religious leaders in Judaism during the Second Temple period. To the extent that their secular overlords allowed it, they also exercised political control. Below the one high priest were chief priests, ordinary priests, and their assistants, the Levites. The ordinary priests together with the Levites probably numbered some twenty thousand in the first century (cf. *C. Ap.* 2.108), though only a tiny fraction of that number served in the temple at any one time. They took up their duties on a rotation of twenty-four courses or shifts for a week at a time (1 Chron. 24:4; *A.J.* 7.365; *m. Sukkah* 5:6). Among their tasks were inspecting and handling animals for sacrifice, butchering the sacrificial victims and cleaning up after the process, offering sacrifices on the altar, burning the appropriate parts and sorting the remaining portions for their own consumption or else that of the worshippers, reciting Scripture, conducting prayers, and burning incense. The Levites assisted them by carrying firewood into the temple precincts, manning the gates, and providing music.

The chief priests were probably comprised of former high priests and members of the principal families from whom the high priests were chosen (cf. *B.J.* 2.243; 6.114). The high priests traditionally stood in the line of Zadok, a succession that lasted with few interruptions until 172 BCE, when Antiochus IV appointed the Hellenophile Menelaus. During the Hasmonean era, the high priesthood was hereditary in the Maccabean family, from Simon's assumption of the office in 142 BCE until Herod began installing those of his own choosing. It is often assumed that the Hasmoneans were not from the line of Zadok, but there is no solid evidence of this.

The high priest presided over worship and sacrifice. He alone was permitted to enter the holy of holies every year on the Day of Atonement to offer mandated sacrifices. In the first century he was also the main political liaison answerable to the Roman prefect, who expected him to keep Jerusalem peaceful and the temple running smoothly. He also functioned as head of the Jewish council, the Sanhedrin, a judicial body that tried cases dealing with high crimes against Jewish law and whose members were drawn from both the clergy and lay orders, including scribes, Pharisees, Sadducees, "elders" (leading lay people from the aristocracy), and priests. According to the Mishnah, it had seventy-one members (*m. Sanh.* 1:6). Josephus reports that it once put the future King Herod on trial (*A.J.* 14.165–67). The Synoptic Gospels highlight the Sanhedrin's role in their narratives of Jesus' passion (Mark 14:53–65 et par.; cf. John 11:47–50), and Acts depicts it putting the apostles on trial (Acts 5:17–42 [cf. 4:1–22]; 22:30; 23:5). Whether the Romans granted the high priest and the Sanhedrin authority to issue the death penalty in capital cases remains disputed (cf. *A.J.* 14.177; John 18:31).

Others. In his treatise *On the Contemplative Life*, Philo of Alexandria describes a group called the *Therapeutae*, Jewish mystics who lived near Lake Mareotis in Egypt. Apart from their avoidance of wine and meat, they resembled the Essenes in several respects, including their practice of asceticism, celibacy, communal worship, and composition of hymns.

The *Samaritans* may be thought of as a Jewish sect, insofar as they shared much of the same Israelite heritage but were at odds with the Judaism practiced in Jerusalem. They called themselves *Shamerim*, "observers [of the Torah]," and claimed to be descendants of the tribes of Joseph. According to 2 Kings 17, though, they were a mixed population comprised of inhabitants of the old northern kingdom and foreign colonists whom the Assyrians forced to settle there when they conquered Israel in 722 BCE.

From the viewpoint of Jews in Judea, the Samaritans were apostates with an improper devotion to Yahweh, led by an illegitimate priesthood that presided over an errant cult centered in an unlawful temple located on the wrong site (Mt. Gerizim). Samaritan feelings for Jews were mutual. In their eyes, Judaism was a heresy that began with the Israelite priest Eli and that was continued by Ezra, whom they accused of corrupting the text of the Pentateuch, and Hillel, to whom they attributed false legal traditions. They revered only the Mosaic Torah, in a distinctive version (the Samaritan Pentateuch) that highlighted the sacred status of Mt. Gerizim, and regarded the second and third divisions of the Jewish Bible as the record of an apostate faith.

According to Ezra, the Samaritans were among those who tried to oppose the resettlement of Judean exiles in and around Jerusalem. In the second century BCE, the Samaritans had supported the Syrians against the Jews, and in 128 BCE John Hyrcanus conquered Samaria and destroyed the temple on Mt. Gerizim.

In Matthew, Jesus forbids his disciples from entering Samaritan territory (10:5), though Luke recounts the unfriendly welcome of some disciples of Jesus in a Samaritan village (9:51–55). According to Acts 8, the Christian mission to Samaria began only after Jesus' death, resurrection, and ascent to heaven. The Fourth Gospel, on the other hand, narrates the famous encounter between Jesus and a woman of Samaria. In its present form John 4 brings something of the post-Easter situation back into the earthly ministry of Jesus (esp. 4:35–38), which may indicate that there was a mission to the Samaritans at some point in the history of the Johannine community.

Conclusion

Attending to the historical context of Scripture is one of the first tasks in its interpretation. Indeed, the validity of an interpretation depends in part on how well it takes into account a biblical text's historical (not to mention literary) context. Thus, the task of engaging the Jewish context of the NT becomes an important hermeneutical responsibility. Such engagement has a theological rationale as well: it is one means of reckoning with the historical particularity of God's self-revelation in Jesus Christ. That context constitutes part of "the fullness of time" in which "God sent his Son, born of a woman, born under the law" (Gal. 4:4 NRSV). So, for examples, Jesus' teaching about the kingdom of God, his debates with Pharisees and Sadducees, his ethical directives in the Sermon on the Mount, and his solidarity with tax collectors and sinners—none of these issues in the Gospels can be comprehended apart from their mooring in first-century Jewish debates. Similarly, the richness and distinctiveness of NT Christology cannot be fully understood apart from its rooting in strands of early Jewish messianism and in reflection on God's Wisdom and Word. Nor, to cite a final example, can Paul's doctrine of justification by faith be understood apart from its setting in early Jewish and Christian disputes over what Gentiles needed in order to become members of God's covenant people. Of course, the word of God cannot be imprisoned in the past. For thoughtful Christians, historical study of Scripture will never be undertaken out of a mere antiquarian interest or regarded as an end in itself. Yet, since every page of the NT points beyond itself to historical realities outside the text, those realities must be taken into account if we are to read the Bible for all its worth.

See also Dead Sea Scrolls; Exile and Restoration; Jewish Exegesis; Messiah/Messianism; Roman Empire

Bibliography

Barclay, J. *Jews in the Mediterranean Diaspora from Alexandria to Trajan (323 BCE–117 CE).* T&T Clark, 1996; Barclay, J., and J. Sweet, eds. *Early Christian Thought in Its Jewish Context.* Cambridge University Press, 1996; Collins, J. *The Apocalyptic Imagination.* 2d ed. Eerdmans, 1998; idem. *Between Athens and Jerusalem.* 2d ed. Eerdmans, 2000; idem. *The Scepter and the Star.* Doubleday, 1995; Dunn, J. D. G. *The Partings of the Ways between Judaism and Christianity and Their Significance for the Character of Christianity.* SCM/Trinity, 1991; Grabbe, L. *Judaism from Cyrus to Hadrian.* 2 vols. Fortress, 1992; Horsley, R., and J. Hanson. *Bandits, Prophets, and Messiahs.* Winston, 1985; Hurtado, L. *One God, One Lord.* 2d ed. T&T Clark, 2003; Nickelsburg, G. W. E. *Ancient Judaism and Christian Origins.* Fortress, 2003; Saldarini, A. *Pharisees, Scribes and Sadducees in Palestinian Society.* Glazier/T&T Clark, 1989. Reprint, Eerdmans, 2001; Sanders, E. P. *Jesus and Judaism.* Fortress, 1985; idem. *Jewish Law from Jesus to the Mishnah.* SCM/Trinity, 1990; idem. *Judaism.* SCM/Trinity, 1992; idem. *Paul and Palestinian Judaism.* SCM/Fortress, 1977; Schürer, E. *The History of the Jewish People in the Age of Jesus Christ.* Rev. ed. Ed. G. Vermes et al. 3 vols. Vol. 3 in 2 vols. T&T Clark, 1973–87; VanderKam, J. *An Introduction to Early Judaism.* Eerdmans, 2000; Wright, N. T. *The New Testament and the People of God.* SPCK/Fortress, 1992.

Daniel C. Harlow

Jewish Exegesis

Jewish exegesis in late antiquity took many forms. It was pursued consciously and methodically, sometimes manifesting itself in informal, almost unconscious ways. There was no purely Jewish exegesis; rather, Jewish exegetes adopted and adapted forms and styles of interpretation of sacred literature practiced throughout the eastern Mediterranean world, including aspects of rhetoric developed in Greek-speaking contexts.

Nevertheless, a distinctive body of materials did emerge in Jewish circles, exemplifying interpretative approaches that are also found in the NT.

Targum

The Aramaic translations of Hebrew Scripture are known as targums (or *targumim*). They shed important light on biblical interpretation in Jewish circles in late antiquity and as such are part of a very important interpretative method that had developed, in which Scripture was translated, paraphrased, and rewritten. There are extant targums of every book of Scripture, with the exceptions of Ezra, Nehemiah, and Daniel. These books may not have been translated because parts of them are already in Aramaic.

How early Hebrew Scripture was translated into Aramaic is unknown. Most of the extant targums are products of the rabbinic period, dating from the fourth to tenth centuries CE. However, the discovery of at least one targum at Qumran (11QtgJob) and possibly two others (4QtgLeviticus; 4QtgJob) demonstrates that some targums existed in the first century BCE, perhaps even earlier. The impulse to translate Hebrew Scripture into Greek (the Septuagint, or LXX) for one Jewish constituency, which began in the third century BCE, may have coincided with a similar impulse to render Scripture into Aramaic for another constituency.

The targums originated in the synagogue and perhaps also the rabbinical academies, as homiletical and interpretative paraphrases of the passage of Hebrew Scripture that was to be read (such as the *haftarah*). Following the Babylonian and Persian exile (ca. 600–500 BCE) many of the Jewish people spoke Aramaic with greater ease than the cognate Hebrew, the language of Scripture. Therefore, it became useful to translate Hebrew Scripture into Aramaic (cf. Neh. 8; cf. *b. Meg.* 3a). The translator was called the *meturgeman* ("translator"). He recited his translation after the reading of the Hebrew passage.

The targums are sometimes literal, but more often they are paraphrastic and interpretative. Targums are part of the phenomenon sometimes called "rewritten Bible," though not identical to it. Rewritten Bible, as seen, for example, in *Jubilees* or Pseudo-Philo's *Biblical Antiquities*, freely omits, rearranges, and radically alters the biblical text. In comparison, targums are more conservative. Concern to update the text, answer questions raised by the text, even correct the text is seen in the targums.

Elements of targumic tradition are present in the NT. At several points Jesus' utterances and interpretation cohere with targumic tradition, especially as seen in the extant Isaiah Targum. Jesus' allusion to Isa. 6:9–10 in Mark 4:12 reflects the targumic diction ("forgive"), not the Hebrew or Greek ("heal"). Jesus' saying about perishing by the sword (Matt. 26:52) reflects Isa. 50:11 in the Aramaic, while linkage of Gehenna with Isa. 66:24 in Mark 9:47–48 also reflects Aramaic tradition. Jesus' admonition to his followers to be "merciful, as your Father [in heaven] is merciful" (Luke 6:36//Matt. 5:48) coheres with Lev. 22:28 in Aramaic (in Pseudo-Jonathan). Jesus' parabolic understanding of Isaiah's Song of the Vineyard (Isa. 5:1–7) and his use of it against the temple establishment in his similar parable (Mark 12:1–12 et par.) once again reflects acquaintance with the Aramaic tradition. The antiquity of this tradition is attested at Qumran (cf. 4Q500). Jesus' allusion to Lev. 18:5 in reference to "eternal life" (cf. Luke 10:25–28) once again reflects the Aramaic and once again is attested at Qumran (CD 3.12–20).

Targumic tradition is echoed in Paul as well. Perhaps the most important instance is seen in Rom. 10, where the apostle creatively applies Deut. 30:11–12 to Christ. At many points Paul's allusive paraphrase and exegesis cohere with the Aramaic paraphrase, especially as seen in *Targum Neofiti* (where instead of crossing the sea to fetch the law, we have reference to Jonah descending into the depths to bring it up).

Midrash

The Hebrew noun *midrash* is derived from the verb *darash*, which means to "search (for an answer)." Midrash accordingly means "inquiry," "examination," or "commentary." The word often refers to rabbinic exegesis, both with respect to method, as well as to form. Scholars therefore refer to midrashic interpretation and rabbinic midrashim. However, in recent years midrash has been discussed against the broader background of ancient biblical interpretation and textual transmission in general. It has become increasingly apparent that portions of the NT itself reflect aspects of midrash. Indeed, there has been considerable recent interest in ascertaining to what extent Jesus and the evangelists may have employed midrashic exegesis.

The verb *darash* occurs in a variety of contexts in the OT, meaning "to seek," "to inquire," or "to investigate." Scripture speaks of seeking God's will (2 Chron. 17:4; 22:9; 30:19; Ps. 119:10), making inquiry of God through prophetic oracle (1 Sam. 9:9; 1 Kings 22:8; 2 Kings 3:11; Jer. 21:2), or investigating a matter (Deut. 13:14; 19:18; Judg. 6:29; cf. 1QS 6.24; 8.26). The nominal form, *midrash*, occurs in the OT twice, meaning "story," "book," and possibly "commentary" (cf. NRSV: 2 Chron. 13:22; 24:27). In later usage there is a shift from seeking God's will through prophetic oracle to seeking God's will through study of Scripture. Later traditions tell us that Ezra the scribe "set his heart to search the law of the LORD" (Ezra 7:10 RSV). Other texts convey similar meanings: "Great are the works of the LORD, studied by all who have pleasure in them" (Ps. 111:2 RSV); "I have sought out your precepts" (Ps. 119:45; cf. vv. 94, 155); "Observe and seek out all the commandments of the LORD" (1 Chron. 28:8 RSV). Although this "searching" of God's law should not in these passages be understood as exegesis in a strict sense, it is only a small step to the later explicit exegetical reference of midrash: "This is the study [*midrash*] of the Law" (1QS 8.15); "The interpretation [*midrash*] of 'Blessed is the man . . .' [cf. Ps. 1:1]" (4QFlor 1.14). Indeed, the Teacher of Righteousness is called the "searcher of the Law" (CD 6.7). Philo urges his readers to join him in searching (*ereunan* = *darash*) Scripture (*Det.* 17 §57; 39 §141; *Cher.* 5 §14). In rabbinic writings midrash becomes standard and its practice as an exegetical method was consciously considered.

In the writings of the rabbis, midrash attains its most sophisticated and self-conscious form. In "searching" the sacred text, the rabbis attempted to update scriptural teaching to make it relevant to new circumstances and issues. This approach was felt to be legitimate because Scripture was understood as divine in character and therefore could yield many meanings and many applications: "'Is not my word like a hammer that breaks the rock in pieces?' [Jer. 23:29]. As the hammer causes numerous sparks to flash forth, so is a verse of Scripture capable of many interpretations" (*b. Sanhedrin* 34a; cf. *m. 'Abot* 5:22).

According to early rabbinic tradition, midrash could be practiced following seven rules (or *middot*) of Hillel the Elder (cf. *t. Sanh.* 7.11; *'Abot R. Natan* [A] §37). All of these rules are utilized in the Gospels.

1. Qal wa-khomer. "Light and heavy" (lit.). According to this rule, what is true or applicable in a "light" (or less important) instance is surely true or applicable in a "heavy" (or more important) instance. This rule is plainly in evidence when Jesus assures his disciples that because God cares for the birds (light), he will surely care for them (heavy; Matt. 6:26//Luke 12:24).

2. Gezerah shawah. "An equivalent regulation" (lit.). According to this rule, one passage may be explained by another, if similar words or phrases are present. Comparing himself to David, who on one occasion violated the law by eating consecrated bread (1 Sam. 21:6), Jesus justifies his apparent violation of the Sabbath (Mark 2:23–28 et par.).

3. Binyan 'ab mikkathub 'ekhad. "Constructing a father [principal rule] from one [passage]" (lit.). Since God is not the God of the dead, but of the living, the revelation at the burning bush, "I am the God of Abraham . . ." (Exod. 3:14–15), implies that Abraham is to be resurrected. From this one text and its implication, one may further infer, as Jesus did (Mark 12:26), the truth of the general resurrection.

4. Binyan 'ab mishene ketubim. "Constructing a father [principal rule] from two writings [or passages]" (lit.). From the commands to unmuzzle the ox (Deut. 25:4) and share sacrifices with the priests (18:1–8), it is inferred that those who preach are entitled to support (Matt. 10:10; Luke 10:7; 1 Cor. 9:9, 13; 1 Tim. 5:18).

5. Kelal upherat upherat ukelal. "General and particular, and particular and general" (lit.). When Jesus replies that the greatest commandment (the "general") is to love the Lord with all one's heart (Deut. 6:4–5) and to love one's neighbor as oneself (Lev. 19:18), he has summed up all of the "particular" commandments (Mark 12:28–34).

6. Kayotse bo mi-maqom 'akher. "To which something [is] similar in another place [or passage]" (lit.). If the Son of Man (or Messiah) is to sit on one of the thrones set up before "the Ancient of Days" (as Rabbi Aqiba interprets the "thrones" in Dan 7:9; cf. *b. Khag.* 14a; *b. Sanh.* 38b), and if Messiah is to sit at God's right hand (Ps. 110:1), then it may be inferred that when the Son of Man comes with the clouds (Dan. 7:13–14), he will be seated at the right hand of God and will judge his enemies. This is evidently what Jesus implied in his reply to Caiaphas (Mark 14:62).

7. Dabar halamed me'inyano. "Word of instruction from the context" (lit.). This rule is exemplified in Jesus' teaching against divorce (Matt. 19:4–8 et par.). Although it is true that Moses allowed divorce (Deut. 24:1–4), it is also true that God never intended the marriage union to be broken, as implied in Gen. 1:27 and 2:24.

Rabbinic midrash falls into two basic categories. These categories are distinguished by objectives, not by method. Halakah (from *halak,* "to walk") refers to a legal ruling (plural: *halakoth*). Hence, a halakic midrash gives legal interpretation. The purpose of halakoth was to build an oral "fence" around written Torah, making violation of it (written Torah) less likely (*'Abot* 1:1; 3:14). Haggadah (lit., "telling," from the root *nagad,* "to draw") refers to the interpretation of narrative and is usually understood as homiletical or nonlegal interpretation (plural: *haggadoth*). Best known is the Passover Haggadah (cf. *b. Pesakh.* 115b, 116b). Haggadic midrash was much more imaginative in its attempts to fill in the gaps in Scripture and to explain away apparent discrepancies, difficulties, and unanswered questions. Legal rulings were not to be derived from haggadic interpretation (cf. *y. Pe'ah* 2:6).

The rabbis of the pre-Mishnaic period (50 BCE–200 CE) are referred to as the Tannaim (the "repeaters"), while the rabbis of the later period ("early": 200–500 CE; "late": 500–1500) are called the Amoraim (the "sayers"). Obviously, the Tannaitic traditions are of the greatest value for NT interpretation.

The legal corpus, in which halakic concerns predominate, is made up of Mishnah ("repetition" or "[memorizable] paragraph"; ca. 200 CE), Tosefta (lit. "supplement [to Mishnah]"; ca. 300), and Talmud ("learning"; Palestinian [or Jerusalem], ca. 500; Babylonian, ca. 600; note that the word for "disciple" is *talmid,* "one who learns"). Many of the halakoth found in the Mishnah date back in one form or another to the time of Jesus (e.g., cf. Mark 2:16 and *m. Demai* 2:3 on being the guest of a nonobservant Jew; Mark 3:1–6 and *m. Shabb.* 14:3–4; 22:6 on healing on the Sabbath; Mark 7:3–13 and *m. Ned.* 1:3 concerning *qorban* ["corban," NIV]). It was believed that the oral law ultimately derives from Moses: "Many rulings were transmitted to Moses on Sinai, [and] . . . all of them are embodied in Mishnah" (*y. Pesakh.* 2:6).

Many of the nonlegal works are called midrashim ("commentaries"). From the Tannaitic period we have *Mekilta de Rabbi Ishmael* (on Exodus), *Sifre Numbers,* *Sifre Deuteronomy,* and *Sifra Leviticus.* From the early Amoraic period we have *Midrash Rabbah* (on the Pentateuch and the Five Scrolls), *Midrash on the Psalms,* *Pesiqta Rabbati,* *Pesiqta of Rab Kahana,* *Seder Eliyahu Rabbah,* and *Midrash Tankhuma.* Tannaitic tradition is often found in these writings as well and is then called a *baraita* (outside teaching).

Pesher

At Qumran, Scripture (usually prophecy) was viewed as containing mysteries in need of explanation. The "pesher" was the explanation of the mystery: "The pesher of this [Scripture] concerns the Teacher of Righteousness to whom God made known all the mysteries of the words of his servants the prophets" (1QpHab 7.4–5). It was assumed that the text spoke of and to the Qumran community, and that it spoke of eschatological events about to unfold. There is also a charismatic element to pesher exegesis, in that the interpreter knows things contained in Scripture that the original author did not. As in NT exegesis (see Mark 12:10–11, citing Ps. 118:22–23; 14:27, citing Zech. 13:7; Acts 2:17–21, citing Joel 2:28–32), pesher exegesis understands specific biblical passages as fulfilled in specific historical events and experiences.

Allegory

Allegorical interpretation involves extracting a symbolic meaning from the text. It assumes that a deeper and more-sophisticated interpretation is to be found beneath the obvious letter of the passage. The allegorist does not, however, necessarily assume that the text is unhistorical or without a literal meaning. His exegesis is simply not concerned with this aspect of the biblical text. The best-known first-century allegorist was Philo of Alexandria, whose many books afford a wealth of examples of the allegorical interpretation of Scripture, primarily of the Pentateuch. Allegorical interpretation is found in Qumran and in the rabbis. There is even some allegory in the NT. The most obvious example is Gal. 4:24–31, where Sarah and Hagar symbolize two covenants. Another example is found in 1 Cor. 10:1–4, where crossing the Red Sea symbolizes Christian baptism (though this aspect may be typological as well), and the rock symbolizes Christ. Jesus' parables are not allegories, but they do sometimes contain allegorical features, as in the parable of the Vineyard Tenants in Mark 12:1–9. There the vineyard owner is God, the vineyard is Israel, the tenant farmers are the religious leaders, and the murdered son of the vineyard owner is Jesus.

Typology

The NT makes several comparisons between various OT and NT individuals and institutions. These comparisons are often expressed, sometimes explicitly, in terms of typology, and as the examples below illustrate, constitute major components of Christology and ecclesiology. But typology offers more than comparisons between specific events and details; it also establishes important links between and within the Testaments themselves. Typology therefore has played an important role in the very formation of the biblical canon. By means of typology, as well as by means of prophetic fulfillment, the NT writers present Jesus and the church as the continuation and completion of the OT.

The biblical concept of typology is based upon the word *typos*, which literally means "impression," "mark" (John 20:25), or "image" (Acts 7:43). Metaphorically it usually means "example" or "model" (Phil. 3:17; 1 Thess. 1:7; 2 Thess. 3:9; 1 Tim. 4:12; Titus 2:7; cf. *hypotypōsis* in 1 Tim. 1:16; 2 Tim. 1:13), or even "warning" (1 Cor. 10:6, cf. *typikōs* in 10:11). In hermeneutical contexts *typos* means something like "pattern" or "figure" (Heb. 8:5). Although the hermeneutical usage of this word, and the related word *antitypos* ("copy" or "counterpart"; Heb. 9:24; 1 Pet. 3:21), is found only in the Pauline and General Epistles, important typologies are also present in the Gospels.

Typology is not unique to the NT. Within the OT itself typological comparisons are made. The exodus story becomes a type of salvation in Second Isaiah (Isa. 40:3–5; 43:16–24; 49:8–13). Psalm 95:7–11 presents the wilderness rebellion (Exod. 17:1–7; Num. 20:1–13) as an example of hardness of heart that Israel is to avoid. Psalm 110:4 mentions Melchizedek, priest of Salem (Gen. 14:18), as a biblical example of the priestly role of the king.

Typology is not to be confused with allegory. Allegorical interpretation assigns, usually rather arbitrarily, "deeper" meanings to biblical stories and their various details. The actual history of the biblical story is unimportant to this method of interpretation. But in typological interpretation, history is essential. It is believed that the original historical event is the "type," and the later corresponding event is the "antitype" that parallels, perhaps fulfills, and sometimes even transcends the type.

Because in the early Jewish and Christian period biblical exegesis was founded on the belief that Scripture contained the ever-relevant will of God, every effort was made to bring its teaching to bear upon the contemporary world and the concerns of the believing community. This effort lies behind all interpretative methods: allegorization, midrash, pesher, and typology. Allegorization discovers morals and theological symbols and truths from various details of Scripture. Pesher seeks to unlock the prophetic mysteries hidden in Scripture. Midrash seeks to update Torah and clarify obscurities and problems in Scripture. And typology represents the effort to coordinate the past and present (and future) according to the major events, persons, and institutions of Scripture. Despite their differences, there is significant overlap between these methods of interpretation. For example, to some extent all four involve a "searching" (midrash) of Scripture. All four find symbolic meaning that transcends the letter of the text (allegory). All four recognize the presence of mystery and hiddenness within the text (pesher). And all four believe that to some extent the present and future are foreshadowed by biblical history (typology). The real difference among these methods is more a matter of what Scripture is essentially taken to be than a matter of method.

Emphasis upon the unity of Scripture and history is the distinctive of typological interpretation. What God has done in the past (as presented in Scripture), he continues to do in the present (or will do in the future). Recent events or future events that are interpreted as salvific are frequently compared to major OT events of salvation. Such comparison does at least two things: (1) It lends credibility to the belief that the newer events are indeed part of the divine plan; and (2) it enables the interpreter to grasp more fully the theological significance of the newer events. Typological interpretation makes it possible for later communities of faith to discern the continuing activity of God in history. It is likely that these ideas lay behind the typologies that Jesus developed.

Typological interpretation is not limited to the NT; it is also found in rabbinical writings. Just as Israel prevailed over Amalek as long as Moses was able to hold his hands high, so also Israel has prospered when the people have obeyed the law of Moses (*Mekilta* on Exod. 17:11). The messianic age is often compared with the exodus, a comparison frequently developed by typological interpretation. For example, when Messiah comes, manna will once again be provided in the wilderness (*Mekilta* on Exod. 16:13, 33).

See also Allegory; Relationship between the Testaments; Targum; Typology

Bibliography

Bowker, J. *The Targums and Rabbinic Literature*. Cambridge University Press, 1969; Drane, J. "Typology." *EvQ* 50 (1978): 195–210; Ellis, E. "Midrash, Targum and NT Quotations." Pages 61–69 in *Neotestamentica et Semitica*, ed. E. Ellis and M. Wilcox. T&T Clark, 1969; Forestell, J. *Targumic Traditions and the New Testament*. SBL Aramaic Studies 4. Scholars Press, 1979; Gertner, M. "Midrashim in the NT." *JSS* 7 (1962): 267–92; Le Deaut, R. "Apropos a Definition of Midrash." *Int* 25 (1971): 259–82; Lieberman, S. *Hellenism in Jewish Palestine*. 2d ed. Jewish Theological Seminary of America, 1962; McNamara, M. *The New Testament and the Palestinian Targum to the Pentateuch*. AnBib 27A. 2d ed. Pontifical Biblical Institute, 1978; idem. *Targum and Testament*. Irish University Press/Eerdmans, 1972; Miller, M. "Targum, Midrash, and the Use of the OT in the NT." *JSJ* 2 (1971): 29–82; Neusner, J. *Midrash in Context*. Fortress, 1983; Patte, D. *Early Jewish Hermeneutic in Palestine*. SBLDS 22. Scholars Press, 1975; Porton, G. "Defining Midrash." Pages 55–92 in *The Study of Ancient Judaism*, ed. J. Neusner. Ktav, 1981; idem. *Understanding Rabbinic Midrash*. Ktav, 1985; Vermes, G. "Bible and Midrash: Early OT Exegesis." Pages 199–231 in *The Cambridge History of the Bible*, ed. P. Ackroyd and C. F. Evans. Cambridge University Press, 1970; Wright, A. *The Literary Genre Midrash*. Alba House, 1967.

Craig A. Evans

Job, Book of

Job presents both great opportunities and peculiar difficulties for those seeking to read it theologically. Why would God cause such disasters to happen to righteous Job? How do Job's protests and accusations against God fit with faith in the rest of Scripture? Are Job's laments still appropriate or permissible after the death and resurrection of Christ?

History of Interpretation

Two trends in early Christian interpretation can be seen in John Chrysostom (ca. 347–407) and Jerome (ca. 347–419). Chrysostom found in Job a model of self-denial for those struggling with the devil, and his perseverance under trial was therefore to be imitated. Yet, it is largely the Job of chapters 1–2 who is Chrysostom's model, not the protesting Job of the dialogue, nor the Job transformed by the Yahweh speeches (Glatzer 24–26). Instead of emphasizing the prologue, Jerome used texts such as 19:23–27 to establish the hope and reality of bodily resurrection as a key to a Christian reading. Thus, Job's trust in his Redeemer is the book's clear and distinctive contribution.

In *Moralia in Job*, Gregory the Great (ca. 540–604) argues for allegorical and moral readings. On the moral level, he seeks to explain away Job's bold words to God, and to portray him as the patient saint of the prologue. His preferred reading is an allegorical one so that, for example, the ostrich in 39:13–14 is the synagogue and her eggs are the apostles "born of the flesh of the synagogue." The book thus outlines the great doctrines of the Christian message, with Job himself being a type of Christ.

The variety of medieval views can be seen by contrasting Maimonides (1135–1204) and Aquinas (1225–74). Both saw that Job centered on the issue of God's providence, but Maimonides in *The Guide to the Perplexed* understands the story as a parable about a nonhistorical person who, though righteous, lacked some wisdom. He suggests that Job had wrong beliefs instigated by Satan, and it was Elihu's role to introduce the concept of the angel of correction and intercession, a kind of counterpart to Satan, who enables the "knowledgeless" Job to hear "the prophetic revelation" of the Yahweh speeches. Aquinas, however, in *The Literal Exposition of Job*, views Job as a real historical figure who, despite his advanced wisdom, was still sinful in his protests. He argued against "spiritual" readings of the story (allegorical, moral, anagogical) and opted for the "literal" or historical sense.

The Reformers strongly affirmed the literal sense rather than the allegorical. Luther (1483–1546), in his preface to the German translation of Job, argues that the theme of the book is whether the righteous can suffer misfortune. He thinks that Job, in his human weakness, spoke wrongly toward God, but was still more righteous than the friends. He does not explore how to read the book christologically. Calvin (1509–64) wrote 159 sermons on the book, but no commentary. He found in Job a resource for enduring suffering, although he often contrasts the more "humble" or submissive approach of the David of the psalms to the angry and impatient outbursts of Job, which cross the line of genuine piety (Schreiner). He found much truth in the words of the friends, but especially in Elihu's view of God's providence and the place of suffering. Despite his pride, Job came to see that God could be trusted to run his world justly.

In more recent times (nineteenth to mid-twentieth century; beyond in Germany), the historical-critical approach has dominated Joban studies, generally focusing on innocent suffering as the central theme of Job, and thus foregrounding the prologue and epilogue. This has led to some clarification of matters of language, date, authorship, and literary parallels in the ancient Near East, but has been accompanied by doubts about the authenticity of many segments in the book (e.g., ch. 28, Elihu, the Yahweh speeches, the epilogue). Such scholars usually assumed that the putative earlier versions of the book offer better clues for the meaning of the book than does its present form.

In the mid-twentieth century, the focus shifted to the dialogue and its discussion of the doctrine of retribution, often seen to be in tension with the prologue and epilogue. This also raised the issue of theodicy, or justifying God's moral governance of the universe. A third movement has been to concentrate on Yahweh's speeches and Job's reply, which makes the key issue the nature of God and how humans can respond to God. A fourth approach has been to explore the message of the book as protesting and unorthodox, calling into question such ideas as retribution or traditional understandings of God (Dell).

More recently, English-speaking scholars have tended to read the book as a literary and theological whole (e.g., Andersen; Habel; Hartley; Janzen; Newsom). Such final-form approaches have sought to give full weight to each section of the book, and they have regained a sensitivity to lament as a legitimate stance before God. Other contemporary interpretations include the liberationist approach of Gutiérrez, deconstructionist readings by Clines, a historicized reading by Wolfers (Job is the nation of Israel), and a variety of feminist, psychoanalytical, and philosophical perspectives.

This brief survey alerts us to several contentious issues. First, where do you look (if at all) for the teaching of the book as a whole? Is it in the prologue and epilogue, the dialogue between Job and his friends, or in the Yahweh speeches? Second, is the book about suffering, the nature of God and his activity in the world, or the appropriate stance for humans to take before God? Third, there is the difficulty with Job's strong laments and protests. Can Job be read in a way that reflects God's verdict in 42:7–8? Finally, how should the book be read as Christian Scripture? Can Job be seen as a person of faith apart from those passages in which he looks for a Redeemer? Does the book point to Christ, and if so, in what way? How is Job to be read as part of the canon? A theological reading of the book is committed to its coherence in its final form, even if there is some tension between the various parts. It will not excise parts that are problematic.

The Message of Job

The popular perception is that Job is a book about suffering, but in what sense? It does not explore why there is suffering, nor the quandary of innocent suffering, but rather the question of how a person can respond in the midst of suffering (Clines). However, this is really to assert that suffering is simply the setting in which the issue of the book is raised. The question of 1:9, "Does Job fear God for nothing?"—whether Job's faith is genuine or based on self-interest—is tested by the losses and suffering in the rest of the prologue. Suffering clarifies and isolates the central issue of faith. In a similar way, the Satan's role in the book is not to inform readers about Satan, who disappears after the prologue (though Fyall suggests that he reappears as Behemoth and Leviathan). The Satan functions simply to implement the testing of Job's faith.

Throughout the dialogue (chs. 3–31), Job's God-directed cries and complaints are best viewed as calls on the seemingly absent God to become present. Though he strongly accuses God (6:4; 13:21; 16:11–14), he longs to speak to God in person (13:15), in a relationship in which God would call and Job would answer (14:15). Job explores imaginative possibilities, including a figure variously described as an arbiter, witness, and Redeemer (9:32–35; 16:18–22; 19:23–27). His oath of clearance (ch. 31) climaxes in a cry that God might answer him (31:35). A legal metaphor is woven through the book (Habel), as Job desperately pleads for justice from God. Job persistently believes that only God can resolve his crisis (7:20–21; 10:1–2; 13:3, 15–19, 22–24; 19:25–27; 23:10–16).

A number of false trails suggest some unsatisfactory answers to Job's dilemma. The first is the advice of the friends. The final verdict of the book is that Eliphaz, Bildad, and Zophar have not spoken about God what is right, but that Job has (42:7–8). This has puzzled many readers since the dialogue is dominated by Job challenging, accusing, and complaining to God, while the friends attempt to defend God's justice and explain Job's suffering. Their trite formulas depict Job as a sinner suffering for his sins (4:17; 5:7, 17–27; 8:3–7; 11:6, 13–16). In the case of Job, their analysis and advice have missed the mark.

Another false trail is the suggestion that the wisdom poem of chapter 28 provides the answer, implying that Job needed to learn to fear God (28:28). However, the prologue has stated that Job already feared God (1:1, 8; 2:3). Furthermore, Job 28 is followed by chapters 29–31, in which Job repeats his complaints and calls for the presence of God. Chapter 28 has not provided the answer, and Job is still calling for a resolution. When God finally does appear, he does not mention fearing him as the way forward.

The final false trail is found in the Elihu speeches (chs. 32–37). While some misunderstand Elihu to be a fourth friend, his function is rather that of an adjudicator. Elihu narrows in on Job's words in the debate (34:3, 5–6, 9, 35–37; 35:16), rather than Job's conduct before the dialogue. His conclusion is that Job has not "spoken of God what is right," a verdict that is thus intentionally set up as a rival to the later words of God. He is thus a foil for the real answer (McCabe).

Job's situation is clarified when chapters 38–41 are seen to provide the answer. There is debate over whether these should be called the Yahweh speeches, drawing attention to what God said, or rather labeled a theophany, which highlights God's appearance. Some of Job's problems (e.g., God's apparent absence) are resolved simply by the arrival of Yahweh. Yet God's speeches also bring about a paradigm shift in the book, and God even needs to speak twice before Job finally understands. His survey of the natural world decisively shifts the issue from Job's question "Why am I not dealt with justly?" to the broader one of how God orders his creation. The dialogue is thus shown to have been telescopic, rather than panoramic. A delicate balance has to be maintained in these chapters, as Yahweh seeks to redirect Job's energies without crushing him. If Yahweh is too harsh, he would appear to endorse the views of the friends; if Yahweh is too soft, then Job will not hear what is needed. The playful irony of the Yahweh speeches preserves a right balance. Job's longings are met, but his broadened understanding has enabled him to persevere in faith.

This change of perspective is exactly what is found in Job's response (42:2–6). He concedes that he spoke of "things too wonderful for me, which I did not know" (v. 3 NRSV; hence the Yahweh speeches). Furthermore, before God's appearance, he had only heard of God "by the hearing of the ear, but now my eye sees you" (v. 5 NRSV; hence the theophany). His new direction is recorded in 42:6, which has often been misunderstood as Job repenting of his sin. This is most unlikely in view of God's endorsement of Job's words (42:7–8, including the honorific title "servant"), and Job's intercession for the friends, leading to their restoration (42:8–10). The Hebrew permits, and the context demands, a translation such as "therefore I reject and turn from the way of dust and ashes" (lamenting as a social outcast). Now that Job's horizons have been expanded and his thinking reconfigured, Job needs to change his perspective in life, which is precisely what he proceeds to do as he rejoins society (42:10–17).

God's appearance and his speeches have enabled Job to move on. Since Job feared God for nothing, genuine human faith is possible.

Job as Part of the Bible

The intellectual or ideological setting of the book is more significant than its historical setting. Job is a part of the wisdom corpus and stands in counterpoint to Proverbs' insistence that the world is regular and ordered, due in part to the presence of wisdom at creation (Prov. 8:22–31; 3:19–20). While Proverbs allows for temporary setbacks (24:15–16), it does proclaim that the righteous will be rewarded and the wicked punished (3:9–10; 10:27–32)—the doctrine of retribution.

The book of Job protests not against Proverbs, but against a fossilized misunderstanding of retribution that had misrepresented the mainstream wisdom tradition of Proverbs (Holmgren). Job's friends are examples of those who have ignored the flexibility of Proverbs (as seen in Prov. 26:4–5), and simply read off a person's spiritual state from their circumstances. The prologue to Job (chs. 1–2) reveals that Job's suffering is not a consequence of his sin, and God's failure to rebuke Job in chapters 38–41 clearly shows that his honest protests throughout the dialogue are seen as legitimate. The book of Job is not rejecting the doctrine of retribution, but simply insisting that retributive justice is not the only principle on which God runs his world.

Job's story is not reflected on at any length in the rest of the Bible, though Job is listed as a righteous person in Ezek. 14:14, 20. However, the issues grappled with in the book have strong echoes in the rest of the OT. The endorsement of Job's lamenting is understandable in the light of a significant OT theme that regards protest addressed to God as legitimate. This can be most clearly seen in the complaints of Lamentations, Jeremiah's laments, and the many lament psalms in the Psalter. These do not picture doubt and protest as illegitimate, but rather as needing to be directed to God, since he has the power to rectify any crisis.

The strong theology of creation in Job also integrates well with the rest of the OT. Genesis 1–11 reminds us that God is king over the whole world that he has created, and not just over Israel. Job is set outside Israel and before the giving of the law (Job 1:1), apparently to give a typically wisdom universal twist to the issues that the book explores. In the Yahweh speeches, Job is confronted with God's kingly rule as sustainer in everyday life, and this broadens his understanding of God's purposes. Until God spoke, he had understood too narrowly how God rules his creation, but now he sees that it is wider than the dispensing of justice. This fits well with the cameos of God's providential involvement in everyday life in books like Ruth and Esther.

The NT affirms many of these OT insights. The legitimacy of lament is reinforced by Christ's uttering the opening words of a lament psalm while hanging on the cross (Matt. 27:46, citing Ps. 22:1; cf. Heb. 5:7–8). Furthermore, God's purposes in Christ are clearly wider than human justice, for in his love and mercy Christ died for undeserving sinners. Yet, while the NT focuses less on the mighty Creator and Redeemer of the OT, and more on God assuming humanity, some full-orbed descriptions of Jesus occur. He was in the beginning, and all things came into being through him (John 1:1–4). Colossians 1:15–23 describes Christ not only as Redeemer but also as the firstborn over all creation, and in him all things were created and hold together. Thus, while there is a focus in the NT on God's sovereignty in redeeming his people, there is certainly no denial of Christ's lordship over creation. All that Yahweh says in Job 38–41, Christ can say too. His mighty control of the created world surfaced in his nature miracles (Mark 4:35–41; cf. Job 38:8–11). Furthermore, the world to come will be a new creation (Rev. 21–22), in which the Lamb's majesty will be fully seen (Rev. 5:11–14; 21:22–23).

The connection between Christ as Lord of creation and the need for persevering faith is also manifest in the NT. At the climax of Col. 1:15–23, Paul's hearers are reminded to "continue securely established and steadfast in the faith" (NRSV). The supremacy of Christ as Creator and sustainer is meant to lead to persevering faith. In the miracle of stilling the storm Jesus asks the disciples, "Where is your faith?" expecting them to keep on trusting him. Significantly, the only time that the NT names Job, it singles out his steadfastness or perseverance (*hypononē*, James 5:11), and it invites us to understand Job's faith in light of his vindication in the end or outcome (*telos*) of his restored situation (1 Pet. 5:6–10).

Job and Theology

The book of Job testifies to a God who is sovereign over all creation. The God of the friends (despite the reference to 5:12–13 in 1 Cor. 3:19) seems to be a hollow and shrunken version of the one who appears and speaks in chapters 38–41. No human dogma, even that God must act with justice, can bind or restrict God (35:7 and 41:11, cited in Rom. 11:35). While God is undoubtedly just, his ordering of the world is broader than a reductionistic human concept of retributive justice in which he can do no more than reward righteousness and punish wickedness.

The picture that emerges in chapters 38–41 is one of God having been involved in his creation from its very beginning, both in the inanimate (38:1–38) and the animal realms (38:39–39:30). He has mastered the mythological forces of cosmic chaos, Behemoth and Leviathan (chs. 40–41), though these may be natural creatures described in hyperbolic terms. God is also sovereign ruler over the creation, so that the Satan must ask permission before afflicting Job (1:6–12; 2:1–6). God is also free to restore Job once the test is over (42:10–15), even though some object that this reestablishes the doctrine of retribution. The book never denies the flexible doctrine of retribution evident in Proverbs, but refuses to distort this into an ironclad dogma that shackles God.

The theology of creation is clearly pivotal in a comprehensive biblical theology. In Job, creation is mentioned in a couple of hymnic (9:5–10; 26:5–14) and other passages (10:3, 8–12, 18) in the dialogue, in chapter 28, and above all in the Yahweh speeches (introduced by Elihu in 36:27–37:24). Job urges his friends to learn from the natural world (12:7–10; 14:7–12, 18–19; 24:5, 19), and God certainly uses it as an object lesson in chapters 38–39. God's delight in his ordered creation is reflected in the leisurely nature of the guided tour, in his care for those bearing young (39:1), and in his evident pleasure in animals such as the warhorse (39:19–25). Yet, there are puzzling elements of God's ordering of creation such as the clumsy and neglectful ostrich (39:13–16) and those animals that devour others (38:39–40). Both order and apparent disorder are manifest.

Furthermore, the way in which God is ordering his creation makes it clear that his concerns are wider than humans alone. The clearest example of this is when he makes rainfall where there are no humans (38:26–27), while the series of impossible questions indicates that God's ordering of his cosmos is beyond human comprehension. These factors have significant implications for contemporary ecological debates, both in their assertion of God's ownership of creation as well as in the breadth of his concerns. The majestic picture of God as the Creator, distinct from his creation, yet involved in freely caring for it, is clearly different from process theology readings.

Job also contributes many insights for a better understanding of humanity. Job's successful passing of the test testifies that he does "fear God for nothing" (1:9), and thus it is humanly possible to have faith in God without ulterior motives. Incidentally, chapter 31 is a classic source of the OT picture of the personal ethics of a righteous person. What emerges from this oath of clearance is an "identikit" picture of unblemished righteousness and integrity. Cultic matters are not at the heart of this (only 31:26–28), nor is keeping the law, for Job's integrity extends to his thoughts and attitudes (31:1, 9, 24–25, 29) and not simply his outward actions.

The nature of human piety is stretched to its extremities within the book. It is Job's strong, accusatory words of protest in the dialogue that seem to sit most awkwardly with his piety in the prologue. Yet, Job's laments and complaints are directed to God and assume God is in control and can alone right the situation. They are ultimately a call for a restored relationship with a seemingly absent God. In such trying circumstances as Job's, they are legitimated as a genuine part of faith. They deal with the hiddenness of God without giving up on the relationship or reducing God to less than God-sized proportions.

Room needs to be made in an understanding of prayer for such words, since God is big enough to take genuine hurt and bewilderment. Job's raw honesty in addressing God is part of a proper expression of faith, not an abandonment of it. His pain and confusion can be communicated openly to his God. Job's struggle is to break through the straitjacketed thinking of his friends to a restored relationship with God, and this only comes through his bold words addressed to the one who can help.

Bibliography

Andersen, F. Job. TOTC. InterVarsity, 1976; Beuken, W. A. M., ed. The Book of Job. BETL. Leuven University Press, 1994; Calvin, J. Sermons from Job. Edited and translated by L. Nixon. Baker, 1952; Clines, D. J. A. Job 1–20. WBC. Word, 1989; Dell, K. J. The Book of Job as Sceptical Literature. BZAW. De Gruyter, 1991; Fyall, R. S. Now My Eyes Have Seen You. NSBT. Apollos, 2002; Glatzer, N. N., ed. The Dimensions of Job. Schocken, 1969; Gutiérrez, G. On Job, trans. M. J. O'Connell. Orbis, 1988; Habel, N. The Book of Job. OTL. SCM, 1985; Hartley, J. The Book of Job. NICOT. Eerdmans, 1988; Holmgren, F. "Barking Dogs Never Bite, Except Now and Then: Proverbs and Job." AThR 61 (1979): 341–53; Janzen, J. G. Job. Interpretation. John Knox, 1985; Lévêque, J. Job et son Dieu. 2 vols.

J. Gabalda, 1970; McCabe, R. V. "Elihu's Contribution to the Thought of the Book of Job." *DBSJ* 2 (1997): 47–80; Newsom, C. "The Book of Job." *NIB* 4 (1996): 317–637; Schreiner, S. *Where Shall Wisdom Be Found?* University of Chicago Press, 1994; Smith, G. V. "Is There a Place for Job's Wisdom in Old Testament Theology?" *TJ* 13 NS (1992): 3–20; Wolfers, D. *Deep Things out of Darkness*. Eerdmans, 1995.

Lindsay Wilson

Joel, Book of

The book of Joel is the second book in the Minor Prophets (the Twelve, MT). The superscription (1:1) connects the prophecy with Joel the son of Pethuel. The name Joel is fairly common, and the father's name is otherwise unknown. The book lacks data that suggest a specific historical context. No chronological setting is provided, and nothing else is known of Joel.

Date

Interpreters vary greatly in dating the book (from the ninth to the second century BCE). The cumulative evidence is suggestive of a date as early as the late sixth or fifth century (Crenshaw, *Joel*), or as late as the late fifth to mid fourth century (Wolff). Calvin's assessment that the theological message of Joel is unaffected by the issue of the date is still relevant.

The Locust Plague

The thematic variation between images of the locusts and the drought (1:4, 5–7, 8–10, 11–12; 2:3–8, 16–20) and warriors (1:6; 2:2–11, 20) has raised the issue of the reality of the locusts. Some rabbinic, patristic, and medieval interpreters understood the locust plague as an image of an enemy attack, such as the Assyrians or Babylonians. Rashi, Calvin, and Luther interpreted the plague as a realistic portrayal of an agricultural disaster that may have evoked memories of foreign invaders ("the northern army," 2:20, 25). Most recent interpreters agree with this conclusion, but Stuart has returned to the metaphorical interpretation and links the prophecy with an invasion by Assyrians (701 BCE) or Babylonians (598 or 588).

Joel among the Twelve

The placement of Joel in the LXX after Micah varies from the MT. The LXX is more chronological throughout, and this is also true for the Twelve: Hosea, Amos, Micah, Joel, Obadiah, Jonah, Nahum, Habakkuk, Zephaniah, Haggai, Zechariah, and Malachi (Crenshaw, *Joel*). The arrangers of the MT paid more attention to literary links between the books of Joel and Amos, such as Yahweh's roaring from Zion (Joel 3:16 [4:16 MT]; Amos 1:2) and the mention of nations (Philistia in Joel 3:4 [4:4] and Amos 1:7; Tyre and Sidon in Joel 3:4 [4:4] and Amos 1:9–10; Edom in Joel 3:19 [4:19] and Amos 1:11). Further, the Zion focus in Joel provides a balance to the Israelite orientation of Hosea and Amos. Each part of the Book of the Twelve makes a contribution to the thematic network of the Minor Prophets and particularly to the theme of the Day of the Lord.

Theological and Literary Unity

Rabbinical, patristic, medieval, and Reformation interpreters viewed the book as unified. The critical analysis of the nineteenth century questioned the book's literary and theological unity (Duhm). The unity of the book has found general acceptance in recent literature except for isolated passages, such as 2:3b; 2:29 (3:2); and 3:4–8 (4:4–8) (Wolff; Crenshaw, *Joel*). The various proposed structures support the unity of the book, but there is little unanimity on the structure.

The Message of Joel

The literary reading of Joel as a unit engages several gaps that open the theological dimensions of the book. First, the text connects the locust plague *in history* with the *eschatological* day of the Lord (1:15–18; 2:2–11). Joel links the real world of human phenomena (1:1–14) with the expectation of the eschatological day of the Lord (2:1–11). The superhuman strength of the locusts dramatically heightens the catastrophe. The images of darkness (2:2), fire (1:19–20; 2:3), and earthquake (2:10) suggest a theophany. God himself is behind the image of the locusts, as he comes to bring devastation on the land and to judge his people (2:10). His coming is near (2:1), cosmic (2:10), and awe-inspiring (2:11). The experience of the locust plague in history is a mirror image of the coming day of the Lord in the future (eschatology).

Second, the language and images of the oracle of salvation (2:18–27) combine what can be conceived in history with what is not readily conceivable (eschatology). The prophecy anticipates that Yahweh's renewal will embrace all aspects of their suffering. The Lord will send rain (2:23), so the crops will provide food and drink (2:19, 21–23, 24, 26). He will protect his people from the disgrace they have suffered from the "northerner" (2:20, 25–27).

The imagery of the renewal is so radical that the oracle conjures up a world unlike the world known to humans: the radical elimination of evil and the absolute presence of God's goodness, resulting in the beneficent joy of his people. The Lord assures them that they will never again suffer (2:19, 26–27). The abundant provisions and the protection offered by the Lord mark the age of a new creation. The whole of creation (humans, fields, animals) shares in the benefits of this renewal (2:21–22). The sound of crying and lament is exchanged for the sound of joy (v. 23) and of praise in Zion (v. 26).

Third, the promise of restoration links up with the coming of the Spirit. But what is the connection between the two? The key to the interpretation lies in the first words of 2:28 (3:1): "And afterward." Is the Spirit's coming subsequent to the era of restoration, or are the two events more closely related? Many take "afterward" to be subsequent to God's act of restoration from the agricultural disaster. The promise of the Spirit (2:28–32 [3:1–5]) confirms God's reversal of fortunes, his goodness, and his presence (2:18–27). The phenomena of God's goodness are not an end in themselves. They evidence God's presence among his people (2:27). The self-declaration, "You will know that I am in Israel" (v. 27), and the recognition formula, "I am the LORD your God," attest to the beneficent presence of Yahweh and to his commitment to bring about all that he has promised. Yahweh alone is God, and he will remove suffering from his people (2:26–27; cf. v. 19; 3:17 [4:17]). The benefits of God's assurance take place in history and extend to the time of the renewal of all things (the new creation).

Fourth, the Spirit comes on the "whole" community ("all flesh," 2:28 [3:1]). The long-expected Spirit (cf. Num. 11:25–29) will come and manifest Yahweh's presence in the new community. Each member in the new community shares in the gift of the Spirit. The democratization by the Holy Spirit transforms the community from a hierocratic (ruled by priests) to a theocratic community. The totality of God's people, nevertheless, is marvelously diverse: male and female, young and old, free and servants. The new community consists of those who "rend [their] heart" rather than their garments (2:13). They are further defined by their "call" (vv. 28, 32 [3:1, 5]). On the one hand, they are "all who call on the name of the LORD" (v. 32 AT). The prophet has already prepared the reader for the importance of this call, because he, too, has called on the Lord (1:19). On the other hand, this group is defined as the remnant "whom the LORD calls" (2:32).

Fifth, Yahweh is sovereign over the nations *in history* (3:1–16 [4:1–16]). This section gives hope to the new community as they still face the real world, with adversaries and enmity. Yahweh promises that he will hold the nations accountable for what they have done to his people and to the land (3:2–4 [4:2–3]). As *time* (the day of the Lord) was the focus in the previous chapters, *space* ("the Valley of Jehoshaphat" = "the Valley where Yahweh judges") is the focus of this section (3:1–2, 14 [4:2, 14]). The principle of judgment is the law of retribution (*lex talionis*; 3:4–8 [4:4–8]). The Lord responds by bringing the nations into judgment ("the Valley of Jehoshaphat," v. 12 [4:12]). The combination of agricultural and war images powerfully presents the bloody nature of the eschatological battle (vv. 10, 13 [4:10–13]), as do the cosmic signs of the day of the Lord (3:15 [4:15]; cf. 2:10, 31 [3:4]). The day of the Lord is terrifying for the wicked nations, but he is the refuge for his people (3:16 [4:16]).

Sixth, the center of Yahweh's promise is his presence in Zion, from which oppressive and evil people are removed (3:17 [4:17]; cf. 2:26–27). Zion is the transcendent reality of Yahweh's dwelling with the new community (3:21 [4:21]). Yahweh's beneficence is expressed in images of the new creation (wine, milk, water, 3:18 [4:18]). The image of water flowing from the temple further reinforces the image of the new creation (3:18 [4:18]; cf. Ezek. 47:1–12; Zech. 13:1; 14:3–9). This oracle, too, comforts God's people in any age, giving hope of a world that far surpasses the present reality. The language of imagination in Joel, as in all the prophets, projects transcendence in images of space and time. The combination of a world in and out of time is characteristic of prophetic speech. The images are best taken as representative of the benefits God's people enjoy throughout redemptive history, as tokens of the renewal of creation. Salvation, the new community, and the new creation are already a present reality, but they also await a greater fulfillment.

Joel and the NT

The book of Joel suggests three major intertextual connections with the NT. First, the day of the Lord imagery is prevalent in the Gospels and in the book of Revelation. The day of the Lord is a general designation for the judgment-to-come (Matt. 24:21, 42; cf. 1 Thess. 5:1–11). The apostles cite or allude to aspects associated with the day of the Lord: the locusts (1:6; 2:2, 4–5; cf. Rev. 9:7–9), the cosmic phenomena (2:10, 31; 3:15 [4:15]; cf. Matt. 24:29 et par.; Rev. 6:12–13; 8:12), the sounding of the trumpet (2:1; cf. Rev. 8:6), and the sickle (3:13; cf. Mark 4:29; Rev. 14:15; cf. 19:15). The question "Who can endure/stand?" in Joel 2:11 occurs in Rev. 6:17. The eschatological day of the Lord is the time of the judgment inaugurated by the coming of Jesus Christ, but it is experienced in the history of the church as well, such as in the fall of Jerusalem in 70 CE.

Second, the coming of the eschatological Spirit (2:28–32 [3:1–5]; cf. Acts 2:17–21), including calling on the name of the Lord and being called by the Lord (2:32 [3:5]; cf. Acts 2:39; 22:16; Rom. 10:13), shapes the book of Acts and the apostolic mission of Paul. The Spirit as the mark of the new community defines the church as the body of Christ and individual believers as members of his body. He constitutes the new community that awaits the coming of Jesus Christ. The coming of the Spirit on Gentile believers evidences the inclusion of Gentiles as copartners with Israel. All who call on the name of the Lord are not only saved (Rom. 10:12–15), but also receive his Spirit (ch. 8; 15:16). The new community of Joel's days is continued in the church, but Israel too will share in this promise (11:28; cf. Acts 2:38–39).

Third, John adopts the image of the fountain flowing (Joel 3:18 [4:18]) from God's throne to describe the new creation (22:1).

Bibliography

Achtemeier, E. *Minor Prophets*. Vol. 1, *Hosea–Micah*. NIBCOT. Hendrickson, 1996; Allen, L. *The Books of Joel, Amos, Obadiah, Jonah, and Micah*. NICOT. Eerdmans, 1976; Barton, J. *Joel and Obadiah*. OTL. Westminster John Knox, 2001; Crenshaw, J. "Freeing the Imagination: The Conclusion to the Book of Joel." Pages 120–47 in *Prophecy and Prophets*, ed. Y. Gitay. Scholars Press, 1997; idem. *Joel*. AB 24C. Doubleday, 1995; idem. "Joel's Silence and Interpreters' Readiness to Indict the Innocent." Pages 255–59 in *Lasset uns Brücken bauen*, ed. K. D. Schunck and M. Augustin; Dillard, R. "Joel." In *An Exegetical and Expository Commentary: Hosea, Joel, and Amos*, ed. T. E. McComiskey. Baker, 1992; Duhm, B. *The Twelve Prophets*, trans. A. Duff. Black, 1912; idem. "Who Knows What YHWH Will Do? The Character of God in the Book of Joel." Pages 185–96 in *Fortunate the Eyes That See*, ed. A. Beck and A. H. Bartelt. Eerdmans, 1995; Garrett, D., and P. Ferris. *Hosea, Joel*. NAC. Broadman & Holman, 1997; Kapelrud, A. S. *Joel Studies*. Almqvist & Wiksells/Harrassowitz, 1948; Marcus, D. "Nonrecurring Doublets in the Book of Joel." *CBQ* 56 (1994): 56–67; Meinhold, A. "Zur Rolle des Tag-JHWHs-Gedichts Joel 2,1–11 im XII-Propheten-Buch." Pages 207–23 in *Verbindungslinien: Festschrift für Werner H. Schmidt zum 65. Geburtstag*, ed. A. Graupner et al. Neukirchener Verlag, 2000; Prinsloo, W. S. *The Theology of the Book of Joel*. BZAW 163. De Gruyter, 1985; Stuart, D. *Hosea–Jonah*. WBC. Word, 1987; Sweeney, M. "The Place and Function of Joel in the Book of the Twelve." *SBLSP* 38 (1999): 570–99; Sweeney, M., et al., eds. *Hosea, Joel, Amos, Obadiah, Jonah*. Berit Olam 1, ed. D. W. Cotter. Liturgical Press, 2000; VanGemeren, W. "The Spirit of Restoration." *WTJ* 50 (1988): 81–102; Watts, J. D. W. *The Books of Joel, Obadiah, Jonah, Nahum, Habakkuk and Zephaniah*. CBC. Cambridge, 1975; Wendland, E. R. *The Discourse Analysis of Hebrew Prophetic Literature*. Mellen Biblical Press, 1995; Wolff, H. W. *Joel and Amos*, trans. W. Janzen et al. Hermeneia. Fortress, 1977.

Willem VanGemeren

Johannine Epistles

Second and 3 John are two short letters from a person who simply calls himself "the elder" to "the elect lady and her children" (either a Christian community or possibly a Christian family) and to his friend Gaius respectively. The letters praise them for their spiritual progress, encourage them to follow love and truth, and urge them to be hospitable to traveling Christian teachers but not to those who do not confess that Jesus Christ has come (or possibly will come) in the flesh. They shed an interesting light on local church life, probably around Ephesus, in the late first century. The unnamed author is known to early tradition as "John," but whether this is John the apostle or another person is not entirely clear.

First John (our focus in the remainder of this article) develops much more fully the theological teaching in these two letters, but it is a tract or written discourse and lacks the form of a letter (including any indication of authorship). The close similarities in style and theological idiom make it most likely that it is by the same author. It is related in the same kind of way to the Gospel of John and is either by the same author (the traditional view) or by somebody in the same Christian circle (an increasingly widely held view). Most hold that it was written subsequent to the Gospel.

History of Interpretation

First John has traditionally been understood as a letter to an unknown group of believers in danger of various problems and errors. These include (1) the danger of claiming freedom from sin; (2) the failure to recognize that Christian love must include not only God but also one's fellow Christians, and must be a matter of deeds as well as words; (3) the problems caused by a group who have left the congregation and denied in some way that Jesus was the incarnate Son of God, the Christ (their thinking resembled that of Cerinthus, a first-century heretic, who claimed that a divine power came upon Jesus at his baptism and departed just before his crucifixion, so that it was only the human Jesus who suffered and died [since a divine being could not do so]); and (4) the difficulty of knowing whether the messages given by prophets claiming inspiration from the Holy Spirit were genuine or otherwise.

These may be identified as the major problems. Side by side with them the author deals with some issues common to any group of Christians: failure to seek forgiveness for sin, the danger of loving sin, uncertainty regarding whether they had true knowledge of God, the danger of assuming that Christians may continue in sin, self-condemnation rather than confidence in approaching God in prayer, problems in pastoral concern for sinful members of the congregation, and the attractions of idolatry. Much of this may be seen as a lack of Christian confidence, and the readers needed encouragement rather than blame. This is what the letter provides; it is meant to strengthen in faith, love, and hope.

Modern critical discussion has raised a number of issues:

1. The identification of the false teaching. It is not identical with that of Cerinthus, and closer parallels have been sought in the teaching opposed by Ignatius or simply in Judaism, denying that the Messiah was Jesus (Griffith). Or it has been argued that there is no other heresy known to us with which it completely corresponds.

2. The relationship of the letter to the Gospel. In various forms it is suggested that the letter endeavors to correct false ideas that may have been held by the readers of the (earlier) Gospel. The problem is complicated by the tendency of some scholars to see various stages in the composition of the Gospel by editors with different agendas and the consequent need to determine where the letter fits into the history of a so-called "Johannine community" (Brown). Some hold that the letter is more "orthodox" than the Gospel and represents a later, more "ecclesiastical" stage in the development of the community. Such a theory assumes that the authors of the Gospel and Epistles were different. More recently, there have been strong criticisms of the whole idea of reconstructing a particular community for whom the Gospel was intended, and it is proposed that all of the Gospels were written for "all Christians." Even if this is so, it is still the case that the author belonged to a particular community

and must have been influenced to some extent by its nature and needs.

3. There have been attempts to uncover earlier material in the letter (such as series of antithetical statements) and, even more, to identify stages in composition (Bultmann), but these have been largely abandoned.

Hearing the Message of 1 John

First John begins with a stately introduction (1:1–4) reminiscent of the prologue to the Gospel, with its focus on the Word of life that was from the beginning, has been revealed, and has been experienced by believers. The Word as Jesus, as the Christian message, and as itself the life that it promises—all three are bound up together in this expression. The writer aligns himself with the original witnesses and servants of the word, whether or not he is an apostle, sharing the message with a wider group who presumably had not the same firsthand experience.

He wants to promote fellowship between his readers and himself that is simultaneously fellowship with the Father and the Son (1:5–2:17). Therefore, the problem of sin must be dealt with by living in the light and seeking forgiveness provided through the atoning death of Christ. Belonging to Christ is seen in keeping his commandments, which appear to be concrete instances of the basic command to love fellow believers. Not loving the world means not being tempted by worldly temptations rather than not loving nonbelievers (although this point lies outside the writer's horizon).

Another danger to the readers is the risk of false belief, which denies that Jesus is the Son of God (2:18–25). The line of thought here is not completely clear. Plainly, the writer believes that if a person does this, they are no longer in fellowship with God, just as a believer may suggest to a Jew that apart from acceptance of Christ they cannot count God as their Father since God has now revealed Jesus as his Son. The belief in the coming of a final adversary of God, an anti-Messiah, before the End (and the second coming of the true Messiah), as reflected in 2 Thess. 2:8–12 and Revelation, is here picked up, with the claim that anybody who denies that Jesus is the Messiah is in effect a manifestation or anticipation of this final foe.

Nevertheless, the readers should not succumb to this deceit because they have been anointed by God (with a gift of discernment from the Spirit or with the knowledge of the gospel). Furthermore, they can look forward to the coming of

Jesus and to their consequent sharing in his glory (2:26–27).

The next part of the letter deals again with the question of sin (2:28–3:10). It emphasizes that the readers should be free from sin because they have a close relationship with Christ and have received a new birth from God; such people do not sin. This leads directly into a reminder that instead of sinning, their positive calling is to love one another, and not to "hate" one another by failing to show genuine, practical love (3:11–24). As they do this, their confidence in prayer will increase.

Yet comes another comment on false teachers, and how to discern the reality or otherwise of messages allegedly given by spiritual inspiration, this time with an assurance that those who are of the truth will not be overcome by false teachings (4:1–6). The rest of chapter 4 reiterates much of what has already been said about the love of God as the pattern for human love, and the confident assurance that God gives to those who love in this way (vv. 7–21). Believers will overcome the world with all its falsity and evil.

Once again, the nature of true belief is spelled out (5:1–12). It is belief in Jesus as the one who came by water (a reference either to his birth or his baptism) and by blood (a reference to his death). This strange expression may be intended to rule out any suggestion that the Son of God had departed from Jesus before his death or simply to emphasize the importance of his atoning death alongside his earlier life.

Finally, there is yet more assurance for the readers (5:13–21). But now specifically they are told that God will hear their prayers for sinful fellow-Christians, except where mortal sin has been committed. "Mortal sin" is generally identified as apostasy.

First John and the Canon

The letters of John are important testimony to the existence of a major stream in early Christianity alongside the Pauline tradition. Together with the Fourth Gospel, they constitute a closely related set of documents with distinctive vocabulary and theology different from that of the Synoptic Gospels and Paul. The book of Revelation is related more closely to this stream than to any other, and it was traditionally thought to be by the same author. This should not be ruled out as entirely impossible, since the apocalyptic genre could have dictated a distinct style of writing, but it is not widely held. It may be safer to see

Revelation simply as another witness to Johannine Christianity in a broad sense.

The similarities between 2 and 3 John and 1 John are clear; the shorter pieces, being real letters, help to relate 1 John to the day-to-day life of actual communities.

The relationship to the Gospel is more complex. A large part of the Gospel is concerned with the relationship of Jesus to nonbelieving Jews, and hence the questions of his messiahship and authority to speak from God are prominent. First John, however, is concerned with problems arising within the Christian community, and the christological error is more concerned with denial of the reality of the incarnation by persons who previously believed in it. There is more stress on the death of Jesus as atonement. It has been argued that this contrasts with the teaching in the Gospel, where (it is claimed) the death of Jesus has significance only as part of the revelation of God in Jesus and not as the means of atonement for sin. But attempts to identify a discontinuity here are fatally flawed by the opening emphasis in the Gospel on Jesus as the Lamb of God who bears sin (John 1:29, 36; cf. 1 John 3:5). The description of the Spirit in the Gospel as "another Comforter" (John 14:16 KJV) is clarified in the light of 1 John 2:1. Within the Gospel the second part especially (John 13–21) is concerned with the disciples after Jesus has left them, and in this part there are closer links with the epistle. As with the other NT letters, there is virtually no reference to the earthly Jesus and his teaching, and this strengthens the hypothesis that the writers leave the straight citation of Jesus almost entirely to the Evangelists. Nor does the letter directly refer to the resurrection and exaltation of Jesus, although the references to abiding in him and to his future coming clearly imply belief in this.

First John and Theology

Within the history of theology, 1 John has occupied an important place in the debate over freedom from sin and Christian perfection. John Wesley is the best-known advocate of the view that there is a call upon believers to perfection (cf. Matt. 5:48) and that it is possible for them to attain it. He was careful to fence his doctrine negatively by insisting that (1) it was freedom from known, deliberate sin; (2) a person might fall away from perfection and regain it; and (3) we should be quite cautious in recognizing examples of it. Positively, he preferred to speak not of sinless perfection but of perfect love that drives out sin. Wesley was largely indebted to 1 John for this doctrine, and he insisted that the promises or declarations in 3:4–10 were to be taken seriously. But his related belief that perfection was a state perhaps attained instantly by faith (rather like baptism with the Spirit in the Pentecostal tradition) would appear to come from elsewhere. His teaching has been largely forgotten in the mainstream Methodist churches but has been cultivated and preserved in the Nazarene tradition.

The crucial teaching in 1 John 3 has been variously interpreted, not least in light of the clear recognition that no believers can say, "We have no sin" (1:8, 10). Part of the problem lies in the juxtaposition of these apparently contradictory teachings. Some think that the "impossible sin" in chapter 3 (esp. v. 9) is solely the sin of apostasy (Griffith), but 3:10 might be thought to suggest otherwise. Most argue, in one way or another, that John is describing an ideal or an eschatological state that believers may claim in this sinful world; the paradox of "already . . . not yet . . ." that characterizes Pauline teaching is also valid here. It is also likely that John is addressing two different tendencies in the congregation, one that claimed sinlessness while not loving their fellow believers, and the other that was content with a low level of Christian living and did not grasp at the higher level promised to them.

The truth is probably that different NT writers use different pictures of the Christian life, including traveling toward a future goal, living by the Spirit, living in love, wrestling with temptation, and so on. These all contain an appeal to progress in Christian living. The danger of not taking 1 John 3 on board is that believers may comfortably resign themselves to mediocrity and fail to realize promises of, and provision for, a life free from sin. In reality, John does not put the point any more strongly than Paul does with his: "sin will have no dominion over you" (Rom. 6:14 NRSV).

Possibly the major, lasting contribution of the letter is its identification of love as the quality shown by God in the self-giving of his Son to atone for human sin and in the call for believers to show a like love for one another, demonstrated in action and not just in words (3:16–17). The letter is silent about loving nonbelievers, possibly because lack of love within the Christian community was a more pressing issue, but the readers are faced with the example of a God who first loved us (before we loved him), and the implication of that is surely clear enough.

Bibliography

Bogart, J. *Orthodox and Heretical Perfectionism in the Johannine Community as Evident in the First Epistle of John*. SBLDS. Scholars Press, 1977; Brown, R. *The Epistles of John*. AB. Doubleday, 1982; Bultmann, R. *The Johannine Epistles*. Hermeneia. Fortress, 1973; Edwards, R. *The Johannine Epistles*. NTG. Sheffield Academic Press, 1996; Griffith, T. *Keep Yourselves from Idols*. JSNTSup. Continuum, 2002; idem. "A Non-polemical Reading of 1 John: Sin, Christology and the Limits of Johannine Christianity." *TynBul* 49, no. 2 (1998): 253–76; Klauck, H.-J. *Der erste Johannesbrief*. EKKNT. Benziger/Neukirchener Verlag, 1991; Lieu, J. *The Theology of the Johannine Epistles*. NTT. Cambridge University Press, 1991; Marshall, I. H. *The Epistles of John*. NICNT. Eerdmans, 1978; Schnackenburg, R. *The Johannine Epistles*. Crossroad, 1992; Smalley, S. *1, 2, 3 John*. WBC. Word, 1984; Strecker, G. *The Johannine Letters*. Hermeneia. Fortress, 1996; Wesley, J. *A Plain Account of Christian Perfection*. Reprint, Epworth, 1952.

I. Howard Marshall

John, Book of

Traditionally, the church has viewed Holy Scripture as divinely inspired and authoritative, read it communally within the context of ecclesial faith and practice, and sought coherence and common ground amid exegetical diversity and disagreement. It is in relation to this rich heritage that we must view the interpretation and influence of the Gospel of John, its message and motifs, its role within the canon, and within the church its ongoing reception as the word of God.

History of Interpretation: John's Role in Church and Scholarship

In the Early Church. Today it is often argued that the earliest interpretations of the Gospel of John are now embedded within the final form of the text, having occurred during the several stages of its composition within a rather isolated and evolving late-first-century "Johannine community." During this process notable contributions would have included those of a "beloved disciple" (13:23; etc.), an "evangelist," and editors and/or "elders" ("we," 21:24), who together sought to shape and safeguard John from secessionist factions and their unorthodox interpretations (cf. 1 John 2:18–19; 4:1). Moreover, it is claimed that the outcome of all such orthodox efforts remained in doubt until well into the second century. Then, early and enthusiastic gnostic use of John, and concomitant wariness and neglect by mainstream Christians, was only finally reversed through the strenuous efforts of Irenaeus (ca. 130–200; esp. *Against Heresies*, ca. 185). In this view, Irenaeus rescued and restored John to the great church (cf. Sanders; Culpepper 107–38).

However, it is likely that such estimations would have puzzled second-century readers themselves, who normally associated the Gospel's origin with the apostle John and the church in Ephesus and Asia Minor. Certainly there was gnostic, more particularly Valentinian, interest in John. This is shown by allusions in writings such as the *Apocryphon of John*, *Gospel of Truth*, *Gospel of Thomas*, and others; citation by Basilides; a commentary on the prologue by Ptolemy; the first complete commentary by Heracleon; and interpretations by Theodotus (all ca. 130–80). Yet, inasmuch as John was clearly inimical to gnostic positions on creation, Christology, and salvation, such interest did not signify ringing endorsement but rather regularly entailed polemic and rejection (see Hill 205–93). Similarly self-serving were Montanist appeals to John in support of their unorthodox views on the Holy Spirit.

Moreover, there is considerable underestimated evidence that together indicates the widespread ecclesial ownership of John during the first half of the second century. This is shown in the writings and teachings of Ignatius, Polycarp, the longer ending of Mark, (John) the Elder, Aristides, Papias, the Shepherd of Hermas, and the *Epistula Apostolorum*. In the later decades John's broad influence and repute is attested by early extant papyri, Justin, Tatian, Apollinarius, Melito, Theophilus, Athenagoras, the *Epistle of Vienne and Lyons*, Hegesippus, Polycrates, the *Muratorian Fragment*, Appollonius, and Tertullian. In sum, familiar and habitual use of John reveals the authoritative, indeed scriptural, role it played within the early church at large, with any dissenting voices (purportedly Gaius of Rome) clearly the exception that proved the rule (on all this, see Braun; Hengel; and now esp. Hill).

In subsequent centuries the church continued to plumb John's theological depths for both pastoral and apologetical purposes. Clement of Alexandria (d. ca. 215), linking John to the Synoptic Gospels and recalling its inspired apostolic and communal context of origin, memorably encapsulated its unique nature: "John, last of all, conscious that the outward facts had been set forth in the Gospels, was urged on by his disciples, and, divinely moved by the Spirit, composed a spiritual Gospel" (in Eusebius, *Hist. eccl.* 6.14.7). Similarly Origen (ca. 185–254), who emphasized John's originality and extolled it as the choicest of the four Gospels, wrote a *Commentary on John*, which attended to both literal and allegorical aspects in seeking to discern its intellectual and spiritual sense. He critiqued Gnostics such as Heracleon for private and arbitrary interpretations, which lacked the church's testimony. For Origen, inasmuch as John disclosed the very Word dwelling with the Father, it exhausted all human interpretation (Schnackenburg 202–3).

John played a significant role in the christological and trinitarian debates of the third and fourth centuries, as attested in the writings of Athanasius, Eusebius of Caesarea, Gregory of Nyssa, and others (Pollard). So, for example, Athanasius countered Arius's subordination of Jesus to God by regarding John 1:1 and 1:14 as complementary rather than contradictory, insisting on both Christ's humanity (incarnation) and divinity, held together in mysterious union. Chrysostom (ca. 347–407) also refuted the Arians in his *Homilies on the Gospel of John*, a quite influential series of pastoral and polemical expositions that stressed the revelatory, theological, and spiritual dimensions of John in service of the practical needs of the church. Commentaries by Theodore of Mopsuestia (d. 428) and Cyril of Alexandria (376–444) also drew much upon John in support of both the divinity of Christ and the distinction between his divine and human natures as upheld by the Nicene Creed (Schnackenburg 204; Wiles 129–47).

Such emphases are also evident in Augustine's important *Tractates on the Gospel of John*, 124 sermons that pastorally appropriate the great mystery of the divinity and incarnation of Christ. Augustine attributes the source of John's profound theology to its author's privileged proximity to Christ (John 13:23), reclining and receiving all his secrets, and issuing in a Gospel that refines the mind so that it may contemplate God. Compared to his Synoptic counterparts, "the Evangelist John, like an eagle, takes a loftier flight, and soars above the dark mist of earth to gaze with steadier eyes upon the light of truth" (*Tractate* 15.1).

From the Middle Ages to the Reformation.
Patristic exegesis of John dominated its interpretation during the Middle Ages, with Chrysostom's *Homilies* and Augustine's *Tractates* especially influential in the East and West respectively. While much medieval commentary took the form of sample collections and epitomes of the patristic materials, we know of a number of notable works devoted to John (Kealy 1). The Venerable Bede (ca. 673–735) wrote a homily on the prologue; Alcuin (ca. 740–804) produced a widely circulated and much revised commentary; John Scotus Eriugena (ca. 810–77) also left a homily

on the prologue ("The Voice of an Eagle") and an unfinished commentary. Later the Byzantine exegete Theophylactus (ca. 1050–1125) wrote a commentary. So too did the Benedictine Rupert of Deutz (ca. 1075–1129); his 800-page work was designed to reconsider and supplement Augustine's efforts, refute all ancient christological heresies, and meditate upon the divinity of Christ. Bonaventure (1217–74) also wrote in response to heresy, with his very popular *Postilla* (a brief commentary and questions) *on the Gospel of John* reflecting upon this "sublime" Gospel in terms of the divine Word in itself (1:1–6) and as joined to human nature (1:7–21:25).

The commentary by Thomas Aquinas (ca. 1225–74) on John is a supreme example of scholastic medieval exegesis. It cites extensively from Origen, Chrysostom, and Augustine; aims to refute all error from the Arians to the Pelagians; and attends carefully to the literal (intended) meaning of the text, while also explicating its threefold spiritual sense. Major themes drawn from John include the all-surpassing love of God; the incarnation, redemption, resurrection, and return of Christ; and the great truth, authority, and contemplative weight of this Gospel, written so that the faithful might be built up into the temple of God. A later commentary by the medieval mystic Meister Eckhart (ca. 1260–1328) employed the now-familiar image of the eagle to portray John the Evangelist as scrutinizing, pondering, and preaching from above, his Gospel of the Word become flesh countering the pretentiousness of a needy humanity (on above, Kealy 1:115–84).

The Gospel of John also played a prominent role in the Reformation period. From 1516 to 1555 alone, some thirty or more authors published works on John in more than 125 separate printings, many of them notable in various respects. Erasmus (1469?–1536), who produced a popular *Paraphrase on John*, caused an uproar with his 1519 Latin version of John 1:1 as "*In principio erat sermo* [in the beginning was the Speech/Discourse]," rather than employing the Vulgate's "*Verbum* [Word]." The also popular first Protestant commentary on John by Philipp Melanchthon (1497–1560) then developed this in the direction of Jesus as the "*oratio* [oration]" of God. An interesting blend of influences, Melanchthon followed Chrysostom and Augustine in his christological and trinitarian readings of certain passages. Yet he was also significantly shaped by Aquinas's scholastic commentary. As a man of his own day, he regarded John as something of a Renaissance historian and Jesus as a divine rheto-

rician. Other important works included those of Martin Bucer (1491–1551), François Titelmans (Franciscus Titelmann, 1502–37), and Wolfgang Musculus (1497–1563; see Farmer).

Martin Luther (1483–1546) never wrote a commentary on John, but he did give it an honored place among NT texts, observing how its focus on the preaching of Jesus served to highlight his divinity and saving significance. Similarly, John Calvin (1509–64) viewed John as the key to understanding the other Gospels, preferring its rich Christology; typically, his commentary attended to the divine intent and transformative impact of the text (Kealy 1:203–74; cf. Larsson).

From the Enlightenment to the Present Day. The increasingly rational, historical, and often skeptical approach toward biblical studies in the centuries succeeding the Enlightenment, not least in relation to Jesus and the Gospels, was also directed toward John in ways that puzzled prejudicially over its historical value and distinctive theological nature. To the extent that a Gospel such as Mark could be seen as taking us closer to the original environment and eyewitnessed activities of a Jewish Jesus, the very different Gospel of John was deemed all the more remote and Hellenistic. Its Jesus was counted as a theologically laden construct of later "Catholic Christianity." Such an outlook was evident in the influential 1820 commentary of K. G. Bretschneider (1776–1848), and more broadly in the wider work of the Tübingen School under F. C. Baur (1792–1860) and D. F. Strauss (1808–74). It resulted in the proliferation of skeptical positions on the authorship, date, purpose, unity, and significance of John.

There were, however, more moderate voices. In his 1832 lectures F. Schleiermacher (1768–1834) regarded John as a trustworthy and realistic eyewitness to a Jesus of "depth and substance." A 1,500-page commentary by Friedrich Lücke (1791–1855) upheld it as an authentic, apostolic Gospel, which combined historical content and spiritual understanding. An 1881 commentary by B. F. Westcott (1825–1901) also defended its apostolic origins and provided a deeply theological analysis of its focus upon Christ's self-revelation to the world (1:19–12:50) and to his disciples (13:1–21:25). Even so, by the beginning of the twentieth century, scholars widely regarded John as a largely second-century Hellenistic presentation of the gospel, theological rather than historical, portraying an "idea" rather than an "actual" Jesus (cf. Kealy 1:357–471).

Over the last century scholarly interpretations of John have often focused on competing and nuanced claims regarding a certain set of interrelated issues: principally, its background, relation to the Synoptic Gospels, sources, composition, and community context. R. Bultmann's influential commentary (1941; ET, 1971; see Ashton) did develop the history-of-religions and Hellenistic approach by arguing for a background in Mandaean Gnosticism. However, most scholars now rightly recognize that the evidence instead points to John's decidedly Jewish setting and traditions. John is far too familiar with the geography, customs, and culture of first-century Palestine; its language and imagery find closer parallels in strands of Judaism such as represented by the Dead Sea Scrolls. Moreover, this same evidence may well indicate that John actually preserves its own early and genuine Jesus materials, and thus can also be seen as emerging reliably and independently of the Synoptic Gospels (e.g., Dodd). While this "new look" at John may reopen basic considerations—such as on dating, apostolic authorship, witness to the historical Jesus (Robinson)—it has largely been taken as clearing the ground for additional proposals. Rather than drawing upon the Synoptics, John may be using common traditions and/or "signs," "discourse," and other sources, all put together by one or more redactors (cf. Fortna). Indeed, as intimated at the outset of this review, rather than requiring the primary eyewitness of an apostolic author, it is usually argued that John unfolded over a multistage compositional and communal process, whether construed as a Johannine community, circle, or school (e.g., Martyn; Brown).

Without depreciating or dismissing any genuine gains arising from these ever-expanding and increasingly nuanced hypotheses, I observe that too often they deflect and defer the essentially theological concerns that earlier commentators regarded as intrinsic to the message of the Gospel of John. Happily, more-recent interest in the narrative, symbolic, theological, and spiritual dimensions of John is beginning to redress the oversight and imbalance (e.g., Kelly and Moloney; Schneiders; Thompson; and others).

Message and Motifs: John and the Drama of the Divine Life

The Gospel of John narrates a two-act divine drama that reveals and enacts the redemption and re-creation of humanity and the world. The prologue unveils the divine life and the entrance into the world of the Word, Jesus the Messiah and Son of God. In the first act the divine will unfolds in the works and words of an obedient if much misunderstood Jesus. The second act displays God's glorification in the departure, death, and resurrection of Jesus. The epilogue charges Jesus' followers with the ongoing embodiment of the divine life in the world.

Prologue: God, Word, and World (1:1–18). The prologue raises the curtain on the divine drama. The opening transcendent and primordial scene discloses the preexistent Word in eternal communion with and as God (1:1–2). This is the divine life, which we later learn also includes the Spirit (1:32). Out of this triune communion has issued the created order, with the co-Creator Word bringing into being all things, including humanity, who thus have in him the divine life and light that sustains and illuminates (1:3–4). Yet, with all this, the Word is also identified as "he/this one" (1:2). In a startling shift in scenes from the heavenly to the earthly realm, we find that in order to overcome a now darkened world (1:5), the co-Creator has entered into creation and history as a human person: the Word has become flesh (1:14). The first witness to this astounding event is John the Baptist, sent by God to testify to the divine light now present so that all might believe through him (1:6–7, 15). However, equally remarkably, the world does not recognize the Word as its Maker; "his own people" do not see that they are his own (1:8–11 NRSV) and that in rejecting him they are denying their true selves.

Yet some do indeed believe in his name—accepting the Word's divine origin, identity, and saving mission—and thus no longer live as those merely "of man" but as "children of God" (1:12–13 NRSV). The manner in which the Word has incarnated the fullness of divine glory and truth is further specified both in relation to God and to the world: he comes as the only Son of the Father and as Jesus Christ (1:18). The prologue thus attests to the primary purpose of the Gospel of John, that its recipients believe Jesus to be Israel's Messiah and the Son of God (20:31). In this way they may be the beneficiaries of "grace upon grace" (1:16 NRSV): the outworking of divine redemption traceable from the giving of the torah to the self-giving of God in Jesus Christ. Given the magnitude of all that is taking place, it is discernible only as disclosure, witness, and confession of faith ("we have seen," 1:14).

Act I: God the Father Revealed in the Works and Words of Jesus the Son (1:19–12:50). The prologue's divine pattern and purpose materializes with the advent and unfolding of Jesus' public ministry within first-century Israel. The first act is focused upon his revelatory and regenerative works and words (signs and discourses). This involves a series of encounters with a range of representative figures and groups, who gradually divide into those who reject or follow him. In the course of these highly charged events, the main issues and themes come into view.

At the outset John the Baptist openly announces the identity and mission of Jesus: "Here is the Lamb of God who takes away the sin of the world!" (1:29 NRSV). The divine life strides onto the earthly stage and will rescue its entire cast by rewriting their script in a wholly unexpected and self-sacrificial way. After calling the first enthusiastic but as yet unenlightened members of his new company (1:35–51), Jesus challenges Israel's usual players and practices in a series of provocative and pregnant episodes. At Cana the Jewish ritual of purification is transformed into the new wine of divine glory (2:1–12). The Jerusalem temple incident foreshadows the replacement of a bankrupt and closed Jewish establishment by a Jesus-centered and Spirit-enriched inclusive community (2:13–22). A representative and too self-assured Nicodemus ("we know," 3:2) has yet to recognize the love of God and receive the eternal life that comes only "from above" in the form of Jesus and the Spirit (3:1–21). The Samaritan woman learns that salvation does indeed come from the Jews, but climactically in Messiah Jesus, who reaches out and includes all faithful worshippers within the divine design (4:1–42). This startling scenario is extended even further in Jesus' ensuing encounter with a believing Gentile official (4:46–54) (cf. Kelly and Moloney 61–114).

There follows a more extensive series of works and words from Jesus, all significantly set against the backdrop of various highly symbolic Jewish festivals. Jesus' healing on the Sabbath critiques "the Jews'" constraint of the holy day and its Lord, and instead enables him as Son to reveal the Father in new, authoritative, and life-giving ways (5:1–47). (In view of later unconscionable anti-Semitic readings of "the Jews," it must be stressed that in John this phrase is a cipher for *all* who are closed and opposed to the divine economy operative in Jesus.) With the Passover in view, the feeding of the five thousand, walking on the water, and accompanying "bread of heaven" discourse—these together display Jesus' divine origin ("I am," 6:35) and limitless provision for his people (6:1–71). The Festival of Tabernacles (or Booths) is the setting for Jesus' ensuing temple teaching and failed arrest; his discourses on the light of the world, coming death, discipleship, and Abraham; and the incident of the man born blind

(7:1–9:41). In all these events it is Messiah Jesus (not the temple) who is associated with true and living water, light, and the glorious divine presence (again, "I am," 8:12, etc.), and God's saving action ("lifted up," 8:28). Jesus' divine work effects true freedom, sight, witness, and worship; this gives rise to children of God, who are characterized by their life, love, and truth.

On either side of a reference to the Festival of Dedication (or Hanukkah, 10:22), we find Jesus' discourse on the Good Shepherd and an account of his rejection by "the Jews" (10:1–42). The latter are aligned with former false leaders in Israel (e.g., Ezek. 34) and contrasted with the selfless outpouring of the Father's love in the Son's atoning self-sacrifice, which overcomes all human pretense and issues in abundant eternal life. Indeed, all this arises out of a divine life in which "the Father and I [Jesus] are one" (10:30 NRSV). This claim incurs charges of blasphemy from those purportedly concerned to safeguard the glory of God and yet failing to recognize that it is revealed only insofar as (says Jesus) "the Father is in me, and I am in the Father" (10:38).

Two complementary scenes—the raising of Lazarus (11:1–57) and Mary's anointing of Jesus (12:1–8)—anticipate his paradoxical death and resurrection, the subject of Act II. But first the current act closes with Jesus' dramatic entrance into Jerusalem, dialogue with both Gentiles and Jews, and his summary reflections upon his much misconstrued mission to date (12:12–50).

Act II: God the Father Glorified in the Death and Resurrection of Jesus the Son (13:1–20:31). The second act finds Jesus focused upon preparing his disciples for his forthcoming departure and their own role thereafter (13:1–17:26). This is immediately followed by a climactic rendering of the events involved in his crucifixion and resurrection (18:1–20:31). Herein the revelation of the Father in the works and words of the incarnate Son is ultimately realized through their shared glorification in Jesus' shameful death, astonishing vindication, and return to the eternal divine life. Again, a rich tapestry of motifs is discernible throughout.

With both the Passover and "his hour" at hand, God's very own Lamb prefigures his self-sacrifice and prepares the disciples for their own share in his servanthood by humbly washing their feet. Attended by Judas's betrayal and the other disciples' lack of understanding, this act expresses Jesus' exemplary and enduring love (13:1–38). It is also a sign of the divine hospitality that will ultimately be given to his followers ("in my Father's house," 14:2). This will be made possible by Jesus' departure and the sending of the Spirit, who in the interim will abide, guide, teach, and comfort the people of God (14:1–31). With all this in view, Jesus, himself "the way and the truth and the life" (14:6), exhorts his disciples to expand their limited horizons ("Rise, let us be on our way," 14:31 NRSV). He thus summons them to follow him homeward into the Father's glorious realm—albeit via the cross and thence the resurrection (Kelly and Moloney 270–306).

Union with Jesus ("the true vine") and his sent Spirit enables his followers to have communion with God and hence a fruitful life of love and joy in one another; this will overcome the barren existence of a hateful and degenerate world (15:1–16:3). Jesus develops these themes as he accounts for his divinely designed yet disturbing death and anticipates its advantages for his disciples. The cross will expose and eradicate the world's sin and injustice, and the Spirit will bring forth the Father's abundant new covenant life in the form of love, joy, and peace (16:4–33). Then in a prayer Jesus binds together all his hopes and fears for himself, his disciples, and all believers, drawing them up into his own eternal communion with the Father. Once again, many interrelated motifs recur, gathered around God's limitless grace, love, holiness, truth, authority, knowledge, protection, unity, and eternal life. All this is found in Jesus' obedient mission, which climaxes in the coming "hour" with the mutual glorification of the Father and the Son (17:1–26) (Kelly and Moloney 307–51).

Paradoxically, in the betrayal, arrest, trial, and death of Jesus, humanity's self-destructive schemes are taken up into God's gracious grand design. At Gethsemane, a remarkably assured Jesus discloses his divine identity ("I am he," 18:6) to the startled authorities and surrenders himself to "the cup the Father has given [him]" (18:11). He is abandoned by his disciples and even denied by Peter ("I am not," 18:17). Behind closed doors Jesus reminds the high priest, Caiaphas, that he has always spoken openly and rightly—of God and of himself in relation with his Father—in the synagogues, the temple, the world (18:19–24). Then a puzzled Roman governor, Pilate ("I am not a Jew, am I?" 18:35 NRSV), also finds himself caught up in this climactic conflict with a strange but seemingly innocent Jewish "Messiah," who pointedly informs him: "My kingdom is not from this world" (18:28–38a NRSV).

The divine logic, which escapes and subverts all concerned, unfolds inexorably: "The Jews" falsely acclaim Caesar as their king; Pilate ironically returns the compliment, calling Jesus "King of the Jews" (19:19–22); and on the cross Jesus truly reveals his identity and destiny, thus also disclosing and glorifying God. Therefore, although the situation seems disastrous to the bereft disciples, the reverse is actually the case. The empty tomb attests to a risen Jesus, who reappears, is acknowledged as "Lord and God," and bequeaths the Spirit, in whose form he will continue to be present with his disciples (20:1–29). From thence he will ascend "to my Father and your Father, to my God and your God" (20:17), to the glory to be enjoyed by all those who believe and receive the divine life given in Jesus, the Messiah and Son of God (20:30–31).

Epilogue: Embodying the Divine Life (21:1–25). In an epilogue, perhaps added later, Jesus again appears and exhorts his gathered disciples, including Peter and "the disciple whom Jesus loved," to remain faithful witnesses and to care for the people of God. This, we are now informed, the beloved disciple has done, not least with the provision of this spiritual Gospel, which invites and enables its audience to join Jesus, the apostles, and all the saints in the divine life.

The Canon: John and the Divine Company

The Gospel of John offers itself as a revelatory and inspired new-covenant document generated by the teaching and deeds of Jesus as recalled through the operation of his Spirit within the witnessing community of faith (cf. 14:25; 20:21–23, 30–31; 21:24–25). On this basis its author (known early on as the apostle John) and its initial audience preserved, transmitted, and proclaimed this divinely authoritative Scripture (cf. 2:22; 19:36–37; 20:31). Despite scholarly claims that this Gospel struggled for acceptance, there is every indication that it was widely received and revered by the early church, and that it played a distinctive, prominent, and indeed canonical role (see Hill). Among the most important elements in this are John's use of the OT and its early associations with both a Johannine corpus of literature and the Synoptic Gospels.

It is according to the OT that John views its own witness to the fulfillment of God's purposes for Israel and the world in Jesus and his Spirit-empowered disciples (5:39, 45–47). This is immediately evident from a range of OT citations, particularly from the Pentateuch, Isaiah, and Psalms, variously quoted by Jesus (1:51; 6:45; 10:34; 13:18; 15:25), his Jewish contemporaries (1:23; 2:17; 6:31; 12:13), and the author (12:15, 38, 40; 19:24, 36–37). Even more impressive is the extent to which John's account of Jesus' message and mission includes a typological and polemical reworking of various OT elements. These include symbols (torah, temple, Sabbath), figures (Moses, Isaiah's Servant, the Psalms' righteous sufferer, Ezekiel's Davidic shepherd), imagery (vine, water, light), and festivals (Passover, Tabernacles). Thus, what John says of the prophet is true of the entire OT: "Isaiah said this because he saw [Jesus'] glory and spoke about him" (12:41). From John's postresurrection perspective, what Isaiah foresaw and the OT prefigured and promised was the startling glory of a cruciform Christ, the very self-expression of God. Above all, this is what lies at the heart of the collective witness of the OT, Jesus, and the Gospel of John.

Yet, not the Gospel of John alone; this document invites comparison with its NT counterparts, not least the Letters and Revelation of John. The well-recognized collocation of so many striking verbal, conceptual, and thematic similarities between the Gospel and especially 1 John is unlikely to be incidental. We may cite, for example, Jesus as Messiah and Son of God; the Paraclete and "S/spirit of Truth"; believers as "children of God"; the love commandment; light and darkness imagery; a stress on truth, witnessing, eternal life; and the exhortation to know, remain in, and love God. All this the recipients of the Letters of John have heard and seen from the beginning, perhaps via the Gospel itself (cf. 1 John 1:1; 2:7, 24; 3:11; 2 John 5, 6). While Revelation is an apocalyptic prophecy in the form of a letter, rather than a Gospel, it too bears notable christological (e.g., Lamb, Logos) and eschatological affinities; it emphasizes similar significant themes (witnessing, commandment-keeping, overcoming, glorification); it also draws extensively and evocatively upon OT language and imagery (cf. Köstenberger 203-5). Moreover, while scholarship has usually considered the origin and identity of the Gospel, Letters, and Revelation of John individually, there is strong evidence from the early second century of an ecclesial awareness that they belonged to an authoritative (even scriptural) corpus. Mention may be made of the common and often intertextual exegesis of two or more Johannine documents; their implicit and explicit attribution to the same author, the apostle John; and the possible existence of codices containing these Johannine works (Hill 451–64).

As noted earlier, the patently distinctive Gospel of John has caused many contemporary scholars to conclude that it emerged independently of and sits rather awkwardly alongside Matthew, Mark, and Luke. Yet, from its outset John presupposes much concerning Jesus, not least as the Word who was Messiah and Son of God, which would only have made sense in the light of the sort of information supplied in documents such as the Synoptic Gospels (Smith). Given the extensive networking between the early and expanding Christian communities, and the probability that each of the Gospels was intended for all Christians (so Bauckham), it is all the more likely that they were correlated with one another. Indeed, second-century evidence (such as from Tatian and Clement) suggests that the church regarded John as written in the full knowledge of Matthew, Mark, and Luke; that it soon circulated in their company; and that it was strategically located last because it could clarify, amplify, supplement, and provide a broader and deeper theological framework for its Synoptic counterparts. In sum, then as now, the reader is invited to read John as a Gospel among the Gospels; and, by extension, to regard it as an integral document within a two-Testament witness to the triune God.

John and Theology: God, Church, and World

From the foregoing it is evident that the Gospel of John is entirely "of God"—in its emanation from Jesus, the Word made flesh, as first witnessed to within its own apostolic and communal context of origin; in its expeditious and widespread reception within an increasingly inclusive and ever-expanding early church; in the mutually interpretative canonical company it has kept from its earliest days as Spirit-shaped Scripture; and in its continued profound effect, explication, and enactment throughout the church historic and universal.

As such, John cannot be constrained by mere human conjecture and self-serving sectarian readings, but must always be embodied ecclesially and thence manifest publicly as a rich and resonant witness to the triune God's self-giving and limitless love for the whole world (3:16; 21:24–25). In God the Father this gracious love precedes and exceeds, creates and generates, sustains and consummates all things. In God the Son this love is incarnate and cruciform as it unmasks and overcomes sin and death, and is vindicated and glorified as it opens up and enables a transformed way of life. In God the Spirit, the continuing presence of the Son, this love also establishes, indwells, abides, witnesses to, and guides all the people of God (cf. Kelly and Moloney 388–94).

It is this all-encompassing divine love and life that governs and authenticates the church and its mission in the world. The church is to be present, faithful, and giving. It is to help, heal, endure, question, confront, and transform. It is to reach out, invite, gather, welcome, and include. Certainly such a calling must not be distorted in the direction of religious pluralism and syncretism (or, conversely, recoil into a peevish parochialism); it is at all times the church of *this* God. Thus, the church must personify God's glory in all its grandeur, with a love and faithfulness that is both vital and vulnerable, disclosing the heavenly horizon and economy within which humanity can know its true identity and destiny. In this way a world that is otherwise enslaved by often unspeakable evil may be providentially rescued and relocated within a new heaven and earth, and so enjoy eternally the divine life.

Bibliography

Ashton, J. *Understanding the Fourth Gospel*. Clarendon, 1991; Bauckham, R., ed. *The Gospel for All Christians*. Eerdmans, 1998; Braun, F.-M. *Jean le théologian et son évangile dans l'église ancienne*. 3 vols. J. Gabalda, 1959; Brown, R. *The Community of the Beloved Disciple*. Paulist, 1979; idem. *The Gospel according to John*. 2 vols. AB 29–29A. Doubleday, 1966–70; Bultmann, R. *The Gospel of John*, trans. G. R. Beasley-Murray. Blackwell, 1971; Culpepper, R. A. *John, the Son of Zebedee*. University of South Carolina Press, 1994; Dodd, C. H. *Historical Tradition in the Fourth Gospel*. Cambridge University Press, 1963; Farmer, C. S. *The Gospel of John in the Sixteenth Century*. Oxford University Press, 1997; Fortna, R. *The Fourth Gospel and Its Predecessor*. Polebridge, 1988; Hengel, M. *The Johannine Question*, trans. J. Bowden. Trinity, 1989; Hill, C. E. *The Johannine Corpus in the Early Church*. Oxford University Press, 2004; Kealy, S. P. *John's Gospel and the History of Biblical Interpretation*. 2 vols. E. Mellen, 2002; Keener, C. *The Gospel of John*. 2 vols. Hendrickson, 2003 (esp. bibliography at 2:1251–1409); Kelly, A. J., and F. J. Moloney. *Experiencing God in the Gospel of John*. Paulist, 2003; Köstenberger, A. J. *John*. BECNT. Baker, 1999; Larsson, T. *God in the Fourth Gospel*. Almqvist, 2001; Martyn, J. L. *History and Theology in the Fourth Gospel*. 2d ed. Abingdon, 1979; Pollard, T. E. *Johannine Christology and the Early Church*. SNTSMS 13. Cambridge University Press, 1970; Robinson, J. A. T. *The Priority of John*, ed. J. F. Coakley. SCM, 1985; idem. *Twelve New Testament Studies*. SCM, 1962; Sanders, J. N. *The Fourth Gospel in the Early Church*. Cambridge University Press, 1943; Schnackenburg, R. *The Gospel according to St. John*. Vol. 1, trans. K. Smyth. Crossroad, 1982; Schneiders, S. *Written That You May Believe*. 2d ed. Crossroad, 2003; Smith, D. M. "Prolegomena to a Canonical Reading of the Fourth Gospel." Pages 169–82 in *"What Is John?"* ed. F. Segovia. Scholars Press, 1996; Thompson, M. M. *The God of the Gospel of John*. Eerdmans, 2001; Wiles, M. *The Spiritual Gospel*. Cambridge University Press, 1960.

S. A. Cummins

Jonah, Book of

Highlights in the History of Interpretation

Y. Sherwood has thoroughly documented the history of interpretation of this popular book that has served as a "cultural hologram" of religious and theological sentiments and trends (71). Early Christian interpretation found its interpretative key in Matt. 12:40 and focused on Jonah and Jesus as "typological twins" (Sherwood 11–21). Jerome and others constructed a web of parallels between the book and the events of Jesus' ministry. Augustine accepted this approach, but alongside it he adopted the idea of the prophet as an embodiment of carnal Israel, inaugurating the second phase of interpretation: Jonah as negative stereotype of Jews. Even into the Reformation, this is evident in Luther's assessment of the book as showing the superiority of Christianity to Judaism. Thus, the book became a lightning rod for anti-Semitic and supersessionistic sentiment and theology (Sherwood 32). The period of the Reformation also saw a shift to a third category, evident in Calvin's treatment of the book as warning against fleeing from God or chiding that people are more important than plants.

Post-Enlightenment exposition focused on the phenomena of the book, whether from a vantage point of skepticism or reacting against it apologetically. Thus, the details of the book came under close scrutiny. Even as the Age of Criticism was dawning and "adolescing," the older modes of interpretation were transmogrified rather than discarded. The eighteenth-century interpreters sermonized about Jewish envy of Gentiles, while the nineteenth century adopted Jonah as the poster child for anti-Semitic sentiment (Sherwood 25–27). As critical study reached the apex of modernism and began the transition to postmodern interpretation, attention turned to deeper discussion of genre, even as more traditional communities continued to argue for the historicity of the book's events.

Contemporary literary analysis is prone to resort to rhetorical labels such as satire (Ackerman 227), parody (Orth), or irony (Simon) to describe the book. Such suggestions are often rejected by evangelical interpreters who view these as modern categories and consider them threatening to biblical authority. On the first count, parody at least has now been identified in ancient literature (Michalowski 84–86), and on the second, it can be observed that satire and parody do not imply fictionalization. The real issue can be framed in the question, "Should the book be categorized as a 'truth-telling' genre or as 'nonrealistic' writing?" Complexity increases if we consider options such as "nonrealistic" writing based on a kernel of historical information, or "truth-telling" tailored so that certain stereotypes surface. While consensus on these questions may exist within particular interpretative communities, a universal consensus has not yet been reached.

The above survey categorizes ways that the book of Jonah has been exploited over the years, commandeered for social, theological, or methodological agendas. Alternatively, the interpretations of the book can be sorted out with relation to its message rather than its use. D. Alexander identified four approaches to the interpretation of the text: that the book was about repentance, about unfulfilled prophecy, about Jewish attitudes toward Gentiles, or about theodicy (Alexander et al. 81–91). U. Simon uses a similar list to represent the history of Jewish interpretation (vii–xiii), all still reflected in interpretive communities today.

Deciding about the theological message of the book concerns what equations it sets up: Israel = Nineveh? Jonah = Israel? Jonah = Jesus? The purpose and message are going to derive from whichever equation is adopted. The challenge interpreters face is arriving at a cohesive reading that would have been recognizable to the author—to arrive confidently at an understanding of what could be called the "face value" of the book.

Literary Structure

The book of Jonah is characterized by a highly artistic literary structure. Chapter 1 parallels chapter 3 as each highlights a non-Israelite audience threateningly confronted by Yahweh. In both cases the response is exemplary, contrasting favorably to the prophet's questionable behavior. God is seen as initiator, non-Israelites as responders, and prophet as foil. Both chapters conclude with God's merciful deliverance. Chapters 2 and 4 are likewise parallel as Yahweh interacts in each with his prophet. These chapters conclude recognizing God's character.

Overview of the Message

The above literary structure highlights many of the major elements that bind the book together. Yet despite parallels, chapter 4 has often been seen as incompatible with the unity of the book. If the persuasiveness of a particular understanding is found in its ability to integrate every aspect into the whole, then the object lesson and the abrupt ending of chapter 4 must be addressed. As the conclusion, it is the key to the book's purpose and message, which in the end is not about Nineveh, Jonah, or Israel, but about God.

The object lesson gives the reader the operative equation by which the book operates: Jonah becomes a surrogate Nineveh. The initial indicator of this is signaled by the variations in the divine name. Through most of the book, Jonah interacts with Yahweh, while the non-Israelites predictably use the term 'elohim (except 1:14–16, after the sailors have been introduced to Yahweh). Consequently, in 4:6 the sudden use of the compound divine name, Yahweh-Elohim, catches the attention of the reader and signals a temporary and meaningful switch. The object lesson then uses Elohim through its conclusion in 4:9. This suggests that Jonah has been relocated among the non-Israelites in the object lesson.

The second indicator is the repetition of the Hebrew root ra'ah in 3:10 and 4:6. For Nineveh, this describes the impending "destruction," from which they are spared. For Jonah, it is the impending "discomfort," from which he is initially spared, but eventually experiences in full. Again, Jonah is thus equated with Nineveh. This opens up the full parallelism incorporated in the object lesson (from Walton 49):

1. Both Nineveh and Jonah have an impending calamity from which they desire to protect themselves (their ra'ah), respectively the prophesied destruction and discomfort of the weather.
2. Both Nineveh (by repentance) and Jonah (by his hut) embark on a course of action to prevent the ra'ah.
3. Both attempts are supplemented and actualized by an act of divine grace: God grants Nineveh a reprieve and provides Jonah a protective plant.
4. At this point there is a change. Rather than allowing his gracious act to continue to protect Jonah, God's protection is removed. A parasite devours the plant, and Jonah is exposed to the full force of the calamity, left only with the protection of his own provision, the hut, which does him no good.

Thus, the object lesson draws out the message of the book. The lesson puts Jonah and Nineveh on the same side, with God on the other side, and establishes its significance relative to God, regardless of the results for Nineveh/Jonah.

What did the incident teach Nineveh? Some consider Jonah as the story of a remarkable conversion of pagan Nineveh to true faith in God, and they focus on what Nineveh learned. Nevertheless, evidence for a conversion to true Yahwism is difficult to find in the text. Unquestionably, they repent of "their evil ways." But there is no mention of turning to Yahweh, being instructed about the covenant, or discarding their other gods. The description of their belief indicates only that they believed what God had said through Jonah about their impending doom (Walton 53–54). It is their action that is commended in 3:10, not their faith.

In addition, once the nature of the object lesson is understood, it becomes clear that Nineveh's response is important for its inadequacy. It is paralleled by Jonah's hut, unable to shelter him from the calamity. In short, then, the Ninevites learned little. But even in their ignorance and paganism, they recognized the need to respond to the word of Deity. They thus offer an important model both to the Israelite audience and to future audiences (Matt. 12:41).

What did the incident teach Jonah? Jonah's function in the narrative is to be the foil—static and recalcitrant. The only "change" in him came simply in response to the inevitable. Once he learned that he had no choice but to go to Nineveh, he did so. He was consistent in self-righteously seeing himself as justified in all his actions and attitudes. We could conclude, then, that he did not learn anything, other than that sometimes God will not take "no" for an answer. The book does not depend on his making progress.

What did the book teach Israel? The purpose of the book, we suggest, focuses on the changes accompanying the period of classical prophecy. The example of Nineveh serves to educate Israel and its prophets regarding the "ground rules" of this era. Through the eighth-century prophets, a new age had dawned in which Israel and Judah were warned of coming judgment in the form of prophetic pronouncement—usually deemed irrevocable. The book of Jonah illustrates that repentance was a proper and acceptable response, and could even turn back the judgment. It worked even for naive, wicked, pagan Nineveh. When Israel faced such warnings, this model for response suggests that even in the shadow of pronounced doom, repentance can bring mercy. It therefore becomes important to recognize the Ninevites' response as shallow and uninformed. The book is counting on that contrast to drive home the point that the response of Israel, God's covenant people, would surely be able to elicit similar compassion from God.

In choosing this interpretation, we reject the popular reading that the book was written to scold Jewish exclusivism in the postexilic period. That view assumes that Jonah was asked to preach repentance and did so. We find no conclusive evidence for such an assumption.

What does the book teach about God? In the interpretation offered here, this is the key, as it should be when we consider Scripture as God's self-revelation. The book ends with God and makes a clear point about his compassion. Jonah is angry that God's grace is stimulated by his compassion rather than requiring a minimal level of theological sophistication or faith. Instead, God's compassion is stimulated by responsiveness. This proclaims a God of second chances, who delights in even small steps in the right direction. Even though Jonah is theologically offended by such grace benefiting Nineveh, he is glad enough of it when his own comfort is at stake, as Israel would be when the classical prophets proclaim their doom-laden oracles. The God of threatening oracles of judgment is a compassionate God, prone to be gracious at the slightest hint of response.

What does the book teach us? We are not receiving messages of doom from prophets, but the judgment of God still threatens the unrighteous. It is most important for us to use the message of the book to deepen our understanding of God. It is not unusual for people to feel that something they have done has put them beyond the reach of God's mercy, disqualified for his grace or compassion. The book of Jonah has encouraging words to offer: God's compassion is boundless. Should anyone feel that their straying has left no way back to God, the encouragement of the book is that God is inclined to respond to even the smallest steps in the right direction. The jump from prodigal to sainthood need not be made in a single leap. We need only to climb the fence out of the pigsty and take a step toward home. A compassionate God waits with open arms and is ready to meet us on our journey.

Discussion of the Book's Contribution to the Canon as a Whole

If the book offers a model response to classical prophecy, it can be seen as canonically integrated with the prophetic corpus. It also offers some nuancing of Deut. 18:22 concerning a prophet's authentication. Jonah qualifies that principle with the allowance for God's grace to postpone judgment if there should be a positive response.

Jonah appears in the Book of the Twelve as a transition between the juxtaposed books of Hosea–Obadiah and the chronologically arranged books, Micah–Malachi. If Jonah serves as conclusion or synthesis of the initial juxtapositions, one can explore them to discover Jonah's role.

Hosea proclaims the impending judgment that grain, new wine, and oil will be taken away (2:9). Joel shows a repentant response to a prophet in whose time this same sort of threat is realized in a locust plague. As a result of the positive response, God restored those commodities (2:19). The juxtaposition of these two books shows the positive result of response by God's errant people. In contrast, Amos pronounces coming judgment on the nations. Edom is not only included in the initial list (1:11–12), but is targeted at the end (9:12). It is logical, then, that Obadiah should follow Amos, illustrating the result of nonresponse found in the destruction of Edom. Joel and Obadiah then serve as postexilic illustrations of the ongoing relevance of preexilic prophetic messages. In the process they exemplify the deliverance that comes when people do respond and the judgment that comes when they do not.

With these two examples juxtaposed for the audience, the book of Jonah provides a synthesis. Even the most pagan of cities, Nineveh, showing even the most uninformed response, experienced mercy at the hands of God. The appropriate response to the prophetic oracles of indictment and judgment is to begin taking steps in the right direction. As Jonah synthesizes the fruits of the juxtaposition of the two previous pairings of books, it also then provides transition to the chronological sequence of prophetic collections. This sequence is concluded and synthesized by Malachi, who summarizes the call and response for the postexilic audience.

The NT connections concern the "sign of Jonah" (Matt. 12:39–41; 16:4; Luke 11:29–32). The Pharisees request a "sign," presumably to authenticate Christ's message, and are told they will receive no sign but the sign of Jonah. In Matt. 12 Christ proceeds with the analogy that as Jonah was three days in the belly of the fish, so the Son of man will be three days in the earth. In both Matt. 12 and Luke 11, Christ comments that the Ninevites will stand up at judgment and condemn the Pharisees for their unbelief. Neither the three-day analogy, nor the future act of the Ninevites, is textually identified as the "sign of Jonah." Luke 11:30 gives the only positive clue: "For just as Jonah became a sign to the people of Nineveh, so the Son of man will be to this generation" (NRSV). We must ask, then, how Jonah "was a sign to the Ninevites." The only indication that the book offers for Jonah to be a sign to the Ninevites (not just to the Pharisees or us) is that he proclaimed a message of judgment. This served as a sign preceding the impending judgment of God.

Bibliography

Ackerman, J. "Satire and Symbolism in the Song of Jonah." Pages 213–46 in *Traditions in Transformation*, ed. B. Halpern and J. Levenson. Eisenbrauns, 1981; Alexander, D., D. Baker, and B. Waltke. *Obadiah, Jonah, Micah*. InterVarsity, 1988; Allen, L. *The Books of Joel, Obadiah, Jonah, and Micah*. Eerdmans, 1976; Clements, R. "The Purpose of the Book of Jonah." *VTSup* 28 (1974): 16–28; Cook, S., and S. C. Winter. *On the Way to Nineveh*. Scholars Press, 1999; Craig, K. "Jonah in Recent Research." *CurBS* 7 (1999): 97–118; Fretheim, T. "Jonah and Theodicy." *ZAW* 90 (1978): 227–37; idem. *Message of Jonah*. Augsburg, 1977; Holbert, J. C. "Deliverance Belongs to Yahweh! Satire in the Book of Jonah." *JSOT* 21 (1981): 59–81; Landes, G. "Jonah: A Mas[h]al?" Pages 137–58 in *Israelite Wisdom*, ed. J. Gammie, W. Brueggemann, et al. Scholars Press for Union Theol. Sem., 1978; idem. "The Kerygma of the Book of Jonah." *Interpretation* 21 (1967): 3–31; idem. "Matthew 12:40 as an Interpretation of 'the Sign of Jonah' against Its Biblical Background." Pages 665–84 in *The Word of the Lord Shall Go Forth*, ed. C. Meyers and M. O'Connor. Eisenbrauns, 1983; Michalowski, P. "Commemoration, Writing, and Genre in Ancient Mesopotamia." Pages 69–89 in *The Limits of Historiography*. Brill, 1999; Orth, M. "Genre in Jonah: The Effects of Parody in the Book of Jonah." Pages 257–82 in *The Bible in the Light of Cuneiform Literature*, ed. W. W. Hallo, B. W. Jones, and G. L. Mattingly. E. Mellen, 1990; Sasson, J. *Jonah*. Doubleday, 1990; Sherwood, Y. *A Biblical Text and Its Afterlives*. Cambridge University Press, 2000; Simon, U. *Jonah*. JPS, 1999; Stuart, D. *Hosea–Jonah*. Word, 1987; Trible, P. *Rhetorical Criticism*. Fortress, 1994; Walton, J. "The Object Lesson of Jonah 4:5–7 and the Purpose of the Book of Jonah." *BBR* 2 (1992): 47–57; Wiseman, D. J. "Jonah's Nineveh." *TynBul* 30 (1979): 29–51.

John H. Walton

Josephus   *See* Jewish Context of the NT

Joshua, Book of

Joshua gives the account of Israel's taking possession of the land promised by God, the division of the land among the tribes, and finally a renewal of the covenant at Shechem (Josh. 24).

History of Interpretation

In precritical Christian interpretation, Joshua was read in light of theology. Since the name Joshua is close to Jesus (identical in the Greek forms in LXX and NT), the figure was readily taken as a type of Christ. In Heb. 4:8–11 the "rest" into which Joshua led Israel is seen as temporary and inferior to the "rest" that still awaits God's people in Christ. Allegorical readings persisted into medieval times (Sæbø 184). In the Reformation it was read with the perspective that God's historical dealings and covenant with Israel were both preparatory for and analogous to his dealings with the Christian church and Christian nations (O'Donovan and O'Donovan 715). Joshua's actions in Canaan could then be exemplary for contemporary rulers (86, 605).

Critical interpretation, no longer looking for Christian doctrine, saw the book rather as evidence of the historical emergence of Israel. Because Joshua relates the taking of the land that was promised in the Pentateuch (Exod. 23:20–33; Deuteronomy passim), early critics thought that the sources they found in the Pentateuch could be traced into Joshua, within a so-called Hexateuch (von Rad 296–305; Fohrer 197). The strength of this view is its recognition of Joshua's continuities with the Pentateuchal books prior to Deuteronomy (e.g., Num. 13–14; 34:17). This kind of approach found links with Israel's actual early history, for example, in memories of conquest kept alive at the sanctuary at Gilgal (Fohrer 200–201).

Recent critical study has placed Joshua within the Deuteronomistic History (Deuteronomy–Kings; Noth). This view rightly observes close affinities between Deuteronomy and Joshua, for example, in the "Deuteronomic" terms in which Joshua succeeds Moses, especially the importance there of "the Book of the Law" (Josh. 1:1–9, cf. Deut. 28:61; 31:26), and also in specific correspondences between the two books (e.g., Deut. 27 and Josh. 8:30–35). Yet there are also contrasts between Deuteronomy and Joshua and, conversely, continuities with Numbers. For example, Joshua has a larger role for the priests than Deuteronomy (Josh. 4:10, cf. Num. 4:1–15). Noth's answer to this was to postulate priestly additions to the Deuteronomistic work. But this underrates the extent to which Joshua follows Numbers as well as Deuteronomy. The role of Joshua himself is prepared for throughout Exodus–Deuteronomy (Exod. 33:11; Num. 27:12–23; Deut. 3:23–29; 31:1–8, 23; 34:9).

Smend's reading of Josh. 1:1–9 found evidence of an exilic "nomistic," or conditional, redaction (1:7–9) of the basic Deuteronomistic account, which had stressed complete victory. A different line derives from the now-dominant view that the basic Deuteronomistic edition stems from the time of Josiah. Here, Joshua is deliberately portrayed as a type of Josiah, and the issue in the book is the need to affirm Yahwistic faith in the context of religious pluralism in late monarchic Judah; this is the condition of Josiah's expansionistic policies (Nelson 21–22).

Form-critically, Joshua has been compared with ancient Near Eastern conquest accounts. Younger has shown that Joshua broadly fits within patterns of such accounts from 1300 to 600 BCE. However, the book may also include other forms, such as toponym lists and boundary descriptions (cf. Nelson 9–11).

Regarding historicity, it is widely argued that Joshua's account of the conquest does not match what is known from archaeology about the patterns of occupation and destruction of the cities in Canaan, such as Ai (Jericho is less of a problem in this respect than sometimes claimed [Mazar 283]). Conservative explanations for these disharmonies include redating the conquest from the generally accepted thirteenth century to the fifteenth century BCE (Bimson), reexamining the identifications of cities in the account (including Ai), and exegetical strategies (e.g., Joshua may not always imply the total destruction of a city; Hess 141, cf. 158–59). In general, the provisional nature of archaeological results is stressed, "etiological" explanations of traditions avoided, and the basic historicity of the text affirmed.

Modern literary approaches draw attention to the dangers of oversimplified readings. Most significantly, a tension is perceived between the claims in the text that Joshua conquered the entire land (11:23; 21:44–45) and the perspective that, even in Joshua's old age, much of the land remained to be conquered (13:1) and certain enclaves still held out (15:6). It is the latter perspective that gave credence to Smend's nomistic redactional layer. The literary approach tends to see the discrepancy as having a function in the meaning of the book, such that, for example, Israel is depicted as undeserving and yet taking the land (Polzin 90).

Finally, sociological readings understand Joshua, not as the history of an actual conquest, but as the delineation of cultural, ethnic, and religious boundaries. Mullen's work provides this new paradigm, and for him the setting is, once again, the time of Josiah, the need being to define carefully who counts as "Israel" (Mullen 87–119).

Hearing the Message of Joshua

The book may be divided into four sections: entry to the land (1:1–5:12), its conquest (5:13–

405

12:24), its division among the tribes (13:1–21:45), and the worship of Yahweh in it (22:1–24:33).

The opening verses of Joshua announce that the time has come for the promises made to Israel through Moses to be fulfilled. The words "After the death of Moses the servant of the LORD" (1:1) not only function as a structural marker of a new beginning, but also recall that Joshua, not Moses, would lead Israel into the land (Deut. 3:23–29). The vision of the land that awaits is reaffirmed (1:4; cf. Deut. 11:24), God's promise of his presence is transferred from Moses to Joshua (1:5), and Joshua is called to "be strong and very courageous" (as Moses had already commissioned him; Deut. 31:7). This courage is to be directed in two ways: first to the battles ahead (v. 6), and second to the keeping of God's commandments, in the form of the "Book of the Law" (1:7–8), which thus stands over the whole action of the book. Joshua is both like and unlike Moses. With respect to God's call and enabling, he is like Moses in taking responsibility to put Israel in possession of the promised land (Moses had begun this with the settlement of the Transjordanian tribes; Deut. 3:12–17), and in his loyalty to Yahweh alone and his obedience to "the Book of the Law." Joshua is unlike Moses in that he is not himself *lawgiver* (but see Josh. 24:25–26), and that his leadership is specifically orientated to the task of land possession. His role as successor to Moses is thus limited, since in a certain sense Moses is succeeded by the "Book of the Law" itself (the written form of his spoken words), and in another sense by the "leaders of the congregation," who make decisions alongside Joshua concerning the status of the Gibeonites (Josh. 9:15, 18 NRSV; see also 23:2). The succession to Moses as prophet (Deut. 18:15–18) is not directly raised in Joshua.

The first section of the book (1:1–5:12) focuses on the crossing into the land. The mission of the spies (ch. 2) recalls a previous, unsuccessful mission (Num. 13–14), but here the cooperation of the Canaanite Rahab and her confession of faith give hope of a better sequel. The crossing of the Jordan (Josh. 3–4) has echoes of that of the Reed Sea at the exodus (Exod. 15). The first Passover in the land (5:10–12) signals the completion of the journey from Egypt to Canaan. Passover structurally marks the departure and the arrival, and theologically the passage from slavery to freedom.

The freedom has yet to be realized in the conquest itself, however. The narrative of this follows in 5:13–12:24. The taking of Jericho furnishes the paradigm for the conquest of a city within the promised land, with the destruction of every living creature in it (6:21), in accordance with the law of Deut. 20:16–18. That this is a victory of Yahweh alone is emphasized by the means by which the city falls. The qualifications of totality in this action are, first, the sparing of Rahab, in fulfillment of the spies' promise to her (2:14), and second, the offense against the ritual proscription of the goods of the city by Achan, which is then nullified by his execution along with his family.

The taking of Jericho is followed by further victories over cities both north and south, these victories being specifically over *kings* (Josh. 12:7–24). In this way a triumph is suggested, not only over enemies as such, but also of a new kind of society over one based (like Egypt) on tyranny. This is another example of the full circle from the exodus.

The account of the conquest is presented first as a clean sweep (11:23), but then as an ongoing work, likely to overspill Joshua's own life (13:1; cf. Judg. 1:1). In the account of the division of the land that follows, there are several indications that this corresponds to reality (15:63; 16:10; 17:12). The stage is thus set for a continuing struggle.

The third section relates the division of the land among the tribes (13:1–21:45). An exception is made for the Levitical (priestly) tribe, who receive towns within the other tribes' territories (14:3–4; ch. 21), following the principle in Deut. 18:2 that "the LORD is their inheritance" (where "inheritance" otherwise entails territory). In practice, they would have towns and land, and in that limited way hold property. But their particular role in relation both to Yahweh and to Israel as a whole is highlighted by this special treatment.

Finally, the commitment of Israel to worship Yahweh alone is reaffirmed, first in a charge by Joshua to "all Israel," represented by its elders, judges, and officers (23:2; cf. Deut. 16:18), then in a formal covenant renewal at Shechem (Josh. 24). This follows a reaffirmation of the obligation of Israel to worship Yahweh alone, including the tribes who had settled in Transjordan (Josh. 22). The people are unified within one land, and the unrivaled place of Yahweh in it is symbolized by the acknowledgment of only one place of worship, at this stage Shiloh, by virtue of the presence of the tabernacle there (18:1).

Can this story of Israel's liberation into its own land have relevance today? The answer lies neither in treating the book's message in a purely spiritualizing way (where, for example, crossing the Jordan is a metaphor for death), nor in finding direct mandates for the warlike behavior of contemporary nations. If there is a mandate for godly nationhood in Joshua, what form does it take? A reading of the NT, with its proclamation of the gospel to all nations, apparently precludes the application of Joshua narrowly to historic Israel and the land it once occupied. On the contrary, the idea of a "Christian nation," which has appeared frequently in the history of Christian thought, in widely differing places (Grosby 213–33), has more credibility. Yet that too has been capable of abuse, to the point of justifying repressive nationalisms and landgrabs. If the dangerous theology of Joshua is to be appropriated somehow for political theology, it must be in such a way as to avoid such extreme and self-regarding realizations.

Joshua and Theology

Joshua continues, in one sense, Deuteronomy's blueprint for nationhood. This consists in an ordering of people under Torah, which is in turn given by God. Joshua himself is called to show the right attitude to this Torah (Josh. 1:7–8), in terms similar to those required of the king (Deut. 17:18–20). And when he comes to pass on responsibility for leadership to "elders and heads, their judges and officers," he urges them in turn to adhere rigorously to it (Josh. 23:2, 6 NRSV). In the covenant renewal at Shechem, Joshua establishes a "statute and ordinance" with the people (24:25 AT; cf. Deut. 5:31), and then writes in the "Book of the Law [Torah] of God" (v. 26). This suggests that the "Book of the Law" is open to allow reaffirmations of Israel's allegiance to God to be added to it (this in qualification of Deut. 4:2). Joshua shows that Torah always informs the people's true leadership.

It is Torah obedience, furthermore, that legitimates the people's possession of territory. The close connection of law and territory is established in Deuteronomy, in which the gift of land is consistently predicated on the people's obedience to Torah (Deut. 17:14–20 is an example). The same connection is made at the outset of Joshua, when Joshua is exhorted to "be strong and courageous" in respect of both law-keeping and land-possession (Josh. 1:6–9). The book of Joshua, therefore, enacts in principle the concept of a people living in a territory, subject to a law that operates within its borders.

Such possession, however, must be legitimate. An important function of Joshua is to demonstrate the legitimacy of Israel's possession of the land of Canaan. The issue is confronted directly, because the land to be possessed is no "land without a people." On the contrary, it is inhabited by peoples who are firmly bedded down in their own places, and who base their own claims, we suppose, on their actual possession, their culture, and their religion. The claim to legitimate possession entails the assertion of the right to take and keep by force, and in principle the need to press the claim against others. This is what is asserted in Yahweh's victory over the peoples of Canaan. It is not only a victory, but also an act of judgment, a claim that it is right that Israel and not others should possess this land. The nature of the war against the Canaanites as a judgment is signaled in several texts outside Joshua (Gen. 15:16; Lev. 20:23; Deut. 9:4–5), and in the frequent characterization of them as acting abominably in God's eyes (Deut. 12:29–32). (For the nexus of victory, judgment, and possession, see also O'Donovan and O'Donovan 36–45.)

The confrontation between Israel and the nations, therefore, is between a nation that lives under Yahweh in obedience to Torah and others that do not. This fundamental difference between Israel and the Canaanite nations is fully present in Joshua only by virtue of the knowledge that Deuteronomy and the Pentateuch generally lie behind it. But it appears at certain points, one hint being in the categorization of the Canaanite enemies repeatedly as "kings" (Josh. 12), a feature that seems to pitch the type of power in the city-states against the kingship of Yahweh, much like the power of Pharaoh in Exodus.

It is against this background that we have to consider the greatest stumbling block for modern readers of Joshua, notwithstanding the rationale just offered. This is the "ban of destruction," or the *kherem*, the command from God to put the inhabitants of Canaan to the sword (6:17). In modern commentary it is common to explain this command as a metaphor for rigorous adherence to Yahweh and separation from other forms of religion (Moberly). This is supported by the historical assessment that in all probability Israel never did to Canaan what the book of Joshua depicts it as having done. The language of *kherem* was borrowed from the conventions of ancient Near Eastern religious war (also known from the famous ninth-century BCE Moabite Stone, on which the Moabite King Mesha claimed to have put *Israel* to the *kherem*).

The problem with a metaphorical understanding is that Joshua speaks about real peoples, land, and politics. The plain force of the language has been felt by those in every age who have used the conquest of Canaan as grounds, by identifying themselves with Israel, for their own subjugation of peoples by war in order to possess land (Collins). The use of a warlike metaphor to speak of a God who abhors war would have to be regarded as a failed strategy!

The issue must be approached differently, by asking whether the book of Joshua as a whole really portrays Israel as matching the criteria of legitimate possession. We have begun to see that the story of the book is not as straightforward as it appears at first glance. Israel permits first Rahab (Josh. 2) and then the Gibeonites (Josh. 9) to live alongside themselves in the land. And the picture of total possession is called in question by the perspective that possession remains to be accomplished (13:1), and has in some cases been frustrated. There are thus questions as to boundaries: what are the actual boundaries of the people? As Hawk (xxii–xxiii) has put it, outsiders (Rahab, Gibeon) become insiders, while insiders (Achan's family) become outsiders. And even the geographical boundary of the Jordan is put in question by the issue of the settlement of some tribes in Transjordan, producing the conflict related in Josh. 22 (Jobling).

On this view the careful constructions of Israelite identity are not finally affirmed in Joshua, but precisely put in question. While the building blocks for a national identity may be put in place here (and thus for nations generally, not just Israel), the picture of Israel in Joshua is part of the wider portrayal in Genesis–Kings of a people that fails to become what it is called to be. Joshua proclaims at Shechem: "You cannot serve the LORD" (24:19 NRSV), a jarring note that corresponds to Deuteronomy's view (9:4–7), ensuring that the story of Israel's possession becomes a critique of the violence that subjugates others without rightly possessing a mandate to do so. In Israel's failure to occupy the land of Canaan in obedience lies the warning that none might claim to make war and dispossess others in the name of God. In Hawk's words: "Joshua should be studied, not shunned, precisely because it holds the mirror up to all who regard themselves as the people of God" (xxxii). Joshua is the counterpart of the prophetic vision for Israel, which consistently resists the identification of "Israel" with an ethnic people and with power that relies on force (see also Jewett and Lawrence). The legitimate possession of warrants to be a nation depends not on unbreakable historic guarantees, but on ongoing commitment to true freedom from tyrannies and idolatries of whatever kind. Joshua, as a document for Israel in its own place and time,

offers a remit for peoples today to conceive their specific traditions of culture and place anew, in light of God's law of liberty.

In the NT, Israel finds its true self in Christ (O'Donovan and O'Donovan 131), and so in the supranational church. This does not mean that God's action of judgment on the nations is revoked, nor the enactment of judgment within political structures (Rom. 13:1–5), both of which can be said to be proposed by the book of Joshua, the latter with warrants that extend to all political authorities. But it does mean the renunciation of all claims to be the people of God in ways that equate with ethnic or national entities.

See also Earth/Land; Political Theology

Bibliography

Bimson, J. *Redating the Exodus and Conquest*. JSOTSup 5. Almond, 1981; Collins, J. "The Zeal of Phinehas: The Bible and the Legitimation of Violence." *JBL* 122 (2003): 3–21; Fohrer, G. *Introduction to the Old Testament*. SCM, 1970; Grosby, S. *Biblical Ideas of Nationality*. Eisenbrauns, 2002; Hawk, L. *Joshua*. Liturgical Press, 2000; Hess, R. *Joshua*. TOTC. InterVarsity, 1996; Jewett, R., and J. Lawrence. *Captain America and the Crusade against Evil*. Eerdmans, 2003; Jobling, D. "'The Jordan a Boundary': Transjordan in Israel's Ideological Geography." Pages 88–134 in *The Sense of Biblical Narrative, II*. JSOTSup 39. JSOT, 1986; Mazar, A. "The Iron Age I." Pages 258–301 in *The Archaeology of Ancient Israel*, ed. A. Ben-Tor. Open University of Israel, 1992; Moberly, R. W. L. "Theological Interpretation of an Old Testament Book: A Response to Gordon McConville's *Deuteronomy*." *SJT* 56 (2003): 516–25; Mullen, E. *Narrative History and Ethnic Boundaries*. SemeiaSt. Scholars Press, 1993; Nelson, R. *Joshua*. OTL. Westminster John Knox, 1997; Noth, M. *The Deuteronomistic History*. JSOTSup 15. JSOT, 1981; O'Donovan, O. *The Desire of the Nations*. Cambridge University Press, 1996; O'Donovan, O., and J. Lockwood O'Donovan, eds. *From Irenaeus to Grotius*. Eerdmans, 1999; Polzin, R. *Moses and the Deuteronomist*. Seabury, 1980; Rad, G. von. *Old Testament Theology*. Vol. 1. Oliver & Boyd, 1962; Sæbø, M. *Hebrew Bible/Old Testament: The History of Its Interpretation*. Vol. 1, part 2, *The Middle Ages*. Vandenhoeck & Ruprecht, 2000; Smend, R. "The Law and the Nations: A Contribution to Deuteronomistic Tradition History." Pages 95–110 in *Reconsidering Israel and Judah*, ed. G. Knoppers and J. G. McConville. SBTS 8. Eisenbrauns, 2000; Younger, K. L. *Ancient Conquest Accounts*. JSOTSup 98. Sheffield Academic Press, 1990.

J. G. McConville

Jude, Book of

The challenge of Jude for theological interpretation is not so much its theology as its ethics: what is the ethical evaluation of such a prophetic denunciation? The second challenge is Jude's use of noncanonical literature and its meaning for our view of the canon.

History of Interpretation

The interpretation of Jude begins with 2 Peter, who edits and adapts Jude, such as removing the direct references to the Pseudepigrapha, to form his second chapter. Unlike 2 Peter, Jude was cited relatively early and included in the early canon lists, only to go through a period of questioning due to his citation of Pseudepigrapha. By the end of the fourth century, most of the church had decided for the canonicity of Jude and thus were using the letter. In the contemporary period Jude again fell out of favor, not because of his use of the Pseudepigrapha, but because of his prophetic denunciation that was viewed as ethically sub-Christian. Normally the work was dated late in the first century or in the first half of the second. Thus it was only after a century and more of neglect that the last thirty years have seen a revival of interest in the letter, as it began to be viewed by some as a representative of Jewish Christianity and appreciated by many for its rhetorical skill.

The Message of Jude

Jude's message is relatively straightforward. He is concerned about traveling teachers who are subverting the local church. His concern is not about doctrinal deviation, but about a rejection of the practical rule of Jesus over Christians in that his teachings were being rejected in the name of grace, which was being used to justify licentiousness. Jude denounces this moral deviation and pronounces a sentence of doom on these teachers, a doom based on illustrations drawn from his understanding of narratives that we find in the OT. Because these teachers also appear to have rejected angelic authority (as well as the authority of the established leaders in the church)—whether of fallen or holy angels is not clear—Jude also accuses them of rebellion, adding to this a third charge of greed. Thus, deviation from the teaching and character of Jesus, in the realms of money, power, and sex, he condemns as practices that doom these Christian teachers to hell.

The response that Jude teaches is twofold. First, the believers are themselves to focus more on growing in their Christian life (prayer in the Spirit, love, Christian practice, and eschatological expectancy). Second, they are to reach out to those caught in the teaching of these teachers, extricate such, and receive them. There is nothing said about dealing with the teachers (no

sentence of excommunication or instruction to have nothing to do with them), but instead they are left to the judgment of "the Lord," who is coming soon.

Jude and the Canon

It is well known that Jude refers to both *1 En.* 1:9 and probably the lost ending of the *Testament of Moses* (known to us from references in the writings of the fathers). What is not as clearly seen is that most of Jude's references to OT narratives reflect the recontextualization of those narratives in Jewish literature. This means that he makes no differentiation between OT texts and *1 Enoch*, nor a differentiation between the canonical form of a story and how that story was told in later Jewish literature. Thus, Jude demonstrates a stage in the development of canon consciousness in which narratives have authority because they are related to the canon, not because they are the canonical form of a narrative. This reminds us that the questions Jews asked about OT works (whether they could be given up to be burned in situations of persecution) were different than later Christian questions about NT works (whether they were to be read in and thereby endorsed by the church).

As Jude's second contribution to the canon, he makes his twin points that ethical deviations are deviations from the faith as much as or more than doctrinal deviations, and that eschatological expectation determines and enforces ethics. Furthermore, he demonstrates in his treatment of those who have followed the intruding teachers his awareness of the present as a time of grace before judgment.

Finally, Jude also demonstrates that the genre of prophetic denunciation was alive and well throughout the first century.

Theological Significance of Jude

Theologically, Jude reveals that neither post-fourth-century concepts of canon nor modern models of biblical interpretation are absolute. His narrative method, which relies on the later development of the biblical narratives, and his loose sense of canonical boundaries show this.

Furthermore, Jude contributes to our understanding of the importance of eschatological, even apocalyptic, expectation. It is the lively expectation of final judgment that for Jude sanctions present ethical behavior.

Jude also shows us the practical application of the doctrine of grace. Upon repentance alone, people are freely received back into the orthodox camp.

Finally, Jude demonstrates the centrality of the concept that Jesus is Lord to the early church. Those who deny his authority in their lives ethically (no matter what their doctrinal confession) are apostate and under sentence of eternal judgment. Heresy for Jude is primarily ethical.

In none of these is Jude unique, but his contribution nonetheless is real.

See also Pseudepigrapha

Bibliography

Bauckham, R. *Jude, 2 Peter.* WBC 50. Word, 1983; idem. *Jude and the Relatives of Jesus in the Early Church.* T&T Clark, 1990; Bray, G., ed. *James, 1–2 Peter, 1–3 John, Jude.* ACCSNT 11. InterVarsity, 2000; Charles, J. D. *Literary Strategy in the Epistle of Jude.* University of Scranton Press, 1993; Chester, A., and R. Martin. *The Theology of the Letters of James, Peter, and Jude.* NTT. Cambridge University Press, 1994; Kelly, J. N. D. *A Commentary on the Epistles of Peter and Jude.* BNTC. Baker, 1981; Kraftchick, S. *Jude, 2 Peter.* Abingdon, 2002; Neyrey, J. *2 Peter, Jude.* AB 37C. Doubleday, 1993; Vögtle, A. *Der Judasbrief, der 2. Petrusbrief.* EKKNT 22. Benziger/Neukirchener Verlag, 1994; Watson, D. *Invention, Arrangement, and Style.* SBLDS 104. Scholars Press, 1988.

Peter H. Davids

Judges, Book of

On the surface Judges seems a straightforward account of Israel's history between the conquest of Canaan and the rise of David, focused on the role of Israel's leadership with respect to the people's increasingly sinful behavior. Along these lines the book breaks quite neatly into three parts:

- an overview story of the failure to complete the conquest (1:1–2:5);
- stories of various judges, which collectively portray a downward spiral of repeated cycles of sin, judgment, distress, and deliverance (2:6–16:31); and
- two final stories of religious and moral depravity (chs. 17–21).

Below the surface, the book is more than simply a negative account of this particular period. The writer of Judges was using past events and experiences of the community of faith and its leadership to exhort his contemporary audience to follow the Lord. Based on theology drawn from Deuteronomy, Judges argued that Israel's leaders were to be constantly reminding Israel to remember the Lord's covenant faithfulness demonstrated by his past action in the exodus and conquest, as well as his ongoing and continued acts of compassion in repeated deliverances of Israel. Therefore, they were to fear the Lord and follow him by keeping covenant (Deut. 4:9–12; cf. Judg. 2:6–10, 20–23; 3:1–6; 6:13). Judges understood this leadership as coming from Judah (1:2–20) and through a king (e.g., 17:6; 18:1; 19:1; 21:25). Judges was pointing, in other words, to King David as the ideal, covenant-keeping leader. For the writer, the right kind of leader—exemplified by King David—was essential for transforming the people of God.

History of Interpretation

Among the historical books in the OT, Judges has perhaps received the least attention in the history of interpretation, except in the modern period.

The events and personages from the period of the judges are barely mentioned in the rest of the OT (only a dozen times outside the book of Judges). The references are of three types: (1) General historical overviews reflect the same negative view (in language similar to Judges) of Israel's covenantal failings in the period of the judges (1 Sam. 12:8–12; Neh. 9:22–37; Pss. 78:54–72; 106:34–46). (2) There are particular accounts of events in Judges (e.g., the victory over Midian [chs. 7–8; Ps. 83:9–12; Isa. 9:4; 10:26], the moral failure of Gibeah [ch. 19; Hos. 9:9; 10:9], and Abimelech's ignominious death [ch. 9; 2 Sam. 11:21]). And (3) there is one positive allusion to the period of the judges (Isa. 1:26), where Isaiah sees the future Zion, purified of sin, as a time of the restoration of judges "as in days of old."

Jewish interpretation in the Second Temple period and Christian interpretation in the NT (and early church period) also show relatively little use of the book, especially in light of much more substantial treatment of other portions of the OT. In the Second Temple period, only a few of the various historical reviews covered the period of the judges. Pseudo-Philo (first century CE) reviewed the period of the judges (*L.A.B.* 25.1–48.5), and spoke of Kenaz, rather than Judah, as the one to lead Israel. (Kenaz is mentioned only in passing in Judges but receives extensive treatment in Pseudo-Philo.) Ben Sirach (175 BCE), as part of a brief review of Israel's history, spoke briefly of the judges in positive tones, suggesting that they did not yield to idolatry (Sir. 46:11–12). During this period the tendency to idealize important figures from Israel's past (e.g., Abraham, Moses, Jacob) was part apologetic against those opposing the Jews of the Second Temple period, and part support for a positive history to encourage national Jewish identity. Not all comments were positive, however. In a passing remark, *The Lives of the Prophets* (early first century CE) refers to the period of the judges as "days of the anarchy" (*Liv. Pro.* 16.3).

In the NT, Acts 13:19–20 and Heb. 11:32–34 are the only clear reflections on the period of the judges. In Acts 13, as Paul reviews Israel's history in a sermon leading up to Christ, he mentions only that the conquest took about 450 years and that God gave Israel judges. (None of the similar sermons in Acts—by Peter, Stephen, and Paul—where a historical review is used even mention the judges; in Acts 7:45–47 Stephen jumps from Joshua to David.)

Hebrews 11:32–34 mentions four judges:

> And what more shall I say? I do not have time to tell about Gideon, Barak, Samson, Jephthah, David, Samuel and the prophets, who through faith conquered kingdoms, administered justice, and gained what was promised; who shut the mouths of lions, quenched the fury of the flames, and escaped the edge of the sword; whose weakness was turned to strength; and who became powerful in battle and routed foreign armies.

This passage comes at the end of the so-called "honor roll of faith," where the writer of Hebrews extols the faith of Abraham, Moses, and significant others. The remark in verse 32—"*I do not have time to tell about* Gideon, Barak, Samson, Jephthah"—sums up (unintentionally) what seems to have been the prevailing attitude among interpreters, that one can pass over Judges quickly, if not skip it altogether.

Between the ancient church and the present day, relatively little has been done with the book of Judges as a whole. Yet in 1615, during the Reformation, Richard Rogers wrote a thousand-page commentary on the book of Judges. He saw the period through the lens of Heb. 11, with his commentary as being for the benefit of "all such as desire to grow in faith and Repentance, and especially of them, who would more cleerely [*sic*] understand and make use of the worthie [*sic*] examples of the Saints, recorded in divine history." Rogers saw the various judges as positive examples of faith. What other work was done on Judges seems to share Rogers's approach of interpreting particular judges as illustrations of theological points. A century later, for example, Jonathan Edwards reflected on Jephthah's vow (Judg. 11:32–40) at length, while addressing issues of his day concerning making vows and covenants.

In the modern period, Judges has been treated as part of a larger, single body known as the "Deuteronomistic History," comprised of Deuteronomy, Joshua, Judges, Samuel, and Kings. Within this grouping of books, scholars have spent more time with Joshua, Samuel, and Kings than with Judges. Only in the contemporary period, where literary—particularly feminist—readings of the Bible have been the focus, has Judges become the object of more intense theological and interpretative scrutiny. In particular, the stories of Acsah, Deborah, Jael, Jephthah's daughter, and the Levite's concubine have received much attention.

When studying any OT passage or book, one should "read the text twice." A "first reading" seeks to understand the text in its own historical setting and on its own terms, without reference to later scriptural or historical developments (e.g., the life, death, and resurrection of Christ). What was the situation of the original audience? How did the author address their concerns and struggles? What did he want them to learn about God and about themselves? How did he want them to respond? A "second reading" looks at how the text fits into the broader picture of the whole sweep of redemptive history, how it appears in light of the climax of the OT story in Christ, and then how it contributes to theology and application.

The book of Judges is not merely a showcase of examples of behavior or belief to imitate or avoid. Rather, it reveals God's plan, purpose, and character (e.g., faithfulness to his covenant and to his people; his patience and compassion in delaying the ultimate judgment of exile from the land). It also reveals the human heart (e.g., its inability to serve God faithfully; its ongoing need to know who God is and what he has done for his people). Judges lays bare the community of faith's need in a certain place and time—the need for godly leadership to lead them in keeping covenant by faith. But like all OT Scripture, it also points forward to Christ, the perfect leader who alone can truly redeem, change hearts, and reveal God.

The Message of Judges

This section reflects a "first reading," as described above, concerned with the message of Judges to its original OT audience. Under the later section entitled "Judges and Theology," a "second reading" of Judges in the light of Christ will come into play.

411

Written *after* the time when David became king, Judges has provided the only extant account of the historical events between the conquest and the rise of David. But the recounting of that history was not its primary purpose. Rather, most simply put, the message of Judges addresses the difficulty that Israel's leadership (the judges) had in leading the people of God to fear the Lord and keep covenant. Failure to follow the Lord by fearing him and keeping his covenant threatened Israel's continued peace and presence in the land. Judges calls the Israelites to consider whom they would follow in terms of both human and divine leaders.

More particularly, Judges' purpose is (1) to demonstrate the failure of Israel's leadership to pass on the knowledge of God to the next generation or to lead them in covenant-keeping (2:10 as it leads into 2:11ff.) and (2) to argue for a better leader: a covenant-keeping king, not a judge; from Judah, not Benjamin; David, not Saul. (David and Saul are never explicitly mentioned in Judges, but the character and behavior of the tribes of Judah and Benjamin are contrasted several times, serving to contrast the character of the leadership of the most famous sons of each tribe—David and Saul.) For Judges, the answer to the crisis in leadership and the increasing Canaanization of Israel was David, the king from Judah, who would lead the people of God in fearing the Lord and keeping covenant.

Judges opens by noting the crisis in leadership created by Joshua's death and God's answer that Judah would lead Israel in completing the conquest (1:1–2). Judges 1 continues by outlining the general success of the tribe of Judah in taking their allotted inheritance (1:2–20) and the almost universal failure of the other tribes to do likewise (1:21–36). Judah is presented as keeping covenant and as a result being the tribe to lead Israel. David, to whom Judges' focus on Judah is pointing, ultimately completed the conquest of Canaan by taking the stronghold of Zion from the Jebusites (2 Sam. 5:6–10). Moreover, he decisively defeated the Philistines (5:17–25), something that even Judah was unable to do in the period of the Judges (Judg. 1:19).

The heart of the book recounts the stories of twelve judges: six are extended accounts and six are short (3:7–16:31). In the extended narratives the problem of the particular leadership of the judges themselves is elaborated. Significantly, the first judge, Othniel, is from Judah, and there is nothing negative recounted about his leadership (3:7–11), both details pointing positively to the role of Judah in leadership, and hence to David. Judges concludes with the accounts of two sordid episodes of religious and moral failure (chs. 17–21). The refrain "in those days Israel had no king; everyone did as he saw fit" (17:6; 21:25; cf. 18:1; 19:1) punctuates the message of Judges, pointing to a king—David in particular—as the solution to Israel's covenant-keeping woes.

Judges showed that not just any king would do. Appealing to the theology of kingship found in Deut. 17:14–20, the writer of Judges is arguing for a covenant-keeping king who would read the Law daily and lead the people in faithful acknowledgment of God (Deut. 4:9, 32–40). Throughout Deuteronomy that obedience is presented as a faith response (fearing the Lord). As Israel knew God, experienced his care and lordship, meditated on his amazing acts on their behalf (particularly the exodus), and rejoiced in being his children, they would *want* to honor him. Hence, it was essential to recall regularly, and teach their children, these things so that each new generation of Israelites would know the Lord and live as his obedient covenant children.

Judges tells repeated tales of what happens when that knowledge of the Lord is not passed on to subsequent generations (e.g., the story of Gideon, who has heard of the Lord from his father; but his father has also built an altar of Baal—Judg. 6:11ff., esp. vv. 13, 25). By focusing on the judges, the book emphasizes the integral role of *leaders* in this process.

Judges 2:16–19 states that Israel will *not listen to their judges* but prostitute themselves after other gods, thus suggesting that the judges may serve prophetic roles (although the accounts portray them almost exclusively as military leaders). And 2:17, read by itself, seems to imply that the judges are righteous and that the problem is simply with Israel at large. The individual stories, however, give more-complex accounts of the judges' faith and failure, elaborating on the problems of their leadership and indicating that their own behavior and struggles with belief have made it difficult for them to remind and teach Israel. They do bring about mighty victories and deliver the people, and they do exercise faith; they are not simply failures. But they fall short and do not establish permanent peace (e.g., 2:19; 3:11; 8:33).

Judges recounts a downward spiral in the pattern of Israel's belief and behavior. The people become increasingly "Canaanized" (Block 58), as shown preeminently in their idolatry, but also in religious (chs. 17–18) and moral (chs. 19–21) failure. The pattern of sin, judgment, crying out in distress, and then deliverance by means of Spirit-anointed judges is not effecting any lasting change. God shows compassion again and again by not sending the nation into exile and by continually delivering the people. But the foreshadowing is there: Israel has to change, or the downward spiral of sin and judgment is going to lead to loss of the land and of God (18:30–31). The judges are not getting that job done. Israel needs to have changed hearts, as Deuteronomy calls for (10:16; 29:2–4; 30:6). They desperately need the right kind of leader—who will remind them of who the Lord is, who will lead them in obeying, and who will help them pass that knowledge on to their offspring. According to Judges, they need a king—from Judah.

By providing mixed accounts of the judges—faith and failure—with the repeated refrain in the closing chapters—"In those days Israel had no king; everyone did as he saw fit" (17:6; 18:1; 19:1; 21:25)—Judges is arguing that a king is a better kind of leader. Not just any king would accomplish this, of course. It is essential that he be a God-fearing, covenant-keeping king, who would help the people themselves keep covenant.

Judges was not written to the people who lived during the time of the judges. It was an account of that time period for a later audience of God's people. For its contemporary audience, Judges is an account of what happens when one generation fails to pass on the knowledge and fear of the Lord, and it is therefore an exhortation to correct that problem among themselves. Its message is to seek and embrace God-fearing, covenant-keeping leadership, which would lead Israel in keeping covenant.

The original setting has been much debated: Was it during David's reign? In the divided kingdom? During the reign of Josiah? In the exile? After the exile? A subtle polemic against Benjamin (and by implication Saul) is found throughout. Benjamin was first in the list of tribes who failed to complete their part of the conquest (1:21). Gibeah in Benjamin (Saul's hometown) was portrayed as a new Sodom (Judg. 19 vs. Gen. 19). Benjamin was the source of a civil war in Israel (Judg. 20), in which all Israel fought against Benjamin. In contrast, Judah, the tribe chosen to lead (1:1–2; 20:18) against Israel's enemies, is the tribe that successfully keeps covenant by driving out the Canaanites (1:2–20). Together the anti-Benjamite polemic and the pro-Judahite apology suggest that Judges may well have been written in the period when there were two viable candidates for the throne—one from the house of David and the other from the house of Saul. That is the period when David was king in the south in Hebron, and Ish-Bosheth, the son of Saul, was king of the ten northern tribes in Ephraim (2 Sam. 2:8–5:10).

In that context, the writer of Judges was encouraging his fellow Israelites to choose and follow King David. One senses the writer hoping that under the leadership of a godly king like David, the people's hearts would at last be changed, they would fear the Lord and keep covenant, and they would avoid the covenant curse of the loss of the land that the Lord had given them.

Judges and the Canon

While Judges may not be reflected upon in great detail elsewhere in the history of interpretation, it does have several important canonical functions. First of all, if not for the book of Judges, almost nothing would be known of this period between the initial entry into the land and the time of Samuel. In that context it provides the first extended picture of problems with covenant-keeping in Israel. It sets a quite different tone than Joshua. Judges repeats the conclusion of Joshua (24:27–31) virtually verbatim rather early (Judg. 2:6–9). Yet, this passage, which served to conclude Joshua on a positive and hopeful note, is used by Judges to introduce the decline of Israel.

The second canonical contribution concerns a particular accent in Deuteronomic theology. As mentioned above, more-recent OT scholarship has most often treated Judges as part of a larger Deuteronomistic History. This DH reflects the particular theological concerns of the late preexilic and exilic periods as refracted through certain key themes: God dealt with Israel by means of the covenant he had made with them (Deut. 4:31). Worship was to be centralized in Jerusalem (ch. 12). Idolatry was the key sin that represented covenant-breaking (4:15–28). And blessing for obedience or judgment for disobedience was the primary expression of covenant in action (ch. 28). It is arguable, however, that Judges was written earlier than the late preexilic period and stands as a unique witness to an earlier Deuteronomic theology with a somewhat different focus. One generation is proclaiming the great and mighty deeds of God to the next and teaching the next generation to fear the Lord (Deut. 4:9–12; Judg. 2:6–10). Judges then becomes an account of what happens when one generation fails to pass on the knowledge and fear of the Lord.

A third canonical contribution concerns the land of inheritance that the Lord had given to Israel. The land's theological significance was underscored by (1) the use of the refrain that "the land had peace" to conclude narratives of deliverance (3:11, 30; 5:31; 8:28) and (2) the recollection of the Lord's gift of the land in covenant lawsuit contexts (2:1–4; 6:7–10). The Lord (appropriately) punished the Israelites for their covenant disobedience by letting them experience captivity to foreigners while they were still in the land, which foreshadowed the eventual captivity of Israel outside it.

A fourth canonical contribution concerns kingship, about which Deuteronomy was reticent (17:14–20). David brought kingship into a prominent position in the theology and tradition of Israel. Judges, written after David had become king, argued for covenant-keeping kingship like David's as a means for leading people in spiritual transformation (echoed by Ps. 78—see esp. vv. 65–72 in light of 56–64). This would help Israel to avoid a continual falling into sin, and instead to enjoy lasting peace. From a perspective of leadership in the community of faith, Judges is perhaps the strongest canonical argument for kingship, although the focus is not on political structure but on spiritual transformation.

Judges and Theology

As has been noted, Judges took its theology primarily from Deuteronomy. Its theology was covenantal. That is, whatever happened to Israel, for good or for ill, was in the hands of the Lord, according to the covenant that he had made with them. When they were oppressed, it was the Lord who sold Israel into the hands of oppressors on account of their sin. When they were delivered, it was the Lord who raised up the judge to deliver them because of his compassion. Both judgment and deliverance (compassion) flowed from God's absolute covenant faithfulness (cf. Deut. 4:31; Judg. 2:18–19).

For the writer of Judges, the immediate hope on the horizon was a king, in particular, David, the king after God's own heart. In later OT history, however, it became obvious that most of the kings were no better at leading the people in keeping covenant than the judges had been. In fact, their perpetual unfaithfulness eventually caused Israel to be cast out of the land. Even the few outstanding, godly kings like David, who brought peace that lasted beyond their own reigns, were not able to change their own hearts or the hearts of the people. Books written by those standing further down the stream of OT history paint substantially the same bleak picture of covenant unfaithfulness on the part of the Lord's people. The OT story as a whole still cries out, like the book of Judges, for a leader who would be faithful to God and lead his people in keeping covenant.

That cry is answered in Christ, who was from the tribe of Judah, descended from David. Deuteronomy shows that Israel's faithfulness would flow from knowing the Lord. Jesus, God himself, became a man and dwelt among the Israelites, revealing the Lord to humankind in an unprecedented way (e.g., John 1:14; 1 John 1:1–2), being the exact radiance of God's glory (Heb. 1:3). Israel was to remember the great deliverance event of the exodus as the ultimate expression of God's care. Jesus brought about an even greater deliverance, saving his people even from sin and death by his own death on the cross. The unfaithfulness of the Israelite kings cost the nation the promised land. Jesus' faithfulness secures heaven itself for his people. The judges did not bring about permanent peace. Jesus, David's son, brought an enduring kingdom and peace that lasts even into eternity. Judges urged the need for a king, from Judah, who would fear God, live in covenant faithfulness, and lead the people in doing the same. Jesus, who was from the tribe of Judah, feared God and lived in perfect obedience to the Father (e.g., Phil. 2:5–8), giving his people an example to follow. Even more, by sending the Holy Spirit, he was able to do what David could not do: break the cycle of sin, judgment, crying out, and deliverance, and actually change the hearts of God's people, enabling them to be faithful to God.

God's compassion during the period of the judges pointed to the greater compassion and permanent peace he would bring through Jesus, the better deliverer. In Jesus, God's repeated acts of compassion in the OT have a foundation; God's mercy, grounded in the cross, extends "backward" as the basis for his compassion in Judges.

Furthermore, in Christ the judges are viewed from a new perspective. As recognized in the history of interpretation, Heb. 11 focuses on the judges as examples of faith, not as examples of failed covenantal leadership. Hebrews is not simply idealizing these characters the way interpreters in the Second Temple period did. Rather, Hebrews' interpretation is grounded in a "second reading," as described earlier, in rereading the OT in light of what has happened in Christ. In the setting of a first reading, the judges are complex characters, sometimes acting in faith, sometimes falling short. But once Christ had come, the struggling faith of the judges was understood as looking forward to Christ. In the end, in Christ, they were seen not as bringing the solution, but as acting in faith that God would bring the solution. Which he did, in Christ.

The book of Judges called its original audience to follow a king who would lead them in knowing and fearing the Lord. In its place in the Christian canon, it issues the same call, except that the king to follow is no longer David but Jesus.

Bibliography

Block, D. *Judges, Ruth.* NAC 6. Broadman & Holman, 2002; Brettler, M. Z. "The Book of Judges: Literature as Politics." *JBL* 108 (1989): 395–418; Davis, D. R. "A Proposed Life Setting for the Book of Judges." Ph.D. diss., Southern Baptist Theological Seminary, 1978; Klein, L. R. *The Triumph of Irony in the Book of Judges.* Almond, 1988; O'Connell, R. H. *The Rhetoric of the Book of Judges.* Brill, 1996; Rogers, R. *A Commentary upon the Whole Booke of Iudges.* T. Man, 1615; Webb, B. G. *The Book of Judges.* JSOT, 1987.

J. Alan Groves

Judgment   *See* Last Things, Doctrine of; Prophetic Writings; Sin, Doctrine of; Violence

Justice

The biblical theme of justice provides a standard and practice for the theological interpretation of Scripture. It exhibits a contrast to modern, post-Enlightenment notions of justice, which focus on the power and freedom of autonomous subjects. It also contrasts with conceptions under the umbrella of postmodernity that consider justice a matter of freedom from the tyranny of the majority, or privilege given to the perspectives of the marginalized. Whether focused on the liberty of individual rational thinkers or various oppressed constituencies, conceptions in modernity and postmodernity both contain primary commitments to the human subject. An aim toward understanding biblical justice in such a way that one hears from God and honors God in practice requires a perspective that places humans beneath the divine.

Justice conceived pan-biblically requires an understanding of the drama of creation and redemption that refuses to drive a wedge between the two. Genesis 1:26–28 and Ps. 8 reveal that God created humans and gave them the responsibility for earthkeeping and cultivation. With this initial responsibility comes the demand of justice: humans are to reflect the character of God in their response to the divine mandate that attends the purpose of human existence, granting God's unique creatures their due regard and proper treatment. This regard and treatment are considered "just" because the resultant social, political,

and relational practices correspond to the righteous character of God as seen, for example, in God's love for the poor and downtrodden as well as in the hospitality God commands his covenant people to extend the stranger and alien. Some traditions also claim that this human responsibility specifically carries with it that justice inheres in the social structure of creation, leading to the view that discoverable divine ordinances exist that correspond to and express the command to love God and neighbor. These latter traditional views present a high view of general revelation as a source for the application of justice, though in concert with special revelation.

The biblical narrative reveals God as a covenant-maker and keeper, self-disclosed as one who will judge rightly and who expects those in covenantal relationship to act justly as one way of expressing fidelity. The Hebrew words for justice and righteousness (*mishpat* and *tsedaqah*, respectively) both reflect significant aspects of the biblical concept of justice. *Tsedaqah* reflects God's righteousness in moral character and his covenant love and faithfulness, as well as the legislative, judicial, and administrative aspects of his action in the world. God's law reflects his perfection in character. He rules justly, and his providential interaction with the world throughout history will ultimately be shown to accord with his righteous character. *Mishpat* and its cognates emphasize God's role as lawgiver and just judge as well as the attribute of rectitude. *Mishpat* and *tsedaqah* commonly appear as a word pair that expresses social justice throughout the OT. *Mishpat* and *tsedaqah* refer to the character trait of justice granted the king by God for the purpose of judging the people rightly, especially the poor and lowly (Ps. 72:1–2), and are found in relationship to the term for "equity" (99:4). As a social ideal, *mishpat* and *tsedaqah* are seen along the lines of kindness, mercy, and truth, and is further considered practically in conjunction with *derek*, "way" of life. To walk in the right way, in the straight and right path, is to practice justice and righteousness in the establishment of laws (99:7), the proper execution of justice, and the institution of social equity for the downtrodden, the poor, and the widow. The pursuit of the way of justice and righteousness is not limited to kings, but it is generally expected of all of God's covenant people as Micah (6:8) requires and Amos asks (5:24). If God's people practice justice, they will be blessed. As the OT narrative reveals, however, God's covenant people repeatedly fail to practice *mishpat* and *tsedaqah*.

Readers of the NT, particularly Protestants, see the failure of God's covenant people to practice justice (*dikaiosynē*—translated as "righteousness" and "justice") as a demonstration of the futility of achieving and practicing righteousness and justice by the power of the law alone. A considerable emphasis in the NT reflects this inability to practice justice, though the requirement remains for God's covenant people (e.g., the righteous in the parable of the sheep and goats practice *mishpat* and *tsedaqah*, even though they do not recognize the significance of their service to God). Part of the Messiah's mission is to meet the righteous requirement for salvation and to exemplify justice for those who would follow him. While the final, eschatological justice where God establishes his reign in full is yet to come, the inaugural presence of the kingdom reflects not only that believing sinners are saved, but also that glimpses of the end come through the practice of justice exhibited by God's new covenant people.

The implications of justice for the theological interpretation of Scripture are vast, especially in light of the legacy of Protestantism. In one sense the Reformation handed the Bible over to the laity, and interpretation became the responsibility not only of the clergy but of all believers. The opposite effect, however, is that the liberation of interpretation has sometimes resulted in anarchy, where the autonomy of the reader (who also "has the same Spirit" as other Christians) leads to reader-response interpretations that often unintentionally do violence to the intent of the text. Interpretative injustice also occurs when autonomous subjects or marginalized groups assume a privileged perspective that implicitly or explicitly displaces the view of the divine author in favor of some human-centered interest. Conservative and liberal interpreters are both guilty of this practice. Unjust interpretations of this sort operate under guises of a rationalistic objectivity that betrays a methodological naturalism or in other cases the hermeneutical equivalent of interest-group politics. To pursue justice in the theological interpretation of Scripture requires the virtue of humility—no interpreter is unaffected by sin, and even the most rigorous may suffer from myopia—as well as charity that yields willingness to listen to other perspectives, even if there is significant disagreement. In addition, interpreters of Scripture must resist the urge toward engagements with the text that render the practice of justice abstract rather than concrete. Justice is rightly a hermeneutical principle beyond the sole purview of liberation theologians

and legal experts. To do justice in the interpretative task requires submission to the triune God, who is the standard for justice, and to the ongoing work of the Spirit, who refines our interpretative perspectives.

See also Ethics; Ideological Criticism; Law; Political Theology

Bibliography

Dengerink, J. *Justice in Christian Perspective*. Wedge, 1978; Reventlow, H. G., and Y. Hoffman, eds. *Justice and Righteousness*. JSOTSup 137. JSOT, 1992; Skillen, J. *A Covenant to Keep*. CRC Publications, 2000.

Vincent E. Bacote

Justification *See* Epistemology; Warrant

Justification by Faith

The Greek word for "justify," like the Hebrew word in the OT, means primarily "to acquit" or "to declare righteous," the opposite of "to condemn." It is a forensic term, taken from the law courts. This does not mean that our relationship to God can be reduced to legal terms but rather that such terms provide one important way among others of describing the salvation that we have in Christ.

Justification in the NT

The theme of justification is developed in three main passages in the NT: Rom. 1:16–5:21; Gal. 2:16–3:24; and James 2:21–25 (cf. Rom. 10:1–13; Phil. 3:7–11). Paul clearly teaches that we are justified or reckoned righteous by God by his grace, through faith and apart from works of the law. This does not mean that Christians can live without performing good works, but rather that their justification or acceptance by God is on the basis of Christ's atoning death for our sins, received by faith.

James appears to contradict this, teaching that we are justified by works and not by faith alone. In fact, however, he acknowledges that Abraham was reckoned righteous (= justified in Pauline terms) by faith (Gen. 15:6), and that later he was justified (seen to be righteous) when he offered Isaac (Gen. 22). Also for James, the faith that alone does not justify is a head knowledge that does not lead to a changed life.

The Historical Understanding of the Doctrine

In the church of the second to fourth centuries, there was little interest in the theme of justification. It was Augustine who brought it into prominence during his dispute with Pelagius in the fifth century. Working in the Latin language, he understood justification to refer not to a "not guilty" verdict but to the making of an unrighteous person righteous. This is clearly demonstrated in a key passage where he discusses Paul's statement (Rom. 2:13 NRSV) that "the doers of the law . . . will be justified" (*Spir. et litt.* 26.45). He recognizes that "justified" here (as in Luke 10:29) means "held to be righteous" or "accounted righteous," but did not recognize that this was also its meaning in the NT as a whole. The Western Catholic doctrine of justification (building on Augustine) is an account of how the unrighteous are transformed by the work of the Holy Spirit and thus become righteous.

With the Reformation the doctrine of justification moved center stage. Renaissance humanism brought a renewed interest in and study of the Greek language. This led to the realization that justification was a forensic term referring to our standing before God, a "not guilty" verdict in the court of God's justice. The Reformers also made a careful distinction between justification (God's declaration that we are righteous) and regeneration or sanctification (the process of inner transformation by which we become righteous). They distinguished between these but did not imagine that they could be separated. One can no more have justification without sanctification, faith without love, than one can enjoy the sun's heat without its light. We are justified or accepted as righteous by God because the righteousness of Christ is reckoned or imputed to our account. They adopted the controversial slogan of justification by "faith alone" (*sola fide*), meaning by this that it is only because of Christ's work, received only by faith, that we are accepted by God. This does not mean that repentance, baptism, love, and good works are unnecessary, but rather that it is not these that lay hold of justification. Justification is not *by* good works, yet it is not *without* good works. The Reformers insisted, however, that even the best works of the believer fall short of perfection and that a Christian remains (in Luther's terms) *simul iustus et peccator* (at the same time righteous and sinner). Alongside this rather austere message, they also affirmed that God in Christ accepts and is pleased with the good works of believers.

In the early years of the Reformation, a number of leading Catholic theologians were sympathetic to the Protestant doctrine of justification, which was possible because there had been no authoritative church pronouncements on the issue. This enabled a historic agreement on the doctrine at the Regensburg Colloquy (1541), where leading theologians on both sides (Melanchthon, Bucer, Eck, and Gropper) agreed on a common statement (art. 5). This affirmed that at conversion we receive both inherent righteousness (inner transformation) and the imputed righteousness of Christ. It is on the latter alone that we should depend before God. Underlying the agreement was a shared perception that converted Christians throughout their lives remain in need of the mercy of God. This article was approved by Calvin and by Cardinal Contarini (who were there), but rejected by Luther (who was not) as a compromising patchwork.

Since the Regensburg Colloquy failed to agree on other doctrines, the Council of Trent was called to define Roman Catholic doctrine in clear contradistinction to Protestantism. The *Decree on Justification* (1547) expounded the doctrine in reaction against the Protestant account. Its exposition of initial justification at conversion is not very different from the Protestant understanding, but the two diverge when it comes to the ongoing justification of the Christian. Christians are acceptable to God and counted as righteous because they truly are righteous, having been transformed by God's grace. At the end they can be said to have truly merited eternal life by their works. Firmly excluded from the decree was any talk of the inadequacy of the inherent righteousness of the Christian or of the need for ongoing mercy or for the imputation of Christ's righteousness. Paul's reference to the justification of "the ungodly" (Rom. 4:5 NRSV) applies only to the initial justification of the unconverted, not to those on the Christian way. Justification was a major theme of the Council of Trent, but it has been far less significant in Catholic teaching, for which the sacramental system is more central.

The Reformers taught that Christ's righteousness is imputed to us, an idea that finds limited support in pre-Reformation Catholic writings. There continues to be another tradition within orthodox Protestantism, however, which is unhappy with this and prefers the alternative phraseology of faith being counted as righteousness (following Rom. 4:5, which echoes Gen. 15:6).

In recent years two main developments have taken place. First, following the pioneering work of Hans Küng in his *Justification* (1957), there has been intensive dialogue between Catholics and Protestants on this issue. The best document produced was the first, entitled *Justification by*

Faith, by American Lutherans and Catholics in 1983. This process culminated in the signing, in 1999, by the Roman Catholic Church and the Lutheran World Federation, of a *Joint Declaration on the Doctrine of Justification*. The declaration claimed not total agreement, but a "consensus in basic truths of the doctrine of justification" such that the condemnations of the Reformation era no longer apply (§§40–41). These dialogues have labored to show not that there is no difference between the two sides but that each side can expound its doctrine in such a way as to answer the fears and meet the concerns of the other side.

The second development is a new approach to the doctrine of justification by a number of NT scholars, often referred to misleadingly as *the* "New Perspective on Paul." This is misleading because it suggests a unity of approach in what are in fact a variety of new perspectives. E. P. Sanders initiated this movement with his *Paul and Palestinian Judaism* (1977), which questioned the idea that first-century Judaism taught a religion of merit and works righteousness. He described it rather as "covenantal nomism," according to which we enter the covenant by grace but remain in it by obedience to the law. Sanders's reassessment of Judaism has been received sympathetically, though not without reservations. Sanders also offered a reinterpretation of Paul, which has met with less favor. Others, such as James Dunn and Tom Wright, have responded to Sanders with their own reinterpretations of Paul. For Dunn, the "works of the law" to which Paul objected were not moral deeds aimed at acquiring merit but Jewish distinctives (such as the Sabbath and the food laws) aimed at excluding Gentiles. What he affirmed has been received with greater sympathy than what he denied. Wright, meanwhile, understands justification in the context of the covenant and as referring not to how one enters the people of God, but how one can tell who belongs to them. There is as yet no consensus about the new perspectives; controversy remains about questions like Paul's attitude to the law and the extent of continuity between Judaism and Paul's doctrine.

Justification and the Hermeneutical Task

The centrality or otherwise of justification is an important hermeneutical issue. Following certain remarks of Luther, some (by no means all) Lutherans have claimed a privileged role for this doctrine. It is *the* central doctrine of the Christian faith. It is the sole criterion by which other doctrines are to be tested and the article

by which the church stands or falls. It is a controlling principle that is to mold all other doctrines. Reformed Protestantism has prized the doctrine, but has never given it this exaggerated prominence. Calvin, for example, declared that it was the main hinge on which religion turns (*Inst.* 3.11.1) and devoted eight chapters of his *Institutio* to it. But he devoted the same number of chapters to sanctification, taking care to give the two doctrines equal weight and to hold them in balance.

It is hard to see how the extreme Lutheran claims can be justified. Given the paucity of mention of justification in the NT and its lack of prominence for most of Christian history, such claims are highly implausible. Paul does not mention it in his account of what is of "first importance" (1 Cor. 15:3–8). In Gal. 1:6–9 Paul condemns those who preach another gospel, but simply to reduce the gospel to justification by faith would be a caricature of Paul's message. Yet justification remains *an* important doctrine. The doctrine of salvation is clearly of major importance for the Bible, and justification is *one* important aspect of that doctrine. It tackles the vital issue of how we can be accepted by God and as such has implications for the interpretation of the whole Bible, not just for passages that use the word "justify."

Understanding the doctrine of justification is not simply a matter of correctly exegeting certain NT passages. It is also about the need to hold together theologically a tension that is found throughout the NT and can be seen in a number of ways:

- In Luke 18:9–14 (the parable of the Pharisee and the tax collector) it is not the one who can point to his works who is justified but the one who prays, "God, have mercy on me, a sinner." Yet shortly before, we hear in Luke 14:25–33 the uncompromising teaching that "any of you who does not give up everything he has cannot be my disciple."
- Paul teaches both justification by faith and judgment by works (Rom. 2:5–11; 2 Cor. 5:10; cf. Rom. 14:7–12; 1 Cor. 3:12–15; 4:4–5; 5:5; 6:9; Gal. 5:19–21; 6:7–9). This tension is closely related to one of the most fundamental tensions of NT theology, that between the already and the not yet. Justification is the anticipation of the final judgment, the declaration of what we will be; yet there is a future judgment by works.

• Paul teaches that we are justified by faith apart from works; James that we are not justified by faith alone.

The hermeneutical task is to allow both sides of this tension to be heard clearly and not to suppress or mute one in the interests of the other. There has always been a danger in Protestantism of so stressing free forgiveness and imputed righteousness as to overlook the call to discipleship and the reality of inner transformation. At a time when the secular world emphasizes openness and individual choice, the threat is greater than ever.

Bibliography

Anderson, H., T. Murphy, and J. Burgess, eds. *Justification by Faith: Lutherans and Catholics in Dialogue VII*. Augsburg, 1985 [key ecumenical document]; Braaten, C. *Justification*. Fortress, 1990 [Lutheran exposition]; Carson, D. A., ed. *Right with God*. Paternoster/Baker, 1992 [from World Evangelical Fellowship study unit]; Carson, D. A., P. O'Brien, and M. Seifrid, eds. *Justification and Variegated Nomism*. 2 vols. Mohr/Siebeck/Baker Academic, 2001, 2004 [large-scale assessment of the New Perspectives]; Husbands, M., and D. Treier, eds. *Justification*. InterVarsity, 2004 [recent conference proceedings]; Jüngel, E. *Justification*. T&T Clark, 2001 [recent theological study]; Lane, A. *Justification by Faith in Catholic-Protestant Dialogue*. T&T Clark, 2002 [on ecumenical debates, with text of the *Joint Declaration*]; McGrath, A. *Iustitia Dei*. 2 vols. 2d ed. Cambridge University Press, 1998 [magisterial history of the doctrine]; Seifrid, M. *Justification by Faith*. Brill, 1992 [important NT study]; Tavard, G. *Justification*. Paulist, 1983 [Roman Catholic study, sympathetic to the Reformation]; Thompson, M. *The New Perspective on Paul*. Grove Books, 2002 [brief account and assessment of the movement].

Anthony N. S. Lane

K

Kant, Immanuel *See* Enlightenment; Epistemology

Kerygma *See* Gospel; Jesus, Quest for the Historical; Oral Tradition and the NT; Preaching, Use of the Bible in

Kingdom of God

The phrase "the kingdom of God" (for which Matthew generally uses the more Jewish equivalent, "the kingdom of heaven," but without any discernible difference in meaning) is generally agreed to have been a characteristic feature of Jesus' teaching style. It encapsulates a (perhaps "the") central focus of his teaching about his own mission and about the life of discipleship. "The kingdom of God" (*hē basileia tou theou*), or an equivalent such as "his kingdom," "your kingdom," occurs some seventy times in the three Synoptic Gospels (not counting parallels). Mark 1:15 tells us that Jesus' public proclamation from the beginning was of the coming of the kingdom of God. In the Fourth Gospel, by contrast, it is found only in John 3:3, 5, and in the rest of the NT less than twenty times.

But it is easier to agree on its importance than to define its nature and scope, and the problem has been made more intractable by the modern habit of using "kingdom" language in connection with a wide range of sometimes-incompatible Christian agendas, from charismatic healing to political activism. Such language serves to commend the matter under discussion as an authentically Christian concern rather than to clarify its nature and aims, and a poll on the meaning of "kingdom" across a representative selection of modern Christians would present a very varied picture.

One reason for this confusion is the English word "kingdom" itself. In the sixteenth century, when this term established its place in the tradition of biblical translation, it appropriately translated the dynamic sense of *basileia* as "kingship" or "rule." But over the centuries that more abstract meaning of "kingdom" has become obsolete, and the term conveys to modern readers the more concrete sense of a place or group of people under the control of a king ("the United Kingdom," "the Kingdom of Saudi Arabia"). Yet, rarely thus far has a modern English version of the Bible had the courage to replace the familiar term "kingdom" with "reign," "rule," "sovereignty." Hence, the term "kingdom" continues to mislead speakers with the idea that some thing or place or group of people is being talked about when the NT speaks of "the kingdom of God." This impression is fostered by the regrettable and widespread tendency to abbreviate "the kingdom of God" into simply "the kingdom" (or worse, to use "kingdom" as an adjective: "kingdom ethics," etc.). But "the reign" has no meaning unless it is stated whose reign is in view. In other words, "the kingdom of God" is not making a statement about a "thing" called "the kingdom," but about *God*, that he is king. Thus, "the kingdom of God has come near" means "God is taking over as king," and to "enter the kingdom of God" is to come under his rule, to accept him as king.

God's Kingship in the OT and Jewish Thought

The phrase "the kingdom of God" does not occur as such at all in most translations of the OT, though "his kingdom" and "your kingdom" are used with God as the subject in Pss. 103:19; 145:11–13; Dan. 4:3, 34; 6:26. In later Jewish literature there are only a few uses of the phrase. But it would be a serious mistake to assume that God's kingship is not therefore an important theme for the OT and later Jewish literature. Many of the psalms celebrate the rule of the Lord as "a great king above all gods" and call on the people of the earth to bow to his authority. It has been rightly observed that God's kingship (in contrast with the pretended kingships of earthly powers) is the controlling theme of the book of Daniel. In such passages God's kingship is stated as an eternal fact, but there are also a number of prophetic passages that, recognizing the extent of human rebellion against God's rule, look forward to a day when his kingship will be more effectively established. In such passages it is possible to speak of God's complete kingship as still future, a hope to be cherished rather than already a fait accompli (e.g., Isa. 45:23; Zech. 14:9).

Both these strands continue in later Jewish literature, so that on the one hand the wisdom writers can speak of "God's kingship" as a basic fact of the present (Wis. 6:4; 10:10; cf. *Pss. Sol.* 17:3: "The kingdom of our God is for ever"). On the other hand, apocalyptic writers speak of a kingship of God yet to be established (*T. Mos.* 10:1: "Then his kingdom will appear throughout his whole creation"; 1QM 6.6: "Kingship shall belong to the God of Israel"). The Qaddish prayer that was in regular use in the synagogue by the time of Jesus (and which is surely echoed in the Lord's Prayer) focused on the petition "May he let his kingdom rule in your lifetime, . . . speedily and soon."

So Joseph of Arimathea, a pious Jew "looking for the kingdom of God" (Mark 15:43), represents a strong strand in first-century Jewish piety. The phrase "the kingdom of God" may not yet have been widely used, but all the raw materials are there. Thus, when Jesus began his mission with the words "The kingdom of God has come near," he would be sure of a ready hearing and would not be misunderstood. He would be heard as saying that the God whose sovereignty over his whole creation was a fundamental belief of Judaism was about to establish that sovereignty in a newly effective way; the king de jure was becoming the king de facto.

What Jesus Meant

In Mark 1:15 Jesus not only declares, "The kingdom of God has come near" (NRSV), but also, "The time has been fulfilled" (AT). This is not, then, as for the prophets, a hope for the future, but the declaration of a new reality. Jesus' exorcisms are a sign that "the kingdom of God has come upon you" (Matt. 12:28). When asked when the kingdom of God is coming, Jesus replies that it is already "among you" (Luke 17:21 NRSV). Yet Jesus can also speak of a future time when people will see that the kingdom of God "has come with power" (Mark 9:1 NRSV); at the Last Supper he looked forward to drinking new wine with his disciples "in the kingdom of God" (Mark 14:25). This tension between the now and the not yet is illustrated by the traditional form of the Lord's Prayer, which bids us pray "Your kingdom come"

and yet concludes with the declaration "Yours is the kingdom."

In a series of parables in Mark 4 and Matt. 13, Jesus explains more about the "mystery of the kingdom of God" (Mark 4:11 KJV). It is not visible to all, but only to those with God-given eyes to see. It is like seed that germinates in some soil but not in others (4:3–8), like a seed growing secretly away from human observation (4:26–29), like the tiny mustard seed that is now so small as to be unnoticed but will one day be a great tree (4:30–32), like the tiny pinch of yeast that will gradually penetrate the whole lump of dough (Matt. 13:33). So God has already established his rule in the coming of Jesus, yet it still has to work itself out to its full potential. In the meantime it remains a secret, a paradox, rejected by some, but for others the one great treasure for which they will sell all they have (13:44–46).

So God's kingship divides people. In Matt. 5:3–10 Jesus sets out the "good life" in terms that sharply differentiate his people (poor in spirit, mourning, meek, hungry for righteousness, merciful, pure, peacemaking, and persecuted) from the world, which despises them. Jesus frames the portrait with the explanation "for theirs is the kingdom of heaven" (5:3, 10). The Sermon on the Mount might be described as a manifesto for life in the kingdom of heaven. When Jesus instructs his disciples on the revolutionary values by which he expects them to live (most notably in Mark 10), it is the phrase "the kingdom of God" that repeatedly sums up this alternative lifestyle. His teaching leads up to the paradox of 10:42–45, where the power structures of this world are contrasted with a regime in which the first are last and the last first.

Jesus is more than the herald of God's kingship. In a few places the subject of *basileia* is not God (or "heaven") but the Son of Man (Matt. 13:41; 16:28; 25:31–34; Luke 22:29–30), who now exercises the kingship he came to inaugurate. And in the last of those passages, even the disciples themselves are to receive a delegated kingship (cf. also Matt. 25:34; Luke 12:32). God rules, but he rules through his Son, and he in turn through those whom he has summoned to accept the kingship of God.

Jesus says that God's rule would come with power during the lifetime of those to whom he speaks (Mark 9:1). And so it has. As the good news was preached, the "powers of the age to come" (Heb. 6:5 NRSV) were experienced, and increasing numbers were brought from darkness into light. But there is still darkness as well as light, and God's people must go on praying "Your kingdom come" until "the kingdom of the world has become the kingdom of our Lord and of his Messiah" (Rev. 11:15 NRSV).

The Kingship of God in Christian Thought

The classical debate among modern theologians as to whether the kingdom of God should be understood as already "realized" in Jesus' ministry (Dodd) or still wholly future (Schweitzer) can thus be seen as a false trail. It is based on the wrong assumption that "the kingdom of God" denoted a particular time or state of affairs within history. Instead, the term is a dynamic expression for any and every situation in which God is king, his authority exercised, and his will done. Even the compromise language of "inaugurated eschatology" (Jeremias) fails to meet the case, since in biblical thought God's kingship is eternal, not just inaugurated in the first century CE. Rather, it operates at different levels as God interacts with human affairs and people respond in their different ways to his kingship. As long as God continues to allow his world to resist his rule, so long will there be tension and paradox built into the language of the "kingdom of God."

This brief survey of the complexity of biblical "kingdom of God" language indicates the danger in much modern "kingdom" talk, which tries to hijack this "feel-good" terminology to the service of one particular Christian agenda. Within certain Christian subcultures the word "kingdom" has a conventional resonance that may have little to do with the essential meaning of such terminology in the Bible. If Christians are to communicate effectively with other Christians outside their own particular subgroup, let alone with a wider world to which the biblical terminology is foreign, they would do well to find other ways of expressing this broad concept of God implementing his eternal sovereignty in the affairs of his world—at least until modern Christians can agree to use the terminology in something more like its biblical sense.

To do so they would be well advised to discard the misleading English translation "kingdom" in favor of "kingship" or "reign" or the like. Thus they could express the basic biblical conviction that God is king and the central concern of Jesus that divine sovereignty should be fully implemented and acknowledged, not only by those who have chosen to "enter the kingship of God," but also by the wider world, which has yet to bow the knee.

Bibliography

Allison, D., Jr. *The End of the Ages Has Come*. T&T Clark, 1985; Ambrozic, A. *The Hidden Kingdom*. Catholic Biblical Association, 1972; Beasley-Murray, G. *Jesus and the Kingdom of God*. Eerdmans, 1986; Chilton, B. *God in Strength*. JSOT, 1987; Chilton, B., and J. McDonald. *Jesus and the Ethics of the Kingdom*. SPCK, 1987; Dodd, C. H. *The Parables of the Kingdom*. Nisbet, 1935; France, R. T. *Divine Government*. SPCK, 1990; Jeremias, J. *New Testament Theology* (part 1). SCM, 1971; Ladd, G. *Jesus and the Kingdom*. Harper & Row, 1964; Perrin, N. *Jesus and the Language of the Kingdom*. Fortress, 1976; idem. *The Kingdom of God in the Teaching of Jesus*. SCM, 1963; Willis, W., ed. *The Kingdom of God in 20th-Century Interpretation*. Hendrickson, 1987; Wright, N. T. *Jesus and the Victory of God*. SPCK, 1996.

R. T. France

Kings, Books of

The books of 1 and 2 Kings provide a theologically laden interpretation of the history of the Israelite monarchy from the death of King David until the end of the monarchy itself. Although some chapters contain administrative records (1 Kings 4), building descriptions (chs. 6–7), rituals (ch. 8), and prophecies and prayers (2 Kings 19), the dominant genre is narrative. For this reason, the primary theological exposition of the text is indirect, through narrative rather than clear exhortative forms. Major theological themes lie behind the narratives and also inform the other types of literature. They concern the nature of God and his relation to his people, including matters such as divine sovereignty and human responsibility, judgment, covenant, worship of God alone, and the Messiah.

Foremost in the books of Kings is the reign of the single God of Israel. Along with it is the habitual practice of God's people, who turn from him to worship other gods. The centers of contrast between the one true God of Israel and the other gods of the nations appear in 1 Kings 11 and 18 and 2 Kings 17. In 1 Kings 11 Solomon reaches the low point of his reign. The king's many foreign wives entice him to leave his devotion to the God who had given him his power, and they divert him to the worship of other gods. This brings about divine judgment: the division of the kingdom and the capitulation to compromise the sole worship of the LORD God in the northern kingdom. A few of the oldest members from that time of division may still have been alive when Elijah challenged the wholesale worship of Baal by Jezebel and Ahab (1 Kings 18). The absolute victory of Israel's God over Baal in the contest and the subsequent execution of all the priests of Baal (and Asherah) demonstrated the uncompromising nature of God's demand for sole worship by his people. The final grand statement of God's sovereignty is that of 2 Kings 17, where the author reflects on the fall of the northern kingdom, attributing it to the worship of other deities and the abandonment of the one true God of Israel. As the writer observes, the consequence of these actions, begun before the time of Solomon, was to bring other nations into the land (through Assyrian deportation and resettlement) so that the countryside became even more polytheistic. This result would contrast with the practice of southern kings, such as Hezekiah and Josiah, who to varying degrees sought to abolish idolatry. The author of Kings praises them for doing so. Nevertheless, the preponderance of kings in the south tolerated the worship of other deities and at times even supported it. Thus, even the righteousness of Josiah was unable to prevent God's judgment for the worship of other deities, as announced by his prophetess (2 Kings 22:17).

Perhaps nowhere more vivid is the contrast between Israel's God and those of other nations than in the verbal challenges that the invading Assyrian king Sennacherib and his representatives raise against Hezekiah and the inhabitants of Jerusalem. In 2 Kings 18:22, 32–35; 19:10–12, 18 appears the Assyrians' charge that the God of Israel cannot deliver from their hand. They suggest that this is the reason Hezekiah closed the outlying worship centers (high places) and brought all formal worship into Jerusalem. The Assyrians point to the inability of all the other national gods to deliver their countries from this superpower. However, it is the response of Hezekiah and of the prophet Isaiah that seals the fate of the enemy. In particular, 19:18–19 brings the matter to a conclusion: "They have thrown their gods into the fire and destroyed them, for they were not gods but only wood and stone, fashioned by men's hands. Now, O LORD our God, deliver us from his hand, so that all kingdoms on earth may know that you alone, O LORD, are God." Thus the collapse of the northern kingdom demonstrates the failure to worship God alone, while the survival of Judah shows how faith in God can bring about unexpected miracles.

It also ties together the theology of God as one, and of God alone with absolute sovereignty over all nations of the world. That power is able to bring the greatest nation of the era, Assyria, to its knees. God's majesty becomes worthy of the greatest of structures that the wealthiest of the kings can build (1 Kings 6–7). The form and structure of this temple, as well as the multitude of sacrifices, represent imports from the surrounding lands—a transformation of the forms and style of the media of worship toward the honoring of the one true Deity.

Solomon's prayer of dedication for the temple sets forth another key theological principle of God's dealings with his people and their kings. In 1 Kings 8:44–53 Solomon prays to God that the nation might receive forgiveness when it sins. If at that time it turns back to God, even if it has been deported to a foreign land, God will forgive and restore the nation to his blessing. This possibility is based upon the sense of Israel as specially chosen by God. God affirms this promise to Solomon in 1 Kings 9:3–10. There he promises that Solomon and his descendants will be treated according to the degree to which they wholeheartedly worship God and refrain from worshipping other gods. God has entered into covenant with them, and their responsibility is to remain faithful to him and refuse the worship of foreign deities. Thus, God promises retribution—punishment for those who turn away from him and blessing for those who follow him. Solomon himself becomes a model of both elements and, in the sequence of blessing followed by judgment, a foreshadowing of the experience of the nation (both northern and southern kingdoms) through the remainder of its history to the exile. Solomon's early search for wisdom from God (1 Kings 3), organization of his kingdom and palace (ch. 4; 7:1–12), and above all his construction and dedication of Yahweh's temple (chs. 5–6; 7:13–9:9)—all indicate a king in obedience to the divine will, leading his people to great prosperity and devotion to God. Nevertheless, his success with other nations, and the consequent diplomatic marriages, compromise his faith and lead to prophecies of judgment (11:1–13). At Solomon's death, the kingdom is divided. Thus, the mixture of some faithfulness with apostasy, characteristic of Solomon's reign and the beginning of the book, anticipates the subsequent history of the monarchy.

Although the title of the books suggests the dominant focus, and the doctrine of retribution is most pronounced with the leaders of the two kingdoms, the prophetic stories that lie in the heart of the books also depict encounters of personal faith and the responses of God. Unlike earlier and especially later prophets, Elijah and Elisha, along with others of their generation, are gifted with amazing abilities to work miracles that complement their verbal messages. Their miracles most often provide life for those to whom they minister.

This could include the miraculous provision of food. As with the story of Solomon, many of these are anticipated in the initial words and acts that introduce the prophet Elijah. In 1 Kings 17, where he first appears, he is kept alive by ravens that feed him. In the same chapter, he preserves alive the widow of Zarephath in Sidon and resurrects her son from death. These miracles would be repeated again and again by Elijah and other prophets who represent living signs of God's power for life. Indeed, even in death the body of the prophet can remain a source of life for others (2 Kings 13:21). The best-known event of Elijah is his challenge of the prophets of Baal, a challenge that ends in their execution (1 Kings 18). This, however, is the other side of the story. God provides signs through his prophets. For those who believe and respond, these are life-giving. For those who reject the signs and turn away from God, they lead to death. The lives of the prophets and the people with whom they deal, kings and commoners, illustrate the love of God for all people (even outside Israel, as at Zarephath), and the need to respond with personal faith. It is this ministry of life that forms the closest living model of Jesus' life and work in the NT. Again and again the miracles that Jesus performs are anticipated by prophets' works in the books of Kings. Further, Elijah ministered in Sidon, outside Israel, and Elisha assisted Naaman the Syrian; these episodes anticipate the mission of Jesus to the Gentiles (Luke 4:25–27).

The theology of the prophetic movement also provides a critique of simple assumptions of retribution. The prophetic word of 1 Kings 13:2, proclaimed against the apostasy of the northern kingdom at the time of the division, names King Josiah, three centuries into the future, as a figure who will bring to an end the sacrifices of the unauthorized northern kingdom altars. Thus the fulfillment of judgment is postponed for three hundred years. In addition, this prophet, one of the first to appear in Kings, is duped by a northern prophet to disobey God's word. As a result, he pays for it with his life. An even greater indictment of the prophets as a group is 1 Kings 22:19–38, which depicts God orchestrating a lying spirit to mislead the court prophets. The prophet Micaiah tells this story, which demonstrates the universal effects of the sin nature on all humanity—even on the prophets (cf. also Gehazi in 2 Kings 5:20–27). No one group or individual is without sin, and the book of Kings makes this clear among kings, commoners, and prophets.

The role of the Lord's anointed, the Messiah, provides a key theological theme throughout the books and ties the whole together. It plays a dominant role in the three great sections of the text: the Solomonic era from David's last days to the division of the united monarchy (1 Kings 1–11); the prophetic challenge from Elijah's conflict with Ahab until the death of Athaliah and the rise of Joash (1 Kings 17–2 Kings 11); and the downfall of the northern kingdom followed by the last kings of Judah (from Hezekiah to Zedekiah) and the destruction of Jerusalem (2 Kings 17–25). The Messiah, or anointed one in Israel, would have been considered the ruling king in Jerusalem, a descendant of the line of David. In each of these sections in the books, that line is threatened. The first book of Kings opens with David near death. As the recipient of the promise of perpetual rule in Jerusalem for his dynasty (2 Sam. 7), the succession is crucial. The establishment of Solomon amid the brutality of the first three chapters demonstrates that God's promise is secure. Solomon's own apostasy ultimately leads to the division of the kingdom, a split that threatens the power of Solomon's successor, Rehoboam. Nevertheless, the line continues. Although Elijah's battle is with the northern kingdom's Ahab and Jezebel, the southern kingdom's ruler, Jehoram, married their daughter Athaliah. Both he and their son, Ahaziah, followed the worship practices of Ahab. Upon Ahaziah's death, Athaliah declared herself ruler and sought to execute the remainder of the royal family. The high priest protected one royal prince, Joash, by hiding him. Despite the attempt to destroy the line of the Messiah, God protects it in the person of young Joash, who becomes king after Athaliah's execution. The collapse of the northern kingdom and then of the southern kingdom, as described in detail at the end of Kings, raises the specter of no continuation of the line. Due to the people's sins, not even the righteousness of kings such as Hezekiah and Josiah can save the kingdom (2 Kings 20:16–19; 23:25–27). Yet, as with Solomon, Rehoboam, and Joash, there remains an heir to the line of David. The book concludes with Jehoiachin alive and well in exile in Babylon. Thus, both hope and God's anointed remain and can be found throughout the books of Kings. The promise of the Messiah is not lost.

See also History of Israel; Kingdom of God; Messiah/Messianism

Bibliography

Hess, R., and G. Wenham, eds. *Zion, City of Our God*. Eerdmans, 1999; Knoppers, G. *The Reign of Jeroboam, the Fall of Israel, and the Reign of Josiah*. Vol. 2 of *Two Nations under God*. HSM 53. Scholars Press, 1994; McConville, J. G. *Grace in the End*. Studies in Old Testament Biblical Theology. Paternoster, 1993; Noth, M. *The Deuteronomistic History*. JSOTSup 15. Sheffield Academic Press, 1981; Provan, I. *1 and 2 Kings*. OTG. JSOT, 1997; Rad, G. von. *Old Testament Theology*. 2 vols. Harper & Row, 1965; Wiseman, D. *1 and 2 Kings*. TOTC. InterVarsity, 1993.

Richard S. Hess

Knowledge *See* Epistemology; Warrant; Wisdom

L

Lamentations, Book of

The book of Lamentations is one of the smallest works in the Bible and yet one of the most powerful and enigmatic. Written in the aftermath of the destruction of Jerusalem and its temple by the Babylonians, Lamentations expresses the grief and disbelief of those who lived through the horror and yet still looked to their God for their hope and deliverance.

Canon, Date, and Authorship

The book of Lamentations is found in the Jewish canon as one of the Megillot, the Five Scrolls. The LXX placed Lamentations after Jeremiah and Baruch, assuming the prophet to be the author, thus leading to its current place in the Christian canon. Wherever its location, its existence within the canon has never been challenged, within either Jewish or Christian tradition.

Almost all scholars agree that the book of Lamentations was written in the years immediately following the destruction of Jerusalem. Certainly these five poems express the kind of shock and despair that we might expect from an eyewitness, yet their form and style demonstrate that they were created as an act of reflection on their tragedy and as a memorial of it. Lamentations does not contain any glimpse of the restoration of Jerusalem and the temple that occurred after Cyrus the Great and the Persians defeated the Babylonians. They allowed the Jews to return and rebuild their holy city in 538 BCE. Thus, the time of composition is set within the years immediately following 586 BCE and before Jerusalem's restoration. Moreover, it is likely that the poet was one of the many who were not exiled to Babylon, but remained in Judah and endured the daily reminders of the Babylonian conquest (Dobbs-Allsopp 4).

Jeremiah has traditionally been ascribed as the author of Lamentations, largely based upon the reference in 2 Chron. 35:25 to Jeremiah's having composed laments for the death of Josiah, but also due to the similarities in message and vocabulary between portions of the books of Jeremiah and Lamentations. The text of Lamentations itself is, in fact, anonymous, and most scholars today agree it is unlikely that it is the work of Jeremiah. In many ways it is the anonymity of the work that provides it with such great power, especially for today's reader. It is not a work by a named and distant prophet; rather, it is a work by "anyone/everyone" who has gone through such tragedy, and the reader is invited to identify with the author's perspective (e.g., Lam. 3, "I am the man . . .").

Form and Genre

The form and genre of Lamentations are unique within the biblical canon and as such deserve some comment. Lamentations is a collection of five poems, each intimately related by both structure and content. The first four are acrostics: the first letter of each stanza is a sequential letter of the Hebrew alphabet. Thus, the first stanza begins with *aleph*, the second with *beth*, and so on. There is variation within this form: chapter 4 has only two couplets per stanza, and chapter 3 has one couplet per stanza and repeats each letter three times (so the first three lines each begin with *aleph*, etc.). The final chapter does not have an alphabetic acrostic but echoes the acrostic form, with 22 lines paralleling the 22 letters in the Hebrew alphabet. The acrostic form is found in other ancient Near Eastern texts and may be merely intended as an aid to memory; however, it is more likely intended to demonstrate the completeness of Judah's grief, which is "from A to Z" (Gottwald).

Another key feature of Lamentations is the rhythm. In biblical Hebrew poetry the fundamental unit is two lines (or units) on each line of text, usually of similar length. In Lamentations and in other lament poems in the Bible, many lines are of unequal length, the first being longer than the second. This "limping" pattern is referred to as *qinah* meter and provides a solemn and mournful rhythm to the recitation of the poem. (For a brief discussion of the poetry of Lamentations and its literary context, see Berlin 2–30.)

The lament genre dominates Lamentations and has particularly strong parallels to the city-lament genre widely attested in Mesopotamian literature (e.g., see Kramer). Some key features of the city-lament genre that have been incorporated into Lamentations include the structure and form, the assigning of responsibility, the abandonment of the city by its patron deity, weeping of the female figure (in this case, Lady Zion), lamentation, and the restoration of the city (see Dobbs-Allsopp 9). As Dobbs-Allsopp has pointed out, however, Lamentations "is no simple Mesopotamian city lament." The author has transformed and adapted the forms and styles available to him, including those well-known from Hebrew poetry, to compose a unique Judean lament of the destruction of Jerusalem.

The most significant departure from the city-lament genre in terms of theological consideration is that the destruction of Jerusalem is *not* attributed to the action of a capricious god. While God is always the primary agent in that he allowed Jerusalem's destruction ("The Lord has destroyed without mercy all the dwellings of Jacob" [2:2 NRSV]), the author of Lamentations makes it abundantly clear this has only come about because of Judah's sin. "Jerusalem sinned grievously, therefore she became filthy" (1:8 RSV; see also 2:14, 17; 3:25–33).

Liturgical Use

The earliest recorded use of these poems is within the Tishah-b'Ab liturgy commemorating the destruction of Jerusalem (see Zech. 7:3–5). They were used and perhaps written as monuments of memorial and continue in such use within Jewish tradition. The early church saw reference to Jesus' messiahship in passages such as Lam. 4:20 ("The LORD's anointed") and his suffering on the cross in 1:12. Portions of the text continue to be used in Christian liturgy such as in the Tenebrae service during Holy Week (1:15).

Interpretation

In seeking a theology of Lamentations, many scholars have failed to take adequate notice of the emotive elements, and instead have focused upon the moments of confession and contrition that employ covenantal language. The language of confession is certainly present within Lamentations and clearly reflects Deuteronomic theology; hence, it fits within the larger canonical context of the Torah and Jeremiah. But Lamentations was written as an expression of grief rather than a systematic theological reflection. These poems are raw and poignant replies to the atrocities that the poet had just survived. Where the book of Job addresses suffering on the personal level, Lamentations addresses it on the national scale. By entering into the text with the author, as *both* the individual (ch. 3) and the nation/church, we may find solace in the deepest despair, even if that solace is long in coming.

Perhaps the most theologically challenging aspect of Lamentations is the presence of God. Where was God during this tragedy? Where is he now, as we seek to make sense of our own tragedies? The book of Lamentations brings this question home with dramatic power. Although the poet repeatedly appeals to God, God never responds; his voice is not heard. "Look, O LORD!" is a repeated refrain (as in 1:11). Yet, even as the personified Zion begs God to see her plight, she has already been ravaged. Zion's cry for God's help and mercy echoes hollowly, and there is no reply. The divine silence is awful. Yet in that silence the poet confronts Israel's responsibility and confesses that "the LORD is in the right, for I have transgressed his word" (1:18 AT).

Even in this confession of responsibility, the poet also asserts throughout Lamentations that God is the active agent. It is the Lord who sent fire from on high that "went deep into my bones" (1:13 NRSV). The Lord "destroyed without mercy all the dwellings of Jacob" (2:2 NRSV). The poet speaks directly to God, declaring, "You have wrapped yourself with anger and pursued us, killing without pity" (3:43 NRSV). Such a direct accusation against God may sound offensive to us, yet it contains within it a powerful statement of faith. In spite of all the famine, torture, and killing, the poet continues to believe that his God, "the LORD" alone, is ruler of the universe and is thus capable of bringing about such utter destruction of his people.

Yet God is silent. This is where life becomes interpretation. Lamentations contains the complaints, prayers, and petitions that any of us might address to God in our grief. God's response is not found in the text, but in history. While the poet recognizes the sin of Israel and declares God just in punishing them, the book ends with a question: "Or have you utterly rejected us and are angry with us beyond measure?" (5:22 AT). God responded to the complaints of Lamentations by fulfilling his word given through Jeremiah (29:10): he restored his people to Judah by the act of Cyrus.

Bibliography

Berlin, A. *Lamentations*. Westminster John Knox, 2002; Dobbs-Allsopp, F. W. *Lamentations*. Interpretation. Westminster John Knox, 2003; Gottwald, N. *Studies in the Book of Lamentations*. SCM, 1954; Kramer, S., trans. "Lamentation over the Destruction of Ur." *ANET* (1950): 455–63.

Christian M. M. Brady

Language, Grammar and Syntax

Grammar is used as a term with reference to several layers of language. The grammar of words, or morphology, refers to the construction of words from certain component parts. Hence "construction" comprises a verbal root and a noun suffix. For example, Greek *hypomenein* (endure, Luke 2:43) is made up of *hypo* (under) + *menein* (remain).

The grammar of sentences, or syntax, analyzes the way sentences are held together according to certain rules. The grammar of discourse focuses on yet larger blocks of text, considering what are the features of a paragraph, chapter, or larger passage that make it coherent as a unit. Nevertheless, grammar as a term is most frequently used to refer to syntax.

There are varying approaches to describing grammatical rules. These include traditional grammatical approaches, structuralist approaches, and functionalist approaches.

From Traditional Grammar to Structuralism

Language analysis was dominated by traditional grammar from the time of the ancient Greeks for over two thousand years. In the early twentieth century the new school of structuralism, founded by the Swiss linguist Ferdinand de Saussure (1857–1913), challenged key assumptions of the traditional grammarians, initiating a dynamic century of debate about diverse approaches to grammatical description.

Traditional grammarians had taken words as their starting point in considering the rules of combination that permitted the forming of correct sentences. For the structuralists, the starting point was the correct sentence, which was then dissected to determine what rules of word combination were permissible.

Furthermore, in concerning themselves with grammatical description, traditional grammarians focused upon literary language, seeing spoken language as secondary in importance. The structuralists, however, insisted that spoken language was primary and grammatical analysis should concern itself with correct spoken forms, on which written forms would be based.

The American structuralist school, which formed around the person of Leonard Bloomfield (1887–1949), advocated the sidelining of semantics in the process of syntactic analysis. The purpose of grammatical description should be to identify the rules built into the minds of language users, which were activated in the production of grammatical sentences. Describing this approach, John Lyons (34) adds, "This part of the grammar was to be a purely *formal* study, independent of semantics."

Noam Chomsky (b. 1928) refined the thinking of the structuralists in producing transformational generative grammar (TGG). He affirmed the structuralist view that semantics should be demoted in the description of grammatical rules, but argued that underlying surface structures were a large set of deep structures in the minds of language users, which were sufficiently uniform across languages to enable the development of a universal grammar. These deep structures depended for their activation on a series of syntactic transformations that would generate grammatical surface structures—hence the name transformational generative grammar.

A further refinement came in the form of case grammar, following the thinking of Charles Fillmore of the University of California at Berkeley. He argued that semantics could not be largely ignored, as proposed by the structuralists and transformational grammarians. Fillmore's case grammar was "a semantic-syntactic grammar model which tries to relate a small number of semantic notions to the syntactic functions in a sentence" (Dirven and Radden 5–6).

From Structuralism to Functionalism

Functionalism represented a revolution in linguistic thinking and had a major impact on how grammar was conceived. Whereas structuralists had focused their efforts to describe language on the workings of the mind, functionalists argued that social context was the driving force in determining the need for linguistic communication and the shape that it took.

Functionalism makes two key assumptions. First, "language has functions that are external to the linguistic system itself." Second, these external functions "influence the internal organisation of the linguistic system" (Schiffrin 22). Although there are a wide variety of functions of language, they nevertheless fall into two broad categories. Transactional functions express language content or transmit information, while interactional functions express social relations and personal attitudes.

For structuralists, study of grammar precedes the study of the use to which language is put; for functionalists, language use precedes and determines the study of grammar. For the former, grammatical structures are arbitrary; for the functionalists, grammatical structure is ethnographically determined.

Grammatical Analysis

The differences in approach described above become evident when linguists from particular schools undertake grammatical analysis of texts.

Classifying Sentences. For traditional grammarians, sentence classification follows long-established grammatical considerations. Sentences may be syntactically unmarked or marked according to word order. For example, in Semitic languages such as Hebrew and Arabic, the unmarked order is represented by verb-initial sentences: VS(O) or V(O)S. For special effect, however, in sentences marked syntactically, the verb is moved away from the initial position on the basis of certain grammatical rules.

Another way of classifying sentences according to traditional grammatical models is on the basis of form. Simple sentences are those consisting of a single proposition centering upon a single verb, such as "Jesus wept" (John 11:35). However, expanded sentences are theoretically capable of indefinite expansion, though they are usually kept to limits as determined by the syntax of the language. These are of two types. Compound sentences, based on coordination, consist of a combination of two or more simple sentences, each of which can stand alone. So (in a sense) Ezek. 18:15—"He does not eat at the mountain shrines or look to the idols of the house of Israel." Complex sentences are based on subordination, where one simple sentence is joined by a subordinate clause that cannot stand alone. So John 3:3—"Unless one is born again, one cannot see the kingdom of God" (AT).

An alternative approach is based upon a twofold classification (Cotterell and Turner 191–92). This approach is essentially structuralist, drawing on the Saussurean distinction between paradigmatic and syntagmatic considerations. Ferdinand de Saussure argued that words achieved both meaning and syntactic role from within a particular language system by way of their relation to other words within that same system, which either could or could not replace them in their sentence context. So in major-pattern sentences (the vast majority), an infinite range of possible sentences may be produced by substitution of alternative nouns, verbs, adjectives, and so forth. So "Jesus came to Nazareth" could be grammatically acceptable as "Peter came to Nazareth," which could then be transformed into "Peter went to Nazareth." In contrast, minor-pattern sentences do not allow for such paradigmatic substitution. This particularly applies to idioms, such as "Not on your life." These minor-pattern sentences pose particular challenges for translators of the biblical materials.

Dissecting Sentences. Traditional grammatical approaches to syntactic analysis focus upon identification of sentence constituents, or parsing. Sentences are parsed into word classes distinguished according to semantic considerations, called form classes, the principal ones being nouns, verbs, adjectives, adverbs, prepositions, and conjunctions. Once parsing is undertaken, traditional grammarians consider grammatical categories, such as number, case, tense, and aspect.

For transformational grammarians, however, a different set of considerations is paramount, including surface and deep structures, identification of kernel sentences, and various other features of language, such as embedding, deletion, and substitution. Langacker (122) points out that "the surface structure of a sentence represents only one facet of its syntactic organisation . . . To give a full account of how a sentence is put together, one must describe not only its surface structure but also its conceptual structure and the step-by-step *derivation* of the former from the latter."

The surface structure refers to the sentence on the page or as spoken. The deep structure relates to cognitive processes that draw on a series of kernel sentences to produce the surface structure shapes of communication. A kernel sentence consists of a single proposition. Multiple kernel sentences are transformed through various processes before appearing as the surface structure sentence. Thus, following Nida and Taber (53–54), the surface structure sentence "For by grace you are saved through faith, and this is not of yourselves, it is the gift of God" (Eph. 2:8 AT) is derived from a series of kernels: God showed grace. God saved you. You believed. You did not save yourselves. God gave it. You did not work for it. No one should boast.

Tree diagrams represent a key device for transformational grammarians in assisting the task of dissecting a sentence into its constituent kernels.

Functional grammarians adopt a very different angle of approach to analysis of sentences. No longer is semantics regarded as of subsidiary importance, as it is by structuralists and transformational grammarians. Furthermore, the functionalist spotlight is placed on pragmatics, an area virtually ignored by structuralists. An understanding of the space between living language and the society that produces it is considered crucial to any exercise in grammatical analysis. This is so true that for functional grammarians, grammatical sentences devoid of context are banished in favor of utterances, or sentences rooted in the contexts that produced them.

The most outstanding example of functional grammar is the systemic functional linguistics model developed by Michael Halliday. Another prominent model is the functional grammar of Simon Dik.

Ongoing Applications to Scriptural Hermeneutics. The above models have all received some attention from biblical scholars. The application of traditional grammatical principles to the study of the biblical text is widespread. Weingreen's widely used reference grammar of biblical Hebrew shows traditional grammatical analysis at its best.

Structuralist approaches, and TGG grammatical concepts, have also made their mark in the world of biblical scholarship. A key name in this regard is Robert Longacre of the Summer Institute of Linguistics. His attention to the grammar of discourse owes much to TGG approaches. Longacre points to certain constituent elements in a block of discourse contributing to a discourse peak, or a zone of grammatical turbulence. Two levels are considered—the surface structure and the notional structure—with the former being the text on the page, and the notional (deep) structure existing in the mind of the author. Furthermore, Longacre's attention to semantic-based constituent roles resonates with Fillmorean case grammar, as seen in the following example:

"Bill received a book from Tom . . .
Bill is agent and goal, *book* is patient, and *Tom* is source." (204)

Two biblical scholars greatly influenced by Longacre are David Dawson in his *Text-Linguistics and Biblical Hebrew* and Ralph Terry in analyzing 1 Corinthians.

The application of functionalist grammatical principles to the study of biblical materials is still in its infancy. Ludwig Wittgenstein laid important foundations with his reference to "theology as grammar," which has stimulated much discussion in later scholarship. His commitment to use, preceding and forming the basis for analysis, is clear from his statement: "One cannot guess how a word functions. One has to look at its use and learn from that" (109).

The reference grammar by Van der Merwe, Kroeze, and Naude provides functionalist perspectives on the description of biblical Hebrew in seeking to take account of syntactic, semantic, pragmatic, and sociolinguistic considerations (11). In various pieces of research, Randall Buth has applied Dik's functional grammar to the study of biblical Hebrew and Aramaic texts. Jean-Marc Heimerdinger produced important pioneering results, adapting various functionalist analytical models in his study of Hebrew narrative texts. The functionalist concerns with moving beyond sentence-level syntax in favor of pragmatic considerations, as well as considering both author and audience perspectives, are clear as Heimerdinger (14) writes: "As information structure deals with the way a speaker tailors an utterance to meet the particular needs of the intended hearer or receiver, it reflects the speaker's hypothesis about the hearer's assumptions and beliefs and it is concerned with the form and structure of utterances in relation to the assumed mental states of speakers and hearers."

Both Buth and Heimerdinger devote dedicated attention to issues of prominence within OT discourse. They seek to identify those clausal and paragraph elements that assist the communication process by foregrounding and backgrounding information, by identifying and changing topic, and by directing focus to a constituent that may have fallen from attention in the communication. Buth (97) offers the following discussion of prominence connected with verb position in relation to Dan. 6:19–20:

6:19 [6:18 ET] Then went the king to his palace [foreground-continuity]
6:20 [6:19 ET] Then the king at dawn got up at sunrise and with haste to the pit of lions he went [background-discontinuity, dramatic pause, peak]

In terms of functionalist attention to the NT, Jeffrey Reed's study of Philippians represents the first comprehensive attempt to apply Hallidayan systemic functional linguistic principles to the study of the Bible. He too is concerned with issues of prominence in his chosen discourse, and demonstrates that these issues cannot be addressed apart from pragmatic factors related to the text in question. Likewise, Cotterell and Turner emphasize the importance of considering text, cotext, and context in analyzing discourse.

These studies have blazed an important trail, but much more needs to be done in order to realize the considerable potential of functional grammar for opening new windows into the study of biblical texts.

See also Etymology; Structuralism; Utterance Meaning

Bibliography

Buth, R. "Functional Grammar, Hebrew and Aramaic: An Integrated, Textlinguistic Approach to Syntax." Pages 77–102 in *Discourse Analysis of Biblical Literature*, ed. W. Bodine. Scholars Press, 1995; Cotterell, P., and M. Turner. *Linguistics and Biblical Interpretation*. InterVarsity, 1989; Dawson, D. *Text-Linguistics and Biblical Hebrew*. Sheffield Academic Press, 1994; Dik, S. *Studies in Functional Grammar*. Academic Press, 1980; Dirven, R., and G. Radden, eds. *Fillmore's Case Grammar*. Groos, 1987; Halliday, M. *Introduction to Functional Grammar*. 2d ed. E. Arnold, 1994; Heimerdinger, J.-M. *Topic, Focus and Foreground in Ancient Hebrew Narratives*. Sheffield Academic Press, 1999; Langacker, R. *Language and Its Structure*. Harcourt Brace, 1973; Longacre, R. *The Grammar of Discourse*. 2d ed. Plenum, 1996; Lyons, J. *Chomsky*. Fontana/Collins, 1970; Nida, E., and C. Taber. *The Theory and Practice of Translation*. Brill, 1969; Reed, J. *A Discourse Analysis of Philippians*. Sheffield Academic Press, 1997; Schiffrin, D. *Approaches to Discourse*. Blackwell, 1994; Terry, R. *A Discourse Analysis of First Corinthians*. Summer Institute of Linguistics, 1995; Van der Merwe, C., J. Kroeze, and J. Naude. *A Biblical Hebrew Reference Grammar*. Sheffield Academic Press, 1999; Weingreen, J. *Practical Grammar for Classical Hebrew*. 2d ed. Oxford University Press, 1959; Wittgenstein, L. *Philosophical Investigations*, trans. G. E. M. Anscombe. 2d ed. Blackwell, 1958.

Peter G. Riddell

Language, Linguistics

Linguistics provides precise ways for people to understand how human languages work. Linguistics as a science has had a remarkable development over the past hundred years. Along with this knowledge explosion has come a plethora of technical terms and specific theoretical perspectives that often bewilder those who begin to study linguistics. Linguistics is a generic way of describing aspects of a language. The sound system (phonetics and phonology), the word shapes (morphology), the formation of sentences (syntax), the relationship of structures of meaning (semantics), and even the formation of whole texts (discourse grammar and text linguistics)—these are all objects of study. Within linguistics, questions are asked that go beyond any one language. Comparisons are regularly made between several languages. Historical linguistics, or the study of the development of related languages, is only one aspect of comparison. Universal grammar is also studied to find out why certain processes recur in languages that are not historically related. Other aspects of linguistics include the study of language learning, reading, cognitive processes, and communication theory.

Phonology and Phonetics

If we remember that approximately one-third of the Hebrew Bible is poetry, it will be immediately apparent that sound plays a role in biblical interpretation and appreciation.

The sound system of Greek in the first century was different from the pedagogy that most NT students are taught. After the time of Alexander the Great (d. 323 BCE), Greek use spread throughout the Near East and Mediterranean world. With the rapid spread and use among second-language users, Greek underwent a series of changes as a result of losing "length" within its phonemic system. This resulted in a vowel system reduced to seven phonemes by the first century (see Horrocks 109 [11a]; 110 [12, 13 iv]; Buth, *Living Koine Greek*, 175–84). These seven vowel phonemes can be grouped according to their graphic representations:

$$\iota = \varepsilon\iota \quad \eta \quad \varepsilon = \alpha\iota \quad \alpha \quad \omega = o \quad o\upsilon \quad \upsilon = o\iota$$

This may influence interpretation when one encounters passages like Rom. 5:1, where the two translation options "we have"/"let us have" and two textual options *echomen/echōmen* both rest on words (textual variants) that were homonyms in the first century.

Morphology, the Shapes of Words

There are historical reasons for whatever is found in a language. However, it is not usually necessary to understand "why" a particular historical development took place in order to use a language. For example, an English speaker does not need to know the history of the forms "to be": *is, am, are, was, were*. In general, what seem like irregularities to a student are historical fossils that have resisted more general changes sweeping through a language and trying to simplify and regularize it. These fossils are able to remain because they are so commonly used.

Hebrew Morphology. Many of the changes in Hebrew vowels are caused by consonants that have guttural features, especially the pharyngeal fricatives, *khet* (voiceless) and *'ayin* (voiced). This often causes a lowering of expected vowels because of the pulling back of the tongue root in *khet* or *'ayin*.

New vocabulary was produced within Semitic languages like Hebrew, Aramaic, and Arabic by altering the pattern of a three-consonant root. This is similar to the way in which Indo-European languages form new vocabulary by adding prefixes, suffixes, or prepositions. Consider for example "produce," "deduce," "reduce," all related to a root "duce" (based on Latin *ducere,* "to lead"). Hebrew had three basic vocabulary building patterns, traditionally called the *Qal, Pi'el,* and *Hiph'il.* Two other common vocabulary-building patterns were the *Niph'al* and *Hithpa'el,* bringing the total productive patterns in ancient Hebrew to five. (The *Pu'al* and *Hoph'al* patterns were only passives; they do not form new vocabulary and may be produced automatically, predictably, as the passives of their respective active pattern.) Examples of vocabulary building patterns: *manah* (מָנָה) meant "he counted"; *minnah* (מִנָּה), "he appointed"; *safar* (סָפַר), "he counted"; but *sipper* (סִפֵּר), "he detailed, reported"; *paqad* (פָּקַד), "he made an accounting"; *hifqid* (הִפְקִיד), "he appointed."

Greek Morphology. A subject sometimes debated among Greek teachers or students is whether Greek had five noun categories or eight. A linguistic framework has a contribution to make. Simply put, the "eight-case" position confuses form and meaning and confuses the protohistory of a language with the language itself. Attic and Hellenistic Greek had five categories of noun forms (nominative, genitive, dative, accusative, vocative). Semantically, those five categories must cover any and all uses of a Greek noun. The number of semantic functions depends on the grammarian's methodology. Thirty to fifty semantic functions may be pedagogically useful for the five formal categories.

Greek and Hebrew Lexical Semantics

Individual words—whether nouns, verbs, or other—contribute a minimal meaning to any one context. They do not carry with them meaning from other contexts. Likewise, they do not carry etymological "original" meanings any more than English "reduce" means "lead back (a horse to its corral)." Lexica and vocabulary studies must be sifted so as to exclude illegitimate importa-

tions from other contexts. In English, a person "charging" a purchase on credit cannot be called "aggressive" simply because a football player can "charge" a defensive line.

Aspect, Greek. A parameter that confronts a user of Greek is "aspect." Aspect is a perspective on an event. An event may be viewed from "inside" a process or state, without specifying the beginning or end of a process/state. In general linguistics, such a perspective is labeled "imperfective." An event may also be viewed from "outside" a process or state, viewing the whole event and specifically including an end point or fixed state. In general linguistics, such a perspective is called "perfective." In English, a simple past "he came" or simple future "he will come" is perfective. English imperfective aspect is signaled with compound structures: "he was coming," "he is coming," "he will be coming." Subcategories of imperfectivity in various languages include repetition (iterativity, "he would visit his aunt") and habituality ("he jogs," "he used to smoke").

The distinction of Greek aspect is that it has entered the morphology of the language to the point where an aspectual choice must be made on virtually every verb. Neutral ambiguity is not an option. A famous example is a line from the Lord's Prayer in both Matthew and Luke.

In English, Hebrew, and Aramaic it is normal to use a simple command and to let the context clarify whether the command is simple and *perfective* or open-ended and *imperfective.*

Et lehem huqqenu ten lanu. (Aramaic)
Give us our allotted food. (Matt. 6:11 AT)

Saying this in Greek requires a distinctive, aspectual choice. Below, we find Matthew with a perfective imperative and Luke with an imperfective imperative. Both writers have properly configured the rest of their sentence to their choice of aspect.

Matt. 6:12—*Ton arton hēmōn ton epiousion dos hēmin sēmeron.*
Give [perfective] us our daily bread today.

Luke 11:3—*Ton arton hēmōn ton epiousion didou hēmin to kath' hēmeran.*
Be giving [imperfective] us our daily bread day by day.

It is possible to make such an aspectual distinction in another language, but doing so requires extra processing energy and extra words.

Greek is a language that lives and breathes aspect. Ironically, its highly aspectual nature is often hidden from students by grammatical terms, by the metalanguage. The various imperfective verbs listed above are traditionally called "present subjunctive," "present optative," "present infinitive," and "present imperative." Grammar books correctly point out to the student that these categories have nothing to do with time, but the name lingers and confusion results more often than not. If an aspectual name like "continuative" were used (continuative subjunctive, continuative optative, continuative infinitive, continuative imperative), students would probably find that they remember and interpret their Greek categories more easily and correctly.

Hebrew "Aspect" and Tense-Mood-Aspect. Hebrew presents the opposite phenomenon from Greek for English users. Instead of a language that requires extra categories for referring to an event, Hebrew uses fewer categories than English. The common terminology in European Hebrew studies has been "imperfect" and "perfect" verbs. As a result of this metalanguage, interpreters have not infrequently assumed that Hebrew was a language where the speakers focused on aspect without reference to time, while Greek was tacitly assumed to be the more temporal, time-oriented language. That inference is quite misleading.

For Hebrew we ask: How many divisions does its TMA (Tense-Mood-Aspect) verb system use? The standard answer is two. (Already in the biblical period the participle had become the default present tense for describing what was happening around a speaker. A volitional system was also in place that partially overlapped with one of the two TMA categories.) While these can be argued to have arisen etymologically from an aspectual category, it would be a logical fallacy to imply that this category in Hebrew did not include both time and modal constraints. For example, a purely "aspectual" Hebrew verb would predict that either verb category, "imperfect" or "perfect," could be used in a future context with *mahar* (מָחָר), "tomorrow." However, none of the 52 occurrences of *mahar* in the Hebrew Bible are used with a so-called perfective; zero out of 52. This is especially diagnostic for linguists because most of the future contexts are "perfective," looking forward to a situation where the future event will be complete. Since Hebrew verbs only have two signals available for marking Times and Aspects and Moods, mapping the categories to cover all potential semantic situations will overlap the three parameters. Ironically, it is specifically aspect that gets the least attention when telling a Hebrew story. Most past events are reported together, mono-aspectually, whether or not the event was still in process. (This is frequent with motion verbs: "He went to X and he saw Y on the way." A language highly sensitive to aspect might say: "He was going to X and saw Y.") Likewise, future events are reported monotonally, usually without differentiating those that will be complete from those that will be in process.

This means that among the biblical languages, Greek is the one that is highly aspectual, while from an Indo-European perspective, Hebrew is not really aspectual but is underdifferentiated, producing a functional fusion of time-aspect-mood. We do not have a good plain-vanilla metalanguage label for the Hebrew system, and until such time as we do, students can comfort themselves with the model of light being both a particle and a wave as the need arises. The biblical Hebrew verb functioned very well over a thousand years for marking time distinctions, mood distinctions, and aspectual distinctions, all with only two distinct TMA categories.

Textuality and Syntax

The use of the lexical, morphological, and syntactical resources of a language is constrained by the context of a larger text in which the pieces sit. Studying these constraints and patterns has given rise to a branch of linguistics called text-linguistics and discourse analysis (on which see the article "Utterance Meaning" in relation to syntax, word order, and the like). Here we note that "Topic," "Comment," and "Focus" are commonly used terms in linguistic literature and are helpful concepts for understanding word-order systems. They are used in various ways by different linguists. We will start with "Comment."

Comment refers generally to the main point of a clause. One linguistic school, Praguian Functional Sentence Perspective (FSP), developed an analytical methodology around this idea. The Comment of a sentence is "what the author wants to say." (In FSP terms, the comment of a sentence is called the "Rheme" of a sentence.)

The "Topic" of a sentence is the noncomment part, and the Topic becomes the framework for predicating the comment. The term "Topic" does not mean syntactic subject. It can refer to any kind of syntactic material as long as it is "nonfocal, noncomment." Consider: "They did it in the morning." Presumably, the salient, new, rhemic information is "in the morning." The whole phrase "they did it" becomes the Topic in this analysis. (In FSP terms, the Topic was called a Theme. Thus started the cycle of terminological confusion because in English something thematic is a generic way of talking about something "focal." So in FSP, the Theme is topical but not thematic, while the Rheme is the salient information, the raison d'être for the sentence.) These concepts of Topic (theme) and Comment (rheme) could be applied to any sentence.

However, there is another kind of information that is specially signaled by the grammar. A specially marked Focus may be a special word-order structure where the salient part of a clause, the Rheme or a part of the Rheme, is put in a special place in the sentence, typically near the beginning. In several linguistic theories the concept of placing special focal information at the beginning of a clause is considered a universal option in human language, though not all languages make use of the phenomenon in the same frequencies.

Topical information, too, can occur in special positions in a sentence. So a reader of a sentence ends up with two kinds of linguistic Topics. One is the generic, unmarked information of a clause that provides more assumed information as a springboard for the comment. The second kind of Topic is when some of this topical information is itself specially marked by placing it near the beginning of a sentence. This special Topic is also hypothesized to be a universal option in human language around the world, to one degree or another.

What the above means is that several linguistic theories have hypothesized that not just one, but two kinds of communicative information ("pragmatic information," in linguistic terms) can be placed in a special order near the beginning of a sentence. Consequently, "emphasis"—a frequently encountered term in Greek and Hebrew grammar books—is insufficient as a guide for interpretation. A reader of Greek and Hebrew texts needs to develop the ability to distinguish a marked Topic from a marked Focus. Greek requires special practice because of its flexibility with word order and multiple marked elements.

Relevance Theory and Interpretation

Relevance Theory is a cognitive theory about how utterances carry meaning. The theory can explain situations from irony to simple questions and answers. The theory stipulates that all statements are encoded and decoded with maximum relevance assumed. An encoder uses as much processing energy as is necessary for the intended audience. An audience assumes that the author thought he had used enough information so that they can reach appropriate strong and weak implicatures about the message. Shared cultural

information will frequently be left out, or if included, it will raise a question in the recipient's mind as to why, and lead them to look for a more complex interpretation. If the implication of a message will take extra processing, the author usually needs to signal this.

Relevance becomes quite complicated in a canonical context because there are two and three audiences. A story in the Gospels takes place between Jesus and his audience, and we regularly see relevance principles at work as various parties in an incident respond to each other. However, there is also the audience of a written Gospel.

> Jesus took the five loaves . . . and blessed. (Matt. 14:19 AT)

The words of the blessing are not given. We may test several hypotheses as readers. Perhaps Matthew did not want us to know the words of blessing. In some cultures this might even suggest that they were special words, powerful words used in a miraculous context. Perhaps the words were irrelevant or distracting to the story line, so Matthew did not record them. Certainly possible, but this leads to the next consideration. The words may not have been recorded by either Matthew or his source because everyone already knew the words to the blessing. Jesus used the traditional wording, so there was nothing to add beyond the mention of blessing itself. To an audience that knew the traditional blessings, that last interpretation has a good claim to be the easiest and first to process for someone who hears the simple "he blessed." (Blessing before eating was part of the oral interpretation of the law and puts Jesus in the camp of the Pharisees on this issue.)

In the Hebrew Bible a reader may also assume relevance. The Joseph story raises a question or two when confronting a reader with Gen. 38, where the story line diverges and follows two generations of Judah's offspring before returning to Egypt in Gen. 39. Whatever reason we come up with, we can assume that the author/editor intended us either to understand or expected us to ask questions about this intervention. (*Genesis Rabbah*, a collection of interpretations and sermons from Talmudic times, understood the story as an example of "measure for measure," poetic justice. Just as the brothers told Jacob to "recognize these things" [Gen. 37:32–33], so did Tamar tell Judah to "recognize these things" [38:25–26]. Robert Alter provides an excellent account of how to read this story carefully.)

Language Learning

Linguists have learned much about what works for human language learning and what impedes language learning. Exciting developments have taken place with listening comprehension theory and with communicative approaches. The development of curricula in theological schools has usually taken place without input from language acquisition studies. This has produced an insular environment where certain questions or tests simply do not arise. What would happen if a Greek professor were asked to explain what she did the week before, in Hellenistic Greek, in the very language in which teacher and students are trying to develop high interpretative skills? This skill is normally expected of a graduate literature instructor or student. Finding efficient methods for teaching a language in a classroom raises the question of how to train the next generation of teachers. Students of canonical literature may take comfort in knowing that Hebrew was used and transmitted as a learned language in a classroom for 1,500 years. The task is doable if made a priority.

See also Etymology; Language, Grammar and Syntax; Utterance Meaning

Bibliography

Alter, R. *The Art of Biblical Narrative*. Basic, 1981; Bar-Asher, M., ed. מחקרים בלשון = *Mehqarim ba-lashon* [Studies in Language]. 9 vols. Hebrew University Press, 1985–2003; Bendavid, A. ולשון הכמים לשון מקרא = *Leshon Miqra' wu-leshon hakhamim* [Biblical Language and Mishnaic Language]. 2 vols. Dvir, 1967; Bickerton, D. *Roots of Language*. Karoma, 1981; Buth, R. "Functional Grammar, Hebrew and Aramaic: An Integrated Text-linguistic Approach to Syntax." In *Discourse Analysis of Biblical Literature*. ed. W. R. Bodine. SemeiaSt. Scholars, 1995; idem. *Living Biblical Hebrew for Everyone*. 2 vols. Biblical Language Center, 2003; idem. *Living Koine Greek for Everyone*. Vol. 1. Biblical Language Center, 2002; Casey, M. *An Aramaic Approach to Q*. SNTSMS 122. Cambridge University Press, 2002; Chomsky, N. *The Minimalist Program*. MIT Press, 1995; Comrie, B. *Aspect*. Cambridge University Press, 1976; Dirven, R., and V. Fried, eds. *Functionalism in Linguistics*. Linguistic and Literary Studies in Eastern Europe 20. John Benjamins, 1987; Fromkin, V., N. Hyams, and R. Rodman. *An Introduction to Language*. 7th ed. Heinle, 2002; Horrocks, G. *Greek*. Longmans, 1997; Hurvitz, A. *A Linguistic Study of the Relationship between the Priestly Source and the Book of Ezekiel*. CahRB 20. Rome, 1982; Krashen, S. D., and T. D. Terrell. *The Natural Approach*. Alemany, 1983; Kutscher, E. Y. *Hebrew and Aramaic Studies*. Magnes, 1977; Porter, S. "Did Jesus Ever Teach in Greek?" *TynBul* 44 (1993): 199–235; Safrai, S. "Literary Languages in the Time of Jesus." *Jerusalem Perspective* 4, no. 2 [= issue 31] (1991): 3–8; idem. "Spoken Languages in the Time of Jesus." *Jerusalem Perspective* 4, no. 1 [= issue 30] (1991): 3–8, 13; Wilson, D., and D. Sperber. "Relevance Theory." Pages 607–32 in *Handbook of Pragmatics*, ed. G. Ward and L. Horn. Blackwell, 2004.

Randall Buth

Language-Game

The concept of "language-game" (*Sprachspiel*) is one of several key concepts belonging to the later philosophy of Ludwig Wittgenstein as preeminently expressed in his classic work *Philosophical Investigations*. The theological significance of the concept for philosophical theology, contemporary hermeneutics, and biblical interpretation stems from the posthumous publication of the *Investigations* in 1953. Nevertheless, Wittgenstein's own thoughts began to crystallize in the 1930s, when he was engaging in intensive reevaluation and criticism of his earlier work, the *Tractatus logico-philosophicus*.

The Later Philosophy

The first occurrence of the concept in Wittgenstein's thought is found in *The Blue Book*:

> I shall in the future again and again draw your attention to what I shall call language-games. These are ways of using signs simpler than those in which we use the signs of our highly complicated everyday life. Language-games are the forms of language with which a child begins to make use of words. The study of language-games is the study of primitive forms of language. If we want to study the problems of truth and falsehood, of the agreement or disagreement of propositions with reality, of the nature of assertion, assumption, and question, we shall with great advantage look at primitive forms of language in which these forms of thinking appear without the confusing background of highly complicated processes of thought. When we look at such simple forms of language the mental mist which seems to enshroud our ordinary use of language disappears. We see activities, reactions, which are clear-cut and transparent. (Wittgenstein, *Blue*, 17)

Here Wittgenstein draws attention to his belief that the study of language-games is central to the study—and dissolution—of philosophical problems. In the *Philosophical Investigations* he gives the clearest indication of what he takes to be such forms of language. The term "language-games," he writes, "is meant to bring into prominence the fact that the *speaking* of language is part of an activity, or of a form of life." He cites as examples of language-games the following: giving orders and obeying them; describing the appearance of an object, or giving its measurements; constructing an object from a description (a drawing); reporting an event; forming and testing a hypothesis; making up a story and reading it; play-acting; guessing riddles; making a joke; telling it; asking, thanking, cursing, greeting, praying (Wittgenstein §23).

In his early view Wittgenstein let logic determine the limits of language; in his later philosophy he assigned that role to the concept of a *private language*. What is a private language? It can be defined in terms of ordinary language itself. It was not a question of language spoken by the ordinary person in the street as compared to the specialized technical vocabulary of the expert. For Wittgenstein, both of these qualified as ordinary language (even logic in this sense was ordinary language in having a definite genuine usefulness to which it could be put). *Ordinary language was language whose rules could be taught in principle to other people.* Beyond the limits of ordinary language lay the realm of private language, the rules of which, Wittgenstein held, *could not be taught in principle from one person to another*. In his battle against the errors of traditional philosophy, such as the philosophical skepticism of a philosopher like Descartes, Wittgenstein's objective is to "bring words back from their metaphysical to their everyday use":

> When philosophers use a word "knowledge," "being," "object," "I," "proposition," . . . one must always ask oneself: is the word ever actually used in this way in the language-game which is its original home?
> What *we* do is bring words back from their metaphysical to their everyday use. (*Philosophical* §116)

This emphasis on meaning as *use*—and the correlative concepts of teachability and learnability—is central to Wittgenstein's understanding of language-games. Language-games that are not teachable or learnable are examples of a private language. Conversely, those that are teachable or learnable are part of the great natural and historical corpus of linguistic behavior and communication. Philosophy will only generate confusion if it seeks to go beyond the limits of these language-games, because then language will not be doing any real work. In epistemology, for example, when Descartes doubts whether we can be sure what anything is, Wittgenstein asks how we could teach—outside of the ordinary everyday context of knowing *what it is* a chair is—what it means to say (pointing to a chair), "That is probably a chair." Wittgenstein's point is this: Try teaching the meaning (or use) of this assertion to a child without first having taught him or her *what it is* a chair is! To know whether something is "prob-

ably a chair" presupposes that one knows *what it is* a chair is (*Zettel* §411). One cannot teach the former without first having taught the latter. This means that—outside of the latter context—one cannot teach (and the child cannot learn) the rule for the use of "That is probably a chair." Saying that the philosopher is to bring words back from their "metaphysical to ordinary everyday use" is saying that they are to be brought back from the realm of the unteachable to that of the teachable. This is why in *Zettel* Wittgenstein makes the remark, "Am I making the connection between meaning and teaching?" (§411). The answer must be "Absolutely yes."

Theology and Religion

The later Wittgenstein is often construed as affirming a "cultural-anthropological" approach to philosophical problem-solving. According to this view, central to the later philosophy is a plethora of language-games, each with its own respective logic and rationality. The philosopher of religion D. Z. Phillips undoubtedly construes Wittgenstein as a "philosophical" cultural anthropologist, albeit an enlightened one. A similar view is held in mainstream theological circles. In common with Phillips's "internalist" approach, George Lindbeck's "intratextual" interpretation of Wittgenstein in *The Nature of Doctrine* advocates a Wittgenstein who maintained that philosophy was limited to describing the grammar of each individual "language-game" or "form of life." In this context "grammar" coincided with rules of truth, intelligibility, reality, and rationality, whose final court of appeal was how these rules were used in each (communal) language-game. Since these rules were different for different language-games, no external critical perspective was possible, each language-game was "self-authenticating," and rationality was an "internal" matter. Lindbeck called his approach "faithfulness as intratextuality." Intratextuality entails that "meaning is constituted by the uses of a specific language rather than being distinguishable from it" (Lindbeck 114).

Though it is not likely that Wittgenstein conceived religion, or for that matter science, as individual and autonomous language-games, the idea that the rules of religious discourse were precisely teachable and therefore learnable repudiated once and for all the view that such discourse was meaningless. As against the kind of positivist conclusions reached by such as A. J. Ayer in his *Language, Truth, and Logic*, one of the implications of the later philosophy was that the charge of meaninglessness was absurd: since the rules of religious language were learnable, it was clearly meaningful.

Nevertheless, it would be a mistake to deduce from this that religious language guaranteed its authenticity in terms of belief, knowledge, and truth. To say that religious and theological discourse have their own epistemological and ontological criteria, for example, that the ontology of God is not the same as the ontology of physical objects, is to say one thing. Saying that the concepts of "true" and "false" are different in the two cases is saying quite another. What is possible is that the rules of religious discourse be only taught *among* believers, in which case believing would be a necessary condition of understanding. This has led to the charge of fideism by such as Kai Neilson and Ernst Gellner.

Hermeneutics and the Bible

The impact of the concept of language-games on biblical hermeneutics has been both theoretical and practical (viz., Shanker's response to Apel). As a hermeneutical approach to the Bible, the concept of the interpretative community has much to commend it. Though the original impetus is undoubtedly Wittgenstein's concept of language-games and forms of life, the church as an interpretative community has been understood in terms of the Aristotelian or Thomistic concept of virtuous readers (Fowl). The hermeneutics of the liturgical life of the church can also be understood in the context of an "ecclesial" language-game.

Noting the resemblance to the concept of language-event in the work of Gerhard Ebeling and Ernst Fuchs, Anthony Thiselton has attempted to apply Wittgenstein's insights about language-games to the field of NT hermeneutics and exegesis with some success (*Two*; *New*; *Promise*). He employs the concept of *communicative action* in order to point to the essentially *performative* nature of an important part of our linguistic behavior.

Conclusion

It may be that Wittgenstein's impact on hermeneutics has been somewhat superseded by current developments in postmodern and "Derridean" hermeneutics. Nevertheless, those in the church who believe that only saving grace can help us understand the concepts of the Bible may gain some validation in Wittgenstein's concept of a language-game. Ironically, the theory of speech acts in the work of Oxford linguistic philosopher John L. Austin may be the true alternative to post-Heideggerian hermeneutics (see Wolterstorff). Yet it is conceivable—in interpreting the word of God—that speech-act theory may constitute merely one practice of many in the life of the church understood as an interpretative community.

Bibliography

Apel, K.-O. "Wittgenstein and the Problem of Hermeneutic Understanding." Pages 70–103 in *Ludwig Wittgenstein*. Vol. 4, ed. S. G. Shanker. Croom Helm, 1986; Austin, J. L. *How to Do Things with Words*. Harvard University Press, 1962; Ayer, A. J. *Language, Truth and Logic*. 2d ed. Victor Gollancz, 1946; Baker, G. P., and P. M. S. Hacker. *An Analytical Commentary on Wittgenstein's "Philosophical Investigations."* Vols. 1–2. Blackwell, 1980–85; Fowl, S. *Engaging Scripture*. Blackwell, 1996; Gellner, E. "Reply to Mr. McIntyre." Pages 71–89 in *Universities and Left Review*, 1958; Hacker, P. M. S. *An Analytical Commentary on Wittgenstein's "Philosophical Investigations."* Vol. 3. Blackwell, 1993; Lindbeck, G. *The Nature of Doctrine*. SPCK, 1984; MacDonald, N. B. *Karl Barth and the Strange New World within the Bible* (ch. 12). Paternoster, 2000; Nielsen, K. "Wittgensteinian Fideism." *Philosophy* 42 (1967): 191–209; Phillips, D. Z. *Belief, Change and Forms of Life*. MacMillan, 1986; idem. *The Concept of Prayer*. Blackwell, 1981; idem. *Faith after Foundationalism*. Routledge, 1988; idem. "Primitive Reactions and the Reactions of Primitives." Pages 103–22 in *Wittgenstein and Religion*. MacMillan, 1993; idem. "Religion in Wittgenstein's Mirror." Pages 135–50 in *Wittgenstein Centenary Essays*, ed. A. P. Griffiths. Cambridge University Press, 1991; Shanker, S. G. "Wittgenstein and the Problem of Hermeneutic Understanding." Pages 104–15 in *Ludwig Wittgenstein*. Vol. 4, ed. S. G. Shanker. Croom Helm, 1986; Thiselton, A. "Communicative Action and Promise in Interdisciplinary, Biblical, and Theological Hermeneutics." Pages 133–239 in *The Promise of Hermeneutics*, R. Lundin, C. Walhout, and A. Thiselton. Eerdmans, 1999; idem. *Language, Liturgy, and Meaning*. Grove Books, 1975; idem. *New Horizons in Hermeneutics*. Paternoster, 1992; idem. *The Two Horizons*. Paternoster, 1980; Wittgenstein, L. *Blue and Brown Books*. Blackwell, 1978; idem. *Culture and Value*, ed. G. H. von Wright in collaboration with H. Nyman. Blackwell, 1980; idem. *Lectures and Conversations of Aesthetics, Psychology and Religious Belief*, ed. C. Barrett. Blackwell, 1966; idem. *On Certainty*, ed. G. E. M. Anscombe and G. H. von Wright, trans. D. Paul and G. E. M. Anscombe. Blackwell, 1969; idem. *Philosophical Investigations*, ed. G. E. M. Anscombe. Blackwell, 1953; idem. *Remarks on Frazer's Golden Bough*, ed. R. Rhees. Brynmill, 1979; idem. *Tractatus logico-philosophicus*. German, 1921. ET, 1922, trans. D. F. Pears and B. F. McGuinness. Routledge & Kegan Paul, 1961; idem. *Zettel*, ed. G. E. M. Anscombe and G. H. Von Wright. Blackwell, 1981; Wolterstorff, N. *Divine Discourse*. Cambridge University Press, 1995.

Neil B. MacDonald

Last Things, Doctrine of

The doctrine of the last things (eschatology) concerns the culmination of God's purposes, focused on the last One, Jesus Christ, "the last Adam" (1 Cor. 15:45), whose (second) coming in judgment and blessing is the focus of Christian hope. Scripture associates the last things with the messianic "last days" or "latter days" or "those days." Scripture portrays the last things in trinitarian style: Christ's return to reign eternally, the fullness of the Spirit's work, and God's presence eternally with his people.

Eschatological Orientation of Re-Creation and Salvation

A broad consensus of contemporary scholarship agrees that the last things should not be understood primarily as a series of events at the end of history, relatively detached from what precedes. The last things are integral to the biblical message for, though culminating at the end, they begin much earlier. Bringing to fulfillment the many story lines and divine promises while exceeding all that we can ask or imagine, this dynamic, transforming rule of God over the entire—and entirely submissive—re-creation culminates the complex scriptural story.

Numerous biblical themes have overtones that confirm the significance of the last things for interpreting Scripture: two themes, creation and salvation, are predominant.

Re-creation culminates the reversal of sin's effects on the fallen, judged creation. The biblical account climaxes with the "new heavens and a new earth, where righteousness is at home" (2 Pet. 3:13 NRSV). The extent and pervasiveness of sin's effects mean that restoring the created order amounts to a re-creation. So drastic a cosmic renewal is regeneration, rebirth, "renewal" (Matt. 19:28). The new birth experienced by God's children, without which they cannot see the kingdom of God, anticipates the created order's renewal.

Jesus brings to fulfillment God's promises for cosmic justice and restoration, and thus is the savior of all humanity. The same enemies threaten humanity's eternal well-being and oppress the created order: injustice and suffering resulting from sin and death, and the devil, "the god of this age" (2 Cor. 4:4 TNIV). Jesus' death and resurrection atones for the sins of the world and conquers these enemies, delivering the created order from bondage. The freedom of the creation, suffering under judgment because of human sin, is integral to the redemption of God's children.

With themes and images pervasively eschatological, salvation is inseparable from the culmination of God's work. Victory over enemies, healing from disease, cleansing from impurity, abundant and satisfying provision for the thirsty and hungry, light for the blind and those in darkness, adoption of the abandoned, reconciliation of the alienated, forgiveness for the guilty, vindication for the wrongly oppressed, restoration of the lost, wholeness and well-being for those who suffer, life for the dead—though God's people often experience foretastes of these blessings, they come fully only in the end. The fullness of redemption culminates God's work for his people. Thus, hope is a preeminent eschatological virtue.

Covenantal Structure of Hope

God embodied his redemptive promises in covenants made with his people, beginning with Abraham (Gen. 12:1–3; 15; 17; 22:15–18; reaffirmed to Isaac in 26:24 and to Jacob in 28:13–15), promising land, seed, and blessing for the world. The Mosaic covenant established at Sinai (Exod. 19–24) and renewed before the Jordan (Deuteronomy) administered the patriarchal promises to Israel, Abraham's multiplied descendants, preparing to enter Canaan. The Davidic covenant (2 Sam. 7; Ps. 89) provided a perpetual dynasty to reign over Israel. The new covenant (Jer. 31:31–34; Ezek. 36:16–37) replaced the broken "old" covenant by granting the Spirit for the covenant community's universal internal renewal and permanently removing sinfulness.

The Day of Yahweh

The day of God's intervention to deliver Israel from oppression became known as the day of Yahweh. Israel experienced many such interventions, but looked for one climactic day of Yahweh at the end of this age, increasingly associated with the Messiah. Though many Israelites rejoiced, anticipating their unqualified victory, Amos warned against seeking that day, for Yahweh would judge his people (5:18–20).

Apocalyptic

The books of Daniel and Ezekiel include a distinctive genre that would flourish during the intertestamental period. Commonly originating during a crisis of oppression, apocalyptic literature consists of angelically mediated divine revelation that humans receive in highly symbolic visions. It announces the climactic triumph of the kingdom of God over hostile earthly kingdoms, calling readers to view contemporary struggles eschatologically.

Jesus, the Covenants, and the Kingdom of God

Jesus' ministry culminates the OT redemptive covenants. He is *the* seed of Abraham (Gal. 3:16), the Savior of the world, in whom the blessings of God become universal, to all who by faith become children of Abraham. He is the final anointed Davidic king, who in righteousness will reign over Israel and all peoples, because the kingdom of this world becomes his kingdom (Rev. 11:15). The crucified, risen, and ascended Messiah has inaugurated the new covenant (Matt. 26:26–30; Mark 14:22–25; Luke 22:14–23; 1 Cor. 11:23–26) and sent the eschatological Spirit (Acts 2). The church experiences this new life in the Spirit while it awaits the fullness in the new earth. Jesus, the priestly mediator offering himself as perfect sacrifice, fulfills the Levitical cultus, incomparably manifesting God's love for the ungodly in conquering his enemies and dealing fully and finally with God's wrath and sin's guilt, alienation, and uncleanness. Jesus unifies in himself God's covenantal promises, far surpassing all expectations.

Echoing John the Baptizer, Jesus proclaimed the nearness of the kingdom of God (Matt. 4:17// Mark 1:15; Matt. 4:23; Luke 4:43–44). His ministry manifested its presence in his person (Luke 11:20), anticipating the Spirit's Pentecostal inauguration. Those who insightfully recognized Jesus' messianic significance evoked his astonished commendation (Matt. 8:5–13; 15:21–28).

Because he conquered sin and death, Jesus received redemptive rule over creation (Phil. 2:6–11). His gift of the Spirit inaugurated God's dynamic, transforming reign mediated through his anointed representative, effected by the Spirit in fullness when Jesus returns. Intermixed with the world, its presence in this age is invisible. Bringing justice and peace and radically reversing this cosmos's priorities, it includes all kinds of people, even the "unclean," but not those expecting honored entrance.

The Spirit's greatest prominence is eschatological. The promise of the Spirit is the promise of kingdom blessings, God's abundant provision for his people, since the Spirit accomplishes them and mediates personal participation in them.

Jesus as Son of Man

Jesus' typical self-designation is "Son of Man," echoing Daniel's vision of "one like a son of man," who comes gloriously from heaven in judgment, receiving an everlasting, universal, indestructible kingdom (7:13–14). Jesus identifies himself as this eschatological judge (Matt. 26:64//Mark 14:62// Luke 22:69).

Present Age and the Age to Come

Like the OT, the NT divides history into two eras, "this age" (the present reign of evil) and "the age to come" ("the last days," Messiah's reign of justice and peace; Matt. 12:32; Mark 10:30; Luke 20:34–35; Eph. 1:21; Heb. 6:5). In Jesus' person and ministry, the age to come has broken into the present age rather than replacing it, so the two ages overlap "between the times" of Jesus' comings (Acts 2:17; 1 Cor. 10:11b; Heb. 1:1–2; 9:26; 1 Pet. 1:20; 1 John 2:18).

Parousia

Christ's parousia (his coming or presence) is his *second* coming. Two comings were not expected by first-century Judaism. The disciples' questions to Jesus on the Mount of Olives suggest that after three years with him, they still expected him to fulfill his work then. His talk of leaving puzzled them, not least because so much was incomplete.

The same Jesus of Nazareth will personally return (Acts 1:11), but gloriously and powerfully (Matt. 24:30) in a disclosure (*apokalypsis*; 2 Thess. 1:7) evident to all (Matt. 24:27). The exalted Jesus will be seen in the splendor now rightfully his at the Father's right hand (Phil. 2:9; Eph. 1:20–23; Heb. 2:9). He will destroy antichrist and evil (2 Thess. 2:8), gather his people, both the dead and the living (Matt. 24:31; 1 Cor. 15:23; 1 Thess. 4:14–17; 2 Thess. 2:1), and judge the world in justice (Matt. 25:31; James 5:9).

Millennialism

The millennium receives its name from Rev. 20, where the phrase "a thousand years" occurs six times. Two disputes concern this phrase: whether it should be read as a specific chronological description and, if so, whether it occurs previous to or subsequent to the parousia.

Amillennialists believe that this period includes Christ's present reign from heaven over the church and the world, not a future distinct from this age and the eternal kingdom. They argue that Christ's present reign and the eternal kingdom fulfill the prophecies, making a distinct period superfluous. Postmillennialists regard the millennium as the glorious fulfillment of OT prophecies, inaugurated through the church's Spirit-empowered preaching of the gospel, followed by the parousia. They argue that the Spirit's blessing of the gospel's worldwide expansion fulfills millennial expectations, in contrast to premillennialism's pessimistic postponement of this until after Christ's return.

Premillennialists regard the millennium as a distinct future period (though they differ regarding its chronological precision, as do some postmillennialists) inaugurated by the glorious coming of Christ. Premillennialists generally believe that a seven-year period ("the great tribulation," Rev. 7:14), Daniel's "seventieth week of sevens" (9:24–27), precedes Christ's premillennial return in judgment and blessing. "Historic premillennialists" affirm that the church remains on earth through the tribulation; "dispensational premillennialists" usually teach that Christ removes the church to heaven before the tribulation. For some premillennialists, especially dispensationalists, the period includes national Israel's (spiritually renewed and Messiah-trusting) participation in Jesus' messianic blessings (fulfilling OT national promises) along with Gentile nations. Recent amillennialists such as A. Hoekema emphasize national Israel's eternal experience of the fulfillment on the new earth, not the present earth during the millennium.

Resurrection of the Body and Life Everlasting

The OT provides little indication of a hope for life after death or beyond the grave. The OT holistic understandings of humans did not suggest that disembodied persons might persist after death. *Sheol* is the place of the dead, primarily the grave. Only in scattered references is conscious life after physical death implied. Yet those indications challenge claims that the OT teaches life ending with bodily death. Cooper rightly distinguishes between indications of conscious human activity after death, on the one hand, and explicit teachings of that life, on the other. The OT may lack the latter, but not the former. Resurrection of the dead seems clearly present in Dan. 12:2–3, 13 and Isa. 26:19.

Jesus' resurrection is victory over death and the grave, bringing life and immortality to light in the gospel (2 Tim. 1:10). Christ is raised as the firstfruits of those who will follow (1 Cor. 15:20, 23). God, who raised Jesus, will also raise us (Rom. 8:11; 1 Cor. 6:14; 2 Cor. 4:14).

The resurrection of the body heralds the completion of redemption, including redemption of the body (not *from* the body). The "fleshly" (sinful)

orientation of the former life is put off, but not human materiality. Denying bodily resurrection imperils the hope of the new creation, making eternal life ethereal, more Platonic than Pauline. God's renewed imagers will fulfill his commission for responsible stewardship of creation, now on the new earth.

The hope of the gospel is bodily resurrection to everlasting life with the triune God, yet this does not exclude an intermediate, apparently disembodied, existence between death and resurrection. Humans are not naturally or essentially immortal, but God grants them enduring conscious existence. In the interim between death and the parousia, the righteous are "with Christ" (2 Cor. 5:6–8; Phil. 1:23) as God grants life even in the unnatural state of disembodiedness, longing with the created order itself for redemption's completion.

The wicked will be raised (Dan. 12:2; John 5:28–29; Acts 24:14–15; Rev. 20:12–15) to judgment in the bodies in which they sinned, enduring "everlasting" punishment. Scriptural depictions of the reality of eternal suffering include apparently conflicting images of "flames of fire," "darkness," and "deepest darkness" (Jude 13 NRSV). Punishment will be physical and also nonphysical (Matt. 8:12; 13:42–43; 22:13; 24:51; 25:30). The majority of the Christian tradition has read this as endless punishment in a conscious state, but a recurring minority reading has recently gained increasing support, including significant evangelicals, arguing that the "everlasting destruction" (2 Thess. 1:9; see Matt. 7:13; Rom. 9:22; Phil. 3:19) of the damned is their annihilation.

Believers will be like Christ (Rom. 8:29; 1 Cor. 15:49; Phil. 3:21; 1 John 3:2) and be with him (John 14:3; 2 Cor. 5:8; Phil. 1:23; Col. 3:4; 1 Thess. 4:17), sharing his glory (Rom. 8:18, 30; 2 Cor. 3:18; 4:17; Col. 3:4; Heb. 2:10; 1 Pet. 5:1) and his reign (2 Tim. 2:12; Rev. 2:26–27; 3:21; 20:4, 6). As children of God they will enjoy perfect fellowship with him (Rev. 21:3, 7), worshipping him (7:15; 22:3) before his face (Matt. 5:8; 1 Cor. 13:12; Rev. 22:4; see Bauckham 339).

Scripture portrays believers in a restored paradise (Luke 23:43; Rev. 2:7; 22:1–5) and the new Jerusalem (Heb. 12:22; Rev. 21). God's people share table fellowship at an eschatological banquet (Matt. 8:11; Mark 14:25; Luke 14:15–24; 22:30) or wedding feast (Matt. 25:10; Rev. 19:9).

Twentieth-Century Revival of Eschatology

For much of church history, study of the last things was limited to bodily resurrection, judgment, heaven, and hell. Nineteenth-century emphasis on the kingdom of God, and classical liberalism's excessive correlation of that with human social progress, precipitated a reversal in A. Schweitzer's and J. Weiss's insistence on Jesus' imminent, apocalyptic, eschatological expectation, later undermined by the delay of the parousia. C. H. Dodd's counterclaim that the NT taught a realized kingdom in turn evoked arguments that it manifests both the presence of and expectation for the kingdom of God, an inaugurated but not consummated kingdom—now a widely acknowledged understanding.

In particular, O. Cullmann, W. Pannenberg, and J. Moltmann have contributed to the return of eschatology as a central Christian doctrine. Cullmann emphasized that Christ, as salvation history's midpoint, must be understood in terms of that entire history, from Abraham to the parousia. Pannenberg argued that Jesus' resurrection can only be understood proleptically, from the end of history. Moltmann's early work made hope an encompassing interpretative lens, understanding eschatologically the church's present life amid unjust suffering and all of theology.

Implications for Theological Interpretation of Scripture

Christians should read Scripture in its relationship to redemptive history and to the measure of proleptic realization of eschatological realities. The blessings and spiritual privileges enjoyed already before the parousia are foretastes and should incite confident expectation. This life's sorrows remind us that it is unjust, marred by sin, and transient. Commands come in light of what has been done in us and as eschatological exhortations to become what we are, as well as to become what we are not yet. One test of faithful discipleship, including scriptural interpretation, is the degree to which it fosters appropriate spiritual dissatisfaction with the present age and corresponding longing for redemption (Rom. 8). Because "what we will be has not been revealed" (1 John 3:2) and "no eye has seen, nor ear heard, nor the human heart conceived, what God has prepared for those who love him" (1 Cor. 2:9 NRSV), hermeneutical humility (not agnosticism) is particularly appropriate in eschatology.

Most fundamental of several demarcating issues is whether the future promised is mythological or historical. Modern defenders of a historical *eschaton* have often debated whether the scriptural depictions should be read "literally" or "spiritually." Recent discussions have instead

asked whether national Israel would be regathered in faith and restored from its dispersion and whether that would take place on this earth or on the new earth. Some covenant theologians argue for Israel's typological relationship to the church, making Israel's national spiritual restoration obsolete. Such questions divided much of recent evangelicalism into "covenant theology" (more amillennial than postmillennial, but sometimes "historic premillennial") and dispensationalism. The church's relation to Israel's promises is symptomatic: Does Israel have promises separate from the church? Does the church participate in the fulfillment of Israel's promises, without exhausting that fulfillment or supplanting Israel? Does Israel find its future only among believers from all nations in the "new Israel" (the church)?

Dispensationalists disagree over the degree of continuity between redemptive history's successive administrations. "Progressive dispensationalists" argue for greater continuity (progress), including an inaugurated kingdom, though the church's participation in Israel's messianic blessings does not supplant Israel's millennial national restoration to faith, while other dispensationalists argue that this blurs or removes the distinction between dispensationalism and covenant theology.

See also Apocalyptic; Covenant; Hope; Kingdom of God; New Creation; Resurrection of the Dead

Bibliography

Bauckham, R. "Eschatology." Pages 333–39 in *New Bible Dictionary*, ed. D. Wood. 3d ed. InterVarsity, 1996; Beasley-Murray, G. R. *Jesus and the Kingdom of God*. Eerdmans, 1986; Bock, D., ed. *Three Views on the Millennium and Beyond*. Counterpoints. Zondervan, 1999; Collins, J. *The Apocalyptic Imagination*. 2d ed. Eerdmans, 1998; Cooper, J. *Body, Soul, and Life Everlasting*. Eerdmans, 2000; Cullmann, O. *Christ and Time*. 3d ed., trans. F. Filson. Westminster, 1964; idem. *Immortality of the Soul or Resurrection of the Dead?* Macmillan, 1958; Fudge, E., and R. Peterson. *Two Views of Hell*. InterVarsity, 2000; Harris, M. *Raised Immortal*. Eerdmans, 1985; Hoekema, A. *The Bible and the Future*. Eerdmans, 1979; Ladd, G. *The Presence of the Future*. Eerdmans, 1974; Moltmann, J. *Theology of Hope*, trans. J. Leitch. Harper, 1967.

Stephen R. Spencer

Latin American Biblical Interpretation *See* Liberation Theologies and Hermeneutics

Law

Definition

The English term "law" covers a much narrower range of literature than the Hebrew term *torah*, which is conventionally translated "law." Hebrew *torah* would be better translated "instruction," and this *torah* comprises the whole of the Pentateuch, Genesis to Deuteronomy, despite the fact that these books contain a fair amount of narrative. Psalm 1:2, inviting the reader to meditate on the *torah* day and night, seems to envisage the book of the Psalms as well as the Pentateuch being the *torah*.

By "law" the English Bible reader understands the legal rulings and moral injunctions found within the Pentateuch, such as the Ten Commandments, the farming regulations of Exod. 22, the laws on sacrifice and purity in Leviticus, and the sermons of Deuteronomy. It is "law" in this sense that is the focus of this article, though I argue that only a broader definition that understands law as *torah* does full justice to the biblical understanding of the term. (There is also "law," of course, in the NT, though its instruction less frequently takes the form of detailed legal stipulations. Regarding law in the Epistles, and their approaches to OT law, see especially articles on Pauline texts.)

History of Interpretation

From the first century the law has been understood in a fairly straightforward literal sense. Among the many NT quotations and allusions to the law, there is only one passage where it appears to be taken allegorically (1 Cor. 9:9). Generally the moral and civil law was taken as binding by the early church; indeed, the ritual obligation to avoid blood was endorsed by the Jerusalem council (Acts 15:29) and still upheld by Tertullian nearly two centuries later. In Christendom the law of the Pentateuch continued to inspire later legislators. King Alfred, father of the English common law, drew inspiration from the laws of Exod. 20–23. The Magisterial Reformers emphasized the positive value of the law. Although the ceremonial law no longer applies to Christians, and the civil law cannot be applied universally, "no Christian man whatsoever is free from the obedience of the Commandments which are called Moral," affirms the seventh of the Anglican Thirty-Nine Articles. As late as 1853 J. L. Saalschütz subtitled his legal study of the Mosaic law as being *For Biblical Scholars, Lawyers and Statesmen*.

But from the late eighteenth century a quite different approach to reading the law began to dominate interpretation: historical criticism became the regnant interpretative paradigm. Instead of focusing on the interpretation and applicability of the law to later societies, scholarship concentrated on trying to work out when and why the different groups of law came into existence. On a straightforward reading of the Pentateuch, all the laws it contains are associated with Moses: they are either said to have been revealed to Moses (Exodus to Numbers) or to be his exposition of the Sinaitic laws (Deuteronomy). A study of these laws should therefore give a clear insight into the constitution and legal principles of early Israel.

However, in the nineteenth century it became the received wisdom that different groups of laws originated in different periods. Generally three main blocks of laws were distinguished: the book of the covenant (Exod. 21–23), the priestly law (most of Exod. 25–Num. 36), and the Deuteronomic code (Deut. 12–26). Early-nineteenth-century scholars such as de Wette held that the different groups of law were written in this order. The Deuteronomic law was dated last, around the time of Josiah's reformation (622 BCE). The other laws preceded Deuteronomy, but whether they went back to the time of Moses was debated.

At the end of the nineteenth century, a drastic change came over this reconstruction, largely as a result of the brilliant advocacy of Julius Wellhausen in his *Prolegomena to the History of Israel* (1878). A Josianic date for the Deuteronomic code was still maintained, but the Priestly material in Exodus to Numbers was dated to the exilic or postexilic eras (sixth–fifth centuries BCE). So instead of these laws being viewed as giving an insight into early Israel's constitution and values, they were now read as the aspirations of tendentious priests or utopian reformers. Great effort was put into distinguishing between earlier and later elements in the law, but because the laws were seen as essentially idealistic and detached from reality, little attention was paid to interpreting them or setting them in their social context.

The twentieth century witnessed a move back to a realistic reading of the laws. Albrecht Alt (*The Origins of Israelite Law*, 1934) distinguished between apodictic laws (Thou shalt not . . .) and case law (If a man does X, he shall suffer Y), arguing that the case law had probably been borrowed from the Canaanites, while the apodictic law was uniquely Israelite and quite early. While he did not link it to Moses, he certainly thought it could be as early as the era of the judges. His disciples Gerhard von Rad and Martin Noth also emphasized the importance of the judges period, holding that some of the key ideas of Israel's unity and covenant with Yahweh could be traced back to that era and have left their imprint on Israel's laws. Though these scholars were trying to recover the original setting of the laws in the Pentateuch, it is now widely acknowledged that their conclusions are quite speculative (Whybray).

The second half of the twentieth century has seen another attempt to read the law realistically. The publication of ancient collections of law from the ancient Near East—such as those of Lipit-Ishtar, Hammurabi, Eshnunna, the Hittites, and the Middle Assyrians—has prompted some distinguished legal commentaries thereon. Commentators on these nonbiblical texts have drawn on many other legal documents from the ancient Near East, including the OT, to illuminate these legal collections and their key ideas.

In turn, OT scholars have drawn on ancient Near Eastern law to clarify the Bible. Many customs in Genesis have been explained on the basis of oriental legal customs. Sometimes these comparisons have been pushed too far, leading to charges of parallelomania. Nevertheless, a number of incidents recorded in Genesis have been helpfully illuminated this way (Selman). Certainly Near Eastern legal texts have shed much light on biblical law. Sometimes these comparisons demonstrate the continuity between biblical and extrabiblical practice, such as in marriage and divorce law or the treatment of homicide (e.g., Westbrook). In other areas, such as the Sabbath and slavery, scholarship has been struck by the discontinuity between the Bible and neighboring cultures. It is neither a case of casual borrowing by the biblical writers nor a wholesale rejection of their neighbors' practices. Instead, these comparisons reveal a principled selection process whereby some oriental laws and customs are endorsed, while others are firmly dismissed.

Another fruitful area of comparison between the biblical legal collections and their oriental parallels has been in the area of covenant and treaty. The pentateuchal laws are not given in a vacuum; rather, they form part of a covenant between "the LORD" and Israel. This is a God-initiated relationship whereby the LORD pledges to make Israel his people and protect them, while Israel responds by pledging to be totally loyal to the LORD their God. In the 1960s many scholars observed that this covenantal relationship corresponds in terminology and ideas to the ancient suzerainty treaties of the Near East. Typically in these treaties, the "Great King," who had conquered his enemy, now made him his vassal. In the treaty the vassal pledged total loyalty to

his suzerain. It was noted that not only was the ideology similar, but also that the structure of oriental vassal treaties was quite similar to the covenant texts in the Pentateuch that contain the laws (McCarthy).

The Message of the Law

Influenced by some apparently disparaging remarks about the law in Romans, many Bible readers have tended to neglect it and miss its true value. Deuteronomy can say, "What great nation is there, that has statutes and rules so righteous as all this law which I set before you this day?" (4:8 RSV). Jesus can say, "Do not think that I have come to abolish the Law or the Prophets; I have not come to abolish them but to fulfill them" (Matt. 5:17). Hence, the law ought to have a vital part in the thinking of the individual, the church, and society.

Its Covenantal Setting. Central to an appreciation of the law is recognition of its covenantal setting. As already mentioned, the lawgiving at Sinai is part of the making of the covenant with Israel, in which the whole nation was constituted the chosen people of God. This was a God-directed relationship. It began with an *act of divine grace,* with the LORD bringing Israel out of Egypt: "You have seen . . . how I bore you on eagles' wings and brought you to myself" (Exod. 19:4 RSV). Israel was expected to respond with *obedience:* "Now therefore, if you will obey my voice and keep my covenant . . ." (19:5 RSV). Such obedience would be rewarded by *blessing,* by an even closer relationship with God: "You shall be my treasured possession out of all the peoples" (19:5 NRSV). Indeed, Israel will mediate divine blessing to the nations through its priestly role: "You shall be to me a kingdom of priests and a holy nation" (19:6 RSV). This short passage shows that the covenant relationship is based on grace, on God's undeserved kindness toward Israel, exhibited in releasing them from Egyptian slavery and bringing them into his presence on Sinai. The laws that follow are not a means of earning divine favor but are part of God's bounty to Israel. By keeping them, Israel shows gratitude to the LORD and brings itself into a closer relationship with its Redeemer.

On the other hand, the covenant, like ancient treaties, also has threats built into it. If the Israelites fail to keep the law, they will be punished: curses will come into play, blighting their future. The covenant will not be terminated by disobedience, but instead of bringing blessing to Israel, it will bring suffering. The key ideas of the covenant may be set out as follows:

1. Divine grace in past history
2. Law
3. Blessing if law obeyed
4. Curse if law disobeyed

Often these ideas are not simply referred to in legal texts, but also structure them to some extent. It has been recognized that the Israelite covenant form is a cross between the form of a typical vassal treaty and a law "code" of the second millennium.

Vassal Treaty	OT Covenant	Law Code
Historical review	History of God's grace	Historical review
Stipulations: Be loyal to suzerain	Laws	Laws
Curses if disloyal	Blessings if obedient	Blessings if obedient
Blessings if loyal	Curses if disobedient	Curses if disobedient

Not only is the OT covenant structurally a hybrid between the vassal treaty and the law code; it is also ideologically a cross between the two. Its centerpiece is numerous laws like a law code, but the most important of these laws is the demand for total loyalty to the LORD, Israel's suzerain, just as in a vassal treaty. The first of the commandments is "You shall have no other gods before me" (Exod. 20:3). The central demand of Deuteronomy is "You shall love the LORD your God with all your heart, and with all your soul, and with all your might" (6:5 NRSV).

The structural dependence of the legal collections on this pattern can be observed at the micro and macro levels. The Ten Commandments are an example of the former. They are prefaced by a historical summary of God's grace: "I am the LORD your God, who brought you out of the land of Egypt, out of the house of slavery" (Exod. 20:2 NRSV). The Ten Commandments are themselves treaty stipulations or laws. Within them there are promises of blessing on the obedient (20:6, 12) as well as warnings of punishment in case of disobedience (20:5, 7). On the macro scale the whole of Exodus to Leviticus is cast in covenant shape. Exodus 1–19 tells the history of redemption from Egypt, and Exod. 20–Lev. 25 gives the laws that should regulate the life of the redeemed people of God. Then Lev. 26 lists blessings that the nation will enjoy if they obey the law (vv. 1–13)

and the curses that will befall them if they fail to keep the law (vv. 14–45). But the best example of a covenantal outline is provided by the book of Deuteronomy: chapters 1–3 give historical retrospect; 4–26, stipulations and laws; and 27–28, blessings and curses. This covenantal thinking pervades the OT. The prophets recall God's saving deeds for Israel, berate them for failing to keep the law, and warn that the threats in the covenantal curses will therefore soon be fulfilled. In Amos's epigram: "You only have I known of all the families of the earth; therefore I will punish you for all your iniquities" (3:2 NRSV).

But this covenantal thinking is not just important for biblical theology in general; it also is vital for interpreting the law. The law is not seen as a means of gaining God's favor: his favor is shown in the redemption of Israel and in his giving them the law. The law shows them how to "be holy, for I am holy" (Lev. 11:45 NRSV). It shows them how to live in a way that will excite the admiration and envy of the nations (Deut. 4:6). Their obedience will make it possible for God to fulfill his promise: "I will walk among you and will be your God, and you shall be my people" (Lev. 26:12).

Its Literary Context. Although covenantal principles pervade the law and the narratives are organized in patterns that reflect treaty-cum-law-code models, the laws in the Pentateuch are not embedded in straight covenant/treaty documents. Rather, the laws form part of a narrative recounting the history of Israel from their enslavement in Egypt to the death of Moses. More exactly, the Pentateuch is a biography of Moses (Wenham, *Exploring*): Exodus 1 tells of his birth and Deut. 34 of his death, and he is the leading human actor throughout these books. Even Genesis may be seen to be part of this biography since it gives vital background material, without which the subsequent four books would not be intelligible.

For instance, the account of creation (Gen. 1:1–2:3) ends with the institution of the Sabbath. "God blessed the seventh day and made it holy, because on it he rested from all the work of creating that he had done" (2:3). The clear implication is that human beings, made in the image of God (1:27), must imitate their Creator by also resting on the seventh day (Exod. 20:11). Genesis 2 portrays the creation of Eve out of Adam's rib and brings her to him in the archetypal marriage. This narrative illustrates many of the principles that underlie the theory of marriage as enshrined in the laws of Leviticus and Deuteronomy: for example, marriage should be monogamous, heterosexual, and permanent. Similarly the stories of sacrifice—by Cain, Abel, Noah, and Abraham—highlight features essential if sacrifice is to achieve its end (Gen. 4:3–7; 8:20–9:17; 22:1–19). These are just a few examples of how Genesis through its narratives inculcates principles that are fundamental to the law.

Nevertheless, in another respect Genesis relativizes the law, or at least some of the laws. Take the issue of violence. Genesis 1 seems to portray a world free of violence, where both humans and animals are vegetarian (1:29–30). However, chapter 4 introduces two murderers, Cain and his descendant Lamech, who actually boasts about his murders (4:23–24). Then as violence envelops the earth, God decides to wipe out all flesh (man and beast), "for the earth is filled with violence through them" (6:13 RSV). The only family to survive is Noah's, who was "blameless in his generation" (6:9 RSV). Genesis 9:11 promises that there will never again be a flood to wipe out all flesh. But how will the problem of violence be dealt with? What is to stop the world being engulfed again in violence?

Genesis 9:6 is the answer: "Whoever sheds the blood of a human, by a human shall that person's blood be shed; for in his own image God made humankind" (NRSV). This is the first remark in the Bible in case-law form. It expresses a principle that applies to most case law. Case law typically deals with problems that in a perfect world would never arise: murder, theft, adultery, and so on. What is to be done in such cases? Genesis 9:6 lays down the principle of proportionate punishment. Ideally, the murderer, made in the image of God himself, should not be put to death. But to stop violence from getting out of hand in the way it did before the flood, or even blood feuds in which tit-for-tat killings may continue over many years, Genesis insists that the murderer be executed. This principle of appropriate punishment runs through the case law of the Pentateuch. Cattle thieves must restore the stolen beast and several extra; arsonists must pay compensation for the damage they cause; seducers must pay the appropriate sum to the girl's father and marry her properly (Exod. 22). Ideally, the Bible would prefer that none of these things happen, that everyone should love his neighbor. But in a sinful world, laws are necessary to preserve order in society and to prevent the strong and ruthless (cf. Lamech in Gen. 4:23–24) from oppressing the weak and innocent. In this sense the literary context of the laws in the Pentateuch relativizes them: they are often compromises between God's ideals for man and the fallenness of human society.

Elements of the Law: (1) The Decalogue and Moral Injunctions

Though we have insisted that many of the case laws in the Pentateuch are essentially compromises, there is much moral idealism expressed in the law as well. Best known of course are the commands to "love the LORD . . . with all your heart" (Deut. 6:5) and "your neighbor as yourself" (Lev. 19:18). But scattered liberally through the law are many other such ethical injunctions, such as these: "If you meet your enemy's ox, . . . you shall bring it back to him" (Exod. 23:4 RSV). "You shall not oppress a resident alien" (23:9 NRSV).

It has been argued (Phillips, *Criminal Law*) that the Ten Commandments are Israel's criminal law: they enshrined the principles of the covenant, and to break any of them was punishable by death. However, this seems improbable. How could someone be convicted in a court of coveting? Rather, the Ten Commandments or the Decalogue reflect the core values of Israel's theology and moral outlook (Exod. 20). At the heart of the faith is total loyalty to the LORD: "You shall have no other gods before me." To protect the family, "honor your father and mother" and "do not commit adultery." Since life is sacred, "you shall not murder." The Ten Commandments, while hinting at God's attitude to those who flout these principles (20:5, 7), do not lay down how society should react to those who break the commandments. This is the concern of many subsequent laws within the Pentateuch.

Elements of the Law: (2) "Love the LORD Your God with All Your Heart"

After the initial section of law largely focused on the Ten Commandments and general moral principles (Exod. 20–23), the central section is devoted principally to the demands of worship. The construction of the tabernacle, in which God would dwell among his people (cf. 40:34; Lev. 26:11–12), is the principal concern of Exod. 25–40. The importance of complete loyalty to God is brought into high relief by the counterpointed episode of the golden calf in Exod. 32–34, in which the first two commandments (no other gods, no graven images) were flouted.

The focus on the correct worship of the LORD continues in Leviticus and Numbers. Laws about the proper way to offer sacrifice dominate Lev. 1–7, and the establishment of the priesthood occupies chapters 8–10. Entry into the holy shrine demands purity, whose exact definition occupies Lev. 11–16, 21–22. Holy days for worship and holy years are the main topics of Lev. 23–25. Further instructions about worship recur in the early chapters of Numbers (e.g., 2–10, 15). In these ways the law emphasizes the centrality and paramount importance of worship. It is the way in which the people of God declare their love for God and through which his love for them is demonstrated in powerful symbols and rites.

Elements of the Law: (3) "You Shall Love Your Neighbor as Yourself"

This command is found in Lev. 19:18 (NRSV), a pithy saying that sums up much of Lev. 18–20 as well as many other elements of the law, especially in the book of Deuteronomy. Moses' exposition of the law in Deut. 12–26 seems to be based in content and order on the Ten Commandments. So from Deut. 17 to 25 the sermon seems to be a reflection on the humanward commandments, applying them to the particular problems that will face Israel in the promised land.

The Future Orientation of the Law

The law ends with Moses looking over the Dead Sea into the promised land. He must die outside the land, but the young Israel will enter the land and enjoy the fulfillment of the promises made to the patriarchs centuries earlier (Deut. 33–34). There in the land, Israel will be able to keep the law, if only they want to. Many of its provisions were quite inapplicable in the wilderness. But in the land flowing with milk and honey, these wise laws and statutes could be implemented and would enable Israel to enjoy peace with God and harmony with each other. This is the great hope of the Pentateuch, though so many of its stories recount the dashing of these hopes on various occasions.

Subsequent history has borne out this ambivalence: the Jews' fidelity to the law over many centuries has preserved them as a people despite dispersal and persecution. But complete fulfillment is as elusive as ever. The LORD promised to write the law of the new covenant on human hearts (Jer. 31:31, 33). But though the Spirit bears fruit in every believer, the church still falls a long way short of perfection. And in a world marred by sin, the law points to ideals for which people should aim and offers a way for them to do justice in situations wrecked by injustice.

Law is in frequent disfavor among many Christians. Luther's sharp law-gospel antithesis contrasts not only portions of Scripture but also approaches to it. Influential upon subsequent Protestants in particular, it may foster both neglect of the OT and ignorance of the gracious character of torah. Perhaps related is the contemporary disfavor, particularly among pacifists, into which the civic aspects of law have fallen. Hauerwas, Yoder, Hays, and others can seem to forbid torah from informing either state or church, in view of strong or even exclusively christocentric and ecclesiocentric hermeneutics. While theonomist approaches must be avoided and the pluralism of contemporary cultures acknowledged, torah must not be simply dismissed. Luther himself saw that torah remains revelation; we must not neglect this provision from God for the care of all in society and the promotion of justice for all societies. This raises the complex but important theological question of whether or how biblical law might reflect a "natural law" within God's creation.

Bibliography

Alt, A. "The Origin of Israelite Law." In *Essays on Old Testament History and Religion*. Blackwell, 1966; Brin, G. *Studies in Biblical Law*. Sheffield Academic Press, 1994; Friedmann, D. *To Kill and Take Possession*. Hendrickson, 2002; Levinson, B., ed. *Theory and Method in Biblical and Cuneiform Law*. Sheffield Academic Press, 1994; McCarthy, D. J. *Treaty and Covenant*. Pontifical Biblical Institute, 1963; Otto, E. *Theologische Ethik des Alten Testaments*. Kohlhammer, 1994; Patrick, D. *Old Testament Law*. John Knox, 1985; Phillips, A. *Ancient Israel's Criminal Law*. Blackwell, 1970; idem. *Essays on Biblical Law*. Sheffield Academic Press, 2002; Roth, M. T., et al. *Law Collections from Mesopotamia*. 2d ed. Scholars Press, 1997; Saalschütz, J. L. *Das Mosaische Recht*. C. Heymann, 1853; Selman, M. "Comparative Customs and the Patriarchal Age." Pages 93–138 in *Essays on the Patriarchal Narratives*, ed. A. Millard and D. J. Wiseman. InterVarsity, 1980; Sprinkle, J. M. *The Book of the Covenant*. Sheffield Academic Press, 1994; Watts, J. W. *Reading Law*. Sheffield Academic Press, 1999; Wellhausen, J. *Prolegomena to the History of Ancient Israel*. 1878. Meridian, 1957; Wenham, G. *Pentateuch*. Vol. 1 of *Exploring the Old Testament*. SPCK, 2003; idem. *Story as Torah*. T&T Clark, 2000; Westbrook, R. *Studies in Biblical and Cuneiform Law*. Gabalda, 1988; Whybray, R. N. *The Making of the Pentateuch*. JSOT, 1987; Wright, C. J. H. *God's People in God's Land*. Paternoster, 1990; idem. *Living as the People of God*. InterVarsity, 1983; idem. *Walking in the Ways of the Lord*. Apollos, 1995.

Gordon J. Wenham

Lectio Divina   *See* Liturgy; Medieval Biblical Interpretation

Lectionary   *See* Liturgy

Leviticus, Book of

In the first five books of the OT, Genesis narrates events before the life of Moses, while Deuteronomy repeats the law given on Mt. Sinai for the generations after Moses. The middle three books detail the career of Moses, with Exod. 1–19 tracing it from his birth until he receives the law, and Num. 10:11–36:13 tracing it afterward until just before his death. The account of the giving of the law runs from Exod. 20:1 to Num. 10:10. The book of Leviticus, therefore, stands in the center of the law and contains many of its most striking provisions.

History of Interpretation

One early interpreter of Leviticus was Jesus, who cited Lev. 19:18: "You shall love your neighbor as yourself" (NRSV). Likewise, the NT book of James makes frequent positive allusions to Lev. 19 (Johnson). Often, though, the NT has to deal with issues from Leviticus that were problematic for the early church: sacrifice (Lev. 1–7), circumcision (12:3), and dietary regulations (ch. 11). Led by Paul, early Christians determined that such works were unnecessary for salvation. In addition, the early church perhaps preserved Mark 5:25–34 because it remembered the church's break with the purity rules found in Lev. 15:19–20.

Jewish interpreters also commented on Leviticus. After the destruction of the temple in 70 CE, the rabbis emphasized prayer and substituted the *study* of the sacrificial laws for performing the *ritual*. Indeed, the medieval scholar Maimonides argued that sacrifice was a concession to human frailty (to give Jews a rite similar to rites practiced by the worshippers of other deities) and never really God's intention.

Post-temple Jews had to address three other issues emphasized in Leviticus: the purity of priests, the Jewish family, and dietary regulations (Levine). Even though there was no further use for priests as officials at sacrifices, priestly families continued to hold to Levitical laws of purity, especially in regard to marriage and contact with the dead. Priests could not marry divorcees, harlots, or daughters born to forbidden unions. Adultery by the wife was the only grounds for divorce. In addition, priests were still to avoid contact with the dead, though members of the immediate family were exempted from this restriction. Preserving the purity of the Jewish family involved observing the ban on a woman's having intercourse for seven days (for her monthly period) and circumcising male babies. The dietary laws in Lev. 11 were not only retained but also carried out strictly in traditional families.

Within Christianity, Origen articulated a theory of Scripture interpretation that distinguished the literal from the more important spiritual meaning discerned by typology. Hence, the sacrifices described in Lev. 1–7 constituted a typology and prediction of Christ, whose sacrifice was superior to and fulfilled the system outlined in Leviticus.

Similar views dominated for over a millennium, but in the last few centuries the interpretation of Leviticus has come under the influence of historical, sociological, and literary theory. Based on stylistic and theological differences, scholars have for years pointed to various alleged sources for the Pentateuch (JEDP) and assigned them different dates, running from the tenth to the fifth centuries BCE. The law codes of the Pentateuch perhaps grew up independently, though often scholars identify their theology with that of a given source. Scholars adhering to this theory generally argue that Leviticus belongs to the postexilic P, or Priestly source, but think Leviticus was comprised of smaller codes, particularly the so-called Holiness Code (chs. 17–26). Among these scholars there has often been a noticeable denigration of Leviticus because of its perceived legalism and ritualism in favor of the prophets, who are thought to have better prepared the way for Jesus and the gospel.

The twentieth century witnessed an explosion of interpretative developments. Hermann Gunkel began a new form of study called form criticism, which utilized an approach to the study of oral literature developed in Germany. For Leviticus, this meant that the original setting for some laws was understood to be priestly judgments on cases brought to them, which became precedents for other people. Other laws or narratives were said to have grown up to regularize sacrifices or in defense of priestly prerogatives. That approach divided biblical books into such small units; however, reaction against it came in the form of attention to the work of editors or redactors and to the rhetorical devices that supply cohesion to books.

Other scholars have taken their cue from sociologists and anthropologists, seeking to interpret Leviticus against the backdrop of societies thought to be comparable to ancient Israel. So, for example, Douglas has subjected the dietary regulations to sociological scrutiny and observes that animals seem to be grouped into what one may call—for a lack of better terms—species and subspecies (not Douglas's terms). If a subspecies conformed wholly to the requirements of the species, it was considered clean and could be eaten. For example, Israel seems to have thought of a species of cloven-footed, cud-chewing farm animals. Subspecies that conformed to both characteristics (e.g., sheep) could be eaten. Subspecies with only one of these characteristics were considered unclean and were not to be eaten: e.g., swine did not chew the cud and camels did not have cloven feet. Similarly, water animals should have scales and fins; those that did were clean, and those that did not were unclean. Animals that died on their own were to be considered unclean; if alive, they could be slaughtered or sacrificed and eaten. Thus, scavengers should be avoided because of their consumption of dead animals. She argues that these distinctions reflect and make specific the worldview of the priestly creation account in Gen. 1:1–2:4a.

Still other scholars advocate abandoning such enterprises altogether and approaching the text of Leviticus simply as a literary product of the postexilic period. For them, it can supply no information about the preexilic period, but can give insights into the thinking of the postexilic author(s) of the Pentateuch and the worship practices current then.

In light of these divergent interpretations, one might approach Leviticus as a book with many laws that no longer apply literally in either a Jewish or a Christian context. Nevertheless, it still retains relevance for its insistence on the worship of God and on moral living in response to God's holiness.

The Message of Leviticus

From the book of Exodus, Leviticus presupposes God as the One who has delivered Israel from bondage in Egypt and covenanted with Israel to be their God. Hence, it conceives of God as somehow resident among the Israelites in their camp (Lev. 1:1). For Israel, the implications of that residency revolve around two pairs of terms: "holy" and "profane," "clean" and "unclean." What is holy has been marked off or set aside for God. In Leviticus, the holy include people (the Aaronic priesthood), space (the tabernacle, which has the peculiar feature that it can be moved), implements used in worship (priestly garb, vessels of various sorts, the altar), and time (festivals, the Day of Atonement). Laws pertaining to these items appear in Lev. 1–10, 16, 23–25, and 27. In addition, things in the world are either clean or unclean. What is holy is supposed to be clean, but can be polluted by what is unclean. Hence, both sacred and nonsacred people have to be careful how they approach the holy, lest they pollute it and bring danger upon themselves and/or others. So, the book of Leviticus contains numerous laws about dealing with impurity, including diet, the purification of women after childbirth, the purification of lepers, and proper sexual relations (Lev. 11, 12, 13–15, and 18 respectively). Either priests or the people can be rendered unholy, with the result that they have to be sanctified before they can again approach the holy (Lev. 18–20; ch. 21 for priests only). Jenson has argued that this worldview actually amounted to a system running from the very holy through the holy, the clean, the unclean, to the very unclean.

One should note, however, that the term "holy" is also used of God, and not only as what is set apart for God (Lev. 19:2 et passim). God is both the source of life and the only being worthy of worship. Hence, idolatry is wrong. Moreover, to be holy as God is holy involves morality in the sense of living in proper communion with God and humans, of recognizing one's dependence upon God and limits to one's desires and rights, and thus the necessity for justice in human affairs. The message of Leviticus, therefore, can be summarized under four sentences that spell out the implications of the residence of the holy God among the people.

First, *the people are to worship God* (Lev. 1–7). This worship will take the form of a variety of sacrifices. In the "burnt offering" (1:1–17), the priests burn the entire carcass of the animal. Reasons for making this offering might include dedicating new altars or worship sites, expressing thankfulness, imploring God's help in times of difficulty, and covering sin. The "grain offering" (2:1–16) can accompany the burnt offering, honor God, or express thanksgiving for the grain crop. In the "peace" or "well-being offering" (3:1–17 NRSV), the worshippers consume a large portion of the animal and share the best parts (fat parts and kidneys) with God. Passover seems to be such an occasion. The "sin offering" (4:1–5:13) atones for inadvertent errors in cultic practice and other inadvertent sins. It is accompanied by confession. The "guilt offering" (5:14–6:7) atones for inadvertent actions where restitution is called for. The sacrificial system does not cover intentional sins (see Num. 15:30), though God nevertheless can forgive people for such behavior.

Second, *the Aaronic priests are to direct the worship* (Lev. 8–10). Leviticus 8 narrates the selection, anointing, and purification of the Aaronic priesthood, while Lev. 9 describes the commencement of Aaron's priesthood. Two of Aaron's sons, however, violate the altar entrusted to the Aaronites and pay for their sin with their lives. Mediating between God and the people is serious business.

Third, *the people are to avoid ritual impurity and make atonement when they fail* (Lev. 11–16). Avoiding ritual impurity covers various aspects of family life, even including, for example, what to do about household mold (14:34–53), which is discussed in connection with leprosy. Actions that render one impure include coming into contact with the dead or with blood. According to Lev. 16, the Day of Atonement arises upon the death of Aaron's two sons, but it becomes a time for public repentance and community cleansing. The liturgy for the day calls upon the high priest to offer a sacrifice for his own sins, and a second one for the people. Then he is to lay his hands upon the scapegoat, symbolically laying the sins of the people upon it. He then sends the scapegoat away into the wilderness, symbolically carrying the sins of the people with it.

Fourth, *the people are to be holy* (Lev. 17–26). The book reaches its pinnacle in the Holiness Code. It derives its name from the oft-repeated phrase "You shall be holy, for I the LORD your God am holy" (as in 19:2). These laws forbid misdeeds ranging from sacrificing in the wrong places to committing incest to worshipping foreign deities. It prescribes the three annual feasts (Passover/ Unleavened Bread, Weeks, Tabernacles). One law deserves particular attention. The so-called *lex talionis* (the law of the talon or claw) seems cruel to moderns who see in it "an eye for an eye, a tooth for a tooth" (24:20). Actually, however, it limits revenge and takes the first step toward leaving revenge to God and ultimately to forgiving one's enemies.

Leviticus and the Canon

The canonical status of Leviticus was established by virtue of its central place in the Pentateuch. The later OT books Chronicles, Ezra, and Nehemiah cited it. A few examples must suffice. Second Chronicles 7:9–10 describes the dedication of Solomon's temple at the festival of Booths as sacrifices offered in accordance with laws such as those in Lev. 23:23–43. It also explains the fall of Jerusalem and the destruction of the temple as the consequence of Israel's failure to observe the Sabbath years as commanded in Lev. 25:1–7 (see 26:27–39 for a warning; 2 Chron. 36:21). Also Ezra 9:11, part of Ezra's penitential prayer, seems to be a fair summary of Lev. 18:24–30 and

Deut. 7:1–6 combined. Ezra 3:5 appears to have in view Lev. 23, and Neh. 8:14–15 refers to the commandment in Lev. 23:42 that the Israelites live in booths during the fall festival.

The author of Hebrews dialogued with the book in his discussion of Jesus' superiority to the old law. First, Jesus the Son of God is superior to Moses, the servant of God who received the law (Heb. 3:1–6). Second, Jesus belongs to a line of priests descended from Melchizedek, which is superior to the Levitical priests. This superiority manifests itself in a number of ways. Jesus is the perfect high priest because he is without sin (2:17–18; 4:15) and did not have to offer sacrifices to cleanse himself as the OT priests did (5:3; cf. Lev. 9:7; 16:2–14). Jesus did not simply offer an animal sacrifice; he offered himself as the perfect sacrifice (Heb. 5:7–8). That sacrifice was superior to the Levitical sacrifice because it was given once for all and did not need to be repeated (9:13–14, 25–26). Finally, Jesus is superior to Levitical priests because he has been raised to the right hand of God, to mediate an eternal covenant superior to the one given at Sinai (8:1–2; 9:15).

Leviticus and Theology

The book of Leviticus (particularly chs. 17–26) emphasizes the holiness of God as the most important theological motif. The holy is *mysterium tremendum et fascinans*, to use Otto's terms. Worshippers confront God as an overwhelming and yet appealing mystery, and then recognize themselves as creaturely. Regardless of the characteristic of God by which worshippers might measure themselves (e.g., power, knowledge, love, moral purity), God is always superior.

Leviticus is about worship. The sacrificial system is the means it outlines by which penitent sinners can express their contrition to God. It is never intended as the vehicle to buy forgiveness, as the prophets made clear (cf. Isa. 1:12–15; Amos 5:21–24). Nevertheless, it speaks the word of God that in worship people should express contrition and ask forgiveness (Lev. 1:1–2:16; 4:1–5:13), share with others and with God (3:1–17), and be prepared to make restitution for losses inflicted on others (5:14–6:7). It has a healthy appreciation for the role of ritual in living the holy life and the possibility of forgiveness when God's people fail.

Bibliography

Budd, P. *Leviticus*. NCB. HarperCollins/Eerdmans, 1996; Douglas, M. "The Abominations of Leviticus."

Pages 41–57 in *Purity and Danger*. 2d ed. Routledge & Kegan Paul, 1969; Elliger, K. *Leviticus*. HAT 1.4. Mohr, 1966; Gerstenberger, E. *Leviticus*. OTL. Westminster John Knox, 1996; Grünwaldt, K. *Das Heiligkeitsgesetz Leviticus 17–26*. De Gruyter, 1999; Hayes, J. "Atonement in the Book of Leviticus." *Int* 52 (1998): 5–13; Jenson, P. P. *Graded Holiness*. JSOTSup 106. JSOT, 1992; Johnson, L. T. "The Use of Leviticus 19 in the Letter of James." *JBL* 101 (1982): 391–401; Levine, B. *Leviticus*. JPS Torah Commentary. Jewish Publication Society, 2003; Milgrom, J. *Leviticus*. AB 3, 3A, 3B. Doubleday, 1991–2001; Noth, M. *Leviticus*. OTL. Rev. ed. Westminster, 1977; Origen. *Homilies on Leviticus 1–16*, trans. G. Barkley. FC 83. Catholic University of America Press, 1990; Otto, R. *The Idea of the Holy*, trans. J. Harvey. 2d ed. Oxford University Press, 1923; Rendtorff, R. *Leviticus*. BKAT. Neukirchener Verlag, 1985; Wenham, G. *Leviticus*. NICOT. Eerdmans, 1979.

Paul L. Redditt

Lexicons, NT

The last half-century has witnessed a heightened interest in NT lexical and linguistic study. This has resulted in a wealth of resources for the study of NT words and idioms. Special attention has been given to the theological vocabulary of the NT, with an important bearing on the theological interpretation of Scripture.

One of the landmark publications of the twentieth century was Kittel's *Theological Dictionary of the New Testament* (*TDNT*). Thorough on issues of background, *TDNT* served the exegetical needs of a generation in which "biblical theology" was in vogue. James Barr's *The Semantics of Biblical Language* questioned some of the assumptions and methods of *TDNT*. Barr exposed the tendency in the dictionary toward "illegitimate totality transfer," in which the exegete assumes the same theological connotation for every occurrence of a word in the NT. He criticized the practice, prevalent in the "biblical theology" movement, of assuming that the root meaning of a word was its basic meaning (the root fallacy). He questioned the common procedure of assigning unwarranted theological overtones to some biblical words, for example, church (*ekklēsia*). Only if the context in which the word occurs permits such an interpretation should the word be considered to carry special theological freight. A generation of commentators and exegetes heeded Barr's perceptive and humorous warnings.

The *New International Dictionary of New Testament Theology* reflects the chastened exegesis in the years following Barr's work. Colin Brown, the editor, notes in his introduction the new situation created by Barr's observation. Nevertheless, the contributors to this dictionary saw the need for continued attention to the theological dimension in NT lexicography. "The dictionary is expressly theological in intention. Historical, geographical and archaeological information, appropriate in a general dictionary of the Bible, is included here only insofar as it is theologically relevant."

Similarly, Baltz and Schneider's *Exegetical Dictionary of the New Testament* "sought to present and work out the implications of the exegetical and theological contexts of the different words, including the necessary historical backgrounds, without commitment to one particular literary theory" (1:vi). The study of a vocabulary of writings that are essentially theological cannot ignore the theological dimension. Nowhere is there a greater need to be alert to the theological element in NT vocabulary than with words and expressions that have entered the NT already theologically freighted. For example, Paul employed the words "righteousness" and "justification" in the context of an already-rich exegetical and theological tradition. This is especially the case for words taken from the LXX and already bearing special connotations. Semitic phrases like *Son of Man* need especially to be noted. Translating such words offers additional challenges.

Another dictionary with theological focus is C. Spicq's *Theological Lexicon of the New Testament*. Spicq states in the preface, "*My intention is theological*. What interests me is not orthographic novelties, idioms, phonetics, or declensions, but the semantics and the religious and moral sense of the language of the NT" (vii). The translator observes that the special value of Spicq's work is the use made of the nonliterary papyri, "still a largely unmined treasure for the study of early Christianity" (xii).

This focus on the papyri was given its initial impetus through the 1935 publication of Moulton and Milligan, *The Vocabulary of the New Testament*. This specialized resource documents the light shed on biblical words through papyri and inscriptions from the Greco-Roman world. Since then, many more documents from the era have been published, and a new and expanded dictionary is now appearing in subsequent issues of the journal *Filologia neotestamentaria* (Horsley and Lee). Attention in these dictionaries has been on background rather than theology.

The most widely used NT lexicon is that of Walter Bauer. First published in Germany in 1937, it appeared in English in 1957 under the editorship of W. F. Arndt and F. W. Gingrich. Subsequent editions appeared in 1979 and 2000, with F. W. Danker as the editor. This dictionary follows the standard philological orientation. The most striking and pleasing departure in the 2000 BDAG is the use of bold roman typeface to highlight the meanings of words and their functional usage. Numerous entries modify some older classifications that were based on mere grammatical or theological distinctions. This indicates that Danker has taken into account recent developments in lexicography and linguistics.

Chief among these lexicographic developments is the approach of Louw and Nida's *Greek-English Lexicon of New Testament: Based on Semantic Domains*. Primarily intended as an aid to translators, this dictionary explores the areas of overlap between similar words, and the distinctive nuances of the different NT words. It seeks to organize words along semantic rather than theological lines. This approach avoids the confusion created when so many different glosses representing diverse meanings are lumped together.

In reviewing the extraordinary achievement and lasting value of Bauer's lexicography, M. Silva nonetheless complained of "a failure to distinguish language and theology" (172). But is such a distinction possible or desirable? The study of literature that is essentially theological cannot ignore the essentially theological character of its vocabulary. The key task in NT lexicography thus remains how to evaluate and interpret the theological content of NT words. Some words have clearly entered the NT already theologically freighted ("beloved," "lift up," "righteousness"). Others will have gained theological dimensions by Christian use or coinage ("Christian"). Still others will have a heightened theological connotation, but sometimes will be used without that sense (*agapē*).

The science and art of discerning where the theological sense is warranted, and where it is not, is a key task facing those engaged in the theological interpretation of Scripture. This is a promising task in light of the richness of resources now available.

See also Biblical Theology; Concept; Etymology

Bibliography

Balz, H., and G. Schneider, eds. *Exegetical Dictionary of the New Testament*. 3 vols. Eerdmans, 1990–93; Bauer, W., et al. *A Greek-English Lexicon of the New Testament and Other Early Christian Literature*. 3d ed. Revised and edited by F. W. Danker. University of Chicago Press, 2000; Brown, C., ed. *New International Dictionary of the New Testament Theology*. 4 vols. Zondervan, 1976–86; Kittel, G., and G. Friedrich, eds. *Theological Dictionary of the New Testament*, trans. G. W. Bromiley. 10 vols. Eerdmans, 1962–76; Louw, J. P., and E. Nida. *Greek-English Lexicon of the New Testament: Based on Semantic Domains*. United Bible Societies, 1988; Silva, M. *Biblical Words and Their Meanings*. Zondervan, 1983; Spicq, C. *Theological Lexicon of the New Testament*. Translated and edited by J. D. Ernest. Hendrickson, 1994.

Peter R. Rodgers

Lexicons, OT

Word studies have long been a standard tool of exegetes for unlocking the truths of Scripture. Lexicons come in two main varieties: traditional philological lexicons and theological dictionaries. Although both types of reference may treat comparative Semitic data and survey the range of meaning and syntactic constructions to a greater or lesser degree, the theological dictionary ultimately aims at treating *theological concepts* organized around certain key words to which these are related. Thus, the theological dictionary stands in a unique, and somewhat precarious, position between that of a philological lexicon (which treats words) and a biblical theology (which treats concepts).

The precariousness of the enterprise was borne out by Kittel's *Theological Dictionary of the New Testament* (*TDNT*), which fosters erroneous approaches to theological word studies. Examples are the assumptions that etymology is an infallible guide to the "basic" meaning of a word, and that every nuance and associated concept for a word is represented in each of its occurrences. These and other criticisms were leveled at Kittel's *TDNT*, among other offenders of the biblical theology movement, by James Barr in *The Semantics of Biblical Language*. The theological dictionaries of the OT that postdate Barr's work have assiduously sought to avoid the pitfalls he outlined.

For example, the *Theological Dictionary of the Old Testament* (*TDOT*), a companion series to *TDNT*, explicitly states that the words are not *directly* related to the concepts with which they are associated, but are merely an avenue to their study: "Thus a comprehensive analysis enables a single word to reveal a bit of history, culture, religion, society, and human self-understanding" (1:v). (The German edition of this project, begun in the early 1970s, was completed in 2000, and the English version has fourteen volumes available in 2004.)

The editors (Harris et al.) of the *Theological Wordbook of the Old Testament* (1980) describe the work as in the tradition of the multivolume TDOT, but more "practical" and "less exhaustive" (just two volumes) than the latter. Another similarly sized theological dictionary is the *Theological Lexicon of the Old Testament* (*TLOT*), edited by Jenni and Westermann. Published in three English volumes (1997), the work originally appeared in German in the 1970s. Writing shortly after Barr's work, the editors show an acute awareness of the pitfalls of theological lexicography. In the preface they discuss the need to avoid the "limitations" of one particular approach to lexicography (e.g., grammatical-philological, diachronic, etc.), claiming instead "to establish and maintain as broad an approach as possible" (1:xi). The editors also acknowledge that the sentence, rather than the word, is the locus of meaning in language, and claim a unique niche for their work in taking into account the findings of form and tradition criticism.

The newest theological dictionary is the *New International Dictionary of Old Testament Theology and Exegesis* (*NIDOTTE*), edited by VanGemeren (et al.)—and its currency is evident especially in its employment of "text" or "discourse" as the locus of meaning instead of the sentence. In several introductory articles, *NIDOTTE* presents the theory behind these lexicographic studies. Kevin Vanhoozer claims, "What is interesting theologically happens on the level not of the letter, nor of the word, but rather of the whole text. In other words, it is not the word or concept alone, but the word/concept as used in the context of the literary whole that is the object of understanding" (1:40). However, since the dictionary is still arranged by *words*, Peter Cotterell warns that "it is clearly important to understand their [i.e., the words'] status as symbols only, to be given their significances by the respective language users" (1:147). Thus, the editors of *NIDOTTE* point out what is true of all the theological dictionaries discussed here: although, following tradition, they are organized by individual words, these words are only "secondary symbols" of the various concepts that may be associated with those symbols by different authors at different times in different literatures of the OT. Thus, recognizing that these dictionaries in practice move from the narrow meaning of individual words to a focus on larger theological concepts allows for their responsible use.

Besides this array of theological dictionaries, there are even more traditional philological lexicons for OT study. Several prominent in English are mentioned here. The most accessible (both in size and price) remains *The Brown-Driver-Briggs Hebrew-English Lexicon* (1906; reprint, Hendrickson, 1979). Because of its age, however, this lexicon does not take into account the textual finds of the twentieth century, such as Ugarit and the Dead Sea Scrolls.

Thus, the recently completed *Hebrew and Aramaic Lexicon of the Old Testament* (translated from the third German edition of the Koehler-Baumgartner lexicon) is important. It has recently become more accessible, published in a two-volume study guide (the standard edition is five volumes), as well as being made available in electronic form.

On the other hand, Sheffield's ongoing *Dictionary of Classical Hebrew* (edited by Clines) is promising to be a mammoth project—"bloated," in the words of one reviewer (O'Connor 204). A notable feature of this dictionary is that it does not restrict its corpus to the OT, but includes Hebrew epigraphs and the Dead Sea Scrolls in its database. Yet, at the same time, it does not include any comparative Semitic data. The entries are organized in concordance-like fashion, by morphological form and syntactic constructions.

Finally, we may mention that a semantic domains lexicon for the OT is currently under way, sponsored by the United Bible Societies, under the leadership of Reinier De Blois. In the meantime, the listing of semantic domains in the *NIDOTTE*'s fifth volume is an aid in carrying out responsible theological word studies.

See also Biblical Theology; Concept; Etymology

Bibliography

Barr, J. *The Semantics of Biblical Language*. Oxford University Press, 1961; Botterweck, G., H. Ringgren, and H.-J. Fabry, eds. *Theological Dictionary of the Old Testament*. 14 vols. Eerdmans, 1974–2004; Clines, D. J. A., ed. *The Dictionary of Classical Hebrew*. Sheffield Academic Press, 1993–; De Blois, Reinier. *Semantic Dictionary of Biblical Hebrew*. United Bible Societies, forthcoming; Gesenius, W., E. Robinson, F. Brown, S. R. Driver, and C. A. Briggs. *A Hebrew and English Lexicon of the Old Testament*. Houghton Mifflin, 1906; Harris, R. L., G. Archer, and B. Waltke. *Theological Wordbook of the Old Testament*. 2 vols. Moody, 1980; Jenni, E., and C. Westermann, eds. *Theological Lexicon of the Old Testament*. Hendrickson, 1997; Kittel, G., and G. Friedrich, eds. *Theological Dictionary of the New Testament*, trans. G. W. Bromiley. 10 vols. Eerdmans, 1962–76; Koehler, L., W. Baumgartner, J. J. Stamm, and M. E. J. Richardson, eds. *The Hebrew and Aramaic Lexicon of the Old Testament*. E. J. Brill, 1994; O'Connor, M. "Semitic Lexicography: European Dictionaries of Biblical Hebrew in the Twentieth Century." Pages 173–212 in *Semitic Linguistics*, ed. S. Izre'el. Israel Oriental Studies 20. Eisenbrauns, 2002; VanGemeren, W., et al., eds. *New International Dictionary of Old Testament Theology and Exegesis*. 5 vols. Zondervan, 1997.

John A. Cook

Liberal Biblical Interpretation

In what ways does liberal biblical interpretation (LBI) differ from other forms of biblical interpretation? An obvious answer would be that LBI is essentially "critical." There is truth in this if it is recognized that biblical interpretation has always been critical. "Critical" scholarship is understood to include studying the transmission of the biblical text, the authorship of the books of the Bible, and the problems of relating the world-view of the Bible to contemporary historical and scientific knowledge. Origen of Alexandria and Caesarea (185–ca. 254) compiled a massive work (the *Hexapla*) on the Greek text of the OT. Papias of Hierapolis (ca. 110) discussed the transmission of the words of Jesus and their relation to the NT Gospels. In *The City of God* Augustine of Hippo (354–430) discusses problems such as the creation of light before the creation of the sun in Gen. 1:3, the lengths of the lives of those who lived to hundreds of years before the flood (Gen. 5), and the existence of giants in 6:4. What distinguished LBI as it began to emerge in the late eighteenth century was not so much its results as its relation to various forms of "rules of faith" that defined Christian orthodoxy. For example, Horne's introduction to the Bible (1:545), while strongly defending the view that there were no errors or inconsistencies in the Bible, argued that passages such as 1 Sam. 17:23–50 were out of order in their present content. In other words, Horne used what many would later consider to be the methods and results of LBI (the detection of inconsistencies and the advocacy of textual rearrangement) in order to defend the infallibility of the Bible.

The essentially thin line dividing LBI from other forms of biblical interpretation can be seen in the case of William Robertson Smith, who was tried for heresy by the Free Church of Scotland, and dismissed from his post at the Free Church College in Aberdeen in 1881. In his defense, Smith maintained passionately that the biblical criticism he practiced (he accepted his own formulation of the so-called Graf-Wellhausen hypothesis) was the continuation and completion of what was begun at the Reformation (Smith 21–24). In his view, biblical criticism was God's gift to the church, to make it possible for the Bible to speak to his generation (see further, Rogerson, *Criticism*). The fundamental issue for Smith's opponents was whether his biblical criticism was compatible with the Westminster Confession of Faith, the basis of belief for the Free Church of Scotland.

Smith's trial and conviction point up the central issue surrounding LBI. Within what doctrinal limits, if any, should biblical interpretation be carried on? The answer is simple, or should be simple, in institutions that have a basis of belief mentioning such things as the inerrancy of Scripture or salvation only through faith in the vicarious, atoning death of Jesus. Such bases of belief provide a broad Christian framework for biblical interpretation in a situation that can also be policed, if necessary. Yet they leave open whether belief in inerrancy commits scholars to accepting the Textus Receptus of the NT as the inspired Greek version of that part of the Bible, or requires scholars to accept, say, that Paul wrote Ephesians. In institutions such as state universities, which lack or prohibit such bases of belief, or in churches where there is no means of trying scholars for heresy or no desire to do so, biblical interpretation may take more diverse forms, some with an explicitly anti-Christian agenda. Examples of the latter would be the types of feminist and liberation scholarship that aim to show how the Bible has led to the silencing of women and to the maintenance of oppressive class structures. On the other hand, biblical interpretation can be carried on in such institutions by scholars who do not feel bound by any particular bases of belief, but who regard themselves as practicing Christians. They may also believe that no sincere search for truth can lead them away from God or be harmful to the Bible, while allowing that there is always a subjective element in ideas of what is true. At the personal level, biblical interpretation may be affected by a scholar's beliefs on whether revelation is propositional or relational, and on whether the Bible primarily reveals truths *about* God or primarily enables God to be encountered and in some senses to be "known." It crucially also depends on beliefs about the nature and extent of divine action, with special reference to claims about the miraculous.

It can be argued that LBI—interpretation unconstrained by bases of belief—whether undertaken by believers or not, has made discoveries that have benefited all biblical interpretation. Inevitably, it has sometimes followed paths leading to conclusions that have not stood the test of time (this is true also of "orthodox" interpretation!). Yet it has ensured that biblical interpretation did not become moribund and stifled by the constraints of orthodoxies. Two hundred years of the most rigorous critical examination to which any set of texts has ever been subjected have not harmed the Bible. Instead, this critical study has brought to light the human circumstances of the Bible's production in such a way as to point to origins that both confound human expectations and confirm the deepest human hopes. The contribution to this process of LBI has been incalculable.

See also Historical Criticism

Bibliography

Horne, T. H. *An Introduction to the Critical Study and Knowledge of the Holy Scriptures*. 5th ed. 5 vols. T. Cadell, 1825; Morgan, R., with J. Barton. *Biblical Interpretation*. Oxford University Press, 1988; Rogerson, J. *The Bible and Criticism in Victorian Britain*. Sheffield Academic Press, 1995; idem. "An Outline of the History of Old Testament Study." Pages 6–24 in *Beginning Old Testament Study*, ed. J. Rogerson. 2d ed. Chalice/SPCK, 1998; Smith, W. R. *The Old Testament in the Jewish Church*. A. & C. Black, 1881.

John W. Rogerson

Liberation Theologies and Hermeneutics

One key feature of the theologies of liberation from Latin America, where the movement started, was their proposal of a new way of reading Scripture from the perspective of the poor. Such a hermeneutical process was part of a new way of developing theology that was defined by Peruvian theologian Gustavo Gutiérrez: "The theology of liberation offers us not so much a new theme for reflection as a *new way* to do theology. Theology as critical reflection on historical praxis" (12). This critical reflection was the result of a new political alignment (praxis) of some Christians in Latin America during the 1960s, and their critical way of reading the history of the church in that region. The Vatican II Council brought to Roman Catholicism the novelty of placing Scripture back at the heart of the theological task; the new theologies added the novelty of reading Scripture "from the underside," from the particular perspective of those who were experiencing political, social, economic, or cultural oppression. As this new form of doing theology made its way in the academic world, it connected with proposals coming from Black, Hispanic, and Amerindian theologies in the United States; theologies in Africa, Asia, and the South Pacific; as well as feminist theologies.

The publication of a revised edition of Gutiérrez's classic work, fifteen years after the first, was an occasion to see the wide repercussions of this theology around the world (Ellis and Maduro),

and the form in which it has been incorporated in a variety of church and missionary situations. Liberation theologians would argue that their own preunderstanding of the text of Scripture includes a commitment to change situations of oppression. With that approach they neither take oppression as an unchangeable given of social reality nor do they accept ways of interpreting the biblical text that do not take into account the facts of oppression.

This new way of reading Scripture may be better perceived, for instance, in the christological proposals of liberation theologies. The Christology of Jon Sobrino, a Jesuit theologian from El Salvador, intentionally starts from the biblical text rather than from the dogmatic statements of the church. He seeks to focus on the historical Jesus in order to provide a basis for Christian action: "The course that Jesus took is to be investigated scientifically, not just to aid in the quest for truth but also in the fight for truth that will make people free" (35). Reading the text of the Gospels, with due attention to the social and political context, Sobrino emphasizes the political dimension of the death of Jesus as the historical outcome of the kind of life he lived. His suffering for the cause of justice becomes the central challenge for discipleship today. Such an approach is to be questioned if, by overemphasizing the political significance of Jesus' death, it would not pay enough attention to the biblical material about the soteriological significance of that death. This is precisely the criticism raised by evangelical scholar René Padilla (Samuel and Sugden 28).

In the development of an ecclesiology from the liberation perspective, Franciscan theologian Leonardo Boff, from Brazil, tried to articulate the experience of the basic Christian communities, the grassroots small groups in which poor people started to revive their Catholic faith, relating it to their daily experience in Latin America. For Boff, "A true 'ecclesiogenesis' is in progress throughout the world, a Church being born from the faith of the poor" (9). The concept of the church as the people of God, emphasized in Vatican II, has been an incentive for new pastoral practices. But according to Boff, "True ecclesiology is not the result of textbook analysis or theoretical hypothesis; it comes about as a result of ecclesial practices within the institution" (1). He has been very critical of hierarchical authoritarianism and clericalism, which he sees practiced in the Roman Catholic Church, and proposes "new ministries and a new style of religious life incarnated in the life of the people" (10). For Boff, the key elements in all these proposals that come from praxis are characteristics of the model of church life that we find in the NT; on the basis of the biblical material, he questions some dogmatic assumptions.

A systematic evaluation of this hermeneutic has been offered by Padilla, who starts by acknowledging a fourfold contribution of liberation theologies to the interpretation of Scripture but also places a critical note at each point. Liberation theologies rightly emphasize the importance of obedience for the understanding of truth, but their pragmatic bent is in danger of seeking to use Scripture in order to justify any practice (provided it seems to work). Second, liberation theologies rightly call our attention to the importance of the historical situation of the interpreter but, turning that situation into "the text" or the primary point of reference, they subordinate Scripture to the context, thus falling into historical reductionism. Third, liberation theologies rightly point to the importance of the social sciences for a better understanding of our contemporary situation as well as some texts of Scripture, but frequently they fail critically to evaluate the ideological presuppositions that shape the social sciences and distort their understanding of biblical texts. Finally, liberation theologies emphasize the importance of recognizing that ideologies condition the theological task anywhere and everywhere, but they fail to hear the word from the biblical text that judges every ideology (Schipani 42–46).

Emphasis on the practice of discipleship as a precondition for true knowledge of God is a common point between Anabaptist and liberation theologies. Working from that starting point, John Howard Yoder has demonstrated that it is possible to approach the book of Exodus while using liberation insights but avoiding pragmatic or historical reductionism. He demonstrates that an understanding of the exodus story in its own context must avoid the ideological approach that dilutes its unique message. If the interpreter is to take seriously the centrality of Exodus in the Hebrew canon, it is impossible to distill from the text of Scripture a timeless idea of liberation that would then be used to ratify all kinds of liberation projects in all places and forms. He reminds us, "God does not merely 'act in history.' God acts in history in particular ways. It would be a denial of the history to separate an abstract project label like liberation from the specific meaning of the liberation God has brought" (Schipani 84).

See also Culture and Hermeneutics; Ideological Criticism

Bibliography

Boff, L. *Church*. Crossroad, 1985; Ellis, M. H., and O. Maduro, eds. *The Future of Liberation Theology*. Orbis, 1989; Gutiérrez, G. *A Theology of Liberation*, trans. C. Inda and J. Eagleson. 2d ed. Orbis, 1988; Padilla, C. R. "Liberation Theology." In *Freedom and Discipleship*, ed. D. Schipani. Orbis, 1989; Samuel, V., and C. Sugden, eds. *Sharing Jesus in the Two Thirds World*. Eerdmans, 1983; Schipani, D., ed. *Freedom and Discipleship*. Orbis, 1989; Sobrino, J. *Christology at the Crossroads*. Orbis, 1978; Sugirtharajah, R. S., ed. *Voices from the Margin*. Orbis, 1991.

Samuel Escobar

Life *See* Holy Spirit, Doctrine of the; Human Being, Doctrine of

Lindbeck, George *See* Language-Game; Narrative Theology; Yale School

Literacy *See* Reading

Literal Sense

"Write in a book what you see and send it to the seven churches" (Rev. 1:11 NRSV). The Bible is written witness to what humans have seen and heard of the God of Israel. The question, of course, is how to read the text. The literal sense has been understood as the authoritative sense of the text on which understanding is based. In the Middle Ages it was understood as the main building block for the other three senses, which were often referred to as the allegorical, tropological or moral, and anagogical. According to the literal sense, Jerusalem is the city of the Jebusites, allegorically it is the church, tropologically it is the law, and anagogically the heavenly city. The literal sense has been alternately understood as the verbal sense (the givenness of the words) or the historical sense (what really happened) or the authorial meaning (what the author really meant). Yet, the three other senses were built up from reading the literal sense and depended upon its solidity and authority for their own fluidity.

During the last decades of the twentieth century, it was the trend to prefer "Antiochene" exegesis over against "Alexandrian" exegesis because Antiochene readings were understood to focus on the literal sense of the biblical text and Alexandrian readings were regarded as "fanciful," not tied to the firm literal sense. Such a hard-and-fast distinction is now thrown into question. And modern literary theory, from structuralism to reader response to deconstruction, has questioned the stability, indeed, even the existence of such a notion as the "literal sense." Instead, the role of the reader and the broader communities of faith that cherish these texts have become of greater interest than any concept of fixity in the literal sense of the text as once understood. Even modern historical criticism of the Bible has begun to lose its authority as "scientific" and "objective," as the sole arbiter of "meaning."

The notion of the literal sense of Scripture has received some attention lately, most notably as it intersects with typological reading. That is, the literal sense, once seen as the "historical" sense, the factual or realistic sense, is now being treated in some quarters under the rubric of "plain sense." Plain sense can mean anything from the community's reading to the interplay between verbal meaning and ruled reading. This second definition bears more fruit for theology and the life of faith. Ruled reading is the reading of the text that lends ultimate authority to the Rule of Faith as outlined in Ignatius, Polycarp, and most notably Tertullian and Irenaeus, for examples. For Tertullian, in his *Veiling of the Virgins*, the Rule of Faith

> is altogether one, alone immovable and irreformable; the rule, to wit, of believing in one only God omnipotent, Creator of the Universe, and His Son Jesus Christ, born of the Virgin Mary, crucified under Pontius Pilate, raised again on the third day from the dead, received in the heavens, sitting now at the right (hand) of the Father, destined to come to judge the quick and the dead through resurrection of the flesh as well (as of the Spirit). The law of faith being constant, the other succeeding points of discipline and conversation admit the novelty of correction. (ch. 1)

This precreedal yet creed-like material disallows both the conflation and separation of the two Testaments of the Bible. That is, it theologically holds together God the Creator and Jesus Christ, and hermeneutically the OT and the NT. It itself is the "law of faith," the fixity often sought in the "literal sense," which allows the judgment of other points of discipline and theological reasoning. That is, when authoritative reading (formerly called "literal sense") is sought, the plain sense disallows certain nonorthodox readings. As such, the Rule of Faith is a basic "take" on the subject matter and plot of the Christian story, which couples the confession of Jesus the Redeemer with God the Creator. Since it is generally understood to be drawn from Scripture, in biblical interpretation it is reapplied to Scripture.

Notice that what becomes important here is not "meaning" or even "sense" but reading. This means that the literal sense itself is no longer the sole authoritative sense. "Literal sense" is often confined to the rubrics of verbal meaning, and plain sense is the construction of reading that takes place in the interplay between verbal sense and ruled reading. Thus, plain sense itself is an authoritative reading that takes with utmost seriousness the confession of the church at one of its earliest points.

A related set of subconcepts to reading according to the plain sense is authority and authoritativeness. Here, the normativity of plain sense reading extends from the authority of the text to the authority of the religious leader, appealing to the plain sense and/or the community in teaching and religious formation of its adherents or members. When plain sense is appealed to as authoritative sense, leaders and teachers diverging from this may lose their extended authority. Likewise, the plain sense of the text functions to control that extended authority: the authority granted to the text can guide, correct, and undercut the authority of the religious leader or community. This was the importance of the plain sense, which played a crucial role in the Protestant Reformation, undercutting the authority of the Roman Catholic leaders by reading Scripture according to the Rule of Faith: *Scriptura sui ipsius interpres* (Scripture interprets itself). Instead of decoupling religious authority from the story line of Scripture, Martin Luther and the great Reformers thus read Scripture according to itself.

See also Allegory; Meaning; Rule of Faith; Typology

Bibliography

Barr, J. "Literality." *Faith and Philosophy* 6 (1989): 412–28; Childs, B. "The Sensus Literalis of Scripture: An Ancient and Modern Problem." Pages 80–93 in *Beiträge zur alttestamentlichen Theologie*, ed. H. Donner, H. Hanhart, and R. Smend. Vandenhoeck & Ruprecht, 1977; Frei, H. "'The Literal Reading' of Biblical Narrative in the Christian Tradition: Does It Stretch or Will It Break?" Pages 36–77 in *The Bible and the Narrative Tradition*, ed. F. McConnell. Oxford University Press, 1986; Froehlich, K. "'Always to Keep the Literal Sense in Holy Scripture Means to Kill One's Soul': The State of Biblical Hermeneutics at the Beginning of the 15th Century." Pages 20–48 in *Literary Uses of Typology*, ed. E. Miner. Princeton University Press, 1977; Halivni, D. *Peshat and Derash*. Oxford University Press, 1991; Loewe, R. "The 'Plain' Meaning of Scripture in Early Jewish Exegesis." In *Papers of the Institute of Jewish Studies London*, ed. J. G. Weiss. Magnus, 1964; Tanner, T. "Theology and the Plain Sense." In *Scriptural Authority and Narrative Interpretation*, ed. G. Green. Fortress, 1987; Williams, R. "The Literal Sense of Scripture." *Modern Theology* 7 (1991): 121–34.

Kathryn Greene-McCreight

Literary Criticism

Although literary criticism of the Bible is most obviously a hermeneutical issue, the purpose of this article is to explore the theological implications of the topic. The rubric of literary criticism has come to encompass a far-flung range of approaches, but the starting point for any legitimate use of the designation is an acknowledgment of the literary nature of the Bible itself. Literary criticism of the Bible approaches the Bible as literature. Accordingly, the discussion that follows defines what it means that the Bible is literary and then delineates the theological implications. The perspective offered is that of traditional literary criticism as practiced by literary scholars in the humanities, with an emphasis on the unity of complete texts, not the dissecting methodology that biblical scholars have tended to mean by literary criticism.

The Bible as Literature

The overall genre of the Bible is that of a literary anthology. This means that the texts comprising the Bible (the word that means "little books") display characteristics that have traditionally been attributed to literature. Four main traits determine that a text is literary.

The Voice of Human Experience. The subject of literature is human experience. Literature aims to get a reader to share an experience, not primarily to grasp ideas. Literature is incarnational. It embodies its ideas or meanings concretely rather than abstractly; it enacts rather than states propositionally.

Instead of stating abstract propositions about virtue and vice, for example, literature presents stories of good and evil characters in action. The command "You shall not murder" is rendered in literary form with the story of Cain and Abel, where neither the word "murder" nor a prohibition against it is explicitly stated. When asked to define "neighbor," Jesus instead told a story about neighborly behavior (the parable of the good Samaritan). Psalm 23 incarnates the reality of God's providence in the imagery of a shepherd's daily provision for his sheep, eschewing the word "providence" and never naming the dominant mood of contentment.

The truthfulness that literature conveys is thus not only ideational but also truthfulness to human experience. Literature always has a cognitive dimension, though its extracognitive dimension is what differentiates it as an art form.

Literary Genres. Through the centuries, literature has been defined by its genres. The theological implications of a literary approach to the Bible do not predominantly lie here, but it is a major consideration in identifying the literary nature of the Bible. We know that the Bible is a literary anthology by the sheer abundance of literary genres that we find in it.

The two largest categories are narrative and poetry. A host of subgenres appear under both master genres—hero stories and parables under narrative, for example, and praise psalms and psalms of lament under poetry. Additional genres fill out the Bible—satire, visionary writing, epistle, proverb, and oratory, to name some leading ones.

Artistry. Literature is an art form, displaying beauty, craftsmanship, and technique. The writer of Ecclesiastes claims that he arranged "proverbs with great care," and further that he "sought to find words of delight" (12:9–10, ESV). Here is tribute to the purely aesthetic side of literature—its attentiveness to artistry and beauty.

Everywhere we turn in the Bible we find evidence of a commitment to the "how" of an utterance and not simply the "what." Repeatedly we find such artistic qualities as pattern, design, repetition, unity, coherence, symmetry, balance, and contrast. The specific form that these artistic qualities take is often related to the genre in which they appear, so that, for example, balance in biblical poetry most obviously manifests itself in the verse form known as parallelism.

Form. The defining principle of literature is that meaning is communicated through form. The concept of form should be construed broadly here as including everything that touches on *how* a writer has expressed the content of an utterance. Form is primary and precedent in the sense that interpretation must begin with it. Before we can extract the theological meaning of a literary text in the Bible, we need to interact with the surface details. These details include the characters and emotions and human experiences that are put in front of us, the genre(s) in which an utterance is embodied, and the artistry that inheres in a text. At its heart literary criticism of the Bible is committed to explicating biblical texts in keeping with their literary nature.

Theological Implications

In turning to the theological implications of literary criticism of the Bible, we do well to note that the Bible itself combines three main authorial impulses and corresponding types of content—the literary, the historical, and the theological. Although one of these usually dominates a given passage, aspects of the other two are usually discernible. For this reason, it is entirely logical that the literary nature of the Bible should produce theological meanings.

A second preliminary point is that the theological principles that flow from the literary nature of the Bible all prove that the medium is the message. All of the theological categories discussed below are rooted in the literary *example* of the Bible, though they can be buttressed by explicit doctrinal passages in the Bible as well. Above all, it is crucial to acknowledge that the Bible is emphatically not a systematic theology book with proof texts attached. It instead is a literary anthology.

Incarnational Theology. The Christian doctrine that has been most often invoked through the centuries as the basis for a Christian aesthetic has been the incarnation of Jesus—God embodied in human form. This incarnation of Jesus has been a convenient model for picturing what a work of literature is, and the Bible itself in its literary form has been offered as a prime illustration. In the Bible, we find the theological truths of the faith embodied in concrete settings, characters, events, and images. As C. S. Lewis noted in a discussion of the parallelism of the Psalms, "Poetry too is a little incarnation, giving body to what had been before invisible and inaudible" (5). The parables of Jesus illustrate incarnational theology in its pure form, inasmuch as they take something as spiritual as "the kingdom of heaven" and embody that theological reality in everyday images, characters, and actions.

The incarnational nature of the Bible serves as a curb against the tendency of theologians to create a system of abstractions when talking about God and spiritual experience. As we immerse ourselves in the literature of the Bible, we are led to see that belief in God does not whisk us away to some ethereal region; instead, we see that it is in the everyday details of life that the great theological issues are lived out and resolved.

Experiential Theology. A tradition extending from the Puritans through such figures as Jonathan Edwards and George Whitefield has made much of "experimental" theology, by which is meant *experiential* theology. In this tradition we find typical statements: "Saints have an experimental knowledge of the work of grace" (Thomas Shepard). "If we were well read in the story of our own lives, we might have a divinity [theology] of our own, drawn out of the observations of God's particular dealing toward us" (Richard Sibbes).

The literary nature of the Bible lends support to such experiential theology. There is no more basic literary principle than that the subject of literature is human experience. Accordingly, every literary text in the Bible is at its heart a specific person's experience of God. This does not mean that those experiences are anything less than normative and universally true at a principal level. It only means that biblical theology is not a collection of free-floating ideas. Instead, it is rooted in people's experiences of God and in God's self-revelation to people, involved in their everyday situations in life.

Narrative Theology. Narrative theology springs from awareness that narrative is the overarching structure of the Bible as a whole, and additionally that stories are the most numerous genre in the literary anthology that comprises the Bible. The phenomenon of narrative theology has consisted primarily of recasting the conventional theological categories in narrative terms, with a view toward viewing theology as the story of what God does in history rather than as a list of doctrines. This is congruent with the way in which we experience God as we assimilate the narrative parts of the Bible, where we primarily understand the nature of God through his role as a character in a series of stories.

Dorothy L. Sayers has expressed in kernel form the principle underlying narrative theology: Christianity "is not primarily an emotional experience, or a set of logical conclusions, or a code of ethics: it is a *story*. . . . It is the story of God's act in history. The whole emotional, rational and ethical structure which we associate with the phrase 'The Christian religion' has to be referred to that story for its explanation and sanction" (84). In the middle of the twentieth century, G. Ernest Wright, in a book whose title summarizes his argument (*God Who Acts: Theology as Recital*), popularized the idea that whatever we say about God is rooted in the actions of God.

Poetic Theology. The privileging of narrative over other genres in recent literary criticism of the Bible has virtually eclipsed nonnarrative forms, particularly as they impinge on theology. But if narrative has its unique way of incarnating people's experiences of God, with attendant theological meanings, poetry also has *its* distinctive way of embodying truth about God as well. Amos N. Wilder coined the term "theopoetic" to denote poetry's contribution to theology, with the term defined as doing justice "to the role of the symbolic and the prerational" (2). Theology based on the poetry of the Bible extracts the intellectual and emotional meanings of the Bible's great images and metaphors, and it encompasses the mystical dimensions of theology, as (for example) in the biblical motif of God and Christ as light.

Theology of Beauty. The literary nature of the Bible implies an aesthetic dimension as well. The word "beauty" remains the best term by which to denote the qualities of artistry and craftsmanship that are important to works of art. In addition to statements about beauty in the Bible, the literary nature of the Bible itself represents an example of artistic beauty. From this example we can infer or deduce a theology of beauty whose main components are these: (1) God is the source of beauty. (2) Beauty is an attribute of God. (3) Beauty is one of God's gifts to the human race. (4) Beauty is a means by which people can experience and worship God. Hans Urs von Balthasar's magisterial seven-volume work on "theological aesthetics" proposes in the preface "to develop a Christian theology in the light of the third transcendental, that is to say: to complement the vision of the true and the good with that of the beautiful."

More specifically, the literary nature of the Bible has been rightly invoked through the Christian centuries among aesthetic theorists who have formulated a biblically based *poetic* (philosophy and defense of literature). At root, such a poetic participates in a theology of the word, based on the premise that the very fact of a literary Bible shows literature to be not merely legitimate but indispensable to the Christian faith. This conclusion is buttressed by the ways in which the parables and discourses of Jesus are literary in nature. Simply put, God chose to reveal himself and his truth through the medium of literature. A literary scholar has rightly claimed that "Christianity is the most literary religion in the world: it is crammed with characters and stories; much of its doctrine was enshrined in poetry—*Job*, the *Psalms*, *Song of Solomon*, *Revelation*. . . . It is a religion in which the word has a special sanctity" (Broadbent 101).

Theology of Culture. Attempts to reach an understanding of how Christians should relate to culture have long sailed under the banner of "theology of culture." The thrust of this has been to answer the question of how God views human culture and accordingly how he wants his followers to view it. Literature is a cultural form. Simply by being a work of literature, the Bible implicitly affirms not only the legitimacy of culture but also its indispensability to the Christian faith. To this we can add the way in which the Bible has been the most important literary source and influence on Western literature and indeed culture.

Additionally, it is well established that biblical writers imitated and adapted literary forms of surrounding ancient cultures. For example, the Song of Solomon bears resemblances to Egyptian love poetry, and the prologue to John's Gospel echoes the Greek hymn to Zeus. At least, the employment and adaptation of pagan literary forms by biblical writers stands as an endorsement of culture in principle. Yet, as a literary model the Bible also contains limits to cultural affirmation (as seen, for example, in the limits that the Bible sets to literary realism, or its prohibition of visual images of God).

Literary Theology

Literary criticism is the analysis of texts in terms of their literary qualities. While such analysis is the scholarly domain of literary specialists, all good expositors of the Bible practice an incipient literary criticism, defined as looking closely at the literary form and content of the Bible. When such analysis is pressed in theological directions as this article has done, it yields something that can accurately be called literary theology. Literary theology is rooted in literary analysis of the biblical text. The fact that the Bible itself is a literary anthology, coupled with the way in which Scripture is the definitive source of Christian doctrine, produces a theology rooted in literature. The final lesson that literary criticism of the Bible holds for theology, therefore, is that for the majority of the Bible, literary analysis must be respected as existing logically prior to any theologizing based on it. We cannot extract theology from a story or metaphor without first interacting with the story or metaphor.

See also Formalism; Narrative Criticism; Narrative Theology; Western Literature, the Bible and

Bibliography

Alter, R. *The Art of Biblical Narrative*. Basic Books, 1981; Balthasar, H. U. von. *The Glory of the Lord*. 7 vols. Ignatius, 1982; Broadbent, J. *Paradise Lost: Introduction*. Cambridge University Press, 1972; Delattre, R. A. *Beauty and Sensibility in the Thought of Jonathan Edwards*. Yale University Press, 1968; Dyrness, W. *Visual Faith*. Baker, 2001; Hauerwas, S., and L. G. Jones, eds. *Why Narrative?* Eerdmans, 1989; Jeffrey, D. L. *People of the Book*. Eerdmans, 1996; Lewis, C. S. *Reflections on the Psalms*. Harcourt, 1958; Lindsey, F. D. "Essays toward a Theology of Beauty, Part I: God Is Beautiful." *BSac* 131 (1974): 120–36; Ryken, L. *Words of Delight*. 2d ed. Baker, 1992; Sayers, D. "Types of Christian Drama: With Some Notes on Production." *Seven* 2 (1981): 84–99; Sternberg, M. *The Poetics of*

Biblical Narrative. Indiana University Press, 1985; Stroup, G. *The Promise of Narrative Theology*. John Knox, 1981; Wilder, A. N. *Theopoetic*. Fortress, 1976; Wright, G. E. *God Who Acts*. SCM, 1952.

Leland Ryken

Liturgy

"O come, let us worship and bow down, let us kneel before the LORD our Maker!" "My soul magnifies the Lord, and my Spirit rejoices in God my Savior." These words from Ps. 95:6 (NRSV) and Luke 1:47 (NRSV) call our attention to a major dimension of the response to God found in both the OT and NT Scriptures. While an ethical response and commitment to a holy life are important, these and other dimensions of faith find their focus and rationale in liturgical worship, or liturgy. By liturgy is meant communal worship offered to God rather than private prayer, though these are closely connected. The Greek words *leitourgein/leitourgia* were used to refer to the public duty, or work, of citizens. The translators of the LXX used these words to describe priestly service of God. In the NT they are sometimes used with a meaning of service to others (2 Cor. 9:12), but also with cultic overtones (Luke 1:23; Rom. 15:16). Closely associated with the latter usage are *proseuchē* (prayer) and *latreia* (adoration).

In the NT, in the account of the temptations, Jesus reminds Satan (and implicitly, all, including Christian disciples) that "You shall worship the Lord your God, and him only shall you serve" (Luke 4:8 RSV; Deut. 6:13). The Gospels portray Jesus' life as a perfect fulfillment of this. He is found in the temple, his Father's house, which he must cleanse and then replace. He prays in synagogue and fulfills the prophetic readings. He teaches his disciples to pray and sets aside time for prayer. His commitment to the divine destiny is one of obedient worship. The letter to the Hebrews asserts that Christ is a high priest and minister (*leitourgos*) in the heavenly sanctuary, who has offered a single sacrifice for sins (chs. 8–10). The hymn in Phil. 2 proclaims that he has been given the Name that is above every name, so that every knee in heaven and earth should bow down to Jesus as Lord. Several NT letters bear testimony to communal gatherings where hymns and psalms are sung, and where thanksgiving, supplication, teaching, instruction, and exhortation all take place. Here at least the *ekklēsia* echoes, and in some sense joins with heaven, both the angelic beings and elders, as depicted in Revelation, worshipping the Father and the Lamb, in, with, and through the Holy Spirit. In other words, Christian liturgy is eschatological in nature; it is an occasion when time and eternity are elided. While liturgy takes the form of human language in all its multiplicity, the people of God nevertheless have their own divine vocabulary. In the events of Pentecost, although everyone heard in their own language, what they all heard and spoke were "the mighty works of God" (Acts 2:11 RSV). Salvation history is this special vocabulary.

Since the NT era, however, churches have evolved widely differing liturgical forms. Some, such as the Eastern and Oriental Orthodox, are quite complex and exotic in their style and content. Roman Catholics, Lutherans, and Anglicans, by comparison, seem to occupy an in-between form and style. Protestant worship through Presbyterianism, Congregationalism, Methodism, to Evangelicalism, Pentecostalism, Quakerism, and the American Shakers and serpent-handlers, by comparison all have simpler forms of worship. This means that any generic description or theology of liturgy becomes difficult. Shakers, for example, communally danced to the Lord, whereas the serpent-handlers have privileged the longer ending of Mark 16, in the King James Version.

Recent ecumenical debate among many of the major churches represented in Faith and Order of the World Council of Churches has respected the many liturgical differences. Yet, there has been concern to identify a common liturgical "ordo," or undergirding structure, of what is to be perceived in the ordering and scheduling of the most primary elements of Christian worship. These are listed as Scripture readings and preaching, yielding intercessions; and, with these, *eucharistia* and eating and drinking together, yielding a collection for the poor and mission in the world. It is formation in faith and baptizing in water, and ministers and community doing these together. How does some of this work out in terms of Scripture and theology?

Liturgies have a beginning, and this may be a call to worship ("Our help is in the name of the LORD," Ps. 124:8, was the old Reformed call), or a greeting or invocation in the name of the divine Trinity (2 Cor. 1:2; Matt. 28:19). Jesus promised that when two or three are gathered in his name, "there am I in the midst of them" (Matt. 18:20 RSV). Here we must not confine our interpretation to the historical *Sitz im Leben*, since at best this leads to binitarianism. Here, across the Scriptures, Jesus' "I am" echoes the "I AM" of Yahweh, the one who causes to be. But since

Jesus returned to the Father so that the Spirit might come, "I am in the midst" can ultimately only be interpreted as the Father, Son, and Spirit being present both with and to the assembled *ekklēsia*. Likewise, in baptism, baptism into the name of Jesus Christ (Acts 2:38) is ultimately into the triune Name (Matt. 28:19). Praise is addressed to the Father, through the Son, and in the Holy Spirit, as well as to the Father, Son, and Holy Spirit as consubstantial. It is true that overly frequent use of the divine names can lead to an empty formula, and the divine persons can also be known by their works. However, the attempt to exclude the divine names as "mere metaphor," in the interests of an inclusive language agenda, seems theologically naive and a cavalier handling of Scripture. Liturgy properly understood is the occasion of an epiphany of the divine Trinity, Father, Son, and Holy Spirit, and where God—who is Creator, Redeemer, and Sanctifier—may speak to the heart, soul, and mind.

Most worship services contain a confession and absolution, or declaration of forgiveness. Any encounter with God leads to fear and unworthiness (Isa. 6:3, 5; Luke 5:8). It is right and proper therefore that in liturgy sins should be confessed, in confidence of the divine grace. Scripture asserts that sin, even unintentional, alienates, and its concealment can render worship insincere or even diabolic. But the NT presents the perfect *leitourgia* of Jesus as being sufficient for the sins of the whole world. Confession and absolution put into words the free forgiveness of sins wrought by the one who gave his life a ransom for many. The ministers/priests never absolve in their own right, but as articulating to the church on its behalf the eternal message of God: "Your sins are forgiven. . . . Go in peace" (Luke 7:48, 50).

In liturgy Holy Scripture is present in many direct and indirect ways, for example, in the singing of psalms and canticles, as well as in the reading of Scripture and preaching. Here the assembly receives both *didachē* and *kerygma*, all in a context of doxology. But the Word heard always gives rise to response. In some assemblies this may be an "altar call," rather like the response called for in some of the sermons in Acts—"What must we do? . . . Repent and be baptized. . . ." Or it may give rise to intercessions, for the church is urged to pray in and out of season, for those of the household of faith, and for all, a concrete expression of which may be giving money or goods as charity. It may result in responding to the command at the Last Supper to do this in remembrance. Many churches have recaptured the full meaning of "thanksgiving," using eucharistic prayers mirrored on those of the rites of the fourth and fifth centuries, and of the *berakot* prayers of Judaism. In such prayers the salvation history of God in Scripture is articulated in doxology, with thanks for creation, for the saving work of Jesus Christ, culminating on the cross, of which the Lord's Supper is the *anamnēsis* (remembrance). It may include the calling of the Spirit on the elements of the bread and wine, that communion may indeed be an encounter with the divine presence and an occasion of divine self-disclosure. Often as immediate preparation the community will pray the Lord's Prayer. Liturgies invariably conclude with blessing, for any worship with God is an occasion of blessing. But there is also usually a sending, for worship is part of the ebbing and flowing rhythm of the Christian life. The church assembles for *leitourgia* of praise only to be dispersed for *leitourgia* in the world, which God created and for which Christ died.

Liturgy encapsulates the good news and challenge of Holy Scripture. Although many Christians read and meditate on Scripture in private and in study groups, worship is the occasion when most Christians encounter Scripture together. It is not practical to read large portions, and not all passages of Scripture have the same urgency or edification. Therefore, a selection has to be made—a canon within a canon, a lectionary. Sometimes this is done by reading through a particular book in course (*lectio continua*); other times selection is made according to what has developed as the liturgical year, separating out the events of the gospel for commemoration and emphasis. In this instance, Scripture is selected according to its relevance. Sometimes readings are thematic, though the danger here is that a predetermined theme may impose itself on the selection and on how the Scripture is understood. Ministers' self-selection can also be a narrowing of the canon to a personal preference of favorite passages. Use of a lectionary such as the three-year Common Revised Lectionary, used in many English-speaking churches, at least enables a wide selection of Scripture to be read.

See also Worship

Bibliography

Allmen, J.-J. von. *Worship*. Oxford University Press, 1965; Bradshaw, P. F. *The Search for the Origins of Early Christian Worship*. Oxford University Press, 2002; Carson, D. A. *Worship*. Baker, 1993; Senn, F. C. *Christian Liturgy*. Fortress, 1997; Spinks, B. *The Sanctus in the Eucharistic Prayer*. Cambridge University Press,

2002; idem. "Trinitarian Theology and the Eucharistic Prayer." *Studia liturgica* 26 (1996): 209–24; Wright, N. T. "Freedom and Framework, Spirit and Truth: Recovering Biblical Worship." *Studia liturgica* 32 (2002): 176–95.

Bryan D. Spinks

Locke, John   *See* Enlightenment

Locutionary Act   *See* Speech-Act Theory

Logic

Logic is primarily concerned with (1) validity of arguments and (2) consistency of propositions. A valid argument is one in which, if the premises are true, the conclusion cannot fail to be true. Two propositions (factual assertions) are consistent if they can both be true at the same time. The science of logic seeks to understand what makes arguments valid or invalid, and what makes propositions consistent or inconsistent.

In the study of any text, including Scripture, logic is an important hermeneutical tool. If a text says that all men are mortal, and Socrates is a man, then we may validly infer from that text that Socrates is mortal. In a sense, the text *asserts*, not only that all men are mortal and Socrates is a man, but also that Socrates is mortal. The conclusion is implicit in the text, and the logical argument makes that conclusion explicit. Logic, then, is a way of understanding the meaning of texts. So the Westminster Confession of Faith (1.6) locates the "whole counsel of God" not only in the things "expressly set down in Scripture," but also in the things that "by good and necessary consequence may be deduced from Scripture."

Human beings have been thinking logically (validly, consistently) since creation. The science of logic, the formal study of logical thought, was largely invented by Aristotle and has continued through the work of such figures as Ockham, Leibniz, Bertrand Russell, and Willard Quine. Sometimes logical theorists have tried to teach logic as a formal system analogous to Euclid's geometry. But these systems have their limitations. For one thing, they deal only with propositions expressed in language. But human beings draw inferences, not only from language, but also from states of affairs. If I keep my car keys in only three places, A, B, and C, and I see they are not in locations A and B, I infer they must be at location C. That is logical reasoning, but I may never think to express it in a syllogism or even in language. Psychologically, it may be nothing more than a feeling that impels me from one location to another. Logical thought, therefore (I am tempted to say "logical feeling"), precedes syllogisms, arguments, and systems. And we have no reason to assume that systems of logic today are rich enough to account for all logical thinking.

Does Scripture itself warrant logic? It does not contain or recommend any particular system of logic, but it does contain logical language, representing logical thought. Further, it recommends consistency and validity as virtues. When James tells us not only to hear God's word but also to do it (1:22–25), he is recommending consistency between our professed beliefs and our actions. When Scripture tells us not to steal, but we steal anyway, we are not permitted to excuse ourselves by renouncing the virtue of consistency. God himself proclaims that his actions are consistent with his promises and threats. When someone claims to be a prophet of God, but events occur that are inconsistent with his prophecies, these events expose the claimant as presumptuous (Deut. 18:15–22). God does not lie or deny himself (2 Tim. 2:13; Titus 1:2). Biblical prohibitions of false witness (Exod. 20:16; Eph. 4:25) emphasize the antithesis between true and false language and the responsibility of God's people to speak consistently with the truth. Passages in which God evidently approves of untruth (as Exod. 1:15–21; Josh. 2:4–6; 8:3–8; Heb. 11:31; James 2:25; etc.) are exceptions that prove the rule: deception of the wicked (not the "neighbor" of Exod. 20:16) in these cases maintains consistency with the purposes of God and the sanctity of human life. Certainly, none of these passages says anything to discourage logical thought and action.

As for inference, we should note that Scripture is often argumentative. It not only states the truth, but it also presents reasons for believing it and acting on it. Don't worship idols, God says through Moses, *because* the Lord is jealous (Exod. 20:5–6) and *because* God chose not to reveal his form when he met with Israel on Mt. Sinai (Deut. 4:15). Paul tells the Colossians that they should seek the things that are above, *because* they have risen with Christ (Col. 3:1), that they should present their bodies as living sacrifices *because* of the "mercies of God" (Rom. 12:1 NRSV). So Scripture presents not only authoritative truths, but also authoritative logical inferences. It is not enough to seek the things that are above; we must seek those things for a particular reason, because we have been raised with Christ. So Paul endorses the syllogism: those raised with Christ should seek the things that are above. The Colossian believers are raised with Christ. Therefore, they should seek the things above.

Logic, therefore, is a valuable tool for theology, a way of understanding meaning from Scripture and applying it to human life. Indeed, one way to look at theological hermeneutics in general is to see it as a group of methods by which we derive logical implications from biblical texts. An interpretation of Scripture is never a mere repetition. An interpretation always uses some words different from the biblical text. But the claim of an interpreter is, in effect, that his interpretation is an expression of meaning logically implicit in the text itself.

If the work of logic in interpretation is done well, the result will preserve the *truth* of the original text. A valid inference from Scripture will be as true as the texts that form the premises of that inference. So the Westminster Confession, as we have seen, locates divine authority both in the express words of Scripture and in truth deduced from Scripture by "good and necessary consequence." One is almost inclined to think that one could greatly enlarge the biblical canon, simply by producing logical inferences from the current canon.

But it is not that easy. There are limitations and dangers in logical inference, sufficient to make clear that such ambitions to enlarge the canon are mere fantasies:

1. Although logic itself preserves truth, human users of logic are fallible. Logic preserves truth only when it is done rightly. But theologians and exegetes make mistakes in their efforts to reason logically. So believers in the infallibility of Scripture must make a sharp distinction between the authority of the biblical texts and that of postcanonical theology. Logical inference ideally preserves the truth of premises in its conclusions, but such inferring, as actually practiced, does not necessarily preserve truth. That limitation pertains to all methods of interpretation. In this respect, logic is no different from textual criticism, translation, paraphrase, commentary, or theological analysis.

2. The fallibility of the practice of logic extends also to logical systems. Like all sciences, the science of logic has a history. Aristotle's system of logic is different at points from those of Ockham, Russell, and Quine, and it sometimes generates different inferences than other systems. There is no reason to suppose that anyone has yet come up with a perfect system of logic.

3. As mentioned earlier, logicians have not yet systematized all forms of logical thinking under axioms, rules, and laws of thought. So there may be legitimate inferences (from Scripture or other texts) that cannot be justified by current logical theory.

4. Sometimes arguments that appear to be logically valid on closer inspection turn out to be invalid. An example would be: All human beings have sinned (Rom. 3:23); Jesus is a human being (1 Tim. 2:5); therefore, Jesus has sinned. The logic here appears valid. But a major rule of logic is that for such a syllogism to be valid the quantifier ("all" in this case) must include the objects to which the conclusion is applied. In this example, it is clear that Paul was not thinking of Jesus when he wrote that "all have sinned." Nor did he mean to deny the sinlessness of Christ, which he affirms in 2 Cor. 5:21 with other NT writers (John 8:46; Heb. 4:15; 7:26; 1 Pet. 2:22; 1 John 3:5). Here "all" does not have the universal force it would need to make the syllogism valid.

Another rule of logic is that in a valid argument the terms must preserve the same meanings throughout the argument. One might argue: everyone who believes in Christ has eternal life (John 3:16); some believers said that Jesus had a demon (8:31, 48); therefore, some who believe Jesus has a demon have eternal life. The argument appears valid, but on closer inspection we note that it equivocates on the word "believe," since the Gospel writer himself uses "believe" in several senses. So, determining logical validity is sometimes more complicated than it may appear on the surface.

5. Indeed, what the above examples prove is that the right use of logic presupposes the right use of other means of interpretation. In the first example, it is not enough to know the rules of logic. One must also understand the language well enough, and indeed know enough about biblical Christology, to know the likely range of "all" in Rom. 3:23. Likewise in the second example: to see what is wrong with it, we must understand that the meaning of "believe" varies in Johannine use, and that it likely has a different meaning in John 3:16 from the meaning it has in 8:31. Hence, right use of logic assumes a right understanding of language. Since I observed earlier that logic itself is a tool in the interpretation of language, we should draw the conclusion that knowledge of logic and language are mutually dependent.

6. Emerging from this discussion is the broader point that logic is in many ways dependent on other kinds of knowledge. Logic itself rarely supplies the premises of logical arguments. Those premises come from many sources, such as ob-

servation, reasoning, imagination, emotion, authority, and study. The use of logic, then, depends on empirical knowledge, among other things. Philosophers have often claimed that logic is entirely a priori, not dependent on experience. Even if that is true of logic as an abstract system, it is not true of logic in actual practice. A logical argument will not yield a true conclusion unless its premises (usually derived from some source other than logic) are true.

7. Is the Bible logical, then? Granted that God is logical, and that Scripture is God's infallible word, the (logical!) conclusion follows that Scripture is logical. That is, its teaching is logically consistent, and its arguments are valid. But given the problems noted above in the actual practice of logic, we should not be surprised to find in Scripture what Cornelius Van Til called "apparent contradictions." These apparent contradictions are due not to logical errors in Scripture itself, but to our fallibility in interpreting and applying Scripture. The examples of number 4 (above) may be reconceived as apparent contradictions: Christ is (Rom. 3:23) and is not (2 Cor. 5:21) a sinner; belief in Christ does (John 3:16) and does not (John 8:31–58) lead to eternal life. Better hermeneutics and logic can resolve these "apparent contradictions." But other apparent contradictions may not be resolvable except in the mind of God. The most difficult logical problems are the doctrine of the Trinity, the relation of divine sovereignty and human responsibility, the goodness of our first parents and the sin they committed, and the problem of evil. I see no reason why theologians should not attempt to resolve these as they have resolved the others, but there is no guarantee that we will be able. Perhaps the resolution of some of these paradoxes awaits the next life, or perhaps only God's perfect logic has the answers.

See also Epistemology; Philosophy; Proof Text; Truth

Bibliography

Clark, G. *Logic*. Trinity Foundation, 1985; Copi, I. *Introduction to Logic*. Macmillan, 1972; Frame, J. *Cornelius Van Til*. P&R, 1995; idem. *Doctrine of the Knowledge of God*. P&R, 1987; Quine, W. V. *From a Logical Point of View*. Harper & Row, 1961; Van Til, C. *A Christian Theory of Knowledge*. P&R, 1969.

John M. Frame

Logion *See* Gospels; Jesus, Quest for the Historical

Logocentrism *See* Deconstruction; Postmodernity and Biblical Interpretation

Lord's Supper

The Lord's Supper—also known to theological discussion as the Mass, the Eucharist, and Holy Communion—has been a contentious practice in the history of the churches. A relatively few clear biblical references to the Supper have provided a platform for a large amount of varied theological superstructure. For example, a difference in understanding the Supper was one of the sticking points between the Reformers of the sixteenth century and their Catholic counterparts and even among themselves. The "Supper strife" between Luther and Zwingli over *Hoc est corpus meum* comes to mind (Mark 14:22 Vulg.). Indeed, some contemporary churches such as the Salvation Army do not celebrate the Supper.

The Lord's Supper in the Biblical Texts

Each of the Synoptic Gospels contains a Last Supper narrative (Matt. 26:17–30; Mark 14:12–26; Luke 22:7–23). In the context of a Passover meal, Jesus took bread, and having given thanks, he broke it and gave it to his disciples and commanded them to eat. Likewise, he did so with the wine and commanded them to drink. He referred to his body given and his blood shed. He spoke of the kingdom of God and his future in it, the forgiveness of sins, and of a new covenant in his blood. John's Gospel has no such narrative. Yet, many have seen, rightly or wrongly, a veiled reference to the Eucharist—from *eucharistia*, used in the NT with the general meaning of "thanksgiving," and first appearing as a technical term for the Lord's Supper in the early-second-century *Didache*—in Jesus' claim to be the bread of life come down from heaven and the necessity of eating his flesh and drinking his blood to have eternal life (John 6:22–59). Some also have seen a eucharistic reference in the Lukan story of Cleopas and friend encountering the risen Christ on the road to Emmaus. The Lord was recognized in the breaking of the bread (24:28–31). There was something familiar about the pattern of the risen Christ's activity.

Acts and Paul's First Letter to the Corinthians are important additional sources. Acts contains three possible eucharistic references. The first is, so some argue, a result of Peter's address at Pentecost. The first converts broke bread together, understood in this view as a regular celebration of the Lord's Supper (2:42), and a later meal at Troas shows the continuation of the practice (20:7). The third is even more allusive. Paul broke bread the night before the ship carrying him under guard to Rome was wrecked (27:35). The Corinthian reference is a fulsome one (1 Cor. 11:17–34). Paul states that in the Lord's Supper—a term we owe to this passage (*kyriakon deipnon*)—Christ's death is proclaimed until he returns. A further possible epistolary source is Jude 12. Jude writes of the abuse of love feasts, and if there is a parallel to the pastoral situation at Corinth with regard to the abuse of the Supper, then the Lord's Supper took place in the context of a fellowship meal in these early churches.

The Theological Interpretation of the Lord's Supper

Dominical command and subsequent Pauline practice suggest that the Lord's Supper is no mere first-century curiosity but an ongoing ordinance of the church. The Pauline presentation in 1 Cor. 11 is of particular importance in showing how the Last Supper has become the Lord's Supper. Paul spells out the moral concomitants of the Supper in a context of abuse. Gluttony and disregard of the body of believers have no place at the meal and had occasioned the Lord's judgment at Corinth. Some of the Corinthians had actually died. The kerygmatic nature of the practice is also highlighted. In Augustine's fine words, the Lord's Supper is a "visible word." The gospel is dramatized for believers in bread and wine as the consumption of the elements preaches (*katangellein*) to our senses the gospel of his once-and-for-all sacrifice for our sins. This kerygma is given an eschatological frame of reference as Christ's death is so proclaimed until his parousia.

The content of the biblical testimonies makes it hard to see any justification for the idea of the Mass as a propitiatory sacrifice (a repetition or representation of Calvary) or notions of eucharistic sacrifice (the sacrifice of praise becoming a part of Christ's eternal offering of praise to the Father, or the rite as a pleading of his sacrifice before the Father). Instead, the biblical accents fall on what God in Christ's death has done for us rather than on what we do—except by way of remembrance. Not that the risen Christ is absent from the Supper. Now at the right hand of the Father, he relates to us by way of sign (sacrament), and we are to meet with him by faith. Over time, the discussion of Christ's words of institution—"This is my body" and "This is my blood"—has generated many sophisticated ideas of Christ's presence, such as the miracle of transubstantiation (as in Aquinas), consubstantiation

(as in Luther), transvaluation (as in Spens), and transignification (as in Schillebeeckx). None of these ideas is obvious in the scriptural record.

At this point, a general challenge to the theologian is the nonpostulational character of Scripture. The biblical writers show no real interest in speculating about the essences of things. Much of the postbiblical theological discussion addresses this lack of interest. Specifically with regard to the Supper, the biblical record leaves much unanswered, such as the relationship between baptism and communion (with regard to ecclesiastical unity, Eph. 4:4–6 lists baptism but not the Lord's Supper, interestingly), the frequency of communion, who should preside at the Supper, and the nature of the wine to employ, to name but a few. Still further, there is surprisingly no explicit connection made in Scripture between the Spirit and the Supper. Yet for Calvin, for example, the Spirit is the key to understanding Christ's presence in the Supper. How the Supper is to be understood trinitarianly in a scripturally well-founded way remains a project.

See also Sacrament

Bibliography

Macquarrie, J. *A Guide to the Sacraments*. SCM, 1997; Marshall, I. H. *Last Supper and Lord's Supper*. Paternoster, 1980; Schillebeeckx, E. *The Eucharist*. Sheed & Ward, 1968; Spens, W. "The Eucharist." In *Essays Catholic and Critical*. SPCK, 1926; Stibbs, A. *Sacrament, Sacrifice and Eucharist*. Tyndale, 1962.

Graham A. Cole

Love

The idea that love should direct the interpretation of Scripture is distinctively Augustinian. Near the end of the first book of *De Doctrina Christiana*, Augustine links Jesus' twofold great commandment (Matt. 22:37–40) with Paul's claims in Romans that "Christ is the end of the law" (10:4) and "love is the fulfilling of the law" (13:10 NRSV). "It is to be understood that the plenitude and the end of the Law and of all the sacred Scriptures is the love of a Being [God] which is to be enjoyed and of a being [our neighbor] that can share that enjoyment with us" (*Doctr. chr.* 1.35.39). He then applies this insight to the interpretation of Scripture:

> So anyone who thinks that he has understood the divine Scriptures or any part of them, but cannot by his understanding build up this double love of God and neighbor, has not yet succeeded in understanding them. Anyone who derives from them an idea which is useful for supporting this love but fails

to say what the writer demonstrably meant in the passage has not made a fatal error, and is certainly not a liar. (1.36.40)

Soon thereafter Augustine shows that he is not unconcerned about "what the writer demonstrably meant":

[If the interpreter] is misled by an idea of the kind that builds up love, which is the end of the commandment, he is misled in the same way as a walker who leaves his path by mistake but reaches the destination to which the path leads by going through a field. But he must be put right and shown how it is more useful not to leave the path, in case the habit of deviating should force him to go astray or even adrift. (1.36.41)

This "going astray" often happens, says Augustine, in the following way. Disregarding the purposes of Scripture's authors—and more importantly, disregarding the purposes of God as the true Author of the whole of Scripture—a reader can reach an interpretation that seems to build up love. But when he then reads further in the Bible, he may find "other things which cannot be reconciled with that original idea." When this happens, he is extremely reluctant to abandon his interpretation, in which he takes prideful satisfaction, and "by cherishing his own idea he comes in some strange way to become more displeased with Scripture than with himself" (1.37.41).

For Augustine, then, love is the sovereign principle of interpretation; however, readers may easily misunderstand what love actually is. In order to grasp the nature of love properly, they must submissively seek to understand the whole of Scripture. Augustine is inscribing a kind of hermeneutical circle here: readers must read lovingly in order to receive the biblical message of love, but the more clearly they receive that message, the more lovingly they will be able to read. As Augustine explains in some detail later in *On Christian Teaching*, an interpreter experienced in charitable reading will be unlikely to attribute absurdity or malice to God, even if a particular passage might seem at first to indicate just that. Familiar, especially to readers of Luther, are the convictions that the meaning of Scripture is whole and unified, and that Scripture interprets itself. For Augustine, these convictions are corollaries or derivatives of the encompassing belief that love is "the end of the commandment" to love God and neighbor, and therefore the end of the whole of Scripture (summarized in *Doctr. chr.* 2.9.14).

Ideas similar to these may be found throughout the history of precritical exegesis, and also in accounts of literary reading. Philo of Alexandria's allegorical interpretations of Genesis establish a pattern of reading (later widely employed among Christian scholars) that "saves" the biblical text from scandal and offense; likewise, Basil the Great counsels an "equitable" way of reading Homer that renders that authoritative text usable for the Christian reader. But Augustine's explicit invocation of love seems to be unique among early theologians.

It has remained, strangely enough, one of the least explored of Augustine's major ideas. "Charity" as a principle of interpretation returns in the twentieth century in the work of the philosopher Donald Davidson, but Davidson is not referring to *caritas*, Christian love; he simply means that we come to a conversation with the assumption that our interlocutor speaks intelligibly. Sometimes we abandon that assumption, but only with great reluctance and only after striving to find some way to reconcile our interlocutor's words with what we take to be intelligible utterance. For Davidson, this is not a discipline we undergo but just what we all *do*, instinctively and universally. Therefore, Davidson's "principle of charity" could scarcely be more different than Augustine's model, which requires spiritual training and discipline and a commitment to obeying God.

Only a few recent scholars (e.g., Fortin; Glidden) have sought even to explore Augustine's idea; still fewer have sought to consider what it might mean to put it into practice. Kevin Vanhoozer has done so in a comment on the interpretation of any text: "General hermeneutics is inescapably theological. Our polluted cognitive and spiritual environment darkens understanding—of *all* texts. . . . Understanding—of the Bible or of any other text—is a matter of ethics, indeed, of spirituality. Indeed, interpretation ultimately depends upon the theological virtues of faith, hope, and love" ("Spirit," 161). Despite this welcome and important point, we must still wait for scholars to consider with full seriousness the idea that interpretation of Scripture—like all other human activities—must be governed by a commitment to Christian love, that love upon which, we should remember, depend all the Law and Prophets.

See also Augustine; Virtue

Bibliography

Augustine. *On Christian Teaching*, trans. R. P. H. Green. Oxford University Press, 1997; Basil. *St. Basil the Great to Students on Greek Literature*, ed. E. R. Maloney. American Book Co., 1901; Davidson, D. "Radical Interpretation." Pages 125–40 in *Inquiries into Truth and*

Interpretation. Clarendon, 1984; Fortin, E. "Augustine and the Hermeneutics of Love: Some Preliminary Considerations." Pages 1–21 in *The Birth of Philosophic Christianity.* Rowman & Littlefield, 1996; Glidden, D. "Augustine's Hermeneutics and the Principle of Charity." *Ancient Philosophy* 17 (1997): 135–57; Jacobs, A. *A Theology of Reading.* Westview, 2001; Vanhoozer, K. "The Spirit of Understanding: Special Revelation and General Hermeneutics." Pages 131–66 in *Disciplining Hermeneutics,* ed. R. Lundin. Eerdmans, 1997.

Alan Jacobs

Lubac, Henri de   *See* Medieval Biblical Interpretation

Luke, Book of

History of Interpretation

Early interpretation of Luke included meditation on its significance as one strand of the fourfold Gospel. Each Gospel was assigned a unique purpose, sometimes linked with a traditional symbol—in Luke's case, the ox. Thus in Ambrose, Augustine, and Bede, a connection is made between the symbol of the ox and the Evangelist's emphasis on the temple, the place of animal sacrifice (1:5–25; 2:22–52; 13:35; 24:53). This is seen as reflecting the truth of Christ's mediation as sacrificial victim and high priest (Wright 68–69).

The discernment of pattern and purpose in Scripture, attributed to divine authorship, reached new sophistication in medieval times and is well represented by Bonaventure's commentary on Luke. His reading of 4:18–21 treats Jesus' "sermon" in Nazareth as not only programmatic for his ministry, but also descriptive of Luke's purpose in writing. Thus, Luke's Gospel itself is read as offering "good news to the poor." Luke's purpose is construed as manifesting truth, healing infirmity, and pointing to eternity. These three are interwoven: it is through knowledge of the truth that we find healing, a healing that will only be complete hereafter. Jesus' ministry is thus represented as being recapitulated by Luke for a far wider public, whose eternal benefit, conversely, finds symbolic expression in the transformations wrought by Jesus while on earth. The traditional identification of the Evangelist with the "beloved physician" of Col. 4:14 assists this rich reading of the many-layered significance of the Gospel (Wright 71).

The historical interest of Luke, clearly stated in 1:1–4 and exemplified in his careful (if not completely accurate) dating statements of 2:1–2 and 3:1–2, naturally started to claim greater attention with the advent of modern historical sensibilities. Some conservative scholars have used this historical interest as an argument for Luke's historical accuracy. Scholars who recognize Luke's careful artistry, however, have tended to see the heavy hand of the theological interpreter in Luke's "historiography." Thus, Luke and its companion volume, Acts, have sometimes been taken as evidence for an "early Catholicism" that supposedly departed from the radical gospel of Paul, accommodating itself to the nonappearance of Christ in glory, and putting greater emphasis on the institution of the church and its organic relation to Judaism.

So Luke's "history" could be seen not so much as a sober record of the facts but as a placement of Jesus and the early church within a framework of "salvation history." This was the position of Rudolf Bultmann and Hans Conzelmann. Conzelmann read in Luke the portrayal of a Jesus who stood "in the middle of time" as the fulfillment of Israel's history and the seed of the church's.

More recently, both "conservative" and "liberal" approaches have given way to more nuanced appreciations of Luke's historical, literary, and theological achievements. The contours of "salvation history," which Conzelmann and others saw as Luke's artifice, Oscar Cullmann saw as, in essence, common to the perspective of early Christianity generally and indeed Jesus himself (Marshall 81–83). It is recognized that theological purposes do not necessarily conflict with historical ones: indeed, the "facts" of Jesus are of fundamental importance for theology, according to Luke. But neither does historical purpose necessarily imply complete accuracy according to modern canons. With literary skill (see esp. Tannehill) Luke weaves together the story as he has received it and its meaning as he believes it to be.

The Message of Luke

Luke's "message" is a story, an "orderly account" of events to give its recipients a secure basis for faith (1:1–4). "For Luke, . . . narration is proclamation" (Green, *Theology*, 19).

The core of Luke's narrative is shared with Matthew and Mark, and its basic shape with John. Jesus of Nazareth proclaimed God's kingdom, called and taught disciples, restored the victims of spiritual, physical, and social dysfunction, encountered opposition, was crucified, and rose from death. We will concentrate on Luke's particular emphasis in telling this story.

The Setting: Jewish and World History. After the elegant Hellenistic prologue in 1:1–4, we are transported back into the world of the Jewish

Scriptures. Chapters 1 and 2 recount the births of Jesus and his precursor John in a manner reminiscent of marvelous OT birth stories (e.g., Judg. 13:2–25; 1 Sam. 1:1–2:10; Drury 46–66). Throughout the Gospel scriptural echoes underscore the continuity between Jesus' story and that of Israel, as well as contrasts (Jesus' virgin birth, for instance, is unique; Green, *Theology*, 24–28).

Luke 2:1–3 and 3:1–3 remind us of the contemporary political context in which these boys were born, that of Roman rule over Palestine. The genealogy (3:23–38), in which the "ancestry" of Jesus (via his foster father, Joseph) is traced all the way back not just to Abraham but to Adam, seals this emphasis. Jesus is the heir to human destiny as well as Jewish hopes (cf. 2:32).

The Anointed One. Like the other Evangelists, Luke testifies that Jesus is Israel's Messiah. In common with Matthew and Mark, he records Jesus' extreme reticence to claim this title for himself before his death, but acceptance of it on the lips of Peter (9:20–21) and of the closely related title "Son of God" from the Sanhedrin (22:70). Unique to Luke are the angels' announcement that "Christ the Lord" is born (2:11), the revelation to Simeon that he would not die before he had seen "the Lord's Christ" (2:25–38), and the explanation by the risen Jesus of how he has fulfilled the true destiny of the Messiah (24:25–27, 45–47). Jesus' coming is the occasion for joyous celebration, the first taste of the longed-for messianic feast (2:10; 13:17; 15:1–2, 7, 10; 19:6, 37; 24:41).

The Vocation of a Prophet. For Luke, Jesus' *prophetic* anointing and calling are central to his messiahship (Tuckett 61–62). By contrast, although Gabriel tells Mary that her child will have an everlasting throne (1:33), Luke's portrayal of Jesus as *King* is ironic. The crowds cry, "Blessed is the *king* who comes in the name of the Lord!" (19:38), but Jesus is on a donkey, not a royal charger. Before Pilate, Jesus is accused of claiming "to be Christ, a king" (23:2)—just before he is led out to die.

But there is no irony in the portrayal of Jesus as the prophet par excellence. His link with the prophetic outpourings of the past is emphasized by the "prophecy" of Zechariah before his birth (1:67–79) and his own implicit self-comparison with Elijah and Elisha (4:25–27). His sense of uniqueness is seen in 4:21, where he declares that Isa. 61:1–2 is fulfilled "today" in his own Spirit-inspired proclamation. After his death he is recalled as "a prophet, powerful in word and deed" (24:19; cf. 7:16).

"Powerful in Word." Jesus comes to "declare good news," "proclaim freedom," "proclaim the year of the Lord's favor" (4:18–19). This "word" ministry is evident throughout the Gospel. Jesus' announcements of what God is doing in salvation and judgment are combined with challenges to join in with God's work.

Luke gives us the largest number of Jesus' narrative parables. These sound a subversive note of both hope and warning. God is pictured at work in surprising ways, to vindicate those who cry out to him in their need for justice and mercy, and disturb those who think they are secure (e.g., 18:1–14). Like Second Isaiah, Jesus discerned light where many saw only gloom. He also, like Jeremiah, discerned judgment impending in the place where many pinned their hopes—the holy city and especially the temple (13:34–35; 19:41–44; cf. Jer. 7:1–11).

Jesus' prophetic words not only concern God's activity. They also contain an immediate challenge for radical generosity and forgivingness, going right against the grain of entrenched social positions and attitudes (Green, *Theology*, 16), as especially seen in 14:7–24.

"Powerful in Deed." Jesus comes "to release the oppressed" (4:18). To reassure John's messengers, he performed many cures there and then (7:21). A typical act was release of a crippled woman from her bondage—physical, social, and spiritual (13:10–17).

Jesus acts as Savior (2:11). Here there are overtones of the leadership and protection that God provided and promised to his people in OT times (cf. 1:69–71). But his "salvation" does not come through military prowess. It occurs as the physically weak, socially ostracized, and morally degraded find a new dignity and place in the community through relating to Jesus. "Your faith has saved you," he says to the "sinful woman" who anoints his feet (7:50). In Jesus, "salvation" comes to Abraham's children, even immoral folk like Zacchaeus, resulting in new justice and generosity (19:1–8).

The forgiveness of sins, especially evident in Luke as central to Jesus' ministry (in particular see 7:41–49; 15:1–32), is much more than restoration of inward peace with God, though it is not less than that. It involves the establishment of a new state of fellowship in the community and signals Israel's renewal. It is not "cheap grace" that demands no repentance, but a forgiveness propelled by a new "economy of grace, inspiring repentance" (Barton). This work of Jesus is to continue, as "repentance and forgiveness of sins" are preached to all nations (24:47).

The Way to and of the Cross. Jesus' calling is that of the *lonely* prophet. He meets rejection among his own countryfolk (4:28–30). In 9:51 he "set[s] his face to go to Jerusalem" (KJV)—for, as he wryly remarks, "no prophet can die outside Jerusalem!" (13:33).

There he will, indeed, meet a lonely death, fulfilling his "exodus" (9:31 Greek) and liberating his people. But Jesus' literal "way *to* the cross" is mirrored in "the way *of* the cross," which he calls *the disciples* to travel. Luke's narrative of the journey to Jerusalem (9:51–19:27) includes much teaching on the nature of discipleship. Jesus takes his people *with him* out of bondage to a new promised land. The travels of Paul in Acts, and especially his final journey to Rome (chs. 27–28), recapitulate Jesus' own journeying and suffering, suggesting the oneness of Christian disciples with their Master.

The disciples are presented in a positive light when compared to Mark and Matthew. Luke does not even mention Peter's objection to Jesus' talk of his death and Jesus' rebuke (cf. 9:18–27 with Mark 8:27–38//Matt. 16:13–18, 20–23). To some extent, therefore, disciples in Luke are exemplary figures for the church. They are those who are traveling the way of Jesus. According to Luke, discipleship means giving up "all" in a quite literal sense (5:11, 28; 14:33; 18:22; Tuckett 96–97). Jesus' way is lonely, but there are others who were at least beginning to accompany him, and Luke wants his readers to join in the journey, taking up the cross "daily" (9:23).

Luke's portrayal of Jesus' suffering and death is well summed up by the centurion's comment: "Surely this was a righteous man" (23:47). Luke accents not so much the anguish of the cross as the innocence and compassion of its victim (23:4, 15, 22, 28, 34). In his dying moments Jesus entrusts himself to the one he had always known as "Father" (23:46; cf. 2:49; Ps. 31:5). Like the other Evangelists, Luke is understated concerning the significance of Jesus' death. But he makes clear that it was utterly undeserved. Therein lies Luke's clue to the resurrection and all that would ensue (cf. Acts 3:14–15).

Luke in the Canon

The Biography of Jesus. To Luke we owe the stories of Jesus' birth in a manger and childhood (ch. 2), his meeting with two disciples on the Emmaus road (24:13–35), and his ascension (24:51). The inclusion of these events gives nar-

rative completeness to his Gospel. It also grounds theological conviction about Jesus in the circumstances of his human life. It is true that belief in the incarnation does not depend on the story of the virgin birth, and that belief in the universal rule of Jesus does not depend on the story of the ascension. Yet these stories remain appropriate and enduring symbols of these truths, and are told with a lack of mythological elaboration that suggests they are based on faithful tradition.

Women. The prominent part played by women throughout the story is one of Luke's unique contributions to our vision of Christian discipleship.

Mary, Jesus' mother, is favored with an angelic visit (1:26–38), actively cooperates (1:38), and praises God (1:46–56). Women make an important contribution to the mission of Jesus and the Twelve (8:1–3). Jesus affirms the (normally male) role Mary of Bethany has chosen as a learner (10:42). A story of a woman is often paired with one of a man (e.g., 7:1–10, 11–17; 15:3–7, 8–10; Donahue 135).

Israel and Church: Continuity and Transformation. Luke's portrayal of the Jewish people and their leaders is in some ways more sympathetic than that of the other Gospels. Some Pharisees are friendly to Jesus (13:31), and he eats with them, even though he also castigates them (7:36–50; 11:37–54; 14:1–24). The disciples' worship in the temple is seen as continuous with that of godly Israelites before Jesus appears (1:8–10; 24:53). Jesus is viewed as respectful of traditions, bringing fulfillment and development rather than an overthrow of old ways (Thielman 135–67).

Nevertheless, Jesus' words and acts in Luke subvert any limitation of God's purposes, or God's people, to the Jewish race. Luke does not read back a full-blown "mission to the Gentiles" into Jesus' ministry. But Jesus suggests that a Samaritan might keep the law (10:30–37; cf. 17:15–18) and forbids the disciples to call down punishment on an unwelcoming Samaritan village (9:51–55). He welcomes those on the margins of Jewish society, tainted by their regular contact with Gentiles, in table fellowship (5:27–32; 15:1–2; 19:1–10) and in narrative (e.g., 15:11–32; 16:1–8; 18:9–14).

A Kingdom of Reversals. Luke's Jesus proclaims "the good news of the kingdom of God" (4:43). Luke, with his accounts of the "acts of Jesus" in both his earthly ministry and his Spirit-filled church, has been seen as toning down the austere apocalyptic expectation evident in Mark. He points to the reality of the kingdom in the present and supposedly makes its future consummation a far-distant event (Conzelmann 101–25; critiqued in Marshall 130–31).

But the difference is simply one of degree. Luke indeed has the saying "the kingdom of God is within you" (or "among you," 17:21 NRSV). But he also has apocalyptic passages (17:22–37; 21:5–38), and as in Matthew and Mark, these have a clear first focus in the disaster that Jesus foresees coming on Jerusalem. Probably Luke's readers, unlike Mark's, would know that this prophecy had been fulfilled—so Luke could place more emphasis on the present evidence of the kingdom, in both judgment and grace. But the kingdom, Luke knew, had not yet come in final fullness (21:9), and in his own day he would have been well aware of the persecutions and temptations that signaled the urgency of the times (12:35–59).

So the distinctive Lukan insights concerning the kingdom of God lie not so much in the issue of the kingdom's *timing*. Rather, Luke particularly stresses the *reversals* entailed in the establishment of the kingdom (1:52–53).

Jesus' blessings and woes (6:20–26) starkly express these reversals: the kingdom belongs to the poor, while the rich have received their comfort. A new perspective on the present is offered in light of certain justice in the future. The parables of 12:16–21 and 16:19–31 warn that reversal may not be far off. Death itself is the first great leveler, and it may strike suddenly.

The kingdom's presence can leave none complacent. Prostitute and Pharisee alike need forgiveness (7:36–50). Yet if that presence is realized, repentance and reconciliation are possible. The rich man's brothers may obey the law, reach out to the poor at their gates, and stay with them on the right side of the great gulf (16:27–31).

Luke and Paul. The relationship between the theologies of Luke and Paul has been much debated. Undoubtedly the two have distinct perspectives. But we may note a fundamental connection.

Luke's emphasis on Jesus' welcome for those whom Israel's moral policemen pushed to the margins is, in Rom. 15:7, linked with Paul's exhortation, on the basis of the grace given to Jew and Gentile alike: "Welcome one another . . . as Christ has welcomed you" (NRSV). The "New Perspective on Paul," by highlighting the social context and implications of Paul's doctrine of justification by faith, has shown that Paul is much closer to the thrust of the Gospels, and especially Luke, than has often been thought.

Luke and Theology

Narrative, History, and Theology. As an early "narrative theologian," Luke raised to new sophistication a genre with which Mark (and maybe Matthew) had already experimented. He does his "theology" through the story he tells of Jesus, carefully linked with that of Israel and the church (Green, *Theology*, 21). The fact that this narrative approach preceded the theological systematizing of later generations should not be lost on us.

Luke's skillful storytelling is not mere spinning of yarns to edify or entertain. His story centers on historical events. It is based on tradition from eyewitnesses and his own careful investigation (1:2–3). More than any other biblical book, Luke reminds us that theology not anchored in history is sub-Christian and docetic.

Supremely among the Evangelists, Luke shows us that Jesus' own "theologizing" was done largely in story. Unlike the Gospel itself, his parables do not depend for their force on any claim to represent actual events. But though they are often surprising and shocking, they depict realistic scenes from the world of Jesus' hearers, inviting them to reconfigure that world in mind and behavior (Wright 182–226). In fictional microcosm they have a similar purpose to Luke's historiographical macrocosm: to enable people to recognize God's activity in the world, and then fall in step with it.

The Plan of God. Luke's concern for the continuity of the story of Jesus and the church with that of Israel warns us to avoid preaching an individualistic gospel of "Jesus and me." Luke summons us to point to the great tradition into which disciples enter. By the grace of God, anyone may become part of his universal purpose, revealed and accomplished through Christ.

While this forbids the marginalization of the OT and/or the Jewish people in Christian theology, it equally forbids interpretations of the OT that regard its prophecies as fulfilled in present-day developments in Israel or elsewhere. With John the Baptist, "the Law and the Prophets" came to an end (cf. 16:16). What was glimpsed in the ministry of Jesus was to be made plain after the resurrection: God's gospel was for "all nations" (24:47).

The immediate prospect for Jerusalem was terrible punishment (21:20–24). The Gentile aggressors would have their "times . . . fulfilled" (21:24)—God would punish them also, as he had promised to punish Israel's aggressors in OT times—but the center of gravity of his plan was shifting. Jerusalem would be the starting point of the disciples' mission (24:47, 52–53). Nevertheless, from now on God's plan would be centered not on a land, a city, a temple, and a nation, but on a message going everywhere, in the name of Christ, through a new multinational people empowered from on high—and all this as "it is written" (24:45–49 NRSV).

Luke does not allow us to underplay the uniqueness of Christ, his pivotal role in God's plan, or the fact that he and all he set in train are the true fulfillment of the OT.

The Scope of the Gospel: The Whole Person and the Whole of Society. Luke does not merely state the universal thrust of the gospel in general terms. He grounds it in vivid portrayals of humans. He demonstrates in narrative that the gospel is for all kinds of people, in the longings, needs, and opportunities of their physical everyday lives, not merely for their "souls" or "spirits." This is especially symbolized by Jesus' coming to people in their homes (7:36; 10:38; 14:1; 19:5–6; 24:29).

So good news comes to an aged couple still bearing the stigma of childlessness (1:5–25), to a fisherman after a fruitless night's fishing (5:4–6), to a bereaved mother (7:11–17), to a harassed cook (10:38–42), to a dying terrorist (23:40–43). But in addressing people where they are, the gospel lifts them far beyond the situation that preoccupies them. Above all, this is seen on the Emmaus road, where far from being merely comforted in their loss, Cleopas and his friend are fired with a new sense of the meaning of the Scriptures and of the one they thought they had lost (24:32).

Moreover, the gospel is for humans *in relationship with each other*. The vision communicated by Jesus in parable, miracle, and table fellowship is not merely of new persons, but of a new society.

Luke's good news remains oriented to the future and offers no easy promises about the certainty of societal transformation in the present (16:19–31). Testing times are to come; ultimate "redemption" is not yet (21:5–36). But the gospel refuses to let the signs of the kingdom be indefinitely postponed. *"Today* this Scripture is fulfilled in your hearing" (4:21). *"Today* salvation has come to this house" (19:9). For Christian theology that seeks to articulate sensitively a gospel of future hope and present opportunity, Luke must surely be the primary resource.

Bibliography

Barton, S. "Parables on God's Love and Forgiveness." Pages 199–216 in *The Challenge of Jesus's Parables*, ed. R. Longenecker. Eerdmans, 2000; Conzelmann, H. *The Theology of St Luke*. Faber & Faber, 1960; Craddock, F. *Luke*. Interpretation. John Knox, 1990; Donahue, J. *The Gospel in Parable*. Fortress, 1988; Drury, J. *Tradition and Design in Luke's Gospel*. Darton, Longman & Todd, 1976; Evans, C., and J. Sanders. *Luke and Scripture*. Fortress, 1993; Green, J. *The Gospel of Luke*. Eerdmans, 1997; idem. *The Theology of the Gospel of Luke*. NTT. Cambridge University Press, 1995; Johnson, L. T. *The Literary Function of Possessions in Luke-Acts*. SBLDS 39. Scholars Press, 1977; Marshall, I. H. *Luke: Historian and Theologian*. Paternoster, 1970; Squires, J. *The Plan of God in Luke-Acts*. SNTSMS 76. Cambridge University Press, 1993; Tannehill, R. *The Narrative Unity of Luke-Acts*. 2 vols. Fortress, 1986; Thielman, F. *The Law and the New Testament*. Herder & Herder, 1999; Tuckett, C. *Luke*. NTG. Sheffield Academic Press, 1996; Wright, S. *The Voice of Jesus*. Paternoster, 2000.

Stephen I. Wright

Luther, Martin

Born, on his mother's side, into the pious Lindemann family, Martin Luther was baptized on November 11, 1483, the day after his birth. He grew up in a world where the words of the Bible were heard often: through preaching and the liturgy, through the psalmody and biblical verses one learned in school, and so on. Later, as an Augustinian friar in the Black Cloister in Erfurt, he listened as the Scriptures were read corporately many times each day, and he diligently studied the red-leather Bible he had received as a novice for personal study and reflection. Ordained a priest in 1507, he began expositing the Scriptures regularly as a preacher. At the insistence of his superior, Johannes von Staupitz, he then undertook academic preparations for a career as professor of Bible. He earned the so-called *baccalaureus biblicus* ("bachelor of Bible" degree) in 1509, after two years of lecturing on assigned biblical texts. In 1512, he was awarded the doctor's cap and ring and installed as professor of Bible in the frontier town of Wittenberg. He began his teaching career with a course on the Psalms (*Dictata super Psalterium*, 1513–15), and lectured on the OT for all but three or four of his thirty-two years in the classroom, including ten years on Genesis (1535–45). More often, however, he preached on the NT. As an old man, he could boast that if the Bible was a forest, then he had shaken every tree in the search for edifying fruit.

Rehearsing the history of Luther's engagement with the Bible suggests continuity. Most fundamentally, he always encountered the text as a baptized Christian. Charged with responsibility for preaching on a regular basis (usually several times each week), biblical exegesis remained for him a spiritual exercise performed in service to God and the church, a task for which one was fitted by the Holy Spirit and by living faith, given in baptism. His career as an expositor, on the other hand, suggests movement. First, he is the celibate young friar preparing biblical lectures in rhythm with the religious life of the cloister. Later, he is the married *Hausvater* leaving home early in the morning to meet a group of eager students, teaching them the Bible, and exhorting them to lives of heroic faithfulness through service in the emerging Protestant ministry. Within this changing and sometimes chaotic context, his classroom exposition slowly evolved from monastic meditation on the "sacred page" (*sacra pagina*)—in which prayer and exegesis were inseparable—toward something more akin to modern university lectures.

Asked how to pray, Luther showed his indebtedness to the *sacra pagina*, instinctively directing his questioner to the Bible. Prayer is human address to God, centered in the Spirit-inspired application of all one's powers to the biblical text, searching for authentic spiritual illumination. This illumination is inevitably followed, however, by testing, the trials faced by the struggling Christian. These trials drive one back to prayer, back to the text, and so on, in a lifelong cycle of prayer, meditation, and temptation (*oratio, meditatio, tentatio*). As the Holy Spirit works in unfailing agreement with Christ, the Word of God, so spiritual experience is tethered to the word in Holy Scripture. The consistent linkage between prayer and Scripture is one of the important links between Luther's biblical interpretation and the patristic traditions of "spiritual exegesis."

Nevertheless, Luther also insisted that interpretation centers on the plain meaning of the text (*sensus literalis*). Understanding requires attention to biblical languages and to history, a conviction he shared with other early modern biblical humanists. Indeed, working with the Wittenberg translation team, what he called his "Sanhedrin," he translated the entire Bible from Greek and Hebrew into German, a process that necessitated careful attention to grammar and history in order to discern the sense of the text. However, translation, and with it interpretation, is a distinctively Christian task, a work of the Spirit and of the mind shaped by Christian truth. Grammatical and historical knowledge alone are insufficient. Translation and interpretation depend on understanding not only the words of Scripture (*verba*) but also the substance (*res scripturae sacrae*). The

reader dare not bracket out Christian beliefs when grappling with a difficult text, either for translation or for interpretation.

Luther often spoke negatively of allegorical interpretation, but his own exegesis remained strikingly sensitive to allegorical and tropological resonances in Scripture, particularly those that could be applied to Christ and faith. The *sensus literalis* is Christ, for the Scriptures are the "swaddling cloths" in which the Christ-child is laid. Interpretation is christocentric because the text unfailingly witnesses to the redemption accomplished by Christ. The exegete searches out the interpretation that emphatically urges Christ the Savior (*was Christum treibet*). Theological exegesis means interpretation in harmony with the loving purposes of the triune God, revealed in the Son's assumption of our humanity, his passion, and resurrection. "Therefore, if the adversaries press the Scriptures against Christ, we urge Christ against the Scriptures" (*LWorks* 34:112). Luther is not speaking hyperbolically. Nor is christocentric interpretation based on the imposition of a presupposition somehow external to the text. To the contrary, it is founded on who God is and on the Christian's experience of God in faith. In its central witness to Christ, moreover, the Bible is clear, and it authenticates its message without dependence on external human authority.

As a reader of the biblical narratives, Luther was remarkably observant and inventive, generously applying a kind of sanctified common sense when attempting to understand the behavior of the characters in biblical stories. He relied extensively on the remarkably thorough exegetical helps developed by his predecessors, particularly the patristic and medieval commentary tradition. Luther felt a deep kinship not only with biblical heroes and heroines, but also with the living tradition of Christian believers who were their faithful followers, the commentators. Together, these saints witnessed to Christ not only by means of their doctrine, but also in their very lives as God shaped them in living faith. One comes to truly understand their stories just as the church fathers did, through prayer, study, and the experience of judgment and grace (law and gospel). Faith, Scripture, and the authentic Christian experience reflected both in the Bible and in the church's exegetical traditions thus illumine one another. This happens in the interplay between the struggle for faith on the part of the living, and the witness of the faithful dead extending in unbroken succession from Adam and Eve down to the present day.

Bibliography

Luther's Works, ed. J. Pelikan and H. Lehmann. American Edition. 55 vols. Concordia/Fortress, 1955–; Bornkamm, H. *Luther and the Old Testament,* trans. E. W. and R. C. Gritsch, ed. V. I. Gruhn. Fortress, 1969; Ebeling, G. *Evangelische Evangelienauslegung.* Chr. Kaiser, 1942. 3d ed. Mohr/Siebeck, 1991; Hagen, K. *Luther's Approach to Scripture as Seen in His "Commentaries" on Galatians, 1519–1538.* Mohr/Siebeck, 1993; Kooiman, W. J. *Luther and the Bible,* trans. J. Schmidt. Muhlenberg, 1961; Mattox, M. *"Defender of the Most Holy Matriarchs."* Brill, 2003; Pelikan, J. *Luther the Expositor.* Concordia, 1959; Preus, J. S. *From Shadow to Promise.* Belknap/Harvard University Press, 1969; Steinmetz, D. *Luther in Context.* 2d ed. Baker, 2002; Wood, A. S. *Captive to the Word.* Paternoster, 1969.

Mickey L. Mattox

LXX   *See* Relationship between the Testaments; Translation

M

Magisterium *See* Catholic Biblical Interpretation

Malachi, Book of

The superscription (1:1) of the book identifies it as an oracle or *massa'* attributed to *mal'aki*, "my messenger/angel." The apparent simplicity of these assertions conceals the debates about the nature of the book and the identity of the one typically called Malachi. It also anticipates issues about the status and place of the book in the prophetic corpus and OT canon. In the Hebrew version, it is the last of the Book of the Twelve or Minor Prophets as well as the final book of Nevi'im, the "Prophets," the second section of the Hebrew Bible. It thus directly precedes the book of Psalms in the Ketubim, "Writings," the third section of the Hebrew Bible. In most English versions, it appears as the last book of the prophetic literature and of the OT, directly preceding the NT (some have the Apocrypha between OT and NT). Most often, the prophetic activity is dated to the fifth-century-BCE context of the Persian period.

History of Interpretation

While there are several notable issues in its interpretive history, the recurrent issues are the structure of the book and the identification of its genre that defines its organization; the function and place of 4:3–6 (3:21–24 MT); and the independent status of the book. These issues build on those of the church fathers. In particular, Tertullian (*Marc.* 4.8.1) observed the placement of the book as a representation of a transition from old to new covenant. Origen (*Comm. Jo.* 2:17; 6:13) saw Mal. 4:2–6 (3:20–24 MT) as the foreshadowing of John the Baptist and Jesus Christ (cf. Hill).

Internal Structure and Genre. The first decades of the twentieth century responded to the nineteenth-century classification of Malachi as prose (Torrey), with some affirming this classification (Smith) and others seeing it as largely poetic (Nowack). Most today affirm the prosaic

nature of the book and the presence of question-answer schema as a characteristic feature. Thus, the characteristic format consists of (1) an assertion (e.g., 1:2a), and (2) a schema formed by a question (e.g., 1:2b) and an answer/response (e.g., 1:2c–5). Pfeiffer introduced this interpretative trend when he categorized the book as prophetic disputation and thus demonstrated his perspective that the book is constituted by one genre. Accordingly, he identifies the macrounits—1:2–5; 1:6–2:9; 2:10–16; 2:17–3:5; 3:6–12; 3:13–4:3 (3:13–21 MT), further noting that 4:4–6 (3:22–24 MT) is generically different from the rest. Inasmuch as its literary form is other than the prophetic disputation and its content is new, 4:4–6 is further classified as an additional rather than an integral part of the book.

While Petersen follows Pfeiffer's lead in asserting a common generic form, he denies that a tripartite structure forms the basic six units. First and foremost, he identifies the book as one of three oracles in the Zechariah–Malachi section of the Book of the Twelve (Zech. 9–11; 12–14). He proposes that the macrounits represent dialogues further identified as "diatribe-like discourses" comparable to Hellenistic diatribe. Petersen further identifies 4:4–6 (3:22–24 MT) as an epilogue that together with Hos. 14:9 (v. 10 MT) is an element of demarcation and a link between the Book of the Twelve and the rest of the Hebrew Bible canon (cf. Hill).

Like Pfeiffer, O'Brien tried to identify common macrounits that exhibit the same generic features and are reflective of the genre. On the other hand, she differs from Pfeiffer in the macrounits and in categorizing the genre of these units and the book as covenant lawsuit with its distinctive parts. She names prologue (1:1–5), accusations (1:6–2:9; 2:17–3:5; 3:6–12; 3:13–4:3 [3:13–21 MT]), admonition (4:4 [3:22 MT]), and an ultimatum (4:5–6 [3:23–24 MT]).

Lescow observes that the form and function of the text are products of the redaction process that transformed the original Torah speeches for didactic and homiletic purposes (e.g., 1:6–2:9).

He takes the question-answer schema as an interchange between the prophet and the one(s) inquiring about a teaching. As to 4:4–6 (3:22–24 MT), he sees it as an appendix or conclusion of the prophetic corpus.

Floyd differentiates between stylistic and generic uniformity, further recognizing the various functions of generically similar units (e.g., 1:10b–14; 2:8–12). He challenges Pfeiffer and others and identifies two macrounits, a superscription (1:1) and the main body, categorized as *massa'* (oracle, 1:1, referring to 1:2–4:6 [3:24 MT]), which further consists of an introduction/prophetic disputation (1:2–5) and exhortation (1:6–4:6). As to the microunits, Floyd notes two units: the first looks at the "cultic corruption," addressing both the priests and the people (1:6–2:16); the second, showing the change from corrupt practices, is addressed to the people (2:17–4:6 [3:24 MT]).

Canonical Place. The first perspective is Malachi's interdependence on Zechariah, evidenced by the presence of the term *massa'* (oracle) in both Malachi (1:1) and Zechariah (9:1a; 12:1; e.g., Petersen; Mason). The second perspective is that Malachi's interdependence includes both Haggai and Zechariah—the latter corpus unified by its representation of the restoration community (e.g., Pierce; Lescow; Hill). With these two perspectives, the place of the book is also represented by the function of 4:4–6 as the conclusion of the Book of the Twelve and the Nevi'im—the prophetic corpus. In a third perspective, Floyd asserts the independent status of Malachi with 4:4–6 seen as an integral part of the microunit 2:17–4:6. It is best to read them as a unit and also as an example of God's interaction with the covenant community to address its concerns about God's love and what that entails for its practices.

Content and Theological Concerns

The fundamental message is God's love for Israel and Israel's response to that love. The book affirms that Israel's practices reflect its love for God. Through the question-and-answer schema, it challenges Israel to understand this and live accordingly. Consequently, the book encompasses several concerns, with multiple dimensions.

Malachi looks at various themes addressed elsewhere in the OT and in doing so suggests that there is an ongoing need to clarify God's requirement for the covenant community. It affirms that being the people of God carries responsibilities that encompass both correct understanding of God's requirements and aligning one's life with them. In particular, it holds the priests accountable for failure to uphold the covenant. Some of the concerns of Psalms and Proverbs concerning God's regard for the wicked (e.g., Pss. 37; 73; Prov. 10) and God's silence in the face of suffering reverberate through Malachi (cf. Ps. 37). These recurring themes signal the perpetual nature of the struggle to make sense of life in the midst of faith in God and the human responsibility to obey God.

God's Love. Israel's understanding of God's love was challenged by the experience of judgment. God's declaration of love for Israel addresses Israel's challenge for proof of that love in light of the turmoil that the restoration community suffered. Consequently, God highlighted love for Israel by contrasting two persons (Jacob, Esau) and the nations that ensued from them (Israel, Edom). The text echoes the Gen. 25:19–26 account of Jacob and Esau, where the choice between the brothers is noted without the stated criteria for the selection of who will serve whom. On the one hand, God loves (*'ahab*) Jacob/Israel and hates (*sane'*) Esau/Edom. God behaves consistently as seen in his covenant with Israel and preservation of Israel as compared to his resolution to destroy Edom and ensure its perpetual demise (1:2–5).

Tithe and Offering. The matter of the tithe and the offerings (*hamma'aser wehatterumah*) addresses the apparent misfortunes of the community (3:8). As a corrective, the people are admonished to stop robbing (*qaba'*) God by giving God the entire tithe (*ma'aser*; cf. Gen. 14:20; 28:18–22; Lev. 27:30–32; Num. 18:21–32; Deut. 14:22–29; Neh. 13:10–12). Several kinds of tithes are indicated: The general tithes of the produce of the land and livestock are designated for the Levites (Lev. 27:30–32; Num. 18:21). The tithe of the produce is annual and seasonal (Deut. 14:22–27). The third-year tithe is designated for the underprivileged (Deut. 14:28–29; cf. Hill; Petersen). Like Mal. 3:10, so also Num. 18:21–32 refers to the entire tithe (cf. Deut. 14:28) and stipulates that it be used to sustain the Levites, who are further required to present to God an offering (*terumah*) of the tithe that they receive. The pairing of the tithes and the offerings (*hamma'aser wehatterumah*) contributes to distinguishing the two (cf. Deut. 12:6, 11; 2 Chron. 31:12). Thus, Hill asserts that the offering (*terumah*) is a gift; others see the offering as a tithe of the tithe (*ma'aser*) or a tithe tax (Num. 18:26; Neh. 10:38; cf. Petersen; Glazier-McDonald).

Divorce. Malachi 2:16 declares that God hates (*sane'*) divorce but does not explain why. It has been interpreted as figurative language representative of the unfaithfulness in the covenant relationship. Some who render a literal interpretation concede that the intermarriage and divorce are the result of the priests' misteachings (cf. Hill). Others note various social and religious consequences of divorce as the reason for God's response. Among the reasons is the apostasy resulting from intermarriage with the foreign women (Ezra 9–10; Neh. 13).

In these cases, the prohibition against Israel's intermarriage with the daughters of other nations is a preventative measure against breaking the covenant with God (cf. Exod. 34:15–16; Deut. 7:3–4). When seen in the intertextual framework of the OT, Mal. 2:16 challenges the Deut. 24:1–4 representation of divorce as a recognized practice within the community (cf. Deut. 22:13–19, 28–29). Within the context of Mal. 2, God's response seems to be generated by the same force that underlies God's displeasure with other practices in the community (e.g., the sacrifices, tithing). In each of these instances, there is a greater ramification of the behavior than a misconstrued teaching. Rather, the practices are as much a detriment to the community as they are offensive to God.

Priests and Sacrifices. The priests are addressed as those who know torah and thus are able to discern and render sound teachings. Even so, they are also presented as deviating from God's requirement (e.g., 2:6–9). For example, God requires sacrifices that meet a specified standard (cf. animal sacrifice, Lev. 22:18–25; firstborn sacrifice, Deut. 15:19–23). Malachi 1:8 represents the unacceptable nature of the sacrifice as including blind, lame, blemished animals (cf. Deut. 15:21), which the priests were offering to God. They are challenged to keep the covenant by honoring God. The contrast is between their concern to please their rulers and the lack of regard for their Deity. Furthermore, their actions depict a disruption of a normative behavior within a relationship; as such, their utter disrespect for the Deity is highlighted.

God's Justice. Fundamentally, the issues in 2:17–3:5 are retribution and theodicy. Why do evildoers prosper? Why does God tolerate evil rather than punish it? While the lament attests to inquiries about God's justice (*mishpat*) and lack of response (cf. Pss. 13:1–3; 22:1; 74:1), there is also intertextual support for the belief in God's justice and response (Isa. 30:18–20). The book of Malachi challenges the character of God to respond in judgment to the evil (*ra'*; 2:17). In calling into question whether or not God is just, the community may have questioned (sarcastically

or genuinely) whether God regards evil (*ra'*) as good (*tob*). This attitude culminates in the perception of God's silence as a lack of judgment, as an overall lack of concern about the practices in the community, and as endorsement of evil (cf. Hab. 1:2–3, 12–13).

Hermeneutical Challenges

The challenges raised here concern the declarations or perspectives within the text that lead to multivalent positions within contemporary settings. These challenges are represented as questions meriting further consideration and reflecting the need to trust God in the midst of life's complexities, without the error of trying to control God or reduce God to ways of being that only conform to one's expectations.

God's Love. God's love and hate represent God's choice and capacity for both. In Mal. 1:2–5 God's hate is a mechanism for demonstrating the particularities of love for Israel. If nothing else, the hermeneutical challenge is to recognize that just as Israel had no choice in being chosen as the object of God's love, so Edom had no choice in being the object of God's hate (cf. Rom. 9:11–14). The quandary is that God's ways in choosing whom to love and hate are complex at best. Having God's love does not exclude one from punishment but is the reason for God's particular response to the covenant community, either to defer or to expedite punishment, and in some cases to use punishment as a form of discipline. Thus, Malachi reminds Israel that God's discipline is a manifestation of love (cf. Deut. 8:5; Pss. 38:2; 94:12; Jer. 31:18; Heb. 12:6, 10). On the other hand, not every form of suffering is either punishment for sin or discipline. Most take for granted that God spoke a word of confirmation to Israel about God's love. However, that God loves the world will remain a paradox for those who continue to experience suffering without such a verifiable confirmation that they are favored by God, that they are not rejected by God and thus experience God's hate. They wonder if God is concerned about their suffering and will rescue them because of the universality of God's love and concern for all.

Tithing and Blessing. Two aspects of the tithe are noteworthy. First, the purpose of the tithe is variously represented in the OT. The tithe was used to maintain the temple and its personnel and to provide for the underprivileged of the community. Do the designated purposes in the OT obligate the same purposes in the modern settings?

Second, the relationship of the tithe to blessings and curses is a complex matter. While the text suggests that there is a relationship, the danger of asserting the numerical quantity and the assurance of that relationship must be met by a caveat. Prosperity is not necessarily a sign of righteous living since evildoers are sometimes prosperous while the righteous endure adversity. Is the relationship between tithing and blessings extended to everyone who tithes? Is there a quantitative requirement that ensures the receipt of positive returns? Are all required to give regardless of their economic resources and obligations? The challenge that the modern reader must face is that everyone addressed in the text should tithe. This is not a prescription for becoming wealthy by obligating God. Even with the observation that God responds to obedience and tithing in particular, the larger significance of this is that God is in control of the resources. That control entails that God may or may not respond according to a mathematical calculation. Fundamentally, the tithe is a response to God's love and not a way of winning that love.

Divorce. Within the OT, divorce is presented as a normative practice, used to address various marital circumstances, including the dissatisfaction of a husband with his wife (Deut. 24:1–4; cf. 22:13–19, 28–29), or a solution to intermarriage (cf. Ezra 9–10; Neh. 13:23–31). Does God hate all divorces? If so, does God hate them equally, regardless of the reasons for divorce? The OT context indicates that some divorces are sanctioned (Deut. 24:1–4) but that in other cases it is not an option (22:29). If the resulting circumstances are the reasons for God's hatred of divorce, would God's response differ based on different resulting circumstances? Whether or not one can justify or condemn modern divorces on the basis of this multivalent perspective, the inescapable consequences of divorce remain. God responds to divorces because they bear evil consequences for the community and reflect violation of commitments. The OT context also sanctions remarriage after divorce but regulates who may enter marriage with a divorced woman without viewing it as adultery (cf. Lev. 21:7, 14; Deut. 24:3–4; Ezek. 44:22 vis-à-vis Matt. 5:32; Luke 16:18).

Bibliography

Bosshard, E., and R. Kratz. "Maleachi im Zwölfprophetenbuch." *BN* 52 (1990): 27–46; Dumbrell, W. "Malachi and the Ezra-Nehemiah Reforms." *RTR* 35 (1976): 42–52; Floyd, M. *Minor Prophets, Part 2.* FOTL 22. Eerdmans, 2000; Glazier-McDonald, B. *Malachi.* SBLDS 98. Scholars Press, 1987; Hill, A. *Malachi.* AB 25D. Doubleday, 1998; Hugenberger, G. *Marriage as Covenant.* VTSup 52. Brill, 1994; Lescow, T. *Das Buch Maleachi.* Calwer, 1993; Mason, R. *The Books of Haggai, Zechariah, and Malachi.* CBC. Cambridge University Press, 1977; Nowack, W. *Die kleinen Propheten.* Vandenhoeck & Ruprecht, 1922; O'Brien, J. *Priest and Levite in Malachi.* SBLDS 121. Scholars Press, 1990; Petersen, D. *Zechariah 9–14 and Malachi.* OTL. Westminster John Knox, 1995; Pfeiffer, E. "Die Disputationsworte im Buche Maleachi." *EvT* 19 (1959): 546–68; Pierce, R. "Literary Connectors and a Haggai-Zechariah-Malachi Corpus." *JETS* 27 (1984): 277–89; Smith, J. M. P. *A Critical and Exegetical Commentary on Haggai, Zechariah, Malachi and Jonah.* ICC. T&T Clark, 1912; Snyman, S. "Antitheses in Malachi 1,2–5." *ZAW* 98 (1986): 436–38; Torrey, C. C. "The Prophecy of Malachi." *JBL* 17 (1898): 1–15; Verhoef, P. *Haggai and Malachi.* NICOT. Eerdmans, 1987; Wendland, E. "Linear and Concentric Patterns in Malachi." *BT* 36 (1985): 108–21.

Mignon R. Jacobs

Male *See* Male and Female

Male and Female

All humanity is embodied as either male or female. All individuals view the world from the perspective of either male or female. One cannot obtain a neutral or androgynous position outside of one's sex. Our identity as male and female stretches beyond our biological identification as beings of one sex or the other, for it is from within our position as persons of a particular sex that we encounter and live in the world around us. Christians have a certain way of understanding the nature of being male or female and the relationship of male and female to each other and to God. This understanding rests on our interpretation of the biblical text, the theology that informs our reading of the text, our experience, and our interaction with science.

The interaction between biblical interpretation and theology is crucial for understanding the topic of male and female. Many biblical scholars and theologians have assumed that collating a catalog of the biblical texts about male and female, men and women, husbands and wives would provide a sufficient understanding of the topic. The introduction of social background to the interpretative mix has been a significant step in showing that our understanding of male and female is deeply embedded in our knowledge of culture and the manner in which it shapes us (Keener). Recognizing that the Bible is a theological book that demands a theological reading is an additional significant directive, for it reminds us that our readings are always particularly situated not only in respect to gender but also in respect to interpretation (Fowl). The theological stance that we take toward the nature of God and the biblical text significantly influences our understanding of male and female in the Bible and its relevance for contemporary discussion (Volf).

Male and Female in the Biblical Texts

The opening chapters of the Bible introduce humanity as male and female, drawing our attention to their relationship to each other and to God. The first creation account ends with the making of humanity in God's own image and instructions given in the plural to the human creation to be fruitful, to multiply, and to have dominion (Gen. 1:26–28). This opening scene portrays the human creature as created in a partnership of male and female, and made to be corulers of the world God created. The second creation account (Gen. 2) and the fall (ch. 3) have been read in multiple ways. Some have seen the creation of Eve after Adam as an indication of her inferior status, while others have seen her designation as "helper" as indicating her subordinate role in relationship to the male (Piper and Grudem). Neither the order of creation nor the designation as "helper" (used elsewhere in the biblical text to refer to God) must necessarily indicate a subordinate status for the female (Jewett). In addition, the argument that the fall and the curses that result from it in Gen. 3 are normative for understanding the relationship between the sexes pays little attention to the theological trajectory of redemption and restoration in the biblical text. In the NT vision Jesus bases the marriage union on the creation of humanity as male and female (Matt. 19:4–5), and Paul declares in Gal. 3:28 that there is no longer "male and female" in the body of Christ (NRSV). This affirms the first portrayal of male and female in the Genesis text. Throughout the canon, men and women are portrayed in partnership with each other and with God. Male and female go into the ark (Gen. 7). The patriarchs and their wives journey and participate in the promise for the future of Israel. The whole nation of Israel is called to be a priestly nation (Exod. 19). Men and women serve God as prophets (Judg. 4; 2 Kings 22; Acts 21; 1 Cor. 11). Men and women follow Jesus (Luke 8) and serve his church (Acts 18; Rom. 16).

Difficult Texts in the Canon. While the biblical text contains a trajectory that understands humanity as male and female corulers who participate equally in the purposes of God, this vision is sometimes obscured by difficult texts in the canon. A good portion of our contemporary difficulty is related to the patriarchal nature of the ancient culture to which Scripture was originally addressed. In a good many places the ancient culture is not called into question. So, for example, in much of the OT women are described in ways that make it clear they are legally subject to either fathers or husbands, and they are excluded from serving God as priests. In the NT, various texts enjoin women to submit to their husbands (Eph. 5; Col. 3), to be silent in the church (1 Cor. 14), and not to teach or exercise authority (1 Tim. 2). All these texts have been the subject of intense study and debate over the last century. This debate has often been focused around the normativity of the texts under discussion. Are these instructions for one time period and culture, or the norm for all cultures and times? These debates over specific texts are almost impossible to resolve solely on the basis of linguistics, genre, sociocultural criticism, or historical analysis. The tension between the trajectory of Scripture outlined above and these difficult passages is also one not easily resolved by recourse to specific interpretative techniques. Ultimately, both debates demand theological reading and response such as those that have been recently offered by Volf and Grenz.

Male and Female: Marriage, Metaphor, and Singleness. The partnership of male and female in marriage is rooted in the creation accounts. Genesis 1 declares the creation of humanity as male and female, and Gen. 2 gives an etiology for marriage. Male and female, men and women, husbands and wives—such language occurs not only in relationship to the literal partnership of male and female in marriage, but also in metaphorical language used to speak of God and his relationship to Israel in the OT and the church in the NT. The OT prophets portray Israel as a woman who is engaged to her bridegroom (Jer. 2:2) and delights God (Isa. 62:5), but the metaphor then develops to include the unfaithfulness of Israel to her covenant relationship (Jer. 3:8). This unfaithfulness is often portrayed as adultery—the breaking of the marriage covenant. God's faithfulness does not depend on Israel's faithfulness, and from his faithfulness comes the possibility of restoration in the relationship. In the NT, the church is portrayed as the bride of Christ (Rev. 21:2), and the union of Christ with his church is the image of ultimate service, love, joy, and unity. Grenz suggests that these metaphorical uses of the marriage relationship in the biblical text can point to one function of male and female partnership in marriage, the portrayal of the union of Christ and the church (63–65).

It is important to recognize that the marriage relationship can be only a limited portrayal of the spiritual reality of Christ's union with the church. In addition, this begs the question: What portrayal of Christ's work is seen in those who remain unmarried? Although there are hardly any portrayals of unmarried people in the OT, singleness is portrayed in the NT as a state that can be good when used for the sake of the kingdom of God (e.g., 1 Cor. 7). While the unmarried state is affirmed in the NT, it is not used metaphorically as part of the description of God and his covenant. However, Grenz argues that singleness resulting in the inclusion of others from a wide circle can be a metaphorical reenactment of God's inclusive calling of the whole world.

Male and Female in the Practice of Theological Interpretation

In the last two centuries, suffragists and feminists have raised anew for us issues related to sex, gender, and gender roles. While feminists have generally focused on issues related to women, their critiques raise significant issues for men as well (Mills). As Jewett writes, "The 'woman question' implies a 'man question.' The one cannot be discussed without the other" (149). It is difficult to answer this question if one of the members, either male or female, insists that their role in the male and female partnership is biblically self-evident. Those who hold that their position or role is self-evident claim the power to define the relationship. It is this very acquisition of power that is critiqued by feminists. This work shows that the prevailing definition of "maleness" as the powerful, patriarchal norm and "femaleness" as the subordinate derivative of that norm can no longer be accepted as the unquestioned standard for defining male and female.

Often biblical scholars and theologians begin their examination of male and female with biblical texts that specifically concern male and female and then proceed to a theological explanation. Volf begins differently by asking how the nature of God should inform the relationships between men and women. He then goes on to show that the generally agreed-upon claim that God is neither male nor female can lead us to the understanding that all of the duties and prerogatives that come from God are not for one gender or the other but for both (173). He follows this with an explanation of the doctrine of the Trinity, carefully retaining both the distinct but equal identities of Father, Son, and Holy Spirit as well as their existence in constant, self-giving relationship to each other

(180). This allows Volf to put forward a model of distinct but equal identity for the genders that is demonstrated and only understood in relationship to the other. "To be a woman means to be a human being of the female sex who is 'not without the man'; to be a man means to be a human being of the male sex who is 'not without woman'" (187). Volf argues that this should lead us to an egalitarian position not based in opposition to, or dominance of, the other sex. Volf's approach recognizes the embodied and subjective nature of our identity as male and female while allowing our understanding of male and female to rest squarely on our knowledge of God's nature.

Other theologians who have explored the relationship between male and female in light of the *imago Dei* have also made an argument for partnership, equality, and mutuality based on a reading of the biblical texts in light of trinitarian theology (Grenz). Those who understand the *imago Dei* as reflecting a social and relational Trinity are able to further the understanding of partnership between the sexes as humanity's means of reflecting the *imago Dei*. The Bible offers a portrayal of male and female created in God's image for the purpose of co-ruling the creation as servants of God's work and each other. Such a portrayal challenges the power paradigms of both ancient and contemporary eras, and calls us to lives of mutuality, respect, and servant-love—even or especially in the midst of our practices of interpretation, as they reflect upon God.

See also Feminist Biblical Interpretation; Image of God

Bibliography

Derksen, M. "The Divine Intention concerning the Role and Relationship of Male and Female as Created and Fallen." *Didaskalia* 11, no. 1 (1991): 31–56; Fowl, S. *Engaging Scripture*. Blackwell, 1998; Grenz, S. *Sexual Ethics*. Westminster John Knox, 1990; Hurley, J. *Man and Woman in Biblical Perspective*. Zondervan, 1981; Jewett, P. *Man as Male and Female*. Eerdmans, 1975; Keener, C. *Paul, Women and Wives*. Hendrickson, 1992; Mills, S., et al. *Feminist Readings/Feminists Reading*. Harvester Wheatsheaf, 1989; Piper, J., and W. Grudem. *Recovering Biblical Manhood and Womanhood*. Crossway, 1991; Volf, M. *Exclusion and Embrace*. Abingdon, 1996; Witherington, B. *Women and the Genesis of Christianity*. Cambridge University Press, 1990.

Ruth Anne Reese

Manuscripts *See* Textual Criticism

Maps of the Biblical World *See* Geography

Marcionism   See Gnosticism; Patristic Biblical Interpretation; Relationship between the Testaments; Scripture, Unity of

Mark, Book of

Mark's Gospel is generally thought to be the earliest. Mainstream opinion is somewhat divided between assuming a date of origin just before the Jewish War or in its immediate aftermath. There is broad agreement that this Gospel became the literary basis for at least two others, Matthew and Luke, and possibly a third (John). Matthew and Luke have considerable overlap with Mark; John's Gospel does not. This is often explained on the assumption that the author wanted to avoid significant overlap with other Gospels, which already enjoyed wide circulation by the time John wrote. The language and the narrative architecture of Mark's Gospel is less sophisticated than those of the other Gospels, but in recent decades there has been a growing appreciation of the theological use of narrative techniques by this author as well. Clearly, Mark was as serious a theologian as any other NT author; characterizing his literary and theological awareness as that of a mere collector of early Christian tradition is no longer a viable option. His linguistic (Greek) capabilities may be limited at times, but his narrative-theological contribution is immense. Mark's significance for the Christian church becomes apparent when it is realized that this Gospel represents the move from oral Jesus tradition (gospel) to a written "Life of Jesus" (Gospel). The likeliest option for genre is that the canonical Gospels should be treated as ancient *bioi*. If so, the recent view that the Gospels did not have specific audiences in mind (Bauckham) ought to be viewed with some caution. There is little doubt that most ancient *bioi* were written to be read or "performed" orally (Bryan) and in specific contexts.

Interpretation and Approaches

Mark's history of reception is by far the least substantial compared to those of the other Gospels, to some extent lingering for centuries in the shadows, particularly of Matthew and John. The situation eventually changed, but not before the last decades of the eighteenth century with the emerging interest in historical questions. Markan priority began to be explored as a real possibility, for it was noticed that Luke and Matthew agree the most in their respective structures where they overlap with Mark. Ironically, this happened at around the same time (1835) when "Q" first emerged as a viable hypothesis. Along with Q, Mark came to be received as a crucial tool needed to rebut Strauss's evaluation of the Gospels as mythical accounts of Jesus. Later, the assumption that Mark preserves some kind of *Urevangelium*, or at least the basis for a definitive historical answer to Strauss, was challenged, but in the nineteenth century it helped propel the Gospel from relative anonymity to the center stage it still commands today.

With hindsight, this rise to prominence toward the end of the nineteenth century was based on positivistic assumptions and motivations that now appear questionable. Mark's Gospel was seen as a historical antidote to the "speculative" nature of John's. But from the perspective of those who enlisted Mark's help in reconstructing a solid "life of Jesus," it was unfortunate that this Gospel proportionally placed more emphasis on miracle stories than any other did. The two-source theory named Mark and Q as the main sources behind Matthew and Luke, with Q denoting the overlap between Matthew and Luke against Mark. Part of this theory's attraction was that Q, with its emphasis on Jesus' teachings, could balance Mark's preoccupation with the miraculous, which was regarded as incompatible with notions of historicity.

It is still against this background of Strauss's challenge to Mark's historical value and the attempt by others to find solid historical ground that Wrede developed his theory of the "messianic secret." According to that theory, the early church attempted to legitimize its understanding of Jesus as Messiah by projecting the secrecy motif back into Jesus' ministry. Historically, Wrede argued, Jesus did not regard himself as Messiah. The disciples' alleged lack of understanding and Jesus' reported enjoinders to them to keep his messianic role and status secret are said to have no historical basis. Instead, they supposedly were introduced into the pre-Markan tradition to explain why belief in Jesus' messiahship only came about as a consequence of the resurrection kerygma. If judged successful, Wrede's argument would undermine the historical value of Mark for reconstructing the life of Jesus, for it was the early church that introduced some of the most theologically significant aspects of this Gospel into the pre-Markan tradition.

In Germany, Wrede's historical skepticism was largely received with approval. Increasingly, Mark's Gospel was viewed as a theological reflection of the early church's perception of Jesus, not Jesus himself. Its role as a historically verifiable source to be used for legitimizing the church's modern christological consciousness began to wane. Form criticism thus tacitly threatened the predominance of Mark in Gospels studies, but then a renewed interest in Mark accompanied the emergence of redaction criticism (Marxsen), though it soon became clear that Matthew and Luke proved more fertile for such studies. Mark's redaction-critical potential was subordinated by some to the continuing interest in the historical Jesus.

Marxsen's assumption that there was substantial continuity between Mark and the earliest days of Christianity meant for some that it would be compelling to compare Mark's theology with that of the early letters of Paul, especially if those letters are the oldest documents in the NT. As such, they present us with a so-called primitive eschatology, not far removed from that of Jesus himself. In addition, there are now significant efforts to reclaim "biography" as a valid category for exploring Mark's genre (Dihle; Hengel). Having said that, few would now want to reduce the theological contribution of Mark to matters of either historicity or "primitive eschatology."

In recent German scholarship the theological focus on the role of the suffering righteous one in the Gospel as a whole (as opposed to just being a component of the passion narrative) is noteworthy (Ruppert; Steichele). In contrast to diachronic and theological concerns, synchronic approaches seek to connect the world in the text with that in front of it and emphasize the likely impact of the text upon the reader. At the postmodern end the interpretive weight tends to be shifted so far in the direction of the reader that stability in interpretation becomes impossible and is perceived as largely undesirable.

Probably the most promising avenue into a theological reading of Mark's Gospel is one that takes its cue from the OT allusions in the opening three verses of the Gospel itself (Watts). At least some recent commentators have recognized the importance of Mark's OT allusions as interpretative keys to unlocking his theology (France; Marcus). The following section demonstrates the importance of this line of inquiry.

Text and Message

Given the relative simplicity of Mark's Gospel, it is ironic to note the sheer diversity of attempts at defining its core theological objectives. Among the obvious main candidates are the kingdom of God, Christology, and discipleship. They are self-evident to the extent that Mark emphasizes all three topics in his opening twenty verses. Form-

critical as well as sociologically inclined scholars often focus on community instruction as an underlying theme (Kee). Gundry reads Mark as an apology for the cross. The list could easily be extended. The difficulty, however, is that none of these topics or approaches are wide enough to cover all of Mark, yet distinct enough to explain Mark's specific purpose. The best approach may well be that chosen by Watts. The starting point of this line of argument is the frequency with which Mark employs Exodus motifs such as the wilderness in the prologue, the two feeding stories, and the mount of transfiguration episode (cloud, dwellings), with its reference to Moses and the sea crossings. Once this is combined with the striking editorial combination of Isa. 40:3 with Mal. 3:1 and Exod. 23:20 in Mark's opening verses, what emerges is an important hermeneutical key to this Gospel. In its original context Isa. 40 is about the inauguration of the long-awaited new exodus (NE), including Yahweh's return. Malachi 3 and Exod. 23:30 are about Yahweh's threat that accompanies his coming at the culmination of the NE.

Isaiah 40 is a word of comfort about the nearing end of Israel's exile (cf. ch. 6, which is partially quoted in Mark 4:10–12), and Isaiah's message is inherently good: Yahweh will return to his people and be enthroned in a restored Jerusalem. Isaiah's comfort culminates in a messenger announcing to Jerusalem the good news (40:9–11) of her redemption and rebuilding (44:26; 45:13; 54:11–12). The link between Mark's prologue and Isaiah is further strengthened by the parallel acclamation of the son in whom God is well pleased (Isa. 42:1//Mark 1:11), for Jesus takes the place of true Israel, the "son."

Malachi 3:1–3 gives the other side of the coin: The coming of the Lord to the temple also means judgment. The reasons are clear: "You are ignoring me" (Mal. 3:7–9). Malachi's setting is the disappointment following the return from the exile; Isaiah's grand promises have still not fully eventuated (cf. Isa. 40–55 and 66). The delay of the Isaianic NE would necessitate the preparation of "the way" in the desert by a messenger. Malachi puts the blame for the delay at the door of both the priests and the people, certainly not God (chs. 1–2), for God is faithful and will eventually return (2:17–3:5).

The middle ground between Isaiah's and Malachi's respective emphases is covered by the third OT component of Mark's prologue, Exod. 23:20: The way of the Lord is being prepared, and Israel must make sure she is ready for it (vv.

21–31). The Exodus text belongs to the Book of the Covenant (20:22–23:33), which is set in the context of Israel's account of her founding moment. The context of v. 20 has the classic covenantal duality of blessings for the obedient (vv. 25–26) and a threat for the disobedient (v. 33). Also, the sins listed in Mal. 3:5 are in breach of either the Decalogue or Exod. 23. In short: Mark quotes the very OT verse that links back to the prototype of the NE, the original exodus, and that emphasizes the duality of God's redemptive faithfulness as opposed to Israel's faithlessness. But there are also close parallels of warnings and promises between Isa. 40:3 and Mal. 3:1 and their respective contexts.

The major advantage of reading Mark in light of his use of OT motifs is that it does justice both to the prologue as well as numerous aspects that are otherwise difficult to fit into an overall purpose. Examples include Mark's emphasis on Jesus' wanderings around Galilee and Judea, which may well have the purpose of reliving the desert wanderings of Israel. The transfiguration is now linked to Sinai, Jesus being the eschatological equivalent of the giver of the law. To be sure, it is not that Mark appeals to the OT a lot. The only time he does so explicitly *as narrator* is in ch. 1. But his allusions to the covenant, the temple, the "way," and the wilderness, along with the symbolism of story elements—such as "by the sea," the point of Israel's deliverance (1:16; 3:7); "on the mountain," Sinai reflection on the renewal of the community (3:13–35); "at home," the golden calf incident (6:1–6); "in the wilderness," Israel's place of rebellion (6:7–31)—all fit well with the exodus/NE scheme. The combination of quotations, allusions, and fragments of OT material (details in Watts) makes the case a strong one.

Mark consciously sets the appearance and ministry of Jesus in the context of the NE. For him, this is the story of the beginning of the renewal of God's covenant people, and Jesus is revealed not just as a protagonist in the NE story, but as Israel's returning God. Once it is set in this theological framework, it becomes clear that Jesus is the embodiment of Israel's returning God, in terms both of good news and ominous threat. Astonishingly, the messenger figure of Malachi is from Mark's perspective not just a prototype of John, but an anticipatory icon of Jesus as the bringer of the NE. Jesus embodies the very presence of Israel's Lord.

For Isaiah, the NE motif involves three main stages: Yahweh's deliverance of his exiled people,

the journey along the "way" (away from captivity), and arrival in Jerusalem, resulting in Yahweh's enthronement. In light of Isaiah's and Mark's deliberate use of the "way" motif, it seems possible that Mark's threefold geographical progression (Galilee, journey, Jerusalem) is designed as a symbolic allusion to Isaiah's NE motif. This itself does not deny the historicity of his account, but it certainly provides a plausible and even powerful theological explanation of the evangelist's selectivity and narrative arrangement. More importantly, it gives the reader a much-needed framework for making sense of Jesus' death and resurrection. Paradoxically, the cross was "the way" of launching the long-promised NE of God's people—a way of seeming defeat but actual vindication.

Mark and Canon

Given the previous section, we are well on the way to situating Mark's Gospel within the biblical canon. It remains to explore its place within the NT. On grounds of probable dating, Mark's relationship with Paul's letters is especially intriguing. If John Mark is the historical author of the Gospel, a view accepted by most, it is interesting that he and Paul both experienced some tension with the Jerusalem church. The main bone of contention for both Paul and Mark was the initial lack of enthusiasm of the "pillars" toward subordinating Jewish tradition to the exalted Jesus (Mark 7:1–23), thus potentially hindering the progress of the gospel among the Gentiles. Together with Paul's letters, it gives us an excellent insight into the early days of Christianity.

The importance of Mark alongside Matthew's and Luke's Q material has been mentioned. Without the evidence of Mark, our appreciation of Jesus' miracles as signs of Israel's eschatological restoration would be significantly poorer, though Luke makes the same theological point. Both Matthew and Luke are deeply indebted to Mark, though Luke in particular replicates Mark's basic outline, possibly because he recognized Mark's allusion to Isaiah's NE. John seems to have taken care not to duplicate Mark's account, for even where he twice presents the same episode as Mark ("feeding" and "sea" episodes—Mark 6 and John 6), he offers different historical details and theological angles. It appears that he took the widespread existence of Mark's Gospel for granted.

Acts begins with what looks like an alternative to Mark's ending, and the theological rationale for the differences appears straightforward. Acts is the second volume of Luke's Gospel and as such connects with Israel's eschatological expectations (such as spiritual restoration) in ways that are replete with Jewish allusions and themes that Mark considered too specific for his Gentile audience. However, both Mark (Isaiah's NE) and Luke-Acts (death-resurrection-ascension-Pentecost cycle) do share an emphasis on the present realization of the kingdom. Even Mark 13 is no exception to the evangelist's interest in pre-70 CE events. It is perfectly plausible to interpret the entire chapter with a first-century referent in mind (France gets close to this).

Peter's greetings in 1 Pet. 5:13 have given rise to speculations about connections between the historical Mark and the author of 1 Peter, even though most literary parallels link 1 Peter to Matthew, not Mark. Perceived ecclesiological (in the general sense of "God's people") differences between Mark and 1 Peter go beyond our purview, for they depend more on exegetical and historical assessments of 1 Peter than Mark's Gospel. Perhaps the most significant overlap between the two documents consists of their common emphasis on Jesus as Isaiah's Suffering Servant (Mark 9:35; 10:45) and their preoccupation with the relationship of faith and suffering.

This last point also closely connects Mark (10:29–30; 13:9–13) to Hebrews. Other common trajectories are their "interior" understanding of purity (Mark 7:1–23), their spiritualized Christian understanding of sacrifice (12:32–34), and their assessment of the Jerusalem temple as a human construction (14:58).

It was implied above that Mark 13 is in its entirety a discourse about the procession toward and climax of the Jewish War. The war and impending fall of the city and temple are presented as another "return" of Jesus, this time as judge (Son of Man; cf. Dan. 7:13). In light of Isaiah's NE motif, Jesus' entry into Jerusalem (Mark 11:1–19) was nothing less than God's return to his people to sacrificially complete Israel's failed mission on her behalf (10:45). The Son of Man's further return to the city as judge (70 CE) brought the negative side of Isaiah's NE to partial fulfillment. In recent scholarship the parousia-oriented eschatology of Revelation has increasingly been interpreted with reference to the first-century experience of the persecuted church, and to that extent Mark's eschatological concern with the first century and the suffering community seems compatible with and similar to that of Revelation.

Mark and Theology

In general terms, Mark's theological agenda can be described as a combination of affirming the faithfulness of Israel's God and the relevance of this for Gentiles. Jesus is the embodiment of Israel's returning God, and as such he enters the city and takes Israel's fate upon himself by becoming the sacrifice for the many (10:45). In the process he pronounces judgment on the corrupt establishment as represented by the temple (11:12–26) and is set to execute the judgment himself, as the Danielic Son of Man, by allowing Jerusalem and the temple to be reduced to rubble (Mark 13). This apparent paradox makes perfect sense once Mark's understanding of Isaiah's NE is taken seriously. Israel is redefined as the renewal movement of those committed to him: The remnant (= disciples) should be able to understand this, Jesus explains. Those outside of this christocentrically defined group, however, experience temporary hardness of heart, thus ensuring that they become subject to the Son of Man's imminent judgment (4:10–12; cf. ch. 13). The Isa. 6 quotation in Mark 4 lays the foundation for the more explicit judgment call of ch. 13. Neither of these texts is about the physical end of the world, yet both are about the end of the (Mosaic) age as humanity knew it. Jesus inaugurated his kingdom decisively, both in self-sacrifice and in judgment, and the clear implication is that his followers should live accordingly. This means readiness for suffering and unfailing loyalty to the One who alone is the defining center of Israel's—and in fact humanity's—renewal. The promise to Abraham is being fulfilled, despite Israel's failure. Jesus and those around him are Israel restored. The responsibility to model authentic creational humanity rests squarely on those who, despite their continuing failures, recognize Jesus as king of Israel and Son of God (15:32–39). Humanity is thus defined christocentrically; ethnicity, social standing, and so forth are transcended in Jesus.

In terms of contemporary relevance, the following selection is suggestive rather than complete (for more discussion, see Telford 214–41). (1) Mark's theology of the cross and self-denial in the name of Jesus stands in stark contrast to modern and postmodern definitions of success in life. Mark's first half (1:1–8:21), which concentrates on glory and success, is followed by an account of the disciples' bitter learning experience in the face of Jesus' self-sacrifice. (2) Jesus' repeated emphasis on the new wine's need for new skins (not always in these words) challenges us to examine and reconfigure the role of religious tradition in our understanding of God's people following the Christ event. Yet, the debates about what was permissible on the Sabbath remind our 24/7 society of the important interplay between covenantal demands and creational values. (3) Politically, Mark's Gospel teaches us a healthy skepticism toward ethnically centered or even nationalistic understandings of God's people. Israel's task was not to overthrow the Roman Empire ("Give to Caesar what belongs to Caesar"), but to reform itself by rendering to God what belongs to him. The one who urges his hearers to pay attention (13:14) also informs us that Jesus' political stance seriously raised some eyebrows in Israel (12:17).

Our final question relates to the contribution Mark has to make in the arena of systematic theology. The most significant challenge falls in the areas of Christology and the Trinity. Traditionally, both have been approached in terms of Aristotelian-inspired substance metaphysics. The issue has often been compounded in NT scholarship by subjecting Mark's christological titles rather exclusively to a history-of-religions approach. It would be anachronistic to expect Mark to frame his theological concerns in this way. From his first-century perspective the most pertinent claim is that somehow Christ embodies the returning God of Israel. Along with his fellow writers, he stops far short of ontological speculations about either the natures of Christ or the inner-trinitarian position of Christ. More importantly for him, Christ is the sole definer of the remnant, the true people of God, for he alone is both the returning God of Israel and the fulfiller of Israel's true destiny. It is at this convergence of *Christ as God* and *true man* throughout Jesus' life that Mark anchors his implied incarnational Jesus theology. For him, this is not an end in itself, but the crucial component in redefining the centerpiece of the Abrahamic project: humanity—that is God's people—in light of the Son of Man's journey to the cross and beyond. Mark's christological titles should not be interpreted as substance-metaphysical indicators, but as powerful narrative ways of connecting *Jesus as God* with the remnant people (Son of Man), whose salvific mission he accomplishes on the cross and in resurrection.

Salvation for Mark is not strictly a concern for the future. In his "already/not yet" scheme, the focus is firmly on the "already." People are rehabilitated spiritually, physically, socially, and emotionally—clear indications that the kingdom has arrived. Life after death starts at the transforming encounter with Jesus, not after physical death. The latter is but a stepping-stone along the way. The disciples experience Israel's eagerly awaited restoration. Mark may not be as interested as Luke in linking Jesus' miracles to the power of the eschatologically awaited Spirit, but he is equally clear that the salvation Jesus brings to repentant sinners is nothing less than Israel's restoration. Consequently, for Mark eschatology is a matter of interpreting the present realization of the kingdom as the climactic renewal of Israel. The future matters primarily in its impact on the present, not as a "not yet" reality. Sinners repent not to await salvation, but to enjoy it by living authentically among God's people. Any systematic-theological correlation of eschatology and soteriology focused on a chronologically final sequence of events will do little justice to Mark's theology.

Mark bases his theological confidence squarely on his reading of the OT, especially the NE motif. His other main source for theological reflection on Christ and his people is the disciples' religious experience of Jesus' divine presence. The two are intimately connected throughout his narrative, for it is God's presence through Jesus with the disciples that, more than anything else, illustrates the arrival of the NE. Instead of walking away from his covenant with an unfaithful people, God through Jesus brings to successful completion the mission of Israel as the model people in the world. God is justified after all. For Mark, the communion meal is not only a powerful reminder of this, but a crucial and appropriate speech-act that re-creates among God's people and in creation this divine faithfulness manifested in Jesus. The Abrahamic recovery project of humanity is alive and well—indeed, it has reached a crucial climax, for "the Son of Man . . . [has given] his life as a ransom for many" (10:45).

See also Exodus/New Exodus

Bibliography

Bauckham, R. "For Whom Were Gospels Written?" In *The Gospels for All Christians*, ed. R. Bauckham. Eerdmans, 1997; Bryan, C. *A Preface to Mark*. Oxford University Press, 1993; Dihle, A. "Die Evangelien und die biographische Tradition der Antike." *ZTK* 80 (1983): 33–49; France, R. T. *The Gospel of Mark*. NIGTC. Eerdmans, 2002; Gundry, R. *Mark*. Eerdmans, 1993; Hengel, M. *Studies in the Gospel of Mark*, trans. J. Bowden. SCM, 1985; Marcus, J. *Mark 1–8*. AB. Doubleday, 2000; Marxsen, W. *Mark the Evangelist*, trans. J. Boyce et al. Abingdon, 1969; Ruppert, L. *Jesus als der leidende Gerechte?* SBS. Katholisches Bibelwerk, 1972; Steichele,

H.-J. *Der leidende Sohn Gottes*. BU 14. F. Pustet, 1980; Strauss, D. F. *The Life of Jesus Critically Examined*. Translated from the 4th German ed. by G. Eliot. Fortress, 1972; Telford, W. *The Theology of the Gospel of Mark*. NTT. Cambridge University Press, 1999; Watts, R. *Isaiah's New Exodus in Mark*. BSL. Baker, 2000; Wrede, W. *The Messianic Secret*, trans. J. C. G. Greig. J. Clarke, 1971.

Thorsten Moritz

Marriage   *See* Male and Female; Sexuality

Mary

In the NT, the texts in which Mary appears are Matt. 1–2; 12:46–50; 13:55; Mark 3:31–35; 6:3; Luke 1–2; 8:19–21; 11:27–28; John 2:1–12; 6:42; 19:25–27; Acts 1:14; and Gal. 4:4. Surely for our understanding of Mary in the Protestant wings of Christendom, the texts that bear Mary in the NT will be of greatest importance and authority for our embrace of her theologically. Mary thus tells the story of Jesus as his mother, as his disciple, as witness of his crucifixion, as grounding his humanity, as witness to his resurrection appearances.

The Roman Catholic Church adds four official dogmas about Mary. The first is Mary as the Bearer of God, or *theotokos*. This was first put forth at the Council of Ephesus in 431. This doctrine is important because it tells the story of Jesus' divinity and paradoxically his humanity as well. The second dogma is the Perpetual Virginity of Mary, accepted by the Lateran Council in 649, which declares that Mary was a virgin before, during, and after Jesus' birth. Here Protestants part with Catholics. The third dogma is the Immaculate Conception, promulgated by Pope Pius IX in 1854. This is often misunderstood to refer to Jesus' conception, but rather refers to Mary's sinless conception. In 1950 Pope Pius XII promulgated the fourth dogma, the Bodily Assumption. It declares that Mary was taken up into heaven and that her body is not under the laws of natural decay and corruption. In addition, there is a corpus of "pious beliefs" that are known as the Marian Theses, not dogmas binding on the faithful, but beliefs acknowledged by the Magisterium. These beliefs hold Mary to be (1) coredemptrix with Christ, (2) mediatrix, (3) the dispensatrix of all graces, (4) the Queen of Heaven, and (5) the prototype of the church.

But what does this mean for Protestants? To consider much of Protestantism alone, today one would think that Mary is nonexistent liturgically, devotionally, and theologically. Insisting that Mary not eclipse Christ, Protestant Churches have come to the almost complete suppression of Mary. However, we must hold on to her not just as a character in the story of Jesus but as the very Mother of God, while eschewing any devotion to Mary herself. Because any statement about Mary must be a christological statement, the Protestant wings of the church must, even while disavowing Mariolatry, hold to the confession of Mary as the "Mother of the Lord," *theotokos*, as upheld by both Luther and Reformed Orthodoxy. Thus, Mary can tell the story of the very gospel of *sola gratia*.

A good illustration of this can be found in the first and largest church of Western Christianity dedicated to Mary, Santa Maria Maggiore, in Rome. It was founded ca. 350 CE by Pope Liberius, and Pope Sixtus III had the church restored in the fifth century to commemorate the declaration of Mary's Divine Motherhood by the Council of Ephesus in 431. In the nave are some of the most spectacular early mosaics of Western Christian art portraying scenes from the OT.

Two particularly significant relics are at this building. One is the remains of Jerome, fourth-century Doctor of the Church, colleague of Augustine, with whom he carried out a vigorous correspondence, and translator of the Bible into Latin. Jerome was one of the only church fathers of his day to know Hebrew well enough (he admitted his knowledge was second only to that of Paula, his colleague) to translate the Bible from the original Hebrew texts of the OT. He lived out his later life in Bethlehem, translating in a cell near the cave where Jesus was said to have been born and which was venerated as a holy place. Also in Sta. Maria Maggiore in Rome is another Bethlehem relic: a piece of the Holy Manger from that cave near Jerome's cell. This network of images at Sta. Maria Maggiore is profound: Holy Mary, Mother of God, Bethlehem, the birth of God-with-us, Jerome's study of the word in the OT, scenes from the OT flanking the nave, the crèche kept here inviting us to have our hearts be crèches ever anew, reminding us of Mary "keeping these things, pondering them in her heart."

The mosaics of the nave of Sta. Maria Maggiore themselves tell a story, and a surprising one in a certain sense: these mosaics all are scenes from the OT. Why would a church dedicated to the Mother of God—the apse mosaic of which depicts Mary being crowned Queen of Heaven by Christ and her Dormition just below—why would these nave mosaics give such prominence to OT stories? The key is the content of the scenes. They are not just any scenes taken at random, but are understood to be among the stories that weave the greater narrative of redemption: Noah, Abraham, Moses, Joshua. They are typologies that point to Christ, and that ultimately tell the story of *sola gratia*, grace alone.

This broad plan that these mosaics of Sta. Maria Maggiore present for us is a sort of family tree of Jesus, or maybe more appropriately a typological tree. And the fit between typology and history is profound: Mary grounds Jesus' humanity and history, without which this typological foreshadowing would have no fulfilling. Yet just as grounding his humanity, she is the mother also of his divinity. Just as she is the Mother of the Son of Man, so she is the Mother of God, for Jesus is confessed to be "truly human and truly divine," indivisibly so.

See also Jesus Christ, Doctrine of; Typology

Kathryn Greene-McCreight

Masoretic Text *See* Translation

Matthew, Book of

The popularity of the Gospel of Matthew enhanced its influence on the theology of the early church and made it an important object of early Christian theologizing. Its Jewish slant combined with its interest in the discipling of "all the nations" to give it universal appeal (28:19 [all ET by author]). Its systematic organization lent it to heavy liturgical use. (To this day, its version of the Lord's Prayer is regularly used instead of Luke's.) And its featuring the ethical teaching of Jesus made it especially suitable for catechetical instruction.

Historical Examples of Interplay between Matthew and Theology

Without evaluation, here are some of the more important instances of interplay between Matthew and theology. The doctrine of the Immaculate Conception grew out of the story of Jesus' virgin birth (1:18–25; also in Luke). The doctrine of Mary's perpetual virginity marked a further development. John the Baptist's saying he needs Jesus to baptize him has played into the doctrine of Jesus' sinlessness, and Jesus' insisting on baptism by John "to fulfill all righteousness" despite his (Jesus') sinlessness played into the doctrine of Christ's imputed righteousness (3:14–17).

The designation of Jesus as God's Son at the baptism contributed to adoptionism, and the temptation of Jesus (4:1–11) raised the theological question whether he was able not to sin

or was not able to sin. His affirmation of every jot and tittle of the Law and the Prophets (5:18) has been used to undergird belief in the verbal, plenary inspiration and inerrancy of Scripture. The nonabolishment of the Law and demand that it be taught and kept (5:17–20) have posed a theological confrontation with Paul's rejection of law-righteousness. Jesus' escalation of the law's demands (5:21–48) led to perfectionism (as in the monastic and Anabaptist traditions), ethical idealism (as in the two-kingdoms doctrine of Lutheranism), the social gospel (as in Protestant liberalism), and limitation to a future millennium (as in dispensationalism).

Matthew's pervasive stress on the kingdom of heaven has gone in the theological directions of consistent eschatology (Jesus thought the end was about to come), ecclesiology (the church represents the kingdom), and millenarianism (Jesus offered the kingdom to the Jewish nation—"the gospel of the kingdom" differing from the Christian gospel—and most Jews refused it, so that the kingdom will arrive in a future millennium only after the interim of the church age). Consistent eschatology produced interim ethics (ethics for only the brief period before the expected end). An ecclesiastical kingdom put emphasis on the visible church as an institution, a mixture of the true and false, a mixture that also raised questions of church discipline. A millennial kingdom led to belief in a restoration of the Jewish nation, complete with a reinstitution of the OT law as interpreted by Matthew's Jesus. Indeed, dispensationalists have often regarded the Gospel of Matthew as not addressed to the church. Parables of the kingdom, such as those of the mustard seed and leaven (13:31–33), have been thought to support the dominance of the church in society at large (as in the Middle Ages), the eventual conversion of the whole world (as in postmillennialism), and the corruption of the institutional church (according to the dispensational understanding of leaven as symbolizing evil, and the birds that nest in mustard branches as symbolizing false teachers).

The prominence of Peter in Matthew, especially in the beatitude pronounced on him by Jesus (16:17–19), has been used to support the Roman Catholic doctrine of the papacy. Nevertheless, "the rock" on which Jesus said he would build his church has also been identified, not with Peter either as the first in a line of popes or by himself, but with his confession of Jesus as the Christ, with Jesus himself, and with Jesus' "words" (cf. 7:24–27). Peter's denying Jesus "before . . . all"

(26:70) combines with Jesus' denying before his Father those who have denied him before others (10:33) and with Matthew's omission of Peter's name from the story of Jesus' resurrection (contrast 28:7 with Mark 16:7) to suggest in Matthew's portrayal of Peter the symbolism of a false disciple.

The eschatological discourse in chs. 24–25 has been referred to the Jewish War of 66–70 CE, to a future tribulation, and to a following return of Christ. The judgmental separation of the nations into sheep and goats has been theologically geared to general humanitarianism on the part of individuals, to true Christians' treatment of their persecuted fellows, and to treatment of the Jewish people by nations qua nations.

Matthew's Christology and Soteriology

A survey of Matthew's Christology and soteriology, with hamartiological, ecclesiological, and eschatological entailments, reveals the extent to which this Gospel and theology can contribute to each other.

Christology. Historic Christology speaks of humanity and deity in the one person Jesus and helps readers of Matthew to see in it just such a Christology, while a reading of Matthew contributes to its construction. Jesus' humanity appears clearly in the genealogy with which Matthew starts. In contrast with Luke's genealogy of Jesus, which goes back to God (Luke 3:38), Matthew's starts with the human being Abraham, gives prominence to David, and prepares for emphasis on Jesus' Davidic ancestry (1:1–2, 6, 17, 20; 9:27; 12:23; 15:22; 20:30–31; 21:9, 15). Apparently written for a Jewish audience, however, Matthew's Gospel lays at least equal emphasis on Jesus' deity, for to Jews this was more unbelievable and objectionable (cf. 26:63–66).

The designation of Jesus as "God-with-us" (1:23) is matched by the replacement of "God" with Jesus' "I" in the promise, "And behold, I am with you all the days till the consummation of the age" (28:20). This designation is also supported in the middle of Matthew's Gospel with Jesus' assurance that where two or three are gathered in his name, there he is "in their midst" (18:20). Because of his reference to "every word coming out through the mouth of God" (4:4, but lacking in the parallel, Luke 4:4), the opening of his mouth to teach (5:2) makes his teaching consist of the very words of God, in consonance with Jesus' being "God-with-us."

God the Father is the first to pronounce Jesus his Son (already in the OT; cf. 2:15 with Hos. 11:1), and in further such pronouncements adds both "beloved" to the designation and the command, "Hear him." This distinguishes Jesus from other sons of God (3:17; 17:5; contrast 5:9, 45), so that the relation between the Father and the Son is unique (11:27). Matthew's changing the baptismal voice from "*You are* my beloved Son" (Mark 1:11// Luke 3:22) to "*This is* my beloved Son" turns an assurance to Jesus into a pronouncement about him. Accordingly, his disciples prostrate themselves before him, even while they are in a boat, and say, "Truly you are God's Son" (14:33). Peter adds to his confession of Jesus as "the Christ" the further identification, "the Son of the living God" (16:16; lacking in Mark 8:29//Luke 9:20). Not as in Mark 15:39 and Luke 23:47, the guards at Jesus' crucifixion join their centurion to declare, "Truly this one was God's Son," upon seeing among other things "the earthquake" that occurred when Jesus "let go" his spirit, an earthquake being typical of theophanies in the OT. Likewise, Jesus has angels just as God does (13:41; 16:27; 24:31), and the kingdom is his as well as the Father's (13:41; 16:28).

At the climactic close of his Gospel, Matthew puts emphasis on Jesus' deity in an incipiently trinitarian passage by sandwiching Jesus as "the Son" between God "the Father" and "the Holy Spirit" in a baptismal formula that features "the name" (singular!) of the three. Even if "the name" were meant to be repeatedly supplied before "of the Son" and before "of the Holy Spirit," the very ellipses would draw the three closely together. The participation of the Father and the Holy Spirit at Jesus' baptism previewed this trinitarian climax.

Matthew does not mention Jesus' preexistence as God's Son, as John, Paul, and Hebrews do. But Matthew does narrate the virginal conception and birth of Jesus (1:18–25), as John, Paul, and Hebrews do not. Considering the whole of the NT canon, then, systematic theologians may legitimately interpret the virginal conception and birth of Jesus as the means by which the preexistent Second Person of the Trinity became incarnate. Thus, both Matthew on the one hand and John, Paul, and Hebrews on the other hand contribute to a larger theological picture. And though Luke mentions Jesus' preexistence no more than Matthew does, perhaps we have the beginnings of this picture already in Luke's tracing of Jesus' genealogy back to God, designating Jesus as God's Son at the annunciation to Mary, and attributing the virginal conception of Jesus to the work of the Holy Spirit (Luke 1:26–38).

Soteriology. Right after presenting Jesus himself, Matthew introduces the topic of salvation, and his first mention of it indicates that salvation consists of deliverance from sins (1:21). The plural "sins" implies that Matthew does not conceive of sin as an external power that has enslaved its victims so as to make them sin against their will (contrast esp. Rom. 7:7–23). By modifying "sins," "their" fixes the blame for sinning on the sinners themselves, so that deliverance from sins means deliverance from punishment for sinful acts, such as those listed in 15:19: "evil designs, murders, adulteries, fornications, thefts, false testimonies, blasphemies" (all plurals in this list). With this view of salvation agree Matthew's references to forgiveness of moral debts (release from having to pay them—6:12; cf. 18:27, 32, 35), forgiveness of trespasses (6:14–15), and forgiveness of sins (9:2, 5–6; 26:28), even every sin and blasphemy except for blasphemy against the Spirit (12:31–32). The plural of "debts," "trespasses," and "sins" is again notable, as is also the modifier "every" when "sin" and "blasphemy" occur in the singular.

On the other hand, salvation consists in rescue from "evil" (neuter) or "the evil one" (masculine, 6:13). The use of the masculine in 13:19 for the "evil one" who snatches the word of the kingdom out of hearers' hearts favors a reference to Satan in both passages (cf. also 5:37, where "the evil one" stands opposite "the Lord," "God," and "the Great King" in the preceding verses; and 13:38–39, where "the evil one" equates with "the devil"). So rescue from the evil one means rescue from the devil, Satan, as the one who tempts people to commit sins (4:1–11; 16:23).

Thus, Matthew portrays human beings as responsible for their sins rather than victimized by sin as a dominating force, as Paul does. But just as Paul does not negate human responsibility, so Matthew does not negate the satanic power of temptation. Systematic theology must take into account the tension between human responsibility and external influences in the matter of sin just as in the matter of repentance and faith.

To the woman who has an issue of blood, Jesus pronounces salvation (9:22); and at his crucifixion chief priests, scribes, and elders say, "He saved others; he cannot save himself!" (27:42). Since the supposed inability of Jesus to save himself has to do with physical deliverance from crucifixion, his antithetically parallel saving of others had to do with deliverance from the physical effects of their sins, just as the woman's salvation had to do with stopping her issue of blood (cf. 4:23–24; 8:16–17; 11:4–5; and other stories of healings, exorcisms,

and the raising of a dead person). Perhaps it is relief from these physical effects of sinning to which Jesus refers in promising rest to the weary and heavy laden who come to him (11:28–30; cf. his miracles mentioned in the earlier part of ch. 11). Such relief raises the question of "healing in the atonement" (as in Pentecostal theology; cf. 8:17) and links up with Paul's description of a better body at the resurrection (1 Cor. 15:42–55; 2 Cor. 5:1–5; Phil. 3:21) and with John the Seer's description of believers' eternal state (Rev. 7:17; 21:4).

For Matthew, however, salvation goes beyond deliverance from the physical effects of sin. It extends to deliverance from condemnation (11:22–24), from being lost and perishing (18:14), from wrath (3:7), from being thrown into a furnace of unquenchable, eternal fire and thus from weeping and gnashing of teeth (3:10–12; 7:19; 13:30, 42, 50; 18:8–9). Positively, salvation extends to justification, being pronounced righteous because of one's words (12:36–37), to entrance into life (18:8–9; 19:17) with the result of having life that is eternal (19:16). This entrance into life comes by way of entrance into the kingdom of heaven (18:3)—through bodily resurrection, if necessitated by prior death (12:41–42; 22:23–33; 27:51b–53). The result is participation in God's heavenly rule on earth, a participation that brings with itself comfort in place of mourning, property in place of poverty, vindication in place of shame, mercy in place of judgment, a vision of God, acknowledgment as God's sons and daughters, and great reward in place of persecution (5:3–12). The links with Johannine soteriology (e.g., John 3:16, 36; Rev. 20:11–15) are obvious, as also the link with Pauline justification. Yet, systematic theologians must forge an accommodation between justification by the quality of the words one speaks and justification by faith, just as they have to forge an accommodation between justification by the quality of one's works (James 2:14–26) and justification by faith. Presumably this accommodation rests on the distinction between an inward state of faith and the outward evidence of faith.

Jesus saves, as his very name indicates (1:21; cf. Peter's outcry in 14:30, "Lord, save me," though he was asking Jesus to save him from drowning). Since salvation includes forgiveness of sins, salvation by Jesus naturally includes *his* forgiveness of sins (9:1–7). And since he acts always in consort with God, salvation naturally includes forgiveness by the Father in heaven as well (6:12 with 6:9). Furthermore, since Jesus' baptizing of people in the Holy Spirit and fire appears in its Matthean context to consist of his Spirit-endowed ministry, the Holy Spirit joins Jesus and God the Father in the act of salvation (3:11–17). This trinitarian cast accords with Matthew's trinitarian formula for baptism, discussed above (28:19; cf. the trinitarian cast of salvation in Eph. 1:3–14).

That Jesus, God the Father, and the Holy Spirit do the saving presents a vertical axis of salvation. But a horizontal axis appears, too. For disciples' restoration of a sinning fellow disciple counts as gaining that fellow disciple so that the straying one does not perish (18:12–18). Thus, we can say that in Matthew disciples save each other. Not only "the Son of Man" but also "human beings" (plural) have "authority" to forgive sins (9:8 with 9:1–7; cf. 18:21–35). Since salvation includes forgiveness, as already noted, and since the authority of human beings to forgive sins parallels the Son of Man's authority to do so, we can say once again that in Matthew disciples save each other.

Matthew does not stop with trinitarian and ecclesial salvation, however. His soteriology proceeds to self-salvation. Those who lose their lives for Jesus' sake will find—save—their lives (16:24–26). Such a losing of life counts as "one's own doing" (16:27), so that you save yourself (cf. Phil. 2:12–13, "With fear and trembling work out your own salvation," though Matthew has nothing corresponding to Paul's addition, "for God is the one working in you"; also John 6:29, where believing is "the work" that God requires). Again, a systematic theological distinction between inward state and outward evidence is required to avoid synergism.

It is Jesus' "people" who are saved (1:21; cf. "my church" in 16:18). They are those who "call his name 'Immanuel,'" those who confess that in him "God [is] with us" (1:23), and who make this confession in public despite the threat of persecution (10:32–33). The third person plural of "they will call" in Matthew's quotation of Isa. 7:14 is text-critically unique. No other known text of the OT passage has the third person plural. Most likely, then, Matthew himself produced this reading by altering a different one so as to define the people whom Jesus saves as those who call his name Immanuel. They are a sinful people; at least they were sinning prior to his saving them from their sins. But he came to call sinners, not the righteous (9:9–13).

For the saved, Matt. 21:43 uses another collective term, "nation." Jesus' having saved them as a people from their sins, they are now a nation that produces the fruits of God's kingdom: good deeds, righteous conduct (see, e.g., 5:16; 21:32).

Comprising this nation are people of faith in Jesus, and of discipleship to him, from all nations (8:10–11; 28:19), plus holy ones, saints, from the past (27:51b–53). This makes an international nation of little people, social nobodies, and mental infants as to human wisdom and prudence (10:42; 11:25; 18:6, 10, 14; 25:40, 45). But the saved are few, the Monaco of nations as far as population is concerned (7:13–14), so few as to be a family (5:22–24, 47; 7:3–5; 10:21; 12:46–50; 18:15, 21, 35; 25:40; 28:10). These are the saved.

Because of their mental infantilism, Jesus' people have to be saved by divine revelation (11:25–26), by God's giving them to know the mysteries of the kingdom of heaven (13:11). Because of their sins, Jesus' people have to be saved by divine mercy (5:7) and generosity (19:30–20:16), and by the service of Jesus in giving his life as a ransom in substitution for them (20:28), by the shedding of his covenantal blood "for the forgiveness of sins" (26:28; contrast the taunt, "Save yourself . . . and come down from the cross" [27:40–42], and Elijah's not coming to save Jesus from death by crucifixion [27:49]). Thence comes the doctrine of substitutionary atonement. So much for what is done on behalf of Jesus' people for salvation.

What do they need to do for themselves? They need to repent of their sins by being baptized, confessing their sins during baptism, and producing fruit worthy of repentance—speaking and acting in a way that shows their baptism in water to have been prompted by genuine repentance (3:6–10; 7:16–20; 12:33–35; 21:43; 28:19–20). They produce such fruit by learning and keeping the law as explained, commanded, and exemplified by Jesus (5:20–48; 11:29; 13:1–23, 51–52; 19:16–19; 28:19–20). Such learning and obedience mean leaving the way of wickedness and going the way of righteousness (21:28–32), speaking good words (12:33–35), doing good deeds (5:16; 16:27; 25:14–30), converting themselves into the lowly position of little children (18:3–4), not causing others to stumble into sin (18:6–7), and not stumbling into sin themselves (18:8–9). The list of specifics goes on and on: meekness, mercy, purity of heart, peacemaking, conciliation, avoidance of lust, maintenance of marriage, truthfulness, love of enemies, prayer for persecutors, secret charity, secret fasting, secret praying, forgiveness of debtors, forgiveness of those who have sinned against you, renunciation of earthly wealth, self-criticism, practice of the Golden Rule (see the whole of the Sermon on the Mount [chs. 5–7] and passages such as 18:21–35; 19:21–30, among others). Matthew will not present salvation apart from these and other evidence—for example, the absence of vices opposite to the foregoing virtues—that repentance was genuine.

Repentance from sins and the practice of virtue do not suffice for salvation, however. One must also believe in Jesus (18:6; cf. 8:25–26; 9:2, 22; 14:31; 16:8; 28:17). Believing in him entails confessing him in public (10:32–33); calling him "Immanuel" (1:23); loving him more than one loves father, mother, son, or daughter (10:37); taking one's cross and following him, which means risking persecution by open discipleship (10:38–39; 16:24–27); persevering under persecution (10:16–23; 24:9–13; cf. 13:18–23; and contrast the denials of Jesus by Peter [26:69–75] and Judas Iscariot's betrayal of Jesus [26:47–57]). Because of double mention by Matthew, it bears emphasis that under persecution one must persevere to be saved: "But the one persevering to the end—this one will be saved" (10:22; 24:13). In contrast is the one who hears the word and receives it immediately and joyfully, but because of tribulation and persecution turns out to be "temporary" and stumbles into sin rather than bearing the fruit of good deeds (13:20–21). Matthew's stress on the necessity of perseverance is not balanced by an equal stress on the comfort of eternal security, so that a systematic theology must supplement Matthew with John and Paul.

Belief in Jesus shows itself not only through perseverance under persecution, but also through endangering oneself by extending hospitality and charity to fellow disciples who are fleeing persecution (cf. 10:41–42; 25:31–46 with 10:11–13, 23, most of this material being unique to Matthew). More generally, genuineness of repentance and belief shows itself in faithful, prudent, and kind treatment of fellow disciples; otherwise, there awaits dichotomization, a fate shared with the hypocrites, and weeping and gnashing of teeth (24:45–51).

Negatively, Matthew takes pains to note that salvation does not come by baptism as such (3:7). To drive this point home, he shifts the phrase "for the forgiveness of sins" from John's baptism (so Mark 1:4//Luke 3:3) to the words of institution (Matt. 26:28). Again negatively, Matthew notes twice that salvation does not come by virtue of Abrahamic ancestry (3:9; 8:11–12).

Forgiveness of sins takes place in the present. "Your sins are being forgiven," Jesus says to a paralytic (9:2). Then he heals the paralytic to prove that as the Son of Man "on the earth," he has authority to be forgiving sins (9:6). Inversely,

blasphemy against the Holy Spirit will not be forgiven "in this age" (12:31–32). But neither will it be forgiven "in the coming [age]." Since forgiveness of sins equates with salvation, then, salvation occurs both now and hereafter. By virtue of repentance and coming to hear the wisdom of Solomon, respectively, the men of Nineveh and the queen of the South will rise up "in the judgment" and condemn Jesus' generation. Corresponding to the condemnation of Jesus' generation, then, the salvation of the men of Nineveh and the queen of the South must take place in the day of judgment, which is also the day of resurrection. Since those who do not turn and become like little children "will by no means enter the kingdom of heaven" (18:3), the entrance of those who do convert will likewise occur in the future. And the going away of the righteous into eternal life (25:46) will occur "when the Son of Man comes in his glory, and all the angels with him," at which time "he will sit on his throne of glory" and judge "all the nations."

Notably, Matthew presents a catchall doctrine of salvation (cf. his catchall Christology: Jesus as the Christ, Immanuel, the Son of God, the Son of Man, Lord, and Wisdom). His is the soteriology of both-and rather than this-but-not-that. In 19:16–30, for example, having eternal life, inheriting eternal life, entering life, entering the kingdom, having treasure in heaven, and being saved—all carry the same soteriological meaning. Fine distinctions mean little to Matthew. Though he distinguishes between repentance and belief on the one hand and evidence ("fruit") on the other hand, he does not distinguish cleanly between salvation as a gift and salvation as a reward, or clearly deny the latter in favor of the former, as Paul does. And it remains unclear what relationship, if any, exists between the covenant in which Jesus' blood is shed for the forgiveness of sins (26:28) and the various covenants that the OT talks about. For answers to these questions, systematic theology requires the letters of Paul and Hebrews.

Within Matthew's soteriological potpourri, however, we can discern certain emphases. For him, salvation consists primarily of forgiveness of sins (though this element is expressed in a variety of terms). But stress falls not so much on God's forgiving mercy, accepted through faith, as on human beings' saving themselves in the sense of demonstrating that they have truly repented of their sins. Thus, it is the righteous who are saved, and they are saved by persevering in the superiorly righteous conduct they have learned from Jesus' teaching and example. Because they must persevere to the end, their salvation occurs mainly in the future.

Matthew's soteriological emphases seem to have grown out of circumstances in which he perceived Jewish Christians to be suffering persecution from fellow Jews who had not become Christians. As a result, and as always happens in times of persecution, some were falling away to save their necks. Matthew saw Christians, Judas-like, betraying other Christians to their persecutors (24:10). He saw Christians, Peter-like, falsifying their earlier profession with public denials of Christ (10:33). He saw their distinctively Christian conduct lapsing in such a way as to make them indistinguishable from their fellow Jews who made no Christian profession (24:12). He saw them failing to evangelize those fellow Jews and failing to make disciples of Gentiles as well, for such evangelistic efforts would mark them for persecution.

Warning! Your salvation depends on perseverance in the Christian life and witness. Otherwise you will be lost along with those who make no profession, many of them your very persecutors. Prove yourselves true. Do not let persecution lead you to hide your connection with Jesus. Flee if you must, but preach the gospel of the kingdom wherever you go. And do your good works as Christians in the full gaze of the public, even to the extent of endangering yourselves by openly ministering to persecuted fellow Christians. The day of judgment is coming. Show yourselves salty, not saltless; wise builders, not foolish ones; wheat, not tares; good fish, not bad; wearing a wedding garment, not lacking one; useful in service, not slothful and useless; wise virgins, not foolish ones. Do not slip into the category of goats rather than sheep. Your salvation is at stake. Make sure you are one of the few that will be saved.

If Matthew's emphasis on salvation by works of righteousness arises out of a need for persecuted Christians to prove the genuineness of their profession, we might ask whether a similar emphasis in the Letter of James arises out of the same need, or out of a different one. If out of a different one, has the difference in need made a difference in the emphasis? In James, the emphasis arises out of a need to quell contentiousness within local assemblies; hence, the works of righteousness have to do with the gaining, or regaining, of harmony in those assemblies. In Matthew, however, the emphasis arises out of a need to prove genuineness of Christian profession under persecution; hence, the works of righteousness have to do with the

risks of open discipleship and Christian evangelism in the larger society.

If Matthew's emphasis arises out of a need for persecuted Christians to prove the genuineness of their profession, we might also ask whether the emphasis has a purpose of combating Paul's doctrine of salvation—or, as he prefers to say, justification—by faith apart from works, or of combating an antinomian aberration of Paul's doctrine. To ask the question in terms of *persecution* is to cast doubt on an affirmative answer. The same is true if we ask whether Matthew's emphasis has the purpose of combating, or competing with, the rabbinic Judaism that was evolving in the last quarter of the first century. For it is one thing to claim superiority over that Judaism for the purpose of keeping persecuted Christians true to the faith, but it would be quite another thing to claim superiority over that Judaism for the purpose of taking command of Jewish religious life. And to suppose a synergy of both purposes founders on the unlikelihood that a persecuted minority thought of taking over the large, persecuting body. On the contrary and as already noted, Matthew underlines the fewness of those who will be saved: "For the gate is small, and the way is narrow that leads to life, and few are those who find it" (7:14):

> These emphases pose the danger of legalism and need balancing by the doctrine of the indwelling Spirit, through whose life and power alone Jesus' disciples can fulfill the righteous requirement of the law (Rom. 8:1–4). But it is good to have Matthew's emphases without that balance; for in some situations to introduce the doctrine of the Spirit quickly is to dull the edge of the demands made on Jesus' disciples. They might fail to feel the pain caused by the sharp edge of those demands. Only when that pain is felt will the Spirit's enablement amount to more than a comfortable sanctification open to the incursion of antinomianism. Wherever the church has grown large and mixed, wherever the church is polarized between the extremes of latitudinarianism and sectarianism, wherever the church feels drawn to accommodation with forces that oppose the gospel, wherever the church loses its vision of worldwide evangelism, wherever the church lapses into smug religiosity with its attendant vices of ostentation, hypocrisy, and haughty disdain for its underprivileged and correspondingly zealous members—there the Gospel of Matthew speaks with power and pertinence. (Gundry 9–10)

Bibliography

Blomberg, C. *Matthew*. Broadman, 1992; Burgess, J. *A History of the Exegesis of Matthew 6:17–19 from 1781 to 1965*. Edwards Brothers, 1976; Carlston, C. "Christology and Church in Matthew." Pages 1283–1304 in *The Four Gospels 1992*, ed. F. Van Segbroeck et al. Leuven University Press, 1992; English, E. *Studies in the Gospel according to Matthew*. F. H. Revell, 1935; Green, H. *The Gospel according to Matthew*. Oxford University Press, 1975; Guelich, R. *The Sermon on the Mount*. Word, 1982; Gundry, R. *Matthew*. 2d ed. Eerdmans, 1994; Hagner, D. "Apocalyptic Motifs in the Gospel of Matthew: Continuity and Discontinuity." *HBT* 7 (1985): 53–82; idem. *Matthew 1–13*. Word, 1993; Luz, U. *Matthew 1–7*. Augsburg, 1989; idem. *Matthew 8–20*. Fortress, 2001; idem. *Matthew in History*. Fortress, 1994; idem. *The Theology of the Gospel of Matthew*. Cambridge University Press, 1995; Meier, J. P. *The Vision of Matthew*. Paulist, 1979; Przybylski, B. *Righteousness in Matthew and His World of Thought*. Cambridge University Press, 1980; Simonetti, M., ed. *Matthew 1–13*. ACCSNT 1a. InterVarsity, 2001; idem. *Matthew 14–28*. ACCSNT 1b. InterVarsity, 2002; Suggs, M. J. *Wisdom, Christology, and Law in Matthew's Gospel*. Harvard University Press, 1970.

Robert H. Gundry

Meaning

Meaning is one of the most disputed notions in contemporary philosophy, and the questions raised about it range over a wide spectrum of topics. Indeed, philosophers from very different traditions have gone so far as to doubt the existence of meaning altogether or the possibility of making sense of it (Quine; Derrida; Oswood). The most pertinent topics in a scriptural context have to do with what meaning is, whether there are limits to it, and what determines textual meaning. These are relevant here in particular because they reveal the important role that theology plays in scriptural interpretation.

What Is Meaning?

There is a sense of meaning that is important in a religious context but that does not especially have to do with language or texts, and therefore with Scriptures. This is the notion of meaning as significance.

Meaning as Significance. In this sense, meaning is taken to involve importance, relevance, and consequences (Hirsch; Gracia, *Theory*). The meaning of X, for example, is the significance that X has for, say, Y. We speak of a particular event as having meaning because it had important historical repercussions, and we refer to something as being meaningful when it is considered to be relevant for something else. On the other hand, we dismiss the meaning of certain events because they have no important consequences or we consider them irrelevant in particular contexts. The sense of meaning as significance is easily applicable to Scriptures, although it is not particularly tied to them, or even to texts or language in general. Anything whatever can have meaning or be meaningful in this sense.

The notion of meaning is also, and particularly, used in the context of linguistic phenomena. We speak about the meaning of words, sentences, or texts, although there are important differences in the views that have been proposed to account for the meaning of these, and not every theory applies to all of them. For example, the so-called Causal Theory is intended to apply to names rather than sentences (Kripke 1987). And the Verificationist Theory proposed by the members of the Vienna Circle, according to which the meaning of a sentence is given in the account of the conditions under which it would be true, is not intended to account for the meaning of words (Ayer). Because of space limitations, this article ignores the differences between theories of meaning applicable to words, sentences, or texts in particular, and addresses meaning generally as it applies to all three kinds of linguistic entities. Most important in a scriptural context, however, are theories that have to do with the meaning of texts, for Scriptures are texts.

The general views of meaning most often proposed fall into at least four main classes, depending on whether they identify meaning with reference, intention, ideas, or use. All four have interesting implications for scriptural meaning.

Meaning as Reference. Some argue that the meaning of a word is the same as its reference or, as it is often put, its extension (Frege). The meaning of "Paul" is Paul, and the meaning of "human being" is the group of human beings. In the case of declarative sentences, their meanings are the facts expressed by the sentences. The meaning of "Christ was born in Bethlehem" is the fact that Christ was born in that town. In this sense, meanings are neither in the mind (psychologism) nor in the head (physicalism) unless they happen to be mental or neurological entities, as is the case with the meanings of "thought" or "neuron."

The referential view of meaning appears to work well when applied to proper names that refer to existing persons. Something similar can be said about definite descriptions, such as "the mother of Jesus" whose meaning is Mary, or certain declarative sentences, such as the one given earlier. But it is more difficult to apply it to proper names of fictitious characters or of abstract nouns, because it is not clear what their reference would be. The case of sentences also poses difficulties, for the status of facts has never been established convincingly. Other troubling cases are commands and exclamations insofar as these have meaning and yet there seem to be no things to which they refer.

Finally, there are cases in which two different words or phrases have the same reference but appear to have different meanings. Consider "the writer of the book of Revelation" and "the apostle who accompanied Mary to Calvary." Assuming that the writer of the book of Revelation is also the apostle who accompanied Mary to Calvary, the reference of these expressions is the same, but still the meaning is quite different.

Meaning as Intention. An alternative to the referential view argues that the meanings of sentences in particular are reducible to the intentions speakers have to produce beliefs in listeners through the recognition of those intentions (Grice). In this sense, meanings are states of mind.

But does it make sense to say that the meanings of texts are intentions? Consider the text, "In the beginning was the Word," which opens the Gospel according to John. Does it make sense to say that the meaning of these words is the intention John had when he wrote the words? Some would say that it is not for at least three reasons: First, the meaning seems to have to do with the words themselves, regardless of any intention John may have had. Second, how can anyone but John have any access to his intention except through the very words in question? And third, the meaning of the words does not seem to be anything in John's mind, whether an intention or any other state; the meaning of "In the beginning was the Word" is that in the beginning was the Word, and this does not appear to be anything mental.

Meaning as Ideas. Other philosophers adopt an ideational view of meaning, according to which meaning consists of ideas, although some of them would object to the use of the terms "idea" and "ideational" to refer to their views. Those who hold versions of this position differ in particular in their understanding of what these ideas or entities are, and whether they are nonmental forms (Plato), abstract objects (Frege), mental concepts or images (Locke), mental or neurological states, or the result of the last two (Fodor).

This view of meaning encounters various difficulties depending on how ideas are interpreted. For example, if they are taken to be forms or abstract objects independent of the mind, then questions arise as to their status, origin, and relation to the mind. And if they are interpreted as mental concepts or images, or as mental or neurological states (or their results), then it is not clear that they account for meaning, as was evident in the intentionalist view. It does not seem to make sense to say that the meaning of "cat" is the idea of cat when this is understood as a mental or physical state, for the mental or physical state whereby I think of cat is something very different from a cat (Quine).

Meaning as Use. Some philosophers propose a conception of meaning as use (Wittgenstein), and this is sometimes taken to mean that understanding the meaning of a sentence, say, is to know the conditions under which it can be asserted (Dummett). One way to understand this view is in relation to an illocutionary act (Austin). Consider an example: When I say to Peter, "Peter, say the Lord's Prayer," I utter a sentence. The act of uttering the sentence is called locutionary. Apart from this act, the sentence may cause certain other acts, such as the act of getting Peter to say the Lord's Prayer, which is also an act I perform. This is called the perlocutionary act. Finally, I also perform the act of ordering Peter to say the Lord's Prayer, and this is an illocutionary act. Now, the meaning of a text may be expressed in terms of the notion of an illocutionary act as follows: The meaning of X is that in virtue of which one who performs a locutionary act also performs a certain illocutionary act. Unfortunately, philosophers disagree on what this is exactly (Searle).

One important disadvantage of this view is that it does not seem to work well with long texts. It is difficult to think of all the illocutionary acts that take place when the locutionary acts involved in reciting or writing the book of Revelation are performed, for example, and this raises questions of indeterminacy. Another is that in an effort to pinpoint the limits of meaning, some philosophers appeal to rules. But the status of these rules themselves and their source become points of contention.

The referential, intentional, ideational, and use views of meaning have interesting implications for the particular case of scriptural meaning, and some of them pose especial issues and problems. Consider, for example, the view that meanings are abstract objects separate from minds and brains. If this is so, then the question arises as to the ontological status and eternity of these objects and of their relation to God. If they are eternal realities, are they caused by God or not? The view that meanings are states of mind poses the questions of whether they are in the mind of God, in the human mind, or in both. If they are in God's mind, a further question arises as to how they are related to God and his attributes.

And if these meanings are considered to be brain states in humans, then one needs to determine what corresponds to them in God's mind insofar as God has no brain.

These questions illustrate how different views of meaning affect religious views and thus how important theology is for the determination of scriptural meaning. Clearly, certain theological doctrines require the adoption of certain understandings of meaning, and certain views of meaning have significant implications for theology.

Are There Limits to the Meanings of Texts?

Regardless of what one takes meanings to be, if one accepts that texts have meanings, one must address the question of whether there are limits to those meanings. Three different answers are generally given to this question. One argues that the meanings of texts have no limits, another that they have strict and narrow limits, and a third tries to find a compromise between these two.

Textual Meanings Have No Limits. According to the first view, there are no limits to the meaning of texts (Gadamer). This is not to say that texts have no meaning, which is a different position altogether. Texts, like words and signs, are polysemous: they are essentially ambiguous in that they do not have a single meaning but can be used to mean different things depending on the circumstances. It is impossible to pinpoint a meaning, or even a range of meanings, for a particular text that would exclude some other meanings for that text for all times and places. The meaning of a text is always open-ended. Indeed, no text can be understood to mean the same thing on two different occasions, for every understanding of it presupposes a different point of view from which the text is approached and its meaning is understood.

The strength of this position lies in the recognition that there is wide disagreement as to the meaning of certain texts, and that often texts are used to mean things their authors and their historical audiences could not have guessed. Frequently, texts are understood by different persons, or even by the same person at different times, to mean different and even contradictory things, and no determination can be reached concerning which is the correct meaning of the text on all occasions.

The weakness of this view is that it does not appear to reflect experience with respect to all texts. Although there is wide disagreement as to the meaning of certain texts, there is little disagreement as to the meaning of others. The NO SMOKING sign posted on my classroom wall means that no smoking is allowed in the room and not that smoking is permitted, a fact with which everyone who knows English agrees. Moreover, this position finds it hard to account for communication through texts, for communication involves the conveyance of meaning, and this in turn presupposes that the meaning in question be determinate in at least some ways.

Textual Meanings Have Strict Limits. The contrary view argues that there are indeed strict, and even narrow, limits to the meanings of texts (Hirsch). The advantage of this view is that, unlike the previous one, it accounts for communication. We communicate effectively because the texts we use have meanings with clear limits that the communicants understand. Indeed, the very use of texts seems to imply that those who use them have in mind specific meanings, with definite boundaries, that they wish to convey. When I say, "Smoking is not permitted," I mean that smoking is not permitted and not something else.

But this position also encounters difficulties. For one thing, it does not account for the mentioned and frequent disagreements we experience concerning the meanings of texts. And disagreements seem to arise because, even in very specific contexts, there appear to be some texts whose meanings are not determinate. Literary texts in particular are generally taken to be open to multiple and equally legitimate interpretations, reflecting the fact that their meanings are not narrow and limited.

Textual Meanings Have Some Limits. The difficulties encountered by the two views examined have led to attempts to find a compromise between them. In working out this compromise, three distinctions have been proposed, although they are not uncontroversial: essential and accidental differences in meaning, meanings and their implications, and meanings and intentions (Gracia, *Theory*). The first distinction helps to show that, although texts may have a well-delimited core of meaning (an essential meaning), they may have other meanings that are the result of contingent conditions, such as changes in context (accidental meanings). This in turn explains disagreements in the understanding of their meanings. The distinction between meanings and their implications is used to make clear that there can be a core of meaning for a text that does not include its implications. This also helps explain why audiences and even authors may disagree on the meaning of a text insofar as some persons may include in the meaning some of its implications, whereas others do not. Finally, the distinction between meanings and intentions is meant to indicate how an author or user of a text may actually have the intention to use a text to mean things that are not part of the meaning of the text. This explains, again, why there are disagreements as to the meanings of texts. In all cases, the strategy is to grant that texts have a well-defined and limited core of meaning, but that they can also be used to mean something else (intentions), they can convey more than they mean (implications), and contextually (by accident) they can mean something more than, or different from, what they essentially mean.

There are interesting implications and questions that result from the three different views about the limits of meaning mentioned when applied to Scriptures. For example: Is the meaning of Scriptures open-ended, so that there is no definite meaning to them? Or is the meaning of Scriptures strictly limited? An affirmative answer to the first question would allow for the kind of flexibility some argue is necessary for the changing understanding of Scriptures throughout history. On the other hand, others object that to allow for so much flexibility would open the doors to complete chaos in interpretation, destroying any unity of message the Scriptures could have. The introduction of the distinction between essential and accidental meaning, meaning and its implications, and meaning and intention helps find a compromise between these views in some cases, but not all cases could be resolved in this way. In particular, the scriptural interpreter needs guidance in this matter, and it makes sense to argue that the source of that guidance can be properly found in theology.

What Determines Textual Meaning?

Regardless of the position one takes with respect to the nature of meaning and the limits of textual meaning, as long as one accepts that texts have meanings, one still needs to establish what it is that determines those meanings. And here again there is wide disagreement. At least eight factors, singly or in combination, have been identified as determining it: authors, audiences, contexts, communities, languages, texts, truth conditions, and cultural functions.

Authors. At first glance nothing would appear more obvious than that the author (utterer, speaker, user, or writer, as others put it) determines the meaning of a text, thus giving rise to the notion of authorial meaning (or utterer, speaker, user, or writer meaning; Grice; Schiffer; Hirsch).

Indeed, because the author produces the text—so the argument goes—it must be the author who determines its meaning. After all, the author selects and arranges the words of which the text is composed in order to convey a specific meaning to an audience. Because the words authors use to compose texts are not naturally tied to particular meanings, or even to any meanings at all, many hold that it is the author's intended meaning that establishes the meaning of a text.

Matters are not so simple, however. Naturally, if the text produced by an author is the result of entirely new words invented by the author, which are stipulatively used to express a specific meaning, then one may be able to claim that the author is fully and singly responsible for both the text and its meaning. However, most texts produced by authors do not fall into this category, for the words authors choose for their texts are already in use prior to that choice, and they belong to natural languages in which they appear to have established meanings. Moreover, the arrangements in which those words are placed follow syntactical rules belonging to those languages and are not creations of the authors. This entails that authors may know less about the meaning of the words they use and the semantic import of the ways they can be arranged than their audiences, and this suggests in turn that texts may have meanings different from those their authors think or intend them to have.

When it comes to Scriptures, matters become more complicated, because not everyone agrees about who the author of these texts is. For some, it is God himself, who worked through individual human persons to produce the texts. But for others, the authors are human and the Scriptures are mere testimonies of their understanding of God's revelation. This, then, can in principle generate two meanings: God's meaning and the human authors' meaning. And this in turn raises questions as to how faithful to God's meaning is the meaning that the human authors understand, and whether these human authors are mere instruments in God's hands or are in fact the authors of texts through which they intend to convey their own understanding of divine revelation (Barth).

Audiences. That the audience (readers, listeners, or interpreters, as others put it) determines the meaning of a text makes sense insofar as it explains the existence of mutually incompatible, but equally acceptable, understandings of the same text, thus giving rise to the notion of audience meaning (or reader, listener, or interpreter meaning; Schleiermacher). Moreover, it also explains how it is possible that in some cases an audience may know the meaning of a text better than its author does.

But there are difficulties. For one thing, the role of an audience appears to be primarily to understand a text, not to establish its meaning. An audience tries to get the point made by an author or user, not to impose a meaning on the text it reads or hears. Audiences feel constrained by the meanings they understand texts to have. This is why they often criticize the views expressed by texts, or modify them to fit their own views. Intentionally, the audience's role is not to create, or to impose, or even to convey meaning, but to grasp it. Moreover, if it were the job of audiences to create or determine meanings, then the purpose of communication would be thwarted. In that case an audience would not be seeking to understand what an author tries to communicate through a text, but rather to impose on a text whatever meaning it thinks fit.

Indeed, to say that audiences are responsible for determining textual meaning entails that the meanings of texts do not in fact have limits. Insofar as meanings would be up to audiences—and the number of possible audiences for any text is potentially infinite—there would be no way of establishing constraints.

In a scriptural context, the audience varies as much as in other contexts. In some cases, the texts themselves pick a particular audience, such as Pharaoh or Christ's apostles, but in most cases they do not. It makes sense, however, to think of the community of believers as the proper audience of Scriptures when these are taken as divine revelation, for the members of this community are the ones who take it to be so. But it makes no sense to say that this particular audience establishes the meaning of Scriptures when in fact they claim that Scriptures contain a divine message for them.

Contexts. It is obvious that context has much to do with the determination of the meaning of at least certain texts, thus giving rise to the notion of contextual meaning (Eco). The shout "Fire!" in a crowded theater means something different from what it means when uttered by an army officer on the front line of battle. But is context what determines textual meaning? A historicist might argue that indeed it is. But what exactly is context? Texts can be part of the context of other texts, and authors and audiences are certainly part of that context. Not to include the author and audience in it makes no sense, for part of

the context of a text is brought in precisely by authors and audiences and their circumstances. On the other hand, if authors and audiences are included in the context, then it is not clear how this position would differ substantially from the previous two. Finally, context is such a broad and changing factor that this could amount to saying that texts have no particular meanings, a fact that seems to prevent effective communication.

The context of Scriptures can be as broad as that of any other text and therefore subject to the same conditions. If believers wish to put some limits on scriptural meaning, context cannot be the exclusive factor.

Communities. Another factor often mentioned as determining the meaning of texts is a community, giving rise to the notion of community meaning (Putnam; Fish). Sometimes the community is taken in general as the speakers of the language of the text in question, but at other times it is identified with a smaller group considered authoritative for purposes of textual understanding—whence the notion of institutional meaning.

A community, however, is nothing but a collection of individual persons who are related to texts as authors or audiences. There is no common entity or mind in a community to which could be assigned the intentions and understandings necessary for the determination of textual meanings. A community can be understood either as authors and audiences, as neither authors nor audiences, or as groups of people composed of authors, audiences, and those who are neither. To say the first is to recognize that texts have authors and audiences and that the limits of their meanings are imposed by them. To say the second entails that there is no relation of the community to the texts, although the community may be responsible for establishing the parameters of word meanings and the rules of grammar for the arrangement of those words. But it is difficult to maintain that a community understood thus establishes the meanings of particular texts, for it is not the community that composes the texts in question.

In the case of Scriptures, the pertinent community is not generally taken to refer to the linguistic community of speakers of the language in which the Scriptures are rendered insofar as the Scriptures are thought to have a special meaning for believers. The pertinent community, then, is identified with the group of believers, or even with a subgroup of persons considered to have the authority to determine scriptural meaning and set the parameters of religious doctrine, such as a group of elders or a general council.

Languages. Language itself is sometimes regarded as sufficient to establish textual meaning, thus giving rise to the notion of linguistic or literal meaning (Katz; Barthes; Davidson). After all, a language is a set of words and a set of rules according to which the words can be legitimately organized so as to produce texts with meaning. In principle, then, one could argue that a language contains virtually all the possible arrangements of the words it has and thus all the possible texts that can be produced in it. If so, then, it would appear that it is the language—the vocabulary and grammatical rules—that establishes the meaning of texts.

However, for at least two reasons one may question the sufficiency of language by itself to establish the meanings of particular texts. In the first place, the meaning of texts, and thus of the words and arrangements that compose a language, depends also on context, and context is not always linguistic or textual. Second, language may virtually contain an infinite number of possible texts and corresponding meanings, but such virtual content does not entail any actual texts or meanings. Decisions are required for the choice of words and the implementation of rules. Languages by themselves are inert; they require users to be actualized into texts. Users are responsible for the production of texts out of languages, and users are not bound by languages, for they introduce modifications, violate rules, and develop innovations. Except for dead languages, or those that are the product of stipulation, languages are in a constant process of change and subject to modification by their users.

This view can easily be applied to scriptural interpretation: The languages used in Scripture determine textual meaning. But Scripture consists of particular texts that presumably are the result of divine revelation. So, the same objections voiced against the position in general apply also to this case.

Texts. The objections raised against the mentioned views lead some to argue that it is texts themselves that establish their own meaning, giving rise to the notion of textual meaning (Beardsley). This view sidesteps several of the problems identified so far. For example, unlike language, texts are not just sets of words that can be arranged in many possible ways in accordance with certain rules, but rather concrete arrangements of words that display particular organizations. Moreover, although this imposes certain limitations on textual meaning, the limitations are not such that the freedom of audiences to understand the same text in incompatible ways is ruled out. There is considerable latitude in the understanding of textual meaning, but not complete license.

This view also encounters difficulties, however. Most important is that it is difficult to see how in fact texts themselves can establish their meanings, for they have no natural connection to those meanings. Why can't a short text be held to mean exactly what a much longer one does? Or vice versa? And how can one choose between two or more equally feasible meanings? If these questions cannot be answered effectively in terms of the text, as they appear not to be, then it would seem that the main purpose of the use of texts, the communication of meaning, is defeated.

The controversy between literal and contextual meanings clearly illustrates the difficulties. Some hold that the meaning of texts is what they say when they are understood in accordance with the common understanding of the terms and rules of arrangement prescribed by the languages in which they are rendered (Katz; Davidson). But others argue that context is essential for their meaning (Gibbs).

In the case of Scriptures this position has had its defenders from the very beginning. According to them, the Scriptures determine their own meaning by interpreting themselves. But does this really work? The controversy between literal and nonliteral meanings (or interpretations) of Scripture clearly indicates that they do not.

Truth Conditions. Truth conditions have been held to be what establishes the meaning of declarative sentences (Frege; Davidson). And this seems to make sense in that the conditions under which a sentence can be true seem to establish what it says. What else could do it?

However, scholars generally identify at least two objections to this position when considered as a general theory of meaning. One is that the meaning in question is only that of declarative sentences. The meaning of linguistic entities that cannot have truth value, such as words, cannot be explained in this way. This requires the elaboration of a more comprehensive view that accounts for the meaning of these entities as well, and it is not easy to relate the truth-conditions theory to this overall view. The second objection is that, even if one accepts that truth conditions determine the meaning of declarative sentences, one must establish, further, the basis on which those conditions are picked. So, clearly there is something else at work in meaning than just truth conditions.

In short, objections can be raised to every one of the seven factors mentioned, taken as a means of establishing scriptural meaning, considered by itself. For example, one may object that the divine author cannot be regarded by a community of believers as determining the meaning of Scriptures for that community because believers have access to what God wishes to say to them only through the Scriptures. A mystical source of knowledge does not work insofar as different persons might claim different things about what Scriptures mean. The case of human authors poses problems because we have no direct access to their intended meaning except through the texts they produce. Context poses problems because Scriptures are read and understood in many different contexts, as their history easily illustrates, giving rise to an endless number of possible meanings. The linguistic community at large encounters difficulties because the Scriptures are supposed to contain messages that make sense only to believers. By itself, the community of believers is controversial unless that community accepts certain rules of understanding that establish the meaning of Scriptures. Language alone seems helpless because it is meaningful only when used, and its use is manifested only in texts. The Scriptures themselves fail because they are no more than certain inscriptions that are not naturally tied to any meanings and that are subject to different understandings. Finally, truth conditions do not work because they require a means of being established.

An alternative to these inadequate views is to combine some of these factors, but where do we find the criteria to pick the relevant ones and to determine the role that each plays? One possibility is to turn to the functions that a text has in a particular culture.

Cultural Functions. According to this view, the determining factor of textual meaning is to be found in the functions that a text has within a culture (Gracia, *Theory*). Texts can be used for a variety of purposes. A text can be used as religious Scripture, a historical source, a literary work, and so on, and it is the uses to which a text is put within a community that determine its meaning. Cultural function goes beyond the factors thus far considered, in that it establishes which of those factors take precedence over the others, and whether they are given any role in the determination of meaning. In particular, it should be distinguished from communities, audiences, and contexts. The cultural function of X within a culture is the use to which X is put in that culture. The culture is the complex system of values, customs, beliefs, and social norms that regulate activities within the community that has the culture, and the community is the group of people involved. Cultural function, then, needs to be distinguished from both the culture and the community. It should also be distinguished from audiences, which consist of any persons with actual or potential access to the text (not just members of the culture of production or use). Likewise, the context of a text is much broader than the cultural function it has in a particular culture, since it includes anything that can affect its meaning.

Like other texts, Scriptures have particular functions, but where do we find the criteria that establish how those functions are to be transformed into a set of rules that determine the meaning of the texts? And what are the roles that the various examined factors play in this determination? The answers to these questions lie in the answer to another more basic question: What establishes the criteria of scriptural meaning? That is, where do we find the rules that establish whether it is the author, audience, context, society, language, truth conditions, or the Scriptures themselves, that determines scriptural meaning? Or, to put it differently, what is the function that the Scriptures have within the community of believers, since that community regards them as Scriptures? The answer is found in theology.

Theology. A theology is primarily a view of the world based on an attempt to understand it in terms of both human knowledge and a particular divine revelation (Gracia, *How?*); theology is the understanding of a religious faith by those who have this faith. As such, theology contains not only interpretations of the world, but also rules that determine the legitimate meaning of the texts regarded as revealed. Consider, for example, the creation of the world as recorded in Genesis. Some Christian groups, committed theologically to the literal interpretation of Scriptures, interpret this description literally. Accordingly, for them creation took place in six days. Other Christian denominations, however, put weight on tradition in the understanding of Scriptures. In keeping with that tradition, they do not accept that scriptural texts need always be interpreted literally, opening the way for a nontemporal, evolutionary understanding of creation.

Theology, then, establishes not only textual meaning, but also the degree to which other factors play roles in the proper interpretation of Scriptures. These rules are both epistemically and ontologically normative: epistemically, because they establish the proper method of finding out the true meaning of Scriptures; ontologically, because they establish legitimate meanings by distinguishing those that are so from those that are not. In this sense, theology is not only a hermeneutical tool for interpretation, but more importantly, it is the ultimate determining factor of scriptural meaning.

Conclusion

In conclusion, the role of theology in scriptural meaning is essential. Theology influences the view of meaning that is required when it comes to Scriptures, it establishes whether Scriptures have limits to their meaning or not, and finally it determines the meaning and the way to acquire it. Theology not only provides the rules for the correct interpretation of Scriptures, but also identifies their correct meaning. A theory of scriptural meaning, then, must begin in theology.

See also Authorial Discourse Interpretation; Exegesis; Hermeneutics; Intention/Intentional Fallacy; Speech-Act Theory; Theological Hermeneutics, Contemporary

Bibliography

Austin, J. L. *How to Do Things with Words*, ed. J. Urmson. Harvard University Press, 1962; Ayer, A. J. *Language, Truth, and Logic*. Dover, 1952; Barth, K. *Church Dogmatics*, trans. G. Thomson et al. 4 vols. T&T Clark, 1960; Barthes, R. "The Death of the Author." Pages 142–48 in *Image, Music, Text*, trans. S. Heath. Hill & Wang, 1977; Beardsley, M. "The Authority of the Text." Pages 16–37 in *Possibility of Criticism*. Wayne State University Press, 1970; Davidson, D. *Inquiries into Truth and Interpretation*. Oxford University Press, 1984; Derrida, J. "Structure, Sign and Play in the Discourse of the Human Sciences." Pages 247–72 in *The Structuralist Controversy*, ed. R. Macksay and E. Donato. Johns Hopkins University Press, 1970; Dummett, M. *Truth and Other Enigmas*. Duckworth, 1978; Eco, U. *The Limits of Interpretation*. Indiana University Press, 1990; Fish, S. *Is There a Text in This Class?* Harvard University Press, 1985; Fodor, J. *Psychosemantics*. MIT Press, 1987; Frege, G. *Collected Papers*. Oxford University Press, 1984; Gadamer, H.-G. *Truth and Method*, trans. G. Barden and R. Cumming. 2d ed. Crossroad, 1975; Gibbs, R., Jr. *Intentions in the Experience of Meaning*. Cambridge University Press, 1999; Gracia, J. *How Can We Know What God Means?* Palgrave, 2001; idem. *A Theory of Textuality*. SUNY Press, 1995; Grice, H. P. "Meaning." *Philosophical Review* 66 (1957): 377–88; Hirsch, E. D., Jr. *Validity in Interpretation*. Yale University Press, 1967; Katz, J. *Propositional Structure and Illocutionary Force*. T. Y. Crowell, 1977; Kripke, S. *Naming and Necessity*. Harvard University Press, 1987; idem. *Wittgenstein on Rules and Private Language*. Blackwell, 1982; Locke, J. *An Essay Concerning Human Understanding*. Dover, 1959; Oswood, C. *Focus on Meaning*. Mouton, 1976; Putnam, H. *Mind, Language and Reality*. Cambridge University Press, 1975; Quine, W. V. O. *Word and Object*. Harvard University Press, 1960; Schiffer, S. *Meaning*. Oxford University Press, 1972; Schleiermacher, F. D. E. *Hermeneutics and Criticism and Other Writings*, ed. and trans. A. Bowie. Cambridge University Press, 1998; Searle, J. *Expression and Meaning*. Cambridge University Press, 1975; Vanhoozer, K. *Is There a Meaning in This Text?* Zondervan, 1998; Wittgenstein, L. *Philosophical Investigations*. Oxford University Press, 1953.

Jorge J. E. Gracia

Medieval Biblical Interpretation

The history of biblical interpretation between the fall of the Western Roman Empire in the fifth century and the Reformation is one of the most important and, until recently, also one of the most neglected areas of Christian thought. For a thousand years, Latin Christendom was shaped by a hermeneutical pattern that affected every area of life, and that has continued to exert considerable influence in the centuries since. But since the Renaissance and Reformation of the sixteenth century, the cutting edge of biblical interpretation has been elsewhere, and the medieval heritage has faded from the picture. The main reason for this neglect is the belief that medieval interpreters worked with a defective text in a series of inappropriate ways, of which allegory is but the most notorious example. Fanciful etymologies abound in the writings of medieval exegetes, as do digressions on subjects like witchcraft and alchemy, neither of which is in much favor among modern biblical scholars. The rediscovery of the original biblical languages in the fifteenth century has often been considered the decisive factor that renders most, if not all, medieval exegesis obsolete and unreliable. As a result, it has been ignored and abandoned, except by medievalists who study it for cultural, rather than theological, reasons.

That the traditionally negative view of medieval exegesis is unfair has only been perceived since the writings of Henri de Lubac, and others have revived a serious interest in it. The recent willingness of some scholars to broaden their horizons and consider alternatives to the historical-critical method has also worked in favor of medieval interpreters. They are sometimes seen as having a contribution to make toward a literary or spiritual interpretation of the text that does not depend on the criteria of historical criticism. Students of the

Reformation have also noticed that Luther and Calvin had more in common with their medieval forebears than we are accustomed to admit, and that too has played a part in stimulating renewed interest in them. However, it must be stressed that this revival of interest is partial and fairly restricted in its scope; there is no question of returning to the medieval outlook in any serious way, or of denying the quite considerable gains in our understanding that have been made since the sixteenth century.

Medieval interpretation is characterized by its virtually complete dependence on the Latin Vulgate translation of the Bible, most of which was made by Jerome in the years 375–400 CE. Jerome worked from original sources in both Hebrew and Greek, and disapproved of the apocryphal additions to the OT found in the Greek LXX, but his scientific spirit was not copied by later generations. They came to regard the Vulgate as an infallible text in itself and seldom made any effort to go behind it to the sources. Fortunately, it is an excellent translation, in some respects superior to the Greek "originals" used by Erasmus and the sixteenth-century humanists. But even so, it is still a translation and therefore unsuited to the minute analysis to which it was often subjected in the Middle Ages. A good example is the way in which Gregory the Great developed the words *vir unus*, used to describe Job. It means no more than "a certain man," but Gregory was convinced that the apparently unnecessary *unus* must have a particular theological significance. To him, it was a pointer to the uniqueness of Christ, the true *vir unus*—an interpretation that obviously has no textual foundation.

In the early Middle Ages, the Latin world still lived in the shadow of ancient Rome, and it is difficult to know whether a writer like Gregory (d. 604) or even Bede (ca. 673–735) can really be called medieval. Bede, for example, despite his geographical isolation in northern England, was fully conversant with patristic exegesis, both Greek and Latin, and wrote commentaries based on it, which became standard works for nearly a thousand years. They are currently being translated into English, and in many instances, they can stand comparison with the most sophisticated modern opinion on textual and historical matters. Yet Bede was also quite clear on the need for maintaining the allegorical interpretation of the Bible, which in his time was acquiring a new lease on life in the monasteries. There, the threefold allegorical scheme of Origen had undergone a permutation, thanks to the work of John Cassian

(360–435), who is generally credited with having added a fourth level of spiritual interpretation by dividing Origen's "spiritual" sense into two distinct parts: The first was allegorical and related mainly to the life of the church militant here on earth. The second (anagogical) sense was proleptic and referred mainly to the life of the church triumphant in heaven. (The "tropological" sense deals with the moral life.) Thus, references to Jerusalem could be differentiated according to whether they applied mainly to the government of the earthly body, or to the blessed state of the redeemed. Which one should be preferred in any given instance was, of course, the task of the interpreter to decide.

The subsequent loss of Latin as a spoken language made grammatical study of the text even more important than it had been before, and medieval commentaries are full of remarks about points of grammar and vocabulary that would have been unnecessary in earlier centuries. From the eleventh century onward, a tradition of grammatical analysis grew up, based in the schools at Paris, that eventually produced the so-called *Glossa ordinaria*, a rambling commentary that by 1150 had become the standard work of biblical interpretation all over Western Europe. The main purpose of the *Glossa* was to remove mysteries in the text, and its authors displayed a remarkable knowledge of ancient law and the teachings of the church fathers. They became aware that there had been different hermeneutical approaches in ancient times, and that occasionally the fathers had contradicted one another, which forced them to make critical choices in their own interpretation.

Gradually commentators became bolder, and Peter Lombard (ca. 1100–1160) added a considerable amount of background detail in his own commentaries, mainly because he thought the *Glossa* was inadequate in that respect. On another front, scholars in the nascent universities launched a series of attacks on the allegorical tendency inherent in traditional monastic interpretation. Many of the leading lights of this development worked in or around the monastery of St. Victor in Paris, where the example of the abbot Hugh (ca. 1096–1141) provided a model for several generations of exegetes. Andrew of St. Victor (d. 1175) worked out a new synthesis of text and meaning; like many of the Victorines, he was English by nationality. Andrew said that because truth is unfathomable, we are not bound to the limited theories of the past, but are free to read and speculate on Scripture for ourselves. His own preference was for the literal rather than the symbolic or allegorical interpretation, with which he had grown up. For example, it was commonly said in his day that Jeremiah and John the Baptist had been free of original sin, because God had "known" them both in the womb. Andrew rejected this on the ground that "know" did not necessarily mean "spiritually accept." Furthermore, the common belief that the womb stood for the synagogue, he regarded as entirely wrong.

Andrew made a serious effort to learn Hebrew and consult Jewish rabbis about their reading of the biblical text. In this way, he came into contact with Talmudic interpretation, which he did his best to understand and integrate into his own exegesis. He had many disciples, of whom the most important was probably Stephen Langton (d. 1228), usually credited with dividing the biblical books into chapters (verse divisions came in the sixteenth century).

Another important interpreter of this period was Peter the Chanter (d. 1197), who compiled a manual for preachers in which biblical interpretation was divided into three parts, which he called *lectio*, *disputatio*, and *praedicatio*. Thomas of Chobham (fl. ca. 1190–1210) developed this structure and claimed that preaching was the highest form of exegesis because it was the application of divine teaching in human words. Thomas distinguished between the meaning of words and the meaning of things (including concepts), restricting his use of allegory to the latter. Thus, for example, he would not find figurative meanings in the name "Jerusalem" (e.g., city of peace, the blessed state of the believer), but he was prepared to use the physical characteristics of the earthly city as guides to its spiritual character (e.g., it was high, beautiful, etc.). Thomas defined *lectio* as the study of how a word is related to the thing it describes. A word like "dog" means only one thing, but a word like "focus" has many meanings. On the other hand, a word like "the" means nothing by itself, whereas a word like "leprechaun" means nothing in reality. Finally, some words have an implicit meaning, which is not self-evident, as when the expression "on high" is used to refer to God. In interpreting the Bible, it was essential to decide which of these categories any particular word fell into, before attempting to determine what its meaning might be in the context.

Disputatio, according to Thomas, was the process by which one part of Scripture was to be harmonized with others. The word of God could not contradict itself, so apparent discrepancies had to be resolved by logical deduction based on what he called the *usus loquendi*, or turns of speech characteristic of particular writers. Thomas concluded that these had changed over the centuries and from one writer to another, so that different usages had to be taken into account. For example, if some writers regarded the "soul" as mortal, and others as immortal, this was not because they disagreed about the nature of the soul, but because they were using the same word in two different senses—in the first instance "life," and in the second "spirit."

Praedicatio was the domain especially reserved for allegory. From this, it appears that Thomas regarded preaching as a means of bringing people to a deeper mystical experience of God, rather than as a form of moral exhortation, and so the connection with the literal sense of the text was less significant. As long as it was largely a monastic activity, that approach remained viable, but the urge to evangelize the laity forced a change of direction, associated primarily (though by no means exclusively) with the order of the preaching friars (Dominicans).

Under their influence, recourse to a special "spiritual interpretation" quite separate from the literal exegesis of a text became less and less common. The imitation of Christ, the ultimate goal of all spiritual reading of Scripture, was interpreted with ever greater literalism, as can be seen from the career of Francis of Assisi, who took the divine commandment to sell all that he had with the greatest seriousness. The new literalism reached its apogee in the movement toward a more extended form of commentary, known as the "postill," whose great master was Hugh of St. Cher (fl. ca. 1230–35). The postillators adhered as closely as possible to the literal sense and frequently criticized the earlier glossators for their flights of fancy and allegory. The postills of Nicholas of Lyra (ca. 1270–1340) were especially popular with preachers and were the first biblical commentaries to be printed in the fifteenth century. They even influenced the early Reformers, whose own work in due course superseded them.

In this atmosphere, the traditional spiritual interpretation retreated into the background, though it enjoyed one last gasp in the eschatological prophesying of Joachim of Fiore (d. 1202). Joachim revived the chiliasm of the early church and gave it a new twist. He believed that the OT and NT represented the first two ages of revelation, and that in the coming third age, the letter of the Bible thus given would be cast aside by the Spirit, proceeding from both Testaments. The book of Revelation would then be fulfilled in a more-or-less literal way, with the appearance of the antichrist and the beginning of the great tribulation of the church. Joachim's theories went through many different recensions over the centuries, with the antichrist being identified with such diverse figures as Emperor Frederick II (1194–1250) and Pope John XXII (1316–34). Despite a history of repeated deception and failure, Joachim's millenarianism has retained its vitality to an astonishing extent.

The separation of the literal from the "spiritual" interpretation of the Bible, so characteristic of the twelfth century, was to some extent arrested and corrected by the rediscovery of Aristotle's writings. Although the church was quite suspicious of these at first, the new insights were eventually absorbed by the theological establishment, which created a new synthesis holding the literal and the spiritual together. Aristotle had taught that body and soul are a unity that cannot be sundered from one another, a doctrine applied to the Bible by saying that the letter and the Spirit must also be seen as a unity. Biblical theology could therefore no longer consist of a purely mechanical exegesis designed to facilitate an allegorical interpretation. Rather, it had to become a speculative science, according to which the spiritual meaning of a text was to be looked for in and through the literal sense—not beyond it.

The significance of this new development can be illustrated from the way in which Exod. 23:19 was interpreted at different times. This verse says: "You shall not boil a kid in its mother's milk" (NRSV), an injunction that Augustine regarded as absurd and unworthy of Scripture as it stood. He claimed that the true meaning was allegorical and meant that the coming Christ would not perish in Herod's slaughter of the innocents at Bethlehem. Andrew of St. Victor pointed out that as the Jews of his day continued the practice, it did have a literal application, however absurd that might have seemed to Augustine. Stephen Langton argued that the prohibition was primarily for hygienic reasons, thereby emptying it of any spiritual content. But Thomas Aquinas (1225–74), who became the leading spokesman of the new synthesis, argued that the prohibition was both to avoid cruelty and to distance the Jews from standard Gentile practice. In this way, it could be seen to have both a moral and spiritual application without departing from its literal meaning.

The emergence of this Thomist synthesis marks the beginning of a recognizably modern type of biblical interpretation, which was picked up and taken further by the Reformation. It also exposed the inadequacies of medieval hermeneutics in a way that would not be satisfactorily resolved before the sixteenth century. For one thing, renewed interest in the literal sense of Scripture underscored the need for a more accurate text, which would not be satisfied until the use of the original languages had been recovered. Similarly, Thomism raised the question of the church's authority as the privileged interpreter of the Bible. If Word and Spirit were to be held together, the interpretative role (if any) accorded to extrabiblical or nonbiblical authorities had to be determined on a new basis. The issue was joined by John Wycliffe (ca. 1330–84), who did not hesitate to accuse the church of having added to the primitive deposit of faith, which was uniquely contained in the Holy Scriptures. He was the first person who specifically advocated the principle of *sola scriptura*, or Scripture alone, as the basis of biblical interpretation, and for this reason he is often regarded as the "morning star" of the Reformation. But Wycliffe's "modernity" should not be exaggerated. He continued to use allegory on occasion, and his practice often fell short of his professed principles. He remained a man of the Middle Ages, and it is symptomatic that, although he wanted to translate the Bible into the vernacular (and his disciples succeeded in doing so), the translation was based on the Latin Vulgate and not on the original texts.

After Wycliffe's time, exegetes came increasingly under pressure from advocates of Renaissance humanism, who demanded a return to the sources and a more critical approach to them. It is perhaps symptomatic of that age that in 1433 the council of Basel received a short treatise on the principles of biblical interpretation composed by John of Ragusa (Dubrovnik). John enunciated a series of maxims, most of which can be construed as an attack on traditional allegorizing. For example, he put great stress on the clarity and perspicuity of the literal sense of the Bible and reminded his hearers that it was this sense, not the figurative ones, that had been inspired by the Holy Spirit and was therefore infallible. This led John to advocate a more intense study of the grammar of the original texts, which in turn made him prefer the witness of the church fathers, who lived closer to the origins of the NT, to the speculations of more recent exegetes. His contemporary Lorenzo Valla (1407–57) was the first person to introduce historical-critical methods of interpretation in a systematic way, and his researches demolished many of the standard assumptions of most medieval exegetes, particularly with regard to the claims of the Roman church. Finally Erasmus of Rotterdam (1466–1536) completed the process when he published his critical edition of the Greek NT, along with a fresh Latin translation, in 1516. This rapidly established itself as the authoritative text, and with the almost simultaneous outbreak of the Protestant Reformation, it signaled the end of the medieval era in biblical interpretation.

The contribution of medieval interpretation to the ongoing history of the church is difficult to assess and continues to be hotly debated. Nevertheless, certain basic features may be said to have survived all the ups and downs of subsequent exegesis, and remain as important today as they were then. The first of these is that it is essential to establish exactly what the text of Scripture is. Variant readings must be weighed and judged against the overall witness of the manuscript tradition, to ensure that we have the most accurate text available. Medieval interpreters lacked the resources needed to perform this task of textual criticism adequately, but when they were finally surpassed, it was by those whose work reflected their underlying principles.

The second fundamental principle is that scholars need to work from an agreed set of assumptions. For most medieval interpreters, that meant the doctrine of the church. But in the writings of the more radical theologians, like Wycliffe, it came to be said that Scripture itself provided the only reliable criteria for its interpretation, a view that continues to be the watchword of Protestant Christianity to this day.

The third lesson we have to learn from our medieval forebears is that the church must be spiritually edified by biblical teaching. To their great credit, they came to see with ever-greater clarity that this meant finding spiritual truth in, rather than under or beyond, the literal sense of the text, which led them to develop an extensive ministry of expository preaching. It was no accident that the friars, to whom this preaching was mostly entrusted, were among the most fervent exponents of the Reformation, which they saw as the fulfillment of their ministry in the wider church.

Finally, the medieval exegetes were aware that biblical interpretation relied on, and had to be integrated with, other branches of learning. There was not a "spiritual" realm totally disconnected from the material world in which we live, and so whatever was said of Scripture had to be consonant with what we know of the law, of history, and of the natural sciences. Harmony between all these disciplines is not always automatic or easy to achieve, but that it must be sought remains axiomatic to the present day. It is this aspect of medieval interpretation, more than anything else, that has inspired Henri de Lubac and his followers in their attempts to recover medieval interpretation for modern use. That the study of the Bible is now an academic discipline, rather than a pattern of mystical contemplation, owes much to the perception of the men who founded the universities in the Middle Ages. Perhaps here, more than anywhere else, their most fruitful legacy is to be found today.

See also Allegory; Literal Sense; Spiritual Sense

Bibliography

Evans, G. R. *The Language and Logic of the Bible*. 2 vols. Cambridge University Press, 1984–85; Lubac, H. de. *Exégèse médiévale*. 4 vols. Paris: Aubier, 1959–64; idem. *Medieval Exegesis*. Vol. 1 trans. M. Sebanc. Vol. 2 trans. E. Macieroweski. Grand Rapids: Eerdmans, 1998–2000; Smalley, B. *The Study of the Bible in the Middle Ages*. 3d ed. Blackwell, 1983; Steinmetz, D. "The Superiority of Pre-Critical Exegesis." Pages 26–38 in *The Theological Interpretation of Scripture*, ed. S. Fowl. Blackwell, 1997; Walsh, K., and D. Wood. *The Bible in the Medieval World*. Oxford University Press, 1985.

Gerald Bray

Messiah/Messianism

Definition

The term "Messiah" is often used in popular expression and in theological discussion to refer to the promised one of Jewish hope. In fact, the Hebrew term *mashiakh*, "messiah" (= the Greek *christos*), simply refers to "an anointed one" and need not point to the promised figure of the end time. Kings could be anointed (1 Sam. 9:16; 16:3), but so could the high priest (Lev. 4:3; 1 Chron. 29:22), priests in general (Exod. 28:41; Lev. 7:36), or prophets (1 Kings 19:16; *TDNT* 9:498–501). In fact, the term used in its later technical sense is rare in the Hebrew Scriptures. The roots of the usage may well be Ps. 2:2 and the hope of an ideal king in Jer. 23:5–6, drawing on the promise of a successful Davidic line of kings in 2 Sam. 7:11–17 (for the theme of regal hope, note also Gen. 49:10; Num. 24:15–19; Isa. 11:1–9; Ezek. 17:3–4, 22–23; 34:23–24; 37:24–25; Amos 9:11; Mic. 5:2–5; Zech. 9:9–10; 12:10). However, Jeremiah does not use the term "Messiah." Otherwise, only Dan. 9:26

uses it in this more technical sense. Thus, although the Jewish hope of a Messiah existed in the time of Jesus, drawing as it did on the end-time hope of the OT, the paucity of explicit texts meant that Judaism had various conceptions of this figure. This variation meant that Jesus had to explain his conception of the figure, for no single portrait was a given in Judaism, although two of the more dominant portraits (regal Messiah and one like a Son of Man) underscored the authority and victory this figure would bring.

Jewish Conceptions of Messiah

Jewish hope certainly was not uniform in the period of Second Temple Judaism. Some works seem to have given up the regal messianic hope. The book of Sirach seems to view the Davidic dynasty and hope as a thing of the past (Collins 33–34). On the other hand, a work like *1 Enoch* looked forward to a transcendent figure of divinely bestowed authority who would share in the judgment of the last days (39–72). This work develops themes from Dan. 7 with its imagery of the authority of one like a son of man. Davidic hope remained expressed in a famous Jewish text, *Pss. Sol.* 17–18, where the hope is for a king who can reverse what Rome had done to Israel in 63 BCE and cleanse the nation of foreign presence. Here appears the term "Christ," the Greek equivalent of "Messiah." *Psalm of Solomon* 17:4 reads, "Lord, you chose David to be king over Israel, and swore to him about his descendants forever, that his kingdom should not fall before you." This Davidic descendant will come and smash the opponents (17:21–25, a description that recalls language from Isa. 11:1–4). In yet another contrast, the hope seen at the Dead Sea community appears to include a political and a priestly Messiah (1QS 9.11), although the portrait of the various documents is highly variegated (Collins 56–67, discussing and rejecting a suffering Messiah image in 4Q285; Collins 74–84, treating the "two Messiahs"). A powerful collection of messianic texts is collected in *Florilegium* (= 4Q174), including 2 Sam. 7:10–14; Ps. 2:1; and Amos 9:11. A Davidic hope appears in 4Q252 1.5. Such a fusion may also appear in the non-Qumranian Jewish text *Testament of the Twelve Patriarchs* (*T. Levi* 18:2–5; also *T. Judah* 21:1–4, where kingship and priesthood are distinguished). An eschatological teacher/prophet of the end is also discussed at Qumran (CD 6.11 and *Florilegium*), but the regal theme is not as prevalent. This expectation of an end-time prophetic figure has precedent in the Hebrew Scriptures (Mal. 3:1; 4:5)

and was picked up in Judaism (Sir. 48:10; 1 Macc. 14:41). So we see four major figures of the end time expected by Jews of one sort or another: a regal, Davidic-like figure; a transcendent figure described as one like a son of man; a priestly figure; and a prophetic teacher. One can make a case that the Davidic and Danielic figures were the most prominent, looking to a political resolution of Israel's plight into a grand era of righteousness, but a uniform Jewish portrait did not exist. The title of one recent messianic work summarizes the situation well, *Judaisms and Their Messiahs* (Neusner, Green, and Frerichs). This variation meant that any messianic associations made by or to Jesus would need explanation, which is exactly what we see in the NT.

Jesus as Messiah-Christ in the Gospels

The title "Christ" is one all the Gospels use within their narratives to discuss Jesus (Matt. 1:16; 2:4; 11:2; Mark 1:1; Luke 2:11, 26; 4:41; 23:2; 24:26, 46; John 1:17, 41; 3:28; 4:29; 7:26–42; 10:24; 11:27; 12:34; 17:3; 20:31). The titulus on the cross marking Jesus as THE KING OF THE JEWS moves in this direction as well (Mark 15:26, 32; Matt. 27:37; Luke 23:38; John 19:19).

Here seven scenes are key. First is Peter's confession at Caesarea Philippi, where the Synoptics share the christological core of the key disciple's confession. Jesus accepts this utterance, especially as it stands in contrast to the populace's view of him as only a prophet. However, Jesus also quickly redefines the confession in terms of his approaching suffering, so that the term is not merely one of glory but takes on overtones of the Servant who suffers as well (Matt. 16:13–23; Mark 8:27–33; Luke 9:18–22). This text may well show Jesus' innovative work on the concept of the Messiah. The one who would represent the hope of the nation would also suffer as the nation had suffered, only now on its behalf and on behalf of all who would identify with him. The need to explain who Messiah is, especially in his suffering, leads Jesus here and in several other places to restrict making a point of the title publicly (Mark 1:25//Luke 4:35; Mark 1:34//Luke 4:41; Mark 3:12// Matt. 4:16; Mark 1:44//Matt. 8:4//Luke 5:14; Mark 8:30//Matt. 16:20//Luke 9:21; Mark 9:9//Matt. 17:9; the parallel in Luke 9:36 only notes they said nothing but does not explain why). The public would be unlikely to appreciate the special way Jesus is using the term, especially given its already variegated use in Judaism.

Second is the Pharisees' attempt to get Jesus to rebuke his disciples for their confession of him as King, a scene unique to Luke (19:39–40). Here Jesus refuses to stop them and says that if they do not speak, creation would. This text is an emphatic rebuke of the Pharisees for their failure to see who Jesus is. What creation sees, they fail to recognize.

Third is the scene at Jesus' examination before the Jewish leadership (Matt. 26:57–68// Mark 14:53–65//Luke 22:66–71). Here the question about whether Jesus is the Christ eventually evokes a positive though qualified response from Jesus in terms of exaltation, appealing to the Son of Man image and the picture of one at God's right hand from Ps. 110:1, another royal psalm. This affirmation not only of messianic authority, but also of exaltation to the side of God, implying his shared equality, is judged by the Jewish leadership as blasphemous. Thus, the public acknowledges Jesus' claim of a messianic role by the end of his ministry, even when they reject it. We also see here yet another element of fusion in Jesus' messianic portrait as Scripture presents it: Jesus is Messiah-Servant-exalted Son of Man.

Fourth is the emphasis that emerges at the examination of Pilate, whether one works with the Synoptics or John (Matt. 27:11–14, 25–26//Mark 15:1–15//Luke 23:1–5, 17–25; John 18:28–38). These accounts all focus on the discussion of Jesus as a "king of the Jews," a point reinforced by the charge hung over the cross. The discussion makes sense since Pilate would not be interested in a religious dispute over Jesus' claims, but if they have regal, political overtones, then his role as governor is to protect Caesar's interests.

As we turn to examples from John alone, Jesus' claims are more direct. Fifth is the discussion in John 4, where Jesus reveals himself as Messiah to the Samaritan woman. Sixth is the discussion with the blind man and his family in John 9, where the confession of Jesus as the "Christ" has yielded a reaction from officials to expel from the synagogue those who make the confession. Seventh is Martha's confession of Jesus to be the Christ, the Son of God, who comes into the world (John 11:27). This is her response when Jesus raises the issue of his authority over resurrection. The Johannine texts are all ways of affirming Jesus as the unique and promised one sent by God.

Put together, we see that Jesus regarded "Messiah" as a foundational term that brings together several portraits into one figure of hope. The confession of Peter that Jesus is the Christ, and not merely a prophet as the crowds claim, is a base from which Jesus can work to bring the disciples to understand who he really is. The disciples' strictly political and victorious preunderstanding of this term is immediately challenged; Jesus makes clear that this messianic figure must and will suffer (as his passion predictions indicate). Jesus is both a righteous and Suffering Servant as well as Messiah, but that suffering will lead to an exaltation to the right hand of God, which also recalls the picture of the Son of Man brought to God's throne. A Messiah who is as exalted as can be is also a Messiah who is humbled unto death. Other images in the Gospels reinforce this imagery, as Jesus speaks of himself as Son of Man in his favorite self-designation, as Shepherd (John 10), and in terms of the Servant (Mark 10:45). What does the rest of the NT do with this portrait?

Messiah in the Rest of the NT

The centrality of the messianic understanding of the early church emerges in its canonical letters and the Acts. Acts 2 presents Peter declaring that Jesus shows himself to be Lord and Christ by his distribution of God's Spirit upon disciples at Pentecost (Acts 2:16–36). In Acts 13, Paul preaches Jesus as the promised Son of David, the messianic figure promised to occupy David's throne and be Son of God (vv. 13–41). Part of the roots of Jesus being God's Son rests in the messianic relationship Jesus has to the Father, as the uses of Ps. 2 in Acts 13 and other NT texts suggest. Paul opens his most focused theological treatise of Romans by an appeal to the gospel promised in the Holy Scriptures (= the OT) concerning his Son, descended from David according to the flesh (1:1–3). This is an inherent messianic claim.

Perhaps nothing shows the centrality of a messianic mentality more than the name by which Jesus came to be referred, Jesus Christ. Jesus' messianic position had become so attached to him that it was the best way to refer to him.

There are communal implications to Jesus' messianic identity. It is this Jesus Christ who has made the community of believers into a kingdom (Rev. 1:4–6), functioning as the ruler of the kings on the earth as well as the provider of forgiveness through his suffering. It is this combination of authority, exaltation, and suffering that makes the messianic portrait of Jesus unique when set against its Jewish background. Jews expected a Messiah of authority and victory, who would come with full divine support, but there was no anticipation of his suffering. The preaching of Acts also highlights how this suffering of the

Christ was anticipated in the OT (Acts 3:18). Paul attributes redemption to the work of this Christ (Rom. 3:24–25; 5:8; 1 Tim. 1:15; 2:5–6; also Peter in 1 Pet. 2:24; and John in 1 John 2:1–2). The work of this messianic figure is so powerfully present in the Spirit that the Christ is said to be "in you" (Rom. 8:10; Gal. 2:20; Col. 1:27) and believers are in him (Col. 1:2). Such imagery is part of what allows Paul to call the church the Messiah's body (1 Cor. 12). This same Messiah is appointed to return and complete the program God has laid out (Acts 3:20; 26:23), as all things will be summed up in him (Eph. 1:10). It is this Christ whom the new community confesses as Lord with God the Father (1 Cor. 8:6). His exaltation allows us to be seated with him so that all hostile spiritual forces can be overcome (Eph. 1:15–23; 2:4–10). One day he as Messiah will transform us as the completion of our citizenship of heaven is made final (Phil. 3:20–21; 1 Pet. 5:10).

His life serves as an ethical example, so that we are said to learn Christ in a way that calls us to live differently from the world (Eph. 4:17–24; Col. 3:1–9). His example of sacrifice leads into a call to humility and working for the unity of the church, even in the face of persecution and rejection (Phil. 2:5–11; 1 Pet. 2:21–24; 3:14–15).

This multifaceted messianic role makes him superior to Moses (Heb. 3:1–6), as well as to any high priest (5:5–10; 9:24–28). The result is that to confess Jesus as the Christ is the testimony of the Spirit of God and is a central affirmation of faith (1 John 4:2–3; 5:1; stated negatively in 2 John 7 and Jude 4).

How do we put together what the NT does with the Messiah in OT texts that are not so explicit? When it comes to theological interpretation, it is important to appreciate how the NT builds on patterns and concepts the OT possesses, rather than simply using titles to describe the figure to come or only using straight prediction. All that a king in any generation should have been as a king of promise, Jesus in fact was, is, or will be. What Israel should have been as Servant, Jesus was in its place. Just as the righteous suffered, so Jesus suffered in a way that made him worthy to take our place. Thus, the messianic portrait of Jesus is not so much a matter of finding a title that is predicated of Jesus, but involves concepts that draw the shape of who he is. The NT puts these pieces together into a coherent whole.

Conclusion

The central role of Messiah is a view rooted in Jewish hope and yet represents an extension and development of it. Here is the central figure of God's promise, who brings righteousness through forgiveness and the Spirit. Messiah's suffering formed the basis for establishing a new relationship with God and with those who shared in the blessing of Messiah entering into their lives. Through faith in that messianic work, believers show themselves to be taught by God's Spirit, members of the messianic body, citizens of heaven, and members of a kingdom that will never end, as the return of Messiah leads to a transformation into full righteousness and immortality.

See also Jesus Christ, Doctrine of; Relationship between the Testaments

Bibliography

Bock, D. *Proclamation from Prophecy and Pattern*. Sheffield Academic Press, 1987; Collins, J. *The Scepter and the Star*. Doubleday, 1995; Cullmann, O. *The Christology of the New Testament*. Rev. ed. Westminster, 1963; Grundmann, W., et al. "Χρίω . . ." *TDNT* 9:493–580; Longenecker, R. *The Christology of Early Jewish Christianity*. SCM, 1970; Neusner, J., W. Green, and E. Frerichs. *Judaisms and Their Messiahs at the Turn of the Christian Era*. Cambridge University Press, 1987; Van Unnik, W. "Jesus the Christ." *NTS* 8 (1961/62): 101–16; Witherington, B., III. *The Christology of Jesus*. Fortress, 1990.

Darrell L. Bock

Metanarrative

"Metanarrative" became a standard term of intellectual discourse when Jean-François Lyotard famously circumscribed postmodernism as "incredulity toward metanarrative" (xxiv). In this usage, "metanarrative" refers to any overarching, universal account of reality and human life that purports to explain everything, and he has in view primarily the modernist claims of the Enlightenment, with its confidence in human reason as the infallible discoverer of universally valid, timeless truths. Lyotard's quote became so widely used that Christian defenses of "metanarrative" have been accused of missing his specific meaning: a story that not only encompasses everything but seeks to explain and legitimate everything in a particular intellectual way.

In Lyotard's (originally French) usage, "incredulity" also has overtones of religious "unbelief." In a derived sense, the term "metanarrative" has been appropriated in biblical hermeneutics to refer to the overall story told by the Christian Scriptures, which is not totalizing or oppressive (Middleton and Walsh), and which makes possible the "redemptive-historical" level of biblical interpretation (Wolters). In this usage, the term has been given a positive rather than a negative valuation, and it has close links with the idea of "worldview."

See also Postmodernity and Biblical Interpretation; Salvation, History of; Worldview

Bibliography

Lyotard, J.-F. *The Postmodern Condition*. University of Minnesota Press, 1984; Middleton, J. R., and B. Walsh. *Truth Is Stranger Than It Used to Be*. InterVarsity, 1995; Wolters, A. "Confessional Criticism and the Night Visions of Zechariah." Pages 90–117 in *Renewing Biblical Interpretation*, ed. C. Bartholomew et al. SHS. Zondervan/Paternoster, 2000.

Albert Wolters

Metaphor

The interpretation of metaphor is often overlooked. Nevertheless, it is one of the most crucial areas in the whole of hermeneutics since so much biblical theology hangs on metaphors, and metaphor is at the heart of philosophical problems with religious language.

At the outset it is worth noting that all language about "imagery" or "symbol" in Scripture is in fact referring to metaphor. Symbols and images belong to the extratextual world of things; their textual counterpart is the metaphor. For example, if I light a candle to express something about the presence of God, then that is a symbol. But if I describe Jesus as the light of the world, then that is a metaphor. For the purposes of this discussion, I will also treat the varieties of language use sometimes called metaphor (A is B), simile (A is like B), and synecdoche (A is used in the place of B, where A is part of B or vice versa, as in "England played France at rugby") all simply as varieties of metaphor. After all, they share the same basic feature whereby two terms are brought together that have different, apparently distinct ranges of meaning to express something new.

The Problem of Metaphor

Aristotle famously declared the central importance of metaphor: "If one wants to master speech, one must master metaphor." Metaphor was seen as a particular way of using language, a use that "carried meaning beyond" (the literal meaning of "metaphor") what was usually meant. As such, it belonged to the arena of rhetoric, though this was in a context where sharp questions about epistemology were not always present.

Metaphor came to be seen as especially problematic during the Enlightenment. Under Kant's separation of knowledge into the two mutually exclusive classes of the "aesthetic" and the "useful," metaphorical language was seen to express the former, over against "literal" or scientific language, which expressed the latter. This had two consequences for metaphor, and by implication for much religious language. In the first place, it meant that metaphor had at very best a questionable claim to be stating "truth" in any form. Since this was the prerogative of "scientific" language, then whatever truth content there is in metaphor could be expressed more effectively in nonmetaphorical language. This led to the second consequence: that metaphor could be seen to be merely ornamental, an emotive (and therefore probably deceptive) and unnecessary addition to language, persuasive in the context of rhetoric, but distracting and unnecessary when it came to seeking truth.

It is worth noting, however, that over the centuries even metaphor's detractors found the use of metaphor irresistible. One of them rejected metaphorical language and called, instead, for a "close, natural, naked way of speaking"!

The move to take language seriously within twentieth-century Western philosophy set the stage for a reconsideration of metaphor. If language is the vehicle of truth, rather than just a window into it, then the form in which language expresses truth needs to be taken into account in thinking about truth. Pioneering rehabilitators of metaphor included Monroe Beardsley, Philip Wheelwright, and Max Black. But the person who, building on their work, has done more than any other to set out the anatomy of metaphor and highlight its importance in language is the French philosopher and phenomenologist Paul Ricoeur.

The Paradox of Metaphor

Black proposed that within a metaphor, the "vehicle" (the term being used to describe the subject, such as "horse" in the phrase "my friend eats like a horse") offers a "grid" through which the subject is seen. Black observed that this is not a simple one-way process; the metaphor could affect the way the vehicle was understood, as well as the subject. To say, for example, that "Man is a wolf," affects my perception of "man" (as being more wolflike in some way), but also my perception of "wolf" (in perhaps embodying some aspect of what it means to be human).

Ricoeur took this idea one step further, by moving from the perceptual to the cognitive. He observed that within a metaphorical predication there was a paradox. In asserting that "A is B," the metaphorical statement is also at the same time claiming that "A is not B"—which is precisely the thing that makes it a metaphorical rather than a literal statement. For example, when I claim that my friend eats like a horse, I am both claiming that he is like a horse in some ways, but also, *at exactly the same time*, that he is unlike a horse in other ways. After all, I still set cutlery for him when he comes round for dinner, rather than filling a nosebag!

So the predication involved in metaphorical statements is only partial, in that only certain aspects of the vehicle are being identified with the subject in order to effect the tenor (the semantic content) of the metaphor. But Ricoeur argues that, far from being merely ornamental, or another way of making propositional statements, metaphor contains an irreducible cognitive content. Metaphors make real and substantial claims about reality that cannot be expressed in alternative propositional forms. This is not to do so much with the effect on individual words, but with the fact that the connections that metaphor makes actually reorganize the perceptive world. Once I begin to describe God as "Father," then I make fundamental connections between human relations and experience and spiritual relations and experience that go beyond a mere collection of propositions about God being "caring" or "authoritative" or "provider." The connection between two realms of life affects both, in this case the spiritual being made accessible, and the human being granted a new dignity and responsibility.

The Significance of Metaphor

Ricoeur's characterization of metaphor in this way offers a convincing description of one of the key ways in which the world that language describes can expand. When new areas of knowledge arise, then the chief way in which language expands to explain this new area is by metaphorical extension of meaning. Until the nineteenth century in Britain, and the growth of the new discipline of "economics," the meaning of the word "inflation" was restricted to the physical expansion of a balloon or other similar object. The term was then carried over (originally in a pejorative sense) to describe what is happening when the money supply increases and currency begins to lose its purchasing value. Nowadays, the use of "inflation" with reference to the economy is seen as within the normal semantic range of the term, and there is no sense of it being a metaphor.

By similar developments of language, our character is understood as being controlled to a large extent by "packets" of information in our body's cells (genes), the universe started with a "big bang," and when life is difficult we suffer from "depression." Terms that started as metaphors have become at most figurative and certainly normal uses, which we will now find in dictionary definitions. But the expansion of semantic range leads to a corresponding expansion of the capacity of language to describe what was previously indescribable, in these cases in the areas of biology, physics, and psychology. Some have argued that this deep structure of metaphor is in fact akin to the process by which hypotheses are conjectured and tested in the development of scientific theory. Hence, the reconfiguration offered by metaphor is closely related to the function of models in science—bringing together the two categories separated by Kant.

This is especially pertinent for Christian theology. How do we describe an encounter with the Transcendent that has only been made possible by the Transcendent's own self-revelation? The answer, at the level of language, is by metaphorical extension. And, in fact, the paradox of "is"/"is not" within metaphorical language corresponds to the tension within Christian thought between the idea that we can know God by analogy (as, e.g., in the work of Thomas Aquinas) and, on the other hand, apophatic theology (in the desert fathers and elsewhere). The latter believes that God is unknowable and can be defined only by negation.

The Context of Metaphor

Understanding the anatomy of metaphor in this way immediately raises two questions of context. The first is that of historical context. If I am to understand the tenor (the effect, the cognitive content) of a metaphor, then I need to understand something of the historical reality of the subject. I need to grasp the semantic range of the vehicle *at the time when the metaphor was coined* in order to have an idea of which parts of the metaphorical identification belong to the "is" and which belong to the "is not." In Laodicea in Asia Minor, the only source of water was thermal springs, laden with calcium deposits, brought in aqueducts from Hierapolis (modern Pammukale). The hot spring water in Hierapolis was therapeutic; cold water, set aside in jars and from which the calcium deposits had settled out, was drinkable. But the water that arrived at Laodicea, now only lukewarm as a result of its journey but also still full of the calcium that had not time to settle out, was good for neither. To be spiritually "hot," "cold," or "lukewarm" in first-century Laodicea (Rev. 3) meant something quite different from common contemporary use.

The second question of context is that of linguistic context. Some metaphors are coined less because of the actual meaning of the terms, but more because of rhetorical considerations (such as the use of alliteration) rather than actual implications. To "sleep like a baby" refers to something other than the frequent waking through the night that is the actual habit of babies (at least in my experience!). Do troopers really swear more than anyone else? Do horses actually have especially large appetites? The question to ask here concerns conventional usage, rather than historical reality. For biblical metaphors, this implies that we must examine the meaning of words in their wider canonical context as well as their historical context. In understanding what it means for Jesus to be the "good shepherd" (John 10), the biblical picture of leaders as shepherds in the OT will be as important as the historical reality of first-century shepherding.

The Power of Metaphor

Why are metaphors so powerful? How are they able to capture the imagination, even transcending time and culture? The answer is, as before, rooted in the paradoxical "is"/"is not" nature of metaphor. The coining of a metaphor implies selectivity. Certain features of the subject, which correspond to features of the vehicle, are identified, and other features are effectively ignored, at least in the context of the metaphor in question. When the connections are made at deeper levels of significance, particularities and details are left behind. It is important to know the historical context in order to see how the metaphor works. Yet, aspects of the historical particularity are often shorn away in revealing features of deeper significance. In Rev. 12 and 13, Roman imperial power is depicted as a beast from the sea, obsessed with image, opposed to the saints, bent on economic control, and acting with totalitarian control. We can see the particular, historical ways in which this might have been true of Rome in the first and subsequent centuries. But these things have also characterized other political systems in other ages, and with the historical details removed, readers have found in this metaphorization a potent description of their own situation.

In this way, the act of coining a metaphor is itself an act of interpretation, of selecting, empha-sizing, and drawing attention to certain aspects of reality, but ignoring, sidelining, or passing over other aspects. This act has a visual counterpart in the drawing of caricatures and other political cartoons. In this respect, metaphor has much in common with narrative, which adds a temporal dimension to the interpretative reconfiguration of the world. Biblical metaphors do indeed often have a narrative context, and narratives in turn can function as metaphors "writ large."

The Interpretation of Biblical Metaphors

The implication of all this is not to suggest a new, separate methodology for interpreting metaphor so much as to require a fresh bringing together of interpretative methods in a distinctively integrative way.

We need to understand the state of language and the historical realities of the subject and vehicle, which implies the need for a historical-critical methodology. But we also need to look at language use and structure, which implies the need for literary analysis. Because of the power of metaphor to transcend time and culture, we are invited to look for a correspondence of relations in our own world, so the horizon of the reader is also in view.

We can see how these elements might interplay by considering some examples.

Father. The metaphor of God as Father is a central one for Christian theology, but it is one that is largely misunderstood in popular reading. There are problems at both ends, as it were, of the reading process. On the one hand, dysfunctional experiences of being fathered can lead contemporary readers to project their perceptions onto the biblical text. On the other hand, positive experiences of being fathered, perhaps leading to an idealization of fatherhood as caring and providing, can displace the historical realities of fatherhood in biblical times. Both of these are engaged by ensuring that the historical dimension of the metaphor is adequately explored. A significant aspect of relations with the father in the family was that the sons engaged in the father's business—something evidenced in business signs today that include "and Son." Addressing God as "Our Father" and asking for the kingdom to come is more like clocking in for work than engaging in a divine embrace.

The feminist and gay critique of gendered language about God asks different questions. Here, metaphor's irreducible cognitive content means that it is far from simple to reduce the metaphor of God as Father to a series of propositions that might even be recast as an alternative metaphor, such as "Life-giver." This is especially important for metaphors such as "father" that have an archetypal significance in human experience. Those wanting to argue for an alternative "root metaphor" for Christian understanding of God may use some other set of criteria to critique every aspect of Christian belief (as with feminist "revolutionaries" such as Mary Daly). Another tack is to use such criteria to prioritize other metaphors present in Scripture but not having such prominent significance (as with feminist "reformers" such as Sallie McFague). In both cases, other sources of authority (in this case, women's experience) need to become prior to Scripture within the hermeneutical circle (see also Soskice).

Bread. "Bread" does not have quite the same transcultural, archetypal significance as "father," and so the question of "translating" or recasting the metaphor arises more sharply. Where another food is the staple source of sustenance, it may be argued that there is some equivalence in using a corresponding term, such as "rice." Here the danger is that we may lose the contours of the original metaphor—in this case the difference between unleavened and leavened bread as an image of holiness and sin. Yet the same danger is present in cultures, like mine, in which only one sort of bread is popularly known.

Warrior. This metaphor is present in the phrase "LORD of hosts" ("Yahweh Sabaoth") as well as being embedded or implied in OT language about God fighting for Israel. Here the horizon of the contemporary reader presents the most challenges, filled as it is both with changing Western ethical thinking about war, and also a quite different idealization of warfare in the Islamic concept of "jihad." If we are to interpret this metaphor aright, we need to look carefully at all the ambiguities in Scripture surrounding this metaphor and how these ambiguities challenge a simplistic appropriation of it in our very different context.

Potter/Clay. This metaphor comes from a particular passage, Jer. 18, but also has echoes in the NT. It is influential in certain strands of Christian piety, but it is often removed from its particular literary context and so misconstrued. In Jer. 18 the metaphor serves to emphasize God's freedom to act as he will. But there is also a contrasting dimension (the "is not" of the metaphorical predication) by which the clay itself is responsible for whether it will be shaped by the potter—something that makes little sense in real-life pottery. The use of this metaphor to imply

that faith is something passive, where we have little or nothing to do with our own shaping and growth, goes against the slightly counterintuitive but prominent aspect of the image in its literary context.

Thus, we can see that the different aspects of interpretation—issues to do with the world behind the text (the historical context), the world of the text (literary concerns), and the world in front of the text (the situation of the reader)—all have significant bearing on how we read biblical metaphors, though in different degrees in different instances.

Bibliography

Black, M. *Models and Metaphors*. Cornell University Press, 1962; Hesse, M. *Models and Analogies in Science*. Sheed & Ward, 1963; McFague, S. *Metaphorical Theology*. Fortress, 1982; Paul, I. *How to Read the Book of Revelation*. Grove Books, 2003; Ricoeur, P. *Interpretation Theory*. Texas Christian University Press, 1976; idem. *The Rule of Metaphor*. Routledge & Kegan Paul, 1978; Soskice, J. M. *Metaphor and Religious Language*. Clarendon, 1985.

Ian Paul

Metaphysics *See* Onto-Theology; Philosophy

Method

In the modern period, method has been perhaps the key theological concept. For a variety of reasons, those who sought to understand Scripture believed that ascertaining the correct method or approach was foundational. In the end, however, preoccupation with method in many ways has been seen as a hindrance to understanding Scripture rather than a help. Hans Frei expressed this problem in terms of "the eclipse of the biblical narrative." Focus on method has caused conservative and liberal Christians alike to neglect the theological meaning of the text itself. A theological approach to Scripture consequently involves a recasting of this role for method. It does not dismiss method, even the most critical, but it does displace critical methodology from being central.

Whether in biblical interpretation per se or in systematic theology, method concerns both the basic rational procedure for yielding and arranging results and, importantly, the presuppositions and conceptual framework that one brings to the task. Modernity itself represents the rise of historical-critical methodology for the interpretation of Scripture, which is consistent with the presupposition that a strict methodology should be followed in any rational discipline. In placing the emphasis upon the text's formation and itself, method displaced the meaning of the text. Stress upon an objective and value-free approach worked against an understanding of the canonical text informed by faith because the latter approach was not methodically controlled.

The dismantling of the hegemony of this modern paradigm more recently has opened up a new intellectual space for a theological interpretation of Scripture and, correspondingly, for method to be understood in a different way. In what may be considered a metatheoretical or metamethodological perspective on method, we will first examine why method became so important in modernity and then how it can be reconceived.

Several features of modernity moved methodology to center stage. One of the most common characterizations of modernity is that it was foundationalist. In other words, in an almost unconscious way, it was assumed that knowledge was structured like a building, so that the foundation had to be secured before something could be built upon it (Murphy 1–2). In an unprecedented way in modernity, this led increasingly to concentration upon the nature of interpretation itself rather than upon the content of interpretation. Alvin Plantinga has more specifically termed this "classical foundationalism" in that the foundations had to be not just sturdy but also certain, indubitable, incorrigible (48). René Descartes's insistence upon truths that are "clear and distinct," as well as beyond doubt, is a classical example (44). Descartes also portrays a classical requirement of a rigorous methodology that must be followed in laying and then building upon the foundation. Richard Bernstein has called the demand for a certain foundation and a rigorous method "objectivism" (8). This objectivism has led to an almost obsessive concentration upon finding and delineating a correct method, for unless the foundation is certain, all the rest is unstable.

A second and related feature of modernity is that in order to secure such a certain foundation, one needs to be rational and objective. This means that scholars must not allow tradition or presuppositions to shape their conclusions, which Hans-Georg Gadamer famously termed the Enlightenment "prejudice against prejudice itself" (270). Obviously, this approach functions itself as a presupposition virtually ruling out a theological interest in Scripture. A theological interpretation inevitably involves commitment and tradition, and thus could not be deemed "rational." The result is that historical-critical methodology reveals great dexterity in uncovering the development and construction of the scriptural text—the world behind the text—but falls silent when it comes to the current theological meaning of the text (Vanhoozer 16–19). In different parlance, method could reveal to some extent what the text "meant," but not what it "means."

The criticism and virtual dismantling of modernity in contemporary thought undermines both of these moves, implying that classical foundationalism is not well founded and an objectivist understanding of reason is not warranted. It is increasingly recognized that an objectively clear foundation is an illusory chimera, and that there is no uninterested reason divorced from its place and tradition. The door is thus open for theologically interested interpretation related to a faith tradition without automatically being labeled as irrational or prejudicial (Thiemann). This does not mean simple fideism or relativism, either. While the public door may be ajar, there is no automatic reception. There is still a place, although chastened, for public evidence and critical methodology.

Moreover, the sharp distinction between what the text meant (traditionally understood as exegesis) and what it means (hermeneutics) is blurred but not abolished. The understanding of the former is already influenced by presuppositions shaped by the latter. Thus, there is no objective or innocent reading; in fact, in this sense all readings are "theological" readings. Methods do not thus stand alone but are shaped by our theological presuppositions. The point is not, as in modernity, to try to rid ourselves of our beliefs; rather, the point is to become more aware and thus self-critical of them. The claim to presuppositionless objectivity in modernity is now seen as ideological deception. Gadamer has pointed out that even the oft-neglected traditional third step of application already affects the first step (274–75). These huge shifts in contemporary thought give permission, in a way not possible since premodern times, for a self-conscious and unapologetic concern to read the scriptural text to discern what Nicholas Wolstertorff calls "divine discourse."

The distinction between premodernity and what in this context we might term "postmodernity" is that critical methodology is not left behind. The gains of historical methods can be appropriated, but they are servants rather than masters of the interpretative task. The various criticisms can open up in intricate ways what Wolterstorff called the "first hermeneutic" of understanding the meaning of the text in light of its time and its author, or authors. The "second hermeneutic" still remains, which is to read a scriptural text for its meaning, within its canonical context, as the word of God (Wolterstorff, chs. 11–12). The latter is not possible apart from some understanding of the entire canon (canonical criticism and biblical theology), the broad theological history of interpretation by the church (historical theology), and contemporary reflection upon the meaning of Scripture (systematic theology). Because of the recognition of the larger influence of one's situation, such reading involves, inevitably, one's own theological and faith tradition. This may be Roman Catholic, Orthodox, Lutheran, Reformed, free church, and so on, as well as larger contexts that are, for example, exemplified in various types of liberation theology, such as African-American, Latin American, and feminist. In addition, most traditions understand that this final discernment of a text's theological meaning includes not only all scholarly aids but also the illumination of the Holy Spirit. This spells the limitations of any method, which cannot ultimately take the place of an individual's and a faith community's personal configuration of meaning as they desire to be faithful to the Word and to the Spirit.

A helpful model for understanding this more subordinate role of methodology may be drawn from Ricoeur's idea of a hermeneutical arc ("Model"; Stiver, ch. 2). He suggests that our understanding is not absolute and certain in the beginning but stems from initial experiences of being grasped by meaning, which is a first naïveté. Rather than remain in an uncritical mode, we should, and usually do, move to a second, critical stage, where we reflect and test our understanding, as consistent with Paul's injunction to "test everything" (1 Thess. 5:21). This is the place not only of critical biblical methodologies but also of systematic theology. Theology itself is not a first-order understanding that takes the place of Scripture, but is second order. It reflects upon Scripture and also primary experiences of faith. Ricoeur, however, appeals for us not to make this critical stage the stopping point, as moderns have tended to do, so that we are caught fast in "the desert of criticism." Rather, we "wish to be called again" and move to a "post-critical naïveté" wherein we reappropriate, with the help of our critical reflection, our first-order sources of faith (*Symbolism*). This should be at the same time a practical application of our faith. In actuality, the hermeneutical arc becomes a hermeneutical

spiral, where we continually reflect upon and reappropriate the substance of our faith.

In this model, method has a place, but it is not foundational nor does it have to be certain. Nor does it, as sometimes happens, become the focus rather than Scripture or the life of faith. For a Christian, any method should point to an understanding of the word of God and thus a theological interpretation of Scripture.

See also Hermeneutical Circle; Hermeneutics; Objectivity; Ricoeur, Paul

Bibliography

Bernstein, R. *Beyond Objectivism and Relativism*. University of Pennsylvania Press, 1985; Descartes, R. *Discourse on Method*. In *Descartes, Spinoza*, ed. R. Hutchins. Great Books of the Western World 31. Encyclopaedia Britannica, 1952; Frei, H. *The Eclipse of Biblical Narrative*. Yale University Press, 1974; Gadamer, H.-G. *Truth and Method*, trans. J. Weinsheimer and D. Marshall. Rev. ed. Crossroad, 1991; Murphy, N. *Beyond Liberalism and Fundamentalism*. Trinity, 1996; Plantinga, A. "Reason and Belief in God." Pages 16–93 in *Faith and Rationality*, ed. A. Plantinga and N. Wolterstorff. University of Notre Dame Press, 1983; Ricoeur, P. "The Model of the Text: Meaningful Action Considered as a Text." Pages 131–44 in *Hermeneutics and the Human Sciences*, ed. J. Thompson. Cambridge University Press, 1981; idem. *The Symbolism of Evil*, trans. E. Buchanan. Religious Perspectives 17. Harper & Row, 1967; Stiver, D. *Theology after Ricoeur*. Westminster John Knox, 2001; Thiemann, R. *Revelation and Theology*. University of Notre Dame Press, 1985; Vanhoozer, K. *First Theology*. InterVarsity, 2002; Wolterstorff, N. *Divine Discourse*. Cambridge University Press, 1995.

Dan R. Stiver

Micah, Book of

Overview

The book of Micah is evidence that the size of a book does not determine its significance to scholars, the quantity of studies focused on its interpretation, or its place in theological discourse. Its content constitutes interpretative challenges to the extent that the various macrounits appear to have different historical contexts, different conceptual foci, and different types of elements signaling the interrelationship of these units.

Sequentially, Micah is sixth in the Book of the Twelve, sandwiched between Jonah and Nahum. Like others (e.g., Amos, Hosea), it opens with a superscription (1:1), a redactional element that relates the prophetic activity to a particular historical context by mentioning rulers of that period. Micah is designated as eighth-century-BCE activity, though some of its content presupposes other historical settings, such as the mention of Babylon (4:10; seventh century BCE). It consists of two macrounits and their microunits: I. 1:1–5:15 (A. 1:2–16; B. 2:1–5:15); and II. 6:1–7:20 (A. 6:1–8; B. 6:9–7:20). Within its seven chapters, it moves from announcement of judgment on Samaria (1:6–7) to declaration of a promise of preservation, of forgiveness for a remnant (2:12–13; 7:18–20).

History of Interpretation

Like much of the OT, Micah has been the focus of various methodological approaches that yielded various interpretative conclusions. Some of the earliest studies centered on questions of authenticity—a question as reflective of the historical context of the interpreters as of the apparent conceptual tensions within the book. As exemplified by Stade, in the nineteenth century, apparent inconsistencies in the extant form of the book (style, historical context, conceptual unity) became the basis for questioning its authenticity. Stade concluded that there are at least three distinct historical contexts—Mic. 1–3 (eighth century); 4–5 and 7:7–20 (sixth century); and 6:1–7:6 (seventh century).

While twentieth- and twenty-first-century scholarship acknowledges the inconsistencies within the book, the concern is not so much about authenticity as about the coherence of the whole. Among the first to look at redactional order of the constitutive units, Haupt observed that the extant order contributes to the incoherence of the book, and that restoration of an original order may restore coherence. Others, including Wolff, Lescow, and Wagenaar, later attempted to discern the composition history of the book through identification of the various redactional accretions, their historical contexts, and the redactional intent.

Mays addressed theological unity in his investigation of the historical context and redactional intention of the book's extant form. Willis and Hagstrom also voiced concerns about coherence and tried to define it by using literary and conceptual elements such as the alternation between judgment (chs. 1–3) and hope (chs. 4–5), and the recurrent concepts within the discernible macrounits (e.g., sin in chs. 1–3; 6–7). Jacobs notes these recurrent concepts in light of their semantic indicators (e.g., *khatta'ah*, "sin"; *pesha'*, "crime/transgression"), genres (e.g., judgment speeches), inquiries about their interrelationship within the book, and also the conceptual framework of the OT.

Multicritical approaches are also part of the methodological orientation toward the book. These methods employ and acknowledge various critical resources in their analysis. Ben Zvi (*Micah*) addressed concerns about the form of the book, identifying the infractions of those against whom judgment is pronounced ("Wrongdoers"). He is also concerned about issues of "readership" as a decisive interpretative element. In this way, he exemplifies others who use the book of Micah to address issues of reader orientation, oppression, and class struggles. In delineating the composition history of chapters 2–5, Wagenaar identified the methodological parameters of her approach: form and redaction criticism. As a part of their historical-critical analysis, Andersen and Freedman employed text criticism in addition to redaction criticism, resulting in a comparative analysis of the LXX and MT editions.

Within all of these approaches, one cannot miss the book's focus on judgment and hope. These are connected with the challenge to correct injustices and to know that God requires one's religious practices to be in line with godly social practices.

Content and Theological Concerns

The message of the book demands that Israel go beyond the external forms of worship and penitence to implement justice, but it does not promise to avert punishment. Rather, it promises to restore Jerusalem after the judgment. To further accentuate the severity of the sins, the priests' abuse of their role resulted in compromises in teaching Torah (cf. Mal. 1:1–9).

Sin and Forgiveness. The pervasive sin is presented through the repeated use of the terminology and depiction of practices: *pesha'* ("crime/transgression," 1:5; cf. 6:7), *khatta'ah* ("sin," 1:5; cf. 3:8; 6:7), *'awen* ("wickedness"), *ra'* ("evil," 2:1–2; cf. 3:1–2), and *'awon* ("iniquity" of the remnant, 7:18). The leaders and other accused are characterized as abusing their power (e.g., 3:1, 5–6) and seizing people's lands and possessions, thus reducing them to poverty (2:1–5). The judgment is extended to the whole nation: *mishpakhah* ("family," 2:3 NRSV). The Deity forgives all types of sins—the terminology may reflect the gamut of forgiveness—taking away iniquity (7:18), overlooking transgression (7:18), trampling upon iniquity (7:19), casting sin into the depth (7:19). Even so, forgiveness is particular to the remnant (*she'erith*—7:18–20), indicating God's selectivity in whom and when to forgive (cf. Jer. 31:34; 36:3; 1 John 1:9).

God's Requirement. One of the challenges encountered by the people is their understanding of God's requirement. First, they assume that God's presence in their midst exempts them from adversity (3:10–11). Second, they believe that God's total requirement is giving sacrifices, and they view this requirement as burdensome (cf. Amos 5:21–25; Isa. 1:11). They thus give sacrifices and expect them to be sufficient to appease if not to please God, rather than seeing that God may be wearied by their sins and sacrifices (6:6–8; cf. 1 Sam. 15:22; Isa. 1:17; 43:22–24; Hos. 6:6; Mal. 1:13). Micah 6 clarifies that God requires doing justice, loving solidarity, and being circumspect in relationship with God (6:8). God does not reject religious rituals; but neither is God pleased simply by the external performances devoid of obedience manifested in repentance and justice (Isa. 1:17; 43:24; Jer. 6:20; Amos 5:21–24; cf. 2 Tim. 3:1–5).

Remnant and Hope. Unlike the book of Amos, which held out the possibility of changing God's resolve to bring judgment, in the book of Micah judgment is inevitable. The identity of *she'erith* (the "remnant") is as much a concern as its relationship to the judgment. First, God promises to restore Jerusalem and inaugurate a new age in the latter days (4:6–7; cf. Isa. 2:2–4). To that end, God promises to restore a remnant identified as those whom God has subjected to adversity (4:6–7). Second, the remnant will be formed without any concern to distinguish between the innocent and the guilty (cf. Isa. 10:20–22; 11:11). Third, the remnant will be forgiven of its sins and will be used to form the new nation in and through which Yahweh will rule. Fourth, the remnant is also identified as the *she'erith ya'aqob* ("remnant of Jacob," 5:7–8 [6–7 MT]), referring to those who survive from Judah, the southern kingdom (cf. Isa. 37:31–32). It appears that 2:12–13; 4:6–8; 5:9 (8 MT); and 7:18–20 may also refer to this group rather than the northern kingdom. Fifth, the remnant is characterized as both a temporary and a destructive presence in the midst of other nations (5:7–9 [6–8 MT]), but not every remnant of Judah will be used in God's plan (cf. Jer. 44:12–14).

Through the concept of remnant, the issue of hope is raised. First, the hope is that through the experience of devastation the nation will be made aware of God's involvement in all phases of its existence (4:1–5:15 [14 MT]). Second, in the eschatological perspective of actualizing the restoration, those to whom the promise is articulated may not live to experience it (cf. Jer. 24; 25:9–14). As with patriarchs waiting for the actualization of the promise, Israel's test of faith is to persist when the present circumstances bear no resemblance to the envisioned future.

Hermeneutical Challenges

Retribution. God punishes people. To some, this sounds like a manifestation of God's justice against the unjust; however, this concerns the nature of judgment, of a God who uses judgment to address sin, and judgment as a prerequisite for actualizing hope. Part of the challenge is that God not only punishes people (e.g., 3:4, 7) but also includes the innocent in the punishment (e.g., 2:3–5; 3:12; Hos. 13:16 [14:1 MT]; cf. Jer. 18:19–23). Consequently, those ravaged by the injustices committed against them are further ravaged by the manifestation of judgment. Additionally, while punishing a nation for its sins, God uses nations to punish each other—such as Babylon versus Judah (Mic. 4:10–11; Jer. 39), and Assyria versus the remnant of Judah (Mic. 5:8–9 [7–8 MT]). This may be viewed as a manifestation of God's sovereignty in its prophetic literary context. Yet, it is problematic within the modern framework for several reasons, at least when it involves (1) discerning God's desires, plans, and involvement in any act that demolishes a nation (cf. Isa. 10:12–14; ch. 13; 43:14; Jer. 50); and (2) distinguishing God's acts and plans from human plans and motives to do harm. There is an inherent danger in unequivocally claiming God's approval for one's own violence.

God's Selectivity. While one may rejoice that in the book judgment is not the final word concerning Jerusalem's existence, one is also haunted by the representation of the remnant—the survivors. God will preserve a group of survivors and forgive its sins, without distinguishing between the innocent and the guilty in forming the remnant (7:18–20; cf. 2:12–13; 4:6–8). On the other hand, Jeremiah reflects God's selectivity in distinguishing between those who will be used to restore Jerusalem (good figs, 24:2–7) and those who will be perpetually rejected (bad figs, 24:8; 29:17; 44:12–14). This divine prerogative to choose or reject persons and nations is fundamental to the election and the covenantal relationship (Gen. 12; 15:2–4; Mal. 1:2–5). Yet God further distinguishes among those who constitute the covenant community: not all of them are to be part of God's chosen (cf. Ezek. 18; Rom. 9:6–9, 11–14). It epitomizes the tension among Christians—the nominal as compared to the committed Christian.

Second, God's selectivity is the timing of the judgment brought against nations, as perceived in the gap between the devastation on Samaria (eighth century BCE) compared to Jerusalem (sixth century BCE). God seems to be more patient and tolerant toward some while readily punishing others. The third aspect of God's selectivity is the choice of nations to be used as instruments and subjects of devastation and the selection criteria—hence, the implications of belief in and pleasing such a Deity.

God's Requirements. The message of Micah confronts any community that extols the virtues of religion while fostering various forms of injustice. The people of Micah's day were accused of oppressing simply because they had the power to do so, and the injustices broke down trust in all arenas of the community. The family bonds are not enough to counter the mistrust in the community (Mic. 7:1–7). As in the Pentateuch, the concern is to protect those who are vulnerable within the community—the widow, orphan, poor (Exod. 22:21–24; Lev. 23:22; Deut. 15; Isa. 9:1–7; 11:1–9; Jer. 7:5–7; 22:3; Ezek. 22:7; Mal. 3:5). The justice accomplished is that those who abuse their power will be deprived of that power, but the modern settings including the church seem to tolerate abuse of power. It becomes difficult to discern God's voice in the midst of misteachings that have become the sanctioned beliefs among Christians and that allow persistent injustices (2 Tim. 4:3).

Bibliography

Andersen, F., and D. N. Freedman. *Micah*. AB 24E. Doubleday, 2000; Ben Zvi, E. *Micah*. FOTL 21B. Eerdmans, 2000; idem. "Wrongdoers, Wrongdoing and Righting Wrongs in Micah 2." *BibInt* 7 (1999): 87–100; Hagstrom, D. *The Coherence of the Book of Micah*. SBLDS 89. Scholars Press, 1988; Haupt, P. "Critical Notes on Micah." *AJSL* 26, no. 4 (1910): 201–52; Jacobs, M. *Conceptual Coherence of the Book of Micah*. JSOTSup 322. Sheffield Academic Press, 2001; Lescow, T. "Redaktionsgeschicht Analyse von Micha 1–5." *ZAW* 84 (1972): 46–85; Mays, J. L. *Micah*. OTL. Westminster, 1976; Stade, B. "Bemerkungen über das Buch Micha." *ZAW* 1 (1881): 161–72; Wagenaar, J. A. *Judgement and Salvation*. VTSup 85. Brill, 2001; Waltke, B. "Micah." Pages 591–764 in *The Minor Prophets*, ed. T. E. McComiskey. Vol. 2. Baker, 1993; Willis, J. T. "The Structure, Setting, and Interrelationships of the Pericopes in the Book of Micah." Ph.D. diss., Vanderbilt University, 1966; Wolff, H. W. *Micah*, trans. G. Stansell. Augsburg, 1990.

Mignon R. Jacobs

Midrash   *See* Jewish Exegesis

Millennium   *See* Kingdom of God; Last Things, Doctrine of

Miracle

The topic of miracle in Scripture involves God showing his power on behalf of his people. Sometimes, especially in Jesus' ministry, they function as an "audiovisual" of deeper spiritual reality. Miracles tend to be concentrated in three periods in Scripture: the exodus, the Elijah-Elisha period of Israel's unfaithfulness, and the time of Jesus and the apostles, although miracles are scattered here and there throughout. In reaction to miracles, often the hearts of those not responsive to God are hardened, as in the case of Pharaoh. Often their impact is limited because they are not fully appreciated for all that they teach. Still, the Gospel of John can call them "signs," an indicator of their role as a witness to God's presence and activity. One's judgment about the issue of whether miracles take place is a function of one's worldview. However, for a God who actively creates the world and engages with it as Scripture insists, miracles are a natural consequence of his presence (Twelftree 38–53). In this article we focus on the theological significance of miracles for Jesus and his ministry, since they reveal all the characteristics of miracles in Scripture and are the key example of the category.

The Scope of Jesus' Miracles

The array of Jesus' miraculous activity is significant because it points to the scope of divine concern. There are twenty miracle accounts in Mark alone, with a few summaries added to the list (Twelftree 57; Mark 1:21–28, 29–31, 32–34 [summary], 40–45; 2:1–12; 3:1–6, 7–12; 4:35–41; 5:1–20, 21–43; 6:30–44 [two miracles present], 45–52, 53–56 [summary]; 7:24–30, 31–37; 8:1–10 [two miracles present], 22–26; 9:14–29; 10:46–52; 11:12–24 with 20–26). They range from various types of healings (of leprosy, bleeding, paralysis, fever, blindness, deafness, withered hand, muteness, epilepsy) to exorcisms to miracles involving nature (calming the storm, cursing the fig tree, walking on the water, providing food) to resuscitation from the dead (Jairus's daughter). To this number, Matthew only adds two more, healing the official's son (Matt. 8:5–13) and supplying a coin in a fish's mouth (17:24–27; Twelftree 102). Luke also has twenty miracle stories and three summaries. Two of his miracles he shares with the Matthean tradition (Luke 7:1–10; 11:14), and six miracles are unique to his Gospel: large catch of fish (5:1–11), raising the widow of Nain's son (7:11–17), freeing a crippled woman on the Sabbath (13:10–17), healing a man with dropsy on the Sabbath (14:1–6), cleansing ten lepers (17:11–19), and replacing the high priest's servant's severed ear (22:51; Twelftree 144). John has eight miracles: changing water to wine (2:1–12), healing the official's son (4:46–54) and the paralytic at Bethsaida (5:1–18), feeding the five thousand (6:1–15//Mark 6:32–44//Matt. 14:13–21//Luke 9:10–17), walking on the sea (6:16–21; cf. Mark 6:45–52//Matt. 14:23–33; cf. stilling the storm, Mark 4:35–41//Matt. 8:23–27//Luke 8:22–25), giving sight to the man born blind (9:1–7), raising Lazarus (11:1–57), and giving the large catch of fish (21:4–14; like Luke 5:1–11).

No other biblical figure has this scope of miraculous activity. The only other figures and periods that are close are the time of the exodus with Moses and the period of high apostasy with Elijah-Elisha. Only then do we see a combination of healing and exercise of authority over the elements. What these older parallels show is that human figures could perform any one of these classes of miracle, although in the OT no one ever gives the blind sight. However, what is impressive is the scope of Jesus' activity, which involves the creation, the healing of the blind, the cleansing of lepers, and the power to raise from the dead. In this variety we see an authority that is unique in scope, a figure who is Moses' equal and more.

However, when given the chance to confess who he is, Jesus points to the miracles as his "witness" and explanation. Several texts are important here.

In Matt. 11:2–5//Luke 7:18–23, when John the Baptist asks if Jesus is "the one who [is] to come," the miracle-worker replies that John should be told what is being done: "The blind receive sight, the lame walk, those who have leprosy are cured, the deaf hear, the dead are raised, and the good news is preached to the poor." Using the language of hope from Isaiah's prophecies, Jesus claims that this is the promised period of God's great work of salvation (Isa. 26:19; 29:18; 35:5–6; 42:18; 61:1). The fulfillment points out his identity and mission. What Jesus is doing shows who he is.

The second and third texts come from John's Gospel, where Jesus' works attest to his claims (John 5:36; 10:38). They represent the Father's work giving attestation to Jesus' claims and person. These Johannine texts conceptually parallel the Synoptics' texts of Jesus' reply to John the Baptist.

The fourth text is associated with Jesus' nature miracles. Here the question is raised after the stilling of the storm: "What sort of man is this, that even the winds and the sea obey him?" (Matt. 8:27 NRSV). The question is raised because the creation was seen to be in the hands of God (Job 40–42; Ps. 107:23–29), a point underscored already by the miracles God performed at the exodus as a sign to Pharaoh. When Jesus walks on the water, the testimony goes beyond what the miracle shows about God; it also helps to show who Jesus is. The resulting confession combined with worship is, "Truly you are the Son of God" (Matt. 14:33).

The fifth text is tied to Jesus' power over life itself. This is most dramatically developed in the story of Lazarus, where Jesus is portrayed as "the resurrection and the life" (John 11). Being the source of life is also another divine prerogative. The raising of Jairus's daughter also points in this direction, but the Synoptics do not develop the idea as John's Gospel does.

Sixth, there is a sequence of texts in Mark 4:35–5:43//Luke 8:22–56. Here the scope of Jesus' miraculous power is summarized in a linked series of four miracles: calming of the sea, exorcism, healing of a woman with a hemorrhage, and raising from the dead. This sequence covers the whole scope of Jesus' power from creation to supernatural forces to human well-being to life itself. It shows Jesus has the power to deliver comprehensively. The sequence points to the "audiovisual" nature of the miracles. It raises the question as well of what human is like this.

Seventh are the Sabbath healings, where God acts through Jesus on the day of rest to show his "support" of Jesus. One dispute closes by making the point, "The Son of Man is Lord even of the Sabbath" (Mark 2:28). So Jesus' authority is seen over the most sacred day of the week as well as over the interpretation of the law. A miracle shows the way to the point.

Eighth is the discussion Jesus engenders about the significance of his miracles in Luke 11:14–23//Matt. 12:22–32. Here he says that if he casts out demons by the "finger" (Luke) or "power" (Matthew) "of God," then the kingdom (promised rule) of God has come upon them. Miracles are signs that point to what God is actively doing and picture that deeper reality. Thus, they are event and metaphor.

Nothing shows this linkage more vividly than the miracle of the miraculous catch of fish in Luke 5:1–11. Here Jesus orchestrates a huge catch of fish and then tells his disciples they will be "fishers of men" (cf. 5:9; Mark 1:17). The miracle illustrates a deeper reality that points to God's relationship to his disciples. In the same way, the healing from leprosy shows God's power to cleanse through Jesus, the healing of a blind man shows Jesus' ability to give sight, and the raising from the dead shows his ability to give life. So miracles are both event and picture of God's saving activity. Miracles that lead to death, as in the plagues of the exodus, underscore God's authority to judge and our accountability to him. Interestingly, Jesus performed only a few miracles of judgment (such as the cursing of the fig tree) and his disciples used them rarely as well (such as the judgment of Ananias and Sapphira, Acts 5:1–11; Paul's judgment of Bar-Jesus, 13:6–12).

Thus, the scope of these miracles suggests the comprehensive extent of God's authority and, in the case of Jesus' miracles, of Jesus' authority as kingdom-bearer. The power over life, demons, and the creation suggests a scope of authority in one person that can exist only because one shares in divine power. So, ultimately miracles serve to reveal the presence, power, and authority of God and those through whom he works. In the case of Jesus, where the scale of miracle is so great, the miracles point to his uniqueness.

Bibliography

Twelftree, G. *Jesus the Miracle Worker*. InterVarsity, 1999.

Darrell L. Bock

Mission   *See* Church, Doctrine of the; Culture and Hermeneutics; Trinity

Model

If interpretation of Scripture is (and should be) theological, it must grapple with the nature, function, and status of models portraying God. In this age we do not know God face-to-face, nor is epistemic access to other theological realities altogether direct (1 Cor. 13). Hence, models play a mediating role in the relatively adequate knowledge of the Christian faith that is presently possible by divine gift.

Models and Metaphors: Depicting Reality?

Models are crucial, not just in theology, but also in any field of abstraction. So Richard Rorty claims, "It is pictures rather than propositions, metaphors rather than statements, which determine most of our philosophical convictions." The model of mind as mirror drove philosophers to conceive of knowledge as accurate representation. Study of models in science, though, has become even more important for their theological use, given the modern prominence of such analysis (Schner 10–12).

For we have learned that (even scientific) models do not speak literally, and they must be in-terpreted carefully. Even physical "models," with evident points of correspondence, lose something in the change of scale—they would be useless if the originals were directly accessible. Models function precisely in mediation.

The frequent assumption, often made explicit, is that models differ from metaphors in degree but not kind: models are developed, sophisticated metaphors that possess considerable explanatory power (Black; Barbour). However, conflating these two categories, argues Janet Martin Soskice, risks not only a confusion of the linguistic (metaphor) and nonlinguistic but also a mistaken view of metaphor, which need not consist of one entity compared to another. "Angry wind" is clearly a figurative expression, yet it is not obvious that wind is being compared to something else, only implicit at most. Because the comparison theory is subject to counterexamples, Soskice defines metaphor instead as speaking of one thing in terms that suggest another. A model, meanwhile, is "an object or state of affairs . . . viewed in terms of some other object or state of affairs" (54–55). It follows that metaphor is language use tied to a model.

For example, Luther unfolds the model of God (the subject: what the model *is of*) as father (the source: what the model *is based upon*) by specifying respects in which God is paternal—making specific demands of us and promises to us (146). Though Luther did not do so in this context, he could have added further implications: if God is Father, then sin is rebellion, and redemption is restoration to the status of child in good standing (McFague, *Models*).

Such classic models have recently become controversial, as especially feminist theologians have inquired into their workings. Sallie McFague suspects that traditional models of God put the world itself in danger: styling the Divine as almighty Father or King means God is distant from the world, his realm. So, if humans imagine themselves in roles parallel to God's, dominion results, whereas if they do not, escapism ensues.

The solution, for McFague, is to reenvision the God-world relation, but not in the sense of more accurate depiction: "What can be said with certainty about Christian faith is very little. . . . Theology is *mostly* fiction" (McFague, *Models*, xi). A theory of indeterminate metaphorical reference fosters this judgment, largely dropping truth from the picture. Specifically, metaphors and models are a matter of what is *and* is not (cf. Ricoeur 7). Just as chess is war (both require strategy) and yet not war (only war involves death), for all we know, God both is and is not how models portray him. According to McFague, scriptural images are exemplars, but not the only possible images theologians may use. Her preferred model for God fosters peace, justice, and an understanding of creation's interdependence. If Christians think of the world as God's body, and act accordingly, they will deeply revere such a sacrament.

Many would agree that theological models motivate action, but are wary of such coyness over reality depiction. If models do not depict reality—or more precisely, if we cannot *know* they do—and theology is a matter of advancing a sociopolitical agenda, then Feuerbach's criticism that religious language simply projects human values has bite (Clayton 17). To be fair, McFague is indeed concerned about that problem, chiding traditional theologies for turning God as Father into something all too human, an "old man with a white beard" (McFague, *Metaphorical*, 97). But in her account, the problem remains unsolved.

From another angle, if models do not depict reality, how should they prompt and regulate action? Christian conduct presupposes the accurate, albeit indirect, reference of metaphorical theological predicates (Barbour; Soskice). Models seem interconnected with, even decisive for, a workable concept of analogy regarding our knowledge of God (McIntyre 58–68). For instance, *if* God is my shepherd, I can rely on God's provision. But nothing follows unless the "if" clause is true. The ambiguity of models in McFague's account is largely a function of their free creation apart from context. The contexts in which biblical authors unfold models help to disambiguate them.

In two ways, then, models are contingent on canonical—historical, literary, and theological—context: (1) For a model *even to be* a model, the figure must play a certain role in a text. Not just any features of the human body model the church, but the essence and extensions of Paul's reference in 1 Cor. 12. This viewing-as, or moment of interpretation, is what constitutes a figure as a model. (2) A biblical model's *meaning* also depends on the dynamics of the text in which it unfolds. Scripture itself must serve as a critical principle by which to check idolatrous use of models, such as confusing sexuality or gender with divine paternity (cf. Mary Daly's line: "If God is male, then male is God").

Models, Traditions, and So On: Construing the Divine?

A theological model, or set of them, drives a tradition. This is so because models suggest ways of seeing relationships as well as modes in which to pursue questions about God, the world, and Christian living. A theological tradition limits the range of acceptable models, although any living tradition will develop. Thus, communicating Calvin's twofold knowledge of God may develop continuities with predecessors, but also creates further discussions (e.g., Barth and Brunner). Yet drastic switches—such as from God as King to God as only a watchmaker who sets the world running—mean moving into a new or alternative tradition.

Meanwhile, in Thomas Kuhn's view science operates with a single model of an object. Since these paradigms are incommensurable, plurality cannot coexist; the new displaces the problematic old. Does this describe theological exegesis vis-à-vis tradition(s)? On the one hand, Robert Shedinger says "no" in his description of how biblical scholarship works. Moreover, theologically, a single model may yield insufficient explanatory power: for example, the church as body felicitously pictures interdependence among church members, and perhaps growth together, but is an awkward way to convey missionary expansion (Clowney). For that purpose, Paul's picture of grafting shoots into a vine is a helpful supplement. Or, for example, the Vatican II text *Lumen gentium* exemplifies a two-model account of the church, including both household of God and body of Christ. Regarding the doctrine of the church (and of revelation also), Avery Dulles pioneered the description of ecclesiological traditions, or their varieties over time, in terms of models. The distinctiveness of each type need not logically exclude others; in fact, it is necessary that all their core affirmations be treated as complementary.

On the other hand, there are reasons to press toward the simplicity of a single model. Some models are able to expand and organize a whole array (Pepper) of doctrines, while it may be jarring to juxtapose disparate models. For instance, God as King may fit with God as Shepherd, but how about God as tower and lion and nesting eagle and rock (Ramsey)? If one purpose of theology is to display the coherence of doctrines, then we must find (1) a model that is remarkably comprehensive (with humility about what remains poorly in focus), (2) an overarching framework such as a symphony (Poythress) that shows how differences may blend harmoniously, or (3) perhaps a combination of these strategies.

Thus, theological models deploy our understanding of Scripture's unity. Ramsey's query illustrates the need to distinguish models (not directly literary) from the metaphors that imply them—from the literary images out of which they may be developed: probably "king" and "shepherd" approach "concept" status (habits of thinking in connection with certain words; Callow), while "tower" and "lion" do not. As regular canonical reality depictions despite particular historical and literary contours, models such as "king" develop to answer questions about, or to portray, particular givens. Within that scope they probably must seek the sort of comprehensiveness (Clayton), however unattainable, that is still true of modest metaphysical claims. But they also produce unintended consequences. We should neither overreach in our expectations of a model's coverage, nor overreact when a model must involve complementary elements (Kaiser) or qualification from other angles.

Thus, theology cannot function like a particular science with an encompassing paradigm, given the scope of its questions. The relation of models to traditions must be many to one, although a tradition might develop from a central model, whereas models increasingly allow conversation across traditions (McIntyre 65–68; e.g., Dulles). Likewise, theological systems must contain and connect multiple models, although dependent perhaps on one inquiry or imaginative act to start with—as a theologian or community tries to communicate and extend their tradition in a particular way.

Though biblical models should be central, and constrain ours, all models involve human construction even if the comparison is something concrete or suggested in the Bible itself (Goldingay 11). Since language becomes involved, theological systems can discern, connect, and deploy biblical models only with "relative adequacy"—no more relevant questions to answer, for a time (so Tracy, following Lonergan). New challenges will evoke ongoing construal of God's presence in relation to biblical patterns and to us (Kelsey). By a process of imagination, inference, hypothesis, testing, and revision (which is abduction more than induction or deduction), "biblical" models can arise and relate systematically across theological inquiry. Systems should be more tensile than traditionally the case, open to complementary models as questions connect

and/or change. Such relative adequacy reflects biblical knowledge of God, which humbly looks forward to fullness of new life but also back to the cross—a scandal for so many theological models then and now.

See also Concept; Critical Realism; Metaphor; Science, the Bible and; Scripture, Unity of; Systematic Theology; Tradition

Bibliography

Barbour, I. *Myths, Models, and Paradigms*. Harper & Row, 1974; Black, M. *Models and Metaphors*. Cornell University Press, 1962; Callow, K. *Man and Message*. University Press of America, 1998; Clayton, P. *The Problem of God in Modern Thought*. Eerdmans, 2000; Clowney, E. "Interpreting the Biblical Models of the Church: A Hermeneutical Deepening of Ecclesiology." Pages 64–109 in *Biblical Interpretation and the Church*, ed. D. A. Carson. Thomas Nelson, 1984; Dulles, A. *Models of the Church*. Rev. ed. Doubleday, 1987; idem. *Models of Revelation*. Doubleday, 1983; Goldingay, J. *Models for Scripture*. Eerdmans, 1994; Kaiser, C. "Christology and Complementarity." *RelS* 12 (1976): 37–48; Kelsey, D. *The Uses of Scripture in Recent Theology*. Fortress, 1975. Reissued as *Proving Doctrine*. Trinity, 1999; Kuhn, T. *The Structure of Scientific Revolutions*. 2d ed. University of Chicago Press, 1970; Luther, M. *The Sermon on the Mount and the Magnificat*. Vol. 21 of *Luther's Works*, ed. J. Pelikan. Concordia, 1956; McFague, S. *Metaphorical Theology*. Fortress, 1982; idem. *Models of God*. Fortress, 1987; McGrath, A. *Science and Religion*. Blackwell, 1999; McIntyre, J. *The Shape of Christology* (ch. 3). 2d ed. T&T Clark, 1998; Murphy, N. *Theology in the Age of Scientific Reasoning*. Cornell University Press, 1990; Pepper, S. *World Hypotheses*. University of California Press, 1942; Poythress, V. *Symphonic Theology*. Zondervan, 1987; Ramsey, I. *Models and Mystery*. Oxford University Press, 1964; Ricoeur, P. *The Rule of Metaphor*, trans. R. Czerny et al. University of Toronto Press, 1977; Rorty, R. *Philosophy and the Mirror of Nature*. Princeton University Press, 1979; Schner, G. "Metaphors for Theology." Pages 3–51 in *Theology after Liberalism*, ed. J. Webster and G. Schner. Blackwell, 2000; Shedinger, R. "Kuhnian Paradigms and Biblical Scholarship: Is Biblical Studies a Science?" *JBL* 119 (2000): 453–71; Soskice, J. *Metaphor and Religious Language*. Clarendon, 1985; Tracy, D. *The Analogical Imagination*. Crossroad, 1981.

Daniel J. Treier with Darren Sarisky

Moltmann, Jürgen   *See* Hope; Last Things, Doctrine of

Monotheism

As used here, "monotheism" designates the belief that one Deity is universally supreme and categorically unique from all other heavenly or "divine" beings, and that worship is properly to be given solely to this one Deity, with worship of any other beings regarded as idolatry. So defined, monotheism can be distinguished from "henotheism," the preference for worshipping one Deity, but without the claim that the worship of other deities by other people or groups is invalid. The distinguishing feature of monotheism is the claim that the one Deity is properly to be recognized and exclusively worshipped universally.

This "monotheism" is the typical religious stance reflected in the Bible, both OT and NT. The God referred to as "Elohim" and "Yahweh" is portrayed as the sole Creator of all things heavenly and earthly (e.g., Gen. 1:1; Ps. 8; Isa. 40:12–17, 28; 44:24; 45:18), and the universal Sovereign, to whom all creation is responsible and from whom alone salvation is possible for all peoples (e.g., Isa. 45:22–25). There are emphatic warnings that God is "jealous" that worship be given to him alone (e.g., Deut. 5:8–9; 6:14–15). Moreover, not only is Israel forbidden to worship any other deity; in the most explicit expressions of monotheism, the biblical texts portray all other nations as misguided in reverencing any other gods, and hold out the aim that all nations should come to the light of the one true God (Isa. 56:6–8; 60:1–16), which the NT presents as fulfilled through the spread of the gospel (e.g., 1 Thess. 1:9–10).

On the basis of archaeological data (e.g., the Elephantine texts) and the witness of the OT itself, however, scholars (e.g., Day; Smith) rightly note that preexilic Israel and Judah were not really monotheistic in dominant belief or worship, although some scholars posit a preexilic "Yahweh-alone party" as a minority voice then (e.g., Lang). Indeed, condemnation of Israel and Judah for worshipping gods other than Yahweh is a major theme in writings such as Hosea (4:12–19; 8:4–6; 10:5–6; 13:1–8; 14:1–3) and the so-called Deuteronomistic narratives (e.g., 2 Kings 17:7–23).

But, whatever vestiges there may be of earlier Israelite religious views and practices, it is clear that the stance advocated in the OT texts in their "final form" as we know them is fiercely monotheistic. This is presupposed and implicit in the Gen. 1 creation account, for example, and is reflected more explicitly in texts such as Deut. 6:4, which forms the heart of what became the traditional Jewish confession of faith in the one God (the Shema). But probably the most sustained and emphatic declarations of monotheism in the OT are passages in Isa. 40–66. In this material Elohim/Yahweh is repeatedly declared to be unique over against all other objects of worship, including those reverenced as gods by other nations, which are mere "idols" (e.g., 40:18–20, 25–26; 43:10–13; 45:5–7, 18, 20–23). And from at least

the fifth century BCE onward and increasingly thereafter, Jewish religion was characteristically expressed as this exclusivist monotheism. What might once have comprised a pantheon of divine beings (as reflected, e.g., in early Canaanite religion) was radically redefined as an entourage of the one God, who presides over them all (e.g., Job 1:6; 2:1; Ps. 82:1) as "the Lord of hosts" (e.g., Pss. 89:8 NRSV; 103:21). The beings of the divine council whose earlier designations were "sons of God" and "holy ones" came to be known more familiarly as "messengers" of God, reflecting their subordinate status and function (Hebrew: mal'akim; Greek: angeloi).

In the NT as well, this exclusivist monotheism is everywhere presumed and affirmed (e.g., Matt. 4:10//Luke 4:8; Eph. 4:4–6; 1 Tim. 1:17; 2:5; Rom. 11:33–36), and is vigorously asserted in particular texts that more directly react against the wider polytheistic culture. In Rom. 1:18–32, Paul's principal indictment against human "ungodliness and wickedness" is that it began in, and continues to involve, idolatry (1:19–23), from which all other sin is depicted as flowing; here Paul echoes Jewish texts such as Wis. 12–15. In 1 Cor. 8 and 10, Paul consistently uses "idols" and "idolatry" to refer to other gods and the reverence given to them in the Roman-era culture; and he insists that Christians must shun the worship of other deities as completely incompatible with their participation in Christ (10:14–22). In Revelation, however, we have the most militant expressions in the NT. The author rails against the widespread idolatry of his time (9:20–21), and in particular warns sternly against worship of "the beast" (14:9–11), urging all to worship solely the true God (14:6–7; 19:10; 21:8–9).

Yet the monotheism reflected in the NT represents also a significant and novel "binitarian" form, in which the resurrected Jesus is confessed as the "Lord" who shares in God's glory and attributes (e.g., 2 Cor. 3:12–4:6), and who is linked with God as recipient of worship (e.g., Rev. 5; Hurtado, *One*). That is, Jesus is defined with reference to God, and God is (re)defined with reference to Jesus as unique agent of God's revealing and redemptive purposes. The roots of post-NT trinitarian thought lie precisely in this binitarian belief and devotional pattern.

Strangely for so central a theme in the Bible, the implications of monotheism have hardly been explored by scholars (but see Peterson; Niebuhr). In the ancient settings, biblical monotheism was expressed as a radical reservation of worship for the one God, a stance that could have profound social consequences for devotees, especially those from Gentile backgrounds, including alienation from friends and family, accusations of antisocial and disloyal attitudes, and even violent persecution. As well, the sharp distinction between the one transcendent God and all creation opens the possibility of a religiously based demythologizing of the state, nation, and all other this-worldly objects for which reverence as divine is demanded.

Monotheism may even have been a major factor contributing to the central place of sacred texts in ancient Jewish tradition and then in Christianity and Islam, for which there is no true analogy in other ancient or contemporary world religions. The true/transcendent God of biblical monotheism cannot be comprehended adequately from nature and its powers (e.g., procreation, death/destruction, seasons, war, etc.), and is more adequately witnessed to in response to God's own acts and words. Perhaps as a consequence of this view, therefore, "Scripture"—as specific words from God (e.g., prophetic oracles) and as testimony to specific acts and attributes of God (narratives, psalms, wisdom)—preserved in written form acquired a unique status and role.

The radical distinction posited between one true God and all other purported divinities also entails the importance of accurate and faithful witness. Insofar as reliable witness to the one God is to be shaped by Scripture, it follows that conscientious exegesis is requisite. Biblical monotheism itself demands the hermeneutical effort and the questions it entails. All the same, however, the transcendent God cannot be fully captured even in Scripture; so, even when testimony about God is conscientiously based in Scripture, it can only amount to human knowledge that, though valid, remains partial (1 Cor. 13:12) and in principle corrigible. The distinctive claim made for Scripture is that it provides a basis for knowledge about the one God that is *sufficient* to guide believers to authentic worship and faithful loving service (1 Cor. 13:13), not that this knowledge is complete or incapable of being revised. To adapt a Reformation formula, theological interpretation shaped by biblical monotheism should be *semper reformanda* (ever reformable). Moreover, because the one God is witnessed to in Scripture, not captured within it, Scripture scholarship properly can only be one servant among others of God and the believing community, not a scribal hierarchy or hegemony over others. And, as inspired human witness to the one God, Scripture itself cannot rightly hold the divinized place given to the Qur'an in Islam.

Because the one God who is most adequately revealed to us in God's own free acts and words has really acted and spoken in historical events and personages, it is unavoidable that these events and the scriptural testimonies to them were historically conditioned by the circumstances in which they first occurred. It follows, therefore, that exegesis should respect and engage the historically conditioned features of the scriptural texts (e.g., language, literary genre, textual transmission, and other factors), and that adequate theological interpretation also involves the attempt to engage the contents of the scriptural texts from, and with concerns for, the specific historical setting of the interpreter and/or those whom the interpretation is meant to serve.

Bibliography

Bauckham, R. *God Crucified*. Eerdmans, 1999; Day, J. *Yahweh and the Gods and Goddesses of Canaan*. JSOTSup 265. Sheffield Academic Press, 2000; Hurtado, L. "First Century Jewish Monotheism." *JSNT* 71 (1998): 3–26; idem. *One God, One Lord*. 2d ed. T&T Clark, 1998; Klauck, H.-J., ed. *Monotheismus und Christologie*. QD 138. Herder, 1992; Lang, B. *Monotheism and the Prophetic Minority*. Almond, 1983; Lang, B., ed. *Der einzige Gott*. Köselverlag, 1981; Niebuhr, H. R. *Radical Monotheism and Western Culture*. Harper & Row, 1970; Peterson, E. *Der Monotheismus als politisches Problem*. Jakob Hegner, 1935; Smith, M. S. *The Early History of God*. Harper & Row, 1987; Thüsing, W. *Per Christum in Deum*. NTAbh 1. Aschendorff, 1965.

Larry W. Hurtado

Moral Sense See Ethics; Ideological Criticism; Liberation Theologies and Hermeneutics; Medieval Biblical Interpretation

Mujerista Interpretation See Feminist Biblical Interpretation

Music, the Bible and

Although music and hermeneutics might at first seem to have little to do with each other, music can offer rich material for the theological interpretation of Scripture. First, biblical references to music can serve to highlight strong theological currents in Scripture, currents in which music is closely caught up. Second, Scripture itself can be interpreted musically. Musical treatments of biblical texts and themes abound, and a range of musical imagery and conceptuality can be (and has been) employed to deepen and advance the hermeneutical task.

Music in the Biblical Texts

The Bible's many references to music need cautious treatment: they are largely in the form of passing comments and incidental allusions, granting only a fragmentary picture of how music was thought about and practiced. Care also needs to be taken not to "read back" assumptions about music drawn from modern Western traditions. For example, most music in biblical times probably took the form of a single line of notes (there was virtually no harmony as we know it), and followed the patterns and rhythms of speech far more closely than much of the music we hear today. Nevertheless, some aspects of musical culture in ancient Israel and the NT period are very clear.

Music in the OT as Social Action. Listening to a "work" of music purely for its own sake, for aesthetic delight, or privately (as we might listen to a CD) was relatively unknown in ancient Near Eastern culture. Music was made by someone (or by a group) for something, and most often was intended to happen between people, in a social setting. It was woven into the fabric of community living, with a huge range of social roles—to help people sleep, celebrate, rest, fight, sow seed, eat, and so on. When music served theological purposes, it did so largely by shaping and strengthening community life, in both cultic and noncultic settings. In Gen. 4:20–22, Jubal, "the ancestor of all those who play the lyre and pipe" (NRSV), is mentioned alongside the first smith (Tubal-cain) and the first cattle-breeder (Jabal), thus testifying to music's embeddedness in daily life. Music was used for greetings and farewells, marriages and burials, coronations and processions, rallying troops and lamenting the dead. Among its more prominent functions was the intense outpouring of emotion, as when music accompanied prophecy and generated ecstatic states (1 Sam. 10:1–12; 2 Kings 3:9–20). The apotropaic use of music—to ward off evil forces and spirits—also finds frequent mention (e.g., Exod. 28:33–35; David's playing to Saul, 1 Sam. 16:23).

Roughly three-quarters of the biblical references to music concern song. Ancient Israel was a singing culture, and the variety of songs seems to be as wide as the variety of human activity. Instruments certainly were available and in use (Braun 8–45). The *kinnor* (lyre) and *nebel* (harp) were the most important string instruments (e.g., Ps. 92:3 [MT, v. 4]). Wind instruments are also cited, especially the *khalil* (pipe or flute). By far the most significant were the *shophar* and *khatso-tsera*—both translated "trumpet." The former, a long horn (of a goat or ram), is the most frequently cited instrument in the OT and was used most often as a signaling and gathering instrument, both culticly and nonculticly. The *khatsotsera* was a tube of beaten or hammered silver with a bell-shaped end, in postexilic times a cultic and priestly instrument of the second temple. Despite these and other references, however, instrumental music seems to have played a relatively marginal role, something almost certainly due to the prominence of the word in Jewish faith, and to the associations of musical instruments with surrounding pagan culture. (In the Canaanite cult, with its strong sexual orientations, instruments seem to have played a conspicuous part.)

This relative lack of interest in musical instruments was later exploited by some early Christians in an effort to prohibit the use of instruments in worship. Also, they drew on a number of OT prophetic texts that seemed hostile to instruments (e.g., Isa. 5:11–12; Amos 5:23–24; 6:4–6). In fact, these passages are attacking music as part of an indulgent lifestyle that masked social injustice, not instrumental music per se. Yet, the church's misreadings of them came to have profound and lasting effects on attitudes to music in Christian history (McKinnon).

Music came to figure prominently in some forms of OT corporate worship. The link between music and praise could be quite strong (exemplified many times in the Psalms). Liturgical music is reported to have become a regular institution in the Davidic and Solomonic eras, along with the establishment of professional musicians drawn from the Levites. John Kleinig has sketched some of the key theological dynamics of music as presented in 1 and 2 Chronicles (ch. 5). On the one hand, singing announced, and became a vehicle of, the presence of the Lord to his people (e.g., 1 Chron. 16:9–11); on the other, singing served to articulate a response of the congregation to the Lord's presence (e.g., 16:35). When instruments were used, they seem to have been caught up in this double movement: from God to his people and from the people to God, a dynamic that seems to have been integral to OT worship as a whole.

Music in the NT Churches. Not surprisingly, much of what applies to pre-Christian Jewish music applies to music in the NT. We can assume that music was intertwined with everyday life, and numerous references suggest that singing was common in the emerging Christian community, with no sign of any negative attitude toward music as such. "The Christian Church was born in song" (Martin 39).

In worship, singing would likely have been relatively informal, involving the whole congregation. Many argue that the NT includes songs or fragments of songs used in worship (e.g., Col. 1:15–20; Phil. 2:6–11; 1 Tim. 3:16). It is probable that singing included the chanting of OT psalms, and fresh Spirit-inspired compositions patterned after the psalms, with a christological focus (Hurtado 88–89).

Ephesians 5:18–20 and Col. 3:16–17 are the two richest NT passages that mention music in the context of corporate worship, with their injunction to sing "psalms, hymns and spiritual songs." Especially striking here is the lack of any negative comment about music, in a context of vigorous ethical concern. Theologically noteworthy is the two-dimensionality of song: it is addressed "to the *Lord*" but is also a means of addressing "*one another*"—in edification, instruction, and exhortation. Singing is a means of mutual upbuilding. This relates to Paul's stress in 1 Corinthians on intelligible singing, as part of a wider concern for intelligibility in worship to ensure the upbuilding of the church (14:14–15). This combination of humanward and Godward finds its main precedent in the Psalter: the writer can extol to others the greatness of God or celebrate what he has done, as well as address God directly in the second person (e.g., Ps. 30).

The christological center of these two passages is unmistakable. In Colossians, the pattern is "to God," and "in the name of" as well as "through" Jesus; in Ephesians, singing is "to the Lord" (most likely the exalted Jesus). Jesus is both the *object* of worship, included in the identity of God, as well as the one *through whom* worship is offered. (A similar pattern is found in Hebrews; Christ is worthy of the worship due to God, *and* the leader of the congregation's song; 1:1–4; 2:12.) In the Ephesians text, this widens into a trinitarian pattern: singing is to be "filled with the Spirit." As with all worship, the personal presence of God the Spirit initiates and sustains the church's singing. Music thus shares in the trinitarian dynamic of worship, which in turn is the dynamic of redemption (cf. Eph. 2:18). The Spirit unites us to Christ and him to us, so that with him, as well as through him, we have access to the Father.

In the NT, instrumental music is neither prohibited nor attacked, and there is no reason to believe that instruments were banned in worship.

Nevertheless, references to musical instruments are few and far between, and are not mentioned in the context of the church's regular worship. If instruments were scarce in worship, it would likely be because of their absence in the synagogue (with the exception of the *shophar*; Foley 48–50). In addition, the centrality of words in the life of the NT church would undoubtedly have played a part in privileging vocal music—it was, after all, a specific and urgent *kerygma* that had led to the formation and mission of the Christian community.

Musical Imagery. Along with literal references to music-making, musical imagery abounds in Scripture and does its own kind of theological work. Creation praises the Creator by "singing" (Pss. 96:12; cf. 65:12–13; 98:7–9). God's covenant people "sing a new song" (Pss. 33:3; 40:3; 96:1; 98:1; 144:9; 149:1; Isa. 42:10)—a potent metaphor of the impact of salvation, and picked up in Revelation (14:3). In the NT, musical imagery frequently has strong eschatological connotations, the most prominent image being the trumpet (*salpinx*), an instrument redolent with overtones of the "last days" (1 Cor. 15:52 NRSV: "The trumpet will sound, and the dead will be raised"). Trumpet symbolism plays a leading part in the drama of the book of Revelation (e.g., 1:10–13; 4:1), evoking the interplay of heaven and earth, bringing together the devastation of earth, the call to penitence, the prophetic associations of judgment, and the announcement of the day of the Lord.

Musical Interpretation

Musical Settings. The interpretation of biblical texts by musicians has been practiced ever since the emergence of the NT writings. These range from direct musical settings of biblical texts (psalm chants, for example), through settings of biblical paraphrases (as with many hymns), settings of biblical texts interspersed among other texts (J. S. Bach's *St. Matthew Passion* or Tebelak and Schwartz's *Godspell*), settings of texts at times loosely connected to biblical writings (Benjamin Britten's *Noye's Fludde*), to purely musical pieces based to a greater or lesser extent on Scripture (Olivier Messiaen's *Visions de l'amen*).

When texts (whether biblical or derived from the Bible) are set by musicians, it is important to regard these as *interpretations*. It is often thought that music will "conform" in a relatively simple way to the meaning of the words it sets, at most adding a kind of transparent varnish, or merely amplifying what is already expressed in the words. If not simply assumed, this kind of model is often urged as an ideal to attain. The Platonic tradition has been highly influential on the church in this regard, not least at the Reformation, when Calvin and others insisted that music must "hug the contours" of biblical texts with point-for-point rigor, especially in worship. This, however (as Calvin himself came to see), is clearly problematic. For music has its own quite distinctive capacities—to move us in particular ways, to create a sense of togetherness-in-distinction through overlapping sounds, to generate a sense of hopefulness through patterns of tensions and resolutions, and so forth. It is perhaps best to speak of music and words *interacting* with each other, music *bringing its own distinctive powers to bear* in the interpretation of texts (Begbie, "Unexplored"; Wright). When J. S. Bach sets the words "And Peter went out and wept bitterly" in *St. Matthew Passion*, the music exercises its own unique capacities as it interacts with the words, enabling us to access and participate in new ways in the reality of which the words speak—the dark depths of Peter's remorse.

Musical Imagery and Conceptuality. Music can also generate imagery, conceptuality, models, and metaphors to enhance the theological interpretation of Scripture. The singing of creation into being by Aslan in C. S. Lewis's *The Magician's Nephew* is an example (as is the musical-evolutionary overture to J. R. R. Tolkien's *Silmarillion*). In *The Art of Performance*, Frances Young compares our interpretation of Scripture to the performance of a musical work, exploring issues of textual authenticity, meaning, "authentic interpretation," "improvisation" for different contexts, and with a firm theological interest throughout. This is an instance of a field sometimes called "performance" hermeneutics (Lash; Barton). The imagery of "polyphony" has been widely used to speak of the diversity-in-unity of the biblical writings (Gowler), and Jeremy Begbie has argued that the metrical wave patterns in music can generate a deeper understanding of patterns of hope, promise, and fulfillment in biblical eschatology (*Theology*).

See also Dialogism; Psalms, Book of; Worship

Bibliography

Barton, S. "New Testament Interpretation as Performance." *SJT* 52 (1999): 179–208; Begbie, J. *Theology, Music and Time.* Cambridge University Press, 2000; idem. "Unexplored Eloquencies: Music, Religion and Culture." Pages 93–106 in *Mediating Religion*, ed. J. Mitchell. T&T Clark, 2003; Braun, J. *Music in Ancient Israel/Palestine.* Eerdmans, 2002; Foley, E. *Foundations of Christian Music.* Grove, 1992; Gowler, D. "Heteroglossic Trends in Biblical Studies: Polyphonic Dialogues or Clanging Cymbals?" *RevExp* (2000): 443–66; Hurtado, L. *At the Origins of Christian Worship.* Eerdmans, 1999; Jones, I. "Music and Musical Instruments." *ABD* 4:930–39; Kleinig, J. *The Lord's Song.* JSOT, 1993; Lash, N. "Performing the Scriptures." Pages 37–46 in *Theology on the Way to Emmaus.* SCM, 1986; Martin, R. *Worship in the Early Church.* Eerdmans, 1975; Porter, W. "Music." Pages 711–19 in *Dictionary of New Testament Background*, ed. C. Evans and S. Porter. InterVarsity, 2000; McKinnon, J. *Music in Early Christian Literature.* Cambridge University Press, 1987; Wright, N. T. "From Theology to Music and Back Again." Pages 177–92 in *Sounding the Depths*, ed. J. Begbie. SCM, 2002; Young, F. *The Art of Performance.* Darton, Longman & Todd, 1990.

Jeremy Begbie

Mysticism, Christian

By the earliest era of Christianity, the Greek term *mystikos* had migrated from a particular usage in the Hellenistic mystery cults into common Mediterranean usage in the ancient world. It had come to mean that which is hidden, that which is beyond the surface level of reality (deriving from the Greek root *my-*, to close). Thus, Paul uses the cognate term *mystērion* (e.g., Rom. 16:25; 1 Cor. 15:51) to denote truth whose unimaginable significance is hidden from the world, apart from the revelation of Christ. The following generations also used the term in reference to Christ, specifically as a way of pointing to the hidden truth of Christ present everywhere in the Scriptures. This sense that the Scriptures testify to Christ, even when texts at the surface level may be speaking of something else, would of course develop into the range of figural and allegorical readings of Scripture that have been so central to the Christian understanding. More than this, however, early Christians held that this sense of a divine more or a hidden presence of Christ in the Scripture was not simply a matter of one text pointing to another or even to truths about Christ; rather, they understood the Spirit as accomplishing a real encounter between the believing community and the risen Christ precisely in the hearing and proclaiming of the word. So for figures like Origen of Alexandria (ca. 185–ca. 254), often identified as the father of Christian mysticism, scriptural exegesis is inherently a mystical process in which the praying community is transformed and through its exegesis of the written word drawn into the hidden or mystical presence of the crucified and living Word.

In the centuries that followed, this perspective was expanded to include other communal practices in which such mystical encounter with God might take place: biblical reflection, worship, and dogmatic understanding all were held not only to point beyond themselves to deeper mysteries but also to open the believing community to the possibility of encounter with the living and hidden presence of God. Importantly, the mystical dimension of Christian life ("mysticism" per se is a term invented in modernity) operated within a fundamentally communal set of activities and referred above all to the hidden presence of God. The mystical dimension did not refer to unusual inner experiences of individuals or to a variety of psychological states among believers but to the reality of God always beyond the power of creaturely forms to express or conceive.

By the time of Maximus the Confessor (ca. 580–662), the process by which believers are fitted for some awareness of this hidden or mystical depth of God's presence comes to be delineated according to stages of moral growth, deep perception of God's handiwork in the world and in history, and finally a contemplation of the divine life itself (this develops into the stages of purgation, illumination, and union in many theories of the mystical life). The ultimate stage involves no achievement of the contemplative but is a gift of God allowing the contemplative to share intimately in God's own knowing and loving. Not surprisingly, it became customary for later thinkers, attempting to direct others along the path of the spiritual life, to attempt some evocation of these stages, often in experiential terms that might give some sense of the unexpected and blessed quality of the contemplative dimension. Bernard of Clairvaux (1090–1153) famously remarked that unless his readers had some experience themselves of what he was explaining, they would never understand him. Sometimes—as in the case of many mystical writers of the later Middle Ages, often writing in the vernacular and outside the learned framework of the monastic or academic worlds—this experiential dimension would be emphasized to a quite high degree. It is this often startling language of such more-popular mystical texts that, in a post-Cartesian modern environment, has led to the mistaken impression that Christian mysticism was preeminently a kind of self-absorption with abnormal inner states.

But even so self-aware a mystical writer as Teresa of Avila (1515–82) constantly warns her readers against placing much emphasis on their spiritual experiences. In her view, what is solely significant is not the self but the transformation of the self into an obedient servant of God. It is this transformational element, intrinsic to any authentic encounter with God, which marks the heart of most mystical texts. For mystical writers as diverse as Bonaventure (ca. 1217–74), Ruusbroec (1293–1381), Julian of Norwich (ca. 1342–ca. 1416), or Catherine of Siena (1347–80), the commonly understood dynamism of the Christian mystical life is the transformation wrought through encounter with the Trinity. The gracious momentum of the trinitarian processions reaches into human existence in Christ and the Spirit, drawing humanity into a transfiguring share in God's own life. Bonaventure, for example, specifically describes this process in terms of Jesus' dying and rising, and identifies the mystical journey as an intensive participation in the paschal mystery.

Understood in this way, the mystical dimension of Christian life is clarified as in fact a way of living into the fullness of the baptismal life, in which believers are brought, through a share in Christ's dying, into a share in his resurrection life (Rom. 6 and 8). The same Spirit who makes Christ alive in the vindicating joy of the Father also works this mystery within the heart of the believing community. What is important for the vast majority of Christian mystical writers is not the experiential "side effects" of this transformation, but the hidden presence of God, who graciously discloses the truth of the divine life precisely through the transformation of human life.

See also Spirituality/Spiritual Formation; Spiritual Sense

Bibliography

Some key primary sources: Bernard of Clairvaux. *Sermons on the Song of Songs*; Bonaventure. *Journey of the Mind into God*; Catherine of Siena. *The Dialogue*; Julian of Norwich. *Revelations of Divine Love;* Origen. *Commentary on the Song of Songs*; idem. *Homilies on the Song of Songs*; Maximus the Confessor. *Centuries on Knowledge.*

Mark A. McIntosh

N

Nag Hammadi

In late 1945 just outside the village of Nag Hammadi (Egypt), a young man came across an earthenware jar containing thirteen leather-bound books. These books, dating from the mid-fourth century CE and fairly well preserved, proved to contain a large number of newly discovered texts. Although the codices—following an intriguing set of circumstances—were eventually made available to scholars for reconstruction and translation, it was not until 1977 that all fifty-two books of the Nag Hammadi library appeared in facsimile edition; the first complete English translation was also published in the same year. Given the relatively recent date of the collection's publication, Nag Hammadi scholarship must still be regarded as being in its early stages. The literary and theological nature of these texts, their sociohistorical location, and their significance for the study of early Christianity and Gnosticism remain sub judice.

Perhaps the most striking feature of the Nag Hammadi library is the diversity of its contents. Some books are little more than translations of Greek philosophical literature; others, often involving elaborate mythologies, seem to derive from Hermetic (see, e.g., *Discourse on the 8th and 9th; Prayer of Thanksgiving*) or Sethian (*Apocryphon of John; Hypostasis of the Archons*) settings. By far the majority of texts appear to reflect a "gnosticized Christianity" (or "Christianized Gnosticism") whereby traditional NT motifs and figures are reinterpreted so as to cohere with a certain sectarian worldview. The Nag Hammadi corpus also offers evidence for a purely Jewish Gnosticism. If the seemingly Jewish *Apocalypse of Adam* could be confidently dated to the first century CE, this would certainly constitute strong evidence for a pre-Christian Gnosticism. A first-century *Sitz im Leben* has been forcefully maintained for the core of Nag Hammadi's most famous writing, the *Gospel of Thomas*. Drawing attention to putative comparisons between the sayings source Q and *Gospel of Thomas*, some (notably Koester and Robinson) have argued that the nature of the Jesus sayings and the relative absence of narrative in the Thomasine gospel indicate its early location in the formation of the canonical Gospels. But this is far from settled, for a renewed case for *Gospel of Thomas*'s second-century origins has also recently been made.

Although the Nag Hammadi find does little toward refining our concept of "Gnosticism" as a heuristic category (on the contrary, the broad array of perspectives contained in the corpus may persuade scholarship to dispense with the designation altogether), it remains the most important source for the study of early gnostic sects. Previously the vast majority of what could have been known about Gnosticism could only be culled from the early church fathers, who were of course its severest critics. Now we are in a position to hear the gnostic writers speak for themselves. Scholarship awaits further investigation into the sects' relationship to mainstream Judaism and early Christianity, and their correspondingly different interpretative frameworks.

See also Gnosticism

Bibliography

Dart, J. *The Jesus of Heresy and History*. Harper & Row, 1988; Evans, C. A., R. Webb, and R. A. Wiebe, eds. *Nag Hammadi Texts and the Bible*. NTTS 18. Brill, 1993; Flory, W. *The Gnostic Concept of Authority and the Nag Hammadi Documents*. Mellen Biblical Press 33. Mellen Biblical Press, 1995; Hedrick, C., and R. Hodgson. *Nag Hammadi, Gnosticism, and Early Christianity*. Hendrickson, 1986; Pagels, E. *The Gnostic Gospels*. Random House, 1979; Perrin, N. *Thomas and Tatian*. Academia Biblica 5. Scholars Press/Brill, 2001; Robinson, J. M., ed. *The Nag Hammadi Library in English*. 3d ed. Harper & Row, 1988; Robinson, J. M., and H. Koester. *Trajectories through Early Christianity*. Fortress, 1971; Scholer, D. *Nag Hammadi Bibliography, 1970–1994*. NHS 32. Brill, 1997; Turner, J. D., and A. McGuire, eds. *The Nag Hammadi Library after Fifty Years*. NHS 44. Brill, 1997; Williams, M. A. *Rethinking "Gnosticism."* Princeton University Press, 1996.

Nicholas Perrin

Nahum, Book of

The book of Nahum is a "prophecy concerning Nineveh, the document of a revelation to Nahum the Elkoshite" (1:1 AT). The revelation concerns the downfall of Nineveh in 612 BCE. The prophetic exposition puts this downfall into a theological framework, focusing on the nature of God, especially his jealous anger and vengeance. Nahum depicts God as powerful and passionate but in a protective rather than possessive way.

The Argument of the Book

Following the superscription (1:1), a hymn describes Yahweh's character and the different fates of two groups, depending on how they relate to Yahweh (1:2–8); to this is added a prophetic challenge (1:9–10) and a statement of the situation that gave rise to the prophecy (1:11). A divine declaration promising liberation from oppression and defeat of the enemy (1:12–14) forms a bridge to images of the fall of Nineveh (2:1–10), which are introduced by a picture of the announcement of victory (1:15). Appended to these images is a rhetorical question stressing defeat (2:11–12) and a prophecy of complete destruction (2:13). In chapter 3 an announcement of doom for a murderous city (3:1–4) precedes a prophecy of complete humiliation (3:5–7). The exposition denounces the city's complacency (3:8–12) before depicting the uselessness of the city's defenses (3:13–17) and the helplessness of the city's ruler (3:18–19). Attempts to separate the message of restoration (for Judah) from the message of destruction (for Nineveh) go against the thrust of the book, which has them closely intertwined. Vengeance executed against the oppressor means liberation for the oppressed.

Addressee and reference of the text are frequently left undetermined (the ambiguity is removed in some translations by insertion of "Judah" and "Nineveh" in 1:7–2:1), suggesting that God's "zealous ardour for the maintenance and promotion of his own legal claims" (Peels 203–4) applies without partiality. The real opposition is not between two nations, but between those who put their trust in a God who loathes injustice and those who are his enemies. The opening hymn ensures that Nineveh is seen as an illustration of God's judgment against all human evil and injustice, an anticipation of God's final triumph against his adversaries.

Nahum within the Canon

The condemnation of imperialism and injustice finds parallels elsewhere in Scripture, as in the judgment on Assyria in Isa. 10:5–15, on Edom in Isa. 34, on Babylon in Jer. 50–51, and on Tyre and Egypt in Ezek. 26–32. The theme is further developed in Rev. 17–18. Nahum makes the fullest link to God's character. It has been argued that the allusion to Exod. 34:6–7 in Nah. 1 is part of a redaction of the Book of the Twelve (Nogalski; cf. Van Leeuwen). This may underestimate the number of links to the creedal language of Exod. 34:6–7 elsewhere in the OT, as well as the close relationship between Nahum and Isaiah, but it is helpful to reflect on the use of Exod. 34:6–7 in the Book of the Twelve. Appeal to God's character functions in Joel 2:13–14 as a motivation for repentance. In Jon. 3:9–4:4, God's compassion is the basis for a change of course regarding Nineveh, just as God is praised in Mic. 7:18 for his grace, which enables his people to be forgiven.

The book of Jonah—with its movement from divine anger to mercy, described with the root to which the name Nahum is related (nakham, "relent"; Jon. 3:9–10; 4:2)—is often considered to have been written in response to Nahum, its message being interpreted as "an outright contradiction of Nahum's prophecy" (Weigl 105). In traditional interpretation, it is commonly assumed that the repentance of the Ninevites was either superficial or short-lived. In any case, both within the Book of the Twelve and as far as the depiction of Nineveh's history is concerned, Nahum speaks the final word on Nineveh. The book of Jonah is more about Israel's vocation than the fate of Nineveh, especially so if the book was written after the demise of the Neo-Assyrian Empire. It reminds us that the judgment on Nineveh should not be reduced to the benefits it brings to Judah. The rhetorical question on which Nahum ends affirms God's concern for other nations as much as the one that concludes Jonah.

The good news of victory of which Nahum speaks (1:15) is of course not limited to the downfall of the Assyrian Empire. Isaiah 52:7 indicates that the return from exile was another instance of God asserting his reign over evil. Supremely, God's victory over evil was won on the cross so that Nah. 1:15 is again fulfilled in the proclamation of the gospel (cf. Rom. 10:15; Eph. 6:15).

Perspectives from the History of Interpretation

The section 1:14–2:1 was particularly popular in Christian interpretation. The traditional fourfold interpretation of the book is neatly summarized in an exposition (wrongly) attributed to Julian of Toledo: "The prophet Nahum is set in the kingdom of the Assyrians. According to the historical sense, he speaks of the destruction of Nineveh, its capital; in the allegorical sense, of the world's being laid waste; in the mystical sense, of the restoration of the human race through Christ; in the moral sense, of the restoring of his first dignified state, or to yet greater glory, of the sinner fallen into wickedness" (from Ball 212).

Modern historical-critical research has been concerned with distinguishing the words of the prophet from those of later editors, and with establishing the setting of the prophet. Particularly, denying Nahum's authorship of the opening hymn would make the prophet's message appear in a quite different light from that of the book. The view that Nahum was one of the false prophets condemned by Jeremiah (J. M. P. Smith) and the view that he was a cult prophet who wrote a liturgy for the celebration of the fall of Nineveh after the event (Humbert; Sellin) are no longer upheld in contemporary scholarship (see Childs; Weigl). Recently, Baumann has read the text as condoning sexual violence against women who are unduly self-confident. But Nineveh is not depicted as an ordinary prostitute making a living, let alone as a sexually liberated and self-confident woman. Rather, she is a source of ensnarement and thinks nothing of selling peoples for her pleasure. The picture of her paying out rather than receiving money (cf. Ezek. 16) distances the metaphor from "ordinary" prostitution and suggests that the text is not intended to be read as saying something about women.

Nahum and the Church Today

Nahum invites a celebration of divine sovereignty and justice, affirming that God's retributive anger is good news. Traditional interpretation is certainly correct to claim that Nahum prefigures the final judgment that will end the cycle of violence: "Everything said to Nineveh is going to happen in the judgment on the devil and his associates" (Haimo of Auxerre, as quoted in Ball 214). This judgment is anticipated in historical events such as the demise of empires and the deconstruction of injustice, not least in the proclamation of the gospel, through which enemies of God become his children. Nahum at the same time expresses a challenge to trust and submit to God, and not to be counted among his adversaries.

Bibliography

Ball, E. "'When the Towers Fall': Interpreting Nahum as Christian Scripture." Pages 211–30 in *In Search of True Wisdom*, ed. E. Ball. JSOTSup 300. Sheffield Academic Press, 1999; Baumann, G. "Das Buch Nahum: Der gerechte Gott als sexueller Gewalttäter." Pages 347–53 in *Kompendium feministische Bibelauslegung*, ed. L. Schottroff and M. Wacker. Kaiser, 1998; Becking, B. "Passion, Power and Protection: Interpreting the God of Nahum." Pages 1–20 in *On Reading Prophetic Texts*, ed. B. Becking and M. Dijkstra. Biblical Interpretation Series 18. Brill, 1996; Childs, B. *Introduction to the Old Testament as Scripture*. Fortress, 1979; Nogalski, J. *Redactional Processes in the Book of the Twelve*. BZAW 218. De Gruyter, 1993; Peels, H. *Vengeance of God*. Brill, 1995; Van Leeuwen, R. "Scribal Wisdom and Theodicy in the Book of the Twelve." Pages 31–49 in *In Search of Wisdom*, ed. L. Perdue et al. Westminster John Knox, 1993; Weigl, M. "Current Research on the Book of Nahum: Exegetical Methodologies in Turmoil?" *CurBS* 9 (2001): 81–130.

Thomas Renz

Narrative Criticism

Narrative is important to Christian theology because the revelation of Yahweh is entwined with the biblical metanarrative and its many subnarratives. There is a widespread recognition that the biblical storywriters were theologians—their tales are not just accounts of what happened but *theological interpretations of what happened* (Long). The study of biblical stories then cannot ignore theology. These narratives give content and nuance to the meaning of theological concepts such as "covenant," "Messiah," "atonement," "love," and "God." For instance, John's concept of "Messiah" cannot be understood simply by examining the cultural and linguistic background of the term. John radically reshapes the messianic concept through his story of the trial and crucifixion, presented as an enthronement ceremony with the cross as the "exaltation" of Jesus as King on his throne (Stibbe 105–13). John's concept of "Messiah" has a narrative shape. Given the place of narratives in Christian theology, narrative criticism will be important in helping us to read them carefully and sensitively.

The Poetics of Biblical Narrative

Narrative criticism has played a key role in the welcome shift of biblical scholarship from the earlier, almost exclusive preoccupation with the sources (literary and oral) and historical events behind biblical stories to an interest in their final form. For Christians, whatever may be fruitfully said of the prehistory of biblical books, the finished texts we possess are the authoritative source for theological reflection (which is *not* to say that historicity is unimportant). Narrative criticism has restored this (misleadingly named) "precritical" focus in academic scholarship.

Narrative criticism will help to clarify the theology of Genesis, Mark, or John, but it will not go far enough to create a biblical theology because the Bible as a whole is not a literary unity *in the same sense* that Genesis is (we cannot see it as having a single narrator's voice, implied readership, etc.). So narrative criticism contributes to the task of a biblical theology but cannot do all the work required. It does, however, go far in helping us read biblical stories theologically.

Biblical studies, following general trends in literary studies, has seen narrative theories develop initially with a focus on the text and more recently with a focus on the reader. Defenders of the New Criticism, which originated in the United States in the 1920s and faded away after the 1960s, argued that it was a mistake to try to get behind a text to the sources or the author's intentions. Instead, the text itself with its structure and form should be the object of interpretation and close reading. Although New Criticism itself has had little direct impact on biblical studies, it has indirectly stimulated fruitful work on the poetics of biblical narrative, sharing its focus on final form and close reading. Particularly worthy of mention are the works (in the 1980s) of Alter, Bar-Efrat, Berlin, and Sternberg. These Jewish scholars have shed considerable light on the grammar underlying the construction of OT narrative. Their work has clarified how dialogues work, the functions of repetition, the use of narrative time and space, the devices used in characterization and in structuring plots, the place of ambiguity, and so on. The art of the biblical storytellers has been revealed, and the exegetical payoff has been enormous.

Narrative criticism can help to identify the central themes of a work. This is so in single narratives and across vast sections of narrative. For instance, David Clines used early narrative-critical methods to identify the unifying theme of the whole Pentateuch: "The partial fulfilment—which implies also the partial non-fulfilment—of the promise to or blessing of the patriarchs" (Clines, *Theme*, 30). Literary devices, such as chiasms and repetition of key words, can help readers identify (the often theological) foci of the narrator. This guides readers away from majoring on minor issues and vice versa, helping interpreters to guard against the oversubjectivism of the "what it means to me" approach.

All the action and speech in a story are mediated via the narrator, and it is the narrator's perspective on the characters and events that a narrative ultimately reveals (Sternberg). It is this narrator's perspective that interpreters are, initially at least, seeking to uncover. A Christian theological interpretation may not end with exposition of a narrator's perspectives but will not ignore it (Moberly). The biblical narrator is usually described as "omniscient." There is no information in the world of the story to which they do not have access—even the inner thoughts of the characters (including God himself). Consequently, biblical narrators are "reliable"—they do not ever lie to readers although they often withhold information either temporarily or permanently for various reasons (see esp. Sternberg, ch. 7). Sternberg argues that the biblical narrators claim to speak with a prophetic-divine voice. This would sit comfortably with a traditional view of the inspiration of Scripture and would have theological implications for the use of narrative. However, it is controversial, and a traditional view of Scripture does not depend upon it.

Another benefit of attention to final form is that the locating of individual stories in wider narrative contexts allows tensions between parts to arise (e.g., on the appropriateness of a monarchy in 1 Samuel). The tensions are often deliberate and theologically significant (regardless of any source-critical explanations that may lie at hand). Sometimes a narrator may wish readers to take a certain stance on an issue and then will overturn it, subverting the readers' judgments. Such strategies are lost when stories are read out of their literary contexts, and they become liable to misuse. Other times the tensions are ones that need preserving in our own theology, such as that running through the Deuteronomistic books between unconditionality and conditionality in Israel's covenant with God (McConville).

Narrative critics also highlight the importance of intertextual allusions in stories, allowing theological and ethical points to be made in subtle ways. Jesus' wilderness sojourn of forty days, by alluding to Israel's forty years, allows making the implicit theological point that Jesus represents Israel and succeeds where they have failed. The Solomon stories at the beginning of 1 Kings are far more critical of Solomon than is often realized once one sees the many allusions to Deuteronomy (Provan). Attention to intertextual allusions has shed considerable new theological light on well-known narratives.

Narrative criticism alerts us to the fact that the very narrative form itself, not simply the propositions that can be distilled from it, can communicate theological points or reinforce the explicit theological content. Robert Alter draws attention to the use of "type scenes"—conventional ways in which scenes of certain types (e.g., betrothal scenes, deathbed scenes) were told (ch. 3). When a biblical narrator breaks with these storytelling conventions, the readers are intended to notice. For instance, the rape of Dinah in Gen. 34 could possibly be seen as a radically twisted telling of a betrothal type scene. The very distortion of the convention indicates the narrator's perspective. Gary Burge has argued that the narrator of John's Gospel employs different storytelling devices, such as withholding crucial information from the readers at key points, in order to tutor his readers in a theological matter: that revelation of Jesus is not accessible to the human mind unassisted by the Spirit of truth. John not only teaches this theology in his text, but also, his very storytelling techniques provide the reader with an experience parallel to that of the actors on stage, provoking them to come to grips with their own lack of understanding. Thus, John's rhetorical strategy reinforces his theology.

Structuralism

The above-mentioned accounts pay close attention to the surface structures of biblical stories. A different approach is embodied in structuralism, which in the field of literature manifested itself in the search to penetrate behind the details at the surface level of individual stories to uncover the so-called deep structures that they share with other stories. Influential in the literary field was the Russian folklorist Vladimir Propp (*Morphology of the Folktale*, in Russian, 1928). Propp argued that underlying all fairy tales was a simple structure like the grammar of a language that all fairy tales obeyed. There are, he wrote, only seven basic roles in fairy tales (villain, donor, helper, sought-for-person, his/her father, dispatcher, hero, false hero) and only thirty-one functions (actions a character can perform to further the plot). A. J. Greimas developed what has been the most influential kind of structuralism in biblical studies: the actantial approach (*Sémantique structurale*, 1966). Greimas sees six actants in narratives (subject, object, sender, receiver, opponent, helper) related along three axes (communication, power, and volition). The essence of narrative grammar is represented in the diagram below.

If we dig below the surface of stories, we have, along the axis of communication, a Sender who initiates an action that communicates a needed

Sender	Object	Receiver
Axis of Communication	↑ *Axis of Volition*	*Axis of Power*
Helper(s)	Subject	Opponent(s)

Object to a Receiver. The Sender gives a Subject the task of bringing the Object to the Receiver. The axis of volition focuses on the Subject's role in fulfilling this commission. The axis of power draws attention to the Opponent, who tries to thwart the Subject in the commission. A Helper provides power to fulfill the commission.

We can illustrate Greimas's relevance to biblical narratives with three brief examples, each of which illustrates a different benefit of the actantial model. First, the model can help in stripping away the details of a narrative to expose its basic structure, and this can be helpful in building up the theology of a text. Andrew Lincoln uses the actantial model to clarify the plot structure of John's Gospel (162–64). God the Father is the Sender, and the world (with Israel as its primary representative) is the Receiver. The Object God wishes to bring to the world is a trial that will issue in the judgment of either eternal life or condemnation. Jesus is the Subject sent to bring the world to trial. The Helpers are the other witnesses (e.g., John the Baptizer, God, Jesus' works, the Scriptures, the disciples, the beloved disciple, and the Holy Spirit). The Opponents are those who do not receive Jesus' witness (the world, the "Jews," Pilate) and the devil.

Second, the model can also help by highlighting when biblical stories take unusual twists that can have theological significance. Roland Barthes analyzed the story in Gen. 32, when Jacob wrestles a stranger. God is the Sender who sends the Subject, Jacob, on the quest of reconciliation with Esau (Object). The night wrestler is the Opponent, but quite unexpectedly, it is revealed that the Opponent *is the* Sender *is the* Helper! This rare twist exposed by Barthes is provocative and provides food for theological thought.

Third, the model can make visible the invisible elements in a story, and this can be theologically useful. David Clines ("Reading") shows how the lack of an explicit Sender in the book of Esther invites the reader to postulate one (God), and this feeds into an implicit theology of divine providence.

Fourth, the focus on binary opposition within plots (Subject-Object, Sender-Receiver, Helper-Opponent) can be helpful in understanding the importance of "contradictions" within the dynamics of a literary work. The theological power of some biblical stories may come from the negotiation of themes in tension. Removing the "contradictions" may remove the message. Although structuralism as a comprehensive theory went into decline after the 1970s, it is still useful as a heuristic tool.

The Place of the Reader

Clearly, readers are free to resist the message of a text, but there is considerable disagreement about how much freedom readers have in the actual *constitution of the meaning of a text*. Some argue that texts have no meanings apart from the reading process, and that there are as many "meanings" in a text as there are readers. Others think that the role of the reader in constituting the meaning is fairly minimal. Sternberg pays considerable attention to the role of the reader and argues that narrators often leave gaps in their stories that readers need to fill in if they are to make sense of the story. The skill of the biblical narrator is such that, however the *responsible* reader fills these gaps, the same verdict on the characters will be produced. Thus, responsible readers can underread or overread a biblical story, but they *cannot misread one* (he calls this "foolproof composition"). This is a bold thesis, and it has been criticized by many other narrative critics who feel that readers have more scope for interpretation than Sternberg suggests (e.g., Fewell and Gunn).

Christian theological readers of stories have taken different stances on this issue. All recognize the importance of the reader, but some are inclined to give a greater role to readers in creating meaning through their interaction with stories (e.g., Fowl; Robert Wall) than others are (e.g., Kevin Vanhoozer). Biblical interpretation needs to navigate between "the Scylla of mechanical replication and the Charybdis of radical polyvalence and unconstrained textual indeterminacy" (Lundin, Walhout, and Thiselton 137). The work of narrative critics can guide readers in this voyage, enabling theological interpretations of biblical narratives to be grounded in close, sensitive readings of those texts.

See also Biblical Theology; Intention/Intentional Fallacy; Intertextuality; Literary Criticism; Metanarrative; Oral Tradition and the NT; Oral Tradition and the OT; Proposition; Reader-Response Criticism; Rhetorical Criticism; Scripture, Authority of; Source Criticism; Structuralism; Text/Textuality

Bibliography

Alter, R. *The Art of Biblical Narrative*. Allen & Unwin, 1981; Bar-Efrat, S. *Narrative Art in the Bible*. Sheffield Academic Press, 1989; Barthes, R. "The Struggle with the Angel: Textual Analysis of Genesis 32:23–33." Pages 21–33 in *Structural Analysis and Biblical Exegesis*, ed. R. Barthes et al. Pickwick, 1974; Berlin, A. *Poetics and Interpretation of Biblical Narrative*. Almond, 1983; Burge, G. "Revelation and Discipleship in St John's Gospel." Unpublished paper presented at Tyndale NT Group, 2002; Clines, D. J. A. *The Theme of the Pentateuch*. 2d ed. Sheffield Academic Press, 1997; idem. "Reading Esther from 'Left to Right': Contemporary Strategies for Reading a Biblical Text." Pages 31–52 in *The Bible in Three Dimensions*, ed. D. J. A. Clines, S. Fowl, and S. E. Porter. Sheffield Academic Press, 1990; Fewell, D. N., and D. M. Gunn. *Narrative in the Hebrew Bible*. Oxford University Press, 1993; Fowl, S. "The Role of Authorial Intention in the Theological Interpretation of Scripture." Pages 71–87 in *Between Two Horizons*, ed. J. Green and M. Turner. Eerdmans, 2000; Lincoln, A. *Truth on Trial*. Hendrickson, 2000; Long, V. P. *The Art of Biblical History*. Zondervan, 1994; Longman, T., III. *Literary Approaches to Biblical Interpretation*. Zondervan, 1987; Lundin, R., C. Walhout, and A. Thiselton. *The Promise of Hermeneutics*. Eerdmans, 1999; McConville, J. G. *Grace in the End*. Zondervan, 1993; Moberly, R. W. L. "Christ as the Key to Scripture: Genesis 22 Reconsidered." Pages 143–73 in *He Swore an Oath*, ed. R. Hess, G. Wenham, and P. Satterthwaite. Baker, 1994; Provan, I. *1 and 2 Kings*. NIBCOT. Hendrickson, 1995; Sternberg, M. *The Poetics of Biblical Narrative*. Indiana University Press, 1987; Stibbe, M. *John as Storyteller*. Cambridge University Press, 1992; Vanhoozer K. "The Reader in New Testament Interpretation." Pages 301–28 in *Hearing the New Testament*, ed. J. Green. Eerdmans, 1995; Wall R. "Reading the Bible from within Our Traditions." Pages 88–107 in *Between Two Horizons*, eds. J. Green and M. Turner. Eerdmans, 2000.

Robin Parry

Narrative Theology

"Narrative theology" refers to a constellation of approaches to the theological task typically joined by their (1) antipathy toward forms of theology concerned with the systematic organization of propositions and grounded in ahistorical principles, and (2) attempt to discern an overall aim and ongoing plot in the ways of God as these are revealed in Scripture and continue to express themselves in history.

A primary impetus for narrative theology comes from Scripture itself. This is true, first, in that the bulk of Scripture comes to us in the form of narratives. Although in the modern period theology has gravitated toward the rational essence of the faith, its dogmatic essentials, scriptural reflections on God's nature, have an altogether different flavor. Rather than enumerating the immutable attributes of God, in the Bible "God's person emerges in a series of contexts. God is a creator, then a destroyer. God relates to a family in the concerns of its ongoing family life, such as the finding of a home, the birth of children, and the arranging of marriages; God then relates to a nation in the different demands of its life, which includes God's becoming a war-maker." That is, "the 'revelation' of God's person is inextricably tied to the events in which God becomes different things, in a way that any person does; it is thus inextricably tied to narrative" (Goldingay 131).

Second, in biblical texts we find the deliberate work of forming God's people by shaping their story. Israel's first "credo" took the form of a narrative: "A wandering Aramean was my father . . ." (Deut. 26:5–10 RSV). The speeches in Acts interpretatively render the history of Israel so as to demonstrate the advent of Jesus as its culmination (e.g., Acts 7:2–53; 13:16–41). And John's Revelation portrays the whole of history from creation to new creation so as to transform the theological imagination of its readers.

Third, the particular narratives related in the biblical books, together with the nonnarrative portions of Scripture, participate in a more extensive, overarching narrative, or metanarrative. This is the story of God's purpose coming to fruition in the whole of God's history with us, from the creation of the world and humanity's falling away from God, through God's repeated attempts to restore his people, culminating in the coming of Jesus of Nazareth and reaching its full crescendo in the final revelation of Christ and the new creation. In an important sense, the Bible is nothing less than the record of the actualization (and ongoing promise) of this purpose of God in the history of the cosmos.

The importance of narrative theology is underscored by the recognition that narrative is central to identity formation; indeed, recent work in neurobiology emphasizes the capacity for and drive toward making *storied sense* of our experienced world as a distinguishing characteristic of the human family. We typically explain our behaviors through the historical narratives by which we collaborate to create a sense of ourselves as persons and as a people. The story we embrace serves as an interpretative scheme that is at once *conceptual* (a way of seeing things), *conative* (a set of beliefs and values to which a group and its members are deeply attached), and *action-guiding* (we seek to live according to its terms; cf. Flanagan 27–55).

In recent times, narrative theology is especially associated with the name of George Lindbeck (building on the thought of Hans Frei), for whom faith is a culture that shapes our individuality, experience, and emotions. Religion, he argues, is not primarily a collection of true propositions or a deeply personal experience of the transcendent, but a language or culture that enables us to characterize the truth and empowers us to experience the Holy. Being Christian therefore involves learning the story of Israel and of Jesus so as to interpret and experience the world on its terms. Hence, the Scriptures are essential in shaping the life-world of God's people. For Lindbeck, the Scriptures are a "world" that supplies the interpretative framework within which believers seek to live their lives and understand reality. The central stories of Scripture tell us who we are as we make the story of the Bible our own. Along similar lines, Gabriel Fackre discusses narrative theology as the linkage of the Christian story to the believer's story through biblical stories. "It is the Christian faith lived at the juncture of personal, ecclesial, and biblical narrative" (194).

Narrative theology has been criticized at various points, three of which invite brief reflection. (1) Some are concerned about Lindbeck's indifference to the historicity of the biblical story, whether externally referential events comprise the biblical narrative. This, of course, is not a problem solely for Lindbeck or biblical narrative in particular, but has been endemic to discourse on the narrative representation of historical events more generally in the last half of the twentieth century (e.g., White). Whether fictional or historical, what mattered most seemed to be the "meaning" provided within and by narrative. More recent work in the philosophy of history has urged that "narrative" need not be so much *creation* of significance through the imposition of interpretative frameworks, but rather the *recognition* of thematic and causal ties among events in the real world (cf. Carter). (2) Others are concerned with the ambiguity of the phrase, "to inhabit a narrative," so central to narrative theology's interest in theological embodiment and performance. This problem has been thoughtfully parsed by Nicholas Wolterstorff, who concludes that the notion of "inhabiting the world of the biblical narrative" is important when it claims that "the story that *most decisively shapes* our lives must be the biblical story" (212).

(3) Still others concern themselves with whether or how a particular narrative can be identified as "the" biblical or "the" Christian narrative. "Inhab-

iting the story" would take on a haunting tone if, for example, the defining story were the direful conquest accounts of Joshua. Taken together, three considerations mitigate this issue. First, since Aristotle, descriptions of the "narrative cycle" have drawn attention to the importance of the narrative's beginning, middle, and end, three "moments" that determine the plot and structure of a narrative by identifying the narrative "need" that must be addressed and resolved. Second, narrative studies distinguish between "satellites" and "kernels"—a logic of hierarchy among narrative events, evaluated according to whether they play a crucial role in the direction the narrative takes, with "kernels" the more pivotal (e.g., Chatman). The question, then, is how one parses the "beginning," "middle," and "end" of the biblical narrative, and so identifies certain events over others as cruxes in the development of the narrative. Although certain constraints are unavoidable (since, by any reckoning, creation and new creation serve as the "beginning" and "end"), it is nonetheless possible to read the biblical narrative in a variety of ways. That not all of these ways would be "Christian" is evident from the intramural disputes among the Jewish people in the first century, leading eventually to the partings of the ways between Jews and Christians; and within the Christian movement, with some groups regarded as heretical even though they based their positions in thoughtful reading of authoritative Scripture. Third, then, the hermeneutical key for a Christian reading of the Scriptures is twofold: its recognition that what holds the two Testaments together is the one aim of God, and its recognition that the character of God (and thus the nature of God's story) is paradigmatically manifest in Israel's release from bondage in Egypt and decisively revealed in Jesus of Nazareth. Accordingly, the Rule of Faith and subsequent creeds of Christian orthodoxy served historically and continue to serve as theological boundary markers for Christian identity, setting the horizons within which the Bible may be read specifically as Christian Scripture (cf. Green; Wall).

One final insight from the study of narrative is crucial: narratives move forward in the service of a central aim, in relation to which all else is oriented. From this perspective, the Bible is not first and foremost "about" humanity, or even about a particular, identifiable segment of humanity, Israel. Nor is the Bible a christological book, in the narrow sense. Rather, its plot is *theo*logically determined. Scripture's subject and focus is God, enfleshed in Jesus Christ, active powerfully and

formatively through word and Spirit. Yahweh's purpose thus determines the shape of this narrative and call upon its readers to choose sides. Hence, engaging with this narrative involves us in a formative and decision-making process. How does this aim beckon us? How will we respond? In this important sense, "narrative theology" is less theological method and more an intrinsically self-involving theological vision of God, church, Scripture, and world, bound together within the economy of salvation, with the people of God cast as pilgrims on a journey whose destination is known and achieved only by indwelling the divine story—which cannot be reduced to principles and rules, but must be embraced and embodied.

See also Narrative Criticism; Ricoeur, Paul; Rule of Faith; Salvation, History of; Yale School

Bibliography

Carter, J. "Telling Times: History, Emplotment, and Truth." *History and Theory* 42 (2003): 1–27; Chatman, S. *Story and Discourse.* Cornell University Press, 1978; Fackre, G. "Narrative Theology from an Evangelical Perspective." Pages 188–201 in *Faith and Narrative,* ed. K. Yandell. Oxford University Press, 2001; Flanagan, O. *The Problem of the Soul.* Basic, 2002; Goldingay, J. "Biblical Narrative and Systematic Theology." Pages 123–42 in *Between Two Horizons,* ed. J. Green and M. Turner. Eerdmans, 2000; Green, G. *Theology, Hermeneutics, and Imagination.* Cambridge University Press, 2000; Green, J. "Scripture and Theology: Failed Experiments, Fresh Perspectives." *Int* 56 (2002): 5–20; Hauerwas, S., and L. G. Jones, eds. *Why Narrative?* Eerdmans, 1989; Lindbeck, G. *The Nature of Doctrine.* Westminster John Knox, 1984; Wall, R. "Reading the Bible from within Our Traditions: The 'Rule of Faith' in Theological Hermeneutics." Pages 88–107 in *Between Two Horizons,* ed. J. Green and M. Turner. Eerdmans, 2000; White, H. *The Content of the Form.* Johns Hopkins University Press, 1987; Wolterstorff, N. "Living within a Text." Pages 202–13 in *Faith and Narrative,* ed. K. Yandell. Oxford University Press, 2001; Yandell, K., ed. *Faith and Narrative.* Oxford University Press, 2001.

Joel B. Green

Nature *See* Earth/Land; Grace; Worldview

Nehemiah, Book of

The book of Nehemiah was originally a continuation of the book of Ezra, with which it is linked both thematically and narratively (see further under "Ezra"). There is little justification for separating the two books apart from the fact that Neh. 1:1 begins a first-person narrative by Nehemiah, who has not previously received mention (the Nehemiah of Ezra 2:2 is a different character). The twelve-year gap between the last events of

Ezra 7–10 and Neh. 1:1 is not sufficient to warrant the break, since a much longer period separates Ezra 7–10 from Ezra 1–6. The separation into two books has done much to hinder a theological interpretation of the whole.

History of Interpretation (see also "Ezra")

A good deal of precritical Christian interpretation focused on the personal qualities of Nehemiah: his humility, his devotion to God's suffering people in spite of his privileged position at the Persian court, and his ability to combine dependence on God with practical forethought. His success at rebuilding Jerusalem was sometimes seen as an example of how to revive the church while being prepared at all times for opposition.

More recently, theological interpretation has tended to be submerged beneath historical-critical issues. As Childs reports, many have approached Ezra-Nehemiah "with the assumption that its proper interpretation depends on establishing an accurate historical sequence of events" (630). To this end, a good deal of debate has centered on the chronological relationship between Nehemiah and Ezra. Many scholars have perceived difficulties with the traditional order of their arrival in Jerusalem, and have amended and reordered the text accordingly. In fact, other approaches to the perceived problems are available, making such drastic solutions unnecessary (Kidner 146–58; Williamson, *Ezra*, 55–69).

Much scholarly contention has surrounded the identity of the law book whose legislation is enacted in Ezra-Nehemiah. Since Ezra was "a scribe skilled in the law of Moses" (Ezra 7:6 NRSV), it is logical to assume that the legislation he set out to teach was contained in "the Book of Moses" referred to in Ezra 6:18 and (with slight variations) in Neh. 8:1, 14; 10:29; and 13:1. The traditional view is that this book was the Pentateuch, but some source critics have doubted whether the complete Pentateuch could have existed as early as the fifth century BCE. Even if the antiquity of the Pentateuch is accepted, questions remain. Some of the legislation enacted in Ezra-Nehemiah seems to have no exact counterpart in the Pentateuch, and this has led Houtman to argue that it was based on a different work, which has not survived. This conclusion would have obvious implications for Ezra-Nehemiah's connection with other parts of the canon. However, it is possible to argue that the application of pentateuchal laws must have undergone development, to adapt them to changed circumstances (Williamson, *Ezra*, 90–98). If this

is accepted, there is no good reason to doubt that the Pentateuch was the book that the postexilic community recognized as authoritative.

A refreshing attempt to read Ezra-Nehemiah as a literary whole is that of Eskenazi. She identifies a tripartite story structure: "potentiality" (Ezra 1:1–4, in which the objective is defined), "process of actualisation" (Ezra 1:5–Neh. 7:73), and "success" (Neh. 8:1–13:31, in which the objective is realized). The main theme is identified as "how the people of God build the house of God in accordance with authoritative documents." Eskenazi goes on to argue that the concept of the "house of God" expands to include the community (175–76)—a suggestive but contentious reading of the text.

A recent interdisciplinary reading of the book of Nehemiah (Tollefson and Williamson) has also contributed to an understanding of the book as a whole. The authors apply a model of cultural revitalization formulated by anthropologist A. F. C. Wallace in the 1950s, thereby finding that the sequence of events in the book of Nehemiah corresponds closely to the six phases described by the model. This explains better than most previous attempts how the various sections of the book cohere, and it removes the ground for suspicion that the present text has suffered serious dislocation. For example, the sequence of events in Neh. 8–10 corresponds well to the "Cultural Transformation Phase" of Wallace's model, and occurs exactly at the point predicted by the model. There thus is no reason to reposition these chapters, as many have suggested. On the other hand, the authors do not claim that the compiler of Ezra-Nehemiah recorded everything exactly as it happened. "Although the compiler may have altered the chronological order of certain specific events, his presentation may yet portray the social process taken as a whole more faithfully than any one of the sources at his disposal in isolation" (Tollefson and Williamson 65).

A recent study by Oded Lipschits, although focusing on Neh. 11, is also fruitful for theological interpretation of the book as a whole. Lipschits sees this chapter as a major climax, full of allusions to other parts of Ezra-Nehemiah, in which Jerusalem's past glory foreshadows a utopian future.

Canonical Context

The book of Nehemiah not only concludes the narrative begun in the book of Ezra; it also contains the latest events to be found in the historical books of the OT (assuming that Esther's

King Ahasuerus = Xerxes and not Artaxerxes I). In the Jewish arrangement of the OT books, Ezra-Nehemiah is usually followed by Chronicles, which concludes the canon. This is surprising in view of the fact that thematically (leaving aside matters of authorship), Ezra-Nehemiah is the sequel to Chronicles. Chronicles may have been placed last because it effectively reviews the whole sweep of OT history, from Adam to the return from exile.

Nehemiah provides an ambivalent conclusion to the OT's historical narratives. On the one hand, Jerusalem has been furnished with a new wall, the population of the city has increased, and various reforms have been instituted to deal with religious and social problems. In view of these successes, the triumphant tone of chapters 8–12 seems entirely appropriate. On the other hand, the final chapter reminds us how easy it is for abuses and failures to recur, even after the most solemn act of dedication. Furthermore, the political context is viewed negatively: although God's people are back in the land God promised to their ancestors, they are "slaves" there. The land's rich yield, instead of being theirs to enjoy, "goes to the kings whom you have set over us because of our sins; they have power also over our bodies and over our livestock at their pleasure, and we are in great distress" (9:36–37 NRSV; cf. Ezra 9:8–9).

In short, many elements that characterized the Babylonian exile (the people's sin, alienation from the land, and oppression by foreign rulers) are shown to be still continuing. This sense of ongoing "exile" also features in the intertestamental literature (e.g., Bar. 2:7–10; 2 Macc. 1:10–2:18), and many aspects of Jesus' message are best understood against this background (Wright 268–72; Evans). In this sense the book of Nehemiah points us forward, as surely as any prophetic book, to God's act of redemption in the NT.

Theology

To discern its theological message, it is important to read Nehemiah not merely as a literary whole but also as a continuation of the book of Ezra. To this end Williamson has helpfully discerned "the overall theological shape" of Ezra-Nehemiah (*Ezra*). He divides the work into five "chapters," of which the book of Nehemiah comprises the last three: Ezra 1–6 has as its focus the rebuilding of the temple in the face of opposition. Ezra 7–10 moves on to a second stage of the restoration project, the definition of the community in accordance with "the law of your God and the law of the king" (7:26). Nehemiah 1–7 echoes

these earlier stages, beginning with God at work through another Persian king (cf. Ezra 1:1; 7:27) and moving on to the completion of Jerusalem's walls, again in the face of opposition. Then Neh. 8–12 brings us to what Williamson calls "the suspended climax" of the earlier achievements, culminating in a united celebration of the work of both Ezra and Nehemiah. However, Neh. 13, by illustrating subsequent setbacks, ends the work on a note of "now and not yet." Williamson concludes: "The narrative structure of the book as a whole thus points to past achievements as a model for future aspiration" (Williamson, "Nehemiah," 981).

The theological perspective of Ezra-Nehemiah explains why chronological concerns take a backseat. This is evident in the compiler's preference for a thematic rather than a chronological ordering of material in Ezra 1–6, and the fact that he can leap almost six decades with the words "after these things" in Ezra 7:1. A twelve-year gap between the events of Ezra 10 and Nehemiah's receipt of news from Jerusalem (Neh. 1:1; 2:1) is passed over in silence. The events of Neh. 1–12 occur within less than a year, and nothing is said of the remaining eleven years of Nehemiah's first term as governor (13:6). Apart from a vague "after some time" (NRSV), no date is given for the events of his second term in 13:6–31. This is frustrating for the historian, but has its own significance for a theological reading. "Historically time-bound events are becoming detached from their chronological moorings in order to be viewed rather as divinely related steps in what may properly be regarded as a history of salvation" (Williamson, *Ezra*, 81).

Bibliography

Childs, B. *Introduction to the Old Testament as Scripture*. SCM, 1979; Eskenazi, T. *In an Age of Prose*. SBLMS 36. Scholars Press, 1988; Evans, C. A. "Jesus and the Continuing Exile of Israel." Pages 77–100 in *Jesus and the Restoration of Israel*, ed. C. Newman. InterVarsity, 1999; Houtman, C. "Ezra and the Law." Pages 91–115 in *Remembering All the Way*, by B. Albrektson et al. Brill, 1981; Kidner, D. *Ezra and Nehemiah*. TOTC. InterVarsity, 1979; Lipschits, O. "Literary and Ideological Aspects of Nehemiah 11." *JBL* 121 (2002): 423–40; Tollefson, K., and H. G. M. Williamson. "Nehemiah as Cultural Revitalization: An Anthropological Perspective." *JSOT* 56 (1992): 41–68; Williamson, H. G. M. *Ezra and Nehemiah*. OTG. JSOT, 1987; idem. "Nehemiah: Theology of." *NIDOTTE* 4:977–82; Wright, N. T. *The New Testament and the People of God*. SPCK, 1992.

John J. Bimson

New Creation

"But a new creation is everything!" (Gal. 6:15b NRSV)

Paul's exclamation indicates that we can hardly overemphasize the importance of "new creation." It was established in the Son's incarnation, human life, death, resurrection, and ascension. By it Christians are presently given new eyes through which to interpret the world: "If anyone is in Christ, behold—new creation!" (2 Cor. 5:17 AT). It is the hope to which we are called—a new heavens and new earth.

The new creation is implied in the gospel story about Jesus—that new human being who retrod the road of humanity, but this time in a new mode, without sin and so as to conquer death. So Luke introduces Jesus as "son of Adam, son of God" (3:38) and then proceeds to show his triumph over the tempter. The climax of the Fourth Gospel presents Jesus as "breathing" upon the apostles after the pattern of the creating God who breathed upon the Edenic couple; now they receive the Spirit, and not simply the gift of life. For explicit teaching, however, we look to the Prophets, Epistles, and Revelation.

Isaiah, Jeremiah, and Ezekiel crescendo toward the new creation from the context of the plight of God's people. Isaiah 40–66 envisions the "regathering" of the chosen people whom the Lord "created" (43:1–7), and their new state of blessing. In the final chapter, God's people emerge through a "new birth" as a joyful nation, nurtured in the holy city, whose population is swelled by foreigners (66:18–21). There will be "a new heavens and a new earth" in which "all flesh" will continually worship God. Jeremiah's vision is less sweeping, but every bit as profound. This prophet glimpses a time when "they shall be radiant over the goodness of the LORD" (31:12 NRSV), when a new covenant will be forged (31:31–34), and when God will create "a new thing" (31:22). Ezekiel pictures the new creation in terms of purity: the people are regathered under the true divine Shepherd (34:1–31), renewed by washing and the gift of a new heart (36:16–37), brought back to life "out of the grave," "inbreathed" by God's Spirit (37:1–28), and placed within an immense temple-garden filled with the divine glory (43:1–47:23).

This new creation is thus portrayed as the prerogative of God's chosen, as a hope to those who suffer at the hands of Gentile superpowers, who long for an end to exile. However, the prophetic vision of the new creation cannot be contained; it overreaches itself beyond the boundaries of Israel: the glory and life-giving power of the LORD will shine upon the "aliens" (e.g., Ezek. 47:22). Thus, Ezekiel's two rivers join to form a huge freshwater sea, adorned with trees supplying "leaves for healing" (47:12), and Isaiah's Zion envisages a remade cosmos. Jeremiah, though not aware of the *extent* of the re-creation, knows of its *depths*: God intends to place his will within his people, so they will innately know his plans for this world.

Thus, the prophets paved the way for the re-creation that was to burst upon the world in Jesus. Paul speaks about the "new creation" as a reality made possible because of the New Man, and as a future hope, with Rom. 8 highlighting the latter. Some have followed Augustine ("Question 67"), who saw Rom. 8:18–25 as limited simply to the hope of the redeemed human "creature" (*ktisis*). It is better, however, to follow John Chrysostom (*Hom. Rom.* 14), who shows that *ktisis* is the "creation"—the created order. In 8:19 the personified creation is pictured as "frustrated" because of the fall (v. 20) but hopeful of deliverance (v. 21). Just as humankind's shame has enslaved creation, so will humankind's "apocalypsed" glory bring release. Sufferings are actually the "birth pangs" that herald the new creation (see also Mark 13:8; 1 Thess. 5:3; *1 En.* 62:4). In particular, God's suffering people play a role, for they are inhabited by the Spirit groaning alongside them as a kind of midwife (Rom. 8:23). Through our prayers, energized by the Holy Spirit, God will bring about a new birth of the whole of creation: all that he has made "will obtain the freedom of the glory of the children of God" (8:20 NRSV). Thus, the salvation that has come to our world in Jesus now through the Spirit is directed from the inside out. We "boast in our hope of sharing the glory of God" (Rom. 5:2), knowing that this will affect the entire creation!

Paul, then, is world-affirming, not world-denying. But does his view of renewal imply universalism in the contemporary sense of the word? Paul frequently uses the term "all" or "world" when speaking about the extent of salvation (e.g., Rom. 11:15; Col. 1:20). Certainly the scope of God's action in Jesus involves the whole of the created order. However, Rom. 1:18–2:16; 14:10; 2 Cor. 5:10; 2 Thess. 1:5–10 and other texts remind us of the judgment to come, just as texts such as 2 Cor. 5:17; Rom. 3:21–31; and Col. 2:9–12 remind us that reconciliation comes by way of faith and baptism, though on the *basis* of what Jesus has done. The Scriptures simply do not reconcile the universal scope of God's salvation with God's demand for human response. Salvation cannot be automatic, since it includes a change in relationship; yet God is sovereign. Does the NT leave the issue deliberately "uncashed" for the sake of our salvation? Judgment must not be denied, or this would cut the nerve of the gospel and undermine the character of God's faithfulness, righteousness, and integrity. Yet the hope for the reconciliation of all remains vivid, for the sovereign God's purposes cannot be thwarted.

We move on to consider the character of the new creation offered to us in the NT—in some ways entirely new and in other ways in continuity with the best that we know. We look for "what no . . . human heart [has] conceived, what God has prepared for those who love him" (1 Cor. 2:9); yet there is some connection with this world, since God himself has entered our physical world in the incarnation, renewed it in the resurrection, and glorified it by the ascension. Our understanding of the new creation must be informed by a thorough understanding of the incarnation, by which God the Son assumed humanity, body and all, not simply to redeem, but also to heal and glorify. So Paul recognizes that corruptible "flesh and blood" cannot inherit; yet he looks not to be disembodied, but to be "reclothed" more gloriously (2 Cor. 5:1–5). We expect neither resuscitation into the same fallible bodies that we now possess, nor a spiritualized existence that is void of the joy of the senses. When that time comes, we will have bodies vivified by the very Spirit of God (*sōma pneumatikon*, "en-Spirited bodies") rather than simply by the breath of life (*sōma psychikon*, "animated bodies," 1 Cor. 15:44).

This is the wonder of the biblical story—that its victory must not be graphed as a "V" but as a check mark! Some still yearn for a return to Eden. The shape of the biblical narrative is otherwise: although the human couple begins in paradise, the final scene is that of an enfoliated, fruitful city, inhabited by a multitude (Rev. 21–22). Despite its condemnation of Babylon, the Apocalypse does not bring its seer or its reader back to an unretouched Eden. The full answer to godless society is not a razing of that city, but a new city, the new Jerusalem, that includes "the glory . . . of the nations" (21:24 NRSV), while it excludes anything "unclean" (21:27 NRSV). Yet by the twelvefold fruits of the tree of life, there shall be "healing [and here John is more explicit than Ezekiel!] of the nations" (22:2).

In the end, God's creation will itself mirror his unity and plurality: the final created order

is seen in all *fullness* and fecundity as *united* in common life and worship (22:1–3). Human culture is bound for transformation so as to share in the glory of God himself; all that we call nature is no mere backdrop for our lives, but a reality of which we are, and will remain, a part. We will not become disembodied spirits, but will retain that link with the material world that God has declared to be "good"—though there will be more substance and glory than we can now imagine.

So we see that our God, who creates ex nihilo and who resurrects, intends to redeem his world. A firm grasp on the new creation will instruct us not to disparage the body, not to leash the Spirit of God, and not to despise the world that God has created. Instead, with new eyes we learn to see the beauty and final end of all God has made. Ecology is given a strong basis, healing is naturalized as part of God's purpose, and salvation is recognized as having an immensely broad scope. Thus, we learn to be grateful not simply for our rescue from sin, but for the shining hope of a new creation: everything around us becomes the gift and sign of God's promise. As Alexander Schmemann puts it, "The world . . . becomes an *epiphany* of God, a means of His revelation, presence and power. . . . We *need* water and oil, bread and wine, in order to be in communion with God and to know him. . . . There is no worship without the participation of the [human] body . . . because the Holy Spirit 'makes all things new'" (120–22).

See also Creation; Last Things, Doctrine of

Bibliography

Augustine. "Question 67." Pages 149–57 in *Eighty-Three Different Questions*, trans. D. Mosher. Fathers of the Church 70. Catholic University of America Press, 1982; Chrysostom, J. "Homily XIV on Romans." *NPNF*[1] 11:439–52; Schmemann, A. *For the Life of the World*. St. Vladimir's Seminary Press, 1973.

Edith M. Humphrey

New Criticism   *See* Formalism; Literary Criticism

New Hermeneutic   *See* Hermeneutics; Literary Criticism; Theological Hermeneutics, Contemporary

New Perspective on Paul   *See* Justification by Faith; Pauline Epistles

Noncanonical Writings   *See* Apocrypha; Canon; Pseudepigrapha

Numbers, Book of

According to Jewish and Christian tradition, Numbers is the fourth book of Moses, relating the history of Israel's desert journey from Mt. Sinai to the dawn of the conquest, a chronological span stretching from the second to the fortieth year after the exodus. Parsed geographically, the book begins with Israel's stay at Sinai (1:1–10:10), chronicles its travels from Sinai to the plains of Moab (10:11–22:1), and then narrates a series of events in Moab (22:2–36:13). The book is known by two Hebrew titles, *Khomesh happequddim* ("the fifth of the census totals") and the more common *Bamidbar* ("in the wilderness" [1:1 MT/NRSV]). The first title, from the Talmud, corresponds to the Greek and Latin names (*Arithmoi* and *Numeri*), from which comes "Numbers." But both Hebrew titles reflect an important feature in the book: the story's setting in the wilderness (hence, *Bamidbar*) and the two censuses that frame the narrative in Num. 1 and 26 (hence, *Khomesh happequddim*).

A Survey of the Book

The book of Numbers is organized around a story that begins with one generation of Israelites (the "exodus generation") and ends with the next (the "conquest generation"). At issue for both generations is their willingness to undertake military operations against stronger, better-equipped forces living in the land that Yahweh has promised Israel. The first generation undertakes a military census in preparation for this engagement and even travels to Kadesh Barnea, a good staging point for the attack. However, after a gloomy reconnaissance report from twelve scouts sent into the land, the Israelites elect not to invade. As a result, God forbids that generation of Israelites from entering the land and condemns them to death in the wilderness. After forty years of nomadic life, during which these Israelites continually make trouble for Moses and thanklessly murmur against God, the last remnants of the exodus generation are destroyed after committing idolatry at Peor in Moab (Num. 25). This final act of disloyalty occasions no surprise since it follows their earlier idolatries at Mt. Sinai (see Exod. 32).

The next generation of Israelites, the conquest generation, immediately took another military census (Num. 26) and made preparations for an invasion of the land, which includes their initial successful military operations in Transjordan. At the same time, Joshua is appointed to succeed Moses as Israel's leader because of Moses'

impiety at Kadesh Barnea (cf. Num. 20, 27). So, Numbers concludes with Israel on the plains of Moab in Transjordan, poised to enter the land under Joshua's leadership.

Numbers in Canonical Context

Because Numbers is only one chapter in the biblical story of Israel, its theological import cannot be properly appraised apart from its narrative context in the "Primary History," which runs from the book of Genesis through 2 Kings. This story has two beginnings, one that focuses on the estrangement between God and humanity (Gen. 1–11), and a second that introduces Yahweh's redemptive plan for humanity through his covenant with Abraham. Because Abraham was a man of faith in word and deed, he received a divine promise of land, progeny, and blessing, blessings that would extend not only to his own children but also to all nations (Gen. 12, 15, 17). The remainder of the Primary History highlights the sometimes happy and sometimes stormy relationship between God and Abraham's children, focused through Yahweh's additional covenants with Israel at Sinai (the Mosaic covenant in Exodus) and with Israel's king, David (2 Sam. 7). The people and their kings eventually broke these covenants, receiving in return the double punishment of exile in Babylon and the destruction of Jerusalem and its temple (2 Kings 25).

If the Primary History is a story of the "ups and downs" in Israel's capricious faith, then the books of Exodus and Numbers vividly portray one of these fickle cycles. According to Exodus, Yahweh has prospered and multiplied the people in Egypt, miraculously delivering them from slavery, providing for them in the desert, and speaking to them in a mighty theophany at Sinai. Israel's response to God's graciousness appears in the book of Numbers, and the response is neither faithful nor pretty. Israel responds no better to God's blessings than does humanity as a whole in the primeval history of Gen. 1–11. So, it appears that the editor of the Pentateuch wishes us to perceive the religious disposition of Israel and of humanity along the same lines: both Jews and Gentiles are rebels (cf. Rom. 1–3). God responds to Israel's rebellion in the wilderness by preserving the nation, but he does not prosper them as in Genesis and Exodus. The count of people in the first census of Numbers (603,550; see 1:46) is actually greater than in the second census taken forty years later (601,730; see 26:51). Numbers, then, is a story that juxtaposes the faithfulness of God with Israel's faithless rebellion.

While the narrative contours of Numbers are clear enough, the unfolding story is generously interspersed with a broad range of ritual and legal materials, which seem to continue the priestly rules found in the book of Leviticus. Indeed, Leviticus also juxtaposes story with law, but its narratives invariably relate to the rituals and so do not seem like an interruption. In Numbers, however, these materials do seem to interrupt the book's narrative flow. The rites and laws are presented as divine prescriptions (Num. 5–10, 15–16, 18–19, 28–30, 35) or in narrative episodes that either illustrate these legal prescriptions (e.g., 15:32–36) or describe the occasion that prompts their creation (e.g., 17; 27:1–11; 36). While these materials cannot be easily integrated with the narrative of Numbers, they share a common focus on the concept of holiness, the special concern being to preserve Israel's purity, and hence to protect its sacred nexus with God.

Numbers presents readers with impressions of narrative unity as well as with diverse ritual and legal materials that do not easily satisfy our hermeneutical thirst for coherence. A good theological reading of this interesting book will need to account for this. Fortunately, our efforts can benefit from the penetrating exegetical and theological work done by our Jewish and Christian forebears.

The Theology of Numbers in Historical Purview

Our earliest theological readings of Numbers, or at least of the traditions now found in Numbers, appear in the Hebrew Bible itself. Deuteronomy relates a summary of Israel's wilderness experience in its first few chapters (1–3). This historical review implicitly accentuates God's faithfulness to Israel in the face of the nation's unfaithfulness, and it explicitly warns Israel not to duplicate the failures of the exodus generation—especially its idolatry—and so reap similar dire consequences (4:1–4). Nevertheless, in Deuteronomy, the piety of the conquest generation shines no brighter than that of its fathers (9:6), and the book predicts a gloomy future for the idolatrous people of Israel (4:30; 30:1–10; 31:14–32:47). The Hebrew prophetic books also allude to Israel's wilderness experience, but in strikingly different ways. Hosea and Jeremiah recall the wilderness with pleasant nostalgia (Hos. 2:14–15 [2:16–17 MT]; Jer. 2:1–7), while Ezekiel remembers it as the first in a litany of Israel's religious rebellions (ch. 20). These positive and negative appraisals of the wilderness also appear in the three psalms that relate Israel's history in hymnic style. Psalm 105 reads the wilderness as an example of God's kind provision for Israel, in contrast to Pss. 78 and 106, where Israel's desert wanderings are a period of ongoing mutiny. The later apocryphal book of 2 Esdras combines these contrasting images of the wilderness experience: "Thus says the Lord Almighty: When you were in the wilderness, at the bitter stream, thirsty and blaspheming my name, I did not send fire on you for your blasphemies, but threw a tree into the water and made the stream sweet" (1:22–23 NRSV).

Thus, the authors of the Hebrew Bible and Apocrypha attend to the wilderness story of Numbers and largely ignore its extensive ritual and legal material. This pattern of exegetical bifurcation, in which interpreters treat the two major genres of Numbers differently by ignoring one or the other, appears in later Jewish exegesis. Philo's work *On the Life of Moses* (first century CE) offers an extensive paraphrase of the wilderness story but touches on the rituals only briefly and under a separate heading (Colson 277–595). His preferred strategy for drawing out the implications of Moses' life is allegory, an interpretative method that suits not only his Hellenistic audience but also his own identity as a Hellenistic Jew. By way of contrast, *Midrash Sifre*, an early commentary on Numbers (second century CE), virtually ignores the narrative in favor of halakic (legal) interpretations of its ritual and legal prescriptions (Levertoff). The few instances of haggadah (illustrative narrative commentary) in *Sifre* only confirm this rule. Rashi's medieval Jewish commentary treats the entire book of Numbers, blending literal interpretation (*peshat*) with free homiletical exegesis (*derash*). But here again one detects an underlying theological concern to show how Numbers informs Jewish traditions of ritual and law.

Early Christian interpreters in the NT allude to Numbers rather sparingly. Two notable exceptions were the writer of Hebrews and Paul, for whom the faithless exodus generation illustrates the ever-present threat of Christian apostasy (Heb. 3–4; 1 Cor. 10:3–14). In briefer allusions, Acts remembers the wilderness as a time of God's divine provision for Israel (7:36), while John's Gospel sees in Moses' bronze serpent an image of the coming Christ (cf. 3:14; Num. 21:4–9). Similar exegetical patterns appear in the patristic evidence, where christological and tropological (moral/behavioral) insights were derived from Israel's story in Numbers (see Lienhard). Not surprisingly, neither the NT nor the church fathers gave much attention to the ritual and legal materials in Numbers.

Two general observations can be culled from early Jewish and Christian readings of Numbers. First, Jewish and Christian interpreters were generally interested in different portions of Numbers. Jewish readers focused on its ritual and legal materials, while Christian readers drew moral and ethical content from its stories. As we will see, in certain respects this generic distinction anticipates modern critical readings of Numbers. Second, in spite of their differing generic interests, both Christian and Jewish commentators viewed Numbers as a manual for achieving holiness in their respective communities. Judaism expressed its holiness through ritual purity (hence the interest in ritual law), and Christian interpreters used Numbers as a guide for moral living (hence their tropological readings of the book's narrative).

Numbers in Modern Biblical Scholarship

Because of the book's ostensible disorganization, modern scholars have been preoccupied with the composition of Numbers rather than with its theology. Although there is continuing debate about the details (Sparks, *Pentateuch*, 22–36), the consensus is that the book was not composed by Moses, as tradition might suggest, but rather by several authors and editors working over a lengthy period of time and at some remove from the so-called Mosaic period. The standard theory is that Numbers owes much of its present shape to at least two major writers, the preexilic or exilic Yahwist (J) and the postexilic priestly writer (P). It is further believed that the basic narrative contours of Numbers were laid down by J (see 10:29–12:15; 20:14–21; 21:12–32; 22:2–25:5), while much of the remaining ritual, legal, and narrative materials—over three-quarters of the book—derives from P. This two-source theory explains the odd combination of law and narrative in the book. It has in its favor both critical and precritical evidence. Critical scholars find similar J/P distinctions elsewhere in the Pentateuch, and precritical Jewish and Christian interpreters focused on one or the other of these two generic segments of Numbers.

Some modern scholars, such as Douglas, Olsen, and Lee, have attempted to peer behind the putative structural confusion in Numbers to discern an underlying coherence in the book's stories and law. Douglas believes that she has discovered a ring structure that alternates between law and story in order to teach a theology of holiness and defilement.

Olsen argues that the final theological shape of Numbers reflects the coherent design of an editor, who has skillfully combined the narrative of J with the rituals, laws, and narratives of P. The resulting structure uses the two censuses in Num. 1 and 26 to frame the story as a tale of two generations, the disobedient exodus generation and the new generation of hope. This tale has as its central themes that God does not tolerate rebellion and that, on the other hand, Israelite rebellions would not frustrate God's plan to bless them according to his promises. Olsen avers that the legal and ritual materials in Numbers do not disrupt the presentation of these themes but rather are editorially integrated into the book to illustrate and reinforce them.

Lee's reading of Numbers is similar to Olsen's, inasmuch as it uses the narrative plot as its organizing principle. According to Lee, the book's conceptual structure is determined by God's responses to Israel, first in punishing the exodus generation because of its disobedience, and then in forgiving Israel and granting the conquest generation success against the Canaanites.

While it is indeed worthwhile to pursue a coherent understanding of the book's combination of law and story, one wonders whether our pursuit of coherence does not apply a modern, post-Enlightenment literary expectation to an ancient anthology of Jewish stories, law, ritual, and priestly lore.

Conclusions

As we have seen, there is a long-standing exegetical tradition in ancient and modern scholarship that either explicitly or implicitly bifurcates the book of Numbers along generic lines, focusing either on the narrative or the legal material. Christians have been interested predominantly in the narrative material because they naturally find themselves tropologically in its powerful story. Whether Israel lived in sin (the exodus generation) or in obedience (the conquest generation), God in all respects was faithful to his people and to his promises to Abraham, Isaac, and Jacob. So, God can be counted on, but we must choose our road. Healthy Christian living does not take the difficulties of life's "wilderness" as evidence for God's absence; rather, we notice God's power as he carries us through it.

Turning to the laws and rituals of Numbers, Christian interpreters have generally neglected this material, largely because of the uniquely Christian viewpoint that the people of God are no longer subject to the minutiae of Jewish law and ritual. Consequently, early Christians did not attempt to directly integrate Jewish rituals and laws into their theology so much as they sought a theological explanation for this conundrum: Why would God command the Jews to observe rites and keep laws that would become obsolete? The standard explanation of the church fathers was that God had accommodated primitive and errant viewpoints of law and ritual in his revelation to Israel, viewpoints that were naturally subject to obsolescence and hence to elimination (Sparks, "Sun"). In some respects this solution only goes halfway, for it fails to assess the function of the laws and rituals in the life of ancient Israel and then to ask what import this function might have for Christians. The most obvious theme that appears in the laws and rituals is God's holiness, which is vividly expressed in these portions of Numbers. Appreciation of divine holiness is, of course, essential to a healthy theological appraisal of what God has done for humanity—and for us—in the person of Jesus Christ.

Bibliography

Ashley, T. *The Book of Numbers*. NICOT. Eerdmans, 1993; Colson, F. H., trans. *Philo*. 10 vols. LCL. Harvard University Press, 1984; Davies, E. W. *Numbers*. NCB. Eerdmans, 1995; de Vaux, J. *Les Nombres*. Gabalda, 1972; Douglas, M. *In the Wilderness*. JSOTSup 158. JSOT, 1993; Drazin, I. *Targum Onkelos to Numbers*. Ktav, 1998; Lee, W. W. *Punishment and Forgiveness in Israel's Migratory Campaign*. Eerdmans, 2003; Levertoff, P. P., trans. *Midrash Sifre on Numbers*. SPCK, 1926; Levine, B. *Numbers*. 2 vols. AB. Doubleday, 1993–2000; Lienhard, J., ed. *Exodus, Leviticus, Numbers, Deuteronomy*. ACCSOT 3. InterVarsity, 2001; Olsen, D. *The Death of the Old and the Birth of the New*, Scholars, 1985; Rashi. *The Metsudah Chumash*, trans. Y. Rabinowitz. Simcha, 2000; Sparks, K. *The Pentateuch*. IBR Bibliographies 1. Baker, 2002; idem. "The Sun Also Rises: Accommodation in Inscripturation and Interpretation." In *Evangelicals and Scripture*, ed. D. Okholm et al. InterVarsity, 2004; Wenham, G. *Numbers*. OTG. Sheffield Academic Press, 1997.

Kent L. Sparks

Obadiah, Book of

The history of Obadiah research mirrors OT studies in miniature. Early Christian interpreters used Edom's fall as a type of the fall of Jerusalem. They also stressed the day of the Lord and final judgment, and treated Mt. Zion and Mt. Edom as types of the church (Ferreiro). Late-nineteenth- and early-twentieth-century historical-critical scholars tended to discuss the book's authorship and date along lines established in analyses of the Pentateuch. Thus, scholars debated how the book was shaped over time, since they did not think it probable that one writer included threats against Edom and hope for Israel's future in the same book (Wellhausen; Bewer). In the first three-quarters of the twentieth century, form-critical experts focused particularly on the book's setting and literary form. Most concluded that the book was a prophetic denunciation from shortly after the fall of Jerusalem in 587/6 BCE, though this opinion was by no means universally accepted (Wolff; Watts). Like historical critics, form critics struggled with the presence of threats and promise in the same short book. In the late twentieth century scholars debated whether Obadiah should be read as a unified construction (Raabe), as part of the Book of the Twelve as a whole (Nogalski), or as a redacted prophetic book (Ben Zvi). Such discussions reflected the trend toward treating the canonical text and reactions to this strategy. By the end of the twentieth century, Obadiah had been the subject of lengthy analyses, but it was still not analyzed as often as longer prophecies.

Even some of the excellent longer studies of Obadiah do not highlight the book's theology. Though understandable, this situation is somewhat regrettable, since a study of the final form of Obadiah provides examples of several of the OT's most significant canonical-theological issues (Barton). These include visionary prophecy as divine revelation, human pride and hatred of one's neighbor as great ethical problems, the day of the Lord, and the significance of Zion.

Visionary Prophecy and Divine Revelation (v. 1)

Of all the prophetic books, only Isaiah's and Obadiah's superscriptions identify the words that follow as "a vision." Isaiah conveys messages related primarily to the present and future of Judah and Jerusalem. In Obadiah's case, messages concerning Edom's current sins and future judgment unfold. The designation of these books as "vision" underscores their divine origins, for this term establishes the belief that Yahweh has given these words to the prophets. Further, having established the term "vision" in verse 1, Obadiah then uses quotation formulas in verses 1, 4, 8, and 18, and utilizes first-person recorded speech in most of 2–18.

Thus, despite the visual implications of "vision," Obadiah consists of words that express what has been seen. These words provide a permanent record of this prophet's personal experiences in a way that benefits the community of faith and calls the sinful into account. This movement from vision to speech (and possibly) to written word given to and accepted by faithful persons mirrors the canonical process of other OT books. Furthermore, Obadiah was considered part of the Book of the Twelve in the Hebrew tradition. As such, it is part of twelve connected prophecies that together express in written word prophecy's great themes: covenant, sin, judgment, renewal, and consummation.

Human Pride (vv. 2–10)

Like Isaiah, Obadiah considers pride the root of other sins. The Edomites' pride is based on their status among the nations (v. 1), their seemingly impregnable capital (vv. 3–4), their famous wise men (v. 8), and their valiant warriors (v. 9). These attainments have led to the self-deception that they are beyond the reach of any higher power (v. 3). Thus, they believe they can act as they wish against Israel (v. 10). In other words, Obadiah depicts Edom in a manner similar to Isaiah's description of Assyria (Isa. 10:1–19). If so, it is ironic that small nations have the same delusions of self-sufficient grandeur as larger ones.

Hatred of Neighbor (vv. 11–14)

Edom's mistreatment of Israel is the reason Obadiah gives for their coming judgment. The Edomites have stood by when invaders ransacked Israel and took captives (vv. 11–12). Worse yet, they rejoiced in Israel's downfall and cut down those trying to flee (vv. 13–14). They did this despite the fact that they were Israel's "brother" (v. 12), a reference to the fact that Jacob and Esau, the patriarchs of Israel and Edom respectively, were brothers. Amos adds the fact that Edom was famous for slave trade (1:9) and for fierce wrath in battle (1:11–12). They have made money from hating their neighbor, and their status and security make them think they can do so forever.

The Day of the Lord and Zion Theology (vv. 15–21)

As in the rest of the prophetic corpus, Obadiah asserts that all nations will be judged on "the day of the LORD" (v. 15). This term signifies a certain, specific event at an unspecified time in the future. It also indicates the Lord's sovereignty over the whole of creation, not just the covenant nation, Israel. The belief that one God rules all nations is indicative of the OT's emphasis on monotheism, and as such it varies greatly from the ancient henotheistic and polytheistic attitudes of most, if not all, of Israel's neighbors. The day of the Lord will remove Edom's proud populace from their secure mountain home and exalt Judah's humble survivors. Edom will experience Yahweh's justice by having their deeds turned against them (v. 15). They will learn the fundamental fact made clear in Joel 3:16–19 and Amos 1:3–2:3 that Yahweh's justice is universal (v. 15).

Further, on the day of the Lord Edom will discover that Zion is special to Yahweh (v. 17), a point underscored in Isa. 4:2–6; Isa. 62; Jer. 30–33; and Ezek. 40–48. There will be deliverance on Mt. Zion, but none on Mt. Seir. There will be deliverance for the house of Jacob, but there will be none for his brother Esau's house (v. 18). Israel's captivity will end (v. 20), and Zion's deliverers will rule Edom (v. 21). Yahweh's rule in Zion on behalf of Israel's survivors constitutes the kingdom of God on earth (v. 21; cf. Isa. 25:6–8). Yahweh is sovereign, and Yahweh fights for Israel, which fulfills the promise made to Abraham to defeat his descendant's enemies (Gen. 12:1–3). Thus, in this last section of Obadiah it is clear that Zion is not simply Jerusalem. Nor is Edom simply a neighboring nation. Rather, Zion is the place where Yahweh lives with his faithful people in the absence of sin and danger. Similarly, Edom represents all nations that threaten Yahweh's redeemed ones. This long-term foe of Israel provides a pattern for what it means to have a determined, harsh enemy.

Like other prophets, Obadiah based his eschatological expectations on concrete historical events. Edom's real acts in history provided a paradigm for how sinful Gentiles behave, and Edom's eventual defeat served as a basis for belief in ultimate redemption for those who please Yahweh. Survival in historical circumstances became the impetus for theological reflection on the future. Therefore, Obadiah provides patterns for theological understanding, not just predictions about the future.

Conclusion

Obadiah's theological significance is at least twofold. First, its significance lies in its ability to present a vision in words that relate common historical events to the larger pattern of eschatology. Concrete events that take place repeatedly at an unspecified point in time prove typical enough to provide a paradigm for the future. Second, its significance lies in its ability to connect with significant OT themes and to adjoining books. One could not reproduce the entirety of prophetic theology from these verses, but one could make a good start. This brief prophecy should therefore be seen for what it is: a tightly packed, theologically rich essay on Yahweh's sovereignty over Israel and Israel's neighbors. When viewed this way, Obadiah highlights the transbiblical belief that Yahweh deserves and demands exclusive worship and service. There are no other gods, so there is no salvation outside of a relationship with Israel's God, who is the Creator and Judge of everyone. Those who deny this exclusive sovereignty place themselves in Edom's precarious position.

Bibliography

Barton, J. *Joel and Obadiah*. OTL. Westminster John Knox, 2001; Ben Zvi, E. *A Historical-Critical Study of the Book of Obadiah*. BZAW 242. De Gruyter, 1996; Bewer, J. *A Critical and Exegetical Commentary on Obadiah and Joel*. ICC. T&T Clark, 1911; Ferreiro, A., ed. *The Twelve Prophets*. ACCSOT 14. InterVarsity, 2003; Nogalski, J. *Literary Precursors to the Book of the Twelve*. BZAW 217. De Gruyter, 1993; idem. *Redactional Processes in the Book of the Twelve*. BZAW 218. De Gruyter, 1993; Raabe, P. *Obadiah*. AB 24D. Doubleday, 1996; Watts, J. *Obadiah*. Eerdmans, 1969; Wellhausen, J. *Die Kleinen Propheten übersetzt und erklärt*.

3d ed. G. Reimer, 1898; Wolff, H. W. *Obadiah and Jonah,* trans. M. Kohl. Augsburg, 1986.

Paul R. House

Objectivity

The history of the idea of "objectivity" has two phases. The first begins with ancient Greek philosophy and is dominant until the seventeenth century. In this phase questions about knowledge are overshadowed by the influence of Aristotle, whose *Physics* was a standard textbook for nearly two millennia. In this view the being or true essence of a thing determines how the thing is known: ontology dictates to epistemology the terms for objectivity.

In this arrangement, the "subject" refers to the true essence of the thing in itself. The "object" is the appearance of the thing as an expression of the essence that is presented to our mind or "intellect." The "problem" of knowledge is how persons should align their intellect with the "object" that is given to it. Aristotle assumes that the objective presentation of the thing is an adequate presentation of its true essence. The dilemma is not whether we have access to the true essence of a thing, but how we should respond to its givenness. "Objectivity," in this premodern view, is the proper aligning of the intellect to the object as the knower sorts out the essence of the thing given in the "objective" appearance. "Knowledge" is the successful alignment of the two.

The modern view begins to emerge in the medieval period and gains purchase in the course of the Renaissance through advancements in science, cosmology, mathematics, and physics (Cassirer). Signaling that the premodern view was being eclipsed was, for instance, the eventual replacement of Aristotle's *Physics* by Francis Bacon's *Novum organum* (1620; Solomon). René Descartes's *Meditations* (1641) is also considered a key work in this development. The full modern expression of objectivity would be made in Immanuel Kant's *Critique of Pure Reason* (1781).

In the modern view, "objectivity" is no longer defined by the essence of the thing as it presents itself to us. Things in themselves are now viewed as being either inaccessible to our senses and intellect (at worst, Kant) or difficult to discern (at best, Bacon). "Objectivity" came to connote the character of the epistemological stance a person assumes while struggling to seek out knowledge of things in their epistemological opacity. That stance is viewed as being, ideally, unaffected by prior beliefs or judgments—in some sense "neu-

tral" or apart from any particular "perspective" (Nagel; Daston). In other words, whereas objectivity formerly was defined by the unproblematic giving of the thing to our intellect, it now is defined by the straining stance of our intellect as an act of "disinterested cognition" (Solomon 45).

This is, in one key respect, the opposite of the view of the premodern phase. In the premodern view, the action of knowledge ran from the essence of the thing to its objective appearance to our intellect. In the modern view, the act of knowing is perceived as running in the opposite direction—the negotiation of our senses *to* the thing, then the action of our reaching out and seeking the thing. Therefore, whereas ontology dictated to epistemology in the premodern phase, that relationship is reversed in the modern (Solomon; Cassirer). Thus, the problem of self-consciousness or self-perception becomes the initiating question. This "reversal" underlies many modern commentaries on the Enlightenment, and on the issues and problems that accompany its hegemony.

Influence of the modern ideal of objectivity reached its apex in the field of science and philosophy with the rise of logical positivism, which accords pure science the cumulative and monolithic authority in the collection and verification of facts and truth. The modern view was also influential on modern developments in history, hermeneutics, and the interpretation of Scripture. This is shown, for one, in that the evolution of modern biblical scholarship mirrors and follows the development of modern historiography and literary and linguistic studies, which all generally accepted modern objectivity as the ideal for knowledge.

In the course of the Enlightenment, modern "objective" readings of Scripture gradually became established as ideal readings (Kümmel). In this sense "objectivity" continues to be a central and controlling idea that underwrites contemporary debates about reading Scripture insofar as they accept the ideal stance of the reader as being on one hand in some sense neutral or impartial with respect to any metaphysical or ontological beliefs or influences, and on the other defined by the action of a reader toward a text. The contemporary adage is that, as far as one is able, one should read Scripture apart from any confessional or theological bias. Theological claims are only properly made if they are the subsequent distillation of an impartial reading of the Bible as a book like any other book.

The acceptance of modern objectivity as an ideal also resulted in the linear arrangement of exegesis to biblical theology to systematic theology that still dominates most curricula of Christian colleges, seminaries, and graduate schools. It highlights the reversal we indicated above, observing that for most of the history of Christianity this line ran in the opposite direction; one studied theology extensively in order to become a capable and discerning reader of Scripture.

It is now generally acknowledged that the modern ideal of objectivity overreaches human capacities. Criticisms arise in the wake of the recognition of the person's location within certain untranscendable epistemological limitations, including time and space. Therefore, for the knower/reader there are only degrees of greater or lesser objectivity, which are always accompanied by a corresponding lesser or greater measure of subjectivity. Postmodernism, poststructuralism, and postphenomenalism focus on these limitations: They are expressions of modern objectivity's self-criticism (Vattimo). They demonstrate the limits and weaknesses as well as the "oppressive" hegemonies (real or otherwise) that modernism engenders. And they signal a crisis in the dominance of modern thought and the pending possibility of its alteration or replacement, but without proposing an alternative (Hutcheon; Vattimo).

Ideal objectivity has come under particular criticism from these late-modern traditions as being both inadequate to account for reading in general and particularly ill equipped to account for the event of reading Scripture. Regarding the former, poststructuralists and postmodernists raise the question of whether it is possible and even harmful to think about the ideal stance of a reader toward a text as being "objective." They draw attention to the social and political forces that shape and underwrite the reader's agency in the act of reading and seek to indicate the inescapable ways that reading is always shaped by the prior influence of these forces and traditions.

Theology and biblical hermeneutics responded by spawning a host of developments that explore the role of the subjectivity of the reader(s) in the production of meaning. Despite their significant differences, both the "Yale" and "Chicago" schools of theology are important moments in this history as it came to bear on the hermeneutics of reading Scripture. In biblical studies as well, a vast array of work has been produced that explores the subjective agency of reader(s), appropriating reader-response critical theories, social-rhetorical studies, and so on.

Critics of these movements have responded by arguing that they have swung the epistemological pendulum from an ideal objectivity to an ideal subjectivity, which hands the responsibility for determining meaning over to the reader or reading community *tout court*. Nevertheless, both advocates and critics of the exploration of subjective readerly action in the determination of meaning remain indebted to modern notions of objectivity insofar as they continue to construe the fundamental problem of reading Scripture in terms of the action of human reader(s) (knower[s]) toward a text (object).

Another result of recognizing the limitations of modern objectivity is reconsideration of the role of theological prejudgments in the reading of Scripture. This has a bearing, in turn, on the relationship between the various exegetical and theological disciplines (Bartholomew et al.; Green and Turner), theological and confessional reading of the Bible (Webster; Davis and Hays; Radner and Sumner), as well as new reflections on the positive roles of communities and traditions (Braaten and Jenson).

The gravity of these reconsiderations turns on the fundamental limitation of the modern ideal of pure objectivity for understanding the dynamics of agency involved in reading Scripture. When we read the Bible, we are not simply examining an object. Rather, we engage a person (author, God) and/or group of persons (reading traditions). That engagement carries with it all the ethical and moral implications that any encounter with others entails. Both we ourselves as readers and the person(s) we encounter in the text possess certain rights and responsibilities in this encounter (Wolterstorff). Modern notions of objectivity that trade on an ideal of neutrality or disinterest in the stance of the subject toward an inert passive object are, at this point, incapable of accounting for the ethical and moral connotations and responsibilities that pertain to the encounter and exchange between the personal voice(s) in the text and the interpretative action of the reader.

This limitation becomes more pronounced when we consider the broader implications of divine agency in the reading of Scripture. In the premodern phase the notion that God is actively speaking in, with, and under Scripture was a given assumption in the self-understanding of reading. In the modern phase this assumption became problematic and was viewed as a dogmatic imposition. The modern view is illusory, however, insofar as it believes that the setting aside of the assumption of God's speaking obtains a nontheological stance. Whatever stance one assumes when one reads Scripture—that God speaks in this text, that God does not speak in this text, that God might speak or will speak—any and all are equally theological and dogmatic. With respect to the reading and hearing of God's Word, therefore, just as human creatures cannot remove themselves from the field of divine agency, so human readers cannot divorce their reading from judgments pertaining to the shape of divine speaking.

For example, the acceptance of the Christian canon as a uniquely authoritative collection entails beliefs regarding both God's action in electing and sanctifying this group of texts as well as the receptive action of the Christian tradition over four hundred years, as it struggled to recognize the canon's shape. Issues related to any kind of study or "criticism" of the origin and shape of Scripture will also entail certain affirmations or denials regarding divine and human action and their relationship. With respect to the recent attention to the role of the reader or reading community, the same implications hold. If one gives preference to the present communities' reading of Scripture over either an authorial-textual meaning or a traditional reading, one is also making a preferential claim regarding the present action of God in relation to the past action of God in either the composition or reading tradition of the Bible.

A refashioned role for objectivity in the theological interpretation of Scripture emerges as a result of these considerations. In the modern sense, objectivity becomes relevant in a necessary but limited and ad hoc fashion. It no longer pertains to an ideal relationship between the reader and text but suggests one aspect of the various relationships, encounters, and exchanges between the human and divine persons that variously inform the task of reading Scripture. Modern objectivity reminds us of the care and precision with which we should reflect on our theological presuppositions. Premodern notions of objectivity speak to another aspect, reminding us to account for the *viva vox Dei* in Scripture—a divine speech action that we acknowledge and receive. Both modes of objectivity only illuminate discrete features of the act of reading Scripture and do not exhaustively define it.

Finally, acknowledgment of the limits of any construal or system of objectivity, including both premodern and modern, for reading Scripture results in retrieval of the constructive role that confessions and theologies necessarily play in the hearing and reading of God's word. The negotiation of hermeneutical problems and disagreements ultimately turns on the recognition, comparison, debate, and resolution of the constructive, material theological assumptions pertaining to the encounter of divine and human persons in the reading and interpretation of Scripture, and not in the sorting out of formal or "objective" methodologies.

See also Method

Bibliography

Bartholomew, C., et al., eds. *Renewing Biblical Interpretation* et al. SHS. Zondervan/Paternoster, 2000–; Bordo, S. *The Flight to Objectivity.* SUNY Press, 1987; Braaten, C., and R. Jenson, eds. *Reclaiming the Bible for the Church.* Eerdmans, 1995; Cassirer, E. "The Subject-Object Problem in the Philosophy of the Renaissance." In *The Individual and the Cosmos in Renaissance Philosophy.* Harper, 1963; Daston, L. "Objectivity and the Escape from Perspective." *Social Studies of Science* 22 (1992): 597–618; Davis, E., and R. Hays, eds. *The Art of Reading Scripture.* Eerdmans, 2003; Green, J., and M. Turner, eds. *Between Two Horizons.* Eerdmans, 2000; Hutcheon, L. *A Poetics of Postmodernism.* Routledge, 1992; Kümmel, W. G. *The New Testament,* trans. S. M. Gilmour and H. C. Kee. Abingdon, 1972; Megill, A., ed. *Rethinking Objectivity.* Duke University Press, 1994; Nagel, T. *The View from Nowhere.* Oxford University Press, 1986; Radner, E., and G. Sumner, eds. *The Rule of Faith.* Morehouse, 1998; Solomon, J. R. *Objectivity in the Making.* Johns Hopkins University Press, 1998; Vattimo, G. *Beyond Interpretation.* Stanford University Press, 1997; Webster, J. *Word and Church.* T&T Clark, 2001; Wolterstorff, N. *Divine Discourse.* Cambridge University Press, 1995.

Mark A. Bowald

Onto-Theology

Kant uses the term "onto-theology" to refer to any attempt to prove the existence of God that "believes that it can know the existence of such a being through mere concepts, without the help of any experience whatsoever" (Kant, A 632 = B 660). He obviously has in mind the ontological argument as developed, for example, by Anselm and Leibniz, against which a few pages earlier he had just developed his famous critique. But in current usage the term derives from Heidegger, sometimes in the form onto-theo-logy, and has a quite different meaning. It is widely bandied about, often with little or no attention to the specifics of Heidegger's definition and critique, as if mere mention of the term were sufficient to discredit any theistic discourse. The matter is much more complicated than that.

Heidegger's Concept 1: The What of Onto-Theology

Heidegger derives the term from the text we know as Aristotle's *Metaphysics*. It starts out to be the theory of being as such, not (like the other sciences) an investigation of this or that particular region of being, but reflection on the totality of being in its universal characteristics (categories). As such it is ontology. But to complete his project, Aristotle finds it necessary to posit a highest being, the Unmoved Mover. As such, metaphysics is theology; or rather, since the theory as a whole requires the two dimensions to cohere in mutual dependence, metaphysics is onto-theology (*Introduction*, 287; *Identity*, 58–61, 69). *It is the affirmation and articulation of the Highest Being who is the key to the meaning of the whole of being.*

But Aristotle's move is unique only in its details. When Heidegger speaks of the onto-theological "constitution" or "essence" of metaphysics (*Identity*, 42–73; *Nietzsche*, 4:210–11), he means Western metaphysics as such, stretching from Anaximander to Nietzsche (*Introduction*, 280), with Plato, Aristotle, Leibniz, and Hegel as especially important instances. To Nietzsche? Yes, his "Highest Being" is the will to power in its eternal recurrence. Once we see, by looking at these proper names, how many different actors have played the role of Highest Being under the direction of various philosophers, we will understand why Heidegger sees science and technology as the metaphysics of modernity, in which the human subject plays the role of Highest Being. We will also see why he thinks both (1) that onto-theology is older than Christian theology, which is onto-theological only because it is metaphysics (*Concept*, 147), and (2) that scholastic theology "is merely a doctrinal formulation of the essence of metaphysics" (*Nietzsche*, 4:209). Theistic discourse is an incidental target because it belongs to the history of metaphysics. The prime target is metaphysics in all its forms because it "determines the history of the Western era. Western humankind, in all its relations with beings, and even to itself, is in every respect sustained and guided by metaphysics" (4:205).

This is only the first part of Heidegger's concept of onto-theology, but it already leads to his first critique. He takes it to be the task of philosophy to think Being in its meaning and truth. He insists that Being is not to be confused with beings, even the Highest Being, and he holds "that beings are thanks to Being, and that Being never is thanks to beings" (4:201). If we object that it is quite unclear what this Being "is" that is to be distinguished from all beings, Heidegger will reply that this is precisely his point. Being is precisely what remains unthought in metaphysics, which occupies itself entirely with understanding beings in relation to various versions of the Highest Being. This is his first critique: Onto-theology is the sustained and systematic forgetfulness of Being.

Obviously, this critique will be found forceful only by those who (1) wish their discourse to qualify as philosophy *and* (2) accept Heidegger's account of the philosophical task. Those who meet the second condition belong to the rather small church of Heideggerian true believers. The theist, whether academic theologian, clergyperson, or lay believer, might well admit, or rather joyfully confess, that belief in God as Creator is belief in a Highest Being, who is the key to the meaning of the whole of being. The theist may well admit that the affirmation of this belief in creed, in witness, in preaching, in liturgy, and even in systematic theology need not worry whether it counts as philosophy in the eyes of a particular philosophical school. Moreover, the Christian philosopher who wants to think about God within a fully theistic framework might well articulate or at least presuppose an alternative conception of philosophy and claim to be doing *philosophical* theology. Heidegger will have a quarrel with the latter, but not with the former. In his own way he recognizes that theology has its own distinctive task.

Heidegger's Concept 2: The How of Onto-Theology

When talking about the more explicitly theological forms of onto-theology, we gather an important further specification of its nature, and it becomes clear that theistic discourse is not inevitably onto-theological. Heidegger asks: "How does the deity enter into philosophy, not just modern philosophy, but philosophy as such?" He answers: "The deity can come into philosophy only insofar as philosophy, of its own accord and by its own nature, requires and determines that and how the deity enters into it" (*Identity*, 55–56). Philosophy, which here means onto-theologically constituted metaphysics, only allows God, or perhaps "God," into its discourse on its own terms and in the service of its own project. It does not merely posit a Highest Being but does so in a certain, self-interested way.

What, then, is the project God must serve if metaphysics is to permit God-talk at all? It is simply to render the whole of reality intelligible to human thought and understanding. Heidegger will often use the terms "calculative thinking" and "representational thinking" to signify the attempt to control the world, both conceptually and practically, through causal, explanatory thinking under the guidance of the principle of sufficient reason (esp. in *Principle*, 28: "God exists only insofar as the principle of reason holds"). We find an important clue to this project when Heidegger notes the abstract, impersonal language onto-theology uses for God, such as *causa prima*, *ultima ratio*, and *causa sui* (*Identity*, 60). But causal explanations set off regresses that threaten to become infinite. So God's task is to be the Self-Explanatory Explainer that brings the regress to a halt and renders comprehension complete. Only a *causa sui* could be a *causa prima* and provide an *ultima ratio*. We can now refine our earlier definition of onto-theology: *It is the affirmation and articulation of the Highest Being, who is the ultimate explanation of the whole of being*. By putting God to work in the service of its project, onto-theologically constituted metaphysics will become the possessor and dispenser of this comprehensive comprehension.

Heidegger can now offer a further critique of onto-theology, one that is no longer linked conceptually to the "ontological difference" between Being and beings. So, it may have a bite where the earlier critique does not. It consists in noting two consequences of the metaphysical project. One is the elimination of mystery from the world and our understanding of it, or at least the attempt to eliminate it, which involves flight from the sources of both anxiety and gratitude (*Postscript*, 235–38). Reality is (to be) compelled to show itself fully. The other consequence, closely related to the first, is that the God of onto-theology is religiously useless. "Man can neither pray nor sacrifice to [the god of philosophy]. Before the *causa sui*, man can neither fall to his knees in awe nor can he play music and dance before this God" (*Identity*, 72).

Here Heidegger sounds a lot like Pascal, contrasting the God of the philosophers with the God of Abraham, Isaac, and Jacob, and like Kierkegaard, contrasting the God of the speculative system with the God of personal existence. His point is no longer just that philosophy should take a step back out of metaphysics (*Identity*, 49–52), but that theology should avoid this trap as well. One who really understands "both the theology of the Christian faith and that of philosophy, would today rather remain silent about God when he is speaking in the realm of thinking. For the onto-theological character of metaphysics has become questionable for thinking, not because of any kind of atheism, but from the experience of a thinking that has discerned in onto-theo-logy the still *unthought* unity of the essential nature of metaphysics" (*Identity*, 54–55). If this silence is not to be permanent, Christian theology, like philosophy, needs to find a postmetaphysical way of thinking and speaking that overcomes its onto-theological tendencies. In the case of theology, this way is to signify a God who remains mysterious but who can evoke prayer and sacrifice and awe and singing and (heaven help us!) even dancing.

Here Heidegger seeks to save theology from itself. With reference to the confluence of Christian theology and Greek philosophy, he notes that whether this has been "for better or for worse may be decided by the theologians on the basis of their experience of what is Christian, in pondering what is written in the First Epistle of Paul the Apostle to the Corinthians . . . 'Has not God let the wisdom of this world become foolishness?' (1 Cor. 1:20) . . . Will Christian theology one day resolve to take seriously the word of the apostle and thus also the conception of philosophy as foolishness?" (*Introduction*, 287–88).

Heidegger clearly thinks that while Christian theology can be and sometimes has been onto-theological, its proper destiny is elsewhere. In the light of his Pascalian, Kierkegaardian, Pauline critique, theology can be postmetaphysical, not by abandoning the notion that God is Creator and as such an uncaused or self-caused cause, but by refusing to make God a means to our ends by subordinating all God-talk to our projects, our systems, and our methods.

Onto-Theology and Hermeneutics

So what does all this have to do with biblical hermeneutics? Quite a bit, if we focus on the How rather than the What of onto-theology. When biblical interpretation is in the service of some theological system, liberal or conservative, or when biblical interpretation is in the service of some hermeneutical method (historical-critical or historical-grammatical), it succumbs to the spirit of onto-theology. The text becomes an object to be mastered by the interpreting subject, individual or communal (Westphal 1–2). The system or the method becomes the Procrustean bed into which the text is required to fit. Its subject matter can enter the interpreter's discourse only on condition and to the degree that it conforms to the interpreter's a priori requirements. Because the language is biblical rather than abstractly metaphysical, the God presented by interpretation may still be worshipped, and Heidegger's critique may seem to have missed its mark. But this God is an idol, created in the human image of a human system or method. It would be clear that "onto-theology" and "fundamentalism" are virtually synonymous if it weren't for the fact that this mode of interpretation can prevail at any point on the theological spectrum.

It is worth noting that Kevin Vanhoozer begins his introduction to this volume by explicitly denying that the theological interpretation of Scripture means subordinating the text either to a theological system or to a hermeneutical method. But interpretation is never free from this dual temptation. How can we guard against it? Doubtless, there is no magic formula (another method?). Perhaps the crucial task is constantly to remember that the Bible is the word of God, not in the Greek sense but in the biblical sense. (In other words, it is not so much logos as an intelligibility out there in the world—in this case in the text, to be discovered by the sufficiently clever interpreter—but rather the voice by whom we are addressed, called, commanded, welcomed, forgiven, guided.) As the word of God, the Bible is not the storehouse of King Midas, in which he hoards and admires his exegetical loot. It is the voice, at once disturbing and comforting, that says, "This is my Son, the Beloved; with him I am well pleased; listen to him!" (Matt. 17:5 NRSV). Systems and methods have their place, but they must always be subordinate to listening.

Bibliography

Heidegger, M. *Hegel's Concept of Reason*. Harper & Row, 1970; idem. *Identity and Difference*. Harper & Row, 1969; idem. "Introduction to 'What Is Metaphysics?'" In *Pathmarks*, trans. and ed. W. McNeil. Cambridge University Press, 1998; idem. *Nietzsche*. 4 vols. Harper & Row, 1979–87; idem. "Postscript to 'What Is Metaphysics?'" In *Pathmarks*, trans. and ed. W. McNeil. Cambridge University Press, 1998; idem. *The Principle of Reason*. Indiana University Press, 1991; Kant, I. *Critique of Pure Reason*. St. Martin's Press, 1961; Westphal, M. *Overcoming Onto-Theology*. Fordham University Press, 2001.

Merold Westphal

Oracle See Prophecy and Prophets in the OT

Oral Tradition and the NT

Jesus announced and taught, the apostles proclaimed, and the gathered community of faith heard. It is thus generally recognized that much of the NT originated as a spoken word, that its formative material was first transmitted by means of oral teachings and traditions concerning Jesus' words and deeds, and that even in their final written form its various documents were delivered orally and received aurally within the common life of the early church. What is less clear, and thus still debated, is precisely how all this took place and what it might mean for any (not least theological) estimation of the NT today.

Jesus and Oral Tradition

Jesus and his first followers lived in the highly oral environment of first-century Judaism and its wider Greco-Roman world (Achtemeier; Wansbrough). As the Gospels well attest, he was a prophetic figure who proclaimed the kingdom of God. On many different occasions he addressed his listeners by using sayings and stories, dialogued with inquiring individuals and groups, and disputed with the increasingly perturbed Jewish authorities. Along the way he also gathered and instructed his disciples. What we know concerning these matters has come to us not because Jesus himself left any written record (apparently he did not), but because his first followers told and retold his message, initially orally and then in writing. Yet, precisely how this process took place, and the degree to which it reliably transmitted the words and voice of Jesus himself, has been the subject of several highly nuanced and often competing proposals.

With reference to folklore traditions, early proponents of form criticism (Bultmann; Dibelius) and recent participants in the Jesus Seminar and others have argued that Jesus traditions were transmitted orally over at least a twenty- to thirty-year period before being written down, and that they existed mainly in the form of (collected) wisdom sayings. Moreover, these traditions would have involved considerable local variation, and entailed the conflation of Jesus' own sayings with the faith-based interpretations and fabrications of the post-Easter church. So viewed, the "very communal, anonymous and changeable nature" of oral transmission (Henaut 15) does not inspire confidence concerning its reliability, notwithstanding more moderate positions balancing variability with reference to more uniform and stable features and patterns (Kelber).

Among early critics of form criticism were those who argued on analogy with rabbinic instruction that in fact oral Jesus traditions were carefully memorized and transmitted by the disciples in formal, fixed, controlled, and corroborated ways (esp. Gerhardsson). Although initially and rather unfairly critiqued, this view has found support in more recent work. R. Riesner has contended that Jesus' proclamation and teachings stood within the Jewish prophetic and wisdom traditions, and were thus seen as reliable and to be safeguarded. Furthermore, like other Jewish rabbis and Greek teachers, Jesus would have prepared his disciples to perpetuate his instruction, with memorization playing a well-recognized role in this respect. S. Byrskog has applied modern studies in oral history to the eyewitness testimony of Greek and Roman historians and to the Gospels, noting the importance of oral recall and that writing was largely seen as a supplement thereto. He concludes that the Gospel narratives concerning Jesus are "the syntheses of history and story, of the oral history of an eyewitness and the interpretative and narrativizing procedures of an author" (305). It is in this nuanced way that we might speak meaningfully of the reliability and historicity of the Jesus tradition.

Other recent approaches have drawn upon K. Bailey's study of oral tradition within modern Middle Eastern village life, specifically his category of "informal, controlled tradition," designating the way in which such communities retain in quite fixed form the important elements in oral retellings. James D. G. Dunn finds this oral paradigm confirmed in his analysis of the combination of stability and flexibility evident in the narrative and teachings of the Jesus traditions in the Synoptic Gospels (Dunn 173–254). Therein may be discerned "a portrayal of the remembered Jesus, of the impact made by his words and deeds on the first disciples as that impact was 'translated' into oral tradition and as it was passed down in oral performance within the earliest circles of disciples and the churches, to be enshrined in due course in the written Synoptic tradition" (254). Dunn's proposal, together with that of Byrskog, attests to the now highly sophisticated state of the discussion, and we hope that their constructive interaction will produce even more fruitful estimations of the crucial interrelated issues involved.

One final issue to be noted here concerns the extent of any interaction between oral Jesus traditions and written texts: How literate were Jesus' disciples? Did they transcribe his words (e.g., using notebooks)? And is the shift from orality to written form to be seen as entailing the loss of a "living" tradition (so Kelber)? On balance, it seems likely that there was a lively and fluid interaction between oral and written elements, with both valued as together witnessing to the words and deeds of Jesus and their unique role in the formation of the new-covenant documentation of the church.

The Apostles, the Early Church, and Oral Tradition

Having been living witnesses to Jesus' own words and deeds (Acts 1:21–22), the post-Pentecost apostles appropriated and applied the Jesus traditions in their own highly oral preaching and teaching of the gospel (Dibelius; Dodd; Bauckham, "Kerygmatic"). In so doing they attested to what God was accomplishing among them: The OT had been fulfilled in the ministry, death, and resurrection of Jesus. A now-exalted Jesus would be present by the Spirit among the messianic people of God until his return. And in the interim all were exhorted to repent and be redeemed (e.g., 2:22–36; 3:12–26). As such, their message bears some comparison to the content and form of the (later) Gospel narratives (cf. 10:36–43). And, given their prominent role, it is likely that the apostles, together with other eyewitnesses, took care to ensure that the Jesus tradition was properly remembered, represented, and retold.

That they did so to significant effect is indicated by Paul, who readily acknowledges the Jesus traditions he has received (1 Cor. 15:1–4; cf. Gal. 2:1–10). Paul's letters also suggest that he was well aware of Jesus' sayings (e.g., Rom. 12:14; 13:8–10; 14:14; 1 Cor. 13:2; 1 Thess. 5:2–3) and teachings (1 Cor. 7:10; 9:14; 11:23–25; 1 Thess. 4:15–17), drawing upon them for his own pastoral purposes. The Letter of James offers another interesting example of the way in which the sayings of Jesus were not simply cited or alluded to, but rather creatively reexpressed in relation to the matters being addressed (e.g., James 1:5–6; 2:5, 13; 5:12; so Bauckham, *James*, 74–93). Certain elements in 1 Peter might be similarly viewed (e.g., 2:7, 12; 4:13–14). From such examples it is evident that Jesus traditions were being impressed upon the lives of early believers and also woven almost imperceptibly into the non-Gospel NT writings.

Finally, it is also apparent that the gospel concerning Jesus found varied oral expression within the worship and common life of the early church. Again, Paul provides a notable case in point. Among various possible examples, reference can be made to confessions and acclamations (Rom. 10:8–9; 1 Cor. 12:3; Phil. 2:11), to songs or hymns (Phil. 2:6–11; Col. 1:15–20), and perhaps to creedal formulations (Rom. 1:3–4; 1 Thess. 1:9–10; Dormeyer 140–54).

Oral Tradition, the NT, and Theology

It is evident that fundamental and wide-ranging issues attend any consideration of oral tradition in relation to the NT, not least the reliability of its witness to Jesus, the nature of its formation and role, and the correlation between Scripture and ecclesial tradition. From the foregoing it can be claimed with confidence that the NT does faithfully represent the words and voice of Jesus and the apostles' testimony thereto, for it is this which is fundamentally constitutive of its very substance and shape. Throughout, the NT indicates the collective and cohesive witness of its divinely governed sources and recipient contexts—from Jesus to the apostles to the early Christian community at large—who together authenticate its contents and urge its receipt as Scripture (cf. Luke 1:1–4; John 21:24–25). And all of this is in service of the unfolding purposes of the triune God, whose word is to be embodied within the lives of his Spirit-empowered people.

See also Form Criticism and the NT; Gospels

Bibliography

Achtemeier, P. "*Omne verbum sonat*: The New Testament and the Oral Environment of Late Western Antiquity." *JBL* 109 (1990): 3–27; Bailey, K. "Informal Controlled Oral Tradition and the Synoptic Gospels." *Them* 20 (1995): 4–11; Bauckham, R. *James*. Routledge, 1999; idem. "Kerygmatic Summaries in the Speeches in Acts." Pages 185–217 in *History, Literature, and Society in the Book of Acts*, ed. B. Witherington III. Cambridge University Press, 1996; Bultmann, R. *The History of the Synoptic Tradition*, trans. J. Marsh. 2d ed. Harper & Row, 1968; Byrskog, S. *Story as History—History as Story*. WUNT 123. Mohr/Siebeck, 2000; Dibelius, M. *From Tradition to Gospel*, trans. B. Woolf. Charles Scribner's Sons, 1935; Dodd, C. H. *The Apostolic Preaching and Its Developments*. Hodder & Stoughton, 1936; Dormeyer, D. *The New Testament among the Writings of Antiquity*, trans. R. Kossov. Sheffield Academic Press, 1998; Dunn, J. D. G. *Jesus Remembered*. Eerdmans, 2003; Gerhardsson, B. *Memory and Manuscript*. Rev. ed. Eerdmans, 1998; idem. *The Reliability of the Gospel Tradition*. Hendrickson, 2001; Harvey, J. *Listening to the Text*. Baker, 1998; Henaut, B. *Oral Tradition and the Gospels*. JSNTSup 82. JSOT, 1993; Kelber, W. *The Oral and Written Gospel*. Indiana University Press, 1997; Riesner, R. *Jesus als Lehrer*. 3rd ed. WUNT 2.7. Mohr/Siebeck, 1988; Wansbrough, H., ed. *Jesus and the Oral Gospel Tradition*. JSNTSS 64. Sheffield Academic Press, 1991.

S. A. Cummins

Oral Tradition and the OT

This addresses the presence of oral material in the literature. To what extent did the OT originate as an oral composition, and to what degree was it composed in a written fashion? Traditionally, oral tradition has been characterized as a body of material with both form and content that was received as property of the community and passed along to the next generation in an oral manner (Knight). The tradition changed to meet new needs. Above all, it was cumulative in the sense that it experienced items added to it.

This question is debated among scholars. Given the wide variety of means by which oral composition could potentially take place, I review the dominant theories, beginning with the earliest, the development of tradition history by H. Gunkel and his students. As a German scholar working at the end of the nineteenth century, Gunkel was influenced by the epic poetry of the Germanic peoples, by the recent discoveries of Babylonian myths that many were comparing with the Bible, especially Gen. 1–11, and by source criticism. Thus, Gunkel compared *Enuma Elish*, the Babylonian creation myth, to the creation accounts found in the Bible. As a result, he felt that he could identify elements in Genesis that betrayed a foreign origin by their disconnected state. This was then traced back to a common origin with the ancient Near Eastern myths. Israel received the myth fragments and incorporated them into their own epic accounts. However, as a monotheistic people, they removed the elements of myth involving other deities: they demythologized the oral traditions. Thus, Gunkel was confident that he could isolate the smallest identifiable units of tradition, determine their origin and milieu, trace their oral composition and development from the earliest periods, and identify the stage at which they became part of the written compositions that formed the Pentateuch and other biblical books.

His students included R. Bultmann in the NT and A. Alt in the OT. The latter focused on the study of Israel's early history. Much of this was believed to have been preserved in the cult and especially in etiologies, legends used to explain the origins of well-known names or customs. Some figures, such as Abram and Jacob, were originally separate and eponymous leaders of tribal groups in various parts of Palestine. Others, such as Joshua, were artificial figures who provided organization to the composition. M. Noth reconstructed Israel's early history as evolving from five tradition complexes transmitted orally: the exodus, the entrance into Palestine, the promise to the patriarchs, the revelations at Sinai, and the wilderness wanderings. These formed the common oral basis from which the composers of the documents drew, according to source criticism.

In Scandinavia, emphasis upon the oral tradition of the Bible was wedded to studies regarding the preliterate composition of northern European epics and stories. Scholars, including Pedersen, Mowinckel, and Engnell, among others, considered the importance of psychological characteristics upon the development of the oral tradition. They also emphasized the cult as the context for the transmission. In particular, Israel's kingship was seen as having a special holiness, at times interpreted in terms of the divine. Thus, the king was somehow recognized as divine.

Meanwhile, in America and elsewhere, there was a rejection of oral tradition as understood in terms of evolution from simpler units to more complex traditions. This was seen as contrary to anthropological findings. In particular, the investigation of Serbo-Croatian bards and their ability to memorize oral traditions on a level with that of the Homeric epics, as well as the discovery of epic poetic texts at Ugarit, from the time of Israel's origins, led some to understand the oral tradition as capable of passing along much larger collections of material without significant alteration. Narrative literature such as the Jacob account in Genesis and historical poems such as Judg. 5 were considered to be examples of oral transmission (Cross; Hendel).

This has led to new investigations into the oral traditions behind the biblical texts. Although many have touched upon this subject in various ways, S. Niditch has attempted to identify evidence for orality in some texts that possess what she calls an "oral register." She identifies evidence for oral traditions in texts that use repetition and certain forms or themes (such as those associated with creation or narratives of battle followed by enthronement). Behind these stated criteria, there is an interconnection with the assumption that writing was absent in ancient Israel before the Persian period (from 539 BCE), or possibly writing appeared in the late seventh century BCE, at the earliest. Thus, for Niditch early texts tend to exhibit oral traits, whereas later texts seem to be more conscious of the literary context in which they were written.

The theological implications for oral tradition have been explored primarily by critics who see the Israelite theology as undergoing a profound transformation that evolved from an early polytheism to a much later, and more literate, monotheism. Nevertheless, the identification of oral sources, particularly in poetry, has value in terms of theological understanding. For example, the early poems of Exod. 15 and Judg. 5 provide parallel accounts of the events found in the prose sections of Exod. 14 and Judg. 4. Perhaps this is an example of oral forms of the prose accounts. It certainly emphasizes the role of Israel's God as a warrior and his leadership of his people from the southern desert into the promised land and victory (Judg. 5:4–5). These theophanic motifs, coupled with the sovereign God as elector and protector of his people and as their defender against their enemies, can also be found in other poetic texts that may have an oral origin (e.g., Ps. 68; Hab. 3). Beyond these, other psalms as well as many proverbs may have had an oral origin. The former were used orally as praise for God's creation and redemption (Ps. 136) and as requests for his assistance (lament psalms, e.g., 13; 80). The proverbs provide a wisdom theology of the role of God in all of creation, and of the integration of nature and human experience within a single meaningful universe under the sovereign hand of its Creator (Prov. 1:7–9). This optimistic view that there is meaning in nature and the world allowed Israelites to live in a world not dominated by evil spirits or the chimera and fears that could be found in polytheism.

However, orality is difficult to prove where it is not explicitly attested. Thus, the repetition found in biblical genealogies may attest to oral origins. Poetry especially has evidence for oral background—as in the Song of the Sea (Exod. 15), David's lament over Saul and Jonathan (2 Sam. 1), and many psalms. On the other hand, the features of repetition and various themes may just as easily appear in what are fundamentally written compositions. The origins of biblical texts are notoriously difficult to identify where they are not explicitly stated. Furthermore, many assumptions about the absence of reading and writing in ancient Israel arise from reinterpreting early texts such as Judg. 8:14 and 1 Kings 21:11, ignoring the dozens of attestations from early in the biblical narrative to written sources (e.g., Josh. 1:8; 8:31–35; 10:13; 23:6; 2 Sam. 1:18; 1 Kings 11:41; et passim), or not evaluating the full implications of the extrabiblical evidence for writing from ancient Israel as well as surrounding cultures.

See also Form Criticism and the OT; Source Criticism

Bibliography

Cross, F., Jr. *Canaanite Myth and Hebrew Epic*. Harvard University Press, 1973; Gunkel, H. *The Legends of Genesis*, trans. W. Carruth. Schocken, 1901; Hendel, R. *The Epic of the Patriarch*. Harvard Semitic Monographs 42. Scholars Press, 1987; Hess, R. "Literacy in Iron Age Israel." Pages 82–102 in *Windows into Old Testament History*, ed. P. Long, D. W. Baker, and G. Wenham. Eerdmans, 2002; Knight, D. *Rediscovering the Traditions of Israel*. 2d ed. Scholars Press, 1975; Millard, A. Review of S. Niditch, *Oral World and Written Word*. *JTS* NS 49 (1998): 699–705; Niditch, S. *Oral World and Written Word*. Library of Ancient Israel. Westminster John Knox, 1996; Noth, M. *The Deuteronomistic History*. JSOTSup 15. Sheffield Academic Press, 1981; Schniedewind, W. "Orality and Literacy in Ancient Israel." *RelSRev* 26 (2000): 327–32; Zevit, Z. "Clio, I Presume." *BASOR* 260 (1985): 71–82.

Richard S. Hess

Origen   *See* Allegory; Hermeneutics; Mysticism, Christian; Patristic Biblical Interpretation; Spiritual Sense

Original Sin

The doctrine of "original sin" conforms to the stereotype of "church dogma": a "rational" theory made authoritative by tradition and institutional decree; a heavy superstructure whose alleged biblical foundations most modern exegetes will not recognize; and literal propositions unpalatable to modern sensitivities (and even more so for late moderns), which can only be "saved" through reinterpretation. One can cite Paul Ricoeur as a model thinker about original sin who mercilessly criticized it as "pseudorational speculations" and as bordering on Gnosticism (*Conflict*, 271, 280, 283, 285), *and* he strove to retrieve its symbolic meaning on his hermeneutical way. The relationship of "original sin" to Scripture, however, may be seen differently from the current picture.

The heart of the matter is the interrelatedness of primeval event and present condition. As the phrase shows, the doctrine binds together the state of humankind, *sin*, and a reference to *origins*. Precisely, traditional theology distinguishes (but also combines) *peccatum originale originans*, the primeval catastrophe that caused the rest, identified with Adam's disobedience, and *peccatum originale originatum*, the innate condition caused by the former event and constituting the seedbed of "actual" sins. Three issues deserve close scrutiny: the extent and significance of the biblical evidence invoked (the "seats," *sedes*, of doctrine); the meaning (*intentio*) of the dogma and whether it is congruous with the "spirit" of Scripture; and the modes and means of sin's transmission, if it is affirmed (*traditio*).

Textual Origin

Critics of the traditional interpretation bemoan the use of very few passages as "seats" of the doctrine, basically Gen. 3 and Rom. 5:12–21, and complain that these are given a weight and signification they do not possess in the texts. It is an odd accident of history (in particular, Augustine's reading of Rom. 5:12) that the Edenic story, that etiological tale (designed to explain why childbirth is painful, weeds grow faster than vegetables, snakes are unpleasant to women, etc.) with almost no echo in the OT, came to exercise such control of Christian thinking! Or, for critics more conservative, that such a skillful myth or symbol of humankind's proneness to evil was (mis)read as teaching about causes. In Rom. 5, Paul is really interested in Christ; Ricoeur (*Symbolism*, 239) argues that Adam's part constitutes "only a flying buttress," "only a false column," to serve homiletical symmetry.

Detailed arguments have been offered in reply. They would show that Paul's logic implies his conviction of a historical Adamic fall and its decisive import; that canonical pride of place, for the Edenic story, reflects Adam's role in the OT view of the human plight; and that reminiscences and allusions are by no means rare in both Testaments (Scharbert; Ligier). Beyond these, the sense of corruption from an early age (Gen. 6:5, *raq ra'*, "only evil"; 8:21), of universal estrangement from God and dreadful subjection to his holy wrath—but for a special move of redemptive mercy—is widely attested indeed. The "natural" dimension of that sinfulness is not ignored, with the notion of "flesh" (in the NT, John 3:6; 1 Cor. 3:3–4; Eph. 2:3; etc.). Not seldom, the OT logic of genealogical continuity is being applied (Hos. 12:3–4; Ezek. 16:44–45; cf. 1 Pet. 1:18) and may reach back to the first patriarch, Adam, as it does in intertestamental writings (Wis. 2:23–24; Sir. 25:24; 1QH 9:13; 2 Bar. 18:2; 23:4; 54:15; 56:8–9; 2 Esd. 7:18–119) and is probably implied in Ecclesiastes. No clear statement, however, of the imputation of an *alien* sin appears (a predicate since Cyprian, *Ep.* 64.5 [58.5 in some editions]).

Dissent and debate bring out the importance of *theological* interest in detecting allusions, of the presupposition of homogeneity within canonical boundaries, of the continuing relevance of intertestamental literature, and of judgments made on literary genres and the relationship of biblical texts to non-Israelite mythologies or wisdom books.

Intention

There is a vast agreement on the dogma's truer intention: it recognizes the universal sway of sin, the deep-seated compulsion and inevitable expression, *yet*, paradoxically, its contingent character as the act of freedom (Brunner 50–51, 74, 100, 103–6; Suchocki 129–30; Ricoeur, *Conflict*, 282–84). If sinfulness equated with metaphysical necessity, sinners would appear as victims and God as the author of evil. In 1960, Ricoeur was able to emphasize the unique separation in the Bible (compared with myths) between the origin of being (goodness) and the origin of sin (abuse of created freedom). He saw the import of a historical fall—"Evil becomes scandalous at the same time as it becomes historical" (*Symbolism*, 203)—as the only way to preserve harmony with the prophetic preaching of ethical monotheism and repentance. Evangelical writers highlight the correspondence with a historical redemption (Rom. 5).

The knot of debate is this: while Brunner, Ricoeur, and others wish to maintain meaning without historical fact, through symbolic interpretation, more orthodox theologians (e.g., the symposium edited by Christoph Schönborn) argue that *as if* constructions cannot stand. Responsible theologizing cannot be satisfied. Involved is the role of theological reason in the interpretation of Scripture: How far is consistency a legitimate goal? Is it part of humility for reason to *receive* historical sequence (without exalting reason above history idealistically)?

Tradition

The spearhead of critiques of traditional dogma is directed against its account of transmission, from Adam to his descendants. Ricoeur denounces the mixture of juridical (ethical) categories with biological ones (*Conflict*, 270, 280). K. Barth (500) rejects the usual German word *Erbsünde* (hereditary sin). It must be recognized that orthodox worthies have made themselves vulnerable here, since they spoke of heredity *as if* original sin were a physical disability, a genetic disease. The *intentio* of the doctrine, as it preserves the dimension of freedom through historical linkage, opposes such category confusion.

Reflection might fruitfully investigate the complexity of *human* transmission and ponder the negative aspects of sin (humankind deprived as well as depraved) in a relational, covenantal, setting. Further work should also sharpen theological hermeneutics of metaphorical language.

Bibliography

Barth, K. *Church Dogmatics*. Vol. IV/1, trans. G. Bromiley. T&T Clark, 1956; Blocher, H. *Original Sin*. Apollos, 1997; Brunner, E. *Dogmatics*. Vol. 2, *The Christian Doctrine of Creation and Redemption*, trans. O. Wyon. Lutterworth, 1952; Ligier, L. *Péché d'Adam et péché du monde*. 2 vols. Aubier, 1960–61; Ramm, B. *Offense to Reason*. Harper & Row, 1985; Ricoeur, P. *The Conflict of Interpretations*, ed. D. Ihde. Northwestern University Press, 1974; idem. *The Symbolism of Evil*, trans. E. Buchanan. Beacon, 1967; Scharbert, J. *Prolegomena eines Alttestamentlers zur Erbsündenlehre*. QD 37. Herder, 1968; Schönborn, C., et al., eds. *Zur kirchlichen Erbsündenlehre*. Johannes, 1991; Suchocki, M. *The Fall to Violence*. Continuum, 1994; Vandervelde, G. *Original Sin*. University Press of America, 1981.

Henri A. G. Blocher

Orthodox Biblical Interpretation

The interpretation of the Bible in harmony with the Bible's own nature and witness achieves its proper goal through the application of the following foundational principles (not necessarily in hierarchical order): (1) There must be fidelity to the witness of Scripture as the word of God, the supreme record of revelation. (2) There must be fidelity to the classical doctrinal tradition of the ancient church, as the tradition of apostolic truth, centered on the gospel of Christ, and enacted in the life of the church through worship, proclamation, teaching, practice, and mission. (3) There must be fidelity to earnest and critical study through the use of reason as a gift of God, yet operative within the horizon of active faith adequate to the apprehension of the transcendent realities testified by the biblical texts. And (4) there must be fidelity to the Holy Spirit, by whose grace alone is the ultimate aim of the reading of Scripture accomplished, that is, the transformation of human lives through the experience of God's holy presence and renewing power, the primary subject matter of Scripture. The integration and practice of the above principles form an authentic and comprehensive interpretative perspective that variously places readers, hearers, and interpreters of the Bible, and their spiritual quest, in unity with the communion of saints. These especially are the prophets, apostles, and great Christian teachers of the past, all faithful servants and authoritative witnesses of God's marvelous deeds for the salvation of the world.

Fidelity to Scripture

The Scriptures constitute "the oracles of God" (Rom. 3:2 NRSV) communicated through inspired men and women "in many and diverse ways" (Heb. 1:1 NRSV), including words, deeds, laws, rites, narratives, dreams, visions, symbols, images, and parables. By such various means God chose to disclose knowledge of his will, his saving wisdom, his summons to human beings, and ultimately personal knowledge of himself, in order freely to draw humanity to be his covenant people. The supreme expression of God's self-disclosure is through the incarnation, life, death, resurrection, ascension, and awaited glorious appearance of his Son, Jesus Christ, "the Lord of glory" (1 Cor. 2:8), who forms the center of revelation and marks the unity of the OT and NT. In view of its nature as the record of the self-disclosure of God and knowledge of his saving will—God himself being in this sense the primary author and subject matter of the Scriptures—the Bible bears intrinsic and undisputed authority for teaching, correction, and the life of righteousness. The church has acknowledged and formalized its authority by the process of its canonization. The primacy of Scripture entails that nothing in the life of the church must contradict the biblical message and spirit. Any usage or interpretation of the Bible apart from the principle of fidelity to the Scripture's witness as the record of God's self-disclosure will fall short of attaining its appropriate hermeneutical efficacy.

But the nature of Scripture also necessarily involves the paradox that the oracles of God are communicated through the words of human beings who spoke and wrote in Hebrew, Aramaic, and Greek. This paradox is an indispensable aspect of the nature of revelation itself that does not occur in a vacuum but rather involves free, willing, thinking, and acting human agents. The OT and NT, in their variety of books, authors, language, style, perspectives, depth of insight, as well as historical origins and development, amply demonstrate the truth of the "humanity" of the Bible. Biblical authors, for example the apostle Paul (2 Cor. 3:6), had some sense of this paradox in that they drew a distinction between letter and spirit in the sacred writings. The theologians of the ancient church—such as Origen, Athanasius, Gregory of Nyssa, John Chrysostom, and Cyril of Alexandria—were confronted by repeated questions of interpretation. They reflected more consciously on the human character of Scripture, a form of divine condescension to human weakness (*synkatabasis*), yet without compromising the authority and essential clarity of Scripture's divine message. In modern times a vast scholarly tradition of literary and historical studies has thoroughly exposed the human contingencies of the biblical books to the extent that academic experts have often rejected the Bible's unity and canonical authority, a cultural trend proved to be as unwise as it is fruitless.

However, grappling with the paradox of Scripture's divine and human character is a necessary part of the interpretative task, a matter that can neither be ignored through pietism, nor evaded through clever answers by well-intentioned defenders of strict forms of verbal inerrancy. The parallel theological paradigm is the mystery of the incarnation—the revelation of the mystery of God in the person and ministry of the unique Son. God's eternal Son was born of a woman, grew in wisdom, suffered hunger and pain, and died a true death as a human being. But the Son also disclosed the reality of God's character and kingdom, rose from the dead in the power of the Spirit, and defeated the forces of evil and death. The challenge is how, by means of interpretative discernment, to keep in balance the divine and human aspects of the mysteries of Christ and Scripture. Interpreters must do so on the basis of and in harmony with the internal evidence of the sacred texts themselves according to their intrinsically bonded theological and historical testimony. This task cannot be fulfilled apart from a dynamic view of inspiration taking into consideration not only the rich variety of authors and texts themselves, but also the community of faith in which the biblical books were generated and gradually gained the status of sacred texts. For another definitive aspect of the nature of the Bible is its communal and traditional character.

Fidelity to Tradition

Just as theology cannot be separated from history, so also Scripture as a holy book cannot be disjoined from the communal context in which it originated, took shape, and was variously used, in Israel and church. The very idea of biblical revelation, indispensably involving active human partners, means that God's self-disclosure created covenant relationships and covenant community. Prior to the composition of texts, God's words and deeds were proclaimed and interpreted by communal leaders and prophets. They were then received and transmitted as oral tradition in the community of faith, and eventually recorded in documents. In Israel, no less than in the early church, diverse claims concerning God's revelation had to be tested and resolved within the life of the community that possessed the discerning and normative criterion of true and false prophecy. The determining factor was not any single individual but the community and its faith tradition, acknowledging the witness of authentic leaders and prophets, preserving their writings, and eventually canonizing them as sacred books. Decisive new claims with extraordinary impact on people's lives, such as in the case of Jesus, created a new community, the early church. In either case, Israel or church, the functional principle remained the same: the ongoing community of faith was the living context of the proclamation, reception, interpretation, transmission, and application of revelation, whether oral or written.

Historical scholarship has indisputably demonstrated the organic bond between the community of faith and its revealed tradition. Already in the oral period, both gospel and sacred rite had attained the status of tradition in the life of the church (1 Cor. 11:23; 15:3). Thus, fidelity to the authority and witness of the Bible is fidelity to the community of faith, its tradition and life, its integrity and mission. Just as without the good news about Christ there could be no church, so also without the church there could be no viable proclamation of the good news. The creation and sustenance of community is a constitutive part of revelation and its interpretation. Moreover, the long process of the canonization of the Scriptures unambiguously attests to the mutually supportive and interdependent relationship between Bible and church. These considerations mean that Bible, church, and tradition cannot be played off against each other. Neither the Bible over church and tradition is a justifiable tradition, nor is church and tradition over the Bible. While the church through its tradition and active discernment gave rise to the biblical canon, the primacy of the biblical canon holds the church accountable to the scriptural witness as the standard of the church's faith and life. In the end, the true problematic of interpretation lies not at the level of formal principles pertaining to the relationships between text, community, and tradition, which are operative consciously or unconsciously in all religious communities. Instead, it lies in the specifics of interpretation at key points such as the understanding of the gospel and the definition of the normative tradition of truth, where critical judgment and discernment become preeminent.

Fidelity to Critical Study

The pursuit of truth necessarily requires discernment and critical judgment. The biblical authors themselves were engaged in discernment and critical assessment at the level of life. For example, the apostle Paul was wholly devoted to the advancement of the gospel and the care of the church through interpretive discernment in preaching and teaching, authoritative appeals to apostolic commission and received traditions, as well as persuasive argumentation and pastoral exhortation. All the NT authors were involved in a similar process of critical judgment, going beyond the mere announcement of the gospel and involving such matters as the christological interpretation of the OT, the formation of creedal confessions, the proper use of the gifts of the Spirit, the relations between Jews and Christians, the meaning of baptism and the Lord's Supper, the role of authority and order in the church, the resolution of internal and external points of conflict, as well as appropriate ethical conduct. These authors and interpreters came to the table with life-defining experiences and convictions that decisively influenced their interpretative stance. Along with their faith in the risen Lord and the guidance of the Spirit, however, they were necessarily engaged in critical reflection. With some disputes and diversity, they needed to work out patterns of faith and life in urgent concern about the truth of the gospel and the unity of the church (e.g., Matt. 18:15–18; Acts 15:22–29; Rom. 6:17; 1 Cor. 4:17; 8:4–6; Gal. 1:9; et al.).

The church fathers, equally faced with numerous theological and pastoral questions, exercised hermeneutical judgment in a more reflective way. At one level, while grounded in Christ and the Spirit as dynamic hermeneutical criteria, they made free and diverse use of known exegetical methods, such as allegorical, typological, grammatical, and textual, derived from both the Jewish and Greek traditions, and in some ways already found in the NT. At another level, having to contend with colossal gnostic distortions of the biblical texts, and much later with Arian and Eunomian rather sophisticated but nonetheless fundamentalist exegesis, the church fathers moved simultaneously toward historical, contextual, and doctrinal approaches to Scripture. They explicated such key principles as the centrality of Christ and the Spirit, the authority of the received apostolic tradition, the church's bond with the Scriptures, the doctrinal sense of the community as a whole (Rule of Faith), as well as the closely related canonization of the Bible. Over against the gnostic and Arian alternatives, a preeminent achievement in patristic exegesis was the focus on the contextual theological meaning of the scriptural texts by means of critical study and discernment of their primary aim (*skopos*) and sequence of thought (*akolouthia*). They interpreted the parts in the light of the whole and the whole in the light of its parts. At stake were not just incidental or technical matters, but the theological core of the apostolic tradition of the gospel. This tradition involved the central teachings of the Bible regarding the Creator God, the true incarnation of his Word, the authenticity of the Spirit's workings, the understanding of salvation of soul and body, the role of sacred rites and unity in the church, the norms of ethical conduct, as well as the acknowledgment of the true Scriptures. The intent was not to stifle variety, with which the patristic literature is rich, but to maintain viable unity on the basis of the truth of the gospel and for the benefit of the nurture of the church, two abiding objectives of biblical interpretation. In this perspective the patristic tradition, largely a tradition of biblical study, through the formation of the scriptural canon and the interpretative tradition that closely accompanied the canon, marks a classic achievement and standard for all ages.

In modern times the dominant biblical criticism, a development of a long and complex academic tradition under the heavy influence of the Enlightenment, has produced a paradox. On the one hand, through formal and systematic studies, biblical criticism has yielded brilliant results, moving far beyond the exegetical work of the church fathers pertaining to the analysis of innumerable literary, historical, and theological aspects of the Bible. It has not only produced a rich array of tools and methodologies, but also elucidated a whole array of biblical institutions, concepts, and themes, such as election and covenant, prophecy and eschatology, kingdom and righteousness. In the process it has shed welcome ecumenical light on major divisive issues such as Bible and tradition, law and gospel, word and sacrament, faith and works. One of its strongest points, in both its modern and postmodern versions, is its insistence on fresh readings of the Scriptures. On the other hand, captivated by philosophical presuppositions and cultural trends, biblical criticism has also been marred by bias, hypercriticism, utterly conflicting proposals, as well as loss of the sense of the theological and spiritual grandeur of the Bible. Not the least

among its flaws has been the arrogance of exclusive claims about "scientific" and "critical" study, judging all other approaches as either "precritical" or "noncritical." The crux of the problem, created by philosophical assumptions as much as the diversity of methodologies, is that while the ideal of biblical criticism is to provide fresh access to the voice of the Bible, it seems to arrive at the chaotic result of dismantling the Scriptures, undermining the authority of their witness, and providing few commensurate benefits to either church or society. This virtual bankruptcy of academic biblical studies can be overcome only by vigorous self-criticism that leads to serious regard for the authority and theological claims of Scripture, the legitimacy of traditional approaches to the Bible such as kerygmatic, devotional, liturgical, and doctrinal, as well as an epistemological humility that autonomous reason and imagination do not necessarily have the last word in what the Scriptures are all about.

Fidelity to the Holy Spirit

Since the Bible calls for faith not in itself but in the living God, the goal of interpretation cannot reach its fullness by intellectual analysis alone, whether literary, or historical, or even theological at a conceptual level. Scripture itself teaches that salvation is by grace, by direct personal encounter with God in his mercy, and not by any privileged body of knowledge, including scholarly erudition. Salvation by grace, however, essentially entails the engagement not only of reason but also of faith, repentance, commitment, love, and holiness of life as ways of knowledge of and communion with the mystery of God. In this hermeneutical context, the usage and interpretation of the Bible requires prayerful fidelity to the Holy Spirit, who alone opens access to the reality of the redeemed life testified by the biblical texts, a vision that decisively qualifies an interpreter's view of the Bible, the church, and everything else.

Hermeneutically, therefore, several levels of interpretation must be distinguished, for example, historical, theological, and mystical, all closely related but having their own hermeneutical aspects and objectives. Historical exegesis, requiring extensive technical training, seeks the original meaning of texts by the canons of historical research, yet without the hidden bias of philosophical and cultural assumptions. The objectives are the analysis and reconstruction of the entire biblical world, its literature, history, theology, institutions, and manners, according to the historical context of each biblical book and author. Such a task is in principle common to all scholars, Orthodox, Roman Catholic, Protestant, and interested and trained others, all mindful and self-corrective about their own presuppositions and the danger of improper interference in the pursuit of historical understanding.

Theological interpretation, also requiring technical training, concentrates on the theological claims and themes of the Bible as normative truth, a task bringing into play an interpreter's faith convictions, philosophical views, cultural sensibilities, and not least one's communal commitments. Although clearly related to the task of historical exegesis, the normative theological task involves its own hermeneutical context and problems, best engaged with awareness of one's presuppositions and an irenic spirit in order that the cogency of theological argumentation itself would provide the criterion of persuasion. For many, of course, what would be argued as the normative teaching of Scripture itself would be of preeminent importance. At this level the church fathers, whose theology was perceived not as an addition to but explication of biblical revelation, have much to teach interpreters about christological, spiritual, ecclesial, doctrinal, and pastoral considerations in essential continuity with the entire biblical tradition. In case of major theological disputes, the final hermeneutical word would belong to the community of faith, whose voice would prove as convincing as the integrity of its actual witness.

Mystical interpretation, a matter having nothing to do with esoteric technique, is related to the above approaches, yet is also of a different order. For one thing, it requires no technical preparation but another kind of training: nurture in the community of faith, where even a child can "interpret" the Bible and absorb its life-changing meaning through the hearing and reading of biblical stories. The paramount point here is neither exactitude in historical understanding, nor erudition in conceptual theological knowledge, but the spiritual receptivity of the believer embracing biblical images, symbols, narratives, and teachings, the Holy Spirit itself being the primary interpreter and teacher. Mystical interpretation is the illumination of grace actualizing the biblical witness in human hearts. The risk of subjectivity is countered by the believer's place in the community, the testing of one's personal faith and experience against the faith and experience of the community—ultimately the community of the biblical authors, as well as the great teachers and saints of the past. At this level, a huge amount of powerful interpretation and appropriation of the Bible's witness occurs in the ordinary stream of the living tradition, which is both conservative and creative, through worship, private devotions, preaching, group Bible studies, and mission outreach. Such activities are far more effective for the lives of ordinary Christians than exposure to the complex world of historical and theological scholarship.

Nevertheless, all three of the above approaches to Scripture are indispensable and mutually supportive. No single approach must be allowed to swallow up any other. The ideal would be the highest degree of integration between them in order that each interpreter at one's level of scriptural study may simultaneously grow as scholar, theologian, and saint in the presence of the living God encountered through Scripture.

Bibliography

Agourides, S. *Hermeneutics of the Sacred Texts*. Artos Zoes, 2000 [in modern Greek]; Breck, J. *The Power of the Word in the Worshipping Community*. St. Vladimir's Seminary Press, 1986; idem. *Scripture in Tradition*. St. Vladimir's Seminary Press, 2001; Burton-Christie, D. *The Word in the Desert*. Oxford University Press, 1993; Florovsky, G. *Bible, Church, Tradition*. Vol. 1. Nordland, 1972; Gamble, H. "Canon: The New Testament." *ABD* 1:852–61; Greer, R. "Biblical Authority in the Early Church." *ABD* 5:1026–28; Hall, C. *Learning Theology with the Church Fathers*. InterVarsity, 2002; idem. *Reading Scripture with the Church Fathers*. InterVarsity, 1998; Hopko, T. "The Bible in the Orthodox Church." *St. Vladimir's Theological Quarterly* 14 (1970): 66–99; Louth, A. *Discerning the Mystery*. Oxford University Press, 1983; Panagopoulos, J. *The Interpretation of Holy Scripture in the Church of the Fathers*. Vol. 1. Akritas Pubns., 1991 [in modern Greek]; Pelikan, J. *Christianity and Classical Culture*. Yale University Press, 1993; Stylianopoulos, T. *Scripture, Tradition, Hermeneutics*. Vol. 1 of *The New Testament: An Orthodox Perspective*. Holy Cross, 1997.

Theodore G. Stylianopoulos

P

Palestinian Judaism *See* Jewish Context of the NT

Pannenberg, Wolfhart *See* Last Things, Doctrine of

Parables

Scriptural parables offer a fascinating study for theological interpretation. Their indirect form has laid them open to a variety of readings. Yet this same *indirectness* has—paradoxically—allowed them to speak with remarkable *directness* to successive generations of Bible readers.

Genre and Texts

"Parable" is a fluid term. Conventionally, it refers to a small number of moral tales or allegories in the OT (e.g., Judg. 9:7–15; 2 Sam. 12:1–7; Ezek. 17:1–10), and to between thirty and forty utterances of Jesus in the Synoptic Gospels, couched in imagistic and/or narrative form. However, Hebrew, Greek, and English terminology does not allow neat demarcation of the genre. The Hebrew *mashal*, which lies behind the NT *parabolē*, is much wider than modern English "parable," including riddles, proverbs, and taunts. (The term does, however, alert us to the family resemblance of parables with wisdom sayings.) Conversely, many of Jesus' sayings generally called "parables" are not given any designation in the NT.

Rather than attempting to define the "ideal" parable genre, we do better trying to catch the force of the texts case by case. This article focuses on the parables of Jesus, upon which most attention has fastened.

No categorization of Jesus' parables lacks arbitrariness. The following subdivisions form a simplified entry point, which will allow us to make some summary statements before proceeding to larger interpretive issues. Items in the bibliography (e.g., Jeremias; Scott) give fuller listings and various more detailed categorizations.

Short Comparisons. These are exemplified by the comparisons of the kingdom of God with a mustard seed (Matt. 13:31–32//Mark 4:30–32//Luke 13:18–19) and with leaven (Matt. 13:33//Luke 13:20–21). Issues of interpretation include the precise point of comparison (e.g., smallness? apparent insignificance? contrast between present and future?) and the extent to which the comparison reshapes standard understandings of God's kingdom. Such sayings do not necessarily concern the kingdom, at least explicitly (cf. Matt. 7:24–27//Luke 6:47–49).

Implied Analogies. These are longer sayings in which Jesus puts a question, implying a similarity between a familiar situation and his own work, and/or the relationship of God to humans. Examples are the shepherd picture in Luke 15:3–7 and that of the friend knocking at midnight in Luke 11:5–10. An important issue here is how far to press the details: in the latter example, clearly no direct comparison between God and a grumpy householder is suggested.

Longer Narratives of the Triple Tradition. Two narrative parables appear in each of the Synoptic Gospels: the sower (Matt. 13:1–9, 18–23//Mark 4:3–9, 14–20//Luke 8:4–8, 11–15) and the wicked tenants (Matt. 21:33–44//Mark 12:1–11//Luke 20:9–18). Both can be interpreted as reflecting Jesus' ministry as God's final messenger, whose word meets resistance but bears ultimate fruit. Both can also be interpreted as pointing away from the speaker: hopefully, to the work of God in a land under judgment (the sower); and warningly, to the danger of rebelling against the Roman authorities (the tenants).

Narrative Parables of Matthew and Luke. Matthew and Luke each contain several longer narrative parables. Two are variations on the same basic story (Matt. 22:1–14//Luke 14:15–24; Matt. 25:14–30//Luke 19:11–27). Mostly, narrative parables are unique to one or other Gospel. Matthew's have a strong focus on warning and judgment (e.g., 18:23–35; 25:1–13). This is not absent in Luke (e.g., 16:19–31), but he tends to present more positive scenes in which people respond aright to the challenge of their situation (e.g., 16:1–8; 18:1–8).

The basic issue with the last two categories concerns how we are to "interpret" *stories* without losing their narrative essence. Although the Evangelists sometimes add interpretative comments, or introductions such as "the kingdom of heaven is like . . . ," and always of course embed the parables in their wider narratives, the stories seem to contain a surplus of meaning that disallows reductive summarizing.

Although all the parables may be seen as fitting into Jesus' proclamation of God's kingdom, with the warning, hope, and present challenge entailed therein, we should be wary about treating them as mere illustrations of a known reality. The words in which they are couched and the literal scenes depicted should be allowed their full weight in communicating new understanding and vision.

History of Interpretation

Three overlapping phases are each characterized by a particular approach to the parables' reference and rhetoric, and the goal of interpretation.

The Early Period. Various elements of a parable were seen to refer "allegorically" to some hidden spiritual truth. Thus Luke 10:30–37 was interpreted in terms of the history of salvation: Christ (the Samaritan) rescues a victim of robbers (humanity seduced by the devil) and delivers him safely to an inn (the church). Moral implications were as important as doctrinal ones.

Rhetorically, the parables were regarded as having *metaphorical* force. Their key functions were felt to be *revelation* or *illustration* of truth to the initiated. According to Jerome, they were not to be used to *establish* doctrine (i.e., in *argument*).

This interpretative strategy was not simply a cultural preference. It was a function of belief in Scripture as God's word, to be plundered for its riches. Early interpreters were interested not in the intention of the historical Jesus, but in the divine significance of the parables.

Such readings flowered in the patristic period and were handed down through medieval times. The Reformers reacted against their excesses, though the approach is still seen in the mid-nineteenth century in Trench. In popular piety, it still flourishes. Allegory in some form has always been a useful preaching tool.

The Modern Period. For Adolf Jülicher (1857–1938), the parables' reference was single, not multiple: their "point" was a moral or religious ideal. C. H. Dodd and Joachim Jeremias followed Jülicher, but read the parables as proclaiming God's kingdom, seen in apocalyptic terms as the inbreaking of his reign.

Jülicher saw the parables' basic rhetorical structure as that of *simile*, not *revealing* hidden truth, but *illustrating* known truth in a way accessible to all. He also paved the way for the notion, developed fully by Jeremias, that the parables were *argument*.

Most importantly, it was Jülicher who first consistently applied to the parables the interpretative *purpose* of seeking Jesus' intention. Recently, readings of this intention have differed widely. The Jesus Seminar regards the parables as products of a quixotic, teasing sage rather than one who issued specific proclamations or commands. N. T. Wright sees them as vehicles of revelation about Jesus' mission, in guarded, allegorical form drawing on, but subverting, standard Jewish imagery. Drury prefers to keep the historical quest on the level of the Evangelists' intention, discerning allegorical patterning in the relationship of a parable to its Gospel context.

Recent Trends. Attention has increasingly turned away from the external reference of the parables to their inner structure (Via; Crossan; Hedrick). This has distanced, though not completely detached, the parables from their historical context. They are seen as reflecting existential questions, disclosures, or demands.

Rhetorically, the parables are now often seen as *metaphorical narratives* (Funk; Crossan; Ricoeur; Scott). Unlike the early period, when they were seen as strings of metaphors, they are now regarded as stories that *as a whole* invite hearers into a world in order to reshape their vision of reality. They are transformative rather than merely illustrative or argumentative. Or instead of reading them as "metaphor," which could imply that earthly scenes simply point to "heavenly" ones, one may read them as synecdoche (offering a "part" of this world, out of which hearers are to make a "whole"; S. I. Wright 182–226) or as an intersection of metonymy (the "horizontal" dimension) and metaphor (the "vertical"; Etchells).

Concurrent with these developments has been a further shift in interpretative goal: away from human intention to *resonance for hearers*. The parables are heard as provocative utterances for their original culture and for today. Bailey and Herzog have reimagined the social web of meaning that acts as their backdrop. Both help us to be attuned to likely original tones in the parables as well as to the contemporary challenge they issue. Neither claims hermeneutical neutrality: their readings are shaped by orthodox Protestant doctrine (Bailey) and Paolo Freire's liberationist approach to pedagogy (Herzog).

Theological Interpretation of Parables Today

What might a properly theological interpretation of the parables look like? Our comments will relate to the three interpretive goals we have noted.

Divine Significance. To regard Scripture as mediating God's voice does not predetermine the manner in which any particular texts may do so. Parables therefore do not have to be interpreted allegorically, with God and his economy as referents. If parables as wholes allow us to glimpse God's kingdom, that is rich theological significance itself.

But this does not preclude us, like the early interpreters, reading the parables in the light of their canonical and doctrinal context. They contain scriptural echoes that are suggestive without the need to determine the extent of their deliberateness. They may also pattern the entire story of Christ. To see him in the Samaritan is not as far-fetched as many have thought. Jesus comes as the "outsider" and identifies with the marginalized, to rescue helpless humanity (McDonald). One does not need to attribute such a thought to Jesus to let the image illumine the meaning of his coming. Similarly, one can recognize the father in Luke 15:11–32 as a human figure in a realistic story, yet still see him as *reflecting* the character of God, disclosed elsewhere in Scripture and by Jesus himself.

Human Intention. The search for the parables' original purpose is theologically necessary. A church that sees Jesus as God's supreme speech-act must ask what he intended in his recorded utterances.

Historical-critical apparatus has often proved inadequate to the task. Yet we must still take seriously not only the Evangelists' interpretation of the parables, but also their sense of bearing witness to Jesus' words.

For example, the parable of the unmerciful servant (Matt. 18:21–35) in canonical context supports teaching about relationships in the church. Theological interpretation will take this seriously. But it will also probe the significance of the parable in Jesus' own setting, as a surprising glimpse of Jubilee in a society dominated by pagan, wealthy Romans. In this case, the impetus is to catch the spirit of the kingdom while it is here—in whatever surprising quarter it may be found.

But "intention" should not be conceived simplistically, as if parables could be decoded into nonparabolic language. Respect for Jesus and the Evangelists implies that our interpretations be grounded in the first-century context, but also that we grasp the importance of narrative as a medium for our own theology. We should further note Jesus' high theology of creation: it was from the everyday world that he drew his scenes and stories.

Resonance for Hearers. Theological interpretation must reckon with the power of parabolic language to resonate differently in different contexts. Attempting to shield people from the parables' puzzles and provocations by offering overly neat explanations is true neither to the text nor to the speaker—nor to the God by whose providence Scripture comes to us.

Theological interpretation will therefore seek to serve the parables' dialectic of pointedness and indirection, rather than master it. Contemporary connections may be drawn out, though not labored, in order to link today's world with the challenge of Jesus.

It is especially important that we allow the parables to continue to question us. We must not be content with fixed, "safe" "meanings" that favor "us" against "them." Some early parable interpretation unfortunately bolstered anti-Judaism—for example, seeing in the parable of the wicked tenants (Mark 12:1–12 et par.) a decree against the Jewish people as a whole. Yet the Evangelists surely want the parable to challenge the church: not least Matthew, whose characteristic emphasis on fruit-bearing emerges here (21:43).

It is precisely a mode of parable interpretation that allows for a *present* hearing, sees ourselves as the objects of their penetrating address, that will most truly represent their intention. For they are not static revelations of truth, but dynamic invitations to transformation.

Bibliography

Bailey, K. *Poet and Peasant.* Eerdmans, 1976; idem. *Through Peasant Eyes.* Eerdmans, 1980; idem. *Poet and Peasant; and, Through Peasant Eyes.* 2 vols. in 1. Eerdmans, 1983; Crossan, J. D. *In Parables.* Harper & Row, 1973; Drury, J. *The Parables in the Gospels.* SPCK, 1985; Etchells, R. *A Reading of the Parables of Jesus.* Darton, Longman & Todd, 1998; Funk, R. *Language, Hermeneutic, and Word of God.* Harper & Row, 1966; Hedrick, C. *Parables as Poetic Fictions.* Hendrickson, 1994; Herzog, W. R., II. *Parables as Subversive Speech.* Westminster John Knox, 1994; Jeremias, J. *The Parables of Jesus,* trans. S. H. Hooke. Rev. ed. SCM, 1963; McDonald, J. I. H. "Alien Grace (Luke 10:30–36): The Parable of the Good Samaritan." Pages 35–51 in *Jesus and His Parables,* ed. V. G. Shillington. T&T Clark, 1997; Ricoeur, P. "Biblical Hermeneutics." *Semeia* 4 (1975): 29–145; Scott, B. B. *Hear Then the Parable.* Fortress, 1989; Trench, R. C. *Notes on the Parables of our Lord.* 1840. John W. Parker & Son, 1853; Via, D. *The Parables.* Fortress, 1967; Wright, N. T. *Jesus and the Victory of God.* SPCK, 1996; Wright, S. I. *The Voice of Jesus.* Paternoster, 2000.

Stephen I. Wright

Passion Narratives

Oral Tradition and the Passion Narrative

Critics have long noted that the Passion Narrative (PN) constitutes the most closely articulated section in each of the Gospels. Elsewhere, we have series of episodes whose connection with each other in terms of narrative logic is often not obvious; in the PN, as Karl Schmidt famously observed, "with compelling logic and necessity one event succeeds another" (303). "The passion 'from Gethsemane to the grave,' . . . is the longest consecutive action recounted of Jesus, quite different from the series of vignettes that constitute the ministry" (Brown, 1:11). What is more, the versions of the PN in the Synoptic Evangelists (Mark 14:1–15:47; Matt. 26:1–27:66; Luke 22:1–23:56) and John (18:1–19:42) all recognizably tell the same story, with the same characters playing the same roles, and the same general sequence of events—Last Supper, Gethsemane, Judas's betrayal, the arrest, Peter's denial, appearances before the Sanhedrin and Pilate, and the rest.

There is a reason for this coherence and uniformity. "We proclaim a Messiah crucified," said Paul (1 Cor. 1:23a AT). That proclamation could never be divorced from another: "He has been raised" (Mark 16:6 NRSV). Yet, it was crucifixion, the shameful death of a slave or rebel, that was a "stumbling block" or "foolishness" to many (1 Cor. 1:23b), and that must therefore be narrated in full. And narrated it clearly was, *orally* narrated. As Paul said, writing in about 56 CE, "faith comes from what is heard" (Rom. 10:17 NRSV). The PN's source in oral tradition is evident. As Albert Bates Lord (one of the pioneers of twentieth-century oral studies) pointed out, the overall form of the PN "resonates" with the patterns of oral heroic narrative: Jesus' death is surrounded by motifs—such as betrayal by someone close and the failure of friends—that occur in other narratives of heroic death: Samson, Heracles, Arthur, and Roland, to name a few. Such heroes are always in some sense greater than the death that overtakes them, and always in some sense die for others (57–58).

But as students of orality also point out, those who listen to oral narrative, and therefore those who create or hand it on, tend to be conservative with regard to structure and content. In an oral or partly oral culture, no narrative intended to be heard can depart very far from accepted tradition—as anyone who has told stories to small children will know. It is likely, then, that when the Evangelists came to write down the passion of their Lord, in distinction from the rest of the story, they found themselves faced with a basic narrative pattern that brooked little change. Something like the Last Supper, the visit to Gethsemane, the arrest, the appearances before the Sanhedrin and Pilate, the scourging, and the crucifixion constituted a structure too familiar to be avoided and too sacred to be altered, even if they had wished to do so—and there is no reason to suppose that they did.

The Question of History

"*Passus est sub Pontio Pilato.* He suffered under Pontius Pilate." So Christians claim, thereby linking their faith to history—the kind of history that could, in principle, be verified by ordinary historical method. What then actually *happened* on the first Maundy Thursday and Good Friday? Some would suggest that nothing happened—or nothing that we can know: the PN is a tale created by various members of the early Christian communities to justify their bids for power. So John Dominic Crossan: "It seems to me most likely that those closest to Jesus knew almost nothing of the details of the event. They only knew that Jesus had been crucified, outside Jerusalem, at the time of Passover, and probably through some conjunction of imperial and sacerdotal authority" (405). Why Crossan thinks this, he does not explain, and his notion that those closest to Jesus knew almost nothing (Did they simply lose interest? Were they *bored*?) may seem to place more strain on our credulity than the alternative. The PN does pose problems, and there certainly are points when we wish we knew more. (What, exactly, was the nature of the trial before Caiaphas? What was the relationship between that trial and the trial before Pilate?) Yet overall the PN is straightforward enough. This is not the place to examine in depth its historical problems and possibilities. As scholars such as Raymond Brown (*Death of the Messiah*) and N. T. Wright (*Jesus and the Victory of God*) have shown in massive detail, one does not have to be a fundamentalist or a literalist—one need only use the ordinary historical-critical criteria of coherence and multiple attestation—to discern behind the PN a scenario that is both coherent and comprehensible.

The Meaning of the Cross

According to the Scriptures. Analysis of the PN in all four Gospels reveals example after example of OT quotation, allusion, or influence. Thus—to pick virtually at random—false witnesses stand up against Jesus at his trial (Mark 14:56–59 et par.), so setting him with the righteous sufferer of the psalms (Pss. 27; 109). Jesus is silent when accused (Mark 14:60–61 et par.; 15:4 et par.; Luke 23:9), as is the Lord's Servant (Isa. 53:7). He is condemned to shameful death, as is the "just one" (Wis. 2:12–20). He is struck and spat upon (Matt. 26:65–68 et par.; Mark 15:7–20 et par.; John 18:22), as is the Servant (Isa. 50:6). Soldiers cast lots for his garment (Mark 15:24 et par.; John 19:24), passersby mock him (Mark 15:27–32 et par.), and when he thirsts, bystanders offer him vinegar (John 19:28–30), all again identifying him with the righteous sufferer (Pss. 22:7–8, 18; 69:3, 21; 109:25; Wis. 2:18). Skeptical critics have viewed this as evidence that the PN lacks historical basis, being merely tissues of invention based on Deutero-Isaiah, the Psalms, and Wisdom. That, of course, is to miss the point. Our choice of style and language is not primarily an indication of the truth or falsehood of what we say, but *of the significance with which we wish to endow our words*. Deutero-Isaiah spoke of Israel's deliverance from exile in terms that recalled the exodus, not because Israel's exile was not real—manifestly it was—but to indicate the significance of its deliverance (Isa. 49:8–11). So it is with the PN. The evangelists use the language of Scripture (as, we may assume, did their sources: see 1 Cor. 15:3–4!) precisely to indicate that the PN is *not* simply the recital of one more execution of a deluded messianic pretender (of which, as is evident from Josephus, there were plenty). Instead, the PN is a description of events that took place, which "let the Scriptures be fulfilled" (Mark 14:49 NRSV// Matt. 26:56; Luke 22:37; 24:44; John 20:9; Acts 13:27), so that these events are in continuity with the story of God's dealing with Israel and the world, God's call and God's promise, from Adam to the exile.

The Son of Man Must Die. Nineteenth- and twentieth-century critics often noted that the various versions of the PN were all of "disproportionate" length in comparison to the rest of the Gospel narratives; and so, by the standards of nineteenth- and twentieth-century biography,

they were. But the Gospels are not nineteenth- or twentieth-century biographies; they are Greco-Roman "lives"—and by the standards of Greco-Roman "lives," the PN is not particularly long, for the ancients took great interest in how notable people died (*exitus illustrium virorum*). How one died showed who one really was. This is the literary tradition in which the Gospels stand (Bryan 27–64; Burridge 164–66, 208–9). So Jesus, facing his death, remains faithful, repeatedly knowing what will happen and that God will vindicate him (Mark 14:8, 18–21, 25, 27–31, 36, et par.). Caiaphas's question at the trial is to the point. "Are you the Messiah, the Son of the Blessed One?" (Mark 14:61 et par.). Is it by *you* that God's kingdom will come? When Jesus replies, "I am," and continues to look for God to vindicate him (Mark 14:62 et par.), it is (for all the ironic echoes of Wisdom) in one sense appropriate that the Sanhedrin hands him over to death. That is, they hand him over to God, to be vindicated or not. *Is* he the Messiah? "Let this Messiah, this King of Israel, come down now from the cross, that we may see and believe" (Mark 15:32 et par.). *That, pace* Nikos Kazantzakis, and not fantasies about married life with Mary Magdalene, is truly the last temptation of Christ. Will he, after all, seek the kingdom in a selfish way rather than God's way? Will he balk when he sees that God has "forsaken" him (15:34)? He will not. Therefore, "when the centurion, who stood facing him, saw how he breathed his last, he said, 'Truly this man was the Son of God!'" (Mark 15:39 AT et par.; John 20:30). *How you die shows who you truly are.*

For Our Sins. Was that the only significance of Jesus' death? Not according to the PN. Nor is it the only reason why his death was (as the Gospels repeatedly say) "necessary [*dei*]" (RSV: Mark 8:31//Matt. 16:21//Luke 9:22; Luke 24:7, 44; John 3:14; 12:34; cf. Mark 9:31; 10:33–34, 45; 12:6–8; 14:24; Acts 2:23). Jesus himself, on the eve of his passion, says that he gives his life "as a ransom for many [*pollōn*]" (Mark 10:45 et par.), echoing Deutero-Isaiah: "Through his suffering, . . . my servant shall justify many [LXX: *polloi*], and their guilt he shall bear" (Isa. 53:11 MT/AT). In both cases, *polloi* implies, not "many as opposed to all," but a contrast between the one who makes the offering and the "many" for whom it avails (cf. Rom. 5:15–19). The earliest forms of the Last Supper narrative—the one part of the PN that Paul tells as fully as do the Gospels—spell out this "ransom" theology (1 Cor. 11:23–26; Mark 14:22–26 et par.). According to Paul, Jesus tells his disciples that his body is offered "for you" (1 Cor. 11:24); in Mark, Jesus' "blood of the covenant" is shed "for many" (14:24 et par.). In both cases the image is still Deutero-Isaiah's picture of the Lord's Servant: "It was our infirmities that he bore, our sufferings that he endured; . . . he was pierced for our offenses, crushed for our sins; upon him was the chastisement that makes us whole; by his stripes we were healed" (Isa. 53:4–5 AT). "Blood of the covenant" implies the new community created by Jesus' death, as was the old at Sinai (Exod. 24:4–8).

The PN, then, makes clear that Christ's death is effective in this way. The question as to *how* it is thus effective—the matter of "theories of atonement"—is never raised, either by the PN or elsewhere in the NT. (Perhaps that is why, of the various theories devised throughout the centuries—juridical, mythical, psychological—the universal church has never recognized any in particular as *the* right one.) What the PN does do, however, is to show us how we may *appropriate* Christ's death. It does this in two ways. First, it *tells the story*. What then? We are to *listen*, for "faith comes by hearing," faith implies baptism, and baptism is "into [Christ's] death," wherein we are "buried with him . . . so that as Christ was raised from the dead, . . . we too might live in newness of life" (Rom. 6:3–4 RSV). That is how *initially* we appropriate Christ's death. Second, our *continuing* appropriation is prescribed in Jesus' instruction at the Supper, "Do this for my *anamnēsis* [EVV: remembrance/memorial]" (Luke 22:19; 1 Cor. 11:24–25 AT), that is, "that God may remember me" (Jeremias 159–65). That, Paul says, means the remembrance of Christ's death: "For as often as you eat this bread and drink the cup, you announce the Lord's death until he comes" (1 Cor. 11:26 AT). Throughout the Scriptures, when God remembers, God acts, with saving grace (Gen. 9:14–17; Exod. 2:24; 6:5; Lev. 26:42; Pss. 9:12; 98:3).

Bibliography

Brown, R. *The Death of the Messiah*. 2 vols. Doubleday, 1994; Bryan, C. *A Preface to Mark*. Oxford University Press, 1993; Burridge, R. *What Are the Gospels?* SNTSMS 70. Cambridge University Press, 1992; Crossan, J. D. *The Cross That Spoke*. Harper & Row, 1988; Jeremias, J. *The Eucharistic Words of Jesus*. Blackwell, 1955; Lord, A. B. *Oral Traditional Literature*. Slavica, 1981; Schmidt, K. *Der Rahmen der Geschichte Jesu*. Trowitzsch, 1919; Wright, N. T. *Jesus and the Victory of God*. Fortress, 1996.

Christopher Bryan

Patriarchal Narratives

The narratives of Gen. 12–50, which portray the patriarchs Abraham, Isaac, Jacob, and Joseph (and others, including the matriarchs, who play an important but smaller role) are among the most memorable and resonant in the whole of Scripture. They are also theologically crucial. For, despite the foundational role of Moses for the Torah as a whole, it is Abraham and his response to God's call that stand at the outset of Israel's story. Deuteronomy in particular reiterates that Yahweh's commitment to Israel is in fulfillment of his antecedent commitment to the patriarchs (Deut. 7:7–8; 9:4–5, 25–29; cf. Exod. 32:11–14). And Paul sees Abraham's response to God as embodying that which identifies Christian faith also (Rom. 4; Gal. 3).

Two common obstacles to theological interpretation of this material need brief mention. First is the ancient and recurring difficulty of the seeming immorality of at least some of what the patriarchs do (see Bainton; Childs 212–14, 218–21), which has recently been exploited to offer an overall negative portrayal of Abraham (Davies; Gunn and Fewell; evaluated in Moberly, *Bible*, 170–76). Part of the difficulty here lies in the lack of specific evaluation on the part of the narrator (so different from the evaluation of kings in 1 and 2 Kings); but, of course, narratives may be meant to invite disapproval as well as approval. More generally, the narratives show God working with recalcitrant material—most obviously, but by no means solely, Jacob/Israel—and slowly molding people to his purposes; this is moral since it involves growth in integrity and faithfulness, but it resists easy moralizing about the process (see Moberly, *Old*, 130–38).

Second, there is the question of genre: how far, and in what way, are the narratives historical, and what difference should this make to their theological interpretation? Even if Moses wrote the patriarchal narratives, their written form would be at a distance of several centuries from the events depicted. The scholarly consensus is that their composition is long after Moses (perhaps in the tenth century BCE, or subsequently; there is little consensus on the specifics). Generally speaking, it seems clear that, although much of the patriarchal material most likely has ancient roots (Moberly, *Old*, 191–98), it has been developed and molded over time and has acquired the coloring of differing historical contexts—a kind of snowballing process that conventionally leads to the literature thus produced being called "legendary." Since this kind of material is widespread and meaningful in most cultures, there need be no objection in principle to its presence in the OT—in theological terms, the validation and appropriation of "legend" by the Spirit. Von Rad (31–43) suggested that "legend" is characterized by deeper existential and symbolic dimensions than conventional history, and that specific narratives may concretize, in a single event, a process of life with God that in fact stretched over many generations, a factor that can give such narratives a sense of depth and lived wisdom.

One fundamental theological issue, felt particularly by Jews (see, e.g., Green), is posed by the pre-Moses context of the patriarchs. If Israel's normative knowledge of God and way of life is given in Mosaic torah, how are those who live pre-torah to be understood? The Genesis narratives themselves do not depict the patriarchs as observant of, say, Sabbath or kashruth (distinguishing clean from unclean animals, and only eating the former), and in general they display a religious ethos with marked differences from that of Mosaic Yahwism (Moberly, *Old*, 79–104; Pagolu). Yet, the predominant Jewish instinct has been to see the patriarchs as religiously observant in accordance with Mosaic norms—as summed up in the rabbinic dictum: "Abraham our Father fulfilled the entire *torah* before it was given, even *'eruv tavshilin* [a rabbinic expedient for permitting the preparation of Sabbath food on the preceding festival day]" (*b. Yoma* 28b). Thus, the earliest retelling of the Genesis narratives that has come down to us, the book of Jubilees (probably ca. mid-second century BCE), introduces extensive Mosaic observances into the text. And it is likely that within the biblical texts themselves, despite their generally distinctive ethos, certain elements of Israel's faith have been utilized to shape and interpret some of the narratives (in accordance with the "snowball" nature of some of the texts). This is most obvious in the explicit depiction of Abraham as keeping God's "charge, commandments, statutes, and laws" (cf. Gen. 26:5 NRSV), but is also apparent in several Abraham narratives, especially Gen. 22 (see Moberly, *Bible*, 71–183).

Here the Jewish concerns are analogous to the Christian concerns as to how, if the normative knowledge of God and life is given in Jesus Christ, Israel's pre-Christ literature should be understood from a Christian perspective (see Moberly, *Old*, esp. ch. 4). Just as the Jewish instinct has been to assimilate the patriarchs to later norms, so too there has been a strong Christian instinct to see key figures in the OT as, in effect, Christians even before Christ. Such a move is given supreme expression in Paul's account of Abraham's faith, which also exploits Abraham's pre-torah context (Gal. 3; Rom. 4). In general, Christians have developed two prime theological concepts for appropriating the OT as Christian Scripture. On the one hand, the notion of promise and fulfillment sees the OT as intrinsically looking beyond itself in terms of the divine purpose it depicts. On the other hand, typology/figuration enables the Christian reader to see OT figures and events as in some way modeling a Christian pattern. It is therefore striking that precisely these two moves seem to have been made by the writers of the Pentateuch when they preserved the patriarchal traditions within the context of Israel's Scriptures. On the one hand, the divine promise that sets the context for Abraham's story (Gen. 12:1–3) looks toward the (postpatriarchal) people of Israel, who are to be, in some sense, a blessing to the nations. On the other hand, Abraham is a type of Israel, whether in a kind of exodus from Egypt (12:10–20) or from Ur of the Chaldeans (15:7—which could resonate with Israel's return from exile in Babylonia), or in demonstrating the kind of total responsiveness to God that should characterize Israel in its obedience to the Ten Commandments (Exod. 20:20; cf. Gen. 22:1, 12, where the key terms "test" and "fear" recur). The theological problem of the appropriate Christian approach to the OT, together with the characteristic Christian resolution, can be seen to be anticipated in Israel's appropriation of the patriarchal traditions. This fact should increase confidence in contemporary renewed attempts to rearticulate the concept of figuration, with a view to the use of the OT within Christian faith (see Seitz; esp. Dawson, ch. 1).

Finally, what are the overarching theological concerns that characterize the narratives about the three prime human figures, Abraham, Jacob/Israel, and Joseph? Abraham's life is framed by the divine promise, primarily of descendants and blessing (Gen. 12:2–3), but also of a land where these are to be realized (12:7). His story can be read as exploring the dynamics of living with promises from God. This involves patience, waiting, endurance—living with apparent lack of fulfillment. As Martin Buber once put it (22), "To believe means to follow in the will of God, even in regard to the temporal realization of His will. (We only grasp the full vitality of the fundamental Biblical insight when we realize the fact of human mortality over against God's eternity)." Also necessary is a supreme trust and obedience when God seems to contradict himself, as when Abraham is required to take Isaac, at long last born as his heir, and reduce him to ashes and smoke in a sacrifice (Gen. 22:1–19).

The most complex figure is Jacob, who from the womb is favored by God over his older twin, Esau, and explicitly personifies the nation/people Israel (25:23). Yet Jacob appears to be a heartless cheat and liar (25:29–34; 27:1–45), who only meets his match in trickery when he stays with his uncle Laban (chs. 29–31). But it is to a fearful Jacob on the run that God appears with promise and without rebuke (28:10–22). And when Jacob fearfully returns to face Esau, his mysterious encounter with God at the Jabbok gives him a new name and anticipates his gracious acceptance by Esau (32:3–33:11). Hereafter, Jacob/Israel at least begins to perform acts of devotion to God (33:20)—though he remains a poor father and a self-pitying old man. Here are some of the deep mysteries of grace and vocation.

The main concern within the lengthy account of Joseph and his brothers is explicitly divine sovereignty over human willfulness and malice: "Even though you [Joseph's brothers] intended to do harm to me [Joseph], God intended it for good, in order to keep alive many people, as is being done today" (50:20 NRSV/AT; cf. 45:5–8). In this, the narrative is comparable to the NT passion narrative, where human fear, treachery, and brutal murder are what they are yet also serve God's purposes (Acts 2:22–24). Yet, the narrative also presents the maturing of Joseph from a foolish and indeed priggish youth (Gen. 37:2–11), through a path beset by malice and abandonment (37:18–36; 39:1–40:23), into a wise and merciful man of power. For Joseph is able to learn to construe his youthful dreams, which at the time seemingly meant only self-promotion at the expense of others, as showing the responsibility of a power used for the benefit of others. Thus, 42:9 shows that Joseph's memory of his dreams does not lead to crowing over his brothers but to his initiating a subtle process of reconciliation.

See also Passion Narratives; Typology

Bibliography

Bainton, R. "The Immoralities of the Patriarchs according to the Exegesis of the Late Middle Ages and the Reformers." *HTR* 23 (1930): 39–49; Buber, M. *Two Types of Faith*, trans. N. Goldhawk. Routledge & Kegan Paul; Childs, B. *Old Testament Theology in a Canonical Context*. SCM, 1985; Davies, P. "Male Bonding: A Tale of Two Buddies." Pages 95–113 in *Whose Bible Is It Anyway?* JSOTSup 204. Sheffield Academic Press, 1995; Dawson, J. D. *Christian Figural Reading and the Fashioning of Identity*. University of California Press, 2002; Green, A. *Devotion and Commandment*. HUCA Press, 1989; Gunn, D., and D. Fewell. *Narrative in the Hebrew Bible*. Oxford University Press, 1993; Moberly, R. W. L. *The Bible, Theology, and Faith*. Cambridge University Press, 2000; idem. *The Old Testament of the Old Testament*. Fortress, 1992; Pagolu, A. *The Religion of the Patriarchs*. JSOTSup 277. Sheffield Academic Press, 1998; Rad, Gerhard von. *Genesis*, trans. J. Marks. 3rd ed. SCM, 1972; Seitz, C. *Figured Out*. Westminster John Knox, 2001.

R. W. L. Moberly

Patristic Biblical Interpretation

Here the patristic period is taken to span the time from the NT to the early fifth century. John Chrysostom in the East and Augustine in the West left massive exegetical resources, which had a lasting influence, and their time provides a fitting terminus.

The Earliest Biblical Interpretation— the Fulfillment of Prophecy

Interpretation was first focused on the books that Christians came to recognize as the Old Testament—there were no other sacred books for them. In the earliest Christian writings—those that became the New Testament—the basic approaches that would shape patristic exegesis are already traceable. The fulfillment of prophecy is the fundamental theme, already present in the allusive way that Gospel narratives are articulated, bringing out for those with knowledge of the Jewish Scriptures the ways in which these narratives replay the stories or act out the prophecies to be found therein. It is made quite explicit in Matthew's Gospel, which repeatedly points out that this (event or saying) was to fulfill what was said by the prophet, followed by a quotation. There can be little doubt that the earliest Christian communities searched the Scriptures to discover the significance of Jesus. They needed to reinterpret traditional messianic prophecies to fit with the person and career of the one they claimed was Messiah; they also needed to find prophecies for the unexpected aspects of his life, such as his death by crucifixion. Rapidly a battery of proof texts was assembled.

Painting with a broad brush, we can state that the outcome of this was a divergence between the key interests of rabbinic and Christian interpreters of the same texts. Within the Jewish tradition halakah predominated, as rabbis sought to explicate the Law in a way that provided clear guidance about the minutiae of everyday life, so that the people would remain obedient to the God who had called them his own and given them the Torah. Within the Christian tradition, however, the ethnic marks of the Jew (circumcision and Torah) rapidly ceased to occupy center stage. The Scriptures, taken over from the Jews in their Greek rendition (the LXX), became almost entirely a work of prophecy. In it could be traced the whole future that had come to pass in Christ, was being enacted in the life of the church, and would be fully consummated at the End. The fulfillment of prophecy was anticipated in Jewish tradition—indeed, the Dead Sea Scrolls have underlined the propensity for Jews of the period to be looking for such fulfillment, and reading the Scriptures in the way the Christians would. Christian reading had its roots in contemporary messianic movements within a diverse Jewish community. Yet the christological reading of the entire Scriptures, and the implied supersession of Judaism by Christianity, would sharply radicalize the outcome of methods adopted from Jewish predecessors.

In the mid-second century, Justin Martyr knew that "memoirs of the Apostles" were read at Christian gatherings; yet in his first *Apology*, he tells the story of Jesus through quotations from the prophetic Scriptures. The argument from prophecy was central to his apologetic enterprise. Another of his works was the *Dialogue with Trypho*. Trypho is the representative Jew who does not accept the Christian reading of the Jewish Scriptures. To neutralize this objection was crucial to Justin's apologetic. Here then, we find examples of Christian prophetic reading that would become persistent throughout the period, such as the following (from Justin, *1 Apol.* 32): In Gen. 49:8–12 Justin takes Judah, the lion, to represent Christ, from whom the scepter will not depart "until tribute comes to him and the obedience of the peoples is his." The Gentiles coming to Christ fulfilled this word. "Binding his foal to the vine and his donkey's colt to the choice vine, he washes his garments in wine and his robe in the blood of grapes." How could this not be a reference to the passion narrative? Throughout the patristic period this text was taken to be christological and eucharistic.

This legacy shaped interpretation of the OT. Always it foreshadowed the truths of the NT. Sometimes it did this through riddling oracles, whose enigmas and symbols had to be teased out to see what they were pointing toward. Often, as in the case of the Delphic oracle, only hindsight revealed the true meaning. This encouraged a piecemeal reading of texts as pregnant sayings, to be lifted out of context and read in the light of a new reality. It also encouraged the treatment of words as tokens and their combination as a code to be cracked. A form of allegory was implicit in this approach.

Sometimes the text prefigured (or provided a "type" of) what was to come. "Typology" has been taken to presuppose the workings of providence in parallel events. The classic example, to be found in paschal homilies throughout the period, from Melito of Sardis to Gregory Nazianzus, is the way the exodus and Passover anticipates salvation in Christ. As the blood of the Passover lamb protected the Israelites from the angel of death and enabled their escape from Pharaoh, so the blood of Christ, "our Passover," protects the church and enables redemption from the devil and his angels. The crossing of the Red Sea anticipates the water of baptism. Already in the Gospels the manna in the wilderness anticipated the stories of Jesus feeding the multitude. The basic reading of the exodus narrative along these lines was elaborated with more and more allegorical detail, but the core of it is a paralleling of saving events, which gives plausibility to the standard account of typology. However, "typology" is a modern coinage, and the ancients saw "types" and "symbols" all over the place, not just in parallel events. As long as Moses held up his arms, the Israelites prevailed against the Amalekites: his outstretched arms were a type of the cross. Ephraim would suggest that a bird could only fly when it made the sign of the cross with its outstretched wings, and call this a type. Job became a "type" of patience. In other words, types were various, but prophetic types were a distinctive feature of early Christian exegesis, with their roots in the Bible itself.

Thus, the fundamental approach to reading the OT was to treat it as prophecy, with symbols foreshadowing future fulfillment. But it was not the only way.

The Homiletic Imperative

The principal place in which the reading and interpretation of Scripture took place was worship. Early Christian worship owed much to precedents from the Jewish synagogue, including the reading and exposition of passages from the sacred texts. The letters and treatises of the earliest period suggest that this too would tease out prophecies and assert Christian truth against Judaism. However, homiletic reading also went in another direction: it was concerned both with detailing a Christian way of life, and with spelling out the consequences of failing to live according to that way. The imminence of judgment and the all-seeing oversight (*episcopē*) of the God who could see even into the heart is a theme that figures strongly in the literature of the second century.

So, in this context the stories of God's people in the OT Scriptures are often treated rather differently. Both the Epistle to the Hebrews and the work known as *2 Clement*, probably the earliest homily we have, are cases in point. The Christian congregation is identified as liable to fall into the same dangers as beset God's people in the past (e.g., Heb. 3:7–4:13). The prophetic warnings to Israel become warnings to the church. Christians should beware lest they deserve the words of Isa. 29:13: "This people honors me with their lips, but their heart is far from me" (*2 Clem.* 3.5). The predominant note is exhortation, enabled by identification with the text: "The Lord says, 'Continually my name is blasphemed among the nations.' . . . Wherein is it blasphemed? In that you do not do what I desire. For when the nations hear from our mouth the oracles of God, they wonder at these good and great sayings; then learning of our [unworthy] deeds . . . , then they are turned to blasphemy, saying this is some myth and delusion" (*2 Clem.* 13.2–3).

The reading of Scripture as exemplary was by far the most common approach in the patristic period. Obedience to God's moral commands was the subject of most preaching, and God's will was discerned in Scripture in a variety of ways. Injunctions in the Gospels and Epistles were set alongside the Ten Commandments and sayings from the Wisdom literature to spell out the way of life and the way of death. Characters in Scripture became "types" of particular virtues—Job as a type of patience has already been mentioned. Scripture became the warrant for the key Christian virtues of charity, humility, and asceticism. This tradition of "ethical reading" would reach its apogee in the two exegetes, John Chrysostom and Augustine, who mark the end of our period. Good examples of the range of tactics adopted to effect an ethical reading may be found in Chrysostom's various homilies on the apostle Paul, as well as his persistent habit of tacking ethical exhortation to each homily in his great commentary series on the various books of the OT and NT.

Gnostic Reading and the Need for Criteria

The second century was a time when forms of early Christianity were very diverse. Toward the end of the century, Irenaeus, Bishop of Lyons, found it necessary to try to articulate what was wrong with "*gnōsis*, falsely so-called." *Gnōsis* is the Greek word for "knowledge," but it came to be associated with a variety of sects eventually rejected as heretical. Christian Gnostics not only produced texts, including gospels such as the *Gospel of Thomas* and the *Gospel of Truth*, but also interpreted texts to suit their ideas. They were fascinated by Genesis as a cosmological text, and seem to have derived some of their ideas from the Epistles of Paul. The first commentary on the Gospel of John that we know of was written by a Gnostic, Heracleon. Marcion seems to have shared some of their ideas, but perhaps arrived at them differently. He thought the God of the Jews had nothing to do with the Father of Jesus Christ, and the Jewish books should be rejected, delimiting Scripture to the (edited) Epistles of Paul and an expurgated version of Luke's Gospel. Prophecy and its fulfillment were not the main interests of Marcion and the Gnostics. Irenaeus had to deal with questions of what texts were authoritative and by what criteria they were to be interpreted properly.

Irenaeus correctly identifies as a major problem the decontextualizing involved in allegory and piecemeal interpretation. What the Gnostics did was to read their own system into the text by abstracting and rearranging the material. They ended up with something that the prophets did not announce, the Lord did not teach, and the apostles did not hand down. They attempted to make ropes of sand in applying the parables of the Lord, or prophetic utterances, or apostolic statements to their plausible scheme, altering the scriptural context and connection. "It is just as if there was a beautiful representation of a king made in a mosaic by a skilled artist, and one altered the arrangement of the pieces of stone into the shape of a dog or a fox, and then could assert that this was the original representation of a king. In much the same manner, they stitch together old wives' tales and wresting sayings and parables, however they may, from the context, [and] attempt to fit the oracles of God into their myths" (*Haer.* 1.8.1). For Irenaeus, it was vital to recognize the unity of the one God revealed in the unity of the Scriptures. In order to ensure this, the diverse Scriptures must be interpreted in the light of the Rule of Faith. Irenaeus gives us the content of this in a variety of different forms—it is clearly not yet fashioned into a fixed creed. Yet the essential features of a creed are there, along with a number of stereotyped phrases. Irenaeus has realized that Scripture cannot simply interpret Scripture, but the theological traditions of the church are necessary to establish a correct reading. He outlines the "overarching story" that the Bible tells in order to provide the right context for reading different scriptural passages. The story begins with creation, tells of the fall and of God's remedies for the situation, and points toward the future. The one God, through the inspiration of the Holy Spirit, foretells redemption in Christ. This is the key to discerning the king's image in the scriptural mosaic.

Irenaeus and others, like Tertullian, challenged Marcion, pointing out that the Christian books becoming known as the NT presuppose the Creator of the world to which the books of the OT bear witness. There is only one God, and the key to God's revelation is the story of promise and fulfillment. In ensuing doctrinal debates, appeal would be made to scriptural texts, often lifted out of context and formed into collages of proof texts. But in the end it would be "the mind of Scripture" that would shape interpretation of details (e.g., in Athanasius's polemic against Arius), and that mind would be summed up in the creeds. Thus, these arguments, which are fundamentally theological, shape the patristic approach to interpretation.

As we have seen, the notion of prophetic fulfillment itself generated allegory, and arguments against heretics rarely appealed to more-literal readings. When methodological debates emerged, appeal is made to the same overarching story of creation and redemption. "Scripture" is a theological concept, and its interpretation was to be guided by theological and moral principles, rather than literary ones. This we find explicit in Augustine.

The Rise of Scholarship and of Questions of Methodology

Scripture is written in human language, and like any other text it requires careful attention from scholars trained in exegetical techniques. The social status of Christians meant that this development was largely deferred until the third century. Not surprisingly, it was in Alexandria, the home of both classical and Jewish scholarship, that the Christian equivalent was born.

The work of Origen was always controversial, and retrospectively many of his ideas were condemned, yet he was also profoundly influential. He was the first to produce commentaries on most of the books of the Bible. He accepted the Rule of Faith as fundamental but thought that it did not offer answers to every legitimate question. Some of his speculations were later treated

as heretical doctrines, his allegorical methods of interpretation were also contested, and modern estimates have sometimes treated his theology as more Platonic than biblical. He was, however, Christianity's first real scholar and intellectual.

In antiquity, education was through the study of classical texts, first with the grammarian as one learned to read, then with the rhetorician as one learned to compose speeches, then, for the privileged few, with the philosopher as one sought the truth about the way things are. What Origen did was to replace the classical texts of Greek culture with the Bible, adopting the philological methods used in the schools. To this day much commentary is concerned with the same questions: What is the original wording of the text? Can we gain understanding by going behind translations to the original Hebrew, or by comparing different versions? Are figures of speech, such as irony or metaphors, employed in the text? What does the text refer to? Is there background information that elucidates it? And so on. Even those who would criticize his allegory would use the same exegetical techniques. Origen professionalized Christian reading of the Bible, while incorporating and systematizing existing Christian traditions, such as the christological reading of the OT.

At bottom, Origen's reading of Scripture was profoundly theological. The Bible being the word of God, the most important thing was to discern the intention of the Holy Spirit. The whole of Scripture was a unity, and not a jot or tittle was without its purpose. Most of the Bible could be taken straightforwardly, and its moral commands were meant to be followed. However, the ceremonial prescriptions of the law, such as circumcision and the practice of sacrifice, were not: these foreshadowed the "bloodless sacrifices" of the new covenant. Indeed, most of the OT prefigured the NT. Thus, Origen adopted the traditional Christian approach to the Jewish Scriptures and took it further. He suggested that there was a deeper, spiritual sense to be read throughout the Bible, and the difficulties (*aporiai*) in Scripture were deliberately placed there to stimulate the soul to search for this deeper meaning. Indeed, using philological techniques, he identified metaphors, enigmas, and parables as signs that the text was not simply to be read "literally," but constantly pointed beyond itself to spiritual realities. Every contradiction or inconsistency could likewise provoke one to discern some profound truth. This was the basis of his allegorical approach to meaning. The Bible was written in code, and one needed the inspiration of the Holy Spirit to read it as intended.

A century later a group often known as the Antiochenes reacted against Origen's position. Yet, they actually had a great deal in common with him. They used philological techniques and looked for "insight" (*theōria*) into the meaning of Scripture, but they insisted that *allēgoria* was but one figure of speech and only to be acknowledged where the text itself indicated it was present. They were most concerned that Origen's allegorical reading of narratives in the Bible undermined the "overarching story" (*historia*). They were as concerned as he was not to take literally things like the talking serpent in Genesis, but they resisted spiritualizing away the event of the fall. God really was the Creator, who had providentially ordered everything; Redemption made no sense without the fall; God's promises were fulfilled in the incarnation of the Son, and would be consummated in the *eschaton*. Their discernment of deeper truths meant finding correct doctrine and morality in the Scriptures. Origen (*Comm. Matt.* 11) had understood the feeding of the multitude in terms of spiritual feeding, the five loaves and two fish symbolizing Scripture and the Logos. John Chrysostom (*Hom. Matt.* 49, on Matt. 14:19) suggested that Christ looked up to heaven to prove he was from the Father; he used the loaves and fish, rather than creating food out of nothing, to stop the mouths of dualist heretics like Marcion and Manichaeus; and he let the crowds become hungry and only gave them loaves and fish equally distributed in order to teach the crowd humility, temperance, and charity. The debate about interpreting Scripture was partly methodological, but strongly colored by theological interest.

Augustine's **De doctrina christiana**

Augustine's intellectual formation meant that he came under influences similar to those affecting Origen a century and a half earlier. He had embarked on a career as rhetor and so knew the philological methods of the schools. His conversion to Christianity came via Platonism. *De doctrina christiana* provides his considered approach to biblical interpretation. Most of the first three books were written thirty years earlier than the rest, but the whole has an impressive consistency.

In this work Augustine set out to give guidance to those who had to interpret Scripture in the church. He refuses to duplicate what people could get from textbooks or from school education, yet everywhere reveals his debt to the philological

tradition. Indeed, he opens the discussion with a distinction that has its roots there. For in composition it was a commonplace that the subject matter (or *inventio*) should be determined first, and its appropriate verbal dress crafted later; in reading the same distinction was used in considering the intention of the author. So Augustine spends the first book of *De doctrina christiana* determining the *res* of Scripture—the "things" Scripture is all about, and in the later books, this sense of what Scripture is all about provides a criterion for solving some of the verbal puzzles that the text presents.

Although Augustine approaches the whole thing in a somewhat novel way, treating language as "signs" pointing beyond themselves, his whole approach is in line with the trends we have observed. It is fundamentally theological and moral. For him, the subject matter of Scripture is love of God and neighbor. The interpretation of every text is to be judged by this criterion. Like Irenaeus, Origen, Athanasius, and the Antiochenes, Augustine affirms the unity of the Bible, and that unity is to be found in its underlying sense, the mind of Scripture, the intent of the Holy Spirit. Exegetical problems are meant to challenge our pride and lead to wisdom and humility. Without the tradition summed up in the creed and lived in Christian practice, it is impossible to discern aright what Scripture is about.

Conclusion

Patristic biblical interpretation was theological through and through. Christology and ethics were primary interests in reading the Bible. Some outcomes—such as the fathers' anti-Judaism, their tendency to assume prophecies were to be found everywhere and to take texts out of context, and their propensity toward allegory—are properly treated with caution in modern scholarship. On the other hand, we would know more about theological reading of Scripture if we could relearn from the fathers the notion that Scripture is a fountain. Many different readers can drink from it without it running dry (an image used by Ephraim the Syrian) because it is God's word, before which we sit judged rather than judging.

See also Allegory; Augustine; Gnosticism; Jewish-Christian Dialogue; Jewish Exegesis; Rule of Faith; Typology

Bibliography

Ackroyd, P., and C. F. Evans, eds. *The Cambridge History of the Bible*. Vol. 1, Cambridge University Press, 1970; Augustine. *Teaching Christianity*, trans. E. Hill.

In vol. 1.11 of *The Works of St. Augustine*, ed. J. Rotelle. New City, 1996; Campenhausen, H. von. *The Formation of the Christian Bible*, trans. J. A. Baker. Fortress, 1972; Dawson, D. *Allegorical Readers and Cultural Revision in Ancient Alexandria*. University of California Press, 1992; Droge, A. *Homer or Moses?* HUT 26. Mohr/Siebeck, 1989; Fishbane, M. *Biblical Interpretation in Ancient Israel*. Clarendon, 1985; Gamble, H. *Books and Readers in the Early Church*. Yale University Press, 1995; Grant, R., with D. Tracy. *A Short History of the Interpretation of the Bible*. 2d ed., revised and enlarged. SCM, 1984; Hanson, R. P. C. *Allegory and Event*. John Knox, 1959. Reprint, introduced by J. Trigg. Westminster John Knox, 2000; Pagels, E. *The Gnostic Paul*. Fortress, 1975. Reprint, Trinity, 1992; Simonetti, M. *Biblical Interpretation in the Early Church*, trans. J. Hughes, ed. A. Bergquist, M. Bockmuehl, and W. Horbury. T&T Clark, 1994; Skarsaune, O. *The Proof from Prophecy*. Brill, 1987; Young, F. *The Art of Performance*. Darton, Longman & Todd, 1990; idem. *Biblical Exegesis and the Formation of Christian Culture*. Cambridge University Press, 1997.

Frances M. Young

Pauline Epistles

The apostle Paul is considered by many to be the first and greatest Christian theologian. No first-generation Christian writings survive that articulate Christian belief to the extent and with the sophistication of Paul's. This article will focus on three crucial aspects of his thought in the history of the interpretation of Paul's letters—God's grace in Christ, Christ's saving death, and the dawn of the new creation in Christ (with illustrative references particularly to the undisputed letters, Romans, 1 and 2 Corinthians, Galatians, Philippians, 1 Thessalonians, and Philemon, as well as the disputed ones, 2 Thessalonians, Colossians, Ephesians, and the Pastoral Epistles).

Theologian of Grace

Paul's Letters. It is hard to identify a single theological theme that ties Paul's letters together. Indeed, their different occasions elicit precisely different thematic developments and emphases. The theme of divine grace in Christ, however, can stake a claim to being the most pervasive and central theological motif in Paul's thought, and has indeed been prominent in the interpretation of Paul's letters from earliest times to the present.

Paul's opening letter greetings and closing benedictions all contain a wish for this grace (*charis*) to the readers (cf. the customary Hellenistic "greetings" [*chairein*]), forming an inclusio and pointing to the main content of his preaching. For Paul "grace" is interchangeable with "gospel" (2 Cor. 4:15; 6:1–2; Col. 1:5–6) and the defining feature of each is Christ crucified and risen for sinners (Gal. 1:6–7). For instance, to imply that "Christ died for nothing" is to "set aside the grace of God" (Gal. 2:20–21); to "have been alienated from Christ" is to "have fallen away from grace" (Gal. 5:4; cf. Titus 2:11). Augustine's epithet for Paul, "theologian of grace," is thus not inappropriate (cf. also Rom. 3:24; 4:4, 16; 5:2, 21; 6:1, 14–15; 11:5–6; 2 Cor. 8:1, 9; 9:14–15; 12:9; Eph. 1:6–7; 2:5, 8; 2 Thess. 1:12).

Grace—defined through Christ's death and resurrection as proclaimed in the gospel—entails the utter unsuitability of its recipients and thus the total gratuity of the gift, attributable only to God's unconditional love. Paul urges the Corinthians not to "receive God's grace in vain," namely, the message that "God was reconciling the world to himself in Christ, not counting people's sins against them" (2 Cor. 5:19; 6:1 TNIV). Those under sin "are justified freely by his grace through the redemption that came by Christ Jesus" (Rom. 3:24). Those under condemnation and death for trespasses have received the life-bringing grace/gift that overflowed through Jesus Christ (Rom. 5:12–21). Christ made the "poor" "rich" by his gracious gift of becoming "poor" for them (2 Cor. 8:9). In terms of salvation, they are entirely on the receiving end: "What do you have that you did not receive?" (1 Cor. 4:7; cf. 1:4–7); "All this is from God" (2 Cor. 5:18; cf. 1 Cor. 15:9–10).

Paul's Earliest Interpreters. While the Pauline theme of divine grace echoes the OT theme of divine favor or mercy, some of Paul's contemporaries were unable to fit his particular slant on the issue together with other cherished Jewish beliefs. Paul echoes their objections in rhetorical questions: Doesn't grace (by his definition) encourage sin (Rom. 6:1)? Doesn't it make the law and the Messiah into sin's instruments by implying that even those under the law, God's people, were sinners in need of grace no differently than Gentiles (Rom. 7:7a, 13a; Gal. 2:17)? Doesn't this also deny the very advantages God has given to the Jews (Rom. 3:1)? And doesn't the Jewish majority's refusal of grace in Jesus Christ impugn God's own faithfulness (Rom. 9:6; 11:1)? At the very least, doesn't grace in Christ need to be paired with the works of the law (as evidence of membership in the covenant) for justification (Gal. 1:6; 2:21)? Then there was the matter of the offensiveness and foolishness—to Jews *and* Greeks—of the message that a man shamefully crucified on a cross and under a curse was a Savior for mere believers (1 Cor. 1:18–4:13). Such grace appealed to few. Even those who accepted it had difficulty adhering to it. The Galatians were quickly captivated by "another gospel" requiring circumcision of Gentile believers and were in danger of "fall[ing] away from grace" (Gal. 5:4). The Corinthians began to gloat over their favorite leaders and became alienated from the unappealing, suffering apostle Paul, who warns them not to "receive God's grace in vain" (2 Cor. 6:1). The Roman Gentile believers, forgetting their own dependence on God's kindness, became boastful over Jews who were cut off from salvation and had to be told that these too will be shown mercy (Rom. 11:17–24, 30–32). Against all these objections Paul defends the grace of God as proclaimed in his gospel (not his opponents'; cf. Rom. 11:5–6) on the grounds that it alone is efficacious for salvation, and so truly in continuity with God's ancient purposes.

Paul claims the mother church in Jerusalem agreed with his views on the sufficiency of grace in Christ and didn't insist on Gentile circumcision, and he criticizes Cephas and Barnabas for acting contradictorily in Antioch (Gal. 2:1–14). Acts (stressing harmony in the early church) basically confirms this agreement (15:1–35), yet also presents Paul as occasionally law-observant (21:20–26). This nevertheless seems consistent with his self-description as a Jew to Jews, as one under the law to those under the law (though not himself under the law) in order to win them (1 Cor. 9:20). So radical grace did not rule out acts of law-observance (including Timothy's circumcision, Acts 16:3) to remove obstacles to evangelism.

Through the third century CE, law-observant Jewish Christian groups opposed Paul. The Ebionites called him a "messenger of Satan" (see *Preaching of Peter* and the *Ascents of James*, excerpted in Eusebius and Epiphanius). Nevertheless, Paul's teaching on grace apart from law-observance prevailed and the church soon became predominantly Gentile. As a result, the polemics over law and grace were replaced by concerns for the church's survival, unity, and moral discipline, and Marcion stood alone as a vociferous proponent of Paul's notion of grace.

Harnack famously commented that Marcion was the only one in the second century to understand Paul—and he misunderstood him! Marcion took God's grace in Christ as proclaimed by Paul to be incompatible with the retributive justice of the OT Creator and Lawgiver, and therefore rejected all texts that identified this God with the God of Jesus (Marcion's canon included only ten of Paul's letters purged of such references, a version of Luke's Gospel, and Marcion's own "Antitheses"). So the orthodox church branded Paul's champion a heretic and produced a counter-emphasis on the law's playing a positive role of preparing for Christ's coming, according to Paul, and on his (implicit) distinction between (nullified) ceremonial laws and (affirmed) moral laws.

Augustine. The Pauline theme of grace did not become prominent in church teaching—but was associated with heretics—until the fifth century CE with Augustine. He saw Paul's quintessential teaching as "justification by grace," which became the dominant view in Western Christianity. Appealing to Paul against Pelagius, Augustine argued that human beings are fallen, resulting in the perversion of the will and inability to believe and love God truly, or even desire to do so, apart from divine grace. Faith and good works are gifts of God (1 Cor. 4:7). Augustine's views carried the day and influenced medieval theologians such as Thomas Aquinas.

Luther. Luther appealed to Paul in challenging medieval Roman Catholic teaching that righteousness, though initially God's gracious gift, becomes believers' own possession: they are transformed by grace into the righteous, and having become righteous by grace, they earn God's favor through righteous deeds (for which the Church granted indulgences). Luther countered that believers remain sinners—*simil iustus et peccator*—and their righteousness is always alien righteousness; they are "reckoned as righteous" or permeated by the righteousness of the indwelling Christ (cf. Finnish Luther scholarship). Thus salvation is solely by grace, from start to finish. Any attempt to earn God's favor through obedience is refusal of grace and tantamount to the ultimate sin of *dis*belief.

Luther read Paul through the lens of his own experience of moral failure, although he was a conscientious monk. The more he tried to measure up to God's demands, the less certainty he had of God's approval and his eternal salvation. He found release from fear and guilt only by casting himself, a sinner, on the grace of God for sinners in Christ. Whether Luther's understanding of Paul was shaped incorrectly (as much current scholarship holds) or correctly by his experience is a matter for debate. Newer Pauline interpretation sees Paul as arguing not against Jewish legalism but the attempt to use God's gracious gifts (e.g., election, the law) to establish a claim on God's favor (see below, on the New Perspective on Paul). Luther similarly criticized the Roman Catholic Church of his day not for works-righteousness that excludes grace but for a synergistic soteriology of grace *and* works that reduces the role of grace. Luther argued, in agreement with Paul, that grace is not "earned," in the sense of being positively correlated with anything in human beings (including the results of God's grace), but "free," as most evident in the justification of the ungodly. Moral transformation also is the work of God/the Spirit that necessarily follows justification (Gal. 5:22–23; Phil. 2:12; Luther: a "good tree" necessarily bears "good fruit"), although not grounding final justification but authenticating faith (contrast Augustine: God rewards believers for the very same good works God grants; cf. Rom. 2:1–16).

The Modern Period. Developments in the nineteenth and twentieth centuries set the stage for a new emphasis on Paul's view of grace by both Barth and, in a very different way, Bultmann. Protestant liberalism had come to see Paul as instantiating its own ideals: universal religion and deep religiosity typified by the yearning of the human spirit for God. When World War I crippled this vision, Barth challenged the prevailing theology with his exposition of Paul's letter to the Romans. The cross represented a divine "No" negating human existence in its present form and destroying all hope of salvation emerging within this world. The resurrection constituted a divine "Yes" reconstituting human existence. This all happened "in Christ," as God's action entirely, apart from human involvement, simply to be accepted in faith. A stronger restatement of Paul's teaching on grace can hardly be imagined.

Bultmann, viewing the biblical claims to God's action in Christ and its salvific results as incompatible with a modern worldview, reinterpreted (in then popular existential categories) Paul's notion of free grace to be received in faith as the demand to renounce all efforts to secure one's own existence. Paul's message, though directed to a Jewish audience, addresses a universal human tendency toward "self (produced)-righteousness" doomed to fail. "Authentic existence" can be realized only in the oft-repeated decision for faith. Bultmann's program of demythologization and his reformulation of the gift of grace in terms of the demand for faith, however, turns Paul's message into its opposite, "salvation" by works (of faith).

The New Perspective on Paul (NPP) and Its Critics. Anticipated by Wrede, Schweitzer, and others, E. P. Sanders brought an end to the dominance of the "Lutheran" Paul. Against the regnant caricature of Judaism as a legalistic, graceless religion—according to which works will be weighed in the balance to determine the covenant member's final destiny, and entering the world to come depends on the good works outweighing the bad—Sanders defines rabbinic Judaism (200 BCE–200 CE) as "covenantal nomism": a "pattern of religion" in which salvation is by grace, and works are the condition of remaining in, but do not earn, salvation. God chose Israel and established the covenant with it by grace. Israel's subsequent submission to God's commands was the appropriate response to God's favor, not the means of earning it. Thus Paul can have no quarrel with Judaism as fostering legalistic works-righteousness, self-righteous boasting, or a despairing uncertainty of salvation. The point of contention between Paul and his fellow Jews, Sanders avers, is the view that Christ is the one way of salvation (which includes Gentiles, whom the Jewish law excluded) in the end time and that other ways are obsolete. Paul may criticize some Jews for boasting in special privileges, but he has no substantive critique of Judaism. Paul agrees that getting in is by grace and staying in is by (the intention to do) works. Sanders summarizes, "This is what Paul finds wrong in Judaism: it is not Christianity."

Further, claims Sanders, Paul argues from solution (Christ as the way of salvation for all) to plight (all are under sin and the law's condemnation). This plight is invented to correspond to the solution instead of reflecting some real problem in Judaism. The Law was *not* impossible to do and did *not* fail to deal with sin, nor did it incite to sin or lead inevitably to self-righteous boasting. Jewish scholars writing before the NPP (Montefiore, Schoeps) had objected that Paul (in his Lutheran guise) misunderstands or misconstrues Judaism (cf. Räisänen). Stendahl anticipated the NPP by labeling the regnant "Lutheran" reading of Paul and Judaism anachronistic and attributing it to Augustine and Luther and "the introspective conscience of the West." The Lutheran Paul mirrors the moral struggles of Augustine and Luther, which ended in dramatic conversions. The authentic first-century Jewish Paul, however, had a "robust conscience" and experienced no conversion away from Judaism, but a call to preach Christ to the Gentiles as their own way of salvation.

Other New Perspectivists who reject the Lutheran Paul argue that the real Paul does have a substantive critique of Judaism, namely, as ethnocentric, or characterized by boasting over other nations on the basis of the practices required by the law (especially circumcision and food laws) that distinguish Jews from Gentiles. Israel's privileges had come to be regarded as badges of superiority (Dunn). Boasting in national righteousness was Israel's meta-sin (Wright). From Paul's salvation-historical perspective such ethnocentrism is ruled out: God established the covenant with Israel in order to redeem *all* of humanity; the promise to Abraham included a blessing for the nations as well. Moreover, the covenant established faith as the principle of acceptance by God. The law served the interim purpose of defining and revealing sin, atoning for sin preliminarily through the sacrificial cult, and separating Israel from the surrounding nations and their immoral practices. Wright stresses the consequences of Israel's law-based ethnocentrism: although Israel was God's chosen instrument of blessing to the nations, it failed to fulfill this role and instead asserted superiority over them based on its privileges as the elect people. Christ had to assume Israel's role toward the nations and died to redeem Israel from the curse of the covenant incurred for unfaithfulness and return Israel from "exile," resulting in the renewal of the covenant and the fulfillment of God's promises to Israel and their extension to the Gentiles. Thereby Christ demonstrated the faithfulness of God in realizing the purpose of the covenant. Jewish Christ-believers who insisted that Gentiles be circumcised in addition to believing in Christ had fallen prey to the same ethnocentrism and misunderstanding of the law as other Jews: they assumed that race mattered for receiving the promised blessings, and failed to recognize that the law played an interim role that had come to an end in Christ.

Similarly, Boyarin argues that Paul confronts ethnocentrism based on the law with monotheistic universalism and in this way resolves a tension within Jewish tradition itself. Christ's (physical) death and (spiritual) resurrection represent the transcendence of universality (in spirit) over particularity (in the flesh), and thus the triumph of oneness and equality over division and inequality—attainable, however, only in a liminal state such as baptism.

For these interpreters the key question Paul is trying to answer is not how the individual can be saved—whether by works or by grace, as in the Lutheran paradigm—since Paul assumes agreement that salvation is by grace. Rather, the question is how to define the boundaries of the people of God, the terms of admission into the people of God. Did the old boundary markers drawn by the law remain valid? No, Paul is said to answer. Faith demarcates the people of God, as is now clear with the coming of Christ, indeed, as foretold in Abraham's righteousness by faith. Paul, in other words, reduces the works of the law to ethnic boundary markers. No believer who lacks such works qua identity markers is excluded from membership in God's universal people. Salvation is by grace through faith apart from the works of the law as identity markers of God's people, not as meritorious deeds that provide access to God's blessings. That is, salvation is ethnically undetermined. Grace is not restricted by race. For the people of God is (now) an entity comprised of different nations, not a Jewish people. The illusion that race matters is overcome. The Jewish sin of ethnocentrism is atoned for. Race-based division is replaced by faith-based unity, reflecting the oneness of God and attesting the faithfulness of God.

Yet some cracks in this reconstruction have appeared. Dunn admits that although the focus of Paul's polemics was the terms of membership in God's people and the extent of God's grace, the apostle also asserted, against his Jewish opponents, that faith rather than the works of the law is the sole means of sustaining the relationship to God—a key emphasis of the Lutheran Paul. Moreover, according to Longenecker, Paul found Jewish ethnocentrism problematic precisely because it underestimated the need for grace (through an overly optimistic view of human beings under the law) and in this way was similar to legalism. Because Paul viewed existence in the "flesh" as bondage to sin, and obedience to the law as therefore always tainted by imperfection (cf. Rom. 7:7–25; Gal. 3:10, 21–22; 4:21–25; 5:16–18), he taught that redemption is through Christ apart from the works of the law, by grace alone, as a sovereign divine initiative. Cf. also Barclay's view that Paul's teaching on grace responds to a Judaism unduly wedded to human cultural and social values. As these scholars show, one can affirm both that grace played an important role in Judaism as such and that Paul himself construed grace and faith differently from many other Jews, not just formally but materially, namely, along the lines associated with the Lutheran Paul. Thus, while the NPP has contributed greatly to our understanding of the occasion for Paul's teaching on grace and law, faith and works—namely, pressure on Gentile Christ-believers to circumcise and identify with physical Israel—the NPP has not replaced, but in some important respects has supplemented, the old perspective.

It is precisely Paul's definition of grace as utterly gratuitous, working independently of, and in contrast to, present human identity and merit, that distinguishes Paul from rabbinic Judaism, argues Westerholm. Rabbinic Judaism *correlated* divine grace and human merit (e.g., the grace of election corresponds to Israel's acceptance of the covenant, in contrast to other nations' rejection of it). Rabbinic Judaism should therefore not be construed in terms of a grace/merit contrast, as in the designation "covenantal nomism" (getting in is by grace while staying in is by works). According to Westerholm, Sanders's reconstruction is an anachronistic reading of Judaism in terms of good Protestantism instead of its own terms. Rabbinic Judaism is more accurately characterized as "synergistic" and in some cases "legalistic" (Gundry)—Pauline value judgments aside. Indeed Scripture itself correlates human merit and final destiny: God placed Israel before the choice of obedience or disobedience, a choice that led to "life" or "death" (Lev. 26; Deut. 28–31; Thielman). Although a sense of failure to do one's part is attested in both Scripture and Jewish sources contemporary to Paul, and although Jewish apocalypticism (e.g., in Qumran) saw divine intervention as the only hope for God's people, Paul's awareness of total dependence on

divine grace came to him through a revelation of Christ (Gal. 1:13–16) in which he experienced God's grace toward him as a persecutor of God's church (1 Cor. 15:9–10). Christ was revealed to him as the grace of God for offenders, to the exclusion of any role for their works, which were those of "sinners" (cf. Gal. 2:17). Hence Paul's apostolic mission to the uncircumcised (and so as such ill-deserving) and his polemics against the circumcised who still maintained that there was necessarily a positive correlation between divine grace and its human recipients.

In conclusion, Paul not only critiqued Jewish ethnocentrism and affirmed the universal extent of salvation—regardless of ethnicity—based on the covenant faithfulness of God and corresponding to God's oneness. Paul also asserted that grace is essential for individuals, not just communities, and is utterly gratuitous for Jews as well as Gentiles, and that faith accompanied by total non-self-regard is the only way of participating in such grace, not just a sign of membership. Paul's arguments about the law and sin support these claims. Even if his opponents themselves were no legalists, he explained that complete observance was the only option the law itself allowed and that it was a doomed one because of sin's dominion over those in the flesh (e.g., Rom. 2:17–3:20; Gal. 3:10–13; 5:1–5). Even the blameless lawkeeper—who also needed the law's provisions for atonement—found no definitive solution for sin through the law (as the universal reign of death over those "in Adam" attested, Rom. 5:12–21) and had to rely on "righteousness that comes from God" and "be found in him [Christ]," or transferred to the lordship of Christ in order to obtain "the prize for which God has called me heavenward," "the resurrection from the dead" (Phil. 3:4b–14). Whatever the gains of the NPP, it has obscured the key difference between Paul and many of his Jewish contemporaries which Luther captured: the nature of God's grace as utterly gratuitous, for sinners without any claim on it, and the crucified Christ as the demonstration of this (insulting) gift of grace.

Theologian of the Cross

Jesus's death (always in conjunction with his resurrection) is for Paul (in agreement with early Christian tradition) the central saving event (1 Cor. 15:3–8) and focus of preaching (1 Cor. 2:2). Precisely how that death and resurrection fulfilled such a crucial function and why it deserved such a prominent role in Christian proclamation are matters of great importance for Paul. The cross is a theme on which he expatiates liberally. More than that, some have argued, it is the starting point for his theology.

The Cross, Justification of the Ungodly, and Revelation of God. Käsemann notes that Paul departs from received tradition by mentioning *how* Jesus died: on a cross, and thus utterly humiliated, cursed, and forsaken by God (1 Cor. 1:17; 2:2; 2 Cor. 13:4; Gal. 3:13). It follows that those for whom Jesus died are "the ungodly," as the uniquely Pauline soteriological formulas state: "Christ died for the *ungodly*" (Rom. 5:6); God "justifies the *ungodly*" (Rom. 4:5). This is polemic against religious self-assertion before God (both legalistic piety and "enthusiasm"), according to Käsemann, whose own polemical intention is to refocus church theology and exegesis by means of the Reformation "theology of the cross" indebted to Paul's teaching that the Son suffered and died on the cross for sinners and so reveals God as the One who loves and justifies the ungodly with faith (cf. Moltmann, Jüngel). For Käsemann, Paul's theology is aptly described as a theology of the cross, and his theological center as justification by faith, or God's victorious setting of a fallen world into right relation to God. This rules out a simple Christology of exaltation or a realized eschatology with no eschatological reservation, and rules in imitation of God's love for the ungodly.

But, while striking some key notes in Paul's theology, Käsemann excludes some important aspects of Pauline teaching on the death of Christ (Stuhlmacher).

The Death of Christ and Pauline Metaphors for Salvation. Paul positively cites early tradition on the atoning death of Christ: "Christ died for our sins" (the "dying formula," 1 Cor. 15:3, etc.), "whom God put forward as a sacrifice of atonement [*hilastērion*] by his blood" (Rom. 3:25–26 NRSV). *Hilastērion* may denote "mercy seat" (where the blood of the sacrifice for sins was sprinkled and atonement was made) or means of atonement. Both imply that Christ's death expiates, or removes, sins. Some argue that it is propitiatory, or averts divine wrath on account of sin. But since Paul explicitly states that Christ's death demonstrates God's love, providing assurance of future salvation from wrath (Rom. 5:8–9), propitiation would have to have the unusual sense of a divine (not human) act of love to avert divine wrath.

Death that atones for others' sins belongs to the larger motif of beneficial death for others that was widespread in Paul's milieu (for Greco-Roman and Jewish parallels, see Hengel). Paul can describe Christ's death as a "righteous act/ obedience" bringing "justification" and "life" to "all/many" (Rom. 5:17–19), as well as accomplishing atonement for sins: ". . . by his blood" (Rom. 5:9); "in my blood" (1 Cor. 11:25; cf. Eph. 1:7; 2:13; Col. 1:20); "God . . . sending his own Son . . . to be a sin offering [cf. Lev. 4 LXX]" (Rom. 8:3); the "surrender formulas," e.g., "delivered over to death for our sins" (Rom. 4:25; cf. Gal. 1:4; Eph 5:2); "Christ, our Passover lamb, has been sacrificed" (1 Cor. 5:7, implying atonement in the light of 11:24–25); "my body, which is for you" read together with "the new covenant in my blood" (1 Cor. 11:24–25). Other uses of the *hyper*-formula—Christ died "for" others (Rom. 5:6–8; 8:32; etc.)—are based on the words of institution. On Isa. 52:13–53:12 as background, see Janowski, ed.

What understanding of sacrificial atonement is presupposed in these interpretations of Christ's death? Gese explains that in postexilic times sacrificial atonement aimed at overcoming a completely forfeit life (due to sin) by bringing this life, represented in the shed blood, into contact (by application to the altar, or mercy seat on Yom Kippur) with the Holy One, who destroys all that is unholy and reconstitutes life as participation in God's glory. Differently, Finlan explains that the pure blood of the blameless sacrificial animal cancels the death charge of sins and purifies the people/temple (alternatively, the sin sacrifice is a tribute payment to a sovereign that liberates the offerers).

It is conceivable that Paul developed his important notion of participation "with Christ" (Rom. 6:3–8; Gal. 2:19–20; etc.) and being "in Christ" (passim) through reflection on Christ's death against such a cultic background. Gese argues that through the ritual of laying a hand on the sacrificial animal's head before slaughter, the offerer was identified with the animal so as to symbolize inclusion in its death as passage to new life in relation to God (depicted in the blood ritual). Sacrificial atonement supplies the notion of "inclusive substitution," which is crucial to Paul: Christ's death for sins includes sinners, who are co-crucified with him (Gal. 2:20) and so reconciled to God and made a "new creation" in him (2 Cor. 5:17; Hofius).

Paul can also construe Christ's death as beneficial even though it is *ignoble* in that he died as a crucified criminal under the law's curse: "Christ redeemed us from the curse of the law by becoming a curse for us" (Gal. 3:13); "God made him who had no sin to be sin for us, so that in him we might become the righteousness of God" (2 Cor. 5:21). The benefit here occurs through an exchange and also has a cultic background, the annual scapegoat ritual, in which an innocent animal exchanged places with the sinful people. The scapegoat bore and removed the people's sin by being brutally victimized and sent out to die, and they assumed its status without sin. (Cf. the "objective" view of the atonement associated with Anselm: Jesus substituted for sinners and they escaped death.)

Paul's cultic language and imagery are used *metaphorically* with respect to Christ's death, which functions like a sin-sacrifice or scapegoat death. "Spiritualization" of literal cultic rituals (this occurred also outside early Christianity) reflects unease with the notion that they actually effect what they intend (Finlan). At best they supply a partial and preliminary solution to the problem of present sin-dominated existence, which must come to an end and be replaced by a new existence under God's rule (cf. Barth: "Man could not be helped other than through his annihilation"). The full, end-time solution to sins/sin is supplied in an eschatological "new creation" through Christ. By his (inclusive) death "for all," Paul says, "in Christ . . . everything old has passed away; see, everything has become new!" (2 Cor. 5:17 NRSV). By this Paul means that believers "have died" (to sin as their master) and "no longer live for themselves but for [Christ]," "to God" in daily service to God/Christ (2 Cor. 5:14–15; Rom. 6:10–14; cf. 7:1–6). Paul's so-called transfer-of-lordship motif is in service of his new creation motif. The "death" and "new life" won by Christ are appropriated individually in Christian baptism (Rom. 6:3–4). In Christ, not the cult, God's grace works more powerfully than sin by effecting the end of the reign of sin and death over those in Adam and bringing about the new reign of righteousness and life for those in Christ, who have become a new humanity for all eternity (Rom. 5:12–21).

Paul also explains the salvific significance of Christ's death metaphorically in terms of justification (acquittal in court, Rom. 3:24), liberation/ redemption/purchase (manumission of slaves, with overtones of the exodus from Egypt, Rom. 3:24; 1 Cor. 6:20; 7:23; Gal. 3:13), adoption to become an heir (Gal. 4:5), reconciliation (sociopolitical language from Paul's Greco-Roman milieu, which he links materially with OT atonement theology, Rom. 5:10–11; 2 Cor. 5:18–19; Eph. 2:16; Col. 1:20), new creation (a Jewish eschatological hope, 2 Cor. 5:17), and triumph (Col. 2:15). The economic metaphor (redemption/purchase) implies the "costliness" of Christ's death both for God, who sends the beloved Son to death (Rom. 8:3, 32), and for Christ, who "became poor" (2 Cor. 8:9), "emptied himself" (Phil. 2:7 NRSV)—not a ransom payment to a particular individual (the devil, *pace* some classical interpretations).

Finally, Paul understands the cross as a divine-human act. Here God is seen demonstrating righteousness (i.e., moral rectitude and saving power congruent with God's promises, Rom. 3:25–26) and love (Rom. 5:8), not sparing the Son (Rom. 8:3, 32), reconciling sinners and enemies to God (the converse of Greco-Roman reconciliation of the offended by the offenders; Rom. 5:10–11; 2 Cor. 5:19), and not counting transgressions (2 Cor. 5:19). Paul's paralleling of God's and Jesus's actions in the cross is striking. Jesus "gave himself" (Gal. 1:4; 2:20), and God "gave him up" (Rom. 8:32); Jesus "loved me" (Gal. 2:20; cf. 2 Cor. 5:14), "sinners, lawbreakers" (Gal. 2:17–18), and God showed "love for us/sinners/enemies" (Rom. 5:8, 10). Jesus's death on the cross is more than an act of obedience (Phil. 2:8); it enacts redemptive love of the kind that distinguishes God from human beings (Rom. 5:7 TNIV: "very rarely will anyone die for a righteous person . . . but God demonstrates his own love"). Acceptance of this extraordinary revelation of God in the cross is enabled by the Spirit, without which it is deemed foolish (1 Cor. 2:6–16; cf. Rom. 5:5). Imitation through love for the "weak" attests genuine discernment of this divine love (1 Cor. 8:1–13; 11:27–34). Cf. the "subjective" view of the atonement associated with Abelard and represented by liberal nineteenth- and early-twentieth-century theology: divine love displayed in the death of Christ effects repentance and responsive love.

Is there a dominant soteriological model in Paul? A juridical model ("justify," "condemn") is prominent in Galatians and Romans (see also

Philippians), polemicizing against the works of the law for justification—but not elsewhere. A participationist model ("with Christ"/"in Christ") has been thought more characteristic of Paul's corpus. Yet his untidy blending of soteriological concepts—for example, Gal. 2:16–21 blends juridical with participationist models, and 2 Cor. 5:14–21 blends these with cultic, reconciliation and new creation models—suggests he treats them as interconnected and complementary. He may highlight one or the other, depending on the context. Thus we should probably not take "justification by faith" as merely forensic, that is, "reckoned" or declarative (the common understanding in Protestant orthodoxy through Melanchthon's influence). Rather, by virtue of believers' relationship with Christ through the Spirit (cf. Rom. 8:9–11; 2 Cor. 3:16–18), we ought to allow for a broader sense of "righteousness by faith" with ethical or ontological connotations. Correspondingly, Luther could speak either of believers' "alien righteousness" or their sanctification through the operation of God's grace in Christ.

Theologian of the New Creation

When Paul received his "revelation of Christ" or Christophany on the road to Damascus, he concluded that despite Jesus's shameful crucifixion he was God's Messiah, and by raising him from the dead God had initiated the eschatological resurrection of the dead (Gal. 1:12, 16, 23): Christ is "the firstfruits of those who have fallen asleep" (1 Cor. 15:20). Other eschatological hopes were also coming to fulfillment: the gift of the Spirit to all (Gal 3:14; cf. Joel 2:28–29) and the Gentiles' thronging to faith in the one true God (Rom. 11:11–12, 25; 1 Thess. 1:9). Thus Paul writes, "on [us] the ends of the ages have come" (1 Cor. 10:11) and "if anyone is in Christ, there is a new creation," for "everything old has passed away; see, everything has become new" (2 Cor. 5:17 NRSV; cf. Gal. 4:4; 6:15). Of course, he had to account for the many inconcinnities: the Messiah's death and resurrection, his heavenly rather than earthly rule, his rejection by most Jews, the non-necessity of circumcision for Gentiles, etc. Still, Paul is sure that future hopes have become present realities in Christ, and this conviction suffuses his thought. In short, he is a "theologian of the new creation."

Paul's sense of present eschatological fulfillment is paired with that of imminent completion. The parousia, last judgment, resurrection of the dead and eternal life are expected soon in 1 Corinthians (7:29; 10:11; 16:22) and 1 Thessalonians (4:13–17; 5:4–10). Later, as a prisoner, he envisions the possibility of his prior martyr death in Philippians (1:20–23). Yet he still pens the words, "the Lord is near" (Phil. 4:5), referring to an "imminent" parousia. It is not the case, therefore, that Paul's eschatology undergoes spiritualization or dehistoricization, e.g., as expressed in the language of present union with Christ (*pace* Dodd, Bultmann). Union with Christ through the indwelling Spirit of Christ enables new life ethically in the present body, and so anticipates its future transformation into a "spiritual," imperishable body (Rom. 8:2–11; 1 Cor. 15:44–49; Gal. 4:6; 5:16–26). Paul can speak of being with Christ immediately after death (2 Cor. 5:6–8; Phil. 1:23) while still affirming future, bodily resurrection (Rom. 8:11, 23; 2 Cor. 1:22; 5:5; Eph. 1:13–14; Phil. 3:11, 20–21). Colossians and Ephesians, on the other hand, speak of believers as already "raised with [Christ]" and "seated . . . with him in the heavenly realms" (Col. 2:12–13; 3:1; Eph. 2:5–6)—one of the reasons for questioning their Pauline authorship. Yet they do not erase future eschatology (see Eph. 6:13–17; Col. 3:4, 6, 24; cf. Eph. 1:13–14). In sum, Paul stresses both present fulfillment and future completion of eschatological hope, with some variance in detail between the letters, possibly pointing to a developing eschatology.

Paul's eschatology cannot be understood apart from Jewish apocalypticism, which Käsemann declared the mother of early Christian theology. Paul shares the Jewish apocalyptic view of the necessity and urgency of divine intervention to wrest control of the world from evil and restore creation under God's sovereignty, marking the end of the present age and the beginning of a new age of blessing for God's people. But what the Jewish apocalypticist hoped for the future, Paul claimed to have taken place in Christ. Thus those in Christ are "no longer" enslaved to sin but "now" free from condemnation (Rom. 6:6; 8:1; etc.). For Beker, Paul has redefined Jewish apocalypticism through Christology: Christ's death and resurrection are the final triumph of God over sin and death. And this apocalyptic interpretation of the Christ-event, according to Beker, constitutes the coherent core of Paul's thought. Each letter is a contingent expression of this interpretation, though the victory motif is not always explicit (e.g., Galatians, see Martyn). Paul is no Hellenizer of originally Jewish apocalyptic ideas (as the once dominant History of Religions School claimed) but himself an apocalyptic theologian. In this regard, it is important to see Paul's letters as a source for first century Judaism (Segal). At the same time, Paul drew on Hellenistic religious and philosophical traditions to communicate his gospel to a primarily Gentile audience familiar with such traditions (Malherbe et al.)—not surprisingly, since, as much recent scholarship has shown, the boundaries between Judaism and Hellenism of Paul's day were porous.

Despite Paul's stress on newness in Christ, he also affirms the continuity between the Christ-event and God's past dealings with Israel. Christ's death and resurrection are the "climax of the covenant" (Wright), the culmination in a series of divine saving initiatives beginning with the election of Israel, and thus the finale in the "sacred story" embedded in Paul's letters (Hays, Wright, Longenecker). Paul's use of Scripture through quotations and allusions emphasizes the connection between the gospel and Christ-believers, on the one hand, and the past saving initiatives of God and those who received them in faith, on the other (Hays). Through Christ Gentiles have become monotheists, participants in the holy "root" together with Jews, and now should live in conformity to God's will (Rom. 9–11; 1 Cor. 1:10–31; 10:1–13; Gal. 2:11–14; Eph. 2:11–22; 1 Thess. 4:3–12) rather than as a separate community apart from the doctrinal and moral impulses of OT-Jewish tradition. How Scripture functions for Paul as theologian is a matter for debate: is it the source of his theology (Watson) or does it shed light on the revelation of Christ (Kim)?

Some have argued that when Paul's converts overemphasized the new (as a result of the powerful experience of the Spirit) Paul tried to curb "enthusiasm" by stressing the "not yet" of salvation and discouraging social change, in the belief that the form of this world was soon to pass away. For example, he advises would-be celibates to have sex with their spouses or marry rather than "burn," and male and female pneumatics to wear gender-specific headdress when they pray and prophesy (1 Cor. 7:2–7; 11:5–7). This has been taken as a retreat from the egalitarianism of the (probably) baptismal tradition in Gal. 3:28 NRSV that in Christ "there is no longer Jew or Greek, . . . slave or free, . . . male and female" (Wire). During the overlap of the ages, believers have to endure the conditions of the old as they live out the new life in Christ.

Yet Paul accepts social change when it is based on the gifts of the Spirit: celibacy based on a spiritual gift (1 Cor. 7:7), women's leadership roles in his churches (Rom. 16; Phil. 4:2), and God's giving greater honor (more prominent gifts) to the less seemly parts of the body of Christ (1 Cor. 11:18–31). What then does Paul rule out? Immorality by those who lack the Spirit's power to resist Satan's temptation (1 Cor. 7:5, 9). Shame incurred by ignoring the distinction between male and female headdress (1 Cor. 11:4–15). Not new social roles but behavior typical of the old age. He may tap Genesis for arguments against shameful behavior (1 Cor. 11:7–9), but he defends mutuality between man and woman "in the Lord" on the basis of his Christian understanding of the Creator's intention (1 Cor. 11:11–12; Gundry-Volf, 1997). Paul calls for greater, authentic eschatological newness based on the Spirit's activity, both individually and corporately, and rejects a "spirituality" which only perpetuates the old order (cf. Rom. 12:2; 1 Cor. 3:1–4; 2 Cor. 5:16; Gal. 3:3; Phil. 3:7–8). (Contrast 1 Tim. 2:11–15, where women are prohibited from teaching or exercising authority over men based on the created order apart from a realized eschatological perspective). Early twentieth-century Pentecostalism and its offshoots—which have emphasized charism-based roles in the body of Christ—reflect Paul's intention.

Empowered by various social forces, the ascetic tradition continued in early Christianity influenced by Paul and armed with his own commendation of celibacy as superior, in the light of the present crisis (1 Cor. 7:26). In Col. 2:18, 21–22 and 1 Tim. 4:1–3 we find evidence of ascetic regulations concerning sex, diet, and wealth, which Colossians opposes as "a shadow of the things that were to come" in contrast to "the reality . . . found in Christ" (consistently with Paul's critique of under-realized eschatology; Col. 2:16–23), and which 1 Timothy opposes on creational (not eschatological) grounds (1 Tim. 4:4–5). The second century CE produced the ascetic follower of Paul, Marcion, and the apocryphal *Acts of Paul and Thecla*, where Paul plays the role of saving the virgin Thecla from the fate of marriage. Against Encratite Christianity's advocacy of an ascetic ethic, the second-fourth-century CE heresiologists argued from Paul's own letters that celibacy is a special grace given to some and marriage is good for others, to satisfy sexual desire and for procreation (despite the fact that Paul himself fails to make the latter argument).

Conclusion. The theological interpretation of Paul's letters spans a variety of periods and circumstances that themselves influence interpreters' grasp of Paul's theological views and emphases. It can be argued that interpreters who have stood within contexts comparable to Paul's have articulated most clearly or persuasively the apostle's distinctive and central theological positions: the centrality of the cross for understanding God, the centrality of Christ for understanding divine grace, the sufficiency of faith for participation in grace, and the eschatological character of God's action in Christ transforming individuals, communities, and all of creation according to the promises of God now coming to fulfillment through the power of the Spirit.

The theological contours, focus, and unity of Paul's letters will doubtless continue to be debated, given the complexity of Paul's thought and difficulty of the issues he raises (cf. 2 Pet. 3:15–16). This discussion stands to be enriched by the fruits of newer methods (including the study of social history and ancient rhetoric; cf. Lampe's proposal of a multi-dimensional interpretation of texts).

Bibliography

Barclay, J. *Obeying the Truth*. Fortress, 1991; Barth, K. *The Epistle to the Romans*, trans. E. Hoskyns. Oxford University Press, 1933; Beker, J. C. *Paul the Apostle*. Fortress, 1984; Boyarin, D. *A Radical Jew*. University of California Press, 1994; Bultmann, R. *Theology of the New Testament*. 2 vols. Charles Scribner's Sons, 1951–55; idem. *Kerygma und Mythos* Vol. 1. Herbert-Reich Evangelischer Verlag, 1960; Carson, D. A., P. O'Brien, and M. Seifrid, eds. *Justification and Variegated Nomism*. 2 vols. Mohr/Siebeck/Baker Academic, 2001, 2004; Cousar, C. B. *A Theology of the Cross*. Fortress, 1990; Dunn, J. D. G. *The Theology of Paul the Apostle*. Eerdmans, 1998; Finlan, S. *The Background and Content of Paul's Cultic Atonement Metaphors*. Society of Biblical Literature, 2004; Gese, H. *Essays on Biblical Theology*, trans. K. Crim. Augsburg, 1981; Gundry, R. H. "The Inferiority of the New Perspective on Paul," *The Old is Better* (Mohr/Siebeck, 2005) 195–224; Gundry-Volf, J. *Paul and Perseverance: Staying in and Falling Away*. Mohr/Siebeck, 1990; idem. "Gender and Creation in 1 Corinthians 11:2–16. A Study in Paul's Theological Method." In *Evangelium, Schriftauslegung, Kirche*, ed. J. Adna et al. Vandenhoeck & Ruprecht, 1997, 151–71; Hays, R. *Echoes of Scripture in the Letters of Paul*. Yale University Press, 1989; Hengel, M. *The Cross of the Son of God*, trans. J. Bowden. SCM, 1986; Hofius, O. *Paulusstudien*. Mohr/Siebeck, 1989; idem. *Paulusstudien II*. Mohr/Siebeck, 2002; Janowski, B., et al. *The Suffering Servant*, trans. D. Bailey. Eerdmans, 2004; Jüngel, E. *God as the Mystery of the World*, trans. D. L. Guder. Eerdmans, 1983; Käsemann, E. *Perspectives on Paul*, trans. M. Kohl. Fortress, 1971; Keck, L. *Paul and His Letters*. 2d ed. Fortress, 1988; Kim, S. *The Origin of Paul's Gospel*. 2d ed. Mohr/Siebeck, 1984; idem. *Paul and the New Perspective*. Eerdmans, 2002; Lampe, P. *From Paul to Valentinus*, trans. M. Steinhauser. Augsburg/Fortress, 2003; Longenecker, B. *The Triumph of Abraham's God*. Abingdon, 1998; idem, ed. *Narrative Perspectives on the Pauline Gospel*. Westminster John Knox, 2002; Malherbe, A. *Paul and the Thessalonians*. Fortress, 1987; Martyn, J. L. *Theological Issues in the Letters of Paul*. Abingdon, 1997; idem. *Galatians*. Doubleday, 1998; Meeks, W., ed. *The Writings of St. Paul*. Norton, 1972; Moltmann, J. *The Crucified God*, trans. R. A. Wilson and J. Bowden. Harper & Row, 1974; Montefiore, C. G. *Judaism and St. Paul*. Max Goschen, 1914; Räisänen, H. *Paul and the Law*. Fortress, 1986; Sanders, E. P. *Paul and Palestinian Judaism*. Fortress, 1977; idem. *Paul, the Law, and the Jewish People*. Fortress, 1983; Schnelle, U. *Apostle Paul*, trans. M. E. Boring. Baker, 2005; Schoeps, H. J. *Paul*. Westminster, 1961; Schweitzer, A. *The Mysticism of Paul the Apostle*, trans. W. Montgomery. Seabury, 1931; Segal, A. *Paul the Convert*. Yale University Press, 1990; Stendahl, K. *Paul among Jews and Gentiles*. Fortress, 1976; Stuhlmacher, P. *Biblische Theologie des Neuen Testaments*. Vol. 1. Vandenhoeck & Ruprecht, 1999; Thielman, F. *Paul and the Law*. InterVarsity, 1994; Watson, F. *Paul and the Hermeneutics of Faith*. T&T Clark, 2004; Westerholm, S. *Perspectives Old and New on Paul*. Eerdmans, 2004; Wrede, W. *Paul*, trans. E. Lummis. American Unitarian Association, 1962; Wright, N. T. *The Climax of the Covenant*. Fortress, 1993.

Judith Gundry-Volf

Peace   *See* Violence

Pentecostal Biblical Interpretation
See Charismatic Biblical Interpretation

People of God   *See* Church, Doctrine of the; Israel

Performance   *See* Dialogism; Music, the Bible and; Theological Hermeneutics, Contemporary

Perlocutionary Act   *See* Speech-Act Theory

Perseverance of the Saints   *See* Apostasy; Assurance; Sanctification

Pesher   *See* Jewish Exegesis

1 Peter, Book of

The First Epistle of Peter purports to be a letter from the apostle Peter to scattered Christians in Asia Minor, who are suffering for the name of Christ. Peter writes to remind them of their redemption through the death of Christ, their living hope through his resurrection, and their new status as God's own people. He encourages them to follow Christ's example and to maintain love for one another and good conduct toward outsiders. Most modern and postmodern commentators have challenged this picture, while some have continued to adhere to it in some form. Theological interpretation may offer a way through this interpretative impasse.

Recent Interpretation

Around the middle of the twentieth century, two important commentaries appeared that set the terms for subsequent interpretation of 1 Peter. E. G. Selwyn's commentary, with extensive additional notes, argued that the apostle Peter authored the letter, with Silvanus (5:12) as the amanuensis. Numerous similarities with other NT documents in catechetical and paraenetic material were presented as evidence that the letter represented mainstream apostolic Christianity at its formative period. For Selwyn, the likely situation that called forth the letter was the fire in Rome and the ensuing persecution of Christians by Nero (63–64 CE).

F. W. Beare, on the other hand, argued that the background to the letter is to be found in the situation described by Pliny the Younger, governor of Bithynia in 112, who wrote to the emperor Trajan about the policy of the empire concerning Christians. Beare saw the letter as a literary fiction, written in the name of the apostle to scattered subapostolic churches in Asia Minor. Beare's thorough textual, lexical, and background studies added weight to his arguments. Subsequent study has lined up behind one or the other, with the majority of commentators positing a pseudepigraphical work written toward the end of the first century (Goppelt; Michaels; Achtemeier; Elliott). Even J. H. Elliott's recent landmark commentary (AB), which posits a date between 73 and 90, does not offer a way beyond the stalemate.

Recent Studies

Compared to the Gospels and the Pauline Letters, 1 Peter has suffered relative neglect. Only a few important commentaries and studies have appeared since 1950. In the last half-century, studies in 1 Peter have demonstrated both the necessity and the opportunity for theological interpretation.

F. L. Cross. Cross argued that 1 Pet. 1:3–4:11 constituted the celebrant's portion of a baptismal rite, and that the actual initiation takes place after 1:21. Cross's view has not been widely accepted, due to forced exegesis and examples drawn from a later date (e.g., the *Apostolic Tradition* of Hippolytus). But his focus on the theme of exodus and Passover as a major emphasis in the letter has not been sufficiently explored. The paschal references in 1 Pet. 1 need to be placed in the context of developing Jewish exegesis of this most important text (Exod. 12) and event in the story of God's people.

J. H. Elliott. Chief among contributors to the study of 1 Peter has been J. H. Elliott. Elliott's *The Elect and the Holy* examines the term "royal priesthood" or "a kingdom of priests" (2:9, citing Exod. 19:6). Elliott concludes that the expression refers not to believers as individual priests, but only to the believing community as community. If Elliott's exegesis and conclusions are sound, 1 Pet. 2 may not be used to support the notion of a priesthood of all believers. However, to insist on a corporate interpretation to the exclusion of an individual one is to miss a narrative element of fundamental importance. No OT passage is more formative for the narrative theology of 1 Peter than Ps. 34. A long quotation from the psalm occurs in 1 Pet. 3, and there are a number of allusions. A citation from Ps. 34:8 immediately precedes the relevant section (2:4–10). A curious and instructive feature of this psalm (and others, notably 130, 22, 69) is the interplay of the individual and the community (Ps. 34:1 "I will bless . . ."; v. 3 "Let us exalt . . ."). The individual righteous sufferer who cries to God for help finds that he or she is not alone. In the narrative movement of Ps. 34, both the individual and the community are distinctive and important. Both are in focus in the story told by the author of 1 Peter, who has meditated deeply on Ps. 34.

The last two decades of the twentieth century have witnessed the rise of social-scientific study of the NT. A pioneering study in 1 Peter has been Elliott's *A Home for the Homeless*. He applies new insights from sociology to the letter, contending that the recipients' strangerhood, their condition of estrangement and alienation, remains social rather than cosmological. Their predicament as "resident aliens and visiting strangers" is contrasted not to having a home in heaven, but to having a home within the Christian community. The reference is more sociological than theological. The trials refer not so much to official persecutions from Rome, but more to local ostracism and pressure due to their strangeness as a new social group. Still, there are important grounds for retaining the NRSV translation "exiles" rather than Elliott's "strangers" in 1:1. N. T. Wright has argued persuasively that the exile is a governing element in the metanarrative all Jewish groups shared in the NT era. The story of deliverance from exile, informed as that story itself is by the foundation of the exodus, is the theological backdrop of the Christian claim that through the death and resurrection of Jesus, Christians have been delivered from bondage into freedom. For early Christians, and especially the writer and recipients of 1 Peter, that deliverance was articulated in terms of Scriptures like Pss. 34 and 39 (v. 12, cited in 1 Pet. 2:11) and Isa. 52–53. Not only the language but also the logic of these passages shaped the theology of the letter. Thus, we must look to its varied use of the OT for an indication of its metanarrative and theology.

W. J. Dalton. Dalton's important monograph, *Christ's Proclamation to the Spirits*, argues that Christ's journey to "preach to the spirits in prison" (3:19) refers not to his "descent into hell," which has been a common assumption from patristic times onward, but to Christ's ascension. During his ascension Christ proclaimed triumph over the rebellious angels, imprisoned in the third heaven of intertestamental Jewish cosmology. Dalton's view has found wide acceptance among commentators. The ascension is certainly fundamental to the whole passage (3:18–22); verse 22 says that Jesus Christ "has gone into heaven, and is at the right hand of God, with angels, authorities, and powers made subject to him" (NRSV). Dalton rightly notes that the influence of Ps. 110:1 is paramount, but he does not develop this line. Psalm 110:1, the most frequently cited OT text in the NT, is probably a conscious echo in 3:22 and fundamental to the theology and ethics of the letter. The same word for the subjection of hostile powers is used to urge slaves and wives to submit, in the household codes. Further study along this line would be fruitful for understanding the theology and ethics of the letter, and elsewhere in the NT.

L. Goppelt. In his commentary, Goppelt, like Elliott, pioneered a social-scientific approach. Surveying the household codes in their cultural setting, he concluded that they represent not the application of an OT and Jewish tradition, but the reworking of a Hellenistic ethos on the basis of principles developed by Jesus and Paul. But such a claim fails to reckon with the theological reflection on Scripture in 1 Peter. The ideas of good behavior are drawn directly from Scriptures like Ps. 34 and Prov. 3. Psalm 34:14 may even have contributed to the unique vocabulary of 1 Peter. His NT *hapax legomenon* for doing good (*agathopoiia*) is probably his own coinage, resulting from meditation on Ps. 34.

D. L. Balch. Balch studied the domestic codes in 1 Peter in the context of attitudes toward husbands and wives in Greco-Roman culture and Hellenistic Judaism. His work, however, does not take sufficient account of the importance of the OT and its interpretation (despite his references to Philo) as the primary influence on the thought and shape of 1 Peter. His Scripture index does not even list Isa. 3:18–24 (as do most commentaries). Epictetus or Seneca may indeed have influenced the argument, but how much more the OT! So with Gen. 18:12 cited at 3:6. Hardly a proof text, this echo may offer some new clues to the background of the letter.

W. L. Schutter. Schutter's *Hermeneutic and Composition in 1 Peter* takes an important step forward. His sustained attention to the hermeneutical presuppositions, methods, techniques, and assumptions in the letter's use of the OT points the way for further study. Especially valuable is Schutter's focus on the OT as a formative influence. The section 1:13–2:10 he takes as a "homiletic midrash," and he offers several parallels from Philo and rabbinic literature for comparison. A sustained study of the use of the OT in 1 Peter, following the lines laid out by Schutter, is certainly needed, and it is likely from this direction that the most valuable work on 1 Peter will emerge in the future.

Theology and OT Hermeneutics

A thorough study of the use of the OT in 1 Peter will concentrate on at least the following six areas:

Form. Careful attention must be paid to places where the text form of the OT citations differs from the MT or LXX. The differences, sometimes slight, have been explained as stylistic, use of a different version, quotation from memory, or targumizing. A special focus on the textual variations within quotations should prove fruitful, especially where the change may be theologically motivated (e.g., 3:14–15 using Isa. 8:12–13; did 1 Peter write "God" or "Christ"?). The reading *Christos* at 2:3 in Papyrus 72 may reflect an important interpretative tradition.

Introduction. First Peter contains both OT texts introduced with a formula (1:16; 2:6) and also passages without them (1:24–25, citing Isa. 40; 3:10–12, citing Pss. 34; 2:21–25, citing Isa. 53). The presence or absence of an introductory formula may indicate the degree of familiarity of writer and readers with the OT and something about background. A study of the formulas, or their absence, would indicate that both writer and recipients were more Jewish than is usually allowed. The echoes of Scripture abound in 1 Peter, and fragments of the OT have been woven artfully into the literary framework. In identifying echoes the interpreter will benefit from applying the criteria developed by R. Hays, which include availability, volume, recurrence, satisfaction, and thematic coherence.

Selection. Listed together, the OT texts in 1 Peter appear as a random selection of quotations. Is there any discernible logic to their selection? Here greater attention is needed to the purpose of 1 Peter as a treatise intended to encourage God's people undergoing persecution for their faith. Special attention to 4 Macc. 18:10–19 (a Jewish persecution document that features both Ps. 34 and Prov. 3) will prove fruitful. This passage holds a number of keys to understanding the letter. In addition, the exegete will ask why several verses were cited from Ps. 34, but surprisingly not 34:20: "He keeps all their bones; not one of them will be broken" (NRSV).

Application. Some OT texts used in 1 Peter are found elsewhere in the NT, where they are applied to other features of the Christian story. For example, phrases from Isa. 53 are employed in 1 Pet. 2:18–25 to encourage Christians to follow the example of Jesus' patient endurance of suffering. Both in 1 Peter and elsewhere in the NT, the passage is applied to the death of Christ and to his healing ministry.

History. OT texts in 1 Peter should be studied in the context of the developing exegesis in the Judaism of the period. Isaiah 28:16, for example, is combined with Isa. 8:14 by both 1 Peter and Paul (1 Pet. 2:3–10; Rom. 9:32–33). But the text has a developed exegetical history before its use by NT writers. It is found in the Qumran texts (1QS 8.7). So 1 Peter is participating in a developed exegetical tradition. This will also be true

in the case of the allusions to Exod. 12 (and the probable allusion to Gen. 22 at 1:20).

Function. Often the OT is assumed to play a supportive or confirming role for the argument of 1 Peter. Texts are brought in, it is argued, as "proof texts." However, careful study demonstrates that the OT has had a much more creative role in the theology of the letter. For 1 Peter, Scripture is not so much plundered as pondered. This proves to be as true for the quotations as for the allusions and echoes of the OT. Elliott has noted the "important and creative role" of Isa. 52–53 for the theology of the letter. Commenting on 2:18–25, Elliott writes, "In its fusion of biblical themes and motifs, kerygmatic formulas, and extensive use of Isaiah 52–53 this passage illustrates both an independence from Pauline thought and a theological formulation that is as creative as it is singular in the NT" (*1 Peter*, 504).

Elliott has called 1 Peter an "exegetical stepchild." Perhaps its relative neglect can now work to its advantage. Sustained study of 1 Peter will bring fresh theological and practical perspective to a discipline that has concentrated primarily on the Gospels and Pauline writings. The letter, which contains more OT relative to its size than any other NT document, except perhaps Revelation, may have much to contribute at a time of renewed interest in the theological interpretation of Scripture.

See also Social-Scientific Criticism

Bibliography

Achtemeier, P. *1 Peter*. Hermeneia. Fortress, 1996; Balch, D. L. *Let Wives Be Submissive*. SBLMS 26. Scholars Press, 1981; Beare, F. W. *The First Epistle of Peter*. 3d ed. Blackwell, 1970; Cross, F. L. *1 Peter*. Mowbray, 1954; Dalton, W. J. *Christ's Proclamation to the Spirits*. 2d ed. Pontifical Biblical Institute, 1989; Elliott, J. *The Elect and the Holy*. NovTSup 12. Brill, 1966; idem. *1 Peter*. AB 37B. Doubleday, 2000; idem. *A Home for the Homeless*. Fortress, 1981; Goppelt, L. *A Commentary on 1 Peter*, ed. F. Hahn. Eerdmans, 1993; Hays, R. *Echoes of Scripture in the Letters of Paul*. Yale University Press, 1989; Michaels, J. R. *1 Peter*. WBC. Word, 1988; Schutter, W. L. *Hermeneutic and Composition in 1 Peter*. WUNT 2.30. Mohr/Siebeck, 1989; Selwyn, E. G. *The First Epistle of Peter*. 2d ed. Macmillan, 1947; Wright, N. T. *The New Testament and the People of God*. Fortress, 1992.

Peter R. Rodgers

2 Peter, Book of

Often seen as one of the "ugly stepchildren" of the NT, 2 Peter has suffered neglect in the modern period. However, 2 Peter makes a significant contribution to help us understand the relationship of eschatology and ethics, and recognize the enculturation of the Christian message in a different culture than the one in which it arose.

History of Interpretation

Second Peter has had a mixed reception in the church. Origen, the first expressly to cite it, had his doubts about the work, as did Eusebius, who said that the church in the East did not consider it canonical. As late as the end of the fourth century, Didymus of Alexandria could cite it as a forgery. On the other hand, it is clear that the work was circulating by the mid-second century, and it does appear along with 1 Peter in the Bodmer papyri. More importantly, not only did Jerome defend it, but also a number of the later church fathers used it, including Chrysostom, Augustine, Hilary of Arles, and Bede. However, for the most part these are brief citations, mined in the service of the teaching or controversies of the time. Martin Luther likewise quoted from the work, and Calvin, as usual, wrote a commentary on it, but for both men Paul was central and 2 Peter of peripheral interest. After the rise of biblical criticism, 2 Peter fell even more out of favor, because the work was viewed as early catholic and because of a rejection of its apocalyptic eschatology. Only in the last two decades of the twentieth century did 2 Peter come into its own as scholars began to appreciate its rhetoric and its theological contribution.

The Message of 2 Peter

The concern of 2 Peter is with licentious teaching that has arisen within certain house churches in one or more city churches of the Christian movement. This licentiousness was being supported by a denial of the parousia and the concomitant final judgment. Ethics and eschatology were going hand in hand negatively. It is also likely that they were using Paul's doctrine of grace to support their licentiousness, claiming that freedom from the law means freedom to break moral boundaries.

Second Peter points out, first, that when called by God to know him, one is freed from the power of desire and made a participant in the divine nature, which should work itself out in increasing virtue. This confirms election and makes one's eschatological hope secure.

Second, the parousia is a secure doctrine in that its prophetic announcement has been confirmed by the proleptic vision given in the transfiguration. Any claim that delay indicates nonreality is negated by the evidence of the flood, where there was also delay before judgment, and an appropriate knowledge of God's nature. His view of time and therefore his patience are not the same as the finite human view of time or human patience. God is patiently waiting, because it is his will that everyone be saved (3:9; yet 2 Peter clearly implies that God will not realize this desire). The end will come, the world will be destroyed, the judgment will happen, and a new and totally righteous heavens and earth will be created (3:10, 12–13). This eschatological hope should motivate believers to moral earnestness (3:11).

The teachers of licentiousness, however, are apostates, for by their pursuit of sex, money, and power they have rejected the teaching of the very Master who bought them. Their doom is sure, as numerous OT examples show. In fact, it would have been better for them never to have been freed by Christ, for having experienced the freedom from desire referred to at the beginning of the letter, they have turned back and have become reenslaved, their last state being therefore worse than their pre-Christian state.

Second Peter and the Canon

Second Peter demonstrates conscious intertextuality within the NT. First, the author is aware of more than one of Paul's letters, which he classes with the "other scriptures" (likely including Pseudepigrapha and early Gospels as well as the canonical OT), demonstrating that Paul's writings have become influential in the church among both the "orthodox" and the "unorthodox." Second, 2 Pet. 2 incorporates most of Jude, but does so by editing the work so as to remove explicit references to the Pseudepigrapha (but not the content drawn from those references, for example, the imprisonment of the fallen angels of Gen. 6) and by expanding some of the other narratives. Thus 2 Peter shows both canon formation and intracanonical interpretation, although both are happening before there is a developed canon consciousness.

Second Peter also witnesses to intertextuality between NT and OT writers. That is, it shows the nascent Christian movement interpreting and applying the Hebrew Scriptures and largely doing so through the lens of Second Temple Jewish tradition, traditions we know from apocalyptic works like *1 Enoch* and *Jubilees*.

The writer's contribution to canonical teaching is largely twofold. First, he explains the nature of the final judgment in different images from those found elsewhere. Second, he explains the idea of salvation as release from control by desire and a participation in the divine nature, which enables virtue. Despite its origin in the call of God, this release is apparently conditional, for one can turn from it and return under the control of desire. This complements teaching found in Paul.

Finally, 2 Peter reveals an early Christian translating received theological concepts into a Greek cultural context, which complements the more non-Hellenistic Jewish conceptual world of works such as Matthew and James.

Theological Significance of 2 Peter

Second Peter underlines the position found in James and Paul that traces the roots of the human predicament to desire. But given the Hellenistic tone of 2 Peter, one suspects that desire has shifted from the Jewish *yetser* (inclination) of the other two writers, which is evil only in that it has no boundaries, to the rejection of desire per se, as found in the Hellenistic world.

God is viewed as good and gracious, so he rescues believers through his promises, by which he makes them participate in the divine nature; this new nature makes human beings now capable of moral growth, since they are freed from the power of desire.

Such freedom is, however, conditional, for if someone fails in moral growth, which would confirm their election by God, he or she may stumble; that is precisely what the teachers 2 Peter condemns have done. Despite having once enjoyed the same freedom and cleansing from sin that the majority in the church still enjoy, these people have turned back to sin and are in a worse state than they were before they got to know Jesus. This conditionality is reminiscent of Hebrews and some teaching of Jesus.

Second Peter's author contributes to a high Christology with his reference to "our God and Savior Jesus Christ" (1:1), although for the most part he refers to Jesus as Lord, as in the parallel expression "our Lord and Savior Jesus Christ" (twice: 1:11; 2:20). This authority of Christ is underlined by his use of "Master," a term that in the NT outside of the *Haustafeln* (household codes) normally refers to God, but that 2 Peter follows Jude in referring to Jesus. While this "Master . . . bought" believers (including the apostate teachers; 2:1 NRSV), the atonement is not otherwise referred to, showing that it was possible in the early church to speak about rescue and redemption without direct reference to the crucifixion.

While the focus of 2 Peter is avoidance of the licentiousness that Peter attributes to the teachers he opposes, his argument revolves around eschatology. Although parousia delay (Christ not returning during the first generation of Christians) is not the main issue, the teachers were using this delay as evidence that there was no final judgment and thus actions done in this world did not have a recompense in the coming one. Second Peter discusses the apparent delay in terms of God's patience. While God does not entirely have his purpose fulfilled (it is clear to 2 Peter that at least the apostate teachers are going to hell), his will is that no one should perish, but that all come to salvation (3:9). Furthermore, picking up on a theme found repeatedly in the OT, 2 Peter observes that God's sense of time is not equivalent to the human perception. The end will come, it will come unexpectedly (like a thief), and when it comes the world will be destroyed by fire. The elements themselves will melt (one cannot be sure whether the elements are earth, air, fire, and water, or whether, like Democritus, he thought in terms of some type of atoms). In this process all hidden things will be revealed: nothing will be shielded from judgment. Some, like the teachers 2 Peter refers to, will go to destruction (the nature of this state is not discussed), while the righteous will receive the new heavens and earth. Because nothing in this world is lasting, it therefore makes sense for the believers to live for the coming age and its values. Eschatology determines ethics.

It should be noted that in 2 Peter there is no reference to an intermediate period between the destruction of the world by fire that ends this age, and the establishment of the age to come. Thus, unlike Revelation, he has no millennium (however one interprets that symbol). His focus is on the destruction of this world (which the teachers apparently think is eternal) and the coming of the new.

Significant is the virtual absence of pneumatology in 2 Peter. While believing human beings participate or share in the divine nature, neither this nor the sanctification that it enables is attributed to the Spirit. The Spirit is mentioned, however, when 2 Peter mentions prophecy. In 2 Peter prophecy is probably OT prophecy, so long as one includes *1 Enoch* and other similar literature along with the canonical OT (since 2 Peter accepts the content that Jude derives from *1 Enoch*). This prophecy is the product of the Holy Spirit rather than human will, and thus it must be interpreted accordingly, which perhaps indicates that 2 Peter does believe that the Spirit is present in the teaching of the church. What is clear is that his other source of authority is the teaching of Jesus and his apostles, including the church's witness to the life of Jesus. There is no evidence in 2 Peter that he knows written Gospels, but it is clear that he knows of several Pauline letters. These he groups with "the other writings," which is a term that 2 Peter uses for the writings that we call the OT (understanding that he likely includes other books that we would not include in this category). These writings, including Paul, are a means of revelation, but they can be twisted (the specific reference is probably to Paul's teaching on grace and freedom from the law), resulting in the destruction of those who do so, not because they twist the meaning of Scripture, but because this twisted meaning leads to behavior that destroys them.

Bibliography

Bauckham, R. *Jude, 2 Peter.* WBC 50. Word, 1983; idem. *Jude and the Relatives of Jesus in the Early Church.* T&T Clark, 1990; Bray, G., ed. *James, 1–2 Peter, 1–3 John, Jude.* ACCSNT 11. InterVarsity, 2000; Charles, J. D. *Virtue amidst Vice.* JSNTSup 150. Sheffield Academic Press, 1997; Chester, A., and R. Martin. *The Theology of the Letters of James, Peter, and Jude.* NTT. Cambridge University Press, 1994; Kelly, J. N. D. *A Commentary on the Epistles of Peter and Jude.* BNTC. Baker, 1981; Kraftchick, S. *Jude, 2 Peter.* Abingdon, 2002; Neyrey, J. *2 Peter, Jude.* AB 37C. Doubleday, 1993; Vögtle, A. *Der Judasbrief der zweite Petrusbrief.* EKKNT 22. Benziger/Neukirchener Verlag, 1994; Wall, R. "The Canonical Function of 2 Peter." *BibInt* 9, no. 1 (2001): 64–81; Watson, D. *Invention, Arrangement, and Style.* SBLDS, 104. Scholars Press, 1988.

Peter H. Davids

Pharisees *See* Jewish Context of the NT

Philemon, Book of

Because of its brevity and relative lack of extended theological reflection, Paul's letter to Philemon has often been overlooked or ignored by those interested in constructing a theology of Paul or the NT. It has not fared much better in the churches or in the devotional life of most Christians. At various times, however, when the political and societal setting was right, this short epistle, with its controversial subject matter, has become a storm center of debate. Some interpreters find in Philemon a liberating message of redemption, while others detect a capitulation to the status quo and a failure to realize the radical implications of the gospel.

Returning a Redeemed Slave

Likely written during Paul's Roman imprisonment, Philemon is a letter of intercession to accompany the return of a slave, Onesimus, to his master, Philemon, in Colossae. In the body of the letter, Paul uses various techniques of persuasion to win Philemon's compliance, including a subtle appeal to his authority as an old man and an apostle, his role in Philemon's salvation, his great love for Onesimus, and his impending visit. The *crux interpretum* is v. 16. Does Paul intend for Philemon to manumit Onesimus? Or is Paul simply telling Philemon to treat Onesimus not just as a slave, but also as a Christian brother (and thus not to pursue legal recourse against him)? The history of interpretation is mostly a record of scholarly grapplings with this question.

History of Interpretation

As early as the fourth century CE, Philemon had become a battleground for the dispute over abolitionism. In theological battles with the gnostic Carpocratians, as well as the Eustatians and the Donatist Circumcellions—all abolitionists—Chrysostom, Jerome, and Theodore of Mopsuestia used Philemon to defend slavery. Likewise, Luther and Grotius held that Paul was not advocating the abrogation of slavery, but the reconciliation of a slave and his master. This interpretation held sway, with notable dissenters (e.g., Calvin), until the nineteenth century, when abolitionists again read Philemon as urging Onesimus's manumission, or at least sowing the seeds of slavery's destruction.

The twentieth century witnessed a bewildering number of new interpretations. J. Knox, for example, questioned the traditional reading at almost every point. He argued that Archippus, not Philemon, was actually the owner of Onesimus, and that the Letter to Philemon is to be identified with the Letter to Laodicea mentioned in Col. 4:16. Paul's purpose in writing to Archippus, Knox contended, was to secure Onesimus's release in order that he might accompany Paul in his labors. Paul was successful, and Onesimus later became bishop of Ephesus (cf. Ignatius of Antioch, who mentions an Onesimus in this connection; *Eph.* 1.3). Philemon's inclusion in the canon was engineered by the grateful Onesimus, who collected the correspondence on his hero, Paul.

While Knox's contributions have met with considerable skepticism, many have followed him in radically rethinking the traditional interpretation. Some have suggested that Onesimus was not a runaway, but may simply have overstayed a leave of absence. Perhaps Philemon had commissioned Onesimus to carry out business in Rome, and

Onesimus had failed to return promptly when his task was completed.

Both P. Lampe and B. Rapske have made the case that Onesimus sought out Paul to serve as *amicus domini* and arbitrate a dispute between Onesimus and his master—a common practice in Roman slavery. This view has garnered many proponents among recent commentators (Dunn; Fitzmyer; Bartchy). S. Winter theorizes that Onesimus was sent as a messenger from the Colossian congregation and was converted during his stay with Paul, where he proved to be quite useful, and that Paul therefore wrote Philemon to request Onesimus's continued service. Others have questioned whether Onesimus was a slave at all (Callahan).

Also influential in recent interpretation has been careful historical research into the nature of slavery in the first century (Bartchy). Roman slavery was by no means equivalent to that of nineteenth-century America. Roman slaves varied widely in their social status, their treatment, and the tasks they performed. Manumission was commonplace, so much so that laws were passed in order to limit and regulate the influx of freed slaves into the economy.

Reading Philemon Theologically

Philemon addresses such a particular historical situation that one might legitimately question whether the letter has any contemporary theological significance. While Philemon is hardly a doctrinal treatise or a sustained theological argument, beneath its surface lies a profound conception of Christian community.

Although the letter is primarily for Philemon, it is also addressed to the church in his house, an indication that Paul saw the situation not merely as a private matter, but one that involved the larger church body, who would in turn encourage Philemon to carry out Paul's wishes. Paul stresses this relational dynamic by identifying Onesimus as his "child" (v. 10 NRSV) and his own heart (v. 12), as well as appealing to his *koinōnia* with Philemon (vv. 7, 17).

If the believing community is to be so integrally connected, it must be characterized, as a reflection of its Lord, by reconciliation and forgiveness. Paul encourages Philemon to go the second mile in receiving Onesimus back (v. 21). As an imitator of Christ, Paul offers to pay Onesimus's debts, if necessary, to effect reconciliation, but it is clear that he expects Philemon also to renounce his rights and make no such demands.

Most importantly, Paul manifests his conviction that, as a new society called forth by God's redemptive act in Christ, the church is to be markedly different from the surrounding society, most notably in the importance commonly attached to social and legal status. Paul's appeal in v. 16 is a natural corollary to his pronouncements elsewhere (Gal. 3:28; Col. 3:11). Within the body of Christ, social distinctions are radically relativized in the light of a common relation to Christ.

The troubling question remains: if Paul held to such a rigorous view of Christian community, how could he have failed to request Onesimus's manumission? Some scholars would argue that he does, in fact, make such a request, pointing to the "even more" of v. 21, as well as the seeming contrast between "brother" and "slave" in v. 16. But even if that is the case, such manumission would be limited to Onesimus and would be specifically in order that Onesimus could return to work with Paul (as Col. 4:9 suggests happened). Philemon was hardly intended to be a manifesto on slavery.

It is evident from Paul's other letters that he did not see ownership of slaves as intrinsically sinful at that moment or inimical to Christian fellowship and community (cf. 1 Cor. 7:21–24; Col. 3:22–4:1), so there would be no ideological reason for him to request Onesimus's manumission. Indeed, Paul's response to the situation can rightly be called "a practical outworking" of the household codes in his other epistles (Barth and Blanke 153).

For the believer, who accepts the letter to Philemon as the word of God, neither a tendentious reading of Paul as an egalitarian hero nor a facile dismissal of Paul as a culture-bound bigot will suffice. Some criticize Paul for shortsightedness or a lack of nerve in not applying his prior magnificent statement of Christian equality (Gal. 3:28) to the situation of Onesimus, but perhaps they have derived their fundamental convictions more from the Enlightenment than from the Scriptures. Such an attempt to be more Pauline than Paul is misguided.

In the final analysis, a focus on slavery has obscured the true theological message of Philemon: The church is to be a radically new society, where divisions founded upon race, gender, and social status are overcome by unity in Christ. In the church the reconciliation and forgiveness modeled by the Lord is manifested in a spirit of agapeic servanthood. Without dispute, this is a message the church in every age needs to hear.

See also Slavery

Bibliography

Bartchy, S. *Mallon Chrēsai*. SBLDS 11. Scholars Press, 1973; Barth, M., and H. Blanke. *The Letter to Philemon*. ECC. Eerdmans, 2000; Callahan, A. *Embassy of Onesimus*. NTC. Trinity, 1997; Dunn, J. *The Epistles to the Colossians and to Philemon*. NIGTC. Eerdmans, 1996; Fitzmyer, J. *The Letter to Philemon*. AB 34C. Doubleday, 2000; Knox, J. *Philemon among the Letters of Paul*. University of Chicago Press, 1935; Lampe, P. "Keine 'Slavenflucht' des Onesimus." *ZNW* 76 (1985): 135–73; O'Brien, P. *Colossians, Philemon*. WBC. Word, 1982; Rapske, B. "The Prisoner Paul in the Eyes of Onesimus." *NTS* 37 (1991): 187–203; Winter, S. "Paul's Letter to Philemon." *NTS* 33 (1987): 1–15.

Daniel R. Streett

Philippians, Book of

Paul's letter to the Christians in Philippi is a small gem. Though it covers a good many well-known theological topics, including particularly Christology, soteriology, and eschatology, its chief and largely unremarked value for theological interpretation is the way in which it hammers out a Christian view of what it means to live within a pagan society. "Let your public behavior be worthy of the gospel of the Messiah" (1:27 AT). This refers not simply to Christian ethics, but also to how Christians behave in the public arena. Most modern readers of Paul have not considered the extraordinary challenge facing the young church, of how to negotiate a totally new way of living. What would it mean to give allegiance, in a city like Philippi, to Jesus as the world's true Lord (2:11)?

The letter is written from prison, to thank the Philippian church for their financial support. Those held in ancient prisons were not provided for by the authorities, and so were utterly dependent on family and friends. In Paul's case, traveling from place to place, this meant that he had to rely on the churches he had founded, and Philippi had come to his help (1:5; 2:25–30; 4:10–19). Many suppose the prison to be in Rome; a good case can be made for Ephesus, though not much turns on this. (Ephesus had its own Praetorian guard; 1:13.) Paul, it seemed, was aware that the charges against him could result in his death (1:18–26), though in prayer he had glimpsed that he still had work to do and so reckoned that he would be released.

The word he uses to describe the "partnership" into which he and the Philippians have entered, the business partnership in which they will support him when he needs their help (1:5, 7), is *koinōnia*, often translated "fellowship." As with some of Paul's other key terms, this word has often been allowed, in the history of interpretation, to slide into referring simply to the way in which Christians feel toward and with one another; but for Paul it was severely practical. It meant a sharing in common life that resulted directly in mutual support; and also it meant that Paul and his supporters belonged to one another with a family identity. What happens to one, happens to all. The fact that in 1:7 it is not clear whether Paul means that he holds them in his heart, or that they hold him in theirs, tells its own story, as does the whole opening paragraph (1:3–11). Initial theological reflection on Philippians ought to focus on the nature of *koinōnia* and the strange fact that so many modern churches manage to ignore it.

So what does it mean for the Philippians that Paul is in prison? Most likely, some kind of threat: if that is what the authorities are doing to our apostle, what will happen to us? This threat was already well known in Philippi, judging from the hints in various parts of the letter (e.g., 1:28–30). Living as Christians in the pagan environment of northern Greece (on the main road from Rome to the East, with a well-established Roman colony supplying some of the leading citizens) must have posed all kinds of problems. Christians would not join in the regular pagan festivals, including those in honor of the emperor. They would not offer sacrifices at pagan shrines, or take part in the other street-level pagan practices. Some of them might already have suffered in business from their newfound faith, as clients became suspicious or scornful and went elsewhere. Others may have run into actual verbal or physical abuse. Does this mean they have made a dreadful mistake? No, replies Paul; but from here on, you need to think through how to live appropriately within the world that has suddenly become strange to you and in turn is likely to regard you as a stranger.

That is what he is praying for the church in Philippi (1:9–11). First, he prays that they will love one another more and more (like *koinōnia*, the word *agapē* refers first and foremost to something you do, not something you feel). Second, he prays that they will do so "with knowledge and all discernment, so that they may be able to make right judgments about things that differ, so that they may be blameless and innocent for the day of the Messiah" (AT). Since Paul more or less repeats and expands this in 2:12–16, it ought to be clear that we are here in touch with one of the key aims of the letter. He is not, again, simply talking about "how to live as good Christians"; he is talking about how to work out what it means to live as a follower of Jesus Christ in a world where there are many things that are good and many things that are not. They are neither to reject everything in the surrounding world nor to embrace everything. They need to develop a keen sense of discrimination. If this set of questions fails to register as a topic in theological interpretation, it is a sign that the Scripture-reading church has forgotten part of its basic calling. It is much easier to decide either to go along with everything in the world or to reject everything in the world than to work out a mature, wise, and discriminating path of loyalty to Jesus as Lord amid the pressures and problems of life and society.

Paul brings them up to date with what has been happening to himself (1:12–26), and in doing so introduces one of the main themes of the letter: the union between the Messiah and his people. He is in prison because of his loyalty to the Messiah, and his life is so bound up with that of Jesus that his sole hope is for whatever happens to him to bring glory to his Lord. It is not entirely clear to whom he is referring when he speaks of some "announcing the Messiah because of envy and rivalry" in 1:15, 17 (AT). They may be rival Christian missionaries, but a good case can be made instead for seeing them as pagans who, affronted that Paul is declaring a crucified Jew to be the Lord of the world, are telling others that this is what he is saying. That, for Paul, would constitute "announcing the Messiah"; for him, "proclaiming Christ" (1:15) does not mean trying to persuade people to accept Jesus, but simply making the announcement, like a herald: Jesus, the Messiah, is Lord! As long as people are saying that, Paul declares, he will be content (1:18).

The main appeal of the letter is stated in 1:27–30. The Philippians must figure out how to live within their surrounding social and cultural world in a manner worthy of the announcement of the Messiah's good news. Central to this will be the unity of Christians, a favorite theme in Paul; opposition and persecution might threaten to split the church, but they must stand firm. Paul then develops this appeal in 2:1–4, which heaps up what to us appear almost impossible demands: think the same thing, have the same love, share the same soul, always seek one another's advantage and not your own. This is the radically different lifestyle that must characterize the Christian community and enable it to stand out, and stand firm, within the watching, curious, and potentially hostile world.

All of this is then undergirded and given specific focus and direction by the spectacular poem of 2:6–11. This is the point at which much of the history of the interpretation of Philippians has been concentrated, and especially on 2:6–7. These verses appear to give an account of the way in which Jesus can be identified with and as the preexistent divine being who became incarnate by "emptying himself" (2:7). Some nineteenth- and twentieth-century Lutheran and Anglican theologians have spoken of "kenotic Christology" (from the Greek *ekenōsen*, "emptied" [2:7 NRSV]) and have used this passage as a key to explore what aspect of Jesus' divinity was abandoned or put on hold when he became a human being. This inquiry goes back to the patristic period, but no special theories were worked out then. However, this is not Paul's concern. For him, as for John, the point is not that we know in advance who "God" is and can then, as it were, fit Jesus into that definition, but that only when looking at Jesus himself do we discover who the true God really is. The second half of the poem (2:9–11) insists, with its opening "therefore" (*dio*, 2:9), that the honor given to Jesus in his exaltation is the result of what has been accomplished in incarnation and crucifixion: he has done what only God can do. For theological as well as grammatical reasons, the key phrase in verse 6 should be translated, "He did not regard his equality with God as something to exploit." Jesus was always equal with God, and, so far from compromising his divinity, expressed that equality in incarnation and crucifixion. This passage stands at the heart of the theological reinterpretation of Jewish traditions in early Christianity. To Jesus is now given the glory that Israel's one and only God declares he will not share with another (Isa. 45:23; 48:11; Phil. 2:10–11).

All this wonderful Christology is placed in the service of Paul's deeply subversive critique of Caesar and his world. The implicit contrast throughout the poem, as in Mark 10:42–45, is between the way in which earthly rulers normally rule and the way in which Jesus expressed his divinity and arrived at his world sovereignty. And this leads back to the appeal of 2:13–14. Over against many interpretative traditions worrying about Paul telling people to "work out your salvation," as though this might compromise justification by faith, Paul means precisely: Therefore, figure out, calculate, and reckon it up, what your kind of "salvation" will mean in practice. Caesar offered one kind of "salvation": live under my rule and I will look after you—a kind of global protection racket. The salvation Jesus offered was of quite a different type, and it is up to communities of Christians to work out how to live within it. More particularly, they must bear in mind their calling to live as lights in the dark world.

The second chapter ends with an extensive recommendation for Timothy, and a warm passage about Epaphroditus, the Philippians' messenger to Paul. Both are held up as examples of the selfless service that Paul commends throughout.

The second half of the letter has sometimes been thought to be a separate composition, and certainly the link in 3:1 feels a bit jerky. But 3:2–21 has so many close thematic and linguistic connections to the earlier chapters, and to 2:6–11 in particular, that it looks as though Paul is consciously building on what he has just said. His appeal in chapter 3 is for the Philippians to be "imitating" him (3:17 NRSV), but this is initially strange. In 3:2–11 he describes in detail how he has abandoned his pride of ancestry and "righteousness under the law" (3:6 NRSV) so that he might find his identity and life as a member of the Messiah's people. He himself follows the pattern of renunciation and resurrection foreshadowed in 2:6–11. This passage integrates closely with the more-developed statements of "justification by faith," rather than by "the works of the law," as in Romans and Galatians. It strengthens the argument for seeing justification not simply as a truth about how sinners get saved but also as a truth about how Jews and Gentiles come together in a single family. The Philippians have no such ancestry or background in the Jewish law. But they do have pride of civic status, as one of the premier Roman cities and colonies in northern Greece. Maybe Paul is saying—this, too, is something with which theological interpretation of Philippians needs to reckon—that they must be prepared to regard their social and civic privileges in the same way that he has regarded his. They need to look at the world in which they live, not in its own terms, but from the perspective of the gospel. According to the gospel, the Lord Jesus, the royal Messiah, will come from heaven with all power vested in him, and will transform both the present situation of the little beleaguered church, surrounded by the wicked and idolatrous world (3:18–19), and the frail, mortal bodies of individual Christians. Paul here applies 2:9–11 to the particular situation of the church in a pagan environment. This is what it means to give allegiance to Jesus, not Caesar, as the world's true Lord.

This is what it means to "stand firm in the Lord" (4:1 NRSV). We should recognize, as a matter of urgently needed theological revision, that when Paul says "our citizenship is in heaven" in 3:20 (NRSV), he does not mean, "Therefore that is where we shall go when we die." That is not how the logic of citizenship worked. Roman citizens living in Philippi would not expect to return to Rome upon retirement, but to be agents of Roman civilization in Philippi and the surrounding countryside.

The central appeal of chapter 4 is, once more, to live within the wider world, not in a state of nervous anxiety at what may happen, but in total trust in the Lord himself (4:4–7) and in readiness to pray about every concern. This leads to the remarkable double command of 4:8–9. On the one hand, they are to think about anything at all that has the stamp of truth, holiness, justice, and so on. Paul is well aware, and wants them to be so aware, that the world is full of beauty and truth, and that they must celebrate it and not pretend that it is all confined to the church. On the other hand, when they think about how to behave, they must once more, as in 3:17, reflect on Paul's own modeling of Christian living in the world. Here is a point of theological interpretation that the twenty-first century church needs more than ever. Christian leaders have an awesome responsibility to model the life that the gospel produces. Others will follow their lead, for better and for worse.

The letter closes, as we saw, with further detailed thanks for the gift the Philippians have sent to Paul, and with reflections on the way in which God works strangely but powerfully to meet the needs of those who live and proclaim the gospel. Philippians, after all, is a severely practical letter, even though the Christology of 2:6–11 and the soteriology of 3:2–11 are among Paul's finest pieces of condensed theology. But that, too, is part of the point. Theological interpretation of Scripture needs constantly to remind itself that we know what true theology is, just as we know who the true God is, by looking at what it means to take the form of a servant.

Bibliography

Bockmuehl, M. *The Epistle to the Philippians.* BNTC. Black/Hendrikson, 1998; Fee, G. *Paul's Letter to the Philippians.* NICNT. Eerdmans, 1995; Oakes, P. *Philippians.* SNTSMS 110. Cambridge University Press, 2001; O'Brien, P. *The Epistle to the Philippians.* NIGTC. Eerdmans, 1991; Wright, N. T. *The Climax of the Covenant.* Fortress, 1992; idem. *What St. Paul Really Said.* Eerdmans, 1997.

N. T. Wright

Philo   *See* Jewish Context of the NT

Philology   *See* Etymology; Language, Linguistics; Lexicons, NT; Lexicons, OT

Philosophical Theology   *See* Philosophy

Philosophy

Philosophy, which etymology suggests to be "the love of wisdom," is perhaps best thought of as the study of abstract and ultimate questions and their answers. What is meant by "abstract and ultimate"? To be philosophical, questions and their answers must be abstract, rather than particular questions of empirical matters of fact: philosophy does not ask what causes the rain to fall, but what causation is. Being abstract on its own is not sufficient for being philosophical, however. After all, pure mathematics is an abstract discipline, though not a philosophical one, because it lacks the required ultimacy or generality. Philosophy is not so much interested in the nature of a triangle as in the nature of geometric objects or of abstract objects in general. The nature of abstract objects is an ultimate question, since abstract objects themselves do not belong to any significant more-general sort save that of existent objects. Much of philosophy is conceptual analysis, the analysis of various abstract concepts, often cashed out in terms of the investigation of the necessary and sufficient conditions for something to fall under that concept. On the other hand, philosophers have also advanced arguments for and against the existence of things falling under particular concepts: the natural theologian's arguments for the existence of God constitute one example.

Philosophy is traditionally divided into different branches, according to the subject matter under investigation. Thus, metaphysics investigates the fundamental nature of reality, including asking what kinds of things are represented in existence (the subdivision of metaphysics known as "ontology"), and the fundamental categories of being: existence, substance, attribute, relation, causation, instantiation, space, time, and so on. Epistemology investigates the nature of knowledge and asks what sorts of thing, if any, feature in our knowledge. Ethics seeks to answer the question of how we should live and also to analyze the various moral notions of goodness and badness, rightness and wrongness. Aesthetics is on a similar tack: it seeks to analyze the aesthetic notions of beauty and ugliness, sublimity and ridiculousness, and to ask what sorts of things have these qualities. Logic seeks to analyze how we should think, and to codify rules of correct thought in a mechanical way that even a computer could follow. In addition to these subdisciplines, there are many subdisciplines concerned with abstract and ultimate questions raised by other disciplines. Thus, philosophy of science deals with the nature of scientific theories, whether science aims at truth, and how to demarcate science from other intellectual activities. Philosophy of mathematics deals with the nature and existence of mathematical entities and mathematical truth. Philosophy of language deals with the nature of language and the associated concepts of meaning, word, concept, and so on. Philosophy of logic, usually though misleadingly known as "philosophical logic," analyzes the fundamental concepts of logic, such as truth, predicate, name, validity, and so on. Political philosophy considers the question of how human society should be organized. And philosophy of religion deals with the meaning and truth of religious claims, such as whether God exists, what God is like, and so on. There are indefinitely many other special branches: the philosophy of history, the philosophy of law, the philosophy of psychology, and so on. Philosophy of mind is often singled out as a special branch, but in truth, since this consists in the study of the nature and existence of the mind, it is part of metaphysics.

Philosophy is usually thought to have begun with Thales in the sixth century BCE, as far as our records tell us. Our sources for these early philosophers, known as the "pre-Socratics," since they precede (or are contemporaries of) Socrates, are largely fragmentary and incomplete until we reach fourth-century BCE Athens. Then we have Plato (and, through him, his mentor Socrates) and Aristotle; their works set the direction of philosophy for two thousand years and still exercise a pervasive influence. Initially, their legacy was taken up by competing schools: the Epicureans, the Stoics, and the Skeptics. In the third century CE these schools were largely transcended in influence by the rise of Neoplatonism, represented in Rome by Plotinus and his disciple Porphyry. In the fifth century this Neoplatonic tradition of thought combined with orthodox Christianity in the works of Augustine, who lived in North Africa. Boethius may fairly be called the last philosopher of the classical period; he died in Italy in 524 CE, five years before the closure of the Athenian schools. Philosophy in the medieval period may be said to have begun with the Irish John Scotus Eriugena in France in the ninth century. He was followed by the Arabic philosophers Avicenna (Ibn Sina) in the eleventh century and Averroës (Ibn Rushd) in the twelfth century, and the latter's contemporary the Jewish philosopher Maimonides. Between Avicenna and Averroës appear the Christian philosophers Anselm and Abelard. The thirteenth century is the high point of medieval philosophy, beginning with Albert the Great and then achieving its acme in Bonaventure and his greater contemporary, Thomas Aquinas. Duns Scotus rounded off this remarkable century, and William of Ockham dominated the first half of the fourteenth century.

Bacon and Hobbes inaugurated the era of modern philosophy in the seventeenth century. But Descartes was its real founder and the first of the so-called rationalists, followed by Spinoza in the Netherlands and Leibniz in Germany. Opposed to the rationalists were the so-called empiricists: Locke from England, Berkeley from Ireland, and Hume from Scotland. It was Hume that awoke Immanuel Kant, the greatest eighteenth-century philosopher, from his "dogmatic slumbers." After Kant came Hegel, Schopenhauer, and (later) Marx, who built their systems in Germany, though they achieved more lasting philosophical influence on the Continent than in Great Britain or North America. The reverse was the case with Gottlob Frege, who is now regarded in English-speaking circles as the founder of analytical philosophy, though he is barely known in his native Germany. Contemporary with Frege in Germany we have such diverse figures as the phenomenologist Edmund Husserl and Friedrich Nietzsche. In the twentieth century the cleavage between Britain and the Continent was embodied in the difference between Wittgenstein, an Austrian who worked in Cambridge under his mentor Russell, and Heidegger, who remained in his native Germany throughout the Nazi period and the Second World War. In the latter half of the twentieth century, after the brief flourishing of "Oxford ordinary language philosophy" and the earlier logical positivist movement, the spotlight of analytical philosophy moved to North America. Continental philosophy turned to France for its leaders: First appeared the existentialists, preeminently Sartre. Later came the deconstructionists and postmodernists, such as Foucault and Derrida, whose work tends to be most influential in English-speaking countries outside departments of academic philosophy, both in the public domain and in other academic disciplines, such as theology.

The divide between analytical and continental philosophy is not so much a difference of subject matter as one of style, though there has been a tendency for continental philosophers to concern themselves with the great questions of the meaning of life and the nature of love; analytic philosophers have tended to concentrate on smaller questions, such as the meaning of "if" and the nature of a name. The analytical tradition places great emphasis on clarity, precision, argument, and logic, whereas the continental tradition has greater affinities with literature and rhetoric. One consequence of this has been that the technical style of much analytical philosophy has prevented its diffusion into other academic departments, whereas continental philosophy has been eagerly embraced by many other such departments, particularly those with long literary associations, such as language and theology departments.

The relationship between philosophy and theology is as contested as anything in philosophy. Opinions range from Sir Alfred Ayer's that theology is meaningless nonsense that philosophy had to expose as such, to the Barthian view that philosophy is captive to the infidel Reason and that theology has a future insofar as, by contrast, it consists in submission to Christ. Some philosophers see their role as being to analyze the concepts that theology makes use of: not just such straightforwardly religious concepts as that of God and the soul, but ancillary concepts such as that of causation, time, and knowledge. More ambitious philosophers think of philosophy as providing a system of ultimate reality, and of theology as the branch of the system that concerns God. Lately there has arisen a movement called "Christian philosophy," centered around the University of Notre Dame and the figure of Alvin Plantinga. This movement consists in the attempt to provide substantive answers to traditional philosophical questions from a distinctively Christian viewpoint. A good example is Plantinga's answer to the age-old philosophical question "What is knowledge?" His answer is that knowledge is a true belief produced by mental faculties that are aimed at truth and working as God intended them to work. The last part of this definition obviously does not appeal to much of the secular philosophical world, but it is a mark of the Christian philosophy movement that its representatives do not care much about what the secular philosophical world thinks. As Plantinga puts it, Christian philosophers are called to do philosophy of the sort that will edify the church. The difference between this and another sort of

Christian philosophy, such as, for example, the work of Herman Dooyeweerd, is that the latter attempts to put forward a systematic interpretation of the whole of reality. Plantinga and his acolytes, however, are content to produce Christian philosophy piecemeal as individual Christian answers to pressing contemporary philosophical questions.

Of particular interest is the connection between philosophy and Scripture. Some Christians, "biblicists," insist that all religious knowledge is gained from Scripture's exact words or what may be inferred from them by "necessary consequence," which leaves no room for additional philosophy of religion. Others insist that human reason is powerless when it comes to the infinite and the transcendent. Others again have claimed that Greek philosophy has sullied the pure gospel truth, and they have attempted to reconstruct theology without the categories of Greek philosophy. At the other end of the spectrum, some Christians of a rationalistic bent, often called "Socinians" after a famous rationalist, insist that only the portion of revelation that is verifiable by human reason may be taken as gospel truth. It seems clear to the present writer that human reason is no match for divine reason. Thus, if there is a divine revelation, it behooves us to believe all of it, even those parts that we cannot justify. Nevertheless, it must also be conceded that the Bible does not define every term it uses, including the term "God." Philosophy comes into play because some terms used in the Bible, such as "free," are capable of more than one explanation, and because more than one philosophical outlook is compatible with the Scriptures. Hence, there is room for genuine philosophical debate among sincere Bible-believing Christians: Scripture in itself does not determine which is the correct philosophy. A cautionary note needs also to be sounded: the fact that the human authors of the Bible had a particular philosophical outlook does not necessarily make that outlook correct any more than the fact that they had a particular scientific outlook makes that correct.

Sometimes Christians misunderstand Paul's warning in Col. 2:8–10, "See to it that no one takes you captive through hollow and deceptive philosophy," as being a declaration that philosophy in general is hollow and deceptive. In fact, Paul is warning the Christians of Colossae to beware of philosophies that are hollow and deceptive—such philosophies do not, alas, carry on them labels marked "hollow and deceptive," so one should be wary of any philosophy lest it be hollow and deceptive. That Paul does not suffer from *odium philosophicum* is clear from his approving use of a quotation from the Greek philosopher Epimenides (Acts 17:28a). It may sound noble to say that one is being purely scriptural and adopting no philosophy at all, but such a statement betrays confusion: it is impossible to have any beliefs about abstract and ultimate matters without having "a philosophy," even if an incomplete and unsystematic one. It is tempting to reply that one gets one's philosophy solely from Scripture; but then one runs up against the point just mentioned that one needs an understanding of the concepts found in Scripture, including the philosophical ones, in order to understand Scripture's overall message. One cannot do this without a prior understanding of the concepts any more than one ignorant of Hebrew and Greek could just sit down and read the original words.

Historically, many of the great philosophers have also been theological interpreters of Scripture: Thomas Aquinas wrote Bible commentaries, as did Augustine, and Bishops Berkeley and Butler also wrote theological as well as philosophical works. Every philosopher up till the time of Hume and La Mettrie believed in God (or the gods, in the case of most of the ancient philosophers). In addition, every Christian theologian was traditionally trained in philosophy, a requirement that was actually encoded in the Westminster Assembly's *Form of Church Government*.

Since the modern age, philosophical analysis and positions have shaped both the form and content of biblical interpretation, especially via "hermeneutics." While these often are theologically loaded (and the distinction between philosophy and theology is always tricky and tenuous), they may be labeled "philosophical" in the sense of being developed without positive reference to Christian doctrine.

For example, Frege's distinction between "sense" and "reference" has been influential within grammatical-historical approaches, especially for conservatives who have held to Hirsch's distinction between a text's "meaning" and "significance." Conversely, continental philosophies such as Gadamer's, or those spawned by Derrida's "deconstruction," have generated other programs of biblical interpretation.

Thiselton in particular has chronicled such influence of Heideggerian existentialism on Bultmann and his followers during the twentieth century. At the dawn of the twenty-first, the interpretative pluralism (or even anarchy) of biblical scholarship no doubt owes in part to philosophical sources (both intentionally borrowed and unintentionally swallowed).

Among theologically interested interpreters, the most influential alternatives may be an ad hoc use of philosophy (following Frei and a more literary emphasis on biblical narrative), and/or the selective integration of analytic and continental styles that characterizes Ricoeur, following up his interests in speech-act philosophy, narrativity, and metaphor. Both streams perhaps need more attention to philosophy of history (beyond the start of N. T. Wright), while both have made varied uses of Wittgenstein (and concepts such as "language-games").

It is not practical for every Christian to be trained in both the theological interpretation of Scripture and in philosophy. This sad fact, however, should not be taken to encourage further diversification between the two disciplines: Christian philosophers need the work of theological interpreters of Scripture, and theological interpreters of Scripture need the work of Christian philosophers.

Bibliography

General Encyclopedias: Craig, E., ed. *Routledge Encyclopedia of Philosophy.* Routledge, 1998; Edwards, P., ed. *Encyclopedia of Philosophy.* 8 vols. Macmillan, 1967. *Supplement,* ed. D. Borchert. Macmillan Reference USA, 1996; Honderich, T., ed. *The Oxford Companion to Philosophy.* Oxford University Press, 1995; *General Dictionaries:* Blackburn, S., ed. *Dictionary of Philosophy.* Oxford University Press, 1996; Flew, A., ed. *A Dictionary of Philosophy.* Pan, 1975; Urmson, J. O., and J. Rée, eds. *The Concise Encyclopedia of Western Philosophy and Philosophers.* Routledge, 1975; *General Introductions:* Blackburn, S. *Think.* Oxford University Press, 1999; Hospers, J. *An Introduction to Philosophical Analysis.* Routledge, 1997; Russell, B. *The Problems of Philosophy.* Oxford University Press, 1959; Scruton, R. *Modern Philosophy.* Penguin, 1996; *Histories:* Copleston, F. *A History of Philosophy.* 8 vols. Burnes, Oates & Washbourne, 1946–66; Parkinson, G. H. R., and S. G. Shanker, eds. *Routledge History of Philosophy.* 10 vols. Routledge, 1993–99; Russell, B. *A History of Western Philosophy.* Allen & Unwin, 1961; Scruton, R. *A Short History of Modern Philosophy.* Routledge, 1984; *Relation to Theology:* Augustine. *City of God;* Plantinga, A. "Advice to Christian Philosophers." *Faith and Philosophy* 1 (1984): 253–71; idem. *Warranted Christian Belief.* Oxford University Press, 1999; Thiselton, A. *The Two Horizons.* Eerdmans, 1980.

Daniel Hill with Daniel J. Treier

Phronēsis *See* Imagination; Practical Theology; Theological Hermeneutics, Contemporary; Wisdom

Play *See* Deconstruction

Plot *See* Narrative Criticism

Poetry

Poetry in the Bible

Even if many Bible translations set their text entirely in prose and do not indicate the presence of poetry in the visual appearance of the page, poetry is present in both the OT and NT—whether in complete poems, fragments, or sayings. In the OT, Psalms and Proverbs are all poetry, Job is largely poetry, and the prophetic books contain significant sections of poetry. Pentateuchal poems are found in Gen. 49, Exod. 15, and Deut. 32–33. In the NT, we find poems in Luke's nativity account and a hymn in Phil. 2:6–11 (Longman 81). Add to these the many of Christ's sayings that are poetic, and the book of Revelation, which contains multiple hymns and numerous figures of speech. Vast portions of the Bible are poems or reflect a poetic use of language.

Western scholars have recognized this for centuries, though not all have agreed on what constitutes biblical "poetry." Modern discussions begin with Bishop Lowth's *Lectures on the Sacred Poetry of the Hebrews* (1753). Bishop Lowth identified parallelism as the essential characteristic of Hebrew poetry and identified several types of parallelism he found in the Bible. James Kugel established the parameters for the modern discussion of Hebrew poetry in general and parallelism in particular in his landmark book, *The Idea of Biblical Poetry.* Tremper Longman discusses semantic parallelism and grammatical parallelism, and in *Words of Delight* Leland Ryken lists four types of parallelism.

In recent years, modern scholars have taken Bishop Lowth's initial definition in new directions. James Kugel galvanized contemporary study with his statements that there is no "poetry" in the Bible—at least no word for it (69)—and that using the term "poetry" "distorts" our understanding of parallelism and is even "damaging" in biblical scholarship (71). C. S. Lewis, on the other hand, claims that "all language about things other than physical objects is necessarily metaphorical" ("Is?" 102). Current scholarship demonstrates that poetry is not easy to define or identify, but that we must continue our work if we are to understand vast portions of the Bible.

Features of Biblical Poetry

Formulating a definition is not as easy as it seems. If we begin with literary glossaries and handbooks, we find only the most general of definitions. *The Bedford Glossary of Critical and Literary Terms* begins by distinguishing poetry from prose, as "any rhythmical or metrical composition" (Murfin and Ray 290). William Harmon and C. Hugh Holman define poetry as "a term applied to the many forms in which human beings have given rhythmic expression to their most intense perceptions of the world, themselves, and the relation of the two" (398). Neither of these definitions takes us very far.

When we turn to biblical scholarship, we find that most scholars usually do not attempt a complete definition of biblical poetry. Rather, they identify a set of features characteristic of biblical poetry. Because most of the material available today relates to Hebrew poetry, I will list the characteristics that modern scholars identify in it and follow this information with a comment on the NT.

The first feature of Hebrew poetry is repetition, or what Robert Alter calls a "dynamics of repetition," in which parallel phrases develop, rather than repeat (as Lowth suggested), an idea introduced in the first phrase (11). Alter emphasizes the subtle shifts in meaning that the parallelisms bring to bear upon the initial colon or phrase. J. P. Fokkelman asserts that repetition, or what he calls "quantity," is the essential feature of biblical poetry, and that it applies at all levels in the poem—cola, strophes, stanzas (including acrostics), and the poem as a whole. A related concept is Kugel's notion of "regularity" (69). These concepts of repetition go beyond Bishop Lowth's idea of simple parallelism and apply to all levels of the poem. Second and third phrases in parallel structure, for instance, modify the initial meaning. Parallelism is no longer seen as a mechanical poetic repetition, as for Bishop Lowth.

The second feature of Hebrew poetry is its terseness (Longman 82; Berlin 5). Poetry is made terse by its simultaneous exercise of several devices, including conciseness, ellipsis, lack of connectives, and figures of speech. Unlike prose, poetry builds on the individual word and line, not the sentence. Much is said in little.

The third characteristic of Hebrew poetry is its "pattern of intensification" (Alter 11), or its "complex of heightening effects" (Kugel 94). Intensification in biblical poetry results from its terseness and parallelisms. Terseness concentrates attention, thereby intensifying poetry over prose, and parallelism arrests the reader's thought, focusing it on one idea for a longer period of time than the rapid reading in prose typically allows. Rather than anticipating the next point in a propositional

argument as we do in prose, the reader ponders and appreciates the idea or image evoked in the poem. When terseness and parallelism work together, as they often do in biblical poetry, the poem magnifies the effect on the reader, involving emotions as well as intellect.

Fourth, Hebrew poetry—like all poetry—uses figures of speech as its stock in trade. Of course, prose often uses figures of speech, but poetry employs them more frequently than prose. Figures of speech include metaphor, imagery, symbol, apostrophe, irony, prosopopoeia, and even the anthropomorphisms so common in the Psalms. Figures of speech are not decorations or crutches for illiterate people; rather, they convey meaning in terms that could not be communicated exactly the same in any other way. The familiar beginning of Ps. 23, "The LORD is my shepherd, I shall not want" (KJV), is more than a comforting image; it is a theological statement framed in terms of the image and its context in the psalm at large. Osborne rightly reminds us, "Theology rarely stems from the metaphor itself but rather from the whole context of which it is a part" (188). Indeed, the rest of Ps. 23 develops the variations on the theme of Yahweh as shepherd of his people.

The final feature of Hebrew poetry is again one that it shares with poetry in all languages—its concreteness. Poetry has a "tendency to concretization" (Alter 21), which allows the reader to see, taste, touch, smell, or hear. Poetry reifies theology, naming concrete objects and using them as images or symbols. Biblical poetry is rooted in the material world and points beyond this world to one that we apprehend by faith. Figures of speech are particularly apt devices in poetry because they are the forms of language in which the disparate is united—object and idea, vehicle and tenor synthesized in one.

A word is in order here about poetry in the NT, for all of the characteristics mentioned above are associated with Hebrew poetry. The NT does contain some poems, but it also uses language poetically even in the prose sections. The nativity hymns of Luke 1–2 derive from Hebrew models and even echo OT hymns. The book of Revelation contains several doxologies that are framed as poems (4:8, 11; 5:9–10, 12, 13; 15:3–4). Apart from these obvious poems, the NT writers often use language poetically. John writes poetically in the multilayered images of Revelation. Christ himself often speaks poetically in the parables, and also in his many "I am's." Leland Ryken comments, "The language of the New Testament is often poetic" (441), and our hermeneutic will do well to account for its poems and poetic passages.

Implications for Interpreting Poetry in Scripture

The language of poetry functions differently than the language of prose and therefore must be examined with appropriate hermeneutical principles. If we read the Psalms the way we read the polemical sections of an epistle like Romans, we run serious risk of misinterpreting them. How then should we read biblical poetry? In *Reflections on the Psalms*, C. S. Lewis tells us that we must read the Psalms as poems: "Most emphatically, the Psalms must be read as poems; as lyrics, with all the licences [*sic*] and all the formalities, the hyperboles, the emotional rather than logical connections, which are proper to lyric poetry" (3). How then do we read poetry as poetry?

Let me suggest four questions to guide an active, engaged reading of biblical poetry (see Travers). Questions are preferable to rules, for questioning requires the reader to participate actively, and poetry of all modes of language requires active reading. The questions:

1. What is the overall effect of the poem? By overall effect, I mean the subject matter in the poem and the tone with which the poet approaches that subject.
2. What is the structure of the poem? As I use it here, "structure" relates to the macrocosmic patterning of the poem and to its genre.
3. What are the figures of speech in the poem? The poet develops his points in the terms of these figures of speech.
4. What are the themes and theology of the poem? This should be the final question we ask, for the answers to it come from developing accurate responses to the first three questions.

Take Ps. 97 as an example. The overall effect is the awesome glory of God and the call to praise him. The structure of Ps. 97 is the tripartite division of a hymn of public praise: a call to praise Yahweh (v. 1); Yahweh's praiseworthy attributes and acts (vv. 2–9); and exhortation to praise Yahweh in the sanctuary (vv. 10–12). Moving from a macrocosmic view in the heavens to the microcosmic in man, Ps. 97 glorifies Yahweh and calls on readers to worship him. There are too many figures of speech to examine here, but we can take vv. 2–6 by way of illustration. The "clouds and thick darkness" (v. 2) show Yahweh to be separate from us, above us, and holy. Righteousness

and justice are associated in a metonymy with Yahweh's throne, underscoring the nature of Yahweh himself. The three images of fire, lightning, and melting mountains (vv. 3–5) all demonstrate Yahweh's power over nature. Fire also suggests holiness, for it consumes Yahweh's (unrighteous) enemies; lightning undoubtedly depicts Yahweh's power over nature; and melting mountains emphasize his prerogative to "de-create" as well as create. In short, Yahweh is sovereign. Verse 6 concludes this picture of Yahweh, reiterating nature's declaration of his glory, and the obligation and privilege it is for all people to praise him. The themes of Ps. 97 relate Yahweh's sovereignty directly to human praise, making the attributes of Yahweh the reason for worship. As with all Scripture, Ps. 97 demands a response from the reader.

Hermeneutically, there is much more that needs to be said. Actively engaging these four simple questions in our reading, however, will go a long way toward helping us read poetry as it was written—and inspired.

Current Issues

Current scholarship on biblical poetry goes in at least two directions—the text and the reader. First, some scholars emphasize the close reading of the text, carried out in "linguistic analysis" (Howard 329). M. O'Connor insists that "syntactical requirements" determine Hebrew poetry. David M. Howard Jr. extends O'Connor's insights on syntax to include "semantics, phonology, and morphology" (350) as necessary elements in a fully developed understanding of the meanings of a biblical poem. Another dimension to the current interest in biblical poems comes from the study of traditional, time-transcending poetic devices as they are used in the Bible (e.g., Longman; Ryken). The reemphasis on the text in current biblical criticism reflects C. S. Lewis's idea in *Reflections on the Psalms*: "Poetry too is a little incarnation, giving body to what had been before invisible and inaudible" (5). Poetry demands close reading.

The second emphasis in modern scholarship is on the reader. This focus is reflected in two recent volumes—*The New Literary Criticism and the Hebrew Bible* (Exum and Clines) and *The New Literary Criticism and the New Testament* (Malbon and McKnight). These volumes demonstrate the increasing influence of such postmodern "literary" approaches in biblical scholarship as deconstruction, feminism, and new historicism.

These reader-centered hermeneutical approaches will provide significant information for biblical scholars, but it is the text-centered interpretations that will extend our understanding of how biblical poetry works.

See also Imagery; Metaphor

Bibliography

Alter, R. *The Art of Biblical Poetry*. Basic Books, 1985; Berlin, A. *The Dynamics of Biblical Parallelism*. Indiana University Press, 1985; Exum, J., and D. Clines, eds. *The New Literary Criticism and the Hebrew Bible*. JSOT-Sup 143. Sheffield Academic Press, 1993; Fokkelman, J. *Reading Biblical Poetry*. Westminster John Knox, 2001; Harmon, W., and C. Holman, eds. *A Handbook to Literature*. 7th ed. Prentice Hall, 1996; Howard, D., Jr. "Recent Trends in Psalms Study." Pages 329–68 in *The Face of Old Testament Studies*, ed. D. Baker and B. Arnold. Baker, 1999; Kugel, J. *The Idea of Biblical Poetry*. Yale University Press, 1981; Lewis, C. S. "Is Theology Poetry?" In *The Weight of Glory and Other Addresses*, ed. W. Hooper, 1996; idem. *Reflections on the Psalms*. Harcourt, Brace, 1958; Longman, T., III. "Biblical Poetry." Pages 80–94 in *A Complete Literary Guide to the Bible*, ed. L. Ryken and T. Longman III. Zondervan, 1993; Malbon, E., and E. McKnight. *The New Literary Criticism and the New Testament*. JSNT-Sup 109. Sheffield Academic Press, 1994; Murfin, R., and S. Ray, eds. *The Bedford Glossary of Critical and Literary Terms*. Bedford Books, 1997; O'Connor, M. *Hebrew Verse Structure*. 2d ed. Eisenbrauns, 1980; Osborne, G. *The Hermeneutical Spiral*. InterVarsity, 1991; Ryken, L. *Words of Delight*. 2d ed. Baker, 1992; Travers, M. *Encountering God in the Psalms*. Kregel, 2003.

Michael E. Travers

Political Theology

The term "political" in "political theology" may be provisionally defined as "pertaining to the nature and purpose of the political community (or polis, or state)." The political community is an authoritative public legal institution responsible for securing justice across a whole society. Maintaining clarity on its nature and purpose is vital in properly grasping the subject matter of political theology.

What goes under the name of "political theology" has experienced a remarkable global resurgence during the last three decades. The fruit of this revival has been the proliferation of contrasting and contending interpretative and substantive perspectives, rather than any clearly discernible movement toward a scholarly consensus on how the Bible speaks politically. On *whether* the Bible speaks politically, there is now little doubt: few would any longer seek to defend a spiritualized, and thereby privatized, reading of Scripture, which arbitrarily confines its authoritative address to the spheres of doctrine, church order, or personal faith and morality. Confronted by twenty-first-century national, regional, and global political orders undergoing rapid transformations, many of them violent and destabilizing, the saliency and urgency of the enterprise of political theology can hardly be overstated.

If there were a contender for primacy among the polyphonous voices of contemporary political theology, it would of course be liberation theology. This school has done more than any other to establish the inescapably political character of the biblical message, and to expose the flawed hermeneutical and ideological factors at work in those who would privatize and thereby muzzle the Bible's prophetic public significance. As a result, many today take "political theology" and "liberation theology" to be synonyms. But there were other forms of political theology before liberation theology, and there have been many since. Liberation theology was forged in the context of widespread economic deprivation and political repression in the Latin America of the 1960s and 70s. Its early manifestations (Gutiérrez) can be seen as a contextualized, if profoundly radicalized, elaboration of the slightly earlier European movement that first took upon itself the name "political theology," and which itself was the outcome of diverse sources (Kee). Since the 1970s liberation theology has spawned an array of regional expressions in Africa, Asia, and also the West. It has also been complemented, or indeed critiqued and superseded, by yet further variations of political theology such as neo-Anabaptism, black theology, feminist theology, postcolonial theology, ecotheology, deconstructionist theology, and, most recently, "Radical Orthodoxy" (Milbank; Bell).

Alongside this proliferation of professedly left-wing forms of political theology has also emerged a revival and renewal of politically more reformist or conservative manifestations, drawing variously on Augustine, Thomas Aquinas, or John Calvin. Thus far these have received much less appreciation from specialists in political theology—or indeed from the World Council of Churches, its national counterparts, and other ecumenical social activist networks, where liberation theology and its affiliates have established a position of clear dominance. Yet they include some of the most biblically responsive and theoretically sophisticated contributions (e.g., O'Donovan). Theological fault lines do not line up neatly with political ones: Many adherents to the radical neo-Anabaptist political theology of John Howard Yoder and Stanley Hauerwas would defend a "conservative" view of scriptural authority. "Radical orthodoxy" is the fruit of a novel postmodern reading of Augustine. Neo-Calvinism began as a theologically conservative movement but has produced some decidedly progressive thinkers (such as Bob Goudzwaard). The "new natural law theory," associated with orthodox Catholic philosophers such as John Finnis and Robert George, has proposed a variant of Thomist political thought justifiable independently of any theological premises. And the most prominent evangelical Augustinian, Oliver O'Donovan, eludes precise political categorization (Bartholomew et al.).

Contemplating the sheer pluriformity of contemporary political theologies can be both exhilarating and disconcerting for those seeking reliable biblical guidance on how to think and act politically in our turbulent times. We can be exhilarated by the richness and challenge of unexpected insights, unearthed by some of the newer forms of political theology, into the political meaning of long-neglected or sidelined scriptural passages or themes. Thus, Lev. 25 gives the meaning of "Jubilee" for economic justice. Daniel and Revelation show resistance in the face of "empire." Luke depicts Jesus' egalitarian attitude toward women. Such resources help in dealing also with other contemporary forms of marginalization and exclusion. Part of the value of these insights is to facilitate a searching ideological criticism of interpretative assumptions hitherto conspiring to silence the prophetic force of such biblical materials. Such contributions greatly enrich the enterprise of political theology.

Yet two aspects of the current pluriformity are disconcerting. First, the enormous diversity of interpretative schools of political theology increasingly threatens to slide from a quite legitimate plurality of foci and accents into a distracting and damaging fragmentation—a Babel of hermeneutical voices urging us in incompatible directions. Second, many of the newer schools proceed as if political theology were a late-twentieth-century invention. But the formidable output of the last thirty years is only a rehabilitation of the project of relating theology to politics as engaged in continuously by the church for two millennia (too often, of course, with profoundly flawed or frankly oppressive results).

Two assumptions ought to guide our response to this situation. The first is that Scripture offers a fundamentally unified testimony about politics and government (Chaplin, "Government," in Atkinson and Field; Marshall; Bauckham). This means that the project of fashioning a truly bibli-

cal theology of politics—in which Scripture is unmuzzled and allowed to speak authoritatively to our own political context—is not only feasible but also urgent. The innovative work of O'Donovan, for example, is charting an exciting pathway in this regard. The second is that the leading—and indeed dissenting—historical traditions of reading Scripture politically must be fully reckoned with today.

Two corresponding challenges then follow. One is to work toward an interpretative framework that honors the unified testimony of Scripture by distinguishing between two kinds of proposals: Some genuinely open up the meaning of Scripture and thus *disclose* its fundamental unity more clearly than the church has hitherto seen. Others threaten to *subvert* the unity of Scripture by forcing a false choice between biblical materials taken to be supportive of one's proposed reading and those seen as obstructing it. A second challenge is to engage in respectful, critical dialogue with the legacy of two thousand years of Christian political reflection (the first fifteen hundred years of which are magisterially represented in O'Donovan and O'Donovan). This implies, additionally, that such dialogue must be ecumenical in scope and sympathy.

An important initial step in meeting these challenges is to explore the definition of the term "political theology" more closely. The proliferation of its diverse schools has led to a progressive expansion of the territory claimed by the term, at the cost of obscuring its meaning. O'Donovan has rightly asserted that "theology must be political if it is to be evangelical" (O'Donovan 3; "evangelical" here means "faithfully responsive to the gospel," rather than in continuity with the movement of that name arising in eighteenth-century Europe and America). All contemporary political theologians would affirm this assertion. A generation ago Alistair Kee stated the point more controversially by questioning "whether anything that is *without* political significance deserves the name of theology" (ix; a formulation that might be read as implying an illegitimate *politicization* of theology). But the immediate question arising is what the term "political" means in these statements. In fact, political theologians have attached diverse and sometimes divergent meanings to the term. Three clarifications are in order.

First, the assertion that theology is "political" has for many meant merely that it is "historical": that is, theology is not rational speculation on timeless truths but reflection on and response to God's saving, liberating action in history with all its implications for political societies. Nor is the gospel an appeal to "faith" as if this functioned in a different realm from the concrete reality of human history. Rather, it is both kerygmatic and eschatological. It is kerygmatic in calling for testimony to God's establishment of a historical people who will bear witness to his name through tangible acts of proclamation, community building, healing, and justice. It is eschatological in summoning us to live now in anticipation of experiencing the promised fullness of the kingdom of God. This twentieth-century rediscovery of the historical character of divine salvation—fatally eclipsed by the idealist and demythologizing liberal theology of the nineteenth—is salutary. But it seems misleading to designate it as "political." Why assume a privileged relationship between "history" and "politics"? A possible explanation for this is a concealed assumption that, among all forms of human action, *political* action is the real motor of history. Yet this is not the case: historical change is multicausal, and to identify just one of the arenas in which humans collectively shape their environments and destinies as uniquely decisive is to fall into historical reductionism. Related to this is a second assumption, that history is the theatre of the assertion of human freedom over against nature, and that the political community is the primary conduit of such assertion. But this is a modernist myth (mediated to the political theology of the 1960s and 1970s through an insufficiently critical appropriation of Marxism). Human freedom can be cultivated as much in any other arena of human social life; and, in any arena, it consists not in "mastering" an inert and passive nature, but rather in respectfully acting to "till and keep it" (Gen. 2:15 NRSV). One contribution of postmodern approaches is to expose the dependence of some earlier schools of political theology on this modernist myth and to disclose its potentially violent consequences (Bell).

Second, the term "political" frequently seems to be used generically to refer to anything and everything related to human collective action, or alternatively, to any context in which power is employed. But such conflations occlude vital distinctions between discrete arenas of such action or distinctive types of power. Not everything that is "social," "familial," "economic," "educational," or "technological" (for example) is necessarily "political" in character (in the sense defined earlier; Stackhouse et al. style these arenas "spheres," "powers and principalities," "authorities," and "regencies"). And not every use of "power" is an exercise of that unique type of political power—coercive legal power pursuant to public justice—which political communities alone enjoy. Nor are the above arenas primarily "public" in character, so that Stackhouse's term "public theology" can also mislead. If theology can be qualified as "political," can it not also equally be qualified by all those other terms? That this is indeed so is increasingly being registered in the emergence of a whole series of specialist subdisciplines referred to as a "theology of . . ." economics, society ("social theology"), education, the family, technology, and so on. Calling for a respect of such boundaries is not to imply that these arenas are *divorced from* politics (or immune from legal regulation) but only that they are not *essentially* political: family, economy, education, and so on are neither parts of nor creatures of the political community. To subsume all arenas of human collective action under the rubric "political" is, perhaps unwittingly, to risk playing into the hands of modern statism. Statism sees the political community as the primary locus of human fulfillment or liberation, and its institutional expression—the state—as the chief guarantor of such goals. It is understandable why political theologies forged out of confrontations with oppressive states, such as liberation theology, might insist that such states, once democratized, should claim extensive powers to overcome social injustice. And where such regimes have supported rampant capitalist excesses, as was true of several Latin American states in the 1960s and 1970s, an extension of state power to regulate the economy is likely to be required. But this is not a necessary implication, as is made clear by the contrasting examples of John Paul II's "personalist" indictments of communism (John Paul II), or seventeenth-century Calvinist theories of resistance. Both insist on setting clear limits to political authority to protect the independent calling of nonpolitical arenas such as the family, "civil society," and the church.

Third, a distinction needs to be drawn between "political theology" and "Christian political philosophy," which have importantly different foci. The former involves systematic reflection on political material in—or the political implications of—*biblical and theological sources* (e.g., Gutiérrez; Moltmann; Forrester, *Theology*; O'Donovan). The latter is systematic reflection on *political reality* as informed by those sources (e.g., Maritain; Dooyeweerd; Mott; Song; Forrester, *Christian*; Plant). While many works quite legitimately engage in both, the distinction between the two enterprises is important because they have different objectives (and may have different audiences). The objective of political theology is to clarify the meaning of revealed truth about politics as an arena of created, fallen, redeemed, and eschatologically destined human existence. It considers various questions: Is political authority grounded in one or another of these four fundamental biblical motifs? What was the normative shape of political order and social justice in Israel, and how might that shape inform what is normative for us today? What can we learn from the responses of the church to the Roman Empire or other forms of political idolatry? And so on. The objective of Christian political philosophy is to address—in the light of a perspective formed by revelation, and drawing on philosophy, history, and a range of empirical disciplines (esp. the social sciences)—the central and recurring problematics of political reality: What is the origin, nature, scope, and purpose of political authority? What is the meaning of law and rights? What are the requirements of distributive justice? What is the nature of representation and consensus? What is the legitimacy of violence and revolution? What are the conditions for civic virtue? And so on. There is a key point in drawing this distinction: it is just as hazardous to move directly from political theology to specific conclusions about the latter range of questions, as it is to embark on the enterprise of Christian political philosophy without a clear apprehension of the totality and coherence of biblical revelation.

See also Augustine; Calling/Vocation; Calvin, John; Deconstruction; Feminist Biblical Interpretation; Ideological Criticism; Justice; Kingdom of God; Liberation Theologies and Hermeneutics; Postmodernity and Biblical Interpretation; Powers and Principalities; Roman Empire; Thomas Aquinas; Violence; Virtue

Bibliography

Atkinson, D. J., and D. H. Field, eds. *New Dictionary of Christian Ethics and Pastoral Theology.* InterVarsity, 1995; Bartholomew, C., et al., eds. *A Royal Priesthood.* SHS. Zondervan/Paternoster, 2002; Bauckham, R. *The Bible in Politics.* SPCK, 1989; Bell, D. *Liberation Theology after the End of History.* Routledge, 2001; Dooyeweerd, H. *Roots of Western Culture.* Wedge, 1979; Forrester, D. *Christian Justice and Public Policy.* Cambridge University Press, 1997; idem. *Theology and Politics.* Blackwell, 1988; Gutiérrez, G. *A Theology of Liberation.* Orbis, 1973; John Paul II. *Centesimus annus.* Catholic Truth Society, 1991; Kee, A., ed. *A Reader in Political Theology.* SCM, 1974; Maritain, J. *Man and the State.* University of Chicago Press, 1951; Marshall, P. *God and the Constitution.* Rowman & Littlefield, 2002; Milbank, J. *Theology and Social Theory.* Blackwell, 1990; Moltmann, J. *On Human Dignity.* SCM, 1984; Mott, S. C. *A Christian Perspective on Political Thought.* Oxford University Press, 1990; O'Donovan, O. *The Desire of the Nations.* Cambridge University Press, 1996; O'Donovan, O., and J. L. O'Donovan, eds. *From Irenaeus to Grotius.* Eerdmans, 1999; Plant, R. *Politics, Theology and History.* Cambridge University Press, 2001; Song, R. *Christianity and Liberal Society.* Clarendon, 1997; Stackhouse, M., et al. *God and Globalization.* 3 vols. Trinity, 2000–2002; Yoder, J. H. *The Politics of Jesus.* Eerdmans, 1974. 2d ed. 1994.

Jonathan Chaplin

Polyphony   *See* Dialogism

Postcolonialism   *See* Asian Biblical Interpretation; Culture and Hermeneutics; Ideological Criticism; Liberation Theologies and Hermeneutics; Political Theology

Postliberalism   *See* Narrative Theology; Yale School

Postmodernity and Biblical Interpretation

Theological interpretation never takes place in a vacuum; it is always historically situated. Thus, theological interpretation requires a deep knowledge not only of Scripture and the tradition but also of the context in which the church lives today. The catchall phrase used to name our time and place in the West today is postmodernity or postmodernism.

The Contours of Postmodernity

"Post" indicates the reaction to modernity that is central to postmodernism and also raises the prospect of the demise of modernity and the arrival of a new era. Such large brushstroke cultural analysis is dangerous. Unless one is careful, it becomes the equivalent of doing surgery with a club rather than a scalpel. From a Christian perspective it also unhelpfully centers the analysis around "modernity," with premodernity and postmodernity encompassing the analytical center of modernity. Provided we are sensitive to these dangers, the postmodern debate remains a helpful way of analyzing our context. "Postmodernism" may, however, be a better term for what we are describing since it names a cluster of tendencies evident today without necessarily suggesting that modernity is over and postmodernity here.

The specifically "postmodern" debate began as a reaction to modernism in the arts in the 1960s and was extended to a critique of Western culture in its entirety in the 1980s as philosophers joined the debate in earnest (Bertens). The social and cultural dimensions of postmodernism must be distinguished from the philosophical.

At a social and cultural level, far from representing the demise of capitalistic modernity, postmodernism indicates its triumph. While the roots of contemporary consumer culture are located in the commercial revolution of early modernity, recent decades have witnessed a massive intensification of consumerism (Bartholomew). Jameson analyzes this cultural logic of late capitalism and argues that there have been three stages in capitalism: market capitalism, the monopoly stage, and our own stage of multinational or consumer capitalism. Increasingly the core values of Western culture derive from consumption rather than the other way around, so that in this respect "postmodernism is consumption" (Storkey). With the communications revolution and consequent technologization of all of life, postmodern Western culture, far from being postmodern, embodies the extension of capitalistic consumerism into all of life. Consumerism is the great characteristic of postmodern culture—appearance is everything, and all is for sale, the only qualifications being desire and profit (cf. Bartholomew and Moritz).

Although not unconnected to consumerism, philosophically postmodernism involves a reaction *against* modernity. Toulmin, for example, asserts: "If an historical era is ending, it is the era of Modernity itself. . . . What looked in the 19th century like an irresistible river has disappeared in the sand, and we seem to have run aground. . . . We are now stranded and uncertain of our location. The very project of Modernity thus seems to have lost momentum, and we need to fashion a successor program" (3). Lyotard defines postmodernity as "incredulity towards metanarratives" (xxiv). Smith sums up the feeling of malaise and crisis: "The Enlightenment is dead, Marxism is dead, and the author does not feel so well either" (quoted in Harvey 325)!

In this respect postmodernity is perhaps better described as "late modernity," for it can be read as the unraveling of tensions hid deep in modernity. In *The Condition of Postmodernity*, Harvey observes that modernity rejected tradition and religious authority but held on to the hope that reason alone would lead us to truth. Postmoderns have given up on the illusion that reason alone will lead us to truth, but they have not recovered tradition and authority. Instead, they courageously celebrate and play amid our limitations and finitude, in a sort of cheerful nihilism. Indeed, by the end of the twentieth century the hubris with which the twentieth century began had been seriously undermined.

The consumerist intensification of modernity and the philosophical reactions to modernity are deeply intertwined; indeed, the very problems of consumerism raise profound questions about modernity. Theorists of the postmodern analyze the problem of contemporary culture in different ways. For Baudrillard, consumer culture, tied in as it is to the communications revolution, has led to the hyperreal replacing and being indistinguishable from what is real so that he is deeply pessimistic about our situation today (via Bertens). Other analysts such as Habermas are more optimistic about getting modernity back on track, with reason playing the appropriate critical role. The important point to note is that postmodernism is a complex social, cultural, and philosophical entity that cannot be reduced to a philosophical reaction to modernity. Perhaps one could say that postmodernism represents a crisis of modernity, as is evident from its key thinkers, who nevertheless respond to this crisis in significantly different ways.

Key Postmodern Thinkers

The influence of the German philosopher *Husserl*, the father of phenomenology, on philosophical postmodernism should not be underestimated; to a significant extent, postmodernism philosophically amounts to *post*-phenomenology. Husserl's phenomenology was a last-ditch attempt to secure the scientific nature of knowledge in human autonomy. Significant tensions appear in his work as a result and it fell to his student *Heidegger* to turn phenomenology in a hermeneutic direction, thereby subverting the strongly Enlightenment character of Husserl's philosophy. Contra Husserl's privileging of intuition as the means to true knowledge, Heidegger asserted that we are always already thrown into the world so that we explore it out of *Dasein*, rather than from a neutral, objective position. In this way Heidegger brought to fruition Dilthey's emphasis on history and understanding. Central to postmodernism is a profound sense that knower and that which is known are historically embedded so that there is no neutral vantage point from which objective, neutral analysis is possible.

Gadamer, a student of Husserl and Heidegger, did the major work in developing phenomenology into a philosophical hermeneutics, particularly in his *Truth and Method*. Gadamer insists on the historical nature of understanding itself: "For Gadamer 'any interpretations of the past, whether they were performed by an historian, philosopher, linguist, or literary scholar, are as much a creature of the interpreter's own time and place as the phenomenon under investigation was of its own time and period in history'" (Mueller-Vollmer 38). In contrast to Enlightenment attitudes, Gadamer sees all interpretation as always guided by its own prejudice. This prejudice is productive and not just negative. The Enlightenment manifests a prejudice against prejudice, whereas Gadamer refuses to set reason in opposition to tradition. Indeed, understanding takes place as an event within a tradition. What makes understanding possible is *Wirkungsgeschichte*. Thus, hermeneutics aims at prejudgments that will foster a fusion of the past with the present, which facilitates the miracle of understanding, the sharing of a common meaning by temporally distant consciousnesses. In this fusing of horizons, distance and critical tension are never completely obliterated; the hermeneutic task is to foreground the tensions. Nevertheless, interpretation always involves application.

Since Gadamer's approach, no other really groundbreaking hermeneutical innovations have appeared, but his hermeneutics has generated numerous debates. Gadamer is definitely a pivotal figure between modern and postmodern paradigms of thinking. Thiselton (*New*, 314) draws attention to Gadamer's role in focusing for hermeneutics and addressing a cluster of metacritical questions concerning the *basis* of understanding and of our possible relation to truth. Gadamer's distinctive way of addressing these questions not only constitutes a point of transition toward a new paradigm of hermeneutical theory; it also places him firmly on the boundary line between modern and postmodern thought.

According to Thiselton, the focus on metacritical issues that one finds in Gadamer emerges from three directions. First is the problem of radical historical finitude. Second is the problem of the constitutive role of language in understanding. Third, unease has beset academic disciplines as they submit to reappraisal what have been regarded as foundations for their methods.

Ricoeur is particularly significant for his understanding of interpretation as a semantic event, of the fusion of text and interpreter through the interplay of metaphor and symbol in a reading along the lines of a second naïveté. In contrast to Gadamer, Ricoeur seeks to bring together explanation and understanding. In Ricoeur's view, Gadamer lets the two collapse into each other so that there tends to be no space for critical testings of understandings. For Ricoeur, "explanation" embodies a hermeneutic of suspicion:

the willingness to expose and to abolish idols, which are mere projections of the human will. Ricoeur is critical of the Enlightenment insofar as it locates meaning in the subject; he professes a permanent mistrust of the pretensions of the subject in posing itself as the foundation of its own meaning. "The reflective philosophy to which I appeal is at the outset opposed to any philosophy of the Cartesian type. . . . The understanding of the self is always indirect and proceeds from the interpretation of signs given outside me in culture and history. . . . The self of self-understanding is a gift of understanding itself and of the invitation from the meaning inscribed in the text" (*Phenomenology*, xv).

However, Ricoeur has no desire to be premodern. We cannot, nor should we, try to escape the lessons of the masters of suspicion, Nietzsche, Marx, and Freud. Hence, "explanation" is an imperative part of interpretation. However, explanation alone is inadequate: "To smash the idols is also to let symbols speak" (*Phenomenology*, 219). Understanding involves a willingness to listen with openness to symbols and to indirect language in such a way that we experience being called again. Narrative orders scattered sequential experiences and events into a coherent structure of human time. This refigured world becomes revelatory and transformative. Narrative constructs a world of the possible.

There is good reason for the positive appropriation of Ricoeur by theologians. Ricoeur's positive stance toward symbol makes him open to religious experience, and although Ricoeur retains a commitment to the autonomy of "responsible thought" (*Essays*, 156), he also wants to secure a fundamental place for religion and theology. Not only has Ricoeur written extensively about literary theoretical and hermeneutical issues; he has also specifically focused on biblical interpretation. Ricoeur has addressed virtually every major theoretical issue in literary criticism, and his irenic approach mediates the interests of Gadamer and Habermas, redirecting hermeneutics away from Derridean extremes (see below).

Habermas has reacted strongly to the postmodern notion of the end of modernity, proposing instead that we think of modernity as an unfinished project. Modernity is in crisis, but the answer is to get it back on track, not to abandon it. Habermas has strongly criticized Gadamer's understanding of hermeneutics as a fusion of horizons leading to consensus because, in Habermas's view, it fails to take account of the possibility of systematic distortion in the communication process. This has led to an ongoing debate between Habermas and Gadamer, which has highlighted the metacritical (or lack thereof) dimension of Gadamer's hermeneutics. Habermas proposes a project of universal pragmatics as he seeks to establish that the possibility of ideal speech is implied in the structure of language. In appealing to reasons, speakers assume that their claims could be substantiated through rational discourse alone. Thus, communication in general points to something like Habermas's ideal-speech situation.

Rorty has expounded a pragmatic version of postmodernity. What is required is not a new quest for legitimation but a detheoreticized sense of community. From such a position one could accept Habermas's privileging of undistorted communication without needing to ground it in a theory of communicative competence. Thus for Rorty, postmodern bourgeois liberalism is "the Hegelian attempt to defend the institutions and practices of the rich North Atlantic democracies without using [the traditional Kantian] buttresses" ("Postmodernist," 584–85). For such postmodern liberalism, morality is stripped of its transcendent grounding and becomes equivalent to loyalty to a society. Rational behavior is simply what conforms to the behavior of other members of a society.

Rorty uses Gadamer to support his view that all knowledge is traditioned and that the idea of the accurate representation of reality underlying the Western concern with epistemology is a myth (*Philosophy*). All forms of knowledge are closer to making than to finding and have this in common with creative enterprises in general. Consequently, the obsession of Western epistemology with legitimation is irrelevant and wedded to an outmoded metaphysics. In place of the epistemological concerns of the Western tradition, Rorty proposes the goal of "edification." Rather than trying to justify our beliefs, we should foster conversations in which we are exposed to and can explore other options and thus find better ways of coping. Rorty thus develops Gadamer's notion that there can be no determinate criteria of interpretation along thoroughly pragmatic lines. For Rorty, hermeneutics is not a way of knowing but a way of coping.

Derrida's type of postmodernism, which also develops out of phenomenology, is called "deconstruction." In response to Husserl and modernity, Derrida's great contribution is to have dismantled the fortress of consciousness through his close analysis of texts. Thereby he exposes in aporia the ever-present "metaphysics of presence." According to Derrida, we cannot ultimately escape metaphysics, and his hermeneutics of deconstruction always therefore operates in two modes at the same time. This is clear with Derrida's textual strategies. On the one hand, the guardrail of authorial intention is indispensable for interpretation. Simultaneously, the aporias in texts enable us to prod them into play, with the result that they are set in motion and flux so that textual meaning can never be saturated or finally constrained.

All these thinkers acknowledge the crisis of modernity, but their responses are plural and diverse; indeed, a significant characteristic of postmodernism is pluralism, as diverse epistemologies compete for attention.

Postmodernism and Textual Interpretation

The philosophical diversity of "the postmodern turn" has been powerfully experienced in biblical hermeneutics, as in virtually all disciplines. Within biblical studies this influence has often been mediated through literary theory, which has itself come to exercise a strong influence far beyond its disciplinary boundaries. The (postmodern) literary turn provides a radical challenge to traditional models.

The very possibility of determinate and true readings of texts has been called into question by much postmodern literary theory. Author, reader, text, and their interrelationships have come under fresh scrutiny, and a variety of positions have developed, particularly as the role of the reader in the construction of meaning has received fresh attention:

> But this latter qualification—the enfranchisement of the viewer's perspective—is precisely the feature which introduces the subversive possibility that each term in the "total situation" is radically unstable or indeterminate, a product of the beholder's gaze. . . . The drift of the "pragmatic" or, as it is nowadays called, reader-response orientation in critical theory challenges the privileged position of the work of art and seeks to undermine its priority and authority not only by displacing the work from the centre and substituting the reader in its place, but [also] by putting in doubt the autonomy of the work and, in certain cases, even causing the work to "vanish" altogether. (Freund 2)

The result is that nowadays there is considerable disagreement over where to anchor textual meaning, if anywhere. Hirsch maintains that textual meaning is inseparable from authorial intention; Barthes, Foucault, and others have pronounced the author dead. Ricoeur and Gadamer see the text as loosed from the author but locate its fixed meaning in its ideality (Wolterstorff, "Promise"). Burke has recently declared the return of the author. The reader and his/her role in the construction of meaning have in the process received close attention with a whole variety of proposals put forward.

In the process the very nature of textuality has become highly problematic. Until recently, the classical-humanist paradigm of textuality had dominated the history of biblical interpretation. According to this tradition, texts are stretches of language that express the thoughts of their authors, and they refer to the extralinguistic world. Texts were seen as mediating interpersonal communication. The new approaches have called every aspect of this tradition into question.

Postmodernism and Biblical Interpretation

As with other disciplines, postmodernism has arrived with a vengeance in biblical studies. It has undermined the dominance of historical criticism, introduced a smorgasbord of new approaches to reading biblical texts, and raised all sorts of foundational questions about biblical interpretation so that biblical studies has become fragmented and pluralistic. Rendtorff's assessment of the current state of OT scholarship rings true of biblical studies as a whole:

> Old Testament scholarship at present is "in crisis." The Wellhausen paradigm no longer functions as a commonly accepted presupposition for Old Testament exegesis. And at present, no other concept is visible that could replace such a widely accepted position. . . . The shaking of this paradigm is part of a far-reaching shaking of the centuries-old fundamentals of Old Testament scholarship. . . . Almost half a thousand years have faded away. (44)

The methodological pluralism now widespread in biblical studies is the most obvious indication of the influence of postmodernism, with a huge variety of approaches and methods being applied in biblical interpretation (see Adam, *Handbook*; idem, *Postmodern . . . Bible*). An example of this pluralist style in action is Clines's "Reading Esther from Left to Right," in which he performs a formalist, structuralist, feminist, materialist, and deconstructionist reading of Esther. He concludes: "I have been impressed in this study by the value of as many strategies as possible for reading a text. As a critic of the text, I should hate to be restricted by a methodological purism. What I have noticed is that different strategies confirm, complement or comment on other strategies, and so help develop an integrated but polychromatic reading" (51).

If a wild methodological pluralism is the surface manifestation of postmodernism in biblical studies, it is important to realize that at a foundational, depth level lies a philosophical and theological diversity informing the surface diversity. Clines's methodological pluralism (mentioned above) is related to his view of textuality and whether or not texts have meanings that can be discovered. Referring to Ps. 23, Clines ("Varieties," 20) concludes: "My experience with Psalm 23 was enough to convince me that 'possible' and 'impossible' are not categories to be applied to interpretations, that, as far as I could see, a text can mean anything at all, and that I myself was (oxymoronically) an absolute indeterminist." Such radical indeterminism is connected philosophically to theorists such as Nietzsche, Derrida, and Foucault and their views of textuality, language, and historicity. Foucault, for example, speaks of the death of the author. The effect of this is to (over)empower the reader in interpretation, often at the expense of the text, which becomes a means for performative interpretation by the reader.

Many other views of language and texts coexist with the sort of radical view (described above) in biblical studies today. Ideological critique—whether of the feminist or postcolonial or queer sort—of the Bible is much in vogue nowadays, and it depends on determinate readings of the text. Thereby one is able to confidently discern the ideology in the biblical texts; from this angle such readers are often more concerned to assert that texts do indeed have meaning that can be discovered. Some experts in biblical hermeneutics such as Sternberg, Thiselton, and Wolterstorff have also resisted textual indeterminism by developing nuanced understandings of the role of the author in textual interpretation. Wolterstorff, for example, advocates authorial-discourse interpretation that aims to discern what the author did in fact say in his/her text. Sternberg appeals to embodied intentionality. Thiselton, Wolterstorff, and Watson have used the resources of speech-act theory to resist the excesses of much postmodern biblical interpretation. Some biblical scholars also lean heavily on Gadamer and Ricoeur, who locate the fixity of meaning in the ideality of texts.

Biblical scholars are not generally trained philosophically, and thus many are unaware of the foundational philosophical diversity informing the plethora of approaches today. However, it is vital in assessing postmodernism in biblical studies to note the swirling philosophical variety that underlies what is going on at the surface. We are now in a situation where diverse epistemologies and anthropologies compete for attention in biblical interpretation.

The great diversity of approaches available today is related to our consumer culture with its supermarkets and endless range of products. In response to our changed context, Clines has even proposed a market theory of interpretation, which is overtly a manifestation of consumerism:

> I want to propose a model for biblical interpretation that accepts the realities of our pluralist context. . . . First comes the recognition that texts do not have determinate meanings. . . . The second axis for my framework is provided by the idea of interpretative communities. . . . There is no objective standard by which we can know whether one interpretation or other is right; we can only tell whether it has been accepted. . . . There are no determinate meanings and there are no universally agreed upon legitimate interpretations.
>
> What are biblical scholars then to be doing with themselves? . . . Biblical interpreters have to give up the goal of determinate and universally acceptable interpretations, and devote themselves to interpretations they can sell—in whatever mode is called for by the communities they choose to serve. I call this "customised" interpretation. ("Possibilities," 78–80)

Such a consumer approach could entail recycling old wasted interpretations, which were thought to have been superseded by the progress model of modernity. These discarded interpretations could be revived in a postcritical form to stock afresh the shelves of the interpretative supermarket. Clines commends feminist and ideology criticism in particular. More than any other form, feminist criticism relativizes the authority of the Bible because it takes its starting point in an ideological position quite different from the patriarchal biblical text. Reading from "left to right" is Clines's slogan for reading the text against its grain and insisting on addressing one's own questions to the text.

Clines's proposals are *a* good example of how consumerism and philosophical antimodernism come together in much postmodernism. Few scholars would be as up front about letting desire and the market control biblical interpretation, and some are vehemently opposed to such a move. Thus, Brueggemann, who is largely positive about postmodernity, says that the dominant infrastructure of consumerism contains little good news for biblical interpretation (27).

Postmodernism and Theological Interpretation

Potentially, at least, postmodernism creates space for theological interpretation. But what should such interpretation look like at this time and place? The diversity of postmodernism at the foundational level means that theological evaluation is crucial and would need to inform theological interpretation today at every point. Works with the range of Gunton's *The One, the Three and the Many* are vital in this context. Gunton ranges across modernity and postmodernity as he seeks to read our times and discern appropriate ways forward from a trinitarian perspective.

Not surprisingly, in our fragmented context theologians articulate a diversity of views about postmodernism. Some are very positive about the ethical emphases of philosophers such as Derrida and Levinas, and they seek to bring theology into close relationship with postmodern emphases. Others are far more skeptical about postmodernism and some alert us to the underlying grip of Gnosticism on much postmodernism, so that caution and critique is where any theological assessment should begin (for postmodernism and Gnosticism, cf. Lundin; Jeffrey).

Graham Ward suggests that Derrida's philosophy of language complements and supports Karl Barth's theology and thus could be of great help to us in theological interpretation. According to Milbank, however, "if Derrida can give a gnostic hermeneutic of the human text in the light of the gnostic logos, then we should have the confidence to give a Christian hermeneutic in the light of the real one" (79). Brueggemann responds positively to the opportunities of postmodernism and suggests that we need a mode of reading the Bible able to fund postmodern imagination. Others are far more critical of postmodernism. Plantinga, for example, relates much of what is called postmodernism to a sort of creative antirealism stemming ultimately from Kant.

Positively, it must be acknowledged that postmodernism has disrupted the hegemony of historical criticism and created room for diverse approaches. In the process, space has been made for the ongoing renewal of theological interpretation. Now that it is acknowledged that all readers bring their interests to the biblical text, it is logically hard to discount all theological interpretation as unscientific and unsuitable for the academy. Indeed, in philosophy postmodernism has led to a renewal of interest in religion. As Vattimo has asserted, there is now no longer any reason for keeping religion out of philosophy (oral comment). Derrida, Kristeva, and others readily engage with biblical texts in their writings, and philosophical conferences are convened on topics such as prayer and forgiveness.

All this is cause for encouragement, and theological interpretation needs to exploit these opportunities. But it is a mistake to interpret this renewed interest in religion necessarily as openness toward the revelation of God in Jesus Christ. Indeed, the historicism latent in so much postmodernism makes such openness unlikely. Vattimo, for example, seeks to recover a hollowed-out version of kenosis beyond Nietzsche. Rorty has come to take more of an interest in religion, yet it is anything but Christian (Boffetti). Derrida has appropriated many Jewish and Christian motifs in his work. Positively, he has contributed in a major way to dismantling the fortress of consciousness, but deconstruction is a long way from a Christian understanding of the world. Derrida's practice of (mis)handling texts, seen clearly in his reading of the tower of Babel narrative, militates strongly against Ward's suggestion that his philosophy of language fits with Barth's theology. And as Steiner rightly notes, deconstruction ultimately confronts us with a choice between nihilism or "In the beginning was the Word":

> It is Derrida's strength to have seen so plainly that the issue is neither linguistic-aesthetic nor philosophical in any traditional, debatable sense—where such tradition and debate incorporate, perpetuate the very ghosts which are to be exorcized. The issue is, quite simply, that of the meaning of meaning as it is re-insured by the postulate of the existence of God. "In the beginning was the Word." There was no such beginning, says deconstruction; only the play of sounds and markers amid the mutations of time. (120)

Some postmodern philosophers are, I suggest, far more compatible with Christian theism than Rorty and Derrida. Levinas, and Ricoeur in particular, have been found by theologians to be fertile thinkers in relation to Christian theology (Vanhoozer; Fodor; Tracy).

However, the different approaches taken to interpretation and hermeneutics by the Chicago (Ricoeur; Tracy) as opposed to the Yale School (Frei; Lindbeck) foreground an important issue for theological interpretation: the role of philosophy and general hermeneutics. The Chicago School is much more positive toward the role of philosophy in biblical hermeneutics than the Yale School. Thiselton, and here he stands with the Chicago School, has argued that transforma-

tive biblical interpretation must attend closely to philosophical hermeneutics. The Yale School, and here its Barthian legacy is clear, is suspicious of the hermeneutical detour and of generalized epistemologies and ontologies, preferring a regional epistemology and wanting to simply get on with reading the Bible for the church. However, it is a moot point as to whether philosophical issues can be ignored in this fashion. The challenge to theological interpretation will be to read the contemporary context aright and to forge theological ways of reading the Bible as Scripture in this context.

Conclusion

Postmodernism presents theological interpretation with tremendous opportunities and real challenges. It has created space for theological interpretation in the academy, but this space will have to be seized without succumbing to the relativism and secularism that is intrinsic to so much postmodernism.

Bibliography

Adam, A. K. M., ed. *Handbook of Postmodern Biblical Interpretation*. Chalice, 2000; idem. *Postmodern Interpretations of the Bible: A Reader*. Chalice, 2001; Bartholomew, C. "Christ and Consumerism: An Introduction." Pages 1–12 in *Christ and Consumerism*, ed. C. Bartholomew and T. Moritz. Paternoster, 2000; Bertens, H. *The Idea of the Postmodern*. Routledge, 1995; Boffetti, J. "How Richard Rorty Found Religion." *First Things* 143 (May 2004): 24–30; Brueggemann, W. *Texts under Negotiation*. SCM, 1993; Burke, S. *The Death and Return of the Author*. Edinburgh University Press, 1992; Clines, D. J. A. "Possibilities and Priorities of Biblical Interpretation in an International Perspective." *BibInt* 1, no. 1 (1993): 67–87; idem. "Reading Esther from Left to Right: Contemporary Strategies for Reading a Biblical Text." Pages 31–52 in *The Bible in Three Dimensions*, ed. D. J. A. Clines, S. Fowl, and S. Porter. JSOT, 1990; idem. "Varieties of Indeterminacy." *Semeia* 71 (1996): 17–27; Fodor, J. *Christian Hermeneutics*. Clarendon, 1995; Freund, E. *The Return of the Reader*. Methuen, 1987; Gunton, C. *The One, the Three and the Many*. Cambridge University Press, 1993; Habermas, J. *The Theory of Communicative Action*, trans. T. McCarthy. 2 vols. Beacon, 1984–87; Harvey, D. *The Condition of Postmodernity*. Blackwell, 1989; Jameson, F. *Postmodernism, or, The Cultural Logic of Late Capitalism*. Duke University Press, 1991; Jeffrey, D. L. *People of the Book*. Eerdmans, 1996; Lundin, R. *The Culture of Interpretation*. Eerdmans, 1993; Lyotard, J.-F. *The Postmodern Condition*. University of Minnesota Press, 1984; Milbank, J. *The Word Made Strange*. Blackwell, 1997; Mueller-Vollmer, K., ed. *The Hermeneutics Reader*. Continuum, 1992; Plantinga, A. "Two (or More) Kinds of Scripture Scholarship." *Modern Theology* 14 (April 1998): 243–78; Rendtorff, R. "The Paradigm Is Changing: Hopes—and Fears." *BibInt* 1, no. 1 (1993): 34–53; Ricoeur, P. *Essays on Biblical Interpretation*. Fortress, 1980; idem. "Foreword." In *Her-*

meneutic Phenomenology. By D. Ihde. Northwestern University Press, 1971; Rorty, R. Philosophy and the Mirror of Nature. Princeton University Press, 1979; idem. "Postmodernist Bourgeois Liberalism." Journal of Philosophy 80, no. 10 (1983): 584–85; Steiner, G. Real Presences. Faber & Faber, 1989; Sternberg, M. The Poetics of Biblical Narrative. Indiana University Press, 1985; Storkey, A. "Postmodernism Is Consumption." Pages 100–117 in Christ and Consumerism, ed. C. Bartholomew and T. Moritz. Paternoster, 2000; Thiselton, A. New Horizons in Hermeneutics. Zondervan, 1992; idem. The Two Horizons. Paternoster/Eerdmans, 1980; Toulmin, S. Cosmopolis. University of Chicago Press, 1990; Tracy, D. The Analogical Imagination. Seabury, 1975; Vanhoozer, K. Biblical Narrative in the Philosophy of Paul Ricoeur. Cambridge University Press, 1990; Watson, F. Text, Church and World. T&T Clark, 1994; Wolterstorff, N. Divine Discourse. Cambridge University Press, 1995; idem. "The Promise of Speech-Act Theory for Biblical Interpretation." Pages 73–90 in After Pentecost, ed. C. Bartholomew et al. SHS. Zondervan/Paternoster, 2001.

Craig G. Bartholomew

Poststructuralism

Although structuralism itself hardly qualifies as a unified movement, the views of poststructuralists are so diverse that it is difficult to speak of "poststructuralism." The term is often interchanged with "postmodernism" (which also defies definition); though there are many overlapping positions and figures, there is no exact congruency. Poststructuralists are probably best described by way of their reaction to the problems of structuralism: (1) its reductionistic tendencies, (2) the focus on formal structure instead of practice, (3) a lack of regard for history, and (4) the assumption of the universality and stability of binary oppositions.

Perhaps the earliest poststructuralist is M. M. Bakhtin (1895–1975), whose work has only become influential in the West in recent years. In his essay "Discourse in the Novel," he speaks of overcoming the "abstract 'formal' approach" and does so by repudiating structuralism's reductionism and emphasizing practice and history. The concept of "dialogue" is central for Bakhtin, since words are alive, constantly evolving, and closely related to both their referents and the persons who use them. As he puts it, "The living utterance . . . cannot fail to brush up against thousands of dialogic threads, woven by socio-ideological consciousness around the given object of an utterance" (276). Bakhtin likewise speaks of the "heteroglossia" of language, that it has a multitude of speakers and contexts, none of which can claim primacy. A similar term for him is that of "carnival," the intersection of language, history,

meanings of author/speaker and reader/listener, and genres. But this play is grounded in what Bakhtin calls "answerability," the ethical responsibility that dialogue partners have to each other ("Art"). And that ethical responsibility is in turn grounded in Bakhtin's theism.

As is typical of Jacques Derrida (1930–2004) in so many respects, both structuralist elements and the questioning of those elements can be found in his thought. Derrida would agree with Ferdinand de Saussure (1857–1913) that language is a system of signs in which meaning is dependent upon difference. Indeed, Derrida elevates "différance" (a term of his own creation) to something like a fundamental metaphysical category, claiming that speaking, understanding, and concepts themselves are characterized by "difference." Thus, interpretation is always a complex mixture that requires understanding words and texts in ways both similar to and different from what the author meant or previous usage or interpretation. Whereas for Saussure the play of signifiers is neat, unchanging, and self-contained, for Derrida it is complex, evolving, and without clear limits. Although he sounds much like a structuralist when he makes his famous claim "there is nothing outside of the text" (Of Grammatology, 158), Derrida later explains that this merely means that there is nothing outside of context (Limited, 136)—a markedly "poststucturalist" claim. Derrida is sometimes read as agreeing with structuralists that signifiers have their meaning apart from referents. But making context central to meaning and connecting signifiers to references seems to indicate a view that is the opposite of structuralism. Derrida claims that signifiers are problematic precisely because they do not give us a "full presence" of that signified. But Derrida uses the notion of the "trace" to indicate that there is still some sort of presence given by signifiers.

Derrida's essay "Structure, Sign, and Play in the Discourse of Human Sciences" is a hallmark in the critique of structuralism; in it he claims that there is no place to "stand" outside of the structure to critique it. Thus, there is no possibility of a "neutral" or "objective" read of the structure itself, or the words and texts that compromise it. In contrast to Saussure, Derrida insists that words and texts are not ideal structures but are thoroughly connected to their historical contexts, and thus subject to temporal change. By way of what he terms "deconstruction," Derrida undermines not only structuralism's ahistoricality, reductionism, and the assumption that language is a closed system, but also the very binary oppositions that provide structuralism's "structure." While Derrida is often read as simply denying binary oppositions (such as light/dark or male/female), it would be more accurate to say that he retains them but questions any simple disjunction between them. Deconstruction has often been construed as promoting hermeneutic and ethical relativism (and there are certainly grounds for such charges). But Derrida strenuously denies that deconstruction necessarily leads to such results, describing the common caricature of the deconstructionist as "skeptic-relativist-nihilist" as simply "false" (*Limited*, 146). Instead, he insists that deconstruction is the "unbuilding" of a complex structure, both to examine its component parts and to consider what is assumed but left unsaid.

Although Derrida claims that deconstruction is something that "happens," it is often considered to be a method for reading texts, one that can be either helpful or highly destructive. In contemporary literary and biblical interpretation, one can find examples of both. An important difficulty in providing examples is that the term "deconstruction" is often either loosely appropriated or employed pejoratively for interpretations with which one does not agree. Considering Derrida's own reading of the Abraham and Isaac narrative (Gen. 22) in *The Gift of Death* is one way around this problem. Following Søren Kierkegaard's account in *Fear and Trembling*, Derrida sees Abraham as suspended between the binary opposition of the demand of universal law and the absolute singularity of responsibility to God's call. For Derrida, it is only in this *moment* of the paradox that true ethical responsibility can be decided. Derrida in no way denies the universality of moral law (and in his later writings he goes so far as to claim that justice is so absolute that it cannot be deconstructed). Yet he resists any reduction of the ethical to universal law. Instead, he argues that the ethical exists precisely in the tension between—on the one hand—the universal, ahistorical, and theoretical and—on the other hand—the singular, historical, and practical.

The move from "archaeology" to "genealogy" in the later work of Michel Foucault (1926–84) also marks a decisive break from structuralism. Archaeology is the search for basic structures or *"epistemes"* (ways of thinking); genealogy is simply the attempt to trace the historical development of thought and practice. Much like human genealogies, it is assumed that there is no "overarching" structure, merely a set of ideas and practices that have no essential unity and

usually are partially contradictory, overlapping, and constantly developing in ways that are unforeseen and disorganized. Strongly influenced by Friedrich Nietzsche (1844–1900), Foucault is particularly concerned with the ways in which practices and discourses are regulated: what can be said, what constitutes a discourse, and who controls discourses (see, e.g., "Discourse" and "Nietzsche"). Reading texts from a Foucaultian viewpoint involves seeking to discover what hierarchies, values, and implied prohibitions are at work both within and behind the text. Genealogy is decidedly diachronic (rather than synchronic) in nature, for it assumes that discourse develops not in a linear, purely rational way but by way of various forces that are diverse and always connected to power in one or more ways.

Although some have accused Foucault of envisioning a "power play" behind everything, he rightly reminds us that language, social practice, and even the search for truth are never simply benign. So images of the "objective scientist" or the "neutral hermeneut" (even of the biblical variety) are simply modern or Enlightenment fantasies. Interpretations, then, must always be subject to such questions: What is an interpreter's point of view? Whose interpretations dominate in literary or biblical fields? What legitimates that dominance? And whose interpretations are excluded as "illegitimate"? One need not agree with Foucault's particular stance or values to realize that such questions cannot simply be ignored. Foucault also reminds us that the very notion of the "author" has its own genealogy, shifting significantly from the Middle Ages to the present day. Although authorship was once taken to be key in scientific texts but not in literary ones, almost the opposite is true today ("What?").

Further poststructuralists include Roland Barthes (1915–80), Jean-François Lyotard (1924–98), and Julia Kristeva (1941–). Barthes began his career as a structuralist but is probably best known for his poststructuralist views regarding the death of the author, the proliferation of textual meaning, and the radical openness of texts. In *The Postmodern Condition* (1979), Lyotard questions the very possibility of constructing an overarching "narrative" (and thus any kind of "universal structure"), though he actually finds support for this view in the decidedly "modern" Immanuel Kant (1724–1804). Along with other feminist poststructuralists, Julia Kristeva has turned attention toward "otherness." For instance, *Strangers to Ourselves* is an examination of the phenomenon of the foreigner, as well as the experience of the "strangeness" within ourselves. Like Derrida's questioning of binary oppositions, such analyses challenge the structuralist assumption of a clear sense of identity of the self or the alien.

See also Deconstruction; Dialogism; Postmodernity and Biblical Interpretation; Structuralism

Bibliography

Bakhtin, M. M. "Art and Answerability." In *Art and Answerability*, ed. M. Holquist and V. Liapunov, trans. V. Liapunov. University of Texas Press, 1990; idem. "Discourse in the Novel." In *The Dialogic Imagination*, ed. M. Holquist, trans. C. Emerson and M. Holquist. University of Texas Press, 1981; Derrida, J. *The Gift of Death*, trans. D. Wills. University of Chicago Press, 1995; idem. *Of Grammatology*, trans. G. Spivak. Corrected ed. Johns Hopkins University Press, 1998; idem. *Limited Inc*. Northwestern University Press, 1988; idem. "Structure, Sign, and Play in the Discourse of the Human Sciences." In *Writing and Difference*, trans. A. Bass. University of Chicago Press, 1978; Foucault, M. "The Discourse on Language." In *The Archaeology of Knowledge*, trans. A. M. Sheridan Smith. Pantheon, 1972; idem. "Nietzsche, Genealogy, History" and "What Is an Author?" In *The Foucault Reader*, ed. P. Rabinow. Pantheon, 1984; Frank, M. *What Is Neostructuralism?*, trans. S. Wilke and R. T. Gray. University of Minnesota Press, 1989; Kristeva, J. *Strangers to Ourselves*, trans. L. S. Roudiez. Columbia University Press, 1981; Lyotard, J. *The Postmodern Condition*. French, 1979, trans. G. Bennington and B. Massumi. University of Minnesota Press, 1984.

Bruce Ellis Benson

Power *See* Ideological Criticism; Powers and Principalities; Racism; Violence

Powers and Principalities

The biblical portrayal of "the principalities and powers" has been badly misconstrued throughout church history. Interpretations have ranged from the extreme of medieval tendencies to confuse the powers with angels or demons to the Enlightenment arrogance of discarding the biblical terms entirely as silly fantasies from an "outdated cosmology" that nobody believes anymore. The first is demonstrated today by the popularity of apocalyptic novels of gruesome spiritual "powers"; on the opposite extreme, a major, current Bible dictionary includes only two sentences on this complex subject.

In contrast, biblical terms for various forces of evil are numerous and complex. Serious study of the relevant texts promotes a proper understanding of the powers' existence and work—crucial for the active engagement of Christians in the world, especially in areas of justice-building and peacemaking.

Biblical Texts concerning the Powers

The language of other evil forces besides angels and Satan first developed in the NT, primarily in the Pauline Epistles. Colossians 1:16 emphasizes that the principalities and powers are created by God in, through, and for Christ. However, the powers share the fracturing of the fallen cosmos, participate in its destructions, overstep their proper vocation, and groan for deliverance (Rom. 8:19–22).

Until Christ's kingdom is consummated, principalities contribute in multiple ways to the world's disorders; yet, however strong they seem to be, they cannot separate us from God's love (Rom. 8:38–39), for Christ has disarmed, exposed, and triumphed over them in the entire work of atonement (Col. 2:9–15). Ultimately, every principality, authority, and power (*archē*, *exousia*, and *dynamis*) will be abolished, including the last enemy, death (1 Cor. 15:24–26).

Meanwhile, Christians must not lose sight of the crucial battle against them, for the principalities were the ones who "crucified the Lord of glory" (1 Cor. 2:8). That text—referring to earthly rulers like Caiaphas, Herod, and Pilate—suggests the powers' functioning in religious, as well as political and economic, spheres. This should caution churches and spiritual leaders, for if they forget their proper vocation and lack essential vigilance, they, too, can become principalities for evil.

The dialectic is difficult to hold—and therefore all the more mandatory. Because we know that the powers and authorities have been made subject to Christ (Eph. 1:21; 1 Pet. 3:22), we can submit to them (Titus 3:1). Simultaneously, however, we must stand against and resist their illegitimate encroachments and enslavements by means of God's armor (Eph. 6:10–20; Yoder Neufeld; the significance of these passages is elaborated in Dawn and Peterson 84–102, 112–19).

The Essence of the Powers

Remarkably, the Bible never examines the powers nor offers any description of their "being"; thus, what the cosmic powers or superhuman potentates are exactly is impossible to say. Rather, Scriptures recognize their mystery by simply naming or briefly displaying their functioning. They are not merely human beings gone amok, but they affect historical events and structures. Contrarily, they are distinguished from supernatural angels and demons, but instruments such as the state, money, the media, technology, and various ideologies bear spiritual powers beyond themselves (Ellul, *Humiliation*).

In the context of 1 Cor. 8, the combination of "there is no such thing as an idol," "no God but one," and "many 'gods' and many 'lords'" (8:4–6 AT/NIV) suggests how entities of God's creation combine with human involvement and supernatural power to become forces for evil. That is, the principalities (since Christ's defeat of them) have no power over us, unless we give it to them in our idolatries.

In this world they have immense scope. They are fallen and will act as fallen unless vigilantly guarded. They thrive in chaos and confusion, cause conflict and dehumanization, act aggressively, enthrall, enslave, and destroy (Stringfellow 77–94).

The Principalities in the Practice of Theological Interpretation

All the earliest formulations of faith (an objective criterion for verifying what the first Christians considered essential) invariably mentioned the powers decisively. The early church accentuated the consequences of Christ's victory over them (Cullmann 103, 192).

However, during Reformation times, misunderstandings by various apocalyptic sects caused Luther and Calvin to avoid the language of "principalities and powers." Later scholars such as Schleiermacher reduced both the powers and God in the trend toward a noncosmic and subjective conception of Christ's kingdom. Both avoidance and subjectivized reductions continue today.

When theological discussions could not name the disastrous events of World Wars I and II in any other way than by restoring the vocabulary of "the principalities and powers," three broadly influential leaders were Johann Christoph Blumhardt, Dietrich Bonhoeffer, and Karl Barth. In contrast to Bultmann, who "demythologized" the concept of "the powers," Barth showed that the apostle Paul himself was demythologizing his culture's notions of hierarchies of intermediaries—and thereby Barth turned the modern hermeneutical problem on its head (Barth, *Church*).

Barth's lecture fragments describe the powers as "spirits with a life and activity of their own, lordless indwelling forces, . . . entities with their own right and dignity . . . as absolutes." Their reality and effectiveness are vague, paradoxical, incomprehensible; they are transitory and assume a variety of forms in different historical epochs, cultural circles, and individuals' lives (Barth, *Christian*, 214–15).

Chiefly, the NT authors, surmounting their contemporaries' cosmology, saw and revealed the powers' presence and potency more clearly than do we, who often ignore them or are hindered by our society's overly rational, scientific worldview. Barth insisted Christians should demythologize not the concept of "the principalities," but the myths that enable modern ones such as politics or mammon to exert their diverse tyrannies (220–33). Colossians 2 and Eph. 6 display this demythologizing: Christ's victory on the cross "exposed" the powers and rendered them vulnerable, and our battle against them similarly begins with Christian truth about their functioning for evil (for examples of exposing and resisting the powers, see Ellul, *Money*; Dawn, *Is?*).

Recently Walter Wink highlighted the powers afresh, but he restricts them to violence, and his reductionistic Christology depreciates Christ's work of atonement and resurrection as the means by which the powers are defeated (instead, see Ellul, *Ethics*; Dawn, *Powers*).

The Theological Significance of the Powers

Several themes in Christian anthropology and the doctrine of the atonement are lost if the power of the principalities is disregarded or reduced. First, our sense of the cosmic battle disclosed in world events is weakened (Stewart 293). Next, we dilute the NT focus on the demonic nature of the evil from which all humankind (and the rest of creation) must be redeemed. The cross was more than a mere "revelation of love and mercy"; rather, it embodied an "objective transaction" that radically transformed the entire cosmos by a "decisive irrevocable defeat of the powers of darkness." Human designs, Christ's will, and God's predestination "met and interlocked" (294–95).

Religious leaders, Jewish and Roman politics, mammon, and the crowds as a social force all served as "agents of more sinister invisible powers" (295–96). Everything in Jesus' life—incarnation, teaching, ministry—was essential to meet "the cosmic forces on the ground of history where they were entrenched" so that Jesus could shatter their power. Only by such lordship could God reconcile the whole universe in Christ (297–300).

The Necessity for Using "the Powers" Language. Since biblical times resemble the present era, biblical language spotlights current manifestations of the powers—an essential tool for fruitful ecclesiology. Similarities between the epochs include a world becoming too complicated too fast; a world in which "little people" feel like playthings of great historical forces; the revival of superstition and religion, contrasted with an escalating sense of fatalism and reckless gambling upon wild chance; the distresses of advancements in warfare; enormous systems of power; immense numbers of people; colossal quantities of material; catastrophic situations that economists and politicians cannot understand; the inexorable bondage of peoples' will; idealistic revolutionary movements; twisted and perverted solidarities and ideologies. Most important, both aeons have been characterized by pessimism, despair, nihilism, and hopelessness because so many approaches to solving the world's problems have failed, so that today there seems to be no way out of the political, economic, and environmental messes (Rupp 13–26).

Theological Clarifications concerning the Powers. Different dominions must be distinguished to understand the powers clearly. Because the Trinity is Lord of the cosmos, in *creation* the powers were only good.

However, the *fall* of humankind was shared by the principalities. Now, just as human beings must guard their sinful nature lest it issue in specific sins, so the powers tend to overstep their proper calling unless confined to it. Thus, governments transgress their appropriate role and become tyrannical; technology controls us instead of serving our goals; money becomes the idol mammon; the media indoctrinate instead of inform.

How can this be if Christ's cross and empty tomb decisively defeated the powers? Jesus' *historical victory* can be compared to D-Day, which established a beachhead and broke Hitler's sovereignty. Though Nazi forces continued to wreak havoc, the limit set to their working was the sign and promise of ultimate defeat (Berkhof 43).

At VE Day total victory was secured. Analogously, when *Christ's kingdom* is culminated at the end of time, all evil powers will be abolished and the cosmos will be recapitulated.

Meanwhile, it makes an enormous difference in the way individuals and churches live if they remember Blumhardt's cry: "That Jesus is conqueror is eternally settled: the universe is his!" (Yoder, *Politics*, 157). Then Christian political, economic, and social involvement operates not from the need to change things, but from the desire to make clear what *really* is the case.

An overly futurist eschatology undervalues Christ's victory and makes him only a potential king. Contrarily, an overstatement of the victory already achieved underestimates the principalities' reality as adversaries and crushes hope if situations do not improve.

The complex relationship of Colossians (proclaiming Christ's creation lordship over the powers in 1:16 and redemption victory over them in 2:14–15) and Ephesians (warning about continuing warfare against the powers in 6:10–20) is rooted in a temporal, not metaphysical, dualism (Cullmann 199). Colossians is not referring to a "heavenly" situation, as opposed to Ephesians' description of an "earthly" struggle. Rather, Colossians displays the abundance of the new aeon, which has already broken into ours, while Ephesians alerts us to the dangers of the old aeon in and with which we still live.

The Church's Tasks in Opposing the Powers

The church proclaims the end of the principalities' dominion and displays the manifold wisdom of God that limits the powers' functioning (Eph. 3:7–10). It celebrates the signs of Christ's ultimate defeat of all evil.

The community seeking to follow Jesus will be the primary social structure by which other powers can be creatively transformed through "revolutionary subordination" (Yoder, *Politics*, 162–92). The powers are neither destroyed, nor "Christianized," but rather "tamed" (Yoder, *He*, 114) because Christ is already their Lord. Such taming requires knowing and loving the powers enough to challenge, resist, reject, or transform them.

Christian worship is crucial. Scriptures and sermons name the powers and expose their perversions. Offerings overthrow money's power. Prayers mobilize believers into their ministry of God's reconciliation. Faith confessions remind disciples of Christ's victory and commit them to living it with resurrection power. Sacraments of baptism and the Lord's Supper confer signs and seals of participation in Christ's triumph and the assurance that principalities have no ultimate control over anyone. Thus, the church's witness is primarily sacramental, rather than moralistic, pietistic, or religious (Stringfellow 138–46, 152).

Most important, the Christian community proclaims the gospel of hope. It does not turn away from darkness, but finds in its midst the light of Christ. The church's unique message is that the only source of hope is God and not the powers.

See also Angels, Doctrine of; Political Theology; Violence

Bibliography

Barth, K. *The Christian Life*. Vol. IV/4 of *Church Dogmatics*. Eerdmans, 1981; idem. *Church and State*. SCM, 1939; Berkhof, H. *Christ and the Powers*. Herald Press, 1962; Cullmann, O. *Christ and Time*. Westminster, 1950; Dawn, M. *Is It a Lost Cause?* Eerdmans, 1997; idem. *Powers, Weakness, and the Tabernacling of God*. Eerdmans, 2001; Dawn, M., and E. Peterson. *The Unnecessary Pastor*. Eerdmans, 1999; Ellul, J. *The Ethics of Freedom*. Eerdmans, 1976; idem. *The Humiliation of the Word*. Eerdmans, 1985; idem. *Money and Power*. InterVarsity, 1984; Rupp, G. *Principalities and Powers*. Abingdon-Cokesbury, 1952; Stewart, J. S. "On a Neglected Emphasis in New Testament Theology." *SJT* 4, no. 3 (September 1951): 292–301; Stringfellow, W. *An Ethic for Christians and Other Aliens in a Strange Land*. Word, 1973; Wink, W. *Engaging the Powers*. Fortress, 1992; Yoder, J. H. *He Came Preaching Peace*. Herald Press, 1985; idem. *The Politics of Jesus*. 1974. 2d ed. Eerdmans, 1994; Yoder Neufeld, T. *Ephesians*. Herald, 2003.

Marva J. Dawn

Practical Theology

In modern theology it was Friedrich Schleiermacher (1768–1834) who first developed the area of practical theology. He was instrumental in the formation of a Protestant chair in that discipline at the University of Berlin in 1821. In this era practical theology first took the form of a theology of the subject. The first practical theologian in an empirical sense was Carl Immanuel Nitzsch (1787–1868), a disciple of Schleiermacher. He defined practical theology as the theory of the church's practice of Christianity. This led to a shift toward the social sciences and the second major emphasis on practical theology as a theology of the way in which the church functions.

Following Schleiermacher and Nitzsch, Philip Marheineke (1780–1846) began with faith as a unity of knowledge and action. He made a distinction between theoretical theology, which thinks from the *possibility* of a relation between life and action, and practical theology, which is based on the *reality* of that relation. As a result, the theory-practice relation became the object of reflection, and practical theology received its own independent status.

In the early twentieth century, drawing upon certain emphases in the Protestant Reformation, a model of practical theology developed more along the lines of pastoral theology. Eduard Thurneysen produced his classic work, *A Theology of Pastoral Care*, which focused on the role of preaching as mediation of God's word to humans so as to effect healing and hope. In North America, Anton T. Boisen (1876–1965) founded

what became known as the Pastoral Counseling Movement, followed by the work of Seward Hiltner. In the late twentieth century the shift from pastoral theology to practical theology took place under the leadership of Don S. Browning, who published a series of essays under this title in 1983. The British scholars Paul Ballard and John Pritchard argue that practical theology must take on the characteristics of theology as such. It too must be a descriptive, normative, critical, and apologetic activity. Practical theology scrutinizes the everyday life of the church, in light of the gospel, in a dialogue that both shapes Christian practice and influences the world.

In his comprehensive survey of the history of practical theology and its most recent developments, Gerben Heitink suggests that practical theology base its method upon the paradigm of the social sciences rather than the humanities. He provides a model of interpretation that links the hermeneutical perspective of the human sciences with the empirical perspective of the social sciences, showing how practical theology can successfully bridge the gap between *understanding* and *explaining*. Practical theology, then, is more than mere applied theory; it is a strategic perspective, which links the hermeneutical with the empirical so as to achieve an *integrative* theological model that underlies the theological task as a whole.

The Relation of Theory to Practice

At the center of the discussion over the nature of practical theology is the relation of theory to practice. Practical theology is both value-directed and theory-laden, according to Browning; it is theory-laden because it includes theory as a vital constituent. It is not just reflective action, but also reflective action that is laden with belief. Practical theology is reflective because it not only engages in and examines actions that seek to achieve particular ends, but also reflects upon the means and the ends of such action to assess the validity of both in the light of its guiding vision. It is important to recognize that doctrine ought to shape the practical work of the church as the ongoing work of God's praxis. Yet, it is also right to say that reflection on the work of God through pastoral and ecclesial praxis leads to interpretation of Scripture and the reconstruction of doctrine.

All forms of ministry practice have some form of theory behind and within them. Thus, theory and practice are drawn together, with each inextricably connected to the other within human praxis. The task of the practical theologian is to discover and lay bare the hidden layers of meaning that indwell the praxis of the church community. Praxis is quite different from the mere application of truth or theory. While the word "practice" ordinarily refers to the methods and means by which we apply a skill or theory, this tends to separate truth from method or action, so one assumes that what is true can be deduced or discovered apart from the activity that applies it. In this way of thinking, truth is viewed as existing apart from its manifestation in an event or an act. Praxis, as Aristotle originally defined it, is an action that includes the telos, the final meaning and character of truth. It is an action in which the truth is discovered, not merely applied or practiced. In praxis, one is not only guided in actions by the intention of realizing the telos, or purpose, but one also discovers and grasps this telos through the action itself.

Praxis reveals theology in its most tangible form. In this sense actions are themselves theological and as such are open to theological reflection and critique. Thus, the praxis of the church is in fact the embodiment of its theology, and is both performative and transformative. Aristotle used the Greek word *phronēsis* to speak of practical wisdom aimed at moral ends. The ministry of the church is grounded in the praxis of God and thus in the *phronēsis* of God's wisdom. Practical theology enables congregations to engage in critical moral reasoning so that the authenticity and moral appropriateness of their praxis can be assessed and tested.

Hence, theory and practice are united within this form of practical knowledge, which works itself out within the praxis of the church. This model of practical theology, with its emphasis on ecclesial praxis and the attainment of practical knowledge, seeks to overcome the rift between theory and practice.

The Hermeneutics of Practical Theology

Practical theology is inherently a hermeneutical discipline insofar as it attempts to interpret situations in terms of the presence and action of the Spirit of God with respect to the word of God. One might say that in practical theology the work of God interprets the word of God in the form of a hermeneutical circle. The practical theologian seeks to interpret Scripture, tradition, and praxis in order that the contemporary life of both church and world can be transformed.

In praxis, God's truth is revealed in the structures of reality by which his actions and presence are disclosed to us through our own actions. It is not our human actions that constitute the praxis of God. Rather, God acts through our human actions to reveal the truth.

The truth of God's word is not merely an idea that can be extracted from the Bible by the human mind so that one can possess this truth as a formula or doctrine. Rather, the purpose of God's word aims at bringing us into the truth in terms of its effect (Isa. 55:11). There is also true doctrine as opposed to false doctrine. But God's truth does not end with our concept of truth, nor is the human mind the absolute criterion for God's truth. Right interpretation of the word of God entails critical engagement with the work of God.

Theology, as an attempt to construct knowledge of God, is inherently practical theology in view of the subject matter, which only emerges through reflection on God's actions as Creator, Reconciler, and Redeemer. There is no knowledge of God that does not include an empirical component in the form of his actions within history as revealed to us through the witness of those who encounter God in his works, first as oral tradition, and then as Holy Scripture.

Theological reflection that begins in the context and crises of ministry seeks to read the texts of Scripture in light of the texts of lives that manifest the work of Christ through the Holy Spirit as the truth and will of God. Present interpretation of Scripture must be as faithful to the eschatological reality and authority of Christ as to the text of Scripture as word of Christ. This is why the hermeneutics of practical theology is a theological hermeneutic, and not merely a spiritual hermeneutic. Practical theology thus includes pastoral theology as those commissioned to practice pastoral care interpret actual human situations with respect to the theological meaning of baptism, the Eucharist, justification, and sanctification, as witness to God's saving activity with his people. The hermeneutics of practical theology seek what is normative in Jesus Christ, as the inspired source of the written word, and seek the objective reality of Christ, as the praxis of the Holy Spirit in the context of ministry.

As discerned in the ministry context, the criterion for the praxis of the Spirit is not determined by cultural relevance or pragmatic expediency. It is the work of the risen Jesus Christ, which becomes the criterion in the praxis of the Holy Spirit. It is this contemporary work (praxis) of Christ through the Holy Spirit that becomes normative and calls the church to repentance

613

where it has imposed its own binding rules. We, of course, are not apostles, nor is Scripture replaced as a normative text by our own experience of the Holy Spirit. Rather, the risen Christ as the true and continuing apostle, through the ministry of the Holy Spirit, binds the word of Christ in Scripture to the work of Christ through the Spirit.

The Mission Focus of Practical Theology

Practical theology maintains the link between God's mission in the world through Jesus Christ and the church's mission in the world through the power of the Spirit. Practical theology is thus inherently a mission theology. Practical theology recognizes the fundamental importance of missiology as a crucial component of ecclesiology.

The mission and nature of the church have their source in the mission of God through the incarnate Messiah, continuing in the world through the Spirit of Christ. This requires a theology that views the nature and mission of the church as a unity of thought and experience. The ongoing ministry of Christ through the power and presence of the Spirit constitutes the praxis of God's mission to the world through the church and its ministry. The context of human praxis in ministry works as a social coefficient with the praxis of God in history as the context for doing theology. This means that practical theology is a task belonging to the mission of the church and a function of those who are involved in that mission.

Practical theology therefore calls theology and the church back to its roots as a fundamentally missionary church with a particular vision and a specific task to perform in the world. One of the primary tasks of the practical theologian is to ensure that the church is challenged and enabled to achieve this task faithfully. The church's nature, as well as its mission and ministry, have their source in the life of the triune God: Father, Son, and Holy Spirit.

The practical theologian is the theologian of the Holy Spirit, who points to and participates in the creative indivisibility of the God who holds all things together. The Holy Spirit is the revelation to us of the inner being of God as constituted by the relations between Father and Son. For this reason, practical theology is grounded in the intratrinitarian ministry of the Father toward the world, the Son's ministry to the Father on behalf of the world, and the Spirit's empowering of the people of God for the work of God.

Bibliography

Anderson, R. "Reading Thomas F. Torrance as a Practical Theologian." Pages 161–84 in *The Promise of Trinitarian Theology*, ed. E. Colyer. Rowman & Littlefield, 2001; idem. *The Shape of Practical Theology*. InterVarsity, 2001; Ballard, P., and J. Pritchard. *Practical Theology in Action*. SPCK, 1996; Browning, D. *A Fundamental Practical Theology*. Fortress, 1996; Forrester, D. *Truthful Action*. T&T Clark, 2000; Heitink, G. *Practical Theology*. Eerdmans, 1999; Hiltner, S. *Pastoral Counseling*. Abingdon-Cokesbury, 1949; idem. *Preface to Pastoral Theology*. Abingdon, 1958; Mudge, L., and J. Poling, eds. *Formation and Reaction*. Fortress, 1987; Thurneysen, E. *A Theology of Pastoral Care*. John Knox, 1962.

Ray S. Anderson

Practice *See* Practical Theology

Pragmatism

Pragmatism is a school of philosophy focused on a cluster of beliefs, attitudes, tendencies, and procedures. In particular, pragmatists have held, via one or the other of its central figures, that (1) the meaning of a concept is a function of its practical consequences, and (2) the truth of a concept is a function of its effects on action. The theory of meaning is foundational; the second proposal applies this thesis to our concept of truth.

Distinctives of Pragmatism

Classic American pragmatists made common cause in their critique of traditional philosophical systems. While drawing elements from their European predecessors, Charles Sanders Peirce, William James, and John Dewey each wrote in response to, first, the scientific achievements and, second, the social developments of the half century following the American Civil War. The sciences, particularly Darwin, highlight process, change, and indeterminacy; pragmatism extends these to human inquiry. Still, pragmatists gained a profound appreciation for progress through the experimental method. The pragmatist, according to Peirce, has "had his mind molded by his life in the laboratory." At the same time, the war highlighted the need to (re)construct social and political structures, along with the devastating effects of absolutism and a priori certainty. Yet, it also suggested a vindication of the American experiment in democracy. In this context arose a method that emphasized the link between thought and action, required ongoing empirical validation of beliefs, construed language and concepts as tools for furthering human values, and recognized the limitations of the social embeddedness of perceptions and judgments, while remaining thoroughly fallibilistic.

C. S. Peirce: The Pragmatic Method

Peirce, the son of renowned Harvard mathematician Benjamin Peirce, had one of the best scientific minds of his time. He considered obvious the superiority of the scientific method to other forms of inquiry, holding in high regard its many accomplishments. From scientific inquiry he learned an experimentalist's respect for observable consequences. Peirce's lasting philosophical contribution centers on problems of method. Philosophical concepts, he argued, have value for their practical role in establishing dispositions to act in specific, salutary ways. Inquiry, then, must begin by carefully examining the very meaning of its terms. "Consider what effects that might conceivably have practical bearings you conceive the object of your conception to have. Then your conception of these effects is the whole of your conception of the object." By shaping expectation of experience, concepts govern the ways we act and respond to our environment. The goal of inquiry is to settle real doubts, those irritating uncertainties about how to act in the world. One must formulate new ideas and modify old ones; these ideas function as hypotheses bearing on future experiences, vindication coming in the form of empirical consequences.

Peirce described this process as abduction or retroduction; he insisted on its general efficacy, even equating this logical process with the essence of pragmatism. Rather than Cartesian or Leibnizian first principles, inquiry begins with a problem. When experience engenders a real doubt, one must draw from those beliefs already in one's possession to formulate a hypothesis that, once confirmed by experimental test, one tentatively accepts. The process is conjectural, and always comparative (recognizing the ubiquity of competing, rival accounts). Its goal is to forge beliefs one is convinced are true, for which one can find no reasons to doubt. To assuage all doubts, testing must involve the entire community of inquirers; satisfaction comes only when each member is satisfied with the adequacy of the proposal relative to his or her own experiences. The process is fully governed by the historical, cultural, social, and even personal contingencies of the community. Peirce believed in the eventual convergence of all belief upon a unified, coherent account. Thus, he proposed that by "true" we mean those beliefs on which the community settles at the end of inquiry. Furthermore, assuming the constraint of the world on inquiry, Peirce maintained that the resulting beliefs describe actual features of a mind-independent reality. While affirming a present fallibilism, he retained hope that community consent constitutes knowledge of the structure of the world.

William James: The Trail of the Human Serpent

James both modified and popularized the relatively obscure and opaque writings of his friend and sometimes colleague. With Peirce, James's pragmatism consisted primarily in "the attitude of looking away from first things, principles, categories, supposed necessities; and looking towards last things, fruits, consequences, facts" (*Pragmatism*, 55). His is a radical empiricism, eschewing abstract, fixed, and absolute principles for concrete facts and action. His most significant break with Peirce centered on the conception of truth; James was wary of the notion of inquiry proceeding along a singular path. He concurred that inquiry is foremost a matter of constructing and choosing beliefs with the greatest potential of utility; he disagreed, however, on the inevitable emergence of a uniquely promising path. His is an unabashed humanism whereby the human is the measure of all things and beliefs are constituted and affirmed for their "cash value" for a particular situation. James's pluralism stems from the variety of experiences that provide the backdrop of inquiry, the mix of prior concepts from which understanding must draw, the contingency of ongoing experiences that guide the process, and even the disparate goals and values that define its proper end. Truth, then, is best construed as neither singular nor fixed; he proposed the notion of truth as a "useful leading," an expedient in the way of thinking. The mind actively selects and organizes experiences, carving out the world so as to fulfill our several needs and desires. Philosophy determines the practical outcomes, the definite differences, of each respective "world-formula," choosing what works best in one's particular circumstances. Evolving circumstances undermine the notion of a fixed or final world version.

John Dewey: Forging Instruments of Change

Dewey's concern for social, political, and educational reform explains his focus on the fundamental role of both beliefs and actions in shaping the world. With James, he emphasized the notion of pragmatism as an attitude toward our beliefs, truth, and reality. On this construal, ideas have value in enabling one to cope with the strain and stress of circumstances. As problems of the world press, one must respond. Yet, action predicated on the settled, staid beliefs of the tradition might not redress the tensions or conflicts one confronts. In a changing, growing, developing world, they may prove ultimately dissatisfying. One desires, rather, a true solution, one providing a satisfactory solution to the situation at hand. We do prize ideas not for their correspondence to reality, but rather for enabling us, in these times, to cope with our circumstances. On Dewey's construal, there is no profit in a fixed reality and absolute truth; there is everything to gain, however, in constantly forging new and better tools for negotiating our practical, moral, and social lives. Once again, specific human consequences provide the provisional test for the very meaning and truth of our concepts. Where Peirce insisted on the democratization of the scientific method, Dewey found the path in democracy itself.

Pragmatics of Belief

While most contemporary Neopragmatist philosophers (Goodman, Davidson, Putnam, Rorty) adopt a nonrealist, social justification theory of truth, insights from pragmatism may shed light on the nature of Christian belief. For instance, the essential tie between belief and action comports well with biblical teaching on disingenuous faith without works. Its empiricism insists that experience, rather than prior intuitions or rationalistic principles, provides the touchstone for justified beliefs, an outlook echoed in the centrality of the historical biblical narrative to Christian theology. Disenchantment with transcendental reasoning and focus on the Word made flesh are foundational to biblical theology. Even while resting on historical truth, the biblical view concurs with pragmatism regarding the ineluctable interpretative effect of background beliefs, expectations, and attitudes. Its fallibilist attitude is reminiscent of Christian humility in belief; its future-oriented experimentalism resonates with Christ's call to a faith whose actions outpace evidence and whose end promises satisfaction. Even a minimalist theory of truth as a reliable, trustworthy way of living captures the frequent use of this notion in Scripture. Lastly, at its very heart, the pragmatist proposal that meaning turns on the definite difference a concept makes in action articulates the central organizing insight for a biblical interpretation.

Bibliography

Several single-volume selections of Peirce's writings include Buchler, J., ed. *Philosophical Writings of Peirce.* Dover, 1955; Wiener, P., ed. *Charles S. Peirce: Selected Writings.* Dover, 1966. James's writings are in Burkhardt, F., F. Bowers, and I. Skrupskelis, eds. *The Works of William James.* 17 vols. Harvard University Press, 1975–88, including *Pragmatism* (1975); *The Meaning of Truth* (1975); *The Will to Believe* (1979). A representative single-volume set can be found in McDermott, J., ed. *The Writings of William James.* Random House, 1967. A sampling of Dewey's work is in Stuhr, J., ed. *Pragmatism and Classical American Philosophy.* 2d ed. Oxford University Press, 2000.

Robert O'Connor

Praxis *See* Liberation Theologies and Hermeneutics; Practical Theology

Prayer

Prayer is language used in relation to God. It is the most universal of all languages, the lingua franca of the human heart. Prayer ranges in form from "sighs too deep for words" (Rom. 8:26 NRSV), to petitions and thanksgivings composed in lyric poetry and stately prose, to "psalms, hymns and spiritual songs" (Col. 3:16), to the silence of a person present to God in attentive adoration (Ps. 62:1, 3).

The foundational presupposition of all prayer is that God reveals himself personally and by means of language. God creates the cosmos with words; he creates us with words; he calls to us, speaks to us, whispers to us, using words. Then he gives us, his human creatures, the gift of language; we not only can hear and understand God as he speaks to us, we can also speak to him—respond, answer, converse, argue, question. We can pray. God is the initiator and guarantor of language both ways, as God speaks to us, as we speak to God. It is a wonder that God speaks to us; it is hardly less a wonder that God listens to us. The biblical revelation is equally insistent on both counts: the efficacy of God's language to us, and the efficacy of our language to God. Our listening to God is an on-again, off-again affair; God always listens to us. The essential reality of prayer is that its source and character are entirely in God. We are most our true selves when we pray. But prayer is not a human-based activity. Psychology does not get us very far in either understanding or practicing prayer. Whether we are aware of it or not (and often we are not), it is theological or nothing.

The Scriptures, read and prayed, are our primary and normative access to God as he reveals himself to us. The Scriptures are our listening post for learning the language of the soul, the ways God speaks to us, and the vocabulary and grammar that are appropriate as we in our turn speak to God. Prayer detached from Scripture, that is, from listening to God, is no longer biblical prayer. Our words to God disconnected from God's words to us short-circuit the relational language that is prayer. Christians acquire this personal and relational practice of prayer primarily under the shaping influence of the Psalms and Jesus.

The Psalms

In most of Scripture we hear God speaking to us; in the Psalms we hear men and women speaking to God. That is why the Christian community continues to use the Psalms as a school of prayer, praying these prayers to gain a feel for what is appropriate to say as we bring our lives into attentive and worshipping response to God. The first thing that we realize from the Psalms is that in prayer anything goes. Virtually everything human is appropriate as material for prayer: reflections and observations, fear and anger, guilt and sin, questions and doubts, needs and desires, praise and gratitude, suffering and death. Nothing human is excluded. The Psalms are an extended refutation that prayer is being "nice" before God. Not at all—it is an offering of ourselves, just as we are. The second thing is that prayer is access to everything that God is for us: holiness, justice, mercy, forgiveness, sovereignty, blessing, vindication, salvation, love, majesty, and glory. The Psalms are a detailed demonstration that prayer brings us into the welcoming presence of God as he generously offers himself, just as he is, to us.

Luther, in his preface to the German Psalter (1528), wrote: "If you want to see the holy Christian Church painted in glowing colors and in a form which is really alive, and if you want this to be done in a miniature, you must get hold of the Psalter, and there you will have in your possession a fine, clear, pure mirror which will show you what Christianity really is; yea, you will find yourself in it and the true *'gnōthi seauton'* ('know thyself'), and God himself and all his creatures, too" (Weiser 20).

Jesus

If the Psalms are our primary text for prayer, Jesus is our primary teacher, the theological and personal center for a life of prayer. But Jesus is more than teacher; Jesus prays for us: "He always lives to make intercession for [us]" (Heb. 7:25). The verb is in the present tense. This is the most important thing to know about prayer, not that

we should pray or how we should pray but that Jesus is praying for us right now (see also Heb. 4:16; John 17). Jesus, the Word that made us, is also among us, teaching us to direct our words personally to God. Mostly, he did this by example; Luke cites nine instances: 5:16; 6:12; 9:18, 28; 11:1; 22:32, 41, 44; 24:30. But we have only a slim accounting of his actual prayers. Some are inarticulate (Mark 7:34; 8:12; John 11:33, 38; Heb. 5:7). Some are quoted verbatim (Matt. 11:25–26; 26:39; 27:46; Luke 23:34, 46; John 11:41–42; 12:27–28; 17:1–26).

The single instance in which Jesus instructed us about prayer was in response to the disciples' request, "Lord, teach us to pray" (Luke 11:1). His answer, "When you pray, say," our so-called Lord's Prayer (Luke 11:2–4//Matt. 6:9–13), is the church's primary text (backed up by the Psalms) for guiding Christians into a life of personal, honest, and mature prayer. The simplicity and brevity of Jesus' first lesson in prayer is striking, a standing rebuke against all attempts to develop techniques or discover the "secret" of prayer. As Jesus practiced and taught prayer, it was not a verbal tool for working on God, nor an insider formula for getting our way with God.

Prayer is shaped by Jesus, in whose name we pray. Our knowledge, our needs, our feelings are taken seriously, but they are not foundational. The God whom we address revealed in Jesus gives both form and content to our prayers. In prayer we are most ourselves; it is the one act in which we can, *must*, be totally ourselves. But it is also the act in which we move beyond ourselves. In that "move beyond" we come to be defined not by the sum total of our experiences but by the Father, Son, and Spirit to whom we pray.

Bibliography

Balthasar, H. U. von. *Prayer*. G. Chapman, 1963; Barth, K. *The Christian Life*. Vol. IV/4 of *Church Dogmatics*, trans. G. Bromiley. Eerdmans, 1981; Ellul, J. *Prayer and Modern Man*, trans. C. E. Hopkin. Seabury, 1973; Forsyth, P. T. *The Soul of Prayer*. Regent, 1995; Houston, J. *The Lord's Prayer*, trans. G. Bromiley. Eerdmans, 1990; idem. *Prayer*. NavPress, 1996; Miller, P. *They Cried to the Lord*. Fortress, 1994; Peterson, E. *Answering God*. HarperSanFrancisco, 1989; Weiser, A. *The Psalms*, trans. H. Hartwell. Westminster, 1962.

Eugene H. Peterson

Preaching, Use of the Bible in

Preaching, the oral proclamation of God's good news, has always been a central impetus and locus for the theological interpretation of Scripture.

Beginnings

The background to the church's use of Scripture in its preaching lies in the use of Hebrew Scripture in the Jewish synagogues. The earliest extant example of this synagogue preaching is the "sermon" of Jesus in Nazareth (Luke 4:16–22). It is hard to deduce much from this occasion, upsetting as it was, about standard practices, but it is clear that it was customary for some passage of Scripture to be read in worship and for someone to comment on it. Thus were formed the targums, Aramaic renderings and expansions of the Hebrew Scriptures. An early precursor of such interpretation is the Levites' explanation of the book of the Law to the people in Neh. 8:7–8.

Jewish methods of interpreting Scripture influenced Christian preaching. These can be grouped under four headings (Longenecker 14–33): (1) literalist; (2) midrashic, disclosing "hidden" meanings in order to make clear the contemporary relevance of the text; (3) pesher, the form of exegesis known especially from Qumran, in which Scripture was read as referring directly to contemporary events; and (4) allegorical, seen in Philo's rereading of Scripture in Stoic and Platonic terms. Jesus' use of Isa. 61 in Luke 4:17–21 is an example of pesher interpretation.

Christian preaching, however, was markedly new. Its central subject was not a book but a person, Jesus Christ. It was the proclamation of an event before it was the explanation of any text. Nevertheless, one of the earliest summaries of Christian preaching (1 Cor. 15:3–8) twice includes the phrase "according to the Scriptures." The belief that Jesus had come to fulfill Israel's history and God's promises meant that preaching must deal not only with oral tradition about Jesus, but also with the written text of Scripture. Christian "theological interpretation of Scripture" was born when Christian preachers started to handle the Hebrew Bible as a text that pointed forward to Christ.

C. H. Dodd distinguished between public proclamation of the message about Jesus (*kerygma*) and "teaching" (*didachē*), which built up the Christian community by applying the teaching of Jesus and the apostles to current concerns. In the early days oral tradition plus the Hebrew Scriptures (often in their LXX form) would have been the staple of a regular teaching ministry. "Exhortation" (*paraklēsis*) gave more immediate encouragement and guidance to the church, based no doubt on Hebrew Scripture and the Jesus traditions, but equally coming in the form of direct Spirit-inspired prophecy.

The NT, as *writing*, does not give us a direct model for *oral* Christian preaching. However, in indirect ways it is very suggestive of the dynamic interplay of Scripture, tradition, and situational freshness that characterizes preaching-as-theological-interpretation at its richest.

First, it preserves much oral teaching of Jesus, with many echoes of Hebrew Scripture, both in content and in its styles of narrative, wisdom, and prophecy; but notably little direct biblical exegesis. The mark of Jesus' teaching, for his hearers, was newness and authority (Mark 1:22, 27). Second, the "Gospels" received that name because they embody the proclamation about Jesus in written form. Explicitly and implicitly, each links the story of Jesus' life to the Scriptures that he fulfilled. Third, Paul's letters apply the proclamation to various pastoral situations, and are grounded in both the story of Jesus and the Scriptures that point forward to it (e.g., Rom. 1:1–5).

Central Issues

Worship and Mission. Scripture took shape as the bipartite collection we know today in the context of worship. The regular rehearsal of the narratives and teaching of both OT and NT kept the early Christian communities rooted in their identity and faith. The preaching of the word took the form of *homilia*, or "conversing," about the texts that had been read, and thus became theological interpretation of *Christian* Scripture.

Dodd's distinctions start to break down as the apostolic era becomes more distant and especially with the birth of Christendom after Constantine's conversion. The homily in Christian worship became *kerygma* as well as *didachē* (or catechesis) and *paraklēsis*, for the Christian congregations needed not only teaching and encouragement, but also a continued grounding in the gospel.

But preaching has always also entailed the evangelization of unchurched peoples. Such preaching has often been characterized by boldness in translating the message of Scripture into the thought forms of the hearers, whereas in-church preaching has often promoted interpretations of Scripture that bolster the institution's authority and make fewer concessions to the hearers (Buttrick 191, 196). This distinction between "worship preaching" and "mission preaching" reflects a basic tension among approaches to theological reading of the Bible. Does one seek to draw hearers into a "biblical" worldview that is in part the construct of a church that sees itself as Scripture's rightful interpreter? Or does one seek to relate the Bible to one's cultural surroundings in such a way as to promote understanding, but risk diluting its message?

Canon and Content. The recognition of Scripture as "canonical" carried an inevitable consequence for its interpretation in the pulpit: its function as boundary marker would be highlighted. Especially in ages of controversy it is natural to find heavily "doctrinal" preaching of Scripture, which underlines a particular interpretation of the boundaries it sets in thought and practice.

The notion of "canon" is problematic if taken to imply that all parts of Scripture should be given equal weight. In practice, the churches have operated with a "canon within the canon" in their public reading of Scripture. They have recognized that some parts of the Bible are more suitable for use in worship than others, being more obviously and directly applicable to hearers. But it can then become too easy for individual churches and preachers to impose their standardized interpretative grid on Scripture, and to cease hearing it as the vehicle for God's challenging address.

In the twentieth century Karl Barth issued a powerful call to the church to hear Scripture afresh in all its strangeness. More recently, Walter Brueggemann has argued for preaching to arise from fresh engagement with the texts, including forgotten or problematic ones, free of any systematizing theological grid. He summons the church to respect the *contents* of the entire canon but to be deeply aware of the danger that its canonical *status* be used as a tool of oppression or the covert imposition of a particular theology.

Literal and Figurative. Preaching has been the natural setting for figurative readings of Scripture. Figural interpretation enabled the OT to be read as pointing forward to Christ, and the entire Bible to be read as pointing forward to the climax of history (Auerbach). Thus, in the light of Scripture the present is made pregnant with meaning, and Christian preachers seek to declare the implications of Scripture for the circumstances of their day. The present is seen reflected in Scripture and vice versa, sometimes with prophetic immediacy.

Such figurative readings are susceptible to fossilization (Stuhlmacher 31), and at the Reformation the time was ripe for a fresh hearing of Scripture's "literal sense." The subsequent development of historical-critical methods of biblical study has given preachers opportunity to keep returning beyond safe, stale theological formulas to a new encounter with the words themselves.

But this emphasis on the literal has had a negative side. The old assumption of a unified world of meaning in which Scripture, the present, and the future were bound up together broke down; the application of Scripture to church and world became increasingly problematic. Preaching has been torn between an arid intellectualism that treats Scripture honestly but has increasing difficulty in hearing it as a living word from God, and a naive fundamentalism that pretends that the literal sense of Scripture can address us immediately without the aid of hermeneutical sensitivity.

It is now recognized that a theologically serious use of Scripture in preaching may invite a revived use of the old categories of figural interpretation (Wilson), without jettisoning all that has been learned through attention to the literal and historical sense.

Oral and Written. The most basic and fertile tension in the relationship of preaching to the Bible is that between the oral and the written word.

In one sense, the oral has priority. The spoken gospel preceded the written Scripture. God lives, and his speech cannot be confined to a written text. Hence, Luther said that the Bible exists for preaching, not preaching for the Bible. Yet, Scripture stands as the perpetual and necessary check on the possible vagaries of preachers.

On the one hand, not only current Roman Catholic teaching, but also distinguished twentieth-century Protestant voices such as P. T. Forsyth and Donald Coggan stress the real sacramental presence of Christ in the preached word. This lends immediacy to biblical interpretation as the congregation is invited to see themselves (for instance) as the very disciples called by Jesus in the Gospels, but invites the danger of simply repeating traditional readings and preventing fresh insights. On the other hand, many modern evangelicals place the written above the oral word, stressing the need for detailed teaching of the text from the pulpit. This lends objectivity to interpretation as the preacher seeks to let Scripture speak, but may make for dryness.

However, the renewed prominence of the Holy Spirit in both Catholic and Protestant thinking has been contributing to the breakdown of these distinctions. Rigid adherence to tradition as the mediator of biblical interpretation and hardened biblicism unwilling to acknowledge the vital role of the oral gospel messengers are both melting.

Contemporary Models

Commitment to the centrality of biblical interpretation in preaching issues today in a variety of homiletic ideals and related forms. Definitions vary, and the following categories should not be taken as watertight, mutually exclusive, or even entirely comparable.

Exposition. Expository preaching may or may not involve verse-by-verse study of a text, be heavily doctrinal in thrust, or be as concerned with the impact of a text as with its meaning. But fundamentally, it aims to "make plain" what is in the text, rather than "imposing" ideas upon it. In addition, exposition must be more than exegesis and is so by including application of the text to hearers' lives. Yet, preachers who regard themselves as "expositors" often take a detached rhetorical posture with respect to the text, speaking *about* it rather than involving themselves *in* it.

Such preaching has been revived since the mid-twentieth century, in reaction to liberalism and to "topical" preaching that seemed to let the world's concerns set preaching's agenda. Its laudable ideal is faithfulness to Scripture. Its danger is the illusion that the "meaning" of Scripture is a readily discoverable entity that can be disclosed to a congregation with minimal self-involvement by speaker or hearer.

Re-Presentation. By contrast with "exposition," "re-presentation" implies that the preacher's task is not to talk *about* Scripture but in some sense to reenact it. Here, "to interpret Scripture" in the pulpit means not "discuss a text and apply it" but "allow its full power to be felt." Whereas "exposition" is often closely associated with the ideal of a "teaching ministry," "re-presentation" sits more comfortably with the proclamatory dimension of preaching. Many aspects of texts may go unexplained, but the attempt is made to let Scripture make its own impact on the minds and hearts of the hearers. Sermons are crafted to reflect the *form* of the text, not only to communicate its content (Long).

Such preaching often revolves around textual images or stories. The preacher may voice more than one standpoint, and thus set up a dialogue—perhaps between a biblical voice and a voice from the present. Contemporary interpretation is triggered as the former is allowed to address the latter, with minimal intrusion from the voice of a "detached" preacher. Re-presentational preaching is greatly assisted by the renewed emphasis on literary and rhetorical questions in biblical studies, though historical sensibility continues to play an important part in enabling texts to be heard with freshness.

Narrative. Narrative preaching may best be seen as a subset of re-presentational preaching, yet as a conception is important in its own right. It means not "preaching as a series of anecdotes," but preaching constructed with *narrative movement*, including such elements as suspense, disclosure, and resolution.

It finds its basis in the narrative shape of Scripture and the desire to catch hearers up into the story. Interpretation of the text may happen through a variety of means. A scriptural answer to a contemporary problem, or the solution to a difficulty perceived in Scripture itself, may be disclosed through a sermon with a "plot" (Lowry). A biblical story may be told with allusions or direct references at various points to the contemporary world. Or contemporary stories may act as echoes or foils to a biblical one.

As with re-presentational preaching generally, much interpretative work is left for the congregation to do. The preacher's task is to help the hearers see and feel the connection between Scripture and our world today, but it is for the hearers to go and work out the implications.

Liturgical. For some, the concept of preaching remains fundamentally shaped by its function within worship. Barth argued that theologically (if not always in practice) preaching takes place between the acts of baptism and Eucharist (*Homiletics*, 60). In the sermon the baptized are reminded of their identity in Christ, which is then enacted in the communion.

In this light, the preacher's task is to take one or more of the appointed readings and to discern and proclaim the gospel that lies at their heart (Fuller). Such preaching is thus distinguished from teaching and exhortation, and also from the expository ideal that can tend toward a focus on Scripture for its own sake.

A re-presentational form often lends itself to "liturgical" preaching, for the sermon can then be felt as one "act" in the "drama" of a service. The theological interpretation of Scripture happens as the preacher helps the congregation see and respond to the "fit" between the readings, the gospel message, and the whole act of worship.

Local Theology. The model of preaching as "local theologizing" takes very seriously the fact that preaching happens in a particular context, and that its biblical interpretation must therefore be thoroughly contextualized (Tisdale).

It assumes that the preacher is becoming familiar with the local congregational culture and yet is able to bring a broader and deeper perspective derived from the wider church and Christian tradition. It implies that it is meaningless to ask whether "text" or "context" should come first in constructing a sermon. Interpretation is a constant process of "negotiating the distance" between text and hearers (Craddock).

As compared with the "liturgical" preaching model, that of "local theology" allows greater latitude in subject matter. The gospel will certainly be informing the sermon, but textual interpretation will not have to focus so narrowly upon the paschal mystery. Scripture may be allowed to affirm, illumine, or challenge many aspects of communal and personal life. This may also turn out to be the most satisfactory umbrella concept for evangelistic preaching.

See also Jewish Exegesis; Liturgy; Oral Tradition and the NT; Targum

Bibliography

Auerbach, E. "Figura." Pages 11–76 in *Scenes from the Drama of European Literature*. Meridian, 1959; Barth, K. *Homiletics*, ed. D. Buttrick. Westminster John Knox, 1991; Brilioth, Y. *A Brief History of Preaching*, trans. K. Mattson. Fortress, 1965; Brueggemann, W. *The Bible and Postmodern Imagination*. SCM, 1993; Buttrick, D. "The Use of the Bible in Preaching." *NIB* 1:188–99; Craddock, F. *Preaching*. Abingdon, 1985; Dodd, C. H. *The Apostolic Preaching and Its Developments*. Hodder & Stoughton, 1936; Fuller, R. *What Is Liturgical Preaching?* SCM, 1959; Long, T. *Preaching and the Literary Forms of the Bible*. Fortress, 1989; Longenecker, R. *Biblical Exegesis in the Apostolic Period*. 2d ed. Eerdmans, 1999; Lowry, E. *The Homiletical Plot*. Rev. ed. Westminster John Knox, 2001; Old, H. O. *The Reading and Preaching of the Scriptures in the Worship of the Christian Church*. 4 vols. Eerdmans, 1998–2002; Stuhlmacher, P. *Historical Criticism and Theological Interpretation of Scripture*, trans. R. A. Harrisville. Fortress, 1977; Tisdale, L. *Preaching as Local Theology and Folk Art*. Fortress, 1996; Wilson, P. *God Sense*. Abingdon, 2001.

Stephen I. Wright

Presence   *See* Deconstruction

Presupposition   *See* Hermeneutical Circle; Hermeneutics; Objectivity

Priesthood/Priests   *See* Jewish Context of the NT

Princeton School

The Princeton School refers to the major conservative theological movement in American Presbyterianism. Its center was at Princeton Theological Seminary, from its 1812 founding under Archibald Alexander's leadership, stretching to J. Gresham Machen's 1929 resignation.

Alexander defended a Protestant scholastic construal of Reformed doctrine derived largely from the eighteenth-century Swiss theologian François Turretin and filtered through the philosophical prism of Scottish Common Sense Realism. He reacted against the challenges of Deism and Unitarianism, centering his argument on the necessity of revealed theology based on Scripture (*Evidences of the Authenticity, Inspiration, and Canonical Authority of the Holy Scriptures*, 1836).

Charles Hodge dominated Princeton from 1822 to his death in 1878, using his editorship of *Biblical Repertory and Princeton Review* (founded in 1825) to advance his views. Hodge wrote informatively about German scholarship in historical criticism, American revivalism, and Darwinism. He defended Reformed doctrine and the plenary inspiration of Scripture in the objectivist manner of Common Sense Realism, and measured the validity of scientific theories by the Baconian method of observation and experiment. In Hodge's view, both liberal theology and emotional evangelicalism are to be treated as suspect because they rely on human experience rather than the clear teaching of the Bible. Darwin's theory of natural selection fails the test of rigorous science because it lacks a clear fossil record. It also contradicts the Christian doctrine of the providence of God.

In Hodge's son Archibald Alexander Hodge, and Benjamin Breckenridge Warfield, the Princeton School continued unabated into the first decades of the twentieth century. In 1881 (the same year that Westcott and Hort published their critical text of the NT), A. A. Hodge and Warfield argued jointly in the *Presbyterian Review* that the "original autographs" of the Bible were without error. This position became the hallmark of the doctrine of "inerrancy," a nineteenth-century neologism that was taken up by conservative Presbyterians during the 1890s and probably contributed to the emergence of fundamentalism in the first decade of the twentieth century.

Fundamentalism's chief (though somewhat ambivalent) defender was J. Gresham Machen, whose *Christianity and Liberalism* (1923) is an eloquent and widely read argument for traditional Reformed teaching against the unwarranted, humanist assumptions of modernist historical criticism. Liberal control of the board of trustees at the seminary led to Machen's resignation in 1929. Machen carried on the work of the Princeton

School at the newly formed Westminster Theological Seminary until his death in 1937.

Princeton continues to influence North American evangelicals today, although the legacy of its doctrine of Scripture is controversial, especially its interface with a primacy of "inductive method" in theological interpretation.

Bibliography

Abraham, W. *Canon and Criterion in Christian Theology* (ch. 12). Clarendon, 1998; Harrisville, R. A., and W. Sundberg. *The Bible in Modern Culture* (ch. 10). 2d ed. Eerdmans, 2002; Kelsey, D. *Proving Doctrine* (ch. 2). Trinity, 1999; Noll, M. *Between Faith and Criticism.* Harper & Row, 1986; Ward, T. *Word and Supplement.* Oxford University Press, 2002; Woodbridge, J., and R. Balmer. "The Princetonians and Biblical Authority: An Assessment of the Ernest Sandeen Proposal." Pages 251–79 in *Scripture and Truth*, ed. D. A. Carson and J. Woodbridge. Baker, 1992.

Walter Sundberg

Promise   *See* Hope; Last Things, Doctrine of; Relationship between the Testaments; Speech-Act Theory

Proof Text

Upon investigation, precise origins of the term "proof text" remain unclear. In current parlance, however, the concept is unremittingly negative. (No one else wanted to write an article on the subject!) Hence, we hear the frequent axiom in many a course on biblical interpretation: "A text without a context is a pretext for a proof text." Proof-texting is not only an accusation lodged against lay reading or preachers' rhetoric (Eidenmuller); it is also the increasing label of choice by which exegetes characterize biblical interpretation among theologians.

The Rise and Fall of Proof-Texting

Popular proof-texting followed the invention of the printing press and the increase of literacy. Lay Bible reading in the West and especially America probably owes much to the spread of inductive "scientific" (Baconian) methodologies coupled with the system of dispensationalism. This happened through the Bible and prophecy conferences of the late nineteenth and early twentieth centuries and the Scofield Reference Bible (Boone; Noll; Hatch and Noll).

Although in this way Bible reading and theological claims were democratized to an unprecedented (and unhealthy! so Hauerwas) degree, such inductive biblical theologizing has had its academic counterpart. Charles Hodge and Lewis

Sperry Chafer, among other systematic theologians, famously wrote of their task as arranging scientifically the various biblical facts or data for any given topic. This proceeded with more or less sophistication depending on a theologian's approach to language—how "literal" interpretation was understood and "word studies" were pursued.

Some theologies might not have lost (especially redemptive) history entirely. Yet, on all sides scholarship was excessively fascinated with a reductive analysis of words and concepts, at least until the "biblical theology movement" ran into the buzz saw of James Barr's *The Semantics of Biblical Language*.

Today's lexical resources are less amenable to such proof-texting (Reese), and theologians at least nominally attend to the linguistic complexity of concept formation. Yet, by induction they have often tried to move rather straightforwardly from the Bible as "propositional revelation" to doctrine in conceptual form. One example would be an actual review in which theologian A claims to have a more "biblical" theology than theologian B, based on counting up verses in parentheses (on a random page from each work) and claiming to have three times as many (I leave out names to protect the guilty).

Not only does such practice generate problems connecting Scripture to salvation history; portions of the canon also tend to be privileged at the expense of others, most especially the Pauline corpus at the expense of the Bible's dominant feature, narrative. This accords with a "monolithic concept of revelation" (Ricoeur). Such privileges have typically been accorded due to a *discrimen* (imaginative construal of what is authoritative; Kelsey) that is pre- or extratextual: the Bible is authoritative as doctrine or as history or as myth, and so on.

The monolithic concept of revelation has then privileged a particular form of theological discourse, the propositional or conceptual. In Paul Ricoeur's unflinching analysis, theologians are tempted thereby to "neutralize" biblical genres in order to "extract their theological content" and "transform these different forms of discourse into propositions." So to interpret is to treat the Bible's literary forms as a "rhetorical facade which it would be possible to pull down in order to reveal some thought content that is indifferent to its literary vehicle" (Ricoeur 75, 90–91; see also Tracy; Vanhoozer).

This resonates with the work of John Goldingay, who links the concept of "revelation" to a particular model: prophetic inspiration and dual authorship—which pertains only to portions of Scripture. He claims that there are multiple models of authority within the biblical text, centrally witnessing tradition, authoritative canon, inspired word, and experienced revelation.

Respecting the Contexts of a "Biblical" Theology

For all its deserved derision, however, some concept of "proof text" seems essential to Christian theology. While their practice may not have been perfect, the Protestant scholastics rightly suggested that if God says what the Bible says, we logically pursue the development and defense of theological claims on such a basis (Muller, esp. 522–23). In addition, canonical practice itself supports the point, both in OT adaptation of earlier theology to later contexts (e.g., complex connections between Torah and Prophets) and in NT appeal to OT texts. A formula such as "it is written" often supports a theological claim, albeit with a richness of context and complex regard for the redemptive-historical situation (e.g., Paul's discussions of the Abraham story), as opposed to simple isolation of word-concepts or "verses."

To be sure, the identity relation between "God says" and "Scripture says" remains in need of careful ontological specification. Especially important is more consistent respect for literary genres as diverse forms of communication from and about God, replacing an exclusively oracular model of divine discourse. Speech-act philosophy, a helpful tool here, also suggests that a communicative act contains "presuppositions," "implications," and "entailments" (Austin 47–48). These will authorize theological development from the Bible beyond its explicit claims or arguments. Caution is required, though, in light of canonical relations to redemptive history and the role of divine vis-à-vis human authorship.

To speak of God we implicitly, if not explicitly, appeal to Scripture for support. In the end, however, "proof text" is probably not the best term. Not only should we avoid its accumulated cultural baggage; modern standards of "proof" carry a burden of certainty that neither we nor our fathers and mothers have been able to bear. Instead, to authorize a theological "judgment" would mean establishing which biblical patterns of communicative action about God ought to become ours, or how those patterns might preclude other possibilities. On the relation of such judgments to words and concepts, see David Yeago, who specifies: "We must ask (1) about the logical subjects of which predicates are affirmed and denied, (2) about the logical type of the particular predicates affirmed or denied within the conceptual idioms they employ, and (3) about the *point* or function of their affirmations or denials within their respective contexts of discourse" (94). On the authoritative roles that the Bible might play within such informal argumentation, see Kelsey (esp. ch. 6).

The selection of relevant biblical texts and their interpretation will be mutually reinforcing, which highlights that theologians must *both* select particular biblical judgments apropos to particular contexts *and* seek consistency or rough coherence between their various judgment-actions. Certain judgments do follow from what God says in Scripture; others are ruled out for inconsistency with what God has said. We must seek the wisdom to recognize the various cases for what they are, and to recognize when "relative adequacy" (frequently in writings from Tracy, following Bernard Lonergan) is reached for a time—when there are no more relevant questions to answer about an interpretation or judgment—until that situation changes.

The Christian reading of biblical texts as Scripture, somehow unified in relation to a redemptive history, will remain essentially contested, requiring an understanding of the Rule of Faith to be used (and perhaps reformed) during interpretation. Apologetics aside, we may nevertheless reach appropriate postcritical standards of public "proof" (1) even when we accept a measure of theoretical underdetermination but achieve the ongoing dialogue of practical reason. (2) We must resist a thoroughly ahistorical approach to the Bible and seek to give textual reasons for theological interpretations, (3) although such reasons will be at the level of canon and may appeal to the revelatory work of the Spirit in hearing the Word. This proper epistemic role of the Spirit—along with possible corollaries in human wisdom and/or Christian virtue—is perhaps the most complex and contested point in today's conversations about "proving doctrine" from Scripture.

Ultimately, we must celebrate the increased attention of all scholars to *literary context*, and commend this to lay readers. We may concede the oft-inadequate attention of theologians to *historical context*. Meanwhile, though, it is perhaps the burden of this dictionary to call exegetes' attention back to the *theological context* of biblical interpretation. What doctrine(s) a text might or might not "prove" can become a material consideration informing exegesis.

See also Biblical Theology; Concept; Logic; Revelation; Systematic Theology

Bibliography

Austin, J. L. *How to Do Things with Words*. Oxford University Press, 1962; Barr, J. *The Semantics of Biblical Language*. Oxford University Press, 1961; Boone, K. *The Bible Tells Them So*. SUNY Press, 1989; Eidenmuller, M. "Evangelicalism, Rhetoric, and the Bible: 'Prooftexting' or 'Scriptural Implant.'" Online: http://www.uttyl.edu/meidenmuller/scholarship/scriptural implant.htm; Goldingay, J. *Models for Scripture*. Eerdmans, 1994; Hatch, N., and M. Noll, eds. *The Bible in America*. Oxford University Press, 1982; Hauerwas, S. *Unleashing the Scripture*. Abingdon, 1993; Kelsey, D. *The Uses of Scripture in Recent Theology*. Fortress, 1975. Reissued as *Proving Doctrine*. Trinity, 1999; Muller, R. *Post-Reformation Reformed Dogmatics*. Vol. 2, *Holy Scripture*. Baker, 1993; Noll, M. *Between Faith and Criticism*. Harper & Row, 1986; Reese, J. "Pitfalls of Proof-Texting." *BTB* 13 (October 1983): 121–23; Ricoeur, P. "Toward a Hermeneutic of the Idea of Revelation." Pages 73–118 in *Essays on Biblical Interpretation*, ed. L. Mudge, trans. D. Pellauer. Fortress, 1980; Tracy, D. "Literary Theory and the Return of the Forms for Naming and Thinking God in Theology." *JR* 74, no. 3 (July 1994): 302–19; Vanhoozer, K. "The Semantics of Biblical Literature: Truth and Scripture's Diverse Literary Forms." Pages 49–104 in *Hermeneutics, Authority, and Canon*, ed. D. A. Carson and J. Woodbridge. Reprint, Baker, 1995; Yeago, D. "The New Testament and the Nicene Dogma: A Contribution to the Recovery of Theological Exegesis." Pages 87–100 in *The Theological Interpretation of Scripture*, ed. S. Fowl. Blackwell, 1997.

Daniel J. Treier

Prophecy and Prophets in the NT

While the significance of prophecy in the NT is affirmed by all, diverse approaches have been used to examine the evidence embedded in both narrative and discourse. Focusing on the source, some have examined prophecy within the broader category of pneumatology. Others have focused on the Jewish and Hellenistic contexts in an attempt to trace the trajectory of prophetic utterances through the Second Temple period. Related to this is emphasis on formal elements that at times leads to the narrowest definition of prophecy. A similar conclusion can be drawn with regard to the use of etymological investigation as the starting point of study. A potentially fruitful approach examines the content of prophetic speeches, but this approach is limited in value for the study of NT prophecy since the content of utterances is often not made explicit. Unsurprisingly, different definitions of prophecy arise respective to these approaches.

Inseparable from God's revelatory acts in history, prophecy naturally lends itself to theological interpretation. Prophecy necessarily assumes that God is able to speak and that the God who speaks is the one who acts (Wolterstorff). Any investigation of NT prophecy and prophets should, therefore, focus on both prophetic utterances and acts. These should in turn be examined within the wider history of God's involvement in history.

Prophecy and the Climax of History

Prophecy is one of the most important themes that highlight the continuity of God's salvific acts in history. The fulfillment formula, used in reference to the fulfillment of OT promises, can be found in Matthew (1:22–23; 2:15, 17–18; etc.). Its related forms also appear throughout the NT (John 13:18; 19:24, 28; Acts 1:16). These prophecies show that the entire history of salvation points to Jesus Christ himself, and in this sense all Scripture is fulfilled in Jesus (Luke 24:44) and he alone can be considered the telos of history (2 Cor. 1:20).

While scholars have pointed to the presence of various types of prophets in the Second Temple period (Aune; Webb), both the intensity and prevalence of prophetic activities in the NT point to the realization that God is acting in a new way. Surrounding the account of the birth of Jesus, one finds the prophetic voices of Elizabeth (Luke 1:42–45), Mary (1:46–55), Zechariah (1:68–79), Simeon (2:29–32), and Anna (2:36–38). These utterances point to the coming of God's salvation. The most significant figure is John the Baptist, who delivers the prophetic call to repentance and the prophetic act of baptism (Matt. 3:1–12; Mark 1:2–8; Luke 3:1–20; John 1:19–28). Many acclaimed John to be a prophet (Matt. 14:5); Jesus considered him to be the conclusion of the period of the Law and the Prophets (11:13). The significance of John as a prophet lies in the anticipatory nature of his ministry as he proclaims the arrival of "the Prophet."

In the Gospels, Jesus is explicitly called a prophet (Matt. 13:57; 21:11; Mark 6:4; Luke 7:16; 9:8, 19; 24:19; John 4:19, 44; 6:14; 7:40; 9:17). Not only does he call the people of God to repentance, but also he is the prophet who will lead his people on the new exodus journey. He is the prophet like Moses (Acts 3:22–23; cf. Deut. 18:18–19), and his journey to Jerusalem is an "exodus" journey (Luke 9:31 Greek). In performing signs and wonders, Jesus embodies the presence of God. As with the prophets of old, he is also characterized by the rejection of his people that ultimately leads to his death on the cross (Luke 13:33). Through the cross and resurrection, he is able to lead his people into the promised "rest" (Heb. 4). In Jesus, therefore, all prophecies find their fulfillment. As the significance of his words and deeds transcends the generation that he addresses, he is clearly recognized as one who is more than a prophet.

The power of the cross and the resurrection forms the center of the messages of many who followed Christ, arguably the most famous of which is the apostle Paul. In the account of his encounter with Christ on the road to Damascus, he uses the prophetic call formula to describe his mission as an apostle to the Gentiles (Gal. 1:15–16; cf. Jer. 1:5; Isa. 49:1). The prophetic message that he proclaims points to the new stage in salvation history: Jesus is now the Lord of all, and Gentiles will be able to participate as God's elected ones (Rom. 16:26–27). His prophetic call to his own people to recognize the dawn of the messianic era also recalls the message of the classical prophets (Rom. 9–11).

Prophecy and the People of the Spirit

The new era initiated through the life and ministry of Jesus is characterized by the renewed work of the Spirit among God's people, as promised in the classical prophets (e.g., Isa. 32:14–17; 44:1–4). The most explicit discussion appears in the context of the Pentecost account in Acts 2, where the quotation from Joel 2:28–32 has been understood as depicting the democratization of the Spirit experience, in which both young and old, male and female will prophesy. This quotation is preceded by a phrase from Isa. 2:2, describing the new era as "the last days" (Acts 2:17). The accounts of the prophetic activities of "maidservants" (Luke 1:38 AT), "daughters" (Acts 21:9), (young) men (11:27; 21:10), and old men (Luke 2:29) confirm the reality of such experiences. This age is one that "all prophets" have spoken of, and the early Christian community is to be considered as "sons of the prophets" (Acts 3:24–25 RSV).

In Paul, the experience of the prophetic Spirit is expressed in terms of the "gifts" of the Spirit. Prophecy appears in every list of gifts (Rom. 12:6; 1 Cor. 12:10, 28; Eph. 4:11). The ecclesiological significance of prophecy is highlighted when Paul claims that the one "who prophesies edifies the church" (1 Cor. 14:4).

The NT also expresses the understanding that the future consummation is yet to come in prophetic terms. As a prophet (Rev. 1:3), John wrote down the revelation of Jesus concerning "what must soon take place" (1:1). This predictive element is complemented by the prophetic call to be faithful as one lives in light of the future (chs. 2–3). Moreover, the presence of the false prophet heightens the need to be alert (Rev. 2:20; 19:20; cf. Matt. 7:15; 24:11; Mark 13:22; Acts 13:6; 1 John 4:1). Nevertheless, John's message is christocentric in nature since prophecy itself is ultimately the testimony of the works of Christ (Rev. 19:10).

Prophecy and Contemporary Interpretation

Prophetic activities testify to the act of God in history. God is the one who reveals himself through words and deeds; prophetic utterances should therefore be considered together with prophetic acts. In terms of salvation history, NT prophecy has to be understood in reference to the definitive revelation in the person of Jesus Christ.

Prophecy cannot be separated from the community of believers. Prophetic utterances affect the life of the community, and the community in turn is responsible to discern the content of such utterances (1 Cor. 14:29). In a broader sense, the community is also called to participate in the prophetic act through witnessing of the person and work of Jesus Christ.

This leads us to the question of authority. With Christ being the goal of OT prophecies, one cannot simply equate the writings of the OT prophets with the utterances of the NT prophets. The distinction between prophets and apostles, on the one hand, and prophetic utterances and canonical witnesses, on the other, has to be articulated (Grudem; Carson).

A carefully constructed understanding of prophetic authority allows one to recognize the possibility of the continuation of the prophetic gift in our times. The fact that Paul affirms the continuation of the gift of prophecy, and the reality of prophetic activities in the early church—both force one to recognize the continuation of prophecy beyond the apostolic period. Whether one wishes to emphasize the kerygmatic (Gillespie), pastoral (Hill), or revelatory (Turner) aspects, one cannot deny that the church is living in the "last days," where the presence of the prophetic Spirit is evident.

Bibliography

Aune, D. *Prophecy in Early Christianity and the Ancient Mediterranean World.* Eerdmans, 1983; Carson, D. A. *Showing the Spirit.* Baker, 1987; Ellis, E. E. *Prophecy and Hermeneutic in Early Christianity.* WUNT 18. Mohr/Siebeck, 1978; Forbes, C. *Prophecy and Inspired Speech in Early Christianity and Its Hellenistic Environment.* WUNT 2.75. Mohr/Siebeck, 1995; Gillespie, T. *The First Theologians.* Eerdmans, 1994; Grudem, W.

The Gift of Prophecy in the New Testament and Today. Rev. ed. Crossway, 2000; Hill, D. *New Testament Prophecy.* Marshall, Morgan & Scott, 1979; Spencer, F. S. "Out of Mind, Out of Voice: Slave-Girls and Prophetic Daughters in Luke-Acts." *BibInt* 7 (1999): 133–55; Turner, M. "Spiritual Gifts Then and Now." *VE* 15 (1985): 7–64; Vanhoozer, K. *First Theology.* InterVarsity, 2002; Webb, R. *John the Baptizer and Prophet.* JSNTSup 62. Sheffield Academic Press, 1991; Wolterstorff, N. *Divine Discourse.* Cambridge University Press, 1995.

David W. Pao

Prophecy and Prophets in the OT

Toward a Definition of Prophecy

The OT uses various terms to refer to the phenomenon of prophecy. The most-common expression, also the most difficult to define, is *navi'*. Its derivation is uncertain, but it is sometimes thought to refer to "someone who calls, proclaims" or to "someone who has been called." The term "seer" (*ro'eh*) stresses the prophets' receipt of visions, which frequently included auditions of the divine word (Num. 23:3–5; Jer. 38:21–23).

The term *khozeh* (seer) similarly reflects the visionary character of prophecy. Yet, since its cognate is used in the headings of some of the prophetic books, which contain prophetic words and visions, it appears to have a wider connotation, denoting a "recipient of divine revelation."

The OT does not always distinguish between these terms (1 Sam. 9:9), nor are they the best guide to defining the nature of prophecy. For this, one needs to turn to the sweep of OT literature, which presents prophets as men and women mediating divine auditions and visions to their audiences (individuals, particular groups, Israel, or foreign nations) by means of speech or symbolic action.

The Ancient Near Eastern Context

Both the OT (Num. 22–24; 1 Kings 18:19; Jer. 27:8–11) and an increasing number of extrabiblical documents indicate that the phenomenon of prophecy was not confined to Israel but was widespread throughout the ancient Near East.

The most important evidence comes from Mesopotamia and includes references to various intermediaries in the Mari letters (eighteenth century BCE), the Old Babylonian Eshnunna oracles, and a variety of Neo-Assyrian documents (seventh century BCE). Additional cuneiform and West Semitic sources confirm the existence of intermediaries throughout the region of Syria-Palestine.

Similarities between Israel and the neighboring cultures—such as the terminology used to refer to prophetic figures, the attestation of professional and lay prophets, the receipt of divine revelation by means of auditions and visions, and prophetic speech forms—are counterbalanced by significant differences. These include the Israelite prohibition of divination (Deut. 13:1–5), the strong ethical drive of the "writing prophets," and Israel's unique corpus of prophetic literature.

The Early Prophets

The Pentateuch traces Israel's history of prophecy back to Moses, the paradigm of the prophetic office (Deut. 34:10). The heirs of Moses' prophetic mantle mentioned in the books of Samuel and Kings include Samuel, Gad, Nathan, Micaiah, Elijah, Elisha, and Huldah. Speaking in the name of Yahweh (2 Sam. 12:7; 1 Kings 21:19), these prophets continue the intermediating role first performed by Moses.

Some of these prophets were important political figures who anointed kings (1 Sam. 16:13; 1 Kings 19:15), acted as their military advisers (1 Kings 22; 2 Kings 3), assumed the role of their God-sent censors (2 Sam. 11–12; 1 Kings 21), and got involved in dethroning some of Israel's rulers (1 Sam. 15:28; 1 Kings 14:7–18; 21:19). Until the mid-ninth century BCE, they were Israel's most important oppositional force (Koch); and as agents and defenders of Yahweh, they opposed religious apostasy and syncretism.

The Prophetic Books

In the Christian canon, the corpus of prophetic books consists of the "major prophets" Isaiah, Jeremiah, Ezekiel, and Daniel, and the smaller books from Hosea to Malachi. It also includes Lamentations, which was added here due to its association with Jeremiah. The period of these "classical" or "writing prophets" stretches approximately from the eighth to the fifth centuries BCE and covers the periods of Neo-Assyrian domination, Babylonian ascendancy, the exile, and the restoration under Medo-Persian rule.

With the exception of Daniel, the prophetic books are anthologies of prophetic oracles whose focus is not on the prophetic personae but on the prophets' divine message. While classical prophecy appears to have evolved out of earlier forms, its announcement of a divine punishment afflicting the entire nation and its production of collections of prophetic speeches are major new developments.

The prophets used a variety of speech forms, including vision reports (Amos 7:1–3), allegories (Isa. 5:1–7), and dirges (Amos 5:1–3). The two main forms or genres, however, are "oracles of judgment," usually consisting of the announcement of judgment and the reasons for it (Isa. 30:1–14), and "oracles of salvation" (Jer. 28:2–4). Many oracles are introduced by a formula such as "thus says Yahweh," which expresses the prophets' claim to speak in Yahweh's name. This claim manifests itself also in "call narratives" like Amos 7:14–15; Isa. 6; Jer. 1; and Ezek. 1–3.

History of Interpretation. "Precritical" readings of the prophetic books, especially those of the early church, which was deeply influenced by the prophetic literature, showed great interest in the prophets' moral exhortations. Prominent examples include their words on fasting (e.g., Joel 1:13–15; 2:12–17) and their exhortations to the watchmen and shepherds of the people (Ezek. 3:17–21; 33:1–9; 34:1–24), which were applied to specific questions of church politics. Most significantly, however, early Christian interpreters adopted a christological model of interpretation, which read the prophets, even including passages that had not been understood christologically by the NT writers, with a view to their fulfillment in Christ (Dassmann).

Modern interpretation of the prophetic literature has followed the general tendencies of the historical-critical study of the OT, while pursuing issues germane to the investigation of prophecy. Important steps along the way include the perception of the "classical prophets" as religious innovators and advocates of an "ethical monotheism," a monotheistic faith marked by ethical imperatives (Wellhausen, Duhm), and an interest in prophetic inspiration and ecstasy (Hölscher, Lindblom). An understanding of the prophets as religious geniuses is also reflected in the quest for their ipsissima verba, their original inspired words, which were thought to have been short poetic sayings (Gunkel).

The development of form criticism and tradition criticism led to a new image that saw the prophets as heirs, transmitters, and developers of traditional convictions and expressions. Various attempts were undertaken to understand the prophets against the backgrounds of the Israelite cult and covenant theology, Israel's legal traditions, or various wisdom circles.

Currently, redaction criticism, which seeks to reconstruct the redactional history of the prophetic books, provides one of the main tools for prophetic research. In offering a positive evaluation of the work of subsequent redactors, it continues to shift the focus away from the prophetic genius and his authentic words, and to the contribution made by Israel's educated elite in adapting the prophetic message to changed historical circumstances.

The postmodern fragmentation of biblical studies has led to the application of a variety of fresh approaches. In contradistinction to the historical-critical interest in the realities "behind the text," these recent approaches have tended to focus on the text itself or the contribution made to the interpretative process by the reader. Important developments include canonical approaches, which find the locus of authority in the final shape of the prophetic books read within the framework provided by the biblical canon as a whole. Rhetorical-critical readings, on the other hand, particularly those in the classical Aristotelian tradition of rhetoric, study prophetic rhetoric as argumentation, as an activity that seeks to alter reality, thus promoting a rhetorical view of religious language that values the communicative force of the biblical texts.

The Message of the Prophetic Books. The prophetic books record the mostly disregarded announcements of divine judgment to a sinful and complacent people together with proclamations of future salvation beyond the divine punishment.

Speaking in the name of Yahweh and against the background of Yahweh's covenant with Israel (Petersen 37), the prophets evaluate the life of God's people from a divine perspective. A characteristic feature of their powerful message is their insistence on love, righteousness, and justice as the proper expressions of Israel's relationship with Yahweh (Amos 5:21–24). Confronting the Israelites with their failure to live up to these standards, the prophets often turn into advocates for the weak and marginalized of society (Isa. 1:16–17; Zech. 7:8–10). Another recurring prophetic criticism concerns Israel's temptation to serve foreign gods (Jer. 7:9; Hos. 13:1–2).

The announcement of divine judgment was meant to induce the prophets' hearers to repentance or served to confirm the finality of Yahweh's decision. In either case, the lack of repentance resulted in tragedy and the conviction that only Yahweh could overcome the corruptness of the human heart (Jer. 31:31–34; Ezek. 36:26–27).

Israel's eventual restoration is another pervasive theme, stressing the reversal of exile (Jer. 3:18) and envisaging life in the land in abundance and prosperity (Amos 9:13–15) under the leadership of a just Davidic king (Isa. 11:1–10; Hos. 3:5).

Yet, speaking in the name of the Creator of all human beings, the prophets' purview extended well beyond Israel. It included the nations, who are the object of both prophetic announcements of judgment (Isa. 13–23; Jer. 46–51; Ezek. 26–32; Amos 1–2; Obadiah) and proclamations of future salvation (Isa. 19:19–25).

The theological significance of the prophetic literature resides in the combination of the vertical and the horizontal dimensions of the prophetic message. As creative speakers and writers, the prophets furnished their contemporaries, as well as countless subsequent generations of readers, with powerful theological reflections and ethical directives. These, though inevitably influenced by their own circumstances, are ultimately based on the divine word (*dabar*, Jer. 1:4; Ezek. 3:16) and revelation/vision (*khazon*, Isa. 1:1; Obad. 1; Nah. 1:1).

Bibliography

Blenkinsopp, J. *A History of Prophecy in Israel*. 2d ed. Westminster John Knox, 1996; Dassmann, E. "Umfang, Kriterien und Methoden frühchristlicher Prophetenexegese." *Jahrbuch für biblische Theologie* 14 (1999): 117–43; Davies, P., ed. *The Prophets*. Sheffield Academic Press, 1996; Gordon, R., ed. *"The Place Is Too Small for Us."* Eisenbrauns, 1995; Gowan, D. *Theology of the Prophetic Books*. Westminster John Knox, 1998; Koch, K. *The Prophets*. 2 vols. SCM, 1982–83; Neumann, P. H. A., ed. *Das Prophetenverständnis in der deutschsprachigen Forschung seit Heinrich Ewald*. Wissenschaftliche Buchgesellschaft, 1979; Nissinen, M., ed. *Prophecy in Its Ancient Near Eastern Context*. SBL, 2000; Nissinen, M., et al., eds. *Prophets and Prophecy in the Ancient Near East*. SBL, 2003; Petersen, D. L. *The Prophetic Literature*. Westminster John Knox, 2002; Rofé, A. *Introduction to the Prophetic Literature*. Sheffield Academic Press, 1997.

Karl Möller

Prophetic Writings

History of Interpretation

The "prophetic writings" in the Christian canon comprise the fifteen books that bear the name of a prophet (Isaiah, Jeremiah, and Ezekiel, and the twelve Minor Prophets), and also Daniel and Lamentations. The Book of the Twelve was counted as a single book in ancient times (in the Babylonian Talmud, for example, *B. Bat.* 14b–15a reckons twenty-four books in the canon) and in some modern treatments (House; Collins). The Hebrew Bible counts only the three major and twelve "minor" prophets in its Nevi'im section.

In the earliest Christian interpretation, such as Justin Martyr's *Dialogue with Trypho*, the prophets afforded an important key to understanding Christian theology, because of the powerful idea that Jesus Christ had fulfilled prophecy. Historical context tended to be secondary, and texts were instead taken as proofs that Jesus was the promised Messiah (Sawyer 42–49). A typological method allowed Jonah, for example, to be taken as a type of Christ (Sherwood, *Biblical*, 11–21). The Reformation saw a return of the historical sense, but this was still subject to a belief in the unified witness of Scripture. For example, Calvin can call the return of the Babylonian exiles "the restitution of the church." And what was promised to Israel in that context is immediately applicable to Christian life (such as need for regeneration by God's Spirit; Calvin 269, 271).

Early critical interpretation, no longer looking directly for Christian doctrine, had two main interests: the prophets' experience and the extent to which they proclaimed a new kind of religion. Literary critics sought the "original" words of the prophets, typically in their poetry, as distinct from the prosaic sections (e.g., Duhm), believing there was a connection between poetic form and prophetic inspiration. Prophets were thought to have had a special religious experience, whether in the apprehension of divine messages, or in prophetic performance, an experience that some called "ecstatic" (Duhm; Lindblom 46). Many scholars believed that prophets introduced a profound new ethical and spiritual dimension to Israelite religion (e.g., Skinner; Eichrodt 345; von Rad 54–55).

Form criticism focused more on typical forms of prophetic speech than on the prophetic experience as such. The dominant forms identified were Oracles of Judgment and Oracles of Salvation. C. Westermann also found third-person accounts (including vision reports) and prayers (Westermann 90–98). The basic division between judgment and salvation oracles raised certain questions. For example, were oracles declarations of unalterable future events (Westermann 65–67), or could an oracle of judgment actually be a threat intended to lead to repentance (Tucker 55–56)?

The form-critical method of inquiry raised a number of other questions. Did the prophets function in the setting of temple worship (Johnson)? Did they originally preach judgment only (as many commentators thought about Amos, for example)? Form criticism therefore led back to questions about the prophets themselves and how their words produced effects. Its unanswered questions therefore led to a next phase, redaction criticism, which focused more firmly on the prophetic book.

Redaction criticism examines the ways in which prophetic words were handed on, added to, and received into new contexts, until they finally took their place in finished books. The structure of certain books gives prima facie evidence for such redactional activity, for example, the alternation of judgment and salvation groups of texts in Isa. 1–12. One version of this process postulates a "rolling corpus" (McKane), in which a core of sayings is gradually expanded in an open-ended way (e.g., Jer. 3:6–11 develops 3:1–5). Another version posits the controlling hand of a final author or redactor, as in Williamson's account of Isa. 1–55, which he thinks was brought to its present form by Deutero-Isaiah.

The redactional process itself is theologically rich. Clements, speaking of the composition of Isaiah, thinks that "through its many stages of growth, intentional connections and interrelationships between the parts were planned" (*Hermeneutical*, 204). The redactional process can explain why the major prophetic corpora, including perhaps the Book of the Twelve (Collins), exhibit similar structures, moving from warnings of judgment to judgment itself, and then announcements of salvation.

In the trend to redaction criticism, the older criteria for identifying "authentic" prophetic words no longer held. The distinction between poetry and prose has been blurred (Kugel; Andersen and Freedman). On some accounts the prophetic figure virtually disappears; for some, the biblical literature has transformed free-thinking "poets" into "prophets" (R. P. Carroll; contrast Duhm!). Others, however, maintain the connection between prophet and book, showing from the ancient world that prophets wrote down their sayings (Barstad 123–24). Some tried to identify the roles of Israel's prophets and of the sociological groups that supported them (Petersen; Wilson).

"Rhetorical criticism" (Patrick and Scult) examines prophetic discourse (whether the prophet's own or as deposited in the book) for its power to persuade an audience. This sheds light on some older questions (such as whether Oracles of Judgment aimed to produce repentance and therefore prevent the threatened evil). It also draws attention to the prophetic *art*: its poetry, metaphors, and other figures of speech (Sherwood, "Of Fruit"), its use of sound (alliteration, assonance), its specifically rhetorical techniques (such as drawing an audience in with an accepted proposition in order to induce acceptance of an unanticipated consequence, as in Amos 1:1–2:8). Such studies can consider the effects of prophetic speech and writing on both "original" and subsequent audiences. This is in keeping with the status of the prophetic writings as canonical literature.

Modern readings have returned to contemporary applications. Some draw out implications for the church's life and ministry (Brueggemann); some have found new contexts, as in Latin America, to apply prophetic social critique in relation to religion and politics (M. D. Carroll R.). Others have sought to identify power concepts inherent in prophetic language, alert to the dangers of using even these texts, so critical of power structures in their day, as pretexts for sustaining such structures today (Weems).

Recovery of the prophetic message does not require a return to precritical methods. Rather, by engaging with literary and historical questions highlighted by modern criticism, it needs to bring the prophetic message to bear on contemporary issues, both within the church and beyond. Such recoveries have to maintain a careful balance between hearing the word of judgment and announcing the hope of liberation.

Overview of Message

The Basic Pattern: Sin, Judgment, and Salvation. The main prophetic corpora share a common broad structure: judgment preached, judgment comes, salvation proclaimed. The first premise of this pattern is the sinfulness of Israel, namely its idolatry (Hosea) and perversion of justice (Amos). The distinction between these two strands is not watertight, and indeed, false worship and injustice are often expressly linked (Jer. 2:33–34; Amos 2:6–8).

The context of the accusation of sin is the expected loyalty of Israel to Yahweh their God. Such loyalty is not generally portrayed as covenantal, though Hosea and Deuteronomy place prophets close to covenantal theology (Nicholson; Andersen and Freedman). Isaiah uses the metaphor of rebellious children (Isa. 1:2–4). Hosea and Jeremiah recall a "golden" wilderness age of faithfulness, in contrast with present idolatry. Amos declares that God will punish Israel because he has "known" them, alone of "all the families of the earth" (Amos 3:2 NRSV).

The falseness of Israel to God leads to an analysis of sin as a powerful tendency to inconstancy. Jeremiah appeals to Judah to "return, faithless children," where "faithless" is a term based on *shub* (turn, return). The moral life is depicted as an intense struggle between turning toward God and turning away to other gods. For the community, the possibilities are either "truth" (*'emeth*) or profound falsehood (*sheqer*; Jer. 8:22–9:9; cf. Zeph. 3:13; Overholt). In the latter situation, the remedy is nothing less than a radical reorientation of loyalties, thought, and practice, or what the prophets call "returning" or "repenting."

However, Israel fails to respond. The only canonical instance of repentance following a prophet's preaching is that of Nineveh to the judgment oracle of Jonah (Jon. 3:4–5)! Otherwise, the prophetic books testify to inevitable judgment due to persistent sin. This, however, becomes a prelude to a dramatic solution—a new act of God, who not only saves the people out of their affliction, but also enables them to do what was previously impossible, to become faithful to God (typified by Jeremiah's new covenant; 31:31–34). The judgment-salvation pattern, therefore, comprises an analysis of the human moral condition, and a soteriology grounded in God's love and mercy.

This transformation from judgment to salvation comes because of God's own commitment to his people's salvation. The classic text expressing, anthropomorphically, God's inner conflict because of the impulse to punish yet overriding compassion is Hos. 11:8–9 (cf. Jer. 31:20). The "incarnational" tendency is expressed also in the "Immanuel" sign ("God with us"; Isa. 7:14). In the prophets, "image of God" becomes incarnational when God's image becomes merged with the prophet's (Mauser, linking Hosea, Jeremiah, and Jesus). Inasmuch as the Suffering Servant of Isa. 40–55 exhibits the divine suffering, this image also lies close to the picture in Jeremiah.

Critical Engagement with Tradition. The themes of the prophetic program may be subsumed under the heading of critical engagement with tradition. As we saw, the prophetic message is addressed to the nation Israel's past with God. Memories of patriarchal origins (Hos. 12:3), exodus from Egypt (Mic. 6:4), entry to the land (Amos 2:9–11), covenant at Sinai (obliquely at Jer. 15:1), and covenant with David (Amos 9:11)—all are found in the prophetic corpus. But either this tradition is used to exhort the people to obedience and gratitude, or their understanding of it is challenged.

A fundamental idea is the impossibility of being truly "Israel" in the absence of a love of righteousness and justice. Paradigmatic are Isa. 5:1–7; Hos. 6:6; Amos 5:24; and Mic. 6:6–8 (cf. Deut. 10:12–13). Temple and king, symbols of Israel's privileged status, have no intrinsic claim to endurance without these qualities. Jeremiah's "temple sermon" outrageously parallels the Jerusalem temple with that of Shiloh, which had succumbed to Philistine ravages generations earlier (Jer. 7:1–15; 26:2–6). Before him, Micah knew that it was vulnerable because of those who "build Zion with bloodshed" (Mic. 3:10, 12). Isaiah holds King Ahaz to account, as "house of David" (Isa. 7:13), to find safety in faith in Yahweh, rather than in alliance with idolatrous Assyria. Failure to be Israel in truth will result in loss of the land, once given in trust to a people who pledged to be faithful.

In this quest of the true Israel, its very boundaries are put in question. First, in a narrowing tendency, the true Israel is sometimes described as a "remnant" of the historic people (Isa. 10:2–23; Jer. 5:10; Joel 2:32 [3:5 MT]). Second, there is a broadening tendency toward an inclusive covenant, incorporating the other nations. The issue is sharply put in Jonah, where God's mercy and compassion—traditional elements in covenantal thought (Exod. 34:6)—are claimed to extend even to the hated Assyrians (Jon. 4:2). The prophetic corpus perhaps conducts an inner dialogue on this, with an echo in Jonah of Joel's more traditional "Divine Warrior" attitude (Joel 2:13). The book of Isaiah also moves toward inclusion of the nations in God's salvation. These will come in pilgrimage to Zion, to learn of God and his torah (Isa. 2:2–4; cf. Mic. 4:1–4). And in Isa. 40–55 the concept of "covenant" itself is reconceived so as to include the nations (Isa. 42:6; 49:6).

Behind the visions of the nations' future inclusion is the belief in God's sovereign power over all nature and history. Ezekiel's visions of Yahweh enthroned over Babylon (Ezek. 1; 10) assert that the God of Israel cannot be confined to one people or city. The universality of Yahweh is a general premise in the prophetic books (Jer. 4:23–26; Joel 3:1–8 [4:1–8 MT]; Amos 1–2; Zeph. 1:2–3).

A special aspect of the belief in God's universality is theodicy. The Oracles against the Nations, which appear in several of the prophetic books (e.g., Isa. 13–23), have at their heart the concept of God's justice. The idea of God bringing a foreign nation in judgment against his people prompts the further proposition that God will in turn punish those nations for their sin (Isa. 10:5–19; Jer. 25:11–12). The prophet Habakkuk laments the potential injustice involved in using a wicked nation to punish God's people (ch. 1). This protest prompts God's famous answer, that "the righteous shall live by his/their faith(fulness)" (Hab. 2:4 AT).

The Shape of the Future. The future hope held out by the prophets is never simply a return to the status quo ante. Since the future always arises out of the catastrophe that destroyed the old order, the prophets visualize possible future communities in that context. The old promises will be fulfilled, but in unexpected ways. The precise concepts vary from prophet to prophet, but the following are found. Holy war is developed into images of total, final conflict, in which the God of Israel triumphs over all enemies (Ezek. 38–39; Joel 3 [4 MT]). In Ezekiel's ideal yet pragmatic vision, future Zion and temple are depicted in Edenic terms (Ezek. 47; cf. Joel 3:17–18 [4:17–18 MT]). In Isaiah, Zion takes on eschatological overtones, with its inclusion of non-Israelite nations, and its depictions of a renewed creation (Isa. 60:17–20). Knowledge of God is no longer confined either to Israel (Hab. 2:14) or to the traditional priestly and prophetic channels (Jer. 31:34; Joel 2:28–29 [3:1–2 MT]). Messianic images involving the Davidic king take diverse forms. He can have a subordinate role (Ezekiel's *nasi'*, "prince," in chs. 44–48), come as a powerful king who establishes justice among the nations (Isa. 11:1–9), or come with both power and humility (Zech. 9:9–10).

Postexilic prophecy lies between two fulfillments, one accomplished already in the restoration from Babylon, and a greater one still in the future. Zechariah's visions celebrate the first restoration (note its announcement that Jeremiah's seventy-year exile is at an end; Zech. 1:12–17), yet that book also proffers further hope, in near-apocalyptic terms (chs. 12–14). In the interim, the currency of the community is justice and righteousness (Isa. 48:17–19; 60:21; Zech. 7:8–10).

Contribution to the Canon

In the canonical prophetic corpus, the location of the writings between fulfillments is definitive. The prophets are put on a par with the Mosaic law, by juxtaposing the expected coming of Elijah with an exhortation to keep the "statutes and ordinances" given at Horeb (Mal. 4:4–6). In this way the prophetic writings continue to call the community to repent, while proclaiming an indefeasible hope based on the faithfulness of God.

Their future orientation is essentially open. This is clear from their diversity on topics such as messianic expectation. Indeed, the canonical form apparently expresses and invites dialogue. An example is the repetition of the formula in Joel 3:16 [4:16 MT] ("The Lord roars from Zion / And utters his voice from Jerusalem"; NRSV) in Amos 1:2, which follows closely in the dominant canonical order. One context is judgment, the other salvation. Similarly, Isaiah's peace text ("They shall beat their swords into ploughshares / And their spears into pruning hooks"; 2:4 NRSV) is precisely reversed in Joel 3:10 [4:10 MT], a text that points to an eschatological holy war. Jonah's affirmation of God's grace to the nations (4:2) echoes Joel's more traditional claim (Joel 2:13). In these pairs of texts none is meant to trump another; rather, they convey diverse aspects of a larger truth.

The prophetic writings as a whole testify to the constant renewal of the grace of God. The "story" underlying them tells of God's readiness to do new things in order to achieve his purpose of creating a faithful people. The trajectory of Jeremiah's seventy-year exile (Jer. 25:11–12; Dan. 9:2; Zech. 1:12–17) traces this, and the new covenant symbolizes it. The NT's re-appropriation of "Israel," Davidic promise, tropes of exile and temple, Spirit (Joel 2:28–29 [3:1–2 MT]), new covenant, Jesus as Suffering Servant, Elijah (as John the Baptist)—all this is in line with the dynamic of development and reapplication that we find in the OT itself.

What the Books Say Theologically

The prophetic writings, along with the Torah, form part of the scriptural Rule of Faith and life. They testify to God's past faithfulness and his ever-present readiness to save again in whatever "day of small things" (Zech. 4:10) we find ourselves. As Zechariah's postexilic community could celebrate deliverance from Babylonian captivity, yet feel that God had greater things in store, so the church hears the prophets between the coming of Christ and his coming again. This invites reinterpretations. The term "exiles"—which can still be applied to the community even after the restoration (Jer. 24:4; cf. Ezra 6:19)—resonates among Christians, who celebrate Easter and yet await the parousia, and in the meantime are "in the world but not of it" (cf. John 17).

In tight tension with such encouragement, however, comes also the call to repent in order to avert judgment. The judgment-salvation pattern, raised to canonical status in the prophetic books, is a pattern of the reality within which we live. Thus, we are called to allow ourselves, individually and as church, to be addressed by the full force of prophetic critique, to explore restlessly the meaning of the call to be God's people, to examine well-established ways of thinking and acting, indeed to question radically all self-serving, complacent attitudes. Above all, we are exhorted to hope in God, not in false objects of trust, to worship in spirit and truth, and to be like Simeon (Luke 2:25 NRSV), "looking forward to the consolation of Israel."

Bibliography

Andersen, F., and D. Freedman. *Hosea*. AB 24. Doubleday, 1980; Barstad, H. "No Prophets? Recent Developments in Biblical Prophetic Research and Ancient Near Eastern Prophecy." Pages 106–26 in *The Prophets*, ed. P. Davies; Barton, J. "The Canonical Meaning of the Book of the Twelve." Pages 59–73 in *After the Exile*, ed. J. Barton and D. Reimer. Mercer University Press, 1996; Brueggemann, W. *Hopeful Imagination*. Fortress, 1986; Calvin, J. *Ezekiel I*, ed. D. F. Wright. Eerdmans/Paternoster, 1994; Carroll R., M. D. *Contexts for Amos*. JSOTSup 132. JSOT, 1992; Carroll, R. P. "Poets Not Prophets: A Response to 'Prophets through the Looking Glass.'" Pages 43–49 in *The Prophets*, ed. P. Davies; Clements, R. "Prophecy as Literature: A Reappraisal." Pages 56–76 in *The Hermeneutical Quest*, ed. D. G. Miller. Pickwick, 1986. Reprint, pages 203–16 in *Old Testament Prophecy*. Westminster John Knox, 1996; Collins, T. *The Mantle of Elijah*. JSOT, 1993; Davies, P., ed. *The Prophets*. The Biblical Seminar. Sheffield Academic Press, 1996; Duhm, B. *Das Buch Jeremia*. Mohr, 1901; Eichrodt, W. *Theology of the Old Testament*. Vol. 1, trans. J. A. Baker. OTL. Westminster, 1961; House, P. *The Unity of the Twelve*. Almond, 1990; Johnson, A. *The Cultic Prophet in Ancient Israel*. University of Wales Press, 1944; Kugel, J. *The Idea of Biblical Poetry*. Yale University Press, 1981; Lindblom, J. *Prophecy in Ancient Israel*. Blackwell, 1962; Mauser, U. *Gottesbild und Menschwerdung*. Mohr, 1971; McKane, W. *A Critical and Exegetical Commentary on Jeremiah*. 2 vols. ICC. T&T Clark, 1986–96; Nicholson, E. *God and His People*. Clarendon, 1986; Overholt, T. W. *The Threat of Falsehood*. SBT. SCM, 1970; Patrick, D., and A. Scult. *Rhetoric and Biblical Interpretation*. Almond, 1990; Petersen, D. L. *The Roles of Israel's Prophets*. JSOTSup 17. JSOT, 1981; Rad, G. von. *Old Testament Theology*. Vol. 2. SCM, 1965; Sawyer, J. F. A. *The Fifth Gospel*. Cambridge University Press, 1996; Sherwood, Y. *A Biblical Text and Its Afterlives*. Cambridge University Press, 2000; idem. "Of Fruit and Corpses and Wordplay Visions: Picturing Amos 8:1–3." *JSOT* 92 (2001): 5–27; Skinner, J. *Prophecy and Religion*. Cambridge University Press, 1922; Tucker, G. *Form Criticism of the Old Testament*. Fortress, 1971; Weems, R. *Battered Love*. Fortress, 1995; Westermann, C. *Basic Forms of Prophetic Speech*. Lutterworth/Westminster John Knox, 1991; Williamson, H. G. M. *The Book Called Isaiah*. Clarendon, 1994; Wilson, R. R. *Prophecy and Society in Ancient Israel*. Fortress, 1980.

J. G. McConville

Proposition

Individual (token) sentences are physical entities: sound waves or marks on paper or sequences of colored flags. J. L. Austin drew attention, however, not just to the act of saying something, which he called the "locutionary act," but also to the act done *in* saying something, which he called the "illocutionary act," and to the act done *by* saying something, which he called the "perlocutionary act." When my wife performs the locutionary act of saying in English "Dinner is ready," she also performs the illocutionary act of affirming that dinner is ready, and the perlocutionary act of drawing me to come downstairs and eat it. There is no finite list of perlocutionary acts, since there is no end of things that one can bring about through speaking, and there are also many different illocutionary acts: we ask questions, express wishes, and issue commands. Even indicative sentences can be used for actions other than affirmation—promising, swearing, naming, apologizing, thanking, pronouncing sentence, and so on.

Nevertheless, affirmation is one of the most important illocutionary acts, since it represents a proposition as true. God cannot affirm a false proposition, so God's affirmation is a particularly important illocutionary act. The principal problem of biblical interpretation is, accordingly, to work out which propositions the divine author is affirming in the sentences of the Bible. Usually the human author and the divine author affirm one and the same proposition in an utterance, but sometimes, as in some cases of prophecy, the proposition affirmed by God may be beyond the understanding of the human author. It may even be the case that the proposition affirmed by the human speaker is false, as seems to be the case with Caiaphas's unwitting prophecy recorded in John 11:49–51.

Occasionally theologians try to contrast a set of propositions and the biblical *narrative*. This is misguided, for in a sense a narrative just is a set of propositions, albeit about events in time. It is, however, important to recognize that the Bible does not contain just propositions; the Bible also contains questions, injunctions, and wishes. Nor need it be slavishly maintained that every indicative sentence affirms a distinct true proposition: perhaps, for example, the parable of the good Samaritan (Luke 10:30–35) is intended as a whole to affirm a single true proposition. In other words, the literary *genre* not only determines what proposition is affirmed—for example, in irony the proposition affirmed is the opposite of the one that the sentence expresses—but also what it is that affirms the proposition, whether an individual sentence or a larger passage.

See also Speech-Act Theory; Truth

Bibliography

Austin, J. L. *How to Do Things with Words*. Oxford University Press, 1961; Searle, J. *Speech Acts*. Cambridge University Press, 1969; Vanhoozer, K. *Is There a Meaning in This Text?* Apollos, 1998; Wolterstorff, N. *Divine Discourse.* Cambridge University Press, 1995.

Daniel Hill

Protestant Biblical Interpretation

The rise of distinctive Protestant biblical interpretation in the sixteenth and seventeenth centuries coincided with the humanistic advances in rhetoric and linguistics of the Renaissance and the Reformers' dogmatic assertions concerning theological authority. This is not to suggest that Protestant interpretation developed ex nihilo, for almost all the exegetical techniques employed by Protestant interpreters in the Reformation and post-Reformation eras have antecedents in medieval exegesis. The theological and ecclesiastical changes brought about by the Reformers did, however, lead to an increased emphasis on the literal sense of the sacred text. The literal sense had also been sought in medieval times by exegetes like Thomas Aquinas, Nicholas of Lyra, and Hugh and Andrew of St. Victor (Smalley; McKim), but it was increasingly important to the Protestant generation in light of the authority they invested in the Bible. The dramatic innovations in academic scholarship and the intellectual milieu of Renaissance humanism enabled Protestant exegetes to pursue that literal sense with increasing precision and confidence. Thus, Protestant biblical interpretation inherited the exegetical legacy of the medieval church and adapted it according to the Reformation's teaching on theological authority, aided by the linguistic and rhetorical insights of the Renaissance.

Development in Protestant Biblical Interpretation

The Reformation's insistence upon the sole authority of the written Word led to an outpouring of material, exegetical and dogmatic, positive and polemical, throughout the Protestant era. Early on, the biblical canon was defined and its integrity defended, the divinity and properties of Scripture were asserted, and its role as *principium cognoscendi theologiae* was clearly affirmed (Muller). In addition to these works that focused upon the nature of the Scripture, material has continued to appear that addresses the question of how the church is to interpret and then use the Bible in its theological reflection (Kelsey).

Protestant exegesis has evolved significantly from its precritical beginnings (1550–1700s), through the modern, historical-critical era (1700s–1900s), to the present postmodern time (1960s–present). The style, purpose, and even much content of biblical commentaries written during the Protestant era vary greatly. This variation is often thought to arise from the application of new exegetical techniques, unknown or ignored by earlier interpreters. However, there is great continuity in the actual practice of biblical interpretation throughout the Protestant era. The differences reflect changes in exegetical methodology (the manner in which interpretative skills and techniques are employed to seek meaning), rather than the creation and implementation of new, previously unknown exegetical practices. There has been some development in techniques and substantial growth in the availability of resources. Yet for the most part, the tools employed in the exegetical task (linguistic and lexical analysis, attention to scope and occasion, the application of the analogies of faith and Scripture, etc.) have not dramatically changed over the centuries.

What have altered are the governing presuppositions that guide the interpretative process—assumptions concerning the nature of the biblical text itself. These assumptions ultimately control how the text is examined for meaning and what authority that meaning eventually carries. As the Protestant community's understanding of the nature of the Bible has evolved, the goal of exegesis and the manner in which the exegetical techniques are used have changed as well.

Initially, in the roughly two centuries of Protestant orthodoxy, theologians shared the precritical conviction that meaning was found in the words of the Bible because it was divinely inspired. The nature of the text itself, being God-breathed, gave rise to its authorial force; Scripture was authoritative for faith and life precisely because it originated with the holy and perfect God. Consequently, the exegetical strategies employed by Reformation era exegetes and their immediate successors presumed a unified biblical message. The literal sense of the text was the sense that was intended by the divine Author and mediated by the words. Interpretative techniques that assumed a unified biblical message and focused primarily on linguistic aspects were decisive during this period.

With the rise of the Enlightenment and the ushering in of the modern era, precritical assumptions concerning the nature of Scripture slowly gave way to empirical and rational critique. It gradually became unacceptable to see absolute authority as grounded in either the divinely ordained Christian tradition (as in medieval times) or in the divinely authored Bible (as in the early

633

Protestant era). The meaning of Scripture derived, not from the divine origin of the received words, but from the "reality" of the persons and historical events to which it attested. The quest for the Bible's "literal sense" became a search for the divine revelation disclosed through time; meaning was found *behind* the text, in the historical situations depicted by the biblical authors.

In modern historical-critical methodology, prominence is given to exegetical techniques that underscore scientifically testable data, where the meaning of the biblical message is to be found. Understanding a text means comprehending the entire world of the human author, using historical, economic, psychological, philosophical, and sociological means of analysis—even prioritizing this extrabiblical material to "correct" the text. In nineteenth-century German scholasticism, this became a search for the historicity of the events described (accurately or not) in the Bible, and the comparative-religions approach. With literary criticism, the focus shifted toward learning about the literary nature of the text and an emphasis on original source material and forms (Ramm). In the extreme, higher criticism came to stand, not just for the scientific examination of the biblical documents, but for the assumption that the exegete has the right to pass judgment upon their truth claims (Kaiser and Silva 236).

Finally, the collapse of modernity cast doubt upon the possibility of objective truth and, consequently, upon the claim that a single, stable meaning may be found in a text; ultimate authority and meaning were removed from the written form and located in its reader (Vanhoozer). Scriptural authority is present (if at all) because it is imputed to the text by the reader and/or community of faith. Postmodern exegesis is ideological and consists of deconstructing the text—identifying the prejudices and preconceptions of its writing and prior interpretation—and construing it along lines set by the reader. While there remains some continuity with previous eras, traditional exegetical tools have much less value in some versions of postmodern biblical interpretation.

Protestant Exegetical Techniques

While differing assumptions concerning the nature of Scripture have greatly influenced the manner in which the biblical text is examined, Protestants throughout the era have employed a fairly consistent set of exegetical skills and tools.

The Spiritual State of the Interpreter. Post-Reformation biblical commentators uniformly affirmed that the true sense of the Bible could only be discovered by the Christian believer who sought the Holy Spirit's assistance throughout the exegetical process. The necessity of the Spirit's role is directly tied to the nature of the text itself—since the Spirit inspired its writing, the Spirit is the most competent to explain its intended meaning. A godly state is also necessary for supernatural enlightenment of the human mind. This belief is rooted in Protestant anthropology and is in no way to be understood as a limitation of Scripture; illumination is needed, not to supply some lack in the character of the text, but due to the spiritual blindness of fallen humanity. Early Protestants recognized that, apart from the Spirit's illumination, one can learn, understand, be proficient, and even teach the meaning of the text to others, yet all the while remain ignorant of its salvific matters and the assurance they bring (Perkins).

The necessity of the Spirit's involvement is explicitly denied in modern historical-critical methodology. Since the text is merely a human record, uncovering its historical referent demands only the scientific examination of the text and related extrabiblical material. Similarly, postmoderns reject a necessary interpretative role for the Holy Spirit when they deem the Spirit to be an external authority insisting on some form of objective textual meaning. On the other hand, as an essential component of many faith communities, the Spirit's impact on that community's referential structure helps determine the reader's interpretative situation.

The Analogy of Faith. It would be difficult to overestimate the importance of the analogy of faith in post-Reformation hermeneutics. Protestant authors consciously followed it, expressed it, and defended it in their theoretical writings. Exegetically, the analogy of faith dictates that no true interpretation of a passage can be contrary to the overall expression of biblical faith. This fundamental presupposition is based on three assumptions concerning Scripture and the doctrine of God: (1) God cannot lie and is not self-contradictory; (2) the divinity of Scripture, its divine origin, means that it also is self-consistent; and (3) core Christian doctrines flow faithfully from the Scripture. As the *analogia fidei* is formulated from the clear, historically and universally accepted sense of the Bible, its exegetical influence ultimately depends upon Scripture itself.

The analogy of faith provides a clear boundary between acceptable and nonacceptable interpretations. Every conclusion is to be tested by this presupposition, and whatever exposition is inconsistent with this analogy must be false. Of course, this does not mean that every possible interpretation of a text that faithfully corresponds to the analogy of faith is exegetically accurate. And, contrary to modern criticism, the analogy of faith does not dictate the interpretation of any particular text; what it does is limit the interpretative options that the exegete may consider as appropriate explanations of a passage; other potential meanings are excluded a priori by the *analogia fidei* assumption.

For early Protestants, the analogy of faith functioned as the framework for all biblical interpretation and served to limit reason's competence in divining theological truth. For these two reasons the *analogia fidei* was largely rejected in the modern era. The analogy was criticized by proponents of a more scientific exegetical strategy as being a restrictive paradigm imposed upon divine revelation by the church, a paradigm that dictates meaning rather than discovers it. Similarly, subjecting the Bible to the traditional theological framework of the Christian faith was perceived as an oppressive limitation upon the freedom of one's use of reason (Farrar). Though there was little reliance upon the analogy of faith in the modern era, assumptions similar to the analogy have paradoxically made an exegetical comeback in some forms of postmodernism. While postmoderns no longer assume an objective meaning or framework such as the analogy of faith, the reader's ideology and the formative structures of the reader's community and experiences do form a coherent framework within which interpretations and meaning are sought (Fish).

The Analogy of Scripture. The analogy of faith, based as it is on the clear and plain passages of the Bible, is simply an extension of the analogy of Scripture. According to the *analogia scripturae*, the truest guide for determining the meaning of a particular text is to seek its explanation within the rest of the Bible—Scripture is its own interpreter. In practice, the exegete, acting in accordance with the analogy of Scripture, analyzes a particular text in relation to other passages. One text is compared and collated with another—the more obscure places with the plainer or less obscure.

As with the *analogia fidei*, justification for the *analogia scripturae* principle is grounded in the assumption of the unity and coherence of the Bible, which itself derives from the divine origin of the written word. Since the Bible teaches a unified truth, one passage cannot logically contradict another. And, since God authored the text via his Spirit-inspired writers, then God himself speaking through his word is its best expositor. The analogy-of-Scripture principle is also intended in part to counter humanity's natural inclination to assert its own authority, and instead to foster looking to God through Scripture for ultimate direction (Flacius).

It is this presupposition of the "harmony and consent" within the biblical text that modern opponents of the *analogia scripturae* principle criticize. Thus, Frederic Farrar objects to this "obscure rule" that Scripture interprets Scripture, "a rule which exegetically considered has no meaning," insisting that "such a view is true only of the simplest essentials of the faith. There is no mechanical unity in the Bible" (332–33n1). Apparent contradictions are not harmonized as a presupposition of the historical-critical method; rather, they are generally seen as evidence of multiple authorship and development of, or even discontinuity within, the human witness to divine revelation.

Original Languages. The most obvious impact of humanism on the development of a distinctive Protestant biblical interpretation was the attention paid to the original source material for Scripture. Biblical study in the original languages allows one to arrive at a more "precise" meaning of a text. Translations are helpful since they provide access to the word for many, yet much of the emphasis, idioms, and nuance of biblical meaning would be evident only through the original languages (Terry). A working knowledge of Greek and Hebrew serves as a guard against misunderstanding and helps expose inadequate interpretations. Exegesis based upon the original languages is the norm for biblical studies in both precritical and modern interpretative methodologies.

In addition to advances in the study of Greek and Hebrew, the Renaissance also brought about a vibrant interest in cognate languages (Syriac, Chaldean, Aramaic, and others) and ancient Near Eastern cultures. Recognizing their value in assessing lexical meaning, uncovering historical data, exploring grammatical and syntactical nuance, and the like, Protestant exegetes urged the use of ancient translations and versions, limited by the assumption that such editions are reliable only insofar as they faithfully express the divine originals. Theologians and exegetes also became increasingly aware of the potential benefits of an in-depth knowledge of the postbiblical Jewish tradition (Weemse). The influence of Hebraic studies in exposing and clarifying the historical occasion of the biblical writing is evident throughout the Protestant era.

These interests obviously increased with the shift toward modern historical-critical methodology. Knowledge of the ancient Near East and growth of the science of archaeology are essential in determining the historical events (and hence, the meaning) of the Bible. The more knowledge gained about the time period referenced in the biblical text, the greater the possibility of discovering the meaning of the event described. In the late modern period, with increased attention on literary issues, cognate languages and studies on Judaism became dominant means in interpretation as meaning was connected with the original, historical literary sources and forms of the text in question.

Linguistic and Contextual Concerns. Under the influence of humanist studies, linguistic and grammatical issues became of paramount importance. Protestant exegetes have universally acknowledged the need for mastering the grammar of the Greek and Hebrew, for in this, Scripture is like other writings and must be understood through the use of language. A vast bulk of exegetical material testifies to the awareness of different literary forms and styles in Scripture, and the need to handle them appropriately (Osborne). The advances in philology initiated by the Renaissance led to the production of lexicons, which, coupled with an increasing availability of classical works, enable the expositor to explore the nuance of individual words.

The context in which the biblical words are found greatly shapes meaning. In precritical and modern methodologies, the exegete seeks the meaning of the words, which the grammar of the passage, understood in its proper context, determines. Of course, that context is understood differently—the entire Bible for the precritical exegete, and the immediate literary and historical context for the modern interpreter. For postmodern studies that seek meaning in the reader, the linguistic character and grammatical nuances of a text are much less significant than in earlier times.

The History of the Biblical Text. The Renaissance heritage is also apparent in Protestant scholars' textual study—their examination of biblical manuscripts, ancient versions, and modern translations. The seventeenth-century debate about the value and role of text criticism, and its companion discussion about the origin of the Hebrew vowel points, has veiled the precritical exegetes' awareness of the need for an examina-

tion of the history of the text. Prominent Protestant exegetes like William Perkins, John Weemse, Johannes Buxtorf, and Louis Cappel were early advocates of a limited textual criticism, which acknowledged the existence of diverse textual variants and codified the steps to be taken in discerning an accurate reading. The most appropriate rendering was identified through a collation of existing texts, an analysis in light of the analogy of faith, the grammatical construction of the immediate context, and the occasion and scope of the passage.

The emerging modern approach to textual criticism, however, was resisted by precritical Protestants because of the perceived assault on the divinity of Scripture. Following the Enlightenment, exegetes accepted textual alterations on the basis of ancient versions (on the grounds that the ancient translations frequently preserved the original, uncorrupted reading), and increasingly, simply on arguments asserted by the scholarly application of reason. In addition, because modern interpretative theory sought the original historical events attested to by the biblical witness, the search for the "original" source material became more influential than the canonical text itself (Childs). In contrast, textual criticism has a limited role in postmodern exegetical strategies, save where such insight is useful in deconstructing the present form of the text.

Scope and Occasion. In precritical exegesis, the scope and occasion of a passage play a crucial role. The scope refers to the focus, design, aim, or intent of a passage, the human author's main goal in writing in the first place. Individual verses and phrases must be interpreted in light of the purposes for which they were written and according to the intent of the whole work. The scope is determined by the immediate literary context of a passage (what precedes and follows the text under examination), the historical occasion for the writing, and the role of the book in the overall redemptive story. As such, the scope and the *analogia fidei* are related; the scope describes how a book or text fits into overall Christian belief. The occasion and circumstance of the text refer to the historical situation that prompted the writing, which frequently includes analysis of the author, date, subject matter, and original recipients. Discovering, and then staying faithful to, the scope and occasion of a passage is crucial.

This precritical view of scope and occasion should not be confused with the modern, critical practice of seeking the author's historic situation and finding the meaning of a text there. The modern method looks at the texts in parts, seeking to discover the historical referent that lay behind the words, whereas the earlier view of scope placed a single passage or book within the larger context of the Bible as a whole. The precritical assumption was that the whole biblical witness determined an author's intent; biblical context (somehow connected to the Rule of Faith) determines the scope, not the historical occasion alone, as in modern hermeneutics. A biblical author's intention was, as guided by the Holy Spirit, to complement the pattern, design, context, and purpose of the whole divine record, and it was this intention that the interpreter sought to explicate.

Contemporary Application. In the early period of Protestant biblical interpretation, it was understood that the scriptural text was directed not only to its original hearers, but also ultimately for the continual benefit of the whole church; the "great end" of the Bible lies in its perpetual witness to contemporary believers (Perkins). Consequently, the task of biblical interpretation was not complete until the text was communicated to the present Christian community. Proper exegesis in precritical hermeneutics demanded a contemporary exposition of the text. The historical information of a pericope was not seen as the ultimate goal, nor did a full understanding of the historical circumstances comprehend the true extent of the divine purpose of the sacred writing. The recognition and assessment of a book's historic circumstances is a necessary but limited step in the complete exposition.

This fundamental understanding—interpreting the biblical documents as containing God's present witness to contemporary situations, while maintaining the importance of the original historical context—was expressly rejected by modern exegetes. Proponents of a modern scientific approach saw prioritizing a contemporary message in the Bible as a denial of the historicity of the texts and a rejection of the pursuit of its "literal sense." True meaning was found only in uncovering the original author's intent and circumstances; any application to modern situations was at best an effort in analogy.

Postmodern hermeneutics has returned with a vengeance to the belief that interpretation and modern application are intimately joined. Now, however, it is no longer viewed as God using the ancient text to communicate an objective message to a contemporary audience, but rather as the audience itself dictating meaning. Application in the present dominates interpretation, even if the application arrived at has no objective connection to the original production of the text.

Conclusion

Throughout the Protestant era, presuppositions concerning the nature of Scripture, its authority, and its location of meaning have changed, leading to an alteration in the methodology employed in the interpretative enterprise. There is significant continuity in the exegetical tools; variation comes because those tools are used toward different ends. Interpretative techniques based upon the presumption of a unified, coherent biblical message were exegetically decisive in early Protestantism; modern exegetes, relying on scientific analytical tools, focused on the historicity of the text; and interpretations that recognize the primacy of the reader predominate in postmodern thought.

The continued viability of a distinctively Protestant exegesis is directly tied to the Protestant view of the sacred text itself. Without a coherent, well-developed understanding of the origin and authority of Scripture, the conclusions reached by exegetes will likely become more and more diverse and possess little of value beyond the individual interpreter. On the other hand, reclaiming precritical assumptions concerning the authority of the biblical text, combined with the increasing technical proficiency in applying exegetical tools, will allow Protestant biblical interpreters to explore the meaning of Scripture in decisive and useful ways, for the good of the entire church.

Bibliography

Childs, B. *Biblical Theology in Crisis*. Westminster, 1970; Farrar, F. *History of Interpretation*. Dutton, 1886. Reprint, Baker, 1961; Fish, S. *Is There a Text in This Class?* Harvard University Press, 1980; Flacius Illyricus, M. *Clavis scripturae sacrae*. Jena, 1674; Frei, H. *The Eclipse of Biblical Narrative*. Yale University Press, 1974; Kaiser, W., and M. Silva. *An Introduction to Biblical Hermeneutics*. Zondervan, 1994; Kelsey, D. *The Uses of Scripture in Recent Theology*. Fortress, 1975; Maier, G. *Biblical Hermeneutics*, trans. R. Yarbrough. Crossway, 1994; McKim, D., ed. *Historical Handbook of Major Biblical Interpreters*. InterVarsity, 1998; Muller, R. *Post-Reformation Reformed Dogmatics*. Vol. 2, *Holy Scripture*. Baker, 1993; Osborne, G. *The Hermeneutical Spiral*. InterVarsity, 1991; Perkins, W. *The Arte of Prophecying, or, A Treatise Concerning the Sacred and Onely True Manner and Methode of Preaching*. In *The Workes of that Famous and Worthy Minister . . . William Perkins*. Vol. 2. London, 1616–18; Ramm, B. *Protestant Biblical Interpretation*. 3d ed. Baker, 1970; Smalley, B. *The Study of the Bible in the Middle Ages*. 3d ed. Blackwell, 1983; Terry, M. *Biblical Hermeneutics*. Zondervan, 1974; Vanhoozer, K. *Is There a Meaning in This Text?* Zondervan, 1998; Weemse, J. *The Christian Synagogue*.

In *The Workes of Mr. John Weemse*. Vol. 1. Thomas Cotes for John Bellamie, 1636.

Henry M. Knapp

Proverbs, Book of

Proverbs is the foundational wisdom book of the Bible, teaching the ABCs of wisdom and introducing more complex issues that are further elaborated in Ecclesiastes, Job, and the wisdom teaching of the NT, such as the Sermon on the Mount. In an extraordinary way, Proverbs raises the theological question of the relation of ordinary life in the cosmos to God the Creator. Moreover, the complexity of interpreting Proverbs has implications for biblical hermeneutics as a whole.

History of Interpretation

A history of reading Proverbs remains to be written, partly because the use of short sayings in Jewish and Christian literature is widely scattered, and systematic exposition of the book in Christian circles was rare until Melanchthon's translation and three commentaries in the sixteenth century (Sick). With rare exceptions, the Eastern and Western exegetical traditions suffered from a lack of Hebrew learning. In contrast, Jewish midrashim regularly interpreted the Torah by juxtaposing texts from Proverbs (e.g., Prov. 8:22, 30 and Gen. 1:1 in *Gen. Rab.* 1.1). Medieval Jewish commentaries richly mined the Hebrew text (cf. Fox 12–13). The twelfth-century Christian *Glossa ordinaria*, with its compilation of observations going back to the fathers, served as a commentary on Proverbs well into the Reformation period (cf. Froehlich).

Proverbs was often exploited for its pithy wisdom by writers ranging from Augustine and Chaucer to Erasmus and Shakespeare (*Henry IV*, 1.2.98–100), while its use in theological debate was sporadic if spectacular. Of particular note was Lady Wisdom's utterance in Prov. 8:22 ("Yahweh *begot* [*qanah*] me as the first of his way") as used in the Arian controversy of the fourth century. Both parties interpreted Wisdom as Christ: the Arians took the Hebrew term *qanah* to mean "created" (so LXX), so that Christ could not properly be God; the Orthodox took it as "possessed" (so other Greek versions and Vulgate; see Clifford 96, 98–99; Pelikan 191–200). Such a direct reading of female Wisdom as Christ was allegorical. In similar fashion, premodern Jewish tradition interpreted Wisdom in Prov. 8 as Torah (cf. Sir. 24:23).

Generally, allegorical reading of Proverbs (apart from the short sayings in chs. 10–29) dominated its use by the church and synagogue until the Reformation, when the great shift to exclusively "literal" reading began to take place (Wolters, *Song*). With the Enlightenment's focus on science and universally true principles, interest especially in the short sayings of Proverbs waned, partly because they seemed internally contradictory (a fact already noted in the Talmud concerning 26:4–5; *b. Šabb.* 30b) and not universally borne out by experience (e.g., the righteous sometimes do hunger, in spite of 10:3; cf. Van Leeuwen, "Wealth").

The 1923 publication of the Egyptian Teaching of Amenemope (with parallels to Prov. 22:17–23:14) gave rise to a resurgence of scholarly interest in Proverbs, focused on the international character of wisdom (Whybray 6–18). Yet ancient Near Eastern wisdom, especially as it appears in Mesopotamian nonwisdom genres, remains a largely ignored gold mine. In spite of gains from ancient Near Eastern studies, the most profound discussion of the theological and human significance of Proverbs remains G. von Rad's *Wisdom in Israel*, which focuses on the text of Proverbs within the biblical canon (unfortunately, the ET is often unreliable).

The Message of the Text

Discerning the "message" of Proverbs is complex because the book is a collection of collections (cf. 10:1; 22:17–20; 24:23; 25:1; 30:1; 31:1) that grew over time (cf. LXX). The book also contains a variety of genres: "lectures" and "speeches" (chs. 1–9), short "sayings" and "admonitions" (chs. 10–29), brief poems (including a prayer, ch. 30), maternal instruction and a "Hymn to a Valiant Woman" (ch. 31). Yet the book forms an edited whole, with an introduction (1:1–7) and a hermeneutical prologue (chs. 1–9), which provide the worldview within which the smaller genres that follow are to be understood. In addition, Prov. 10–15 teaches the elementary patterns of acts and consequences, while chs. 16–29 develop the exceptions to the rules (Van Leeuwen, "Proverbs"). But the complexity of the book's interpretation, especially of the short sayings whose contextual relations are not always clear, has important implications for reading Scripture as a whole, since the Bible itself is a collection of books composed over time. Consequently, not every word of the Lord is valid for every time and place (contrast the fate of Jerusalem according to Isaiah and Jeremiah!). Wise interpretation is always needed.

It is generally acknowledged that 1:7 and 9:10 ("the fear of the LORD is the beginning of knowledge/wisdom") form the thematic inclusio of chs. 1–9 and the motto for the entire book (cf. 31:30, an inclusio with 1:7 for the whole book). For Israel, knowledge (of the world and human affairs) and wisdom are inextricably related to God (von Rad, *Wisdom*, 53–73). The point is fundamental, for Wisdom concerns the relation of creation to God, in every aspect of creation, and the implications of this relation for human piety and conduct in the ordinary affairs of life, whether high (8:15–16; 16:1–15; 31:1–9) or low (25:11; 27:8, 14). This is an essential point of the "Hymn to a Valiant Woman" (31:10–31), whose fear of the Lord (her "religion") is demonstrated precisely in her wise conduct in the areas of life considered by many moderns to be merely "secular" (Wolters, "Nature"; Wolters, *Song*).

The purpose of the whole book is stated in 1:2–7. It is to help the young become wise and the mature wiser, to help them interpret wise sayings, using them to think and act in real-life circumstances, and for general discipline and instruction (*musar* means both, as the Greek translation *paideia* suggests) in "righteousness, justice, and equity" especially in socioeconomic and judicial relations (1:3 NRSV; cf. 11:1; 14:31, 34; 16:11–13; 25:18; 28:5, 8–9; 29:4, 7, 12, 14; and the general opposition of "righteous" and "wicked" in chs. 10–15).

In addition to the general concern for justice and righteousness in all areas of life, the art of understanding "a proverb and a figure, the words of the wise and their riddles" (1:6 NRSV) suggests that the book itself is aware of the hermeneutical task (cf. 8:9; 26:7). The wise use of sayings requires interpretation of people and situations as well as of texts. In the modern period, proverbial wisdom has fallen into disrepute (except among advertisers) partly because of its contradictory, local, and "unscientific" character (cf. Toulmin). Moreover, its apparent generalizations do not always appear true to specific cases. But this fact is an essential characteristic of sayings and makes them hermeneutically significant. Vernacular proverbs of all cultures present patterns of reality that are frequently observed, but which have exceptions. One son is advised to "Look before you leap," another is told, "He who hesitates is lost." "Birds of a feather flock together," but also, "Opposites attract." Consequently, "He who knows one, knows none." Proverbs is a repository of many observations, some of which are true in the majority of cases, others only in a minority

or even exceptionally. The wise person knows which saying or admonition is "fitting" or proper for the right person at the right time, in the right circumstances, and in the right way.

In a certain sense, it takes wisdom to use wisdom. A few examples from Proverbs will illustrate. Proverbs 17:17–18 say contradictory things about "friends." The contradiction is obscured in most translations because the word for "friend" (*re'a*) in v. 17 is translated as "neighbor" in v. 18. Read instead, "A *friend* loves at all times, and a brother is born for adversity. A man who lacks sense strikes a deal, becoming a guarantor for his *friend*" (AT). The contradiction concerns the ambiguity of those we designate as "friends," and how we relate to them, wisely or unwisely. It is not wise to cosign a loan for every "friend." But other "friends" will lay down their life for you, and perhaps you for them, as Jesus showed in word and deed. The ambiguity of friendship is captured in English by other proverbial sayings: "He's a fair-weather friend" (who will not stick with you in adversity) and "A friend in need is a friend indeed." Similarly, 17:27–28 explores the contradictory and ambiguous character of silence.

The most famous contradiction in Proverbs is 26:4–5, which contains contradictory admonitions about whether to speak or be silent when dealing with a fool. The Talmud already wrestled with the problem, arguing whether Proverbs, containing such a contradiction, belonged among the sacred books. The medieval *Glossa ordinaria* solved the problem correctly by explaining that the verses apply to different matters. Most wisdom utterances are situational: they need to be applied fittingly to the contradictory and complex circumstances of life. One may compare the contradictory sayings of Jesus (Matt. 5:16; 6:1; 7:1, 6; Ridderbos) and Paul (Gal. 6:2, 5; Hays). Like many utterances of Scripture, the full truth of a saying like 11:4 will only be resolved eschatologically. This means that the promises of Proverbs (e.g., righteousness leads to prosperity and well-being) are not always realized in this life. The wicked sometimes do prosper, while the godly suffer unjustly (cf. Van Leeuwen, "Wealth").

The range of topics covered in Proverbs, especially in the short genres of chs. 10–30, reminds us that wisdom and folly involve all of life. Every human endeavor from farming (12:10–11; 28:19) and metallurgy (17:3) to politics (16:10–15; chs. 25, 28–29), economics (11:1; 16:11), and psychology (12:25; 14:10, 13) is fair game. What is more, these sayings have a metaphorical applicability far beyond their literal concerns.

Proverbs 1–9 is designed to provide the underlying worldview and theology for understanding the diverse sayings of chs. 10–29. Here we find "lectures" addressed by a parent to a "son" ("child" in NRSV is misleading), who is on the verge of adult responsibilities, including marriage. There are also speeches by cosmic Wisdom herself, personified as a woman (1:20–33; 8:1–9:6). Rather than focusing on the complexities of life (as esp. chs. 16–29 do), these chapters show life as lived in a structured world of boundaries. This world has a fundamental opposition of good and bad, represented primarily by the opposition of two ways, and the two (types of) women and houses at the end of the ways, one a doorway to Sheol, the other to life. The opposition of wisdom and folly in 1–9 finds its correlate in the opposition of righteous/ness and wicked/ness in 10–15. One can be morally righteous without being wise, but one cannot be wise without being righteous, for sin is a fundamental breach of the cosmic order. The contrary ways, women, and houses are both literal and symbolic. The young man can be seduced by the "strange" (*zarah*) or "other" (*nokriah*) woman ("loose woman," RSV; "adventuress/adulteress," RSV/NRSV). But the literal wife (5:15–19; cf. 31:10–31) also symbolizes Lady Wisdom (cf. 8:35; 18:22), while the other woman represents the attractive seductions of Lady Folly (9:13–18). Especially significant are the passages where the imagery of ways, women, and houses come together. This happens usually with reference to folly and death (2:16–19; 5:3–6, 8; 7:24–27; 9:1–18), but also with reference to life (5:15–19, where cistern and well imply house, and water implies life; 9:1–6).

These passages, however, teach more than the contrast of deadly versus life-enhancing sexuality. The imagery of woman, ways, and houses implicitly teaches about the nature of the cosmic "house" that God created with wisdom (3:19–20; 8:22–31; 9:1–6; Van Leeuwen, "Book"), in which we humans live. The "ways" convey the communal and traditional character of life: humans follow good and bad paths laid down by previous generations, whether in the language they speak or the ethics they live. Moreover, life is ultimately a journey toward, and determined by, the object of our desire: godly wisdom or deadly folly. The desirable "women" that entice the young man on the way to their respective houses are metaphors for *all* created goods that humans desire, whether

properly and within created bounds, or wrongly and out-of-bounds—like my neighbor's property or good name.

Proverbs 1–9 presents our world as one of boundaries and limits, shown most powerfully by the division of sea and dry land (8:29; cf. Job 38:8–10; Ps. 104:9; Jer. 5:22). The waves of the sea may play within that limit, but when they flood dry land, death and destruction result. This cosmic principle has its cultural aspect as well, symbolized in the sexual teaching of 1–9. The "waters" of sexuality are good within the limits of marriage, but destructive outside of it (5:15–20). The worldview of Prov. 1–9 insists on freedom within form, life within law, and love within limits. Practically, this means that wise persons are constantly aware of the boundaries and limits that separate wise from foolish behavior and excess from enough. They are also aware that behaviors need to be appropriate to the specifics of situations, and to the nature and kinds of persons and things we relate to (Van Leeuwen, "Liminality"). In this world, the acts, habits, and eventually character that are a human "way" have consequences that lead ultimately to life or death (von Rad, *Wisdom*, 124–37).

Proverbs and the Canon

Modern scholarship has exaggerated the differences between Proverbs and the rest of Scripture. For example, the lack of salvation history in Proverbs is a function of its genre and purpose, rather than of differences in worldview and theology. And the affinities of Proverbs with other ancient Near Eastern literatures are by no means unique to this book (cf. Roberts). Proverbs thus forces us to think about the reality of "common grace" and the general human condition that is common to Christians and non-Christians alike. Wisdom "speaks" to all humans in the cosmos (ch. 8), even those who do not have special revelation, so that all human cultures respond with varying degrees of *relative* wisdom, much of which finds counterparts in biblical Proverbs. The attempt to deny the significance of the Wisdom literature for Christian theology (Preuss 186–90) has more to do with a fear of "natural theology" and a focus on salvation history narrowly conceived than it does with a proper understanding of Proverbs and its role in the canon. This view is belied by the NT's frequent quotation of Proverbs and its use of Lady Wisdom to articulate Christ's role in creation (cf. John 1:1–18; Rom. 1:18–20; 2:14–15; Col. 1:15–20). Similarly, Christ's insistence that he is "the way" cannot be understood except against the background of Proverbs. An adequate treatment of the NT's use of Proverbs remains to be written.

Theology and Significance for the Church

Proverbs provides the church with a spirituality of the ordinary, not unlike Paul's insistence that Christians "glorify God in your body" (1 Cor. 6:20 NRSV). Here, life's daily actions take place in the presence of the Creator. Moreover, the creation is humanity's partner, the correlate of our humanity. Israel did not separate reason and revelation, religion and knowledge. "Experiences of the world were for [Israel] always experiences of God as well, and experiences of God were for her experiences of the world"—without confusing God and world. Again, "Humans are always entirely in the world, yet are always entirely involved with Yahweh" (von Rad, *Wisdom*, 62, 95; my translation of *Weisheit*, 87, 129). Scholarly attempts, on form-critical grounds, to separate the cosmology of Prov. 1–9 from the anthropological focus of chapters 10–29 (Doll; Westermann) underestimate the wisdom of the book's final redaction, which establishes the nature of the world as stage and criterion for human actions before dealing further with human conduct. Likewise, Gen. 1–3 does this for the Bible as a whole, and Rev. 21–22 for the world to come. Proverbs guides the church in serving God wisely and righteously in all its doings and interactions with creatures (12:10) and fellow humans alike (14:31).

See also Wisdom; Wisdom Literature

Bibliography

Clifford, R. *Proverbs*. OTL. Westminster John Knox, 1999; Doll, P. *Menschenschöpfung und Weltschöpfung in der alttestamentlichen Weisheit*. SBS. Verlag Katholisches Bibelwerk, 1985; Fox, M. *Proverbs 1–9*. AB 18A. Doubleday, 2000; Froehlich, K. "Glossa ordinaria." Pages 449–50 in *Dictionary of Biblical Interpretation*, ed. J. Hayes. Abingdon, 1999; Hays, R. "The Letter to the Galatians." *NIB* 11:183–348; Pelikan, J. *The Emergence of the Catholic Tradition (100–600)*. Vol. 1 of *The Christian Tradition*. University of Chicago Press, 1971; Preuss, H. *Einführung in die alttestamentliche Weisheitsliteratur*. Kohlhammer, 1987; Rad, G. von. *Weisheit in Israel*. Neukirchener Verlag, 1970. ET, *Wisdom in Israel*. Abingdon, 1972; Ridderbos, H. "The Significance of the Sermon on the Mount." Pages 26–43 in *When the Time Had Fully Come*. Eerdmans, 1957; Roberts, J. *The Bible and the Ancient Near East*. Eisenbrauns, 2002; Sick, H. *Melanchthon als Ausleger des Alten Testament*. Mohr/Siebeck, 1959; Toulmin, S. *Cosmopolis*. Macmillan, 1990; Van Leeuwen, R. "The Book of Proverbs." *NIB* 5:17–264; idem. "Liminality and Worldview in Proverbs 1–9." *Semeia* 50 (1990): 111–44; idem. "Proverbs." Pages 256–67 in *The Complete Literary Guide to the Bible*, ed. L. Ryken and T. Longman III. Zondervan, 1993; idem. "Wealth and Poverty: System and Contradiction in Proverbs." *HS* 33 (1992): 25–26; Westermann, C. *Roots of Wisdom*. Westminster John Knox, 1995; Whybray, R. *The Book of Proverbs*. Brill, 1995; Wolters, A. "Nature and Grace in the Interpretation of Proverbs 31:10–31." *CTJ* 19 (1984): 153–66; idem. *The Song of the Valiant Woman*. Paternoster, 2001.

Raymond C. Van Leeuwen

Providence

The doctrine of providence affirms an ongoing divine concern for and activity in the world subsequent to its original creation. The way in which one interprets Scripture theologically will have much to do with one's view of the God-world relation, and vice versa. Biblical depictions of divine action will have one sense when interpreted in the context of classical theism, for example, and quite another sense when interpreted according to some other model of the God-world relation.

Theologians have traditionally formulated the doctrine in terms of a threefold distinction: *conservatio* (God is active in preserving creation and, according to Barth, the canon!); *concursus* (God is coactive in all that comes to pass); *gubernatio* (God orders all that comes to pass according to his final purpose). Apart from the doctrine of providence, the idea of God would be largely irrelevant to what is happening in the world. Though there is no single biblical term for providence, the doctrine is intimately connected to the way in which one conceives God's relation to Scripture. Hence, it is connected to theological interpretation of Scripture since one's doctrine of Scripture is inextricably tied up with one's doctrine of God (Kelsey). Moreover, one's doctrine of providence has a decisive bearing on the way in which Christians approach prayer and action. To affirm providence is to confess with the apostle that "in everything God works for good with those who love him, who are called according to his purpose" (Rom. 8:28 RSV).

Providence in the History of Christian Thought

Christian theologians have traditionally affirmed both general providence (God's universal care and control of the cosmos as a whole) and special providence (God's particular interaction with specific events and individuals).

Augustine. Against the Epicurean notion that the universe is the result of chance, Augustine contends that the cosmos is an ordered whole. And against the Stoic conception of the cosmos as ordered by an impersonal, immanent *ratio*, he affirms the truth that the world is guided and governed by a personal transcendent being. God's providence culminates in the event of Jesus Christ and in the subsequent history of the church, which establishes the city of God. Providence is to be distinguished from fortune and fate and identified with the form of Jesus Christ. God is at work on an eschatological project: forming a people for himself by conforming them to Christ through the Spirit. Note that Augustine was able to read secular history as well (e.g., the decline and fall of Rome) as an aspect of God's overarching providential plan.

Thomas Aquinas. Thomas views providence as divine prudence—God's wise plan for the world—and employs Aristotelian categories to explain how God acts and interacts with creatures. God is the "First Cause" of all things, but secondary causes (e.g., creatures) bring about specific events in nature and history. The concept of "First Cause" is not intended to insinuate God in a system of causality in which he would be the biggest cog. On the contrary, "the purpose of the distinction between First Cause and second cause was to avoid any pantheistic notion which might identify the two, making God a part of the causal system of nature" (Berkouwer 154). In Thomas's words: "The one action does not issue from two agents on the same level" (Ia, q. 105). Noteworthy too is his insistence that God always works with things/persons according to their created natures.

Calvin. Calvin insists that God's sovereign will holds sway over all things—natural occurrences (Matt. 10:29) as well as human freedom, including sinful human actions (Acts 2:23)—not as some blind force but as the result of personal deliberation and specific direction. Calvin does not take the easy way out of distinguishing divine permission from divine willing; he insists that God governs and even cooperates (in the sense of communicating the energy and opportunity) in human sinning while simultaneously remaining holy. The difference lies in the motive and the intended outcome: "you meant evil against me; but God meant it for good" (Gen. 50:20 RSV).

Modern and Postmodern Views. The doctrine of providence has not fared as well in modernity and postmodernity, where teleological accounts of the cosmos have given way to explanations in terms of scientific causality and historical consciousness. Schleiermacher viewed the doctrine of providence as an expression of our feeling of absolute dependence on God, specifically, our feeling that in nature—not a stage for God's further interventions but a display of his original wisdom—all things are "interdependent." Divine providence is simply a poetic-religious way of talking about causal occurrences. For Hegel, the world process is itself an unfolding of a purely immanent divine purpose.

Though some twentieth-century theologians continued to speak of God's "mighty acts," most modern theologians came to the conclusion that the notion of an "act" of God could not be taken literally (Gilkey, "Cosmology"). Liberal Protestant theologians declared the end of the "royal metaphor," the idea that God rules the cosmos like a monarch (Hodgson), not least because the notion of an all-determining sovereignty runs counter to modern historical consciousness (Gilkey, *Reaping*, 242). While process theologians (see below, on "Divine Action and Science") continued to preserve some measure of divine providence, postmodern theologians claimed that the demise of the theistic notion that God rules "over" the world entailed the end of meaningful history as well (Taylor).

Barth. K. Barth resists extrabiblical notions of providence as raw causal power, eschewing general concepts and preferring rather to let the revelation of God in Jesus Christ define this and every aspect of God's being. Accordingly, a doctrine of providence must take its bearings not from philosophies, whether Stoic or process, but only from the event of loving freedom enacted in the incarnation, cross, and resurrection of Jesus Christ. God is preserving, cooperating with, and governing the created order and humanity in and through Jesus Christ. As in Augustine, the meaning and order of creation is a function of its being the stage for the theater of Christ—the performance of covenant grace.

Providence: Biblical Sources

Though there is no single technical term for providence in Scripture, the concept of the care and control of God for individuals, for Israel and the nations, and for the church is everywhere assumed and displayed.

The substance of the doctrine of providence is most clearly seen in the way in which God guides and superintends the lives of certain individuals who form part of God's chosen people: Abraham, Moses, Joseph, David, Esther, and so on. The Joseph narrative (Gen. 37–45) is exemplary in this regard.

Biblical Wisdom literature offers rich variations on the theme of divine providence. Proverbs defines wisdom as living in accordance with the created order that God actively sustains. Ecclesiastes goes further, suggesting that neither meaning nor purpose is immanent to life's processes but instead depends on God's active giving (Eccles. 2:24, 26; 3:13; 5:19; 6:2; 8:15). The book of Job affirms God's providence even when no pattern or purpose can be discerned in innocent human suffering. Scripture enjoins trust in the care and control of God despite the realities of evil and death, thus suggesting that some providential outcomes are eschatological, mysteries reserved for the last days, when evil will be no more (Rom. 8:28).

God's care and control of nature is a consequence of his being the Creator of all things. As Author of the universe, almighty God possesses both the authority, wisdom, and power to work his will. Similarly, the sense that history is teleological—linear rather than cyclic—is a function of the prophets' conviction that their covenant God keeps his promises, and that the Abrahamic promise will eventually result in a blessing to all nations (Gen. 12:2–3). That God cares for and controls history is the underlying assumption that fuels Israel's hope for the messianic age of the new kingdom of God.

Christ, we might say, is the wisdom and providence of God made flesh—the culmination of God's ongoing work with creation, the incarnation of the Father's distinctive care and control (Eph. 1:9–13). God works out his final purpose for Israel and the whole world through the life and fate of Jesus. The Spirit, too, is the providence of God. In the book of Acts in particular, it is the Spirit who superintends the spread of the gospel and the growth of the church, thus ensuring God's care and control for his new creation and his special people.

Providence as Material Principle: The Ongoing God-World Relation

Perhaps the main interpretative question raised by the doctrine of providence concerns the nature of the God-world relation. Does God control the world-historical process, and if so, how? Can the world-historical process frustrate the divine purpose?

Divine Action and Science. A number of models have been proposed for conceiving God's relation to the world. Some have marginalized God's role, locating him in the remaining gaps of an Einsteinian universe, working at the subatomic level as a determiner of quantum indeterminacies (Pollard; Murphy 119). Others, preferring an interactionist rather than interventionist model, liken the God-world relation to the inputting of information into a system (Peacocke). In chaos theory an infinitesimal input of information can produce higher-level structural changes in the system (Polkinghorne). Still others wonder whether the communication of the Logos is best conceived along the lines of information processing (Barbour 167).

Process theologians adopt a panentheistic model in which the world is in God, who nevertheless is greater than the world. God is both distinct from and necessarily related to the world, participating creatively (though noncoercively) in its processes. What God provides to the world process is not being or energy but aims and objectives. Process theologians contend that God's creative love (not causality) accounts for novelty in the world process. God's persuasive influence is but one factor in what happens, however; the other factor is an entity's "freedom." It follows that God's will is loving, but not efficacious.

Divine Action and Human Freedom. Scripture treats the theme of the freedom of the will not as an abstract philosophical problem (determinism) but in terms of the conflict between sin and grace. The biblical narrative encourages the belief that human beings make their own choices such that their actions are really their own. At the same time, Scripture also portrays God as being in control of everything that happens, including the nefarious work of Satan and the more pedestrian evil acts of characters such as Pharaoh and Judas. One aspect of divine control is foreknowledge, the concept captured by the Latin root of the term providence (*providentia* = "seeing before"). In some cases, the future is not only foreseen but also decreed by God.

In the broad interpretative framework of the history of redemption, however, divine action is essentially liberative, not coercive. General and special providence alike work to maintain creation's integrity, not against it. It is a caricature of providence, therefore, to construe it in terms of divine puppetry. God rules creation precisely by renewing it, releasing it from corruption, and enabling creatures to be all that they were supposed to be. Again, it is the divine nature that defines the nature of the divine determining. God's sovereignty is not that of an impersonal principle but of an infinitely wise, loving, and just person. In sum, God's being and action is the basic reality behind the existence of the universe and its workings. It is this fundamental insight, rather than the details of the mechanics, that is the special interest of Scripture.

Providence as Formal Principle: The Doctrine of Scripture

Typology and inspiration are examples of special providence and provide a basis for affirming the special authority of Scripture as opposed to other texts. They contribute to the unity of redemption's drama and the concomitant notion of Scripture's unity, under the signs of the Son and Spirit respectively.

Typology: Providence and Redemptive-Historical Interpretation.
The canonical connection between various types and antitypes (e.g., persons, things, events) finds its ground and justification in a belief in divine providence, in the continuity of God's plan as it unfolds in the history of redemption. The doctrine of providence does not justify interpreters' seeing Christ in every detail; it pertains not to the details but to the whole pattern of redemptive history, and in particular, to Christ's recapitulating the history of Adam and of Israel.

The importance of typology stems from its concern to interpret the OT and NT as a unity, as twin aspects of a single plan of salvation worked by the one God of Israel and of Jesus Christ. The OT is fulfilled in Jesus Christ because he is the full flowering of divine providence and the summation of the history of redemption. The two-beat rhythm of salvation history (judgment and restoration) reaches a climax in Jesus' death (his "exodus") and resurrection (his return from "exile"; his restoration to David's throne).

Inspiration: Dual Agency.
One's understanding of inspiration and illumination—the way in which the Spirit is at work in the origin and reception of Scripture—is also closely connected to one's understanding of divine providence. Inspiration speaks of the divine activity in ordering the creaturely reality of Scripture—its composition, redaction, and canonization—to play a role in the divine economy of communicative action (Webster 30–39). Here too, the practical implication of the doctrine is to raise the interpreter's expectation that broad patterns unifying the Scriptures may indeed be discerned. The canon is the "providence of God put into writing," and as such displays God's preserving, cooperating, and governing purpose, especially in the relation of its parts to its center, the gospel of Jesus Christ.

As we have seen above, divine providence is not a matter of overriding human freedom but of guiding and governing it in a way that accords with its nature. Accordingly, there is no reason to associate verbal inspiration with a mechanical dictation theory, which wrongly construes providence in an interventionist rather than interactionist mode. The latter is well articulated by M.-J. Lagrange, who argues that God as the ultimate author of Scripture nevertheless respected the personalities and intellects of the human authors, the secondary means/agents of God's communicative will.

Scripture and Providence in the Triune Economy

Typology, inspiration, and illumination are not merely examples of divine providence but may themselves be paradigmatic instances of the way in which God cares for and controls the creature and creation. Their contrast with fate and chance (whether quantum or chaos) could not be greater. For they remind us that providence is best exposited not in terms of the Father's will alone (this way fate, causality, and Stoicism lie) but in terms of Word and Spirit. Providence is a triune work discerned with the eye of faith, especially when it is wearing the spectacles of faith (e.g., the Scriptures as framework for interpreting the world).

What is needed is a notion of the triune provider: the Father makes provision for the world through the Word in the power of the Spirit. Framing the doctrine in terms of Word and Spirit means contrasting a merely mechanical or causal view of providence with a richer and more personal communicative notion. It also follows that providence and Scripture, as both means and product of God's care and control of his covenant people, find their proper place in the triune economy of redemption.

Though almighty God has causal power, there is ample biblical evidence that, in working with human creatures, God does not manipulate from the outside so much as transform from the inside, for example, by converting natures, sanctifying spirits, and renewing minds. Process theology sees God's providence as always and only persuasive (e.g., never purely causal or coercive). Yet, the doctrine of the effectual call, wherein the Spirit efficaciously ministers the Word, suggests that God can act communicatively in a way that does not violate human nature but nonetheless brings about the intended result (cf. Isa. 55:11).

To the extent that Scripture itself is our paradigm for understanding the workings of providence, the emphasis will be not on the divine causality but on the divine communicative action. Speech is a form of action, but not the sort of action that can by itself deprive another of his freedom. God's infinite freedom meets finite human freedom not primarily in terms of causal action and reaction (the latter is too impersonal), but rather in a communicative interaction that respects the integrity of the creature in addressing itself specifically to its rational and spiritual nature.

The ministry of the word in the power of the Spirit is a helpful way of understanding God's relation to human beings, and perhaps the doctrine of providence in general as well. Finally, an emphasis on providence as triune communicative action clarifies the way in which Christian disciples can participate in God's drama of redemption through their own ministry of the same word that the Spirit uses to create and govern the church.

Bibliography

Barbour, I. *When Science Meets Religion*. HarperCollins, 2000; Berkouwer, G. C. *The Providence of God*. Eerdmans, 1952; Calvin, J. *Institutes*. Book I, chs. 16–18; Farley, B. *The Providence of God*. Baker, 1988; Gilkey, L. "Cosmology, Ontology, and the Travail of Biblical Language." Pages 29–43 in *God's Activity in the World*, ed. O. Thomas. Scholars Press, 1983; idem. *Reaping the Whirlwind*. Seabury, 1976; Gorringe, T. *God's Theatre*. SCM, 1991; Hodgson, P. *God in History*. Abingdon, 1989; Kelsey, D. *Proving Doctrine*. Trinity, 1999; Murphy, N. *Anglo-American Postmodernity*. Westview, 1997; Peacocke, A. *Theology for a Scientific Age*. SCM, 1993; Polkinghorne, J. *Belief in God in an Age of Science*. Yale University Press, 1998; Pollard, W. *Chance and Providence*. Faber & Faber, 1958; Saunders, N. *Divine Action and Modern Science*. Cambridge University Press, 2002; Taylor, M. C. *Erring*. University of Chicago Press, 1984; Thomas Aquinas. *Summa Theologiae*; Webster, J. *Holy Scripture*. Cambridge University Press, 2003.

Kevin J. Vanhoozer

Psalms, Book of

Contemporary resources on worship generally describe readings from the Psalms as *responses* to the OT lesson, suggesting at least implicitly that the book of Psalms is something other than Scripture itself. This perspective is sometimes reinforced by homileticians who resist preaching on the Psalms because, in their view, the Psalms originated as liturgical materials and should be used accordingly. To be sure, the book of Psalms may well have been "the hymnbook/prayerbook of the second temple" (or the first temple) but, in addition, "it became eventually something like an instruction manual for the theological study of the divine order of salvation" (Seybold 27). Or, as Martin Luther put it, the Psalms are "a little Bible" (Luther 254), a prime source for learning about God, God's will for the world, and life lived under God's claim.

History of Interpretation

In all probability, the early church continued to sing and pray the Psalms (see Eph. 5:19; Col. 3:16), but the extensive use of the Psalms in the NT indicates that they were also read as a source of illumination and instruction. In particular, the early church read the Psalms messianically, an interpretative practice that had already begun in postexilic Judaism. This makes sense, since David's name is associated with seventy-three psalms, and since the "anointed" (the Hebrew *mashiakh* or, more usually, *messiah* = the Greek *christos*) is featured in the book as early as Ps. 2:2 (see also Pss. 18; 20; 21; 45; 72; 89; 110; 132; 144, often categorized as royal). In any case, it is clear that the early church could not understand or proclaim its faith in Jesus Messiah/Christ without frequent use of the Psalms (see esp. Pss. 22; 32; 69).

Like all Scripture in the precritical era of interpretation, the Psalms were read on more than one level. But in every instance, the Psalms functioned as Scripture, a source for theological illumination and proclamation. Augustine's *Enarrations* [*Expositions*] on the Psalms are a prime example, as are both Luther's and Calvin's commentaries. In the preface to his commentary, for instance, Calvin maintains not only that the Psalms teach us how to pray and how to praise God, but also that they "principally teach and train us to bear the cross" (Calvin xxxix). In a sense, Calvin and others read the Psalms historically, although not in the modern sense—they found in the Psalms information about David's life and trials. But Calvin and others also read the Psalms prophetically—finding the life and trials of David, the "anointed," prefigured the experiences of Jesus, the "anointed." From this perspective, Jesus could be heard praying the Psalms.

Early critical interpretation of the Psalms has been called "the personal/historical method" (Bellinger 15). Attempts were made (and are still being made) to date individual psalms and to discern in them information about David and other persons, groups, or events. In the early twentieth century Hermann Gunkel, the pioneer of form criticism, took a decisive step beyond this personal/historical approach. Although he still maintained that the Psalms as we have them are products of pious individuals, he claimed that they are based on cultic prototypes. These prototypes can be described and classified; Gunkel suggested the following major types, along with several others: hymns (songs of praise), community laments, individual songs of thanksgiving, and individual laments (30–39). Gunkel's work still exerts a profound influence on contemporary Psalms scholarship. Sigmund Mowinckel took the next logical step, suggesting that the Psalms as we have them are the actual materials produced by and for use in the worship of Israel and Judah (with the exception of "The Learned Psalmography," or wisdom psalms). Like Gunkel, Mowinckel's cult-functional approach still influences contemporary scholarship, although his proposal that many psalms find their setting-in-life in a New Year festival no longer commands a consensus. More recent scholars have modified and extended the form-critical and cult-functional approaches, capitalizing especially upon advances made in the fields of sociology and cross-cultural anthropology. Erhard Gerstenberger, for instance, locates the life-setting of many psalms in small-group or familial settings rather than in large-group gatherings that would have taken place in the temple or later synagogues.

While the form-critical and cult-functional approaches continue to flourish, the most recent interpretation of the Psalms has partaken of the general movement in biblical studies toward more literary approaches. Rhetorical criticism attempts to explore and identify what is unique rather than typical; scholarship on the shaping of the Psalter investigates its possible meaningfulness, including how the placement of particular psalms may affect their message and the whole.

While any method may yield theological results, proponents of the literary approaches in recent years have shown the most interest in theological conclusions. For instance, in his commentary, James L. Mays refuses to provide the standard list of psalms by form-critical category, so as not to distract readers from matters of content and theology. In subsequent sections of this article, I shall rely heavily on insights derived from study of the Psalter's shaping.

Hearing the Message of Psalms

It is a nearly unanimous consensus that Ps. 1 was either written or very intentionally chosen to be the introduction to the Psalter, and many interpreters also conclude that Pss. 1–2 constitute a paired introduction. This conclusion is extremely important because it means that Pss. 1–2 provide an interpretative agenda for the entire book. More specifically, Ps. 1 invites attention to God's *torah*, "instruction" (twice in 1:2; NIV/NRSV "law"), claiming that genuine happiness derives from constant attentiveness to God and God's "instruction" (1:1–2). The traditional translation of *torah* as "law" has meant that Ps. 1 has often been understood to commend some form of legalism, but torah in the broadest sense connotes God's will. Not surprisingly, Ps. 1 features two Hebrew roots that constitute a concise summary of God's will—*shapat* and *tsadaq*, which underlie the words "justice" and "righteous(ness)." The interpretation of Ps. 1:5 is disputed, but it is possible to translate v. 5a as follows: "Therefore the wicked will not stand up for justice." In any case, the appearance of these two key roots, in a psalm that highlights God's "instruction" or will, serves to anticipate Pss. 93 and 95–99, which have aptly been described as "the theological 'heart'" of the Psalter (Wilson 92; see below).

These so-called enthronement psalms all address God as "King" (95:3; 98:6; 99:4) or explicitly assert "The LORD reigns" (93:1; 96:10; 97:1; 99:1) or "The LORD is king" (NRSV). In short, God's sovereignty is world-encompassing; what God wills for God's world is clear—"justice" (see the root *shapat* in 96:13 [2x]; 97:2; 98:9 [2x]; 99:4 [2x]) and "righteousness" (see the root *tsadaq* in 96:13; 97:2, 6, 11, 12; 98:2 [NRSV: "vindication"], 9; 99:4). The two descriptions of God's "coming" (96:13; 98:9) are particularly revealing. God's presence in the world is marked by justice and righteousness: God "is coming to establish justice (on) earth . . . with righteousness" (96:13 AT; 98:9; NRSV: "is coming to judge the earth . . . with righteousness"). To be sure, God's intention to set things right in the world will mean opposition to those who oppose God's will. From this perspective, the root *shapat* means "judgment"; but the translation "justice" captures in a positive sense the harmony and order that God intends among "the nations" (96:10; 98:2; see also "families of the peoples" in 96:7) and among the entire creation (96:11–12; 98:7–8), which participate joyfully in the celebration of God's presence and the working out of God's will in the world. Given the focus on torah in Ps. 1, along with its anticipation of the enthronement psalms and their emphasis on God's will for justice and righteousness, it is not surprising that Ps. 2 features God's "anointed" (v. 2, *messiah*). God's "anointed" is the Judean king, entrusted with the earthly implementation of God's justice and righteousness toward the realization of God's will for world-encompassing *shalom*, "peace." This is especially evident in Ps. 72:1–7, which features the repetition of "justice/judge" and "righteousness" along with the repetition of *shalom*, which NRSV translates as "prosperity" in v. 3 and "peace" in v. 7. As Ps. 72:1–7, 12–14 make clear, the king's vocation of establishing justice and righteousness gives him a special responsibility for "the needy" (vv. 4, 12–13), "the poor" (vv. 2, 4, 12), and "the weak" (v. 13). The establishment of God's justice and righteousness takes the form of judgment only over against those who position themselves in relation to God and others as "the oppressor" (v. 4; cf. v. 14).

In any case, the king's administration is to have creation-encompassing effects (see 72:5–6, 8, 16). It is to benefit not only the king himself (vv. 8–11, 15–17), along with the weak and poor and needy (vv. 1–4, 12–14), but also ultimately everyone: "May all nations be blessed in him" (v. 17 NRSV). This world-encompassing extension of the king's vocation recalls Gen. 12:1–3, the beginning of Israel's story with Abraham and Sarah that is set in a context affirming God's sovereignty over the whole universe and all its people (Gen. 1–11). Not coincidentally, the king, whose administration of justice and righteousness will effect blessing for "all nations," is to be pronounced by them as "happy" (v. 17 NRSV). Thus, not only does the featuring of the king at the beginning of Ps. 72 recall Ps. 2, but also the conclusion of Ps. 72 recalls Ps. 1, especially 1:1–2. As Ps. 1 has already suggested, it is precisely the implementation of God's will—the concrete embodiment of justice, righteousness, and peace—that makes one "happy." The word "happy" also serves to link Pss. 1 and 2 with an envelope structure (see 1:1; 2:12). The occurrence of "happy" in 2:12 is explicitly associated with taking "refuge" in God. The necessity of taking refuge in God highlights another feature common to Pss. 1, 2, and 72—God, God's "anointed," and God's people are persistently opposed. These opponents are variously named—"the wicked" in 1:1, 5–6; "the nations," "the peoples," "the kings of the earth," and "the rulers" in 2:1–2; "the oppressor" in 72:4. As it turns out, these "foes" (3:1) or "enemies" (3:7) are a regular feature in the Psalter,

especially in Pss. 3–72, which consist mostly of prayers generally known as psalms of lament or complaint.

In fact, the situation at the beginning of Ps. 3, the first prayer in the Psalter, is typical. The psalmist is surrounded by enemies, who say, "There is no help for you in God" (3:2 NRSV). This assertion, of course, is a direct contradiction of Ps. 2:12. The psalmists are sometimes tempted to join the wicked in their arrogant self-assertion and self-sufficiency (see Ps. 73:1–15, which includes a quotation of the wicked in v. 11; see also the speech of the wicked in 10:4, 6, 11, 13), but they always steadfastly resist this temptation. The conclusion of Ps. 3, again typically, demonstrates the commitment of the assailed psalmists to stand with God. Using the same Hebrew word that the foes had used in v. 2, the psalmist prays, "Help me, O my God!" (v. 7; "Deliver me . . . ," NRSV). Then the psalmist affirms, "Help comes from the LORD" (v. 8; "Deliverance belongs to the LORD," NRSV). This confidence that God stands with the persecuted psalmist, and this commitment to continue standing with God, is what the Psalms mean by taking refuge in God. Given the predominance of prayers in Books I–II (Pss. 1–72), it is not surprising that "refuge" is a major theme (Creach; Pss. 7:1; 11:1; 14:6; 16:1; 17:7; 18:2, 30; 31:1–2, 19; 34:8, 22; etc.).

The fact that the prayers are typically composed of complaint (3:1–2; 13:1–2), petition (3:7; 13:3–4), and expressions of trust and/or praise (3:8; 13:5–6) is extremely important. In each prayer the effect is to juxtapose the realities of hurt and hope, pain and praise, suffering and glory. Of course, it is possible to conclude that pain and praise represent separate moments or movements in a psalm. For instance, some scholars conclude that the praise/trust sections of the prayers were spoken or written later than the complaint sections, after the threat had been removed or after conditions had improved. Others conclude that the psalmist moves through the pain and comes out safely, as it were, at the praise end of the psalm, perhaps with the assistance of some sort of cultic intervention that the psalm leaves unmentioned. But it is more likely that the pain and praise are meant to be understood as *simultaneous* realities. In other words, the psalmists complain and celebrate at the same time; the theological import is profound. As Mays concludes ("Psalm 13," 282), the prayers thus teach us about what it means to live as people of God: "The agony and the ecstasy belong together as the secret of our identity." In any case, as Mays again concludes, Ps. 3 and the other prayers in the Psalter demonstrate that prayer is "the ultimate act of faith in the face of the assault on the soul" (*Psalms*, 53). Prayer, in essence, represents the renunciation of self-sufficiency and self-help as one fully entrusts life and future to God (see Ps. 31:5, 14–15). To be sure, one could conclude that praise too is an act of faith. The Hebrew title of the Psalter is *Tehillim*, "Praises," and there are a significant number of psalms in which praise stands alone without the expression of pain. Even so, it is clear that the songs of praise should be heard in the context of the prayers, so as to avoid the temptation for praise to become merely a celebration of the status quo. Of course, the content of the songs of praise should be sufficient to avoid this temptation. As the central verse of Ps. 100 makes clear, praise is a matter of knowing "that the LORD is God . . . and not we ourselves" (v. 3, NRSV margin). Not coincidentally, Ps. 100 follows the aforementioned enthronement collection (Pss. 93, 95–99) that explicitly asserts God's universal sovereignty and celebrates God's will for world-encompassing justice and righteousness. In essence, then, praise is both the liturgy and the lifestyle of those who, denying self-sufficiency and self-assertion, entrust themselves to God and commit themselves to God's ways in the world. Praise is "lyrical self-abandonment" (Brueggemann 67) expressed in constant gratitude to God (see "thanksgiving/thanks" in the title of Ps. 100 and twice in v. 4) and constant commitment to the justice, righteousness, and *shalom* that God wills for individual lives and the life of the whole creation. Quite appropriately, the final verse of the Psalter envisions a world-encompassing community of praise: "Let everything that breathes praise the LORD!" (150:6 NRSV).

As we have seen, however, the Psalter is not naively optimistic about the existence of such a universal community of praise and obedience. From its very beginning in Pss. 1–2, the Psalter is well aware of the persistent opposition to God, God's will, and the community that God has gathered to represent God's purposes in the world. This persistent opposition serves to explain another prominent feature of the Psalter evident already in Pss. 1–3—namely, the request for God to destroy the wicked, or the confidence expressed that God does or will destroy the wicked (see Pss. 1:6; 2:8–12; 3:7; 5:10; 7:12–16; 9:5–6; 11:6; 12:3–4; passim). Indeed, the theme of retribution or vengeance is so prominent in some psalms that they have traditionally been known as imprecatory

psalms, or more simply, as psalms of vengeance (Zenger; see Pss. 12, 44, 58, 83, 109, 137, 139).

This aspect of the Psalms often proves to be particularly problematic for Christian readers, who are genuinely and rightly troubled by the violent imagery and the portrayal of God as fiercely wrathful. Indeed, the psalms of vengeance are often effectively ignored in Christian circles; or sometimes, they are edited for use in Christian worship by removing the "objectionable" portions (e.g., Ps. 137:8–9). But a careful reading of the Psalter reveals that God simply does *not* act unilaterally to wipe out God's enemies. If God did so, the enemies of God and God's will would not be such a pervasive feature of the Psalms (or of contemporary life!). What message, then, is to be derived from the expressions of vengeance in the Psalms?

In the first place, these expressions function to communicate the pervasiveness of the opposition to God and God's will, as well as the hurtful consequences of injustice and unrighteousness. Pastorally and ethically speaking, victimization needs to be acknowledged, articulated, and opposed. The worst possible response to evil would be divine and human silence. The psalms of vengeance thus voice both the human and divine objection to the injustice and unrighteousness that creates victimization. The vengeance psalms are the outcries of victims, the theological thrust of which is to affirm that God stands with the victimized. Or, as the conclusion to Ps. 109 puts it: "For he [God] stands at the right hand of the needy" (v. 31; also 9:8; 12:5; 40:17; 140:12).

From this perspective, the psalms of vengeance, as well as the pleas for vengeance throughout the Psalter, can be seen as essentially prayers for justice, righteousness, and *shalom*. In Christian terms, they amount to praying the prayer that Jesus taught his disciples, "Your will be done on earth as it is in heaven" (Matt. 6:10), a petition immediately following the request that also echoes the Psalter's affirmation of God's universal sovereignty, "Your kingdom come" (6:10). That the psalmists regularly pray for God to set things right in the world is entirely in keeping with the Psalter's initial focus on the centrality of God and God's will for the experience of human happiness (see above on Ps. 1:1–2). It is theologically revealing that at a key point the Psalter includes the end of Book III, a psalm that articulates God's wrath against God's "anointed" (Ps. 89, esp. vv. 38–51, noting the repetition of "anointed" in vv. 38, 51). In short, Ps. 89 indicates that God shows no partiality, except to stand with the victimized (see Pss.

72, 82). When God's own "anointed" one fails to be a servant of God's justice and righteousness, as he was supposed to be (Ps. 72), then the "anointed" one is as much a target of God's wrath as anyone else is when they oppose God.

Historically and canonically speaking, the appearance of Ps. 89 at the end of Book III probably reflects the rupture represented by the Babylonian exile. In any case, it is almost certainly not coincidental that Book IV (Pss. 90–106) begins with the only psalm attributed to Moses, who presided over the people of God before they had a land, a temple, or a monarch. Not coincidentally too, Book IV goes on to feature the theological perspective first articulated explicitly by Moses and the people at the conclusion of the Song of the Sea: "The LORD will reign for ever and ever" (Exod. 15:18). This is precisely the message of Pss. 93, 95–99, the enthronement psalms. Because they follow and seem to respond to the crisis articulated in the pivotal Ps. 89, they constitute "the theological 'heart'" of the Psalter (see above).

The remainder of the Psalter seems also to have been shaped to address the theological crisis of exile and its aftermath. For instance, Book V gives a prominent, pivotal place to the massive Ps. 119, as if to represent that matters pertaining to both exodus (Pss. 113–118, the Egyptian Hallel used at Passover) and Zion (Pss. 120–134, the Psalms of Ascents that focus attention on Jerusalem) find their focal point in relation to *torah* (the key word in Ps. 119, occurring twenty-five times). This is but one more way that the Psalter continues to indicate the pervasive significance of *torah* (see Ps. 1:1–2)—that is, God's will, which directs human life toward the happiness (Ps. 1:1) or peace God desires for humankind and the creation.

Given the prominence of the "anointed" one as early as Ps. 2, plus at key points elsewhere in the Psalter (Ps. 72, at the end of Book II, and Ps. 89, at the end of Book III), it is also quite revealing that Ps. 149 recalls Ps. 2. After the exile, the monarchy never reappeared, thus raising the question of which earthly agency was to be responsible for the concrete enactment of God's will in the world. Psalm 149 offers a response to this question, for here it is God's "faithful" (vv. 5, 9), who, recognizing God as their "King" (v. 2), are entrusted with the vocation formerly assigned to the monarchy and articulated as such in Ps. 2 (cf. Ps. 149:7–9 and Ps. 2:8–9). To be sure, the imagery in both cases is shockingly violent; but as Ps. 149:9 makes clear, the issue is essentially *mishpat*, "justice" ("judgment," NRSV). Particularly when heard in relationship to Ps. 89, with

its reminder that God's chosen agents are also subject to God's wrath (see above), Ps. 149 is a crucial affirmation that God entrusts God's "faithful" with the enactment and embodiment of God's will in the world—in a word, with God's "justice." Thus, Ps. 149 maintains the Psalter's ubiquitous focus on God's *torah*—God's will for justice, righteousness, and *shalom*—that was introduced in Pss. 1–2 and celebrated at the Psalter's theological heart (Pss. 93, 95–99). Along the way, of course, the prayers protest the absence of God's justice and righteousness, articulate the hurtful effects of disobedience, and plead that God's will be done. The songs of praise invite all peoples and nations to submit themselves to the sovereign God, who wills their well-being and, indeed, nothing short of peace on a cosmic scale.

The Psalms and the Canon

Given Luther's description of the Psalms as "a little Bible," it is not surprising that the messages of the Psalms resonate throughout both the OT and NT. Indeed, Psalms is the OT book most quoted in the NT.

The affirmation at the heart of the Psalter—that God reigns, and wills justice, righteousness, and peace on a universe-encompassing scale—might itself be considered a sort of summary of the Bible's fundamental message. As suggested above, Israel understood the exodus from Egypt to be decisive evidence of God's eternal reign. But, as Terence Fretheim points out, the exodus event aims at the fulfillment of God's creational purposes. To affirm God as Creator of the universe (Gen. 1–11) already affirms God's sovereign claim, including all peoples and nations. When the story appears to narrow from all humankind to Abraham and Sarah and their descendants, the intent of God is still to effect a blessing for "all the families of the earth" (Gen. 12:3 NRSV). This creation-wide perspective is especially evident in the songs of praise, including not only in the enthronement psalms (Pss. 93, 95–99) that explicitly assert God's sovereignty, but also in other songs of praise that regularly invite "all the earth" (66:1; 100:1), "all you nations" and "all you peoples" (117:1), and ultimately "everything that breathes" (150:6) to praise God. The apostle Paul apparently understood the practical theological implications of this expansive view of God's claim on the world. As part of his warrant for including the Gentiles (nations) in the church, Paul cites Ps. 117:1 (Rom. 15:11).

Of course, the Psalter's representation of God's will for justice, righteousness, and peace, along with its featuring of the "anointed" and his responsibility for enacting God's will (see esp. Pss. 2, 72, 89), puts the Psalms in conversation with major portions of the OT, including key texts like 1 Sam. 8 (Israel's request for a king and God's granting of this request) and 2 Sam. 7 (God's promise to David and his descendants; cf. Ps. 89). When the kings failed to do what God had entrusted to them, it fell upon prophets to call king and nation back to God's will. The prophets often articulated this call in terms of justice and righteousness (e.g., Isa. 1:21, 27; 5:7; 9:7; 32:1, 16–17; Jer. 22:13–17; Amos 5:24). Not surprisingly, a psalm like Ps. 82 sounds as if a prophet could have written it. As for postexilic prophecy, there are major connections between the enthronement psalms (Pss. 93, 95–99) and the material in Isa. 40–55, including the affirmation that God reigns (Isa. 52:7; Pss. 96:10; 97:1; 99:1) and the invitation to sing "a new song" (Isa. 42:10; Pss. 96:1; 98:1). Then too, the book of Isaiah as a whole portrays God in the same way as the Psalms—a God whose sovereign claim upon the whole creation means that God wills nothing short of universal peace on earth (Isa. 2:2–4; 42:1–9; 49:1–6).

This same complex of theological affirmations—God's sovereignty, God's will, and the agency of God's "anointed" in enacting it—plays a major role in the NT as well, especially in the Synoptic Gospels and their presentation of Jesus Christ (the Greek *Christos* is the translation of Hebrew *Messiah*, "anointed"). The titles for Jesus at the beginning of the Gospel of Mark, "Christ" and "Son of God," are the same ones found in Ps. 2 ("anointed" in v. 2 and "son" in v. 7). When Jesus is baptized (Mark 1:11), the heavenly voice recalls Ps. 2:7, "You are my son." Jesus' fundamental proclamation of "the kingdom of God" (Mark 1:15//Matt. 4:17) echoes the message that lies at the Psalter's theological heart; according to the Gospel of Matthew, Jesus' teaching begins with the same word that begins the Psalter: "Happy" or "Blessed" (Matt. 5:3). In fact, the Beatitudes of Jesus in Matt. 5:3–11 pronounce "happy" or "blessed" precisely the same kind of people who regularly appear as the pray-ers of the Psalms—the poor, the meek (cf. Matt. 5:5 with Ps. 37:11), the persecuted. In a real sense, the Beatitudes reinforce the affirmation of the Psalms that God stands with the dispossessed, the suffering, and the victimized, an affirmation further illustrated by the whole thrust of Jesus' ministry among the poor, weak, and needy. This whole direction, according to Matt. 5:17, serves to fulfill the Torah and the Prophets; it is the fullest expression of the will of God, the greater "righteousness" that "exceeds that of the scribes and Pharisees" (Matt. 5:20 NRSV). As suggested above, the Psalter also begins with a focus on *torah* (Ps. 1:2), commending constant orientation to God's will, which is subsequently described as righteousness and justice (see esp. Pss. 96–99).

Not surprisingly, therefore, the Gospel writers cannot tell the story of Jesus, especially Jesus' passion, without using the Psalms as a major source. Jesus' entry into Jerusalem recalls Ps. 118, thus suggesting that Jesus' upcoming death and resurrection continue God's salvific activity in the exodus and other OT deliverances (Mark 11:9 cites parts of Ps. 118:25–26). And the passion narratives in all four Gospels echo Pss. 22 and 69. In Matthew and Mark, Jesus' words from the cross are drawn from Ps. 22:1 (Matt. 27:46//Mark 15:34). Luke's account differs, but it is another psalm that supplies Jesus' words from the cross (Luke 23:46; see Ps. 31:5).

Not coincidentally, Pss. 22, 31, and 69 are the three longest and most intense prayers in the Psalter. The canonical effect is to portray Jesus' passion as the fullest expression of one whose suffering communicates not divine punishment, but rather oneness with God. Indeed, as is the case with the psalmist in Ps. 69, it is clear that Jesus suffers precisely *because* he is faithful to God and God's purposes. The profound theological significance of this reality will be considered further below.

While Pss. 22, 31, and 69 are more clearly related to the story of Jesus' suffering and death, their hopeful and praise-filled conclusions may also have helped the Gospel writers appreciate the meaning of Jesus' ministry and even his resurrection. Psalm 22, for instance, portrays the psalmist gathering around himself a community of grateful praise, beginning with the afflicted (v. 24) and the poor (v. 26), but eventually extending to "all the families of the nations" (v. 27) and including the dead (v. 29) and "people yet unborn" (v. 31). While Ps. 22 should not be understood as a prediction of Jesus' ministry among the outcast or the reality of his resurrection, it certainly anticipates Jesus' expansive ministry to all people, as well as his proclamation and embodiment of a communion with God that even death itself cannot destroy (Davis).

Theology in the Psalms

The preceding sections have already begun to discuss theological dimensions, but it is appropriate in this concluding section to consider more explicitly the Psalter's portrayal of God and some of its implications. Of paramount importance is the Psalter's affirmation of God's universal sovereignty and its simultaneous recognition that God has enemies (Ps. 2). This situation, of course, virtually forces the reader to explore the nature of God's sovereignty or power. If God's power is simply force, then God should have no enemies, at least not for long. But God always does, as do the people committed to God's justice, righteousness, and peace in the world. Thus, God's power must be understood not as sheer force, but rather as something like sheer love.

As contemporary Reformed theologians are pointing out, the Bible portrays a loving God who wills authentic relationship with humankind. Because love cannot be coerced, human beings must genuinely be able to choose to obey or disobey God (Hall 71–72; Placher). The Psalter's portrayal of God conforms to this understanding. Because God loves the world and wills to be in relationship with it (note that justice, righteousness, and peace are all relational terms), God simply will not coerce obedience. This explains why opposition to God is possible, and indeed, why the Psalms are full of such opposition (even from God's own people; see Pss. 32, 51, 130).

All this does not mean that God is powerless, however. The good news that God stands with the poor and needy (see Pss. 22:24; 31:21–22; 34:18; 109:31; 140:12) serves to energize and empower them to resist oppression, and to pursue for themselves and others the life that God wills. Such resistance and pursuit are powerful, and it is *God's* power. But this is the power of incarnational love, not coercion or enforcement. God loves the world into obedience.

This portrayal of God certainly has profound implications for understanding the human situation, including suffering. Most dramatically, perhaps, suffering cannot simply be understood as divine punishment. Although the psalmists themselves sometimes seem to view their suffering as punishment (Pss. 6:1; 38:1), they actually undercut this view by claiming God's presence with themselves and with other sufferers. Like the book of Job, the Psalter finally obliterates any comprehensive doctrine of retribution. The psalmists suffer, not because God wills or causes it; rather, they suffer because they themselves or their enemies have chosen not to enact and embody the justice, righteousness, and peace that God wills. Injustice and unrighteousness always have bad consequences; they hurt people, and they anger God. If the negative consequences of injustice and unrighteousness are considered divine "punishment," then one must at least stipulate that such "punishment" does not necessarily correspond to what one might deserve, and that its occurrence is actually an indication that God's will is *not* being accomplished.

To put it slightly differently, only when the doctrine of retribution has been obliterated is there any logical space for grace, which by definition means that the guilty do *not* get what they deserve. Thus, the Psalms finally participate with the rest of the canon in portraying God as essentially "merciful and gracious, slow to anger, and abounding in steadfast love and faithfulness" (Exod. 34:6 NRSV). Given this portrayal of God, it is entirely understandable not only that certain psalms echo Exod. 34:6 (86:15; 103:8; and less directly, 25:10; 36:5; 40:10–11; 57:3; 61:7; 85:10; 89:14; 115:1; 138:2), but also that God's *khesed*, "steadfast love," is regularly celebrated in the songs of praise (as in 33:5; 100:5; 103:11, 17; 106:1; 107:1, 8, 15, 21, 31, 43; 117:2; 118:1–4, 29; 136:1–26), appealed to in the prayers for help (6:4; 17:7; 25:7; 26:3; 31:16; 51:1), and cited as ground for trust in psalmic professions of faith (5:7; 13:5; 23:6 NRSV, "mercy"; 33:18; 63:3).

From the Christian perspective, the portrayal of a gracious God, whose love makes God vulnerable to the disobedience of humankind, reaches its culmination in the incarnation, life, death, and resurrection of Jesus. As suggested above, the Gospel writers could not tell the story of Jesus without the Psalms. The Psalter's regular juxtaposition of pain and praise, hurt and hope, suffering and glory anticipates the death and resurrection of Jesus, who then and now calls people to experience the glory of life by taking up a cross to follow him (see Mark 8:34–35). As Calvin discerned, the Psalms do finally "teach and train us to bear the cross."

See also Messiah/Messianism; Music, the Bible and; Worship

Bibliography

Bellinger, W., Jr. *Psalms*. Hendrickson, 1990; Brown, W. *Seeing the Psalms*. Westminster John Knox, 2002; Brueggemann, W. "Bounded by Praise and Obedience: The Psalms as Canon." *JSOT* 50 (1991): 63–92; Calvin, J. *Commentary on the Book of Psalms*. Vol. 1. Calvin Translation Society, 1845; Creach, J. *Yahweh as Refuge and the Editing of the Hebrew Psalter*. JSOTSup 217. Sheffield Academic, 1996; Davis, E. "Exploding the Limits: Form and Function in Psalm 22." *JSOT* 53 (1992): 93–105; Fretheim, T. *Exodus*. Interpretation. John Knox, 1991; Gerstenberger, E. *Psalms, Part 1, with an Introduction to Cultic Poetry*. FOTL 14. Eerdmans, 1988; idem. *Psalms, Part 2, and Lamentations*.

FOTL 15. Eerdmans, 2001; Gunkel, H. *The Psalms*. Fortress, 1967; Hall, D. J. *God and Human Suffering*. Augsburg, 1986; Limburg, J. *Psalms*. Westminster Bible Companion. Westminster John Knox, 2000; Luther, M. *LWorks*. Vol. 35. Fortress, 1960; Mays, J. L. *The Lord Reigns*. Westminster John Knox, 1994; idem. "Psalm 13." *Int* 34 (1980): 279–83; idem. *Psalms*. Interpretation. John Knox, 1994; McCann, J. C., Jr. "The Book of Psalms: Introduction, Commentary, and Reflections." *NIB* 4:641–1280; idem. *A Theological Introduction to the Book of Psalms*. Abingdon, 1993; Mowinckel, S. *The Psalms in Israel's Worship*. Vols. 1–2. Abingdon, 1962; Placher, W. *Narratives of a Vulnerable God*. Westminster John Knox, 1994; Seybold, K. *Introducing the Psalms*. T&T Clark, 1990; Tate, M. *Psalms 51–100*. WBC. Word, 1990; Wilson, G. H. "The Use of the Royal Psalms at the 'Seams' of the Hebrew Psalter." *JSOT* 35 (1986): 85–94; Zenger, E. *A God of Vengeance?* Westminster John Knox, 1996.

J. Clinton McCann Jr.

Pseudepigrapha

The word "Pseudepigrapha" refers to a vast body of literary works, a good number of which originate from the Second Temple period by Jewish writers/communities. "Pseudepigrapha" is a wholly artificial category; the texts contained therein are of diverse origins, spanning several centuries, and written for diverse purposes. Broadly speaking, what holds this voluminous corpus together is the fact that they all purport to be written by some figure of biblical stature (or that they are given through divine revelation), claim some level of authority, and are explicitly connected to some biblical idea, theme, event, and so on. Moreover, in modern Western thinking the term implies an element of deception on the part of the community of origin. This is almost certainly not the case. Rather, many of these texts should be understood as the products of believing communities, who, faced perhaps with some crisis or challenge, appeal to the authoritative past (their Scriptures) to substantiate their point. When defined in this way, one sees some similarities with a number of biblical books, including Ecclesiastes and Chronicles.

Moreover, how the genre of pseudepigrapha was understood in the ancient world can profitably come into play for certain NT books, such as 2 Peter. Given the popularity of pseudepigraphal writing in the ancient world, it should not be assumed that NT books cannot participate in the same literary convention. On the other hand, it must also be kept in mind that the appeal of a Second Temple writer to a *long past* figure like Solomon or Moses is qualitatively different from a contemporary—or near contemporary—appealing to the authority of Peter or Paul. In any event, purely ideological or doctrinal commitments cannot preclude the possibility that pseudepigraphal works exist in the Christian canon.

According to Charlesworth's *The Old Testament Pseudepigrapha*, sixty-three texts are included in this collection (Charlesworth counts 3 and 4 Maccabees and *Prayer of Manasseh*, which are often included among the Apocrypha). Some of the earliest texts are *Jubilees* (mid-second century BCE); *Ahiqar* (seventh to sixth century BCE); *Letter of Aristeas* (perhaps as early as 250 BCE); *1 Enoch* (as early as second century BCE). Others are dated well into the Christian era: *Greek Apocalypse of Ezra* (second to ninth century CE); and *Vision of Ezra* (fourth to seventh century CE). Some of these later writings, although of Jewish origin, show clear indications of Christian influence at some later stage (e.g., *Sibylline Oracles*, second century BCE through seventh century CE).

In recent decades, the study of the Pseudepigrapha has taken on a new fervor. This can be attributed to two interrelated factors. First, the discovery of the Dead Sea Scrolls has brought subsequent generations of scholars into conversation with Second Temple Judaism. Many of the Pseudepigrapha are invaluable sources to filling out the picture of Jewish life and thought during this period (e.g., *Jubilees*, Pseudo-Philo's *Book of Biblical Antiquities*, *1 Enoch*). What has become quite clear from these texts is that Judaism in the centuries following the exile was a diverse phenomenon: there are *Judaisms* but no "Second Temple Judaism." This is an important lesson for both Christians and Jews to keep in mind. The line from biblical Israelite religion does not run straight to either of its two heirs, Judaism or Christianity. Rather, the Second Temple evidence in general shows a number of varied and competing trajectories, all of which claim biblical precedent. The fact that these texts are noncanonical for both faiths is irrelevant to the point being made here. The Pseudepigrapha open windows through which to view the world out of which both Judaism and Christianity arose.

Study of these texts reveals a world where Jews demonstrated commitment to their past in the midst of changing cultures and conflict. The Israelites were a people whose fortunes were often at the whim of competing kingdoms; their struggles with self-identity vis-à-vis the influence of Persia, Greece, and later Rome are well known. Such struggles were felt on varied levels, such as religious ideology among competing Jewish groups, and political status in a world of the surrounding superpowers. Any of these conflicts was answered differently by different groups, evidence of which is preserved for us in some of the Pseudepigrapha. For example, *Jubilees* offers a polemic in favor of a 364-day calendar, rather than the lunar month. For this community, it was evidently quite important to maintain a regular rhythm to the festal year, assuring that the festivals would occur on the same day each year. Although this is only one example, it illustrates a principle that can be extended to many of the Pseudepigrapha: they are categorized by varied attempts to answer the question "What does it mean to be a Jew here, today?"

Second, what many of the Pseudepigrapha share with other texts of antiquity is a close interaction with biblical texts and themes. In other words, in addition to their *historical* importance, these texts have also a profound *hermeneutical* importance. The ways in which both rabbinic Judaism and the NT authors interact with their Scripture did not arise in a vacuum. Rather, both demonstrate hermeneutical methods and conclusions that are demonstrable in many, many Second Temple texts, including the Pseudepigrapha. In fact, similar hermeneutical trajectories were already set within the Hebrew Scriptures (the Chronicler's interpretation of Israel's history; Daniel's interpretation of Jeremiah's seventy years as seventy "sevens" of years). How the rabbis and the apostles handled their Scripture must be understood within the context of earlier interpretative activity. With respect to the NT, for example, the *Book of Biblical Antiquities* (along with other Second Temple texts) contains the tradition of a well following the Israelites through the desert (Exod. 17; Num. 20–21). Such a tradition certainly informs our understanding of Paul's "the spiritual rock that accompanied them" (1 Cor. 10:4). *Jubilees* reflects the notion of angels being actively involved in the revelation to Moses on Sinai, an event without explicit OT support but that also seems to find its way into Acts 7:53; Gal. 3:19; and Heb. 2:2. The Pseudepigrapha, therefore, contribute to the church's own understanding of its Bible, insofar as they outline general interpretative trajectories adopted by NT authors.

In addition, a number of theological themes discussed in the Pseudepigrapha are of interest to anyone wishing to discuss the religious beliefs of postexilic Judaism. In view of the many struggles and conflicts mentioned above, it is not surprising to see theodicy as a recurring concern. The flip side of this coin is the question of Israel's sin and what God is doing, or will do, to his people as a result. Current debates regarding the so-called New Perspective on Paul, which revolve around this question of sin and justification, are really derivatives of a larger issue, the New Perspective on Second Temple Judaism, specifically as it affects our understanding of the nature of sin and judgment. Related matters include the role of the Messiah in bringing to a closure the period of Israel's expectation of God's justice, and the use of the apocalyptic genre to portray those anticipated events.

See also Jewish Context of the NT; Pauline Epistles

Bibliography

Charles, R. H. *The Apocrypha and Pseudepigrapha of the Old Testament in English*. 2 vols. Clarendon, 1913; Charlesworth, J. H., ed. *The Old Testament Pseudepigrapha*. 2 vols. Doubleday, 1983–85; idem. *The Old Testament Pseudepigrapha and the New Testament*. SNTSMS 54. Cambridge University Press, 1987; idem. *The Pseudepigrapha and Modern Research with a Supplement*. SBLSCS 75. Scholars Press, 1981; Charlesworth, J. H., and C. A. Evans. *The Pseudepigrapha and Early Biblical Interpretation*. JSOT, 1993; Cohen, S. *From the Maccabees to the Mishnah*. Westminster, 1987; Nickelsburg, G. W. E. *Jewish Literature between the Bible and the Mishnah*. Fortress, 1981; Russell, D. S. *Between the Testaments*. SCM, 1960; Stone, M. E. *Jewish Writings of the Second Temple Period*. CRINT 2.2. Van Gorcum/Fortress, 1984; idem. *Scripture, Sects, and Visions*. Fortress, 1980.

Peter Enns

Pseudonymity *See* Pseudepigrapha

Psychological Interpretation

Psychological interpretation of the Bible is less a methodology or set of principles than a way of reading the Bible that is critically attentive to psychological factors. Psychology is the systematic study of human behavior, such as cognition, personality, and motivation. Every human encounter with the biblical text—in its origins and composition, its transmission and translation, its interpretation and expression—involves a psychological dimension.

Psychology and Theology

Psychology's roots lie in theology; its name derives from the Greek word for "soul." The Bible has much to say about the qualities, tendencies, and transformation of the psyche, and early theologians wrote extensively on the subject. Luther's student Philipp Melanchthon brought the term "psychology" into general use. With the rise of modern scientific psychology in the late nineteenth century came serious conflict between contemporary psychology and theology. Both study the nature of human beings and propose sometimes-competing norms for behavior.

Four general models of the relationship of psychology and theology have emerged. Some assert that the two disciplines simply are entirely different and cannot be meaningfully related to each other. Others are hostile; advocates on either side insist that one must choose and consider the other illegitimate and dangerous. A third approach involves setting one in subservience to the other—reading the Bible only as an illustration of a psychological theory, or summoning psychological theories to support biblical concepts. Finally, some seek to keep the two fields in a dialogue that can potentially inform and deepen both disciplines. One's attitude about the relationship between psychology and theology will determine to a great extent whether one finds psychological interpretation of the Bible valid or useful.

Psychology and the Bible

Wayne Rollins has outlined several broad areas for psychological interpretation (*Soul*). These include exploring biblical psychology, exegesis, hermeneutics, description of biblical phenomena, the effects of the Bible on readers and communities, and developing contemporary models.

Biblical Psychology. Though the Bible certainly deals with psychological phenomena, it does not offer a systematic exploration or explanation of them. From Tertullian and Augustine to present-day pastoral counselors, people have made an effort to systematize and correlate biblical psychology with contemporary understanding. In 1855, Franz Delitzsch suggested that biblical psychology was similar to secular theories, but was fundamentally revelational, rather than empirical. Others have argued that biblical psychology is entirely dissimilar, and that reference to secular sources is neither useful nor desirable.

Exegesis. The Bible is not "psychological" in the modern sense. There is scant material for psychobiography of biblical figures. Early psychological interpretation received a deservedly bad reputation for efforts to psychoanalyze the prophets, Paul, or Jesus, often concluding that they were pathological or that their faith could be explained in purely psychological terms.

Psychology has little to offer as a historical method; it can, however, illuminate how biblical characters are depicted and how they interact. Biblical imagery and symbolism may reveal unconscious connections and significance; psycho-

logical dynamics of narratives provide insight into human motivation and behavior. Psychological perspectives can illuminate the context of the biblical text—the social psychology of self-identity, family and group relations, the nature of human motivation and emotions. In exegesis, it is important to recognize significant differences between the world of the Bible and our own, and not to apply modern psychological models indiscriminately.

Hermeneutics. Scholars have long recognized the significance of presuppositions in interpretation. A psychologically informed hermeneutics will alert us to presuppositions that arise from the personality and are not conscious to the interpreter. Recognition of these unconscious dynamics has led to a "hermeneutics of suspicion," which questions the objectivity of interpretation. In its most radical form, this suspicion is one of the underpinnings of postmodernism—the assertion that everything is only subjective, and there is no objective knowledge.

One need not accept such absolutism to acknowledge that people do bring themselves to the text in ways that affect understanding. Personality factors and psychological tendencies will lead readers to focus on different aspects of the Bible and to understand its authority differently. Without recognition of psychological factors in perception, cognitive processes, and social conformity, biblical interpretation can become little more than a projection of the reader's own biases.

Human transformation rests ultimately with God's initiative, yet it is still possible to discern how psychological dynamics in reading, cognition, memory, and interrelationships of individual and community may enable or hinder that transformation. Even those interpretative approaches that claim skepticism of psychological insight base themselves on assumptions about human reading, learning, and behavior that are fundamentally psychological.

Psychological Description of Biblical Phenomena. Psychological interpretation may also help contemporary readers better to understand biblical experiences such as dreams, healing, speaking in tongues, or conversion. It can provide another avenue for grasping the meaning of biblical symbols and images, understanding that they are not merely reflective of ancient cultures, but are powerfully linked to our own inner psyches.

The Bible's Effect on Readers and Communities. Pastors and counselors have long been aware of the Bible's healing power in guiding people through life's challenges. They may also notice how problems in an individual's self-image or relationships may be revealed in their interpretation of Bible passages. Recognition of psychological dimensions of interpretation can help in understanding why some misreadings of Scripture are destructive and yet so persistent and attractive.

Models for Psychological Criticism. For psychological interpretation to be fruitful, there must be a good fit between psychological insight and the biblical text. Psychological methods should be used in tandem with other exegetical and hermeneutical principles. A psychological interpretation that does not take into account the insights of linguistic, structural, genre, and historical study runs the risk of psychologizing the text.

It is impossible for interpreters in our psychological era to avoid psychological interpretation. From the sacred experience to the sacred text, from inspiration to writing to collecting and canon, the Bible engages, shapes, and interacts with human beings and their psyches. Psychological interpretation helps us to be conscious of those interactions and to journey further in understanding ourselves and our communities in the light of the Bible.

See also Human Being, Doctrine of

Bibliography

Delitzsch, F. J. *A System of Biblical Psychology*, trans. A. E. Wallis. 2d ed. Baker, 1966; Everding, H. E., Jr., M. Wilcox, L. Huffaker, and C. Snelling Jr. *Viewpoints: Perspectives of Faith and Christian Nurture*. Trinity, 1998; Francis, L. *Personality Type and Scripture*. Mowbray, 1997; Johnson, C. *The Psychology of Biblical Interpretation*. Zondervan, 1983; Kille, D. A. *Psychological Biblical Criticism*, ed. G. Tucker. GBS (OT). Fortress, 2001; Rollins, W. *Jung and the Bible*. John Knox, 1983; idem. *Soul and Psyche*. Augsburg Fortress, 1999; Theissen, G. *Psychological Aspects of Pauline Theology*. Fortress, 1987; Wink, W. *The Bible in Human Transformation*. Fortress, 1973.

D. Andrew Kille

Public Theology *See* Political Theology

Q *See* Gospels; Redaction Criticism; Source Criticism

Qumran *See* Dead Sea Scrolls; Jewish Context of the NT

Quotation *See* Intertextuality; Relationship between the Testaments

R

Racism

A general definition of this social and personal vice can be framed as a belief that human groups can be validly grouped in races on the basis of their biological and cultural traits, which in turn determine their behavior and social value (Banks 74–75). The underlying assumption of this categorical organization of human groups by race is that some human groups are superior to others. This type of categorical distribution of human groups cannot (and should not) be understood without considering the connection between the social value assigned to each group and the social power of the group determining the categorical value—in this case, race. In other words, the roots of racism are found in the abuse of social power and location of the dominant group as, consciously and unconsciously, defining the value of certain human groups, categorized by race, by comparing them to the dominant group as the norm. In this way all other groups are judged based on the dominant group's norm; thus, groups that do not fit the norm imposed by the dominant group are deemed inferior.

Interpretations of history and current practices show that some groups have had, and still have, unequal power in the decision-making process. For this reason, every decision made by the dominant group enhances, legitimizes, and reinforces their own norm, and in this case their categorical distribution of human groups by race disenfranchises, minimizes, and devaluates groups that do not fit the norm and/or are not part of the dominant group. Furthermore, the assumptions of the dominant group are not only false and morally pernicious; in a devastating way its evil manifestations also affect the identity and self-understanding of those who are considered inferior. Individuals in their process of self-construction and self-identity develop a picture of themselves primarily informed by their interaction with their social environment. Occasionally groups of individuals will be identified, either voluntarily or involuntarily, in subcategories, often named "ethnic" groups. A biblical example of this process is the naming and value distribution to the Israelites, Canaanites, Jews, and so on. In any case, persons' social context and its interpretation heavily influence their identity and self-understanding. But when the interpretation of their social context is almost always defined and determined by the dominant group, the individual in this condition "accepts" this imposed reality and develops a self-consciousness, self-understanding, and identity of inferiority.

Sadly, Christians whose social location and power have placed them in a privileged position are not exempted from this self-centered and socially located practice. A clear example of the consequences of racism has been the use of the Scriptures in the affirmation of slavery as a valid Christian practice. This example shows that biblical interpreters and scholars, as well as Christian communities, are not exempt from falling into the trap of abusing their power and social location to determine the meaning and moral value of the Scriptures. They thus provide interpretations that affirm the practices of the dominant group and their self-centered motivations. Interpretations like these are often justified by allusions and exegetical work that intend to capture the "original" meaning of the text, by placing it in its social context and providing a careful examination of that context. But this approach does not consider the reader's and interpreter's social context and location, consequently imposing their own biases, and in this case their own categorical distribution of human groups by race. Perhaps a good way to avoid this self-centered practice is to spend the same amount of time and energy in exploring the social context and location of the person(s) in charge of the interpretative task, and in fostering reciprocal and meaningful dialogue with readers and interpreters from the global Christian community. In doing so, perhaps, one will become self-aware of one's own limitations and bias.

Furthermore, contrary to this self-centered categorical distribution of human groups by race, the biblical creation narrative provides a solid ethical foundation for the affirmation of all humans. In the creation narrative it is clear that humans were created equal (Gen. 1:26–27). As bearers of God's image, humans have the capacity and responsibility to reflect divine moral attributes in every action and decision, but particularly in relating to each other. In the same way that the three persons of the Trinity relate to each other in a harmonious and egalitarian relationship we, as humans, are called to reflect this type of relationship as we relate to each other. Additionally, God's creation is a concrete expression and reflection of God's goodness and holiness, in which humans and God live in perfect harmony and humans reflect God's character by living in an egalitarian and harmonious relationship with each other. Humans, male and female, are blessed and given equal responsibilities to care for the earth, preserving and replicating God's harmonious relationship with it (Gen. 1:28–30). Humans are created and called to enter into a just and equal partnership with God and with each other, in this way providing a living testimony and a reflection of God's character. Thus, harmony and equality are signs present in God's creation and implicit in the image of God imprinted in all humans. When these signs and values are pursued and embraced by humans and expressed in their relationships with one another, they are striving to reflect God's character and image as depicted in the creation narrative. But when these signs and values are ignored and/or neglected, global harmony and equality are replaced with systematic and structural oppression of certain groups by the dominant group. For this reason, racism is an anticreation tendency and a reality that has become inherent to our human condition and a manifestation of our sinful nature—selfishness and self-centeredness.

Nevertheless, the biblical narrative offers a solution to this inherent human tendency, by providing sufficient teaching that affirms the value of all races and the importance of equality among them, condemning self-centered interpretations and racial discrimination. Not only in the creation narrative do we find these affirmations; they are also present throughout Scripture and particularly in the morally shaping and formative stories. In the story of Abram's call, God promises him and his descendants that *all nations* will be blessed through them, not few nations or certain ethnic groups but all nations. Isaiah, later quoted by Gospel writers, reminds Israel that the temple, the house of prayer, should be called a house of prayer for *all nations*, a statement that is later affirmed by Jesus in the cleansing of the temple. Perhaps the conclusion of this trajectory and affirmation of all races and ethnic groups as equal and valuable is found in Gal. 3:28 and Eph. 2:11–19. There Paul clearly follows the trajectory that begins in Genesis and culminates in Revelation with the eschatological gathering of *all nations* before the Lord. In the light of this holistic narrative projection, some of the passages that seem to provide a justification for slavery and racism (ironically Paul's writings) should be read. Therefore, by exploring our own social-context location, by dialoguing with the global Christian community, and by following the trajectory of the all-nations-centered biblical narrative, we will be able to avoid the pitfalls of racist biblical interpretation. We will also be challenged to promote racial equality as we reflect God's character and holiness—by living in harmony and treating with respect and dignity all humans, regardless of their ethnic and cultural background.

See also Culture and Hermeneutics; Ideological Criticism; Slavery; Violence

Bibliography

Bailey, R., and T. Pippin. "Race, Class, and the Politics of Bible Translation." *Semeia* 76, no. 1 (2001): 1–40; Banks, J. *Teaching Strategies for Ethnic Studies*. Allyn & Bacon, 1991; Emerson, M., and C. Smith. *Divided by Faith*. Oxford University Press, 2000; Feagin, J., and H. Vera. *White Racism*. Routledge, 1995; Feagin, J., and C. Booher Feagin. *Racial and Ethnic Relations*. Prentice Hall, 1996; Felder, C. H., ed. *Stony the Road We Trod*. Fortress, 1988; Horsman, R. *Race and Manifest Destiny*. Harvard University Press, 1981; Mosala, I. "Race, Class, and Gender as Hermeneutical Factors in the African Independent Churches' Appropriation of the Bible." *Semeia* 73, no. 1 (2001): 43–57; Pagan, S. "Poor and Poverty: Social Distance and Bible Translation." *Semeia* 76, no. 1 (2001): 69–79.

Hugo Magallanes

Radical Orthodoxy *See* Political Theology; Violence

Reader-Response Criticism

One over-simplified but useful narrative concerns the shift in twentieth-century literary theory away from a concern with authorial intention (textual meaning lying "behind the text"). Instead, readers focus on the text itself (textual meaning as encoded "within the text," ready for them to "discover" it), and finally on readers' present interest (readers actualize textual meaning "in front of the text"). Reader-response theory is not a single theory but a family of diverse hermeneutical theories that share a focus on the *active role* of the reader (or communities of readers) in interpretation. The various theorists disagree on a range of issues: how much control texts exercise in interpretation, the role of communities within which readers live, the role of the interpretative histories of texts, whether the readers they speak of are experts or ordinary readers, and so on. We shall consider the theories in two broad categories, radical theories and moderate theories; but it must be understood that this categorization is only one way to cut the cake.

Radical Reader-Response Theories

Radical theories are those that emphasize the reader in the creation of meaning over against any constraints the text may place upon interpretation. The best-known radical is Stanley Fish. In his later work Fish came to believe that the idea that meaning resides "in" the text or that texts exercise control over interpretation was an illusion. Instead, reading communities determine what counts as an interpretation, and their response to texts is not a response to some preexistent meaning in those texts but rather *is the meaning of those texts*. Prior to such a response there is no meaning and there is no text. This does not mean that individual readers can do anything they like with texts because critical readers are trained and authorized to read texts by their communities. It does mean that there are as many meanings of a text as there are community responses to that text. Norman Holland's psychological reader-response theory sees individual readers (not communities) as projecting themselves into texts and using literary works to symbolize and replicate themselves. The ego-unification achieved through reading texts *is* the meaning of the text.

Moderate Reader-Response Theories

Moderate theories desire to mediate between the claim that a text means only one thing and the claim that a text can mean anything. In the words of Paul Ricoeur: "It is true that there is always more than one way of construing a text, it is not true that all interpretations are equal. . . . The text is a limited field of possible constructions. . . . It is possible to argue for or against an interpretation, to confront interpretations, to arbitrate between them, and to seek for an agreement, even if this agreement remains beyond our reach" (175). For Ricoeur, texts have a "surplus of meaning" that goes beyond any authorial intentions. He says, "A text means all that it can mean" (176), but it cannot mean *anything* a reader wants. So inter-

pretation takes place "in front of the text," but the text places limits on legitimate interpretation.

Wolfgang Iser argues that *potential* meanings do reside within texts and readers "actualize" or "concretize" dimensions of meaning by reading the text. So *actual* meanings are neither in the text nor in the reader but are realized in the act of reading. Different readers may actualize different meanings, but all such meanings are guided by the structures of the text. Iser famously speaks of how all texts necessarily include "gaps"—missing information that readers need to fill in to "complete" the text. Different readerly gap-fillings actualize different meanings.

The "Reception Theory" of Hans Robert Jauss adds a crucial historical dimension to the mix. He opposes "timeless" reader-response theories that do not appreciate the role of traditions of interpretation inherited by readers. Christian readers of Romans cannot come to the text without its effect on them being shaped by its effect on past Christian interpretations of that text. Past reception history sets boundaries on interpretation but also creates fertile ground for innovative interpretations.

Reader-Response Theories and Theological Interpretation

Christian Bible-readers (who have thought about the issues) have been divided on quite what attitude to take toward reader-response theories. Some have hailed them as a breakthrough that creates space for Christian theological interpretations of biblical books to regain legitimacy alongside other interpretations (e.g., feminist, neocolonialist, Marxist); others have seen them as a major threat to biblical authority.

Radical theories do seem to be deeply problematic, for they are not merely philosophically implausible but, as Thiselton argues, they betray the function that hermeneutics arose to perform—they *"collapse the 'two horizons' of hermeneutics* [i.e., those of the text and the reader] *into one single horizon*. This violates the concern for listening, openness, and dialogue which stands at the heart of hermeneutical theory" (546). For Holland, the text is, at best, a trigger that sets *self-discovery* in motion. For Fish, there is no prophetic challenge from "beyond" the community. The inability of such theories to allow the text to confront us as "other" throws theological interpretation into crisis, for how can we conceive of God addressing and transforming the community through the text? "The Reformation then becomes a dispute over alternative community life-styles.

It has nothing to do with retrieving authentic meanings of biblical texts" (Thiselton 549)!

However, moderate reader-response theories do provide liberating insight. They allow "more Light and Truth to . . . break forth out of [God's] Holy Word" without yielding to extreme relativism. It is helpful to think of texts on a scale of varying degrees of openness, with some quite open to diverse legitimate interpretations while others are relatively closed to such diversity, allowing readers less room for maneuver. No texts would be completely open or completely closed.

The attempt to discern an author's communicative intent is both perfectly intelligible and important (Vanhoozer). Another important task is to seek to discern the range of reader responses that one might expect of the text's implied readers. Implied readers are not the original readers but a theoretical construct: "an imaginary set of people who may be assumed to read a given text in the way they are expected to read it, bringing to their reading experience the knowledge, competence, beliefs and values that appear to be presupposed for the text in question" (Powell 64). Such a project allows us to try to discern the range of responses we can say a text "expects" from its ideal readers, and it allows us to discern the grain of the text.

It may be thought that theological interpretation can stop with authorial intention or expected readings—that simply expositing the intentionality of a biblical text brings out *the* theological meaning. Things are not so simple. Real flesh-and-blood readers of texts, even the original audiences, are not the implied readers, and the greater the historical and/or social gap between a real reader and the implied reader, the less we are able to stand in those shoes. Obviously, the implied readers of biblical books are believers in Yahweh, as are Christian readers today, so we can stand closer to the implied reader than, say, an atheist can. However, the implied reader of Leviticus, for example, is Jewish and is expected to see the text as commanding him or her to keep the laws found there, but *I* cannot read the text in that way.

Odd as it may seem, the very creation of the canon as a controlling context for the Christian interpretation of any biblical book means that Christian theological interpretation cannot simply be collapsed into the expected reading of a text (i.e., with the implied reader). The human redactor of Leviticus did not have the completed canon of the Christian Bible in mind when he shaped his text, but a theological interpretation of Leviticus would not be Christian if it did not read from a different "location" than that of the implied reader. The canon-as-context opens up various potential directions for the interpretation of individual books and closes down others.

In the ways that NT authors read their Jewish Scriptures, one can see that the "meaning" of those Scriptures could not be limited to the intentions of the original (human) authors or to the expected readings of implied readers. If the meaning of a text was *exhausted* by authorial intention, then NT writers were doing something other than telling us what their Scriptures meant.

It is not simply that the canon creates a new literary and theological context for reading biblical texts. It is also that the historical, theological, and social location of actual readers is often very different from that of the implied readers. David Steinmetz famously defended the superiority of precritical exegesis on such grounds:

> How was a French parish priest in 1150 to understand Psalm 137, which bemoans captivity in Babylon, makes rude remarks about Edomites, expresses an ineradicable longing for a glimpse of Jerusalem, and pronounces a blessing on anyone who avenges the destruction of Jerusalem by dashing Babylonian children against a rock? The priest lives in Concale, not Babylon, has no personal quarrel with Edomites, cherishes no ambition to visit Jerusalem (though he might fancy a holiday in Paris), and is expressly forbidden by Jesus to avenge himself on his enemies. Unless Psalm 137 has more than one possible meaning, it cannot be used as a prayer by the Church and must be rejected as a lament belonging exclusively to the piety of ancient Israel. (28)

The community of the church had reading strategies enabling such "alien" texts to be reappropriated as Christian Scripture in very different contexts. Although Ps. 137, taken in isolation, can be interpreted in many ways, legitimate *Christian* interpretations are constrained by the canonical context (including the biblical metanarrative), the Rule of Faith (Wall), the gospel (Powell), the interpretation's discipleship-forming power (Fowl), the text's Christian reception history (Lundin, Walhout, and Thiselton), and authorial intention (Vanhoozer). But even within such constraints considerable diversity of appropriation is legitimated by diverse sociohistorical contexts. People receive texts differently for many reasons, influenced by their race, gender, age, social class, income, education, personality, career, self-image, and so on. Such factors can open our eyes to some of the textual "surplus of meaning" not perceived by others. Mark Allan

Powell notes how in the West most people think that the point of the parable of the Good Samaritan is, "We should be like the Samaritan and help the needy." In Tanzania people are more likely to think the point is, "People who are in need cannot afford the luxury of prejudice." The Tanzanians empathize more readily than Westerners with the needy person in the story. In fact, the Tanzanian interpretation is closer to Luke's intended meaning, but the Western reading is also surely a legitimate understanding even if Luke may not have foreseen it. Plurality in biblical interpretation is partly due to misunderstandings resulting from our lack of relevant knowledge or of appropriate interpretative skills, partly due to human sin but *also* partly to do with the very structures of God's good creation. Interpretative pluralism is partly funded by the fact that God has created us as creatures who are finite and understand reality perspectivally. There would have been some pluralism in interpretation before the fall, as there will be in the new heavens and earth (Smith). Resurrected and sinless humans will still be finite and bring their cultural distinctiveness with them to the never-ending task of interpretation.

One crucial question concerns the connection required between authorial intention and later Christian appropriations of texts in different sociohistorical contexts. I maintain that we ought ordinarily to seek a recognizable organic relationship between the intentionality of a text and the variety of theological interpretations that emerge from reader engagements with it (*pace* Fowl). Thus, NT readings of the OT are usually connected at deep levels with the structures and trajectories of the original texts. Those deep structures are reread in the light of developments in salvation history that reconfigure the original texts and draw out some of the "surplus of meaning," but they do not do this, for the most part anyway, by sidestepping the structure or context of the original texts. Theological interpretations that run roughshod over authorial intention saw off the branch they are sitting on.

Christians can concede that different acts of reading are undertaken with different goals in mind and that theological interpretation is not the *only* goal a Bible-reader, even a Christian Bible-reader, may have. For instance, I may read Scripture in order to attempt a historical reconstruction of the events narrated, or to explore the gender relations encoded in the text. Such differing goals will yield different results and must be judged by criteria relevant to their goal. For the Christian, theological interpreta-tion *is* the supreme goal for Bible-reading, and it too has its own rules of assessment (canonical context, the Rule of Faith, the gospel, etc.). Faith will also guide Christians in discerning which other goals may be legitimate *subservient* Christian projects (e.g., discerning a text's redaction history) and which produce inappropriate ways of handling Holy Scripture (e.g., materialist interpretations).

See also Authorial Discourse Interpretation; Community, Interpretative; Meaning; Postmodernity and Biblical Interpretation; Reading; Text/Textuality

Bibliography

Aichele, G., et al., The Bible and Culture Collective. "Reader Response Criticism." Pages 20–69 in *The Postmodern Bible*, ed. E. Castelli et al. Yale University Press, 1995; Fish, S. *Is There a Text in This Class?* Harvard University Press, 1980; Fowl, S. "The Role of Authorial Intention in the Theological Interpretation of Scripture." Pages 71–87 in *Between Two Horizons*, ed. J. Green and M. Turner. Eerdmans, 2000; Fowl, S., and L. G. Jones. *Reading in Communion*. SPCK, 1991; Holland, N. *Poems in Persons*. W. W. Norton, 1973; Iser, W. *The Act of Reading*. Johns Hopkins University Press, 1978; Jauss, H. R. *Toward an Aesthetic of Reception*, trans. T. Bahti. University of Minnesota Press, 1982; Lundin, R., C. Walhout, and A. Thiselton. *The Promise of Hermeneutics*. Eerdmans, 1999; McKnight, E. "Reader Response Criticism." Pages 230–52 in *To Each Its Own Meaning*, ed. S. McKenzie and S. Hayes. Rev. ed. Westminster John Knox, 1999; idem. "Reader Response Criticism." Pages 370–73 in *Dictionary of Biblical Interpretation*, ed. J. Hayes. Abingdon, 1999; Meadowcroft, T. "Relevance as a Mediating Category in the Reading of Biblical Texts: Venturing beyond the Hermeneutical Circle." *JETS* 45 (2002): 611–27; Powell, M. A. *Chasing the Eastern Star*. Westminster John Knox, 2001; Ricoeur, P. "Metaphor and the Central Problem of Hermeneutics." In *Hermeneutics and the Human Sciences*, ed. J. B. Thompson. Cambridge University Press, 1981; Smith, J. K. A. *The Fall of Interpretation*. InterVarsity, 2000; Steinmetz, D. "The Superiority of Pre-Critical Exegesis." Pages 26–38 in *The Theological Interpretation of Scripture*, ed. S. Fowl. Blackwell, 1997; Stiver, D. *Theology after Ricoeur*. Westminster John Knox, 2001; Thiselton, A. *New Horizons in Hermeneutics*. HarperCollins, 1992; Treier, D. "The Superiority of Pre-Critical Exegesis? *Sic et non*." *TJ* 24 NS (2003): 77–103; Vanhoozer, K. *Is There a Meaning in This Text?* Zondervan/Apollos, 1998; Wall, R. "Reading the Bible from within Our Traditions." Pages 88–107 in *Between Two Horizons*, ed. J. Green and M. Turner. Eerdmans, 2000.

Robin Parry

Reading

Reading is ordinarily understood as one component of the technical skill of literacy. When it is so understood, the reader is seen as someone who exercises the skill of interpreting (decoding)

a written text, ideally in silence and without intermediary or audience. Readers may read with ease or with difficulty, at speed or slowly; but reading is, for those who understand it as part of literacy, a single skill with a single purpose—the extraction of meaning from a written text. This assimilation of reading to literacy also typically carries with it the implication that the only way to understand a written text is by applying the skill of literacy to it.

These are not, at first blush, very sensible ideas. It is better to think that reading does and should vary according to the nature of what is read. For Christians, the Bible is not the same kind of book as any other: it is God's word in a sense that no other book is, and this means that it must be read with different expectations and in a different way than is the case for any other book. Christians also cannot easily assent to the claim that literacy is necessary (or even preferred) as a means for coming to understand a written text. This is because only a tiny minority of Christians have been literate or are so now (though it is probable that premodern Christians, as also Jews, had higher literacy rates than most other groups). Also, there is no good reason to think that those without literacy understand the Bible less well than those who are literate.

Understanding reading simply as the exercise of literacy has not helped Christians to grasp what it is they ought to be doing when reading the Bible. Quite the contrary: when biblical reading is assimilated to the exercise of literacy, and when it comes to be thought that the Bible is essentially a printed book to be read by the literate in silence and in solitude, the almost inevitable result is a decline in Bible-reading as Christians should do it. Fortunately, the idea that reading is essentially a component of literacy has been challenged and modified by recent scholarship on the practice of reading, and by specifically Christian attention to the history of Christian thought about and practice of reading. This body of work, while certainly not free from the lively disagreements that characterize all specialized scholarship, does exhibit some deep-going agreements.

Among these agreements is the view that there is no clear-cut distinction between the textual habits of cultures in which most are literate and those in which few are. Large and complex bodies of literature can be transmitted from mouth to ear to memory over long periods of time without use of literacy's skills. The memory has capacities that often seem incredible to those educated in Western schools and universities during the last century or so. What is held in the memory can be retrieved therefrom, meditated upon, and produce understanding of a depth that at least rivals and often exceeds that available to the literate. It is also now clear that successive technologies for composing, producing, storing, and displaying texts (voice, memory, pen, paper, print, book, computer) tend to coexist rather than serially to displace other technologies. Ours is, no doubt, a culture in which the two dominant technologies of text-composition and text-transmission are, first, paper- and print-based; and, second, electronic. But it seems unlikely that one or the other will vanish, and both coexist with methods of communicating and understanding texts that are largely or entirely oral and aural. These last will likely become more important as literacy in the West decreases. Technology, then, does not determine how texts will be transmitted and understood.

This scholarship opens some space for attention to, and partial recovery of, what premodern Christians have said about reading in general and biblical reading in particular.

Reading of biblical texts is sometimes depicted in the Bible. Such depictions usually present an individual reading aloud to a group, as part of a public act of worship. This is followed by interpretation or exhortation so that those who have heard the reading may grasp its meaning (see Ezra's reading of "the Book of the Law of Moses" in Neh. 8, and Jesus' reading from Isa. 61 in Luke 4). Coming to understand the Bible in such a context requires literacy of almost no one; it does require capacity to hear, attend, consider, and recall on the part of listeners; and it does presuppose that the biblical text requires interpretation by a community.

The private, solitary, silent reading of a biblical (or any other) text is rarely depicted in the Bible, and even when it is, the account tends to conform to the model just mentioned. In Acts 8:26–40, for example, an Ethiopian is alone in his chariot reading from Isa. 53; Philip approaches and asks him whether he understands what he's reading. The Ethiopian says he does not, and that without guidance he cannot. Philip explains that this chapter is about Jesus; the Ethiopian is illuminated and is at once baptized by Philip. The episode begins with solitary reading that produces puzzlement and ends with understanding produced by a community of interpretation in the person of Philip. It is an implication of this way of understanding biblical reading that not all meanings of the biblical text are easily or directly accessible; some require communal guidance if they are to be grasped.

Christian theorists from late antiquity until the high Middle Ages wrote a good deal about scriptural reading, for which the standard Latin term is *lectio*. They were not, however, writing about the private exercise of the skill of literacy upon a printed book. They were writing about the repeated hearing of the Bible in the context of its exposition by a community of interpretation, the church, and about its memorization and repeated meditative consideration in order that its meanings should become increasingly apparent to the reader.

These premodern theorists took the Bible to be God's word and therefore fundamentally different from every other written text. This meant for them that the Bible had layers of meaning and an inexhaustible richness of content not found in any other text, and that reading it must take this into account. The text must be read and reread (heard and reheard), inscribed on the tablets of memory, meditated upon repeatedly like a cow chewing the cud (this image is everywhere in medieval works on reading). It must be incorporated into its readers. As this is increasingly done, they will be increasingly conformed to its meanings and thus to the will of God. The Bible must therefore be read with the knowledge and love of God always in mind.

Biblical reading so understood is a transformative spiritual discipline practiced by a community. All other reading (of literature, philosophy, science, and so on) is ancillary to it. Hearing, memorization, and repeated contemplation are more important to such reading than literacy, and this is because they issue in a moral relation between reader and text, a relation in which the text is the main agent and the reader a humble, patient, and reverential recipient of a gift.

See also Reader-Response Criticism

Bibliography

Carruthers, M. *The Book of Memory*. Cambridge University Press, 1990; Gavrilov, A. K. "Techniques of Reading in Classical Antiquity." *CQ* 47 (1997): 56–73; Goody, J. *The Interface between the Written and the Oral*. Cambridge University Press, 1987; Griffiths, P. *Religious Reading*. Oxford University Press, 1999; Illich, I. *In the Vineyard of the Text*. University of Chicago Press, 1993; Manguel, A. *A History of Reading*. Viking, 1996; Ong, W. *The Presence of the Word*. Yale University Press, 1967; Steiner, G. *Real Presences*. University of Chicago Press, 1989; Stock, B. *After Augustine*. University of Pennsylvania Press, 2001; idem. *Augustine the Reader*. Belknap, 1996; Vander Weele, M. "What Is Reading For?" *ChrLit* 52, no. 1 (2002): 57–83.

Paul J. Griffiths

Realism *See* Critical Realism; Semiotics

Redaction Criticism

Redaction criticism is a literary discipline that studies the way a biblical author/editor altered his sources to develop his unique theological message. The school is best known for NT studies but is utilized in OT research as well. For instance, G. von Rad used it in his Genesis commentary to ascertain the theological threads of what he called the Yahwist editor. In NT studies it is used primarily on the Synoptic Gospels.

Origins of the Movement

There were several precursors. In 1901 W. Wrede wrote *The Messianic Secret*, saying the author of Mark changed his sources to explain why the disciples failed to realize Jesus was Messiah during his life (he told those who began to grasp this not to tell anyone). In his Bampton Lectures of 1934, R. H. Lightfoot traced Mark's theological reworking of his sources. In *The Witness of Matthew and Mark to Christ* in 1944, N. B. Stonehouse studied the christological emphases of each. Yet the movement proper did not begin until the late 1940s as a result of weaknesses inherent in form criticism. That movement, begun in 1919, studied the individual pericopes of each Gospel to ascertain which aspects went back to the historical Jesus and which were the result of changes introduced by the early church during the oral period as the stories and sayings developed. However, the Gospels themselves were seen as the end result of an artificial scissors-and-paste compilation of the traditions. The evangelists were virtually ignored. Redaction criticism brought back the evangelists themselves as the creative compilers of their respective works. G. Bornkamm was the first with his 1948 article on the stilling of the storm, later incorporated into his *Tradition and Interpretation in Matthew* (1963). For him, Matthew has changed Mark's miracle story into a discipleship episode centering on the "little faith" journey of the disciples in light of the trials of the church (the boat). Then came H. Conzelmann, *Theology of Luke* (German, 1954) and W. Marxsen, *Mark the Evangelist* (German, 1956). Marxsen was the first to use the term *Redaktionsgeschichte* ("history of redaction" or editing as Mark called the church to flee the terrible events of the Jewish War, 66–70 CE). But Conzelmann is generally considered the more important work, arguing that Luke explained the "delay of the parousia" by replacing Mark's imminent eschatology with a salvation-historical scheme involving three stages—the time of Israel, the time of Jesus, and the time of the church. Thus the parousia is no longer the focus of Luke but is replaced by the timeless "kingdom of God" that is already here.

The Methodology Employed

In short, the student uses a Gospel synopsis and analyzes the passage by "reading horizontally" (comparing the way it is presented in other Gospels and noting the differences) and "reading vertically" (looking down the column to see how the author has composed the passage). Thus one may discover the writer's individual theological emphases (Blomberg, *Jesus*, 93). In so doing most critics assume the consensus view of source criticism, that Mark was the first Gospel and was used by Matthew and Luke along with Q (from the German *Quelle* [source], referring to a hypothetical document or oral tradition that contained the 250 verses with sayings of Jesus that are common to Matthew and Luke but missing from Mark). So redactional study is most relevant for Matthew and Luke and not as useful for Mark and John since we do not know their sources.

The goal of most such critics is to separate the tradition (inherited from their sources) from redaction (the changes made by the evangelist). This is accomplished by looking for several possible changes: (1) One may identify what has been added to the tradition (e.g., Matt. 14:28–32 adds Peter walking on the water to Mark's account of stilling the storm) or subtracted from it ("their hearts were hardened," omitted by Matthew from Mark 6:52), and then draw a theological conclusion (Peter as a model of "little faith" but also of the beginning of faith due to the presence of Jesus "the Son of God," in Matt. 14:33). (2) One may study the seams (transitions), introductions, and conclusions to ascertain how the author arranges the pericope (e.g., Matt. 9:35–38, where Jesus asks the disciples to pray for workers, while in 10:1–2 the disciples become the answers to their own prayer as the "workers" for "the harvest"). (3) One may observe changes in the arrangement of the material (e.g., Luke 6:20–26 has four beatitudes followed by four woes [cf. Matt. 5:3–12; they parallel each other exactly, showing that Luke is presenting a "reversal of roles" in which the poor will have everything and the rich nothing in the kingdom). (4) One may recognize changes in the setting or placement of a story (e.g., Mark 3:20–35 sandwiches the Beelzebub incident into the episode where Jesus' family wants to take him home, believing he has lost his mind

[stressing the extent of the opposition to Jesus], while Luke 11:14–26 has it much later, following the sayings on prayer [stressing the authority of Jesus]). (5) One may identify changes in the words used—this has to be done carefully, for in the past some scholars have assumed theological intent in every single difference, while in fact many changes are merely stylistic, so one must ask whether the terms have theological implications in their respective Gospels (e.g., "poor in spirit" in Matt. 5:3 stresses the spiritual aspect and "poor" in Luke 6:20 stresses the economic aspect of Jesus' original speech [which stressed both aspects]). (6) One may discover how two traditions are combined in a single episode (e.g., the temptation narratives, where Matthew and Luke combine Mark [Matt. 4:1–2; Luke 4:1–2] with Q [Matt. 4:3–11; Luke 4:3–13]). (7) One may see how the evangelist provides explanations for readers (e.g., Mark explaining Jewish customs for Gentile readers in 7:3–4, 11). (8) One may find changes in order to avoid misunderstanding (due to the possible implications of Mark 10:18, "Why do you call me good? . . . No one is good—except God alone," Matt. 19:17 alters it to "Why do you ask me about what is good? . . . There is only One who is good").

In the early decades of the movement, scholars assumed the theology was inherent in the changes alone, so they would examine only the immediate context to see what the changes added. Now, however, it is realized that theology is also contained in the tradition accepted, for the author chose to keep that portion intact. In the 1970s this began to be called "Composition Criticism" because the emphasis was no longer just on the redactional changes but on the composition as a whole. So now theology is determined to combine the micro- and macrolevels. The student studies not only how the change affects the immediate context, but also how it fits into the whole context and how that theological point is developed through the book as a whole. For instance, take the beatitudes and woes of Luke 6:20–26 and the "reversal of roles" theme inherent in it. At the microlevel, it adds a sense of social concern to the "Sermon on the Plain" in Luke 6:20–49. There is a distinct countercultural air about this sermon, with the switch from rich to poor in 20–26, the command to "love your enemies" in 27–36, the injunction to forgive rather than judge in 37–38 and to look to one's own sins rather than the sins of others in 41–42. At the macrolevel it is part of a major theme relating to material things and the poor in Luke (see 1:51–53; 3:8–14; 4:18–19;

6:20–26; 7:22; 9:3–5; 10:30–36; 11:39–42; 12:13–21, 22–34; 14:12–14, 21–24; 15:11–32; 16:1–14, 19–31; 18:18–25; 19:1–9, 12–27; 20:22–26; 21:1–4; 22:25–27). From this it is clear that the theme discovered in 6:20–26 is part of a major motif in the Gospel of Luke.

The Weaknesses of Redaction Criticism

The major problem with the discipline is its origins in a skeptical view of the historicity of the Gospels. Many practitioners are still controlled by form and tradition criticism, with an assumption that the Gospels are primarily the product of the early church and have only a minimal amount of historical data. So for them redaction means that the evangelist created material. However, expansion, omission, wording, and rearrangement are aspects of style; in and of themselves, they do not necessarily mean that the author is uninterested in history. This radical skepticism is fueled by a presupposition that theology must exclude history—claiming that if a writer is producing a theological point, that must involve a lack of interest in history. Yet there is no basis for such an assumption. It has long been realized that no one can study history without an interest in its implications for the current situation. In fact, the term "gospel" means not just "good news" but also (in its verb form) the proclamation of that good news for today. The Gospels in one sense are sermons about Jesus, or "history with a message." That does not require a lack of interest in what happened but rather the significance of what happened for the church (see Blomberg, *Reliability*).

Next, the vast majority bases their approach on the two-document hypothesis (Mark and Q being the tradition behind Matthew and Luke). Though it is the consensus position today, it is still hypothetical, and many assume Matthean priority, resulting in quite different decisions. Therefore, it may be best not to depend too much on source-critical discussions and simply center on the differences between the Gospels, Mark and John as well as Matthew and Mark.

Redaction critics have often been so focused on the differences that they have assumed that the theology flows entirely from the changes made to the traditions. However, the theology of the Gospels actually flows from the whole story, tradition as well as redaction, and the interaction within the whole work. The movement in Gospels study has been from redaction to composition to narrative criticism, more and more from the parts to the whole. The redactional changes are quite helpful as a control on how the evangelist has shaped his material, but the theological emphases come from studying the theological threads that are woven together to form the whole tapestry of the individual Gospel.

Scholars have also assumed that a major goal of Gospels research is to discover the *Sitz im Leben* (situation in life) or the community each Gospel is addressing. The problem is that the entire pursuit is based on a false premise, that each evangelist was writing for a small group of churches that belonged to their peculiar circle of ministry. But studies to that effect are very speculative, stemming from the assumption that the Gospels do not reflect the situation of Jesus' day but that of the evangelist's time. Bauckham has shown that this is not true to the situation. Scholars assume the Gospels are like the Epistles, addressing an individual community, but there is no evidence for such. Rather, they were written to the church as a whole, meant for wide distribution.

The Strengths of Redaction Criticism

Of all the schools of criticism in the last two centuries, none have done better at developing the theology of the individual Gospels. Yet it must be done with great sensitivity, lest the theological task be reduced to subjectivity and speculation. The key is not to make redactional analysis an end in itself but to blend it with other disciplines, especially narrative criticism. The latter deals with the text as a whole and acts as a control against the tendency of redaction criticism to center only on the parts. Narrative criticism considers the plot and setting, the atmosphere within which the evangelist tells his story. Yet redactional analysis corrects the error of narrative criticism, that the author no longer is present in his story. So together they enable the student to discover the theology of the whole (tradition and redaction taken together) as intended by the author/evangelist.

While some critics consider redaction criticism a thing of the past along with form and tradition criticism, replaced by narrative and reader-response approaches, many still recognize the value of redactional analysis. It provides greater accuracy in determining the theological emphases, for it tells us how the biblical author has used his sources, which parts he has accepted and which parts he has altered to highlight different aspects of what Christ said and did. The evangelists did not just gather and string together the traditions they received, but interpreted them and chose aspects that fit the theological nuances they wished to highlight.

Finally, redaction criticism properly construed is the friend rather than the enemy of historical investigation. There is no need for wholesale creation of sayings and events in the life of Jesus, for redactional analysis shows how each evangelist chose certain details to highlight and omitted other details to bring out their theological nuances. History and theology work together to produce the unique Gospels.

See also Form Criticism and the NT; Gospels; Narrative Criticism; Source Criticism

Bibliography

Bauckham, R. ed. *The Gospel for All Christians*. Eerdmans, 1997; Blomberg, C. *Historical Reliability of the Gospels*. InterVarsity, 1987; idem. *Jesus and the Gospels*. Broadman & Holman, 1997; Carson, D. A. "Redaction Criticism: On the Legitimacy and Illegitimacy of a Literary Tool." Pages 119–42 in *Scripture and Truth*, ed. D. A. Carson and J. Woodbridge. Zondervan, 1983; Kelber, W. "Redaction Criticism: On the Nature and Exposition of the Gospels." *PRSt* 6 (1979): 4–16; McKnight, S. *Interpreting the Synoptic Gospels*. Baker, 1988; Osborne, G. "The Evangelical and Redaction Criticism: Critique and Methodology." *JETS* 22 (1979): 305–22; idem. "Redaction Criticism." Pages 662–69 in *Dictionary of Jesus and the Gospels*, ed. J. Green, S. McKnight, and I. H. Marshall. InterVarsity, 1992; Perrin, N. *What Is Redaction Criticism?* Fortress, 1969; Stein, R. "Redaction Criticism (NT)." *ABD* 5:647–50; idem. "What Is Redaktionsgeschichte?" *JBL* 88 (1969): 45–56; Wenham, D., and S. Walton. *A Guide to the Gospels and Acts*. Vol. 1 of *Exploring the New Testament*. SPCK, 2001.

Grant R. Osborne

Reference *See* Critical Realism; Meaning

Relationship between the Testaments

"Old Testament" and "New Testament" are Christian terms that carry heavy theological connotations. They express a theology of a continuing purpose of God that runs through the history and religion of Israel as God's chosen people, on into the life and ministry of Jesus Christ and the community that he founded, the Christian church. They presuppose a single salvation history within which pre-Christian Israel represents the first and preliminary stage, with Jesus and his church the second, climactic stage, the time of fulfillment. The term "Testament" (an old-fashioned translation of the Greek *diathēkē*, more usually translated "covenant") speaks of the special relationship between God and his chosen people.

But the addition of "Old" and "New" suggests that the pre-Christian phase of that relationship has now been superseded by a new and (by implication) final phase. In it, that relationship is focused not on the Israelite nation but on the person of Jesus and those, of whatever nation, who have been called to follow him. Jeremiah's prophecy of a "new covenant" (Jer. 31:31–34) is taken up by Jesus' words at the Last Supper, "This cup is the new covenant in my blood" (Luke 22:20), and expounded in Heb. 8:7–13 by the claim that the "old covenant" is now past its sell-by date. To speak of OT and NT at all is thus to commit oneself to a distinctively Christian view of salvation history; it is little wonder that Jews object to this apparently dismissive way of describing the Hebrew Scriptures. In this article, which has as its subject the relationship between the two Testaments, it would be too cumbersome to abandon the familiar terminology, but it must be understood that it is written from a self-consciously Christian perspective.

Not all Christians have been happy with this takeover of the Hebrew Scriptures to be part of a single "Christian Bible." Ever since the Gnostic Marcion in the second century, there have been those who are hostile to or embarrassed by the OT, and who speak of the OT God as a stern and vengeful deity, unlike the loving God of Jesus. While today there are few theoretical Marcionites, there are many who in practice reflect his teaching, confining the reading of Scripture in public and in private almost entirely to the NT. (For a full study of the range of Christian attitudes to the relationship between the Testaments, see Baker.)

Among those who do acknowledge the two Testaments together as "Scripture," however, there are two fundamentally different approaches to assessing the nature and extent of their relationship. On the one hand, it is possible to take the Hebrew Scriptures as our starting point and to look for aspects of those Scriptures that have an inherently forward-looking character. This may be through explicit prediction of what is still to come or by displaying a provisionality that in itself cries out for future development in a new situation. This is an exegetical enterprise in which Jews and Christians can engage together, though they are likely to differ as to the nature of the fulfillments or extrapolations that are envisaged. But, on the other hand, we may note places in which the NT implicitly or explicitly draws on the OT, and trace elements of continuity and of discontinuity between the two phases of God's work and revelation. This is a more specifically Christian enterprise. The two enterprises are not at all the same, since many of the NT's uses of the OT are of passages that in themselves carry no clear forward-looking dimension. Their relevance to the Christian situation has been perceived not by objective exegesis of the original sense of the OT text, but by hindsight in the light of the new situation that Christ has brought. At times this "heuristic" use of the OT by the apostolic Christian writers appears arbitrary and even irresponsible, and it raises questions as to the theology of "fulfillment" that has given rise to it. At such points modern Western interpreters of the NT tend to become embarrassed and apologetic. This article aims to explore how far such embarrassment is justified.

NT Use of the OT

There are nearly four hundred direct quotations of the OT in the NT. Not all of them are introduced by explicit quotation formulas ("As it is written," etc.), and not all are in verbatim agreement with the wording of the OT text as we know it, but all are clearly deliberate citations of a specific OT text. That statistic is relatively uncontroversial. But there is less agreement on the incidence of less-formal allusions, places where the NT writer's language echoes or apparently refers to that of the OT, but without quoting it directly. For instance, the book of Revelation contains not a single formal quotation from the OT, yet its language and imagery are totally impregnated with that of Ezekiel, Daniel, and so on, and whole sections of the book are clearly modeled on familiar OT visions. There is an inevitable subjectivity about how deliberate or how significant an interpreter judges such echoes to be: how long is a piece of string? But a representative listing of allusions and verbal parallels, which errs on the side of caution, gives well over two thousand. (These figures draw on the lists of OT quotations and allusions printed at the back of the United Bible Societies' *Greek New Testament*.)

The majority of these quotations and allusions are to what were then the familiar Greek translations of the OT books, which we now know collectively as the Septuagint (LXX). This was only to be expected, just as present-day writers in English normally quote a known English version of the Bible rather than go back to the original languages. The LXX translators varied in their approach, some being excessively literal while others were quite free in their renderings, and this range is reflected in the NT quotations. Where the NT version differs from extant LXX texts, there are a number of possible explanations. The NT writer may be using a Greek version that differs from what we now have in the LXX. Or he may be giving his own version of the Hebrew or Aramaic text with which he was familiar and that was not represented in the LXX. Or he may not be intending to quote verbatim at all, but giving a free rendering of what he takes to be the sense of the OT passage (or, sometimes, a combination of related passages). This last option is important and needs further elaboration.

The ideal of "accurate" quotation is quite a modern one. It belongs to a culture in which written texts are easily accessible for reference. But in the NT world, in which literacy was perhaps no higher than 20 percent, a scroll of a single OT book, whether in Hebrew or Greek, was an expensive luxury, available to few apart from the Hebrew texts kept in the synagogues. It was also more inconvenient to consult than the compact, paged books we know, and there were no chapters and verses to guide readers through the scroll. The Scriptures were therefore known and experienced primarily through oral repetition and quoted normally from memory.

In a preliterate society oral memory can be much more accurate and extensive than we would expect in our literate world today. But there is the further question whether exact quotation was always intended, even if it could be achieved. The Aramaic targumim, which represent the traditional versions of the Hebrew Scriptures as presented in the synagogues, are often far from literal translations. At times they are significantly expanded with explanatory material, and sometimes they "angle" the text in the direction of a preferred interpretation. Several of the LXX translators do the same. This is not a matter of "distortion" of the sense of Scripture, but rather a self-conscious attempt to help the reader to grasp its full meaning, as this has been perceived by the person who is translating and interpreting it (and all translation is, necessarily, interpretation). Many of the variations from the known OT text that we find in NT quotations are of this nature.

To take a simple example, when Matt. 2:6 quotes Mic. 5:2 in relation to the birth of Jesus in Bethlehem, Micah's description of Bethlehem as "little among the clans of Judah" becomes in Matthew "by no means the least among the leaders of Judah" (AT). This apparent contradiction of Micah's description is Matthew's way of pointing out to his readers that Micah's prophecy has been fulfilled: the insignificant village has become "by no means the least" because it is now the birthplace of the Messiah. This is exactly what Micah was saying would happen; Matthew's wording neatly points out that now it has happened, not by an explanatory comment or footnote, but by a subtle adaptation of the quotation itself. This may not seem to follow our normal conventions for quotation. But anyone who listens carefully to the use of biblical quotations and allusions in the pulpit even today will notice that when the preacher is not actually reading directly from the open Bible, the quotation is often "angled" in such a way as to emphasize the interpretation which is being drawn from it. No one would dream of complaining that this is an illegitimate use of the biblical text—unless, of course, they disagree with the preacher's interpretation!

The modern reader needs to be prepared to recognize that simple verbatim quotation is not the only appropriate way to use Scripture, and to work within the communication strategies of the first-century world. Then the "embarrassing" uses of the OT by the NT become a fruitful field for uncovering the theological presuppositions of Christian leaders and thinkers in the apostolic period. Some examples from one of the more "creative" NT interpreters of the OT, Matthew, may help to illustrate this theme.

The Gospel of Matthew

An overriding theme of Matthew's Gospel is the fulfillment of the OT in the coming of Jesus the Messiah and in the new community that results.

Formal Quotations with Fulfillment Formula. This theme is most prominent in the formula repeated with minor variation ten times in the Gospel: "All this took place in order to fulfill what the Lord had spoken through the prophet." The OT texts that follow this formula vary considerably. Some are what we (but perhaps not all Jewish interpreters) would recognize as messianic: Matt. 2:6 (Mic. 5:2); 4:15–16 (Isa. 9:1–2); 8:17 (Isa. 53:4); 12:18–21 (Isa. 42:1–4); 21:5 (Zech. 9:9); others reveal a more "creative" approach.

Matthew 1:22–23 claims the fulfillment of Isa. 7:14 in the birth of Jesus from a virgin mother. But in its original context 7:14 belongs to a prediction of political events in the eighth century BCE. In that context it had already been fulfilled. The child was probably Isaiah's own son, Maher-Shalal-Hash-Baz, and the "young woman" (so the Hebrew) who bore him was not a virgin. But in the wider context of Isa. 7–11, this specific birth is taken up into the developing theme of a wonder-child, Immanuel ("God with us"), who transcends all normal expectations and who will be hailed as "Mighty God" (9:6). It was probably to reflect this wider dimension that the LXX translated the rare word for "young woman" as "virgin," and Matthew uses this earlier interpretation as his basis for claiming a second fulfillment of the prophecy on a quite different level from the first. The recognition that a single OT prophecy may be seen to have more than one level of fulfillment casts light on several surprising NT quotations.

Matthew 2:15 finds in Jesus' childhood refuge in Egypt a fulfillment of Hos. 11:1, "Out of Egypt I called my son." The "son" in Hosea is Israel, and the OT passage is not a prediction of the future but a reminiscence of the past event of the exodus. But for Matthew, Israel's status as "son of God" finds its ultimate embodiment in Jesus, who is God's Son in a much fuller sense (see below, on 4:1–11). Hosea's words thus point (even though Hosea himself had no such thought) beyond their immediate reference to a new exodus and a new and greater Son of God.

The quotation attributed to Jeremiah in Matt. 27:9–10 is in fact most closely parallel to Zech. 11:12–13 with its "thirty pieces of silver" thrown to the enigmatic "potter" in the house of the Lord. For Matthew, this prophecy of the rejected shepherd and his derisory wages is fulfilled in Judas's betrayal of Jesus and his subsequent return of the money to the temple, together with the buying of "the potter's field." But where does Jeremiah come in? Jeremiah was famous for his visit to the potter (Jer. 18:1–11), his use of a potter's jug to prophesy Judah's destruction in the Valley of Hinnom, the site of Aceldama, the "potter's field" (19:1–13), and for his own purchase of a field (32:6–15). Echoes of these passages are woven into Matthew's free rendering of Zech. 11:12–13, as well as into the narrative that leads up to it, and the whole composite quotation is attributed to the greater prophet Jeremiah. This is not simple quotation of a proof text, but the result of some very subtle and sophisticated reflection on a variety of prophetic texts, related by key words and woven together into a creative prophetic package in which Matthew could see the events of his day foreshadowed. What we might have expressed by means of footnotes and cross-references, he has achieved by a single pregnant "quotation" that demands imaginative exploration on the part of his readers. It is the sort of use of the OT that Jewish interpreters of the time would have found attractive and familiar, however much they might have disputed the specific application.

Typological Allusions. Such explicitly signaled quotations are only the tip of the iceberg. Among the many less-formal allusions to the OT, one prominent feature is what is often described as "typology," though definitions of this term have varied. It is used here to mean an NT writer's perception of models or foreshadowings of Jesus and his work in passages of the OT that in themselves have no predictive or forward-pointing intention. We have seen an example in Hos. 11:1, a reminiscence of the exodus, which Matthew sees "fulfilled" in Jesus. Again, a few examples must suffice.

Matthew 12:40 draws an explicit parallel between Jonah and Jesus: "As Jonah . . . , so the Son of Man . . ." The OT story of Jonah gave no hint of a future repetition, but Jesus makes the link on the basis not of the OT text itself but of a perceived parallel in his own experience. Yet it is not a simple repetition on the same level: rather, "something greater than Jonah is here" (Matt. 12:41 NRSV). The same formula is repeated in the next verse with regard to Solomon, and back in 12:6 Jesus has defended his authority to override legal convention with the observation that "something greater than the temple is here" (NRSV). Thus, in response to a challenge to justify his authority (12:38), Matthew's Jesus places himself in the succession of the prophets (Jonah), the kings (Solomon, the wise man), and the temple and its priesthood. Yet he does so not as merely recapitulating their role as mediators between God and his people but rather as "something greater" (12:41 NRSV). Typology thus takes the people and institutions of sacred history and traces not only a repetition in principle of what God has done in the past but also its fulfillment. The patterns of God's working in the OT have reached their climax in the coming of "something greater," in which/whom the various strands of OT authority and mediation are finally brought together.

The account of Jesus' testing in the wilderness (Matt. 4:1–11) focuses on three quotations from Deut. 6–8. This is Moses' speech reminding Israel of their experiences in the wilderness and the lessons it had been designed to teach them: see Deut. 8:2–5, culminating in the statement that "As a man disciplines his son, so [Yahweh] your God disciplines you." Now Jesus, who at his baptism has been declared "Son of God" (see the repetition of this title as the introduction to the devil's proposals in vv. 3 and 6), in his turn undergoes a wilderness testing, and takes to himself the lessons that God's "son" Israel should have learned. But where Israel failed to learn its lessons, and only partially succeeded in taking over the promised land, here is a "Son of God" who is fully in tune with his Father's will and whose mission will succeed. The typological identification of Jesus with Israel already presupposed in 2:15 ("Out of Egypt I called my son") is here more fully set out, again not simply as a repetition but as a climax. Here at last is the true Israel, and the new exodus spoken of by the prophets.

None of this could have been arrived at simply by an objective reading of the stories of Jonah and Solomon or of Israel's wilderness experience. But as Jesus' own awareness of his mission developed, and as his followers meditated on it, it was possible to perceive patterns running through God's earlier dealings with his people that were now coming together in one great climactic act of deliverance. Such typological perceptions come to the surface repeatedly in Matthew's story, and throughout the NT, coming to their climax in the argument of the Letter to the Hebrews—that in Jesus we have something even "better" than all that God's people have rightly celebrated with pride in their OT heritage.

Interpreters have often spoken of a *sensus plenior*, a "fuller meaning" in the OT texts, which the NT writers are able to perceive. Perhaps that is not the best way to put it. This new meaning is not something inherent in the OT texts themselves, so that any objective exegesis, Jewish or Christian, ought properly to perceive it. Rather, it is a new level of relevance, going beyond what the OT writer and the original readers could have perceived, which is now discovered by retrospective reflection in the light of NT events. Typology depends not so much on exegesis of the original meaning as on a theological hindsight informed by commitment to Christ as the climax of God's work of salvation. It proceeds from faith rather than from objective literary analysis.

Continuing Fulfillment. This concept of the repetition of God's work on a higher level perhaps explains also the fact recognized above that the NT writers, and particularly Matthew, seem able to find more than one point of fulfillment for a given OT prophecy (see above, on Matt. 1:22–23). For instance, prophecies of the destruction and desecration of the temple, already fulfilled in the sixth or the second century BCE, remain as pointers to an even more devastating event still to come (Matt. 23:38, echoing Jer. 12:7; 22:5; Matt. 24:15, echoing Dan. 11:31; 12:11).

Perhaps the clearest example of such multiple or continuing fulfillment of prophecy is seen in Matthew's various allusions to the vision of "one like a son of man" in Dan. 7:13–14. It is *already* fulfilled in Jesus' postresurrection authority (Matt. 28:18). It will be seen to be fulfilled in a variety of ways during the lifetime of Jesus' contemporaries (Matt. 10:23; 16:28; 24:30 with 34; 26:64). But it is also a model for describing the ultimate sovereignty of the Son of Man at "the renewal of all things" (19:28) and at the final judgment (25:31–34).

So, Christian interpretation has traditionally thought of OT prophetic oracles as pointing forward to a single identifiable "fulfillment." Yet it may be more appropriate to see the prophet as setting up a model that, even if specifically fulfilled in a given historical event or situation, remains as a continuing pointer to God's way of fulfilling his purposes of judgment and of blessing. Like the nonpredictive models that are the traditional province of typology, predictions too can have a continuing relevance as God's work moves forward toward its ultimate climax. In that ongoing process *the* climactic point is the coming of Jesus the Messiah, but there remains a "not yet" together with the "already" of Christian fulfillment. Since God does not change, neither do the principles of his working adumbrated in the OT and brought fully to light in the NT.

Jesus and God. The use of Dan. 7:13–14 in Matthew raises a significant issue in NT Christology. In Matt. 25:31–34 the Son of Man is "the King" acting as universal judge. In the OT these are the prerogatives of God himself, and indeed the wording of that vision includes also echoes of OT passages that speak of God himself as the judge (Joel 3:1–12; Zech. 14:5; Dan. 7:9–10, with the Ancient of Days sitting on the throne of judgment). The NT writers had become so used to thinking of Jesus as in the place of God that it seemed natural for them to apply to him passages that in the OT spoke of God. Thus, Malachi's prophecy of a forerunner for God's coming to judgment (Mal. 3:1; 4:5–6) is applied to John the Baptist as the herald of *Jesus'* coming (Matt. 11:10, 14). Jesus justifies the children's welcome to him by an OT text about the praise of *God* (Matt. 21:16; Ps. 8:2). He asserts the permanence of his own word in terms that recall what Isa. 40:8 said about God's word (Matt. 24:35).

In Matthew this tendency is relatively undeveloped; in Hebrews it is blatant. Hebrews 1:6, 10–12 simply applies to "the Son" OT texts about God the Creator (Deut. 32:43; Ps. 102:25–27),

and does not feel the need to explain. His way is eased by similar use of another quotation in 1:8–9, in which the OT text itself describes the king as "God" (Ps. 45:6–7). It is also eased by the fact that the Greek translation of "Yahweh" was *Kyrios*, the same title applied to Jesus as "Lord." It seems that early Christians were so convinced of the divinity of Jesus that they found it natural to equate the one "Lord" with the other, and so to apply to Christ what the OT said of Yahweh (cf. Rom. 10:9–13).

A Theology of Fulfillment

Our study of Matthew has illustrated some significant features of NT use of the OT, and similar examples could have been drawn from many parts of the NT; but it remains to discuss their theological implications.

Continuity. Clearly, Marcion was quite wrong. The NT is full of the OT. It takes over the OT writers' understanding of God and his ways, and reasserts their ethical and spiritual norms. Jesus sums up the essential relationship in the words "not to abolish them but to fulfill them" (Matt. 5:17). The careful drawing of connecting lines between the OT and the Christian situation, not only in terms of specific predictions fulfilled but also in a more far-reaching network of typological interpretation, testifies to an overriding sense of continuity. The new covenant established in Christ is understood precisely as the successor to the old covenant under Moses, not as its repudiation. It is the next, and final, phase of the saving purpose of the same covenant God.

Discontinuity. But the covenant is *new*; Jeremiah had said it "will not be like the covenant that I made with their ancestors" (Jer. 31:32 NRSV). Things are going to be different. Not only is there a pervading sense of climax, of "something greater" about the new as compared with the old. There are also elements of the old covenant that will no longer apply. As Heb. 8:7–13 argues, the coming of the new means the pensioning off of the old. It has served its purpose and may now pass into honorable retirement.

The most obvious (and most uncontroversial) example of this discontinuity is the abandonment of the whole sacrificial system that was so central to the old covenant. But Jesus' illustrations of what it means to "fulfill the law" in Matt. 5:17–48 indicate that not only the ceremonial aspects of the law need to be rethought. The "greater righteousness" set out in that passage moves away from a legalistic concern with keeping rules and regulations to a more far-reaching ideal of being "perfect . . . as your heavenly Father is perfect." Paul rejoices in being no longer "under the law" (Rom. 8:2; Gal. 4:21; 5:1–18), which was our custodian to lead us to Christ (3:24), who is himself "the end of the law" (Rom. 10:4).

The focus has thus moved from a written code to a person, Jesus the Messiah; in relationship with him rather than in membership of a law-based community, God's purpose of salvation is now being fulfilled. This means that the people of God is no longer to be defined in terms of the national community of Israel, but will embrace people of all nations who have become disciples of Jesus the Messiah (Matt. 28:18–20). The change that has taken place, and the complementary elements of continuity and discontinuity that it involves, are explained in Paul's famous allegory of the olive tree in Rom. 11:17–24. Some branches of the olive tree (Israel) have been broken off because of unbelief, while branches from a wild olive tree (the Gentiles) have been grafted in. But it remains the same olive tree, and the broken-off branches may yet be regrafted into the parent stock "if they do not persist in unbelief." Thus, by the amazing (and horticulturally impossible!) providence of God, "all Israel will be saved" (11:26), not now as an exclusive community of the descendants of Abraham, but as a worldwide community of all who by faith have become Abraham's children (Rom. 4).

Supersessionism. The Letter to the Hebrews sets out an extended comparison of all that was best in the old covenant with the "better" things that have now taken their place with the coming of Christ. Its theology is often described as "supersessionist": Jesus supersedes the OT, his church supersedes Israel. Such language must be used with care; its potential misuse to fuel anti-Jewish prejudice is clear. The more positive term "fulfillment" is more typical of the NT perspective. For all his dismissal of aspects of the old covenant (especially its priesthood and sacrifices) as no longer relevant, the writer of Hebrews is second to none in his love for the OT and his desire to do justice to its role in the ongoing purpose of God. The question is how its undoubtedly central role in God's revelation of himself should now be taken forward.

By the first century CE the religion of the OT had come to a parting of the ways. After the destruction of the temple in 70 CE and the consequent cessation of sacrifice, it could not continue as it had been. Two contrasting visions emerged, each in their own way equally a development away from and yet a "fulfillment" of the traditional religion of Israel. On the one hand, what we call rabbinic Judaism developed a new law-based spirituality that remained largely within the ethnic boundaries of Israel. On the other hand, Christianity found the way forward in a personal focus on Jesus the Messiah, which opened the riches of Israel's tradition to a worldwide community of faith. Each was a new way of religion, yet each was organically related to the OT, out of which it sprang. Each had a new set of religious texts to supplement the Hebrew Scriptures: on the one hand, the rich expansion of Talmud and midrash; on the other, the Christian NT. Modern Judaism and Christianity are each in their different ways "supersessions" of the OT.

A Move away from Literal Fulfillment. Three books published over a forty-year period and from different theological perspectives form an interesting and significant trilogy on the NT adaptation of OT images. R. J. McKelvey, *The New Temple* (1969), traces the NT concept of Jesus and his people as constituting "something greater than the temple," which renders the building in Jerusalem theologically redundant. W. D. Davies, *The Gospel and the Land* (1974), shows how NT writers systematically transfer OT ideals and prophecies concerning the literal land of Israel to a nonterritorial and international people of God. P. W. L. Walker, *Jesus and the Holy City* (1996), demonstrates how the NT writers, following the lead of Jesus himself, see no future for the literal city as the center of God's purposes, but rather look for a new Jerusalem. There is a consistency about this aspect of NT biblical interpretation that Christians must not ignore in favor of a "Christian Zionism" that reads the OT as if nothing has changed with the coming of Jesus.

See also Anti-Semitism; Intertextuality; Jewish-Christian Dialogue; Jewish Exegesis; Targum; Translation; Typology

Bibliography

Baker, D. L. *Two Testaments, One Bible*. InterVarsity, 1976; Beale, G., ed. *The Right Doctrine from the Wrong Texts?* Baker, 1994; Carson, D. A., and H. G. M. Williamson, eds. *It Is Written*. Cambridge University Press, 1988; Davies, W. D. *The Gospel and the Land*. University of California Press, 1974; Ellis, E. E. *Paul's Use of the Old Testament*. 1957. Baker, 1981; idem. *The Old Testament in Early Christianity*. Mohr, 1991. Reprint, Baker, 1992; Evans, C. A., ed. *The Interpretation of Scripture in Early Judaism and Christianity*. Sheffield Academic Press, 2000; Evans, C. A., and J. Sanders, eds. *Early Christian Interpretation of the Scriptures of Israel*. Sheffield Academic Press, 1997; France, R. T. *Jesus and the Old Testament*. Tyndale, 1971; Goppelt, L. *Typos*. Eerdmans, 1982; Hanson, A. *The Living Ut-

terances of God. Darton, Longman & Todd, 1983; Hawthorne, G., and O. Betz, eds. *Tradition and Interpretation in the New Testament.* Eerdmans, 1987; Hays, R. *Echoes of Scripture in the Letters of Paul.* Yale University Press, 1989; Juel, D. *Messianic Exegesis.* Fortress, 1988; Lindars, B. *New Testament Apologetic.* SCM, 1961; Longenecker, R. *Biblical Exegesis in the Apostolic Period.* Eerdmans, 1975; McKelvey, R. J. *The New Temple.* Oxford University Press, 1969; Moo, D. *The Old Testament in the Gospel Passion Narratives.* Almond, 1983; Moyise, S., ed. *The Old Testament in the New Testament.* Sheffield Academic Press, 2000; Satterthwaite, P., et al., eds. *The Lord's Anointed.* Baker, 1995; Walker, P. W. L. *Jesus and the Holy City.* Eerdmans, 1996.

R. T. France

Relevance Theory *See* Language, Linguistics; Translation

Religion

"Religion" is a term of art now deeply woven into the fabric of our theological and political thought. This is perhaps especially true in the United States, where the term is enshrined in the country's Bill of Rights and therefore also in the jargon of legislative, bureaucratic, and judicial procedures. The First Amendment guarantees freedom of religion (or at least that Congress shall neither establish it nor prevent its free exercise). The IRS must often decide whether an institution is sufficiently religious to be granted tax privileges. And, most obviously, the state and federal courts must often rule as to whether some belief or practice is or is not religious.

Christians, too, are now likely automatically and naturally to think of themselves as religious people—people whose religion is Christianity. The same is true, mutatis mutandis, of Jews and Judaism, Buddhists and Buddhism, and so on. This kind of talk suggests that "religion" picks out a type of which there are many tokens such as Christianity, just like "currency" is a type whose tokens are dollars, pounds, yen, and so on. However, there is fairly widespread agreement about what makes it reasonable to say that dollars and deutsche marks are tokens of the same type (and about what type they are a token of). But there is much less about what makes it reasonable to say that Islam and Buddhism are tokens of the same type (and about what type they are a token of). This is why there are few impassioned arguments about whether something is or is not a currency, but many about whether something is or is not a religion and even more about whether some action, event, or belief does or does not merit the label "religious."

At present there is no broad or deep agreement—either among those who would call themselves religious or among those who would not—about what the category "religion" should be taken to embrace. Disagreements about these things are in fact among the liveliest sources of difficulty in public life, both nationally and internationally. It is also the case that "religion" has not historically been of much importance to Christian self-understanding, and that the importance it did have before the fifteenth century is in many respects at odds with that it has now. A little history will explain both points.

The History of "Religion"

The Latin word *religio,* from which comes "religion," was not an especially important term for pre-Christian thinkers who used that language, and there is no single Greek word for which it is the obvious translation. This lack of importance is reflected, too, in early Christian literature. Jerome's fourth-century Latin version of the NT, for instance—the Vulgate which, with some revisions, was the standard text for Western Christians for a thousand years—uses *religio* and its derivatives only eight times (Acts 2:5; 10:2; 13:50; 26:5; Col. 2:18; James 1:26–27), rendering a number of different Greek words thereby. The word is simply not an important part of the biblical lexicon, and this is evident, too, in the decisions made by early translators of the Bible into English. The King James Version (1611), for instance, uses "religion" or "religious" only seven times in translating the NT from Greek (Acts 13:43; 26:5; Gal. 1:13–14; James 1:26–27), and for three different Greek terms (not always the same ones that Jerome chose to render with *religio*).

Christians sometimes used the term in late antiquity. Augustine, for instance, gave detailed attention to it at the end of the fourth century in his work *De vera religione (On True Religion),* and occasionally in other works as well. For him, *religio* meant worship, the patterns of action by which, in public, we self-consciously turn ourselves toward God in homage and praise. There could, he thought, be a right and proper ("true") way of worshipping God, just as there could be improper and damnable ("false") ways of doing so; and so there could be a true and many false "religions." Since Augustine was a Catholic Christian, he also thought that Catholic worship was, on the whole, identical with true religion; and that, although true religion (proper public and communal worship) was not found only within the bounds of the Catholic Church, it was found preeminently and most perfectly there.

This equation of religion with public and communal worship was not unique to Augustine (he adopted its essentials from Cicero). It was almost standard in the pre-Christian Mediterranean world, and it became the ordinary understanding of *religio* among the Christians of late antiquity who thought and wrote in Latin. This understanding of the word is evident, too, in the etymology of *religio* most commonly given by Latin-using intellectuals (Christian and otherwise) in late antiquity. They derived *religio* from *re + ligare*, "to bind back," or "to rebind," meaning to reestablish by worship a lost or broken intimacy between God and worshippers. There are other etymologies, defended by a minority both ancient and modern, the most interesting of which derives *religio* from *re + legere*, "to reread"; but this etymology has entered less deeply into the soul of the West.

Western Christians from the fourth century onward had little occasion to think or write about things we now usually call religions. Islam did not come into existence until the seventh century, and until the Renaissance, Christians most often thought of it as a Christian heresy rather than a non-Christian religion. The religions of India, China, Japan, Africa, and America were effectively unknown until the sixteenth century; and Judaism, in spite of the many lively Jewish communities in Europe, was a topic of interest to Christians largely as a precursor to Christianity, a *praeparatio evangelica*. So Christians rarely, if ever, thought of Christianity as one religion among many: the idea that there is a type called "religion" of which there are many tokens did not gain much currency until the sixteenth century. It is mostly a modern invention.

Insofar as there was a standard use of *religio* in Europe between the effective end of Roman hegemony in the fifth century and the cataclysm of the Reformation in the sixteenth, it was to denote the activities and members of the monastic orders. These were typically called "religious orders," and their members were simply "the religious." This usage has survived, in somewhat attenuated form, in the Catholic Church, where it is possible still to hear people speak of "the religious life" and mean by it life within a vowed monastic order.

Modern (post-Reformation) understandings of religion differ from these premodern uses most dramatically in that they see religion exactly as a type of which there are many tokens. One influence upon the acceptance of this idea was the pressing necessity in the seventeenth century to create political forms of life in Europe that could peacefully accommodate a wide variety of Christian groups. These groups had incompatible understandings of what it means to be a Christian, and often a deep hatred of one another. The Thirty Years' War in Europe (1618–48) and the Civil War in England (1642–48), in which such differences showed themselves clearly in large-scale and long-lived violence, made it clear that the political forms that had served Europe fairly well for the preceding millennium would no longer do. Any new ones would have to find a way of dealing with the violent splintering of Christendom brought about by the Reformation.

The political solutions that emerged were of two kinds. The first affirmed the idea that a sovereign state could and should accommodate only one Christian group, and that one's religion (now it began commonly to be called that) should therefore be determined by geography, by where one happened to live. Calvin's Geneva provides one instance of this solution, as does the English settlement of 1688. Both use the idea that there are many religions, and that the state should establish and give special privileges to one among them. The second kind of political resolution preferred the idea that the state should be neutral with respect to religion (which usually meant neutral with respect to the various brands of Protestant Christianity; Jews and Catholics were typically beyond the pale, and Buddhists and Muslims did not enter into consideration). The passage of the First Amendment to the American Constitution in 1791 provides a paradigm here. This second kind of political resolution, like the first, required (usually in quite explicit terms) the view that religion is a type with many tokens—although in all these cases "religion" had Protestant Christianity as its ideal type.

But it was not only the division of Christianity into many different and often warring "religions" in the sixteenth and seventeenth centuries that contributed to the idea that religion is a type with many tokens. Almost equally important was the vast increase in European knowledge of the history, languages, and practices of non-European civilizations. Beginning in the fifteenth century (and increasing almost exponentially in the sixteenth and seventeenth), reports of the habits and practices of the Indians, the Chinese, the Japanese, and the inhabitants of Meso-America began to be available to the literati of Europe. Among these early reports, Catholic missionaries wrote the most extensive ones for the use of the church in its efforts to propagate itself. But these were soon followed by work sponsored by the European states with interests in empire-building, first the Portuguese, Spanish, and Dutch, and later the English and French. By the seventeenth century, grammars and lexicons of hitherto exotic and unknown languages (Sanskrit, Chinese) began to become available, and throughout the eighteenth and nineteenth centuries works in these languages were translated in ever-increasing numbers into those of Europe.

Much of the information gathered in these ways seemed to European intellectuals, Christian and otherwise, to reveal forms of life and patterns of belief both deeply like and importantly unlike Christian forms and patterns. The Indians wrote hymns and prayers to many gods, and they seemed to worship images and statues of them; the Chinese had temples, sacred works, and a highly developed ritual system; and so on. It began to seem natural to European historians, philosophers, and theologians to think of these forms of life as the religions of India and China, and also to think of Christianity as the religion of Europe. Nicholas of Cusa in the fifteenth century is perhaps the first Christian thinker to approach this view. It was then not difficult to move to the more abstract theoretical view that there is a type called religion of which there are many tokens. This was effectively the standard position among Christians by the eighteenth century.

But here again "religion" meant "things like (mostly Protestant) Christianity." The likeness often became quite strained. Yet the controlling power of the paradigm case can be seen clearly in the endless nineteenth- and early-twentieth-century debates about whether such things as Buddhism (no God?) or State Shinto (the Japanese Emperor as God and no theology?) are really religions—for they really are not much like Christianity. Such resolutely anti-Christian figures as David Hume (in the *Natural History of Religion*, 1757) or quasi-Christian thinkers as Immanuel Kant (in *Religion within the Bounds of Reason Alone*, 1793) and G. W. F. Hegel (in *Lectures on the Philosophy of Religion*, first delivered in 1821) analyzed "religion." Yet they did so by a process of abstraction from features of Protestant Christianity.

Contemporary Difficulties about "Religion"

"Religion," as should now be evident, is a term of art fraught with difficulties. For non-Christians, and especially for those who must administer states whose public life is ordered around the idea that there is a multiplicity of religions, what

is needed is an understanding of religion that will discriminate the religious from the nonreligious. This needs to be done without appealing only to the particulars of Christianity. This continues to prove exceedingly difficult, as a glance at U.S. Supreme Court rulings on the religion clauses of the First Amendment will abundantly show.

For scholars of religion, what is wanted is an understanding of religion that is theologically neutral, and that will nonetheless be sufficiently substantive and interesting to make possible the development of an intellectual discipline. The historian of religion Jonathan Z. Smith puts the matter clearly: "'Religion,'" he writes, "is not a native term; it is a term created by scholars for their intellectual purposes and therefore is theirs to define. It is a second-order generic concept that plays the same role in establishing a disciplinary horizon that a concept such as 'language' plays in linguistics or 'culture' plays in anthropology. There can be no disciplined study of religion without such a horizon" (281–82). Smith might have added, though he does not, that such a horizon is, as a matter of fact, largely lacking. Its lack explains why the scholarly study of religion shows one of two tendencies: to slip back into theology, which it was founded to avoid; or to devolve into anthropology and cultural studies.

For Christians, too, the term is deeply problematic. Thinking of Christianity as a religion almost inescapably tends, given the history just sketched, to carry with it the implication that Christianity is a species of a genus. Hence, this also implies that it is in some significant respects on a par with other "religions" such as Islam or Buddhism. This claim is rightly seen by many Christians as an offense against Christianity's self-understanding as a sui generis phenomenon. They count themselves as the community of those gathered in public worship of the triune God, responsive in their worship to the incarnation, death, and resurrection of the Second Person of that triune God as Jesus the Christ. On this view what is significant about Christianity is not what it shares with the religions (in most of the ordinary understandings of that term), but precisely what it does not. One version of this point can be seen in John Wycliffe's fourteenth-century objections to calling Christianity a religion (discussed in Despland 139–42). A more sophisticated one is argued by Karl Barth in his *Church Dogmatics*, who identifies religion (and Christianity insofar as it is a religion) with human piety. He opposes piety to God's revelatory action, which has picked out the Christian religion (and perhaps also its

Jewish progenitor) for transfiguration into truth, but which has done so not because but in spite of Christianity's religiosity.

Given all these difficulties, it may reasonably be doubted that a concept of religion usable for Christian thought can be salvaged. One is scarcely needed for biblical exegesis, and its introduction into Christian theological thought tends to create more problems than it solves. The usual premodern antonym of *religio* is *superstitio* (and its close relative, *impietas*). On this understanding, there are not many religions: there is only (true) religion and its simulacra, which are all characterized by superstitious impieties of various kinds. This is likely to prove a more productive understanding for Christian thought than the problematic modern synthesis. It leaves open and in fact makes pressing the vital question of whether the church's worship is the only place piety is to be found. And it offers for consideration, as well, the even more fundamental question of how much of what the church itself does is true religion.

Bibliography

Augustine. *De vera religione/On True Religion*. Composed in the 380s, trans. J. H. S. Burleigh. LCC 6. Westminster, 1953; Barth, K. "God's Revelation as the Sublation of Religion." Section 17 (in part I/2) of *Church Dogmatics*, trans. G. Bromiley. T&T Clark, 1982; Cicero. *De natura deorum/On the Nature of the Gods*, ed. and trans. H. Rackham. LCL 268. Harvard University Press, 1994; Crawford, R. *What Is Religion?* Routledge, 2002; Despland, M. *La religion en Occident*. Éditions Fides, 1979. Gothóni, R. "Religio and Superstitio Reconsidered." *Archiv für Religionspsychologie* 21 (1994): 37–46; Harrison, P. *"Religion" and the Religions in the English Enlightenment*. Cambridge University Press, 1990; Hegel, G. W. F. *Lectures on the Philosophy of Religion*. First delivered in 1821. Translated (from the 1827 version) by R. F. Brown et al., as *Hegel: Lectures on the Philosophy of Religion*. University of California Press, 1988; Hume, D. *The Natural History of Religion*. 1757. In Hume, *Four Dissertations*. Thoemmes, 1995 (facsimile ed. of the first printing); Kant, I. *Religion within the Bounds of Mere Reason*. 1793, trans. G. di Giovanni (from the 1794 ed.), in *Immanuel Kant: Religion and Rational Theology*. Cambridge University Press, 1996; Lash, N. *The Beginning and the End of "Religion."* Cambridge University Press, 1996; Nicholas of Cusa. *De pace fidei/The Peace of Faith*. Composed in 1453, trans. J. Hopkins. In *Nicholas of Cusa's De pace fidei and Cribratio Alkorani*. 2d ed. Banning Press, 1994; Smith, J. "Religion, Religions, Religious." Pages 269–84 in *Critical Terms for Religious Studies*, ed. M. C. Taylor. University of Chicago Press, 1998; Ward, G. *True Religion*. Blackwell, 2003.

Paul J. Griffiths

Resurrection Narratives

Each of the four canonical Gospels (though not, significantly, the various noncanonical writings sometimes called "gospels," such as Thomas) concludes with stories about the discovery of the empty tomb and of Jesus' appearances to his followers. There is also a brief further mention at the start of Acts, and a summary statement, which must be seen in parallel with the other accounts, in 1 Cor. 15:3–8. These stories possess certain features making it more or less certain that, though they were written down as part of the Gospels a generation or so after the events, they are not late inventions. Instead, they likely go back largely unaltered, apart from a light editorial touch, to the quite early oral memory of the first disciples.

First, the portrait of Jesus is extraordinary and unprecedented. Despite the strong background presence of Dan. 12:3, Jesus is not described as "shining like a star," but appears initially as an ordinary human being. However, even in those accounts (especially in Luke and John), which insist that he is real, physical, and capable of being touched, breaking bread, cooking breakfast, and eating fish, there is something strange about him. He is not immediately recognized; he can come and go at will through locked doors; he vanishes into thin air, and finally ascends into heaven.

Second, the stories are remarkably free of OT quotation, allusion, and echo. Whereas the accounts of Jesus' entry into Jerusalem through to his death are full of interpretative biblical material, the resurrection stories are almost entirely empty of it. They read not as narratives that have been mulled over in the light of sustained scriptural reflection (which was already sophisticated by Paul's day) but as breathless and unreflective.

Third, nobody inventing such stories would have allowed women pride of place, since women were not regarded as credible witnesses in that world. The formal, stylized account in 1 Cor. 15 has carefully removed them.

Fourth, in all other early Christian writings (and a good deal of later liturgy and hymnody), the connection is regularly made between Jesus' resurrection and that of Christians. But the resurrection narratives themselves never mention this. Instead, they emphasize that a new stage has opened in God's purposes, which the disciples must carry forward.

All this means that the stories are to be taken seriously as extremely early memories of what happened at Easter. They make sense as the origin of the later, developed theology we find in Paul and elsewhere. But they cannot be explained as the back-projection of such developed thought—not least because all four accounts share all these features while being extremely unlike in other ways, so as to make it difficult to reconstruct the detail of the events. Even when they tell the same story, there is remarkably little overlap of words. The authors had certainly not colluded in making up a story and sticking to it.

The question of how the present narratives came to be written has become bogged down in the debate as to whether the stories of the empty tomb and those of the appearances of Jesus can be separated, and if so, whether one is primary and the other secondary and separate. Various theories have been advanced as to how the accounts might have grown up in response to needs and beliefs in the church. However, historical investigation of the rise of resurrection belief indicates that both the empty tomb and the appearances were necessary for that belief to begin and to be sustained. If the tomb had been found empty but Jesus had not appeared, it would have been assumed that someone had taken the body. If people had reported appearances of Jesus but his body had still been in the tomb, the disciples would have believed they had seen a ghost or a vision, such things being well known in their world. Only the combination—missing body plus appearing Jesus—would produce the early Christian belief. This makes it intrinsically unlikely that the stories would have developed with only one of these elements, and the other one becoming attached at a later stage.

Mark's resurrection account has almost certainly been cut short. Many have argued that he did indeed conclude his Gospel at 16:8, but there are good reasons to suppose that it originally continued beyond that (vv. 9–20 as we now have them are later attempts to fill in the gap). Mark has repeatedly stressed that Jesus will die and be raised; now, after a chapter on Jesus' death, he has written a chapter on the resurrection, of which we only have the first part.

Matthew's account (whose ending may perhaps reflect what stood originally in Mark) has the disciples go to Galilee, where they meet Jesus on a mountain and are commissioned to be witnesses of his rule on earth and in heaven.

Luke's account highlights the incomparable story of the disciples on the road to Emmaus, whose hearts burn within them while Jesus, incognito, expounds the Scriptures to them. Then they recognize him as he breaks bread. Luke's story, continuing in Acts, has Jesus commission the disciples to be his witnesses in all the world, in the power of the Spirit.

John 20 corresponds broadly to these, emphasizing that Easter is the first day of the week (20:1, 19) and hence the beginning of the new creation. The disciples are to share in this new creation by being equipped with the Spirit and sent into the world as Jesus was sent to Israel (20:19–22). There are vivid portraits of Jesus' meeting with Mary Magdalene and Thomas. In John 21, it is Peter's turn, with a lengthy exchange in which Jesus both forgives and recommissions Peter following his triple denial.

In all these stories, different though they are, the emphasis is the same. With Easter, God's new creation has begun; Jesus' followers are to be its agents, not merely its beneficiaries. The stories, clearly and often artlessly recounting the extraordinary memories of the first Easter itself, are told in such a way as to lay the foundation for the continuing witness and life of the church.

Bibliography

Alsup, J. *The Post-Resurrection Stories of the Gospel Tradition.* Calwer, 1975; Catchpole, D. *Resurrection People.* Darton, Longman & Todd, 2000; Dodd, C. H. "The Appearances of the Risen Christ." Pages 9–35 in *Studies in the Gospels,* ed. D. E. Nineham. Blackwell, 1967; Evans, C. F. *Resurrection and the New Testament.* SCM, 1970; Fuller, R. H. *The Formation of the Resurrection Narratives.* Macmillan, 1971; Lüdemann, G. *The Resurrection of Jesus.* SCM, 1994; McDonald, J. I. H. *The Resurrection.* SPCK, 1989; Moule, C. F. D., ed. *The Significance of the Message of the Resurrection for Faith in Jesus Christ.* SCM, 1968; Wright, N. T. *The Resurrection of the Son of God.* Fortress, 2003.

N. T. Wright

Resurrection of the Dead

In ancient pagan or Jewish thought, "resurrection" was never a synonym (as it often is today) for "life after death." It always denoted the idea that people once dead could subsequently be raised to new bodily life. This was regarded as ridiculous in ancient worldviews, as in modern ones. From Homer and Aeschylus to Plato and Pliny, pagan writers glanced at the idea, only to dismiss it with scorn. The discovery that dead people stay dead was not an achievement of modern science.

But in Second Temple Judaism, something different happened. Key passages like Dan. 12 and 2 Macc. 7, written in a context of persecution and martyrdom, built on the older celebration of Yahweh as Creator and Judge, and on ancient

Israel's insistence on the essential goodness of the material universe. Thereby they affirmed that all the dead, and especially those who had died in loyalty to God and his law, would be raised again. Since this belief encouraged zealous resistance to tyranny, it is not surprising that it was embraced and expounded by the Pharisees, a popular-level pressure-group insisting on law-based reforms. It was rejected by the Sadducees, the Jerusalem-based aristocracy. The rabbis (successors to the Pharisees) continued to discuss the coming resurrection as part of their vision of the promised "age to come."

Belief in resurrection, though, was not a major element in their thinking—just as Jesus himself did not say much about it, with only occasional mentions in the Gospels apart from the one head-on discussion with the Sadducees (Mark 12:18–27 et par.). Nor is it clear within Jewish thought whether resurrection will mean a return to a body identical with the present one, or transformation into something different (a shining star, for instance). In these and other respects, the early Christian belief in resurrection marked a significant mutation in the Jewish belief.

Resurrection took center stage and would involve the transformation of the present body into a new type of physicality, incapable of corruption (and hence immortal; "immortality" need not mean, and as used in 1 Cor. 15:52–54 does not mean, "disembodied immortality"). Moreover, "resurrection" was no longer simply a large-scale, last-minute future event. It had already happened in one instance, that of Jesus himself, an event to be repeated at the last for all his people (1 Cor. 15:23).

The early Christian belief in future resurrection, then, was based on Jesus' own resurrection, which they rightly saw as an event within history, bringing to birth God's future world in advance of its full appearing. Paul drew out the significance of this, not least in terms of the renewal and redemption of the entire cosmos (Rom. 8:18–25). He understood baptism in terms of dying and rising with Christ, so that the Christian ethic consists not of rule-keeping from within the old creation, but of learning in the present to live the life that will characterize God's new creation (6:1–11; 1 Cor. 6:12–20).

All this generates a view of the ultimate future with which the church has struggled to come to terms. The early fathers insisted on the bodiliness of the future life over against the spiritualizations of dualistic Gnosticism. Resurrection posed a threat to paganism, not least to empire,

a threat that Gnosticism toned down completely. Resurrection, and the consequent theology and spirituality, have remained central in the Eastern Orthodox churches.

But in the Roman Catholic West, and in the churches of the Reformation, resurrection ceased to play a major role. Great theologians like Bernard, Thomas Aquinas, Luther, and Calvin all emphasized the bodily resurrection of Jesus and the future resurrection of believers. But the massive emphasis on Jesus' death as the means of salvation, and the spirituality of passion-devotion that it engendered, pushed resurrection out of the frame. The development of an "equal and opposite" view of heaven and hell made it difficult to see what ultimate bodily resurrection might mean. What we miss in this period is the robust NT sense of renewed heavens and earth, of God's kingdom coming, and of Jesus' saving sovereignty being exercised, not in a remote "heaven," but throughout the whole creation. In this situation, the Deism of the seventeenth and eighteenth centuries and the skepticism of the Enlightenment began to suggest that Jesus' bodily resurrection had never happened, and that the future resurrection of believers was simply a metaphor for some kind of spiritual survival. Thus, the church found it difficult to do more than capitulate (in its liberal mode) or proceed with shrill reaffirmations unconnected to the central matters of the faith (in its conservative mode). In both cases the church failed to see how resurrection itself challenges the very split between faith and reality that has been endemic in post-Enlightenment worldviews, including those of much Western Christianity.

But then came renewed historical investigation of Jesus' own resurrection, and the reappropriation of the theology that the NT writers developed around it. This opened the way for the church to speak of God's ultimate future for his people in terms, not of "going to heaven," but of the two-stage future that first-century Jews would have assumed. Except for those still alive at the Lord's return, those who die go to be "with Christ," in a state of conscious and blissful rest (Luke 23:43; John 14:2–3; Phil. 1:23). But when the Lord reappears, joining heaven and earth into one, the dead will be given new bodies like the one he already has (Rom. 8:11; Phil. 3:20–21).

The hope for the resurrection of the dead is thus to be distinguished from the normal language about "life after death"; it denotes, instead, a new bodily life after "life after death." The fact that most Western Christians are unaware of this

677

indicates a serious weakness in the biblical formation of the modern church, which has corollaries in the difficulties often felt in imitating the early church's integration of faith and public life. Resurrection is about the Creator God reclaiming, judging, and renewing the created world. The Christian who believes in resurrection should also believe that working for God's kingdom in the present is therefore "not in vain" (1 Cor. 15:58).

Bibliography

Avemarie, F., and H. Lichtenburger, eds. *Auferstehung—Resurrection*. WUNT 135. Mohr, 2001; Bieringer, R., et al., eds. *Resurrection in the New Testament*. Peeters, 2002; Bynum, C. *The Resurrection of the Body in Western Christianity, 200–1336*. Columbia University Press, 1995; Davis, S. T., et al., eds. *The Resurrection*. Oxford University Press, 1997; Lapide, P. *The Resurrection of Jesus*. Augsburg, 1983; Longenecker, R., ed. *Life in the Face of Death*. Eerdmans, 1998; Moule, C. F. D., ed. *The Significance of the Message of the Resurrection for Faith in Jesus Christ*. SCM, 1968; O'Collins, G. *Easter Faith*. Darton, Longman & Todd, 2003; O'Donovan, O. *Resurrection and Moral Order*. 2d ed. Eerdmans, 1994; Perkins, P. *Resurrection*. Doubleday, 1984; Porter, S., et al., eds. *Resurrection*. Sheffield Academic Press, 1999; Segal, A. *Life after Death*. Doubleday, 2004; Torrance, T. F. *Space, Time, and Resurrection*. Handsel Press, 1976; Williams, R. *Resurrection*. Darton, Longman & Todd, 1982; Wright, N. T. *The Resurrection of the Son of God*. Fortress, 2003.

N. T. Wright

Revelation

The word "revelation" can be used in a variety of ordinary, biblical, and theological senses. As a comprehensive theological category, "revelation" covers a variety of phenomena that we encounter in Scripture. There is divine speech and there are mighty acts of God in history; there is theophany, dream, prophecy, revelation in nature, revelation in Christ, the revelation of the gospel, and eschatological manifestation. This is neither an exhaustive nor an ordered account. It involves concepts that may deeply interlock or that are relatively separate. The concepts may be on the scriptural surface or the product of our broader theological construction; they may or may not be correlated with specific Hebrew, Aramaic, and Greek words, whose semantic ranges may or may not be close to each other. A cluster of things in Scripture, therefore, can be put under the rubric of "revelation." They are held together by the biblical claim that there is a God who has personally communicated with humanity, and this warrants talk of revelation in a comprehensive way.

"Communication" suggests speech, but the overarching concept of revelation that emerges from the biblical account includes action also in the sense of deeds. (Speech is a form of action, of course, and the point may be particularly important to make in relation to God, but I am distinguishing them familiarly for our purposes.) As regards the connection between speech and revelation, there is some analogy with human agency. In speech, humans disclose or reveal things, which may include facts unknown or unknowable in any other way. There can also be direct or indirect disclosure of one's identity or character. All this applies to God. Two things are peculiar in this case. First, since God is not accessible to the empirical senses in the way that humans are, particular importance attaches to the revelation that God is and who God is. Second, what God reveals is of unsurpassed and unsurpassable significance for everyone without exception, since the nature, purpose, and destiny of humankind is at stake, and salvation is at issue.

In reporting divine speech, the OT generally neither analyzes the concept nor even describes the experience underlying the predication. The experience may occasionally be similar to or even identical with the physical hearing of a physical voice, but there is no reason to assume that it is always or normally like this. Rather, there appears to be an inner conviction that God has spoken, an inward hearing, or a dream or vision in which the impression is unmistakably conveyed. Despite some disanalogies here with normal human experience of interhuman communication, the analogy between divine speech and human speech holds in relation to the concept of revelation—both are, or can be, its media.

It may be harder to apply analogy in the case of divine action. Human action can be described in a variety of ways, such as according to its external and manifest aspect or according to its scientifically precise physiological mechanism. Divine action is also known in its external, apparent aspect, but Scripture does not probe its ontological mode. This also applies to speech; however, the range of things covered by divine "action" appears greater. Scripture may not consistently distinguish, for example, between providential and miraculous activity. But there is a manifest difference between the external aspect of the action involved when God providentially gives children (which can apparently be described in purely natural terms) and when water is miraculously turned into wine (which apparently cannot). Extraordinary action is itself of different kinds. It may be explained in terms that defy natural explanation or in terms of "coincidence" (the Israelites are able to cross the Red Sea on account of an unusual, but partially scientifically explicable occurrence, the rising of a mighty east wind). So divine action appears to be more varied in its outward aspects than divine speech, and analogy with human action is looser.

How exactly does revelation enter into this? Divine action, as well as divine speech, can be revelatory. Roughly speaking, acts take on a revelatory character when they are interpreted by the word of God. And belief that a divine word has been spoken is warranted by the concomitant act. The relations of word and event form a nexus of revelation. This pattern, established in the OT, is broadly maintained in the NT. It applies in the case of both the ordinary and the extraordinary event. The crucifixion of Jesus can be called an ordinary event, but its significance is ultimately revealed, so that God's action in Christ is revealed. Resurrection is an extraordinary event per se, but its significance is unintelligible apart from the apostolic word that interprets it, so that it becomes a revelation of divine power.

Of the many questions that arise in connection with our broad concept of revelation, two in particular can be selected for comment, on account of their theological significance. The first concerns the centrality of Christ and of Christology. Karl Barth, whose influence on discussion of revelation (as of much else) has been so massive upon modern theology, appeared to rule out sources of revelation outside Christ, though this move was fundamentally integrated into, not separated from, a theology that gave centrality to Trinity, pneumatology, and Scripture. Irrespective of how we interpret Barth himself, the question of the relation of special revelation (in Christ or Scripture) to general revelation (in nature, by reason, or through religious experience) is hard to adjudicate in a short compass. If we may and should speak of a general revelation, it does not necessarily follow that we can construct a whole natural theology on its basis. And if we may and should speak of the possibility of salvation outside the explicit knowledge of God in Christ, it does not necessarily follow that this is because general revelation abounds.

Talk of revelation and talk of salvation are, in fact, inextricably connected. Oscar Cullmann, for example, in *Christ and Time*, did not want to distinguish significantly between *Heilsgeschichte* (salvation history) and *Offenbarungsgeschichte* (the history of revelation). These themes dominate the Gospel accounts of Jesus Christ, which lie at the center of the entire biblical narrative. This story conveys the public aspect of revelation. When Jesus pronounced blessed those "who have not seen and yet have believed" (John 20:29), he was not denigrating the importance of the empirical, nor of the empirical as the medium of revelation. He was attending to the fact that the generation of eyewitnesses will pass away, not suggesting that faith is not grounded in what that generation saw. Inasmuch as reason is implicated in seeing, hearing, and judging, revelation and faith are not set in opposition or in sharp contrast to reason.

In another respect, revelation is not public. Early in 1 Corinthians Paul makes the point with force. From the subjective point of view, the Spirit illuminates the believer, revealing the things of God; in the wider NT context, he reveals Christ. So a theological interpretation of Scripture compels us to distinguish roughly between the grounds for believing and the causes of conviction. The public aspect of revelation through Christ provides grounds for believing that are within the objective capacity of human reason to apprehend—this is the significance of the empirical emphasis in the Gospel reports. But the cause of personal conviction and certainty lies in the operation of the Spirit of God—he testifies to Christ, who is the revealer.

The second question concerns the connection between revelation and the scriptural text. The issues here are too many to enumerate, let alone to allow comment. From questions of canon, church, and tradition, arising in the patristic era, to questions of speech and writing, text and language, in postmodernity; from Enlightenment questions about faith and history to contemporary questions about discourses of truth and power—we are faced with the question of this connection. The massive shadow of the issue of hermeneutics, whose subject matter expanded particularly after the work of Schleiermacher in the early nineteenth century, is cast over the whole. That the broad question of revelation is somehow at the heart of all these issues shows its multidimensionality.

It is evident that Scripture bears witness to revelation. But we must go further than this. The word spoken by God to the prophets, for example, was transmitted in writing because its content was of divine, not human, origin and was revealed. From the perspective of the Bible itself, the text can and should be regarded as the word of God. Whether the Bible as a whole is to be considered the word of God, and what we should make of ecclesiastical disagreements on what constitutes the Bible, are further questions. But the spoken word of God can be textually inscribed and enjoy in salient respects the same status of revelation, even when its originating accompaniments have disappeared. Indeed, speech and prophecy are just examples of revelation; the Pauline ascription of inspiration to Scripture (2 Tim. 3:16) offers a more comprehensive connection between revelation and text, however we interpret the notion of inspiration in detail.

Does it make conceptual sense to speak of revelation contained in a text with an objective and perspicuous meaning? It does. Objective meaning is not exhaustive meaning, as though all the meaningful layers and ramifications must be captured in the act of truly understanding a text. Rather, to ascribe objective meaning to the biblical text qua revelation is to say that an agent (God or prophet or scribe) intended to convey something determinate, disclosed by revelation. Perspicuity is logically assignable to textual meaning, though the relation of word and Spirit has to be teased out. The Bible invites us to connect revelation and text closely, and all we do here is to note the conceptual possibilities.

The theological discussion of revelation is completely unbalanced unless it keeps two connected things in view. First, the root of the matter is the conviction that God is to be conceived of as a personal agent. Jesus is the exegesis of that claim. His appearance confirms the fact that the personal attributes predicated of Yahweh in the OT are not personified ways of speaking of a deity who is unknowable or who is not personal in any sense remotely analogous to our own personal being. These ways of speaking may be literal, anthropomorphic, or metaphorical; Christian theologians have embarked on cataphatic and apophatic approaches to knowledge of and speech about God. However we elucidate matters, the Son reveals the nature of God as personal in terms of his character and ways, not the metaphysics of his form. Incarnation is the definitive disclosure of the personal reality of God; in that respect, incarnation is the heart of revelation.

Second, revelation aims not only at intellectual response or cognitive acknowledgment, but also at personal repentance and transformation. The broad line of a biblical theological anthropology is that active will and understanding, which are mutually conditioning, are rooted in the profound religious affection or disaffection of the heart. Both the disposition to obey and the exercise of obedience can be conditions of receiving disclosure (John 14:21). As John Baillie put it: "In the last resort the determining conditions of religious belief are moral conditions" (363), although "moral" is perhaps too weak a word here to describe our basic orientation. Revelation is a divine initiative in the sphere of interpersonal relations, and as such is ultimately ordered to the achievement of communion, not to the imparting of information.

See also Analogy; Anthropomorphism; God, Doctrine of; Scripture, Authority of

Bibliography

Baillie, J. *The Interpretation of Religion*. Scribner, 1928; Barr, J. *The Bible in the Modern World*. SCM, 1973; idem. *Biblical Faith and Natural Theology*. Oxford University Press, 1993; idem. *Old and New in Interpretation*. SCM, 1966; Barth, K. *Church Dogmatics* Vol. I/1. T&T Clark, 1975; idem. Vol. I/2. T&T Clark, 1956; Fackre, G. *The Doctrine of Revelation*. Edinburgh University Press, 1997; Gunton, C. *A Brief Theology of Revelation*. T&T Clark, 1995; Jensen, P. *The Revelation of God*. InterVarsity, 2002; Pannenberg, W. *Systematic Theology*. Vol. 1. T&T Clark, 1991; Wolterstorff, N. *Divine Discourse*. Cambridge University Press, 1995.

Stephen N. Williams

Revelation, Book of
("The Apocalypse of Saint John the Divine")

Revelation and the Canon

The Christian Bible concludes with an apocalypse, but like Waterloo, the victory of this "last battle" was a close run. The vicissitudes of the canonization of John's Apocalypse were related to three linked factors, (1) its authorship, (2) its tendency to inspire millennialist fervor, and (3) the question of how this strange vision fits into the NT. The Apocalypse is atypical in that, having achieved recognition as Sacred Scripture, it did not retain it, remaining peripheral to the Western canon until the late fourth century and being ejected from the Eastern canon until the fourteenth century.

An early-second-century Bishop of Hieropolis, Papias, thought the apostle John wrote the Fourth Gospel, (First) Epistle (of John), and Revelation. Irenaeus believed Papias to have been a "hearer of John and a friend of Polycarp," who had also known John. On Papias's say-so, Irenaeus considered Revelation and John's Gospel as artifacts of the same personality. Justin Martyr (ca. 100–ca. 165) also thought Revelation was apostolic. The primitive church used two other apocalypses, the Shepherd of Hermas and the *Apocalypse of*

Peter. The *Muratorian Canon/Fragment* (ca. 170) describes the author of Revelation as Paul's "predecessor," identifying him with the "eyewitness and hearer" who wrote the Gospel. It rejects the Shepherd as written "recently" and accepts "the apocalypses of John and Peter, though some of us are not willing that the latter be read in church."

Thirty years later, when Montanists turned to the Apocalypse for scriptural legitimation, their opponents discredited the apocalypticism of this Phrygian sect by disparaging the authorship of their favored text. In about 200, a Roman presbyter named Gaius attributed the Apocalypse to the Gnostic Cerinthus because of its teaching a "millennial" (thousand-year) worldly kingdom. Writing around 247, Dionysius, bishop of Alexandria, contended that its stylistic differences from the Fourth Gospel, and its bad Greek, indicate that John the Presbyter wrote it, not John the Evangelist. Eusebius of Caesarea (ca. 260–ca. 339) quotes Dionysius's queries in salacious detail. Eusebius undermines the evidence for Papias's acquaintance with John the Evangelist-Apostle. He describes Papias as "a man of very little intelligence," who taught that "there will be a millennium after the resurrection of the dead, when the kingdom of Christ will be set up in material form on this earth" (*Hist. eccl.* 3.39).

The notion of an earthly millennial kingdom derives from Rev. 20:1–6, in which an angel seized the dragon/devil and "bound him for a thousand years. He threw him into the Abyss, and locked and sealed it over him. . . . After that, he must be set free for a short time. I saw thrones on which were seated those who had been given authority to judge. And I saw the souls of those who had been beheaded because of their testimony to Jesus. . . . They came to life and reigned with Jesus for a thousand years. . . . This is the first resurrection." Those who share in the first resurrection "will be priests of God and of Christ and will reign with him for a thousand years." Like his Montanist adversaries, Gaius the Presbyter read Revelation literally, but he found the implication that Christ will return to set up an earthly kingdom of a thousand years' duration ridiculous.

The manuscript of the Codex Sinaiticus, contemporary with Eusebius, contains Revelation. Cataloging the texts aspiring to canonical status under three headings—"Recognized," "Disputed," and "Spurious"—Eusebius puts Revelation into both first and second categories: "For, as I said, some reject it, but others count it among the Recognized Books" (*Hist. eccl.* 3.25). Eusebius's

empiricism binds him to recording that Revelation was widely read in churches; the rationalist in him deprecated millennial enthusiasm.

Eusebius speaks highly of Gaius's reasoning powers. Gaius had asked rhetorically: What "good does" Revelation "do me when it tells me of seven angels and seven trumpets, or of four angels who are to be let loose at the river Euphrates?" Theologians made sense of such images by allegorizing them. The Egyptian bishop Nepos wrote a *Refutation of the Allegorists*, which claimed, according to his critical friend, Dionysius of Alexandria, "that there will be a kind of millennium on this earth devoted to bodily indulgence." Dionysius did not follow those who "rejected and altogether impugned" Revelation because of its literalist interpreters. He "should not dare to reject the book, since many brethren hold it in estimation. . . . For although I do not understand it, yet I suspect that some deeper meaning underlies the words."

The Apocalypse fell under a cloud in the East. It was rejected by Cyril of Jerusalem and Gregory of Nazianzus, and accepted by other bishops, including Athanasius, whose Festival Letter of 367 lists the canonical books. Jerome observed in 414 that "if the usage of the Latins does not receive [Hebrews] among the canonical Scriptures, neither indeed by the same liberty do the churches of the Greeks receive the Revelation of John. And yet we receive both in that we follow . . . the authority of ancient writers, who for the most part quote each of them . . . as canonical and churchly."

The author of Revelation insists on his work's inspired character. He claims that "the Spirit" speaks through him to the church (2:7, 11, 17, 29; 3:6, 13, 22; cf. 22:6; etc.), and concludes with an anathema seldom matched by any framer of canonical lists. "I warn everyone who hears the words of the prophecy of this book: If anyone adds to them, God will add to him the plagues described in this book. And if anyone takes words away from this book of prophecy, God will take from him his share in the tree of life and in the holy city, which are described in this book. He who testifies to these things says, 'Yes, I am coming soon.' Amen. Come, Lord Jesus!" (22:18–20; cf. the injunctions in Deuteronomy, last book in the Torah: 4:2; 12:32). As the only apocalypse to overcome ecclesiastical resistance to apocalypticism, Revelation must have resonated with ecclesiastical needs. Who wrote it mattered to primitive and patristic Christians because John-the-Gospel-writer stood foursquare within the church. Revelation was canonized once exegetes

681

were able to read it synoptically with the rest of Sacred Scripture. Theologians analyzed Revelation alongside apocalyptic sayings in other NT books and in Daniel. So, for example, although "antichrist" does not figure in the Apocalypse, its dragon (12:3), sea beast (13:1), and earth beast (13:11) have been cross-identified with the figure of the Johannine Epistles. Irenaeus, Augustine of Hippo, and Bede understood the lion, calf, man-faced beast, and eagle (4:7) to represent the authors of the four Gospels: conversely, the church sees itself in the Apocalypse when finding it to inform the whole Christian drama. It is "like an onion," said Mr. Tumnus, "except that as you go in and in, each circle is larger than the last" (Lewis 169). Western medieval manuscripts of the Apocalypse were often prefaced by a pictorial biography of John, emphasizing its ecclesial origin. Although the linguistic asymmetries are an obstacle to joint authorship of Gospel and Apocalypse, the uncovering of realized eschatology in both texts harmonizes the Apocalypse with the Johannine corpus.

History of Interpretation

Distinguishing Eschatology and Apocalyptic. A fourth-century scribe wrote "A Revelation of John" at the head of his page, and added in the margin, *tou theologou*, "the theologian." A successor copyist moved the words to center page; ever since, the author has been known as "John the theologian," or "John the Divine" in the Authorized Version (KJV). Today, most scholars see both Gospel and Apocalypse as works of theology. The theology of Revelation flows into *two* elements of Christian thought, eschatological historiography and apocalyptic. Do the two overlap? To what extent should the promises and threats of the Apocalypse be taken as *predicting* history-like events? Is the End datable, and will the world to come have a chronology?

Irenaeus's *Against Heresies* concludes with an apocalyptic vision of the kingdom of Christ on earth. The Irenaean apocalyptic is pictorial and "millennial": "It is fitting," he writes, "that the creation itself, being restored to its primeval condition, should without qualification be under the dominion of the righteous." During Diocletian's persecution, Victorinus read the Apocalypse in a historical and millenary sense, and took its "things that must *shortly* come to pass" (1:1 KJV) to show that the End was imminent. Commenting on Daniel, Jerome forswore a *historical* eschaton: "The saints will in no wise have an earthly kingdom, but only a celestial one;

thus must cease the fable of one thousand years." In his Isaiah commentary, Jerome indicated why there was "much difference . . . among men . . . about the way in which John's Apocalypse is to be understood": "To take it according to the letter is to Judaize. If we treat it in a spiritual fashion, as it was written, we seem to contradict the views of many older authorities: Latins such as Tertullian, Victorinus, and Lactantius; Greeks such as Irenaeus, to pass over the others." Jerome rewrote Victorinus's commentary, saving Victorinus's insight that the Apocalypse's eschatology is realized recurrently throughout the history of the church. As Victorinus and Jerome have it, Revelation's seven trumpets blew over the Babylonian Empire and will sound again; its dragon/antichrist depicts Roman emperors and emperors yet to come. The eternity seen in Revelation becomes *always* when it is reflected back into history.

Eusebius of Caesarea compared Constantine's construction of the church of the Holy Sepulchre in Jerusalem to the promise of 21:2 that the heavenly Jerusalem will come down to earth. Did he contradict his own aversion to apocalyptic when he noted God's historical design in the Christianizing of the Roman Empire? Only if we fail to distinguish eschatology, or the philosophy of history, from apocalypse, the ending of time. To do so, one must grapple with the fact that Revelation is a dualistic text. Steeped in OT prophecy, the author summed up his book's symbolic battle in the two cities: Babylon, whoring after power, and Jerusalem, the eternal city. Augustine (354–430) interpreted Babylon and Jerusalem as the city of man and the city of God. He traced their passage through biblical, extrabiblical, and postbiblical history. Stating that "the kingdoms of men are established by divine providence," Augustine saw God's benevolent plan in the reigns of Constantine and Theodosius (5, preface; 25; 26). Postbiblical history is no emptier of theological design for Augustine than for Eusebius. But Augustine is able to put the eschatological philosophy of history that he draws out of Revelation, and its apocalyptic, on different planes. The first is concerned with the "six days" of creation, the ages of history from its origins to the end of time. Christ's Incarnation inaugurated the sixth day in which humanity will live until the end of time. The second coming of Christ, which brings with it the "seventh day," the "eternal Sabbath," ruptures the temporal, numbered series. All history is eschatological, but the Apocalypse is transhistorical.

Augustine stigmatizes the millenarians' pictorialization of the kingdom as a round of "material feasts in which there will be so much to eat and drink that not only will those supplies keep within no bounds of moderation but will also exceed the limits even of incredibility" (20.7). The uncharacteristic stylistic clumsiness indicates that millennialist literalism affected the bishop of Hippo's digestion much as it did that of the bishop of Caesarea.

The Donatist Tyconius (330–90) devised a *Book of Rules* for interpreting Scripture. These exegetical principles enabled him to demillennialize Donatist proof texts. Rule 1 says that Scripture references to "the Lord" sometimes indicate Christ, sometimes his *ekklēsia*-body. Tyconius argues that biblical references to the "coming of the Lord" can mean the advent of the church. Rule 4 states that references to individuals sometimes have a wider application. Augustine used Tyconius's *Rules*. Applying rule 4 to the binding of the devil in Rev. 20, he finds that the devil will not be "thrown into the abyss" just once, but is constantly driven into the "abyss" of the hearts of the impious. Rule 5 regulates for a nonarithmetical reading of biblical statements about time. Tyconius had used it against a literal-temporal reading of the thousand-year kingdom. Augustine likewise advised against taking the "thousand years" as a countable series: he took them to symbolize "totality," since multiples of ten produce a "solid figure," such as a "cube" (ibid.).

Augustine takes the "first resurrection" of Rev. 20 to refer to baptism. He distinguishes this from the resurrection to judgment that will occur after the end of time. "It follows," he says, "that the Church even now is the kingdom of Christ and the kingdom of heaven. And so even now his saints reign with him, though not in the same way as they will then reign; and yet the tares do not reign with him, although they are growing in the Church side by side with the wheat. . . . Ultimately, those people reign with him who are in his kingdom in such a way that they themselves *are* his kingdom" (20.9). The "city of God" is not in the temporal future: the eternal Jerusalem is folded into the past and present church on earth. Nor is the kingdom a cosmic "place," but rather a state of being: "they themselves *are* his kingdom." By detaching apocalyptic from chronology, Augustine deterred Christians from seeing *endings*, such as that of the Roman Empire, as signs of the End. Apocalyptic is more elusive than the philosophy of history, for Augustine: Constantine *is* part of God's providence; the present-day church *is and is not* the kingdom of the saints.

Both the North African bishop of Justiniapolis, Primasius (540s), who knew Victorinus-Jerome's commentary, and the Spanish Beatus of Liébanus (c. 780) treat Revelation as a book about Christ and the church. Where Primasius relates the woman giving birth (12:2) to the Virgin Mary, Beatus identifies her with a feminine *Ekklēsia*. Beatus initiates a line of commentarial cross-reference of Revelation to the Song of Songs. Drawing on *The Book of Rules* and the commentaries of Jerome and Primasius, the Venerable Bede uses Tyconius's rule 1 to interleave Revelation and the Song. In his eighth-century *Explanatio Apocalypsis*, Bede states that it is the church that says, "I am dark and comely" (Song 1:5). For Bede, both the Song and Revelation are allegories of the church's mission. The woman in labor is "the Church, in a spiritual sense, bring[ing] forth those with whom it travails"; "she brought forth a man child" (12:5 KJV) means the church "ever" giving birth to Christ.

Bede notes that Tyconius's rule 6 concerns "recapitulation." Chronological *"sequence"* sometimes enfolds flashbacks to earlier events. Revelation does not progress in a straight line. After the seventh seal has been opened (8:1), Bede finds that "now he recapitulates from the beginning, as he is about to say the same things in another manner"; the "sequence" cycles around to begin again with the first of the seven trumpets (8:2).

Primasius had broken the text down into sections: (1) seven churches; (2) seven seals; (3) seven trumpets and the woman of Rev. 12; (4) beasts of land and sea, and seven bowls with seven plagues; (5) new heaven and earth. Such sectional divisions became standard. Bede read Revelation as the recurrent story of the "seven days" of history. He created *seven* sections within Revelation, adding two to Primasius's five by giving the woman's labor and conflict with the dragon its own section, and separating the fate of Babylon (Rev. 17:1–20:5; sec. 6) from the wedding of Jerusalem and the Lamb (chs. 21–22; sec. 7). For Bede, the sections of the book of Revelation are isomorphic with the divisions of time. He organizes the apocalypse into the sevenfold division of history. Although he quotes Augustine verbatim on Rev. 20, Bede smoothes the transition from eschatology to apocalypse. The Revelation commentaries of Charlemagne's court theologian, Alcuin (ca. 800), and Haimo (ca. 840) adopt Bede's septilinear periodization of history. Augustine's *City of God* inspired Charlemagne's desire that his empire would reflect the new Jerusalem. Medieval theologians were in line with Augustine when Revelation informed their perception of history, as with Bede observing bad monks, heretics, and Arians in the four horses of Rev. 6:1–8. Reading the signs of the times providentially, or eschatologically, is Augustinian; reading history apocalyptically is not.

The Benedictine Berengaudus (840–92) builds on the sense of optimism that had accumulated within Western commentaries on Revelation. His *Expositio super septem visiones libri Apocalypsis* connects the Lamb of Rev. 5–7 and 21:9 with John the Baptist's "Behold, the Lamb of God" in John 1:29 (RSV). John continues, "Happy are those who are called to his supper" (Rev. 19:9 AT). For Berengaudus, Revelation is a vision of the marriage feast of the Lamb and his *Ekklēsia*. He downplays its conflictual element to the extent of reading the four horses of Rev. 6 as figures of "the Lord," rather than harbingers of the devil. Writing in the reign of Charles the Bald, Berengaudus positions the "persecutions" of Rev. 16 in the past; nowadays, he notes, emperors promote true worship.

A tenth-century Spanish illuminated copy of Beatus of Liébanus's commentary states: "I have depicted the wonderful words of the story in sequence, so that those who know of them will be terrified by the events of the future judgment." Revelation 3:12 promises, "Him who overcomes I will make a pillar in the temple of my God." Following Bede, Berengaudus read Rev. 3:12 as a reminder that "the heavenly [city], . . . unlike the old, is not built of stones but is daily constructed by the saints." He found that promise *fulfilled* in the *present*, in the Saint-City of Rev. 21. Medieval Christians walked into church under the statue of *Christ in Judgment* in the west porch, where the damned departed to the left, the saved to the right; thus, the worshipper entered paradise. Bernard Guinée remarked that "Paradise was the Christian's country in the Middle Ages." Their ecclesiastical interpretation of Revelation came quite naturally. The number of surviving illuminated copies of Berengaudus's commentary shows how popular it was. Illustrated versions of his commentary on Revelation influenced the churches on the pilgrimage route to Compostella. Romanesque sculptures represent John's elders in burlesque postures, in which scholars struggle to find Christian value. In the choir frieze at Marignac, the elders of Rev. 4 frolic naked with domesticated dragons. Derk Visser suggests that this is the expression of Revelation as read beside the Song of Songs, indicating a "medieval mind-set which saw *salvation promised* as

reality believed," and which "therefore focussed less on the *Last Judgement* than on the blessed life that came after." Revelation's marriage feast, already enjoyed at Mass, was the basis not of fearful predictions of antichrist, but of "utopian expectation" (Visser 182–83).

Apocalypse as History. Joachim of Fiore (1135–1202) described the Apocalypse as "the key of things past, the knowledge of things to come; the opening of what is sealed, the uncovering of what is hidden." Joachim's *Expositio in Apocalysism* is the most influential work of biblical exegesis of all time. Historians of ideas have traced its spore from the Spiritual Franciscans to Hitler's Third Reich. The Calabrian hermit's long lineage is paradoxical, in that he retrenched himself against the intellectual developments of his time. He was a visualizer of Scripture when the figural syntheses of the patristic era were giving way to the discursive analyses of the scholastic *Summae*.

At Easter of 1183, Joachim's efforts to penetrate Revelation were rewarded: "Suddenly something of the fullness of this book and of the entire harmony of the Old and New Testaments was perceived with clarity of understanding in my mind's eye" (*Expositio*). For Joachim, Revelation is the wheel within the wheels of history, as mapped out by the two Testaments. The "seven times" that Joachim discerned in OT and NT are recapitulated in the seven epochs he pictured in the Apocalypse. These "epochs" correspond to a linear sequence of events in world history, down to his own time. Most earlier exegetes had seen correspondences between past or present events and those described in Revelation. Joachim made a *science* of theological historiography, using Revelation to predict future events and persons: the Apocalypse "embraces the fullness of history" (*Expositio*). The seven epochs of Joachim's Apocalypse depict three sequential "states": the Status of the Father (Rev. 1:1–11:18), the Status of the Son (Rev. 11:19–19:21), and the Status of the Spirit (Rev. 20:1–10). The third age of grace would commence around 1200–1260. It will be an age of "Spiritual men," in which the "everlasting gospel" (Rev. 14:6) shall be preached by a suprainstitutional church. The Sabbath will come on this earth, after the defeat of antichrist, anticipating the descent of the new Jerusalem. Joachim's eighth era, eternity, melts into the seventh temporal epoch; eschatology and apocalyptic are effectively equated. The "third status of the Spirit" will not last a thousand years; Joachim was not technically a "millennialist."

Joachim related Revelation's twin cities to Scripture scholars, the Babylonian, bestial-*carnal* exegetes, and Jerusalem's *spiritual* interpreters. The first wave of Joachimism, from the thirteenth to the sixteenth century, addressed itself to separating the carnal and the spiritual within the church. In his 1297 Apocalypse commentary, the Spiritual Franciscan Peter Olivi enlarged upon Joachim, adding a fiercer conception of antichrist, with whom Revelation's true witnesses would soon be embattled. Olivi spoke of "spiritual" and "carnal" churches. A cult of Spiritual Franciscanism, with a special devotion to Olivi, emerged in Languedoc. In 1326, Pope John XXII had Olivi's commentary condemned. After studying Olivi and the Apocalypse, the Franciscan John of Rupescissa predicted the coming of antichrist in 1366, followed by a thousand-year kingdom. He claimed the right to reject Augustinian amillennialism on the basis of an "intellectual vision," revealing to him the meaning of Rev. 16–20. Thomas Aquinas observed: "Although the state [*status*] of the New Testament in general is foreshadowed by the state of the Old, it does not follow that individuals correspond to individuals. . . . [This] would seem applicable to the statements of the Abbot Joachim" (*Summa theologiae* III, Q. 77, Art. 2, Reply Obj. 3). Yet Aquinas's comment did not deter the spread of Pseudo-Joachimite prophecies, identifying antichrist with this and that emperor.

Joachimism inspired the fifteenth-century Bohemian Taborites, who rose in rebellion against the church's leaders. The Taborites were the first "Rapturists," expecting that, once the earth had been cleansed by massacre, the elect would soar into the sky to greet their Christ, whereupon the third age of grace would dawn on earth. Thomas Müntzer (1488–1525) picked up Joachimite apocalypticism on his travels in Bohemia. Preaching on Daniel before Duke John of Saxony, he advised: "Drive Christ's enemies out from among the Elect. . . . The sword is necessary to exterminate them. . . . At the harvest-time one must pluck the weeds out of God's vineyard. . . . The angels who are sharpening their sickles for that work are . . . the . . . servants of God." In response to Luther's *Letter to the Princes of Saxony*, Müntzer denoted the author as the beast and Babylonian whore of Revelation. Luther reserved such appellations for the pope—not necessarily a mark of apocalypticism, since "antichrist" had become a general term of abuse. The Anabaptist Hans Hut identified Müntzer and Heinrich Pfeiffer as the two witnesses of Rev. 11. Hut used Revelation as a calendar to date the last judgment (Pentecost, 1528). The Anabaptist "calendarizer" Melchior Hoffmann applied Revelation to the events of 1520–30. Faced with the millennialism of Thomas Müntzer and the Münster Anabaptists, Luther relegated Revelation to the outskirts of his German NT, complaining that "this writer recommends his own book much too highly and does not show Christ clearly." Seventeenth-century Protestant theologians like Cocceius nonetheless understood prophecy, like that of Revelation, as future-related historiography. The "innocently licentious" English Ranters and Muggletonians inherited the myth of the Apocalypse as predicting a third age of the Spirit (Kermode).

Joachim of Fiore entrenched history in sacral patterns at a time when the human sciences were gaining a measure of secularity. His was an evolutionist history, conceiving the three "states" as three trees growing from one root. His Apocalypse exegesis flowered in the secular utopias of the Enlightenment. Joachim's "three ages," culminating in earthly fulfillment, return in Comte's theological, metaphysical, and positivist "states"; in Hegel's idea of a growth of freedom from oriental despotism, through the aristocratic Middle Ages, to modernity, in which all are free; and in the Marxist-Leninist triad of primitive communism, bourgeois society, and the classless Jerusalem of communism. Gaius the Roman Presbyter might feel that his hypothesis of the Gnostic Cerinthus fathering the Apocalypse has been verified by its ideological progeny.

Time Shall Be No More? In *The End of All Things* (1794), Kant commented aversely on the angel's pronouncement "that there shall be time no longer" (Rev. 10:6). "If we are to assume that this angel . . . was crying nonsense, he must have meant that there shall be change no longer." This, Kant felt, is "a contradictory notion that revolts the imagination." Notwithstanding his pessimistic conception of human nature, Kant translated the Joachimite Apocalypse tradition into a "rational" belief in humanity's *temporal* progress. One strand of contemporary Apocalypse commentary shares the pessimism of the German philosopher, and the sense that Revelation must be about *time*. In the 1830s, John Nelson Darby created a premillennial, "dispensationalist" theology. Dispensationalist Apocalypse interpreters were in the late twentieth and early twenty-first century as widely consulted as astrologers, identifying modern politicians with the agents of Revelation, as in Hal Lindsey's *The Late Great Planet Earth* (1970). With the Gnostics, and in some sense with

Revelation, Darby had divided humanity in twain. He believed that once having been beamed up into heaven, the "heavenly church" would reign over the "earthly people"—left behind after the rapture. Tim LaHaye's Left Behind series is a fictional account of events occurring during the rapture/millennium; with forty million volumes in print, these are the best-selling Christian novels in history.

Some contemporary biblical scholars employ the notion of recapitulation to make sense of Revelation's nonsequential "narrative." David Barr finds "three one-act plays" in the text: (1) Christ's dictation of seven letters, (2) the Lamb's opening of the sealed book, and (3) the war between the dragon and the faithful, culminating in the triumph of bride over whore. This manifests the "three dimensions" of Christ's work—(1) the salvific/judgmental, (2) the enabling of worship, and (3) the overthrow of evil—"not three consecutive actions" (Barr, "Transformation").

The Message of Revelation

Pictorializers and Hearers. Historically, Revelation exegetes have tended either to pictorialize the text or to listen to it. Jacques Ellul claimed, "The apocalypticist is first of all a seer while the prophet is a hearer. . . . The apocalypticist also receives words, but he is first of all the one who sees the personages, the scenes, the scenario, the events" (21). Most narrative "pictorializers" see John's visions as weaving God's design for history down to its conclusion, thereby providing a "sense of an ending," the rounded rationale of history. On the other hand, there are those for whom the "*orality* of the book is an essential element of its hermeneutic" (Barr, "Enactment"). This takes account of the fact that Revelation is more like a dream than a progressive story. Its agents and objects are not set on a single visual plane; it builds up expectations of order by taking the reader through numbered sequences, and then abruptly spins off rhythm into nightmare. The nonrepresentationalists receive the book as primarily a rendition of *eternity*, in which created past, present, and future are heard *simultaneously*, or polyphonically, in the voices of the liturgy before the throne of God. In the *Messiah*, Handel's librettist integrated Revelation with the resurrection themes of biblical prophecy. Treated as a self-standing lyric, Revelation is a popular source of Christian rock music. Are its choral hymns the home key of the Apocalypse? Somewhere in the middle, between pictoralizations and hearings, stand nonrepresentational picturings,

such as the surreal features of the medieval Last Judgments, or the conception of Rev. 14 in Jan van Eyck's *Adoration of the Lamb* (1420s), its horizon of seven church buildings indicating past, present, and future time. When painters view *eternity* scenically, they eschew visual *narrative*. Is Revelation analogous to a *movie*, a visual narrative of *time* and its close, or is it using quasi-*musical* modes to render *timelessness*?

Since the eighteenth century the techniques of Western music have expressed temporal progression. The French composer Olivier Messiaen (1908–92) abandoned them, replacing counterpoint with heterophony, progressive development with symmetry, ordered change with repetition, and resolved diatonic chords with tritones. His first organ work, *Le banquet céleste*, opens with a chord of seven seconds' duration. Messiaen inscribed the score: "He that eateth my flesh and drinketh my blood, dwelleth in me, and I in him" (John 6:56). The piece evokes the participation of Christ's eternity in time, in what the Catholic Messiaen believed to be the supratemporal sacrifice of the Mass. Messiaen's *Quartet for the End of Time* (first performed in a German prison camp in 1941) is dedicated "in homage to the Angel of the Apocalypse, who raises his hand heavenwards saying: 'There will be no more Time.'" The effects of this musical exegesis of the Apocalyse work against unilinear clock time, and in favor of multitemporality or timelessness. It lets us hear eternity as stasis and as playfulness.

Resurrection. Revelation teaches that the end point of history is cosmic catastrophe. In his first words to the narrator, Christ announces that he has defeated death (1:18). Each of the promises made by the resurrected Christ to the seven churches in Rev. 2–3 is about eternal life. The message of Revelation is resurrection. From the seven days of Gen. 1, createdness in the Bible signifies temporality. With the "new heaven and new earth" of Rev. 21, the created cosmos is lifted into eternity. Resurrection to eternal life is the transposition of temporal-created life into eternal-created life. Revelation's apocalyptic fulfills rather than overthrows its eschatological philosophy of history. According to Aquinas, "The being of the creature cannot wholly come to an end"; "even if it is transient, the creature will never fall back into nothingness." Revelation's "new Jerusalem" is made from the precious stones of paradise; resurrection is the regaining to eternity of what was given in the Garden of Gen. 1–3. The "kings of the earth" will bring "their glory into" the new Jerusalem (21:24 RSV). Christ says, "Behold,

I make all things new" (21:5 RSV), not "Behold, I make a new set of things" (von Balthasar, 5:200). "Our faith tells us that this 'new' reality was already present in the 'old,' in our drama," the old Narnia present in the new (Lewis 170).

Fire. Exegetes from Augustine to the present have thought it appropriate that the Apocalypse brings history to a close in *fire*. "The Apocalypse, convulsed with lightning, blazing with conflagration, provides us only with final, perpendicular excerpts of the last stages of dramatic action between heaven and earth, God and his creation. There is no other way of portraying this final act. This drama, in which God's absoluteness (understood as power of love) touches the sphere of the fragile creature, can only be a fiery event, a history of fire, made up either of devouring or of healing flames" (von Balthasar, 4:59).

Revelation and Theology

God. A 1422 Sienese antiphonal illustrates "[God] will wipe every tear from their eyes" (Rev. 21:4) with a picture of the Lord bending to wipe a pilgrim's eye. The warmth of such depictions comes from their comicality. Revelation does not contain anthropomorphic images of God. But it does show God. The narrator sees, not only the throne of God, but also "one seated on the throne," a multicolored being around whom is wrapped "a rainbow . . . like an emerald" (4:2–3 RSV).

The Trinity. Revelation's salutation makes reference to God ("who is, and who was, and who is to come"; cf. Isa. 44:6; 48:12), to "the seven spirits before his throne," and to "Jesus Christ, . . . the faithful witness" (Rev. 1:4b–5). It thus is the most "trinitarian" book in the Bible. In Rev. 22:13 Christ says, "I am the Alpha and the Omega, the First and the Last, the Beginning and the End" (cf. 1:8; 1:17; 21:6; etc.). As divine self-designations, "Alpha and Omega," "the First and the Last," and "the Beginning and the End" occur seven times, a number that signifies completeness for the author. Primasius and Beatus of Liébanus used Revelation against the christological heresies of Arianism and Adoptionism. The angel of Rev. 19:10 refuses the narrator's prostration, telling him to worship Christ alone. In his Revelation commentaries and *God Crucified*, Richard Bauckham contends that Revelation is pragmatically "trinitarian," in that Christ is included in the "monotheistic liturgy" of the heavenly agents. In practice, Christ is worshiped as God.

Worship of the Lamb. Revelation was probably composed for oral reading at a Christian service of worship. Each of the three scrolls in Revelation mentions true worship of God. The "last battle" is not between good and evil as abstractly conceived but between worshippers of the beast and worshippers of God. The leitmotif of the Apocalypse is worship combined with judgment. The one who is thus worshipped is not simply a conquering hero, a symbol of power, but "a Lamb standing, as though it had been slain" (5:6 RSV). The "true witnesses" who participate in this triumphal paean are those who have "conquered [the devil] by the blood of the Lamb and by the word of their testimony, for they loved not their lives even unto death" (12:11 RSV). The judgment of the world is the sacrifice of the Lamb.

See also Apocalyptic

Bibliography

Augustine. *Concerning the City of God against the Pagans*, trans. H. Bettenson. Penguin, 1972; Balthasar, H. U. von. *Theo-Drama*. Vol. 4, *The Action*. Ignatius, 1994. Vol. 5, *The Last Act*. Ignatius, 1998; Barr, D. "The Apocalypse as a Symbolic Transformation of the World: A Literary Analysis." *Int* 38, no. 1 (1984): 39–50; idem. "The Apocalypse of John as Oral Enactment." *Int* 40 (1986): 243–56; Bauckham, R. *The Climax of Prophecy*. T&T Clark, 1993; idem. *God Crucified*. Paternoster, 1998; idem. *The Theology of the Book of Revelation*. Cambridge University Press, 1993; Bede. *The Explanation of the Apocalypse*, trans. E. Marshall. J. Parker, 1878; Campenhausen, H. von. *The Formation of the Christian Bible*. Black, 1968; Carey, F., ed. *The Apocalypse and the Shape of Things to Come*. British Museum Press, 1999; Cohn, N. *The Pursuit of the Millennium*. Secker & Warburg, 1957; Collins, A. Y. *The Combat Myth in the Book of Revelation*. Scholars Press, 1976; Ellul, J. *Apocalypse*. Seabury, 1977; Emmerson, R., and B. McGinn, eds. *The Apocalypse in the Middle Ages*. Cornell University Press, 1992; Eusebius of Caesarea. *The Ecclesiastical History*, trans. K. Lake. LCL. Heinemann, 1926; Griffiths, P. *Olivier Messiaen and the Music of Time*. Faber & Faber, 1985; Kermode, F. "Millennium and Apocalypse." Pages 11–27 in *The Apocalypse and the Shape of Things to Come*, ed. F. Carey. British Museum Press, 1999; Lewis, C. S. *The Last Battle*. Bodley Head, 1956; Metzger, B. *The Canon of the New Testament*. Clarendon, 1987; Olson, C. "No End in Sight." *First Things* 127 (November 2002); Peterson, E. *Reversed Thunder*. Harper, 1988; Pieper, J. *The End of Time*, trans. M. Bullock. Faber & Faber, 1954; Thomas Aquinas. *Summa theologiae*. Vol. IIIa, qq. 79–90; Visser, D. *Apocalypse as Utopian Expectation (800–1500)*. Brill, 1996; Voegelin, E. *Science, Politics and Gnosticism*. H. Regnery, 1968.

Francesca Aran Murphy

Rhetoric

Detailed study of rhetoric, now commonplace in biblical studies, is not a modern phenomenon but a classical discipline going back to Aristotle

(384–322 BCE), whose *Rhetoric* is probably the most influential ancient textbook on the subject. However, what has come to be known as the *ars rhetorica* (the art of rhetoric) goes back even further, to the writings of Homer (ninth–eighth century BCE), whose heroes were masters of the *rhetorikē technē* (the Greek equivalent of *ars rhetorica*). Because Homer's writings predate the formal study of rhetoric, his heroes' skillful speech is best described as "preconceptual" rhetoric (Kennedy).

The English language makes a clear distinction between *rhetoric*, the art of composition by which written or spoken language becomes persuasive, and *oratory*, the art of effective public speech; but in Greek and Latin no such distinction is made. The terms *rhetorikē technē* and *ars rhetorica* both refer to the art of the public speaker, which includes both notions.

Conceptualized rhetoric first emerged in the handbooks on judicial rhetoric produced by Corax of Syracuse and his pupil Tisias (fifth century BCE). Their aim was to train orators for their tasks in the law courts by teaching principles of logic and persuasion as well as effective delivery. Tisias's pupil Gorgias (483–378 BCE) was responsible for the development of "epideictic" or ceremonial rhetoric, with its focus on emotive appeal and rhetorical effects.

Plato's (ca. 428–348 BCE) criticism of the lack of moral purpose in the relativistic oratory of Sophists such as Gorgias and Protagoras (ca. 485–410 BCE), which was aimed solely at persuasion, marks the beginning of the critical evaluation of the *rhetorikē technē*. But it was Plato's pupil Aristotle who devoted himself to the detailed study of rhetoric and the development of a practical rhetorical theory. This included the distinction of three types of rhetoric (judicial, epideictic, and deliberative) and of three modes of persuasion (*ethos*, *pathos,* and *logos*), as well as a theory of rhetorical topoi, stock topics or arguments that could be employed in the speech.

By the beginning of the first century BCE, rhetoric was well established in Rome, having become an important part of Roman education. Its most important advocate and theorist was Cicero (ca. 106–43 BCE), who wrote seven books on rhetorical techniques. He is most remembered for his notion of the rhetorician's three "duties" and the concomitant "styles" appropriate to each. Thus, while the task to instruct (*docere*) required the "plain" style, the attempt to move one's audience (*movere*) was best accomplished by reverting to the "grand" style. If, however, the orator sought to delight (*delectare*), the most appropriate style would have been the "intermediate" one.

Another important Roman rhetorician was Quintilian (ca. 35–100 CE), whose *Institutio oratoria* is the most extensive treatise on rhetoric to have survived from antiquity. In subsequent centuries, however, especially from the fourth century onward, Roman rhetoric and oratory suffered a dramatic decline, due partly to the tendencies criticized by Plato several centuries earlier and partly to oratory's degeneration into mere declamation and entertainment. This degenerated form of rhetoric continued to be criticized by philosophers educated in the classical tradition.

In the Christian tradition, the influence of Greek rhetoric can be seen especially in the works of Gregory of Nazianzus, Gregory of Nyssa, and Basil of Caesarea (fourth century). While these Cappadocian fathers excelled in the sophisticated application of rhetorical devices, the development of a theory of Christian rhetoric was left to Augustine of Hippo (354–430). Influenced by Roman rhetoric and especially by Cicero, Augustine's *De doctrina christiana* instructs Christian rhetoricians to be concerned with truth rather than mere persuasion, and with defending the Christian faith.

Yet, the Cappadocian fathers and Augustine were not the only Christian interpreters influenced by ancient rhetoric. Tertullian (ca. 160–220), Cyprian (ca. 200–258), Arnobius (ca. 248–327), and Lactantius (ca. 240–320) all had been professional rhetoricians before they were converted to Christianity (Kennedy 146). Many of the Greek church fathers were similarly trained in rhetoric and the "art of persuasion."

Despite the later decline of rhetoric, mention must be made of Judah ben Jehiel's *Book of the Honeycomb's Flow*, an important medieval *ars rhetorica* (published in 1475/76) that offers "a rhetorical interpretation of the 'plain meaning' . . . of the Hebrew Scriptures" (Rabinowitz lx). Ben Jehiel's study indicates that ancient rhetoric was not completely neglected in medieval times, yet it was employed much more frequently during the period of the Renaissance and the Reformation.

The author of three handbooks on the subject, Philipp Melanchthon (1497–1560), who did much for the study of ancient rhetoric and its use for interpreting of the Bible, deserves particular mention (Classen 8–16, 99–177). Although Melanchthon was fully cognizant of the ancient tradition of rhetoric, he did not hesitate to modify it, introducing new elements where he deemed the traditional concepts deficient. Before Melanchthon, Lorenzo Valla (1405–57) appears to have been the first humanist to apply the ancient resource of rhetoric to the study of the NT.

The modern application of rhetoric to the interpretation of the biblical texts is often traced back to two seminal lectures: OT rhetorical critics are much indebted to James Muilenburg's 1968 presidential address to the Society of Biblical Literature, published as "Form Criticism and Beyond." Hans Dieter Betz's 1974 lecture "The Literary Composition and Function of Paul's Letter to the Galatians" provided an important impetus to NT studies. But Carl Joachim Classen rightly stresses that the application of rhetorical categories to the study of the biblical literature had in fact never been given up completely (16).

See also Rhetorical Criticism

Bibliography

Andersen, O. *Im Garten der Rhetorik*. Wissenschaftliche Buchgesellschaft, 2001; Aristotle. *The Art of Rhetoric*, ed. and trans. J. H. Freese. Harvard University Press, 1926; Augustine. *De doctrina christiana*, ed. and trans. R. P. H. Green. Clarendon, 1995; Betz, H. D. "The Literary Composition and Function of Paul's Letter to the Galatians." *NTS* 21 (1975): 353–79; Classen, C. J. *Rhetorical Criticism of the New Testament*. Brill, 2002; Kennedy, G. A. *New Testament Interpretation through Rhetorical Criticism*. University of North Carolina Press, 1984; Muilenburg, J. "Form Criticism and Beyond." *JBL* 88 (1969): 1–18; Porter, S., ed. *Handbook of Classical Rhetoric in the Hellenistic Period, 330 B.C.–A.D. 400*. Brill, 2001; Quintilian. *The Orator's Education*, ed. and trans. D. Russell. 5 vols. Harvard University Press, 2001; Rabinowitz, I. "Introduction." Pages xv–lxx in *The Book of the Honeycomb's Flow* (1475/1476), ed. and trans. I. Rabinowitz. Cornell University Press, 1983. *See also* the editions of Greek and Latin rhetoricians in the Loeb Classical Library.

Karl Möller

Rhetorical Criticism

The last three decades have seen a growing interest among biblical scholars in rhetorical-critical approaches. To some extent, this tendency reflects the increasing disillusionment with historical criticism. Yet, rhetorical criticism does not have to be construed as a complete move away from historical criticism's interest in the realities "behind the text" (such as the author or the "real" events). Indeed, one of the approach's defining features is that it promises to combine the three foci on the author ("the world behind the text"),

the discourse ("the world of the text"), and the reader ("the world in front of the text").

Rhetorical criticism, which goes back to the ancient study of the *rhetorikē technē* or *ars rhetorica*, also has the potential to contribute to the current endeavor to rejuvenate the discipline of biblical theology. Already the American classicist George A. Kennedy, one of the founding fathers of the rhetorical-critical revival, recognized that "all religious systems are rhetorical" (7). And Wilhelm Wuellner, whose 1987 article provided another important impetus for applying rhetorical-critical categories to study of the NT, called rhetoric "religion's closest ally" (449).

The link with theology is clearest in Don Compier's call for a "rhetorical theology," but rhetorical criticism can also help biblical theology to adopt a view of religious language that appreciates the communicative force of the biblical texts.

Two Definitions of Rhetorical Criticism

Rhetorical criticism can take many different forms, but in biblical studies its two most dominant orientations are what have been called the "art of composition" and the "art of persuasion" (Trible 32, 41).

The former is associated with James Muilenburg and those following in his footsteps. Muilenburg's conception of rhetorical criticism is largely an attempt to overcome the shortcomings of form criticism by paying increased attention to a text's unique stylistic or aesthetic qualities. This focus on a text's unique features was meant to complement and correct form criticism's penchant for the typical and conventional.

Studies exemplifying an "art of persuasion" approach, by contrast, belong to the classical Aristotelian tradition and its modern revival in the "new rhetoric" (e.g., Perelman and Olbrechts-Tyteca), which combines the Greco-Roman model with modern approaches such as literary criticism, hermeneutics, structuralism, semantics, and linguistics. The focus of the "art of persuasion" approach is on rhetoric as argumentation, and its interest is properly characterized as sociolinguistic in nature, because it regards all discourse as *social* discourse, which is inseparable from the wider social relations between writers or orators and their audiences. In this model, human discourse is an activity that seeks to alter reality and is largely unintelligible outside the social purposes and conditions in which it originated (Eagleton, *Theory*, 179).

Rejecting the Muilenburg approach as "rhetoric restrained" and as *"letteraturizzazione,"* Kennedy and Wuellner regard the "new rhetoric" as the revaluation and reinvention of rhetoric, which is finally being restored to all its ancient rights.

Rhetorical-Critical Procedures

In developing a rhetorical-critical approach to biblical interpretation, scholars have tended to adopt Kennedy's scheme, which presents a lucid and systematic model for rhetorical-critical exegesis that is undergirded by classical erudition and proceeds in five distinct steps (Kennedy 33–38; Wuellner 455–60). First, based either on the final text or (less often in current biblical scholarship) on any of its supposed preliminary stages, the critic identifies the text's *rhetorical unit(s)*, understood as argumentative units that affect the audience's reasoning and imagination. Next, the focus is on the specific *rhetorical situation* and *the "imperative stimulus"* or exigency that the discourse is designed to modify (Bitzer) and that determines the choices made by the rhetorician.

The third step consists in identifying the *rhetorical genre(s)* employed by the rhetorician. Following Aristotle, biblical rhetorical critics usually distinguish (1) judicial rhetoric, which expects hearers or readers to judge past events; (2) deliberative rhetoric, where the audience is invited to assess expedient or beneficial actions for future performance; and (3) epideictic rhetoric, which treats the audience as spectators, seeking to reinforce certain beliefs and values. The conventional concentration on these genres can become problematic, however, if the text in question is a hybrid or does not fit any of the argumentative genres identified by Aristotle (Black).

Following Kennedy, it is also too often taken for granted that the predominant rhetorical genre is indicative of the rhetorician's major purpose (19). What is not usually considered is the possibility that the genre of the discourse may reflect not the purpose but the main communicative strategy of the rhetorician.

Fourth, the text's *style* and *rhetorical strategy*, chosen by the rhetorician to address the specific rhetorical problem that occasioned the discourse, become the objects of investigation. Integral to Aristotle's system of rhetoric are the "proofs," among which he lists ethos, pathos, and logos. These correspond respectively to the rhetorician's moral character, the ability to put the hearer into a certain frame of mind, and the speech itself (*Rhet.* 1.2.4). Rhetorical criticism thus investigates the *whole* range of appeals embraced by rhetoric:

the rational and cognitive, the emotive and the imaginative (Wuellner 461).

In a final step, the critic then considers the discourse's *rhetorical effectiveness*, seeking to establish whether, or to what extent, it is a fitting response to the original exigency.

Some Criticisms of Rhetorical Criticism

Rhetorical criticism has been criticized on various grounds. One pertinent objection concerns the disquieting tendency of some biblical rhetorical critics to press texts such as prophetic oracles or the NT epistolary literature into elaborate and sometimes rather contrived schemes of organization.

However, the oft-repeated criticism that rhetorical-critical study of texts such as the OT is anachronistic, because its authors would not have been familiar with the system of classical Greco-Roman rhetoric and thus could not have been guided by its conventions, is less convincing. Indeed, the use of "anachronistic" conceptual tools such as modern linguistics is the norm in the study of ancient literature. Rhetorical critics therefore rightly insist that any discourse, whether written or oral, ancient or modern, can be investigated and assessed using the categories of classical rhetoric, provided the critic is sensitive to the unique qualities of the discourse under investigation.

Rhetorical-Critical Interpretation of the Bible

NT. Rhetorical criticism understood as the "art of persuasion" has been applied to the NT, and especially the Pauline Epistles, since the mid-1970s. Hans Dieter Betz's work on Galatians provided an important early influence, even though his conclusions have not gone unchallenged. Another significant impetus came from the studies of Kennedy and Wuellner. In recent years, the flood of rhetorical-critical studies has been unceasing, as the approach has been adopted by an increasing number of scholars and applied to the entire spectrum of the NT literature.

The following example, taken from *The Postmodern Bible* (see also Wuellner 458–60), illustrates how Kennedy's five steps of rhetorical-critical inquiry might be applied to a passage such as 1 Cor. 9:1–10:13. This digression from Paul's main argument in 1 Cor. 8–10 has often been subjected to source-critical operations. The whole passage constitutes a large-scale *rhetorical unit* consisting of an apology (9:3–27), an exhortation or paraenesis (10:1–11), and a brief conclusion or peroration (10:12–13).

The *rhetorical situation* of 1 Cor. 8–10, where Paul deals with divisive social practices generated by the use of meat sacrificed to idols, "is a mixed one because he partly supports existing social behavior . . . but seeks even more to . . . promote changed behavior" (Bible and Culture Collective 151). The choice of Paul's *rhetorical genre*, labeled an "apology" (*apologia*, 9:3), introduces an ironic mood because the speech in fact functions as a parody of an apology, "assigning praise and blame in the guise of offering a judicial defense" (152). In stressing that his response to Christ has led him to refuse payment for his teaching and thereby to reverse a universal cultural norm, Paul seeks to incite the Corinthians to follow his example and live by the eschatological norms that encompass all cultural ones.

Paul's *rhetorical style* in 1 Cor. 9 is dominated by rhetorical questions, which aim at dissociation and the depreciation of accepted values. The *effectiveness* of Paul's rhetorical strategy in 1 Cor. 9:1–10:13 is illustrated by the fact that it conforms to the educational intention of the epistle's epideictic rhetoric, which urges the Corinthians to maintain unity in the face of all kinds of distractions or distortions.

OT. Muilenburg's initial influence on OT rhetorical criticism was significant, but recent years have witnessed an increasing interest among OT scholars in persuasive rhetoric. Dale Patrick and Allen Scult's *Rhetoric and Biblical Interpretation* illustrates this revival of the classical Aristotelian definition. But mention must be made especially of Yehoshua Gitay, who pioneered the application of classical rhetorical categories to the OT prophetic literature. As of now, the approach has also been applied to the study of the Pentateuch, OT narrative, the Psalms, and Wisdom literature, but it has not yet engendered quite the same profusion of analyses as in NT studies.

Rhetorical criticism's potential to contribute to the theological interpretation of Scripture can be illustrated vis-à-vis traditional historical-critical readings of the book of Amos, which tend to regard the prophet as a messenger of unconditional doom. It has even been said that the radicalization of Amos's message, achieved by means of literary-critical operations, has turned the prophet into the messenger of a nation-murdering God, who may safely be seen as theologically outdated.

However, historical criticism's radical conclusions appear to be the result of its literalistic fixation on the surface text to the neglect of the text's strategy and purpose. Applying a communication-theoretical perspective and paying attention to the exigency occasioning the discourse as well as the text's rhetorical genre and strategy, rhetorical criticism transcends historical criticism's literalism, thus opening up new possibilities of interpretation (see Möller).

Applying the aforementioned observation that a text's predominant rhetorical genre may reflect the rhetorical strategy rather than the purpose of the discourse, Amos's chiefly judicial nature (notice the abundance of accusations and announcements of judgment) does not necessarily suggest that the prophet merely sought to bring his audience under judgment.

Combining rhetorical criticism with speech-act theory and investigating Jonah's diatribe against Nineveh (Jon. 3:4–9), Terry Eagleton ("Austin") and Walter Houston have shown that unconditional announcements of punishment could in fact be taken by the audience as warnings to repent. It is therefore conceivable that Amos focused on Israel's wrongdoings, painting a picture of unfolding death and calamity, in order to cause the people to repent in the face of the impending divine judgment. In this case, the rhetorician's purpose would be deliberative despite the judicial nature of the surface text.

The example illustrates rhetorical criticism's value for the theological interpretation of a book such as Amos. All too often, interpreters have naively assumed that the book's (supposedly utterly gloomy) theology can simply be read off the pages of the OT. However, this literalistic approach fails to do justice to the nature and function of human language. It also necessitates a variety of literary-critical and redaction-critical maneuvers in order to come to terms with the passages that do not fit the suggested interpretation.

Unleashing Rhetorical Criticism's Full Potential

Rhetorical criticism does not have to be construed along the lines suggested by the majority of biblical scholarship; nor does it have to follow Kennedy's five steps of rhetorical-critical inquiry. Indeed, Amador has criticized biblical rhetorical critics for their antiquarian outlook, which leads them to focus exclusively on ancient rhetorical textbooks. He also objected that the approach too often is synthetic, failing to distinguish between different ancient rhetorical theories, and that it is too preoccupied with the identification of argumentative structures and compositional styles.

To unleash rhetorical criticism's full potential, Amador rightly urges that considerably more work is needed on genres, social movements, sociolinguistics, metaphor, narrative, argumentation theory, feminist critical rhetorics, critical rhetoric, and the rhetoric of inquiry, all of which receive sustained attention in university rhetoric and communication departments.

See also Rhetoric

Bibliography

Amador, J. D. H. "Where Could Rhetorical Criticism (Still) Take Us?" *CurBS* 7 (1999): 195–222; Betz, H. D. "The Literary Composition and Function of Paul's Letter to the Galatians." *NTS* 21 (1975): 353–79; The Bible and Culture Collective. "Rhetorical Criticism." Pages 149–86 in *The Postmodern Bible*, ed. E. Castelli et al. Yale University Press, 1995; Bitzer, L. F. "The Rhetorical Situation." Pages 247–60 in *Rhetoric*, ed. W. R. Fisher. Michigan State University Press, 1974; Black, E. *Rhetorical Criticism*. Macmillan, 1965; Compier, D. *What Is Rhetorical Theology?* Trinity, 1999; Eagleton, T. "J. L. Austin and the Book of Jonah." Pages 231–36 in *The Book and the Text*, ed. R. Schwartz. Blackwell, 1990; idem. *Literary Theory*. 2d ed. Blackwell, 1996; Gitay, Y. *Prophecy and Persuasion*. Linguistica Biblica, 1981; Houston, W. "What Did the Prophets Think They Were Doing?" Pages 133–53 in *"The Place Is Too Small for Us,"* ed. R. P. Gordon. Eisenbrauns, 1995; Kennedy, G. A. *New Testament Interpretation through Rhetorical Criticism*. University of North Carolina Press, 1984; Möller, K. "Words of (In-)Evitable Certitude?" Pages 352–86 in *After Pentecost*, ed. C. Bartholomew et al. SHS. Zondervan/Paternoster, 2001; Muilenburg, J. "Form Criticism and Beyond." *JBL* 88 (1969): 1–18; Patrick, D., and A. Scult. *Rhetoric and Biblical Interpretation*. Almond, 1990; Perelman, C., and L. Olbrechts-Tyteca. *The New Rhetoric*. University of Notre Dame Press, 1969; Trible, P. *Rhetorical Criticism*. Fortress, 1994; Watson, D. F., and A. J. Hauser. *Rhetorical Criticism of the Bible*. Brill, 1994; Wuellner, W. "Where Is Rhetorical Criticism Taking Us?" *CBQ* 49 (1987): 448–63.

Karl Möller

Ricoeur, Paul

One of the most influential thinkers of the twentieth century, P. Ricoeur (1913–2005), "philosopher of the word," is along with H.-G. Gadamer best known for his hermeneutic philosophy. Dual appointments at the Universities of Paris (Nanterre) and Chicago through the 1970s and 1980s led Ricoeur to mediate the worlds of Anglo-American analytic philosophy, with its concern for clarity and conceptual precision, and Continental philosophy, with its concern for human subjectivity. Creative mediation is the operative term throughout Ricoeur's thought. He mediates between disciplines as diverse as psychology, social theory, history, literary theory, and religious studies—by demonstrating previously unseen connections, formal and material, between them—and he mediates between diverse interpretative approaches by finding a place for each in his hermeneutical arch, which spans explanation and understanding.

Ironically, the discipline for which Ricoeur appears to have the least sympathy is systematic theology, at least to the extent that this latter is guilty of rushing to conceptual abstractions (e.g., doctrines) too quickly, to the detriment of the original forms of biblical discourse. For example, Ricoeur thinks that Augustine's doctrine of original sin reduces the Adamic myth to a forensic concept: the concept, however, is nothing more than "pseudo-knowledge, grafted onto myth, interpreted literally, and dressed up in pseudo-history" ("'Original Sin,'" in *Conflict*, 285).

Also of importance for the interpretation of Scripture is his mediation of suspicion and belief: in marked contrast to the historical, critical, and deconstructionist distrust of appearances, Ricoeur retrieves the power of creative language (e.g., metaphor, narrative) and makes possible a reading of the Bible that is existentially deep. There is some debate, however, as to whether Ricoeur's respect for the limits of philosophy ever allows his interpretations of the Bible to move beyond anthropology to speak of God.

Hermeneutic Philosopher of the "I Am"

Ricoeur's project is first and foremost one of philosophical anthropology. He stands squarely in the tradition of the philosophy of the subject, whose goal is ultimately self-understanding. While an ontology of the self is the goal, however, hermeneutical reflection is the means. Descartes's "*Cogito, ergo sum* [I think, therefore I am]" errs in thinking that human subjectivity can be directly inspected, as it were. Hermeneutics is the "long route" to the "promised land" of ontology (*Conflict*, 24). The manifesto of hermeneutic philosophy is "existence via semantics": self-understanding via textual interpretation.

Ricoeur's fundamental conviction that language discloses human being leads him to engage the so-called "masters of suspicion" (e.g., Freud, Marx, Nietzsche), who argue that language conceals as much if not more than it reveals. Ricoeur concedes their critical point, but he insists that self-understanding remains possible; hence, "consciousness is not a given but a task."

Ricoeur similarly incorporates Nietzsche's and Feuerbach's accusation that talk of "God" is simply a projection of the human will to power. Ricoeur's is a postcritical faith, one that has to endure the chastening effect of various forms of criticism, especially the suspicion that images of God are being used to serve some ideological project, such as enforcing a particular moral order.

Finally, Ricoeur transcends the historical-critical preoccupation with "the world behind the text." He does this by bringing a variety of literary approaches to bear on Scripture's diverse genres ("the world of the text") and by focusing on the way in which the text engages and transforms the situation of the reader ("the world in front of the text"). "Beyond the desert of criticism, we wish to be called again" (*Symbolism of Evil*, 349). Called, yes: but by whom, and to what end?

The Second Naïveté: Appropriating the World of the Text

Ricoeur challenges Heidegger's decision to take anxiety as the fundamental "mood" of human being, arguing that joy and hope have equal claim to be regarded as the basic clue to the meaning of humanity. There is a positive charge to Ricoeur's hermeneutic philosophy: a belief in transcendence, a desire to say "Yes" in spite of the negative aspects of human existence.

Like Kant, who claimed to have abolished knowledge in order to make room for faith, Ricoeur abolishes the first naïveté, a faith in what the text literally says. He does this to make room for a second naïveté: "To smash the idols is also to let the symbols speak" ("Critique of Religion," in *Philosophy*, 219). A hermeneutical "wager" funds his philosophical work: "The symbol gives rise to thought. . . . I believe [in symbol] in order to understand [the self]."

For Ricoeur, the text, as written discourse (e.g., something said to someone about something), is neither a mirror to the past, nor a self-contained entity, but rather a world-bearing or world-projecting dynamism. Texts, by virtue of being written, gain autonomy from their authors and original situations and launch out on a career of their own. Textual interpretation must explain the text's structure (sense) and understand the text's world (reference). Interpretation is less a matter of recovering the author's original discourse than it is an exploration of a text's trajectory of meaning. (For an important critique of Ricoeur's preference for "textual sense" rather than "authorial intention," see Wolterstorff 130–52.)

Ricoeur's preferred texts range from metaphors to narratives. He discerns a parallel between the ways metaphors and narratives refer: both are types of creative language that project a meaning beyond any possible literal reference. Metaphors, for example, are not literally true, but they do open up new ways of seeing the real. They suspend the first-order reference to empirical actuality (the focus of the first naïveté) in order to liberate a second-order reference to new existential possibilities (the focus of the second naïveté). Narratives are like metaphors in that they do not simply picture empirical reality but configure it, emplotting persons and events in patterns in order to display possible ways of human being-in-time. Together, stories and histories display the full panoply of human possibilities. In his Gifford Lectures, Ricoeur completes his project by arguing that self-understanding comes precisely by appropriating a narrative identity (*Oneself*).

Philosophical or Theological Hermeneutics?

"I believe that the fundamental theme of Revelation is this awakening and this call, into the heart of existence, of the imagination of the possible. The possibilities are opened before man which fundamentally constitute what is revealed. The revealed as such is an opening to existence, a possibility of existence" ("Language of Faith," in *Philosophy*, 237). The Bible, similarly, is revelatory to the extent that its being-in-the-world is a new kind of being, a creative possibility for human existence. If not only the Bible but also all poetic texts "reveal" the "transcendent"—in the sense that the worlds they project open up possible ways of being-in-the-world that, if appropriated, can transform the world of the reader—what then is unique about Scripture? And what might Ricoeur mean by "theological interpretation"?

Led by H. Frei, the erstwhile Yale School criticized Ricoeur for subjecting his biblical interpretation to an all-encompassing extratextual philosophical framework. All self-understanding is mediated through the ensemble of texts that refigure human existence; hence, for Ricoeur biblical interpretation is at one and the same time self-interpretation. The purpose of biblical narrative is not to convey knowledge about what God has done in Jesus Christ so much as to enlarge our understanding of human existence. On this view, biblical hermeneutics is merely a regional instance of general hermeneutics, a variation on the theme of self-understanding—with devastating consequences for Christology (Vanhoozer, chs. 7–9). Others, however, point out that Ricoeur seeks only to provide philosophical "approximations" of theology and that his hermeneutic philosophy may be employed by a variety of theological perspectives (Stiver 245–46).

What distinguishes biblical interpretation from general hermeneutics in Ricoeur's view is the particular referent of Scripture—"limit" or ultimate existential possibilities—and the concern of Scripture to "name" God. "God" is the referent of the medley of biblical genres, taken together in all their irreducible diversity. Yet God is not a univocal concept so much as the index of incompleteness of human discourse and hence of the ineluctable mystery of being.

Commentators disagree about the kind of theology to which Ricoeur's hermeneutics give rise; some draw comparisons with Bultmann (Vanhoozer), others with Barth (Wallace) and Hauerwas (Fodor). What remains beyond dispute is Ricoeur's belief that the human being is constituted by the "word" that summons it. The philosopher cannot ultimately say, however, whether this word—and the possibility of transformed life projected by the biblical text—is human or divine. More recently, Ricoeur has stressed the importance of the interpretative community for biblical interpretation: "The text exists, in the final analysis, thanks to the community, for the use of the community, with a view to giving shape to the community" (*Thinking*, xiii).

While Ricoeur scrupulously keeps theology and philosophy separate (the one arising from historical testimony, the other from universal experience), there are several aspects of his interpretation theory (e.g., the revelatory world-of-the-text, the wager of faith) that approximate Christian themes. Moreover, he has written provocative interpretations of the opening chapters of Genesis, the book of Job, the parables, and the Gospel narratives, as well as a number of essays on other biblical texts and themes (e.g., revelation, time, testimony). He treats Jesus' parables as metaphoric narratives that redescribe the kingdom of God and hence open up new possibilities for human social existence ("Biblical Hermeneutics").

Ricoeur describes his position as a "post-Hegelian Kantianism." With Kant, Ricoeur carefully respects the limits of reason; with Hegel, he explores reason's many forms, both figurative and conceptual (e.g., of history, poetry, culture, and religion). Against Hegel, however, Ricoeur refuses to let conceptual language swallow up figurative language. It is just here, in the rehabilitation of the imagination and the closely related notion of literary form, that Ricoeur advances beyond the Yale School's preoccupation with narrative

and makes what is perhaps his most significant contribution to the project of theological interpretation of Scripture.

As with narrative, each of the literary genres in Scripture "refigures" the world in its own irreducible manner, all of which "call for thought." A hermeneutic philosophy does not try to prove the existence of God but instead attends to the diverse literary strategies for "naming" God in Scripture. Theological interpretation is not a matter of pure but of hermeneutic reason—of reason reflecting on historical testimonies to the divine in a way that does justice to the plurality of the literary forms in which these testimonies are embedded. The "language of faith" is not objectifying; unlike historical and scientific discourse, which describes empirical actuality, the language of faith awakens the imagination, that "prophet of our existence," to "eschatological" possibilities.

Conclusion: Toward What Kind of Eschatological Possibility?

What are the consequences of Ricoeur's "second naïveté" for the theological interpretation of Scripture? Ricoeur takes the literal reading of Scripture to yield what he calls a "moral vision" of the world in which human beings are caught in an economy of guilt and punishment. Ricoeur's postcritical, metaphorical interpretation, by contrast, yields an "eschatological vision" that allows us to refigure existence as a gift from something greater than ourselves, to be cherished "in spite of" our fallibility and faults, "in spite of" suffering and evil.

Some have compared Ricoeur's hermeneutics to Barth's on the basis that each is fundamentally committed to the subject matter of the text (Wallace). However, it is not entirely clear just what Ricoeur thinks the Bible is fundamentally about. Is his "eschatological" vision about divinely inaugurated possibilities, or about human existential possibilities that have been forgotten and need to be recovered? Philosophy may approximate the eschatological event that is the object of Easter preaching, though what it knows and what it says must remain within the limits of reason.

Ricoeur's own second naïveté is apparently compatible with his nonbelief in a literal resurrection. Despite his being a believing philosopher who trusts testimony, Ricoeur understands the resurrection to be about (1) the victory over death through service to others, and (2) Jesus' acquiring a historical body in the church that continues his self-giving way of being-in-the-world. So, while theologians may helpfully employ aspects of

Ricoeur's hermeneutic philosophy on an ad hoc basis, we must question the wisdom of a wholesale appropriation of an interpretation theory that proceeds from a "Christianity of the philosopher" (*Critique*, 152–53).

See also Hermeneutics; Method

Bibliography

Primary, by Ricoeur, in Chronological Order: *The Symbolism of Evil*. Beacon, 1967; *The Conflict of Interpretations*. Northwestern University Press, 1974; "Biblical Hermeneutics." *Semeia* 4 (1975): 27–148; *Interpretation Theory*. Texas Christian University Press, 1976; *The Philosophy of Paul Ricoeur*, ed. C. E. Reagan and D. Stewart. Beacon, 1978; *Essays on Biblical Interpretation*. Fortress, 1980; *A Ricoeur Reader*, ed. M. J. Valdes. Harvester Wheatsheaf, 1991; *Oneself as Another*. University of Chicago, 1992; *Figuring the Sacred*. Fortress, 1995; *Thinking Biblically*. With A. Lacocque. University of Chicago Press, 1998; *Critique and Conviction*. Columbia University Press, 1998. **Secondary:** Fodor, J. *Christian Hermeneutics*. Clarendon, 1995; Kearney, R. *On Paul Ricoeur*. Ashgate, 2004; Laughery, G. *Living Hermeneutics in Motion*. University Press of America, 2002; Stiver, D. *Theology after Ricoeur*. Westminster John Knox, 2001; Vanhoozer, K. *Biblical Narrative in the Philosophy of Paul Ricoeur*. Cambridge University Press, 1990; Wallace, M. *The Second Naïveté*. Mercer University Press, 1990; Wolterstorff, N. *Divine Discourse*. Cambridge University Press, 1995.

Kevin J. Vanhoozer

Roman Empire

Early Christianity began within the Roman Empire, and many of its early writings bear the marks of reflection on, and sometimes resistance to, what it was, how it operated, and what it stood for. Failure to recognize this leads not only to under-exegesis of the NT, but also under-application to subsequent imperial rhetoric, ideology, and demands.

Rome had an empire long before it had an emperor. The ancient Roman republic, proud of its refusal to grant anyone supreme power for more than a short emergency period, had steadily conquered lands in all directions from the capital. By the middle of the first century BCE, its large network of provinces and client regimes had become increasingly difficult to govern by the system of rotating magistrates, and it was vulnerable to the ambitions of powerful individuals. The best known of these, Julius Caesar, was effectively becoming sole ruler when he was murdered by angry republicans (44 BCE), precipitating factional civil wars. From these there emerged Caesar's adopted heir, Octavius, who took the name Augustus and ruled the entire Roman world from 31 BCE to his death in 14 CE.

Flattering poets like Virgil and historians like Livy told the story of the transition to imperial rule in terms of a long historical process coming at last to fulfillment. The older Roman ideology—according to which Rome was naturally free and had a responsibility to bring this kind of "freedom" to the rest of the world through its superior military might—was transferred to the claims of Augustus and his family. Rome believed that its own system of justice was the fairest in the world ("Iustitia" became a goddess during Augustus's reign). Rome also, of course, sat at the center of an economic empire, using its own "freedom" and "justice" to rake in profits from around the world. Since his accession followed the end of civil war, Augustus was hailed also as the bringer of peace and "salvation" (= rescue). His accession and his birthday were hailed throughout the empire as "good news" (*euangelion* in Greek). Most important for the rise of Christianity, a religious cult of Augustus began to spring up. This did not happen in Rome itself, where the citizens would have objected, but certainly in the Greek East, from Greece right round the eastern Mediterranean to Egypt, where local and international rulers had long been regarded as divine. Cities competed for the honor (and the tax-exemption status) of building and looking after temples to Augustus and his family. Statues were made of him and his family, often in the guise of some of the ancient pagan gods and goddesses. In Rome itself and on his coins, Augustus described himself as "son of the god Julius," having conveniently declared his adopted father to be divine after his death.

Augustus's successor Tiberius (14–37 CE) carried on the same ideology, as did the mad Gaius (37–41) and the weak but crafty Claudius (41–54). Nero (54–68) copied Gaius in making the recognition of his own divinity mandatory and widespread. After his suicide, the "year of the four emperors" (69) saw Galba, Otho, and Vitellius come and go in quick succession, before Vespasian, who had been besieging Jerusalem, stopped the rot by marching to Rome and claiming the crown (69–79). He began a new dynasty, the Flavians, being succeeded by Titus (79–81), whom he had left to complete the capture of Jerusalem in 70. Titus was succeeded by his brother Domitian (81–96), who has had bad press from Roman as well as Christian sources. This gives the empire's shape and something of its flavor, under which Christianity was born, spread, and—despite persecution—flourished.

The Jewish people had a long tradition of theological and practical reflection on living under imperial rule. In exile in Babylon, Jeremiah had told them both that Babylon was wicked and ripe for God's judgment, and that they should settle down there, pray for the city, and seek its welfare (29:7). The book of Daniel recounts the regular clashes between the pagan empire and those loyal to Israel's God. Yet, when the Jewish heroes escape from pagan persecution, they resume their work as high-ranking imperial civil servants. In the political thought that follows from Jewish monotheism, the one God calls rulers to account but does not want the world to collapse into anarchy. Sometimes first-century Jews emphasized the first of these, not least in the various kingdom movements ("no king but God") that flourished during Jesus' boyhood. Sometimes they went for the second, hoping to live by their own laws and negotiate a truce with Rome. Julius Caesar had allowed the Jews to practice their own religion, and part of the tension within early Christianity concerned whether this privilege would be extended to followers of Jesus. This complex theological and political tradition, reshaped around Jesus and the Spirit, informs the early Christian thought and life under the Roman Empire.

This is the setting for Jesus' cryptic saying about the tribute penny (Mark 12:13–17 et par.). "Pay back the pagans as they deserve," said the rebel Mattathias to his sons (1 Macc. 2:68), "and keep the law's commands." "Pay Caesar what belongs to Caesar," said Jesus, "and give God what belongs to God" (AT). This could be heard either as a cryptic call to revolt, or as an instruction to be a good citizen, or both. The clash between Jesus and Rome reaches its height in the remarkable conversation with Pilate (John 18:33–19:16). Jesus acknowledges that Pilate's power over him comes from God, while continuing to challenge him with news about a kingdom from beyond the world (18:36).

Paul echoes the entire range of Roman imperial rhetoric in several passages. In Phil. 2:6–11 he tells the story of Jesus as the truth of which Caesar's proud boast is a mere parody. And in 3:20–21 he ascribes to Jesus the titles King, Lord, and Savior, and credits him with the power to subject all things to himself, exactly as Caesar would have claimed for himself. In 1 Thess. 4:15–17 he draws a vivid picture of the reappearance of Jesus on the model of Caesar paying a state visit to a colony (coupled, confusingly for us, with language drawn from Dan. 7 about God's people being vindicated, caught up on the clouds). In Rom. 1:3–5 he describes the "good news" of Jesus as being about God's Son, raised from the dead by God's power, claiming obedient loyalty from the whole world. And in 1:16–17 he declares that through this gospel "salvation" is available for all, because in it God's "justice" is revealed (1:17 JB). At the end of the letter's theological exposition, he speaks again of the root of Jesse, the royal Messiah "who will arise to rule the nations" (15:12). Paul's implicit critique of Caesar, his empire, and all that he stood for is the foundation for the more explicit resistance we find a generation or two later in figures like Polycarp.

Romans 13:1–7 is not a charter for political quietism, but a warning against the wrong sort of resistance. In the NT, it corresponds to Jer. 29, as also does 1 Pet. 2:13–17. The book of Revelation articulates the most explicit early Christian critique of Roman imperial ideology and resistance to it. As a measure of the inability of the post-Enlightenment Western church to grasp the necessity for such critique, Revelation has been either a closed and puzzling book or merely a quarry for strange theories about the future. From the vision of the worship going on in heaven (Rev. 4–5) to the final vision of the new Jerusalem, the true eternal city, the book constantly and kaleidoscopically insists that God the Creator and Jesus the Lamb are the true objects of worship. Whatever human empire may do, God's people must stay faithful. The NT remains rooted in the Jewish critique of pagan empire, articulating that critique afresh in the light of Jesus and the Spirit in the new circumstance of worldwide Roman rule, and thereby providing a model for the church in our own day.

Bibliography

Alexander, L., ed. *Images of Empire*. JSOTSup 122. JSOT, 1991; Bowman, A., et al., eds. *The Cambridge Ancient History*. 2d ed. Vol. 10, *The Augustan Empire, 43 BC–AD 69*. Cambridge University Press, 1996; Bowman, A., et al., eds. *Representations of Empire*. Oxford University Press, 2002; Goodman, M. *The Roman World, 44 BC–AD 180*. Routledge, 1997; Lintott, A. *Imperium Romanum*. Routledge, 1993; Millar, F. *The Emperor in the Roman World (31 BC–AD 337)*. 2d ed. Cornell University Press, 1992; idem. *The Roman Near East, 31 BC–AD 337*. Harvard University Press, 1993; Price, S. R. F. *Rituals and Power*. Cambridge University Press, 1984; Zanker, P. *The Power of Images in the Age of Augustus*. University of Michigan Press, 1990.

N. T. Wright

Romans, Book of

Genre

The book of Romans is a Greco-Roman letter. It contains elements characteristic of a family letter, notably, Paul's expressed desire to visit his addressees (1:1, 7, 8–10, 13) and his lengthy concluding salutations (16:3–16, 21–24); and it briefly takes the form of a letter of commendation when he speaks of Phoebe (16:1–2). But by far its greater part (1:16–15:13) consists of what the ancients would have called *logos protreptikos*—"a persuasive discourse." In philosophical tradition, such discourse was associated with the choice of a particular school, or with the choice of philosophy itself. Philosophers used protreptic to strengthen believers and convert outsiders. Ever since Aristotle's *Protrepticus* there had been a tradition of putting such discourses into letter form—as, for example, Lucian's *Nigrinus*. Philon of Larissa (ca. 160–80 BCE) identified two main elements in protreptic: dissuasion or refutation (*apelegmos*), and demonstration (*endeiktikos*). To those we should probably add a third: normally, such discourses involved personal appeal and exhortation (*parainesis*).

Occasion, Place, and Date of Writing

Paul wrote Romans on the eve of his final visit to Jerusalem, where he intended to deliver in person a collection that he had taken up from Gentile churches (15:25; cf. 1 Cor. 16:1). Though he evidently viewed the outcome of the projected visit with some uncertainty (15:30–31), the gift would, he hoped, show to the Jerusalem church the solidarity in Christ that existed between her "poor" and the Gentile believers of Achaia, Galatia, and Macedonia (15:26–27). That visit aside, and having preached Christ "from Jerusalem all the way round to Illyricum" (15:19), Paul evidently considered that his apostolate in the area of the eastern Mediterranean was complete. He now contemplated a mission to Spain, and he planned to go there by way of Rome, partly so that he might use the Roman church as a base (15:22–24, 28). (Note that in 15:24 Paul hopes "to be sent on [his] way [*propemphthēnai*]" by the Romans; Paul uses the word *propempein* elsewhere to speak of being sent on by a community with its support, as in 1 Cor. 16:6; 2 Cor. 1:16.)

Paul refers to Gaius as his host (16:23), so it is likely that Romans was composed in Corinth or Cenchreae (see 1 Cor. 1:14), perhaps during the winter of 56–57. This date would also fit with the positive view of Roman *imperium* in 13:1–4: at this period Nero was still under the influence of Burrus and Seneca, and he was generally regarded with high hopes.

Outline

In tracing the outline of Romans, it is easy to discern the three main elements of protreptic identified above.

Following the epistolary opening (1:1–15), the first part of the document (1:16–4:25) is a dissuasive, or refutation (*apelegmos*). These chapters seek, on the basis of Scripture, to dissuade Paul's hearers from a view of God's relationship with the world or with Israel that would see it as ever at any time or in any situation founded on anything except God's justice and grace. This is the point, not only of the long discussion of Abraham that concludes the section (3:27–4:25), but also of the entire denunciation of human sin (Jewish and Gentile) that runs from 1:18 to 3:20. This denunciation culminates at 3:21–26 with the affirmation of God's saving justice/righteousness "manifested apart from the law, although testified to by the Law and the Prophets" (3:21 AT). In other words, Paul claims that what he refers to as "my gospel" (2:16)—the proclamation of a God who, through the long-promised coming of the Messiah, has chosen to be gracious to all, Jew and Gentile alike—manifests the saving justice/righteousness of God promised through the prophets. Paul's gospel says nothing about that justice that was not implicit in the law given to Israel from the beginning.

This dissuasive involves Paul in making two other points. (1) The proclamation of God's universal graciousness does *not* strip Israel of her "special relationship" with God. The unshakable basis of that relationship is clear in Israel's possession of the Law (3:1–4). (This is important, for if God's graciousness *did* strip Israel of her privilege, then the universally gracious God would not be trustworthy, since God *promised* a special relationship to Israel.) (2) The God who is gracious to all is *not* on that account a God who is morally indifferent, so that in proclaiming such a God, Paul is *not* saying, in effect, "Let us do evil, that good may come" (3:5–8 NRSV).

The second part of the letter (5:1–11:36) is a positive demonstration (*endeiktikos*) of God's justice and grace at work in the life of faith—a life lived at "peace with God through our Lord Jesus Christ" (5:1). This demonstration involves defense, which means further reflection on the falsity of the two charges that Paul has already summarily denied. First, he considers the question of moral indifference (6:1–8:39). One who is "in Christ" no longer lives under the dominion of sin (6:14), has been "put to death to the law" (7:4 AT), and is freed from "condemnation" (8:1). Far from leading, however, to a life of moral indifference (6:1, 15), this leads to being "led by the Spirit of God" (8:14). Thereby we "put to death the deeds of the flesh" (8:13 AT) on the basis of a new relationship, as "heirs of God and joint heirs with Christ" (8:17 NRSV). Even suffering may be endured cheerfully (8:18; cf. 5:1–5), for Christians know that nothing can finally separate them from "the love of God in Christ Jesus our Lord" (8:39 NRSV). Second, Paul considers the question of God's special relationship to Israel (9:1–11:36). Paul argues that the fulfillment of the law in Christ (10:4), far from meaning that God has abandoned the promised special covenant relationship with Israel, means on the contrary that God is being faithful to *all* the promises, *including* the promises to Israel. Despite the disobedience of all—Jew *and* Gentile—it is God's will finally to "have mercy upon all" (11:32 RSV).

The third part of the letter (12:1–15:13) is taken up with appeal and exhortation (*parainesis*)—an exhortation springing directly out of the demonstration that preceded it. Those who know that they live only "by the mercies of God" (12:1 NRSV) certainly cannot lead lives of moral indifference. Far from conforming themselves "to this age," those who live "by the mercies of God" will look to be "transformed" by the "renewal" of their minds (12:2–3 AT). Within the life of the Christian community, this is going to mean mutual acceptance among those who feel called to obey the law in one way, and those who feel called to obey it in another (14:1–12). The basis of their actions will be plain—the example offered by Christ himself: "Welcome one another, therefore, as Christ welcomed you, for the glory of God" (15:7 RSV; cf. 12:1; 15:2–3).

The remainder of the letter is taken up with Paul's commendation of Phoebe, a deacon of the church at Cenchreae, his patron, and presumably the bearer of the letter (16:1–2), with final greetings and salutations (16:3–16, 21–24), and a note that was perhaps written in Paul's own hand (16:17–20).

Style

Ever since Rudolf Bultmann produced his dissertation in 1910 (*Der Stil der paulinischen Predigt und die kynisch-stoische Diatribe*), it has been common to associate Romans with

diatribe. This is helpful, if "diatribe" is understood in accordance with ancient usage—which, unfortunately, has not always been the case. In connection with the kind of literature we are considering, the word "diatribe" (*diatribē*: "a way of passing the time," "an occupation") is properly used with reference either to the activity of teaching in a school or to texts describing that activity. Examples are Epictetus's *Discourses*—records of his lectures, noted down "so far as possible in his own words" by his student Arrian. By extension, "diatribe" is also applied to texts using rhetoric and pedagogy, which characterized education. As such, written diatribe has identifiable characteristics of both subject matter and style.

Regarding subject matter, diatribe is generally concerned with serious philosophical or moral issues. Clearly, Romans would be at home in such company. Regarding style, diatribe is marked by a whole battery of characteristics. Frequently there is discussion with an imaginary partner, whose role is to raise objections, offer false conclusions, and pose difficult questions. The teacher turns from his real audience to respond to such objections with direct, second-person discourse (9:19–20). False conclusions and suggestions may be set aside with a scornful *mē genoito!* "Of course not!" (3:4, 31; 6:2; 11:1). Suggestions and conclusions regarded as correct may be supported by citations from sources considered authoritative. In Epictetus, this means allusions to Homer, Plato, and others of the "canon" of Greek *paideia*; in Paul, naturally, it means appeals to Scripture. Some composers of diatribe like to personify abstractions, and so, at times, does Paul: "For Sin, seizing an opportunity in the commandment, deceived me and through it put me to death" (7:11 AT). Some use sarcasm, and so, at times, does Paul: "Will what is made say to its maker, 'Why have you made me so?' Or does not the potter have a right over the clay?" (9:20–21 AT). There are lists of virtues and vices (1:29–30).

This then is the style in which the Letter to the Romans is written: a style designed, above all, for leading those who heard it to the truth—often by correcting their assumptions or pretensions. It is a style not to be associated, as was at one time supposed, with public preaching on street corners to the masses, but with the lecture hall, the classroom, and the school—in other words, with education and instruction. It was a style, therefore, eminently suited to protreptic, which, as a genre, had the same associations.

Destination, Purpose, and Strategy

As his opening salutation shows (1:1–15), Paul is writing to a church that he does not know personally. On the other hand, if his closing salutations are to be taken seriously, he was acquainted with a good many individuals in it (16:3–16). There is no reason to suppose that he would not, through them, have come to know something of the situation at Rome, regarding both the believers' attitudes to each other, and their reactions to Paul or what they had heard of Paul's gospel. In addressing the Romans, then, Paul seems particularly to have been aware of two groups. First were some—mostly but not necessarily all of Jewish descent—who had accepted Jesus as Messiah but believed that Paul's admission of uncircumcised Gentiles to full fellowship simply on the basis of faith in Jesus was an abandonment of God's law. They saw in Paul's gospel of "grace for all" both an implicit denial of Israel's calling and a proclamation of moral indifference. Second were those—mostly but not necessarily all of Gentile origin—who resented the claims of the former group and felt, or claimed to feel, superior to those who were so hung up on questions of law and obedience. In Romans, Paul sought to address both groups, not with "a compendium of Christian doctrine" (as Philipp Melanchthon suggested), but with an account of how the gospel (which was also "my gospel" [2:16]) accorded with God's promises to restore creation (8:18–25) and redeem Israel (chs. 9–11), and how that should affect the attitude of believers to each other (12:1–15:13).

A strategic reason for Paul's undertaking to address the Roman congregations in this way is not difficult to see. He hoped for support from them for his projected mission to the West (15:23–24): clearly, the better they understood and accepted his apostolate, the sounder that support would be. Yet finally, it was more than a matter of strategy. Paul was convinced that an approach to the gospel that founded it on *anything* other than the justice and grace of God available for all who would put their trust in the Son of God amounted in fact to rejection of the gospel. "You who want to be justified by the Law," he wrote on another occasion, "have cut yourselves off from Christ; you have fallen away from grace" (Gal. 5:4 NRSV; cf. 1:6–9). Equally, Paul was convinced that those who did accept the gospel were committed by it to emulating the grace by which they were saved: "Welcome one another, therefore, just as Christ has welcomed you, for the glory of God" (Rom.

15:7 NRSV). In other words, not simply strategy, but the thing itself was at stake.

Genre is a tool of meaning. Protreptic was a form of address associated with the choice of a particular philosophical school, or with the choice of philosophy itself. Just why, then, did Paul choose to present his defense of the gospel in this form? Partly, he may have acted in the light of Jewish precedent. The Wisdom of Solomon, which appears to have influenced him in other respects (e.g., 1:24–32; cf. Wis. 14:22–27), certainly seems to have protreptic features. More decisive, however, was perhaps something in the nature of the gospel itself as the ancient world, including Paul, would have perceived it. The ancients generally seem to have understood what we call "religion" in terms of experience and ritual, whereas ultimate truth claims and demands for appropriate living were associated with philosophy. So Seneca:

> Who can doubt, my dear Lucilius, that life is the gift of the immortal gods, but that living well is the gift of philosophy? Hence the idea that our debt to philosophy is greater than our debt to the gods, in proportion as a good life is more of a benefit than mere life, would be regarded as correct, were not philosophy itself a boon which the gods have bestowed upon us. They have given the knowledge thereof to none, but the faculty of acquiring it they have given to all. . . . [Philosophy's] sole function is to discover the truth about things divine and things human. From her side awe of the divine (*religio*) never departs, nor duty, nor justice, nor any of the whole company of virtues which cling together in close united fellowship. (*Ep.* 90.3, altered)

Hence, joining a philosophical school involved many of the ideas, and even the emotions, that we associate with religious conversion. And so for the ancients, Christianity (like Judaism) was a confusing phenomenon. Insofar as it involved ritual and cult, it might naturally be described in Latin as *superstitio*—the usual disparaging term for a foreign cult in the first century, as used by Pliny in his rescript to Hadrian about Christians in Bithynia (*Ep.* 10.96.10). On the other hand, insofar as Christianity presented itself as teaching doctrines describing what is ultimately true and requiring appropriate activity, it appeared to be a philosophical school. This, no doubt, was precisely the point. Paul's purpose in Romans was to persuade his hearers to a favorable view of his beliefs about God and God's promise—"my gospel." By using the protreptic form, he immediately declared to his contemporaries that he regarded what he was presenting *not* simply as an invitation to religious experience, but rather, and much more importantly, as also a witness to ultimate truth. It is "the power of God for salvation" (1:16 NRSV), in response to which no "rational worship" is possible other than total obedience, the presentation of one's whole being "as a living sacrifice" (12:1 AT; cf. NRSV margin).

In this connection, it is interesting finally to consider how Paul's pagan contemporaries might have reacted to Romans. No doubt they would have found it very Jewish, full of "questions about words and names and your own law" (Acts 18:15). If they were like Galen a century or so later, they might have said that while its "philosophy" could lead people to behavior "not inferior to that of genuine philosophers" (*Summary of Plato's Republic: Fragment*), yet it was full of "talk of undemonstrated laws" (*On the Pulse* 2.4). Nevertheless, in broad terms, they would not have been in any doubt about what Paul was trying to do. He was, in his own way, a "philosopher," seeking to persuade hearers to his particular "school."

Romans throughout Christian History

In August 386 a professor of rhetoric sat in his friend Alypius's garden in Milan and heard a child singing in a neighboring house, "Take up and read, take up and read!" Taking the scroll that lay at Alypius's side, he found himself reading Rom. 13:13b–14, "not in orgies and drunkenness, not in promiscuity and licentiousness, not in rivalry and jealousy. But put on the Lord Jesus Christ, and make no provision for the desires of the flesh" (AT). Augustine's reaction was immediate. "No further would I read, nor did I need to: at once, at the end of this sentence, a clear light flooded my heart, and all the darkness of doubt vanished away" (*Conf.* 8.29).

In November 1515, Martin Luther began lecturing to his students at Wittenberg (Germany) on the Letter to the Romans. He went on with his expositions until the following September; and as he did so, his own understanding changed.

> I greatly desired to understand Paul's Letter to the Romans, and nothing barred the way, save one expression, "the righteousness of God"—for I understood it to signify that righteousness whereby God is righteous and acts righteously in punishing the unrighteous. . . . Night and day I thought about this, until . . . I took hold of the truth, that the righteousness of God is that righteousness whereby, through grace and sheer mercy, he justifies us by faith. At which I felt myself to be born again, and to have passed through open doors into Paradise. The whole of Scripture took on a new significance, and whereas before "the righteousness of God" had filled

> me with hate, now it became for me indescribably sweet in greater love. This passage of Paul became for me a gateway to heaven. (WA 54:179–87)

In his journal John Wesley tells us how, in the evening of May 24, 1738, he "went very unwillingly to a society in Aldersgate Street [London], where one was reading Luther's Preface to the Epistle to the Romans. About a quarter before nine, while he was describing the change which God works in the heart through faith in Christ, I felt my heart strangely warmed. I felt I did trust in Christ, Christ alone, for my salvation; and an assurance was given me that he had taken my sins away, even mine, and saved me from the law of sin and death."

At the end of World War I, and in the chaotic years immediately following, Karl Barth, pastor in Safenwil (Switzerland), looked for a theology that might enable him to function amid the turmoil around him. "I sat under an apple tree and began to apply myself to Romans with all the resources that were available to me at the time. I had already learned in my confirmation instruction that this book was of crucial importance. I began to read it through as I had never read it before. . . . I read and read and wrote and wrote" ("Nachwort," 294). The result was *Der Römerbrief*, Barth's commentary on Romans. The first edition, published in 1919, fell (in Karl Adams's well-known words) "like a bombshell on the playground of the theologians."

These four vignettes may serve to illustrate the effect that Paul's Letter to the Romans has had, and continues to have, on Christian history. Other major interpreters throughout that history have included Chrysostom, Origen, Theodore of Mopsuestia, John Damascene, Oecumenius, Theophylact, Ambrosiaster, Hugh of St. Victor, Abelard, and Thomas Aquinas. To this day Romans continues to challenge the finest minds in Christendom. Certainly, there are differences over details of interpretation. But in general, all who listen to Romans agree as to what it is overall: a proclamation of Christian freedom. Not surprisingly, then, it has again and again been a factor in the renewal of the church.

Theological Significance

Gratia sola: *The Gift of Salvation.* According to Paul, there is "no distinction; for all have sinned and come short of the glory of God, being justified [*dikaioumenoi*] by his grace as a gift, through the redemption [*apolytrōseōs*] that is in Christ Jesus: whom God set forth to be a propitiation [mercy seat; *hilastērion*], by his own blood, through faith (*dia pisteōs*)" (3:22b–25a AT). It is possible, though not certain, that Paul was here adapting a formula already familiar to the Roman church. In any case, the three metaphors that now fly past us like changing images on a cinema screen enable him to make his point with a force that has echoed through the centuries.

The first metaphor, "justified," is about law and judgment. "Justify" (Greek: *dikaioō*) means "to treat as just," or more simply, "to acquit." For Paul, "justification" (*dikaiōsis*) is God's declaration that we are not condemned, even though we are sinners; and through that declaration we are holy (set apart for God), for by it we are set in a positive relationship with the One who is holy. Hence, the believer is, in Luther's matchless phrase, *simul iustus et peccator,* "simultaneously justified and a sinner." This, as Karl Rahner finely said, is "God's justice, that in fact divinises us, [being] an unmerited gift of God's incalculable favor" (6)—and this is the justification that is brought about "through the redemption . . . in Christ Jesus" (3:24 NRSV).

"Redemption (*apolytrōsis*)" is a metaphor from the slave market, but has roots in Scripture. The cognate verbs *apolytroō* and *lytroō* (both meaning "obtain release on payment of a ransom") are used in the Septuagint (LXX) to speak of God's redemption of Israel from Egypt (e.g., Exod. 6:6; Deut. 7:8) and from Babylon (Isa. 51:11). "Redemption" therefore speaks of those who have been handed over, or fallen, into the power of something they cannot control—the dominant metaphor of Rom. 1:18–32, which has repeatedly spoken of humankind "handed over" into the power of sin.

Finally, "propitiation" (RSV: "expiation"; NRSV: "sacrifice of atonement") involves a metaphor from the cult. Greek *hilastērion* is a neuter noun formed from the (somewhat rare) adjective *hilastērios,* meaning "propitiatory" or "offered in propitiation." In the LXX this noun occurs regularly—and in the context of very important passages—in reference to the mercy seat in the temple (e.g., LXX: Exod. 31:7; 35:12). Since this seems to have become an accepted usage in Greek-speaking Judaism of the early Christian era (cf. Heb. 9:5; Philo, *Cher.* 25), there seems little reason to question that Paul, too, uses it in this way. If there was one thing in Judaism that was evidently forbidden to uncircumcised Gentiles, it was to come anywhere near the holy of holies, the place of the mercy seat, where once a year the high priest entered to make atonement by the sprinkling of blood (Lev. 16:14–16). There was

therefore a peculiar poignancy in Paul's seeing Christ himself as a true mercy seat, "set forth" by God the Father for Jews and Gentiles to approach together—and that, not by the blood of animal victims, but "by his blood," the blood of the Messiah.

On what basis is Christ so "set forth"? It is "through faith" (*dia pisteōs*). Whose faith? God's faith? Christ's faith? Ours? Here is a question that continues to occupy the scholars. But the answer, as Barth saw, is surely "Yes," to all (42). Rooted in the faithfulness of God, the faithfulness of Jesus Christ invites our faithfulness in return: indeed, there is nothing else we can offer, no other basis on which we can stand with regard to God. Paul, as a good rhetorician, brings us full circle. In "his gospel," as he said from the beginning, "God's justice is revealed from faith for faith; as it is written, 'the just shall live by faith'" (1:17 AT).

We have, then, a hope of salvation, but it is solely on the basis of God's justice and mercy. Therefore, all human boasting is absurd—indeed, it is denial of the one God (3:27–30). Surely paganism—the deification of powers or forces within creation—undermines Hebrew monotheism from one side; but a claim to status before God that is based on something other than God's justice and God's mercy undermines it from the other side. It makes no difference whether the claim is (as among some whom Paul addressed at Rome) based on knowledge of God's law, or (as among some he addressed at Corinth) on knowledge of another kind, or on wisdom, or on gifts—*any* such claim undermines Hebrew monotheism. Any such claim asserts, by implication, that God is in some sense and in some measure *not* God of a part of the created order, or that there is something inherently wrong with a part of that order. In short, such a claim asserts a dualism (Rom. 3:27–31; 10:12; cf. 1 Cor. 8:4–6). Therefore, paganism and dualism alike must be confronted by the unyielding confession that none stand before God, save on the basis of God's justice and mercy (3:30).

On this basis Paul declares (among other things) that "all Israel will be saved" (11:26)—not thereby claiming that every single Jew will go to heaven, but certainly affirming his conviction that Israel as a whole, ethnic Israel, will find there is a place for her in the final salvation. Indeed, Paul went further, for he claimed finally, and on the same basis, that "God has consigned all . . . to disobedience, that he may have mercy upon all" (cf. 11:32). As to *how* that was to happen, Paul did not say. Like Dame Julian of Norwich centuries later, his confidence was simply in God's promise in Jesus Christ: "This is the great deed intended by our Lord God from the beginning, cherished and concealed in his blessed breast, known only to himself, through which deed he will make all things well" (*Revelations of Divine Love* 32).

Una ecclesia sancta: *Unity in Christ*. If none of us has any standing before God save on the basis of God's justice and mercy, what does that say about our relationships with each other, within the fellowship of faith? Paul's discourse to the Romans did not take only the form of a protreptic, but also that of a "family letter." Why? Because he regarded those whom he addressed not merely as individuals, but also as a household, God's household, and therefore unavoidably bound to each other, even if they disagreed with or disliked each other. For Paul, proclaiming and hearing the gospel led directly to forming communities "in Christ"—communities of the new age, which had begun with the Messiah's victory (Gal. 3:13–14). In short, the gospel led to the church (Rom. 12:1–5). Therefore, the important question for Paul about behavior was always not, "Does this square well with your conscience?" but, "Does this serve to build up your brothers and sisters in the community?" *Especially* is this the case if you happen to consider your brothers and sisters to be weaker than you are (14:1–15:13). And in any case, "Who are you to pass judgment on someone else's servant? Before his own master he stands or falls. And he will be upheld, for the Lord is able to make him stand" (14:4 RSV adapted).

The ancients, and presumably Paul among them, were as well aware as we are of the violence of the world (see 2 Cor. 11:24–25). Rome itself was a frightening and violent city. Yet Paul thought it possible for believers to create among themselves what François Bovon has called "zones of peace" (371)—caring for one another "with mutual affection" (12:10 NRSV). In Rom. 12:1–15:13 (and notably at 14:1–15:13) the apostle insists on continuing fellowship in the church among groups who evidently differed widely among themselves in a range of significant matters of faith and practice. This continues to challenge not only the behavior of Christians toward each other *within* congregations, communities, and denominations. It also challenges the feeble ecumenism that marks all major Christian denominations in their relationships toward each other at the beginning of the twenty-first century.

Vita venturi saeculi: *Christian Hope*. Protreptic is more than exhortation to a way of living. Protreptic bases its exhortation on a perception of how the world is and how it will be. "For you did not receive the spirit of slavery to fall back into fear, but you have received the Spirit of adoption, through whom we cry 'Abba! Father!' The same Spirit bears witness in support of our spirit that we are children of God, and if children, then also heirs, heirs of God and coheirs with Christ, given that we suffer with him, in order that we may be glorified with him" (8:15–17 AT). "For the creation waits with eager longing for the revealing of the children of God; for creation was made subject to futility, not of its own accord, but because of the one who subjected it, in hope—because the creation itself will be set free from the bondage of corruption and obtain the liberty of the glory of the children of God" (8:19–21 AT). Paul's hope, we should recognize, is not merely for the individual, or the church, or even humanity, but for "the creation." Only with the redemption and restoration of the whole creation will God's promises be fulfilled (Isa. 11:6–9).

To be "in Christ" is therefore by definition to "live in this hope" (Rom. 5:1–5; 8:24–25). Such hope (eschatology) is not simply an interesting idea, to be contemplated when we have leisure from more-pressing business (as one might indeed suppose from much of our contemporary preaching, even in the season of Advent). We do not have two lives, one transient and one (later on) that will be eternal. We have a single life, designed from eternity to be life in Christ Jesus. Because of that, it is worthwhile now to engage in the creative subversion that is Christian witness. Because of that, it is already "high time for you to awake from sleep. For now is our salvation nearer than when we first believed" (13:11 AT).

Bibliography

Barth, K. *The Epistle to the Romans*, trans. E. Hoskyns. Oxford University Press, 1933; Bovon, F. "The Child and the Beast." *HTR* 92 (1999): 369–92; Bryan, C. *A Preface to Romans*. Oxford University Press, 2000; Byrne, B. *Romans*. SP 6. Liturgical Press, 1996; Cranfield, C. E. B. *A Critical and Exegetical Commentary on the Epistle to the Romans*. 2 vols. ICC. T&T Clark, 1975–79; Dunn, J. D. G. *Romans*. 2 vols. WBC 38A–B. Word, 1988; Fitzmyer, J. *Romans*. AB 33. Doubleday, 1993; Julian of Norwich. *Revelations of Divine Love*; Käsemann, E. *Commentary on Romans*, trans. G. Bromiley. Eerdmans, 1980; Moo, D. *The Epistle to the Romans*. NICNT. Eerdmans, 1996; Rahner, K. *Theological Investigations*. 23 vols. Darton, Longman & Todd, 1961–92; Seneca. *Ad Lucilium epistulae morales*. Vol. 2, *Letters 46–92*, trans. R. Gummere. LCL 76. Heinemann, 1920; Wesley, J. *Journal from February 1, 1738–August 12, 1738*. Online: http://www.godrules.net/

library/wesley/274wesley_a6.htm; Wright, N. T. "The Letter to the Romans." *NIB* 10:393–770.

Christopher Bryan

Rorty, Richard   *See* Epistemology; Hermeneutics; Postmodernity and Biblical Interpretation; Pragmatism

Rule of Faith

Kanōn tēs pisteōs, or *tēs alētheias*, the *regula fidei*, or *regula veritatis* are the oldest terms used by the Ante-Nicene fathers, Ignatius, Polycarp, and in particular Irenaeus and Tertullian, to refer to the sum content of apostolic teaching. The Rule of Faith is a confession of faith for public use in worship, in particular for use in baptism, and it outlines the authoritative articles of faith. For the most part it was not written down, other than in the above authors for the purpose of its defense, and was not revealed until baptism. To be noted, "faith" here in the Rule of Faith does not refer to subjective, individual experience but the faith of the church, received from apostolic preaching. As such, the Rule of Faith functions as a hermeneutical key for the interpretation of Scripture.

We can find early kernels of the Rule of Faith, which expand upon NT statements about Jesus and his relation to the Father, in Ignatius's *Letter to the Ephesians* and *Letter to the Trallians*, and in Polycarp's *Letter to the Philippians*. References to and longer summaries of the Rule of Faith can be found in Tertullian's (160–225) *Veiling of Virgins* (1), where we see the similarities between the Rule of Faith and the creeds:

> The Rule of Faith, indeed, is altogether one, alone immoveable and irreformable, the rule, to wit, of believing in one only God omnipotent, Creator of the Universe, and His Son Jesus Christ, born of the Virgin Mary, crucified under Pontius Pilate, raised again the third day from the dead, received in the heavens, sitting now at the right of the Father, destined to come to judge the quick and the dead through resurrection of the flesh as well [as of the Spirit]. The law of faith being constant, the other succeeding points of discipline and conversation admit the novelty of correction.

Again, in the *Prescription against the Heretics*, Tertullian summarizes the Rule of Faith as

> that which prescribes the belief that there is one only God, and that He is none other than the Creator of the World, who produced all things out of nothing through His own Word, first of all sent forth; that this Word is called His Son, and under the name of God was seen in diverse manners by the patriarchs, heard at all times in the prophets, at last brought down by the Spirit and Power of the Father into the Virgin Mary, was made flesh in her womb, and being born of her, went forth as Jesus Christ; thenceforth He preached the new law and the new promise of the Kingdom of Heaven, worked miracles, having been crucified, He rose again the third day; having ascended into the heavens, He sat at the right hand of the Father; sent instead of Himself the Power of the Holy Ghost to lead such as believe; will come with glory to take the saints to the enjoyment of everlasting life and of the heavenly promises, and to condemn the wicked to everlasting fire, after the resurrection of both these classes shall have happened, together with the restoration of the flesh.

We also find similar material in Irenaeus, who as early as 180 in his treatise *Against the Heretics* declares the church's understanding of the faith. This understanding can be expressed in different words, but the content remains the same: a trinitarian creedal affirmation that later develops into the fixed forms like the Apostles' Creed and the Nicene Creed. The Rule of Faith, says Irenaeus, is like a rich man who puts his money in a bank: so the apostles deposited in the church their faith by bequeathing to the church the Rule of Faith and the Scriptures (*Haer.* 3.4.1). Irenaeus illustrates the relationship between the Rule of Faith and Scripture by using the metaphor of a mosaic (*Haer.* 1.8.1), which can be arranged to form the portrait of a king or that of a dog. In the ancient world, unassembled mosaics were shipped with the plan or key (*hypothesis*) according to which they were to be arranged. The Rule of Faith is like the key, he says, which explains how the Scriptures are to be arranged, to render the portrait of the King, whereas the heretics arrange the Scriptures wrongly to form the picture of a dog or fox. Thus, the Rule of Faith assures a correct reading of Scripture, indeed a christological reading (in accordance with the "King").

In a subsequent passage, Irenaeus points out how the heretics are exactly like the readers of Homer's poetry who take bits and pieces of text and string them together in their own fashion, taking them out of context such that they now form a new narrative (*Haer.* 1.9.4). (Tertullian also refers to these Homeric textual distortions, in *Praescr.* 39.)

> So the person who holds to himself unswervingly the Canon of Truth he received in baptism, will recognise the names and terms and parables as being from the scripture, but will not recognise this blasphemous *hypothesis* of theirs. Though he will detect the mosaic pieces, he will not accept the fox instead of the king's image. Restoring each of the expressions to its own rank, and accommodating it to the body of

truth, he will expose as naked and unsubstantiated their fiction. (Irenaeus, *Haer.* 1.9.4)

The *hypothesis* is characterized implicitly as the "king's face," or the christological referent. The "plan" is christological, as we see in Irenaeus's *Demonstration of the Apostolic Preaching*. He links the Father and the Son, insisting that the Word is active in creation, that the Creator God is the God of both OT and NT (*Epid.* 6). This is precisely what the heretics do not acknowledge. The Rule of Faith, then, forms a hermeneutical circle, inside of which are many possible, not overdetermined, readings of Scripture, while outside are the readings of the heretics. Again, "The law of faith being constant, the other succeeding points of discipline and conversation admit the novelty of correction" (Tertullian, *Virg.* 1).

The Rule of Faith thus functions hermeneutically to hold together theologically the confessions of God the Creator and Jesus Christ the Son, and thus also to bring together in a dialectical relation the two Testaments. The Rule is thus a basic "take" on the subject matter and plot of the Christian story, which couples the confession of Jesus the Redeemer with the confession of God the Creator, and thus "rules out" heretical statements that do not honor the content of the Rule. Understood to have been drawn from Scripture (Tertullian claims that this rule was taught by Christ himself), in biblical interpretation it is reapplied to Scripture. Thus, it circumscribes a potential set of interpretations while disallowing others.

Later in the history of the church, the Rule of Faith came to be hermeneutically important again in defining the role and scope of what becomes known as the "literal sense" of Scripture, especially as we see it in Reformation interpretation. The literal sense for the Reformers, against any notion of multiple meaning of Scripture such as threefold or fourfold meaning, takes on the authority of the Rule of Faith. Where the Rule of Faith is not followed, the Reformers deem that reading of Scripture as inadequate and therefore as not adhering to the literal sense. All readings that (the "law of faith being constant") honor the Rule of Faith are therefore deemed authoritative or "literal." In this sense the Rule of Faith is key to the Reformation's reaction against Roman multiple meanings in its interpretation of Scripture, and is key to the sense in which Scripture is authoritative for the church catholic. Ultimately, it is the Rule of Faith that is behind the statement that Scripture is *sui ipsius interpres*, the conviction that Scripture is its own interpreter.

See also Literal Sense; Patristic Biblical Interpretation; Scripture, Unity of

Bibliography

Blocher, H. "The Analogy of Faith in the Study of Scripture." *Scottish Bulletin of Evangelical Theology* 5 (1987): 17–38; Blowers, P. "The 'Regula Fidei' and the Narrative Character of Early Christian Faith." *ProEccl* 6 (1997): 199–228; Countryman, W. "Tertullian and the Regula Fidei." *Second Century* 2 (1982): 208–27; Hägglund, B. "Die Bedeutung der 'regula fidei' als Grundlage theologischer Aussagen." *ST* 12 (1958): 1–44; Osborn, E. "Reason and the Rule of Faith in the Second Century AD." Pages 40–61 in *The Making of Orthodoxy*, ed. R. Williams. Cambridge University Press, 1989; Yeago, D. "The New Testament and the Nicene Dogma: A Contribution to the Recovery of Theological Exegesis." *ProEccl* 3 (1994): 152–64.

Kathryn Greene-McCreight

Ruth, Book of

The book of Ruth tells how a Bethlehemite family of Elimelech and Naomi, with sons Mahlon and Chilion, migrates to Moab to escape famine. All the males die there, leaving Naomi with two widowed daughters-in-law. The story develops around the return of Naomi with Ruth to Bethlehem, and the events leading to Ruth's marriage to Elimelech's kinsman, Boaz, and the birth of Obed, forming part of David's genealogy.

History of Interpretation

Various theories for the book's purpose have been proposed, such as the following:

In Praise of **Khesed.** This has ancient rabbinic support; according to R. Ze'ira, it was written to "teach how great is the reward of those who do deeds of *kindness*" (*Ruth Rabbah* 2.14). Some modern scholars concur (such as Würthwein; Rebera, "Ruth"; Bush). If *khesed* were the main theme, however, then the word might be expected at more focal points, particularly 2:11–12; 4:14–15. God is petitioned to do *khesed* (1:8), while Boaz (2:20) and Ruth (3:10) are praised for showing it. The actors are praised for behavior conforming to an accepted ideal, rather than the ideal itself being encouraged or praised. *Khesed* is an important but auxiliary motif to the purpose of the story.

To Encourage Performance of the Levirate. This is unlikely. Regardless of whether the story of Ruth is truly an instance of levirate marriage, we observe that the social customs are neither evaluated nor praised but are simply background to the story.

As a Defense of Mixed Marriage. This would counter the exclusiveness of Ezra and Nehemiah by showing that even the great David had Moabite ancestry—suggested as long ago as 1816 by Bertholdt (Rowley 173n1) and widely accepted in the early twentieth century, but rarely today. Lacocque is a modern exponent (84–116). If this view were correct, then Ruth must be dated late; but many scholars believe the book is preexilic. Rowley explains that Ruth might as easily be read as supporting Ezra and Nehemiah, since Ruth is shown to be a true convert.

To Support Inclusion of Gentiles. Ruth is viewed not as a defense of mixed marriage per se, but as encouraging acceptance of believing Gentiles. Though it was considered important to uphold the exclusiveness of Israel's monotheism, the book of Ruth demonstrates the possibility of Gentiles truly converting to Yahwism (cf. Herbert 271). Sakenfeld (4) sees the story as "legitimizing an inclusive attitude towards foreigners, perhaps especially towards foreign women." Irrespective of whether we accept an inclusivist purpose for the book, Ruth's ethnicity and inclusion are clearly significant motifs. But it should be recognized that in contexts where her Moabite ancestry receives mention, it is followed by a corresponding note, either of her relationship as daughter-in-law of Naomi (Ruth 2–3 passim), or, in Ruth 4:5, 10, that she is wife of Mahlon. So, while Ruth's Moabite ancestry *is* seen as a problem, her marriage to Boaz is legitimated by its intention to continue Mahlon's lineage. Rather than defending mixed marriages in general, the book of Ruth is defending one particular marriage. Hence, the inclusion motif is important but is not the central purpose of the book.

To Demonstrate Divine Providence. The book may intend to show God's hand in events giving rise to the Davidic monarchy. Theological elements are certainly found in the story, such as the providential answering of prayer, the reversal motif, the practice of *khesed*, and so on (see "Theological Aspects of Ruth," below). But the paucity of *narrative* theological statements suggests that the theological dimension is in some respects auxiliary to the purpose.

Nontheological Readings. Various literary readings have appeared in the last quarter century, such as Sasson's formalist-folklorist approach, focusing on the literary artistry of Ruth while playing down "theology" (qualified in the foreword to Sasson's second edition). It is true that narrative statements of Yahweh's activity are rare in Ruth and the exceptions (1:6; 4:13) could be interpreted as part of Israelite belief in Yahweh's general providence over matters of fertility. Thus, Rebera's discourse analysis (esp. "Ruth," 181–244) shows that Ruth, like the author of the succession narrative, prefers to embed theological evaluation in dialogue. The author appears reluctant to show his or her own *tendenz*, if there is one.

"Realistic" Readings. Against a long tradition of interpreting Naomi, Ruth, and Boaz as "ideal" characters worthy to be emulated, some recent studies have highlighted the gritty realism of the story (e.g., Fewell and Gunn). Naomi is viewed as a self-centered character, whose silence after Ruth's magnificent vow of loyalty indicates her hardness of heart. Moreover, she ignores Ruth when lamenting her emptiness before the women of Bethlehem, thus showing that she considers Ruth a liability. Likewise, Boaz has been portrayed as protective of his own interests in a self-righteous manner, needing a push before he is prepared to act as redeemer.

However, while the story *is* realistic, Naomi's behavior in the first chapter conforms better to the effects of depression. It may be Naomi's concern for Ruth that leads to her attempt to persuade her to stay in Moab, recognizing that a Moabite might not be welcome in Bethlehem. As for Boaz, he treats Ruth kindly enough, but in view of the age difference, he may have considered himself an unlikely candidate for Ruth's amour. When she did signal her availability, he responded with alacrity, but also with restraint, out of respect for the nearer kinsman.

As an Apology for David. This may be necessary because of David's Moabite ancestry. According to Deuteronomy, Moabites were prohibited from entering the congregation till the tenth generation (Deut. 23:3–6). However, Ruth shows that despite her Moabite ancestry, she was a person of great worth, loyal to Mahlon's kinsfolk, loyal to his memory in seeking marriage to his kinsman Boaz, and a true believer in the God of Israel. Moreover, the events leading to the marriage of Boaz to Ruth, followed by the birth of Obed, were providential. The portrayal of the marriage as leviratic also served as part of its justification. The information that this concerned David's ancestry is kept to the end so as not to arouse audience prejudice prematurely (cf. 2 Sam. 12:1–7).

The advantages of interpreting Ruth as "Davidic apologetic" are that it incorporates and accounts for the focus on *khesed* and explains the preponderance of kin terms, especially where Ruth's Moabite ancestry receives mention. Thus, in Ruth 2 the inclusion motif is emphasized, and Ruth 4 settles the legal basis of the marriage. Further, it accounts for the inclusion of theological elements, including providential answers to prayer and Ruth's conversion, as well as the restraint of the author in making narrative theological statements. Finally, the apologetic interpretation accounts for a feature unique in Hebrew narrative—a genealogy placed at the end rather than the beginning.

Canonical Context

Ruth's canonical position was fluid. The MT locates Ruth in the *Ketubim* (Writings) but with divergent order. The Babylonian Talmud (*B. Bat.* 14b) places Ruth ahead of Psalms. The Ben Asher family of Masoretes (see *BHS*) place Ruth at the head of the Megillot, directly after Proverbs, perhaps answering the question, "Who can find a worthy woman?" (Prov. 31:10 AT). A later tradition found in the Ben Hayyim family of manuscripts has Song of Songs first, since it is read at Passover, followed by Ruth, read at the Feast of Weeks/Pentecost.

The LXX, followed by the Latin Vulgate and Christian tradition, sets Ruth between Judges and Samuel. This appears to be supported by Josephus (*C. Ap.* 1.8), who speaks of a twenty-two-book Hebrew canon. Jerome in his prologue to Samuel and Kings knows of a twenty-four-book canon but claims a twenty-two-book canon was accepted by most Jews, this being achieved by combining Judges with Ruth and Lamentations with Jeremiah. By contrast, the Babylonian Talmud (*B. Bat.* 14b–15a) and 2 Esd. 14:44–46 hold to a twenty-four-book canon; Ruth and Lamentations are separated from Judges and Jeremiah respectively and included with the Megillot.

These two traditions—one setting Ruth in the Former Prophets (so Moore 294–95; Linafelt xviii–xxv), the other among the Writings (so Campbell 32–36; Bush 5–9)—each have ancient support. Any preference must be tentative, but it is worth recognizing the interpretive consequences. The setting in the Writings would attribute to Ruth a liturgical purpose, including a fertility motif. Placing Ruth between Judges and Samuel sets Ruth in the transition from tribal federation to monarchy, emphasizing Ruth's role in salvation history.

The sorry tale of Judg. 17–18 is set in Ephraim, the territory of Jeroboam, and the terrible events of 19–21 relate to Gibeah, the home of Saul. Both

stories are replete with cultic elements, but cult gone awry. By contrast, Ruth, set in Bethlehem, lacks cultic elements. Instead, we find a community of ordinary people serving Yahweh as they go about the business of everyday life and showing *khesed* to those in need. This reflects favorably on the origins of David, while showing us a better way.

Theological Aspects of Ruth

Prayer and Blessing. Ruth has been thought theologically sparse since only 1:6 and 4:13 provide narrative statements of Yahweh's activity, but as Rebera observes, Ruth mostly embeds theological evaluation in dialogue ("Ruth," esp. 181–244). This has significance for seeing that prayer constitutes a significant part of the "theology." Prayers or blessings include (1) 1:8–9; (2) 1:20–21; (3) 2:11–12; 3:10; compare Gen. 15; 30:16, 18; and Ps. 127:3, where reward is linked with progeny; (4) 2:19–20; (5) 3:10–11; (6) 4:11–12; (7) 4:14–15. All these prayers/blessings have fulfillment in the marriage of Ruth to Boaz, and a lineage leading to David. The author of Ruth expected readers to be alert to the work of God in answering prayer, as should we today. Like Boaz, we too may be called to participate in answering our own prayers.

Providence. As well as the divine activity suggested by answered prayer, providence is discerned in the reversal of the famine (1:6), leading to Naomi's return with Ruth. While chapters 2 and 3 lack overt narrative theological statements, chapter 2 first introduces us to Boaz and tells us that Ruth "happened" upon the field of Boaz, hinting at divine overruling. This echoes the meeting of Abraham's servant and Rebekah (Gen. 24, also overruled by Yahweh). There is *concurrence* between divine and human activity. Although God is the unseen actor, this is very much a human story, about "people, living as they are to live under God's sovereignty, who proceed to work it out" (Campbell 29). Thus, Naomi counsels Ruth to act boldly to achieve marriage with Boaz. Ruth plays her part, but after she returns home in the morning, Naomi counsels her to wait to see how the matter falls out. While Boaz can be relied on, ultimately the result is in the hand of God. Chapter 4 likewise points to concurrence. Boaz does his part by marrying Ruth, but we are told that it is Yahweh who gives conception (4:13).

Reversal Motif. In the OT, it is Yahweh who "sends poverty and wealth," who "lifts the needy from the ash heap" (1 Sam. 2:7). In the book of Ruth, there is a movement from emptiness to fulfillment. Elimelech migrates to escape famine, but dies; his sons marry, and die. Naomi, widowed and childless, is left with two childless widows. News of Yahweh's providence prompts her return, commencing a movement from deprivation to restoration. In the remainder of the story, Naomi's immediate needs are met through Ruth's industry and Boaz's generosity. The levirate marriage of Boaz and Ruth plus the birth of Obed restores the lineage.

Conversion/Inclusion. Ethnicity is first mentioned when the sons of Elimelech marry Moabite women (1:4). Once Ruth arrives in Bethlehem, it becomes a key issue because there she is a foreigner (Rebera, "Ruth," 156–59), being mentioned at 1:22; 2:2, 6, 10, 21, and twice during the legal case (4:5, 10). But it is important to observe a countermovement for Ruth's inclusion. When Naomi counsels Ruth to return to her god(s) and people, Ruth vows allegiance to Naomi in life and death, declaring, "Your people shall be my people and your God my God" (1:16 NRSV), showing that she is a convert to Yahwism. Whenever Ruth's Moabite origins are mentioned in the remainder of the story, there are kin terms linking her to her Judahite family. She is described as "daughter-in-law of Naomi," and by both Naomi and Boaz as "my daughter" (2:2, 8). Chapter 2 highlights Boaz's actions to include Ruth; he approves her actions and gives her protection (2:8–16). Ethnicity is not an issue in chapter 3 but arises again in 4. Twice in the legal case, Ruth is described as Moabite, but the countering fact of her marriage to Mahlon is then immediately mentioned. Hence, the marriage of Boaz and Ruth is viewed as leviratic and legally justified. When the women give their final blessing at the birth of a son, Ruth's inclusion is complete. Now she is "your daughter-in-law who loves you, who is [worth] more to you than seven sons" (4:15 NRSV).

Kindness **(Khesed).** This motif has long been recognized (1:8; probably 2:11; definitely 3:10; 2:20, supported by Rebera ["Yahweh or Boaz?"]). Earlier studies of the Hebrew word *khesed* pointed to the loyalty expected in reciprocal relationships, implying obligation. But in the OT *khesed* contains a gracious element: in human relationships it "mainly describes exceptional acts of one human to another, meeting an extreme need outside the normal run of perceived duty, and arising from personal affection or goodness" (Andersen 81). The KJV comes close to this sense with "loving-kindness." God in his grace and mercy shows such kindness to humans; he does not owe salvation but gives it freely. The nature of the divine-human relationship means

we cannot give *khesed* to God. But if we have experienced God's loving-kindness, we can, like Ruth and Boaz, demonstrate it in our relationships with others (cf. Mic. 6:8; Matt. 25:34–40; 1 John 4:7–12).

The Place of Women. Whether or not we posit a female author (cf. Campbell 22–23), Ruth's story is unique among ancient literature in celebrating female friendship (cf. Daube 35–37). The power of the story lies largely in the hands of female characters. Elimelech, his wife, and sons commence the story, but the males soon die. Thereafter, Ruth and Naomi are the main characters, with Boaz being given third place. In a sense, his is a supporting role, and the heroine receives the larger role, highlighted by the fact that it is Ruth, not Boaz, who proposes marriage in 3:9. Boaz has the lead role in the legal case, but it is the women who again take the lead in 4:13–17. In the patrilineal genealogical material (4:18–22), Ruth drops from view, but this should not be viewed negatively. The outsider has now been integrated into Israelite history. The story of Ruth is a reminder of how much women with chutzpah can achieve even in a society that restricts their roles.

Davidic Messianic Role. The marriage of an Israelite to a Moabite and the genealogy of David are key elements in understanding the book of Ruth. The book seeks to justify the marriage of Boaz to Ruth, a believing Gentile, and hence to defend the claim of the Davidic line to the throne. There is a move in recent scholarship to favor some such view (e.g., Gerleman; Gow; Hubbard; Nielsen; Block), although with a variety of views as to the possible historical setting for such an apologetic. As part of the lineage of the Davidic king, the story becomes messianic in character, partially fulfilled in the Davidic monarchy, but widened out to bring blessing to the whole world through a future descendant of David (cf. Gen. 12:1–3; Matt. 1; Rom. 1:3).

Bibliography

Andersen, F. I. "Yahweh, the Kind and Sensitive God." Pages 41–88 in *God Who Is Rich in Mercy*. Anzea, 1986; Atkinson, D. *The Message of Ruth*. InterVarsity, 1983; Block, D. *Judges, Ruth*. NAC. Broadman & Holman, 1999; Bush, F. *Ruth, Esther*. WBC 9. Word, 1996; Campbell, E. F. *Ruth*. AB 7. Doubleday, 1975; Daube, D. *Ancient Jewish Law*. Brill, 1981; Farmer, K. *The Book of Ruth*. NIB. Abingdon, 1998; Fewell, D. N., and D. M. Gunn. "'A Son Is Born to Naomi': Literary Allusion and Interpretation in the Book of Ruth." *JSOT* 40 (1988): 99–108; Fisch, H. "Ruth and the Structure of Covenant History." *VT* 32 (1982): 425–37; Gerleman, G. *Ruth*. Biblischer Kommentar, Altes Testament Bd. 18. Neukirchener Verlag, 1981; Gow, M. *The Book of*

Ruth. Apollos, 1992; idem. "Prayer and Providence in the Book of Ruth." *Journal of the Christian Brethren Research Fellowship* 101 (1985): 9–25; Hals, R. M. *The Theology of the Book of Ruth*. Fortress, 1969; Herbert, A. "Ruth." Pages 271–72 in *Peake's Commentary on the Bible*, ed. M. Black and H. Rowley. T. Nelson, 1962; Hubbard, R., Jr. *The Book of Ruth*. NICOT. Eerdmans, 1988; idem. "Ruth, Theology of." *NIDOTTE* 4:1153–57; Lacocque, A. *The Feminine Unconventional*. Fortress, 1990; Larkin, K. J. A. *Ruth and Esther*. OTG. Sheffield Academic Press, 1996; Linafelt, T. *Ruth*. Berit Olam. Liturgical Press, 1999; Merrill, E. "The Book of Ruth: Narration and Shared Themes." *BSac* 142 (1985): 130–41; Moore, M. S. *Ruth*. NIBCOT 5. Hendrickson, 2000; Nielsen, K. *Ruth*. OTL. SCM/Westminster John Knox, 1997; Porten, B. "The Scroll of Ruth: A Rhetorical Study." *Gratz* 7 (1978): 23–49; Prinsloo, W. S. "The Theology of the Book of Ruth." *VT* 30 (1980): 330–41; Rebera, B. "The Book of Ruth." Ph.D. diss., Macquarie University (Sydney, Australia), 1981; idem. "Yahweh or Boaz? Ruth 2.20 Reconsidered." *BT* 36 (1985): 317–27; Rowley, H. H. "The Marriage of Ruth." Pages 171–94 in *The Servant of the Lord and Other Essays on the Old Testament*. Blackwell, 1965; Sakenfeld, K. D. *Ruth*. Interpretation. John Knox, 1999; Sasson, J. M. *Ruth*. 2d ed. JSOT, 1989; Trible, P. *God and the Rhetoric of Sexuality*. Fortress, 1978; Van Wolde, E. *Ruth and Naomi*, trans. J. Bowden. SCM/Smyth & Helwys, 1997; Wegner, P. "Ruth." *EDBT*, 694–96; Younger, K. L., Jr. *Judges, Ruth*. NIVAC. Zondervan, 2002.

Murray D. Gow

S

Sacrament

The English word "sacrament" derives from the Latin word for "sign" (*sacramentum*) for the Greek word "mystery" (*mystērion*). In secular contexts, *mystērion* referred to a religious rite or oath, as *sacramentum* was used especially in military contexts when individuals were inducted into the army. It is difficult to locate a topic more illustrative of the deep inner connections of faith and practice.

The History of Exegesis

In understanding the sacraments, considerable latitude prevailed during the patristic period and the Middle Ages (between Bernard and Thomas Aquinas). The thirteenth century (Fourth Lateran Council and Thomas), however, saw the development of the sacramentology that would culminate in the decrees of the Council of Trent, when the doctrine of transubstantiation became settled and binding. Although the elements still retained the accidental properties of bread and wine, they were in reality transubstantiated into the substance of Christ's body and blood. At Trent (1545–63), the sacraments (now formally established as seven in number) were regarded as conferring grace *ex opere operato* (by doing it, it is done). Baptism effects the "first justification" (regeneration and forgiveness), and the increase in grace occurs through penance, confirmation, the Supper, marriage, ordination, and extreme unction (last rites).

Martin Luther's protest encountered two fronts: Rome and the "enthusiasts" or, as they came to be called (especially by their critics), Anabaptists. Against the former, Luther argued the importance of faith, denied that the Mass was a perpetual sacrifice of Christ, and affirmed only those sacraments that he believed had dominical sanction and were evangelical in character: baptism, the Supper, and absolution. With respect to the Supper, Luther so emphasized the union of the two natures in Christ that the properties of deity were transferred to the humanity of Christ (his understanding of the *communicatio idiomatum*). "Thus, what is true in regard to Christ is also true in regard to the Sacrament" (*LWorks* 36:35). This was extended to include the notion of the *genus majestaticum* (genus of majesty: according to his *human* nature Jesus possessed all the attributes of deity at birth). Thus, the ascended Christ can be physically present at every altar by means of an illocal rather than local presence. This last point is often overlooked by non-Lutheran theologians who erroneously attribute to the Lutheran view the doctrine of ubiquity (see Mueller).

The Zurich Reformer Ulrich Zwingli appealed to John 6 as a spiritual rather than carnal eating (in line with Augustine's exegesis), and emphasized Christ's bodily ascension. But it is evident from Zwingli's writings that at least as fundamental as his exegesis was his commitment to a Neoplatonic body-soul dualism, which colored his Christology and his view of the Supper. For Zwingli, influenced in part by Erasmus's interpretation, the sacraments were primarily pledges of the believer toward God, rather than vice versa.

Strasbourg's Martin Bucer (who had also helped shift the Church of England from a Zwinglian to a more "Calvinian" view) embraced a mediating position, which reached its mature articulation in his disciple, John Calvin. Philipp Melanchthon, author of the Augsburg Confession and Apology, who had steadied Luther's hand against Zwingli at the Marburg Colloquy (1529), nevertheless saw in the young reformer of Geneva a potential ally. Rejecting what it regarded as Melanchthon's compromise, the Book of Concord (1580) returned to the unaltered version of the Augsburg Confession and added statements clarifying what became the orthodox Lutheran position.

Insisting that believers truly feed on Christ's body and blood in the sacrament, Calvin had described Zwingli's view of the Supper as "wrong and pernicious." At the same time, he rejected both transubstantiation and Luther's account of an illocal presence in and under the elements. He agreed with Zwingli about Christ's ascension to the Father's right hand but, unlike the Zurich

Reformer, emphasized the role of the Holy Spirit in bringing together mysteriously what is distant. Thus, the work of the Spirit in effecting union with Christ became crucial to Calvin's eucharistic theology. "I would rather adore the mystery than explain it," Calvin concluded (*Inst.* 4.17.32). As for baptism, God's action was again central: "And as the instruments of the Holy Spirit are not dead, God truly performs and effects by baptism what he figures" (*Second Defense* 2.319; cf. *Inst.* 4.16.3). Sacraments were necessary because of our weakness, and here Calvin rejected Zwingli's view that faith needed no props. Far different from Zwingli's philosophical objection to the view that spiritual riches can be given or received through physical means, Calvin states, "Here our merciful Lord . . . leads us to himself even by these earthly elements" (*Inst.* 4.1). To deny the real presence of Christ and a true feeding on his body and blood in the Supper "is to render this holy sacrament frivolous and useless—an execrable blasphemy unfit to be listened to" (Calvin, *Short Treatise*, 170).

The sixteenth-century Belgic, French, and Scots' confessions and the Thirty-Nine Articles, as well as the Westminster Confession and Catechisms (1645), regard the sacraments as "effectual means of salvation . . . only by the working of the Holy Spirit, and the blessing of Christ by whom they are instituted" (W. Larger Catechism, Q. 161). The *reality*, however, must be *received*. The sacraments are therefore "signs and seals" of God's favor to us and, in the case of infant baptism, to our children. In the Supper believers receive nothing less than the true body and blood of Christ, *with*, though not *in* and *under*, the bread and wine. Consequently, Calvin, against the practice of infrequent communion, urged a weekly celebration.

Despite the modern rationalism that continues to downplay the importance of the sacraments, renewed attention and consensus have also been in evidence. Some (e.g., Bloesch; Webster) have explored the sacramental character of biblical interpretation (as a mediation of revelation), and others (e.g., Wolterstorff; Vanhoozer) have appropriated speech-act theory as a way of underscoring the performative function of the sacraments as divine discourse. Catholic as well as Protestant reflection is marked by a wide range of views. Although Karl Barth (1886–1968) seems to have preferred more Zwinglian views, the reforms of Vatican II and the exegetical studies generated during the height of the ecumenical movement have contributed to a greater consensus.

Biblical-Theological Issues

While no specific biblical passage identifies baptism or the Lord's Supper by the word *mystērion*, Scripture does assign the terms "sign and seal," as Paul referred to circumcision under the old covenant (Rom. 4:11). And although there is no set of passages defining the nature of a sacrament in general, there are many describing the nature of baptism and the Lord's Supper. By working our way inductively from the exegesis of these passages, we are able to arrive at a broader understanding of sacraments.

Jesus, of course, was baptized by John (Matt. 3:13–17), but would himself baptize with the Spirit (v. 11). In his Great Commission, Jesus declared, "Go into all the world and preach the gospel to every creature. He who believes and is baptized will be saved; but he who does not believe will be condemned" (Mark 16:15–16 NKJV). The disciples are to baptize with water "in the name of the Father and of the Son and of the Holy Spirit" (Matt. 28:19). Baptism is described in the NT as the sealing of the promise to believers and their children, and indeed, even to strangers who will embrace it (Acts 2:39). When his audience asks what they must do to be saved, Peter replies, "Repent, and let every one of you be baptized in the name of Jesus Christ for the remission of sins; and you shall receive the gift of the Holy Spirit" (v. 38 NKJV). This seems to be a settled answer, since we meet with it again in Acts 22:16: "Be baptized, and wash away your sins, calling on the name of the Lord" (NKJV). The salvation of Noah and his family through water was a type of which baptism is the antitype (1 Pet. 3:20–22).

Similarly, the Lord's Supper is described as the "body" of Christ and "new covenant in my blood" (Matt. 26:26–29; Luke 22:14–21), "a participation [*koinōnia*] in the blood . . . and . . . body of Christ" (1 Cor. 10:16). Those who eat and drink unworthily are guilty of sinning not simply against bread and wine but against "the body and blood of the Lord" (1 Cor. 11:27 NKJV). We dare not underestimate the realism in these declarations. Yet God's freedom and sovereignty are checks on our tendencies to have God at our disposal (John 3:5, 8; Rom. 4:11; 9:6–18).

In the light of such passages, and a larger biblical-theological treatment, we may perhaps understand the sacraments first and foremost as covenantal rituals: a cutting ceremony (circumcision), with analogies in ancient treaty-making, and a bonding meal (Passover). In the Passover meal, even those descendants who were not themselves present in the exodus from Egypt are united to their ancestors as one people liberated from bondage.

The NT explicitly picks up these redemptive threads in the institution of baptism and the Lord's Supper. The unity of the church is found in "one Lord, one faith, one baptism" (Eph. 4:5). Jesus instituted the Supper with the words, "Take and eat; this is my body. . . . This is my blood of the new covenant" (Matt. 26:26–29 NIV margin; Luke 22:14–21). We have been baptized into Christ just as Israel had been baptized into Moses through the cloud and in the sea, and they "all ate the same spiritual food, and all drank the same spiritual drink. For they drank of that spiritual Rock that followed them, and that Rock was Christ" (1 Cor. 10:1–4 NKJV). Paul appeals to baptism as a new circumcision (Col. 2:11–12), being buried and raised with Christ (Rom. 6:3–9; Gal. 3:27). Like the Passover, the Lord's Supper is not merely a memorial of a past event but also participation in that event, and in the ongoing work of the Spirit.

This raises the importance of eschatology: the sacraments are signs and seals of God's *promise*, which means the *word* of the gospel. It is not just the memory of a past event, but participation in its ongoing reality as well as a proclamation of Christ's saving work until he returns (1 Cor. 11:26). Like Israel in the wilderness, the church in between the two advents experiences the "already" and "not yet" of redemption—the inbreaking of Christ's new creation through word and sacrament (Heb. 6:4–5). Whichever view of the sacraments we embrace, it should be able to affirm the real tension between sign and reality, faith and sight, hope and presence.

See also Baptism; Lord's Supper

Bibliography

Augustine. *Of Baptism, Against the Donatists*. Vol. 4 of *NPNF*[1]; idem. *On Christian Doctrine*. Vol. 2 of *NPNF*[1]; Calvin, J. *Institutes of the Christian Religion*. 1536, trans. F. L. Battles. John Knox, 1975; idem. *Short Treatise on the Supper of Our Lord*. Pages 163–98 in vol. 2 of *Selected Works of John Calvin*, ed. H. Beveridge and J. Bonnet. Baker, 1983; Cross, F., ed. *St. Cyril of Jerusalem's Lectures on the Christian Sacraments*. St. Vladimir's Seminary Press, 1995; Faith and Order Commission. *Baptism, Eucharist, and Ministry 1982–1990*. WCC Publications, 1990; Kelly, J. N. D. *Early Christian Doctrines*. Rev. ed. Harper & Row, 1978; Kline, M. *By Oath Consigned*. Eerdmans, 1968; Luther, M. *Word and Sacraments*. Vols. 1–4 of *LWorks*; McDonnell, K. *John Calvin, the Church, and the Eucharist*. Princeton University Press, 1967; Melanchthon, P. *Loci communes*, trans. J. A. O. Preus. Concordia, 1992; Mueller, J. T. *Christian Dogmatics*. Concordia, 1934; Schillebeeckx, E. *Christ, the Sacrament of the Encounter with God*. Sheed & Ward, 1963; Schlink, E. *Theology of the Lutheran Confessions*, trans. P. Koehneke and H. Bouman. Fortress, 1961; Schulte, R. "Sacraments." Pages 378–84 in vol. 5 of *Sacramentum mundi*, ed. K. Rahner et al. Herder & Herder, 1968; Thomas Aquinas. *Summa theologica*, trans. Fathers of the English Dominican Province. Vol. 5. Christian Classics, 1981; Zwingli, U. *Commentary on True and False Religion*, ed. S. Jackson and C. Heller. Labyrinth, 1981.

Michael S. Horton

Sadducees   *See* Jewish Context of the NT

Salvation, Doctrine of

Salvation is a central concept within Christian theology, and a disputed one. Both the importance and the arguments have deep roots within the biblical tradition. Within the OT, at least one of the basic identifications of God is as the one who saved Israel: "Yahweh your God, who brought you up out of Egypt, out of the land of slavery." While the "God of Abraham, Isaac, and Jacob" formula and the covenant formula ("I will be your God, and you will be my people") are less straightforwardly about salvation than about election, the covenant, at least, should probably be seen in soteriological terms. For Israel to be God's people means that God has saved and will save Israel. In the NT, the message of salvation is even more central. "You are to name him Jesus, for he will save his people . . ." (Matt. 1:21 NRSV) is the fundamental announcement, and the Pauline corpus regularly describes Christians as those who are being saved. We need to take seriously the warnings that Jesus' own teaching was less about salvation than the coming of the kingdom, and that the center of Pauline theology is incorporation in Christ, not some Lutheran account of guilt and forgiveness. Yet the kingdom and being in Christ are both, when examined, soteriological categories.

These reflections immediately raise the disputes. "Salvation" is a concept that demands further specification: people are not just "saved"; they must, it would seem, be saved from something; and mechanisms and agents of salvation also need identifying. Unquestionably, biblically, God saves, but this might mean many things. God's salvation might mean that he delivers the oppressed from their captivity into a new socioeconomic situation in the exodus, or that he removes the disgrace of the barren woman who cries out to him for a child, as in the case of Hannah. Again, God's saving acts can be an intervention on the side of his people in political and military conflict, allowing them to be those who oppress others, forcing them to be "hewers of wood and drawers of water" (Josh. 9:21 NRSV); or it can be a deliverance of the nation from its ruler's guilt (1 Chron. 21). The list could go on.

It is historically difficult to judge how widespread or varied Jewish messianic expectation was at the time of Jesus. But the Gospels certainly witness to a series of debates about the nature of the salvation that he will bring, and the way he will bring it. The temptation narratives (Luke 4:1–13 et par.) can be read in this light, as can John's account of the people's desire to make Jesus king (6:15), and even the mocking at the cross: "He saved others; let him save himself!" (Luke 23:35). In each case, what is in dispute is the nature of the salvation that God's Christ will bring.

This complexity, combined with the recent fashion in certain schools of biblical studies for atomized readings of the canonical texts, leads to a multiplicity of accounts of salvation. On such readings, there is no biblical (and hence no theological) account of salvation; rather, there are competing accounts within the canon that witness to different visions of salvation, and to which different theological constructions may appeal. In this area the basic challenge for a theological reading of Scripture is to recognize the real diversity present in the Scriptures, which drives such particularizing tendencies, while seeking a rich account of the fundamental unity of all the different pictures and emphases.

Historical study of the OT suggests that the earliest understanding of God in the life of the people of Israel was an account of salvation: God is the God of the patriarchs, who brought up his people out of Egypt and rescued them from the land of slavery. This recognition is central to the worship of God's people in the Psalms, and to the regulation of their shared life in the law codes. The Decalogue itself begins with an announcement of this salvation, and the laws that follow flow from it. Notably, in the various canonical forms of the exodus narrative, there is no suggestion of a connection between salvation and morality: God's people are not in need of salvation because of their failings; they are not saved because of (or even through) their repentance. The covenant relation between God and Israel is presented in this foundational story as utterly amoral, in the sense that Israel's part is to be the passive recipients of God's promises. (God's actions are, of course, profoundly moral,

in that he acts to keep his promises.) The giving of the law, which follows covenant and salvation, introduces the issue of Israel's faithfulness into the situation.

In the Deuteronomic history, Joshua and Judges (and, indeed, the later books) continue this message of God's salvation as a political, social, and economic reality, but it is now intimately linked to the obedience of God's people. Disobedience to the covenant stipulations, spelled out in explicitly moral terms ("Israel did what was evil in the sight of Yahweh"), brought military defeat and political subjection. Discovering and removing the source of pollution (e.g., in the case of Achan), or a national return to Yahweh ("Israel cried to Yahweh for help"—a repeated refrain in Judges), produced deliverance through military success and brought political autonomy. Within this narrative, however, the repeated implicit criticism of the charismatic theocracy of the judges ("In those days Israel had no king; everyone did as [they] saw fit" [e.g., Judg. 21:25]) perhaps suggests an awareness of a salvation less ephemeral than mere military success.

Many of the historical narratives demand and repay attention to the detail of their canonical forms in developing theological readings of Scripture. To take only one example, the way the exodus story is narrated in the canon has suggested a liturgical context to some, with stylized representations of a sequence of conflicts between God and Pharaoh, testing their power in a climactic battle for control of the world. The anonymity of Pharaoh marks him out as a type of every oppressive and unjust government, every temporal power that sets itself up against God. The final act of the drama, the parting of the sea, suggests that the cosmic forces of evil—which Hebrew writings commonly personify as the sea (see, e.g., Ps. 74:12–14)—are in league with Pharaoh. The final celebration of deliverance comes in the Song of Moses and Miriam as God's power achieves total salvation by throwing the opposing evil alliance into such confusion that Pharaoh is destroyed by the sea.

Salvation in the pentateuchal and historical texts is not just on a national level, however. God's saving action is also seen in the lives of the poor, forgotten, and oppressed. God is the one who sees and rescues Hagar and Ishmael, who guides Ruth and Naomi to their kinsman-redeemer, who hears the inarticulate prayers of barren Hannah. This theme too is prominent in the Psalms, where the poor and needy cry to God, their only savior. The writing prophets turn this belief in God's deliverance of those who suffer under oppression into an ethical demand: God's people are called to be those whose laws and lives demonstrate an understanding of, and a commitment to, God's salvation. This ringing proclamation of the prophets can be traced through the law, where concern for "the widow, the orphan, and the stranger in your midst" is repeatedly stressed, debtors and slaves are regularly liberated, the very land is given a Sabbath, and Jubilee is proclaimed for all once in fifty years.

Within the wider ancient Near Eastern wisdom tradition, salvation is perhaps not a central concern, but the particular emphases of the biblical Wisdom texts bring it more to the fore. The practical advice for right living is present but placed in a wider context suggesting that such right living is related to soteriological themes (Prov. 1–3 develops this context, as does Wisdom's song in Prov. 8). Again, the speculative wisdom, examining existential conundrums, was common to the wider tradition, but the particular answers given within Israel's canonical literature are often soteriological (Ps. 73 is an example of this, as is Job's continued insistence that redemption, vindication, and salvation will eventually come to him from God).

The exile both refocused expectations of salvation into the future political, social, and economic prosperity of Israel and strengthened the sense of the linkage between the need for salvation and moral failure. The disappointing events that followed the return from exile led to the development of the final soteriological emphasis in the OT: eschatology. The final realization of salvation began to be seen as something both larger and more remote than previously. It was no longer merely individual or national, but also cosmic: the whole universe would one day be transformed, with natural relationships reordered to bring an end to violence even also in the animal kingdom, poverty, oppression, and all other manifestations of sin and evil. As a result, while moments of individual and national salvation could still be looked for and celebrated, the final reality of salvation was deferred to a coming "day of the LORD," when a decisive intervention would result in the saving transformation of the entire cosmos. The development of apocalyptic writing, prefigured in Zechariah, parts of Daniel, Isa. 24–27, parts of Ezekiel, and so on, came to fullest flower in the intertestamental period (although one or two of the disputed books regarded as canonical by Roman Catholic and other traditions, such as 2 Esdras, are full-blown apocalypses). Apocalyptic pictures salvation as a climactic cosmic battle resulting in the final salvation and vindication of God's people.

There are passages within NT books that are clearly apocalyptic in genre: Revelation, Mark 13 (and parallels), and 2 Thess. 2 are the most obvious. The influence of this apocalyptic tradition on the visions of salvation within the NT writings, however, is far more profound. In the resurrection of Christ, the decisive salvific events that will inaugurate the eschatological kingdom of God have begun, and although there is a deferral of their completion until the return of Christ, the final cosmic salvation has begun.

Within the Synoptic Gospels, the first theme of Christ's preaching is the coming of this eschatological moment of conflict and salvation, and the need to choose sides within the conflict: "Repent, for the kingdom of God/heaven is at hand!" Miracles of healing and particularly exorcism are themselves moments of salvation, and also graphic illustrations of both the conflict and on which side decisive power lies. The forgiveness of sin, and moral transformation, are also decisive salvific events (e.g., Luke 5:17–32; 19:1–9). Acts develops similar themes. In the Fourth Gospel, salvation is central to the message of Jesus, who is sent by the Father to "save the world" (3:17). The gift of "life" and the promised relationship with the Father through Jesus are particular conceptions of salvation that are important in this Gospel.

In the Pauline corpus, salvation is understood as what God has done through Christ, and particularly his death and resurrection, to bring about deliverance from sin and death, wholeness, health, moral and physical transformation, and enduring new life. Believers are united with Christ, and so will share in his sufferings, and finally his glory. The Catholic Epistles and Revelation point to the eschatological cosmic salvation, presently made visible and available (at least in prospect) in the person of Jesus.

A theological interpretation of Scripture will, when faced with an issue like salvation, refuse the too-easy decision that these varying biblical pictures are simply incommensurate. Against the fashion for finding irreconcilable divergences, it is necessary to assert that God, who has one purpose, has one salvation, and so to seek a single vision of salvation that unites the biblical testimony. Equally, theological accounts of salvation that privilege one particular strand of the biblical witness (whether political and economic liberation or deliverance from sin), to the effective exclusion of all others, must be challenged to take the genuine diversity of the canonical accounts more seriously, and so find a richer theology.

The assertion that God brings salvation in Jesus Christ will be foundational to adequate theological interpretation, as will the strong NT witness to the coming eschatological fullness of salvation. Within these overarching themes, other themes may take their proper place. Deliverance from sin and death, and a final end to oppression and injustice, are alike components of the promised eschatological wholeness. Miracles of physical healing and of political deliverance alike can be genuine moments of salvation, foretastes of what is to come. The place of the people of God, as those who experience a foretaste of salvation and so witness to its coming fullness, will also be central, although exactly how the relationship of Israel and the church will be constructed in this context is open to debate.

Bibliography

Dillistone, F. W. *The Christian Understanding of Atonement*. Westminster, 1968; Gunton, C. *The Actuality of Atonement*. T&T Clark, 1988; Wright, N. T. *Jesus and the Victory of God*. Fortress, 1996.

Stephen R. Holmes

Salvation, History of

Central to both the unity of the Bible and its theological interpretation is what is sometimes called sacred or redemptive history, but more commonly, salvation history. By any reading, salvation and history are both key facets of Scripture. God is portrayed preeminently as "a God who saves" (Ps. 68:20), in the OT above all at the exodus (Deut. 6:21–23) and in the NT at the cross (Col. 1:19–20). And attempts to summarize the Bible's teaching as a whole frequently choose the theme of salvation (e.g., Caird). As for the second term, OT narratives regularly claim the status of history (Sternberg). In like manner, the NT Gospels are best compared with a recognized category of Hellenistic historical writing, the *bios*, or biography (Burridge), and the book of Acts similarly with Greek historiography (Sterling). Even those parts of the NT not overtly writing history evince a keen interest in history (Dodd).

Although linked in the nineteenth century with the German Protestant J. C. von Hofmann, attention to salvation history (*Heilsgeschichte*) can be traced back to the Reformers' rejection of Alexandrian allegorical exegesis and their recovery of the historical sense of the OT. Twentieth-century interest in the subject grew out of dissatisfac-

tion with the reduction of biblical theology to the history of religious ideas, devoid of reference to events in human history.

Some authors who doubt the historicity of the biblical account of Israel and Jesus Christ use the term "salvation history" either to characterize the individual's personal journey to faith (e.g., Bultmann), or to understand the Bible as the history of the proclamation of salvation (e.g., von Rad), rather than as a history of the events themselves.

Nonetheless, for many the major tenets of salvation history are (1) that God has acted in human history; and (2) that the books of the Bible, while not uniformly historical in form, all relate to an unfolding narrative of these events. It follows not only that salvation is historic, but also that history is salvific, itself revelation.

Salvation History: A Theological Affirmation

The following selective survey seeks to trace the main lines of the history of salvation in both Testaments with an emphasis on the way the various strands of the NT relate to the OT.

The OT. In the OT, revelation is tied to a particular national history, the history of Israel as the chosen people. The key points include the covenant promises to Abraham, which eventually lead to his descendants being released from the Egyptian bondage in the exodus; the Mosaic covenant at Sinai, constituting them as the people of God; a new generation of Israelites entering the promised land under Joshua; the rule of the judges and the prophet Samuel, leading to the establishment of kingship; King David capturing the Jebusite city of Jerusalem, which becomes the holy city of Zion; God's covenant with David, establishing David's dynasty in relation to the temple and the throne; the "rest" in the land enjoyed under David and Solomon; the decline and division of the kingdom under Solomon's son, Rehoboam; the outworking of the covenant curses against both kingdoms through enemy invasion and eventual exile to Assyria (the northern kingdom) and Babylonia (the southern kingdom); and the return from Babylon under Nehemiah, Ezra, and Zerubbabel.

This account of biblical history is based on the narrative and prophetic books. The Psalms, with their many references to incidents in Israel's history, Zion, the king, and especially the figure of David could be used to complement the picture. Yet the relation of the Wisdom literature to salvation history, which hardly ever refers to such persons or events, is less obvious. The answer may lie in the link between wisdom and Solomon, especially in 1 Kings 3–10, where in midpericope about Solomon's wisdom is the account of building the temple. Only when Israel is firmly planted in the land with God in the midst and the anointed king on the throne does wisdom flower (Goldsworthy).

The Gospels. When we come to the NT Gospels, the question salvation history urges us to ask is, How do Matthew, Mark, Luke, and John carry forward the narrative of God's saving activity? Even a cursory survey indicates that each of the Gospels is firmly yet distinctively embedded in Israel's story through its respective selection and use of OT texts.

Matthew. The Gospel's opening words allude to Israel's opening book (cf. 1:1 with Gen. 2:4), and a genealogy ensures continuity of "Jesus Christ the son of David, the son of Abraham" (1:1) with the story of Israel. Hence, Matthew can hardly be more explicit about the importance of Jesus to salvation history and vice versa. Jesus, the Davidic Messiah, has come to announce that "the gospel of the kingdom" (4:23 RSV), the promised rule of God, is now to be realized in history. Matthew includes more than sixty OT quotations to forge unmistakable links with God's saving activity in the past and to identify Jesus as the Christ, who must suffer. Ten of these are introduced with the slightly varied formula, "This took place to fulfill . . ." More allusively, through intricate typology, discerning escalated patterns or analogies in history, Jesus is depicted as a new Moses, who demands a "higher righteousness" (Allison), and a new Israel. Jesus recapitulates the nation's history (rescued from Egypt, tempted in the wilderness, etc.), but without failure, and fulfills her destiny.

Mark. Mark describes the good news in terms of the fulfillment of Isaiah's prophecy of a new exodus (1:2–3; cf. Isa. 40:3; Mal. 3:1; Watts). Less overt than Matthew, Mark has explicit citations of the OT only at the opening of his account, in the passion narrative, and occasionally on the lips of Jesus. Yet his message that the climax of Israel's story has been reached is no less compelling. Echoing the words of Ps. 2:7, "You are My beloved Son, in whom I am well pleased," Jesus' messianic identity is made clear at his baptism (1:11 NKJV). The "tearing" open of the heavens in this scene (only in Mark; in Matthew and Luke the heavens are merely "opened") indicates that at last God has acted decisively to make good on his promises of salvation (cf. Isa. 64:1). OT passages and themes frequently underlie Mark's narrative.

Luke(-Acts). Perhaps more than any other Gospel, Luke presents Jesus as the continuation of biblical history (Rosner). His style of Greek, especially at the beginning of the Gospel (and also Acts), is reminiscent of the LXX. Though the OT for Matthew is largely a book of prophetic predictions, Luke emphasizes that God has bound himself to Israel with words of promise (e.g., to David, 1:30–32, 68–71 [2 Sam. 7:14]; to Abraham, 1:54–55, 72–73 [Gen. 12:1–3; etc.]), which are being accomplished in Jesus. Jesus is also depicted as the interpreter of Scripture himself (24:25–49), for "all things which were written about [him] in the Law of Moses and the Prophets and the Psalms must be fulfilled" (cf. NKJV). In Acts, a salvation-historical approach to reading the OT is modeled in the speeches of Peter (2:16–36), Stephen (7:2–56), and Paul (13:16–41).

John. OT antecedents also define the shape of the Christ and his mission in John. The final revelation from God that Jesus brings and embodies is compared and contrasted with that received and mediated by Moses. The signs he performs, recalling the "signs and wonders" of Moses, point to a new exodus. Jesus eclipses the great Jewish feasts and institutions that marked God's saving work in the past. As the "light of the world" and "living water," he fulfills the torch-lighting and water-pouring ceremonies of the Feast of Tabernacles. He replaces the Jerusalem temple and, by dying during Passover week, is the ultimate Jewish Passover sacrifice. He is also seen as the long-awaited "prophet like Moses" (6:14; 7:40; cf. Deut. 18:15).

Paul. According to Paul (e.g., in Gal. 3:15–29), salvation history is rooted in God's promise to Abraham, a promise fulfilled in Christ. The law of Moses was only a temporary stage used by God to preserve Israel until God would make good on his promise. God's dealings with Israel recorded in the Bible lead to Christ, who is the turning point of history. In fact, for Paul, history divides into two epochs, the old age of sin, death, and the Torah; and the new age, which eclipses it (see esp. Ridderbos). From another perspective, the decisive act in the ending of Israel's exile and the restoration of God's people has now taken place in Christ (Wright).

Revelation. No book in the Bible underscores the sovereignty of God in the affairs of human history more profoundly than Revelation. It opens with a vision in chapters 4–5 of a heavenly world where God and the Lamb's throne are at the center of everything. Gathering many themes of the rest of the NT, it closes in chapters 21–22 with a vision of a new Jerusalem and temple (21:2; 21:9–22:5), a new covenant (21:3–4), and even a new Israel. Both the "names of the twelve tribes of Israel" (21:12) and "the names of the twelve apostles of the Lamb" (21:14) are found on the gates and walls of the city. However, the most comprehensive theme is the new creation, climaxing all of these as the goal of both salvation and history (Dumbrell).

Salvation History: A Principle of Scriptural Interpretation

The Unity of Scripture. As can be seen from this selective survey, a salvation-historical hermeneutic understands the later parts of the Bible to take the form they do by building on earlier parts. This is seen not only through the familiar schemas of the fulfillment of prophecy and promise. In addition, God has saved his people in the past by redeeming them through an exodus, raising up prophets (like Moses), establishing a Davidic dynasty, and instituting a temple and sacrifices. Therefore, his ultimate deed of salvation in Jesus Christ recalls and climaxes all of these.

The Knowledge of God. A salvation-historical perspective speaks about God in the concrete rather than relying on philosophical and abstract terms of reference. God can be known not as some impersonal prime mover or a vague creative force, but as the God of Abraham, Isaac, and Jacob, the Father of the Lord Jesus Christ. The knowledge of God comes not in a set of ideas or even via a mystical experience, but primarily by the great things he has done in human history, culminating in the gospel. The biblical account gives us a narrative framework, a continuing story, in which we may locate ourselves, come to know God, and find meaning in life.

Stages in the History of God's Saving Acts. In tracing the history of salvation, a number of dispensations or epochs, periods of history with distinctive characteristics, have been discerned. Hermeneutical significance is sometimes attached to these various stages, which can help open up the Bible's diversity as well as its unity. However, little consensus has been achieved. Proposals are numerous, ranging from twelve (Van Gemeren) to seven (the *Scofield Reference Bible* [1917], representing classic dispensationalism) or six periods of redemptive history (Clowney).

To give a specific example, Donald Robinson's schema of three major epochs takes the kingdom of God as its unifying concept and is explicitly gospel-based. The first movement goes from the divine choice of Abraham, and the making of promises to him, to the realization of those promises in the kingdom of Solomon, and the subsequent decline. The second, the epoch of prophetic eschatology, sees the prophets from the eighth century onward proclaiming a message about a future salvation and a future coming of the kingdom. This future is to recapitulate what has already happened in the first phase (a new captivity, new exodus, new redemption, new covenant, new Davidic rule in a new Zion with a new temple). The third epoch is signaled by the appearance of Jesus, who preaches that the time is fulfilled and the kingdom of God is at hand.

The Corporate Dimension of Salvation. The framework of salvation history draws attention to the fact that it is God's intention to save a people and not just individuals. Christ and Adam have inclusive significance, representing new and old humanity respectively. The place of Jews and Gentiles in God's saving purposes is an important focus.

Salvation is thought of both individually and corporately. If Christ is in the individual believer, correspondingly all believers together are in Christ. The believer is a temple of the Holy Spirit, just as the church as a whole is such a temple. As well as a judgment of individuals, there will also be a judgment of nations. And if individuals long for salvation, no less does the whole creation. Salvation history makes it clear that God's purposes loom larger than my personal fulfillment, are bigger than me and my God, and embrace a universalistic vision.

A Tension with Eschatology? If eschatology is the end of history, this creates a potential problem for salvation history. A final cataclysmic intervention of "apocalyptic" proportions might seem to militate against an emphasis on God's less-dramatic activity in history. However, the conflict is only apparent. In the book of Revelation, as we saw above, God's determination to make Christ all in all in the future, even if more "earth-shattering," will be built upon and recall what he has done in the past. Furthermore, implicit in the whole notion of God's acting in history is the goal toward which this history is moving. Thus, as Cullmann insists, history, to be salvation history, must involve eschatology. Salvation history is heading somewhere, and the end is always in mind.

See also Biblical Theology; Exile and Restoration; Last Things, Doctrine of; Metanarrative; Scripture, Unity of; Typology

Bibliography

Allison, D. *The New Moses.* T&T Clark, 1993; Bultmann, R. *The Old Testament and Christian Faith,* ed. B. Anderson. SCM, 1964; Burridge, R. *What Are the Gospels?* Cambridge University Press, 1992; Caird, G. B. *New Testament Theology.* Oxford University Press, 1994; Clowney, E. *Preaching and Biblical Theology.* P&R, 1961; Cullmann, O. *Salvation in History.* SCM, 1967; Dodd, C. H. *History and the Gospel.* Nisbet, 1938; Dumbrell, W. *The End of the Beginning.* Homebush West, 1985; Goldsworthy, G. *Gospel and Wisdom.* Exeter, 1987; Rad, G. von. *Old Testament Theology.* 2 vols. Harper & Row, 1962–64; Ridderbos, H. *Paul.* Eerdmans, 1974; Robinson, D. *Faith's Framework.* New Creation, 1985; Rosner, B. "Acts and Biblical History." Pages 65–82 in *The Book of Acts in Its Ancient Literary Setting,* ed. B. Winter and A. Clarke. Vol. 1 of *The Book of Acts in Its First-Century Setting,* ed. B. Winter. Eerdmans, 1993; Satterthwaite, P. "Biblical History." Pages 43–51 in *New Dictionary of Biblical Theology,* ed. T. D. Alexander and B. Rosner. InterVarsity, 2000; Sterling, G. *Historiography and Self-Definition.* Brill, 1992; Sternberg, M. *The Poetics of Biblical Narrative.* Indiana University Press, 1985; Van Gemeren, W. *The Progress of Redemption.* Zondervan, 1988; Watts, R. *Isaiah's New Exodus and Mark.* Mohr/Siebeck, 1997; Wright, N. T. *The Climax of the Covenant.* Fortress, 1992.

Brian S. Rosner

Samuel, Books of

Samuel was originally one book that was divided into two when the Hebrew text was translated into Greek, to accommodate the work to the length of scrolls typically used in classical antiquity. The books of Samuel are concerned primarily with the establishment of the monarchy in Israel under Saul, followed by the rise and reign of David. The prophet Samuel oversees the introduction of the monarchy, as kingmaker to both Saul and David. Through the actions of these three, the order of Israel's life and faith is fundamentally changed, with reverberations felt throughout the rest of the Bible.

Highlights in the History of Interpretation

A dominant approach of patristic and medieval exegesis was to seek out the "spiritual" senses of Scripture as a strategy for reading the OT as a prophetic Christian book. These methods entailed imaginative typological and eschatological interpretations of the text. Thus, David's career and rejection, then subsequent elevation as king in Jerusalem, were seen as prefiguring Christ, who was crucified, then enthroned in glory in heaven.

Reformation exegesis was much more restrained in any typological comparisons it drew between David and Christ. The Reformers essentially affirmed the Antiochene approach to Scripture, insisting that "the literal sense *is* the spiritual sense." Thus, in Calvin's *Sermons on 2 Samuel* the moral and theological meaning of the text is deduced primarily from historical exegesis and close attention to the literary context. For Calvin, of course, the OT's witness was to Christ, and the NT authoritatively interpreted the OT. David's kingdom and God's promises to him had their proper meaning within that context and anticipated their fulfillment in Christ's kingdom.

Much scholarly work in the nineteenth and twentieth centuries concentrated on literary source-critical approaches as a way of dealing with perceived tensions and doublets in the text. Thus, Wellhausen (1871) argued that an early promonarchic stratum (1 Sam. 9:1–10:16; chs. 11, 13–14) had been combined with a postexilic, antimonarchic stratum (1 Sam. 8; 10:17–27; chs. 12, 15) to produce a hybrid text of conflicting attitudes. The view that the present text has arisen from numerous expansions and elaborations of earlier sources has remained influential up to recent years (see, e.g., McCarter's commentary).

Rost (1926) strongly advocated the view that older, originally separate documents had been combined to produce the present work. Rost identified 1 Sam. 4:1b–7:1 + 2 Sam. 6 as an independent "Ark Narrative," 1 Sam. 16:14–2 Sam. 5 as an original "History of David's Rise," and 2 Sam. 9–20 + 1 Kings 1–2 as a "court history" (the "Succession Narrative" [SN]) detailing how Solomon became king. This last work Rost considered to be one of the world's earliest examples of eyewitness historiography.

Noth's (1943) hypothesis of a "Deuteronomistic History" (DH) understood 1–2 Samuel to be part of a continuous narrative (Deuteronomy–2 Kings) composed by a single exilic writer using traditional materials. The extent of pre- and postexilic redactions of DH and additions thereto (and even the existence of such a work) remains a hotly debated subject. In Noth's view, the underlying documents of 1–2 Samuel were incorporated into DH with comparatively little redaction. Noth held that 2 Sam. 21–24 was an "appendix" of miscellaneous Davidic materials added to the narrative after DH was divided into separate books.

Rost's basic identification of documents is still broadly accepted, although the precise bound-

aries, dating, genre, and theme of these postulated documents (especially SN) are now much
more disputed. Gunn, for example, defines SN
as a novella rather than historiography. Keys rejects the inclusion of 1–2 Kings in the narrative
on grounds of style and content, and holds that
the real theme of 2 Sam. 9–20 is not succession
but David's sin and punishment. Complementary
observations are made by Stoebe (2 Sam. 9–20
shows that despite David's failings, the kingship
perdured under God's hand) and Provan (the narrative unmasks pretensions to "wisdom" that are
not rooted in God and the divine Torah).

Gunn's work signaled a turn from a concern
with source criticism and historiography to final-
form literary approaches concentrating on the
poetics and ideology of the book. Brueggemann's
postliberal commentary follows this approach in
focusing on the imaginative force and rhetoric of
the presentation, and the relationship between religious faith and political power. More adventur-
ous is Jobling's postmodern handling of 1 Samuel,
which presents an eclectic set of subversive readings engaged with contemporary issues (including class, polity, gender, ethnicity).

Recent writing in a more conservative vein
argues against the older documentary theories
(that differing outlooks in the text arose from the
untidy growth and conflation of various traditions over time), holding instead that 1–2 Samuel
should be read as a complex, intentional unity
with a coherent theological message.

Long's study of Saul's reign rejects Wellhausen's
thesis of conflicting pro- and antimonarchic documents underlying 1 Sam. 8–15 by distinguishing
the narrator's voice from that of the characters
(some of whom express anti-Saul rather than
antimonarchic views). Following Halpern and
Edelman, Long argues next that the complex
account(s) of Saul's election as king is comprehensible and not confused, once we grasp the
different stages involved in king-making in the
ancient world. Finally, Saul's rejection as king
makes sense as well, when we adopt the appropriate reading strategy for deducing the author's
intent. Saul's rejection arises from his unwilling-
ness to submit to the new authority structure of
the theocracy, whereby the king must obey the
word of the Lord mediated through God's prophet
(cf. 1 Sam. 12:13–15, 24–25).

On the structural level, Klement concentrates
on the ending (2 Sam. 21–24), arguing that it is
no "appendix" or miscellany but a carefully composed conclusion to the work as a whole. The
conclusion provides the key to the grand, chiastic

structure of the book and its basic theological
message. Klement identifies other structural
patterns throughout the book as evidence of a
sophisticated and intentional artistic design.

The advantage of these recent approaches is
that they support a final-form reading of the
text that is not arbitrary but takes seriously the
original literary integrity of the Samuel scroll.
(In contrast, it must be remembered that DH is
a scholarly postulate without any manuscript
basis.) This allows the message of 1–2 Samuel
to be heard on its own terms, and not just as an
episode within a larger narrative.

Message of 1–2 Samuel

The two major themes of the work are monarchy and Yahweh's word. The offices of king and
prophet (along with the priesthood in its oracular
activity) exist by God's election and call (1 Sam.
2:28; 3:4; 10:24; 13:14; 2 Sam. 6:21; 7:8) for the
protection and rule of his people.

On monarchy, Klement identifies the message
at the center of the chiasm of 2 Sam. 21–24 (and
thus the summative message of the book) as an affirmation of Yahweh's covenant with David as an
institution for Israel's good. David utters the two
poems in this section (2 Sam. 22:2–51; 23:1–7),
which celebrate Yahweh's "everlasting covenant"
and "steadfast love to David and his descendants
forever." At its outset this work shows Israel to be
afflicted both by the corrupt priesthood in Shiloh
and the oppression of the Philistines. Yahweh
acts to reverse the unhappy state of his people,
first by answering Hannah's prayer for a son. The
birth of Samuel, the faithful prophet and kingmaker, sets in train the course of actions that will
culminate in David's kingship. Hannah's song of
thanksgiving (1 Sam. 2:1–10), with its prayer that
Yahweh "will give strength to his king and exalt
the horn of his anointed one," has close verbal and
thematic correspondences with the concluding
poems. Thus, these two poetic sections function
as chiastic bookends for the whole work.

Hannah's prayer is fulfilled in the achievements
of David's reign at its best (2 Sam. 5–10; cf. 23:3–
4), where he appears as the ideal ruler. Monarchy as such is not really faulted in the book (cf.
Deut. 17:14–20). The issue turns rather on the *type*
of king. Shall he be a figure of human political
conceiving and choice ("a king for ourselves,"
1 Sam. 8:18–20; 12:19 NRSV), or one of Yahweh's
choice and for his purpose ("I have provided for
myself a king [David]," 1 Sam. 16:1 NRSV)? Saul
is rejected as king because of his failure in the
fundamental matter of obedience to God's word

as mediated by his prophet Samuel. (A parallel theme to this is the rejection of the priestly family of Eli for dishonoring God; 1 Sam. 2:31.) With the departure of Yahweh's spirit (1 Sam. 16:14), Saul declines into depression and madness. David, on the other hand, is presented as Yahweh's chosen king, Spirit-endowed and Saul's "better" (1 Sam. 13:14; 15:28; 16:13). Pious, brave, and innocent of treachery against Saul, David gains the throne through Yahweh's choice and Israel's willing assent (2 Sam. 5:1–3). He subjugates the neighboring states, thus securing "rest" for the people (2 Sam. 5:17–25; 8:1–14). David's conquest of Jerusalem provides a capital for his kingdom and a final resting place for the ark of the covenant, uniting in one place the religious and political symbols of the nation (2 Sam. 5:6–14; 6:1–23). In turn, Yahweh's commitment to David extends to his descendants in the gracious promise of a secure and enduring dynasty and kingdom (2 Sam. 7:16; 23:5).

David thus appears as a worthier and more effective ruler than Saul, whose reign ends in apostasy and national disaster (1 Sam. 28, 31). The apogee of David's obedient reign (and the sign of divine blessing upon it) is indicated in 2 Sam. 8:15–18, the brief note on his administration, and in 2 Sam. 9, his exemplary treatment of Mephibosheth. Overall, however, David's reign has an ambiguous character. Blessing turns to curse in the following chapters, where David's later disobedience and decline are candidly revealed, along with the destructive consequences these have, both for his family and for the nation (2 Sam. 11–20). Thus, David in his later years fails to realize the blessings promised to his own kingship. His rule is beneficial only insofar as he submits himself to Yahweh and his commands. The various intrigues involving a wayward David and his equally wayward sons indicate that politics (both sexual and power) posited on a calculating worldly wisdom leads only to disaster. Nevertheless, Yahweh's covenant grace prevails. Unlike Saul, David himself is not rejected (cf. 1 Sam. 15:26), nor is Yahweh's promise done away with.

The theme of Yahweh's word is presented in two major ways. First, the narrative shows that Yahweh's word, mediated by his prophets or the priestly oracle, determines the course of history, in declaring blessing or judgment. We are informed that early in this period "the word of Yahweh was rare" (1 Sam. 3:1 AT), but everything is changed for Israel by the time Samuel reaches adulthood (1 Sam. 3:19–4:1a). What Yahweh's messengers declare will surely happen (cf. Deut. 18:21–22). Thus, Samuel first anoints Saul as "leader" (*nagid*) in obedience to Yahweh's word, with confirming signs to follow (1 Sam. 9:16; 10:1–9), then David as his successor, again as Yahweh directs (1 Sam. 16:12, fulfilled in 2 Sam. 5:1–3). Through Nathan, David also receives the promise of a dynastic line and the assurance that his successor will build a temple (2 Sam. 7:11–16), matters whose fulfillment lies outside this book (1 Kings 2:12; ch. 6).

Conversely, the word of divine judgment is given in the declarations against Eli's house and descendants and is fulfilled in subsequent events (1 Sam. 2:31–36; 3:11–14; cf. 4:11; 22:18–19); in the rejection of Saul (15:26, specifically for spurning Yahweh's word, v. 23; cf. 31:6; 2 Sam. 6:21); and against David (2 Sam. 12:10–12; 24:13; cf. chs. 13–20; 24:15).

Second, Yahweh's word is given to admonish and guide. Samuel reproaches the sinful people in Yahweh's name (1 Sam. 8:10; 10:18–19), as well as giving specific instructions to Saul (9:27; 10:3–8; 15:2–3, 17–19). Nathan and Gad are also specifically sent by Yahweh to counsel David or rebuke him with God's word (2 Sam. 7:4–5; 12:1; 24:11–12, 18), and David responds fittingly on each occasion. In addition, David inquires of God through the oracles given by Ahimelech and Abiathar (1 Sam. 22:10; 23:2, 4; 30:8; 2 Sam. 2:1; 5:19, 23), and enjoys success. By contrast, a disobedient Saul is denied a word from God and has recourse instead to necromancy (1 Sam. 28:6–7). In these ways, the book teaches that the exercise of kingship within Israel must be subject to Yahweh's word.

Notwithstanding its final canonical location (within a history extending from Genesis to 2 Kings), 1–2 Samuel can be read on its own terms as a reflection of the early days of the Judahite monarchy (cf. 1 Sam. 27:6). The work holds up the Davidic covenant as the grounds for national and dynastic confidence, along with the necessity of royal obedience to the prophetic word. Hence, it perhaps sought to inculcate a similar response from the first descendants of David and his people, in the difficult days that followed the division of the kingdom (cf. 1 Kings 14:8).

1–2 Samuel and the Canon

The book has close connections with many other parts of the canon. First, whatever we make of Noth's hypothesis (DH), 1–2 Samuel is the natural narrative bridge from Judg. 17–21, when "there was no king in Israel" (21:25 NRSV), to the history of the monarchy in 1–2 Kings. Kings also reflects many of the themes in Samuel, such as the fulfillment of the dynastic promise (cf. 1 Kings 2:4; 8:25; 9:4–5), Solomon as the appointed temple builder (5:5), and the backward look to David as the standard for evaluating his successors (3:14; 11:6, 38; 2 Kings 14:3; 15:3; 18:3; 22:2).

The closest canonical connection is with 1 Chron. 10–21, which is directly dependent on 1–2 Samuel in recounting the narratives of Saul and David. The Chronicler significantly recast and modified his sources, omitting most of the material on Saul and on David's rise to power and subsequent family problems. The Chronicler's chief interest here was to extol the public role of David as king and cofounder with Solomon of the Jerusalem cult. At the same time, David's sinful census, with its disastrous consequences for Israel (2 Sam. 24) has a pivotal place in the Chronicler's presentation (1 Chron. 21)—recognition that David could be a source of ill for the nation as well as good.

The presentation of David as musician and composer of psalms (1 Sam. 16:18, 23; 18:10; 2 Sam. 22:1–51; 23:1–7) was no doubt a fountainhead of the tradition that ascribes large parts of the Psalter to David (whether by or about him). The superscriptions on many of the Psalms (3, 7, 18, 34, 51, 52, 54, 56, 57, 59, 60, 63, 142) associate these compositions with incidents in 1–2 Samuel and indicate how these psalms were anciently understood and related (perhaps midrashically) to David as the model worshipper of Yahweh.

1–2 Samuel and Theology

The historical development of messianism is especially dependent on this work. In its presentation of David and the Davidic covenant, the book provided the soil for later messianic hopes and conceptions. As Yahweh's "anointed" (*mashiakh*, 1 Sam. 2:10; 2 Sam. 22:51; 23:1), David is elected and upheld by God for the blessing of his people. As the ideal king and recipient of the promise, David becomes the archetype of prophetic hopes for a successor in the troubled later centuries of Judah's existence (Mic. 5:2–5; Isa. 11:1–2; Jer. 23:5; Ezek. 37:24). That trajectory continues throughout the NT in its expectation of a Messiah in David's line (cf. Matt. 1:1; 21:9; Luke 1:32; John 7:42; Rom. 1:3; Rev. 5:5). However, the NT goes beyond comparisons, emphasizing that Jesus as Messiah also surpasses and *contrasts* with David, a great but flawed human being (cf. Acts 2:25–36).

Historically speaking, 1–2 Samuel has played a significant role in the articulation of political theology, especially in medieval and early modern reflection on the meaning of Christian kingship. In portraying the (Davidic) king as the representative and mediator of God's own kingship, charged with securing the continued identity of the people through military leadership against external threats and by ensuring justice and right worship at home, 1–2 Samuel presents data on the political task with which Christians must constantly reckon. Yet the book is also skeptical (at least) about human kingship, which is not fundamental to Yahweh's rule or Israel's identity, and is sometimes inimical to these, especially when the prophetic word is spurned. Similarly, while no state today understands itself as a Christian theocracy, the exercise of political and judicial power must always be tempered by the church's proclamation of the gospel (which centers on the present and coming kingship of Christ). Otherwise, the state will lose sight of its own identity and the concept of right that it exists to defend.

See also History of Israel; Kingdom of God; Messiah/Messianism; Narrative Criticism; Source Criticism

Bibliography

Brueggemann, W. *First and Second Samuel.* John Knox, 1990; Edelman, D. *King Saul in the Historiography of Judah.* Sheffield Academic Press, 1991; Gordon, R. P. *1 and 2 Samuel.* Zondervan, 1986; Gunn, D. *The Story of King David.* Sheffield Academic Press, 1978; Halpern, B. *The Constitution of the Monarchy in Israel.* Scholars Press, 1981; Jobling, D. *1 Samuel.* Liturgical Press, 1998; Keys, G. *The Wages of Sin.* Sheffield Academic Press, 1996; Klement, H. *II Samuel 21–24.* P. Lang, 2000; Long, V. P. *The Reign and Rejection of King Saul.* Scholars Press, 1989; McCarter, P. K. *I Samuel.* Doubleday, 1980; idem. *II Samuel.* Doubleday, 1984; McConville, J. G. "Law and Monarchy in the Old Testament." In *A Royal Priesthood?*, ed. C. Bartholomew et al. SHS. Zondervan/Paternoster, 2002; Provan, I. "On 'Seeing' the Trees While Missing the Forest: The Wisdom of Characters and Readers in 2 Samuel and 1 Kings." Pages 153–73 in *In Search of True Wisdom*, ed. E. Ball. JSOTSup 300. Sheffield Academic Press, 1999; Rost, L. *The Succession to the Throne of David.* German, 1926, trans. M. D. Rutter and D. M. Gunn. Sheffield Academic Press, 1982; Stoebe, H. J. *Das zweite Buch Samuelis.* Chr. Kaiser, 1994.

Brian E. Kelly

Sanctification

Sanctification is a key element in the order of salvation (*ordo salutis*) and is usually placed between justification and glorification. Some theologians further distinguish between definitive or positional sanctification and progressive or conditional sanctification. The former concerns the believer's being set apart for God's service and as God's person. The latter concept refers to the believer's growth in Christlikeness and has its ultimate completion in the believer's glorification in the age to come. In classic Protestant thought sanctification, in this second sense, is clearly distinguished from justification. In classic Catholic thought the distinction is not observed. This was an issue of theological dispute during the Reformation period and remains so. There are remaining disputes too concerning the role of the Holy Spirit in sanctification. The Holiness and Pentecostal traditions have often argued the importance of a second work of grace in the believer's life after conversion, before sanctification in the progressive sense may really proceed. Lutheran and Reformed theologians generally beg to differ.

Sanctification in the Biblical Texts

The Scriptures present a holy God, who is both set apart from the world as its Creator and is morally pure (Gen. 1:1; Hab. 1:12–13). God expects his people to be set apart for him and to exhibit his moral character. They are to be holy as he is holy. This idea appears in both Testaments (Lev. 19:2; 1 Pet. 1:16). The canonical plotline reveals the story of God's reclaiming a fallen world and establishing a new heavens and earth in which righteousness is at home (2 Pet. 3:11–13). That new world will see God's holy people living in God's holy presence in God's holy city in God's holy way (Rev. 21:1–4). The activity of God in sanctifying a people for himself is integral to that story.

In the OT presentation the idea of sanctification in the sense of being set apart to be God's holy people or for God's use is found in many different contexts. The tent of meeting could be sanctified as the setting for God's meeting with his people (Exod. 29:43). In Joel, a fast could be sanctified for the purpose of calling upon God in repentance (Joel 1:13–15). Indeed, in the OT, people, places, objects, and times could be so sanctified.

In the NT, Jesus is the sanctified one par excellence. In his humanity, as God's Holy One, he perfectly instantiates God's holy character and is perfectly able to bring others to the place where they too mirror God's holiness (John 6:69; 17:17–19; Acts 2:27; Heb. 2:10–11).

Paul's contribution to the theology of sanctification is particularly important. The Corinthians were saints ("holy or sanctified ones"). God had set them apart for himself. They were now located in Christ (1 Cor. 1:2–3). They belonged to him.

Yet they were hardly sanctified in the progressive sense. In fact, the church was problematic in the extreme. The letter speaks of congregational disunity (chs. 1–4), sexual immorality within the congregation (ch. 5), lawsuits among believers (ch. 6), impropriety at the Lord's Supper (ch. 11), problems with the exercise of spiritual gifts (chs. 12–14), and wrong ideas about the resurrection (ch. 15). Some recent theological commentary suggests that positional or definitive sanctification is the major NT idea (Peterson).

With regard to the notion of progressive sanctification, Paul's Thessalonian correspondence is a rich source of instruction. In his brief ministry at Thessalonica he left the new converts with a gospel (1 Thess. 1:9–10) and an ethic (4:1–12). God's will is their sanctification (4:3). At the personal level such sanctification involves the maintenance of sexual purity. After all, they have God's Holy Spirit (4:8). In ever-widening circles, the sanctified life also involves love for other believers (1:9–10) and proper behavior toward outsiders (4:11–12). Paul urges the Thessalonians to live like this more and more (4:1, 10). This suggests progression. Paul recognizes that God needs to sanctify his people, and he prays for the Thessalonians to that end (5:23). The other main idea of sanctification as a definitive act of God in setting apart a people for himself is also in the Thessalonian correspondence (e.g., 2 Thess. 2:13).

Sanctification and the Theological Interpretation of Scripture

The Theological Interpretation of Scripture Recognizes the Need for Extrabiblical Distinctions to Make Sense of the Biblical Record. Paul, for example, does not write in terms of definitive and progressive sanctification per se. But the ideas are there as his Thessalonian correspondence, other Pauline texts, and the wider NT deposit show (1 Cor. 1:30; Phil. 3:12–14; Heb. 2:11; 12:14; 1 Pet. 1:15–16; 2 Pet. 3:18).

The Theological Interpretation of Scripture Acknowledges the Distinction between Biblical and Technical Usages of Words. The exegete's temptation is not to see ideas of sanctification in biblical texts because certain specific words are not used (e.g., "saint," "sanctification," "sanctified," "holy"). The theologian's temptation is to read back into the biblical texts one's more-complex understandings of sanctification and fail in the duty of exegetical care. An example of the latter is the theologian who cited 1 Cor. 6:11 as a proof text for the doctrine of progressive sanctification. Part of the problematic is that translators—working with the *qdsh* (Hebrew) and *hagi-* (Greek) word groups—use the same English words as the theological textbooks do. However, biblical literature is pretechnical; in contrast, the theological texts are products of a profession with a long history. And so the word "sanctification" in the latter refers to a master concept that the history of theological discussion has made both more complex (with its subcategories) and nuanced (with its distinctions) than the biblical concepts themselves.

The Theological Interpretation of Scripture Reckons with Double Agency. With regard to progressive sanctification, Paul tells a double story. There is a God story (1 Thess. 5:23), but also the story of believers' own efforts (4:12). The paradox of both God's agency at work and believers' work was captured beautifully by Paul when he wrote to the Philippians: "Work out your own salvation with fear and trembling; for it is God who is at work in you, enabling you both to will and to work for his good pleasure" (2:12–13 NRSV). Progressive sanctification is a cooperative venture.

Bibliography

Alexander, D., ed. *Christian Spirituality*. InterVarsity, 1988; Boyd, G., and P. Eddy. *Across the Spectrum*. Baker, 2002; Dieter, M. *Five Views on Sanctification*. Academie, 1987; Peterson, D. *Possessed by God*. Eerdmans, 1996.

Graham A. Cole

Satan   *See* Angels, Doctrine of; Powers and Principalities

Schleiermacher, Friedrich   *See* Hermeneutical Circle; Hermeneutics; Practical Theology

Science, the Bible and

There are any number of interpretative issues arising at the interface of Scripture and science. Clearly, specific findings of cosmology, origins, evolution, neuroscience, and genetics, among others, bear strongly on biblical theology. Some of these findings may actually serve as a resource for proper interpretation of Scripture, possibly contributing to a reformulation of traditional thought. In other cases, biblical teachings may provide grounds for formulating and assessing specific scientific proposals. In either case, the interpretative dynamic requires the reader to have a confident sense of the relative merits of the claims put forth in each respective discipline. Sound biblical interpretation demands at least a rudimentary grasp of the methodologies utilized in scientific inquiry in order to determine how much weight to grant their respective results. Apparent conflict between the teachings of science and the teachings of Scripture serves to raise, not to settle, the interpretative question of meaning and reliability. Even understanding an infallible word requires input from the fallible findings of science.

A New Humility

There are a number of reasons for caution regarding the specific results of scientific research. Recent work on the methods of science indicates several direct challenges to the objectivity, even reliability, of the process. For instance, it has become something of a truism to point out that perception, the very foundation of the discipline, requires the contribution of background concepts, beliefs, and expectations as well as the actions of the external world on sensory organs. Observational bias, in the form of prior experience, expectation, and training, indelibly skews sensory data, infecting the objectivity of research at the start. In its most radical form, personal, nonempirical, idiosyncratic beliefs appear to undermine the edifice of science at its very foundations. Although some forms of subjectivity may be ameliorated at the level of the broader scientific community, the initiation process for membership in that community must inevitably propagate certain biases.

The problem of the empirical base is compounded by problems central to the logic of theory confirmation. The very notion, for instance, that a fulfilled prediction verifies a hypothesis either requires untested assumptions, or simply commits the fallacy of affirming the consequences. With the persistent possibility of rival accounts, there can be no crucial experiment to provide definitive proof. Neither will an inductive approach help to save this notion of confirmation. Absent specific unsupported assumptions, a finite number of positive outcomes adds nothing in support of a universal law. Even falsification stumbles on the inherent complexity of scientific proposals; any hypothesis can be modified so as to save the appearances.

This latter observation has been generalized in the Duhem-Quine underdetermination thesis: however much evidence one gathers, there will always be more than one theory capable of accounting for that data. Since there will always be a competitor with equal empirical support, then the probability, construed as a function of observational data, can never rise above 50 percent. There can never be sufficient empirical evidence to judge a theory, rather than some rival, more likely than not. Preference for a specific theory, then, must appeal to nonempirical, nonepistemic considerations such as the elegance, simplicity, beauty, familiarity, or internal coherence of the hypothesis. Such preference may simply reflect our aesthetic sensibilities, cultural tastes, or even the vested interests of the governing body. More charitably, preference may be conferred on accounts that merely promote such pragmatic virtues as prediction, manipulation, and technological power, with no particular concern for their truth.

Support for this severely chastened view of the sciences is available from historians and sociologists of science who, following T. S. Kuhn, insist that the numerous revolutionary changes in scientific theories, and especially the terms of scientific analysis, undermine its claim to rationality. Why suppose that contemporary science embodies a rational, truth-tracking procedure when the scientific community periodically and radically revises its understanding of the natural world? In fact, the internal dynamics of theory change, where even the very criteria of assessment undergo revision, suggest that these theory changes are more akin to conversion experiences than to careful, step-by-step, reason-guided developments. Furthermore, because these shifts are so comprehensive, there is no support for the assumption that this process is on a progressive track. If there were common grounds for comparing each successive framework, or stable standards of evaluation, we might speak of scientific progress. As it stands, the incommensurability of each distinct view of the world undermines the very notion of a cumulative or progressively better grasp of reality.

A Reasonably Similar Interpretative Task

These several considerations have served well to support the broader philosophical theses often cited by postmodern critiques of rationality, realism, and truth. If this analysis were to carry the day, then the authority of science would be so weakened as to completely undercut its interpretative relevance to Scripture. Nonetheless, even as the postmodern critique challenges the epistemic authority of the sciences, it invariably proceeds to completely defuse any normative force carried by Scripture.

Yet it should be noted that reasons exist to resist this pessimistic posture. One response takes the primary aim of the sciences as providing an explanatory account of experience, often by appeal to unobserved, even unobservable, entities, processes, mechanisms, forces, structures, and so forth. It also acknowledges the reciprocal dynamic between observational data and the theoretical commitments of the community, recognizes the often-vague and imprecise terms by which scientists judge the relative superiority of a hypothesis, and embraces the role of nonempirical criteria for theory appraisal. In spite of these features, scientific realists maintain that the ongoing historical success of the best of our scientific accounts suggests that to some extent they do represent some features of the natural world. While embracing the foibles of scientific inquiry, critical realists argue that the best explanation for the evident historical success of the very human endeavors of science is the proposal that its results do approximate a mind-independent world.

Taking scientific inquiry as primarily an explanatory, or interpretative, process also provides a framework for sorting out those cases where it interfaces with biblical scholarship. Scientists and theologians each face interpretative challenges. The interpretative accounts offered by each are likewise assessed according to similar standards and values. Each process constitutes a fallible endeavor to understand a broad range of experience, often by appeal to unobservable, explanatory posits—the existence of which would account for otherwise inexplicable phenomena. Judging the relative authority of their respective claims will be an extremely complex process; nevertheless, common terms of appraisal provide grounds for their mutual development. The trails blazed in various ways by figures such as theologian Bernard Ramm and scientist Michael Polanyi—and traveled more recently by Ian Barbour, John Polkinghorne, Arthur Peacocke, Nancey Murphy, and others—still seek destinations that are not obvious. But they may lead to greater convergence between biblical theology and science on matters such as divine action and physics, or human nature and genetics, or technology, bioethics, and the like.

Bibliography

Several texts present these proposals in accessible form: Brown, J. R. *Who Rules in Science?* Harvard University Press, 2001; Giere, R. *Science without Laws.* University of Chicago Press, 1999; Kitcher, P. *The Advancement of Science.* Oxford University Press, 1993 (with a sustained and detailed argument for a critical-realist interpretation of science); Newton-Smith, W., ed. *A Companion to the Philosophy of Science*. Blackwell, 2000 (analyzing many issues mentioned above). Among those exploring the relation between science and theology, John Polkinghorne's prolific writings spell out many of the details, as seen in his Gifford Lectures: *The Faith of a Physicist*. Princeton University Press, 1994. For a fine example of biblical scholarship drawing heavily and explicitly on scientific methodologies, see Wright, N. T. *Christian Origins and the Question of God*, esp. chs. 2–5 of vol. 1, *The New Testament and the People of God*. Fortress, 1992.

Robert O'Connor

Scribes   *See* Jewish Context of the NT

Scripture, Authority of

Talk of the authority of Scripture indicates that the texts of the Christian canon are normative for the speech, thought, and practice of the church, because these texts mediate God's self-revelation. As the instrument through which divine authority is present and operative in the church, Scripture is primary in the church's governance and fundamental to instruction in the Christian religion as well as to the church's theological self-articulation and its processes of discernment and judgment.

History

The literature of the patristic era contains little formal treatment of the nature of biblical authority. The normative character of Scripture is largely assumed; patristic attitudes to Scripture are visible primarily in exegetical practice and in recommendations about the virtues appropriate to knowing God through Scripture. Thus, the hermeneutical discussion in Augustine's *On Christian Teaching* includes reflections on fear of God, piety, and teachableness as the most fitting characteristics of the godly reader of the divine wisdom encountered in Scripture. Moreover, patristic theology does not generally treat Scripture as a juridical norm from which can be drawn exegetical warrants for theological proposals, since theology and exegesis are largely coterminous. Scripture is not so much a source or norm of theology as its idiom.

Systematic reflection on the nature of Scripture takes its rise in the latter part of the twelfth century; it should not be thought to begin with the sixteenth-century Reformation. Much Reformation and post-Reformation theology of Scripture is anticipated in the teaching of, for example, Alexander of Hales, Bonaventure, or Thomas Aquinas; the emphasis upon Scripture's authority in the magisterial Reformers is thus not a new departure. What is innovative in the Reformers lies rather in their insistence (with some appeal to humanistic methods of text-interpretation) on the priority of the grammatical sense of the Bible over elaborate fourfold exegesis. They had radical commitment to the supremacy of Scripture's authority over other claims to normativity in the church, whether those of ecclesiastical office or of individual spiritual experience. Thus, Calvin sees scriptural authority as standing against claims to immediate access to God on the part of Christian enthusiasts, and also against official church claims to have competence to "authorize" Scripture or to impose a particular interpretation. Scripture's authority, though it is exercised in the church, does not derive from the church. In this way, Scripture's authority consists in its capacity to outbid and relativize human judgment, and to deliver a normative revelation that overthrows idolatry. Knowledge of its authority is not a rational deduction from external evidences, but is rooted in Spirit-generated persuasion. Furthermore, though Scripture's authority is a basis of appeal in matters of controversy, it is primarily at work in the exegetical and homiletical tasks, through which Scripture is brought to bear on the life of the church. Thus, the authority of Scripture is seen in Calvin's *Institutes of the Christian Religion* not simply in formal affirmations of its primacy but also in the entire conception of the work as a guide to the content and implications of Scripture's testimony to the word and work of God. More formal conceptualization of Scripture's authority can be found in the theology of high Protestant orthodoxy. There the cognitive normativity of Scripture for theology is stated with considerable precision through an elaboration of the origin and properties of Scripture. Though it is common to judge Protestant orthodoxy as replacing a dynamic view of Scripture's authority with a static account, such a reading scarcely does justice to the Protestant scholastic texts.

From the end of the seventeenth century, mutations in European civic and intellectual culture had a profound effect on conceptions of the authority of Scripture. Among these changes, the rise of modern understandings of undetermined liberty as basic to intellectual and political responsibility is the most important. Premodern Christian theology assumed that the authority of Scripture is beneficent instruction in given truth; modern views of freedom came to regard that authority as implicated in malevolent theocratic practices that inhibit free inquiry and self-responsibility. "Authority" and "truth" are antithetical, the former being the province of arbitrary power, the latter that of critical freedom. For Spinoza, one of the early formative figures in the history of critical biblical study, this political critique of biblical authority acts as one of the chief motivations for demoting Scripture by "naturalizing" it, regarding it as a humanly produced text bearing no intrinsic power to command assent. As historical study of the Bible gained currency, Scripture was drawn into the sphere of human religion, and no longer handled with the assumption of its mediation of divine authority. The remarkable explanatory power of historical study of the Bible in part depended upon a dualistic assumption that a historical text cannot mediate divine authority, so that claims to textual authority are in fact bids for power on the part of interpreters. This dualism was, of course, exacerbated by the heavy supernaturalism of some orthodox Protestant theology of Scripture, which appeared to leave little room for the historical and human character of the biblical materials.

Some strands of modern Christian theology responded to such critiques of biblical authority by grounding an account of that authority in considerations such as the moral or religious superiority of the biblical materials or their veracity in reporting history. Others sought to reason toward the authority of Scripture on the basis of a general notion of inspiration, of which the Bible is shown to be the supreme instance. Though formally similar to earlier Protestant positions, these strategies are primarily apologetic in character, and so differ substantially from more classical Reformation positions by appealing to external warrants for biblical authority.

The dominant contemporary conventions of historical biblical scholarship are mostly sophisticated variations on Spinoza's "natural history" of the Bible, though allowing considerably more complexity about the nature of that history. On such accounts, affirmations of Scripture's authority are generally considered to be religious or theological evaluations that do not indicate anything objective about the texts, and have no exegetical import. Libertarian critiques of the politics of biblical authority have been reinforced with especial stringency in feminist interpretation of the Bible. This interpretation has considered the authority of the canon to be an instrument of patriarchy, both in its enforcement of certain patterns of thought and practice, and in its exclusion of other traditions of experience from the church. Comparative studies of sacred texts in different religious traditions have com-

monly stressed that scriptural authority may be explained as a function of social practice, without any reference to the relation of authoritative texts to divine revelation. More drastically, deconstructive abandonment of textual determinacy makes Scripture into pragmatics on the part of readers, and so undercuts the possibility of any theological account of the Bible's normativity. A somewhat different hermeneutical tradition has given greater attention to the authority of texts as classics that command attentiveness on the part of readers by their cultural resourcefulness and their ability to transcend any one reading. Some modern theological accounts of Scripture, both Protestant and Roman Catholic, have made much use of this tradition, and in particular have reflected on the ecclesial character of Scripture's authority as the source of the stock of common meanings in the Christian community.

Theology

The authority of Scripture lies in its reference to the church's God and his gospel. Scripture is authoritative because it is instrumental in bringing the word of God to bear upon the thought and practices of the church. In this context, God's "word" refers to God's self-communicative presence, through which he establishes the knowledge of himself in the face of defiance and ignorance; Scripture is the creaturely means through which the Word's activity is extended into the church.

Accordingly, a theological account of the authority of Scripture has to be located in the context of a wide spread of Christian doctrinal affirmations about God's communicative presence and activity. It may not be isolated as a quasi-independent topic in Christian doctrine, and should not be expounded prior to or apart from primary Christian doctrines. This isolation often happened in the post-Reformation era, when the theology of Scripture was caught up within the more general inflation of the theology of revelation. Teaching about revelation migrated away from the Christian doctrine of God to the beginning of dogmatics as the pretheological cognitive "foundation" of theological teaching. Over against this, the theology of Scripture is consequent upon the doctrine of God. Most of all, this means that Scripture is a function of the triune God's self-manifestation, especially his presence in the risen Christ, who through the Holy Spirit instructs the church. The primacy of christological and pneumatological doctrine prevents the detachment of the theology of Scripture from a wider account of the economy of God's dealings with creatures.

It does this by integrating teaching about the nature and authority of Scripture with substantive doctrine about God's saving self-manifestation to creatures. Moreover, a theology of Scripture is properly inseparable from soteriology, and especially Christian teaching about ignorance and idolatry as forms of human rejection of the given truth of God. This, in turn, means that a theology of Scripture is to be related to sanctification—the healing and renewal of human life through the work of the Holy Spirit—and of the doctrine of the church as the sphere in which God's communicative activity is encountered and confessed. Theological teaching about the authority of Scripture is thus best seen in relation to the full scope of a theology of God's fellowship with creatures. The adequacy of any such teaching about Scripture will in part depend upon its reference to all the elements outlined, and not simply to a partial selection of features.

Within such an account, Scripture's authority lies in its reference to God and the gospel. Its authority does not lie within itself, any more than the sacraments have any inherent effectiveness, but in its testimony to the authority of the one who appoints Scripture as his servant. Scripture's authority is therefore that of a commissioned witness or herald. One consequence here is that the authority of Scripture is the authority of its content, that which it sets forth in its function as witness to the Word. Only as the bearer of this particular truth is Scripture able to function as the "law" of the Christian community. That to which the church submits in its obedience to the authority of Scripture is not a contentless norm, a purely formal statute, but rather the commanding force of its truth-content.

As testimony to the self-manifesting truth of God in the gospel, Scripture is authoritative because it indicates the sovereignty and perfection of God's self-communication. This indication is reliable, and therefore authoritative, because God acts in, with, and over the human authors, ordering their acts of communication in such a way that they are caused to bear fitting and effective testimony. In the theological tradition, this divine oversight is usually termed "inspiration." By this is meant God's superintending of the processes of creaturely text-production. Though some restrict inspiration to the personality of the biblical authors, it may also be extended to all the processes of the composition of the text, including not only the choice of words ("verbal inspiration") but also preliterary tradition and such processes as canonization. Some prefer to distinguish between inspiration as a work of the Spirit in respect to the text, and illumination as the Spirit's work of enabling apprehension of and assent to divine truth in inspired Scripture. Alongside inspiration, Scripture is also usually affirmed to have other properties that bear upon its authority. Chief among these are clarity and sufficiency. The clarity of Scripture is not so much its self-evidence as its given capacity to illuminate the godly, meaning the Spirit-directed, reader; the sufficiency of Scripture is its adequacy as a presentation of the gospel, which renders other sources of instruction supplementary or superfluous.

The sphere of biblical authority is the church as the community that is generated and sustained by the Word. The church confesses Scripture's authority, but Scripture does not depend upon the church's approbation. One of the chief contentions of Reformation doctrines of Scripture was that the church has no competence to bestow authority upon Scripture or to command particular interpretations as universally binding, and that any such attempts subvert the primacy of the Bible. Hence, the process of canonization is properly to be understood, not as an act in which the church creates an authority for itself by determining a set of normative texts, but as an act of acknowledging antecedent authority imposed upon the church from without. Further, although the authority of Scripture is contextless and inoperative without the church as the sphere in which it is recognized, this should not be taken to mean that its authority is simply de facto and not de jure. The rule of Scripture is not simply the consequence of use or veneration, but it is legitimate authority because of its relation to the revealing acts of God. However, this should not be stressed in such a way that Scripture's authority is conceived in purely formal terms, as if it were a property independent of the relation that the text has to the common life of the Christian community. Authority is not independent of use; the authority of Scripture is the lawfulness with which it may command and elicit patterns of thought and action on the part of the church. Hence, the demonstration of accepting the authority of Scripture is primarily practical, and only secondarily theoretical (in, e.g., a theological account of the nature and properties of Scripture).

Accordingly, the authority of Scripture stands in close relation to the practice of interpretation. The act of interpreting an authoritative text involves the adoption of specific attitudes and virtues, as well as the performance of certain operations, as appropriate to the character of the text and its authoritative claim. Thus, for example, to interpret an authoritative text is not simply to be an agent acting upon a passive text that we summon before our minds and question; nor is it to handle the text as if it were an inert historical artifact. Because the text has authority, it makes certain claims upon the reader, claims to which the reader must attend if an appropriate response is to be made to the text. An appropriate response will be one of subordination, deference, or compliance as one stands beneath the claim that the text presents. Such a response will not exclude attention to the contingent features of the text (such as its historical matrix, linguistic or genetic features, or relation to other texts). Instead, it will also consider attention to these matters preliminary to the chief task of attending to the text as herald of its particular content. Further, because the text is authoritative, the text will be inexhaustible by any one reading, not only because it has a surplus of meaning, but also because the text's claim upon the church's attention is perpetual and cannot be disposed of in a single act of interpretation.

Nevertheless, the authority of Scripture is not such that no acts of interpretation are required: what is authoritative is a text, and texts elicit acts of reading. Scripture's authority is not exercised apart from the work performed upon the text by its readers; its authority is not a formal property, but an aspect of the interaction between God's self-revelation and its hearers. Authority quickens action, directing it in ways that are fitting to the truth that is declared. The authority of Scripture thus includes its capacity to stimulate and direct interpretative action. Interpretative action is, however, rarely an end in itself; it is engaged in order to enable other kinds of action and judgment—intellectual, moral, political. In this way, therefore, the authority of Scripture is formative of the life of the Christian community in which it presents the divine claim.

Scripture is authoritative for all the activities of the church. It has an especial authority with respect to the church's articulation of its beliefs in doctrine. This theological authority of Scripture is not first and foremost to be seen in formal statements about its authority, nor simply in a theological method that adduces biblical warrants for theological positions. It is chiefly evident in deference to Scripture, in which the Bible determines the range, content, and limits of Christian doctrine, and thus governs the overall shape of a theological account of Christian belief. Within such deference, patterns of interpretation may be quite varied; but they will find their center in a certain transparency to the biblical texts. Doctrines are not best understood as conceptual improvements upon or reorganizations of biblical material, nor is Scripture best thought of as a body of raw material awaiting theological conceptualization. Rather, doctrines are conceptual statements that both sum up tracts of the biblical materials and also enable fresh exegesis. Doctrines may guide the interpretation of Scripture; but they can do so only if they derive from and promote the authoritative Word that is encountered through Scripture's service.

See also Canon; Revelation; Scripture, Clarity of; Scripture, Sufficiency of; Word of God

Bibliography

Abraham, W. *The Divine Inspiration of Holy Scripture*. Oxford University Press, 1981; Barr, J. *Holy Scripture*. Clarendon, 1983; Barth, K. *Church Dogmatics*. Vol. I/2. T&T Clark, 1956; Berkouwer, G. C. *Holy Scripture*. Eerdmans, 1975; Cantwell Smith, W. *What Is Scripture?* SCM, 1993; Ebeling, G. "The Significance of the Critical Historical Method for Church and Theology in Protestantism." Pages 17–61 in *Word and Faith*. SCM, 1963; Farley, E. *Ecclesial Reflection*. Fortress, 1982; Kelsey, D. *Proving Doctrine*. Trinity, 1999; Muller, R. *Post-Reformation Reformed Dogmatics*. Vol. 2, *Holy Scripture*. Baker, 1992; Preus, J. S. *Spinoza and the Irrelevance of Biblical Authority*. Cambridge University Press, 2001; Preus, R. *The Inspiration of Scripture*. Oliver & Boyd, 1957; Reventlow, H. G. *The Authority of the Bible and the Rise of the Modern World*. SCM, 1980; Scholder, K. *The Birth of Modern Critical Theology*. SCM, 1990; Warfield, B. B. *Revelation and Inspiration*. Oxford University Press, 1927; Webster, J. *Holy Scripture*. Cambridge University Press, 2003; Wenz, A. *Das Wort Gottes—Gericht und Rettung*. Vandenhoeck & Ruprecht, 1996; Young, F. *Biblical Exegesis and the Formation of Christian Culture*. Cambridge University Press, 1997.

John Webster

Scripture, Clarity of

The "doctrine" of Scripture's clarity is associated with the Reformers, but the conviction that Scripture has the capacity to address and transform the human being, and to offer a reliable guide to human action, has permeated the Christian tradition. This conviction, however, has always been accompanied by an acknowledgment of the need for divine aid; Scripture is clear to the mind enlightened by the Holy Spirit to perceive the revelation offered in Christ. This does not obviate the need for interpretation or teaching within the church, but it does imply that Scripture stands over rather than under its interpreters, academic or clerical. Behind the affirmation of the clarity, or perspicuity, of Scripture stands a conviction that, through the Holy Spirit, Scripture communicates sufficiently clearly to guide one with faith to knowledge of what is pleasing to God.

While the *claritas* or *perspicuitas* of Scripture was a key principle of the Reformers, similar concerns surface in the earliest strata of Christian tradition. The issue arises because, as Luther acknowledges, some texts are not immediately clear. Scripture is vulnerable to twisting by the unscrupulous, and to misunderstanding by the uneducated. Surfacing already in the NT are various ways of interpreting the OT and acknowledged complexity in interpreting what is now the NT. On the one hand, 2 Pet. 3:16 declares that some of Paul's teaching is hard to understand and susceptible to misuse by insincere people. On the other hand, 2 Tim. 3:16–17 asserts that all Scripture is profitable for teaching that equips the disciple, even as it acknowledges a certain skill in handling the Scripture that makes the good teacher comparable to a workman. Paul asserts that the Holy Spirit unveils the meaning of the OT, which is Christ (2 Cor. 3:15–18). He sometimes appeals to the straightforward literal meaning of OT texts; but, reading in light of the coming of Christ, he also finds in the Hebrew Scriptures what he explicitly refers to as "allegory" (Gal. 4:24 NRSV). All this indicates that the NT itself gives a complex picture of the interpretative process.

The early commentator with perhaps the greatest impact on later debates over Scripture's clarity is Augustine. In *On Christian Teaching*, devoted to the principles of biblical exegesis, Augustine holds that Scripture is perspicuous, yet not easy to interpret. The difficulty of interpretation serves a divine purpose: "to wear out pride with hard work and to keep intelligence from boredom" (*Doctr. chr.* 2.14–15). The "hard work" for Augustine includes the rigorous employment of the most important exegetical tools: grammar, rhetoric, knowledge of languages, and the rudimentary "critical" tools (2.34–58). On one hand, he stresses grammatical and philological work to uncover the authorial intention of the text. On the other hand, he acknowledges the final author to be God, who may make one thing in salvation history a sign of another, and may allow for a multiplicity of meanings to enrich the text beyond the human author's conscious intention (3.84–86).

Augustine allows a certain flexibility in interpretation, distinguishing between lying and mistakenly failing to grasp the intention of the author. The true end of all Scripture is love of God and neighbor, issuing from a pure heart, genuine faith, and a good conscience (1.95). There is no danger in giving more than one interpretation of a difficult passage, as long as each finds backing elsewhere in the Scripture (3.83). Augustine's aim is the instruction and upbuilding of the church; so he moves easily from a christological interpretation to an ecclesiological or hortatory one (Simonetti 106).

In 1524 Erasmus of Rotterdam wrote a treatise entitled *On Freedom of the Will*, arguing that the Bible does not give sufficient grounds for certainty about whether human choice after the fall remains free or is bound by sin. In this, as in many disputes, he claims, Scripture does not speak clearly, so one does best to defer to the weight of tradition (*De libero arbitrio* 38–40). It is the method and presuppositions, as well as the material conclusions in Erasmus's diatribe, to which Luther objects. Against the claim that Scripture is inherently obscure, he asserts two ways in which the Bible is clear. The first of these is "internal" and results from the action of the Holy Spirit to enlighten the understanding obscured by sin; apart from such aid, the human interpreter has no capacity to grasp the truth that Scripture is intended to convey (*De servo arbitrio* 159). "External clarity" claims that the text itself, when interpreted according to the public rules of language, offers a clear account of the truth it is intended to convey (Vanhoozer 315). Luther maintains that apparently obscure passages become clear when viewed in the light of Scripture as a whole. Scripture is thus self-glossing. When disputes over doctrine arise, they may thus be settled "at the bar of Scripture" (*Serv. arb.* 159). While Luther derides Erasmus's "skepticism" and "sophistry," he objects most strongly to the potential of Erasmus's argument to bolster papal authority by frightening people away from putatively obscure Scripture (*Serv. arb.* 159).

Luther thus does not deny the need for teachers or claim that Scripture is a matter of private judgment; this was the crux of his debate with the *Schwärmer*, "enthusiasts" who made inner experience the norm of interpretation (*Serv. arb.* 158; cf. Luther's *Against the Heavenly Prophets*). Luther's claim is that Scripture is clear enough that one need not rely on the official magisterium of the church to mediate its meaning. One can expect human beings guided by the Holy Spirit to arrive at consensus on the interpretation of the text. This has several consequences.

First, Scripture is to be available to all. The spread of literacy and education of clergy are key planks in Luther's reforming platform (Thiselton 189). Second, Luther holds to an ecclesiology that is not hung on bishops holding an authoritative teaching office in succession from the apostles. The church is rather an assembly of men and women holding right doctrine, expressed in right preaching and celebration of the sacraments. Third, against Erasmus, Luther insists that the Bible clearly teaches that the human will is in bondage to sin, and only divine grace frees the will at any moment; this issue is a test case for what one can affirm clearly on biblical grounds. Thus, Luther's view of the clarity of Scripture goes hand in hand with a set of doctrinal commitments derived from the text of the Bible. The church, then, is where those who read the Bible in this way and preach in accord with those doctrines are gathered.

In a polemical context in which multiple senses were sometimes invoked in support of disputed doctrinal positions, on the grounds that Scripture is multivalent, Calvin responded that Scripture is *simplex*, bearing only a single sense (*Commentary on Gal.* 5:22). Its clarity is rooted in the accessibility of that single, literal sense. Calvin's exegesis is marked by several important features: a humanist approach to the letter of the text, which prizes knowledge of the original languages, close attention to the historical context of any given passage, separation of doctrinal discussions from exposition of the text ("Epistle to the Reader," in *Inst.*, 2d ed., cited in Thiselton 189), and a christocentric narrative/historical framework for the whole of the Bible. He builds on a christocentric vision of salvation history drawn from Scripture as a whole, which enables him to draw a number of hortatory or theological implications from a text that looks much like the multiple "senses" of earlier theologians (Parker 44).

Thus, as Anthony Thiselton points out, the principle of Scripture's clarity has a fourfold function for the Reformers: christological; critical; epistemological; ecclesiological. By no means was it meant to sideline ecclesial tradition or disavow the need for the sometimes-messy work of interpretation. The better Catholic apologists, such as Peter Canisius, agreed with the Reformers in holding that Scripture is self-interpreting and invoked magisterial authority for interpretation sparingly, only as a necessary role of adjudication in the face of exegetical disagreements (Thiselton 404–8). Positions on both sides hardened in the following century, however, with many Protes-

tants virtually eliminating the role of ecclesial interpretative tradition, and Catholic bishops shielding laypeople from the Bible and instead offering putative distillations of its message (Berkouwer 267–98; Callahan 156–59; Congar 177–221).

In light of the polemical context of much of the discussion of Scripture's clarity, it is worth recognizing some developments in Roman Catholic teaching over the last fifty years or so and also some philosophical developments that place this discussion in a new context. First, in the face of liberal historical-critical ideology, Pius XII strongly affirmed the inspiration of the Scripture in its entirety; this was coupled with active promotion of biblical studies making use of critical tools (*Divino afflante Spiritu* [1943]). Second, the Second Vatican Council's declaration that the bishops stand under the Word of God and serve it enshrines the principle that the official magisterium is subject to the word of God and accountable to it (*Dei verbum* §2.10). Third, that same council affirmed that access to the Bible is to be wide open to the faithful (*Dei verbum* §6.22), and that preaching is to take exposition of the Bible as its material focus (6.25). While disputes over doctrine remain, one can see a certain convergence in the approach to Scripture that has undergirded progress in doctrinal dialogues between Roman Catholics and representatives of Reformation traditions.

At the same time, the late twentieth century saw what Kevin Vanhoozer calls "the literary turn" in philosophy, often characterized by a deep suspicion of the capacity of any text to convey its object to a reader. The affirmation of Scripture's clarity in the present context is an expression of confidence that this text, like all human texts vulnerable to the misunderstanding and deception that mark communication among sinful human beings, will still be used by God to speak. In the present context, one may make a reasonable argument that the primary differences in approach to Scripture's clarity are no longer between Roman Catholics and descendants of the Reformation tradition. Instead, the basic differences are between those who hold that God speaks to the church through the Bible by the action of the Holy Spirit, and those varied postmodern theorists who hold a basic suspicion of the capacity of any text to communicate its object.

Bibliography

Beisser, F. *"Claritas scripturae" bei Martin Luther.* Vandenhoeck & Ruprecht, 1966; Berkouwer, G. C. *Holy

Scripture. Eerdmans, 1975; Callahan, J. *The Clarity of Scripture*. InterVarsity, 2001; Congar, Y. *Tradition and Traditions*. Burns & Oates, 1966; *Constitution on Divine Revelation*. In *The Documents of Vatican Council II*, ed. A. Flannery, OP. Costello, 1987; Lubac, H. de. *Exégèse médiévale*. 4 vols. Aubier, 1959–64; idem. *Medieval Exegesis*. Vol. 1 translated by M. Sebanc. Vol. 2 translated by E. Macieroweski. Eerdmans, 1998–2000; Parker, T. H. L. *Calvin's New Testament Commentaries*. SCM, 1971; Ramm, B. *Protestant Biblical Interpretation*. 3d ed. Baker, 1970; Simonetti, M. *Biblical Interpretation in the Early Church*. T&T Clark, 1994; Thiselton, A. *New Horizons in Biblical Hermeneutics*. Zondervan, 1992; Vanhoozer, K. *Is There a Meaning in This Text?* Zondervan, 1998.

John Yocum

Scripture, Inerrancy of *See* Scripture, Authority of; Truth

Scripture, Infallibility of *See* Scripture, Authority of; Truth

Scripture, Inspiration of *See* Scripture, Authority of

Scripture, Sufficiency of

The doctrine of the sufficiency of Scripture is at heart an assertion of the nature of God's relationship to Scripture, and consequently of its authoritative significance. It is regularly distinguished into two aspects. "Material sufficiency" asserts that Scripture contains everything necessary to be known and responded to for salvation and faithful discipleship. This is so because God has identified himself and his communication with the meaning (or better: the actions—"speech acts"—performed by means of the words) of Scripture, in a way that he has done with no other text or speech in the world (see Vanhoozer; Ward; Wolterstorff). "Formal sufficiency" claims that Scripture as the word of God ought not ultimately to be subject to any external interpretative authority, such as the teaching authority of the church or a Spirit-filled individual, and so is significantly "self-interpreting."

The Bible as "Sufficient"

Scripture claims its own sufficiency and witnesses to the theological bases of its sufficiency in a number of ways. It claims that its content is "breathed-out," spoken by God ("breathed-out" being quite likely a better translation of *theopneustos* in 2 Tim. 3:16 than "inspired"), and is sufficient to equip one "for every good work" (2 Tim. 3:17). John warns that anyone who adds to or subtracts from his prophecy will be subject to divine judgment (Rev. 22:18–19), alluding to a similar charge given in the OT (Deut. 12:32). The OT assumes that to obey the Lord's revealed law is to live blamelessly and to remain in close fellowship with him (Ps. 119:1, 8–10).

The latter observation leads us beyond individual references to the overall relationship between God and Scripture. God fundamentally relates to humankind as a covenant-making (promise-speaking) God. For God to be knowable, he must express his covenant in the words of human language. The nature of a covenant is such that for a person to put one's trust in those words is simply to put trust in God (Wolterstorff). Thus, Abraham enters into covenant with God simply by responding to his command to leave Haran (Gen. 12:1–3), and Christ abides in his followers, and they in him, to the extent that his words abide in them (John 15:1–11). The canon of Scripture functions as God's "book of covenant": it is the semantic means by which he offers himself to the world as a covenant-making God. Scripture is therefore sufficient for the performance of the divine promise of salvation in Christ.

The doctrine of scriptural sufficiency claims neither that God has ceased to prompt, guide, and direct ("speak to") disciples and the church, nor that he has told us everything about himself and every question we face. Rather, it asserts that, when responded to in trust and love by us, the revelatory, covenant-making act that God performs in and through Scripture can confidently be believed to be sufficient for salvation and for truthful, faithful discipleship of Christ.

Hermeneutical Implications of the Sufficiency of Scripture

The sufficiency of Scripture is sometimes thought, by both opponents and proponents, to entail more in practice than it really does. Such misunderstanding is so common that it is important to state clearly what the doctrine does not necessarily imply. First, it is a statement about the sufficiency of Scripture, not about the sufficiency of any single interpreter or community of interpreters. Thus, it does not entail the beliefs that interpreting the Bible is simple and that faithful doctrine and practice can easily be read off every page by a single interpreter or community. Nor does it exalt individualistic and sometimes eccentric biblical interpretation, neglecting the contributions of scholarship and of interpretative traditions. Groups of Christians who adhere strongly to scriptural sufficiency have often, it is true, been suspicious of both scholarship and the traditions of biblical interpretation, but that is certainly not true of the mainline Reformation and post-Reformation theologians who expounded the doctrine with greatest clarity (Mathison). Second, the sufficiency of Scripture claims that Scripture is sufficient only for a particular divinely intended purpose. Thus, it claims neither that Scripture speaks directly to every conceivable question of faith and practice, nor that it speaks unequivocally on every topic it addresses. Nor does it imply that Scripture necessarily gives exhaustive knowledge of God, the world, ourselves, history, or protological and eschatological events.

To put it positively, to claim "the sufficiency of Scripture" is at heart to claim that (1) God is knowable. For the Protestant Reformers, Scripture provided, epistemologically, "a ground on which we may confidently proceed," and theologically, "a witness to Christ to which we may confidently respond" (Thiselton 184–85). This is sometimes alleged, in its post-Reformation manifestations, to be a Christianized version of the modernist quest for reason-based certainty. However, at its best it is a faithful response to the fact that God has chosen to make himself known, and to communicate Jesus Christ to us, in comprehensible human language. (2) Text and interpretation are fundamentally separate. Interpreters and interpretative communities will always tend to use Scripture to legitimate their own beliefs and biases, thereby silencing some of what Scripture says. The Christian church stands in constant need of reformation—that is, in constant need of the God who indwells the church also to speak from outside in words that call it back to faithfulness to its head, Jesus Christ. The text through which God supremely does this, and whose content funds the meaning of every other means through which God does this, is Scripture. (3) Ultimately, the meaning of Scripture can at no point be definitively decided by the declaration either of a particular church magisterium or of an individual claiming special and decisive divine revelation, presenting themselves as the contemporary mouthpiece of the Holy Spirit. Instead, the Spirit's ongoing speaking activity is consistent with the meaning of the biblical texts, which he once inspired. This is what is meant by the principle that "Scripture interprets itself": again, not that every question of interpretation can be easily settled just by reading the Bible, but that no external institution or individual may impose final interpretive fiat on Scripture. Any act of biblical interpretation is only truly authoritative to the extent that it demonstrates its legitimacy with careful and thoughtful reading of Scripture itself.

See also Canon; Scripture, Authority of; Tradition

Bibliography

Helm, P., and C. Trueman, eds. *The Trustworthiness of God*. Apollos, 2002; Mathison, K. *The Shape of Sola Scriptura*. Canon, 2001; Thiselton, A. *New Horizons in Hermeneutics*. HarperCollins, 1992; Vanhoozer, K. *First Theology*. InterVarsity, 2002; Ward, T. *Word and Supplement*. Oxford University Press, 2002; Wolterstorff, N. *Divine Discourse*. Cambridge University Press, 1995.

Timothy Ward

Scripture, Unity of

Christian faith faced two crucial external challenges from the modern age. Empirical commitments raised doubts about the Bible's purported history, especially of supernatural events. Rationalists raised doubts not only about access to such a (redemptive) history, but also about its significance for universal reason (Lessing's infamous ugly ditch) or even its consistency with such truths. These external challenges led critics either to reject the Bible's claims or else to rescue its truth by changing its meanings (as chronicled by Frei).

Just as crucial over the long haul, however, has been the internal challenge to Christian teaching from critical fragmentation of the Bible. Can Christians reach coherent theological claims on their own terms? Or does the legacy of the modern West show the impossibility of any Christian consensus based upon Scripture, apart from an ecclesiastical authority imposed somewhat arbitrarily? In response to this complex problem, we may suggest some key biblical texts and hermeneutical strategies, resulting in a confessional and post- (but not anti-) critical standpoint.

Unity in the Scriptural Texts?

The obvious diversity in the canon falls roughly along "synchronic" or literary lines, involving various genres and word-concept relationships, and "diachronic" or historical lines, involving various relationships between textual "sense" and extra-textual "reference." Thus, biblical texts not only can function differently in terms of authority across time; they also differ in proximity to the formation of theological concepts in the first place (as emphasized by Barr).

On the literary difficulties, see (among other articles herewith) "Proof Text," with its discussion of Ricoeur and various models of biblical authority (Goldingay). As an illustration here, we may mention the constant tendency of "biblical theology" to marginalize the Wisdom literature in favor of an organizing theme such as salvation history, or conversely to focus Wisdom theology excessively upon creation.

We may also highlight texts that are prominent illustrations in current discussions of Scripture's diversity (see, e.g., Fowl; Johnson; essays in Green and Turner). How are we to read Ps. 137, which pronounces a blessing on those who would dash Babylonian children against the rocks, in light of the Sermon on the Mount? Or to what extent is Acts 15, where at least certain OT laws are set aside in light of redemptive-historical progression (plus, as often neglected, in light of reading Amos 9!), a model for our own theological interpretation, even of the NT?

Hermeneutical Strategies That Support Scriptural Unity

Premodern interpreters were not unaware of the Bible's diversity: Marcion should make that fairly obvious. Moreover, we must admit that some practiced allegory because they found the literal sense problematic in places. Nevertheless, biblical theology, as an academic discipline constituted by preoccupation with human authorship, has tended to canonize more extreme conclusions about that diversity than the church has traditionally accepted.

The most central problems concern whether or how Christians may read the OT with reference to the triune God's self-revelation in Jesus Christ, whether or how those Scriptures of Israel relate to the church, and whether the NT can coherently support the teaching of the orthodox creeds about Jesus Christ or traditions of Christian ethics.

The Rule of Faith. A long-standing solution, from the days of Irenaeus's opposition to Gnosticism onward, lies in the Rule of Faith, which has come into various creedal forms such as the Nicene. The Rule expresses certain central "judgments of identity" between the Testaments, the most important of which are

> (1) that the one who sent Jesus, and raised him from the dead, is self-identically the God of Israel, the God attested in the Old Testament Scriptures; (2) that the church of Jesus Christ is continuous, to be sure across massive and radical transformation, with the covenant people of the Old Testament; and (3) binding these together, that Jesus Christ is the *one* word that God speaks to his people, so that whatever is "word of God" in the Old Testament must be read as

a moment within the protracted utterance of what is conclusively articulated only in the paschal mystery of Good Friday and Easter—in "the resurrection which has now taken place." . . . [It is true that] there is no "method" of a *formal* kind—historical or literary, critical or allegorical or typological—by which the unity of the Christian canon can be set forth in abstraction from theological argument and judgment. (Yeago, "Bible," 72)

It is also true that the Rule of Faith is considered a derivation from and description of the Bible's own unity (Blowers).

Typology and/or Allegory? Moreover, the medieval fourfold sense, which developed from earlier Christian allegorizing, did not simply pursue spirituality, but more centrally a redemptive-historical unity in reading the Bible. Despite excesses, the approach was not entirely unlike Calvin's method (cf. Steinmetz 29; Muller 11): we ought to read Scripture for what the church should believe (correspondence between the allegorical sense and the virtue of faith), for what Christians should do (correspondence between the tropological sense and the virtue of love), and for what we should hope (corresponding to the anagogical sense). As we seek these virtues today with more hermeneutical precision, evaluating typology vis-à-vis allegory is crucial. To what extent may the necessary redemptive-historical connections be discerned from within the Bible itself (typology)? Or must the narrative(s) be imposed partially from outside (allegory)? Depending on how one understands the historical distinctions involved, "figural reading" may be the more apt terminology for following in Calvin's footsteps (so Frei 47; Dawson). Recovering such a reading strategy may be essential for contemporary church life, not merely for connecting the Testaments à la the ancients (Lindbeck, *Interpretation*, 31; Seitz, *Figured Out*).

The Analogy of Faith/Scripture. While in addition to the Rule of Faith Eastern Orthodox interpreters will then involve Tradition, and Roman Catholics the magisterium (tending also to accept allegory), Protestants confess Scripture's basic clarity (tending to accept typology only). But Protestants can still deploy hermeneutical summaries of the Bible's scope and coherence as well. Seeking to follow Augustine, Luther and Calvin held that one could interpret difficult passages in light of clearer texts or dominant ideas of biblical teaching. These two versions of an *analogia fidei* need not contradict but could supplement an apostolic version à la the Rule of Faith (Blocher 18–23).

Expecting coherence between every part of Scripture, which has often been the developed "formal" Protestant understanding, seems like an even stronger version, challenging to accept. Arguably, though, it is a necessary safeguard against using the *analogia fidei* to privilege a passage or guard a doctrine that seems clear enough—but only to us (Blocher 27). Coherence with other parts of Scripture could be a criterion by which we prematurely flatten the historical unfolding or literary contours of God's self-disclosure, or foist upon the Bible a plainly impossible standard of unity. Chastely applied, however, such a criterion need not force artificial coherence, but could function as a helpful gateway into the hermeneutical circle.

Cacophony or Polyphony? How then should we approach contemporary criticism? The problems and possibilities of "biblical theology" are discussed in depth elsewhere. B. B. Warfield's analogy of an army—comparing exegesis to the work of a recruiting officer, biblical theology to the organization of companies and regiments and corps, and systematic theology to their combination as a fighting force (cited in Abraham 325–26)—is surely too optimistic. Yet his accusation that critics overemphasize biblical diversity is probably accurate. Hence, more dynamic concepts of unity are being sought (Welker 239), most prominently the "dialogical" borrowed from the Russian Mikhail Bakhtin: multiple voices may not contradict each other or compete chaotically. Instead, they cohere in a dialogue that balances and expresses together truths that cannot be held all at once in a single consciousness (Vanhoozer).

Thus, for instance, having raised the question of cacophony or polyphony regarding NT ethics, Richard Hays seeks a complex unity through complementary "focal lenses." Or consider the practice of NT theology: we must take more seriously the need for four Gospels, not one, and the General Epistles vis-à-vis the Pauline. Perhaps this could be modeled after an "apostolic conference table" (Turner 54). Further, while appropriately sensitive to Judaism, a Christian biblical theology probably cannot or should not avoid reading the OT in relation to the NT (Watson, *Truth*; Watson, "Scripture"). Yet we must remember that the NT itself reveals an early struggle over Christian identity vis-à-vis Israel (Lindbeck, "Church," 44), since they were reading the OT as their "canon" with its own integrity (Seitz, "Interpretation"). Thus, a concept of unified teaching is needed in which the complexity of revelation corresponds to the unity of divine action in history (Lints 74).

Concepts and Judgments. Accordingly, difficulties for biblical unity will constantly center on the identity of Jesus Christ. Continuing defenses will even be needed for the correspondence between the Rule of Faith and coherent NT teaching. In response to James Dunn on that point, David Yeago ("Dogma"; cf. Carson) demonstrates the possibility of similar theological "judgments" taking different conceptual forms. The *judgments* of Paul and John may be expressed differently, but both support the preexistence of God's Son, thus sharing continuity with Nicene dogma.

Conversely, another question about diverse content arises when similar conceptual forms are involved. Consider Paul (Rom. 4) and James (ch. 2): they use the same vocabulary ("faith"), and indeed the same OT passage regarding Abraham (Gen. 15:6), in markedly different ways. Yet if each addresses different questions, it is plausible that their voices are complementary rather than contradictory.

Intracanonical Criticism. A hermeneutical strategy for diversity, then, might learn from Acts 15, or from our Lord's example in handling divorce (Matt. 19:1–12). Such examples suggest that the doctrinal and/or ethical teaching of a passage must be set in canonical, redemptive-historical context, its authority shaped or perhaps even set aside by balancing it with other biblical truths. Such balancing will also be needed at broader literary levels, as in the ways Job, Proverbs, and Ecclesiastes are read together. Still, intracanonical criticism of this sort must respect the finality of God's self-revelation in Jesus Christ. Though the Spirit will not complete God's perfecting work until the second advent ushers in the fullness of the kingdom, the NT may not be handled in all respects as early Christians read the OT.

Thus, it is doubtful whether intracanonical criticism licenses a "canon within a canon" (as alleged, e.g., of Luther or later of Käsemann), equals a largely unbridled "reading with the Spirit" (as, e.g., Fowl on Acts 15), or even functions exactly like more contemporary "law-gospel" hermeneutics (e.g., Watson, *Church*, part 3).

Scriptural Unity Confessed in "Faith Seeking Understanding"

If Scripture is not at all unified, then "the canon threatens to become a grab-bag in which searchers pick and choose according to whim or, less pejoratively, in accordance with extra-biblical principles" (Lindbeck, "Interpretation," 38–39). Christians are committed by their Rule of Faith to reading Scripture as ultimately united around God's story in Jesus Christ. The strangely wonderful story of the disciples traveling to Emmaus in Luke 24, a passage so vital to this issue, makes tangible our tension. We only see the OT's connection to Jesus of Nazareth with divinely opened eyes of faith, yet such faith is only possible if Christ is essential to understanding the OT (Moberly, esp. 51).

Combined elements of several hermeneutical strategies can explicate such a commitment. While Scripture's unity is a conviction that Christians confess in faith, we seek to understand not only biblical texts in its light, but also implications of the conviction itself. For this, careful encounters with critical scholarship remain essential, even if we cannot be utterly subject to its skeptical excesses.

Contemporary struggles especially concern how to unfold an intracanonical criticism without question-begging. Even when Scripture's unity is embraced, challenges remain. Robert Gundry rightly wonders whether we should seek all-embracing systems of theology, or instead employ certain biblical texts or themes or truths in situation-specific ways (95). Perhaps that practice would often display a more "dialogical" and defensible concept of Scripture's unity—without denying its narrative coherence or the complementarity of its concepts. For these authorize continued exegetical interaction with theologies of a modestly "systematic" kind.

See also Allegory; Biblical Theology; Dialogism; Proof Text; Relationship between the Testaments; Rule of Faith; Systematic Theology; Typology

Bibliography

Abraham, W. *Canon and Criterion in Christian Theology*. Clarendon, 1998; Alexander, T. D., and B. Rosner, eds. *New Dictionary of Biblical Theology*. InterVarsity, 2000; Barr, J. *The Concept of Biblical Theology*. Fortress, 1999; Blocher, H. "The 'Analogy of Faith' in the Study of Scripture." Pages 17–38 in *The Challenge of Evangelical Theology*, ed. N. M. de S. Cameron. Rutherford House, 1987; Blowers, P. "The *Regula Fidei* and the Narrative Character of Early Christian Faith." *ProEccl* 6, no. 2 (1997): 199–228; Carson, D. A. "Unity and Diversity in the New Testament: The Possibility of Systematic Theology." Pages 65–95 in *Scripture and Truth*, ed. D. A. Carson and J. Woodbridge. Baker, 1992; Dawson, J. D. *Christian Figural Reading and the Fashioning of Identity*. University of California Press, 2002; Dunn, J. D. G. *Unity and Diversity in the New Testament*. Westminster, 1977; Fowl, S. *Engaging Scripture*. Blackwell, 1998; Frei, H. *The Eclipse of Biblical Narrative*. Yale University Press, 1974; Goldingay, J. *Models for Scripture*. Eerdmans, 1994; Green, J., and M. Turner, eds. *Between Two Horizons*. Eerdmans, 2000; Gundry, R. *Jesus the Word according to John the Sectarian*. Eerdmans, 2002; Hays, R. *The Moral Vision of the New Testament*. HarperCollins, 1996; Johnson, L. T. *Scripture and Discernment in the Early Church*. Rev. ed. Abingdon, 1996; Lindbeck, G. "Postcritical Canonical Interpretation: Three Modes of Retrieval." Pages 26–51 in *Theological Exegesis*, ed. C. Seitz and K. Greene-McCreight. Eerdmans, 1999; idem. "The Story-Shaped Church: Critical Exegesis and Theological Interpretation." Pages 39–52 in *The Theological Interpretation of Scripture*, ed. S. Fowl. Blackwell, 1997; Lints, R. *The Fabric of Theology*. Eerdmans, 1993; Moberly, R. W. L. *The Bible, Theology, and Faith*. Studies in Christian Doctrine. Cambridge University Press, 2000; Muller, R. "Biblical Interpretation in the Era of the Reformation: The View from the Middle Ages." Pages 3–22 in *Biblical Interpretation in the Era of the Reformation*, ed. R. Muller and J. Thompson. Eerdmans, 1996; Seitz, C. "Christological Interpretation of Texts and Trinitarian Claims to Truth: An Engagement with Francis Watson's *Text and Truth*." *SJT* 52, no. 2 (1999): 209–26; idem. *Figured Out*. Westminster John Knox, 2001; Steinmetz, D. "The Superiority of Pre-Critical Exegesis." Pages 26–38 in *The Theological Interpretation of Scripture*, ed. S. Fowl. Blackwell, 1997; Turner, M. "Historical Criticism and Theological Hermeneutics of the New Testament." Pages 44–70 in *Between Two Horizons*, ed. J. Green and M. Turner. Eerdmans, 2000; Vanhoozer, K. *First Theology*. InterVarsity, 2002; Watson, F. "The Old Testament as Christian Scripture: A Response to Professor Seitz." *SJT* 52, no. 2 (1999): 227–32; idem. *Text and Truth*. Eerdmans, 1997; idem. *Text, Church, and World*. Eerdmans, 1994; Welker, M. "Biblical Theology and the Authority of Scripture." Pages 232–41 in *Theology in the Service of the Church*, ed. W. Alston Jr. Eerdmans, 2000; Yeago, D. "The Bible: The Spirit, the Church, and the Scriptures." Pages 49–93 in *Knowing the Triune God*, ed. J. Buckley and D. Yeago. Eerdmans, 2001; idem. "The New Testament and the Nicene Dogma: A Contribution to the Recovery of Theological Exegesis." Pages 87–100 in *The Theological Interpretation of Scripture*, ed. S. Fowl. Blackwell, 1997.

Daniel J. Treier

Scripture Principle *See* Scripture, Authority of; Word of God

Semantics *See* Meaning; Semiotics

Semiotics

Communication in all forms—whether between humans, plants, animals, or in other contexts—draws on a series of signaling systems. The study of these systems is *semiotics*, also known in European circles as *semiology*. Daniel Chandler points to the vast scope of this field: "Semiotics involves the study not only of what we refer to as 'signs' in everyday speech, but of anything which 'stands for' something else. In a semiotic sense, signs take the form of words, images, sounds, gestures and objects" (2).

Semiotics comprises three broad disciplines. *Semantics* is based on a study of the signs themselves. *Syntax* studies relations between the signs, or rules of permissible combinations. *Pragmatics* is concerned with relating signs to their users, taking account of the effects of sociocultural and linguistic contexts.

The study of semiotics can be traced back to the ancient Greeks (BCE), who developed a strong interest in signs as a communication device. Key names were Plato (ca. 427–347), Aristotle (384–322), and the Stoic school of philosophers, pioneered in about 300 in Athens by Zeno (ca. 345–263) of Citium. These great Greek thinkers sought to explain the process by which signs acquired and transmitted meaning. Their debate surrounded an essentially *realist* position, whereby signs such as "man" and "table" were considered to represent extramental concepts that exist. Thus, their approach was based on an ontological construct. Objective universal concepts, such as "manness" and "tableness," were connected by various means to the signs that made communication possible.

In response to the realist position emerged that of the *nominalists*, who took an epistemological view focusing on signs as a means of knowing the world. Key names in this regard were the medieval philosophers William of Ockham (ca. 1285–1349) and John Locke (1632–1704). The latter, in his *Essay concerning Human Understanding* (1690), first established semiotics as a science of signs. The nominalists insisted that sign names such as "man" were usually arrived at arbitrarily. There were no objective extramental universals; that is, there is no such entity as "redness," but only red things.

The early Greek and medieval thinkers laid the foundations of the modern field of semiotics. The twentieth century witnessed the flourishing of this field within two major traditions. Ferdinand de Saussure (1857–1913) developed a theory of the linguistic sign that was key in stimulating the study of semiotics, which he proposed should be a discrete field of study in a way not previously conceived: "A science that studies the life of signs within society is conceivable; it would be a part of social psychology and consequently of general psychology; I shall call it *semiology*. . . . Since the science does not yet exist, no one can say what it would be; but it has a right to existence, a place staked out in advance. Linguistics is only a part of the general science of semiology" (16).

Saussure's thinking, much developed by his disciples, is essentially nominalist. It insists that signs necessarily mediate our engagement with the world and prevent us from understanding reality in an absolute sense. In order to explain this method of engagement, Saussure proposed a *dyadic* relationship between a *signifier* and a *signified*. Thus, the sign "roses" calls to mind "passion" for Europeans; the roses are the *signifier*, passion is the *signified*, and the relationship itself is termed *signification*.

Importantly, Saussure pointed out that signification did not result from a direct connection between signifier and signified, but rather from the contrasts between signs. Thus, "white" acquires its meaning through contrast with "black," "yellow," and so forth.

The second major tradition within the modern study of semiotics emerged from the United States. Saussure's contemporary, the American philosopher Charles S. Peirce (1839–1914), felt similarly challenged to explain the process by which signs acquired meaning. However, in contrast with the Saussurean view, Peirce worked on the basis of a triad. It is a *triadic* view that has come to predominate in modern semiotics, especially through the triangle of signification developed by Ogden and Richards (11), which depicts the relationship between *sign*, *concept*, and *significatum* or *referent*.

Peirce also developed a threefold classification of signs. A *symbol* is a sign for which the relationship between concept and form is arbitrary. This applies to most linguistic signs. For example, English "tree," French "arbre," and Indonesian "pohon" are all signs for the same concept. The link is arbitrary; none are naturally representative of characteristics of trees. Peirce's second sign type is the *icon*, which is a nonarbitrary sign. A clear example of this is provided by the phenomenon of onomatopoeia, such as English "cuckoo," French "coucou," and Indonesian "tekukur."

The third type of sign in the Peirce classification is the *index*. Like the symbol, this is an arbitrary sign, but it additionally expresses a material, factual correlation in space and time between sign and concept. So "smoke" is an index of "fire," "footprints in snow" are an index of "walker," "slurred speech" is an index of "a drunk speaker," "black" is an index of mourning, and the color saffron is an index of detachment for Buddhists. So index tells us something about the source. The most common indexes in linguistics are *deictic* words pointing to referents: I, your, this, here, now.

During the second half of the twentieth century, the rise of functionalism in modern linguistics had an impact on semioticians. Umberto Eco (b. 1932) was critical of Saussure's approach in certain respects: "Saussure did not define the signified any too clearly, leaving it half way between a mental image, a concept and a psychological reality." In this regard Eco is more inclined to Peirce's ideas: "The definition given by Peirce seems to me more comprehensive and semiotically more fruitful" (14–15). Eco has devoted considerable attention to using semiotics in literary interpretation.

The pioneer of *systemic functional linguistics*, Michael Halliday (b. 1925), sought to move beyond the preoccupation of the structuralists with the workings of the mind to consider broader contextual issues. He pointed out that the early Greeks tended to study signs in isolation, while Saussure, in spite of his view of language as a network of relationships, still focused on "a rather atomistic conception of the linguistic sign" (Halliday and Hasan 3). Halliday reinforced semiotics as the study of sign systems, emphasizing that linguistics was merely one aspect of semiotics. Also included were other sign systems, especially cultural systems used to impart meaning: painting, sculpture, music, dance, modes of exchange, dress, and family structure. Thus, in order to understand how these sign systems operate, Halliday points to the importance of considering social context as a starting point. This has resulted in Hallidayan social semiotics emerging as a major approach within semiotics.

Applications to Scriptural Hermeneutics

Semiotics as a field of study has received some bad press over the years. Trask (271) comments that "in spite of its deliberate emphasis upon the social nature of the sign systems examined, semiotics tends to be highly abstract and at times seemingly impenetrable." Nevertheless, the emerging scholarly rigor associated with semiotics has had a striking effect on the methods of those biblical scholars interested in exploring new approaches to Scripture.

James Barr's forceful critique of traditional methods of interpretation in his *Semantics of Biblical Language* was influenced by advances in thinking from semioticians. His call for a more scientific method in analyzing biblical languages, taking account of findings from modern linguistics, was to have a major impact on applying a key subdiscipline of semiotics, that of semantics, to study of the biblical text. The fruit can be seen in the studies of lexical semantics (Louw; Silva; Cotterell and Turner).

At the level of lexis, Peirce's threefold classification of signs bears consideration as one device for analyzing biblical words. As with all written texts, the Bible depends most heavily on the symbols that link sign and concept in an arbitrary fashion. However, icons can also be found. Examples from the Revised Standard Version are "wail" (Isa. 13:6; Matt. 2:18), "gnash" (Job 16:9; Matt. 13:42), and "roar" (1 Chron. 16:32; Luke 21:25). Furthermore, indexes are found prolifically in the biblical text. Several instances are "clouds," which evoke theophany; "cross," which evokes Christ; and "fire," which evokes the punishment of hell.

Another semiotic principle providing potential for biblical analysis relates to the signs that depend not on individual words but on paralinguistic signals. This can include intonation patterns and stress, although it is not always possible to retrieve such clues from a text like the Bible, so far removed in time from the original communities that produced it. However, the biblical text provides important clues as to other paralinguistic signs, including facial expressions (smiling, frowning, raised eyebrows, winking, etc.) and gestures (nodding, pointing).

In Esther 5:1–2, multiple signaling systems are used by the main actors. Esther puts on her royal robes, signaling both her own status and her respect for that of the king. The locations where Esther stands and the king sits both significantly signal in themselves. The king's holding out of the gold scepter, and Esther's touching it, carry the nonverbal communication further. A semiotic analysis focusing on such data yields much information without a single spoken word having been considered. Similarly, Prov. 16:30 ("He who winks his eyes plans perverse things, he who compresses his lips brings evil to pass" [RSV]) clearly illustrates the communicative force of facial gestures.

The application of semiotics to scriptural hermeneutics does not stop at the level of lexis. The contribution of Halliday's social semiotics to discourse-level research has direct relevance. Cobley and Jansz (165) summarize Halliday's thinking: "It is here, between speaker and hearer, that language is generated, and the social context actually appears within the utterance rather than existing externally in a system." So consideration of contextual features should not be an afterthought, but it should be fully integrated with any semiotic analysis at the discourse level.

This approach is making its mark on scriptural hermeneutics at the turn of the twenty-first century. Jeffrey Reed's study of Philippians represents the first significant attempt to apply Hallidayan methods to the study of a whole book of the Bible. More studies of this type, based on both OT and NT, are currently under way.

There are also increasing scholarly efforts to develop analytical criteria for applying semiotic principles to wide-ranging text types. Daniel Chandler has developed a semiotic analytical framework that is helping to crystallize methods in what has at times been regarded as a field of "abstract and 'arid formalism'" (209). Chandler identifies macrothemes that should be taken into account in conducting a semiotic analysis of text, including genre identification, modality, paradigmatic analysis, syntagmatic structure, rhetorical tropes, intertextuality, and social factors. Each of these is considered in terms of a set of guiding questions, which help the analyst to relate semiotic theory to real texts. This approach, though developed from study of secular materials, offers considerable potential for refining the application of semiotic theory to the biblical text.

See also Etymology; Language, Linguistics; Poststructuralism; Structuralism

Bibliography

Barr, J. *The Semantics of Biblical Language*. Oxford University Press, 1961; Chandler, D. *Semiotics*. Routledge, 2002; Cobley, P., and L. Jansz. *Semiotics for Beginners*. Icon Books, 1997; Cotterell, P., and M. Turner. *Linguistics and Biblical Interpretation*. InterVarsity, 1989; Eco, U. *A Theory of Semiotics*. Indiana University Press, 1979; Halliday, M., and R. Hasan. *Language, Context, and Text*. Deakin University, 1985. Reprint, Oxford University Press, 1989; Halliday, M. *Language as Social Semiotic*. E. Arnold, 1978; Louw, J. P. *Semantics of New Testament Greek*. Fortress, 1982; Lyons, J. *Semantics*. Vol. 1. Cambridge University Press, 1977; Ogden, C. K., and I. A. Richards. *The Meaning of Meaning*. Routledge & Kegan Paul, 1923; Peirce, C. S. *Collected Papers of Charles Sanders Peirce*. Vols. 1–6, ed. C. Hartshorne and P. Weiss. Harvard University Press, 1931–35; Reed, J. *A Discourse Analysis of Philippians*. Sheffield Academic Press, 1997; Saussure, F. de. *Course in General Linguistics*. Rev. ed. Collins, 1974; Silva, M. *Biblical Words and Their Meaning*. 2d ed. Zondervan, 1994; Trask, R. L. *Key Concepts in Language and Linguistics*. Routledge, 1999.

Peter G. Riddell

Sense   *See* Literal Sense; Meaning; Ricoeur, Paul; Spiritual Sense

Sensus Plenior   *See* Allegory; Meaning; Medieval Biblical Interpretation; Spiritual Sense; Typology

Sentence   *See* Language, Grammar and Syntax; Language, Linguistics; Proposition; Utterance Meaning

Sermon on the Mount

Genre and Setting

The most significant division among interpreters of the Sermon on the Mount (SM) has been between those who see it as a vision of life for all (e.g., the *Didache*; John Chrysostom, *Hom. Matt.* 16.3; 16.5; 18.4) and those who see it as counsel for those seeking "perfection" (poverty, celibacy, and obedience—e.g., Bonaventure, *Apologia pauperum* 3.8; Maldonatus, *In Quattuor Evangelistas* 1).

The evangelist's intention lies broadly with the former group. SM is an address to "the crowds" (5:1a; 7:28); the "disciples" (5:1b) merely represent the church. SM is *public* teaching, wherein the Messiah points out the "road" for those calling him "Lord!" (7:13–14, 21). That is why SM stands where it does in the narrative. What precedes it prepares us to know who Jesus is and what grace he brings (1:1–4:25). Now we hear his first major teaching, wherein he begins to tell us of life in that sphere of grace, and the part we are called to play. Of course we will fail, and God is merciful: at SM's center is the prayer, "Forgive us our debts" (6:12). But that does not dilute SM's challenge.

It is not difficult to discern in SM's structure what contemporaries would have heard as an exercise in deliberative rhetoric: it is designed to lead its audience to a decision for action (Kennedy 39–63). The evangelist is probably responsible for this structure, but the content mostly has its source in Jesus' own teaching.

Structure and Argument

Proem. Matthew 5:3–16 functions to secure goodwill. It describes as "happy" or "fortunate" (*makarioi*; "blessed" in most ET) various groups—the poor in spirit, the merciful, peacemakers, the pure in heart, those persecuted for righteousness' sake—with whom Jesus' hearers will identify or wish to identify (5:3–12). Notably, the *Proem* is not exhortation, but proclamation. Those identified *are* "fortunate." They may not *seem* fortunate in the world's eyes, but they are, for "theirs is the kingdom of heaven" (5:10). The emphasis is not on "reward" but on God's faithfulness: God will keep God's promise. Similarly the passages on "salt" and "light" (5:13–16) are not exhortations to *become* those things but promises that those who seek to follow Jesus *are* these things. As always with grace, however, response is invited. The essence of this response is stated immediately (5:16), and so prepares us for the next part of SM.

Proposition. Matthew 5:17–20 emphasizes that Jesus came to fulfill the law's promises. Therefore, not only must his followers observe the least of Torah's commands; their obedience also must exceed even that required by recognized authorities (the Pharisees). Matthew has specifically in mind *Jewish* followers of Jesus who, while supportive of the Gentile mission (28:19–20), remain committed to halakah as their way of response to God's grace (see 23:1–3; cf. Acts 15:22–29). This qualifies our understanding of certain specific aspects of SM (see on 5:31–32, below), though not affecting its main challenge.

The *Proposition* stated, SM moves to *Headings* (5:21–7:27), the arguments and illustrations supporting the *Proposition.*

First Heading: How the Law Must Be Taken More Seriously Than Ever (5:21–48). First are pericopes interpreting the OT. Jesus' method is similar to the rabbis: "You have heard . . . [you might understand the Scriptures to be saying . . .], but I say to you . . . [you should understand like this . . .]."

At 5:21–26, "judgment," "council," and "fire of hell" involve a climax, paralleled by being "angry," calling someone "*Raca*" (an Aramaic term of abuse), and calling someone "*Mōe*." Most ET render the third of these as if it were *mōros* (fool), but the Greek probably transliterates an Aramaic word meaning "rebel" (against God)—thus making this the most serious insult of the three. Matthew 5:23–24 speaks of a situation where your fellow has a just claim against you. R. Eleazar ben Azariah (ca. 80–120 CE) taught, "For transgressions between a man and his fellow the Day of Atonement does not effect atonement until he shall have first placated his fellow" (*m. Yoma* 8:9). Then 5:25–26 adds a note of urgency: it is the last hour!

Matthew 5:27–30 is not about sexual attraction, but desire without concern. The Greek word (also in the LXX) translated "commit adultery" frequently has the force of "debauch" and is so understood here. Hence, "causes you to stumble" (5:29 AT) focuses not on the man's fate, but on what he has done to the woman and so also to himself.

With 5:31–32 compare Mark 10:10, noting, however, qualifications added in 5:32. Possibly these reflect views attributed to R. Zechariah ben ha-Katzav (ca. 80–120 CE): in cases of adultery,

divorce is not only allowed but also commanded, and *the adulteress may not marry her paramour.* "Just as she is prohibited to the husband so she is forbidden to the adulterer" (*m. Sotah* 5:1). The Matthean community, looking for an obedience exceeding that of others, might have footnoted Jesus' saying in this way. (Here then is an example of NT teaching, ad hoc and ad hominem, which cannot be applied without remainder to other Christian situations, and doubtless could not have been so applied even when the Gospels were written: both Mark and Luke lack the provision.)

At 5:33, "swear falsely" (RSV) is problematic: better would probably be "You shall not break your oath." The attitudes implied at 5:34–37 resemble those of Essenes (Josephus, *B.J.* 2.135) and classical antiquity generally (Sophocles, *Oed. col.* 648–51).

Matthew 5:38–42 is (*pace* Horsley, *Spiral*) antifreedom fighters. Under Roman law a Roman soldier had the right to require a noncitizen to carry his equipment one mile. Similarly, in the following pericope about loving the neighbor (5:43–48), a call to "hate your enemy" is not part of any known Jewish ethic, but would be understandable as an interpretation of Lev. 19:18 by freedom fighters. Matthew 5:48 echoes Deut. 18:13 and Lev. 19:2: the emphasis is not on "flawlessness" but on the parallel between God's compassion and the compassion for enemies and strangers to which disciples are called (cf. 5:45). *Pace* Yoder theologically and Horsley (*Empire*), Jesus does not counsel rejecting Roman rule, violently or nonviolently (see Bryan).

Second Heading: Behaviors (6:1–18). Almsgiving, prayer, and fasting form a characteristically Jewish triad, particularly associated with penitence. Before and after 70 CE, Jews were enjoined in times of distress: "Three things cancel out the harsh decree: prayer, almsgiving, and repentance" (*y. Ta'an.* 2.1).

Matthew 6:1–18 stresses that Jesus' disciples must not be "as the *hypokritai*" (6:2, 5, 16). The ET "hypocrites" (people pretending to be something they aren't) may mislead here and makes scant sense at other places (e.g., 23:24–25). Matthew's *hypokritai* probably means the same as the Qumran sectaries' *doreshey khalaqot* (interpreters of smooth/false things; cf. Isa. 30:10 MT/NRSV; 1QH 2.32; 4.7–12; CD 1.18–20). In both cases the accusation is that those referred to are wrongly interpreting Torah. Thus, those who give alms, pray, or fast *only* to be "praised" or "seen" (6:2, 5, 16) have forgotten the essence of these things, and so are disobeying Torah.

Matthew 6:7–15 digresses, but appropriately. It places the Lord's Prayer and God's forgiveness at the heart of the SM. Since God's forgiveness is the basis of our hope, forgiving others must be the basis of our behavior (6:12, 14–15).

Third Heading: Other Examples of Righteousness (6:19–7:20). Sayings about treasure in heaven (6:19–21), the light of the body (6:22–23), and God and mammon (6:24) continue to revolve around getting priorities right. In rabbinic texts "mammon" denotes "property" and is not pejorative: what is criticized here is not the notion of property, but devoting such attention to property as is proper toward God alone.

At 6:22–23, "sound" (RSV; *haplous*) implies wholehearted commitment to God. "Evil eye" (KJV; *ophthalmos poneros*) was an expression denoting meanness (cf. 20:15, RSV margin). Matthew 6:22–23 therefore contrasts wholehearted devotion to God with that spiritual niggardliness that always looks for ways to limit love's demands.

Matthew 6:25–34 assumes that those addressed *do* have something to wear, eat, and drink. The passage does not invite the oppressed to assume that God wills their suffering, nor invite oppressors to justify their oppressing actions. If oppressors take seriously Jesus' invitation here, they will not need to oppress.

Matthew 7:1, "Judge not!" (RSV), is hyperbole. Sometimes we *must* make judgments (cf. 1 Cor. 6:1–6). Priorities are still the issue: the danger is that we *enjoy* judging, and so indulge in it beyond what is necessary. At 7:3–5, "you that are mistakenly interpreting Torah" again makes good sense of *hypocrita*, "hypocrite." Priorities are still the issue.

These *Headings* conclude with words about perseverance in prayer (7:7–11), and the Golden Rule, summarizing "the Law and the Prophets" (7:12).

Epilogue (7:21–27), Restating the Proposition and Encouraging Action. Matthew 7:13–14 echoes Deut. 30:15–20 and stresses the need for decision. Then 7:15–23 points to "fruits" as the mark of true prophecy. Mere "preaching" or "miracles" (the showier types of "Christian action"!) are not enough. Matthew 7:24–27 emphasizes the need to *act* upon Jesus' words, facing his hearers with the question, "What kind of disciple am I?"

Bibliography

Betz, H. D. *Essays on the Sermon on the Mount*, trans. L. L. Welbourne. Fortress, 1985; Bryan, C. *Render to Caesar*. Oxford University Press, forthcoming; Davies, W. D., and D. Allison. Pages 429–731 in vol. 1 of *A Critical and Exegetical Commentary on the Gospel according to Saint Matthew*. 3 vols. T&T Clark, 1988–97; Fitzgerald, J. "The Problem of Perjury in Greek Context: Prolegomena to an Exegesis of Matthew 5.33, 1 Timothy 1.10, and *Didache* 2.3." Pages 156–77 in *The Social World of the First Christians*, ed. L. M. White and O. L. Yarborough. Fortress, 1995; Horsley, R. *Jesus and Empire*. Fortress, 2003; idem. Pages 261–64 in *Jesus and the Spiral of Violence*. Fortress, 1993; Kennedy, G. Pages 39–63 in *New Testament Interpretation through Rhetorical Criticism*. University of North Carolina, 1984; Luz, U. Pages 209–460 in *Matthew 1–7*, trans. W. C. Linss. Fortress, 1992; Schnackenburg, R. *All Things Are Possible to Believers*, trans. J. Currie. Westminster John Knox, 1995; Yoder, J. H. Pages 1–20 in *The Politics of Jesus*. Eerdmans, 1972.

Christopher Bryan

Setting   *See* Ancient Near Eastern Background Studies; Archaeology; Context; Culture and Hermeneutics

Sexuality

To say that sexuality is one of the most contested areas of biblical theology is to state the obvious. The chief reason is that societal views have undergone significant shifts.

Scripture regards the urge to gratify intensely pleasurable sexual desires as part of God's good creation. Nevertheless, given their often-insatiable quality, Scripture also recognizes a constant threat to the Creator's norms—even when there is clear communal consensus about proper behavior and strong social sanctions reinforce conformity, which today can no longer be assumed.

Truth claims about sexuality have suffered from the rise of various intellectual currents and values: historical-critical analysis, postmodernism, deconstructionist thought, and absolutist versions of pluralism, diversity, and tolerance. Beyond that and the obvious need to justify pleasurable desires, women's roles, rights, and opportunities have expanded, challenging traditional patriarchal structures and beliefs. Birth control has made possible decoupling the pleasures of sexual intercourse from the responsibilities of childbearing. This in turn has minimized the importance of reserving sexual intercourse for marriage; no-fault divorce laws have challenged the permanence of marriage, further diminished by easy access to pornography, the welfare state, and even economic affluence.

A militant gay-rights movement has taken the ultimate step of demanding an end to "heterosexism." This has called into question the very foundation of biblical sexuality: that sexual differentiation matters for the complementary sexual merging of two persons into one. Fueled also by some radical feminist trends, this questioning has led further to arguments for bisexuality and even transgenderism.

The advancement of a homosexual agenda is not the originating cause for all of society's sexual dysfunctions, but in many ways the unfortunate logical end result. In effect, the acceptance of homosexual practice heralds the eventual demise of any structural prerequisites for a sexual relationship (sex, number, degree of blood relatedness, age), inasmuch as homosexual practice is defended on the grounds of the self-validating character of affective bonds.

The current climate of confusion makes it essential that the church develop theological clarity regarding sexual expression. The appropriate starting point in any attempt at a biblical-theological definition of sexuality is Jesus. Jesus' treatment of divorce and remarriage in Mark 10:2–12// Matt. 19:3–12 and in Matt. 5:31–32//Luke 16:18 (Q) is pivotal (cf. 1 Cor. 7:10–11, where Paul alludes to Jesus' prohibition of divorce).

Jesus and Scripture on Sexuality

Making the Creation Model of Marriage Normative and Prescriptive. Jesus understood the stories about the creation of humans in Gen. 1–2 not merely as descriptive but also as texts that supplied a prescriptive model for subsequent human sexual behavior (Mark 10:6–9//Matt. 19:4–6, 8b). This is clear from his remark "From the beginning of creation it was not so" (cf. Mark 10:6; Matt. 19:8). It is also clear from his back-to-back citations of Gen. 1:27 ("The Creator 'made them male and female'") and 2:24 (NRSV: "For this reason a man shall leave his father and mother and be joined [attached, glued] to his wife, and the two shall become one flesh"). Jesus did not emphasize the openness of creation to change but rather a binding standard that critiqued all postcreation compromises. Malachi (2:15–16) may be making a similar normative allusion to Gen. 2:24, though there are difficult translation issues: "Did he [God] not make [you/them] one? . . . Do not act faithlessly against the wife of your youth. If one hates and divorces . . . , he covers his garment with violence" (so Hugenberger 151–67, 341–43; ESV; alternatively: "Did not One [God] make [her/all]? . . . For he hates/I hate divorce . . .").

Closing Loopholes and Inconsistencies in the Law of Moses. Jesus believed that Moses had made concessions to human (chiefly male) "hard-

ness of heart" (*sklērokardia*), thereby compromising the will of God as expressed in creation (Mark 10:5–6//Matt. 19:8 RSV). In the particular case of divorce, Moses had given men an exemption from God's creation standard that for the most part had not been given to women. In view of the anticipative inbreaking of the kingdom of God (the end time is like the primal time [*Endzeit* = *Urzeit*]), Jesus was now revoking this concession.

In an important recent book, Instone-Brewer sees things a bit differently. Based on the occurrence of *sklērokardia* in Jer. 4:4 LXX (not the same sense as in MT), he understands "hardness of heart" as a reference to the stubbornness of the *adulterous* partner, who refuses to give up adulterous ways (144–46, 176–77). According to Instone-Brewer, who relies more on Matt. 19:3–12 than Mark 10:2–12, Jesus interprets Moses rather than overrides him. Against the Pharisees, Jesus insists that Moses did not "command" but only "permitted" divorce (Matt. 19:7–8); moreover, Moses did not allow divorce "for any . . . reason" (19:3), but only when an adulterous spouse remained impenitent (142–43, 180–81). The Matthean exception clauses—"except for a matter of indecency [*porneia*]" (5:32 AT) and "unless for indecency" (19:9 AT)—reinforce that Jesus was essentially siding with the Shammaite interpretation. In Deut. 24:1, the Shammaites took the phrase *'erwat dabar* (lit., "nakedness of a thing" or "indecency of a matter") as adultery, and the Hillelites took it to mean "indecency or any matter" (*m. Git.* 9:10; Instone-Brewer 110–13, 158–59, 185–86).

While Instone-Brewer argues well, there are problems. First, the context for "*your* hardness of heart" in Mark 10:5 favors reading it as a reference to *men* who divorce their wives in spite of God's will enshrined in creation. Second, a better echo than Jer. 4:4 LXX may be Mal. 2:14. Just before a possible allusion to Gen. 2:24 (above), Mal. 2:14 refers to "the wife of your youth, to whom you have been faithless [in divorcing her], though she is your companion and your wife by covenant" (NRSV). The critique is against the callousness of men who divorce their wives. Third, Mark 10:4–9, on which Matthew's version depends, gives the impression that Jesus' appeal to Gen. 1:27 and 2:24 is revoking the Mosaic permission, not just interpreting it in Shammaite fashion. While "Moses *permitted* a man to write a certificate of divorce and send her away," God's will "from the beginning of creation" was different, not *permitting* divorce (cf. Mark 10:4, 6; Matt. 19:8). Jesus apparently understood himself to be amending the Torah itself, to close a loophole inconsistent with the Creator's will (similarly, his stance against oaths in Matt. 5:33–37). This, in turn, raises a question as to whether the Matthean exception clause accurately reflects a permission Jesus would have granted.

Jesus' amendment strategy introduces an important theological principle. Regarding the sexual standards for men and women, OT law contains some inequities and double standards, and not just over the question of divorce. Although by Jesus' day Jewish women had some options for initiating divorce (Instone-Brewer 72–74, 85–90, 151–52), these were still limited in comparison to those granted men. For example, laws prohibiting men from committing adultery focus on having intercourse with another man's fiancée or wife, not with women unattached to other men (cf. the seventh and tenth commandments, Exod. 20:14, 17; Deut. 5:18, 21; also, Exod. 22:16–17; Lev. 18:20; 20:10; Deut. 22:22–29). Christians are not unfaithful to Scripture when they criticize such imbalances in OT law.

Intensifying Sexual Ethics. Rather than loosening the demands of the law in the area of sexual ethics, Jesus intensified them and closed loopholes. The sexual equity that Jesus established between men and women was equity in sexual restraint, not freedom. He took an already circumscribed sexual ethic given in the Hebrew Scriptures and narrowed it further, for both sexes.

In the sayings on *divorce and remarriage*, Jesus lifted up marriage's indissolubility over the principle of sexual "rights" and self-fulfillment. For Jesus, remarriage after divorce constituted adultery because, in God's eyes, the original marriage was still valid, irrespective of a divorce certificate. Jesus even warned against marrying divorced women, stating that a man who "marries a divorced woman commits adultery" (Matt. 5:32 NRSV//Luke 16:18). Sexual purity took precedence over gratification.

Paul and Matthew tinker with Jesus' prohibition of divorce, but not by much. Paul, who explicitly alludes to Jesus' "command" on divorce (1 Cor. 7:10–11), allows for an exception in the case of marriage to an unbelieving person—but only when the unbelieving spouse insists on leaving (7:12–16). A believer who initiates divorce is to "remain unmarried or else be reconciled" (7:11; cf. Rom. 7:3). Matthew, with his exception clause allowing divorce of an adulterous spouse and, presumably, remarriage, surmises that adultery dissolves the original union, at least potentially (Matt. 5:32; 19:9). Even with this exception, Matthew recognizes

the intensity of Jesus' prohibition of divorce and remarriage (hence, the disciples' reported comment in 19:10: if marriage is this hard to dissolve, "it is not expedient to marry" [RSV]). In the end, both Matthew and Paul strongly maintain Jesus' radical opposition to divorce over against a broader cultural environment that is much more permissive.

What then should the church do today with believers who, in opposition to Jesus' teaching, divorce and remarry? There are reasons for believing that Jesus would not have insisted on dissolution of the second marriage, including the fact that such an insistence would replicate the problem of divorce (see further, Gagnon, "Sex Precepts?" 119–22).

The sayings on divorce and remarriage also imply a prohibition of *polygyny* (many wives). A man who "divorces his wife and marries another woman commits adultery *against her*" because the first marriage is treated as still intact (Mark 10:11//Luke 16:18). The underlying principle is that having two wives rather than one constitutes adultery. If this applies even when the husband thinks he has dissolved the prior union, then it certainly applies to a union not yet dissolved in the husband's eyes. In the OT, a man did not commit adultery against his wife by taking another wife or concubine. Rather, he committed adultery when he had intercourse with another's wife, and then the offense was against the other man. Here Jesus indicates that the wife has as much claim to her husband's monogamy as the husband to his wife's faithfulness (as in Mark 10:12). His emphasis on the number "two"—"so they are no longer two, but one [flesh]" (Mark 10:8//Matt. 19:6)—speaks against polygamous unions. Paul's discussions of marriage, including in 1 Cor. 7, presume a principle of monogamy. Even the OT, though permitting poly*gyny*, foreshadowed a case against poly*gamy*, not only in Gen. 2:20–24, but also in the implicit prohibition of poly*andry* (many husbands), the norm of one wife in Israelite society, and stories of internal disputes in polygynous households.

Jesus' intensification of sexual ethics also comes across in his saying about *adultery of the heart* (Matt. 5:27–28). The point is not to trivialize external acts of adultery by inferring that the heart's intent matters more than conformity to behavioral rules. Instead, Jesus expands the reach of God's will, from regulating outward behavior to interiorizing the demand as well (cf. Matt. 5:21–26). So adulterous behavior remains a serious offense, and even entertaining adulterous thoughts violates God's will. Jesus' hyperbolic statement about what defiles a person at first glance seems to prioritize intent over behavior, but a closer look indicates otherwise (Mark 7:14–23//Matt. 15:10–20). It is not so much food entering the stomach from the outside that defiles a person, but rather the inward desires that lead one to commit what Scripture regards as "sexually immoral acts [*porneiai*] . . . adulteries . . . sexual licentiousness [*aselgeia*]" (Mark 7:21–22 AT). Jesus was not saying that the morality of an action is ultimately settled by a person's subjective motivation, as if persons could violate a command of God regarding sexuality without repercussion so long as their heart was "in the right place." Instead, he was saying that sex is not like food; the former is never a matter of indifference (cf. 1 Cor. 6:12–20, where Paul makes a similar point). The active desire for what God deems to be immoral sexual activity is already defiling, even before the act is committed.

Jesus' sayings about divorce and remarriage have implications for sexual purity in other areas. *Fornication*, sexual intercourse between unmarried persons, is obviously ruled out of bounds since Jesus' sayings on divorce and remarriage aim at restricting sexual intimacy to one person in marriage until the death of the partner dissolves the union (cf. Rom. 7:1–3; 1 Cor. 7:39–40). Allowing premarital or nonmarital sexual intercourse would essentially inflict a "marriage penalty," encouraging persons to stay unmarried so they could avoid Jesus' rigorous expectations. This would be the same kind of hypocrisy based on the "letter of the law" that Jesus criticized in some of the Pharisees' teachings (Matt. 23). Jesus' own disciples, after hearing his rigorous teaching, did not conclude that it was expedient to form sexually intimate relationships outside of marriage, but rather that it was expedient to abstain from all sexual relationships (19:10). Jesus qualified this observation but still maintained celibacy or marriage as the only options open to the people of God (19:11–12). Similarly, Paul advised unmarried believers to get married if they did not feel capable of controlling desires for sexual intimacy (1 Cor. 7:9, 36; cf. 7:2, 5; also, Paul's assumption that the engaged women believers are virgins, in 7:25–38).

Citing Gen. 2:24 ("the two shall become one flesh"), Paul warned that even the most impersonal and noncommittal of sexual "relationships," sex with a prostitute, created a certain "joining," a one-flesh bond (1 Cor. 6:15–16). Paul could say, albeit perhaps with hyperbole,

that "every sin, whatever a person commits, is outside the body [perhaps in partial agreement with a Corinthian slogan], but the one who commits sexual immorality sins against the body" (6:18 AT). Sexual intercourse engages persons holistically, even when they pretend that the relational dimension is meaningless. In ancient Israel, women were expected to be virgins at the time of marriage. According to Exod. 22:16–17, a man who had intercourse with an unbetrothed virgin was expected to pay the bride-price and marry her, unless the father refused permission. In that case the man still had to pay (cf. Deut. 22:28–29, which says nothing about the father's right of refusal, but adds "he shall not be permitted to divorce her" [NRSV]). Jesus' practice of equalizing sexual purity requirements for men and women would speak for the same expectation of virginity for men at the time of marriage.

Obviously, the points raised above tell against *prostitution* and *sex with prostitutes*. It is possible that Jesus' statement about cutting off one's hand (Matt. 5:30; cf. Mark 9:43//Matt. 18:8) refers to *masturbation*. The inference is suggested by rabbinic parallels (e.g., *b. Nid.* 13b) and by the proximity of Matt. 5:30 to the saying about adultery of the heart (5:27–28). Certainly Jesus' views are clearly against masturbation facilitated by sexual fantasies about persons other than one's spouse.

Although there is no mention of *incest* in the extant sayings of Jesus, there can be no doubt about Jesus' acceptance of the incest laws in Lev. 18 and 20 (cf. Deut. 22:30; 27:20, 22–23). The basic problem with incest is implicit in the general prohibition stated in Lev. 18:6: "No one shall approach any flesh of his flesh to uncover nakedness" (AT). In other words, sexual intercourse with another who is too much of a familial "same" is inappropriate. A "one-flesh" union—establishment of kinship across bloodlines—cannot be created by a sexually intimate union of two people who are already of the same "flesh" (close blood relations). So seriously are incest laws taken that they extend to in-law relations. In dealing with incest between a man and his stepmother in 1 Cor. 5, Paul did not have to deliberate about "What would Jesus do [WWJD]?"—despite absence of an explicit saying of Jesus. He asserted "in the name of our Lord Jesus" that when the community at Corinth gathers together "with . . . the power of our Lord Jesus," they must temporarily disfellowship the incestuous believer in hope of reclaiming him ultimately for the kingdom of God (5:3–5; cf. 6:9–10).

The issue of *homosexual practice* is dealt with separately (below).

Making Sexual Ethics a Life-and-Death Concern. Jesus plainly demonstrated that sexual purity was a major concern. In between Jesus' sayings on adultery of the heart and divorce/remarriage, Matthew sandwiches a dire warning: If your right eye or hand should threaten your downfall, cut it off. "For it is expedient for you that one of your members be lost/destroyed and that your whole body not be thrown into Gehenna [hell]" (5:29–30 AT; cf. Mark 9:43–48//Matt. 18:8–9; *b. Nid.* 13b). In Jesus' view, sexual misbehavior could send a person to hell. Although extant sayings of Jesus devoted to sexual matters are few in number, particularly compared with those against materialism and economic exploitation, their generally countercultural character underscores their significance. Jesus did not naively imbibe from the cultural well but made demands that in some respects exceeded even those of the Pharisees. That he did not say more about sexual matters can be attributed to the fact that first-century Jewish Palestinian society already maintained a fairly exacting standard.

Paul, however, operated in a Gentile milieu, where such standards could no longer be presumed. Consequently, his warnings about sexual conduct consume a more significant portion of his overall message. Pauline literature suggests that, soon after Gentiles converted, Paul gave them the commands of God regarding sexual purity. He repeatedly and solemnly warned that violating these commands would be tantamount to rejecting God, putting at serious risk their inheritance of God's kingdom (Rom. 1:24–27; 6:19; 13:12–14; 1 Cor. 5; 6:9–20; 10:8, 12; 2 Cor. 12:21; Gal. 5:19–21 [cf. 6:7–9]; Eph. 4:17–19; 5:3–6; Col. 3:5–10; 1 Thess. 4:1–8; 1 Tim. 1:9–11; outside the Gospels and Pauline literature: the apostolic decree in Acts 15; Heb. 12:16; 13:4; 1 Pet. 4:2–5; 2 Pet. 2:4–10, 13–16; Jude 7; Rev. 2:14, 20–21; 9:20–21; 21:8; 22:15).

Reaching Out in Love to Violators. For Jesus, the significance of sexual ethics goes hand in hand with loving outreach to sexual sinners (Matt. 21:31–32; Luke 7:36–50; John 4:16–18; 7:53–8:11). Jesus undertook the same type of outreach on behalf of the biggest economic exploiters of his immediate context, tax collectors (Mark 2:15–17; Matt. 11:19//Luke 7:34; Luke 15; 19:1–10). From Jesus' outreach to sexual sinners, the inference is often drawn that sexual sin is a relatively minor matter. However, Jesus' outreach to tax collectors suggests rather that outreach to sexual sinners correlates precisely with the seriousness of sexual sin. For his followers, Jesus modeled an intensified sexual ethic and warnings, combined with aggressive outreach in love to those who most violated this ethic. Moreover, he coupled this outreach with a joyous and generous readiness to forgive (Matt. 20:1–16; Luke 15:22–24; 18:9–14), even when professed repentance followed a ridiculously high number of repeat offenses (Matt. 18:21–22; Luke 17:3–4).

It would be a mistake, however, to regard such ministry as necessarily incompatible with ecclesiastical discipline for professed followers of Jesus (cf. Matt. 18:15–20 with 1 Cor. 5; 2 Cor. 2:6–11; 7:8–13; 2 Thess. 3:6, 14–15). For discipline, too, aims at recovery of the offender. Jesus himself could pronounce harsh judgments on the impenitent and those who rejected his outreach (e.g., Matt. 11:22–24//Luke 10:13–15; Matt. 12:39–41//Luke 11:29–32; Mark 6:11; Matt. 10:14//Luke 9:5; 10:10–11).

The story of Jesus and the woman caught in adultery in John 7:53–8:11—probably not of Johannine authorship but rather a later insertion—has had enormous influence. Some have read Jesus' statements about not casting a stone (8:7, 11) as criticism of any judgment about another's sexual behavior. This assumption misreads the story. In context, "condemn" means to "execute the sentence of stoning," literal stoning, not mere judgment. The problem with stoning is that it has a terminal effect. Apparently, Jesus thought the risk of eternal forfeiture of God's kingdom was so serious that it required every last option for repentance in this life (cf. Matt. 10:28//Luke 12:4–5). Jesus' remarkable display of mercy, saving her from a punishment stipulated by the Mosaic law (Deut. 22:23–24), was designed to stimulate gratitude and obedience, lest a worse fate befall the woman on judgment day. "From now on sin no more" (8:11 AT). On love and righteousness in Jesus' ministry, see further works by Gagnon (*Homosexual Practice*, 210–28; Gagnon and Via, 50–52, 70–71).

The Value of Sexual Intimacy in Marriage. There are no sayings of Jesus that extol the joys of sex in marriage—perhaps not surprisingly, in view of Jesus' own celibacy. But he was slandered as "a glutton and a drunkard" (Matt. 11:19//Luke 7:34; cf. Mark 2:18–20) and did not view the command to procreate in Gen. 1:28 as binding on all (Matt. 19:11–12). Hence, it seems unlikely that

Jesus viewed sexual intercourse as serving the purpose solely of procreation.

The same is true of Paul. Some scholars argue, based largely on 1 Cor. 7 and 1 Thess. 4:4–5, that Paul thought sexual passion per se was dishonorable (e.g., Fredrickson 207–9, 222; Balch, passim). However, this confuses Paul's position on sexual desire with the ascetic stance of some Corinthian believers, who were arguing they had become so "spiritual" (*pneumatikoi*) that they could do without intercourse in marriage (1 Cor. 7:1; cf. 1 Tim. 4:3a). Perhaps they held conscious awareness of a saying of Jesus on the unmarried state of angels (Mark 12:25) and the baptismal formula "there is no 'male and female'" (Gal. 3:28 AT; cf. its omission in 1 Cor. 12:13; Col. 3:11). It was Paul who exhorted married believers not to abstain from sexual relations. Indeed, he contends, men and women owe it to each other *equally* to fulfill the other's sexual needs (1 Cor. 7:3; cf. 11:11). He repeatedly states that getting married, and thus satisfying sexual desires, is no sin (7:28, 36–38; cf. 1 Tim. 4:3b–5; 5:14). It is particularly significant that 1 Cor. 7 shows relatively little concern for procreation; satisfying the sexual desire of one's spouse has value in its own right. Paul's expressed preference for singleness was motivated more by pragmatic missionary considerations, particularly in light of perceived nearness of the end, than by antipassion bias (7:26–35).

Furthermore, Paul's promotion of sexual activity within marriage was probably conditioned, at least in part, by Corinthian arguments. Since they stressed that their exalted spiritual status had enabled them to transcend tempting sexual urges, Paul countered by focusing on marriage as an institution given by God for the responsible release of such desires. First Corinthians 7 probably does not record everything Paul believed about marriage. There are no substantial grounds for assuming he dispensed with the vibrant image of marital intimacy put forward by Gen. 2:18–24; 29:9–30; Deut. 24:5; Prov. 5:15–23; Eccles. 9:9; Mal. 2:13–16; and, of course, the sensual poetry of the Song of Solomon. Paul was not a strict ascetic (Phil. 4:12). It is not likely that he was unmarried, or promoted singleness, because he wanted to deny himself and others all sexual pleasures. Even 1 Thess. 4:4–5 is not an exhortation to passionless sex, but rather not to make physical beauty the paramount consideration for mate selection.

The Penultimate Value of Sex. Paul's remarks about the value of single life given over to service underscore the penultimate significance of sexual intimacy. Jesus expressed a similar point in Matt. 19:11–12. Partly agreeing with his disciples that "it is not expedient to marry" (19:10 RSV), he also qualified their conclusion by saying: "Not everyone can accept this message, but only those to whom it has been given" (AT). This specifically means "those who [make] . . . themselves eunuchs for the sake of the kingdom of heaven" (19:12 NRSV; cf. Luke 18:29). Paul agreed with Jesus (1 Cor. 7:7): God has given some persons special capacity to forgo marriage, with its attendant sexual pleasures and obligation to procreate. Jesus also noted that in their resurrected state people "neither marry nor are given in marriage, but are like angels in heaven" (Mark 12:25 NRSV//Matt. 22:29//Luke 20:34–36; cf. 1 Cor. 7:29, 31). Even the human institution of marriage will one day be subsumed by the heavenly marriage of the people of God to Christ or God (Isa. 54:5; 62:4–5; Jer. 2:2; 3:20; Ezek. 16:8; Hos. 2:19–20; Matt. 22:1–14; 25:1–13; Mark 2:19–20; John 3:29; 2 Cor. 11:2; Eph. 5:27, 31–32; Rev. 19:7–9; 21:2, 9).

None of this meant that sexual differentiation and sexual norms no longer mattered in this age. To the contrary: Precisely because sexual fulfillment was not a necessity, Jesus and his followers could maintain and even intensify OT prerequisites and rules. In the context of discussing sexuality issues in 1 Cor. 7, Paul, the apostle of grace, could insist that what counted was "keeping God's commands" (v. 19). Even reference to celibacy as gift (v. 7) could not be turned into a wedge for prying loose binding prerequisites for sexual behavior. So long as one could not find a partner who met the prerequisites for marriage, one could assume God's empowerment to chastity in singleness. There is a difference between imposing a celibacy requirement and maintaining prerequisites for a valid sexual relationship. Scripture provides a conditional opportunity for sexual intimacy, not an opportunity by right. Sexual purity is a necessity; sexual gratification is not.

Jesus and Scripture on Homosexuality

Jesus' View. There is little historical doubt about Jesus' view of homosexual practice. Although focused on the indissolubility of marriage, in Mark 10:5–9 he clearly *presupposed* that the presence of a "male and female" was an important prerequisite of marriage (Gen. 1:27). Only a "man" and a "woman" are structurally capable of being "joined" through a sexually intimate relationship into a one-flesh union (2:24). The explicit mention of a two-sex pairing in these texts is not incidental but rather expresses the most essential intrahuman requirement for sexual relations. Of special note is Jesus' back-to-back linking of Gen. 1:27 and 2:24, which suggests that Jesus meant "for this reason" (in Mark 10:7) to introduce Gen. 2:24 as a back-reference to the gender differentiation established in 1:27. *For this reason*—because God made them "male and female," complementary sexual beings (1:27)— man and woman may be joined in a permanent one-flesh union (2:24). For Jesus, then, the Creator ordained marriage—it was not just a social construct—as a lifelong union of one man and one woman. Both the Scriptures Jesus cited with approval and the audience addressed—indeed, the whole of early Judaism, so far as extant evidence indicates (Gagnon, *Homosexual Practice*, 159–83)—presumed the male-female prerequisite as critical. Had Jesus wanted his disciples to think otherwise, he would have had to state such a view clearly. As it is, we know of no dissenting opinions on the issue in earliest Christianity.

In addressing marriage's permanence, Jesus was not making lifelong monogamy a more important consideration for sexual relations than the heterosexual or other-sex dimension. The latter remained the unalterable prime prerequisite for all considerations of fidelity. Certainly, no reasonable person would argue that Jesus prioritized monogamy and permanence over the nonincestuous and nonbestial character of normative sexual relationships. Because Jesus' conviction about a male-female prerequisite at creation was shared throughout early Judaism, he could focus on other facets over which disputes existed in his cultural context.

There are other sayings of Jesus besides Mark 10:6–9 that, taken in the context of early Judaism, implicitly forbade same-sex intercourse. For example, he speaks against "sexual immoralities" (*porneiai*) in Mark 7:21, a term that for Jews of the Second Temple period called to mind the forbidden offenses in Lev. 18 and 20, particularly incest, adultery, same-sex intercourse, and bestiality. This is reinforced in the prohibition of *porneia* in the apostolic decree in Acts 15:20, 29; 21:25, which was formulated with Lev. 18 in view (Gagnon, *Homosexual Practice*, 435–36). In Mark 10:17–22 Jesus affirmed the seventh commandment, against adultery (Exod. 20:14; Deut. 5:18), which presupposes preservation of the male-female marital bond (cf. the tenth commandment, on not coveting a neighbor's wife). Early Judaism could use this commandment as a rubric for treating sex laws in the Bible, including proscriptions of male-male intercourse (cf. Philo,

Spec. 3). Jesus' acknowledgment of Sodom's role in Scripture is the prime example of abusing visitors in Matt. 10:14–15//Luke 10:10–12, which in the context of other early Jewish texts indicates special revulsion for the attempt at treating males sexually as females (cf. Philo, *Abr.* 133–41 and *QG* 4.37; Josephus, *A.J.* 1.194–95, 200–201 and *B.J.* 4.483–85; 5.566; *T. Naph.* 3:3–4; *2 En.* 10:4; 34:1–2). Within Scripture, Ezek. 16:50; 2 Pet. 2:6–10; and Jude 7 also point in this direction (Gagnon, *Homosexual Practice*, 79–91; Gagnon and Via 57–59, with online notes 33–36). Jesus warns against giving "what is holy to dogs" (Matt. 7:6 NRSV), a likely echo of Deut. 23:17–18 (18–19 MT). That text forbids any Israelite from using the wages of a "dog" or *qadesh* (the self-styled "holy man," "sacred one," but often translated "male temple prostitute") to pay a vow to the "house of Yahweh" (for "dog," cf. Rev. 22:15 with 21:8; on the subject of the *qedeshim*, cultic "men-women" who sometimes served as the receptive partners in male-male intercourse, see Gagnon, *Homosexual Practice*, 100–110).

Jesus did not advocate that the law of Moses be abrogated (Matt. 5:17–18//Luke 16:17). He did not even abolish minute rules about tithing herbs (Matt. 23:23//Luke 11:42), to say nothing of sexual laws about which Jesus apparently cared a great deal. Jesus was a much less vigorous critic of the law of Moses than Paul, and we know what Paul's view of same-sex intercourse was. (See further: Gagnon, *Homosexual Practice*, 185–209; Gagnon and Via 68–74, with online notes 59–73, esp. 59.)

Paul's View. Paul understood same-sex intercourse as an affront to the Creator's stamp on gender in Gen. 1–2. In Romans, Paul cites two prime examples of humans suppressing the truth about God evident in creation/nature: idolatry and same-sex intercourse (1:18–27). Paul first talks about humans exchanging the Creator's glory for worship of idols made "in the *likeness* of the *image* of a perishable *human* and of *birds* and *animals* and *reptiles*" (1:23 AT). Then he writes about "*females* [who] exchanged the natural use" and "*males* leaving behind the natural use of the female" to have intercourse with other "males" (1:26–27 AT). This obviously echoes Gen. 1:26–27. There are not only eight points of correspondence between Gen. 1:26–27 and Rom. 1:23, 26–27, but also a threefold sequential agreement: (1) God's likeness and image in humans, (2) dominion over the animal kingdom, and (3) male-female differentiation. What is the point of this echo? Idolatry and same-sex intercourse oppose the work of the

Creator. Those who have suppressed the truth about God transparent in creation were more likely to suppress the truth about the complementarity of the sexes transparent in nature, choosing instead to gratify contrary innate impulses (on Rom. 1:24–27, see further Gagnon, *Homosexual Practice*, 246–303, 361–80; Gagnon and Via 76–81, with online notes 76–95, esp. 76, 88; Gagnon, "Review Essay 2," 182–87, 206–26).

Paul's readers would pick up these echoes. But Paul's argument goes further. Even Gentiles unaware of Scripture have enough revelation in creation/nature to know that males with females, not females with females or males with males, are complementary sexual beings. In effect, Paul is saying: Start with the obvious fittedness of human anatomy; when done with that, consider procreative design as a clue; then move to a broad range of interpersonal differences that define maleness and femaleness. These are much better clues to God's will for human sexuality than preexisting, controlling passions—which can be warped by the fall and shaped by socialization factors.

In 1 Cor. 6:9 (AT; cf. 1 Tim. 1:10) Paul mentions "men who lie with a male" (*arsenokoitai*)—a term formed from the absolute prohibitions of men lying with a male in Lev. 18:22 and 20:13—in a list of offenders that risk not inheriting the kingdom of God. Just as Rom. 1:26–27 has Gen. 1:27 in view, so too 1 Cor. 6:9 has Gen. 2:24 in view about a "man" and a "woman" joining to become "one flesh" (partially cited in 1 Cor. 6:16). In the background of references to homosexual behavior, Paul lifts up the same two texts, Gen. 1:27 and 2:24, that Jesus cited as normative. Paul recognizes the obvious implication of these texts for prohibiting all forms of same-sex intercourse. Taken in the context of remarks in 1 Cor. 5 (a case of adult incest) and 7 (male-female marriage), there is little doubt that Paul understood the offense of "men who lie with males" in 1 Cor. 6:9 (AT) as substitution of another male for a female in sexual activity. Put differently, it is abandonment of an other-sex structural prerequisite to a holistic sexual union (on 1 Cor. 6:9 and 1 Tim. 1:10, see further Gagnon, *Homosexual Practice*, 303–36; Gagnon and Via 81–88 [with online notes 96–111, esp. 97, 99]; idem, "Review Essay 2," 226–39).

That Paul did not limit his opposition to homosexual practice only to certain exploitative forms is evident both from his indictment of lesbian intercourse in Rom. 1:26 and from advocacy for nonexploitative homoerotic behavior that persisted in many quarters of the Greco-Roman world (Gagnon, *Homosexual Practice*, 347–61). Moreover, modern views about "homosexual orientation" would have made little difference to Paul's critique. There were "pagan" moralists and physicians who both posited something akin to homosexual orientation and held such desires to be "contrary to nature" even when given "by nature" (Gagnon, *Homosexual Practice*, 380–95; "Intrinsically Sinful?" 141–52). We know that Paul viewed sin as an innate impulse, operating in the members of the human body, passed on by an ancestor, and never entirely within human control (Rom. 7:7–23).

Genesis and Rationale. The main problem with same-sex intercourse is that it does not restore the original sexual unity portrayed in Gen. 1:27 and 2:21–24. Genesis 1:27 brings into close connection creation "in God's image" and creation as "male and female." When humans engage in sexual activity, they engage another in their sexual particularity, as only one incomplete part of a two-faceted sexual whole. Ignoring this particularity effaces that part of the divine image stamped on human sexuality. Procreative capacity (1:28) is an important dimension of male-female complementarity, but only one among others. The Priestly material gives attention to structural congruity or "kinds" (1:11–12, 21, 24–25; 6:20; 7:14) and likely would not have equated an infertile male-female union with a homoerotic union. In the Yahwistic material of Gen. 2:18–24, a binary, or sexually undifferentiated, human is split down the "side" (a better translation than "rib") into two constituent parts, man and woman. Sexual relations are pictured as reconstitution or remerger of these two parts into a sexual whole. Homoerotic unions are precluded as a matter of course. One's sexual counterpart, complement, or "other half" is still missing.

Men and women are different in ways that complement—fill in the gaps of and moderate—the sexuality of the other. It is one of the great ironies of the modern prohomosexual lobby that it often argues for the insignificance of sexual differentiation while insisting that most homosexual persons have an "orientation"—not mere tastes or preferences—solely toward persons of the same sex. If men and women are really not all that different, why is there little attraction to the opposite sex on the part of many who claim homoerotic attraction? Throw in exclusively oriented heterosexuals, and over 95 percent of the population in Western society limits selection of mates to persons of a particular sex. No other criterion for mate selection comes even close to this consideration. Clearly, there is a basic human acknowledgment that a person's sex matters.

This brings us to the point. Sexual attraction for persons of the same sex amounts to sexual narcissism or self-deception. There is either conscious recognition that one desires in another what one already possesses as a sexual being (anatomy, physiology, sex-based traits) or self-delusion of sorts in which the sexual same is perceived as some kind of significant sexual other. Sexual intimacy is not just about more intimacy. If it were, Jesus' love commandment would imply that we should have sexually intimate relationships with all believers rather than restrict sexual relationships to lifelong monogamy. One should be intimate with parents, siblings, and children, but not *sexually* intimate. Sexual intimacy is a special kind that involves *merging* with another who is structurally compatible to oneself, manifesting the right degree of likeness and unlikeness to make the merger truly complementary. Homoerotic relationships represent a misguided attempt at completing the sexual self with a sexual same when true integration requires a complementary sexual "other." Concerns about fidelity, monogamy, permanence, and love come into play only once prerequisites for an acceptable sexual union have been met.

The Rest of Scripture. Given adequate space, it is possible to show, through examination of literary and historical contexts as well as the history of interpretation, that the stories of Sodom in Gen. 19:4–11, of the Levite at Gibeah in Judg. 19:22–25, and of Ham's act against Noah in Gen. 9:20–27—these all include an indictment of male-male intercourse per se, not just of coercive acts (Gagnon, *Homosexual Practice*, 63–100; Gagnon and Via 56–62). One could show that the prohibitions in Lev. 18:22 and 20:13 are not antiquated purity laws (Gagnon, *Homosexual Practice*, 111–46; Gagnon and Via 62–68, 100–101, online rejoinder to Via, 22–28). Indeed, every text in Scripture having anything to do with sexual relations (laws, moral exhortations, narratives, poetry, prophetic speech metaphors) presupposes a heterosexual requirement (Gagnon, *Homosexual Practice*, 432–39). It is relatively easy to demonstrate that in ancient Israel, early Judaism, and early Christianity the only form of "consensual" sexual behavior consistently regarded as a more severe infraction than homosexual practice was bestiality (Gagnon and Via, online note 17). Historical evidence indicates that every author of Scripture, as well as Jesus, would have been appalled by homosexual relationships, committed or otherwise. This assessment does not absolve the church of obligation to love those who seek to gratify homosexual desire, but rather informs believers on how the church should love such persons.

The Hermeneutics of the Gentile Inclusion Analogy. The narrative in Acts 10:1–11:18 and chapter 15, which recounts the inclusion of Gentiles into the church apart from circumcision and, implicitly, some food laws, is often cited as precedent for disregarding the Bible's prohibition of homosexual practice. The argument is that the Spirit contravened Scripture, and so why not now also be free from Scripture?

There are many reasons why the alleged analogy is unworkable, some of which have already been suggested. (1) Jesus grounded the two-sexes prerequisite for marriage in the will of God, established at creation—a fact that gave it preeminent significance for him. Circumcision is not grounded in creation structures. Paul correctly understood this (Rom. 1:24–27; 2:25–29; ch. 4; 6:19; 1 Cor. 6:9; 7:18–19). (2) The alleged analogy treats as comparable distinctively *Jewish ritual* requirements that affect the body *superficially* and *universal standards* for sexual ethics that affect the body *holistically*. While Jesus gave diminished significance to diet and Sabbath regulations, he intensified God's demands in sexual ethics. He rejected an equation between food that enters the body and desires for prohibited sexual conduct that proceed from the body (Mark 7:14–23). Paul likewise contended that sexual behavior could not come unreservedly under the slogan "all things are permissible for me" (1 Cor. 6:12–20; cf. Rom. 13:13–14:23). Immoral sexual behavior—unlike Gentile failure to observe laws regarding circumcision, diet, and calendar—could lead to exclusion from God's kingdom (1 Cor. 6:9; 7:18–19). (3) The alleged analogy confuses what Acts 15 clearly distinguishes: welcoming *persons* and accepting *behaviors*. The apostolic decree forbade continued participation in *porneia* (15:20, 29; 21:25) and did so with the Lev. 18 sex laws in view. Paul similarly welcomed Gentiles into the household of faith while commanding them not to live like (unbelieving) Gentiles, especially with regard to engaging in sexual behavior that Scripture categorically forbids (Rom. 6:19; 1 Thess. 4:3–8; cf. Eph. 4:17–24; 5:3–5).

(4) The alleged analogy between prescribing circumcision and proscribing homosexual practice overlooks the degree to which Scripture and the putative new work of the Spirit are in tension. Embrace of uncircumcised Gentiles has significant OT precedents and uniform NT sup-

port, whereas embrace of homosexual practice constitutes a radical departure from Scripture. (5) The justifications for such claims tend to be naive. Advocates of homosexual practice wrongly assume that evidence of the Spirit's outworking in one area of a person's life (for example, in exhibiting care for a same-sex partner) necessarily validates other areas (having sex with that partner). They also presuppose that any behavior that does not produce scientifically measurable harm to all participants in all circumstances must be acceptable in some circumstances, thereby ignoring the implication for some adult incest, polygamy, and even adult-child sex. (6) The alleged analogy sidesteps completely the reason why Scripture regards same-sex intercourse as wrong: a dishonoring of the sexual self's integrity through attempted completion with what one already is as a sexual being. Finally, (7) the alleged analogy disregards the significant differences between ethnicity and "sexual orientation." Whereas the former is culturally immutable and intrinsically benign, the latter is a condition that is neither genetically predetermined nor transparently neutral. As with alcoholism or pedophilia, there is good indication that macrocultural (society) and microcultural (familial, peer) influences, as well as incremental choices, can influence the intensity and even incidence of homosexual development. (On this analogy, see further Gagnon, *Homosexual Practice*, 460–69; Gagnon and Via 43–44, with online notes; on the high rates of harm, see Gagnon, *Homosexual Practice*, 452–60, 471–85; Gagnon and Via online note 167.)

Bibliography

Allison, D. *Jesus of Nazareth*. Fortress, 1998; Balch, D., ed. *Homosexuality, Science, and the "Plain Sense" of Scripture*. Eerdmans, 2000; Brawley, R., ed. *Biblical Ethics and Homosexuality*. Westminster John Knox, 1996; Brooten, B. *Love between Women*. University of Chicago Press, 1996; Campbell, K., ed. *Marriage and Family in the Biblical World*. InterVarsity, 2003; Carr, D. *The Erotic Word*. Oxford University Press, 2002; Collins, R. *Sexual Ethics and the New Testament*. Crossroad, 2000; Deming, W. *Paul on Marriage and Celibacy*. Cambridge University Press, 1995; De Young, J. *Homosexuality*. Kregel, 2000; Fredrickson, D. "Natural and Unnatural Use in Romans 1:24–27: Paul and Philosophic Critique of Eros." Pages 197–222 in *Homosexuality, Science . . .* , ed. D. Balch. Eerdmans, 2000; Gagnon, R. "Are There Universally Valid Sex Precepts? A Critique of Walter Wink's Views on the Bible and Homosexuality." *HBT* 24 (2002): 72–125; idem. *The Bible and Homosexual Practice*. Abingdon, 2001; idem. "A Comprehensive and Critical Review Essay of [D. Balch's] *Homosexuality, Science, and the 'Plain Sense' of Scripture*, Part 1" and "Part 2." *HBT* 22 (2000): 174–243; 25 (2003): 173–275; idem. "Does the Bible Regard Same-Sex Intercourse as Intrinsically Sinful?" In *Christian Sexuality*. Kirk House, 2003; Gagnon, R., and D. Via. *Homosexuality and the Bible*. Fortress, 2003. Online notes: http://www.robgagnon.net/TwoViews.htm (additional articles by Gagnon online: www.robgagnon.net); Greenberg, D. *The Construction of Homosexuality*. University of Chicago Press, 1988; Grenz, S. *Sexual Ethics*. Word, 1990; idem. *Welcoming but Not Affirming*. Westminster John Knox, 1998; Hays, R. *The Moral Vision of the New Testament*. HarperCollins, 1996; Hugenberger, G. *Marriage as a Covenant*. Brill, 1994; Instone-Brewer, D. *Divorce and Remarriage in the Bible*. Eerdmans, 2002; Keener, C. *And Marries Another*. Hendrickson, 1991; Nissinen, M. *Homoeroticism in the Biblical World*. Fortress, 1998; Satlow, M. *Jewish Marriage in Antiquity*. Princeton University Press, 2001; Schmidt, T. *Straight and Narrow?* InterVarsity, 1995; Scroggs, R. *The New Testament and Homosexuality*. Fortress, 1983; Swartley, W. *Homosexuality*. Herald Press, 2003; Watson, F. *Agape, Eros, Gender*. Cambridge University Press, 2000; Webb, W. *Slaves, Women, and Homosexuals*. InterVarsity, 2001; Winter, B. *After Paul Left Corinth*. Eerdmans, 2001.

Robert A. J. Gagnon

Significance   See Meaning

Sin, Doctrine of

Ancient Christian interpreters of the Bible developed a scheme to unify the heterogeneity of scriptural texts into a single, overall reading. Following suggestions in Paul's letters, early Christian readers understood the Bible as an account of the unfolding dispensation or economy of God. To use more modern terms, the Bible depicts an unfolding "salvation-history" (von Rad), "narrative" (Frei), or "drama" (Balthasar). In each case, theological interpretation involves placing individual texts into a temporal scheme structured by divine purpose. This method of interpretation has intrascriptural warrant. The structuring role of a historical or narrative scheme is already present in the Scriptures themselves (cf. Neh. 9; Deut. 6:20–24).

The schemes for framing a unified reading of Scripture are diverse. Modern scholars have noted, for example, that Greek patristic theology tends to view the drama of Scripture as an ascent to participation in God, while Latin patristic theology tends to treat the narrative as a story of justice and debt payment. Moreover, the conceptual techniques for describing the unfolding dispensations vary (e.g., promise/fulfillment, carnal/spiritual, shadow/substance). Within this diversity, however, Christian theological interpretation has consistently identified sin as the crucial inner-worldly reality that shapes the economy presented in Scripture. Numerous patristic figures summarize the scriptural narrative according to a scheme of creation-fall-redemption (cf. Irenaeus). Like Macbeth's murder of Duncan, the transgression of Adam and Eve sets in motion the chain of events that stretches from Genesis through Revelation. Sin is the singular fact over and against which God acts.

The Essence of Sin

Although universally acknowledged by the tradition, theological interpreters have developed no consensus about the nature and root of sin, and there are no ecumenical doctrines that define the essence of sin. In the late patristic period, divergent accounts of the origin or foundation of sin developed. The Eastern monastic tradition identified eight "evil thoughts" that ascended from temptations of the flesh to spiritual dangers such as sloth and pride (Cassian). In contrast, the Western pastoral tradition formulated the sequence from a foundational pride to the outworkings of sin in lust and gluttony (Gregory the Great). In the post-Reformation West, definitions of sin were seen as church-dividing issues (cf. Trent, *Sessio* V; The Formula of Concord, art. 1).

The lack of consensus about the essence of sin reflects the diversity of scriptural terminology: *hamartia* (missing the mark), *parabasis* (transgression), *adikia* (unrighteousness), *asebeia* (impiety), *anomia* (lawlessness), *ponēria* (depravity), and *epithymia* (evil desire). Furthermore, the rich OT vocabulary of prostitution and other forms of idolatrous defilement adds distinctive color to biblical depictions of human sinfulness. Finally, the Scriptures offer divergent descriptions of the root or cause of sin: pride goes before the fall (Prov. 16:18); love of money is the root of all evil (1 Tim. 6:10); the evil tongue is the source of iniquity (James 3:6).

Two narrative moments in Scripture exemplify the difficulty of specifying the nature of sin. Genesis 3:1–7 depicts the original transgression of Adam and Eve. In a homily on this passage, the influential patristic interpreter John Chrysostom retells the story without settling on a single explanation for the fall. He moves from serpent, to Eve, to Adam, drawing in envy, negligence, ignorance, disobedience, and pride. The fall has no single, identifiable cause. The multiple directions of temptation are present in the threefold temptation of Jesus, which the patristic tradition linked to the triad of evil itemized in 1 John 2:16. An even greater plurality characterizes the Gospel accounts of Jesus' passion. An atmosphere of blindness, deception, complicity, fear, greed, collective madness, and menace characterizes the scene in Jerusalem, and the narrative resists efforts to resolve sin into a single form or cause.

The diverse and allusive biblical witness to the reality of sin encourages a fundamentally negative definition. Sin is not an ontological category. It is not a function of embodiment or finitude. For Augustine, sin is disordered desire, not desire itself. Sin is perverse love. Nor can sin be reduced to a single, fundamental motive, such as pride. Instead, sin is a temporal category. Augustine uses the image of weight, describing human personality as dynamic and always moving either upward to God or downward toward corruption. This image captures a patristic consensus that sin is a direction of life away from God. For this reason, as Karl Barth has argued most forcefully, sin is most visible and evident in contrast to the righteousness and holiness of God, revealed in Jesus Christ. The idolatry described by Paul in Rom. 1 is revealed by the possibility of true worship.

Although sin is a personal and not ontological reality, a function of will and not nature, the role of sin in the drama of salvation has definite features.

The Universality of Sin

The universality of redemption presupposes the universality of sin. Paul's genealogy of sin in the first chapters of Romans sets the stage for the universal role of Christ. Neither Jew nor Gentile escapes the stain of sin. "There is no distinction, since all have sinned and fall short of the glory of God" (Rom. 3:22–23 NRSV). The universality of sin even extends to the created order, which is subjected to futility and bondage to decay (8:20–21). The cosmic scope of sin sets the stage for a cosmic redemption: "Turn to me and be saved, all the ends of the earth" (Isa. 45:22 NRSV). The universal need for redemption, not particular passages in Scripture that suggest the ubiquity of sin (Ps. 14), presses theological interpreters to emphasize original sin. For Paul, the destiny of the entire created order turns on the death and resurrection of Jesus Christ, and this entails presuming that sin penetrates all aspects of life.

Sin Is Unnatural

It is very tempting to imagine that sin is a consequence of embodiment. Paul warns of the "passions of our flesh" (Eph. 2:3 NRSV), speaks of "the law of sin that dwells in my members" (Rom. 7:23 NRSV), and consistently uses the word "carnal" to describe the path of sin. Yet, a theological reading of the Scriptures blocks a "carnal reading" of these and other passages as indicating that sin is an upshot of our embodied, natural existence. Any suggestion that instinct or bodily needs cause sin is inconsistent with Gen. 1. The universality of sin cannot be linked to the shared, embodied condition of human beings (cf. Jenson's clear discussion in *Human*). On the contrary, sin is a perversion or disorder of human nature. For this reason, the reality of sin does not require a theological reading of Scripture that portrays the gospel as disembodied. The drama of redemption takes place within a created order that is intrinsically good and therefore fit for sanctification. The Roman Catholic rejection of the Reformation doctrine of total depravity was motivated by the fear that the Reformers were defining sin as destroying or replacing the human nature that God had created and called good. The concern is linked to criticisms of forensic justification, raising the objection that Reformation doctrines of sin and salvation do not permit an inner-worldly drama of salvation. Unless theological exegesis presumes that sin is unnatural, accounts of salvation will tend to become otherworldly or purely eschatological.

Sin Is Determinative

The universality of sin is not peripheral to human identity. Sin shapes life. To use Paul's language, sin enslaves, dictating the direction of human life. The direction is dynamic, gaining speed and intensity, leading to greater and greater iniquity (Rom. 6:19). However intrinsically good the created reality, sin has perverted life to its very marrow. For this reason, the very identity of the sinner is defined by sin, and that identity must be destroyed. Echoing Paul again, the old man must die and a new man must be born if one is to turn from a life defined by sin to a life of righteousness (Rom. 6:6–8). A redemptive change in direction will come as a blow of judgment that ends this perverted life. For this reason, theological interpretation of redemption must be structured by the radical disjunction of death and resurrection. The Reformation insistence on the doctrine of total depravity was motivated by the fear that Roman Catholic accounts did not make sin determinative of the identity of persons, softening the blow of judgment and eliminating the disjunction of new life in Christ. Unless one understands sin as determinative, theological exegesis cannot portray the life-and-death drama of redemption.

Sin Can Be Transferred

Each person rightly bears the consequences for his or her sin. Those who sin "deserve to die" (Rom. 1:32 NRSV). Here, the language of payment and debt is prominent in the theological tradition. When the Son of Man comes in glory, the Father "will repay everyone for what has been done" (Matt. 16:27 NRSV). We rightly merit punishment, for sin is determinative; it characterizes who we are. In the history of theology about original sin, its nature and transmission, a great deal of the debate stems from the desire to explain how each of us can be held accountable for the sinfulness that is universal and inescapable. Some explanations are more persuasive than others. The important point, however, is that a theological interpretation of Scripture must define sin as a personal liability, but also as a transferable liability, a debt that can be taken up by another. For the crux of the biblical drama of redemption is the *pro-nobis* (for-us) role of Jesus Christ. He can take the blow of judgment in our place. However determinative of each person's life, the weight and power of sin can be assumed by another.

The possibility of the transfer of sin is presupposed in the ritual dynamics of atonement, both in its OT (Leviticus) and NT (Hebrews) uses. This transfer is not limited to ritual contexts and language. Isaiah 53 and Rom. 4 presume the possibility of one assuming the sin of another, with Paul concerned about the even more important possibility of the transfer or "reckoning" of righteousness. The history of theology in the West has been characterized by extensive debate about the specific conditions for such a transfer (e.g., substitutionary atonement) and the proper vocabulary for expressing the currency of transfer (e.g., debt, punishment). This debate presumes that the most personal of realities—sin—can be assumed by another. This presumption must characterize theological interpretation. For without the possibility of transfer of sin, the redemptive economy of the entire sweep of the biblical witness cannot turn on the identity of one man, Jesus Christ, on whom is concentrated the sin of the whole world, that all might die to their sin and rise in his righteousness.

See also Human Being, Doctrine of; Original Sin

Bibliography

Augustine. *On True Religion*. In *Augustine: Earlier Writings*. Westminster, 1953; Balthasar, H. U. von. *Theodrama*. Vol. 1. Ignatius, 1988; Barth, K. *Church Dogmatics*. Vol. IV/1, trans. G. Bromiley. T&T Clark, 1956; Bloomfield, M. *The Seven Deadly Sins*. Michigan State

Press, 1952; Cassian, J. *The Conferences*. Paulist, 1997; Chrysostom, J. *Homilies on Genesis* 1–17. Catholic University of America Press, 1986; Frei, H. *The Eclipse of Biblical Narrative*. Yale University Press, 1974; Hodge, C. *Systematic Theology*. Vol. 2. Scribner, Armstrong, 1872; Irenaeus. *Against the Heresies*. Book 1. Newman, 1992; Jenson, R. *On Thinking the Human*. Eerdmans, 2003; idem. *Systematic Theology*. Vol. 2. Oxford University Press, 1999; Menke, K.-H. *Stellvertretung*. Johannes, 1991; Nellas, P. *Deification in Christ*. St. Vladimir's, 1987; Rad, G. von. *Old Testament Theology*. 2 vols. Westminster John Knox, 2001; Soulen, R. K. *The God of Israel and Christian Theology*. Fortress, 1996.

R. R. Reno

Slavery

The biblical texts dealing with slavery have much to teach the church about how to understand and apply the Bible. One must make a crucial distinction between (1) a *redemptive-movement* appropriation of Scripture, which encourages movement beyond the original application of the text in the ancient world; and (2) a more *static* or *stationary* appropriation of Scripture. The latter understands the words of the text in isolation from their canonical and cultural context and aside from, or with minimal emphasis upon, their underlying spirit. It thus restricts contemporary application of Scripture to how the words of the text were applied in their original setting. While beyond the focus of this article, it is important to note that both aspects of redemptive-movement meaning contained in canonical movement and cultural movement provide an essential, though often overlooked, part of textual meaning within the words of Scripture themselves (Webb).

An opening illustration from the slavery texts of these different approaches might be helpful. For instance, Deuteronomy instructs Israel to provide safety and refuge to slaves fleeing harsh treatment from a foreign country (Deut. 23:15–16). Upon crossing Israel's borders, a fleeing slave was to be given shelter, was permitted to live in any of Israel's cities, and was not to be handed over to his/her master. The redemptive dimension of this slavery legislation sparkles brightly in comparison to the surrounding nations. Most ancient Near Eastern countries had extradition treaties and administered severe punishment to runaway slaves, to their families, and to those who aided in their escape.

A static hermeneutic would apply this slavery-refuge text by staying exactly with the words on the page, words read in isolation from their movement meaning. It would not use the spirit-

movement meaning in this text to cry out for the abolition of slavery today. Rather, it would permit slavery in our modern culture, but simply adopt some form of leniency toward runaway slaves within the church. Proponents of a stationary hermeneutic would support or at least permit the institution of slavery, but seek to give refuge to slaves in abusive relationships. Such an approach to applying the Bible emphasizes the words of the text in a highly isolated sense, while missing the spirit of the text.

Problems with the Slavery Texts

As one reads the biblical texts on slaves, an overwhelming impression emerges: *a less-than-ultimate ethic in the treatment of slaves is a major part of our Bibles*. If we clear away the technical language, we might simply say that there is a problem with the treatment of slaves in the Bible. There exist numerous "not so pretty" components within the slavery texts that illustrate a less-than-ultimate ethic in the treatment of slaves/people:

1. Human beings are considered to be property (Exod. 12:44; 21:20–21, 32; Lev. 22:11).
2. Foreign slaves in Israel did not experience the seventh year of release (Lev. 25:39–46).
3. Slaves within Israel were used to produce offspring for their infertile owners (Gen. 16:1–4; 30:3–4, 9–10; cf. 35:22).
4. Sexual violation of a betrothed slave woman led not to death, as in the case of a free woman (Deut. 22:25–27), but to a mere payment/offering for damages (Lev. 19:20–22).
5. Slave owners were permitted to beat their slaves without any penalty provided the slave survived by a couple of days (Exod. 21:20–21).
6. Biblical legislation contains inequality in the value placed on a slave's life compared to a free person's life (Exod. 21:28–32).

To call the biblical treatment of slaves "abusive" in terms of the original culture would be anachronistic. Relative to that culture, many of these texts were in some measure redemptive. Nevertheless, the above practices are problematic and in need of movement toward an ultimate ethic. A much more humane treatment of persons can be legislated and lived out in our modern civil-law settings. The theological implication is not that God himself has somehow "moved" in his thinking or that Scripture is in any way less than God's word. Rather, it means that God in a pastoral sense accommodates himself to meeting people and society where they are in their existing social ethic, and (from there) he gently moves them with incremental steps toward something better. Moving large, complex, and embedded social structures along on an ethical continuum is by no means a simple matter. Incremental movement within Scripture reveals a God who is willing to live with the tension between an absolute ethic in theory and the reality of guiding real people in practice toward such a goal.

Redemptive Movement Yields an Ultimate Ethic

Fortunately, there exists a "wonderful and inspiring" side to the biblical portrait of slaves. It is this positive side that establishes *redemptive movement as crucial meaning within the biblical text*. This movement meaning or redemptive-spirit meaning must profoundly shape the course of our contemporary appropriation of the Bible in a way that often carries us beyond the bound-in-time components of meaning within the biblical text. In the next set of examples the task of theological interpretation is to "listen" to the slavery texts within their cultural context (relative to the ancient world) and their canonical context (with movement to the NT):

1. The holidays for festivals and for the weekly Sabbath rest, compared to the ancient world, were generous (Deut. 16:10–12; Exod. 23:12).

2. In both Testaments slaves are included in the worship setting (Exod. 12:44; Deut. 12:12, 18; cf. Col. 3:22–4:6), and the NT church community profoundly raised a slave's status yet further to equality "in Christ" (Gal. 3:28). Some ancient cultures (such as the Roman Empire) restricted slaves from involvement in the sacred rituals and religious festivals because they were thought to have a defiling or polluting influence.

3. No-interest loans within Israel were an attempt to reduce the occurrence of debt slavery (Lev. 25:35–36; Deut. 15:1–2, 7–11); this compares with loan rates within the surrounding nations that were often well in excess of 20 percent interest.

4. The release of Hebrew debt slaves after a certain number of years compared with the ancient world is unique (excepting the code of Hammurabi) and a highly redemptive aspect to biblical legislation (Lev. 25:39–43; cf. Jer. 34:8–22).

5. Material assistance for released slaves stands out as a generous act of biblical law (Deut. 15:12–18).

6. Limitations were placed upon the severity of physical beatings (Exod. 21:20–21), and freedom was granted to any slave who was physically damaged (21:26–27). Other cultures did not limit the slave owner's power in this way; torturous abuse of select slaves often became an object lesson for others.

7. Masters are admonished to turn away from harshness and to show genuine care for their slaves (Col. 4:1; Eph. 6:9), transforming the slave-master relationship with a new sense of Christian brotherhood (Philem. 16).

8. Scripture denounces foreign countries (Gaza and Tyre) for stealing people in order to trade them as slaves (Exod. 21:16; Deut. 24:7; cf. 1 Tim. 1:10; Rev. 18:13).

9. In a radical departure from prevalent views, Israel became a safety zone or refuge for foreign runaway slaves (Deut. 23:15–16; cf. Isa. 16:3–4).

When the Bible's slavery texts are read against their contexts, redemptive movement becomes increasingly clear. These biblical modifications to the existing social norms brought greater protection and dignity for the slave. This improvement in the conditions of slaves relative to the original culture was clearly a redemptive action on the part of Scripture. Admittedly, it was not redemptive in any absolute sense. Scripture only moved the cultural "scrimmage markers" so far. Yet, that movement was sufficient to signal a clear direction in terms of further improvements for later generations. Redemptive-movement meaning was (and is) absolutely crucial to contemporary application.

If Christians are willing to listen to the underlying spirit of the slavery texts, these passages will (as was the case in the 1800s in Britain and the United States) persuade God's people toward the total abolition of slavery. Today the same redemptive spirit continues to speak to our modern work world even where slavery itself is no longer present. That voice calls for Christians to champion the cause of those less fortunate, to better the working conditions of those most vulnerable to abuse, and to be concerned in some collective way for the economic well-being of all people within our society.

See also Culture and Hermeneutics; Racism

Bibliography

Bradley, K. *Slavery and Society at Rome*. Cambridge University Press, 1994; Chirichigno, G. *Debt-Slavery in Israel and the Ancient Near East*. JSOTSup 141. Sheffield Academic Press, 1993; Garlan, Y. *Slavery in Ancient Greece*, trans. J. Lloyd. Cornell University Press, 1988; Giles, K. "The Biblical Argument for Slavery: Can the Bible Mislead? A Case Study in Hermeneutics." *EvQ* 66 (1994): 3–17; Meeks, W. "The 'Haustafeln' and American Slavery: A Hermeneutical Challenge." Pages 232–53 in *Theology and Ethics in Paul and His Interpreters*, ed. E. Lovering Jr. and J. Sumney. Abingdon, 1996; Mendelsohn, I. "Slavery in the Old Testament." *IDB* 4:383–91; Swartley, W. *Slavery, Sabbath, War, and Women*. Herald Press, 1983; Thompson, D. "Women, Men, Slaves and the Bible. Hermeneutical Inquiries." *Christian Scholar's Review* 25 (1996): 326–49; Tise, L. *Proslavery*. University of Georgia Press, 1987; Webb, W. *Slaves, Women and Homosexuals*. InterVarsity, 2001; idem. "The Limits of a Redemptive-Movement Hermeneutic: A Focused Response to T. R. Schreiner." *EvQ* 75, no. 4 (Oct. 2003): 327–42.

William J. Webb

Social-Scientific Criticism

Definition and Description

Social-scientific criticism of the Bible is "that phase of the exegetical task which analyses the social and cultural dimensions of the text and of its environmental context through the utilization of the perspectives, theory, models, and research of the social sciences" (Elliott 7). As such, it is part of the wider enterprise of historical criticism of the Bible. Its presupposition is that validity in interpretation of texts from the past like the Bible involves disciplined attention both to the intentions of the original author and to the meaning(s) of the text in its original historical setting.

However, whereas historical criticism focuses traditionally on questions of sources, dating, authorship, language, genre, history of tradition, historical background, and the history of the reception and interpretation of the text, social-scientific criticism attends to questions of a different but related kind. These are concerned not so much with diachronic aspects as with synchronic aspects, the typical social patterns and taken-for-granted cultural conditions and conceptions most likely to have characterized the biblical world and influenced the biblical writers. The kinds of questions posed in social-scientific interpretation include questions about (1) boundary markers and their role in the definition and preservation of individual and social identity; (2) authority and the interpretation and regulation of power in social relations, not least in the ordering and discipline of the human body; (3) status and role,

including the ways these are played out in relation to wealth, education, age, gender, race, and class; (4) ritual as an aspect of the symbolic construction of meaning through time, especially in relation to moments of crisis or change; (5) texts and other media of communication and their production and social effects; (6) group functions, including the function of conflict and how the group deals with experiences of cognitive dissonance; and (7) the symbolic universe and the social construction of reality, including a society's understanding and representation of history and of the relation between worlds divine and human (Kee 65–69).

The claim of social-scientific criticism is that, by asking a different set of questions, aspects of the text usually hidden from view by the more traditional methods of historical interpretation are allowed to come to the surface. This is a significant aid to interpretations of the Bible that seek to take its embeddedness in time, space, and the lives of societies and cultures with full seriousness. Furthermore, since biblical interpretation involves *readers* as well as texts—the reading of Scripture by reading communities in time and over time (cf. Fowl and Jones)—the potential contribution of social-scientific criticism is greater still. Put differently, social-scientific criticism is able to deepen our understanding, not only of the world *behind* the text (the world of the author), but also of the world *within* the text (the world of narrated persons and events) and of the world *in front of* the text (the world of the readers of the text down through the ages, including ourselves; cf. Tate).

Impact and Roots

From at least the 1970s onward, social-scientific criticism has had a significant impact on biblical interpretation. Numerous bibliographies, surveys, and collections of essays testify to this (e.g., Barton; Elliott 138–74; Horrell; Lang), as do developments in professional scholarly organizations, such as the founding of the Context Group by Bruce Malina and other (primarily) North American scholars in 1986. Now there are entire biblical commentaries (e.g., Malina and Rohrbaugh) and scholarly monographs (e.g., Elser; Rogerson) written from a social-scientific perspective. Clearly, then, we have to do with a weighty development in academic biblical interpretation.

One reason for its considerable impact is that the roots of social-scientific criticism go deep and wide. Contributory factors include (1) the relative failure of form and redaction criticism to deliver fully on their promise to correlate scriptural texts with historical and social contexts (*Sitz im Leben*) in the life of Israel and the early church; (2) the rise in prominence and prestige of the social sciences (sociology, anthropology, and psychology) and of the scientific study of religion from the nineteenth century onward, developments grounded in ways of seeing legitimated by models of scientific reason associated with the Enlightenment; (3) the influence on the Western intellectual and cultural tradition—including traditions of interpreting texts like the Bible—of the "hermeneutics of suspicion" characteristic of modernity and represented above all by Feuerbach, Nietzsche, Durkheim, Marx, Freud, and more recently by feminism; (4) shifts in historiography generally, away from the great-man view of history typical of Romanticism to one more attentive to history "from below," with a much stronger popular, cultural, and social dimension; (5) the surfacing of different kinds of questions to put to the scriptural text in the light of developments in twentieth-century theology and history, not least the crisis in liberal theology and the urgent concerns (often of a social and political kind) raised by fundamentalism (of various kinds) on the one hand and by liberationist and feminist theologies on the other.

Strengths and Weaknesses

One of the main contributions of social-scientific criticism has been the revitalization of scriptural interpretation by enlarging the agenda so that the reality—human and divine, material and spiritual—to which the text bears witness may be grasped more fully. As Robin Scroggs put it in an early contribution:

> To some it has seemed that too often the discipline of the theology of the New Testament (the history of *ideas*) operates out of a methodological docetism, as if believers had minds and spirits unconnected with their individual and corporate bodies. Interest in the sociology of early Christianity is no attempt to limit reductionistically the reality of Christianity to social dynamic; rather it should be seen as an effort to guard against a reductionism from the other extreme, a limitation of the reality of Christianity to an inner-spiritual, or objective-cognitive system. In short, sociology of early Christianity wants to put body and soul together again. (Scroggs 165–66)

This new "hermeneutics of social embodiment" (Meeks) has brought a new appreciation of the material and corporate dimensions of biblical

faith along with their attendant implications for its appropriation today.

Such an approach does have potential or real weaknesses. Some argue that the danger of anachronism in using methods and models from a quintessentially modern discipline like sociology is too great and results in a necessarily reductionist account. Or alternatively, they argue that the tools of the social sciences are just too blunt to do justice to the startling novelty and historical particularity of aspects of Israelite religion or of the movement inaugurated by Jesus. On the other hand, Ernst Troeltsch's sect-church typology, Max Weber's theory of charisma and its routinization, Mary Douglas's interpretation of the social and religious significance of ritual purity, Edmund Leech's structural interpretation of sacrifice, or J. G. Peristiany's account of honor and shame as pivotal values in Mediterranean societies—any of these may nevertheless draw attention (working by analogy) to significant features of biblical and early Christian social dynamics that might otherwise go unnoticed (cf. Lang for OT examples; Rohrbaugh for NT examples).

A related concern arises from a particular construal of the genealogy of the social sciences in post-Enlightenment rationalism and atheistic positivism. Recently, John Milbank has argued powerfully that, historically speaking, the social sciences are attempts to "police the sublime." They are parasitic on Christian orthodoxy and represent modern heretical deviations grounded in an ideological and methodological atheism (Milbank 51–143). However, not all theologians share Milbank's hostility to the social sciences nor his construal of the genealogy of the social sciences (e.g., Flanagan; Williams). It is also worth recognizing that significant analyses of biblical material from a social-scientific perspective have come from practitioners who are themselves religiously committed (e.g., Davies; Douglas; Theissen).

The Social Sciences and Theological Hermeneutics

A particularly robust defense of the role of social-scientific criticism in relation to theology, partly in response to Milbank's alternative and hostile narrative, has come from Richard Roberts. Acknowledging the problematic nature of the relation between theology and the social sciences, he traces no less than five "strategies of appropriation" that have pertained historically. (1) In the various forms of religious fundamentalism characteristic of modernity, the tendency is for theology to repel the social sciences except when they can be used instrumentally to support the attempt to reconquer the world by bringing about personal conversion. (2) By contrast, the work of Ernst Troeltsch, one of the founders of the sociology of religion, represents sociology's conquest of theology resulting from Troeltsch's acceptance of the claims of historicism. As a consequence, in Troeltsch's church-sect typology and its elaboration, belief and religious behavior are liable to relativization as the (mere) corollaries of the social structure of the religious organization. (3) In the work of Dietrich Bonhoeffer, on the other hand, sociology is drafted into the service of theology in a way that preserves the dialectical tension between the disciplines. This first appears in his study of what it means to be the church in the modern world (*Sanctorum Communio*, ET, 1963), and second, expressing his theological engagement with secularization, in his *Letters and Papers from Prison* (ET, 1967). (4) More recently, Edward Farley's phenomenological approach represents the "mutual absorption" of theology and sociology. In his two works, *Ecclesial Man* (1975) and *Ecclesial Reflection* (1982), social-scientific insights are assimilated into a method that overcomes what many would see as the necessary divergence between sociology and theology and (arguably) blunts their respective contributions in favor of a phenomenology of "ecclesial being." (5) The last strategy is that of John Milbank, in his *Theology and Social Theory* (1989). According to Roberts, Milbank is determined to drive a wedge between theology and the social sciences and to interpret the latter as heretical deviations from Christian truth and practice. This effort gives to his work the character of a "postmodern quasi-fundamentalism," whereby a fundamental choice has to be made between two competing, incompatible, totalizing practices: either Christianity or secular reason.

This typology of forms of engagement between theology and the social sciences is very apropos since social-scientific interpretation of the Bible is one of the arenas where that engagement takes place. If we repel social-scientific criticism in the theological interpretation of the Bible, we risk the cultural marginalization of the church and its Scriptures and blindness to "the real" in relation to changing understandings of, for example, power, wealth, and gender, not to mention transcendence itself. And if we allow theological interpretation to be supplanted by sociology or subsumed within phenomenology, we risk both the silencing of the Bible as witness to the Word-made-flesh and the emasculation of those vibrant faith communities who maintain and embody that witness. To sustain theological interpretation in critical dialogue with the social sciences (and with the human sciences generally), after the manner of Bonhoeffer, we need to refuse premature foreclosure on the truth and to keep alive the possibility of ongoing attention and obedience to the word. We can do this while disciplined by the resources and practices of the faith tradition on the one hand, and by the often-abrasive but sometimes exhilarating encounter with modernity on the other.

Bibliography

Barton, S. "The Communal Dimension of Earliest Christianity: A Critical Survey of the Field." *JTS* 43, no. 2 (1992): 399–427; Davies, D. *Anthropology and Theology.* Berg, 2002; Douglas, M. *Purity and Danger.* Routledge & Kegan Paul, 1966; Elliott, J. *Social-Scientific Criticism of the New Testament and Its Social World.* SPCK, 1995; Esler, P. *Community and Gospel in Luke-Acts.* Cambridge University Press, 1987; Flanagan, K. "Sublime Policing: Sociology and Milbank's City of God." *NBf* 73 (1992): 333–41; Fowl, S., and L. G. Jones. *Reading in Communion.* SPCK, 1991; Horrell, D., ed. *Social-Scientific Approaches to New Testament Interpretation.* T&T Clark, 1999; Kee, H. C. *Knowing the Truth.* Fortress, 1989; Lang, B. *Anthropological Approaches to the Old Testament.* SPCK, 1985; Malina, B., and R. Rohrbaugh. *Social-Science Commentary on the Synoptic Gospels.* Fortress, 1992; Meeks, W. *The First Urban Christians: The Social World of the Apostle Paul.* 2d ed. Yale University Press, 2003; Milbank, J. *Theology and Social Theory.* Blackwell, 1990; Roberts, R. H. *Religion, Theology and the Human Sciences.* Cambridge University Press, 2002; Rogerson, J. *Anthropology and the Old Testament.* Blackwell, 1978; Rohrbaugh, R., ed. *The Social Sciences and New Testament Interpretation.* Hendrickson, 1996; Scroggs, R. "The Sociological Interpretation of the New Testament: The Present State of Research." *NTS* 26 (1980): 164–79; Tate, W. R. *Biblical Interpretation.* Hendrickson, 1991; Theissen, G. *The Social Setting of Pauline Christianity.* T&T Clark, 1982; Williams, R. "Saving Time: Thoughts on Practice, Patience and Vision." *NBf* 73 (1992): 319–26.

Stephen C. Barton

Societies, Scholarly

Scholarly societies consist of members in diverse geographical configurations with a variety of missions and a fairly similar set of activities. These organizations have shaped, if not changed, the theological interpretation of Scripture since they began in the last half of the nineteenth century. They have flourished during the twentieth century, with signs of increasing strength at the beginning of the twenty-first. For their members they provide solidarity benefits, professional/

academic standards, and opportunities for intellectual debate. For the general public and the academic world they publish journals, books, and increasingly provide a variety of digital resources over the Internet. Indirectly, they promote the theological interpretation of Scripture for confessional communities.

Two definitional issues require comment. First, while definitions of "scholarly" exist, the use and meaning of the term is wide-ranging. "Scholarly" can describe a group or individual who has developed a specific set of methods, or it can refer to qualities or attitudes of the group or individual. Yet any taxonomy of these societies is shaped by an understanding of "scholarly." Individuals associated with universities and seminaries have developed the organizations that have flourished through the twentieth century. This academic context has played an important role in shaping the contributions of these scholarly societies to the theological interpretation of Scripture.

Second, the adjective "theological" also carries a variety of connotations and denotations. "Theological" can refer to specific confessional, religious, or praxis matters. Within one stream of American jurisprudence, in debates over the relationship between "church and state," theology has been understood as only having to do with training for a specific religious group's ministry. Some scholarly societies promote the interpretation of Scripture within a specific context of faith even though they may permit membership outside the particular confessional perspective. Other scholarly societies explicitly avoid any one context of faith, do not promote any particular confessional perspective, and understand "theological" as one approach to the interpretation of Scripture alongside a multiplicity such as historical and literary interpretations. The more-general practice of the scholarly societies and the academic world is to understand "theological" with this broader meaning.

Three factors influence the shape of scholarly societies: geographical makeup of the members, the relationship between mission and Scripture, and the activities promoted by the organization. One must remember that, just as all groups of people, scholarly societies are made up of individuals whose lives have been shaped by diverse intellectual, social, religious, political, and personal factors.

Geography

Currently scholarly societies may be geographically categorized into regional, national, and international. The regional organizations range from informal gatherings to formalized entities that maintain membership lists, and some have publications. In areas where one or more graduate programs in theology, religion, and Bible exist, there are frequently informal gatherings of professors and sometimes students. They come together to share research, so are usually focused on scholarly interests and in some social context. Other organizations such as the Chicago Society of Biblical Research were founded in a specific area, but over the years have come to include scholars who reside at some distance from the core geographical area. The regional groups of the Society of Biblical Literature and American Academy of Religion have met since the mid-twentieth century. Some of these gatherings have formed their own separate regional consortia of societies, such as the Southeastern Consortium for the Study of Religion.

Many scholarly societies are nationally based, such as the Finnish Exegetical Society and the Canadian Society of Biblical Studies/Société canadienne des Études Bibliques. Others have developed multinationally, such as among the Scandinavian countries and the Australian and New Zealand Society for Theological Studies. Outside the European and North American contexts, a growing number of groups have emerged in Asia, such as the Ecumenical Association of Third World Theologians and the Congress of Asian Theologians.

Few if any scholarly societies began with an international constituency. However, since the last quarter of the twentieth century, the Society of Biblical Literature has encouraged international participation and seen a growing number of international members, culminating in the establishment of its international meeting in 1983. Some groups are established by invitation only and include senior scholars from several continents (e.g., Studiorum Novi Testamenti Societas/Society for the Study of the New Testament). The International Organization for Masoretic Studies and the International Organization for Septuagint and Cognate Studies are membership organizations that are international not only in name but also in outlook and membership. Their contribution to theological interpretation is viewed by some as minimal since their focus is narrowly defined to a specific text of Scripture.

New regional, national, and international scholarly societies continue to emerge. As new scholarly societies develop, they reshape the existing ones, so the map of scholarly societies is in flux.

Mission

In addition to geographical factors, scholarly societies may be categorized by their missions. The intellectual distinctions and disciplinary/area studies concerns in the university and seminary world more heavily influenced the missions than the confessing communities' perspectives on Scripture. Nevertheless, a growing tendency to encourage interaction between the academic and confessional communities seems to be emerging.

No identification of "scholarly societies" that have shaped the theological interpretation of Scripture at the beginning of the twenty-first century is complete without recognizing that few, even those with a specific mission related to biblical studies, focus on all of Scripture. The Society of Biblical Literature is one of the few international organizations whose mission is to foster scholarship related to the entire Bible. The mission of many scholarly societies in biblical studies is on either the OT (Hebrew Bible) or the NT (Early Christian Literature). This fact can be noted in any list of their organizational names. The Catholic Biblical Association of America's mission does promote the study of the entire Scripture (and this includes the Roman Catholic understanding of canon) within a confessing community; the interdependence of the academy and a religious body can be seen in this type of mission.

A series of explicitly Christian theological organizations and institutes adds further weight to the remarkable richness, diversity, and complexity of persons gathered to advance the theological interpretation of Scripture. Among these groups one must mention the Evangelical Theological Society, Institute for Biblical Research, Academy of Homiletics, Society for Pastoral Theology, American Bible Society, Ecumenical Institute, Center of Theological Inquiry at Princeton, American Theological Society, and United Bible Societies.

Societies that interface with the theological interpretation of Scripture include those whose missions are focused in a variety of specializations seen in almost every discipline/area study of the university world. A list of nearly 1,500 organizations has occasional or standing groups that engage the interpretation of Scripture. These include the following North American organizations, many with counterparts in other regions of the world: North American Society of Christian Ethics, Association of Jewish Studies, the American Theological Library Association, American Academy of Religion, Society for the Scientific Study of Religion, American Schools of Oriental Research, Biblical Archaeology Society, American Society of Church History, American Society of Papyrologists, Middle Eastern Studies Association, North American Patristic Society, and even an enormous disciplinary organization like the Modern Language Association.

Activities

Another way to categorize the scholarly societies is to look at the range of activities they promote. These activities are diverse and depend almost entirely on the staff infrastructure of the organization. The influence of scholarly societies is frequently gauged by the quantity or range of activities they manage. Quantity and range of activities, however, do not address the quality of those activities, and quality is important to every scholarly society even if its measurement is diverse.

The range of scholarly society activities is incredibly broad and dynamic. Publication is often thought to be the hallmark activity of these scholarly societies. In fact, many of the organizations were founded for the purpose of publishing a journal. The range of societal publications has gone beyond journals to include books, reference works, translations of the Bible, and an increasing number of digital products available through organizational Web sites. The scholarly standards emerge from this activity of publications.

Increasingly, studies of the scholarly societies have indicated that another hallmark is the solidarity benefit, providing opportunities for members to gather socially and to share their work. Most have annual meetings that provide an opportunity for members to gather for the sharing of research, ideas, and the opportunity to see the latest books and software for the interpretation of Scripture.

Closely connected to this networking benefit is fulfilling the professional needs of members, whether teachers, religious leaders, students, or librarians. While these societies have central missions related to the interpretation of Scripture, they have increasingly recognized that members need jobs and seek advancement in their occupations. Professional and ethical standards have begun to develop as a central concern.

Finally, only a few of these scholarly societies are involved in public policy issues. Certainly, far fewer of the scholarly societies entrusted with the theological interpretation of Scripture are as engaged in the significant contemporary public debate as their counterparts in other university and seminary disciplines/areas of study.

Conclusion

The scholarly societies involved centrally or peripherally in the theological interpretation of Scripture have extended the voices speaking on these texts and traditions beyond the confessing communities. The historical perspective of these scholarly societies is minimal compared to the long history of the confessing communities who have interpreted the Bible. Yet, since individuals often reside in both communities, a synergy has frequently emerged. As the twenty-first century begins, things look bright for interdependence, without loss of identities, among those involved in the theological interpretation of Scripture. More awareness and analysis of the interrelationships is needed, however, given the increasing hermeneutical prominence of "interpretative communities" after the work of Stanley Fish and others.

Kent Harold Richards

Song of Songs

From beginning to end, the Song of Songs contains poetic speeches of the most sensuous kind. An unnamed woman and an unnamed man speak lovingly to each other and also occasionally describe their love to an anonymous group of women, often referred to as the chorus. The topics of the poems are love and intimacy between a man and a woman, with no reference at all to God, the covenant, the history of Israel, or anything that has explicitly theological significance. What then does theological interpretation mean when it comes to the Song of Songs?

History of Interpretation

The history of the interpretation of the Song of Songs begins around 100 CE with the earliest preserved comments on the book. The voice that breaks the silence is that of Rabbi Aqiba, who famously stated: "Whoever sings the Song of Songs with a tremulous voice in a banquet hall and (so) treats it as a sort of ditty has no share in the world to come" (quoted from Murphy 13). Though brief, this statement says much about the early understanding of the book. First, those who were singing it with a tremulous voice obviously treated the Song's sensual imagery literally, while

Aqiba, certainly representative of institutional sentiments, sought to repress such readings.

Aqiba himself treated the Song in a manner similar to that which dominated synagogue and church until relatively recently, as an allegory. Approaching the Song as an allegory is a way of understanding its message as different from its surface meaning. The most commonly held form of allegorical interpretation of the Song in the synagogue understood the man to represent God and the woman to represent Israel. The story of the relationship of the man and the woman in the Song was actually a veiled way to present the history of God's redemption of Israel.

The targum to the Song (ca. 700–900 CE) is a case in point. The targum paraphrases the first unit of the Song (1:2–4), in which the woman, understood as Israel, begs the man, God, to take her into his chamber; it interprets this request as Israel's desire that God bring it into the promised land. In other words, the Song begins with the exodus from Egypt. From this point, the targum's allegorical interpretation follows Israel through its history.

Christian interpretation followed this strategy, only making necessary adjustments for its distinctive religious beliefs. Interpreters such as Hippolytus, Origen, Jerome, and Bernard of Clairvaux read the Song as an allegorical expression of the love between Jesus (the man) and the church or individual Christian (the woman). Often the details of the text were pressed into the service of a theological reading. This is illustrated by Cyril of Alexandria's comment on 1:13, that the woman's two breasts represented the OT and NT, and the sachet of myrrh that lodges between them stood for Jesus Christ, who spanned the two parts of the Bible.

Historical allegory was the interpretative method of choice from the earliest witnesses down to the mid-nineteenth century, but it was not the only type of allegorical interpretation. Also popular, particularly among some Jewish interpreters, was a mystical or philosophical allegorical understanding of the book. From the medieval period we have the example of the interpretation of Levi ben Gershom (thirteenth century), an Aristotelian, who distinguished between the material intellect, the acquired intellect, and the Active Intellect (Kellner). The last stood for God, and the first was the capacity for God's creatures to learn. The acquired intellect was knowledge accumulated through life. Levi read the Song as an allegory on two levels. The man represents the Active Intellect and the woman the material intellect; the Song shows them in dialogue, and their union is "a human being's highest perfection and greatest felicity" (Kellner xxi).

One further twist on the allegorical approach to the Song is provided by Don Isaac Abravanel, a rabbi from the sixteenth century (Pope 110–11). In his reading, the man is Solomon, and the woman stands for wisdom. Thus, their union represents Solomon.

No matter what the particular brand, the evidence is overwhelming that the dominant interpretative approach to the Song up to the mid-nineteenth century was allegorical. On the rare occasion that a theologian objected to the traditional interpretation and concluded that the Song was really about the intimate love of a man and a woman, this conclusion was typically accompanied by the argument that the book was not worthy of the canon. Theodore of Mopsuestia (350–428 CE) was such a theologian, and his interpretation was judged "not fitting the mouth of a crazy woman" by his own student Theodoret (Davidson 3).

Though allegorical interpretation of the Song held almost exclusive sway over the synagogue and church for many centuries, the nineteenth century saw a dramatic swing toward the position that the Song concerned human, rather than divine, love. Three factors led to this shift.

In the first place, allegory lost force as an interpretative strategy. To be sure, ancient and modern literature has allegories. Perhaps the best-known allegory, particularly to Christian audiences, is *Pilgrim's Progress*, by John Bunyan. As this book illustrates, however, true allegories do not hide their "deeper meaning." After all, the main character is a man named Christian, who is journeying toward the Celestial City, encountering obstacles like the Slough of Despond. On the other hand, the Song of Songs never hints at another level of meaning. Why take the two breasts of 1:13 as a reference to the OT and NT? For that matter, are there any indications within the text that the man represents God and the woman represents Israel? The answer is obviously negative. The allegorical interpretation was kept alive by the force of tradition, and in the post-Enlightenment period, this was not adequate to sustain it.

In the second place, the nineteenth century witnessed the rediscovery of ancient Near Eastern cultures, as the architecture and literature of Sumer, Babylon, Assyria, and Egypt, among others, were excavated and interpreted. Among that literature were a number of love poems that shared many of the themes, poetic devices, and metaphors of the Song of Songs. These texts were nonreligious, and this fact led many to conclude that the Song of Songs was also human love poetry (Watson; White; Fox; Westenholz; Cooper).

Finally, the nineteenth century was also a time of increased Western political involvement in the Middle East. In new ways biblical scholars became aware of Arab customs, and often connections were made. As relates to interpretation of the Song, there is a famous interchange between a German consul to Damascus named J. G. Wetzstein and the well-known Lutheran commentator Franz Delitzsch. Wetzstein attended weddings of local Arab leaders and noted in amazement that the songs they sang at their celebrations sounded similar to the Song. Delitzsch cites Wetzstein's correspondence in his commentary.

During this period the conclusion of most scholars was that the Song had been fundamentally misunderstood in the preceding centuries. It was read as an allegory when in reality it was love poetry. In retrospect, it appears that the synagogue and the church imbibed a form of Neoplatonic philosophy that created a contrast between spirituality and sexuality (so Davidson). The body and its desires were something to be repressed as inimical to one's relationship with God. If this is true, how could there be a book as sensual as the Song in the canon? To resolve the tension, an allegorical strategy of interpretation was adopted to shift the meaning of the text from what it seemed to say to what it "really" said (Phipps). The Song of Songs is an unfortunate example of the tendency to use theology/philosophy to skew the interpretation of a text.

For the past century and a half, interpretation of the Song has moved away from allegory, but what has replaced it? Further, and more central to the purpose of this essay, if the Song is not about the relationship between God and his people, then what is the theological contribution of this book?

As the allegorical approach began to fade, most scholars adopted what has been called the dramatic approach to the Song. Delitzsch himself argued that the poetry of the Song told a story about Solomon and a woman named the Shulammite (6:13). He believes that the Shulammite is an actual historical figure. But, unlike many before and after him, he does not think she is the Egyptian princess or any prominent woman. Instead, he sees her as "a country maiden of humble rank, who, by her beauty and by the purity of her soul, filled Solomon with a love for her which drew him away from the wantonness of polygamy, and made for him the primitive idea of marriage, as it is described in Gen. ii 23ff., a self-experienced reality" (Delitzsch 3). He treats the story as a drama consisting of six acts, each with two scenes.

While Delitzsch represents the so-called two-character dramatic approach, the more recent commentary by Provan argues in favor of another popular interpretation that sees three characters. The Song is not a story about the love between a man and a woman, pure and simple, but rather concerns a love triangle. In Provan's own version of the story, the Shulammite has already entered Solomon's harem, but she has preserved her love for the young shepherd boy back home. The moral of the story is that true love overcomes coerced legal love.

Scholars have suggested other approaches to the book. The cultic interpretation of Pope (anticipated by Meek), the political interpretation of Stadelmann, and the psychological interpretation of Landy have not won many adherents. The main competitor to the dramatic approach today is the anthological interpretation of the Song. Since this view represents my own opinion (see Longman), I will describe it in the next section, though that discussion should be seen as completing our survey of the history of interpretation.

Hearing the Message of the Song of Songs

The problem with the dramatic approach is highlighted by its inability to settle on a single story. There are as many permutations of the drama, even to the point of disagreement over whether there are two or three main characters, as there are scholarly advocates. Every story has gaps that the reader must fill in, but the gaps in the Song are too large to be filled in with confidence. It appears that scholars are not reading a story from the text, but rather creating a story.

The Song of Songs is, thus, what its title implies: a single song constructed from a number of different songs. It is an anthology of love poems, bound together by a unity of purpose, consistency of character, and a few repeated refrains. The goal of the interpreter is not to describe the story, but rather to unpack the rich metaphors and explore the strong emotions expressed by the poet.

To be sure, those who recognize the anthological nature of the Song disagree about the number of individual poems. My own conclusion that there are twenty-three poems is closer to Falk than to Goulder, who believes there are only fourteen songs, or Landsberger, who does not give us a full study but gives us the impression that virtually every verse is a separate song. But in reality it does not really matter how many poems there are since the number does not affect interpretation.

Whether there are fourteen or a hundred poems, the Song's primary significance relates to love and sexuality, an important aspect of our humanity. The Song affirms human love, intimate relationship, sensuality, and sexuality. According to the Song, love is mutual, exclusive, total, and beautiful (Hubbard 260–63). The Song not only celebrates love; it also warns its readers not to hurry love (2:7; 3:5; 8:4) because sometimes the desire for intimacy brings pain (5:2–6:3; so Schwab).

Song of Songs and the Canon

The Song is one of only a handful of OT books whose canonicity was questioned (Beckwith 1–2, 275–76, 279, 282–84, 308–22). Those questioning its authority did so because they doubted that a book of such sensuality could be sacred. The fact that God's name is not found in the book (the supposed occurrence in 8:6 is unlikely) added to the skepticism. Their doubts, as we have suggested above, rested on a problematic contrast between spirituality and sexuality. Even those early witnesses that demonstrate the Song was widely accepted as canonical (2 Esdras, Josephus, Aquila, Melito, Tertullian) did so based on a faulty understanding of the book's interpretation. Unfortunately, the book's immediate reception is lost in obscurity.

In any case, once the false dichotomy between body and spirit is rejected, it becomes clear why such a book might be found in the canon. God loves his human creatures as whole people, not just as temporarily embodied spirits. Love is a powerful emotion and sexuality a large part of the human experience, bringing great joy and pain. The book's affirmations and warnings about love express God's concern for his people. As the last section explains, the book also makes a powerful contribution to biblical theology.

Song of Songs and Theology

Contrary to preconceptions, the Song of Songs fits into the rest of the canon as an integral part of a biblical theology of love and sexuality. As Trible has pointed out, the story begins in the Garden. Adam and Eve are there, naked, and feeling no shame. The implication is that, before sin, the two are completely open with one another, not only sexually, but also psychologically and spiritually. Genesis 3, however, narrates the fall, at which time the alienation between God and his human creatures has repercussions in the relationship between Adam and Eve. They cover themselves from the gaze of the other, and God removes them from the Garden. Reading the Song of Songs, in which many poems present the man and the woman in the Garden, enjoying one another's nakedness, makes one think of Eden and understand that the Song is about the redemption of sexuality. However, it is an already-not yet redemption because of the continuing problems acknowledged by some of the poems (5:2–6:3).

Furthermore, when understood within the context of the canon as a whole, the Song makes yet another important theological contribution. To be sure, God is not named or even alluded to within the book. Nonetheless, by celebrating the intimacy of the male-female relationship, it reminds us of the pervasive use of the marriage metaphor to throw light on God's relationship with his people. In the OT, that metaphor is used negatively, in that Israel's apostasy is often likened to adultery (Ezek. 16, 23; Hos. 1–3), but behind this negative use stands the positive statement that God's relationship with his people is like a marriage (see Jer. 2:1). Accordingly, the more we understand the depth of desire and the power of marital intimacy, the more we will understand our relationship with God. The exclusivity of the marriage relationship, as opposed to other human relationships, also makes it an appropriate vehicle to give insight into the divine-human relationship. Of course, in the NT the Christian's relationship with Jesus is compared to the relationship of a husband and wife (Eph. 5:21–33), and our ultimate union with our Lord at the end of days is described as a wedding (Rev. 19:6–8).

See also Allegory; Sexuality

Bibliography

Beckwith, R. *The Old Testament Canon of the New Testament Church*. SPCK, 1985; Cooper, J. S. "New Cuneiform Parallels to the Song of Songs." *JBL* 90 (1971): 157–62; Davidson, R. "Theology of Sexuality in the Song of Songs: Return to Eden." *AUSS* 27 (1989): 1–19; Delitzsch, F. *Proverbs, Ecclesiastes, Song of Solomon*. German, 1885, trans. M. Easton. Eerdmans, 1975; Falk, M. *Love Lyrics in the Bible*. Almond, 1982; Fox, M. "Love, Passion, and Perception in Israelite and Egyptian Love Poetry." *JBL* 102 (1983): 1–14; idem. *The Song of Songs and the Ancient Egyptian Love Poetry*. University of Wisconsin Press, 1985; Goulder, M. *The Song of Fourteen Songs*. JSOTSup 36. JSOT, 1986; Hubbard, D. *Ecclesiastes, Song of Solomon*. Communicator's Commentary. Word, 1991; Kellner, M. *Commentary on the Song of Songs: Levi ben Gershom (Gersonides)*. Yale University Press, 1998; Landsberger, B. "Poetic Units within the Song of Songs." *JBL* 73 (1954): 513–28; Landy, F. *Paradoxes of Paradise*. Almond, 1983; Longman, T., III. *The Song of Songs*. NICOT. Eerdmans, 2001; Meek, T. "Babylonian Parallels to the Song of Songs." *JBL* 43 (1924): 245–52; idem. "Canticles and the Tammuz Cult." *AJSL* 39 (1922–23): 219–28; Murphy, R. *The Song of Songs*. Hermeneia. Fortress, 1990; Phipps, W. "The Plight of the Song of Songs." *JAAR* 42 (1974): 82–100; Pope, M. *Song of Songs*. AB 7C. Doubleday, 1977; Provan, I. *Ecclesiastes and Song of Songs*. NIVAC. Zondervan, 2001; Schwab, G. *The Song of Songs' Cautionary Message concerning Human Love*. P. Lang, 2002; Stadelmann, L. *Love and Politics*. Paulist, 1990; Trible, P. *God and the Rhetoric of Sexuality*. Fortress, 1978; Watson, W. G. E. "Some Ancient Near Eastern Parallels to the Song of Songs." Pages 253–71 in *Words Remembered, Texts Renewed*, ed. J. Davies et al. Sheffield Academic Press, 1995; Westenholz, J. "Love Lyrics from the Ancient Near East." Pages 2471–84 in vol. 4 of *Civilizations of the Ancient Near East*, ed. J. Sasson. Charles Scribner's Sons, 1995; Wetzstein, J. "Die syrische Dreschtafel." *Zeitschrift für Ethnologie* 5 (1873): 270–301; White, J. *A Study of the Language of Love in the Song of Songs and Ancient Egyptian Love Poetry*. Scholars Press, 1975.

Tremper Longman III

Soul   *See* Human Being, Doctrine of

Source Criticism

Source criticism, which has also gone by the name "Literary Criticism," is an attempt to uncover written documents lying behind a given text (e.g., 2 Kings 18:13–20:19; cf. Isa. 36:1–39:8), a biblical book (e.g., Isaiah), or several books (e.g., the Pentateuch, Joshua through 2 Kings, or the Synoptic Gospels). Source critics take as indicators of such documents the presence of alleged contradictions between texts (e.g., how many pairs of animals did Noah take on board the ark? cf. Gen. 6:19 with 7:2), of doublets or triplets (multiple versions of a narrative with the same basic plot: cf. Gen. 12:10–13:1 with 20:1–18 and 26:6–11), and of diverse styles (cf. the simple narrative style of 2:4b–25 with the more flowing style of 1:1–2:4a). Source critics also look for recurrences of these styles, finding the simple narrative styles of 2:4b–25 in places in the rest of Genesis, as well as in parts of Exodus and Numbers. The style of Deuteronomy is said to appear as well in Joshua, Judges, Samuel, Kings, and Jeremiah, but not elsewhere (or else rarely) in the Pentateuch. Consequently, source critics offer as an explanation for these problems the Documentary Hypothesis, with its conclusion that as many as four (or more) narrative documents and a number of separate law codes stand behind the Pentateuch.

Another well-known hypothesis from source critics is the so-called Four-Source Hypothesis, designed to explain the relationships among the Synoptic Gospels. It is well known that Matthew, Mark, and Luke (though not John) describe many of the same actions and teachings of Jesus. The question rises, therefore, of why the Synoptics share so much material (sometimes nearly word for word). The Four-Source Hypothesis provides answers.

The first source typically is said to be the Gospel of Mark, which provided the framework, many of the narratives, and some of the teachings of Jesus—the biblical texts common to the three Synoptic Gospels. Source critics note that Matthew shares about 90 percent of Mark and Luke about 55 percent. In the areas where they overlap, one sometimes diverges from the other two (cf. Mark 13:14 and Matt. 24:15 versus Luke 21:20). Matthew and Mark may agree against Luke, or Luke and Mark may agree against Matthew, but rarely if ever do Matthew and Luke agree against Mark. The remaining material in Matthew and Luke is ascribed typically to three sources. The first, called Q (for the German word *Quelle*, "well"), is a hypothetical source consisting mainly of sayings of Jesus, sometimes with short narratives providing the setting for the sayings. Accordingly, the teachings and narrative material *common* to Matthew and Luke but *missing* from Mark are attributed to Q (e.g., the Sermon on the Mount/Plain). In addition, both Matthew and Luke report sayings (cf. Matt. 18:23–35; Luke 10:29–37) and narratives (cf. Matt. 1:18–2:23; Luke 1:5–2:52) unique to each. Hence, scholars further hypothesize sources M and L for Matthew and Luke respectively. (Some scholars, however, think that the materials unique to Matthew and Luke also may have been taken from Q, so they speak of a Two-Source Hypothesis.)

Such theories are not theologically neutral. For one thing, they depend on a view of Scripture that allows for differences in presentation, and perhaps even outright contradictions between passages. Moreover, they argue that "contradictions" and diverse styles imply different authors for the different sources lying behind the received form of the biblical text. The theories cast doubt, therefore, on such widely held, traditional views as the Mosaic authorship of the Pentateuch, single authorship of prophetic books (Isaiah, Jeremiah, Ezekiel, and many of the Minor Prophets as well), and of the Psalter plus other books. Differences in style and theology within the Pauline corpus cause some source critics to question whether Paul wrote Ephesians, Colossians, 2 Thessalonians, 1 and 2 Timothy, and Titus. Thus, source criticism typically is not neutral toward traditional views about the authorship of books in the Bible. Further, the suggestion that the Bible contains "contradictions" (or historical or other kinds of errors) is incompatible with certain views of its inspiration. For some people, therefore, source criticism, or at least many of its results, is simply unacceptable.

It need not be, however. Since, for example, Gen. 6:19 records that God told Noah to take one pair of every kind of animal on board the ark and 7:2 records that God told Noah to take one pair of unclean animals and seven pairs of clean animals, that difference demands an explanation. By means of the Documentary Hypothesis, source critics offer a plausible explanation for the quandary, that the author of the Pentateuch (Moses or someone later) employed sources that did not always agree in detail though they were compatible at some other level. In this particular case both texts say Noah preserved representatives from each animal species. On the other hand, the distinction between clean and unclean animals in Genesis may foreshadow the distinction in Lev. 11. Hence, the final author preserved both versions of the Flood narrative and their distinctive insights into God's work without forcing the versions to agree. If the resulting Scripture is less tidy than modern readers might be comfortable with, the benefit in keeping all views would seem to source critics to outweigh the loss.

Another example is the suggested use of sources in 1 and 2 Samuel with conflicting views as to whether Israel should have a king like the other nations. Some narratives praise Saul as a man who stood head and shoulders above others (1 Sam. 10:20–27), God's choice for Israel's king (9:1–10:16; 11:1–15). Others condemn the monarchy in general (ch. 8; 10:17–19) and Saul in particular (13:1–15a). Why does this difference exist? Perhaps they derived from different hands. Why did the author use them both? Perhaps it was because the monarchy was a complex institution. On the one hand, kings could muster armies and lead them to battle against enemies, in particular the Philistines. On the other hand, kings would tax the people, take their sons for soldiers and their daughters for servants, concubines, or wives. The author of 1 and 2 Samuel, therefore, included narratives showing both sides of the issue, but came down in favor of the Davidic monarchy (2 Sam. 7). He had arrived at a compromise in which monarchy under God was acceptable, but

Israel's monarchy had gotten off on the wrong foot with the wrong king. Ultimately, of course, the NT sided with the author of 2 Sam. 7, seeing Jesus as the fulfillment of the Davidic dynasty.

See also Gospels

Bibliography

Beardslee, W. *Literary Criticism of the New Testament.* Fortress, 1970; Eissfeldt, O. "The Prophetic Literature." Pages 115–61 in *The Old Testament and Modern Study,* ed. H. H. Rowley. Oxford University Press, 1961; Farmer, W. *The Synoptic Problem.* Macmillan, 1964; Grant, R. Pages 59–73, 107–18, 171–202 in *Historical Introduction to the New Testament.* Harper & Row, 1963; Griesbach, J. "Inquisitio in fontes, unde evangelistae suas de resurrectione Domini narrationes hauserint." 1783. Pages 241–56 in vol. 2 of *Griesbachii opus.* Acad. Jena, 1789; Habel, N. *Literary Criticism of the Old Testament.* Fortress, 1971; Kee, H. C. Pages 81–101, 221–305 in *Understanding the New Testament.* 5th ed. Prentice Hall, 1993; Kümmel, W. G. Pages 33–59, 237–72 in *Introduction to the New Testament.* 14th ed. Abingdon, 1966; North, C. R. "Pentateuchal Criticism." Pages 48–83 in *The Old Testament and Modern Study,* ed. H. H. Rowley. Oxford University Press, 1961; Soggin, J. A. *Introduction to the Old Testament.* 3d ed. Westminster John Knox, 1989.

Paul L. Redditt

Special Revelation   *See* Revelation

Speech-Act Theory

The idea that language is fundamentally concerned with the stating of facts and the representing of "states of affairs" has exerted something of a stranglehold over the modern mind through the last two centuries, evidenced in the distinctively modern style of "historical-critical" commentary so beloved of professional biblical interpretation. In the words of Wittgenstein, it is almost as if "a picture held us captive. And we could not get outside it" (§115). In his 1955 William James lectures at Harvard, philosopher of language J. L. Austin began to work at undermining this picture. The lectures, posthumously published as *How to Do Things with Words,* gave birth to the contemporary study of "speech acts": acts performed by, in, or with speech.

In particular, Austin sought to distinguish between the act performed *in* saying something and the act performed *by* saying something, labeling these "illocutionary" and "perlocutionary" acts respectively. When John Searle formalized Austin's essentially oral tradition into a written theory of *Speech Acts,* he turned it into a logical structure of five fundamental kinds of illocutionary acts, whereby all language uses are, or are combina-

tions of, assertive, directive, commissive, expressive, or declarative acts (*Expression,* 1–29).

Speech-act theory, the resultant subdiscipline of the philosophy of language, still encompasses a wide range of views on precisely how pragmatic, logical, formal, or rhetorical its concerns are supposed to be. Corresponding to such diversity, one finds an equally varied range of applications of the theory to the various hermeneutical and theological tasks of biblical interpretation.

The Central Concerns of Speech-Act Theory

The first point to clarify is just how far speech-act theory moves from the idea that all language is fact-stating. In an approach that guaranteed confusion on this issue, Austin's work begins by distinguishing between the descriptive (or "constative") use of language to describe states of affairs, and the "performative" use of language, which does a variety of other things, only to conclude that no such distinction could be maintained (91). The constative use turns out in fact to be a kind of performance after all, and "the class of exceptions thus swallows the supposedly normative class" (Fish 231). Austin concludes that there are five different kinds of language use, of which the constative is one, and this scheme is essentially adopted by Searle, albeit considerably tidied up. The point often missed here is that Austin and Searle are both allowing the "descriptive" use of language to be a performative act, like any other use of language, but demonstrating ways in which it is not the same type of performative act as other types. Differing views on this issue largely explain the differing uses of speech-act theory in biblical and theological studies.

A second feature of speech-act theory is its isolation of the illocutionary act as one of the most important aspects of language use. An illocution is an act performed *in* saying something, and examples might include "I promise to be there tomorrow," or "I believe in God the Father, maker of heaven and earth." The act in question is not so much the result of the spoken words, as an act performed instantaneously in the uttering of the words, by virtue of what the words are taken to mean in context. The person who says "I do" at the appropriate point in a wedding ceremony (in certain cultures only, of course) cannot follow it up moments later with "Actually, I don't." The conventions that make the first utterance a promise of marriage are not in place to make the second utterance an undoing of that promise.

The illocution is probably the most significant analytical tool offered by speech-act theory, but again is interpreted in widely differing ways. Austin's first example of an illocution was "He urged me to shoot her" (102), although few would now accept that "urging" is an illocution. Austin also focused on heavily institutionalized instances of illocutions, such as the wedding ceremony or the conventions whereby a queen is entitled to name a ship. While these have had a memorable pedagogical value, they obscure the more fundamental point that most speech acts operate outside of institutionalized settings, and thus invite consideration of just how it is (and by whom) that words are taken in a certain way.

It is also clear that one "locution" (the simple uttering of certain words) can typically be the vehicle of several illocutions, whether intended or unintended. "It's hot in here" can be a statement, a complaint about the heating, a request to open the window, and so forth. Indeed, most locutions are multilayered in some way, and will often admit of unintended illocutions when approached from angles or agendas not envisaged. This is the bread and butter of historical criticism when it attempts to unravel "I permit no woman to teach or to have authority over a man" (1 Tim. 2:12 NRSV): one way to express the matter at stake is to ask which illocution(s) the text supports. Indeed, it has been argued that the meaning of a text is best understood as its "illocutionary act potential" (Alston), and this does clarify certain issues in interpretation, although debate will continue over the question of how far the speaker/author's intended illocution should govern interpretation.

If there is any agreement on what illocutionary analysis achieves, it is that it draws together the issues of authorial (or speaker's) intention and the audience's understanding, by examining what conventions exist within the public domain of both the author and the audience. Speech-act theory insists that language does not exist idly to make certain sounds, but is always language in action, and usually communicative action. The conventions in place then set certain constraints within any given situation on how a communicative speech act can be understood or interpreted. It is in balancing the various elements of this communicative process that disagreement exists among speech-act theorists.

A third matter, of importance especially to biblical and theological critics, is the vexed question of how far the criteria of speech acts can be transferred to written texts. The greater "distance" introduced here between the author's "act" and the reception of that act by some future reader clearly allows for a greater role to be played by the conventions in place in the reader's situation. Different theological views typically view this as either a problem or an opportunity, but as the development of secular literary-critical "speech-act criticism" demonstrates, there are no reasons in principle why speech-act theory cannot apply to written texts (Briggs, *Words*, 73–103).

Once this has been established, a further distinction then occurs between those who focus on the text itself as a communicative act between the author and the reader, and those who utilize speech-act theory to examine the workings of performative acts that occur within the world of the text, such as from one character to another within a narrative (Buss 125). In theological circles this is the watershed between those seeking a communicative account of the nature of Scripture (Wolterstorff; Vanhoozer; Ward) and those seeking clarification of certain hermeneutically interesting qualities of particular illocutions that occur in Scripture (Evans; Thiselton, *New Horizons*, 272–312; Neufeld; Briggs). The dividing line between these two approaches is blurred, with most authors having an interest in both of them, but it is a significant methodological distinction, which results in an emphasis on different aspects of speech-act theory.

The notion that language is performative in some sense is now well accepted, but the significance of this insight remains widely disputed. It needs to be noted that an emphasis on the idea that "descriptive" speech acts are also performative finds itself very much at home in avowedly postmodern philosophies and criticisms. Both Stanley Fish and Jacques Derrida have found Austin's work (though less so that of Searle) congenial to their own concerns. For Fish, the reading community determines what speech act was performed in the text (197–245, 268–92). For Derrida, the absence of the author to judge this issue allows performative acts to freewheel in the deconstructive space between conventionalized acts and readerly presence (1–23). Postmodernism pulls speech-act theory toward the perlocutionary, arguing that what matters with texts is what effect they have on readers, and in this connection biblical criticism has sometimes wanted to harness speech-act theory to aid the concerns of rhetorical criticism (e.g., Botha). It seems unlikely that the ever-burgeoning industry of reading the Bible rhetorically either needs or wants such help. One recent survey of the many and various uses of speech-act theory in biblical interpretation reveals an extraordinary diversity of aims and achievements in this area (Briggs, "Uses"). Here we shall simply consider some of the ways in which the theological interpretation of Scripture might be served by speech-act considerations.

Speech-Act Theory and the Theological Interpretation of Scripture

As long ago as 1932 Karl Barth wrote of "The Speech of God as the Act of God" (Barth 143–62). Then throughout *Church Dogmatics*, he demonstrated what it would mean to take the biblical text as the vehicle of the word of God, at every point allowing God to be the one at work in and through the words of the text. In many ways, Nicholas Wolterstorff's 1995 work *Divine Discourse* represents a long-overdue attempt to explore just how far the conceptuality of speech-act theory can clarify such concerns. Wolterstorff argues that divine illocutions can be carried by human locutions, and that since the performing of illocutions in the public domain is what it is to speak, it can thus be literally true that God speaks in Scripture (75–129). He in fact concludes that God's speaking is a topic generally obscured (even in Barth) by the idea of God's self-revelation, and he sets out something of a manifesto for viewing the biblical text as divine speech, understood as God's speech actions. Since Scripture is evidently also human speech actions, he advocates the notion of "double discourse" and calls for a corresponding double hermeneutic: to interpret the mediating human discourse for human illocutions, and also the mediated divine discourse for divine ones (183–222).

It is debatable how far this manifesto moves us forward in practice when confronted with the task of interpreting particular passages of Scripture, although it does certainly offer clearly articulated ways of understanding the Bible as God's own voice. Wolterstorff is weaker at explaining how (if at all) one should arbitrate between differing construals of what it is that God was intending to say through a scriptural passage. Arguing that "the goal of interpretation . . . is to discover what counts as what," he ultimately appeals to the idea that the "speaker and audience *ought to* count X as Y" (84, 183); but the evidence of biblical interpretation, even within self-confessedly Christian communities, is that actual agreement can be thin here.

Working within a similar framework to that which Wolterstorff outlines, interest has turned in recent years to the notion of Scripture as God's communicative act with its readers. To this end Kevin Vanhoozer has pursued the idea of "Scripture acts": the communicative action of God in Scripture seen in "covenantal terms" (*First Theology*, 159–203). By this he means that the author and reader are parties to a "covenant of discourse," with all the rights and obligations which that covenantal language suggests.

These approaches frequently suggest that interpretation is an ethical act in which the interpreter is morally responsible for their use of the text, and their handling of the "rights" of the author. Such concerns situate texts within a communicative context of author, text, and reader, and this too invites a speech-act approach by way of correlating the textual locution with the authorial illocution, and even with the perlocutionary effect upon the reader. This approach is to some extent still a general theory of interpretation, albeit focused on the specific case of the Christian community reading the biblical text (thus Vanhoozer, *Meaning*, parts 1 and 2, an account entirely structured around this communicative triad).

Vanhoozer goes further in offering the intriguing, if speculative, possibility that the word of God as locution corresponds to the Father, while as illocution it corresponds to the Son, and in perlocutionary effect it is the domain of the Spirit (*First Theology*, 148–58; *Meaning*, 455–59). His concern to articulate an appropriate doctrine of Scripture as divine communicative action further allows him to explore various creative possibilities with respect to speech-act interpretations of actual texts. Moving increasingly toward an explicitly theological hermeneutic, he develops the idea of a "canonical illocution," noting that different illocutions come into focus when a text is considered in its entirety rather than as a series of separate speech acts. For example, the book of Jonah as a whole may have the illocutionary function of critiquing ethnocentrism (*First Theology*, 192), which occurs not at the level of any specific locution but in terms of the whole text. John's Gospel also proves to be fertile soil for such a consideration of theological communicative action (*First Theology*, 236–308). The doctrine of Scripture has most recently been treated in speech-act terms in relation to the notion of the "sufficiency" of Scripture. Speech-act theory provides sharp critical tools for examining in what sense a text can be sufficient in itself, and in what sense such sufficiency has necessarily to be seen within some communicative framework such as speech-act theory indicates (Ward).

A recent symposium on philosophy of language and biblical interpretation demonstrated both this theological/doctrinal appeal of speech-act concerns as well as the relevance of speech-act theory for the interpretation of specific texts (Bartholomew et al.). It is evident that when scriptural texts concern themselves with performative utterances (in a "strong" sense, as other than assertions), speech-act theory will elucidate the hermeneutical issues involved. Work in this area has been sporadic, but includes the christologically oriented confessions, boasting, and slogans of 1 John (Neufeld); the speech acts of confession, forgiveness, and teaching (Briggs, *Words*); and the conventions surrounding blessing and cursing in the OT (Thiselton, "Power").

On a hermeneutical level, it is significant to note that the successful performance of an illocutionary act requires an investment of the speaking/writing self in the communicative act, an investment with certain public commitments and entailments. This led Donald Evans to describe a "logic of self-involvement," which commits the biblical interpreter to various theological claims. Reformulated as "a hermeneutic of self-involvement" (Briggs, *Words*, 147–82), it offers considerable scope for exploring how the illocutions remain effective among us in the process of personal involvement and transformation in the reading of Scripture.

As Anthony Thiselton has observed ("Promise," 223–39), the suitably open-ended phrase "the promise of hermeneutics" invites us to hold together the biblical notion of divine promise, the paradigmatic role of promise as an illocutionary act, and readerly self-involvement. This is the task of an expectant reading of Scripture that can do justice to the many forms and functions of the speech acts, both divine and human, found within it.

Bibliography

Alston, W. *Illocutionary Acts and Sentence Meaning.* Cornell University Press, 2000; Austin, J. L. *How to Do Things with Words.* Oxford University Press, 1962; Barth, K. *Church Dogmatics.* Vol. 1, *The Doctrine of the Word of God,* Part 1. 1932. Reprint, T&T Clark, 1975; Bartholomew, C., et al., eds. *After Pentecost.* SHS. Zondervan/Paternoster, 2001; Botha, J. E. *Jesus and the Samaritan Woman.* NovTSup 45. Brill, 1991; Briggs, R. "The Uses of Speech-Act Theory in Biblical Interpretation." *CurBS* 9 (2001): 229–76; idem. *Words in Action.* T&T Clark, 2001; Buss, M. "Potential and Actual Interactions between Speech Act Theory and Biblical Studies." *Semeia* 41 (1988): 125–34; Derrida, J. *Limited Inc.* Northwestern University Press, 1988; Evans, D. *The Logic of Self-Involvement.* SCM, 1963; Fish, S. *Is There a Text in This Class?* Harvard University Press, 1980; Neufeld, D. *Reconceiving Texts as Speech Acts.* BIS 7. Brill, 1994; Searle, J. *Expression and Meaning.* Cambridge University Press, 1979; idem. *Speech Acts.* Cambridge University Press, 1969; Thiselton, A. "Communicative Action and Promise in Interdisciplinary, Biblical, and Theological Hermeneutics." Pages 133–239 in *The Promise of Hermeneutics.* By R. Lundin, C. Walhout, and A. Thiselton. Eerdmans, 1999; idem. *New Horizons in Hermeneutics.* HarperCollins, 1992; idem. "The Supposed Power of Words in the Biblical Writings." *JTS* 25 (1974): 283–99; Vanhoozer, K. *First Theology.* InterVarsity, 2002; idem. *Is There a Meaning in This Text?* Zondervan, 1998; Ward, T. *Word and Supplement.* Oxford University Press, 2002; Wittgenstein, L. *Philosophical Investigations.* Blackwell, 1967; Wolterstorff, N. *Divine Discourse.* Cambridge University Press, 1995.

Richard S. Briggs

Spirituality/Spiritual Formation

The biblical word translated "spirit" in English means wind or breath. It is frequently used in the biblical languages as a metaphor for the life-giving God breathing life into his creation and creatures. It is the Invisible that is behind and gives energy to the visible: "The wind blows where it chooses, and you hear the sound of it, but you do not know where it comes from or where it goes. So it is with every one who is born of the Spirit [Wind]" (Jesus in John 3:8 NRSV). In the biblical revelation "Spirit" is the Third Person of the Trinity, God personally and creatively present and at work in his world. Three representative texts mark the contours of the formative work of Spirit in our world.

Genesis 1:1–3 (RSV): Creation by the Spirit accounts for everything there is, visible and invisible, "the heavens and the earth." The Spirit takes noncreation, or anticreation, that which is "without form and void," that which is without light ("darkness . . . upon the face of the deep") and makes something of it, gives it form and content, and floods it with light.

Mark 1:9–11 (RSV): The same Spirit of God, so lavishly articulated in words that create everything that is, descends on Jesus as he comes up from the waters of baptism and is identified as God's "beloved Son." The baptism is a replay of the Genesis creation in the formation of salvation.

Acts 2:1–4 (RSV): After Jesus' ascension, 120 of his followers wait to be "baptized with the Holy Spirit" (1:5 RSV), as he had instructed them. The continuity with God's life-giving breath in the Genesis creation and the Markan baptism is evident but also augmented—the holy breathing becomes a holy wind, "the rush of a mighty wind" (2:2). It fills the room and then fills them. Then the sign of fire is added. For them, fire was altar fire, associated with the active presence of God. Here each person is an "altar" signed with a tongue of fire, God's active presence. The breathing of Genesis creation and Jesus' baptism swells into a wind; old altar fires multiply into personalized fires above each waiting man and woman, each now a sign of God alive, present, and active.

The three texts are a tripod, grounding every aspect of life—creation, salvation, community—in the living (breathing) God: God alive makes alive, God the Spirit empowers our spirits. God's Spirit is not marginal to the main action, but *is* the main action.

In discussing spirituality and spiritual formation, it is essential that God's Spirit be understood as the root of the meaning of spirituality. "The Spirit is God's way of being present" (Fee xxi). The human spirit exists in continuity with God's Spirit but is not identical with it.

Spirituality

Spirituality was once used exclusively in religious contexts; it is now used indiscriminately by all sorts of people in all sorts of circumstances and with all sorts of meanings. This once pristine word has been dragged into the rough-and-tumble dirt of marketplace and playground.

In contemporary usage, that which has to do with spirit, that is, spirituality, has lost virtually all connection with God's Spirit. The term "spirituality" has become a net that, when thrown into the sea of contemporary culture, pulls in a vast quantity of spiritual fish, rivaling the resurrection catch of 153 "large fish" that John reports (21:11). Spirituality, de-Spirited, has become secularized into a major business for entrepreneurs and a recreational pastime for the bored. For others, whether many or few (it is hard to tell), it is still a serious and disciplined commitment to breathe deeply and live fully in and by God's Holy Spirit.

The attempt to reclaim the word for exclusively Christian or other religious usage usually begins with a definition. But attempts to define "spirituality"—and they are many—are futile. The term has escaped the disciplines of the dictionary. The current usefulness of the term is not in its precision but rather in the way it names something indefinable yet quite recognizable—Transcendence vaguely intermingled with Intimacy. Transcendence: a sense that there is more, a sense that life extends far beyond me, beyond what I get paid, beyond what my spouse and children think of me, beyond my cholesterol count. And Intimacy: a sense that deep within me there is a core being inaccessible to the probes of psychologists or the examinations of physicians, the questions of the pollsters, and the strategies of the advertisers. "Spirituality," though hardly precise, provides a catchall term that recognizes an organic linkage between this Beyond (transcendence) and Within (intimacy) that is part of everyone's experience. As such, by throwing every intimation of Beyond and Within into one huge wicker basket, the term can still be useful.

The word "spirituality" is a relative latecomer to our dictionaries and only recently has hit the streets in common, everyday speech. Paul used the adjective "spiritual" (*pneumatikos*) to refer to actions or attitudes derived from the work of the Holy Spirit in all Christians, people of the Spirit. He never used it to refer to "the interior life of a believer" (Fee 28–32). It was only later, in the medieval church and primarily in the context of monasticism, that the word was used to name a way of life restricted to an elite class of Christians—monks and nuns vowed to celibacy, poverty, and obedience, who worked at a higher level than ordinary Christians. "Spiritual" Christians were viewed in contrast to the muddled lives of men and women who married, had babies, and got their hands dirty in fields and markets. In that context spirituality came to designate the study and practice of a perfect life before God, a specialized word having to do with only a small number of people and never a part of everyday life.

The word entered our everyday language more or less through the back door. A movement developed among Roman Catholics in seventeenth-century France with the then-radical notion that the monasteries had no corner on the Christian life well lived. They insisted that the ordinary Christian was quite as capable of living the Christian life as any monk or nun—and living it just as well. Archbishop Fenelon, Madam Guyon, and Miguel de Molinos, prominent voices in this movement, were silenced under the condemnation of "quietism." The official church attempted to silence them, but it was too late; the cat was out of the bag. The term *la spiritualité* was used by the detractors as a term of derogation for laypeople who practiced their devotion too intensely—a snobbish dismissal of upstart Christians who did not know what they were doing, writing, thinking, and practicing. These were things best left in the hands of the church's religious experts. But it was not long before the word lost its pejorative tone. Among Protestants, lay-oriented spiritual seriousness came to be expressed in Puritan "godliness," Methodist "perfection," and Lutheran "pietism."

Spirituality, a loose "net" word, is now used on the streets with general approval. Now anybody can be spiritual.

Interestingly, some are again using the term dismissively. Because there appears to be a widespread and faddish use of the term by men and women judged to be misguided, ignorant, and undisciplined, some critics and "experts" are once again taking a condescending stance toward spirituality in its popular forms.

Living and living well is at the heart of all serious spirituality. At this time in our history, spirituality seems to be the term of choice to refer to this vast and intricate web of "livingness." It may not be the best word, but it is what we have. Its primary weakness is that in English it is an abstraction, even though the metaphor "breath" can be detected just beneath the surface. But the metaphor has been eroded into an abstraction so that "spirituality" frequently obscures the very thing it is intended to convey: God alive and active and present. The more the word is secularized, the less useful it is. Still, it does manage to convey a sense of living as opposed to dead. When we sense that the life has gone out of things and people, institutions and traditions, eventually, and sometimes this takes us a while, we notice the absence. We look for a file-drawer kind of word in which to store the insights and desires for just exactly what it is we are missing. "Spirituality" works about as well as anything for such filing purposes.

Spiritual Formation

The Christian community counters the vagueness associated with "spirituality" by addressing spiritual formation. Spiritual formation is not in the first place or for the most part what we do; it is what the Spirit of God does; it is the formation of life by the Spirit. God the Holy Spirit conceives and forms the life of Christ in us. Our spirits are formed by Spirit. Spirituality is never a subject that we can attend to as a thing-in-itself on our own, but requires formation by God's Spirit, a complex and lifelong way of being. It is always an operation of God the Spirit in which our human lives are pulled into and made participants in the life of God, whether as lovers or rebels.

We give careful attention to spiritual formation because we have learned, from long experience, how easy it is to get interested in ideas of God and projects for God while at the same time losing interest in God alive, deadening our lives with the ideas and projects. It is the devil's work to get us worked up in thinking and acting for God and then subtly detach us from a relational obedience and adoration, substituting our selves, our god-pretentious egos, in the place originally occupied by God.

Spiritual formation places Jesus at the center to keep us out of the center. Jesus keeps us attentive to the God-defined, God-revealed life that we are created to live. The amorphous limpness so often associated with spirituality is given skeleton, sinews, definition, and shape by Jesus. The Spirit that conceived Jesus in Mary's womb (Luke 1:31, 35) will also conceive Jesus in us (Gal. 4:19). Jesus is the central and defining figure in spiritual formation.

By accepting Jesus as the final and definitive revelation of God, the Christian church makes it impossible to make up our own customized variations of the spiritual life—not that we don't try. But we can't get around him or away from him: Jesus is the incarnation of God, God among and with us. This is the life, this Jesus life, the Spirit forms in us.

When we become more interested in ourselves than in the Spirit forming the life of Christ in us, we typically attempt to take over the work of formation, which always results in malformation. Three forms in which these "takeovers" often express themselves are in projects of self-improvement, the imposition of codes of conduct, and ventures into spiritual technology.

When spiritual formation is a project in self-improvement, the narratives and prayers of Scripture, and the guidance of theology, are replaced by the insights of psychology. Ideas and insights are begged, borrowed, and stolen indiscriminately, put to use as the person sees fit. Spiritual is all about my spirit and has nothing to do with Holy Spirit. Narcissus on his knees.

When spiritual formation is the imposition of a code of conduct, a respectable, moral life is cobbled together in order to become good without dealing personally with God. The Ten Commandments is the usual place to start, supplemented by Proverbs, salted by the Golden Rule and then capped off by the Beatitudes. Or something of that order. The Pharisee in stereotype.

When spiritual formation is a venture into spiritual technology, in a culture defined by information and technology, our spirits are formed unawares by impersonal knowing and efficient doing. In seeming innocence, we venture into a world of abstract principles, depersonalizing programs, and functionalized roles empty of Spirit. The devil in the desert.

The fundamental inadequacy of these ways of formation is that they put us in charge (or, which is just as bad, put someone else in charge) of something that we know next to nothing about. The moment that we take charge, "knowing good and evil," we are in trouble and almost immediately start getting other people in trouble, too.

But if we are not to turn spiritual formation into a project that we take over and manage, what do we do? This question needs to be delayed for as long as possible. We hold back on the question because spiritual formation mostly involves paying attention and participating in who God is—Father, Son, and Holy Spirit—and what he does. If we get too interested too soon in what *we* do and are, we go off the rails badly. Still, we are part of it and need a term to designate the human side of spiritual formation, something that accurately names what we do, but does not make us the center of the subject.

The term of choice is "fear-of-the-Lord," the stock biblical phrase for the way of life that is lived responsively and appropriately before God as he is and what he does as Father, Son, and Holy Spirit.

Despite its prominence in the Bible, the term does not find wide use among Christians today. "Fear" apparently gets us off on the wrong foot. Grammarians help us regain our biblical stride by calling attention to the fact that fear-of-the-Lord is a "bound" phrase (syntagm). The four words in English (two in Hebrew) are bound together, making a single word. The bound word cannot be taken apart, analyzed, and then defined by adding up the meanings of the parts. But when biblical contexts provide the conditions for understanding the word, we find that it means something more like a way of life in which human feelings and behavior are fused with God's being and revelation. There are upward of 138 occurrences of the term across a wide range of OT books (Waltke 17–33). God is active in the term; the human is active in the term. "Fear-of-the-Lord" is a new word in our vocabularies and a key to spiritual formation; it marks the way of life appropriate to our creation and salvation and blessing by God.

Question: So what is my part in spiritual formation?

Answer: "Fear the LORD, you his saints" (Ps. 34:9). Cultivate fear-of-the-Lord.

Fear-of-the-Lord is not studying about God but living in reverence before God; not specializing in "spiritual things" but attentively following Jesus where he leads; not merely maintaining moral standards, a subset of human behavior, but living the whole of life in prayerful conversation with God. Fear-of-the-Lord is the cultivation of everything we do as we are "breathing God."

The primary way in which we cultivate fear-of-the-Lord is in prayer, worship, and obedience: personal prayer, corporate worship, and sacrificial obedience. We deliberately interrupt our preoccupation with ourselves and attend to God, place ourselves intentionally in Sacred Space, in Sacred Time, in the Holy Presence. We become silent and still in order to listen and respond to what and who is Other than us. This is spiritual formation. In actual practice we find that it can occur any place and any time. But prayer, worship, and obedience provide the base.

A world has been opened up to us by revelation; we find ourselves walking on holy ground and living in sacred time. The moment we realize this, we feel shy, cautious. We slow down, we look around, ears and eyes alert. Like lost children happening on a clearing in the woods, and finding elves and fairies singing and dancing in a circle around a prancing two-foot-high unicorn. We stop in awed silence to accommodate this wonderful but unguessed revelation. But for us it isn't a unicorn; it is Sinai and Tabor and Golgotha.

See also Holy Spirit, Doctrine of the; Human Being, Doctrine of; Religion; Sanctification; Spiritual Sense

Bibliography

Augustine. *Confessions,* trans. A. Outler. Westminster, 1955; Bass, D., ed. *Practicing Our Faith.* Jossey-Bass, 1997; Berry, W. *A Timbered Choir: The Sabbath Poems, 1979–1997.* HarperCollins, 1998; Bonhoeffer, D. *Life Together,* trans. J. Doberstein. Harper & Bros., 1954; Borgmann, A. *Technology and the Character of Contemporary Life.* University of Chicago Press, 1984; Buechner, F. *Now and Then.* Harper & Row, 1983; Fee, G. *God's Empowering Presence.* Hendrickson, 1994; Ford, D. *The Shape of Living.* Baker, 1997; Foster, R. *Celebration of Discipline.* HarperSanFrancisco, 1978; Hauerwas, S. *A Community of Character.* University of Notre Dame Press, 1981; Lewis, C. S. *Till We Have Faces.* G. Bles, 1956; Miles, M. R. *Practicing Christianity.* Crossroad, 1990; Rad, G. von. *Wisdom in Israel.* Abingdon, 1972; Tugwell, S. *Ways of Imperfection.* Templegate, 1985; Waltke, B. "The Fear of the Lord." Pages 17–33 in *Alive to God,* ed. J. I. Packer and L. Wilkenson. InterVarsity, 1996; Williams, R. *Christian Spirituality.* John Knox, 1979.

Eugene H. Peterson

Spiritual Sense

The expression "spiritual sense" is the English equivalent of ancient designations that referred to a Spirit-conferred understanding of the biblical text. In this way the biblical text could become the sacrament of a faith experience of the divine realities mediated by its words. A more technical understanding of the term "spiritual sense," in use from the very beginning but codified in the Middle Ages, referred to the understanding of the events and personages of the OT that sees them in the light of Christ. In practice, especially in patristic exegesis, the term was also loosely employed to refer to other procedures that could range from moral application to exuberant fantasy.

An Epistemology of the Spirit

Hans-Georg Gadamer cites a relevant phrase of Martin Luther: "He who does not understand the realities cannot extract the meaning from the words" (frontispiece to part 2). After a detour of centuries Christian philosophy has retrieved and placed in a more profound context this type of critical and realistic epistemology. Knowledge, says Aquinas, is the effect of truth, and truth is the "assimilation of the knower to the thing known" (*De veritate* 1.1). In terms of revelation this means that, by the action of the Holy Spirit in and through the sacred text, divine reality, and ultimately the word of God himself, discloses God assimilating the believer to the divine truth and thus creating the effect of that truth: knowledge. And this "spiritual understanding," according to Augustine, "saves the believer" (*Enarrat. Ps.* 33.1, 7). It is for this reason, according to the ancient adage referred to by Vatican II in *Dei verbum* §12, that Scripture must be read and interpreted "in the same Spirit in which it was written."

The Spiritual Understanding of the OT

The inspired authors of the NT instinctively referred and alluded to the authoritative texts of what is now the OT. However, it took centuries before a beginning was made in a reflexive articulation of the manner in which the reality and mystery of Christ related to the Scriptures of Israel, and the task is not yet complete. Following the study of Joseph Lienhard, we can observe that the fundamental attitude of the NT writers was that of continuity and contrast. Paul accented the dimension of law without, however, ignoring the importance of prophetic teaching (Rom. 9–11), and even initiated the notion that the realities recounted in the OT had a figurative role in anticipating the realities of the NT (e.g., 1 Cor. 10:1–11). Once (Gal. 4:24) he adapted an expression (*allēgoroumena*) for this procedure that has often been pressed into service in ways unwar-

ranted by his text (Young, ch. 8). The Gospels, while replete with allusions to events, themes, and persons in the OT, place most of their accent on the prophetic texts, which already in Israel were understood to refer to a work of God in the future. It is here particularly that we find the term "fulfill." The subtlety and depth of the views of the Letter to the Hebrews would require a treatment of its own.

By the middle of the second century, the number of Gentile readers of the OT forced people to try to express fundamental questions regarding the relevance of the *whole* of the OT to Christian life and thought. At about this time rabbinic Judaism faced the same challenge in another way. Among Christians, two extremes of thought emerged: both paid minute attention to the OT, but both were unfaithful to the NT. On the one hand, Marcion read the OT literally and concluded that it was irrelevant, assigning its events and texts to the realm of an inferior and unstable god. On the other hand, the author of the *Letter of Barnabas* read the whole of the OT allegorically, using the text as a springboard for his own notions in a classical "this stands for that" reading of the OT text.

The foundational theoretical solution was elaborated by Irenaeus of Lyons (Lienhard; Simian-Yofre) with his notion of "recapitulation." Irenaeus saw clearly that both the continuity and discontinuity between the two dispensations lay in the relationship between the *events* and the *persons* and their situation within God's overall plan for history. For this relationship, he often used the term "recapitulation" (*anakephalaiōsis*), which he derived and developed from Eph. 1:10.

It was, however, Origen who developed this understanding of history and employed it in his exposition of the OT, and it is from him that we receive a consistent reading of the OT in the light of Christ. Whatever be made of Origen's exaggerations and flaws, there is no doubt that the church owes to him a fundamental attitude toward the OT that, despite the eclipse of recent centuries, is still the most faithful to the viewpoint of the NT. This is true because the church reads with faith the mystery of Christ already present in an anticipated manner in the history of Israel.

In this technical sense just discussed, the development of the spiritual understanding of the OT was marked, as exegesis has always been, by figures of great genius, such as Augustine and Chrysostom, as well as by a generous number of solid scholars and much repetition and error. Finally, at one point Augustinus Dacius (1260) summed up the tradition in a brief formula that found many imitators (de Lubac 1:1): "The literal meaning teaches you the events; how you are to understand them in faith is the allegorical (christological) meaning; the moral teaching in the text is its *tropological* meaning; while the as yet unfulfilled dimension of an OT or NT text is its *anagogical* (eschatological) meaning." The scholar who finally expressed the heart of the insight in theological terms was Thomas Aquinas (de Lubac 2:2). In the *Summa theologiae* (I/1.10) Aquinas builds upon a phrase of Gregory the Great (*Moral.* 20.1) to the effect that "Scripture transcends other bodies of knowledge in its way of speaking since with one and the same expression it both tells an event and makes known its relation to God's plan [dum narrat gestum, prodit mysterium]." The two words *gestum* and *mysterium* refer in turn to the literal sense, the event, and then the spiritual sense, the same event that is now seen to have been a participating anticipation of the mystery of Christ. Augustine has much the same to say: "We must seek out the plan of God in the event itself and not only in the text" (*Enarrat. Ps.* 68).

Aquinas's own answer is basically the same. He responds that God is able to have not only words signify, as humans can do, but also "res ipsas," which must be taken to mean "events" and not merely "things." He then goes on to say that the first signification, that of the words, belongs to the first meaning (*sensum*) "which is its historical or literal meaning/understanding." The signification by which "res [realities] signified by the words in turn signify other realities [the realities of the Christ event]" is called the "sensus spiritualis, which is founded upon the literal sense and presupposes it." It is obvious that the context of this discussion is that of the relation between the OT and the NT. Yet, for Aquinas as for the tradition preceding him, the realities of the NT have their own way of signifying and containing the eschatological realities yet to come and thus have an anagogical sense.

The West began its "passage to modernity" (Dupré) and began to be content with a nontranscendent understanding of history and of the act of thinking itself. In this transition, Christians lost the theological vision that provides the underpinning for the spiritual sense and considered it to be an arbitrary imposition from the outside on something that required only an immanent explanation. Thus, in achieving what is now called the "literal sense," an understanding of texts hitherto unattainable, something was gained and something was lost. On the side of history, what was gained was the development of a "science" of history: an ordered and critical assembling of knowledge about the past that enables one to contextualize the text and its author. On the side of knowledge itself there has been a greater appreciation of the role of the thinking subject in the act of knowledge. What has been lost and must be recovered is a sense of the depth, the interior dimension, of history and the direction being given to it by God, as well as the metaphysical nature of the act of knowledge itself.

On the Way to Recovery

The widespread dissatisfaction with the historical-critical method is leading people to search more deeply for a way of defining the reality attained by this method and locating it within the spectrum of knowledge. This can only be achieved by the development of an understanding of the Word incarnate as the objective center, cause, and goal of history. In tandem with the deficiencies of the historical-critical method itself is the neo-Kantian bias of its approach to reality. This is so profound that "reading the text in the light of the paschal mystery" has come to mean comparing texts in the light of a concept, rather than comparing realities mediated by the Holy Spirit through the texts, happening in the context of a faith experience of Jesus Christ. Only the latter merits to be called spiritual meaning or understanding.

It is often objected that reading the OT in this way results in a superficial imposition of preexisting notions upon the text in a way that ignores the profound spiritual depths already present there. That such an error has been committed in both past and present is undeniable. Continued modern study of the OT by both Jewish and Christian scholars such as Levenson, Lohfink, and Beauchamp serves to reveal what Augustine called the *mira profunditas* of the text, what we may call, in this context, its ongoing religious sense. These depths, valuable in themselves, are also refractions of the white light of Christ, enabling us to grasp more of his mystery.

It is also objected that searching for resemblances serves to parcel out the text into fragments and lose its own intrinsic meaning. Again, this has happened and continues to happen. The more reflexive achievements of literary and historical criticism (Sternberg) enable us to appreciate the subordinate role of certain aspects of a text that contribute to its overall meaning, as well as images and symbols. This may enable us to respond to the question of Origen, that lover of the OT who looked for Christ everywhere in its pages. Commenting on Gen. 18:8 ("Abraham . . . stood under a tree"), he writes: "What does it help me to hear what the Holy Spirit teaches the human race, if I hear that 'Abraham was standing under a tree'?" Our historical and epistemological knowledge has undoubtedly developed. It remains for us now to have that knowledge urged on by faith to mature into that living and experiential knowledge of divine realities that alone merits the name "spiritual sense."

See also Allegory; Literal Sense; Medieval Biblical Interpretation; Mysticism, Christian; Patristic Biblical Interpretation

Bibliography

Beauchamp, P. L'un et l'autre Testament. Éditions du Seuil, 1976; Dupré, L. Passage to Modernity. Yale University Press, 1993; Gadamer, H.-G. Truth and Method, trans. J. Weinsheimer and D. Marshall. Seabury, 1989; La Potterie, I. de. "The Spiritual Sense of Scripture." Comm 23 (1996): 738–56; Levenson, J. "The Universal Horizon of Biblical Particularism." Pages 143–69 in Ethnicity and the Bible, ed. M. Brett. Brill, 1996; Lienhard, J. "Origen and the Crisis of the Old Testament in the Early Church." ProEccl 9 (2000): 355–66; Lohfink, N., and E. Zenger. The God of Israel and the Nations, trans. E. R. Kalin. Liturgical Press, 2000; Lubac, H. de. Exégèse médiévale. 4 vols. Aubier, 1959–64; idem. Medieval Exegesis. Vol. 1 translated by M. Sebanc. Vol. 2 translated by E. Macieroweski. Eerdmans, 1998–2000; Martin, F. "St. Matthew's Spiritual Understanding of the Healing of the Centurion's Boy." Comm 25 (1998): 161–77; Michaud, J. "Des quatre sens de l'Écriture: Histoire, théorie, théologie, herméneutique." ÉgT 30 (1999): 165–97; Simian-Yofre, H. "Old and New Testament: Participation and Analogy." Pages 267–98 in Vatican II, ed. R. Latourelle. Paulist, 1988; Sternberg, M. The Poetics of Biblical Narrative. Indiana University Press, 1985; Young, F. Biblical Exegesis and the Formation of Christian Culture. Cambridge University Press, 1997.

Francis Martin

State   See Political Theology

Structuralism

Simply put, structuralism is the view that meaning in language and culture is based upon internal relations within the linguistic or cultural system as a whole, rather than something outside the system that is substantial. As a methodology, structuralism can be applied to any cultural phenomenon, whether language, individual texts, or societal practices. Structuralist elements can be found in a wide variety of movements and figures, only a few of which can be mentioned here.

Structuralism and semiotics (the study of signs) can be traced back to Ferdinand de Saussure (1857–1913), who radically reoriented linguistics. His Course in General Linguistics (1916) defines language as a system of signs that have meaning only by way of relation to one another. Whereas previous linguists had studied the historical development of language (diachronically), Saussure proposes that language be studied primarily as a systematic whole (synchronically). Focusing on language as langue (an objective structure) rather than as parole (actual, historical language), structuralist linguistics is thus purely formal in nature, concerned with "signifiers" rather than "referents" (the object to which a signifier refers). From a structuralist viewpoint, the meaning of signifiers is based on arbitrary convention and the play of signifiers, so that "in the language itself, there are only differences" (166, French pagination).

Roman Jakobson (1896–1982), who coined the term "structuralism," developed Saussure's ideas and applied them to literary texts. In his influential essay "Linguistics and Poetics: Closing Statement" (1960), Jakobson claims that all communication has the same structure. An addresser (speaker or writer) communicates a message (meaning) to an addressee (listener or reader) by way of a point of contact (speech or writing) that presumes a code (language) and context (which "frames" the message). Concentrating on any one of these elements gives an act of communication or interpretation a distinct orientation.

Lévi-Strauss expands structuralism by examining what he takes to be the universal code of cultures. In Structural Anthropology (1958), he claims (echoing Saussure) (1) that all languages share a structure that can be articulated in terms of binary oppositions (not only for such phonemes as "d" and "t" but also for such signifiers as "light" and "dark") and (2) that this binary structure can be found in all cultures. In The Savage Mind (1962), he attempts to ground the structure of language and culture in what he takes to be the universal unconscious structure of the human mind. Lévi-Strauss's most important claim is that, while myths clearly have diachronic elements, synchronically they have the same basic structure. He attempts to substantiate this claim in studies of a wide variety of cultures.

Roland Barthes (1915–80) and Michel Foucault (1926–84) are difficult to classify, in many ways. Both began as structuralists, even though they became increasingly uneasy with structuralism's underlying assumptions. In "Introduction to the

Structural Analysis of Narratives" (1966), Barthes presents a conception of narrative that assumes a universal structure to all narratives. But there is a significant reversal of structuralist ideas in his later thought. For instance, he later came to think that individual texts were primary, instead of the linguistic system itself. Similarly, although Foucault explicitly opens *The Order of Things* (1966) by denying that the book has anything to do with structuralist methods, his attempt to articulate the *epistemes*—the limits or structures governing thought and speech in given eras—is very much a structuralist project. *The Archaeology of Knowledge* (1969) is likewise an attempt to describe the rules of a discourse. Foucault's later texts, though, represent a sharp reversal, in which the genealogical (diachronic) method replaces archaeology (which is synchronic), and attention to the ways in which power is exercised becomes prominent.

One can easily apply structuralist methods to biblical texts, either as an exclusive way of interpretation or as merely one method among many. What distinguishes structuralist interpretations is the concern with structure over content and a particular (even though not necessarily exclusive) focus on the text itself. A text is read as exemplifying a narrative structure, linguistic pattern or genre, or cultural expression (such as the text's "story world"). For instance, an essay by Barthes presents a reading of Jacob's struggle in Gen. 32:22–32 that interprets the sequence of events as a pattern of passage, struggle, and nomination. Another example is the essay "Myth in Theology," in which Maurice Wiles claims that the four basic Christian myths are (1) creation, (2) fall, (3) incarnation and atonement, and (4) resurrection and judgment. Both "narrative criticism" and "form criticism" can be termed "structuralistic," at least to some degree.

The deficiencies of structuralism should be readily apparent, and it has come under increasing attack since the 1960s. First, structuralist analyses are inherently reductionistic, since particularity (of persons and entire cultures) is subsumed under the universal. But it is at least open to question whether such languages as Hebrew and English (for instance) are really structurally "the same," or whether the cultures that gave rise to those languages have—at root—an identical "deep structure." Second, whether the almost exclusive focus on *langue* instead of *parole* (formal structure over actual practice) gives us an accurate picture of either language or culture is likewise questionable. Third, although Saussure and other structuralists admit historical change in language and culture, structuralist analyses tend to be ahistorical in nature. Finally, the entire "structure" of structuralism depends upon the universality and stability of binary oppositions and "differences," a stability that may not be quite as rigid as structuralists assume. Not surprisingly, the recognition of these problems has given rise to what is known as poststructuralism.

See also Form Criticism and the NT; Form Criticism and the OT; Narrative Criticism; Poststructuralism; Semiotics

Bibliography

Barthes, R. "Introduction to the Structural Analysis of Narratives" and "The Struggle with the Angel: Textual Analysis of Genesis 32:22–32." In *Image—Music—Text*, ed. and trans. S. Heath. Hill & Wang, 1978; Caws, P. *Structuralism*. Humanities, 1988; Foucault, M. *The Archaeology of Knowledge*, trans. A. M. Sheridan Smith. Pantheon, 1972; idem. *The Order of Things*. French, 1966. ET, Vintage, 1970; Greenwood, D. C. *Structuralism and the Biblical Text*. Mouton, 1985; Jakobson, R. "Linguistics and Poetics: Closing Statement." In *Style in Language*, ed. T. Sebeok. Technology Press of MIT, 1960; Lévi-Strauss, C. *The Savage Mind*. University of Chicago Press, 1966; idem. *Structural Anthropology*. French, 1958, trans. C. Jacobson and B. Grundfest Schoepf. Basic, 1963; Saussure, F. de. *Course in General Linguistics*. French, 1916, trans. R. Harris. Open Court, 1986; Wiles, M. "Myth in Theology." In *The Myth of God Incarnate*, ed. J. Hick. Westminster, 1977.

Bruce Ellis Benson

Subjectivity   *See* Objectivity

Symbol   *See* Imagery; Metaphor; Semiotics

Synoptic Problem   *See* Gospels; Source Criticism

Syntax   *See* Language, Grammar and Syntax; Semiotics

Systematic Theology

Systematic theology is the cognitive and passionate enterprise that seeks to know and love the God of the gospel and to demonstrate its understanding in forms of obedient speech and practice.

Given the subject matter of the Bible—the words and works of God—it seems only fitting that systematic theologians would occupy a prominent role in conversations about Scripture's meaning and truth. Such, however, has not generally been the case in the modern academy, where biblical studies is seen to be an enterprise of neutral and objective historical description. In contrast, theology is thought to be a confession-based prescriptive activity that reads Scripture through the conceptual grid of doctrinal frameworks. The exegete says what people in the past—the biblical authors—thought about God; the theologian says what the church should believe about God today.

What for R. Bultmann was a question—Is exegesis without presuppositions possible?—has become the starting point for postmoderns, who contend that all interpretations show the signs of their historical, cultural, and political situatedness. The vaunted universal viewpoint of Enlightenment scholars has dissolved into a multiplicity of perspectives. Theology has not remained unaffected; once the queen of the sciences, theology has become as weak as any other form of tradition-based rationality, so much so that the very notion of "systematic" theology has become problematic.

Any adequate account of the role of systematic theology in the interpretation of Scripture must address the following issues: (1) the nature and method of theology as a form of God-centered biblical interpretation; (2) the way in which systems of theology seek to articulate the unity of the Scriptures; (3) the nature of doctrine, theology's best-known product; (4) how theology best serves the church, as a theoretical science and form of knowledge (*scientia*), or as a practical wisdom and form of life (*sapientia*).

The Unity and Diversity of Theologia: Historical Overview

Theology is as old as the proclamation, explication, and application of the Scriptures as the word of God. The fragmentation of the theological disciplines into specialized compartments (biblical, systematic, historical, philosophical, practical) is, by contrast, a later development.

Patristic Theologies. Perhaps the most important theological development in the early church was the ecumenical creeds. They sought to summarize the main substance of the biblical "faith that was once for all entrusted to the saints" (Jude 3) and hence to define orthodoxy: "what is to be believed by everyone, everywhere, at all times," said Vincent of Lérins. Creeds such as the Nicene (325) and Chalcedonian (451) helped to solidify the ancient Rule of Faith. The latter was itself a summary of the main story line of Scripture and a crucial hermeneutical tool for reading the OT and NT as referring to the words and acts of one and the same God, and for seeing Jesus Christ as part of the divine identity narrated in Scripture (Pelikan 369–96).

The creeds emerged from a process of following the biblical *signa* (signs) to the divine *res* ("thing," subject matter) to which they point. From the first, however, theologians differed as to their readings of the fundamental Christian thing. Tertullian and the Latin fathers interpreted with a framework influenced by categories taken from Roman law. Greek-speaking Alexandrian theologians like Origen, by contrast, were influenced by Hellenistic philosophies and discovered metaphysical, not moral, principles in Scripture. Yet a third type of theology, represented by Irenaeus, was motivated by pastoral interest and conceived the unity of Scripture in terms of redemptive history rather than in a system of truths (González 3–16).

Medieval Theologies. The beginnings of a distinct discipline of systematic theology are concomitant with the birth of the university, where the hitherto informal reading of Scripture (*lectio*) was transformed into a formal method of argumentation on the basis of Scripture (*disputatio*). Abelard's *Sic et non* demonstrated that it was not enough to cite the church fathers to settle theological questions because the authorities disagreed (for a detailed analysis of the twelfth-century origins of theology as an academic discipline, see Evans).

The academic lingua franca of the medieval university was Latin, but the categories were Aristotle's. The latter were mediated to the West via Spain, courtesy of Arabic scholarship. Aristotle's *Categories* set forth the universal principles of logic and a universal system of classification in terms of "substance" (a thing's essential nature) and "accidents" (the nonessential qualities that characterize a particular thing's actual existence). The challenge of theology, as the science of God, was to interpret the biblical description of God in terms of these metaphysical categories, a challenge that yielded several sophisticated accounts of the nature of theological language.

At this time theology was every bit as comprehensive and rational as the new philosophy, the main difference being that theology has recourse to the truths of special revelation, but natural philosophy does not. Such was the governing assumption behind the *Summa theologiae* of Thomas Aquinas, the crowning work of medieval "scholasticism" (a theological method that seeks the rational and systematic presentation of revealed truth on the basis of a set of concepts). His so-called golden synthesis combined classical learning and biblical revelation, supplementing what can be known of God, the world, and ourselves by natural reason, with what can be known only through the revealed truths of Scripture. At the same time, he made the perhaps fateful decision to exposit these biblical truths largely through syllogistic reasoning and with categories drawn from Aristotle (such as substance, form, matter, cause).

Reformation Theologies. Reformation theologians, riding the crest of the Renaissance wave of scholarship into the original languages of the Bible, eschewed abstract speculation and examined anew the relation of theologies to the original sources on which they were supposedly based. Luther, for example, proposed to base his theology on the Bible and Augustine rather than on the scholastic tradition and Aristotle. The Reformers rejected tradition as a supplement to the Scriptures, viewing it instead as an authoritative interpretation of Scripture. Moreover, tradition's authority was ministerial only; the Bible and the Bible alone enjoyed magisterial authority as the locus of the word of God written.

The Reformation emphasis on the clarity and authority of Scripture went hand in hand with its view of theology as a more or less direct exposition of the text. However, agreement upon the authoritative source of theology did not entail a necessary agreement as to how this source was to be interpreted. Accordingly, diverse theologies associated with the Lutheran and Reformed churches were set forth systematically, each with its own set of proof texts.

Historians of doctrine commonly portray post-Reformation Protestant theology as exchanging its birthright—the revealed truths of the gospel—for a mess of rationalistic pottage. Yet the scholastic character of confessionally driven Protestant theology in the seventeenth century may not be a function of indebtedness to Aristotle's metaphysics (or to any philosophical scheme, for that matter). Instead, it may be more committed to detailed analysis and to passing on the Reformers' insights to succeeding generations (Muller 17–27). Like tradition, reason played a ministerial, not a magisterial role: "Reason never proves faith, but only elaborates faith toward understanding" (Muller 93).

Modern and Postmodern Theologies. The success of science in the early modern era, counterpoised with the incessant wars of religion, prompted the following question: Is there a single universal method that can be employed by every intellectual discipline and religious faction? Descartes's method of "universal doubt"—not believing anything that was not based on an indubitable foundation—combined with Kant's inquiry into the limits of human reason resulted in the project of Enlightenment criticism: not "faith seeking understanding" but "reason seeking evidence." Critical reason was autonomous and neither tradition-based nor confession-bound.

Ironically, most "autonomous" liberal and revisionist theologians busied themselves commending Christianity to contemporary culture by interpreting the Bible in terms of the latest theories and intellectual movements. The result was systems of theology without dogma—isms for thinking about God on the basis of human religious experience, including the religious experience recorded in what was now generally thought of as a humanly authored Bible. R. Bultmann's demythologizing and P. Tillich's method of correlation, with their wholesale translation of biblical terms into concepts taken from existentialism, represent the high-water mark of modern theology's quest for a single universally applicable system of theological interpretation.

If modern theology sought a universal "view from nowhere," the first principle of postmodern theology is "location, location, location." The situatedness of the theologian trumps his or her supposedly neutral methodology. What was previously thought of as a candidate for metanarrative status is now seen as merely one more community narrative expressing a particular group's interpretative interest. From this vantage point, the whole history of Western theology is only a series of "local theologies" (Schreiter).

Theological Systems

Whereas philosophical theology seeks to understand God truly on the basis of reason and universal human experience, systematic theology—a church-based rather than academy-based discipline—works with material provided by general and especially special revelation. Biblical theologies set forth the unity of Scripture by unfolding the single history of redemption or by tracing the historical development of certain biblical themes. Systematic theologies set forth the unity of Scripture in terms of a different kind of order—more suitable for displaying the overall conceptual consistency of the biblical witness as a finished and complete work. Traditionally, systematicians have claimed to provide a scientific ordering of the Bible's content.

The systematic understanding that faith seeks is nothing less than a grasp of the relation of the parts to the whole, the inherent connections of the faith, where the whole is the completed story of God's relation to the world from its original creation to its final consummation. However, there is more than one system for configuring the various biblical parts.

On the Very Idea of a Theological System. The raw materials for building systems of theology—what E. Gilson called "cathedrals" of the mind—include Scripture, tradition, human experience (both individual and corporate, which is culture), and reason. A system is a way of ordering and coordinating these raw materials. The key question thus becomes this: What are the principles by which we will organize what the Bible says? Where do the categories that comprise one's interpretative framework come from? The task of biblical theologians is to discern such categories in Scripture itself, in apparent contrast to those systematic theologians who borrow categories from philosophy or who at the least order their accounts in some kind of logical rather than chronological fashion.

Theological systems may be "hard" and "strong," or "soft" and "weak." "Strong" theological systems resemble geometries and exposit Scripture with a comprehensive set of categories and a definite logic (Gunton 7). Typically, this means interpreting the meaning and truth of Scripture in terms of some comprehensive conceptual scheme. T. Aquinas, for example, interpreted the biblical depiction of God with categories taken from Aristotle (e.g., "uncaused cause").

While "hard" theological systems enjoy a high degree of intelligibility vis-à-vis the intellectual framework of the day, the danger of such systems is that they are governed by a conceptual scheme—by some ism, like Platonism or existentialism—that ends up being imposed upon the text. H. Frei warns against such "extratextual" theologies, observing that they invariably end up distorting the identity of Jesus Christ and hence the gospel itself. There are thus properly theological reasons for heeding the prophetic warning of postmodern thinkers about the violence wreaked on the texts by such Procrustean conceptual schemes.

Not every theological system needs be totalitarian. A kinder, gentler version of systematicity requires only that one take responsibility for the overall consistency of one's beliefs. Such quests for coherence do not necessarily kowtow to a particular philosophy; they merely strive for intellectual honesty, where honesty means both being consistent within one's own thinking and doing

justice to the particular subject matter. For example: "The intrasystematic relations with which Irenaeus is concerned are chiefly those of the economy of divine actions" (Gunton 9). Irenaeus's system consists in recognizing the distinction-in-unity of creation and redemption, along with the typological connections that bind the history of Israel to the history of Jesus Christ. As such, it is more intra- than extratextual, a (narrative) network of truths rather than a static and hierarchical structure.

Systems of Theology: A Brief Miscellany. Theologians differ as to starting points and the relative weight given to the various loci or doctrines. Some contend that there is a single order and a necessary hierarchy of truths (e.g., from divine cause to created effects). In general, disparate systems of theology emerge from one of three sources: (1) competing worldviews (e.g., rival metaphysics); (2) different privileged human experiences (e.g., rival anthropologies); (3) different interpretations of the main story line of the Bible (e.g., rival theologies).

Some authors use metaphysical interpretative frameworks. One need only compare and contrast the systems of classical and process theism to appreciate the difference an underlying metaphysics makes. Classical theism, using Aristotelian categories as modified by Aquinas, thinks of God as a being of infinite perfection, immutable, impassible, and eternal. The Westminster Shorter Catechism similarly weds biblical and Aristotelian categories when it defines God as "a Spirit—infinite, eternal, and unchangeable—in his being, wisdom, power, holiness, justness, goodness, and truth" (Q. 4).

In contrast to classical theism, with its underlying substantival metaphysics, process theism conceives of God in terms of an underlying process metaphysics. For the latter, "event" and "becoming," not "being" and "substance," are the fundamental categories for thinking about and classifying reality, and for which "persuasion" and "influence," not cause and effect, characterize the God-world relation. On the process view, the world is God's "body," and God is the "creativity" of the world. As in classical theism, other Christian doctrines are worked out in terms of this overarching process metaphysic.

Other authors use anthropological interpretative frameworks. F. Schleiermacher's fateful decision to view theology as the science of faith rather than the science of God gives rise to a very different tradition of system-making, this time based not on metaphysics but on analyses of human experience. For Schleiermacher himself, Christian doctrines are "accounts of the religious affections set forth in speech." R. Bultmann's theology is the epitome of such anthropological systems, providing as it does a comprehensive set of categories, taken from existentialist philosophy, for explicating the self-understanding that accompanies faith in the proclaimed word of God. In this view, theological statements are clarifications of inauthentic (e.g., sinful) or authentic (e.g., saved) human existence.

So-called advocacy theologies—done from the perspective (and for the benefit) of a certain social or ethnic group (e.g., women, the poor, Black, Native American) or combinations thereof (e.g., womanist, *mujerista*)—make race, gender, and class into lenses through which to filter theology. As such, they are anthropological; yet, unlike Bultmann, they do not attempt to describe the universal human experience of a particular people group. The experience of a particular community serves as a vantage point from which to read and critically reexamine Scripture and Christian tradition. The emphasis is less on doctrine and orthodoxy than on justice and orthopraxis. "System" in the present context thus refers more to a method than to a finished set of connected doctrines. Given the sheer scope of human diversity, there is almost no end to the proliferation of such systems. This fact renders increasingly problematic various expressions of the unity and catholicity of theological truth, not to mention criteria for truth.

Many authors use biblical/theological interpretative frameworks. Not all theological systems rely on conceptual or experiential frameworks. K. Barth departs from arbitrarily chosen starting points in sources outside Scripture on the basis that merely human standpoints fail to come to the real subject matter of theology—God in self-revelation—on its own terms: "If I have a system, it is limited to a recognition of what Kierkegaard called the 'infinite qualitative distinction' between time and eternity" (Barth, *Romans*, "Preface" to 2d ed.). The material insight behind the whole of Barth's theology is that everything there is to know about God is revealed in the event of Jesus Christ, in which we see that God is "for us" as Father, Son, and Spirit.

Some theological systems may similarly be distinguished on the basis of their different material insights into the logic governing the story line of the Bible. Reformed theology differs from its Arminian counterpart on the basis of their respective soteriologies, in particular, their rival

conceptions of the relation between (and the relative priority of) human freedom and divine grace. In this connection, some have suggested that there are only two self-consistent systems of theology possible: Pelagianism and Augustinianism (Hodge 96).

Other material theological insights give rise to certain hermeneutical principles that generate still more systems. Luther's insight into justification by faith, for example, developed into a law/gospel distinction that became the key organizing principle of Lutheran theology. Similarly, classic dispensational theology is based on a hard-and-fast distinction between Israel and the church, and on a reading of Scripture that stresses the discontinuity of God's dealings with humans in different ages or dispensations.

The State of the Systematic Art: Doctrine in Contemporary Theology

The Bible is an indispensable resource in the theologian's attempt to set forth an orderly account of Christian belief. Accordingly, every theology must be prepared to give an account of the way in which it moves from Scripture to doctrine.

Doctrines of God and Doctrines of Scripture. D. Kelsey has convincingly demonstrated that not all theologians who profess biblical authority practice it in the same way. Even those who may agree on "what it meant" may disagree about "what it means" for the church today (Kelsey 202–3). In short, systems of theology differ not only in their basic material insights, but also in the formal patterns that distinguish their uses of Scripture. Various theologians construe the Bible "as" history or "as" myth or "as" doctrine in a way that correlates with their imaginative discernment of the mode of God's presence and activity in and with the believing community. Kelsey thus calls our attention to the importance of what we might term the "theological-hermeneutical circle": one's use of Scripture in theology is related to one's doctrine of God, and one's doctrine of God is related to the church's use of Scripture.

Doctrine and Narrative. As the title of Kelsey's work itself indicates, one of the most common uses of Scripture in systematics is to substantiate theological claims: to prove doctrine. How does Scripture generate and exercise control over doctrine? "The genesis of doctrine lies in the exodus from uncritical repetition of the narrative heritage of the past" (McGrath 7). On this view, one obtains doctrine by thinking through the logic and implications of the biblical story.

The doctrine of the atonement, for example, is not metaphysical speculation but an answer to the question "How is Jesus' death 'for us'?" Doctrine results from faith seeking understanding of the biblical narrative. The Reformation cry of *sola scriptura* is an assertion of "the primacy of the foundational scriptural narrative over any framework of conceptualities which it may generate" (McGrath 64). Yet certain doctrinal differences remain even between traditions that profess *sola scriptura*.

Doctrine and Church Practice. One recent development deserves special note. G. Lindbeck, in a much-discussed 1984 work, argues that doctrines are neither truth claims about objective realities nor symbolic expressions of subjective religious experience, but rather rules for inter-subjective—which is to say, ecclesial—language and practice. Theology thus explicates the "grammatical" rules that govern Christian speech and action. Though Lindbeck defines "Christian" language in relation to the biblical narrative, what theology actually ends up describing is the logic of ecclesial practice.

This cultural-linguistic turn represents an important sea change in Protestant theology. The new focus for theology is not the Bible as such but the Bible-as-used-in-the-church, which is another way of saying tradition. On this, postliberals, Radical Orthodox, and Catholic-evangelical theologians appear to agree: "Knowing the triune God is inseparable from participating in a particular community and its practices—a participation which is the work of God's Holy Spirit" (Buckley and Yeago 1). Being in a community of interpretation is, in this view, the only way to know what God means in Scripture (Gracia). The relevant question to be asked of this approach is whether such descriptions get us beyond sociology to theology proper.

Theodramatic Systematics

Too sharp a dichotomy between theory and practice (e.g., systems of doctrinal knowledge vs. forms of community life) is just as toxic to the project of faith seeking understanding as it is to the theological interpretation of Scripture. Accordingly, systematic theology needs to take its bearings by attending to (1) the subject matter of the history of redemption that culminates in Jesus Christ, and (2) the way in which the church can demonstrate its understanding of this subject matter by the way it continues to follow Jesus Christ in new cultural contexts.

The Gospel, the Theodrama, and the Script. At the heart of Christian theology is a series of divine words and divine deeds, historical sayings and enactments: a drama of redemption. Theology must respond and correspond to this prior divine speech and action, this theodrama (Balthasar). And it has. The earliest doctrinal reflection sought to clarify the divine *dramatis personae*. Subsequent doctrinal reflection sought to clarify the meaning and significance of the divine action.

The Bible is the normative specification of the gospel: a divinely authorized and commissioned account of the words and deeds that comprise the theodrama. For this reason Scripture is the church's authoritative script, the final criterion of theological understanding. At the same time, the script needs to be taken into new situations. What is called for is not mere repetition, but creative understanding.

Doctrine as Direction. Christian doctrine provides direction for the church's fitting participation in the drama of redemption (Vanhoozer, *Drama*). This "directional" model focuses on doctrine's role in enabling believers to be competent participants in the continuing theodrama.

Doctrinal claims about what is fit action for the church today rest on claims about what God has done. The directional model of doctrine thus integrates cognitive-propositional understanding with practical understanding (e.g., knowing what to say and do now as faithful disciples). Doctrine is a statement of "performance knowledge," a direction given for assuming one's proper place in the drama of redemption. Doctrine is direction for scripted and spirited performances of the gospel's truth in concrete contexts.

Conclusion: Toward a Sapiential Systematics

"Systems" of theology, at their best, are more than theoretical; they are "designs for living" (Gunton 11) that embody the wisdom of God revealed in Jesus Christ. A systematic theology oriented to practical wisdom rather than theoretical knowledge only seeks theodramatic understanding, a grasp of both the biblical script and the contemporary situation, in order to participate fittingly in the drama of redemption: "Given what we have heard and seen as the gospel, what shall we next say and enact?" (Jenson 21).

Systematic theology is a matter of understanding the church's situation in its cultural-historical context in light of the gospel in its canonical context. Though all systems this side of the *eschaton* will be provisional (because the church's situation varies), Christian wisdom can be learned through an apprenticeship to Scripture that is attentive to the particularities of its canonical forms and cultural situations (Vanhoozer, *Drama*).

A Plurivocal Systematics. The polyphonic Scriptures speak in many and diverse ways of what God was doing in Jesus Christ. Systematic theology must resist reducing the many authorial voices and literary forms of Scripture to a single set of concepts. As M. Bakhtin has argued, literary genres are more than rhetorical packages that can be unwrapped to get their content; instead, genres are modes of experience and cognition that cannot be reduced without significant loss to the propositional information they convey. Some truths, for example, can only be articulated dialogically—an insight that casts new light on why the NT includes four Gospels.

Similarly, it is unlikely that a single interpretative community or scheme will discern all that there is to be gleaned from Scripture. A canonically bounded polyphonic tradition that includes Western and non-Western voices, ancient and modern, best corresponds to the nature of the Scriptures themselves. To acknowledge such plurality is not to leave systematic theology bereft of criteria. On the contrary, both the "canonic" and "catholic" principles that should govern theology are simultaneously plural and yet bounded.

A Phronetic Systematics. For much of its history, systematic theology has been conceived as a kind of science that aims at *epistēmē*: theoretical knowledge. However, if doctrine is to exercise a directive and a pastoral function (Charry), it would do well to recover *phronēsis*: practical reason, the ability to deliberate well about what to say and do in particular situations to the glory of God. Scripture remains the supreme authority for systematic theology, not as an epistemic norm that caters to modernity's craving for theoretical certainty and completeness, but as a sapiential norm that provides direction for fitting participation in the ongoing drama of redemption.

In conclusion, a sapiential systematics proceeds from faith seeking theodramatic understanding, displays both canonic sense and catholic sensibility, and aims at bearing faithful witness in word and deed to the truth of God, world, and self made known "in Christ."

See also Biblical Theology; Model; Providence; Rule of Faith; Theological Hermeneutics, Contemporary; Truth; Word of God

Bibliography

Balthasar, H. *Theo-Drama*. 5 vols. Ignatius, 1988–98; Buckley, J., and D. Yeago, eds. *Knowing the Triune God*. Eerdmans, 2001; Charry, E. *By the Renewing of Your Minds*. Oxford University Press, 1997; Evans, G. R. *Old Arts and New Theology*. Clarendon, 1980; Evans, G. R., A. McGrath, and A. Galloway, *The Science of Theology*. Vol. 1 of *The History of Christian Theology*. Eerdmans, 1996; Ford, D., ed. *The Modern Theologians*. 2d ed. Blackwell, 1997; Ford, D., and G. Stanton, eds. *Reading Texts, Seeking Wisdom*. Eerdmans, 2003; Frei, H. *Types of Christian Theology*. Yale University Press, 1992; González, J. *Christian Thought Revisited*. Orbis, 1999; Gracia, J. *How Can We Know What God Means?* Palgrave, 2001; Green, G. *Theology, Hermeneutics, and Imagination*. Cambridge University Press, 2000; Grenz, S., and J. Franke. *Beyond Foundationalism*. Westminster John Knox, 2001; Gunton, C. "A Rose by Any Other Name? From 'Christian Doctrine' to 'Systematic Theology.'" *IJST* 1 (1999): 4–23; Hodge, A. A. *Outlines of Theology*. Zondervan, 1972; Holmes, S. *Listening to the Past*. Baker, 2002; Horton, M. *Covenant and Eschatology*. Westminster John Knox, 2002; Jenson, R. *Systematic Theology*. Vol. 1. Oxford University Press, 1997; Kelsey, D. *Proving Doctrine*. Trinity, 1999; Levering, M. *Scripture and Metaphysics*. Blackwell, 2004; Lindbeck, G. *The Nature of Doctrine*. Westminster John Knox, 1984; McGrath, A. *The Genesis of Doctrine*. Eerdmans, 1990; Muller, R. *Post-Reformation Reformed Dogmatics*. Vol. 1. Baker, 1987; Pelikan, J. *Credo*. Yale University Press, 2003; Schreiter, R. *Constructing Local Theologies*. Orbis, 1985; Schwöbel, C. "Doing Systematic Theology." *King's Theological Review* 10 (1987): 51–57; Vanhoozer, K., *The Drama of Doctrine*. Westminster John Knox, 2005; idem, ed. *Cambridge Companion to Postmodern Theology*. Cambridge University Press, 2003; Wainwright, G. *Doxology*. Oxford University Press, 1980.

Kevin J. Vanhoozer

T

Targum

The Hebrew term "targum" (plural: "targumim") literally means "translation," but in the rabbinic period (ca. first–seventh centuries CE) the term came to refer specifically to the written Jewish Aramaic translations of the Hebrew Bible (OT). Targumim exist for every book of the Bible except Ezra, Nehemiah, and Daniel, possibly because these books already contain significant portions in Aramaic. Like the Septuagint, there are actually several different textual traditions within the corpus of targumim. Thus, there are three primary groups of targumim that are translations of the Pentateuch: Targum Onqelos, Targum Pseudo-Jonathan, and Targum Neofiti. Fragmentary targumim to the Pentateuch also appear in at least five different groups, in addition to the Cairo Geniza fragments. Targum Jonathan is the targum to the Prophets (within the Jewish canon these books include Joshua, Judges, 1–2 Samuel, 1–2 Kings, and the Major and Minor Prophets, but *not* Daniel). Finally, targumim exist for the Jewish canonical division of the Writings. These are often later translations (probably from the sixth–eighth centuries CE), and different textual traditions are sometimes attested for individual books, such as two quite different targumim to Ruth.

The origins of the targumim can probably be traced back to the liturgical practices in the synagogue. The Mishnah (ca. 200 CE) states that the reading of the biblical text in a synagogue is to be accompanied with an appropriate translation so that all might understand the text being read (*m. Meg.* 4:4). Rabbinic texts make it clear that the *meturgeman*, the one who translates the biblical text into Aramaic during the synagogal service, is not allowed to read from a written text. Thus, the congregation will not confuse the translation with the actual holy, written word. This leads to the possibility that the physical texts we study today may not, in fact, represent the actual targum as recited in the synagogue. Nonetheless, the written targumim that we can study share this same

respect for the Bible as God's word and exhibit this in the nature of the genre.

The targumim are at once both translation and commentary. As translation a targum is engaged in the task of faithfully representing God's word by rendering into Aramaic every word of the biblical text in its proper order. (This is in contrast with midrash, rabbinic exegetical commentary, which often comments only upon select verses.) Yet in the targumim commentary is also frequently woven into the translation and thus moves targum beyond what we might define in modern terms as a "simple translation." This is most often found as simple glosses or additional words and phrases added to the text for explanation, but occasionally larger sections of material will be spliced into the text.

For example, Gen. 15:1 reads, "After this, the word of the LORD came to Abram in a vision." In one targum tradition, Targum Onqelos, the text reads, "After these matters, the word of the LORD *was before* Abram in a *prophecy*." (The italics indicate material added to the base translation of the Hebrew text.) Here the targumist has avoided referring to God's revelation to Abram as a vision, possibly to avoid an anthropomorphic attribution to God, while emphasizing that the message Abram received was indeed from God and was prophetic. Yet another targum tradition of the same passage, Targum Pseudo-Jonathan, is much more expansive. I offer only a small portion of it here. "After these words, *when the kings had gathered together, and had fallen before Abram; and four kings had been slain, and nine hosts brought back, Abram reasoned in his heart, and said, Woe to me, because I have received the reward of my appointments in this world, and have no portion in the world to come. . . .*" In this targumic version several lines precede the actual translation of Gen. 15:1 and place the biblical passage of God reassuring Abram that his own child shall be his heir in what the targumist understands as the proper context. Even this brief example illustrates that the exegetical activity of the targum is similar to that of midrash, but its mode is significantly different since it is confined within the context of translation.

See also Commentary; Jewish Exegesis; Translation

Christian M. M. Brady

Temple

Biblical tradition identifies the temple as the place of *sacrifice* and of *vision*. The connections among these three elements are so intimate that, not only is the temple the ordained site of offering to God and of seeing God disclosed, but this sacred space is also delineated by vision, by sacrifice.

When Moses ascends Sinai with Aaron, Nadab, and Abihu, they see the God of Israel on his sapphire throne, and eat a meal in God's presence. The covenantal sacrifice of pouring blood on the altar and over the people prepares for that encounter (Exod. 24:3–11). Moses remains on the mountain; God gives him commandments for all the items necessary to worship in the temple.

The vision of God is fraught with danger. "You cannot see my face, for no one may see me and live" (Exod. 33:20), Yahweh tells Moses in the same book that also recounts Moses' vision of the divine throne and his specification of what he saw and heard on Sinai. Those who would prepare for a visionary encounter must be pure, and must be ready to understand that they see partially, not yet face-to-face (1 Cor. 13:12).

Prophetic vision often takes precedence over the assignment of any established site of God's temple. Jacob sees the entry to heaven at Bethel ("House of God," Gen. 28:10–22), for example, and Elijah's sacrifice on Mt. Carmel trumps all the nationalistic pretensions of Ahab and Jezebel's cultic innovations in Israel (meaning the northern kingdom; 1 Kings 18). Later, in this kingdom that has separated from Judah, Amos assails all worship—particularly at Bethel—as systematic oppression (Amos 2:6–5:27); he sounds the perennial prophetic warning that worship without justice is synonymous with idolatry.

Even the settled establishment of Solomon's temple is subjected to prophetic criticism. Isaiah sees the seraphim and God's royal apparel streaming into the sanctuary (Isa. 6:1–5), yet then disciplines a king whose role is to protect the temple (7:1–17). Jeremiah trenchantly insists (7:4 AT), "Do not trust in these lying words: 'This is the temple of the LORD, the temple of the LORD, the temple of the LORD!'" Prophetic wisdom insists that the site of offering is not a place with physical coordinates only, but also a focus of the sacrificial worship and dedicated vision that pleases God.

Acceptable sacrifice occasions divine pleasure. When Noah sacrificed of his clean animals, the "pleasing odor" delighted God (Gen. 8:21 RSV), and although it was obvious that imagination of the human heart was no better after the flood than before, this offering put humanity in a new light. They could not be perfect, but they could be pleasing. People felt honest enjoyment in the act of feasting—normally a vital aspect of sacrifice in Israel, especially during the great festivals of Passover, Weeks, and Booths. God also enjoyed a good sacrifice, the gathering of God's people with the yield of their labor and appropriate concern for their ritual and ethical purity.

Vision and sacrifice not only made the temple, but also restored it. God's presence went with his people into exile. His Spirit inspired Ezekiel, with the deported Judeans in Babylonia, to describe his vision of God's chariot-throne in detail, and to specify the dimensions of the new temple that was to replace what the Babylonians had destroyed in 587 BCE (Ezek. 1, 40–48). God would move heaven and earth to have his house among his people again, and this time the prophetic ambition for worship there extended beyond historic Israel. This was to be a house of prayer for all nations (Isa. 56:6–7). People from outside Israel, non-Jews, would come to that temple and take part in sacrifice there, especially at the feast of Booths, the biggest, lushest sacrifice of the annual cycle (Zech. 14).

That vision of Zechariah, who promoted the building of the second temple, also played a pivotal role in Jesus' actions in Jerusalem. Zechariah foresaw a time when, because peoples of the world were freely to enter the temple for sacrifice, there would be no trade, no merchants whatever involved in the sanctuary (14:20–21). When Jesus saw that the high priest Caiaphas had in fact permitted trade in the temple, he took action, clearing the outer court of animals and their vendors (Matt. 21:12–13; Mark 11:15–17; Luke 19:45–46; John 2:13–17), and prompting the mortal enmity of Caiaphas.

Jesus' response to a temple that put trade in the place of purity was that it was a "cave of thugs," in the words of Jeremiah (7:11 AT); it did not deserve to stand. In his vehement insistence on the priority of prophetic sacrifice and vision over literal place, Jesus also claimed that his meals with his disciples—which had long been designed as celebrations of God's kingdom—amounted to better offerings than what Caiaphas sanctioned in the temple. The meal became a visionary sacrifice, with wine taking the place of literal "blood" and bread replacing an animal's "body" or "flesh" (Matt. 26:26–28; Mark 14:22–24; Luke 22:17–19; John 6:53; 1 Cor. 11:23–25). Jesus' meals became a prophetic challenge to the temple establishment, which replied with Rome in executing Jesus and dispersing his followers.

Jesus' resurrection emboldened his disciples to return to Jerusalem, despite the continuing opposition of the high priesthood. Every day they worshiped in the temple and "broke bread in their homes" (Acts 2:46). The living presence of the Lord was their assurance that Jesus' vision of a universal sacrifice on Mt. Zion would be vindicated. Until then, his meals held the place of Zechariah's prophecy. In addition to Peter, and eventually supplanting Peter in a position of leadership in the holy city, James (Jesus' brother) occupied a prominent place in temple worship, especially in his encouragement of the Nazirite vow (Acts 21:17–26) among Jesus' followers.

Paul was also involved in the support of the community that worshiped in the temple, and he saw this as his own priestly service for the "offering of the nations" (Rom. 15:16 AT). At the same time, Paul described Jesus as the *hilastērion* (Rom. 3:25), the place of delight where God meets his people. Commentators continue to dispute whether this word here means "mercy seat" (the throne over the ark of the covenant) or "propitiation" more generally. Either way, the focus on the delight God takes in meeting his people in Jesus is evident. Once the Roman army in 70 CE destroyed the second temple, the way was open for thinkers such as the author of Hebrews to see Jesus as the definitive replacement of any physical temple for all time. The vision of God and the giving of oneself in imitation of Christ's sacrifice once-for-all (Heb. 9:23–28) took the place of any literal altar of sacrifice. There would be a new heaven, a new earth, a new Jerusalem, but one would see "no temple in the city, for its temple is the Lord God the Almighty and the Lamb" (Rev. 21:1–2, 22).

Bibliography

Anderson, G. A. *Sacrifices and Offerings in Ancient Israel*. HSM 41. Scholars Press, 1987; Brandon, S. G. F. *The Fall of Jerusalem and the Christian Church*. SPCK, 1957; Brown, J. R. *Temple and Sacrifice in Rabbinic Judaism*. Seabury-Western Theological Seminary, 1963; Büchler, A. *Studies in Sin and Atonement*. Ktav, 1967; Busink, T. A. *Der Tempel von Jerusalem von Salomo bis Herodes*. Brill, 1980; Caillois, R. *L'homme et le sacré*. Gallimard, 1989; Chilton, B. *Redeeming Time*. Hendrickson, 2002; Daly, R. J. *Christian Sacrifice*. SCA 18. Catholic University of America Press, 1978; Grappe, C., and A. Marx. *Le sacrifice*. Essais bibliques 29. Labor & Fides, 1998; Haran, M. *Temples and Temple-Service in Ancient Israel*. Oxford University Press, 1978; Levine, B. *In the Presence of the Lord*. SJLA 5. Brill, 1974; Mazar, B. *The Mountain of the Lord*, trans. G. Cornfield. Doubleday, 1975; Milgrom, J. *Studies in Cultic Theology and Terminology*. Brill, 1983; Roth, C. "The Cleansing of the Temple and Zechariah XIV 21." *NovT* 14 (1960): 174–81; Smith, W. R. *Lectures on the Religion of the Semites*. Black, 1901; Westcott, B. F. *The Epistle to the Hebrews*. Macmillan, 1909; Yerkes, R. K. *Sacrifice in Greek and Roman Religions and Early Judaism*. Scribner, 1952.

Bruce Chilton

Tertullian See Patristic Biblical Interpretation; Rule of Faith; Scripture, Unity of

Testimonia See Intertextuality

Text Linguistics See Language, Linguistics; Text/Textuality; Utterance Meaning

Text/Textuality

Readers of any edition of the Bible are confronted with a canonical collection of *texts*. Although these texts have been heard and read since their composition and collection by every generation of Christians, only since the early nineteenth century has their textuality been explored in greater detail within the larger framework of hermeneutical thinking. Theologians, philosophers, text-linguists, and literary scholars have advanced this critical reflection upon the textuality of texts and its implications for their reception.

The aim of biblical interpretation is not to decipher particular sentences, though this task is a necessary part of the overall exercise, but understanding the meaning of larger communicative units: texts. A "biblical text" may refer to a particular book of the Bible or parts thereof (such as the readings in a church service or any other religious reading program); it may refer to the OT, the NT, the Apocrypha, or the entire Bible. In whatever extension a biblical text is heard or read, it is received as a *text*.

A text is more than the sum of its sentences. A text is a linguistic composition that is read or heard as a relatively coherent communicative unit, a structured whole (Schleiermacher); it invites recipients to become engaged in its communicative potential through an act of reading or hearing. The text has a surplus of meaning over against its constitutive parts. It opens a world for the reader (Ricoeur). Every text is organized on three levels at once: on a semantic level of creating a meaning, on a syntactic level of structuring linguistic parts into a whole, and on a pragmatic level that indicates textual beginning and end. Hence, the pragmatic dimension of the text's textuality defines the external extension of the text, whereas the combination of syntactic and semantic dimensions produces the internal communicative dynamics of the text.

The discipline of text-linguistics, which pays special attention to general linguistic strategies in the production and reception of texts, could show how a number of different aspects—such as thematic progression, cross-referentiality, pronominal substitution, conventional genre, and particular style—together contribute to the emerging textuality of a text. The unfolding of the text's communicative potential in the act of reading or hearing can then be described as a dynamic process whose energy stems from the encounter between recipient and text. The text comes to life in a process that is always initiated by a recipient. Without recipients who are prepared to invest their skillful attention to this process, texts remain ink on paper—mere communicative potentials. The biblical text is no exception.

Biblical texts reach today's reader in the form of *written* texts. Even when read aloud during an act of personal or communal worship, they are still written texts, though performed now in this particular way. Written texts differ from oral texts insofar as the latter emerge in an actual meeting between people in a particular communicative situation. Biblical texts, however, are written texts that can be read at any time by anybody, individuals and communities, capable of deciphering the textual code and willing to enter into the world that these texts are evoking in the reader during the act of reading. The written text has been described as "a discourse fixed by writing"; as such, it now owns a communicative autonomy (Ricoeur). Knowledge of the text's author and of the situation of its origin is therefore not a necessary condition for a successful process of biblical reading. Yet these matters will be of particular interest to readers who wish to pay attention to the fact that these texts can function both as documents of significant religious developments in Israel and the early church, and as carriers of divine revelation for all generations to come.

The *genre* of a text refers to traditional rules and conventions of human communication (e.g., letter, psalm, historical account, aphorism, narrative, prophecy, law, apocalypse, etc.) according to which a textual expression is normally shaped. A

text's *style* refers to the individual characteristics of the composition. Of course, stylistic decisions in text-composition and -reception are always conditioned as well by a complex network of circumstances and traditions that organize communicative expectations. Genre and style of a text provoke in the reader a corresponding genre and style of reading. In this encounter between general forms of communication and particular features of expression, a reader or group of readers can unfold a written communication. A text can thus be defined as an "individual universal" (Frank).

At times, the need for new ways of expression becomes so pressing that a mere change of style will no longer suffice. Then a new genre of expression may become necessary in order to allow for the realization of new communicative perspectives. The birth of the genre "gospel" was the result of the first Christians' experience of God's action and presence in the life, death, and resurrection of Jesus of Nazareth. The communication of their experience demanded a new genre of writing; this new genre in turn has been calling for a new genre of reading, a christological reading. However, no reader can be expected to relate adequately to totally new forms of expression. Hence, even a new genre, such as *gospel*, will always need to employ a sufficient measure of conventional aspects in order to achieve its communicative purpose for the reader and thus to be understood to be a new genre of expression in the first place.

The production of texts employs one or more textual strategies, such as narration, argumentation, description, and instruction, depending on the principal function of a text in a particular communicative situation. Readers need to identify a text's overall communicative strategy in order to disclose the text's meaning appropriately. Only following such a basic assessment, after developing an initial grasp of the text's overall strategy as text, is the reader in a position to follow the concrete communicative dynamics of the text and to move toward the disclosure of meaning—which in turn may lead to a reassessment of the initial grasp. Thus, the concern for adequate reading of a biblical (or any other) text as text demands first of all the grasp and subsequent application of the most adequate reading perspective.

A reading perspective is adequate only when it corresponds to the text's own communicative perspectives and potential. If it does not, the text will be misread. The communicative potential of most biblical texts is theological: it reflects upon experiences of the creative and redemptive presence of God in Israel, the world, Jesus Christ, the church, and eternal life. Although all kinds of perspectives have been applied to read and examine biblical texts, no reading genre appears to be fully adequate that is not open to the texts' own particular theological potential. Depending on the function of a biblical text in particular religious contexts, additional strategies of reading will be added to this basic approach to the textuality of the text.

See also Genre; Utterance Meaning

Bibliography

Frank, M. *Das individuelle Allgemeine*. Suhrkamp, 1977; Jeanrond, W. *Text and Interpretation as Categories of Theological Thinking*. Crossroad, 1988; idem. *Theological Hermeneutics*. Crossroad, 1991; Ricoeur, P. *Hermeneutics and the Human Sciences*, ed. J. Thompson. Cambridge University Press, 1981; idem. *Interpretation Theory*. Texas Christian University Press, 1976; Schleiermacher, F. *Hermeneutics*, ed. H. Kimmerle. Scholars, 1977; Thiselton, A. *New Horizons in Hermeneutics*. Zondervan, 1992; Vanhoozer, K. *Is There a Meaning in This Text?* Zondervan, 1998; Watson, F. *Text and Truth*. T&T Clark, 1997.

Werner G. Jeanrond

Textual Criticism

Textual criticism is the science of discovering where a document has been corrupted, and the art of restoring it (Housman 325). In the study of Scripture, textual criticism is the interpreter's response to the reality that there are thousands of manuscripts of the biblical texts with tens of thousands of variations, and no extant autographs to establish once for all the original readings. Textual criticism analyzes the available evidence in order to understand the transmission history of a text and to determine the most authentic reading where manuscripts differ. While the task of the textual critic is usually considered a step prior to interpretation, it is properly an integral part of that task. This article considers the textual criticism of both Testaments, first separately and then together. It also explores new directions in the discipline and their significance for exegesis and theology.

Role in the Interpretative Task

Textual criticism arises out of the need for a reasonably reliable text as the basis for interpretation. Most textual critics proceed both with a high degree of confidence that in many cases the original text is attainable, and awareness that often there are interpretive and theological issues at stake in decisions on the text. In addition to the primary goal of establishing the original text, textual critics have given increased attention to the history of interpretation, literary layers in the production of texts, theologically or ethically motivated changes, and the impact of canon on textual issues. None of these areas should be isolated; they are interdependent in the interpretative task. Epp is correct to insist on "expanding our horizons and making the discipline more broadly relevant than previously to related fields, such as literary-critical, hermeneutical and church historical studies" (Epp 270). To Epp's list we should add the terms "theological" and "ethical."

Traditionally OT textual critics have privileged the Masoretic Text (MT), but recent discoveries and research have challenged its position as a Textus Receptus. The discovery of the Dead Sea Scrolls shows a pluriformity of the Hebrew Bible in the Second Temple period. Some Qumran readings agree with the Septuagint (LXX) against MT, while others are clearly superior to MT (Tov 24). The LXX itself often witnesses to interpretative traditions. The questions of the origins and textual variety within the LXX texts and versions (Aquila, Theodotion, Symmachus) offer special challenges and opportunities for the textual critic. Another tradition is reflected in the Samaritan Pentateuch, which contains theologically motivated changes. Discoveries of divergent manuscripts for the MT itself (Leningrad Codex, the basis of the *BH* [*Biblia Hebraica*] and *BHS* [*Biblia Hebraica Stuttgartensia*] texts; the Aleppo Codex forms the basis of the Hebrew University Bible) further challenge the position of MT. Moreover, the Kethib-Qere practice (notes to ignore what is written and substitute the marginal reading) bears witness to ancient interpretative techniques in the rabbinic tradition. This situation of manuscript and textual diversity offers opportunity for creative engagement of the textual critic of the OT and the NT.

The NT textual critics work with an embarrassment of riches. From earliest times Christians have noted textual variations in the NT (Origen, Jerome, Ibn al-'Assal). Since Erasmus produced the first modern critical edition (1516) by drawing on six manuscripts, the number of known Greek manuscripts of the NT has grown to almost six thousand. Together with lectionaries, versions, and patristic quotations, this constitutes a great mass of material to be collated and evaluated. Recent discoveries of more than 115 NT papyri, some from the second century, enhance our knowledge of the earliest transmission of the text. The NT textual critics have sorted this mass of data into text types (Metzger 95–146). Of the three main groups of manuscripts, the Alexandrian is characterized by restraint, the Western by expansion, and the Byzantine by conflation. The standard critical editions, Nestle/Aland[27] and UBS[4], with identical text but different apparatuses, offer the opportunity for truly scientific study of textual criticism. But debate over methods demonstrates that textual criticism is art as well as science.

The Methods

Textual critics of both the OT and NT face challenges in methodology and can learn from each other. For the OT, a primary challenge in method is the relation of textual to literary criticism in a situation where texts have developed over a long period of time and manifest different versions: Jeremiah, Joshua, Ezekiel, Proverbs (Tov 313–50). NT textual critics debate the relative value of external (manuscript) and internal (an author's style and theology) criteria for making judgments (Kilpatrick; J. K. Elliott in Black; Ehrman and Holmes). Decisions are made on the basis of age and affinity of manuscripts, and on transcriptional and intrinsic probabilities. All follow an eclectic method. Kilpatrick and Elliott represent thoroughgoing eclecticism in which style, Atticism, and other features are more significant for making text-critical judgments (Elliott in Black 101–24).

Established rules for textual decisions—such as a preference for the more difficult or shorter reading, or the reading that best explains the rise of the others (Aland and Aland 275–77)—should be applied "sparingly and with full recognition of their subjective nature" (Tov 308). Tov states: "Common sense should be the main guide of the textual critic" (296). But sense is not necessarily common (Housman).

The Goals

Ancient and modern textual critics seek to discover the original reading where there is variation in a biblical text. Postmodern critics have questioned whether this is an attainable or desirable goal. NT textual criticism has been especially influenced by these developments. The focus has shifted to an interest in "subsequent forms of the text for understanding the history of exegesis" (Ehrman 29). Parker's assertion summarizes the shift: "There is no original text, there are just different texts from different stages of production"

(4). This shift of emphasis from the "original text" to the early transmitters and interpreters reflects the broader postmodern cultural shift away from the text, its meaning, and the author's intent and toward the readers' response to and use of the text. Recent philosophical and literary theories, such as proposed by Rorty, Derrida, and Fish, find meaning not in the author or in the text but in the reader (Vanhoozer). The original text becomes an illusion; discerning the theological crosscurrents in early Christianity and their influence on the text has become the goal.

Ehrman assumes Bauer's picture of diversity within earliest Christianity, with no single primitive stream, but competing Christian movements, more Gnostic or heretical than orthodox in some places. The party (and their scribes) represented by Irenaeus, Tertullian, Hippolytus, and others, dubbed "proto-orthodox," was not original, primitive, or true, but merely successful, and sealed its victory at Nicea. They not only won the struggle, but also changed the texts to make them say what they were known to mean. The addition of "The Son of God" at Mark 1:1 and the suppression of "the chosen one" at John 1:34 supply for Ehrman clear illustrations of this view. Bauer overstates his case, often making claims without evidence, but the phenomenon of textual diversity cannot be denied. The motive for an early Christian scribe's selection or creation of a different reading is still much a matter of debate.

Parker's incisive review of the sayings of Jesus on marriage and divorce leads him to conclude that recovery of an original saying of Jesus is impossible. What is available is not the original texts but "a collection of interpretive rewritings of the tradition" (92–93). The implications of these observations are of critical importance for the exegete, theologian, and church leader. Parker points to two facts, "that the Gospel texts exist only in a manuscript tradition, and that from the beginning the text grew freely. It is from these facts that all questions of interpretation and all theological formulations must start. Concepts of biblical inspiration, or any other doctrinal formulations, which fail to take account of these two key facts are based on a priori theorizing or prejudice, and not on the actual character of the writings" (203).

Did the text grow freely, or were there some controls and constraints? To answer this question, the student of the text must reckon with several factors that have recently surfaced in the study of early Christianity.

1. The relative ease of travel in the earliest Christian centuries meant that early Christians communicated with one another and knew each other's manuscripts. Roman scribes knew Alexandrian readings and vice versa. A Greek fragment of Irenaeus, written in Gaul, around 200 CE, turned up in Egypt "not long after the ink was dry" (Roberts 53).

2. Most NT textual critics, not known to embrace each other's views, agree that all significant variations in the NT textual tradition were in place before 200 CE (Ehrman 44). This means that the second century, from which our earliest papyri are dated, can provide clues as to how the NT (and OT) was copied and preserved in the context of the culture and its theological and ethical crosscurrents.

3. It is increasingly clear that the church remained more Jewish far longer than has formerly been allowed. Therefore, the attitudes toward the text and the motives and methods of textual alteration in the OT should be studied more closely in assessing changes in the NT text in the most critical period before 200 CE. For example, the two textual types in the Acts of the Apostles should be studied in light of similar phenomena in the book of Esther, with two distinct Greek versions, the LXX and the Alpha-Text (Jobes and Silva 227–35).

4. "Proto-orthodox" teachers and scribes retained in their texts some readings that were potentially embarrassing to them. P.Oxy. 405, a fragment of *Against Heresies*, and possibly from the hand of Irenaeus himself, shows that he cited a form of Matt. 3:17 (*"You are . . ."* rather than *"This is* my beloved Son") that would have been useful in the hands of the adoptionists. Luke 23:34a ("Father, forgive them . . .") is omitted in some early manuscripts (P^{75} B D W etc.). The omission accords with the common claim of the second and third centuries that the Jews were responsible for Jesus' death, and thus denied forgiveness. Origen makes such a claim (*Cels.* 4.22). It is surprising that Origen quoted the contested words several times, though he must have known manuscripts that lacked the reading. These are words he would have preferred not to have in Scripture. Despite temptations to alter the text, Irenaeus, Origen, and others faithfully copied the Scriptures they had

received. Controls to the free growth of the text are evident.

F. J. A. Hort had stated that there are no variations in the NT textual tradition that were altered by orthodox scribes for doctrinal purposes (Hort and Westcott 42); Ehrman, Parker, and others have demonstrated that such intentional theological and ethical changes did occur. However, there is no evidence of such intentional alteration being sanctioned by the church leadership or practiced by official scribes of the church. No doubt zealous scribes took matters into their own hands; Eusebius's brief citations from Dionysius of Corinth (ca. 170 CE) show that church leaders were alert to such dangers. This very awareness indicates controls on the free growth of the texts. Despite undue pessimism regarding establishing the original text, Ehrman and Parker have done a valuable service by insisting that the textual critic is a necessary partner with the exegete, church historian, and theologian in the enterprise of interpreting Scripture.

The two parallel phenomena of control and freedom in the transmission of the text can be found in both OT and NT textual traditions. The two disciplines should therefore be studied together, especially where the material overlaps, as in the OT quotations in the NT. Claims that the NT text grew because it was not yet considered canonical must reckon with the reality that the canonical status of the OT within Judaism did not prevent continued interpretive rendering. Furthermore, from the privileged position of the MT the NT textual critic can gain respect for the Byzantine text.

The study of NT textual variations within quotations from the OT provides a useful point of departure for the practice of textual criticism with a theological focus. The following verses promise to be especially fruitful in this exploration: Matt. 3:3; 13:35; 27:43; Mark 1:3; 7:6; 10:7, 19; 12:36; 15:34; Luke 3:22; 4:4, 18; 19:38; John 10:34; 13:18; Acts 2:30; 15:18; Rom. 8:28; 9:28, 33; 10:5, 15; 13:9; 1 Cor. 15:55; Gal. 3:17; Eph. 4:8; 5:31; Phil. 2:11; 2 Thess. 2:4, 8; Heb. 1:8, 12; 2:7; 3:2; 10:38; 1 Pet. 2:3; 3:15; Rev. 4:7; 15:3.

The OT textual critic will be careful to assess a variety of aspects of the NT quotation (form, introduction, selection, application, history, and function) in the context of the range of developing interpretations in intertestamental Judaism. The NT textual critic should be careful to look beyond the confines of Christian manuscripts and developments in the early church. One needs to assess the form and function of the text in the MT, LXX and versions, Qumran, Samaritan Pentateuch, and Hellenistic Judaism in Alexandria and elsewhere, and to view the NT's use of OT texts as a part of this larger stream of developing interpretations. What is shared with that stream and what is uniquely Christian will come clearly into focus. The textual critic, then, as full partner in the interpretative task, offers some of the earliest and best data for the theological interpretation of Scripture.

Bibliography

Aland, K., and B. Aland. *The Text of the New Testament*, trans. E. F. Rhodes. Eerdmans, 1987; Bauer, W. *Orthodoxy and Heresy in Earliest Christianity*, trans. G. Strecker. Fortress, 1971; Black, D. A., ed. *Rethinking New Testament Textual Criticism*. Baker, 2002; Ehrman, B. *The Orthodox Corruption of Scripture*. Oxford University Press, 1993; Ehrman, B., and M. Holmes. *The Text of the New Testament in Contemporary Research*. Eerdmans, 1995; Epp, E. J. "The Multivalence of the Term 'Original Text' in New Testament Textual Criticism." *HTR* 92 (1999): 245–81; Hort, F. J. A., and B. F. Westcott. *The New Testament in the Original Greek*. Cambridge University Press, 1882; Housman, A. "The Application of Thought to Textual Criticism." In *Selected Prose*, ed. J. Carter. Cambridge University Press, 1961; Jobes, K., and M. Silva. *Invitation to the Septuagint*. Baker, 2000; Kilpatrick, G. *The Principles and Practice of New Testament Textual Criticism*, ed. J. Elliott. BETL 96. Louvain University Press/Peeters, 1990; Metzger, B. *The Text of the New Testament*. 3d ed. Oxford University Press, 1992; Parker, D. *The Living Text of the Gospels*. Cambridge University Press, 1997; Roberts, C. *Manuscript, Society and Belief in Early Christian Egypt*. Oxford University Press, 1979; Tov, E. *Textual Criticism of the Hebrew Bible*. 2d rev. ed. Fortress/Royal Van Gorcum, 2001; Vanhoozer, K. *Is There a Meaning in This Text?* Zondervan, 1998.

Peter R. Rodgers

Theme *See* Language, Linguistics

Theological Hermeneutics, Contemporary

At its broadest, "hermeneutics" is an effort to understand the nature of human understanding. Often, though not necessarily, this takes the particular form of understanding the understanding of texts, or else all forms of understanding in terms of "texts"—whether a person, a poem, a play, or a painting, and so on is being understood, it is understood *as* a text. However, in the modern age focus shifted from the practice of textual interpretation to its ontological possibility via human historicity (Heidegger's influence, especially via Gadamer).

The broader history and significance of that philosophical project is chronicled elsewhere. "Theological hermeneutics," however, is fast becoming a term with its own history, which may designate at least two projects for Christians to undertake. (1) They need to develop an account of text interpretation or even human understanding in interaction with Christian doctrine(s). (2) They also need to develop an account of how biblical interpretation should shape, and be shaped by, Christian theology. For the former project, the adjective "theological" designates the mode in which *general* hermeneutics are pursued; for the latter, "theological" designates not only a mode of pursuit, but also the material aims of *special* hermeneutics regarding the Bible. The two projects may be undertaken simultaneously, or distinctly, or even separately—as if the interpretative interests of each are uninteresting to the other. The following chronicle leads to a suggestion for their interrelationship.

Appealing to Precedents

Theological hermeneutics frequently appeal to precedent(s) favoring their work. In particular, many concerned with "theological interpretation of Scripture" have been motivated by admiration for premodern exegetes, perhaps even by nostalgia for their "religious reading" (Griffiths) and adherence to a unified Bible.

Premodern Readers. Accordingly, many appeal to precritical models and to the Rule of Faith, championed by Irenaeus, Tertullian, and other patristic interpreters. Appeals are also made to the medieval fourfold sense (Steinmetz).

Origen has been frequently studied, given his influence upon allegorical exegesis as well as his general intrigue. However, the practices of Augustine, Thomas Aquinas, Martin Luther, and John Calvin have the most potential for present influence.

Augustine's *De doctrina christiana* (*On Christian Teaching*) influenced Christian pedagogy and exegetical practice even into the Reformation period (examined, e.g., in English). As noted below, efforts have been made to recover a hermeneutic of charity that follows in his footsteps (Jacobs), while his understanding of Scripture's "plain sense" has also been studied comparatively (Greene-McCreight). Augustine is sometimes said to be the father of semiotics (e.g., Jeanrond 22, who probably overemphasizes such traditional connections to general hermeneutics).

When appeals are made to the medieval fourfold sense, or conversely to the Reformers' rejection of allegorical interpretation, we must remember that Thomas Aquinas (and others) had already begun to recover a priority upon the literal sense (Rogers's essay has become influential). The late medieval growth of grammatical exegesis, and of humanism generally, did indeed flower in the Reformers' hermeneutics, whether they lean more toward the premodern or the modern (about which there is much discussion). Their connection to the Protestant scholastics and the extent to which the latter are protomodern figure here. Whereas a certain consistency with the fathers is evident (so, e.g., Greene-McCreight), many fault the Reformation both for individualism (the "priesthood of the believer" run amok à la American democracy; e.g., Hauerwas) and "foundationalism," as an outgrowth of *sola scriptura* (Abraham) coupled with the modern turn to method (Louth). Conversely, however, Frei—no friend of modernity—seems to appreciate Calvin's approach to Scripture, differentiating the early Protestant "figural reading" (the literal sense extended to the whole canonical story) from a later, eighteenth-century shift.

Modern Reactions. If premodern interpreters have inspired theological hermeneutics (along with debates over the Protestant legacy), so has a perceived archenemy of the modern, whose appropriation of the Reformers was at points critical—Barth. Not only does Barth loom large in Jeanrond's chronicle *Theological Hermeneutics*, but he has also inspired studies such as Cunningham's *What Is Theological Exegesis?* and figures in Greene-McCreight's comparative study.

It would appear that Barth's understanding and use of critical biblical scholarship developed over time. Oddly enough, he "had no significant place for any such thing as 'biblical theology,'" yet stimulated certain of its forms (Barr 73). In any case, it appears that the early Barth held a generally negative theory of the compatibility between historical criticism and theological exegesis. However, his position grew toward a more ad hoc approach: historical criticism provides "a starting point for the interpretive exercise and at a later stage in the hermeneutical process helps to safeguard against subjective excess" (McCormack, cited in Cunningham 16n37).

Whereas much has been made of Barth's legacy, Bultmann's has been more modest or even negative within the "theological interpretation of Scripture" movement. Appreciative of Heidegger's existential philosophy, Bultmann distinguished "presuppositions" (indispensable) from "prejudice" (inappropriate) in study of the NT. Famously suggesting the impossibility of believing in miracles while using lightbulbs, he defended a program of "demythologization" in which the true theological significance of supernatural claims was the crux of interpretation. Thus would the gospel's claim on the modern human be clarified; Bultmann used supposedly historical criteria to separate faith from history (which would, in his particular Lutheran view, constitute reliance upon something besides the word of God). In any case, as Jeanrond notes, both Barth and Bultmann "tried to overcome the ideological limitations of historicist interpretation of the Bible" (157), but opposed each other concerning proper interaction with philosophy.

Addressing General Hermeneutics

Yet Bultmann seems to have set the stage for biblical scholarship to interact with general hermeneutics more intentionally, especially via the "New Hermeneutic." For a long time, however, such interaction meant basically adopting or adapting general hermeneutics to the task of biblical interpretation, albeit sometimes in the shadow of a "word of God" theology (e.g., Ebeling). More recently, efforts have been made in the reverse—to assess the influence of biblical interpretation upon general hermeneutics, or even to address general hermeneutics by way of understanding biblical interpretation.

Philosophy. Jeanrond, in fact, strongly advocates special hermeneutics only following, *then* contributing to, general hermeneutics: "Our narrative of the history of philosophical hermeneutics began with a theologian, Friedrich Schleiermacher, who discovered that theological interpretation needed a thorough foundation in philosophical hermeneutics. Now the development of philosophical hermeneutics by Ricoeur has revealed the need to include the interpretation of religious texts in an adequate human existential reflection. The symmetry between the theological endeavours of Schleiermacher and the philosophical enterprise of Ricoeur is striking!" (Jeanrond 77). Accordingly, Jeanrond celebrates the work of Tracy and others who follow in Schleiermacher's footsteps and lean heavily on Ricoeur. Meanwhile, he criticizes not only Barth but also the likes of Ebeling for their failure to interact with, or contribute to, philosophical hermeneutics (e.g., Jeanrond 158).

The British NT scholar Thiselton burst upon the scene with *The Two Horizons*. Critically appreciative of philosophers such as Gadamer and Ricoeur, he has maintained the possibility of scholarly exegesis but also personal and theological engagement with the biblical text. He has written widely, from a significant commentary on 1 Corinthians to a hermeneutical recovery of "selfhood." Thiselton has drawn upon speech-act philosophy, especially its significance for divine "promising" in relation to the Bible.

Wolterstorff has also applied speech-act philosophy, defending the possibility of "divine discourse" and developing aspects of such a model. He suggests that God appropriates the human discourse of biblical texts, unless we have good reason to think otherwise (based on an exceptional principle, that God would only tell the truth and promote love for neighbor). We therefore approach the Bible with a first hermeneutic (for the human discourse), and then a second (for the divine). Perhaps this illuminates our larger point: Wolterstorff almost thoroughly borrows concepts from general hermeneutics for biblical interpretation, and *then* addresses its particularities. But he does not critically or constructively address general hermeneutics from a theological perspective, or with biblical interpretation in mind.

Literary Criticism. Besides philosophical hermeneutics, again the traffic moves largely one way with literary theory (e.g., the importance of Fish and Stout for Fowl's *Engaging Scripture*, or the variety of literary influences upon Callahan's *The Clarity of Scripture*).

Lundin and Walhout have, however, collaborated with Thiselton. In those projects, as well as his *The Culture of Interpretation*, Lundin offers theologically informed assessments of modern literary hermeneutics' cultural history. The idea that Christian faith itself, by interacting with the Bible, developed a distinctive literary culture is demonstrated in Jeffrey's *People of the Book*. Jeffrey seems intent on defending such a culture not only against deconstructionists who charge the West with "logocentrism," but also against individualized Western Christians who internalize everything besides the word.

Likewise, Jacobs is concerned to recover the relationality of Christian reading. Unfolding a hermeneutic of charity that recalls Augustine, he appeals to Bakhtin as a resource for exploring the "dialogical" nature of reading practice. Largely eschewing theoretical procedure for charitable practical reason (see his prelude), in a rich tapestry of example and reflection he demonstrates that "we need not choose between a self-absorbed hedonism and a diligently politicized interpretation that gradgrindingly forces every text and every author into a fixed place in the political grid." A hermeneutics of love "will be both flexible and responsible, . . . will have *universal obligations but highly particular forms of attention*" leading to shalom (Jacobs 138).

The Bible. Vanhoozer shares the interest of Thiselton and Wolterstorff in speech-act philosophy, as well as the idea of a Christian literary culture and Augustinian hermeneutics of love. In *Is There a Meaning in This Text?* Vanhoozer pursues the development and defense of "the morality of literary knowledge" (his subtitle) by exploring biblical interpretation. He argues that readers are obligated to do justice to the communicative actions of authors, that texts do not contain but just *are* communicative actions. Vanhoozer seems intent on general hermeneutics, suggesting that Christians start with the Bible as a way to learn about interpretation. His subsequent work focuses more upon special hermeneutics, perhaps responding to worries about neglecting the specific problems and possibilities in reading the Bible as Scripture, with the Holy Spirit. His 1998 book is probably read too much for special hermeneutics—hence comes misunderstanding about what is not addressed.

Articulating Special Hermeneutics

We may assess specifically Christian contributions to hermeneutics as modest but promising, having begun to move from uncritical adoption of reigning general hermeneutics to (more recently) critical appropriations of them for biblical interpretation. Yet the legacy of a Christian literary culture, along with modern and postmodern reactions to it, is still assessed variously regarding its particular relevance for biblical interpretation.

"Canonical Approach." The Yale OT scholar Childs, in some respects building on the tradition-historical approach of von Rad, responded to the demise of the so-called biblical theology movement by developing what has been called a canonical approach. While intricacies are treated elsewhere, we note here its importance. Childs's practice (exemplified in a famous commentary on Exodus) has been to interact with precritical exegetes such as Calvin and theologians such as Barth, plus critical scholarship. The goal is treatment of the text's final form, but in light of its canonical status, and thus what the traces of its formative processes shed on its meaning. He has tried to do biblical, not just OT or NT, theology, but still to grant the OT some integrity as canonical. Methodological shifts or inconsistencies have been traced even by the appreciative (e.g., Watson), while Barr has tenaciously attacked idiosyncrasies. Perhaps Childs's program could only achieve stability with a doctrine of biblical inspiration added (Noble). Regardless, his legacy of inspiring theological exegesis is secure, as a *Festschrift* evidences (Seitz and Greene-Mc-Creight).

"Biblical Theology." Watson has authored two daring catalysts to theological hermeneutics. The first, *Text, Church, and World*, tries to return theological questions to biblical interpretation, treating textuality (part 1) and hence postmodernism (part 2), feminist critique (part 3), and finally the relation of theology, hermeneutics, and exegesis more explicitly (part 4). Watson appreciates the synchronic and literary emphases often associated with the "Yale School"; he interacts with both Childs and Frei, whose critique of modern Gospels interpretation (*Eclipse*) has been influential. Yet he insists that the biblical texts themselves demand engagement with historical and especially ethical concerns. Thus the "intratextuality" called for by Lindbeck in *The Nature of Doctrine* must give way to an "intratextual realism," which emerges from interactions with both postmodernism and feminism. In the resulting theological hermeneutics (Watson, *Church*, ch. 13), access to Jesus is textually mediated; work with the canonical form does not immunize the text from criticism, due to a law-gospel hermeneutic; thus, insights from the secular world may assist the church's reading of its Scripture.

The second book, *Text and Truth*, has tried to redefine biblical theology (as the subtitle suggests) to be "an interdisciplinary approach to biblical interpretation which seeks to dismantle the barriers that at present separate biblical scholarship from Christian theology, . . . a theological, hermeneutical and exegetical discipline" (Watson, *Truth*, vii). Watson claims that the demarcation between OT and NT studies stems from a similar line between biblical studies and systematic theology, which has become normative, not just pragmatic for dividing up labor. Opposing this requires that Watson respond to critics, as well as Barr at points. Contra Childs, Watson denies the OT integrity as a canon, a debate that has since continued (Seitz; Watson, "Response"). The book continues Watson's trend of developing hermeneutical positions while practicing exegesis on particular issues—such as the Gospels as multiple narrated histories, and the doctrine of creation over against Barr's defense of natural theology.

Others are pursuing a renewal of biblical theology as well. For instance, Moberly has written *The Bible, Theology, and Faith*, a captivating study of connections between Abraham and Jesus via a modified canonical approach increasingly characteristic of some OT scholars. The more traditionally critical Stuhlmacher and others are represented in a recent collection of essays (Hafemann), as is the salvation-historical emphasis of many Australian, British, and American evangelicals reflected in the *New Dictionary of Biblical Theology* (Alexander and Rosner).

"Underdetermined" Hermeneutics. Yet Hafemann's *Biblical Theology* volume also contains a rejection of biblical theology by Fowl. Arguing partly from history, he sees its integrity as an academic discipline lying in a historical approach of the sort Barr champions. By contrast, Fowl's *Engaging Scripture* illustrates three claims fairly common to "theological interpretation of Scripture" as a movement: (1) Scriptural exegesis belongs in the church. (2) Practical reasoning will be needed (which, like Watson, Fowl exemplifies by providing extended theological interpretations). (3) Thus, Christians are not compelled to accept the reigning practices and ideologies of critical biblical scholarship, which tends to splinter theology into discrete disciplines and the Bible into discrete Testaments.

Fowl's own model, however, does not represent the entire movement, as he acknowledges. He tells three "stories of interpretation." The "anti-determinate" approach of deconstruction is the parasitic opposite of "determinate" interpretation, (1) which has the aim of "rendering interpretation redundant." (2) "It views the biblical text as a problem to be mastered" (32). (3) "It sees the biblical text as a relatively stable element in which an author inserts, hides, or dissolves (choose your metaphor) meaning." (4) It assumes "that matters of doctrine and practice are straightforwardly determined by biblical interpretation and never the other way around" (34). (5) It trumps others by showing how "opponents have allowed theological concerns, prejudices, or preferences to determine their interpretation" (35). And (6) it is linked to "method," implying a "professional ethic" that snatches the Bible from ordinary Christians (47). Fowl criticizes Watson and Childs for following this approach, but instead advocates "underdetermined" interpretation, believing that "there is no theoretical way to determine how these interactions [of Christians and biblical texts] must work in any particular context" (8).

Fowl's composite "determinate interpretation" can only describe traditional biblical scholarship or even a worst-case modern scenario. Watson and others who champion the literal sense of Scripture, often in connection with authorial discourse interpretation, also champion churchly reading and practical reason; they simply understand biblical authority and general hermeneutics somewhat differently.

A better-told story would connect three modes of "postcritical canonical interpretation" (Lindbeck, "Three Modes") with three hermeneutical understandings of biblical authority (Buckley). (1) Advocates of authorial discourse interpretation tend to be "revelationalists" (emphasizing God's presence related to the Bible's subject matter). (2) Advocates of interpreting for the Bible's witness to Jesus Christ tend to be "textualists" (emphasizing the final form). And (3) advocates of interpreting for narrationally structured symbolic worlds tend to be "functionalists" (emphasizing the interpretive context). Of course, these are generalizations; the first two categories tend to run together, as Lindbeck himself and probably Watson illustrate. Fowl seems to take functionalism as a thoroughly normative position, beyond its more descriptive analysis of how theologians use the Bible (Kelsey, *Uses*). Missing is any discussion of "word of God." Many other theological hermeneutics, by contrast, are less enamored of Fish's emphasis on interpretive communities, because they understand the Bible as Scripture to communicate divine discourse.

Precisely because of commitment to "canon," Webster worries about correlating biblical interpretation with general hermeneutics. Ultimately the doctrine of the Trinity must be involved, and theories of textuality can have only ad hoc usefulness so as to avoid the secular anthropology underlying hermeneutics. The Bible and Word of God are related sacramentally: "God's agency is real and effective yet indirect" (Webster 74). This enables a priority of divine action over the reading situation that, while embracing communal and ethical concerns over against hermeneutical domination, still depicts the church responding to an external word.

The preceding discussion illustrates the dependence of theological hermeneutics on dogmatic positions, in addition to disciplinary locations and practical concerns. For example, further specification of Webster's sacramental theology would be needed, but might prompt rejection of this correlation with the nature of the Bible, unless scriptural warrant were provided. Though fraught with perils, the possible analogy between the human texts of the Bible as divine discourse and the hypostatic union of Jesus Christ, God's final Word, deserves continued hermeneutical attention, in concert with the trinitarian doctrine Webster prioritizes. If Scripture is revelatory, then theology will be hermeneutically decisive; yet that can be defended as appropriate for such a text, without entailing iconoclastic relativism (Gracia).

Attempting to Connect the General and Special

This survey of theological approaches to biblical interpretation is scarcely comprehensive. While these are prominent in Western academic literature, openness is needed to postcolonial and non-Western insights. Perhaps more basic still is a certain personal openness to reading with and for the Christian virtues. One needs to be attentive via practical reason (*phronēsis*) or imagination not only to the particulars of the text but also to the context, especially the church's historical commitments along with its call to serve in the contemporary world. Yet these persistent themes of special hermeneutics—now frequently tied to a "performance" model on analogy with music or drama (surveyed in Barton)—could perhaps be understood non-Christianly or undertaken non-theologically in "postmodern" fashion. Meanwhile, they also pertain when reading texts in general! So a fresh Christian contribution to hermeneutics is unlikely without deciding what is distinctive about reading the Bible *as word of God*.

Should we seek a hermeneutic that will cover understanding generally, and then apply this more specifically to how we understand God's self-disclosure? Or should we seek a hermeneutic that applies only select insights from that special case to texts in general?

However we nuance, we tend to privilege one or the other. The burden on those who take very seriously general hermeneutics is "to do justice to what is essential for Christian communal identity, and avoid the reduction of Christian knowledge to a mere 'case in point' of some more general kind of knowing." The burden on those who take very seriously a starting point in special hermeneutics is "to relate the singular Christian knowledge of God to other human knowing, and avoid the isolation of the knowledge of God in a special 'religious' sphere" (Buckley and Yeago 7). General hermeneutics, though, always foster our understanding of what is special about knowing God via the Bible, since they offer the languages within which, and the cultural "others" against which, we articulate Christian concerns.

If the triune God chose to create others with whom to share the communion of the divine life, and if God communicates to fallen creatures through the redemptive action of Son and Spirit, then human understanding will be a relational affair intimately connecting knowledge and love. For ancients like Augustine, these were as inseparably related as their parallel in the Word and Spirit of the Holy Trinity (Williams). "Understanding" might then be characterized in terms of various "capacities for action in relation to something" (Kelsey, *Understand*, 124–29), specifically communicative action.

Consequently, we should be predisposed toward a Christian version of a "virtue epistemology," in which understanding is dialogical, undertaken with our character formed in community—ultimately with the God who is love. This accords with the general but Christianly informed sensibilities of Bakhtin, but can be articulated in "virtue" categories according to the biblical theme of "discernment" or "judgment." Wise Christian reading is possible in Christ, patterned after him, and then pursued as people develop in community the capacity to recognize what situations call for, and respond accordingly. Via *phronēsis*, virtue properly deploys sciences and skills.

A Christian hermeneutic for the Bible will nevertheless be special in at least two senses. (1) God in the person of Jesus Christ is freely communicated in Scripture, and forms our character through the active accompaniment of the Holy Spirit, as covenanted through no other book. (2) This communication takes the form of various writings that were composed spanning a complex history of revelation and redemption, yet are collected as human forms faithfully speaking one word. We read Scripture with a submissive, trusting expectation to encounter God in the truth, goodness, and beauty of Christ, as no other book can match. By God's grace the Christian virtues are necessarily conducive to grasping the meaning of biblical Truth in particular.

However, O'Donovan reminds us that people outside the Christian faith may understand and even obey many divine ordinances because God created with order, and has reaffirmed this in Christ's resurrection—hence, for example, the Wisdom literature and its connection to other cultures. In terms of special hermeneutics, these others fail to match the moral whole—they cannot respond with integrity (in the full sense Wisdom calls for) because they do not know and love the God of cruciform wisdom. Yet they may have insight into many particulars, and help us recognize how beautiful and good patterns of Truth cohere in Scripture; often we will mistake these connections or need criticism when we do not connect our own living with what we see.

The lesson is that strong similarity can obtain between special and general hermeneutics. Often non-Christian interpreters will understand—that is, develop various capacities for communicative action in relation to—texts far better than Christians will. With various virtues they will perhaps read charitably to a degree, even Scripture—but not in the fullest sense of integrity or imagination, for they do not know and love the One who is love, the form knowledge takes in its fullest connections and freedom. To the degree that the whole shapes the parts, there may be misunderstanding.

Such communicative action has not yet fully accounted for reaction to the Spirit over time and across place: God's communicative action takes human forms, with the Spirit giving freedom for our communicative actions to correspond fittingly with God's in Christ. Perhaps the most contested aspect of theological hermeneutics must concern the form our corresponding action takes *in the church*, and therefore the respective roles of Word and Spirit.

Human persons are agents; communities are not, except in a more abstract and complex sense. Ultimately, however, the NT teaches that the Spirit effects the new creation of *one new humanity*—that the local church, the concrete shape of catholicity, would correspond corporately to "the measure of the stature of the fullness of Christ" (Eph. 4:13 RSV). The goal is a community united in growth to maturity, which connects truth and love. Given biblical texts regarding discernment, such as Phil. 1:9–11, for example, practical reason must be a gift in which we pray to grow together.

Our personal actions, and even the communication of congregations, are but subplots in the effect of God's one act, in the growing creation of a new humanity conformed—with knowledge corresponding—to the Son. This does not disregard personal actions as unimportant, or deny that communities are unfaithful. Sometimes particular people (like Luther) must read against the grain. Yet doctrinal development, cultural difference, and therefore ethical discernment are not always problems but possibly a "Pentecostal plurality" in relation to Scripture (Vanhoozer, *Meaning?* 419–21; Smith).

The Spirit's new creation has a developmental identity across time and a dialogical unity across place that entails discernment—figuring out in what ways the church grows in faithfulness, free to take cultural form in correspondence to the Word. If this is right, then parallel to general hermeneutics, understanding and *moral* formation are possible in many particular ways for persons outside the Christian faith and communities outside the church. But parallel to special hermeneutics, the fullest sense of understanding and *spiritual* formation is not. General and special hermeneutics will therefore share much overlapping territory, including many scholarly criteria and reading skills, even as biblical interpretation constitutes a distinct province. Despite its church *polis*, Christian reading of Scripture may not have to address general hermeneutics either by "plundering the Egyptians" or by defending against a Trojan horse. Indeed, since its entire realm concerns living virtuously in communion with God, all understanding will have a theological component—and so the interpretation of Scripture may have abundant hermeneutical gifts to share, in a developing story of fair trade.

See also Hermeneutics; Virtue; Wisdom

Bibliography

Abraham, W. *Canon and Criterion in Christian Theology.* Clarendon, 1998; Alexander, T. D., and B. Rosner, eds. *New Dictionary of Biblical Theology.* InterVarsity, 2000; Barr, J. *The Concept of Biblical Theology.* Fortress, 1999; Barton, S. "New Testament Interpretation as Performance." *SJT* 52, no. 2 (1999): 179–208; Buckley, J. "Beyond the Hermeneutical Deadlock." Pages 187–203 in *Theology after Liberalism,* ed. J. Webster and G. Schner. Blackwell, 2000; Buckley, J., and D. Yeago, eds. *Knowing the Triune God.* Eerdmans, 2001; Callahan, J. *The Clarity of Scripture.* InterVarsity, 2001; Cunningham, M. K. *What Is Theological Exegesis?* Trinity, 1995; English, E., ed. *Reading and Wisdom.* Notre Dame University Press, 1995; Fowl, S. *Engaging Scripture.* Blackwell, 1998; Frei, H. *The Eclipse of Biblical Narrative.* Yale University Press, 1974; Gracia, J. *How Can We Know What God Means?* Palgrave, 2001; Greene-McCreight, K. *Ad Litteram.* P. Lang, 1999; Griffiths, P. *Religious Reading.* Oxford University Press, 1999; Hafemann, S., ed. *Biblical Theology.* InterVarsity, 2003; Hauerwas, S. *Unleashing the Scripture.* Abingdon, 1993; Jacobs, A. *A Theology of Reading.* Westview, 2001; Jeanrond, W. *Theological Hermeneutics.* Crossroad, 1991; Jeffrey, D. *People of the Book.* Eerdmans, 1996; Kelsey, D. *To Understand God Truly.* Westminster John Knox, 1992; idem. *The Uses of Scripture in Recent Theology.* Fortress, 1975. Reissued as *Proving Doctrine.* Trinity, 1999; Lindbeck, G. *The Nature of Doctrine.* Westminster John Knox, 1984; idem. "Postcritical Canonical Interpretation: Three Modes of Retrieval." Pages 26–51 in *Theological Exegesis,* ed. C. Seitz and K. Greene-McCreight. Eerdmans, 1999; Louth, A. *Discerning the Mystery.* Clarendon, 1983; Lundin, R. *The Culture of Interpretation.* Eerdmans, 1993; idem, ed. *Disciplining Hermeneutics.* Eerdmans, 1997; idem. *The Promise of Hermeneutics.* Eerdmans, 1999; Lundin, R., C. Walhout, and A. Thiselton. *The Responsibility of Hermeneutics.* Eerdmans, 1985; Moberly, R. W. L. *The Bible, Theology, and Faith.* Cambridge University Press, 2000; Noble, P. *The Canonical Approach.* Brill, 1995; O'Donovan, O. *Resurrection and Moral Order.* 2d ed. Eerdmans, 1994; Rogers, E., Jr. "How the Virtues of an Interpreter Presuppose and Perfect Hermeneutics: The Case of Thomas Aquinas." *JR* 76, no. 1 (January 1996): 64–81; Seitz, C. "Christological Interpretation of Texts and Trinitarian Claims to Truth: An Engagement with Francis Watson's *Text and Truth.*" *SJT* 52, no. 2 (1999): 209–26; Seitz, C., and K. Greene-McCreight, eds. *Theological Exegesis.* Eerdmans, 1999; Smith, J. K. A. *The Fall of Interpretation.* InterVarsity, 2000; Steinmetz, D. "The Superiority of Pre-Critical Exegesis." Pages 26–38 in *The Theological Interpretation of Scripture,* ed. S. Fowl. Blackwell, 1997; Thiselton, A. *Interpreting God and the Postmodern Self.* Eerdmans, 1995; idem. *New Horizons in Hermeneutics.* Zondervan, 1992; idem. *The Two Horizons.* Eerdmans, 1980; Vanhoozer, K. *First Theology.* InterVarsity, 2002; idem. *Is There a Meaning in this Text?* Zondervan, 1998; Watson, F. "The Old Testament as Christian Scripture: A Response to Professor Seitz." *SJT* 52, no. 2 (1999): 227–32; idem. *Text and Truth.* Eerdmans, 1997; idem. *Text, Church, and World.* Eerdmans, 1994; Webster, J. *Word and Church.* T&T Clark, 2001; Williams, A. "Contemplation: Knowledge of God in Augustine's *De trinitate.*" Pages 121–46 in *Knowing the Triune God,* ed. J. Buckley and D. Yeago. Eerdmans, 2001; Wolterstorff, N. *Divine Discourse.* Cambridge University Press, 1995; Wood, C. *The Formation of Christian Understanding.* Trinity, 1993.

Daniel J. Treier

Theology   *See* Doctrine; Systematic Theology

Theology, NT   *See* Biblical Theology

Theology, OT   *See* Biblical Theology

Theophany   *See* Revelation

Theory   *See* Practical Theology; Wisdom

1 Thessalonians, Book of

First Thessalonians holds a unique place among the writings of the NT in the view of many contemporary scholars because it is widely believed that 1 Thessalonians is not only Paul's first extant letter, but also the earliest extant writing of Christianity. If this is correct then 1 Thessalonians gives us our earliest window on the theology of nascent Christianity. Strikingly, this theology is communicated in the form of a letter and through the medium of apocalyptic discourse. Both of these points are significant. Beker (*Paul;* and "Recasting") argues that Paul's letters are characterized by contingency and coherence. The contingency results from the unique situation addressed by each letter; the coherence derives from Paul's interpretation of the Christ event through the master symbolism of Jewish apocalyptic thought. A proper interpretation of 1 Thessalonians requires that both of these points be kept in mind.

History of Interpretation

The earliest extant commentaries on 1 Thessalonians come from the Antiochene school of theology in the fourth and fifth centuries. The school approached Scripture as a historical document and as a result sought the meaning intended by the inspired author. This posed a problem for them since in 4:15 Paul seems to place himself among the living at the time of the parousia, but if this is what he intended, history proved him wrong. As a result the tendency was simply to deny that Paul referred to himself in order to avoid the apostle being wrong. Some contemporary commentators follow the same approach.

During the Middle Ages commentators often merely reproduced the church fathers or resorted to allegorical exegesis. With the Protestant Reformation allegorical interpretation was replaced by grammatical and literal interpretations. The legacy of the early Reformers meant that scholars became interested in historical questions with respect to the Bible. In the case of 1 Thessalonians Hugo Grotius in the early seventeenth century raised questions regarding the order in which Paul wrote the Thessalonian letters, arguing for a reversed sequence to the canonical order. The issue that he first posed, the relation between the Thessalonians letters, has remained a significant part of Thessalonians studies to this day. Grotius's arguments for the priority of 2 Thessalonians have been developed significantly during the last two centuries. But others have claimed that 2 Thessalonians is a post-Pauline forgery.

In the nineteenth century Baur questioned the Pauline authorship of 1 Thessalonians, but his view failed to carry conviction. More recently some (e.g., Richard, *Thessalonians*) have claimed that it is a compilation of two or more letters based on form-critical considerations regarding the multiple thanksgivings. Several scholars (e.g., Pearson) have claimed that 2:14–16 is a Deutero-Pauline interpolation because of its anti-Jewish character. A recent debate has also emerged over whether 2:1–12 is an apostolic apology against opponents criticizing Paul (Weima), or whether the apostle was employing a self-description

derived from the ideal philosopher (Malherbe, *Paul*). As with other Pauline letters, interpreters have been interested in the question of whether Paul was making use of various Jewish and Christian traditional materials in composing his letter. In the last twenty years rhetorical analysis has been employed extensively in the interpretation of 1 Thessalonians in order to understand Paul's persuasive strategy (e.g., Jewett), and Malherbe (*Paul*) has attempted to show that the pastoral nature of Paul's letter was indebted to the tradition of moral philosophers of antiquity.

Hearing the Message of 1 Thessalonians

The message of 1 Thessalonians originally addressed a community of recent converts from paganism (1:9–10). Following their acceptance of Paul's gospel, they experienced serious opposition from their fellow citizens (1:6; 2:14; 3:3). In spite of persecution and the premature departure of Paul (2:17), they remained faithful to Christ and loyal to Paul (3:6). In this situation the essential message of the letter served the twin pastoral functions of encouraging and exhorting the Thessalonians. Paul presented his message through a carefully constructed introduction (1:2–10) that introduces the main themes of the letter, an extended narrative of his relationship with the Thessalonians (2:1–3:10), and an exhortative section (4:1–5:22), which includes an eschatological clarification regarding the resurrection (4:13–18).

Much of 1 Thess. 1–3 reads like a narrative devoted to recounting aspects of Paul's and the Thessalonians' experience. Beneath the surface, however, Paul seeks to encourage his readers by reminding them of how they impressed other Christians by their response to persecution (1:4–10), and by showing them that through suffering they became imitators of himself and the Lord (1:6), as well as the Judean Christians (2:14–16). He also indicates that he has a special affection for them (2:7b–12, 19–20; 3:1–10). In 2:1–12 Paul's account of his ministry among the Thessalonians functions to reconfirm the Thessalonians in the pattern of Christian behavior that they had seen him demonstrate in his ministry.

In the main exhortative section Paul introduces a discussion about how the readers should live as Christians. His first topic concerns sexual ethics appropriate for those called to holiness (4:3–8), while in 4:9–12 he directs them to love one another as God has taught them to do and to behave appropriately toward those outside the community of faith. Paul then offers an important theological clarification regarding participation in the parousia of Christ (4:13–18), followed by an exhortation to ethical and religious vigilance as they wait for the coming of their Lord, through whom they are to obtain salvation (5:1–11). Before concluding the letter, Paul offers a series of short exhortations on how to live the Christian life (5:12–22).

1 Thessalonians and the Canon

Among the letters of Paul, 1 Thessalonians does not appear to be a very significant theological writing because it primarily served a pastoral function and as such contains little doctrinal material on topics like sin and the law, justification by faith, and the cross and resurrection of Christ. Nevertheless, 1 Thess. 4–5 does have theological importance within the context of the canon of Scripture. First, these chapters contain a great deal of ethical exhortation and community instruction that contribute to our understanding of what Christian identity is and how Christians should live lives of holiness in order to please God. Second, 4:13–17 contains an important discussion of the parousia, or return of Christ. In a number of respects 4:13–17 shows conceptual connections with the eschatologically charged passages of Mark 13, Matt. 24, and Luke 17. The fact is that Paul identifies what he is saying in 4:15–17 as "the word of the Lord" (NRSV). The close verbal similarities between these verses and Matt. 24:29–31 and 40–41, in particular, suggest that this passage may be a reference to the Jesus tradition regarding the coming of the Son of Man from heaven. The coming of the day of the Lord "like a thief in the night" (5:2) may also derive from the apocalyptic tradition of the coming of the Son of Man found in Matt. 24:23–27.

Although the OT is nowhere directly cited, there are allusions to it, particularly in the apocalyptic eschatological sections. For example, the expression "the day of the Lord" in 5:2 was taken over from the OT "day of Yahweh" (e.g., Amos 5:18–20; Joel 1:15; 2:31–32). Similarly, the metaphor of judgment coming like "sudden labor pains" in 5:3 is well attested in judgment passages in the OT (e.g., Isa. 13:6–8; Jer. 6:22–30), as is the light and darkness metaphor in 5:4–5 (e.g., Job 22:9–11; Ps. 82:5; Isa. 2:5; 9:2). Thus, Paul either directly or through Jewish apocalyptic traditions makes important use of the OT.

1 Thessalonians and Theology

At the center of the theological thought of 1 Thessalonians stands the belief that God elects (1:4) and then calls (2:12; 5:24) believers through the message of the gospel (1:5; 2:13), and that he appoints them to future salvation through Jesus Christ, who died for them so that they might live with him at his victorious coming from heaven (5:9–10). The future salvation to which they are called means that, unlike those who do not believe, they will not be subject to divine wrath on the day of judgment (1:9–10). From this central theological point flow several other key considerations.

First, faith represents the necessary response to the message of the gospel for those who would be saved (1:5–10). But it is more than this. It designates the trust, commitment, and loyalty that form the core elements in the Christian's relationship with God and Jesus Christ. The Thessalonians demonstrated their faith in God by remaining loyal in the face of persecution by their fellow citizens. Such faith, maintained under adverse circumstances, can provide encouragement to others (3:7). But more importantly, God reciprocates with faithfulness toward those whom he has called. Therefore, those who trust in God may rely upon God to keep them safe and without blame until the parousia of the Lord Jesus Christ (5:23–24).

Second, God wills that believers should be holy or sanctified (4:3). Malherbe (*Thessalonians*, 343) identifies this theological theme, along with the election and call of believers, as the two main themes of the letter. Fundamental to the concept of sanctification is the idea of separation from what is impure (4:7). This separation involves both divine action and human effort. God's call through the gospel of Christ involves believers' sanctification by God (4:7). Nevertheless, God will only complete the process of sanctification at the parousia of Jesus Christ (3:13; 5:23). At the same time sanctification requires moral endeavor on the part of believers. In 4:3 sanctification, separation from all forms of immorality, constitutes the ethical response of believers as they seek to please God (4:1). It also serves to distinguish them from their pagan neighbors (4:5). To reject this requirement of the faith is to reject divine authority itself (4:7–8). Positively, sanctification is closely associated with the love that Christians are called to show toward fellow members of the community, as well as to outsiders (3:12–13). Just as much as maintaining ethical purity separates Christians from those who are not believers, so doing deeds of love toward one's brothers and sisters in the faith also distinguishes and therefore separates Christians from outsiders (4:9–10; 1:3; Yarbrough 86–87).

Third, the theme of hope suffuses the letter. In introducing the main topics to be covered, Paul twice alludes to his readers' eschatological hope (1:3, 9–10). The main body of the letter, 2:1–5:22, is bracketed by 1:9–10 and 5:23, in which Paul stresses the eschatological hope of the Thessalonians. In 3:13 Paul invokes the theme of eschatological hope in the transition to the main exhortative section of the letter. Elsewhere in the letter Paul refers to eschatological hope in 2:12, 19; 4:13–18; 5:1–4, 9–10. With so many references, particularly at crucial points in the structure of the letter, it is clear that the eschatological hope of apocalyptic thought plays a fundamental role in the letter. Like moral purity and love for the family of God, Christian hope also serves to separate the followers of Christ from outsiders (4:13). First Thessalonians 4:15–17 offers a word from the Lord Jesus himself regarding the coparticipation in the parousia by both living and deceased Christians and the promise of eternal life in his presence. Knowledge of this hope means that death has lost its power for the believer in Christ, unlike those who lack this hope. The hoped-for salvation of Christians stands in complete contrast to the destiny of those without faith, who will be subject to divine wrath at the coming of the Lord. Theologically, hope for eternal life requires vigilance and ethical preparedness on the part of Christ's followers (5:1–11).

Finally, and often unnoticed, 1 Thessalonians provides resources for a theology of ministry. Paul sets out the character of his own ministry in 2:1–12. The goal of his ministry was to declare the gospel in order to please God, not other humans (2:2–4), and to build up his converts in the faith (2:11–12). The passage also underscores the ethical qualities of his ministry as well as the exemplary character of his commitment to the Thessalonians (2:3–8, 10–11). All of this is every bit as relevant today as in Paul's time, as is his instruction to the community to love and respect those who minister to them (5:12–13).

From this brief discussion of the themes in 1 Thessalonians, we may conclude that the theological value of 1 Thessalonians for Christians today is perhaps much greater than has often been recognized. It speaks to how Christians should live in the world while waiting with hope for the parousia of Christ.

Bibliography

Beker, J. C. *Paul the Apostle*. 1980. Reprint, T&T Clark, 1989; idem. "Recasting Pauline Theology: The Coherence-Contingency Scheme as Interpretive Model." Pages 15–24 in *Thessalonians, Philippians, Galatians, Philemon*, ed. J. Bassler. Vol. 1 of *Pauline Theology*. Fortress, 1991; Chapa, J. "Is First Thessalonians a Letter of Consolation?" *NTS* 40 (1994): 150–60; Collins, R., ed. *The Thessalonian Correspondence*. BETL. Leuven University Press, 1990; Donfried, K. *Paul, Thessalonica, and Early Christianity*. Eerdmans, 2002; idem. "The Theology of 1 Thessalonians." Pages 1–79 in *The Theology of the Shorter Pauline Letters*, ed. K. Donfried and I. H. Marshall. Cambridge University Press, 1993; Jewett, R. *The Thessalonian Correspondence*. FF. Fortress, 1986; Lyons, G. *Pauline Autobiography*. SBLDS. Scholars Press, 1985; Malherbe, A. *The Letters to the Thessalonians*. AB 32B. Doubleday, 2000; idem. *Paul and the Thessalonians*. Fortress, 1987; Marshall, I. H. *1 and 2 Thessalonians*. NCB. Eerdmans, 1983; Meeks, W. "Social Function of Apocalyptic Language in Pauline Christianity." Pages 687–705 in *Apocalypticism in the Mediterranean World and the Near East*, ed. D. Hellholm. Mohr, 1983; Pearson, B. "1 Thessalonians 2:13–16: A Deutero-Pauline Interpolation." *HTR* 64 (1971): 79–94; Plevnik, J. *Paul and the Parousia*. Hendrickson, 1997; Richard, E. J. "Early Pauline Thought: An Analysis of 1 Thessalonians." Pages 39–51 in *Thessalonians, Philippians, Galatians, Philemon*, ed. J. M. Bassler. Vol. 1 of *Pauline Theology*. Fortress, 1991; idem. *First and Second Thessalonians*. SP 11. Liturgical, 1995; Wanamaker, C. "Apocalyptic Discourse, Paraenesis and Identity Maintenance in 1 Thessalonians." *Neot* 36 (2002): 131–45; idem. *The Epistles to the Thessalonians*. NIGTC. Eerdmans, 1990; Weima, J. "The Function of 1 Thessalonians 2:1–12 and the Use of Rhetorical Criticism: A Response to Otto Merk." Pages 114–31 in *The Thessalonians Debate*, ed. K. Donfried and J. Beutler. Eerdmans, 2000; Wiles, G. *Paul's Intercessory Prayers*. SNTSMS 24. Cambridge University Press, 1974; Yarbrough, O. *Not like the Gentiles*. SBLDS 80. Scholars Press, 1985.

Charles A. Wanamaker

2 Thessalonians, Book of

In the modern period the interpretation of 2 Thessalonians has proved far more controversial than 1 Thessalonians because of three related uncertainties. First, the letter's relationship to 1 Thessalonians has been the subject of considerable debate. Second and closely related to the first, scholars have frequently contested the Pauline authorship of the letter. Third, because of the first two uncertainties and the limited information in the text, the precise situation addressed by the letter has proved elusive. Naturally, the position taken on these issues has a significant bearing on the general interpretation of the letter and more specifically on its theological interpretation (Bassler, "Peace").

History of Interpretation

The general history of commentating on 2 Thessalonians closely parallels the history for 1 Thessalonians. The elusive nature of the apocalyptic discourse in 2 Thess. 2:1–12 has made it a fertile ground for exegetical speculation from the patristic period onward. Because most interpreters up until the modern period understood the passage to be prophetic, they linked their explanations of 2:1–12 to historical circumstances of their own period. The "man of lawlessness" (2:3–4) was early identified with the antichrist of the Johannine letters. Tertullian thought that the figure would arise on the ruins of the Roman state. He, like Chrysostom, believed the restraining force mentioned in 2:6–7 to be the Roman Empire, though Chrysostom mentions that some thought the restrainer was the Holy Spirit. The reference to the temple of God (2:4) was often taken literally, and some interpreters therefore believed that the temple in Jerusalem would have to be rebuilt for the prophecy to be fulfilled. Others understood the temple metaphorically as a reference to the church.

For the Reformers, 2:1–12 proved an invaluable scriptural weapon in their attack on the papacy. Calvin, for example, regularly referred to the pope as the antichrist, citing 2:3–4. He claimed that the papacy had arrogated to itself the honor and glory due to God alone, fulfilling the prophecy in 2:4. Some Protestants even claimed that the seat taken by the antichrist in the temple was the seat of the apostle Peter, usurped by the pope.

In the seventeenth century Hugo Grotius set the course for the modern study of 2 Thessalonians when arguing that 3:17, with its reference to Paul's own signature, only made sense if written at the end of Paul's first letter to the Thessalonians, not his second letter. His study raised the wider issue of the relationship of 1 and 2 Thessalonians.

Around 1800 J. Schmidt maintained that 2 Thess. 2:1–12 was an interpolation into an otherwise authentic letter. He based his conclusion on two points. First, he claimed that a contradiction existed between the sequence of events prior to the parousia of Christ in 2:1–12 and the suddenness of the parousia in 1 Thess. 4:13–5:11, and second that the antichrist fantasy in 2:1–12 was un-Pauline in character. The supposed tension between the eschatology of 1 and 2 Thessalonians has been a recurring feature in subsequent claims rejecting Pauline authorship of 2 Thessalonians.

In 1839 F. Kern rejected the authenticity of 2 Thessalonians. He maintained that 2 Thessalonians showed signs of literary dependence on 1 Thessalonians, and that 3:17 was part of the attempt by a forger to secure acceptance of his work in the name of Paul. At the turn of the twentieth century Wrede further developed Kern's literary approach. His work largely set the parameters of the debate for those rejecting Pauline authorship until the work of Trilling in 1972. Trilling consolidated and further developed the argument against Pauline authorship to the extent that, it is fair to say, a majority of critical scholars now reject the Pauline origins of 2 Thessalonians. Trilling's case, however, is far less compelling under scrutiny than is often appreciated (see Wanamaker, *Epistles*, 17–28; Malherbe, *Letters*, 364–70).

Hearing the Message of 2 Thessalonians

The starting point for hearing the message of 2 Thessalonians, like all of Paul's letters, begins with the recognition that the message of the letter is contingent upon the circumstances that Paul believed himself to be addressing. The message that we hear when listening to 2 Thessalonians depends heavily on the assumptions we make regarding the three uncertainties mentioned in the first paragraph. In this article I assume the following: (1) Paul wrote 2 Thessalonians. (2) He did so prior to writing 1 Thessalonians. (3) He did so at a time when he believed that the Thessalonian Christians were experiencing persecution on account of their new faith in God and Jesus Christ (see Wanamaker, *Epistles*, 17–28, 37–45).

The letter deals with three main issues. First, in 1:4–12 we find the theme of retributive justice, in which an eschatological reversal is promised. The current persecutors of the community are threatened with divine vengeance on the judgment day, while the persecuted are promised relief from their affliction. The promise of retributive vengeance to bring comfort and encouragement is unusual in Paul. Since he addressed it to a community that was powerless in the face of persecution and believed that God was just, it is at least understandable. Second, in 2:1–2 Paul exhorts the readers not to believe that the day of the Lord has already come. Presumably their experience of persecution may have led some to believe that the woes associated with the parousia of the Lord had come (Aus, "Relevance," 260–65). Paul presents evidence in 2:3–12 that the day of the Lord cannot have come yet by outlining an apocalyptic, eschatological scenario leading up to the day of the Lord. As part of this, Paul includes an etiology for the lawlessness or evil that has led to the persecution of the Thessalonians (2:7–12). The apocalyptic scenario in 2:3–12 is unparalleled in Paul or anywhere else in the NT for that matter (Malherbe, *Letters*, 427).

Finally, in 3:6–15 Paul both instructs and exhorts regarding the problem of idleness among some members of the community who were not making any effort to provide for themselves. Russell has shown that the problem may have had its origins in the poor entering into client relations with better-off members of the community, thereby putting their Christian patrons under financial pressure. Paul begins by instructing the readers not to have fellowship with believers who are refusing to work for a living (3:6, 10–11). Such behavior, he indicates, runs contrary to the example that he set when preaching in Thessalonica (3:7–9). He then both commands and exhorts those who are living in idleness to mend their ways by working for a living and living quietly (3:12). In closing, he exhorts the hearers of the letter to break fellowship with any who do not obey what he has instructed, but also to continue admonishing such people to reform themselves (3:14–15).

Apart from the main points, Paul seeks to encourage and comfort his readers in their difficult circumstances through thanksgivings in 1:3–4 and 2:13–14, as well as through his wish-prayer in 2:16–17 and his prayer-request and promise of assurance in 3:1–5.

2 Thessalonians and the Canon

In the modern era 2 Thessalonians has not been considered a very significant writing. Its limited and highly contextual message, colored by apocalypticism, has marginalized it within the canon.

Not surprisingly, 2 Thessalonians is most closely related in vocabulary, content, and function to 1 Thessalonians. Several of its features, however, are connected to other canonical writings. The theme of the avenging retribution of God, which plays an important role in the book of Revelation (Collins), derives from the OT. Aus ("Relevance"), for example, has demonstrated a close relation between 2 Thess. 1 and Isa. 66, where the theme of divine vengeance occurs. Paul himself employs this theme in Rom. 12:17–21, although the context is quite different from 2 Thessalonians, and Rev. 6:9–17 and 19:2 utilize the theme of retributive vengeance specifically in relation to the persecution and martyrdom of the people of God. Although no OT passage is directly quoted, Bruce (149–53) has identified a number of OT passages parallel in thought or wording to various phrases and ideas found in 1:5–10. The judgment scene in 1:9–10 has some affinities with the coming of the Son of Man in

the Gospel tradition (Wenham 347–49), and with the separation and destruction of the unrighteous in Matt. 25:31–46.

The eschatological gathering of Christians mentioned in 2:1 is redolent of a number of OT passages (e.g., Isa. 43:4–7), but the apocalyptic scenario of 2:3–12 is unparalleled in the canon. Nevertheless, several of the individual features of the scenario are connected to the OT. For example, the lawless one who defiles the temple of God should be read against Dan. 11:31, 36. His arrogation of divine status is perhaps modeled on Ezek. 28:1–10 and Isa. 14:4–20. The idea that God sends a deluding influence (2:11) is well known from the OT (e.g., 2 Sam. 24:1), and occurs in the NT (Rom. 1:24–32).

2 Thessalonians and Theology

The highly contextual and pastoral character of the letter means that Paul's theological thought is narrowly focused on addressing specific issues for his readers, issues that do not resonate very well with many Christians today. This naturally has limited the theological value of 2 Thessalonians for the contemporary church.

In relation to 1:4–12 and 2:8–12, Donfried points to a theology of divine justice, typical of Jewish and Christian apocalyptic thought, but this is a component of what Aus and Bassler ("Enigmatic Sign") have called a theology of suffering. In their account, the theology of suffering emerged in Judaism during the second and first centuries BCE. This theology believed in God's retributive justice and understood the present suffering of the righteous as the means by which they satisfied the just demands of God for their own sins in order to be made worthy of future salvation. Malherbe (*Thessalonians*, 408) suggests that Paul selectively employs this tradition. In 1:4–5 (part of the sentence running from 1:3–11 in the Greek) the suffering of the Thessalonians is not described as satisfying God's justice for their own sins; instead, it makes them worthy of the divine kingdom. In doing so it demonstrates God's justice toward them. A second component of this suffering theology maintains that God will send affliction to punish the godless, who currently afflict the righteous, leading to a just reversal of current unjust circumstances. In 1:6–10 Paul makes this very point. The combination of future blessing for the suffering righteous and punishment for evildoers because they afflict the righteous has often provided encouragement to the oppressed people of God, but Collins rightly warns of the potential dehumanizing effects of the desire for vengeance.

The scenario in 2:3–12, which demonstrates that the day of the Lord has not come (2:1–2), takes us to the heart of Paul's own apocalyptically oriented eschatology. The obscure thought of the mythic-symbolic language occurring in the passage is theologically difficult for contemporary Christians to deal with at face value. For example, the temple of God (2:4) has not existed for nearly two millennia. If the mystery of lawlessness (anarchy) was already at work in Paul's day (2:7), and Paul expected the return of Christ during his lifetime (1 Thess. 4:17), what are we to make of the last 1,900 years of human history? One possibility is to look at what led to Paul's apocalyptic eschatology. The answer seems to be a sense of powerlessness and alienation caused by pervasive evil within the social, economic, political, and religious structures of the day. This same sense is not unknown to contemporary Christians in many parts of the world, as is the refusal of people to accept the truth of the gospel and instead to engage in evil without constraint (2:10–12). In the face of this, 2:3–12; 2:13–17; and 3:1–5 provide a reminder that God is ultimately in control of human destiny. Those who perpetrate evil will suffer God's recompense of condemnation; those who receive the gospel will share in the glory of the Lord Jesus Christ at his coming. Christian hope assures us that God's justice will ultimately triumph over all forms of evil, and that God's elect who already have "eternal comfort and good hope" in the present (2:16 NRSV) will be empowered for Christian living (2:17).

Bibliography

See also bibliography for "1 Thessalonians, Book of"; Aus, R. "God's Plan and God's Power: Isaiah 66 and the Restraining Factors of 2 Thess 2:6–7." *JBL* 96 (1977): 537–53; idem. "The Relevance of Isaiah 66:7 to Revelation 12 and 2 Thessalonians 1." *ZNW* 67 (1976): 252–68; Bassler, J. "The Enigmatic Sign: 2 Thessalonians 1:5." *CBQ* 46 (1984): 496–510; idem. "Peace in All Ways: Theology in the Thessalonian Letters: A Response to R. Jewett, E. Krentz, and E. Richard." Pages 71–85 in *Thessalonians, Philippians, Galatians, Philemon*, ed. J. Bassler. Vol. 1 of *Pauline Theology*. Fortress, 1991; Bruce, F. F. *1 and 2 Thessalonians*. WBC 45. Word, 1982; Collins, A. Y. "Persecution and Vengeance in the Book of Revelation." Pages 729–49 in *Apocalypticism in the Mediterranean World and the Near East*, ed. D. Hellholm. Mohr/Siebeck, 1983; Donfried, K. "The Theology of 2 Thessalonians." Pages 88–113 in *The Theology of the Shorter Pauline Letters*, ed. K. Donfried and I. H. Marshall. Cambridge University Press, 1993; Giblin, C. *The Threat to Faith*. AnBib 31. Pontifical Biblical Institute, 1967; Jewett, R. "A Matrix of Grace: The Theology of 2 Thessalonians as a Pauline Letter." Pages 71–85 in *Thessalonians, Philippians, Galatians, Philemon*, ed. J. Bassler. Vol. 1 of *Pauline Theology*. Fortress, 1991; Krentz, E. "Through a Lens: Theology and Fidelity in 2 Thessalonians." Pages 71–85 in *Thessalonians, Philippians, Galatians, Philemon*, ed. J. Bassler. Vol. 1 of *Pauline Theology*. Fortress, 1991; Rigaux, B. *Saint Paul les épitres aux Thessaloniciens*. ÉBib. Gabalda, 1956; Russell, R. "The Idle in 2 Thess 3.6–12: An Eschatological or a Social Problem?" *NTS* 34 (1988): 105–19; Trilling, W. *Untersuchungen zum zweiten Thessalonischerbrief*. St. Benno, 1972; Wenham, D. "Paul and the Synoptic Apocalypse." Pages 345–75 in vol. 2 of *Gospel Perspectives*, ed. R. T. France and D. Wenham. JSOT, 1981.

Charles A. Wanamaker

Thiselton, Anthony   *See* Hermeneutical Circle; Hermeneutics; Speech-Act Theory; Theological Hermeneutics, Contemporary

Thomas Aquinas

Thomas Aquinas (1225?–74) is recognized as one of the most influential philosophical and theological thinkers of the Middle Ages. Besides the *Summa theologiae* (*ST*) and the *Summa contra gentiles*, the two works for which he is best known, Aquinas's works include commentaries on Aristotle, biblical commentaries, and numerous treatises on particular topics. This entry will focus on Aquinas as an interpreter of Scripture (a subject often overlooked) rather than on his thought in general. (For the most current information on Aquinas's life and works, see Torrell. Also helpful in this regard: Weisheipl; Tugwell in Thomas Aquinas, *Albert and Thomas*; Kretzmann and Stump.)

Biblical Commentaries

While Aquinas is justly remembered for his contributions to philosophy and systematic theology, it is not often realized that the exposition of Scripture constituted one of his principal academic duties. Aquinas produced commentaries on Isaiah, Jeremiah, Lamentations, Job, Matthew, John, all the Pauline epistles (including Hebrews), and the Psalms. He also compiled the *Catena aurea* (the Golden Chain), a verse-by-verse commentary on all four Gospels made up of exegetical passages from Greek and Latin church fathers. (Of these works, all that have been translated into English are indicated in the bibliography below. For translations into other modern languages, see Torrell.)

The commentaries on Isaiah, Jeremiah, and Lamentations are rather brief expositions, focusing on the literal sense of the text, together with references to related biblical passages. Parts of the Isaiah commentary, however, contain "great riches on certain points" (Torrell 27). The commentary on Job is highly developed and is especially noteworthy for its treatment of divine providence. Quite developed, too, is the commentary on Matthew. The commentary on John, considered by Weisheipl to be unsurpassed among Thomas's writings on Scripture, includes lengthy reflections on the Trinity, the beatific vision, and the love of God, among other subjects (Stump, "Biblical," 254). Of the commentaries on Paul, those on Romans, 1 Corinthians, and Hebrews are especially rewarding. In Stump's words: "The commentary on Hebrews contains detailed discussion of Christ as the incarnate Savior, as the second person of the Trinity, and as the fulfiller of the Old Testament promises; and, besides the well-known discussion of the nature of love, the commentary on 1 Corinthians includes intriguing discussions of Christian relations within the family, within the church, and with secular authority" ("Biblical," 255). According to Weisheipl, the Romans commentary "reveals how deeply he [Aquinas] was committed to the Pauline doctrine of justification by faith, gratuity of grace, predestination, merit, good works, and the doctrine of original sin" (Weisheipl 249). Aquinas's Psalms commentary (which covers only Pss. 1–54) can accurately be described as christocentric, since Aquinas makes a special effort to indicate the ways in which the Psalms prefigure Christ and his church.

Characteristics of the Commentaries. Four characteristics of Aquinas's biblical commentaries are worth mentioning: (i) the *divisio textus*, (ii) the copious references to other passages of Scripture, (iii) the frequent use of the church fathers, and (iv) the use of philosophy. First, Thomas's commentary on a passage usually begins with a *divisio textus* (division of the text), a passage that sets forth the logical order in the text. Second, he uses Scripture to explain Scripture; his commentary on a given passage typically includes numerous references to passages from elsewhere in the Bible. Third, Aquinas draws heavily on the insights of the church fathers, both Greek and Latin. Among those cited most frequently are Augustine, Chrysostom, and Jerome. Fourth, Aquinas utilizes the terminology and insights of pagan philosophers (most notably Aristotle) in his exposition of the biblical text.

The Senses of Scripture. With his contemporaries, Aquinas holds that a text of Scripture can have a spiritual sense as well as a literal (or historical) sense (*ST* I.1.10). The spiritual sense is itself divided into the allegorical, moral (or tropo-logical), and anagogical senses. The literal sense is signified by the words of Scripture. (On Aquinas's view, the literal sense includes metaphor; when Scripture speaks of God's arm, for example, the literal sense is not that God has an arm, but only that God has operative power [*ST* I.1.10 ad 3].) The spiritual sense is signified not by the words of Scripture but by the persons, things, or events described by those words (as when the Passover lamb described in the OT signifies Christ). The allegorical sense is present when a thing signified by the text in turn signifies something of Christ or his church. The moral sense is present when a thing signified by the text signifies something relating to right action. And the anagogical sense is present when a thing signified by the text signifies something relating to the next life.

Principles of Interpretation

When we seek the most general principles of scriptural interpretation to which Aquinas subscribes, the following four emerge. First, Aquinas holds that there are no contradictions in Scripture, and, in fact, that whatever is contained in Scripture is true (*Questiones quodlibetales* [*QQ*] XII q. 17; *Commentary on Titus*, ch. 3, lect. 2; Stump, "Revelation," 172). Second, Thomas recognizes that Scripture is sometimes obscure, and that the successful interpretation of Scripture is aided by "long study and practice" (*ST* II-II.1.9). Third, the Holy Spirit can assist believers in understanding Scripture (*QQ* XII q. 17). For example, the gift of understanding (one of the seven gifts of the Holy Spirit) aids believers in penetrating or grasping whatever things come under the assent of faith (*ST* II-II.8.6), i.e., whatever is contained in divine revelation. Since the things that come under the assent of faith are manifested in Scripture and the teaching of the church (*ST* II-II.5.3), it follows that the gift of understanding aids believers in grasping the things contained in Scripture. (Furthermore, in some places Thomas indicates that the Holy Spirit can give to some members of the church a special ["gratuitous"] grace for the interpretation of difficult passages of Scripture [*Commentary on 1 Cor.* 12:10; *QQ* XII q. 17].) Sin, however, can block the assistance of the Holy Spirit (see, e.g., *ST* II-II.11.1); thus, it is not inaccurate to say that on Thomas's view virtue is a hermeneutical aid. Fourth, the teaching of the universal church provides an interpretative guide. Because it is guided by the Holy Spirit, the universal church cannot err (*ST* II-II.1.9; 2.6 ad 3). The church, therefore, has the right interpretation of Scripture and of revelation (*ST* II-II.5.3 ad 2; see also *QQ* III q. 4 a. 2). The sovereign pontiff, in whom the authority of the church chiefly resides, plays a special role in the church's teaching (*ST* II-II.11.2 ad 3; II-II.1.10; II-II.39.1).

Bibliography

Johnson, M. F. "Another Look at St. Thomas and the Plurality of the Literal Sense of Scripture." *Medieval Philosophy and Theology* 2 (1992): 117–41; Kretzmann, N. and E. Stump, eds. *The Cambridge Companion to Aquinas.* Cambridge University Press, 1993; Stump, E. "Biblical Commentary and Philosophy." Pages 252–68 in *The Cambridge Companion to Aquinas,* ed. N. Kretzmann and E. Stump. Cambridge University Press, 1993; idem. "Revelation and Biblical Exegesis: Augustine, Aquinas, and Swinburne." Pages 161–97 in *Reason and the Christian Religion: Essays in Honour of Richard Swinburne,* ed. A. Padgett. Clarendon, 1994; Thomas Aquinas. *Albert and Thomas: Selected Writings.* The Classics of Western Spirituality. Translated, edited, and introduced by S. Tugwell. Paulist, 1988; idem. *Catena aurea,* trans. and ed. J. H. Newman. Saint Austin Press, 1997; idem. *Commentary on the Gospel of Saint John, Part I.* Aquinas Scriptures Series 4, trans. J. Weisheipl and F. Larcher. Magi Books, 1980; idem. *Commentary on Saint Paul's Epistle to the Ephesians.* Aquinas Scriptures Series 2, trans. M. Lamb. Magi Books, 1966; idem. *Commentary on Saint Paul's Epistle to the Galatians.* Aquinas Scriptures Series 1, trans. F. Larcher. Magi Books, 1966; idem. *Commentary on Saint Paul's First Letter to the Thessalonians and the Letter to the Philippians.* Aquinas Scriptures Series 3, trans. F. Larcher and M. Duffy. Magi Books, 1969; idem. *The Literal Exposition on Job.* AAR Classics in Religious Studies 7, trans. A. Damico. Scholars Press, 1989; idem. *Thomas Aquinas—The Gifts of the Spirit: Selected Spiritual Writings,* ed. B. Ashley, trans. M. Rzeczkowski. New City Press, 1995; Torrell, J.-P. *Saint Thomas Aquinas:* Volume I: *The Person and His Work,* trans. R. Royal. Catholic University of America Press, 1996; Weisheipl, J. *Friar Thomas d'Aquino.* 2d ed. Catholic University of America Press, 1983.

Michael W. Rota

1 Timothy, Book of

With 2 Timothy and Titus, 1 Timothy is one of the three "Pastoral Epistles" addressed by Paul to his co-workers rather than to congregations. It deals with the task of Timothy as overseer of the congregation(s) in Ephesus and is largely concerned with the danger of opposition and heresy in the church, the need for measures to ensure the proper maintenance of congregational life (including care for widows and the conduct of elders), the development of reliable leadership (overseers and deacons), the responsibilities and personal life of Timothy as local pastor, and the curbing of disturbing influences (unacceptable teaching by both male teachers and women). It is not primarily concerned with articulating theology, but nevertheless has considerable theological importance.

History of Interpretation

The origin of the letter is disputed. Until modern times it was accepted as a letter of Paul, probably written toward the end of his life around the same time as 2 Timothy and Titus, with which it has close links in style and content. Recognition of its unusual style and the impression that it reflects a post-Pauline situation led to the hypothesis that it is a pseudonymous composition, possibly from the early second century. In it a partisan of Paul endeavors to call the church back to a Pauline position, although in so doing he presents a theology that has developed beyond Paul in an early catholic direction. Thus, it is counted as emphasizing the static reproduction of tradition; the creation of a fixed church order, with leadership by appointed officers replacing the less-structured, informal charismatic ministry of an earlier period; and the development of a way of life that conforms more to the patterns of secular society and wards off criticism and persecution.

Alongside this majority position that the document is substantially later and reflects interests around the turn of the first century, strong support is still being expressed for composition by Paul himself (perhaps with an active amanuensis). A related option is for the use of Pauline materials (oral or written) by a close associate in the immediate post-Pauline period via a letter intended to maintain Paul's influence without any attempt to deceive readers. Since in my view there is no compelling evidence for a late date, 1 Timothy should be read as a document that belongs to the period around the close of Paul's life, whether from his lifetime or soon afterward.

Hearing the Message of 1 Timothy

First Timothy reflects an understanding of the gospel that centers on God as Savior, who wants all people to be saved and to know the truth (2:4). The purpose of God makes universal provision for salvation even though it is clear that salvation becomes a reality only in the case of believers (4:10). The presupposition is that all people are sinners and therefore need to be delivered from sin and its consequences. Christ Jesus came into the world to save sinners; he is depicted as the mediator between God and humankind, the implication being that sinners stand under divine judgment (1:15; 2:5). The statement that Jesus gave himself as a ransom for all (2:6, echoing Mark 10:45) constitutes the gospel to which people respond in faith. Paul himself is an example of such belief; he was shown mercy and forgiven because he had sinned ignorantly in unbelief (1:12–13). The clear implication is that to continue knowingly in sin and unrepentance leads to judgment. It is not stated whether people who have sinned ignorantly can be forgiven without hearing the gospel or coming to faith.

The letter is opposed to the kind of idle speculations that lead to heterodox views. Nevertheless, it contains an important statement enshrining the remarkable revelation by God that constitutes the truth at the heart of the faith. This is the cryptic description of Christ: "He was revealed in flesh, vindicated in spirit, seen by angels, proclaimed among Gentiles, believed in throughout the world, taken up in glory" (3:16 NRSV). This statement affirms the reality of Christ's incarnation (and so probably implies his preexistence) and then of God's affirmation of him, presumably in response to his humiliation and death, "in spirit" (which probably refers to the sphere in which it happened, in contrast to his earthly life "in flesh"). The vindication continues in that he was seen (acknowledged) by angels in heaven. Back on earth he was the object of preaching far and wide, and this led to people believing in him everywhere (possibly in contrast to the comparative lack of belief among the Jews). Finally, he was taken up to be with God in glory; although this clause comes after the mention of the worldwide mission, it can only refer to the ascension. The whole statement emphasizes the vindication of Christ in both heaven and earth, and implicit in it is the church's task of participating in that vindication by preaching Christ to the Gentiles, among whom there will be a positive response to him.

God's purpose for the church as "the pillar and bulwark of the truth" (3:15 NRSV) leads to the calling of specific people to be heralds, charged with making it known. This is the role of Paul himself, who emphasizes his mission especially to the Gentiles (2:7; cf. 2 Tim. 1:11). He also encourages the right people to take on responsibility in the congregations. Normative requirements for overseers (or bishops) and deacons (including "women," who are probably female deacons rather than the wives of deacons) are laid down (3:1–13). These are a mixture of freedom from anything that would give them a bad reputation in and outside the church, competence in leadership skills, and a firm hold on the faith (3:9 of deacons, and implicitly also expected of overseers). Later in the letter (5:17–25) instructions are given regarding proper recognition of the "elders" in the congregation and appropriate disciplinary measures if any fall into sin. It is to be presumed that the elders are identical with the overseers, or perhaps the term embraces both overseers and deacons.

The task of the church is to be faithful to the Christian message. Misguided teachers have been sidetracked into strange speculations based on Jewish myths and have developed commandments based on the Jewish law that they are promulgating as the conduct required of Christians. Paul regards all this as nonsense, with which it is difficult to have any useful debate (1:7); although pursuit of it is spiritually fatal (1:19), the victims are not beyond the hope of repentance and restoration (cf. 2 Tim. 2:23–26).

In place of fruitless controversy he advocates the place of prayer in the congregation, both for peaceful conditions in which evangelism is possible, and for people of all kinds to be saved (2:1–10). In this connection Paul warns against the danger of the men in the congregation behaving inappropriately by quarreling, probably as a result of the false teaching. He then warns against the women dressing extravagantly and possibly also seductively. As a kind of appendix to this (2:11–15), he further requires that a woman should not teach or have authority over a man but should be "silent" (or quiet).

1 Timothy and the Canon

First Timothy is part of a canon that includes the earlier letters of Paul. If the letter is genuinely by Paul, it forms part of the total evidence for his theology, and it can be argued that his other letters should be read in the light of it. Such a reading of both 1 Timothy and the other letters would need to bear in mind any special circumstances attaching to their individual composition. If, for example, 1 Timothy were the work of Paul in old age and there had been a decisive shift in his manner of thinking and theological position, then this would have a bearing on the exercise. However, there is no evidence whatever that Paul's age (still less an aging process) is a factor to be considered. If the letter is substantially distanced from Paul, then it can be interpreted on its own. The question that then arises is whether it differs from, or even contradicts, Paul. I see no signs that it is attempting to provide a normative reinterpretation of Paul for a much later situation. Rather, it provides appropriate teaching for a specific situation that stands in the tradition of the earlier Pauline letters. It does lack much of the kind of theologizing that is characteristic of the earlier letters, and like Luke-Acts it might be thought to show less depth of theological thinking. But it does an appropriate job in its own setting.

1 Timothy and Theology

1. For a letter that is of necessity much concerned with false teaching and congregational order, 1 Timothy contains a warm theology of salvation that preserves the mystery of the gospel and emphasizes the primacy of grace. Like 2 Timothy and Titus, it inculcates an attitude to Christian living that stresses the need for obedience to a conscience operating in close conjunction with faith and on the basis of sound teaching. This lifestyle produces an orderly and self-controlled life that wins respect from non-Christians, commends the gospel, and gives us important insights into the character and duties of Christian leaders. The author holds to an essentially missionary theology in which apostles are church planters, but the responsibility of the church planter includes the continuing care of the church and its preservation from error. It can be safely assumed that, had it not been for the demands of this necessary task, the need for active evangelism would have been closer to the forefront of his concerns.

2. First Timothy significantly develops the concept of the church as the household of God. Whereas the metaphor of the body, as expressed in Rom. 12 and 1 Cor. 12, has little to say about leadership and structure in the congregation (though 1 Cor. 12:28 should not be overlooked), the household metaphor does recognize the need for direction in the church. It was perhaps inevitable that such structuring would resemble the pattern in the society of the time, but the letter does not imply that this particular form is appropriate for all time. A solution to the problems of congregational organization today will be found by holding together the concepts of the body and the household in a fruitful and creative tension, not by assuming that either is necessarily superior to the other and following either model exclusively.

3. The instruction to women to learn in silence remains controversial. Some congregations today accept women into "ministry," specifically the ordained pastoral ministry, with the authority that accompanies it. There are debates over whether a woman can function as a priest in denominations where the ordained ministry is understood as a form of priesthood confined to males. Apart from that, there is strong resistance to women taking an active part in preaching and ordained ministry in some congregations where high regard is paid to what is regarded as the "plain teaching" of Scripture.

In the first-century situation with its generally patriarchal society, where women played little part in public affairs, teaching by women could be regarded as an unacceptable breach of behavior patterns, whether among Jews or also among some Gentiles. Accordingly, the restriction can be interpreted as a culturally shaped prohibition that is no longer binding in a different setting.

The difficulty is in the appeal to Scripture that is used to back up the prohibition. It has a twofold argument that Adam was created prior to Eve (and therefore is superior), and that it is Eve who was deceived by the serpent (with the implication that women are still more likely to be deceived than men). This seems to be a doctrinal rather than a cultural consideration and is decisive for those who believe that the authority of a passage of Scripture must be accepted even when it seems to run against the grain of NT teaching generally (e.g., Gal. 3:28).

Other factors must be brought into consideration. (1) If it were not for the presence of this passage (together with 1 Cor. 14:33–36, though its significance is not agreed upon), probably nobody today would hold that women should be prohibited from teaching. (2) In an ancient society, where illiteracy and lack of education were common, it was especially the women who would suffer from these disadvantages. (3) The evidence of 1 Tim. 5:13 and 2 Tim. 3:6–7 suggests that women were especially susceptible to the prevalent false teaching in these specific congregations. (4) The argument that women are for all time more likely to be deceived than men because Eve was deceived is groundless. In any case, there is no way of knowing whether, if the serpent had spoken to Adam rather than to Eve, he would not have fallen just as readily as she had. (5) The argument that priority in creation places men in such a position of superiority over women (or a husband over a wife) that a woman should not teach is untenable. (6) Eunice and Lois are commended for teaching the faith to the boy Timothy; evidently, therefore, it is not the teaching that is at fault, but rather the implication that the teaching woman is exercising authority over a man. (7) The very rare verb "have authority over" (Gk. *authenteō*) most probably expresses an unacceptable form of dominance. (8) Some women may have been arguing that they needed to teach in order to be saved, whereas the writer insists that this is not so, and reminds them that bearing children (which may also have been an issue; see 4:3) was a proper fulfillment of their Christian calling.

One possible interpretation is that, even if a woman should not have authority over a man, the exercise of teaching or the holding of ministerial office in the church should not be regarded as infringing this principle in contemporary society. Another possibility is that there may have been women teaching that women were superior to men on the basis of a faulty interpretation of Genesis, and the author is concerned simply to refute this and to stop the women giving false teaching. Hence, nothing more may be involved than a correction of a false interpretation of Genesis in a specific situation.

Certainty in interpretation of this difficult passage is difficult to achieve, but there is at least sufficient doubt concerning the validity of the patriarchal interpretation as a ruling for practice today to make it very unwise to impose it upon the church.

4. There is no uncertainty, however, over the full-scale treatment of the dangers of wealth, both the desiring of it and the misuse of it (6:3–19; cf. 2:9–10; 5:6). The author is quite clear that these are real dangers, against which Christians must be extremely vigilant, and he is very serious about the right use of income and possessions and the dangers of greed and envy. In a world where many Christians cannot avoid earning relatively high incomes, where there are many opportunities for lavish expenditure, and where equally many people are living in various degrees of poverty—the lesson of 1 Timothy is uncomfortably relevant and challenging.

Bibliography

See also bibliography for "Titus, Book of"; Campbell, R. *The Elders*. Studies of the New Testament and Its World. T&T Clark, 1994; Donelson, L. *Pseudepigraphy and Ethical Argument in the Pastoral Epistles*. HUT 22. Mohr/Siebeck, 1986; Kidd, R. *Wealth and Beneficence in the Pastoral Epistles*. SBLDS 122. Scholars Press, 1990; Köstenberger, A., et al., eds. *Women in the Church*. Baker, 1995; Oberlinner, L. *Die Pastoralbriefe*. HTKNT 9/2. Herder, 1994; Quinn, J., and W. Wacker. *The First and Second Letters to Timothy*. ECC. Eerdmans, 2000; Roloff, J. *Der erste Brief an Timotheus*. EKKNT. Benziger/Neukirchener Verlag, 1988; Webb, W. *Slaves, Women and Homosexuals*. InterVarsity, 2001.

I. Howard Marshall

2 Timothy, Book of

With 1 Timothy and Titus, 2 Timothy is classified as a "Pastoral Epistle"; it is addressed to an individual engaged in mission and oversight, dealing with his personal lifestyle as a pastor and his relationships with the congregations under his supervision. Unlike the other two letters, it has no formal material on congregational structures and leadership. It reflects Paul facing up to the impending end of his life and deals primarily with the future mission of his younger colleague Timothy without supervision. It considers the nature of apostleship, the incipient dangers from within the church, and the need to respond to them, plus the external threats of persecution and even martyrdom.

History of Interpretation

From earliest times 2 Timothy was accepted as the last surviving letter of Paul, written from imprisonment in Rome, whether that described in Acts 28 or a subsequent imprisonment after a presumed further period of missionary activity (Eusebius, *Hist. eccl.* 2.22). Critical scholarship in the nineteenth century called into question the authenticity of all the so-called Pastoral Epistles on grounds of style and apparent reflection of a later period of composition. Some regard 2 Timothy as entirely fictitious. Others hold that it includes substantial fragments of Pauline material. Scholars who hold that it is fully Pauline generally hold to the traditional dating; some place it earlier (from prison in Ephesus or Caesarea), but the necessary reinterpretation of 1:17 is unconvincing. This is the Pastoral Epistle that has the strongest claims to be genuine or at least to be a reworking of Pauline material, including a letter from prison to Timothy. The closeness in style and content to 1 Timothy and Titus strongly suggests the final composition was from a hand other than Paul's (whether an amanuensis in his lifetime or a later compiler).

On the traditional understanding, 2 Timothy is an authentic or near-authentic expression of the mind of Paul as he faces the end of his active career and is concerned for the continuation of his mission, possibly through Timothy as his successor. If it is a later fiction, it is thought to be patterned on Jewish testament literature, in which a godly person is represented as facing impending death and conveying memorable last instructions and encouragement to his family or successor. This context distinguishes 2 Timothy to some extent from 1 Timothy and Titus, which convey instructions ("mandates") from an active apostle to his colleagues in mission.

Hearing the Message of 2 Timothy

The message is summed up nicely as "do the work of an evangelist" (4:5). Timothy is a member of Paul's mission team, which carried out evangelism, involving both the planting of congregations and their nurture. The letter is largely concerned with Timothy himself; the self-references by Paul function by way of example and stimulus, although in chapter 4 they are also concerned with his own situation and requirements.

Even in a letter to a close colleague and friend, Paul writes self-consciously as an apostle with a calling related to the "life that is in Christ Jesus" (1:1). Apostleship is the key to Paul's self-understanding, the position of a missionary authorized by the risen Lord to preach and teach (1:11), but also called to the possibility of suffering for the sake of the gospel like any other believer (3:12). He therefore leads a life that should be exemplary for other missionaries, both in the things that happened to him but also in the way that he lived (3:10–11).

Timothy was apparently tempted to lack of courage and thus to maintaining a low profile. Paul still refers to him as his child, which may imply that he was comparatively young (2:1). He had a pious upbringing by his mother and grandmother; his father (Acts 16:1) is not mentioned. As a young believer, Paul took him along as a junior colleague. At some point Paul prayed and laid hands upon him for his work as a fellow missionary, so that he might have the appropriate gifts of the Spirit, in this case "a spirit of power and of love and of self-discipline" that needed to be kept burning brightly (1:6–7 NRSV).

Paul's opening exhortation (1:3–18) is backed up by an appeal first of all to the power of God and to Timothy's colleagueship with Paul. Through participating with Paul in a ministry carrying the risk of suffering, Timothy shares in the power of God. The thought is developed through using a traditional formulation of the gospel that is quite similar to the teaching in Titus, with its correlation of what God did before ages began and what he has now revealed through the epiphany of Christ. Here the stress, however, is more on the "life and immortality" brought by the gospel (1:10), probably to provide an incentive in the face of threats of death against the missionaries (cf. 2:11–12). Paul comments on the suffering that he endures as a missionary but declares his trust in God, who delivers him from being "ashamed,"

from the feeling of shame that results from failure. His concern is not for his own resurrection but for the safe preservation of the gospel, no matter what happens to himself. God will guard to the last day what Paul has entrusted to him: the gospel (rather than Paul's own self; but the interpretation of 1:12 is disputed).

Against this background, Paul appeals to Timothy to hold fast to the faith, in the sense of proclaiming and transmitting it faithfully, and especially of standing up to corrupting influences within the church. At the same time, he can be told to "be strong in the grace that is in Christ Jesus" (2:1). There is an irreducible tension between the appeals to human faithfulness and the promises of divine empowerment.

Timothy is called to total commitment to his pastoral work (2:1–26). His tough assignment demands self-denial, self-discipline, and self-commitment. There is a broad appeal to the example of Jesus, who was "raised from the dead" (2:8), an expression doubtlessly implying that first he submitted to death, but God was faithful in raising him. There is a further appeal to the pattern of Paul in his suffering and commitment, so that God's people may attain to salvation without falling away; here is the reminder that, although the messengers may be imprisoned, the word of God cannot be fettered. And there is the sure knowledge that those who are prepared to suffer with Christ will share in his resurrection and reign. This trustworthy statement also warns against the consequences of falling away and again insists that even if some of God's people are faithless, he will continue faithfully to uphold them, since that is his very nature (2:11–13). Further reassurance is provided by the fact that, despite the activity of false teachers, the church has a firm foundation laid by God himself. Here again the tension recurs. God knows his people and (it is implied) watches over them; at the same time it is their responsibility to turn aside from wickedness. Even if people do turn aside, nevertheless, the opportunity for repentance and escape from the shackles imposed by the devil remains, and the faithful pastor will continue to persuade them to repent.

In the remaining instruction (3:1–4:5), the context for Timothy's work is the further spread of godlessness and error in the church but with the assurance that it will not triumph. Once again, he is reminded of how Paul's mission was not free from opposition and persecution, but the Lord rescued him. The stress now is on the danger of error, into which even Timothy might fall. The antidote lies in holding firmly and faithfully to the original Christian teaching received from people whom he knows to be reliable. It is rooted in the sacred writings, the Scriptures.

The conclusion of the letter (4:6–22) offers a further picture of Paul as the representative missionary, who is assured of his reward from the Lord. Deliverance in this situation is not only protection from the attacks of enemies, but also preservation of Paul in the faith so that he will reach God's heavenly kingdom.

2 Timothy and the Canon

This letter makes a distinctive contribution to the canon in various ways.

1. Even more than 1 Timothy, it is concerned with the personal life of the Christian and especially of the congregational leader. It may seem strange that a letter to a close colleague should be couched in this rather formal style and give advice with which Timothy would have been already familiar. However, Ignatius writes to Polycarp as a fellow Christian leader in a similar manner. And although the letter is addressed to Timothy himself, in its canonical form the letter is to be read by a wider audience, doubtlessly including both church leaders and members (cf. "you" [plural!], 4:22).

2. It gives a fuller picture of Paul himself, his own situation, and his self-consciousness. To some scholars it reads like an ideal picture of a missionary who is beginning to be a legend, an exaggerated portrait from a later date. Paul, it is said, has here become almost part of the gospel, a paradigm of conversion and perseverance. Certainly, the picture can be read exemplarily, just as Paul presents himself implicitly as an example in Philippians, but it may also well be authentic.

3. The importance of preserving the gospel unchanged and sharing Paul's message with a wider circle of teachers is appropriate at this later stage in the growth of the church. Although the admonition (2:2) has been interpreted solely in terms of passing on the message to the next generation of leaders, there is also a concern for widening the influence by equipping local congregations with leaders so that they are not dependent upon a teacher like Timothy himself.

4. The place of the Holy Spirit in equipping congregational leaders is stressed. With the growth of a leadership of people appointed to serve, perhaps with little previous Christian experience and no training, it was vital to emphasize the provision of divine enabling for leaders. Yet, although the leaders are doubtlessly especially in mind, the gift of the Spirit is common to all believers.

2 Timothy and Theology

1. A major contribution of this letter is its statement of the inspiration and usefulness of Scripture. It contains the only biblical use of the term *theopneustos*, "breathed by God," which is applied to "all" or "every [passage of] Scripture." There is no mention of the Holy Spirit in this connection (contrast 2 Pet. 1:21). Nor do we have the suggestion that God "played" on the human writers like a musician playing on an instrument. The point is rather that Scripture teaches the Christian understanding of salvation and provides whatever the believer needs for instruction in Christian living. The corollary of the inspiration of "all Scripture" is that any passage may have value for the Christian. Its origin in God implies its authority, truthfulness, and usefulness. The extension of applying the text to apply to the NT is fully justified, and there is at least the possibility that some early Christian writings were being regarded as Scripture by this date.

2. The Christian life is understood to be empowered and guaranteed by God and yet dependent on the faith and commitment of the believer. The author places these two facts side by side without saying anything to suggest that the believer is automatically brought safely through every danger and temptation to a heavenly reward, or that everything depends on the believer's personal commitment and effort. Alongside the falling away of some Christians like Demas, there is the assured conviction of Paul himself. Perseverance to the end is expressed in terms of trust in God's faithfulness.

Bibliography

See also bibliography for "Titus, Book of"; Oberlinner, L. *Die Pastoralbriefe*. HTKNT 11/2. Herder, 1995; Prior, M. *Paul the Letter-Writer and the Second Letter to Timothy*. JSNTSup 23. JSOT, 1989; Quinn, J., and W. Wacker. *The First and Second Letters to Timothy*. ECC. Eerdmans, 2000; Stott, J. *Guard the Gospel*. InterVarsity, 1973.

I. Howard Marshall

Titus, Book of

With 1 Timothy and 2 Timothy, Titus is one of three letters ostensibly addressed to missionary colleagues of Paul and collectively known since the eighteenth century as the "Pastoral Epistles." Although its brevity and similarity in content to 1 Timothy have encouraged its neglect, it has its own distinctive and valuable contribution to make to the theology of the NT.

History of Interpretation

Until the nineteenth century Titus was understood as a letter of Paul, written during the final period of his life to his junior companion, Titus, in charge of the congregations in Crete (1:5). They were less developed than those in Ephesus (as reflected in 1 Timothy). Negatively, the letter is concerned with the danger caused by "rebellious people" teaching material eccentrically based on Jewish mythology and commandments; they are criticized for their greed, deceit, and general immoral behavior (1:10–16). Positively, the letter advocates the appointment of local congregational leaders of good character and sound faith (1:5–9) and the inculcation of a respectable way of life characterized by self-control, submission to authority, abstention from time-wasting controversy, and devotion to good works (2:1–15; 3:1–11). This exhortation is backed up by two reminders of the way in which God acted graciously in Christ to achieve the redemption of believers and to save them personally from their previous sinful way of life (2:11–14; 3:3–7). The letter is a mature statement of Pauline theology and ecclesiology that encourages an orderly way of life but is redeemed from dullness by its inspirational teaching on the nature of salvation.

This traditional understanding has been challenged by a different view, based on the increasingly severe objections raised against Pauline authorship (especially by Holtzmann). Titus, along with its companion letters, was held to be a pseudonymous composition of a considerably later date (perhaps even from the early second century). Its general purpose was to rehabilitate Paul during a period of declining influence by presenting the kind of teaching that he would have given if still alive and encouraging people to be loyal to his brand of Christianity. However, the teaching actually presented is significantly different from that of Paul, it was alleged. Detachment from the hypothesis of Pauline authorship allowed modern critical scholars to emphasize the differences and see the three letters in their own light rather than to conform them to the pattern of the earlier Paul. At the same time there is the danger of seeing the letters as different facets of a common agenda, although some scholars are now recognizing that each must be appreciated for its own worth. Two things characterize the new outlook.

1. Later books of the NT were regarded as "early catholic" in their outlook. They represented and promoted the type of ecclesiology found in second-century Christianity, with an emphasis on fixed traditions handed down from the past. The theology has become static. Pauline creativity has disappeared. The church is the dispenser of salvation and is developing a fixed, hierarchical church structure, in which "office" has replaced the less-formal charismatic congregational ministry (e.g., prophecy) of an earlier period. The Holy Spirit's activity is increasingly confined to the ordained leaders.

2. Dibelius characterized the way of life in the Pastoral Epistles as "bourgeois," by which he meant that the church was adopting the patterns of Hellenistic-Roman society, living according to its ideals and becoming so innocuous as to avoid persecution. The ethic is characterized by sobriety, self-control, and good works. Orderliness and submission to authority are paramount. Slaves, in particular, are to be obedient and submissive. There is little that is specifically Christian.

Such an evaluation of Titus is essentially negative and pejorative. Superficially, it may seem to be plausible. For example, the actual amount of theological teaching in the letter is small in comparison with the ethical and ecclesiastical material. Nevertheless, there has been a justified reaction against it.

On the one hand, there is a continuing and vigorous defense of Pauline authorship (whether directly or through an amanuensis) by scholars who cannot be accused of a blind traditionalism (Fee; Johnson; Knight; Mounce; Spicq). They have demonstrated the essential harmony of the letter with Paul's earlier writings.

On the other hand, there has been recognition of the creative, theological character of the letter by scholars who find it hard to recognize the literary style and manner of thinking as those of Paul himself (so variously Marshall; Oberlinner; Quinn). One approach attempts to do justice to the Paulinism of the letter by seeing it as a nondeceptive presentation of what Paul would have said to the church in the period fairly soon after his death. It is conveyed by a follower who makes use of the kind of things that Paul actually did say to his colleagues. This view and that which attributes the letter to Paul himself, assisted by an amanuensis, are not far apart.

The result has been a recognition of a much more vigorous theology in Titus than earlier scholars detected, whether through their seeing Titus in the shadow of the major Pauline letters or through assessing it as typical of early catholicism. At the same time there has developed recognition of the contribution that literary and social-scientific approaches can make to a fuller appreciation of the letter.

Hearing the Message of Titus

In the lengthy opening salutation (1:1–4), the self-description of Paul as an apostle becomes a mini-statement of the gospel, setting out the correlation between the eternal plan of God the Savior and its realization in the proclamation of the gospel. The apostle is concerned to promote knowledge of the truth and faith in God's people as leading to a life characterized by godliness and hope. The Father's character and purpose are summed up in his title of "Savior," and his purpose for humankind is salvation. Jesus Christ stands alongside him as "Savior" (1:4).

The "proclamation" is an integral part of the accomplishment of God's plan of salvation; the saving act is the revelation of God's grace (2:11), which includes both the coming of Christ and the apostolic mission. Special importance attaches to the work of the apostles and those who share in their work by continuing it where the apostles are absent, whether geographically or no longer active.

The growth of error leads to great emphasis on "sound doctrine" (2:1). Knowledge figures prominently alongside faith as a characteristic of God's people, and there is a greater tendency than in earlier literature to see faith not only as a relationship of personal trust and commitment to God, but also as acceptance of the true teaching enshrined in Christian tradition.

The first doctrinal passage (2:11–14) complements the salutation. The word "grace," which could have been dismissed as a formal element in a stereotyped greeting (1:4), is now forefronted as the key quality of God. The whole of what God has done and is doing to save people is "grace," and in a remarkable statement it is "grace" that has been revealed rather than God's Son (contrast Gal. 1:15–16). A further clarification appears in 3:4 (NRSV), where "the goodness and loving kindness" of God appears; the language of human benefaction is used to explain in simple terms the beneficence of God. The term "appeared," related to the noun "epiphany," picks up on language used to express the saving intervention of divine beings in the world. The same terms are used both for the future coming of the Savior to wind up God's saving action in the world and for the historical action in the incarnation of Jesus and the associated events.

The saving action is also described in traditional language as redemption (2:14), quite deliberately echoing Ps. 130:8 and Mark 10:45. God acts to rescue people from a sinful life (rather than simply from the penal consequences of sin) to live a life of goodness worthy of himself.

Such a life looks forward to the end of the present age in which we live in a sinful world, and eagerly longs for the manifestation of the glory of Christ. But here there is a surprise: the awaited one is "our great God and Savior, Jesus Christ." This explicit application of the term "God" to Jesus Christ has been challenged by some who would render the phrase "of the great God and our Savior Jesus Christ," but the evidence strongly favors the former interpretation. Although anticipated earlier (Rom. 9:5), this statement is the climax in the growing recognition that Jesus Christ is alongside the Father in the complex identity of God.

The second doctrinal passage (3:4–7) shifts the emphasis to the way in which God has acted savingly in the lives of believers. The Pauline stress on "not by works" is affirmed; this is probably in response to Jewish stress on the commandments as the means of salvation, and it reiterates that salvation is entirely dependent upon God's action. A picture is painted of people living such sinful lives that they do not in fact have any goodness that might count in their favor; they are justified by divine grace. They are entirely dependent on divine mercy, and mercy is exercised in a radical change, like being born again, brought about by the agency of the Holy Spirit. The Spirit is said to be poured out on them, echoing the language of Pentecost, but acts inwardly to renew them. Thus, as in Romans, justification and regeneration by the Spirit are brought together as the two essential aspects of God's saving work. Out of this fundamental saving action of God, the obligation to a new way of life emerges. The practical teaching that Titus is to give is to be "consistent with sound doctrine" (2:1 NRSV).

Titus and the Canon

1. The doctrinal teaching in Titus, though expressed in new ways, is in fundamental agreement with that of the earlier Pauline letters in its teaching about the gracious saving action of God, justification by grace and not by works, and regeneration by the Spirit. The unity of the saving revelation in Christ and in the proclamation of the gospel is likewise already present (2 Cor.

5:18–21). The Christology, implicit and explicit, ranks God the Father and Jesus Christ together as the sources of salvation and draws the logical conclusion that the term "God" is equally applicable to both. Nevertheless, the term "Son" is not used.

2. Ethical teaching is addressed to the different groups in the congregation (rather than in the family): older men and women, younger women and men, and slaves. The instruction to slaves is particularly significant in that, while inculcating the need for submission to their masters, it nevertheless insists that the lowest class in society can be "an ornament to the doctrine of God our Savior" (2:10 NRSV).

3. There are the first detailed instructions regarding the choosing of local congregational leaders. Here only elders are mentioned, functioning as overseers or "bishops" (1:5, 7), with no mention of deacons (contrast 1 Tim. 3). The importance of their being able to teach positively and also to refute error is highlighted. However, the appointment of local leaders is nothing new (cf. Phil. 1:1). There is the risk here that addressing leaders like Titus and concentrating on the work of local church leaders could promote an early "catholic" type of ecclesiology; within the canon the teaching in the Pastoral Epistles must be balanced by the more "charismatic" ecclesiology found elsewhere.

Titus and Theology

Like its companions, the letter to Titus is brief and written in a specific situation. Therefore, care must be taken in appropriating its theological message for today, and it must be seen as part of Scripture as a whole. Nevertheless, it sets an important precedent in two ways.

1. Titus is an important example of recontextualizing the gospel within the NT and its first-century context. The author holds fast to the apostolic doctrine and institutes measures in the church to maintain it in pure form against the inroads of opposition and incipient heresy. Teaching based on the gospel is crucial. So too is the careful appointment of congregational leaders who are of sterling Christian character, possess the gifts of leadership, and are able to teach. It is probable that a plurality of leaders in each local situation is in mind rather than one for each Christian group.

2. While the author holds fast to the Pauline teaching, it is expressed in new ways, using a fresh vocabulary that will speak meaningfully and so communicate successfully in the Hellenistic world. Christian communication today not only takes over the language of Titus (as well as that of the NT generally) but also follows its example in searching out relevant ways of expressing the gospel and the imperatives of Christian living in the contemporary world.

Bibliography

See also bibliography for articles on "1 Timothy" and "2 Timothy"; Dibelius, M., and H. Conzelmann. The Pastoral Epistles. Hermeneia. Fortress, 1972; Fee, G. 1 and 2 Timothy, Titus. NIBCNT. Hendrickson, 1988; Harding, M. What Are They Saying about the Pastoral Epistles? Paulist, 2001; Holtzmann, H. Die Pastoralbriefe, kritisch und exegetisch behandelt. Engelmann, 1880; Johnson, L. T. Letters to Paul's Delegates. NTC. Trinity, 1996; Knight, G., III. Commentary on the Pastoral Epistles. NIGTC. Eerdmans/Paternoster, 1992; Lau, A. Manifest in Flesh. WUNT 2.86. Mohr/Siebeck, 1996; Marshall, I. H. (with P. Towner). A Critical and Exegetical Commentary on the Pastoral Epistles. ICC. T&T Clark, 1999; Mounce, W. The Pastoral Epistles. WBC. Word, 2001; Oberlinner, L. Die Pastoralbriefe. HTKNT 22/2. Herder, 1996; Quinn, J. The Letter to Titus. AB 35. Doubleday, 1990; Spicq, C. Les Épîtres Pastorales. ÉBib. J. Gabalda, 1948, 1969; Stott, J. The Message of 1 Timothy and Titus. InterVarsity, 1996; Towner, P. The Goal of Our Instruction. JSNTSup 34. Sheffield Academic Press, 1989; Young, F. The Theology of the Pastoral Letters. NTT. Cambridge University Press, 1994.

I. Howard Marshall

Topical Preaching See Preaching, Use of the Bible in

Totality Transfer, Illegitimate See Etymology

Tradition

Tradition refers to the handing down of the Christian faith from generation to generation. At its broadest it is the sum total of the Christian heritage passed down from previous ages, of which Scripture is just one item. But since discussions of tradition usually concern its relation to Scripture, it is normal to exclude Scripture from the definition. This is not inappropriate since the NT predates almost every other surviving item of Christian tradition.

In the NT a twofold attitude to tradition can be discerned. The tradition of the (Jewish) elders is rejected, together with other human tradition (Matt. 15:1–9; Mark 7:1–13; Gal. 1:13–14; Col. 2:8). At the same time there is a good apostolic tradition, which is simply the Christian faith as proclaimed and transmitted by the apostles and their associates (1 Cor. 11:2, 23; 15:3; 2 Thess.

2:15; 3:6; 2 Tim. 2:2). The NT writings sprang out of this latter tradition at different stages in its history, as for example did Luke's Gospel (1:1–4). There thus is an important sense in which (apostolic) tradition precedes Scripture.

The emergence of the NT canon is a complex process, but by the last quarter of the second century the NT was seen as a more or less well-defined corpus of Scripture alongside the OT. This posed the question of the relation between Scripture and tradition, a question that always to a greater or lesser extent involves the current teaching of the church, as will become apparent below. In the early years tradition was primarily oral, but by the end of the second century, oral tradition had nothing reliable to offer, outside of long-standing liturgical practices. Apart from the liturgy, it was to written tradition that appeal was made from the third century.

The Relation between Scripture, Tradition, and Church

How do Scripture, tradition, and the teaching office of the church relate to one another? Over the course of history a number of different positions have been held.

The Coincidence View. The first clear position to emerge is found in Irenaeus and Tertullian, in their opposition to Gnosticism. Different gnostic groups each claimed to have received a secret tradition from one or another apostle. This raised the question of where genuine apostolic teaching was to be found. Irenaeus and Tertullian taught that the apostles committed their teaching to writing (the NT) and also committed it orally to their churches, in which it has been handed down in an open tradition of public teaching. These apostolic churches teach the apostolic message that has reached them both through apostolic tradition and through the apostolic Scriptures. The purpose of apostolic tradition is not to add to Scripture but to show how it is to be interpreted. Apostolic tradition in this context means the Rule of Faith, a basic outline of beliefs that later grew into the Apostles' Creed. Thus, there is a harmony or *coincidence* between Scripture, tradition, and the teaching of the church. This was the dominant position in the early church.

The Supplementary View. A rival position emerged that gave to tradition the role of *supplementing* Scripture, of adding to it. If liturgical and ceremonial tradition be included, the Supplementary View can be traced to the earliest times. The *Didache* (or *Teaching of the Twelve Apostles*) and *The Apostolic Tradition* (of Hippolytus) both claim to derive from the teaching of the apostles, and Tertullian explicitly and at length argues for apostolic ceremonial traditions. The problem is that the innovation of one generation becomes the apostolic tradition of the next. Augustine argued that there are many practices observed by the whole church that can therefore fairly be held to have been enjoined by the apostles, although not found in their writings (*Bapt.* 5.23.31). This makes the church a de facto source of binding tradition.

Can one appeal to tradition for doctrines not found in Scripture? The first significant instance of this came when Basil the Great appealed to the liturgical tradition in defense of the deity of the Holy Spirit, although this was not the only argument that Basil used. Some of the beliefs and practices of the church are found in written teaching, he claimed, and others in a mystery (the liturgy) received by tradition from the apostles. Both have the same force (*Holy Spirit* 27.66–67; 29.71).

The Supplementary View gained ground throughout the Middle Ages. As time went on, the official teaching of the church included beliefs (about the Virgin Mary, for example) that were not found in Scripture. Supplementary tradition was then invoked to make good the deficiencies of Scripture. In most cases the tradition appealed to was ceremonial: the principle of *lex orandi lex credendi* (worship guides theology) was the basis of the Supplementary View. But in due course it became clear that the problem was not just that the church taught *more* than was found in Scripture, but also that its teaching in places was *contrary* to Scripture. This realization gave rise first to medieval "heresy" and in due course to the Reformation.

Protestantism: The Ancillary View. The Reformation was at heart a dispute not about tradition but about the teaching of the church. The Reformers were convinced that the current Roman Church had perverted the gospel and accused it of heresy in the name of Scripture. They sought to recover the purity of the gospel and to reform the church by Scripture. The root issue was whether the church defines the gospel or vice versa. The Reformers were opposed not to tradition but to the teaching of the contemporary (Roman) Church. For support, they appealed extensively to the early church fathers in general and Augustine especially, but did not regard such tradition as infallible or irreformable. It had to be measured by the yardstick of God's word in the Bible. This was not a return to the Coincidence View of the early church; instead, the unity of Scripture, tradition, and church teaching had been shattered. Nor did this view involve a rejection of either tradition or the teaching authority of the church. Both had a vital role to play, but *ancillary* or subordinated to the supreme authority of Scripture and open to correction in the light of it.

The Solitary View. The Reformation view is often identified by the slogan *sola scriptura*; but while *sola fide* was already a recognized slogan by the 1530s, *sola scriptura* did not emerge until the post-Reformation era. It means not that we have no need for tradition or for the teaching authority of the church, but rather that these are both subordinated to the supreme authority of Scripture. In due course, however, there arose an attitude in Protestantism that questioned the value of tradition with or without the teaching authority of the church. The Anabaptists in the sixteenth century and the Brethren in the nineteenth century were alike hostile to tradition—and repeated the crude second-century heresy that Mary was only Jesus' host mother. Many Protestant groups emerged that saw no value in tradition and sought to return to the NT as if nothing had happened since then. A similar position is taken by much modern theological study. The OT and NT are carefully studied in their original contexts, attention is devoted to studying today's context, and the biblical message is then applied to the current context—as if the Bible were a book recently discovered in the sands of Egypt!

The Catholic Reformation. The Roman Catholic Church fought to defend its teaching against the Reformers. Scripture and tradition alike could only be interpreted in line with the defined teaching of the (Roman Catholic) Church. The Council of Trent decreed that no one should presume to interpret the Scriptures contrary to Holy Mother Church. Faced with the need to defend doctrines whose connection with the Bible is tenuous at best, most Roman Catholics adopted the Supplementary View, appealing to tradition as a source for such doctrines. Until recently, the Council of Trent was widely held to have taught the Supplementary View in its *Decree on the Canonical Scriptures* (1546), but it is now widely recognized that the issue was left undefined. The Second Vatican Council, in its *Dogmatic Constitution on Divine Revelation* (*Dei verbum*), took care to remain neutral on this question (§2.8–9).

The Unfolding View and the Contextual View. Hesitations about supplementary tradition in modern Catholic theology do not spring from a renewed confidence in the ability to prove Catholic doctrine from Scripture alone. With the rise of modern historical studies, it became clear that many Roman Catholic doctrines receive as little support from early tradition as from Scripture. Just as the failure of Scripture to validate Catholic doctrines required an appeal to supplementary tradition, so the failure of Scripture and early tradition alike to support some doctrines gave birth to the idea that doctrines develop over time. One of the first to wrestle with this issue was John Henry Newman in his *Essay on the Development of Christian Doctrine* (1845). He was aware of the difference between the primitive church and the contemporary Roman Catholic Church and explained this in terms of a process of development. The Second Vatican Council sanctioned the idea of the development of doctrine (*Divine Revelation* 2.8). Protestants would also recognize a process of development of some doctrines (e.g., the Trinity) but would require a more solid biblical foundation than can be claimed for doctrines such as the Immaculate Conception and Assumption of the Virgin Mary.

More recently, Protestants and Catholics alike have recognized the need to relate Christian teaching to specific cultural contexts by a process of contextualization. While for some this has involved making the modern context the norm by which to test doctrine, there is no reason why Scripture should not remain the final norm. There is nothing new about this process (except the name) and it can be seen in the outworkings of the Christian faith in the Platonist context of the early church and the Aristotelian context of the late Middle Ages. Both were serious attempts to relate the Christian faith to the context of the time and were remarkably successful, albeit not perfect.

The Role of Tradition

It is impossible to read Scripture without tradition, save in the rare examples of those with no prior contact with the Christian faith who pick up a portion of Scripture—hardly a paradigm for the Christian exegete! We bring to the Bible a preunderstanding of the Christian faith that we have received from others, thus by tradition. There is nothing wrong with this; in fact, it is God's purpose: "The things you have heard me say in the presence of many witnesses entrust to reliable men who will also be qualified to teach others" (2 Tim. 2:2). Since, like it or not, we are molded by twenty centuries of Christian tradition, it is wisest to be aware of this influence, remembering the adage that "those who are ignorant of history are condemned to repeat it."

Valuable as tradition may be, it is not infallible and must be tested by Scripture. Scripture is well suited to this normative role since it remains fixed, while tradition is constantly changing. Scripture stands over against tradition as the norm by which it is to be tested. Karl Barth aptly saw the authority of both church and tradition in the light of the Fifth Commandment, to honor our father and mother. This authority is real but limited, in that both are subject to the word of God in Scripture. They are open to be reformed and corrected, while Scripture is not.

What practical use does tradition have in the task of hermeneutics? First, it should not be forgotten that we are indebted to tradition for the canon of Scripture. The one page of the Bible that is not the word of God is the contents page! Of course, the role of the church and of tradition was to *recognize* the various books as the word of God, not to *make* them such—any more than the church made Jesus God by recognizing his deity. Second, it must be acknowledged that earlier, precritical tradition is of limited value for the exegetical task of discerning the original meaning of the texts, though there are a few gifted exegetes like Calvin whose works are still valued today for this purpose. Third, when it comes to the application of Scripture, as in preaching, the insights of the past are of greater and more abiding value, as Steinmetz has argued. Finally, when it comes to the task of synthesizing the biblical message as a whole, the modern theologian would be foolish to ignore the fruits of past endeavors. There is no virtue in reinventing the wheel in every generation and even less in repeating the errors of the past. "Experience is the wisdom of fools"—the wise learn from others' mistakes.

See also Creed; Hermeneutical Circle; Hermeneutics; Patristic Biblical Interpretation; Rule of Faith

Bibliography

Bauckham, R. "Tradition in Relation to Scripture and Reason." Pages 117–45 in *Scripture, Tradition and Reason*, ed. R. Bauckham and B. Drewery. T&T Clark, 1988; Bruce, F. F. *Tradition Old and New*. Paternoster, 1970; Bruce, F. F., and E. G. Rupp, eds. *Holy Book and Holy Tradition*. Manchester University Press, 1968; Congar, Y. *Tradition and Traditions*. Burns & Oates, 1966; Fourth World Conference on Faith and Order. "Scripture, Tradition and Traditions." Pages 50–61 in *The Fourth World Conference on Faith and Order*, ed. P. C. Rodger and L. Vischer. SCM, 1964; Lane, A. N. S. "Scripture, Tradition and Church: An Historical Survey." *VE* 9 (1975): 37–55; idem. "Sola scriptura? Making Sense of a Post-Reformation Slogan." Pages 297–327 in *A Pathway into the Holy Scripture*, ed. P. Satterthwaite and D. F. Wright. Eerdmans, 1994; Steinmetz, D. "The Superiority of Pre-Critical Exegesis." Pages 26–38 in *The Theological Interpretation of Scripture*, ed. S. Fowl. Blackwell, 1997; Thiselton, A. *New Horizons in Hermeneutics*, ch. 4. Harper Collins, 1992; Williams, D. H. *Retrieving the Tradition and Renewing Evangelicalism*. Eerdmans, 1999.

Anthony N. S. Lane

Trajectory *See* Culture and Hermeneutics; Ideological Criticism; Slavery

Translation

Because most Christians read the Bible in translation, and generally identify their translation with the word of God, the quality and character of the translations people read have an extraordinary importance for shaping worldview and theology—whether for good or ill. The last century has seen an explosion of Bible translations into many languages and multiple versions in the same language (Metzger 8–10). Thus, awareness of the nature of Bible translation and its limitations is crucial for the church's well-being (Barr).

"Translation" is defined here as the attempt to communicate what was first expressed in one language by expressing it in another. The words of the target language (= TL; e.g., Dutch, English, or Kingandou) "map" the words of the source language (= SL; e.g., biblical Hebrew, Aramaic, and Greek) so that readers may, as much as possible, discern what was said and infer what was meant in the original. Our discussion is focused on written translation of the Bible. We consider translation a communicative *process* in which the translator in effect "quotes" (directly or indirectly) what was first written in an SL in a TL. The communicative goal is that readers in the TL will understand what Isaiah, Matthew, or Paul wrote in a SL, and ultimately what God said over many generations to Israel and the human race through them. Crucial here is that readers of translated Bibles expect the translator to give them, as faithfully as possible, *what God said* through the human biblical authors (cf. Wolterstorff). The relevance and power of Scripture is found not in its immediate address to a reader's perceived needs, but rather in the fact that *in times past God spoke in many and various ways by the prophets* (i.e., in Scripture). Then he spoke to humanity in his Son, Jesus the Messiah (cf. Heb. 1:1; 2 Tim. 3:15–17). A Bible translation's relevance is found in its status as a *quotation* of the divine word across language barriers.

To understand translation itself, some basic principles of communication must be kept in mind. Verbal communication occurs when something is *said or written* with the intent of conveying some *meaning*, and the hearer or reader *infers* a meaning (rightly or wrongly) from what is said or written. When a communication is successful, we say something has been *understood*. With large, composite, complex artistic communications like the Bible, the process of inference and understanding is never complete. Nor is it *immediate*, for readers today live in a different cultural, historical world than Paul or Amos.

The task of biblical translation is thus an enormous responsibility. It is also extraordinarily difficult. In fact, it can never be perfectly done, given the nature of human languages and communication. Translation must always be supplemented by preaching, teaching, and commentary from those who know the original languages.

Thus, translation does not claim to say something original. Rather, translation implies a contract between the translator and the audience that the translator will faithfully communicate what the original author wrote (cf. Robinson 194–258). The faithful translator does not rewrite Amos to bring Amos into the present. Rather, she puts Amos's language into a TL so that, as much as possible, the reader can enter Amos's strange world and meet him as he is. The translator is a "secondary author" who speaks to her contemporaries in their own tongue. Strictly speaking, the translator has authority to write nothing but what the "primary author" has written, for the authority of Scripture resides in the original text. In practice, the cultural, contextual, and linguistic differences between the SL and the TL make it impossible to write in a TL exactly what was first written in the SL. Hence, the goal of a "literal translation" is a chimera. *There are and can be no truly "literal" translations* in which the TL reflects the SL "word for word." For nonlinguists, this statement may seem questionable, but for competent linguists it is an obvious fact, though they also are tempted to ignore its implications. We may suggest, instead, that TL words and phrases are verbal *metaphors* for the words and phrases of the SL (cf. Barnstone).

A Paradigm Shift in Translation

Discussion of translation today is made especially difficult because a "paradigm shift" (Kuhn) is occurring in translation theory and practice, and there currently seem to be two main models for translation (Smith). Over the last half century, one theory of translation has, with few exceptions, dominated the practice of Bible translation around the world. This theory is most prominently associated with the name of Eugene Nida, and has had a series of names: "dynamic equivalence," "functional equivalence," and most recently, "meaning-based" translation (Nida; Nida and Tabor; de Waard and Nida; Larson). The current paradigm conflict concerns how verbal meaning is communicated and appropriated. The Nida tradition believes that meaning and form are largely independent, and that translators must translate meaning rather than words. This tradition thus opposes "formal equivalence" (sometimes caricatured as "word-for-word" translation) and argues that one must translate meaning rather than words, so that the *effect* on the TL reader is "equivalent" to that of the SL on its first readers. Nida's theories have been largely institutionalized in translation projects around the world (for critique, see Porter and Hess).

The other main translation paradigm is based on a linguistic model called "Relevance Theory" (Sperber and Wilson; cf. Goatly). In biblical translation, its main proponent has been E.-A. Gutt (cf. Smith). A simplified version of this theory is presented in the present article (cf. Van Leeuwen). Gutt argues that we are dealing with competing paradigms, and not merely with intraparadigm disputes, because practitioners of the older Nida paradigm appear not to understand essential aspects of the Relevance paradigm, much as Newtonian physicists were once hostile to the new Einsteinian theories (Gutt, *Translation*, 202–38).

What Translation Can and Cannot Do

Though our focus is on Bible translation, the general principles and problems of translation apply also to Sacred Scripture. Understanding is possible only when three types of *relevant* knowledge are present. That is, communication is relevant to us if it interacts with what we already know, believe, or assume. The three types of knowledge are

1. Knowledge of the language system
2. Knowledge of the context: situation and cotext
3. Background schematic knowledge: factual and sociocultural (Goatly 137–38)

Obviously, without knowledge of a shared language, we cannot understand what is said. Translation seeks to overcome this sort of knowledge gap by "remapping" what was said in an SL in terms of the TL. Translation accommodates what was said to the "language system" of readers, because that is what they already know. Many readers of the Bible are unable or unwilling to learn the original biblical languages. Translation attempts to communicate what is written in the Bible by compensating for this lack of linguistic knowledge. But for understanding to take place, readers need knowledge of the immediate context (2, above) and of background schematic factual and sociocultural factors (3). Translation by itself cannot make up for lack of the second and third types of knowledge. For example, when Jesus is called "Christ," readers need to know that *Christos* is the NT Greek translation of Hebrew "*mashiakh*/messiah," both meaning "anointed" (1 Sam. 16:6, 12–13; cf. Ps. 2:1–2; Matt. 26:63–64; Acts 4:25–6; etc.). They also need to know that anointing was the means through which God appointed and empowered a person by his Spirit to fill a particular office, whether of prophet, priest, or Davidic king, and that Jesus' "anointing" occurred at his baptism by John. All this knowledge is necessary for understanding something as simple as anointing and the identity of Jesus the Christ. A major limitation of biblical translation is that translation by itself cannot provide such information, and without such information, understanding of what is meant is not possible. The letter by Rehum and Shimshai to the Persian king (Ezra 4:11–16) requires knowledge of Judah's conflicted local situation and of Rehum's dishonest agenda. Moreover, the letter is written in Aramaic—though most of the book is written in Hebrew—because Aramaic was the language of diplomacy in the Persian Empire. Finally, understanding of the letter in its historical and literary context requires knowledge of Israelite religion, in which Yahweh had promised the land of Israel and then the city of Jerusalem to the faithful descendants of Abraham and of David, characters found in Genesis, Samuel, Kings, and Chronicles! Since many Bible translations begin with a portion of Scripture, usually an NT Gospel, the crucial question becomes, How do readers acquire the necessary *background* knowledge to understand the texts they read?

Bible translations cannot avoid this central question. Two options exist. One may attempt to provide contextual and background material in the translated text itself. In a sense, this involves not only writing the original in a new language, but also actually rewriting, in the form of explanatory paraphrase, what was said in the original. This practice may give readers a text that is easily understandable, but it has the deficit of breaking the implicit contract between translator and reader that the former should say in the TL what was said in the SL. It also imposes the translator's interpretation of the text on the reader, sometimes with serious theological consequences. For example, the NIV in Ecclesiastes (and *only* in Ecclesiastes) translates the important keyword *hebel* as "meaningless" (passim). *Hebel* is here a metaphor meaning something like "breath, vapor, mist." To translate *hebel* as "meaningless" forces a certain interpretation of the book on the reader, an interpretation that many scholars consider incorrect (Van Leeuwen, "New Translation"). Alternately, one may provide help in the form of notes, commentary, teaching, or preaching on the translated text. The NT does something similar when it explains the meaning of Hebrew "Immanuel" by adding "which means, 'God with us'" (Matt. 1:23; Isa. 7:14). Thus, it is fair to conclude that while translation is necessary, it is never enough. The church needs pastors, teachers, and laity who search the Scriptures in the original languages, to help translators and readers dependent on translations by bringing out of Scripture "treasures new and old" (cf. Matt. 13:52).

See also Culture and Hermeneutics; Hermeneutics; Language, Linguistics; Meaning

Bibliography

Barnstone, W. *The Poetics of Translation*. Yale University Press, 1993; Barr, J. "Modern English Bible Versions as a Problem for the Church." *QR* 14 (1994): 263–78; Goatly, A. *The Language of Metaphors*. Routledge, 1997; Gutt, E.-A. *Translation and Relevance*. St. Jerome, 2000; idem. "Urgent Call for Academic Reorientation." *Notes on Sociolinguistics* 5 (2000): 47–56; Kuhn, T. *The Structure of Scientific Revolution*. 2d ed. University of Chicago Press, 1970; Larson, M. L. *Meaning-Based Translation*. University Press of America, 1997; Metzger, B. *The Bible in Translation*. Baker, 2001; Nida, E. *Toward a Science of Translating*. Brill, 1964; Nida, E., and C. Tabor. *The Theory and Practice of Translation*. Brill, 1969; Porter, S., and R. Hess, eds. *Translating the Bible*. Sheffield Academic Press, 1999; Robinson, D. *The Translator's Turn*. Johns Hopkins University Press, 1991; Smith, K. G. "Bible Translation and Relevance Theory." Diss. University of Stellenbosch, 2000; Sperber, D., and D. Wilson. *Relevance*. Harvard University Press, 1986; Van Leeuwen, R. "On Bible Translation and Hermeneutics." Pages 284–311 in *After Pentecost*, ed. C. Bartholomew. SHS. Zondervan/Paternoster, 2001; idem. "We Really Do Need a New Translation of the Bible." *Christianity Today* 22, no. 11 (October 2001): 28–35; Waard, J. de, and E. Nida. *From One Language to Another*. T. Nelson, 1986; Wolterstorff, N. *Divine Discourse*. Cambridge University Press, 1995.

Raymond C. Van Leeuwen

Trinity

The Christian faith is inalienably trinitarian. Baptism "in the name of the Father and of the Son and of the Holy Spirit," administered by command of the risen Christ (Matt. 28:18–20), is the ground and seal of a faith that responds to a gospel proclaimed from NT times in embryonically trinitarian terms (Acts 2:22–38). By the end of the second century the kerygma and the faith were formulated according to a "canon of truth" or "regula fidei" and expressed in early creeds. Thus Irenaeus in his *Demonstration of the Apostolic Preaching*:

> This then is the order of our faith, the foundation of our building, and the support of our conduct: God the Father, uncreated, uncontainable, invisible; one God, the creator of all things: this is the first point of our faith. The second point is this: the Word of God, Son of God, Christ Jesus our Lord, who appeared to the prophets, each characteristically and according to the Father's ways of disposing; through Christ all things were made, and he also at the end of the times, to complete and gather up all things, was made man among men, visible and tangible, in order to abolish death and show forth life and effect communion between God and man. And the third point is: the Holy Spirit, through whom the prophets prophesied, the patriarchs learned the things of God, and the righteous were led into the way of righteousness; and who in the end of the times was poured out in a new way upon the human race, renewing man in all the earth unto God. (*Epid.* 6 [SC 406:90–93, 242]; cf. *Haer.* 1.10.1 [SC 264:154–59]; 4.33.7–8 [SC 100:818–21]; and Tertullian, *Praescr.* 13.1–6 [SC 46:106]; *Prax.* 2 [in *Tertulliani Adversus Praxean liber*, ed. E. Evans (SPCK, 1948), 90–91, 131–32])

According to the *Epistula Apostolorum*, Christians profess faith "in the Father, the Ruler of the universe; and in Jesus Christ, our Savior; and in the Holy Spirit, the Paraclete; and in the holy church; and in the forgiveness of sins" (5 [16], in Duensing 7). What we know as the Apostles' Creed "betrays in its form and language its direct descent from the primitive apostolic Preaching" (Dodd 73–74). In the fourth century, to ward off Arian heresies, the ecumenical councils of 325 and 381 introduced more precise phraseology, drawing transformatively upon Greek ontology to achieve a sharper statement of what was to be taught and believed concerning the being, character, action, and purposes of God. These councils thus produced the Niceno-Constantinopolitan Creed, which has remained the most widely affirmed statement of trinitarian faith in both East and West.

The classic creeds were being formulated at the same time as the canon of the Scriptures was being recognized and determined; there was interaction between the two processes, and the Scriptures and the creeds continue to function reciprocally. In the one direction, the story that the Scriptures tell and the history they record find summary statement in the creeds. In the other direction, the creeds serve as the key to the interpretation of the complex Scriptures. The narrative begins, "In the beginning," with the creative speech-act of God's Word and the life-giving energy of God's Spirit (Gen. 1:1–2:7; cf. Ps. 33:6–9). The narrative reaches its paradoxical climax when "the Word became flesh" as Jesus Christ (John 1:14), the "only Son," who "for our salvation came down from heaven, and by the power of the Holy Spirit became incarnate from the Virgin Mary, and was made man" (Nicene Creed; cf. Matt. 1:18–23; Luke 1:30–35). On the cross Jesus offered himself to the Father through the eternal Spirit (Heb. 9:14), and by the same Spirit the Father raised him from the dead (Rom. 1:4; 8:11). The narrative looks forward to a conclusion when "the Spirit and the bride" will cry "Come, Lord Jesus" (Rev. 22:17, 20), and at his return Christ will inaugurate the definitive kingdom in which God will be praised and enjoyed by God's people forever. In its preaching and its liturgical rehearsal of the narrative in Scripture readings, creeds, and eucharistic anaphoras, the church invites and enacts the participation of each new generation until the final denouement of the divine drama.

Given the trinitarian faith, traditional Christians see the historical composition of the Scriptures as a trinitarian work. Thus, John Wesley, for instance, in the preface to his *Explanatory Notes upon the New Testament* (1754–55), gives the following succinct account of the historical origins of the Scriptures:

> Concerning the Scriptures in general, it may be observed, the word of the living God, which directed the first patriarchs also, was, in the time of Moses, committed to writing. To these were added, in several succeeding generations, the inspired writings of the other prophets. Afterwards, what the Son of God preached, and the Holy Ghost spake by the apostles, the apostles and evangelists wrote. . . . The Scripture, therefore, of the Old and New Testament is a most solid and precious system of divine truth. (*Works* 14:238)

The God of Israel, who "directed" the patriarchs and "inspired" the prophets, is the holy Trinity, who has now been clearly revealed as such in the incarnation of the Son, the Word made flesh, and in the Holy Spirit. This Spirit was seen to rest upon Jesus and heard to speak through the apostles at Pentecost and beyond. Wesley clearly recognized a human role of various kinds—differing according to historical circumstances—in the writing down of God's word by Moses and his successors, and by the apostles and evangelists. In his account of that role, Wesley, like much of the Christian tradition, oscillates between the reception of a divine dictation—whereby certain parts of Scripture at least were given to the human writer by "particular revelation"—and the allowance that the writers used their human judgment in a more general accordance with "the divine light which abode with them, the standing treasure of the Spirit of God" (*Explanatory Notes*, ad 1 Cor. 7:25).

The trinitarian origin of the Scriptures is to be matched in our appropriation of them. Correspondingly, traditional Christians go about their reading of the Scriptures in a trinitarian way. This is well expressed in *The Catechism of the Catholic Church*, drawing on the Vatican II *Constitution on Divine Revelation (Dei verbum)*. First, "Sacred Scripture must be read and interpreted in the light of the same Spirit by whom it was written" (*Catechism* §111). Here we may think of the prayer of Hilary of Poitiers. In his work *On the Trinity*, he asks the Father for "participation in the prophetic and apostolic Spirit, so that we may grasp their words in no other sense than (the prophets and apostles) uttered them" (*De trinitate* 1.38 [CCSL 62:36]). Second, "Scripture is a unity by reason of the unity of God's plan, of which Christ Jesus is the center and heart, open since his Passover" (*Catechism* §112; cf. §134). Here we may think of Luther's words concerning Christ himself as the *res* or "substance" of the Scriptures, now clearly revealed. "What more august thing," he asks Erasmus, "can lie hidden in the Scriptures, now that the seals have been broken and the stone rolled away from the mouth of the tomb, and that the supreme mystery has gone forth, that Christ the Son of God became a human being, that God is one and triune, that Christ suffered for us and will reign eternally? . . . Remove Christ from the Scriptures and what more will you find in them?" (*De servo arbitrio* [WA 18:606]). Third, "In the sacred books, the Father who is in heaven comes lovingly to meet his children, and talks with them" (*Catechism* §104, citing *Dei verbum* §21).

The divine descent is for the purpose of lifting God's human creatures (cf. 2 Cor. 1:18–22). The Scriptures play their part in this upward movement also in trinitarian fashion. Through Christ we have access to the Father in the Spirit (Eph. 2:18; cf. Rom. 8:14–17; Gal. 4:6). The ultimate consequence of that, as the Cappadocian theologians recognized, is that the Father, the Son, and the Holy Spirit are properly worshipped and glorified together, "three persons" of "one nature," "one in essence." Liturgically, that occurs, for instance, through the acclamation "Gloria Patri et Filio et Spiritui Sancto," which concludes the recitation of psalms. It confirms an understanding of the Psalms as a prophetic telling of the entire story of God with the world, as the NT writers imply by their citations from the Psalter at crucial points. This move is endorsed and developed by traditional Christian commentators on the Psalms.

The present "praise of the Lord" as—according to a hymn of Isaac Watts—both our "duty" and our "delight" is a foretaste of our final salvation. Wesley's sermon 43, "The Scripture Way of Salvation," is trinitarian through and through. This is true from "the first dawning of grace in the soul" by the "drawings of the Father" (John 6:44), the "light" of the Son and Word (John 1:9), and the "convictions" of the Spirit (John 16:8). It continues through justification on account of the merits of Christ and sanctification by the renewing work of the Holy Spirit. And it finds fulfillment in the consummation in glory. "To crown all, there will be a deep, an intimate, an uninterrupted union with God; a constant communion with the Father and his Son Jesus Christ, through the Spirit; a continual enjoyment of the Three-One God, and of all the creatures in him" (Wesley, Sermon 64, "The New Creation"). The Scriptures are consonant with other elements in the church's life, particularly preaching and the sacraments, and are norming in appropriate ways these other elements. They are God-given means for the Holy Spirit to bring us to Christ and through him to the Father.

In sum, by their content, their composition, their use, and their functions in worship and proclamation, the Scriptures are thoroughly trinitarian. In the aftermath of the deistic trends of the Enlightenment, twentieth-century Protestant theology was aided toward the recovery of this fundamental fact of the classic Christian faith by Karl Barth's massively important *Church Dogmatics*. In it the threefold structure of the divine self-revelation—which occurs for us by the Son and in us by the Spirit—corresponds to the very being of the triune God and Lord, to whom the Bible bears permanent and normative witness.

In a rich and comprehensive treatment of "Scripture in the economy of salvation," Telford Work sees the Scriptures at the service of the triune God, who employs them to reveal and achieve his purposes. Each person of the Trinity plays his appropriate part in and through them in the undivided work of salvation. "Christian Scripture reflects and accomplishes the will of the Father, through the ministry of the Son, in the power of the Holy Spirit and the humanity of God's chosen people" (11; cf. 319–20).

The traditional trinitarian hermeneutic of Scripture, such as sketched thus far, has more recently been challenged on two fronts, particularly with regard to the OT. Historical critics bring the charge of anachronism against finding the Trinity in the OT; given the history of European anti-Semitism, there is now also a desire to avoid any supersessionistic account of the continuing Jewish people that would move from the level of theological judgment to that of racial hostility. In face of the first point, C. Kavin Rowe has argued that a genuinely canonical reading of the Bible will respect the sequential unfolding of the external story. Thereby the very newness of the incarnation and Pentecost will exert a "pressure" that gives Christians the clue for a christological and indeed trinitarian understanding of the internal story and its God from its very beginnings. There is no need to read conscious trinitarian thinking "anachronistically" into the minds of the OT authors. In face of the second point, Bruce Marshall realizes that to deny OT Israel access to the triune God would be to saw off the branch on which Christianity sits, since Christians have always claimed that the God revealed in Jesus Christ is "the God of Abraham, Isaac, and Jacob." Nevertheless, he wishes to avoid the dangerous conclusion that the continuing Jewish people do not have such access. That would risk misinterpreting what the apostle Paul says in Rom. 11:25–32 concerning God's fidelity to his promises and the salvation of "all Israel." It also might be used to condone the unconscionable behavior of many historic Christians toward Jews over the centuries. Marshall observes that traditional Christian hermeneutics oscillates in its interpretation of "the LORD" in the OT between Christ as the Son or Word, the Father, the Spirit (occasionally), and the entire Trinity. From "the lack of referential fixity in Christian discourse about the God of Israel," he concludes that "the Father is the God of Israel, the Son is the God of Israel, and the Holy Spirit is the God of Israel, yet they are not three Gods of Israel, but one God of Israel" (258). According to Marshall, "Knowledge of the Trinity, while not necessary in order to identify God, completes and perfects the identification of Israel's God" (263). "By giving descriptions that enable us to distinguish and relate the Father, the Son, and the Holy Spirit, Christian liturgy and Scripture render to us God's very identity, his inmost personal reality. Themselves instruments of the eternal Spirit, they put us in touch with 'the deep things of God' (1 Cor. 2:10)" (263–64).

Augustine recognized the difficulties in a trinitarian distribution of the theophanies of the OT when he systematically explored the relevant passages (*Trin.* 2.7.12–2.18.35 [CCSL 50:96–126]). In my judgment, there is still a broad wisdom to be found in Augustine's dictum that "the new testament lies latent in the old, and the old stands revealed in the new" (*Quaest. Hept.* 2.73 [CCSL 33:106]). This by no means excludes what the Orthodox theologian Boris Bobrinskoy calls "intimations" of the Trinity before the incarnation and Pentecost. Thereby OT saints and prophets may already have glimpsed what was to be more fully revealed of the Godhead later (John 5:46; 8:56–58; 12:41; 1 Cor. 10:4; 1 Pet. 1:10–12). In Eastern iconography, the scene from Gen. 18 depicting the three visitors to Abraham and Sarah under the oaks at Mamre becomes a visual means for offering worship to the triune God rendered present.

Patristically, it is possible to read the increasing clarity of trinitarian revelation in ways that may on the surface seem contradictory but which, in fact, each and together preserve the differentiated unity of the stages in one history of salvation. According to Gregory Nazianzus, "The Old Testament proclaimed the Father openly, and the Son more obscurely; the New manifested the Son, and suggested the deity of the Spirit; now the Spirit himself dwells among us, and supplies us with a clearer demonstration of himself" (*Fifth Theological Oration* 26 [SC 250:326–27]). In the reverse direction, Irenaeus declared that God, "having been seen in bygone days through the Spirit prophetically, and then seen through the Son adoptively, shall be seen in the kingdom of heaven paternally, the Spirit preparing man for the Son of God, the Son leading him to the Father, and the Father giving him the incorruptibility and eternal life that come from the vision of God" (*Haer.* 4.20.5 [SC 100:638–41]). This latter sequence corresponds to what, evangelically and experientially, is already the case as those who are being saved anticipate the "ascent through the Spirit to the Son, and through the Son to the Father" (5.36.2 [SC 153:458–61]; cf. *Epid.* 7 [SC 406:92–93]). For it is also, according to Basil the Great, the direction of Christian prayer, being the counterpart to the bestowal of divine blessing from the Father through the Son in the Spirit (*On the Holy Spirit* 7 [16]; 16 [37]; 18 [47] [SC 17 bis:298–301, 374–77, 412–15]).

Bibliography

Blowers, P. "The *Regula Fidei* and the Narrative Character of Early Christian Faith." *ProEccl* 6 (1997): 199–228; Bobrinskoy, B. *The Mystery of the Trinity.* St. Vladimir's Seminary Press, 1999; Catholic Church. *Catechism of the Catholic Church,* §§101–41. Paulist, 1994; Davis, S., D. Kendall, and G. O'Collins, eds. *The Trinity.* Oxford University Press, 1999; Dodd, C. H. *The Apostolic Preaching and Its Developments.* Hodder, 1960; Duensing, H., ed. *Epistula Apostolorum.* A. Marcus & E. Weber, 1925; Leslie, B. *Trinitarian Hermeneutics.* P. Lang, 1991; Marshall, B. "Do Christians Worship the God of Israel?" Pages 231–64 in *Knowing the Triune God,* ed. J. Buckley and D. Yeago. Eerdmans, 2001; Potterie, I. de la. "Interpretation of Holy Scripture in the Spirit in Which It Was Written (*Dei verbum* §12c)." Pages 220–66 in vol. 1 of *Vatican II,* ed. R. Latourelle. Paulist, 1988; Rowe, C. K. "Biblical Pressure and Trinitarian Hermeneutics." *ProEccl* 11 (2002): 295–312; Wainwright, A. *The Trinity in the New Testament.* SPCK, 1962; Wainwright, G. "The Ecumenical Rediscovery of the Trinity." *OiC* 34 (1998): 95–124; idem. "Psalm 33 Interpreted of the Triune God." *ExAud* 16 (2000): 101–20; idem. "Wesley's Trinitarian Hermeneutics." *Wesleyan Theological Journal* 36 (2001): 7–30; Wesley, J. "The Scripture Way of Salvation." Sermon 43. Online: http://www.godrules.net/library/wsermons/wsermons43.htm; idem. "The New Creation." Sermon 65. Online: http://www.godrules.net/library/wsermons/wsermons64.htm; idem. *The Works of John Wesley,* ed. T. Jackson. 14 vols. Zondervan, 1958–59; Work, T. *Living and Active.* Eerdmans, 2002; Yeago, D. "The New Testament and the Nicene Dogma: A Contribution to the Recovery of Theological Exegesis." *ProEccl* 3 (1994): 152–64; idem. "The Spirit, the Church, and the Scriptures: Biblical Inspiration and Interpretation Revisited." Pages 49–93 in *Knowing the Triune God,* ed. J. Buckley and D. Yeago. Eerdmans, 2001.

Geoffrey Wainwright

Trope *See* Imagery; Metaphor

Tropological Sense *See* Medieval Biblical Interpretation; Typology

Truth

To ascribe "truth" to a text or interpretation is to confer the ultimate accolade. On this, Scripture and philosophy agree, for truth is a prominent theme in each. No such consensus obtains, however, with regard to the nature and function of truth—to what kind of accolade truth is. Ancient and medieval philosophers were prone to think of truth in relation to goodness and beauty under the rubric of metaphysics (truth as a theory about ultimate reality). Modern thinkers cast lots for the concept according to their respective philosophical preferences. For science and epistemology in general, truth became a function of human methods for knowing facts. For existentialists, truth became a function of subjectivity in the throes of decision-making. For hermeneutics, the experience of the work of art became the paradigm for thinking about truth as an aesthetic experience and ontological event that enlarges one's self-understanding (Gadamer). Postmoderns, following Nietzsche, are more likely to view the concept with suspicion, a Western subterfuge for various forms of ideological and social oppression (Foucault). Guilty by association with politics and power ploys, the concept of truth has now entered strange new philosophical territory, joined at the hip with the rhetoric and sophistry from which Plato had originally sought to distinguish it.

Philosophical Theories of Truth

J. Barr's analysis of conservative theology aptly illustrates the effect of presuppositions about truth on biblical interpretation. The conservative tendency to tie the authority of the Bible to its inerrancy—its being without error in everything on which it speaks—results in a "fundamentalism" that insists on seeing the truth of biblical narrative in terms of its historical veracity. Barr opines that fundamentalism is less a strategy for reading the Bible literally than it is a program for ensuring the inerrancy of Scripture. Hence, a theory of truth as correspondence to empirical actuality is the presupposition that governs conservative exegesis (Barr 40–55). However, to presuppose inerrancy or historical factuality imposes a nonbiblical theory of truth on the Bible, leading conservatives to read the Bible wrongly—against the textual grain, against even the literal sense.

H. Frei generalizes Barr's point in convincing fashion by displaying how modern theologians, conservative and liberal alike, let extratextual theories about the nature and criteria of truth govern their interpretations of biblical narrative (*Eclipse*). The truth of narrative was thought to refer either to the historical events behind the text or to existential truths about human nature. But to force Scripture to conform to modern ideas of what its truth should be is to make the biblical narrative as "weak" as any other history or myth. The challenge is to let the Bible present its truth in its own terms. Frei himself suggested that this requires reading the Bible as realistic narrative (which means what it says), but later changed his mind and claimed that it required reading the Bible in the context of the community of faith (*Theology*, 94–116).

"Thy word is truth" (RSV: Ps. 119:160; John 17:17). Yes, but "What is truth?" asks Pilate (John 18:38). Aristotle captures our pretheoretical intuition about truth: "To say of what is that it is, or of what is not that it is not, is true" (*Metaph.* 4.7, 1011b.25–28). Truth names the relation that confers the authority of reality on what we say. We speak truly when an extralinguistic state of affairs "corresponds" to our linguistic formulations. Though intuitive, this view is not without its problems. First, interpreters must still determine to what language corresponds. To insist that language must always correspond to empirical actuality is to assume a modern reductionistic view of that to which true language corresponds. Second, and more significant, is the problem of describing the nature of such correspondence: how exactly does language correspond to the world? The so-called picture theory, where words name objects and sentences represent facts, is too severe and limited a theory of meaning and fails to account for what speakers and writers actually do with words.

While correspondence may be the intuitive meaning of truth, there is no shortage of alternative theories. Perhaps the chief rival in the context of theological interpretation of Scripture is the coherence theory, favored by nonfoundationalists, which focuses on reading in community according to the Rule of Faith and conceives of truth as a relation between statements. Some nonfoundationalists prefer a more pragmatic theory, in which the true is a matter of successfully serving some end (e.g., fostering love of God and neighbor).

Given the core Christian kerygma ("Christ is risen"), however, the best way forward is to follow those who advocate a minimalist correspondence/realist account of truth (Clark; Alston). Truth concerns the relation of a potential truth-bearer to a reality beyond itself: "Truth is always about something, but reality is that about which truth is" (Lewis 66). The distinguishing feature of a "chastened" correspondence view is that it leaves the exact nature of the correspondence relation unfinalized. Such minimalism, far from being a feeble evasion of the issue, is in fact the enabling condition of an enlarged sense of correspondence, one that actually does greater justice to the full panoply of biblical literature (see below).

Biblical Images of Truth

Scripture itself employs a rich and varied vocabulary of truth. The Hebrew term *'emeth* connotes what is firm, reliable, trustworthy, and faithful and expresses the character of a person's speech, thought, or action. As such, truth is opposed to hypocrisy. The Greek term *alētheia* (used regularly in the LXX to translate *'emeth*) carries these connotations into the NT as well as conveying the more cognitive Hellenistic sense of reality (as opposed to appearance). Truth in this sense is opposed to falsehood.

Note that faithfulness, reliability, and integrity are every bit as much properties or qualities of persons as well as propositions (Thiselton). We fail to do justice to the biblical use of terms for truth if we do not preserve the tie between factuality and faithfulness (Nicole). In biblical usage, promises as well as propositions are privileged truth-bearers. Accordingly, a true statement is not just accurate, a matter of mere intellectual assent; it is also reliable, deserving of personal commitment.

"But the LORD is the true God" (Jer. 10:10). Theologically, truth is first and foremost an attribute of God that emphasizes divine reliability and steadfastness. Truth is grounded in who God is, especially in relation to his covenant word. God is trustworthy just because he acts faithfully, and God's word is God's bond. God's word is true in the sense that it can be relied on, come hell or high water: "Heaven and earth will pass away, but my words will not pass away" (Matt. 24:35; cf. 5:18).

No biblical books speak of truth more than the Johannine writings. The Fourth Gospel opposes the light of truth to the darkness of the world, thus situating truth eschatologically. The truth of the gospel belongs to the new age inaugurated by the advent of Christ and is perceived through faith only by those who have received the Spirit of truth. Jesus is God's embodied truth claim, a covenant proposition made personal (John 14:6), whose history displays how things ultimately are (or will be). In the meantime, those who seek to speak and do the gospel must be prepared to suffer for the truth, just as Jesus, God's embodied truth, suffered on the cross (Vanhoozer, "Trials").

Truth and Theological Interpretation of Scripture: Further Issues

Three further issues are of particular relevance for the theological interpretation of Scripture.

Can Interpreters Gain "Objective" Knowledge of Truth?

The "traditional Western concept" of truth (Hicks 10)—with its stress on objectivity (truth is outside us), universality (truth is the same for all people), and eternity (truth lasts forever)—fails to address the postmodern emphasis on human situatedness and hence the inaccessibility of objective truth. If the issue is whether truth can be known in a value-neutral way apart from prejudices and presuppositions, the answer Scripture gives, at least with regard to the knowledge of God, is clearly "no." The apostle Paul gives the lie to such objectivism when he states that the truth is actively suppressed in unrighteousness (Rom. 1). From a different angle, Gadamer has argued that human situatedness in history, language, and tradition, together with the prejudices that such situatedness entails, is not an obstacle but an enabling condition of understanding truth, which progressively comes to light during the course of an ongoing conversation.

Kierkegaard's "truth is subjectivity" is not a capitulation to subjectivism, but rather a call to go beyond a mere intellectual apprehension of the truth; truth demands passionate commitment, or to use the biblical term, that truth be done. A desire for truth is necessary for one's being motivated to cultivate the intellectual virtues, truth-conducive habits of the mind that are apt to result in cognitive contact with reality (Zagzebski). Accuracy and sincerity, for example, are twin "virtues of truth" (Williams 11). The point to appropriate for theological interpretation is that biblical truth is not merely a storehouse of propositional facts to be mastered, but also something that persons must desire and appropriate—something to which persons must wholeheartedly submit.

Must the Loss of Epistemological Objectivity Entail the Loss of Objective Truth?

Truth theory has traditionally been a "metaphysical project" (Kirkham), an attempt to specify what it is for a proposition to be true. The trend among a good number of contemporary philosophers and theologians is to abandon the attempt to say how reality satisfies the condition for truth. Instead, they favor reducing truth to an "epistemic project," according to which truth becomes a function of knowledge: what we are warranted in asserting or ideally justified in believing. The main appeal for the antirealist is that, in contrast to the correspondence view, truth—warrant, not world—becomes accessible.

Theological interpreters, however, must resist reducing truth to "our best efforts." One should not confuse what it is for something to be true with how one comes to know something as true. Some things (e.g., that God is triune) are true, even though they are in principle beyond the reach of what Enlightenment thinkers require in terms of sufficient evidence or verifiability. The chastened correspondence view presented above does not depend on the assumption that truth is always susceptible of demonstration. The realist concept of truth nevertheless matters because it is important for human beings to relate their theoretical and practical concerns to the way things really are (Alston 235–40). Indeed, the biblical dichotomy between the way of the wise and the way of the foolish is not unrelated to the truth and falsity of their respective beliefs.

Are Statements the Primary Bearers of Truth?

A third issue concerns the bearers of truth. Strictly speaking, individual words can be neither true nor false. Words are inert and say nothing until someone uses them to say something in a sentence or speech act. Moreover, not all sentences or speech acts make assertions. Accordingly, philosophers identify statements—or propositions, the technical name for the cognitive content of statements—as the primary truth-bearers (Alston 9–17).

The assumption that truth pertains to statements has far-reaching implications for the theological interpretation of Scripture. At one extreme, it is conducive to proof-texting—to abstracting individual statements of Scripture out of their historical, literary, and canonical context and insisting that they nonetheless are true. Second, the focus on statements makes it difficult to take seriously the contention of the Fourth Gospel that Jesus is the truth (John 14:6). Finally, to reduce truth to what can be stated in individual assertions is to lose the richness of truth's expression through metaphors and through various forms of literature. Are the forms of biblical literature simply vessels into which is poured propositional content, or are the forms themselves statements? The issue is whether truth is always transparent to the indicative mood of reason, or whether some truths can be mediated only via certain forms of the poetic imagination (e.g., narrative, poetry, myth).

Truth and Theological Interpretation of Scripture: Contemporary Proposals

As we have seen, many modern theologians, conservative and liberal alike, tend to interpret Scripture theologically with some extratextual theory of truth already in hand. Other contemporary theologians seek to do justice to theological truth on its own terms.

Karl Barth. For K. Barth, truth is not propositional, nor does it refer to a fixed state of affairs; rather, it is "a predicate of God's own living reality as the Lord" (Hunsinger 67). Similar to Gadamer, who also insisted that truth cannot be limited to what is confirmable by method, Barth stresses the subject matter, or *Sache,* of Scripture—the living Word of God—which "commandeers" the human words so that they effectively and truthfully refer. Truth is not a static relation but a dynamic event of correspondence between human words and divine truth. Exegetical methods cannot master such truth; on the contrary, the exegete must prayerfully submit to the sovereignty of divine truth. Truth appears in theological interpretation, then, at the moment of personal encounter, when interpreters come both to recognize and actively to participate in the truth of Jesus Christ by becoming witnesses to the truth (Hunsinger 152–84).

Postliberal. G. Lindbeck's cultural-linguistic theology sees truth as a function of coherence with the overall Christian system, which is constituted not merely by axioms and definitions but more centrally by stories and social practices (64). We cannot know whether or not first-order statements correspond to reality because we lack epistemic access. For all theological intents and purposes, "intrasystematic" truth (e.g., coherence) suffices. To the extent that theological statements do correspond to reality, such correspondence is a function not of the statements considered in and of themselves, but as a function of their role in an ecclesial form of life. It is the whole form of life, not merely the isolated statements, that corresponds to divine reality (65).

In response to criticisms that Lindbeck's view fails to get beyond a version of social coherentism or consensus, where the truth is simply what people agree it is, other postliberals have turned to the doctrine of the Trinity. Thereby they give a distinctly Christian theological account of truth, in which Jesus is the primary truth-bearer and Christian doctrines are the primary criteria of truth (Marshall). To give primacy to any other set of truth commitments (e.g., science, existentialism, Marxism) determines the meaning one assigns to Scripture and hence inhibits the Bible's making sense on its own terms. Theology must reject the "dependence thesis," according to which Christian beliefs depend for their meaning and truth on some other set of beliefs (Marshall 98). An intratextual approach thus demands that

the gospel enjoy epistemic primacy; the story of Jesus becomes the interpretative framework for making sense of all other beliefs. The Father's will decides what is and what will be; the Son mediates what is and what will be; the Spirit, largely by empowering practices that are truth conducive, enables us to will true beliefs. In sanctifying us, the Spirit conforms us to the triune God. The correspondence that ultimately counts is that of self, not sentences, to God. Correspondence here means not theoretical mirroring but participatory likeness (cf. Milbank and Pickstock 1–18).

Postconservative. Finally, what for lack of a better term (and by way of contrast with the preceding) we may call postconservative theology continues to look to the biblical text as a bearer of theological truth, but not as a deposit of atomized statements. While postconservatives affirm the truth of Scripture, they understand language as other than primarily pictorial and theological truth as more than empirically factual. A postconservative theology recognizes the cognitive significance of literary forms other than assertorical statements and is thus less prone to reduce doctrine to propositional paraphrases of Scripture's content. On the contrary, it seeks to do justice to the multiple forms of Scripture (Vanhoozer, *Drama*), and above all, to the canonically attested form of Jesus Christ.

Postconservative theology works with a chastened correspondence view but also with an enlarged view of the correspondence relation. To take literary forms seriously, as more than mere rhetorical packaging, means affirming a multiform correspondence relation that takes account of the diverse ways in which different types of speech acts and types of literature engage and render reality. Together, the canonical texts map the way of truth and life, though not every biblical map highlights the same features of reality in the same way. As with maps, one must study the key and the legend in order to determine just how the text corresponds to reality.

Christ and Canon: Truth as Covenantal Relation

God's triune communicative action—whereby God's Word and Spirit correspond to the Father and to one another—is the paradigm of truth. God is true because his actions are consistent with his word—because he keeps his word. Jesus is the truth because he is God's "kept" word: "The truth . . . is in Jesus" (Eph. 4:21). The primary form of theological truth is the person and history of Jesus Christ, the one in and through whom all things have been created and redeemed. Christ is the splendor of truth: the finite human form of the infinite divine glory. Jesus is the light, and in his face is summed up the truth, goodness, and beauty of God himself.

God's truth made known in Jesus Christ goes hand in hand with his *khesed* or covenant love (Exod. 34:6). In Jesus, the reality of the covenant—and hence the truth of God, humanity, and the relation between them—is made manifest in an utterly reliable way. This truth is "the truth of the gospel" (Gal. 2:5), the truth that sets one free from the old order of sin and death for the eschatological flourishing of the created order. Truth in the context of theological interpretation must never be merely theoretical (a correspondence relation) but practical, transformative, and relational as well. In short, truth is not a bare correspondence but a covenantal relation. To say that truth is covenantal is to acknowledge that it is not simply something to be believed, but also something to be done (the good), appreciated (the beautiful), and adored. Note that truth as a covenantal relation between language and reality allows us to see propositions and persons alike as truth-bearers, for truth is a matter of keeping one's word.

In Jesus Christ, God, the infinite, assumes finite form, and it is precisely the particularities of this form, not some abstract universal principle, that disclose the nature of ultimate reality. Truth is what conforms to the form of Jesus Christ, the submission of language before the Word made flesh. Truth has commissioned its own authorized witnesses. The canon is ultimately the self-attestation of Jesus Christ, the most reliable word that is. The truth of Scripture is not a function of the genius of its authors but of its role in the triune economy of communicative action. The biblical texts are creaturely realities sanctified by the Spirit, co-opted for the sake of facilitating covenantal contact with the triune God. The splendor of truth revealed in Christ is diffused throughout the canon; the white light of the infinite divine form is refracted in a variety of canonical colors and literary forms: song, history, parable, apocalyptic, law, prophecy, and so forth. Hence "the truth of being is 'poetic' before it is 'rational'" (Hart 132).

"Thy word is truth." No other text is as truth-conducive as Scripture. No other texts are the normative specification of truth as those of the canon. If homiletics is a matter of speaking the truth in love, hermeneutics must surely be a matter of searching for the truth (of Scripture) in love. Nothing less than the desire for truth—the desire to know God as God has made himself known in Christ and in the Scriptures that attest him—is a sufficient motivation for cultivating the epistemic and interpretative virtues.

The Spirit employs the biblical texts to minister truth, to bring about covenantal contact with reality. To be in covenant relation with God, keeping his words in obedience as God keeps them in faithfulness, corresponding to the word of God in Christ, is to live in spirit and in truth. It is precisely in coming to know the truth of God in Christ and canon that humans are able to glorify God and enjoy him forever.

Bibliography

Alston, W. *A Realist Conception of Truth*. Cornell University Press, 1996; Barr, J. *Fundamentalism*. Westminster, 1978; Clark, D. *To Know and Love God*. Crossway, 2003; Feinberg, J. "Truth: Relationship of Theories of Truth to Hermeneutics." Pages 3–50 in *Hermeneutics, Inerrancy, and the Bible*, ed. E. Radmacher and R. Preus. Zondervan, 1984; Frei, H. *The Eclipse of Biblical Narrative*. Yale University Press, 1974; idem. *Theology and Narrative*. Oxford University Press, 1993; Gadamer, H.-G. *Truth and Method*. 2d ed. Continuum, 2002; Hart, D. B. *The Beauty of the Infinite*. Eerdmans, 2003; Hicks, P. *Evangelicals and Truth*. Apollos, 1998; Hunsinger, G. *How to Read Karl Barth*. Oxford, 1991; Kirkham, R. *Theories of Truth*. MIT Press, 1995; Lewis, C. S. "Myth Became Fact." Pages 63–67 in *God in the Dock*. Eerdmans, 1970; Lindbeck, G. *The Nature of Doctrine*. Westminster, 1984; Marshall, B. *Trinity and Truth*. Cambridge University Press, 2000; Milbank, J., and C. Pickstock. *Truth in Aquinas*. Routledge, 2001; Nicole, R. "The Biblical Concept of Truth." In *Scripture and Truth*, ed. D. A. Carson and J. Woodbridge. Zondervan, 1983; Thiselton, A. "Truth." *NIDNTT* 3:874–902; Vanhoozer, K. *The Drama of Doctrine*. Westminster John Knox, 2005; idem. "The Trials of Truth." Pages 337–73 in *First Theology*. InterVarsity, 2002; Williams, B. *Truth and Truthfulness*. Princeton University Press, 2002; Zagzebski, L. *Virtues of the Mind*. Cambridge University Press, 1996.

Kevin J. Vanhoozer

Tübingen School

This intellectual movement, centered in Schwabian (southwest) Germany at the University of Tübingen, can be dated 1835–60. It is associated first of all with F. C. Baur (1792–1860). Other prominent figures include Eduard Zeller, Albert Schwegler, and Adolf Hilgenfeld. Baur's student David Friedrich Strauss (1808–74) also bears mention. For it was Strauss's *The Life of Jesus Critically Examined* (1835) that marked a clear break with the orthodox and supernaturalist reading of Scripture still widely affirmed at that time in Tübingen and other German Protestant faculties. Strauss's work exemplified a mode of biblical interpretation that rejected cardinal Christian doctrines. Instead, the Bible was understood using categories provided by ethical and philosophical convictions rooted in German idealism. Controversy ensued, engulfing both Strauss (whose academic future was ruined) and Baur (whose university post was already secure). It continued until Baur's death, by which time theological fashion had turned in the direction of Albrecht Ritschl, who studied at Tübingen but then rejected many of Baur's key tenets. Yet even after Baur's passing, aspects of his method continued to develop. "As a practising historian Baur stands closer to . . . Troeltsch than to Hegel" (Morgan 273). Among scholars who carried Baur's legacy into the twentieth century are Franz Overbeck (1837–1905), Otto Pfleiderer (1839–1908), and B. W. Bacon (1860–1932). The Tübingen School's legacy retains influence in NT study today.

Baur approached the NT based on a doctrine of God rooted in Hegel's dialectical panentheism. The NT message was the realization of a philosophical ideal, not the proclamation of God's incarnate self-disclosure through Jesus in accordance with Scripture (cf. Rom. 1:2; 16:26). The chief historical dynamic for the unfolding of this ideal, which covered the better part of two centuries, was internecine strife. An early Jewish (Petrine) Christianity focusing on Jesus' messianic consciousness was opposed by Gentile (Pauline) Christianity, which focused on Jesus' ethical idealism and universalism. Only the four Pauline Epistles that reflect this warfare are authentic (Romans, Galatians, 1–2 Corinthians); the sole first-century document reflecting the Petrine party's outlook is Revelation. Later, well after the apostles' time and into the second century, documents were produced that display a reconciliation between the two factions; these include Acts, Hebrews, James, 1 Peter, the Synoptic Gospels, and the rest of the (pseudo-) Pauline letters (but not the Pastorals). The apex of ecclesial and christological formation is found in the Pastorals, 2 Peter, and John's Gospel, all placed near the close of the second century.

Few of Baur's historical and literary judgments have stood the test of time. All the NT writings can be dated comfortably within the first century. The Petrine-Pauline controversy is too slender a cord to bear the whole weight of early Christian development. John's "high" Christology is ubiquitous in the NT, and the Fourth Gospel was not written in the late second century, since a papyrus attests its existence by around 125 CE. In other words, rationalistic German idealism provided an unsuitable platform for exegeting the NT either theologically or historically. Despite such miscues, Baur's work remains a monument to the power of an integrated hermeneutical vision. Theological interpretation of Scripture that avoids Baur's erroneous critical judgments and antitraditional animus would do well to strive for the erudition, clarity, and creativity of the synthetic reading of Scripture for which the Tübingen School is remembered.

Bibliography

Baird, W. History of New Testament Research. Vol. 1, From Deism to Tübingen. Vol. 2, From Jonathan Edwards to Rudolf Bultmann. Fortress, 1992–2002; Harris, H. The Tübingen School. Clarendon, 1975; Harrisville, R. A., and W. Sundberg. The Bible in Modern Culture. 2d ed. Eerdmans, 2002; Hodgson, P. The Formation of Historical Theology. Harper & Row, 1966; Köpf, U. "Ferdinand Christian Baur als Begründer einer konsequent historischen Theologie." ZTK 89, no. 4 (1992): 440–61; Morgan, R. "Ferdinand Christian Baur." Pages 261–89 in vol. 1 of Nineteenth Century Thought in the West, ed. N. Smart et al. Cambridge University Press, 1985; Neill, S., and T. Wright. The Interpretation of the New Testament, 1861–1986. 2d ed. Oxford University Press, 1988; Rollmann, H. "From Baur to Wrede: The Quest for a Historical Method." SR 17, no. 4 (1988): 443–54; Strauss, D. F. The Life of Jesus Critically Examined, ed. P. Hodgson. Translated from the 4th German ed. by G. Eliot. Fortress, 1972.

Robert W. Yarbrough

Two Horizons *See* Hermeneutical Circle; Hermeneutics

Typology

Decisions about the definition and propriety of "typological" exegesis have decisive consequences for theological hermeneutics. Not only will they affect how we describe inner-biblical exegesis (NT use of the OT in particular). Such decisions will also affect how we prescribe a contemporary hermeneutic for moving between texts and theology or application. They will influence whether or not we should find in the interpretative practices of NT authors a pattern to follow for handling such "analogical" movement.

Definition among Biblical Scholars

Typology, according to a representative and concise definition, relates "the past to the present in terms of a historical correspondence and escalation in which the divinely ordered prefigurement finds a complement in the subsequent and greater event" (Ellis 106). Types in this strict sense have to do with persons, institutions, or events (Baker, ch. 7; Davidson; Goppelt). For example, the NT seems to view *persons* such as Moses and David to pattern fulfillments in Jesus Christ as prophet, leader of Israel, Son of God, and so on. *Institutions* such as the tabernacle or sacrificial system foreshadow the substance of Christian realities. And as to *events*, the Noahic flood prefigures Christian baptism.

Not all scholars would agree that the prefiguration provides advance notice or leaves evidence in the "typical" text (as argued by, e.g., Davidson; and Kaiser; on the other side, France; for representatives of each, see Moo 196n63). Neither do all scholars accept the historicity of the types, so approaches to salvation history affect discussions about what would count as evidence for typological hermeneutics. For the moment, whatever modern convictions might be, we must admit that the NT authors took the precedents of the canonical salvation history to anticipate patterns of further divine action.

Development in the Bible and Church History

We should point out that "typology" is not really a biblical term, since it implies developed study of types, which may not really characterize the texts themselves (so Ostmeyer; nonetheless, here I accede to common use). For a long time, the standard bearer on *typos* has been Goppelt, but his work is somewhat problematic due to its tendency to discover phenomena within the Bible that match an assumed definition (Davidson 53–55). Accordingly, Davidson has countered by seeking to provide a thoroughly inductive understanding. He shows that *typos* may basically denote (1) any matrix or *Vorbild* that leaves its impress; (2) an impression or *Nachbild*, the impression left by the matrix; or (3) a matrix or *Vorbild* that is at the same time an impression or *Nachbild*. Three cognates of *typos* also appear in the NT: *antitypos*, *typikos*, and *hypotypōsis* (131–33).

Among NT appearances of this vocabulary, Davidson argues for these hermeneutically relevant passages: Rom. 5; 1 Cor. 10; Heb. 8; Heb. 9; and 1 Pet. 3 (188). Several "structures" are common to them: historical, eschatological, christological-soteriological, ecclesiological, and prophetic. However helpful these are, (1) ironically enough (given the inductive effort), the appearance of each structure is probably not demonstrated adequately for all the texts. (2) Nor will word usage alone suffice to select texts for the NT's "typological" hermeneutics if *typos* is not a technical term

(which appears somewhat doubtful). (3) This is all the more true if it is correct that, for example, "typological" interpretations offered by Jesus, according to the Gospels, are often "most implicit," involving a "far looser method" than type and antitype. "More often the parallels, though present, are unexpressed, and the typological intention must be inferred from the selection of that particular Old Testament passage for that particular occasion" (France 76). (4) Moreover, arguably Paul's "allegory"—typological or not?—regarding Hagar and Sarah is a vital limit-case with which to assess his hermeneutic for canonical persons and events connected to salvation history.

Indeed, Gal. 4 and other texts became a basis for the early Christians' recourse to allegorical interpretation, which few distinguished from typology in their need for Christian readings of the OT. Early on, such reading strategies were often apologetically motivated (e.g., Justin's *Dialogue with Trypho* representatively dealing with Jewish objections to Christian claims). However, Origen and others were also pedagogically oriented to "spiritual" reading. Such exegesis was perhaps not intended to dismiss the particularity of the original so much as being dependent on a conception of history that moderns (such as Auerbach and others who accuse Origen of antihistorical allegorizing) do not understand (so Dawson).

Nevertheless, the "Alexandrian" school was perceived by the "Antioch" school, back in that very day, to read ahistorically. The Antiochenes were not really quibbling over whether to use the word "allegory" to describe what Paul does in Gal. 4, but wanted to defend its legitimate relation to the letter of the OT (Young 180). However, the influence of Origen, Augustine, and Gregory the Great won out, so that allegory was taken up into the medieval development of the Bible's "fourfold sense"—literal, allegorical (corresponding to faith), tropological (corresponding to love), and anagogical (corresponding to hope). The Reformation's rejection of this—in theory if not entirely in practice—followed by the development of critical biblical scholarship and its domination of the public square requires historical and theological assessments of typology in relation to allegory.

Distinction from Allegory?

Such theological assessments differ. At each end of a spectrum are those who find no substantial difference between typology and allegory, or find that unimportant.

1. On what I shall call the *"inspiration"* end, some conservative scholars find many NT readings of OT texts unacceptable by current standards of "meaning" (usually, the human author's "intention"), and may see such "allegorizing" or spiritual exegesis not really to be interpretative. Anyway, such uses of the text are covered by the privilege of divine inspiration, which leads us to accept the NT theological assertions without necessarily adopting their methods (e.g., Longenecker, who has clarified recently that NT readings of the OT are acceptable but distinct from their "methods," which are unnecessary).

2. On what I shall call the *"illumination"* end, typically less conservative scholars also find many NT readings of the OT to be allegorical, or do not substantially distinguish typology and allegory. Whether or not the older Roman Catholic *sensus plenior* approach is adopted (in which there is a fuller divine or spiritual sense when biblical texts are read canonically), such churchly scholars permit contemporary imitation of NT interpretative practice. Claiming the leading of the Holy Spirit, they may go beyond or even against the verbal sense of a particular passage (e.g., Hays; Fowl).

Historical and/or literary approaches often fund such theological assessments. The literary truism of a New Critic such as Northrop Frye, that all reading involves a certain dimension of "otherness" (e.g., Young 3) intruding due to contextual differentiation, has helped to foster construals of all the "typological" as "allegorical" (which derives from the Greek word *allos* for "other"). Perhaps such a truism, however, becomes virtually tautological, which (so Whitman) should chasten many of us who have been guilty of repeating it as if the point were conceptually vital. Meanwhile, we must grant the historical fuzziness of the boundary between typology and allegory in practice, but not as if we know entirely better than the patristic ("Antioch" vs. "Alexandria") or later (Reformers vs. various Roman Catholics) disputants that nothing was at stake. A rough distinction between "typology" and "allegory," then, might be reformulated around different kinds of mimesis (representation of reality or "world"). An "iconic" version may correspond to typology and preserve a "narrative coherence" between referents. On the other hand, "symbolic" versions may correspond to allegory, which arbitrarily imposes a thoroughly ahistorical connection (so Young).

3. Some such distinction is theologically important for those toward the middle of our spectrum. They believe that we may imitate NT interpretative practices *and* that those practices may be construed as consistent with the OT verbal sense, *at least* when that is read as—and in the context of—a canonical whole. This whole canon shapes and is shaped by the narrative coherence just mentioned, and ties together the particular texts.

3a. More conservative scholars, who tend more toward emphasizing a doctrine of biblical inspiration, also tend toward an author-centered construal of "verbal sense." They can be inclined to find (as much as possible) verbal evidence in particular OT passages of prophetic anticipation for NT typological fulfillment.

3b. Meanwhile, reader-oriented theories tend toward the "illumination" emphasis mentioned above, along with some text-centered theories. (Other, more centrist, text-oriented theories distinguish between [at least some that would count as] allegorical excess and canonically warranted typological or "figural" readings.)

Deployment in "Figural Reading"

Hans Frei's influential *The Eclipse of Biblical Narrative* contrasts modern with pre-eighteenth-century hermeneutics in this way: "Figural reading had been literalism extended to the whole story or the unitary canon containing it. But now figural sense came to be something like the opposite of literal sense. . . . Literal reading came increasingly to mean two things: grammatical and lexical exactness in estimating what the original sense of a text was to its original audience, and the coincidence of the description with how the facts really occurred" (7). Figural interpretation for the Reformers held together the Bible as a book projecting the one coherent world/story as it really is. Something like typology allowed for biblical interpretation to be both literal and Christian. Calvin, Frei's prime example, held *both* that the Spirit enabled Christian experience to illuminate (newly) the meaning of OT types, *and* that such interpretation "is in no sense a material contribution on the part of the interpreter" (Frei 34). This contrasts subtly but significantly with the characterizations in Hays and others of the Spirit's influence over NT use of the OT—that this allowed a reading in what (in a sense) was not really there.

Arguably, we must admit that many NT typological readings were not fully possible until after Christ's first advent, and the outpouring of his Spirit (so even Moo). But we need not stipulate experience as their interpretative warrant if, following Calvin broadly, we trust that God's

825

speech in Scripture and actions in salvation history manifest a sort of unity and consistency with each other. Experience of Christ via the Spirit may have been necessary for recognition of the reality about which the biblical texts spoke—may in a sense have been the reality about which they spoke—without being *the* grounds for such recognition. When it comes to typological reading, experience may be hermeneutically significant, but not solely decisive.

The significance of experience also concerns an ethical dimension of NT readings, which may have been underdeveloped by scholars to date. According to George Lindbeck, "Traditionally expressed, one could perhaps say that typological tropology or tropological typology was the chief interpretative strategy for making the Bible contemporary, for absorbing one's own world into the world of the text" (31). Paul's reading of Israel's story as "typical" for the Corinthians concerning testing and idolatry depends on aforementioned typological structures (e.g., the ecclesiology of 1 Cor. 10:1–4, along with the eschatology in 10:11) but is strikingly ethical in its focus. While his depiction of their reality is grounded in *extrapolating* from past to present divine action, what is typical for the Corinthian decision concerns Israelite patterns that they should or should not *emulate*. For an event to be written is to enable its encouragement of our proper response to God (Rom. 15:4).

Biblical "typology" cannot be treated, therefore, simply as a prophetic matter of extrapolating the *indicative*—divine action and associated realities (such as connections between Jesus, Israel, and church) that are already set. It also involves discerning the *imperative*: prudential discernment of such realities in light of their divinely prepared application to God's people in the present. However important it is to distinguish divine action and human response, so that we respond with discernment about what God has really said and done, such realities may not be separated. Hebrews, perhaps the typological reader par excellence, is a prime example of this point (e.g., see the end of ch. 5). Our moral growth (or lack of it) affects discernment, which affects what relationships we will hear, taste, and see between God's covenant realities.

If Scripture indeed involves divine action, then we may not allegorize to our heart's content, as if determining or creating God's action in the present or downplaying the particular reality of the past with which the Spirit will somehow be consistent. (See, e.g., Seitz contra examples in Fowl and others concerning spiritual reading and Acts 15; while another interesting "figural reading," which may or may not live up to textual details, comes from Radner.) Moreover, it is entirely appropriate for scholars to attempt defenses of NT typological readings, describing their *warrant* in terms that might satisfy a modern public. This might work if that public were to apply historical and literary criteria with a heuristic openness to the plausibility of the readings, given a framework of Christian assumptions about salvation history.

Nonetheless, such "typology" might not do entire justice to NT reading strategies for *discovery*, with their ethical allowance—indeed necessity—for recognizing anew divine realities and authorized patterns of life via prudence in a given moment (previously those patterns would have been impossible to foresee). We may focus on warrant at one moment (especially when studying NT hermeneutics prescriptively), but then on strategies for discovery at another (which might do NT hermeneutics more descriptive justice); in any case, these reinforce each other. Thus, while we may want to distinguish between them, in the end they may not be separated because they are mutually implicating. If this broadens a "typological" hermeneutic to cover discovery as well as warrant, still it also constrains "analogical" moves from Bible to context, by tying such "applications" more tightly to textual realities.

For there is interrelationship between patterns of divine action we extrapolate typologically, and patterns of human response we should or should not emulate figurally. That we should expect, since NT "typology"—while deploying a pattern of interpretation with precursors in the OT itself—is fundamentally a Christ-centered development, and in him the divine and human connect. Both particular OT persons and Israel the people of God anticipate Christ by being divine action with a human vocation; OT events and institutions likewise foreshadow his work. Thus, the regathering Israel—both particular new covenant persons and the one people of God they comprise—may extrapolate divine action from biblical patterns read through Christ. Moreover, churchly readers find in Jesus the biblical pattern of human life to emulate. He is the measure of fullness to which a new humanity is being conformed and therefore through which all other scriptural patterns must be read. Jesus Christ is both the fulfillment of promised divine action that precedes our discernment, and the faithful pattern through which humans discover afresh our proper future. God has spoken the final communicative act—we now have all the patterns to emulate. Yet we await full realization of the happy ending, so we must continue to extrapolate from prior patterns how God is wrapping up our final scenes. This significance of Christology for ecclesiology and eschatology (as well as vice versa) answers why and how tropology and "typology" must work together for theological interpreters of Scripture: *typoi* have to do with the interrelation between reading of who God is for us and who we shall be.

See also Allegory; Jewish Exegesis; Relationship between the Testaments

Bibliography

Auerbach, E. "Figura." Pages 11–76 in *Scenes from the Drama of European Literature*. Meridian, 1959; Baker, D. L. *Two Testaments, One Bible*. Rev. ed. InterVarsity, 1991; Beale, G. K., ed. *The Right Doctrine from the Wrong Texts?* Baker, 1994; Davidson, R. *Typology in Scripture*. Andrews University Press, 1981; Dawson, J. D. *Christian Figural Reading and the Fashioning of Identity*. University of California Press, 2002; Ellis, E. E. *The Old Testament in Early Christianity*. Baker, 1991; Fowl, S. *Engaging Scripture*. Blackwell, 1998; France, R. T. *Jesus and the Old Testament*. Tyndale Press, 1971; Frei, H. *The Eclipse of Biblical Narrative*. Yale University Press, 1974; Glenny, W. E. "Typology: A Summary of the Present Evangelical Discussion." *JETS* 40, no. 4 (December 1997): 627–38; Goppelt, L. *Typos*, trans. D. Madvig. Eerdmans, 1982; Hanson, R. P. C. *Allegory and Event*. Westminster John Knox, 2002; Hays, R. *Echoes of Scripture in the Letters of Paul*. Yale University Press, 1989; Johnson, S. L., Jr. *The Old Testament in the New*. Zondervan, 1980; Kaiser, W., Jr. *The Uses of the Old Testament in the New*. Moody, 1985; Lampe, G. W. H., and K. J. Woolcombe. *Essays on Typology*. SBT 22. A. R. Allenson, 1957; Lindbeck, G. "Postcritical Canonical Interpretation: Three Forms of Retrieval." Pages 26–51 in *Theological Exegesis*, ed. C. Seitz and K. Greene-McCreight. Eerdmans, 1999; Longenecker, R. *Biblical Exegesis in the Apostolic Period*. Rev. ed. Eerdmans, 1999; Moo, D. "The Problem of Sensus Plenior." Pages 179–211 in *Hermeneutics, Authority, and Canon*, ed. D. A. Carson and J. Woodbridge. 2d ed. Baker, 1995; Ostmeyer, K.-H. "Typologie und Typos: Analyse eines schwierigen Verhältnisses." *NTS* 46 (2000): 112–31; Radner, E. *The End of the Church*. Eerdmans, 1998; Seitz, C. *Figured Out*. Westminster John Knox, 2001; Treier, D. "The Superiority of Pre-Critical Exegesis? Sic et Non." *TJ* 24 NS (2003): 77–103; Whitman, J., ed. *Interpretation and Allegory*. Brill's Studies in Intellectual History 101. Brill, 2000; Young, F. *Biblical Exegesis and the Formation of Christian Culture*. Cambridge University Press, 1997.

Daniel J. Treier

U

Ugarit and the Bible *See* Ancient Near Eastern Background Studies

Underdetermined Meaning *See* Meaning; Theological Hermeneutics, Contemporary

Understanding *See* Hermeneutical Circle; Hermeneutics; Theological Hermeneutics, Contemporary

Unity *See* Church, Doctrine of the; Culture and Hermeneutics; Dialogism; Scripture, Unity of

Use of the OT in the NT *See* Intertextuality; Jewish Exegesis; Relationship between the Testaments; Scripture, Unity of; Typology

Utterance Meaning

At the very heart of modern debates about the meaning of texts, including biblical texts, is a threefold question: How are the words of such writings expected to relate to "reality" out there? How can we perceive what they say? And how, if at all, is what they say "meaningful" (= "significant") to us? Here we deal only with the first two questions.

Introduction

The choice of the title "utterance meaning" requires some clarification. In linguistics and semantics it signals the sharp and useful difference between contextless sentences, and real, situationally embedded ones (Cotterell and Turner, chs. 1–3). A contextless sentence such as "Beautiful Virginia is in an awful mess!"—written on a blackboard merely as an example of English usage—tells us *nothing* about *anything* in the real world, because it refers to nothing in particular, nor anything in general. The same sentence could be used on countless different specific occasions with utterly different meanings. Spoken by a heckling politician, it may say "The State of Virginia is in serious financial danger; vote for me, instead!" Spoken in a different situation, it may say: "The yacht, Beautiful Virginia, is greatly storm-damaged (or its crew 'close to mutiny,' or 'the boat is unforgivably untidy')," and so forth. But when Mr. Black utters the same words to his wife, about the mistreatment of their beloved daughter, then the despairing conversation's *context* in which he makes the statement (including, perhaps, the sad tone in which he says it, and the sorrowful shaking of his head as he does so) unambiguously clarifies that he thereby expresses a lament over the emotional turmoil of dear Virginia. *And that is thereby conventionally established as "the determinate meaning" of what he has said.*

An "utterance" is a particular, and contextually defined, communicative use of language, of whatever length (from the briefest exclamation to a book-long speech, or more), and whether written or spoken. Romans thus contains many utterances by Paul; but at a different level, the *whole* letter might be analyzed as a single utterance to the churches in Rome, introducing his gospel, and advocating related behavioral outcomes. To call Romans Paul's "utterance," then, is to make the significant claim that (unlike contextless sentences) this text had (at least at *one* stage) determinate meaning: the meaning that the apostle *intended* and can have reasonably expected to be conveyed by what he wrote to his first-century readers, given their shared presuppositions and conventions of language use. In short, the "utterance meaning" of Romans, understood as a speech event between the apostle and the congregations to which he wrote, *is (by definition) neither more nor less than Paul's meaning.*

At another quite different level, confessing Christians may also wish to insist that in appropriating Paul's Letters and giving them to the church as part of the canon, God has in some analogous way performed a *new* (and different) "utterance" of the text of Romans (and of everything else in Scripture). The difference between the original authorial utterance meaning and God's might be seen as sharpest in, say, the imprecatory psalms; perhaps least in the apostles' letters (once due allowance is made for the fact that God speaks only indirectly, through an authorized representative).

But such discussion would take us beyond the confines of this article (for different perspectives see, e.g., the essays by Fowl, Turner, and Wall in Green and Turner; also Wolterstorff; Vanhoozer; Ward).

In what follows, this article examines first the components that make up utterance meaning at sentence level; only subsequently will we turn to the higher levels of paragraph and above. It is surprisingly difficult to find agreement between linguistic experts on what a sentence is, but one criterion is that sentences should be grammatically complete (except for ellipsis) and independent. They may be simple and short (e.g., "Jesus wept," John 11:35) or compound (coordinated) and/or complex (subordinated). Ephesians 1:3–14 is analyzed by the ESV translators as consisting of five sentences, and by GNT as no fewer than fifteen sentences. But in the Greek original, it is just *one* sentence: a striking cascade of coordinations and subordinations. In understanding the utterance meaning of even relatively simple sentences, a variety of factors interplay: both formal (lexical, grammatical, structural) and occasional (cotext, context).

Formal Factors in Sentence Meaning

Lexical. Sense is fundamentally communicated by stringing *words* together in linguistically competent ways. *Precision* of sense, however, is quite substantially afforded by lexical choice between partially synonymous terms. There are many verbs an author might use to say that "Stephen (of Acts 7) was 'killed.'" Among them are put to death, stoned, lynched, executed, slaughtered, martyred, sacrificed, and so on. Choice of wording to fill the sentence-slot, here represented by the connotationally neutral verb "killed," helps map the hearer/reader onto the speaker's much more specific intended sense or spin about the death in question. So it is always important to understand the *subtle network of closely related words* available to biblical speakers in their particular language-system. It is then not entirely surprising that much scholarly energy has been put into "word studies," though unfortunately many of these have been seriously flawed in method (see Barr; Cotterell and Turner, chs. 4–5).

The most common errors are (1) the assumption that word meaning is transparent from its formation (often partly true, e.g., for "black-bird"; but not for "ladybird," "butterfly," etc.; and what climber confuses a "hangover" with an "overhang," despite the similarity of their formation?); (2) the assumption that a word's "original meaning" is necessarily significant for its later usage (the fact is that, with time, words usually develop a plurality of new senses, and these are not necessarily closely related to original meaning, or to each other; cf. the seventy-or-so quite different senses of the English word "run" or, e.g., the misleading analysis of *ekklēsia* to mean that the church is the people "called out" of the world by God); (3) the confusion of word senses with "concepts": John may have a clear "concept" of authentic love as selfless and Christlike, but we must not confuse that with the *sense* of the Greek noun *agapē* ("love") or its corresponding verb (*agapaō*). When John says, "People loved darkness, rather than light" (John 3:19), he means quite the opposite of "selfless, Christlike love" (cf. also 12:43; 1 John 2:15; etc.).

Grammatical. The main verb lies at the heart of the sentence's meaning. As in English, so also in Hebrew and Greek, the way the "verb" word is written can be coded for *mood* (indicative, imperative, or infinitive, etc.), *voice* (active or passive [but in Greek also "middle"]), *tense* (various forms of present, future, and past), *aspect* (how the writer presents the events: as complete or continuing, etc.), and *person* (I/she/they/you). The question of whether, say, "aorist" forms of the verb represent "tense" (expressing the event[s] as past-present-future) or "aspect" (viewing events either "completed" [aorist] or "in progress" [as in present and imperfect forms], or "with immediate consequences" [as in perfect and pluperfect forms]) is a major debate (see Porter, *Aspect*). The vast majority of sentences in all texts and many languages, however, involve the complexity of relating main to subordinate clauses.

Word Order. Since Hebrew and Greek are inflected languages, word order is less important for their sentences than for English. If one were to change the order of the words "One of the officers struck Jesus on the face" (cf. John 18:22) to "Jesus struck one of the officers on the face," the result would be a completely different assertion. In Greek, however, the fact that the officer is the grammatical subject and Jesus is the object is marked by case endings, which we could represent as "Struck [*verb*] the officer [*subject*] Jesus [*object*]." These words could be placed in *any* order (such as this "unmarked" one [in the previous sentence]) without confusion concerning what happened. That said, we should not conclude that the order is arbitrary. Greek sentences place the most semantically prominent element first (usually the verb), and leave the least semantically marked to the end. The typical, so neutral, word order would be Verb-Subject-Object and so on (as above). So the word order in the Greek of John 11:35, "Wept[-he] Jesus," is neutral. If John had written the Greek words in the order "Jesus wept[-he]," that would make "Jesus" semantically prominent in ways that would raise questions in the mind of the hearer. Does it signal a change of topic or a contrast (as if the narrative had been saying, "The others were enjoying their meal, but what was Jesus doing? *He* was weeping"), or what? In Luke 13:16, most translations follow the Greek word order. But in English, leaving the words "on the Sabbath day" to the end of the sentence could mark emphasis: "*especially* on the Sabbath day" (i.e., the Sabbath is a particularly appropriate day for this poor woman to be released from Satan's bondage). In Greek, however, to make that point the sentence would need to be written in an order more like "On the sabbath . . . ought not be loosed . . . this woman . . . ?"

Semantic Structure. Most real sentence utterances have relatively complex meaning relations between the parts (clauses, complement, prepositional phrases, etc.). In narrative, the relations are normally temporal and/or explicative, and so relatively transparent. In an argumentative letter, such as Romans, however, the "logic" may become quite dense. In such cases we map sentence "meaning" by trying to express the relationship of the subordinate clauses to the main verb. So Rom. 5:1–2 has a main clause: "We have peace with God," with a satellite of dependent clauses, expressing "reason" ("since we are justified by faith": 5:1 NRSV) and qualification ("through our Lord Jesus," in turn qualified by "through whom we have . . . access to this grace" [NRSV]). The analysis of the semantic structure of the sentence, where complex, is, to a comparative degree, subjective. For example, Eph. 3:14–19 might be analyzed (as it is by Hoehner's massive commentary) as a prayer that believers may be strengthened in their inner being *in order* that Christ may dwell in their hearts, *so that* (as a *result*) they may be able to comprehend the dimensions of God's love, *so that* (as a further *consequence*) they be filled with the fullness of God. Alternatively, we can (preferably?) read the prayer as expressing mutually explanatory/complementary outcomes: that the readers may be innerly strengthened, *that is,* that Christ may dwell in them, *that is,* that they may comprehend the dimensions of God's love, *that is,* that they may be filled with the fullness of God. The kind of propositional and semantic analysis

involved here is most conveniently elucidated in Cotterell and Turner (ch. 6).

"Occasional" or Situational Factors in Sentence Meaning. Formal factors, such as discussed above, always contribute to the meaning of a sentence, but other factors may be just as important. If, in a particular situation, I say to my son, "Oh, I *do* like the look of your back!" he will correctly decode it not as a true assertion but as an ironical way of *requesting* that he move so that he does not block my view of the television. This request could hardly be deduced from the linguistic *form*. Irony is a relatively extreme example of how sentence meaning and utterance meaning may differ, and of how much of the latter depends on contextual factors. The utterance meaning of a sentence depends on a variety of cotextual (= surrounding "text"), contextual (= situational aspects), and "co-operative discourse-conventional" factors. Grice has summarized these last as: You are expected to speak as briefly, clearly, truthfully, and relevantly as possible (see Cotterell and Turner 259–66). When you flout any of these maxims, you are making a point. My son detects the true utterance meaning of my sentence because he knows (1) I do not normally make such an uninvited interjection while watching TV (flouting Grice's criterion of relevance), and (2) I do not particularly admire his back, far less the sweaty T-shirt he is wearing (additionally flouting Grice's criterion of truth). So he knows I *must* mean something else. And the *context* provides the meaning: he has just stood in front of me and his back obscures my view.

The *most* significant contribution to the utterance meaning of a sentence, or of *any* discourse, however long, is made by what is called its (shared) "presupposition pools": the information, conventions, views, or understandings that the writer/speaker feels *no* need specifically to state, because one can assume they are common assumption. Arguably, most of our normal discourse rests on unstated information (see Cotterell and Turner 90–97; Green and Turner 47–52). For example, Mark's brief sentence "And they crucified him" (15:24) does not need him to explain to his readers that it means they executed Jesus in the most public and degrading way possible. They nailed him naked to a cross-tree, a way usually reserved for the lowest form of political enemy. Mark can assume that everyone in the Roman Empire is aware of that form of execution (see further below).

Utterance Meaning at the Level of the Paragraph/Pericope

The basic semantic unit in *all* our communication is the *paragraph*, rather than the sentence. What makes a paragraph is semantic cohesion and appropriate "closure." A paragraph "talks" about a "concept" (an event or a topic) and closes in a way that says to the reader, "move on!" This sort of change is probably most obvious in the Gospels. For example, Luke 4:14–30 is a programmatic passage about Jesus' teaching in Nazareth. The opening (4:14–15) has Jesus return to Galilee from his trial in the wilderness. The incident itself epitomizes his central teaching (4:18–19, 21). It closes with "he went . . . on his way." So the reader naturally switches to a new expectation. In the NT letters paragraphing is not quite so easy to detect. But, for example, Phil. 2:5–11 seems to be a semantically distinct portion that some regard as a pre-Pauline hymn, precisely because it seems not quite to fit the cotext, but to be a digression from it. In Galatians, the text of 1:18–24 is marked off, as a paragraph, by the initial "then" of 1:18 and the new beginning "then" of 2:1 (NRSV). But other paragraphs are marked by their relatively sharp change from the previous unit (e.g., "I am astonished . . ." in Gal. 1:6; etc.). *Within* the paragraph, meaning is essentially provided by linguistic markers indicating sense relationships between the various "propositions" advanced, in the same way as it is within a sentence (for how this is analyzed, see Cotterell and Turner, ch. 6).

Utterance Meaning and Cotext

In linguistics, the term "cotext" has a usefully specialized sense. It means the total verbal "text" immediately and uniquely around the unit under consideration. Such cotext may help us understand the text in question, where its meaning is problematic. For example, some scholars take Luke 4:17–21 to mean the Spirit on Jesus is purely the "Spirit of prophecy," and has nothing to do with healing or other works of power. Others would point out the "cotextual" evidence of such passages as Luke 7:21–23 and Acts 10:38 to suggest that Luke intentionally attributes Jesus' healing miracles to the Spirit. In the case of Rom. 7:7–25, the cotext (7:4–6 and 8:1–4) strongly suggests this element is a parenthesis in Paul's argument. A cotext establishes its own "world" and expects you to read its text within the worldview that it presents: real or imaginary.

Utterance Meaning and Context

"Context," as opposed to "cotext," refers to the outside world—the real one out there (or at least as we perceive it)! So while the cotext of Rev. 3:14–22 is about other churches in the area west of Turkey, the "context" is more specific. The town of Laodicea was between Hierapolis, which has hot cleaning and healing waters, and Colossae, which has cold refreshing streams. The water supply to the then newly industrialized Laodicea was piped in from several miles away. As a result it was like lukewarm sludge: it clogged the pipes, and was just fit to be spewed out. So Rev. 3:14–22, in its real context, unfavorably compares the church supply of that city with the healing warm waters and the refreshing cool ones of neighboring towns. The point is that the Laodicean church neither refreshes nor heals. The church would undoubtedly have hoped the risen Lord would compare it with the city's rich banking facilities or its famous eye salves. Instead, with deep irony, the Lord says they need to come to *him* for gold and eye salve, and he compares their works not with any of the city's strengths but with its most prominent weakness: its notorious water supply!

There is a fundamental difference between the variety of meanings any particular sentence "may" have, and what the same sentence definitely and concretely does actually mean when uttered by a particular person in a specified context.

Utterance Meaning and Argument

Theology has often been dominated by what is called the "argument" of an author. But it must be noted that most biblical books are not "argument(s)" in any formal sense. The large proportion is actually *narrative*, or "*story*," depicting the "world" within which we live, and thereby implicitly or explicitly providing strong indications of how we should live within it. When scholars talk about the "argument" of Gen. 1–3, they are actually using that word as a very specialized and potentially misleading metaphor. They mean that the "story" narrated in those chapters is deliberately constructed so as (polemically) to contrast with the competing global stories of Near Eastern mythologies. When we are dealing with the narratival "histories" (including the Gospels and Acts), it is better to elucidate the utterance meaning in terms of "development of themes/ characters," than to speak of the "argument" of such works. The Psalms, Wisdom literature, the prophetic books, and the Apocalypse all *contain* arguments, but we need to analyze them with the tools of "Discourse Analysis" (see below), not as "argument." For example, anyone who tried to state the "argument" of Job by appeal to the many arguments of his "comforters" would find oneself utterly unwound in the last chapter, where God essentially says they were wrong. Similarly, the Psalms contain arguments but are not themselves arguments: indeed, their utterance meaning is perhaps deliberately left *open* so that users may take them over to express their *own* circumstances, feelings, and worship.

The writings that come formally closest to real argument are Romans and Galatians, and it is probably the historical centrality of these, in the thinking of the church, that has led scholars to speak of them and of other epistolary writings as "arguments." But we need to note that most Pauline letters are *not* primarily argument: for example, Philippians, 1–2 Thessalonians, and 1–2 Corinthians are simply multitheme friendship letters (see esp. Reed); Philemon is a typical "request letter"; Ephesians is a celebratory exhortation. Even such a "logical" letter as Paul's to the church in Rome is essentially not a brick-on-brick argument—not *even* in 1:17–3:31, where the apostle is rhetorically most tight (see Moores). Rather, Paul normally works more "as an artist, who covers the whole canvas quickly with very broad strokes and then returns to fill in the details" (Seifrid 107). The whole of the letter could be seen as a recurrent exploration of the themes adumbrated in 1:1–6, and, at a different level, chapters 9–11 may be analyzed as a more specific discussion of the apostle's claims made in 3:1–8, and so on.

What is nevertheless perhaps fundamentally helpful about speaking of the "argument" and of its contribution to the understanding of "utterance meaning" is that it suggests a situationally conditioned, deep and very *deliberate* coherence between the various parts of the discourse. The parts may together constitute an internally coherent "message," even if not precisely an "argument."

Discourse Analysis and Utterance Meaning

Discourse analysis is a branch of the more general discipline of semantic linguistics, methodologically devoted to elucidating how spoken or written "texts" (whether "one-liners" or whole books) signify "meaning" to readers/hearers (see Cotterell and Turner; Hurford and Heasely; Brown and Yule; Halliday and Hasan; Reed; et al.). Surprisingly, it is largely ignored by biblical scholars, for whom the discipline should (arguably)

be *central*. There are essentially two main (and entirely complementary) divisions in academic discourse analysis. One, "text-linguistics," examines texts in terms of the strictly *internal* markers of textual meaning indicated in the actual wording: the explicit or implicit verbal indications of argument, indications of "cohesion," of development of themes, of carefully parallel structuring, of deixis (indications like "here," "those people"), or whatever (see Porter and Carson; Porter and Reed). The other, "pragmatics," deals more with how utterances are (expected to be) understood to *function* in the world in which they are spoken/written, including the hermeneutically quite important theoretical area of speech-act theory (on which, see the related article, and Alston). From the perspective of text-linguistics, the quite complex sentence of Eph. 1:3–14 (Greek) can fairly objectively be divided into a cascading pattern of shorter and dependent strophes, each with similar structure marked by (e.g.) a main participle, qualifying "according to" clauses, the repetition of some variant of "to the praise of his glorious grace," and so on. From the perspective of pragmatics, however, Eph. 1:3–14 is not merely a "statement" of Paul's own blessing of God, but functionally also *counts as* a deliberate "invocation" corporately to share in the same eulogy, when Paul's letter is publicly read in and to the congregation. That is its contextual utterance meaning, and, more important, that is (arguably) the utterance meaning of the same passage in its canonical context, which thus addresses us today.

See also Concept; Etymology; Language, Grammar and Syntax; Language, Linguistics

Bibliography

Alston, W. *Illocutionary Acts and Sentence Meaning.* Cornell University Press, 2000; Barr, J. *The Semantics of Biblical Language.* Oxford University Press, 1961; Brown, G., and G. Yule. *Discourse Analysis.* Cambridge University Press, 1983; Cotterell, P., and M. Turner. *Linguistics and Biblical Interpretation.* InterVarsity, 1989; Green, J., and M. Turner, eds. *Between Two Horizons.* Eerdmans, 2000; Halliday, M. A. K., and R. Hasan. *Language, Context and Text.* Oxford University Press, 1989; Hoehner, H. *Ephesians.* Baker, 2002; Hurford, J., and B. Heasley. *Semantics.* Cambridge University Press, 1983; Moores, J. *Wrestling with Rationality in Paul.* SNTSMS. Cambridge University Press, 1995; Porter, S. Ch. 20 in *Idioms of the Greek New Testament.* Sheffield Academic Press, 1992; idem. *Verbal Aspect in the Greek New Testament.* Lang, 1989; Porter, S., and D. A. Carson, eds. *Discourse Analysis and Other Topics in Biblical Greek.* JSNTS 170. Sheffield Academic Press, 1995; Porter, S., and J. Reed, eds. *Discourse Analysis and the New Testament.* JSNTS

170. Sheffield Academic Press, 1999; Reed, J. *A Discourse Analysis of Philippians*. JSNTS 136. Sheffield Academic Press, 1997; Seifrid, M. "Unrighteous by Faith: Apostolic Proclamation in Romans 1:18–3:20." Pages 105–45 in *Justification and Variegated Nomism*, ed. D. A. Carson, P. O'Brien, and M. Seifrid. Mohr/Siebeck, 2004; Vanhoozer, K. *Is There a Meaning in This Text?* Zondervan, 1998; Ward, T. *Word and Supplement*. Oxford University Press, 2002; Wolterstorff, N. *Divine Discourse*. Cambridge University Press, 1995.

Max Turner

V

Validity   *See* Exegesis; Hermeneutics; Logic; Meaning; Proof Text

Vanhoozer, Kevin   *See* Speech-Act Theory; Theological Hermeneutics, Contemporary

Violence

Violence as a Theological Issue

Disagreement over the justifiability of violence often goes back to different ways of defining or describing violence. Violence is perhaps best defined as "an act which *causes injury* to the life, property, or person of a human being" (Burt 162). As such, violence can be divine or human, physical or nonphysical, personal or institutional, incidental or structural. By this definition—one commonly used or at least assumed—an ethical stance of absolute nonviolence would require the renunciation of all right to cause any kind of injury to human beings. Such a position would imply the rejection of all punishment and of all coercion or force, ranging from military intervention to economic blockades, punishments, and enforcing speed limits (since these all injure people in some fashion, either physically or nonphysically). Therefore, we have two options: If we wish to legitimize any of these kinds of activities ethically, we must insist that some violence can be justified. If we are unwilling to do that, we are forced to employ a different definition of violence (for example, one that defines it as causing *excessive* injury or as *unjustifiable* injury). In either case, we recognize that it can sometimes be morally justified to cause some kind of injury. Using the common definition given above, the conclusion must be that most people recognize that violence can sometimes be morally justified.

Many Christians, of course, do not recognize the right to violence and so tend to define it (whether consciously or subconsciously) by qualifying the kind of injury that a particular activity causes. Although philosophical and theological issues surrounding violence have resurfaced with particular intensity over the last few decades, theological reflection on and objections to violence go back to the early church. The second-century heretic, Marcion, is well known for his rejection of divine violence. To protect God's moral integrity, he sharply distinguished between the violent creator God of the OT and the peaceful God of the NT. Some of the early church's allegorizing hermeneutics (particularly in Clement and Origen) tied in with their fears of attributing violence to God. Several of the church fathers rejected the idea that God used violence in order to accomplish human redemption (Irenaeus; *Epistle to Diognetus*; Gregory of Nyssa). Many in the early church rejected the use of the sword, at least in a literal sense, and in the sixteenth century, the Radical Reformation continued this tradition of disavowing military violence.

Several contemporary developments have resulted in renewed awareness of the pervasive character of the issue of violence and of its problematic nature. First, hermeneutical theory has emphasized the ubiquity of violence. Friedrich Nietzsche's insistence that the "will to power" is the ultimate human drive, followed by Martin Heidegger's position that interpretation is always violent, have left deep traces in recent postmodern philosophy. One of the most influential scholars in this regard is Emmanuel Lévinas, who has seriously critiqued the Western metaphysical tradition for its preoccupation with issues of being (ontology) instead of ethics. Lévinas argues that such imposition of rational categories on the external world implies a penchant for totality rather than infinity: in a totalizing fashion we have tended to interpret the world in ways that conform to our own standards, thereby doing violence to the integrity of others. Lévinas demands that we cease such attempts to reshape the world in our own image, and that instead we take our starting point in the infinity or absolute transcendence of the other. In this way, we would learn to respect their alterity and come to a renewed appreciation of hospitality: "The other facing me makes me responsible for him/her, and this responsibility has no limits" (Lévinas, *Totality*, 194). Of course, such radical or boundary-less hospitality implies that others may, in turn, violate my personal integrity. Such interruption, Lévinas is forced to acknowledge, is a form of "good violence" that stems from my absolute obligation toward the other (Lévinas, *Otherwise*, 43).

Jacques Derrida's understanding of deconstruction draws on Lévinas. In reaction against the history of the religious violence of the determinate messianic religions, Derrida wants to avoid violence by means of the demand for absolute or unconditional hospitality. At the same time, however, he is aware that this indeterminate messianic future remains unrealizable (always still to come, *à venir*; Boersma, "Irenaeus"). Derrida's view that violence and narcissism are embedded in the very nature of things leaves little room for a possible future of peace (Smith) and has popularized the notion that we live in a "tragically violent" universe.

Second, minority voices have drawn attention to the violence and oppression that have been used to subdue them. In particular, the heritage of the West (e.g., in crusades, colonization, globalization) and of the church (e.g., regarding women, homosexuals, heretics) is often criticized for complicity in violence (e.g., Cone; Ray; Snyder; Weaver). Third, something of a theological consensus appears to be building that the use of military force is never a good way to solve our problems. Not only traditional Anabaptists but also the Roman Catholic Church and mainline denominations have spoken out forcefully in recent decades against the use of all military force (except, perhaps, for humanitarian reasons).

Theological Approaches to Violence

Among some of the most influential theological approaches to violence are the following:

Jesus as Example of Nonviolence. The tradition of nonviolence, most ably represented by John Howard Yoder and Stanley Hauerwas, regards Jesus as the ultimate revelation of God and as such the peaceful social and political model for us to imitate. Some, closely allying themselves with this tradition, would nonetheless insist that while God does indeed engage in violence, this does not necessarily make it right for human beings to do so; and that while it may not always be possible to avoid violence, when we do engage in it, we should not seek a religious legitimation for it (Volf 301–6). The strength of these approaches is that they take seriously God's revelation in Jesus Christ and refuse to limit his significance to matters of personal salvation. Moreover, by taking the

"politics of Jesus" as the ethical starting point, this tradition has tended to generate creative peacebuilding activities. Some of the problems with this approach, however, are the sharp disjunction that sometimes results between the OT and the NT. This may produce a one-sided picture of Jesus as nonviolent (cf., e.g., Mark 11:15; Matt. 8:12; 11:24; Luke 7:36–50; 11:37–52) and a tendency to oppose the Christian faith to politics and cultural involvement.

The Cross as Unmasking the Scapegoat Mechanism. René Girard's theory of mimetic desire has become quite influential in the last few decades. Girard argues that a scapegoat mechanism lies at the origin of all human culture: by imitating other people's desires, we end up in a mimetic spiral of confrontation that can only be broken when we substitute an innocent scapegoat and direct our violence against this scapegoat. Subsequent to the murder of the victim, we maintain the peace through ritualistic sacrifices, mythological accounts, and religious taboos. Girard sees Christ as the ultimate scapegoat, whose nonresistance and resurrection expose the violence of the scapegoat mechanism. Despite his genius and popularity, I believe Girard errs by rejecting (or, perhaps, radically reinterpreting) all traditional atonement models, by placing violence rather than peace at the origin of human culture (cf. Milbank, *Theology*, 395–96), and by insisting on absolute nonviolence as a distinct Christian possibility.

Participation in Divine Peace. John Milbank, as the most prominent spokesman for Radical Orthodoxy, believes that the violent nihilism of modern and postmodern accounts of reality stems from theological deviations in the thirteenth century. Starting with Duns Scotus, theologians began to separate nature and grace, and to grant a degree of autonomy to the former. The result was the loss of a participatory vision in which all of nature and all of humanity shared in the abundance of God's peace. Like Yoder and Hauerwas, Milbank regards Jesus' way of life as one founded on "non-rivalry, non-retaliation and mutual sharing" (Milbank, *Word*, 312), and he insists that the church is to continue Jesus' life of forgiveness. Milbank argues that his participatory vision is built on an "ontology of peace." Despite his apprehension about coercive power, however, Milbank realizes the need for at least some coercion for pedagogical reasons. But he always regards such use of violence as tragic. Milbank's theological opposition to modern and postmodern accounts of reality is eminently insightful. At the same time, his ambiguity on the justifiability of violence remains unfortunate and ultimately does not answer questions regarding the relationship between violence and peace.

Opposing Authorial Intent. Phyllis Trible, in dealing with what she terms "texts of terror," and Chris Heard, in his account of divine violence in Habakkuk, both insist that at times we need to read against the intentions of the narrator and the plot of Scripture. These postmodern readings of the text end up insisting that we need to see ethical obligations toward those whom the text has forced outside the margins. While such deconstructive approaches allow us to have a compassionate eye for the weak and marginalized in society, this comes at the cost of a loss of normative standards by which we determine which cause to take up and which one to reject. If Scripture loses its normative status in judging human violence, we are left with our own desire or will to power, which hardly represents a higher moral standard.

Augustinian Just-War Theory. The traditional Augustinian understanding insists that there are certain circumstances under which it is just to go to war (*jus ad bellum*), and certain criteria that determine whether a war is fought justly (*jus in bello*). The former criteria are those of a just cause, the right authority, the right intention, proportionality of ends, and last resort; the latter are those of the proportionality of means and the noncombatant protection/immunity (Johnson). Despite the fact that much of today's theological consensus seems to oppose the Augustinian view, and despite the difficulties in determining whether a particular act of violence fulfills the criteria, the Augustinian view rightly insists that violence should not be universally condemned, and that it can be redemptive in character. As we see below, the theology of Scripture appears to operate on the principle that under certain circumstances divine (as well as human) violence is justified.

Divine Violence: Election and Atonement

Biblically, the pervasive character of divine violence seems hard to avoid. Several scholars have recently pointed out that both the OT and the NT present God, at least some of the time, as a violent God (Boyd; Longman and Reid). This is not to say that, according to Scripture, God is a God of wrath in the same way that he is a God of love. Rather, it seems that according to the Bible, God expresses wrath precisely because he is passionately committed to the redemption of the world (Peels 293). Divine violence, in other words, accompanies divine redemption.

This is evident particularly in the two areas where divine violence appears most problematic: predestination and atonement theology. In Reformed theology, predestination has traditionally been interpreted as God's dual decree from eternity to save some people for eternal life (election) and to condemn others to eternal death (reprobation). Calvinism has often been criticized for the arbitrary divine violence that this framework appears to entail. Many scholars today would argue that election is better interpreted as a historical act of God to choose his people Israel for the sake of the world, and that we today are included in this election when we are in Christ as the representative of Israel (Wright). The latter interpretation regards election as a historical and corporate act of God. It does not, however, obviate all violence: the destruction of the nations around Israel is still the result of God's election of Israel. For example, the classic election passage of Deut. 7:6–8 is preceded by a passage insisting on the destruction of the nations around Israel by means of a ban (*kherem*) (7:2–5), leading several scholars to reject the violence of the Bible's election theology (e.g., Schwartz). Yet it seems impossible to remove all divine violence from election theology. Likewise, in atonement theology, each of the three traditional models regard God as involved in the death of Christ. In the classic or Christus Victor model, God is seen as either making a deal with the devil (paying him a ransom for the freedom of human beings), as deceiving him (tricking the devil into thinking that Jesus was merely human), or as actually fighting the principalities and powers. In the penal substitutionary model, God punishes his Son for the sins of the world. And in the moral influence model, God sacrifices his Son to evoke a human response of love. As a result, contemporary attempts to present nonviolent models of the atonement can only be successful by abandoning each of the traditional models (e.g., Weaver).

We can legitimately use several strategies to alleviate the difficulties. As noted above, it is not possible to avoid making decisions about the use of violence (causing injury) in concrete situations. In other words, we would be hard pressed to argue that all use of divine violence is necessarily wrong. Scripture itself gives indications of some of the criteria justifying the violence accompanying divine election in the OT: (1) Election is meant to safeguard the practice of monotheism as expressed in the Shema of Deut. 6:4–6 (cf. 7:3–4;

20:16–18). (2) The ban of destruction is meant to punish the nations for their immorality (Gen. 15:16; Deut. 9:5). (3) God's election seems to favor Israel because of her marginalized status (Deut. 7:7; 8:17–18; 9:6). (4) God's harsh treatment of the nations is not restricted to them; he can apply the same to his own people if need be (Lev. 18:24–28; Deut. 31:16–18). (5) And perhaps most significantly, God's election of Israel was missiological in character in that it was ultimately intended for the salvific benefit also of the nations (Gen. 12:3). None of these five considerations gives a comprehensively adequate justification of the violence of "reprobation" that accompanies God's election of his people. They do, however, give some insight into the mystery of God's love, by which he also judges it just to engage in violence.

Much the same appears to be the case with God's involvement in the cross. The traditional atonement models quite rightly emphasize God's involvement not just in the life but also in the death of Jesus (Acts 2:23; 4:27–28). We must recall that the question is not How can *any* divine violence (*any* causing of injury) be justified? but How can *this* particular act of divine violence (*this* particular injury) be justified? The early church father Irenaeus interpreted Christ's work of redemption in terms of recapitulation, meaning that Christ represented, faithfully retraced, and so healed the sinful and broken existence of human life (Boersma, "Redemptive"). N. T. Wright, using a similar imagery, reads Christ's work of redemption in terms of reconstitution, meaning that Christ is the one who in representative fashion retraces the life, death, and resurrection of the nation Israel. Although punishment is part of this picture (with Christ on the cross suffering the exilic curse of the law), it is punishment as a last resort (not each of Israel's transgressions leads to exile or to the cross). And it is punishment for the sake of restoration, healing, or shalom (restorative justice; Marshall 69). In short, we need to bracket our moral reservations regarding particular divine acts of violence because of our inability to comprehend God's right intention and the proportionality of ends, or put differently, because we cannot fully grasp the glory of the resurrection life (cf. Rom. 11:33). God's right to violence is not ours but is his to judge. Whether or not particular human acts of violence are justifiable depends on how they fit the Augustinian criteria.

The inevitably difficult questions, particularly surrounding the right intention and the proportionality of ends, can only be tentatively answered today; the ultimate justification of human violence can only be found in the resurrection. It is ultimately the resurrection glory that determines whether this or that particular act of violence has truly been redemptive and therefore justifiable.

See also Atonement

Bibliography

Boersma, H. "Irenaeus, Derrida and Hospitality: On the Eschatological Overcoming of Violence." *Modern Theology* 19 (2003): 163–80; idem. "Redemptive Hospitality in Irenaeus: A Model for Ecumenicity in a Violent World." *ProEccl* 11 (2002): 207–26; Boyd, G. *God at War.* InterVarsity, 1997; Burt, D. *Friendship and Society.* Eerdmans, 1999; Cone, J. *God of the Oppressed.* Rev. ed. Orbis, 1997; Derrida, J. *Of Hospitality,* trans. R. Bowlby. Stanford University Press, 2000; Girard, R. *The Girard Reader,* ed. J. Williams. Crossroad, 1996; Hauerwas, S. *The Hauerwas Reader,* ed. J. Berkman and M. Cartwright. Duke University Press, 2001; Heard, C. "Hearing the Children's Cries: Commentary, Deconstruction, Ethics, and the Book of Habakkuk." *Semeia* 77 (1997): 75–89; Johnson, J. T. *Morality and Contemporary Warfare.* Yale University Press, 1999; Lévinas, E. *Otherwise than Being,* trans. A. Lingis. Duquesne University Press, 1998; idem. *Totality and Infinity,* trans. A. Lingis. Duquesne University Press, 1969; Longman, T., and D. Reid. *God Is a Warrior.* Zondervan, 1995; Marshall, C. *Beyond Retribution.* Eerdmans/Lime Grove House, 2001; Milbank, J. *Theology and Social Theory.* Blackwell, 1993; idem. *The Word Made Strange.* Blackwell, 1997; Peels, H. G. L. *The Vengeance of God,* trans. W. Koopmans. Brill, 1995; Ray, D. K. *Deceiving the Devil.* Pilgrim, 1998; Schwartz, R. *The Curse of Cain.* University of Chicago Press, 1997; Smith, J. K. A. *The Fall of Interpretation.* InterVarsity, 2000; Snyder, T. R. *The Protestant Ethic and the Spirit of Punishment.* Eerdmans, 2001; Trible, P. *Texts of Terror.* Fortress, 1984; Volf, M. *Exclusion and Embrace.* Abingdon, 1996; Weaver, J. D. *The Nonviolent Atonement.* Eerdmans, 2001; Wright, N. T. *Jesus and the Victory of God.* Vol. 2 of *Christian Origins and the Question of God.* Fortress, 1996; Yoder, J. H. *The Politics of Jesus.* 2d ed. Eerdmans/Paternoster, 1994.

Hans Boersma

Virgin Birth   *See* Infancy Narratives

Virtue

There seem to be two basic ways of thinking about the relationship between virtue and theological interpretation of Scripture. The first has to do with the ways in which theological interpretation aids in the cultivation of virtue. The second has to do with the ways in which virtue aids in the practice of theological interpretation. I will call the former virtue-through-interpretation and the latter virtue-in-interpretation.

Before discussing each of these, however, it will be important to say a few words about the ways in which virtue might be understood. In fact, most of the scholarly literature in this area usually speaks of the virtues rather than virtue in the singular (MacIntyre; Hauerwas and Pinches). One might say that the person of virtue is someone who successfully displays the virtues over the course of his or her life. The virtues can be thought of, then, as those habits of seeing, feeling, thinking, and acting that, when exercised in the right ways and at the right times, will enhance one's prospects of both recognizing, moving toward, and attaining one's proper end. Thus, all questions of virtue and the virtues depend on prior answers to questions about the proper end of human life. Diverse and conflicting accounts of the proper end of human life will generate diverse and conflicting accounts of the virtues.

Virtue through Interpretation

The role of virtue in the theological interpretation of Scripture must be closely tied to the ends and purposes for which Christians are called to read Scripture (Fowl). Those ends and purposes are themselves tied to the ultimate end of the Christian life. When it comes to articulating a concise statement of the end of life in Christ, the Westminster Confession speaks in terms of glorifying God and enjoying God forever. Thomas Aquinas speaks in terms of ever-deepening friendship with God. Eastern Orthodox Christians tend to speak of being drawn up into the life of God. These formulations are really much less different than they may first appear. God's purpose in creating humans is that we might enjoy eternal fellowship with God. Despite the damages of sin, God has enabled this purpose to be fulfilled in and through the life, death, and resurrection of Jesus. In Christ, Christians can ultimately be brought to their proper end. Thus, all Christian groups assume that the followers of Jesus are called into ever-deeper communion with God.

The Christian life, then, is a journey, guided and enabled by the Holy Spirit, into ever-deeper communion with God. If this, or something much like it, is the chief end of life in Christ, then it is not surprising that Christians have traditionally considered love (or *agapē* or charity) as the primary virtue. Of course, Scripture itself confirms this in such passages as Matt. 22:36–40, where Jesus affirms that the greatest commandments are those calling believers to comprehensive, self-giving love of God and neighbor; and 1 Cor. 13:13, where Paul is seen to identify love as the foremost virtue.

In this light, Scripture plays a dual role. It articulates the shape and nature of the virtues. Further, as Christians interpret and embody their interpretations of Scripture, Scripture becomes a vehicle to help in the formation of virtues so that Christians are moved ever closer to their true end. Perhaps the clearest statement of the relationship between scriptural interpretation and the formation of virtue is found in Augustine's *On Christian Doctrine*. There Augustine emphasizes both Scripture's role as a vehicle to move Christians toward their true end, and that all true interpretation of Scripture must cultivate the double love of God and neighbor.

Virtue in Interpretation

Given that Christians are called to interpret Scripture as part of their ongoing journey into ever-deeper communion with God, it is not surprising that those who have grown and advanced in virtue will tend to be masterful interpreters of Scripture. This is not to deny that the novice or the outsider will sometimes offer superior interpretations of any particular text. Rather, it simply stands to reason that those who have advanced in the Christian life will tend to offer the best interpretations for those whose primary aim is to advance in the Christian life.

In particular, those who are well practiced at interpreting Scripture in ways that enhance the love of God and neighbor will tend to demonstrate just such love in the very act of interpretation. Such demonstrations of love will appear in the way one's own position is formulated and presented, and will particularly appear in the ways in which one deals with the arguments of others (Fowl). This becomes crucial in the present time, when Christians "see in a mirror dimly" (1 Cor. 13:12 NRSV). Short of the eschatological perfection of our knowledge of God, Christians should expect that their interpretation and embodiment of Scripture will be matters of debate, discussion, and argument. If such argument is to advance and enhance Christians' prospects of deeper communion with God, then Christians must manifest love as well as all other virtues in their interpretation of Scripture.

See also Love; Wisdom

Bibliography

Augustine. *On Christian Doctrine*, trans. D. Robertson. Macmillan, 1958; Fowl, S. *Engaging Scripture*. Blackwell, 1998; Hauerwas, S., and C. Pinches. *Christians among the Virtues*. University of Notre Dame Press, 1997; MacIntyre, A. *After Virtue*. 2d ed. University of

Notre Dame Press, 1984; Rogers, E. "How the Virtues of the Interpreter Presuppose and Perfect Hermeneutics: The Case of Thomas Aquinas." *JR* 76 (1996): 64–81; Thomas Aquinas. *Summa theologiae*, Pt. I–II, esp. qq. 49–70.

Stephen E. Fowl

Virtue Epistemology   *See* Epistemology; Theological Hermeneutics, Contemporary; Virtue; Wisdom

Vulgate   *See* Medieval Biblical Interpretation; Translation

W

War *See* Violence

Warrant

Warrant is that quality or quantity enough of which makes the difference between knowledge and mere true belief. Imagine that you ask me to guess which playing card you are holding and I correctly guess that it is the ace of clubs. I could not truly be said to have *known* that you held the ace of clubs. On the other hand, if you hold it up so that I can see it, then I can correctly be said to know it, since my belief that it is the ace of clubs is true and warranted by my experience of seeing it. But what precisely is warrant?

Until the 1960s the standard answer was "justification." Plato considers the definition of knowledge as true belief with a *"logos"* (*Theaet.* 201c–d; 202c). This definition, with *"logos"* understood in the sense of "justification," was adopted as standard for two and a half thousand years. What does it mean to be justified in believing a proposition? A justified belief is a belief that one cannot be blamed for holding. Some beliefs are not justified for particular believers in particular circumstances. For example, we might say that somebody today who believed that the Earth was flat was not justified in holding such a belief since there is abundant available evidence to the contrary. But a peasant who in the Middle Ages believed that the Earth was flat might have been justified in holding that false belief since there was not so much evidence available then to the nonscholar. Clearly, one can be justified in holding a false belief, since sometimes there can be a lot of deceptive evidence for a falsehood.

This account of warrant in terms of justification went unchallenged until the 1960s, when Edmund L. Gettier published his seminal paper, "Is Justified True Belief Knowledge?" He answered the question of his title with a resounding "No," putting forward cases of justified true belief that did not amount to knowledge. A simple example would be the following: I want to know what time it is, so I look at a clock. I see that it says it is noon, so I form the belief that it is noon. By a fluke the clock stopped exactly 24 hours previously, so my belief is true. But it is true by a fluke and does not qualify as knowledge, since it lacks warrant.

Most philosophers accepted that Gettier had disposed of the idea that warrant was justification, and so the search resumed for a more satisfactory analysis of warrant. In particular, there has been division between *internalists* and *externalists* over warrant: *internalists* claim that, whatever warrant is, it is something internal to the knower, a mental state of the knower. Historically, the leading example of internalism was classic foundationalism. This was the theory that a belief was warranted if it was either properly basic (not based on another belief, and did not have to be) or properly based on a belief that was itself warranted. A belief was properly basic if it was self-evident (e.g., the belief that two and two make four), incorrigible (e.g., the belief that I am now in pain), or evident to the senses (e.g., the belief that my lawn is green). All other beliefs, in order to be warranted, had to be deduced or induced from these. Recently, this theory has been rejected not just because of problems with Gettier-style counterexamples, but also because it has been seen to be self-referentially incoherent. In other words, the theory proclaims that belief in itself is not warranted.

Externalists, by contrast, claim that warrant is, at least in part, external to the knower: it is, at least in part, something outside the knower's mind. The most recent externalist idea to come onto the market is one of particular interest to Christians. This is Plantinga's idea, that a belief is warranted if and only if it is produced by a properly functioning mental faculty that is directed at truth. A cognitive faculty functions properly if and only if it functions as it was designed to do, and the matter of the design of a cognitive faculty is a matter that is external to the cognitive faculty itself. Most controversially of all, Plantinga claims that we have a "God module" or, as he calls it (following John Calvin), a *sensus divinitatis*. This is a cognitive faculty that is designed by God to produce beliefs in him. Plantinga applies the definition to the case of this faculty and concludes that we can know God exists if indeed he does, and our belief in him is produced by a properly functioning *sensus divinitatis*.

Plantinga goes further and argues that specifically Christian beliefs are warranted if they are true and if they are produced by what he calls, again following Calvin, the internal instigation of the Holy Spirit. So, for example, my belief in the teaching of the Bible may still be warranted if it is produced by the Holy Spirit (and is true), even if unbelieving scholars say that such beliefs cannot be derived from a strictly "scientific" historical-critical reading of the text. The Christian in the pew has a source of belief open to him or her that may not be open to the scholar. This notion of warrant as proper function, however, does not tell us in itself, of course, which particular beliefs are warranted when it comes to Bible interpretation or any other area of life.

See also Epistemology

Bibliography

Gettier, E. "Is Justified True Belief Knowledge?" *Analysis* 23 (1963): 121–23; Plantinga, A. "Two (or More) Kinds of Scripture Scholarship." Pages 81–116 in *Theology and Scriptural Imagination*, ed. L. G. Jones and J. Buckley. Blackwell, 1998; idem. *Warrant*. Oxford University Press, 1993; idem. *Warrant and Proper Function*. Oxford University Press, 1993; idem. *Warranted Christian Belief*. Oxford University Press, 1999; Plato. *Theaetetus*, trans. R. Waterfield. Penguin, 1987; Vanhoozer, K. Ch. 6 in *Is There a Meaning in This Text?* Zondervan, 1998.

Daniel Hill

Watson, Francis   *See* Theological Hermeneutics, Contemporary

Western Literature, the Bible and

It will be apparent that, from the earliest stages of Christian history, theological interpretation of Scripture has been the task not only of theologians in the formal sense, but also of fiction writers, poets, dramatists, and graphic artists. Just as from the eighteenth century certain Protestant theologies of original sin and the process of redemption and sanctification reveal the influence of Milton and Bunyan on the popular Christian mind, so too there is a kind of vernacular theology being done by novelists and filmmakers today. Like it or not, the Left Behind series of apocalyptic fictions, with their speculative and often eccentric Americanizations of biblical apocalyptic, are becoming formative for eschatology in many quarters of the contemporary church. Similarly, novels such as Dan Brown's *Da Vinci Code*, a calculated attack on the divinity of Jesus and an attempt to subvert the canonical Gospel narratives, are significant shapers of theological interpretation for many. Films such as *Jesus Christ Superstar*, *Jesus of Montreal*, *The Gospel of John*, and Mel Gibson's *The Passion of the Christ* are rather diverse. Yet each has an inherent theology, an informing conviction about the nature of God as revealed in Christ Jesus, which bids to inform (or deform) received understandings of Scripture, both in the church and in the dominant culture.

The role of the arts in relation to Scripture has generally been to interpret so as to enhance our sense of Scripture. In one respect Scripture, in which the language is generally terse and the narrative gaps frequent, may seem to invite this sort of imaginative elaboration. It has long been a tendency of Christian preaching to extrapolate somewhat speculatively upon the bare details of the text. But as with preaching, all such interpretative expansion entails a speculation informed by or productive of a theological position: fictive elaboration is typically predicated on some order of presumptive knowledge about the character of God and/or specific revelation concerning his purposes and action in history. Even putatively "playful" fictionalizing *supra scriptura* implies or makes explicit such predilections.

Thus, literature occasioned by a passage of Scripture becomes a "reading" (a *lectio*) of that Scripture, but one colored-in by a context and predisposition concerning the status of Scripture and the character of God as revealed in Scripture. For example, early Christian poets made much use of the erotic language of the Song of Solomon to allegorize the relationship between Christ as Bridegroom and the contemplative or mystically inclined poet as metonymically his bride. Thus, the resulting poem became a "love song" of the redeemed church—made poignant as well as intelligible because medieval theology, like some Jewish targums beforehand, had so "theologized" this Hebrew epithalamion. Certain songs of Bernard of Clairvaux (e.g., "Rosa sine spina") elaborate the allegory of the church as bride (Rev. 19–22), fusing it with the Annunciation to Mary (Luke 1) and the incarnation. In so doing, he lets Mary represent the gathered and expectant church, awaiting the fullness of its redemption in the Bridegroom's triumphant return to the Beloved. Similarly, the language of Thomas Aquinas in his "Adoro te devote," a eucharistic hymn, is replete with analogies to the marriage supper of the Lamb. The symbolic reach of the poet's language depends absolutely on the poet's typological reading of the OT in the light of the NT, and his anticipation that the *historia humanae salvationis* achieves its consummation in Christ the King's return for his bride. Many vernacular medieval lyricists adapt this language, as does Dante most famously in his *Paradiso*.

During the Middle Ages in Europe, the process of translation into vernacular languages was in itself a way of doing theology. In an English example, the Anglo-Saxon poet of "Genesis B," in a very loose paraphrase, treats the story of the fall. Along the way, he makes the conflict between God and Satan (much in the style of Job) central to his audience's understanding of the subversive temptation of Eve and Adam. His Satan is a strutting, arrogant exemplar of the "warrior hero" in the might-makes-right pagan Viking world, with which the audience is familiar. His purpose is to cause his audience, in the light of Christ, to deconstruct their notion of the "heroic," and to see the ruthless ambition of a crudely "Darwinian" politic as dark and demonic. So also Cynewuf, in "Christ and Satan," in which the temptation of Christ (Luke 4) reveals the overcoming strength of Christ to be expressed not in violence but in a firmly obedient understanding of the sovereign will of God. In the justly famous lyric "Dream of the Rood," this radical transposition of pagan notions of the heroic is further advanced. The poem presents the willingness to sacrifice oneself to death by torture—the utmost in repugnant shame for a Nordic culture—as essential to our understanding of what "almightig God" has done for us in Christ.

These examples, like the great medieval cycle dramas that vernacularize, paraphrase, and render dramatically the biblical narrative of human salvation (Genesis to Revelation), are all a species of theological interpretation of Scripture in which the text is more or less immediately present to the memory and imagination of the audience. The literary treatment is a kind of exposition, and the resulting text a free paraphrase in terms culturally comprehensible to medieval Europeans.

With the expansion of biblical translation of a more literal character, in England especially following Wycliffe and his heirs in the fourteenth and fifteenth centuries, other possibilities were occasioned. The printing of the Bible in translations by Tyndale, Coverdale, and eventually the committee who, under King James I, produced the 1611 Authorized Version, meant that the Bible itself could be read by laypeople *like a book*—or

better, perhaps, a library of books. The result was a rise in biblical literacy, especially in England, to levels unapproached anywhere in Europe or North America today (perhaps only among Christians in China is there anything now like it). This meant that writers no longer needed so much to paraphrase Scripture (though some Protestant playwrights, such as John Bale, continued to do so for polemical and theological purposes), but were free to *depend* upon it as a literary foundation upon which their own fictions might with more freedom build. What is "learned" allusion for us was, in effect, commonplace allusion for a Renaissance dramatist, and Shakespeare, Johnson, or Marlowe could count upon even the "groundlings" (unsophisticated spectators) to "get it."

Thus, when the possibly atheist divinity student Christopher Marlowe wrote his *Tragicall Historie of Doctor Faustus*, he could incorporate a high order of theological critique in his dramatization of a Wittenberg professor's pact with the devil and subsequent damnation. It would seem that Faustus, like his Wittenberg "colleague" Luther, sets a high premium on personal freedom, including freedom to interpret the Bible as he chooses—however erratically. Though he claims, among other accomplishments, to have mastered theology, his reading of certain passages theologically crucial to all sides of the Reformation debate is partial and willfully incomplete. "The reward of sinne is death," Faustus reads. "That's hard." But he fails to read the rest of the verse: "but the gift of God is eternal life through Jesus Christ our Lord" (Rom. 6:23 KJV). Then he flips the pages and reads, "If we say we have no sinne, we deceive ourselves, and there is no truth in us," and interjects without finishing the sentence, "Why then belike we must sinne, and so consequently die." On these grounds he rejects his calling as a theologian and proceeds to magic and sorcery. But the whole of his audience knows what he has left out: "If we confess our sins, he is faithful and just to forgive us our sins, and to cleanse us from all unrighteousness" (1 John 1:8–9 KJV). That is, they know Faustus has made a decision to foreclose on the grace held out to him, and that it was a real choice. Atheist or not, Marlowe has elaborated in his play a sound traditional soteriology and, in heightening the horror of Faustus's damnation, has made a strong theological case for the NT view of graceless consequences. Much the same sort of reflection is invited by Oscar Wilde in his novel *The Picture of Dorian Gray*.

In a similar way Milton depends upon familiarity with the Bible (not merely Genesis) to allow him in *Paradise Lost* to write a theodicy, "to justifie the ways of God to man." He seems to have read the Anglo-Saxon "Genesis B" and to have understood its point about the inferiority of the triumphantly egotistical Satan to the self-effacing and obedient-unto-death Christ. The use of poetry or fiction to conduct a form of Christian apologetic is not, moreover, without high literary practice in more recent times. C. S. Lewis in his space trilogy, *Till We Have Faces* (notably in the Miltonesque *Voyage to Venus*), and in the Narnia tales for children, and also J. R. R. Tolkien in *The Lord of the Rings*—these works similarly engage in apologetics, that species of theological reflection that embraces theodicy and soteriology alike. They can depend much less upon biblical literacy than Reformation-era writers such as Marlowe, John Donne, or even eighteenth-century and nineteenth-century authors such as Samuel Johnson, Henry Fielding, Charlotte Brontë, or the Brownings. Hence, they tend to build in their theological interpretation through combinations of symbol, allegory, and deft, intermittent verbal recollection. One sees this also, for example, in G. M. Hopkins, Charles Williams, T. S. Eliot, W. H. Auden, R. S. Thomas, Richard Wilbur, and playwright/screenwriter Horton Foote (*Tender Mercies*).

Occasionally allegory emerges as a means of "coding" theology for those "within," while leaving the possibility of a less-textual understanding for those "without" the community of informed Christian faith. This technique, highly developed in the Middle Ages as a means of reaching readers of varying stages of spiritual and theological maturity, is particularly exemplified in Dante, in whose *Commedia* is found also a kind of political allegory (or "coding"). For Dante, even where the Bible is not immediately visible in the weave of his text, it is a kind of "absent text" upon which his own poem is not greater than a "present gloss" or, as we might say, a situated reading. In a Christian perspective, all literature, for Dante, is "chiosata da altro testo," glossed by another text (the Bible), until the ending of time.

In our time it may be that, for works such as C. S. Lewis's Narnia tales or even (though less allegorically) Tolkien's trilogy, the reading and "theological understanding" projected from the works for Christian readers is either invisible or, when made visible, entirely repugnant to secularist readers who enjoy the works on other grounds. This "two-level" option is not so available to readers of John Bunyan's great allegory, *Pilgrim's Progress*. Its secular readers and scholars

(and they are many) are obliged to read the Bible and wrestle with Bunyan's theology to comprehend and appreciate this book. After the English Bible, it is probably still the most influential work of literature in the English language.

No account of the theological interpretation of Scripture in Western literature (even one so introductory and partial as this must be) could be balanced without noting the contribution literary figures have made to a revisionist, secularizing, or even atheist antitheology. To take only two examples: William Blake's elaborate myth is an antitheology (*Marriage of Heaven and Hell, Four Zoas*), even in some respects an infernal reading of both Scripture and earlier literary theologizing built upon it. Famously, he derides Milton for "being of the devil's party without knowing it," and praises Milton's Satan in *Paradise Lost* for being in fact the true hero of the poem, more admirable than Jehovah (contra, e.g., "Genesis B"). Blake is unable to accept that the new Jerusalem is of God, not man, and must, as in Revelation and Milton's *Paradise Regained*, descend to earth at *God's* choosing. He demands (in "Jerusalem") that the new Jerusalem be built now, by man, in "England's green and pleasant land." In this, he presages many a modern theologian (some of whom, ever since Cotton Mather, might substitute "America").

Another figure at the threshold of modern literary studies is Matthew Arnold. For Arnold, literary theory and criticism was a substitute for theology, and great secular literature, in effect, a substitute for Scripture. In *Literature and Dogma* (1873), *God and the Bible* (1875), and *St. Paul and Protestantism* (1870) in particular, he sets out to demythologize (in almost precisely the same fashion as, later, would Rudolf Bultmann) the scriptural account of salvation and its representation of God. In so doing, he was influenced by Blake and the Romantics, particularly Shelley, but also (as were Coleridge and George Eliot) by German idealist philosophy and rationalist biblical criticism. Both Blake and Arnold are foundational for that species of contemporary literary criticism that sees itself as an enlightened substitute for a naively orthodox, Bible-based theology. This kind of "demythologizing" or "detheologizing" criticism of literature takes many forms, but in a figure like Northrop Frye (*A Fearful Symmetry* [1947], *The Secular Scripture* [1976], *The Great Code* [1981]), the confluence of Blake, Arnold, and Bultmann is transparent. Similarly, in Terry Eagleton, a leading British theorist and a prominent Marxist, a line from the skepticism of Enlightenment Catholic thinkers to modern post-Catholic commentators is direct, and his own work is essentially a secularized version of liberation theology (e.g., *Introduction to Literature* [1982], *After Theory* [2003]). Frye was at one time ordained to the Methodist ministry, and Eagleton to the Roman Catholic priesthood. It might reasonably be argued that today the effort to counter orthodox Christian theological content in the canon of Western literature is at least as pronounced among critics and theorists as among the more sensational writers of fiction and filmmakers.

But that would be to tell only part of the story. Interest in the spiritual and theological dimensions of human reflection has, if anything, sharply increased in the past two decades. This is abundantly evident to the filmgoer and novel-reader alike. It is also clear that in much of this art there is bad theology. In some, there is arrestingly orthodox theological interpretation of Scripture, often indirect and imaginatively arresting to a degree that takes a thoughtful reader, on faithful trajectories, back into the Scriptures themselves most profitably. Some of the recent films on the life and passion of Christ, and novels—such as Michael O'Brien's *Father Elijah* (1999), or Lief Enger's *Peace Like a River* (2001), or short stories such as Wendell Berry's volume *Fidelity* (1992)— move us into a realm of theological reflection. Their orthodoxy is as refreshing as it is radical—which makes it refreshing. A brief article of this nature can do little but hint at the riches of theological reflection contained in so many works, most necessarily unmentioned here, both past and present. The appended bibliography will assist in opening up a wealth of resources for theological reflection.

Bibliography

Bercovitch, S. *The American Jeremiad*. University of Wisconsin Press, 1978; Brantley, R. *Locke, Wesley, and the Method of English Romanticism*. University of Florida Press, 1984; Damrosch, L. *God's Plot and Man's Stories*. University of Chicago Press, 1985; idem. *Symbol and Truth in Blake's Myth*. Princeton University Press, 1980; Fisch, H. *The Biblical Presence in Shakespeare, Milton, and Blake*. Clarendon, 1999; Frei, H. *The Eclipse of Biblical Narrative*. Yale University Press, 1974; Frye, N. *The Great Code*. Routledge, 1982; Gunn, G., ed. *The Bible and American Arts and Letters*. Fortress, 1983; Jeffrey, D. L., ed. *A Dictionary of Biblical Tradition in English Literature*. Eerdmans, 1992; idem. *Houses of the Interpreter*. Baylor University Press, 2003; idem. *People of the Book*. Eerdmans, 1996; Prickett, S. *Words and the Word*. Cambridge University Press, 1986; Steiner, G. *Real Presences*. University of Chicago Press, 1989; Ziolkowski, T. *Fictional Transfigurations of Jesus*. Princeton University Press, 1972.

David Lyle Jeffrey

Wisdom

The theme of wisdom bears on the context, aims, and norms of interpreting Scripture theologically. Our postmodern age is suspicious of "ideologies" in traditional Christian texts, and of the modern critical "ideology" that rejects all tradition. Biblical wisdom is pertinent, both by ordering society around the communication of tradition formed in past experience, and by fostering inquiry about tradition's ongoing viability in lived experience.

Indeed, the postmodern lure of the immanent and the local has pitfalls of its own, for biblical wisdom does not legitimize just any community or just any practice of a community. Biblical wisdom seeks to form a *sensus communis* around the fear of the Lord. Wisdom therefore bears not only on the current postmodern context but also on the aims and norms of biblical interpretation. Thus, consideration of wisdom in the practice of theological interpretation must follow a treatment of wisdom in the biblical texts.

Wisdom in the Biblical Texts

In manifold forms, the Bible evinces a tension over wisdom. Was the particularity of Israel's covenant relationship with God through the Torah compatible with the exercise of human judgment—with prudence, or with reflection on the created order, or with the more universal "wisdom" gleaned from other cultures? After the primal fall, does a life wisely lived anticipate a just recompense in the here and now or a deferral to future hope? When the Bible speaks of "wisdom," is it talking about cleverness or instrumental skill, about human moral judgment, about a quest to live in harmony with the order of creation, or about a prudence incorporating all of the above *after* beginning with "the fear of the Lord" (Prov. 1:7; 9:10)? Did seeking wisdom keep us from the tree of life (Gen. 2–3), or is wisdom itself a tree of life (Prov. 3:13–18)?

OT Wisdom Literature: Life in Israel and the Order of Creation. As a biblical genre, wisdom involves fairly stable forms of relating language to life. The degree to which this body of biblical literature reflects a particular wisdom "school" or "tradition" within Israel is a matter of ongoing debate. The corollary debate has concerned how distinctive is wisdom's emphasis on creation when compared with the rest of the OT.

Recent scholarship is acknowledging that the wisdom approach to reality was not alien to the typical Israelite, even if the people who composed the literature were distinctly literate and aware of other cultures. Indeed, Proverbs has affinities with a covenantal document such as Deuteronomy (e.g., in orienting wisdom to the "fear of the LORD"), whereas the Genesis narratives of creation and fall have both sapiential and covenantal motifs: Adam and Eve failed a test that paralleled Israel's. In each case, God had intended that obedience would display the definitive wisdom (e.g., Deut. 4:5–6), but the covenanters failed by seeking life autonomously. Fusions of Torah and wisdom (e.g., in Sirach) make sense as a strong reaction against the tempting autonomy afforded by "wisdom."

Obeying God's law, however, requires character (the unifying theme of Wisdom literature, says William Brown, *Character*), so that people will choose wisdom over folly and thereby gain prudence. Consider Prov. 26:4–5 as a paradigm for law more generally: we must have a sense of which rule applies to which case. Prudent character, Proverbs emphasizes, must be formed in an ethos that is both communal and cosmic. Wisdom teaches subsequent generations that life flourishes in a harmony of societal and creation orders. When this order breaks down due to the folly of waywardness—when the adulteress is pursued rather than Woman Wisdom—the consequences are deadly. Success might still be found instrumentally in small parts of life because of the way God's creation works, but life on the whole will be lost (O'Donovan).

Other wisdom material, especially Job and Ecclesiastes, wrestles with and qualifies this teaching. After the fall, the relationship between successful life and good character is not always direct. The person who expects to master creation by way of wisdom will often be disappointed; true wisdom knows its limitations.

NT Wisdom: Word and Spirit. Although its significance for Christology remains debated, wisdom is an NT theme as well, again pressing home human limitations. Jesus was partly a teacher of wisdom, as portrayed by the Gospel records of his parables and aphorisms. Moreover, the Gospel of John arguably presents him as Wisdom incarnate, and Matthew's Gospel seems to present Jesus as not only teaching but also somehow embodying wisdom. This extends the OT emphasis on wisdom (to whatever extent personified) as God's initiative of communication to humanity. The christological implications are complex and the

problems knotty. Yet wisdom apparently figures on the divine rather than the human side of the divide between Creator and creature, the Worshipped and the not worshipped.

Paul's bracing critique of worldly wisdom in 1 Cor. 1:18–2:16 continues, in a Christ-centered key, the OT suspicion of autonomous human reason arrogating life to itself. Paul does not deny that God speaks in the created order, yet God will confound the worldly "wisdom" that picks and chooses strategic benefits from what is immanent. By a transcendent communicative action in Jesus Christ, God has broken into our world and brought a new Word near to us.

Jesus Christ *is* our God-given wisdom (1 Cor. 1:30), and he *enables* us to become wise as we have his mind by the Spirit (2:7–16). Unlike the Greek version focused on immanence, Christian wisdom is offered not to a heroic few, nor by way of recollection. Unlike the former Jewish version, wisdom has an aspect of transcendence, not as a gift of the law, but as a gift to people who have failed to follow the law. Christian wisdom is cruciform—the eschatological mystery of Christ revealed by the Spirit; the Christ fulfills the Torah as the embodiment of wisdom, while the Spirit fulfills the Torah as the enablement for wisdom. Yet the NT still contains "wisdom literature" as well, notably in James and in the *Haustafeln* that flesh out Paul's appeals for discernment.

The Bible finally manifests, therefore, a pluriform unity on the theme of wisdom. There is a redemptive-historical thrust, as the OT consolidation of wisdom toward the Torah gives way to NT fulfillment in the Word and the Spirit. Yet the theme of character formed in response to communication—communication of what prior generations have heard from God and learned of God's creation—persists. God's new communication, Jesus Christ, fulfills anticipations of OT wisdom and reorders our lives so that we will keep covenant and eat from the tree of life. This reordering includes a wholeness of vision that glimpses a unity of canonical teaching by which to live in God's world.

Wisdom in the Practice of Theological Interpretation

Contemporary appeals to wisdom may be energized less by these biblical themes than by the complexities of cultural change for the Christian tradition. Wisdom is a wedge against modernity's narrowly instrumental and procedural reason, which runs like the machines we build. It stands against modernity's excessively critical orientation, which (ironically) degenerates into parroting traditional criticisms. It is against modernity's persistent reduction of the natural order into observable parts, which loses the enchantment of the world's hidden structures, moral implications, and wholeness. And it critiques modernity's obsession with dilemmas of moral obligation, which precludes living by virtue of an orientation to the true, the good, and the beautiful. Especially for our purposes, wisdom turns us against the exclusively procedural, excessively critical, reductionist rationality of modern biblical scholarship.

Wholeness and Particularity in Theological Epistemology. In other words, wisdom pushes for wholeness while attending to the particular. We have learned that our lives are ongoing stories of exercising practical reason (prudence, or Aristotle's *phronēsis*) in a quest to envision the good (related to Aristotle's *sophia*, but not an unchanging abstraction that is contemplated; Christian *sophia* is embodied in Jesus Christ). One does not simply apply a Christian vision in particular situations; discernment in each case works back onto understanding of the rule, producing fresh construals of the vision. For theology, this accords with Ellen Charry's claim that premodern theological proposals took their shape due to situated pastoral concerns. In another sense, it accords with John Calvin that knowledge of God is mutually implicated with knowledge of our selves.

The way of wisdom might foster a Christian theism that maintains transcendence via doctrines of creation and prevenient divine action without ignoring the immanent. The postmodern hope is that, in this manner, tensions connected to biblical wisdom—transcendence and immanence, divine and human action, creation and redemption, command and common sense—might be embraced in their movement rather than denied by prioritizing one side or the other in some linear procedure. Usually, such procedures have made God remote to, or expelled from, what is rational.

Likewise, wisdom could hold together epistemology and ethics but, more pointedly, avert the modern fixation with *epistemē* (scientific knowledge) and *technē* (technique or skill). Epistemologies that (attempt to) detach knowledge from other actions and dispositions of embodied and social beings should be rejected; the oscillation of *sophia* and *phronēsis* provides the Christian judgment whereby sciences and skills can be appropriated where needed.

Vision and Discernment in Theology's Hermeneutical Circle. How, then, would Christian wisdom shape the aims and norms of biblical interpretation? Advocates for theological interpretation of Scripture can agree that its aim is knowledge of God, ingredient to which is the formation of Christian identity and virtue, unto human flourishing and God's glory. This aim might recover wholeness to the theological disciplines and to "theory" and "practice"—to whatever extent that theological scholarship can serve Christian living. To read the Bible with Christian vision ultimately means reading the corpora of the OT and NT together, against sometimes imperious practices of "biblical theology" as defined in the academic guild. And to read the Bible with Christian discernment means attending to the questions of church and world, against some "scholarly" claims that all particularity and subjectivity be avoided.

Yet if wisdom's "hermeneutical circle" oscillates between vision and discernment, what does that aim imply about the norms of biblical interpretation? On this question, advocates of theological interpretation are less agreed. Among several who advocate the recovery of practical reason (*phronēsis*), Stephen Fowl virtually equates the norms of biblical interpretation with Christian aims. Interpretation is theoretically underdetermined; the church must engage in ongoing discussion and debate concerning which interpretation(s) foster Christian virtue and human flourishing before God. Interpretations are to be measured by their fruitfulness rather than by textually based criteria.

Conversely, Kevin Vanhoozer retains a robust role for the human authors' enacted communicative intentions in norming biblical interpretation. Christian virtues are an interpretative aim and a necessity in approaching the Bible; practical reason is needed to indwell the worlds of canonical language, and to bear faithful witness about what God says in Scripture as canon.

Similarly, Nicholas Wolterstorff (in *Divine Discourse* and later articles) relates practical reason to two levels of biblical interpretation. First is the level of reaching judgments about the human discourse. Second is the level of reaching judgments about God's appropriation of that human discourse. These judgments involve imaginative construals about what an author *would* say. So to the principle "Scripture interprets Scripture" must be added a Christian vision—while taking the canon as a whole—of what God would be saying when we read some particular text.

If theological interpretation of Scripture could be theoretically determined, then it would be an enterprise of *epistemē* and *technē*; wisdom would be (at best) an applied by-product. So to speak of *sophia* and *phronēsis* makes biblical interpretation partially underdetermined, taking up sciences and skills in ad hoc fashion; we trust the Spirit both to form and to free our imagination. Yet Christian virtue cannot be the only, or even primary, norm of interpretation, lest an immanent *sensus communis* preempt "hearing" God's communicative action. For we do not love as we ought, nor would we know what love is, apart from God's final Word in Jesus Christ and the Spirit's witness to that Word in the texts of Holy Scripture. The scandal of Christian wisdom is not finally its communal but its cruciform character.

See also Theological Hermeneutics, Contemporary; Virtue; Wisdom Literature

Bibliography

Barton, S., ed. *Where Shall Wisdom Be Found?* T&T Clark, 1999; Brown, W. *Character in Crisis.* Eerdmans, 1996; idem. *The Ethos of the Cosmos.* Eerdmans, 1999; Charry, E. *By the Renewing of Your Minds.* Oxford University Press, 1997; Ford, D., and G. Stanton, eds. *Reading Texts, Seeking Wisdom.* Eerdmans, 2003; Fowl, S. *Engaging Scripture.* Blackwell, 1998; Johnson, L. T. *Scripture and Discernment in the Early Church.* 2d ed. Abingdon, 1996; Kelsey, D. *To Understand God Truly.* Westminster John Knox, 1992; O'Donovan, O. *Resurrection and Moral Order.* 2d ed. Eerdmans, 1994; Vanhoozer, K. *First Theology.* InterVarsity, 2002; Wolterstorff, N. *Divine Discourse.* Cambridge University Press, 1995; Wood, C. *Vision and Discernment.* Scholars Press, 1985.

Daniel J. Treier

Wisdom Literature

In the nineteenth century, when Job and Ecclesiastes played a prominent role in intellectual life (Smend 254), the term "Wisdom Literature" came to designate Proverbs, Job, and Ecclesiastes, in addition to Sirach and Wisdom of Solomon in the LXX. The grounds for this designation were laid in antiquity, partly because Proverbs, Ecclesiastes, and the Song of Songs were attributed to Solomon, Israel's wisest king (Leanza). Wisdom Literature (WL) in this essay will refer to the canonical Proverbs, Job, and Ecclesiastes. As a neutral designation, WL may designate the books that focus on "wisdom" (*khokmah*) and employ macro- and microgenres appropriate to that focus. In this regard, biblical WL is generically and conceptually unique in the ancient Near East, for nowhere else is the nature of wisdom itself made an object of reflection (Lambert 1; Fox, *Proverbs*, 346).

Unfortunately, the term "Wisdom Literature" has been theologically problematic because it isolated these books from the rest of Scripture. Though Job and Ecclesiastes were at times ignored or disdained, for most of church history the WL was considered an integral part of Scripture, essential for faith and practice. Among the church fathers, Christ was widely described as the Word and Wisdom of God, particularly with regard to his role in ordering the cosmos (e.g., Athanasius, *C. Gent* 40; Lantantius, *Inst.* 4.9; cf. John 1:1; Col. 1:15–20) or his role in salvation (e.g., Augustine, *Doctr. chr.* 1.11–14; cf. 1 Cor. 1:17–2:8). Proverbs 8:22–31 played a major role in the Arian controversy (Hanson 440–43; Pelikan 191–200).

In the last two hundred years, as WL was set over against the rest of the canon, so was Proverbs set against Job and Ecclesiastes. Proverbs was considered a simplistic dogmatism, in which good behavior resulted in prosperity and bad resulted in poverty and death. Job and Ecclesiastes, however, were presumed to result from a "crisis of wisdom" because history and innocent suffering proved the dogmatism of Proverbs false. Proverbs, however, presents the ABCs of wisdom, in which one *generally* reaps what one sows, while Job and Ecclesiastes present "graduate-school wisdom," in which the "exceptions to the rules" and the limits of human life and knowledge are radically explored (Van Leeuwen, "Wealth").

For Augustine and the Western tradition after him, the *entire* Bible was read as a "wisdom" book for humanity (Jeffrey 88). This ancient view of Scripture had its roots in the Bible itself, since the purpose of Scripture as a whole was in this life to make readers "wise (*sophisai*) for salvation" and to train them in righteousness, a requisite for wisdom (2 Tim. 3:15–16; cf. Prov. 10–15, 28–29). But with the triumph of historicism and the concomitant neglect or misconstrual of creation in theology (Wingren; Knierim), WL became isolated from the operative theological "canon within a canon" because it did not treat Israel's historical traditions such as exodus, covenant, conquest, prophecy, and exile. In the twentieth century salvation history became the heart of the "biblical theology movement" (Childs). Theological interest in WL waned, even as scholars in the history of religions began a quest comparing Israelite wisdom texts with ancient Near Eastern and Egyptian literature, spurred by the probable use of Amenemope in Prov. 22:17–23:11 (Römheld). Some went so far as to claim that the WL was a "foreign body" in Scripture, more akin to ancient Near Eastern literature than to the rest of the biblical canon (cf. Preuss). While scholars noted that WL was different in genre than most of the canon, they generally failed to notice that lack of reference to Israel's history was a *function of its generic purposes*. The WL did not mention history because it was not generically germane. Rather, WL in its final form *presupposed* "canonical" religion and its traditions, as is evident from many verbal and thematic links (*pace* Crenshaw 13). It provided a necessary complement, not duplicate, to the rest of the canon.

The term WL was also problematic because, though Proverbs, Job, and Ecclesiastes focused on "wisdom," they were not of one type generically, nor was their purpose the same. Moreover, they employed a wide variety of generic subtypes, such as (autobiographical) instruction, prayer and hymn, admonition and saying. The question of the relation of various genres to wisdom as a concept remained unresolved, further clouding the problem of "wisdom" in the canon as a whole (Van Leeuwen, "Form Criticism").

Though the term WL rightly highlighted these books' focus on wisdom and their generic differences from other scriptural macrogenres, it concealed a more fundamental, unresolved question: "What is biblical wisdom?" An adequate answer must take into account the fact that wisdom is not genre bound, but appears in all areas of life and in various literary genres. Wisdom genres are not the same as wisdom per se. Thus, we must see how the OT actually uses wisdom terms and also how wisdom functions throughout the OT and in comparable ancient literatures. Scholarship is far from finished with these questions. What follows is necessarily a provisional attempt at a theory of OT wisdom, for the Bible itself does not provide such a theory.

Wisdom is difficult to define because it is a *totality concept*. That is, the idea is as broad as reality and constitutes a culturally articulated way of relating to the entire world. The absence of wisdom is "folly," which like "wisdom" is expressed in a variety of Hebrew terms (Fox, *Proverbs*, 28–43). Thus, in the OT good sailors, metalworkers, weavers, counselors, scribes, and builders—all may be described as "wise" (*khokmah*). Originally, concepts of "wisdom" generally referred to any human craft, skill, or competence. The WL did not abandon such usages, but focused on articulating the religion-based, sociomoral aspects of human competence and virtue in relation to Yahweh. Ancient wisdom thought and

practice are never "secular," even where God is not mentioned. Thus, even farming is an aspect of religion (Isa. 28:23–29). Ancient Greece followed a similar, culturally specific development in the use of the term *sophia*, leading to *philosophia* (Gladigow). Human wisdom and folly are forms of action in the world, including actions of thought or speech—important topics throughout Proverbs and Job. The wide referential range of wisdom terms like *khokmah* is perhaps the most important clue to their meaning, a phenomenon for which any adequate description of biblical wisdom must account. To conclude from the wide range of "wisdom" that there are fundamentally competing notions in the OT overlooks the totality character of *khokmah*. Yet, the Hellenistically influenced works of Sirach (also in Hebrew) and Wisdom of Solomon make clear that the influence of worldviews (or philosophies) in the articulation of wisdom must also be carefully discerned.

The theological reason for the totality character of terms like "wisdom" and "folly" (like that of "good" and "evil") is that they are rooted in divine creation. This is the import of Prov. 8, where cosmic wisdom, personified as a woman, addresses all humanity in the midst of life (von Rad, ch. 9). She has the right to do so because she was present with God at the creation of all things. The Lord has "built" the universe "with wisdom" (Prov. 3:19–20; Ps. 104:24). Thus, any human activity (including worship) can be done wisely or foolishly, well or poorly. Human activities are wise and good inasmuch as they are in harmony with the wisdom by which God created the world (cf. Prov. 3:19–20; 14:1; 24:3–4; Exod. 31:1–3; 1 Kings 7:13; Van Leeuwen, "Building"). Though the Wisdom of Solomon frames OT thought in a Platonic way, its comprehensive description of human wisdom rooted in God's cosmic wisdom offers profound insight into the scope and character of biblical wisdom (Wis. 7:15–22).

For our purposes, wisdom may be described as the sum of several aspects, none of which may be lacking. First, wisdom presupposes the "fear of Yahweh/God" (Prov. 1:7; 9:10; Job 1:1; 28:28; Ps. 111:10; see above, on creation). This concept has its origins in numinous awe at God's mighty works (cf. Exod. 14:31), but comes in time to be OT shorthand for "religion" in the sense of *all of life*, not just worship, as service to Yahweh, Creator and redeemer of the world through Israel. This concept, in various verbal formulations, appears throughout the OT (e.g., Deut. 10:12; Pss. 25; 86:11), and is one way in which the authors of the WL connected their works to the larger biblical worldview, even when they did not take up historical themes so prominent elsewhere. The fear of the Lord is the key to Israel's epistemology (von Rad, ch. 2), for knowing the Creator puts one in position appropriately to know the creation and humans with their divinely given possibilities and limits.

Second, wisdom entails insight into and practice of the *generic* patterns and norms for creation and creatures. Both natural and cultural things are to be dealt with according to their "kinds" (cf. Wenham). In a very focused way, WL thinks resolutely in terms of biblical "creation theology" (Zimmerli), in which nature and culture are not split in a post-Kantian dichotomy. All human activities are delimited by conditions that God ordered in the beginning. Knowledge of the cosmic order requires the knowledge not only of how things work, but also of how all things fit together and relate in one whole, all to the glory of God. Cosmic order is a matter both of factually existing creatures, functions, and relations within the cosmos, but equally of the *divinely ordained laws and norms* that hold for them (laws for nature, norms and relative freedom for human culture). In Scripture, such laws and norms can take the form of God's creative, governing word ("Let there be . . ."). Secondarily, Israel's written law codes and wisdom are culturally specific articulations of cosmic norms, accommodated to treat the complications of sin and history (cf. Matt. 19:1–12). The created limits for human conduct permit a good deal of freedom within those limits for societies, groups, and persons alike. Such norms are also designated as the *Wisdom* of God, personified in Prov. 8 as a woman who addresses humankind (von Rad, ch. 9). In this regard, Israel's wisdom thinking is comparable to ancient Near Eastern concepts of cosmosocial order such as the Sumerian ME and Egyptian Ma'at (Schmid; contrast Fox, "Ma'at").

Third, wisdom entails knowledge of and appropriate action with reference to *particular* circumstances, institutions, persons, and other creatures. For example, to marry is a general human institution under created norms (Gen. 2:24; Prov. 5:15–19; Matt. 19:3–9). But to marry requires knowledge of individuals (both of self and the other) and of the circumstances in which marriage is good or not. Similarly, the human pattern of work is both general and particular: What calling is right for this person in these circumstances? Questions like "Whom shall I marry?" and "What work shall I do?" require knowledge both of culturally articulated creational patterns

and of relevant particulars. Wisdom behavior is always "fitting" or appropriate to the concrete, particular circumstances (Van Leeuwen, "Proverbs," on 26:1–12). Part of the folly of Job's "friends" is that they know the general "rules" of theological wisdom, without recognizing that they do not apply to Job's particular, indeed unique, case. It is possible to speak the truth in ways that are false.

Fourth, wisdom is traditional. Knowledge of generic patterns and their re-cognition in particular situations is mediated generationally, whether in a profession or the general affairs of life. Traditions permit humans to discern and deal with the "new" in terms of what was learned in the past, and to relate particulars to the generic patterns within which they fall. The biblical image for tradition is the "way" or the "path" (Ps. 1; Prov. 1–9). A "way" is an enculturated means of negotiating the human journey through created reality. "Ways" have traditional staying power because they seem to work; they effectively get us from point A to B, sparing those who come later the onerous task of clearing a path for the first time. Nonetheless, ways can be good or bad, inasmuch as they conform to the divine norms for reality or not (see Proverbs). Thus, in Acts "the way" designates the one true path of Christianity. Augustine appropriated this insight in a profoundly christological way: "Though Wisdom [Christ] was Himself our home, He made Himself also the way by which we should reach our home" (*Doctr. chr.* 1.11.8).

This insight of Augustine reminds us that in Jesus Christ are found "all the treasures of wisdom and knowledge" (Col. 2:3). The NT as a whole shares in the general movement of early Judaism toward a sapiential understanding of revelation (1 Tim. 3:15–16). For the NT, the Redeemer of all things is the incarnate Word or Wisdom, through whom the Father created all things (John 1:1–18; cf. Prov. 8; Col. 1:15–20; Heb. 1:1–14; 1 Cor. 1:24, 30). Moreover, the life and teaching of Jesus embody and advance the principles of OT wisdom. Here only an example or two must suffice. Thus, the Sermon on the Mount is largely proverbial teaching in genre and content (cf. Eccles. 5:18–20 and 9:9–10 with Matt. 6:25–34; Ps. 37:11, 22 with Matt. 5:5; etc.). Jesus also repeatedly befuddles his opponents by answering and not answering fools according to their folly (Prov. 26:4–5; Matt. 19:3–9; 21:23–27; 22:15–22). On the ethical level, the NT repeatedly urges Christians not only to cross-bearing and virtue, but also to wisdom (Acts 6:3, 10; 1 Cor. 2:6; Eph. 1:9, 17; Col. 3:16; etc.).

Though wisdom in the NT has become a topic of scholarly discussion, much more needs to be done to make it part of the pastor's toolkit, so that the church may have the mind of Christ in all wisdom.

See also Wisdom

Bibliography

Childs, B. *Biblical Theology in Crisis*. Westminster, 1970; Crenshaw, J. "Murphy's Axiom: Every Gnomic Saying Needs a Balancing Corrective." Pages 1–17 in *The Listening Heart*, ed. K. Hoglund et al. JSOT, 1987; idem. *Old Testament Wisdom*. Westminster John Knox, 1998; Fox, M. *Proverbs 1–9*. AB. Doubleday, 2000; idem. "World Order and Ma'at: A Crooked Parallel." *JNES* 23 (1995): 37–48; Gladigow, B. *Sophia und Kosmos*. G. Olms, 1965; Hanson, R. P. C. "Biblical Exegesis in the Early Church." Pages 412–53 in *The Cambridge History of the Bible*, ed. P. R. Ackroyd and C. F. Evans. Cambridge University Press, 1970; Jeffrey, D. L. *People of the Book*. Eerdmans, 1996; Knierim, R. "Cosmos and History." Pages 171–224 in *The Task of Old Testament Theology*. Eerdmans, 1995; Lambert, W. G. *Babylonian Wisdom Literature*. Clarendon, 1960; Leanza, S. "Wisdom Books." Pages 878–81 in vol. 2 of *Encyclopedia of the Early Church*, ed. A. Di Berardino. Oxford University Press, 1992; Murphy, R. *The Tree of Life*. Eerdmans, 2002; idem. "Wisdom—Theses and Hypotheses." Pages 35–42 in *Israelite Wisdom*, ed. J. Gammie et al. Scholars Press, 1978; Pelikan, J. *The Christian Tradition: A History of the Development of Doctrine*. Vol. 1, *The Emergence of the Catholic Tradition (100–600)*. University of Chicago Press, 1971; Preuss, H. *Einführung in die alttestamentliche Weisheitsliteratur*. Urban-Taschenbücher 383. Kohlhammer, 1987; Rad, G. von. *Wisdom in Israel*. Abingdon, 1972; Römheld, D. *Wege der Weisheit*. BZAW 184. De Gruyter, 1989; Schmid, H. H. *Gerechtigkeit als Weltordnung*. BHT 40. Mohr/Siebeck, 1968; Smalley, B. *The Study of the Bible in the Middle Ages*. University of Notre Dame Press, 1964; Smend, R. "The Interpretation of Wisdom in Nineteenth-Century Scholarship." Pages 257–68 in *Wisdom in Ancient Israel*, ed. J. Day et al. Cambridge University Press, 1995; Steiert, F.-J. *Die Weisheit Israels—ein Fremdkörper im Alten Testament?* FThSt 143. Herder, 1990; Van Leeuwen, R. "The Book of Proverbs." *NIB* 5:17–264; idem. "Building God's House: An Exploration in Wisdom." Pages 204–11 in *The Way of Wisdom*, ed. J. I. Packer and S. Soderlund. Zondervan, 2000; idem. "Form Criticism, Wisdom, and Psalms 111–112." In *The Changing Face of Form Criticism for the Twenty-First Century*, ed. M. Sweeney and E. Ben Zvi. Eerdmans, 2003; idem. "Wealth and Poverty: System and Contradiction in Proverbs." *HS* 33 (1992): 25–26; Wenham, G. *The Book of Leviticus*. NICOT. Eerdmans, 1979; Wingren, G. *Flight from Creation*. Augsburg, 1971; Zimmerli, W. "The Place and Limit of the Wisdom in the Framework of the Old Testament Theology." *SJT* 17 (1964): 146–58.

Raymond C. Van Leeuwen

Wittgenstein, Ludwig   *See* Language-Game

Wolterstorff, Nicholas   *See* Authorial Discourse Interpretation; Speech-Act Theory; Theological Hermeneutics, Contemporary

Womanist Interpretation   *See* Feminist Biblical Interpretation; Ideological Criticism

Word of God

At the core of theological interpretation of Scripture is the conviction that the Bible—the words of human authors—is somehow also the word of God. Many liturgical traditions have the reader of the OT lesson and epistle end with "the word of the Lord." Other churches encourage their congregations to "listen for the word of God." These diverse liturgical practices pose the central theological issue of the present article: Is the Bible itself the word of God written, or is it the vehicle through which the church may on occasion hear the word of God? To what extent do these liturgical expressions affirm the "Scripture principle"—that what Scripture says, God says—and to what extent do they carry over into theological hermeneutics?

There are three parts to this overarching question: (1) Is the Bible (a form of) the word of God? (2) What exactly do biblical authors and later theologians mean by "word of God"? (3) What ought theological interpreters of Scripture assume about the relation of the Bible to the word of God?

Scripture as a Form of God's Word: Sic et non

K. Barth. It is fitting to begin with a theologian who opens his dogmatics with a massive analysis of the word of God. For Barth, theology begins with the self-presentation of the triune God, a free and gracious act, never a static thing waiting to be discovered. Only God can make God known, and God remains the active sovereign subject of his revelation, regardless of the particular form it takes. The Son is the essential and objective form of God's self-communication to the world; the Spirit is the subjective power of the word without which the word is not recognized or received. Hence, the word of God is not a static message, but a dynamic event—less propositional content than personal address.

Barth distinguishes the essential word (e.g., the Son as revelation of God's being) from its two further forms, the only two forms in which the church today meets the word of God: Scripture and preaching. There is thus a unity-in-differentiation of the one word just as there is a unity-in-differentiation of the one God: the revelation itself (the Son), the witness to that revelation (the prophetic and apostolic testimony), and the preaching of that witness. The Bible and human preaching *become* God's word when God actively communicates himself to human recipients through the divinely appropriated human discourse: "The Word of God is God Himself in Holy Scripture" (Barth 457). At the same time, "A real witness is not identical with that to which it witnesses, but it sets it before us" (Barth 463).

In sum, the Bible becomes the word of God when it serves as the creaturely medium of the self-presentation of Christ through the Spirit and becomes a witness to revelation, when its substance or *Sache*—the living Word—graciously makes himself known. The witness *indicates* but is not *identical* with that to which it witnesses. The substance of the revelation—the Son—retains his sovereign freedom precisely by refusing to be equated with the human words. The Word of God is not an attribute of the biblical text (this would violate divine freedom) but commandeers the human words of the Bible and so directs readers to its true subject matter (Barth 513).

J. Barr and J. Barton. While Barth espouses an indirect identity thesis, most modern biblical critics hold to a nonidentity thesis. To insist that the Bible is the word of God is to invoke a dogmatic category, one moreover that alienates the Bible from the world of scholarly exegesis. For Barr, the authority of the Bible stems not from its divine origin but from its ecclesial function as a classic model for understanding God. As a humanly formulated model, however, the Bible is rife with imperfections—chronological, historical, even theological. In the final historical-critical analysis, the Bible is not the word of God but the "word of Israel" or "word of leading early Christians" (Barr 119–20).

Other modern biblical scholars worry that identifying Scripture with the word of God commits bibliolatry and elevates the Bible above Jesus Christ: "As long as we have the Bible (it seems) Jesus need not really have existed, for it is the text that reveals the truth about God, not Jesus himself" (Barton 37). Critics typically find it difficult to conceive of a literal communication from God: "The text of Scripture is not God's word spoken to us; it reveals God as the one *about* whom, not *by* whom, various types of literature are written" (Barton 72; cf. Barr 131). Modern biblical criticism's agnosticism as to the divine origin of Scripture is likewise agnosticism, or perhaps outright denial of God as a living, breathing, and speaking communicative agent. Such a critically emasculated Bible leaves us with only "human reflection on the mystery of God. . . . This literature is not of divine origin" (Barton 46).

"Word of God" in Scripture and Theology

The poet Goethe pictures his protagonist Faust puzzling over the translation of *logos* in the prologue to the Fourth Gospel: "In the beginning was the . . ." Faust considers several possibilities—word, thought, power, deed—each of which seems to capture something of the biblical idea.

Biblical Sources. The OT is replete with hundreds of instances of God "saying" or "speaking," from the command of bringing light into existence or the boy Samuel hearing an audible voice (1 Sam. 3:4) to messages mediated by various types of go-betweens (e.g., prophets, Balaam's ass). The pentateuchal literature prefers more specific terms to describe the *kind* of divine speech (e.g., "covenant," "command," or "instruction"). The whole Deuteronomistic History presents a theology of the word of God at work in history and of Israel's response to it. The formula "the word of the Lord came" (*dabar Yahweh*) belongs especially to the prophetic literature, where Yahweh tends to speak through the prophets rather than directly to individuals. What is authoritative is not the human messenger but the divine message (Deut. 18:18–19).

Though God reveals himself in creation and history, his covenantal purposes are ultimately unintelligible apart from his accompanying interpretative speech acts (e.g., promises, commands, blessings, curses). The word of God is reliable and efficacious, not because words themselves contain magical power, but because the divine speech agent is faithful, wise, and able (Isa. 55:11). One of the telltale marks of false gods (idols) is that they are dumb: they cannot speak and so cannot bring about any effect through speech acts.

In the NT, as in the LXX, the word *logos* is often used to translate the Hebrew *dabar*. The NT speaks of the word of God, the words of Jesus, and of Jesus as the Word of God. In the parable of the sower, the seed sown is explicitly identified in Luke 8:11 as the word of God, thus linking the word and the gospel message about the kingdom coming in the person of Jesus. The term thus refers both to the teaching of Jesus and to the apostolic preaching and teaching about Jesus (1 Thess. 2:13). Moreover, this word about Jesus—the gospel—does more than convey propositional content; it is a dynamic word that acts upon the lives of its listeners (Heb. 4:12; 1 Pet. 1:23), just as the words of Jesus themselves are "spirit and . . . life" (John 6:63).

Most strikingly, John 1:1–4 and the whole Fourth Gospel identify the word of God with the preexistent Son of God made flesh in Jesus Christ, and identify Jesus' words with the word of God (Gundry 1–50; cf. Rev. 19:13). Jesus' person and work become the definitive mode of God's communication (Heb. 1:1–2). Nevertheless, the word of God is often identified with the words of Scripture as well (John 10:35; 2 Cor. 6:16–17; 2 Tim. 3:16–17; Heb. 3:7; 2 Pet. 1:19–21; 3:15–16).

Theological Formulations. From the rich storehouse of biblical images and instances of God's speaking, theologians have harvested what essentially amounts to a doctrine of revelation.

Given the virtually unquestioned conviction in the early church that the Bible is God's word, some patristic exegetes felt the need to offer allegorical interpretations in order to discover something worthy of God and applicable to new situations in texts that seemed either trivial or immoral. The Bible's status as word of God thus stimulated and legitimated a millennium and more of "spiritual" interpretation, based largely on the assumption that the whole body of biblical texts makes up a consistent message, thanks to the Spirit's authorship.

Renaissance and Reformation theologians were still precritical in their acceptance of the direct identity thesis between the words of the biblical authors and the word of God. Yet their "rediscovery" of the original languages of Scripture and their interest in philology led to a renewed interest in the grammatical-historical sense.

Some scholars contend that Luther maintained a distinction between the biblical text and the word of God. Nevertheless, later Lutheran and most Reformed theologians (together with their respective communities' confessions of faith) agreed with Augustine, for whom theology consisted primarily in interpreting the Bible as God's word. They likewise affirmed a strong version of the identity thesis. The Thirty-Nine Articles of the Church of England, for instance, state that the Bible is "God's word written" (art. 20).

Calvin argued that the main task of the interpreter consists in "lucid brevity": the commentator should remain as inconspicuous as possible so as to unfold the mind of the author. The human authors retain their personal and intellectual integrity even though the Spirit so superintends the writing process that what the authors wrote could be said ultimately to proceed from God

himself. Scripture deserves the epithet "word of God" not because the church decided to count it as such but because of the ministry of the Spirit, who enables the church to see the Bible for what it truly is (Calvin, *Inst.* 1.6–9).

It is precisely the direct identification between the biblical texts and the word of God that modern biblical scholarship has called into question. Biblical critics examine the grammatical-historical sense of the text in relation to historically reconstructed culturally conditioned contexts rather than the canonical context that had enabled earlier interpreters to read Scripture as the unified word of God. The privileged locus of biblical interpretation shifts from special to general hermeneutics, and from the church to the academy—so much so that we may now wonder what biblical studies has to do with theology (Barr).

Theologians of the so-called New Hermeneutic (Fuchs, Ebeling) espouse another version of the indirect identity thesis, following Bultmann (and before him, Heidegger). They claim that the word of God is an event of personal encounter (a "language-" or "word-event"), occasioned by the reading or preaching of Scripture, not an intrinsic property of the Bible itself. Theological conservatives, faced with this and other twentieth-century emphases on noncognitive revelation, have defended the Bible as God's word under the rubric of propositional revelation (Henry).

The modern preoccupation with epistemology—the possibility, limits, and methods of knowledge—led theologians to elevate the doctrine of revelation into the virtual first principle of theology. Accordingly, the discussion about the Bible's relation to the word of God focused—in thinkers as diverse as Barr and Barth, Fuchs and Henry—on whether (and how) the Bible is *revelatory* of God. In postmodernity, the skeptical trend with regard to the possibility of knowledge through or about texts led to two results. First is an awareness that all texts, including the Bible, *conceal* as much (if not more) as they reveal. Hence comes the typical deconstructive strategy of exposing the multivalent signifiers and structural inconsistencies that undermine determinate textual meaning. Second is an aversion to a theological foundationalism that treats the Bible as divinely revealed propositional data.

The widespread connection between Scripture, "word of God," and revelation in modern theology is telling. Yet there are lingering questions as to whether revelation is the fittest rubric. Designating the whole Bible as "revealed"—or for that matter, "inspired," "witness," or "authority"—is problematic in that it fails to do justice to all that the Bible is (Goldingay).

Also problematic is the assumption that the basic unit of meaning is the individual word, an inert item in a system of *langue*, rather than a word-in-use, or *parole*. The latter better accords with the biblical depiction of the word of God as dynamic and transformative rather than merely static and informative. Yet, while we may welcome the recent emphasis on the performative rather than merely informative aspect of language, certain things that authors do with words depend upon the truth value of their cognitive content (Thiselton 326).

In light of these concerns, we do well to consider one option overlooked by Goethe's Faust for the translation of *logos*: *discourse*, "something someone says to someone about something." Discourse includes more than "revealing." It is needlessly reductionistic to insist that "revealing" is the only thing God does with biblical words. Strictly speaking, "revelation" pertains to the disclosure of something hidden. As such, it is a particular kind of discourse: a making known of something that would otherwise remain unknown (Wolterstorff 19–36). To be sure, there is revelation in the Bible. The relevant question, however, is whether "revelation" is the best concept with which to capture everything relevant that falls under the rubric "word of God."

"Word of God" and the Theological Interpretation of Scripture

Interpreting Scripture theologically means assuming that there is something about Scripture that is "of God," but what? Revealed information? Personal encounter? Disclosure of a new way of seeing the world? What dogmatic conclusions may we draw from the church's confessing "the word of the Lord" after the Scripture reading and from the Bible's own self-attestation?

Instead of asking whether the words of human beings might convey the word of God, perhaps we should ask, with Barth, whether the word of God employs words of human beings. An affirmative answer implies some notion of double agency in which God works in and with and through the human mind, not to violate but to perfect its natural capacities. Such sanctifying work includes making use of reason and imagination alike. Yet, to interpret Scripture theologically is ultimately not a matter of solving historical and intellectual puzzles about what certain people thought in the past, but of engaging in various ways with the many things that God does with the language and literature of the Bible. It is a matter of engaging the communicative economy of the triune God, whose word ministers and administers right covenantal relations and so brings about communion.

Divine Discourse. For those who continue to espouse the Scripture principle ("what Scripture says, God says"), the way forward is to move beyond the narrow identification of the Bible, and of God's word, with propositional revelation (e.g., the information conveyed). Divine discourse is the better rubric, and this is true for several reasons: (1) It overcomes the personal/propositional dichotomy inasmuch as discourse is both a "saying" and a "doing." (2) It corresponds to the biblical depiction of God as a communicative agent who does many things with words besides transmitting knowledge. (3) It better accounts for the diversity of Scripture itself, especially for the plurality of its literary forms. (4) It enriches the notion of canonical authority by insisting that the church attend not only to propositional content (e.g., revealed truths) but to all the things God is doing communicatively in Scripture to administer his covenant. (5) It encourages us to view the Bible as a means by which we relate personally to God and commune with God.

While interpreters may have other interests—for example, in reconstructing the historical context of the author or the history of the text's composition, or in examining the text's literary structure or rhetoric—those who have a theological interest will read to discern the divine discourse. As commissioned divine-human discourse, the Bible is not only authorized but, in providential fashion, *authored* by God. Illocutions—what one *does* in speaking—are the key discursive acts. The Bible is the word of God, not simply because of the information it conveys, but also because it is the means by which God promises, commands, warns, guides, and yes, reveals.

The fundamental principle in reading Scripture to hear the word of God is to assume that the human discourse is the divinely authorized and appropriated discourse unless there is good reason to do otherwise (Wolterstorff 204). Another important principle is to regard the Bible as one book whose parts are ultimately understood only in light of the larger unified whole. It follows that theological interpretation of Scripture will pay particular attention to the biblical texts in their canonical context.

Scripture in the Triune Communicative Economy: Illocutions Accomplished and Applied.

The word of God is God in creative, communicative, and self-communicative action, doing things in and with the word written and the word made flesh. We need to distinguish the "internal" word of the Father from its "externalization" in the humanity of Jesus and in the spirited Scriptures. The eternal Son is the immanent Word that was with God and is God; Jesus and the Scriptures figure as "economic" words, the word of God as it enters created reality.

To be sure, the Bible is not a divine person, but a creaturely reality chosen by God to play a special role in the economy of the Word, an economy of triune communicative action. The theological significance of the Bible "is derived not from any of its immanent characteristics—its value as a historical source, its literary qualities, its religious insights, its influence on Western culture—but from the indispensable role assigned to it in the outward movement of the divine communicative action into the world" (Watson 61).

The Spirit is of special importance in the triune communicative economy of the Word. While the Father is the original speaker or locutor and the Son the decisive word-deed to whom the various biblical illocutions ultimately point, the Spirit is the "entelechy," or power of completion, the "perlocutionary" efficacy and effect, the breath that ministers and applies the word to the listening/reading subject. The Word of God is thus a word incarnate (enfleshed), a word inscripturate (written), a word "incardiate" (taken to heart).

Trading on the key speech-act distinction between what one does in saying and the effect one brings about by saying, one could say both that the Bible, as comprised of divinely authorized illocutions, *is* the word of God, and that it *becomes* the word of God if and when the Spirit renders it perlocutionarily efficacious (Vanhoozer). Hence, one can agree with Barth that the being of the Bible in its richest sense—that of a full-blown divine speech act comprised of illocution and perlocution alike—is in its becoming (McCormack).

Conclusion. In its fullest sense the "Word of God" is something that God *says*, something that God *does*, and something that God *is*. The Bible is the word of God in the sense that it is a field and form of divine communicative action. More precisely, it is a medium of divine illocutionary acts, the creaturely means that God has set aside (e.g., made "holy") for his own use. Scripture therefore is the word of God, but this means more than divinely revealed information. For God does many things with words, not just transmit information. Scripture is the word of God because it is the chosen means through which the triune God presents Christ, ministers and administers the covenant of grace, and makes all things new through the ministry of the Word in the power of the Spirit.

Bibliography

Barr, J. *The Bible in the Modern World*. SCM, 1973; Barth, K. *The Doctrine of the Word of God*. Vol. I/2 of *Church Dogmatics*. T&T Clark, 1956; Barton, J. *People of the Book?* Westminster John Knox, 1988; Brueggemann, W. *Theology of the OT*. Fortress, 1997; Calvin, J. *Institutes of the Christian Religion*. Westminster, 1960; Fanning, B. "Word." Pages 848–53 in *New Dictionary of Biblical Theology*, ed. T. Alexander and B. Rosner. InterVarsity, 2000; Fretheim, T., and K. Froehlich. *The Bible as Word of God in a Postmodern Age*. Fortress, 1998; Goldingay, J. *Models for Scripture*. Eerdmans, 1994; Gundry, R. *Jesus the Word according to John the Sectarian*. Eerdmans, 2002; McCormack, B. "The Being of Holy Scripture Is in Becoming." Pages 55–75 in *Evangelicals and Scripture*, ed. V. Bacote, L. Miguélez, and D. Okholm. InterVarsity, 2004; Packer, J. I. *Fundamentalism and the Word of God*. InterVarsity, 1958; Thiselton, A. "The New Hermeneutic." Pages 308–33 in *New Testament Interpretation*, ed. I. H. Marshall. Eerdmans, 1977; Vanhoozer, K. "God's Mighty Speech Acts." Pages 127–58 in *First Theology*. InterVarsity, 2002; Warfield, B. B. *Inspiration and Authority of the Bible*. P&R, 1979; Watson, F. "The Bible." Pages 57–71 in *Cambridge Companion to Karl Barth*, ed. J. Webster. Cambridge University Press, 2000; Webster, J. *Holy Scripture*. Cambridge University Press, 2003; Wolterstorff. N. *Divine Discourse*. Cambridge University Press, 1995.

Kevin J. Vanhoozer

Word Study   See Concept; Etymology; Language, Linguistics; Utterance Meaning

Worldview

The English word "worldview" is a translation of the German *Weltanschauung*, a word first coined by Immanuel Kant. It has become a key term in Western intellectual discourse since the beginning of the nineteenth century, generally denoting a global outlook on life and the world—like philosophy in its scope, but without philosophy's claims of universal rational justification. Since the end of the nineteenth century, it has also become common to speak of a specifically *Christian* worldview. This denotes an overall Christian view of things that is broader and less discipline-specific than "theology." It also highlights aspects of Christianity where it provides an alternative to culture-transformative secular ideologies like Marxism and liberalism. As such, it has become an important category in Christian strategies of cultural engagement, both in the academy and beyond. See Naugle, *Worldview*, for an extensive treatment of the term, its use, and its history.

As applied to biblical interpretation, "worldview" is significant in three principal ways. First, it fulfills a kind of deconstructive function in highlighting the foundational assumptions brought to the interpretative task. Much of classical historical criticism, for example, is based on a worldview that separates faith and reason, and postulates a closed universe that does not allow for miracles or prophetic prediction. In the tradition of avowedly Christian interpretation, by contrast, the undergirding worldview seeks to integrate faith and reason, and postulates an open universe. Examples of other significant worldview issues informing biblical interpretation are the questions of the determinacy of meaning, the hermeneutical role of gender and class, the relation of history and revelation, and the unity of Scripture. To a significant extent, worldview commitments on these and similar issues, whether openly acknowledged or not, shape the interpretative practices of biblical exegetes. In the interests of hermeneutical clarity and transparency, much is to be gained by foregrounding the worldview dimension of all interpretation, both in one's own way of reading Scripture and in that of others.

Second, "worldview" has been used as a category for integrating the diverse aspects of first-century Judaism and first-century Christianity. Here we think especially of N. T. Wright in his *The New Testament and the People of God* and in subsequent writings. Wright defines worldview as being constituted by the answers to four basic questions: "Who are we?" "Where are we?" "What is wrong?" and "What is the solution?" For first-century Israel, the answers have to do with being the chosen people, residing in the Holy Land, having the wrong rulers, and looking to God to liberate them through his own kingship. For the church, the answers have to do with a modified form of the Jewish worldview, centered on the person of Jesus Christ. Who are we? We are a new group, but in continuity with Israel. Where are we? We are in the midst of a pagan world. What is wrong? Paganism still rules the world. What is the solution? The work of Jesus the Messiah, in his death and resurrection and coming again. By applying this kind of worldview analysis to the Judaism and Christianity of NT times, it is possible to make coherent sense of a wide array of symbols, practices, and writings that might otherwise appear diffuse and contradictory.

Finally, "worldview" can be used in a more specific sense to refer to differences among Christians with respect to their attitude to the "world" as a religious category. At bottom, this has to do with one's paradigm for relating the classical Christian categories of "nature" and "grace." "Nature" here is a shorthand formulation for everything involved in the "world" as God's good but fallen creation (including human culture). "Grace" is a similar designation for everything involved with the redemption in Christ or the kingdom of God (including human culture). Within the tradition of historic Christian orthodoxy (defined in terms of adherence to the ecumenical creeds of the early church), it is possible to discern four such paradigms or worldviews. Three of these can be called dualistic, in that they conceive of grace as either opposing, supplementing, or flanking nature. In varying degrees, these Christian worldviews allow for a dichotomy or separation between a sacred and a secular realm of life. The fourth, in the tradition of Irenaeus, Augustine, and Calvin, construes grace as *restoring* nature, of entering into it as a medicine in order to reclaim its original health. For the interpretation of Scripture, worldview in this sense is especially important insofar as reason and faith (often aligned with "critical scholarship" and "theology") are correlated with nature and grace in a dualistic way, thus providing a religious justification for the epistemological separation—à la Kant—of knowledge and belief. Alternatively, the more integral conception represented by the fourth worldview provides a religious critique of the Kantian legacy, and a spur to let faith play its role in the heart of the academic study of Scripture, from textual criticism to ideological criticism. In addition, an interpreter's conception of the nature-grace relation is often projected onto the Scriptures themselves, so that, for example, "secular" proverbs are assigned to a different date from "religious" ones, or the entire category of Wisdom literature is considered secular as compared to prophetic and priestly literature. But it is doubtful whether "religion" or the service of God was something less than comprehensive for the Bible writers themselves. In fact, a strong case can be made for the view that the Scriptures themselves, taken together as a canonical whole, embody and promulgate a nondualistic worldview (see Wolters, *Creation*). If that is so, then in the dynamics of the hermeneutical circle, the Bible's own worldview ought to inform the way it and its component parts are interpreted.

See also Grace

Bibliography

Marshall, P. A., et al. *Stained Glass*. University Press of America, 1989; Naugle, D. *Worldview*. Eerdmans, 2002; Wolters, A. *Creation Regained*. Eerdmans, 1985; idem. "Nature and Grace in the Interpretation of Proverbs 31:10–31." *CTJ* 19 (1984): 153–66; Wright, N. T. *The New Testament and the People of God*. Fortress, 1992.

Albert Wolters

Worship

In common English usage, the word "worship" is typically used to refer to a public gathering of people to perform religious activities. For Christians, this will mean the regular assembly of the church, day by day or week by week, meeting to engage directly with the triune God of Jesus Christ, and with each other in God's name.

A theological interpretation of these occasions as referred to in Scripture, however, demands that we first consider a much wider and more general sense of "worship."

Worship in the Biblical Texts

The Whole-of-Life Setting. The importance of a broader context is evident in that the biblical words customarily translated "worship" (and associated terms) often have a reference far beyond what God's people are to do when they meet together, sometimes embracing all that humans are, say, think, and do before God. For example, in the OT the vocabulary of cultic worship can be picked up and used in a noncultic way to denote a lifestyle, flowing out of a heart humbled before God (Ps. 51:17), and there are frequent attacks on empty cultic acts divorced from appropriate behavior. In the NT, *leitourgeō* and its cognates, used of duties performed toward God, can be employed noncultically as well as cultically—of aid given to the poor (Rom. 15:27) or from one Christian to another (Phil. 2:25). The *latreuō* word group, connoting service, is not restricted to regular gatherings but can also be used of serving God in quite general ways (2 Tim. 1:3; Heb. 9:14). Paul uses sacrificial terminology ("present," "sacrifice," "holy," "acceptable") to speak of the people of God giving their entire lives to God as "reasonable worship" (Rom. 12:1; cf. Phil. 2:17; 4:18).

The Whole-of-Creation Setting. Interpretation of this "whole-life" worship demands taking account of even broader contexts still. In particular, it means the affirmation that creation as a whole offers worship and praise to God (Pss. 69:34; 98:7–8; 148). The vocation of human beings is not only to know this but also to gather and articulate creation's praise in God-dedicated lives. Humans are to "hallow God's name" as his representative vice-regents and image-bearers, exercising wise dominion over the earth (Gen. 1:26–31). Put differently, humans, as creatures, are called to render and reflect back to God, and to the world, the "holy love" God longs to share (Hart).

The tragedy of humankind issues from the catastrophe of misplaced worship, a refusal to hallow God's name through lives of praise, a disobedient honoring of creature rather than Creator. Multiple calamities result (Rom. 1:18–32), affecting God's chosen people as well as humanity at large (1:18–3:20). The whole creation, frustrated and groaning, longs for the liberation of the children of God, for Adam's original calling as God's faithful image-bearer to be restored (Rom. 8:19–23).

The Reversal of Idolatry in Christ. In Jesus Christ, this faithful one is provided, the true Israelite and child of God, the image-bearer par excellence (2 Cor. 4:4). Here the saving project initiated in Abraham's faithful worship finds its climax. He is the true worshipper, from our side offering a life of unbroken, loving obedience to God, even to the point of death on a cross, where the root cause of humanity's catastrophe is borne and taken away. In Christ, the idolatry of sinful humanity is reversed, sin defeated, and God's name at last hallowed. Revelation 4 and 5 (echoing Gen. 1) offer a spectacular portrayal of this: the entire creation pours forth unending praise before God, and twenty-four elders (the people of God from old and new covenants) fall down and declare God the Creator as the only one worthy of worship. This corporate worship springs from, and is only possible because of, the victorious death of the Lamb, who occupies, alongside God, the center of the vision.

Christ is thus portrayed in the NT as the climactic fulfillment of all prior worship—in the narrow as well as in the wide sense. He belongs to the unique identity of the God of Israel (Bauckham), the God to whom exclusive reverence as Creator is due. He is the true temple, the "place" where God dwells in the midst of his people, and through whom worship of the Father in spirit and truth is possible (John 2:13–25; 4). He is both priest and sacrifice, affording access by his blood to the very throne room of God (Heb. 8:1–13; 10:1–10).

Only through Christ, then, by whose death and resurrection humanity is reconciled to the Father, is genuine worship possible. Only through him can humanity's original vocation as God's image-bearer and vice-regent advance again, now with a redeeming dimension. Only through him can the self-destructive, downward-spiraling idolatry of Rom. 1 be reversed to generate the authentic worship of Rom. 12 (Thompson 124–27). Only through him can a reconciled community emerge that can truly honor God, the church of Jew and Gentile, slave and free, man and woman, embodying and reflecting back to God his own covenant love.

Worship as Trinitarian. In the NT, the repeated inclusion of Christ in the identity of God and an understanding of the Spirit as distinct divine agent (Fee) throw into question undifferentiated unitarianism, while at the same time being faithful to Jewish monotheism. The Fourth Gospel in particular opens up a vision in which the worship Jesus offers God is grounded in the eternal Son's loving communion with the Father. Here and elsewhere, the trinitarian "grammar" of worship begins to be evident (J. Torrance). The church's worship is united with the one perfect response of the incarnate Son, with his once-for-all offering of worship on the cross, and with his ongoing worship of the Father in our midst as High Priest (Heb. 4:14; cf. Rom. 8:34). This is possible through the same Spirit who enabled and undergirded Christ's own earthly self-offering. The Spirit is the enabler of worship, empowering God's people to be conformed to the image of his Son and cry "*Abba*, Father" (Rom. 8:15–17; Gal. 4:6–7; cf. Eph. 5:18–20). The dynamics of worship and salvation are thus seen to be inextricably intertwined (Hart).

Corporate Gatherings. There is every reason to understand the theological dynamic of "whole-life worship" as intrinsic to the regular, corporate and public gatherings of the church. To hold that mutual edification was the pivotal center of such gatherings in the NT (Richardson) is unconvincing (Thompson; Campbell). These occasions—in both OT and NT—are best interpreted as events when "whole-life" worship is concentrated in relation to God in a conscious and directed way, when the people of God are realigned with God and his purposes, and through this realignment, with each other. More fully, in Christian terms, the church faces and engages with God directly, being built up as a fellowship by sharing in the worship of Christ through the Spirit's indwelling. Thus, in the Spirit's communion with the Father, the church anticipates the end of creation, when the whole world will fulfill its telos in Christ and hallow the Father's name.

It is notoriously hard to determine the precise content of these assemblies in the NT period, not least because of their considerable diversity (Bradshaw). But the gatherings seem to have included praise of God and thanksgiving for all he had done, the reading of Sacred Scripture, speech in the name of God, mutual encouragement, prayer, singing, and (when required) baptism. Further, many would interpret the Lord's Supper as embodying worship's trinitarian dynamic in a particularly comprehensive way, both in the NT churches and today (Cocksworth, ch. 6). Through sharing as one people in bread and wine, the church is given to share in Christ, the risen High Priest. As the Spirit binds us to Christ in his offering of himself to the Father, the church is directed back to the once-made sacrifice of Christ, remembering his victory over sin and evil. In being drawn back, the church is also pointed forward: the risen and ascended Christ to whom the church is united is the one who is yet to come, offering now through his Spirit a foretaste of the final, messianic feast (1 Cor. 11:26; Luke 22:16).

The corporate assemblies, however, cannot be separated from worship in its wider sense. To insist that only the name of *this* God is to be hallowed is to refuse to give allegiance to any other god. And it is a commitment to honor this God (and no other) *publicly*—worship is potentially a political and costly act. To be realigned to God means being sent into the world. The church goes with Christ in the power of the Spirit, to fulfill the mission entrusted to him by the Father. It witnesses to Christ in word and deed, calls others to know him, serves all men and women in his name, and works unceasingly for the establishment of his love and justice. Regular corporate worship and ongoing mission are inseparable; worship generates mission just as mission drives the church to deeper worship.

Worship and Scriptural Interpretation

For the church, to read Scripture means interpreting it with a view to worship in its widest sense—the hallowing of God's name through sharing in the life and mission of the triune God. Scripture is to inform, shape, and promote lives of faith and obedience in the world. Clearly, Scripture also shapes the church's worship in the narrower sense, not only by providing instructive glimpses of the earliest Christian communities as they gathered together, and some of the concerns that shaped such gatherings, but also and more centrally through its unique and unsurpassable testimony to the gospel. The reading and preaching of Scripture in worship (some would say, supremely in eucharistic worship) normatively "realign" the church to the gospel of the triune God.

In addition, many have argued that worship—in both wide and narrow senses—provides the primary and most appropriate hermeneutical "posture" and "situation" for the reading of Scripture (Fodor). To interpret Scripture faithfully entails an openness to being addressed and transformed through reading and hearing it. Much scholarship has been critical of a stance toward Scripture that aims to suspend commitment and defer obedience in the interests of "objective" truth. It is argued that to read Scripture aright is to be oriented to the God of whom Scripture speaks and who speaks through Scripture, and thus to be caught up in the trinitarian drama of God's self-communication, through which God claims his people and sustains their agency in the world.

A trinitarian account of worship in turn presses us to give an integrally theological account of scriptural language, centered in the true Worshipper, Jesus Christ. The adoption of fallen human words by the incarnate Son, their re-formation by him, their being-made-appropriate to God, is intrinsic to salvation, and thus to the establishment of true worship of the Father through him. Semantic adequacy is not a property of our language per se, but is realized in Christ alone, and given to the church inasmuch as it is incorporated into him by the Spirit, given to share in his eternal worship of the Father. Scripture arose within, embodies, and can be a vehicle of this doxological, dynamic transformation of language. "Doxological participation" and "semantic participation" through the language of Scripture are thus intrinsically related (A. Torrance).

See also Music, the Bible and

Bibliography

Bauckham, R. *God Crucified*. Paternoster, 1998; Bradshaw, P. *The Search for the Origins of Christian Worship*. SPCK, 1992; Campbell, A. "Once More: Is Worship Biblical?" *Chm* 110 (1995): 131–39; Cocksworth, C. *Holy, Holy, Holy*. Darton, Longman & Todd, 1997; Fee, G. "Paul and the Trinity." Pages 49–72 in *The Trinity*, ed. S. Davis, D. Kendall, and G. O'Collins. Oxford University Press, 1999; Fodor, J. "Scripture Reading: Rehearsing Identity/Practicing Character." In *The Blackwell Companion to Christian Ethics*, ed. S. Hauerwas and S. Wells. Oxford University Press, 2004; Hart, T. "Atonement and Worship." *Anvil* 11 (1994): 203–14; Hurtado, L. *At the Origins of Christian Worship*. Eerdmans, 1999; Marshall, I. H. "How Far Did the Early Christians Worship God?" *Chm* 99 (1985): 216–29; Martin, R. "Worship." Pages 982–91 in *Dictionary of Paul and His Letters*, ed. G. Hawthorne and R. Martin. InterVarsity, 1993; Peterson, D. *Engaging with God*. InterVarsity, 2002; Richardson, J. "Is Worship Biblical?" *Chm* 109 (1995): 197–218; Thompson, M. "Romans 12:1–2 and Paul's Vision for Worship." Pages 121–32 in *A Vision for the Church*, ed. M. Bockmuehl and M. Thompson. T&T Clark, 1997; Torrance, A. *Persons in Communion*. T&T Clark, 1999; Torrance, J. *Worship, Community and the Triune God of Grace*. Paternoster, 1996; Volf, M. "Worship as Adoration and Action: Reflections on a Christian Way of Being-in-the-World." Pages 203–11 in *Worship*, ed. D. A. Carson. Baker, 1993.

Jeremy Begbie

Writing   *See* Deconstruction; Postmodernity and Biblical Interpretation

Y

Yale School

Never intended to describe a unified program and single hermeneutical method, the appellation "Yale School" usefully designates common themes and related approaches to biblical interpretation among various theologians at Yale University and Yale Divinity School. The immediate difficulty in employing the term is determining the roster of Yale School theologians and biblical scholars. At least, however, theologians Hans Frei, George Lindbeck, and David Kelsey ought to be acknowledged as the key figures. The primary contribution made by these theologians of the Yale School is methodological, for although their seminal work provides noteworthy suggestions for theological exegesis, instances of the exegetical practice are few (although their colleague Brevard Childs is perhaps somewhat related). Briefly stated, the methodological proposals address three issues: first and foremost, the character of the text of Scripture; second, the role of the church in biblical interpretation; and third, the agency and activity of God in the church's reading and interpretation of the Scripture.

Hans Frei (1922–88)

Hans Frei studied at Yale (B.D., 1945; Ph.D., 1956) under H. Richard Niebuhr and served in Yale's department of Religious Studies from 1957 until his death in 1988.

Arguably, Frei may be considered the unintentional founder of the Yale School, given his groundbreaking and influential study of the history of biblical interpretation in modern theology (*Eclipse*) and numerous constructive essays addressing biblical interpretation. Frei's basic contribution to theological exegesis is his insistence on reading Scripture as a realistic narrative centered on the particular story of Jesus Christ. Frei describes and seeks to correct the modern shift in the way the Bible is approached both in the church and in academic theology. Rather than beginning with contemporary human experience and determining the meaning of the biblical text on the basis of this experience, Frei insists that readers must begin with the particularity of the biblical text. They must focus interpretative investigation on its meaning, rather than on a search for general truths on the one hand or historical accuracy and reference on the other. In short, the text of Scripture must be interpreted on its own terms.

Frei resists allowing general theories of hermeneutics and anthropology to determine the shape and scope of biblical interpretation. He insists that the interpreter attend to the particularity of the biblical text as rendering the concrete and particular identity of Jesus Christ and, further, the identity of God. Frei's preference for the literal sense (the *sensus literalis*) of Scripture, as the consensus form of interpretation in the history of the church, corresponds to his insistence on the inseparability of meaning and truth. The meaning of the Gospel narratives, for example, cannot be separated from the formal structure of the narrative as narrative. The Gospel narratives, Frei maintains, are stories about Jesus, not something else. The Gospel narratives are unique testimonies to Jesus Christ and his unique relationship to God as the incarnate, crucified, and risen Savior. Given the uniqueness of Scripture and the uniqueness of the person to whom they witness, Frei contends that we cannot determine the meaningfulness and truthfulness of Scripture by extratextual categories and conceptual schemes. On this particular point, Frei concludes that the preoccupation of liberal biblical interpretation with uncovering universal moral lessons or insights, and that of conservative biblical interpretation with verifying historical accuracy, both distort the literal sense of Scripture. Although Frei acknowledges and highlights the importance of the church for biblical interpretation, his colleague George Lindbeck offers the most sustained and penetrating account of the communal context within which the biblical text is read and interpreted.

George Lindbeck (b. 1923)

George Lindbeck earned his B.D. (1946) and Ph.D. (1955) degrees from Yale. He taught in the areas of medieval philosophy, historical theology, and comparative doctrinal theology at Yale from 1952 until his retirement in 1993.

Lindbeck's contribution is an emphasis on the community of the church as the location for theological exegesis. While Lindbeck follows Frei in matters of the character of the biblical text, realistic narrative, canon, and precritical hermeneutics (which he dubbed "intratextuality"), his stress on the ecclesial context of biblical interpretation is his distinguishing feature. For Lindbeck, theological exegesis takes place by the community and in the community, leading to the constitution of the community as the church. By attending to the *sensus fidelium*, the consent of the faithful, the theological exegesis of the church seeks and achieves community-building consensus.

Lindbeck insists that the Bible is the community's book, and that the reading and interpretation of this book is not to be reserved for a small elite class, whether academic or clerical. Consensus must be achieved through reading and interpretation that spans from bishops, priests, and academics to all faithful laity. His emphasis on the *sensus fidelium* coupled with his insistence on exegesis as constitutive of the church leads to pragmatic criteria for evaluating the church's interpretation of Scripture. "What builds up the Church is what counts" (Lindbeck, "Scripture," 221). The proof of any theological exegesis will not be theoretical but practical. According to Lindbeck, community-forming exegesis depends upon the existence of communities of interpretation "in which pastors, biblical scholars, theologians and laity together seek God's guidance in the written word for their communal as well as individual lives" (Lindbeck, "Scripture," 220). Lindbeck's suggestions for theological exegesis risk being ecclesiocentric, with scant attention to divine agency and activity. Nevertheless, his colleague David Kelsey complements both Frei's work on realistic narrative and Lindbeck's emphasis on the communal character of biblical interpretation. Kelsey gives a constructive proposal for a properly *theological* account of the church's exegesis.

David H. Kelsey (b. 1932)

Like Frei and Lindbeck before him, David Kelsey received both a B.D. (1958) and Ph.D. (1964) from Yale, and he has taught theology at Yale Divinity School since 1965.

Kelsey contributes to the Yale School emphasis on narrative, as seen in his depiction of the Bible as nonfiction narrative that renders the particular identity of Jesus Christ (Kelsey, *Uses*, 39–50). Additionally, he underscores the relationship between the Bible and church by describing how the Bible as Scripture functions within the common life of the church to shape and transform persons' identities (Kelsey, *Uses*, 90–92). Further, though this aspect of his work has been overlooked and underdeveloped, Kelsey extends his descriptive ("functional") analysis of *how* Scripture is in fact used by theologians and within the church by offering a constructive proposal for *why* Scripture *ought* to be used in the church. This proposal is Kelsey's distinct contribution, since it focuses the church's attention on the significance and necessity of God's action in theological exegesis. Kelsey suggests that attention be paid to God's use of the church's use of Scripture for the purpose of forming communal and individual identity. Here, a doctrine of Scripture is located within the doctrine of God. The authority of Scripture, which determines the shape of exegesis, is attributed specifically to the activity and agency of the Holy Spirit, who as sanctifier transforms and empowers human identities (Kelsey, "Bible," 396).

Conclusion

Focusing reflection on Scripture's use, the Yale School offers suggestive methodological guidance for theological exegesis centered on the Bible as a unique text, the church as a particular community, and the activity of God as a necessary component of the church's interpretation. The lasting significance of the Yale School has yet to be determined and will be decided by the actual practice of theological exegesis informed by these proposals.

See also Canonical Approach; Language-Game; Narrative Theology

Bibliography

Frei, H. *The Eclipse of Biblical Narrative*. Yale University Press, 1974; idem. *The Identity of Jesus Christ*. Fortress, 1975; idem. *Theology and Narrative*, ed. G. Hunsinger and W. Placher. Oxford University Press, 1993; idem. *Types of Christian Theology*, ed. G. Hunsinger and W. Placher. Yale University Press, 1992; Hunsinger, G. "Postliberal Theology." Pages 42–57 in *Cambridge Companion to Postmodern Theology*, ed. K. Vanhoozer. Cambridge University Press, 2003; Kelsey, D. "The Bible and Christian Theology." *JAAR* 48 (1980): 385–402; idem. *The Uses of Scripture in Recent Theology*. Fortress, 1975. Reissued as *Proving Doctrine*. Trinity, 1999; Lindbeck, G. "Barth and Textuality." *ThTo* 43 (1986): 361–76; idem. *The Nature of Doctrine*. Westminster, 1984; idem. "Postcritical Canonical Interpretation: Three Modes of Retrieval." Pages 26–51 in *Theological Exegesis*, ed. C. Seitz and K. Greene-McCreight. Eerdmans, 1999; idem. "Scripture, Consensus and Community." Pages 201–22 in *The Church in a Postliberal Age*, ed. J. Buckley. Eerdmans, 2003.

David Lauber

Z

Zealots *See* Jewish Context of the NT

Zechariah, Book of

The book of Zechariah has often been called one of the most difficult books of the Bible. With the exception of the middle section (chs. 7–8), which consists of a series of relatively straightforward ethical and religious exhortations, the book is obscure for a variety of reasons. The first section (chs. 1–6) is obscure because it consists largely of dreamlike visions accompanied by apparently unconnected oracles, and the third section (chs. 9–14) because it is composed almost entirely of a kaleidoscope of divine threats and promises regarding the future of Jerusalem, the nations, and the cosmos, but often having no clearly identifiable historical referents. On the other hand, the book has many messianic predictions, which in the light of the NT clearly find their fulfillment in Jesus Christ.

History of Interpretation

Much of patristic exegesis (e.g., the recently rediscovered commentary by Didymus the Blind) was characterized by an uninhibited allegorical interpretation. The great exception is Theodore of Mopsuestia, who espoused a more literal and historical reading. He and a number of Syriac commentators (notably Ephraim Syrus) interpreted the predictions of chapters 9–14 as referring primarily to the history of Israel before the coming of Christ, especially the time of the Maccabees. Jerome wrote an influential commentary on two levels: one "literal," in which he drew on the Hebrew text and Jewish sources, and one "spiritual," which was heavily dependent on Didymus's allegorical commentary.

Jerome's commentary overshadowed the interpretation of Zechariah in the Latin West until the time of the Reformation. Early modern interpretation is dominated by Protestant exegetes, and by a turn away from allegory toward a philological and historical understanding of the Hebrew text. Nevertheless, it was still characterized by great diversity, especially regarding the historical referents of chapters 9–14. Zechariah 14, for example, was taken to refer to the fortunes of God's people at the time of the Maccabees (Hugo Grotius), in the church age (Luther), in the period between the exile and Christ (Calvin), or in the end times and preceding the last judgment (Oecolampadius). Until the late eighteenth century, there nevertheless was broad agreement (also among those who, on the basis of Matt. 27:9, assigned part or all of Zech. 9–14 to Jeremiah) that the canonical book of Zechariah was a divinely inspired part of Holy Scripture, spoke the truth about future events, and portrayed the coming Messiah in terms that were fulfilled in Jesus Christ.

All of this changed with the rise of historical criticism, which began to exclude such confessional commitments from biblical scholarship, and to focus on questions of multiple authorship and dating. Zechariah 9–14, for example, was attributed to as many as four different authors, and assigned to dates ranging from the eighth to the second century BCE. The constituent parts of Zechariah were read, not with a view to hearing the voice of God, but to hearing a diversity of human voices, which each reflected its own milieu and agenda. Among confessional interpreters of Scripture in the nineteenth and twentieth centuries, the chief innovations have been the detailed defense of traditional positions (e.g., unity of authorship) against the results of mainline historical criticism, and the rise of a dispensationalist hermeneutic. The latter stressed literal fulfillment of Zechariah's prophecies and thus saw many of these as fulfilled, not in the church, but in a future separate group of converted Jews (Unger). Of significance in recent decades have been discussions of the category "apocalyptic" (variously said to apply to all, part, or none of Zechariah), the analysis of literary structure (leading to widely divergent results), and the softening of the classical dispensationalist hermeneutic (Merrill). A remarkable development in the tradition of historical criticism is the recent trend in dating chapters 9–14 ("Deutero-Zechariah"). After a time (most of the nineteenth century) when these chapters were almost unanimously assigned a preexilic date, there had followed a time (from about 1880 to 1960) when almost all critical scholars assigned them to the Hellenistic period. Since then, a growing consensus has emerged that "Deutero-Zechariah" should be dated to the early postexilic period (Hanson; Meyers and Meyers; Petersen; Sweeney). Thus, there is currently widespread agreement that the entire book of Zechariah could have been written during the lifetime of the sixth-century prophet whose name it bears.

The Message of the Text

In coming to a theologically responsible reading of the message of Zechariah, we must take seriously its literary and canonical unity, its embeddedness in an authoritative canon that culminates in the Christ of the NT evangelists and apostles, and the historic Christian claim that Scripture in all its parts communicates the word of God to every generation of believers in their own situation.

Despite the obscurity and apparently jumbled character of much of Zechariah, there are broad themes that come through clearly. Among such themes we find the centrality of Jerusalem ("Jerusalem" and "Zion" occur a total of forty-seven times, quite evenly distributed throughout the book). It is to Jerusalem that Yahweh returns in mercy (1:16); it is Jerusalem that he chooses again (2:12), where his temple is to be rebuilt (1:16), and where he himself will take up residence (2:10). It is to Jerusalem that the remaining exiles are exhorted to return (9:12), and it is to Jerusalem that all nations will eventually come to serve Yahweh (14:16). Other themes are the future inclusion of all nations in Yahweh's covenant (2:11 [15 MT]; 8:20–23), and the continuity with earlier prophecy (passim). As in so many of the prophets, overshadowing all these themes is the emphasis on the sovereignty of God in both judgment and grace. Terrible judgment is threatened both against the nations (1:21; 2:9; 6:7–8; 9:1–7; 12:3–4, 9; 14:3, 12) and against God's own disobedient people (11:3, 6; 13:8–9; 14:1–2). Particularly chilling is the passage where God promises to send two shepherds to rule over his people, both of whom will eventually abandon and ruin them (11:4–16). But inexplicable grace is the dominant note. It is not only manifested in the present, as God returns in mercy to his people after the scourge of the exile (1:16–17), but also promised for the future (8:1–5, 12–13; 9:8, 16–17; 10:6). Especially prominent among these promises of grace are the predictions concerning a coming messianic figure called the Branch (3:8; 6:12–13), a figure later described in four remarkable passages (9:9–12; 12:1–2; 12:10–13:1; 13:7–9). These texts appear to echo and amplify Isaiah's accounts of the Suffering Servant (Lamarche 125–47).

Zechariah and the Canon

Zechariah was one of the last OT prophets, and he wrote at a time when the OT canon was near completion. As a result, his prophecies are laced with allusions (sometimes direct quotations, as in 9:10b, citing Ps. 72:8) to the canonical writings that preceded him, especially the books of Isaiah, Jeremiah, and Ezekiel. He clearly sees himself as standing in the tradition of what he calls "the former prophets" (NRSV: 1:4; 7:7, 12). At the same time he points forward to the NT fulfillment of the messianic prophecies that he has delivered, and to the ultimate restoration of all things. The NT often quotes Zechariah, especially with reference to the passion of Christ (Matt. 21:5; 26:31; 27:9–10; Mark 14:27; John 12:15; 19:37).

Theological Significance

In light of the foregoing, it is clear that the book of Zechariah is both deeply rooted in the preceding history of revelation, and is itself revelatory of the messianic and cosmic future. In it God promises to reclaim Jerusalem as the center of his empire, and to rebuild the temple as his royal dwelling. Meanwhile, he reassures his people that, through a long history marked by judgment and grace, the coming future Messiah will expand the significance of both Jerusalem and the temple into unprecedented and unimagined dimensions. In a word, Zechariah is all about the world-historical and indeed cosmic coming of the kingdom of God (Webb).

Bibliography

Baldwin, J. G. Haggai, Zechariah, Malachi. TOTC. InterVarsity, 1972; Hanson, P. D. The Dawn of Apocalyptic. Rev. ed. Fortress, 1979; Lamarche, P. Zacharie IX–XIV. Lecoffre, 1961; Merrill, E. Haggai, Zechariah, Malachi. Moody, 1994; Meyers, C. L., and E. M. Meyers. Zechariah 9–14. AB 25C. Doubleday, 1993; Petersen, D. L. Zechariah 9–14 and Malachi. OTL. Westminster John Knox, 1995; Sweeney, M. A., ed. Micah, Nahum, Habakkuk, Zephaniah, Haggai, Zechariah, Malachi. Vol. 2 of The Twelve Prophets, ed. D. W. Cotter. Berit Olam. Liturgical Press, 2000; Unger, M. Zechariah. Zondervan, 1963; Webb, B. G. The Message of Zechariah. InterVarsity, 2003; Wolters, A. "Confessional Criticism and the Night Visions of Zechariah." Pages 90–117 in Renewing Biblical Interpretation, ed. C. Bartholomew et al. SHS. Zondervan/Paternoster,

2000; idem. "Zechariah 14: A Dialogue with the History of Interpretation." *Mid-America Journal of Theology* 13 (2002): 39–56; idem. "Zechariah 14 and Biblical Theology: Patristic and Contemporary Case Studies." In *Out of Egypt*, ed. C. Bartholomew et al. SHS. Zondervan/Paternoster, 2004.

Albert Wolters

Zephaniah, Book of

The concept of the day of Yahweh as a day of decisive punishment permeates the book of Zephaniah, which nevertheless ends on a note of joy for those who have come through the judgment. From the sweeping declaration at the beginning onward, Zephaniah is characterized by its use of comprehensive language for the scope of this judgment (see esp. 1:2–3, 18; 2:11; 3:8). This scope is reflected in twenty-three occurrences of the phrase "all/the whole" (the highest use of the phrase in relation to words in a book). Key issues in the interpretation of the book are the identification of the "people humble and lowly" (3:12 NRSV; cf. 2:3) and the historical setting with regard to Josiah's reforms in the seventh century.

The Argument of the Book

Zephaniah is often thought to follow a tripartite pattern, as also presumed for other prophetic books: punishment of Jerusalem and Judah (1:1–2:3), followed by punishment of other nations (2:4–3:8), and finally the promise of redemption for Jerusalem and the whole world (3:9–20). This pattern is understood to outline an eschatological sequence of events and is usually considered to be the product of a postexilic redaction. Yet the pattern does not do justice to the arrangement of Zephaniah (cf. Sweeney; Weigl). The book opens with an announcement of a comprehensive punitive action, which is subsequently focused on particular groups in Jerusalem (1:2–18). The call to Judah's humbled population in 2:1–3, to escape the judgment through submission to Yahweh, is supported by the observation that the Philistine cities will certainly be devastated (2:4; cf. 3:6–7). The words of doom over other nations are in two parts. The first is shot through with promises for the remnant (!) of Judah (2:5–11); the second is addressed against Assyria's claim to be the force that matters (2:12–15). The Assyrian defeat of the Cushite dynasty that governed Egypt until 663 BCE was in fact Yahweh's doing (2:12), and thus the word against Assyria (2:13–15) underlines the point that not Assyria but Yahweh is the force next to which there is no other.

Chapter 3 juxtaposes condemnation of Jerusalem's leadership with Yahweh's punitive intervention in other nations (3:1–7). Yet Jerusalem's punishment is only alluded to; it appears to be a consequence of Yahweh's universal decree to have the whole world experience his anger and be transformed to true worship (3:8–13). In isolation, the concluding section (3:14–20) could be read as a summons to rejoice after an oppressive enemy has been defeated. Yet in the context of the book, the victory is won not only against taunting Moabites and domineering Assyrians, but also against the oppressive regime of unbelief in Jerusalem itself. There is ambiguity within the book as to whom Judah regards as its king (cf. 1:5). The day of Yahweh is the day when Yahweh executes his decision and establishes himself as king (cf. 3:15).

Zephaniah within the Canon

There are numerous links between Zephaniah and other parts of the Bible, with literary influence going both ways (cf. Berlin 13–17, 117–24). The judgment in chapter 1 is reminiscent of the flood, survived by only a remnant. The claim on foreign land made in chapter 2 may be based on Gen. 10 and Deuteronomy as well as the contemporary political situation (cf. Berlin 117–24). The promise in 3:9 of unity and pure speech for the peoples may be considered a reversal of Gen. 11 (Berlin 14). What at first sight looks like complete annihilation is seen in the light of these links as a purifying judgment, which restores the original design. Zephaniah's hope for the emergence of a spiritually humble remnant among those of a materially, or at least politically, humble background found an application among those left behind by the Babylonians (cf. 2 Kings 24:14; 25:12; Jer. 39:10; 40:7). It is part of the common biblical motif of God's election of the disregarded. The restoration of Israel through a humble remnant was again enacted in Christ who, unlike Zephaniah's poor, ensures this by taking the judgment upon himself. This enables the reversal of Babel's confusion at Pentecost, and extends Yahweh worship beyond the confines of ethnic Israel; yet it affirms the division of humanity into the humble, who inherit the world, and the proud, upon whom the judgment remains. This judgment constitutes "the day of the LORD"—a time when God executes his decision about the fate of a community. Such a day is described in many other places as a cosmic upheaval, even when applied to specific historical events. Zephaniah's universalistic language prepares the way for an understanding of "the day of the LORD" (1:14) as an eschatological event, the day when God's purposes for all peoples are executed.

Regarding the trappings of wealth and power, Zephaniah's message is reflected in Jesus' warning that it is hard for the rich to enter God's kingdom (Mark 10:23 et par.). As elsewhere in Scripture, poverty is neither an ideal to aspire to nor a guarantee for favor with God, but wealth may well be a hindrance (cf. James 1:9–11; 2:5–6; 5:1–6).

Perspectives from the History of Interpretation

Luther thought that among the Minor Prophets, Zephaniah "makes the clearest prophecies about the kingdom of Christ" (319). He saw in the prophet someone who, like himself, proclaimed a divine message unacknowledged as such by the authorities. For Luther, Zephaniah ruthlessly rejects human righteousness and religion, preparing the kingdom of Christ. The gathering of kingdoms and nations he sees fulfilled through the spread of the gospel (355), which is a message declaring the outpouring of God's wrath and calling for repentance (356). Zephaniah agrees with all of Scripture in its battle against "the powerful, the wise, and the holy" (326), and in addressing the promise to the "humble, oppressed, . . . those who lack honor and wealth," like Christ and Mary in the NT (339).

Key issues discussed in modern research are Zephaniah's relationship to Josiah's reforms and the literary history of the book, which often affects the understanding of the "poor"—with the socioeconomic interpretation favored for an early date, a religious interpretation with a postexilic date. Along with the presumed tripartite structure (see above), talk of a remnant and return from exile are often thought to reflect a postexilic setting, but this need not be the case. The remnant motif is an integral aspect of the concept of inevitable disaster, and return from exile has been an issue ever since the deportation of northern Israelites by Assyria. Christensen's attempt to link 2:4–15 specifically to Josiah's policies has problems, but it is clear that Zephaniah's message fits with the aims of Josiah's reforms. Yet, with different emphases, it remains relevant for the postexilic community and beyond.

Zephaniah and the Church Today

The history of interpretation reminds us of the need to find our place within the drama that unfolds in Zephaniah, as well as the fact that the same message looks somewhat different from within different contexts, whether or not the book was reshaped after the exile. The church in the Western world is warned that being implicated in a syncretistic and oppressive regime makes it hard to escape the judgment of God, and that God may again choose to continue his history with those who are despised and rejected. The oppressed church is encouraged to trust God's ability to act on a large scale for those who belong to him who became poor so that we might become rich (2 Cor. 8:9). Together we are challenged to seek first God and his righteousness (2:3; cf. Matt. 6:33) and to order all our doings accordingly.

Bibliography

Berlin, A. *Zephaniah*. AB 25A. Doubleday, 1994; Christensen, D. "Zephaniah 2:4–15: A Theological Basis for Josiah's Program of Political Expansion." *CBQ* 46 (1984): 669–82; Dietrich, W. "Die Kontexte des Zefanjabuches." Pages 19–37 in *Der Tag wird kommen*, ed. W. Dietrich and M. Schwantes. SBS 170. Katholisches Bibelwerk, 1996; Floyd, M. *Minor Prophets, Part 2*. FOTL 22. Eerdmans, 2000; Luther, M. "Lectures on Zephaniah." *LWorks* 18:317–64; Sweeney, M. "A Form-Critical Reassessment of the Book of Zephaniah." *CBQ* 53 (1991): 388–408; Veijola, T. "Zefanja und Joschija." Pages 9–18 in *Der Tag wird kommen*, ed. W. Dietrich and M. Schwantes. SBS 170. Katholisches Bibelwerk, 1996; Weigl, M. *Zefanja und das "Israel der Armen."* ÖBS 13. Österreichisches Katholisches Bibelwerk, 1994.

Thomas Renz

LIST OF ARTICLES BY CATEGORY

Hermeneutics

Historical

Literary

Philosophical

Interpreters and Interpretative Communities

TOPICAL INDEX

This index is an alphabetical listing of all topics discussed in the *Dictionary for Theological Interpretation of the Bible*. Each topic is followed by a list of all articles that provide substantive discussion of the topic. Boldface type identifies topics that are also titles of dictionary articles, which are accompanied by the relevant page numbers.

SCRIPTURE INDEX